1982 WRITER'S MARKET®

WHERE TO SELL WHAT YOU WRITE

Edited by P.J. Schemenaur & John Brady

Writer's Digest Books

Cincinnati, Ohio

Writer's Market. Copyright© 1981. Published by Writer's Digest Books, 9933 Alliance Rd., Cincinnati, Ohio 45242. Printed and bound in the United States of America. All rights reserved. No part
of this book may be reproduced in any manner whatsoever without written permission from the
publisher, except by reviewers who may quote brief passages to be printed in a magazine or
newspaper.

Library of Congress Catalog Number 31-20772
International Standard Serial Number 0084-2729
International Standard Book Number 0-89879-052-2/6x9

Contents

The Profession

The Markets

Services

Appendix

Glossary

Index

The Profession

Introduction

How to Use This Book. *Writer's Market*, like any tool, must be used properly to be effective. This book is more than a compendium of names and addresses; it is a chronicle of information a writer *must* know in order to sell to a particular market. Close examination of the book as a whole and of individual listings is, therefore, essential.

Start by reading the material in the front portion of the book introducing you to the writing field. Here you will find information on writing query letters, preparing manuscripts, copyright, and many of the basics of professional writing. Learn those basics, because even the best word-crafter won't make a sale by behaving unprofessionally in the market.

After reading the introductory material, move on to The Markets section. Listed here are thousands of places that will consider freelance work, ranging from play producers to magazines to book publishers. Markets are categorized according to their type, and, often, according to their subject needs. Almost 170 categories compose the trade journals and consumer publications sections alone; obviously a market exists for almost *any* kind of writing. Many of the sections have detailed introductory sections with tips on how to sell to those particular markets. *Read the section intros* before plunging into the market listings, and you stand a better chance of succeeding.

Diversification Pays. Don't limit your marketing to a single category. Editorial needs often overlap, so a writer might make a sale in any number of places. An article about a film star who jogs, for example, could be sold to a general-interest magazine, a sports publication, the city magazine where the star lives, etc. With sufficient rewriting and new information, the same article can be sold to *all* three publications. Because some publications accept previously published work, you can resell the article printed in the general-interest magazine to a sports publication that reprints material, if you still own the rights to the piece.

Letting you know if a particular magazine accepts previously published submissions—and all other needs and requirements of any market—is the purpose of *Writer's Market*. Listings are designed to relate a buyer's policies, requirements and editorial needs. Each listing is stuffed with information, and is a how-to manual in itself.

All information in the listings has been provided, reviewed, and approved by the buyer/editor (or a member of his staff). Consider each market listing carefully before putting anything on paper. The value of some statements—such as preferred word length, required article slant, how to contact the market, preferred subject matter—is obvious. But other facts should be considered, too. You will find specific selling information under the "Tips" subhead—pointers about subject matter, audience, research, etc. You might also read between the lines—look for what *isn't* there. For example, if a listing includes only a Nonfiction subhead, this means you should limit your submissions to articles.

What Editors Dislike. Don't take wild swings at markets. If you swing an ax at a tree and miss, you can wound yourself. You can wound your freelance career by swinging wildly at a market by submitting *anything* to it, hoping that it *might* sell. Editors make mental notes about freelancers who have submitted material way off the mark. If a listing states that the publication or firm wants queries only, *don't* expect to beat the crowd by sending in a completed manuscript, no matter how extraordinary you might think it is. Violation of the guidelines in listings rarely brings more than a rejection slip—and not even that if the editor asks you to enclose a self-addressed, stamped envelope (SASE) and you haven't.

Missing in Action. Information in listings is as current as possible, but editors come and go, companies and publications move, and editorial needs change between the publication date of *Writer's Market* and the day you buy it. Listings for new markets and changes in others can be found throughout the year in *Writer's Digest*, the monthly magazine for freelancers. If you know of a market not listed in this book, write us and give the market's name and address: we will solicit it for the next edition.

When looking for a specific market, check the index. A market might not be listed for one of these reasons: 1) It doesn't solicit freelance material. 2) It has gone out of business. 3) It doesn't pay for material (we have, however, included nonpaying listings in the journalism, literary, alternative, and poetry categories because publication in those magazines could be valuable to a writer). 4) It has failed to verify or update its listing for the 1982 edition. 5) It requests not to be listed. 6) Complaints have been received about it, and it hasn't answered *Writer's Market* inquiries satisfactorily.

Protect Your Rights. One major trend that we have observed in the past year is the increased value of subsidiary rights for the writer. Many magazine articles, for instance, are now the subject of movie scripts; and numerous magazines are going into cable television—using material that appeared originally in their pages. Therefore, it is imperative that all writers hold on to as many secondary rights as possible when negotiating with publishers. Such "windfalls" after publication can be worth thousands of dollars—but only when a writer has *not* sold "all rights" to the publisher. Watch out.

We research, review and update all listings in WM annually. This edition includes 550 new listings, 1,927 changes in editorial requirements, 488 changes in editors, and 294 changes in address. It excludes 300 listings detailed in last year's book.

We wish you a productive, rewarding year on the writing trails ahead, and we look forward to meeting you again next year at this editorial crossroad. Excelsior!

P.J. Schemenaur & John Brady

Using Your Writer's Market

How to Read a Market Listing

A good writer is a careful reader, especially when consulting *WM* market listings. Each listing must be read carefully and *interpreted* before you jump to your typewriter. Remember these tips:

● Information regarding the emphasis and audience of a publication gives important clues to the slant and style your submissions should take.

● Figures listing the number of freelance manuscripts purchased are approximations, but they indicate a market's openness.

● Figures for manuscript lengths preferred by editors are limits to keep in mind when submitting material or suggesting manuscript length in a query letter. However, a story should be told in the space it requires—no more and no less.

● Look for markets that pay on acceptance, *not* "on publication." Payment here is immediate, and not dependent on when your story appears in print.

● Look, too, for markets that don't buy all rights, and don't make "work-for-hire" contract agreements (in which the market, and not the author, owns the article's copyright). Retain rights you might be able to resell. (Information regarding a publication's openness to previously published work is also listed.)

● Don't abuse openness to simultaneous submissions or phone queries. Use these routes only when your "hot" story will be chilled by usual submission procedures. Also, openness to photocopied submissions *does not* imply that simultaneous submissions are OK.

● Listed reporting times are approximate. Give editors about six extra weeks before following up politely on queries or submissions.

● Enclose a self-addressed, stamped envelope (SASE) in *any* correspondence with editors.

● If a listing instructs you to query, please query. If it instructs you to send a complete manuscript, send a complete manuscript. If either is OK, a query may save you time and labor on a manuscript.

● Listings are based on editorial questionnaires and interviews. They are *not* advertisements, nor are markets reported on here endorsed by *WM* editors.

● Finally, don't abuse the editor's willingness to distribute free sample copies. Purchase samples at newsstands if possible, but *always* get a sample copy before querying or making a submission. A good writer is a careful reader, and a sample of your target publication should be at the top of your reading list.

Life in the Writing Lane

A successful freelance writer in Florida recently told a class of writing students, "When I was 25 years old, one morning on my way back from the mailbox with yet another fistful of rejection slips I was suddenly struck with despair by the deep down awareness that I might never ever publish a word. For the first time it was painfully clear to me that I could write and write my heart out until I was an old and bitter man and die at 82, broke, unknown, never having seen a single word of mine in print. That was a scary feeling, and it almost made me quit writing. Almost."

That writer was 29 before publishers started buying his material. Now he says, "Even though I was selling my stories and articles to national magazines pretty regularly, I was aware that I might never have a book published. That, too, was a scary feeling."

Since then he has had three books published. Now when he fantasizes about greater fame and riches, as writers do, he delights himself with visions of writing screenplays for major feature films that will flicker across the screen at his neighborhood theater. But no doubt there are times when other possibilities startle him from his reverie and he says to himself, "Gee, I might never sell a screenplay."

The point is that life in the writing lane is not some safe and secure journey, wherein the writer confidently looks back and laughs about how rough things were along the way. No, a writing career, whether part- or fulltime, is in constant motion, more like a train than a series of train stations. It is an often exciting, and sometimes discouraging process that is nourished by triumphs and enriched by goals. But the true writer never stops and says, "There, I have accomplished all that I want in writing," for to end the quest is to give up being a writer.

While the emerging writer looks forward to his first sale with a sense of impending victory, and justifiably greets it with celebration, he should see it for what it is. The first writing sale is not a watershed that divides those who are succeeding from those who are failing. It is a single important step along the way on a writing journey that is as promising and as uncertain as life itself. All of this is important for the would-be writer to know, because he often comes to think of himself as a different sort of animal from the published writer. He is not. He is simply at a different point along the journey.

Desire. The journey begins with desire, the desire to write. The need to communicate is not unique. It is encoded in the genes, and its manifestations can be found everywhere—from the walls of ancient caves to the walls of high school restrooms. But the true writer has a desire to communicate that burns much hotter. He is willing to take on a Goliath of resistance to his efforts because he is not content simply to scrawl some primitive message on a wall where it *might* be seen. He needs more. He needs to communicate in a special and beautiful way with many people. He needs to draw from the mishmash of life a single vision and organize words in such a way as to flash that vision on the minds of his readers. His desire is not unique, but his commitment to it is a rare and dynamic quality. It is the intensity of that vision and the persistence of his efforts more than anything else that determine whether he will survive or fail as a writer.

Learning to Write. To continue his writing journey, the writer must acquire knowledge to go with his desire. He must learn how to write well.

There are people who seriously believe that you cannot learn to write and they will not hesitate to share that ignorance with you. They think that writing ability is something you are born with, like blue eyes or a club foot. Don't let them discourage you. If you need to be convinced that writing can be learned, break into the home of any good writer and wrest from his files some of the stories he wrote as a dewy-eyed adolescent. You will see at a glance how much his work has improved. And if his work has improved, it means he has *learned* to write better. So yes, writing can be taught and writing can be learned by the open, inquiring mind that has the desire.

Unlike the prospective brain surgeon, the questing writer has a variety of educational paths he can follow. He can read books about writing technique, and then write.

He can take writing courses in high school and college, and then write. He can drive off to adult education courses immediately after supper on cold winter nights, and then write. He can send away for correspondence courses, and then write. He can attend conferences, join workshops, ask questions of other writers, and then write. He can encounter a life worth telling others about, and then write.

Perhaps there are no absolutes of good writing technique, but a few things come close. There are rules of grammar and rules of writing style to which the writing instructor can point and with almost certainty say, "This will work better than that."

But there is a larger area of good writing, an artistic, intuitive area that no one can lead you through. You must explore it yourself by listening and reading.

Cock an ear to the sounds of language all around you. Listen for the rhythms and combinations of words that make you lift your head and lean forward to hear. Catch the phrases, the sentences that sketch fascinating pictures in your mind. And note also the droning weary language that sets your eyelids drooping and your brain fleeing for the solace of daydreams. As you read, study the writer's work. Why did he use this word instead of that? How did he make this character so vivid in so few words? When the writer's thoughts are unclear, ask yourself why. How would you change the language to bring his vision to life?

Beware of growing arrogant about your knowledge of good writing. Your journey should be a constant unfolding of new knowledge, new understandings of how language works. Professional writers read the instructional articles in the writer's magazines. Professional writers buy books on writing technique. They never "know it all," and what they do know needs constant repeating.

Ideas. The raw material of the writer's craft is ideas, those nebulous, sometimes foolish, bits of brilliance that flash on the brain at the darnedest times.

"How do you come up with ideas?" new and exasperated writers often ask established professionals, and the established pros, sometimes equally exasperated, often reply, "How do you *stop* getting ideas?"

The idea-producing mechanism of the brain is like a muscle: The more you use it, the stronger it becomes. Many writers have brains glutted with more ideas than they can possibly use in a lifetime.

Some new writers fail to find strong ideas for stories and articles because they are looking too far away for them. They suspect that anything close and familiar can't be valuable. They are reaching for something, but as soon as they discover that it is within their grasp, they dismiss it as trivial.

Where do good story and article ideas come from? The simple and honest answer is, "Everywhere," but for the beginning writer who craves specifics that is not good enough.

For Ron Trahan, a freelance writer in Massachusetts, a specific answer might be: Ideas come from the things you pass on your way to work.

Five years ago Trahan didn't know a fetlock from a daily double, but every morning, while driving to his job as an English teacher in Shrewsbury, Ron Trahan passed a horse farm. Every morning he observed people out in the morning mist working with the horses. Every morning he asked himself, "What exactly are they *doing* out there?"

One morning Ron Trahan stopped his car and chatted with the horse people. From their expertise he concocted dozens of article ideas. Within a year he was selling articles to national horse magazines regularly. Within three years he had a contract from a major publisher to write and photograph a book for young adults about careers working with horses.

Ron Trahan is no longer an English teacher. He's a professional writer because he knew that an idea could be anywhere, even at a horse farm on the way to work. He had a writer's curiosity—even snoopiness—before he even knew he had the makings of a writer.

Ideas for stories, articles and books come from the people you meet. That woman at the party who teaches men to operate heavy construction equipment might make a good topic for a feature article. Ideas can be seen from your kitchen window. That woman who staggers home at midday, why does she drink? What might her story be?

Ideas come from asking yourself questions. How can I better organize my slides? How has my religion changed in the past ten years? One writer in New Mexico sold over 20 articles about professions, and created many fictional story characters from his knowledge of those professions. His source of ideas? He thumbs through the Yellow Pages.

You will meet many ideas along your writing journey. Flirt with them. Sleep with them. But do not fall in love with them. Or if you do, don't promise them fidelity. Many writers cling foolishly to an idea, forsaking all others, though it fails them again and again. This is neither practical nor professional and it can lead to writing despair. There is a limitless supply of ideas once you open your mind to them. They are not so precious as you think and they should be discarded when they fail you. Only when you have executed an idea in a fresh and daring way is it precious.

Marketing. The writer who has latched onto an idea he cares about must ask himself who else would care. Who would want to read about it? Then he enters into a phase of his writing journey that is closer to science than to art: marketing his work. His primary marketing tools are common sense—and the book you are now reading. He uses the first to imagine the reader of his work, and the latter to find out who is publishing what for those readers. If the writer has written the story of a child caught in a blizzard, then the science fiction buffs who read *Isaac Asimov's Science Fiction Magazine* would not as a group be enthralled, but the mothers who read *Lady's Circle* and the children who read *Jack & Jill* might be. Do you want to write a profile of an 80-year-old deaf veteran in your community who teaches children to dance? His story might be of interest to the readers of *Modern Maturity, The Deaf Canadian Magazine, V.F.W. Magazine*, the local newspaper, and *Dance Scope*.

Though it is not so obvious to the layperson, the writer must know that book publishers, too, tend to focus on specific audiences of readers. Certainly there are the giants, like New American Library, that publish books on every subject; but far more numerous are the smaller publishers who seek a limited range of material, like Paladin Press, which publishes books on military science, weaponry and self-defense; and Broadman Press, which publishes only religious books.

Query. Once you have what you think is a good idea and an audience you're sure would like to read it, you must get an editor to agree with you. If you want to write an article, you can try to convince him with a query letter. In your query tell the editor:

● Your idea: *telephone conversations* (for example).

● Your slant, or special way of looking at the subject: *How telephone conversations are different from in-person conversations.*

● Why his readers would care: *The teenagers who read* Seventeen *conduct a good part of their social life by phone, and their failure to understand how the telephone affects voice tones and conversational dynamics often results in hurt feelings, misunderstandings, and missed opportunities to pursue relationships.*

● Why you are qualified to write the piece: *I am a freelance writer whose work has appeared in* The Louisville Courier, Louisville Today, Country Journal, Dynamic Years *and other national and regional magazines. I also spent three years working as a telephone operator.*

● Some of your sources: *My primary source for this piece will be Prof. Harold Wingley of the University of Kentucky's Social Science Center, who has made an extensive study of telephone conversational dynamics.*

Also include a suggested word length (though, if you get an assignment, the editor will probably suggest a word length of his own) and photo possibilities. If you have no writing credits, ignore the issue. Don't write something like, *I've never published anything, but I'm trying to break in as a freelancer.* That will only encourage the editor to reject you.

Your letter, in effect, is an application for a job. Just as you would be well-spoken and well-groomed for an in-person interview, make certain that your letter is carefully written and visually attractive. Also make it direct and brief—no more than a page, if possible. The editor has a lot to read and he appreciates succinctness.

Include a self-addressed stamped envelope with your query letter. Within six weeks you should receive one of three things:

● 1. A form or letter saying, *We're not interested.*

● 2. A letter saying, *We're interested. Would you please write the piece on specu-lation and send it to us?* (The editor is not committing himself to using it or paying you for your work if he doesn't, but if you write it well he'll probably buy it. Though this might seem unfair, the wise beginner will take the assignment, and write the piece as well as he possibly can.)

● 3. A letter saying, *We're interested. Please write it for us and if for some reason we don't use it, we will pay you a "kill fee"* (usually 20 percent of the purchase price) *and you will have the right to sell your article somewhere else.* This is as firm as a writing assignment gets. Take it.

For the writer of fiction or personal essays, no such scouting ahead is possible. The form and content of stories and essays are so hopelessly entwined that an editor cannot possibly tell the unproved writer he would like to publish a story or essay "about something." He must see it. If you have a story or essay to write, simply write it. Find an appropriate place to send it in *Writer's Market*, and send it with a self-addressed stamped envelope (SASE). If not purchased for publication, it will most likely come back with a form rejection slip, though sometimes you will get an en-couraging letter, or even some advice on improving the story for possible sale.

Rejection Slips. In any case it is important to remember that a form rejection slip cannot be interpreted to mean any one statement. Many writers look at a rejection slip and read, "You did a poor job," but it might be saying, "We just bought something similar," or "It's good, but we don't publish this sort of thing. Read your *Writer's Market* more carefully," or it's too long or too short or too technical or too topical or too liberal or too conservative, etc. If you want your writing judged, take it to someone who can judge writing—but don't let it be judged by a rejection slip that was printed before you even wrote the piece it's judging.

Bookwriting. Once a freelancer has survived his baptism by fire in magazine writing, he may itch to move on to books; more thoughtful, more lasting work than articles—and more steadily paying, providing they sell well. If so, you draw royalties over a long period of time, which is like money in the bank.

In the search for book ideas, timing is crucial. Today's fad may fade tomorrow. The trick, of course, is to anticipate tomorrow's lively interests.

Once you have a book idea in mind, try to measure its salability by:

● *Checking for similar books listed in the* Subject Guide to Books in Print. BIP is a standard reference tool in libraries. Don't wait for your editor to run the check. Know your competition beforehand, and slant your book to fill an editorial niche.

● *Reading* Publishers Weekly *assiduously*—particularly its book evaluations, PW Forecasts. If you read them regularly, you begin to see what the flow of ideas is, what's coming. And maybe your idea *is* unique.

● *Studying the publisher's catalog.* It's a handy guide to that house's personality and strengths.

Write a query to the publisher in which you state the name of your proposed project, a summary of its themes, its commercial value in the current book market, and your qualifications for writing it. The query should run about 1½ pages unless the subject is so complex it demands more. For a nonfiction book idea, add a proposed table of contents; for a work of fiction, add up to fifty pages of sample writing you have already done on the book. You may simultaneously submit your book proposal to several publishers if you feel it justifies quick publication. However, you must advise the editor accordingly in your cover letter: "I am submitting this project to several publishing houses simultaneously because of the timely nature of this project." If you are writing a novel, even if your sample fifty pages engage an editor, you may have to submit the completed novel to that same editor before the publishing house makes a decision. Publishers rarely give unknown novelists a contract without seeing the finished manuscript.

The consolidation of big publishing houses has pushed the agent into a role of increasing prominence in book manuscript decisionmaking. Many publishing houses no longer have "reading" departments—first readers whose job it is to plow through the unsolicited manuscripts looking for that rare over-the-transom gem. Instead, many of those readers are now agents, and publishing houses rely more on agents to prescreen the material from beginning or unknown writers. Therefore, if you can get an agent interested in handling your book idea or your book-length manuscript, you may have an edge that is worth the 10% or 15% of your proceeds from a book sale an agent will cost you. (See the section on **Authors' Agents** for more information on the agent's role in book marketing, and suggestions on how to get an agent to represent your work.)

Scriptwriting. Writing theatrical, film and TV scripts is a highly glamorous, and often highly lucrative field. But such writing is also among the most competitive of writing genres.

Of the three types of scriptwriting, playwriting offers the freelancer the easiest access and most opportunity. Every community has one or more theater groups—from children's theater companies to high school drama departments to semi-professional troupes—and most will consider original material. Regional professional theater is growing, and some of the best new plays in the country are premiering in such places as Louisville, Dallas and Minneapolis. New York's Broadway, however, remains at the top of the theatrical heap, and the top of every playwright's goal list.

Breaking onto the Broadway stage—or even the Off-Broadway stage—is a worthy dream, but only hard work, talent, familiarity with current theater, and a smidgeon of luck will accomplish that for you. Residence in New York helps, too. Therefore, it's best to work with community groups first, and work up. Check the **Scriptwriting** section of this book for more information on theater.

Whereas you can find playwriting opportunities in your hometown, opportunities in writing feature films and television scripts are virtually nonexistent unless you live in Los Angeles. Film and TV producers confer frequently with the writers they work with, making an L.A. location convenient and, often, essential. (However, opportunities in documentary/educational scriptwriting do not depend on a West Coast location.)

You can't simply sit down and write a television or film script and hope to sell it over the transom to a producer. Most if not all these scripts are sold through agents—and usually what is sold is not the script itself, but the idea for a script, which the writer develops into final form once he has the contract. Teleplays are rarely completed before the idea is approved.

The usual procedure for selling teleplays is this: The writer, through his agent, submits a "treatment," which is a synopsis of the proposed script. If he likes the treatment, the producer will commission the final script.

The procedure is often the same for screenplays, though many writers, through their agents, submit completed drafts.

In all types of scripts, form is important, because producers will deem scripts not typed in standard format to be amateurish. Check your local library for books on scriptwriting, and for published scripts. You can also study unpublished scripts by consulting the communications department of the local university, which may maintain archives of unpublished scripts and related material, or a special library of useful texts. For example, the UCLA Theater Arts Library (Room 22478, Research Library, UCLA, Los Angeles 90024) collects screenplays and TV scripts, as does the Wisconsin Center for Film and Theater Research (816 State St., Madison 53706), associated with the University of Wisconsin and the State Historical Society of Wisconsin.

L.A.-area writers can consult the Charles K. Feldman collection of the American Film Institute. The scripts aren't loaned off the premises and the library isn't open to the public, though writers, researchers, graduate students and members of the entertainment industry are welcome to use the materials. Materials can *not* be duplicated. Address: 2021 N. Western Ave., Los Angeles 90027.

Once you have completed your script, it is wise to register it with the Writers Guild of America. For details, contact the Guild at 8955 Beverly Blvd., Los Angeles 90048, or 555 W. 57th St., New York City 10019.

Short Fiction. Despite the license it affords the writer, fiction may require *more* market study than nonfiction does. The writer may have a passable grasp on the slant of, say, *Prehistoric Wordworking* after studying two issues; then he need only check back copies to see whether his story idea has been recently covered. But the would-be science fiction writer must read not only the magazines (and more than two issues a piece; as many, in fact, as he can get his hands on), but also the books: Bradbury, Clarke, Silverberg, Pohl and Kornbluth—all of them. It's the only way to discover what is new ground and what is as old as the stars; what will bring a check and an editorial shout, and what will bring a crisp note: "Heinlein was here thirty years ago." Even beyond that, editors and writers agree that to write great stories one must read great stories and develop a *wide* knowledge of contemporary literature.

Despite the workload—and the limited markets in major consumer magazines today—short stories are well worth tackling. The beginner is advised to check the literary and little magazine markets, which often encourage the fledgling writer and even offer personal criticism. The pay is sometimes erratic to negligible, but the opportunities are greater and include a large range of specialized subjects, interests, and styles. There are no set patterns for the creative and the innovative; the plotless short short or the prose poem may be just as acceptable as the plotted novella.

Submit your manuscripts (not queries) to as many publications as possible. If you can say you have published a few short stories, your manuscripts are more likely to be read and given consideration. Editors scout large and small magazines for new talent in short fiction, which may just lead to the sale of that novel in your drawer. Also, check *Fiction Writer's Market* (Writer's Digest Books) for how-to articles and hundreds of additional markets for fiction.

Poetry. Poetry pays poorly—or exceedingly well. Poets, unlike nonfiction and fiction writers, cannot play the market. Most of the magazines that matter in the career of a poet pay little or nothing beyond contributor's copies, and quality book publication usually pays nothing beyond a small advance, if that. Poets cannot depend upon their writing for economic support, though once their names are known, many derive some income from readings and related benefits.

Your best resource is a good bookstore with a rack of poetry magazines. There you can detect which poetry magazines publish poems similar in style to the free verse or traditional forms you write. Try to mail your poems, from the first, to the better poetry magazines; in the field of poetry, there is some snobbery and in-fighting between factions. If you start publishing poems in a good poetry magazine, it may be easier to get published by mentioning your credits to other magazines. You can also protect your ego from the rejections by keeping a minimum of fifty poems in the mails or in the unsolicited manuscript piles of poetry magazines. This blitz attack on poetry outlets was the practice of a poet who eventually had a book published in the Yale Series of Younger Poets. The few commercial successes in poetry (e.g., Rod McKuen, Ogden Nash) tend not to be taken seriously by the literary establishment. Many regard this as snobbism. Whether the situation is just or not, a poet should be aware of it. The most dependable markets for commercial poetry are greeting-card manufacturers and poster publishers. Some successful commercial poets have syndicated newspaper columns or contracts with popular magazines. Some combine their writing with singing or other forms of performance.

A beginning poet usually starts in the little literary magazines—of which there are dozens open to (some begging for) contributions from unknown writers. When he has a string of credits in such magazines, he may begin submitting book manuscripts to quality publishers or to the few contests of literary significance. Sometimes the life span of literary magazines is brief. Most pay nothing. They tend to be edited and published by dedicated individuals or groups who are passionately involved—as artists have always been—in the exciting current (and often ephemeral) trends in experimental writing. For regular announcements of reputable contests and good magazines and book publishers (as well as other information pertinent to poetry), subscribe to *Coda: Poets & Writers Newsletter*, 201 W. 54th St., New York City 10019—write for current subscription rates. As one reader put it, *Coda* is for poets (and other writers) what the *Wall Street Journal* is for bankers. Request *The Cultural Post* free from the

National Endowment for the Arts, Washington, D.C. 20506.

Fillers. Many publications buy filler items, which can be thought-provoking quotations, short verse or catchy sayings. Or they can be short nonfiction pieces of 100 to 750 words. A practical short feature of this type is a single idea, tightly written, telling the reader how to: a.) save time; b.) increase business; c.) do something more easily; d.) improve his personality; or e.) improve human relations. Your ideas can come from your own experiences as a gardener, national guardsman, hot rodder or expectant mother—the range is infinite. The biggest markets for fillers are popular mechanics-type publications, confession magazines, shelter publications, and hobby books.

Other fillers are written for entertainment or inspiration. They often consist of historical anecdotes, general interest items on unique people, business, and community programs, or humor. Many men's magazines buy "party" jokes. The religious press is the ideal starting marketplace for the inspirational filler. From there, you will find many other outlets.

When submitting fillers, double-space, regardless of the length of the piece. Type on full-size paper. Some editors don't return very short pieces because they get so many. Check the market listings carefully so you will know which ones they are. It is not necessary to enclose SASE with such submissions.

Pictures. Photographs are a powerful method of communication, and the writer who adds them to his article package is helping to guarantee sales that might otherwise be lost.

A single-lens reflex is one of the best types of cameras for the writer who wishes to take his own pictures for these reasons: You can get a good model for under $300; it is a camera which is easy to use; its system is such that many kinds of lenses can be used with it interchangeably; and faster lenses permit pictures in poorer available light.

When you start an assignment, work first as a writer. Gather your material and write your article. Then read your article, taking note of the picture possibilities. Go back and concentrate entirely on photography. Don't compromise the quality of the total package because of the time advantage in doing both photography and research at once.

Your pictures should illustrate the important points of the article. Compress your article's highlights into a few pictures. When taking them, don't be fancy. Try for straight, honest photographs without gimmicks. The simple presentation is not only the easiest, but, unless you are an expert, the most effective.

It is wise to send your films to a lab for processing. This way you avoid the expense of setting up a darkroom, you save time for writing, and you take advantage of the skills of technicians who have had years of experience in developing film. When you have a roll of 35mm film developed, ask the lab for a "contact sheet," from which you may select the photos you want enlarged. A contact sheet is a single 8x10 photo reproducing every shot on the roll in "miniature"—or negative size. Many writers enlarge a few good shots from a roll, and send the contact sheet to an editor for review as well. Editors will often find value in shots a writer may overlook.

Of course not all writers are photographers. If you don't care to take your own pictures, try to interest a good local freelance photographer in working with you on speculation. You'd get paid for text; he for pix.

Many public service agencies, public relations offices, and industrial companies offer good quality photos free to writers. These pictures are usually connected with some commercial venture or public service project, but are often well-suited for magazine and newspaper feature articles. Your best bet is to pick the association or firm dealing in some aspect of your article's subject and ask exactly what they have available. These photographs are often loaned, usually with a request for credit.

Pictures for publication should be brilliant in tone and contrast and sharply focused. Acceptable sizes range from 5x7 to 11x14, although there is no strict rule. Snapshot size is usually too small, although a few trade journal editors will accept Polaroid prints in special cases. Editors usually prefer 8x10 prints on glossy paper, although a smooth, nontextured paper is acceptable. Do not send tinted, toned or mounted prints. Color pictures should be submitted as transparencies and not as prints.

Research. To fortify his idea into a compelling story or an informative article, the writer needs information, facts. The acquisition of those facts is known as research, a term that is often intimidating to new writers, who feel inadequate because they have not penetrated secret rooms in big city libraries or peered through microscopes at major universities. But "doing research" really means nothing more than finding out facts, and that includes anything from opening a letter to telephoning a senator. The most complete, logical and accessible research tool you have is the local library. Use it often, and don't be afraid to ask a librarian for help. That's one of the things he gets paid for, and helping people like you find facts is often the most interesting part of his job.

But along your writing road you will find that libraries are only a small part of a world that is filled with research tools. There are companies, associations, clubs, and organizations of all sorts that are anxious to supply you with information on their specialty. There's the man down the street who's an expert on your subject. There's a guest on a talk show. Tape it or take notes. There's an article in the new issue of *Reader's Digest*; there's a feature in this morning's paper; there's your friend Linda who remembers a childhood incident involving your topic. Keep your eyes and ears open and you will be constantly doing research for articles and stories you haven't even thought of writing yet.

Though the nonfiction writer can rarely convince himself that he doesn't need to learn more about his subject, beginning fiction writers often overlook the value of research, thinking they are engaged in pure art which requires no facts to sustain it. But the fiction writer must do research. He is trying to convince the reader of a reality that is not there. With only black lines on white paper he must create a full-blown, three-dimensional world, and so he must paint that world in the most vivid and authentic colors. What were streetcars like in 1930? How would a man move after a hip operation? The fiction writer must watch, he must listen, and he, too, must lug those books home from the library.

Interviews. One of the most exciting aspects of your journey is that you will meet and interview hundreds of people along the way. You will drink coffee with them, you will learn from them, you will listen to their anger, their hope, their confusion, and you will give to them the opportunity to tell friends, "I know this writer."

For various reasons, the interviewer and the interviewee are almost always happy to see each other. And yet, as with the librarians, freelancers often think they are "bothering" somebody by asking for an interview. This uneasiness is often magnified when the interview subject is famous. But think for a moment: How many famous people don't grant interviews? A handful of ax murderers and a few reclusive writers is about it. The reason is that you can often define "famous person" as "someone who gets his name in the paper and magazines by granting interviews." So famous people need to grant interviews to continue being famous. And if the person you want to question is not famous, you are doing him a favor by asking for an interview. This might be his one chance in life to see his name in print.

Of course, not everybody you interview will show up in print. You interview people you are going to write about, but you also interview experts for information on the *subject* you are writing about. One interview with an expert can save you hours of reading—though background reading can save you hours of shallow interviewing and thin results. Best to blend both.

Getting an interview is a fairly straightforward business. Simply call up and ask. Tell the person what you want to talk about and why, how much time you need, and agree on a time and place. Then show up on time, well prepared, and friendly.

In addition to all these formal planned interviews for stories and articles, remember that every conversation you have is an interview. If you chit chat with a carpenter about his work this afternoon, and create a carpenter character in a story next year, it might be because you interviewed an expert. For in-depth tips and strategies on the wily craft of interviewing, see *The Craft of Interviewing*, by John Brady (Writer's Digest Books).

Money. Aside from that burning desire to communicate, the writer writes for another reason. Money. He wants to earn his living, or part of it, from putting words on paper.

Money is a trauma-ridden subject in general. For the writer it can be terribly confusing and deceptive. We are brought up to expect a consistent relationship between the amount of money we are paid, and the number of hours we have worked or the number of things we have produced. For the writer this logic does not apply. The writer can write for a week and get $20. He can write for three hours and get $850. In the first case, he feels drained. In the second, he might even feel guilty.

The levelheaded writer usually thinks of money as being generated by his entire being, by his totality, not by the specific amount of time he puts in on a specific assignment. After all, a writer could receive a thousand dollars for a reprint sale of an article without doing any work at all, except cashing the check. The writer's paycheck is affected by such a variety of factors—advertising revenue, magazine circulation, his own reputation, etc.—that he will only earn frustration if he tries to measure himself by the usual monetary yardsticks. As a writer in North Carolina observed: "I once was paid $500 for an hour of writing. Was I overpaid almost to the point of immorality, with people starving in the ghettos? No. I got the assignment in the first place because I had accumulated special knowledge in one area over a period of years. The $500 helped to pay for some of the time I put in acquiring that knowledge."

"How much do freelancers make?" the new writer often asks. Because of these strange economic factors, an average figure is meaningless. Most of the listings in this edition of *Writer's Market* include payment to writers. Read them. Get a sense of what's being offered. Then with each assignment and each submission decide whether the amount of work you have done or will do is worth the amount of money you will receive. Learn to ask for larger fees as your writing talents grow; and say no to editors who ask you to write for terms too low to lift your bank account (not to mention your self-esteem).

The Writing Life. Whether or not you have been paid for your writing, you are a writer if you write. You have begun the writing journey.

It is a journey that brings more rewards than most. It brings people, knowledge, money and fame in doses small and large. Few people in this world get to have their work admired by thousands, even millions of people, as the writer does.

But the writing journey is also fraught with emotional pain and piercing doubts not found in many other professions. Writing is a lonely business. It is generally done by one self-motivated person who must look out entirely for himself. Because writing is a glamor field, it draws to the writer not just the effusive praise that comes with success, but the sometimes chilling criticism inspired by failure: *You should have known you couldn't make a living as a writer. Who do you think you are, Ernest Hemingway?* The ego-stretching, required to begin such a journey in the first place, inevitably leads to a kind of self doubt that never haunts, say, a plumber. And writing is an intensely personal endeavor. Each piece of writing is different because of the writer whose hand and heart created it. The writer's work is much more wound up in who he is, his self-esteem, his identity, than is the work of, say, the man who drills holes in umbrella handles for a living.

In many ways the writer's world is constructed to reinforce insecurity, self-doubt, expectations of failure, and he must move forward forcefully to fight these negative influences.

Secretaries don't receive rejection slips.

Ministers don't have parishioners buttonholing them at the back of the church and saying, "Your sermon needs a little more development before it will be ready for this particular market."

Policemen are never told to make an arrest on speculation, with payment to come later if the defendant is found guilty.

It is beyond argument that writers, and artists in general, are not always treated fairly. They are a breed apart, and the penalties as well as the rewards for sticking to their art are out of proportion.

Let none of this slow you down or swerve you from the course you have chosen. Unlike other treks, the writer's journey is most arduous at the beginning. As you move along you will become familiar with the landscape, and you will acquire your pace and strengthen your muscles. The path will feel smoother. Difficulties will diminish. You will need talent, desire and knowledge on your journey. But the single most valuable quality you can bring with you is perseverance. The success of the journey lies most of all in your dogged determination to keep on keeping on.

Markets

Advertising Copywriting

Advertising copywriting was the entrée to the writing profession for several literary notables, among them F. Scott Fitzgerald, James Dickey and Joseph Heller. That is not to say that copywriting is fiction—or poetry. Writing and selling ad copy means writing copy that *sells*. It requires a willingness to do market research, possibly meet with the advertiser, then inform the consumer and motivate him to act in a positive way. Sometimes this is done in the space of a few seconds, as in the case of a TV spot; or it can occur over a period of months, as in a direct mail campaign.

If you are a beginning copywriter, it is unlikely that you will get assignments on the basis of a flashy business card. Instead, you'll need to do some work on speculation (without pay). In other words, familiarize yourself with the agency's accounts (through the *Standard Advertisers Directory*, the "Red Book"), and write some appropriately targeted ads to round out your portfolio. That's right—portfolio.

A portfolio is a notebook, a sample of actually produced ads you have created "on spec" as examples of the type of work you can do. Until you have actually had some ads produced, you will have to rely on this method of presenting your work. And remember, less is more, so compile your best work, not a book filled with mediocrity.

A phone call or letter to the agency you're interested in working with should be your first contact with the agency. Preferences will vary, so do consult the *WM* listing first.

If you have already had ads produced, a business card, résumé, samples and brochures may be sufficient presenting material for the creative director to make a hiring decision. On the other hand, the agency may decide they want to see more of your work in the form of your portfolio. Always be prepared to show it, and update it as you gain experience.

If you have never written ad copy, you will certainly be put to the test writing samples about products the agency represents. That's where research enters in. Find out as much as you can about the advertiser—talk to your reference librarian and find out what trade directories are available on advertising. Agencies look for basic competency in the English language and an expertise in their account areas. It's a real plus to have an innovative spirit—even if the product is a ball bearing.

Stay current by reading *Advertising Age*, the trade biweekly, and *Standard Rate & Data Services*. To familiarize yourself with the very specialized language of advertising, read Crain Books' *The Dictionary of Advertising Terms* and *Sell Copy*, by Webster Kuswa (Writer's Digest Books).

ADLER, SCHWARTZ INC., 140 Sylvan Ave., Englewood Cliffs NJ 07632. (201)461-8450. Creative Director: Peter Adler. Clients: automotive and industrial. Works with 3-5 local writers/year. Submit resume, samples and tearsheets for future assignments. Buys all rights. Does not return material.
Needs: Consumer magazines, direct mail, newspapers, radio and trade magazines. Arrange interview to show portfolio or query with samples. Pays by the job.

AMERICAN TALENTWORLD CO., 639 Teaneck Rd., Teaneck NJ 07666. (201)836-1530. Talent Director: Chip Miller. Clients: entertainment, motion pictures and television. Works with 4-6 local writers/year by phone, mail, etc. Submit resume, business card and samples for future assignments. Buys all rights. SASE.
Needs: Direct mail, 16mm films, newspapers, radio, television and trade magazines. Arrange interview to show portfolio or play demo tapes. Pays by the job.

AURELIO & FRIENDS, INC., 11110 SW 128th Ave., Miami FL 33186. (305)595-0723. Creative Directors: Aurelio and Nancy Sica. Clients: resorts, fashion, shopping centers, medical facilities, and retail. Works with 5-7 local and national writers/year. Submit resume, tearsheets and samples for future assignments. Buys all rights. SASE.
Needs: Brochures, consumer magazines, direct mail, newspapers, radio, television, and trade magazines. Query with resume of credits and samples. Pays by the job.

BAUERLEIN, INC., 615 Baronne St., New Orleans LA 70113. (504)522-5461. Chief Copywriter: Tom Voelker. Clients: mostly industry and finance. Works with 2 local and national writers/year. "Mr. Voelker will make arrangements to see New Orleans people. Out-of-towners can send resumes and/or samples." Submit resume, business card and samples for future assignments. Buys all rights. Free client list.
Needs: Brochures, annual reports and collateral material. Pays negotiable fee.

BB&W ADVERTISING, 1106 W. State St., Boise ID 83701. (208)343-2572. Creative Director: Jack Ewing. Clients: financial institutions, political, development companies, dairies, insurance companies, automotive sales/service, business and industry, entertainment, and copiers/word processors. Works with 4-6 writers/year—"mostly lyricists for jingles." Works with local and national writers by phone/mail. Submit résumé, business card, samples, and "reel-to-reel dubs with samples/lyrics if you also perform or announce," for future assignments. Buy all rights. SASE.
Needs: Consumer magazines, direct mail, 35mm films, foreign media, newspapers, radio, television and trade magazines. "Most of the above, however, are handled in-house." Query with samples, send material by mail for consideration, or submit portfolio or tapes for review. Payment "depends strictly upon talent of writer, amount of experience, and scope of job."
Tips: "Learn the English language well. Have at least 3 years' experience in writing advertising for agencies, radio stations, etc. Present a professional-looking portfolio and/or reel; have reasonable rates; be willing to wait patiently between assignments. We have little need for freelance writers at the present time. When we do employ them it is generally either as lyricists in conjunction with production facilities, or on short-term basis for special projects. Preference is usually given to those who can offer more than one skill, especially an announcer—quality voice, radio/television production experience, or graphic abilities. Freelancers should, however, keep trying us as future project may require the use of outside writers to a greater degree. And we're always interested in seeing the efforts of talented people."

JACK D. BERMAN CO., 50 E. 8th St., New York NY 10003. Creative Director: Jack D. Berman. Clients: "all kinds." Works with 10+ local and national writers/year by mail only. Submit samples for future assignments. Rights purchased vary. Does not return material.
Needs: Billboards, consumer magazines, direct mail, films, foreign media, newspapers, radio, television, and trade magazines. Query with samples. Pays variable fee.

BOZELL & JACOBS, INC., 2440 Embarcadero Way, Palo Alto CA 94303. (415)856-9000. Creative Director: C. Scott McSwain. Clients: primarily very technical computer and semi-conductor-related. Works with 1-10 local writers/year. Submit resume, brochure and tearsheets; "photocopies only, so we can keep them." Buys all rights.
Needs: Trade magazines and brochures, etc. Query with resume and samples. Pays negotiable fee "based on size and difficulty of the assignment."
Tips: "Be sure to show work where the consumer benefit surfaces above the technical jargon."

E.H. BROWN ADVERTISING AGENCY, INC., 20 N. Wacker Dr., Chicago IL 60606. (312)372-9494. Creative Director: Sheldon Wasserman. Clients: business and industry, data pro-

cessing, office equipment, life insurance, aviation aftermarket, and technical trade schools. Works with 3 local writers/year. Submit resume and samples for future assignments. Buys all rights. SASE.
Needs: Consumer magazines, direct mail, newspapers, radio and television. Pays by the job.

CANON & SHEA ASSOCIATES, INC., 31 E. 28th St., New York NY 10016. (212)683-0855. Creative Director: John E. Shea. Clients: industrial advertising/PR/marketing. Works with 15-20 local writers/year. Submit samples and brochure for future assignments. Buys all rights. Does not return material.
Needs: Trade magazines. Query with resume of credits; query with samples or send material for consideration. Pays by the hour, job or day.
Tips: "Know the industrial marketplace. Possibly have an engineering or technical background, particularly in material handling and building products."

CARTER ADVERTISING, INC., 1810 Elizabeth Ave., Shreveport LA 71101. (318)227-1920. Creative Director: Dan Baldwin. Clients: industrial, financial, business and retail. Works with 1-5 local and national writers/year by telephone and mail. Submit resume and samples for future assignments. Buys all rights. SASE.
Needs: Billboards, consumer magazines, direct mail, newspapers, radio, television, and trade magazines. Arrange interview to show portfolio or play demo tapes; or query with resume of credits. Pays flexible fee—"arrangements made according to nature of job, client, talent, etc."
Tips: "Make initial contact by letter with resume and samples; follow up with in-person interview if possible; stay in touch providing *carefully selected* samples for your file."

COPY OVERLOAD, (RE: JOHN BORDEN ADVERTISING AGENCY), 5841-73rd Ave., N, 102, Minneapolis MN 55429. (612)566-4515. Creative Director: James P. Richardson. Clients: business, industry, financial, recruitment for personnel departments. Works with 5 writers/year. Works with local writers only. Submit résumé, brochure and samples for future assignments. Buys all rights. SASE.
Needs: Consumer magazines, direct mail, newspapers, radio, trade magazines and client literature. Arrange a personal interview to show portfolio or play demo tapes, or send material by mail for consideration. Payment "depends on experience."

CUNDALL/WHITEHEAD ADVERTISING, INC., 3000 Bridgeway, Sausalito CA 94965. (415)332-3625. Creative Director: Alan Cundall. Clients: general consumer and business/industrial. Works with 10 writers/year. "Prefer local writers, but there could be exceptions." Submit resume and samples for future assignments. Buys all rights. SASE.
Needs: Consumer magazines, direct mail, films, newspapers, radio, trade magazines and collateral/brochures/AV. Arrange interview to show portfolio or play demo tapes. "Calling and discussing with us is the best way for us." Pays "by the job, usually, based on estimated number of hours we both agree it might take."
Tips: "Call and see if we have any needs at the moment. Then, send us a resume and samples, if any, which we will keep on file until such time as we have a need for freelance help."

DIEGNAN & ASSOCIATES, RD 2, Lebanon NJ 08833. (201)832-7951. Clients: business and industry. Works with 6 local and national writers/year. Submit brochure, flyer, tearsheets and samples for future assignments. SASE.

THE DR GROUP, 10 Post Office Square, Boston MA 02109. Senior Vice President/Creative Director: Brian Turley. Clients: industry, finance, and publishing. Large, fulltime copy and art staff. Very seldom need freelance assistance. Free client list.

DANIEL J. EDELMAN, INC., 1730 Pennsylvania Ave., NW, Washington DC 20006. (202)393-1300. Contact: John Meek or Pat Pellerin. PR firm. Clients: trade associations, foreign manufacturers and foreign governments. Works with 3-4 writers/year.
Needs: Newspapers, trade magazines, and brochure copy. Query with resume of credits and "copy letter explaining freelance status." Pays daily or weekly sum.

EVANS WYATT ADVERTISING, 3833 S. Staples St., Corpus Christi TX 78411. (512)854-1661. Creative Director: E. Wyatt. Clients: business, industry, retail, general. Works with 12 local writers/year by mail and phone. Submit resume, business card, brochure, flyer, tearsheets and samples; "any and all" for future assignments. Buys all rights. SASE.
Needs: Billboards, consumer magazines, direct mail, films, foreign media, newspapers, radio,

television, and trade magazines. Arrange interview to show portfolio or play demo tapes. Pays by the job.
Tips: "Prepare yourself for a full-scale interview in all respects—total time: 15 minutes."

MICHAEL FAIN ADVERTISING, 156 5th Ave., New York NY 10010. (212)243-6825. Creative Director: M. Fain. Clients: industrial accounts (hard goods). Works with 1-2 local writers/year. Submit resume, business card, and samples for future assignments. Buys all rights. Does not return material.
Needs: Consumer magazines, direct mail, newspapers, and trade magazines. Query with resume of credits. Pays $25-200/job.
Tips: "Have experience and knowledge of accounts in the industrial field."

FRYE-SILLS, INC., Division of Young & Rubicam, 5500 S. Syracruse Circle-Englewood, Denver CO 80110. (303)773-3900. Contact: Creative Director. Clients: financial, industrial, general consumer. Works with 2-3 primarily local writers/year. Free client list.
Needs: Consumer magazines, films, foreign media, newspapers, radio, television, trade magazines and collateral. "Phone the Creative Director and ask if you can send a resume and inquire about what jobs maybe coming up, etc."

GOODWIN, DANNENBAUM, LITTMAN & WINGFIELD, 7676 Woodway, Houston TX 77063. (713)977-7676. Creative Director: Cliff Gillock. Clients: retail, industrial, real estate, and financial. Works with 2-3 local writers/year. Submit samples for future assignments. Buys all rights. SASE.
Needs: Brochures and sales materials. Arrange interview to show portfolio or play demo tapes. Pays negotiable fee.

THE GRAPHIC EXPERIENCE, INC., 341 Madison Ave., New York NY 10017. (212)867-0806. Creative Director: John Marinello. Clients: direct response, consumer goods, publications and business to business. Works with approximately 10 local writers/year. Submit samples for future assignments. Buys all rights. SASE.
Needs: Consumer magazines, direct mail and catalogs. Send material for consideration. Pays by the job.

GREENSTONE & RABASCA ADVERTISING, One Huntington Quadrangle, Melville NY 11746. (516)249-2121. Creative Director: Jack Schultheis. Clients: industrial and consumer. Works with 5-6 local and national writers/year. Free client list.
Needs: Billboards, direct mail, newspapers, radio, and trade magazines. Query with resume and samples. Pays by the hour and job.

THE GRISWOLD-ESHLEMAN CO., 55 Public Square, Cleveland OH 44113. (216)696-3400. Associate Creative Director: Mike Atwell. Clients: consumer and industry. Works with 1-2 local ("sometimes others") writers/year. Free client list.
Needs: Direct mail and collateral. Query with samples. Pays negotiable fee.

HEPWORTH ADVERTISING CO., 3403 McKinney Ave., Dallas TX 75204. (214)526-7785. Creative Director: S.W. Hepworth. Clients: banks, insurance, stock brokers and industrial metal working. Works with variable number of local writers/year; "others considered." Submit business card and samples for future assignments.

IMAGE DYNAMICS, INC., 1101 N. Calvert St., Suite 1406, Baltimore MD 21202. (301)539-8555. Creative Director: Jenny Kline. Clients: bank, hotels, restaurants, beverage distributor, cemetery, hospital, etc. Works with 1-5 local writers/year. Free client list.
Needs: Consumer magazines, direct mail, newspapers, radio, television, trade magazines and public relations. Call Ms. Kline to find out what material she wants sent in. Pay "depends on job."

GEORGE JOHNSON, ADVERTISING, 755 New Ballas Rd., S., St. Louis MO 63141. (314)569-3440. Creative Director: George Johnson. Clients: financial, fast food, drug evaluation publication, real estate, brake and carburetor repair parts, pollution control devices, political, etc. Works with 1-2 local writers/year. Submit resume, samples and "a letter stating personal objective(s)" for future assignments. Buys all rights. SASE.
Needs: Billboards, consumer magazines, direct mail, newspapers, radio, television, trade magazines and audiovisual presentations. Query with resume of credits. Pays by the job. "Amount paid depends entirely on our ideas of value of the work to our client."
Tips: "Quality of work continues to deteriorate. We see fewer free spirits, fewer landmark ideas. Everybody seems to be playing it safe."

F. SCOTT KIMMICH & CO., 17 Washington St., South Norwalk CT 06854. Contact: Don Brown, copy chief, or President. Clients: pharmaceutical only. Works with 5-6 writers/year. Buys all rights "usually." Free client list.
Needs: Direct mail and technical (scientific and medical) magazines. Prefers letter before phone contact. Pays by the hour; day; or job, depending upon the particular job.

KLEMTNER ADVERTISING, INC., 1185 Avenue of the Americas, New York NY 10036. (212)869-8200. Creative Director: Fred Mann. Clients: pharmaceutical only. Works with 5-6 writers/year. Free client list.
Needs: Direct mail, films, foreign media, monographs, salesmen's visual aids, "and may rarely use writer in a campaign." Query with resume first, then follow up with phone call to show portfolio. Pays by the hour or by the project, "depending on job."

MANDABACH & SIMMS, 20 N. Wacker, Chicago IL 60606. (312)236-5333. Creative Director: Burt Bentkover. Copy Director: Art Clifton. Clients: business, industry, the nation's largest food service, finance and graphic arts. Works with 4 local writers/year. Submit resume, business card and "photocopies of best work" for future assignments. Buys all rights. Does not return material "unless requested." SASE.
Needs: Billboards, consumer magazines, direct mail, 16mm films, newspapers, radio, television, and trade magazines. Arrange interview to show portfolio or play demo tapes. Pays by the job.

LLOYD MANSFIELD CO., INC., 900 Main-Seneca Bldg., Buffalo NY 14203. (716)854-2762. Vice President: Norwood T. Smith. Clients: business, industry, commerical, consumer, and retail. Works with 3-4 writers/year. Works with local and national writers by "mail, phone and occasional contract." Submit resume, tearsheets and samples for future assignments. Buys all rights. SASE.
Needs: Consumer magazines, films, brochures, folders, and articles. Arrange interview to show portfolio or play demo tapes. "We prefer first contact by phone or mail." Pays $15-60/hour; $100 minimum/job.
Tips: "There is a need for very flexible, multi-purpose writing abilities, i.e., writers who are writers *first* and specialists *second* and can handle varied writing assignments."

MARKETAIDE, Box 1645, The United Building, 8th Floor, Salina KS 67401. (913)825-7161. Creative Director: Russ Norwood. Production Manager: Walter Hern. Clients: agricultural, industrial and financial. Works with "very few" freelance writers/year. Works with local writers only. Submit resume, business card, tearsheets and samples for future assignments. Buys various rights, "depending on job." SASE. Does not return material.
Needs: Features a "marketing-oriented program, market research, and direct mail services." Direct mail, foreign media, newspapers, radio, television, trade magazines—"virtually any media." Send material for consideration. Pay is "negotiated on a per-job basis."

MOLNER & COMPANY ADVERTISING, INC., 21500 Greenfield Rd., Oak Park MI 48237. (313)968-2770. Creative Director: Bob Molner. Clients: financial, industrial and retail. Works with 3-5 writers/year. Works with local and national writers by "mail, phone or facsimile." Submit resume, brochure, tearsheets and samples for future assignments. Buys all rights. Does not return material.
Needs: Direct mail, 16mm films, foreign media and television. Query with resume of credits. Pays $25 minimum/job.

NATIONWIDE ADVERTISING SERVICE, 1900 W. Loop South, Houston TX 77027. (713)960-8008. Creative Director: Frank Rouser. Clients: various. "We specialize in recruitment advertising only." Submit business card for future assignments. Buys all rights. SASE. Works with 2-3 writers/year.
Needs: Billboards, direct mail, newspapers, trade magazines, brochures, catalogs, and posters. Query with resume of credits and samples. Pays by the job.

NEWMARKS ADVERTISING AGENCY, 183 Madison Ave., New York NY 10016. (212)725-7200. Creative Director: Al Wasserman. Clients: business, industry, resort. Works with 3-4 local writers/year. Submit resume and samples for future assignments. Does not return material.
Needs: Billboards, consumer magazines, direct mail, 16mm films, foreign media, newspapers, radio, television, and trade magazines. Query with samples. Pays $200 minimum/day; $75 minimum/job; pay "depends on extent of job."
Tips: "Avoid the temptation to be too 'cute' at the sacrifice of content."

OGILVY & MATHER, INC., 2 E. 48th St., New York NY 10017. (212)688-6100. Administrative Supervisor of the Creative Department: Mary Mahon. Clients: various. Works with 4-5 writers/year. Free client list.
Needs: Consumer magazines, direct mail, films, newspapers, radio, television, and trade magazines. Phone first, then drop off samples for review. Pays by the day.

PRINGLE DIXON PRINGLE, 3340 Peachtree Rd., NE, Atlanta GA 30326. (404)261-9542. Creative Director: Mike Hutchinson. Clients: fashion, finance, fast food, industry. Works with 3-4 local writers/year. Free client list.
Needs: Billboards, consumer magazines, direct mail, films, newspapers, radio, television, and trade magazines. Arrange interview to show portfolio or play demo tapes. Pays by the hour.

PRO/CREATIVE COMPANY, 25 W. Burda, Spring Valley NY 10977. Creative Director: D. Rapp. Clients: package goods, publications, financial, sports, and entertainment. Works mostly with local writers. Submit rates, resume, business card and photocopies of samples for future assignment. SASE.
Needs: Consumer magazines, direct mail, newspapers, radio, trade magazines and P-O-P displays. Query with resume of credits. Pays by the hour or by the job—"varies with the client and the project."

THE RUSS REID CO., 80 S. Lake Ave., Pasadena CA 91101. (213)449-6100. Vice President/Creative Director: Gary Evans. Clients: religious and cause-related organizations. Works with 5 writers/year.
Needs: Direct mail, television scriptwriting and fundraising. Query with resume of credits. "We have a set fee for direct mail package and a set fee for TV script package, depending upon package."

RFM ASSOCIATES, INC., 35 Atkins Ave., Trenton NJ 08610. (609)586-5214. Creative Director: Rodney F. Mortillaro. Clients: retail and industrial. Works with 50 local writers/year. Submit business card and samples for future assignments. Does not return material.
Needs: Billboards, consumer magazines, direct mail, newspapers, radio, and trade magazines. Send material by mail for consideration. Pays $25-300/job.
Tips: "Get the reader to respond, buy or take action no matter what media is used."

ROSS ROY OF CANADA, LTD., 2 Carlton St., Toronto 2, Ontario, Canada. (416)977-2270. Vice President/General Manager: Robert Hobbs. Clients: beverage and alcohol. Works with 4 writers/year. Free client list.
Needs: Consumer magazines, direct mail, newspapers, trade magazines, and PR releases and/or promotional material. Pays by the hour or by the day. "Even when we pay by the day, it is calculated on an hourly basis."

JOE SNYDER & COMPANY, LTD., 155 W. 68th St., New York NY 10023. (212)595-5925. Creative Director: Joe W. Snyder. Clients: Fortune 500s. Works with "several" writers/year. Works with local writers only. Submit resume and brochure for future assignments. Buys all rights. SASE.
Needs: Direct mail, films, newspapers, and trade magazines. Send material by mail for consideration. Pays by the job.

J.J. SPECTOR & ASSOCIATES, 2900 N.E. 30th St., Ft. Lauderdale FL 33306. (305)563-4093. President/Creative Director: Julius J. Spector. Publishing-insurance-services-all things sold by "direct response in direct mail and mail order. We are direct response specialists—designers, creators, and writers of direct mail packages." Works with local and national writers by mail. Submit resume, business card, brochure, flyer, tearsheets and samples for future assignments. Buys all rights. Does not return material unless accompanied by SASE.
Needs: Consumer magazines, direct mail, newspapers, radio, television, and trade magazines. Send material by mail for consideration. Pays $100-1,000/job.
Tips: "Send samples of sales letters and direct mail packages written and produced."

NEAL SPELCE ASSOCIATES/MANNING, SELVAGE & LEE, Box 1905, Austin TX 78767. (512)476-4644. Creative Director: Hank T. Smith. Clients: trade associations, real estate, financial institutions, professional offices and retailers. Works with 1-2 local writers/year by phone. Submit resume, business card, and samples for future assignments. Buys all rights. SASE.
Needs: "We try to give a strong conceptual mailing to every job." Consumer magazines, direct mail, 16mm films, foreign media, newspapers, radio, television, and trade magazines. Query with resume of credits and samples. Pays $250-1,500/job.

VANGUARD ASSOCIATES, INC., 15 S. Ninth St., Minneapolis MN 55402. (612)338-5386. Creative Director: Ira Frank. Clients: fashion, food, packaging and government. Free client list. **Needs:** "We use writers in 2 ways: 1) call in at the beginning of the project and then do writing on all media; and 2) assign work on a specific job basis—usually newspapers or brochures. Local people can arrange personal interview; out-of-towners can send samples." Pays by the job.

VINYARD & LEE & BRIDWELL ADVERTISING, 7701 Clayton Rd., St. Louis MO 63117. (314)725-2277. Creative Director: Rick L. Anello. Clients: various. Works with a variable number of writers/year. Works with local and national writers by phone or mail. Submit resume, business card, and samples for future assignments. Buys all rights. SASE. **Needs:** Billboards, consumer magazines, direct mail, films, foreign media, newspapers, radio, television, and trade magazines. Send material by mail for consideration. Pays on the basis of "individual project by project arrangement."

H. WILSON COMPANY, 555 W. Taft Dr., South Holland IL 60473. (312)339-5111. Creative Director: B.J. Bond. Clients: business and industry. Works with 6 local writers/year. Submit resume, brochure, flyers, tearsheets and samples for future assignments. Buys all rights. SASE. **Needs:** Consumer magazines, direct mail, foreign media, and trade magazines. Query with samples. Pays by the job. **Tips:** "There is a trend toward more concise and creative direct mail packages, and more efficient copy for smaller space ads. Do some homework on the company and its marketplace before presenting ideas."

WOMACK/CLAYPOOLE/GRIFFIN, 2997 LBJ Business Park, Dallas TX 75234. (214)620-0300. Art Director: Matthew Gleason. Clients: petroleum, aviation, finance, insurance and retailing. Works with 24 writers/year. **Needs:** Billboards, newspapers, collateral and print material. Query with samples, "then Mr. Gleason will contact freelancer if interested." Pays by the hour or by the job.

Book Publishers

Book publishing enjoys good health despite escalating production costs and other economic problems that plague the industry. Sales for nonfiction and fiction are up over last year in both specialty and general publishing. All this bodes well for the writer—*if* you have the right manuscript for the right editor.

Before you roar off into the gilt-edged sunset, however, you need more than simply a professionally prepared manuscript. To ensure your manuscript's survival beyond the mail drop, run a safety check. Does it have a fresh point of view (for nonfiction)? Compelling characters (for fiction)? Will it stand the test of time? Have you enclosed adequate postage and a mailer large enough to handle the manuscript? If you answered "no" to any of these questions, get ready for the inevitable rejection slip.

The best way to reduce manuscript rejection is to conduct adequate market research *before you write the first paragraph of your book*. Read the "trades": *Library Journal* and *Publishers Weekly* (look for fall and spring announcement issues listing upcoming titles, available in February and September, respectively). A trip to the library can save future anguish. Check *Subject Guide to Books in Print* for already-published titles that yours might duplicate. If reading the listings that follow reveals that the publisher will supply you a book catalog, write for it—and study it.

Make sure your subject matter is neither too narrow, nor too autobiographical—unless, of course, your name is Prince Charles.

Keep your proposal focused, whether you're writing a complete manuscript or an outline and sample chapters. Don't keep the editor guessing. A table of contents, along with brief chapter descriptions in outline form, is more useful than a free-floating list of two-word chapter headings that *you* think is self-explanatory. And pay attention to the submission method preferred by the individual editor, as expressed in the following listings. If an editor asks for a synopsis/outline, don't send 60,000 words.

A synopsis should summarize the chapters of the book you're proposing, and tell what you hope the book will accomplish. One to two pages should do the job.

If a query is called for instead, state your proposal in one and a half pages or less, describe your related background, describe your target audience, and explain how close you are to completing the manuscript.

To further improve your manuscript's chances, take a critical look at it. Editors note that manuscripts are often rejected because they simply are not ready for publication. They lack the authority that research gives them, or, in the case of novels, they are poorly plotted with unconvincing characters. Ask a published writer/friend to read the manuscript and offer constructive criticism.

Summing up, don't send your manuscript out before its time. No editor wants to be burdened with a book that needs work in order to be published. That editor cannot persuade a marketing director or a publisher to buy your manuscript if you have not done your homework or have not developed a story that moves the reader.

Some other points: Avoid turning into a book or novel the idea that really belongs in a magazine article or short story. If your subject pertains to the concession business at the Indianapolis 500, for example, better interest a magazine editor in it, rather than a book publisher.

If you have published articles, books, short stories or poems, you may want to interest an agent in representing you to a publisher. See the Authors' Agents section for some possibilities.

Although forecasting trends is risky, there are a few directions some publishing houses have taken in the last year or so that are worth mentioning (and perhaps you'll want to consider these in focusing your manuscript).

- Computer technology developments have increased the need for books about home computing and computer management.
- Educational publishers are seeking more manuscripts for both specialized and general audiences, with an eye to improved bookstore sales.
- Historical Biblical fiction and problem-solving nonfiction are on the rise in religious publishing circles.
- In adult fiction, interest in contemporary fiction continues. Genre fiction needs change regularly. Follow writers club newsletters and *Writer's Digest* and *Publishers Weekly* for regular reports.
- Movement is away from children's and young adult fiction that concentrates on problems, and is toward humorous realism. Young adult romantic fiction has received favorable responses recently. Interest in picture books is declining. Publishers rely on reprints more and more in this category.
- Special markets—including those covering medical, science, health and natural health topics—offer opportunity to qualified authors.
- Publishers are increasingly concerned with finding the "big book" that can head the bestseller lists—and command a higher cover price (*big*, meaning 100,000-200,000 words). The marginal "little" book has lost its appeal to many commercial publishers. See individual listings for variations, and *Fiction Writer's Market* (Writer's Digest Books) for requirements of small-press publishers.
- Fewer unsolicited manuscripts are sought, with some exceptions. Staffs are getting smaller, and they cannot handle the bulk of unsolicited manuscripts. Consult individual *WM* listings for further guidelines.

A&P BOOKS, A division of The Atlantic & Pacific Commerce Co., Inc., 8105 Edgewater Dr., Oakland CA 94621. Chief Editor: Dee Lillegard. Publishes hardcover and paperback originals (90%) and reprints (10%). Averages 41 + titles/year. Pays 4-16% royalty "depending upon marketing methods used. Advances paid before or on date of publication." Simultaneous and photocopied submissions OK. SASE. Reports in 4 weeks. Free book catalog.
Nonfiction: Animals; health; how-to; juveniles; recreation; history and travel. "We specialize in top quality children's books." Submit outline/synopsis and sample chapters.
Recent Nonfiction Title: *The Amazing Fact Books* (12 volumes).
Fiction: Children's books, picture story books, plays and poetry. Submit outline/synopsis and sample chapters; or complete manuscript.
Recent Fiction Title: *According to Amos*, by Ginny Benson.

A & W PUBLISHERS INC., 95 Madison Ave., New York NY 10016. (212)725-4970. Imprints include A&W Visual Library and Gallahad Books. Executive Editor: Carolyn Trager. Publishes hardcover and paperback originals (80-90%) and hardcover and paperback reprints (10-20%). Published 50 titles in 1980, 50 in 1981; plans 60 in 1982. Pays standard royalty; offers variable advance. Simultaneous and photocopied submissions OK. SASE. Reports in 1 month. Free book catalog.
Nonfiction: Beauty, fitness, child care, humor, women's interest, financial advice and self-help. Needs include all areas of general nonfiction. Preferably submit complete ms; outline/synopsis and sample chapters are acceptable. "Do not send photos or artwork that are irreplaceable."
Recent Nonfiction Titles: *Image Impact, Getting Rich* and *Lasting Relationships*.
Fiction: Mainstream. Needs trade books of general interest. Submit complete ms.

AARON PUBLISHERS, INC., Box 2572, Sarasota FL 33578. (813)365-6212. President: Kenneth Matthews. Estab. 1979. Publishes mass market paperback originals. Averages 4 titles/year. Pays 12% minimum royalty on wholesale price; no advance. Simultaneous submissions and photocopied submissions OK. SASE. Reports in 2 weeks on queries; 3 weeks on mss.
Nonfiction: Biography, cookbook, how-to, history and nature. Subjects include animals, art, cooking and foods and recreation. "Florida community histories, Florida animals and wildlife." No mss on "anything without a Florida interest." Query.

Recent Nonfiction Titles: *The Unlikely Legacy*, by Mathews/McDevit (history); and *Florida Birds*, by Hewitt (bird guide).

ABBEY PRESS, St. Meinrad IN 47577. (812)357-8011. Editor: John T. Bettin. Publishes original paperbacks. Averages 14 titles/year. Pays variable royalty on wholesale or retail price; offers variable advance. Query with outline and sample chapter. Reports in 3 weeks. SASE.
Nonfiction: "Primarily books aimed at married and family life enrichment."
Recent Nonfiction Titles: *When Your Marriage Goes Stale*, by James and Mary Kenny; *When Your Teenager Stops Going to Church*, by James J. DiGiacomo; and *When You Are a Single Parent*, by Robert DiGiulio.

ABC-CLIO, INC., 2040 A.P.S., Santa Barbara CA 93103. (805)963-4221. Associate Editor: Elizabeth McNamara. Acting Publisher: Myrt Leimer. Publishes hardcover originals (95%) and paperback reprints (5%). Averages 15-20 titles/year. Pays 10-12% royalty on retail price; no advance. Photocopied submissions OK. Reports in 2 months. SASE. Free book catalog.
Nonfiction: Guides, reference books, bibliographies in the field of history and political science (specifically in ethnic studies, war/peace issues, comparative and international politics, women's studies, environmental studies, library science—acquisition guides, collection guides for the reference librarian, or for the el-hi market). Mss on comparative politics should be forwarded directly to the series editor, Prof. Peter H. Merkl; bibliographies on war/peace issues may be forwarded to Prof. Richard D. Burns; reference guides may be forwarded to Gail Schlachter. Query or submit outline/synopsis and sample chapters.
Recent Nonfiction Titles: *World Hunger: A Guide to the Economic and Political Dimensions*, by Nicole Ball; *U.S. Diplomats in Europe, 1919-1945*, by K. Paul Jones; and *Guide to the History of American Foreign Relations*, by Richard D. Burns.

ABINGDON PRESS, 201 8th Ave. S., Nashville TN 37202. (615)749-6403. Editorial Director: Ronald P. Patterson. Managing Editor: Robert Hill Jr. Senior Editor/Professional Resources: Paul M. Pettit. Senior Editor/Reference Resources: Carey J. Gifford. Editor of Lay Resources: Mary Ruth Howes. Editor of Academic Resources; Pierce S. Ellis Jr. Editor of Children Resources: Ernestine Calhoun. Publishes paperback originals and reprints. Published 120 titles last year. Pays royalty. Query with outline and samples. Write for ms preparation guide. Reports in 6 weeks. SASE.
Nonfiction: Religious-lay and professional, children's books and academic texts. Length: 32-200 pages.
Recent Nonfiction Titles: *Introduction to Old Testament Study*, by J. Hayes; *Contagious Congregation*, by G. Hunter (evangelism); and *If I Were Starting My Family Again*, by J. Drescher.
Fiction: Juveniles only.
Recent Fiction Titles: *A Sweetheart for Valentine*, by L. Balian (baby adopted by entire village); and *The Devil's Workshop*, by K. Marcuse (historical fiction about Johann Gutenberg).
Tips: "A short, pithy book is ahead of the game. Long, rambling books are a luxury few can afford."

HARRY N. ABRAMS, INC., 110 E. 59th St., New York NY 10022. (212)758-8600. Subsidiary of Times Mirror Co. Editor-in-Chief/Executive Vice President: Paul Gottlieb. Publishes hardcover and "a few" paperback originals. Published 65 titles in 1979; 60 in 1980; plans 60 in 1981. "We are one of the few publishers who publish almost exclusively illustrated books. We consider ourselves the leading publishers of art books and high quality artwork in the US." Offers variable advance. Prefers no simultaneous submissions; photocopied submissions OK. SASE. Reports in 3 months. Free book catalog.
Nonfiction: Art, nature and science and outdoor recreation. Needs illustrated books for art and art history, museums. Submit outline/synopsis and sample chapters.
Recent Nonfiction Titles: *Broadway Musicals* (an illustrated survey); *Jacques Cousteau-The Ocean World*, by J. Cousteau (photo-educational); and *Gnomes*, by Poortuliet (bestseller).

ABT BOOKS, Subsidiary of Abt Associates, Inc., 55 Wheeler St., Cambridge MA 02138. (617)492-7100. Editor-in-Chief: Robert Erwin. Publishes hardcover and trade paperback originals. Averages 20 titles/year. Pays 10-20% royalty on receipts; offers negotiable advance. Photocopied submissions OK. SASE. Reports on queries in 3 weeks; 2 months on mss. Free book catalog.
Nonfiction: Technical, textbook, social science and public affairs. Subjects include business and economics, health, politics, psychology, sociology and research methods. "Social policy studies based on extensive research; how-to books on research methods; and business strategy. Our readers are professional and business groups with the 'need to know'; e.g., how housing programs work, how to conduct survey research, how to meet the public-involvement requirements under

state and federal law." No belles-lettres. Submit outline/synopsis and sample chapters.
Recent Nonfiction Titles: *The Winding Passage*, by Daniel Bell (social theory); *On Social Welfare*, by Henry Aaron (national policy); and *Overhead*, by Jack Fultz (business practice).

ACADEMIC PRESS, INC., 111 5th Ave., New York NY 10003. (212)741-6836. Editorial Vice President: E.V. Cohen. Pays variable royalty. Publishes over 400 titles/year. Reports in 1 month. SASE.
Nonfiction: Specializes in scientific, mathematical, technical and medical works. Textbooks and reference works only in natural, behavioral-social sciences at college and research levels. Submit outline, preface and sample chapter.
Recent Nonfiction Titles: *Handbook of Optical Holography*, by Caulfield; *Millimeter and Submillimeter Waves*, by Button; and *Ion Implementation*, edited by J. Hironen (materials science).

ACADEMY CHICAGO LIMITED, (formerly Academy Press Limited), 360 N. Michigan Ave., Chicago IL 60601. (312)782-9826. Editorial Director/Senior Editor: Anita Miller. Publishes hardcover and paperback originals (35%) and reprints (65%). Publishes 10 titles/year. Pays 7-10% royalty; no advance. Photocopied submissions OK. Reports in 4 weeks. SASE.
Nonfiction: "We are interested in feminist books: children's and adult; travel, historical, etc." No how-to, cookbooks, self-help, etc. Query or submit sample chapters. "Do *not* send whole books."
Recent Nonfiction Titles: *Masquerade: An Adventure in Iran*, by Sarah Hobson; *Flaubert in Egypt*, edited and translated by Francis Steegmuller; and *Forbidden Sands*, by Robert Tunsh (trip across the Sahara).
Fiction: "We would consider mysteries with one detective for series." No "romantic" fiction, or religious or sexist material; nothing avant-garde.
Recent Fiction Titles: *They Hanged My Saintly Belly*, by Robert Graves; *Case for Three Detectives*, by Leo Bruce; and *Pelican Rising*, by Elizabeth North (a wry look at an English marriage).
Tips: "We are very interested in good nonfiction history and biography."

ACCENT BOOKS, a division of Accent Publications, 12100 W. 6th Ave., Box 15337, Denver CO 80215. (303)988-5300. Managing Editor: Mrs. Edith Quinlan. Publishes evangelical Christian paperbacks targeted to the average man or woman. "This person may have problems and concerns for which he is seeking a solution." Pays royalty on retail price. "Manuscripts for Accent must be written out of a personal relationship with Christ." SASE. Reports in 2 months. Free author's information sheet.
Nonfiction: Biography, how-to, self-help, marriage and family, other contemporary subjects, written in easy-to-read style containing Christian message and offering help to people in troubled specific areas. All mss considered must appeal to the contemporary reading public while maintaining Christian standards. Submit outline/synopsis and sample chapters or complete ms.
Recent Nonfiction Titles: *Taking Charge*, by Gordon N. McMinn with Larry Libby (the dynamics of personal decision making and self management); and *How to Handle Life's Hurts*, by James A. Nelson.
Fiction: All fiction must be developed out of a contemporary, conservative Christian point of view, presenting Jesus Christ or Biblical teachings as ultimate solution to contemporary problems. No poetry, children's stories, science fiction or Biblical novels. Query. Submit outline/synopsis and sample chapters or submit complete ms.
Recent Fiction Titles: *Search for the Avenger*, by Lee Roddy (historical Hawaiian adventure and intrigue); and *Cult Sunday*, by William D. Rodgers.

ACE BOOKS, Editorial Department, 51 Madison Ave., New York NY 10010. Publishes paperback originals and reprints. "Terms vary; usually on royalty basis." Published more than 200 titles last year. Fiction only. Query with detailed outline. "Do not send completed manuscripts." Reports in 4-8 weeks. SASE.
Fiction: Contemporary romance, western, science fiction and action/adventure. Length: 75,000-140,000 words. Recently published *The Magic Goes Away*, by Larry Niven; and *The Masquers*, by Natasha Peters.

ACE TEMPO BOOKS, A Division of Grosset and Dunlap, 51 Madison Ave., New York NY 10010. (212)689-9200. Executive Editor: Ms. Sarah Ashman. Editor: Ms. Kathy O'Hehir. Sports Editor: Ms. Wendy Wallace. Publishes hardcover and paperback originals. Averages 90 titles/year. Pays 6-8% royalty on retail price; also buys manuscript for outright purchase: $1,000+. Average advance. Simultaneous and photocopied submissions OK. SASE. Reports in 1 month.
Nonfiction: Biography, humor and sports for ages 12 and up. "Please, only popular nonfiction. No bios of George Washington." Submit outline/synopsis and sample chapters.
Recent Nonfiction Titles: *Bill Adler's All-Time Great Classic Letters From Camp*, by B. Adler; and

Something for Nothing (Great Giveaways for Teen Age Girls), by Betty Lou Phillips and Roblyn Herndon (catalog).

Fiction: Contemporary romances and problem novels for ages 12 to 16. "We are looking for contemporary young adult fiction dealing in all subjects." Submit outline/synopsis and sample chapters.

Recent Fiction Titles: *The Lottery Rose*, by J. Hunt; *Willow Farm*, by Alison Prince; and *A Matter of Time*, by Roni Schotter.

ACROPOLIS BOOKS, LTD., Subsidiary of Colortone Press, 2400 17th St., NW, Washington DC 20009. (202)387-6805. Publisher: Alphons J. Hackl. Publishes hardcover and trade paperback originals. Averages 20 titles/year. Pays "individually negotiated" royalty on retail price. SASE. Reports in 2 months. Free book catalog.

Nonfiction: Cookbook, how-to, juvenile, reference and self-help. Subjects include Americana, animals, cooking and foods, health, nature, beauty/fashion and human development. "We will be looking for manuscripts dealing with fashion and beauty, and self development. We also will be continuing our teacher books for early childhood education. Our audience includes general adult consumers, professional secondary school teachers and children." Submit outline/synopsis and sample chapters.

Recent Nonfiction Titles: *Color Me Beautiful*, by Carole Jackson (fashion beauty); *The Collector's Dictionary of Quilt Names & Patterns*, by Yvonne Khin (hobbies); and *The Touchlings*, by Michael W. Fox (children's fantasy creatures).

ADDISON-WESLEY PUBLISHING CO., INC., Children's Book Department, Jacob Way, Reading MA 01867. Assistant Editor, Children's Book: Cyrisse Jaffee. Publishes hardcover originals and trade paperbacks. Pays royalty on retail price. Simultaneous and photocopied submissions OK. SASE. "Please send one manuscript at a time only." Reports in 3-4 weeks.

Nonfiction: The arts, sciences, the environment, biography and picture books for grades K-12. Submit complete ms.

Recent Nonfiction Title: *A Show of Hands*, by Mary Beth Sullivan and Linda Bourke (sign language).

Fiction: Contemporary and young adult fiction, science fiction, mystery, adventure and picture books. No adult fiction. Submit complete ms.

Recent Fiction Titles: *Made in America*, by M. Suid and R. Harris; *Sara and the Door*, by V.A. Jensen (picture book); and *Once Upon a Time in a Pigpen*, by Margaret Wise Brown.

ADDISON-WESLEY PUBLISHING CO., INC., General Books Division, Jacob Way, Reading MA 01867. Editor-in-Chief: Ann Dilworth. Adult Trade Editors: Dorothy Coover, Harriet Rubin. Publishes hardcover and paperback originals. Publishes 45 titles/year. Pays royalty. Simultaneous and photocopied submissions OK. SASE. Reports in 3-4 weeks. Free book catalog.

Nonfiction: Biography, business/economics, health, how-to, juveniles, nature, photography, politics, psychology, recreation, science, self-help, sociology and sports. "Also needs books on 'tools for living' related to finance, everyday law, health, education, and parenting by people well-known and respected in their field. No cookbooks or books on transactional analysis." Submit outline/synopsis and sample chapters.

Recent Nonfiction Titles: *The Joy of Photography*, by the editors at Eastman Kodak Company; *Theory Z*, by William Ouchi; and *The ABC Monday Night Football Book & Calendar*.

AERO PUBLISHERS, INC., 329 W. Aviation Rd., Fallbrook CA 92028. (714)728-8456. President: Ernest J. Gentle. Editor: Craig S. Avery. Publishes hardcover and paperback originals. Pays 10% royalty. Simultaneous and photocopied submissions OK. Reports in 1 month. SASE. Free catalog.

Nonfiction: "Manuscripts submitted must be restricted to the fields of aviation and space and should be technical or semitechnical or historical in nature. Manuscripts should be 50,000-100,000 words in length and well illustrated." No personal biographies. Submit outline/synopsis and sample chapters.

Recent Nonfiction Titles: *Aviation and Space Dictionary, 6th Edition*, by Gentle and Reithmaier; *Space Shuttle: America's Wings to the Future*, by M. Kaplan; and *Seven Decades of Progress: The Story of General Electric Aircraft Engine Division*, by W. Schoneberger.

*ALASKA NATURE PRESS, Box 632, Eagle River AK 99577. Editor/Publisher: Ben Guild. Senior Editor: Mary Malpass. Box 103, Poway CA 92064. Publishes hardcover and paperback

---

* *Asterisk preceding a listing indicates that individual subsidy publishing (where author pays part or all of publishing costs) is also available. Those firms that specialize in total subsidy publishing are listed at the end of the book publishers' section.*

originals. Plans to offer subsidy publishing "as needed—estimated 10%." Averages 2 titles/year. Pays 10% royalty on retail price; no advance. Simultaneous and photocopied submissions OK. SASE. Reports in 2 months.

Nonfiction: Alaska material only: animals, biography, history, how-to, juveniles, nature, photography, poetry, recreation, wildlife, nature and self-help. No hunting or fishing tales. Query or submit outline/synopsis and sample chapters or complete ms.

Fiction: Alaska material only: adventure, historical, romance and suspense. Query senior editor: M. Malpass, Box 103, Poway CA 92064. "SASE, please." Reports in 2 months.

ALASKA NORTHWEST PUBLISHING CO., Box 4-EEE, Anchorage AK 99509. Editor and Publisher: Robert A. Henning. Publishes primarily paperback originals. Averages 12 titles/year. Most contracts call for straight 10% of sales. Free book catalog. "Rejections are made promptly, unless we have 3 or 4 possibilities in the same general field and it's a matter of which one gets the decision. That could take 3 months." SASE.

Nonfiction: "Alaska, northern British Columbia, Yukon and Northwest Territories are subject areas. Emphasis on life in the last frontier, history, outdoor subjects such as hunting and fishing. Writer must be familiar with the North first-hand. We listen to any ideas." Length: open.

ALBA HOUSE, 2187 Victory Blvd., Staten Island, New York NY 10314. (212)761-0047. Editor-in-Chief: Anthony L. Chenevey. Publishes hardcover and paperback originals (90%) and reprints (10%). Specializes in religious books. "We publish shorter editions in our field than many publishers." Pays 10% royalty on retail price. Averages 15 titles/year. Query. State availability of photos/illustrations. Simultaneous and photocopied submissions OK. Reports in 2-4 weeks. SASE. Free book catalog.

Nonfiction: Publishes philosophy, psychology, religious, sociology, textbooks and Biblical books.

Recent Nonfiction Titles: *Bible Sharings*, by J. Burke (Biblical); *Celibacy, Prayer and Friendship*, by C. Kiesling (on spirituality); and *Pope John XXIII*, by Robert Bonnut.

ALLANHELD OSMUN & CO. PUBLISHERS, Division of Littlefield Adams & Co., 81 Adams Dr., Totawa NJ 07512. Executive Editor/Editorial Director/Marketing Associate: Sara H. Held. Editorial Director: Matthew Held. Publishes hardcover and paperback originals (95%) and hardcover and paperback reprints (5%). Pays 5-12½% royalty on net sales; offers no advance. Simultaneous submissions OK. SASE. Reports in 2 months. Free book catalog.

Nonfiction: Art, business/economics, health, photography, politics, psychology, reference, science, sociology, technical and textbooks. "We publish scholarly studies in these fields with special emphasis on international studies (development, 3rd World, trade, finance, agricultural), labor economics and agricultural science. Our authors are typically academics writing for other professionals, for government bodies and other organizations which utilize primary research." Submit outline/synopsis and sample chapters.

Recent Nonfiction Titles: *Banks and the Balance of Payments*, by Benjamin J. Cohen in collaboration with Fabio Basagni (private lending in the international adjustment process).

ALLEN PUBLISHING CO., 5711 Graves Ave., Encino CA 91316. Publisher: Michael Wiener. Publishes paperback originals. Published 2 titles in 1979, 2 in 1980. Averages 3 titles/year. Pays 10% royalty on net price; no advance. Simultaneous and photocopied submissions OK. "Author queries welcome from new or established writers. Do not send manuscript or sample chapter." Reports in 3 weeks. SASE "essential." One-page author guidelines available for SASE.

Nonfiction: "Self-help material, 25,000-50,000 words, aimed at wealth-builders. We want to reach the vast audience of opportunity seekers who, for instance, purchased *Joe Karbo's Lazy Man's Way to Riches*. Material must be original and authoritative, not rehashed from other sources. Most of what we market is sold via mail order in softcover book form. No home fix-it, hobby hints, health or 'cure' books, or 'faith' stories, poetry or fiction. We are a specialty publisher and will not consider any book not fitting the above description."

Recent Nonfiction Titles: *Making it Rich in the 1980's*; *Follow Me to the Money Tree*; and *How to Find Your Fortune*, by Eric Getsch.

ALLEN & UNWIN INC., 9 Winchester Terrace, Winchester MA 01890. (617)729-0830. Executive Vice President: Mark Streatfeild. Publishes hardcover and paperback originals. Averages 150 titles/year. Simultaneous and photocopied submissions OK. SASE. Reports in 2-3 weeks. Book catalog for SASE.

Nonfiction: Biography; business/economics; history; literature; literary criticism; philosophy; politics; psychology; reference; religion; science; sociology; technical; textbooks. Especially needs advanced university material; must be of international interest. Submit outline/synopsis and sample chapters.

ALLYN AND BACON, INC., 470 Atlantic Ave., Boston MA 02210. Editors: Gary Folben (college texts), Tab Hamlin (el-hi texts), John Gilman (professional books). Publishes hardcover and paperback originals. Published 200 titles last year. "Our contracts are competitive within the standard industry framework of royalties." Reports in 1-3 months. SASE.
Nonfiction: "We are primarily a textbook, technical and professional book publisher. Authoritative works of quality. No fiction or poetry." Will consider business, medicine, reference, scientific, self-help and how-to, sociology, sports, technical mss and other course related texts. Letter should accompany ms with author information, ms prospectus, etc. Query or submit complete ms.

ALMAR PRESS, 4105 Marietta Dr., Binghamton NY 13903. Editor-in-Chief: A.N. Weiner. Managing Editor: M.F. Weiner. Publishes hardcover and paperback originals and reprints. Averages 6 titles/year. Pays 10-12-15% royalty; no advance. Prefers exclusive submissions; however, simultaneous (if so indicated) and photocopied submissions OK. Reports in 1 month. SASE. Catalog for SASE.
Nonfiction: Publishes business, technical, and consumer books and reports. "These main subjects include general business, financial, travel, career, technology, personal help, hobbies, general medical, general legal, and how-to. *Almar Reports* are business and technology subjects published for management use and prepared in 8½x11 and book format. Publications are printed and bound in soft covers as required. Reprint publications represent a new aspect of our business." Submit outline/synopsis and sample chapters.
Recent Nonfiction Titles: *Directory of Dividend Reinvestment Plans,* by D.L. Fox; *How To Live With Your Children,* by D.H. Fontenelle; and *Jan's Consumer Guide,* by Jan Leasure.

THE ALMARK COMPANY, Box 2036, Hollydale Stn., South Gate CA 90280. (213)633-1780. President E. Ronald Fishman. Publishes paperback originals. Published 7 titles in 1979, 10 in 1980. Pays 10% minimum royalty; also buys mss by outright purchase. "Average purchase order is $80. Material is usually bought in quantities for employees or union members." Simultaneous and photocopied submissions OK. SASE. Reports in 1 month. Free book catalog.
Nonfiction: Business/economics, health, reference, technical and textbooks. Especially needs "manuals used in large number training viz.: retail, nursing, restaurant, etc." Query.
Recent Nonfiction Titles: *Toran,* by E.R. Fishman (motivational); *Holistic Nursing,* by N. King (nurse training); and *The Thalco Self Trainer for Waitresses,* by E.R. Fishman (restaurant training).

ALPINE PUBLICATIONS INC., 1901 S. Garfield St., Loveland CO 80537. Managing Editor: B.J. McKinney. Publishes hardcover and paperback originals. Published 4 titles in 1979, 4 in 1980. Pays 7-15% royalty; "occasionally a small advance is offered." Simultaneous and photocopied submissions OK if so indicated. SASE. Reports in 6 weeks. Free catalog for SASE.
Nonfiction: "Alpine Publications is seeking book-length nonfiction mss with illustrations on the care, management, health, training or characteristics of various breeds of dogs, horses, and cats. We specialize in books for the serious owner/breeder, so they must be written by persons knowledgeable in these fields or be well-researched and documented. Our books provide in-depth coverage, present new techniques, and specific 'how-to' instruction. We are not interested in the typical 'pet shop' type of book, nor in books about reptiles or exotic pets." Query. Submit outline/synopsis and sample chapters or submit complete ms.
Recent Nonfiction Titles: *Sheltie Talk,* by McKinney and Rieseberg (breed book on Shetland Sheepdogs); and *Beardie Basics,* by Rieseberg (breed book on Bearded Collie dogs); *Canine Hip Dysplasia; Your Dog: Companion & Helper.* "Upcoming titles include several books on dog breeds and on Arabian Horses."

ALYSON PUBLICATIONS, INC., 75 Kneeland St., #309, Boston MA 02111. (617)542-5679. Publisher: Sasha Alyson. Publishes trade paperback originals and reprints. Averages 12 titles/year. Subsidy publishes 10% of books. Pays 3-10% royalty on retail price; buys some mss outright for $200-1,000; offers average $400 advance. SASE. Reports in 2 weeks on queries; 3 weeks on mss. Book catalog for business size SAE and 2 first class stamps.
Nonfiction: Biography and general nonfiction. Subjects include health, history, politics, sociology, and gay/lesbian/feminist. "We are especially interested in nonfiction providing a positive approach to gay/lesbian and feminist issues." Submit outline/synopsis and sample chapters.
Recent Nonfiction Titles: *The Men With the Pink Triangle,* by Heinz Heger (history); *Coming Out in the Seventies,* by Dennis Altman (essays); and *Energy, Jobs and the Economy,* by R. Grossman (current events).
Fiction: Historical and gay novels. Submit outline/synopsis and sample chapters.

AMERICAN ASTRONAUTICAL SOCIETY, (Univelt, Inc., Publisher), Box 28130, San Diego CA 92128. (714)746-4005. Editorial Director: H. Jacobs. Publishes hardcover originals. Averages

8-10 titles/year. Pays 10% royalty on retail price; no advance. Simultaneous and photocopied submissions OK. Reports in 4 weeks. SASE. Free book catalog.

Nonfiction: Proceedings or monographs in the field of astronautics, including applications of aerospace technology to Earth's problems. "Our books must be space-oriented or space related. They are meant for technical libraries, research establishments and the aerospace industry world-wide." Submit outline/synopsis and sample chapters.

Recent Nonfiction Titles: *Soviet Lunar and Planetary Exploration*, by N.L. Johnson; and *Guidance and Control 1980*, by L.A. Morine.

AMERICAN BABY BOOKS, Harlequin Enterprises, 11315 Watertown Plank Rd., Milwaukee WI 53226. (414)771-2700. President: Don Wood. Publishes hardcover and trade paperback originals and reprints. Averages 20 titles/year. Pays variable royalty; offers variable advance. Reports in 2 months. Book catalog for 9x12 SAE and 2 first class stamps.

Nonfiction: How-to, reference and self-help. Subjects include parenting. "We're looking for material on such topics as getting ready for a baby, adjusting to the baby, growth of toddlers—including their habits, recreational ideas, how-to, learning aids, clothing information, diet and nutrition information, getting ready for school, caring for the handicapped child, and anything of possible interest to parents of children six years of age or younger." Query "with concept" or submit outline/synopsis and sample chapters or complete ms.

Recent Nonfiction Titles: *What Shall I Name the Baby*, *Keepsake Record Book*, *The First Year of Life*, *New Mother's Cookbook*, and *American Baby Handbook*, by American Baby Editors.

AMERICAN CATHOLIC PRESS, 1223 Rossell Ave., Oak Park IL 60302. (312)386-1366. Editorial Director: Father Michael Gilligan. Publishes hardcover originals (90%) and hardcover and paperback reprints (10%). Published 4 titles in 1979, 2 in 1980. "Most of our sales are by direct mail, although we do work through retail outlets." Pays by outright purchase of $25-100; no advance. Simultaneous and photocopied submissions OK. Reports in 2 months. SASE. Free book catalog.

Nonfiction: "We publish books on the Roman Catholic Liturgy, for the most part books on religious music and educational books and pamphlets. We also publish religious songs for church use, including Psalms as well as choral and instrumental arrangements. We are very interested in new music, meant for use in church services. Books, or even pamphlets, on the Roman Catholic Mass are especially welcome. We have no interest in secular topics at all, and are not interested in religious poetry of any kind." Query. Recently published *The Role of Music in the New Roman Liturgy*, by W. Herring (educational); *Noise in Our Solemn Assemblies*, by R. Keifer (educational); and *Song Leader's Handbook*, by W. Callahan (music).

AMERICAN PHILATELIC SOCIETY, Box 800, State College PA 16801. (814)237-3803. Editor: Richard L Sine. Publishes hardcover originals (85%), and hardcover reprints (15%). Averages 6 + titles/year. Pays 5-10% royalty. Photocopied submissions OK. SASE. Reports in 2 weeks on queries; 3 + months on mss. Free book catalog.

Nonfiction: How-to, reference and technical. Subjects include hobbies. "We're interested in anything showing solid research into various areas of stamp collecting." Query "if not a member of our society" or submit complete ms.

Recent Nonfiction Titles: *U.S. Cancellations 1845-1869*, by Amos Eno and Hubert Skinner (reference); *Postal History of A.E.F.*, by a group of authors (reference); and *Postal History of U.S. POWs*, by Norman Gruenzner (reference).

AMERICAN POETRY PRESS, Box 634, Claymont DE 19703. (302)798-7441. Editor: J. Topham. Publishes trade paperback originals. Averages 5-7 titles/year. Pays 10-15% royalty on retail price; no advance. Simultaneous and photocopied submissions OK. ("Many authors are still not sending SASE, especially with query letters. We hold their mss hoping they will send one, or, we send them a post card. We *never* discard any mss. until after a year.") Reports in 2 weeks on queries ("if there is SASE"); 1 month on mss. Book catalog for business size SAE and 1 first class stamp.

Poetry: "We publish only traditional poetry. At present, we want war poems and/or political poems written by Vietnam or Korean veterans. Our organization specializes in publishing writing by the handicapped under section 504 of the Rehabilitation Act of 1973, but this does not exclude writing by authors in general (the public). No light verse, humor, children's, nature poems, domestic (family) poems, folk poems, dialect. No poems by amateurs. Above all, *no free verse*." Submit complete ms; "include list of places previously published."

Recent Poetry Titles: *DiVersity Poems*, edited by R. McKinney and J. Hollis (traditional); *Morning's Come Singing*, by James Facos (lyrics, traditional); and *Vietnam Poems: The War Poems of Today*, by J. Hollis (traditional).

Tips: "Our books are read by college students, the general public, and high school students. We sell books overseas in Malaysia, Australia, The Hague, Amsterdam and Canada. Write honestly about your reaction to events in the world today that affect the common people, with compassion for their suffering. Write about the tragedy of war and its effects. Try to write poetry books that would exert an influence for good in the world. We would prefer to receive publishable mss from agents as we now receive much amateur work. However, we do not wish to restrict ourselves to receiving mss through agents only. We would like to get in touch with well-known, established poets."

AMERICAN UNIVERSAL ARTFORMS CORP., Box 4574, Austin TX 78765. Editor-in-Chief: R.H. Dromgoole. Hardcover and paperback originals. Pays 10% (of net invoice) royalty. Possibility of advance "depends on many factors." Send sample print if photos and/or artwork are to accompany ms. Simultaneous submissions OK (if so advised); photocopied submissions OK. Reports in 2-4 weeks. SASE. Book catalog for SASE.
Nonfiction: Publishes textbooks (bilingual educational material, K-12; Spanish/English); books on hobbies; how-to; humor; and politics. Submit complete ms.

AMPHOTO, 1515 Broadway, New York NY 10036. (212)764-7300. Editorial Director: Harbert T. Leavy. Managing Editor: Virginia Croft. Publishes hardcover and paperback originals. Published 40 titles in 1979, 50 in 1980. Pays royalty, or by outright purchase; offers variable advance. Simultaneous and photocopied submissions OK. Reports in 1 month. SASE. Free book catalog.
Nonfiction: "Photography only. We cover all aspects of photography—technical and how-to. Few portfolios or picture books." Submit outline/synopsis, sample chapters and sample photos.
Recent Nonfiction Titles: *Professional Fashion Photography*, by Robert Farber (how-to); *The Fine 35mm Portrait*, by Jack Manning (portraiture with a small camera); and *The Encyclopedia of Practical Photography* (14 volumes of photography A to Z.)
Tips: "Consult the photo magazines for book ideas."

AND BOOKS, 702 S. Michigan, South Bend IN 46618. (419)232-3134. Editor: Janos Szebedinszky. Publishes trade paperback originals and trade paperback reprints. Averages 20-30 titles/year. Subsidy publishes some books based on "tactical decision making through statistical marketing analysis." Pays 50% maximum royalty on retail price; buys some mss outright. "We make mutually rewarding arrangements ranging from royalty to copublishing." Simultaneous and photocopied submissions OK. SASE. Reports in 5 weeks on queries; 1 week on mss. Free book catalog.
Nonfiction: Biography ("depends on who"); coffee table book; cookbook; how-to; humor; illustrated book; and self-help. Subjects include business and economics, music, philosophy, psychology, recreation, sociology and sports. "Material must be literate and salable." No college theses, found-out descriptions, autobiographies of Civil servants, pet stories, hunting and fishing guides, technical journals, investment guides or family genealogy." Query or submit complete ms.
Recent Nonfiction Titles: *Bailout: Chrysler Story*, by R. Stuart (current events); *Bonzo Goes to Washington*, by E. Krause (humor); and *Eating What Grows Naturally*, by K. Gay (nutrition).
Fiction: Adventure (fantasy); confession (popular); erotica (soft porn, philosophy); ethnic (Transylvanian, Italian); experimental ("salable"); fantasy ("must be original"); humor ("must be original"); mainstream; and mystery (epic). Query or submit complete ms.
Poetry: "We're looking for epic poetry."

ANDERSON PUBLISHING CO., 602 Main St., Suite 501, Cincinnati OH 45201. (513)421-4393. Editorial Director: Jean Martin. Publishes hardcover and paperback originals (98%) and reprints (2%). Publishes 12 titles/year. Pays 15-18% royalty; "advance in selected cases." Simultaneous and photocopied submissions OK. Reports in 6 weeks. SASE. Free book catalog.
Nonfiction: Law, and law-related books, criminal justice texts (justice administration legal series), social studies. Query or submit outline/chapters with vitae.
Recent Nonfiction Titles: *An Issues Approach*, by M.D. Schwartz/T.R. Clear/L.F. Travis; *Justice As Fairness*, by D. Fogel/J. Hudson; and *The Law Dictionary*, by W. Gilmer.

AND/OR PRESS, Box 2246, Berkeley CA 94702. Executive Editor: Peter Beren. Paperback originals (90%); hardcover and paperback reprints (10%). Specializes in "nonfiction works with youth market interest. We function as an alternative information resource." Pays 5-10% royalty; offers advance of 10% of first print run. Published 8 titles in 1979, 6 in 1980; plans 8 in 1981. Reports in 2 weeks to 3 months. SASE. One-page queries only. Book catalog $1.
Nonfiction: Publishes appropriate technology, human potential, the future, health and nutrition, travel and psycho-pharmacology books. Also alternative lifestyle books.
Recent Nonfiction Titles: *Holistic Health Lifebook*, by Berkeley Holistic Health Center; and *Vagabonding In the U.S.A.*, by Ed Buryn.

ANDREWS AND McMEEL, INC., 4400 Johnson Dr., Fairway KS 66205. Editorial Director: Donna Martin. Publishes hardcover and paperback originals. Publishes 30 titles annually. Pays royalty on retail price. "Not currently reading unsolicited mss. Publishing program mainly related to features of Universal Press Syndicate, parent company of Andrews & McMeel."

APPALACHIAN MOUNTAIN CLUB BOOKS, 5 Joy St., Boston MA 02108. (617)523-0636. Director of Publications: Arlyn S. Powell Jr. Publishes hardcover and paperback originals (80%) and reprints (20%). Published 6 titles in 1979, 8 in 1980; plans 8 in 1981. Offers 5-10% royalty on retail price; offers average advance: $1,000. Simultaneous and photocopied submissions OK. SASE. Reports in 2 months. Free book catalog.
Nonfiction: How-to; nature; recreation; and sports. "The Appalachian Mountain Club is a non-profit public service organization dedicated to outdoor recreation and conservation, primarily in the Northeast. Most of our books to date have been hiking and canoeing guidebooks to specific regions. We have also done 'how-to' books on trail building, canoeing, growth planning. Others include mountaineering, memoir, historical reprint, mountain photography, environmental primer, ski touring. Any book we do must fall under the charter of the AMC." Does *not* want to see mechanized sports (e.g., snowmobiling and "no 'how to save the world' essays." Query first.
Recent Nonfiction Titles: *Wilderness Search and Rescue*, by Tim J. Setnicka; and *White Water Handbook*, by John Urban and T. Walley Williams.

APPLE PRESS, 5536 SE Harlow, Milwaukie OR 97222. (503)659-2475. Senior Editor: Judith S. Majors. Publishes paperback originals. Averages 3-5 titles/year. Pays 7-10% royalty on retail price; offers average advance $200-500. SASE. Reports in 4-6 weeks.
Nonfiction: Health; juveniles; self-help; Christian attitudes and ideals. Query first. SASE.
Recent Nonfiction Titles: *Sugar Free Kid's Cookery* (calculated youth cookbook); *Diet Out Oregon*; and *Sugar Free Microwavery*.
Fiction: Mainstream (juvenile) and suitable for Christian youth.
Recent Fiction Title: *Mr. Fix-it* (juvenile humor).

APPLE-WOOD BOOKS, INC., Box 2870, Cambridge MA 02139. (617)964-5150. Editorial Director: Phil Zuckerman. Publishes hardcover and trade paperback originals. Average 8 titles/year. Pays 10-15% royalty on wholesale price; offers $250-2,500 advance. Simultaneous and photocopied submissions OK. SASE. Reports in 3 weeks on queries; 3 months on mss. Book catalog for 8½x11 SAE and 2 first class stamps.
Nonfiction: Subjects include history, politics and sociology. "Books concerning social themes and New Englandia. We publish for a young, literary audience." No how-to or cookbooks. Query.
Recent Nonfiction Titles: *Cocktails at Somoza's*, by Richard Elman (political); and *Crossing Over*, by Richard Currey (political journal).
Fiction: "We don't consider fiction by category, but by quality. We publish the future great American writers." Query or submit outline/synopsis and sample chapters.
Recent Fiction Titles: *P-town Stories*, by R.D. Skillings; *Candace & Other Stories*, by Alan Cheuse; and *Death By Dreaming*, by Jon Manchip White.

APPLEZABA PRESS, 410 St. Louis, Long Beach CA 90814. (213)434-7761. Publisher: D.H. Lloyd. Publishes trade paperback originals. Averages 3-4 titles/year. Pays 8-15% royalty on retail price "plus a few author copies." Photocopied submissions OK. SASE. Reports in 2 weeks on queries; 4 months on mss. Free book catalog.
Fiction: Erotica, experimental, fantasy, mainstream, short story collections and translations. Submit outline/synopsis and sample chapters.
Recent Fiction Titles: *Someone Else's Dreams*, by John Yamrus (novella); *The Cure*, by Gerald Locklin (novella); and *Mog & Glog*, by d.h. lloyd (short stories).
Poetry: "We would like to see more poetry that has both humor and depth to it. No poetry that is didactical or has awkward rhymes." Submit complete ms.
Recent Poetry Titles: *Video Poems*, by Billy Collins (humor); *Frenchwoman Poems*, by Nichola Manning (surrealistic) and *If Gravity Wasn't Discovered*, by d.h. lloyd (humor).

THE AQUARIAN PUBLISHING CO. (LONDON) LTD., Denington Estate, Wellingborough, Northamptonshire MN8 2RQ England. Editor-in-Chief: J.R. Hardaker. Hardcover and paperback originals. Pays 8-10% royalty. Photocopied submissions OK. SAE and International Reply Coupons. Reports in 2-4 weeks. Free book catalog.
Nonfiction: Publishes books on astrology, magic, witchcraft, palmistry and other occult subjects. Length: 15,000-60,000 words.

ARCHER EDITIONS PRESS, Box 562, Danbury CT 06810. Editorial Director: Wanda Hicks. Publishes hardcover and paperback originals (60%) and paperback reprints (40%). Pays 15% royalty on wholesale price; occasionally offers $250-750 advance. Published 2 titles in 1979, 5 in 1980; plans 6 in 1981. Simultaneous and photocopied submissions OK. Reports in 2-3 months. SASE. Free book catalog.
Nonfiction: "We are interested in books that could go to the academic and public library market in the fields of history, literature and art. We would especially like biographies in this field." Query.
Recent Nonfiction Titles: *Thomas Francis Meagher,* by W.F. Lyons (Civil War reprint); and *Lost Sandstones and Lonely Skies,* by Jesse Stuart (essays).
Fiction: "We are doing a limited amount of fiction of a somewhat academic nature by established authors."
Recent Fiction Titles: *The Autobiography of Cassandra; Princess and Prophetess of Troy,* by Ursule Molinaro.

ARCHITECTURAL BOOK PUBLISHING CO., INC., 10 E. 40th St., New York NY 10016. (212)689-5400. Editor: Walter Frese. Royalty is percentage of retail price. Prefers queries, outlines and sample chapters. Reports in 2 weeks. SASE.
Architecture and Industrial Arts: Publishes architecture, decoration, and reference books on city planning and industrial arts. Also interested in history, biography, and science of architecture and decoration.

ARCO PUBLISHING, INC., 219 Park Ave. S., New York NY 10003. Editorial Director: Robin Little. Hardcover and paperback originals (70%) and reprints (30%). Pays 10-12½-15% royalty on retail price; advance averages $1,500. Published 160 titles in 1979, 180 in 1980. Simultaneous and legible photocopied submissions OK. Reports in 4-6 weeks. SASE (manuscripts and materials submitted without postage will not be automatically returned). Book catalog for 50¢ for postage and handling.
Nonfiction: Publishes (in order of preference) crafts and collecting; pet care and training; self-help (medical, mental, financial); career guidance; medicine and psychiatry (technical and authoritative); test preparation and study guides; sports instruction (no spectator sports: baseball, football, etc.); specialized cookbooks in health food and nutrition areas only; how-to; medical review books; military history; reference. "Our readers are people who want information, instruction and technical know-how from their books. They want to learn something tangible." No fiction, poetry, religion or personal "true" accounts of persons or pets. Query or submit outline/synopsis and sample chapters.
Recent Nonfiction Titles: *The Age of Enlightenment Cookbook,* by Miriam Kasin (vegetarian cooking); *Illustrated Index to Traditional American Quilt Patterns,* by Susan Winter Mills (reference); *Weekend Mechanic's Handbook,* by Paul Weissler (how-to); and *Graduate Management Admission Test,* Third Edition (test preparation).

*ARLINGTON HOUSE PUBLISHERS, 333 Post Rd., W., Westport CT 06880. President: Robert T. Enos. Senior Editor: Richard Bishirjian. Publishes hardcover originals (80%) and reprints (20%). Published 22 titles in 1979, 25 in 1980; plans 30 in 1981. Pays 10% royalty on retail price—escalating based on sales; offers advance. Reports in 3-4 weeks.
Nonfiction: Biography, business/economics, health, history, politics, self-help, investing, Americana, films, TV and entertainment. No religious books. Query, submit outline/synopsis and one sample chapter.
Recent Nonfiction Titles: *The Candidates 1980,* by Aram Bakshian Jr. (social commentary); *The Great Money Panic,* by Martin Weiss (investment); and *The Real Oscar,* by Peter Brown (entertainment).

E.J. ARNOLD & SON LTD., 64 Greenfield Gardens, London NW2 1HY England. Children's Editor: Brenda Gardner. Publishes hardcover originals. Average 20 titles/year. Pays 7½-10% royalty; offers average $750 advance. Simultaneous and photocopied submissions OK. SASE. Reports in 6 weeks. Free book catalog.
Imprints: *Educational Books for Children* (nonfiction).
Nonfiction: Biography, how-to, humor and juvenile. Subjects include animals, business and economics, cooking and foods, history, hobbies, nature, sports, travel and science. "We're looking for nonfiction for the 5-8 age group and for older age groups." No natural history. Submit outline/synopsis and sample chapters.
Recent Nonfiction Titles: *Project: Bridges* and *Project: Skyscrapers,* by MacGregor (for 9-and-older age group, b&w illustrations with models to make); and *Abilene 1870: A Quest for the Past,* by MacGregor (for 6-9 age group; through fiction, facts of everyday western life are revealed).
Fiction: Adventure, humor, mystery, science fiction, suspense and Western. "We especially need

picture books for the 5-8 age group." No historical mss. Submit outline/synopsis and sample chapters.
Recent Fiction Titles: *Chilly Billy*, by Peter Mayle (humorous fiction for 6-8 age group).
Tips: "Try to find a topic that has not been properly covered or considered. Look in bookshops to see the most successful approaches to similar topics. Then write with a synopsis to a publisher whose list seems sympathetic with your topic, or approach someone who is starting to build a list."

ART DIRECTION BOOK COMPANY, 10 E. 39th St., New York NY 10016. (212)889-6500. Editorial Director: Don Barron. Senior Editor: Lawrence Oberwagor. Publishes hardcover and paperback originals. Published 9 titles in 1979, 10 in 1980; plans 12 in 1981. Pays 10% royalty on retail price; offers average advance: $1,000. Photocopied submissions OK. SASE. Reports in 3 months. Free book catalog.
Nonfiction: Commercial art; ad art how-to; and textbooks. Query first. "We are interested in books for the professional advertising art field—that is, books for art directors, designers, et. al; also entry level books for commercial and advertising art students in such fields as typography, photography, paste-up, illustration, clip-art, design, layout and graphic arts."
Recent Nonfiction Titles: *How to Get a Job in Advertising*, by Ken Haas; *How to Prepare a Portfolio*, by John Marquand; and *The Illustrations of Murray Tinkelman*, by Murray Tinkelman.

ARTECH HOUSE BOOKS, 610 Washington St., Dedham MA 02026. (617)326-8220. Editor: Carol McGarry. Publishes hardcover originals. Published 12 titles in 1979, 15 in 1980; plans 18 in 1981. Offers 15-20% royalty on net price. No advance. Simultaneous and photocopied submissions OK. SASE. Reports in 1½ months. No book catalog.
Nonfiction: Technical. "High quality treatments of the state-of-the-art in electronic technologies, including radar, microwave, telecommunications, and medical subjects. We do *not* want anything non-scientific or technical in any area not cited above." Submit outline/synopsis and sample chapters or complete ms.
Recent Nonfiction Titles: *Intro to Synthetic Array and Imaging Radar*, by S.A. Horanessian, Ph.D. (radar); and *Gaas Fet Principles and Technology*, by T.V. DiLorenzo, Ph.D. (circuit design).

ARVIN PUBLICATIONS, Box 758 Tavernier FL 33070. (305)852-9558. Publishes trade paperback originals. Averages 3 titles/year. Pays 20% maximum royalty on retail prices; no advance. Simultaneous and photocopied submissions OK. SASE. Reports in 1 month. Sample booklet $1.
Nonfiction: Self-help on child welfare. "We publish monographs dealing with child welfare. Material must develop and enhance professional skills. Authors must be professionally qualified to teach others in the field of child welfare." Submit complete ms.
Recent Nonfiction Titles: *Professional Parenthood*, by V. Scheppler (monograph on foster care); *The Adoption Dilemma*, by V. Scheppler (monograph on adoption); and *Be Your Own Therapist*, by E. Kirchner (self-help manual).

ASI PUBLISHERS, INC., 127 Madison Ave., New York NY 10016. Editor-in-Chief: Henry Weingarten. Publishes hardcover and paperback originals and reprints. Pays 7½% royalty based on retail and wholesale price; no advance. Published 7 titles in 1979, 10 in 1980; plans 12 in 1981. Book catalog for SASE. Will consider photocopied submissions. Query. Submit outline and sample chapters. Mss should be typed, double-spaced. SASE. Reports in 1-3 months.
Nonfiction: "We specialize in guides to balancing inner space, e.g., natural healing, astrology, new age consciousness, etc. Our editors are themselves specialists in the areas published. We will accept technical material with limited sales potential." Healing Arts Editor: Barbara Somerfield. Astrology Editor: H. Weingarten.
Recent Nonfiction Titles: *Synastry*, by R. Davison (astrology); *Person-Centered Astrology*, by Dane Rudhyar and Color Therapy, by Dr. Amber (healing).

*ASSOCIATED BOOKSELLERS, 147 McKinley Ave., Bridgeport CT 06606. (212)366-5494. Editor-in-Chief: Alex M. Yudkin. Hardcover and paperback originals. Averages 8 titles/year. Pays 10% royalty on wholesale or retail price; advance averages $500. Subsidy publishes 10% of books. Subsidy publishing is offered "if the marketing potential is limited." Query. Simultaneous and photocopied submissions OK. Reports in 2-4 weeks. SASE. Book catalog for SASE.
Nonfiction: Publishes how-to, hobbies, recreation, self-help, and sports books.
Recent Titles: *Key to Judo*; *Ketsugo*; and *Kashi-No-Bo*.

ASSOCIATED BOOK PUBLISHERS, INC., 1015 Howard Ave., Box 6219, San Mateo CA 94403. Editor: Ivan Kapetanovic. Publishes hardcover and paperback originals. "Offer outright payment or standard minimum book contract. We have not made a practice of giving advances." Averages 3-4 titles/year. Will consider photocopied submissions. Submit outline and sample chapters, or submit complete ms. Reports in 3 weeks. "We are not responsible for unsolicited materials unless return postage is enclosed."

Nonfiction: "We would especially consider publication of books suitable for elementary, junior high and high school students, in the field of guidance, including occupational information, college entrance and orientation, personal and social problems and how to pass tests of all kinds. In addition to the categories listed below, we are interested in bibliographies in all subject areas and in textbooks for elementary through high school grades. Books published in following categories: economics, linguistics, dictionaries, education, children's books, cooking and nutrition, gardening, history, hobby and crafts, self-help and how-to, sociology and guidance. No strict length requirements."

Recent Nonfiction Titles: *Croatian Cuisine*, by Kapetanovic.

ATHENEUM PUBLISHERS, 597 5th Ave., New York NY 10017. Editor-in-Chief: Thomas A. Stewart. Published 170 titles in 1979. Simultaneous and photocopied submissions OK. Reports in 6 weeks. SASE.

Nonfiction: General trade material dealing with politics, psychology, popular health, cookbooks, sports, biographies and general interest. Length: 40,000 words minimum. Query or submit outline/synopsis and a sample chapter.

Recent Nonfiction Titles: *Diaghilev*, by Richard Buckle; and *Prince Charles*, by Anthony Holden.

Fiction: "We are not interested in unsolicited fiction."

ATHENEUM PUBLISHERS, INC., Juvenile Department, 597 5th Ave., New York NY 10017. Editor: Jean Karl. Publishes hardcover originals and paperback reprints. Published 58 titles in 1979, 64 in 1980; plans 60 in 1981. Reports in 6 weeks. SASE.

Nonfiction: Juvenile books for ages 3-16. Picture books for ages 3-8. "We have no special needs; we publish whatever comes in that interests us."

Tips: "Most submissions are poorly conceived, poorly written. Think deeper and learn how to write."

ATHENEUM PUBLISHERS, INC., College Department, 597 5th Ave., New York NY 10017. College Dept. Editor: Mrs. E. Soschin. Publishes paperback reprints. Averages 15 titles/year. Pays royalty on wholesale or retail price. Free book catalog.

Nonfiction: "We will not seek to acquire books, relying on our own backlist for our paperback list at least for the next several seasons."

Recent Nonfiction Titles: *Confessions of an Advertising Man*, by David Ogilvy; *Jung: Man and Myth*, by Vincent Brome (psychology); and *Venice: A Thousand Years of Culture & Civilization*, by Peter Lauritzen.

ATHLETIC PRESS, Box 2314-D, Pasadena CA 91108. (213)283-3446. Editor-in-Chief: Donald Duke. Publishes paperback originals. Specializes in sports conditioning books. Pays 10% royalty; no advance. Averages 3 titles/year. Query or submit complete ms. "Illustrations will be requested when we believe ms is publishable." Simultaneous and photocopied submissions OK. Reports in 2-4 weeks. SASE. Free book catalog.

Nonfiction: Publishes sports books.

Recent Nonfiction Title: *Flexibility for All Sports*, by John Beleau (sports conditioning).

ATLANTIC MONTHLY PRESS, 8 Arlington St., Boston MA 02116. (617)536-9500. Director: Upton Birnie Brady. Children's Book Editor: Melanie Kroupa. Averages 36 titles/year. "Advance and royalties depend on the nature of the book, the stature of the author, and the subject matter." SASE.

Nonfiction: Publishes, in association with Little, Brown and Company, general nonfiction, biography, autobiography, science, philosophy, the arts, belles lettres, history and world affairs. Length: 70,000-200,000 words.

Recent Nonfiction Titles: *America Revised*, by Frances FitzGerald; *Walker Percy*, by Robert Coles; and *Walter Lippman and the American Century*, by Ronald Steel (biography/history).

Fiction: Publishes, in association with Little, Brown and Company, general fiction, juveniles and poetry. Length: 70,000-200,000 words.

Recent Fiction Titles: *The Sending*, by Geoffrey Household; *Fire Watch*, by Alan Dennis Burke; *Yearwood*, by Paul Hazel; and *Brother Enemy*, by Speer Morgan (international spy thriller set in the Caribbean).

THE ATLANTIC MONTHLY PRESS, Children's Books, 8 Arlington St., Boston MA 02116. (617)536-9500. Editor of Children's Books: Melanie Kroupa. Publishes hardcover and some simultaneous hardcover/paperback originals. Published 13 titles in 1979. Photocopied submissions

OK. No query letters. SASE. Reports in 1 month.

Nonfiction: Picture books through young adult. Subjects include animals, art, biography, history, hobbies, how-to, humor, music, nature, photography, poetry, psychology, recreation, science and sports. Submit outline/synopsis and sample chapters. Recently published *Next Year in Jerusalem*, by Robert Goldston; and *Inside Animals*, by Dr. Gale Cooper.

Fiction: Contemporary fiction, adventure, fantasy, historical, humor, mystery, romance, science fiction and picture books. Submit complete ms only. Recently published *Far From Home*, by Ouida Sebestyen; *Humbug Mountain*, by Sid Fleischman; *Here Comes Alex Pumpernickel!*, by Fernando Krahn; and *Arthur's Valentine*, by Marc Brown.

AUGSBURG PUBLISHING HOUSE, 426 S. 5th St., Minneapolis MN 55415. (612)332-4561. Director, Book Department: Roland Seboldt. Publishes hardcover and paperback originals (95%) and paperback reprints (5%). Publishes 45 titles/year. Pays 10-15% royalty on retail price; offers variable advance. Simultaneous and photocopied submissions OK. Reports in 6 weeks. SASE.

Nonfiction: Health, psychology, religion, self-help and textbooks. "We are looking for manuscripts that apply scientific knowledge and Christian faith to the needs of people as individuals, in groups and in society." Query or submit outline/synopsis and a sample chapter or submit complete ms.

Recent Nonfiction Titles: *The Friendship Factor*, by Alan Loy McGinnis; *Adventure Inward*, by Morton T. Kelsey (Christian growth through personal journal writing); and *Stress/Unstress*, by Keith W. Sehnert, MD.

Fiction: "We are looking for good religious fiction with a Christian theme for the young readers age 8-11." Submit complete ms.

*AUTO BOOK PRESS, 1511 Grand Ave., San Marcos CA 92069. (714)744-2567. Editorial Director: William Carroll. Publishes hardcover and paperback originals. Publishes 3 titles/year. Subsidy publishes 25% of books based on "author's exposure in the field." Pays 15% royalty; offers variable advance. Simultaneous and photocopied submissions OK. Reports in 2 weeks. SASE. Free book catalog.

Nonfiction: Automotive material only: technical or definitive how-to. Query. Recently published *Brief History of San Marcos*, by Carroll (area history); *Honda Civic Guide*, by Carroll; and *How to Sell*, by Woodward (sales hints).

AUTUMN PRESS, INC., 1318 Beacon St., Brookline MA 02146. (617)738-5680. President/Editor-in-Chief: M. Nahum Stiskin. Publishes hardcover and paperback originals and paperback reprints. Averages 8 titles/year. Standard royalty on retail price; sometimes offers a small advance. Simultaneous and photocopied submissions OK. "No unsolicited manuscripts, please." Reports in 1-3 months. SASE. Free book catalog.

Nonfiction: "We are interested in books on holistic health, natural foods cooking, alternative lifestyles, psychology and growth, philosophy, humor, Eastern and Western thought, ecology, and environmental concerns. No poetry. Submit outline/synopsis with query letter.

Recent Nonfiction Titles: *The Book of Whole Meals*, by Annemarie Colbin; *The Great American Tofu Cookbook*, by Patricia Gaddis McGruter; and *Headaches: The Drugless Way to Lasting Relief*, by Harry Ehrmantraut.

Fiction: "We may be interested in fiction that reflects the above themes."

AVALON BOOKS, Thomas Bouregy & Co., Inc., 22 E. 60th St., New York NY 10022. Editor: Rita Brenig. "We like the writers to focus on the plot, drama, and characters, not the background." Publishes hardcover originals. Publishes 60 titles/year. Pays $400 advance which is applied against sales of the first 3,500 copies of the book. SASE. Reports in 12 weeks. Free book list for SASE.

Fiction: "We want well-plotted, fast-moving light romances, romance-mysteries, gothics, westerns, and nurse-romance books of about 50,000 words." Query or submit one-page synopsis or submit complete ms. No sample chapters or long outlines. SASE.

Recent Fiction Titles: *Nurse Whitney's Paradise*, by Betty Rose Gunn (nurse-romance); *The Magic of Paris*, by Berta LaVan Barker (light romance); *Pictures of Fear*, by Lucy Fuchs (gothic); and *Gunfire at Flintlock*, by Terrell L. Bowers.

*AVI PUBLISHING CO., 250 Post Rd. E., Box 831, Westport CT 06881. (203)226-0738. Editor-in-Chief: Norman W. Desrosier, PhD. Hardcover and paperback originals. Specializes in publication of books in the fields of food science and technology, food service, nutrition, health, agriculture and aquaculture. Pays 10% royalty, based on list price on the first 3,000 copies sold; $500 average advance (paid only on typing and art bills). Subsidy publishes 2% of titles (by professional organizations) based on "quality of work; subject matter within the areas of food, nutrition, agriculture and health, endorsed by appropriate professional organizations in the area of our

specialty." Published 50 titles in 1980, 45 in 1981; plans 52 in 1982. Reports in 2-4 weeks. SASE. Free book catalog.
Nonfiction: Publishes books on foods, agriculture, nutrition and health, scientific, technical, textbooks and reference works. Query or "submit a 500-word summary, a preface, a table of contents, estimated number of pages in manuscript, when to be completed and a biographical sketch."
Recent Nonfiction Titles: *Nutrition and Medical Produce*, by Barness; *World Fish Farming, 2nd Ed.*, by Brown; *Microeconomics*, by Redman and Redman; and *Food Process Engineering*, by Heldman and Singh.

AVIATION BOOK CO., 1640 Victory Blvd., Glendale CA 91201. (213)240-1771. Editor: Walter P. Winner. Publishes hardcover and paperback originals and reprints. Published 5 titles in 1979, 7 in 1980. Pays royalty on retail price. No advance. Free book catalog. Query with outline. Reports in 2 months. SASE.
Nonfiction: Aviation books, primarily of a technical nature and pertaining to pilot training. Young adult level and up. Also aeronautical history. Recently published *Airmen's Information Manual*, by Winner (pilot training); *Their Eyes on the Skies*, by Martin Cole (aeronautics history); *"Upside-Down" Pangborn*, by Cleveland (aeronautics history); and *Corporate Flying*, by King (aeronautics and transportation).

AVON BOOKS, 959 8th Ave., New York NY 10019. Executive Vice President and Publisher: Walter Meade. Editorial Director: Robert Wyatt. Executive Editor: Susan Moldow. Publishes paperback originals (40%) and paperback reprints (60%). Publishes 380 titles/year. Pay and advance are negotiable. Simultaneous and photocopied submissions OK. SASE. Reports in 8 weeks. Free book catalog for SASE.
Nonfiction: Animals, biography, business/economics, cookbooks/cooking, health, history, hobbies, how-to, humor, juveniles, music, nature, philosophy, photography, poetry, politics, psychology, recreation, reference, religion, science, self-help, sociology, and sports. Submit outline/synopsis and sample chapters.
Fiction: Adventure, fantasy, gothic, historical, mainstream, mystery, religious, romance, science fiction, suspense, and western. Submit outline/synopsis, sample chapters and SASE.
Recent Fiction Titles: *Lost Love, Last Love*, by Rosemary Rogers; *Emperor of the Amazon*, by Mavcio Souza; and *Sea Trial*, by Frank DeFelitta.

AZTEX CORP., 1126 N. 6th Ave., Box 50046, Tucson AZ 85703. (608)882-4656. Publishes hardcover and paperback originals. Published 19 titles in 1979, 12 in 1980. Pays 10% royalty. SASE. Reports in 3 months. Free catalog. *Author-Publisher Handbook* $3.95.
Nonfiction: "We specialize in transportation subjects, how-to and history of automobiles, trucks, fire engines, sailboats, powerboats, motorcycles and motor sports. We also use material on railroading military and wargaming subjects." Submit outline/synopsis and sample chapters or complete ms.
Recent Nonfiction Titles: *Daytona USA*, by William Neely, (auto racing history); *Mack-Revised* and *Bulldog*, by J.B. Montville (both truck histories); *Collecting Model Farm Toys of the World*; and *How to Buy a Boat* (powerboats).

BAHAMAS INTERNATIONAL PUBLISHING CO., LTD., Box 1914, Nassau, The Bahamas. (809)322-1149. Editorial Director: Michael A. Symonette. Publishes paperback originals. Averages 18-24 titles/year. Buys mss outright for $250-1,000; offers average $250 advance. Simultaneous and photocopied submissions OK. SASE. Reports in 6 weeks. Book catalog $3.
Imprints: *The Island Press, Ltd.* and *The Herold, Ltd.*
Nonfiction: Biography. Subjects include history. Query or submit outline/synopsis and sample chapters.
Recent Nonfiction Title: *Discovery of a Nation* (illustrated history of The Bahamas).
Fiction: Mainstream. "We will consider only mainstream fiction of the highest literary quality, suitable for European as well as North American readers. We are not really interested in fiction built around the standard commercial formula of today. We are concerned with substantial themes and the development of ideas. There should be strong characterization and a meaningful story line. Ours is a limited but highly literate international market. *Absolutely no* romances, gothics, science fiction, confessions, occult, fantasy, or variations on these themes in any form." Query or submit outline/synopsis and sample chapters.
Recent Fiction Titles: *The Best of the Herald (Anthology); The Stone Kings; The Sunlit Wheel; Something a Little Like Love;* and *Refugees.*
Poetry: "We are considering poetry for the first time."

*BAKER BOOK HOUSE COMPANY, Box 6287, Grand Rapids MI 49506. (616)676-9185. Editorial Director: Dan Van't Kerkhoff. Publishes hardcover and paperback originals (40%) and paperback reprints (60%). Published 150 titles in 1979, 150 in 1980. Subsidy publishes 1% of books. Subsidy contract is offered "if title is in harmony with our line" and author has religious writing experience. Pays 5-10% royalty. Also buys mss by outright purchase: $250-500. No advance. Simultaneous and photocopied submissions OK. SASE. Reports in 4 weeks. Book catalog for SASE.

Nonfiction: Humor; juveniles; philosophy; psychology; religion; self-help; and textbooks. "All must be of religious nature." Submit outline/synopsis and sample chapters or submit complete ms.

Recent Nonfiction Titles: *Taming Tension*, by P. Keller (self-help); *Happiness is a Choice*, by P. Meier and F. Minirth (psychology); and *Money in the Cookie Jar*, by E. Kilgo (money making business at home for wives).

Fiction: "Juvenile adventure with religious flavor." Submit complete ms.

Recent Fiction Titles: *Anaku: True Story of a Wolf*, by J. DeJonge; and *Mystery at Red Rock Canyon*, by E. Vogt.

BALE BOOKS, Box 2727, New Orleans LA 70176. Editor-in-Chief: Don Bale Jr. Publishes hardcover and paperback originals and reprints. Offers standard 10-12½-15% royalty contract on wholesale or retail price; "no advances." Sometimes purchases mss outright for $500. Published 6 titles in 1979, 10 in 1980. "Most books are sold through publicity and ads in the coin newspapers." Book catalog for SASE. Will consider photocopied submissions. "Send ms by registered or certified mail. Be sure copy of ms is retained." Reports usually within several months. SASE.

Nonfiction: "Our specialty is coin and stock market investment books; especially coin investment books and coin price guides. We are open to any new ideas in the area of numismatics. The writer should write for a teenage through adult level. Lead the reader by the hand like a teacher, building chapter by chapter. Our books sometimes have a light, humorous treatment, but not necessarily."

Recent Nonfiction Titles: *How to Find Valuable, Old Scarce Coins*; and *A Gold Mine in Gold*, by Bale.

BALLANTINE BOOKS, Division of Random House, 201 E. 50th St., New York NY 10022. "Science fiction and fantasy should be sent to Judy-Lynn editor-in-chief of Del Rey Books at Ballantine. Proposals for trade books, poster books, calendars, etc., should be directed to Joelle Delbourgo, editor of trade books. Proposals including sample chapters for contemporary and historical fiction and romances should be sent to Pamela Strickler, senior editor." Publishes trade and mass market paperback originals and reprints. Royalty contract varies. Published 350 titles last year; about 25% were originals.

General: General fiction and nonfiction, science fiction and fantasy. "Not interested in poetry or books exclusively for children or young adults; books under 50,000 words are too short for consideration. We do very few biographies, and we are not interested in collections of short stories, or books that depend largely on photographs. Since we are a mass market house, books which have a heavy regional flavor would be inappropriate for our list."

Recent Titles: *Shelley*, by Shelley Winters (biography); *Peter the Great*, by Robert Massie (historical); *Ordinary People*, by Judith Guest (fiction); and *Skye O'Malley*, by Bertrice Small (historical romance).

BALLINGER PUBLISHING CO., 17 Dunster St., Harvard Square, Cambridge MA 02138. (617)492-0670. Editor: Carol Franco. Publishes hardcover originals. Published 80 titles in 1979, 80 in 1980; plans 80 in 1981. Pays royalty by arrangement. Simultaneous and photocopied submissions OK. SASE. Reports in 1 month. Free book catalog.

Fiction: Professional and reference books in social and behavioral sciences, energy, criminal law and criminal justice, psychology, housing and real estate, health policy, and administration business and finance and economics. Submit outline/synopsis and sample chapters or submit complete ms.

Recent Nonfiction Titles: *Energy: The Next 20 Years*, by Hans H. Landsberg; and *Coal: Bridge to the Future*, by Carroll L. Wilson.

BANKERS PUBLISHING CO., 210 South St., Boston MA 02111. (617)426-4495. Editor: Celeste Ronciglione. Publishes hardcover originals. Average 3-5 titles/year. Pays 10-15% royalty on both wholesale and retail price; buys some mss outright for negotiable fee; offers negotiable advance. SASE. Reports in 1 month. Book catalog for 5½x8½ SAE and 1 first class stamp.

Nonfiction: How-to reference texts on banking only for banking professionals. "Because of their nature, our books remain useful for many years (it is not unusual for a title to remain in print for 5-10 years). Our titles also are revised and updated frequently."

Recent Nonfiction Titles: *Accounts Receivable & Inventory Lending, 2nd ed.*, by David A. Robinson; *Getting Ready for NOW Accounts*, by Bob Hall; and *Bank Audits and Examination*, by John Savage.

Tips: "As long as a book contains technical, necessary information about doing a particular banking job, it does well. We try to provide bankers with information and guidance not available anywhere else. Most of our writers are experienced bankers, but we are willing to consider a professional researcher/writer for some projects."

BANTAM BOOKS, INC., 666 5th Ave., New York NY 10019. Imprints include Perigord Press. (212)765-6500. Chairman & CEO: Louis Wolfe. Vice President & Editor-in-Chief: Rollene W. Saal. Vice President & Associate Editor-In-Chief: Allan Barnard. Publishes mass market and trade paperback books for adults, young adults (ages 12-17), and young readers (ages 8-12), fiction and nonfiction reprints and originals. Pays variable royalty and advance. Queries must be accompanied by outline and sample chapter, but publisher does not accept unsolicited manuscripts. SASE.
Nonfiction: Material will be returned unread unless sent at Bantam's request. Please query as appropriate. Grace Bechtold, Vice President & Executive Editor, Religious & Inspiratonal Publishing; Toni Burbank, Executive Editor (women's studies, school and college); Senior Editors: Linda Price (cookbooks, health), Kathleen Moloney (general nonfiction), under the Perigord Press imprint. Queries will be considered for joint hardcover/paperback imprint. Executive Editor: Peter Gethers (general adult fiction and nonfiction).
Fiction: Senior Editors: Kathleen Moloney (general), Linda Price (mysteries); Executive Editor, Science Fiction & Fantasy: Sydny Weinberg; Editorial Director, Young Readers Books: Ron Buell; Senior Editor: Cathy Camhy (women's fiction); Associate Editor, General Books: Linda Clark.

BANYAN BOOKS, INC., Box 431160, Miami FL 33143. (305)665-6011. Director: Ellen Edelen. Publishes hardcover and paperback originals (90%) and reprints (10%). Published 8 titles in 1979, 10 in 1980. Specializes in Florida regional and natural history books. Pays 10% royalty on retail price; no advance. Subsidy publishes 10% of books; "worthwhile books that fill a gap in the market, but whose sales potential is limited." Send prints if illustrations are to be used with ms. Photocopied submissions OK. Reports in 1 month. SASE. Free book catalog.
Nonfiction: Publishes regional history and books on nature and horticulture. Submission of outline/synopsis, sample chapters preferred, but will accept queries.
Recent Nonfiction Title: *Trees of Central Florida*, by Lakela and Wunderlin.
Tips: "Look for gaps in material available in bookstores and libraries; ask booksellers and librarians what they are asked for that is not readily available. Read *Publishers Weekly* and *Library Journal*; be aware of trends and what is being accepted for publication."

A.S. BARNES AND CO., INC., 11175 Flintkote Avenue, San Diego CA 92121. (714)457-3200. President: Charles C. Tillinghast. Vice President/Editorial Director: Cynthia B. Tillinghast. Managing Editor: JoAnn Fisher. Publishes hardcover and paperback originals and reprints; occasionally publishes translations and anthologies. Contract negotiable: "each contract considered on its own merits." Advance varies, depending on author's previous works and nature of book. Averages 80-100 titles/year. Will send a catalog. Query. Reports in 1 month. SASE.
Nonfiction: "General nonfiction with special emphasis on cinema, antiques, sports, and crafts."
Recent Nonfiction Titles: *Film Noir*, by Foster Hirsch (cinema); and *Chromos*, by Francine Kirsch (paper collectibles).

BARNES & NOBLE, Division of Harper & Row. 10 E. 53rd St., New York NY 10022. (212)593-7000. Editors: Nancy Cone and Jeanne Flagg. Editoral Director: Irving Levey. Publishes paperback originals (25%) and paperback reprints (75%). Published 149 titles in 1979. Pays standard paperback royalties for reprints; offers variable advance. Simultaneous and photocopied submissions OK. SASE. Reports in 1 month.
Nonfiction: Education paperbacks including "College Outline Series" (summaries of college subjects) and Everyday Handbooks (self-teaching books on academic subjects, and skills and hobbies). Query or submit outline/synopsis and sample chapters.
Recent Nonfiction Titles: *Energy Saving Handbook*, sold to various States in the US; and language books including conversational French, Spanish and Italian.

BARRE PUBLISHERS, Valley Rd., Barre MA 01005. Publisher: Jane West. Publishes hardcover and paperback originals. Offers standard book contract. Free book catalog. Photocopied submissions OK. Submit outline and sample chapters or complete ms. Reports in 4 weeks. SASE.
Nonfiction: "We specialize in books on fine craftsmanship and design. History, Americana, art, photography, travel, cooking and foods, nature, recreation and pets. No length requirements; no restrictions for style, outlook, or structure. Our emphasis on quality of manufacture sets our books apart from the average publications. Particularly interested in art and folk art." Recently published *The Log Cabin, Molas, Running the Rivers of North American* and *Pamper Your Possessions*.

BARRON'S EDUCATIONAL SERIES, INC., 113 Crossways Park Dr., Woodbury NY 11797. Publishes hardcover and paperback originals. Publishes 170 titles/year. Pays royalty, based on both wholesale and retail price. Simultaneous and photocopied submissions OK. Reports in 3 months. SASE. Free book catalog.
Nonfiction: Adult education, art, cookbooks, foreign language, review books, sports, test preparation materials and textbooks. Query or submit outline/synopsis and a sample chapter.
Recent Nonfiction Titles: *How to Prepare for the Minimum Competency Examination in Mathematics*, by Angelo Wieland (test preparation); *Man Ray: The Photographic Image*, by Janus (art photography); and *The Big Book of Mountaineering*, by Bruno Moravetz.

BASIC BOOKS, INC., 10 E. 53rd St., New York NY 10022. (212)593-7057. Editoral Director: Martin Kessler. Publishes hardcover originals (90%) and paperback reprints "of own hardcovers" (10%). Publishes 65 titles/year. Pays standard royalty; negotiates advance depending on projects. SASE. Reports in 1 month.
Nonfiction: Political, social, behavorial and economics for universities and trade. Prefers submission of complete ms; outline/synopsis and sample chapters acceptable.
Recent Nonfiction Titles: *Godel-Escher-Bach*, by D. Hofstadter (thinking computers and their relation to culture); *Who Gets Ahead?*, by C. Jenks (a social study); and *Freud-Biologist of the Mind*, by F. Sulloway (intellectual biography of Freud).

BEACON PRESS, 25 Beacon St., Boston MA 02108. (617)742-2110. Director/Editor-in-Chief: MaryAnn Lash. Publishes hardcover originals (50%) and paperback reprints (50%). Averages 20 titles/year. "Our audience is composed of liberal/religious and other book readers interested in a wide variety of subjects pertaining to the social and political issues facing contemporary society." Pays 7½% royalty on retail price (paperback); 10% on hardbound; advance averages $3,000. Photocopied submissions OK. Reports in 6 weeks. SASE. Free book catalog.
Nonfiction: General nonfiction, religion, world affairs, social studies, history, psychology, art, literature, and philosophy. Query.
Recent Nonfiction Titles: *Civil Wars*, by June Jordan (contemporary essays); and *Atomic Soldiers: American Victims of Nuclear Experiments*, by Howard Rosenberg (contemporary affairs).
Tips: "Write about complex and important issues for the average reader."

BEAR WALLOW BOOKS, Box 579, Nashville IN 47448. (812)988-2342. Publisher/Editorial Director: Janet S. Collester. Publishes hardcover and paperback originals. Averages 5 titles/year. Pays royalty on both wholesale and retail price, and buys some mss outright. "Price negotiable, based on book." Offers negotiable advance. Simultaneous and photocopied submissions OK. SASE. Reports in 3 weeks. Free book catalog.
Nonfiction: Americana (especially Indiana and Midwest), cookbooks, cooking and foods, history, how-to, nature, recreation and travel. "Particularly interested in material with a Southern Indiana orientation. No fiction, poetry or juveniles." Query. "Unsolicited mss will be returned unopened."
Recent Nonfiction Titles: *Old Shaker Recipes; Old Amish Recipes; Old-Fashioned Mushroom Recipes;* and *Old-Fashioned Tomato Recipes*.

BEAU LAC PUBLISHERS, Box 248, Chuluota FL 32766. Publishes hardcover and paperback originals. SASE.
Nonfiction: "Military subjects. Specialist in the social side of service life." Query. Recently published *The Officer's Family Social Guide*, by M.P. Gross; and *Military Weddings and the Military Ball*, by M.P. Gross.

BEAUFORT BOOKS, INC., 9 E. 40th St., New York NY 10016. (212)685-8588. Editorial Director: Susan Suffes. Publishes hardcover and trade paperback originals (100%). Averages 40-50 titles/year. Pays 7½-15% royalty on retail price; offers variable advance. Simultaneous and photocopied submissions OK. SASE. Reports in 2 weeks on queries; 1 month on mss. Book catalog for 6x9 SAE and 2 first class stamps.
Nonfiction: Biograhpy, cookbook, how-to, illustrated book, self-help and young adult. Subjects include cooking and foods, health, history, hobbies, psychology and recreation. Query, or submit outline synopsis and sample chapters or complete ms.
Recent Nonfiction Titles: *The Alexander Technique*, by Stransky/Stone (health/self-help); *Farming the Waters*, by Limburg (natural science); and *Lemon-Aid*, by Edmonston (car advice).
Fiction: Adventure, and contemporary thrillers. "No first novels, no science fiction." Query or submit complete ms.
Recent Fiction Titles: *Minerva's Stepchild*, by Forrester (young adult/adult/women); *Periscope Red*, by Rohmer (oil thriller); and *The Flowered Box*, by Green (mystery).

BELL SPRINGS PUBLISHING, Box 640, Laytonville CA 95454. Editorial Director: S.K. Bear. Publishes hardcover and paperback originals. Averages 3 titles/year. Pays 8-10% royalty (negotiable) on retail price; sometimes offers advance. Simultaneous and photocopied submissions OK. SASE. Reports in 1 week. Book catalog for SASE.

Nonfiction: Business and music. "We have 2 divisions, how-to business books and music books. In music, we're interested in popular, jazz, rock & roll—about the music, the musicians and the instruments as well as the music itself. We do not publish sheet music." Query.

Recent Nonfiction Titles: *Small Time Operator*, by Kamoroff (starting your own business); *We Own It*, by Beatty (co-ops and collectives); and *The 1982 Rock & Roll Calendar*.

THE BENJAMIN COMPANY, INC., One Westchester Plaza, Elmsford NY 10523. (914)592-8088. Executive Vice President: Ted Benjamin. Publishes hardcover and paperback originals. Averages 10-12 titles/year. Buys mss by outright purchase. Offers advance. Simultaneous and photocopied submissions OK. Reports in 2 months.

Nonfiction: Business/economics, cookbooks, cooking and foods, health, hobbies, how-to, self-help, sports and consumerism. "Ours is a very specialized kind of publishing—for clients (industrial and association) to use in promotional, PR, or educational programs. If an author has an idea for a book, and close connections with a company that might be interested in using that book, we will be very interested in working together with the author to 'sell' the program and the idea of a special book for that company. Once published, our books do get trade distribution, through a distributing publisher, so the author generally sees the book in regular book outlets as well as in the special programs undertaken by the sponsoring company. Normally we do not encourage submission of mss. We usually commission an author to write for us. The most helpful thing an author can do is to let us know what he or she has written, or what subjects he or she feels competent to write about. We will contact the author when our needs indicate that the author might be the right person to produce a needed ms." Query. Submit outline/synopsis and sample chapters.

Recent Nonfiction Titles: *Complete Dessert Cookbook* (C&H Sugar); *What Have You Done for Me Lately?*, by A. Perlow (labor union activity); and *A Century of Light*, by J. Cox (General Electric's 100th anniversary of light bulb).

BENNETT PUBLISHING CO., 809 W. Detweiller Dr., Peoria IL 61615. (309)691-4454. Editorial Director: Michael Kenny. Publishes hardcover and paperback originals. Specializes in textbooks and related materials. Pays 10% royalty for textbooks "based on cash received, less for supplements"; no advance. Averages 25 titles/year. Query "with a sample chapter that represents much of the book; not a general introduction if the ms is mostly specific 'how-to' instructions." Send prints if photos/illustrations are to accompany the book. Photocopied submissions OK. Reports in 2-4 weeks. SASE. Free book catalog.

Nonfiction: Publishes textbooks and related items for home economics, industrial education, and art programs in schools, junior high and above.

Recent Nonfiction Titles: *Finding My Way*, by Dr. Audrey Riker and Dr. Charles Riker (sex education); *Graphic Reproduction*, by Dr. William P. Spence and Dr. David Vequist (printing and related processes); and *Professional Cooking and Baking*, by Mary Ray and Beda Dondi (vocational foods textbook).

BERKLEY PUBLISHING CORP., 200 Madison Ave., New York NY 10016. Editorial Director: Bill Grose. Editor-in-Chief: Roger Cooper. Publisher: Rena Wolner. "We do very little original paperback publishing; most of our books are reprints of hardcovers." Publishes about 190 titles/year. Simultaneous and photocopied submissions OK. Reports in 1-2 months. SASE.

Nonfiction: Biography, psychology (popular), self-help, health and nutrition. Submit through agent only. State availability of photos or illustrations.

Recent Nonfiction Titles: *Ordeal*, by Linda Lovelace; and *A Handbook for New Parents*, by Dr. Alvin Eden.

Fiction: Fantasy, historical, mainstream, mystery, romance, science fiction, suspense and western. Submit through agent only.

Recent Fiction Titles: *Children of Dune*, by Frank Herbert (science fiction); and *Whispers*, by Dean Koontz.

THE BERKSHIRE TRAVELLER PRESS, INC., Stockbridge MA 01262. (413)298-3636. Editorial Director: Norman T. Simpson. Senior Editor: Virginia Rowe. Publishes paperback originals (95%) and reprints (5%). Publishes 5 titles/year. Pays 10% royalty on wholesale or retail price; offers average $300-800 advance. Simultaneous submissions OK. SASE. Reports in 2-3 months. Book catalog for SASE.

Nonfiction: Americana; biography (light, early America); cookbooks, cooking and foods; history (early America); how-to (related to country architecture; energy conservation); humor (related to specific subjects); nature (energy conservation); recreation (travel); and travel (related and off-beat with wide appeal). Does *not* want to see technical or scholarly treatises or textbooks. Submit outline/synopsis and sample chapters. All unsolicted mss are returned unopened.

Recent Nonfiction Titles: *Country Inns & Back Roads, North America*, by N.T. Simpson (travel); *A Guide to Music Festivals in America*, by C.P. Rabin (travel/music); *Apple Orchard Cookbook*, by J. Christensen and B. Levin; and *A Guide for Solotravel Abroad*, by E.A. Baxel.

BETHANY FELLOWSHIP, INC., 6820 Auto Club Rd., Minneapolis MN 55438. (612)944-2121. Managing Editor: Carol Johnson. Publishes hardcover and paperback originals (85%) and paper-back reprints (15%). "Contracts negotiable." Averages 50 titles/year. Simultaneous and photocopied submissions OK. Reports in 1-2 months. Free book catalog on request.

Nonfiction: Publishes biography (evangelical Christian), devotional (evangelical, charismatic) and self-help books. "No poetry, please." Query.

Recent Nonfiction Titles: *Book of Bible Lists*, by Joel Meredith (reference); *Developing Spiritually Sensitive Children*, by Olive Alexander (family); *Today I Feel Like a Warm Fuzzy*, by William Coleman (devotional); and *If God Loves Me Why Can't I Get My Locker Open?*, by Lorraine Peterson (teen devotional).

Fiction: Well-written stories with a Christian message. Submit outline and 2-3 sample chapters.

Recent Fiction Titles: *The Jordan Intercept*, by J. Alexander McKenzie (adventure/intrigue); *Love Comes Softly*, by Janette Oke (prairie romance); and *Little Princess of the Flowers*, by Bonnie Clement (children's fantasy).

BETTER HOMES AND GARDENS BOOKS, 1716 Locust St., Des Moines IA 50336. Editor: Gerald Knox. Publishes hardcover originals and reprints. Published 18 titles in 1979, 20 in 1980. "Ordinarily we pay an outright fee for work (amount depending on the scope of the assignment). If the book is the work of one author, we sometimes offer royalties in addition to the fee." Prefers outlines and sample chapters, but will accept complete ms. Will consider photocopied submissions. Reports in 6 weeks. SASE.

Nonfiction: "We publish nonfiction in many family and home service categories, including gardening, decorating and remodeling, sewing and crafts, money management, entertaining, handyman's topics, cooking and nutrition, and other subjects of home service value. Emphasis is on how-to and on stimulating people to action. We require concise, factual writing. Audience is primarily husbands and wives with home and family as their main center of interest. Style should be informative and lively with a straightforward approach. Stress the positive. Emphasis is entirely on reader service. We approach the general audience with a confident air, instilling in them a desire and the motivation to accomplish things. Food book areas that we have already dealt with in detail are currently overworked by writers submitting to us. We rely heavily on a staff of home economist editors for food books. We are interested in non-food books that can serve mail order and book club requirements (to sell at least for $9.95 and up) as well as trade. Rarely is our first printing of a book less than 100,000 copies. Publisher recommends careful study of specific *Better Homes and Gardens* book titles before submitting material."

BILINGUAL EDUCATIONAL SERVICES, INC., 1607 Hope St., South Pasadena CA 91030. (213)682-3456. General Manager: Joann N. Baker. Publishes hardcover and paperback originals. Averages 2 titles/year. Negotiates royalty; offers no advance. Simultaneous and photocopied submissions OK. SASE. Reports in 3 months. Book catalog for 9x12 SASE.

Nonfiction: Publishes adult and juvenile nonfiction. Interested in "anything which will appeal to Spanish-speaking people, especially Chicano and Southwest US topics—high-interest low-vocabulary—easy to translate into Spanish." Submit outline/synopsis and sample chapters. Submit complete ms if intended for translation.

Recent Nonfiction Titles: *Knowledge Aid Picture Dictionary*; *450 Years of Chicano History*; and *US Government in Action* (Spanish translation of English textbook).

Fiction: Publishes adult and juvenile fiction. Same subject requirements as nonfiction.

*BINFORD & MORT, PUBLISHERS, 2536 SE 11th Ave., Portland OR 97202. (503)238-9666. Editor-in-Chief: L.K. Phillips. President: Thomas Binford. Publishes hardcover and paperback originals (80%) and reprints (20%). Pays 10% royalty on retail price; offers variable advance (to established authors). Occasionally does some subsidy publishing, "when ms merits it, but it does not fit into our type of publishing." Publishes about 24 titles annually. Reports in 2-4 months. SASE. Free book catalog.

Nonfiction: Publishes books about the Pacific Northwest, mainly in the historical field. Also Americana, art, biography, cookbooks, cooking and foods, history, nature, photography, recreation, reference, sports, and travel. Query.

Recent Nonfiction Titles: *Northwest Conifers*, Dale N. Bever; *Portland Names and Neighborhoods*, by Eugene Snyder; and *China Doctor of John Day*, by Jeffrey Barlow and Christine Richardson. **Fiction:** Publishes historical and western books. Must be strongly laced with historical background.

BIOMEDICAL PUBLICATIONS, Box 495, Davis CA 95617. (916)756-8453. General Manager: L. Mak. Average 3-5 titles/year. Pays 10-20% royalty on wholesale or retail price; offers average $300 advance. Simultaneous and photocopied submissions OK. SASE. Reports in 1 week on queries; 3 weeks on mss. Free book catalog.
Nonfiction: Reference, technical and textbook. Subjects include health and biomedical sciences. "Manuscripts on industrial toxicology, environmental contamination, drug and chemical toxicology, forensic science. Our readers include toxicologists, phamacologists, clinical pharmacists, pathologists, forensic scientists and attorneys." Query or submit outline/synopsis and sample chapters.
Recent Nonfiction Titles: *Biological Monitoring Methods for Industrial Chemicals*, by Baselt (laboratory manual); *Forensic Toxicology*, by Cravey (textbook); and *Studies on Psychoactive Drug-Involved Deaths*, by Gottschalk (reference).

*BIWORLD PUBLISHERS, INC., 671 N. State, Orem UT 84057. (801)224-5803. Vice President: Al Lisonbee. Publishes hardcover and trade paperback originals. Average 12-20 titles/year. Subsidy publishes 10% of books, based on each individual case. Pays 8-12% royalty on retail price; no advance. Simultaneous and photocopied submissions OK. SASE. Reports in 2 weeks on queries; 1 month on mss. Free book catalog.
Nonfiction: Cookbook, how-to, reference, self-help and textbook. Subjects include cooking and foods, health and nature. "We're looking for reputable, professionally-done, well-researched manuscripts dealing in health, natural medicine, etc." Submit outline/synopsis and sample chapters or complete ms.
Recent Nonfiction Titles: *The Treatment of Cancer With Herbs*, by John Heinerman (health); and *The Herbal Connection*, by Ethan Nebelkoff ("drug addiction and use of herbs to get off").
Tips: "The health field is just now dawning. Health-related books of quality research are in demand."

THE BLACKSBURG GROUP, INC., Blacksburg VA 24060. (703)951-9030. President: Jonathan A. Titus, PhD. Editorial Director: Christopher A. Titus, PhD. Senior Editor: J.R. Smallwood. "Our group writes and edits books from outside authors. Our books are published by technical publishers. We offer competitive royalties, advances for technical works, and we offer our writers many advantages not found with most technical publishers. We are not agents and do not take any portion of the author's royalties for our publishing efforts." Publishes paperback originals. Publishes 12 titles/year. Pays 7½-13% royalty; offers average $800 advance. Photocopied submissions OK. SASE. Reports in 1 month. Free book catalog.
Nonfiction: Electronics and ham radio hobbies; how-to (electronic projects); reference, technical and textbooks (computers, electronics, and computer programming). Especially interested in "microcomputer applications (hardware and software), digital and analog electronics, word processing, telephone applications, fiber optics, books with experiments/projects/hands-on learning, robotics, home satellite TV and home solar control." Query, submit outline/synopsis and sample chapters or complete ms.
Recent Nonfiction Titles: *Programming & Interfacing the 6502*, by M.L. DeJong; *Guide to CMOS Basics*, by H.M. Berlin; and *TRS-80 Interfacing*, by J.A. Titus (all technical electronic).

JOHN F. BLAIR, PUBLISHER, 1406 Plaza Dr., Winston-Salem NC 27103. (919)768-1374. Editor-in-Chief: John F. Blair. Publishes hardcover originals; occasionally paperbacks and reprints. Royalty to be negotiated. Published 6 titles in 1979, 6 in 1980. Free book catalog. Submit complete ms. Reports in 2 months. SASE.
Nonfiction: Especially interested in well-researched adult biography and history. Preference given to books dealing with Southeastern United States. Also interested in environment, politics, recreation, humor, education.
Recent Nonfiction Titles: *The New River Controversy*, by Thomas J. Schoenbaum; *A Cuban Story*, by Marcia Del Mar; and *The Learning-Disabled Child*, by Suzanne Stevens.
Fiction: "We are most interested in serious novels with high literary merit for adults. No category fiction. Juveniles should be for ages 10-14; no picture books. We are not accepting poetry mss at this time."
Recent Fiction Titles: *The Epic of Alexandra*, by Dorothy Dayton; and *The Tessie C. Price*, by Jean Heyn.

THE BOBBS-MERRILL CO., INC., 4 W. 58th St., New York NY 10019. Publisher: Grace G. Shaw. Publishes hardcover originals and some trade paper originals and reprints. Pays variable royalties and advances depending on author's reputation and nature of book. Publishes 30 titles/year. Query. No unsolicited mss. Reports in 4-6 weeks. SASE.
General Fiction and Nonfiction: Little fiction; publishes American novels. Emphasizes nonfiction: publishes history, biography/autobiography, health, medical, diet, how-to, self-improvement, military, gardening and crafts. No poetry.
Recent Nonfiction Title: *Public Speaking for Private People*, by Art Linkletter.

THE BOND WHEELRIGHT COMPANY, Box 296, Freeport ME 04032. (207)865-6045. Editor: Mary Louise Morris. Pays 10% royalty on retail price. No advance. Published 8-9 titles in 1980. Query. SASE.
Nonfiction: "We are interested in nonfiction only—books with New England regional topics or specialized subject matter, or calligraphy books."
Recent Nonfiction Titles: *The Nubble*, by C. Shattuck (local lightstation history); and *Illustrated Dictionary of Lobstering*, by K. Merriam.

BOOKCRAFT, INC., 1848 W. 2300 South, Salt Lake City UT 84119. Senior Editor: H. George Bickerstaff. Publishes (mainly hardcover) originals and reprints. Averages 25 titles/year. Pays standard 10-12½-15% royalty on retail price; "we rarely make an advance on a new author." Published 28 titles in 1979, 28 in 1980; plans 25 in 1981. Will send a catalog and a copy of information for authors to a writer on request. Query. Will consider photocopied submissions. "Include contents page with ms." Reports in about 2 months. SASE.
Nonfiction: "We publish for members of The Church of Jesus Christ of Latter-Day Saints (Mormons) and do not distribute to the national market. All our books are closely oriented to the faith and practices of the LDS church. We will be glad to review such mss, but mss which have merely a general religious appeal are not acceptable. Ideal book lengths range from about 64 pages to 160 or so, depending on subject, presentation, and age level. We look for a fresh approach—rehashes of well-known concepts or doctrines not acceptable. Mss should be anecdotal unless truly scholarly or on a specialized subject. Outlook must be positive. We do not publish anti-Mormon works. We don't publish poetry, plays, personal philosophizings, family histories, or personal histories. We also publish short and moderate length books for Mormon youth, about ages 14 to 19, mostly nonfiction. These reflect LDS principles without being 'preachy'; must be motivational. 20,000-30,000 words is about the length, though we would accept good longer mss. This is a tough area to write in, and the mortality rate for such mss is high. We only publish 1 or 2 new juvenile titles annually."
Recent Nonfiction Titles: *Simplified Husbandship, Simplified Fathership*, by Richard M. Eyre; *The Love Book*, by Marvin Payne (youth); *The Prophet Teaches Little Saints*, by Marsha Jacobson (juvenile); and *Love is Easy . . . Love is Hard*, by Pat M. Allen (juvenile).
Fiction: Must be closely oriented to the LDS church.
Recent Fiction Titles: *My Enemy, My Love*, by Susan Evans McCloud (historical romance); and *The Bishop's Horse Race*, by Blaine and Brenton Yorgason (humorous adventure).

BOOKS FOR BUSINESS, INC., 1100 17th St. NW, Washington, D.C. 20036. (202)466-2372. Publishes hardcover and paperback originals (80%) and reprints. Specializes in high-priced books on business or international trade. Published 3 titles in 1979, 10 in 1980; plans 20 in 1981. "Looking for a unique content area geared to business and/or the entrepreneur. New and different concepts are welcomed. Usually royalties start at 10%; sometimes 5% for anthologies, but this is not a fixed rule." No advance. Send contact sheets for selection of illustrations. Simultaneous and photocopied submissions OK. Reports in 1-2 months. Book catalog for SASE.
Recent Nonfiction Titles: *Legal Barriers to Solar Heating and Cooling of Buildings*; *How to Develop & Manage a Successful Condominium*; *It's Your Money: A Consumer's Guide to Credit*.
Tips: "Reference and how-to books should not date themselves. Their main purpose should be years of survival."

BOREALIS PRESS, LTD., 9 Ashburn Dr., Nepean, Ontario, Canada K2E 6N4. Editorial Director: Frank Tierney. Senior Editor: Glenn Clever. Publishes hardcover and paperback originals. Averages 20 titles/year. Pays 10% royalty on retail price; no advance. Reports in 8 weeks. SAE and International Reply Coupons. Book catalog $1.
Nonfiction: "Only material Canadian in content." Query.
Recent Nonfiction Titles: *Seated with the Flighty*, by John Adams (biography of Sir Gilbert Parker); *Horace Walpole, the Critic*, by Rex Barrell (study of Walpole's criticism of French literature); and *French Correspondence of Lord Chesterfield*, edited by Rex Barrell (literary criticism).

Fiction: "Only material Canadian in content." Query.
Recent Fiction Titles: *Prairie Symphony*, by Wilfrid Eggleston; *Thistle Creek*, by Nell Hanna; and *Threat Through Tibet*, by Elgin Duke (undercover army patrol in China).

THE BORGO PRESS, Box 2845, San Bernardino CA 92406. (714)884-5813. Publisher: R. Reginald. Publishes hardcover and paperback originals. Averages 12 titles/year. "About 80% of our line consists of The Milford Series: Popular Writers of Today, critical studies on modern popular writers, particularly science fiction writers." Pays royalty on retail price: "10% of gross, with a 12% escalator." No advance. "Most of our sales are to the library market." Reports in 1-2 months. SASE. Free book catalog for SASE.
Nonfiction: Publishes literary critiques, historical research, interview volumes and reference works for library and academic markets. Query with outline/synopsis and sample chapters. "We appreciate people who've looked at our books before submitting proposals; all of the books in our Milford series, for example, are based around a certain format that we prefer using." Recently published *The Rainbow Quest of Thomas Pynchon*, by Douglas A. Mackey; *Science Fiction and Fantasy Statistics*, by R. Reginald (reference); and *The Analytical Congressional Directory* (reference).

THOMAS BOUREGY AND CO., INC., 22 E. 60th St., New York NY 10022. Editor: Rita Brenig. Offers advance on publication date. Published 60 titles in 1980, 60 in 1981; plans 60 in 1982. Reports in 3 months. SASE.
Fiction: Romances, nurse/romances, westerns and gothic novels. Avoid sensationalist elements. Query with SASE. No sample chapters. Length: about 50,000 words. Also publishes Airmont Classics Series.
Recent Fiction Titles: *Nurse Whitney's Paradise*, by Betty Rose Gunn (nurse-romance); *The Magic of Paris*, by Berta LaVan Barker (light romance); *Pictures of Fear*, by Lucy Fuchs (gothic); and *Gunfire at Flintlock*, by Terrell L. Bowers.

R.R. BOWKER CO., 1180 Avenue of the Americas, New York NY 10036. (212)764-5100. Editor-In-Chief, Book Division: Judith S. Garodnick. Senior Editor, Prefessional and Reference Books: Nancy Volkman. Managing Editor, Directories: Olga S. Weber. Pays negotiable royalty. Reports in 2 months. SASE.
Nonfiction: Publishes books for the book trade and library field, reference books and bibliographies. Query; "send in a very thoroughly developed proposal with a table of contents, representative chapters, and analysis of the competition with your idea."

BOWLING GREEN UNIVERSITY POPULAR PRESS, Popular Culture Center, Bowling Green State University, Bowling Green OH 43403. Editors: Ray B. Browne, Pat Browne. Publishes hardcover and paperback originals. Offers variable royalty; no advance. Published 15 titles last year. Free book catalog. SASE.
Nonfiction: "Popular culture books generally. We print for the academic community interested in popular culture and popular media." Interested in nonfiction mss on "folklore, black culture, popular literature, detective fiction and westerns." Will consider any book-length mss. "No multiple submissions." Submit complete ms.
Recent Nonfiction Titles: *Beams Falling: The Art of Dashiell Hammett*, by Peter Walfe; and *Fallen Angel: The Unchaste Women in Fiction*, by Sally Mitchell.

BRADBURY PRESS, INC., 2 Overhill Rd., Scarsdale NY 10583. (914)472-5100. Editor-in-Chief: Richard Jackson. Publishes hardcover originals. Published 11 titles in 1979, 19 in 1980; plans 20 in 1981. "We're distributed by E.P. Dutton." Pays 10% royalty or 5% on retail price to author, 5% to artist; advance averages $1,000. Photocopied submissions OK. Reports in 3 months. SASE. Book catalog for 28¢
Fiction: Contemporary fiction; adventure and humor. Also "stories about real kids; special interest in realistic dialogue." No fantasy or religious material.
Recent Fiction Titles: *Tiger Eyes*, by Judy Blume; and *Tunnel Vision*, by Fran Arric.

BRADT ENTERPRISES, INC., 54 Dudley St., Cambridge MA 02140. President: George N. Bradt. Publishes trade paperback originals. Averages 3 titles/year. Pays 5-7½% royalty on retail price; offers average $500 advance. Simultaneous and photcopied submissions OK. SASE. Reports in 2 weeks on queries; 1 month on mss. Book catalog for SAE and 1 first class stamp.
Nonfiction: Travel. Subjects include animals, nature and travel. "In the near future, we'll stay in travel, but we will consider scripts outside the narrow backpacking field. We're highly specialized." No material that does not pertain to international travel. Query ("post card fine"); then submit outline/synopsis and sample chapters.
Recent Nonfiction Titles: *Backpacking Venezuela*; *Backpacking Peru*; and *South America River*

Trips, by Bradt (travel).
Tips: "Travel, do something original (not kinky), and tell us about it. Or do mainline travel from a new perspective."

BRANDEN PRESS, INC., 21 Station St., Box 843, Brookline Village, Boston MA 02147. (617)734-2045. Editor-in-Chief: B.J. Levin. Publishes hardcover and paperback originals (70%) and reprints (30%). Pays 10% royalty up to 5,000 copies; 15% thereafter. "We offer an advance only on important books and cannot give an average amount. We publish some scholarly books." Publishes about 30 titles annually. Photocopied submissions OK. Reports in 6 weeks. SASE. Free book catalog.
Imprints: *Masterworks Series* (art and music); *International Pocket Library* (reprints of classics); *Findhorn Publications* (new age/inspirational, Scotland); and *Popular Technolgies, Inc.* (microcomputer books).
Nonfiction: "We publish books of all sorts and kinds and are willing to consider any ms, but are not interested in fiction or poetry." Query.
Recent Titles: *Fundamentals of Applied Industrial Management*, by J. Glasser (educational); *Two-Language Battery of Tests*, by A. Caso (bilingual); *Myopia Myth*, by Donald Rehm (health); and *Earth at Omega V*, by Donald Keys (handbook).

CHARLES T. BRANFORD CO., Box 41, Newton Centre MA 02159. (617)924-1020. Editor-in-Chief: I.F. Jacobs. Hardcover and paperback originals (80%) and reprints (20%). Offers 10% royalty on retail price. No advance. Publishes about 4 titles annually. Photocopied submissions OK. Reports in 2 weeks. SASE. Free book catalog.
Nonfiction: Hobbies; how-to; recreation; and self-help. Query first.
Recent Nonfiction Title: *The Constance Howard Book of Stitches.*

GEORGE BRAZILLER, INC., 1 Park Ave., New York NY 10016. Offers standard 10-12½-15% royalty contrat; Offers variable advance depending on author's reputation and nature of book. No unsolicited mss. Reports in 6 weeks. SASE.
General Fiction and Nonfiction: Publishes fiction and nonfiction; literature, art, philosophy, history. Query.

BREITENBUSH BOOKS, Box 02137, Portland OR 97202. Executive Editor: James Anderson. Publishes hardcover and trade paperback originlas. Averages 4-6 titles/year. Pays negotiable royalty on retail price; offers average $250 advance. SASE. Reports in 3 weeks on queries; 3 months on mss. Free book catalog.
Poetry: Needs are limited. No "concrete or overtly confessional poems." Submit 5 samples with query.
Recent Poetry Titles: *Collected Poems*, by Mary Barnard (formal/modern lyric); *Different Ways To Pray*, by Naomi Shihab Nye (contemporary lyric); and *Jabon*, by Gary Gildner (parable/contemporary).
Tips: "Know what kind of book you are trying to market, what segment of the book-buying population would be interested, and investigate publishers who have had success with your kind of book."

BREVET PRESS, INC., Box 1404, Sioux Falls SD 57101. Editor-in-Chief: Donald P. Mackintosh. Managing Editor: Peter E. Reid. Publishes hardcover and paperback originals (67%) and reprints (33%). Published 4 titles in 1979, 6 in 1980. Specializes in business management, history, place names, historical marker series. Pays 5% royalty; advance averages $1,000. Query; "after query, detailed instructions will follow if we are interested." Send copies if photos/illustrations are to accompany ms. Simultaneous and photocopied submissions OK. Reports in 1-2 months. SASE. Free book catalog.
Nonfiction: Publishes Americana (A. Melton, editor); business (D.P. Mackintosh, editor); history (B. Mackintosh, editor); and technical books (Peter Reid, editor). Recently published *Illinois Historical Markers and Sites* (nonfiction historical series); and *Challenge*, by R. Karolevitz (history).

BRIARCLIFF PRESS PUBLISHERS, (formerly Dorison House Publishers), 11 Wimbledon Ct., Jericho NY 11753. Editorial Director: Trudy Settel. Senior Editor: J. Frieman. Publishes hardcover and paperback originals. Publishes 8 titles/year. Pays $4,000-5,000 by outright purchase; average advance of $1,000. "We do not use unsolicited manuscripts. Ours are custom books prepared for businesses and assignments are initiated by us."
Nonfiction: How-to, cookbooks, sports, travel, fitness/health, diet, gardening, and crafts. "We want our books to be designed to meet the needs of specific business." Query.
Recent Nonfiction Title: *Amana Microwave Oven Cookbook*, by C. Adams.

BRICK HOUSE PUBLISHING CO., 3 Main St., Andover MA 01810 (617)475-9568. Publisher: Jack D. Howell. Publishes hardcover and paperback originals. Averages 12 titles/year. Pays 7-10% royalty on paperback and 10-15% on hardcover. Photocopied submissions OK. Reports in 4 weeks. SASE. Free book catalog.

Nonfiction: Trade paperbacks generally in the $6-12 range. Alternative sources of energy material; "and would like to diversify into other how-to and alternative lifestyle books. We will consider any quality nonfiction trade material."

Recent Nonfiction Titles: *Passive Solar Energy*, by Bruce Anderson and Malcolm Wells; and *Solar Retrofit*, by Dan Reif.

Tips: "Include complete prospectus telling why and for whom you are writing, listing all aspects, graphs, photos, line drawings, length, etc."

BRIGHAM YOUNG UNIVERSITY PRESS, University Press Bldg., Provo UT 84602. Director: Ernest L. Olson. Acting Managing Editor: Louise Hanson. Publishes hardcover and paperback originals (85%) and reprints (15%). Averages 17-22 titles/year. "We subsidy publish 15% of our books. If a book has scholarly merit but little potential for repaying the cost of publication, we encourage the author to seek a subsidy from an institution or foundation." Pays royalties based on estimated market potential, ranging 0-15% of wholesale price; offers very small advances. Reports in 3-6 weeks. SASE. Free book catalog.

Nonfiction: Scholarly nonfiction, textbooks, and high-level popularizations. "We are interested in high-quality work from any discipline, but we focus mainly on Western regional studies, preschool education, outdoor recreation, and the social sciences, especially anthropological studies dealing with the American Indian. No length preferences. We do not publish fiction or children's literature." Query.

Recent Nonfiction Titles: *Indeh: An Apache Odyssey*, by Eve Ball; *Japanese Woodblock Prints*, by Lucille Webber; and *On Being a Christian and a Lawyer*, by Thomas Shaffer.

BROADMAN PRESS, 127 9th Ave. N, Nashville TN 37234. Editorial Director: Thomas L. Clark. Publishes hardcover and paperback originals (85%) and reprints (15%). Averages 100 titles/year. Pays 5-10% royalty on retail price; no advance. Photocopied submissions OK "only if they're sharp and clear." SASE. Reports in 2 months.

Nonfiction: Religion. "We are open to freelance submissions in the children's and inspirational area. Materials in both areas must be suited for a conservative Protestant readership. No poetry, biography, sermons, or anything outside the area of Protestant religion." Query, submit outline/synopsis and sample chapters, or submit complete ms.

Recent Nonfiction Titles: *From Night to Sunlight*, by Thomas Whitfield; *The Wise Woman*, by Joyce Rogers; and *What Every Husband Should Know*, by Jack Taylor.

Fiction: Religious. "We publish almost no fiction—less than five titles per year. For our occasional publication we want not only a very good story, but also one that sets forth Christian values. Nothing that lacks a positive Christian emphasis; nothing that fails to sustain reader interest." Submit complete ms.

Tips: "Bible study is very good for us, but our publishing is largely restricted in this area to works that we enlist on the basis of specific author qualifications."

WILLIAM C. BROWN CO., PUBLISHERS, 2460 Kerper Blvd., Dubuque IA 52001. Vice President, Director of Product Devlopment: Raymond C. Deveaux. Publishes 80 titles/year. Pays variable royalty on wholesale price. SASE. Query.

Nonfiction: College textbooks. "Be aware of the reading level for the intended audience."

Recent Nonfiction Titles: *Anatomy and Physiology*, by Hole; and *Principles of Modern Management*, by Certo, et al. (introductory management).

BRUNSWICK PUBLISHING CO., Box 555, Lawrenceville VA 23868. (804)848-3865. Publisher: Marianne S. Raymond. Publishes hardcover originals, trade and mass market paperback originals. Average 6-10 titles/year. Subsidy publishes 75% of books based on "author-publisher dialgue." Payment is based on "individual contracts according to work." Photocopied submissions OK. SAE. Reports in 2 weeks on queries; 3 weeks on mss. Book catalog for business size SAE.

Nonfiction: Biography, coffee table book, cookbook, how-to, humor, illustrated book, juvenile, reference, self-help, technical and textbook. Subjects include Americana, animals, business and economics, cooking and foods, health, history, hobbies, music, nature, philosophy, politics, psychology, religion, sociology, travel, biography, black experience and ethnic experience. "Not limited to any particular subject, but interested in Third World authors and subjects to continue Third World Monograph series." Query or submit outline/synopsis and sample chapters

Recent Nonfiction Titles: *Dictionary of Politics*, by Walter J. Raymond, S.J.D., Ph.D. (reference); *Philosophy of Education and Third World Perspective*, by Festus C. Okafor, Ph.D. (textbook); *The*

Nkrumah Regime, by Charles Jarmon, Ph.D. (monograph); and *Ali A. Mazrui*, by Sulayman S. Nyang (monograph).
Fiction: "Will consider fiction mainly on subsidy basis—not limited to special topics." Adventure, erotica, ethnic, historical, humor, mainstream and romance. Query or submit outline/synopsis and sample chapters.
Poetry: "Poetry published only on subsidy basis as of now—not limited to any particular subject."
Recent Poetry Titles: *The Footprints of Jesus*, by Isabel H. Lancaster (religious).
Tips: "Try to be either very original or very funny in material or presentation. Offer your readers excellent advice (how-to, self-help). Don't take one person's opinion of what constitutes a 'good' or 'bad' manuscript as final."

THE MARTIN BUBER PRESS, Subsidiary of The Revisionist Press, Box 2009, Brooklyn NY 11202. Editor: Bezalel Chaim. Publishes hardcover originals. Averages 12 titles/year. Pays "10% of the net selling price on each copy sold." Simultaneous and photocopied submissions OK. SASE. Reports in 2 weeks.
Nonfiction: Biography and scholarly. Subjects include business and economics, history, philosophy, politics, psychology, religion, sociology and dissertations. "We're looking for books dealing with peace movements, libertarian philosophy and social movements and international understanding." Query.
Recent Nonfiction Titles: *Proudhon's Solution of the Social Problem*, by Henry Cohen; *Max Stirner versus Karl Marx*, by Philip B. Dematteis; and *Germany's Poet-Anarchist: John Henry Mackay*, by Thomas A. Riley.

BUCK PUBLISHING CO., 2409 Vestavia Dr., Birmingham AL 35216. (205)979-2296. Editor and Publisher: Janie B. Buck. Publishes hardcover originals. Averages 2 titles/year. Pays 10% royalty on retail price; no advance. Photocopied submissions OK. SASE. Reports in 2 weeks on queries; 1 month on mss. Free book catalog.
Nonfiction: Coffee table book, illustrated book, and books about the South. Subjects include Americana (pertaining to the South); history; religion; and the South. "We especially need Southern history, books about the South." Submit outline/synopsis and sample chapters.
Recent Nonfiction Titles: *Sad Earth Sweet Heaven*, by Lucy P. Buck (Civil War diary); and *Taming of the Buck*, by William P. Buck (answers for fathers on how to live with their teenagers).
Fiction: Historical, religious and Southern. No confession, erotica, horror, western, romance or mystery. Submit outline/synopsis and sample chapters.
Recent Fiction Titles: *My Country Roads* by Lou Brown (essay on life in the deep South); and *The Old Trund*, by Mary K. Butler ("a little girl's gowing up during the depression after her father died and left her mother with 5 children").

BUSH PRESS, Bush Press Communications Ltd., Box 32-037, Devonport, Auckland 9, New Zealand. Editor and Publisher: Gordon Ell. Publishes trade paperback originals. Averages 7 titles/year. Pays 7½-12½% royalty on retail price; offers "expenses only" as advance. Photocopied submissions OK. SASE. Reports in 1 month. "Brochures available, SAE appreciated."
Nonfiction: How-to, humor, illustrated book, juvenile, reference, self-help, technical, textbook, travel and guidebooks. Subjects include animals, history, hobbies, nature, photography, recreation, sports and travel. "Bush Press is a regional publishing house with a specific interest in New Zealand and the Pacific. We're looking for readable books about the natural sciences and New Zealand history. Will consider commissions in the fields of travel and nature guides. Interested in lively, accurate prose—usually illustrated—on most aspects of New Zealand life and the region in general." Preferred length for mss is 15,000-50,000 words. Query or submit outline/synopsis and sample chapters.
Recent Nonfiction Titles: *Encouraging Birds in the New Zealand Garden*, by Gordon Ell with color photo guide by Geoff Moon (wildlife guide); *Kawau, The Governor's Island*, by Tessa Duder (local history and track guide); and *Children's Guide to Birds of the NZ Seashore* (color photo guide).
Tips: "Start by discussing the needs of the market with a sympathetic publisher. Books need to be concise, well-researched and readable, with good illustrations and suitable presentation."

BYLS PRESS, Department of Bet Yoatz Library Services, 6247 N. Francisco Ave., Chicago IL 60659. (312)262-8959. President: Daniel D. Stuhlman. Publishes trade paperback originals. Averages 3 titles/year. Pays 7½-15% on wholesale price; no advance. Photocopied submissions OK. SASE. Reports in 1 week on queries; reporting time on mss "depends on material." Free book catalog.
Nonfiction: How-to (for teachers); and juvenile. Subjects include cooking and foods and religion ("stories aimed at children for Jewish holidays"). "We're looking for children's books for Jewish holidays that can be made into computer personalized books. In particular we need books for

Sukkot, Shabbat, and Purim. We also need titles for our teacher education series." Query; "no agents, authors only. Do not submit ideas without examining our books."

Recent Nonfiction Titles: *How Can I Best Manage My Classroom*, by Martha McCarthy (trade); *My Own Hanukah Story*, by D. Stuhlman (children's); and *My Own Pesah Story*, by D. Stuhlman (children's).

Fiction: Religious (stories for Jewish children). No pure fiction. All unsolicited mss are returned unopened."

CALEDONIA PRESS, Box 245, Racine WI 53401. (414)637-6200. Senior Editor: John Kingsley Shannon. Publishes trade paperback originals, and hardcover and trade paperback reprints. Averages 8 titles/year. Pays royalty on retail price; buys some mss outright; "very flexible." Simultaneous ("if identified as such") and photocopied submissions OK. SASE. Reports in 2 weeks on queries; 1 month on mss. Book catalog 50¢.

Imprints: Harting Grange Library (fiction). Kids Complete Guide to Pet Care (nonfiction).

Nonfiction: How-to, juvenile and technical. "We are interested only in books which satisfy all of the following conditions: 1) The title is part of a potential series; 2) The potential series appeals to a specialized, identified, delimited audience; 3) The series has long-term sales appeal; and 4) The series is marketable through both non-traditional and traditional outlets, e.g., *Bean Sprout Cuisine* can be sold through both health food stores and regular bookstores. If you have an idea for a series of books, and if you have the first three titles firmly identified, with at least seven more directly-related books in mind, write us a query letter. We will consider anything meeting the above criteria. We will consider a new book series, or a reprint books series; fiction or nonfiction." No "one-shot books." Query.

Recent Nonfiction Title: *Thomas Edison*, by Hubbard (biography).

Tips: "We are a niche publisher, not a general publisher. We discover and nurture an audience; we are not interested in topical one-week bestsellerdom."

CALIFORNIA BOOKS, Box 9551, Stanford CA 94305. Contact: Editor. Publishes trade paperback originals. Averages 4 titles/year. Pays 10-15% royalty on retail price; offers variable advance. SASE. Reports in 1 month.

Nonfiction: How-to and self-help. Subjects include health, psychology and medical. "Projected releases filled 1½ years; other 6 months open. We prefer material related to psychology or medicine by holders of MD or PhD degrees." Query.

Recent Nonfiction Title: *Consumer's & Layman's Guide To Psychotherapy & Counseling: Everything About Headshrinking Without Getting Psyched Out*, by Dr. Dennis Lee (psychology).

CALIFORNIA INSTITUTE OF PUBLIC AFFAIRS, Box 10, Claremont CA 91711. (714)624-5212. President/Director: T.C. Trzyna. Assistant: Kim Mueller. Publishes paperback originals. Published 8 titles in 1979, 6 in 1980. Negotiates royalties and outright purchases; also for some types of mss authors are not paid. Rarely offers advance. Simultaneous and photocopied submissions OK. SASE. Reports in 3 weeks. Free book catalog.

Nonfiction: "The California Institute of Public Affairs is a research foundation affiliated with The Claremont Colleges. Most of our books are written by our staff; however, we are open to publishing material by other writers that fits into our program and several titles have come to us 'over the transom.' Our list is very specialized. We do not want to see mss that do not fit exactly into our very specialized fields of interest and format. We publish in two fairly narrow fields and all submissions must fit into one of them: (1) California reference books, that is, either directories or bibliographies relating to California; and (2) reference books on global environmental and natural resource problems. Several titles have been co-published with such houses as Marquis Who's Who, Inc. and the Sierra Club. A prospective author should request and examine our list before submitting an idea or outline." Query or submit outline/synopsis and sample chapters (biographic information useful).

Recent Nonfiction Titles: *California Energy Directory*, by Michael Paparian (information guide); *The United States and the Global Environment: A Guide to American Organizations*, by staff (information guide); *California Museum Directory*, by Kimberly Mueller (guidebook); *World Directory of Environmental Organizations*, by Trzyna et al. (information guide).

CAMARO PUBLISHING CO., Box 90430, Los Angeles CA 90009. (213)837-7500. Editor-in-Chief: Garth W. Bishop. Publishes hardcover and paperback originals. Pays royalty on wholesale price. "Every contract is different. Many books are bought outright." Published 5 titles last year. Query. SASE.

Nonfiction: Books on travel, food, wine, health and success.
Recent Nonfiction Titles: *Success Training for Children*, by Pat McCormick.

CAMBRIDGE BOOK COMPANY, 888 Seventh Ave., New York NY 10106. (212)957-5300. Vice President Editorial: Brian Schenk. Publishes paperback originals in Work-a-Text TM format. Averages 25 titles/year. Pays 6-8% royalty on institutional net price; offers small advance. Photocopied submissions OK. SASE. Reports in 1 month. Free book catalog.
Nonfiction: Basic skills—adult education only—emphasizing alternative programs. Vocational, pre-GED, ESL. Submit prospectus and sample lesson only.
Recent Nonfiction Titles: Best known for GED preparation material. Recently published *Basic Skills With Math*, by Jerry Howett.

CAMBRIDGE UNIVERSITY PRESS, 32 E. 57th St., New York NY 10022. Editor-in-Chief: Walter Lippincott. Publishes hardcover and paperback originals. Publishes 400 titles/year. Pays 10% royalty on retail price; 6% on paperbacks; no advance. Query. Reports in 2 weeks to 6 months. SASE.
Nonfiction and Textbooks: Anthropology, economics, psychology, upper-level textbooks, academic trade, scholarly monographs, biography, history, music. Looking for academic excellence in all work submitted. Department Editors: Kyle Wallace (biology, earth science); Steven Fraser (economic history, American history, social and political theory); Susan Milmoe (psychology); Colin Day (economics); and Richard Ziemaki (history of science, chemistry).
Recent Nonfiction Title: *States and Social Revolution: A Comparative Anaylsis of France, Russia and China.*

CAMELOT BOOKS, Children's Book Imprint of Avon Books, a division of the Hearst Corp., 959 8th Ave., New York NY 10019. (212)262-7454. Senior Editor: Jean Feiwel. Publishes paperback originals (25%) and reprints (75%). Averages 48 titles/year. Pays 6-10% royalty on retail price; minimum advance $1,500. Query or submit outline/synopsis and sample chapters. Simultaneous and photocopied submissions OK. SASE. Reports in 6 weeks. Free book catalog.
Nonfiction: Animals, health, history, how-to, humor, and self-help.
Recent Nonfiction Titles: *How Did We Find Out About Outer Space?*, and *How Did We Find Out About Earthquakes?*, by Isaac Asimov.
Fiction: Adventure, fantasy, humor, mainstream, mystery, science fiction, picture books and suspense.
Recent Fiction Titles: *Bridge to Terabithia*, by Katherine Paterson; *The Westing Game*, by Ellen Raskin; *Good Work, Amelia Bedelia*, by Peggy Parish; and *Bunnicula*, by James and Deborah Howe.

CANADIAN MUSEUMS ASSOCIATION, 331 Cooper St., Suite 400, Ottawa, Ontario, Canada K2P 0G5. (613)233-5653. Head, Publications and Documentation: Andree Champagne. Publishes hardcover and paperback originals. Published 5 titles in 1978. Pays negotiable royalty. Simultaneous submissions OK. Reports in 3 months. SASE. Free book catalog.
Nonfiction: Must be related to the museum and art gallery field, primarily Canadian. Museology, museography, care of collections, security, environmental control, museum architecture, exhibition care and design, cataloguing and registration, conservation methods, glossaries of terminology, staff training, extension and educational services, and technical skills. Primarily concerned with the Canadian scene, with a view to the international market. Submit outline/synopsis. Consult Chicago *Manual of Style*. Recently published *Handbook for the Travelling Exhibitionist*, by V. Dickenson/B. Tyler; *Fellows Lecture*, by E. Turner; and *Cataloguing Military Uniforms*, by D. Ross/R. Chartrand.

CAPRA PRESS, 631 State St., Santa Barbara CA 93101. Editor-in-Chief: Noel Young. Publishes hardcover and paperback originals. Specializes in documentary lifestyle books, and biographies (no fiction). Pays 8% royalty on wholesale price; advance averages $1,000. Averages 14 titles/year. State availability of photos and/or illustrations to accompany ms. Simultaneous submissions OK "if we are told where else it has been sent." Reports in 1 month. SASE. Book catalog for SASE.
Nonfiction: Publishes western contemporary nonfiction (30,000 words); biography (30,000 words); how-to; and nature books "for the more serious reader with an exploring mind." Submit outline/synopsis and sample chapters. Recently published *The World of Lawrence*, by Henry Miller (an appreciation of D.H. Lawrence); *Farmers Markets of America*, by Robert Sommer; and *Los Angeles: The Enormous Village*, by John Weaver (popular history).

*CARATZAS BROTHERS, PUBLISHERS, Box 210, 481 Main St., New Rochelle NY 10802. (914)632-8487. Editorial Director: Aristide D. Caratzas. Publishes 80% hardcover and paperback originals and 20% hardcover and paperback reprints. Published 13 titles in 1979, 10 in 1980. Subsidy publishes 5% of books based on ms "commercially marginal, though of importance to a particular field." Pays 10% royalty. Photocopied submissions OK. SASE. Reports in 3 months. Free book catalog on request.

Nonfiction: Subjects include art, history, philosophy, photography, politics, religion and travel. Query first, or submit outline/synopsis and sample chapters. All unsolicited mss are returned unopened; "we cannot be responsible for lost unsolicited mss."

Recent Nonfiction Titles: *The Gardens of Pompeii,* by W.F. Jashemski (art history and archeology); *The Eternal Olympics,* by N. Yalouris (art history, history and sport); and *Armenian Art Treasures of Jerusalem,* by B. Narkiss, and M. Stone (art history).

CAREER PRESS, Division of Singer Communications, 1500 Cardinal Dr., Little Falls NJ 07424. (201)256-4712. Chief Editor: Don Bolander. Publishes hardcover and paperback originals. Publishes 2-10 titles/year. Pays in royalties, or more often, in outright purchase, "which varies with size and complexity of project." No advance. Simultaneous and photocopied submissions OK. SASE. Reports in 2-4 weeks. Free book catalog.

Nonfiction: "Primarily self-study education materials or programs, or how-to-do-it books (i.e., photography, locksmithing, dress design, interior decoration, and similar subjects). Also reading programs for children and adults." Query or submit complete ms.

CAREER PUBLISHING, INC., 931 N. Main St., Box 5486, Orange CA 92667. (714)998-8471. Contact: Senior Editor. Publishes paperback originals. Published 18 titles in 1979; plans 21 in 1980, 23 in 1981. Pays 10% royalty on wholesale price; no advance. Simultaneous (if so informed with names of others to whom submissions have been sent) and photocopied submissions OK. Reports in 2 months. SASE. Book catalog 25¢.

Nonfiction: "Textbooks should provide core upon which class curriculum can be based: textbook, workbook or kit with 'hands-on' activities and exercises, and teacher's guide. Should incorporate modern and effective teaching techniques. Should lead to a job objective. We also publish support materials for existing courses, and are open to unique, marketable ideas with schools in mind. Reading level should be controlled appropriately—usually 8th-9th grade equivalent for vocational school and community college level courses. Any sign of sexism or racism will disqualify the work. No career awareness masquerading as career training." Submit outline/synopsis and sample chapters or complete ms.

Recent Nonfiction Titles: *Medical Office Management,* by G.E. Bonito (allied health textbook); *Medical Sound-Alikes,* by L. Rowe; and *Dictionary of Motorcycle Terminology,* by William Kosbab.

Tips: "Authors should be aware of vocational/career areas with inadequate or no training textbooks, submit ideas and samples to fill the gap."

CAROLINE HOUSE PUBLISHERS, INC., Box 738, Ottawa IL 61350. Editorial Director: Jameson Campaigne Jr. Senior Editor: Richard W. Wheeler. Publishes originals (85%) and reprints (15%) and distributes for other publishers. Published 50 titles in 1979. Pays 6-15% royalty; outright purchase averages $2,500. Advance averages $2,000. Simultaneous and photocopied submissions OK. Reports in 2 months. SASE. Book catalog for SASE.

Nonfiction: Racquet sports, how-to, guides and biographies (of major subjects). No autobiographies, fiction or "nostrum-peddling." Query; all unsolicited mss are returned unopened. Recently published *Watch the Ball, Bend Your Knees, That'll Be $20 Please,* by E. Collins (tennis instruction); *Successful Community Fundraising,* by S. Petersen; and *I Didn't Do It Alone,* by Art Linkletter (humor).

CARSTENS PUBLICATIONS, INC., Hobby Book Division, Box 700, Newton NJ 07860. (201)383-3355. Publisher: Harold H. Carstens. Publishes paperback originals. Published 8 titles in 1979. Pays 10% royalty on retail price; offers average advance. SASE. Book catalog for SASE.

Nonfiction: Model railroading, toy trains, model aviation, railroads and model hobbies. "We have scheduled or planned titles on several railroads as well as model railroad and model airplane books. Authors must know their field intimately since our readers are active modelers. Our railroad books presently are primarily photographic essays on specific railroads. Writers cannot write about somebody else's hobby with authority. If they do, we can't use them." Query.

Recent Nonfiction Titles: *Susquehanna: NYS & WRR,* by Krause and Crist; *Colorado Memories of the NG Circle,* by Krause and Grenard; and *Design Handbook for Model RR,* by Paul Mallery.

CATHOLIC TRUTH SOCIETY, 38/40 Eccleston Square, London, England SW1V 1PD. (01)834-4392. Editorial Director: David Murphy. Publishes hardcover and paperback originals (70%) and reprints (30%). Published 50 in 1980; plans 60 in 1981, 70 in 1982. Pays in outright purchase of $50-400; no advance. Simultaneous and photocopied submissions OK. Reports in 4 weeks. SASE. Free book catalog.

Nonfiction: Books dealing with how to solve problems in personal relationships, parenthood, teen-age, widowhood, sickness and death, especially drawing on Christian and Catholic tradition for inspiration; simple accounts of points of interest in Catholic faith, for non-Catholic readership; and books of prayer and devotion. Query, submit outline/synopsis and sample chapters, or submit complete ms.

Recent Nonfiction Titles: *Natural Family Planning*, by Jean Johnson; *A Miracle for Jason?*, by Ruth Chambers; and *Thomas Merton—A Pictorial Biography*, by James Forest.

CATHOLIC UNIVERSITY OF AMERICA PRESS, 620 Michigan Ave. NE, Washington DC 20064. (202)635-5052. Director: Dr. David J. McGonagle. Manager: Miss Marian E. Goode. Averages 5-10 titles/year. Pays 10% royalty on wholesale or retail price. Query with sample chapter plus outline of entire work, along with curriculum vita and list of previous publications. Reports in 2 months. SASE.

Nonfiction: Publishes history, biography, languages and literature, philosophy, religion, church-state relations, social studies. No doctoral dissertations. Length: 200,000-500,000 words.

Recent Nonfiction Titles: *Ecclesiastical Office and the Primacy of Rome: An Evaluation of Recent Theological Discussion of First Clement*, by John Fuellenbach; *Thomas Aquinas and Radical Aristotelianism*, by Fernand Van Steenberghen; and *The Philosophy of Baruch Spinoza*, edited by Richard Kennington.

*CAVEMAN PUBLICATIONS LTD, Box 1458, Dunedin, New Zealand. Contact: Editor-in-Chief. Publishes hardcover and paperback originals (80%) and reprints (20%). Pays 10% royalty; advance depends on circumstances. Subsidy publishes 50% of books "from government grants only, *not* from authors." Publishes 5 titles/year. Photocopied submissions OK. Reports in 2 months. Enclose cheques. Free book catalog.

Nonfiction: Publishes books on the environment, conservation, energy systems, technical, UFO-logy and speculative science, nature, self-help, how-to, cooking and foods, economics, hobbies, medicine, health and welfare, biography/autobiography, politics, science, humor and art. Query first.

Recent Nonfiction Titles: *The Drug Book*, by Ray Gardner; *New Zealand for Beginners*, by Howard/Higginson; and *Life in New Zealand*, by Ed T. Reeves.

Fiction: Publishes experimental, fantasy, humorous and science fiction. Query first.

Recent Fiction Titles: *The Primal Therapy of Tom Purslane*, by G. Billing (novel); *Mixed Singles*, by B. Southam (short stories); and *Beethoven's Guitar*, by P. Olds (poetry).

CBI PUBLISHING CO., INC., 51 Sleeper St., Boston MA 02210. (617)426-2224. Vice-President and Editorial Director: Norman A. Stanton. Publishes hardcover and paperback originals. Published 34 in 1979; plans 46 in 1980, 55 in 1981. Pays 10-15% royalty on wholesale price; offers $500-1,000 advance. Simultaneous and photocopied submissions OK. SASE. Reports in 2 weeks. Free book catalog.

Nonfiction: Business/economics, cookbooks/cooking, health, reference, technical, textbooks, and travel. "We would like to see more professional and reference in foodservice, management training, consumer cookbooks, health care planning and management, textbooks in hospitality, and business computer service." Submit outline/synopsis and sample chapters.

Recent Nonfiction Titles: *Classical Cooking the Modern Way*, by Eugene Pauli (professional food service); *Design Application Handbook for Distribution Systems*, by Robert Patrick (management information processing); and *Supervising Today*, by Martin Broadwell (management training).

CDE, Box 41551, Atlanta GA 30331. President: Charles Edwards. Publishes trade and mass market paperback originals, and trade and mass market paperback reprints. Averages 5+ titles/year. Pays on negotiable basis. Simultaneous and photocopied submissions OK. SASE. Reports in 1 month.

Nonfiction: Subjects include business and economics; music (including records); and radio.

Fiction: Erotica, ethnic and fantasy.

CELESTIAL ARTS, 231 Adrian Rd., Millbrae CA 94030. Managing Director: Richard Baltzell. Imprints include Les Femmes. Publishes hardcover and paperback originals, adult and children's books. Publishes 20 titles/year. Simultaneous and photocopied submissions OK. SASE. Reports in 3 months. Book catalog for SASE.

Nonfiction: Celestial Arts publishes biography, cookbooks/cooking, health, humor, psychology, recreation, self-help and sports. No poetry. "Sample chapters and outline accepted, no original copy. If return requested, include postage."

Recent Nonfiction Titles: *Love Is Letting Go of Fear*, by Jerry Jampolsky; *The Psychic Is You*, by Kay Rhea; and *High Steel*, by Dillon, Moulin and DeNevi (building of the Bay and Golden Gate bridges).
Fiction: "We have published very few fiction titles and have no plans to develop fiction list."
Recent Fiction Title: *On the 8th Day*, by Lawrence Okum, M.D.

CENTER FOR NONPROFIT ORGANIZATIONS, Subsidiary of Venture Publishing Co., 155 W. 72nd St., New York NY 10023. (212)873-7580. Vice President: R. Hess. Publishes trade paperback originals. Simultaneous and photocopied submissions OK. SASE. Reports in 2 weeks "with SASE." Book catalog for SAE and 1 first class stamp.
Nonfiction: How-to, reference and self-help. Subjects include business and economics, hobbies, nonprofit organizations, tax exemption, management and fundraising. "We seek articles for periodicals relating to hobby-into-career, fundraising, nonprofit organizations, community development, arts management, volunteers, board development, etc." Submit outline/synopsis and sample chapters.
Recent Nonfiction Title: *Contacts*, by H. Fischer (individual management).

*CENTRAL CONFERENCE OF AMERICAN RABBIS, 790 Madison Ave., New York NY 10021. (212)734-7166. Director of Publications: Rabbi Elliot L. Stevens. Publishes hardcover and trade paperback originals. Averages 5-8 titles/year. Subsidy publishes 15% of books based on whether "work is of direct benefit to rabbis or, less, of direct benefit or interest to segments of the Jewish community." Buys some mss outright. Pays "fee plus negotiated royalty based on either wholesale or retail price." Simultaneous and photocopied submissions OK. SASE. Reports in 1 week on queries; "a few" weeks on mss. Free book catalog.
Nonfiction: Reference, self-help, Judaica and liturgy. Subjects include religion (Judaica) and Judaica art. "The CCAR Press, publishing arm of the Central Conference of American Rabbis, will be interested to review submissions or queries relating to all aspects of Jewish interest. Smaller articles may also be submitted for our quarterly scholarly journal, the *Journal of Reform Judaism*."

*CENTURY HOUSE PUBLISHERS OF ALF, Watkins Glen NY 14891. Editor: Larry Freeman. Averages 5 titles/year. Pays standard royalty contract on retail price, "but many books are house written. Query first to see if editor is interested in seeing ms." SASE.
Americana and Hobbies: Publishes Americana and books on American decorative arts: history, historical biography, American arts, books on antiques and other collector subjects; hobby handbooks. Pictorial preferred. Query.
Recent Nonfiction Titles: *Cavalcade of Dolls: A Basic Source Book for Collectors*, by Ruth S. Freeman (hobbies); *Wish You Were Here: Centennial Guide to Postcard Collecting*, by Dr. Lang Freeman (hobbies); and *Spa Fever*, (the water cures of New York and other states).

*CHAMPION ATHLETE PUBLISHING COMPANY, Box 2936, Richmond VA 23235. Editor: Dr. George B. Dintiman. Publishes hardcover and paperback originals. Averages 3 titles/year. Pays 15% royalty on wholesale or retail price. Offers occasional advance. Simultaneous and photocopied submissions OK. SASE. Reports in 4 weeks. Brochure for $1.
Nonfiction: Health, sports and textbooks (physical education/athletics). Especially needs diet, health-related and sports books for the trade market. Exercise texts for the college class market and other texts targeted for a specific course. Books are published for the participant and not the coach. "We are only interested in health and sports areas or texts designed for physical education service or major classes." Submit outline/synopsis and sample chapters or submit complete ms.
Recent Nonfiction Titles: *Doctor Tennis*, by J. Myers (tennis conditioning and injury prevention guide); *How to Run Faster*, by G. Dintiman; and *P.E. Activities Manual*, by Barrow, et al.

CHARIOT BOOKS, David C. Cook Co., 850 N. Grove, Elgin IL 60120. (312)741-2400. Children's Editor: Janet Hoover Thoma. Publishes hardcover and paperback originals and paperback reprints. Averages 35-40 titles/year. Pays 6-10% royalty on retail price. Photocopied submissions OK. "We prefer a 2-to 4-page synopsis and first four chapters." SASE. Reports in 3 months. Free book catalog.
Nonfiction: "We maintain high standards of quality in art and literature, as well as requiring integral spiritual content in manucripts. In nonfiction we want stories of outstanding Christians, written for young people. We are particularly interested in books for 3- to 10-year old children."
Recent Nonfiction Titles: *Sometimes I Get Lonely*, by Elspeth Campbell Murphy (Psalm 42 for children); and *Jesus My Forever Friend*, by Bill Coleman/Ken Taylor (life of Jesus plus fun facts and probing questions).
Fiction: "We want books with a spiritual dimension that is an integral and inevitable part of the story. They must be entertaining—a good story for the sake of a good story—but they must have a

theme that conveys truth about the Christian faith. Our average reader comes from a home in which a high value is placed on church and Christianity. However, we do not want preachy books in which the characters are super-evangelists. We want to see faith portrayed as a part of daily living. We look for plots in which there is spiritual as well as an external conflict, and where the characters resolve those conflicts though faith in God." Submit outline/synopsis and sample chapters.

Recent Fiction Titles: *The Crooked Gate*, by Marilyn Cram Donahue (adventure); *To Catch A Golden Ring*, by Marilyn Donahue (inner-city girl and boy have dreams shattered, then rebuilt); and *The Sword And The Sundial*, by Phyllis Prokop (fictionalized adventure biography of Old Testament king Hezekiah). Submit outline/synopsis and sample chapters. '

CHARLES RIVER BOOKS, 1 Thompson Sq., Charlestown MA 02129. Senior Editor: B. Comjean. Editorial Director: Dennis Campbell. Publishes hardcover originals and reprints and paperback originals. Pays 4%-10% royalty; offers a "modest" advance. Simultaneous and photocopied submissions OK. Reports in 6 weeks. Book catalog for SASE.
Nonfiction: Most needed are how-to and sports books. Also sought are Americana, New England topics, biography, health, history, humor, nature, psychology, recreation, reference, sociology and textbooks. Submit outline/synopsis.
Recent Nonfiction Titles: *Short History of American Rowing*, by Thomas Mendenhall; *Rowing for the Fun of It*, by Peter Raymond; and *Flora Tristan's London Journal*, by Flora Tristan.
Fiction: Query.
Recent Fiction Title: *It Will Take a Lifetime*, by F. Sweeney (short stories).

CHARTER BOOKS, 51 Madison Ave., New York NY 10010. (212)889-9800. Executive Editor: Michael Seidman. Editor: Pat Crain. Publishes paperback originals (50%) and reprints (50%). Published 85 titles in 1979, 96 in 1980; plans 96 in 1981. Pays royalty on retail price; average advance $3,000 on most titles; some series are purchased outright. Simultaneous and photocopied submissions OK. Reports in 4 weeks. SASE. Catalog for SASE.
Fiction: General fiction, suspense, adventure, espionage, epic/saga, and westerns. No gothics, romances, short stories or novellas. Query or submit outline/synopsis and sample chapters or submit complete ms. Submit "chapters that show best development of the character and with examples of both dialogue and narrative styles."
Recent Fiction Titles: *The Trinity Factor*, by Sean Flannery; *Casca: The Eternal Mercenary*, by Barry Sadler: *Death of a Borgia*, by C.J. Stevermer; and *The Judas Gene*, by Albert and JoAnn Klainer.

THE CHATHAM PRESS, a subsidiary of Devin-Adair, 143 Sound Beach Ave., Old Greenwich CT 06870. Publishes hardcover and paperback originals, reprints, and anthologies. "Standard book contract does not always apply if the book is heavily illustrated. Average advance is low." Averages 15 titles/year. Free book catalog. Query with outline and sample chapter. Reports in 2 weeks. SASE.
Nonfiction: Publishes mostly "regional history and natural history, involving almost all regions of the US, all illustrated, with emphasis on conservation and outdoor recreation, photographic works, and the arts."
Recent Nonfiction Titles: *The Winter Woods*, by John Quinn; and *The House on Nauset Marsh*, and *A Book of Cape Cod Houses* (reprints).

CHICAGO REVIEW PRESS, 820 N. Franklin, Chicago IL 60610. (312)644-5475. Editor: Linda Matthews. Publishes hardcover and trade paperback originals. Averages 12 titles/year. Pays 7-15% royalty on retail price; offers average $2,000 advance. Simultaneous and photocopied submissions OK. SASE. Reports in 3 weeks on queries; 2 months on mss. Free book catalog.
Nonfiction: Cookbook, how-to, reference, self-help and guidebooks. Subjects include cooking and foods, health, hobbies, recreation, sports and travel. "We especially need Chicago guidebooks, national-interest, popular how-to or self-help books, career guides, books on writing, and trendy nonfiction with strong subrights possibilities." Query or submit outline/synopsis and sample chapters.
Recent Nonfiction Titles: *SyberVision: Muscle Memory Programming for Every Sport*, by Steven DeVore and Dr. Gregory DeVore (sports training); *How to Write Your Own Life Story*, by Lois Daniel (how-to on creative writing); and *The Test Yourself Book*, by Dr. Harry E. Gunn (popular psychology).

CHILDRENS PRESS, 1224 W. Van Buren St., Chicago IL 60607. (312)666-4200. Editorial Director: Fran Dyra. Pays in outright purchase or offers small advance against royalty. Averages 80-100 titles/year. Reports in 6 weeks. SASE.
Juveniles: For supplementary use in elementary and secondary schools; easy picture books for

early childhood and beginning readers; high-interest, easy reading material. Specific categories include careers, social studies, science and special education. Length: 50-10,000 words. For picture books, needs are very broad. They should be geared from preschool to grade 3. "We have a strong tendency to publish books in series. Odds are against a single book that couldn't, if sales warrant, develop into a series." Length: 50-1,000 words. Send outline with sample chapters; complete ms for picture books. Do not send finished artwork with ms.

Recent Nonfiction Titles: *World of Racing Series* (4 titles); *Airplanes That Work for Us*; and *Prime Time Adventure Stories* (ten hi-low adventures).

Fiction: For supplementary use in elementary and secondary schools. Length: 50-10,000 words. Picture books from preschool to grade 3. Length: 50-1,000 words. Send outline with sample chapters; complete ms for picture books. Do not send finished artwork with ms.

Tips: Submissions often "lack originality. Too often authors talk 'down' to young readers. First it must be a good story, then it can have an educational or moral point."

CHILTON BOOK CO., Chilton Way, Radnor PA 19089. Editorial Director: Alan F. Turner. Publishes hardcover and trade paperback originals. Publishes 65 titles/year. Pays royalty; average advance. Simultaneous and photocopied submissions OK. SASE. Reports in 3 weeks.

Nonfiction: Business/economics, health, hobbies, how-to and technical. "We only want to see any manuscripts with informational value." Query or submit outline/synopsis and sample chapters.

Recent Nonfiction Titles: *The Quality System*; *Handbook of Radio Advertising*; *Tax Saving*; *Emeralds and Other Beryls*; and *Living Better: Recipes for a Healthy Heart*.

CHOSEN BOOKS, Lincoln VA 22078. (703)338-4131. Executive Director: Leonard E. LeSourd. Hardcover and paperback originals. Published 7 titles in 1980; 7 in 1981. Pays 10-12½-15% royalty; advance averages $1,000. Free book catalog for SASE.

Religion: Seeks out teaching and personal experience books of Christian content with high quality. Length: 40,000-60,000 words. Query.

Recent Nonfiction Titles: *Life Sentence*, by Charles Colson; *Where Eagles Soar*, by Jamie Buckingham; and *Bathsheba, by Roberta Dorr.*

Tips: "Write a book that grips the reader in the first pages and then holds them through all chapters. Give the reader a 'you are there feeling.' "

CHRISTIAN CLASSICS, Box 30, Westminster MD 21157. (301)848-3065. Director: John J. McHale. Publishes hardcover originals (5%), and hardcover reprints (95%). Averages 5 titles/year. Pays 10% royalty; buys some mss outright for $500-2,000. Photocopied submissions OK. SASE. Reports in 2 months. Free book catalog.

Nonfiction: Subjects include psychology and religion. "We're looking for general books of religious interest." Query.

Recent Nonfiction Titles: *Creed and Catechetics*, by Rev. Eugene Kevane (religious); *Lives of the Saints*, by Alban Butler (religious); and *The Angels and Their Mission*, by Jean Danielou, S.J. (religious).

Tips: "Think about mass market paperback possibilities."

CHRISTIAN HERALD BOOKS, 40 Overlook Dr., Chappaqua NY 10514. (914)769-9000. Editorial Director: Mr. Leslie H. Stobbe. Publishes hardcover originals. Published 14 titles in 1979, 20 in 1980, 20 in 1981. Emphasizes Christian themes. Pays 10% royalty on retail price; offers negotiable advance. State availability of photos and/or illustrations to accompany ms. Simultaneous and photocopied submissions OK. Reports in 2-3 months. SASE. Book catalog for SASE.

Nonfiction: Publishes Christian evangelical books. "Our target reader shops in a Christian bookstore; is a conservative evangelical (meaning he accepts the *Bible* as inerrant); and is aware of world events." Query or submit outline/synopsis and sample chapters.

Recent Nonfiction Titles: *Forgive, Forget, and Be Free*, by Jeanette Lockerbie; *Managing Your Emotions*, by Erwin Lutzer; and *Once Through the New Testament*, by Thomas McCall and Zola Levitt.

Fiction: Publishes biblical novels only.

Recent Fiction Title: *Abigail*, by Lois Henderson (biblical fiction).

Tips: "Book buyers are purchasing fewer personality books, are extremely selective in books on marriage and family. The future may well show a new interest in one-on-one relationships."

CHRONICLE BOOKS, 870 Market St., San Francisco CA 94102. Editorial Director: Larry L. Smith. Publishes hardcover and paperback originals. Publishes 25 titles annually. Pays 6-10% royalty on retail price; negotiates advance. Simultaneous and photocopied submissions OK. SASE. Reports in 1 month.

Nonfiction: West Coast regional and recreational guidebooks; West Coast regional histories; art and architecture; and natural history. No fiction, science fiction, drama or poetry. "Our readers are literate, somewhat sophisticated and interested in the world around them. Writers should, for this audience, shun tired topics and stay somewhat future-oriented." Query or submit outline/synopsis and sample chapters.

Recent Nonfiction Titles: *Literary L.A.*; *1906: Surviving San Francisco's Great Earthquake and Fire*; and *An Illustrated History of Bay Area Theater*.

CITADEL PRESS, 120 Enterprise Ave., Secaucus NJ 07094. (212)736-0007. Editorial Director: Allan J. Wilson. Publishes hardcover originals and paperback reprints. Published 42 titles in 1979. Pays 10% royalty on hardcover, 5-7% on paperback; offers average $1,000 advance. Simultaneous and photocopied submissions OK. Reports in 2 months. SASE.

Nonfiction: Biography, film, psychology, humor and history. Also seeks "off-beat material," but no "poetry, religion, politics." Query.

Recent Nonfiction Titles: *Moe Howard and the Three Stooges*, by M. Howard (filmography); *The Great American Amusement Parks*, by G. Kyriazi (Americana); and *Documentary History of the Negro People in the U.S.* , by H. Aptheker (history).

*CITIZENS LAW LIBRARY, INC., 7 S. Wirt St., Box 1745, Leesburg VA 22075. (703)777-2007. Editorial/Senior Director: J.S. Lanning. Publishes hardcover and paperback originals. Subsidy publishes 5-10% of books; determined by "doing marketing studies and surveying the depth of the potential audience for the type of work. Also how well the author knows what he is writing about is a major factor for us." Published 12 titles 1979, 21 in 1980; plans 12 in 1981. Offers 5% net-17% royalty based on wholesale and retail price; also buys mss by outright purchase: $500. Average advance: $500. No simultaneous submissions; photocopied submissions OK. SASE. Reports in 4 weeks. Free book catalog.

Nonfiction: How-to (legal, tax, financial); self-help (tax, financial areas); and law for laymen titles. "Rather than limiting competent authors to a specific area(s), we would rather have them submit original mss in the above areas and take each one on a case-by-case basis. Don't want to see anything *not* pertaining to the above areas." Submit outline/synopsis and sample chapters or complete ms.

Recent Nonfiction Titles: *The No-Fault Divorce Guide* (legal, self-help); *Tax Shelters for Everybody* (financial, self-help); and *How To Do Your Own Legal Work*, by Charles F. Abbott.

CLARION BOOKS, Ticknor & Fields: a Houghton Mifflin Company. 52 Vanderbilt Ave., New York NY 10017. Editor and Publisher: James C. Giblin. Senior Editor for Nonfiction: Ann Troy. Publishes hardcover originals. Averages 20-25 titles/year. Pays 5-10% royalty on retail price; $1,000-2,000 advance, depending on whether project is a picture book or a longer work for older children. Photocopied submissions OK. No multiple submissions. SASE. Reports in 6-8 weeks. Free book catalog.

Nonfiction: Americana, biography, hi-los, holiday, humor, nature and photo essays. Prefers books for younger children. Query.

Recent Nonfiction Titles: *A Christmas Feast*, compiled by Edna Barth (holiday anthology); *Junk Food, Fast Food, Health Food*, by Lila Perl (nutrition); and *Light Another Candle*, by Miriam Chaikin (Hanukkah).

Fiction: Adventure, fantasy, humor, mystery, science fiction and suspense. "We would like to see more humorous contemporary stories that young people of 8-12 or 10-14 can identify with readily." Query on ms of more than 50 pages.

Recent Fiction Titles: *Cute is a Four-Letter Word*, by Stella Pevsner (teenage story); *Tangled Butterfly*, by Marion Dane Bauer (contemporary drama); and *The People Therein*, by Mildred Lee (historical romance).

ARTHUR H. CLARK CO., Box 230, Glendale CA 92109. (213)245-9119. Editorial Director: Robert A. Clark. Publishes hardcover originals. Averages 8 titles/year. Subsidy publishes 10% of books based on whether they are "high-risk sales." Pays 10% minimum royalty on wholesale prices. Photocopied submissions OK. SASE. Reports in 1 week on queries; 2 months on mss. Free book catalog.

Nonfiction: Biography, reference and historical nonfiction. Subjects include Americana and history. "We're looking for documentary source material in western American history." Query or submit outline/synopsis and sample chapters.

Recent Nonfiction Titles: *Only One Man Died*, by E.G. Chuinard (historical); *Seeking the Elephant*, by Shirley Sargent (historical); and *Fur Trade Letters of Ermatinger*, by Lois McDonald (historical).

T&T CLARK LTD., 36 George St., Edinburgh Scotland EH2 2LQ. (031)225-4703. Editorial Director: Geoffrey Green. Publishes hardcover and paperback originals (25%) and reprints (75%).

Published 40 titles in 1979; 60 in 1980; plans 60 in 1981. Pays 5-10% royalty based on wholesale or retail price. May offer 250 pounds advance. Simultaneous and photocopied submissions OK. SASE. Reports in 4 weeks. Free book catalog.

Nonfiction: Religion; philosophy; and history. Top level academic. Query first.

Recent Nonfiction Titles: *A History of Christian Doctrine*, by H. Cunliffe-Jones (religion/theology/history student textbook); *Great Themes of the New Testament*, by W. Barclay (popular commentary); and *Ethics*, by Karl Barth (theology).

CLARKE, IRWIN & CO., LTD., 791 St. Clair Ave., W., Toronto, Ontario, Canada M6C 1B8. Publishes hardcover and paperback originals (90%) and reprints (10%). Specializes in Canadian subjects. Pays variable royalty, minimum of 10%. Publishes about 25 titles a year. Submit outline/synopsis and sample chapters or complete ms. Must be typed double-spaced. "Don't send only copy." Send samples of prints for illustration. Photocopied submissions OK. Reports in 2 months. SASE.

Nonfiction: Publishes juveniles and books on Canadiana, art, biography, history, how-to, music, nature, politics, recreation, sports, textbooks, travel.

Recent Nonfiction Titles: *Drapeau*, by Brian McKenna and Susan Purcell; *Vanishing Canada*, by Rick Butler; and *Paper Boy*, by Stuart Keate.

Fiction: Publishes juveniles, adventure, historical, humorous, and mainstream books.

Recent Fiction Titles: *The Suicide Murders*, by Howard Engel; *Far From Shore*, by Kevin Major; and *Hag Head*, by Susan Musgrave and Carol Evans.

CLIFFS NOTES, INC., Box 80728, Lincoln NE 68501. (402)477-6971. Editor: Michele Spence. Publishes trade paperback originals. Averages 10 titles/year. Pays royalty on wholesale price. Buys some mss outright; "full payment on acceptance of ms." SASE. Reports in 1 month. Free book catalog.

Nonfiction: Self-help, textbook. "We publish self-help study aids directed to junior high through graduate school audience. Publications include *Cliffs Notes, Cliffs Test Preparation Guides, Cliffs Speech and Hearing Series*, and other study guides. Most authors are experienced teachers, usually with advanced degrees. Some books also appeal to a general lay audience." Query.

COBBLESMITH, Box 191, RFD 1, Freeport ME 04032. Editor-in-Chief: Gene H. Boyington. Publishes hardcover and paperback originals (90%); hardcover and paperback reprints (10%). Published 2 titles in 1979, 3 in 1980; plans 2 in 1981. Pays 8½% royalty on list price; no advance. Simultaneous and photocopied submissions OK. SASE. Query. *"Unsolicited mss often are treated as though only a little better than unsolicited third class mail."* Reports in 4 months. Free book catalog.

Nonfiction: Americana and art topics (especially New England and antiques); law (popular, self-help); cookbooks, cooking and foods; gardening; psychology (applied—not theory); how-to (home and homestead crafts); philosophy (educational and new developments); sociology (applied—not theory); material on alternative life styles; nature, travel (offbeat guide books); and self-help.

Recent Nonfiction Titles: *Across the Running Tide* (environment);and *Our Classroom is Wild America*, by Michael Cohen; and *The Day the White Whales Came to Bangor*, by Gerald Hausman (children/environment).

COLES PUBLISHING CO., LTD., 90 Ronson Dr., Rexdale, Ontario, Canada M9W 1C1. (416)249-9121. Vice President/Editorial Director: Jeffrey Cole. Publishes hardcover and paperback originals (20%) and reprints (80%). Averages 300 titles/year. "We are a subsidiary company of 'Coles, the Book People,' a chain of 235 bookstores throughout America." Pays by outright purchase of $500-$2,500; advance averages $500. Simultaneous and photocopied submissions OK. Reports in 3 weeks. SAE and International Reply Coupons.

Nonfiction: "We publish in the following areas: education, language, science, math, pet care, gardening, cookbooks, medicine and health, occult, business, reference, technical and do-it-yourself, crafts and hobbies, antiques, games, and sports." No philosophy, religion, history or biography. Submit outline/synopsis and sample chapters.

Recent Nonfiction Titles: *The Complete Works of William Shakespeare*; and *Marketing*, by J. Stapleton (business).

COLGATE UNIVERSITY PRESS, Hamilton NY 13346. Editor-in-Chief: R.L. Blackmore. Publishes hardcover originals, reprints, and an annual journal about the Powys family of writers and their circle. No other subjects at this time. Pays standard royalty contract on retail price: "rarely an advance." Averages 0-4 titles/year. Free book catalog. Will consider photocopied submissions. Query first. Reports in 1 month. SASE.

Biography: "Books by or about the Powyses: John Cowper Powys, T.F. Powys, Llewelyn Powys. Our audience is general and scholarly." Length: open.
Recent Titles: *Rodmoor*, by John Cowper Powys (reissue of his 2nd novel); and *Welsh Ambassador*, by Louis Marlow (biography of Powyses).

COLLECTOR BOOKS, Box 3009, Paducah KY 42001. Editor: Steve Quertermous. Publishes hardcover and paperback originals. Pays 5% royalty on retail; no advance. Publishes 25-30 titles/ year. Send prints or transparencies if illustrations are to accompany ms. SASE. Reports in 2-4 weeks. Free book catalog.
Nonfiction: "We only publish books on antiques and collectibles. We require our authors to be very knowledgeable in their respective fields and have access to a large representative sampling of the particular subject concerned." Query. Recently published *Collector's Encyclopedia of Depression Glass*, by G. Florence; *Madame Alexander Collector Dolls*, by P. Smith; and *Primitives and Folk Art, Our Handmade Heritage*, by Catherine Thuro.

COLLIER MACMILLAN CANADA, LTD., 1125 B Leslie St., Don Mills, Ontario, Canada. Publishes both originals and reprints in hardcover and paperback. Advance varies, depending on author's reputation and nature of book. Published 35 titles last year. Reports in 6 weeks. SAE and International Reply Coupons.
General Nonfiction: "Topical subjects of special interest to Canadians." Query.
Textbooks: Mathematics, language arts, and reading: mainly texts conforming to Canadian curriculum requirements. Also resource books, either paperback or pamphlet for senior elementary and high schools. Length: open.

COLORADO ASSOCIATED UNIVERSITY PRESS, Box 480, University of Colorado, 1424 15th St., Boulder CO 80309. (303)492-7191. Editor: Frederick Rinehart. Publishes hardcover and paperback originals. Averages 10 titles/year. Pays 10-12½-15% royalty contract on wholesale or retail price; "no advances." Free book catalog. Will consider photocopied submissions "if not sent simultaneously to another publisher." Query. Reports in 3 months. SASE.
Nonfiction: "Scholarly and regional." Length: 250-500 ms pages.
Recent Nonfiction Titles: *Chemicals and Cancer*, by Matthew S. Meselson (biology); *The Virginius Affair*, by Richard H. Bradford (history); and *Imperial Science and National Survival*, by David Montgomery (general science; politics).

*COLUMBIA PUBLISHING CO., INC., Frenchtown NJ 08825. (201)996-2141. Editorial Director: Bernard Rabb. Publishes hardcover originals. Published 6 titles in 1979. Pays 10% royalty; offers average advance. "Subsidy publishing is rarely offered and then only if we feel the book to be worthy to have our name on it." Simultaneous and photocopied submissions OK. Reports in 6 months. SASE.
Nonfiction: Biography, theater, film, dance, classical music, political science, business, recreation, and nature/ecology. "We do not want fad books, religious titles, sex guides, photography books, or academic books not applicable to a lay audience." Submit complete ms.
Recent Nonfiction Titles: *The Deathday of Socrates*, by Eckstein; *Wayside Simples and Grateful Herbs*, by Abraitys; and *Conductors on Conducting*, by Jacobson (classical music).
Fiction: Literary novels only. Submit complete ms.
Recent Fiction Title: *Cousin Drewey and the Holy Twister*, by Sinclair.

COLUMBIA UNIVERSITY PRESS, 562 W. 113th St., New York NY 10025. (212)678-6777. Director and Editor-in-Chief: John D. Moore. Publishes hardcover and paperback originals. Pays negotiable royalty. Query. SASE.
Nonfiction: "General interest nonfiction of scholarly value."
Scholarly: Books in the fields of literature, philosophy, fine arts, Oriental studies, history, social sciences, science, law.

COMMONERS' PUBLISHING, 432 Rideau St., Ottawa, Ontario, Canada K1N 5Z1. (613)233-4997. Editorial Director: Glenn Cheriton. Senior Editors: Lucille Shaw, Maridee Winters. Publishes hardcover and paperback originals. Published 6 titles in 1979, 7 in 1980; plans 8 in 1981. Royalties paid yearly based on 10% of sales, list. Photocopied submissions OK. "We do not like simultaneous submissions." Reports in 4 months. SAE and International Reply Coupons. Book catalog for SAE and International Reply Coupons.
Nonfiction: Self-help, alternative lifestyles and crafts books. Submit complete ms.
Recent Nonfiction Titles: *Ottawa Historic Calendar*, by Herbert; and *Apple II*, by Cheriton (historical).
Fiction: Canadian short stories, plays and fiction; also full-length novels with Canadian themes,

locations, and authors; and Canadian poetry. Submit complete ms.
Recent Fiction Titles: *Stations*, by P. White (poetry); *Hard Road*, by G. Forbes (humor); and *Still Close to the Island*, by Dabydeen (short stories).

COMMUNICATION SKILL BUILDERS, INC., Box 42050, Tucson AZ 85733. (602)327-6021. Editorial Manager: Linda Nadell. Publishes hardcover and paperback originals. Averages 12 titles/year. Offers 5-10% royalty on wholesale or retail price. Average advance: $1,000. "Advance is not offered, but given if requested." No simultaneous submissions; photocopied submissions OK. SASE. Reports in 4-6 weeks. Free book catalog.
Educational Material: Articulation, learning disabilities, reading, speech therapy and speech language development. "We publish materials (books and kits) for educators of/and adults/children with special needs." Query first or submit outline/synopsis and sample chapters.
Recent Nonfiction Titles: *King Louie Holiday Stories for Speech and Language Development*, by D.J. Soule; and *Hands On, A Manipulative Curriculum*, by Potocki and Miller (education).

COMPUTER SCIENCE PRESS, INC., 11 Taft Ct., Rockville MD 20850. (301)251-2050. President: Barbara B. Friedman. Publishes hardcover originals. Averages 10 titles/year. Pays royalty on wholesale price; no advance. Simultaneous and photocopied submissions OK. Reports ASAP. SASE. Free book catalog.
Nonfiction: "Technical books in all aspects of computer science, computer engineering, computer chess, electrical engineering and telecommunications. Both text and reference books. Will also consider public appeal 'trade' books in computer science." Also publishes bibliographies in computer science areas and the quarterly *Journal of Digital Systems.* Query or submit complete ms. "We prefer 3 copies of manuscripts."
Recent Nonfiction Titles: *Principles of Database Systems*, by Jeffery D. Ullman (text and reference book); *Assemblers, Compilers and Program Translation*, by Peter Calingaert (text and reference book); and *Reliability and Maintainability of Electronic Systems*, by Arsenault and Roberts.

CONCORDIA PUBLISHING HOUSE, 3558 S. Jefferson Ave., St. Louis MO 63118. Pays royalty on retail price; outright purchase in some cases. Published 65 titles in 1979, 60 in 1980; plans 60 in 1981. Submit outline and sample chapter for nonfiction; complete ms for fiction. Reports in 3 months. SASE. Free book catalog.
Nonfiction: Publishes Protestant, general religious, theological books and periodicals, music works and juveniles. "As a religious publisher, we look for mss that deal with ways that readers can apply Christian beliefs and principles to daily living. Any ms that deals specifically with theology and/or doctrine should conform to the tenets of the Lutheran Church-Missouri Synod. We suggest that, if authors have any doubt about their submissions in light of what kind of mss we want, they should first correspond with us."
Recent Nonfiction Titles: *I Wonder—Answers to Religious Questions Children Ask*, by Jahsmann (religious/reference); and *Family Evening Activity Devotions*, by Brusius.
Fiction: Publishes adult fiction, juvenile picture and beginner books. "We look for mss that deal with Bible stories, Bible history and Christian missions."

CONGRESSIONAL QUARTERLY PRESS, 1414 22nd St., N.W. Washington DC 20037. (202)887-8642. Deputy Director, Book Department: Jean Woy. Publishes hardcover and paperback originals. Averages 35 titles/year. Pays standard college royalty on wholesale price; offers college text advance. Simultaneous and photocopied submissions OK. SASE. Reports in 6 months. Free book catalog on request.
Nonfiction: "We are probably the most distinguished publisher in the area of Congress and US government." College texts American politics. Submit outline and prospectus. "Virtually all our books are written by experienced scholars."
Recent Nonfiction Titles: *Congress Reconsidered, Second Edition*, by Dodd and Oppenheimer; *Mass Media and American Politics*, by Doris A. Graber; and *Congressional Elections*, by Professor Barbara Hinckley.

CONSUMER REPORTS BOOKS, Subsidiary of Consumers Union. Subsidiaries include *Consumer Reports* magazine and *Penny Power, A Magazine for Children 8-12.* 256 Washington St., Mt. Vernon NY 10550. (914)664-6400. Director, Consumer Reports Books: Jonathan Leff. Publishes trade paperback originals (50%), and trade paperback reprints (50%). Averages 5-10 titles/year. Pays royalty on retail price; buys some mss outright. Simultaneous and photocopied submissions OK. Reports in 1 month on queries; 2 months on mss. Free book catalog.
Nonfiction: Cookbook, how-to, reference, self-help and technical. Subjects include business and economics, cooking and foods, health, music and consumer guidance. Submit outline/synopsis and sample chapters.

Recent Nonfiction Titles: *The Consumers Union Report on Life Insurance* (buying guidance); *Health Quackery* ("information on worthless remedies"); and *The Medicine Show* ("practical guide to health problems and products") all by Editors of Consumer Reports Books.

CONTEMPORARY BOOKS, 180 N. Michigan Ave., Chicago IL 60601. (312)782-9181. Publisher: Harvey Plotnick. General Interest Editor: M.M. Carberry. Sports Editor: N. Crossman. Adult Education Editor: L. Fleming. Publishes hardcover and trade paperbacks. Published 110 titles in 1979, 100 in 1980; plans 100 in 1981. Pays sliding scale of royalties for cloth; most frequently 7½% for paperback. Offers small advance. Simultaneous submissions OK, if so advised. Reports in 3 weeks, longer on complete ms.
Nonfiction: Sports instructional, fitness and health, how-to, self improvement, leisure activities, hobbies, practical business, women's interest, and cookbooks. Also publishes test preparation guides such as CLEP and GED and adult basic education materials. Prefers query first with outline/synopsis and sample chapter. "We look at everything; and we do, in fact, publish occasional titles that come in over the transom."
Recent Nonfiction Titles: *Male Practice*, by Dr. Robert Mendelsohn; *Winning Body Building*, by Franco Columbu; *How We Made a Million Dollars Recycling Great Old Houses*, by Sam and Mary Weir; and *Brass*, by Kathleen Fitzgerald.
Fiction: An occasional unusual title. Seldom more than one fiction book per list.

THE CONTINUUM PUBLISHING CORPORATION, 18 E. 41st St., New York NY 10017. (212)683-1300. Contact: The Editors. Estab. 1980. Publishes hardcover originals and paperback reprints. Publishes 30 titles/year. Pays in royalties; offers an advance. Photocopied submissions OK. SASE. Reports in 6-8 weeks. Free book catalog.
Nonfiction: Current affairs, social and educational concerns, psychology, philosophy, sociology, literary criticism, history, biography and self help. Query.
Recent Nonfiction Titles: *On Being a Teacher*, by Jonathan Kozol (education); *Crisis Counseling*, by Eugene Kennedy (behavior); and *Making America Work*, by James O'Toole (current affairs).

DAVID C. COOK PUBLISHING CO., Adult (General) Division, 850 N. Grove, Elgin IL 60120. (312)741-2400. General Titles Managing Editor: Mrs. Janet Hoover Thoma. Assistant Editor: Randall Nulton. Publishes hardcover and paperback originals (98%) and paperback and hardcover reprints (2%). Published 30 titles in 1980, 30 in 1981; plans 30 in 1982. Pays 8-15% royalty on retail price; offers variable advance. Simultaneous and photocopied submissions OK (only if so indicated in a letter). SASE. Reports in 4 months.
Nonfiction: Religious. Our primary emphasis is in the nonfiction area. We are interested in inspirational books which help people to grow in their Christian faith and which minister to people's needs when they hurt, i.e., loss of a loved one; depression; etc. The spiritual element must be evident and Bible-based, but it doesn't necessarily need to dominate the story. Be careful not to get too preachy. We are interested in biographies of famous or unusual people who have a faith which can challenge the reader. Also, books on current topics from a Christian viewpoint are given serious consideration, e.g., abortion; personal finances; sex; the occult; marriage; etc. Submit outline/synopsis and first four chapters. In your cover letter, include the theme of your proposed book and its uniqueness, who you think will buy the book, and something about your spiritual, literary, educational, and professional background. Query first.
Recent Nonfiction Titles: *Crossroads*, by Leon Jaworski (autobiography); and *The Fragile Curtain*, by Karen Burton Mains.
Fiction: Religious; "We are looking for good manuscripts that follow the popular romance, mystery, or gothic formula and have a religious theme. Send for guidelines. We also publish serious religious novels from time to time."
Recent Fiction Titles: *Master of MacKenzie Station*, by Kathleen Yapp; and *Olympia*, by Dr. Elgin Groseclose.
Tips: "Write in popular style. Make people want to read more."

DAVID C. COOK PUBLISHING CO., Chariot Books, Book Division, 850 N. Grove, Elgin IL 60120. (312)741-2400. Editor: Janet Hoover Thoma. Assistant Editor: Susan Zitzman. Publishes hardcover and paperback originals and paperback reprints. Published 39 titles in 1979. Pays 6-10% royalty on retail price. Simultaneous and photocopied submissions OK. "We prefer a 2- to 4-page synopsis and first four chapters." SASE. Reports in 3 months. Free book catalog.
Nonfiction and Fiction: Religious. "We're particularly interested in books that teach the child about the Bible in fun and interesting ways—not; just Bible story rehashes. Also books that help children understand their feelings and problems; books about animals, sports, or boy adventures; true stories of young people whose Christian faith is a vital part of an interesting life."
Fiction: "We want books with a spiritual dimension that is an integral, inevitable part of the story.

However, we don't want preachy books in which the characters are super-saints and offer sermons. But the plot should involve spiritual as well as external conflict, and the characters should resolve these conflicts through faith in God. Yet the stories should be entertaining and compelling. We are always looking for books that are humorous and books that can be part of a series. We are also interested in fiction for 10- to 14-year-old boy, and romances for 10- to 14-year-old girls."
Recent Nonfiction Titles: *Who What When Where Book About The Bible*, by William Coleman.
Recent Fiction Title: *Dear Angie, Your Family's Getting A Divorce*, by Carol Nelson.

COPPLE HOUSE BOOKS, Road's End, Lakemont GA 30552. (404)782-2134. President: Ed O'Neal. Publishes hardcover originals and trade paperback originals and reprints. Averages 5 titles/year. Pays 10-15% royalty on retail price; no advance. Simultaneous and photocopied submissions OK. SASE. Reports in 1 month; "sometimes sooner." Book catalog for business size SAE and 1 first class stamp.
Nonfiction: "Coffee table" book, cookbook, how-to, illustrated book, juvenile and regional. Subjects include Americana, art, cooking and foods, history and regional. "Books for readers interested in our American heritage." No "religion, politics, weight reduction, diet, sex, sales manuals, technical, psychology, homespun philosophy, how-to-fix faucets." Query. All unsolicited mss are returned unopened.
Recent Nonfiction Titles: *Herk: Hero of the Skies*, by Joseph Dabney (aviation); *Places of Discovery I-Asheville*, by Lou Harshaw (200-year history of Asheville NC).

CORDOVAN CORP., 5314 Bingle Rd., Houston TX 77018. (713)688-8811. Editor-in-Chief: Bob Gray. Publishes hardcover and paperback originals and reprints under the Cordovan Press, Horseman Books and Fisherman Books imprints. Pays minimum book contract of 10-12½-15%. Published 5 titles in 1979; 6 in 1980. Marketed heavily by direct mail and through various consumer and trade periodicals. Photocopied submissions OK. Query or submit outline and sample chapters. Reports in 1 month. SASE.
Nonfiction: Cordovan Press, a trade book division, seeks books on Texas history for the history buff interested in Texana. Horseman Books are practical, how-to books on horse training, grooming, feeding, showing, riding, etc., either by experts in the field or as told to a writer by an expert. "Fisherman Books are how-to, where-to, when-to books on fishing in Texas and/or the Southwest. Author must be noted expert on fishing, or be retelling what a noted expert told him. The emphasis is on plain language in all of these lines. Short sentences. Make the verbs sing the song. Pungent quotes. Don't try to snow the readers; they are too sharp and already know most of the score in all areas. Use humor when it isn't forced." Length: 150 ms pages. Recently published *Rick Clunn's Championship Bass Fishing Techniques*, by R. Clunn; *Eyes of Texas Travel Guide*, by R. Miller; and *The Cowgirls*, by J.G. Roach (Americana).

CORNELL MARITIME PRESS, INC., Box 456, Centreville MD 21617. Managing Editor: Willard A. Lockwood. Publishes original hardcover and quality paperbacks. Published 9 titles in 1979, 9 in 1980; plans 11 in 1981. Payment is negotiable but royalties do not exceed 10% for first 5,000 copies, 12½% for second 5,000 copies, 15% on all additional. Revised editions revert to original royalty schedule. Free book catalog. Send queries first, accompanied by writing samples and outlines of book ideas. Reports in 2-4 weeks. SASE.
Nonfiction: Marine subjects, highly technical; manuals; how-to books on maritime subject. Tidewater Publishers imprint publishes books on regional history, folklore and wildlife of the Chesapeake Bay and the Delmarva Peninsula.
Recent Nonfiction Titles: *Commercial Transportation (6th ed.)*; *Compact Sight Reduction Table*; and *Dangerous Marine Animals (2nd ed.)*.

CORNERSTONE BOOKS, 9825 W. Roosevelt Rd., Westchester IL 60153. (312)345-7474. Editor-in-Chief: Jan P. Dennis. Averages 13-18 titles/year. Pays royalty; offers standard advance. Simultaneous and photocopied submissions OK. SASE. Reports in 2 weeks on queries; 3 months on mss.
Nonfiction: "Writers for Cornerstone Books must be dedicated Christians who have something genuinely fresh and important to say and can say it in a high-quality way."
Fiction: Fantasy (must be informed by Christian perspective); religious (must not be preachy or didactic); science fiction (must be informed by Christian outlook); and sacramental naturalism (in the vein of Flannery O'Connor, Walker Percy, John Cheever, etc.). "We are developing a line of religious fantasy and mainstream fiction that will be good enough to sell in the general market, but still appropriate for the religious market." Query or submit complete ms.

R.D. CORTINA CO., INC., 136 W. 52nd St., New York NY 10019. General Editor: MacDonald Brown. Pays on a fee or a royalty basis. Published 27 titles last year. "Do not send unsolicited mss; send outline and sample chapter." Reports in 2 months or less.

Textbooks: Publishes language teaching textbooks for self-study and school; also publishes language teaching phonograph records and tapes. Materials of special ESL interest. Word length varies.

COUGAR BOOKS, Box 22246, Sacramento CA 95822. Editorial Director: Ruth Pritchard. Publishes paperback originals and trade paperbacks. Averages 5 titles/year. Pays 7% royalty on wholesale or retail price; outright purchases negotiable. Offers limited advance. Simultaneous and photocopied submissions OK. SASE. Reports in 2 months. Book catalog sent for #10 SASE.
Nonfiction: Specifically needs contemporary social issues, topical issues, trends in nutrition. "We're picking up subject areas in which California is pioneering." Query first or submit outline/synopsis and sample chapters.
Recent Nonfiction Titles: *Mommy, I'm Hungry-How to Feed Your Child Nutritiously*, by P. McIntyre; *Alternative Birth*, by K. Anderson; and *Midwife Murder Case*, by J. Bowers and Rosalie Tarpening.

COUNTRY JOURNAL, 205 Main St., Brattleboro VT 05301. (802)257-1321. Special Projects Director: Judy Oliver. Publishes hardcover and paperback originals. Averages 4 titles/year. Pays 10-12½% royalty on wholesale or retail price; offers "fair and competitive" advances. Simultaneous and photocopied submissions OK if so indicated. SASE. Reports in 1 month. Writer's guidelines for SASE.
Nonfiction: Specifically needs books relating to self-sufficiency, woodworking, gardening, home design and repairs, woodburning and how-to. "The character of the *Country Journal*, a monthly magazine, determines the nature of the books we publish." Submit outline/synopsis and sample chapters.
Recent Nonfiction Titles: *The Country Journal New England Weather Book*, by D. Ludlum (weather history and predictions).

COWARD, McCANN & GEOGHEGAN, INC., 200 Madison Ave., New York NY 10016. (212)765-8900. President: David Braunstein. Editor-in-Chief: Joseph Kanon. Publishes hardcover originals. "We publish about 60 adult titles a year." Pays 10-15% royalty on retail prices; offers $5,000 average advance on first book. Query before submission. Simultaneous and photocopied submissions OK. SASE. Reports in 6 weeks. Free book catalog.
Nonfiction: Animals, biography, health, history, how-to, juveniles, nature, politics, psychology, recreation, science, self-help, sociology and sports. "We are looking for nonfiction books on topics of current and/or lasting popular interest, for general, not specialized audiences. Our scope is broad; our needs are for quality manuscripts marketable in the hardcover arena. We do not want manuscripts in specialized or technical fields that require extensive design and art work that lead to high cover prices." Query.
Recent Nonfiction Titles: *The Great American Waistline*, by Chris Chase; and *Great Expectations*, by Landon Jones.
Fiction: Adventure, historical, humor, mainstream, mystery, occult, romance and suspense. "We also want historicals, family sagas, espionage thrillers, and novels for and about contemporary women. We also want gothics and mysteries, although the market for these is not as strong as it once was. We do not want science fiction, fantasy or experimental novels." Query with SASE only.
Recent Fiction Titles: *Loitering With Intent*, by Muriel Spark; and *Shadowland*, by Peter Straub.

COWARD, McCANN & GEOGHEGAN, Books for Boys and Girls, 200 Madison Ave., New York NY 10016. (212)576-8900. Editor-in-Chief, Books for Boys and Girls: Refna Wilkin. Pays royalties on juvenile. Advances are competitive. Query. SASE.
Nonfiction: "Our publishing program is small and selective but we will consider nonfiction for ages 4 and up."
Fiction: Fiction for ages 4 and up.

CRAFTSMAN BOOK CO. OF AMERICA, 542 Stevens Ave., Solana Beach CA 92075. (714)755-0161. Editor-in-Chief: Gary Moselle. Publishes paperback originals. Pays royalty of 12½% of gross revenues, regardless of quantity sold. Averages 12 titles/year. "More than 60% of our sales are directly to the consumer, and since royalties are based on gross revenues the author's share is maximized." Will send free catalog and author's submission guide on request. Will consider photocopied submissions. Submit outline and sample chapters. Reports in 2 weeks. SASE.
Nonfiction: "We publish practical references for professional builders and are aggressively seeking manuscripts related to construction, the building trades, civil engineering, construction cost estimating and construction managments. Ours are not how-to books for homeowners. Emphasis

is on step by step instructions, illustrations, charts, reference data, checklists, forms, samples, cost estimates, estimating data, rules of thumb, and procedures that solve actual problems in the field or in the builder's office. Each book covers a limited subject fully, becomes the owner's primary reference on that subject, has a high utility to cost ratio, and helps the owner make a better living in his profession. We like to see ideas and queries for books in their early stages, and we work with first-time authors."

Recent Nonfiction Titles: *Building Layout*, by W.P. Jackson and *Basic Plumbing Illustrated*, by Howard C. Massey.

CRAIN BOOKS, 740 Rush St., Chicago IL 60611. Director: Kathryn Sederberg. Publishes hardcover and paperback originals. Averages 10-15 titles/year. Pays royalty on net revenues, makes an advance only under exceptional circumstances. Send contact sheet if photos/illustrations are to accompany ms. Reports in 2-4 months. SASE. Free book catalog.

Nonfiction: Publishes business books exclusively both for the professional and academic market. Subject areas: advertising and marketing; insurance and finance and investment; business management, international business. Basically interested in practical, nuts and bolts, how-to approach by experts in the field."

Recent Nonfiction Titles: *Media Planning: A Quick and Easy Guide*, by Jim Summanek; *Getting New Business Leads*, by David Lockett; and *Essentials of Advertising Creativity*, by Don Schulz.

CRANE, RUSSAK & CO., INC., 3 E. 44th St., New York NY 10017. Editor-in-Chief: Ben Russak. Publishes scientific journals and scientific and scholarly books. Published 22 titles (17 journals) in 1979, 20 (journals) in 1980; plans 20 (journals) in 1981. Pays royalty on net sales income.

Technical and Reference: "We publish scientific and scholarly works at the graduate and reference level: postgraduate textbooks and reference books for scholars and research workers. Our publications also appeal to members of professional societies. No esoteric subjects. Please do not submit material. Our publishing program is full for the next two years."

Recent Nonfiction Title: *Geological Oceanography*, by Francis Shepard (submarine geology).

CREATIVE ARTS BOOK COMPANY, Modern Authors Monograph Series; Black Lizard Books; CA Communications Books. 833 Bancroft Way, Berkeley CA 94710. (415)848-4777. Publisher: Donald S. Ellis. Senior Editor: Barry Gifford. Sales Director: Joan L. Low. Publishes hardcover and paperback originals (50%) and paperback reprints (50%). Averages 10-12 titles/year. Pays 5-10% royalty on retail price or buys some mss outright for $500-$10,000. Offers minimum $500 advance. Simultaneous and photocopied submissions OK. SASE. Reports in 3 weeks. Free book catalog.

Nonfiction: Biography, cookbooks, cooking & foods; how-to; sports; and travel. Does *not* want to see poetry. Query first.

Recent Nonfiction Titles: *Obituaries*, by W. Saroyan (memoirs); *Tofu Primer*, by Joel Andersen (cookbook); and *Outwitting Arthritis*, by Isabel Hanson (interviews).

Fiction: Mystery; literature; serious fiction. Query first.

Recent Fiction Titles: *Fathers*, by H. Gold; *The Horn*, by J.C. Holmes; and *Port Tropique*, by Barry Gifford.

CREATIVE BOOK CO., 8210 Varna Ave., Van Nuys CA 91402. (213)988-2334. Editor-in-Chief: Sol H. Marshall. Publishes paperback originals. Published 20 titles in 1979, 20 in 1980. Pays $50-200 in outright purchase. Simultaneous and photocopied submissions OK. SASE. Reports in 2 weeks. Book catalog for SASE.

Nonfiction: Cookbooks/cooking, fund raising, public relations, and promotion for education and community services. Query or submit outline/synopsis and sample chapters or submit complete ms.

Recent Nonfiction Titles: *Public Relations for Community Organizations*, by Sol H. Marshall; *Public Relations for Theatre*, by Steven F. Marshall; and *How to Publish an Organization Newsletter*, by Linda Nanfria.

CRESCENDO PUBLISHING, 132 W. 22nd, New York NY 10011. Publishes hardcover and paperback originals and reprints. Offers standard 10-12½-15% royalty contract; "advances are rare; sometimes made when we seek out an author." Published 20 titles last year. Free book catalog. Will look at queries or completed mss. SASE. Address submissions to Gerald Krimm. Reports in 6 weeks.

Music: Trade and textbooks in music. Length: open.

CRESTWOOD HOUSE, INC., Box 3427, Mankato MN 56001. (507)388-1616. Editorial Director: Karyne Jacobsen. Publishes hardcover originals. Published 29 titles in 1979, 30 in 1980; plans

35 in 1981. "All fees are negotiated based upon subject matter, length of publication, and additional work furnished." Occasionally offers advance. Simultaneous and photocopied submissions OK. Reports will be furnished. SASE.

Nonfiction: "Crestwood House publishes high-interest, low-vocabulary books for children with a reading level of grades 2-5. Our books are always published in series which have related subject matter (probably 5-10 titles per series). We do current topics on sports, recreation, and other current topics of high interest to children and young adults. Books are generally between 32-48 pages; no mss accepted under 5,000 or over 10,000 words. All books include a generous number of photographs." Submit complete ms.

Recent Nonfiction Titles: *Desperate Search*, by East (outdoor survival); *Future Communication*, by Abels.

Fiction: Same basic requirements as nonfiction. Science fiction; adventure; and sports. No preschool through 1st grade material.

Recent Fiction Title: *Green Invasion*, by Abels (science fiction).

THE CROSSING PRESS, Box 640, Trumansburg NY 14886. Co-Publishers: Elaine Gill or John Gill. Publishes hardcover and trade paperback originals. Averages 10-12 titles/year. Pays royalty. Simultaneous and photocopied submissions OK. Reports in 2 weeks on queries; 1 month on mss. Free book catalog.

Nonfiction: Cookbook, how-to, literary and feminist. Subjects include cooking and foods (vegetarian and natural foods only) health; and feminism. Submit complete ms.

Recent Nonfiction Title: *Voices from Three Mile Island*, by Robert Leppzen (anti-nuclear).

Fiction: Feminism (good literary material). Submit complete ms.

Recent Fiction Titles: *Mother, Sister, Daughter, Lover; The Shameless Hussy;* and *On the Line, New Gay Fiction*.

CROWELL JUNIOR BOOKS, 10 E. 53rd St., New York NY 10022. (212)593-7011. Editorial Director: Patricia Allen. Publishes hardcover originals. Averages 45-48 titles/year. Pays standard royalty on retail price. Photocopied submissions OK. SASE. Reports in 6-8 weeks. Free book catalog for self-addressed label.

Nonfiction: Science and history. Submit outline/synopsis and sample chapters or submit complete ms.

Recent Nonfiction Titles: *Party Politics, Party Problems*, by Weiss; *Digging up Dinosaurs*, by Aliki; and *Locks and Keys*, by Gibbon.

Fiction: "All kinds for all ages.

Recent Fiction Titles: *Pearl In The Egg*, by Van Woerkom; *My Friend the Monster*, by Bulla; and *Onions, Onions*, by Horman and Stanley.

CROWN PUBLISHERS, INC., 1 Park Ave., New York NY 10016. (212)532-9200. Imprints include Clarkson N. Potter, Barre, Harmony and Julian Press. Editor-in-Chief: Carol Baron. Publishes hardcover and paperback originals. Publishes 250 titles/year. Simultaneous and photocopied submissions OK. SASE. Reports in 6 weeks.

Nonfiction: Americana, animals, art, biography, cookbooks/cooking, health, history, hobbies, how-to, humor, juveniles, music, nature, philosophy, photography, politics, psychology, recreation, reference, science, self-help, and sports. Query or submit outline/synopsis and sample chapters. Recently published *Cambridge Encyclopedia of Archeology*, by Andrew Sherratt (science); *The Cook Book*, by Terrence Conran and Caroline Conran (culinary); and *How to Avoid Probate (updated)*, by Norman Dacey.

CURTIN & LONDON, INC., 6 Vernon St., Somerville MA 02145. (617)625-1200. Publishes hardcover and paperback originals. Published 9 titles in 1979; 8 in 1980. Pays 5-15% royalty on wholesale price; offers minimum $500 advance. Simultaneous and photocopied submissions OK. SASE. Reports in 1-2 weeks. Free book catalog.

Nonfiction: How-to; photography; technical; and textbooks for beginning to advanced photographers. Especially needs "any how-to books in photography and the graphic arts." Does not want "picture" books. Query first.

Recent Nonfiction Titles: *Darkroom Dynamics*, by Stone (advanced darkroom techniques); *Photojournalism: The Professional's Approach*, by Kobne (technical book on photojournalism); and *A Short Course in Photography*, by London (basic how-to).

DANCE HORIZONS, 1801 E. 26th St., Brooklyn NY 11229. (212)627-0477. Editorial Director: A.J. Pischl. Publishes hardcover and paperback originals (40%) and paperback reprints (60%). Published 8 titles in 1980; plans 10 in 1981. Pays 10% royalty on retail price; offers average $500 advance. Simultaneous and photocopied submissions OK. SASE. Reports in 1 month. Free book catalog.

Nonfiction: "Anything dealing with dance." Query first.

Recent Nonfiction Titles: *Behind Barres: The Mystique of Masterly Teaching,* by Joseph Gale; *Modern Dance: Techniques and Teaching,* by Gertrude Shurr and Rachael Dunaven Yocom; *Black Dance in the United States From 1619 to 1970,* by Lynn Fauley Emery; and *Both Sides of the Mirror: The Science and Art of Ballet,* by Anna Paskevska.

DANTE UNIVERSITY OF AMERICA PRESS, INC., Box 843, 21 Station St., Brookline Village MA 02147. Contact: Manuscripts Editor. Publishes hardcover originals and reprints, and trade paperback originals and reprints. Averages 3-5 titles/year. Pays royalty; offers negotiable advance. Simultaneous and photocopied submissions OK. SASE. Reports in 6 weeks on queries; 2 months on mss. Book catalog for business size SAE and 1 first class stamp.

Nonfiction: Biography, reference, reprints and translations. Subjects include general scholarly nonfiction, Renaissance thought and letter, Italian language and linguistics, Italian-American history and culture and bilingual education. Query first.

Recent Nonfiction Titles: *Lives of the Italian-Americans: 50 Illustrated Biographies,* by Caso; *An Ode to America's Independence: A Bilingual Edition,* by Alfieri; and *Italian Panel Paintings of the 14th and 15th Centuries,* by Boskovits.

Poetry: "There is a chance that we would use Renaissance poetry translations."

DARTNELL CORP., 4660 N. Ravenswood Ave., Chicago IL 60640. (312)561-4000. Senior Vice-President: Norman F. Guess. Publishes manuals, reports, hardcovers. Royalties: sliding scale based on wholesale or retail price. Published 7 titles last year. Send outline and sample chapter. Reports in 4 weeks. SASE.

Business: Interested in new material on business skills and techniques in management, supervision, administration, advertising sales, etc. Recently published *Employee Fringe Benefits,* by Sesco Associates; and *Technical Marketing to the Government,* by Robert Rexrood.

MAY DAVENPORT, PUBLISHERS, 26313 Purissima Rd., Los Altos Hills CA 94022. (415)948-6499. Editor/Publisher: May Davenport. Hardcover and trade paperback originals. Averages 3-4 titles/year. Pays 10-40% royalty on retail price; no advance. Photocopied submissions OK. SASE. Reports in 2 weeks. Paperback book with listings of title $2.50.

Imprints: md Books (nonfiction and fiction), May Davenport, editor.

Nonfiction: Humor, juvenile and textbook. Subjects include Americana, animals, art, music and nature. "We're looking for manuscripts which reflect personal contact of human beings with animals, art, music, nature, and the joy and interest about it which other people could share. Our readers are students in elementary and secondary public school districts, as well as correctional institutes of learning, etc." No "hack writing." Query.

Recent Nonfiction Titles: *That Reminds Me . . . ,* by Questa Kaiser (journalist's writings for children); *Courage,* edited by May Davenport (anthology of short stories, poems, articles); and *Involvement* edited by May Davenport (anthology of short stories, poems, articles).

Fiction: Adventure, ethnic, fantasy, humor, mystery and suspense. "We would like children's stories with imaginative flair for storytelling—animal point of view of society we live in. Vocabulary should be elementary school level and fun reading." No sex or violence. Query.

Recent Fiction Titles: *Pigalee Pink,* by Evelyn Dorio; *The Mouse Who Didn't Believe,* by Marguerite Atcheson; and *A Time to Fantasize,* by May Kapela Davenport (book of closet plays—to be read rather than performed).

Tips: "Make people laugh. Humor has a place, too."

F.A. DAVIS CO./PUBLISHERS, 1915 Arch St., Philadelphia PA 19103. (215)568-2270. President and Senior Editor: Robert H. Craven. Editor-in-Chief: Karen R. Emilson. Advertising Manager: James C. Mills. Publishes hardcover and paperback originals. Published 25 titles in 1980, 20 in 1981. Pays 8-15% royalty; offers $1,000 average advance. Simultaneous submissions OK. SASE. Reports in 3 weeks. Free book catalog on request.

Nonfiction: Medicine, nursing and allied health. "We evaluate all mss for potential publications provided they are authored by professional personnel in these categories." Query first and submit outline/synopsis and sample chapters.

Recent Nonfiction Titles: *Office Cardiology,* by R. Brandenburg (professional medical text); *Modern Legal Medicine, Psychiatry, and Forensic Science,* by W. Curran, A. McGarry and C. Petty (professional medical text).

DAVIS PUBLICATIONS, INC., 50 Portland St., Worcester MA 01608. Published 10 titles last year. Pays 10-15% royalty. Write for copy of guidelines for authors. Submit complete ms. Enclose return postage.

Art and Reference: Publishes art and craft books. "Keep in mind the reader for whom the book is written. For example, if a book is written for the teacher, avoid shifting from addressing the teacher to addressing the student. Include illustrations with text. All illustrations should be collated separately from the text, but keyed to the text. Photos should be good quality original prints. Well-selected illustrations can explain, amplify, and enhance the text. It is desirable for the author's selection of illustrations to include some extras. These may be marked 'optional.' The author should not attempt to lay out specific pages. Poorly selected illustrations or too many competing illustrations in a short space can mar a book. For instance, if you are planning a 125-150 page book and you have over 300 photos (more than 2 photos per page, average), you probably have too many."

DAW BOOKS, INC., 1633 Broadway, New York NY 10019. Editor: Donald A. Wollheim. Publishes science fiction paperback originals (80%) and reprints (20%). Publishes 62 titles/year. Pays 6% royalty; $2,500 advance and up. Simultaneous submissions "returned at once unread." SASE. Reports in 6 weeks. Free book catalog.
Fiction: "We are interested in science fiction and fantasy novels only. We do not publish any other category of fiction. We are not seeking collections of short stories or ideas for anthologies. We do not want any nonfiction manuscripts." Submit complete ms.
Recent Fiction Titles: *Yurth Burden*, by Andre Norton (science fiction); *Stormqueen!*, by Marion Zimmer Bradley; and *Interstellar Empire*, by John Brunner.

JOHN DE GRAFF, INC., Distributed by International Marine Publishing Co., Camden ME 04843. Editorial: Clinton Corners NY 12514. (914)266-5800. President: John G. DeGraff. Publishes hardcover originals. Averages 2-3 titles/year. Pays 10% royalty on retail price. Simultaneous and photocopied submissions OK. SASE. Reports in 2 weeks on queries; 1 month on mss. Free book catalog.
Nonfiction: Nautical (pleasure boating). "Our books are for yachtsmen, boat builders and naval architects. We're interested in the how-to aspects, rather than boating experiences." Submit complete ms.
Recent Nonfiction Titles: *Yachtsmen's Legal Guide to Co-ownership*, by Odin; *Sailing Years, a Memoir*, by Coles; and *Marine Survey Manual for Fiberglass Boats*, by Edmunds.

DELACORTE PRESS, 245 E. 47th St., New York NY 10017. (212)832-7300. Imprints include Seymour Lawrence and Eleanor Friede. Editorial Director: Ross Claiborne. Publishes hardcover originals. Published 70 titles in 1979; plans 70 in 1980. Pays 10-12½-15% royalty; average advance. Simultaneous and photocopied submissions OK. SASE. Reports in 1 month.
Fiction and General Nonfiction: Query or outline or brief proposal, or complete ms accepted only through an agent; otherwise returned unopened.
Recent Nonfiction Titles: *Men in Love*, by Nancy Friday (sexuality); *Kilgallen*, by Lee Israel (biography); and *Number 1*, by Billy Martin and Peter Gollenbeck (autobiography).
Recent Fiction Titles: *Random Winds*, by Belva Plain (family saga); and *Change of Heart*, by Sally Mandel (contemporary fiction).

DELL PUBLISHING CO., INC., 1 Dag Hammarskjold Plaza, New York NY 10017. Imprints include Dell, Delacorte Press, Delta Books, Yearling and Laurel Leaf. Publishes hardcover and paperback originals and reprints. Publishes 500 titles/year. Pays royalty on retail price. "General guidelines for unagented submissions. Please adhere strictly to the following procedure: 1) Do not send manuscript, sample chapters or art work; 2) Do not register, certify or insure your letter; 3) Send only a 3-page synopsis or outline with a cover letter stating previous work published or relevant experience." Simultaneous and photocopied submissions OK. Reports in 3 months. SASE.
Nonfiction: "Because Dell is comprised of several imprints, each with its own editorial department, we ask you to carefully review the following information and direct your submission to the appropriate department. Your envelope must be marked "Attention: (blank) Editorial Department—Proposal." Fill in the blank with one of the following: Delacorte: Publishes in hardcover. Looks for popular nonfiction (*My Mother, Myself; Elvis We Love You Tender*). Delta: Publishes in trade paperback; rarely publishes original fiction; looks for useful, substantial guides (*Feed Your Kids Right*); entertaining, amusing nonfiction (*Junk Food*); serious work in the area of modern society (*Children of Crisis*). Laurel Leaf: Publishes in paperback and hardcover for young adults, grades 7-12. Yearling: Publishes in paperback and hardcover for children, grades K-6. Purse: Publishes miniature paperbacks about 60 pages in length on topics of current consumer interest, e.g., diet, exercise, coin prices, etc.
Fiction: Refer to the above guidelines. Delacorte: Publishes top-notch commercial fiction in hardcover (e.g., *Class Reunion; Evergreen*). Dell: Publishes mass-market paperbacks; rarely

publishes original nonfiction; looks for family sagas, historical romances, sexy modern romance, adventure and suspense, thrillers, occult/horror and war novels. Especially interested in submissions for our Candlelight (light romances and regencies) and Western categories. Not currently publishing original mysteries. Laurel Leaf: Publishes in paperback and hardcover for young adults, grades 7-12. Yearling: Publishes in paperback and hardcover for children, grades K-6.

DELMAR PUBLISHERS, Subsidiary of Litton Educational Publishing, Inc., 50 Wolf Rd., Albany NY 12205. (518)459-1150. Director of Publications: Gerald O. Stoner. Publishes hardcover and paperback originals, and hardcover and paperback reprints. Averages 50 titles/year. Pays royalty on wholesale price. SASE. Reports in 2 weeks on queries; 2 months on submissions. Free book catalog.
Nonfiction: Cookbook, how-to, self-help, technical and textbook. Subjects include business and economics; cooking and foods; health; nursing texts; music; nature; psychology; and textbooks for most vocational and technical subjects. Books are used in secondary and postsecondary schools. Query or submit outline/synopsis and sample chapters.
Recent Nonfiction Titles: *The Commerical Greenhouse*, by James W. Boodley (agricultural textbook); *Children in Your Life*, by Deanna Radeloff and Roberta Zechman (home economics textbook); and *Electrical Writing—Residential*, by Ray C. Mullin (electrical trades textbook).

DELTA BOOKS, Division of Dell Publishing Co., 1 Dag Hammarskjold Plaza, New York NY 10017. (212)832-7300. Editor-in-Chief: Christopher J. Kuppig. Publishes trade paperback originals and reprints. Published 40 titles in 1980, 35 in 1981; plans 23 in 1982. Pays 6-7½% royalty; average advance. Simultaneous and photocopied submissions OK. SASE. Reports in 5-6 weeks. Book catalog for 8½x11 SASE.
Nonfiction: Americana, consciousness, cookbooks/cooking, health, how-to, humor, music, New Age, photography, politics, recreation, reference, science, self-help, and sports. "We would like t see books of The New Age, popular music, social history, social criticism and analysis, and child care. We do not want to see biography, philosophy, academic books, textbooks, juveniles, or poetry books." Query or submit outline/synopsis and sample chapters.
Recent Nonfiction Titles: *Parent's Magazine Mother's Encyclopedia*; *Sun*, by John Gribbin; and *Holistic Medicine*, by Kenneth Pelletier.
Fiction: "We are looking for original, innovative and contemporary novels." Submit through an agent.
Recent Fiction Titles: *Going After Cacciato*, by Tim O'Brien; *Black Tickets*, by Jayne Anne Phillips (collection of powerful short stories); *Legends of the Fall*, by Jim Harrison; and *A Dove of the East*, by Mark Helprin.

RED DEMBNER ENTERPRISES CORP., 1841 Broadway, New York NY 10023. (212)265-1250. Editorial Director: S. Arthur Dembner. Senior Editor: Anna Dembner. Imprints include Dembner Books. Publishes hardcover originals. Averages 6-8 titles/year. Offers royalty on retail price. "Advances are negotiable—from bare bones on up." Simultaneous and photocopied submissions OK. SASE. Reports in 2-3 weeks.
Nonfiction: Biography, business/economics; health; history; hobbies; how-to; nature; philosophy; politics; psychology; recreation; reference; science; and self-help. "We're interested in upbeat, intelligent, informative mss. No cult, fad, or sex books. We prefer books that are worth reading, and even keeping." Submit outline/synopsis and sample chapters.
Recent Nonfiction Titles: *Isaac Asimov's Book of Facts*, by I. Asimov (compilation); *Run the Cat Roads*, by L.L. Edge (history); and *The Second Time Around*, by Otty Lippi (autobiography).
Fiction: Adventure; historical; mainstream; mystery; and suspense. "We are prepared to publish a limited number of well-written, non-sensational works of fiction." Submit outline/synopsis and sample chapters.
Recent Fiction Titles: *Like Father*, by D. Black (novel); and *Broken Vows*, by Robert J. Charles.

*DENEAU PUBLISHERS & CO. LTD., 281 Lisgar St., Ottawa, Ontario, Canada K2P 0E1. (613)233-4075. Editorial Director: Denise Schon. Publishes 93% hardcover and paperback originals and 7% paperback reprints. Averages 12 titles/year. Negotiates royalty and advance. Simultaneous and photocopied submissions OK. SASE. Reports in 2 months. Free book catalog.
Nonfiction: Business/economics, how-to, recreation, self-help and travel. Submit outline/synopsis and sample chapters.
Recent Nonfiction Titles: *Working People*, by Desmond Morton; *The Canadian Wood Heat Book*, by G. Flagler (how-to); and *Nahanni-Trailhead*, by Joannne Ronan Moore (outdoors).
Fiction: Mainstream. Submit complete ms.
Recent Fiction Titles: *From A Seaside Town*, by Norman Levine (short Stories); *Five Hundred Keys*, by Michael Carin (novel); and *Cock-Eyed Optimists*, by Dorothy O'Connell (short stories).

T.S. DENISON & CO., INC., 9601 Newton Ave., S. Minneapolis MN 55437. Editor-in-Chief: W.E. Rosenfelt. Publishes hardcover and paperback originals. Specializes in educational publishing, textbooks, supplemental textbooks, and teacher aid materials. Royalty varies, usually $80-100 per 1,000 copies sold; 10% on occasion; no advance. Send prints if photos are to accompany ms. Photocopied submissions OK. Reports in 2-4 weeks. SASE. Book catalog for SASE.
Nonfiction: Publishes textbooks and teaching aid books. Query.

THE DEVIN-ADAIR CO., INC., Subsidiary: The Chatham Press, 143 Sound Beach Ave., Old Greenwich CT 06870. (203)637-4531. Editor-in-Chief: Alan Cross. Publishes hardcover and paperback originals (90%) and reprints (10%). Royalty on sliding scale, 7-12½%; advance averages $100-3,500. Averages 10 titles/year. Send prints to illustrate ms. No simultaneous submissions. SASE. Free book catalog.
Nonfiction: Publishes Americana, business, how-to, politics, history, medicine, nature, economics, sports and travel books. Query or submit outline/synopsis and sample chapters.
Recent Nonfiction Titles: *The IRS vs. the Middle Class*, by Martin A. Larson; *The Save-Your-Life Defense Handbook* (how-to); and *Roosevelt, Churchill and the World War II Opposition*, by George Eggleston (politics).

*DHARMA PUBLISHING, 2425 Hillside Ave., Berkeley CA 94704. Editorial Director: Tarthang Tulku. Managing Editor: Merrill Peterson. Publishes hardcover and paperback originals (90%) and paperback reprints (10%). Published 10 titles in 1979, 12 in 1980. Pays 5-7% royalty on retail price; no advance. Subsidy publishes 5% of books. SASE. Reports in 1-2 months. Free book catalog.
Nonfiction: Art (Tibetan and other Buddhist); biography (Buddhist); history (Asia and Buddhism); philosophy (Buddhist); photography (Buddhist); psychology (Buddhist); religion (Buddhism); and self-help. "We want translations of Buddhist texts from Tibetan or Sanskrit. Please no original discussions of Buddhist topics." Query. Recently published *Life and Liberation of Padmasambhava*, by Yeshe Tsogyal (biography); *Time, Space, and Knowledge*, by Tarthang Tulkv (philosophy/religion); *Tibet in Pictures*, by LiGotami Govinda (photography); and *Buddha's Lions*, by Abhayadatta (biography).

THE DIAL PRESS, 1 Dag Hammarskjold Plaza, New York NY 10017. (212)832-7300. Publishes hardcover and paperback originals. Pays royalty on retail price. Simultaneous and photocopied submissions OK. Reports in 4 weeks. SASE. Free book catalog.
Nonfiction: "All general trade nonfiction is of interest." Submit outline/synopsis and sample chapters.
Recent Nonfiction Titles: *Off Center*, by Barbara Grizzuti Harrison.
Fiction: All general adult categories. Submit outline/synopsis and sample chapters.
Recent Fiction Titles: *The Ants of God*, by W.T. Tyler; and *Real Presence*, by Richard Bausch.

DILITHIUM PRESS, 11000 SW 11th St., Suite E, Beaverton OR 97005. (503)646-2713. Editorial Director: Merl Miller. Publishes paperback originals. Averages 20 titles/year. Pays 5-25% royalty on wholesale or retail price; average advance. Photocopied submissions OK. SASE. Reports in 2 months. Free book catalog.
Nonfiction: Textbooks and books about small computers. "We are looking for manuscripts in the field of microcomputers. Topics should be geared to general information, hardware and software." Query.
Recent Nonfiction Titles: *Small Computers for the Small Businessman*, by Nicholas Rosa and Sharon Rose; *Computers for Everybody*, by Merl Miller and Jerry Willis; and *32 Basic Programs for the Apple*, by Tom Rugg and Phil Feldman.

DILLON PRESS, INC., 500 S. 3rd St., Minneapolis MN 55415. (612)336-2691. Editorial Director: Uva Dillon. Senior Editor: Linda Kusserow. Publishes hardcover originals. Published 16 titles in 1979, 20 in 1980; plans 20-25 in 1981. Pays royalty and by outright purchase. Contract to be negotiated. Submit complete ms or outline and sample chapters. Reports in 6 weeks. SASE.
Nonfiction: "We are actively seeking manuscripts for the juvenile, educational and adult trade markets. Careers, American Indians, contemporary biographies, 'high-low' biographies of popular modern personalities, how-to books on original crafts and outdoor activities, environmental action, and ethnic heritage are some areas of interest for juvenile books. Ethnic heritage, cookbooks, fishing, popular history, and contemporary issues are adult trade specialties. We prefer complete ms." Recently published: *Paper by Kids*, by Arnold Grummer (juvenile); *Eight Words for Thirsty, a Story of Environmental Action*, by Ann Sigford (juvenile); *Mother Teresa*, by Betsy Lee; *Ishi, The Story of an American Indian*, by Kathleen Allan Meyer (juvenile); *Of Dutch Ways*, by Helen Colijn (adult Heritage); and *Verna Meyer's Menu Cookbook*, by Verna Meyer (adult).

Tips: "Writers can best tailor their material to our needs by making themselves aware of the subjects and people who appeal to today's youngsters."

DIMENSION BOOKS, INC., Box 811, Denville NJ 07834. (201)627-4334. Contact: Thomas P. Coffey. Publishes 35 titles/year. Pays "regular royalty schedule" based on retail price; advance is negotiable. Book catalog for SASE. Reports in 1 week on requested mss. SASE.
General Nonfiction: Publishes general nonfiction including religion, principally Roman Catholic. Also psychology and music. Query. Length: 40,000 words minimum. Recently published *Looking for Jesus*, by A. van Kaam; *Called By Name*, by P. van Breemen; and *Jesus, Set Me Free!*, by G. Maloney.

DOANE AGRICULTURAL SERVICE, INC, 8900 Manchester Road, St. Louis MO 63144. (314)968-1000. Editor, Books and Special Projects: Tom Corey. Publishes hardcover and paperback originals. Averages 3 titles/year. Pays 8% of the gross sales. "Policy on advances has been quite liberal to authoritative authors." Submit outline/synopsis and sample chapter. Reports in 1-2 months. SASE.
Nonfiction: Publishes books written for farmers and ranchers and others involved in agribusiness. Most titles are guides, handbooks, references or how-to books. Books that sell to this audience offer specific advice and assistance, not overviews or general interest.
Recent Nonfiction Titles: *Buying & Selling Farmland*, by Jundt; and *Farm Buildings: From Planning to Completion*, by Phillips.

DODD, MEAD & CO., 79 Madison Ave., New York NY 10016. (212)685-6464. Executive Editor: Allen T. Klots. Royalty basis: 10-15%. Advances vary, depending on the sales potential of the book. A contract for nonfiction books is offered on the basis of a query, a suggested outline and a sample chapter. Write for permission before sending mss. Averages 150 titles annually. Adult fiction, history, philosophy, the arts, and religion should be addressed to Editorial Department. Reports in 1 month. SASE.
General Fiction and Nonfiction: Publishes book-length mss. Length: 70,000-100,000 words. Fiction and nonfiction of high quality, mysteries and romantic novels of suspense, biography, popular science, travel, yachting and other sports, music and other arts. Very rarely buys photographs or poetry.
Juveniles: Length: 1,500-75,000 words. Children's Books Editor: Mrs. Joe Ann Daly.

THE DONNING COMPANY/PUBLISHERS, INC., 5041 Admiral Wright Rd., Virginia Beach VA 23642. Editorial Director: Robert S. Friedman. Publishes hardcover and paperback originals. Averages 25-30 titles/year. Pays 10-12½-15% royalty on retail price, up to 50% discount (hardcover titles); 8-10-12% royalty on paperback; advance "negotiable." Simultaneous (if so informed) and photocopied submissions OK. Reports in 12 weeks. SASE. Book catalog for SASE.
Nonfiction: Wants material for 3 series: 1) Portraits of American Cities Series (pictorial histories of American cities with 300 illustrations, primarily photographs, with fully descriptive captions and historical overview text of approximately 10,000 words. "The intent is to capture the character of a community in transition, from earliest known settlers to the present. Author need not be a professional historian, but must have close ties to the community and cooperation of local historians and private and public photo archives); 2) Regional Specialty Books (specialty, regional cookbooks, popular history and art collections); and 3) Unilaw Library imprint (Editor: Stefan Grunwald. Religious, inspirational, metaphysical subjects and themes). Query or submit complete ms.
Recent Nonfiction Titles: *Portland (OR): A Pictorial History*, by Harry Stein, Kathleen Ryan and Mark Beach; and *The Krone Chronicles*, by Sam Harrison (metaphysics).
Fiction: Starblaze Editions imprint. Editors: Kelly and Polly Freas.
Recent Fiction Titles: *Castaways in Time*, by Robert Adams (science fiction); *Web of Darkness*, by Marion Zimmer Bradley (science fiction); and *Voices? Voices!*, by Stefan Grunwald (metaphysical fiction).
Tips: "Beginning writers are finding it harder to get published because of the increasing number of copies needed to break even. Regional appeal books are easier to place, and authors should consider doing more of them to break into print."

DOUBLEDAY & CO., INC., 245 Park Ave., New York NY 10167. (212)553-4561. Managing Editor: Karen Van Westering. Publishes hardcover and paperback originals; publishes paperback reprints under Anchor, Dolphin and Image imprints. Offers standard 10-12½-15% royalty on retail price; offers variable advance. Reports in 1 month. Published 640 in 1980, 550 in 1981 plans 500 in 1982. Special submission requirements outlined below. Query with outline and sample chapters for both fiction and nonfiction. "Your letter of inquiry should be addressed to the Editorial Department. The letter may be as short as one page, but no longer than six pages (double-spaced).

Use a separate letter for each submission. The first sentence should tell us whether your book is a novel, a biography, a mystery, or whatever. The first paragraph should give us an idea of what your book is about. This description should be clear and straightforward. If your book is a novel, please give us an engaging summary of the plot and background, and a quick sketch of the major characters. If you have already been published, give us details at the end of your letter. You should also tell us of any credentials or experience that particularly qualify you to write your book. For a nonfiction book, it will be helpful to you to consult the *Subject Guide to Books in Print* (available in most libraries) so that you are aware of other books on the same or similar subjects as your own, and can tell us how your book differs from them. Finally, letters of inquiry should be inviting and typed with a good ribbon. If we ask to see your ms, it should be submitted double-spaced on white paper. You should retain a carbon copy, since we cannot assume responsibility for loss or damage to mss. Sufficient postage, in the form of loose stamps, should accompany your submission to insure the return of your ms in the event it is not accepted for publication."

Nonfiction and Fiction: "Doubleday has a policy concerning the handling of manuscripts. We return unopened and unread all complete manuscripts, accompanied by a form telling how we would like submissions made. However, in 2 areas, we will accept complete manuscripts: mysteries and science fiction. These mss should be addressed to the appropriate editor (for example, Science Fiction Editor) and not just to Doubleday. We presently have a moratorium on Western books for young readers, and poetry publishing and are not accepting mss."

DOUBLEDAY CANADA, LTD., 105 Bond St., Toronto, Ontario, Canada M5B 1Y3. (416)977-7891. Editorial Director: Richard Archbold. Publishes hardcover originals. Publishes 15-20 titles/year. Pays royalty on retail price; advance "varies." Simultaneous and photocopied submissions OK. Reports in 2 months. Free book catalog.
Nonfiction: General interest. "We do not specialize, but the major part of our list consists of biography, popular history, and subjects of contemporary interest. Our main concern is to publish books of particular interest to the Canadian market, although our books are published in the US as well. We will consider any nonfiction proposal." Query, submit outline/synopsis and sample chapters, or submit complete ms. Recently published *Sable Island, Nova Scotia's Mysterious Island of Sand*; *Lester Pearson and the Dream of Unity*, by Peter Stursberg (oral history); and *Men in the Shadows, The RCMP Security Service*, by John Sawatsky.
Fiction: "No particular preferences as to style or genre. We publish both 'literary' and 'commercial' books. Once again, we are most interested in fiction with a Canadian angle (author, setting, subject). Of course, we hope they have North American potential as well." Query or submit outline/synopsis and opening chapters. Recently published *The Musk Ox Passion*, by T. York; *Me Bandy, You Cissie*, by Donald Jack; and *Laughing War*, by Martyn Burke.

DOUGLAS & McINTYRE, 1615 Venable St., Vancouver, British Columbia, Canada V5L 2H1. (604)254-7191. President: J.J. Douglas. General Manager: Scott McIntyre. Managing Editor: Marilyn Sacks. Averages 20-25 titles/year. Pays 10% royalty on retail price; $500 average advance. State availabilty of photos and/or illustrations. "Query only." Reports in 3 weeks. SAE with International Reply Coupons.
Nonfiction: Publishes books on Canadian history, recreation and sports, cooking and foods, music and art books and juveniles.
Recent Nonfiction Titles: *Sacred Places*, by Barry Downs (historical architecture); *The World of Canadian Writing*, by George Woodcock (essays); and *The Ancient Jews: How They Lived in Canaan*, by Linda Matchan (juvenile history).
Fiction: Publishes occasionally.
Recent Fiction Title: *Icequake*, by Crawford Kilian (adventure/disaster).

DOW JONES-IRWIN, 1818 Ridge Rd., Homewood IL 60430. (312)798-6000. Executive Editor: Ralph Rieves. Publishes originals only. Royalty schedule and advance negotiable. Publishes 40 titles annually. Reports in 2 weeks. SASE.
Nonfiction: Business and industrial subjects. Query with outline.
Recent Nonfiction Titles: *Money Market: Myth, Reality and Practice*, by Marcia Stigum; *Hour Power*, by John Lee and Milton Pierce (time management); and *Modern Portfolio Theory*, by Robert Hagen (investing).

DRAGONSBREATH PRESS, Rt. 1, Sister Bay WI 54234. Editor: Fred Johnson. Publishes hardcover and trade paperback originals. Averages 3 titles/year. Payment conditions "to be arranged"; no advance. Simultaneous and photocopied submissions OK. SASE. Reports in 1 week on queries; 1 month on mss.
Nonfiction: Biography, humor, illustrated book and juvenile. Subjects include Americana, art, history and photography. "We're interested in anything suited to handmade book production—

short biography, history, original artwork, photography." "The Dragonsbreath Press is a small press producing handmade limited edition books including original artwork meant for collectors of fine art and books who appreciate letterpress printing. This audience accepts a handmade book as a work of art." Query or submit complete ms.

Fiction: Adventure, erotica, experimental, fantasy, historical, horror, humor, mystery, science fiction, suspense and western. "We are looking for short, well-written stories which lend themselves to illustration and deserve to be made into fine, handmade books." No long, novel-length manuscripts. Query or submit complete ms.

Recent Fiction Title: *How I Became Popular Overnight*, by F.W. Johnson (mystery/humor).

Poetry: "We're looking for good readable poetry relating emotions, feelings, experiences." Submit 3 samples with query; submit complete ms "when requested."

DRAMA BOOK SPECIALISTS (PUBLISHERS), 150 W. 52nd St., New York NY 10019. (212)582-1475. Contact: Ralph Pine. Publishes hardcover and paperback originals. Pays 10% royalty on retail price; advance varies. Published 25 titles in 1979, 40 in 1980; 30 in 1981; 400 titles in print. Reports in 4-8 weeks. SASE.

Nonfiction: "Theatrical history, texts, technical books and books dealing with the performing arts. Highly technical nuts-and-bolts books." Query; no complete mss.

DUQUESNE UNIVERSITY PRESS, 600 Forbes Ave., Pittsburgh PA 15219. (412)434-6610. Averages 9 titles/year. Pays 10% royalty on both wholesale and retail price; no advance. Query. Reports in 3 months. Enclose return postage.

Nonfiction: Scholarly books in the humanities, social sciences for academics, libraries, college bookstores and educated laypersons. Length: open. Recently published *Milton's Poetry*, by Edward W. Tayler (literature); *Melancholy*, by H. Tellenbach; *Social Theory at a Crossroads*, by William L. McBride (social science/philosophy); and *Health Care: Its Psychosocial Dimensions*, by J. Bergsma (medical psychology).

DUSTBOOKS, Box 100, Paradise CA 95969. (916)877-6110. Publisher: Len Fulton. Publishes hardcover and paperback originals. Published 8 titles in 1979, 6 in 1980. Offers 15% royalty; also buys mss by outright purchase: $500-1,000. Offers average $500 advance. Simultaneous and photocopied submissions OK if so informed. SASE. Reports in 1-2 months. Free book catalog.

Nonfiction: Technical. "DustBooks would like to see manuscripts dealing with microcomputers (software, hardware) and water (any aspect). Must be technically sound and well-written. We have at present no titles in these areas. These represent an expansion of our interests." Submit outline/synopsis and sample chapters.

E.P. DUTTON, 2 Park Ave., New York NY 10016. (212)725-1818. Editor-in-Chief, General Books: Charles P. Corn. Editor, Juvenile Department: Ann Durell. Editor, Dutton Paperbacks: Cyril Nelson. Imprints include Dutton Paperbacks, Everyman Library. Averages 75 titles/year. Pays royalty on list price; offers variable advance. No unsolicited mss. "Pleas send query letter first."

Nonfiction: Americana, animals, biography, business/economics, history, juveniles, nature, photography, politics, psychology, science, sociology, sports, fine arts, memoirs, and belles-lettres translations. Query.

Recent Nonfiction Titles: *Max Perkins, Editor of Genius*, by A. Scott Berg (biography); *States of Desire*, by Edmund White (gay lifestyles); and *Ambition*, by Joseph Epstein (ambition).

Fiction: Novels of "permanent literary value," quality paperbacks and juveniles. Mainstream. Query.

Recent Fiction Titles: *Winter Journey*, by T. Alan Broughton; *Bellefleur*, by Joyce Carol Oates; and *Abbey's Road*, by Ed Abbey.

EAKIN PUBLICATIONS, Drawer A6, Burnet TX 78611. (512)756-6911. Imprints include Nortex. Editorial Director: Edwin M. Eakin. Publishes hardcover and paperback originals (95%); and reprints (5%). Published 9 titles in 1979, 20 in 1980; plans 30 in 1981. Pays 10-12½-15% in royalty. No advance. Simultaneous and photocopied submissions OK. SASE. Reports in 3 months. Free book catalog sent on request.

Nonfiction: History, juvenile history and folklore. Specifically needs biographies of well-known southwestern people, current Texas politics and history for the grades 3-9. Query first or submit outline/synopsis and sample chapters.

Recent Nonfiction Titles: *Fred Gipson Before Old Yeller*, by F. Gipson; *My Years with Bob Wills*, by A. Stricklan (about Texas Playboys-swing band); *Six Central Texas Auto Tours*, by M. McIlvain; *Books for Young Texans* (4 biographies for junior high); and *The Lady Cannoneer*, by C. Richard King (Texas history).

Fiction: Historical fiction for school market. Specifically need juveniles that relate to the Southwest and historical fiction for Texas gradeschoolers. Query or submit outline/synopsis and sample chapters.
Recent Fiction Titles: *Cannon Boy of the Alamo*, by L. Templeton; *Shag Chacota*, by J. Watson and *Seed of a New Land*, by V. Gholson.

THE EAST WOODS PRESS, (Trade name of Fast & McMillan Publishers, Inc.), 820 E. Blvd., Charlotte NC 28203. Editorial Director: Sally Hill McMillan. Publishes hardcover and paperback originals for "travelers and seekers of alternative lifestyles." Publishes 10 titles/year. Pays 8-10% royalty on retail price; 5% on wholesale price. Reports in 2-4 weeks. SASE. Book catalog for SASE.
Nonfiction: "We are mainly interested in travel and the outdoors. Regional guidebooks are our specialty, but anything on travel and outdoors will be considered." Submit outline/synopsis and sample chapters. "A list of competitive books should be submitted, along with specific reasons why this manuscript should be published. Also, maps and art should be supplied by the author."
Recent Nonfiction Titles: *Sea Islands of the South*, by Diana and Bill Gleasner; *Wild Places of the South*, by Steve Price; *Train Trips: Exploring America by Rail*, by William Scheller (travel); and *Hosteling USA*, by Michael Frome.

*EDEN PRESS WOMEN'S PUBLICATIONS, 245 Victoria Ave., #12, Montreal, Quebec, Canada H3Z 2M6. (514)931-3910. Editor: Sherri Clarkson. Publishes hardcover and trade paperback originals. Averages 10 or more titles/year. Subsidy publishes 10% of books based on "the quality of the manuscript." Pays 10-15% royalty. Photocopied submissions OK. SAE and International Reply Coupons. Reports in 2 weeks. Free book catalog.
Nonfiction: Biography, reference, textbook and scholarly. Subjects include Americana, animals, art, business and economics, cooking and foods, health, history, philosophy, politics, psychology, religion, sociology and women. "Original scholarly work on any aspect of women in society. Our audience is intelligent, well-educated, interested in women and their role in society, nature, history. Usually university-affiliated, but non-specialists, as well as specialist, readers. We are a highly specialized press, with an exclusive interest in academic women's studies. That field is extremely broad in its interests and a multitude of titles are anticipated." No material that is unrelated to women or unscholarly. Query or submit outline/synopsis and sample chapters.
Recent Nonfiction Titles: *Sex Roles: Origins, Influences & Implications for Women*, by Dr. C. Stark-Adamec (scholarly/psychology); *Birth in Four Cultures*, by Dr. Brigitte Jordan (health/anthroplogy/women); and *Primate Paradigms: Sex Roles & Social Bonds*, by Dr. L. Fedigan (anthropology/natural history).
Tips: "Our readers are intelligent, well educated, interested in women and their role in society, nature, history. Usually university-affiliated, but non-specialists, as well as specialist readers. Do sound, original, careful scholarly research, write it up intelligently, with style and wit, and package it nicely for ease of evaluation. Simple."

EDITS PUBLISHERS, Box 7234, San Diego CA 92107. (714)488-1666. Editorial Director: Robert R. Knapp. Publishes hardcover and paperback originals. Published 3 titles in 1979, 3 in 1980; plans 4 in 1981. Pays variable royalty on retail price; no advance. Photocopied submissions OK. Reports in 1-2 months. SASE. Book catalog for SASE.
Nonfiction: "Edits publishes scientific and text books in social sciences, particularly counseling and guidance, psychology, statistics and education." Query. Recently published *Actualizing Therapy*, by E. Shostrom (therapy text); *Naked Therapist*, by S. Kopp; and *Handbook in Research and Evaluation*, by S. Isaac.

WILLIAM B. EERDMANS PUBLISHING CO., Christian University Press, 255 Jefferson Ave. SE, Grand Rapids MI 49503. (616)459-4591. Editor: Marlin J. Van Elderen. Associate Editor: Jon Pott. Publishes hardcover and paperback originals (80%) and reprints (20%). Published 50 titles in 1979; 60 in 1980; plans 60 in 1981. Pays 7½-10% royalty on retail price; no advance. Simultaneous and photocopied submissions OK. SASE. Reports in 3 weeks for queries and 4 months for ms. Free book catalog.
Nonfiction: History, philosophy, psychology, reference, religion, sociology and textbooks. "Approximately 80% of our publications are religious—specifically Protestant and largely of the more academic or theological (as opposed to devotional, inspirational or celebrity-conversion type of book) variety. Our history and 'social studies' titles aim, similarly at an academic audience; many of them are 'documentary' histories. We prefer writers take the time to notice if we have published anything at all in the same category as their manuscript before sending it to us." Query.
Recent Nonfiction Titles: *Alaska: A History of the 49th State*, by Claus M. Naske and Herman Slotnick; *A Hospice Handbook*, by Michael Hamilton and Helen Reid (essays); *Paul: Apostle of the Heart Set Free*, by F.F. Bruce (theology/biography); *Faith and Fiction: The Modern Short Story*, by Glenn Meeter (literature/faith); and *Christian Life*, by Karl Barth (theology).

*EFFECTIVE LEARNING, INC., 7 N. MacQuesten Pkwy., Box 2212, Mt. Vernon NY 10550. (914)664-7944. Editor: William Brandon. Publishes hardcover and paperback originals (95%) and reprints (5%). Averages 6-10 titles/year. Subsidy publishes 2% of books. Simultaneous submissions OK. Query. SASE. Reports in 1-2 months. Free book catalog.
Nonfiction: Americana, biography, business, cookbooks, cooking and food, economics, history, hobbies, how-to, multimedia material, nature, philosophy, politics, reference, religious, scientific, self-help, sociology, technical, textbooks and travel. "All manuscripts should be sent to the editorial review committee. Recently published *The Middle East: Imperatives & Choices*, by Alon Ben-Meir (politics).

ELSEVIER/NELSON BOOKS, 2 Park Ave., New York NY 10016. (212)725-1818. Editor-in-Chief: Virginia Buckley. Hardcover originals. Publishes 50 titles/year. Pays royalty on retail price; advance offered. State availability of photos and/or illustrations. Photocopied submissions OK. Reports in 2-4 months. SASE. Book catalog for 59¢ postage and 6x9 SAE.
Nonfiction: Publishes juveniles, young adults, fiction and nonfiction. Query or submit outline/synopsis and sample chapters.
Fiction: Publishes adventure, experimental, fantasy, historical, humorous, mainstream, mystery, science fiction, suspense and western books. Submit complete ms.

EMC CORP., 180 E. 6th St., St. Paul MN 55101. Senior Editor: Northrop Dawson Jr. Production Editor: Rosemary Barry. Publishes hardcover and paperback originals (90%) and reprints (10%). "We publish for the school (educational) market only, in limited runs as compared to trade publishers. Writers should not have expectations of huge quantity sales." Contract and advance "open to negotiation." Reports in 4 weeks. Free book catalog for large SASE.
Nonfiction: Career Education. Consumer Education. "Topics of interest to juvenile readers: sports; the media; popular entertainers; outdoor life and activity (wild animals, outdoor sports such as cross-country skiing, ballooning, etc.); "the unexplained" (supernatural, esp, etc.); unusual occupations; and biographies of achievers surmounting great odds. No how-to, religious, or travel material." Query; "send resume and one or more samples of previously published work." Unsolicited manuscripts not accepted.
Recent Nonfiction Title: *Whales*, by George Shea.
Fiction: Juvenile fiction: mystery; "the unexplained"; young detectives; stories focusing on non-stereotyped, active, aggressive girls; adventure stories involving young people; sports fiction involving juvenile athletes, both male and female; outdoor and wildlife adventure involving juveniles; realistic stories of juveniles overcoming handicaps; science fiction geared to juveniles; and stories involving animals. No religious material. Query, "send one or more samples of previously published work. After we have indicated interest in initial query, submit outline and sample chapters." Unsolicted manuscripts not accepted.
Recent Fiction Title: *Finding A Job*, by John J. McHugh Jr. (career education).

ENSLOW PUBLISHERS, Bloy St. and Ramsey Ave., Box 777 Hillside NJ 07205. (201)964-4116. Editor: Ridley Enslow. Publishes hardcover and paperback originals. Published 12 titles in 1979, 15 in 1980; plans 24 in 1981. Pays 10-15% royalty on retail price; offers $500-5,000 advance. Query. Photocopied submissions OK. SASE. Reports in 2 weeks. Free book catalog.
Nonfiction: Business/economics, health, hobbies, how-to, juveniles, philosophy, psychology, recreation, reference, science, self-help, sociology, sports and technical.
Recent Nonfiction Titles: *Amateur Astronomer's Handbook*, by Sidgwick (science); *Breastfeeding Handbook*, by Goldfarb (medical); and *Inside the Cell*, by Pines.

ENTELEK, Ward-Whidden House/The Hill, Portsmouth NH 03801. Editor-in-Chief: Albert E. Hickey. Publishes paperback originals. Offers royalty on retail price of 5% trade; 10% textbook. No advance. Published 4 titles in 1980, 4 in 1981; plans 6 in 1982. Free catalog. Photocopied and simultaneous submissions OK. Submit outline and sample chapters or submit complete ms. Reports in 1 week. SASE.
Nonfiction: Publishes computer, math, and business and books and programs. "We seek books that have not been undertaken by other publishers." Length: 3,000 words minimum.
Recent Nonfiction Titles: *Genetics With the Computer*; *Physics with the Computer;* and *Sullivan's Guide to Learning Centers in Higher Education.*

ENTERPRISE PUBLISHING CO., INC., 725 Market St., Wilmington DE 19801. (302)654-0110. Editor and Publisher: T.N. Peterson. Publishes hardcover and paperback originals. Published 2 titles in 1979, 14 in 1980; plans 20 in 1981. Pays royalty on wholesale or retail price. Advance averages $1,000. Simultaneous and photocopied submissions OK, but "let us know." Reports in 1 month. SASE. Catalog and writers' guidelines for SASE.

Nonfiction: "Subjects of interest to small business owners/entrepreneurs. They are highly independent and self-sufficient, and of an apolitical to conservative political leaning. They need practical information, as opposed to theoretical: self-help topics on business, including starting and managing a small enterprise, advertising, marketing, raising capital and public relations." Business/economics, legal self-help, and business how-to. Query; all unsolicited mss are returned unopened.

Recent Nonfiction Titles: *How to Get Out of Debt*, by Ted Nicholas; *How to Totally Avoid Estate Taxes*, by Gilbert M. Cantor; *How to Set Up a Business Office*, by Norma Morris; *How to Profit From Condominium Conversions*, by Paul Bullock; and *Partners in Business*, by Dr. Melvin Wallace.

ENVIRONMENTAL DESIGN & RESEARCH CENTER, 142 Lowell Ave., Newtonville MA 02160. (617)965-5910. Director: Dr. Kaiman Lee. Publishes hardcover originals. Averages 5 titles/ year. Pays 15-18% royalty. SASE. Reports in 2 weeks on queries; 3 weeks on submissions. Free book catalog.
Nonfiction: Reference, technical, textbook and encyclopedic. Subjects include business and economics (personal finance); architecture; energy; and environment. "We're looking for mss on personal financial and survival planning. Our books are highly technical but of current material." Submit complete ms.
Recent Nonfiction Titles: *Encyclopedia of Financial and Personal Survival: 650 Coping Strategies*, by K. Lee and R. Yang; *Kaiman's Encyclopedia of Energy Topics*, by K. Lee; and *Environmental Court Cases Related to Buildings*, by K. Lee.

*PAUL S. ERIKSSON, PUBLISHER, Battell Bldg., Middlebury VT 05753. (802)388-7303. President: Paul S. Eriksson. Publishes hardcover and paperback trade originals (99%) and paperback trade reprints (1%). Averages 5-10 titles/year. Pays 10-15% royalty on retail price; advance offered if necessary. Subsidy publishes 5% of books. "We have to like the book and probably the author." Photocopied submissions OK. SASE. Reports in 3 weeks. Free book catalog.
Nonfiction: Americana, animals, art, biography, business/economics, cookbooks/cooking/foods, health, history, hobbies, how-to, humor, juveniles, music, nature, philosophy, photography, politics, psychology, recreation, self-help, sociology, sports and travel. Submit outline/synopsis and sample chapters.
Recent Nonfiction Titles: *Steinbeck and Covici*, by Thomas Fensch; *It's A Pig World Out There*, by Phyllis Demong; and *The Best Years of My Life*, by Harold Russell.
Fiction: Mainstream. Submit outline/synopsis and sample chapters.
Recent Fiction Title: *The Silkies*, by Charlotte Koplinka (novel of the Shetlands).

EROS PUBLISHING CO., INC., 9172 Eton Ave., Chatsworth CA 91311. (213)709-1160. Editor-in-Chief: Charles Anderson. Publishes paperback originals (90%) and reprints (10%). Published 138 titles in 1979 and 138 in 1980. Buys mss by outright purchases for $1,000 minimum; offers average $1,000 advance. Simultaneous and photocopied submissions OK if readable. SASE. Reports in 3 weeks. Free book catalog.
Nonfiction: Americana, biography, business/economics, health, history, hobbies, how-to, humor, philosophy, psychology, recreation, self-help, sociology and travel. Subjects must be applicable to mass market with aim toward adult interest well-developed and well-researched. Query, submit outline/synopsis and sample chapters.
Recent Nonfiction Titles: *A Guide to Travel in America*, by R. Ward (self-help); *Illustrated Encyclopedia Sexualis*, by E. Johnson (self-help); and *A Guide to Transvestism*, by E. Podolsky (self-help).
Fiction: Adventure, confession, erotica, experimental, gothic, historical, mystery, romance, suspense and western. 50,000 word mss within contemporary mainstream that explore the wide variety of psychological and otherwise contemporary problems that are typical of adult experience today. Query, submit outline/synopsis and sample chapters.
Recent Fiction Titles: *Daphne*, by R. Slatzer (story of a career woman); *Lost Temptations*, by T. Simpson (female spy story); and *Grand Prix for Lovers*, by D. Benson (first woman Formula I driver).

ESSCO, Akron Airport, Akron OH 44306. (216)733-6241. President/Editorial Director: Ernest Stadvec. Publishes paperback originals. Averages 14 titles/year. Pays 10% royalty on retail price for the first 1,000 and 15% thereafter; no advance. Simultaneous and photocopied submissions OK. SASE. Reports in 2 weeks. Free book catalog.
Nonfiction: Biography, history, hobbies, how-to, technical and textbooks, all on aviation. Specifically needs aviation related subjects, aircraft guide books, training manuals, aircraft picture books, historical books and military aviation. Query.

Recent Nonfiction Titles: *Encoupe-Twin Tail Tiger*, by L.J. Buffardi (aircraft guide); *Inflatoplane*, by E. Stadvec (technical); and *The Rubber Flying Machines*, by E. Stadvec (historical).

*ETC PUBLICATIONS, Drawer 1627-A, Palm Springs CA 92263. (714)325-5352. Editorial Director: Leeona S. Hostrop. Senior Editor: Dr. Richard W. Hostrop. Publishes hardcover and paperback originals. Subsidy publishes 5-10% of books. Averages 12 titles/year. Offers 5-15% royalty, based on wholesale and retail price. No advance. Simultaneous and photocopied submissions OK. SASE. Reports in 3 weeks. Book catalog $2.
Nonfiction: Biography; business/economics; how-to; psychology; recreation; reference; self-help; sociology; sports; technical; and textbooks. Submit complete ms.
Recent Nonfiction Titles: *How To Write for the Religion Market*, by J. Moore (how-to); *Nellie's Boardinghouse: A Dual Biography of Nellie Coffman and Palm Springs*, by M. Bright (biography); and *Making Changes: A Futures-Oriented Course in Inventive Problem Solving*, by J. Thomas (textbook).
Tips: *"ETC.* is particularly interested in new nonfiction titles that have film or television potential."

EVANS AND CO., INC., 216 E. 49 St., New York NY 10017. Editor-in-Chief: Herbert M. Katz. Publishes hardcover originals. Royalty schedule to be negotiated. Averages 30 titles annually. Will consider photocopied submissions. "No mss should be sent unsolicited. A letter of inquiry is essential." Reports in 6-8 weeks. SASE.
General Fiction and Nonfiction: "We publish a general trade list of adult fiction and nonfiction, cookbooks and semi-reference works. The emphasis is on selectivity since we publish only 30 titles a year. Our fiction list represents an attempt to combine quality with commercial potential. Our most successful nonfiction titles have been related to the behavioral sciences. No limitation on subject. A writer should clearly indicate what his book is all about, frequently the task the writer performs least well. His credentials, although important, mean less than his ability to convince this company that he understands his subject and that he has the ability to communicate a message worth hearing."
Recent Titles: *Domestic Arrangements*, by Norma Klein; and *Pain Erasure*, by Bonnie Prudden.
Tips: "Writers should review our catalog or the *Publishers Trade List Annual* before making submissions."

EVEREST HOUSE, PUBLISHERS, 33 West 60th St., New York NY 10023. (212)764-3400. Senior Editor: William Thompson. Publishes hardcover and paperback (trade) originals. Published 45 titles in 1979, 50 in 1980; plans 60 for 1981. Usually pays standard royalty rates; advance varies. Simultaneous and photocopied submissions OK. SASE. Reports in 6 weeks. Book catalog for $1.
Nonfiction: General trade books in the areas of biography, history, how-to, humor, music, psychology, self-help and sports. No juvenile or poetry. Submit outline/synopsis and sample chapters.
Recent Nonfiction Titles: *Stephen King's Danse Macabre*, by Stephen King; *Presenting Mark Russell*, by Mark Russell, *The Cola Wars*, by J.C. Louis and H. Yazijian; *Help 1981*, by A. Rouse and Consumer News, Inc.
Fiction: Mainstream, romance and suspense. No science fiction.
Recent Fiction Titles: *Razzmatazz*, by P.D. Wheaton; and *Lady Susan*, by P.A. Karr.

EXANIMO PRESS, 23520 Hwy 12, Segundo CO 81070. Editor: Dean Miller. Publishes hardcover and trade paperback originals. Averages 6-10 titles/year. Pays 10% minimum royalty on retail price; buys some mss outright for $500-1,500; no advance. Photocopied submissions OK. SASE. Reports in 1 month on queries; 2 weeks on mss. Book catalog for SAE and 1 first class stamp.
Nonfiction: How-to and technical. Subjects include prospecting; small mining; treasure hunting; self-employment; dowsing (water witching); and self- or family-improvement from an economical point of view. "We would like to publish one book per month in our particular field which is mining, prospecting, and treasure hunting. Our style and format is approximately 8x10" pages with books running from 40 to 104 pages. We prefer a profusely illustrated book and our artist will make finished sketches from rough drawings. Our books are aimed at the adventuresome person or family and people who want to get out of the rat race and get into a profitable activity that relieves them of audits, inspections and red tape. No copy-artistry, please, and no read-and-rewrites; we want hard-core mining material from people with at least 10 full years of experience." Query.
Recent Nonfiction Titles: *Beachcomber's Handbook*, by Warren Merkitch; *Gold Rocker Handbook*, by Tron Miller; *Gold Dredger's Handbooks*, by Karl von Mueller; *Placer Miner's Manual* 3 volumes, by Karl von Mueller; and *Mysteries of Treasure Hunting*, by R.J. Santschi.
Tips: "Investigate the market and find a publisher whose specialty is in accord with your proposed

book or books. Most try to create a good working relationship and pave the way for future books which will obviously pave the way for a higher financial return for you. The secret is to get a first book published in order to give leverage for future books. Specialize in 1 field and develop a reputation for technically accurate books and get 2 or 3 titles into print and then look forward to an ascending career in writing."

FACTS ON FILE, INC., 119 W. 57th St., New York NY 10019. (212)265-2011. Editorial Director: Eleanora Schoenebaum. Publishes hardcover originals (75%) and reprints (25%). Averages 60-70 titles/year. Offers "usually 15% royalty of net proceeds, sometimes 10% of list price." Also buys some mss by outright purchase: $2,000-50,000. Advance averages $7,000. Simultaneous and photocopied submissions OK. SASE. Reports in 4 weeks. Book catalog for SASE.
Nonfiction: Reference for libraries and trade in art; biography; business/economics; history; music; nature; energy; politics; psychology; science; self-help; sociology; and travel. "All books must be essentially reference or information-oriented, but given that, the subject matter can be almost anything." Does *not* want "juvenile books, textbooks, Ph.D. thesis, opinionated books." Submit outline/synopsis and sample chapters.
Recent Nonfiction Titles: *The World Directory of Multinational Enterprises*, by John M. Stopford, John H. Dunning and Klaus O. Haberich (business reference); *America's Paychecks: Who Makes What*, by David Harrop (reference); and *Performing Arts*, by Michael Billington (reference).

FAIRCHILD BOOKS & VISUALS, Book Division, 7 E. 12th St., New York NY 10003. Manager: E.B. Gold. Publishes hardcover and paperback originals. Offers standard minimum book contract; no advance. Pays 10% of net sales distributed twice annually. Published 12 titles last year. Photocopied submissions OK. Free book catalog. Query, giving subject matter and brief outline. Enclose return postage.
Business and Textbooks: Publishes business books and textbooks relating to fashion, electronics, marketing, retailing, career education, advertising, home economics, and management. Length: open. Recently published *Fairchild's Designer's/Stylist's Handbook*, by Gioello; and *Fashion Advertising and Promotion*, by Winters/Goodman.

FAIRMONT PRESS INC., Box 14227, Atlanta GA 30324. (404)447-5314. Director of Operations: V. Oviatt. Publishes hardcover originals. Averages 4-8 titles/year. Pays 5-12% royalty; offers advance. SASE. Reports in 6 weeks. Free book catalog.
Nonfiction: How-to, reference, science, self-help, technical, energy, plant engineering, environment, safety. Submit outline/synopsis and sample chapters.
Recent Nonfiction Title: *Guide to Efficient Burner Operation*, by Faulkner.

FARNSWORTH PUBLISHING CO., INC., 78 Randall Ave., Rockville Centre NY 11570. (516)536-8400. President: Lee Rosler. Publishes hardcover and paperback originals. "Standard royalty applies, but 5% is payable on mail order sales." Publishes 20 titles/year. Reports in 2 months. SASE.
General Nonfiction, Business and Professional: "Our books generally fall into 2 categories: books that appeal to executives, lawyers, accountants and life underwriters and other salespeople (subject matter may cover selling techniques, estate planning, taxation, money management, etc.); and books that appeal to the general population—generally in the financial and self-improvement areas—and are marketable by direct mail and mail order, in addition to bookstore sales."
Recent Nonfiction Titles: *Tax Shelters in Plain English*, by Robert Daniel Fierro; *Negotiate Your Way to Success*, by David Seltz and Alfred Modica; and *Esop for the Eighties*, by Robert Frisch.

FARRAR, STRAUS AND GIROUX, INC., 19 Union Square West, New York NY 10003. Children's Editor: Stephen Roxburgh. Publishes hardcover originals. Published 24 titles in 1979, 24 in 1980. Pays royalty; advance. Photocopied submissions OK. SASE. Reports in 2 months. Catalog for SASE.
Nonfiction: History, humor, juveniles, philosophy, psychology and sociology. "We are not interested in nonfiction for the under 12-18 age group unless the book is specifically keyed to young adult readers—no biography or nature books of a general nature for that age group." Submit outline/synopsis and sample chapters.
Recent Nonfiction Titles: *The Forbidden Experiment: The Story of the Wild Boy of Aveyron*, by Roger Shattuck; and *South Africa: Coming of Age Under Apartheid*, by Jason and Ettegale Lauré.
Fiction: Adventure, fantasy, historical, humor, mainstream, mystery, romance, science fiction, suspense and western. "We particulary want to see contemporary fiction for 7-10 and 10 and up age group." Submit outline/synopsis and sample chapters.
Recent Fiction Titles: *A Ring of Endless Light*, by Madeleine L'Engle; *The Iceberg and Its Shadow*, by Jan Greenberg; and *A Place Apart*, by Paula Fox.

FAWCETT BOOKS GROUPS, CBS Publications, The Consumer Publishing Division of CBS Inc., 1515 Broadway, New York NY 10036. Averages 350 titles/year. Fawcett Books Group consists of five imprints: *Fawcett Crest* (generally reprints); contact Arlene Friedman (212)975-7867; *Columbine* (trade paperback/reprints and originals), *Juniper* (Young Adult/ reprints and originals); *Fawcett Gold Medal* (generally paperback originals); contact Maureen Baron (212)975-7673; and *Coventry Romances* (reprints and originals), contact: Barbara Dicks (212)975-7688.
Recent Titles: *Kane & Abel*, by Jeffrey Archer (contemporary popular fiction); and *Donahue: My Story*, by Phil Donahue & Co. (autobiography).

F.W. FAXON CO., INC., 15 Southwest Park, Westwood MA 02090. (617)329-3350. Publisher: Albert H. Davis Jr. Editor-in-Chief: Beverly D. Heinle. Editor: Sandra Conrad. Publishes hardcover originals. Publishes 10 titles/year. Offers 10% of sales net price for each book sold, payable at the end of each fiscal year. No advance. Books are marketed through advertising, mail campaigns, book reviews, and library conventions. Will send catalog to writer on request. Mss must be original copy, double-spaced, and must be accompanied by a copy. They should contain reference material useful to library users throughout the world. Query. Reports in 2 months. SASE.
Reference: "We publish library reference books. These are primarily indexes but we would also consider bibliographies and other material useful to library users. Develop proposals for reference works in subject areas where there is a need for organized access to a body of information. Such reference works should be of particular value to libraries (school, college, university and public)."
Recent Nonfiction Titles: *Collector's Index*, by Pearl Turner; and *Index to Nutrition and Health*, by Joseph W. Sprug.

FREDERICK FELL PUBLISHERS, INC., 386 Park Ave., S., New York NY 10016. (212)685-9017. Editor: Cornelia Guest. Publishes hardcover and paperback originals (90%) and reprints (10%). Pays 10% royalty, based on wholesale or retail price. Published 21 titles in 1979, 19 in 1980; plans 24 in 1981. Query. Send sample prints or contact sheet if photos/illustrations are to accompany ms. Photocopied submissions OK. Reports in 2 months. SASE. Free book catalog.
Nonfiction: Diet, business, hobbies, how-to, law, medicine and psychiatry, pets, psychology, recreation, reference, inspiration, self-help and sports books. Especially needs Pet Lovers Library; Home Medical Library.
Recent Nonfiction Titles: *The Complete Guide to Cosmetic Facial Surgery*, by John A. McCurdy Jr., MD, F.A.C.S.; and *How to Hypnotize Yourself and Others*, by Rachel Copelan.

THE FEMINIST PRESS, Box 334, Old Westbury NY 11568. (516)997-7660. Publishes paperback and hardcover originals and historical reprints. Published 8 titles in 1979, 8 in 1980; plans 10 in 1981. Pays 6½% royalty on retail price; no advance. Simultaneous and photocopied submissions OK. Reports in 3 months. Query or submit outline/synopsis and sample chapters.
Adult Books: Elsa Dixler, Editor. Feminist books for a general trade and women's studies audience. "We publish biographies, reprints of lost feminist literature, women's history, bibliographies and educational materials. No material without a feminist viewpoint. No contemporary adult fiction, drama, or poetry." Recently published *I Love Myself When I am Laughing . . . and Then Again When I am Looking Mean and Impressive: A Zora Neale Hurston Reader*, edited by Walker (anthology); *Moving the Mountain*, by Cantarow (oral history); and *In Her Own Image*, by Hedges and Wendt (literary and visual anthology).
Children's Books: "We publish juvenile fiction and biographies. No picture books." Recently published *Tatterhood and Other Tales*, E. Phelps (folklore); and *The Lilith Summer*, by H. Irwin.
Tips: "Submit a proposal for an important feminist work that is sophisticated in its analysis, yet popular in its writing style. Both historical and contemporary subjects will be considered. We are especially interested in works that appeal to both a trade audience and a women's studies classroom market."

FFORBEZ ENTERPRISES, LTD., 2133 Quebec St., Vancouver, British Columbia, Canada V5T 2Z9. (604)872-7325. Editor-in-Chief: P.W. Zebroff. Manuscript Editor: Janice Strong. Publishes paperback originals. Specializes in how-to and health-oriented books. Pays 10% royalty on retail price; no advance. Published 9 titles in 1979, 15 in 1980; plans 15 in 1981. Markets books through health and book stores, food and drug chains, sponsoring organizations and direct mail. Send at least 1 copy of illustration and 1 print. Simultaneous submissions OK if exclusive to Canada. Photocopied submissions OK. Reports in 2-4 weeks. SAE and International Reply Coupons. Free book catalog.
Nonfiction: Concise self-help health books (medical or nursing credentials an asset): entertaining, educational activity coloring books; pictorial histories for companies and other sponsoring organi-

zations. Submit outline/synopsis, sample chapters and table of contents, including illustrations. Recently published *Fitness Over Forty*, by Kareen Zebroff; *Kids! Kids! Kids! Famous Rhymes*, by Bob Masse and Jim Wright (activity book); and *Pacific Pilgrims*, by Lyndon Grove (pictorial history of a diocese).

*THE FILTER PRESS, Box 5, Palmer Lake CO 80133. (303)481-2523. Editorial Director: Gilbert L. Campbell. Senior Editor: Lollie W. Campbell. Publishes hardcover and paperback originals (50%) and reprints (50%). Publishes 8 titles/year. Subsidy publishes about 20% of titles/year. "These are usually family histories in short runs, although subjects have ranged from preaching, ranching, history debunking, to a study of UFOs. If we feel we can market a book profitably for us and the author, and it is a good book and the author feels he needs it published, we will consider it." Pays 10% royalty on net price; no advance. Simultaneous and photocopied submissions OK. Reports in 2-3 weeks. "Must have SASE." Book catalog for SASE.
Nonfiction: "Cookbooks must appeal to Westerners, campers, and tourists. We have one on game cookery, one on pancakes, one on camp cooking, one on Southwestern Indian recipes, one on Mexican cooking for the Anglo bride. Also Western legends, and other Western Americana, as we are quite regional. We must stay at or near our 64-page limit, as most booklets are sold softbound, saddle stitched. We have done some verse of Western interest. Our morgue of antique wood engravings is used extensively, so books with a Western Victorian feel fit in best. Western Americana on our list includes Indians, explorations, lawmen, and bandits. We have Butch Cassidy and Pat Garrett. Family histories and very local history have not done well for us. Writers must remember we are small, publish few books, and they must be things that a tourist will buy to take home, although we are in many Eastern bookstores." Query; "it is much cheaper to send a query and SASE than to send the manuscript to us cold."
Recent Nonfiction Titles: *Genuine Navajo Rug: How to Tell*, by Noel Bennett; *Pueblo Crafts*, by Ruth Underhill; and *Blond Chicana Bride's Mexican Cookbook, by Helen Duran.*
Fiction: "Practically all our fiction has been reprinted from 19th century authors, a distinguished group who never ask for an up-to-date royalty statement! Our poetry is evenly divided between old and new. I suppose if something very short and imaginative should come along on the 19th-Century West, we might do it, but. . . ."

FITZHENRY & WHITESIDE, LTD.,150 Lesmill Rd., Don Mills, Ontario, Canada M3B 2T5. Editor-in-Chief: Robert Read. Publishes hardcover and paperback originals and reprints. Chiefly educational materials. Royalty contract varies; advance negotiable. Publishes 50 titles/year. Photocopied submissions OK. Reports in 1-3 months. Enclose return postage.
General Nonfiction, Drama and Poetry: "Especially interested in topics of interest to Canadians, and by Canadians." Biography, business, history, medicine, nature and politics. Submit outline and sample chapters. Length: open.
Recent Titles: *Tom Longboat*, by Bruce Kidd; *The One-Room School in Canada*, by Jean Cochrane; and *The North*, by Stan Garrod.
Textbooks: Elementary and secondary school textbooks, materials in social studies, language arts and science. Submit outline and sample chapters.

FLARE BOOKS, Young Adult Imprint of Avon Books, a division of the Hearst Corp., 959 8th Ave., New York NY 10019. (212)262-7454. Senior Editor: Jean Feiwel. Publishes mass market paperback originals (50%) and reprints (50%). "We have published young adult books under the *Avon* imprint. Beginning August, 1981 those books are under the *Avon-Flare* imprint." Pays 6-10% royalty; offers average $1,500 advance. Simultaneous and photocopied submissions OK. SASE. Reports in 6 weeks.
Nonfiction: Self-help. Subjects include health and psychology. Query or submit outline/synopsis and sample chapters.
Recent Nonfiction Titles: *Why Am I So Miserable, If These Are the Best Years of My Life?*, by Andrea Boroff Eagan (self-help).
Fiction: Adventure, ethnic, experimental, fantasy, humor, mainstream, mystery, romance, science fiction, suspense and contemporary. Mss appropriate to age 12-20. Submit outline/synopsis and sample chapters.
Recent Fiction Titles: *Sooner or Later*, by Bruce and Carole Hart.

FLEET PRESS CORP., 160 5th Ave., New York NY 10010. (212)243-6100. Editor: Susan Nueckel. Publishes hardcover and paperback originals and reprints. Royalty schedule and advance "varies." Published 11 titles in 1980. Free book catalog. Reports in 6 weeks. Enclose return postage with ms.
General Nonfiction: "History, biography, arts, religion, general nonfiction, sports." Length: 45,000 words. Query with outline; no unsolicited mss.

Juveniles: Nonfiction only. Stress on social studies and minority subjects; for ages 8-15. Length: 25,000 words. Query with outline; no unsolicited mss.

FOCAL PRESS INC., 10 E. 40th St., New York NY 10016. (212)679-1777. President: C. Hudson. Publishes hardcover and paperback originals. Publishes 45 titles/year. Offers 10% royalty; also buys mss by outright purchase. No advance. Simultaneous and photocopied submissions OK. SASE. Reports in usually 3 weeks. Free book catalog.
Nonfiction: "We publish only in the fields of photography, cinematography, graphic arts, printing, audiovisual and television—for beginning amateur to advanced research level monographs." Does *not* want to see books of pictures or portfolios. Submit outline/synopsis and sample chapters or complete ms.
Recent Nonfiction Titles: *The Minolta Way*, by C. Reynolds (use of photographic equipment and techniques); *Technique of TV Production*, by G. Millerson (professional and student book on producing TV programs); and *Story of Photography*, by Michael Longford.

FODOR'S MODERN GUIDES, 2 Park Ave., New York NY 10016. (212)340-9800. President and Publisher: James Louttit. Executive Vice President/Editorial: Alan Tucker. Publishes hardcover and paperback originals. Published 68 titles in 1980.
Nonfiction: "We are the publishers of dated travel guides—religious, countries, cities, and special tourist attractions. We do not solicit manuscripts on a royalty basis, but we are interested in travel writers and/or experts who will and can cover an area of the globe for Fodor's for a fee." Submit credentials and samples of work.
Recent Nonfiction Titles: *Fodor's Colorado; Fodor's Washington, DC*; and *Fodor's Pennsylvania.*

FOLCRAFT LIBRARY EDITIONS/NORWOOD EDITIONS, 842 Main St., Darby PA 19023. (215)583-4550. President: Hassie Weiman. Publishes hardcover originals (library bound). Publishes 300 titles/year. Pays standard royalty rates; offers variable. Simultaneous and photocopied submissions OK. SASE. Reports in 3 months.
Nonfiction: Scholarly materials in the humanities by scholars and active researchers associated with universities. Submit complete ms.
Recent Nonfiction Titles: *The Communal Future*, by Prof. J. Blasi; *Music As Culture*, by Prof. M. Herndon; and *Bibliography of Books on Sleep, Dreams and Insomnia*, by M. Weiman.

FOLLETT PUBLISHING CO., Children's Books, 1010 W. Washington Blvd., Chicago IL 60607. (312)666-5858. Editor: C. McGuire. Publishes hardcover originals and some paperback reprints. Pays negotiable royalty and advance. "Photocopied manuscripts are OK, but simultaneous submissions are not accepted." Reports in 4-6 weeks. SASE. Book catalog for SASE.
Fiction: "We are interested in quality fiction that children in grades one through six can read themselves. We're adding at the Beginning-To-Read level and are also looking for juvenile novels. We are not accepting picture-story book manuscripts, poetry, or novels for teenaged readers." Submit outline/synopsis or complete ms.

FORDHAM UNIVERSITY PRESS, University Box L, Bronx NY 10458. (212)933-2233, ext. 366. Director: H.G. Fletcher. Published 8 titles in 1979, 9 in 1980; plans 8 in 1981. Pays royalty on sales income. Photocopied submissions OK. SASE. Reports in 1 week. Free book catalog.
Nonfiction: Humanities. "We would like the writer to use the *MLA Style Sheet*, latest edition. We do not want dissertations or fiction material."
Recent Nonfiction Titles: *The Value of Justice*, edited by Charles A. Kelbley; *The Metaphysics of Experience* by Elizabeth M. Kraus; and *Conservative-Millenarians*, by Paul Gottfried.

FORTRESS PRESS, 2900 Queen Lane, Philadelphia PA 19129. (215)848-6800. Editorial Director: Norman A. Hjelm. Publishes hardcover and paperback originals. Published 52 titles in 1979, 60 in 1980. Specializes in general religion for laity and clergy; academic texts and monographs in theology (all areas). Pays 7½% royalty on paperbacks; 10% on hardcover; modest advance. Mss must follow *Chicago Manual of Style* (13th edition). Photocopied submissions OK. Reports in 90 days. SASE. Free book catalog.
Nonfiction: Publishes philosophy, religious and self-help books. Query. No religious poetry or fiction. Recently published *Introduction to the Old Testamental Scripture*, by B. Childs; *Paul and Palestinian Judaism*, by E.P. Sanders; and *Prism or Paradise? The New Religious Cults*, by James and Marcia Rudin.

FRANCISCAN HERALD PRESS, 1434 W. 51st St., Chicago IL 60609. (312)254-4455. Editor: The Rev. Mark Hegener, O.F.M. Senior Editor: Marion A. Habig. Imprints include *Synthesis Booklets* and *Herald Biblical Booklets*. Publishes hardcover and paperback originals (90%) and reprints (10%). Published 52 titles in 1979, 55 in 1980; plans 60 in 1981. Pays 8-12% royalty on both wholesale and retail price; offers $200-1,000 advance. Photocopied submissions OK. SASE. Reports in 2 weeks. Free book catalog.

Nonfiction: "We are publishers of Franciscan literature for the various branches of the Franciscan Order: history, philosophy, theology, Franciscan spirituality and biographies of Franciscan saints and blessed." Query or submit outline/synopsis and sample chapters. Recently published *The Franciscan Book of Saints*, by M. Habig; *The Credo of Pope Paul* VI: *Theological Commentary*, by C. Pozo, S.J.; and *The Principles of Catholic Moral Life*, edited by William E. May.

FRANKLIN PUBLISHING CO., INC., Box 765, Palisade NJ 07024. (201)567-6477. Editor: Irene E. Berck, Ph.D. Publishes hardcover originals. Pays 10% maximum royalty on published price, less discount. Simultaneous and photocopied submissions OK. SASE. Reports in 1 week on queries; 1 month on mss. Free book catalog.

Nonfiction: Biography, how-to, illustrated book, reference, self-help, technical, and textbooks (on science subjects for elementary, high, and college libraries). Query or submit outline/synopsis and sample chapters.

Recent Nonfiction Titles: *Below the Belt*, by John G. Deaton, MD (a book about the pelvic organs); *Scientific Instruments*, by Sam Epstein; (how-to build and use them); and *Computer Science and Technology*, by Tom Logsdon.

THE FREE PRESS, Division of the Macmillan Publishing Co., Inc., 866 3rd Ave., New York NY 10022. President: Edward W. Barry. Editor-in-Chief: Charles E. Smith. Royalty schedule varies. Send sample chapter, outline, and query letter before submitting mss. Reports in 3 weeks. SASE.

Nonfiction and Textbooks: Publishes college texts and adult educational nonfiction in the social sciences, business and humanities.

RICHARD GALLEN & CO., 8-10 W. 36th St., New York NY 10018. Imprints include Parallax, Confucian Press, James Bryans Books, Tor Books, Full Moon Books, Richard Gallen Romances. Vice President: Judith T. Sullivan. Editorial Director: Richard T. Gallen. "The nature of our business is primarily publishing packaging." Publishes hardcover and paperback originals (98%) and paperback reprints (2%). Averages 124 titles/year. Pays 6-12% royalty; offers average $5,000 advance. Simultaneous and photocopied submissions OK. SASE. Reports in 1 month.

Nonfiction: How-to, psychology, recreation and self-help. "We are interested in nonfiction only if we feel it is a very special idea and believe it will have mass market potential. We do very little nonfiction." Query first. All unsolicited mss are returned unopened.

Recent Nonfiction Titles: *Superlearning*, by Ostrander and Schroeder (how-to do stress free learning through relaxation).

Fiction: Historical, suspense, disaster, occult and science fiction. "We are looking for women's historicals, contemporary love stories, topical suspense and disaster novels. All must have definite mass market possibilities. Most, but not all our books are original paperbacks." Query first. All unsolicited mss are returned unopened.

Recent Fiction Titles: *The Velvet Promise*, by Jude Deveraux; *The Homesteaders*, by Lee Davis Willoughby; and *The Fallon Pride*, by Reagan O'Neal.

GAMBLER'S BOOK CLUB, GBC Press, Box 4115, Las Vegas NV 89106. (702)382-7555. Editorial Director: John Luckman. Publishes paperback originals (67%) and reprints (33%). Published 24 titles in 1979, 20 in 1980; plans 20 in 1981. Pays 10% royalty on sales income; advance averages $300. Photocopied submissions OK. Reports in 1 month. SASE. Book catalog for SASE.

Nonfiction: 20,000-word mss pertaining to gambling or to games on which people wager money. Submit complete ms. Recently published *Theory of Blackjack*, by Peter A. Griffin; *Class in Thoroughbred Racing*, by Chuck Badone; *7 Card Stud: The Waiting Game*, by George Percy; *Betting the Bases*, by Mike Lee (baseball betting); *Craps—A Smart Shooter's Guide*, by Thomas Midgley (shooting craps to win); and *The Tote Board is Alive and Well*, by Milt Gaines (gambling, pari-mutuel betting).

GUY GANNETT BOOKS, Subsidiary of Guy Gannett Publishing Co., 390 Congress St., Portland ME 04101. (207)775-5811. Editorial Director: Allan A. Swenson. Publishes hardcover originals and trade paperback originals and reprints. Averages 10 titles/year. Pays 6-14% royalty on retail price; offers average $1,500 advance. Simultaneous and photocopied submissions OK. SASE. Reports in 1 month on queries; 6 weeks on mss. Free book catalog.

Nonfiction: Biography, cookbook, how-to, humor, juvenile and self-help. Subjects include Americana, animals, cooking and foods, history, nature and travel. "We're looking for books of wide appeal based on Maine and New England themes and topics. We publish the 'Best of Maine' books—expanding to be the 'Best of New England.' Our audience is a broad base of readers interested in New England history, traditions, folklore, heritage and outdoors." Submit outline/synopsis and sample chapters.

Recent Nonfiction Titles: *Wilderness Journal*, by Dorothy Boone Kidney (outdoor); *Secrets of a Salt Marsh*, by John Snow (nature); *Over to Home & From Away*, by Jim Brunelle (humor); and *Housewarming*, by Bob Cummings (energy saving).

Fiction: Historical and mainstream. "We're looking at 1983-84 prospects."

GARDEN WAY PUBLISHING, Charlotte VT 05445. (802)425-2171. Editor: Roger Griffith. Publishes hardcover and paperback originals. Publishes 12 titles/year. Offers a flat fee arrangement varying with book's scope, or royalty, which usually pays author 6% of book's retail price. Advances are negotiable, but usually range from $1,500 to $2,000. "We stress continued promotion of titles and sales over many years." Emphasizes direct mail sales, plus sales to bookstores through salesmen. Photocopied submissions OK. Enclose return postage.

Nonfiction: Books on gardening, cooking, animal husbandry, homesteading and energy conservation. Emphasis should be on how-to. Length requirements are flexible. "The writer should remember the reader will buy his book to learn to do something, so that all information to accomplish this must be given. We are publishing specifically for the person who is concerned about natural resources and a deteriorating life style and wants to do something about it." Would like to see energy books with emphasis on what the individual can do. Query. Recently published *At Home in the Sun*, by Davis and Lindsey (solar homes).

GARLAND PUBLISHING, INC., 136 Madison Ave., New York NY 10016. (212)686-7492. Executive Editor: Richard Newman. Publishes hardcover originals. Averages 125 titles/year. Pays 10-15% royalty on wholesale price. "Depending on marketability, some copies may be royalty-exempt, or author may prepare camera-ready copy." Simultaneous and photocopied submissions OK. Reports in 2 weeks on queries; 1 month on mss. Free book catalog.

Nonfiction: Reference. Subjects include Americana, animals, art, business and economics, cooking and foods, health, history, hobbies, music, nature, philosophy, photography, politics, psychology, recreation, religion, sociology, sports and travel. "We're interested in reference books—bibliographies, sourcebooks, indexes, etc.—in all fields." Submit outline/synopsis and sample chapters.

Recent Nonfiction Titles: *A Directory of Religious Bodies in the US*, by Melton (directory); *Folk Song Index*, by Brunnings (index to 1,000 books); and *Afro-Americans in Sports Bibliography*, by Gilmore (comprehensive annotated bibliography).

GARLINGHOUSE COMPANY, 320 SW 33rd St., Box 299, Topeka KS 66601. (913)267-2490. President: Whitney Garlinghouse. Publishes trade paperback originals. Averages 2-5 titles/year. Pays 5-10% royalty on retail price; no advance. Simultaneous and photocopied submissions OK. SASE. Reports in 1 month.

Nonfiction: How-to. Subjects include home building and remodeling. "We want books of use to individuals and professionals involved in building or remodeling homes. Of particular interest are books dealing with underground homes, passive solar energy, or energy conservation; or instructive assistance for those building their own home. Our books are read by individuals interested in planning and building a new home. Also, some professionals in the home builders industry read them. Authors must be able to demonstrate technical competence in their subject area. No books that do not relate specifically to home building or remodeling." Submit outline/synopsis and sample chapters. "Please list credentials with submissions."

Recent Nonfiction Titles: *Multi-level, Hillside & Solar Home Plans* and *Single-level, & Underground Home Plans*, both by Garlinghouse (new home plans).

*GASLIGHT PUBLICATIONS, 112 E. 2nd St., Bloomington IN 47401. (812)332-5169. Publisher: Jack Tracy. Estab. 1979. Publishes hardcover originals (50%) and hardcover reprints (50%). Averages 6-8 titles/year. Pays 10% minimum royalty on retail price; no advance. "Individual subsidy publishing is available. We have yet to do any subsidy work, but we would make it available for worthwhile Sherlockian projects which do not fit the rather narrow confines of our Sherlock Holmes Monograph/Reference Series." Simultaneous and photocopied submissions OK. SASE. Reports in 1 month.

Nonfiction: "Studies in A. Conan Doyle, Sherlock Holmes and related Victoriana. Serious, well-researched, not necessarily for the specialist. 12,000 words minimum. State availability of illustrations." No ephemera, parodies, pastiches or "untold tales." Query or submit outline/synopsis, sample chapters or complete ms.

Recent Nonfiction Titles: *"You Know My Method": A Juxtaposition of Charles S. Peirce and Sherlock Holmes*, by T. Sebeok and J. Umiker-Sebeok (semiotics); *The Sherlock Holmes Book of Quotations*, by B. Beaman (quotes); and *Jack London and Conan Doyle: A Literary Kinship*, by Dale L. Walker (comparative literature).

*GENEALOGICAL PUBLISHING CO., INC., 111 Water St., Baltimore MD 21202. (301)837-8271. Editor-in-Chief: Michael H. Tepper, Ph.D. Publishes hardcover originals and reprints. Offers straight 10% royalty on retail price. Does about 10% subsidy publishing. Averages 90-100 titles/year. Will consider photocopied submissions. Prefers query first, but will look at outline and sample chapter or complete ms. Reports "immediately." Enclose SAE and return postage.

Reference, Textbooks and History: "Our requirements are unusual, so we usually treat each author and his subject in a way particularly appropriate to his special skills and subject matter. Guidelines are flexible and generous, though it is expected that an author will consult with us in depth. Most, though not all, of our original publications are offset from camera-ready typescript. Since most genealogical reference works are compilations of vital records and similar data, tabular formats are common. We hope to receive more ms material in the area of census indexes, specifically indexes to statewide censuses. We also anticipate mss documenting the Revolutionary War service of large numbers of early Americans. We would like to have an on-going Revolutionary War genealogy project." Family history compendia, basic methodology in genealogy, and advanced local history (for example, county histories, particularly those containing genealogy); heraldry: dictionaries and glossaries of the art and science, armorials of families entitled to bear coat armor, manuals and craftbooks describing heraldic painting, etc. Recently published *Index to the 1820 Census of Virginia* , by J. Felldin; *Heraldic Design*, by H. Child; and *Genealogies of Virginia Families*, 5 volumes.

THE K.S. GINIGER COMPANY, INC., 235 Park Ave., S., New York NY 10003. (212)533-5080. President: Kenneth Seeman Giniger. Book publisher and independent book producer/packager. Publishes hardcover, trade, and mass market paperback originals. Averages 10 titles/year. Pays royalty on wholesale or retail price. SASE. Reports in 2 weeks.

Nonfiction: Biography, cookbook, how-to, juvenile, reference and self-help. Subjects include Americana, art, cooking and foods, health, history, hobbies, religion, sports and travel. Query with SASE. All unsolicited mss are returned unread "if postage is enclosed."

Recent Nonfiction Titles: *Churchill and the Generals*, by Barrie Pitt (history); *The Complete Gymnastics Book*, by Frank Bare (sports); *The Duchess of Windsor*, by Diana Mosley (biography); and *European Detours*, by Nino Lo Bello (novel).

GINN AND CO., 191 Spring St., Lexington MA 02173. Publisher: Dr. James R. Squire. Royalty schedule: from 10% of net on a secondary book to 4% on elementary materials. Averages 300-400 titles/year. Sample chapters, complete or partially complete mss will be considered. Reports in 2 to 6 weeks. Enclose return postage.

Textbooks: Publishers of textbooks and instructional materials for elementary and secondary schools. Recent titles: *A History of the United States*, by Dan Boosten and Brooks Kelly (American history); and *Ginn Elementary Science*, by J. Myron Atkins (elementary school science).

GLOBE MINI MAGS, 220, E. 42nd St., Suite 2800, New York NY 10017. (212)953-9630. Associate Editor: Toby Hempel. Averages 120 titles/year. Buys some mss outright; "negotiated individually." No advance. SASE. Reports in 1 month.

Nonfiction: "We publish 64-page mini mag handbooks sold at variety stores, supermarkets, and gift shops." Subjects include cooking and foods, health and diets and exercises.

Recent Nonfiction Title: *Aerobic Dancing* (exercise); and *Herbal Diets*, by Wade (weight loss).

THE GLOBE PEQUOT PRESS, INC., Old Chester Rd., Box Q, Chester CT 06412. (203)526-9572. Publications Director: Linda Kennedy. Publishes hardcover and paperback originals (95%) and paperback reprints (5%). Published 14 titles in 1978; 20 in 1979; 15 in 1980. Offers 7½-10% royalty on retail price; advance offered occasionally "for specific expenses only." Simultaneous and photocopied submissions OK. SASE. Reports in 2 weeks. Book catalog for SASE.

Nonfiction: Americana; recreation (outdoor books); and travel (guide books). Some light history and how-to books. "Guide books are especially promising today; people are finding with a guide book they can plan travel activities in advance and consequently save precious gasoline. All books should have a New England focus." No doctoral theses, genealogies or textbooks. Submit outline/synopsis and sample chapters.

Recent Nonfiction Titles: *The New England Indians*, by C. Keith Wilbur (New England crafts and history); *Short Bike Rides in Rhode Island*, by Howard Stone (outdoors recreation); *Guide to the Recommended Country Inns of New England*, by S. Chapin and E. Squier (New England guide/travel book); and *Historic Walk In and Around Old Boston*, by John Harris.

GOLDEN BOOKS, Western Publishing Co., Inc., 850 3rd Ave., New York NY 10022. Publisher: Walter Retan. Editorial Director, Juvenile Books: Janet B. Campbell.

Nonfiction: Adult nonfiction, especially family-oriented. Children's Books, including picture-books, concept books, novelty books, information books. Query before submitting ms.
Fiction: Children's picturebooks and young fiction. Query before submitting ms.

GOLDEN WEST BOOKS, Box 8136, San Marino CA 91108. (213)283-3446. Editor-in-Chief: Donald Duke. Managing Editor: Jeff Dunning. Publishes hardcover and paperback originals. Published 7 titles in 1979, 5 in 1980, 6 in 1981. Pays 10% royalty contract; no advance. Simultaneous and photocopied submissions OK. Reports in 2-4 weeks. SASE. Free book catalog.
Nonfiction: Publishes selected western Americana and transportation Americana. Query or submit complete ms. "Illustrations and photographs will be examined if we like ms."
Recent Nonfiction Title: *The Super Chief*, by Stan Repp.

GOODYEAR PUBLISHING CO., INC., 1640 5th St., Santa Monica CA 90401. (213)393-6731. Editor-in-Chief: John F. Pritchard. Publishes hardcover and paperback originals. Averages 40 titles/year. Pays varying royalty; advance, "available on certain projects, varies." Simultaneous and photocopied submissions OK. SASE. Reports in 2 months. Free book catalog.
Nonfiction: Reference (on education; for elementary and secondary teachers); and textbook. "We're looking for college textbooks especially in business, math and science, economics, sociology, political science, education, physical education and health recreation. Also need reference books for elementary and secondary teachers." Query.
Recent Nonfiction Titles: *Organizational Behavior and Performance*, 2nd ed., by Szilagyi and Wallace (college text); *Financial Management*, 2nd ed., by Solomon and Pringle (college text); *Calculus and Analytic Geometry*, by Shenk (college text); and *Biology: The World of Life*, 2nd ed., by Wallace (college text).
Tips: "Look at the leading sellers and attempt an evolutionary improvement."

GORDON PRESS PUBLISHERS, Box 459, Bowling Green Station, New York NY 10004. Editor: R. Gordon. Publishes hardcover originals (45%); and reprints (55%). Averages 50 titles/year. Pays 5% royalty on retail price. Photocopied submissions OK. SASE. Reports on queries in 2 weeks; mss in 10 weeks. Book catalog for $3 in stamps.
Imprints: *Krishna Press (nonfiction), R. Gordon, editor.*
Nonfiction: Biography, reference, self-help and technical. Subjects include Americana, art, business and economics, cooking and foods, health, history, hobbies, music, nature, philosophy, photography, politics, psychology, recreation, religion, sociology, travel, and parapsychology and occult. "We mainly need scholarly dissertations and monographs. We reject many manuscripts because of inadequate or undocumented research. Some writers are lazy about this." Query.
Recent Nonfiction Titles: *The Crucifixion in American Painting*, by Robert Henkes (art); *W.W. Griffith: Titan of Film Art*, by Leona Phillips (films); *The Hero & the Class Struggle in the Contemporary Spanish Novel*, by Scott Jonson (criticism); and *Puerto Rican Historiography*, by Allen Woll (Puerto Rican history).

GRAPHIC ARTS CENTER PUBLISHING CO., 3019 NW Yeon Ave., Box 10306. Portland OR 97210. (503)224-7777. General Manager: Betty A. Sechser. Assistant Publisher and Editor: Douglas Pfeiffer. Publishes hardcover originals. Averages 10-15 titles/year. Pays outright purchase averaging $3,000 (less for paperbacks); no advance. Simultaneous and photocopied submissions OK. Reports in 3 weeks. SASE. Free book catalog.
Nonfiction: "All titles are pictorials with text. Text usually runs separately from the pictorial treatment. State and regional book series are published under the imprint name (D.B.A.) Belding. Several theme series of pictorial books have also been begun and length and style are more flexible." Query.

GRAY'S PUBLISHING LTD., Box 2160, Sidney, BC, Canada V8L 3S6. (604)656-4454. Editor: Maralyn Horsdal. Publishes hardcover and paperback originals and reprints. Offers standard royalty contract on retail price. Averages 5-8 titles/year. Free book catalog. Query with outline. Reports in 6-10 weeks. SAE and International Reply Coupons.
Nonfiction: Wants "nonfiction, Canadiana," especially Pacific Northwest. Biography, natural history, history, nautical. Length: 60,000-120,000 words.
Recent Nonfiction Titles: *Evergreen Islands*, by Doris Andersen (history); *Herstory: The Canadian Women's Calendar*, by the Saskatoon Women's Calendar Collective (history/biography); and *Yukon Places & Names*, by R.C. Coutts (history/biography).

GREAT OUTDOORS PUBLISHING CO., 4747 28th St. N., St. Petersburg FL 33714. (813)522-3453. Editor-in-Chief: Charles Allyn. Publishes paperback originals. Offers royalty of 5% on retail price. No advance. Published 8 titles last year. Will send free catalog to writer on request. Will consider photocopied submissions and simultaneous submissions. Query for nonfiction. Reports in 1 month. Enclose return postage.

Nonfiction: Books of regional interest. Fishing, gardening, shelling in Florida. Also publishes some cookbooks of Southern emphasis. Should be straightforward, how-to style with consideration for the hobbyist or sportsman who needs the basic facts without flowery phrasing. "No other publisher is geared to the tourist market in Florida. Our books are low-cost and especially suited to their market." Would like to see more shell books with illustrations. No personal narratives. Department editors: Joyce Allyn, cooking, nature, recreation; Charles Allyn, self-help and how-to. Length: cooking, 9,000-17,000 words; nature, 52,000-90,000 words; self-help, how-to, sports, hobbies, recreation and pets, 9,000-17,000 words.

WARREN H. GREEN, INC., 8356 Olive Blvd., St. Louis MO 63132. Editor: Warren H. Green. Publishes hardcover originals. Offers "10-20% sliding scale of royalties based on quantity distributed. All books are short run, highly specialized, with no advance." About 5% of books are subsidy published. Averages 90 titles/year. "37% of total marketing is overseas." Will send a catalog to a writer on request. Will consider photocopied submissions. Submit outline and sample chapters. "Publisher requires 300- to 500-word statement of scope, plan, and purpose of book, together with curriculum vitae of author." Reports in 60-90 days.

Medical and Scientific: "Specialty monographs for practicing physicians and medical researchers. Books of 160 pages upward. Illustrated as required by subject. Medical books are non-textbook type, usually specialties within specialties, and no general books for a given specialty. For example, separate books on each facet of radiology, and not one complete book on radiology. Authors must be authorities in their chosen fields and accepted as such by their peers. Books should be designed for all doctors in English-speaking world engaged in full or part-time activity discussed in book. We would like to increase publications in the fields of radiology, anesthesiology, pathology, psychiatry, surgery and orthopedic surgery, obstetrics and gynecology, and speech and hearing. **Education:** "Reference books for elementary and secondary school teachers. Authors must be authorities in their fields. No textbooks."

Recent Nonfiction Titles: *Insect Allergy*, by Frazier; *Cerebral Circulation and Stroke*, by McHenry; and *Psychodynamics of the Emotionally Uncomfortable*, by Shave.

GREEN TIGER PRESS, 7458 La Jolla Blvd., La Jolla CA 92037. (714)238-1001. Editor: Harold Darling. Publishes hardcover and trade paperback originals and reprints. Averages 18 titles/year. Pays 5-15% royalty on retail price; offers average $350 advance. Simultaneous and photocopied submissions OK. SASE. Reports in 2 weeks on queries; 2 months on mss. Book catalog $3.95.

Nonfiction: Coffee table book, illustrated book and juvenile. Subjects include religion. Query.

Recent Nonfiction Titles: *Song of Songs* (religion); *Humpty Dumpty* (literary-historical); and *Circle of Bears* (memoir).

Fiction: Experimental and fantasy. "We need mss dealing with the imaginative, the visual and the fantastic." Submit complete ms.

Recent Fiction Titles: *The Catalog, One Day Scene through a Leaf*, and *Little Mouse Trapped in a Book*.

THE STEPHEN GREENE PRESS, Box 1000, Brattleboro VT 05301. (802)257-7757. Editorial Director: Mary E. Metcalf. Publishes hardcover and paperback originals (99%); hardcover and paperback reprints (1%). Averages 20 titles/year. Royalty "variable; advances are small." Send contact sheet or prints to illustrate ms. Photocopied submissions OK. Reports in 6 weeks. SASE. Book catalog for SASE.

Nonfiction: Americana; biography; cookbooks, cooking and foods; history; how-to (self-reliance); nature and environment; recreation; self-help; sports (outdoor and horse); popular technology; and regional (New England). "We see our audience as mainly college-educated men and women, 30 and over, living in the country, suburbs or small towns. They are regular book buyers and readers. They probably have pronounced interests, hobby or professional, in subjects that our books treat. Authors can assess their needs by looking critically at what we have published."

Recent Nonfiction Titles: *The Small Computer in Small Business*, by Smith; *Successful Cold Climate Gardening*, by Hill; and *Central Heating With Coal & Wood*, by Larry Gay (self sufficiency).

GREENLEAF CLASSICS, INC., Box 20194, San Diego CA 92120. Editorial Director: Douglas Saito. Publishes paperback originals. Specializes in adult erotic fiction. Publishes 360 titles/year. Pays by outright purchase about 2½ months after acceptance. Photocopied submissions OK. Reports in 2-4 weeks. "NO mss will be returned unless accompanied by return postage." Writer's guidelines for SASE.

Fiction: Erotic novels. "All stories must have a sexual theme. They must be contemporary novels dealing with the serious problems of everyday people. All plots are structured so that characters must get involved in erotic situations. Write from the female viewpoint. *Request our guidelines before beginning any project for us.*" Preferred length: 35,000 words. Complete ms preferred.

GREGG DIVISION, McGraw-Hill Book Co., 1221 Avenue of the Americas, New York NY 10020. Vice President and General Manager: Charles B. Harrington. Publishes hardcover and paperback originals. "Contracts negotiable; no advances." Query. "We accept very few unsolicited mss." Reports in 1-2 months. Enclose return postage with query.
Textbooks: "Textbooks and related instructional materials for the career education market." Publishes books on typewriting, office education, shorthand, accounting and data processing, distribution and marketing, agriculture, trade and industrial education, health and consumer education and adult/continuing education.
Recent Nonfiction Titles: *Fashion Merchandising*, by Troxell and Stone; *Getting Involved With Business*, by Poe, Hicks, and Church; and *Automotive Engines*, by Crouse and Anglin.

GREGG PRESS, 70 Lincoln St., Boston MA 02111. (617)423-3990. Imprints include G.K. Hall Co. Publishes hardcover reprints. Publishes approx. 30 titles/year. Pays standard royalty based on the book and advance. Simultanous submissions OK. SASE. Reports in 1 month. Free book catalog.
Fiction: Children's, mystery, science fiction and western. Hardcover reprints mainly for libraries. "We usually get a list from consultants. Then we acquire rights to books no longer in print. We don't often publish books submitted to us." Submit complete book.
Recent Fiction Titles: *The Floating Admiral*, (mystery); *The Lone Ranger*, by F. Striker (children's); and *Double Star*, by R. Heinlein (science fiction).

GROSSETT AND DUNLAP, INC., (Adult Trade Division), 51 Madison Ave., New York NY 10010. (212)689-9200. Editor-in-Chief: Robert Markel. Publishes hardcover and paperback originals and reprints. Royalty on retail price and advance terms generally vary. Published "close to 100 adult trade" titles last year. Will send a catalog to a writer on request (with SASE). Send query letter, outline, or sample chapter only; do not send complete ms. "We do not accept unsolicited manuscripts." Reports in 3-5 weeks. SASE.
General Nonfiction: Sports, health, cooking, general reference. Favors writers with strong experience and good credits.
Recent Nonfiction Titles: *The Pritikin Program*, by N. Pritikin (health and cookbook); *Vitamins and You*, by Robert Benowicz (health); and *Eat Well, Get Well, Stay Well*, by Carlton Fredericks (health).
Juveniles and Teen: Editor-in-Chief, Children's Picture Books: Doris Duenewald.

GROUPWORK TODAY, INC., Box 258, South Plainfield NJ 07080. Editor-in-Chief: Harry E. Moore Jr. Associate Editor: Joseph B. Hoffmier. Publishes hardcover and paperback originals. Averages 4-6 titles/year. Offers $100 advance against royalties on receipt of contract and completion of ms ready for publication; 10% of gross receipts from sale of book. Books are marketed by direct mail to Groupwork Agency executives and professionals (YMCA, YWCA, Scouts, Salvation Army, colleges, directors of organized camps, and libraries.) Will send catalog to a writer for SASE with 28¢ in stamps. "Also will answer specific questions from an author considering us as a publisher." Will not consider simultaneous submissions. Submit outline and sample chapters for nonfiction. Reports in 6-8 weeks. Enclose return postage.
Nonfiction: "We are publishers of books and materials for professionals and volunteers who work with people in groups. Titles are also used by colleges for texts and resources. Some of our materials are also suited to the needs of professionals who work with individuals. Groupwork agency management, finance, program development and personnel development are among the subjects of interest to us. Writers must be thoroughly familiar with 'people work' and have fresh insights to offer. New writers are most welcome here. Lengths are open but usually run 40,000-60,000 words." Readers are mainly social agency administrators and professional staff members. Groupwork materials are also read by volunteers serving in the social agencies. Mss are judged by experienced professionals in social agencies. The company is advised on policy direction by a council of advisors from national agencies and colleges across the nation. "We also are publishing our 'Seminar' series to deal with the most important problems with which social work agencies must deal today."
Recent Nonfiction Titles: *Helping Women: Counseling Girls and Women in a Decade of Change*, by Gloria Sklansky and Linda Algazi; and Guide to Creative Giving, by Bernard P. Taylor.
Tips: "If a writer will send material only on which he or she has done as much work as possible to make a good outline, a sample chapter or two to indicate writing ability, and the idea is a

contribution to our field, we will spend all kinds of time guiding the author to completion of the work."

GROVE PRESS, 196 W. Houston St., New York NY 10014. Editoral Director: Barney Rosset. Senior Editor: Kent Carroll. Editors: Claudia Menza and Lisa Krug. Imprints include Evergreen and Black Cat books. Publishes hardcover and paperback originals (50%) and paperback reprints (50%). Published 40 titles in 1978; 50 in 1979; 40 in 1980. Simultaneous and photocopied submissions OK. SASE. "We accept no phone calls concerning mss, requests for catalogs and other information." Free book catalog.
Nonfiction: Biography; business/economics; health, history, how-to; poetry; philosophy; politics; psychology; self-help; and sports.
Recent Nonfiction Titles: *The Cancer Syndrome*, by Ralph Moss (medicine, current affairs, investigative report on the cancer industry); *Nutrition and Vitamin Therapy*, by Michael Lesser, MD (health, nutrition); and *The Story of Motown*, by Peter Benjamin.

GRYPHON HOUSE, INC., 3706 Otis St., Box 217, Mt. Rainier MD 20822. (301)779-6200. President Editor: Larry Rood. Publishes trade paperback originals. Averages 3 titles/year. Pays 10-12½% royalty on retail price; offers average $300 advance. Photocopied submissions OK. SASE. Reports in 2 weeks. Book catalog for 9x12 SAE and 2 first class stamps.
Nonfiction: How-to and creative educational activities for parents and teachers to do with preschool children, ages 1-5. "We are specialty publishers and do not consider anything at present out of the above category. Our audience includes parents and teachers in preschools, nursery schools, day care centers and kindergartens." Query or submit outline/synopsis and sample chapters.
Recent Nonfiction Titles: *A Parent's Guide to Day Care; Bubbles, Rainbows and Worms: Science Experiments for Pre-School Children*, by Brown; and *Easy Woodstuff for Kids*, by Thompson.

GUIDANCE CENTRE, Faculty of Education, University of Toronto, 1000 Yonge St., Toronto, Ontario, Canada M4W 2K8. (416)978-3210. Editorial Director: S.J. Totton. Senior Editor: Hazel Ross. Publishes hardcover and paperback originals. Published 20 titles in 1978. Pays in royalties. Reports in 1 month. Submissions returned "only if Canadian postage is sent." Free book catalog.
Nonfiction: "The Guidance Centre is interested in publications related to career planning and guidance and in measurement and evaluation. Also general education. No manuscripts which have confined their references and illustrations to United States material." Submit complete ms. Consult Chicago *Manual of Style*.
Recent Nonfiction Titles: *Growing Old*, by Peter J. Naus; and *Get the Job*, by Gerald Cosgrave.

*GULF PUBLISHING CO., Box 2608, Houston TX 77001. (713)529-4301. Vice President: C.A. Umbach Jr. Editor-in-Chief: B.J. Lowe. Publishes hardcover and large format paperback originals. Pays 10% royalty on net income; advance averages $300-2,000. Averages 40-50 titles/year. Subsidy publishes 1-2 titles a year. Simultaneous and photocopied submissions OK. Reports in 1-2 months. SASE. Free book catalog.
Nonfiction: Business, reference, regional trade, regional gardening, scientific and self-help. "We are the world's largest specialized publisher to the energy industries."
Recent Nonfiction Titles: Backroads of Texas, by Ed Syers; and *Creative Worklife*, by Don Scobel (management).

H.P. BOOKS, Box 5367, Tucson AZ 85703. Senior Editor: Jonathan Latimer. Publishes hardcover and paperback originals. Specializes in how-to books in several fields, all photo-illustrated. Pays royalty on wholesale price; advance negotiable. Averages 35-40 titles/year. Simultaneous and photocopied submissions OK. Reports in 2-4 weeks. SASE. Free book catalog.
Nonfiction: Cookbooks, cooking and foods; hobbies; how-to; leisure activities; photography; automotive; recreation; self-help; art techniques; and technical books. All books are 160 pages minimum; "word count varies with the format." Query and state number and type of illustrations available. Recently published *Chocolate Cookery*, by Mabel Hoffman; *Nikon Cameras*, by Carl Shipman; *Roses*, by Ray/MacCaskey (gardening); and *How to Rebuild Your Small-Block Ford*, by Tom Monroe.

HAMMOND, INC., 515 Valley St., Maplewood NJ 07040. (201)763-6000. General Trade Editor: Warren Cox. Hardcover and paperback originals. "Books are negotiated from flat fee for outright purchase to advances against standard royalties, depending on subject." Published 50 titles in 1979. Submit outline/synopsis and sample chapters. State availability of photos/illustrations. Simultanous submissions OK. Reports in 2-4 weeks. SASE. Book catalog for SASE.
Nonfiction: Publishes Americana, art, business, cookbooks, cooking and foods, history, hobbies, how-to, humor, nature, photography, recreation, reference, sports and travel books.

Recent Titles: *Western Memorabilia*, by Wm. C. Ketchum, Jr.; *Volcanoes*, by Katia and Maurice Krafft; *The Big Book of Small Needlework Gifts*, by Annette Feldman; *The All-American Chinese Cookbook*, by L.C. Mchale and J. Goldberg; *The Hammond Almanac; Home Inspection Workbook*, by Steve Hunter; and *European Detours*, by Nino LoBello.

HANCOCK HOUSE PUBLISHERS LTD., 10 Orwell St., North Vancouver, British Columbia, Canada V7J 3K1. Editor-in-Chief: David Hancock. Managing Editor: Michael Campbell. Hardcover and paperback originals (85%) and reprints (15%). Pays 10% royalty on list price; $500 minimum advance. Publishes 20 titles/year. State availability of photos and/or illustrations to accompany ms. Reports in 1-2 months. SAE and International Reply Coupons. Free book catalog.
Nonfiction: Publishes (in order of preference): craft, anthropology, sport, nature, history, biography, reference, Americana (Canadian), cookbooks, cooking and foods, hobbies, how-to, juveniles, photography, recreation, self-help, and travel books. Query.
Recent Nonfiction Titles: *Guide to Eastern Wild Flowers*, by Barrie Kavasch; *Guide to Orchids of North America*, by Dr. Petrie; and *Lady Rancher*, by Gertrude Minor Rogers.

HARCOURT BRACE JOVANOVICH, 757 3rd Ave., New York NY 10017. Director of Trade Books Department: Peter Jovanovich. Publishes hardcover and paperback originals and reprints. SASE.
Adult Trade Hardcovers: "We regret that all unsolicited mss for hardcover trade publication must be returned unread. Only mss submitted by agents or recommended to us by advisors or actively solicited by us will be considered."
Adult Trade Paperbacks: Editor-in-Chief: John Ferrone. Publishes original and reprint trade paperbacks under the Harvest imprint.

HARCOURT BRACE JOVANOVICH, INC., Children's Books, 757 3rd Ave., New York NY 10017. (212)888-3947. Editorial Director: Anna Bier. Associate Editor: Nancy Rockwell. Assistant Editor: Pamela Hastings. Publishes hardcover and paperback originals. Published 30 titles in 1978; 40 in 1979; 30 in 1980. Pays 8-10% royalty; offers $1,000 minimum advance. Simultaneous (if indicated) and photocopied submissions OK. SASE. Reports in 2 months. Free catalog.
Nonfiction: "Easy-reading" nonfiction for juveniles. Length: 2,500-60,000 words. "Before submitting your manuscript, write to the Children's Book Editor and describe it briefly. Give its approximate word length and the age group for which it is planned."
Recent Nonfiction Titles: *Geothermal Energy: A Hot Prospect*, by Augusta Goldin; *Safeguarding the Land: Women at Work in Parks, Forests, and Rangelands*, by Gloria Skurzynski; and *The Young Tycoons*, by Gloria D. Miklowitz and Madeleine Yates.
Fiction: Picture-book texts and middle-grade and junior-high fiction. Length: 15,000-60,000 words. Query.
Recent Fiction Titles: *The Marzipan Moon*, by Nancy Willard; *The Comic Adventures of Old Mother Hubbard and Her Dog*, illustrated by Tomie dePaola; *The Man Who Kept House*, retold by Kathleen and Michael Hague; and *Luke and Angela*, by Christine Nostlinger.

HARLEQUIN BOOKS, Harlequin Publishing Corporation, 6525 Sunset Blvd., Hollywood CA 90028. (213)464-6444. Subsidiary of Harlequin Enterprises Ltd., Toronto, Ontario, Canada. Editorial Director: Andrew Ettinger. Senior Editor: Evelyn Grippo. Publishes mass market paperback originals (100%). Averages 35 titles/year. Pays 6-10% royalty on retail price; offers $3,000-10,000 advance, "depending on category, length, etc." Simultaneous and photocopied submissions OK. Reports in 3 weeks "average" on queries; 2 months "average" on mss. Submissions Requirements Memos and Editorial Guidelines available.
Imprints: *Gold Eagle* (fiction).
Fiction: "Adventure (action-oriented); gothic; historical (romantic or saga); romance; western; and regency romance. "We're looking for books that fit into solid category areas, and/or series." Query (first); submit outline/synopsis and sample chapters (after query). All unsolicited mss are returned unopened.
Tips: "Study the bestselling original novels within popular categories, particularly those by new and unknown authors. For specifics regarding the various categories originating from 'Harlequin West,' such as word length, general direction, etc., please write for our Authors' Guidelines, specifying the category(s) wanted and including an SASE. If submitting material, include outline or synopsis and first two or three consecutive chapters."

HARLEQUIN BOOKS, LTD., 225 Duncan Mill Rd., Don Mills, Ontario, Canada M3B 3K9. (416)445-5860. Editorial Manager: George Glay. Imprints include Harlequin Romances, Harlequin Presents and Raven House Mysteries. Publishes paperback originals. Published 191 titles in 1978, 240 in 1979, 288 in 1980. Pays royalty on retail price; offers advance. Photocopied submis-

sions OK. SAE and International Reply Coupons. Reports in 3 months.
Fiction: "Harlequin Romances and Harlequin Presents should be sent to Alice Johnson, senior editor." Submit outline/synopsis and sample chapters. Also interested in mysteries of approximately 60,000 words. Submit outline/synopsis and sample chapters of mysteries to Wallace Exman, senior editor.
Tips: "This is a tough market. The odds against you are high but the rewards are great if you hit."

HARMONY BOOKS, 1 Park Ave., New York NY 10016. (212)532-9200. Division of Crown Publishers. Publisher: Bruce Harris. Senior Editor: Manuela Soares. Publishes hardcover and paperback originals (95%) and reprints (5%). Publishes 40 titles/year. Royalties vary with project; advance varies. Simultaneous and photocopied submissions OK. SASE. Reports in 8 weeks. Free book catalog.
Nonfiction: Art, cookbooks, cooking and foods, music and photography. Need popular topics for adults. Submit outline/synopsis and sample chapters. Unsolicited mss will not be accepted.
Recent Nonfiction Titles: *Flowers*, by I. Penn (photography); *The Dance Catalogue*, by N. Reynolds (encyclopedia of dance); and *Working Outside*, by P. Hardigree (pictures and text); *In Performance*, by Nancy Evans and Susan Reimer-Torn; *Blake's Dante*, by Milton Klunsky (Wm. Blake); and *The Complete Guide to Home Video*, by Leonard Malten and Alan Greenfield.
Fiction: Mainstream. Needs contemporary fiction. No mystery, romance or science fiction. Unsolicited mss will not be accepted.
Recent Fiction Titles: *Charting by the Stars*, by L. Abrams (growing up in the 50s); and *The Hitchhiker's Guide to the Galaxy*, by Douglas Adams.

HARPER & ROW PUBLISHERS, INC., 10 E. 53rd St., New York NY 10022. (212)593-7000. Executive Editors: Aaron Asher, M.S. Wyeth and Larry Ashmead. Imprints include T.Y. Crowell; J.B. Lippincott; Barnes & Noble; and Harper & Row—San Francisco (religious books only: Perennial; Colophon; and Torchbooks). Publishes hardcover and paperback originals, and paperback reprints. Publishes 300 titles/year. Pays 7½%-15% royalty; "advance ranges from $3,000 to five and sometimes six figures. Query with letter "describing the ms, outlining or summarizing the content, and asking whether we would be interested." SASE. Reports on queries in 6 weeks.
Nonfiction: Americana, animals, art, biography, business/economics, cookbooks, health, history, how-to, humor, music, nature, philosophy, photography, poetry, politics, psychology, reference, religion, science, self-help, sociology, sports and travel. "No technical books."
Recent Nonfiction Titles: *William E. Donoghue's Complete Money Market Guide*, by William E. Donoghue (economics); *Cosima Wagner*, by George Marek (biography); *Off the Record: The Private Papers of Harry S. Truman*, by Robert H. Ferrell (political writings); and *An Imagined World*, by Jane Goodfield (science).
Fiction: Adventure, fantasy, gothic, historical, mainstream, mystery, romance, science fiction, suspense, western and literary. "We look for a strong story line and exceptional literary talent. No self-indulgent, autobiographical fiction."
Recent Fiction Titles: *The Chaneysville Incident*, by David Bradley; *Free Fall in Crimson*, by John D. MacDonald; *Balancing Acts*, by Lynne Sharon Schwartz; *Clear Light of Day*, by Anita Desai; and *Close Relations*, by Susan Isaacs.

HARPER JUNIOR BOOKS, 10 E. 53rd St., New York NY 10022. (212)593-7000. Vice President/ Associate Publisher/Editorial Director: Charlotte Zolotow. Pays varied royalty depending on whether it is a picture book, story book or novel. Offers variable advance, depending on each individual book. Simultaneous submissions OK. SASE. Reports in 3 months. Free book catalog.
Nonfiction: Anything well done for children. "We have no specific needs but look for anything original and well done." Prefers whole ms but will consider outline/synopsis and sample chapters. "We want unsolicited mss."
Recent Nonfiction Titles: *All Times, All People*, by Milton Meltzer; and *Born in Fire*, by John Rublowsky.
Fiction: Adventure, experimental, fantasy, gothic, historical, humor, mystery, romance, science fiction, suspense and western. "All sorts—picture books through young adult novels. It is quality writing—humor, characterization, atmosphere and fine prose we look for. Submit outline/synopsis and sample chapters; we prefer complete books. We want unsolicited mss."
Recent Fiction Titles: *Arthur for the Very First Time*, by Patricia MacLachlan; *Two Blocks Down*, by Jina Delton; and *Sunday Morning We Went to the Zoo*, by Deborah Ray (picture book).
Tips: "Harper Junior Books range from zany, wonderful picture books, to good stories for the 8-12 year olds to fine young adult novels. The common factor is good writing, originality and a fine quality. Write on something you care about deeply and submit it to us."

HART PUBLISHING CO., INC., 12 E. 12th St., New York NY 10003. (212)260-2430. Book packagers.. Hardcover and paperback originals. Pays on royalty on list price for paperbacks and hardcovers. Averages 30 titles/year. Reports in 2-3 weeks. SASE.
Nonfiction: Publishes only nonfiction books on education, hobbies, how-to, psychology, recreation, reference, self-help and sociology. Query, submit outline and sample chapter or submit complete ms.
Recent Nonfiction Title: *Mammoth Book of Fun & Games.*
Tips: "We need crossword puzzles with reproducible art, quizzes, puzzles and original word games. We pay anywhere from $15-25 per piece, depending on length and merit. Payment is made immediately upon acceptance. All material must be accompanied by SASE. Replies will be made within 2 weeks."

HARVARD UNIVERSITY PRESS, 79 Garden St., Cambridge MA 02138. (617)495-2600. Director: Arthur J. Rosenthal. Editor-in-Chief: Maud Wilcox. Publishes hardcover and paperback originals and reprints. Publishes 120 titles/year. Free book catalog.
Nonfiction: "We publish only scholarly nonfiction." No fiction.

HARVEY HOUSE PUBLISHERS, 20 Waterside Plaza, New York NY 10010. Publisher: L.F. Reeves. Publishes hardcover originals. Published 11 titles in 1979, 22 in 1980; plans 25 in 1981. Pays 5% minimum royalty based on wholesale or retail price; advance "depends on the manuscript." Simultaneous (if so informed) and photocopied submissions OK. Reports in 3 weeks. "Manuscripts and queries without SASE will be destroyed."
Nonfiction: Juvenile leisure-time activity books. "We have successful books on skateboards, minicycles, hang gliding, etc. Our biography series 'Star People' covers athletes; we have books on Dorothy Hamill, Tracy Austin, Janet Guthrie, Reggie Jackson and people in the news. Also occasional science books." No religious, self-help, strictly adult textbooks or travel books. Query.
Recent Nonfiction Title: *Kitty O'Neil*, by Ireland (biography).
Fiction: "We publish only a couple of novels a year. Recently, we have opted toward realistic fiction about contemporary problems, e.g., foster children, American Indians, etc." No science fiction, romances, fantasy, talking animal stories or rehashed fairy tales. Query.
Recent Fiction Title: *Hot Wire*, by William Butterworth (teenage employment problems).
Tips: "The children's book market (school libraries, public libraries) is an endangered species."

HASTINGS HOUSE PUBLISHERS, INC., 10 E. 40th St., New York NY 10016. (212)689-5400. Editor: Walter Frese. Hardcover and paperback originals (80%) and reprints (20%). 10% minimum royalty. Reports in 1-2 weeks. SASE. Free book catalog.
Nonfiction: Publishes Americana, biography; cookbooks, cooking and foods; history, humor, juveniles, photography, recreation, sports and travel. Query or submit outline/synopsis and sample chapters. Recently published *Food Processor Magic*, by Hemingway/DeLima (cooking); *Inside ABC-American Broadcasting Company's Rise to Power* by Sterling/Quinlan; *Martha's Vineyard in Color* by Lazarus/Vuillevmier (travel).

*HAVEN PUBLICATIONS, Box 2046, New York NY 10001. (212)886-6753. Editor: Harvey Sachs. Publishes hardcover and trade paperback originals. Averages 10-15 titles/year. Subsidy publishes 5% of books (subsidized by federal funds), based on content: "logic books only and this is rare." Pays 10-15% royalty on both wholesale and retail price; no advance. Photocopied submissions OK. SASE. Reports in 2 weeks on queries; 1 month on mss.
Nonfiction: Biography, reference, technical, textbook and original monographs. Subjects include art, business and economics, health, history, philosophy, psychology and religion. "We're looking for nonfiction books on philosophy and literature, philosophy and art, drama and sculpture. Submit outline/synopsis and sample chapters.
Recent Nonfiction Titles: *Evolving Theories*, by R. Gumb (logic); *Science and Psychotherapy*, by Stern (science); and *Pathology and Consciousness*, by Myers (psychology).
Fiction: Experimental, fantasy and mainstream. Query.

*HAWKES PUBLISHING, INC., 3775 S. 5th W., Salt Lake City UT 84115. (801)262-5555. President: John Hawkes. Publishes hardcover and trade paperback originals. Averages 24 + titles/year. Subsidy publishes 25% of books/year based on "how promising they are." Pays 10% maximum royalty on retail price; no advance. Photocopied submissions OK. SASE. Reports in 1 month on queries; 3 months on mss. Free book catalog.
Nonfiction: Cookbook, how-to and self-help. Subjects include cooking and foods, health, history, hobbies and psychology. Query or submit outline/synopsis and sample chapters.

HAYDEN BOOK CO., INC., 50 Essex St., Rochelle Park NY 07662. (201)843-0550. Editorial Director: Michael Violano. Publishes hardcover and paperback originals. Publishes 60 titles/year.

Pays 12% royalty; offers "minimal" advance. Simultaneous (if so identified) and photocopied submissions OK. Reports in 6 weeks. SASE. Free book catalog.
Technical: Publishes technician-level and engineering texts and references in many subject areas (emphasis on electronics and computer science); text and references for hotel, restaurant and institution management and other personnel (emphasis on management, food service); texts and references for senior high schools, technical institutes and community colleges in English (literature and composition), computer sciences, mathematics and other subject areas.

HEALTH PROFESSION PUBLISHING, McGraw-Hill Book Co., 1221 Avenue of the Americas, New York NY 10020. Publisher: J. Dereck Jeffers. Publishes 60 titles/year. Pays on royalty basis. SASE.
Textbooks: Publishes textbooks, major reference books and continuing education materials in the fields of medicine, dentistry, nursing and allied health.

D.C. HEATH & CO., 125 Spring St., Lexington MA 02173. (617)862-6650. College Division Editor-in-Chief: Robert Runck. School Division Editor-in-Chief: Robert Marshall. Lexington Books and Collamore Press: Michael McCarroll. Publishes hardcover and paperback textbooks and professional reference books. Published 189 titles in 1979, 183 in 1980. Offers standard royalty rates. Query. "Final revised mss accepted are published within 1 year." SASE.
Textbooks: "Texts at the college level in sociology, psychology, history, political science, chemistry, math, biology, physics, economics, education, modern languages and English. Also publishes professional reference books: "Advanced-level research studies in the social sciences, library science, and in technical fields (Lexington Books) and medical books (Collamore Press)." Length varies.

HEIAN INTERNATIONAL, INC., Box 2402, South San Francisco CA 94080. (415)658-1615. Publishes hardcover and paperback originals (95%) and paperback reprints (5%). Averages 20 titles/year. Pays 5-15% in royalty on wholesale or retail price. Average advance: $500. Simultaneous and photocopied submissions OK. SASE. Reports in 1-2 months. Book catalog for SASE.
Nonfiction: Animals; art; cookbooks, cooking & foods; health; juveniles; philosophy; photography; psychology; religion; and Orientalia (religion, philosophy, art, poetry, literature). "We are interested in well-written and well-illustrated juveniles. We are also looking for nonfiction books (translations acceptable) on any subject that assists man through the development of his inner potentials or search. Interested in books on Orientalia and world scriptures. We do not want text books, technical or hobbies." Query first, then submit outline/synopsis and sample chapters.
Recent Nonfiction Titles: *Haiku, Volumes 1 & 2*, by R.H. Blyth (literature); *Exploring Kittens*, by N. Honda (photographic); *Matsuri: Festival*, by N.K. Araki & J.M. Horii (Japanese-American customs); and *Textiles of the Andes*, by Y. Tsunoyana (art).
Fiction: "We are looking for well-written and well-illustrated juveniles. We are also interested in books with a religious, oriental theme, or one that deals with man's inner search." Query first, then submit outline/synopsis and sample chapters.
Recent Fiction Titles: *The ABC Book*, by J. Harada; *Wally the Whale Who Loved Balloons*, by Yuichi Watanabe; and Pocket Pop-Up Series: *Monkey, The Mermaid, Cinderella, Hansel and Gretel, The Emperor's New Clothes and Gulliver's Travels.*

HEINLE & HEINLE PUBLISHERS, INC., Subsidiary of Science Books International, Inc., 51 Sleeper St., Boston MA 02210. (617)451-1940. Editor-in-Chief: Charles H. Heinle. Averages 15 titles/year. Pays 6-15% royalty on net price; no advance. SASE. Reports in 3 weeks on queries; 3 months on mss. Free book catalog.
Nonfiction: Textbook. "Foreign language and English as a second or foreign language and English as a second or foreign language text and non-text materials. Before writing the book, submit complete prospectus along with sample chapters, and specify market and competitive position of proposed text."
Recent Nonfiction Titles: *Toward a Philosophy of Second Language Learning and Teaching*, by Kenneth D. Chastain (teaching methods); *How to Learn a Foreign Language*, by Paul Pimsleur (foreign language learning); and *Vida y voces del mundo hispanico*, by P. Smith, H. Babbitt, H. Frey and A. Tejeda (Spanish textbook).
Fiction: "Education materials in foreign language." Query.

HEMKUNT PRESS, E-1/15, Patel Rd., New Delhi, India 110008. Tel. 587149. Senior Editor: Mr. Menon. Publishes hardcover and paperback originals (85%) and reprints (15%). Averages 15 titles/year. Pays 5-10% royalty on list price; no advance. Photocopied submissions OK. SASE.

Reports in 2 months. Free book catalog.
Nonfiction: Health, how-to, self-help and textbooks. Query.
Recent Nonfiction Titles: *Tales of the Great*, by H. Bhatt (general supplementary book); *Action Chemistry*, by G. Mayer (textbook); and *Discovering Geography V*, by D.P. Gupta (textbook).
Fiction: Erotica, humor, romance and science fiction. Query.
Recent Fiction Titles: *Tales From Indian Classics*, by R. Gupta; *Aesop's Fables*, by V. Thomas; and *Story of Buddha*, by J. Landaw.

HENDRICKS HOUSE, INC., Main St., Putney VT 05346. (802)387-4425. Editor: Hildamarie Hendricks. Publishes hardcover originals and hardcover and paperback reprints. Pays royalty on wholesale or retail price. Publishes 5 titles/year. Free book catalog. Photocopied submissions OK. Submit complete ms. Reports in 1 month. SASE.
Nonfiction: "Mainly educational." Publishes Americana, biography, history, philosophy, reference and college level textbooks.

*HERALD PRESS, Mennonite Publishing House, 616 Walnut Ave., Scottdale PA 15683. (412)887-8500. Book Editor: Paul M. Schrock. Publishes hardcover and paperback originals and reprints. Published 30 titles in 1979, 35 in 1980; plans 35 in 1981. Several titles a year are subsidized by church organizations. "Subsidy is accepted only for books sponsored by an official board or committee of the Mennonite Church to meet discriminating needs when a book is not otherwise economically feasible." Pays 10-15% royalty on retail price; no advance. Photocopied submissions OK. SASE. Catalog 50¢. Reports in 3 weeks.
Nonfiction: Biography (religious); cookbooks; history (church); how-to; juveniles; devotional/ inspirational; psychology (religion); reference (Mennonite); religion; missions and evangelism; self-help (Christian); sociology (of religion); peace and social issues; and textbooks (Christian). Query.
Recent Nonfiction Titles: *Living More with Less*, by Doris Longacre; *Christ and Violence*, by Ronald J. Sider; *Caring Enough to Forgive*, by Donald Augsburger (personal relationships); and *Soviet Evangelicals Since World War II*, by Walter Sanatsky (modern church history).
Fiction: Adventure (juvenile); historical and religious. Query.
Recent Fiction Titles: *Caught in the Crossfire*, by Levi Keidel; and *Mystery at Indian Rocks*, by Ruth Nulton Moore.

*HERITAGE BOOKS, INC., 3602 Maureen, Bowie MD 20715. (301)464-1159. Editorial Director: Laird C. Towle. Publishes hardcover and paperback originals (20%) and reprints (80%). Averages 5 titles/year. "Quality of the book is of prime importance; next is its relevance to our fields of interest." Pays 10% royalty on retail price; occasional advance. Simultaneous and photocopied submissions OK. Reports in 1 month. SASE. Free book catalog.
Nonfiction: "We particularly desire nonfiction titles dealing with history and genealogy including how-to and reference works, as well as conventional histories and genealogies. The titles should be either of national interest or restricted to New England. Other subject matter will be considered provided that it is of either national or New England interest. We prefer writers to query, submit an outline/synopsis, or submit a complete ms, in that order, depending on the stage the writer has reached in the preparation of his work."
Recent Nonfiction Titles: *Genealogical Periodical Annual Index, Vol. 17*, by Mayhew and Towle; *Newspaper Genealogical Column Directory*, by Milner; *Provincetown, Massachusetts Cemetery Inscriptions*, by Cook, et. al.; and *New England Annals, Vol. 1*, edited by Towle.

HERMAN PUBLISHING, 45 Newbury St., Boston MA 02116. Editor: S.M. Herman. Publishes hardcover and paperback originals. Averages 20 titles/year. "Standard 10% royalty (7% on paperbacks) up to break-even point; higher beyond." Advance varies, depending on author's reputation and nature of book. Will send copy of current catalog on request. Send query, outline and sample chapter to C.A. Herman. Reports in 2 months, "longer if jammed up." SASE.
Nonfiction: Business, technical reference, the arts, health, self-improvement, psychiatry, psychology, regional, careers, electronics, architecture, communications arts, engineering, commerce, finance, technology, food service and home economics, health care, management, manufacturing, marketing and selling. "It might be worth noting that we also perform a unique service. We will market books that may have been privately published by the author or by a small publisher. Naturally, we must first see a sample copy and be satisfied that we can market it." Writing must be factual and authoritative. No length limits.
Recent Nonfiction Titles: *Professional Engineer's License Guide*, by Joseph D. Eckard; *The Manufacturer's Representative*, by Frank LeBell (marketing and selling); and *Trade Shows in the Marketing Mix*, by Hanlon.

HIGH/COO PRESS, Route #1, Battle Ground IN 47920. (317)567-2596. Editors: Randy and Shirley Brooks. Publishes trade paperback originals. Averages 5 titles/year. Pays 15% minimum royalty on retail price. SASE. Reports in 2 weeks on queries; 2 months on mss. Book catalog for 5x7 SAE and 2 first class stamps.
Nonfiction: Reference. Subjects include haiku books. "Every two years we publish a directory of haiku in English called *Haiku Review.* We list and review haiku books in print along with other haiku bibliography information. We have an international audience of poets and haiku enthusiasts. We do not seek or desire any mass market, but rather an informed, astute readership." Query.
Recent Nonfiction Title: *Haiku Review '80,* edited by Randy and Shirley Brooks (haiku directory).
Poetry: "We publish a chapbook of short poetry every 6 months. Each chapbook is 24-48 pages. We also publish 3-4 mini-chapbooks every year. Each mini is 12-24 pages. No poems with more than thirteen lines." Submit complete ms.
Recent Poetry Titles: *Walking With the River,* by Bob Boldman (Zen haiku); *The Dawn That Bleeds,* by Edward Tick (short lyrics); and *It's Ok if You Eat Lots of Rice,* by Wayne Westlake (senryu).

HILL & WANG, 19 Union Sq., W, New York NY 10003. (212)741-6900. Division of Farrar, Straus Giroux, Inc. Assistant Editor: Marcia Johnston. Editor-in-Chief: Arthur W. Wang. Publishes hardcover and paperback originals (99%) and reprints (1%). Publishes 19 titles/year. Pays standard royalty; advance varies. Photocopied submissions OK. SASE. Reports in 6 weeks.
Nonfiction: History. Submit outline/synopsis and sample chapters.
Recent Nonfiction Titles: *Many Reasons Why,* by Michael Charlton and Anthony Moncrieff; *Crisis in Command,* by Richard Gabriel and Paul Savage; *A Lover's Discourse,* by R. Barthes; *Frontier Women,* by J. Jeffrey (history); *The Woman Within,* by E. Glasgow (autiobiography).
Fiction: Submit complete ms.
Recent Fiction Titles: *The Sheltered Life,* by E. Glasow; and *The Sacred Stones Trilogy,* by M. Caldecott.

HOLIDAY HOUSE, 18 E. 53rd St., New York NY 10022. (212)688-0085. Editorial Director: Margery Cuyler. Publishes hardcover originals. Averages 25-30 titles/year. Pays in royalties based on retail price; offers variable advance. Photocopied submissions OK. Reports in 2 months. SASE. Free book catalog.
Nonfiction and Fiction: General fiction and nonfiction for young readers—pre-school through high school. "It's better to submit the ms without art." Submit outline/synopsis and sample chapters or complete ms. "No certified, insured or registered mail accepted."
Recent Titles: *Picking Up the Pieces,* by Betty Bates (romance); and *Horses of America,* by Dorothy Hinshew Patent.

HOLLOWAY HOUSE PUBLISHING CO., 8060 Melrose Ave., Los Angeles CA 90046. (213)653-8060. Editorial Director: Robert Leighton. Publishes paperback originals (95%) and reprints (5%). Averages 30 titles/year. Pays royalty based on retail price. Photocopied submissions OK. SASE. Reports in 6 weeks. Free book catalog for SASE.
Nonfiction and Fiction: "Holloway House is the largest publisher of Black Experience literature. We are in the market for hard-hitting contemporary stories with easily identifiable characters and locations. Dialogue must be realistic, with authentic slang and current 'street' language. A strain of sex is acceptable but not essential. Action, people and places must be thoroughly depicted and graphically presented. Now launching a new series of original paperbacks relating to the Hispanic experience in the United States. We are searching for fast-paced contemporary stories set in realistic situations. The dialogue must contain authentic bilingual elements." Black Experience Biography/Commentary-biographies of big-name personalities such as Joe Louis, Jesse Jackson, Louis Armstrong and Andrew Young. Not interested in 'This is My Story' treatments. Gambling and Game Books-from time to time publishes gambling books along the line of *How to Win, World's Greatest Winning Systems, Backgammon, How to Play and Win at Gin Rummy,* etc. Send query letter and/or outline with one sample chapter. SASE. Length: 60,000 words.
Recent Nonfiction Titles: *Lena,* by Brett Howard (biography of Lena Horne); and *Richard Pryor,* by Joseph Nazel (biography).
Recent Fiction Titles: *Double Dunk,* by Barry Beckham (basketball player); and *Cadillac Square,* by Sadie Tillman (black community).

HOLMES & MEIER PUBLISHING, INC., 30 Irving Place, New York NY 10003. (212)254-4100. Promotion: K. Brooks and M. Simmerman. Senior Editor: Emily Ganvud. Publishes hardcover and paperback originals and reprints. Publishes 120 titles/year. Pays variable royality. SASE. Reports in 3 months. Free book catalog.

Nonfiction: Americana, art, biography, business/economics, history, music, nature, politics, psychology, reference, sociology and textbooks. "We are noted as a scholarly publishing house and are pleased with our reputation of excellence in the field. However, while we will continue to publish books for academic and professional audiences, we are expanding our list to reach a broader readership. We will continue to build on our strengths in the social sciences, humanities and natural sciences. We do not want how-to and self-help material." Query first and submit outline/synopsis, sample chapters and curriculum vitae and idea of intended market/audience.
Recent Nonfiction Titles: *Elites in American History, Vols. 1-3,* by Philip H. Burch Jr. (history, contemporary); *Gender and Literary Voice,* edited by Janet Todd (women's studies); *A History of Africa 1840-1914,* edited by Tidy and Leeming (Africana, politics); and *The Modernization of Turkey,* by Walter F. Weiker (history).

HOLT, RINEHART & WINSTON, 521 5th Ave., New York NY 10017. (212)688-9100. Publishes hardcover and paperback (trade) originals (95%) and reprints (5%). Averages 100 titles/year. Contracts and advances vary with projects. Simultaneous and photocopied submissions OK. SASE. Reports in 1 month.
Nonfiction: Biography, American and World history, science and sports. Contemporary affairs. Submit samples.
Fiction: Mainstream and science fiction. Submit samples.
Recent Fiction Titles: *Year Of The French,* by T. Flanigan; *Horn of Africa,* by P. Caputo; *The Hastings Conspiracy,* by A. Coppel; and *the Ringword Engineers,* by L. Niven.

HOLT, RINEHART & WINSTON OF CANADA, LTD., 55 Horner Ave., Toronto, Ontario Canada M8Z 4X6. (416)255-4491. School Editor-in-Chief: William Park. College Acquisitions Editor: Joe McKeon. Publishes hardcover and paperback text originals. Published 20 titles in 1979, 40 in 1980. Royalty varies according to type of book; pays $200-500 for anthologies. No advance. Simultaneous and photocopied submissions OK. Reports in 1-3 months. SAE and International Reply Coupons. Free book catalog.
Nonfiction: Education texts. Query.
Recent Nonfiction Titles: *Essentials of Canadian Managerial Finance,* by Weston, Brigham, Halpem (college finance text); and *Inside, Outside,* by Jack Booth (elementary language arts text).

HORIZON PRESS, 156 5th Ave., New York NY 10010. Pays royalty based on both wholesale and retail price. Royalty schedule standard scale from 10% to 15%. Averages 24 titles/year. Free book catalog. Reports in 3 months. SASE.
Nonfiction: History, literature, science, biography, the arts, general. Length: 40,000 words and up. Query with full description. Recently published *The Poem Itself,* by Stanley Burnshaw; *Those Drinking Days,* by D. Neulgue; *Passion For Jazz,* by L. Feather; *Pissarro: His Life & Work,* by R. Shikes and P. Harper; *The Garden & The Wilderness,* by Charles Pratt; and *Lawsuit,* by S. Speiser.
Fiction: Query with full description. Recently published *Against the Stream,* by James Hanley. "We rarely publish fiction."

HOUGHTON MIFFLIN CO., 2 Park St., Boston MA 02107. (617)725-5000. Editor-in-Chief: Austin G. Olney. Managing Editor: Linda L. Glick. Hardcover and paperback originals (90%) and paperback reprints (10%). Royalty of 7½% on retail price for paperbacks; 10-15% on sliding scale for standard fiction and nonfiction; advance varies widely. Publishes 150 titles/year. Simultaneous submissions and photocopied submissions OK. Reports in 6 weeks. SASE.
Nonfiction: Americana, natural history, animals, biography, cookbooks/cooking/food, health, history, how-to, juveniles, poetry, politics, psychology and self-help. Query.
Recent Nonfiction Titles: *The Silent Intruder,* by Charles Panati (science); *A Life in Our Times,* by John Kenneth Galbraith; and *Alice James: A Biography,* by Jean Strouse.
Fiction: Historical, mainstream, mystery, science fiction and suspense. Query.
Recent Fiction Titles: *American Rose,* by Julia Markus; *A Sense of Shadow,* by Kate Wilhelm; and *After Eli,* by Terry Kay.

HOUSE OF ANANSI PRESS, LTD., 35 Britain St., Toronto, Ontario, Canada M5A 1R7. (416)363-5444. Editorial Director: James Polk. Publisher: Ann Wall. Publishes Canadian authors only. Hardcover and paperback originals 99% and paperback (out-of-print important Canadiana) reprints 1%. Averages 6 titles/year. Royalty "varies, depending whether we publish the book first in hardcover or paperback or both; not less than 8%;" advance averages $500, "but we also participate in the author subsidy plan of the Ontario Arts Council, and through them can offer up to $4,000." Query, submit outline/synopsis and sample chapters or complete ms. "We're flexible, but prefer for nonfiction to have a pretty good idea of what we're going to get. Don't send photos or illustrations with first submission. Tell us about them and if we are interested in the writing, we'll talk about those later." Photocopied submissions OK. Reports in 1-2 months. SASE. Free book catalog.

Nonfiction: Publishes biography; history; law; medicine and psychiatry; music; philosophy; poetry; politics; pyschology; and sociology books. "We have no length requirement. A book should be as long as it has to be to cover its topic adequately, and no longer. The slant should be toward the general reader with some university education who still likes to think when he reads. We like well-researched but not heavy or over-footnoted books." Recently published *The Art of Margaret Atwood: Essays in Criticism*, edited by A.E. and C.N. Davidson; and *Six Journeys: A Canadian Pattern*, by Charles Taylor (biographies).

Fiction: Publishes experimental books. Recently published *Basic Black With Pearls*, by Helen Weinzweig.

HOUSE OF COLLECTIBLES, INC., 1900 Premier Row, Orlando FL 32809. Publishes hardcover and trade paperback originals. Royalty is based on the stature of the author, the subject and the ms. Average advance is $1,000. Published 25 titles last year. Exclusive publisher of official price guides. Complete distribution and marketing range in all fields with heavy coverage on the collectible markets. Will consider photocopied submissions. Mss must be typed, double spaced with sample illustrations, when necessary. Reports in 2 months. Enclose return postage. Will send catalog to writer on request.

Nonfiction: "On the subject of collectibles (antiques, numismatics, philatelics) and how-to-do books. We prefer an author who knows his or her subject thoroughly. Style and general format are left entirely to the author. Any special treatment of emphasis is a matter of decision for the author." Submit outline and sample chapters.

HOWARD UNIVERSITY PRESS, 2900 Van Ness St. NW, Washington DC 20008. (202)686-6696. Publicity Director: Donna Ennis. Publishes hardcover and paperback originals (90%), and hardcover reprints (10%). Averages 14 titles/year. Pays 5-15% royalty; offers average $500 advance. Simultaneous and photocopied submissions OK. SASE. Reports in 2 months. Free book catalog.

Nonfiction: Biography and reference. Subjects include Americana, art, business and economics, health, history, music, philosophy, photography, politics, psychology, religion, sociology, sports, science and literary criticism. "We would be pleased to receive inquiries concerning projects of an original, scholarly, conceptual nature on the above subjects as they pertain to minorities in the US or to people in the Third World. Biography is very popular and, more broadly, anything which is based on a particular person, personality or clash of personalities. In Black studies, works that relate Black Americans to the Diaspora and, continually, works that serve to integrate Black history from slavery to WWII." No dissertations, anthologies, textbooks, or personal revelations having no foundation in scholarly or journalistic methods."

Recent Nonfiction Titles: *Meanness Mania: The Changed Mood*, by Gerald Gill (political science); *Profile of the Negro in American Dentistry*, by Dr. Foster Kidd (history); and *A Knot in the Thread: The Life and Works of Jacques Roumain*, by Dr. Carolyn Fowler (literary criticism).

Fiction: Experimental and mainstream. "Our needs in this area are minimal. We will probably be aware of and seek out any projects we would do in this area. No mss by unpublished writers." Query.

Tips: "Visit bookstores and college campuses, and tune in to what is being bought, read, researched and argued."

HOWELL-NORTH BOOKS, 11175 Flintkote Ave., San Diego CA 92121. (714)457-3200. President: Charles C. Tillinghast III. Vice-President: Cynthia B. Tillinghast. Publishes hardcover and paperback originals (95%) and hardcover reprints (5%). Averages 6-10 titles/year. Offers 12½% royalty on wholesale or retail price; no advance. Simultaneous submissions OK. Reports in 6 weeks. SASE. Free book catalog for 41¢ postage.

Nonfiction: "We would like to see manuscripts in the transportation field—railroads and marine preferred. In the Western Americana field, we would like to see books on mining, but ones with general appeal rather than those too restricted in area or subject." Query.

Recent Nonfiction Titles: *MoPac Power*, by J. Collias; *Our City: The Jews of San Francisco*, by Irene Narell (history); and *Western Maryland Railways*, by Karl Zimmermann.

HUDSON HILLS PRESS, INC., Suite 4323, 30 Rockefeller Plaza, New York NY 10112. (212)247-3400. President/Editorial Director: Paul Anbinder. Publishes hardcover and paperback originals. Averages 6-8 titles/year. Offers royalties of 5-8% on retail price. Average advance: $10,000. Simultaneous and photocopied submissions OK. SASE. Reports in 4 weeks. Free book catalog.

Nonfiction: Art and photography. "We are only interested in publishing books about art and photography, or collections of photographs (photo essays or monographs)." Query first, then submit outline/synopsis and sample chapters.

Recent Nonfiction Titles: *Exploring Photography*, by Campbell; *American Masterpieces From the National Gallery of Art*, by John Wilmerding; and Behind the Lines, by R.O. Blechman.

HUMAN SCIENCES PRESS, INC., 72 5th Ave., New York NY 10011. (212)243-6000. Promotion Manager: Peter Katz. Vice President/Editor-in-Chief: Norma Fox. Publishes hardcover and paperback originals. Published 49 titles in 1979, 52 in 1980; plans 55 in 1981. Pays standard royalites; sometimes offers advance. No simultaneous submissions; 3 photocopied submissions OK. SASE. Reports in 1 month. Free book catalog.
Nonfiction: Behaviorial and social sciences for professional text references. Submit complete ms.
Recent Nonfiction Titles: *Becoming A Family Therapist*, by C. Kramer; and *The Abusing Family*, by B. and R. Justice; *I Have Feelings Too*, by T. Berger; and *Me And Einstein: Breaking Through The Reading Barrier*, by R. Blue.

CARL HUNGNESS PUBLISHING, Box 24308, Speedway IN 46224. (317)244-4792. Editorial Director: Carl Hungness. Publishes hardcover and paperback originals. Published 7 titles in 1979. Pays "negotiable" outright purchase; advance averages $500. Reports in 3 weeks. SASE. Free book catalog.
Nonfiction: Stories relating to professional automobile racing. No sports car racing or drag racing material. Query. Recently published *Indianapolis 500 Yearbook*, by C. Hungness and others (historical); and *The Mighty Midgets*, by J.C. Fox (historical).

*HUNTER HOUSE, INC., Subsidiary of Servire, B.V. the Netherlands, 748 E. Bonita, Suite 105, Pomona CA 91767. (714)624-2277. General Manager: Hugh Grubb. Publishes hardcover and trade paperback originals. Averages 4 titles/year. Subsidy publishes 10-25% of books based on "commercial non-viability yet sound content and editorial familiarity." Pays 7½% average royalty on retail price; offers average $750 advance. Simultaneous submissions OK. SASE. Reports in 2 weeks on queries; 3 months on mss.
Nonfiction: How-to. Subjects include psychology and sociology. "Psychology and psychotherapy—especially in area of marital therapy—written for professionals/academics." Query or submit outline/synopsis and sample chapters.
Recent Nonfiction Titles: *LSD Psychotherapy*, by Dr. Stan Grof (text and general); *Once a Month*, by Dr. Katharine Dalton; and *Questioning Techniques*, by Dr. Artur Kaiser.

HURTIG PUBLISHERS LTD., 10560 105th St., Edmonton, Alberta, Canada T5H 2W7. (403)426-2359. Editorial Manager: José Druker. Hardcover and paperback originals (80%) and reprints (20%). Averages 12 titles/year. Pays 10% royalty on first 7,000 copies; 12% on next 7,000; 15% thereafter. Advance averages $500-1,000. State availablity of photos and/or illustrations to accompany ms. Photocopied submissions OK. Prefers letter of inquiry first. Reports in 1-2 months. SASE. Free book catalog.
Nonfiction: Publishes biographies of well-known Canadians; Canadian history; humor; nature; topical Canadian politics and economics; reference (Canadian); and material about native Canadians "aimed at the nationalistic Canadian interested in politics, the North and energy policy." No poetry or original fiction. Query or submit outline/synopsis and sample chapters; or submit complete ms.
Recent Nonfiction Titles: *The Art of Canadian Nature Photography*, by J.A. Kraulis (nature); *Canadian Newspapers/The Inside Story*, edited by Walter Stewart (socio-economic, current events); and *Pitseolak: A Canadian Tragedy*, by David F. Raine.

*HWONG PUBLISHING CO., 10353 Los Alamitos Blvd. Los Alamitos CA 90720. Editor-in-Chief: Hilmi Ibrahim. Managing Editor: Sarah Keating. Specializes in college textbooks, minorities literature, and Chinese publications. Textbook areas: social sciences, history, humanities, business, and science. Some fiction, biographies and other subjects published on a subsidy basis. Submit complete manuscript. Include any prints of photos and/or illustrations. Simultaneous and photocopied submissions OK. Reports in 2-4 weeks. SASE. Publishes paperback originals and some hardcover. Averages 15 titles/year. Pays royalty on wholesale price. Recently published: *White Winds*, by Joe Wilcox (mountaineering); *Polynesian Twilight*, by Juanita Ritchie (poetry); *Survival is the Bottomline*, by Phil Potts (small business); *Khalil and All of Lebanon*, by S.I. Salem (Lebanon); and *Condemned to Live*, by Waldo Zimmermann (population control).

ICARUS PRESS, INC., Box 1225, South Bend IN 46624. (219)291-3200. Editorial Director: Bruce M. Fingerhut. Publishes hardcover and paperback originals. Published 4 titles in 1979, 9 in 1980; plans 15 in 1981. Offers 10-15% royalty based on wholesale or retail price. Average advance:

$2,000. Simultaneous and photocopied submissions OK (if so indicated). SASE. Reports in 1 month. Free book catalog.

Nonfiction: Americana; biography; history; recreation; sports; and travel (regional). "We have been going into regional, popular books in Americana, sports, festivals, etc. (in all aspects—folk arts, heritage, historical, agricultural, music, arts and crafts, etc.), and we shall expand our total output in these fields across the country in regional books. Our interests in sports, whether of the self-help, coaching, or history genre, remain high. As to history, biography, current affairs, etc., such manuscripts as we publish must be real trade titles—with national appeal. Our interest in religion (traditional Christian) and politics (and philosophy) will be growing during the next few years. We do *not* want to see poetry, photography, art, hobbies (other than those immediately connected with sports), or cookbooks." Query first, then submit outline/synopsis and sample chapters.

Recent Nonfiction Titles: *The Book of Festivals in the Midwest, 1980 & 1981* , (guide) by Akin and Fingerhut; *A Trial of Generals*, by Lawrence Tayler (history); and *The Game Is Never Over*, by Jim Langford (sports).

Fiction: Mainstream. "We shall probably not be publishing any fiction for the next year or two, although our intention is to publish fiction as soon as possible." Does *not* want to see confession, romance, science fiction, mystery, or western. Query first, then submit outline/synopsis and sample chapters.

*IDEAL WORLD PUBLISHING CO., Box 1237-EG, Melbourne FL 32935. New Idea Publishing Co. is a division of Ideal World Publishing Co. Publisher: Harold Pallatz. Editor: Leona Rudman. Publishes hardcover and paperback originals and reprints. Averages 3 titles/year. Offers subsidy publication of "difficult-to-place" manuscripts. "If your book has marketing potential which major publishers have failed to recognize due to their own business strategy, we can help you get published. We offer you a special subsidy plan which includes typing, printing, binding and distribution. Fee starts at $50 for short runs, depending upon number of pages, copies, etc. "Will consider photocopied submissions. "Query, first, please." Reports in 2-4 weeks. *"No material will be returned unless SASE is attached."*

Health: "Natural approaches to good health through nutrition, herbs, vegetarianism, vitamins, unusual medical approaches for specific ailments, particularly from authorities in the field. Any style is acceptable, but it must hold the reader's attention and make for fairly smooth nonintensive (no brain taxation) requirements. Ideas should be in a simple, easygoing pace." Also publishes energy—related books: alternative energy themes, particularly do-it-yourself hybrid vehicles. "The scope of our publishing is confined to health and energy nonfiction; we do not accept fiction or poetry."

Recent Nonfiction Title: *Hybrid Manual*, by Harold Pallatz (electric cars).

IDEALS PUBLISHING CORP., 11315 Watertown Plank Rd., Milwaukee WI 53226. Editorial Director: James A. Kuse. Imprints include *Good Friends* (juvenile) and *Successful* (how-to books for the homeowner). Publishes hardcover and paperback originals, and greeting booklets. Published 75 titles in 1979, 80 in 1980. Pays variable royalty; offers advance only on assigned projects. Photocopied submissions OK. SASE. Reports in 4-6 weeks.

Nonfiction: Cookbooks. Length: 300 recipes. *Sucessful* imprint includes books of approximately 60,000 words on do-it-yourself home projects. Often buys manuscripts with illustrating photographs.

Recent Nonfiction Titles: *Thank You, Lord*, by Gigi Graham Tchividjian (family life); *A Time for Giving*, by Jill Briscoe (religious); and *Candy Cookbook*, by Mildred Brand.

Fiction: Juveniles under the *Good Friends* imprint. "Stories which are fun to read, entertaining yet instructive without being overly didactic. Often buys illustrated children's manuscripts. Query. Length varies.

Recent Fiction Titles: *Alex in Wonderland*, by David Schansberg; and *Dugan the Duck*, by Gale Brennan.

INDIANA UNIVERSITY PRESS, 10th & Morton Sts., Bloomington IN 47405. (812)337-4203. Director: John Gallman. Publishes hardcover and paperback originals (75%) and paperback reprints (25%). Averages 75-80 titles/year. Pays 10% royalty on retail price; offers occasional advance. Photocopied submissions OK. Reports in 2 months. SASE. Free book catalog.

Nonfiction: Scholarly books on humanities, history, philosophy, translations, semiotics, public policy, film, music, linguistics, social sciences, regional materials, African studies, women's studies, and serious nonfiction for the general reader. Query or submit outline/synopsis and sample chapters. "Queries should include as much descriptive material as is necessary to convey scope and market appeal to us."

Recent Nonfiction Titles: *Eisenhower's Lieutenants: The Campaign of France and Germany,*

1944-1945, by Russell F. Weigley; *Speech, Writing and Sign: A Functional View of Linguistic Representation*, by Naomi S. Baron; and *The Fantasy Tradition in American Literature: From Irving to Le Guin*, by Brian Attebery.
Fiction: Query or submit outline/synopsis.

INSTITUTE FOR BUSINESS PLANNING, Division of Prentice-Hall, IBP Plaza, Englewood Cliffs NJ 07632. (201)592-3080. Managing Editor: Anthony Vlamis. Publishes hardcover originals and paperback reprints. Averages 18 titles/year. Pays 5% maximum royalty (direct mail) and 15% royalty (trade retail). Average advance: $1,500-2,000. No simultaneous submissions; photocopied submissions OK. SASE. Reports in 4-6 weeks. Free book catalog.
Nonfiction: Business/economics; how-to ("high level professional audience; not how to make money in mail order or other pedestrian books"); and reference. "We seek practical professional reference books in the following areas: accounting, business management, small business management and operations, estate planning and administration, real estate, law and finance. Areas open for future considerations are: banking, insurance, paralegal and finance planning." Does *not* want inspirational and selling mss. Query first or submit outline/synopsis and sample chapters.
Recent Nonfiction Titles: *Real Estate Appraiser's Kit*, by Barbara Miller (real estate appraisals); *Accounting Desk Book*, by W. Behrenfeld (accounting); *Paralegal's Litigation Handbook*, by C. Bruno (law); and *Successful Pension Design*, by Robert Slimmon.

*INSTITUTE FOR THE STUDY OF HUMAN ISSUES, (ISHI Publications), 3401 Market St., Suite 252, Philadelphia PA 19104. (215)387-9002. Director of Publications: Betty C. Jutkowitz. Editor: Douglas C. Gordon. Managing Editor: Janet Greenwood. Publishes hardcover and paperback originals (85%) and hardcover reprints (15%). Published 15 titles in 1979; 16 in 1980, 20 in 1981. Subsidy publishes 10% of books. Pays 10-12½% royalty on wholesale price; no advance. Photocopied submissions OK. Reports in 3 months. SASE. Free book catalog.
Nonfiction: Books on political science, history, anthropology, folklore, sociology, narcotics and macro-economics, suitable for scholars in these fields. Submit outline/synopsis and sample chapters. Recently published *Jews in the Eyes of the Germans*, by Alfred D. Low (intellectual/social history); *Revolutionary Cuba in the World Arena*, edited by Martin Weinstein (Cuban politics and diplomacy); and *Pastoralists of the Andes*, by Jorge A. Flores-Ochoa (ethnography).

INTERCULTURAL PRESS, INC., 70 W. Hubbard St., Chicago IL 60610. (312)321-0075. Contact: David S. Hoopes, Editor-in-Chief, 130 North Rd., Vershire VT 05079. (802)685-4448. Publishes hardcover and trade paperback originals. Averages 5-15 titles/year. Pays royalty; occasionally offers small advance. Simultaneous and photocopied submissions OK. SASE. Reports in "several weeks" on queries; 2 months on mss. Free book catalog.
Nonfiction: How-to, reference, self-help, textbook and theory. Subjects include business and economics, philosophy, politics, psychology, sociology, travel, or "any book with an international or domestic intercultural, multicultural or cross-cultural focus, i.e., a focus on the cultural factors in personal, social, political or economic relations. We want books with an international or domestic intercultural or multicultural focus, especially those focusing on business operations (how to be effective in intercultural business activities) and education (textbooks for teaching intercultural subjects, for instance). Our books are published for educators in the intercultural field, business people who are engaged in international business, and anyone else who works in an international occupation, or has had intercultural experience. No mss that don't have an intercultural focus." Query "if there is any question of suitability (we can tell quickly from a good query)," or submit outline/synopsis. All unsolicited mss are returned unopened.
Recent Nonfiction Titles: *Survival Kit for Overseas Living*, by Robert Kohls (how-to); *Multicultural Education: The Cross-Cultural Training Approach*, edited by Peggy Pusch (text); and *American Cultural Patterns: A Cross-Cultural Perspective*, by Edward Stewart (theory/text). "Will consider any fiction with an intercultural focus." Query "if there is any question of suitability," or submit outline/synopsis. All unsolicited mss are returned unopened.

INTERGALACTIC PUBLISHING CO., 221 Haddon Ave., Westmont NJ 08108. (609)854-0499. Contact: Samuel W. Valenza, Jr. Publishes trade paperback originals. Averages 2 titles/year. "We have a unique setup for teachers: 50% royalty paid on 1st edition after costs; 60-40 split on subsequent editions after costs." Pays royalty on both wholesale and retail price; offers average $100 advance. Simultaneous and photocopied submissions OK. SASE. Reports in 1 month on queries; 2 months on mss. Free book catalog.
Nonfiction: Technical and textbook. Subjects include "educational methods and motivational materials in the areas of math and science. Materials, texts and how-to vehicles that accent mathematics and sciences at the K-12 level in an 'applied' sense, particularly mss developed in

classrooms by teachers of mathematics. We also produce games, and AV materials related to these areas. Our readers include academia on a secondary and junior college level; also high school and junior libraries, and media centers." Submit complete ms.

Recent Nonfiction Titles: *The Mathematics of the Energy Crisis*, by R. Gagliardi; *The Mathematics Laboratory In the Elementary School, How? What? and Who?*, by F. Swetz; and *Geometrical Theorems in Slides*, by V. Madan (21 slides plus 16-page booklet).

Fiction: "Math and science if related to teachable concepts. A title is applicable only if it is uniquely suited to our list; e.g., 'Professor Googol's Math Primer.' " Submit complete ms.

Tips: "Our market is limited, but books accenting the *application of learned material* on the secondary level are doing best, since our market as a whole is concerned with *motivation* in education."

INTERNATIONAL MARINE PUBLISHING CO., 21 Elm St., Camden ME 04843. President: Roger C. Taylor. Managing Editor: Kathleen M. Brandes. Publishes primarily hardcover originals and reprints. Averages 15 titles/year. "Standard royalties, based on retail price, with advances." Free book catalog. "Material in all stages welcome. Query preferred. More often than we like, we receive complete manuscripts over the transom, and the authors expect us to reply immediately with a decision. We prefer queries first. We like unsolicited manuscripts as long as the authors are patients." Reports in 6 weeks. Return postage necessary.

Marine Nonfiction: "Marine nonfiction only—but a wide range of subjects within that category: fishing, boatbuilding, boat design, yachting, seamanship, boat maintenance, maritime history, etc.—anything to do with boats, lakes, rivers, seas, and the people who do things on them, commercially or for pleasure." Recently published *Plank on Frame*, by Paul Lipke; *Still More Good Boats*, by Roger C. Taylor; and *Traditions and Memories of American Yachting, Complete Edition*, by W.P. Stephens.

INTERNATIONAL SELF-COUNSEL PRESS, LTD., 306 W. 25th St., North Vancouver, British Columbia, Canada V7N 2G1. (604)986-3366. Editorial Director: Diana R. Douglas. Legal Editor: Lois Richardson. Publishes paperback originals. Publishes 50 titles/year. Pays 10% royalty on wholesale price; no advance. Simultaneous and photocopied submissions OK. Reports in 2 weeks. SASE. Free book catalog.

Nonfiction: "Books only on law and business for the layperson (how-to)." Submit outline/synopsis and sample chapters. Follow Chicago *Manual of Style*. Recently published *Mike Grenby's Tax Tips*, by Mike Grenby; *Immigrating to the USA*, by Dan P. Danilov; and *The Word Processing Handbook: A Step by Step Guide to Automating Your Office*, by Katherine Aschner (office practice).

INTERNATIONAL WEALTH SUCCESS, Box 186, Merrick NY 11566. (516)766-5850. Editor: Tyler G. Hicks. Averages 10 titles/year. Pays 10% royalty on wholesale or retail price. Usual advance is $1,000, but this varies, depending on author's reputation and nature of book. Will consider photocopied submissions. Query. Reports in 4 weeks. Enclose return postage.

Self-Help and How-to: "Techniques, methods, sources for building wealth. Highly personal, how-to-do-it with plenty of case histories. Books are aimed at the wealth builder and are highly sympathetic to his and her problems." Financing, business success, venture capital, etc. Length 60,000-70,000 words.

Recent Nonfiction Title: *How to Grow Rich in Real Estate*, by Nielsen.

Tips: "Concentrate on practical, hands-on books showing people how to build wealth today, starting with very little cash. Most of the manuscripts we get today assume that everyone has money to invest in gold, rare coins, stocks, etc. This is not so! There are millions who haven't made it yet. This is *our* audience, an audience that can build great wealth for a writer who tells these people what to do, where to do it and how to do it. Forget theories; concentrate on the day-to-day business of making money from one's own business and you've got it made!"

THE INTERSTATE PRINTERS & PUBLISHERS, INC., 19-27 N. Jackson St., Danville IL 61832. (217)446-0500. Acquisitions: Russell L. Guin. Managing Editor: Ronald L. McDaniel. Hardcover and paperback originals. Usual royalty is 10% of wholesale price; no advance. Publishes about 50 titles/year. Markets books by mail and exhibits. Reports in 1-2 months. SASE. Free book catalog.

Nonfiction: Publishes textbooks; agriculture; special education; trade and industrial; home economics; athletics; career education; outdoor education; school law; marriage counseling; and learning disabilities books. "We favor, but do not limit ourselves to, works which are designed for class-quantity rather than single-copy sale." Query or submit outline/synopsis and sample chapters. Recently published *Speech and Language Rehabilitation*, by Robert L. Keith; *The Meat We Eat*, by John R. Romans and P. Thomas Ziegler; *Flower and Plant Production in the Greenhouse*, by Kennard S. Nelson; *Producing Farm Crops*, by Lester V. Boone, et al. (agriculture); and *The Big Book of Sounds*, by Ann M. Flowers (speech-language pathology).

INTERVARSITY PRESS, Box F, Downers Grove IL 60515. (312)964-5700. Editorial Director: James W. Sire. Publishes hardcover and paperback originals. Averages 40 titles/year. Pays 10% royalty on retail price; advance averages $500. "Indicate simultaneous submissions." Photocopied submissions OK. Reports in 16 weeks. SASE. Free book catalog.
Nonfiction: "InterVarsity Press publishes books geared to the presentation of Biblical Christianity in its various relations to personal life, art, literature, sociology, psychology, philosphy, history and so forth. Though we are primarily publishers of trade books, we are cognizant of the textbook market at the college, university and seminary level within the general religious field. The audience for which the books are published is composed primarily of university students and graduates; stylistic treatment varies from topic to topic and from fairly simplified popularizations for college freshmen to extremely scholarly works primarily designed to be read by scholars." Query or submit outline/synopsis and sample chapters. Recently published *Out of the Saltshaker: Evangelism as a Way of Life*, by Rebecca Manley Pippert; *Rich Christians in an Age of Hunger*, by R. Sider (practical theology); and *God Has Spoken*, by F.I. Parker.

*IOWA STATE UNIVERSITY PRESS, S. State Ave., Ames IA 50010. (515)294-5280. Director: Merritt Bailey. Managing Editor: Judith Gildner. Hardcover and paperback originals. Pays 10-12½-15% royalty on wholesale price; no advance. Subsidy publishes 10-50% of titles, based on sales potential of book and contribution to scholarship. Averages 35 titles/year. Send contrasting b&w glossy prints to illustrate ms. Simultaneous submissions OK, if advised; photocopied submissions OK if accompanied by an explanation. Reports in 2-4 months. SASE. Free book catalog.
Nonfiction: Publishes biography, history, recreation, reference, scientific technical, textbooks and Iowana books. Submit outline/synopsis and sample chapters; must be double-spaced throughout. Recently published *Pilot's Log Book*, by William Kershner; *Basic Technical Writing*, by Freeman; *The 5-string Banjo*, by Joe Taschetta; and *West to the Sunrise*, by Grace Harris.

ISLAND PRESS, Star Route 1, Box 38, Covelo CA 95428. Executive Director: Barbara Dean. Publishes paperback originals. Publishes 4 titles/year. Pays 10-15% royalty on retail price; offers $1500-3000 average advance. Simultaneous and photocopied submissions OK. SASE. Reports in 3 months. Free book catalog for SASE.
Nonfiction: Animals, biography, health, history, how-to, nature, philosophy, psychology, religion, self-help, sociology and travel. "We specialize in books on the environment and on human experience. We would welcome well-researched, technically accurate material on particular aspects of nature, conservation, animal life; also on true, personal experiene in nature or personal growth. Emphasis on protection of wilderness, living with nature and human experience as means of spiritual growth. No poetry, children's books or textbooks. Also we are not interested in new age fads or trendy material." Query or submit outline/synopsis and sample chapters.
Recent Nonfiction Titles: *Headwaters: Tales Of The Wilderness*, by Ash, Russell, Doog and Del Rio (experience of 4 men in the wilderness); *Wellspring: A Story From The Deep Country*, by B. Dean (personal experience on a remote piece of land); *A Citizen's Guide to Timber Harvest Plans*, by M. Bytheriver (layperson's guide to the timber harvest procedures in California); and *Building an Ark*, by Phillip M. Hoose (strategies for natural diversity through land protection).
Fiction: Historical (regional) and religious. "We are interested only in the unusual fiction that would merge with our primarily nonfiction list; fiction dealing with environmental consciousness or with human experience leading to personal/spiritual growth. No gothic, science fiction, romance, confession, etc. Query or submit outline/synopsis and sample chapters.
Recent Fiction Titles: *The Christmas Coat*, by R. Jones (story of a family discovering itself); *The Search For Goodbye-To-Rains*, by P. McHugh (young man's odyssey across America to find himself); and *No Substitue for Madness*, by Ron Jones (six stories from a teacher and his unusual kids).

JANEVAR PUBLISHING CO., Rt. 11, Box 129, Muncie IN 47302. (317)289-3137. Publisher: Jane Elsmere. Publishes hardcover and trade paperback originals. Averages 3 titles/year. Pays 10% royalty on wholesale price; no advance. Simultaneous and photocopied submissions OK. SASE. Reports in 2 weeks on queries; 1 month on mss.
Imprints: *Brindale Books* (nonfiction), Jane Elsmere, publisher.
Nonfiction: Biography, textbook and scholarly. Subjects include Americana; history (of the US). "We're looking for mss on US history (biography, bibliography, family, local, state, and nation)." Submit outline/synopsis and sample chapters.
Recent Nonfiction Title: *Justice Samuel Chase*, by J.S. Elsmere (biography).

JANUS BOOK PUBLISHERS, 2501 Industrial Pkwy., W., Hayward CA 94545. (415)785-9625. Vice President: Charles Kahn. Averages 10-12 titles/year. Pays 4-10% royalty on retail price or buys some mss by outright purchase; average advance. Query or submit outline/synopsis and sample chapters. SASE. Reports in 3 weeks. Free book catalog.
Nonfiction: "We publish work texts written at a 2.5 reading level for young adults with limited reading ability."
Recent Titles: *The Last Goodbye*, by Mark Jameson and Al Nist (short stories about growing into adulthood; and *Using the Phone Book*, by Pat Gundlach and Keenan Kelsey.

JH PRESS, Box 294, Village Station, New York NY 10014. (212)255-4713. Publisher: Terry Helbing. Publishes trade paperback originals. Averages 3 titles/year. Pays 6-10% royalty on retail price; offers average $100 advance. Simultaneous and photocopied submissions OK. SASE. Reports in 2 weeks. Free book catalog.
Nonfiction: Subjects include drama and theater. "Studies of gay theater or gay plays." Query.
Recent Nonfiction Title: *Gay Theatre Alliance Directory of Gay Plays, by Terry Helbing.*
Fiction: Drama and theater. "Gay plays that have been produced but not previously published." Query.
Recent Fiction Titles: *Forever After*, by Doric Wilson (play); and *News Boy*, by Arch Brown (play).

JOHNS HOPKINS UNIVERSITY PRESS, Baltimore MD 21218. Editorial Director: Anders Richter. Publishes mostly clothbound originals and paperback reprints; some paperback originals. Publishes 100 titles/year. Payment varies; contract negotiated with author. Reports in 2 months. SASE.
Nonfiction: Publishes scholarly books and journals, biomedical sciences, history, literary theory and criticism, wildlife biology and management, psychology, political science, regional material, and economics. Query. Length: 50,000 words minimum.
Recent Nonfiction Title: *Cancer Care: A Personal Guide*, by H. Glucksberg and J. Singer.
Fiction: Occasional fiction by invitation only.

JOHNSON PUBLISHING COMPANY, 1880 S. 57th Ct., Boulder CO 80301. (303)443-1576. Editorial Director: Michael McNierney. Publishes hardcover and paperback originals and reprints. Publishes 8-10 titles/year. Royalties vary. SASE. Reports in 1-2 months. Free book catalog.
Nonfiction: General non-fiction, how-to, western regional history, contemporary issues, science, geology, nature, outdoor recreation, guidebooks. "We are primarily interested in books for the informed popular market, though we will consider vividly written scholarly works. As a small publisher, we are able to give every submission close personal attention." Query first or call.
Recent Nonfiction Titles: *The Electric Vegetarian: Natural Cooking the Food Processor Way*, by Paula Szilard and Juliana J. Woo; *Front Range Restaurants: The 100 Best*, by Richard Fetter, et al.; *Kinnikinnick: The Mountain Flower Book*, by Millie Miller; *Train Robbery*, by Richard Patterson; and *To Kill an Eagle: Indian Views on the Last Days of Crazy Horse*, by Edward and Mabell Kadlecek (western history).

JONATHAN DAVID PUBLISHERS, 68-22 Eliot Ave., Middle Village NY 11379. (212)456-8611. Editor-in-Chief: Alfred J. Kolatch. Publishes hardcover and paperback originals. Averages 25-30 titles/year. Pays 10-15% royalty on wholesale or retail price, or by outright purchase of $1,000-3,000. Reports in 3 weeks. SASE.
Nonfiction: Adult nonfiction books for a general audience. Americana, cookbooks, cooking and foods, how-to, recreation, reference, self-help and sports. "We specialize in Judaica." Query. Recently published *The Baseball Catalog*, by D. Schlossberg; *The Household Book of Hints and Tips*, by D. Raintree; and *Cooking Kosher: The Natural Way*, by Jadne Kinderlehrer.

JOSSEY-BASS, INC., PUBLISHERS, 433 California St., San Francisco CA 94104. (415)433-1740. Editorial Director: Allen Jossey-Bass. Senior Editors: JB Hefferlin, Higher Education; William E. Henry, Social and Behavioral Science. Publishes hardcover and paperback originals. Averages 100 titles/year. Pays 10-15% royalty on net receipts; no advance. Simultaneous (if so informed) and photocopied submissions OK. Reports in 4 weeks. SASE. Free book catalog.
Nonfiction: Professional, scholarly books for senior administrators, faculty, researchers, graduate students, and professionals in private practice. Research-based books developed for practical application. "We do not want undergraduate texts or collections of previously published materials." Submit outline/synopsis and sample chapters. Recently published *Encyclopedia of Clinical Assessment*, edited by R. H. Woody (social and behavioral science); *Achieving Optimal Enrollments and Tuition Revenues*, by W. Ihlanfeldt; and *The Modern American College*, by Arthur W. Chickering and Associates (higher education).

JOVE PUBLICATIONS, 200 Madison Ave., New York NY 10016. Contact: Editorial Department. Publishes paperback originals. Publishes 150 titles/year. Pays 6-8% royalty; offers advance. SASE. Reports in 6 months.
Fiction: Adventure, historical, mystery, suspense and western, occult, romance. Submit outline and 2 chapters only through agent. Recently published *Girl of Golden Hair*, by Leslie Deane; *The Women's Room*, by Marilyn French; and John Jakes's bicentennial series *The Bastard, The Lawless, Furies* and *The Rebels, The Americans* (historical saga).

JUDSON PRESS, Valley Forge PA 19481. (215)768-2116. General Manager: Harold L. Twiss. Publishes hardcover and paperback originals. Generally 10% royalty on retail price. "Payment of an advance depends on author's reputation and nature of book." Publishes 40 titles/year. Free book catalog. Query with outline and sample chapter. Reports in 3 months. Enclose return postage.
Religion: Adult religious nonfiction of 30,000-80,000 words. "Our audience is mostly church members who seek to have a more fulfilling personal spiritual life and want to do a better job as Christians in their church and other relationships." Recently published *Mid-Life: A Time to Discover, a Time to Decide*, by R.P. Olson; *A Taste of Creation*, by V. Stem Owens (inspirational); and *Lay Shepherding*, by Rudolph Grantham.

K & R BOOKS LTD., Edlington Hall, Edlington, Horncastle, Lincs, England. Contact: Director/ Senior Editor. Publishes hardcover and paperback originals. Published 10 titles in 1979, 50 in 1980. Pays negotiable royalty; also buys mss by outright purchase "dependent on title and series." Photocopied submissions OK. SASE. Reports in 2 months "depending on size of ms and on subject."
Nonfiction: Animals, hobbies (dogs, birds [avicultural] pets) and nature. Needs "any title from paperback material through to monographs on natural history—preferably on specific animals or groups. These should ideally refer to mammals, though others will be considered." No topics that are in story form. No biographies or poetry on animals. Query or submit outline/synopsis and sample chapters or complete ms.
Recent Nonfiction Titles: *The Afghan Hound: A Definitive Study*, by M. Niblock (monograph); *Dog Shows and Show Dogs: A Definitive Study*, by C.G. Sutton (monograph); *Lovebirds: Their Care & Breeding*, by D. Alderton (handbook); *Pheasants: Their Breeding & Management*, by K.C.R. Houwman (introductory guide); and *Goats: Their Care & Breeding*, by P. Mintere and F. Rogers (handbook).
Tips: "We would like to see more completed manuscripts or at least chapters which would indicate writer's ability and depth of research. While it would still not be any guarantee of publication it greatly inceases the chances. Where good color illustrations are offered with ms, this also increases chances."

KALMBACH PUBLISHING CO., 1027 N. 7th St., Milwaukee WI 53233. (414)272-2060. Editorial Director: David P. Morgan. Books Editor: Bob Hayden. Publishes hardcover and paperback originals (80%) and paperback reprints (20%). Averages 10 titles/year. Offers 3-10% royalty on retail price. Average advance: $750. No simultaneous or photocopied submissions. SASE. Reports in 4 weeks. Free book catalog.
Nonfiction: Hobbies; how-to; and recreation. "Our book publishing effort is in railroading and how-to-do-it titles *only*." Especially needs "at least one title in each of the following hobby subject areas: radio-controlled models; plastic model planes; powered aircraft models; wargaming primer; and plastic car and truck models." Query first. "I welcome telephone inquiries. They save me a lot of time, and they can save an author a lot of misconceptions and wasted work."
Recent Nonfiction Titles: *Basics of Model Rocketry*, by Doug Pratt (model rocketry hobby); and *How to Build Dioramas*, by Shep Paine (hobby book on diorama building).
Tips: "Our books are about half text and and half illustrations. Any author who wants to publish with us must be able to furnish good photographs and rough drawings before we'll consider contracting for his book."

WILLIAM KAUFMANN, INC., 1 1st St., Los Altos CA 94022. Editor-in-Chief: William Kaufmann. Hardcover and paperback originals (90%) and reprints (10%). "Generally offers standard minimum book contract of 10-12½-15% but special requirements of book may call for lower royalties"; no advance. Published 12 titles in 1979; 15 in 1980, plans 15 in 1981. State availability of photos and/or illustrations to accompany ms. Simultaneous and photocopied submissions OK. Reports in 1-2 months. SASE. Free book catalog.
Nonfiction: "We specialize in not being specialized; we look primarily for originality and quality." Publishes Americana; art; biography; business; economics; history; how-to; humor; medicine and psychiatry; nature; psychology; recreation; scientific; sports; and textbooks. Does not want to

see cookbooks, novels, poetry, inspirational/religious or erotica. Query.
Recent Nonfiction Titles: *The Almanac of American Letters*, by Randy Nelson.

KEATS PUBLISHING, INC., 36 Grove St., Box 876, New Canaan CT 06840. Editor: Ms. An Keats. Publishes hardcover and paperback originals and reprints, and two magazines on health and nutrition. Offers standard royalty contract. Advance varies. Free book catalog. Query with outline and sample chapter. Reports in 3 months. Enclose return postage.
Nonfiction: "Natural health, special interest. Also, mss with promotion and premium potential. In natural health, anything having to do with the current interest in ecology, natural health cookbooks, diet books, organic gardening, etc." Length: open.
Religion: "Largely in the conservative Protestant field."

J.J. KELLER & ASSOCIATES, INC., 145 W. Wisconsin Ave., Neenah WI 54956. (414)722-2848. Editor George McDowell. Research Librarian: John Breese. "Keller provides *updated* regulatory compliance information in a format which can be easily understood and applied in 'how-to-do-it' situations." Averages 10-12 titles/year. Pays by arrangement. Query. SASE.
Technical and Reference: "Working guides, handbooks and pamphlets covering the regulatory requirements for the motor carrier industry at both the federal and individual state levels. Technical and consumer publications pertaining to the International System of Units (Metric system of measurement); environmental publications pertaining to occupational health and safety." Recently published *Hazardous Waste Guide Series* (reference); and *1980 Emergency Response Guide* (D.O.T handbook).

KENT STATE UNIVERSITY PRESS, Kent State University, Kent OH 44242. (216)672-7913. Director: Paul H. Rohmann. Publishes hardcover and paperback originals and some reprints. Standard minimum book contract on net sales; rarely offers advance. Averages 10-12 titles/year. Free book catalog. "Always write a letter of inquiry before submitting mss. We can publish only a limited number of titles each year and can frequently tell in advance whether or not we would be interested in a particular ms. This practice saves both our time and that of the author, not to mention postage costs." Reports in 10 weeks. Enclose return postage.
Nonfiction: Especially interested in "scholarly works in history of high quality, particularly any titles of regional interest for Ohio. Also will consider scholarly biographies, literary studies, archeological research, the arts, and general nonfiction."
Recent Nonfiction Titles: *Hopewell Archeology*, by David S. Brose and N'omi Greber (archeology); *An Ohio Schoolmistress*, by Irene Hardy (19th century memoir); and *Lucy Breckinridge of Grove Hill*, by Mary D. Robertson (Civil War diary).

KERN PUBLICATIONS, Subsidiary of Data Dynamics, Inc., 190 Duck Hill Rd., Box 1029, Duxbury MA 02332. (617)934-0445. Senior Editor: Pam Korites. Publishes trade paperback originals. Averages 3 titles/year. Pays 15-25% royalty on wholesale price. Simultaneous and photocopied submissions OK. SASE. Reports in 2 weeks. Free book catalog.
Nonfiction: How-to, technical, textbook and computer software in book form. Subjects include business and economics, and computer software marketing and development. "We publish two lines of books: 1) computer software marketing, and 2) computer software development and computer programming. Our needs in the first category include anything that relates to the marketing of computer software. Examples are *Free-Lance Software Marketing* and *1981 Software Writers Market* (which we presently publish), case studies of successful software entrepreneurs, legal tips for software marketers, descriptions of specific markets for computer software, etc. In the second category, we are interested in books that include computer program listings. Of special interest are how-to books in this area, such as *How to Write Programs for Computer Graphics on a Microcomputer* and *Finite Element Analysis on Microcomputers*. We are also interested in nontechnical applications such as business applications, as long as they relate to microcomputers. Of special interest are computer-aided design and manufacturing, robotics, computer graphics, and computer-aided instruction. These last four topics need not relate exclusively to microcomputers. Also, our publications must be of immediate interest to the computer industry and must be highly professional in technical content. No mss of merely academic interest." Query or submit outline/synopsis and sample chapters.
Recent Nonfiction Titles: *Free-Lance Software Marketing*, by B.J. Korites (technical/reference); *Vector Methods in Computer Graphics*, by B.J. Korites (technical/reference); and *1981 Software Writer's Market*, staff-written (technical/reference).

KIRKLEY PRESS, INC., 8753 Mylander Ln., Baltimore MD 21204. Editor: Jay Weitzel. Publishes paperback 16-page booklets and paycheck stuffer folders. "We buy mss outright and pay upon acceptance. Payment (total) varies between $200 and $300, depending on subject and strength with which written. Sample of our material sent on request." Send complete ms. "We try to answer in 2 weeks." Enclose return postage.

Business: "We publish small booklets which are sold to businesses for distribution to the employee. They attempt to stimulate or motivate the employee to improve work habits. Basically they are pep talks for the employee. We need writers who are so close to the problems of present-day employee attitudes that they can take one of those problems and write about it in a warm, human, understanding, personal style and language that will appeal to the employee and which the employer will find to his advantage to distribute to the employees." Length: 2,400-2,600 words.

Recent Nonfiction Titles: *Get the Breaks*, by W. Hallstead; *The I in Inflation*; and *If You Were the Boss*, by D. Shiel.

B. KLEIN PUBLICATIONS, Box 8503, Coral Springs FL 33065. (305)752-1708. Editor-in-Chief: Bernard Klein. Hardcover and paperback originals. Specializes in directories, annuals, who's who type of books; bibliography, business opportunity, reference books. Published 10 titles in 1979; plans 10-15 in 1980, 15-20 in 1981. Pays 10% royalty on wholesale price, "but we're negotiable." Advance "depends on many factors." Markets books by direct mail and mail order. Simultaneous and photocopied submissions OK. Reports in 1-2 weeks. SASE. Catalog for SASE.

Nonfiction: Business, hobbies, how-to, reference, self-help, directories and bibliographies. Query or submit outline/synopsis and sample chapters or complete ms.

Recent Nonfiction Titles: *Reference Encyclopedia of the American Indian*; *Your Business, Your Son and You,* by J. McQuaig (nonfiction); *Guide to American Directories*; and *Mail Order Business Directory.*

ALFRED A. KNOPF, INC., 201 E. 50th St., New York NY 10022. (212)751-2600. Senior Editor: Ashbel Green. Children's Book Editor: Ms. Frances Foster. Publishes hardcover and paperback originals (90%) and paperback reprints (10%). Published 139 titles in 1981. Royalties and advance "vary." Simultaneous (if so informed) and photocopied submissions OK. Reports in 2-4 weeks. Book catalog for SASE.

Nonfiction: Book-length nonfiction, including books of scholarly merit on special subjects. Preferred length: 40,000-150,000 words. "A good nonfiction writer should be able to follow the latest scholarship in any field of human knowledge, and fill in the abstractions of scholarship for the benefit of the general reader by means of good, concrete, sensory reporting." Query.

Recent Nonfiction Titles: *The Mapmakers*, by J. Wiford (geography); *Peter The Great*, by R. Massie (biography); and *The Winning Weapon*, by G. Hekken (history).

Fiction: Publishes book-length fiction of literary merit by known or unknown writers. Length: 30,000-150,000 words. Submit complete ms.

Recent Fiction Titles: *Tar Baby*, by T. Morrison; and *The Rat on Fire*, by G.V. Higgins.

KNOWLEDGE INDUSTRY PUBLICATIONS, INC., 701 Westchester Ave., White Plains NY 10604. (914)694-8686. Editor-in-Chief: E. Sigel. Publishes hardcover and paperback originals. Averages 30 titles/year. Offers 5%-10% royalty on wholesale price; also buys mss by outright purchase for minimum $500. Offers minimum $500 advance. No simultaneous submissions; photocopied submissions OK. SASE. Reports in 2 weeks. Free book catalog.

Nonfiction: Business/economics. Especially needs "communication and information technologies, TV and video, library and information science." Query first, then submit outline/synopsis and sample chapters.

Recent Nonfiction Titles: *Who Owns the Media*, by Conpaine; *Video Discs*, by Sigel; and *Library Information Manager's Guide to Online Services*, by Hoover.

THE KNOWLEDGE TREE GROUP, INC., 360 Park Ave. S., New York NY 10010. (212)689-1500. Contact: Marc D. Zarowin. Averages 50 titles/year. Buys some mss outright for $50-600. Book catalog for 5x7 SAE and 2 first class stamps.

Nonfiction: Subjects include Americana, animals, health, history, hobbies, nature, psychology, recreation, sports and travel. Query. All unsolicited mss are returned unopened.

Fiction: Adventure, fantasy, historical, humor, mystery, science fiction and suspense. Query. All unsolicited mss are returned unopened.

JOHN KNOX PRESS, 341 Ponce de Leon Ave. NE, Atlanta GA 30308. (404)873-1531. Director: Richard A. Ray. Publishes hardcover and paperback originals and paperback reprints. Publishes 42 titles/year. Pays royalty on retail price; no advance. Photocopied submissions OK. SASE. Free book catalog.

Nonfiction: "We publish books dealing with Biblical studies, Christian faith and life, family relationships, Christian education, and the relationship of faith to history and culture." Query or submit outline/synopsis and sample chapters to R. Donald Hardy, associate editor. Recently published *Biblical Ethics*, by R.E.O. White; *Survival Papers for Young Mothers*, by D. Aydt Holmes; and *You Can Become Whole Again: A Guide to Healing for Christians*, by Jolonda Miller.

KODANSHA INTERNATIONAL, LTD., 12-21, Otowa 2-chome, Bunkyo-ku, Tokyo 112, Japan. Hardcover originals and a limited number of paperback originals. Pays 3-8% royalty, either against sales or printing; determined case by case. Advance varies. Published 38 titles in 1979, 43 in 1980; plans 50 in 1981. Markets trade books through Harper & Row and by direct mail to Asian studies specialists. State availability of prints or transparencies to illustrate ms. Photocopied submissions OK. SAE and International Reply Coupons. Reports in 2-4 months. Free book catalog from 10 E. 53 St., New York NY 10022.
Nonfiction: "Books about Japan and the Far East of interest to American general readers or specialists. Translations of Japanese classics in all fields. Books on arts and crafts of highest quality." Oriental arts and crafts of the world, especially ceramics. Books on Oriental cooking; on economics related to Japan and Asia; how-to on arts and crafts and Oriental martial arts. Biography, philosophy, photography, politics, psychology, comparative religion, reference and sociology. Query. "We especially welcome innovative approaches to arts and crafts subjects. Currently, we are actively soliciting translations of previously untranslated modern Japanese fiction and classics of modern Japanese political science and sociology."
Recent Nonfiction Titles: *Shigaraki, Potters' Valley*, by L.A. Cort (crafts); *A History of Japanese Literature*, by S. Kato; *Javanese Silat: The Fighting Art of Perisai Dili*, by Q. Chambers and D.F. Draeger (martial arts).
Recent Fiction Title: *Into a Black Sun*, by T. Kaiko (Vietnam at war as witnessed by a neutral Asian bystander).

KARL KRAMER GMBH & CO., Rotebuhlstrasse 40, D-7000, Stuttgart, Germany. 49-711-62-08-93. President/Editorial Director: Karl H. Kramer. Senior Editor: Annemarie Bosch. Publishes hardcover and paperback originals. Published 13 titles in 1979 and 12 in 1980. Pays 10% minimum royalty; offers $500-$1,000 average advance. SASE. Reports in 2 months. Free book catalog.
Nonfiction: Architecture. Submit outline/synopsis and sample chapters or complete ms.
Recent Nonfiction Titles: *Architektur in Umbruch*, by J. Joedicke (methods in modern architecture); *Bent Wood Furniture*, by G. Candilis (history of this furniture); and *Hans Scharoun*, by P.B. Jones (monograph).

LAKEWOOD BOOKS, 4 Park Ave., New York NY 10016. Editorial Director: Donald Wigal, PhD. Publishes 96- and 64-page paperback originals. Publishes 38 titles/year. Pays on a work-for-hire basis. "Few exceptions." Simultaneous and photocopied submissions OK. Reports in 2 months.
Nonfiction: "Our books are apparently bought by women who have families, or are attracted to a rather middle-of-the-road life style. Our titles are mainly self-help (exercise, diet) and informational (finances, how-to). We avoid controversial topics. Nonfiction which ties in with specific products welcomed by query. (e.g., '100 Tips on Using Brand X in the Garden')." No fiction, poetry, astrology, puzzle, cookbook or sport titles needed at present (1981-2)."
Recent Nonfiction Title: *Your Teenager's Diet*, by Joseph Duffy, PhD (nutrition).
Tips: "Consider the competition and see what seems to be working. Find a slightly new approach and blend the tried-and-true with the innovative. An entertaining, yet informative book with a single concept sells the best, e.g., 'The Flat Tummy Book.' "

LAME JOHNNY PRESS, Box 66, Hermosa SD 57744. (605)255-4466. Publisher: Linda M. Hasselstrom. Publishes hardcover and trade paperback originals (98%), and hardcover reprints (2%). Average 1-6 titles/year. Pays 30-50% royalty on wholesale price. Photocopied submissions OK. SASE. Reports in 6 weeks. Book catalog for business size SAE and 2 first class stamps.
Nonfiction: How-to and self-help. Subjects include Americana and history. "We do not search for nonfiction titles; accept only occasional rare ones that originate in the Great Plains." Submit complete ms.
Recent Nonfiction Titles: *The Book Book: A Publishing Handbook (for Beginners & Others)*, by L.M. Hasselstrom (how-to); and *Next-Year Country: One Woman's View*, by Alma Phillip (informal history).
Fiction: Historical (on the Great Plains only) and western. "We consider only works by/about Great Plains, loosely defined. Quality determines acceptance." Submit complete ms.
Recent Fiction Titles: *The Indian Maiden's Captivity/Heart of the Country*, by E.R. Zietlow (historical; 2 novels in 1 vol.); and *A Country for Old Men and Other Stories*, by Zietlow (Great Plains short stories).

Poetry: "Quality determines acceptance; must be by/about the Great Plains." Submit complete ms.

Recent Poetry Titles: *Mato Come Heal Me*, by Craig Volk (based on history; Indian youth, 1880's); *Delivery*, by Carolyn Bell (on woman's awakening); and *Where is Dancer's Hill?*, by Robert Schuler (short poems, influenced by Indian history and myth).

Tips: "Our readers in the Great Plains seek cultural pride. Readers outside the plains seek information, entertainment, and high-quality writing. Our authors participate in the publishing of their books; sometimes by helping finance the book (but we're *not* a subsidy publisher); sometimes in other ways. The entire process remains personal, with the writer involved in every step if he/she wishes to be."

LANCASTER-MILLER PUBLISHERS, 3165 Adeline St., Berkeley CA 94703. (415)845-3782. Editor and Publisher: Richard Schuettge. Publishes trade hardcover and paperback originals. Averages 6-7 titles/year. Pays 6-8% royalty on paperbacks; 10-12% on hardcover; offers $3,000-30,000 advance. Simultaneous and photocopied submissions OK. SASE. Reports in 2 weeks. Free book catalog.

Imprint: *Asian Humanities Press* (scholarly books, art and thought).

Nonfiction: Picture books, art books for trade and special markets. "Full color, black and white when appropriate." Art, photography, graphic design, architecture, industrial design for worldwide market. (Also picture books for western region.)

Recent Nonfiction Titles: *California Murals*, by Clark, Myers and Gordon (color photo book of mural art); *Woody Guthrie and Me*, by E. Robbin (intimate reminiscence); *Women in Buddhism*, by D. Paul (scholastic Buddhist tales and commentary); and *Joy of Automobile Repair*, by C.J. Becker (basic how-to auto repair).

LANDMARK BOOKS, 7847 12th Ave. S., Minneapolis MN 55420. Director: Robert A. Hill. Editor-in-Chief: Joyce Hovelsrud. Publishes hardcover and paperback originals. Pays standard royalty on retail price; no advance. Averages 6-10 titles/year. Photocopied and simultaneous submissions OK if so indicated. SASE. Reports in 6 weeks. Free book catalog and writer's guidelines.

Nonfiction: "We're a religious market looking for manuscripts which present tangible solutions to problems faced by the individual in society today and which address current issues as they can be related to the Bible. Material must be scripturally sound. We believe in a life-changing, dynamic gospel and are interested in material with impact. We do *not* publish watered-down religion." Query or submit complete ms.

Recent Nonfiction Titles: *Gift of Years*, by M. Wyatt and L. Woodward; *Blessed Fools*, by C. LeNoir; and *Letter to the Pope*, by Mary Eillen Twyman.

Fiction: Needs are limited. Query first.

LANE AND ASSOCIATES, INC., P.O. Box 3063, La Jolla CA 92038. (714)488-0747. President: Gloria J. Lane. Editorial Director: Dr. D.G. Shadwell. Publishes hardcover and paperback originals (90%) and paperback reprints (10%). Averages 15 titles/year. Pays 10-15% royalty on wholesale or retail price; offers average $200 advance. Buys some mss outright for $200-$500. Simultaneous and photocopied submissions OK. SASE. Reports in 6 weeks. Free book catalog for SASE.

Nonfiction: Americana, art, business/economics, history, how-to, philosophy, photography, psychology, reference, science, self-help, sociology, sports, technical and textbooks. Looking for technically-oriented books on any subject. Also, interested in unique self-help mss. No religion, fiction, politics or poetry. Submit outline and synopsis.

Recent Nonfiction Titles: *Unlock Your Mind and Be Free*, by Dr. E. Barnett (self-help); *Strategies, Structures and Systems Theory*, by Dr. R. Kuehne (self-help); and *Positive Concepts For Success (For Women Only)*, by G. Lane (business self help).

LARKSDALE PRESS, 133 S. Heights Blvd., Houston TX 77007. (713)869-9092. Publisher: James Goodman. Editor-in-Chief: Nancy Buquoi Adleman. Production Editor: Brad Sagstetter. Publishes hardcover and paperback originals. Published 3 titles in 1979, 8 in 1980; plans 10 in 1981. Pays standard royalty contract; no advance. Simultaneous (if so indicated) and photocopied submissions OK. "SASE, or no reply." Reports in 3 months.

Imprints: *The Linolean Press* (religious). *The Lindahl Press* (general). *Harle House* (mass market paperback).

Nonfiction: Religion (Christian doctrine). General trade publisher. No poetry, children's or humorous. Submit complete ms to Brad Sagstetter.

Recent Nonfiction Titles: *Search for Truth*, by Natasha Rawson; *How You Can Get Straight A's in College*, by Dale Rich; and *The End, The End*, by Bob Robin.

LAW-ARTS PUBLISHERS, 453 Greenwich St., New York NY 10013. Editorial Director: Joseph Taubman. Publishes hardcover and paperback originals (90%) and paperback reprints (10%). Published 10 titles in 1979. Pays 10% royalty; no advance. Simultaneous and photocopied submissions OK. Reports in 1 month. SASE. Free book catalog.
Nonfiction: Legal-related, in-depth textbooks; books on creative work, audiovisual techniques, management, publicity, etc. No photography books. Submit outline/synopsis and sample chapters. Recently published *Performing Arts Management and Law*, by J. Taubman; and *Professional Sports and the Law*, by L. Sobel.

SEYMOUR LAWRENCE, INC., 61 Beacon St., Boston MA 02108. Publisher: Seymour Lawrence. Editor: Merloyd Ludington Lawrence. Publishes hardcover and paperback originals. Seymour Lawrence books are published in association with the Delacorte Press. Royalty schedule: 10% to 5,000 copies; 12½% to 10,000; 15% thereafter on adult hardcover books. Published 15 titles in 1979, 9 in 1980; plans 15 in 1981. Send outline and sample chapters. SASE.
Nonfiction: Child care and development and behavioral science books for the general reader; no textbooks.
Recent Nonfiction Title: *Helen and Teacher*, by Joseph P. Lash (biography).
Fiction: Adult fiction.
Recent Fiction Title: *Jailbird*, by Kurt Vonnegut.

LE BEACON PRESSE, 621 Holt Ave., Iowa City IA 52240. (206)322-1431. Editorial Coordinator: Keith S. Gormezano. Publishes trade and mass market paperback originals and reprints. Averages 5-8 titles/year. Pays 20-25% royalty; buys some mss outright for $100-1,000. Simultaneous and photocopied submissions OK. SASE. Book catalog for business size envelope and 1 first class stamp (available after January, 1982).
Nonfiction: Humor, reference and technical. Subjects include Americana, art, business and economics, cooking and foods, photography, politics, recreation and travel. "In the near future, we will need 5 reference books, 3 books with political themes, and 3 autobiographical novels. Query. All unsolicited mss are returned unopened.
Recent Nonfiction Titles: *Who's Who Among Hispanic-Americans*, staff-written (reference); *Who's Who in Iowa*, staff-written (reference); and *Name Identification*, by Keith S. Gormezano (political).
Fiction: Adventure, erotica, ethnic, experimental, historical, horror, humor, mystery, science fiction and suspense. "Four fiction titles are being planned for 1983." Query. All unsolicited mss are returned unopened.
Poetry: "Will publish 3, 36-page poetry books." Submit maximum 3 poems.
Recent Poetry Titles: *36 Flavours*, by Gormezano (ethnic).

LEBHAR-FRIEDMAN, 425 Park Ave., New York NY 10022. (212)371-9400. Executive Editor: Barbara Miller. Marketing Director: Joseph Morse. Publishes hardcover and paperback originals (100%). Averages 17-20 titles/year. Pays royalty on wholesale price; no advance. Photocopied submissions OK. Reports in 4-8 weeks. SASE. Book catalog for SASE.
Nonfiction: "Most of our books published are for the retail business field (food service and supermarket). Our market is directed at both the retailer, administrator, and the college and junior college student wishing to enter the field and needing a good hard look at the facts and how-to's of the business. We are not interested in the generalist approach but with specifics that will be of importance to the business person." Submit outline/synopsis and sample chapters. Recently published *Wage & Hour Handbook*, by Branch and Swann (restaurant); *Food Merchandising*, by Leed & German (supermarket); and *Fast Food: The Endless Shakeout*, by Emerson.

LEISURE BOOKS, (formerly Belmont Tower Books/Leisure Books) Nordon Publications, Inc., 2 Park Ave., New York NY 10016. (212)679-7707. Editor-in-Chief: Milburn Smith. Publishes paperback originals (70%) and reprints (30%). Published 168 titles in 1980, 170 in 1981. Pays 4-6% royalty or $500-1,500 for outright purchase; average advance $1,500. Simultaneous and photocopied submissions OK. SASE. Reports in 2-3 months. Book catalog for SASE.
Nonfiction: Biography, history, humor, self-help, and sports. "We publish very little nonfiction, but what we do publish must be timely and popularly oriented with a core of solid information. We do not want to see manuscripts on crafts, technical or texts." Query or submit outline/synopsis and sample chapters.
Recent Nonfiction Titles: *Daddy Cooles*, by Martin Rugoff; *Investment Tips for Today's Woman*, by Roslyn Nemet (Tiara); *Merv*, by Michael B. Druxman.
Fiction: Adventure, astrology, fantasy, gothic, historical, humor, mainstream, mystery, romance, science fiction, suspense, western, and war. "Of the books we publish each year, most are category novels, so we have a continual need for category fiction of nearly all sorts. We are also interested in

seeing general novels of a popular nature. We do not want any juvenile or young adult manuscripts." Send 1-page synopsis and entire ms, or synopsis and sample chapters.
Recent Fiction Titles: *Island Flame*, by Karen Robards (historical romance); *Straw Boss*, by Stephen Longstreet (novel); Timequest series, by William Tedford (science fiction); *Through Eyes of Evil*, by Alpha Blair (occult).

LESTER AND ORPEN DENNYS, LTD., PUBLISHERS, 78 Sullivan St., Toronto, Ontario M5T 1C1, Canada. (416)863-6402. President: Malcolm Lester. Vice President: Louise Dennys. Publishes hardcover and trade paperback originals. Offers standard minimum book contract of 10-12½-15% on retail price. Averages 20 titles/year. Free book catalog. Will consider photocopied submissions. Query with outline and one sample chapter showing style and treatment. Submit complete ms only for fiction, or if writer has been published before. Reports in 2 months. SAE and International Reply Coupons.
General Fiction and Nonfiction: "Our basic philosophy of publishing only carefully selected books is stronger than ever; each and every title reflects a uniqueness in concept, careful and imaginative editing and design, and powerful and creative promotion." Publishes adult trade fiction, biography, sociology, economics and philosophy.
Recent Titles: *Images: Contemporary Canadian Realism*, by Marci and Louise Lipman; *Ways of Escape*, by Graham Greene; and *Upon This Rock*, by Philippe van Rindt (fiction).

LIBERATOR PRESS, Box 7128, Chicago IL 60680. (312)243-3791. Vice-President: Douglass Rowe. Publishes hardcover and paperback originals (80%) and paperback reprints (20%). Averages 6 titles/year. Pays 5-11% royalty on retail price. Average advance: $500. Simultaneous and photocopied submissions OK. SASE. Reports in 2 months. Free book catalog.
Nonfiction: History; politics; Afro-American; sociology (American labor movement); women; and Asia (modern China). No self-help; how-to; or technical. "Our audience is primarily concerned with current events and the political arena. They want to learn about the real world and what makes it tick." Submit outline/synopsis and author biography.
Recent Nonfiction Titles: *China Notebook*, by J. Myrdal; *Battered Women: Shattered Lives*, by Kathleen H. Hofeller (wife abuse); and *The Mossadegh Era*, by Sepehr Zabih (Iran).

****LIBRA PUBLISHERS, INC.**, 391 Willets Rd., Roslyn Heights NY 11577. (516)484-4950. Publishes hardcover and paperback originals. Specializes in the behavioral sciences. Averages 15 titles/year. 10-15% royalty on retail price; no advance. Subsidy publishes a small percentage of books (those which have obvious marketing problems or are too specialized). Simultaneous and photocopied submissions OK. Report in 1-2 weeks. SASE. Free book catalog.
Nonfiction: Mss in all subject areas will be given consideration, but main interest is in the behavioral sciences. Submit outline/synopsis and sample chapters. Recently published *Emotional Aspects of Heart Disease*, by H. Giest, Ph.D.; *The Counseling Process: A Cognitive Behavioral Approach*, by J. Lembo, Ph.D.; and *The Underachievers*, by Paul Freidman (New York City teaching problems).

LIBRARIES UNLIMITED, Box 263, Littleton CO 80160. (303)770-1220. Editor-in-Chief: Bohdan S. Wynar. Publishes hardcover and paperback originals (95%) and hardcover reprints (5%). Averages 20 titles/year. Specializes in library science and reference books, 10% royalty on net sales; advance averages $500. Marketed by direct mail to 40,000 libraries in this country and abroad. Query or submit outline/synopsis and sample chapters. All prospective authors are required to fill out an author questionnaire. Query if photos/illustrations are to accompany ms. Reports in 2 months. SASE. Free book catalog.
Nonfiction: Publishes reference and library science text books. *Introduction to Cataloging and Classification*, by Bohdan S. Wynar; *Images in a Crystal Ball*, by Lillian B. Wehmeyer (world futures in novels for young people); and *US Copyright Documents*, by Jerome K. Miller.

LIGHT BOOKS, Box 425, Marlton NJ 08053. Publisher: Paul Castle. Publishes hardcover and paperback originals. Averages 4-6 titles/year. Pays 10-15% royalty on wholesale or retail price; no advance. Simultaneous and photocopied submissions OK. SASE. Reports in 4 weeks.
Nonfiction: Photography. "We are always interested in good mss on technique and/or business of photography. We especially want mss on *marketing* one's photography as art or home decor. We don't want mss on art criticism of photography, collections of art photos, basic photo teaching books, or anything other than books on the technique and/or business of photography. Query, if the idea is good, we'll ask for outline/synopsis and sample chapters." Recently published *How to Produce and Mass Market Your Creative Photography*, by Kenneth Townend; and *Outdoor Photography How to Shoot it, How to Sell it*, by Robert McQuilkin.
Tips: "We need more anecdotes and illustrations (word) to amplify the writer's points."

LIGUORI PUBLICATIONS, Book and Pamphlet Dept., 1 Liguori Dr., Liguori MO 63057. (314)464-2500. Editor-in-Chief: Rev. Christopher Farrell, C.SS.R. Managing Editor: Roger Marchand. Publishes paperback originals. Specializes in Catholic-Christian religious materials. Published 33 titles in 1980. Pays 8% royalty on books; flat fee on pamphlets and teacher's guides; no advance. Query or submit outline/synopsis and sample chapter; "never submit total book." State availability of photos and/or illustrations. Photocopied submissions OK. Reports in 6-8 weeks. SASE. Free book catalog.
Nonfiction: Publishes doctrinal, inspirational, Biblical, self-help and educational materials.
Recent Nonfiction Titles: *How to Deal with Difficult People*, by Anthony Costello; *The Illustrated Catechism*; and *Communidades Eclesiales de Base.*
Tips: "People seek light on real-life concerns. Writers lead and educate in light of Good News shared in faith-community."

*LION BOOKS, 111 E. 39th St., New York NY 10016. Editorial Director: Harriet Ross. Publishes originals (80%) and reprints (20%). Averages 16 titles/year. Pays 7-12% royalty based on wholesale price or retail price, or pays $500-30,000 outright purchase price; advance varies. Photocopied submissions OK. Reports in 4 weeks. SASE.
Nonfiction: Biography (in all areas, especially political); African crafts; black historical nonfiction; and sports (how-to on gymnastics, swimming, riding). Query or submit complete ms.
Recent Titles: *Phillis Wheatey, Negro Slave*, by Jensen; *Good Morning, Please!*, by Sullivan; and *Winning With Science*, by Loiry (grants, scholarships for college).

LIPPINCOTT JUNIOR BOOKS, 10 E. 53rd St., New York NY 10022. Editorial Director: Patricia Allen. Submit all manuscripts to Patricia Allen. Publishes trade books for kindergarten through high school. Standard royalty schedule on retail price. Reports in 8-10 weeks. Free book catalog.
Fiction and Nonfiction: For children of all ages. Particularly interested in social sciences and self-help.
Recent Titles: *Lots of Rot*, by V. Cobb (science); *Computers in Your Life*, by Berger (science); and *The Waiting Game*, by Bunting (hi-lo fiction).

LITTLE, BROWN AND CO., INC., 34 Beacon St., Boston MA 02106. Publishes hardcover and paperback originals and paperback reprints. Publishes 105 titles/year. "Royalty and advance agreements vary from book to book and are discussed with the author at the time an offer is made." Reports in 6-8 weeks for queries/proposals. SASE. Free book catalog.
Nonfiction: "Some how-to books, select and distinctive cookbooks, biographies, history, science and sports." Query or submit outline/synopsis and sample chapters.
Recent Nonfiction Titles: *Male Sexuality: A Guide to Sexual Fulfillment*, by B. Zilbergeld, Ph.D.; *Connections*, by James Burke; *American Caesar: Douglas MacArthur 1880-1964*, by William Manchester; and *Crockett's Indoor Garden*;, by James Underwood Crockett.
Fiction: Contemporary popular fiction as well as fiction of literary distinction; some mysteries, suspense novels and adventure novels. "Our poetry list is extremely limited; those collections of poems that we do publish are usually the work of poets who have gained recognition through publication in literary reviews and various periodicals." Query or submit outline/synopsis and sample chapters.
Recent Fiction Titles: *War and Remembrance*, by Herman Wouk; and *The Executioner's Song*, by Norman Mailer.

*LLEWELLYN PUBLICATIONS, Box 43383, St. Paul MN 55164. (612)291-1970. President: Carl L. Weschcke. Publishes hardcover and trade paperback originals. Averages 6-12 titles/year. Subsidy publishes 5% of books "if it appears to be a viable preposition with too limited a market for our economics to justify, and if the author has the resources." Pays 10% maximum royalty on both wholesale and retail price. Simultaneous and photocopied submissions OK. SASE. Reports in 2 weeks on queries; 2 months on mss. Book catalog 50¢.
Nonfiction: "Coffee table" book, how-to, reference, self-help and textbook. Subjects include nature, philosophy, psychology and religion. "We specialize in astrology and the occult, broadly defined. We cater to sincere students and professionals in astrology, students and intelligent lay-people interested in the reality of astrology and occultism, the self-help and the farming and gardening market (for lunar and organic planting). We only want astrology or occult—but not 'pop' stuff! No 'celebrity' stuff! No satanist or devil possession, etc." Submit outline/synopsis and sample chapters or complete ms.
Recent Nonfiction Titles: *The Llewellyn Practical Guide to Astral Projection*, by Melita Denning and Osborne Phillips (occult; parasychology: out-of-body-experience); *Voudoun Fire: The Living Reality of Mystical Religion*, by Denning and Phillips (religion or occult or parapsychology:

phenonmena of mysticism); and *The Secret Science*, by John Baines (occult philosophy).
Fiction: Erotica ("possible—with a Tantric theme"); mystery ("possible—with an occult theme"); science fiction (possible—with an occult theme); and suspense (possible—with an occult theme). "We're booked up pretty solid, but will consider exceptional works. No 'satanist,' 'devil-worship,' 'demon possession,' 'saved from witchcraft,' or material from writers not actually—and really—knowledgeable about the occult or parapsychological theme or data included in faction, or nonfiction." Query.
Recent Fiction Title: *The Secrets of Dr. Taverner*, by Dion Fortune (short stories of ceremonial magic and psychotherapy with the aid of supersensible knowledge).

*LONE STAR PUBLISHERS, INC., Box 9774, Austin TX 78766. (512)255-2333. Editorial Director: A.J. Lerager. Publishes hardcover and paperback originals. Averages 3 titles/year. Subsidy publishes approximately 1 title/year based on "the subject matter, the author's reputation, the potential market, the capital investment, etc." Pays 12½-15% royalty on wholesale or retail price; no advance. Simultaneous and photocopied submissions OK. Reports in 3 weeks. SASE. Free book catalog.
Nonfiction: College textbooks; how-to; cookbooks; self-help and sports. No poetry. Query. Recently published *The Texas Press Women's Cookbook,* by D. Hunt, K. Pill and B. Field (cookbook); *Poverty, Manpower, & Social Security,* by P. Brinker and J. Klos (college text); and *Business Policy*, and *Economics for the Voter*, by M.L. Greenhut and Charles Stewart.

LONGMAN INC., 19 W. 44th St., New York NY 10036. (212)764-3950. President: Lothar Simon. Editorial Director, College Division: Lane Akers. Senior Editor, College Division: Irving Rockwood. Editorial Director, English as a Second Language: Larry Anger. Publishes hardcover and paperback originals. Publishes 60 titles/year. Pays variable royalty; offers average $1,000 advance. Photocopied submissions OK. SASE. Reports in 6 weeks.
Nonfiction: Textbooks only (college and professional). History, music, politics, psychology, reference, sociology and English as a second language. No trade, art or juvenile. Query.
Recent Nonfiction Titles: *Education in a Free Society*, Fourth Edition, by Rippa; *Clinical Supervision*, by Acheson and Gall (education); and *Elections in America*, Second Edition, by Pomper (political science).

LOTHROP, LEE & SHEPARD BOOKS, (a division of William Morrow Company), 105 Madison Ave., New York NY 10016. (212)889-3050. Editor-in-Chief: Dorothy Briley. Hardcover original children's books only. Royalty and advance vary according to type of book. Averages 50 titles/year. State availability of photos and/or illustrations to accompany ms. Photocopied submissions OK, but originals preferred. Reports in 4-6 weeks. SASE. Free book catalog.
Juveniles: Publishes picture books, biography, hobbies, and sports books. Submit outline/synopsis and sample chapters for nonfiction. Juvenile fiction emphasis on contemporary novels, but also includes adventure, fantasy, historical, humorous, fiction. Recently published *The Kissimmee Kid*, by Vera and Bill cleaver; *You Can't Be Timid*, by Betty Lou English (photoessay on orchestra); and *Can't Catch Me, I'm the Gingerbread Man*, by Jamie Bilson

LOUISIANA STATE UNIVERSITY PRESS, Baton Rouge LA 70803. (504)388-2071. Editor: Beverly Jarrett. Director: L.E. Phillabaum. Averages 60 titles/year. Pays royalty on wholesale price; no advance. Photocopied submissions OK. SASE. Reports in 2 weeks (queries); 1-6 months (mss). Free book catalog.
Nonfiction: "We would like to have mss on humanities and social sciences, with special emphasis on Southern history and literature; Southern studies; French studies; political philosophy; music, especially jazz." Query.
Recent Nonfiction Titles: *The Achievement of Robert Penn Warren*, by James Justus (Southern literature); and *Rice and Slaves*, by Dan Littlefield (Southern history).

LOYOLA UNIVERSITY PRESS, 3441 N. Ashland, Chicago IL 60657. (312)281-1818. Director: the Rev. Daniel Flaherty. Assistant Director: Mary FitzGerald. Published 8 titles in 1978; 10 in 1979. Pays 10% royalty; no advance. Simultaneous and photocopied submissions OK. SASE. Reports in 1 month.
Nonfiction: History and religion. Query. Recently published *Reading of the Wreck*, by Milward; and *Abortion: Development of Catholic Perspective*, by Connery.

MAC PUBLISHING, INC., Box 7037, Colorado Springs CO 80933. (303)687-6453. Editor: Claude A. Wiatrowski. Publishes hardcover and trade paperback originals and reprints. Averages 2 titles/year. Pays 8-12% royalty on wholesale price. Simultaneous and photocopied submissions OK. SASE. Reports in 1 month.

Nonfiction: Cookbook, how-to, illustrated book and reference. Subjects include cooking and foods, history, hobbies, photography and travel. "We cover these subjects only as they relate to railroads, model railroading, and western US and Canada. We prefer railroad subjects but will consider any western subject. Must be illustrated with photos. We especially need specific railroad histories and will consider rewrites of college theses. No topics other than railroads, model railroading and western subjects." Query or submit outline/synopsis and sample chapters.

Recent Nonfiction Titles: *RR Maps East*, (reference); *RR Maps West* (reference); and *The Colorado and Wyoming RR*, by William McKenzie (pictorial history).

Tips: "Supply as much well-researched *information*, both written and pictorial, as possible on *new subjects.*"

McCLELLAND AND STEWART, LTD., 25 Hollinger Rd., Toronto, Ontario, Canada M4B 3G2. Editor-in-Chief: J.G. McClelland. Publishes hardcover and paperback originals. Offers sliding scale of royalty on copies sold. Advance varies. Free book catalog. Submit outline and sample chapters for nonfiction and fiction. Reports in 6 weeks, average. SAE and International Reply Coupons.

Nonfiction, Poetry and Fiction: Publishes "Canadian fiction and poetry. Nonfiction in the humanities and social sciences, with emphasis on Canadian concerns. Coffee table books on art, architecture, sculpture and Canadian history." Will also consider general adult trade fiction, biography, history, nature, photography, politics, sociology, textbooks.

McCORMICK-MATHERS PUBLISHING CO., 135 W. 50th St., New York NY 10020. President: Joseph W. Berkery. Publishes supplementary materials, mostly workbooks, for classroom use grades kindergarten through 12. Contract negotiated by flat fee or royalty. Averages 75 titles/year. Will consider photocopied submissions. Submit outline and sample chapters. Reports as soon as possible. Enclose return postage.

Nonfiction: Text materials within the el-hi age range geared to classroom use, with general appeal: inner-city, rural suburban settings. Reading level primarily at or below grade level. All materials rewritten.

Recent Nonfiction Title: *Read On*, by W. Valmont (reading). "We do not use short stories, juvenile fiction or adult fiction. Such submissions are returned. Class room-use materials only."

MARGARET K. McELDERRY BOOKS, Atheneum Publishers, Inc., 597 5th Ave., New York NY 10017. Editor: Margaret K. McElderry. Publishes hardcover originals. Publishes 25-30 titles/year. Pays royalty on retail price. Reports in 6 weeks. SASE.

Nonfiction and Fiction: Quality material for preschoolers to 18-year-olds.

Recent Titles: *The Dark is Rising*, by Susan Cooper (sequence of fantasy titles); and *On the Land*, by Elinor Horowitz (history of US agriculture).

McFARLAND & COMPANY, INC., PUBLISHERS, Box 611, Jefferson NC 28640. (919)246-4460. President: Robert Franklin. Publishes hardcover and trade paperback originals. Averages 12 titles/year. Pays 10-15% royalty on gross sales income; no advance. Simultaneous and photocopied submissions OK. Reports on queries "same day"; 1 week on mss. Free brochure.

Nonfiction: Biography, reference, technical and professional. Subjects include Americana, art, business and economics, health, film/cinema/radio/TV, history, literature, hobbies, librarianship, music, politics, parapsychology, psychology, recreation, religion, and sociology. "We will consider *any* scholarly book. Reference books are particularly wanted—fresh material (i.e., not in head-to-head competition with an established title). Librarianship. Scholarly monographs in women's studies, literature, world affairs, drama/theater, film/TV, health care, chess. We don't like mss of fewer than 200 double-spaced typed pages. Our audience consists of libraries, mainly. Also professional schools' textbook users, and some individuals such as college professors. Our film books are the only ones going to bookstores." No memoirs, poetry, children's books, collections of personal essays. Query or submit outline/synopsis and sample chapters.

Recent Nonfiction Titles: *Free Magazines for Libraries*, by Adeline M. Smith (reference); *Dental Care in Society*, by Fredericks et al. (professional textbook); *Brezhnev: Soviet Politician*, by Paul J. Murphy (biography); and *Films Ex Libris: Literature on 16mm and Video*, by Salvatore J. Parlato (reference).

Tips: "Don't worry about 'writing skills'—we have editors. What we want is real *knowledge* of an area in which there is not good information coverage at present. Plus reliability (so we don't feel we have to check everything)."

McGRAW-HILL BOOK CO., 1221 Avenue of the Americas, New York NY 10020. Hardcover and paperback originals, reprints, translations and anthologies. Pays 10-12½-15% royalty. Submit outline and sample chapter; unsolicited mss rarely accepted. Reports in 3 weeks. SASE.

General Trade Division: "McGraw-Hill Trade Division is no longer assessing unsolicited manuscripts. Rising costs have made it uneconomical for us to employ skilled editors to read all manuscripts without consideration of the company's area of interest or the chances of achieving success on publication. All mss not sought by McGraw-Hill will be returned unopened to the sender via 4th-class manuscript rate, regardless of the postal rate selected by the sender."

Professional and Reference: Publishes books for engineers, architects, scientists and business people who need information on the professional level. Some of these books also find use in college and technical institute courses. This division also publishes multi-volume encyclopedias (which are usually staff-prepared using work from outside contributors who are specialists in their fields) and one-volume encyclopedias prepared by experts in a given field. The professional books are usually written by graduate engineers, architects, scientists or business people (such as accountants, lawyers, stockbrokers, etc.) Authors of the professional books are expected to be highly qualified in their fields. Such qualifications are the result of education and experience in the field; these qualifications are prerequisite for authorship. The multi-volume encyclopedias rarely accept contributions from freelancers because the above education and experience qualifications are also necessary. Single-volume encyclopedias are usually prepared by subject specialists; again freelancers are seldom used unless they have the necessary experience and educational background. Publisher: Tyler G. Hicks; Multi/volume Encyclopedia Editor-in-Chief: Sybil Parker; Behavioral Science Editor-in-Chief: Thomas Quinn; Business Editor-in-Chief: William Sabin; Architecture and Engineering Editor-in-Chief: Jeremy Robinson; Handbooks and Technical Books Editor-in-Chief: Harold B. Crawford.

College Textbooks: The College Division publishes textbooks. The writer must know the college curriculum and course structure. Also publishes scientific texts and reference books in business, economics, computers, engineering, social sciences, physical sciences, mathematics. Material should be scientifically and factually accurate. Most, but not all, books should be designed for existing courses offered in various disciplines of study. Books should have superior presentations and be more up-to-date than existing textbooks. Editorial Director: P.D. Nalle; Editor-in-Chief, Business, Economics, and Computing: David M. Edwards; Editor-in-Chief, Engineering: B.J. Clark; Editor-in-Chief, Arts and Sciences: Donald E. Chatham. *Health Professions:* Medical and nursing. Publisher: J. Dereck Jeffers.

High School and Vocational Textbooks: The Gregg Division publishes instructional materials in two main areas, business and office education (accounting, data processing, business communication, business law, business mathematics and machines, management and supervision, secretarial and clerical, records management, shorthand, typing, adult basic education) and career and vocational education (career development, marketing and distribution, public and personal services, applied arts and sciences, technical and industrial education, consumer education, health occupations, and agribusiness). Materials must be accurate, with clearly stated objectives, and should reflect a structuring of technical and interpersonal skills which mesh with both career clustering and course content. D. Cripps, Editor-in-Chief, Accounting, Computing, and Data Processing; D.E. Hepler, Executive Editor, Trade and Technical Education; Gail Modlin, Executive Editor, Shorthand and Typing; Cynthia Newby, Executive Editor, Business and Office, Distributive, and Adult Basic Education.

DAVID McKAY CO., INC., 2 Park Ave., New York NY 10016. Editor: James Louttit. Publishes hardcover and paperback originals. "No unsolicited manuscripts or proposals considered or acknowledged."

MACMILLAN OF CANADA, 146 Front St., W., Suite 685, Toronto, Ontario, Canada M5J 1G2. Publisher: Douglas M. Gibson. Executive Editor: Colleen Dunsen. Publishes hardcover originals and paperback reprints. Averages 25 titles/year. 10% royalty on retail price. Sample chapters and outlines only acceptable form of submission. Reports in 6 weeks. SAE and International Reply Coupons. Book catalog for SAE and International Reply Coupons.

Nonfiction: "We publish international and Canadian books of all kinds. Biography; history; art; current affairs; how-to; and juveniles. Particularly looking for good topical nonfiction."

Recent Nonfiction Titles: *Lawyers,* by Jack Batten (general nonfiction); *The Back Doctor,* by Dr. Hamilton Hall (medical advice); and *The Little Immigrants,* by Kenneth Bagnell (child immigration to Canada 1870-1930).

Fiction: Query. Recently published *From the Fifteenth District,* by Mavis Gallant; *The Resurrection of Joseph Bourne,* by Jack Hodgins; and *Voices In Time,* by Hugh MacLennan.

MACMILLAN PUBLISHING CO., INC., 866 3rd Ave., New York NY 10022. Publishes hardcover and paperback originals and reprints. Published 128 titles in 1979, 145 in 1980. Will consider photocopied submissions. Send query letter before sending ms. Address all mss except juveniles to

Mrs. R. Simons, Trade Editorial Department; children's books to Children's Book Department. Enclose return postage.
Fiction and Nonfiction: Publishes adult fiction and nonfiction. Length: 75,000 words minimum.
Juveniles: Children's books.

MADRONA PUBLISHERS, INC., 2116 Western Ave., Seattle WA 98121. (206)624-6840. President: Daniel J. Levant. Editorial Director: Sara Levant. Publishes hardcover and paperback originals (90%) and paperback reprints (10%). Averages 15 titles/year. Pays 7½-15% royalty on wholesale or retail price; offers $1,000 average advance. Simultaneous and photocopied submissions OK. SASE. Reports in 6 weeks. Free book catalog.
Nonfiction: Americana, biography, cookbooks, cooking and foods, health, history, hobbies, how-to, humor, photography, politics, psychology, recreation, self-help and travel. Query, submit outline/synopsis and sample chapters or complete ms.
Recent Nonfiction Titles: *Color & Design in Macrame*, by Virginia Harvey; and *The Cider Book*, by Lila Gaut and Betsy Sestrap (cookbook).
Fiction: Mainstream. Query.
Recent Fiction Title: *Sheltered Lives*, by Mary Hazzard (woman's self discovery).

MAJOR BOOKS, 21335 Roscoe Blvd., Canoga Park CA 91304. (213)999-4100. Editor-in-Chief: Harold Straubing. Publishes paperback originals (90%) and reprints (10%). Averages 40 titles/year. Pays 4-6% royalty on retail price; average advance. SASE. Reports in 1-2 months. Book catalog for SASE.
Nonfiction: History (World War II). "We want strong biographies and new angles on World War II. Untold stories with drama and action, photographs if available." Submit outline/synopsis and sample chapters. Recently published *Don't Die on My Shift*, by William F. Sayers (personal experience of a hospital patient); *Wake Island*, by Gen. J.P. Devereux (experience on war-torn Wake Island); and *White Teacher in a Black School*, by Robert Kendall.
Fiction: Science fiction, western, and historical romance. "We are looking for westerns, science fiction, science fantasy and fast-paced adventure. Stories should be set in solid backgrounds. Romance and historical romance should have solid emotional impact. No erotica, please." Submit outline/synopsis and sample chapters. Recently published *Satan Help Me*, by B.W. Battin (occult); *The Black Chapel File*, by L. Christian Balling (historical novel); and *Payment in Lead* by Cortes (western).

*MANYLAND BOOKS, INC., 84-39 90th St., Woodhaven NY 11421. Editor-in-Chief: Stepas Zobarskas. Publishes hardcover and paperback originals. Pays 5-10-12½-15% royalty on wholesale price; offers $250-500 average advance. About 25% of books are subsidy published. Averages 20 titles/year. Photocopied submissions OK. Submit complete ms. Reports in 6-8 weeks. Enclose return postage with ms.
Fiction, Nonfiction, Poetry, and Juveniles: "Manyland is concerned primarily with the literature of the lesser known countries. It has already published a score of novels, collections of short stories, folk tales, juvenile books, works of poetry, essays, and historical studies. Most of the publications have more than local interest. Their content and value transcend natural boundaries. They have universal appeal. We are interested in both new and established writers. We will consider any subject as long as it is well-written. No length requirements. We are especially interested in memoirs, biographies, anthologies." Recently published *The Soviet Genocide in Lithuania*, by Juozas Pajaujis-Javis (a study); *The House of a Stranger*, by Gerald E. Bailey; and *Prague Diptych*, by Marija Petzovska.

*MEDCO BOOKS, 1646 S. La Cienega Blvd., Los Angeles CA 90035. Editor-in-Chief: Gil Porter. Hardcover and paperback originals. Specializes "primarily in sex, health, wealth topics, popular medicine such as dealing with diabetes, weight, arthritis, etc." Pays $500-1,500 for outright purchase; advance averages ⅓-½ on contract, balance on acceptance. Subsidy publishes 1% of books. Subsidy publishing offered "if writer has a viable means of selling his book himself, such as personality with media access, etc. We charge our cost plus about 20% for each step of production as a working average." Query. Send prints if photos are to accompany ms. Simultaneous submissions OK. Reports in 1-2 weeks. SASE.
Nonfiction: Publishes erotica, how-to, medicine and psychiatry, and self-help.

MEDICAL BUSINESS SERVICES (IMS COMMUNICATIONS, INC.), Division of IMS America, 426 Pennsylvania Ave., Fort Washington PA 19034. (215)643-0400. Publisher: Calvin Probst. Publishes trade paperback originals. Averages 1-2 titles/year. Pays royalty; buys some mss outright. SASE. Reports in 2 weeks on queries; 1 month on submissions.
Nonfiction: Consumer-oriented medical books. Subjects include health. "We're looking for mate-

rial on any subject suitable for sale at busy prescription counters. Our audience is made up of concerned homemakers." Query.

Recent Nonfiction Titles: *Is It Poisonous?*, by Helen Dauncey; *Your Prescription and You*, (4th edition), by Steven Strauss; and *Hospital Purchasing Guide*, (5th edition), by Calvin Probst.

MEDICAL EXAMINATION PUBLISHING CO., INC., 969 Stewart Ave., Garden City NY 11530. Editors: Dana Dreibelbis and Kenneth I. Werner (for clinical medicine); Joseph M. Cahn (for nursing and allied health). Royalty schedule is negotiable. Free catalog. Submit outline. Reports in 1 month.
Medical: Medical texts and medical review books; monographs and training material for the medical, nursing and allied health professions.

MED-PSYCH PUBLICATIONS, Box 19746, West Allis, WI 53219. (414)546-2310. Editorial Director: Patricia Wick. Publishes hardcover and paperback originals. Averages 3-5 titles/year. Pays 10% royalty on wholesale price; no advance. Simultaneous and photocopied submissions OK. SASE. Reports in 2 months. Book catalog $1.
Nonfiction: Health, how-to psychology, and self-help. "We would like to see more parapsychology, folk medicine and counseling material. We do not want any text books." Query. Recently published *Elements of Contemporary Counseling*, by Liebman (how-to psychology counseling); and *What is Love and How to Find It*, by Liebman (self-help and/or counseling handbook).

*MEMPHIS STATE UNIVERSITY PRESS, Memphis State University, Memphis TN 38152. (901)454-2752. Editor-in-Chief: J. Ralph Randolph. Publishes hardcover and paperback originals. Averages 12 titles/year. Each contract is subject to negotiation. Does about 10% subsidy publishing. Free book catalog and writer's guidelines. Will consider photocopied submissions. Query. Reports in 3-6 months. SASE.
General Nonfiction: Regional emphasis. "We publish scholarly and trade nonfiction, books in the humanities, social sciences, and regional material. Interested in nonfiction material within the lower Mississippi River Valley. Tennessee history, and regional folklore."
Recent Nonfiction Titles: *A Guide to Wildflowers of the Mid-South*, by Arlo I. Smith (natural history), *Memphis Memoirs*, by Paul Coppock (history); and *Home Place*, by Robert Drake (growing up in west Tennessee).

MERIT PUBLISHING, INC., 610 NE 124th St., N. Miami FL 33161. (305)895-3030. Editor: Louise Hinton. Publishes paperback originals. Published 10 titles in 1979, 12-15 in 1980; plans 25 in 1981. Pays 5¢/word for outright purchases; negotiates advance. Simultaneous and photocopied submissions OK. #10 SASE. Reports in 1 month. Free book catalog for SASE.
Nonfiction: Animals (care of pets), crafts, cookbooks, cooking and foods, health (nutrition, exercise, mental health), history, hobbies, photography, psychology, recreation, reference, self-help and sports. Submit outline/synopsis and sample chapters.
Recent Nonfiction Titles: *Complete Baby Care*, by Dr. D. Kullman; *A-2 Astrology*, by M. Adler; and *Complete Guide to Wines and Mixing Drinks*, by R. Trimnell.

ARTHUR MERIWETHER, INC., 1529 Brook Dr., Downers Grove IL 60515. Editor-in-Chief: Arthur L. Zapel Jr. Publishes paperback originals on how-to subjects relating to youth activities or communication arts. Published 7 titles in 1979, 10 in 1980; plans 10 in 1981. Payment by royalty arrangement, based on wholesale and retail price. Marketed by direct mail. Book catalog 75¢. Editorial guidelines also available. Query. "Do not send ms until after query response from us." Reports in 1 month. Enclose return postage.
Education: Mss for educational use in schools and churches. Subjects include speech, drama and English. Mss for business and staff training on subjects related to business communications and advertising. Religious, self-help, how-to, sociology, Bible-study are also published.
Recent Nonfiction Titles: *Stage Lighting in the Boondocks*, by James Hull Miller; *An Introduction to Mime*, by E. Reid Gilbert; and *101 Ways to Cure Cabin Fever*, by Rosemary Hines.
Drama: Plays, satire and comedy. 1-act plays only. "We publish 25-30 yearly."

THE MERRIAM-EDDY COMPANY, INC., Box 25, South Waterford ME 04081. Executive Vice President: Eleanor M. Edwards. Published hardcover and trade paperback originals. Averages 3 titles/year. Pays 10% royalty on "gross sales, less returns"; no advance. Simultaneous and photocopied submissions OK. SASE. Reports in 3 weeks on queries; 6 weeks on mss. Free book catalog.
Nonfiction: Biography, illustrated book, juvenile, self-help and textbook. Subjects include music, math, reading, audiovisual—all related to special education. "We're looking for any materials relating to special education, work with handicapped, stories about handicapped; also texts suit-

able for children or adults in special education. Special education materials of good quality are especially needed. Emphasis is on the deaf and hard-of-hearing." Query.

Recent Nonfiction Titles: *Math Can Be Easy*, by Mary G. Santos (high school math text for adults); *Santa's Problem*, by Myra Jordan and Roy Grant (musical play, special education); and *Floppy Rabbit*, by Myra Jordan and Roy Grant (musical play, special education).

Fiction: Adventure (concerning handicapped); fantasy, historical, humor, mystery, science fiction and materials suitable for special education. Query.

Recent Fiction Titles: *I Hear the Day*, by Catherine Johnston (illustrated story book, juvenile); and *The Deaf Experience*, by Trenton Batson and Eugene Bergman (high school, college, adult anthology of literature re: deaf).

Tips: "This company is now working along two lines: 1) textbooks and production of materials for special education, 2) book production for any person or company who wishes to have a book typeset, designed and printed for their own distribution. We market and sell our own books, i.e., the books in our catalog. The other books, unless they applied to our field, would be marketed by the authors."

CHARLES E. MERRILL PUBLISHING CO., a Bell & Howell Co., 1300 Alum Creek Dr., Columbus OH 43216. Publishes hardcover and paperback originals. "Royalties and contract terms vary with the nature of the material. They are very competitive within each market area. Some projects are handled on an outright purchase basis." Publishes approximately 200 titles/year. Submit outline/synopsis and sample chapters. Reports in 4-12 weeks. Will accept simultaneous submissions if notified. SASE.

Education Division: Editor: Ann Turpie. Publishes texts, workbooks, instructional tapes, overhead projection transparencies and programmed materials for elementary, junior high and high schools in all subject areas, primarily language arts and literature, mathematics, science and social studies (no juvenile stories or novels).

College Division: Executive Editor, Education and Special Education: Roger Williams; Executive Editor, Business, Mathematics, Science and Technology: Greg Spatz. Publishes texts and multi-media programs in college areas which include Education and Special Education, Business and Economics, Math and Science, and Technology.

General Trade Division: Editorial Manager: Gwen Hiles. A recently formed division publishing general interest adult and juvenile fiction and nonfiction and children's picture books. "We are looking for quality works with broad appeal to the retail bookstore market. Fiction works should be of literary quality and be submitted by an agent or recommended by a reviewer. No short stories or religious books."

JULIAN MESSNER,(Simon & Schuster Division of Gulf & Western Corp.), 1230 Avenue of the Americas, New York NY 10020. Editor-in-Chief: Iris Rosoff. Senior editor for elementary grades: Madelyn Klein Anderson. Senior Editor for junior and senior high school: Jane Steltenpohl. Hardcover originals. Published 52 titles in 1979, 70 in 1980; plans 70 in 1981. Royalty varies. Advance averages $2,000. State availability of photos and/or illustrations to accompany ms. "Propose book ideas to start with. If the editor is interested, we will ask for detailed outline and sample chapters." Reports in 2-3 months. SASE. Free book catalog.

Juveniles: Nonfiction books only for young people.

Recent Nonfiction and Fiction Titles: *Allergies and You*, by Sheila Burns; *Girls Can Be Anything They Want*, by Patricia Foot; *Solar Energy in Tomorrow's World*, by Reed Millard; and *The Stop Smoking Book for Teens*, by Curtis W. Casewit.

MILLER BOOKS, 2908 W. Valley Blvd., Alhambra CA 91803. (213)284-7607. Subsidiaries include *San Gabriel Valley Magazine*, Miller Press and Miller Electric. Publisher: Joseph Miller. Publishes hardcover and trade paperback originals, and hardcover reprints. Averages 4 titles/year. Pays 10-15% royalty on retail price; buys some mss outright. Simultaneous and photocopied submissions OK. SASE ("no returns on erotic material"). Reports in 2 weeks on queries; 2 months on mss. Free book catalog.

Nonfiction: Cookbook, how-to, self-help, textbook and remedial textbooks. Subjects include Americana, animals, cooking and foods, history, philosophy and politics. "Remedial manuscripts are needed in most fields." No erotica. Submit complete ms.

Recent Nonfiction Title: *Republican Chaos*, by J. Miller (political textbook).

Fiction: Adventure, historical, humor, mystery and western. No erotica. Submit complete ms.

Recent Fiction Titles: *The Magic Story*, by F.V.R. Dey (positive thinking); *Republican Chaos*, by J. Miller (political textbook); and *Headless Horseman*, by H. Boye (mystery and adventure).

Tips: "Write something good about people, places and our country. Avoid the negative—it doesn't sell."

*MIMIR PUBLISHERS, INC., Box 5011, Madison WI 53705. Editor-in-Chief: Henry H. Bakken. Hardcover and paperback originals. Specializes in books in the social sciences at college level. Averages 3-10 titles/year. 15% royalty on list price, "but nearly all titles are determined on a special contract." No advance. Subsidy publishes 50% of books. Subsidy publishing is offered "if the author wishes to proceed on our 50/50 type contract and share in the proceeds. Under this contract the author gets all the proceeds until he recovers his venture capital." Query or submit complete ms. Simultaneous ("if indicated") and photocopied submissions OK. Reports in 2-4 months. SASE. Free book catalog.
Nonfiction: Publishes Americana; biography (limited); business; economics; history; law; philosophy; politics; sociology; and textbooks.
Recent Nonfiction Titles: *The Hills of Home*, by Bakken; and *Wisconsin Income Tax Guide for Individuals*, by J.B. Bower.

MIT PRESS, 28 Carleton St., Cambridge MA 02142. (617)253-1624. Acquisition Dept. Averages 100 titles/year. Published 105 titles in 1979, 120 in 1980. Pays 8-10% royalty on wholesale or retail price; $500-1,000 advance. SASE. Reports in 4-6 weeks Free book catalog.
Nonfiction: Computer science/artificial intelligence, civil engineering/transportation, nutrition, neuroscience, work and quality of life, public policy, history, linguistics/psychology/philosophy, architecture, design, film, visual communication, economics, management, business, international affairs, physics, math, biochemistry, history of science and technology, urban planning and energy studies. "Our books must reflect a certain level of technological sophistication. We do not want fiction, poetry, literary criticism, education, pure philosophy, European history before 1920, belles-lettres, drama, personal philosophies and children's books." Submit outline/synopsis and sample chapters.
Recent Nonfiction Titles: *John Von Neumann & Norbert Wiener: From Mathematics to the Technologies of Life and Death*, by Steve J. Heims; *Venetian Architecture of the Early Renaissance*, by John McAndrew; and *Freight Transport Regulation: Equity, Efficiency and Competition in the Rail and Trucking Industries*, by Ann F. Friedlaender and Richard H. Spady (economics).

MONITOR BOOK CO., INC., 195 S. Beverly Dr., Beverly Hills CA 90212. (213)271-5558. Editor-in-Chief: Alan F. Pater. Hardcover originals. Pays 10% minimum royalty or by outright purchase, depending on circumstances; no advance. Send prints if photos and/or illustrations are to accompany ms. Reports in 2-4 months. SASE. Book catalog for SASE.
Nonfiction: Americana, biographies (only of well-known personalities); law and reference books. Recently published *What They Said in 1981: The Yearbook of Spoken Opinion* (current quotation); *Anthology of Magazine Verse for 1981*; and *United States Battleships: A History of America's Greatest Fighting Fleet*.

MOODY PRESS, 2101 W. Howard St., Chicago IL 60645. (312)973-7800. Administrative Editor: Beverly J. Burch. General Editor: Charles E. Phelps. Publishes hardcover and paperback originals (90%) and reprints (10%). Averages 70 titles/year. Pays 5-10% royalty on wholesale or retail price; rarely offers advance. Simultaneous and photocopied submissions not encouraged. SASE. Reports in 3 months.
Nonfiction: Religious. "We publish only books which are Evangelical Christian in nature. Christian education, Christian living, inspirational, theology, missions, and missionaries, pastors' helps. Conservative theological position. Clothbound: 45,000-60,000 words. Paper: 20,000-450,000 words." Submit an outline, synopsis, sample chapter and biographical data.
Recent Nonfiction Titles: *When Mom Goes to Work*, by Mary Beth Moster; *Jesus' Pattern of Prayer*, by John MacArthur; and *What Happens When We Die?*, by Carolyn Nystrom (children).
Fiction: Religious. "We do not encourage Biblical fiction but will accept historical and contemporary fiction." Submit synopsis and sample chapters.
Recent Fiction Titles: *Margo*, by Jerry Jenkins; *Of Wrath and Praise*, by Tom Taylor; and *"Really, Marty!"*, by Bettilu Davies (youth).

*MOREHOUSE-BARLOW CO., INC., 78 Danbury Rd., Wilton CT 06897. Editorial Director: Theodore A. McConnell. Publishes hardcover and paperback originals. Averages 30 titles/year. Pay 10% royalty on retail price. Simultaneous and photocopied submissions OK. SASE.
Nonfiction: Specializes in Anglican religious publishing. Theology, ethics, church history, pastoral counseling, liturgy and religious education. No fiction, poetry or drama.
Recent Nonfiction Titles: *The Spirit of Anglicanism*, by William J. Wolf; *A Faithful Church*, by O.C. Edwards and John Westerhoff; and *The Episcopal Church Annual*.

WILLIAM MORROW AND CO., 105 Madison Ave., New York NY 10016. Editor-in-Chief: Hillel Black. Payment is on standard royalty basis. Published 321 titles in 1980. Query letter on all

books. No unsolicited mss or proposals. Mss and proposals should be submitted through a literary agent.
Imprints: *Greenwillow Books* (juveniles), Susan Hirschman, editor. *Lothrop, Lee and Shephard* (juveniles), Dorothy Briley, editor. *Morrow Junior Books* (juveniles), Connie C. Epstein, editor. *Quill* (trade paperback), James D. Landis, publisher.
General Trade: Publishes adult fiction, nonfiction, history, biography, arts, religion, poetry, how-to books and cookbooks. Length: 50,000-100,000 words.
Recent Titles: *The Key to Rebecca*, by Ken Follett; *Shelley: Also Known as Shirley*, by Shelley Winters; and *Century*, by Fred Mustard Stewart.

MORROW JUNIOR BOOKS, 105 Madison Ave., New York NY 10016. (212)889-3050. Editor-in-Chief: Connie Epstein. Senior Editor: Elizabeth D. Crawford. Publishes hardcover originals. Publishes 40 titles/year. All contracts negotiated separately; advance varies. No simultaneos or photocopied submissions. SASE. Reports in 6 weeks. Book catalog for $1.
Nonfiction: Juveniles (trade books). No textbooks. Query.
Fiction: Juveniles (trade books).

MOTORBOOKS INTERNATIONAL PUBLISHERS & WHOLESALERS, INC., Box 2, Osceola WI 54020. Director of Publications: William F. Kosfeld. Senior Editor: Barbara K. Harold. Hardcover and paperback originals. Offers 10-15% royalty on wholesale or retail price. Average advance: $1,000. Averages 6-8 titles/year. Simultaneous and photocopied submissions OK. Reports in 2-3 months. SASE. Free book catalog.
Nonfiction: Publishes biography; history; how-to; photography; and motor sports as they relate to cars, trucks, motorcycles and motor sports (domestic and foreign). Submit outline/synopsis, sample chapter and sample of illustrations. "State qualifications for doing book." Prefers not to see repair manuals and texts.
Recent Nonfiction Titles: *Tootsie Toys: World's First Diecast Models*, by James Wieland and Ed Force; *Pontiac: The Postwar Years*, by Jan Norbye and Jim Dunne; and *Chevy Super Sports 1961-1976*, by Terry V. Boyce (illustrated automotive history).

MOTT MEDIA, 1000 E. Huron, Milford MI 48042. Associated with Evangelical Book Club. Hardcover and paperback originals (65%) and paperback reprints (35%). Publishes 12-20 titles/year. Specializes in religious books, including trade and Christian school textbooks. Pays variable royalty on retail, depending on type of book. Query or submit outline/synopsis and sample chapters. Photocopied submissions OK. Reports in 1 month. SASE. Free book catalog.
Nonfiction: Publishes Americana (religious slant); biography (for juveniles on famous Christians, adventure-filled; for adults on Christian people, scholarly, new slant for marketing); how-to (for pastors, Christian laymen); juvenile (biographies, 30,000-40,000 words); politics (conservative, Christian approach); religious (conservative Christian); self-help (religious); and textbooks (all levels from a Christian perspective, all subject fields). No preschool materials. Main emphasis of all mss must be religious.
Recent Nonfiction Titles: *By Their Blood*, by James and Marti Hefley; and *Asking Questions*, by Bruce Lockerbie.

*MOUNTAIN PRESS PUBLISHING CO., 279 W. Front, Missoula MT 59801. Publisher: David P. Flaccus. Hardcover and paperback originals (90%) and reprints (10%). Royalty of 12% of net amount received; no advance. Subsidy publishes less than 5% of books. "Top-quality work in very limited market only." Averages 12 titles/year. State availability of photos and/or illustrations to accompany ms. Simultaneous submissions OK. Reports in 2-4 weeks. SASE. Free book catalog.
Nonfiction: Publishes history (western Americana); hobbies, how-to (angling, hunting); nature (geology, habitat and conservation); outdoor recreation (backpacking, fishing, etc.); technical (wood design and technology); and textbooks.
Recent Nonfiction Titles: *A Brush With the West*, by Dale Burk; *Packin' In On Mule and Horses*, by Smoke Elser and Bill Brown; and *Plants of Big Basin State Park and the Coastal Mountains of Northern California*, by Mary Beth Cooney-Lazaneo and Kathleen Lyons.

MOUNTAIN STATE PRESS, c/o University of Charleston, Charleston WV 25304. (304)346-9471. Managing Editor: Ira Herman. Publishes hardcover and trade paperback originals, and hardcover reprints. Averages 5-10 titles/year. Pays 10-30% royalty on retail price; no advance. Simultaneous ("if informed") and photocopied submissions OK. SASE. Reports in 2 weeks on queries; 2 months on mss. Free book catalog.
Nonfiction: Biography. Publishes books in all categories about Appalachia. Subjects include Americana. "We're especially looking for reference books, tourist guides, cookbooks and how-to; (all material must be Appalachia-related). No material that presents stereotyped view of the

Appalachian region." Submit complete ms.

Recent Nonfiction Titles: *Peaceful Patriot: The Story of Tom Bennett,* by Bonni McKeown (biography); *As I Remember It,* by Stanley Eskew (autobiography); and *Tale of the Elk,* by W.E.R. Byrne (WV history).

Fiction: "We will consider novels and short story collections of any category, that have an Appalachian flavor or setting. We do not want material that is not Appalachian-related in some way." Submit complete ms.

Recent Fiction Titles: *Life at an Early Age,* by Jack Welch (WV novel); *A Tree Full of Stars,* by Davis Grubb (WV Christmas novel); and *Six Miles Out,* by Barbara Smith (WV novel).

Poetry: "Our poetry needs are limited to Appalachian poetry by Appalachian poets. We plan only one or two books of poetry per year. We do not want poetry without an Appalachian connection." Submit complete ms.

Recent Poetry Title: *Anse on Island Creek,* by Paul C. Steele (Appalachian).

Tips: "The smaller presses offer a needed chance for unknown writers to break into print and to build up credits. Even here, the competition is stiff. The key word is perseverance."

THE MOUNTAINEERS BOOKS, 719-B Pike St., Seattle WA 98101. (206)682-4636. Director: John Pollock. Publishes hardcover and paperback originals (85%) and reprints (15%). Averages 15-25 titles/year. Offers 10-15% royalty based on wholesale or retail price. Offers advance on occasion. Simultaneous (depending upon circumstances) and photocopied submissions OK. SASE. Reports in 6-8 weeks. Free book catalog.

Nonfiction: Recreation; sports; and textbooks. "We specialize only in books dealing with mountaineering, hiking, backpacking, skiing, snowshoeing, canoeing, bicycling, etc. These can be either how-to-do-it, where-to-do-it (guidebooks), or accounts of mountain-related experiences." Does *not* want to see "anything dealing with hunting, fishing or motorized travel." Submit outline/synopsis and sample chapters.

Recent Nonfiction Titles: *Trekking in Nepal,* by Stephen Bezruchka (guidebook); *The Last Step,* by Rick Ridgeway (expedition account); and *Snowshoeing,* by Gene Prater (how-to).

Fiction: Adventure and humor. "We might consider an exceptionally well-done book-length manuscript on mountaineering. It could be humorous and/or could be aimed at the juvenile audience." Does *not* want poetry or mystery. Query first.

MUDBORN PRESS, 209 W. De la Guerra, Santa Barbara CA 93101. Editor: Erasmus Newborn. Publishes paperback originals. Royalty schedule varies with project. Averages 5 titles/year. Query with project outline. Will consider photocopied submissions. Reports in 6 weeks. SASE.

General: International fiction and humanities. We will consider multi-author projects with a specific literary or cultural focus.

Recent Titles: *The Poetry of Jurge de Sena,* edited by Frederick G. Williams (collection from the lifework of an internationally famous Portuguese poet, with ten translations); and *Autobiographies,* by Richard Kastelaretz (large-scale experimental work).

MULTIMEDIA PUBLISHING CORP., (affiliates: Steinerbooks, Rudolf Steiner Publications, Sprititual Fiction Publications, Biograf Publications), 7 Garber Hill Rd., Blauvelt NY 10913. (914)359-9292. Editor: Paul M. Allen. Publishes hardcover and paperback originals and reprints. Averages 15 titles/year. Pays 5-7% royalty on retail price; advance averages $1,000. Free book catalog. Query with outline and sample chapters for nonfiction. Will consider photocopied submissions. Reports in 2 months. SASE.

Nonfiction: "Spiritual sciences, occult, philosophical, metaphysical, ESP. These are for our Steiner books division only. Scholarly and serious nonfiction. How-to-do or make books using our patented format of Biograf Books. Examples: origami, breadbaking, calendar." Department Editor, Multimedia Materials and Self-Help: Beatrice Garber; Department Editor, Philosophy and Spiritual Sciences: Bernard J. Garber.

Recent Nonfiction Titles: *Citizens of the Cosmos,* by Beredene Jocelyn (astrology and life after death); *Maps of the Soul,* by Richard Kingsbury (astrology and psychology); and *Graphology: The Science of Handwriting,* by Henry Frith.

Fiction: "A new affiliate has been added called Spiritual Fiction Publications. We are now looking for original manuscripts or rewrites of classics in modern terms."

Recent Fiction Titles: *Zanoni,* by Sir Edward Bulwer-Lytton; and *Romance of Two Worlds, Seraphita,* by Honoré Balzac.

MUSEUM OF NEW MEXICO PRESS, Box 2087, Santa Fe NM 87503. (505)827-2352. Editor-in-Chief: Sarah Nestor. Director: James Mafchir. Hardcover and paperback originals (90%) and reprints (10%). Published 6 titles in 1980, plans 4 in 1981. Royalty of 10% of list after first 1,000 copies; no advance. Prints preferred for illustrations; transparencies best for color. Sources of photos or illustrations should be indicated for each. Simultaneous and photocopied submissions OK. Submit complete mss, addressed to James Mafchir, Publisher. Mss should be typed double-spaced, follow Chicago *Manual of Style* and *Words Into Type,* and be accompanied by information about the author's credentials and professional background. Reports in 1-2 months. SASE. Free book catalog.

Nonfiction: "We publish both popular and scholarly books on regional anthropology, history, fine and folk arts; geography, natural history, the Americas and the Southwest; regional cookbooks. Art, biography (regional and Southwest); music, nature, reference, scientific and technical. Recently published *Cuentos, Tales of the Spanish Southwest,* by José Griego and Rudolfo Anaya; *On the Trail,* by Jean M. Burroughs; and *Taos Adobes,* by Bainbridge Bunting.

Fiction: Historical, and other regional (New Mexico/Southwest) fiction.

MUSIC SALES CORP., 33 W. 60th St., New York NY 10023. (212)246-0325. Imprints include *Quick Fox, Acorn, Amsco, Anfor, Ariel, Award, Consolidated, Embassy, Oak, Yorktown.* Editor-in-Chief: Peter Pickow. Publishes paperback originals (95%) and reprints (5%). Publishes 75 titles/year. Standard royalty contracts; advance offered. Simultaneous and photocopied submissions OK. SASE. Reports in 2 weeks. Free book catalog.

Nonfiction: General trade books: instructional music books on blues, bluegrass, classical, folk and jazz; also technical, theory, reference and pop music personalities. "We publish and distribute a complete line of quality music instruction books for every musician from beginner to professional. We do not publish original music or songs. We are looking for instruction books or collections that will be readily salable in educational or pop/commericial music markets." Submit outline/synopsis and sample chapters.

Recent Nonfiction Titles: *Jazz Violin,* by Stephane Grappelli and Matt Glaser (history, technique, transcriptions); and *Fingerpicking Gershwin,* by John Miller (guitar arrangements).

THE NAIAD PRESS, INC., Box 10543, Tallahassee FL 32302. (904)539-9322. Editorial Director: Barbara Grier. Publishes paperback originals. Averages 8 titles/year. Pays 50% royalty on wholesale or retail price; no advance. Reports in 6 weeks. SASE. Book catalog for SASE.

Fiction: "We publish lesbian fiction, preferably lesbian/feminist fiction. We are not impressed with the 'oh woe' school and prefer realistic (i.e., happy) novels." Query.

Recent Fiction Titles: *Outlander,* by Jane Rule; *The Black and White Of It,* by Ann Allen Schockley; and *Sapphistry, The Book of Lesbian Sexuality,* by Pat Califia.

*NATIONAL ASSOCIATION OF COLLEGE AND UNIVERSITY BUSINESS OFFICERS, One Dupont Circle, Suite 510, Washington DC 20036. (202)861-2500. Director, Information and Publications: Mr. Abbott Wainwright. Publishes hardcover and trade paperback originals. Averages 5 titles/year. Subsidy publishes 40% of books based on "relevance to publisher's subject needs." Buys mss outright for $500-2,000. Simultaneous and photocopied submissions OK. SASE. Reports in 1 week on queries; 3 weeks on mss. Free book catalog.

Imprints: *NACUBO,* (nonfiction), Mr. Abbott Wainwright, Director, Information and Publications.

Nonfiction: Technical and textbook. Subjects include business and economics. "We're looking for mss on the effects of demographic changes in the traditional college-age population on colleges and universities; also, mss on college and university planning, management, accounting, costing, investments, real estate, financial reporting, and personnel administration. We publish books that provide immediate help with real problems, as opposed to conceptual studies. Our audience is made up of college and university senior administrators." Query or submit outline/synopsis and sample chapters or complete ms. "We have a narrow audience, so recommend queries if there is any doubt."

Recent Nonfiction Titles: *Financial Self-Assessment: A Workbook for Colleges,* by Dickmeyer & Hughes; *A Planning Manual for Colleges,* by Dozier et al.; and *Personnel Practices for Small Colleges,* by Bouchard.

NATIONAL BOOK COMPANY, 333 S.W. Park Ave., Portland OR 97205. (503)228-6345. Imprints include Halcyon House. Editorial Director: Carl W. Salser. Senior Editor: John R. Kimmel. Manager of Copyrights: Lucille Fry. Publishes hardcover and paperback originals (95%) and paperback reprints (2%). Published 25 titles in 1979 and 30 in 1980. Pays 5-15% royalty on wholesale or retail price; no advance. Simultaneous and photocopied submissions OK. SASE. Reports in 2 months. Free book catalog for SASE.

Nonfiction: Art, business/economics, health, history, music, politics, psychology, reference, science, technical and textbooks (materials suitable for educational uses in all categories). "The vast majority of titles are individualized instruction programs for educational consumers. Prospective authors should be aware of this and be prepared for this type of format, although content, style and appropriateness of subject matter are the major criteria by which submissions are judged. We are most interested in materials in the areas of the language arts, social studies and the sciences." Query, submit outline/synopsis and sample chapters or complete ms.

Recent Nonfiction Titles: *Chemistry Problem Solving*, by J. Wheeler; *U.S. Government-Executive Branch*, by R. Adam; *Food Additives*, by R. Froehlich; and *Personal Shorthand for the Journalist*, by Blum and Yerian.

THE NATIONAL GALLERY OF CANADA, Publications Division, Ottawa, Ontario, Canada K1A 0M8. (613)995-6526. Head: Peter L. Smith. Publishes hardcover and paperback originals. Published 10 titles in 1979, 20 in 1980; plans 15 in 1981. Pays in outright purchase of $1,500-2,500; advance averages $700. Photocopied submissions OK. Reports in 3 months. SASE. Free sales catalog.

Nonfiction: "In general, we publish only solicited manuscripts on art, particularly Canadian art, and must, by the way, publish them in English and French. Exhibition catalogs are commissioned, but we are open upon approval by Curatorial general editors' to mss for the various series, monographic and otherwise, that we publish. All mss should be directed to our Editorial Coordinator, who doubles as manuscript editor. Since we publish translations into French, authors have access to French Canada and the rest of Francophonie. Also, because our titles are distributed by University of Chicago Press, authors have the attention of European as well as American markets."

Recent Nonfiction Titles: *Annual Bulletin 2*, by Myron Laskin and Jean-René Ostiguy: *Reflections in a Quiet Pool, the Prints of David Milne*, by Rosemarie L. Tovell; and *Canada Video*, by Bruce Ferguson.

NATIONAL TEXTBOOK CO., 8259 Niles Center Rd., Skokie IL 60077. Editorial Director: Leonard I. Fiddle. Mss purchased on either royalty or buy-out basis. Averages 9 titles/year. Free book catalog and writer's guidelines. Send sample chapter and outline or contents. Reports in 4 months. Enclose return postage.

Textbooks: Major emphasis being given to language arts area, especially secondary level material. Donna Anthony Drews, Language Arts Editor.

Recent Nonfiction Titles: *Reading by Doing*, by Simons & Palmer (critical reading); *The Mass Media Workbook*, by Hollister (mass media); and *Student Congress & Lincoln-Douglas Debate*, by Fryar and Thomas (forensics).

NATUREGRAPH PUBLISHERS, INC., Box 1075, Happy Camp CA 96039. (916)493-5353. Editor: Barbara Brown. Quality trade books. Averages 5 titles/year. "We offer 10% of wholesale; 12½% after 10,000 copies are sold. To speed things up, queries should include: 1)summary, 2)detailed outline, 3)comparison to related books, 4)sample of text, 5)availability and samples of any photos or illustrations, 6)author background. Send ms only on request." Photocopied submissions OK. Reports in 1-2 months. SASE. Free book catalog.

Nonfiction: Primarily publishes nonfiction for the layman in 8 general areas: natural history (biology, geology, ecology, astronomy); American Indian (historical and contemporary); outdoor living (backpacking, wild edibles, etc.); land and gardening (modern homesteading); crafts and how-to; holistic learning (resources for alternative and home education); holistic health (natural foods and healing arts); PRISM Editions (Baha'i and other new age approaches to harmonious living). Fictional treatment of these subject areas will be considered. All material must be well-grounded; author must be professional, and in command of effective style. Our natural history and American Indian lines can be geared for educational markets." Recently published *The Earthshapers*, by Speerstra (about the Mound Builder culture); *Everyone's Guide to Food Self-Sufficiency*, by Gullett and Gullett; and *Edible, Incredible Pondlife*, by Marjorie Furlong and Virginia Pill.

NAVAL INSTITUTE PRESS, Annapolis MD 21402. Acquisitions Editor: Richard R. Hobbs. Press Director: Thomas F. Epley. Averages 45 titles/year. Pays 14-18-21% royalty based on net sales; modest advance. Simultaneous and photocopied submissions OK. SASE. Reports in 2 weeks (queries); 6 weeks (others). Free book catalog.

Nonfiction: "We are interested in naval and maritime subjects: navigation, naval history, biographies of naval leaders and naval aviation." Query. Recently published *Double-Edged Secrets*, by W. J. Holmes (history of naval intelligence in the Pacific during WWII); *American Flying Boat*, by Richard C. Knott (history of American seaplane); and Battleship Bismarck: A Survivor's Story, by Baron Burkard von Mullenheim-Rechberg.

NAZARENE PUBLISHING HOUSE, Box 527, Kansas City MO 64141. Trade name: Beacon Hill Press of Kansas City. Betty Fuhrman. Publishes hardcover and paperback originals and reprints. Offers "standard contract (sometimes flat rate purchase). Advance on royalty is paid on first 1,000 copies at publication date. Pays 10% on first 10,000 copies and 12% on subsequent copies at the end of each calendar year." Averages 60-65 titles/year. Query. Follow *Chicago Manual of Style*. Address all mss to Book Editor. Reports in 2-5 months. "Book Committee meets quarterly to select, from the mss which they have been reading in the interim, those which will be published." Query. SASE.

Nonfiction: "Basically religious, (inspirational, devotional, Bible study, beliefs) but of wide scope from college textbook level to juvenile. Doctrinally must conform to the evangelical, Wesleyan tradition. Conservative view of Bible. Personal religious experience. We want the accent on victorious life, definitely upbeat. Social action themes must have spiritual base and motivation. Popular style books should be under 128 pages." Interested in business and professional books on church administration, Sunday school, etc. Textbooks are "almost exclusively done on assignment. Send query first." Length: 10,000-30,000 words.

Recent Nonfiction Titles: *God, Man, and Salvation,* by W.T. Purkiser, R. Taylor and W. Taylor (Biblical theology); *Get Ready to Grow,* by P.R. Orjala (church growth); and *The Year of the Locust,* by David Nixon.

Fiction: "Must have religious content germane to plot not artificially tacked on. At the same time not preachy or moralistic." Publishes 1 adult fiction and 1 juvenile a year. "Currently a moratorium on adult fiction."

NC PRESS, 24 Ryerson Ave., Toronto, Ontario, Canada M5T 2P3. (416)368-1165. Editorial Director: Caroline Walker. Publishes hardcover and paperback originals and reprints. Averages 10-15 titles/year. Pays royalty on wholesale price. Simultaneous and photocopied submissions OK. SASE. Free book catalog.

Nonfiction: "We generally publish books of social/political relevance either on contemporary topics of concern (current events, ecology, etc.), or historical studies. We publish primarily Canadiana." Submit outline/synopsis and sample chapters.

Recent Nonfiction Titles: *This Thing of Darkness,* by Norman Elder (travel/anthropology); *Beginnings,* edited by John Moss (literary criticism); and *Columbo's Book of Marvels and Names and Nicknames,* by John Robert Colombo (trivia).

NELLEN PUBLISHING CO., INC., Box 18, Newton NJ 07860. (201)948-3141. Editorial Director: Nancy W. Dunn. Senior Editor: M.F. Valentine. Publishes hardcover and paperback originals. Published 10 titles in 1979, 10 in 1980. Pays 10-12½-15% royalty on wholesale price; no advance. Photocopied submissions OK. Reports in 2-4 weeks. SASE. Free book catalog.

Nonfiction: "We are seeking titles of interest to both trade and scholarly markets. Our emphasis is on the trade. If a book is addressed to the scholarly or technical market we may ask the author to rewrite with the larger market in mind. Our subject areas are wide: history, politics, economics, health, crime, self-help, management, the arts, etc. We are especially interested in Americana books on names (like our Smith book) and genealogy. Submit outline/synopsis and sample chapters. "With a clear synopsis of the book we appreciate knowing something about the author. We prefer authors with published works to their credit. If not books, at least magazine or journal articles."

Recent Nonfiction Titles: *The Book of Smith,* by Edson C. Smith (fact book); *Managing Change,* by John Flaherty (management); and *Roots of Crime,* by Thomas Marsh.

Fiction: "We will consider all types of novels. Submit outline/synopsis and sample chapters. Recently published *On a Field of Black,* by Gerald Tomlinson (suspense).

THOMAS NELSON PUBLISHERS, 407 7th Ave. S., Nashville TN 37203. (615)244-3733. Editor: Lawrence M. Stone. Publishes hardcover and paperback originals (95%) and hardcover reprints (5%). Published 160 titles in 1979, 55 in 1980; plans 55 in 1981. Pays royalty or by outright purchase; sometimes an advance. Wants no fiction. Photocopied submissions OK. SASE. Reports in 6-8 weeks. Book catalog for SASE.

Nonfiction: Reference, and religious (must be orthodox Christian in theology).

Recent Nonfiction Titles: *The Bible Almanac,* by Merrill Tenney, J.J. Parker and William A. White (reference); *Three Steps Forward, Two Steps Back,* by Charles Swindall (religious); and *Ireland Portrayed,* by Gordon Wetmore (gift book/art book).

NELSON-HALL PUBLISHERS, 111 N. Canal St., Chicago IL 60606. (312)922-0856. Editorial Director: Harold Wise, Ph.D. Publishes hardcover and paperback originals. Averages 105 titles/year. Pays 15% royalty on retail price; average advance. Photocopied submissions OK. SASE. Reports in 1 month. Free book catalog.

Nonfiction: Americana, biography, business/economics, cookbooks/cooking, health, history, hobbies, how-to, music, philosophy, photography, politics, psychology, recreation, reference, religion, science, self-help, sociology, sports, technical and textbooks. "We do not want essays, opin-

ions, speculations, memoirs or armchair ruminations." Query.
Recent Nonfiction Titles: *Think Like a Lawyer*, by Dudley (advocacy skills); *Stock Market Strategy*, by Righetti (profitable investing); and *Plumes in the Dust*, by Walsh (love affair of Edgar Allan Poe).

NEW AMERICAN LIBRARY, 1633 Broadway, New York NY 10019. (212)397-8000. Imprints include Signet, Mentor, Classic, Plume and Meridian. Associate Publisher: Elaine Koster. Editor-in-Chief/Paperback: Diana Levine. Editor-in-Chief/Hardcover: Joan Sanger. Publishes hardcover and paperback originals and hardcover reprints. Publishes 350 titles/year. Royalty is "variable;" offers "substantial" advance. Simultaneous and photocopied submissions OK. Reports in 2 months. SASE. Free book catalog.
Nonfiction: "We will consider all nonfiction sent—educational, mystic, self-help, inspirational, topical, etc. Submit outline/synopsis and sample chapters.
Recent Nonfiction Titles: *Music for Chameleons*, by Truman Capote; *The Clam Plate Orgy*, by Wilson Bryan Key; and *Bittersweet*, by Susan Strasberg.
Fiction: "We will consider all fiction. We publish romance sagas, gothics, romances, science fiction, contemporary, suspense, thrillers, family sagas, etc." Submit outline/synopsis and sample chapters.
Recent Fiction Titles: *The Booze & Rachel*, by Joel Gross; *Hungry as the Sea*, by Wilbur Smith; and *The Girl in a Swing*, by Richard Adams.

NEW ENGLAND PRESS, 45 Tudor City, #1903, New York NY 10017. Chief Editor: G. Dorset. Publishes trade paperback originals. Averages 5 titles/year. Pays 7-10% royalty on wholesale price and in outright purchase; no advance. Photocopied submissions OK. SASE. Reports in 1 month.
Imprints: *Bina Books* (fiction).
Fiction: Experimental, novellas and short stories. "Our audience includes young college adults." Query. All unsolicited mss are returned unopened.
Recent Poetry Titles: *Water Hills*, by Mike Finley (post modern); *NY Geopoems*, by G. Dorset (art-realism); and *Video Tapes*, by G. Dorset (surrealism).

NEW HAMPSHIRE PUBLISHING CO., 9 Orange St., Somersworth NH 03878. (603)692-3727. Publishes hardcover and paperback originals (75%) and hardcover reprints (25%). Published 13 titles in 1979, 15 in 1980. Pays 5-10% royalty on retail price; advance varies. Simultaneous and photocopied submissions OK. Query. SASE. Reports in 4-8 weeks. Free book catalog.
Nonfiction: Health (related to outdoor sports only); history (New England reprints only); how-to (related to outdoors recreation only); nature; recreation; sports and travel (guides to Northeastern areas only). "We do not want to see anything that is not related in some way to those areas we have mentioned." Query or submit outline/synopsis and sample chapters along with resume or author biographical information. Recently published *Fifty Hikes in the Adirondacks*, by McMartin (outdoor recreation guidebook); *25 Ski Tours In Maine*, by Beiser; and *Canoeing Massachusetts, Rhode Island and Connecticut*, by Weber.

NEW LEAF PRESS, INC., Box 1045, Harrison AR 72061. Editor-in-Chief: John Boneck. Hardcover and paperback originals. Publishes 10 titles/year. Specializes in charismatic books. Pays 10% royalty on first 10,000 copies, paid once a year; no advance. Send photos and illustrations to accompany ms. Simultaneous and photocopied submissions OK. SASE. Reports in 3 months. Free book catalog.
Nonfiction: Biography; self-help. Charismatic books; life stories; how-to live the Christian life. Length: 100-400 pages. Submit complete ms.
Recent Titles: *Run to the Roar*, by Tammy Bakker with Cliff Dudley (fear); *Released to Reign*, by Charles Trombley (the Christian's place); and *Supreme Commander*, by Col. Henry C. Godman with Cliff Dudley (testimony and history).

NEW READERS PRESS, Publishing division of Laubach Literacy International, Box 131, Syracuse NY 13210. Editorial Director: Caroline Blakely. Assistant Editorial Director: Kay Koschnick. Publishes paperback originals. Averages 18-24 titles/year. "Most of our sales are to public education systems, including adult basic education programs, with some sales to volunteer literacy programs, private human-services agencies, prisons, and libraries with outreach programs for poor readers." Pays royalty on retail price, or by outright purchase. "Rate varies according to type of publication and length of ms." Advance is "different in each case, but does not exceed projected royalty for first year." Photocopied submissions OK. Reports in 2 months. SASE. Free book catalog.
Nonfiction: "Our audience is adults and older teenagers with limited reading skills (6th grade level and below). We publish coping skills materials that are of immediate practical value to our readers

in such areas as consumer education, career education, health, family life, parenting skills, self-awareness, life-span development (adolescence through old age), legal rights, community resources, and adapting to US culture (for functionally illiterate English-as-a-second-language students). We are particularly interested in mss written at the 3rd-4th grade level or below. Mss must be not only easy to read but also adult in tone and concepts, and sensitive to the needs and circumstances of low-income adults. We also publish basic education materials in reading and writing, math, and English-as-a-second-language for double illiterates. Our *basic* programs are usually commissioned by us, but we would consider submissions of materials in areas like reading comprehension, composition, and practical math or materials for specialized audiences of non-readers, such as the learning disabled or speakers of nonstandard dialects. We prefer proposals for a cluster of related titles; we are interested in isolated titles only if they could fit in existing clusters. We are not interested in biography, poetry, or anything at all written for children." Recently published *Help Yourself to Health*, by Nancy Raines Day; *Your Rights When You're Young*, by Maxine Phillipps; and *Focus on Phonics-2B*, by Gail Rice (student workbook and teacher's edition).

Fiction: "We're looking for original, realistic fiction written for adults, but written at a 3rd-grade reading level. We want well-developed believable characters in realistic situations. We want mss of approximately 10,000 words that can be published as short novels. We are not interested in formula fiction but would consider adventure, mystery, or romance of interest to the adult or teenager. We do not want simplified versions of already published works." Query.

Recent Fiction Titles: *The Other Side of Yellow*, by Jessie Redding Hall.

NEW REVIEW BOOKS, Box 31, Station E, Toronto, Ontario, Canada M6H 4E1. (416)536-5083. Editorial Director: Dr. Oleh S. Pidhainy. Senior Editor: Dr. Alexander S. Pidhainy. Publishes hardcover and paperback originals. Publishes 10 titles/year. 10% royalty to 2,000 copies, 15% thereafter; no advance. Photocopied submissions OK. Reports in 3 months. SAE and International Reply Coupons. Free book catalog.

Nonfiction: Academic works in bibliography, archeology, history, literature, international relations, sociology, politics and etc., in regard to Eastern Europe/Soviet Union and northern Asia. No propaganda or improperly researched works. Interested primarily in academic monographs (revised dissertations will be considered). Consult Chicago *Manual of Style*. Submit outline/synopsis and sample chapters.

NEWBURY HOUSE PUBLISHERS, INC., 54 Warehouse Lane, Rowley MA 01969. Editor-in-Chief: R.H. Ingram. Publishes paperback originals (90%) and reprints (10%). Pays 10% royalty. Pays $500 maximum advance against royalties "in special cases." Published 25 titles in 1980. State availability of photos and/or illustrations to accompany ms. Photocopied and simultaneous submissions OK. Reports in 1-2 months. SASE. Free book catalog.

Nonfiction: "Any topic of motivating interest to students (adult and near-adult) of English as a second/foreign language." Query.

Fiction: "These materials are intended for students of English as a second language; wanted are materials created especially for the purpose, or simplified and abridged versions of already published materials. Avoid topics that may give offense to persons overseas and topics that are dated or provincial."

NEWCASTLE PUBLISHING CO., INC., 13419 Saticoy, North Hollywood CA 91605. (213)873-3191. Editor-in-Chief: Alfred Saunders. Publishes trade paperback originals and trade paperback reprints. Averages 8 titles/year. Pays 5-10% royalty on retail price; no advance. Simultaneous and photocopied submissions OK. SASE. Reports in 3 weeks on queries; 6 weeks on mss. Free book catalog.

Nonfiction: How-to, self-help and metaphysical. Subjects include health (physical fitness, diet and nutrition); psychology; and religion. "Our audience is made up of college students and college-age non-students; also, adults aged 25 and up." No biography or travel. Query or submit outline/synopsis and sample chapters.

Recent Nonfiction Titles: *Tarot: A Handbook for the Apprentice*, by E. Connolly; *How to be a Couple & Still be Free*, by Tessina & Smith (psychology); and *Handwriting Analysis: The Complete Basic Book*, by Amend & Ruiz (occult/psychology).

R & R NEWKIRK, ITT Publishing, Box 1727, Indianapolis IN 46036. (317)297-4360. Contact: William L. Willard. Publishes trade paperback originals. Averages 12 titles/year. Pays 10-15% royalty on retail price. Simultaneous and photocopied submissions OK. SASE. Reports in 2 weeks on queries; 1 month on mss. Free book catalog.

Nonfiction: Self-help/motivational, technical, and sales techniques/methods. Subjects include how-to for life insurance selling. "Our books are written for life insurance agents, managers and trainers. We publish 1 softcover book per month—have scheduled prospective mss through June, 1982, but this is not an inflexible schedule and we can alter it in consideration of a publishable ms. Material must pertain to sales." Submit outline/synopsis and sample chapters or complete ms.

Recent Nonfiction Titles: *If This is a People Business . . . Why All This Paperwork?*, by Jean Walterson (training); *Time Management*, by Dennis Hensley (motivation/how-to); and *Profitable Prospecting*, by Gordon Hawkins (training).

Tips: "Research *thoroughly* your intended audience and direct your work to their needs."

NICHOLS PUBLISHING CO., Box 96, New York NY 10024. Editorial Director: Linda Kahn. Publishes hardcover originals. Averages 25-30 titles/year. Simultaneous and photocopied submissions OK. Reports in 6 weeks. SASE. Book catalog for SASE.

Nonfiction: Professional/academic materials in architecture, business, education, engineering, international affairs, marine reference, and energy topics. Query.

Recent Nonfiction Titles: *The Future of Oil*, by Peter Odell and Kenneth Rosing; *Peacemaking and the Consultant's Role*, by C.R. Mitchell; and *The World Food Book*, edited by David Crabbe and Simon Lawson.

NIGHTHAWK PRESS, Box 813, Forest Grove OR 97116. (503)357-0327. Editor: J. Saunders. Publishes hardcover and trade paperback originals. Averages 2 titles/year. Pays 10-15% royalty on wholesale price; offers variable advance. Simultaneous and photocopied submissions OK. SASE. Reports in 2 weeks on queries; 3 weeks on mss. Book catalog for business size SAE and 2 first class stamps.

Nonfiction: Biography and reference. Subjects include music. "Comprehensive music criticism, history, biography and discography mainly in the area of rock, jazz, blues, ethnic and minority music, folk, etc." Musical material only. "Our readers include the interested layperson, teachers, musicologists and sociologists." Submit outline/synopsis and sample chapters.

Recent Nonfiction Titles: *Rhythm & Blues Records 1943-75*, by Scott and Martin; *Slide Guitar—A History*, by Martin; and *Reggae—History*, by Smith.

Tips: "Try to be both simple and wise in your writing, while remaining sincere."

NORTH COUNTRY BOOKS, INC., Box 506, Sylvan Beach NY 13157. (315)762-5140. Editor: Robert B. Igoe. Publishes hardcover and trade paperback originals, and hardcover reprints. Averages 2-3 titles/year. Pays 10% royalty on retail price; no advance. Simultaneous and photocopied submissions OK. SASE. Reports in 3 weeks on queries; 3 months on mss. Free book catalog.

Nonfiction: Biography and history. Subjects include Americana; history (of the New York State region); railroads; and nostalgia. "We presently have manuscripts or proposed manuscripts for 1981-1982. We can always use good Adirondack/upstate New York history." No personal histories, autobiographies, poetry or children's books. Query or submit outline/synopsis and sample chapters.

Recent Nonfiction Titles: *The Fairy Tale Railroad*, by Henry Harter (railroad history); *The Great and the Gracious*, by Kathryn O'Brien (biographies and homes); and *The Old Line Mail*, by Richard Palmer (history of stage coach business in upstate New York).

NORTHEASTERN UNIVERSITY PRESS, 17 Cushing Hall, Northeastern University, 360 Huntingon Ave., Boston MA 02115. (617)437-2783. Editor: Robilee Smith. Publishes hardcover originals and hardcover reprints. Averages 10 titles/year. Pays 7-10% royalty on wholesale price. Simultaneous and photocopied submissions OK. SASE. Reports in 1 month on queries; 3 months on mss.

Nonfiction: Biography, reference and scholarly. Subjects include business and economics, history, music, politics, French literature, criminal justice, literary criticism, architecture, New England regional and scholarly material. "We are looking for scholarly works of high quality, particularly in the field of American history, criminal justice, business, economics, literary criticism, French literature, music and architecture. Our books are read by scholars, students, and a limited trade audience." Submit outline/synopsis and sample chapters.

Recent Nonfiction Titles: *Lightning: The Poetry of René Char*, by Nancy Kline Piore (criticism/French literature); *Prelude to Independence*, by Arthur Schlesinger (history/reprint); and *The Strands Entwined*, by Samuel Bernstein (drama/criticism).

Poetry: "We will consider translations, particularly of French poetry." Submit complete ms.

Recent Poetry Title: *Roof Slates and Other Poems of Pierre Reverdy*, by Mary Ann Caws and Patricia Terry (verse and prose translations of the French).

NORTHERN ILLINOIS UNIVERSITY PRESS, DeKalb IL 60115. (815)753-1826. Director: M.L. Livingston. Published 5 titles in 1979, 10 in 1980. Pays 10-15% royalty on wholesale price; $250 advance offered. SASE. Free catalog.

Nonfiction: "We are interested in history, literary criticism and regional studies. We do not want a collection of previously published articles, essays, etc., nor do we want unsolicited poetry." Query with outline/synopsis and sample chapters.

NORTHLAND PRESS, Box N, Flagstaff AZ 86002. (602)774-5251. Hardcover and paperback originals (80%) and reprints (20%). Advance varies. Publishes 12-20 titles/year. Pays royalty on wholesale or retail price. Transparencies and contact sheet required for photos and/or illustrations to accompany ms. Simultaneous and photocopied submissions OK. Reports in 6-8 weeks. SASE. Free book catalog.
Nonfiction: Publishes Western Americana, Indian arts and culture, Southwestern natural history and fine photography with a western orientation. Query. "Submit a proposal including an outline of the book, a sample chapter, the introduction or preface and sample illustrations. Include an inventory of items sent."
Recent Nonfiction Titles: *Of Earth & Little Rain: the Papago Indians*, by Bernard L. Fantana and John P. Scharfer; and *Photography of the West: A State-by-State Guide*, by Erwin and Peggy Bauer.

W.W. NORTON CO., INC., 500 5th Ave., New York NY 10036. (212)354-5500. Managing Editor: Sterling Lawrence. Pays 10-12½-15% royalty on retail price; advance varies. Publishes 200 titles/year. Photocopied and simultaneous submissions OK. Submit outline and/or sample chapters for fiction and nonfiction. Return of material not guaranteed without SASE. Reports in 4 weeks.
Nonfiction and Fiction: "General, adult fiction and nonfiction of all kinds on nearly all subjects and of the highest quality possible within the limits of each particular book." Last year there were 60 book club rights sales; 10 mass paperback reprint sales; "innumerable serializations, second serial, syndication, translations, etc."
Recent Titles: *Shadow of Cain*, by Vincent Bugliosi and Ken Hurwitz; *The Medicine Calf*, by Bill Hotchkiss; *Jane Brody's Nutrition Book*, by Jane Brody; *Texas Rich*, by Harry Hurt III; and *Human Options*, by Norman Cousins.
Tips: "Long novels are too expensive—keep them under 350 pages (manuscript pages)."

NOYES DATA CORP., (including Noyes Press and Noyes Medical Publications), Noyes Bldg., Park Ridge NJ 07656. Publishes hardcover originals. Published 55 titles in 1979, 60 in 1980; plans 65 in 1981. Pays 10%-12% royalty on retail price; advance varies, depending on author's reputation and nature of book. Free book catalog. Query Editorial Department. Reports in 1-2 weeks. Enclose return postage.
Nonfiction: "Art, classical studies, archeology, history. Material directed to the intelligent adult and the academic market."
Technical: Publishes practical industrial processing science; technical, economic books pertaining to chemistry, chemical engineering, food, textile, energy, pollution control, primarily those of interest to the business executive. Length: 50,000-250,000 words.

OAK TREE PUBLICATIONS, INC., 11175 Flintkote Ave., San Diego CA 92121. (714)452-8676. Editorial Director: Cynthia Tillinghast. Publishes hardcover and paperback originals. Published 15 titles in 1979, 15 in 1980. Pays 10-15% royalty; offers variable advance. Simultaneous and photocopied submissions OK. SASE. Reports in 6 weeks. Book catalog for SASE (9x12) plus 35¢ postage.
Nonfiction: Publishes books for children and parents. Query or submit outline/synopsis and sample chapters.
Recent Nonfiction Titles: *What You Think of Me Is None of My Business*, by Rev. T. Cole-Whittaker; and *I Wish I Had A Computer That Makes Waffles*, by Dr. Fitzhugh Dodson.
Fiction: Educational and informational children's books.
Recent Fiction Title: *Carnival Kidnap Caper*, by Dr. F. Dodson and P. Reuben.

OCCUPATIONAL AWARENESS, Box 948, Los Alamitos CA 90720. Editor-in-Chief: Edith Ericksen. Publishes originals for career education. Offers standard minimum book contract; advance varies. Photocopied submissions OK. Submit outline and sample chapters for books and textbooks. SASE.
Nonfiction: Materials should relate to students, careers, personnel, teachers, counselors and administrators. "We are an educational publishing company, relating occupations to curricula."

OCEANA PUBLICATIONS, INC., 75 Main St., Dobbs Ferry NY 10522. (914)693-1394. Acquisitions Editor: Ms. Heike Fenton. Publishes hardcover originals. Published 160 titles in 1980; 160 in 1981; plans 180 in 1982. Pays 10% royalty on retail price; no advance. Simultaneous and photocopied submissions OK. SASE. Reports in 6 weeks. Free book catalog.

Nonfiction: Business/economics, politics and reference. "We are mostly concerned with international and comparative law and most especially with reference books in this area." Submit outline/synopsis. Recently published *New Directions in Law of the Sea*, by M. Nordquist; *Living Together*, by I.J. Sloan (legal almanac); and *World Shipping Laws*, by J. Jackson.

ODDO PUBLISHING, INC., Box 68, Beauregard Blvd., Fayetteville GA 30214. (404)461-7627. Managing Editor: Genevieve Oddo. Publishes hardcover and paperback originals. Scripts are usually purchased outright. "We judge all scripts independently." Royalty considered for special scripts only. Book catalog 50¢. Send complete ms, typed clearly. Reports in 3-4 months. "Ms will not be returned without SASE."
Juveniles and Textbooks: Publishes language arts, workbooks in math, writing (English), photophonics, science (space and oceanography), and social studies for schools, libraries, and trade. Interested in children's supplementary readers in the areas of language arts, math, science, social studies, etc. "Texts run from 1,500 to 5,000 words. Ecology, space, oceanography, and pollution are subjects of interest. Books on patriotism. Ms must be easy to read, general, and not set to outdated themes. It must lend itself to full color illustration. No stories of grandmother long ago. No love angle, permissive language, or immoral words or statements."
Recent Titles: *Bobby Bear Meets Cousin Boo*; *Timmy Tiger and the Masked Bandit*; and *Let's Walk Safely*.

OHIO STATE UNIVERSITY PRESS, 2070 Neil Ave., Columbus OH 43210. (614)422-6930. Director: Weldon A. Kefauver. Pays royalty on wholesale or retail price. Averages 12-20 titles/year. Query letter preferred with outline and sample chapters. Reports in 2 months. Ms held longer with author's permission. Enclose return postage.
Nonfiction: Publishes history, biography, science, philosophy, the arts, political science, law, literature, economics, education, sociology, anthropology, geography, and general scholarly nonfiction. No length limitations.

*OHIO UNIVERSITY PRESS, Scott Quad, Ohio University, Athens OH 45701. (614)594-5505. Imprints include *Ohio University Press* and *Swallow Press*. Director: Patricia Elisar. Managing Editor: Holly Panich. Publishes hardcover and paperback originals (97%) and reprints (3%). Averages 40-45 titles/year. Subsidy publishes 6% of titles, based on projected market. Pays in royalties starting at 1,500 copies based on wholesale or retail price. No advance. Photocopied submissions OK. Reports in 3-5 months. SASE. Free book catalog.
Nonfiction: "General scholarly nonfiction with particular emphasis on 19th century literary criticism. Also history, social sciences, philosophy, business, western regional works and miscellaneous categories and the hard sciences." Query or submit complete ms.
Recent Nonfiction Titles: *Shawnee!*, by James Howard (sociology); *Riotous Victorians*, by Donald C. Richter (history); and *Mountain Dialogues*, by Frank Waters (myths and legends).
Fiction: Scholarly fiction, poetry and miscellaneous categories.
Recent Fiction Titles: *Night Studies*, by C. Colter; and *Seasons Such as These*, by N. Petesch.

THE OLD ARMY PRESS, Box 2243, Ft. Collins CO 80524. (303)484-5535. Editor-in-Chief: Michael J. Koury. Hardcover and paperback originals (90%) and reprints (10%). Specializes in western Americana. Pays 10% royalty; no advance. State availability of photos and/or illustrations to accompany ms. Simultaneous and photocopied submissions OK. SASE. Free book catalog.
Nonfiction: Publishes Americana (60,000 words or less); and history (60,000 words or less). Query. Recently published *Washington's Eyes*, by B. Loescher; *Legend Into History*, by C. Kulhman (western Americana); and *Dust to Dust*, by J. Gaddy.

101 PRODUCTIONS, 834 Mission St., San Francisco CA 94103. (415)495-6040. Editor-in-Chief: Jacqueline Killeen. Publishes paperback originals. Offers standard minimum book contract on retail prices. Averages 12 titles/year. Free book catalog. Will consider photocopied submissions. Query. No unsolicited mss will be read. SASE.
Nonfiction: All nonfiction, mostly how-to: cookbooks, the home, gardening, outdoors, travel. Heavy emphasis on graphics and illustrations. Most books are 192 pages.
Recent Nonfiction Titles: *Fitness First*, by J. Jones and K. Kientzler; *Best Restaurants Philadelphia*, by Elaine Tait (travel); and *More Calculated Cooking*, by Jeanne Jones (diet cookbook).

OPEN COURT PUBLISHING CO., Box 599, LaSalle IL 61301. Publisher: M. Blouke Carus. General Manager: Howard R. Webber. Averages 5-10 titles/year. Royalty contracts negotiable for each book. Query. Reports in 6-8 weeks. Enclose return postage.
Nonfiction: Philosophy, psychology, mathematics, comparative religion, education, chemistry, orientalia and related scholarly topics. "This is a publishing house run as an intellectual enterprise,

to reflect the concerns of its staff and as a service to the world of learning."
Recent Nonfiction Titles: *Philosophy of Jean-Paul Sartre*, edited by Paul Schilpp (philosophy); *Philosophy of Brand Blanshard*, edited by Paul Schilpp (philosophy); *Kant, The Architectonic and Development of His Philosophy*, by W. Werkmeister (philosophy); and *Projection and Re-Collection in Jungian Psychology: Reflections of the Soul*, by M. von Franz (psychology).

OPTIMUM PUBLISHING INTERNATIONAL INC., 511 Place D'Armes. Montreal, Quebec, Canada H2Y 2N7. (514)844-8468. Managing Director and Editor-in-Chief: Michael S. Baxendale. Hardcover and paperback originals and reprints. 10% royalty on retail price. Published 17 titles in 1979, 20 in 1980; plans approximately 25 in 1981. Publishes in both official Canadian languages (English and French). Query or submit outline/synopsis and sample chapters. Photocopied submissions OK. Reports in 2-4 weeks. SAE and International Reply Coupons.
Nonfiction: Biography; cookbooks, cooking and foods; gardening; history; natural history; how-to; health; nature; crafts; photography; art; self-help; crime; sports; and travel books.
Recent Nonfiction Titles: *Who Killed Lynne Harper?*, by B. Trent with S. Truscott (crime); *Children of the North*, by F. Breummer (general interest, native peoples, anthropology, photography); and *The Scots*, by Clifford Hanley.

ORBIS BOOKS, Maryknoll NY 10545. (914)941-7590. Editor: Philip Scharper. Publishes paperback originals. Publishes 30 titles/year. 10-12½-15% royalty on retail prices; advance averages $1,000. Query with outline, sample chapters, and prospectus. Reports in 4 to 6 weeks. Enclose return postage.
Nonfiction: "Religious developments in Asia, Africa, and Latin America. Christian missions. Justice and peace. Christianity and world religions."
Recent Nonfiction Titles: *Archbishop Romero: Martyr of Salvador*, by Placido Erdozain; *Exodus: A Hermeneutics of Freedom*, by J. Severino Croatto; and *New Ministries: The Global Context*, by William R. Burrows.

OREGON STATE UNIVERSITY PRESS, 101 Waldo Hall, Corvallis OR 97331. (503)754-3166. Hardcover and paperback originals. Averages 5-10 titles/year. Pays royalty on wholesale price. No advance. Submit contact sheet of photos and/or illustrations to accompany ms. Reports in 4 months. SASE. Free book catalog for SASE.
Nonfiction: Publishes Americana; biography; economics; history; nature; philosophy; energy and recreation; reference; scientific (biological sciences only); technical (energy); and American literary criticism books. Emphasis on Pacific or Northwestern topics. Submit outline/synopsis and sample chapters.
Recent Nonfiction Titles: *Contemporary Northwest Writing*, by R. Carlson (anthology); and *Salmonid Ecosystems of the North Pacific*, by W. McNeil and D. Himsworth (marine biology).

ORYX PRESS, 2214 N. Central Ave., Phoenix AZ 85004. (602)254-6156. President/Editorial Director: Phyllis B. Steckler. Publishes hardcover and paperback originals. Published 14 titles in 1979, 23 in 1980; plans 26 in 1981. Pays 10-15% royalty on net receipts; no advance. Simultaneous and photocopied submissions OK. SASE. Reports in 6 weeks. Free book catalog.
Nonfiction: Bibliographies; directories; education; popular reference; library and information science; and agriculture monographs. Publishes nonfiction for public, college and university, junior college and special libraries; education faculty members; agriculture specialists. Query or submit outline/synopsis and sample chapters, or complete ms.
Recent Nonfiction Titles: *Meeting the Needs of the Handicapped*, by Thomas (resource for teachers and librarians); *Joy of Cataloging*, by Berman (library information science monograph); and *Current Index to Journals in Education* (educational reference).

OTTENHEIMER PUBLISHERS, INC., 300 Reisterstown Rd., Baltimore MD 21208. (301)484-2100. President: Allen Hirsh Jr. Publishes hardcover and paperback originals. Publishes 250 titles/year. Negotiates royalty and advance. Photocopied submissions OK. Reports in 1 month.
Nonfiction: Cookbooks, reference, gardening, home repair and decorating, and automotive. Submit outline/synopsis and sample chapters or complete ms.

OUR SUNDAY VISITOR, INC., 200 Noll Plaza, Huntington IN 46750. (219)356-8400. Managing Editor: Paul Zomberg. Publishes paperback and hardcover originals and reprints. Pays variable royalty on net receipts; offers average $500 advance. Averages 20-30 titles a year. Reports in 1 month on most queries and submissions. SASE. Free author's guide and catalog.
Nonfiction: Catholic viewpoints on current issues; reference and guidance; Bibles and devotional books; Catholic heritage books.

Recent Nonfiction Titles: *Strange Gods: Contemporary Religious Cults in America*, by William Whalen; and *Forever Family: Our Adventures in Adopting Older Children*, by Ruth Piepenbrink.
Fiction: Juveniles only. Submit 2-page annotated outline and sample chapter (minimum).
Recent Fiction Titles: *God Sends the Seasons (1981)*, by Katherine Allan Meyer (preschool picture book).

OWLSWOOD PRODUCTIONS, INC., 1355 Market St., San Francisco CA 94103. (415)626-2480. Editor: Susan H. Herbert. Publishes trade paperback originals. Averages 4 titles/ year. Buys some mss outright; offers advance. Simultaneous and photocopied submissions OK. SASE. Reports in 1 week.
Nonfiction: Cookbook. Subjects include cooking and foods. "Our books are for anyone interested in good, wholesome foods." Query or submit outline/synopsis and sample chapters.
Recent Nonfiction Titles: *Versatile Vegetables* and *The Low Calorie Way*, by Kyte and Greenberg (cookbooks); and *Chicken Favorites*, by MK Hollander (cookbook).

OXFORD UNIVERSITY PRESS, INC., 200 Madison Ave., New York NY 10016. (212)679-7300. Editor-in-Chief: Sheldon Meyer. Publishes hardcover originals and paperback reprints. Publishes over 100 titles/year. Pays standard royalty; offers variable advance. Photocopied submissions OK. SASE. Free book catalog.
Nonfiction: American history, music and political science. Submit outline/synopsis and sample chapters.
Recent Nonfiction Titles: *Franklin D. Roosevelt and American Foreign Policy* (political history); *Jerome Kern* (biography); *American Musical Theatre* (popular history); and *The Majority Finds Its Past* (women's history).

OXMOOR HOUSE, (a division of The Progressive Farmer Co.), Box 2262, Birmingham AL 35202. Director: Don Logan. Editor: John Logue. Publishes hardcover and paperback originals. Pays on royalty basis or fee. Published 12 titles in 1979; 13 in 1980. Submit outline and sample chapter. Reports in 1 month. SASE.
Nonfiction: "Publishes books of general interest to Southern readers—cookbooks, garden books; books on crafts, sewing, photography, art, outdoors, antiques and how-to topics.
Recent Nonfiction Titles: *The American South; Naturecrafts*; and *Quick and Easy Cookbook*.

P. A. R., INC., Abbott Park Place, Providence RI 02903. (401)331-0130. President: Barry M. Smith. Hardcover and paperback originals. Specializes in textbooks for business schools, junior or community colleges, and adult continuing education programs. Pays 10% royalty. Markets through fall and winter workshops throughout the country with special seminars that are periodically held by authors and sales staff. State availability of photos or illustrations to furnish at a later date. Simultaneous submissions OK. Reports in 2-4 months. SASE. Free book catalog.
Nonfiction: K. L. Short, Department Editor. Business, economics, law, politics, psychology, sociology, technical, textbooks.
Recent Titles: *Library of Adult Basic Educations*; *The Person You Are* (personal development); *Concepts of Business* (management); and *Principles of Marketing* (management).

P.S. ENTERPRISES, 1627 Moody Ct., Peoria IL 61604. (309)674-2008. Contact: Paul T. Jackson. Publishes trade paperback originals and trade paperback reprints. Averages 2 titles/year. Pays 10-33% royalty on retail price; buys some mss outright; "will work 3-way split with author/ associations/publisher after expenses." Simultaneous and photocopied submissions OK. SASE. Reports in 2 weeks on queries; 1 month on mss. Free book catalog.
Imprints: *Re: mark* and *Recorded Sound Research* (nonfiction), Paul T. Jackson, owner.
Nonfiction: How-to, reference, self-help and seminar loose-leaf manuals. Subjects include hobbies (record collecting, discography and bibliography of sound). "Re: mark, 'making your mark,' is a marketing service which has launched a series of self-help/how-to outline manuals for direct and seminar sales; subjects can be anything relating to attaining success in business activities. We're looking for annotated bibliographies on the marketing, advertising, or business fields—especially for the hotel-motel-convention-meeting-seminarsindustry. We're also looking for self-help/how-to-make-your-mark material related to various phases of business, and suitable for use in half- to two-day seminars. We will look at any book on recorded sound." Query or submit outline/ synopsis and sample chapters.
Recent Nonfiction Titles: *Collector's Contact Guide* (directory/bibliography); *Sound Search* (collection of subject guides); and *Interview Manual* (outline for seminars), all by Paul T. Jackson.
Tips: "Costs of book production, inventory and mailing are eating away at much of the market; however, self-help books, manuals, outlines and reference guides will do well if they can be done inexpensively. A 20-page book with 'meat' is better than a 'made-up' book with everything. 'Less is better,' since comprehensiveness is usually unusable and too expensive to produce."

PACIFIC BOOKS, PUBLISHERS, Box 558, Palo Alto CA 94302. (415)856-0550. Editor: Henry Ponleithner. Royalty schedule varies with book. No advance. Averages 8 titles/year. Will send catalog on request. Send complete ms. Reports "promptly." SASE.
Nonfiction: General interest, professional, technical and scholarly nonfiction trade books. Specialties include western Americana and Hawaiiana.
Recent Nonfiction Titles: *What Comes After You Say, "I Love You?"*, by James R. Hine (marriage); and *Mountain Climber: George B. Bayley, 1840-1894*, by Evelyn Hyman Chase (biography).
Textbooks and Reference: Text and reference books; high school and college.

PADRE PRODUCTIONS, Box 1275, San Luis Obispo CA 93406. Editor-in-Chief: Lachlan P. MacDonald. Publishes hardcover and paperback originals (90%) and reprints (10%). Pays 6% minimum royalty; advance ranges from $200-1,000. Published 4 titles in 1979, 26 in 1980, 6 in 1981. State availability of photos and/or illustrations or include contact sheet or stat. Simultaneous submissions OK. Reports in 2-4 months. Mss and queries without SASE are not answered. Book catalog for SASE.
Nonfiction: Publishes Americana (antiques); art; business opportunities; collectibles; cookbooks; history (local California); hobbies; how-to; investments for the layman; nature (with illustrations); photography; poetry; psychology; publishing; recreation; reference; self-help; and travel books. Query or submit outline and sample chapters. "Ample packaging; type all material; don't send slides unless asked." Recently published *Nature Walks on the San Luis Coast*, by H. Wieman (nature); *With Love, From Jo*, by J. Bolivar (inspirational story of a young woman's faith in the face of cancer); and *Bright Eyes*, by J. Unruh (baby jackrabbit tale).
Fiction: Publishes (in order of preference): adventure; fictional treatment of entertainment world. Juvenile titles only for 10-14 year readers, about 160 pages with strong illustrative possibilities. Submit complete ms.

PAGURIAN PRESS LTD., Suite 1106, 335 Bay St., Toronto, Ontario, Canada M5H 2R3. Editor-in-Chief: Christopher Ondaatje. Publishes paperback and hardcover originals and reprints. Offers negotiable royalty contract. Advance negotiable. No titles published in 1980. Photocopied submissions OK. Submit 2-page outline, synopsis or chapter headings and contents. Reports "immediately." SAE and International Reply Coupons.
Nonfiction: Publishes general interest trade and art books. Will consider fine arts, outdoor and cookbooks. Length: 40,000-70,000 words.

PALADIN PRESS, Box 1307, Boulder CO 80306. (303)443-7250. President/Publisher: Peder C. Lund. General Manager: Timothy J. Leifield. Editorial Director: Devon M. Christensen. Publishes hardcover and paperback originals (80%) and paperback reprints (20%). Averages 23-25 titles/year. Pays 10-12-15% royalty on net sales. Simultaneous and photocopied submissions OK. Reports in 1 month. SASE. Free book catalog.
Nonfiction: "Paladin Press primarily publishes original manuscripts on military science, weaponry, self-defense, survival, police science, guerrilla warfare and fieldcraft. Survival and how-to manuscripts, as well as pictorial histories, are given priority. Manuals on building weapons, when technically accurate and cleanly presented, are encouraged. If applicable, send sample photographs and line drawings with outline and sample chapters." Query or submit outline/synopsis and sample chapters.
Recent Nonfiction Titles: *Survival Poaching*, by Ragnar Benson (hunting); and *The Revenge Book*, by Bob Smith (humor).

PAN AMERICAN NAVIGATION SERVICE, INC., 16934 Saticoy St., Box 9046, Van Nuys CA 91409. (213)345-2744. Editorial Director: John Dohm. Publishes hardcover and paperback originals. Averages 5-6 new or revised editions/year. Offers 8-10% royalty on retail price. No advance. No simultaneous submissions; photocopied submissions OK. SASE. Reports in 8 weeks. SASE.
Nonfiction: How-to; reference (aviation); technical (aeronautical); textbooks; and all civil aviation work. "Exclusively, on general (non-military) aviation (i.e., private, business, executive and airline aviation). Mostly the training of air crew members to fly and service these aircraft. Specializing in preparation of airmen for their Federal examination ratings, but also aviation (civil) in general. We have no proscriptions on treatment or specific topics in our general field, actually; the only criterion is one of fairly high general interest to private and commercial civilian pilots and crewmembers." Query first or submit outline/synopsis and sample chapters.
Recent Nonfiction Titles: *The New Private Pilot*, staff-written (how to obtain a private pilot license); *Airline Transport Pilot*, by staff (study text and exams for the FAA ATP license); *Powerplant Mechanics Manual*, staff-written (preparing for the Federal license); and *How to Be a Flight Steward/Stewardess*, by Johni Smith (handbook and training manual for airline cabin attendants).

THE PAN-AMERICAN PUBLISHING COMPANY, Subsidiary of The Pan-American Industrial Loan Company, Box 1505, Las Vegas NM 87701. Editor-in-Chief: Rose Calles. Publishes hardcover and trade paperback originals (50%), and reprints (50%). Averages 10 titles/year. Pays 10-15% royalty on retail price. Simultaneous submissions OK. SASE. reports in 1 month on queries; 6 weeks on mss. Free book catalog with SASE.
Nonfiction: Biography, cookbook, how-to, illustrated book and self-help. Subjects include Americana, art, cooking and foods, history and hobbies. "Historical writing of general interest and readership, controversial subjects, and topics with wide appeal, will all receive top priority during our forthcoming publishing seasons." No erotic, scholarly, regional, science, law, or highly technical manuals. Query.
Recent Nonfiction Titles: *Padre Martinez & Bishop Lamy*, by Ray John de Aragon (history); *The Complete Camper's Cookbook*, by Alberta G. Vigil (cookbook); and *The Great Lovers*, by Ray John de Aragon (history).
Fiction: Adventure, confession, fantasy, gothic, historical, horror, mystery, romance, science fiction, suspense and western. "We will consider most types of fiction. We are particularly interested in books of mass-market appeal." No pornography or homosexual material. Query.
Recent Fiction Titles: *Saints and Sinners*, by Marian Ackerman (historical); *The Pearl*, by Maximo de Aragon (poetry); and *The Legend of La Llorona*, by Ray John de Aragon (horror-romance).

PANTHEON BOOKS, Division of Random House, Inc., 201 E. 50th St., New York NY 10022. Managing Editor: Betsy Amster. Published more than 60 titles last year. Pays royalty on retail price. Address queries to Don Gutenplan, Adult Editorial Department (15th Floor). Enclose return postage.
Nonfiction: Books mostly by academic authors. Emphasis on Asia, international politics, radical social theory, history, medicine, and law. Recreational guides and practical how-to books as well. Query.
Juveniles: Publishes some juveniles. Address queries to Juvenile Editorial Department (6th floor).
Recent Nonfiction Titles: *"Watch Out For the Foreign Guests!"*, by O. Schell; *The Success and Failure of Picasso*, by J. Berger; and *American Dreams: Lost and Found*, by S. Terkel.
Fiction: Publishes fewer than 5 novels each year, primarily mysteries. Query. Recently published *A Killing Kindness*, by R. Hill; *Seagull*, by Y. Kemal; and *Macho Camacho's Beat*, by L.R. Sánchez.

PARENTS MAGAZINE PRESS, A division of Parents' Magazine Enterprises, Inc., 685 3rd Ave., New York NY 10017. (212)878-8700. Editor: Stephanie Calmenson. Publishes hardcover originals. Averages 20 titles/year. Pays flat fee for Parents' book club edition; royalty for trade and library editions which are distributed by Elsevier-Dutton. Photocopied submissions OK. SASE. Reports in 6-8 weeks.
Nonfiction: "We are not doing any nonfiction at this time."
Fiction: "We are publishing only easy-to-read, full color picture books for children 2-7. Average text/art pages about 38, in a 48-page self-ended book. Approximately 400-800 words. Emphasis is on humor, action, and child appeal." Submit complete ms.
Recent Titles: *But No Elephants*, by Jerry Smath; *Henry's Awful Mistakes*, by Robert Quackenbush; and *Detective Bob and the Great Ape Escape*, by David Harrison, pictures by Ned Delaney.

PARKER PUBLISHING CO., West Nyack NY 10994. Publishes hardcover originals and paperback reprints. Pays 10% royalty; 5% mail order and book clubs. Publishes 85 titles/year. Will send catalog on request. Reports in 3-5 weeks.
Nonfiction: Publishes practical, self-help, how-to books. Subject areas include popular health, letterwriting, electronics, education, secretarial, selling, personal and business self-improvement. Length: 65,000 words.
Recent Nonfiction Titles: *Hawaiian and Polynesian Miracle Health Secrets*, by Stone and Stone; and *101 PupilsParentsTeacher Situations and How to Handle Them*, by Mamchak and Mamchak.

PAULIST PRESS, 545 Island Road, Ramsey, N.J. 07446. (201)825-7300. Imprints include Newman Books, Deus Books, and Exploration Books. Editorial Director: Kevin A. Lynch. Managing Editor: Donald Brophy. Publishes hardcover and paperback originals (90%) and paperback reprints (10%). Published 120 titles in 1979, 110 in 1980. Pays royalty on retail price; sometimes an advance. Photocopied submissions OK. SASE. Reports in 4 weeks.
Nonfiction: Philosophy, religion, self-help, and textbooks (religious subject). "We would like to see theology (Catholic and ecumenical Christian), popular spirituality, liturgy, and religious education texts." Submit outline/synopsis and sample chapters.
Recent Nonfiction Titles: *Healing Life's Hurts*, by Dennis and Matthew Linn (spirituality); *Jesus

the Christ, by Walter Kasper (theology); *The Community of the Beloved Disciple*, by R. Brown (New Testament studies); and *Invisible Partner*, by John Sanford (psychology).

PEACE PRESS, INC., 3828 Willat Ave., Culver City CA 90230. President: Bob Zaugh. Publishes paperback originals and reprints. Specializes in how-to; socio-political history; cultural analysis; health; appropriate technology; and psychology books. Pays 5% royalty on retail price; offers small advance. Averages 6-8 titles/year. Submit outline/synopsis and sample chapters. State availability of photos and/or illustrations. Simultaneous and photocopied submissions OK. Reports in 2-3 months. SASE.
Nonfiction: Editorial: Deborah Lott. Publishes how-to; psychology; socio-political history; alternative energy; serious nonfiction; self-help; religious; cookbooks; ecology; and health.
Recent Nonfiction Titles: *Earthquake Ready*, by Virginia Kimball (safety-health); and *Guide to Stress Reduction*, by Dr. L. John Mason (health).

PELICAN PUBLISHING CO., INC., 1101 Monroe St., Gretna LA 70053. (504)368-1175. Imprints include *Pelican Publishing House*, *Paddlewheel Publications*, *Dixie Press*, *Hope Publications*, *Friends of the Cabildo*, *Sam Mims*, *Jackson Square Press*, and *Mississippi Library Association*. Editor-in-Chief: James Calhoun. Editor: Frumie Selchen. Publishes hardcover and paperback originals (90%) and reprints (10%). Publishes 25 titles/year. Pays 10-15% royalty on wholesale price; sometimes offers advance. Photocopied submissions preferred. SASE if manuscript is to be returned. Reports in 3 months. Book catalog for SASE.
Nonfiction: Art; cookbooks/cooking; self-help (especially motivational); inspirational and travel (guidebooks). Submit outline/synopsis and sample chapters.
Recent Nonfiction Titles: *The Maverick Guide to New Zealand*, by Robert W. Bone; *Best Editorial Cartoons of the Year* (annual series); and *La Bouche Creole*, by Leon E. Soniat Jr.
Fiction: Novels. "We only publish one title per year." Query.
Recent Fiction Title: *The Catalyst*, by Nelda Gavlin (suspense).

PENGUIN BOOKS, 625 Madison Ave., New York NY 10022. Editorial Director: Kathryn Court. Publishes paperback originals (5-10%) reprints (90-95%). Publishes 200 titles/year. Pays standard royalty on retail price; offers variable advance. Photocopied submissions OK. SASE. Reports in 4 weeks. Free book catalog.
Nonfiction: Educational handbooks on health and humor. "We do not publish original fiction or poetry." Submit outline/synopsis and sample chapters.
Recent Nonfiction Titles: *The Bank of Terms*, by M. Witte (puns and humor); *Travelling Healthy*, by S. and R. Hillnia; and *Zero-Sum Society*, by Lester Thurow (economics).

THE PENNSYLVANIA STATE UNIVERSITY PRESS, 215 Wagner Bldg., University Park PA 16802. (814)865-1327. Editor-in-Chief: Jack Pickering. Hardcover and paperback originals. Specializes in books of scholarly value, and/or regional interest. Averages 40 titles/year. Pays 10% royalty on wholesale price; no advance. Maintains own distribution company in England which serves the British Empire, Europe, etc. Submit outline/synopsis and sample chapters or complete ms. Send prints if photos/illustrations are to accompany ms. Simultaneous and photocopied submissions OK. Reports in 2-4 months. SASE. Free book catalog.
Nonfiction: Publishes art, biography, business, economics, history, hobbies, medicine and psychiatry, multimedia material, music, nature, philosophy, politics, psychology, recreation, reference, religious, scientific, sociology, technical, textbooks, women's studies, black studies, agriculture books and *Keystone Books* (a paperback series concentrating on topics of special interest to those living in the mid-Atlantic states.) Recently published *Rivers of Pennsylvania*, by T. Palmer (nature, conservation, history); *Clouds and Storms*, by F.H. Ludlam (meteorology); and *The Development of Plato's Metaphysics*, by Henry Teloh (philosophy).

PEREGRINE SMITH, INC., Box 667, Layton UT 84041. (801)376-9800. Editorial Director: Richard A. Firmage. Publishes hardcover and paperback originals (50%) and reprints (50%). Pays 10% royalty on wholesale price; no advance. Photocopied submissions OK. Reports in 3 months. SASE. Book catalog 28¢.
Nonfiction: "Western American history, natural history, American architecture, art history, arts and crafts (including how-to) and fine arts. We consider biographical, historical, descriptive and analytical studies in all of the above. Much emphasis is also placed on pictorial content. Many of

our books are used as university texts." Query or submit outline/synopsis and sample chapters. Consult *Chicago Manual of Style*. Recently published *Rodin*, by R. Rilke (aesthetic criticism); *The Simple Home*, by C. Keeler (simple philosophy); and *A Photographic Vision*, edited by Peter Neumeyer (photographic history).

Fiction: "We have mainly published reprints or anthologies of American writers; but are very interested in expanding in the areas of serious fiction: novels, short stories, drama and poetry. This will include reprints of important work as well as new material." Query or submit outline/synopsis and sample chapters. "No unsolicited manuscripts accepted. Query first." Recently published *Homage to John Clare*, by P. Neumeyer (poetry); and *Trout Madness*, by R. Traver (short stories).

Tips: "Write seriously. If fiction, no potboilers, bestseller movie tie-in type hype books. We like Pynchon and Gaddis. If nonfiction, only serious, well-researched critical, historical or craft-related topics. No self-help books."

THE PERFECTION FORM CO., 8350 Hickman Rd., Suite 15, Des Moines IA 50322. (515)278-0133. Senior Editor: Wayne F. DeMouth. Publishes paperback originals. Publishes 10 titles/year. Pays $200-850 outright purchase; no advance. Simultaneous and photocopied submissions OK. SASE. Reports in 1 month. Free book catalog.

Fiction: Adventure, humor and mainstream. "Original manuscripts of approximately 30,000-40,000 words written for young adult audiences ages 12-18. Content should be appropriate for average young people. We do not want stories with heavy moral overtones, offensive language, sex, etc." Submit complete ms. Recently published *The Ghost Boy*, *The Vandal* and *An Alien Spring*, by Anne Schraff (young adult).

PERIGEE BOOKS, A Division of the Putnam Publishing Group, Subsidiary of MCA, Inc., 200 Madison Ave., New York NY 10016. (212)576-8900. Editorial Director: Samuel A. Mitnick. Publishes trade paperback originals (50%) and reprints (50%). Averages 50-75 titles/year. Pays starting 6-7% royalty "on retail price through normal channels; sometimes different on special sales, etc. Sometimes we purchase finished books from packagers as an outright, royalty inclusive deal." Offers average $3,500 advance "for unagented mss, but it's gone much higher for some titles." Simultaneous and photocopied submissions OK ("if clear and legible"). SASE. Reports in 1 month.

Nonfiction: How-to, humor, reference and self-help. Subjects include animals, health, hobbies, music, recreation, sociology, sports, and women's studies. "We'd like to see reference, how-to. beauty and health, humor, and 'youth market'—oriented books (for 16-35 year olds). Absolutely *no* cookbooks, no religious mss, no autobiography, no art books. Unlikely subjects are history, biography, rock-n-roll (either 'fan' books or surveys)." Query or submit outline/synopsis and two sample chapters. All unsolicited full mss are returned unopened.

Recent Nonfiction Titles: *How to Help Your Child Start School*, by Bernard Ryan, Jr (how-to/parenting); *The Golden Turkey Awards*, by Harry and Michael Medved (humor/film); and *The New Massage*, by Gordon Inkeles (self-help/sports).

Fiction: "We are categorically uninterested in original fiction at this time. We will be looking for hardcover literature to reprint in trade paper, similar in nature to our recent publication of 5 books each by Yasuanri Kawabata, Junichiro Tanazaki, Kobo Abe and Yukio Mishima. No material that hasn't already been published and highly recognized (i.e., Nobel Prize material, etc.)" Submit through agent only.

Recent Fiction Titles: *The Deer Park*, by Norman Mailer (novel); *The Makioka Sisters*, by Junichiro Tanazaki (novel); and *The Box Man*, by Kobo Abe (novel/science fiction).

*PERIVALE PRESS, 13830 Erwin St., Van Nuys CA 91401. (213)785-4671. Publisher: Lawrence P. Spingarn. Publishes trade paperback originals and trade. paperback reprints. Averages 2-3 titles/year. Subsidy publishes 25% of books. "If the book's appeal is limited, we ask a subsidy to cover printing that is returnable from proceeds after one year." Pays 10-15% royalty or through grants. Simultaneous and photocopied submissions OK. SASE. Reports in 1 week on queries; 2 months on mss. Book catalog for business size SAE and 1 first class stamp.

Nonfiction: Humor and criticism. Subjects include criticism. "We are open to any new ideas that come along, particularly cook books, herbals and humor." Query.

Recent Nonfiction Title: *Not-so-Simple Neil Simon*, by Edythe McGovern (criticism of dramatic work of Neil Simon).

Fiction: Experimental and mainstream; "open." " We are fully scheduled until 1983." No novels over 120 pages. Query.

Recent Fiction Titles: *Rice Powder*, by Sergio Galindo (novella; translation); *Mountainhouse*, by Patt McDermitt (novella; regional fiction, California); and *The Blue Door*, by Lawrence Spingarn (stories).

Poetry: "Schedule is complete until 1982." No rhymed traditional lyrics, love poems or juvenile poetry. Submit complete ms.
Recent Poetry Titles: *Open to the Sun*, edited by Nora Wieser (anthology of Latin-American women poets by women); *Birds of Prey*, by Joyce Mansour (surrealist French poetry in translation); and *The Dark Playground*, by Lawrence Spingarn (satirical and polemical poetry).
Tips: "Study the trends in one particular field. Length is a factor. In all cases we hope for either grants from foundations or a returnable author subsidy written into the contract."

PERSEA BOOKS, 225 LaFayette St., New York City NY 10012. (212)431-5270. Editorial Director: Karen Braziller. Publisher: Michael Braziller. Publishes hardcover and paperback originals and reprints. Published 9 titles in 1979, 8 in 1980. Pays 6-15% royalty. Offers average $500 advance. Simultaneous and photocopied submissions OK. SASE. Reports in 2 months. Free book catalog.
Nonfiction: Poetry, critical essays and literary criticism. "Authors must send query letters first. If no query letter is sent unsolicited manuscripts will not be considered."
Recent Nonfiction Title: *Looking for LaForgue*, by D. Arkell.
Fiction: Experimental; historical; mainstream; and autobiographical fiction. Submit complete ms.
Recent Fiction Titles: *A Season in Paradise*, by B. Breytenbach; and *The Open Cage*, by A. Viezienska.

PERSEPHONE PRESS, Box 7222, Watertown MA 02172. (617)924-0336. Executives: Pat McGloin and Gloria Z. Greenfield. Publishes trade paperback originals. Averages 8 titles/year. Pays 12% maximum royalty on retail price. Simultaneous and photocopied submissions OK. SASE. Reports in 2 weeks on queries; 2 months on mss. Free book catalog.
Nonfiction: Lesbian/women's books. Subjects include history, philosophy, politics, psychology, religion, sociology and lesbian/women's issues. "Persephone Press is interested in publishing innovative and provocative books by women with a strong lesbian sensibility. Our audience is general, but mainly consists of women, both lesbians and straights. We do not publish manuscripts by men." Query. All unsolicited mss are returned unopened.
Recent Nonfiction Titles: *Woman, Church and State*, by Matilda Joslyn Gage (reprint); and *A Feminist Tarot*, by Sally Miller Gearhart and Susan Rennie.
Fiction: Adventure, confession, erotica, ethnic, experimental, fantasy, historical, humor, mystery, romance, science fiction and women's/lesbian. "Innovative and provocative fiction by women with a strong lesbian sensibility. No fiction by men." Query. All unsolicited mss are returned unopened.
Recent Fiction Titles: *Choices*, by Nancy Toder (novel about lesbian love); and *The Wanderground: Stories of the Hill Women*, by Sally Gearhart (Utopian novel).
Poetry: "Innovative and provocative poetry by women with a strong lesbian sensibility. We do not publish poetry by individual authors, nor do we publish works by men." Query.
Recent Poetry Titles: *Claiming An Identity They Taught Me To Despise*, by Michelle Cliff (prose-poetry); and *The Lesbian Anthology of Poetry*, by Elly Bulkin/Joan Larkin Eds. (lesbian poetry).

PETERSEN PUBLISHING COMPANY, 6725 Sunset Blvd., Los Angeles CA 90028. (213)657-5100. Sales Promotion Manager: Linda Marcus. Submit ms to Director, Book Division: John Carrington. Editorial Director: Lee Kelley. Publishes hardcover and paperback originals. Published 10 titles in 1979, 12 in 1980. Pays royalty. Photocopied submissions OK. SASE. Reports in 4 weeks. Free book catalog for SASE.
Nonfiction: How-to and nonfiction works relating to automotive, photography, Americana, art, sports and hobbies. Size and format variable. Particularly interested in titles in any field written by an acknowledged expert in that area. Query or submit outline/synopsis and sample chapters.
Recent Nonfiction Titles: *Method Modeling*, by Valerie Cragin; *Toyota Tune-Up*, (in-house on auto repair); and *A Gallery of Waterfowl and Upland Birds*, paintings by D. Maas and essays by G. Hill (combination art and outdoor essays by recognizable experts in hunting and nature art).

PETERSON'S GUIDES, INC., Box 2123, Princeton NJ 08540. (609)924-5338. Publisher/President: Peter W. Hegener. Editorial Director: Karen C. Hegener. Publishes paperback originals. Averages 12 titles/year. Pays 8% royalty on "net price after discount," buys some mss outright; offers advance. Photocopied submissions OK. SASE. Reports in 2 months. Free book catalog for SASE.
Nonfiction: Educational reference works. Submit complete ms or outline.
Recent Nonfiction Title: *Jobs for English Majors and Other Smart People*, by John Munschauer.

PETROCELLI BOOKS, INC., 1101 State Road, Princeton NJ 08540. (609)924-5851. Editorial Director: O.R. Petrocelli. Senior Editor: Roy Grisham. Publishes hardcover and paperback originals. Publishes 18 titles/year. Offers 12½-18% royalties. No advance. Simultaneous and photoco-

pied submissions OK. SASE. Reports in 4 weeks. Free book catalog.
Nonfiction: Business/economics; reference; technical; and textbooks. Submit outline/synopsis and sample chapters.
Recent Nonfiction Titles: *Management Fraud*, by Elliot and Willingham (business); *Computer Optimization Techniques*, by W. Conley (computer/mathematics); and *Sexual Harassment*, by Mary C. Meyer.

S.G. PHILLIPS, INC., 305 W. 86th St., New York NY 10024. (212)787-4405. Editor: Sidney Phillips. Publishes hardcover originals. "Graduated royalty schedule varies where artists or collaborators share in preparation." Published 3 titles in 1979. Will send a catalog to a writer on request. "Query; no unsolicited mss." Reports in 30-60 days. SASE.
General and Juvenile: "Nonfiction for adults and young people. Particular interests—informational books. Length depends on age group."

PHILOMEL BOOKS, Division of The Putnam Publishing Group, 200 Madison Ave., New York NY 10016. (212)889-5422. Editor-in-Chief: Ann Beneduce. Editors: Sarah Crane, Linda Falken, Joan Knight. Publishes quality hardcover originals. Publishes 30 titles/year. Pays standard royalty. Advance negotiable. Simultaneous and photocopied submissions OK. SASE. Reports in 2 months. Free book catalog on request.
Nonfiction: Young adult and children's picture books. Submit text. Does not want to see alphabet books or workbooks. Submit complete ms to Sarah Crane. Prefers query first.
Recent Nonfiction Title: *Columbia and Beyond: The Story of the Space Shuttle*, by Franklyn Branley.
Fiction: Young adult and children's book on any topic. Submit complete ms to Sarah Crane.

THE PICKWICK PRESS, 5001 Baum Blvd., Pittsburgh PA 15213. Editorial Director: Dikran Y. Hadidian. Publishes paperback originals and reprints. Averages 3-6 titles/year. Pays 8-10% royalty on wholesale or retail price; no advance. Photocopied submissions OK. Reports in 2 months. SASE. Free book catalog.
Nonfiction: Religious and scholarly mss in Biblical archeology, Biblical studies, church history and theology. Also reprints of outstanding out-of-print titles and original texts and translations. No popular religious material. Query. Consult *MLA Style Sheet* or Turabian's *A Manual for Writers*.
Recent Nonfiction Titles: *Reformed Roots . . .*, by Irena Bachus (historical-Biblical); and *Orientation by Disorientation*, by Spencer (literary and Biblical literary criticism).

PICTORIAL PRESS, Communications Institute, 1550 Bryant St., San Francisco CA 94103. Editor-in-Chief: T.S. Connelly. Publishes paperback originals. Royalty contract on wholesale price; offers negotiable advance. Averages 2-3 titles/year. Photocopied and simultaneous submissions OK. Query first and include research outline. Reports in 45 days. SASE.
Nonfiction and Art: Publishes children's art; books about cable television; broadcast radiation; radiation and electromagnetic subjects.
Recent Nonfiction Titles: *BCTV: Bibliography on Cable Television*; and *CINCOM: Courses in Communications*.

PILGRIMAGE, INC., Route 11, Box 553, Jonesboro TN 36759. (615)753-4887. Editor: Michael Braswell. Publishes hardcover and trade paperback originals, and trade paperback reprints. Average 10-15 titles/year. Pays 10% royalty on wholesale price. Simultaneous and photocopied submissions OK. SASE. Reports in 1 month on queries; 2 months on mss. Free book catalog.
Nonfiction: Reference, textbook, bibliography, journal and monograph. Subjects include business and economics, health, history, philosophy, politics, psychology, religion, sociology and "most other academic and professional subject areas. We are interested in reviewing monographs (30-100 pages) and book proposals in all academic and professional areas, particularly in the behavioral and social sciences. Our publications are for the academic community, human service agency professionals and an informed lay audience." Query or submit outline/synopsis and sample chapters.
Recent Nonfiction Titles: *Behavior Change Research*, by Michael Lambert and Lorraine Lauper (bibliography); *Psychotherapy for Offenders*, by David Lester (correctional counseling); *Understanding American Government*, by Raymond Chambers (American studies/political science); and *Organized Crime in Africa*, by James Opolot (comparative criminal justice).

PILOT BOOKS, 347 5th Ave., New York NY 10016. (212)685-0736. Publishes paperback originals. Offers standard royalty contract based on wholesale or retail price. Usual advance is $250, but this varies, depending on author's reputation and nature of book. Averages 20-30 titles/year. Send outline. Reports in 4 weeks. Enclose return postage.

General Nonfiction, Reference, and Business: "Publishes financial, business, travel, career, personal guides and training manuals. Our training manuals are utilized by America's giant corporations, as well as the government." Directories and books on moneymaking opportunities. Wants "clear, concise treatment of subject matter." Length: 8,000-30,000 words. Recently published *Innovative Strategies for Locating, Recruiting and Hiring the Handicapped*, by R. Rabby; and *A Woman's Guide to Starting a Small Business*, by Mary Lester.

PINNACLE BOOKS, 1430 Broadway, New York NY 10018. Editorial Director: Patrick O'Connor. Publishes paperback originals and reprints. "Contracts and terms are standard and primarily competitive." Publishes 160 titles/year. Pays royalty on retail price. Catalog and requirements memo for SASE. "Will no longer accept unsolicited mss. Most books are assigned to known writers or developed through established agents. However, an intelligent, literate and descriptive letter of query will often be given serious consideration." SASE.
General: "Books range from general nonfiction to commercial trade fiction in most popular categories. Pinnacle's list is aimed for wide popular appeal, with fast-moving, highly compelling escape reading, adventure, espionage, historical intrigue and romance, science fiction, western, popular sociological issues, topical nonfiction. Seems to be a better acceptance of nonfiction and good commercial contemporary romance—both in the Helen Van Slyke and Jacqueline Susann style." Recently published *Bee Gees Biography*, by D. Leaf; *How to Sell Your Film Project*, by H. Beckman; *Love's Raging Tide*, by P. Matthews (romance); *Windhaven Saga*, by M. de Jourlet (historical romance); and *Executioner Series*, by D. Pendleton (action/adventure).
Tips: "Become familiar with our list of published books, and follow our instructions. It is a difficult market—paperbacks—with publishers competing for rack space. Watch what sells best and follow the trends as closely as possible. Study the original books that work as well as the reprints. Good, persuasive query letters are the best and fastest tools you have to get an editor's attention. The idea, or angle is vital . . . then we trust the author has or can complete the manuscript."

PIONEER PUBLISHING CO., subsidiary of Book Publishers, Inc., 8 E. Olive Ave., Fresno CA 93728. (209)485-2631. President: Charles W. Clough. Publishes hardcover and trade paperback originals and reprints. Averages 12 titles/year. Subsidy publishes 100% of books based on subject matter of the book, marketing potential and projected audience. Pay is based on book sales. Photocopied submissions OK. Reports in 2 weeks on queries; 1 month on mss.
Nonfiction: Biography, how-to, humor, reference and technical. Subjects include Americana (Californiana); history; nature; philosophy; politics; religion; genealogies and family histories. "We are looking for authors whose markets may be limited but whose talents and ideas decidedly are not. While our orientation has been toward histories, we are receptive to a spectrum of subjects. No professional journal article derivations, dissertations, or trade-type publications." Submit outline/synopsis and sample chapters.
Recent Nonfiction Titles: *The Fortune Seekers*, by Doris Scovel (California history); *The Good 'Uns*, by H.C. Jackson (autobiography/agriculture); and *Fresno County California*, by M. Theo. Kearney (historical reprint).
Fiction: Adventure; ethnic; historical (especially folklore); humor; mainstream; science fiction; and western (with a strong California bent). No plays, film scripts or television scripts. Submit outline/synopsis and sample chapters.
Recent Fiction Titles: *The Imprisoned Sun*, by John J. Fayne (Eastern religion); *Curse of the Feathered Snake*, by Angus MacLean (California folklore); and *Gray Shadow*, by Arthur Shipley (animals/nature).
Poetry: "By the nature of what we do, our needs are flexible. No poems dealing with the extremely esoteric." Submit complete ms.
Recent Poetry Titles: *The Young Man & The Poet*, by D.L. Robbins (epic); *God's Valentine*, by Lois Rose Taaffe (religious); and *The Unweeded Garden*, by Jo Doris Hibner (romance).
Tips: "We see a trend toward autobiography. Writers should seriously consider subsidy publishing as a means of retaining control over their work and still obtaining a return on their investments."

PIPER PUBLISHING, INC., 400 Butler Square Bldg., Minneapolis MN 55403. President: Paul C. Piper. Editorial Director: John M. Sullivan Jr. Publishes hardcover and paperback originals and reprints. Published 15 titles in 1980. Pays royalty and occasional advance. Simultaneous and photocopied submissions OK. SASE. Reports in 6-10 weeks.
Nonfiction: Americana, art, biography, business/economics, cookbooks/cooking/foods, health, history, hobbies, how-to, humor, photography, politics, psychology, restaurant guides, sports and travel. Submit outline/synopsis and sample chapters. Recently published *High and Dry, How to Discover, Understand, and Love the Alcoholic, Family and Friends*, by D. Riley and D. Selvig; and *Offical Special Olympics Celebrity Cookbook*, by K. Buursma and M. Stickney.

PITMAN LEARNING, (formerly Fearon/Pitman Publishers, Inc.), 6 Davis Dr., Belmont CA 94002. Vice President, Editorial: Joan Wolfgang. Averages 50-70 titles/year. Pays royalty on wholesale price or fee outright. Photocopied submissions OK. SASE. Query or submit outline/synopsis and sample chapters. Reports in 1 month. Free book catalog.
Nonfiction: "We don't want to see material for the general trade market—our basic-skills and life-skills books are sold to elementary, secondary and adult basic education schools. Query.
Recent Nonfiction Title: *That's Life*, by Reiff/Clews (life skills/basic skills program).
Fiction: "We are looking for easy-to-read fiction written to a vocabulary scale we provide and suitable for the junior high school through adult basic education market. We are not looking for juvenile fiction, but prefer the major characters to be adults in adult situations. Sex role stereotyping is taboo." Fiction list is full through 1982. Recently published *Laura Brewster Books* (6 young adult mysteries, including teacher's guides); *Man in the Cage*, by Lisa Eisenberg (mystery); and *Buying With Sense* (consumer work/text for the high school or adult student reading at the 4th grade level).

PLATT & MUNK PUBLISHERS, Division of Grosset & Dunlap, 51 Madison Ave., New York NY 10010. Editor: Rosanna Hansen. Publishes hardcover and paperback originals. Published 25 titles in 1979, 25 in 1980; plans 40 in 1981. Pays $1,000-3,500 in outright purchase; no advance. Simultaneous and photocopied submissions OK. SASE. Reports in 6 weeks.
Nonfiction: Juvenile. "We want picturebook manuscripts for children 4-12 describing how the world works—demystification of machinery and natural processes, and animal nonfiction." Submit complete ms.
Recent Nonfiction Titles: *Wolves and Coyotes*, by R. Hansen; and *Gorilla Mysteries*, by M. Elting.
Fiction: Fantasy. "We want original picturebook manuscripts for children ages 3-7." Submit complete ms.
Recent Fiction Titles: *Trolls*, by D. Cushman; *Witches*, by Ann Iosa; and *The Littles to the Rescue*, by John Peterson.

PLAYBOY PAPERBACKS, Division of Playboy Enterprises, Inc., 1633 Broadway, New York NY 10019. (212)688-3030. Editorial Director: Irma Heldman. Publishes paperback originals and reprints. Royalty contract to be negotiated. Query. SASE.
General: Fiction and nonfiction slanted to the adult male who reads *Playboy Magazine*.

PLENUM PUBLISHING CORP., 227 W. 17th St., New York NY 10011. Imprints include Da Capo Press, Consultants Bureau, IFI/Plenum Data Corporation, Plenum Press, Plenum Medical Book Company, Plenum Scientific. President: Martin Tash. Publishes hardcover and paperback reprints. Publishes 300 titles/year. Offers standard minimum contract of 7½-10%. Query. SASE.
Nonfiction: Scientific, medical and technical books including the social and behavioral sciences, physics, engineering and mathematics. Da Capo division publishes art, music, photography, dance and film.

POCKET BOOKS, 1230 Avenue of the Americas, New York NY 10020. Paperback originals and reprints. Published 300 titles last year. Pays royalty on retail price. Reports in 3 months. Enclose return postage.
Imprints: *Washington Square Press* (high-quality mass market). *Timescape* (science fiction and fantasy). *Archway* (children and young adults).
General: History, biography, general nonfiction and adult fiction (mysteries, science fiction, romance, westerns). Reference books.
Recent Nonfiction Titles: *Heartsounds*, by Martha Lear; *Crisis Investing*, by Douglas Casey; and *Get Really Rich in the Coming Super Metals Boom*, by Gordon McLendon.
Recent Fiction Titles: *If There Be Thorns*, by V.C. Andrews; *Save the Last Dance For Me*, by Judi Miller; and *This Calder Sky*, by Janet Dailey (contemporary romance).

POET GALLERY PRESS, 224 W. 29th St., New York NY 10001. Editor: E.J. Pavlos. Publishes paperback originals. Pays standard 10-12½-15% royalty contract. Published 4 titles last year. Submit complete ms only. Enclose return postage with ms.
Nonfiction: "We are a small specialty house, and we place our emphasis on publishing the works of young Americans currently living in Europe. We are interested in creative writing rather than commercial writing. We publish for writers who live overseas, who write and live, who produce writings from the self. Our books might turn out to be commercial, but that is a secondary consideration. We expect to emphasize poetry; however, our list will be concerned with all aspects of literature: the novel, plays, and cinema, as well as criticism. We urge that authors recognize our imposed restrictions; we cannot, and do not wish at this time to compete with major publishing

companies." Recently published *Sarah*, by Gamela; *Iris Elegy*, by Hakim; and *Balancing Act: A Congruence of Symbols*.

Tips: "The major problem with submissions is that while the works submitted are works of 'love,' the writers have not learned their craft! Read, write, study. Economic difficulties have made it more and more difficult to achieve a break even point. Audiences raised on TV and instant image without the need for interpretive thought have meant a reduction of the potential market."

POLARIS PRESS, 16540 Camellia Terrace, Los Gatos CA 95030. (408)356-7795. Editor: Edward W. Ludwig. Paperback originals; considers reprints, depending upon reputation of author. Specializes in college-level books with appeal to general public. Averages 3 titles/year. Pays 6% royalty on retail price; advance averages $100-300. Send contact sheets or prints if photos and/or illustrations are to accompany ms. Simultaneous and photocopied submissions OK. Reports in 1-2 weeks. SASE. Free book catalog.

Fiction: Publishes some fantasy and science fiction "Please, *no* mss which require extensive (and expensive) use of color in inner pages." No juvenile or general fiction. Sample book copy $2.50. Query. Recently published *The Seven Shapes of Solomon; Bean & Eleven Others*, by Ludwig (anthology of previously published science and science fantasy stories); *A Mexican American Coloring Book*, by Rascon; and *The California Story: A Coloring Book*, by Bernal.

Tips: "Query to determine immediate needs, which are usually specialized. List briefly main interests and qualifications. There is little chance that a nonsolicited manuscript will be accepted spontaneously."

PORTER SARGENT PUBLISHERS, INC., 11 Beacon St., Boston MA 02108. (617)523-1670. Publishes hardcover and paperback originals, reprints, translations and anthologies. Published 3 titles in 1980; 4 in 1981; plans 4 in 1982. Pays royalty on retail price. "Each contract is dealt with on an individual basis with the author." Free book catalog. Send query with brief description, table of contents, sample chapter and information regarding author's background. Enclose return postage.

Reference, Special Education, and Academic Nonfiction: "Handbook Series and Special Education Series offer standard, definitive reference works in private education and writings and texts in special education. The Extending Horizons Series is an outspoken, unconventional series which presents topics of importance in contemporary affairs, viewpoints rarely offered to the reading public, methods and modes of social change, and the framework of alternative structures for the expansion of human awareness and well-being." This series is particularly, although not exclusively, directed to the college adoption market. Nonfiction only. Contact Christopher Leonesio.

Recent Nonfiction Titles: *Social Power and Political Freedom*, by G. Sharp (political science); and *Workplace Democracy and Social Change*, by F. Lindenfeld and J. Rothschild-Whitt (sociology).

G. HOWARD POTEET, INC., Box 217, Cedar Grove NJ 07009. Publishes paperback originals. Published 3 titles in 1979, 5 in 1980; plans 7 in 1981. Pays 10% royalty on retail price; no advance. Simultaneous submissions OK. Reports in 1-2 weeks. SASE. Book catalog for SASE.

Nonfiction: How-to books in the areas of business, hobbies, multimedia material; photography; technical material and education. Query or submit outline/synopsis and sample chapters. Recently published *Between the Lines in the Mail Order Game*, by Matt Dol; and *Inside Guide to Flea Market Profits*, by C. Ross.

Tips: "Try to speak to the reader as clearly, simply and directly as possible on an interesting topic supplying precise information."

POTENTIALS DEVELOPMENT FOR HEALTH & AGING SERVICES, 775 Main St., Suite 325, Buffalo NY 14203. (716)842-2658. Vice President: Mary V. Kirchhofer. Publishes paperback originals. Averages 12 titles/year. Pays 5-10% royalty on wholesale or retail price. Simultaneous submissions OK. SASE. Reports in 6 weeks. Free book catalog for SASE.

Nonfiction: Human development mss with emphasis on mental, physical and emotional health for all ages. "We seek material of interest to those working with residents and staffs of long term care facilities; counselors in all areas of human service. We need instructional materials for crafts, exercise, recreational activities; mss dealing with job change, divorce, retirement, death and dying; and textbooks for gerontological education." Query or submit outline/synopsis and sample chapters.

Recent Nonfiction Title: *Activities for the Frail Aged*, by P.M. Cornish.

CLARKSON N. POTTER, INC., 1 Park Ave., New York NY 10016. (212)532-9200. Vice President/Publisher: Jane West. Executive Editor: Carol Southern. Publishes hardcover and paperback originals. Pays 10% royalty on hardcover; 5-7½% on paperback, varying escalations; advance depends on type of book and reputation or experience of author. Published 20 titles in 1979, 28 in 1980; plans approximately 35 in 1981. Samples of prints may be included with outline.

Photocopied submissions OK. Reports in 2-4 weeks. SASE. Free book catalog.
Fiction: Quality and commercial.
Nonfiction: Publishes Americana, art, autobiography, biography, cookbooks, cooking and foods, decorating, history, how-to, humor, nature, photography, politics, self-help and annotated literature. "Mss must be cleanly typed on 8½x11 non-erasable bond; double-spaced. Chicago *Manual of Style* is preferred." Query or submit outline/synopsis and sample chapters. Recently published *High Tech*, by Joan Kron and Suzanne Slesin (decorating); *Larry Rivers' Drawings and Digressions* (art); *O Thou Improper Thou Uncommon Noun*, by Willard R. Espy (humor/etymology); *A Cornish Childhood*, by A.L. Rowse (literature); *J.M. Barrie and the Lost Boys*, by A. Birkin; and *Throw a Tomato*, by J. Erskine and G. Moran.

PRECEDENT PUBLISHING, INC., 520 N. Michigan Ave., Chicago IL 60611. (312)828-0420. Editorial Director: Louis A. Knafla. Senior Editor: Henry Cohen. Publishes hardcover and paperback originals. Pays 10% royalty on wholesale price; advance averages $400. Reports in 2 weeks on queries; 2 months on mss. SASE. Free book catalog.
Nonfiction: Scholarly books: history and historical methodology, Afro-American life, philosophy and science. No fiction or poetry. Query, including outline of chapters, synopsis of book, maximum number of words projected and tentative date of ms. Recently published *Envelopes of Sound*, by Grele (oral history); *Perception, Theory, Commitment*, by Brown (philosophy/science); *US Diplomatic Codes*, by Weber (history); and *Heidegger, Man and Thinker*, edited by Sheehan.

PRENTICE-HALL, Juvenile Division, Englewood Cliffs NJ 07632. Manuscripts Editor: Rose Lopez. Publishes hardcover and paperback originals (90%) and paperback reprints (10%). Publishes 50 titles/year. Pays royalty; average advance. SASE. Reports in 2 weeks. Book catalog for SASE.
Nonfiction: Americana (8-12 in short chapters), "star" biography (7-10 of outlaws, magicians and other characters), current events (7-10 and 9-12), health (teenage problems by MDs only), history (any unusual approaches), humor (no jokes or riddles but funny fiction), music (keen interest in basic approaches, no biographies), sociology (8-12), and sports (6-9), puzzle and participation (6-8). Query.
Recent Nonfiction Titles: *A Kid's Guide to the Economy*, by Riedel; *Museum People*, by Thomson; and *Grains*, by Brown.
Fiction: Gothic, humor, mainstream and mystery. Submit outline/synopsis and sample chapters.
Recent Fiction Titles: *Haunted House*, by Hughes (bubblegum gothic); *Go Ask Alice* (documentary); and *Flat On My Face*, by First (8-12 sports humor).

PRENTICE-HALL, INC., General Publishing Division, Englewood Cliffs NJ 07632. Editor-in-Chief: John Grayson Kirk. Publishes hardcover and paperback originals and reprints. Free book catalog. Will consider photocopied submissions. "Always keep 1 or more copies on hand in case original submission is lost in the mail." Reports in 4-6 weeks. SASE.
Nonfiction: "All types of trade nonfiction, save poetry, drama and westerns. Average acceptable length: 80,000 words. The writer should submit his work professionally and be prepared to participate to the extent required in the book's promotion." Publishes business, history, medicine and psychiatry, music, nature, philosophy, politics, reference, religion, science, self-help and how-to, sports, hobbies and recreation. Submit outline and sample chapters.

THE PRESERVATION PRESS, National Trust for Historic Preservation, 1785 Massachusetts Ave. NW, Washington DC 20036. Publishes nonfiction books and periodicals on historic preservation (saving and reusing the "built environment"). Averages 4-8 titles/year. Books are almost entirely commissioned by the publishers. Subject matter encompasses architecture and architectural history, neighborhood preservation, regional planning, preservation law, building restoration and rural area conservation. No local history. Query.
Recent Nonfiction Titles: *Old and New Architecture: Design Relationship*; *Fabrics for Historic Buildings*; and *American Landmarks: Historic Properties of the National Trust*.

PRESIDIO PRESS, Box 3515, San Rafael CA 94902. (415)457-5850. Editor-in-Chief: Adele Horwitz. Senior Editor: Joan Griffin. Publishes hardcover and paperback originals (90%). Published 25 titles in 1979, 25 in 1980. Pays 10-15% in royalty; offers variable advance. Photocopied submissions OK. SASE. Reports in 3 months. Free book catalog.
Nonfiction: Californiana, popular history, politics, and military. No scholarly. Query or submit outline/synopsis and sample chapters.
Recent Nonfiction Titles: *San Francisco: Story of a City*, by J. McGloin (history); *Strategy for Defeat*, by U.S. Sharp (popular military affairs); and *We Led the Way: Darby's Rangers*, by W. Baumer (popular WW II history).

PRESS PACIFICA, LTD., Box 1227, Kailua HI 96734. Publisher: Jane Wilkins Pultz. Publishes hardcover and paperback originals (50%) and reprints (50%). Published 5 titles in 1980. Pays 10% royalty "with escalations" on retail price; advance averages $100. Simultaneous and photocopied ("if on good white paper and very readable") submissions OK. Reports in 4 weeks-3 months. SASE. Book catalog for 50¢.
Nonfiction: Publishes Hawaii authors only. History (especially women and Hawaii); Hawaiiana; women (history, biography, anthologies, feminist theory); self-help; and how-to. "We are open to new authors who have expertise in their field." No technical or supernatural material. Submit outline/synopsis and sample chapters. Recently published *Guide to Independent Schools in Hawaii*; *This Fragile Eden* (poetry); and *What to Say After You Clear Your Throat*, by J. Gochros (guide to sex education).

PRESSWORKS, INC., Suite 249, 2800 Routh St., Dallas TX 75201. (214)749-1044. President: Anne Dickson. Publishes hardcover originals. Averages 12 titles/year. Pays variable royalty on retail price; offers variable advance. Simultaneous and photocopied submissions OK. SASE. Reports in 2 weeks on queries; reporting time varies on mss. Free book catalog.
Nonfiction: Reference. Subjects include Americana, art, business and economics, history, and other branches of the humanities. Consumers are libraries and scholars. Submit outline/synopsis and sample chapters or complete ms.
Recent Nonfiction Title: *First Printings of Texas Authors*, by Cameron Northouse (reference).

PRICE/STERN/SLOAN INC., PUBLISHERS, 410 N. La Cienega Blvd., Los Angeles CA 90048. Imprints include *Cliff House Books*, *Serendipity Books* and *Laughter Library*. Executive Editor: L.L. Sloan. Publishes trade paperback originals. Averages 100-120 titles/year. Pays royalty on wholesale price, or by outright purchase; small or no advance. Simultaneous and photocopied submissions OK. SASE. Reports in 2-3 months. Book catalog for SASE.
Nonfiction: Humor; self-help; and satire (limited). Submit outline/synopsis and sample chapters. "Most titles are unique in concept as well as execution and are geared for the so-called gift market."
Recent Nonfiction Titles: *Mr. Men Series*, by R. Hargreaves (juvenile); and *Trapped in the Organization*, by J. Fox (humor).

PRINCETON BOOK CO., PUBLISHERS, Box 109, Princeton NJ 08540. (201)297-8370. Editorial Director: Charles Woodford. Publishes hardcover and paperback originals (70%) and reprints (30%). Averages 5-7 titles/year. Pays 10% royalty; no advance. Simultaneous and photocopied submissions OK. Reports in 6 weeks. SASE. Free book catalog.
Nonfiction: Professional books and college textbooks on education, physical education, dance, sociology and recreation. No "books that have a strictly trade market." Submit outline/synopsis and sample chapters with vita. Recently published *Making it Till Friday: A Guide to Successful Classroom Management*, by Long/Frye (college textbook); *Recreational Leadership*, by Shivers (professional book); and *Principles and Techniques of Supervision in Physical Education*, by Humphrey (professional book).

PRINCETON UNIVERSITY PRESS, 41 William St., Princeton NJ 08540. (609)542-4900. Associate Director and Editor: R. Miriam Brokaw. Publishes hardcover and trade paperback ("very few") originals and reprints. Averages 130 titles/year. Subsidy assists 50% of books, "when we don't break even on the first printing." Pays 15% maximum royalty on retail price; offers $1,000 advance ("but rarely"). Simultaneous (rarely) and photocopied submissions OK. SASE. Reports in 1 week on queries; 1 month on mss "if unsuitable" or 4 months "if suitable."
Nonfiction: Biography, reference and technical. Subjects include art, literature, history, music, politics, religion, sociology and poetry. "We're looking for any scholarly book." Query.
Recent Nonfiction Titles: *Bertolt Brecht in America*, by James K. Lyon (literature); *Japan Over Two Centuries*, by Marius B. Jansen (Asian history); and *Japan Before Tokugawa*, by John W. Hall (Japanese history).
Poetry: "Poetry submissions (original and in translation) are judged in competition. Write Mrs. Marjorie Sherwood." Submit complete ms.

PROGRAMMED STUDIES, INC., Box 113, Stow MA 01775. (617)897-2130. Director: R. Whitson. Publishes hardcover and trade paperback originals. Averages 3-6 titles/year. Buys some mss outright for $200-250; no advance. Simultaneous and photocopied submissions OK. SASE. Reports in 1 month. Free book catalog.
Nonfiction: How-to, humor, reference, self-help and technical. Subjects include business and economics, travel and aviation. "We're looking for articles on airport noise pollution and aviation problems in general." No cookbooks. Query.

Recent Nonfiction Titles: *Airplanes, Airports & Noise Pollution*; *General Aviation: Arrogant, Ignorant, Unsafe, Noisy Bastards*; and *Airports: Today's Small Airfield, Tomorrow's Neighborhood Nightmare*, all by Dick Amann.
Tips: "Price is becoming inconsequential: books must be able to help. Write how-to material."

PROMETHEUS BOOKS, INC., 700 E. Amherst St., Buffalo NY 14215. (716)837-2475. Editor-in-Chief: Paul Kurtz. Director: Jerry Koren. Publishes hardcover and trade paperback originals. Averages 24 titles/year. Pays 5-10% royalty on wholesale price; offers average $500 advance. SASE. Reports in 1 month. Free book catalog.
Imprints: *Critiques of the Paranormal, Library of Liberal Religion,* and *The Skeptic's Bookshelf* (all nonfiction), Victor Gulotta, director of advertising and promotion.
Nonfiction: Textbook and trade. Subjects include philosophy, politics, psychology, religion, sociology, medical ethics, and criticism of paranormal phenomena. "We especially need books in medical ethics, critiques of paranormal and philosophy texts. Serious studies of paranormal phenomena seem to be quite popular; they sell especially well for us (we are the only publisher specializing in this area). We publish books in new fields such as gerontology and biomedical ethics—there is a trend in these areas. Fields will become increasingly specialized warranting new and specialized texts." Submit outline/synopsis and sample chapters.
Recent Nonfiction Titles: *Science: Good, Bad and Bogus*, by Martin Gardner (critique of paranormal); *The Politics of Procrustes*, by Antony Flew (philosophy); *Israel's Defense Line*, by I.L. Kenen (foreign affairs); and *The UFO Verdict: Examining the Evidence*, by Robert Sheaffer (critique of paranormal).
Tips: "Present original material. The writer should come up with marketing suggestions and help his publisher as much as possible."

PRUETT PUBLISHING CO., 2928 Pearl, Boulder CO 80302. Managing Editor: Gerald Keenan. Averages 25-30 titles/year. Royalty contract on wholesale price. No advance. "Most books that we publish are aimed at special interest groups. As a small publisher, we feel most comfortable in dealing with a segment of the market that is very clearly identifiable, and one we know we can reach with our resources." Free catalog on request. Mss must conform to the Chicago *Manual of Style*. Legible photocopies acceptable. Query. Reports in 2-4 weeks. SASE.
General Adult Nonfiction and Textbooks: Pictorial railroad histories; outdoor activities related to the Intermountain West; some Western Americana. Textbooks with a regional (Intermountain) aspect for pre-school through college level. Does not want to see anything with the personal reminiscence angle or biographical studies of little-known personalities. "Like most small publishers, we try to emphasize quality from start to finish, because, for the most part, our titles are going to a specialized market that is very quality conscious. We also feel that one of our strong points is the personal involvement ('touch') so often absent in a much larger organization." Recently published *N&W: Giant of Steam*, by Jeffries (railroadiana); *Montana: Our Land and People*, by Lang and Myers; and *Evening Before the Diesel*, by Fass.

PSG PUBLISHING CO., INC., 545 Great Rd., Littleton MA 01460. (617)486-8971. President/Editor-in-Chief: Frank Paparello. Hardcover and paperback originals. Published 43 titles in 1979, 45 in 1980; plans 45-50 in 1981. Pays royalty on net revenues. Specializes in publishing medical and dental books for the professional and graduate student market. Pays 10-15% royalty; no advance. Send prints of photos to accompany ms. Simultaneous submissions OK. Reports in 2-4 weeks. SASE. Free book catalog.
Nonfiction: Publishes medical books and ones on dentistry and psychiatry. Query or submit complete ms.
Recent Nonfiction Titles: *Cancer: Signals and Safeguards*, by Murphy; *Sports Injuries*, by Haerner and Vinger; and *Prescribing for the Elderly*, by Lamy.

PULSE-FINGER PRESS, Box 488, Yellow Springs OH 45387. Editor-in-Chief: Orion Roche. Publishes hardcover and paperback originals. Published 8 titles in 1979, 9 in 1980; plans 8-10 in 1981. Offers standard minimum book contract on wholesale price for books; less for poetry. Advance varies, depending on quality. "Not less than $100 for poetry; or $500 for fiction." Query. Absolutely no unsolicited mss. Reports in 3 months. "SASE must accompany inquiries, or they will not be acknowledged."
Fiction and Poetry: "We're interested in subjects of general concern with a focus on fiction and poetry. All types considered; tend to the *contemporary-cum-avant-garde*. No length requirements. Our only stipulation is quality, as we see it." Recently published *Twelve Muscle Tones*, by L.C. Phillips; *The Margate Mysteries*, by N. Kazinsky; and *Rising Son*, by H. Swale.
Tips: "Concentrate on fiction, poetry and drama of the highest quality. We are not interested in how-to books or commercial formula for fiction. We are not interested in fiction which is a

disguised form of 'fact.' We want prose which is vivid but not overblown; poetry which is dramatic and daring in terms of image and metaphor."

PURDUE UNIVERSITY PRESS, South Campus Courts, D., West Lafayette IN 47907. (317)749-6083. Director: William J. Whalen. Managing Editor: Verna Emery. Publishes hardcover and paperback originals. Specializes in scholarly books from all areas of academic endeavor. Pays 10% royalty on list price; no advance. Publishes 6 titles/year. Photocopied submissions OK "if author will verify that it does not mean simultaneous submission elsewhere." Reports in 2-4 months. SASE. Free book catalog.
Nonfiction: Publishes agriculture, Americana, art (but no color plates), biography, communication, engineering, history, horticulture, nature, philosophy, poetry, political science, psychology, reference, scientific, sociology, technical, and literary criticism. "Works of scholarship only."
Recent Nonfiction Titles: *Radical Reflection and the Origin of the Human Sciences*, by Calvin O. Schrag; *Ruined Eden of the Present: Hawthorne, Melville, and Poe, (Critical Essays in Honor of Darrel Abel)*, edited by G.R. Thompson and Virgil L. Lokke; and *Ultimately Fiction: Design in Modern American Literary Biography*, by Dennis W. Petrie.

Q.E.D. INFORMATION SCIENCES, INC., Box 181, 180 Linden St., Wellesley MA 02181. (617)237-5656. Editor: Mark Walsh. Publishes trade paperback originals. Averages 10 titles/year. Pays 10-15% royalty on retail price. Photocopied submissions OK. SASE. Reports in 1 week on queries; 3 weeks on mss. Free book catalog.
Nonfiction: Technical. Subjects include computers and database technology. "Our books are read by data processing managers and technicians." Submit outline/synopsis and sample chapters.
Recent Nonfiction Titles: *Managing Systems Maintenance*, by W. Perry (technical); *Design Guide for CODASYL DBMS*, by R. Perron (technical); and *Managing for Productivity in Data Processing*, by J. Johnson (technical).

QUALITY BOOKS, INC., 400 Anthony Trail, Northbrook IL 60062. (312)498-4000. Vice President: Dan Blau. Publishes hardcover and paperback originals. Publishes 10 titles/year. Offers royalty; also buys mss by outright purchase. Offers advance. Simultaneous and photocopied submissions OK. SASE. Reports in 4 weeks. Free book catalog.
Nonfiction: Biography; how-to; recreation; sports; and technical. Needs "major, highly noticeable consumer trends." Submit outline/synopsis and sample chapters.
Recent Nonfiction Titles: *Official Guide to Outdoor Skating*, by Simcoe (illustrated how-to); *Country Music Stars*, by David (photo/biography); and *Complete Book of Electric Vehicles*, by Shacket (illustrated technical).

QUARTET BOOKS, INC., 360 Park Ave. S., New York NY 10010. (212)689-1500. Editorial Director: Marilyn Warnick. Publishes hardcover and paperback originals. Averages 25 titles/year. Offers 8-12% royalty on wholesale or retail price; average advance: $5,000. Simultaneous and photocopied submissions OK. SASE. Reports in 4 weeks. Free book catalog.
Nonfiction: Biography and memoirs; health; modern history; philosophy; politics; psychology; photography; and sociology. "Our head office is in London, England so we are looking for titles to print in both countries." Query first.
Recent Nonfiction Titles: *Eat Well, Live Longer*, by M. Westberg; *Bisexuality*, by C. Wolff; *The Indispensable Rousseau*, compiled by John Hope Mason; and *Terence Rattigan: The Man and His Work*, by Michael Darlow and Gillian Hodson.

QUICK FOX, 33 W. 60th St., New York NY 10023. Editor-in-Chief: Jim Charlton. Managing Editor: Ruth Flaxman. Publishes paperback originals. Averages 50 titles/year. Pays 10% royalty on retail price; advance varies. Simultaneous and photocopied submissions OK. Reports in 1 month. SASE. Free book catalog.
Nonfiction: "We publish general interest books in a special way—contemporary culture and society; practical and instructional books; photo/biographies; and photography and art books." Query or submit outline/synopsis and sample chapters with resume.
Recent Nonfiction Titles: *Sportshealth*, by Marshall Hoffman and William Southmayd, MD; *John Lennon in His Own Words*, compiled by Miles (photo biography); *Interiors*, by Tim Street-Porter (home design); *Ten Point Plan for College Acceptance*, by Lawrence Graham; *Buck Rogers in the 25th Century*, by Gray Morrow and Jim Lawrence; and *Recipe Cards From the Pages of Kitchen Detail*, by Herb Wise.

R & E RESEARCH ASSOC., 936 Industrial Ave., Palo Alto CA 94303. (415)494-1112. Publisher: R. Reed. Publishes trade paperback originals. Averages 60 titles/year. Pays 10-15% royalty on retail price; no advance. Photocopied submissions OK. SASE. Reports in 1 month. Free book catalog.

Nonfiction: How-to, reference, self-help, textbook and scholarly. Subjects include Americana, business and economics, health, history, politics, psychology, sociology and education. "We would like how-to books, manuals for educators, self-help books, and reference materials." Query or submit outline/synopsis and sample chapters.
Recent Nonfiction Titles: *Inequality in the Military*, by Butler; *Black Power Brokers*, by Ellis; and *Educational Computer Technology*, by Sidman.

RAINBOW BOOKS, Box 27028, Tempe AZ 85282. Editorial Director: Frank Hardman. Vice President of Sales: Frank L. Hardman. Publishes paperback originals. Averages 15-20 titles/year. Pays 5-10% royalty on wholesale price; no advance. Simultaneous and photocopied submissions OK. SASE. Reports in 2 months. Free book catalog.
Nonfiction: Biography, health, how-to, psychology, recreation, religion, self-help and texbooks. Need "books that have a definite Christian message. Books for the Evangelical Christian market having to do with marriage and family, youth and children, evangelism, Christian living, inspirational, theology, missions and missionaries and pastor's helps. Submit outline/synopsis and sample chapters or complete ms.
Recent Nonfiction Titles: *Children's Church Manual*, by Sullivan; and *All Kinds of Help.*

RAND McNALLY & CO., Adult Division, Box 7600, Chicago IL 60680. Editor: Elliott H. McCleary. Publishes hardcover and paperback originals and paperback reprints. Averages 20 adult titles/year. Pays royalty on wholesale or retail price ("usually"); advance varies. Photocopied submissions OK. SASE. Reports in 1 month. Free book catalog.
Nonfiction: Travel, personal adventure, how-to, Americana and some sports. "We do not want any personal travel stories unless they're unique." Query.
Recent Nonfiction Titles: *Winging It!* (personal adventure); *Photographing Sports* (photography, sports); and *Never Make a Reservation In Your Own Name* (how-to; travel; humor).

RAND McNALLY & CO., Juvenile Division, Box 7600, Chicago IL 60680. Trade Editor: Dorothy Haas. Mass Market Editor: Roselyn Bergman. Publishes hardcover and paperback originals and paperback reprints. Averages 24 juveniles/year. Pays royalty on retail price, or by outright purchase for trade books; by outright purchase for mass market books; advance varies. Photocopied submissions OK. SASE. Reports in 10 weeks. Free book catalog.
Nonfiction: "We are interested in natural science, humor, preschool subjects, subjects of broad interest, all of which should lend themselves well to illustration. We do not want any ABC's, counting books, holiday stories, poetry or biographies." Submit outline/synopsis and sample chapters. Recently published *Album of Whales*, by Tom McGowen (scientific, readable, ages 8-12); and *Words in My World*, by Yvonne Russel (categories of words, an easy-to-look-up word book).
Fiction: "We use preschool books of broad national and wide personal appeal. Humor for the 8- to 12-year olds and facts presented in an interesting way." Submit complete ms. "Query on longer manuscripts only. Do not query on picture book manuscripts." Recently published *A Time to Keep*, by Tasha Tudor (the holidays in another lifestyle); and *A Mouse Family Album*, by Pamela Sampson (illustrated highlights in the life of the woodmouse family).

RAND McNALLY, Trade Publishing Division, Box 7600, Chicago IL 60680. Variable royalty and advance schedule. Trade books payment on royalty basis or outright; mass market juveniles outright. Reports in 10 weeks (juvenile); 1 month (adult).
General Nonfiction: Adult manuscripts should be sent to Elliott H. McCleary, Editor, Adult Books, Trade Division, but query first on the subjects including travel, sports, natural history, personal adventure or how-to. Contracts are sometimes offered on the basis of outline and sample chapter.
Trade Juveniles: Dorothy Haas, Editor. Picture books ages 3-8; fiction and nonfiction ages 8-12; special interest books (no fiction) for young adults. Send picture book manuscripts for review. Query on longer manuscripts.
Mass Market Juveniles: Roselyn Bergman, Editor. Picture book scripts, six years and under; Jr. Elf Books, Elf Books, activity formats. Realistic stories, fantasy, early learning material; not to exceed 600 words and must present varied illustration possibilities.

RANDOM HOUSE, INC., 201 E. 50th St., New York NY 10022. Also publishes Vintage Books. Publishes hardcover and paperback originals and reprints. Payment as per standard minimum book contracts. Query. SASE.
Fiction and Nonfiction: Publishes fiction and nonfiction of the "highest standards."
Poetry: Some poetry volumes.

RANDOM HOUSE, INC., Juvenile Division. 201 E. 50th St., New York NY 10022. (212)751-2600. Managing Editor: Elma Otto. Publishes hardcover and paperback originals (90%) and reprints (10%). Published 80 titles in 1979, 85 in 1980; plans 80 in 1981. Pays royalty; average advance depending on book. Free book catalog for SASE.
Nonfiction and Fiction: No unsolicited mss. Query will be answered only if we wish to see ms."

*RANGER ASSOCIATES, INC., Box 1357, Manassas VA 22110. (703)369-5336. Publications Director: Sharon M. Lane. Publishes hardcover and trade paperback originals and reprints. Averages 5 titles/year. Subsidy publishes 25% of books based on "the literary quality of the manuscript and a board decision as to the profitability of the book for the client. We will not print a book which we feel will not sell." Pays 5-12% royalty on wholesale price; on retail price for those sold at retail. Simultaneous and photocopied submissions OK. SASE. Reports in 2 weeks on queries; 1 month on mss. Free book catalog "when available."
Imprints: *Ranger Press* (fiction and nonfiction) Sharon M. Lane, director, publications.
Nonfiction: Biography, how-to, humor, illustrated book, juvenile and self-help; "will consider all types." Subjects include business and economics, history, hobbies, recreation, sports and travel; "will consider others. We are particularly interested in manuscripts about elite military units and leaders, e.g., rangers, paratroopers, commandos and irregular forces. We would like to receive original works on the Ranger Battalions of WWII, the Ranger Companies of the Korean War, and Ranger/Special Forces Advisors in Vietnam. Our audience is the mass of American readers searching for well researched, well written books on elite military units and leaders. We address our advertising to soldiers, veterans and their families." Query or submit outline/synopsis and sample chapters.
Recent Nonfiction Titles: *Rudder's Rangers*, by Ronald L. Lane (history); *Look What I Wrote!*, by Dr. Bonnie N. Miller (how-to); and *Lead the Way, Rangers!*, by Henry S. Glassman (history).
Fiction: "Our preference is for nonfiction during the coming year; however, we will consider exceptional work in some areas of fiction." No erotica. Query or submit outline/synopsis and sample chapters.
Recent Fiction Title: *Goodness Gracious*, by Harry P. Levitt (juvenile).

REALTORS NATIONAL MARKETING INSTITUTE, Affiliate of National Association of Realtors, 430 N. Michigan Ave., Chicago IL 60611. (312)440-8500. Book Editor: Barbara M. Gamez. Publishes hardcover and trade paperback originals. Averages 12 titles/year. Pays 10% maximum on retail price; offers advance: "50% of estimated royalties from sales of first printing." Simultaneous and photocopied submissions OK. SASE. Reports in 2 months. Free book catalog.
Nonfiction: How-to, reference, self-help and technical. Subjects include business and economics (realty-oriented) and professional real estate. "We're interested in real estate-oriented mss on commercial-investment-(basic how-to); residential-creative; and management strategies and motivation for real estate professionals." Submit outline/synopsis and sample chapter.
Recent Nonfiction Titles: *Real Estate Data—Your Market & Your Firm*, by George D. Herman; *Home Buying—The Complete Illustrated Guide*, by Henry Harrison; and *The Condominium Home—A Special Marketing Challenge*, by Janet Scavo.

RED DUST, INC., 218 E. 81st St., New York NY 10028. Editor: Joanna Gunderson. Publishes hardcover and paperback originals and translations. Specializes in quality work by new writers. Books printed either simultaneously in hard and paper covers or in hardcover alone, in editions of 1,000 copies. Pays 10-12-15% royalty; offers $300 average advance. Catalog for 1st class stamp.
Fiction: Novels and short stories. Query preferred. Sample of 10 pages (photocopied preferred) can be sent as a preliminary. Please: no full length manuscripts. We can fall behind and will make no time commitments about return of manuscript. That is why photocopied pages should be sent so manuscript will not be held up in our office and can be submitted elsewhere. Specialty experimental fiction. SASE required for return of ms. Failure to enclose SASE will delay return immeasurably. Sending stamps or money order is not the same."
Poetry: Specialty experimental poetry. Query.

REGAL BOOKS, Division of Gospel Light Publications, 2300 Knoll Dr., Ventura CA 93003. Senior Editor: Donald E. Pugh. Publishes hardcover and paperback originals and paperback reprints. Averages 35 titles/year. Pays 6-14% royalty on paperback titles, 10% net for curriculum books. Photocopied submissions OK. Reports in 2-6 wkeks. SASE.
Nonfiction: Missions (gift books); Bible studies (Old and New Testament); Christian living; counseling (self-help, the future); contemporary concerns (biographies); evangelism (church growth); marriage and family; youth; handcrafts; communication resources; teaching enrichment resources; Bible commentary for Laymen Series; and material for the International Center for Learning. Query or submit outline/synopsis and sample chapters.

Recent Nonfiction Titles: *Preparing for Parenthood*, by H. Norman Wright; *Measure of a Marriage*, by Gene Getz (Christian life); and *No Fear In His Presence*, by Dr. David Dawson (mission).

THE REGENTS PRESS OF KANSAS, 303 Carruth-O'Leary, Lawrence KS 66045. (913)864-4154. Managing Editor: Yvonne Willingham. Hardcover and paperback originals. Averages 12 titles/year. "No royalty until manufacturing costs are recovered." No advance. Markets books by direct mail, chiefly to libraries and scholars. "State availability of illustrations if they add significantly to the ms." Photocopied submissions OK. Reports in 4-6 months. SASE. Free book catalog.
Nonfiction: Publishes biography, history, literary criticism, philosophy, politics, regional subjects, and scholarly nonfiction books. "No dissertations." Query.
Recent Nonfiction Titles: *Economics and the Truman Administration* (history); *Walt Whitman's Western Jaunt* (literary history); and *Poisonous Plants of the Central United States* (regional).

REGENTS PUBLISHING CO., INC., 2 Park Ave., New York NY 10016. Averages 12 titles/year. Pays royalty on wholesale or retail price. Prefers complete proposals. Reports in 3 to 4 weeks.
Textbooks: Publishes English as a Second Language text; and related materials.
Recent Nonfiction Titles: *React Interact*, by Byrd and Clemente-Cabetas (communication activities); and *Words, Words, Words*, by Sheeler and Markley (vocabulary building).

*REGNER/GATEWAY, INC., 116 S. Michigan Ave., Suite 300, Chicago IL 60603. (219)232-5911. Assistant to the Editor: Karen Chassin. Publisher: Douglas Hofmeister. President: Henry Regnery. Senior Editor: John Stoll Sanders. Publishes hardcover and paperback originals (50%) and paperback reprints (50%). Averages 12-15 titles/year. Pays royalty; offers advance. Simultaneous and photocopied submissions OK. SASE. Reports in 1 month. Free book catalog.
Nonfiction: Biography, business/economics, history, philosophy, politics, psychology, religion, science, sociology, travel and education (teaching). "We are looking for eight books on current affairs—of either political, legal, social, environmental, educational or historical interest. Books heavy on sex and obscene brutality should not be submitted. Please, no fiction, verse, or children's literature." Inquries preferred, or submit outline/synopsis and sample chapters.
Recent Nonfiction Titles: *Fat City: How Washington Wastes Your Taxes*, by D. Lambro (investigative report on federal government); *Target America: The Influence of Communist Propaganda on the U.S. Media*, by James L. Tyson; and *From Under the Rubble*, by Alexandr Solzhenitsyn (essays from six dissidents).

*RESOURCE PUBLICATIONS, INC., Box 444, Saratoga CA 95070. Editorial Director: William Burns. Publishes paperback originals. Publishes 6 titles/year. Has subsidy published 1 title; "if the author can present and defend a personal publicity effort, and the work is in our field, we will consider it." Pays 8% royalty; no advance. Photocopied submissions (with written assurance that work is not being submitted simultaneously) OK. Reports in 2 months. SASE.
Nonfiction: "We look for creative source books for the religious education, worship and religious art fields. How-to books, especially for contemporary religious art forms, are of particular interest (dance, mime, drama, choral reading, singing, music, musicianship, bannermaking, statuary, or any visual art form). No heavy theoretical, philosophical, or theological tomes. Nothing utterly unrelated or unrelatable to the religious market as described above." Query or submit outline/synopsis and sample chapters.
Recent Nonfiction Title: *Banners and Such*, by Ortegel (how-to).
Fiction: "Light works providing examples of good expression tj rough the religious art forms. Any collected short works in the areas of drama, dance, song, stories, anecdotes or good visual art. Long poems or illustrated light novels which entertain while teaching a life value which could be useful in religious education or to the religious market at large." Query or submit outline/synopsis and sample chapters. Recently published *Keeping Festival*, by Suzanne Toolan, SM (collected songs); *Winter Dreams*, by Joseph Juknialis (stories); and *God of Untold Tales*, by Mike Moynahan, SJ (poetry).
Tips: "Prepare a clear outline of the work and an ambitious schedule of public appearances to help make it known and present both as a proposal to the publisher. With our company a work that can be serialized or systematically excerpted in our periodicals is always given special attention."

RESTON PUBLISHING CO., Subsidiary of Prentice-Hall), 11480 Sunset Hills Rd., Reston VA 22090. President: Matthew I. Fox. Publishes hardcover originals. Offers standard minimum book contract of 10-12-15% on net sales; advance varies. Published 170 titles last year. Free catalog on request. Will consider photocopied submissions. Submit outline and sample chapters. Reports immediately. Enclose return postage.
Textbooks: "We look for titles in agriculture; business and real estate; engineering; computer

science; paramedical field; nursing. Primarily for the junior college and vocational/technical school market. Professionally oriented books for in-service practitioners and professionals. All material should be written to appeal to these markets in style and subject. We are able to attract the best experts in all phases of academic and professional life to write our books. But we are always seeking new material in all areas of publishing; any area that is represented by courses at any post-secondary level."
Recent Nonfiction Title: *Money Dynamics for the 1980's*, by Van Caspal.

FLEMING H. REVELL CO., Central Ave., Old Tappan NJ 07675. Imprints include Power Books and Spire. Editorial Director: Dr. Victor L. Oliver. Managing Editor: Norma F. Chimento.Publishes hardcover and paperback originals and reprints. Publishes 80 titles/year. Wants no poetry. Pays royalty on retail price; sometimes an advance. Simultaneous and photocopied submissions OK. SASE. Reports in 2 months. Book catalog for SASE.
Nonfiction: Religion and inspirational. "All books must appeal to Protestant-evangelical readers." Query.
Recent Nonfiction Titles: *Woman*, by Dale Evans Rogers; *Hide or Seek (Expanded and Updated)*, by Dr. James Dobson; *Whatever Happened to the Human Race?*, by Francis A. Schaeffer and C. Everett Koop, M.D.; and *Hold Me Tight*, by Beth Jameseon (inspirational).

REVIEW AND HERALD PUBLISHING ASSOCIATION, (formerly Southern Publishing Association), 6856 Eastern Ave. NW, Washington DC 20012. Editor-in-Chief: Richard W. Coffen. Publishes hardcover and paperback originals. Specializes in religiously oriented books. Averages 60-70 titles/year. Pays 5-10% royalty on retail price; advance averages $100. Simultaneous and photocopied submissions OK. SASE. Reports in 2-4 months. Free brochure.
Nonfiction: Juveniles (religiously oriented only; 20,000-60,000 words; 128 pages average); nature (128 pages average); and religious (20,000-60,000 words; 128 pages average). Query or submit outline/synopsis and sample chapters.
Recent Nonfiction Titles: *The Rise and Fall of Superwoman*, by Carole Sheron; *Don's California Canary*, by Mabel Latsha; and *Become Your Own Ideal*, by Carol Behrman.
Tips: "Familiarize yourself with Adventist theology because Review and Herald Publishing Association is owned and operated by the Seventh-day Adventist Church."

THE REVISIONIST PRESS, PUBLISHERS, Subsidiaries include The Martin Buber Press and The Mutualist Press, Box 2009, Brooklyn NY 11202. Editor: Bezalel Chaim. Publishes hardcover originals (50%) and reprints (50%). Averages 20 titles/year. Pays 10% royalty on the net selling price of each copy sold." Simultaneous and photocopied submissions OK. SASE. Reports in 3 weeks on queries; 6 weeks on mss.
Imprints: *The Martin Buber Press* (nonfiction), Bezalel Chaim, editor.
Nonfiction: Biography, reference, technical and textbook. Subjects include Americana, art, business and economics, cooking and foods, health, history, music, philosophy, photography, politics, psychology, recreation, religion, sociology, travel and cinema. "We need many titles in these listed areas. Our audience includes university faculty." Query or submit outline/synopsis and sample chapters.
Recent Nonfiction Titles: *Dream Street: The American Movies*, by Edward Ifkovic (film history); *Tolstoy the Man*, by Leo Hecht (critical biography); and *The Revisionist Historians & German War Guilt*, by Warren B. Morris Jr. (history).

REYMONT ASSOCIATES, 29 Reymont Ave., Rye NY 10580. Editor-in-Chief: D.J. Scherer. Managing Editor: Felicia Scherer. Paperback originals. Pays 10-12-15% royalty on wholesale price; no advance. Submit outline/synopsis and sample chapters. Simultaneous and photocopied submissions OK. Reports in 2 weeks. SASE. Book catalog for SASE.
Nonfiction: Publishes business reports; how-to; self-help; unique directories; bibliographies. "Aim for 7,500-10,000 words."
Recent Nonfiction Titles: *Improving EDP Software Production*; *Preventing Misuse of EDP Systems*; and *How to Make Money With Pen & Ink Drawings*.

RICHARDS ROSEN PRESS, 29 E. 21st St., New York NY 10010. (212)777-3017. Editors: Ruth C. Rosen and Roger Rosen. Publishes hardcover originals. Averages 36 titles/year. Pays royalty; no advance. Simultaneous and photocopied submissions OK. SASE. Reports in 3-4 weeks.
Nonfiction: Arts, health, history, hobbies, psychology, science, self-help, sociology and sports. "Our books are geared to the young adult audience whom we reach via school and public libraries. Most of the books we publish are related to guidance-career and personal adjustment. We also publish material on the theater, science and women, as well as journalism for schools. Interested in supplementary material for enrichment of school curriculum." Query.

Recent Nonfiction Titles: *Learning to Control Stress*, by Buchalew; *Your Future in Big Business*; and *Your Future: A Guide for the Handicapped Teenager*, by Feingold and Miller.

ROSS BOOKS, Box 4340, Berkeley CA 94704. President: Franz Ross. Publishes hardcover and paperback originals (85%) and paperback reprints (15%). Averages 7-10 titles/year. Offers 8-12% royalties on retail price. Average advance: 10% of the first print run. Simultaneous and photocopied submissions OK. SASE. Reports in 1 month. Free book catalog.
Nonfiction: General career finding, bicycle books, popular how-to science, garden books, music, general how-to, some natural foods and eastern religion. Especially wants general career finding, popular how-to science and how-to's. No political, fiction, poetry or children's books. Submit outline/synopsis and sample chapter with SASE.
Recent Nonfiction Titles: *Living on Two Wheels*; *Holography Handbook*; and *Rock, Water & Marsh Gardens."*

ROSS-ERIKSON, INC., PUBLISHERS, 629 State St., Santa Barbara CA 93101. (805)962-1175. Publicity Director: Alma Hecht. Publishes hardcover and trade paperback originals, and hardcover and trade paperback reprints. Averages 8 titles/year. Pays 10-15% royalty; offers average $500 advance. Simultaneous and photocopied submissions OK. SASE. Reports in 2 months on queries; 6 months on mss. Free book catalog.
Nonfiction: Coffee table book, how-to, self-help, literary, anthropology, history, philosophy, poetry and comparative religion. Subjects include art; health; history; philosophy; psychology; religion (comparative); travel; and literary criticism. Query or submit outline/synopsis and sample chapters or complete ms.
Recent Nonfiction Titles: *The Don Juan Papers*, by Richard deMille (anthropology, philosophy and science); *Maria Sabina: Her Life and Chants*, by Alvaro Estrada (oral autobiography of Mazatec Indian Shaman); and *Unstress Yourself!*, by Stuart Litvak (self-help).
Fiction: Ethnic, historical, mystery, Western and literary works. Query or submit outline/synopsis and sample chapters or complete ms.
Recent Fiction Title: *St. Mick*, by Jack Challenge (homosexual novel).
Poetry: Consulting Poetry Editor: Jerome Rothenberg. "Our poetry is pretty full for the next year or two." Submit 3-5 poems.
Recent Poetry Titles: *Representative Works*, by Jackson MacLaw (performance); *Poetry For Crazy Cowboys*, by Raymond Coffin (humorous, "profound poetry"); and *New Wilderness Letter*, edited by Jerome Rothenberg (collection of contemporary works).

ROUTLEDGE & KEGAN PAUL, LTD., 9 Park St., Boston MA 02108. Publishes hardcover and paperback originals and reprints. Pays standard 10-12½-15% wholesale royalty contract "on clothbound editions, if the books are not part of a series"; usual advance is $250-2,500. Averages 200 titles/year. Query with outline and sample chapters. Submit complete ms "only after going through outline and sample chapters step." Reports in 2-3 months. Enclose check for return postage.
Nonfiction: "Academic, reference, and scholarly levels: English and European literary criticism, social sciences, philosophy and logic, psychology, parapsychology, oriental religions, history, political science and education. Our books generally form a reputable series under the general editorship of distinguished academics in their fields. The approach should be similar to the styles adopted by Cambridge University Press, Harvard University Press and others." Interested in material for the International Library of Sociology, International Library of Philosophy, and International Library of Psychology. Length: 30,000-250,000 words.

ROYAL PUBLISHING CO., Subsidiary of ROMC (Recipes of the Month Club), Box 5027, Beverly Hills CA 90210. (213)277-7220. President: Mrs. Harold Klein. Publishes hardcover, trade, and mass market paperback originals (100%). Averages 4 titles/year. Pays 8-12% royalty on retail price; buys some mss outright. Simultaneous and photocopied submissions OK. SASE. Free book catalog.
Nonfiction: Cookbook. Subjects include cooking and foods. "We especially need cookbooks, diet, food history and specialty cookbooks." Submit complete ms.
Recent Nonfiction Titles: *Joy of Eating*, *Love of Eating*, and *Joy of Eating French Food*, all by Darling (cookbooks).
Fiction: Historical, humor, mystery, romance and suspense. "We are looking to include fiction titles on our list in the next year or two." Submit complete ms.

RUSSICA PUBLISHERS, INC., 799 Broadway, New York NY 10003. (212)473-7480. Contact: Valery Kuharets. Publishes trade paperback originals (50%) and reprints (50%). Averages 15 titles/year. Pays 10-15% royalty on retail price. Photocopied submissions OK. SASE. Reports in 2 weeks. Free book catalog.

Nonfiction: Biography and humor. Subjects include history. "We're looking for biographies of prominent Russians or Slavs and histories of Russian art and culture. Manuscripts in Russian are always wanted." Submit complete ms.
Recent Nonfiction Titles: *Uncensored Russian Limericks*, by Kobronsky (folklore); and *The Fate of Traitor*, by Nikolaevsky (history).
Fiction: Adventure, erotica, ethnic, horror, humor, mystery and suspense. "Russian language manuscripts only." Submit complete ms.
Recent Fiction Titles: *Poetry*, by Marina Tsvetaeva; *Prose* (2 volumes), by M. Tsvetaeva; and *The Hand (Ruka)*, by Iuz Aleshkovsky.
Poetry: Modern Russian poetry. No political or historical. Submit complete ms.
Recent Poetry Titles: *The Nets (Seti)*, by M. Klizmin; *Anthology of Russian Lyrics*, compiled by Sviatopolk—Mirsky; and *Collection of Poems*, by V. Khodasevich.

RUTGERS UNIVERSITY PRESS, 30 College Ave., New Brunswick NJ 08903. Averages 20 titles/year. Pays royalty on retail price. Free book catalog. Final decision depends on time required to secure competent professional reading reports. Enclose return postage.
Nonfiction: Scholarly books in history, literary criticism, anthropology, sociology, political science, biography and criminal justice. Regional nonfiction must deal with mid-Atlantic region with emphasis on New Jersey. Query. Length: 60,000 words minimum.
Recent Nonfiction Titles: *Sergei Nechaev*, by Philip Pomper; *Informed Consent in Medical Therapy and Research*, by Bernard Barber; *Politics in Renaissance Venice*, by R. Finlay.

S. C. E.-EDITIONS L'ETINCELLE, 3449 Rue St-Denis, Montreal, Quebec, Canada H2X 3L1. (514)843-7663. President: Robert Davies. Publishes trade paperback originals. Averages 12 titles/year. Pays 8-12% royalty on retail price; offers average $1,000. Simultaneous and photocopied submissions OK. SASE. Reports in 3 weeks on queries; 2 months on mss. Free book catalog.
Imprints: *L'Etincelle* (nonfiction and fiction), Robert Davies, President.
Nonfiction: Biography, cookbook, how-to, humor, reference and self-help. Subjects include animals, business and economics, cooking and foods, health, history, hobbies, nature, philosophy, politics, psychology, recreation, sociology, sports and travel. "We would be looking for about 5 translatable works of nonfiction, in any popular field. Our audience includes French-speaking readers in all major markets in the world." No "topics of interest only to Americans." Query or submit outline/synopsis and sample chapters.
Recent Nonfiction Titles: *Openings and Short Games of Chess*, by H. Tranquille (hobby); *When God Was a Woman*, by M. Stone (history/feminism); and *The Book of Solar Houses*, by D. Watson.

SAIL BOOKS, Subsidiary of Meredith Corp., 34 Commercial Wharf, Boston MA 02110. Director: R. Mamis. Publishes hardcover originals. Averages 8 titles/year. Pays 10-15% royalty on retail price; 5% on price received by mail order; offers average $3,500 advance. Simultaneous and photocopied submissions OK ("must be clear"). SASE. Reports in 1 month on queries; 6 months on mss.
Nonfiction: How-to and adventure. Subjects include sports (sailing only). "We're interested in instructional texts with illustrations—some real adventure." Query.
Recent Nonfiction Titles: *Blown Away*, by Payson (how-to/adventure); *Blue Water*, by Griffith (how-to/adventure); and *Cooking On the Go*, by Groeme (shipboard cooking).

ST. ANTHONY MESSENGER PRESS, 1615 Republic St., Cincinnati OH 45210. Editor-in-Chief: The Rev. Jeremy Harrington, O.F.M. Publishes paperback originals. Averages 14 titles/year. Pays 6-8% royalty on retail price; offers $500 average advance. Books are sold in bulk to groups (study clubs, high school or college classes) and in bookstores. Will send free catalog to writer on request. Will consider photocopied submissions if they are not simultaneous submissions to other publishers. Query or submit outline and sample chapters. Enclose return postage.
Religion: "We try to reach the Catholic market with topics near the heart of the ordinary Catholic's belief. We want to offer insight and inspiration and thus give people support in living a Christian life in a pluralistic society. We are not interested in an academic or abstract approach. Our emphasis is on the popular writing with examples, specifics, color and anecdotes." Length: 25,000-40,000 words.
Recent Nonfiction Titles: *Making the Family Matter: A New Vision of Expanded Family Living*, by James and Mary Kenny; *Brokenness: The Stories of Six Women Whose Faith Grew in Crises*, edited by Carol Leubering; and *Mary and Inner Healing*, by Gloria Hutchinson.

ST. MARTIN'S PRESS, 175 5th Ave., New York NY 10010. Averages 550 titles/year. SASE. Reports "promptly."

General: Publishes general fiction and nonfiction; major interest in adult fiction and nonfiction, history, self-help, political science, popular science, biography, scholarly, popular reference, etc. "No children's books." Query.
Recent Titles: *Trade Wind*, by M.M. Kaye (romantic historical); *The Lord God Made Them All*, by James Herriot; and *Comparisons* (popular reference).
Textbooks: College textbooks. Query.

HOWARD W. SAMS & CO., INC., 4300 W. 62nd St., Indianapolis IN 46268. Manager, Technical Books and Acquisitions: C.P. Oliphant. Payment depends on quantity, quality, salability. Offers both royalty arrangements or outright purchase. Prefers queries, outlines, and sample chapters. Usually reports within 30 days. SASE.
Nonfiction: Technical, scientific and how-to. "Publishes technical and scientific books for the electronics industry and the amateur radio field."

SCARECROW PRESS, INC., 52 Liberty St., Metuchen NJ 08840. Senior Editor: Gary Kuris. Publishes hardcover originals. Averages 110 titles/year. Pays 10-15% royalty on gross receipts; no advance. Photocopied submissions OK. SASE. Reports in 2 weeks. Free book catalog.
Nonfiction: Music. Needs reference books, bibliographies, women's studies and movies. Query.

SCHENKMAN PUBLISHING CO., INC., 3 Mt. Auburn Place, Cambridge MA 02138. (617)492-4952. Editor-in-Chief: Alfred S. Schenkman. Publishes hardcover and paperback originals. Specializes in textbooks. Published 40 titles in 1979; 60 in 1980; plans 60 in 1981. Royalty varies on net sales, but averages 10%. "In some cases, no royalties are paid on first 2,000 copies sold." No advance. State availability of photos and/or illustrations. Simultaneous and photocopied submissions OK. Reports in 1-2 months. SASE. Free book catalog.
Nonfiction: Publishes economics, history, psychology, sociology and textbooks. Query.
Recent Nonfiction Titles: *The Westernization of Asia*, by F. Darling (political science/history); *Harassment Therapy*, by Don Stannard-Friel; and *The Minority Administrator in Higher Education*, edited by G. Mims.

SCHIFFER PUBLISHERS, LTD., Box E, Exton PA 19341. (215)363-7275. Editorial Director: Peter Schiffer. Publishes hardcover and paperback originals (80%) and reprints. (20%). Published 8 titles in 1979; 9 in 1980. Offers 10-15% royalty on wholesale price. No advance. No simultaneous or photocopied submissions. SASE. Reports in 4 weeks. Book catalog for SASE.
Nonfiction: Americana; art; cookbooks, cooking and food; history; and gardening. Especially needs books on antiques, art, cooking and collectibles. Submit outline/synopsis and sample chapters.
Recent Nonfiction Titles: *Chef Tell Tells All*, by T. Erhardt (cookbook); and *The Garden of Eden*, by J. Eden.

SCHIRMER BOOKS, Macmillan Publishing Co., Inc., 866 3rd Ave., New York NY 10022. Editor-in-Chief: Ken Stuart. Editor, Music Education: Abigail Sterne. Publishes hardcover and paperback originals (90%) and paperback reprints (10%). Pays royalty on wholesale or retail price; small advance. Publishes 20 books/year. Submit photos and/or illustrations "if central to the book, not if decorative or tangential." Photocopied and simultaneous submissions OK. Reports in 6 weeks. SASE. Book catalog for SASE.
Nonfiction: Publishes books on the performing arts: ; college texts; coffee table books; biographies; reference; and how-to. Submit outline/synopsis and sample chapters.
Recent Nonfiction Titles: *Pavlova*, by John and Roberta Lazzarini (coffee table); *Recorded Classical Music, A Critical Guide to Compositions and Performances*, by Arthur Cohn; and *Teaching Woodwinds*, by Gene Saucier.

SCHOCKEN BOOKS, INC., 200 Madison Ave., New York NY 10016. (212)685-6500. Editorial Director: John Simon. Publishes hardcover and paperback originals and paperback reprints and simultaneous. Publishes 56 titles/year. Pays standard royalty; offers variable advance. Photocopied submissions OK. SASE. Reports in 6 weeks. Free book catalog.
Nonfiction: Needs books of Jewish interest, academic sociology, and children's (mythology and folktales). Submit outline/synopsis and sample chapters.
Recent Nonfiction Titles: *Continuing the Good Life*, by H. and S. Nearing; *Jewish Holiday Kitchen*, by J. Nathan; and *The Magic Orange Tree*, by D. Wolkstein.

SCHOLARLY RESOURCES, INC., 104 Greenhill Ave., Wilmington DE 19805. (302)654-7713. Managing Editor: Philip G. Johnson. Publishes hardcover and trade paperback originals (60%). Averages 20 titles/year. Pays 5-15% royalty on retail price. Simultaneous and photocopied submis-

sions OK. SASE. Reports in 2 weeks on queries; 2 months on mss. Free book catalog.
Nonfiction: Reference. Subjects include history and sociology. "We are interested in bibliography and other reference material as well as historical research and interpretative works on modern America, modern China, and diplomatic history. Our audience includes university and public libraries; some course adoption." Query or submit outline/synopsis and sample chapters.
Recent Nonfiction Titles: *The People's Republic of China: A Documentary Survey* (5 vols.), by Harold C. Hinton (reference); *The Gallup Poll: Public Opinion, 1979*, by George Gallup (reference); and *NATO After Thirty Years*, edited by Kaplan and Clawson (scholarly essays).

SCHOLIUM INTERNATIONAL, INC., 265 Great Neck Rd., Great Neck NY 11021. Editor-in-Chief: Arthur L. Candido. Publishes hardcover and paperback orignals. Published 8 titles in 1979. Standard minimum book contract of 12%. Free book catalog. Will consider photocopied submissions. Query. Reports in 2 weeks. SASE.
Science and Technology: Subjects include cryogenics, electronics, aviation, medicine, physics, etc. "We also publish books in other areas whenever it is felt the manuscript has good sales and reception potential. Contact us prior to sending ms, outlining subject, number of pages and other pertinent information which would enable us to make a decision as to whether we would want to review the manuscript."

*ABNER SCHRAM LTD., 36 Park St., Montclair NJ 07042. (201)744-7755. Editorial Director: Sara Held. Senior Editor: Frances Schram. Publishes hardcover originals. Published 32 titles in 1979, 30 in 1980; plans 30 in 1981. Subsidy publishes 3-4% books. Offers 7½-10% royalty; very limited advance. Simultaneous and photocopied submissions OK. SASE. Reports in 2 months. Book catalog for 8x10½ SASE.
Nonfiction: "Our main thrust is art and art history." Also interested in the slight outer periphery of art history and wants some idea of photos that could illustrate the book. Query first.
Recent Nonfiction Titles: *Medieval Calligraphy*, by Mark Grogin; *Ashile Gorky*, by Harry Rand; and *Religious Paintings of Jan Steen*, by B. Kirschenbaum (art history).

CHARLES SCRIBNER'S SONS, 597 5th Ave., New York NY 10017. Director of Publishing: Jacek K. Galazka. Publishes hardcover originals and hardcover and paperback reprints. Averages 300 titles/year. "Our contract terms, royalties and advances vary, depending on the nature of the project." Reports in 1-2 months. Enclose return postage.
General: Publishes adult fiction and nonfiction, practical books, garden books, reference sets, cookbooks, history and science. Queries only.
Recent Titles: *Innocent Blood*, by P.D. James (mystery); and *Of Wolves and Men*, by Lopez (natural history).

CHARLES SCRIBNER'S SONS, Children's Books Department, 597 5th Ave., New York NY 10017. (212)486-4035. Editorial Director, Children's Books: Lee Anna Deadrick. Senior Editor, Children's Books: Clare Costello. Publishes hardcover originals and paperback reprints. Averages 40 titles/year. Pays royalty on retail price; offers advance. Photocopied submissions OK. SASE. Free book catalog.
Nonfiction: Animals, art, biography, health, hobbies, humor, nature, photography, recreation, science and sports. Query.
Recent Nonfiction Titles: *A Natural History of Raccoons*, by Dorcas MacClintock (natural history); and *I'm Dancing!*, by Michael Spector, Alan McCarter and Glenn Reed (ballet).
Fiction: Adventure, fantasy, historical, humor, mainstream, mystery, science fiction and suspense. Submit outline/synopsis and sample chapters.
Recent Fiction Titles: *The Leaving*, by Lynn Hall (contemporary); *Anna to the Infinite Power*, by Mildred Ames (futuristic); and *That's Not Fair*, by Jane Sarnoff and Reynold Ruffins (picture book).

THE SEABURY PRESS, 815 2nd Ave., New York NY 10017. (212)557-0500. Publishes hardcover and paperback originals (85%) and paperback (adult only) reprints (15%). Publishes 75 titles/year. Pays 7-10% royalty; offers variable advance. Photocopied submissions OK. SASE. Reports in 6-8 weeks. Free book catalog.
Nonfiction: Theology, inspiration, liturgy, religious education. Query.
Recent Nonfiction Titles: *John Paul II: Pilgrimage of Faith; The Easter Moment*, by J.S. Spong; *Sharing the Vision*, by R.G. Cheney; and *Anne and the Sand Dobbies*, by J.B. Coburn (juvenile).

SERVANT PUBLICATIONS, Box 8617, 840 Airport Blvd., Ann Arbor MI 48107. (313)761-8505. Managing Editor: James D. Manney. Publishes hardcover, trade and mass market paperback originals (80%), and hardcover, trade and mass market paperback reprints (20%). Averages 25 titles/year. Pays 10% royalty on retail price. "Queries only." Reports in 1 month. Free book catalog.

Nonfiction: Subjects include religion. "We're looking for practical Christian teaching, Scripture, current problems facing the Christian Church, and inspiration." No heterodox or non-Christian approaches. Query or submit outline/synopsis and sample chapters. All unsolicited mss are returned unopened.

Recent Nonfiction Titles: *Man and Woman in Christ*, by Stephen B. Clark (theology); *The Angry Christian*, by Bert Ghezzi (teaching); and *Mark: Good News for Hard Times*, by George Montague (Scripture).

'76 PRESS, Box 9925, Atlanta GA 30319. (404)458-8340. Editor-in-Chief: Wallis W. Wood. Publishes hardcover and paperback originals. Publishes 4 titles/year. Pays 10% royalty; offers $2,500 average advance. Simultaneous and photocopied submissions OK. SASE. Free book catalog.

Nonfiction: "Economics, politics and international relations written from conservative, anti-big government perspective. Information on author's credentials on subject matter is very important." Submit outline/synopsis and sample chapters. Recently published *The War on Gold*, by A.C. Sutton; *Chelation Therapy*, by Dr. M. Walker; and *Tax Target: Washington*, by G. Allen.

HAROLD SHAW PUBLISHERS, Box 567, 388 Gundersen Dr., Wheaton IL 60187. (312)665-6700. Senior Editor; Luci Shaw. Publishes hardcover and paperback originals (80%) and paperback reprints (20%). Published 18 titles in 1979; 15 in 1980; plans 20 in 1981. Offers 5-10% royalty on retail price. Average advance (with established authors): $300-1,000. Simultaneous and photocopied submissions OK. SASE. Reports in 1 month. Free book catalog.

Nonfiction: How-to; juveniles; poetry; religion; and self-help. Especially needs "manuscripts dealing with the needs of Christians in today's changing world. We are specially looking for mss on guilt, forgiveness, marriage (if it is handled in an original and creative way), pain and suffering. Also any well done books on doctrine or Biblical exposition. If it is not for the Christian market, we don't want to see it. We do not want to see poetry unless the poet is already established and has a reading audience. Mss must be high in quality and creativity." Query first, then submit outline/synopsis and sample chapters.

Recent Nonfiction Titles: *Double Take*, by G. Hardy (pop apologetics); *How to Win the War*, by D. Watson (Biblical exposition and practical application); *The Achievement of C.S. Lewis*, by Thomas Haward (literary criticism); *Song For Sarah*, by P. D'Arcy (personal experience); *Adam*, by D. Bolt (retelling of Genesis 1-3); and *Walking on Water*, by Madeleine L'Engle.

SHOAL CREEK PUBLISHERS, INC., Box 9737, Austin TX 78766. (512)451-7545. Senior Editor: Ruth Steyn. Publishes hardcover and paperback originals (90%) and reprints (10%). Averages 4-8 titles/year. Pays 10% royalty on retail price; no advance. Simultaneous and photocopied submissions OK. Reports "as soon as practical." SASE. Free book catalog.

Nonfiction: Historical, biographical and character studies. Also interested in how-to and popular reference materials. Submit outline/snyopsis and sample chapters.

Recent Nonfiction Titles: *Ambush: The Real Story of Bonnie and Clyde*, by Ted Hinton, as told to Larry Grove; *Fred Gipson: Texas Storyteller*, by Mike Cox; and *Texas Woman: Interviews and Images*, by Patricia Lasher.

Fiction: Children's stories. Submit manuscript and sample artwork.

THE SHOE STRING PRESS, (Archon Books, Linnet Books, Library Professional Publications), 995 Sherman Ave., Hamden CT 06514. (203)248-6307. Distributor for the Connecticut Academy of Arts and Sciences. President: James Thorpe III. Publishes 60 titles/year. Royalty on net; no advance. Reports in 4-6 weeks. SASE.

Nonfiction: Publishes scholarly books: history, biography, literary criticism, reference, geography, bibliography, military history, information science, library science, education and general adult nonfiction. Preferred length: 40,000-130,000 words, though there is no set limit. Query with table of contents and sample chapters.

Recent Nonfiction Title: *Devil Wagon in God's Country: Automobile and Social Change in Rural America*, by Michael L. Berger (social history).

SIERRA CLUB BOOKS, 530 Bush St., San Francisco CA 94108. (415)981-8634. Editor-in-Chief: Daniel Moses. Publishes hardcover and paperback originals (95%) and reprints (5%). Published 12 titles in 1979; 15 in 1980; plans 15 in 1981. Offers 8-12½% royalty on retail price. Average advance: $7,000. Simultaneous and photocopied submissions OK. SASE. Reports in 2 months. Free book catalog.

Nonfiction: Animals; health; history (natural); how-to (outdoors); juveniles; nature; philosophy;

photography; recreation (outdoors, nonmechanical); science; sports (outdoors); and travel (by foot or bicycle). "The Sierra Club was founded to help people to explore, enjoy and preserve the nation's forests, waters, wildlife and wilderness. The books program looks to publish quality trade books about the outdoors and the protection of natural resources. Specifically, we are interested in undeveloped land (not philosophical but informational), nuclear power, self-sufficiency, natural history, politics and the environment, and juvenile books with an ecological theme." Does *not* want "personal, lyrical, philosophical books on the great outdoors; proposals for large color photographic books without substantial text; how-to books on building things outdoors; books on motorized travel; or any but the most professional studies of animals." Query first, submit outline/synopsis and sample chapters, or submit complete ms.

Recent Nonfiction Titles: *The Integral Urban House,* by the Farallones Institute (self-sufficient, nonwasteful living in the city); *Fifty Classic Climbs of North America,* by S. Roper and A. Steck (mountaineering); and *Sierra Club Naturalist's Guide to the Sierra Nevada,* by S. Whitney (one of a series of guides to the terrain, flora and fauna of a specific geographical area).

Fiction: Adventure; historical; mainstream; and science fiction. "We do very little fiction, but will consider a fiction manuscript if its theme fits our philosophical aims: the enjoyment and protection of the environment." Does *not* want "any ms with animals or plants that talk; apocalyptic plots." Query first, submit outline/synopsis and sample chapters, or submit complete ms.

Recent Ficton Title: *The Sacred Hoop,* by B. Broder (myths and historical tales about men and nature).

SIGNPOST BOOKS, 8912 192nd SW, Edmonds WA 98020. Editor-in-Chief: Cliff Cameron. Publishes paperback originals. Averages 5-6 titles/year. Offers standard minimum book contract of 8% on retail price. Free book catalog. Query. Reports in 3 weeks. SASE.

Nonfiction: "Books on outdoor subjects emphasizing self-propelled activity such as hiking, canoeing, bicycling, camping and related interests. Books should have strong environmenal material for a general audience, where applicable."

Recent Nonfiction Titles: *Stehekin: The Enchanted Valley,* by Fred Darvill Jr. (hiking and nature guide); and *177 Free Oregon Campgrounds,* by Ed and Christina Bedrick (camping guide).

SILHOUETTE BOOKS, Subsidiary of Simon & Schuster/Pocket Books, 1230 Avenue of the Americas, New York NY 10020. (212)586-6151. Editor-in-Chief: Karen Solem. Publishes mass market paperback originals. Averages 144 titles/year. Pays royalty; buys some mss outright. Photocopied submissions OK. SASE. Reports in 3 weeks on queries; 6 weeks on mss. "Tip-sheets are available upon request."

Imprints: *Silhouette Romances* (contemporary adult romances); 50,000-55,000 words. *Silhouette Special Editions* (contemporary adult romances); 70,000-75,000 words. *Silhouette First Loves* (contemporary young adult romances); 50,000-55,000 words.

Fiction: Romance (contemporary romance for adults and young adults). "We are particularly interested in seeing mss for the longer adult romance line and YA line, though we will consider submissions for all 3 lines. No mss other than contemporary romances of the type outlined above. No mystery, gothic or medical." Submit complete ms.

Recent Fiction Titles: *Island Conquest,* by Brooke Hastings; *Promises from the Past,* by Donna Vitek; and *A Touch of Magic,* by Elizabeth Hunter (all contemporary romance).

SILVER BURDETT, Subsidiary of SFN Companies, Inc., 250 James St., Morristown NJ 07960. Editor-in-Chief: Barbara Thompson Howell. Publishes hardcover and paperback originals. Publishes 180 titles/year. "Textbook rates only, el-hi range." Query. SASE.

Education: Produces educational materials for preschoolers, elementary and high school students and professional publications for teachers. Among materials produced: textbooks, teachers' materials, other print and nonprint classroom materials including educational games, manipulatives and audiovisual aids (silent and sound 16mm films and filmstrips, records, multimedia kits, overhead transparencies, tapes, etc.). Assigns projects to qualified writers on occasion. Writer must have understanding of school market and school learning materials.

SIMON & SCHUSTER, Trade Books Division, 1230 Avenue of the Americas, New York NY 10020. Administrative Editor: Daniel Johnson. "If we accept a book for publication, business arrangements are worked out with the author or his agent and a contract is drawn up. The specific terms vary according to the type of book and other considerations. Royalty rates are more or less standard among publishers. Special arrangements are made for anthologies, translations and projects involving editorial research services." Published over 300 titles in 1979. Free book catalog. "All unsolicited mss will be returned unread. Only mss submitted by agents or recommended to us by friends or actively solicited by us will be considered. In such cases, our requirements are as follows: All mss submitted for consideration should be marked to the attention of the editorial department. Mystery novels should be so labeled in order that they may be sent to the proper editors without delay. It usually takes at least three weeks for the author to be notified of a decision—often longer. Sufficient postage for return by first-class registered mail, or instructions for return by express collect, in case of rejection, should be included. Mss must be typewritten, double-spaced, on one side of the sheet only. We suggest margins of about one inch all around and the standard 8"x11" typewriter paper." Prefers complete mss.

General: "Simon and Schuster publishes books of adult fiction, history, biography, science, philosophy, the arts and popular culture, running 50,000 words or more. Our program does not, however, include school textbooks, extremely technical or highly specialized works, or, as a general rule, plays. Exceptions have been made, of course, for extraordinary mss of great distinction or significance." Recently published *Sideshow*, by William Shawcross (history/current affairs); *The Second Ring of Power*, by C. Castaneda (anthropology); and *White Album*, by Joan Didion.

CHARLES B. SLACK, INC., 6900 Grove Rd., Thorofare NJ 08086. (609)848-1000. Associate Publisher: Richard N. Roash. Executive Editors: Kaye Coraluzzo, Diana Wheeler, Peg Carnine, Eric Baloff. Promotion Manager: Peter Slack. Publishes hardcover and paperback originals (90%) and reprints (10%). Specializes in medical and health education texts. Pays 10% (of net proceeds) royalty; advances are discouraged. Averages 10 titles/year. State availability of photos and/or illustrations to accompany ms. Simultaneous submissions OK. Reports in 1-2 months. SASE. Free book pamphlet for SASE.

Nonfiction: Publishes medicine and psychiatry, psychology, scientific and textbooks. Query, submit outline/synopsis and sample chapters, or submit complete ms. All queries, outlines and mss should be sent to the attention of Peter N. Slack.

Recent Nonfiction Titles: *The Retinoscopy Book: A Manual for Beginners*, by John M. Corboy, M.D. (opthalmology); and *Creativity in Nursing*, by S. Steele.

Tips: "We specialize in publications for the allied health and educational fields, consequently a strong English background with a specialized knowledge in your chosen field is necessary. As more publishers realize the need for specialization, the writer today should direct his education to complement the publishing industry to increase his chances of marketing his skills."

*SLAVICA PUBLISHERS, INC., Box 14388, Columbus OH 43214. (614)268-4002. President/Editor: Charles E. Gribble. Publishes hardcover and paperback originals (90%) and reprints (10%). Averages 15 titles/year. Subsidy publishes ⅓-½ of books. "All manuscripts are read for quality; if they pass that test, then we talk about money. We *never* accept full subsidies on a book, and we *never* publish anything that has not passed the scrutiny of expert readers. Most subsidies are very small (usually in the range of $200-800)." Offers 10-15% royalty on retail price; "for some books, royalties do not begin until specified number has been sold." No advance. "Only in exceptional circumstances will we consider simultaneous submissons, and only if we are informed of it. We strongly prefer good photocopied submissions rather than the original." SASE. Reports in 1 week to 4 months (more in some cases). Free book catalog.

Nonfiction: Biography; history; reference; textbooks; travel; language study; literature; folklore; and literary criticism. "We publish books dealing with almost any aspect of the peoples, languages, literatures, history, cultures of Eastern Europe and the Soviet Union, as well as general linguistics and Balkan studies. We do not publish original fiction and in general do not publish books dealing with areas of the world other than Eastern Europe, the USSR and the Balkans (except for linguistics, which may deal with any area)." Query first.

Recent Nonfiction Titles: *Brain and Language*, by Roman Jakobson (linguistics); *Guide to the Slavonic Languages (Third Edition)*, by R.G.A. de Bray (language study and linguistics); and *Sologub's Literary Children: Keys to a Symbolist's Prose*, by Stanley J. Rabinowitz.

Tips: "A large percentage of our authors are academics, but we would be happy to hear from other authors as well. Very few of our books sell well enough to make the author much money, since the field in which we work is so small. The few that do make money are normally textbooks."

SLEEPY HOLLOW PRESS, (imprint of Sleepy Hollow Restorations, Inc.), 150 White Plains Rd., Tarrytown NY 10591. (914)631-8200. Editor-in-Chief: Saverio Procario. Managing Editor: James R. Gullickson. Publishing hardcover and paperback originals (85%) and hardcover reprints (15%). Pays 5-10% (net) royalty; no advance. Averages 3-4 titles/year. State availability of photos and/or illustrations to accompany ms. Simultaneous and photocopied submissions OK. Reports in 1-2 months. SASE. Free book catalog.

Nonfiction: Publishes Americana; art (American decorative arts); biography; cookbooks; cooking and foods (regional, historical); history (especially American, New York state and colonial through modern times); technical (17th- to 19th-Century technology); travel (regional and New York state); American literature and literary criticism (especially 19th-Century). Query the Managing Editor.

Recent Nonfiction Titles: *An Emerging Independent American Economy, 1815-1875*, edited by Joseph R. Frese, S.J. and Jacob Judd; and *Party and Political Opposition in Revolutionary America*, edited by Patricia U. Bonomi.

THE SMITH, 5 Beekman St., New York NY 10038. Publishes hardcover and paperback originals. The Smith is now owned by the Generalist Association, Inc., a nonprofit organization, which gives to writers awards averaging $500 for book projects. Averages 8 titles/year. Free book catalog. Send query first for nonfiction; sample chapter preferred for fiction. Reports in 2 months. SASE.
Nonfiction and Fiction: "Original fiction—no specific schools or categories; for nonfiction, the more controversial, the better." Editor of Adult Fiction: Harry Smith. Nonfiction Editor: Sidney Bernard.
Recent Titles: *Forever and Ever and a Wednesday*, by Menke Katz (Lithuanian folk tales); and *Cosmologists of the Word*, by Donald Phelps, Dick Higgins and Richard Morris (literary criticism).

SOCCER ASSOCIATES, Box 634, New Rochelle NY 10802. Editor: Irma Ganz. Published 124 titles in 1979, plans 150 in 1980; 175 in 1981. Pays royalty on wholesale price. SASE.
Nonfiction: Publishes sports, recreation, leisure time and hobby books under *Sport Shelf* and *Leisure Time Books* imprints. Most titles are British and Australian although they do have a special service for authors who publish their own books and desire national and international distribution, promotion and publicity. Query with outline.
Recent Nonfiction Titles: *Soccer*, by Arpad Csanadi; and *Official Rules of Sports and Games*.

SOCIAL SCIENCE EDUCATION CONSORTIUM, INC., (SSEC), 855 Broadway, Boulder CO 80302. (303)492-8154. Publications Manager: Ann M. Williams. Publishes trade paperback originals. Averages 12-15 titles/year. Pays up to $600 honorarium. Photocopied submissions OK. SASE. "At the end of each calendar year we establish a forthcoming list for the whole year. Before that time, we can only respond tentatively to prospective authors. Definite 'nos' receive responses within 30 days." Free book catalog.
Nonfiction: Reference and professional books for educators. Subjects include economics, history, politics, psychology, sociology and education. "We are always looking for useful, original resources that social studies educators can use in the classroom and in planning curriculum and staff-development programs. We also publish some scholarly research in social science education." No material "that would not be of direct interest to social studies educators, administrators, teacher educators, and preservice teachers." Query or submit outline/synopsis and sample chapters.
Recent Nonfiction Titles: *Teachers Have Rights, Too: What Educators Should Know About School Law*, by Leigh Stelzer and Joanna Banthin (review of educators' legal rights, status); *Data Book of Social Studies Materials and Resources*, vol. 6 (annual), edited by Laurel Singleton (analyses and descriptions of new social studies materials); and *Global Issues: Activities and Resources for the High School Teacher*, by Kenneth A. Switzer and Paul T. Mulloy (lessons and student materials).
Tips: "The SSEC is a not-for-profit educational service organization. One of our ongoing activities is a small, short-run publications program. All of our publications are designed for professionals in some aspect and at some level of education, particularly social studies/social science education. In fact, without exception, all of our publications are written and edited by people who fit that description. Our books are sold exclusively by direct mail. Thus, a freelance writer whose main motivation is to make money by selling manuscripts probably would not find us to be an attractive market. We pay only a modest honorarium, although some royalty arrangements will also be forthcoming; most of our authors are motivated by desire for professional growth, prestige, and service."

SOUTHERN ILLINOIS UNIVERSITY PRESS, Box 3697, Carbondale IL 62901. (618)453-2281. Director: Kenney Withers. Averages 50 titles/year. Pays 10-12.5% royalty on net price; offers advance. Simultaneous and photocopied submissions OK. SASE. Reports in 1 week. Free book catalog.
Nonfiction: "We are interested in humanities, social sciences and contemporary affairs material. No dissertations or collections of previously published articles." Query.
Recent Nonfiction Title: *Thomas Pynchon*, by Cowart (literary criticism).

SOUTHERN METHODIST UNIVERSITY PRESS, Dallas TX 75275. (214)692-2263. Director: Allen Maxwell. Associate Director and Editor: Margaret L. Hartley. Published 6 titles in 1980, 8 in 1981; plans 10 in 1982. Payment is on royalty basis: 10% of list up to 2,500 copies; 12% for 2,500-5,000 copies; 15% thereafter; no advance. Free book catalog. Appreciates query letters, outlines and sample chapters. Reports "tend to be slow for promising mss requiring outside reading by authorities." Enclose return postage.

Nonfiction: Regional and scholarly nonfiction. History, Americana, economics, banking, literature and anthropology. Length: open. Recently published *Freedom and Fate in American Thought: From Edwards to Dewey*, by Paul F. Boller Jr.; *Mexican Folktales from the Borderland*, by Riley Aiken; and *Unconventional Methods in Exploration for Petroleum and Natural Gas: II*, edited by B.M. Gottlieb.

SRS ENTERPRISES, INC./SCIENTIFIC RESEARCH SERVICES, 1018 N. Cole Ave., Hollywood CA 90038. (213)461-3366. Book Department: Bruce Plopper. Publishes hardcover and trade and mass market paperback originals. Averages 2 titles/year. Pays 10-15% royalty on retail price; no advance. Simultaneous and photocopied submissions OK. SASE. Reports in 6 weeks on queries; 3 months on mss.
Nonfiction: How-to. Subjects include gambling. "We're looking for books on all types of gambling and gambling-related activities." Submit outline/synopsis and sample chapters.
Recent Nonfiction Titles: *Million Dollar Blackjack*, by Ken Uston (how to play and win at 21); and *Winning Blackjack*, by Stanley Roberts.
Fiction: Query.

STACKPOLE BOOKS, Box 1831, Harrisburg PA 17105. (717)234-5091. Editor: Ruth Dennison-TeDesco. Publishes hardcover and quality paperback originals. Publishes approximately 35 titles/year. "Proposals should include a 2- to 4-page outline and 2 or 3 sample chapters, plus a summary of the book's contents and appeal and author's credentials." Simultaneous and photocopied submissions OK. SASE. Free author's guidelines describing publishing program and submissions procedure.
Nonfiction: Firearms, fishing, hunting, military, wildlife, outdoor skills, space exploration, and crafts.

STANDARD PUBLISHING, 8121 Hamilton Ave., Cincinnati OH 45231. (513)931-4050. Publishes hardcover and paperback originals (85%) and reprints (15%). Specializes in religious books. Averages 60 titles/year. Pays 10% usual royalty on wholesale or retail price. Advance averages $200-1,500. Query or submit outline/synopsis and sample chapter. Reports in 1-2 months. SASE.
Nonfiction: Publishes how-to; crafts (to be used in Christian education); juveniles; reference; Christian education; quiz; puzzle and religious books; and college textbooks (religious). All mss must pertain to religion.
Recent Nonfiction Titles: *My Child on Drugs?*, by Art Linkletter, George Gallup Jr. (youth and the drug culture); *The Power of the Christian Woman*, by Phyllis Schlafly (women's influence, responsibility); and *Frankly Feminine*, by Gloria Hope Hawley (God's idea of womanhood).
Fiction: Publishes religious, devotional books.
Recent Fiction Titles: *6 Thorne Twin Adventure Books*, by Dayle Courtney (teen adventure).

STANFORD UNIVERSITY PRESS, Stanford CA 94305. (415)497-9434. Contact: Editor. Published 25 titles in 1979; 34 in 1980. Pays 10-15% royalty; "rarely" offers advance. Photocopied submissions OK. SASE. Reports in 3 weeks. Free book catalog.
Nonfiction: Books on European history, the history of China and Japan, anthropology, psychology, taxonomy, literature and Latin American studies. Query.
Recent Nonfiction Titles: *Lionel Trilling*, by Chace; and *Marriage and Adoption in China, 1845-1945*, by Wolf and Huang.

*STATE HISTORICAL SOCIETY OF WISCONSIN, 816 State St., Madison WI 53706. (608)262-9604. Editorial Director: Paul H. Hass. Senior Editor: William C. Marten. Publishes hardcover and paperback originals (75%) and hardcover reprints (25%). Publishes 2 titles/year. Subsidy publishes 66% of titles based on "an educated guess on the availability of a subsidy from some source and the strength of the market for the title." Pays 10% royalty; no advance. Photocopied submissions OK. Reports in 8 weeks. SASE. Free book catalog.
Nonfiction: "Research and interpretation in history of the American Middle West—broadly construed as the Mississippi Valley. Must be thoroughly documented but on topics of sufficient interest to attract the layman as well as the scholar. 150,000-200,000 words of text, exclusive of footnotes and other back matter. No extremely narrowly focused monographs on non-Wisconsin subjects."
Recent Nonfiction Titles: *The Documentary History of the Ratification of the Constitution: Volume III*, edited by Merrill Jensen; *Wisconsin Indians*, by Nancy Oestreich Lurie; *Danes in Wisconsin*, by Frederick Hale; and 12 pamphlets in the *Wisconsin Stories* series, by various authors.

STEIN AND DAY, Scarborough House, Briarcliff Manor NY 10510. Published 105 titles in 1979, 100 in 1980; plans 100 in 1981. Offers standard royalty contract. No unsolicited mss without querying first. Nonfiction, send outline or summary and sample chapter. *Must* furnish SASE with all fiction and nonfiction queries.
General: Publishes general adult fiction and nonfiction books; no juveniles or college. All types of nonfiction except technical. Quality fiction. Length: 65,000 words. Recently published *The Hargrave Deception*, by E. Howard Hunt; *The History of American League Baseball*, by Glenn Dickey; and *A Life in Two Centuries*, by Bertram D. Wolfe.

STERLING PUBLISHING, 2 Park Ave., New York NY 10016. (212)532-7106. Publisher: Charles Nurnberg. Publishes hardcover and paperback originals (75%) and reprints (25%). Published 25 titles in 1979, 80 in 1980. Pays royalty; offers advance. Simultaneous and photocopied submissions OK. Reports in 4-6 weeks. SASE. Book catalog for SASE.
Nonfiction: Americana, business, foods, economics, history, hobbies, how-to, humor, law, medicine, nature, pets, photography, psychology, recreation, reference, self-help, sports, technical and woodworking. Query or submit outline/synopsis and sample chapters. Recently published *Underground Houses*, by R. Roy (how-to); *Complete Diabetic Cookbook*, by M. Finsand (health); and *Biggest Riddle Book in the World*.

STRAWBERRY HILL PRESS, 2594 15th Ave. San Francisco CA 94127. President: Jean-Louis Brindamour, Ph.D. Senior Editors: Donna L. Osgood, Renee Renouf, Jane Cormack. Publishes paperback originals. Publishes 12 titles/year. "We are a small house, proud of what we do, and intending to stay relatively small (that does not mean that we will do a less-than-professional job in marketing our books, however). The author-publisher relationship is vital, from the moment the contract is signed until there are no more books to sell, and we operate on that premise. We do no hardcovers, and, for the moment at least, our format is limited strictly to 6x9 quality paperbacks, prices between $4.95-10.95. We never print fewer than 5,000 copies in a first printing, with reprintings also never falling below that same figure." Pays 10-20% royalty on wholesale price; no advance. Photocopied submissions OK. Reports in 2 months. SASE. Book catalog for SASE.
Nonfiction: Self-help; inspiration (not religion); cookbooks; health and nutrition; aging; diet; popular philosophy; metaphysics; alternative life styles; Third World; minority histories; oral history and popular medicine. No religion, sports, craft books, photography or fine art material. Submit outline/synopsis and sample chapters.
Recent Nonfiction Titles: *Excalibur Briefing*, by Thomas E. Bearden; *A Surti Touch: Adventures in Indian Cooking*, by Malvi Doshi; and *The Sound of One Mind Thinking*, by Eugene M. Schwartz.

STRUCTURES PUBLISHING CO., Ideals Publishing Corp. Box 1101, Milwaukee WI 53201. Editor: David Schansberg. Publishes paperback originals. Published 9 titles in 1979, 12 in 1980; plans 13 in 1981. Offers standard 10-12% royalty contract on selling price. Advance varies, depending on author's reputation and nature of book. Will send a catalog to a writer on request. Submit outline and sample chapters. Photocopied submissions OK. Reports in 4-6 weeks. Enclose return postage.
Technical and How-To: Books related to home remodeling, repair and building. Successful Series published for the do-it-yourself homeowners. Will consider structure, construction, building, remodeling, home improvement, and decorating-related topics. "Manuscripts are commissioned, usually. Book illustration and photography expertise of interest."
Recent Nonfiction Titles: *Successful Homeowners Tools*, by James Ritchie; *Putting it All Together*, by Robert Scharff (fastening materials together); and *Successful Home Electrical Wiring*, by Larry Mueller.
Tips: "Manuscripts must be comprehensive, well researched and written and reflect the most current trends of the home improvement and construction markets."

LYLE STUART, INC., 120 Enterprise Ave., Secaucus NJ 07094. (201)866-0490, (212)736-1141. Subsidiaries include Citadel Press and University Books. President: Lyle Stuart. Publishes hardcover and trade paperback originals, and trade paperback reprints. Averages 70 titles/year. Pays 10-12% royalty on retail price; offers "low advance." SASE. Reports in 1 week on queries; 3 weeks on mss. Free book catalog.
Nonfiction: Biography, "coffee table" book, how-to, humor, illustrated book and self-help. Subjects include Americana, art, business and economics, health, history, music and politics. "The percentage of acceptable over-the-transom mss has been so low during the years that we no longer invite unsolicited submissions." Query.
Recent Nonfiction Titles: *Ordeal*, by Linda Lovelace (biography); *You Can Negotiate Anything*, by Herb Cohen (self-help); and *Casino Gambling for the Winner*, by Lyle Stuart (self-help).

SHERWOOD SUGDEN & COMPANY, PUBLISHERS, 1117 Eighth St., La Salle IL 61301. (815)223-1231. Publisher: Sherwood Sugden. Publishes hardcover and trade paperback originals and reprints. Averages 8 titles/year. Pays 4-12% royalty. Simultaneous and photocopied submissions OK. SASE. Reports in 3 weeks on queries; 3 months on mss. Book catalog for business size SAE.

Nonfiction: Subjects include history; philosophy; politics; religion (Christian, especially Roman Catholic); and literary criticism. "We're looking for lucid presentations and defenses of orthodox Roman Catholic doctrine, Church history and lives of the Saints aimed at the average intelligent reader. (Possibly one or two scholarly works of the same sort as well.) Works of criticism of British or American authors: perhaps a biography or two; also a work in elementary syllogistic logic. The audience for our books ranges from the bright high school student with a curiosity about ideas through the mature general reader. Certain of our titles (perhaps 30% of our annual output) will appeal chiefly to the advanced student or scholar in the relevant disciplines." Submit outline/synopsis and sample chapters.

Recent Nonfiction Titles: *Dynamics of World History*, by Christopher Dawson (cultural history); *The Impatience of Job*, by George W. Rutler (extended meditation); and *Why Flannery O'Connor Stayed Home: Vol. 1 of The Prophetic Poet & the Spirit of the Age*, by Marion Montgomery.

SUMMIT BOOKS, Division of Simon & Schuster. 1230 Avenue of the Americas, New York NY 10020. (212)246-2471. Publishes hardcover originals. Published 25 titles in 1979, 30 in 1980; plans 30 in 1981. Pays standard royalty; offers variable advance. Simultaneous and photocopied submissions OK. SASE. Reports in 2 months.

Nonfiction: General trade list; no poetry. Query or submit outline/synopsis and sample chapters.
Fiction: General trade list; no short stories, no category books.

*SUN PUBLISHING CO., Box 4383, Albuquerque NM 87196. (505)255-6550. Editor-in-Chief: Skip Whitson. Publishes hardcover and paperback originals (40%) and reprints (60%). Pays 8% royalty; no advance. Will subsidy publish "if we think the book is good enough and if we have the money to do it, we'll publish it on our own; otherwise, the author will have to put up the money." Query or submit outline/synopsis and table of contents. Send photocopies if photos/illustrations are to accompany ms. Simultaneous and photocopied submissions OK. Reports in 2-4 months. SASE. Book list for SASE.

Nonfiction: Publishes Americana, art, biography, cookbooks, history, how-to, politics, scientific, self-help, metaphysical, Oriental and new age books. "40-200-page lengths are preferred." Recently published *Science and Art of Hot Air Ballooning*, by Dichtl/Jackson (science/sports); *Meditation for Healing*, by J. F. Stone (metaphysical); and *Rolling Thunder: The Coming Earth Changes*, by J.R. Jochmans.
Fiction: Publishes some science fiction books.
Tips: "We are looking for manuscripts on the coming Earth changes, for outright purchase."

THE SUNSTONE PRESS, Box 2321, Santa Fe NM 87501. (505)988-4418. Editor-in-Chief: James C. Smith Jr. Publishes paperback originals; "sometimes hardcover originals." Publishes 12 titles/year. Pays royalty on wholesale price. Free book catalog. Query. Reports in 2 months. Enclose return postage.

Nonfiction: How-to series craft books. Books on the history of the Southwest; poetry. Length: open. Recently published *Terra Dulce*, by Rosemary Nusbaum (history); *The Great Kiva*, by Phillips Kloss (epic poems); and *August in Abiquiu*, by Diane Jackson (poetry).
Fiction: Publishes "for readers who use the subject matter to elevate their impressions of our world, our immediate society, families and friends."
Recent Fiction Titles: *Searching for Fifth Mesa*, by Juana Foust (Southwest fiction); and *Lord How Different*, by Carolyn Pomonis (Southwest fiction).

SUPERIOR PUBLISHING, Box 1710, Seattle WA 98111. (206)282-4310. Publisher: Joseph Salisbury. Publishes hardcover and trade paperback originals and reprints. Averages 10 titles/year. Pays 5% of retail on paperbacks; 10% of retail on hardcovers; no advance. Simultaneous submissions OK; photocopied submissions "preferred." SASE. Reports in 45 days on queries; 3 months on mss. Free book catalog.

Imprints: Hangman Press and Salisbury Press (nonfiction).
Nonfiction: Only historical biographes, coffee table book, illustrated book and pictorial history. Subjects include Americana, art, history, hobbies, nature and photography (all pictorial); also recreation. "No family (personal) histories." Submit outline/synopsis and sample chapters.
Recent Nonfiction Titles: *Rails North*, by Howard Clifford; *When Timber Stood Tall*, by Joseph Pierre (logging history); and *Train Watchers Log*, by Pat Dorin.
Tips: "Complete your ms before attempting to land a publisher, as I (the publisher) receive many book ideas but few complete mss."

SUSANN PUBLICATIONS, INC., 3110 N. Fitzhugh, Dallas TX 75204. (214)528-8940. Editorial Director: Susan Goldstein. Managing Editor: Jon Caswell. Publishes paperback originals. Averages 3 titles/year. Offers 10-15% royalty on retail price. No advance. Simultaneous and photocopied submissions OK. SASE. Reports in 4 weeks.
Nonfiction: Cookbooks, cooking and foods; health; how-to; humor; political exposés; and self-help. "We are interested in how-to books which specifically help us toward self improvement or gratification of our desires. We are a female-owned company. We do not want to see sexist, chauvinistic or anti-woman material." Query first "always!"
Recent Nonfiction Titles: *The Underground Shopper Series: Dallas/Fort Worth, New York City, Houston, Austin/San Antonio*, staff-written (shopping guides); *Greatest Little Bachelor Book in Texas*, staff-written (guide to bachelors).
Fiction: Humor or mainstream. "We are interested in seeing works that are fast paced and humorous that can be readily transformed into other media. No science fiction, please. We like stories based on personal experiences."
Tips: "Take some time with your query letter. Mistakes are very unappealing. Include biographical information (limit to one paragraph) with an eye to what is promotable about yourself."

THE SWALLOW PRESS, INC., 811 W. Junior Terrace, Chicago IL 60613. (312)781-2760. Senior Editor: Donna Ippolito. Publishes hardcover and paperbacks (95%) and reprints (5%). Averages 20 titles/year. Pays 10% royalty on wholesale price (7½% on paperback, 10% on hardcover). Rarely offers advance. Photocopied submissions OK. SASE. Reports in 3 months.
Nonfiction: Biography (Western); cookbooks/cooking; history (Western); nature; poetry; politics; recreation; reference (literary); self-help; travel; Western Americana and books on Chicago; particularly unusual guide books; restaurant guides; etc. "We do not want to see books on religion, sports, juvenile, technical or art books." Query or submit outline/synopsis and sample chapters. SASE.
Recent Nonfiction Titles: *Buffalo Bill*, by Nellie Snyder Yost; and *Make Your Own Backpack and Other Wilderness Gear*, by Hugh Nelson.
Fiction: "We're interested in quality fiction, not genre fiction. No unsolicited fiction manuscripts considered." Query or submit outline/synopsis and sample chapters. SASE. Recently published *There Must Be More to Love Than Death*, by Charles Newman; *Night Studies*, by Cyrus Colter; and *Cities of the Interior*, by Anais Nin.
Recent Fiction Title: *Seasons Such as These: Two Novels*, by Natalie L.M. Petesch.

SYBEX, INC., 2344 6th St., Berkeley CA 94710. (415)848-8233. Editor-in-Chief: Dr. Rudolph S. Langer. Publishes hardcover and paperback originals. Published 8 titles in 1979, 12 in 1980. Subsidy publishes some books. Offers 10% royalty. Also buys mss by outright purchase for $5,000-50,000. Average $2,500 advance. Simultaneous and photocopied submissions OK. Word-star word processor diskettes preferred. SASE. Reports in 1 month. Free book catalog.
Nonfiction: Computer and electronics. "Manuscripts most publishable in the field of microprocessors, microcomputers, hardware, LSI, programming, programming languages, applications, automation, telecommunications." Submit outline/synopsis and sample chapters.
Recent Nonficton Titles: *Programming the 78000; Introduction to Pascal, the Pascal Handbook*; and *Fifty Basic Exercises, Pascal Programs for Scientists and Engineers*.

SYLVAN PRESS, Box 15125, Richmond VA 23227. Editor-in-Chief: Sylvia Manolatos. Editorial Director: Joyce H. Wright. Senior Editor: Frederica D. Garcia. Publishes hardcover and paperback originals. Published 2 titles in 1979, 6 in 1980. Pays 10% royalty; no advance. Photocopied submissions OK. SASE. Reports in 2 months.
Nonfiction: Poetry. "We want to see collections of serious poetry for possible publication as paperback and hardcover originals, preferably not to exceed 60 pages. Also, we are interested in individual poems for consideration in a yearly anthology, *Sylvan Sequence*. We do not want to see trite verse of any kind." Submit complete ms.
Recent Nonfiction Titles: *Citadels of Sun*, by Manolatos (poetry); and *Sylvan Sequence* (poetry anthology).
Tips: "Sylvan Press is trying to create a market for serious poets who want to see their works in print without resorting to vanity publishers. We are a small specialty publisher. We put our emphasis on literary quality rather than popular demands for triteness. At present, we are in the process of publishing an anthology of poetry as well as two individual collections of verse."

*SYMMES SYSTEMS, Box 8101, Atlanta GA 30306. Editor-in-Chief: E.C. Symmes. Publishes hardcover and paperback originals. Pays 10% royalty on wholesale price. "Contracts are usually written for the individual title and may have different terms." No advance. Does 40% subsidy publishing. Will consider photocopied and simultaneous submissions. Acknowledges receipt in 10 days; evaluation within 1 month. Query. SASE.

Nonfiction and Nature: "Our books have mostly been in the art of bonsai (miniature trees). We are publishing quality information for laypersons (hobbyists). Most of the titles introduce information that is totally new for the hobbyist." Clear and concise writing style. Text must be topical, showing state-of-the-art and suggestions on how to stay on top. All books so far have been illustrated with photos and/or drawings. Would like to see more material on bonsai and other horticultural subjects, photography and collecting photographica. Length: open.

Recent Nonfiction Title: *Physician's Guide to Nutritional Therapy*, by Anderson.

SYRACUSE UNIVERSITY PRESS, 1011 E. Water St., Syracuse NY 13210. (315)423-2596. Director/Editor: Arpena Mesrobian. Published 15 titles in 1979, 20 in 1980. Pays royalty on net sales. Simultaneous and photocopied submissions OK "only if we are informed." SASE. Reports in 2 weeks on queries; "longer on submissions." Free book catalog.

Nonfiction: "The best opportunities for freelance writers are in our nonfiction program of books on New York state. A catalog is available. We have published regional books by people with limited formal education, but they were thoroughly acquainted with their subjects, and they wrote simply and directly about them. No vague descriptions or assumptions that a reference to a name (in the case of a biography) or place is sufficient information. The author must make a case for the importance of his subject." Query. Recently published *Adirondack Fishing in the 1930's*, by Vincent Engels (collection of fishing stories); *Canal Boatman*, by Richard Garrity (semiautobiographical reminiscences of growing up on the Erie Canal); and *A Farm and Village Boyhood*, by Fred Lape (autobiographical reminiscences about growing up on a small farm at the turn of the century).

TAB BOOKS INC., Blue Ridge Summit PA 17214. (717)794-2191. Vice President: Anthony R. Curtis. Publishes hardcover and paperback originals and reprints. Publishes 200 titles per year. Pays variable royalty and advance. Buys some mss outright for a negotiable fee. Photocopied submissions OK (except for art). Reports in 6 weeks. SASE. Free book catalog and manuscript preparation guide.

Nonfiction: TAB publishes titles in such fields as computer hardware; computer software; solar and alternate energy; marine life; aviation; automotive; music technology; consumer medicine; electronics; electrical and electronics repair; amateur radio; shortwave listening; model railroading; toys; hobbies; drawing; animals and animal power; practical skills with projects; building furniture; basic how-to for the house; building large structures; calculators; robotics; telephones; model radio control; TV servicing; audio, recording, hi-fi and stereo; electronic music; electric motors; electrical wiring; electronic test equipment; video programming; CATV, MATV and CCTV; broadcasting; photography and film; appliance servicing and repair; advertising; antiques and restoration; bicycles; crafts; farmsteading; hobby electronics; home construction; license study guides; mathematics; metalworking; reference books; schematics and manuals; small gasoline engines; two-way radio and CB; and woodworking.

TAFT CORP., 1000 Vermont Ave. NW, Washington DC 20005. (800)424-9477; (202)347-0788. Publisher: Tracy D. Connors. Publishes paperback originals. Specializes in publishing and marketing books directed toward nonprofit industry. Averages 15 titles/year. Pays 9% royalty on first 3,000 copies, 11% on next 2,000, 14% over 5,000; advance of $250-500. State availability of photos and/or illustrations to accompany ms "and whether right to use has already been obtained." Simultaneous and photocopied submissions OK. Reports in 1-2 months. SASE. Free book catalog.

Nonfiction: Publishes directories, technical books and periodicals on subjects related to the nonprofit, human services sector. "All dealing with fund raising, management, and topics of importance to other elements of the nonprofit industry." Query or submit outline/synopsis and sample chapters.

Recent Nonfiction Titles: *Taft Corporate Directory, the Nonprofit Executive*; and *Swipe File III*.

TALON BOOKS, LTD., 201/1019 E. Cordova, Vancouver, British Columbia, Canada V6A 1M8. (604)255-5915. Editors: David Robinson (fiction and drama), Karl Siegler (poetry). Publishes paperback originals and reprints. Royalty. Simultaneous and photocopied submissions OK. No unsolicited mss; query. Reports in 3-6 months. SASE. Free book catalog.

Nonfiction: Occasionally publishes nonfiction (local history and geography, cookbooks and books about native peoples). Recently launched a new series of children's drama scripts and a book about the growth of theater for young audiences.

Fiction: Publishes David Fennard, Britt Hagarty, Ken Mitch, Howard O'Hagan, Jane Rule, George Ryga, Michel Tremblay and Audrey Thomas. Poetry by Canadian and American poets (Bill Bissett, George Bowering, Frank Davey, Edward Dorn, Barry Gifford, Duncan

McNaughton, Daphine Marlatt, B.P. Nichol, Fred Wah and Phyllis Webb, among others). Recently launched a series of six *Selected Poems/Writing.*
Drama: "Talon Books is the major publisher of plays in Canada (Michael Cook, David Fennario, James Reaney, George Ryga, Beverley Simons, Michel Tremblay among others) and is now expanding to include American and international drama with the acquisiton of works by Israel Horovitz, David Rudkin and Sam Shepard (for Canada)."

TAMARACK PRESS, Box 5650, Madison WI 53705. (608)831-3363. Editor: Howard Mead. Publishes hardcover and paperback originals (75%) and reprints (25%). Averages 4 titles/year. Pays 14% royalty on net cash receipts, "if the author supplies all materials needed for book." Advance averages $500. Photocopied submissions OK if not simultaneous. Reports in 1 month on queries, 2 months on outline/synopsis and sample chapters. SASE. Author/illustrator guidelines.
Nonfiction: "We are seeking adult nonfiction books that deal in a positive way with the state of Wisconsin. We are willing to review a broad range of subjects and approaches, but we do not want religious, academic or technical titles. No book should deal with an area smaller than the entire state, though titles dealing with Wisconsin and neighboring states are welcome. We reach a general audience, but one that's well-educated and environmentally minded." Query. Recently published *Wild Things*, by D. Henderson (nature essays); *Yarns of Wisconsin*, edited by Jill Dean; and *Wisconsin Country Cookbook*, by Heth.

TANDEM PRESS PUBLISHERS, Box 237, Tannersville PA 18372. (717)629-2250. Editor-in-Chief: Judith Keith. Hardcover originals. Averages 4 titles/year. 10-12½-15% royalty on retail price. Sometimes offers an advance. "This is handled with each author individually." Photocopied submissions OK. SASE. Reports in 2-4 weeks. Book catalog for SASE. Does not accept multiple submissions. Also handles sales of original paperback to major houses.
Nonfiction: Cookbooks, cooking and foods; how-to; multimedia material; nature; pets; psychology; recreation; self-help; and sports books. Query.
Recent Nonfiction Title: *I Haven't a Thing to Wear*, by J. Keith (how-to on clothes and accessories).
Fiction: Adventure; confession; fantasy; historical; mainstream; mystery; religious; romance; and suspense. Submit outline/synopsis and sample chapters to Judith Keith.
Recent Fiction Title: *Desires of Thy Hearts*, by Joan Cruz (historical romance).

TAPLINGER PUBLISHING, CO., INC., 132 W. 22nd, New York NY 10011. (212)741-0801. Imprints include Crescendo (music), Pentalic (calligraphy), and Pivot (quality fiction in paperback). Executive Editor: Ms. Bobs Pinkerton. Publishes hardcover originals. Publishes 75 titles/year. Pays standard royalty; offers variable advance. Simultaneous and photocopied submissions OK. SASE. Reports in 6 weeks. Free book catalog.
Nonfiction: Art, biography, history, current affairs, theatre, general trade and belles-lettres. No juveniles. Query.
Fiction: General trade, interesting contemporary and new fiction. No juveniles.

J.P. TARCHER, INC., 9110 Sunset Blvd., Los Angeles CA 90069. (213)273-3274. Editor-in-Chief: Jeremy P. Tarcher. Publishes hardcover and trade paperback originals. Pays 10-12½-15% royalty on retail price; offers advance "competitive in the industry." Published 25 titles in 1979, 30 in 1980; plans 35 in 1981. State availability of photos and/or illustrations to accompany ms. Simultaneous and photocopied submissions OK. Reports in 3-5 weeks. SASE. Free book catalog.
Fiction and Nonfiction: Publishes popular psychology, sociology, health and fitness, alternative medicine, consciousness. Submit outline/synopsis and sample chapters. Recently published *Drawing on the Right Side of the Brain*, by B. Edwards, Ph.D.; *The Aquarian Conspiracy*, by M. Feruson; and *Joy's Way*, by W. Joy, M.D.

TEACHER UPDATE, INC., Box 205, Saddle River NJ 07458. (201)327-8486. Editorial Director: Donna Papalia. Senior Editor: Nick Roes. Editorial Assistant: Nancy Roes. Publishes hardcover and paperback originals. Published 5 titles in 1979, 10 in 1980. Pays royalty; buys some mss outright by arrangement; offers variable advance. Photocopied submissions OK. SASE. Reports in 2 months. Free book catalog for SASE.
Nonfiction: Education, consumer and general interest. Query, submit outline/synopsis and sample chapters or complete ms.
Recent Nonfiction Titles: *Helping Children Watch TV*, by N. Roes (handbook); *America's Lowest Cost Colleges*, by N. Roes (directory); *Poems For Young Children*, by editors of *Teacher Update* (poetry); and *The Do Nothing Way To Beauty And Health*, by Mimi (beauty and health).

TEACHERS COLLEGE PRESS, 1234 Amsterdam Ave., New York NY 10027. (212)678-3929. Director: Thomas M. Rotell. Publishes hardcover and paperback originals (90%) and reprints

(10%). Royalty varies; "very rarely" offers advance. Averages 45 titles/year. Reports in 3-6 months. SASE. Free book catalog.

Nonfiction: "This university press concentrates on books in the field of education in the broadest sense from early childhood to higher education: good classroom practices, teacher training, special education, innovative trends and issues, administration and supervision, film, continuing and adult education, all areas of the curriculum, comparative education, guidance and counselling and the politics, economics, philosophy, sociology and history of education. The press also issues classroom materials for students at all levels, with a strong emphasis on reading and writing." Submit outline/synopsis and sample chapters.

Recent Nonfiction Title: *Reading Without Nonsense*, by Frank Smith.

TEMPLE UNIVERSITY PRESS, Broad and Oxford Sts., Philadelphia PA 19122. (215)787-8787. Editor-in-Chief: Kenneth Arnold. Publishes 30 titles/year. Pays royalty on wholesale price. Photocopied submissions OK. SASE. Reports in 3 months. Free book catalog.

Nonfiction: American history, public policy and regional (Philadelphia area). "All books should be scholarly. Authors are generally connected with a university. No memoirs, fiction or poetry." Uses University of Chicago *Manual of Style*. Query.

Recent Nonfiction Titles: *Charlotte Perkins Gilman*, by Mary A. Hill; and *Policy and Politics in Britain*, by Douglas Ashford.

TEN SPEED PRESS, Box 7123, Berkeley CA 94707. Editor: P. Wood. Publishes hardcover and paperback originals and reprints. Offers royalty of 8% of list price; 12½% after 100,000 copies are sold. Offers average $3,000 advance. Averages 15 titles/year. Will send catalog to writer on request for SASE. Submit outline and sample chapters for nonfiction. Reports in 2 weeks. Enclose return postage.

Nonfiction: Americana, book trade, cookbooks, cooking and foods, history, humor, law, nature, self-help, how-to, sports, hobbies, recreation and pets and travel. Publishes mostly trade paperbacks. Subjects range from bicycle books to William Blake's illustrations. "We will consider any first-rate nonfiction material that we feel will have a long shelf life and be a credit to our list." No set requirements. Some recipe books and career development books.

Recent Nonfiction Titles: *Don't Use a Resume*, by Lathrop (job finding); and *Wellness Workbook*, by John Travis (medical self care).

TEXAS A&M UNIVERSITY PRESS, Drawer C, College Station TX 77843. (713)845-1436. Director: Lloyd G. Lyman. Publishes 20 titles/year. Pays in royalties. Photocopied submissions OK. SASE. Reports in 1 week (queries); 1 month (submissions). Free book catalog.

Nonfiction: History, natural history, economics, agriculture and regional studies. "We do not want fiction and poetry." Query. Recently published *The Shadow of Pearl Harbor*, by Martin V. Melosi (history); *The Central Texas Gardener*, by C. Hazeltine and J. Filvaroff (guide on vegetable and landscape gardening in Central Texas); and *The March to Zion*, by K. Bain.

TEXAS CHRISTIAN UNIVERSITY PRESS, Box 30783, TCU, Fort Worth TX 76129. (817)921-7822. Editorial Director: Dr. James Newcomer. Editor and Distribution Manager: Emilie White. Publishes hardcover and paperback originals. Averages 6 titles/year. Pays royalty; no advance. Simultaneous and photocopied submissions OK. Reports "as soon as possible." Free book catalog.

Nonfiction: Americana, art, biography, history, music, nature, philosophy, politics, religion, sociology, textbooks, literature and criticism. "We are looking for good scholarly monographs, other serious scholarly work and regional titles of significance. No bone-dry dissertations, scholarly research of little import." Query.

Recent Nonfiction Titles: *Interpretation Theory: Discourse and the Surplus of Meaning*, by Paul Ricoeur (rhetoric); and *Kiowa Voices: Ceremonial Dances, Ritual and Song*, edited by Maurice Boyd (Indian culture and history).

TEXAS MONTHLY PRESS, INC., Subsidiary of Mediatex Communications Corp., Box 1569, Austin TX 78767. (512)476-7085. Editor: Barbara Reavis. Publishes hardcover and trade paperback originals (80%), and trade paperback reprints (20%). Averages 16 titles/year. Pays royalty on retail price; offers average $2,500 advance. Simultaneous and photocopied submissions OK. SASE. Reports in 2 weeks on queries; 1 month on mss. Free book catalog.

Imprints: *Texas Monthly Press* and *New West Press* (fiction and nonfiction) Barbara Reavis, editor.

Nonfiction: Biography, "coffee table" book, cookbook, humor, guidebook, illustrated book and reference. Subjects include Americana, art, business and economics, cooking and foods, history, nature, photography, politics, recreation, sports and travel. Texas and California-related subjects only. Query or submit outline/synopsis and sample chapters.

Recent Nonfiction Titles: *Texas Statehouse Blues*, by Ben Sargent (humor); *The Only Texas Cookbook*, by Linda Eckhardt; and *Texas Folk Art*, by Cecilia Steinfeldt (art).

Fiction: Adventure, ethnic, historical, mainstream, mystery, suspense and western. "All stories must be set in Texas or California." Query or submit outline/synopsis and sample chapters.

Recent Fiction Titles: *The Gay Place*, by William Brammer (political); and *The Power Exchange*, by Alan Erwin (suspense).

Poetry: Need for poetry in the next two years will be slight. No inspirational poems. Submit 5-10 samples.

TEXAS WESTERN PRESS, The University of Texas at El Paso, El Paso TX 79968. (915)747-5688. Publishes hardcover and paperback originals. Publishes 7 titles/year. "We are a university press, not a commercial house; therefore, payment is in books and prestige more than money. Most of our books are sold to libraries, not to the general reading public." Published 8 titles last year. Will send a catalog to a writer on request. Query. Will consider photocopied submissions. Follow *MLA Style Sheet*. Reports in 1 to 3 months.

Nonfiction: "Scholarly books. Historic accounts of the Southwest (west Texas, southern New Mexico, and northern Mexico). Some literary works, occasional scientific titles. Our *Southwestern Studies* use mss of 20,000 words. Our hardback books range from 30,000 words up. The writer should use good exposition in his work. Most of our work requires documentation. We favor a scholarly, but not overly pedantic, style. We specialize in superior book design."

Recent Nonfiction Titles: *To Be Alive*, by Elroy Bode; and *Pass of the North II*, by C.L. Sonnichsen.

*THE THEOSOPHICAL PUBLISHING HOUSE, Subsidiary of The Theosophical Society in America, 306 W. Geneva Rd., Wheaton IL 60187. (312)665-0123. Senior Editor: Rosemarie Stewart. Publishes trade paperback originals. Averages 12 titles/year. Subsidy publishes 40% of books based on "author need and quality and theme of manuscript." Pays 7½-12% royalty on retail price; offers average $1,500 advance. Simultaneous and photocopied submissions OK. SASE. Reports in 1 week on queries, 2 months on mss. Free book catalog.

Imprints: *Quest* (nonfiction), Rosemarie Stewart, senior editor.

Nonfiction: Self-help. Subjects include health, philosophy, psychology (trans-personal), religion and occultism. "TPH seeks works on philosophy, psychology, comparative religion, etc., which are compatible with the theosophical philosophy. Our audience includes the 'new age' consciousness community plus all religious groups, professors, general public." No "material which does not fit the description of needs outlined above." Query or submit outline/synopsis and sample chapters.

Recent Nonfiction Titles: *Practical Guide to Death & Dying*, by John White; *Judaism*, by Jay G. Williams; and *Astrology of Transformation*, by Dane Rudhyar.

A. THOMAS & CO., LTD., Denington Estate, Wellingborough, Northamptonshire England NN8 2RQ. Editor-in-Chief: J.R. Hardaker. Publishes hardcover and paperback originals and reprints. Specializes in inspirational, practical psychology and self-improvement material. Pays 8-10% royalty. Photocopied submissions OK. SAE and International Reply Coupons. Reports in 2-4 weeks. Free book catalog.

Nonfiction: Publishes books on how-to methods, psychology and self-help. Submit outline/synopsis and sample chapters.

*THE THORNDIKE PRESS, One Mile Rd., Thorndike ME 04986. (207)948-2962. Senior Editor: Timothy A. Loeb. Publishes hardcover and paperback originals (75%) and reprints (25%). Averages 80 titles/year. Subsidy publishes 5-10% of books. Offers 10-15% of wholesale receipts; also buys mss by outright purchase: $100-1,000. Average advance: $500. Simultaneous and photocopied submissions OK. SASE. Reports in 2 months. Free book catalog.

Nonfiction: Americana (especially Maine and the Northeast); animals; humor; nature; and all subjects of regional interest. Especially needs "manuscripts relating to the wilderness and oudoor recreation (hunting, fishing, etc.) in the Northeast US." No poetry. Submit outline/synopsis and sample chapters.

Recent Nonfiction Titles: *Fly Fishing in Maine*, by A. Raychard (guide); *Go Light—A Guide to Equipment for Hiking in the East*, by J. Gibson (guide); and *Canoeing Maine*, by E. Thomas (guide).

Fiction: Adventure; humor (New England); nostalgia; and regional interests (Maine and New England). "We will always consider exceptional manuscripts, but currently have enough for general plans. Prefer short works." Submit outline/synopsis and sample chapters.

Recent Fiction Titles: *Puffin Island*, by Ada and Frank Graham (young adult nature); *Adventure in a Model T*, by Arthur Macdougall (Dud Dean stories); and *Neighborly Relations*, by Edwin Merry (growing up in the 1920s).

THORSONS PUBLISHERS, LTD, Denington Estate, Wellingborough, Northamptonshire NN8 2RQ England. Editor-in-Chief: J.R. Hardaker. Publishes hardcover and paperback originals and reprints. Specializes in health books, psychology, self-improvement, hypnotism, self-sufficiency; alternative medicine and business success books. 5-10% royalty. Photocopied submissions OK. SAE and International Reply Coupons. Reports in 2-4 weeks. Free book catalog.
Nonfiction: Business; cookbooks, cooking and foods; philosophy, psychology, self-help themes. Submit outline/synopsis and sample chapters.

THREE CONTINENTS PRESS, 1346 Connecticut Ave. NW, Washington DC 20036. Editor-in-Chief: Donald E. Herdeck. Publishes hardcover and paperback originals (90%) and reprints (10%). Pays 10% royalty; advance "only on delivery of complete ms which is found acceptable; usually $150." Query. Prefers photocopied submissions. State availability of photos/illustrations. Simultaneous submissions OK. Reports in 6 months. SASE. Free book catalog.
Nonfiction and Fiction: Specializes in African, Caribbean and Middle Eastern (Arabic and Persian) literature and criticism in translation, third world literature and history. Scholarly, well-prepared mss; creative writing. Fiction, poetry, criticism, history and translations of creative writing. "We search for books which will make clear the complexity and value of African literature and culture, including bilingual texts (African language/English translations) of previously unpublished authors from less well-known areas of Africa. We are always interested in genuine contributions to understanding African and Caribbean culture." Length: 50,000 words. "Please do not submit ms unless we ask for it." Recently published *Fire: Six Writers from Angola, Mozambique, and Cape Verde*, by D. Burness; *Black Shack Alley* (from Joseph Zobel's Martiniquian novel, La rue Cases-Negres); and *Harlem, Haiti & Havana*, by Martha Cobb (criticism).

TIDEWATER PUBLISHERS, Box 456, Centreville MD 21617. Managing Editor: Willard A. Lockwood. An imprint of Cornell Maritime Press, Inc. Publishes hardcover and paperback originals and reprints. Offers standard 10-12½-15% royalty contract. SASE. Reports in 2-3 weeks. Free book catalog.
Nonfiction: "General nonfiction on Maryland and the Delmarva Peninsula." Query with outline and sample chapters. Recently published *Birdlife at Chincoteague*, by B. Meanley.

TIMBER PRESS, Box 1631, Beaverton OR 97075. (503)243-1158. Editor: Richard Abel. Publishes hardcover and paperback originals. Publishes 10 titles/year. Pays 10-20% royalty; "sometimes" offers advance. Photocopied submissions OK. SASE. Reports in 2 months. Free book catalog.
Nonfiction: Arts and crafts, natural history, Northwest regional material, forestry and horticulture. Query or submit outline/synopsis and sample chapters. Recently published *Japanese Maples*, by J.D. Vertrees (horticulture); *Without a Thorn*, by Stuart Mechlin and Ellen Bonanno (horticulture); and *The Mud Pie Dilemma*, by John Nance (arts and crafts).

TIME-LIFE BOOKS INC., 777 Duke St., Alexandria VA 22314. (703)960-5000. Managing Editor: Jerry Korn. Publishes hardcover originals. Publishes 40 titles/year. "We have no minimum or maximum fee because our needs vary tremendously. Advance, as such, is not offered. Author is paid as he completes part of contracted work." Books are almost entirely staff-generated and staff-produced, and distribution is primarily through mail order sale. Query to the Director of Planning. SASE.
Nonfiction: "General interest books. Most books tend to be heavily illustrated (by staff), with text written by assigned authors. We very rarely accept mss or book ideas submitted from outside our staff." Length: open.
Recent Nonfiction Titles: *The Healthy Heart (Health Series); The First Aviators (Epic of Flight Series); and Japan at War* (WWII Series).

TIMELY BOOKS, Box 267, New Milford CT 06776. Co-Publisher: Yvonne MacManus. Publishes trade paperback reprints. Publishes a varying number of titles/year. Pays 7% royalty on retail price. Photocopied submissions OK. SASE. Reports in 2 weeks on queries; 6 weeks on mss.
Nonfiction: "Areas are relatively 'open'—prefer books with feminist appeal. No 'coffee table' books, humor, illustrated books, juvenile, technical or textbooks. Our books are read by enlightened women and non-macho men, as well as by persons on college campuses (they are being used at a growing number of universities)." Query.
Fiction: "We're interested in any area of fiction written from the feminist perspective. No 'typical women's fiction; nothing that portrays women in stereotypical roles." Query.
Recent Fiction Titles: *By Sanction of the Victim*, by Patte Wheat (child abuse); and *Love is Where You Find It*, and *Edge of Twilight* both by Paula Christian (lesbian fiction).
Poetry: "We're interested in poetry written from the feminist perspective—but chances for acceptance are slim." Submit complete ms.

TIMES BOOKS, The New York Times Book Co., Inc., 3 Park Ave., New York NY 10016. (212)725-2050. Vice President and Editorial Director: Edward T. Chase. Senior Editors: Hugh G. Howard, Patrick Filley. Publishes hardcover and paperback originals (75%) and reprints (25%). Publishes 35 titles/year. Pays royalty; average advance.
Nonfiction: Business/economics, cookbooks/cooking, self-help and sports. "We do not want technical, textbook or poetry manuscripts." Accepts only solicited manuscripts.
Recent Nonfiction Titles: *Craig Claiborne's Gourmet Diet*, by Craig Claiborne with Pierre Franey (diet cookbook); *The Last Mafioso*, by Ovid Demaris (biography of a Mafia killer); and *On Language*, by William Safire (word book by Pulitzer-prizewinning NY *Times* columnist).

TIMES MIRROR MAGAZINES, INC., BOOK DIVISION, (Subsidiary of Times Mirror Co.) 380 Madison Ave., New York NY 10017. Publishing books in the Popular Science and Outdoor Life fields. Editor: John W. Sill. Royalties and advance according to size and type of book. Wants outlines, sample chapters, author information. Enclose return postage.
How-To and Self-Help: Publishes books in Popular Science field: energy saving, home renovation, repair and improvement, workshop, hand and power tools, automobile how-to. In the Outdoor Life field: wildlife, especially big game and deer; fishing, camping, firearms. Small books to 35,000 words; large books to 150,000 words.

TL ENTERPRISES, INC., Book Division, 29901 Agoura Rd., Agoura CA 91301. (213)991-4980. Vice President/Editor-in-Chief: Patrick J. Flaherty. Publishes hardcover and trade and mass market paperback originals. Averages 5 titles/year. Pays 5-10% royalty on retail price; offers average $6,000 advance. Reports in 1 month.
Nonfiction: Cookbook, how-to, reference, technical and travel/touring. Subjects include cooking and foods, hobbies, nature, recreation and travel. "We have 9 mss in our publishing pipeline at present, so our immediate needs are satisfied. But we *do* read all queries, we will direct mail-test titles of promise, and we will give test winners an immediate home. At present, our book market consists of RV owners and motorcycle touring enthusiasts—so we want to see nothing that does not have a specific interest to one group or the other. For now, our book audience is our magazine audience—the million or more people who read *Trailer Life*, *Motorhome Life*, *Rider*, et al.— together with the 400,000 families who belong to our Good Sam (RV owners') Club." Query with outline/synopsis and sample chapters ("3 chapters only"). All unsolicited mss are returned unopened.
Recent Nonfiction Titles: *TL's RV Repair & Maintenance Manual*, by John Thompson (technical guide); *TL'S RV Travel & Atlas*, by Bob Longsdorf (RV touring guide); and *TL'S Secrets of Successful RVing*, by John Thompson (RVing how-to).

THE TOUCHSTONE PRESS, Box 81, Beaverton OR 97075. (503)648-8081. Editor-in-Chief: Thomas K. Worcester. Publishes paperback originals. Specializes in field guide books. Royalty of 10% of retail price; seldom offers an advance. Averages 4 titles/year. Photocopied submissions OK, "but don't expect response without SASE." Reports in 1-2 months. SASE. Free book catalog. No fiction or poetry.
Nonfiction: Cookbooks, cooking and foods; history, hobbies, how-to, recreation, sports and travel books. "Must be within the range of our outdoor styles." Query.
Recent Nonfiction Titles: *35 Hiking Trails, Columbia River Gorge*, by Don and Roberta Lowe; and *U Pick, U Profit*, by Diana Burnell (food selection and preparation).

TOWER PUBLICATIONS, INC., 2 Park Ave., New York NY 10016. (212)679-7707. Editor-in-Chief: Milburn Smith. Publishes paperback originals (75%) and reprints (25%). Published 312 titles in 1980, 320 in 1981. Offers 4-6% royalty on originals; buys reprints outright for $500-1,500. Average advance: $1,500. Simultaneous submissions OK, but "we must be told"; photocopied submissions OK. SASE; "without SASE, we do not return the manuscript." Book catalog for SASE. Reports in 3 months.
Nonfiction: History of World War II, self-help, sports, crime and sex. "Our nonfiction program is very limited. We're willing to consider something that's particularly timely or especially interesting. Any really strong and popular idea is worth a query letter. No personalities or crafts manuscripts." Query.
Recent Nonfiction Titles: *The Gossip Wars*, by Milt Machlin; *The Body Book*, by Julius Fast; and *In Search of the Lindbergh Baby*, by Theon Wright.
Fiction: Adventure, fantasy, gothic, historical, mainstream, mystery, romance, science fiction, suspense, western and war. "Most of what we publish is category fiction. We do not publish juvenile fiction or confessions." Query.
Recent Fiction Titles: *Season of Power*, by Sam Tanenhaus and Gregory Tobin (novel); *The Entry*, by Hans Holzer (occult); and *Brak* series, by John Jakes (sword & sorcery).

Tips: "We happen to be very open to first novels, since we try to build up a long-term relationship with an author. We feel that, as a small publishing house, we are an ideal market for the first-time novelist who might not even be considered by a larger house, particularly if he is not represented by an agent. We prefer receiving synopsis and entire mss, and typescript must be legible and double-spaced."

TRADO-MEDIC BOOKS, (Division of Conch Magazine, Ltd., Publishers), 102 Normal Ave. (Symphony Circle), Buffalo NY 14213. (716)885-3686. Editorial Director: Dr. S.O. Anozie. Senior Editor: Dr. Philip Singer. Publishes hardcover and paperback originals. Published 4 titles in 1979, 4 in 1980; plans 6-10 in 1981. "Terms vary from book to book, though they often do involve a royalty on the retail price. No simultaneous submissions; photocopied submissions OK. Reports in 1-2 months. Book catalog for SASE.
Nonfiction: Health; psychology; reference; and sociology. "Trado-Medic Books serves the informational needs and interests of an international academic community in the fields of medical anthropology, medical sociology, social psychiatry, ethnopsychiatry, community health, health-care delivery and the libraries and institutions that serve it." Query first. All unsolicited mss are returned unopened.
Recent Nonfiction Titles: *Scientific Insights Into Yoruba Traditional Medicine*, by James I. Durodola, MD; *Psyche Versus Soma: Traditional Healing Choices in Jamaica*, by Joseph Long, PhD; and African Traditional Medicine and Pharmacopaeia, edited with an introduction by Professor J. Ki-Zerbo.

TRANSACTION BOOKS, Rutgers University, New Brunswick NJ 08903. (201)932-2280. Book Division Director: Kerry Donnelly Kern. Publishes hardcover and paperback originals (65%) and reprints (35%). Specializes in scholarly social science books. Publishes 60 titles/year. Royalty "depends almost entirely on individual contract, we've gone anywhere from 2-15%." No advance. Photocopied submissions OK "if they are perfectly clear." Reports in 2-4 months. SASE. Free book catalog.
Nonfiction: Americana, art, biography, economics, history, law, medicine and psychiatry, music, philosophy, photography, politics, psychology, reference, scientific, sociology, technical and textbooks. "All must be scholarly social science or related." Query or submit outline/synopsis and sample chapters. "Send introduction or first chapter and conclusion or last chapter. Use Chicago *Manual of Style*." State availability of photos/illustrations and send one photocopied example. Recently published *Contemporary Anarchism*, by T. Palin (political science); *Television as an Instrument of Terror*, by A. Berger (sociology/pop culture); *The New Class?*, by B. Briggs (sociology); and *Children's Rights and the Wheel of Life*, by E. Boulding (sociology).

TRANS-ANGLO BOOKS, Box 38, Corona del Mar CA 92625. Editorial Director: Spencer Crump. Pays 5-10% royalty. Publishes 4 titles/year. Reports in 3-4 weeks. Enclose return postage. Free book list on request.
Nonfiction: Americana, Western Americana and railroad books. Also planning to enter the college text field. "In regard to texts, they should be written by working college instructors and should be ones that are required at the freshman and sophomore level. We are not interested in books for teachers, but books for students that will be adopted by teachers. We are not interested in family histories or local history that lacks national appeal." Most books except texts are 8½x11 hardcover with many photos supplementing a good text of 5,000-15,000 words. Query. Recently published *Rails to the Minarets*, by H. Johnston (railroad history); *The Stylebook for Newswriting*, by S. Crump (journalism text); and *Gold and Where They Found It*, by C. and J. Martin (gold ghost towns).

TREACLE PRESS, Box 638, New Paltz NY 12561. Editor: Bruce McPherson. Imprints include Documentext. Publishes hardcover and paperback originals. Averages 5 titles/year. Pays royalty. Simultaneous and photocopied submissions OK. Query first. SASE. Reports in 3 weeks to 2 months.
Fiction: "Treacle Press publishes novels, short fiction, and literary criticism of innovative and expressive character. We are only interested in serious fiction, with particular emphasis on experimental works. *Documentext* is an imprint specifically for the publication of books about avant-garde artists and art movements of the past 20 years. Query. Recently published *Bastards: Footnotes to History*, by U. Molinaro; *Shamp of the City-Solo*, by J. Gordon; and *Toward a Phenomenology of Written Art*, by G. Burns.

TREASURE CHEST PUBLICATIONS, Box 5250, Tucson AZ 85703. (602)623-9558. Contact: Sterling Mahan. Publishes paperback originals. Publishes 4 titles/year. Pays 5% minimum royalty; advance "depends on the situation." Simultaneous and photocopied submissions OK. Reports in 6 weeks. SASE. Free book catalog.

Nonfiction: "We specialize in books concerning the lifestyle, culture, history and arts of the Southwest, and especially would like to see related works. We are particularly interested in manuscripts by and/or about Native Americans, and works about Native American artists. Also art, history, biography, and photography with a Southwestern theme. Recently published *Indian Jewelry Making*, by O. Branson; and *Wild Brothers of the Indians*, by A. Wesche.

TREND HOUSE, Box 611, St. Petersburg FL 33731. (813)821-5800. Chairman: Eugene C. Patterson. President: John B. Lake. General Manager: Andrew P. Corty. Publishes hardcover and paperback originals and reprints. Specializes in books on Florida—all categories. Pays 10% royalty; no advance. Books are marketed through *Florida Trend* magazine. Photocopied submissions OK. Reports in 2-4 weeks. SASE.
Nonfiction: Business, economics, history, law, politics, reference, textbooks and travel. "All books pertain to Florida." Query. State availability of photos and/or illustrations. Recently published *All About Wills for Florida Residents*, by R. Richards (legal information).

*TRIUMPH PUBLISHING CO., Box 292, Altadena CA 91001. (213)797-0075. Editor-in-Chief: William Dankenbring. Hardcover and paperback originals. Pays 5-10% royalty; no advance. Subsidy publishes occasionally "depending upon the merits of the book." Published 6 titles in 1981. State availability of photos and/or artwork to accompany ms. Simultaneous and photocopied submissions OK. Reports in 1-2 months. SASE. Free book catalog.
Nonfiction: History, science, theological, biblical, family and health.
Recent Nonficiton Titles: *Health Secrets From the Bible*, by Wlodyga; *Beyond Star Wars*, by Dankenbring; and *In Search of the Lost Ten Tribes*, by McNair.

TROUBADOR PRESS, 385 Fremont St., San Francisco CA 94105. (415)397-3716. Publisher: Malcolm K. Whyte. Manuscript Submissions: Karen Schiller. Publishes hardcover and paperback originals. Averages 10-15 titles/year. Pays 4-12% royalty on wholesale or retail price. Advance averages $500-1,000. Simultaneous and photocopied submissions OK. Reports in 1 month. SASE. Book catalog for SASE.
Nonfiction: "Troubador Press publishes project, activity, entertainment, art, game, nature, craft and cookbooks. All titles feature original art and exceptional graphics. Primarily nonfiction. Current series include creative cut-outs; in-depth, readable cookbooks; mazes and other puzzle books; color and story books; how-to-draw and other art and entertainment books. Interested in expanding on themes of 85 current titles. We like books which have the potential to develop into series." Query or submit outline/synopsis and sample chapters.
Recent Nonfiction Titles: *Travels with Farley*, by Phil Frank; *3-Dimensional Maze Art*, by Larry Evans; and *Robots (To color, Cut Out & Fly)*, by Yoong Bae.

TURNSTONE BOOKS, Denington Estate, Wellingborough, Northamptonshire, England NN8 2RQ. Editor-in-Chief: Alick Bartholomew. Hardcover and paperback originals and reprints. 7½% royalty on paperbacks; 10-15% on hardcovers. Photocopied submissions OK. SASE. Reports in 1-2 months. Free book catalog.
Nonfiction: Pre-history and ancient wisdom; holistic medicine, Jungian psychology, alternative technology and ecology, mysticism and self-sufficiency topics. Query first or submit outline/ synopsis and sample chapters.

CHARLES E. TUTTLE CO., INC., Publishers & Booksellers, Suido 1-chome, 2-6, Bunkyo-ku, Tokyo, Japan. Publishes originals and reprints, "handles all matters of editing, production and administration including royalties, rights and permissions." Pays $500 against 10% royalty on retail price; advance varies. Averages 30 titles/year. Book catalog $1. Send complete mss or queries accompanied by outlines or sample chapters and biographical data. US and Canada distributors: Publishers and Booksellers, Drawer F, 26-30 Main St., Rutland VT 05701. Reports in 4-6 weeks. SASE.
Nonfiction: Specializes in publishing books about Oriental art, culture and sociology as well as history, literature, cookery, sport and children's books which relate to Asia, the Hawaiian Islands, Australia and the Pacific areas. Also interested in Americana, especially antique collecting, architecture, genealogy and Canadiana. No poetry and fiction except that of Oriental themes. Normal book length only.
Recent Nonfiction Titles: *Techniques of Vigilance*, by K. Parsons (martial arts for police); and *The Ninja and Their Secret Fighting Art*, by Stephen K. Hayes.

TWAYNE PUBLISHERS, A division of G.K. Hall & Co., 70 Lincoln St., Boston MA 02111. (617)423-3990. Editor: Caroline L. Birdsall. Payment is on royalty basis. Publishes 120 titles/year. Query. Reports in 5 weeks. Enclose return postage.

Nonfiction: Publishes scholarly books and volumes for the general reader in series. Literary criticism, biography, history of immigration, film and theater studies, musical criticism, women's studies, scholarly annuals and critical editions.

Recent Titles: *Carson McCullers*, by M. McDowell; *Howard Nemerov*, by R. Labrie; *Alexander Solzhenitsyn*, by A. Kodjak; and *Sam Peckinpah*, by D. McKinney.

TYNDALE HOUSE PUBLISHERS, INC., 336 Gunderson Dr., Wheaton IL 60187. (312)668-8300. Editor-in-Chief and Acquisitions: Wendell Hawley. Managing Editor: Virginia Muir. Publishes hardcover and trade paperback originals (90%) and hardcover and mass paperback reprints (10%). Publishes 100 titles/year. Pays 10% royalty; negotiable advance. Simultaneous queries OK; prefers original submissions. Reports in 6 weeks. SASE. Free book catalog.

Nonfiction: Religious books only: personal experience, family living, marriage, Bible studies and commentaries, Christian living, devotional, inspirational, church and social issues, Bible prophecy, theology and doctrine, counseling and Christian psychology, Christian apologetics and church history. Submit table of contents, chapter summary, preface, first two chapters and one later chapter.

Fiction: Bible and contemporary novels. Submit outline/synopsis and sample chapters.

UNITY PRESS, 235 Hoover Rd., Santa Cruz CA 95065. (408)427-3344. Publisher: Craig Caughlan. Publishes paperback originals; (occasional simultaneous cloth publications). Pays standard royalty on cover price; prefers to put advance money into promotion. Averages 8-10 titles/year. Simultaneous and photocopied submissions OK. Reports in 6 weeks. SASE. Free book catalog.

Nonfiction: "Our editorial direction could be defined as follows: books that bring an individual to a better understanding of self and environs. Prefer books that are on the leading edge of the social sciences and human behavior/trade-oriented and non-academic. With each submission, author should state in 50 words or less the purpose of his/her book, and what makes it better than others that are available on similar subjects." Query or submit outline/synopsis and sample chapters.

Fiction: "Our editorial direction includes fiction as well. Would like to see books on futurism." No poetry, mysteries, or romances. Query or submit outline/synopsis and sample chapters.

Recent Nonfiction Titles: *The Way of Herbs*; and *Feeling Great!*

Tips: "We would also like to see a good spoof on the 'new age', humor and satire."

UNIVELT, INC., Box 28130, San Diego CA 92128. (714)746-4005. Editorial Director: H. Jacobs. Publishes hardcover originals. Averages 8 titles/year. Pays 10% royalty on actual sales; no advance. Simultaneous and photocopied submissions OK. Reports in 4 weeks. SASE. Free book catalog.

Nonfiction: Publishes in the field of aerospace, especially astronautics, and technical communications, but including application of aerospace technology to Earth's problems. Submit outline/synopsis and sample chapters.

Recent Nonfiction Titles: *Handbook of Soviet Manned Space Flight; Space—New Opportunities For International Ventures*; and *Space Shuttle: Dawn of an Era*.

*UNIVERSE BOOKS, 381 Park Ave. S., New York NY 10016. (212)685-7400. Editorial Director: Louis Barron. Publishes hardcover and paperback originals (95%) and reprints (5%). Published 50 titles in 1979, 40 in 1980; plans 40 in 1981. Offers 10-15% royalty on retail price (hardbound books). "On a few extra-illustrated art books and on special studies with a limited market we may pay a smaller royalty." Average advance: $1,000-4,000. Subsidy publishes 5% of books; "if a book makes a genuine contribution to knowledge but is a commercial risk, we might perhaps accept a subsidy from a foundation or other organization, but not directly from the author." Simultaneous and photocopied submissions OK. "Will not return material without postage-paid SAE." Reports in 2 weeks. Book catalog if 35¢ in stamps (not SASE) is enclosed.

Nonfiction: Animals, art, history, nature, performing arts, politics, reference and science. Universe also pays secondary attention to biography, health and how-to. Also uses "discussions of specific animal, bird or plant species; social histories of specific types of artifacts or social institutions; art histories of specific types of artifacts or symbols. We publish books in the following categories: antiques, crafts and collectibles, art, architecture and design, history, life, physical and agricultural sciences, the performing arts, social sciences (especially books on survival, appropriate technology, and the limits to growth). We do not publish fiction, poetry, cookbooks, criticism or belles lettres." Submit outline/synopsis and sample chapters.

Recent Nonfiction Titles: *The Ballerina*, by S. Montague; *The Ice-Skating Book*, by Sheffield and Woodward (ice skating-not a how-to-do-it); *Goya*, by Fred Licht (art history); and *Enterprise Zones*, by Stuart M. Butles.

UNIVERSITY ASSOCIATES, INC., Box 26240, 8517 Production Ave., San Diego CA 92126. (714)578-5900. President: Leonard D. Goodstein. Publishes paperback originals (65%) and reprints (35%). Specializes in practical materials for human relations trainers, consultants, etc. Pays 10-15% royalty; no advance. Markets books by direct mail. Simultaneous submissions OK. SASE. Reports in 2-4 months. Free book catalog.
Nonfiction: Marion Mettler, Vice-President, publications. Publishes (in order of preference) human relations training and group-oriented material; management education and community relations and personal growth; business; psychology and sociology. No materials for grammar school or high school classroom teachers. Use *American Psychological Association Style Manual.* Query. Send prints or completed art or rough sketches to accompany ms. Recently published *The 1981 Annual Handbook for Group Facilitators*, by J.W. Pfeiffer and J.E. Jones; *Preparing for Retirment*, by Leland Bradford; and *Learning Through Groups*, by Phillip G. Hanson.

UNIVERSITY OF ALABAMA PRESS, Box 2877, University AL 35486. Director: Malcolm MacDonald. Assistant Director: Paul R. Kennedy. Publishes hardcover originals. Published 28 titles last year. "Maximum royalty (on wholesale price) is 12%; no advances made." Photocopied submissions OK. Enclose return postage. Free book catalog.
Nonfiction: Biography, business, economics, history, music, philosophy, politics, religion and sociology. Considers upon merit almost any subject of scholarly interest, but specializes in linguistics and philology, political science and public administration, literary criticism and biography, philosophy, and history. Also interested in biology, ecology, medicine, and agriculture. Submit outline/synopsis and sample chapters.
Recent Nonfiction Title: *A History of Metals in Colonial America*, (US history); and *Judge Frank Johnson*, by Yarbrough (biography).

UNIVERSITY OF ARIZONA PRESS, Box 3398, Tucson AZ 85722. (602)626-1441. Director: Marshall Townsend. Publishes hardcover and paperback originals and reprints. "Contracts are individually negotiated, but as a 'scholarly publishing house' operating primarily on informational works, does not pay any advances. Also, royalty starting point may be after sale of first 1,000 copies, by virtue of the nature of the publishing program." Published 23 titles in 1980, plans 25-30 in 1981. Marketing methods "are based on 'what is considered best for the book,' giving individual treatment to the marketing of each book, rather than a generalized formula." Free catalog and editorial guidelines. Will consider photocopied submissions if ms is not undergoing consideration at another publishing house. "Must have this assurance." Query and submit outline and sample chapters. Reports on material within 90 days. SASE.
Nonfiction: "Significant works of a regional nature about Arizona, the Southwest and Mexico; and books of merit in subject matter fields strongly identified with the universities in Arizona; i.e., anthropology, arid lands studies, space sciences, Asian studies, Southwest Indians, Mexico, etc. Each ms should expect to provide its own answer to the question, 'Why should this come out of Arizona?' The answer would be that either the work was something that ought to be made a matter of record as a service to Arizona and the Southwest, or that it was presenting valuable information in a subject matter field with which the Arizona institutions hold strong identification. The University of Arizona Press strongly endorses 'the target reader' concept under which it encourages each author to write for only *one* reader, then leave it up to the publisher to reach the thousands—as contrasted with the author's trying to write for the thousands and not 'hitting home' with anyone. The press believes this approach helps the author come to a consistent level of subject matter presentation. The press also insists upon complete departure of 'time-dating' words such as 'now,' 'recently,' and insists that the author consider how the presentation will read three years hence." Americana, art, biography, space sciences, history, nature, scientific, technical. Length: "what the topic warrants and demands." No "personal diary types of Western Americana, mainly directed only toward family interest, rather than broad general interest."
Recent Nonfiction Titles: *Lightning and Its Spectrum: An Atlas of Photographs*, by Leon A. Salanave; and *Planets and Pluto*, by William G. Hoyt.

UNIVERSITY OF CALIFORNIA PRESS, 2223 Fulton St., Berkeley CA 94720. Director: James H. Clark. Assistant Director: Stanley Holwitz. New York Office, Room 513, 50 E. 42 St., New York NY 10017. London Office CCJ, Ltd., Ely House, 37 Dover St., London W1X 4HQ, England. Publishes hardcover and paperback originals and reprints. "On books likely to do more than return their costs, a standard royalty contract beginning at 10% is paid; on paperbacks it is less." Published 199 titles last year. Queries are always advisable, accompanied by outlines or sample material. Send to Berkeley address. Reports vary, depending on the subject. Enclose return postage.
Nonfiction: "It should be clear that most of our publications are hardcover nonfiction written by scholars." Publishes scholarly books including art, literary studies, social sciences, natural sciences

and some high-level popularizations. No length preferences.

Fiction and Poetry: Publishes fiction and poetry only in translation, usually in bilingual editions.

*UNIVERSITY OF IOWA PRESS, Graphic Services Bldg., Iowa City IA 52242. (319)353-3181. Editor: Art Pflughaupt. Publishes hardcover and paperback originals. Averages 7 titles/year. Pays 10% royalty on retail price. Subsidy publishes 5% of books. Subsidy publishing is offered "if a scholarly institution will advance a subsidy to support publication of a worthwhile book. We market mostly by direct mailing of fliers to groups with special interests in our titles." Query or submit outline/synopsis and sample chapters. Use University of *Chicago Manual of Style*. State availability of photos/illustrations. Photocopied submissions OK. Reports in 2-4 months. SASE. Free book catalog.

Nonfiction: Publishes art; economics; history; music; philosophy; reference; and scientific books. "We do not publish children's books. We do not publish any poetry or short fiction except the Iowa Translation Series and the Iowa School of Letters Award for short fiction."

Recent Nonfiction Titles: *Modern Hebrew Poetry*, translated by Bernhard Frank (Iowa Translations Series); *Impossible Appetites*, by James Fetler (Iowa Short Fiction Award); *The Iowa Writers' Workshop: Origins, Emergence, and Growth*, by Stephen Wilbers; and *Windows on the World: World News Reporting 1900-1920*, by Robert W. Desmond.

*UNIVERSITY OF MASSACHUSETTS PRESS, Box 429, Amherst MA 01004. (413)545-2217. Editorial Director: Leone Stein. Senior Editor: Richard Martin. Publishes hardcover and paperback originals (95%) and reprints (5%). Averages 25-30 titles/year. "Royalties depend on character of book; if offered, generally at 10% of list price. Advance, if offered, averages $250." Subsidy publishes 10% of books; "Press specifies subsidy requirement on basis on estimated edition loss." No author subsidies accepted. Simultaneous (if advised) and photocopied submissions OK. Preliminary report in 6 weeks. SASE. Free book catalog.

Nonfiction: Publishes art, biography, criticism, history, nature studies, philosophy, poetry, politics, psychology, science and sociology in original and reprint editions. Submit outline/synopsis and sample chapters.

Recent Nonfiction Titles: *Henry David Thoreau: What Manner of Man?*, by Edward Wagenknecht (literature and language); *From the Ashes of Disgrace: A Journal from Germany, 1945-1955*, by Hans Speier (history); and *Powerline: The First Battle of America's Energy War*, by Barry M. Casper and Paul D. Wellstone (sociology).

UNIVERSITY OF MICHIGAN PRESS, 839 Greene St., Ann Arbor MI 48106. (313)764-4394. Editorial Director: Walter E. Sears. Senior Editor: Mary C. Erwin. Publishes hardcover and paperback originals (95%) and reprints (5%). Averages 35-40 titles/year. Pays 10% royalty on retail price but primarily on net; offers advance. Simultaneous and photocopied submissions OK. SASE. Reports in 2 weeks. Free book catalog.

Nonfiction: Americana; animals; art; biography; business/economics; health; history; music; nature; philosophy; photography; psychology; recreation; reference; religion; science; sociology; technical; textbooks; and travel. No dissertations. Query first.

Recent Nonfiction Titles: *Nuclear Power: Technology on Trial*, by J. Duderstadt and C. Kikuchi; *Wind Power and Other Energy Options*, by D.R. Inglis; and *Code of the Quipu*, by Marcia and Robert Ascher (mathematics and culture).

UNIVERSITY OF MISSOURI PRESS, 200 Lewis Hall, Columbia MO 65211. (314)882-7641. Director: Edward D. King. Managing Editor: Susan E. Kelpe. Publishes hardcover and paperback originals and paperback reprints. Published 22 titles in 1979, 24 in 1980; plans 30 in 1981. Pays 10% royalty on net receipts; no advance. Photocopied submissions OK. Reports in 6 months. SASE. Free book catalog.

Nonfiction: "Scholarly publisher interested in history, literary criticism, political science, social science, music, art, art history, and original poetry." Also regional books about Missouri and the Midwest. "We do not publish very much in mathematics or hard sciences." Query or submit outline/synopsis and sample chapters. Consult Chicago *Manual of Style*. Recently published *Infinite Jest: Wit and Humor in Italian Renaissance Art*, by Paul Barolsky; *The Fierce Embrace: A Study of Contemporary American Poetry*, by Charles Molesworth (literary criticism); and *The Peregrine Falcon in Greenland*, by J. Harris.

Fiction: "Will not be reading fiction manuscripts again until February, 1983. We publish original short fiction in Breakthrough Series, not to exceed 35,000 words. May be short story collection or novella. We also publish poetry and drama in the same series. No limitations on subject matter." Query. Recently published *Dowry*, by Janet Beeler; *Van Gogh Field and Other Stories*, by William Kittredge; and *Light and Power: Stories*, by I. MacMillan.

UNIVERSITY OF NEBRASKA PRESS, 901 N. 17th St., Lincoln NE 68588. Editor-in-Chief: Stephen Cox. Publishes hardcover and paperback originals (60%) and hardcover and paperback reprints (40%). Specializes in scholarly nonfiction; some regional books; reprints of Western Americana; natural history. Royalty is usually graduated from 10% on wholesale price for original books; no advance. Averages 35 new titles, 30 paperback reprints (*Bison Books*)/year. SASE. Reports in 2-4 months. Free book catalog.
Nonfiction: Publishes Americana, biography, history, nature, photography, psychology, sports, literature, agriculture and American Indian themes. Query.
Recent Nonfiction Titles: *The Chisholm Trail*, by Don Worcester (Western history); and *Deadwood: The Golden Years*, by Watson Parker (Western history).

UNIVERSITY OF NEVADA PRESS, Reno NV 89557. (702)784-6573. Director: Robert Laxalt. Editor: Nicholas M. Cady. Publishes hardcover and paperback originals (90%) and reprints (10%). Averages 5 titles/year. Pays 10-15% royalty on retail price; advance depends on title. Simultaneous (if so indicated) and photocopied submissions OK. Preliminary reports in 2 months. Free book catalog.
Nonfiction: Specifically needs regional history, anthropology, biographies and Basque studies. "We are the first sustaining university press with a sound series on Basque studies—New World and Old World." No juvenile books or cookbooks. Submit outline/synopsis and sample chapters.
Recent Nonfiction Titles: *The Witches Advocate: Basque Witchcraft and the Spanish Inquisition*, by Gustav Henningsen; *Will James: The Last Cowboy Legend*, by A. Amaral (regional biography); and *Sierra Summer*, by M. Marshall (regional natural history).

THE UNIVERSITY OF NORTH CAROLINA PRESS, Box 2288, Chapel Hill NC 27514. (919)933-2105. Editor-in-Chief: Iris Tillman Hill. Publishes hardcover and paperback originals. Specializes in scholarly books and regional trade books. Royalty schedule "varies." No advance. Averages 50 titles/year. "As a university press, we do not have the resources for mass marketing books." Send prints to illustrate ms only if they are a major part of the book. Photocopied submissions OK. Reports in 2-5 months. SASE. Free book catalog.
Nonfiction: "Our major fields are American and European history." Also scholarly books on Americana, classics, biography, political science, philosophy, psychology and sociology. History books on law and music. Books on nature, particularly on the Southeast; literary studies. Submit outline/synopsis and sample chapters. Must follow University of Chicago *Manual of Style*. Recently published *A Revolutionary People at War*, by C. Royster; *The French Veteran From the Revolution*, by I. Woloch; and *Women of the Republic*, by Linda Kerber (early American history and women's studies)."

UNIVERSITY OF NOTRE DAME PRESS, Notre Dame IN 46556. Editor: Ann Rice. Publishes hardcover and paperback originals and paperback reprints. Pays 10-12½-15% royalty; no advance. Publishes 30-35 titles/year. Free book catalog. Will consider photocopied submissions. Query. Reports in 2 months. SASE.
Nonfiction: "Scholarly books, serious nonfiction of general interest; book-length only. Especially in the areas of philosophy; theology; history; sociology; English literature (Middle English period, and modern literature criticism in the area of relation of literature and theology); government; international relations; and Mexican-American studies.
Recent Nonfiction Titles: *Philosophy and Social Issues*, by Richard Wasserstrom; *Five Biblical Portraits*, by Elie Wiesel; and *Race and Class in the Southwest*, by M. Barrera.

*UNIVERSITY OF OKLAHOMA PRESS, 1005 Asp Ave., Norman OK 73019. (405)325-5111. Editor-in-Chief: John Drayton. Publishes hardcover and paperback originals (85%); and reprints (15%). Averages 50 titles/year. Royalty ranges from 0-15% on wholesale price, "depending on market viability of project"; no advance. Subsidy publishes 5% of books. "If a book has scholarly merit, but is destined to lose money, we seek a subsidy." Does not accept subsidy from author. Submit sample photos or 8x10 glossy prints. Photocopied submissions OK. Reports in 2-4 months. SASE. Book catalog for SASE.
Nonfiction: Publishes Americana and art (Western and Indian); biographies of major Western and Indian figures; history; hobbies; how-to; music; nature; politics; reference; sociology; technical; textbooks; archeology (Mesoamerican); classics; and anthropology books. Query. Recently published *Bat Masterson*, by DeArment (Western Americana); *The Potawatomis*, by Edmunds (Indian history); and *The Toltec Heritage*, by Davies (Mesoamerican archeology).

*UNIVERSITY OF PENNSYLVANIA PRESS, 3933 Walnut St., Philadelphia PA 19104. (215)243-6261. Director: Maurice English. Hardcover and paperback originals (90%) and reprints (10%). Pays 10% royalty on wholesale price for first 5,000 copies sold; 12½% for next 5,000 copies sold; 15% thereafter; no advance. Averages 30 titles/year. Subsidy publishes 10% of books. Subsidy publishing is determined by: evaluation obtained by the press from outside specialists; work approved by Press Editorial Committee; subsidy approved by funding organization. State availability of photos and/or illustrations to accompany ms, with copies of illustrations. Photocopied submissions OK. Reports in 1-3 months. SASE. Free book catalog.

Nonfiction: Publishes Americana; biography; business (especially management); economics; history and psychiatry; philosophy; politics; psychology; reference; scientific; sociological; technical; folklore and folk life books. "Serious books that serve the scholar and the professional." Follow the University of Chicago *Manual of Style*. Query with outline and sample chapter addressed to the editor.

Recent Nonfiction Titles: *Presence of Ford Maddox Ford*, by Stans (Americn literature); and *Forms of Talk* (socio linguistics).

UNIVERSITY OF PITTSBURGH PRESS, 127 N. Bellefield Ave., Pittsburgh PA 15260. (412)624-4110. Director: Frederick A. Hetzel. Managing Editor: Catherine Marshall. Publishes hardcover and paperback originals. Publishes 30 titles/year. Pays 12½% royalty on hardcover, 8% on paperback; no advance. Photocopied submissions OK. Reports in 1-4 months. SASE. Free book catalog.

Nonfiction: Scholarly nonfiction. No textbooks or general nonfiction of an unscholarly nature. Submit outline/synopsis and sample chapters. Recently published *Improbable Fiction: The Life of Mary Roberts Rinehart*, by J. Cohn; *Clifford W. Beers: Advocate for the Insane*, by Norman Dain; and *Nationalism in Iran*, by R. Cottam.

UNIVERSITY OF PUERTO RICO PRESS (UPRED), Box X, UPR Station, Rio Piedras PR 00931. Manager: Felix Rodriquez Garcia. Published 50 titles in 1979, 45 in 1980. Pays 10% royalty. Photocopied submissions OK. SASE. Reports in 1-3 months. Free catalog.

Nonfiction: Special interests are Puerto Rican topics and literature and studies relevant to the Caribbean and Latin America. Recently published *Puerto Rico: Cien anos de lucha politica*, 5 vols. *(Puerto Rico: A Hundred Years of Political Struggle)*, by R. Bothwell; *Bibliografia de teatro puertorriqueno (Bibliography of Puerto Rican Theater)*, by N. Gonzalez; and *On Text and Context: Methodological Approaches to the Contexts of Literature*, edited by E. Brashci et al.

THE UNIVERSITY OF TENNESSEE PRESS, 293 Communications Bldg., Knoxville TN 37916. Contact: Acquisitions Editor. Averages 25 titles/year. Pays negotiable royalty on retail price. Photocopied submissions OK. SASE. Reports in 1 week on queries; "in 1 month on submissions we have encouraged." Free catalog and writer's guidelines.

Nonfiction: American history, political science, film studies, sports studies, literary criticism, anthropology, folklore and regional studies. Prefers "scholarly treatment and a readable style. Authors usually have PhDs. No fiction, poetry or plays." Submit outline/synopsis, author vita, and sample chapters.

Recent Nonfiction Titles: *Victims: A True Story of the Civil War*, by Phillip Paludan (history); and *The Wild and the Tame: Nature and Culture in the American Rodeo*, by Elizabeth Atwood Lawrence (anthropology).

Tips: "Our market is in several groups: scholars; educated readers with special interests in given scholarly subjects; and the general educated public interested in Tennessee, Appalachia and the South. Not all our books appeal to all these groups, of course. But any given book must appeal to at least one of them."

UNIVERSITY OF TEXAS PRESS, Box 7819, Austin TX 78712. Published 55 titles in 1979, 65 in 1980; plans 65 in 1981. Pays royalty based on net income; occasionally offers advance. Photocopied submissions OK. SASE. Reports in 8 weeks. Free catalog and writer's guidelines.

Nonfiction: General scholarly subjects: human social science, economics, anthropology, archeology, political science, psychology, linguistics, photography and comparative literature. Also uses specialty titles related to the Southwest, national trade titles, regional trade titles and studies in the sciences and humanities. "No popular psychology or popular books." Query or submit outline/synopsis and sample chapters. Recently published *Rites of Fall*, by G. Winningham (photography); *Skywatchers of Ancient Mexico*, by A. Aveni (archeoastronomy); and *Manufacturing the News*, by M. Fishman (journalism).

Tips: "It's difficult to make a ms over 400 double spaced pages into a feasible book. Authors should take special care to edit out extraneous material." Looks for sharply focused, in-depth treatments of important topics.

UNIVERSITY OF UTAH PRESS, University of Utah, 101 University Services Bldg., Salt Lake City UT 84112. (801)581-6771. Director: Norma B. Mikkelsen. Publishes hardcover and paperback originals and reprints. Pays 10% royalty on wholesale price on first 2,000 copies sold; 12% on 2,001 to 4,000 copies sold; 15% thereafter. Royalty schedule varies on paperback editions. No advance. Averages 12 titles/year. Free book catalog. Query with outline and sample chapter. Reports in 6-8 months. SASE.

Nonfiction: Scholarly books on Western history, philosophy, religion, anthropology, the arts and general nonfiction. "We encourage submission of high quality mss in the fields of energy development, Middle Eastern studies and Mormonia." Author should specify page length in query.

Recent Nonfiction Titles: *Saints of Sage and Saddle: Folklore Among the Mormons,* by Austin and Alta Fife; *Remembering: The University of Utah,* edited by Elizabeth Haglund; and *Cowboy Cave* (University of Utah Anthropological Paper No. 104), by Jesse D. Jennings.

UNIVERSITY OF WISCONSIN PRESS, 114 N. Murray St., Madison WI 53715. (608)262-4928 (telex: 265452). Director: Thompson Webb. Acquisitions Editor: Peter J. Givler. Publishes hardcover and paperback originals, reprints and translations. Pays standard royalties on retail price; no advance. Averages 30-40 titles/year. Send complete ms. Follow *Modern Language Association Style Sheet.* Reports in 3 months. Enclose return postage with ms.

Nonfiction: Publishes general nonfiction based on scholarly research. "Among University publishers, geographical orientation and environmental emphasis distinguishes this university press."

Recent Nonfiction Titles: *Politics of Land-Use Reform,* by Frank J. Popper (land-use, zoning); *The Prairie Garden,* by J.R. and B.S. Smith (botany, horticulture); and *The American Jeremiad,* by Sacvan Bercovitch (American history and literature).

UNIVERSITY PRESS OF AMERICA, 4720 Boston Way, Lanham MD 20801. (301)459-3366. Editorial Director: James E. Lyons. Publishes hardcover and paperback originals (95%) and reprints (5%). Published 275 titles in 1979, 350 in 1980; plans 400 in 1981. Pays 5-15% royalty on wholesale price; no advance. Simultaneous and photocopied submissions OK. Reports in 6 weeks. SASE. Free book catalog.

Nonfiction: Scholarly monographs, college, and graduate level textbooks in history, economics, business, psychology, political science, African studies, black studies, philosophy, religion, sociology, music, art, literature, drama, and education. No juvenile or el-hi material. Submit outline. Recently published *African Society, Culture, and Politics,* edited by C. Mojekwu; *The Weimar in Crisis: Cuno's Germany,* by A. Cornebise; and *Thirteen Thinkers: An Introduction to Philosophy,* by G. Kreyche.

UNIVERSITY PRESS OF KENTUCKY, 102 Lafferty Hall, Lexington KY 40506. (606)258-2951. Director: Kenneth Cherry. Editor-in-Chief: Jerome Crouch. Managing Editor: Evalin F. Douglas. Hardcover originals (95%); paperback reprints (5%). Pays 10% royalty after first 1,000 copies; no advance. State availability of photos and/or artwork to accompany ms. "Author is ultimately responsible for submitting all artwork in camera-ready form." Reports in 2-4 months. SASE. Free book catalog.

Nonfiction: Publishes (in order of preference): history, political science, literary criticism and history, politics, anthropology, law, philosophy; medical history and nature. "All mss must receive an endorsement (secured by the press) from a scholar in the appropriate area of learning and must be approved by an editorial board before final acceptance." No original fiction, poetry, drama or textbooks. Query or submit outline/synopsis with sample chapters. Recently published *Finley Peter Dunne & Mr. Dooley: The Chicago Years,* by Charles F. Fanning (American studies); *Bomber Pilot: A Memoir of World War II,* by Philip Ardery; and *The Secretary of Defense,* by Douglas Kinnard (political science).

*UNIVERSITY PRESS OF MISSISSIPPI, 3825 Ridgewood Rd., Jackson MS 39211. (601)982-6205. Director: Barney McKee. Publishes hardcover and paperback originals (90%) and reprints (10%). Averages 18 titles/year. Subsidy publishes 5% of books. Pays 10% net royalty on first printing and 12% net on additional printings. No advance. Photocopied submissions OK. SASE. Reports in 1 month. Free book catalog.

Nonfiction: Americana; art; biography; business/economics; history; philosophy; photography; politics; psychology; sociology; literary criticism; and folklore. Especially needs regional studies (Mississippi architecture, art, historical figures), and literary studies, particularly mss on William Faulkner and Eudora Welty. Submit outline/synopsis and sample chapters.

Recent Nonfiction Titles: *Enclave: Vicksburg and Her Plantations, 1863-1970,* by J. Currie; *Poulenc's Songs: An Analysis of Style,* by V. Wood; and *Sense of Place: Mississippi,* edited by P. Prenshaw and J. McKee.

UNIVERSITY PRESS OF NEW ENGLAND, Hanover NH 03755. (603)646-3349. "University Press of New England is a consortium of university presses. Some books—those published for one of the consortium members—carry the joint imprint of New England and the member: Dartmouth, Brandeis, Brown, Tufts, Clark Universities of New Hampshire, Vermont and Rhode Island." Director: Thomas L. McFarland. Publishes hardcover and paperback originals (95%) and reprints (5%). Averages 24 titles/year. Pays 10-15% royalty on wholesale or retail price; offers $500 average advance. Photocopied submissions OK. SASE. Reports in 1 month. Free book catalog.

Nonfiction: Americana, art, biography, business/economics, history, music, nature, philosophy, politics, psychology, reference, religion, science, sociology, technical, textbooks and regional (New England). No festschriften, memoirs or unrevised doctoral dissertations. Only a few symposium collections accepted. Submit outline/synopsis and sample chapters.

Recent Nonfiction Titles: *Robert Frost and Sidney Cox; Forty Years of Friendship*, by W. Evans (collected letters); *A Good Poor Man's Wife*, by C. Bushman (biography); and *Greece in the 1940's; A Nation in Crisis*, by J. Iatrides (history).

UNIVERSITY PRESS OF THE PACIFIC, INC., Box 66129, Seattle WA 98166. Publishes hardcover and paperback originals (50%) and reprints (50%). Published 10 titles in 1979, 15 in 1980. Pays 5-10% royalty; buys some mss outright; no advance. Simultaneous and photocopied submissions OK. SASE. Reports in 2 months. Book catalog for SASE.

Nonfiction: Americana, animals, art, biography, business/economics, history, how-to, photography, politics, reference, science, technical and textbooks. "We would be delighted to receive all nonfiction submissions. We are looking for scholarly and reference books which are unique in contents. Our advertising media concentrates on the library marketplace, yet we do sell to the trade. We are not interested in unsubstantiated popular trade books." Query.

Recent Nonfiction Titles: *World Within Worlds*, by I. Asimov (historical account of science); *Business in 1990*, by A. Starchild (anthology on business); *Powerhouse of the Atom*, by K. Gladkov (science); and *Science Fiction of Konstantin Tsiolkovsky*, by K. Tsiolkovsky.

Tips: "We will also consider text for specialized courses where a professor can identify a specific market at his own or at other institutions."

*UNIVERSITY PRESS OF VIRGINIA, Box 3608, University Station, Charlottesville VA 22903. (804)924-3468. Editor-in-Chief: Walker Cowen. Publishes hardcover and paperback originals (95%) and reprints (5%). Averages 45 titles/year. Royalty on retail depends on the market for the book; sometimes none is made. "We subsidy publish 40% of our books, based on cost vs. probable market." Photocopied submissions OK. Returns rejected material within a week. Reports on acceptances in 1-2 months. SASE. Free catalog.

Nonfiction: Publishes Americana, business, history, law, medicine and psychiatry, politics, reference, scientific, bibliography, and decorative arts books. "Write a letter to the director, describing content of the manuscript, plus length. Also specify if maps, tables, illustrations, etc., are included. Please, no educational or sociological or psychological manuscripts." Recently published *The Immigrant in Industrial America*, by R.L. Ehrlich; *The New Humanism*, by J.D. Hoeveler Jr; and *Unmentionable Cuisine*, by Calvin Schwabe (cookery).

URIZEN BOOKS, INC., 66 W. Broadway, New York NY 10007. Editor: Michael Roloff. Publishes paperback and hardcover originals. Offers standard minimum book contract of 10-12½-15%. Average advance is $3,000. Book catalog $1. Will consider photocopied submissions. Query for nonfiction. Reports in 6 weeks. Enclose return postage.

Fiction, Nonfiction, Drama, Poetry: Social and behavioral sciences and humanities, "first-class fiction." High caliber writing necessary.

Recent Titles: *Wedding Feast*, by Michael Brodsky; *Literature and Evil*, by Georges Bataille; and *Railway Journey*, by Wolfgang Schivelbusch.

VAN NOSTRAND REINHOLD, LTD., 1410 Birchmount Rd., Scarborough, Ontario, Canada M1P 2E7. (416)751-2800. Executive Editor: Phyllis Bruce. Publishes hardcover and paperback originals. Averages 25 titles/year. Pays 10% royalty on wholesale or retail price. Simultaneous and photocopied submissions OK. SASE. Reports in 2 months. Free book catalog.

Nonfiction: Art, cookbooks, cooking and foods, health, how-to, humor, music, nature, photography, sports, technical, textbooks and Canadiana. Submit outline/synopsis and sample chapters.

Recent Nonfiction Titles: *The Book of Insults*, by N. McPhee; *The Montreal Canadiens*, by Claude Mouton (sports); and *Path of the Paddle*, by Bill Mason (hobbies).

VANGUARD PRESS, INC., 424 Madison Ave., New York NY 10017. Editor-in-Chief: Mrs. Bernice S. Woll. Publishes hardcover originals and reprints. Publishes 20 titles/year. Offers 7½-15% royalty on retail price; also buys mss outright; pays variable advance. Simultaneous and photocopied submissions OK. SASE. Reports in 5 weeks.

Nonfiction: Animals; art; biography (especially of musicians, artists and political figures); business (management, making money, how-to); cookbooks (gourmet and diet books); cooking and foods; history (scholarly, but written with flare); hobbies (crafts, especially sewing); how-to; humor; juveniles (folk stories, nature and art topics); music (no scores, but anything pertaining to the field—also, jazz); nature (ecology and nature adventure); philosophy; poetry; politics (current issues); psychology; religion in literature and society (no tracts); current sociology studies; sports; travel; juvenile science; and literary criticism. "No textbooks, reference books or technical material." Query or submit outline/synopsis and sample chapters.

Recent Nonfiction Titles: *Act II*, by N. Baker (mid-career changes); *The Pillow Book*, by C. Blackburn (craft); and *Pleasures of Walking*, by E. Mitchell.

Fiction: Believable adventure, experimental, humor, mystery, modern suspense and "good literature." No confessions, erotica or gothics. Query or submit outline/synopsis and sample chapters.

Recent Fiction Titles: *To Keep Our House Clean*, by E. McDowell (military training); and *The Fence*, by B. McGinnis.

*VESTA PUBLICATIONS, LTD., Box 1641, Cornwall, Ontario, Canada K6H 5V6. (613)932-2135. Editor-in-Chief: Stephen Gill. Paperback and hardcover originals. 10% minimum royalty on wholesale price. Subsidy publishes 5% of books. "We ask a writer to subsidize a part of the cost of printing; normally, it is 50%. We do so when we find that the book does not have a wide market, as in the case of university theses and the author's first collection of poems. The writer gets 50 free copies and 10% royalty on paperback editions." No advance. Publishes 15-20 titles/year. State availabiliy of photos and/or illustrations to accompany ms. Simultaneous submissions OK if so informed. Photocopied submissions OK. Reports in 1 week on queries; 1 month on mss. SAE and International Reply Coupons. Free book catalog.

Nonfiction: Publishes Americana, art, biography, cookbooks, cooking and foods, history, philosophy, poetry, politics, reference, religious. Query or submit complete ms. "Query letters and mss should be accompanied by synopsis of the book and biographical notes."

Recent Nonfiction Titles: *A Crack in the Mosaic: Canada's Race Relations in Crisis*, by David Lazarus; *Wheels for Life*, by Raguhbir Singh; and *Music & Spirituality*, by Richard Hickerson.

VGM CAREER HORIZONS, (Division of National Textbook Co.), 8259 Niles Center Rd., Skokie IL 60077. (312)679-4210. Editorial Director: Leonard Fiddle. Senior Editor: Barbara Wood Donner. Publishes hardcover and paperback originals. Averages 20-30 titles/year. Mss purchased on either royalty or buy-out basis. Average advance: $500. No simultaneous submissions; photocopied submissions OK. SASE. Reports in 6 weeks. Book catalog for large SASE.

Career Guidance Books: "We are interested in all professional and vocational areas. Our titles are marketed to a senior high school, college and trade audience, so readability and reading level (10-12) of books in the series is especially important. VGM books are used by students and others considering careers in specific areas, and contain basic information of the history and development of the field; its educational requirements; specialties and working conditions; how to write a resume, interview, and get started in the field; and salaries and benefits. Additionally, we expect to be producing more general career guidance and women's career development materials in the next year or two. We are open to all suggestions in this area, although all proposals should be of relevance to young adults, as well as to older career changers. Since our titles are largely formatted, potential writers should always query first, requesting information on already-publised titles and format and structure."

Recent Nonfiction Titles: *Opportunities in Architecture*, by R.J. Piper; *Opportunities in Carpentry*, by Roger Sheldon; and *Opportunities in Journalism*, by J. Tebbel.

Tips: "On most projects, we prefer writers who have considerable knowledge of their subjects, although freelance writers who research well are also considered. Although the content of most titles is similar, the ability to present fairly cut-and-dried information in an upbeat, interesting manner is heavily in an author's favor."

VICTOR BOOKS, Box 1825, Wheaton IL 60187. (312)668-6000. Editorial Director: James R. Adair. Paperback originals. Averages 30 titles/year. Pays 7½-10% royalty on retail price; occasionally offers an advance. Prefers outline/synopsis and sample chapters, but queries are acceptable. Reports in 1-2 months. SASE. Free book catalog and author's brochure.

Nonfiction: Only religious themes. "Writers must know the evangelical market well and their material should have substance. Many of our books are by ministers, Bible teachers, and seminar speakers. Freelancers can team with nonwriting experts to ghost or co-author books to fit our line." Recently published *Loving One Another*, by G. Getz; *The Success Fantasy*, by A. Campolo; and *How to Say No to a Stubborn Habit*, by Erwin W. Lutzer (Christian living).

THE VIKING PENGUIN, INC., 625 Madison Ave., New York NY 10022. Published over 300 titles last year. Pays royalty. Query letter only. Manuscripts considered only when sent through agent or intermediary to specific editor. Reports in 6 weeks.

Imprints: *Studio Books* (art, photography, etc.). *Viking Junior Books. The Viking Press* (adult fiction and nonfiction).

VISAGE PRESS, INC., 2333 N. Vernon St., Arlington VA 22207. (703)528-8872. Editor-in-Chief: Emilio C. Viano. Managing Editor: Sherry Icenhower. Hardcover and paperback originals. "At this time, interested in particular in how-to books and books about sports, particularly written by and for women athletes." Pays 10% royalty on first 5,000 hardcover; 12% next 5,000; 14% thereafter. Paperback royalty depends on the run. "Average advance is $1,000, generally given upon receipt of acceptable ms; rarely given on basis of outline alone. For scholarly works, please follow the style of the *American Sociological Review* (see their *Notice to Contributors*), or send for style sheet." Published 8 titles in 1979, 10 in 1980. Send contact sheets (if available) or prints to illustrate ms. Pictures must always be captioned and accompanied by proper releases. Photocopied submissions OK. Reports in 1-2 months. SASE. Book catalog for SASE.

Nonfiction: Publishes business; hobbies, medicine and psychiatry (particularly about emergencies, crisis, rape, child abuse, other victimizations, prevention of victimization); pets (a consumer guide to pet books; "gourmet" foods for pets); psychology (particularly in the area of the rapist, sex offender and victims repeatedly victimized); recreation (soccer, in particular); religious (books about the coming millennium sought); sports (for the woman athlete in particular); and sexuality "after 50." Query or submit outline/synopsis and sample chapters.

Tips: "We're in need of series on skiing of the travel book variety, telling people where to go, what to expect in terms of facilities, schools, lifts, accommodations, etc. Also books on soccer."

VULCAN BOOKS, INC., Division of Trinity-One, Inc., Box 25616, Seattle WA 98125. Publisher: Michael H. Gaven. Publishes hardcover and paperback originals and reprints. Pays royalty on retail price. "Advances offered only in special cases." Published 5 titles in 1979, 5 in 1980; plans 7 in 1981. "Our books are marketed by all major occult distributors and we sell them to practically every store in America dealing with our subject matter." Submit outline and sample chapters for nonfiction; complete ms for fiction. Reports in 4-8 weeks. SASE.

Nonfiction: "We are expanding into all areas of truth, even a bit into fiction. We are still committed to our original field of astrology, and are especially searching for books on computers & astrology, astrocartography, astropyschology. We will accept a few highly selected religious books that are nondenominational, truly nondenominational, that will appeal to people of all the world. Books covering the new mutation of mankind into a global consciousness are encouraged. We are at the end of an age where we must group together to survive to fight those who think that freedom only belongs to a few. Books on these subjects, without fire and brimstone preaching are needed.

Recent Nonfiction Titles: *Philip's Cousin Jesus: The Untold Story*; and *Moongate: The Great NASA Cover-up.*

Tips: "We are now interested in books covering basic survival skills; alternative energy sources, different approaches to gardening, etc. All areas of self-help are examined."

J. WESTON WALCH, PUBLISHER, Box 658, Portland ME 04104. (207)772-2846. Managing Editor: Richard S. Kimball. Senior Editor: Jane Carter. Publishes paperback originals. Averages 120 titles/year. Offers 10-15% royalty on gross receipts. Buys some titles by outright purchase; offers $100-1,000. No advance. No simultaneous submissions; photocopied submissions OK. SASE. Reports in 3 weeks. Free book catalog.

Nonfiction: Art; business; economics; English, foreign language; government; health; history; music; psychology; recreation; science; social science; sociology; and sports. "We publish only supplementary educational material for sale to secondary schools throughout the United States and Canada. Formats include books, posters, ditto master sets, visual master sets (masters for making transparencies), cassettes, filmstrips, and mixed packages. Most titles are assigned by us, though we occasionally accept an author's unsolicited submission. We have a great need for author-artist teams and for authors who can write at third- to tenth-grade levels. We do *not* want basic texts, anthologies or industrial arts titles. Most of our authors—but not all— have secondary teaching experience. I cannot stress too much the advantages that an author-artist team would have in approaching us and probably other publishers." Query first.

Recent Nonfiction Titles: *My Problem Is . . . ,* by Margaret Dewey (teenagers' problems); *Exploring Business Education*, by June Dostal (high school business course); and *Cartooning for Beginners*, by Lafe Locke (art).

WALKER AND CO., 720 5th Ave., New York NY 10019. Editor-in-Chief: Richard Winslow. Senior Editor: Ruth Cavin. Hardcover and paperback originals (90%) and reprints (10%). Averages 92 titles/year. Pays 10-12-15% royalty on retail price or by outright purchase; advance averages $1,000-2,500 "but could be higher or lower." Publishes 80 titles annually. Query or submit outline/synopsis and sample chapters. Submit samples of photos/illustrations to accompany ms. Photocopied submissions OK. SASE. Free book catalog.

Nonfiction: Publishes Americana; art; biography; business; cookbooks, cooking and foods; histories; hobbies; how-to; juveniles; medicine and psychiatry; multimedia material; music; nature; pets; psychology; recreation; reference; popular science; self-help; sports; travel; and gardening books. Recently published *The New York Philharmonic Guide to the Symphony*, by E. Downs (music nonfiction); *How to Make Your Child a Winner*, by Dr. Victor B. Cline (parenting); and *The Collapsing Universe*, by Isaac Asimov (nonfiction).

Fiction: Mystery; science fiction; suspense; gothics; regency books; and westerns.

Recent Fiction Title: *The Twelve Deaths of Christmas*, by Marian Babson (mystery).

WALLACE HOMESTEAD BOOK CO., 1912 Grand Ave., Des Moines IA 50309. (515)243-6181. Editorial Director: Don Brown. Publishes hardcover and paperback originals. Averages 20 titles/year. Offers 10% royalty on wholesale price. No advance. Simultaneous and photocopied submissions OK. SASE. Reports in 6 weeks. Free book catalog.

Nonfiction: Antiques and collectibles. Query first, submit outline/synopsis and sample chapters or submit complete ms.

Recent Nonfiction Titles: *You Can Be A Super Quilter*, by Hassel; *WH Price Guide to Oriental Antiques*, by Andacht, Garthe and Mascarelli; and *Victorian Furniture Styles and Prices Book II*, by Swedberg.

WANDERER BOOKS, Division of Simon & Schuster, 1230 Avenue of the Americas, New York NY 10020. (212)245-6400. Editor-in-Chief: Wendy Barish. Publishes hardcover, trade and mass market paperback originals (80%), and mass market paperback reprints (20%). Averages 50-60 titles/year. Pays 2-6% royalty on retail price; buys some mss outright. Simultaneous submissions OK. SASE. Reports in 2 weeks on queries; 2 months on mss. Book catalog for SAE.

Nonfiction: Juvenile. Subjects include art, health, hobbies and recreation. "We are looking for special humor, activity or solid backlist nonfiction for the next year or so, for ages 8-14. No science, nature, history, or other school- and library-oriented nonfiction. We are a trade and mass market publishing imprint for children."

Recent Nonfiction Titles: *The Complete Babysitter's Handbook*, by Barkin and James; and *I Can Draw Monsters* and *Puzzleback* series, by Fallarico.

Fiction: Adventure, humor, mystery and science fiction. "We are looking for novels for young people ages 8-14, in light, humorous style, or mystery/adventure style." No heavy, topical, social issue-oriented teenage fiction. Query or submit outline/synopsis and sample chapters or complete ms.

Recent Fiction Titles: *Secret in the Old Lace*, by Carolyn Keene (Nancy Drew series); *Old Fashioned Children's Story Book* (collected stories); and *The City in the Stars*, by Victor Appleton (Tom Swift series).

FREDERICK WARNE & CO., INC., 2 Park Ave., New York NY 10016. Editor, Books for Young People: Meredith J. Charpentier. Publishes juvenile hardcover originals. Offers 10% royalty contract. Published 15 titles in 1979, 20 in 1980. Minimum advance is $1,000. Submit outline and sample chapters for nonfiction and fiction. "Ms will not be considered unless requested." Reports in 10 weeks.

Juveniles: Hardcover trade books for children and young adults. Picture books (ages 4-7), fiction and nonfiction for the middle reader (ages 7-12) and young adults (ages 11 and up). Mss must combine a high-interest level with fine writing. Prefers to see fewer picture books and more submissions for 8- to 12-year-olds.

Recent Titles: *Part-Time Boy*, by Elizabeth Billington; *The Last of Eden*, by Stephanie Tolan; and *An Eye on the World: Margaret Bourke-White, Photographer*, by Beatrice Siegel.

WATSON-GUPTILL PUBLICATIONS, 1515 Broadway, New York NY 10036. Imprints include Whitney Library of Design. Publishes originals. Pays 10-12½-15% royalty; usual advance is $1,000, but average varies, depending on author's reputation and nature of book. Published 70 titles in 1979, 65 in 1980; plans 65 in 1981. Address queries (followed by outlines and sample chapters) to Herbert T. Leavy, Editorial Director. Reports on queries within 10 days. Enclose return postage.

Art: Publishes art instruction books. Interested only in how-to books in any field of painting, crafts, graphic design, etc. Length: open.

WAYNE STATE UNIVERSITY PRESS, 5959 Woodward Ave., Detroit MI 48202. (313)577-4601. Editor-in-Chief: B.M. Goldman. Managing Editor: J. Owen. Publishes hardcover and paperback originals. "Standard royalty schedule" on wholesale price; no advance. Publishes 30 titles/year. Reports in 1-6 months. SASE. Free book catalog.

Nonfiction: Publishes Americana, biography, economics, history, law, medicine and psychiatry, music, philosophy, politics, psychology, religious, and sociology books. Query or submit outline/synopsis and sample chapters. "Do not send photos unless requested, or send photocopies."
Recent Nonfiction Titles: *German Churches Under Hitler*, by Ernst Helmreich (history); and *Life of Music in North India*, by Daniel Neuman (musicology).

WEBSTER DIVISION, McGraw-Hill Book Co., 1221 Avenue of the Americas, New York NY 10020. Vice-President/General Manager: Lawrence A. Walsh. Royalties vary. "Our royalty schedules are those of the industry, and advances are not commonly given." Photocopied submissions OK. Reports in 2-4 weeks. SASE.
Textbooks: Publishes instructional materials for elementary and secondary schools. Subject areas served include social studies, science, reading and language arts, industrial education, home economics, health, foreign languages, the arts, mathematics. "Material is generally part of a series, system, or program done in connection with other writers, teachers, testing experts, et al. Material must be matched to the psychological age level, with reading achievement and other educational prerequisites in mind."

WESLEYAN UNIVERSITY PRESS, 55 High St., Middletown CT 06457. Director: Jeannette Hopkins. Publishes 15-25 titles/year. Photocopied submissions OK. SASE. Reports in approximately 2 months.
Nonfiction: Concentration on American history and American studies, public affairs, dance, theater, and the philosophy of history. Query.

WESTERN ISLANDS, 395 Concord Ave., Belmont MA 02178. Editor: C.O. Mann. Publishes hardcover and paperback originals (75%) and reprints (25%). Published 3 titles in 1979, 1 in 1980; plans 6 in 1981. Pays 10% of list price royalty on hardcover, 5% on paperback; no advance. Simultaneous and photocopied submissions OK. Reports in 2 months. SASE. Book catalog for SASE.
Nonfiction: "We are interested in conservative books on current events: economics, politics, contemporary history, etc. We are not interested in biographies, autobiographies (unless by a famous conservative), fiction, poetry, etc. Anti-communist books, if not overly autobiographical, are welcome." Query or submit complete ms. Recently published *To Covet Honor,* by H. Alexander; *The Siecus Circle,* by C. Chambers; *The Age of Inflation*, by H. Sennholz; and *Nicaragua Betrayed*, by A. Somoza as told to Jack Cox.

WESTERN PRODUCER PRAIRIE BOOKS, Box 2500, Saskatoon, Saskatchewan, Canada S7K 2C4. Manager: Rob Sanders. Publishes hardcover and paperback originals (95%) and reprints (5%). Specializes in nonfiction historical works set in Western Canada by Western Canadian authors. Pays 10% (of list price) royalty. Published 14 titles in 1979, 15 in 1980; plans 15 in 1981. Submit contact sheets or prints if illustrations are to accompany ms. Simultaneous submissions OK. Reports in 2-4 months. SAE and International Reply Coupons. Free book catalog.
Nonfiction: Publishes history, nature, photography, biography, reference, agriculture, economics, politics and cookbooks. Submit outline, synopsis and sample chapters. Recently published *Our Nell*, by C. Savage (biography); *Out West*, by R. Phillips; and *Butter Down the Well*, by R. Collins.

WESTERN TANAGER PRESS, 1111 Pacific Ave., Santa Cruz CA 95060. (408)425-5758. Editor: Michael S. Gant. Publishes hardcover and trade paperback originals (50%), and hardcover and trade paperback reprints (50%). Averages 10 titles/yeqr. Pays 10-15% royalty on retail price; also works through "various contractual agreements"; offers average $200-400 advance. Simultaneous and photocopied submissions OK. SASE. Reports in 1 week on queries; 2 months on mss. Free book catalog.
Nonfiction: Biography and history. Subjects include Americana, history, California and the West. "We are looking for works of local and regional history dealing with California and Western America. This includes biography, natural history, art and politics. Also interested in travel." Query.
Recent Nonfiction Titles: *Oildorado*, by William Rintoul (history); *Sidewalk Companion to Santa Cruz Architecture*, by John Chase (history and architecture); and *Tribute to Yesterday*, by Sharron Hale (history).
Fiction: Historical, mainstream, mystery, suspense and western. "Our needs are minimal, but we will consider submissions." No juvenile books or romances. Query.

WESTERNLORE PRESS, Box 35305, Tucson AZ 85740. Editor: Lynn R. Bailey. Publishes 6-12 titles/year. Pays standard royalties on retail price "except in special cases." Query. Reports in 60 days. Enclose return postage with query.

Americana: Publishes Western Americana of a scholarly and semi-scholarly nature: anthropology, archeology, historic sites, restoration, and ethnohistory pertaining to the greater American West. Republication of rare and out-of-print books. Length: 25,000-100,000 words.

THE WESTMINSTER PRESS, Department CBE, 925 Chestnut St., Philadelphia PA 19107. (215)928-2700. Children's Book Editor: Barbara S. Bates. Publishes hardcover originals. Publishes 12 titles/year. Royalty on retail price and advance "vary with author's experience and credentials, and the amount of illustration needed." Photocopied submissions OK if not simultaneous. Reports in 3 months. SASE. Book catalog for SASE.
Nonfiction: Juvenile only, for readers 8-12. Career; consumer education; ecology and nature; science and math; social studies; recreation and how-to; and sports and hobbies. Query or submit outline/synopsis and sample chapters.
Recent Nonfiction Titles: *My Diary—My World*, by Elizabeth Yates (social studies/career); *The Team Behind Your Airline Flight* (social studies resource and career interest); and *This Time Count Me In*, by Phyllis Anderson Wood (personal relationships and high suspense).
Fiction: Juvenile only, for ages 8-13. Adventure; humor; mystery; family; science fiction; and suspense. No picture books or stories in verse. Submit outline/synopsis and sample chapters.
Recent Fiction Titles: *The Pig at 37 Pinecrest Drive*, by Susan Fleming (humor); *Summer of the Green Star*, by Robert C. Lee (science fiction); and *Skateboard Scramble*, by Barbara Douglass (tale of friendship, rivalry and family relationships).

*WESTVIEW PRESS, 5500 Central Ave., Boulder CO 80301. (303)444-3541. Publisher: F.A. Praeger. Associate Publisher/Editorial Director: Lynne Rienner. Hardcover and paperback originals (90%), lecture notes, reference books, and paperback texts (10%). Specializes in scholarly monographs or conference reports with strong emphasis on applied science, both social and natural. Zero to 12½% royalty on retail price, depending on market. Accepts subsidies for a small number of books, "but only in the case of first class scholarly material for a limited market when books need to be priced low, or when the manuscripts have unusual difficulties such as Chinese or Sanskrit characters; the usual quality standards of a top-flight university press apply, and subsidies must be furnished by institutions, not by individuals." Averages 175 titles/year. Markets books mainly by direct mail. State availability of photos and/or illustrations to accompany manuscript. Reports in 1-4 months. SASE. Free book catalog.
Nonfiction: Agricultural/food, public policy, energy, natural resources, international economics and business, international relations, area studies, geography, science and technology policy, sociology, anthropology, reference, military affairs, health. Query and submit sample chapters. Use University of Chicago *Manual of Style*. "Unsolicited manuscripts receive low priority; inquire before submitting projects."
Recent Nonfiction Titles: *Animal Agriculture*, edited by Wilson G. Pond; and *Renewable Resources*, edited by Dennis Little.

WHITAKER HOUSE, Pittsburgh and Colfax Sts., Springdale PA 15144. (412)274-4440. Editor: Victoria L. Mlinar. Paperback originals (40%) and reprints (60%). "We publish only Christian books." Royalty negotiated based on the cover price of the book. Advance only under certain circumstances. Publishes about 15-20 titles annually. "We market books in Christian book stores and in rack-jobbing locations such as supermarkets and drug stores." Looking for teaching books with personal experiences used throughout, typed, double-spaced, about 200 pages in length. Simultaneous and photocopied submissions OK. Reports in about 6 weeks. SASE.
Nonfiction: Publishes only very select biography or autobiography (testimony of spirit-filled Christians; 60,000 words); publishes mostly how-to books ("how to move on in your Christian walk"; 60,000 words); religious ("don't want heavy theology"; 60,000 words). "Please note that we want teaching books that give the author's life experiences as well as solid Christian teaching."
Recent Nonfiction Titles: *Victory Over Depression*, (teaching-how-to); *How To Conquer Fear* (teaching-how-to); and *Of The Imitation of Christ*, by Thomas aKempis (reprint).

ALBERT WHITMAN & CO., 560 W. Lake St., Chicago IL 60606. Editorial Director: Kathleen Tucker. Senior Editor: Ann Fay. Publishes hardcover originals. Publishes 21 titles/year. Royalty, advance, and outright purchase vary. Photocopied submissions OK. SASE. Reports in 2 months. Free book catalog for SASE.
Nonfiction: Juveniles. Need easy craft books, easy joke and/or riddle books, easy how-to books on cooking, gardening, etc. No science or social studies. Query or submit outline/synopsis and sample chapters.
Recent Nonfiction Titles: *Behind the Scenes at the Horse Hospital*, by F. Brown; *More Codes for Kids*, by B. Albert (easy codes for kids to crack); and *City Trucks*, by Robert Quackenbush (picture book).

Fiction: Juvenile only. "We are looking for simple picturebook mss about children coping with real-life situations. We are also looking for novels (realistic, humorous and upbeat) for 8-10 year olds and easy-to-read mysteries for all ages." No young adult novels, alphabet books or poetry. Submit outline/synopsis and sample chapters of long novels and submit complete ms of picture books.

Recent Fiction Titles: *Nobody's Perfect, Not Even My Mother*, by N. Simon (picture book); *Come Home, Wilma*, by M. Sharmat (picture book); and *Black Magic at Brillstone*, by F. Heide and R. Heide (easy mystery).

WHITMORE PUBLISHING CO., 35 Cricket Terrace, Ardmore PA 19003. Vice President/Editorial: Linda S. Peacock. Offers "standard royalty contract, profit-sharing contract, or outright purchase." Published 6 titles last year. Reports in 1 month. Send queries and sample chapters or poems. SASE.

General Nonfiction and Poetry: "Books that will provide the reader with insight and techniques to manage his or her life more effectively. Interests include education, nutrition, community life, philosophy, self-improvement, family study and planning, career planning; explanations of significant science and technology not broadly understood."

Recent Titles: *Human Values Teaching Programs for Health Professionals*, by McElhinney; and *The Ice King*, by Casolaro.

THE WHITSTON PUBLISHING CO., Box 958, Troy NY 12181. (518)283-4363. Editorial Director: Stephen Goode. Publishes hardcover originals. Published 30 titles in 1979, 30 in 1980; plans 40 in 1981. Pays 10-12-15% royalty on wholesale price; no advance. Simultaneous and photocopied submissions OK. Reports in 1 year. SASE. Free book catalog.

Nonfiction: "We publish scholarly and critical books in the arts, humanities and some of the social sciences. We also publish reference books, bibliographies, indexes and checklists. We do not want author bibliographies in general unless they are unusual and unusually scholarly. We are, however, much interested in catalogs and inventories of library collections of individuals, such as the catalog of the Evelyn Waugh Collection at the Humanities Research Center, the University of Texas at Austin; and collections of interest to the specific scholarly community, such as surveys of early black newspapers in libraries in the US, etc." Query or submit complete ms. Recently published *Marcel Duchamp: Eros C'est la Vie*, by A. Marquis (biography); *The Letters of Randolph Bourne*, by E. Sandeen; *A Proust Dictionary*, by M. Vogely; *Women Poets of Pre-Revolutionary America, 1650-1775*, by P. Cowell; and *W.B. Yeats and the Emergence of the Irish Free State*, by R. Krimm.

WILDERNESS PRESS, 2440 Bancroft Way, Berkeley CA 94704. (415)843-8080. Editorial Director: Thomas Winnett. Publishes paperback originals. Averages 7 titles/year. Pays 8-10% royalty on retail price; advance averages $200. Simultaneous and photocopied submissions OK. Reports in 2 weeks. SASE. Book catalog for SASE.

Nonfiction: "We publish books about the outdoors. Most of our books are trail guides for hikers and backpackers, but we also publish how-to books about the outdoors and perhaps will publish personal adventures. The manuscript must be accurate. The author must research an area thoroughly in person. If he is writing a trail guide, he must walk all the trails in the area his book is about. The outlook must be strongly conservationist. The style must be appropriate for a highly literate audience." Query, submit outline/synopsis and sample chapters, or submit complete ms.

Recent Nonfiction Titles: *Sawtooth National Recreation Area*, by L. Linkhart; and *Arizona Trails*, by David Mazel.

JOHN WILEY & SONS, INC., 605 3rd Ave., New York NY 10158. (212)850-6000. Publishes hardcover and paperback originals. Publishes 800 titles/year. Pays variable royalties on wholesale price. Follow *MLA Style Sheet*. Simultaneous and photocopied submissions OK. Reports in 6 months. SASE. Free book catalog.

Nonfiction: Publishes college textbooks, professional reference titles, trade books and journals in engineering, social science, business, life sciences, politics, medicine and psychology. Query or submit outline/synopsis and sample chapters.

Recent Nonfiction Titles: *America's Technology Slip*, by Ramo; *Winning the Salary Game*, by Chastain; and *Architectural Graphic Standards, 7th edition*, by Ramsey and Sleeper.

WILSHIRE BOOK CO., 12015 Sherman Rd., North Hollywood CA 91605. (213)875-1711. Editorial Director: Melvin Powers. Publishes paperback originals (50%) and reprints (50%). Publishes 50 titles/year. Pays 5% minimum royalty; "advance varies with nature of the book." Simultaneous and photocopied submissions OK. SASE. Reports in 2 weeks. Catalog for SASE.

Nonfiction: Calligraphy, health, hobbies, how-to, psychology, recreation, self-help and sports.

"We are always looking for self-help and psychological books, such as *Psycho-Cybernetics* and *Guide to Rational Living*. We need manuscripts teaching mail order, advertising, and calligraphy. We publish 70 horse books and need books dealing with instruction and teaching circus tricks." Query. "All that I need is the concept of the book to determine if the project is viable. I welcome phone calls to discuss manuscripts with authors."

Recent Nonfiction Titles: *How to Get Rich in Mail Order*; by Melvin Powers; *How to Write a Good Advertisement*, by V. Schwab; and *World Wide Mail Order Shopper's Guide*, by E. Moller

WIMMER BROTHERS BOOKS, 4210 B.F. Goodrich Blvd., Box 18408, Memphis TN 38181. (901)362-8900. Editorial Director: Richard Anderson. Senior Editor: Janine Buford Earney. Publishes hardcover and paperback originals. Published 4 titles in 1979, 4-5 in 1980; plans 5-6 in 1981. Offers 10-15% royalty on wholesale price. No advance. SASE. Reports in 2 months. Book catalog for SASE.

Nonfiction: Cookbooks, cooking and foods; and how-to. Especially needs specialized cookbooks and how-to books dealing with home entertainment. Submit complete ms.

Recent Nonfiction Titles: *The Pastors' Wives Cookbook*, by S. DuBose (cookbook); and *Forgotten Recipes*, by Jaine Rodack (cookbook).

B.L. WINCH & ASSOCIATES, 45 Hitching Post Dr., Bldg. 2, Rolling Hills Estates CA 90274. (213)547-1240. Editorial Director: B.L. Winch. Senior Editor: J. Cooper. Publishes paperback originals (60%) and reprints (40%). Published 4 titles in 1979, 8 in 1980; plans 8 in 1981. Offers 5-15% royalty on wholesale or retail price. No advance. Simultaneous and photocopied submissions OK. SASE. Reports in 6 weeks. Free book catalog.

Nonfiction: Self-help; educational/early childhood; and textbooks. "All published materials are based on researched topics and data." Especially needs "curriculum-oriented books for early childhood education, special education, staff development and parent programs." Submit outline/synopsis and sample chapters.

Recent Nonfiction Titles: *Two Years Old—Play and Learning*, by Dr. M. Segal and D. Adcock (early childhood); *Communicating to Make Friends—A Social Acceptance Program for the Elementary School Teacher*, by Dr. C. Lynn Fox (mainstreaming, social acceptance); and *Handicapped—How Does It Feel*, by Gregory LaMore (mainstreaming).

WINCHESTER PRESS, Box 1260, Tulsa OK 74101. (918)835-3161. Editor-in-Chief: Robert Elman. Vice President/General Manager: Don Karecki. Publishes hardcover and paperback originals. Pays 10-12½-15% royalty on retail price; offers $2,500 average advance. Averages 20 titles/year. "Submit sample photos and some idea of total number projected for final book." Simultaneous and photocopied submissions OK. Reports in 3 months. SASE. Free book catalog.

Nonfiction: Main interest is in leisure activities, outdoor sports, crafts and related subjects. Publishes cookbooks (if related to their field); how-to (sports and sporting equipment); pets (hunting dogs); recreation (outdoor); sports (hunting, fishing, etc.); and technical (firearms, boats and motors, fishing tackle, etc.). Submit outline/synopsis and sample chapters.

Recent Nonfiction Titles: *The Duck-Huntingest Gentlemen*, by Keith C. Russell and Friends; *Penny Pinching Guide to Bigger Fish and Better Hunting*, by Clair Rees and Hartt Wixom; and *Handbook of Metallic Cartridge Reloading*, by Edward Matunas.

Tips: "The writing of leisure-activities books—particularly how-to books—has vastly improved in recent years. Mss must now be better written and must reflect new ideas and new information if they are to be considered for publication by Winchester Press. Recreational equipment and opportunities have expanded, and writers must also be up-to-date journalists."

WINDSOR PUBLICATIONS, 21220 Erwin St., Woodland Hills CA 91365. Editorial/Photographic Director: Glenn R. Kopp. Senior Publications Editor: Rita Johnson. "We publish pictorial civic publications, business directories, and relocation guides for chambers of commerce, boards of realtors, etc. Our audience is anyone considering relocating or visiting another part of the country, and our publications document in pictures and words every aspect of a city or area. Writers, photographers and photo/journalists work on assignment only, after having demonstrated ability through samples. Publications are annual or biennial, vary in size and are titled with thu name of a city. Circulation is controlled. Writers and writer/photographers with strong interview, reporting and travel writing experience are especially sought." Queries, stating writing and/or photography experience and including tearsheets, are welcome. Reports in 2 weeks. SASE. Sample copy, writer's and photographer's guidelines sent on request.

Nonfiction: "All mss assigned. Unsolicited manuscripts and/or photos not wanted." Buys 150-200/year. Length: 3,000-10,000 words. Pays $500-2,400 on acceptance for all rights.

Photos: Photography for each publication usually assigned to photographer or photo/journalist on per-day rate plus expenses. Also purchase stock, speculative and existing photos on one-time use basis if they pertain to future publications. 35mm and larger color transparencies, b&w contact sheets and negatives or b&w prints (5x7 to 8x10) are acceptable; no color prints. Complete captions required. Photo guidelines, sample copy and upcoming photo needs will be sent in response to all queries. SASE.

WINSTON PRESS, INC., CBS Educational Publishing, 430 Oak Grove, Minneapolis MN 55403 (612)871-7000. Imprints include Winston House (backlist audiovisual). Editorial Director: Susan Canning Stochl. Publishes hardcover and paperback originals (90%) and reprints (10%). Publishes 35 titles/year. Pays 10-12½-15% royalty; advance varies. Photocopied submissions OK. SASE. Reports in 2 months. Book catalog for SASE.
Nonfiction: "Religion and human development: most titles are done on request. Curriculum materials for preschool through adult education. Specialized and general trade books, gift and photography books. Also, audiovisual material." Query or submit outline/synopsis. Recently published *Permanent Love*, by Edward E. Ford and Steven Englund; *The Christmas Pageant*, by Tomie de Paola (children's storybook); and *An Irish Blessing* and I Am of Ireland, by Cyril A. Reilly and Renee Travis Reilly.

WINSTON-DEREK PUBLISHERS, INC., Pennywell Dr., Box 90883, Nashville TN 37209. (615)356-7384. President: James W. Peebles. Publishes hardcover, trade and mass market paperback originals (5%). Averages 10-12 titles/year. Pays 10-15% royalty on retail price; offers average $1,500 advance. Simultaneous and photocopied submissions OK. SASE. Reports in 3 weeks on queries; 6 weeks on submissions.
Nonfiction: Biography, cookbook, illustrated book, juvenile and poetry. Subjects include Americana; cooking and foods; philosophy (contemporary format); religion (non-cultism); travel; poetry; and inspirational. "We are looking for material concerning education end desegregation, minority sensitivity, bicultural education (Black, Asian, Appalachian), and the Third World countries." No sexist, political or technical material. Submit complete ms.
Recent Nonfiction Titles: *Car Trek*, by Catherine Trowbridge (educational travel); and *A Survey of African and Black American Theology*, by Jamamogi Watumbi (theology).
Fiction: Ethnic (non-defamatory); religious (theologically sound); suspense (highly plotted); and Americana (minorities and whites in positive relationships). "We can use fiction with a semi-historical plot; must be based or centered around actual facts and events—Americana, religion, gothic, etc." No fantasy, science fiction or erotica. Submit complete ms.
Recent Fiction Title: *Strange Paradox*, by Marjorie S. Staton (Americana).
Poetry: "We are looking for poetry that's inspirational and divine—poetry that is suitable for meditation. We will also accept poetry that is about nature and life. No simple, plainsong, etc." Submit complete ms.
Recent Poetry Titles: *Ransom From a Poet*, by Jerry W. Elkins (theo-philosophical); and *Once Upon a Memory*, by James W. Winston (early American life).
Tips: "The American audience is looking for less violent material. Outstanding biographies are quite successful, as are books dealing with the simplicity of man and his relationship with his environ."

*ALAN WOFSY FINE ARTS, 150 Green St., San Francisco CA 94111. Publishes hardcover and paperback originals (50%) and hardcover reprints (50%). Specializes in art reference books, specifically catalogs of graphic artists; bibliographies related to fine presses and the art of the book. Pays negotiable fee on retail price; no advance. Publishes 5 titles annually. SASE. Reports in 2-4 weeks. Free book catalog.
Nonfiction: Publishes reference books on art. Query.

WOLF HOUSE BOOKS, Box 209-K, Cedar Springs MI 49319. (616)696-2772. Editorial Director: Richard Weiderman. Publishes hardcover and paperback originals (50%) and reprints (50%). Published 5 titles in 1979. Offers 10% royalty. No advance. Simultaneous and photocopied submissions OK. Reports in 4 weeks. SASE. Book catalog for SASE.
Nonfiction: Literary criticism and biography and other studies (e.g. bibliography, etc.) on Jack London. Query.
Recent Nonfiction Titles: *Alien Worlds of Jack London*, by D.L. Walker; *White Logic: Jack London's Short Stories*, by J.I. McClintock; and *Jack London at Yale*, by A. Irvine.

WOODBRIDGE PRESS PUBLISHING CO., Box 6189, Santa Barbara CA 93111. Editor-in-Chief: Howard B. Weeks. Publishes hardcover and paperback originals. Standard royalty contract. Rarely gives an advance. Published 11 titles in 1979. Will consider photocopied submissions. Query. Returns rejected material as soon as possible. Reports on material accepted for publication in 3 months. Enclose return postage with query.

General Nonfiction: "How-to books on personal health and well-being. Should offer the reader valuable new information or insights on anything from recreation to diet to mental health that will enable him to achieve greater personal fulfillment, with emphasis on that goal. Should minimize broad philosophy and maximize specific, useful information." Length: Books range from 96 to 300 pages. Also publishes cookbooks and gardening books. Recent titles include *The Oats, Peas, Beans and Barley Cookbook* (Cottrell); *More Food From Your Garden* (Mittleider); and *Butterflies in My Stomach* (Taylor).

WORLD ALMANAC, 200 Park Ave., New York NY 10166. (212)557-9653. Editorial Director: Hana Umlauf Lane. Publisher of *The World Almanac.* Publishes hardcover and paperback originals. Averages 5 titles/year. Pays 5-15% on retail price; offers minimum $5,000 advance. Buys some mss outright for minimum $3,000. No simultaneous or photocopied submissions. SASE. Reports in 3 weeks. Free book catalog.
Nonfiction: Reference. "We especially need reference books, like *The World Almanac,* but popular and entertaining." Submit outline/synopsis and sample chapters.
Recent Nonfiction Titles: *The World Almanac; The World Almanac Book of Who;* and *The World Almanac Book of Buffs, Masters, Mavens and Uncommon Experts.*

WORLD NATURAL HISTORY PUBLICATIONS, A division of Plexus Publishing, Inc., Box 550, Marlton NJ 08053. (609)654-6500. UPS address: Anderson House, Stokes Rd., Medford NJ 08055. Editorial Director: Thomas Hogan. Publishes hardcover and paperback originals. Averages 4 titles/year. Pays 10-20% royalty on wholesale price, buys some booklets outright for $250-1,000; offers average $500-1,000 advance. Simultaneous and photocopied submissions OK. SASE. Reports in 2 months. Book catalog for SASE.
Nonfiction: Animals, biography of naturalists, nature and reference. "We are looking for mss of about 300-400 pages for our series *Introduction to ...* some group of plants or animals designed for high school and undergraduate college use and for amateur naturalists. We will consider any book on a nature/biology subject, particularly those of a reference (permanent) nature. No philosophy or psychology; no gardening; generally not interested in travel, but will consider travel that gives sound ecological information." Also interested in mss of about 20 to 40 pages in length for feature articles in *Biology Digest* (guidelines for these available with SASE). Always query.
Recent Nonfiction Titles: *The Naturalist's Directory and Almanac,* (reference); *Introduction to the Study of Spiders,* by W.H. Whitcomb; and *Taxonomists' Glossary of Mosquito Anatomy,* by R. Harbach and K. Knight.
Tips: "Write a book that is absolutely accurate and that has been reviewed by specialists to eliminate misstatement of fact."

WORLD WIDE PUBLISHING CORPORATION, Box 105, Ashland OR 97520. (503)482-3800. Editor: Helen M. Wathne. Publishes hardcover, trade and mass market paperback originals (75%), and hardcover, trade and mass market paperback reprints (25%). Pays 5-15% royalty on retail price; buys some mss outright for $100-5,000. Photocopied submissions OK. SASE. Reports in 6 weeks on queries; 2 months on submissions. Book catalog for small SAE and 1 first class stamp.
Nonfiction: Cookbook (health only); how-to; self-help; and survival (financial, physical and spiritual). Subjects include animals; cooking and foods (health only); health; hobbies; nature; religion; inflation/l epression-proof investments; wilderness/retreat-survival; best areas in the world to live; and cheap traveling. "We're looking for how-to books related to free market business subjects (investments that beat inflation and recessions and depressions, including foreign investments; how to start a successful business of your own with the least amount of paper work and personnel problems). How-to books on country and wilderness living, gardening, animal husbandry, homesteading, alternate lifestyles and energy conservation. We are trying to reach the people that are alarmed about the declining standard of living, prospects of war, governmental taxation and regulations, the ravages of inflation, and a depressed economy, and that want to do something about it—those that want to escape the rat race of civilization in order to enjoy maximum freedom and liberty through a self-sufficient lifestyle." Query or submit outline/synopsis and sample chapters. "No unsolicited mss please."
Recent Nonfiction Titles: *Timely and Profitable Help for Troubled Americans,* by Hans J. Schneider; *Official U.S. Air Force Survival Manual,* by Department of the Air Force; and *Flying to be Free,* by Hans J. Schneider.
Tips: "Although we appreciate credentials and experiences that particularly qualify the author to write the book, we are more interested in the subject than in the author's name or potential reviewer's comments. Practicality is what counts. Write on a subject of universal appeal—or at least of appeal to a large segment of the population—that is foremost on the minds of a lot of people and that tells them what they can do about it and how they can do it. Author should retain a carbon copy of ms, since we cannot assume responsibility for loss or damage. Sufficient postage either by

check or in the form of loose stamps must accompany query and ms as well as SAE to ensure return of ms in the event it is not accepted for publication and to ensure our answer to the query. Subject matters must be well-researched and authentic. We do not accept immoral material and do heavy editing on repetition and jargon as well as slang. We solicit books that have a market value for many years, as we will promote titles for quite a long time."

WRITER'S DIGEST BOOKS, 9933 Alliance Rd., Cincinnati OH 45242. (513)984-0717. Senior Book Editor: Carol Cartaino. Publishes hardcover and paperback originals (nonfiction only) about writing, photography, songwriting, art, crafts, related fields; selected trade titles. Pays variable royalty depending upon type of book; offers $3,000 average advance. Published 18 titles in 1981. Simultaneous (if so advised) and photocopied submissions OK. Reports in 3 months. Enclose return postage. Book catalog for SASE.
Nonfiction: "We're seeking up-to-date, instructional treatments by authors who can write from successful experience—how-to, reference, and other books about writing, photography, and other categories are described. Should be well-researched, yet lively and anecdotal." Query or submit outline/synopsis. "Be prepared to explain how the proposed book differs from existing books on the subject." Recently published *How to Make $20,000 a Year Writing, No Matter Where You Live*, by Nancy Edmonds Hanson; *Make Every Word Count*, by Gary Provost; *The Scriptwriter's Handbook*, by Alfred Brenner; *How to Write Best-Selling Fiction*, by Dean Koontz; *The Complete Handbook for Freelance Writers*, by Kay Cassill; *Sell & Re-Sell Your Photos*, by Rohn Engh; and *Is There Life After Housework*, by Don Aslett.

YALE UNIVERSITY PRESS, 92A Yale Station, New Haven CT 06520. Editor-in-Chief: Edward Tripp. Publishes hardcover and paperback originals (96%) and reprints (4%). Averages 100 titles/ year. Pays 5-10% royalty on retail price; seldom offers advance. Photocopied submissions OK. Reports in 2-3 months. SASE. Book catalog for SASE.
Nonfiction: Works of original scholarship in the humanities, social sciences and hard sciences. No fiction, cookbooks or popular nonfiction. Query or submit outline/synopsis and sample chapters.
Recent Nonfiction Titles: *Social Justice in the Liberal State*, by B. Ackerman; *Man, The Promising Primate*, by P. Wilson; and *Russia in the Age of Catherine the Great*, by I. de Madariaga.

ZIFF-DAVIS BOOKS, 1 Park Ave., New York NY 10016. (212)725-7894. Publisher: Tinoo Puri. Editorial Director: Jeanne Fredericks. Publishes hardcover and paperback originals (95%) and reprints (5%). Published 25 titles in 1980; plans 28 in 1981. Pays 10-15% royalty; offers variable advance. Photocopied submissions OK. SASE. Decisions in 2 months. Free book catalog.
Nonfiction: How-to in areas of photography, sailing, aviation, skiing, and fishing. Submit tight outline/sample chapters.
Recent Nonfiction Titles: *Laser Sailing*; *The 35mm Handbook*; *Complete Guide to Cibachrome Photography*; and *Air Power*.

Subsidy Book Publishers

The following listings are for book publishing companies who are totally subsidy publishers, meaning they do no standard trade publishing, and will publish a work only if the author is willing to underwrite the entire amount of the venture. This can be costly, and may run into thousands of dollars, usually returning less than 25% of the initial investment.

Read any literature or contracts carefully and thoroughly, being sure that all conditions of the venture (binding, editing, promotion, number of copies to be printed, number of copies to be bound, etc.) are spelled out specifically.

Dorrance & Company, Cricket Terrace Center, Ardmore PA 19003.

Exposition Press, 325 Kings Hwy., Smithtown NY 11787.

Mojave Books, 7040 Darby Ave., Reseda CA 91335.

Vantage Press, 516 W. 34th St., New York NY 10001.

Company Publications

The average reader of a company publication has certain needs that must be met. He turns to his company's publication for information (about benefits, among other things), motivation and inspiration. Writing for this reader, therefore, must be focused and knowledgeable. The writer should be well informed about both the specific company sponsoring the publication and the industry at large.

At the same time, this audience is like any gathering of readers: It likes to have fun. Editors want their publications to be read again and again—but they don't want to sound like every other sponsored publication. So they're interested in writers who can break out of this starched, statistic-laden mold and entertain the reader, as well as serve up the facts.

This is not to devalue research. You will need to be dogged in your approach. Don't be surprised if you have to travel to a plant site, for instance, to learn something about a company's other operations. But an unusual angle will often cinch a sale. Look for it.

Basically, six kinds of company publications exist: 1) employee magazines published to keep employees abreast of company policy and the goings-on of their co-workers; 2) customer magazines edited to remind customers of the desirability of owning or using that company's products or services; 3) stockholder or corporate magazines put out for the shareholder to inform him of financial or policy matters; 4) sales magazines telling the company's field representatives how to better push their wares; 5) dealer magazines published to maintain open channels of communication between manufacturer and independent dealers; and 6) technical service magazines sponsored by companies to which technical data are important in the use and application of products. A single company may publish any or all of these types, enlarging their need for well-written information regarding their products, employees and services.

The trick to successful (meaning selling) writing in the field is the word *company*. These magazines are published as a service to the sponsor, whether in an internal publication (a controlled circulation magazine distributed only among the employees of a company) or an external publication (published for the public relations benefits to the company and circulated among the customers and users of that company's products or services). These publications vary in emphasis, some giving more space to company production-related information, and others highlighting the interesting activities or unique doings of company personnel. Manuscripts lacking a strong company tie-in, or containing derogatory material about the company or its goods are worthless to company publication editors.

Article ideas for company publications are as numerous as the number of companies that publish magazines. Stay alert for new businesses or unique applications of company's products in your own hometown. This is, however, the type of story that a staff writer might normally handle—unless the story takes place in a location so far away from the publication's offices that sending a staffer to cover it would be too expensive.

Because you can't be sure what type of story is normally staff-written, querying these editors instead of sending the complete manuscript unsolicited is wise.

Quite often, an out-of-the-ordinary use of a company's product is the way to a sure sale. Due to the limited nature of the publication, and the fact that editors have run stories on the use of their company's goods in all the conventional ways, an article about some merchant in your town who uses products in an offbeat manner will catch the editor's eye.

Showing recreational and other benefits of a product can also lead to sales, but avoid gimmicks.

Other possible topics you can cover for these magazines include human interest stories about company executives and employees, service articles that help employees work more efficiently or plan their recreation time more constructively, and general interest articles that serve only to entertain.

Photos are a must for most company publications. Shoot photos that prominently display the company's product. Show off the product in a manner that compliments its qualities.

For names and addresses (but no marketing information) of company and in-house publications, see *Gebbie House Magazine Directory* (The National Research Bureau, Inc.).

AMERICAN YOUTH MAGAZINE, Ceco Publishing Co., Campbell-Ewald Bldg., 7th Floor, 30400 Van Dyke, Warren MI 48093. Editor: Betsey Hansell. Emphasizes free enterprise, basic economics, driver safety, career opportunities, celebrities in entertainment and sports for high school students. Magazine published 4 times during school year. Circ. 900,000. Buys all rights. SASE. Reports in 6 weeks.
Nonfiction: Basic economics presented in a lively fashion using young people as examples where possible; career opportunities written by well-known professionals; inspirational, about young people who have successfully started a business or have overcome obstacles to special achievement; driver safety, presented in a unique and non-preachy way; how to get a job, improve self-image, deal with pressure, decide about the future; some general interest and entertainment." *American Youth* is distributed to high school teachers across the country for classroom use. Our goal is to provide informative material in a lively, concise and interesting way. Excellent writing style and accuracy are musts. First-time queries must include clips of published work or a manuscript. Length: 1,000-2,000 words plus a teacher's guide of 500 words where applicable. Pays $350-700.
Photos: B&w contact sheets or negatives, or color transparencies. Payment is negotiated with story. Captions and model releases required.

ASHLAND NOW, Ashland Oil, Inc., Public Relations Dept., Box 391, Ashland KY 41101. (606)329-3780. Editor: Melinda Hamilton. 80% freelance written. Emphasizes issues, stockholder communications and features related to the company's work for an audience of stockholders, employees, opinion makers and community leaders. Quarterly magazine. Circ. 80,000. Pays on acceptance. Buys all rights. Phone queries OK. Previously published submissions OK. Reports in 2 weeks.

BAROID NEWS BULLETIN, Box 1675, Houston TX 77001. Editor-in-Chief: Virginia L. Myers. Editorial Assistant: Ava A. King. 50% freelance written. Emphasizes the petroleum industry for a cross-section of ages, education and interests, although most readers are employed by the energy industries. Quarterly magazine; 36 pages. Circ. 20,000. Pays on acceptance. Buys first North American serial rights. Byline given. Submit seasonal/holiday material 1 year in advance. SASE. Reports in 3 weeks. Free sample copy and writer's guidelines.
Nonfiction: General interest and historical. No travel articles or poetry. Buys 12 mss/year. Submit complete ms or query. Length: 1,000-3,000 words. Pays 8-10¢/word.
Photos: "Photos may be used in the publication, or as reference for illustration art." Submit b&w prints. No additional payment for photos accepted with ms. Captions preferred. Buys first North American serial rights.
Tips: Manuscripts accompanied by good quality photos or illustrations stand a much better chance of acceptance.

BARTER COMMUNIQUE, Full Circle Marketing Corp., Box 2527, Sarasota FL 33578. (813)349-3300. Editor-in-Chief: Robert J. Murely. Emphasizes bartering for radio and TV station owners, cable TV, newspaper and magazine publishers and select travel and advertising agency presidents. Semiannual tabloid; 48 pages. Circ. 30,000. Pays on publication. Rights purchased vary with author and material. Phone queries OK. Simultaneous, photocopied and previously published submissions OK. SASE. Reports in 4 weeks. Free sample copy and writer's guidelines.
Nonfiction: Articles on "barter" (trading products, goods and services, primarily travel and advertising). Length: 1,000 words. "Would like to see travel mss on southeast US and the Bahamas, and unique articles on media of all kinds. Include photos where applicable." Pays $30-50.

THE BLOUNT BANNER, Blount International, Ltd., 4520 Executive Park Dr., Box 4577, Montgomery AL 36116. (205)277-8860. Editor: Victor R. McLean. Emphasizes construction and engi-

neering for a business and professional audience that includes company employees. Bimonthly magazine; 20-24 pages. Circ. 5,000. Pays on publication. Buys all rights. Byline given. Phone queries OK. Photocopied submissions OK. Reports in 3 weeks. Free sample copy.
Nonfiction: Articles on company projects and photo features on project sites and company projects. Query. Length: 1,500-2,500 words. Pays $50-250.
Photos: "All features in our publication require photographic coverage." State availability of photos. Pays $5-50/5x7 b&w glossy print; $25-125/35mm color transparency. Captions required. Buys all rights. Model release required.
Tips: "Writers interested in doing work for our publication should simply write the editor and include a brief summary of experience. Most freelance work is on assignment."

BRISTOL-MYERS NEW YORK, 345 Park Ave., New York NY 10022. (212)644-3956. Editor: Chris Arrington. Emphasizes consumer and pharmaceutical products for employees. Monthly magazine. Circ. 2,000. Pays on publication. Buys first rights. Simultaneous and photocopied submissions OK. SASE. Reports in 3 weeks. Free sample copy.
Nonfiction: Company news, employee news, humor, job safety, new products, photo features and profiles. "Company tie-in essential. We emphasize stories that help employees understand the company and its operations better." Buys less than 1 ms/issue. Query. Length: 350-750 words. Pays $100-300.

BUCKEYE MONITOR, Buckeye Pipe Line Co., 201 King of Prussia Rd., Radnor PA 19087. Editor: Stephen D. Hibbs. Emphasizes petroleum transportation for "blue-collar and technical employees and retirees of petroleum products pipeline. Many readers live in rural areas." Quarterly magazine. Circ. 1,500. Pays on acceptance. Not copyrighted. SASE. Reports in 3 weeks. Free sample copy.
Nonfiction: Employee features based on a personal experience of an employee and in-depth employee profiles; job safety features both on-the-job and off-the-job. Company tie-in is essential. Buys 6 mss/year. Query with clips of published work. Length: 600-1,200 words. Pays $300-500 plus expenses.
Tips: "Writer must be located in our operational area which covers: Middle Atlantic States and the Midwest, east of the Mississippi River. Writer has a better chance if he is willing to travel to remote locations to conduct in-person employee interviews. An increase in our staff has reduced our needs for freelance help at this time."

BUSINESS ON WHEELS, Box 13208, Phoenix AZ 85002. (602)264-1579. Editor: Frederick H. Kling. "External house organ of Goodyear Tire and Rubber Company for distribution to owners and operators of truck fleets, both common carrier trucking systems and trucks used in connection with businesses of various types." Quarterly. Not copyrighted. Pays 25% kill fee. Byline given. Pays on acceptance. "Stories on assignment only. We like to choose our own subjects for case history stories." Query. SASE.
Nonfiction and Photos: "Freelance writers and photographers (especially writer-photographer teams or individuals) are invited to send in their qualifications for assignment of articles on truck-fleet operators in their territory. Pays from $300-350, plus expenses, for complete editorial-photographic coverage, additional for color, if used."

CAL-TAX NEWS, 921 11th St., Suite 800, Sacramento CA 95814. (916)441-0490. Editor: Pam McNally. Emphasizes state and local government expenditures in California for corporate tax managers, local government officials, local taxpayer organizations and California media outlets. Bimonthly newsletter. Circ. 5,500. Pays on acceptance. Not copyrighted. Simultaneous, photocopied and previously published submissions OK. SASE. Reports in 1 week. Free sample copy.
Nonfiction: "Scholarly essays related to public expenditure control." Buys 2-3 mss/year. Query or submit complete ms. Length: 500-2,000 words. Pays $50-250.

CATERPILLAR WORLD, Caterpillar Tractor Co., 100 NE Adams AB1D, Peoria IL 61629. (309)675-5829. Editor-in-Chief: Tom Biederback. 10-25% freelance written. Emphasizes "anything of interest about Caterpillar people, plants, or products. The magazine is distributed to 110,000 Caterpillar people and friends worldwide. It's printed in French and English. Readers' ages, interests and education vary all over the map." Quarterly magazine; 32 pages. Circ. 110,000. Pays on acceptance. Buys one-time rights in 3 languages. Pays 50% kill fee and expenses; "however, we've never had to pay it." Byline given. Phone queries OK. "We rarely use seasonal or holiday material. All material has at least a 3-month lag time." Simultaneous and previously published submissions OK. First submission is usually on speculation. "It's unfortunate, but our experience has shown we need to establish a 'track-record' with freelance writers before we assign articles." Reports in 4 weeks. Free sample copy and writer's guidelines.

Nonfiction: "Everything must have a Caterpillar tie. It doesn't have to be strong, but it has to be there. How-to (buy one piece of equipment and become a millionaire, etc.); general interest (anything that may be of interest to Cat people worldwide); humor (it's hard to find something humorous yet interesting to an international audience; we'd like to see it, however); interview (with any appropriate person: contractor, operator, legislator, etc.); new product (large projects using Cat equipment; must have human interest); personal experience (would be interesting to hear from an equipment operator/writer); photo feature (on anything of interest to Cat people; should feature people as well as product); and profile (of Cat equipment users, etc.). We don't want anything that has not been read and approved by the subjects of the article. Their written approval is a must." Buys 10 mss/year. Query. Length: "Whatever the story is worth." Pays $200 minimum.

Photos: "The only articles we accept without photos are those obviously illustrated by artwork." State availability of photos. Pays $50 minimum for color. Submit transparencies, contact sheets or negatives. Captions required; "at least who is in the picture and what they're doing." Model release required.

Tips: "Best way to get story ideas is to stop in at local Cat dealers and ask about big sales, events, etc."

THE COMPASS, Mobil Sales and Supply Corp., 150 E. 42nd St., New York NY 10017. Editor-in-Chief: R. Gordon MacKenzie. 60% freelance written. Emphasizes marine or maritime activities for the major international deep sea shipowners and ship operators who are Mobil's marine customers. 40 pages. Circ. 20,000. Pays on acceptance. Buys one-time rights. Byline given. Simultaneous, photocopied and previously published submissions OK. SASE. Reports in 2 weeks. Free sample copy. Currently overstocked on stories through 1981.
Nonfiction: Marine material only. General interest, historical, nostalgia, new product, personal experience and technical. No travelogues. Query or submit complete ms. Length: 2,000-4,000 words. Pays $125-250.
Photos: Purchased with accompanying ms. Submit 5x7 or larger b&w prints or 35mm color transparencies. Offers no additional payment for photos accepted with ms. Captions preferred. Buys one-time rights. Model release required.

CORRESPONDENT, Aid Association for Lutherans, Appleton WI 54919. (414)734-5721. Editor: Linda J. Peterson. Emphasizes fraternal insurance for Lutherans and their families. Quarterly magazine. Circ. 750,000. Pays on publication. Buys one-time rights. Simultaneous and photocopied submissions OK. SASE. Reports in 1 month. Free sample copy.
Nonfiction: Profiles of Lutherans doing unusual jobs. Company tie-in essential. Buys 2-3 mss/year. Query. Length: 500-1,500 words. Pays 10¢/word.
Photos: Pays $5 for b&w glossy prints; $10 for color prints or slides.

CORVETTE NEWS, c/o GM Photographic, 3001 Van Dyke, Warren MI 48090. Managing Editor: Jack Alden. For Corvette owners worldwide. Bimonthly magazine. Circ. 265,000. Buys all rights. Pays on acceptance. Free sample copy and editorial guidelines. Query. SASE.
Nonfiction: "Articles must be of interest to this audience. Subjects considered include: (1) Technical articles dealing with engines, paint, body work, suspension, parts searches, etc. (2) Competition, 'Vettes vs. 'Vettes, or 'Vettes vs. others. (3) Profiles of Corvette owners/drivers. (4) General interest articles, such as the unusual history of a particular early model Corvette, and perhaps its restoration; one owner's do-it-yourself engine repair procedures, maintenance procedures; Corvettes in unusual service; hobbies involving Corvettes; sports involving Corvettes. (5) Celebrity owner profiles. (6) Special Corvette events such as races, drags, rallies, concourse, gymkhanas, slaloms. (7) Corvette club activities. We're willing to consider articles on Corvette lifestyles. This could include pieces not only about the mechanically-minded (who own Corvettes) but also about the fashion-conscious and people seeking the active good life. Send an approximately 100-word prospectus on the proposed article and add a statement about how you are prepared to supplement it with drawings or photographs." Length: 1,200-3,600 words. Pays $150-400.
Photos: Color transparencies required. Offers no additional payment for photos accepted with ms.

CREDITHRIFTALK, CREDITHRIFT Financial, Box 59, Evansville IN 47701. (812)464-6638. Editor-in-Chief: Gregory E. Thomas. Emphasizes consumer finance. All readers are employees of CREDITHRIFT Finanical or one of its financial or insurance subsidiaries, age range 18-65, with most in the 25-45 bracket. Most are high school graduates with one year of college, interested in company advancement. Monthly magazine; 12-16 pages. Circ. 3,000. Pays on acceptance. Not copyrighted. Pays 100% kill fee. Byline given only if requested. Submit seasonal/holiday material 5 months in advance of issue date. Simultaneous, photocopied and previously published submissions OK. Reports in 2 weeks. Free sample copy for SASE.

Nonfiction: Interview (must be with company employee; subject need not be limited to consumer finance and could center on employee's personal experience, hobby, volunteer work, etc.); personal opinion; photo feature (employee engaged in a unique activity); profile (employee); and finance industry trends. Query. Length: 800-3,000 words. Pays $35 minimum.
Photos: State availability of photos. Pays $15 minimum/b&w photo; submit contact sheet. Captions preferred. Buys one-time rights. Model release required "in some cases where a non-employee is included in the photo."

CROSSROADS MAGAZINE, Signature Publications, 2020 Dempster, Evanston IL 60602. Editorial Director: Michael J. Connelly. Emphasizes travel, automotive subjects, recreational vehicles (RVs) and camping for middle-income readers, 25-65 years old. Bimonthly magazine; 64 pages. Circ. 1,200,000. Pays on acceptance. Buys first North American serial rights. Reports in 1 month. Free sample copy and writer's guidelines to published writers.
Nonfiction: How-to, informational, historical, humor, interview, nostalgia, profile, travel, photo feature and semi-technical. "Author must demonstrate why he is best qualified to handle subject; subject should be unusual or surprising—not a cliché." Buys 9 mss/issue. Query with clips of published work. Length: 600-2,500 words. Pays about 20¢/word.
Photos: Pays $25 for b&w and $50 minimum for color. Captions required; model releases preferred.

THE ENERGY PEOPLE, PSE&G, 80 Park Place, Newark NJ 07101. (201)430-5989. Editor: Eugene Murphy. For employees. Quarterly magazine. Circ. 19,000. Pays on acceptance. Not copyrighted. Simultaneous, photocopied and previously published submissions OK. SASE. Reports in 3 weeks. Free sample copy.
Nonfiction: Company news, employee news and humor (industry-related). Company tie-in preferred. Buys 3 mss/year. Query with clips of published work. Pays $75-200.

THE ENTHUSIAST, 3700 W. Juneau, Milwaukee WI 53208. (414)342-4680. Editor: Bob Klein. 35% freelance written. Published by Harley-Davidson Motor Co., Inc. for "motorcycle riders of all ages, education, and professions. Our publication is read by a 'following' of people who live, eat and die Harley-Davidson. They want to know what is happening with new designs and what people are doing with present-day bikes." Circ. 170,000. Quarterly magazine. Not copyrighted. Pays on publication. Free sample copy and writer's guidelines. Photocopied submissions OK. Submit seasonal material 2 months in advance. Reports in 6-8 weeks. SASE.
Nonfiction and Photos: "Stories on motorcycling—humor, technical, racing, touring, adventures, competitive events. All articles should feature Harley-Davidson products and not mention competitive products. We do not want stories concerning sex, violence, or anything harmful to the image of motorcycling. We use travel stories featuring Harley-Davidson motorcycles, which must be illustrated with good quality photos of the motorcycle and travelers with scenic background taken on the trip. Also needed are stories of off-road usage, e.g., scrambles, racing, trail riding, or any other unusual usage." Informational articles, how-to's, personal experience articles, interviews, profiles, inspirational pieces, humor, historical articles, photo features, travel articles, and technical articles. "No stories that say, 'then we went north, to St. Louis and built a campfire,' or 'Bill Jones has been riding for 200 years.' " Query or submit complete ms. Length: 3,000 words. Pays 5¢ "per published word, or as previously agreed upon."
Photos: Submit photos that blend with the story. Emphasis is on "people with their bikes, not a bike that has some people tagging along." Photos purchased with mss and without mss; captions optional. Uses "quality b&w or color 35mm transparencies or larger." Pays $7.50-25.

EUA SPECTRUM, EUA Service Corp., Box 212, Lincoln RI 02865. (401)333-1400. Editor: Ms. D. Switzer. Monthly. Circ. 2,500. Pays on publication. Not copyrighted. Submit seasonal or holiday material 2 months in advance. SASE. Reports monthly.
Nonfiction: How-to articles, humor, think pieces, new product coverage, photo, and travel and safety articles. Length: open.

THE FLYING A, Aeroquip Corp., 300 S. East Ave., Jackson MI 49203. (517)787-8121. Editor-in-Chief: Wayne D. Thomas. 10% freelance written. Emphasizes Aeroquip customers and products. Quarterly magazine; 24 pages. Circ. 32,000. Pays on acceptance. Buys all rights. Phone queries OK. Simultaneous submissions OK. Reports in 1 month.
Nonfiction: General interest (feature stories with emphasis on free enterprise, business-related articles); interview (by assignment only); and human interest. "An Aeroquip tie-in in a human interest story is preferred." No jokes, no sample copies; no cartoons. Buys 1 ms/issue. Query with biographic sketch and clips of published work. Length: 1-2 printed pages. Pays $50 minimum.
Photos: "Photos are generally by specific assignment only."
Fillers: Human interest. Pays $50 minimum for a one-page article.

FRIENDLY EXCHANGE, Webb Company, 1999 Shepard Rd., St. Paul MN 55116. (612)690-7383. Editor: Adele Malott. Quarterly magazine "designed to encourage the sharing or exchange of ideas, information and fun among its readers, for young, traditional families between the ages of 19 and 39 who live in the western half of the United States." Estab. 1981. Circ. 4.5 million. Pays on acceptance. Offers 25% kill fee. Buys first North American serial rights and non-exclusive reprint rights for use in other Webb publications. Submit seasonal/holiday material 6 months in advance. Simultaneous queries and photocopied submissions OK. SASE. Reports in 6 weeks. Sample copy free for 9x12 SASE and 93¢ postage; writer's guidelines free for business size SAE and 1 first class stamp.
Nonfiction: General interest (family activities, sports and outdoors, consumer topics, personal finance); historical/nostalgic (heritage and culture); how-to (decorate and garden); travel (domestic); and lifestyle. "Whenever possible, a story should be told through the experiences of actual people or families in such a way that our readers will want to share experiences they have had with similar activities or interests. No product publicity material." Buys 36 mss/year. Query. Length: 1,000-2,500 words. Pays $250-500/article.
Photos: Contact: Art Director, Webb Company. Send photos with ms. Pays $150-400 for 35mm color transparencies; and $75 for 8x10 b&w prints. Pays on publication.
Columns/Departments: The Family Treasury (money saving and household hints); Behind the Scenes (how things work); and Whatever Happened To? (public personalities). Buys 20 mss/year. Pays $150-250/article.

FRIENDS MAGAZINE, Ceco Publishing Co., 30400 Van Dyke Blvd., Warren MI 48093. (313)575-9400. Managing Editor: Bill Gray. 75% freelance written. "The only common bond our audience shares is they own Chevrolets." Monthly magazine; 32 pages. Circ. 2,000,000. Pays on acceptance. Rights vary. Submit seasonal/holiday material 6 months in advance. Simultaneous and photocopied submissions OK. SASE. Reports in 4 weeks. Free sample copy and writer's guidelines.
Nonfiction: General interest (lifestyle); historical (when story has contemporary parallel); how-to (service features for families, especially financial topics); humor (any subject); travel; and photo feature (strong photo essays that say something about American lifestyle, especially focusing on family life). "We're looking for freelancers who can spot lifestyle trends in their areas that have potential national impact. We're looking for fresh ideas and different ways of telling familiar stories."
Photos: State availability of photos. Pays $50 for b&w contact sheets and $75 for 35mm color transparencies. Captions and model releases required.

GEMCO COURIER, Lu Gem Advertising, 6565 Knott Ave., Buena Park CA 90620. (714)739-2200. Articles Editor: Susan Spies, 390 Santa Monica Blvd. #309, Santa Monica CA 90401. Monthly magazine covering how-to and product-related articles for a national audience of employees of a discount department store chain. Circ. 5.5 million. Pays on acceptance. Byline given. Pays 10% kill fee. Buys one-time rights ("6-months exclusive"). Submit seasonal/holiday material 4½ months in advance. SASE. Reports in 1 month. "We cannot officially accept articles until the actual Table of Contents for a given month's issue is approved by Gemco." Sample copy for SAE and 4 first class stamps; writer's guidelines for SAE and 1 first class stamp.
Nonfiction: General interest, how-to, money-saving ideas, energy articles, and product-use pieces for merchandise carried at Gemco/Memco stores. "*Courier* articles are based on fact and on sound ideas for improving our readers' quality of life. Do remember money counts and don't send queries on subjects like 'Cooking with Truffles' or 'How to Avoid Jet Lag on your 'Round the World Vacation'. Instead, consider an article like 'Working Wonders with Leftovers' or 'Great Gifts to Make Instead of Buy.' Bright ideas really count with us." Especially needs holiday-related pieces. No humorous, first-person, or short-on-fact pieces. "The currently popular 'psychological genre' is not for us." Buys 150 mss/year. ("No editorial in the December and January issues.") Query with clips of published work. Length: 225-1,000 words. Pays $75-400. "Note: Do not send correspondence to publisher's address; send to Susan Spies."
Tips: "All editorial sections of the *Courier* are open to freelancers, except the medical column, which is written by an M.D. Write for guidelines; then send a specific query and samples of your previously published work. We look for fresh, practical ideas that will interest our readers. Please don't send broad topic queries; instead look for one tight, unusual angle that will render real information to our readership."

HANDS ON, Shopsmith, Inc., 4530 Wadsworth Rd., Dayton OH 45414. (513)276-5201. Editor: Nick Engler. Bimonthly magazine featuring woodworking for an audience of novices and skilled woodworkers primarily between the ages of 35 and 65, half with a college degree and most of whom make $15,000 and over/year. Circ. 1,000,000. Pays on acceptance. Buys all rights. Submit

seasonal material 6 months in advance. Simultaneous, photocopied and previously published submissions OK. SASE. Reports in 4 weeks. Free sample copy and writer's guidelines.
Nonfiction: General interest (design ideas); historical (history of tools and woodworking); how-to (woodwork, care for shop and tools); humor; interview (of craftsmen and pro woodworkers); profile; new product (tools, inventions, better ways of performing shop operations); photo feature (on architecture and wood design). "No ideas for extremely complicated or costly projects." Buys 24 mss/year. Query. Length: 1,500 words maximum. Pays $25-500. "From time to time we do 'theme books.' Examples are issues on children's toys and building your own home. If a good freelancer expresses an interest in writing for these theme books, we'll send him our game plan."
Photos: Send photos with ms. Pays $10-25 for 8x10 b&w glossy prints and color transparencies. Reviews contact sheets. Captions required. Buys one-time rights.
Columns/Departments: Money Makers (simple projects that can be sold in craft shops); For Young Hands (describes woodworking projects for kids); MAKE-IT-FIX-IT (short how-to's and shop tips, 200 words maximum). Buys 12 mss/year. Send complete ms. Pays $25-50.
Fillers: Anecdotes, short humor and newsbreaks (woodworking news). Buys 12 mss/year. Length: 50-200 words. Pays $25 maximum.
Tips: "Become familiar with the Shopsmith tool line. Send us a project idea that can be built on our tools. We're more interested in imagination, ingenuity and good, clean craftsmanship than we are in your writing ability. Describe your workshop to show us how serious you are about woodworking."

HNG MAGAZINE, Houston Natural Gas, Box 1188, Houston TX 77001. (713)654-6814. Editor: Elaine McCasland. Emphasizes the energy industry—oil, gas, coal, industrial gases and river commerce—for employees, through articles about its subsidiary companies. Quarterly magazine. Circ. 9,000. Pays on acceptance. Buys all rights. Reports in 1 month. Query first.
Nonfiction: Company tie-in mandatory. "We have locations worldwide and would consider articles that relate to our company through these locations. These might be of historical, unusual event or human interest."

INLAND, The Magazine of the Middle West, Inland Steel Co., 30 W. Monroe St., Chicago IL 60603. (312)346-0300. Managing Editor: Sheldon A. Mix. 25% freelance written. Emphasizes steel products, services and company personnel. Quarterly magazine; 24 pages. Circ. 12,000. Pays on acceptance. Buys one-time rights. Kill fee: "We have always paid the full fee on articles that have been killed." Byline given. Submit seasonal/holiday material at least a year in advance. Simultaneous submissions OK. SASE. Reports in 6-8 weeks. Free sample copy.
Nonfiction: Articles, essays, humorous commentaries and pictorial essays. "We encourage individuality. Half of each issue deals with staff-written steel subjects; half with widely ranging nonsteel matter. Articles and essays related somehow to the Midwest (Illinois, Wisconsin, Minnesota, Michigan, Missouri, Iowa, Nebraska, Kansas, North Dakota, South Dakota, Indiana and Ohio) in such subject areas as history, folklore, sports, humor, the seasons, current scene generally; nostalgia and reminiscence if well done and appeal is broad enough. But subject is less important than treatment. We like perceptive, thoughtful writing, and fresh ideas and approaches. Please don't send slight, rehashed historical pieces or any articles of purely local interest." Personal experience, profile, humor, historical, think articles, personal opinion and photo essays. Length: 1,200-5,000 words. Payment depends on individual assignment or unsolicted submission.
Photos: Purchased with or without mss. Captions required. "Payment for pictorial essay same as for text feature."
Tips: "Our publication particularly needs humor that is neither threadbare nor in questionable taste, and shorter pieces (800-1,500 words) in which word-choice and wit are especially important. A writer who knows our needs and believes in himself should keep trying."

LIVING TRENDS, Webb Company, 1999 Shepard Rd., St. Paul MN 55116. (612)690-7304. Editor: Don Picard. Quarterly magazine covering mobile home living for people who live in mobile homes and are insured by Foremost Insurance Company. Estab. 1980. Circ. 200,000. Pays after acceptance by client. Byline given. Offers 25% kill fee. Buys first North American serial rights and non-exclusive reprint rights. SASE. Reports in 1 month on queries. Sample copy free for 9x12 SAE and 2 first class stamps; writer's guidelines free for business size SASE and 1 first class stamp.
Nonfiction: Interview/profile (mobile home owners); travel (domestic and inexpensive) and service pieces for mobile home owners on maintenance, decorating and storage. Buys 28 mss/year. Query. Length: 500-1,200. Pays $200-$350/article.
Photos: State availability of photos. Reviews 35mm color transparencies and 8x10 b&w prints. Pays $100 inside color; $50 inside b&w; $300 color cover. Captions and model releases required. Buys first rights and non-exclusive reprint rights for other Webb publications.

MARATHON WORLD, Marathon Oil Co., 539 S. Main St., Findlay OH 45840. (419)422-2121. Editor-in-Chief: Norman V. Richards. 20% freelance written. Emphasizes petroleum/energy for shareholders, educators, legislators, government officials, libraries, community leaders, students and employees. Quarterly magazine; 28 pages. Circ. 72,000. Pays on acceptance. Buys first North American serial rights. Pays 20% kill fee. Byline given on contents page, not with article. Photocopied submissions OK. SASE. Reports in 3 weeks. Free sample copy and writer's guidelines.
Nonfiction: Informational, interview and photo feature. Especially needs "articles on subjects to help readers live better, handle problems (economic, social, personal, medical) more effectively, and generally get more out of life. We like articles on self-awareness, science, cultural events, outdoor sports and activities, and Americana in areas where Marathon operates. No articles promoting travel by car. Freelancers should not attempt to sell articles on Marathon or oil industry operations; these are staff written." Buys 2-3 mss/issue. Query. Length: 800-1,500 words. Pays $300-1,000.
Photos: Photos purchased with accompanying ms or on assignment. Pay negotiable for b&w and color photos. Total purchase price for a ms includes payment for photos.
Tips: "Because of the special nature of the *World* as a corporate external publication and the special limits imposed on content, the best approach is through initial query. Include as many details as possible in a 1-2 page letter."

MORE BUSINESS, 11 Wimbledon Court Jerico, New York 11753. Editor: Trudy Settel. "We sell publications material to business for consumer use (incentives, communicaton, public relations)—look for book ideas and manuscripts." Monthly magazine. Circ. 10,000. Pays on acceptance. Buys all rights. SASE. Reports in 1 month. Free writer's guidelines.
Nonfiction: General interest, how-to, vocational techniques, nostalgia, photo feature, profile and travel. Buys 10-20 mss/year. Word length varies with article. Payment negotiable. Query. Pays $4,000-7,000 for book mss.

NAUTILUS MAGAZINE, Nautilus/Virginia, Box 160, Independence VA 24348. (703)773-2881. Editor: James P. Martin. Emphasis is on enjoying life through physical fitness. We are written for "Every Active Body!" Published bimonthly. Estab. 1979. Circ. 70,000. Pays on publication. Byline given. Buys all rights. Phone queries OK. Closing date for manuscripts is 3 months prior to cover date. Photocopied and previously published submissions OK. SASE. Reports in 3 weeks. Sample copy $1; free writer's guidelines.
Nonfiction: "We are very receptive to articles that are entertaining, informative, and inspirational, with the focus on physical fitness. We are not a muscle-builder magazine, but instead concentrate on the benefits of physical fitness to persons in every sport (professional and amateur), recreation, and area of human interest. We seek articles dealing with people of all ages, occupations, and avocations. Articles should not dwell primarily on Nautilus equipment or technique, but on people enjoying life through physical fitness." Buys 50 mss/year. Query. Length: 300-3,000 words. Pays $3.50 per published column inch (about 10¢ per word).
Photos: State availability of photos or send with ms. We prefer color slides or color transparencies. B&w given low priority. Photos must be of good to excellent quality. Pays $20-40 for color, up to $300 for cover photo. Captions preferred. Rights vary.
Columns/Departments: Fitness & Senior Citizens, Fitness & Handicapped, The International Scene, Men and Women in Sports, Fitness in the Armed Forces, For Women Only, Fitness in Industry, Fitness and Youth, Nonfiction Humor, Sports/Medicine, Nutrition and Diet, Fitness Trends. Query. Length: 300-2,000 words. Pays same as above.
Tips: "We will not consider articles highlighting competitor equipment, fitness fads, or fitness information based upon other than proven scientific fact. We publish only the truth! Competent, reliable, interesting writers can expect to become regional field editors."

PGW NEWS, Philadelphia Gas Co., 1800 N. 9th St., Philadelphia PA 19122, (215)796-1260. Communications Administrator: William B. Hall, III. Monthly magazine covering gas utility; for employees, retirees, their families, suppliers, other utility editors in US and abroad. Circ. 5,000. Pays on acceptance. Buys one-time rights. Submit seasonal/holiday material 3-4 months in advance. Articles should relate to Greater Philadelphia or Pennsylvania—New Jersey regions. SASE. Reports in 2 months. Free sample copy.
Nonfiction: How-to (be a better employee); informational; inspirational (from a job viewpoint). Send complete ms. Length: 1,000-2,000 words. Pays $25 minimum.

PORT OF BALTIMORE MAGAZINE, The World Trade Center Baltimore, Baltimore MD 21202. (301)659-4550. Editor: L. Cromwell McDaniel. Monthly magazine published by the Maryland Port Administration covering maritime industry for freight forwarders, customhouse brokers, shippers and port service industries. "This publication's slant is the advantages and capabilities of the port of Baltimore." Circ. 12,000. Pays on acceptance or publication. Not copyrighted. Free sample copy.

Nonfiction: Company news (on firms involved in the maritime industry); historical (maritime facets of the port of Baltimore); job safety; vocational techniques; new product (maritime-related products); profile (on companies involved in the maritime industry); and technical. Company tie-in essential. Buys 4 mss/year. Query. Length: "depends on topic—will advise." Pays $100-$150.

Photos: B&w for inside of magazine; color for cover. Payment negotiable.

Tips: "Write an article of 750 words or more (1500 limit) that is about maritime matters and somehow can be applied to the port or to the Baltimore maritime community."

THE PRESS, The Greater Buffalo Press, Inc., 302 Grote St., Buffalo NY 14207. Managing Editor: Janet Tober. Bimonthly tabloid for advertising executives at Sunday newspapers, ad agencies, retail chains and cartoonists who create the Sunday funnies. Circ. 3,000. Pays on acceptance. Buys all rights. Submit seasonal/holiday material 2 months in advance. Photocopied submissions and previously published submissions OK. SASE. Reports in 2 weeks. Sample copy 50¢; free writer's guidelines.

Nonfiction: Short biographies of people in advertising, retailing, business, or unusual occupations. No travel/leisure articles. Back issues sent upon written request. Buys 4-6 mss/issue. Query. Length: 800-1,500 words. Pays $100-125.

Photos: State availability of photos (with ms only). Uses negatives or prints (color preferred). Offers no additonal payment for photos accepted with ms. Captions optional. Photos are usually returned after publication. "We do not accept photographs or artwork unless they accompany a ms."

RAYTHEON MAGAZINE, Raytheon Company, 141 Spring St., Lexington MA 02173. (617)862-7600, ext 413. Editor-in-Chief: Robert P. Suarez. Quarterly magazine for Raytheon stockholders, employees, customers, suppliers, plant city officials, libraries, interested persons. "Ours is a company publication that strives to avoid sounding like a company publication. All stories must involve some aspect of Raytheon or its products." Estab. 1981. Circ. 175,000. Pays on acceptance. Byline given. Free sample copy.

Nonfiction: General interest, humor, interview/profile, new product, nostalgia, photo feature, technical and travel. "This is a corporate publication designed to illustrate the breadth of Raytheon Company in a low-key manner through six general-interest articles per issue. Photos are used liberally, top quality and exclusively color. Stories are by assignment only." Buys 6 mss/issue. Query with clips of published work, stating specialities, credentials and other publication credits. Length: 800-1,000. Pays $400-$1,000/article.

Columns/Departments: Send clips of published work.

Tips: "Submit resume and magazine-style writing samples. We are looking for established writers who are capable of crisp, interesting magazine journalism. We are not looking to promote Raytheon, but rather to inform our audience about the company, very subtly. Heavy marketing-style or house organ writing is of no interest to us."

REVIEW, North American Benefit Association, 1338 Military St., Call Box 69, Port Huron MI 48060. (313)985-5191. Editor: V.E. "Jean" Farmer. Associate Editor: Patricia Pfeifer. Bimonthly magazine of general interest, family oriented, for people of all ages and walks of life who are members of fraternal insurance associations in the United States and Canada. Circ. 42,000. Pays on publication. Buys one-time rights. Phone queries OK. Submit seasonal material 5 months in advance. "Manuscripts and art material will be carefully considered, but received only with the understanding that North American Benefit Association shall not be responsible for loss or injury." Simultaneous, photocopied and previously published submissions OK. SASE. Reports in 1 month. Free sample copy.

Nonfiction: General interest (American customs); historical (United States); humor (on daily living); inspirational (slice of life stories); nostalgia (family oriented holiday features); profile (of interesting ordinary people); and personal experience. Buys 1 ms/issue. Query with clips of previously published work. Length: 1,000-1,500 words. Pays up to 5¢/word.

Photos: State availability of photos. Pays $15 minimum/5x7 b&w glossy print. Captions and model release required.

ROSEBURG WOODSMAN, Roseburg Lumber Co., 1221 SW Yamhill, Portland OR 97205. (503)227-3693. Editor: Shirley P. Rogers. Monthly magazine for wholesale and retail lumber dealers and other buyers of forest products, such as furniture manufacturers. Emphasis on company products. Publishes a special Christmas issue. Circ. 10,000. Buys all rights. No byline given. Buys approximately 10-12 mss/year. Pays on publication. Free sample copy and writer's guidelines. No photocopied or simultaneous submissions. Submit seasonal material 6 months in advance. Reports in 1 week.

Nonfiction: Features on the "residential, commercial and industrial applications of wood products, such as lumber plywood, prefinished wall paneling, and particleboard, particularly Roseburg Lumber Co. products. We look for unique or unusual uses of wood stories and stories on hobbyists and craftsmen. No 'clever', 'wise' or witty contributions unless they tell a fascinating story and are well-illustrated." Query or submit complete ms. Length: 250-500 words. Pays $50-$100.

Photos: "Photos are essential. Good pictures will sell us on a story. B&w photos immediately relegate a story to secondary position." Prefers 120 color transpaencies but 35mm is acceptable. Pays $25-$50/color transparency or color-corrected print; more for cover photo. Pays $10-$15/b&w glossy print purchased with ms.

Tips: "I sometimes hire a freelancer 'on assignment' at a higher rate. Send letter specifying experience, publications, types of stories and geographic area covered. We have an absolute need for good, striking, interesting photos."

ROWAN GRAPEVINE, Rowan Companies, Inc., 1900 Post Oak Tower, 5051 Westheimer, Houston TX 77056. (713)621-7800. Editor: Linda M. Copley. Quarterly magazine for workers on drilling rigs, pilots of rotor/fixed wing craft, mechanics for aircraft and administrative personnel. Circ. 3,500. Pays on publication. Not copyrighted. SASE. Reports in 2 weeks. Free sample copy.

Nonfiction: General interest (public service such as health and finance); job safety; technical (on petroleum/aviation); and travel (Southeast Asia, Scotland, the Middle East and Latin America). Query. Length: 500-1,500 words. Pays $50-250.

RURALITE, Box 557, Forest Grove OR 97116. (503)357-2105. Editor: Ken Dollinger. Monthly magazine primarily slanted toward small town and rural families, served by consumer-owned electric utilities in Washington, Oregon, Idaho, Nevada and Alaska. "Ours is an old-fashioned farm-house publication, with something for all members of the family." Circ. 196,000. Buys first North American rights. Byline given. Pays on acceptance. Submit seasonal material at least 3 months in advance. Query. SASE. Sample copies 50¢.

Nonfiction: Walter J. Wentz, nonfiction editor. Primarily human-interest stories about rural or small-town folk, preferably living in areas (Northwest states and Alaska) served by Rural Electric Cooperatives. Articles emphasize self-reliance, overcoming of obstacles, cooperative effort, hard or interesting work, unusual or interesting avocations, odd or unusual hobbies or histories, public spirit or service, humor, inspirational. Will also consider how-to, advice for rural folk, little-known and interesting Northwest history, people or events. "Looking specifically for energy (sources, use, conservation) slant and items relating to rural electric cooperatives." No "sentimental nostalgia or subjects outside the Pacific Northwest." Length 500-1,500 words. Pays $20-80, depending upon length, quality, appropriateness and interest, number and quality of photos.

Photos: Reviews b&w contact sheets. Offers no additional payment for photos accepted with ms.

SAVER, First Federal Savings and Loan Association of Chicago, Box 4444, Chicago IL 60680. Editor-in-Chief: Marilyn Hopkins. Managing Editor: Chester Myszkowski. Quarterly magazine covering saving, mortgage, and lending news of the savings and loan industry for Chicago area families with middle and upper-middle incomes. Circ. 300,000. Pays on publication "or acceptance if story is done a year in advance." Buys one-time rights. Submit seasonal/holiday material 1 year in advance of issue date. Simultaneous and photocopied submissions OK. Reports in 8 weeks. Free sample copy.

Nonfiction: "Articles of general interest to families in the Chicago area: travel, arts/crafts, things to do, etc." Historical (Chicago, Illinois or closeby features); interview (with well-known figure in the world of budgeting/personal finance); and travel (Chicago, Illinois, or nearby). "We are always looking for clearly written, topical financial stories for the average consumer. No general interest articles about a holiday, etc." Buys 2 mss/issue. Query with clips of previously published work. Length: 1,000-3,000 words. Pays $250 minimum.

SEVENTY SIX MAGAZINE, Box 7600, Los Angeles CA 90051. Editor: Sergio Ortiz. Bimonthly publication of the Union Oil Company for employees, retirees, elected officials and community leaders. Circ. 42,000. Not copyrighted. Buys 5-6 mss/year. Pays on acceptance. Free sample copy and writer's guidelines. Reports "as soon as possible." SASE.

Nonfiction: Buys informational, profile, humor historical articles about the petroleum industry, Union Oil Company, or Union Oil's employees or retirees. No articles about service stations or dealers. No travel features. "Please query first." Pays 15¢/word minimum.

Photos: 8x10 b&w glossy prints and 35mm color transparencies purchased with mss for extra payment. Captions required.

SMALL WORLD, Volkswagen of America, 818 Sylvan Ave., Englewood Cliffs NJ 07632. Editor: Burton Unger. Magazine published 5 times/year for Volkswagen owners in the United States.

Circ. 400,000. Buys all rights. Byline given. Buys about 20 mss/year. Pays on acceptance. Free writer's guidelines. Reports in 6 weeks. SASE.
Nonfiction: "Interesting stories on people using Volkswagens; useful owner modifications of the vehicle; travel pieces with the emphasis on people, not places; Volkswagenmania stories, personality pieces, inspirational and true adventure articles. VW arts and crafts, etc. The style should be light. All stories must have a VW tie-in, preferably with a new generation VW model, i.e., Rabbit, Scirocco, Jetta, Vanagon or Dasher. Our approach is subtle, however, and we try to avoid obvious product puffery, since *Small World* is not an advertising medium. We prefer a first-person, people-oriented handling. "If you have a long feature possibility in mind, please query first. Though queries should be no longer than 2 pages, they ought to include a working title, a short, general summary of the article, and an outline of the specific points to be covered. We strongly advise writers to read at least 2 past issues before working on a story." Length: 1,500 words maximum; shorter pieces, some as short as 450 words, often receive closer attention." Pays $100 per printed page for photographs and text; otherwise, a portion of that amount, depending on the space allotted. Most stories go 2 pages; some run 3 or 4.
Photos: Submit photo samples with query. Photos purchased with ms; captions required. "We prefer color transparencies, 35mm or larger. All photos should carry the photographer's name and address. If the photographer is not the author, both names should appear on the first page of the text. Where possible, we would like a selection of at least 40 transparencies. It is recommended that at least one show the principal character or author; another, all or a recognizable portion of a VW in the locale of the story. Quality photography can often sell a story that might be otherwise rejected. Every picture should be identified or explained." Model releases required. Pays $250 maximum for front cover photo.
Fillers: "Short, humorous anecdotes about Volkswagens." Pays $15.

SPERRY UNIVAC NEWS, Box 500, Blue Bell PA 19424. (215)542-4215. Editor: Pete Sigmund. Emphasizes computers for "all US employees of Sperry Univac." Monthly newspaper. Circ. 40,000. Buys all rights. Photocopied submissions OK. Reports in 1 week.
Nonfiction: Company news, employee news, general interest, and how-to. Company tie-in preferred. Query. Pay negotibable.

SUN MAGAZINE, Sun Co., 1608 Walnut St., Philadelphia PA 19103. Editor: Elaine Reba Rose. Quarterly magazine for "local, state and national government officials; community leaders; news and financial communicators; educators, shareholders, customers, and employees of Sun Company." Circ. 140,000. Not copyrighted. Byline given. Buys 1-2 mss/year. "Most are staff-written." Pays on acceptance. Free sample copy. Reports in 6 weeks. Query.
Nonfiction: "Articles only. Subject matter should be related to Sun Company, oil industry or national energy situation. Articles should be directed toward a general audience and written in magazine-feature style and a nontechnical approach. Travel themes are currently being overworked." Buys informational articles, interviews, profiles, historical articles, think pieces, coverage of successful business operations. Length: 1,000-3,000 words.
Photos: Purchased on assignment; captions optional. "We do not buy photos on spec."

SUNSHINE SERVICE NEWS, Florida Power & Light Co., Box 529100, Miami FL 33152. (305)552-3891. Editor: Jay Osborne. Monthly employee newspaper for the electrical utility industry. Circ. 12,000. Pays on publication. Not copyrighted. Reports in 1 week. Free sample copy.
Nonfiction: Company news, employee news, general interest, historical, how-to, humor and job safety. Company tie-in preferred. Query. Pays $25-100.

TAXING TIMES MAGAZINE, Tax Information Center, R.D. 1, New Concord OH 43762. Editor: Carol W. Miller. Monthly magazine about taxes, real estate and investment for the fee-paying clients of the Tax Information Center and medical practitioners throughout the United States. Estab. 1979. Controlled Circ. Pays on acceptance. Buys all rights. Submit seasonal material 2 months in advance. SASE. Reports in 3 weeks. Free sample copy and writer's guidelines.
Nonfiction: Exposé (related to taxes, real estate and investment); how-to; interview (of prominent tax legislators, tax accountants and tax collectors); and personal experience (with the I.R.S.). "We're still in the process of planning our editorial calendar and are open to any suggestions related to tax and estate planning subjects, the world of real estate investment and the broad spectrum of personal finance. Seek out subjects that appeal to a well-educated, affluent readership with considerable discretionary income and major tax and estate planning problems. Double check all the facts and try to impart the the information in a terse, lucid and interesting manner." Buys 2 mss/issue. Query. Length: 3,000-5,000 words. Pays $100-$500.
Photos: State availability of photos or send photos with ms. Pays $10-$25/5x7 and 8x10 b&w

glossy prints. Pays $10-25/2¼x2¼ color transparencies. Captions and model release required. Buys one-time rights.

Columns/Departments: Editor: Daniel Kaczmarski. Taxing Times (news briefs dealing with taxes, real estate and finance); People (items about individuals involved with tax problems and movements); Sheople (about people who practiced tax evasion and were caught); Tax Watch (current, important legislation or possible legislation); Books (reviews of books dealing with taxes, real estate and investment); and "IRS" at Work (current, important I.R.S. rulings and tax court decisions). Buys 5 mss/issue. Send complete ms. Length: 150-500 words. Pays $10-$25.

Tips: "A freelancer can break in by becoming knowledgeable about tax, financial and inflationary trends, underscored by factual and accurate reporting. For an initial submission, a writer should submit a detailed query of up to 250 words, supplemented by a list of his academic and writing credits."

TIME BREAK, GeoSpace Corp., Box 36374, Houston TX 77036. (713)666-1611. Editor: Lee C. Dominey. Semiannual magazine published in winter (Jan-Feb) and summer (July-Aug)."The purpose of *Time Break* is to inform 'friends and customers' about new products and applications plus trends and items of interest in the geophysical exploration field. It includes technical and semitechnical articles." Circ. 4,000. Pays on acceptance. Buys all rights. Byline given. Submit seasonal/holiday material 3 months in advance of issue date. Simultaneous and previously published submissions OK. SASE. Reports in 1 month. Free sample copy.

Nonfiction: "All articles need to be related to seismic exploration." General interest (to people engaged in seismic exploration); historical; interview; and nostalgia. Query. Length: 500-5,000 words. Pays $50-250.

Photos: "Hopefully, *all* articles in the magazine have photos." State availability of photos. Pays $10-50 for b&w photos. Captions preferred. Buys all rights. Model release required.

Tips: "Some knowledge of the seismic exploration industry is a *must*."

WDS FORUM, Writer's Digest School, 9933 Alliance Rd., Cincinnati OH 45242. (513)984-0717. Editor: Kirk Polking. Bimonthly magazine covering writing techniques and marketing for students of seven courses in fiction and nonfiction writing offered by Writer's Digest School. Pays on acceptance. Buys all rights. Pays 25% kill fee. Byline given. Phone queries OK. Submit seasonal/holiday material 3 months in advance of issue date. Simultaneous, photocopied and previously published submissions OK. SASE. Reports in 3 weeks. Free sample copy.

Nonfiction: How-to (write or market short stories, articles, novels for young people, etc.); and interviews (with well-known authors of short stories, novels and books). Buys 10 mss/year. Query. Length: 500-1,500 words. Pays $10-30.

Photos: Pays $2-5 for 8x10 b&w prints of well-known writers to accompany mss. Captions required. Buys all rights.

Consumer Publications

The past year heralded a new look for many consumer publications—and made new marketing demands on writers. A number of covers familiar to the newsstand racks have undergone radical facelifts and/or name changes, along with changes in format and editorial style. *Apartment Life*, for example, is now *Metropolitan Home*; and *Decorating Magazine* is now *Great American Home Designs*.

To keep pace with such changes, a regular part of the magazine writer's regimen should be a trip to the local bookstore/newsstand and a perusal of the goods thereon. If a newsstand, bookstore or library does not stock the magazine in question, you can often write the publisher for a sample copy (see instructions in the listings that follow). In any case, research today is an increasingly important part of marketing to magazines as competition increases among writers. You can't conduct research half-heartedly. Know your audience. Study the magazine—over several issues—to determine style, content and slant. Look for gaps in the editorial mix. Remember, you want your manuscript to be fresh six months from now, to satisfy the editor's needs and the reader's interest.

Know your subject. Nothing earmarks a manuscript quicker for the reject file than a lack of familiarity with the subject at hand. This does not necessarily mean you have to be an encyclopedic writer to succeed with a consumer publication. In fact, you should write in a popular style that appeals to readers with a variety of interests.

Another trend should be noted. Leisure time (and income!) are on the downswing, according to the American Council for the Arts, while interest in the arts—especially lifestyles reflecting integration of the arts—is rising. Thus, new listings in this section reflect those interests: music, video machines, visual arts, home decorating and crafts. Sports magazines, often geared to a specific city or geographical region, are gaining popularity, as are new women's and entertainment publications that cater to residents in a specific city or state.

So much for the new. What follows may sound familiar, but is worth repeating.

Let the listings be your guide. Editors state their submission requirements clearly: They either want to see the entire manuscript, or a query, possibly with clippings of published work. One to three clips should exemplify your output without being credential overload.

Product quality is often reflected in the packages on the supermarket shelves, and submitting written matter to an editor is no different. Put your cover letter or manuscript in the best possible shape before mailing it. You want to make a good first impression on the editor (and that doesn't mean blowing your budget on stationery). Be sure you are complying with the editorial guidelines; a complete manuscript instead of a personalized query to an editor who specifically prefers the latter may tie up your manuscript for months, whereas a query would be answered in a week.

Address the editor correctly. It is not necessary to know the contact person's marital status. If the name is gender-uncertain, you're safe using the full name in your greeting without a title, i.e., "Dear Robin Jones." Unless otherwise indicated, "Ms." is acceptable.

Most importantly, spell the editor's name correctly. A misspelling in this instance can raise editorial doubts about the care with which you prepared your manuscript.

A professional-looking manuscript will certainly get more attention than a besmudged one full of typos, strikeovers and incomplete erasures. Margins should be at least one and a quarter inch on all pages except the first one (see

Manuscript Mechanics in the Appendix for more specifics).

Your major concern, however, should be with your content and style. There is not much an editor can do with a manuscript that lacks substance—and a distinctive style will hold the attention of the readers, the people you ultimately want to win over.

For articles, keep files of other articles on the same subject; know your competition. If you write fiction, research locales and scenery so you can give your story verisimilitude.

After you've done your best work, take one final look at your query or manuscript. Have you answered every question the editor might have? Are you vague, glossing over what rightfully needs to be drawn out?

If you are satisfied, the next step should be directed to the mailbox. Bear in mind that in dealing with a new listing and/or new editor, you may not receive a response within the stated time in the listing. Editors are often seasonally swamped, so allow a few weeks' lag time before dropping a cordial note asking for a progress report, if you have waited longer than the reported time.

For the latest marketing tips and information, including reports on new markets, read *Writer's Digest* magazine (9933 Alliance Rd., Cincinnati 45242). *WD* has five columns—The Markets, New York Market Letter, L.A. Market Report, Poetry, and Market Update—designed to keep you up-to-date on the changing publications scene.

Alternative

Publications listed here cover a wide range of special interests. They offer writers a forum for expressing unconventional or minority ideas and views that wouldn't necessarily be published in the commercial or "establishment" press. Included are a number of "free press" publications that do not pay except in contributor's copies. Writers should be aware that some of these publications remain at one address for a limited time or prove unbusinesslike in their reporting on, or returning of, submissions. However, the writer will also find a number of well-established, well-paying markets in this list.

THE ADVOCATE, Liberation Publications, Inc., 1730 S. Amphlett, Suite 225, San Mateo CA 94402. Editor-in-Chief: Robert I. McQueen. For gay men and women, aged 21-40; middle-class, college-educated, urban. Biweekly tabloid. Circ. 65,835. Pays on publication. Rights purchased vary with author and material. Byline given. SASE. Reports in 6 weeks.
Nonfiction: "Basically, the emphasis is on the dignity and joy of the gay lifestyle." News articles, interviews, lifestyle features. "Major interest in interviews or sketches of gay people whose names can be used." Informational, personal experience, profile, humor, historical, photo feature, spot news, new product. Query with "concrete description and writing sample." Length: open.
Photos: "Payment for b&w photos purchased without ms or on assignment depends on size of the reproduction."

ASCENSION FROM THE ASHES, The Alternative Magazine, AFTA Press, 153 George St., Suite #1, New Brunswick NJ 08901. (201)846-0226. Editor: Bill-Dale Marcinko. Quarterly magazine covering popular culture (TV, film, books and music) political and sexual issues for young adults (18-30) who are interested in rock music, films, literature and political and sexual issues. Circ. 20,000. Pays in copies. Acquires one-time rights. Phone queries OK. Submit seasonal material 1 month in advance. Simultaneous, photocopied and previously published submissions OK. SASE. Reports in 2 weeks. Sample copy $3.
Nonfiction: Humor (satires on popular books, TV, films, records and social issues); interview (of authors, TV/film writers or directors, rock musicians and political movement leaders); opinion (reviews and reactions); profile; personal experience; and photo feature (on the making of a movie or TV program, coverage of a rock concert or political demonstration). AFTA also buys investiga-

tive articles on political, consumer, and religious fraud. Buys 50 mss/year. Query with clips of previously published work. Pays in copies.

Photos: State availability of photos. Reviews b&w prints. Pays in copies.

Columns/Departments: Books, Etc. (book reviews, fiction and nonfiction of interest to a young counterculture audience); Demons in Dustjackets (horror and science fiction book reviews); and Medium Banal (TV reviews); Sprockets (film reviews); and Slipped Discs (record reviews). "We use short (3-4 paragraphs) reviews of comic books, underground comix, alternative magazines, recent books, television programs, films and rock albums, especially on gay, lesbian, and politically controversial small press magazines and books. Buys 50 mss/year. Query with clips of previously published work. Length: 100-1,000 words. Pays in copies.

Fiction: Short stories only. Experimental, erotic, humorous, science fiction, suspense and mainstream. Buys 10 mss/year. Query with clips of previously published work. Length: 3,000 words maximum. Pays in copies.

Fillers: "We buy editorial cartoons and comic strips and panels. Send photocopies. Payment from $5-100. We print folk/rock songs on social issues with music. Buys 8 mss/year. Pays in copies. We also have a section in which readers describe their first-time sexual experiences (gay or straight)."

Tips: "Sending for a sample copy is probably the best way to familiarize yourself with the kind of writing in *AFTA*. Write with humor, simplicity, and intensity, first person if possible. Avoid being formal or academic in criticism. Write for a young adult audience. The short stories accepted generally have a style similar to the works of Vonnegut or Tom Robbins, very loose, playful and humorous. AFTA doesn't censor language in any submissions, and is known for printing material other magazines consider sexually and politically controversial."

BLACK MARIA, Box 25187, Chicago IL 60625. Collective editorship. Magazine published 1-3 times/year for women who are writers, students or feminists interested in redefining women's position in society. Circ. 1,000. Rights acquired vary with author and material. Byline given. Uses about 80 mss/year. Pays in contributor's copies and a subscription. Sample copy $2. Photocopied submissions OK. Simultaneous submissions OK if so designated. Reports in 6 months. SASE.

Nonfiction: "Articles must be written by women. Subjects include those pertinent to women. Articles should be pro-woman and define her as active, intelligent; a complete human being. Profiles of women artists, writers, or pioneers in various careers and situations are welcomed but we prefer a more subtle approach than political rhetoric. We do not want immediate, newsy articles about specific events. We prefer more general, nontransitory themes for articles."

Fiction: Written by women. Subject matter should particularize women. Experimental, mainstream, science fiction, fantasy, humorous and historical fiction.

Poetry: Traditional forms of poetry, free verse, light verse and avant-garde forms. Submit 3-10 poems at one time.

Photos: Uses 5x7 or 8x10 b&w with mss or independently.

Tips: "Everything that is sent to us is given careful attention. Materials are judged according to their quality, not packaging or presentation. Be creative and unique!"

THE BOSTON PHOENIX, 100 Massachusetts Ave., Boston MA 02115. (617)536-5390. Editor: Richard M. Gaines. 40% freelance written. For 18-40 age group, educated middle-class and post-counterculture. Weekly alternative newspaper; 124 pages. Circ. 125,000. Buys all rights. Pays at least 50% kill fee. Byline given. Pays on publication. Sample copy $1. Photocopied submissions OK. Reports in 6 weeks. Query letter preferable to ms. SASE.

Nonfiction: Sections are: News (investigative, issues, some international affairs, features, think pieces and profiles), Lifestyle (features, service pieces, consumer-oriented tips, medical, food, mental health, some humor if topical, etc.), Arts (reviews, essays, interviews), Supplements (coverage of specific areas, e.g., stereo, skiing, automotive, education, apartments with local angle). Query Section Editor. "Liveliness, accuracy and great literacy are absolutely required." No fiction or poetry. Pays 4¢/word and up.

CO EVOLUTION QUARTERLY, Whole Earth Catalog, Box 428, Sausalito CA 94966. (415)332-1716. Editor: Stewart Brand. Assistant Editor: Stephanie Mills. Quarterly magazine; alternative publication reviewing media for "everybody and anybody. Large concentration of readers are in San Francisco Bay area. Others are in rural and in metropolitan areas all over." Circ. 42,000. Pays on publication. Byline given. Buys first North American serial rights. Submit seasonal/holiday material 3 months in advance. Reports in 2 months. Writer's guidelines for business size SAE and 1 first class stamp.

Nonfiction: "There is *no* unifying theme. That's the unifying theme." Buys 50-60 mss/year. Send complete ms. Length: 20,000 words. Pays $150-300, "depending on importance, illustrations and clarity."

Photos: Pays $25 for 8x10 b&w glossy prints. Identification of subjects required. Buys one-time rights.
Columns/Departments: "Letters, reviews, first suggestions of any item published." Buys dozens mss/year. Send complete ms. Pays $15 minimum.
Fiction: Buys 4 mss/year. Send complete ms. Length: open. Pays $150-300.
Poetry: Avant-garde, free verse, haiku, light verse and traditional. Buys 6 mss/year. Pays variable fee.
Fillers: Clippings, jokes, gags, anecdotes, short humor and newsbreaks. Buys dozens/year. Length: open. Pays $15.

COMMUNITY, 1746 W. Division St., Chicago IL 60622. (312)227-5065. Editor: Hal Wand. For teachers, religious students and movement types (high school age up) interested in social change through nonviolent action. Quarterly magazine. Circ. 1,000. Acquires all rights. Byline given. Uses about 40 mss/year. Pays in contributor's copies. Sample copy $1. Photocopied submissions OK. Occasionally considers simultaneous submissions. Reports in 2 months. Query. SASE.
Nonfiction: "All types of material concerning the reconciliation and liberation of peoples and how to achieve such through scripturally-based nonviolence. Our approach is from the viewpoint of the Catholic left. We like to publish material extracted from personal experience whether theoretical or practical, also transcripts of talks and interviews. No term paper types. We also use book reviews, poetry and photo essays." Length: 2,400 words.
Photos: 8x10 glossy or matte photos are used with mss.
Poetry: Johnny Baranski, poetry editor. Nothing trite. Traditional forms. Blank verse, free verse, avant-garde forms and haiku. Length: 3-30 lines.

COSMOPOLITAN CONTACT, Pantheon Press, Box 1566, Fontana CA 92335. Editor-in-Chief: Romulus Rexner. Managing Editor: Nina Norvid. Assistant Editor: Irene Anders. Magazine irregularly published 2 or 3 times a year. "It is the publication's object to have as universal appeal as possible to students, graduates and others interested in international affairs, cooperation, contacts, travel, friendships, trade, exchanges, self-improvement and widening of mental horizons through multicultural interaction. This polyglot publication has worldwide distribution and participation, including the Communist countries. As a result of listing in *Writer's Market*, more and better literary material is being contributed and more space will be allocated to literary material relevant to the philosphy and objectives of Planetary Legion for Peace (PLP) and Planetary Universalism. Our magazine has worldwide circulation; writers participate in its distribution, editing and publishing." Circ. 1,500. Pays on publication in copies. Byline given. Simultaneous, photocopied and previously published submissions OK. SASE. Reports in 6 weeks. Sample copy $2.
Nonfiction: Exposé (should concentrate on government; education; etc.); how-to; informational; inspiration; personal experience; personal opinion and travel. Submit complete ms. Maximum 500 words. "Material designed to promote across all frontiers bonds of spiritual unity, intellectual understanding and sincere friendship among people by means of correspondence, meetings, publishing activities, tapes, records, exchange of hospitality, books, periodicals in various languages, hobbies and other contacts."
Poetry: Haiku and traditional. Length: Maximum 40 lines.
Tips: "Most of the material is not written by experts to enlighten or to amuse the readers, but it is written by the readers who also are freelance writers. The material is didactic, provocative, pragmatic—not art-for-art's sake—and tries to answer the reader's question, 'What can I do about it?' If a writer wants us to be interested in him, he/she should also be interested in our aims. The addresses of all contributors are published in order to facilitate global contacts among our contributors, editors and readers/members. Instead of writing, e.g. about Lincoln or history, it is better to be an emancipator and to make history by promoting high ideals of mankind. Consequently, the material submitted to us should not be only descriptive, but it should be analytical, creative, action—and future-oriented. We are not interested in any contribution containing vulgar language, extreme, intolerant, pro-Soviet or anti-American opinions."

EARTH'S DAUGHTERS, Box 41, Central Park Station, Buffalo NY 14215. Collective editorship. For people interested in literature and feminism. Publication schedule varies from 2-4 times a year. Circ. 1,000. Acquires first North American serial rights. Reverts to author after publication. Byline given. Pays in contributor's copies. Sample copy $2.50. Clear photocopied submissions and clear carbons OK. Reports "very slowly. Please be patient." Submit complete ms. SASE.
Fiction: Feminist fiction of any and all modes. "Our subject is the experience and creative expression of women. We require a high level of technical skill and artistic intensity, and we are concerned with creative expression rather than propaganda. On occasion we publish feminist work by men." Length: 1,500 words maximum. Pays in copies only.

Poetry: All modern, contemporary, avant-garde forms. Length: 40 lines maximum preferred with occasional exceptions.

EAST WEST JOURNAL, East West Journal, Inc., 17 Station St., Brookline MA 02146. (617)734-1000. Editor: Alex Jack. Emphasizes natural living for "people of all ages seeking balance in a world of change." Monthly magazine. Circ. 50,000. Pays on publication. Buys one-time rights. Byline given. Phone queries OK. Submit seasonal/holiday material 5 months in advance. Simultaneous, photocopied and previously published submissions OK. SASE. Reports in 1 month. Free sample copy.
Nonfiction: Bobbi Joels, nonfiction editor. Exposé (of agribusiness, modern medicine, the oil and nuclear industries) and features (on solar and alternative energies, natural foods and organic farming and gardening, ecological and energy-efficient modes of transportation, natural healing, whole food and technology). No negative, politically-oriented, or new-age material. "We're looking for original, first-person articles without jargon or opinions of any particular teachings; articles should reflect an intuitive approach." Buys 15 mss/year. Query. Length: 1,500-2,500 words. Pays 5-7¢/word.
Photos: Send photos with ms. Pays $15-40 for b&w prints; $15-175 for 35mm color transparencies (cover only). Captions preferred; model release required.
Columns/Departments: Body, Food, Healing, Gardening, Alternative Energy and Spirit. Buys 15 mss/year. Submit complete ms. Length: 1,500-2,000 words. Pays 5¢/word.
Fillers: Jokes, anecdotes, puzzles and short humor relating to renewable energy, natural food, health or the meeting of East and West."

FARMSTEAD MAGAZINE, Box 111, Freedom ME 04941. (207)382-6200. Editor-in-Chief: George Frangoulis. Magazine published 8 times/year covering gardening, small farming, homesteading and self-sufficiency. "We combine a practical, how-to approach with an appeal to aesthetic sense and taste." Circ. 120,000. Pays on publication. Buys first serial and reprint rights. Phone queries OK. Submit seasonal/holiday material 3 months in advance. SASE. Reports in 3 months. Free sample copy and writer's guidelines.
Nonfiction: General interest (related to rural living, gardening and farm life); how-to (gardening, farming, construction, conservation, wildlife livestock, crafts, and rural living); interview (with interesting and/or inspirational people involved with agriculture, farm life or self-sufficiency); new product (reviews of new books); nostalgia (of rural living; farm life self-sufficiency); and occasionally travel (agriculture in other lands). No recipes, food, sentimentality or nostalgia. Buys 60 mss/year. Submit complete ms. Length: 1,000-5,000 words maximum. Pays $50-250.
Photos: State availability of photos with ms. Pays $5-10 for each 5x7 b&w print used. Buys all rights.
Tips: "Contribute a thorough well-researched or first-hand-experience type article. B&w photos of good quality or careful diagrams or sketches are a boon. We look for an unusual but practical how-to article. An article sent in a folder is helpful. Presentation is important. We appreciate material from those who have lived and done what they are writing about. We like the how-to, hands-on approach; no theorizing." Send short factual pieces with good photos.

FOCUS: A JOURNAL FOR LESBIANS, Daughters of Bilitis, 1151 Massachusetts Ave., Cambridge MA 02138. A literary journal for lesbians of all ages and interests. Bimonthly magazine. "This is a magazine by lesbians for lesbians. We do not publish work by men, nor will we consider work that is male-centered. We are interested in writing that is relevant to our audience and which is also of high artistic quality." Circ. 400. Pays in contributor's copies. Obtains first rights. Byline given. Submit seasonal/holiday material 3 months in advance. Simultaneous and photocopied submissions OK. SASE. Reports in 3 months. Sample copy $1.35.
Nonfiction: Historical; humor; informational; interview; personal experience; personal opinion; profile and book reviews. Send complete ms. Length: 3,000 words maximum.
Fiction: Relating to magazine theme. Confession; erotica; fantasy; historical; humorous; romance; and science fiction. Send complete ms. Length: 3,000 words maximum.
Poetry: Avant-garde; free verse; haiku; light verse; and traditional. Length: 200 words maximum.
Fillers: Cartoons and short humor. Length: 200 words maximum.
Tips: "Be professional. Type your work, include a SASE, proofread, etc. We are very open to new writers; but sloppy, careless work is a real turn-off. Also, check out the magazine before submitting. Although we do accept nonfiction pieces, we prefer fiction. The tone of the journal is definitely literary. We are looking for quality writing rather than political correctness. Our primary concern is to bring together material that reflects all aspects of lesbian life and experience."

FREE FOR ALL, BETTER WORLD EDUCATION CORP., Box 962, Madison WI 53701. (608)255-2798. Editor: Sarah Schuyler. For the student community—university students; large, liberal-to-radical readership; and craftspeople/artists. Biweekly tabloid. Circ. 12,000. Byline given. No payment to writers. Phone queries OK. Simultaneous, photocopied and previously published submissions OK. SASE. Sample copy 35¢.

Nonfiction: Exposé; general interest; humor; analytical (socialist-feminist perspective on culture, news, economy, etc.); interview; and photo feature. "We do not want any racist, sexist, anti-gay/lesbian or anti-labor articles." Buys 20/year. Send complete ms. Length: 50-700 words.

Photos: State availability of photos with ms or send photos with ms. Offers no additional rights. Captions preferred.

Columns/Departments: Culture (reviews, news releases, socio-political angles); education; minorities and national/international. Also humor. Open to suggestions for new columns/departments.

FRUITFUL YIELD NEWSLETTER, The Fruitful Yield, Inc., 721 N. Yale, Villa Park IL 60181. (312)833-8288. Editor: Doug Murguia. Bimonthly national newsletter covering natural foods, vitamins and living. Features subjects ranging from prenatal care to health and nutrition for all age groups. Circ. 15,000. Pays on publication. Buys first rights. Phone queries OK. Submit seasonal material 2 months in advance. Photocopied submissions OK. SASE. Reports in 6 weeks. Free sample copy and writer's guidelines.

Nonfiction: Exposé (of drugs, chemicals, food processing and related companies); general interest (health and exercise); historical (food history and vitamin research); how-to (use natural foods, vitamins, exercise, save energy and overcome disease); interview; nostalgia (whole foods of yesteryear); new product; personal experience; technical (plain, natural cooking, including recipes); and book reviews. "No articles handled in a too general or unspecific manner. Articles that promote medicine, drugs, chemicals are always bad." Buys approximately 100 mss/year. Send complete ms. Length: 250-500 words. Pays $10-20.

Columns/Departments: Energy Conservation; How Natural Foods Helped Me; Health Happenings. Buys 20 mss/year. Send complete ms. Length: 250-500 words. Pays $10-20.

Poetry: "We are not using poetry now, but are open to submissions. Poetry should be short and humorous and deal with health." Length: 30 lines maximum. Pays $10-15.

Fillers: Short humor, newsbreaks and inspirational health lines or quotes. Buys 12 mss/year. Length: 100 words maximum. Pays $5-10.

HARROWSMITH MAGAZINE, Camden House Publishing, Ltd., Camden East, Ontario, Canada K0K 1J0. (613)378-6661. Editor-in-Chief: James M. Lawrence. Published 8 times/year "for those interested in country life, nonchemical gardening, solar and wind energy, folk arts, small-stock husbandry, owner-builder architecture and alternative styles of life." Circ. 170,000. Pays on acceptance. Buys first North American serial rights. Pays 50% kill fee. Byline given. Submit seasonal/holiday material 6 months in advance. SASE. Reports in 1 month. Sample copy $1.95; free writer's guidelines.

Nonfiction: Frank B. Edwards, nonfiction editor. Exposé; how-to; general interest; humor; interview; photo feature; and profile. "We are always in need of quality gardening articles geared to northern conditions. No articles whose style feigns 'folksiness.' No how-to articles written by people who are not totally familiar with their subject. We feel that in this field simple research does not compensate for lack of long-time personal experience." Buys 10-15 mss/issue. Query. Length: 500-4,000 words. Pays $75-750, but will consider higher rates for major stories.

Photos: State availability of photos with query. Pays $25-75 for 8x10 glossy b&w prints; $35-200 for 35mm or larger color transparencies. Captions required. Buys all rights. "We regularly run photo essays for which we pay $250-750."

Tips: "We have standards of excellence as high as any publication in the country. However, we are by no means a closed market. Most of our material comes from unknown writers. We welcome and give thorough consideration to all freelance submissions. Magazine is read by Canadians who live in rural areas or who hope to make the urban to rural transition. They want to know as much about the realities of country life as the dreams. They expect quality writing, not folksy clichés."

HIGH TIMES, Trans-High Corp., 17 W. 60th St., New York NY 10023. (212)974-1990. Editor: Larry Sloman. Monthly magazine for persons under 35 interested in lifestyle changes, cultural trends, personal freedom, sex and drugs. "Our readers are independent, adventurous, free-thinkers who want to control their own consciousness." Circ. 400,000. Pays on acceptance. Buys all rights or second serial (reprint) rights or first North American serial rights. Submit seasonal/holiday material 5 months in advance. SASE. Reports in 2 months. Sample copy $2.50.

Nonfiction: Exposé (on political, government or biographical behind the scenes); general interest (political or cultural activities); historical (cultural, literary, dope history, political movements); how-to (that aids the enhancement of one's lifestyle); interview (of writers, scientists, musicians, entertainers and public figures); new product (on dope-related or lifestyle enhancing); nostalgia (cultural or dope-related); opinion (only from public figures); photo feature (on dope- or travel-related topics); profile, technical (explorations of technological breakthroughs related to personal lifestyle); travel (guides to places of interest to a young hip audience). "We want no material on 'my drug bust.'" Buys 5 mss/issue. Query with clips of published work. Length: 3,000-5,000 words. Pays $500-750.

Photos: Send photos with ms. Pays $25-150 for 8x10 glossy print per page; and $50-250 for 35mm color transparencies per page. Captions preferred; model releases required. Buys one-time rights.

Tips: "Think of article ideas that are too outrageous, visionary, radical or adventurous for any other magazine."

INTEGRITY FORUM, Box 891, Oak Park IL 60303. (312)386-1470. Editor: David R. Williams. Theological journal published 6 times/year for "gay Episcopalians and friends. About one-fourth of our readers are clergy, many of them gay themselves, and others of them trying thereby to become more informed of our basically gay point of view. Readers are Christians interested in human rights, non-Christian gays seeking to be informed of our Christian witness and chapter members in over 35 cities." Circ. 1,200. Rights acquired vary with author and material. Byline given. Usually acquires all rights. Uses 15 to 20 mss/year. Pays in contributor's copies. Sample copy $1. Photocopied submissions OK. Simultaneous submissions OK only if other distribution is explained. Reports in 2 weeks. SASE.

Nonfiction: "Theological and moral discussion items, particularly with a Christian (but not sentimental) focus, and particularly with the poignancy to be forceful about the truth of the gay experience. We like materials that discuss gay sexuality in the broader context of human sexuality." Book reviews welcome. Query or submit complete ms. Length 25-1,000 words.

THE MOTHER EARTH NEWS, Box 70, Hendersonville NC 28791. (704)692-0211. Editor: Bruce Woods. Emphasizes "back-to-the-land self-sufficiency for the growing number of individuals who seek a more rational self-directed way of life." Bimonthly magazine. Circ. 1,000,000. Pays on acceptance. "We buy any rights we might ever need, while leaving the author free to resell the same material as often as he or she pleases." Byline given. Submit seasonal/holiday material 5 months in advance. Simultaneous, photocopied and previously published submissions OK if so indicated. SASE. Reports in 3 months. Sample copy $3; free writer's guidelines.

Nonfiction: Roselyn Edwards, submissions editor. How-to, home business, alternative energy systems, low cost—$100 and up—housing, energy-efficient structures, seasonal cooking, gardening and crafts. "We're overstocked on cooking, but will *look* if the article has exceptionally good photos as in holiday material." Buys 150-200 mss/year. Query or send complete ms. "A short, to-the-point paragraph is often enough. If it's a subject we don't need at all, we can answer immediately. If it tickles our imagination, we'll ask to take a look at the whole piece. No phone queries, please." Length: 300-3,000 words. Pays $80/minimum/published page; $25-50 for Profiles and Newsworthies; $7.50-25 for shorties.

Photos: Purchased with accompanying ms. Captions and credits required. Send prints or transparencies. Uses 8x10 b&w glossies; any size color transparencies. Include type of film, speed and lighting used. Total purchase price for ms includes payment for photos.

Columns/Departments: "Contributions to *Mother's* Down-Home Country Lore; and Successful Swaps are rewarded by a one-year subscription; Bootstrap Business pays a two-year subscription; Profiles and Newsworthies; pays $25-50."

Fillers: Short how-to's on any subject normally covered by the magazine. Query. Length: 150-300 words. Pays $7.50-25.

Tips: "Probably the best way to break in is to send a tightly written, short (1,000 words), illustrated (with color transparencies) piece on a slightly offbeat facet of gardening, alternative energy, or country living. It's important that the writer get all the pertinent facts together, organize them logically, and present them in a fun-to-read fashion. "Study our magazine, digest our writer's guidelines, and send us a concise article illustrated with color transparencies that we can't resist. We want articles that tell what real people are doing to take charge of their own lives. Articles should be well-documented and not just another repeat of something we've just done."

NATURAL LIFE MAGAZINE, Natural Dynamics, Inc., Box 640, Jarvis, Ontario, Canada N0A 1J0. Editor-in-Chief: Wendy Priesnitz. Emphasizes "new age and ecology matters for a readership (both rural and urban) interested in natural foods, alternate energy, do-it-yourself-projects and self-sufficiency. Bimonthly magazine. Circ. 30,000. Pays on acceptance. Buys all rights. Byline given. Submit seasonal/holiday material 3 months in advance. SASE. Reports in 3 weeks. Sample copy $1.50; free writer's guidelines.

Nonfiction: How-to (on becoming self-sufficient, e.g., organic gardening, vegetarian cooking, homestead carpentry, useful crafts, etc.); interview (ecology-oriented, new age personalities/natural healers, alternate energy people); personal experience (with homesteading, self-sufficient lifestyle); and technical (solar and wind energy). Buys 30 mss/year. Query with clips of published work. Length: 2,000 words maximum. Pays $25-100.

Photos: State availability of photos with query. "Our readers want to see how everything is done, or built, etc." Offers no additional payment for photos accepted with ms. Uses b&w prints mainly. Captions preferred. Buys all rights.

NEW FARM MAGAZINE, Rodale Press, Inc., 33 E. Minor St., Emmaus PA 18049. (215)683-3111. Editor: Steve Smyser. Bimonthly magazine on alternative agriculture for farmers who are interested in using less energy, biological alternatives to chemical pesticides and in using land economically. Estab. 1979. Circ. 85,000. Pays on publication. Buys first North American serial rights. Phone queries OK. Submit seasonal material 4 months in advance. Simultaneous, photocopied and previously published submissions OK. Reports in 1 week on queries; in 2 weeks on mss. Free sample copy and writer's guidelines.

Nonfiction: General interest (alternatives to conventional tillage, stretching the equipment budget); how-to (make marginal farmland productive, use biological alternatives in weed and insect control, use energy conserving techniques); opinion; personal experience (on controversial farm issues); and semi-technical (of a research nature). Buys 4 mss/issue. Query. Length: 1,800-2,000 words. Pays $250-350.

Photos: Editor: Thomas Gettings. State availability of photos. Reviews contact sheets and any b&w glossy prints. Offers no additional payment for photos accepted with ms. Captions preferred; model release required. Acquires one-time rights.

Fillers: Newsbreaks and agricultural updates. Buys 2 mss/issue. Length: 500-700 words. Pays $100 minimum.

PRAIRIE SUN, Box 885, Peoria IL 61652. (309)673-6624. Editor-in-Chief: Bill Knight. Weekly tabloid for music listeners who are also interested in films, books and general entertainment. "We have a consciously Midwest orientation, and combine music and current events." Circ. 35,000. Pays on publication. Buys all rights. Byline given. Phone queries OK. Simultaneous, photocopied and previously published submissions OK. SASE. Reports in 3 weeks. Sample copy 50¢.

Nonfiction: Exposé (government and corporate interests); how-to (back to nature; gardening; living with less; alternative energy systems); interview (especially cultural and entertainment personalities); and profile (music personalities). Buys 20 mss/year. Query with outline. Length: 400-1,000 words. Pays $15-40.

Tips: "Creatively select themes."

SAN FRANCISCO BAY GUARDIAN, 2700 19th St., San Francisco CA 94110. (415)824-7660. Editor: Bruce Brugmann. Department Editors: Louis Dunn (photos); Alan Kay (articles). Weekly paper for "a young liberal to radical, well-educated audience." Circ. 40,000. Buys first rights. Byline given. Buys 200 mss/year. Pays two months after publication. Photocopied submissions. SASE.

Nonfiction: Publishes "investigative reports, features, analysis and interpretation, how-to and consumer reviews. All stories must have a Bay Area angle in the consumer, neighborhood, environmental and lifestyles areas." Freelance material should have a "public interest advocacy journalism approach."

Photos: Purchased with or without mss. B&w full negative prints, on 8x10 paper. Pays $15 per published photo, $40 minimum/photo essay.

Tips: "Work with our volunteer projects in investigative reporting. We teach the techniques and send interns out to do investigative research. We like to talk to writers in our office before they begin doing a story."

THE SECOND WAVE, Box 344, Cambridge A., Cambridge MA 02139. (617)491-1071. Editors: Women's Editorial Collective. Biannual magazine for women concerned with issues of feminism. Circ. 5,000. Acquires first serial rights. Byline given. Uses 40 mss/year. Pays in contributor's copies. Sample copy $2.50. Photocopies OK. Reports in 1-2 months. Query or submit complete ms. SASE.

Nonfiction: *The Second Wave* is intended to be a forum for diverse feminist perspectives, both from a large societal scale and from women's personal experiences. We try to integrate the personal, political, and artistic through a balance of articles, fiction, poetry, and graphics. We are committed to the eradication of sexism and heterosexism and to a radical transformation of society as a whole, and so we emphasize radical, socialist, and anarchist feminism. We want to explore the differences and similarities between these perspectives in a productive and supportive way." Length varies.

Photos: B&w photos are used with or without accompanying mss. Captions optional.

Fiction: Must relate to feminist themes. Experimental, mainstream, science fiction, fantasy.
Poetry: Structured verse and free verse.
Tips: "We encourage and like to publish work of women who have never been published before. We don't look for 'clever' things, rather we appreciate honesty and clarity of expression. We appreciate quality writing that shows skill and thoughtfulness."

SIPAPU, Route 1, Box 216, Winters CA 95694. Editor: Noel Peattie. For "libraries, editors and collectors interested in Third World studies, the counterculture and the underground press." Semiannual. Circ. 500. Buys all rights. Byline given. Pays on publication. Sample copy $2. Will consider photocopied submissions. Reports in 3 weeks. Query with article ideas; indicate professional background. SASE.
Nonfiction: "Primarily book reviews, interviews, descriptions of special libraries and counterculture magazines and underground papers. We are an underground 'paper' about underground 'papers.' We are interested in personalities publishing dissent; counterculture; Third World material; and the peace movement, whether secular or religious, with allied subjects such as disarmament, opposition to nuclear power or weapons, etc. Informal, clear and cool. We are not interested in blazing manifestos, but rather a concise, honest description of some phase of dissent publishing, or some library collecting in this field, that the writer knows about from the inside." Personal experience, interview, successful library operations. "No unsolicited reviews. We do our own reviews or occasionally solicit them. Payola we don't need." Pays 5¢/word.

THE UNSPEAKABLE VISIONS OF THE INDIVIDUAL, INC., Box 439, California PA 15419. Editors-in-Chief: Arthur Winfield Knight, Kit Knight. For "an adult audience, generally college-educated (or substantial self-education) with an interest in Beat (generation) writing." Annual magazine/book. Circ. 2,000. Payment (if made) on acceptance. Buys first North American serial rights. Reports in 2 months. Sample copy $3.
Nonfiction: Interviews (with Beat writers), personal experience, photo feature. Uses 20 mss/year. Query or submit complete ms. Length: 300-15,000 words. Pays 2 copies, "sometimes a small cash payment, i.e., $10."
Photos: Used with or without ms or on assignment. Captions required. Send prints. Pays 2 copies to $10 for 8x10 b&w glossies. Uses 40-50/year.
Fiction: Uses 10 mss/year. Submit complete ms. Pays 2 copies to $10.
Poetry: Avant-garde, free verse, traditional. Uses 10/year. Limit submissions to batches of 10. Length: 100 lines maximum. Pays 2 copies to $10.

THE WASHINGTON BLADE, Washington Blade, Inc., 930 F St. N.W., Suite 315, Washington DC 20004. (202)347-2038. Managing Editor: Donald J. Michaels. Biweekly tabloid covering the gay community for "gay men and women of all ages, oriented to living within the mainstream of society. Articles (subjects) should be written from or directed to a gay perspective." Circ. 20,000. Pays on publication. Byline given. Pays $15 kill fee. Buys first North American serial rights. Submit seasonal/holiday material 1 month in advance. Photocopied and previously published submissions OK. SASE. Reports in 1 month. Free sample copy and writer's guidelines.
Nonfiction: Expose (of government, private agency, church, etc., handling of gay-related issues); historical/nostalgic; humor (primarily satire); interview/profile (of gay community/political leaders; persons—gay or non-gay—in positions to affect gay issues; outstanding achievers who happen to be gay; those who incorporate the gay lifestyle into their professions); photo feature (on a nationally or internationally historic gay event); and travel (on locales that welcome or cater to the gay traveler). "*The Washington Blade* basically covers three areas: News (on DC area gay community, local and federal government, etc., with some national reports); major features on current events. The news/feature articles in this section are primarily staff-written, on assignment, but queries are welcome; Community features (such as a services directory, bar guide, calendar of events, etc.); Entertainment/Lifestyle (columns on health and restaurant reviews; articles on stage, music, film and books, interviews). "This is the area in which we offer the most opportunity for freelancers—queries encouraged." Special issues include: Annual gay pride issue (early June); annual parody/satire issue (April 1). No sexually explicit material. Buys 30 mss/year, average. Query with clips of published work. Length: 500-1,500 words. Pays 3-5¢/word.
Photos: "A photo or graphic with entertainment/lifestyle articles is particularly important. Photo(s) with news stories are appreciated." State availability of photos. Reviews b&w contact sheets. Pays $20 minimum for 8x10 b&w glossy prints or 5x7 color glossy prints. Captions preferred. Model releases required. On assignment, photographer paid hourly rate plus film, expenses reimbursement. Publication retains all rights.

WOMEN: A JOURNAL OF LIBERATION, 3028 Greenmount Ave., Baltimore MD 21218. (301)235-5245. Collective editorship. Quarterly magazine for women; specifically feminists. Circ.

20,000. Payment in contributor's copies. Acquires all rights. Byline given. Phone queries OK. Simultaneous and photocopied submissions OK. SASE. Reports in 5 months. Sample copy $1.25.
Nonfiction: "All articles should be related to upcoming themes and reflect nonsexist and, hopefully, a socialist/feminist approach." Uses 60 mss/year. Submit complete ms. Length: 1,000-3,000 words.
Photos: Photos used with or without mss or on assignment. Uses 5x7 or larger b&w.
Columns/Departments: Uses reviews of feminist press books about women.
Fiction: Adventure, experimental, fantasy, historical, humorous, mainstream, mystery, suspense and science fiction. Uses 6 or more/year. Length: 4,000-5,000 words.
Poetry: Avant-garde and traditional forms; free verse, blank verse, haiku and light verse. Submit complete ms. Length: open.

WOMEN'S RIGHTS LAW REPORTER, 15 Washington St., Newark NJ 07102. (201)648-5320. Legal journal emphasizing law and feminism for lawyers, students and feminists. Quarterly magazine; 64-80 pages. Circ. 1,300. No payment. Acquires all rights. SASE. Sample copy $4.00.
Nonfiction: Historical and legal articles. Query or submit complete ms with published clips and education data. Length: 20-100 pages plus footnotes.

WOODSMOKE, Burnt Fork Publishing Co., Box 15754, Colorado Springs CO 80935. Editor: Richard Jamison. Quarterly magazine covering survival and primitive living for people of all ages with an outdoor interest. Circ. 1500. Pays on publication. Buys one-time rights. Byline given. Submit seasonal/holiday material 2 months in advance. Photocopied and previously published submissions OK. SASE. Reports in 1 month. Sample copy $1.
Nonfiction: Historical (on pioneer and Indian historical trips and hardships); how-to (on self-sufficiency theme, cooking, homestead etc.); and personal experience (how-to and interesting experiences in the outdoors, true survival experiences). "We do not want any *researched* articles on edible plants or herbal medicines. Actual experiences OK." Buys 12-14 mss/year. Send complete ms or query. Length: 500-3,500 words. Pays 2¢/word.
Photos: State availability of photos with ms. Offers no additional payment for photos accepted with ms. Uses b&w prints. Captions preferred.
Columns/Departments: Wild and Free (wild edible plants and herbs); Recipe Box (natural and outdoor recipes); Survival Journal (true life survival experiences); and Who's Who (people with expertise in survival education or outdoor experience). Buys 6 columns/year. Send complete ms. Length: 500-1,000 words. Pays 2¢/word.
Poetry: Light Verse and traditional. "We are open to verse that will fit our outdoor, homestead format." Submit in batches of 3. Pays $3 each.
Fillers: Jokes, gags, anecdotes, short humor and outdoor recipes. Buys 2/issue. Length: 50-100 words.
Tips: "Send a brief but thorough outline of the subject matter. We need qualifications—a biography or references. Please send for a sample before submitting. We get a lot of mss that just don't fit our format."

Animal

These publications deal with pets, racing and show horses, and other pleasure animals. Magazines about animals bred and raised for the market are classified in Farm Publications. Publications about horse racing will be found in the Sport and Outdoor section.

ALL CATS, Pet Pride, Inc., 15113 Sunset Blvd., Suite 7, Pacific Palisades CA 90272. (213)454-4531. Editor: Will Thompson. Managing Editor: Celia Heriot. Bimonthly magazine covering cats. "*All Cats* carries authentic, authoritative and informative articles on cats, their care, health, environment and owners. Includes news on cat organizations, cat clubs, cat shows, humane groups and cat magazines. Caters to persons involved with various kinds of cats (stray, pet and show)." Circ. 26,000. Pays on publication. Byline given. Buys all rights. Submit seasonal/holiday material 6 months in advance. Simultaneous, photocopied, and previously published submissions OK. SASE. Reports in 2 weeks. Sample copy for 11x14 SAE and 5 first class stamps; writer's guidelines for 4x9 SAE and 1 first class stamp.
Nonfiction: Diane Danehy, articles editor. General interest, humor, personal experience, and

technical. No "articles that dwell on the maudlin or the negative aspects of the way cats are treated (we are all too fully aware of these facts)." Buys 10 mss/year. Send complete ms. Length: 500-1,500 words. Pays $15-50.

Photos: Send photos with accompanying ms. Pays $5 for b&w or color prints. Identification of subjects required.

Fiction: Diane Danehy, fiction editor. Humorous and mainstream. No "stories that are supposedly written from a cat's point of view, as they tend to be ridiculous." Buys 25 mss/year. Send complete ms. Length: 500-1,500 words. Pays $15-50.

Poetry: Diane Danehy, poetry editor. Light verse and traditional. Buys 10 poems/year. Submit maximum 5 poems. Length: 4-40 lines. Pays $5-25.

Tips: "The fiction area is most open to freelancers. The stories should be upbeat in their dealings with cats and should appeal to a wide audience. I see more and more specialization in magazine publication. There seems to be a magazine out there for every interest group; thus, the market for writers is constantly expanding."

AMERICAN FARRIERS JOURNAL, Box L, Harvard MA 01451. Editor-in-Chief: Henry Heymering. Strictly professional horseshoeing. Magazine published 5 times/year. Circ. 2,400. Pays on publication. Buys all rights. Byline given. Submit material 6 months in advance of issue date. SASE. Reports in 3 weeks.

Nonfiction: Historical (old tools and methods); how-to; informational; technical; research findings (especially equine anatomy and care); and news coverage of contests and competitions. Query. Length: 800-2,000 words. Pays minimum $1/column inch.

Photos: State availability of photos with query. Pays $5-25 for b&w prints. Also interested in vintage photographs of farriers at work.

ANIMAL KINGDOM, New York Zoological Park, Bronx NY 10460. (212)220-5121. Editor: Eugene J. Walter Jr. Bimonthly magazine for members of zoological societies, individuals interested in wildlife, zoos and aquariums. Buys first North American serial rights. Usually pays 25% kill fee but it varies according to length, amount of work involved, etc. Byline given. Pays on acceptance. Reports in 3 months. SASE.

Nonfiction: Wildlife articles dealing with wildlife, natural history, conservation or behavior. Articles should be scientifically well-grounded, but written for a general audience, not scientific journal readers. No pets, domestic animals, or botany. Length: 1,500-3,000 words. Pays $100-500 (average is $350-500). State availability of photos. Payment for photos purchased with mss is negotiable.

Tips: "It helps to be a working scientist dealing directly with animals in the wild, or a scientist working in a zoo such as a staff member here at the New York Zoological Society. I cannot be too encouraging to anyone who lacks field experience. Most of the authors who send us unsolicited mss are nonscientists who are doing their research in libraries. They're simply working from scientific literature and writing it up for popular consumption. There are a fair number of others who are backyard naturalists, so to speak, and while their observations may be personal, they are not well grounded scientifically. It has nothing to do with whether or not they are good or bad writers. In fact, some of our authors are not especially good writers, but they are able to provide us with fresh, original material and new insights into animal behavior and biology. That sort of thing is impossible from someone who is working from books."

ANIMALS, MSPCA, 350 S. Huntington Ave., Boston MA 02130. Editor: Susan Burns. Bimonthly magazine for members of the MSPCA. 40 pages. Estab. 1868. Circ. 20,000. Pays on publication. Buys all rights. Photocopied and previously published submissions OK. Reports in 2 weeks. Sample copy $1.25 with 8½x11 SASE; writer's guidelines for SASE.

Nonfiction: Uses practical articles on animal care; humane/animal protection issues; animal profiles; true pet stories (*not mawkish*) and research essays on animal protection. Nonsentimental approach. Length: 300-3,000 words. Pays 2¢/word.

Photos: Pays $10 for 5x7 or larger b&w prints; $30 for color transparencies; with accompanying ms or on assignment. Uses photo essays and original photos of artistic distinction for "Gallery" department.

APPALOOSA NEWS, Box 8403, Moscow ID 83843. (208)882-5578. Monthly magazine covering Appaloosa horses for Appaloosa owners and breeders, and people interested in horses. 186 pages. Circ. 29,000. Buys all rights. Byline given. Phone queries OK. Seasonal/holiday material should be submitted 3 months in advance. SASE. Reports in 2 months. Free sample copy.

Nonfiction: How-to (horse-related articles); historical (history of Appaloosas); informational; interview (horse-related persons—trainer, owner, racer, etc.); photo feature; profile (must be authentic); and technical. No western artist features or general horsemanship articles. Submit complete ms. Pays $35-125, however, "most are gratis by owners."

Photos: Reviews 8x10 or 5x7 b&w glossy prints or color transparencies for cover. Offers no additional payment for photos accepted with accompanying ms. Captions required.

Columns/Departments: For regional reports for Appaloosa Horse Club, horse shows or sales. Send complete ms. No payment.

Tips: Write "feature stories about top youth, trainers and breeders involved in Appaloosas are especially liked by our readers—especially those with tips on how they got to where they are today. Mss with photos are more likely to be used. Although we use a few first- and second-person articles, third-person, professionally presented articles are definitely preferred."

CALIFORNIA HORSE REVIEW, The Largest All-Breeds Horse Magazine in the Nation, Related Industries Corp., Box 738, Lodi CA 95241. (209)334-5533. Managing Editor: Bill Shepard. Monthly magazine covering all equines, for "professional trainers, breeders and amateurs whose main interest is in caring for, showing and riding their horses. Articles provide entertainment and factual information to these readers. Emphasis is on equines in the West and most particularly in California." Circ. 7,500. Pays on acceptance. Byline given. Pays $50 kill fee. Buys all rights; "will reassign rights after publication upon written request by the author." Submit seasonal/holiday material 3 months in advance. Photocopied submissions OK. SASE. Reports in 3 weeks. Sample copy $1; writer's guidelines for business size SAE and 1 first class stamp.

Nonfiction: Historical/nostalgic, how-to, humor, inspirational, interview/profile, personal experience, photo feature, technical and travel. "Thirty to forty percent of the magazine is freelance written. We want material for major articles concerning health, training, equipment and interviews with well-known personalities in the equine field. No general-interest articles or articles not aimed at Western horse owners, trainers or breeders." Buys 120 mss/year. Query with clips of published work. Length: 1,200-3,000 words. Pays $35-125.

Photos: "Photos are purchased as a part of the editorial package; however, we do buy cover photos for $75."

Fiction: Adventure, condensed novels, historical, humorous, mainstream, novel excerpts, serialized novels and western. No general interest fiction. Buys 5-6 mss/year. Length: 1,200-2,500 words. Pays $45-125.

Tips: "We are more apt to purchase material from horsemen who have some writing skill than from writers who have little horse knowledge. Interviews of trainers, breeders or others well-known in the horse world are always sought. Readers want factual information written in clear, understandable fashion. Photos are necessary to illustrate many nonfiction articles. A writer in this field should also be a photographer and should continually work to sharpen writing skills."

THE CANADIAN HORSE, 7240 Woodbine Ave., Suite 210, Markham, Ontario, Canada L3R 1A4. (416)495-7722. Editor: Leslie Thomas. For thoroughbred horsemen. Monthly magazine. Circ. 5,500. Buys all rights. Pays on publication. Query first. "With a letter that demonstrates your knowledge of and familiarity with our magazine." Enclose SAE and International Reply Coupons.

Nonfiction: Material on thoroughbred racing and breeding. Length: 2 pages. Pays $50/page.

CAT FANCY, Fancy Publications, Inc., Box 4030, San Clemente CA 92672. (714)498-1600. Editor: Linda Lewis. Monthly magazine for men and women of all ages interested in all phases of cat ownership. 48 pages. Circ. 80,000. Pays after publication. Buys first American serial rights. Byline given. Submit seasonal/holiday material 4 months in advance. SASE. Reports in 3 months. Sample copy $2; free writer's guidelines.

Nonfiction: Historical; medical; how-to; humor; informational; personal experience; photo feature and technical. Buys 5 mss/issue. Send complete ms. Length: 500-3,500 words. Pays 3¢/word.

Photos: Photos purchased with or without accompanying ms. Pays $7.50 minimum for 8x10 b&w glossy prints; $50-100 for 35mm or 2¼x2¼ color transparencies. Send prints and transparencies. Model release required.

Fiction: Adventure; fantasy; historical and humorous; nothing written with cats speaking. Buys 1 ms/issue. Send complete ms. Length: 500-3,500 words. Pays 3¢/word.

Poetry: Avant-garde, free verse, haiku, light verse and traditional. Buys 4 poems/issue. Length: 5-50 lines. Pays $10.

Fillers: Short humor. Buys 10 fillers/year. Length: 100-500 words. Pays 3¢/word.

CATS MAGAZINE, Box 4106, Pittsburgh PA 15202. Executive Editor: Jean Amelia Laux. Box 37, Port Orange FL 32019. Co-Editor: Linda J. Walton. Monthly magazine for men and women of all ages; cat enthusiasts, vets and geneticists. Estab. 1945. Circ. 75,000. Buys first North American serial rights and Japanese first rights. Byline given. Buys 50 mss/year. Pays on publication. Free sample copy. Submit seasonal Christmas material 6 months in advance. Reports in 6-8 weeks. SASE.

Nonfiction: "Cat health, cat breed articles, articles on the cat in art, literature, history, human culture, cats in the news. Cat pets of popular personalities. In general how cats and cat people are contributing to our society. We're more serious, more scientific, but we do like an occasional light or humorous article portraying cats and humans, however, as they really are. No talking cats! Would like to see something on psychological benefits of cat ownership; how do cat-owning families differ from others?" Length: 800-2,500 words. Pays $15-75. Photos purchased with or without accompanying ms. Captions optional. Pays $10 minimum for 4x5 or larger b&w photos; $100 minimum for color. Prefers 2x2 minimum, but can use 35mm (transparencies only). "We use color for cover only. Prefer cats as part of scenes rather than stiff portraits." Send transparencies to Box 37, Port Orange FL 32019. Please mark each transparency with name and address.

Fiction and Poetry: Science fiction, fantasy and humorous fiction; cat themes only. Length: 800-2,500 words. Pays $15-$100. Poetry in traditional forms, blank or free verse, avant-garde forms and some light verse; cat themes only. Length: 4-64 lines. Pays 30¢/line.

DOG FANCY, Fancy Publications, Inc., Box 4030, San Clemente CA 92672. (714)498-1600. Editor: Linda Lewis. Monthly magazine for men and women of all ages interested in all phases of dog ownership. 48 pages. Circ. 65,000. Pays after publication. Buys first American serial rights. Byline given. Submit seasonal/holiday material 4 months in advance. Sample copy $2; free writer's guidelines. SASE.

Nonfiction: Historical, medical, how-to, humor, informational, interview, personal experience, photo feature, profile and technical. Buys 5 mss/issue. Length: 500-3,500 words. Pays 3¢/word.

Photos: Photos purchased with or without accompanying ms. Pays $7.50 minimum for 8x10 b&w glossy prints; $50-100 for 35mm or 2¼x2¼ color transparencies. Send prints and transparencies. Model release required.

Fiction: Adventure, fantasy, historical and humorous. Buys 5 mss/year. Send complete ms. Length: 500-5,000 words. Pays 3¢/word.

Fillers: "Need short, punchy photo fillers and timely news items." Buys 10 fillers/year. Length: 100-500 words. Pays 3¢/word.

FAMILY PET, Box 22964, Tampa FL 33622. Editor-in-Chief: M. Linda Sabella. Quarterly magazine about pets and for pet owners in Florida. "Our readers are all ages; many show pets, most have more than one pet, and most are in Florida." Averages 12 pages. Circ. 2,500. Pays on publication. Buys one-time rights. SASE. Reports in 6-8 weeks. Free sample copy and writer's guidelines.

Nonfiction: Historical (especially breed histories); how-to (training and grooming hints); humor (or living with pets); informational; personal experience; photo feature; and travel (with pets). Buys 1-2 mss/issue. Send complete ms. Length: 500-1,000 words. Pays $5-20. Maximum $20 for article/photo package.

Photos: Purchased with or without accompanying ms. Captions required. Pays $3-5 for 5x7 b&w glossy prints uses inside. Send prints. Pays $10 for photos used on cover.

Columns/Departments: New Books (reviews of recent issues in pet field). Send complete ms. Length: 200-400 words. Pays $3-5. Open to suggestions for new columns/departments.

Poetry: Light verse, prefers rhyme. Buys 1/issue. Length: 12-16 lines preferred. Pays $3-5.

Fillers: Jokes, gags, anecdotes, puzzles and short humor. Buys 4-5 fillers/year. Length: 100-350 words. Pays $2-5.

HORSE AND HORSEMAN, Box HH, Capistrano Beach CA 92624. Editor: Mark Thiffault. 75% freelance written. For owners of pleasure horses; predominantly female with main interest in show/pleasure riding. Monthly magazine; 74 pages. Circ. 96,000. Buys all rights. Byline given. Buys 40-50 mss/year. Pays on acceptance. Sample copy $1.50 and writer's guidelines free with SASE. Submit special material (horse and tack care; veterinary medicine pieces in winter and spring issues) 3 months in advance. Reports in 1 month. Query or submit complete ms. SASE.

Nonfiction and Photos: Training tips, do-it-yourself pieces, grooming and feeding, stable management, tack maintenance, sports, personalities, rodeo and general horse-related features. Emphasis must be on informing, rather than merely entertaining. Aimed primarily at the beginner, but with information for experienced horsemen. Subject matter must have thorough, in-depth appraisal. Interested in more English (hunter/jumper) riding/training copy, plus pieces on driving horses and special horse areas like Tennessee Walkers and other gaited breeds. More factual breed histories. Uses informational, how-to, personal experience, interview, profile, humor, historical, nostalgia, successful business operations, technical articles. Length: 2,500 words average. Pays $75-200. B&w photos (4x5 and larger) purchased with or without mss. Pays $4-10 when purchased without ms. Uses original color transparencies (35mm and larger). No duplicates. Pays $100 for cover use. Payment for inside editorial color is negotiated.

HORSE, OF COURSE, Derbyshire Publishing Co., Temple NH 03084. (603)654-6126. Editor: John G. Grow. Monthly magazine for horse owners and horse enthusiasts. Circ. 135,000. Pays on publication. Buys all rights. Submit seasonal/holiday material 6 months in advance. SASE. Reports in 2 months. Sample copy $2; free writer's guidelines.

Nonfiction: How-to (about all aspects of horsemanship, horse care and horse owning); newsworthy items (on breeds, famous horse related people, etc., would be particularly salable if you include some tips on riding and horse care); interview (with trainers, riders giving their methods); and short photo feature (profiles, personalities). Buys 80-100 mss/year. Submit complete ms. Length: 500-2,000 words. Pays $50-200.

Photos: Purchased with accompanying ms. Captions required. Submit prints. Pays minimum $5 for 4x5 or larger b&w glossy prints; pays $50-100 for 35mm or 8x10 glossy color prints (for cover). Model release required.

Tips: Send ms to Editorial Dept. If style and talent are right, other assignments may be made. "Queries which give multiple article suggestions are most appealing. They suggest a more well rounded talent." Mss. with excellent photos have better chance of being purchased than mss with no photos.

HORSE PLAY, Box 545, Gaithersburg MD 20760. (301)840-1866. Editor: Cordelia Doucet. Monthly (except combined issue January and February) magazine covering horses and horse sports for a readership interested in horses, especially people who show, event and hunt. 60-80 pages. Circ. 53,000. Pays within 30 days after publication. Copyrighted. All rights reserved. Pays negotiable kill fee. Byline given. Phone queries OK. Submit all material 2 months in advance. SASE. Reports in 6 weeks. Sample copy $2; free writer's guidelines.

Nonfiction: How-to (various aspects of horsemanship, course designing, stable management, putting on horse shows, etc.); humor; interview; photo feature; profile and technical. Buys 40 mss/year. Length: 1,000-3,000 words. Pays $35-100.

Photos: Margaret Thomas, photo editor. Purchased on assignment. Captions required. Query or send contact sheet, prints or transparencies. Pays $7.50 for 8x10 b&w glossy prints; $125 maximum for color transparencies (cover only). Book Reviews: pays $10.

Tips: "Write requesting our writer's guidelines and a sample copy. Study both. No fiction, western riding, or racing articles."

HORSE WOMEN, Rich Publishing, Inc., 41919 Moreno, Temecula CA 92390. Editor: Ray Rich. Annual magazine covering western and English riding for those interested in taking better care of their horse and improving their riding. 120 pages. Pays on publication. Buys all rights. Pays 100% kill fee. Byline given. Phone queries OK. Submit seasonal/holiday material 3 months in advance. SASE. Reports in 1 month. Sample copy $3; free writer's guidelines.

Nonfiction: How-to (anything relating to western and English riding, jumping, barrel racing, etc.); humor; interview (with well-known professional trainers); new product (want new product releases, description of the product and b&w photo, featuring the latest in western and English tack and clothing) and photo feature (preferably foaling). Buys 10-15 mss/issue. Query or send complete ms. Length: 1,000-2,500 words. Pays $40-50/printed page depending on quality and number of photos.

Photos: Send photos with ms. Offers no additional payment for 5x7 or 8x10 b&w glossy prints. Captions preferred.

HORSEMAN, 5314 Bingle Rd., Houston TX 77092. (713)688-8811. Editor: David Gaines. Monthly magazine for people who own and ride horses for pleasure and competition. Majority own western stock horses and compete in western type horse shows as a hobby or business. Many have owned horses for many years. Circ. 160,000. Rights purchased vary with author and material. Buys all rights, first North American serial rights, or second serial (reprint) rights. Byline given unless excessive editing must be done. Pays on publication. Free sample copy and writer's guidelines. Submit seasonal material 4 months in advance. Reports in 3 weeks. Query. SASE.

Nonfiction and Photos: "How-to articles on horsemanship, training, grooming, exhibiting, horsekeeping, and history dealing with horses. We really like articles from professional trainers, or articles about their methods written by freelancers. The approach is to educate and inform readers as to how they can ride, train, keep and enjoy their horses more." Length: 1,000-2,500 words. Pays up to 7¢/word. Photos purchased with accompanying ms or on assignment. Captions required. Pays $10 minimum for b&w 5x7 or 8x10 prints; 35mm or 120 negatives. Pays $25 for inside color. Prefers transparencies. Buys all rights.

Tips: "Send article ideas with very narrow focus. Indicate depth. Use know-how from top experts or send us good, concise articles about specific training problems with detailed explanation of correction. Otherwise, stick to fringe articles: humor, photo essay, Horseman Travelog. The articles need to be packed with information, but we don't always mean step-by-step how to. Make them readable."

HORSEMEN'S YANKEE PEDLAR NEWSPAPER, 19 Harvard St., Worcester MA 01609. (617)753-1467. Publisher: Christine S. Dillard. Associate Editor: JoAnn Griffin. "All-breed monthly newspaper for horse enthusiasts of all ages and incomes, from one-horse owners to large commercial stables. Covers region from New Jersey to Massachusetts." Circ. 12,000. Pays on publication. Buys all rights for one year. Submit seasonal/holiday material 3 months in advance of issue date. SASE. Reports in 1 month. Sample copy $1.25.

Nonfiction: Humor, educational and interview about horses and the people involved with them. Pays $2/published inch. Buys 50-60 mss/year. Submit complete ms or outline. Length: 1,500-2,500 words.

Photos: Purchased with ms. Captions and photo credit required. Buys 1 cover photo/month; pays $10. Submit b&w prints. Pays $5.

Columns/Departments: Area news column. Buys 85-95/year. Length: 1,200-1,400 words. Pays 75¢/column inch. Query.

Tips: "Query with outline of angle of story, approximate length and date when story will be submitted. Stories should be people-oriented and horse focused. Send newsworthy, timely pieces, such as stories that are applicable to the season, for example; foaling in the spring or how to keep a horse healthy through the winter. We like to see how-to's, features about special horse people and anything that has to do with the preservation of horses and their rights as creatures deserving a chance to survive."

HORSES ALL, Rocky Top Holdings, Ltd., Box 550, Nanton, Alberta, Canada T0L 1R0. (403)486-2144. Editor: Jacki French. Monthly tabloid for horse owners, 75% rural, 25% urban. Circ. 9,833. Pays on publication. Buys one-time rights. Phone queries OK. Submit seasonal material 3 months in advance. Simultaneous, photocopied (if clear), and previously published submissions OK. Reports on queries in 2 weeks; on mss in 3 weeks. Free sample copy.

Nonfiction: Interview, humor and personal experience. Query. Pays $20-100.

Photos: "A good pic is worth 1,000 words." State availability of photos. Pays $2.50-$10 for 5x7 b&w glossy prints; $2.50-$10 for 5x7 color glossy prints. Captions required.

Columns/Departments: Length: 1-2 columns. Query. Open to suggestions for new columns/departments. Query Doug French.

Fiction: Historical and western. Query. Pays $20-100.

Fillers: Jokes, anecdotes, short humor, and word puzzles. Length: 5-100 words. Pays $1-$10/set.

HUNTING DOG MAGAZINE, 9714 Montgomery Rd., Cincinnati OH 45242. (513)891-0060. Editor-in-Chief: George R. Quigley. Monthly magazine covering sporting dogs. 56 pages. Circ. 31,000. Pays on publication. Buys all rights. Byline given. Phone queries OK. Submit seasonal/holiday material 6 months in advance. Photocopied submissions OK. Reports in 1 month. Free sample copy and writer's guidelines.

Nonfiction: How-to (training dogs, hunting with dogs, building dog-related equipment), informational, interview (with well-known outdoor and dog-related persons), opinion (by the experts), profile, new product, photo feature, technical (guns, dog-related items). Our magazine is technical; therefore, we accept few freelance submissions. Material must be of a technical nature, i.e., no "Joe-and-his-dog" articles. Buys 175-200 mss/year. Query or submit complete ms. Length: 1,500-2,200 words. Pays 3¢/word minimum.

Photos: Purchased with or without accompanying ms. Captions required. Send contact sheet, prints or transparencies. Pays $5 minimum for 8x10 b&w glossy prints; $50 for 35mm or 2¼x2¼" transparencies (for cover).

Fillers: "Short (200-700 words) pieces about hunting dogs or new uses for equipment." Buys 100 mss/year. Submit complete ms. Pays 3¢/word.

Tips: "Send a good manuscript that shows the writer knows the sporting dog world or how to write from the expert's-eye view."

PAINT HORSE JOURNAL, American Paint Horse Association, Box 18519, Fort Worth TX 76118. (817)439-3400. Editor: Henry King. For people who raise, breed and show paint horses. Monthly magazine. 200 pages. Circ. 11,000. Pays on acceptance. Normally buys all rights. Pays negotiable kill fee. Byline given. Phone queries OK. Submit seasonal/holiday material 3 months in advance. Photocopied and previously published submissions OK. SASE. Reports in 1 month. Free sample copy and writer's guidelines.

Nonfiction: General interest (personality pieces on well known owners of paints); historical (paint horses in the past—particular horses and the breed in general); how-to (training and showing horses); and photo feature (paint horses). Buys 4-5 mss/issue. Send complete ms. Pays $50-250.

Photos: Send photos with ms. Offers no additional payment for photos accepted with accompanying ms. Uses 3x5 or larger b&w glossy prints; 3x5 color transparencies. Captions preferred. Normally buys all rights.

Tips: "*PHJ* needs breeder-trainer articles from areas far-distant from our office. Photos with copy are almost always essential. Well-written first person articles welcome. Humor, too. Submit well-written items that show a definite understanding of the horse business. Use proper equine terminology and proper grounding in ability to communicate thoughts."

PET PARADE MAGAZINE, 6045 Huntington SE., Grand Rapids MI 49506. Editor: Nancy Jeanne Larson. Bimonthly magazine covering all household pets (no wildlife). Estab. 1979. Circ. 10,000. Pays on acceptance. Byline given. Buys first rights. Submit seasonal/holiday material 4 months in advance. SASE. Reports in 1 month on queries and mss. Sample copy $1; writer's guidelines for business size SAE and 1 first class stamp.
Nonfiction: How-to (make pet items with diagrams, care for pets—specific first aid, nutritional, psychological, and grooming hints); inspirational (stories of animals that have done exceptional things); interview/profile (of people doing somthing extra to help pets, animals); and personal experience (lessons learned that will help other pet owners). "All material is written from a humane and affectionate, but practical point of view. "We always need short, concise articles (100-350 words) to use as bright features to supplement the pet care articles. These features can be about interesting pets, interesting pet-related groups or projects or how-to plans for making pet items at home. Good examples that we have used in 1981: Project Earthquake Watch (how pets in California are monitored to predict earthquakes), a summer camp for dogs, the Bay Area Turtle & Tortoise Society, how to take pet photos, etc." No "articles about specific dog and cat breeds or in-depth articles about care of specific pets, such as guinea pigs, parakeets or goldfish; these are all staff-written." Buys 40 mss/year. Query or send complete ms. Length: 100-750 words. Pays 5¢/word.
Photos: Send photos with ms. Pays $10 for b&w 5x7 prints. Identification of subjects required. Buys one-time rights.
Columns/Departments: "All columns are staff-written. The 'People Who Care' section uses 12 freelance stories a year. These stories are about people doing something extra to help pet animals (not wildlife). Photo should accompany manuscript."
Poetry: Free verse and traditional. Buys 20/year. Submit maximum 10 poems. Length: 4-24 lines. Pays $10.

PRACTICAL HORSEMAN, The Pennsylvania Horse, Inc., 225 S. Church St., West Chester PA 19380. Articles Editor: Miranda Lorraine. Monthly magazine for knowledgeable horsemen interested in breeding, raising and training thoroughbred and thoroughbred-type horses for show, eventing, dressage, racing or hunting, and pleasure riding. 88-96 pages. Circ. 42,000. Pays on publication. Buys all rights. Simultaneous and photocopied submissions OK, but will not use any submission unless withdrawn from other publishers. SASE. Reports in 2 months. Free sample copy and writer's guidelines.
Nonfiction: How-to interviews with top professional horsemen in the hunter/jumper field; veterinary and stable management articles; photo features; and step-by-step ideas for barn building, grooming, trimming, and feeding and management tips. Buys 3-4 mss/issue. Query with sample of writing or complete ms. Length: open. Pays $200.
Photos: Purchased on assignment. Captions required. Query. Pays $7.50 minimum for b&w glossy prints (5x7 minimum size); $75 maximum for 35mm or 2¼x2¼ color transparencies for covers.

THE QUARTER HORSE JOURNAL, Box 9105, Amarillo TX 79105. (806)376-4811. Editor-in-Chief: Audie Rackley. Official publication of the American Quarter Horse Association. Monthly magazine; 650 pages. Circ. 81,199. Pays on acceptance. Buys all rights or first rights. Phone queries OK. Submit seasonal/holiday material 2 months in advance. SASE. Reports in 2 weeks. Free sample copy and writer's guidelines.
Nonfiction: Historical ("those that retain our western heritage"); how-to (fitting, grooming, showing, or anything that relates to owning, showing, or breeding); informational (educational clinics, current news); interview (feature-type stories—must be about established people who have made a contribution to the business); new product; personal opinion; and technical (medical updates, new surgery procedures, etc.). Buys 30 mss/year. Length: 800-2,500 words. Pays $50-200.
Photos: Purchased with accompanying ms. Captions required. Send prints or transparencies. Uses 5x7 or 8x10 b&w glossy prints; 2¼x2¼ or 4x5 color transparencies. Offers no additional payment for photos accepted with accompanying ms.

THE QUARTER HORSE OF THE PACIFIC COAST, Pacific Coast Quarter Horse Assn., Box 254822, Gate 12 Cal Expo, Sacramento CA 95825. Editor-in-Chief: Jill L. Scopinich. Monthly magazine covering quarter horses for owners, breeders and trainers on the West Coast. 150 pages. Circ. 8,200. Pays on acceptance. Buys all rights or first North American serial rights. Pays 50% kill fee. Byline given. Simultaneous submissions OK. SASE. Reports in 1 month. Sample copy $2.

Nonfiction: How-to; informational; interview; personal experience; photo feature; and profile. Buys 2 mss/issue. Send complete ms. Length: 500-3,000 words. Pays $35-250.
Photos: Photos purchased with or without accompanying ms. Captions required. Pays $5-10 for 8x10 b&w glossy prints. Model release required.
Columns/Departments: Of Course, A Horse; Racing Room; and The Stable Pharmacy. Buys 3 mss/issue. Send complete ms. Length: 500-2,000 words. Pays $35-100.
Tips: "Readers are owners, breeders, trainers of show, race and performance Quarter horses on the West Coast. We emphasize knowledge, laws and activities involving them. We need breeding, feeding, legislative information and humorous articles."

TODAY'S ANIMAL HEALTH, Animal Health Foundation, 1905 Sunnycrest Dr., Fullerton CA 92635. Editor-in-Chief: Richard Glassberg, D.V.M. Managing Editor: Jane Wright. Bimonthly magazine covering animal health, nutrition and care for people who own animals. 32-40 pages. Circ. 26,000. Pays on publication. Buys all rights. Submit seasonal/holiday material 6 months in advance. Simultaneous, photocopied and previously published submissions OK. SASE. Reports in 2 months. Sample copy $1.50; writer's guidelines for SASE to: Mr. Harry Maiden, 8338 Rosemead, Pico Rivera CA 90660.
Nonfiction: Expose, how-to, general interest, interview, photo feature, profile and technical. Buys 6/issue. Submit complete ms. Length 250-2,000 words. Pays $5-25.
Photos: D.M. Diem, photo editor. Submit photo material with accompanying ms. Pays $5-25 for 8x10 b&w glossy prints and $5-25 for 5x7 color prints. Caption preferred. Buys all rights.

TROPICAL FISH HOBBYIST, 211 W. Sylvania Ave., Neptune City NJ 17753. Editor: Marshall Ostrow. Monthly magazine for tropical fish keepers. 100 pages. Circ. 40,000. Rights purchased vary with author and material. Usually buys all rights. Byline given. Buys 50 mss/year. Pays on acceptance. Sample copy $1. No photocopied or simultaneous submissions. Query or submit complete ms. SASE.
Nonfiction and Photos: "Don't submit material unless you're an experienced keeper of tropical fishes and know what you're talking about. Offer specific advice about caring for and breeding tropicals, amphibians, reptiles and about related topics. Study the publication before submitting." Informal style preferred. Can use personality profiles of successful aquarium hobbyists, but query first on these.
Photos: Submit b&w prints.

THE WESTERN HORSEMAN, Box 7980, Colorado Springs CO 80933. Editor: Chan Bergen. Monthly magazine covering western horsemanship. Circ. 177,532. Pays on acceptance. Buys one-time rights. Byline given. Submit seasonal/holiday material 3 months in advance. SASE. Reports in 3 weeks. Sample copy $1.50.
Nonfiction: How-to (horse training, care of horses, tips, etc.); and informational (on rodeos, ranch life, historical articles of the West emphasizing horses). Buys 15-20/issue. Submit complete ms. Length: 1,500 words. Pays $85-135; "sometimes higher by special arrangement."
Photos: Send photos with ms. Offers no additional payment for photos. Uses 5x7 or 8x10 b&w glossy prints and 35mm transparencies. Captions required.
Tips: "Submit clean copy with professional quality photos. Stay away from generalities. Writing style should show a deep interest in horses coupled with a wide knowledge of the subject."

Art

THE AMERICAN ART JOURNAL, Kennedy Galleries, Inc., 40 W. 57th St., 5th Floor, New York NY 10019. (212)541-9600. Editor-in-Chief: Jane Van N. Turano. Scholarly magazine of American art history of the 17th, 18th, 19th and 20th Centuries, including painting, sculpture, architecture, decorative arts, etc., for people with a serious interest in American art, and who are already knowledgeable about the subject. Readers are scholars, curators, collectors, students of American art, or persons who have a strong interest in Americana. Quarterly magazine; 96 pages. Circ. 2,000. Pays on acceptance. Buys all rights. Byline given. Photocopied submissions OK. SASE. Reports in 2 months. Sample copy $7.
Nonfiction: "All articles are historical in the sense that they are all about some phase or aspect of American art history." No how-to articles or reviews of exhibitions. No book reviews or opinion pieces. No human interest approaches to artists' lives. No articles written in a casual or "folksy" style. *Writing style must be formal and serious.* Buys 25-30 mss/year. Submit complete ms "with

good cover letter." Length: 2,500-8,000 words. Pays $300-400.
Photos: Purchased with accompanying ms. Captions required. Uses b&w only. Offers no additional payment for photos accepted with accompanying ms.
Tips: "Actually, our range of interest is quite broad. Any topic within our time frame is acceptable if it is well-researched, well-written, and illustrated. Whenever possible, all mss must be accompanied by b&w photographs which have been integrated into the text by the use of numbers."

ARTS MAGAZINE, 23 E. 26th St., New York NY 10010. (212)685-8500. Editor: Richard Martin. A journal of contemporary art, art criticism, analysis and history, particularly for artists, scholars, museum officials, art teachers and students, and collectors. Monthly, except July and August. Circ. 28,500. Buys all rights. Pays on publication. Query. SASE.
Nonfiction and Photos: Art criticism, analysis and history. Topical reference to museum or gallery exhibition preferred. Length: 1,500-2,500 words. Pays $100, with opportunity for negotiation. B&w glossies or color transparencies customarily supplied by related museums or galleries.

ARTS MANAGEMENT, 408 W. 57th St., New York NY 10019. (212)245-3850. Editor: A.H. Reiss. For cultural institutions. Published five times/year. Circ. 6,000. Buys all rights. Byline given. Pays on publication. Mostly staff-written. Query. Reports in "several weeks." SASE.
Nonfiction: Short articles, 400-900 words, tightly written, expository, explaining how art administrators solved problems in publicity, fund raising, and general administration; actual case histories emphasizing the how-to. Also short articles on the economics and sociology of the arts and important trends in the nonprofit cultural field. Must be fact-filled, well-organized and without rhetoric. Payment is 2-4¢/word. No photographs or pictures.

CONNECTICUT ARTISTS MAGAZINE, Connecticut Artists, Inc., Box 131, New Haven CT 06501. (203)787-4106. Publisher: Salvatore Rascati. Editor: David Alvarez. Associate Editor: Donald Faulkner. Quarterly magazine covering literature, visual arts, performing arts, and photography for an audience in Connecticut, Massachusetts, New York and Rhode Island. Circ. 10,605. Pays on publication. Byline given. Buys all rights. Phone queries OK. Submit seasonal/holiday material 3 months in advance. Photocopied and previously published submissions OK. SASE. Reports in 1 month on queries; in 6 weeks on mss. Sample copy $2; writer's guidelines for SASE.
Nonfiction: Historical (retrospective features on past Connecticut artists); interview (of prominent and/or emerging Connecticut artists); opinion (guest editorials on issues concerning art in Connecticut); profile; photo feature (on art/photography); and essays. No technical, human interest, expose. Buys 4-7 mss/issue. Query with clips of previously published work. Length: 300-3,500 words. Pays $25 minimum.
Photos: John Spalding, photo editor. "Since many articles concern visual artists, photos do help. Also, with non-visual artists, it helps to have photos of people being interviewed." State availability of photos. Reviews 8x10 b&w prints and 2¼x2¼ color transparencies. Offers no additional payment for photos accepted with ms. "There are exceptions—staff photographer is available." Captions preferred; model release required. Buys one-time rights.
Columns/Departments: "Around the State," (short articles concerning events/issues of interest around the state of Connecticut); "Retrospect" (articles on past work of distinction by Connecticut artists; includes artists who work in literature and crafts as well). Query. Length: 250-1,000 words. Pays $25 minimum. Open to suggestions for new columns/departments. Query David Alvarez.
Fiction: David Alvarez, fiction editor. Drama, fantasy, humor, mystery, experimental, mainstream, science fiction. "Nothing pornographic, overly political or defamatory." Buys 1-3 mss/issue. Send complete ms. Length: 250-5,000 words. Pays $25 minimum.
Poetry: Avant-garde, free verse, haiku, light verse, traditional and narrative, concrete. Buys 12 mss/issue. Submit in batches of 7-8. Length: open. Pays $5 minimum.
Tips: "All areas are equal, however, short fiction is always in demand. Profiles on Connecticut artists are always welcome (with these, query). *Connecticut Artists* follows a seasonal pattern: literature (spring); photography (summer); performing arts (fall); visual arts (winter). While emphasis is placed on these areas, all are dealt with in each issue."

CRAFT RANGE, the Mountain Plains Crafts Journal, Colorado Artist Craftsmen, 6800 W. Oregon Dr., Denver CO 80226. (303)986-4891. Editor: Carol M. Hoffman. Bimonthly tabloid covering artists, shows, galleries, institutions and issues related to contemporary crafts and arts for and about artists, teachers, and art lovers in areas west of the Mississippi River, excluding the West Coast states. Circ. 1,000. Pays on publication. Byline given. Buys one-time rights. Simultaneous queries, simultaneous, photocopied and previously published submissions OK. SASE. Reports on queries and mss in 1 month. Sample copy free; writer's guidelines free for business size SASE and 1 first class stamp.

Nonfiction: General interest (art related); interview/profile (artists or people); personal experience; photo feature; and book reviews. No how-to-do crafts, or business/marketing. Query. Length: 250-1,500 words. Pays $15 minimum/article.

Photos: State availability of photos. Reviews 5x7 or larger b&w glossy prints. Cost of photos are reimbursed. Model releases and identification of subjects required. "Try to get public relation photos from the gallery or artist."

THE CULTURAL POST, National Endowment for the Arts, 2401 E St. NW., Washington DC 20506. Editor: George Clack. The official newspaper of the Arts Endowment, a federal agency that gives grants to nonprofit cultural institutions and individual artists. Read by arts administratiors and artists seeking grants from the Arts Endowment. Bimonthly newspaper. Buys all rights. Pays 10% kill fee. Byline given. Reports in 1 month.

Nonfiction: "Interested in carefully researched articles on the financial or administrative side of Arts Endowment grantees, examinations of important trends or problems in various art fields, and reports on arts activities at the state and community level." Buys 20 mss/year. Query. Length: 1,000-3,000 words. Pays $300-500, including photos.

Tips: "Send us a resume and outstanding writing sample on the administrative side of the arts. Be located somewhere other than New York, Washington or San Francisco. Have a lively, reportial writing style in the samples submitted and an unusual story idea with some specific connection to the Art Endowment."

DESIGN FOR ARTS IN EDUCATION MAGAZINE, Heldref Publications, 4000 Albemarle St. NW, Washington DC 20016. (202)362-6445. Publisher: Cornelius W. Vahle. Managing Editor: Jane Scully. "For teachers, art specialists, administrators, and parents who work with children in education." Bimonthly magazine. Byline given. Accompanying photographs encouraged. SASE. Reports in 8-10 weeks. Sample copy $3. Editorial guidelines for SASE.

Nonfiction: *Design* deals with architecture, dance, the environmental arts, folk arts, literature, media, museums, music, opera, theatre and the visual arts, as well as their relationships with each other. The articles are aimed at teachers, administrators, parents and professionals both within and outside of the arts fields. Articles will range from theory to practice, from exemplary programs to learning theory in and among the arts disciplines and other curricular areas. Emphasis will be on information about the arts and their place, focus, and impact on education and the educational process. Submit complete ms. Length: 1,000-2,000 words.

FORMAT: ART & THE WORLD, Seven Oaks Press, 405 S. 7th St., St. Charles IL 60174. (312)584-0187. Editor: Ms. C.L. Morrison. Quarterly magazine covering art and society. "Our audience consists of three groups: young artists wanting to know more about survival in the current art system (visual and other arts); married and unmarried women who are interested in the role, position, opportunities for, and situation of women in the art world; and writer/editors involved in the small-press literary magazine community. We are non-romantic, practical, straight-talking and non-sexist. Subscribers are 40% midwest, 10% west coast, 10% east coast, with the rest scattered in the US and a tiny segment of Europe." Circ. 1,000. Pays on publication. Byline given. "We copyright for the author; some assignments are on a work-for-hire basis. Submit seasonal/holiday material 4 months (long); 2 months (short) in advance. Photocopied and previously published submissions OK. SASE. Reports in 1 month on queries and mss. Sample copy $1.50.

Nonfiction: Opinion and personal experience. "Special theme issues usually evolve out of receiving a lot of material on one interesting subject. Recently we printed our special 'Rejection' issue. We are always interested in material about artist-survival, what it means to be a critic, and the education of and existence of artists. Opinions about government funding, how artists get along with one another, artists and money, how current society affects current art, and artists' personal experiences with one thing or another—i.e., real-life episodes, particularly women's real-life episodes." No "exhibition reviews or publicity-oriented monographs on individual artists. We're not interested in the kind of article that says 'I don't understand modern art—it's all a bunch of ridiculous stuff,' and variations on that theme." Send complete ms. Length: 300-3,000 words. Pays $5-15 plus 6 or more contributor's copies.

Fiction: "Art-related, or 'odd' subjects." Buys 60 mss/year. Length: 250-1,000 words. Pays $5-15/article.

Poetry: Avant-garde, free verse and traditional. No "romantic, organic sense-impressions, word-pictures, pure language, and so forth. Poem subjects are social critique, art and women's issues. Buys 25 mss/year. Submit maximum 10 poems. Length: 8-50 lines. Pays 6 contributor's copies.

Tips: "A writer can break in with us by being honest, outspoken, well-informed, individualistic, concerned. Our general tone, however, is not what I would call angry. We are often quite light and humorous. Nonetheless, most of the features would be considered intelligent critiques with very astute political consciousness. Articles and poetry are the departments most open to freelancers. Articles should be well-written and not repeats of information published 1,000 times before in history books, magazines, and so forth. We are documenting the current time, and the particular forces at work now, and so presentations of applicable material should be considered in terms of real-life experience, now. If the writer has no real-life experience, i.e., is all text-books and academia, forget it. Poetry, also, should be subject-oriented."

FUNNYWORLD, THE MAGAZINE OF ANIMATION & COMIC ART, Box 1633, New York NY 10001. For animation and comic art collectors and others in the field. Quarterly magazine; 56 pages. Circ. 7,000. Pays on publication. Buys all rights. Photocopied and previously published work OK. SASE. Reports in 1 month. Sample copy $3.50.
Nonfiction: Historical (history of animation and its creators; history of comic books, characters and creators); interview (with creators of comics and animated cartoons); and reviews (of materials in this field). Buys 4 mss/issue. Query. Pays $20 minimum.
Photos: "Photos of creators, film stills, comic strips and art used extensively." State availability of photos. Pay varies for 8x10 b&w and color glossy prints. Offers no additional payment for photos accepted with ms. Captions preferred.

GLASS STUDIO, Box 23383, Portland OR 97223. Editor: Maureen R. Michelson. For artists working in blown glass, stained glass, conceptual glass, collectors, museum curators, gallery and shop owners, art critics, students in the arts, and hobbyists. Monthly. Circ. 30,000. Pays 1 month after publication.
Nonfiction: "We are looking for technical articles, features on artists and 'how-to' pieces for artists, craftspersons and hobbyists." Pays $500 maximum.
Photos: No additional payment for b&w prints used with mss.

HORIZON, The Magazine of the Arts, Boone, Inc., Drawer 30, Tuscaloosa AL 35402. Editor: Gray Boone. Managing Editor: Kellee Reinhart. Monthly magazine covering the arts (fine arts, architecture, literature, theater, dance, film, music, photography, television). "*Horizon* is a graphically rich arts magazine aimed at the intelligent layperson who is as likely to live in a small town as in New York." Pays on publication. Byline given. Offers kill fee. Buys first North American serial rights. Submit seasonal/holiday material 2½ months in advance. "This is important, as many of our articles are timed with openings, etc." SASE. Reports in 1 month. Sample copy $2; free writer's guidelines.
Nonfiction: David Roberts, articles editor. Book excerpts ("relatively few"); expose ("if sound and well-documented"); historical/nostalgic ("rarely"); profile ("perhaps half our articles are profiles"); personal experience ("rarely, unless by famous artist"); and photo feature ("only with strong text"). "We get mistaken for a travel magazine. We publish no original fiction or poetry." Buys 100 mss/year. Query with clips of published work or send complete ms ("only if offbeat but well-written or strong. Articles accompanied by good photographs or comprehensive photographic research more likely to be accepted." Length: 1,500-3,500 words. Pays $350-600.
Photos: Robin McDonald, photo editor. State availability of photos or send photos with ms. Reviews any size color transparencies or 8x10 prints. Identification of subjects required. Buys one-time rights.
Tips: Most open to "feature articles. We're rarely interested in merely regional pieces, but encourage a wide diversity of cultures (not just US) among the ms we'll run. The most important quality for freelancers wanting to publish in *Horizon* is good prose. Query letters should be to the point (not two pages long) and are best supported with clips of the writer's other publications. Timeliness and a unique angle are vital also. We take queries in writing only. Phone queries are counterproductive, because they annoy our editors, who are working on other things. Flexibility and promptness at deadlines endear writers to us."

METALSMITH, Society of North American Goldsmiths, 8589 Wonderland NW, Clinton OH 44216. (216)854-2681. Editors: Mark Baldridge and Sarah Bodine. Editorial address: 35 W. 84th St., New York City NY 10024. Quarterly magazine covering craft metalwork and metal arts for people who work in metal and those interested in the field, including museum curators, collectors and teachers. The magazine covers all aspects of the craft including historical and technical articles, business and marketing advice and exhibition reviews. Estab. 1980. Circ. 2,300. Pays on publication. Byline given. Buys first North American serial rights. Submit seasonal/holiday material 6 months in advance. Photocopied and previously published submissions (foreign) OK. SASE. Reports in 1 month on queries; 6 weeks on mss. Free sample copy and writer's guidelines.
Nonfiction: Expose (metals, markets, theft); historical/nostalgic; how-to (advanced-level metalsmithing techniques); humor; inspirational; interview/profile; opinion (regular column); personal experience; photo feature; technical (research); travel (Metalsmith's Guides to Cities). Special

issues include: Annual Summer Program Listing and Suppliers Listing. Buys 15 mss/year. Query with clips of published work and indicate "experience in the field or related fields." Length: 1,000-3,500 words. Pays $25-100/article.

Columns/Departments: Exhibition reviews, Issues: Galleries, Marketing and Business Advice, Metalsmith's Guides to Cities and Regions, and Book Reviews. Buys 20 mss/year. Query with clips of published work. Length: 250-3,000 words. Pays $10-50/article.

Tips: "The discovery of new talent is a priority—queries about innovative work which has not received much publicity are welcome. Almost all our writing is done by freelancers. Those knowledgeable in the field and who have previous experience in writing analysis and criticism are most sought after. *Metalsmith* is looking to build a stable of crafts writers and so far have found these few and far between. Those who both have a feeling for metalwork of all kinds and a sharp pencil are sought. Articles have some substance. We do not go for two-page spreads, so an idea submitted must have thematic unity and depth. We are not looking for pretty pictures of metalwork, but analysis, presentation of new or undiscovered talent and historical documentation. A few lines of explanation of a story idea are therefore helpful."

THE METRO, Libre Press, Inc., Suite 529-530, Connell Bldg., Scranton PA 18503. (717)348-1010. Managing Editor: Joseph Skorupa. Executive Editor: John White. Monthly magazine featuring cultural material on art, sculpture, theater, film and a limited amount of social commentary. Pays on publication. Byline given. Buys First North American serial rights. Submit seasonal material 2 months in advance. Simultaneous, photocopied and previously published submissions OK. SASE. Reports in 2 weeks on mss. Sample copy and writer's guidelines free for SASE.

Nonfiction: General interest (financing art and anything that encourages art in Pocono Northeast, pertaining to cultural personalities); historical; opinion (commentary on the arts); profile (cultural personalities); and how-to (make a living as an artist). Send complete ms. Length: 600-800 words. Pays average $25.

Photos: Reviews 5x7 or 8x10 glossy prints. Captions and model release required. Buys one-time rights.

NEW YORK ARTS JOURNAL, Manhattan Arts Review, Inc., 560 Riverside Dr., New York NY 10027. (212)663-2245. Editor-in-Chief: Richard Burgin. Emphasizes the arts: fiction, poetry, book reviews, music and visual arts. Bimonthly tabloid; 44 pages. Circ. 25,000. Buys one-time rights. Phone queries only. Sample copy $1.

Nonfiction: Historical, informational, interview, photo feature and profile. "We publish full-page portfolios of photos which stand on their own, not necessarily as illustration." Buys 3-6 mss/issue. Send complete ms with SASE. Pays $3/page.

NEWORLD: THE MULTI-CULTURAL MAGAZINE OF THE ARTS, Los Angeles Cultural Center, 1308 S. New Hampshire Blvd., Los Angeles CA 90006. (213)387-1161. Editor-in-Chief: Fred Beauford. Managing Editor: Jan Alexander-Leitz. Bimonthly magazine; 60 pages. Circ. 15,000. Pays on publication. Buys all rights. Pays $25 kill fee. Byline given. Phone queries OK. Submit seasonal/holiday material 4 months in advance. Photocopied submissions OK. SASE. Reports in 3 weeks. Sample copy $1.25.

Nonfiction: "Only articles related to dance, theater, photography, visual arts, music, poetry, literature, film and television, and issues that affect the arts." How-to; general interest; historical; interview; opinion; photo feature; and profile. Buys 3 mss/issue. Submit complete ms. Length: open. Pays $50-75.

Photos: State availability of photos with ms. Submit contact sheets. Pays $5-10/b&w photo. Captions and model release required. Buys one-time rights.

Poetry: Avant-garde; free verse; light verse; and traditional. Buys 7/issue. Limit submissions to batches of 3. Length: 42 lines maximum. No payment.

THE ORIGINAL ART REPORT, Box 1641, Chicago IL 60690. Editor and Publisher: Frank Salantrie. Emphasizes "visual art conditions for visual artists, art museum presidents and trustees, collectors of fine art, art educators, and interested citizens." Monthly newsletter; 6-8 pages. Pays on publication. Buys all rights. SASE. Reports in 2 weeks. Sample copy $1.25.

Nonfiction: Exposé (art galleries, government agencies ripping off artists, or ignoring them), historical (perspective pieces relating to now), humor (whenever possible), informational (material that is unavailable in other art publications), inspirational (acts and ideas of courage), interview (with artists, other experts; serious material), personal opinion, technical (brief items to recall traditional methods of producing art), travel (places in the world where artists are welcome and honored), philosophical, economic, aesthetic, and artistic. Query or submit complete ms. Length: 1,000 words maximum. Pays 1¢/word.

Columns/Departments: New column: "In Back of the Individual Artist in which artists express their views about non-art topics. After all, artists are in this world, too!;" WOW (Worth One Wow), Worth Repeating, and Worth Repeating Again. "Basically, these are reprint items with introduction to give context and source, including complete name and address of publication. Looking for insightful, succinct commentary." Submit complete ms. Length: 500 words maximum. Pays ½¢/word.

Tips: "I get excited when ideas are proposed which address substantive problems of individual artist in the art condition and as they affect the general population. Send original material that is direct and to the point, opinionated and knowledgeable. Write in a factual style with clarity."

SOUTHWEST ART, Box 13037, Houston TX 77019. (713)850-0990. Editor: Susan Hallsten McGarry. Emphasizes art—painting and sculpture. Monthly; 162 pages. Controlled circ. Pays on 10th of the month of publication. Buys all rights. Photocopied submissions OK. SASE. Reports in 2 months. Sample copy $6.

Nonfiction: Informational, interview, personal opinion, and profile. "We publish articles about artists and art trends, concentrating on a geographical area west of the Mississippi. Articles should explore the artist's personality, philosophy, artistic values, media and techniques, and means by which they convey ideas." Buys approximately 100 mss/year. Must submit 20 color prints/ transparencies along with a full biography of the artist. If artist is accepted, article length is 2,000 words minimum. Pays $150 base.

Tips: "Submit both published and unpublished samples of your writing. An indication of how quickly they work and their availability on short notice is helpful."

TODAY'S ART & GRAPHICS, 6 E. 43rd St., New York NY 10017. Editor: George A. Magnan. For professional and fine artists, commercial artists and illustrators, printmakers, artists working in 2- and 3-dimensional forms, and art teachers. Monthly. Circ. 86,000. Buys first rights. Byline given. Pays on publication. Query. SASE.

Nonfiction and Photos: Step-by-step art demonstrations, interviews with fine and commercial artists, features on art materials and technical applications; business of art. Color illustrations of art with some b&w. Step-by-step demonstrations. Length: 500-1,000 words. Fee from $75; negotiable.

Tips: "Please send story idea in a letter or in outline form first. Include color slides of the artwork which best typifies the artist. We are most interested in interviews or how-to stories that reveal the artist's approach to technical and aesthetic problems, that reveal the special personality of this artist, and that provide the reader with practical direction. We don't want art history or philosophizing about art. With rare exceptions, we won't do stories on unknown artists."

WESTART, Box 1396, Auburn CA 95603. (916)885-0969. Editor-in-Chief: Martha Garcia. Emphasizes art for practicing artists and artist/craftsmen; students of art and art patrons. Semimonthly tabloid; 20 pages. Circ. 7,500. Pays on publication. Buys all rights. Byline given. Phone queries OK. Photocopied submissions OK. Sample copy 50¢; free writer's guidelines.

Nonfiction: Informational; photo feature and profile. No hobbies. Buys 6-8 mss/year. Query or submit complete ms. Length: 700-800 words. Pays 30¢/column inch.

Photos: Purchased with or without accompanying ms. Send b&w prints. Pays 30¢/column inch.

Tips: "We publish information which is current—that is, we will use a review of an exhibition only if exhibition is still open on date of publication. Therefore, reviewer must be familiar with our printing deadlines and news deadlines."

Association, Club, and Fraternal

These publications keep members, friends and institutions informed of the ideals, objectives, projects, and activities of the sponsoring club or organization. Club-financed magazines that carry material not directly related to the group's activities (for example, *Manage* magazine in the Management and Supervision Trade Journals) are classified by their subject matter in the Consumer and Trade Journals sections of this book.

CALIFORNIA HIGHWAY PATROLMAN, California Association of Highway Patrolmen, 2030 V St., Sacramento CA 95818. (916)452-6751. Editor: Richard York. Monthly magazine; 100 plus pages. Circ. 18,000. Pays on publication. Buys all rights. SASE. Reports in 2 months. Free sample copy.

Nonfiction: Publishes articles on transportation safety and driver education. "Topics can include autos, boats, bicycles, motorcycles, snowmobiles, recreational vehicles and pedestrian safety. We are also in the market for travel pieces and articles on early California. We are *not* a technical journal for teachers and traffic safety experts, but rather a general interest publication geared toward the layman." Pays 2½¢/word.

Photos: "Illustrated articles always receive preference." Pays $2.50/b&w photo. Captions and model releases required.

D.A.C. NEWS, Detroit Athletic Club, 241 Madison Ave., Detroit MI 48226. Editor: John H. Worthington. For business and professional men. Much of the magazine is devoted to member activities, including social events and athletic activities at the club. Magazine published 9 times/ year. Pays after publication. Buys first rights. Byline given. SASE. Reports in 1 month. Sample copy for 9x12 SASE.

Nonfiction: General interest articles, usually male-oriented, about sports (pro football, baseball, squash, golf, skiing and tennis); travel (to exclusive resorts and offbeat places); drama; personalities; health (jogging, tennis elbow, coronary caution); and some humor, if extremely well-done. Some nostalgia (football greats, big band era are best examples). "We would like to see articles on eccentric millionaires, sunken treasure, the world's biggest yacht, old English pubs, Arab money and where it's going, the economy, football's greatest games, offbeat resorts and gourmet foods." Buys 1 ms/issue. Send complete ms. Length: 750-3,000 words. Pays $50-250.

Photos: Send photos with ms. Offers no additional payment for photos accepted with mss.

Tips: "Tell us your story idea and where you have been published previously. Give us a brief synopsis of one idea. Express a cheerful willingness to rewrite along our lines."

THE ELKS MAGAZINE, 425 W. Diversey, Chicago IL 60614. Managing Editor: Donald Stahl. Emphasizes general interest with family appeal. Monthly magazine; 56 pages. Circ. 1,600,000. Pays on acceptance. Buys first North American serial rights. SASE. Reports in 6 weeks. Free sample copy and writer's guidelines.

Nonfiction: Articles of information, business, contemporary life problems and situations, or just interesting topics, ranging from medicine, science, and history, to sports. "The articles should not just be a rehash of existing material. They must be fresh, provocative, thought-provoking, well-researched and documented. No fiction, travel or political articles, fillers or verse. Buys 2-3 mss/issue. Written query a must. No phone queries. Length 2,000-3,500 words. Pays $150-500.

Photos: Purchased with or without accompanying manuscript (for cover). Captions required. Query with b&w photos or send transparencies. Uses 8x10 or 5x7 b&w glossies and 35mm or 2¼x2¼ color transparencies (for cover). Pays $250 minimum for color (cover). Offers no additional payment for photos accepted with mss.

Tips: "Since we continue to offer sample copies and guidelines for the asking there is no excuse for being unfamiliar with *The Elks Magazine*. A submission, following a query letter go-ahead would do best to include several b&w prints, if the piece lends itself to illustration."

THE KIWANIS MAGAZINE, 101 E. Erie St., Chicago IL 60611. Executive Editor: Scott Pemberton. Magazine published 10 times/year for business and professional men and their families. Circ. 300,000. Buys first North American serial rights. Pays 20-40% kill fee. Byline given. Pays on acceptance. Free sample copy. Reports in 1 month. SASE.

Nonfiction and Photos: Articles about social and civic betterment, business, education, religion, domestic affairs, etc. Emphasis on objectivity, intelligent analysis and thorough research of contemporary problems. Concise writing, absence of clichés, and impartial presentation of controversy required. Especially needs "articles on business and professional topics that will directly assist the readers in their own businesses (generally independent retailers and companies of less than 25 employees) or careers. In addition, we have an increasing need for articles of international interest, especially in the area of world health." Length: 1,500-3,000 words. Pays $300-600. "No fiction, personal essays, fillers or verse of any kind. A light or humorous approach welcomed where subject is appropriate and all other requirements are observed. Detailed queries can save work and submission time. We often accept photos submitted with mss, but we do not pay extra for them; they are considered part of the price of the ms. Our rate for a ms with good photos is higher than for one without." Query.

LEADER, The Order of United Commercial Travelers of America, Box 159019, 632 N. Park St., Columbus OH 43215. (614)228-3276. Editor-in-Chief: James R. Eggert. Emphasizes fraternalism for its officers and active membership. Magazine published 8 times/year; 32 pages. Circ. 25,000. Pays on publication. Buys all rights. Byline given. Submit seasonal/holiday material 3 months in

advance. SASE. Reports in 1 week. Free sample copy and writer's guidelines.
Nonfiction: General interest; how-to; humor; interview; and profile. Buys 1 ms/issue. Submit complete ms. Length: 500-3,000 words. Pays 1½¢/word.
Photos: State availability of photos with ms. Pays $5 for 5x7 b&w glossy prints. Captions preferred. Buys all rights. Model release required.
Fiction: Humorous. Buys 2 mss/year. Submit complete ms. Length: 500-1,500 words. Pays 1½¢/word.
Tips: "Submit a letter, along with the ms itself. We are looking for travel/leisure articles pertaining to the US and Canada."

THE LION, 300 22nd St., Oak Brook IL 60570. (312)986-1700. Editor-in-Chief: Roy Schaetzel. Senior Editor: Robert Kleinfelder. Covers service club organization for Lions Club members and their families. Monthly magazine; 36 pages. Circ. 670,000. Pays on acceptance. Buys all rights. Byline given. Phone queries OK. Photocopied submissions OK. SASE. Reports in 2 weeks. Free sample copy and writer's guidelines.
Nonfiction: Humor; informational (stories of interest to civic-minded men); and photo feature (must be of a Lions club service project). Buys 4 mss/issue. Query. Length: 500-2,200. Pays $50-400.
Photos: Purchased with or without accompanying ms or on assignment. Captions required. Query for photos. B&w and color glossies at least 5x7. Total purchase price for ms includes payment for photos, accepted with ms. "Be sure photos are clear and as candid as possible."
Tips: "The Lions Club project proposed for assignment should be large enough in scope to warrant feature-length treatment. Ascertain first the amount of money raised or the number of people who benefit as a result of the project."

NATIONAL 4-H NEWS, 7100 Connecticut Ave., Washington DC 20015. (301)656-9000, ext. 219. Editor: Suzanne C. Harting. For "young to middle-aged adults (mostly women) who lead 4-H clubs; most with high school, many with college education, whose primary reason for reading us is their interest in working with kids in informal youth education projects, ranging from aerospace to swimming, and almost anything in between." Monthly. Circ. 90,000. Buys first serial or one-time rights. Buys about 25 mss/year. Pays on acceptance. Free sample copy and writer's guidelines. Query with outline. "We are very specialized, and unless a writer has been published in our magazine before, he more than likely doesn't have a clue to what we can use. When query comes about a specific topic, we often can suggest angles that make it usable." Submit seasonal material 1 year in advance. Reports in 1 month. SASE.
Nonfiction: "Education and child psychology from authorities, written in light, easy-to-read fashion with specific suggestions how the layman can apply them in volunteer work with youth; how-to-do-it pieces about genuinely new and interesting crafts of any kind. This is our primary need now but articles must be fresh in style and ideas, and tell how to make something worthwhile . . . almost anything that tells about kids having fun and learning outside the classroom, including how they became interested, most effective programs, etc., always with enough detail and examples, so reader can repeat project or program with his or her group, merely by reading the article. Speak directly to our reader (you) without preaching. Tell him in a conversational text how he might work better with kids to help them have fun and learn at the same time. Use lots of genuine examples (although names and dates are not important) to illustrate points. Use contractions when applicable. Write in a concise, interesting way. Our readers have other jobs and not a lot of time to spend with us. Will not print stories on 'How this 4-H club made good' or about state or county fair winners. Reasons for rejection of freelance submissions include: failure of the writer to query first; failure of the writer to study back issues; and mss submitted on subjects we've just covered in depth." Length: 3-8 pages, typewritten, doublespaced. Payment up to $100, depending on quality and accompanying photos or illustrations.
Photos: State availability of photos. "Photos must be genuinely candid, of excellent technical quality and preferably shot 'available light' or in that style; must show young people or adults and young people having fun learning something. How-to photos or drawings must supplement instructional texts. Photos do not necessarily have to include people. Photos are usually purchased with accompanying ms, with no additional payment. Captions required. If we use an excellent single photo, we generally pay $25 and up."
Tips: "Familiarity with the 4-H program and philosophy is most helpful. Write for sample copy. I judge a writer's technical skills by the grammar and syntax of query letter; seldom ask for a ms I think will require extensive reorganization or heavy editing."

THE OPTIMIST MAGAZINE, Optimist International, 4494 Lindell Blvd., St. Louis MO 63108. (314)371-6000. Editor: Dennis R. Osterwisch. Monthly magazine about the work of Optimist clubs and members for the 135,000 members of the Optimist clubs in the United States and Canada.

Circ. 135,000. Pays on acceptance. Buys first North American serial rights. Submit seasonal material 3 months in advance. Photocopied and previously published submissions OK. SASE. Reports in 1 week. Free sample copy.

Nonfiction: General interest (people, places and things that would interest men dedicated to community service through volunteer work); inspirational (up-beat stories on members who have overcome hardships or setbacks because of an optimistic attitude toward life); interview (members who have in some way distinguished themselves). No articles of a negative nature. "A well-written article on some unusual Optimist-related activity with good action photos will probably be purchased, as well as, upbeat general interest articles that point out the good side of life, anything that promotes fellowship, international understanding, respect for the law, and anything that highlights what's good about the youth of today." Buys 2-3 mss/issue. Query. "Submit a letter that conveys your ability to turn out a well-written article and tells exactly what the scope of the article will be and whether photos are available." Length: 500-1,500 words. Pays $50-100.

Photos: State availability of photos. Payment negotiated. Captions preferred. Buys all rights. "No mug shots or people lined up against the wall shaking hands. We're always looking for good color photos relating to Optimist activities that could be used on our front cover. Colors must be sharp and the composition must be suitable to fit an 8½x11 cover."

Tips: "We are mainly interested in seeing general-interest articles from freelancers because most club activities are better covered by club members. We're open to almost any idea, that's why all queries will be carefully considered. We don't want stories about a writer's Uncle Clem who 'had a rough life but always kept a smile on his face.' If you don't know about Optimist International, ask for our free sample magazine."

PERSPECTIVE, Pioneer Clubs, Inc., Box 788, Wheaton IL 60187. (312)293-1600. Editor: Julie Smith. "All subscribers are volunteer leaders of clubs for girls and boys in grades 1-12. Clubs are sponsored by evangelical, conservative churches throughout North America." Quarterly magazine; 32 pages. Circ. 20,000. Pays on acceptance. Buys first North American serial rights. Submit seasonal/holiday material 9 months in advance. Simultaneous submissions OK. SASE. Reports in 3 weeks. Sample copy $1; writer's guidelines for SASE.

Nonfiction: How-to (projects for clubs, crafts, cooking, service), informational (relationships, human development, mission education, outdoor activities), inspirational (Bible studies, adult leading youths), interview (Christian education leaders), personal experience (of club leaders). Buys 4-12 mss/year. Byline given. Query. Length: 200-1,500 words. Pays $5-50.

Columns/Departments: Storehouse (craft, game, activity, outdoor activity suggestions—all related to club projects for any age between grades 1-12). Buys 8-10 mss/year. Submit complete ms. Length: 150-250 words. Pays $8-10.

Tips: "Submit articles directly related to club work, practical in nature, i.e., ideas for leader training in communication, Bible knowledge, teaching skills. They must have practical application. We want substance—not ephemeral ideas. In addition to a summary of the article idea and evidence that the writer has knowledge of the subject, we want evidence that the author understands our purpose and philosophy."

PORTS O' CALL, Box 530, Santa Rosa CA 95402. (707)542-0898. Editor: William A. Breniman. Newsbook of the Society of Wireless Pioneers. Society members are mostly early-day wireless "brass-pounders" who sent code signals from ships or manned shore stations handling wireless or radio traffic. Biannually. Not copyrighted. Pays on acceptance. Reports on submissions "at once." SASE.

Nonfiction: Articles about early-day wireless as used in ship-shore and high power operation; radar, electronic aids, SOS calls, etc. Early-day ships, records, etc. "Writers should remember that our members have gone to sea for years and would be critical of material that is not authentic. We are not interested in any aspect of ham radio. We are interested in authentic articles dealing with ships (since about 1910)." Oddities about the sea and weather as it affects shipping. Query. Length: 500-2,000 words. Pays 1¢/word.

Photos: Department Editor: Dexter S. Bartlett. Purchased with mss. Unusual shots of sea or ships. Wireless pioneers. Prefers b&w, "4x5 would be the most preferable size but it really doesn't make too much difference as long as the photos are sharp and the subject interests us." Fine if veloxed, but not necessary. Pays $2.50-10; "according to our appraisal of our interest." Ship photos of various nations, including postcard size, if clear, 25¢-$1 each.

Poetry: Ships, marine slant (not military), shipping, weather, wireless. No restrictions. Pays $1-$2.50 each.

Tips: "Material will also be considered for our *Ports O'Call* annual and *Sparks Journal*, a quarterly tabloid newletter. *Sparks* (next volume is IV, published yearly) takes most of the contents used in *Port O'Call*, published now every 2 years in encyclopedic format and content. *The Sparks Journal*, published quarterly in tabloid form carries much of the early days, first hand history of wireless (episodes and experiences). Also this year (1981) we will publish our first *Wireless Almanac*. This will also contain much nautical data relating to radio and wireless used at sea. The *Sparks Journal* is normally 32 to 40 page tabloid printed and 50 pound bookstock."

THE ROTARIAN, 1600 Ridge Ave., Evanston IL 60201. (312)328-0100. Editor: Willmon L. White. 50% freelance written. For Rotarian business and professional men and their families; for schools, libraries, hospitals, etc. Monthly. Circ. 458,000. Usually buys all rights. Pays on acceptance. Free sample copy and editorial fact sheet. Query preferred. Reports in 1 month. SASE.
Nonfiction: "The field for freelance articles is in the general interest category. These run the gamut from inspirational guidelines for daily living to such weighty concerns as world hunger, peace, and preservation of environment. Recent articles have dealt with international illiteracy, salary, energy, dehumanization of the elderly, and worldwide drug abuse and prevention. Articles should appeal to an international audience and should in some way help Rotarians help other people. An article may increase a reader's understanding of world affairs, thereby making him a better world citizen. It may educate him in civic matters, thus helping him improve his town. It may help him to become a better employer, or a better human being. We are interested in articles on unusual Rotary club projects or really unusual Rotarians. We carry debates and symposiums, but we are careful to show more than one point of view. We present arguments for effective politics and business ethics, but avoid expose and muckraking. Controversy is welcome if it gets our readers to think but does not offend ethnic or religious groups. In short, the rationale of the organization is one of hope and encouragement and belief in the power of individuals talking and working together." Length: 2,000 words maximum. Payment varies.
Photos: Purchased with mss or with captions only. Prefers 2¼x2¼ or larger color transparencies, but also uses 35mm. B&w prints and photo essays. Vertical shots preferred to horizontal. Scenes of international interest. Color cover.
Poetry and Fillers: "Currently overstocked on serious poetry, but will look at short, light verse." Pays $2 a line. Pays $10 for brief poems. "We occasionally buy short humor pieces."

SERTOMAN, Sertoma International, 1912 E. Meyer Blvd., Kansas City MO 64132. (816)333-8300. Editor: Ginger Graham. Director of Public Relations: Patrick Burke. Bimonthly magazine with "service to mankind" as its motto edited for business and professional men. Circ 35,000. Pays on acceptance. Byline given. Buys one-time rights. Submit seasonal material 3 months in advance. Simultaneous, photocopied and previously published submissions OK. SASE. Reports in 2 weeks. Free sample copy and writer's guidelines.
Nonfiction: General interest (social civic issues, energy, finance, retirement, alcohol, drug abuse); and humor (in daily living). "We're especially interested in articles on speech and hearing, Sertoma's international sponsorship." Buys 2 mss/issue. Query with clips of previously published work. Length: 500-2,000 words. Pays $25-100.
Photos: Pays $5 minimum/5x7 b&w glossy prints. Captions and model release required. Buys one-time rights.

THE TOASTMASTER, 2200 N. Grand Ave., Box 10400, Santa Ana CA 92711. (714)542-6793. Editor-in-Chief: Sherry Angel. Covers communication and leadership techniques; self-development for members of Toastmasters International, Inc. Monthly magazine; 32 pages. Circ. 75,000. Pays on acceptance. Buys all rights. Phone queries OK. Byline given. Photocopied submissions and previously published work OK. SASE. Reports in 3 weeks. Free sample copy and writer's guidelines.
Nonfiction: How-to (improve speaking, listening, thinking skills; on leadership or management techniques, meeting, planning, etc., with realistic examples), humor (on leadership, communications or management techniques), interviews (with communications or management experts offering advice that members can directly apply to their self-development efforts; should contain "how to" information). No articles on fear of speaking, time management, basic speaking techniques. Buys 20-30 mss/year. Query. Length: 1,800-3,000 words. Pays $25-150.
Photos: Purchased with or without ms. Query. Pays $10-50 for 5x7 or 8x10 b&w glossy prints; $35-75 for color transparencies. Offers no additional payment for photos accepted with ms.
Tips: "Study our magazine and send us (after a query) material that is related. Since we get a number of articles from our members on 'how to build a speech,' freelancers should concentrate on more specific subjects such as body language, time management, etc. We're a nonprofit organization, so if they're looking to get rich on one article, they can probably forget it. But we do offer inexperienced freelancers an opportunity to get published in a magazine that will give their work international exposure. Offer ideas on subjects that haven't been covered in the past two years (membership turnover period), interviews with celebrities discussing their speaking techniques and success secrets. We prefer a lively writing style with lots of quotes and anecdotes rather than an academic appoach."

V.F.W. MAGAZINE, Broadway at 34th St., Kansas City MO 64111. (816)561-3420. Editor: James K. Anderson. 30-50% freelance written. For members of the Veterans of Foreign Wars, men who served overseas, and their families. They range in age from the 20s to veterans of World War I and the Spanish-American War. Interests range from sports to national politics. Magazine published 10 times/year. 48 pages. Circ. 1,800,000. Buys all rights. Buys 40 mss/year. Pays on acceptance. Sample copy 50¢; free writer's guidelines. Seasonal material should be submitted 3 months in advance. Query. SASE. Reports in 1 week.

Nonfiction and Photos: "Nonfiction articles on sports, personalities and history. Special emphasis within a subject, special outlook related to veterans. The Veterans of Foreign Wars organization is geared to the man who has served overseas, a distinction that other veterans organizations do not make." Buys informational, how-to, personal experience, interview, profile, historical, think articles, and travel articles. "Appropriate illustrations should be included when possible." Length: 1,000-1,500 words. Pays 5-10¢/word. B&w and color photos purchased with accompanying ms. Captions required. Pays $5 each.

WOODMEN OF THE WORLD MAGAZINE, 1700 Farnam St., Omaha NE 68102. (402)342-1890, ext. 302. Editor: Leland A. Larson. 20% freelance written. Published by Woodmen of the World Life Insurance Society for "people of all ages in all walks of life. We have both adult and children readers from all types of American families." Monthly. Circ. 460,000. Not copyrighted. Buys 25 mss/year. Byline given. Pays on acceptence. Will send a sample copy to a writer on request. Will consider photocopied and simultaneous submissions. Submit complete ms. Submit seasonal material 3 months in advance. Reports in 5 weeks. SASE.

Nonfiction: "General interest articles which appeal to the American family—travel, history, art, new products, how-to, sports, hobbies, food, home decorating, family expenses, etc. Because we are a fraternal benefit society operating under a lodge system, we often carry stories on how a number of people can enjoy social or recreational activities as a group. No special approach required. We want more 'consumer type' articles, humor, historical articles, think pieces, nostalgia, photo articles." Length: 10-1,800 words. Pays $10 minimum, 5½¢/word depending on count.

Photos: Purchased with or without mss; Captions optional "but suggested." Uses 8x10 glossy prints, 4x5 transparencies ("and possibly down to 35mm"). Payment "depends on use." For b&w photos, pays $25 for cover, $10 for inside. Color prices vary according to use and quality with $100 maximum. Minimum of $25 for inside use; up to $100 for covers.

Fiction: Humorous and historical short stories. Length: 600-2,000 words. Pays "$10 or 5½¢/word, depending on count."

Astrology and Psychic

The following publications regard astrology, psychic phenomena, ESP experiences, and related subjects as sciences or as objects of serious scientific research. Semireligious, occult, mysticism, and supernatural publications are classified in the Alternative category.

AMERICAN ASTROLOGY, Clancy Publications, Inc., 2505 N. Alvernon Way, Tucson AZ 85712. (602)327-3476. Editor: Joanne S. Clancy. 50% freelance written. For all ages, all walks of life. Monthly magazine; 112 pages. Circ. 265,000. Buys all rights. Buys 50-75 mss/year. Pays on publication. Free writer's guidelines. Reports in 1 month. Submit complete ms. SASE.

Nonfiction: Astrological material, often combined with astronomy. More interested in presenting results of research material and data based on time of birth, instead of special Sun-sign readings. Source of birth data must be included. Length: 3,500 words. "Payment is made according to the astrological knowledge and expertise of the writer."

Tips: Clancy Publications also publishes a 158-page yearbook, *American Astrology Digest*. Articles of about 3,500 words based on astrology that concern environment, sports, vocation, health, etc., will be given prompt consideration for the yearbook.

BEYOND REALITY MAGAZINE, 30 Amarillo Dr., Nanuet NY 10954. Editor: Harry Belil. 75% freelance written. Primarily for university students interested in astronomy, archeology, astrology, the occult (the whole range), UFOs, ESP, spiritualism, parapsychology, exploring the unknown. Bimonthly magazine; 64 pages. Estab. 1971. Circ. 83,000. Buys all rights. Buys 30-35 mss/year. Pays on publication. Sample copy $1; writer's guidelines for SASE. Photocopied submissions OK. Query or submit complete ms. SASE.

Nonfiction and Photos: Interested in articles covering the range of their readers' interests, as well as any new discoveries in parapsychology. How-to, interview, inspirational, historical, think pieces, spot news. Length: 2,000-3,000 words. Pays 3¢/word maximum, or "whatever the editor feels such a feature warrants." Offers no additional payment for photos accepted with ms.

Fillers: "We pay $1 for clippings used."

Tips: "Show me some pieces you've written and if I like your style, I'll provide you with the subjects to write on. Also looking for current ideas from the campuses, so student writers should give us a try." Lack of research documentation, or re-hashing old material will bring a rejection here.

DAILY PLANETARY GUIDE, Llewellyn Publications, Box 43383, St. Paul MN 55164. (612)291-1970. Editor: Carl L. Weschcke. Emphasizes astrology for everyday guidance to better living. Annual book; 300 pages. Circ. 20,000. Pays 1 month after publication. Buys all rights. Phone queries OK. Photocopied submissions OK. SASE. Reports in 6 months. Free sample copy and writer's guidelines.

Nonfiction: How-to and technical. "No cartoons, fun or amusing articles."

Photos: State availability of photos with ms. Buys b&w and color contact sheets. Pay varies.

FATE, Clark Publishing Co., 500 Hyacinth Place, Highland Park IL 60035. Editor: Mary Margaret Fuller. 70% freelance written. Monthly. Buys all rights; occasionally North American serial rights only. Byline given. Pays on publication. Query. Reports in 2 months. SASE.

Nonfiction and Fillers: Personal psychic experiences, 300-500 words. Pays $10. New frontiers of science, and ancient civilizations, 2,000-3,000 words; also parapsychology, occultism, witchcraft, magic, spiritual healing miracles, flying saucers, etc. Must include complete authenticating details. Prefers interesting accounts of single events rather than roundups. "We very frequently accept manuscripts from new writers; the majority are individuals' first-person accounts of their own psychic experience. We do need to have all details, where, when, why, who and what, included for complete documentation." Pays minimum of 5¢/word. Fillers should be fully authenticated. Length: 100-300 words.

Photos: Buys good glossy prints with mss. Pays $5-10.

HOROSCOPE GUIDE, 350 Madison Ave., Cresskill NJ 07626. (201)568-0500. Editor: Jim Hendryx. For persons interested in astrology as it touches their daily lives; all ages. Monthly. Circ. 60,000. Buys all rights. Byline given. Buys 40 mss/year. Pays on acceptance. Sample copy for $1. Photocopied submissions OK. Submit seasonal material 5 months in advance. Submit complete ms. SASE.

Nonfiction, Poetry and Fillers: Wants anything of good interest to the average astrology buff, preferably not so technical as to require more than basic knowledge of birth sign by reader. Mss should be light, readable, entertaining and sometimes humorous. Not as detailed and technical as other astrology magazines, "with the astro-writer doing the interpreting without long-winded reference to his methods at every juncture. We are less reverent of astrological red tape." Wants mss about man-woman relationships, preferably in entertaining and occasionally humorous fashion. No textbook-type material. Does not want to see a teacher's type of approach to the subject. Length: 900-4,000 words. Pays 2-3¢/word. Buys traditional forms of poetry. Length: 4-16 lines. Pays $2-$8.

Tips: "Best way to break in with us is with some lively Sun-sign type piece involving some area of man-woman relationships—love, sex, marriage, divorce, differing views on money, religion, child-raising, in-laws, vacations, politics, life styles, or whatever."

MOON SIGN BOOK, Box 43383, St. Paul MN 55164. (612)291-1970. Editor: Carl L. Weschcke. For "persons from all walks of life with interests in gardening, natural living and astrology." Annual Book; 500 pages. Annual. Circ. 200,000. Buys all rights. Byline given. Pays on publication. Phone queries OK. Photocopied and previously published submissions OK. SASE. Reports in 6 months.

Nonfiction: How-to and photo features. "We can use material in natural medicine, healing, and living in intelligent cooperation with nature. We are a yearly publication dealing with farming, gardening, yearly forecasts for all types of activities, with informative articles applying astrology to better living. We try to be educational as well as practical." Buys 5-10 mss/issue. Query. Length: 3,000-10,000 words. Pays 3¢/word.

Photos: State availabiltiy of photos with ms. Buys b&w and color contact sheets. Pay varies. Captions and model releases required.

Tips: "The *Moon Sign Book* is a farming and gardening almanac emphasizing astronomical effects on planting, growing, harvesting and using crops to maximum advantage. Since a good portion of the book is taken up with tables and in-house material, we have room for only a few outside articles. Those articles should have something to do with either astrology or gardening (we are also interested in herbs and herbal remedies). Since most freelancers are not astrologers I would suggest that they concentrate on the many aspects of organic gardening or possibly how-to-do features that relate in some way to farming and gardening. Short articles on the occult phenomena (enhancing growth psychically), are also good possibilities for the beginning writer. We are continually looking for astrologers capable of writing Sun sign predictions and features on "planetary planting" for *Moon Sign Book*. Also astrological predictions for weather, stock and commodity markets, news and political developments, etc. We generally stick with one, but we find that quality depends on a variety, and would like to find a few more writers to back us up. We want to expand our coverage of lunar and organic gardening and related aspects of healthful living."

NEW REALITIES, 680 Beach St., Suite 408, San Francisco CA 94109. (415)776-2600. Editor: James Bolen. 20% freelance written. For general public interested in total wellness and personal growth and in holistic approach to living and being—body, mind, and spirit—as well as straightforward, entertaining material on parapsychology, consciousness research, and the frontiers of human potential and the mind. Bimonthly. Buys all rights. Pays on publication. Reports in 6 weeks. Query. SASE.
Nonfiction and Photos: "Documented articles on mental, physical and spiritual holistic dimensions of humankind. Balanced reporting, no editorializing. No personal experiences as such. Accept profiles of leaders in the field. Must have documented evidence about holistic leaders, healers, researchers. Short bibliography for further reading." Length: 1,500-3,500 words. Pays $75-250.

SADIC MAGAZINE, Box 2026, North Hollywood CA 91602. (213)762-6995. Editor-in-Chief: S.E. Adlai. Managing Editor: T.L. Adlai. Monthly magazine; 41 pages. Circ. 35,000. All staff written.

TRUE OUTER SPACE & PARANORMAL WORLD QUARTERLY, Histrionic Publishing, 23 W. 26th St., New York NY 10010. (212)689-3933. Editor: Herbert McLean Furlow. Quarterly magazine. Pays on publication. Byline given. Buys first North American serial rights. SASE. Reports in 3 weeks.
Nonfiction: "Unusual outer space, UFO or paranormal subjects are used." Buys 5-10 mss/year. Length: 2,000-3,000 words. Pays $50-150, depending on picture availability and rewriting necessities.
Photos: Send photos with ms. Reviews 5x7 b&w glossy prints. Captions required. "Payment is part of article payment."

Automotive and Motorcycle

Publications listed in this section detail the maintenance, operation, performance, racing and judging of automobiles and motorcycles. Publications that treat vehicles as a means of transportation or shelter instead of as a hobby or sport are classified in the Travel, Camping, and Trailer category. Journals for teamsters, service station operators, and auto dealers will be found in the Auto and Truck classification of the Trade Journals section.

AMERICAN MOTORCYCLIST, American Motorcyclist Association, Box 141, Westerville OH 43081. (614)891-2425. Editor: Bill Amick. For "enthusiastic motorcyclists, investing considerable time and money in the sport. Unlike most motorcycles magazines, we never publish road tests or product evaluations unless they are related to safety or anti-theft. We emphasize the motorcyclist, not the vehicle." Monthly magazine; 56-96 pages. Circ. 126,000. Pays on publication. Rights purchased vary with author and material. Pays 25-50% kill fee. Byline given. Query. Submit seasonal/holiday material 4 months in advance. SASE. Reports in 1 month. Free sample copy.
Nonfiction: How-to (different and/or unusual ways to use a motorcycle or have fun on one); historical (the heritage of motorcycling, particularly as it relates to the AMA); interviews (with interesting personalities in the world of motorcycling); photo feature (quality work on any aspect of motorcycling); and technical (well-researched articles on safe riding techniques). Buys 10-20 mss/year. Query. Length: 500 words minimum. Pays minimum $2/published column inch.
Photos: Greg Harrison, Art Director. Purchased with or without accompanying ms, or on assign-

ment. Captions required. Query. Pays $15 minimum per photo published.

Tips: "Just deal with us in a professional manner. Deliver the goods as promised and on time. Acuracy is critical. We have terminated relationships with promising freelancers over accuracy."

AUTOMOBILE QUARTERLY, 221 Nassau St., Princeton NJ 08540. (609)924-7555. Editor-in-Chief: L. Scott Bailey. Emphasizes automobiles and automobile history. Quarterly hardbound magazine; 112 pages. Circ. 40,000. Pays on acceptance. Buys all rights. Pays expenses as kill fee. Byline given. SASE. Reports in 3 weeks. Sample copy $12.95.

Nonfiction: Authoritative articles relating to the automobile and automobile history. Historical, humor, interview and nostalgia. Buys 5 mss/issue. Query. Length: 2,000-10,000 words. Pays $200-600.

Photos: Purchased on assignment. Captions required. Query. Uses 8x10 b&w glossy prints and 4x5 color transparencies. "Payment varies with assignment and is negotiated prior to assignment."

Tips: "Familiarity with the magazine a *must*."

AUTOWEEK, Crain Consumer Group, Inc., 965 E. Jefferson, Detroit MI 48207. (313)567-9520. Managing Editor: Paul Lienert. Emphasizes automobile racing and the auto industry, domestic and international. Weekly tabloid; 40 pages. Circ. 100,000. Pays on publication. Byline "generally given!" Buys first North American Serial rights or by agreement with author. Submit seasonal/holiday material 2 months in advance. SASE. Reports in 2-4 weeks. Free sample copy and writer's guidelines.

Nonfiction: Informational (group-based vs. assembly line system; does Volvo/Kalmar plant really work?, etc.); historical (the first Indy race, first successful Ferrari, first European assembly line, etc.); nostalgia ("we'd have room for 2-3/month if we had them on tap"). Technical articles on radical design changes. News reports on auto racing. "Any literate auto racing enthusiast can offer articles to *AutoWeek*. If the beginner is at a local race and he sees no *A W* reporter around, he might try covering the event himself. If he's going to a big race, he should query first since we undoubtedly already have it covered. A number of stringers got started just that way. Industry stories may range from General Motors to consumerists. In either case, remember we're not the auto section in a family paper." Buys 24 mss/year. Length: 1,000 words maximum. Query. Pays $75-100.

Photos: Purchased with or without mss, or on assignment. "Photo rates by arrangement." Captions and model release required. Buys first-time right.

BMW JOURNAL, A. Christ Zeitschriftenverlag GmbH, Goethestrasse 68, 8000 Munich 2, W. Germany. (089)53.96.07. USA editorial office: 2540 Bonita Way, Laguna Beach CA 92651. Editor: Ron Wakefield. Editor-in-Chief: Udo Wuest. An automobile customer magazine for owners and enthusiasts of BMW automobiles; upper income audience; generally, people with active life styles and an eye for the unusual. Bimonthly magazine. Estab. 1962. Circ. 50,000. Pays on publication. Buys all rights. Phone queries OK. SASE. Reports in 1 month.

Nonfiction: Historical (having to do with places or with history of automobiles if related to BMW); informational; nostalgia, photo features; profiles (of interesting BMW owners); travel (by automobile, BMW in photos). Buys 3-5/issue. Query. Length: 500-1,500 words. Pays $150-185/printed page.

Photos: Used with or without ms, or on assignment. Captions required. Query. No additional payment for 5x7 b&w glossy prints or 35mm minimum (larger preferred) color transparencies. Model release required. Need not relate to publication's subject matter; can encompass a broad range of life style themes.

Fiction: Adventure, experimental, historical, mystery, science fiction, suspense. Buys 1 ms/issue. Query. Length: 500-1,500 words. Pays $75-150/printed page.

Tips: "Author must know the magazine, available at local BMW dealers. Articles must be submitted with excellent photos, captioned."

CAR AND DRIVER, 2002 Hogback Rd., Ann Arbor MI 48104. (313)994-0055. Editor/Publisher: David E. Davis Jr. For auto enthusiasts; college-educated, professional, median 26-28 years of age. Monthly magazine; 100 pages. Circ. 730,000. Rights purchased vary with author and material. Buys all rights or first North American serial rights. Buys 10-12 unsolicited mss/year. Pays on acceptance. Submit seasonal material 4 months in advance. Query with clips of previously published work. Reports in 2 months. SASE.

Nonfiction and Photos: Non-anecdotal articles about the more sophisticated treatment of autos and motor racing. Exciting, interesting cars. Automotive road tests, informational articles on cars and equipment; some satire and humor. Personalities, past and present, in the automotive industry and automotive sports. "Treat readers as intellectual equals. Emphasis on people as well as hardware." Informational, how-to, humor, historical, think articles, and nostalgia. Length: 750-

2,000 words. Pays $200-$1,000. B&w photos purchased with accompanying mss with no additional payment. Also buys book reviews for book review department, and mini-features for FYI department. Length: about 500 words. Pays $50-150.

Tips: "It is best to start off with an interesting query and to stay away from nuts-and-bolts stuff since that will be handled in-house or by an acknowledged expert. Probably the very best way for a new writer to break in with us is with a personal, reasonably hip approach which shows a real intimacy with what we are trying to do. A while back, for instance, we ran a freelance piece on automobiles in Russia, which was the product of an interesting query. We are not like other automotive magazines inasmuch as we try to publish material that could just as well appear in the general magazines. We're not interested in antique cars or hot rods. To us the Ford Mustang is infinitely more important than a 1932 Ruxton wicker-seat five-passenger touring car. Good writing and unique angles are the key."

CAR COLLECTOR/CAR CLASSICS, Classic Publishing, Inc., 346 Carpenter Dr., Suite 3, Atlanta GA 30328. Editor: Donald R. Peterson. For people interested in all facets of classic, milestone, antique, special interest and sports cars; also mascots, models, restoration, license plates and memorabilia. Monthly magazine; 76 pages. Circ. 55,000. Pays on publication. Submit seasonal/holiday material 4 months in advance. Photocopied submissions OK. SASE. Reports in 2 months. Sample copy: $2 and free writer's guidelines.

Nonfiction: General interest, historical, how-to, humor, inspirational, interview, nostalgia, personal opinion, profile, photo feature, technical and travel. Buys 50-75 mss/year. Query with clips of published work. Length: 300-2,500 words. Pays 5¢/word.

Photos: State availability of photos with ms. Offers no additional payment for photos with accompanying mss. Uses b&w glossy prints; color transparencies. Pays $75 for cover and centerfold color; $10 for inside color; $5 for inside b&w. Buys one-time rights. Captions and model releases required.

Columns/Departments: "Rarely add a new columnist but we are open to suggestions." Buys 36/year. Query with clips of published work. Length: 2,000 maximum; prefer 1,000-2,000 words. Pays 5¢/word.

Fiction: "We buy very little fiction, but would not exclude a well-written fiction piece directed to our market."

CAR CRAFT, Petersen Publishing Co., 8490 Sunset Blvd., Los Angeles CA 90069. (213)657-5100, ext. 345. Editor: Jon Asher. For men and women, 18-34, "enthusiastic owners of 1949 and newer muscle cars." Monthly magazine; 124 pages. Circ. 415,000. Study past issues before making submissions or story suggestions. Buys all rights. Buys 12 mss/year. Pays generally on publication, on acceptance under special circumstances. Query. SASE.

Nonfiction and Photos: How-to articles ranging from the basics to fairly sophisticated automotive modifications. Drag racing feature stories and some general car features on modified late model automobiles. Especially interested in do-it-yourself automotive tips, suspension modifications, mileage improvers and even shop tips and homemade tools. Stories about drag racing personalities are generally of more interest than stories about racing machinery. Length: open. Pays $100-200/page. Art director: Joe Martinez. Photos purchased with or without accompanying text. Captions suggested but optional. Reviews 8x10 b&w glossy prints; 35mm or 2¼x2¼ color negotiable. Pays $30 for b&w, color negotiable. "Pay rate higher for complete story, i.e. photos, captions, headline, subtitle: the works, ready to go."

CAR EXCHANGE MAGAZINE, Krause Publications, 700 E. State St., Iola WI 54990. Editor: R. Chris Halla. Monthly magazine devoted to postwar automotive hobby (especially cars between 1953 and 1968) for 18-40 year old automobile collectors and enthusiasts with average to above average education. Estab. 1979. Circ. 137,000. Pays on acceptance. Submit seasonal material 4 months in advance. SASE. Reports in 1 month on queries. Free sample copy; free writer's guidelines with SASE.

Nonfiction: Historical; how-to (restore, buy, sell, store, transport); humor; interview (past designers who worked on cars); nostalgia (love affair with the car); opinion; new product (products for collectors, calendars, tools, polishing); photo feature (car collector, meets, shows); technical (repairs). "No 'local club does this or that' or 'local man restores car.'" Buys 80-120 mss/year. Query. Length: 300-2,000 words. Pays 5¢/word.

Photos: "We do not accept manuscripts without accompanying art." Send photos with ms. Pays $5/5x7 b&w glossy prints. Pays $50 minimum/2¼x2 or 4x5 color transparencies.

Columns/Departments: Book reviews, short subjects, personal experience. Buys 24 mss/year. Send complete ms with dust jacket. Length: 100-500 words.

Fiction: Adventure, experimental, historical and mainstream. "Must have emphasis on postwar collectible cars." Length: 500-2,000 words. Pays 4¢/word.

Tips: "The best way to break in is to know the subject and consider the audience carefully. Write short, lively prose."

CARS MAGAZINE, Arden Communications, Inc., Box 99, Amawalk NY 10501. (914)962-7570. Publisher: John McCluskey. Covers automotive high performance: factory muscle cars, hot street machines, drag race cars, and racing. For enthusiasts from early teens through thirties, some older, who have fairly technical knowledge of cars. Bimonthly magazine. Circ. 80,000. Pays on publication. Buys one-time or all rights. Byline given. Phone queries OK. SASE. Reports in 3 months. Sample copy $1.50.
Nonfiction: How-to (budget hop-ups, speed tricks, suspension modification, customizing, repair, body work, or race car building); informational and new product offerings; high-performance or automotive humor; interviews and profiles (of prominent people in drag racing or automotive field); historical and nostalgia (looking back on hot rods, muscle cars of the '50s and '60s); technical (drivetrain and suspension subjects); and some drag race coverage. "We're currently looking for new (auto) products performance reports, substantiated with reputable facts and figures, and photos." Buys 12 mss/issue. Submit complete ms. Length: 500-3,000 words. Pays $100-500.
Photos: Pays $25 for b&w 8x10 glossy prints and $50 for 35mm or larger transparencies without accompanying mss. Offers no additional payment for photos accompanying mss. Model release required.
Tips: "Having a background in the automotive field and knowing how to package a story with photos and captions are plusses."

CORVETTE FEVER, Prospect Publishing Co., Inc., Box 407, Triangle VA 22172. (703)221-8064. Publisher: Patricia E. Stivers. Bimonthly magazine; 64-84 pages. Circ. 43,000. Pays on publication. Buys all rights. Byline given. Phone queries OK. Submit seasonal/holiday material 4 months in advance. Photocopied submissions OK. SASE. Reports in 4 weeks. Sample copy and writer's guidelines $1.
Nonfiction: General interest (event coverage, personal experience); historical (special or unusual Corvette historical topics); how-to (technical and mechanical articles, photos are a must); humor (special section Schlick Shift is devoted to Corvette-related humor); interview (with important Corvette persons, race drivers, technical persons, club officials, etc.); nostalgia (relating to early Corvette car and development); personal experiences (related to Corvette car use and experiences); profile (prominent and well-known Corvette personalities wanted for interviews and articles); photo feature (centerspread in color of Corvette and Vette owner; photo essays on renovation, customizing and show cars); technical (any aspect of Corvette improvement or custom articles); and travel (relating to Corvette use and adventure). Buys 7-10 mss/issue. Query or send complete ms. Length: 500-3,000 words. Pays $40-300.
Photos: Send photos with ms. Pays $5 for 5x7 b&w glossy prints; $10 for color contact sheets and transparencies. Captions preferred; model release required.
Columns/Departments: Innovative Ideas, In Print, Model Shop, Pit Stop, Schlick Shift and Tech Vette. Buys 5 mss/issue. Send complete ms. Length: 300-800 words. Pays $24-200.
Fiction: "Any type of story as long as it is related to the Corvette." Buys 1-2 mss/issue. Send complete ms. Length: 500-2,500 words. Pays $40-200.
Fillers: Clippings, jokes, gags, anecdotes, short humor and newsbreaks. Buys 2-3/issue. Length: 25-150 words. Pays $2-15.

CYCLE, Ziff-Davis Publishing, Co., 780-A Lakefield Rd., Westlake Village CA 91361. (213)889-4360. Editor: Phil Schilling. Managing Editor: Don Phillipson. Monthly magazine covering motorcycles for motorcycle owners (mostly men). Circ. 450,000. Pays on publication. Byline given. Buys first North American serial rights. Submit seasonal/holiday queries 4 months in advance. Simultaneous queries and photocopied submissions OK. SASE. Reports in 1 month. Free sample copy.
Nonfiction: Investigative, historical, interview/profile (of racing personalities or others in the industry); photo feature; technical (theory or practice); travel (long-distance trips anywhere in the world); reports on racing; and investigative articles. Buys 10-20 mss/year. Query "with references." Length: 2,000-4,000 words. Pays $400-700.
Photos: Pays $500 for 35mm color transparencies. Model releases and identifiction of subjects required. Buys one-time rights.

CYCLE NEWS, WEST, 2201 Cherry Ave., Box 498, Long Beach CA 90801. (213)427-7433. Managing Editor: Charles Morey. Publisher: Sharon Clayton. Emphasizes motorcycle recreation for motorcycle racers and recreationists west of Mississippi River. Weekly tabloid; 48 pages. Circ. 60,000. Pays on 15th of month for work published in issues cover-dated the previous month. Buys all rights. SASE. Reports in 1 month. Free writer's guidelines.

Nonfiction: Exposé; how-to; historical; humor; informational; interview (racers); personal experience (racing, nonracing with a point); personal opinion (land use, emission control, etc.); photo feature; profile (personality profiles); technical; and travel (off-road trips, "bikepacking"). Buys 1,000 mss/year. Submit complete ms. Pays $1/column inch.

Photos: Purchased with or without accompanying manuscript. Captions required. Submit contact sheet, prints, negatives or transparencies. Pays $5 minimum for 5x7 or 8x10 glossy prints; $10 minimum for 35mm slides or 2¼x2¼ color transparencies. Model release required. No additional payment for photos accepted with accompanying ms.

CYCLE WORLD, 1499 Monrovia Ave., Newport Beach CA 92663. Editor: Allan Girdler. For active motorcyclists, "young, affluent, educated, very perceptive." Subject matter includes "road tests (staff-written), features on special bikes, customs, racers, racing events; technical and how-to features involving mechanical modifications." Monthly. Circ. 350,000. Buys all rights. Buys 200-300 mss/year from freelancers. Pays on publication. Sample copy $1; free writer's guidelines. Submit seasonal material 2½ months in advance. Reports in 6 weeks. Query. SASE.

Nonfiction: Buys informative, well-researched, technical, theory and how-to articles; interviews; profiles; humor; and historical pieces. Taboos include articles about "wives learning to ride; 'my first motorcycle.'" Length: 800-5,000 words. Pays $75-100/published page. Columns include Competition, which contains short, local racing stories with photos. Column length: 300-400 words. Pays $75-100/published page.

Photos: Purchased with or without ms, or on assignment. "We need funny photos with a motorcycle theme." Captions optional. Pays $50 for 1-page; $25-35 for half page. 8x10 b&w glossy prints, 35mm color transparencies.

Fiction: Humorous stories. No racing fiction or "rhapsodic poetry." Length: 1,500-3,000 words. Pays $75 minimum/published page.

DUNE BUGGIES & HOT VWS, Wright Publishing Co., Inc., Box 2260, Costa Mesa CA 92626. Editor: Tom Chambers. Monthly magazine; 100 pages. Circ. 60,000. Pays on publication. Buys one-time rights. Submit seasonal or holiday material 3 months in advance. SASE. Free sample copy.

Nonfiction: Technical how-to and informational articles. No first person articles. Buys 6-8 mss/issue. Submit complete ms. Length: 500-2,000 words. Pays $60/published page.

Photos: Purchased with ms. Captions required. Send contact sheet. Pays $12.50 maximum for 8x10 b&w glossy prints; $15 minimum for color negs or slides.

EASYRIDERS MAGAZINE, Entertainment for Adult Bikers, Box 52, Malibu CA 90265. (213)889-8701. Lou Kimzey. For "adult men—men who own, or desire to own, expensive custom motorcycles. The individualist—a rugged guy who enjoys riding a chopper and all the good times derived from it." Monthly. Circ. 488,000. Buys all rights. Buys 36-48 mss/year. Pays on acceptance. Sample copy 25¢. Reports in 2-3 weeks.

Nonfiction, Fiction, and Fillers: Department Editor: Louis Bosque. "Masculine, candid material of interest to men. Must be bike-oriented, but can be anything of interest to any rugged man. It is suggested that everyone read a copy before submitting—it's not *Boy's Life*. Light, easy, conversational writing style wanted, like men would speak to each other without women being around. Gut level, friendly, man-to-man. Should be bike-oriented or of interest to a man who rides a motorcycle. *Easyriders* is entirely different from all other motorcycle magazines in that it stresses the lifestyle and good times surrounding the owning of a motorcycle—it's aimed at the rider and is nontechnical, while the others are nuts and bolts. Not interested in overly technical motorcycle articles. We carry no articles that preach or talk down to the reader, or attempt to tell them what they should or shouldn't do." Buys personal experience, interviews, especially humor, expose of (Big brother, big government, red, white and blue, motorcycle-oriented) articles. Length: 1,000-3,000 words. Pays 10¢/word minimum, depending on length and use in magazine. "It's the subject matter and how well it's done—not length, that determines amount paid." Risque jokes, fillers, short humor. Length: open. Pays on acceptance.

Photos: Department Editor: Pete Chiodo. B&w glossy prints, 35mm color, 2¼x2¼ color transparencies purchased with mss. "We are only interested in *exclusive* photos of exclusive bikes that have never been published in, or photographed by, a national motorcycle or chopper publication. Bikes should be approved by editorial board before going to expense of shooting. Submit sample photos—Polaroids will do. Send enough samples for editorial board to get good idea of the bike's quality, originality, workmanship, interesting features, coloring." Payment is $50-$250 for cover, $100-350 for centerspread, $20 for b&w and $35 for color for "In the Wind," $25 up for arty, unusual shots, and $100 to $225 for a complete feature.

Fiction: "Gut level language okay. Any sex scenes, not to be too graphic in detail. Dope may be implied, but not graphically detailed. Must be biker male-oriented, but doesn't have to dwell on that fact. Only interested in hard-hitting, rugged fiction." Length: 2,000-3,500 words. Pays 10¢/word minimum, dpending on quality, length and use in magazine.

Tips: "There is no mystery about breaking into our publications as long as the material is aimed directly at our macho, intelligent, male audience. We suggest that the writer read the requirements indicated above and seriously study a current copy of the magazine before submitting material."

THE EJAG NEWS MAGAZINE, EJAG Publications, Box J, Carlisle MA 01741. (617)369-5531. Editor: Lori R. Toepel. Monthly magazine covering "everything about Jaguar and Daimler autos for readers ranging from corporate presidents to local car-fixers; Sunday mechanics—all Jaguar-Daimler fans." Circ. 24,000. Pays on acceptance. Byline given. Offers $10-25 kill fee. Buys all rights unless otherwise negotiated. Submit seasonal/holiday material 3 months in advance. SASE. Reports in 1 month. Free sample copy and writer's guidelines.

Nonfiction: General interest (on auto field in general); historical/nostalgic (on Jaguars of previous eras, in USA and abroad); how-to (do it yourself pieces in depth for maintenance, repair, restoration); interview/profile (of Jag owners, racers, factory people, collectors); new product (anything applicable to Jaguars); personal experience ("A Funny Thing Happened on the Way . . ." in a Jag-regular feature with reader participation); photo feature (on beautiful Jaguars, technical procedures, restorations); technical (do-it-yourself or general tech background); and travel (long distance driving techs. How to manage a Jag in the city; where to park, what to see). "No club news or club meets (we have direct lines to these). No technical articles that sound like manuals." Buys 24+ mss/year. Query. Length: 1,200-5,000 words. "Longer article accepted—for splitting into several months installments." Pays 3-10¢/word.

Photos: State availability of photos. Pays $5 maximum for 35mm, 3x3 color transparencies and 3x5 and 5x7 prints. Caption, model release and identification of subjects (if possible) required. Buys one-time rights.

Columns/Departments: Calling all Cars—"1,200-1,600 words on British or European cars—history, interesting anecdotes or the like. This is a non-Jaguar section. We're looking for 2 or 3 new columns in the coming year." Buys 3-4 mss/year. Query. Length: 1,200-1,600 words. Pays 4-10¢/word.

Fiction: Serialized novels. "We're looking for a serialized mystery with a Jaguar base. Needs much Jag knowledge (we can help)." Query.

Tips: "We welcome unpublished writers *but* you must know the subject. Material from standard Jag books is not enough. No 'How the Jaguar got its name' stories. Technical writers need to know nuts and bolts and add enough details for the novice Sunday mechanic."

FOUR WHEELER MAGAZINE, 21216 Vanowen St., Canoga Park CA 91303. (213)992-4777. Publisher: Jack Pelzer. Editor: Bill Sanders. Emphasizes four-wheel-drive vehicles. Monthly magazine; 108 pages. Circ. 170,000. Pays on publication. Buys all rights. Phone queries OK. Submit seasonal/holiday material at least 4 months in advance. SASE. Reports in 1 year. Free sample copy and writer's guidelines.

Nonfiction and Photos: 4WD trip articles from the East, as well as an occasional vehicle feature about a unique 4WD vehicle. Query or send complete ms. Length: 2,500 words. Pay varies from $150/article with b&w photos to $300 with color.

Photos: Requires excellent quality photos.

Fillers: Newsbreaks and 4WD outings.

Tips: "Technical material is difficult to come by. A new writer has a better chance of success with us if he can offer new technical articles, maintenance tips, etc. Also, we like unique custom vehicle features."

HOT ROD, Petersen Publishing Co., 8490 Sunset Blvd., Los Angeles CA 90069. (213)657-5100. Editor: Leonard Emanuelson. For readers 10 to 60 years old with automotive high performance, street rod, truck and van, drag racing and street machine interest. Monthly magazine; 120 pages. Circ. 900,000. Buys all rights. Buys 30 mss per year. Byline given. Pays on acceptance. Free sample copy and editorial guidelines. Submit seasonal material 4 months in advance. Reports on accepted and rejected material "as soon as possible." SASE.

Nonfiction and Photos: Wants how-to, interview, profile, photo, new product and technical pieces. Length: 2-12 ms pages. Pays $100-225/per printed page. "Freelance quantity at *Hot Rod* will undoubtedly decline; staff will originate most material. Foresee more need for photo essays, less for the written word." Photos purchased with or without accompanying ms and on assignment. Sometimes offers no additional payment for photos accepted with ms. Captions required. Pays $25 for b&w prints and $25 minimum for color.

Tips: "Freelance approach should be tailored for specific type and subject matter writer is dealing with. If it is of a basic automotive technical nature, then story slant and info should be aimed at the backyard enthusiasts. If the story is dealing with a specific personality, then it must include a major portion of human interest type of material. What we do is attempt to entertain while educating and offering exceptional dollar value."

KEEPIN' TRACK OF CORVETTES, Box 5400, Reno NV 89513. (702)329-4519. Editor: Frank Kodl. For Corvette owners and enthusiasts. Monthly magazine; 68-84 pages. Estab. 1976. Circ. 58,000. Pays on publication. Buys all rights. Byline given. Submit seasonal/holiday material 2-3 months in advance. Photocopied and previously published submissions OK. SASE. Reports in 3-4 weeks. Free sample copy and writer's guidelines.
Nonfiction: Exposé (telling of Corvette problems with parts, etc); historical (any and all aspects of Corvette developments); how-to (restorations, engine work, suspension, race, swapmeets); humor, informational; interview (query); nostalgia; personal experience; personal opinion; photo feature; profile (query); technical; and travel. Buys 4-5 mss/issue. Query or submit complete ms. Pays $50-200.
Photos: Send photo with ms. Pays $10-35 for b&w contact sheets or negatives; $10-50 for 35mm color transparencies; offers no additional payment for photos with accompanying ms.

MOTOCROSS ACTION MAGAZINE, 16200 Ventura Blvd., Encino CA 91436. (213)981-2317. Editor: Dick Miller. For "primarily young and male, average age 12 to 30, though an increasing number of females is noticed. Education varies considerably. They are interested in off-road racing motorcycles, as either a profession or a hobby." Monthly magazine; 72 pages. Circ. 100,000. Buys all rights. Buys 20-25 mss/year. Pays on publication. Sample copy $1.50; free writer's guidelines. Will consider photocopied but no simultaneous submissions. Reports in 1-6 months. Query. SASE.
Nonfiction and Photos: Wants "articles on important national and international motocross events, interviews with top professionals, technical pieces, and in-depth investigative reporting. Short stories and/or poetry will be greeted with a heartfelt yawn. It's best to obtain a copy of the magazine and read recent stories. Stories should be brief and to the point, though flair is appreciated. Top photography is a must. No blatant hero worship. For the coming year, we want to see articles on the evolution of Motocross from a backyard to a big-time, multi-million dollar sport and business." Takes informational, how-to, profile, humor and photo pieces. Length: 500-2,000 words. Pays $25-$200. Photos purchased with accompanying ms with extra payment and on assignment. Captions optional. Pays $8-$10 for b&w, 8x10 glossy prints. $25-$50 for 35mm or 2¼x2¼ color slides.

MOTOR TREND, 8490 Sunset Blvd., Los Angeles CA 90069. (213)657-5100. Editor: John Dianna. For automotive enthusiasts and general interest consumers. Monthly. Circ. 750,000. Buys all rights. "Fact-filled query suggested for all freelancers." Reports in 30 days. SASE.
Nonfiction: Automotive and related subjects that have national appeal. Emphasis on domestic and imported cars, roadtests, driving impressions, auto classics, money-saving ideas for the motorist, and high-performance features for the enthusiast's news tips on new products, pickups, long-term automotive projects. Packed with facts.
Photos: Buys photos, particularly of prototype cars and assorted automotive matter. Pays $25-250 for b&w glossy prints or 2¼x2¼ color transparencies.
Fillers: Automotive newsbreaks. Any length.

MOTORCYCLIST MAGAZINE, Petersen Publishing, 8490 Sunset Blvd., Los Angeles CA 90069. (213)657-5100. Editor-in-Chief: Art Friedman. Emphasizes motorcycles or motorcycle enthusiasts. Monthly magazine; 100 pages. Circ. 200,000. Pays on publication. Buys all rights. Byline given. Written queries preferred. SASE. Reports in 1 month. Free writer's guidelines.
Nonfiction: How-to, humor, informational, interview, new product, photo feature, profile and technical. Buys 12 mss/year. Length: 500-2,000 words. Pays $100/published page.

OFF-ROAD, Argus Publishing, 12301 Wilshire Blvd., Suite 316, Los Angeles CA 90025. (213)820-3601. Editor: Dave Epperson. Managing Editor: Joe R. Hicks. Monthly magazine covering off-pavement vehicles, particularly 4-wheel drive, utility, and pickup trucks; and off-road racing and rallying vehicles. Readers are owners and people who aspire to own off-road vehicles, as well as those who intend to modify engines and other components for off-road use. Circ. 120,000. Pays on publication. Byline given. Buys all rights, "but may reassign rights upon request. Submit seasonal/holiday material 4 months in advance. SASE. Reports in 1 month. Writer's guidelines for business size SAE and 1 first class stamp.
Nonfiction: Technical (modification); travel (and adventure in the continental US); off-road groups; and land-closures. "The key to writing for us is technical expertise. You must be knowl-

edgeable on the subject." Buys 50 mss/year. Send complete ms and photos or diagrams. Length: 2,00-3,000 words. Pays $125-300.
Photos: Send photos with ms. Reviews 35mm color transparenices and 8x10 b&w glossy prints.
Fillers: Fix it, How-to. Buys 25/year. Length: 750-1,000 words. Pays $50-100.

OFFROAD EAST, Intra-South Publications, 6637 Superior Ave., Sarasota FL 33581. (813)921-5687. Managing Editor: George Haborak. Monthly tabloid covering 4- wheel drive vehicles and events for owners and enthusiasts, club members, and accessory industry people. Circ. 50,000. Pays on publication. Byline given. Buys first North American serial rights. Phone queries OK. Submit seasonal material 1 month in advance. Photocopied submissions OK. SASE. Reports in 1 month on queries; in 1 month on mss. Free sample copy and writer's guidelines.
Nonfiction: Interview (of celebrities and outstanding drivers); profile (of outstanding drivers); travel (trade shows); how-to (related to mechanics, equipment and the uses of accessories); personal experience (caravan); photo feature; technical (4 wheel drive vehicle related) and race results, rallies, fundraising, conservation cleanups, and truck and tractor pulls. Query with clips of previously published work. Length: 1,000 words. Pays $20 minimum.
Photos: Reviews 5x7 and smaller b&w glossy prints and 5x7 and smaller color glossy prints. Captions required. Buys one-time rights.

PETERSEN'S 4-WHEEL & OFF-ROAD, Petersen Publishing Company, 8490 Sunset Blvd., Los Angeles CA 90069. (213)657-5100. Editor: Craig Caldwell. Managing Editor: Michael Coates. Monthly magazine covering automotive four-wheel drive vehicles. "We appeal to the off-road enthusiast who plays hard and likes to have fun with his or her 4x4. Our approach is slanted towards showing how to do-it-yourself when it comes to maintaining or modifying an off-road vehicle." Circ. 175,000. Pays on acceptance. Byline given. Pays 50% kill fee. Buys all rights. Submit seasonal/holiday material 6 months in advance. SASE. Reports in 3 weeks.
Nonfiction: How-to (modify a vehicle); interview/profile (of racers, engineers); photo feature (modified vehicles); and technical (modification of a vehicle). Buys 12-18 mss/year. Query or send complete ms. Length: 300-1,500 words. Pays $50-500.
Photos: Barry Wiggins, photo editor. Pays $10-75 for color transparencies; $5-25 for 8x10 b&w prints. Captions, model releases, and identification of subjects required. Buys all rights.
Columns/Departments: Tailgate (miscellaneous automotive news). Buys 6 mss/year. Send complete ms. Length: 20-100 words. Pays $10-25.
Tips: "The best way to break in is with a well photographed, action feature on a modified vehicle. Study our magazine for style and content. We do not deviate much from established editorial concept. Keep copy short, information accurate, and photos in focus."

PICKUP, VAN & 4WD MAGAZINE, CBS Consumer Publishing, 1499 Monrovia Ave., Newport Beach CA 92663. (714)646-4451. Associate Publisher/Editor: Don E. Brown. Managing Editor: Jon Thompson. Covers pick-ups, vans and off-road vehicles. Monthly magazine; 104 pages. Circ. 260,000. Pays on publication. Buys all rights. Pays kill fee "depending on assignment." Byline given. Submit seasonal/holiday material 3-4 months in advance. Photocopied submissions OK. Query and request writer's guidelines, "Contributor's Memo." SASE. Reports 1-2 months. Free writer's guidelines.
Nonfiction: How-to (modifications to light duty trucks, such as extra seats, tool storage; 4WD repairs, modifications, etc.), historical, nostalgia (old restored trucks and 4-wheel drives), technical and travel (4-wheel drive travel only, must show vehicle being used). Buys 4-5 mss/per issue. Submit complete ms. Length: 1,000-3,000 words. Pays $75/published page.
Photos: Purchased with accompanying manuscript or on assignment. Captions required. Query for photos. Pays $12.50-75 for 8x10 b&w glossy prints; $25-75 for 35mm or 2¼x2¼ color transparencies; offers no additional payment for photos accepted with ms. Model release required.

RIDER, 29901 Agoura Rd., Agoura CA 91301. Editor: Bill Estes. For owners and prospective buyers of motorcycles to be used for touring, sport riding, and commuting. Bimonthly magazine; 100-160 pages. Buys all rights. Pays on publication. Sample copy $1. Free writer's guidelines. Submit seasonal material 3 months in advance. Photocopied submissions OK. Query. Reports in 1 month. SASE.
Nonfiction and Photos: Articles directly related to motorcycle touring, camping, commuting and sport riding including travel, human interest, safety, novelty, do-it-yourself and technical. "Articles which portray the unique thrill of motorcycling." Should be written in clean, contemporary style aimed at a sharp, knowledgeable reader. Buys informational how-to, personal experience, profile, historical, nostalgia, personal opinion, travel and technical. Length is flexible. Pays $150-300. Offers no addtional payment for photos purchased with ms. Captions required. "Quality photographs are critical. Graphics are emphasized in *Rider*, and we must have photos with good visual impact."

ROAD & TRACK, 1499 Monrovia Avenue, Newport Beach CA 92663. Editor: John Dinkel. For knowledgeable car enthusiasts. Monthly magazine. Buys all rights. Query. Reports in 6 weeks. SASE.

Nonfiction: "The editor welcomes freelance material, but if the writer is not thoroughly familiar with the kind of material used in the magazine, he is wasting both his time and the magazine's time. *Road & Track* material is highly specialized and that old car story in the files has no chance of being accepted. More serious, comprehensive and in-depth treatment of particular areas of automotive interest." Pays 12-25¢/word minimum depending upon subject covered and qualifications and experience of author.

Tips: "Freelancer must have intimate knowledge of the magazine. Unless he can quote chapter and verse for the last 20 years of publication he's probably wasting his time and mine."

ROAD KING MAGAZINE, 233 E. Erie, Chicago IL 60611. Editor-in-Chief: George Friend. 10% freelance written. Truck driver leisure reading publication. Quarterly: 48 pages. Circ. 213,855. Pays on acceptance. Buys first rights. Byline given "always on fiction—if requested on nonfiction— copyright mentioned only if requested." Submit seasonal/holiday material 3 months in advance. Simultaneous and photocopied submissions OK. Sample copy for 7x10 SASE with 50¢ postage or get free sample copy at any Union 76 truck stop.

Nonfiction: Trucker slant or general interest, humor, and photo feature. No articles on violence or sex. Name and quote release required. Submit complete ms. Length: 500-2,500 words. Pays $50-100.

Photos: Submit photos with accompanying ms. No additional payment for b&w contact sheets or 2¼x2¼ color transparencies. Captions preferred. Buys first rights. Model release required.

Fiction: Adventure, historical, humorous, mystery, suspense and western. Especially about truckers. No stories on sex and violence. Buys 4 mss/year. Submit complete ms. Length: 2,500 words maximum. Pays $100.

Poetry: Light verse and traditional. No avant-garde poetry. Buys 2 poems/year. Submit 1 poem/ batch. Length: 250 words maximum. Pays $50-100.

Fillers: Jokes, gags, anecdotes and short humor. Buys 20-25/year. Length: 50-500 words. Pays $5-100.

Tips: No collect phone calls or postcard requests. "We don't appreciate letters we have to answer." No certified, insured or registered mail. No queries. "Do not submit mss or art or photos using registered mail, cerfified mail or insured mail. Publisher will not accept such materials from the post office. Publisher will not discuss refusal with writer. Nothing personal, just legal. Do not write and ask if we would like such and such article or outline. We buy only from original and complete mss submitted on speculation. Do not ask for "writer's guidelines." See above and/or get copy of magazine and be familiar with our format before submitting anything. Never phone for free copy as we will not have such phone calls."

ROAD RIDER, Box 678, South Laguna CA 92677. Editor/Publisher: Roger Hull. Covers touring and camping on motorcycles for a family-oriented audience. Monthly magazine; 96 pages. Circ. 35,000. Pays on acceptance. Buys all rights. Submit seasonal/holiday material 6 months in advance. "We schedule seasonal material 1 year in advance." SASE. Reports in 2-3 weeks. Sample copy $1.50; free writer's guidelines with SASE.

Nonfiction: "We will consider any articles providing they are of sound base so far as motorcycling knowledge is concerned. Must be cycle-oriented. On expose we need documentation. How-to's usually are of technical nature and require experience. We would love to see more humorous cycle experience type of material. Cycling personalities are also big here. We try to do three or four historical pieces per year. All evaluation/testing pieces are done in house. Travel pieces need good photos; same thing is true on historical or nostalgia material." Buys 48 mss/year. Query or send complete ms. Length: 300-2,000 words. Pays $100-150.

Photos: Send photos with ms. Offers no additional payment for photos accepted with accompanying ms. Uses 5x7 b&w glossy prints; 35mm or 2¼x2¼ color transparencies. Captions and model releases required.

Fiction: "We are open for good, motorcycling fiction which is slanted toward a family-type audience. No erotica." Buys 2-3 mss/year. Send complete ms. Length: 300-2,000 words. Pays $100-150.

Poetry: "We use very little poetry." Buys 3-4/year. Pays $10-15.

Tips: "We are an enthusiast publication—as such, it is virtually impossible to sell here unless the writer is also an enthusiast and actively involved in the sport. A good, well-written, brief item dealing with a motorcycle trip, accompanied by top quality b&w photos receives prime time editorial attention. We are always on the lookout for good material from eastern seaboard or Midwest. Best way to hit this market is to buy and study a sample issue prior to submitting. Most of our contributors are Road Rider People. If you are unsure as to what Road Rider People refers, you will probably not be able to sell to this magazine. We continue to be overstocked on following: beginner articles (all ages, sexes, etc.), journal-format travel articles (not welcome) and travel articles from Southwestern US."

STOCK CAR RACING MAGAZINE, 67 Peach Orchard Rd., Burlington MA 01803. Editor: Dick Berggren. For stock car racing fans and competitors. Monthly magazine; 100 pages. Circ. 120,000. Pays on publication. Buys all rights. Byline given. SASE. Reports in 6 weeks.
Nonfiction: "Uses primarily nonfiction on stock car drivers, cars, and races. We are looking for Canadian and California people. We are interested in the story behind the story in stock car and sprint car racing. We want interesting profiles and colorful, nationally interesting features." Query. Buys 100 mss/year. Length: 100-6,000 words. Pays $10-350.
Photos: State availability of photos. Pays $20 for 8x10 b&w photos; $50-150 for 35mm or larger color transparencies. Captions required.
Tips: "We get more queries than stories. We just don't get as much material as we want to buy. Almost everyone who writes fails to finish the story. The world is filled with would-be's. We need material and pay a fair price."

STREET RODDER MAGAZINE, TRM Publications, Inc., 2145 W. LaPalma, Anaheim CA 92801. Editorial Director: Bud Lang. For the automotive enthusiast with an interest in street-driven, modified old cars. Monthly magazine. Circ. 105,000. Buys all rights. Buys 80-90 mss/year. Pays on publication. Sample copy $2.00; free writer's guidelines. No photocopied or simultaneous submissions. Reports in 1 month. Query or submit complete ms. SASE.
Nonfiction and Photos: "We need coverage of events and cars that we can't get to. Street rod event (rod runs); how-to technical articles; features on individual street rods. We don't need features on local (Southern California) street rods, events or shops. We stress a straightforward style; accurate and complete details; easy to understand (though not 'simple') technical material. Need good, clear, complete and well-photographed technical and how-to articles on pertinent street rod modifications or conversions. We very seldom accept a story without photos." Length: 250-1,500 words. Pays $50-70/page. Average payment for 2-page feature using 5x7 or 8x10 b&w photos is $100. "We demand good close-ups of details and 10-20 views, so that we can pick 5 or 6 for the photo layout."
Tips: "We regularly encourage new freelancers to submit material to us. They must have a knowledge of the street rod itself and how it is built. Our readers build and own pre-1949 cars that are modernized with late model engines, etc. We would like to see more photo features on non-Ford rods."

SUPER CHEVY, Argus Publishing, 12301 Wilshire Blvd., Suite 316, Los Angeles CA 90025. (213)820-3601. Editor: Doug Marion. Feature Editor: Pete Pegtrre. Monthly magazine covering Chevrolet automobiles for anyone associated with Chevys-owners, mechanics, car builders and racing drivers. Circ. 160,000. Pays on acceptance. Byline given. Buys all rights. Submit seasonal/holiday material 4 months in advance. Simultaneous queries OK. Reports in 2 weeks on queries; 1 week on mss. Free sample copy.
Nonfiction: Historical (classic Chevy); interview; race coverage (drage, stock and sprint car). Buys 25 mss/year. Query by phone or letter. Length: 300-1,500 words. Pays $100-300.
Photos: State availability of photos. Pays $25-60/35mm color transparency; $15 minimum/5x7 or 8x10 b&w glossy print. Captions and model releases required.

SUPER STOCK AND DRAG ILLUSTRATED, Lopez Publications, 602 Montgomery St., Alexandria VA 22314. Editor: Steve Collison. Monthly magazine for "mostly blue-collar males between 18-40 years old; high performance, drag racing oriented." Circ. 85,000. Pays on publication. Buys all rights. Byline given. Simultaneous and photocopied submissions OK. SASE. Reports in 6 weeks. Sample copy $1.50.
Nonfiction: Interview (with prominent drag racers); profile (on local or national drag cars); photo features (on drag racing cars or racing events); and technical. Buys 120 mss/year. Query or submit complete ms. Length: 500-5,000 words. Pays $50-250.
Photos: Purchased with accompanying ms. Captions required. Submit prints or transparencies. Pays $10 for 8x10 b&w glossy prints; $50-150 for 35mm color transparencies.
Fiction: Adventure, humorous. Must be drag racing oriented. Submit complete ms. Length: 500-5,000 words. Pays $50-250.

VW & PORSCHE, Argus Publishers, 12301 Wilshire Blvd., Suite 316, Los Angeles Ca 90025. (213)820-3601. Editor: Greg Brown. Bimonthly magazine covering VW and Porsche and Audi cars for owners of VW's and Porsches. Estab. 1979. Circ. 65,000. Pays one month before publication. Byline given. Kill fee varies. Buys one-time rights. Submit seasonal/holiday material 4 months in advance. SASE. Reports in 2 weeks on queries. Free sample copy.

Nonfiction: How-to (restore, maintain or tune-up); Special, modified or restored VW's and Porsches. Buys 30-35 mss/year. Query. Length: 1,000-2,500 words. Pays $60-75/printed page. "More if color pictures are used."

Photos: State availability of photos. Reviews 8x10 glossy prints. Identification of subjects required. "Photo payment included in page price."

Tips: "Whoever writes for a 'nut' book should research their material extremely well. Our readers want straight, honest, new information. Errors are caught at once."

Aviation

Publications in this section aim at professional and private pilots, and at aviation enthusiasts in general. Magazines intended for passengers of commercial airlines are grouped in a separate In-Flight category. Technical aviation and space journals, and publications for airport operators, aircraft dealers and others in aviation businesses are listed under Aviation and Space in the Trade Journals section.

AIR LINE PILOT, 1625 Massachussetts Ave. NW, Washington DC 20036. (202)797-4176. Editor-in-Chief: C.V. Glines. Managing Editor: Anne Kelleher. Covers commercial aviation issues for members of Air Line Pilots Association (ALPA). Monthly magazine; 56-64 pages. Circ. 45,000. Pays on acceptance. Buys all rights. Submit seasonal material 4 months in advance. SASE. Reports in 1 month. Free sample copy and writer's guidelines.

Nonfiction: Historical (aviation/personal or equipment, aviation firsts); informational (aviation safety, related equipment or aircraft aids); interview (aviation personality); nostalgia (aviation history); photo feature; profile (airline pilots; must be ALPA members); and technical. Buys 25 mss/year. Query. Length: 1,000-2,500 words. Pays $100-500.

Photos: State availability of photos with query. Purchased with or without accompanying ms. Captions required. Pays $10-25 for 8x10 b&w glossy prints; $20-250 for 35mm or 2¼x2¼ color transparencies. Covers: Pays $250.

Tips: "Unless a writer is experienced in the technical aspects of aviation, he is more likely to score with a pilot profile or aviation historical piece."

THE AOPA PILOT, 7315 Wisconsin Ave., Washington DC 20014. (301)654-0500. Editor: Edward G. Tripp. For plane owners, pilots, and the complete spectrum of the general aviation industry. Official magazine of the Aircraft Owners and Pilots Association. Monthly. Circ. 258,000. Pays on acceptance. Reports in 2 months. SASE. Sample copy $2.

Nonfiction: Factual articles up to 2,500 words that will inform, educate and entertain pilots and aircraft owners ranging from the student to the seasoned professional. These pieces should be generously illustrated with good quality photos, diagrams or sketches. Quality and accuracy essential. Topics covered include maintenance, operating technique, reports on new and used aircraft, or avionics and other aviation equipment, places to fly (travel), governmental policies (local, state or federal) relating to general aviation. Additional features on weather in relation to flying, legal aspects of aviation, flight education, pilot fitness, and aviation history are used occasionally. Short features of 100-300 words written around a single photograph, and strong photo features. Pays $400 maximum.

Photos: Pays $25 minimum for each photo or sketch used. Original b&w negatives or color slides should be made available.

AVIATION QUARTERLY, Box 606, Plano TX 75074. Publisher and Editor: Brad Bierman. Managing Editor: Glenn Bierman. For the serious aviation enthusiast, interested in the history of aviation. Quarterly; hardbound volume with four-color illustrations. Circ. 7,000. No advertising. Buys all rights. Pays 50% kill fee. Byline given. Pays on publication. Phone queries OK. Submit seasonal/holiday material 5 months in advance. Simultaneous, photocopied and previously published submissions OK. SASE. Reports in 4-6 weeks. Sample copy $10; free writer's guidelines.

Nonfiction: Historical (on any historical aspect of aviation—past, present or future); interview (with aviation pioneers, those connected with aviation's history); nostalgia (on any aviation-oriented piece); personal experience (on any historical piece); photo feature (especially photo essays on any of the classic airplanes); and profile (on any aviation/history-oriented person). Buys

20 mss/year. Query or send complete ms. Length: 1,500-10,000 words. Pays $100-600.
Photos: Send photos with ms. Buys any size b&w or 35mm and 4x5 color transparencies. Payment for all photography work varies, and is negotiated. Captions required.
Tips: "All our articles must be well-written and well-documented with historical photos. Articles supported by fewer than a dozen photographs have little chance of making it. Good photo support is essential. Poor color will result in the rejection of a good article if the subject matter calls for color. No personal modern day experiences."

AVIATION TRAVEL & TIMES, Box 606, Plano TX 75074. Managing Editor: Glenn G. Bierman. For owners of business and private aircraft. Buys all rights. Buys about 50-60 mss/year. Pays on publication. Sample copy $2. Will consider photocopied submissions. Submit seasonal material 3-4 months in advance. Query or submit complete ms. Reports in 2 months. SASE.
Nonfiction and Photos: Buys general aviation informational articles, how-to's, personal flying experience articles, humor, historical articles, photo features travel pieces, aircraft flight reports, new developments in general aviation, and other technical flying articles. Travel stories must be short, informational, and specific enough to be helpful to the traveler. Destinations must be emphasized, rather than flight. Dates, admission, what to take, etc., increase the value of a story. We're interested in fly-in wilderness, fishing, hunting, golfing and camping stories at specific locations. Length: 500-3,000 words. Pay "varies: about 5¢ per word, depending on subject and quality. Photos must accompany articles requiring photo support." Photos purchased with or without mss; captions required. Pays $5 and up, depending on photo, for b&w glossy prints 5x7 and larger. Pays $5 and up, "depending on photo and use for transparencies only."

FLYING, Ziff-Davis Publishing Co., 1 Park Ave., New York NY 10016. (212)725-3799. Editor-in-Chief: Richard L. Collins. Editorial Coordinator: Peter Boody. 5% freelance written. For private and commercial pilots involved with, or interested in, the use of general-aviation aircraft (not airline or military) for business and pleasure. Monthly magazine; 116 pages. Circ. 370,000. Pay on acceptance. Buys all rights and first North American serial rights. Submit seasonal/holiday material 4 months in advance of issue date. SASE. Reports in 3 weeks.
Nonfiction: How-to (piloting and other aviation techniques); and technical (aviation-related). No articles on "My Trip" travel accounts, or historical features. Buys about 12 mss/year. Submit complete ms. Length: 750-3,500 words. Pays $50-1,000.
Columns/Departments: "I Learned About Flying From That" personal experience. Pays $100 minimum.
Tips: "New ideas and approaches are a must. Tone must be correct for knowledgeable pilots rather than the non-flying public. Facts must be absolutely accurate."

GENERAL AVIATION NEWS, Drawer 1416, Snyder TX 79549. (915)573-6318, 1-800-351-1372 (Texas 1-800-592-4484). Editor-in-Chief: Norval Kennedy. 20% freelance written. For pilots, aircraft owners, mechanics, aircraft dealers and related business people. Weekly tabloid; 40 pages. Circ. 40,000. Pays on acceptance. Buys all rights. Byline given "only on features and short features, not on straight news stories." Phone queries OK. Submit seasonal/holiday material 1 month in advance. Photocopied submissions OK. SASE. Reports in 1 month. Sample copy $1; writer's guidelines for SASE.
Nonfiction: General aviation articles that would be of interest to nationwide audience; articles and features of interest to corporate aviation (businesses and people that own and operate one or more business aircraft). No articles on commercial or military airplanes. Buys up to 50 mss/year. Submit complete ms. Length: 2,000 words maximum. Pays $25/1,000 words.
Photos: Send photo material with accompanying ms. Pays $3-5 for 4x5 b&w or color prints. Captions required. Buys all rights.
Tips: "Knowing about business aviation is helpful, but the freelancer who can put together a good story about an aspect of it could also have a good chance of selling. I would be happy to discuss specifics on phone. Follow the advice in the front of *Writer's Market!*"

PLANE & PILOT MAGAZINE, Werner & Werner Corp., 606 Wilshire Blvd., Suite 100, Santa Monica CA 90401. (213)451-1423. Editorial Director: Steve Werner. 75% freelance written. Emphasizes all aspects of general aviation—personal and business. Monthly magazine; 80 pages. Circ. 75,000. Pays on publication. Buys all rights. Phone queries OK. Submit seasonal/holiday material 6 months in advance. SASE. Reports in 1 month. Sample copy $1.50.
Nonfiction: How-to articles (emergency procedures; weather); informational (proficiency; aircraft reports; jobs and schools; avionics); humor; personal experience (regular features on "Flight I'll Never Forget;" Travel). Buys 150 mss/year. Query. Length: 1,000-3,000 words. Pays $100-300.
Photos: State availability of photos in query. Offers no additional payment for photos accepted with ms. Only uses 8x10 b&w. Prefers 2¼x2¼ or 35mm slides. Query.

PRIVATE PILOT, Macro/Comm Corp., Box 4030, San Clemente CA 92672. (714)498-1600. Editor: Dennis Shattuck. 60% freelance written. For owner/pilots of private aircraft, for student pilots and others aspiring to attain additional ratings and experience. "We take a unique, but limited view within our field." Circ. 90,000. Buys first North American serial rights. Buys about 30-60 mss/year. Pays after publication. Sample copy $2; writer's guidelines for SASE. Will consider photocopied submissions if guaranteed original. No simultaneous submissions. Reports in 1 month. Query. SASE.
Nonfiction: Material on techniques of flying, developments in aviation, product and specific airplane test reports, travel by aircraft, development and use of airports. All must be related to general aviation field. No personal experience articles. Length: 1,000-4,000 words. Pays $75-250.
Photos: Pays $15 for 8x10 b&w glossy prints purchased with mss or on assignment. Pays $100 for color transparencies used on cover.
Columns/Departments: Business flying, homebuilt/experimental aircraft, pilot's logbook. Length: 1,000 words. Pays $50-125.
Tips: "Freelancer must know the subject about which he is writing; use good grammar; know the publication for which he's writing; remember that we try to relate to the middle segment of the business/pleasure flying public. We see too many 'first flight' type of articles. Our market is more sophisticated than that. Most writers do not do enough research on their subject. Would like to see more material on business-related flying, more on people involved in flying."

WINGS MAGAZINE, Division of Corvus Publishing Group, Ltd., Suite 158, 1224 53rd Ave., NE, Calgary, Alberta, Canada T2E 7E2. (403)277-2337. Editor-in-Chief: Wayne D. Ralph. Covers private, commercial and military aviation. Readers are age 15-70 and are predominantly people employed in aviation or with a hobbyist's interest in the field. Bimonthly magazine. Circ. 10,000. Pays on publication. Buys first rights. Phone queries OK. SASE. Sample copy $1.50.
Nonfiction: Historical (mainly Canadian history); how-to (technical); informational (technical aviation); interview (Canadian personalities in aviation circles); new product, photo feature; profile (Canadian individuals); technical; travel (flying-related); aircraft handling tests and technical evaluation on new products. No poetry or cartoons. Query; include phone number (with area code). Length: 500-2,000 words. Pays $50-200.
Photos: State availability of photos in query. Purchased with or without accompanying ms. Captions required. Offers no additional payment for photos accepted with SASE. Pays $5-20 for 5x7 b&w glossy prints; $25-50 for 35mm color transparencies.
Tips: The writer must have a technical grounding in aviation, be employed in aviation, be a knowledgeable buff or a licensed pilot. Be sure story idea is unique and would be of interest to a Canadian audience. The audience has a high level of technical insight and needs reading material that is newsworthy and informative to the industry, executive, aviation expert and worker.

Black

General interest publications for blacks and other minorities are listed in this category. Additional markets for black-oriented material are in the following sections: Business and Finance, Confession, Juvenile, Literary and Little, Men's, Poetry, Politics and World Affairs, Sport and Outdoor, Teen and Young Adult, Theater, Movie, TV and Entertainment, Scriptwriting, Book Publishers, Greeting Card Publishers, and Syndicates.

AFRO-DENVER, Box 22557, Denver CO 80222. (303)399-2500. Editor/Publisher: R. Mason Hawkins. Associate Editor: Jack Jones. Monthly magazine. "This is a Rocky Mountain magazine covering minorities." Circ. 10,000. Pays on publication. Byline given. Buys first North American serial rights. Phone queries OK. Submit seasonal material 3 months in advance. Simultaneous, photocopied and previously published submissions OK. Reports in 2 weeks on queries; in 1 month on mss. Sample copy $1. Buys 8-10 features and 12 short features/issue.
Nonfiction: General interest; interview (with prominent people around Denver or minority members or people involved with minorities); profile (people of national significance); travel (in the Colorado area); and photofeature (scenic photography in or around Denver). Buys 3 mss/issue. Query with clips of published work or send complete ms. Pays $30-100.
Photos: State availability of photos. Reviews 8x10 b&w glossies and color prints and 35mm

transparencies. Offers no additional payment for photos accepted with ms. Captions and model release required. Buys one-time rights.

Fiction: Adventure, humorous, mystery, romance, suspense, historical, mainstream and western. "We want fiction that appeals to both men and women and something minorities can identify with." Buys 1 ms/issue. Query. Length: 1,000-3,000 words. Pays $30-100.

Poetry: Free verse, light verse, and traditional "with appeal to a general audience. No abstract poetry." Buys 2 mss/issue. Pays $25 minimum.

BLACK ENTERPRISE MAGAZINE, For Black Men and Women Who Want to Get Ahead, Earl G. Graves Publishing Co., 295 Madison Ave., New York NY 10017. (212)889-8220. Editor: Earl G. Graves. Executive Editor: Joel Dreyfuss. Monthly magazine covering black economic development and business for a highly-educated, affluent, black, middle-class audience interested in business, politics, careers and international issues." Circ. 230,000. Pays on acceptance. Byline given. Offers 25% kill fee. Buys all rights. Submit seasonal/holiday material 4 months in advance. Simultaneous queries OK. Reports in 2 weeks on queries; 1 month on mss. Sample copy and writer's guidelines free.

Nonfiction: Exposé, general interest, how-to, interview/profile, technical, travel and short, hard-news items of black interest. "We emphasize the how-to aspect." Special issues include: Careers, February; Black Business, June; and Money Management, October. "No fiction or poetry; no 'rags-to-riches,' ordinary-guy stories, please." Buys 30-40 mss/year. Query with clips of published work. Send "a short, succinct letter that lets us know the point of the piece, the elements involved, and *why* our readers would want to read it." Length: 600-3,000 words. Pays $100-800/article.

Columns/Departments: Emile Milne, senior editor. In the News (short, hard-news pieces on issues of black interest); and Personal Finance (aimed at middle-income readers). Buys 50-60 mss/year. Query with clips of published work. Length: 300-1,000 words. Pays $75-300/article.

Tips: "We have stayed away from trivia and first-person pieces on the belief that our readers want hard-nosed reporting and innovative analysis of issues that concern them. *Black Enterprise* has a mission of informing, educating and entertaining an upscale, affluent audience that wants issues addressed from its unique perspective. We are most open to 'In the News,' an expression of a sensitivity to issues/events/trends that have an impact on black people."

BLACK FUTURE, VSC Inc., Box 4989, Atlanta GA 30301. (404)241-2712. Editor: Cecil J. Williams. Quarterly magazine covering trends, with emphasis on people achieving. Estab. 1979. Circ. 60,000. Pays on acceptance. Byline given. Buys all rights "but we will consider buying other rights." Submit seasonal/holiday material 3 months in advance. Simultaneous queries, and simultaneous, photocopied, and previously published submissions OK. SASE. Reports in 2 weeks. Sample copy $1.75; free writer's guidelines. "Write for an editorial calendar that outlines specific editorial needs."

Nonfiction: How-to (home repair, decorating, saving money); humor; inspirational; interview/profile; new product; opinion; personal experience; photo feature; and travel. Buys 4-6 mss/year. Query with outline or send complete ms. Length: 3,000 words maximum. Pays $25-350.

Photos: Send photos with ms. Reviews b&w or color 35 mm transparencies and 8x10 b&w prints. Captions and model releases required. Buys one-time rights. Pays negotiable fee.

Columns/Departments: Spectrum (news bits and short pieces); People Shaping the Future; and Modern Living (food, travel, habitat). Buys 15-20 mss/year. Send complete ms. Length: 500-1,000 words. Pays $25.

Fiction: "We're looking for stories of a sociological nature." Buys 2-4 mss/year. Send complete ms. Length: 1,000 words minimum. Pays $100.

Tips: "A writer should get our magazine and become familiar with it before submitting anything."

BUFFALO MAGAZINE, For the Black American Military Professional, Buffalo Publishing Co., Box 35606, Fayetteville NC 28303. (919)864-4706. Editor: Ariel P. Wiley. Monthly magazine covering life in the military, or black community. "Our magazine publishes articles and pieces that concern military life, and most specifically, black viewpoints on the military. Contributions are welcome from any racial group. Our only request is that the material submitted be pertinent to our readership—which is a very specific group in itself. Since the black service person's family is part of our audience, we do print things that would concern the military spouse, and articles on education . . . things that concern the adult reader about their children. News on trends in the black community and politics is welcome, since our readers are part of that larger ethnic group." Estab. 1980. Circ. 10,000. Pays on publication. Byline given. Offers 20%-of-commission kill fee. Buys one-time rights. Submit seasonal/holiday material 3 months in advance. Simultaneous queries and simultaneous submissions OK. SASE. Reports in 2 weeks on queries and mss. Sample copy 50¢ ("covers our postage and stationery costs"); free writer's guidelines.

Nonfiction: Book excerpts (historical research on black military personnel); exposé (only concerning military problems that could be brought to the attention of the chain of command); general interest (to the black community); how-to (on military skills and survival or best bargains on tour); interview/profile (on interesting or unique black, military-related persons); opinion (only from service people); personal experience (of or concerning black service people); technical (concerning military skills); travel (by or concerning blacks on tour of duty). No articles "unconcerned with the black community or military life." Query with clips of published work. Length: 1,300-8,000 words. Pays $25-100/article; "depends on length, quality, how much editing is needed, and photos supplied."

Fiction: Adventure (military in nature; must concern the black military); historical (on the black military); mainstream (with black protagonists); western (on black presence in the West). "We consider all fiction of quality as long as it is directed toward our readership, as blacks, or as military." No "stories that bear no, or little, relation to the concerns of the black military community, or sections of the black community at large that would concern the black service person." Buys 6 mss/year. Send complete ms. Length: 4,000-10,300 words. Pays $50-150/article.

Poetry: Avant-garde, free verse, haiku, light verse and traditional. "We will accept most forms." Buys 20/year. Submit maximum 3 poems. Length: 10-60 lines. Pays $30-75.

Fillers: Clippings, anecdotes and newsbreaks. Buys 9/year. Length: 500-1,300 words. Pays $20-50.

Tips: "The best tip to breaking into *Buffalo*, is to avoid extraneous material. We print a lot of black historical material, (i.e., Bill Pickett a black rodeo star and inventor of steer wrestling, a small piece on Tuskegee Airmen and we're looking for more material). . . . A perspective on the racial climate of the times is needed with historical material. Any piece on a well-known black personality is a possibility. Our publishing point is to show the black military professional *and* his job/career in a positive light. We aren't trying to be *Ebony*. The best hint is to keep the interest of the black service person and family in mind, that is: Would it interest them as military personnel, family people, or voting members of the black community, or parents interested in showing their children the range of black achievements to instill pride and a sense of accomplishment. We prefer to print fiction and poetry from members of the armed forces along with their rank, names and duty stations. Our readership has a very limited interest in reading about the white community, or military matters that relate to Hispanics, other ethnic groups, or strictly Caucasian personalities and military campaigns."

CORE, 1916-38 Park Ave., New York NY 10037. (212)690-3678. Editor: Doris Innis. Publication of the Congress of Racial Equality. Bimonthly. Circ. 30,000. Rights acquired vary with author and material. Uses about 60 freelance articles/year. "Most of our articles are donated." Free sample copy. Will consider photocopied submissions. Submit seasonal/holiday material at least 2 months in advance. Query. Reports in 6 months. SASE.

Nonfiction and Photos: "Articles about or related to the black movement, black people's oppression, projected or attempted solutions. Also profiles of Black Movement people. Interviews. Health, food, books, sports. Also interested in travel, fashion, movies or African affairs. The writer's style and emphasis is up to him. We like variety. Of course, it helps if his outlook is black nationalist, but it's not mandatory. We try to make black nationalism (a little understood concept) digestible for the common man as well as the intellectual." Length: 500-5,000 words. Pays $25 for b&w photos on assignment. Captions optional.

Poetry and Fillers: Free verse and avant-garde forms. Length: open. Short humor and anecdotes. Length: 500-1,500 words. "Most are donated."

EBONY MAGAZINE, 820 S. Michigan Ave., Chicago IL 60605. Editor: John H. Johnson. Managing Editor: Charles L. Sanders. For black readers of the US, Africa, and the Caribbean. Monthly. Circ. 1,300,000. Buys all rights. Buys about 5 mss/year. Pays on publication. Submit seasonal material 2 months in advance. Query. Reports in 1 month. SASE.

Nonfiction: Achievement and human interest stories about, or of concern to, black readers. Interviews, profiles and humor pieces are bought. Length: 1,500 words maximum. "Study magazine and needs carefully. Perhaps one out of 50 submissions interests us. Most are totally irrelevant to our needs and are simply returned." Pays $150 minimum.

Photos: Purchased with mss, and with captions only. Buys 8x10 glossy prints, color transparencies, 35mm color. Submit negatives and contact sheets when possible. Offers no additional payment for photos accepted with mss.

ESSENCE, 1500 Broadway, New York NY 10036. (212)730-4260. Editor-in-Chief: Susan L. Taylor. Executive Editor: Audrey Edwards. Senior Editors: Rosemary L. Bray, Jennie Bourne. Emphasizes black women. Monthly magazine; 150 pages. Circ. 650,000. Pays on acceptance. Makes assignments on work-for-hire basis. 3 month lead time. Pays 25% kill fee. Byline given. Submit seasonal/holiday material 6 months in advance. SASE. Reports in 2 months. Sample copy $1.25; free writer's guidelines.

Nonfiction: "We're looking for articles that challenge and inform black women. Our readers are interested and aware; the topics we include in each issue are provocative. Every article should move the *Essence* woman emotionally and intellectually. We welcome queries from good writers on a wide range of topics: general interest, historical, how-to, humor, interview, personal experience, political issues, personal opinion." Buys 200 mss/year. Query. Length: 1,500-4,000 words. Pays $300-850.

Photos: Ron Albrecht, art director. State availability of photos with query. Pays $50-300 for b&w contact sheets; $100-600 for color transparencies. Captions and model release required.

Columns/Departments: Query department editors: Entertainment, Jennie Bourne; Health, Stephanie Renfrow Hamilton; Travel, Cheryl Everette; Work, Alice Jones-Miller. Query. Length: 1,500-3,000 words. Pays $100 minimum.

Fiction: Rosemary L. Bray. Looking for serious, experimental, humorous or romantic fiction with a positive outlook about black women. The ending doesn't have to be happy, but characters should experience growth or change in the course of the story. Buys 33 mss/year. Submit complete ms. Length: 1,500 words. Pays $200 minimum.

JET, 820 S. Michigan Ave., Chicago IL 60605. Executive Editor: Robert E. Johnson. For black readers interested in current news and trends. Weekly. Circ. 750,000. Pays 100% kill fee. No byline. Study magazine before submitting. SASE.

Nonfiction: Articles on topics of current, timely interest to black readers. News items and features: religion, education, African affairs, civil rights, politics and entertainment. Buys informational articles, interviews, profiles, spot news and personal experience articles. Length: varies. Payment negotiated.

Photos: Photo essays. Payment negotiable.

SEPIA, 1220 Harding St., Ft. Worth TX 76102. Editor: Willie Johnson. For "a young, mobile, black audience, ages 21-45." Monthly. Circ. 160,000. Buys all rights. Buys about 75 mss/year. Pays on publication. Free sample copy. Submit seasonal material 3 months in advance. Reports in 1 month. Query. SASE.

Nonfiction: Sports figures; finance/money management; interviews; career advancement; regional dining; political; hobbies (e.g., collecting Oriental rugs or Oriental jewelry); fashion; photo essays—"anything relevant to a national audience." Length: 1,500 words minimum. Pays $150-300.

Photos: Send photos with ms, if possible. B&w glossy prints, color transparencies.

Columns/Departments: Accepts reviews of records, books, movies and plays.

UMOJA SASA NEWS JOURNAL, Pre-Professional Publications, 512 E. State St., Ithaca NY 14850. (607)272-0995. Editor: Tyrone Taborn. Managing Editor: Eric Steele. Bimonthly magazine covering world and current events for black and minority students. Estab. 1979. Circ. 10,000 Pays on publication. Byline given. Offers $25 kill fee. Buys first rights. Submit seasonal/holiday material 2 months in advance. Simultaneous queries and simultaneous submissions OK. SASE. Reports in 1 month on queries; 2 months on mss. Free sample copy and writer's guidelines.

Nonfiction: Cathie LaMarr. Exposé (of landlord, police, equal employment); inspirational (on coping with crime, poverty and social injustice); interview/profile (with black personalities); new product; and political. Needs "good news stories on urban problems. We prefer a fresh approach to problems like crime and unemployment." No travel or how-to. Buys 7 mss/year. Send complete ms. Length: 750-2,000 words. Pays $25-200/article.

Photos: Norris Smith. Send photos with ms. Pays $5-10 for b&w 8x10 prints. Buys one-time rights.

Tips: "Need good news stories on urban problems. Use a fresh approach to problems like crime and unemployment."

Business and Finance

National and regional publications of general interest to business executives form below. Those in the National grouping cover national business trends, and include some material on the general theory and practice of business and financial management. Those in the Regional grouping report on the business climates of specific regions.

Magazines that use material on national business trends and the general theory and practice of business and financial management, but which have a technical or professional slant, are classified in the Trade Journals section, under the Business Management, Finance, Industrial Management, or Management and Supervision categories.

National

B&E INTERNATIONAL, Borgen Publishing Company, 4040 Milam, Suite 105, Box 66098, Houston TX 77006. (713)526-7400. Publisher: Erik T. Borgen. Monthly newspaper covering business, industry, finance and government for chief executive officers, chairmen, presidents, vice presidents, and managing directors of major international business, industry, energy, transportation, and finance, and heads of state, ministers, and other principal government leaders around the world. Circ. 83,000. Average issue includes approximately 20 articles. Pays on publication. Offers 33⅓% kill fee. Buys all rights. Photocopied submissions OK. SASE. Reports on queries in 1 week; on mss in 2 weeks. Sample copy $5.
Nonfiction: Interview. "We seek only one-on-one interviews with presidents, chairmen, and chief executive officers of major international corporations and with heads of state and principal ministers of foreign governments. Nothing else will be accepted, or should be either queried or submitted." Buys 10-12 mss/year. Length: 250 words. Query with clips of previously published work. Pays $25 minimum for articles, $100 for interviews.
Photos: State availability of photos. Pays $25 for 5x7 b&w glossy prints. Buys all rights.
Tips: "We seek regular contributors in major world cities who can be given assignments for both interviews and articles. To be considered, resumes and samples of best work would be the first step. Chances of an unknown writer being granted an interview with the sort of persons we feature are slim, therefore, it is best to let us see samples of writing skills first. Writers should not represent themselves as members of our staff unless permission to do so is given in writing."

BARRON'S NATIONAL BUSINESS AND FINANCIAL WEEKLY, 22 Cortlandt St., New York NY 10007. (212)285-5245. Editor/Publisher: Robert M. Bleiberg. For business and investment people. Weekly. Free sample copy. Buys all rights. Pays on publication. SASE.
Nonfiction: Articles about various industries with investment point of view; shorter articles on particular companies, their past performance and future prospects as related to industry trends for News and Views column. "Must be suitable for our specialized readership." Length: 2,000 minimum. Pays $500-750 for articles. Articles considered on speculation only.
Columns/Departments: News and Views. Pays $200-350.
Tips: "News and Views might be a good way to break in, but the key thing to remember here is these pieces must be fully researched and thoroughly documented."

BUSINESS WEEK, 1221 Avenue of the Americas, New York NY 10020. Does not solicit freelance material.

COLLECTOR-INVESTOR, Crain Communications, 740 Rush St., Chicago IL 60611. (312)640-5406. Editor: Mark K. Metzger. News Editor: Beverly J. Montgomery. Monthly magazine covering the practical aspects of the top levels of collecting for chief executive or chief financial officers of United States companies and professional money managers in the United States and abroad. Estab. 1980. Circ. 30,000. Pays on acceptance. Buys all rights. Submit seasonal material 3 months in advance. SASE. Reports in 2 weeks. Sample copy $2; free writer's guidelines.
Nonfiction: Expose (thefts, frauds and illegal or unethical practices in the collecting field); State of the Market (examines one part of the collecting field, such as the Oriental carpet or lithograph market, explaining the dynamics of the market generally, and details what is going on now); Ardent Collectors (profiles of a major collector of art or antiques). "We do not want stories about off-beat collections or about collection items like beer cans or barbed wire. We cover the top end of the collecting world." Buys 2-3 mss/issue. Query with clips of previously published work. Length: 600-2,500 words. Pays $50-50¢/word plus potential bonus.
Columns/Departments: Newsfronts (news tips and stories and important developments that affect the collector). Buys 2-3 mss/issue. Query. Pays $50-50¢/word.
Tips: "With a particular emphasis on investment angles, we cover all practical aspects of collecting paintings, sculpture, antique furniture, books, rare coins, objects of art, stamps, classic autos, musical instruments, the whole gamut of investment grade collectibles. We apply the expertise and the sensibilities of good business journalists to the realm of collecting."

COMMODITY JOURNAL, American Association of Commodity Traders, 10 Park St., Concord NH 03001. Editor: Arthur N. Economou. For investors interested in commodity trading based on cash, forward and option markets, alternative energy sources and foregin currencies. Monthly tabloid. Circ. 165,000. Pays on publication. Buys all rights. Byline given. Written queries OK.

Photocopied and previously published submissions OK. SASE. Reports in 1 month. Free sample copy and writer's guidelines.

DOLLARS & SENSE, National Taxpayers Union, 325 Pennsylvania Ave. SE, Washington DC 20003. Editor-in-Chief: M.E. Hubbard. 10% freelance written. Emphasizes taxes and government spending for a diverse readership. Monthly newspaper; 8-12 pages. Circ. 90,000. Pays on publication. Buys all rights. Submit seasonal/holiday material 1 month in advance. Previously published submissions OK. SASE. Free sample copy and writer's guidelines.
Nonfiction: Exposé dealing with wasteful government spending and excessive regulation of the economy. Buys 10 mss/year. Query. Length: 500-1,500 words. Pays $25-100. "We look for original material on subjects overlooked by the national press and other political magazines. Probably the best approach is to take a little-known area of government mismanagement and examine it closely. The articles we like most are those that examine a federal program that is not only poorly managed and wasteful, but also self-defeating, hurting the very people it is designed to help. We are also interested in the long-term harm done by different kinds of taxation. Articles on IRS harassment and abuses are always needed and welcome. We have no use for financial or investment advice or broad philosophical pieces."

DUN'S REVIEW, Dun & Bradstreet Publications Corp., 666 5th Ave., New York NY 10103. (212)489-2200. Editor: Clem Morgello. Emphasizes business, management and finances for a readership "concentrated among senior executives of those companies that have a net worth of $1 million or more." Monthly magazine. Circ. 284,000. Pays on acceptance. Buys all rights. Submit seasonal/holiday material 3 months in advance. Photocopied submissions OK. Reports in 1 month. Sample copy $2.25.
Nonfiction: Exposé (business and government), historical (business; i.e., law or case history), management (new trends, composition), finance and accounting, informational (business and government), interview (assigned only), personal opinion (submitted to The Forum, opinion from high-ranked sources), and profile (companies, turnarounds, etc). Buys 12 mss/year. Query. Length: 1,500-3,000 words. Pays $200 minimum.
Photos: Art Director. Purchased with accompanying ms. Query. Pays $75 for b&w photos; $150 for color.
Columns/Departments: Footnote (historical or important issues impacting business world), Spotlight, Forum, and The Economy (by invitation only). Buys 1 ms/issue. Query. Length: 1,000-1,500 words. Pays $200.
Tips: "Make query short and clearly to the point. Also important—what distinguishes proposed story form others of its type."

THE EXECUTIVE FEMALE, NAFE, 485 Fifth Ave., Suite 401, New York NY 10017. (212)697-6544. Executive Editor: Karin Abarbanel. Managing Editor: Susan Strecker. Emphasizes "upbeat and useful career and financial information for the upwardly mobile female." Bimonthly magazine; 60 pages. Circ. 50,000. Byline given. Pays on publication. Submit seasonal/holiday material 6 months in advance. Simultaneous and photocopied submissions OK. SASE. Reports in 3 months. Sample copy $1.50; free writer's guidelines.
Nonfiction: Profile (of successful working women and the story of their careers), and technical (stories of women entrepreneurs, and career advancement and financial planning for women). "Articles on any aspect of career advancement and financial planning for women are welcomed." Sample topics: investment, coping with inflation, money-saving ideas, financial planning, business communication, time and stress management, and career goal setting and advancement. No negative or radical "women's lib" material. Buys 1-2 mss/issue. Queries preferred. Length: 800-1,500 words. Pays $50 minimum.
Columns/Departments: Profiles (interviews with successful women in a wide range of fields); Entrepreneur's Corner (successful female business owners with unique ideas); Horizons (career planning personal and professional goal-setting); and $$$ and You (specific financial issues, social security, tax planning). Buys 1-2/issue. Queries preferred. Length: 800-1,200 words. Pays $50 minimum.

EXPRESS, The Magazine Amtrak, East/West Network, 5900 Wilshire Blvd., Los Angeles CA 90036. Editor: Helen Newton. Monthly magazine emphasizing business and service pieces for passengers of Amtrak trains—oriented toward executives on the East Coast. Estab. 1981. Circ. 100,000. Pays on acceptance. Byline given. Pays varying kill fee. Buys first North American serial rights. Submit seasonal/holiday material 4 months in advance. Previously published submissions OK ("indicate where and when published"). SASE. Reports in 1 month. Sample copy $2; writer's guidelines for business size SAE and 1 first class stamp.
Nonfiction: Profile, travel, money, health, and sports. "We commission articles, generally. We find

writers to carry out ideas that we generate." Buys 60 mss/year. Query with clips of published work; "make the query very sharp." Length: 1,500 words minimum. Pays $500.
Photos: State availability of photos.

FINANCE, The Magazine of Money & Business, 25 W. 39th St., 15th Floor, New York NY 10018. (212)221-7900. Publisher/Editor: James C. Burke. 50% freelance written. For senior executives and decision-makers in the business and financial communities. Magazine; 48 pages. Circ. 30,000. Pays on publication. Buys all rights. Phone queries OK. Submit seasonal/holiday material 6 weeks in advance of issue date. Simultaneous and photocopied submissions OK. SASE. Reports in 3 months. Free sample copy and writer's guidelines.
Nonfiction: Survey articles of banking and corporate finance trends. Interviews and profiles with high ranking business and financial executives. "No nuts-and-bolts or lower/middle management-related how-to articles." Query. Length: 1,000-5,000 words. Pays $100-500.
Photos: State availability of photos with query. Pays $10 for 5x7 glossy b&w prints; $10 for color transparencies. Captions preferred. Buys all rights.
Columns/Departments: Buys 3 mss/year. Query. Length: 1,000-2,000 words. Pays $100. Open to suggestions for new columns/departments.

FINANCIAL WORLD, Macro Communications, Inc., 150 E. 58th St., New York NY 10155. (212)826-4396. Editor: Stephen W. Quickel. Semimonthly magazine covering Wall Street opinions and investment possibilities for predominantly sophisticated investors. Circ. 100,000. Pays on publication. Buys all rights. SASE. Reports in 1 month. Sample copy $1.50.
Nonfiction: General interest (of an investigative nature, such as how stocks progressed after the company cut dividends); interview (of Wall Street people who are successful or influential in investment); profile (of individual companies in terms of investment possibilities); and implications of government spending on investments. Buys 75-100 mss/year. Query. Length: 1,000-4,000 words. Pays $200-1,500.
Tips: "A freelancer must be able to demonstrate that he can write fluently and entertainingly, and that he isn't frightened by numbers."

FORBES, 60 5th Ave., New York NY 10011. "We occasionally buy freelance material. When a writer of some standing (or whose work is at least known to us) is going abroad or into an area where we don't have regular staff or bureau coverage, we have given assignments or sometimes helped on travel expenses." Pays negotiable kill fee. Byline usually given.

FORTUNE, 1271 Avenue of the Americas, New York NY 10020. Staff-written, but does buy a few freelance articles (by Irwin Ross, for example) and pays well for them.

INC., Inc. Publishing Company, Inc., 38 Commercial Wharf, Boston MA 02110. (617)227-4700. Editor: Milton D. Stewart. Executive Editor: Stewart Alsop II. Monthly management magazine for top executives of smaller companies with $1-30 million in annual sales. 120-190 pages. Estab. 1979. Circ. 400,000. Pays on acceptance. Byline given. Negotiates kill fee. Buys all rights. Submit seasonal material 3 months in advance. Photocopied submissions OK. SASE. Reports in 6 weeks. Free sample copy and writer's guidelines.
Nonfiction: How-to (manage, market, finance, operate a company, with either experts or executives as the source); reader experience (analysis of a specific case); profile (of an interesting or unusual entrepreneur or company); think piece (opinion generally written by specialist); Inc. 100 profile (of a fast-growth company from magazine's annual ranking); special report (comprehensive report usually staff-written). "We are an analytical management magazine, not a reporting news magazine, so you need to understand business to write for us." Buys 4-6 mss/issue. Query, Jeff Tarter, Senior Editor. Length: 1,000-3,000 words. Pays $250-1,500.
Columns/Departments: People & Innovations (brief profiles), News and Trends (short items); Time Out (leisure), Marketing Finance, Health, Management, Law (all columns on specific strategies), INC. Interview (Q&A with opinion leader). Buys 4-6 columns and 10-12 short items/issue. Query Christopher Leach, Senior Editor. Length: 600-1,200 words for columns; 250-500 words for short items. Pays $50-1,000.
Tips: "Get the guidelines, read the magazine, and query us in detail. Show us in the query how much you know about business management and the problems of small companies. Tell us who you will talk to and how you will get the right information. Tell us why our readers will use their limited time to read the proposed article. Freelancers can help us most with stories on a single company or entrepreneur."

MONEY, Time-Life Bldg., Rockefeller Center, New York NY 10020. Managing Editor: Marshall Loeb. "For the middle to upper income, sophisticated, well-educated reader. Major subjects:

personal investing, financial planning, spending, saving and borrowing, careers, travel. Some freelance material.

OUTPUT, Technical Publishing, 666 5th Ave., New York NY 10019. (212)489-3474. Editor: Laton McCartney. Monthly magazine covering information systems for executives from major private and public industries who use internal and external information processing and communication. Estab. 1980. Circ. 70,000. Pays on acceptance. Byline given. Offers 50% kill fee. Buys first North American serial rights. Submit seasonal material 4 months in advance. Simultaneous and photocopied submissions OK. SASE. Reports in 2 weeks. Free sample copy.
Nonfiction: Articles on computers, word processing and communications. "Although the subject matter is technological, we have technical advisors. It is more important that the writer be able to write in the style of a consumer business magazine. A good look at the publication will give the writer an idea of the wide range of articles from personal computers to phenomenal decision making systems." Buys 2 mss/issue. Query. Length: 1,500-3,000 words. Pays $500-1,500.
Photos: Reviews b&w prints and color transparencies. Payment negotiable.
Columns/Departments: Emerging Technologies (the future of computing); and Random Access (newsbreaks). Buys 4 mss/issue. Length: 500-1,000 words. Pays $150-300.
Tips: "Query with an outline of a case history of an unusual way new technology is being used in the public or private sector and include short personal introduction with samples of previously published articles. A demonstrated interest in technology is desirable. Strong writing and reporting skills are even more important. Nearly all stories are assigned, so a personal letter is most important."

WEEKDAY, Enterprise Publications, 20 N. Wacker Dr., Suite 3417, Chicago IL 60606. For the average employee in business and industry. Circ. 30,000. Buys all rights. Byline given. Pays on acceptance. SASE.
Nonfiction and Photos: Uses articles slanted toward the average man, with the purpose of increasing his understanding of the business world and helping him be more successful in it. Also uses articles on "How to Get Along with Other People," and informative articles on meeting everyday problems—consumer buying, legal problems, community affairs, real estate, education, human relations, etc. Length: approximately 1,000 words maximum. Pays $25-50. Uses b&w human interest photos.

Regional

ALASKA CONSTRUCTION & OIL MAGAZINE, 109 W. Mercer St., C#19081, Seattle WA 98119. Executive Editor: Christine A. Laing. For management level personnel in construction/oil/ timber/mining. Monthly magazine; 70 pages. Circ. 9,500. Pays on publication. Buys first North American serial rights. Submit seasonal/special interest material 3-4 months in advance. Previously published work OK. SASE. Reports in 2 weeks. Sample copy $1.
Nonfiction: "Only informational articles on the fields we cover. Articles must deal only with Alaska." Buys 10-15 mss/year. Query. Length: 500-2,000 words. Pays $1.50/column inch.
Photos: Purchased with mss. Pays $15-25/5x7 or 8x10 b&w glossy prints; $5-100/color positives of any size.

ALBERTA, INC., Alberta's Business Magazine, Pacific Rim Publications Ltd., 601-510 W. Hastings St., Vancouver, British Columbia, Canada V6B 1L8. (604)689-2021. Editor: J.R. Martin. Managing Editor: Len Webster. Monthly magazine covering general business for residents of the province of Alberta. Estab. 1980. Circ. 20,000. Pays on publication. Byline given. Makes work-for-hire-assignments. Simultaneous queries OK. SASE. Reports in 2 weeks. Sample copy and writer's guidelines free.
Nonfiction: Interview/profile (queries only). "Corporate profiles and industry state-of-the-art reports are the areas most accessible to freelancers." Special issues include franchising. No "how-to articles; no subjects not directly related to our geographic market." Buys 100 mss/year. Query with clips of published work. Length: 500-5,000 words. Pays $50-800.
Photos: Send photos with accompanying ms. Pays $10-25 for 5x7 b&w prints. Captions, model releases, and identification of subjects required. Buys one-time rights.
Columns/Departments: Personal Investing and, Travel; "all by Alberta freelancers." Buys 24 mss/year. Query. Length: 500-900 words. Pays $75-125.
Tips: "Read the product; query with an idea—sell your story; no form letters; understand the magazine's needs."

ATLANTA BUSINESS CHRONICLE, 1750 Century Circle, Atlanta GA 30345. (404)325-2442. Editor: Carol Werneck Carter. Emphasizes Atlanta business for upper-income executives. Weekly tabloid; 24 pages. Circ. 10,000. Pays on publication. Buys all rights. Phone queries OK. Submit seasonal/holiday material 2 months in advance. SASE. Reports in 1 month. Sample copy $1.
Nonfiction: Exposé, how-to, humor and photo feature. "All articles should relate to business in Atlanta." Buys 2 mss/issue. Query. Length: 1,000-2,500 words. Pays $2.50/column inch.
Photos: State availability of photos. Pays $10 for 8x10 glossy b&w prints. Captions and model releases required.
Columns/Departments: Comparison Shopping, Car Repairs, Executive Lifestyle, Gourmet and Profile. Buys 100 columns/year. Query. Length: 750-2,500 words. Pays $2.50/column inch.
Tips: "Writer may query by phone; or send resume, clips with solid local angle story ideas; business writing experience important."

AUSTIN MAGAZINE, Austin Chamber of Commerce, Box 1967, Austin TX 78767. Editor: Hal Susskind. A business and community magazine dedicated to telling the story of Austin and its people to Chamber of Commerce members and the community. Magazine published monthly by the Chamber; 72-128 pages. Circ. 9,500. Copyrighted. Pays kill fee. Byline given "except if the story has to be completely rewritten; the author would be given credit for his input but he may not be given a byline." Sample copy for $1. Will consider original mss only. Reports in 1 month. SASE.
Nonfiction and Photos: Articles should deal with interesting businesses or organizations around town with emphasis on the Austin community and Chamber of Commerce members. Articles are also accepted on Austin's entertainment scene and the arts. Length: 1,000 to 2,000 words. Pays $30-200. B&w photos are purchased with mss.

B.C. BUSINESS MAGAZINE, 601-510 W. Hastings St., Vancouver, British Columbia, Canada V6B 1L8. (604)685-2021. Editor-in-Chief: J. R. Martin. Managing Editor: Len Webster. Magazine emphasizing British Columbia business. Circ. 23,000. Pays on publication. Buys all rights. Phone queries OK. Simultaneous and photocopied submissions OK. Reports in 2 weeks. Sample copy $1.75.
Nonfiction: Interview (B.C. business people); profile (B.C. business people); and general business (in B.C.). No items unrelated to business in British Columbia and no how-to business articles. Buys 6 mss/issue. Query. Length: 500-2,500 words. Pays $50-500.
Photos: Offers no additional payment for photos accepted with mss. Uses 5x7 or 8x11 b&w prints. Captions required.

BUCKEYE BUSINESS JOURNAL, Praex Corp., Box 222, Worthington OH 43085. (614)888-6005. Publisher: Paul Parshall. Editor: Glenn Clayman. Emphasizes business in Columbus for an upper and middle class management audience. "Our publication is feature-oriented, containing stories for and about successful Columbus businesses. Monthly tabloid. Circ. 20,000. Pays on publication. Buys all rights. Phone queries OK. Submit seasonal material 3 months in advance. SASE. Reports in 2 weeks on queries. Free sample copy and writer's guidelines.
Nonfiction: Expose (business environment); interview (with top executives of successful Columbus companies, telling how company started, where it is now, and where it is heading); profile (past and future of given company); new product (how it affects a Columbus company); and technical (breakthrough which affects business in terms of manufacturing, computers). Buys 24 mss/year. Query or send clips of previously published work. Length: 650-800 words. Pays $25.
Photos: State availability of photos. Pays $5/5x7 b&w glossy prints. Captions required. Buys one-time rights.
Columns/Departments: "We occasionally run guest columns about a particular aspect of business (financial planning, how to start an investment club, etc.) but there is no payment for these."
Tips: "Each issue has a particular theme, and we run 3-4 stories along those lines. The themes are insurance, real estate and construction, transportation, financial institutions, energy, franchising, restaurants, new year forecast, recreation and wholesale-retail. Either call for an assignment or find a successful Columbus business in your area and call or send in a query. A story geared to one of our special issues is ideal."

BUFFALO BUSINESS REVIEW, The Voice of Business, New York Business Publications, 237 Main St., Buffalo NY 14203. (716)845-6260. Editor: Richard B. Landers. Managing Editor: Stephen F. Brady. Biweekly tabloid covering trends in business of Western New York. Estab. 1980. Circ. 15,500. Pays on publication. Byline given. Buys one-time rights. Submit seasonal/holiday material 2 months in advance. SASE. Reports in 2 weeks. Sample copy $1; free writer's guidelines.
Nonfiction: General interest (business-related); interview/profile (of business persons); new product; and technical. "An article about an issue directly related to the business community of western

New York is always of interest to our publication." Buys varying number of mss/year. Query. Length: 300-750 words. Pay varies.
Photos: State availability of photos. Pays varying fees for 5x7 b&w prints. Captions required.

CALIFORNIA BUSINESS, 6420 Wilshire Blvd., Suite 711, Los Angeles CA 90048. (213)653-9340. Editor: Mike Harris. Emphasizes Western business for business executive, businessmen, market analysts, etc. Monthly magazine. Pays on publication. Buys first rights. Pays negotiable kill fee. Byline usually given. Simultaneous submissions OK. SASE. Reports in 6 weeks. Sample copy $1; SASE for writer's guidelines.
Nonfiction: "General business pieces both with California/Western states focus. We also do trends for industries, company features and an occasional piece on business men and women who've done something unique or have something to say relating to their field of expertise. No material on entrepreneurs." Buys 2-3 mss/issue. Query. Length: 1,000-2,000 words. Pays $200-350.
Photos: State availability of photos. Pay negotiable for b&w prints and color transparencies. Captions and model releases required.
Tips: Query should be 2-3 paragraphs with samples of writing.

CANADIAN BUSINESS, CB Media, Ltd., 56 Esplanade, Suite 214, Toronto, Ontario, Canada. (416)364-4266. Editor-in-Chief: Alexander Ross. Editor: Peggy Wente. Managing Editor: John Partridge. Emphasizes general business. Monthly magazine; 150 pages. Circ. 81,000. Pays on acceptance. Buys first North American serial rights. Pays 50% kill fee. Byline given. Submit seasonal/holiday material 3 months in advance. Photocopied submissions OK. SASE. Reports in 1 month. Sample copy $2.
Nonfiction: How-to. Buys 6 mss/issue. Query. Length: 500-5,000 words. Pays $150-1,000.
Tips: "Freelancers will find it easiest to sell us short pieces for the front and back of the book. The magazine is feature, rather than news oriented. Quality of writing is just as important as content."

CARIBBEAN BUSINESS NEWS, 111 Queen St. E., Suite 332, Toronto, Ontario, Canada M5C 1S2. (416)368-6404. Managing Editor: Colin Rickards. 3% freelance written. Emphasizes business and financial news affecting the entire Caribbean area for upper- and middle-echelon business/management people worldwide. Monthly magazine, 32-40 pages. Circ. 32,000. Pays on publication. Buys all rights. Byline given "but there might be a circumstance, at our discretion, where a byline would not be given." Phone queries OK. Photocopied and previously published submissions OK. SASE. reports in 2 weeks. Free sample copy.
Nonfiction: General interest, interview and business/financial articles on Caribbean topics. No travel material. Buys 8 mss/year. Query. Length: 500-1,000 words. Pays $50-250.
Photos: Pays $25 minimum for 5x7 or 8x10 b&w prints. Captions required.
Tips: "We are looking for the offbeat in business. Recent articles include the business side of treasure diving in Dominica and the business side of being a beauty queen. Emphasis must be on business/finance."

COMMERCE MAGAZINE, 130 S. Michigan Ave., Chicago IL 60603. (312)786-0111. Editor: Gordon A. Moon II. For top businessmen and industrial leaders in greater Chicago area. Also sent to chairmen and presidents of *Fortune* 1,000 firms throughout United States. Monthly magazine; varies from 100 to 400 pages, (8½x11½). Circ. 12,000. Buys all rights. Buys 30-40 mss/year. Pays on acceptance. Query. SASE.
Nonfiction: Business articles and pieces of general interest to top business executives. "We select our freelancers and assign topics. Many of our writers are from local newspapers. Considerable freelance material is used but almost exclusively on assignment from Chicago—area specialists within a particular business sector." Pays 4-8¢/word.

CONNECTICUT BUSINESS TIMES, Connecticut Business Times, Inc., 544 Tolland St., East Hartford CT 06108. (203)289-9341. Managing Editor: Deborah Hallberg. Monthly tabloid covering business and financial news within Connecticut for "the top executive or business owner in Connecticut." Circ. 20,000. Pays on publication. Byline given. Pays 30% kill fee. Buys exclusive rights within Connecticut. Phone queries OK. Submit seasonal/holiday material 1 month in advance. Simultaneous queries and previously published submissions OK. SASE. Reports in 1 month. Sample copy $1.
Nonfiction: Book excerpts (of books on business, money, finance, taxes, etc.); how-to (improve efficiency, generate sales, etc.); interview/profile (of a Connecticut business person with a unique story); new product (pertaining to Connecticut only). "Features include legislative updates, state-of-the-economy analysis, industry profiles, etc. We use very little national news. It helps if out-of-state freelancers specialize in one area, e.g., real estate. Articles should be written with the business *owner*—not the office manager or secretary—in mind, the one who calls the shots and makes the

decisions." Special monthly supplements include: computers, CPAs, office design, word processing, copiers, real estate, tax shelters, transportation service, telecommunications, banking & finance, energy. "We have a need for material for our monthly advertising supplements. These are usually nuts & bolts kind of articles—state-of-the-art, etc." No articles on improving sales techniques. Buys 8-12 mss/year. Query with clips of published works. Length: 800-1,500 words. Pays $1/column inch.

Photos: State availability of photos. Reviews 8x10 &w prints. Pays $15/first photo, $10 each additional photo. Captions required. Buys exclusive rights within Connecticut.

Columns/Departments: Tax ideas (tax shelters, loopholes, advantages businessmen should consider); Profitsense (how to increase profits, generate sales, improve efficiency); Bookshelf (reviews of new releases, business, finance, money, economics). "For 'Profitsense,' be specific. The ideas have to work; they have to be immediately valuable to a reader, e.g., 'How to be Your Own Public Relations Man.' For 'Bookshelf,' stick to new releases and accessible books." Buys 10-12 items/year. Query with clips of published work. Length 600-1,300 words. Pays $15-75, "depending on nature of column. One-time only is our freelance rate, $1/column inch."

Tips: "The best thing to do is study our style and then try to match it."

CRAIN'S CLEVELAND BUSINESS, 140 Public Square, Cleveland OH 44114. (216)522-1383. Editor: Jacque Neher. Biweekly tabloid about business in the 7 county area surrounding Cleveland, Akron and Canton for upper income executives, professionals and entrepreneurs. Estab. 1980. Circ. 25,000. Average issue includes 7-10 features and 2-3 analytical news pieces. Pays on publication. Byline given. Buys first North American serial rights. Phone queries OK. Simultaneous, photocopied and previously published submissions OK, if so indicated. Reports in 3 weeks on queries; in 2 weeks on mss.

Nonfiction: "We are interested in business and political events and their impact on the Cleveland area business. We also want news developments and trends of significance to business life in the Cleveland-Akron-Lorain area." Buys 5-8 mss/issue. Query. Length: 500-1,200 words. Pays $5 column inch.

Photos: State availability of photos. Reviews 5x7 b&w glossy prints. Payment varies. Captions required. Buys one-time rights.

DELAWARE VALLEY BUSINESS MAGAZINE, 105 Chestnut St., Philadelphia PA 19106. Editor: James Smart. Emphasizes general business-oriented local material. Local writers preferred. Articles usually require some human interest angles, for anyone in business in the Delaware Valley. Monthly magazine. Pays on publication. Buys first North American serial rights. SASE.

Nonfiction: "New trends in business; exclusive reports on subjects relating to the business of the Delaware Valley; health and quality of life articles; technical articles of general interest—like 'How to Sell Your Business'; a fresh look or unique perspective on area problems." Mostly staff written. Query. Length: 800-2,000 words. Payment negotiated if query is accepted.

Tips: "We are buying virtually nothing from writers we don't already know. We get more good queries than we can handle from local writers. We are not a good market for freelancers at this time."

FINANCIAL POST, Maclean-Hunter, Ltd., 481 University Ave., Toronto, Ontario, Canada M5W 1A7. Editor: Neville J. Nankivell. Executive Editor: Dalton S. Robertson. News Editor: Michael Fox. 10% freelance written. Emphasizes Canadian business, investment/finance and public affairs. Weekly newspaper. Circ. 190,000. Pays on publication. Buys one-time rights. Pays 100% kill fee. Byline given. Reports in 2-3 weeks. Sample copy $1.

Nonfiction: Useful news and information for executives, managers and investors in Canada. Buys 3 mss/issue. Query. Length: 700-800 words. Pays 15-20¢/word.

Photos: State availability of photos with query. Pays $25-50 for 8x10 b&w glossy prints. Captions required. Buys one-time rights.

HOUSTON BUSINESS JOURNAL, Cordovan Corp., a Scripps-Howard Company, 5314 Bingle Rd., Houston TX 77092. (713)688-8811. Editor: Bill Schwadewald. Emphasizes Houston business. Weekly tabloid; 40-64 pages. Circ. 20,000. Pays on publication. Buys all rights. Byline given. Phone queries OK ("but prefer mail"). Submit seasonal/holiday material 2 months in advance. SASE. Reports in 1 month. Sample copy $1.

Nonfiction: Exposé (business, if documented), how-to (finance, business, management, lifestyle), informational (money-making), interview (local business topics), nostalgia (possible, if business), profile (local business executives), personal experience and photo feature. Buys 3 mss/issue. Length: 500-2,000. Pays $3/column inch.

Photos: State availability of photos or send photos with ms. Pays $10 for b&w prints. Buys all rights. Captions required.
Columns/Departments: Automotive Review, Profile and Restaurants. Query. Pays $2.50. Open to suggestions for new columns/departments.

INDIANA BUSINESS, (formerly *Indiana Business and Industry*), 1100 Waterway Blvd., Indianapolis IN 46202. (317)634-1100. Editor: H.A. Wernle. Monthly magazine. Pays on publication. Rights negotiable. SASE. Reports in 3 weeks. Free sample copy.
Nonfiction: "All articles must relate to Indiana business and must be of interest to a broad range of business and professional people." Buys 2-3 mss/issue. Query or send complete ms or send clips of published work. Pay negotiable.
Photos: State availability of photos. Pay negotiable for b&w or color photos. Captions and model releases required.
Tips: "A query letter must show that the author is familiar with our publication. It should also be concise but catchy. Be willng to submit samples and/or articles on speculation. We are very interested in articles that flow well—business-like but not dry."

KANSAS BUSINESS NEWS, Kansas Business Publishing Co., Inc., Box 511, Lindsborg KS 67456. (913)227-3330. Editor: Dan Bearth. Monthly magazine about Kansas business for the businessman, executive and professional who wants to learn how to become more efficient, save money and net more profit. Estab. 1979. Circ. 15,000. Pays on publication. Buys all rights. Phone queries OK. Submit seasonal material 3 months in advance. Simultaneous and previously published submissions OK. SASE. Reports in 1 week. Free sample copy.
Nonfiction: How-to, humor, interview, profile, and technical. Send complete ms. Length: 500-1,500 words. Pays $25-100.
Photos: Editor: Chester Peterson, Jr. State availability of photos or send photos with ms. Reviews b&w contact sheets and negatives. Offers no additional payment for photos accepted with ms. Captions preferred; model release required. Buys all rights.
Columns/Departments: Business law, Finance, Government, Personnel management, Taxes and Insurance. Buys 6 mss/issue. Send complete ms. Length: 750-1,250 words. Pays $25 minimum.

KENTUCKY BUSINESS LEDGER, Box 3508, Louisville KY 40201. (502)589-5464. Editor: Dot Ridings. 60% freelance written. Emphasizes Kentucky business and finance. Monthly tabloid; 32-48 pages. Circ. 11,000. Pays on publication. Buys all rights. Byline given at editor's option. Phone queries OK. Submit seasonal/holiday material 1 month in advance of issue date. Simultaneous, photocopied and previously published submissions OK. SASE. Reports in 2 weeks. Sample copy $1; free writer's guidelines.
Nonfiction: How-to (tips for businesses on exporting, dealing with government, cutting costs, increasing profits); interview (government officials on issues important to Kentucky businesspersons); new product (new uses for coal); profile (of Kentucky businesspersons); and articles on the meanings of government laws and regluations to Kentucky businesses. "We get too much industry-wide trend stories, which we use hardly at all. We must have a strong Kentucky link to any story." Buys 15-20 mss/issue. Query. Length: 1,250 words maximum. Pays $1.25/inch.
Photos: State availability of photos with query. Pays $10 up for b&w glossy prints.
Tips: "On technical subjects from unknown freelancers, we need a statement of expertise and /or previous work within the subject area."

LOS ANGELES BUSINESS JOURNAL, Cordovan Corp., 611 S. Catalina St., Los Angeles CA 90005. Editor: David Rees. Weekly tabloid covering business developments within the Los Angeles area for business executives, managers and entrepreneurs in a five county area. The publication is designed to help the decision-making process for businessmen in the areas of new trends and ideas important to commerce and industry. Estab. 1979. Circ. 15,000 guaranteed. Pays on publication. Buys all rights. Submit seasonal material 6 weeks in advance. SASE. Reports in 2⅗ weeks. Sample copy $1.
Nonfiction: "We are interested in Los Angeles area industry or business trend stories based on at least four and preferably more sources. No one-source articles. Illustrate trends with specific figures; they are the backbone or skeleton of the article. Then flesh out the article with examples and quotes." Buys 1-2 mss/issue. Query. Pays $3/column inch.
Tips: "Submit a story line query of two-three-or four sentences. List the specific points expected to be covered in the article and write a headline for the story subject."

MANITOBA BUSINESS, Canasus Publications, Ltd., 201-177 Lombard Ave., Winnipeg, Manitoba, Canada R3B 0W5. Editor: Donald Aiken. Bimonthly emphasizing provincial business con-

ditions. Estab. 1979. Circ. 10,000. Buys all rights. Phone queries OK. SASE. Reports in 2 weeks. Free writer's guidelines.
Nonfiction: General interest (business); humor; inspirational; interview/profile; travel; photo feature; and lifestyle. Buys 8 mss/issue. Length: 800-2,400 words. Query. Pays $100-300.
Photos: State availability of photos with query letter. Pays $25-30 for 5x7 b&w; $35-40 for color photos. Captions required. Buys one-time rights.
Columns/Departments: Provincial Affairs and National Affairs only. Buys 3 mss/issue. Query with clips of previously published work. Length: 800-1,000 words. Pays $100.

NEW JERSEY BUSINESS, Hotel Robert Treat, 50 Park Place, Newark NJ 07102. (201)623-8359. Editor: James Prior. Emphasizes business in the State of New Jersey. Monthly magazine. Pays on acceptance. Buys all rights. Simultaneous and previously published work OK. SASE. Reports in 3 weeks. Sample copy $1.
Nonfiction: "All freelance articles are upon assignment, and they deal with business and industry either directly or more infrequently, indirectly pertaining to New Jersey." Buys 6 mss/year. Query or send clips of published work. Pays $150-200.
Photos: Send photos with ms. Captions preferred.

NORTHWEST INVESTMENT REVIEW, 534 SW 3rd Ave., #400, Portland OR 97204. (503)224-6004. Editor-in-Chief: Shannon P. Pratt. Associate Editor: John MacKellar. For investors, advisors and corporate leaders who pay $195 a year to read about the 400 Northwestern publicly held corporations covered by this and a companion publication. "Newsletter published at least 50 times/year (weekly). Pays on publication. Query. Reports in 1 month.
Nonfiction: "We need top highly regional articles, covering public companies headquartered or having major operations in Hawaii, Alaska, Oregon, Washington, Idaho, Montana, Colorado, Wyoming, Utah and the two western provinces of Canada. Must appeal to investors. Length: 500-2500 words. Pay negotiable. Many are done for a fee; no set minimum."
Tips: "All work must be well-researched. Ideally, freelancers should be from business page writing or finance/security backgrounds."

PHOENIX BUSINESS JOURNAL, Cordovan Corp., 1817 N. 3rd St., Phoenix AZ 85004. (602)271-4712. Editor: Jack Mayne. Weekly tabloid covering business economics for CEOs and top corporate managers. Estab. 1980. Circ. 6,100. Pays on publication. Byline given. Buys one-time rights. Submit seasonal/holiday material 1 month in advance. Simultaneous queries ("if so indicated") and previously published submissions OK. SASE. Reports in 1 week. Sample copy free.
Nonfiction: How-to (solve management problems); interview/profile (of entrepreneurs); and "news affecting all types of corporations, large and small." "Our audience is all local. We need people who understand the problems of Phoenix area executives." Buys 250 mss/year. Query by phone. Length: open. Pays average 7¢/word.

REGARDIES, The Magazine of Washington Business and Real Estate, 1010 Wisconsin Ave. NW., Washington DC 20017. (202)342-0410. Assistant Editor: Mary Jo Egler. Editor: Henry Fortunato. Bimonthly magazine covering business and real estate in the Washington DC metropolitan area for Washington business executives. Estab. 1980. Circ. 27,000. Pays on publication. Byline given. Pays variable kill fee. Buys all rights. Submit seasonal/holiday material 3 months in advance. Reports in 1 week. Sample copy free.
Nonfiction: Interview (of business leaders); investigative reporting; real estate; advertising; labor issues; and financial issues—all on the Washington business scene. Buys 35 mss/year. Length: 4,000 words average. Pays "generally 20¢/word."
Fillers: Newsbreaks. Buys 60/year. Length: 500 words maximum. Pays 20¢/word.

SAN DIEGO BUSINESS JOURNAL, Cordovan Business Journals, 3444 Camino Del Rio N., Suite 204, San Diego CA 92108. (714)283-2271. Editor: Denise Carabet. Weekly tabloid covering business for business and professional people. Estab. 1980. Circ. 5,000. Pays on publication. Byline given. Buys first North American serial rights. Submit seasonal/holiday material 6 weeks in advance. Photocopied and previously published submissions ("if indicated where and when published") OK. SASE. Reports in 2 weeks. Free sample copy.
Nonfiction: How-to (run a business better); and interview/profile (of entrepreneurs). "We look for local perspectives on national business issues of sophisticated handling of everyday business topics. Corporate profiles or high-finance pieces done in-house." Buys 100 mss/year. Query with clips of published work. Length: 1,500-2,000 words. Pays average $200.
Photos: State availability of photos. Pays $25 for 5x7 or 8x10 b&w glossy prints. Model releases and identification of subjects required. Buys one-time rights.

Fillers: Newsbreaks. Buys 50/year. Length: 50 words minimum. Pays $10.

SAN FRANCISCO BUSINESS JOURNAL, Cordovan Corp., 745 Stevenson St., San Francisco CA 94103. (415)552-7690. Editor: Bill Doyle. Weekly tabloid about business and finance of the San Francisco Bay area for a primarily male audience between 40-45 in middle management. Estab. 1979. Pays on publication. Buys all rights. SASE. Reports in 3 weeks. Free Sample copy.
Nonfiction: How-to (overcome obstacles to create a successful business); interview (personality sketches of business executives and entrepreneurs); and stories on businesses which produce an unusual product. Length: 1,000-1,500 words. Pays $3/inch.

SEATTLE BUSINESS MAGAZINE, Seattle Chamber of Commerce, 215 Columbia St., Seattle WA 98104. (206)447-7214. Editor-in-Chief: Ed Sullivan. Emphasizes regional socio-economic affairs. For business and government leaders, civic leaders, regional businessmen, educators, opinion makers, and the general public. Monthly magazine; 56 pages. Circ. 7,100. Pays on publication. Buys all rights. Submit seasonal/holiday material 2 months in advance. Previously published submissions OK. SASE. Reports in 2 weeks. Free sample copy.
Nonfiction: Informational (socio-economic affairs) and technical. Buys 1-2 mss/issue. Query. Length: 500-2,500 words. Pays $50-300.
Photos: Purchased with accompanying ms or on assignment. Captions required. Pays $50-100 for b&w photos. Total purchase price for ms includes payment for photos. Model release required.
Tips: "The freelancer must be able to write—and have a basic awareness of and sympathy for—the interests and problems of the business community as these relate to the community at large."

SOUTH BUSINESS, Southern Business Publishing Co., Inc., Box 16267, Mobile AL 36616. Contact: Editor. Emphasizes the Southern business community and climate. Monthly magazine; 64-96 pages. Circ. 50,000. Pays on acceptance. Buys first North American serial rights. SASE. Reports in 6 weeks. Sample copy $1; free writer's guidelines.
Nonfiction: No articles on how-to. Buys 8 mss/issue. Query. Length: 300-1,800 words. Pays $45-300.
Photos: State availability of photos with query. No additional payment for 5x7 b&w glossy prints or 35mm color transparencies. Captions required. Buys one-time rights. Model release preferred.

TIDEWATER VIRGINIAN, Box 327, Norfolk VA 23501. Editor: Marilyn Goldman. 90% freelance written. Published by six Tidewater area chambers of commerce. Monthly magazine for business management people. Circ. 7,300. Byline given. Buys 60 mss/year. Pays on publication. Sample copy $1.25. Photocopied and simultaneous submissions OK. Reports in 3 weeks. Query or submit complete ms. SASE.
Nonfiction: Articles dealing with business and industry in Virginia primarily; the surrounding area of southeastern Virginia (Tidewater area). Profiles, successful business operations, new product, merchandising techniques and business articles. Length: 500-2,500 words. Pays $25-125.

Child Care and Parental Guidance

The publications below highlight child care and parental guidance. Other categories that include markets that buy items about child care for special columns and features are: Confession, Religious, and Women's in Consumer Publications; Education Journals in Trade Journals.

AMERICAN BABY MAGAZINE, 575 Lexington Ave., New York NY 10022. (212)752-0775. Editor-in-Chief: Judith Nolte. 30% freelance written. Emphasizes how-to and medical information for expectant and new parents. Monthly magazine. Circ. 1,000,000. Pays on acceptance. Buys one-time rights. Byline given. Submit seasonal/holiday material 5 months in advance. Simultaneous, photocopied and previously published submissions OK. SASE. Reports in 1 month. Writer's guidelines and sample copy with SASE only.
Nonfiction: How-to (on pregnancy and child-related subjects); interview (with medical authority on some subject of interest to expectant and new parents); personal experience; personal opinion; and profile (well-known figure in child care). No breast-feeding, natural childbirth experiences or poetry. Buys 5 mss/issue. Submit complete ms. Length: 1,000-2,000 words. Pays $100-300.
Tips: Send very brief biography with submissions.

BABY TALK, 185 Madison Ave., New York NY 10016. Editor: Patricia Irons. For new and expectant parents. Monthly. Circ. 850,000. Buys first North American serial rights. Pays on acceptance. Submit complete ms. SASE.
Nonfiction and Photos: Articles on all phases of baby care. Also true, unpublished accounts of pregnancy, life with baby or young children. B&w and color photos are sometimes purchased with or without ms. Payment varies.

BEST WISHES, 37 Hanna Ave., Toronto, Ontario, Canada M5S 2P1. Managing Editor: Ruth Weinstock. Quarterly magazine "distributed in 495 Canadian hospitals to women who have just given birth. Not for pregnant women; for new mothers." Circ. 300,000. Pays on publication. Rights "depend on the article." SAE and International Reply Coupons.
Nonfiction: How-to (care for your baby; cope with being a new mother/father). Query or send complete ms. Length: 750-2,500 words. Pays negotiable fee.
Photos: Pays negotiable fee for 5x4 b&w prints and 5x4 color transparencies.
Tips: "Don't send articles describing a wonderful American program that remedies such-and-such a problem; you'll only be acting as a PR agent for the institution in question, when what you're after is selling an article. Think 'universally.' Delete inappropriate local references."

EXCEPTIONAL PARENT, 296 Boylston St., Boston MA 02116. (617)536-8961. Editor-in-Chief: Dr. Maxwell J. Schleifer; Editor: Dr. Stanley D. Klein; Associate Publisher: Joanne Tangredi. Magazine provides practical information for parents and professionals concerned with the care of children with disabilities (physical disabilities, emotional problems, mental retardation, learning disabilities, perceptual disabilities, deafness, blindness, chronic illness, etc.). Bimonthly. Circ. 22,000. Buys all rights. Buys about 20 mss/year. Pays on publication. Sample copy for $2.50; writer's guidelines for SASE. No queries. Reports in 6-12 months. SASE.
Nonfiction and Photos: "The general intent of the magazine is to provide practical information for the parents and professionals concerned with the care of children with disabilities. We print articles covering every conceivable subject within this area, including legal issues, tax and economic information, recreation programs, adaptive aids, parent groups, personal experience and instructional advice, etc. This is a consumer publication within a very specialized market. Articles should be comprehensible for the layperson. Articles within special areas are checked by an advisory board in the medical and allied professions. There is no other magazine of this type." Length: 2,500-3,000 words maximum. Pays $25/printed page. Flat fee for professionals: $25. Photos accompanied by signed releases are of interest.

EXPECTING, 685 3rd Ave., New York NY 10017. Editor: Evelyn A. Podsiadlo. Assistant Editor: Grace Lang. Issued quarterly for expectant mothers. Circ. 1,000,000. Buys all rights. Pays 100% kill fee. Byline given. Pays on acceptance. Reports in 2-4 weeks. Free writer's guidelines. SASE.
Nonfiction: Prenatal development, layette and nursery planning, budgeting, health, fashion, husband-wife relationships, naming the baby, minor discomforts, childbirth, expectant fathers, working while pregnant, etc. Length: 800-1,600 words. Pays $100-200 for feature articles, somewhat more for specialists.
Fillers: Short humor and interesting or unusual happenings during pregnancy or at the hospital; maximum 100 words, $10 on publication; submissions to "Happenings" are not returned.
Poetry: Occasionally buys subject-related poetry; all forms. Length: 4-24 lines. Pays $5-10.

FAMILY JOURNAL, W.J. Wheeler Publishing, RD 2, Box 165, Putney VT 05346. (802)257-1044. Editor: Whitman Wheeler. Managing Editor: Cheryl Wilfong. Bimonthly magazine covering families with children up to about 8 years of age, for "the educated parent, aged 28-45, who desires sensible, useful information and advice. The reading audience is assumed to be sophisticated, and includes women who have pursued successful careers before becoming mothers. Fathers are also readers of *Family Journal*, and are active in all decisions affecting the welfare of the child." Estab. 1980. Circ. 12,000. Pays on publication. Byline given. Pays 15% kill fee. Buys all rights. Submit seasonal/holiday material 6 months in advance. Simultaneous queries, and simultaneous, photocopied, and previously published submissions OK. SASE. Reports in 1 month. Sample copy and writer's guidelines free.
Nonfiction: General interest, how-to, humor, interview/profile, personal experience, pregnancy, childbirth, and childrearing through preadolescence. "We look for articles that deal with the above subject areas in a lucid style. The magazine is pro-family, and it addresses such topics as single parents, parents who adopt, infertility, and the many cultural influences on families. No mush, hippie writing, joyous birthing experiences, or sexist viewpoints. The magazine does not take a feminist position, or a political or religious stand. Buys 40-45 mss/year. Send complete ms. Length: 1,000-2,500 words. Pays $20-250.
Photos: Pays $10 maximum for 8x10 b&w prints. Model release required. Buys one-time rights.

Columns/Departments: Family Counsel, Books for Parents, Adoption, Food, Books for Children. Buys 15 mss/year. Send complete ms. Length: 1,000-1,500 words. Pays $20-150.
Fillers: Practical information. Buys 5/year. Length: 700-1,000 words. Pays $20-50.
Tips: "One's professional background in terms of the article, writing ability, and the magazine's editorial needs are taken into consideration in deciding payment. However, it should also be stressed that one's professional background is of less importance than the actual writing. *Family Journal* looks for writers who can articulate an experiential viewpoint as a parent."

GIFTED CHILDREN NEWSLETTER, For the Parents of Children with Great Promise, 530 University Ave., Palo Alto CA 94301. (415)982-5113. Editor: Morton Malkofsky. Managing Editor: Bruce Raskin. Monthly newsletter covering parenting and education of gifted children for parents. Estab. 1979. Circ. 40,000. Pays on acceptance. Byline given. Pays variable kill fee. Buys all rights and first rights. Submit seasonal/holiday material four months in advance. Simultaneous queries, and simultaneous, photocopied, and previously published submissions OK. SASE. Reports in 1 month on queries; 2 months on mss. Sample copy and writer's guidelines for SAE.
Nonfiction: Book excerpts; historical/nostalgic; how-to (on parenting of gifted kids); humor; inspirational; interview/profile; new product; opinion; and personal experience. "Our Special Reports section is most accessible to freelancers." Buys 24 mss/year. Query with clips of published work or send complete ms. Length: 1,000-2,500 words. Pays $25-200.
Fillers: David Grady, fillers editor. Newsbreaks. Length: 50-500 words. Pays $5-25.

GREAT EXPECTATIONS, Professional Publishing Associates, 45 Charles St., E., Toronto, Ontario, Canada M4Y 1S2. (416)964-8903. Editor: H.N. Haken. Quarterly newspaper for expectant mothers. "We try to publish material on all aspects of pregnancy, birth, parenting and human sexuality that will help, educate and perhaps even amuse our readers." Circ. 81,000. Pays on publication. Byline given. Offers $100 kill fee. Buys first North American serial rights. Submit seasonal/holiday material 3 months in advance. SAE and International Reply Coupons. "We cannot use US stamps." Reports in 3 weeks on queries; 6 weeks on mss. Free sample copy for 9x12 SAE; free writer's guidelines for #9 SAE.
Nonfiction: Humor, personal experience, photo feature, and technical ("We would particularly welcome submissions from physicians, nurses or others in the health professions"). No articles on "anything relating to children over 2 years of age." Buys 25-30 mss/year. Query. Length: 1,000-3,000 words. Pays $100/printed page (about 1,100 words).
Photos: State availability of photos. Reviews color transparencies and 8x10 b&w prints. "Photos are paid at the same rate: $100/page." Captions, model releases and identification of subjects are required. Buys one-time rights.
Tips: "Remember that our readers are expectant mothers—60% of them having their first baby, and generally speaking, ignorant of what is happening to them. Realize that Canada is not part of, or an appendage to the US. We are most open to educational material on such subjects as breast-feeding, hormonal changes, pre-natal instruction, Leboyer deliveries, etc."

HOME LIFE, Sunday School Board, 127 9th Ave., N., Nashville TN 37234. (615)251-2271. Editor-in-Chief: Reuben Herring. Emphasizes Christian family life. For married adults of all ages, but especially newlyweds and middle-aged marrieds. Monthly magazine; 64 pages. Circ. 800,000. Pays on acceptance. Buys all rights. Byline given. Phone queries OK, but written queries preferred. Submit seasonal/holiday material 10 months in advance. SASE. Reports in 6 weeks. Free sample copy and writer's guidelines.
Nonfiction: How-to (good articles on marriage and child care); informational (about some current family-related issue of national significance such as "Television and the Christian Family" or "Whatever Happened to Good Nutrition?"); personal experience (informed articles by people who have solved family problems in healthy, constructive ways). Buys 10 mss/month. Submit complete ms. Length: 1,200-2,400 words. Pays 3½¢/word.
Fiction: "Our fiction should be family-related and should show a strong moral about how families face and solve problems constructively." Buys 12 mss/year. Submit complete ms. Length: 1,600-2,400 words. Pays 3½¢/word.
Tips: "Study the magazine to see our unique slant on Christian family life. We prefer a life-centered case study approach, rather than theoretical essays on family life. Our top priority is marriage enrichment material."

MOTHERS' MANUAL MAGAZINE, 441 Lexington Ave., New York NY 10017. Editor-in-Chief: Janet Spencer King. Emphasizes pregnancy and parenting of young children. Bimonthly magazine; 60-72 pages. Circ. 900,000. Pays on publication. Buys all rights. Pays 20% kill fee. SASE required. Reports in 6 weeks. Sample copy 75¢.
Nonfiction: Well-researched, and well-documented how-to, humor, informational, inspirational,

personal experience and opinion stories. Read the magazine before submitting complete ms. Length: 500-2,000 words. Pays $50-650.

Poetry: Lyn Roessler, Poetry Editor. Free verse, light verse and traditional. "We are looking for good humor; short, crisp poetry, upbeat, amusing poetry as well as narrative." Pays $10-30.

Tips: "Send a short finished piece written in the first person. Follow with a query for a second piece on a different subject. We like to cultivate good writers."

PARENT'S CHOICE, Parents' Choice Foundation, Box 185, Waban MA 02168. (617)332-1298. Editor: Diana Huss Green. Emphasizes reviews of children's media, designed to alert parents to trends and events in books, TV, records, films, toys and educational issues. Pays on publication. Buys all rights. Phone queries OK. SASE. Reports in 1 month. Sample copy $2; writer's guidelines $1.

Nonfiction: General interest (to parents interested in uses of the media); how-to (use books, films, TV, toys, games and records); humor; essays (on social and political issues related to media); interview (with writers of fiction for young adults and children, and directors, producers of films and TV); personal experience; photo feature (of parents and children, grandparents and children) and profile. Buys 10 mss/issue. Query. Pays $25 minimum.

Photos: State availability of photos. Offers no additional payment for photos accompanying ms. Uses b&w prints. Captions preferred.

Columns/Departments: A Parent's Essay, Choice Books and Full Platter. Send complete ms. Length: 1500-1700 words.

PARENTS MAGAZINE, 685 3rd Ave., New York NY 10017. Editor: Elizabeth Crow. 25% freelance written. Monthly. Circ. 1,500,000. Usually buys first North American serial rights; sometimes buys all rights. Pays $100-350 kill fee. Byline given "except for 'Parents Report' or short items for which we pay only $20-75 and purchase all rights." Pays on acceptance. Reports in approximately 3 weeks. Query. SASE.

Nonfiction: "We are interested in well-documented articles on the development and behavior of preschool, school-age, and adolescent children and their parents; good, practical guides to the routines of baby care; articles which offer professional insights into family and marriage relationships; reports of new trends and significant research findings in education and in mental and physical health; articles encouraging informed citizen action on matters of social concern. Especially need articles on women's issues, pregnancy, birth, baby care and early childhood. We prefer a warm, colloquial style of writing, one which avoids the extremes of either slang or technical jargon. Anecdotes and examples should be used to illustrate points which can then be summed up by straight exposition." Length: 2,500 words maximum. Payment varies; pays $300 minimum.

Fillers: Anecdotes for "Parents Exchange," illustrative of parental problem-solving with children and teenagers. Pays $20 on publication.

SESAME STREET PARENTS NEWSLETTER, Children's Television Workshop, 1 Lincoln Plaza, New York NY 10023. (212)595-3456. Editor: Ira Wolfman. Assistant Editor: Jan Carr. Monthly magazine covering parenting for parents of children ages 2-8. Estab. 1981. Circ. 50,000. Pays within 30 days of acceptance. Byline given. Pays ½ kill fee. Buys all rights "with provision for payment for reuse." Submit seasonal/holiday material 4 months in advance. Simultaneous queries OK. Reports in 3 weeks. Sample copy $2; writer's guidelines for business size SAE and 1 first class stamp.

Nonfiction: General interest (reading and creativity in children); interview/profile (of child-rearing experts); personal experience (by parents); development, health, and special needs of children. Buys 100 mss/year. Query with clips of published work. Length: 450-1,500 words. Pays $125-200.

YOUR BABY, (service section of *Modern Romances* magazine), *Modern Romances*, Macfadden Women's Group, 215 Lexington Ave., New York NY 10016. Editor: Jean Sharbel. Buys all rights. Byline given. Pays on publication. Reports in 4 months. SASE.

Nonfiction: Uses warmly written, genuinely helpful articles of interest to mothers of children from birth to three years of age, dealing authoritatively with pregnancy problems, child health, child care and training. Editors recommend you study this market before trying to write for it. Length: 1,000 words maximum. Pays "special rate, depending on merit."

Market conditions are constantly changing! If this is 1983 or later, buy the newest edition of *Writer's Market* at your favorite bookstore or use the back-of-the-book order form.

College, University, and Alumni

The following publications focus on students, graduates, and friends of the particular institution involved. Publications for college students in general are found in the Teen and Young Adult category.

ALCALDE, Box 7278, Austin TX 78712. (512)476-6271. Editor: Gail Chavez. Bimonthly magazine. Circ. 38,000. Pays on acceptance. Buys all rights. Submit seasonal/holiday material 5 months in advance. SASE. Reports in 2 weeks. Free sample copy and writer's guidelines.
Nonfiction: General interest; historical (University of Texas, research, and faculty profile); humor (humorous University of Texas incidents or profiles that include background data); interviews (University of Texas subjects); nostalgia (University of Texas traditions); profile (students, faculty or alumni); and technical (University of Texas research on a subject or product). "We do not want subjects lacking taste or quality or not connected with the University of Texas." Buys 30 mss/year. Query. Length: 1,000-1,800 words. Pays 10¢/word.

BOSTONIA/INSIGHT, Boston University, 25 Buick St., Boston MA 02215. (617)353-3081. Editor: Laura T. Freid. Quarterly magazine covering education and research for a college educated audience from 26-60 years old. Circ. 150,000. Pays on acceptance. Buys all rights. Submit seasonal material 4 months in advance. Reports in 3 weeks. Sample copy $2.20; free writer's guidelines.
Nonfiction: Feature (written about Boston University graduates or about Boston University research); historical (medicine, nutrition); interview (of graduates and professors); profile; photo feature (of people and research); technical (related to current Boston University research); and interpretation of academic research. Buys 10 mss/issue. Query or send clips of 3 articles of previously published work. Length: 1,000-1,500 words. Pays 10¢/word or flat fee depending on the amount of research.
Photos: State availability of photos. Pays $30-40 for 5x7 glossy prints. Buys one-time rights. Model release required.

DePAUW UNIVERSITY ALUMNUS MAGAZINE, Greencastle IN 46135. (317)653-9721, ext. 2626. Editor-in-Chief: Patrick Aikman. Assistant Editor: Char Alexander. 25% freelance written. Emphasizes alumni activities and institutional developments. Read by alumni and parents. Quarterly magazine; 40 pages. Circ. 28,000. Pays on publication. Buys all rights. Submit seasonal/holiday material 3 months in advance. SASE. Reports in 3 weeks. Sample copy $1. •
Nonfiction: General interest; historical; humor; inspirational; interview; nostalgia; personal experience; opinion; photo feature; and profile (interesting careers, hobbies and perspectives of alumni). Stories must be DePauw-related. Buys 2 mss/issue. Query with clips of published work. Length: 1,000-2,500 words. Pays $50-150.
Photos: State availability of photos with query. Pays $5-25 for b&w 8x10 prints or contact sheets; $2-25 for 35mm color transparencies. Captions required. Buys all rights.

MISSISSIPPI STATE UNIVERSITY ALUMNUS, Mississippi State University, Alumni Association, Editorial Office, Box 5328, Mississippi State MS 39762. (601)325-3442. Editor-in-Chief: Lin H. Wright. Emphasizes articles about Mississippi State graduates and former students. For well-educated and affluent audience. Quarterly magazine; 36 pages. Circ. 15,071. Pays on publication. Buys one-time rights. Pays 25% kill fee. Byline given. Phone queries OK. Submit seasonal/holiday material 3 months in advance. Simultaneous, photocopied and previously published submissions OK. SASE. Reports in 1 month. Free sample copy.
Nonfiction: Historical, humor (with strong MSU flavor; nothing risque), informational, inspirational, interview (with MSU grads), nostalgia (early days at MSU), personal experience, profile and travel (by MSU grads, but must be of wide interest to other grads). Buys 2-3 mss/year ("but welcome more submissions.") Send complete ms. Length: 500-2,500 words. Pays $50-150 (including photos, if used).
Photos: Offers no additional payment for photos purchased with accompanying ms. Captions required. No additional payment for photos accepted with accompanying ms. Uses 5x7 and 8x10 b&w photos and color transparencies of any size.
Columns/Departments: Statesmen, "a section of the *Alumnus* that features briefs about alumni achievements and professional or business advancement. We do not use engagements, marriages or births. There is no payment for Statesmen briefs."
Tips: "We welcome articles about MSU grads in interesting occupations and have used stories on off-shore drillers, miners, horse trainers, etc. We also want profiles on prominent MSU alumni and have carried pieces on Senator John C. Stennis, comedian Jerry Clower, professional football

coach Ray Malauasi and Eugene Butler, editor-in-chief of *Progressive Farmer* magazi
feature three alumni in each issue, alumni who have risen to prominence in their fields or who are
engaged in unusual occupations or who are involved in unusual hobbies."

NATIONAL FORUM: THE PHI KAPPA PHI JOURNAL, The Honor Society of Phi Kappa Phi,
East Tennessee State University, Box 19420A, Johnson City TN 37614. (615)929-5347. Editor:
Stephen W. White. Managing Editor: Elaine M. Smoot. Quarterly interdisciplinary, scholarly
journal. "We are an interdisciplinary journal that seeks crisp, nontechnical analyses of issues of
social and scientific concern as well as scholarly treatments of different aspects of culture." Circ.
90,000. Pays on publication. Byline given. Buys all rights. Submit seasonal/holiday material 6
months in advance. SASE. Reports in 6 weeks on queries; 2 months on mss. Free sample copy and
writer's guidelines.
Nonfiction: General interest, interview/profile and opinion. Each issue is devoted to the exploration of a particular theme. Upcoming theme issues: Perspectives on the Future, Women in the
Professions, Sports in America, Aging & the Aged, The Quality of Work Life, Leisure & Entertainment, The Scientific Imagination, Science and Religion. Buys 50-60 mss/year. Query with clips of
published work. Length: 1,500-2,500 words. Pays $50-200.
Photos: State availability of photos. Identification of subjects required. Buys one-time rights.
Columns/Departments: Educational Dilemmas in the 80s and Book Review Section. Buys 8
mss/year for Educational Dilemmas, 40 book reviews. Length: Book reviews-400-800 words.
Educational Dilemmas-1,500-1,800 words. Pays $15-25 for book reviews; $50/printed page, Edu-
cational Dilemmas.
Fiction: Humorous and short stories. Buys 2-4 mss/year. Length: 1,500-1,800 words. Pays
$50/printed page.
Poetry: Poetry Editors: Professor Van K. Brock, Professor Daniel Fogel. Avant garde, free verse,
haiku, light verse, traditional. No love poetry. Buys 20 mss/year. Submit 5 poems maximum.
Prefers shorter poems.

OSU OUTREACH, Room 007 Student Union, Oklahoma State University, Stillwater, OK, 74078
(405)624-6009. Editor: Doug Dollar. Quarterly magazine for OSU alumni. Circ. 11,000. Pays on
acceptance. Byline given. Buys one-time rights. Submit seasonal/holiday material 3 months in
advance. Simultaneous, photocopied and previously published submissions OK. SASE. Reports
in 2 weeks. Free sample copy for 9x12 SASE.
Nonfiction: General interest; humor (with strong OSU tie); interview (with OSU grads);
historical/nostalgic (OSU traditions, early days events, people, the campus); interview/profile
(OSU subjects); personal experience; and photo feature. "Subjects must have strong connection to
OSU, and must be of interest to alumni." Buys 5 mss/year. Query with clips of published work or
send complete ms. Length: 500-2,000 words. Pays $15-25 (including photos, if used).
Photos: State availability of photos. Pays $5-15 for 5x7 b&w prints; reviews b&w contact sheets.
Captions required. Buys one-time rights.
Columns/Departments: Campus, sports, alumni. Buys 30 mss/year. Send complete ms. Length:
100-300 words. Pays $5-10.
Tips: "Items on alumni personalities are of great value if they have strong human-interest appeal.
We prefer a tight style."

Confession

If you think confession magazines promote the "sin, suffer and repent" syndrome, you haven't read one lately. Today's confession story centers around a
"character flaw"—so abandon the old formula, all ye who would enter this market.

Pick up a current issue of a confession magazine and you'll see that the
modern confession reflects social issues and real-life situations. But beware of
trying to change societal attitudes; the confession reader still has fairly traditional
values, and some situations (such as incest) are taboo, unless handled with extreme sympathy and understanding.

For a closer look at writing for this specialized market, see *The Confession
Writer's Handbook*, by Florence K. Palmer (revised by Marguerite McClain,
Writer's Digest Books).

BRONZE THRILLS, 1220 Harding St., Ft. Worth TX 76012. Editor: Jeanette Barret. Monthly magazine; 82 pages. Circ. 80,000. Buys all rights. Buys 60 mss/year. Pays on publication. Sample copy and writer's guidelines free. Reports in 90 days. Submit complete ms to Willie Johnson, managing editor.
Fiction: All material must relate to blacks. Romance or confession; black-oriented. Interested in true romance, confession material. Length: 4,000-6,000 words. Pays $40.
Photos: B&w and color photos are purchased on assignment. 8x10 b&w glossy prints, 2¼x2¼ or 4x5 color transparencies. Pays $50 for b&w.

INTIMATE ROMANCES, Rolat Publishing Corp., 667 Madison Ave., New York NY 10021. Editorial Director: Ilene Dube. Requirements same as *True Secrets*.

INTIMATE SECRETS, Rolat Publishing Corp., 667 Madison Ave., New York NY 10021. Editorial Director: Ilene Dube. Requirements same as *True Secrets*.

INTIMATE STORY, 2 Park Ave., New York NY 10016. Editor: Janet Wandel. 95% freelance written. For women 14-70 years old; small minority of readership composed of men; blue-collar. Monthly magazine; 66 pages. Circ. 250,000. Buys all rights. No byline. Buys about 120 mss/year. Pays on publication. Rarely sends sample copies. No photocopied or simultaneous submissions. Submit seasonal material 6 months in advance. Reports in 3 months. SASE.
Fiction: "Sex-oriented and human interest stories; all types of fictional confession stories. Always first person; always enough dialogue. Our stories are within the realm of the believable. Story themes encompass whatever is of interest to women today." No stories with the theme of hopelessness or depressing situations. Most titles are house-generated. Length: 2,000-7,000 words. Pays 3¢/word; $160 maximum.

MODERN ROMANCES, Macfadden Women's Group, Inc., 215 Lexington Ave., New York NY 10016. Editor: Jean Sharbel. 100% freelance written. For blue-collar, family oriented women, 18-35 years old. Monthly magazine; 88 pages. Circ. 200,000. Pays within 30 days after publication. Buys all rights. Byline given on nonfiction. Submit seasonal/holiday material 4 months in advance. SASE. Reports in 12-16 weeks.
Nonfiction: General interest; how-to (homemaking subjects); humor; inspirational; and personal experience. Submit complete ms. Length: 200-1,500 words. Pay "depends on merit."
Fiction: "Confession stories with reader identification and a strong emotional tone. No third person material." Buys 14 mss/issue. Submit complete ms. Length: 1,500-8,500 words. Pays 5¢/word.
Poetry: "Light, romantic poetry, to 24 lines." Buys 36/year. Pay "depends on merit."

PERSONAL ROMANCES, Ideal Publishing Corp., 2 Park Ave., New York NY 10016. Editor: Ronnie Nina Mann. Monthly. Buys all rights. No byline. Pays on publication. Reports on submissions in 8-10 weeks. SASE. "Query letter not necessary."
Fiction: First-person stories told in strong up-to-date terms by young marrieds, singles, and teens revealing their emotional, sexual, and family conflicts and their search to resolve personal problems. Blue-collar, white collar group identification. "We are interested in fresh ideas, and occasionally buy supernatural and macabre stories if they fit in with the confession format, and have plausible explanations." Length: 2,000-6,000 words. Pays $160 maximum, based on 3¢/word.

REAL STORY, 23 W. 26th St., New York NY 10010. (212)689-3933. Editor: Ardis Sandel. For housewives, teenagers, and working women. Monthly magazine; 64 pages. Buys all rights. Buys about 200 mss/year. Pays on publication. Sample copy $1.25. Reports in 6-8 weeks. Submit seasonal or holiday material 6 months in advance. SASE.
Nonfiction and Fiction: "First-person confession stories and service articles on sex, decorating, arts and crafts, fashions, homemaking, beauty, cooking, children, etc. Stories must be well-plotted, have real situations, motivation and characterization." Writer should read several issues for style and approach. Strong emphasis on realism. No racial stories. "Sexy passages and dialogue are okay if integral part of the story." Mss should feature a different twist or angle to make the story usable. Lengths from short-shorts to 7,500 words maximum. Pays $150 maximum, depending on length.

SECRETS, 0Macfadden Women's Group, 215 Lexington Ave., New York NY 10016. (212)983-5644. Editor: Jean Press Silberg. For blue-collar family women, ages 18-35. Monthly magazine. Buys all rights. Buys about 150 mss/year. Pays on publication. No photocopied or simultaneous submissions. Submit seasonal material 4-5 months in advance. Submit only complete ms. Reports in 6 weeks. SASE.

Nonfiction and Fiction: Wants realistically told, strongly plotted stories of special interest to women: family, marriage and romance themes, "woman-angle articles," or self-help or inspirational fillers. "No pornographic material; no sadistic or abnormal angles." Length: 300-1,000 words for nonfiction; 1,500-7,500 words for full-length mss. Occasional 10,000-worders. Pays 3¢/word for story mss. Greatest need: 2,000-5,000 words.

TRUE CONFESSIONS, Macfadden Women's Group, 215 Lexington Ave., New York NY 10016. Editor: Barbara J. Brett. For high-school-educated, blue-collar women, teens through maturity. Monthly magazine. Circ. 350,000. Byline given on poetry and articles. Buys all rights. Pays within 30 days after publication. No photocopied or simultaneous submissions. Submit seasonal material 6 months in advance. Reports in 4 months. Submit complete ms. SASE.
Stories, Articles, and Fillers: Timely, exciting, emotional first-person stories on the problems that face today's young women. The narrators should be sympathetic, and the situations they find themselves in should be intriguing, yet realistic. Every story should have a strong romantic interest and a high moral tone, and every plot should reach an exciting climax. Careful study of a current issue is suggested. Length: 2,000-7,000 words; 5,000 word stories preferred; also book-lengths of 10,000-12,000 words. Pays 5¢/word. Also, articles, regular features, and short fillers.
Poetry: Romantic poetry, free verse and traditional, of interest to women. Limit submissions to batches of 4. Pays $10 minimum.

TRUE EXPERIENCE, Macfadden Women's Group, 215 Lexington Ave., New York NY 10016. Contact: Helene Eccleston. For your marrieds, blue-collar, high school education. Interests: children, home, arts, crafts, family and self-fulfillment. Monthly magazine; 80 pages. Circ. 225,000. Buys all rights. Byline given. Buys about 100 mss/year. Pays within 30 days after publication. "Study the magazine for style and editorial content." No photocopied or simultaneous submissions. Submit seasonal material 5 months in advance. Reports in 3 months. Submit complete ms. SASE.
Fiction and Nonfiction: Stories on life situations, e.g., death, love and sickness. Romance and confession, first-person narratives with strong identification for readers. Articles on health, self-help or child care. "Remember that we are contemporary. We deal with women's self-awareness, and consciousness of their roles in society." Length: 250-1,500 words for nonfiction; 1,000-7,500 words for fiction. Pays 3¢/word.
Poetry: Only traditional forms. Length: 4-20 lines. Payment varies.

TRUE LOVE, Macfadden Women's Group, 215 Lexington Ave., New York NY 10016. Editor: Lois E. Wilcken. For young, blue-collar women. Monthly magazine; 80 pages. Circ. 225,000. Buys all rights. Byline given for nonfiction. Buys about 150 mss a year. Pays within 30 days after publication. Submit seasonal material at least 6 months in advance. Reports in 12-16 weeks. Submit complete ms. SASE.
Fiction: Confessions, true love stories (especially young romance); problems and solutions; supernatural; health problems; marital and child-rearing difficulties. Avoid graphic sex. Stories dealing with reality, current problems, everyday events, with emphasis on emotional impact. Length: 1,500-8,000 words. Pays 3¢/word.
Nonfiction: Informational and how-to articles. Length: 250-800 words. Pays 5¢/word minimum.
Tips: "The story must appeal to the average blue collar woman. It must deal with her problems and interests. Characters—especially the narrator—must be sympathetic. Since we always have an eye out for a true story, it sometimes helps when the author indicates in a brief note, where he or she got the story idea. Was it from one's personal experience or from the experience of one's friend? We tend to get a lot of short stories under 3,000 words. I'm interested in seeing more long pieces—5,000 to 8,000 words—in which some dramatic development can take place."

TRUE ROMANCE, Macfadden Women's Group, 215 Lexington Ave., New York NY 10016. (212)983-5644. Editor: Susan Weiner. "Our readership ranges from teenagers to senior citizens. The majority are high school educated, married, have young children and also work outside the home. They are concerned with contemporary social issues, yet they are deeply committed to their husbands and children. They have high moral values and place great emphasis on love and romance." Monthly magazine. Circ. 225,000. Pays on publication. Buys all rights. Submit seasonal/holiday material at least 5 months in advance. SASE. Reports in 3 months.
Nonfiction: How-to and informational. Submit complete ms. Length: 300-1,000 words. Pays 3¢/word, special rates for short features and articles.
Fiction: Confession. Buys 13 stories/issue. Submit complete ms. Length: 2,000-7,500 words. Pays 3¢/word; slightly higher flat rate for short-shorts.
Poetry: Light verse and traditional. Buys 15/year. Length: 4-20 lines. Pays $10 minimum.
Tips: "The freelance writer is needed and welcomed. A timely, well-written story that is told by a

sympathetic narrator who sees the central problem through to a satisfying resolution is all that is needed to 'break into' *True Romance*. We are always looking for good love stories."

TRUE SECRETS, Rolat Publishing Corp., 667 Madison Ave., New York NY 10021. Editorial Director: Ilene Dube. Magazine for women between the ages 15-35. Circ. 170,000. Pays on acceptance. Buys all rights. Submissions addressed to *True Secrets* are also considered for publication for *Intimate Romances* and *Intimate Secrets*. Reports in 4-6 weeks. Free writer's guidelines with SASE only.
Nonfiction: "Though we do not purchase much nonfiction, if the subject is of interest, relevance, and handled appropriately for our readership, we'll consider it. Please do not submit ms. Send a brief paragraph decribing story, 2-4 sample pages, and SASE. No material will be returned when SASE is not included." Length: 3,000-5,000 words. Pays $125-150.
Fiction: "We look primarily for tender love stories, touching baby stories, and stories dealing with identifiable marital problems, particularly sexual. We are interested in realistic teen stories, and, on occasion, male-narrated stories and tales with occult and gothic overtones. Stories should be written in the first-person. They should deal with a romantic or emotional problem that is identifiable and realistically portrays how the narrator copes with her conflict and resolves it. We reject stories based on hackneyed themes and outdated attitudes. In our contemporary society, stories condemning premarital sexual experience, abortion, and those that preach chastity, etc., are unsuitable for our needs." Length: 1,500-7,000 words. Pays $75-150.
Tips: "Avoid the 'sin-suffer-repent' syndrome. Tailor your needs to suit a young, rural audience who, though unsophisticated, no longer live by puritanical values. Buy a copy of one of our books and study it. Don't think that all confessions are the same. They're not."

TRUE STORY, Macfadden Women's Group, 215 Lexington Ave., New York NY 10016. Editor: Helen Vincent. 80% freelance written. For young married, blue-collar women, 20-35; high school education; increasingly broad interests; home-oriented, but looking beyond the home for personal fulfillment. Monthly magazine; 104 pages. Circ. 1,700,000. Buys all rights. Byline given "on nonfiction only." Buys about 125 full-length mss/year. Pays on publication. No photocopied or simultaneous submissions. Submit seasonal material 4 months in advance. Make notation on envelope that it is seasonal material. Query for nonfiction. Submit only complete mss for fiction. Reports in 2-3 months. SASE.
Nonfiction, Fiction and Fillers: "First-person stories covering all aspects of women's interest: love, marriage, family life, careers, social problems, etc. Nonfiction would further explore same areas. The best direction a new writer can be given is to carefully study several issues of the magazine; then submit a fresh, exciting, well-written story. We have no taboos. It's the handling that makes the difference between a rejection and an acceptance." How-to, personal experience, inspirational. Length: 1,000-2,500 words. Pays 5-10¢ or more/word. Also seeks material for Women are Wonderful column. Length: 1,500 words maximum. Pays 5¢/word. Pays a flat rate for column or departments, announced in the magazine. Query Art Director, Gus Gazzola, about all possible photo submissions. Length: 1,500-8,000 words. Pays 5¢/word; $100 minimum. Regular departments—New Faces and Children's Corner—bring $5/item.

Consumer Service and Business Opportunity

These publications tell readers how to get the most for their money—either in goods purchased or in earnings from investment in a small business of their own. Publications for business executives are listed under Business and Finance. Those on how to run specific businesses are classified in Trade, Technical and Professional Journals.

BEST BUYS, the Magazine for Smart Shoppers, (formerly *New York Shopper*), 150 5th Ave., New York NY 10011. (212)675-4777. Editor: Carol J. Richards. Publisher: Jon J. Bloomberg. Magazine published 8 times/year covering various products/goods for consumers. Circ. 30,000. Pays on publication. Byline given for original stories. Buys all rights. Submit seasonal/holiday material 4 months in advance. Original plus photocopied submissions OK. SASE. Writer's guidelines free for business size SAE and 1 first class stamp.

Nonfiction: General interest (educational articles for consumers); and how-to (bargain, find good buys). Buys 30-40 mss/year. Query with brief biography plus b&w photos. Length: 650-1,200 words. Pays $50 per 650 word page.

Photos: State availability of photos. Reviews 5x7 b&w glossy prints. Captions, model releases, and identification of subjects required.

Fillers: Short humor (about shopping). Length: 200-500 words. Pays up to $50.

Tips: "We look for research oriented people who can write with an unbiased slant, correctly and with meticulous care to accuracy of copy."

CANADIAN CONSUMER, Consumers' Association of Canada, 200 1st Ave., Ottawa, Ontario, Canada K1S 5J3. (613)238-4840. Editor: David Shaw. Emphasizes consumer information for a "very broad readership." Monthly magazine. Circ. 152,000. Pays on publication. Buys one-time rights. Phone queries OK. Simultaneous and photocopied submissions OK. SASE. Query first. Reports in 1 month. Free sample copy.

Nonfiction: "Anything of specific interest to consumers." Exposé and how-to. Buys 18 mss/year. Query first. Length: 1,200-2,700 words. Pays $50.

Photos: State availability of photos with ms. Pays $10-25 for 8½x11 b&w glossy prints. Captions preferred. Buys one-time rights.

CAPITAL SHOPPER, Box 72, Fairfax VA 22030. (703)281-7350. Editor/Publisher: Seth Allan Bloomberg. Magazine published every 6 weeks covering price comparisons for consumers in the Washington DC area. Estab. 1980. Circ. 50,000. Pays on publication. Byline given. Buys all rights. Submit seasonal/holiday material 3 months in advance. Photocopied submissions OK. SASE. Reports in 1 week on queries. Unsolicited material not returned.

Nonfiction: Exposé (of products or services); how-to (do-it-yourself articles that help people save money or get the most for their dollar); interview/profile (of purveyors); new product; travel; and consumer-oriented material. Buys 40-50 mss/year. Query, send complete ms or phone. Pays $75-300/article.

Photos: Send photos with ms. "Photos are paid for with payment for ms." Captions and model release required.

CASH NEWSLETTER, Box 1999, Brooksville FL 33512. Editor-in-Chief: G. Douglas Hafely Jr. Managing Editor: K.R. Baker. Emphasizes "making, saving and investing money." Monthly newsletter. Pays on acceptance. Buys all rights. Usually no bylines unless requested on outstanding articles. Regular contributors are listed as "contributing editors." Submit seasonal/holiday material 2 months in advance. Simultaneous and photocopied submissions OK. SASE. Reports in 2 weeks. Sample copy 50¢.

Nonfiction: Small businesses (ones the average person could start with little or no capital, preferably from home); exposé (rags to riches, how the little guy got started and made it big; need full details on how); humor (pertaining to making and saving money); how-to (make, save, keep, use and invest money; how to get services, information and goods free); informational (ways for anyone to succeed); inspirational (hope for the small man); interview (with successful people who started small); new product (hot items for resale, new items of interest to mass audience, how to buy and save); personal experience (if from small to successful); technical (on interesting new ways to invest; market projections and contacts); and travel (any inexpensive and/or unusual vacations). Buys 2-10 mss/issue. Submit complete ms. Length: 100-1,000 words. "Omit puffery and flowery phrases; write in telegraphese, short and to the point. No grocery, cooking or household tips used." Pays $2-10.

Photos: Purchased with or without accompanying ms. Captions required. Send prints. Pays $2-5 for 4x5 b&w glossy prints. No additional payment for photos accepted with accompanying ms.

Fillers: Clippings and newsbreaks. Buys 1-10/issue. Length: 5-50 words. Pays 50¢-$2.

CONSUMER LIFE, The Webb Co., 1999 Shepard Rd., St. Paul MN 55116. (612)647-7383. Editor: Adele Malott. Managing Editor: Jim Carney. Quarterly magazine for perceptive members of Unity Buying Service who are primarily "working women with a family who like to shop by mail." Circ. 1,000,000. Pays on acceptance. Byline given. Offers 25% kill fee. Buys first North American serial rights. Submit seasonal material 14 months in advance. Simultaneous, photocopied, and previously published submissions OK. If previously published, writer should hold rights and specifiy where and when published. Reports in 6 weeks on queries; in 1 month on mss. Free sample copy; free writer's guidelines with SASE.

Nonfiction: General interest (any story with a mail order-slant good recent articles: health organizations; home maintenance: tax and legal angles of starting a business; shopping for garden supplies and equipment by mail); travel (luggage; brochures; travel agents); how-to (do your own repairs; and shop for materials); products (criteria in shopping for a product—no brand names);

and technical (purchasing oriented articles, such as shopping for stereo equipment). Buys 4-7 mss/issue. Query with clips of published work. Length: 1,200-2,200 words. Pays $250-400.
Photos: Pays $25 minimum for b&w prints. Captions and model release required. Buys one-time rights.
Columns/Departments: Readers' Tips (household hints and shopping ideas). Buys 30 mss/issue. Send complete ms. Length: 50 words minimum. Pays $5 minimum.

CONSUMER REPORTS, 256 Washington St., Mt. Vernon NY 10550. Editor: Irwin Landau. Staff-written.

CONSUMERS DIGEST MAGAZINE, Consumer Digest, Inc., 5705 N. Lincoln Ave., Chicago IL 60659. (312)275-3590. Editor: Larry Teeman. Emphasizes anything of consumer business interests. Bimonthly magazine. Circ. 1,000,000. Pays on publication. Buys all rights. Phone queries OK. Submit seasonal/holiday material 3 months in advance. SASE. Reports in 1 month. Free writer's guidelines. Sample copy $1.
Nonfiction: Exposé; general interest (on advice to consumers and consumer buying products, service, health, business, investments, insurance and money management); how-to; news product and travel. "Writers *must* be experts in fields they write about. We do *not* want general articles." Buys 10 mss/issue. Query. Length: 2,500-3,500 words. Pay negotiable.
Tips: Send query with summary and outline.

CONSUMERS' RESEARCH MAGAZINE, Box 168, Washington NJ 07882. Technical Editor: F.J. Schlink. Monthly. Byline given "except when the article as written requires extensive editing, improvement, amplification, which may occur when a nontechnical person writes in a field where engineering or physical science knowledge is essential." Limited amount of freelance material used. Query. SASE.
Nonfiction: Articles of practical interest to consumers concerned with tests and expert judgment of goods and services they buy. Must be accurate and well-supported by chemical, engineering, general science, medical, or other expert or professional knowledge of subject. Pays approximately 5¢/word.
Photos: Buys b&w glossy prints with mss only. Pays $5 minimum. "Photos are accepted only if they are clearly relevant to the article being published or essential to understanding of points made or discussed."

ECONOMIC FACTS, The National Research Bureau, Inc., 424 N. 3rd St., Burlington IA 52601. Editor-in-Chief: Betty Beck. Magazine for industrial workers of all ages. Published 4 times/year. Circ. 30,000. Pays on publication. Buys all rights. Byline given. Submit seasonal/holiday material 3-4 months in advance of issue date. Previously published submissions OK. SASE. Reports in 1 week. Free sample copy and writer's guidelines.
Nonfiction: Barbara Boeding, articles editor. General interest (private enterprise, government data, graphs, taxes and health care). Buys 2-3 mss/issue. Query with outline of article. Length: 400-600 words. Pays $20 minimum.

ENTREPRENEUR MAGAZINE, 2311 Pontius, Los Angeles CA 90064. Publisher: Chase Revel. Editor: James Bartel. For a readership looking for highly profitable opportunities in small businesses, as owners, investors or franchisees. Monthly magazine. Circ. 175,000. Pays on publication. Buys all rights. Byline given. Submit seasonal/holiday material 3 months in advance of issue date. Photocopied submissions OK. SASE. Reports in 1 month. Sample copy $3; free writer's guidelines.
Nonfiction: How-to (in-depth start-up details on 'hot' business opportunities like tanning parlors or computer stores). Buys 12 mss/year. Query with clips of published work. Features—Length: 5,000-10,000. Pays $500-1,500; Operating Articles—Length: 1,000-2,500 words. Pays 10¢/word; Featurette—Length: 500-1,000 words. Pays $100 or 10¢/word, whichever is more.
Photos: "We need top quality color transparencies and 8x10 b&w glossy prints to illustrate articles." Offers no additional payment for photos accepted with ms. Caption information required. Buys all rights. Model release required. Query.

FDA CONSUMER, 5600 Fishers Lane, Rockville MD 20857. (301)443-3220. Editor: Roger W. Miller. For "all consumers of products regulated by the Food and Drug Administration." A federal government publication. Monthly magazine. December/January and July/August issues combined. Circ. 20,000. Not copyrighted. Pays 50% kill fee. Byline given. "All purchases automatically become part of public domain." Buys 4-5 freelance mss a year. Pays on publication. Query. "We cannot be responsible for any work by writer not agreed upon by prior contract." SASE.
Nonfiction: "Articles of an educational nature concerning purchase and use of FDA regulated

products and specific FDA programs and actions to protect the consumer's health and pocket-book. Authoritative and official agency viewpoints emanating from agency policy and actions in administrating the Food, Drug and Cosmetic Act and a number of other statutes. All articles subject to clearance by the appropriate FDA experts as well as the editor. The magazine speaks for the federal government only. Articles based on facts and FDA policy only. We cannot consider any unsolicited material. All articles based on prior arrangement by contract. The nature and subject matter and clearances required are so exacting that it is difficult to get an article produced by a writer working outside the Washington DC metropolitan area." Length: average, 2,000 words. Pays $750.

Photos: B&w photos are purchased on assignment only.

GOOD IDEAS NEWSLETTER, G. Howard Poteet, Inc., Box 217, Cedar Grove NJ 07009. SASE. **Nonfiction:** Money making and money saving ideas. Query. Pays $10/typeset page.

INCOME OPPORTUNITIES, 380 Lexington Ave., New York NY 10017. Editor: Joseph V. Daffron. Managing Editor: Frances Freilich. For all who are seeking business opportunities, full- or part-time. Monthly magazine. Buys all rights. Buys 50-60 mss/year. No photocopied or simultaneous submissions. Two special directory issues contain articles on selling techniques, mail order, import/export, franchising and business ideas. Reports in 2 weeks. Query with list of sources and outline of article development. SASE.

Nonfiction and Photos: Regularly covered are such subjects as mail order, direct selling, franchising, party plans, selling techniques and the marketing of handcrafted or homecrafted products. Wanted are ideas for the aspiring entrepreneur; examples of successful business methods that might be duplicated. No material that is purely inspirational. Length: 800 words for a short; 2,000-3,000 words for a major article. "Payment rates vary according to length and quality of the submission."

Tips: "Study recent issues of the magazine. Best bets for newcomers: Interview-based report on a successful small business venture."

IT'S THE LAW, Lawmedia Associates, Drawer 390, Charlottesville VA 22902. Editorial Director: Elaine Hadden. Monthly publication covering law for upscale, well-educated, professional persons. Readers are physicians, dentists, accountants, business executives, real estate and insurance professionals, etc. Estab. 1981. Circ. 300,000. Pays on acceptance. Photocopied and previously published submissions OK, if so indicated. SASE. Reports in 1 month on queries; 6 weeks on mss.

Nonfiction: General interest (on legal topics only—e.g., how government agencies work, law in the news, etc.); how-to (use the law for one's own benefit, work through legal documents, etc.); interview/profile (of persons, important or little-known, who have an impact on the legal system); and a balanced pro and con treatment of controversial issues in law will be considered if they accurately reflect the current state of the law. Query with clips of published work or send complete ms. "We want to know that the writer is familiar with the topic in advance. Also, one or two ideas at a time are better than a string of quick thoughts off the top of the writer's head." Length: 2,000-4,000 words. Pays $200-800/article.

Photos: State availability of photos. Pays $5-50 for b&w contact sheet and $5-75 for color transparencies. Model release required.

Columns/Departments: Legal Briefs (deals with 16 specific areas of law). "These are short, informative columns (750-1,200 words) on questions derived from law which arise in everyday situations and are of interest to an educated, affluent readership. They must be readable and non-technical; must contain examples, preferably taken from real situations; must be documented for in-house review. These columns are a possibility for legally-knowledgeable writers with developed research skills. Information on specific areas and typical topics." Length: 750-1,200 words. Pays $75-125/article.

Tips: "We need writers who understand the intricacies and subtleties of legal points and issues well enough to express them clearly and accurately to non-lawyers; hence, some background in law or legal work is very helpful. Materials and ideas submitted should be well-thought-out, specific, and plainly and neatly submitted. If the writer is suggesting and outlining a piece rather than submitting a draft, clips of published works are essential. Good examples are critical to enliven copy and to relate the legal points to real life situations. Articles on legal issues and on aspects of the legal system will obviously require knowledge of the law. Writers should be interested in the law, but should not view us as an opportunity to promote a viewpoint. Think first about practical yet interesting aspects of law which would interest educated, affluent readers. Don't try to tackle an intricate, technical legal issue beyond your expertise. Look for real examples that are typical rather than extraordinary. We are not anti-lawyer or anti-legal system, but that does not mean we don't look for pieces which are constructively critical."

NEW VENTURES NEWSLETTER, The Entrepreneur's Newsletter of Business Opportunities, 9003 Reseda Blvd., Suite 205B, Northridge CA 91324. Assistant Editor: Lois Sapio. Publisher: Arnold Van Den Berg. Monthly newsletter covering "unique new business opportunities created by changes in technology, lifestyles and the economy." Buys all rights. Pays on acceptance. Photocopied submissions OK. SASE. Reports "immediately." Free sample copy.
Nonfiction: "How-to start, operate, grow in a unique new business that has potential of earning $50,000 per year and can be started with under $10,000. No costly franchise deals or material on management advice, mail order business, or import-export articles." Buys 104 mss/year. Query. Length: 1,200-1,500 words. Pays $100-500.
Tips: "In query state unusual business opportunity idea which meets guideline requirements. Interview someone in that business and outline costs and profit potential. Writer must have ideas which are unique or unusual and haven't been written about frequently in other business opportunity publications. Writer must be willing to get additional information or do additional research if requested."

PUBLIC CITIZEN, Public Citizen, Inc., Box 19404, Washington DC 20036. Editor: Richard Pollock. Quarterly magazine covering consumer issues for "members of Public Citizen, a consumer group established by Ralph Nader in the public interest. Our readers have joined the group because they believe the consumer has a voice in the products he buys and in the country. Our slant is toward consumer power." Estab. 1980. Circ. 45,000. Pays on publication. Byline given. Buys first rights. Submit seasonal/holiday material 4 months in advance. Photocopied submissions OK. SASE. Reports in 1 month on queries; 2 months on mss. Sample copy available.
Nonfiction: Exposé (of government waste and inefficiency of big business); general interest (features on how consumer groups are helping themselves); how-to (starting consumer groups such as co-ops, etc.); interview/profile (of big business figures or consumer figures, or of government figures in positions that affect consumers); and photo feature (dealing with consumer power). "We are looking for stories that go to the heart of an issue and explain how it affects the consumer. Articles must be in-depth investigations that expose poor business practices or bad government. Send us stories that consumers will feel they learned something important from or that they can gain inspiration from to continue the fight for consumer rights. All are facts double checked by our fact-checkers. Misinformation or slanting the truth to fit the story is the best way never to get into *Public Citizen*." No "fillers, jokes or puzzles." Query or send complete ms. Length: 500-2,500 words. Pays $50 maximum/article.
Photos: State availability of photos. Reviews 5x7 b&w prints. "Photos are paid for with payment for ms." Captions required. Buys one-time rights.
Columns/Departments: Notes (short features on consumer issues); Keeping Score ("500-1,000 words on issues concerning consumers that have already been decided or taken effect; should examine an issue to see if the right decision was made"); Reviews ("books only—anything dealing with consumer issues"). Query or send complete ms—"no clips please." Length: 500-1,000 words. Pays $125 maximum/article.
Tips: " 'Features,' 'Notes' and 'Keeping Score' are all very much open to freelancers."

SUBURBAN SHOPPER, Box 208, East Millstone NJ 08873. (201)874-8857. Editor-in-Chief: Kevin K. Kopec. For convenience shoppers, working women who are interested in savings and unusual gadgets/home items. Quarterly tabloid. Pays on publication. Buys one-time rights. Phone queries OK. Submit seasonal/holiday material 1 month in advance. Simultaneous, photocopied, and previously published submissions OK. SASE. Reports in 3 weeks. Sample copy $1.25; free writer's guidelines.
Nonfiction: General interest (any aspect of mail order shopping-buying tips, etc.); and new product (mail order product reviews). Buys 5 mss/issue. Submit complete ms. Length: 500-1,000 words. Pays $5-10.

SUPERMARKET SHOPPER, American Coupon Club, Inc., Box 1149, Dept. WD, Great Neck NY 11023. President: Martin Sloane. Managing Editor: Ruth Brooks. Emphasizes smart supermarket shopping and the use of cents-off coupons and refund offers for "a wide audience of supermarket shoppers who want to save money. The editorial slant is definitely consumer-oriented." Monthly; 52 pages. Circ. 50,000. Pays on publication. Buys all rights. Byline given. Simultaneous, photocopied and previously published submissions OK. SASE. Reports in 8 weeks. Free sample copy; writers guidelines for SASE.
Nonfiction: Lee Shore, editor. General interest; exposé (of supermarket operations, management, coupon misredemption); how-to (save money at the supermarket, tips, dollar stretchers; etc.); humor; interview (of top management, food manufacturers or supermarkets); new product (food, household products); and personal experience (couponing and refunding). Buys 2-3 mss/issue. Send complete ms. Length: 750-2,500 words. Pays 5¢/published word.

Fiction: "We have not used fiction, but we might be interested if the events are in context of supermarket shopping." Query. Length: 750-2,500 words. Pays 5¢/published word.
Fillers: Jokes, short humor and newsbreaks. Buys 1-2/issue. Length: 50-200 words. Pays $5-10.
Tips: "The best way to break in is to read a copy of our magazine and get an idea of the type of material we publish. The consumer viewpoint is utmost in our minds."

VENTURE, THE MAGAZINE FOR ENTREPRENEURS, Venture Magazine, Inc., 35 W. 45th St., New York 10036. Editor: Carl Burgen. Monthly magazine about entrepreneurs for people owning their own businesses, starting new businesses and people wanting to start a new business. Estab. 1979. Pays on acceptance. Buys all rights. SASE. Free sample copy.
Nonfiction: "We are looking for stories on new startups of companies and current news on venture capital and entrepreneurs." No respectives. Buys 15 mss/issue. Query with clips of previously published work. Length: 1,200-3,000 words. Pays $250-800.

WINNING, National Reporter Publications, Inc., 15115 S. 76th E. Ave., Bixby OK 74008. (918)366-4441. Editor: Gerald S. Pope. Monthly tabloid covering "winning in all its aspects to help you cash in on the best things in life." Circ. 200,000. Pays on publication. Byline given. Buys all rights. Submit seasonal/holiday material 3 months in advance. Simultaneous queries and submissions OK. SASE. Reports in 1 month. Free sample copy.
Nonfiction: How-to (succeed/win); inspirational; and articles on winning/winners. Buys 48+ mss/year. Length: 300-900 words. Pays 5¢/word maximum.
Photos: State availability of photos. Pays $15 maximum for 5x7 b&w prints. Identification of subjects required.

Detective and Crime

Publications listed in this section provide markets for nonfiction accounts of true crimes. Markets for criminal fiction (mysteries) are listed in Mystery Publications.

DETECTIVE CASES, Detective Files Group, 1440 St. Catherine St. W., Montreal, Quebec, Canada H3G 1S2. Editor-in-Chief: Dominick A. Merle. Art Director: Art Ball. Bimonthly magazine. See *Detective Files.*

DETECTIVE DRAGNET, Detective Files Group, 1440 St. Catherine St. W., Montreal, Quebec, Canada H3G 1S2. Editor-in-Chief: Dominick A. Merle. Art Director: Art Ball. Bimonthly magazine; 72 pages. See *Detective Files.*

DETECTIVE FILES, Detective Files Group, 1440 St. Catherine St. W., Montreal, Quebec, Canada H3G 1S2. Editor-in-Chief: Dominick A. Merle. Art Director: Art Ball. Bimonthly magazine; 72 pages. Pays on acceptance. Buys all rights. Submit seasonal/holiday material 4 months in advance. Photocopied submissions OK. SASE. Reports in 4 weeks. Free sample copy and writer's guidelines.
Nonfiction: True crime stories. "Do a thorough job; don't double-sell (sell an article to more than one market); and deliver, and you can have a steady market. Neatness, clarity and pace will help you make the sale." Query. Length: 3,500-6,000 words. Pays $175-300.
Photos: Purchased with accompanying ms; no additional payment.

FRONT PAGE DETECTIVE, INSIDE DETECTIVE, Official Detective Group, R.G.H. Publishing Corp., 235 Park Ave. S., New York NY 10003. Editor-in-Chief: Albert P. Govoni. Editor: Joshua Moroz.
Nonfiction: The focus of these two publications is similar to the others in the Official Detective Group, but concentrates more on pre-trial stories. Byline given. For further details, see *Official Detective.*

HEADQUARTERS DETECTIVE, Detective Files Group, 1440 St. Catherine St. W., Montreal, Quebec, Canada H3G 1S2. Editor-in-Chief: Dominick A. Merle. Art Director: Art Ball. Bimonthly magazine; 72 pages. See *Detective Files.*

MASTER DETECTIVE, Official Detective Group, R.G.H. Publishing Corp., 235 Park Ave. S., New York NY 10003. Editor-in-Chief: Albert P. Govoni. Managing Editor: Art Crockett. Monthly. Circ. 350,000. Buys 9-10 mss/issue. See *Official Detective.*

OFFICIAL DETECTIVE, Official Detective Group, R.G.H. Publishing Corp., 235 Park Ave. S., New York NY 10003. Editor-in-Chief: Albert P. Govoni. Managing Editor: Art Crockett. "For detective story or police buffs whose tastes run to *true,* rather than fictional crime/mysteries." Monthly magazine. Circ. 500,000. Pays on acceptance. Buys all rights. Byline given. Phone queries OK. SASE. Reports in 2 weeks.

Nonfiction: "Only *fact* detective stories. We are actively trying to develop new writers, and we'll work closely with those who show promise and can take the discipline required by our material. It's not difficult to write, but it demands meticulous attention to facts, truth, clarity, detail. Queries are essential with us, but I'd say the quickest rejection goes to the writer who sends in a story on a case that should never have been written for us because it lacks the most important ingredient, namely solid, superlative detective work. We also dislike pieces with multiple defendants, unless all have been convicted." Buys 150 mss/year. Query. Length: 5,000-6,000 words. Pays $250.

Photos: Purchased with accompanying mss. Captions required. Send prints for inside use; transparencies for covers. Pays $12.50 minimum for b&w glossy prints, 4x5 minimum. Pays $200 minimum for 2¼x2¼ or 35mm transparencies. Model release required for color photos used on cover.

Tips: Send a detailed query on the case to be submitted. Include: locale; victim's name; type of crime; suspect's name; status of the case (indictment, trial concluded, disposition, etc.); amount and quality of detective work; dates; and availability and number of pictures. "We're always impressed by details of the writer's credentials."

STARTLING DETECTIVE, Detective Files Group, 1440 St. Catherine St. W., Montreal, Quebec, Canada H3G 1S2. Editor-in-Chief: Dominick A. Merle. Art Director: Art Ball. Monthly magazine; 72 pages. See *Detective Files.*

TRUE DETECTIVE, Official Detective Group, R.G.H. Publishing Corp., 235 Park Ave., S., New York NY 10003. Editor-in-Chief: Albert P. Govoni. Managing Editor: Art Crockett. Monthly. Circ. 500,000. Buys 11-12 mss/issue. Byline given. See *Official Detective.*

TRUE POLICE CASES, Detective Files Group, 1440 St. Catherine St. W., Montreal, Quebec, Canada H3G 1S2. Editor-in-Chief: Dominick A. Merle. Art Director: Art Ball. Bimonthly magazine; 72 pages. See *Detective Files.*

Education

Magazines here cover education for parents and the general public. Journals for professional educators and teachers are included in the Education category in the Trade Journals section.

AMERICAN EDUCATION, Department of Education, 400 Maryland Ave. SW, Washington DC 20202. (202)245-8907. Editor: Richard Elwell. Managing Editor: Gertrue Mitchell. Presents successful education programs with some federal involvement for readership of educators and others with special interest in the field. Published 10 times/year (2 combined issues). Circ. 12,000. Pays on acceptance. Buys all rights. Pays $100-150 kill fee. Byline given. Submit seasonal/holiday material 4 months in advance. SASE. Reports in 3 weeks. Free sample copy and writer's guidelines.

Nonfiction: Should have educational substance written in lively journalistic style. Buys 30 mss/year. Query. Length: average 2,500 words. Pays $350 minimum, depending on quality.

Photos: Alyce Jackson, Photo Editor. Pay negotiable. Submit b&w glossy prints and contact sheet. Pays $15 minimum.

CAREER WORLD, Curriculum Innovations, Inc., 3500 Western Ave., Highland Park IL 60035. (312)432-2700. Editor: Bonnie Bekken. 60% freelance written. Emphasizes career education for junior and senior high school students at approximately 7th grade reading level. Monthly (September-May) magazine. Pays on publication. Buys all rights. Byline given. Submit seasonal/holiday material 5 months in advance. SASE. Reports in 4-6 weeks.

Nonfiction: How-to, informational, interview, profile. Buys 18 mss/year. Query with brief outline and opening paragraphs. Length: 750-1,500 words. Pays 5¢/word minimum.

Columns/Departments: Lifestyle (worker profile), Offbeat Job (unusual occupation), New Careers. Buys 9/year. Query. Length: 300-1,500 words. Pays 4¢/word and up.

Tips: Articles must emphasize self-awareness and career exploration for students. "We like to see articles on specific occupations—preferably new or unusual—or on job getting and job holding. Follow-up activities are useful. Copy must be written simply, clearly and in a manner that appeals to young readers. We look for writing that excites the reader's imagination."

DAY CARE AND EARLY EDUCATION, Day Care Council of America, 711 14th St. NW, Washington DC 20005. Contact: LaVisa Wilson, editor (5086 Haley Center, Auburn University, Auburn AL 36849). For day care professionals—teachers, paraprofessionals, administrators, family day care providers and parents. Quarterly magazine. Circ. 20,000. Photocopied submissions OK—2 copies. SASE. Writer's guidelines.
Nonfiction: Activities, articles on model programs, child development, public policy for nonprofit and proprietary centers and day care homes. Avoid jargon. Use practical examples. No articles on child abuse. Length: 1,000-2,000 words. No payment.

Food and Drink

Magazines appealing to readers' appreciation of fine wines and fine foods are classified here. Journals aimed at food processors, manufacturers, and retailers will be found in Trade Journals.

BON APPETIT, Knapp Communications, 5900 Wilshire Blvd., Los Angeles CA 90036. Editor-in-Chief: Paige Rense. Managing Editor: Marilou Vaughan. Emphasizes food, cooking and wine "for affluent young, active men and women, interested in the good things of life." Monthly magazine; 120 pages. Circ. 1 million. Pays on acceptance for first rights. Submit seasonal/holiday material 6 months in advance. Reports in 6 weeks.
Nonfiction: William J. Garry, articles editor. How-to cook, and food articles with recipes. No historical food pieces. "We use only highly skilled food and wine writers." Query. Length: 2,000 words. Pay varies.

CHOCOLATE NEWS, The World's Favorite Flavor Newsletter, Zel Publishing Company, Box 1745, New York NY 10150. (212)750-9289. Editor: Boyd Hunter. Bimonthly newsletter covering chocolate; "we publish only chocolate-related information." Estab. 1980. Circ. 10,000+. Pays on publication. No byline given. SASE. Reports in 2 weeks. Sample copy $2.
Nonfiction: General interest; how-to (recipes); humor; and personal experience. "*Chocolate News* rarely accepts unsolicited material as the newsletter is compiled by our editor and the staff. We do accept and publish those chocolate-product recipes we deem unusual enough to interest our readership and are interested in personal-experience stories and chocolate-related humor. For these, we can pay an honorarium of $10 per piece or a one-year subscription to *Chocolate News*. The queries we would consider, without much encouragement to offer, are stories we could normally not cover ourselves, i.e., a chocolate tour of Los Angeles, California; or Chicago, Illinois. Payment would depend on what we published, but some agreement would be reached beforehand."
Tips: "We emphasize the infrequency with which we would use outside writers."

CUISINE, 52 Vanderbilt Ave., New York NY 10017. Editor: Patricia Brown. "The magazine of fine foods and creative living." Monthly. Study several issues of the publication and query first. SASE. Unsolicited mss not accepted.

EPICURE, Hazelton Publications, Ltd., York Square, 49 Avenue Rd., Toronto, Ontario, Canada M5R 2Y3. (416)968-3359. Editor: Diana Watts. Magazine published 10 times/year about food, wine and travel for well educated, sophisticated adults from 25-45 years old. Estab. 1980. Circ. 70,000. Average issue includes 10-12 articles and shorter pieces on motoring, and design. Pays on acceptance. Byline given. Offers 50% kill fee. Buys first North American serial rights. Phone queries OK. Submit seasonal material 5 months in advance. SAE with International Reply Coupon. Reports in 3 weeks. "American SASEs are not valid in Canada, and nothing will be returned or answered without an International Reply Coupon."
Nonfiction: Interview (with people in food and wine industries); nostalgia (great food stores, restaurants and hotels); profile; travel (either traditional destination pieces or articles having a well-defined and different approach; also travel to offbeat places); how-to (food pieces and wine guides); humor (whimsical pieces); new product (food, wines, spirits and kitchen equipment);

personal experience (visits to great restaurants); and photo feature (query first). "No scholarly 'wine snob' articles; no history of food or recipes for or stories about time-saving foods." Buys 5 mss/issue. Send query (preferably) or complete ms. Length: 1,000-3,000 words. Pays $250-1,200. Special issues on Christmas food and travel, Easter and Thanksgiving.

Photos: State availability of photos. Pays $5-15 for 4x5 b&w glossy prints. Pays $5-50 for color transparencies. Captions and model release required.

Columns/Departments: "Departments are all freelanced, though most are from regular contributors." Query with clips of previously published work. Length: 600-1,200 words. Pays $200-500.

Tips: "Study the magazine, then submit a query of about 200 words. We are looking for fresh approaches to the enjoyment of food and wine. We like personal reflections on great dinners, on restaurants, but we want them to contain a lot of specific information. The wine, spirits and foods should be accessible to our readers. We are interested in destination travel pieces, including destinations in North America. Writers should discuss food in the travel pieces whenever possible."

FINE DINING, Connell Publications, Inc., 7300 Biscayne Blvd., #333, Miami FL 33138. Editor: Sean O'Connell. Emphasizes restaurant dining and gourmet cuisine. Bimonthly magazine; 68 pages. Circ. 31,000. Pays on publication. Buys all rights. Byline given. Submit seasonal/holiday material 3 months in advance. Photocopied submissions OK. SASE. Reports in 2 months. Sample copy $2.41.

Nonfiction: Historical, interview, nostalgia, and travel, (prefer FL or NY vicinity), recipes, particularly from restaurants. Buys 2 mss/issue. Query with clips of published work. Length: 1,500-2,000 words. Pays $200.

Photos: Send photos with ms. Offers no additional payment for photos accepted with ms. Captions preferred.

Columns/Departments: *Taking Off With Fine Dining* (short travel getaways); *Cooking Class (recipes for complete meals); From the Grapevine* (international news and gossip about wine); and *Celebrity Cooks* (the favorite food and recipes of celebrities). Query.

Poetry: Humorous. Buys 5 mss/year. Limit: 3 submissions. Pays $10.

Fillers: Food quiz. Pays $10.

FOOD & WINE, Int. Review of Food & Wine Association, an affiliate of American Express Publishing, 750 3rd Ave., New York NY 10017. (212)599-5959. Editor: William Rice. Managing Editor: Warren Picower. Monthly magazine covering food and wine for "an upscale audience who cooks, entertains, dines out and travels stylishly." Circ. 300,000. Pays on acceptance. Byline or "signer" at the end is given. Pays 25% kill fee. Buys one-time rights. Submit seasonal/holiday material 6 months in advance. Simultaneous queries and photocopied submissions OK. SASE. Reports in 1 month; "letters of agreement are issued on every ms."

Nonfiction: Contact: Catherine Bigwood. How-to (equip or remodel a home or restaurant); interview/profile (of chefs, restaurateurs, or persons who entertain well and are especially knowledgeable in food and wine); and "very specialized articles on food and wine worldwide." Contact John and Elin Walker on all wine queries. Buys 75 mss/year. Query, "detailing an idea with a special slant for our magazine." Length: 1,000-2,200 words; "2,200-word maximum with or without a recipe." Pays $1,000-2,000, "depending on length, amount of work involved, stature of writer and quality."

Columns/Departments: Contact: Catherine Bigwood. Postcards (pegged to an event or place worldwide). Query. Length: 200-500 words. Pays $200.

Fillers: Short humor; and newsbreaks ("one-page articles of topical interest"). Buys 10/year. Length: 800 words. Pays $500-600.

Tips: "A number of pieces are bought cold from writers we are not familiar with."

GOURMET, 560 Lexington Ave., New York NY 10022. Managing Editor: Miss Gail Zweigenthal. For moneyed, educated, traveled, food-wise men and women. Monthly. Purchases copyright, but grants book reprint rights with credit. Pays on acceptance. Suggests a study of several issues to understand type of material required. Reports in 2 months. Query. "We prefer published writers, so if you haven't written for us before, you should enclose some samples of previous work." SASE.

Nonfiction: Uses articles on subjects related to food and wine—travel, adventure, reminiscence, fishing and hunting experiences. Prefers personal experiences to researched material. Recipes included as necessary. Not interested in nutrition, dieting, penny-saving or bizarre foods, or in interviews with chefs or food experts, or in reports of food contests, festivals or wine tastings. Buys recipes only as part of an article with interesting material to introduce them and make them appealing. "Gourmet Holidays" written by staff contributors only. The same is true for material including specific hotel or restaurant recommendations. Sophisticated, light, nontechnical.

Length: 2,500-3,000 words. Current needs include American regional pieces (no restaurants). Pays $650 minimum.

Poetry and Verse: Light, sophisticated with food or drink slant. Pays $50 minimum.

Tips: "Personal reminiscences are the easiest way to break in, since we always use staff writers when recommending hotels or restaurants. Our biggest problem with freelancers is that they are not familiar with our style or that they fail to treat their material with enough sophistication or depth. We don't want pieces which sound like press releases or which simply describe what's there. We like to really cover a subject and literary value is important. We'd very much like to see more regional American material. It seems to be much easier to get people traipsing around Europe."

GREAT RECIPES OF THE WORLD, Makes Simple Meals Great and Great Meals Simple, Digest Publishing, Inc., 333 Sylvan Ave., Englewood Cliffs NJ 07632. (201)569-2424. Editor: Holly Garrison-Repp. Monthly magazine covering food for Middle America. Estab. 1981. Circ. 350,000. Pays within 30 days of acceptance. Byline given. Pays 50% kill fee. Buys first North American serial rights. Submit seasonal/holiday material 6 months in advance. Simultaneous queries, and simultaneous and photocopied submissions OK. SASE. Reports in 3 weeks on queries; 1 week on mss. Sample copy 50¢.

Nonfiction: "This is a working magazine for people who shop in supermarkets. Category articles include recipes that are simple but interesting. Our magazine is meant to be taken into the kitchen, not left on the coffee table." No travel articles. Buys "up to 50 mss/year. Query with clips of published work. Length: 500-4,000 words. Pays $200 minimum.

Photos: "Writer is responsible for getting photos from food companies or other sources." State availability of photos. Reviews 2¼x2¼ color transparencies. Identification of subjects required. Buys one-time rights.

Tips: "I'm very interested in giving writers a first chance."

THE WINE SPECTATOR, Tasco Publishing Corp., 8170 Ronson Rd., Suite O, San Diego CA 92111. (714)569-7858. Editor: Gerald D. Boyd. Biweekly newspaper covering wine. Circ. 25,000. Byline given. Not copyrighted. Buys first rights. Submit seasonal/holiday material 3 months in advance. Simultaneous queries and photocopied submissions OK. SASE. Reports in 2 weeks. Sample copy $1; free writer's guideline.

Nonfiction: General interest (about wine or wine events); historical (on wine); how-to (build a wine cellar, taste wine, decant, etc.); humor; interview/profile (of wine; vinters, wineries); opinion; and photo feature. "Writers should query about special issues since we have an extensive list." No "winery promotional pieces, travel pieces or articles by writers who lack sufficient knowledge to write below just surface data." Buys 200 mss/year. Query or query with clips of published work. Length: 750 words maximum. Pays $50-150.

Photos: Send photos with ms. Pays $10 minimum for b&w contact sheets and 4x5 prints. Identification of subjects required. Pays one-time rights.

Tips: "A solid knowledge of wine is a must. Query letters help, detailing the story idea. New, refreshing ideas which have not been covered before stand a good chance of acceptance. *The Wine Spectator* is a consumer-oriented *newspaper*. We are not interested in trade stories, and brevity is essential."

WINE WORLD MAGAZINE, 6308 Woodman Ave., Suite 115, Van Nuys CA 91401. (213)785-6050. Editor-Publisher: Dee Sindt. For the wine-loving public (adults of all ages) who wish to learn more about wine. Bimonthly magazine; 48 pages. Buys first North American serial rights. Buys about 50 mss/year. Pays on publication. Send $1 for sample copy and writer's guidelines. No photocopied submissions. Simultaneous submissions OK, "if spelled out." Reports in 30 days. Query. SASE.

Nonfiction: "Wine-oriented material written with an in-depth knowledge of the subject, designed to meet the needs of the novice and connoisseur alike. Wine technology advancements, wine history, profiles of vintners the world over. Educational articles only. No first-person accounts. Must be objective, informative reporting on economic trends, new technological developments in vinification, vine hybridizing, and vineyard care. New wineries and new marketing trends. We restrict our editorial content to wine, and wine-oriented material. Will accept restaurant articles— good wine lists. No more basic wine information. No articles from instant wine experts. Authors must be qualified in this highly technical field." Length: 750-2,000 words. Pays $50-100.

WOMEN'S CIRCLE HOME COOKING, Box 1952, Brooksville FL 33512. Editor: Barbara Hall Pedersen. For women (and some men) of all ages who really enjoy cooking. "Our readers collect and exchange recipes. They are neither food faddists nor gourmets, but practical women and men trying to serve attractive and nutritious meals. Many work fulltime, and most are on limited budgets." Monthly magazine; 72 pages. Circ. 225,000. Pays on acceptance. Buys all rights. Submit seasonal/holiday material 6 months in advance. SASE. Reports in 2-8 weeks. Sample copy for large SASE.

Nonfiction: Expose, historical, how-to, informational, inspirational, nostalgia, photo feature and travel. "We like a little humor with our food, for the sake of the digestion. Keep articles light. Stress economy and efficiency. Remember that at least half our readers must cook after working a fulltime job. Draw on personal experience to write an informative article on some aspect of cooking. We're a reader participation magazine. We don't go in for fad diets, or strange combinations of food which claim to cure anything." Buys 50 mss/year. Query. Length: 50-1,000 words. Pays 2-5¢/word.

Photos: State availability of photos. Pays $5 for 4x5 b&w or color sharp glossy prints; $35 minimum for 35 mm, 2¼x2¼ and 4x5 transparencies used on cover.

Fiction: Humorous fiction, related to cooking and foods. Length: 1,200 words maximum. Pays 2-5¢/word.

Poetry: Light verse related to cooking and foods. Length: 30 lines. Pays $5/verse.

Fillers: Short humorous fillers. Length: 100 words. Pays 2-5¢/word.

General Interest

Publications classified here are edited for national, general audiences and carry articles on any subject of interest to a broad spectrum of people. Other markets for general interest material will be found in the Black, In-Flight, Men's, Newspapers and Weekly Magazine Sections, Regional magazines and Women's classifications in the Consumer section. Some company publications cover general-interest topics.

THE AMERICAN LEGION MAGAZINE, Box 1055, Indianapolis IN 46206.(317)635-8411. Editor: Dan Wheeler. Monthly. Circ. 2,600,000. Reports on submissions "promptly." Buys first North American serial rights. Byline given. Pays on acceptance. SASE.

Nonfiction: Query first, but will consider unsolicited mss. "Submit an outline query with no 'cutsey' stuff. Just get to the point. Relate your article's thesis or purpose, tell why you are qualified to write it, the approach you will take and any authorities you intend to interview. War remembrance pieces of a personal nature (vice historic in perspective) should be in ms form." Uses current world affairs, topics of contemporary interest, little-known happenings in American history and 20th century war-remembrance pieces. Buys 50 mss/year. Length: 2,000 words maximum. Pays $100-750.

Photos: Chiefly on assignment.

Poetry: Short, humorous verse. Pays $4.50/line, minimum $10.

Fillers: Short, tasteful jokes of interest to veterans, humorous anecdotes and epigrams. Pays $10-20.

Tips: "Query should include author's qualifications for writing a technical or complex article. Also include: thesis, length, outline and conclusion. Send a thorough query into which some thought has obviously gone. Submit material which is obviously suitable for us, showing that you have at least read a couple of issues. Attach a few clips of previously published material. Radiate professionalism from the first request for a copy of our writer's guidelines to the return of the author's release form. *The American Legion Magazine* is a general-interest publication which puts a premium on good taste and well-written articles about subjects of wide interest (subjects which have not been beaten to death by 10,000 writers)."

THE ATLANTIC MONTHLY, 8 Arlington St., Boston MA 02116. (617)536-9500. Editor-in-Chief: William Whitworth. For a professional, academic audience interested in politics, arts and general culture. Monthly magazine. Circ. 325,000. Pays on acceptance. Buys first North American serial rights. Pays negotiable kill fee "though chiefly to established writers." Byline given. Phone queries OK. Submit seasonal/holiday material 3-5 months in advance. Simultaneous and photocopied submissions OK, if so indicated. SASE. Reports in 2-6 weeks. Sample copy $1.75.

Nonfiction: General interest, historical, humor, interview, nostalgia, personal experience, personal opinion, profile and travel. Query with clips of published work or send complete ms. Length: 1,000-6,000 words. Pays $200 and up minimum/published page.

Fiction: Mainstream. Buys 2 mss/issue. Send complete ms. Length: 2,000-6,000 words. Pays $200 and up/page.

Poetry: Avant-garde, free verse, light verse and traditional. "No concrete or haiku poetry." Buys 2-3 poems/issue. Submit in batches of 8 or less. Length: 100 lines maximum. Pays $2 and up/line.

CAPPER'S WEEKLY, Stauffer Communications, Inc., 616 Jefferson St., Topeka KS 66607. (913)295-1108. Editor: Dorothy Harvey. Emphasizes home and family for readers who live in small towns and on farms. Biweekly tabloid. Circ. 414,000. Pays for poetry and cartoons on acceptance; articles on publication. Buys first North American serial rights. Submit seasonal/ holiday material 2 months in advance. SASE. Reports in 3 weeks, 2 months for serialized novels. Sample copy 45¢.
Nonfiction: Historical (local museums, etc.), inspirational, nostalgia, travel (local slants) and people stories (accomplishments, collections, etc.). Buys 2-3 mss/issue. Submit complete ms. Length: 700 words maximum. Pays $1/inch.
Photos: Purchased with accompanying ms. Submit prints. Pays $5 for 8x10 b&w glossy prints. Total purchase price for ms includes payment for photos. Limited market for color photos (35mm color slides, please).
Columns/Departments: Heart of the Home (homemakers' letters, recipes, hints), Hometown Heartbeat (descriptive). Submit complete ms. Length: 300 words maximum. Pays $2-10.
Fiction: Novel-length mystery and romance mss. Buys 2-3 mss/year. Query. Pays $200.
Poetry: Free verse, haiku, light verse, traditional. Buys 7-8/issue. Limit submissions to batches of 5-6. Length: 4-16 lines. Pays $3-5.
Tips: "Study a few issues of publication. Most rejections are for material that is 1) too long; 2) unsuitable (as short stories which we never use) or 3) out of character for our paper (too sexy, too much profanity, etc.). On occasion we must cut material to fit column space."

CHANGING TIMES, The Kiplinger Magazine, 1729 H St. NW, Washington DC 20006. Editor: Sidney Sulkin. For general, adult audience interested in personal finance, family money management and personal advancement. Monthly. Circ. 1,500,000. Buys all rights. Pays on acceptance. Reports in 1 month. SASE.
Columns/Departments: "Original topical quips and epigrams for our monthly humor feature, 'Notes on These Changing Times.' Almost all other material is staff-written." Pays $12.50 for Notes.

COMMENTARY, 165 E. 56th St., New York NY 10022. Editor: Norman Podhoretz. Monthly magazine. Circ. 50,000. Buys all rights. Byline given. "All of our material is done freelance, though much of it is commissioned." Pays on publication. Query, or submit complete ms. Reports in 1 month. SASE.
Nonfiction: Editor: Brenda Brown. Thoughtful essays on political, social and cultural themes; general, as well as with special Jewish content. Informational, historical and think articles. Length: 3,000 to 7,000 words. Pays approximately $75/printed page.
Fiction: Editor: Marion Magid. Uses some mainstream fiction. Length: varies.

EASY LIVING MAGAZINE, The Webb Co., 1999 Shepard Rd., St. Paul MN 55116. (612)647-7304. Editor: Don Picard. Managing Editor: Paula Kringle. "The publication's editorial goal is to inform and entertain the readers, with emphasis on the former." Emphasizes financial topics, personal improvement, lifestyles, family activities, consumer and food articles, plus occasional international travel; for an audience between 45 and 75; fairly high income. Distributed by Creative Marketing Enterprises, Inc. Quarterly magazine. Circ. 250,000. Pays on acceptance. Buys one-time rights and nonexclusive reprint rights. Submit seasonal/holiday material 1 year in advance. Photocopied submissions OK. SASE. Reports on queries in 3 weeks; on mss in 6 weeks. Free sample copy and writer's guidelines.
Nonfiction: Informational (about personal financial topics, real estate, taxes, new trends), profile (of unknown), and international travel. Query. Length: 800-1,500 words. Pays $200-500.
Photos: Photos purchased with or without accompanying ms (but only to illustrate ms already purchased). Pays $50 for 8x10 b&w glossy prints; $100 for color photos; $300 for color cover photos. 35mm acceptable. Captions required; model release preferred, "but in some circumstances may be dispensed with."

EASY TIMES MAGAZINE, Fantasma Productions, Inc. of Florida, 3713 South Dixie Hwy., West Palm Beach FL 33405. (305)832-6397. Editor: Debra Montgomery. Emphasizes general interest features for a young adult readership interested in the entertainment media, sports, health, travel and clothes. Quarterly magazine. Circ. 62,500. Pays on publication. Buys simultaneous rights, second serial (reprint) rights or first North American serial rights. Byline given. Submit seasonal/ holiday material 4 months in advance. Simultaneous, photocopied and previously published submissions OK. SASE. Reports in 6 weeks. Sample copy 9x12 SASE with 50¢; writer's guidelines for #10 SASE.

Nonfiction: General interest (music, sports, latest fads); how-to (make money, save money or get credit); interview (researched and highly informative interviews/profiles with famous young adults); profile (of young adults across the nation who are doing exciting things—changing laws, leading people, living new lifestyles—in all the fields of science, medicine, law and the arts); and travel (true accounts with story angle). Buys 20 mss/year. Query or submit complete ms. Length: 400-1,250 words. Pays $25-40.

Photos: "Each feature is illustrated in some way. Sending photos along makes our job easier." Submit photo material with accompanying ms. Pays $5-10 for 8x10 b&w prints. Captions preferred; model releases required. Buys all rights. Cover photos: pays $100/35mm color transparency.

Tips: "Keep the writing concise and light, with a strong identification for the young adult. Keep an 'up' attitude and entertain as well as inform. Articles that contain personal experiences as well as informative reading are great. Don't have to overdose with factual writing, but give the readers enough meat to chew on."

THE EVENT MAGAZINE, The Quarterly Documentary in Print, Four Points Productions, Inc., 9 E. 32nd St., New York NY 10016. (212)685-5255. Editor: Els Sincebaugh. Quarterly magazine. Estab. 1979. Circ. 85,000. Pays on publication. Byline given. Pays 50% kill fee. Submit seasonal/holiday material 3 months in advance. Photocopied and previously published submissions OK. Reports in 2 weeks. Sample copy $2.50; free writer's guidelines.

Nonfiction: General interest, interview/profile, opinion and technical. "All our issues are essentially one-shots because they deal with one topic each: state of religion, space shuttle, crime, education, audiovisual revolution, etc. Topics available by calling the magazine. Writers must be specialists in the field of inquiry. Our readers expect real substance, clear analysis of trends in the field of our inquiry. We need, for this new public, writing that has the precision and depth of a serious book—in clean, informative magazine style." Buys 50 mss/year. Query with clips of published work. Length: 1,200-2,000 words. Pays $350-750.

Photos: State availability of photos. Reviews b&w contact sheets. Captions, model releases, and identification of subjects required. Buys one-time rights.

Fiction: Same topics as nonfiction. Buys 8 mss/year. Query with clips of published work. Length: 1,200 words minimum, no maximum. Pays $100-800.

Poetry: "We need good poetry pertaining to our documentary topics, e.g., state of religion, crime, education, audiovisual revolution, etc."

Tips: "Contact us for topics of our documentaries."

EXCLUSIVELY YOURS, Patten Co., 161 Wisconsin, Milwaukee WI 53203. (414)271-4270. Editor: Wallace Patten. Magazine published 15 times/year covering general interest topics for upper-middle-class persons. Circ. 40,000. Pays on publication. Byline given. Buys first North American serial rights. Submit seasonal/holiday material 6 months in advance. Photocopied and previously published submissions OK ("indicate where and when published"). Reports in 1 month. Sample copy $1; writer's guidelines for business size SAE and 1 first class stamp.

Nonfiction: General interest ("anything of interest to upper-middle-class persons"). No mss pertaining to religion, politics or travel. Buys 45-50 mss/year. Query or send complete ms. Length: 1,000-2,000 words. Pays 5¢/word, $100 maximum.

Photos: State availability of photos or send photos with ms. Reviews any size b&w glossy prints. "We do not pay extra for photos." Captions and model release required. Buys one-time rights.

FAMILIES, Readers Digest, Pleasantville NY 10570. Editor: Jerry Dole. Monthly magazine emphasizing articles and features condensed from books, newspapers, magazines and television for parents, single parents and step parents. Estab. 1981.

Nonfiction: "Early issues will rely for the most part on previously published material. As our needs change, we will let freelancers know."

FAMILY IDEAS EXCHANGE, Families Helping Families, 7230 Mimosa Dr., Carlsbad CA 92008. (714)438-4190. Editor: John Ramuno. Monthly newsletter based on the theme: "No success in life can compensate for failure in the home." For parents, religious leaders, clinical psychologists and community leaders dealing with parents. Estab. 1980. Circ. 15,000. Pays on publication. Byline given. Buys first North American serial rights, second serial (reprint) rights, and "right to trade item with other publications." Submit seasonal/holiday material 2 months in advance. Simultaneous, photocopied, and previously published submissions OK. SASE. Reports in 1 month on mss. Sample copy free for business size SAE and 1 first class stamp.

Nonfiction: How-to. We're looking for "upbeat stories on family life that will give parents ideas on

how to have fun and hold activities with their children." Buys 12 mss/year. Send complete ms. Length: 500-1,000 words. Pays $25-200/article.
Columns/Departments: 24 columns on aspects of family living. "Sending a profile of a family for the department 'Special Families' is a good way to break in." Send complete ms. Length: 250-500 words. Pays $25/article or 5¢/word.
Fiction: Material for preschoolers to read aloud. Buys 12 mss/year. Send complete ms. Length: 500-1,000 words. Pays 5¢/word.
Poetry: Needs "upbeat poems encouraging positive feeling toward the family." Buys 12-36 poems/year. Submit maximum of 5 poems.
Tips: "Write as though you were writing a short, personal letter from your family to another family. We emphasize how-to articles on such topics as family activities, relationships and teaching moments. We especially need everyday traditions carried on within families. All articles fall under department heading with easily recognized logos and fast reading."

FAMILY WEEKLY, 641 Lexington Ave., New York NY 10022. Executive Editor: Arthur Cooper. Managing Editor: Tim Mulligan. No longer accepting unsolicited mss, but will consider queries. SASE.
Fillers: Will consider short jokes and humor items. Pays $10.

FORD TIMES, Ford Motor Co., Box 1509-B, Dearborn MI 48121. Managing Editor: Richard L. Routh. "Family magazine designed to attract all ages." Monthly magazine. Circ. 1,500,000. Buys first serial rights. Pays 30% kill fee. Byline given. Buys about 125 mss/year. Pays on acceptance. Free sample copy and writer's guidelines. Query with specific angle for exploring a town or city, region or point of interest. "Too many queries are general." Submit seasonal material 6 months in advance. Reports in 2 months. SASE.
Nonfiction: "Almost anything relating to American life, both past and present, that is in good taste and leans toward the cheerful and optimistic. Topics include motor travel, sports, fashion, where and what to eat along the road, vacation ideas, character sketches, big cities and small towns, the arts, Americana, and the outdoors. We strive to be colorful, lively and engaging. We are particularly attracted to material that presents humor, anecdote, first-person discourse, intelligent observation and, in all cases, superior writing. We are committed to originality and try as much as possible to avoid subjects that have appeared in other publications and in our own. However, a fresh point of view and/or exceptional literary ability with respect to an old subject will be welcomed." No reminiscences or nostalgia. Length: 1,500 words maximum. Pays $300 minimum for full-length articles.
Photos: "Speculative submission of good quality color transparencies and b&w photos with mss is welcomed. We want bright, lively photos showing people. We need publicity releases for people whose identity is readily apparent in photos. Writers may send snapshots, postcards, brochures, etc., if they wish."
Tips: "We also welcome fresh perspective on old subjects."

GEO, Gruner and Jahr, 450 Park Ave., New York NY 10022. (212)223-0001. Contact: David Maxey. Monthly magazine giving "a new view of our world in terms of science, environment, places and issues for sophisticated people with wide ranging international interests." Estab. 1979. Circ. 250,000. Pays on acceptance. Buys first North American serial rights. Submit seasonal material 4 months in advance. Simultaneous and photocopied submissions OK. SASE. Reports in 2 months. Sample copy $5.
Nonfiction: Exposé (of nongovernmental or political issues, such as a recent feature on dogfighting); historical (natural history); interview (of authorities in fields of *Geo*'s interest); opinion (essays); personal experience; photo feature (of recent topics, such as the tops of New York skyscrapers or machine parts as art); technical (frontiers of technology, science and medicine); and new scientific thinking, top level scientific research, such as studying the squid to learn about the human nervous system. "No pure travel pieces." Buys 5 mss/issue. "It is relatively rare that we use an unsolicited manuscript, and we do not encourage their submission. We prefer concise, clearly stated queries, explaining the story idea, the proposed approach and the photographic possibilities. Short clips from other publications are helpful. *Geo* stories often require a hefty investment, so it is unusual that we send an inexperienced writer on assignment." Query with clips of published work. Length: 3,500-8,000 words. Pays $2,500 minimum. "The writer does not need to be an authority but must get to the top people in science, the environment and current issues."
Photos: Editor: Alice George. State availability of photos. Reviews all sizes color prints and transparencies. Gives guarantee upon acceptance against $250/page upon publication. Captions and model release required. Buys one-time rights.
Columns/Departments: "Our new *Geo* sphere section, which contains only brief items, is open to

suggestions." Pays $10-100. Buys 1 ms/issue. Query with clips of previously published work. Length: 1,000-2,000 words. Pays $1/word.

Tips: "All story ideas must have a very strong photo tie-in. You need not take photos. *Geo* will provide the photographer."

GLOBE, Box 711, Rouses Point NY 12979. Executive Editor: Cliff Barr. "For everyone in the family over 18. *Globe* readers are the same people you meet on the street, and in supermarket lines, average hard-working Americans who prefer easily digested tabloid news." Weekly national tabloid newspaper. Circ. 2,000,000. Byline given. SASE.

Nonfiction, Photos and Fillers: Photo Editor: Alistair Duncan. We want upbeat human interest material, of interest to a national audience. Stories where fate plays a major role are always good. Always interested in features on well-known personalities, offbeat people, places, events and activities. Current issue is best guide. Stories are best that don't grow stale quickly. No padding. Grab the reader in the first line or paragraph. Tell the story, make the point and get out with a nice, snappy ending. Don't dazzle us with your footwork. Just tell the story. And we are always happy to bring a new freelancer or stringer into our fold. No cliques here. If you've got talent, and the right material—you're in. Remember—we are serving a family audience. All material must be in good taste. If it's been written up in a major newspaper or magazine, we already know about it." Buys informational, how-to, personal experience, interview, profile, inspirational, humor, historical, exposé, nostalgia, photo, spot news. Length: 1,000 words maximum; average 500-800 words. Pays $250 maximum (special rates for "blockbuster" material). Photos are purchased with or without ms, and on assignment. Captions are required. Pays $50 minimum for 8x10 b&w glossy prints. "Competitive payment on exclusives." Buys puzzles, quizzes.

Tips: "*Globe* is constantly looking for human interest subject material from throughout the United States and much of the best comes from America's smaller cities and villages, not necessarily from the larger urban areas. Therefore, we are likely to be more responsive to an article from a new writer than many other publications. This, of course, is equally true of photographs. A major mistake of new writers is that they have failed to determine the type and style of our content and in the ever-changing tabloid field, this is a most important consideration. It is also wise to keep in mind that what is of interest to you or to the people in your area may not be of equal interest to a national readership. Determine the limits of interest first. And, importantly, the material you send us must be such that it won't be 'stale' by the time it reaches the readers."

GOOD READING, Henry F. Henrichs Publications, Litchfield IL 62056. (217)324-2322. Monthly magazine. Circ. 12,000. Buys 100-125 mss/year. Buys first North American serial rights. Pays on acceptance. SASE.

Nonfiction: Accurate articles on current or factual subjects, adventure or important places. Material based on incidents related to business or personal experiences that reveal the elements of success in human relationships. Humorous material welcome. Uses some quizzes. All published material is wholesome and noncontroversial. "We particularly enjoy historical travel articles or foreign travel articles with clear, b&w glossy photos, and we avoid material that emphasizes the financial aspects of traveling." No biographical material; no "over emphasized or common topics." Length: 500-900 words. Pays $20-60.

Photos: Good quality b&w glossy prints illustrating an article are desirable and should be submitted with the article.

Fillers: 200-500 words. Pays $10-20.

Poetry: Does not pay for poetry, but publishes 4-5/month. Prefers pleasantly rhythmic humorous or uplifting material of 4-16 lines.

GOODSTAY, Hart, Inc., 22 Throckmorton St., Freehold NJ 07728. (201)780-4278. Publisher/Editor: S. Harvey Price. Executive Editor: Arthur S. Schreiber. Features human interest for patients in hospitals (adults only). "We want to help them 'escape' their present environment. Tell them how to buffer the time between discharge and return to normal routine." Monthly magazine. Circ. 100,000. Byline given. Pays on acceptance. Makes work-for-hire assignments. Phone queries OK. Submit seasonal/holiday material 3 months in advance. Simultaneous, photocopied and previously published submissions OK. SASE. Reports in 2 months. Writer's guidelines available—send SASE.

Nonfiction: General interest (hobbies, second careers, interesting careers, educational opportunities); how-to (understand everyday activity: weather forecasting, hobbies); travel; and photo feature. "No overseas travel, how to care for indoor plants, nostalgia. No discussion of diseases or disorders." Buys 6 mss/issue. Send complete ms. Length: 250-1,500 words. Pays $50-150.

Photos: State availability of photos or send photos with ms. High quality b&w. Offers no additional payment for photos accepted with ms. Captions preferred; model release required. Buys one-time rights.

Columns/Departments: Away (travel for one week or less), and Living Plants (how to care for seasonal plants, flowers in patient's room). Buys 2 mss/issue. Query. Length: 250-1,500 words. Pays $50-150.

Tips: Articles should be "upbeat diversion for adult patients, mostly in suburban communities. They can be on most any subject, except disease or disorders and religion, and we most appreciate those that are written very well, showing intelligence and a good sense of humor. A refreshing new glance at a familiar subject is what we are looking for. Try to imagine patient reading the article. If article is tedious or offensive in any way, or suggests hobbies that are too expensive or too strenuous for a convalescing person, it should not be submitted."

GREEN'S MAGAZINE, Green's Educational Publishing, Box 313, Postal Substation 40, University of Regina, Regina, Saskatchewan, Canada S4S 0A2. Editor: David Green. For a general audience; "the more sentient, literate levels." Quarterly magazine. Circ. 700. Buys first North American serial rights. Byline given. Buys 48 mss/year. Pays on publication. Sample copy $2. Reports in 2 months. Submit complete ms. SAE and International Reply Coupons.

Fiction: Mainstream, suspense, humorous, must have a realistic range in conflict areas. Slice of life situations enriched with deep characterization and more than superficial conflict. Avoid housewife, student, businessmen problems that remain "so what" in solution. Open on themes as long as writers recognize the family nature of the magazine. Length: 1,000-3,000 words. Pays $15-$25.

Poetry: Haiku, blank verse, free verse. Length: about 36 to 40 lines. Pays $2 to $3.

GRIT, 208 W. 3rd St., Williamsport PA 17701. (717)326-1771. Editor: Terry L. Ziegler. For a general readership of all ages in small-town and rural America. Tabloid newspaper. Weekly. Circ. 1,011,039. Buys first serial rights and second serial (reprint) rights. Byline given. Buys 1,000-1,500 mss/year. Pays on acceptance for freelance material; on publication for reader participation feature material. Sample copy $1; free writer's guideline. Reports in 2-4 weeks. Query or submit complete ms. SASE.

Nonfiction and Photos: National Editor: Naomi L. Woolever. Wants mss "about individuals and groups who are making important contributions to their neighbors, community, and/or the American way of life." Also wants patriotic stories which have an immediate tie-in with a patriotic holiday. Avoid sermonizing, but mss should be interesting and accurate so that readers may be inspired. Also mss about men, women, teenagers and children involved in unusual occupations, hobbies, athletic endeavors, or significant personal adventures. "*Grit* seeks to present the positive aspect of things." No mss promoting alcoholic beverages, immoral behavior, narcotics, unpatriotic acts. Wants good Easter, Christmas and holiday material. Mss should show some person or group involved in an unusual and/or uplifting way. "We lean heavily toward human interest, whatever the subject. Writing should be simple and down-to-earth." Length: 300-800 words. Pays 12¢/word for first or exclusive rights; 6¢/word for second or reprint rights. Photos purchased with or without ms. Captions required. Size: prefers 8x10 for b&w, but will consider 5x7. Transparencies only for color. Pays $25 for b&w photos accompanying ms; $60 for accompanying color transparencies.

Fiction and Poetry: Mrs. Fran Noll. Buys reprint or original material for fiction. Western, adventure, mystery, romance. Length: 1,500-12,000 words. Pays variable rates. "Fiction stories must be wholesome with interesting plots and believable characters. No explicit sex, profanity, drugs or immorality." Buys traditional forms of poetry and light verse. Length: preferably 20 lines maximum. Pays $6 for 4 lines and under, plus 50¢/line for each additional line.

Tips: "The freelancer would do well to write for a copy of our Guidelines For Freelancers. Everything is spelled out there about how-to's, submission methods, etc. All manuscripts should include in upper right-hand corner of first page the number of words and whether it's first or second rights."

HARPER'S MAGAZINE, 2 Park Ave., Room 1809, New York NY 10016. (212)481-5220. Editor: Lewis H. Lapham. 90% freelance written. For well-educated, socially concerned, widely read men and women and college students who are active in community and political affairs. Monthly. Circ. 325,000. Rights purchased vary with author and material. Buys approximately 12 non-agented, non-commissioned, non-book-excerpted mss/year. Pays negotiable kill fee. Byline given. Pays on acceptance. Sample copy $1.50. Will look only at material submitted through agents or that which is the result of a query. Reports in 5 weeks. SASE.

Nonfiction: "For writers working with agents or who will query first only, our requirements are: public affairs, literary, international and local reporting, humor." Also buys exposes and essays. Length: 1,500-6,000 words. Pays $250-1,500.

Photos: Art director: Sheila Wolfe. Occasionally purchased with mss; others by assignment. Pays $35-400.

Columns/Departments: Publishes pieces between 1,000 and 2,000 words as columns in both the front and back of the magazine. "These should be construed as topical essays on all manner of

subjects (politics, the arts, crime, business, etc.) to which the author can bring the force of passionately informed statements."
Fiction: On contemporary life and its problems. Also buys humorous stories. Length: 1,000-5,000 words. Pays $500-1,000.
Poetry: 60 lines and under. Pays $2/line.

IDEALS MAGAZINE, 11315 Watertown Plank Rd., Milwaukee WI 53226. Vice-President, Publishing: James A. Kuse. Editor: Colleen Gonring. Family-oriented magazine of general interest published 8 times/year with seasonal themes: Valentine's Day, Easter, Mother's Day, Father's Day, friendship, Americana, Thanksgiving Day and Christmas. Pays on publication. Byline given. Buys one-time rights. Submit seasonal material 6 months in advance. Photocopied and previously published submissions OK. Reports on mss in 6 weeks. Sample copy for 50¢ postage; free writer's guidelines for SASE.
Nonfiction: General interest (holidays, seasons, family, nature, crafts); nostalgia (family oriented); profile (notable people); and travel. Buys 8-10 mss/issue. Length: 2,000 words minimum. Query or send complete ms. Pays $100-300.
Photos: State availability of photos with ms. Buys one-time rights.
Fiction: Length: 2,000 words minimum.

IN-CRUISE NETWORK: EMBARK, GOLDEN ODYSSEY, SUNWAY, SEASCENE, TL Enterprises, Inc., 29901 Agoura Rd., Agoura CA 91301. (213)991-4980. Editor: Bob Howetts. Annual magazine covering luxury cruising. "We're geared to a generally upscale audience—those aboard luxury cruise ships. We're after general interest articles of appeal to that audience. All travel articles—e.g., ports of call—are prepared in-house." Estab. 1979. Pays on publication. Byline given. Offers ½ of agreed-upon fee for kill fee. Buys all rights. Submit all seasonal/holiday material by late winter. SASE. Reports in 6 weeks on queries and mss. Free writer's guidelines for legal size SASE and 1 first class stamp.
Nonfiction: General interest (of interest to upscale audience: the good life, fine food, clothing, etc.); and humor (pertaining to cruising). No travel or destination articles. Buys 10 mss/year. Query. Length: 500-1,500 words. Pays $150-300/article.
Photos: State availability of photos. Reviews 35mm color transparencies. Captions, model releases and identification of subjects required. Rights purchased are negotiable.
Fillers: Jokes, gags, and anecdotes. Buys 5 mss/year. Length: 25-100 words. Pays $25.
Tips: "Always query first. Remember that our magazines are already on board ship when our readers see them; don't try to sell them on the joys of cruising. We're after clever articles of interest to an upscale audience. These should be relevant for an entire year. We don't care what you've done in the past; we're interested in what you can do now. First-timers and veterans receive equal consideration. The section most open to freelancers is a common section that runs in all our books. Articles thus should not be specific about particular cruise lines or destinations; all those articles are handled in-house. Ours are class books, color throughout. Articles must be accompanied by color photos or illustrations. Can't emphasize enough that we are NOT a travel magazine. We carry articles of interest to travelers, but NOT destination pieces."

KNOWLEDGE, Research Services Corp., 5280 Trail Lake Dr., Drawer 16489, Ft. Worth TX 76133. (817)292-4272. Editor: Dr. O.A. Battista. For lay and professional audiences of all occupations. Quarterly magazine; 60 pages. Circ. 1000. Pays on publication. Buys all rights. Byline given. Submit seasonal/holiday material 6 months in advance. SASE. Reports in 2 weeks. Sample copy $2.
Nonfiction: Informational—original new knowledge that will prove mentally or physically beneficial to all lay readers. Buys 4 mss/issue. Query. Length: 1,500 words maximum. Pays $100 minimum.
Columns/Departments: Journal section uses maverick and speculative ideas that other magazines will not publish and reference.

LIFE, Time-Life, Time-Life Bldg., Rockefeller Center, New York NY 10020. (212)841-4661. Editor: Phil Kuhnhardt. Articles Editor: Robert E. Ginna, Jr. Monthly general interest picture magazine for people of all ages, backgrounds and interests. Circ. 1.2 million. Average issue includes 2 features and pictures with captions. Pays on acceptance. Byline given. Offers $500 kill fee. Buys first North American serial rights. Submit seasonal material 2 months in advance. Simultaneous and photocopied submissions OK. SASE. Reports in 6 weeks on queries; immediately on mss.
Nonfiction: "We've done articles on anything in the world of interest to the general reader and on people of importance. It's extremely difficult to break in since we buy so few articles. Most of the magazine is pictures. I'm lookin for very high quality writing. We select writers who we think

match the subject they are writing about." Buys 1-2 mss/issue. Query with clips of previously published work. Length: 2,000-5,000 words. Pays $3,000 minimum.
Columns/Departments: Portrait (photo and 1,200 word essay on a well-known person); "We like to do these on people in the news." Buys 1 ms/issue. Query with clips of previously published work. Length: 1,200 words. Pays $2,000.

MACLEAN'S, 481 University Ave., Toronto, Ontario, Canada M5W 1A7. (416)596-5328. Editor: Peter C. Newman. For news-oriented audience. Weekly newsmagazine; 90 pages. Circ. 650,000. Very occasionally buys first North American serial rights. Pays on acceptance. "Query with 200- or 300-word outline before sending material." Reports in 2 weeks. SAE and International Reply Coupons.
Nonfiction: "We have the conventional newsmagazine departments (science, medicine, law, art, music, etc.) with slightly more featurish treatment than other newsmagazines, and specialize in subjects that are primarily of Canadian interest. We buy short features, but most material is now written by staffers or retainer freelancers. Freelancers should write for a free copy of the magazine and study the approach." Length: 400-3,500 words. Pays $300-1,000.

MODERN PEOPLE, 11058 W. Addison St., Franklin Park IL 60131. Managing Editor: Larry Henkle. Emphasizes celebrities, consumer affairs and offbeat stories for white lower- and middle-class, blue-collar, non-college educated people with religious, patriotic, conservative background. Monthly magazine. Circ. 200,000. Pays on acceptance. Buys all rights. Byline given. Submit seasonal/holiday material 3 months in advance. Photocopied submissions OK. SASE. Reports in 2 weeks. Free sample copy and writer's guidelines.
Nonfiction: Exposé (consumer ripoffs); how-to (get rich, save money, be healthy, etc.); interviews (celebrities); stories on real people who do offbeat things (life style); photo feature (offbeat subjects), diets and the singles lifestyle. Buys 15 mss/issue. Query. Length: 150-500 words. Pays $25-150.
Photos: Photos purchased with accompanying ms. Pays $25-40 for 8½x11 b&w glossy prints; $50-200 for 8x5.5-pica color slides or transparencies. Total purchase price for ms includes payment for photos. Model release required.
Columns/Departments: Psychic Prediction, Real People, Celebrity Gossip and Dieting. Buys 10 mss/issue. Query. Length: 15-300 words. Pays $25-50. Open to suggestions for new columns/departments.
Tips: "We've just started two new publications and are particularly in need of stories on diet and the singles lifestyle."

NATIONAL ENQUIRER, Lantana FL 33464. Executive Editor: Michael Hoy. Weekly tabloid. Circ. 6,000,000. Pays on acceptance at executive level, or negotiable kill fee. Query. "Story idea must be accepted first. We're no longer accepting unsolicited mss and all spec material will be returned unread." SASE.
Nonfiction and Photos: Any subject appealing to a mass audience. Requires fresh slant on topical news stories, waste of taxpayers' money by government, the entire field of the occult, how-to articles, rags to riches success stories, medical firsts, scientific breakthroughs, human drama, adventure and personality profiles. "The best way to understand our requirements is to study the paper." Pays $325-500 for most completed features, plus separate lead fees; more with photos. "Payments in excess of $1,000 are not unusual; we will pay more for really top, circulation-boosting blockbusters." Uses single or series b&w and color photos that must be attention-grabbing. Wide range; anything from animal photos to great action photos. "We'll bid against any other magazine for once-in-lifetime pictures."

NATIONAL EXAMINER, Box 711, Rouses Point NY 12979. (514)866-7744. Editor-in-Chief: John Vader. For a contemporary, upbeat audience, 50% male. Weekly color tabloid. Pays on publication. Buys first North American serial rights. Phone queries OK. SASE.
Nonfiction: Ron Lee, features editor. Informational, diets, medical, how-to, personal experience, interview, profile, inspirational, humor, historical, exposé, nostalgia, photo feature, spot news and new product. Especially interested in pieces on ghosts, psychics and astrology. No cartoons. Query.
Photos: Purchased with or without accompanying ms. "Celebrities, off-beat shots, humorous and spot news photos always in demand." Send prints or transparencies; "b&w photos (b&w publication) preferred."

NATIONAL GEOGRAPHIC MAGAZINE, 17th and M Sts. NW, Washington DC 20036. Editor: Wilbur E. Garrett. Address queries to Senior Assistant Editor, James Cerruti. For members of the National Geographic Society. Monthly. Circ. 10,700,000. 50% freelance written. Buys first publication rights for magazine, with warranty to use the material in other National Geographic Society copyrighted publications for additional compensation. Pays 50% kill fee. Byline given. Buys 40-50 mss/year. Pays on acceptance. Reports in 2-4 weeks. Query by letter. Writers should study several recent issues of *National Geographic* and send for leaflets "Writing for *National Geographic*" and "*National Geographic* Photo Requirements." SASE. Sample copy $1.45.

Nonfiction and Photos: "First-person narratives, making it easy for the reader to share the author's experience and observations. Writing should include plenty of human-interest incident, authentic direct quotation, and a bit of humor where appropriate. Accuracy is fundamental. Contemporary problems such as those of pollution and ecology are treated on a factual basis. The magazine is especially seeking short American place pieces with a strong regional 'people' flavor. The use of many clear, sharp color photographs in all articles makes lengthy word descriptions unnecessary. Potential writers need not be concerned about submitting photos. These are handled by professional photographers. Historical background, in most cases, should be kept to the minimum needed for understanding the present." Length: 8,000 words maximum for major articles. Shorts of 2,000-4,000 words "are always needed." Pays $3,000-6,000 (and, in some cases, more) for acceptable articles. "A paragraph on an article idea should be submitted to James Cerruti, senior assistant editor. Please do not phone. If the idea is appealing, he will ask for a one- or two-page outline for further consideration." Photographers are advised to submit a generous selection of photographs with brief, descriptive captions to Bruce A. McElfresh, Assistant Editor.

Tips: "Send 4 or 5 one-paragraph ideas. If any are promising, author will be asked for a one- to two-page outline. Read the latest issues to see what we want."

THE NEW YORKER, 25 W. 43rd St., New York NY 10036. Editor: William Shawn. Weekly. Circ. 500,000. Reports in 2 months. Pays on acceptance. SASE.

Nonfiction, Fiction and Fillers: Single factual pieces run from 3,000-10,000 words. Long fact pieces are usually staff-written. So is "Talk of the Town," although ideas for this department are bought. Pays good rates. Uses fiction, both serious and light, from 1,000-6,000 words. About 90% of the fillers come from contributors with or without taglines (extra pay if the tagline is used).

THE OLD FARMER'S ALMANAC, Yankee, Inc., Dublin NH 03444. (603)563-8111. Editor: Judson D. Hale. Annual magazine; "a traditional collection of astronomical information, weather forecasts, and feature articles related to country living, for a general audience." Circ. 3.5 million. Pays on acceptance. Byline given. Rights purchased are negotiable. Submit material for the next year's issue by February. Photocopied submissions OK. SASE. Reports in 2 weeks. Sample copy free "while supply lasts."

Nonfiction: Historical, humor, biography, gardening, science and philosophy. "We want fresh and unusual material. This is a national magazine with a nationwide readership." Buys 5-10 mss/year. Query with clips of published work. Length: 2,000 words average. Pays $300 minimum.

Columns/Departments: Anecdotes and Pleasantries (short, self-contained items); and Rainy Day Amusements (puzzles, word games, quizzes). Buys 10 mss/year. Send complete ms. Length: 250-500 words. Pays $50.

Fillers: Anecdotes. Length: 300 words minimum.

PARADE, Parade Publications, Inc., 750 3rd Ave., New York NY 10017. (212)573-7000. Editor: Walter Anderson. Weekly magazine for a general interest audience. Circ. 23 million. Pays on acceptance. Kill fee varies in amount. Buys first North American serial rights. Submit seasonal/holiday material 2 months in advance. Photocopied submissions OK. SASE. Reports in 2 weeks on queries. Writer's guidelines free for 4x9 SAE and 1 first class stamp.

Nonfiction: General interest (on science, business or anything of interest to a broad general audience); interview/profile (of news figures, celebrities and people of national significance); and "provcative topical pieces of news value." No fashion, travel, poetry, quizzes, or fillers. Address queries to articles editor. Length: 800-1,500 words. Pays $1,000 minimum.

Photos: Send photos with ms.

Columns/Departments: Query or send complete ms. Length: 100-300 words. Pays $50-200.

Tips: "Send a well-researched, well-written query targeted to our market. Please, no phone queries. We're interested in well-written exclusive manuscripts on topics of news interest."

PEOPLE ON PARADE, Meridian Publishing Co., 1720 Washington Blvd., Box 2315, Ogden UT 84404. (801)394-9446. Editor: Dick Harris. For employees, stockholders, customers and clients of 2,000 business and industrial firms. 90% freelance written. Monthly magazine; 28 pages. Circ. 450,000. Pays on acceptance. Buys first North American rights. Byline given. Submit seasonal/holiday material 10 months in advance. SASE. Reports in 3-4 weeks. Sample copy 50¢; free writer's guidelines with SASE.

Nonfiction: "*POP* focuses on people—active, interesting, exciting, busy people; personality profiles on people succeeding, achieving, doing things." Humorous, informational, inspirational. "We want material from all regions of the country and about all types of people. Big-name writers are fine, but we know there is a lot of talent among the little knowns, and we encourage them to submit their ideas. We read everything that comes in, but writers will save their time and ours by writing a good, tantalizing query. *POP* has a strong family-community orientation. Without being maudlin or pious, we cherish the work ethic, personal courage and dedication to the American dream. So we look for material that reflects positively on the man/woman who succeeds through diligence, resourcefulness and imagination, or finds fulfillment through service to community or country. Tell us about people whose lives and accomplishments inspire and encourage others. We are still looking for personality profiles on successful people. We also have a Celebrity Chef page—we like featuring a well-known person with his favorite recipes. We like humor and nostalgia. We want tight writing, with lively quotes and anecdotes. We're overstocked with stories on handicapped people (blind TV repairmen, etc.) and senior citizens with new hobbies. Pictures should be fresh, sharp, unposed, showing action, involvement." Buys 10 mss/issue. Length: 400-1,000 words. Pays 10¢/word.

Photos: State availability of photos. Purchased with or without mss or on assignment. Captions required. Pays $20 for 8x10 b&w glossy print; $25 for 35mm, 2¼x2¼ or 4x5 color used inside; up to $300 for cover color. Model release required.

Columns/Departments: Wit Stop (humor pieces). Length: 600-800 words.

Fillers: "We welcome fillers and shorts with a humorous touch, featuring interesting, successful, busy people." Buys 1-2/issue. Length: 200-300 words. Pays 10¢/word.

Tips: "*People on Parade* has started a celebrity cooking section. We feature a celebrity each month with his/her favorite foods or recipes, meal planning, dieting tips, etc. Length should be 500-600 words, and we need at least one photo of the celebrity in the kitchen, dining, etc.—preferably a color transparency. Pay 10¢/word, $25 for a color photo, $20 for b&w. We pay on acceptance. Everything comes to us on spec. Send for a sample copy or guidelines so you know what we're looking for—our word limits, photo requirements etc. Don't send snap shots or manuscripts that are over our word limit. *Always include SASE.* No phone queries, please. We're always looking for humor pieces for our 'Wit Stop' feature. Subtle humor—not forced."

PEOPLE WEEKLY, Time, Inc., Time & Life Bldg., Rockefeller Center, New York NY 10020. Editor: Richard B. Stolley. For a general audience. Weekly. Circ. 2,300,000. Rights purchased vary with author and material. Usually buys first North American serial rights with right to syndicate, splitting net proceeds with author 50/50. Pays on acceptance. Query. SASE.

Nonfiction and Photos: "Nearly all material is staff-produced, but we do consider specific story suggestions (not manuscripts) from freelancers. Every story must have a strong personality focus. Payment varies from $200 for Lookouts to $1,000 for Bios. Photo payment is $200/page for b&w, minimum $75. Prefer minimum size of 8x10 from original negatives."

QUEST/82, 33 West 60th St., New York NY 10023. Executive Editor: Arnold Ehrlich. Senior Editors: Jonathan Black, Laura Bergquist. Emphasizes "the pursuit of human excellence for an educated, intelligent audience, interested in the positive side of things; in human potential, in sciences, the arts, good writing, design and photography. We have no connection with the feminist magazine, *Quest*." 10 issues/year; 112 pages. Circ. 300,000. Pays on acceptance. Buys all rights. Pays negotiable kill fee. Byline given. Submit seasonal/holiday material 4 months in advance. Photocopied submissions OK. Free writer's guidelines.

Nonfiction: Humor (short pieces deflating or satirizing world views or "good" things), interviews (with fascinating individuals in government, the arts, business, science), personal experience (adventures, unusual experiences), profiles (of risk-taking people, great craftsmen, adventurers), reviews (books, products, thoughts, places, etc.), and technical (new inventions, applications of science). Query with writing samples. Length: 500-2,500 words. Pays $600-1,200.

Tips: Read several issues of the magazine carefully before submission. Try to target ideas for specific magazines. Send queries rather than manuscripts.

READER'S DIGEST, Pleasantville NY 10570. Monthly. Circ. 18 million. Includes general interest features for the broadest possible spectrum of readership. "Items intended for a particular feature should be directed to the editor in charge of that feature, although the contribution may later be referred to another section of the magazine as seeming more suitable. Query in writing to: "The Editors" for original or reprint submissions. Buys all rights to original mss. Also buys second serial rights. Manuscripts cannot be acknowledged, and will be returned—usually within eight or ten weeks—only when return postage accompanies them." Byline given. Offers variable kill fee.

Nonfiction: "*Reader's Digest* is interested in receiving First Person articles. An article for the First Person series must be a previously unpublished narrative of an unusual personal experience. It may be dramatic, inspirational or humorous, but it must have a quality of narrative and interest comparable to stories published in this series. Pays $3,500 on acceptance. Address: First Person Editor.

Columns/Departments: "Life in These United States contributions must be true, unpublished stories from one's own experience, revelatory of adult human nature, and providing appealing or humorous sidelights on the American scene. Maximum length: 300 words. Address Life in U.S. Editor. Payment rate on publication: $300. True and unpublished stories are also solicited for Humor in Uniform, Campus Comedy and All in a Day's Work. Maximum length: 300 words. Payment rate on publication: $300. Address Humor in Uniform, Campus Comedy or All in a Day's Work Editor. Toward More Picturesque Speech: The first contributor of each item used in this department is paid $35. Contributions should be dated, and the sources must be given. Address: Picturesque Speech Editor. For items used in Laughter, the Best Medicine, Personal Glimpses, Quotable Quotes, and elsewhere in the magazine, payment is made at the following rates: to the *first* contributor of each item from a published source, $35. For original material, $15 per *Digest* two-column line, with a minimum payment of $35. Address: Excerpts Editor."

Tips: Send a good nonfiction general interest article, preferably in print and on a subject not recently discussed in *Reader's Digest*. "This is a digest of leading articles and books of general interest that have appeared in other publications, plus original articles developed by staff writers. We are also willing to consider a well developed query on an original article."

READERS NUTSHELL, Allied Publication, Drawer 189, Palm Beach FL 33480. Editor: Anita M. Kirchen. Bimonthly magazine with general interest articles for the middle class man and woman. Circ. 40,000. Pays on acceptance. Buys one-time rights. Phone queries OK. Submit seasonal material 6 months in advance. Simultaneous, photocopied and previously published submissions OK. SASE. Reports in 2 weeks on queries; in 1 month on mss. Sample copy $1; free writer's guidelines.

Nonfiction: General interest (non-controversial home, family, children, and safety article); humor; interview (of famous people); nostalgia. Buys 2 mss/issue. Send complete ms. Length: 400-800 words. Pays 5¢/published word. "We have seasonal special issues. Freelancers should limit submissions to 600 words, with good black and white photos."

Photos: Send photos with ms. Pays $5 for 8x10 b&w glossy prints. Captions preferred; model release required.

Fillers: Puzzles. Pays $10.

THE SATURDAY EVENING POST, The Curtis Publishing Co., 1100 Waterway Blvd., Indianapolis, IN 46202. (317)634-1100. Editor-in-Chief: Cory Ser Vaas M.D. Associated Editor/Publisher: Fredrick Birmingham. For general readership. Magazine published 9 times/year; 144 pages. Circ. 535,000. Pays on publication. Buys all rights. Simultaneous and photocopied submissions OK. SASE. Reports in 1 month. Free writer's guidelines for SASE.

Nonfiction: Curt Smith, nonfiction editor. How-to (health, general living); humor; informational; people; (celebrities and ordinary but interesting personalities); inspirational (for religious columns); interview; personal experience (especially travel, yachting, etc.); personal opinion; photo feature; profile; travel and small magazine "pick-ups." Buys 5 mss/issue. Query. Length: 1,500-3,000 words. Pays $100-1,000.

Photos: Photo Editor: Patrick Perry. Photos purchased with or without accompanying ms. Pays $25 minimum for b&w photos; $50 minimum for color photos. Offers no additional payment for photos accepted with mss. Model release required.

Columns/Departments: Editorials ($100 each); Food ($150-450); Medical Mailbox ($50-250); Religion Column ($100-250) and Travel ($150-450).

Fiction: Fiction editor: Ted Kreiter. Adventure; fantasy; humorous; mainstream; mystery; romance; science fiction; suspense; western; and condensed novels. Buys 5 mss/issue. Query. Length: 1,500-3,000 words. Pays $150-750.

Fillers: Fillers Editor: William Barton. Jokes, gags, anecdotes, cartoons, postscripts and short humor. Buys 1 filler/issue. Length: 500-1,000 words. Pays $10-100.

Tips: "Interested in topics related to science, government, the arts, personalities with inspirational careers and humor. We read unsolicited material."

SATURDAY NIGHT, Saturday Night Publishing Ltd., 69 Front St. E., Toronto, Ontario, Canada M5E 1R3. (416)362-5907. Editor: Robert Fulford. Managing Editor: Bernadette Sulgit. 70% freelance written. Emphasizes "politics, business/economics, lifestyles and the arts scene for readers 18 and up, with most ranging in age between 18-49; well-educated, with a high percentage in managerial/professional occupations." Monthly magazine; 88 pages. Circ. 120,000. Pays on acceptance. Buys first North American serial rights in French and English. Phone queries OK. Submit seasonal/holiday material 4 months in advance of issue date. Photocopied submissions OK. SAE and International Reply Coupons. Reports in 4 weeks. Sample copy $1.50.

Nonfiction: General interest (Canadian politics, business, the arts, academe, the media, sports); profiles (in-depth profiles of interest to Canadians). Buys 3 mss/issue. Query with samples and "outline that contains a strong point of view." Length: 1,000-4,500 words. Pays $500-2,000.
Fiction: "High quality writing by new or established writers. No restrictions on theme but should appeal to a fairly sophisticated audience who do not read literary journals. Buys 12 mss/year. Submit complete ms. Length: 1,500-4,000 words. Pays $1,200 maximum.

SATURDAY REVIEW, 150 East 58th St., New York NY 10155. Editor: Carll Tucker. Managing Editor: Henry Weil. "A review of literature and the arts." Monthly. 100 pages. Circ. 550,000. Pays on publication. Buys all rights. Pays one-third kill fee. Byline given. No writer's guidelines.
Nonfiction: Investigative pieces on the world of literature, and the arts. Buys 50 mss/year. Query with "a description of an article that has a point beyond 'isn't that interesting!' ". Length: 2,500 words. Negotiates pay.
Tips: "The writer must suggest that the material he or she is proposing will be of national interest and will not be the sort of common-garden reporting that any competent writer can produce."

SIGNATURE—The Diner's Club Magazine, 880 3rd Ave., New York NY 10016. Managing Editor: Horace Sutton. For Diners' Club members—"businessmen, urban, affluent, traveled, and young." Monthly. Circ. 625,000. Buys first rights. Buys 75 mss/year. Pays on acceptance. Write for copy of guidelines for writers. Submit seasonal material at least 3 months in advance. Returns rejected material in 3 weeks. Query. SASE.
Nonfiction: "*Signature* will accept its natural franchise entertainment in the broadest sense of the word." Articles on travel, dining out or eating in, sports, self-improvement, learning, exercise, cultural events. "Travel pieces require a *raison d'etre,* a well-defined approach and angle. Eschew destination or traditional travel piece. Feature articles run 2,500-3,000 words. Also buy shorter 800- 1,200-word pieces which are a slice of some travel experience. It's important that writer be familiar with our magazine." Pays $500 minimum for shorts; $800 minimum for longer articles.
Photos: "Picture stories or support are usually assigned to photographers we have worked with in the past. We rarely ask a writer to handle the photography also. But if he has photos of his subject, we will consider them for use." Pays $50 minimum/photo; $200/page.

SMILES MAGAZINE LIMITED, 3887A Bathurst St., Toronto, Ontario, Canada M3H 5V1. (416)751-2568, Monday-Friday 9-5; (416)635-1586, Tuesday-Thursday 7-10. Managing Editor: Paul McLean. Biweekly magazine covering general interest topics. "*Smiles* is a humorous, light-hearted consumer magazine aimed at 18-35-year-old men and women. It is more upbeat than *Reader's Digest* and aimed at a younger market than *Homemakers Magazine*." Estab. 1980. Circ. 75,000. Pays on publication. Buys first North American serial rights. Submit seasonal/holiday material 3 months in advance. Simultaneous queries and simultaneous submissions OK. "Writers responsible for queries whether by phone or mail." SASE. Reports in 3 weeks on queries; 2 weeks on mss. Sample copy free.
Nonfiction: General interest, humor, interview/profile, new product, photo feature, travel, and "lighthearted information and entertainment pieces. No articles of a distasteful or pornographic nature." Query. Length: 500-1,500 words. Pays 7-10¢/word.
Photos: Georges Haroushin, photo editor.
Columns/Departments: Politics, Business, Television, Media, Interviews, Profiles, Crossword Puzzles. Buys 260 mss/year. Query. Length: 500 words minimum. Pays 7-10¢/word.
Fiction: Adventure, experimental, fantasy, humorous, mainstream, mystery, romance, science fiction, serialized novels, suspense, and "lighthearted and humorous articles." Buys 85 mss/year. Query. Length: 1,500 words maximum. Pays 7-10¢/word.
Poetry: Humorous.
Fillers: Clippings, jokes, anecdotes, short humor and newsbreaks. Buys 260/year. Length: 250 words/maximum. Pays $25.
Tips: "Our magazine is lighthearted and humorous, but we cannot stress enough that we would like the writing to be solid and professional. Articles should appeal equally to both men and women."

THE STAR, 730 3rd Ave., New York NY 10017. (212)557-9200. Editor/Publisher: Ian Rae. Executive Editor: Phil Burton. Managing Editor: Leslie Hinton. 25-40% freelance written. "For every family; all the family—kids, teenagers, young parents and grandparents." Weekly tabloid; 48 pages. Circ. 3.5 million. Buys all rights, second serial (reprint) rights, and first North American serial rights. Pays negotiable kill fee. Byline given. Submit seasonal/holiday material 2-3 months in advance of issue date. SASE. Free sample copy and writer's guidelines.
Nonfiction: Malcolm Abrams, news editor. Exposé (government waste, consumer, education, anything affecting family) general interest (human interest, consumerism, informational, family

and women's interest); how-to (psychological, practical on all subjects affecting readers); inspirational (off-beat personal experience, religious, and psychic); interview (celebrity or human interest); new product (but not from commercial interests); personal experience (adventure, human drama, etc.); photo feature; profile (celebrity or national figure); travel (how-to cheaply); health; medical; and diet. Buys 50 mss/issue. Query or submit complete ms. Length: 500-1,200 words. Pays $50-1,500.

Photos: State availability of photos with query or ms. Pays $25-100 for 8x10 b&w glossy prints, contact sheets or negatives; $125-1,000 for 35mm color transparencies. Captions required. Buys one-time, or all rights.

Fillers: Statistical-informational. Length: 50-400 words. Pays $15-100.

SUNSHINE MAGAZINE, Henry F. Henrichs Publications, Litchfield IL 62056. (217)324-2322. 75% freelance written. For general audience of all ages. Monthly magazine. Circ. 90,000. Buys 125-150 mss/year. Buys first North American serial rights. Pays on acceptance. Sample copy 50¢; free writer's guidelines. Complimentary copy sent to included authors on publication. Submit seasonal material 6 months in advance. Reports in 1-2 months. Submit complete ms. SASE.

Nonfiction: "We accept some short articles, but they must be especially interesting or inspirational. *Sunshine Magazine* is not a religious publication, and purely religious material is rarely used. We desire carefully written features about persons or events that have real human interest—that give a 'lift'. No reminiscent articles or lead stories." Length: 100-300 words. Pays $10-50.

Columns/Departments: My Most Extraordinary Experience—Yes, It Happened to Me. Must be in first person, deal with a very unusual or surprising situation and have a positive approach. Length: 350-600 words. Payment: $25.

Fiction: "Stories must be wholesome, well-written, with clearly defined plots. There should be a purpose for each story, but any moral or lesson should be well-concealed in the plot development. Humorous stories are welcome. Avoid trite plots that do not hold the reader's interest. A surprising climax is most desirable. Material should be uplifting, and noncontroversial." Length: 400-1,000 words. Youth story: 400-700 words. Pays $20-100.

Poetry: Buys one poem for special feature each month. Payment: $15. Uses several other poems each month but does not purchase these. Prefers pleasantly rhythmic, humorous or uplifting material. Length: 4-16 lines.

Fillers: 100-200 words. Payment: $10.

Tips: "We prefer not to receive queries. Enclose a SASE, be neat, accurate and surprising, but wholesome."

TOWN AND COUNTRY, 717 5th Ave., New York NY 10022. Managing Editor: Jean Barkhorn. For upper-income Americans. Monthly. Not a large market for freelancers. Always query first. SASE.

Nonfiction: Department Editor: Frank Zachary. "We're always trying to find ideas that can be developed into good articles that will make appealing cover lines." Wants provocative and controversial pieces. Length: 1,500-2,000 words. Pays $300. Also buys shorter pieces for which pay varies.

US, Peters Publishing, 215 Lexington Ave., New York NY 10016. (212)340-7577. Editor-in-Chief: Richard Kaplan. Biweekly magazine featuring personalitites for readers from 18-34. Circ. 800,000. Pays on publication. Buys all rights. Simultaneous and photocopied submissions OK if so indicated. Reports in 2 weeks.

Nonfiction: General interest (human interest pieces with political, sports and religious tie-ins, fashion, entertainment, science, medicine); interview (of Hollywood figures); profiles (of trend and style setters, political personalities, sports figures) and photo feature (personalities, not necessarily celebrities). "We are looking for the odd story, the unusual story, featuring colorful and unusual people." Buys 5 mss/issue. Query with clips of previously published work. Length: 750-800 words. Pays $350-400.

Photos: State availability of photos. Reviews b&w prints. "Color is OK, but we will convert to black and white. We've got to have stories with pictures."

Tips: "We do what we call anticipatory journalism. That means you should peg the story to a specific date. For example, a story about an unusual track star would work best if published close to the date of the star's most important race. The editors work 3-4 weeks ahead on stories. Query with a one-paragraph description of the proposed subject."

WEEKLY WORLD NEWS, 600 S. East Coast Ave., Lantana FL 33462. (305)586-0201. Editor: Richard Long. Weekly tabloid edited for a general audience. Estab. 1979. Circ. 600,000. Pays on publication. Byline given sometimes. Buys one-time rights. Phone queries OK. Submit seasonal material 1 month in advance. Simultaneous and photocopied submissions OK. SASE. Reports in 2 weeks.

Nonfiction: Expose (of celebrities, something really astonishing and exclusive); interview (of TV and movie celebrities); humor (true-to-life); inspirational (miraculous recovery); personal experience (adventure, survival); and kids' news (precocious kids doing unusual things). No articles on health or medicine. Buys 10-20 mss/issue. Send complete ms. Length: 300-800 words. Pays $75-200.
Photos: Pays $35-150/5x7 and larger b&w glossy prints.
Columns/Departments: Weird World, Mad Mad World, and Health. Buys 3 mss/issue. Send complete ms. Length: 50-100 words. Pays $25 minimum.
Tips: "We like unique, unusual and adventurous survival stories. We also like humorous, wacky and offbeat stories and psychic and celebrity stories. Everything has to be true to life and should be accompanied by pictures."

Health

Nearly every publication is a potential market for an appropriate health article, particularly the General Interest publications. Bodybuilding magazines list in the Sport/Miscellaneous section.

ACCENT ON LIVING, Box 700, Bloomington IL 61701. (309)378-2961. Editor: Raymond C. Cheever. For physically disabled persons and rehabilitation professionals. Quarterly magazine; 128 pages. Circ. 19,000. Buys all rights unless otherwise specified. Byline usually given. Buys 20 mss/issue. Pays on publication. Sample copy $1.50; free writer's guidelines. Photocopied submissions OK. Reports in 2 weeks. SASE.
Nonfiction: Betty Garee, assistant editor. Articles about new devices that would make a disabled person with limited physical mobility more independent; should include description, availability, and photos. Medical breakthroughs for disabled people. Intelligent discussion articles on acceptance of physically disabled persons in normal living situations; topics may be architectural barriers, housing, transportation, educational or job opportunities, organizations, or other areas. How-to articles concerning everyday living giving specific, helpful information so the reader can carry out the idea himself. News articles about active disabled persons or groups. Good strong interviews. Vacations, accessible places to go, sports, organizations, humorous incidents, self improvement, and sexual or personal adjustment—all related to physically handicapped persons. Length: 250-1,000 words. Pays $200 maximum for feature articles with photos. Query.
Photos: Pays $15 minimum for b&w photos purchased with accompanying captions.
Tips: "We read all manuscripts so one writer won't get preferred treatment over another. Make sure that you are writing to disabled people, not a general audience. We are looking for upbeat material. Hint to writers: ask a friend who is disabled to read your article before sending it to *Accent*. Make sure that he understands your major points, and the sequence or procedure."

BESTWAYS MAGAZINE, Box 2028, Carson City NV 89701. Editor/Publisher: Barbara Bassett. Emphasizes health and nutrition. Monthly magazine; 120 pages. Circ. 180,000. Pays on publication. Buys all rights. Byline given. Submit seasonal/holiday material 6 months in advance. SASE. Reports in 6 weeks. Sample copy and writer's guidelines for SASE.
Nonfiction: General interest (nutrition, preventive medicine, vitamins and minerals); how-to (natural cosmetics, diet and exercise); personal experience; profile (natural life style); and technical (vitamins, minerals and nutrition). "No direct or implied endorsements of refined flours, grains or sugar, tobacco, alcohol, caffeine, drugs or patent medicines." Buys 6 mss/issue. Query. Length: 2,500 words. Pays $50.
Photos: State availability of photos with query. Pays $5 for 4x5 b&w glossy prints; $15 for 2¼x2¼ color transparencies. Captions preferred. Buys all rights. Model release required.

BODY FORUM MAGAZINE, Cosvetic Laboratories, 470 E. Paces Ferry Rd., Atlanta GA 30305. Editor: Louis Rinaldi. Emphasizes "health and beauty from standpoint of nutrition for an audience ranging from mid 20s to 60s with 50% below age 38, and educational levels from high school to post-grad. Average income is $16,000." Monthly magazine; 54 pages. Circ. 2.2 million. Pays on acceptance. Buys all rights. "We only assign articles to professional writers. Interested professionals can send queries." Free sample copy.
Nonfiction: Exposé, how-to, informational, interview and technical. Length: 1,500-1,800 words. Pays $500 minimum. Pays for "specialist articles at negotiated rates."

CORPORATE FITNESS NEWSLETTER, Corporate Fitness, Inc., 11570 Betlen Dr., Dublin CA 94566. (415)829-6151 or (415)285-2708. Editor: Bernard Levine. Monthly newsletter covering fitness for employees of large organizations with practical tips for working people. Estab. 1980. Circ. 2,000. Pays on publication. Byline given. Buys one-time rights, first rights or second serial (reprint) rights. Submit seasonal/holiday 3 months in advance. Previously published work OK. SASE. Reports in 2 weeks on queries; 1 month on mss. Sample copy 50¢ for #10 SAE and 1 first class stamp.

Nonfiction: Book excerpts (health or fitness related; how-to (exercise, stop smoking, organize company sports team); new product (health or fitness related-include photo); personal experience (life style changes, company fitness program); photo feature (exercise, fitness program); and recipes (easy and low-calorie). "Practical tips for working people. Must be simple, brief and clear. Holiday or seasonal material welcome." No "fad diets or exaggerated claims." Buys 20 mss/year. Query with clips of published work or send complete ms. Length: 250-750 words. Pays $15-50.

Photos: State availability of photos or send photos with accompanying ms. Pays $3-10 for 5x7 and 8x10 b&w prints. Caption and model release required. Buys one-time rights.

Fillers: Clippings and newsbreaks. "Health or fitness news only." Length: 75 words maximum. Pays $1-10.

Tips: "Be innovative, practical, factual, clear, brief, and upbeat. Newspaper style is fine, but articles *must* have substance. Read, understand, and obey Strunk & White."

HEALTH, 149 5th Ave., New York NY 10010. Editor: Hank Herman. For health-minded men and women. Magazine; 58 pages. Monthly. Circ. 850,000. Rights purchased vary with author and material. Pays 20% kill fee. Byline given. Pays within 8 weeks of acceptance. Sample copy $1.75. Reports in 6 weeks. Query with fresh, new approaches; strongly angled. Submit complete ms for first-person articles. SASE.

Nonfiction: Articles on all aspects of health: physical; sexual; mental; emotional advocacy articles; and medical breakthroughs. No "all about" articles (for example, "All About Mental Health"). Informational (nutrition, fitness, diet and beauty), how-to, personal experience, interview, profile, think articles, exposé; book reviews. Length: 500-2,500 words. Pays $200-1,000.

Tips: Query with one-page sample of style intended for the whole story, and include an outline and author's background. "We don't often buy an unsolicited story or idea, but we often get back to a freelancer who has queried us when we get an idea that they might be qualified to write."

HEALTHWAYS MAGAZINE, 2200 Grand Ave., Des Moines IA 50312. Editor: Tracy Mullen. 75% freelance written. Emphasizes chiropractic and a natural approach to health and well-being. Bimonthly magazine, 50 pages. Circ. 96,000. Pays on publication. Buys one-time rights. Byline given. Submit seasonal/holiday material 6 months in advance. Simultaneous submissions OK. SASE. Reports in 3 weeks. Free sample copy and writer's guidelines.

Nonfiction: General interest and humor, articles on chiropractic, nutrition, environment and exercise. Buys 30 mss/year. Query or submit complete ms. Length: 400-1,200 words. Pays $10-75.

Photos: State availability of photos with query or ms. Pays $2.50-25 for 8x10 b&w glossy prints and $15-50 for 35mm color transparencies. Captions required. Buys one-time rights. Model release required.

Poetry: Light verse. "No long, maudlin stuff." Buys 8 mss/issue. Length: 4-10 lines. Pays $1-5.

HEALTH SCIENCE, 698 Brooklawn Ave., Bridgeport CT 06604. Executive Director: Jo Willard. Emphasizes the importance of one's habits and one's environment to one's health. Bimonthly magazine; Circ. 6,000. Pays on publication. Buys second serial (reprint) rights, first North American serial rights and one-time rights. Byline given. Phone queries OK. Submit seasonal/holiday material 4 months in advance. SASE. Reports in 2 months. Free sample copy and writer's guidelines.

Nonfiction: "We particularly encourage how-to articles on such subjects as avoiding air and noise pollution, stress, radiation, etc.; living more healthfully on the job; relaxing; and making the home environment more healthful. We would like to see articles relating health to sound, light, climate, architecture, geography, interpersonal relationships and food. We are also interested in explanation and application of new discoveries in physiology, anatomy and biochemistry; reports of remarkable examples of the endurance and resiliency of the human organism; ideas and inspiration for conquering addictions and other habits; suggestions for organizing life so that it is more efficient, creative and satisfying; safety recommendations and advice for first aid. We do not want articles pertaining to religion or the occult." Buys 6 mss/issue. Send complete ms. Length: 1,200-3,600 words. Pays $20-50.

Photos: Send photos with ms. Pays $3-10 for negatives and 5x7 b&w glossy prints. Captions and model releases are required.

Columns/Departments: Buys 6/issue. Query with clips of published work. Length: 750-2,500 words. Pays $15-50.

Fillers: Newsbreaks and short humor on health. Buys 6/issue. Length: 100-600 words. Pays $5-15.

LET'S LIVE MAGAZINE, Oxford Industries, Inc., 444 N. Larchmont Blvd., Los Angeles CA 90004. (213)469-3901. Managing Editor: William Koester. Associate Publisher: Peggy Mac-Donald. Emphasizes nutrition. Monthly magazine; 160 pages. Circ. 140,000. Pays on publication. Buys all rights. Byline given unless: "it is a pen name and author fails to furnish legal name; vast amount of editing is required (byline is then shared with the editors of *Let's Live*); it is an interview by assignment in which 'questioner' is *LL (Let's Live)*." Submit seasonal/holiday material 4 months in advance. SASE. Reports in 3 weeks for queries; 6 weeks for mss. Sample copy $1.50; free writer's guidelines.

Nonfiction: Exposé (of misleading claims for benefits of drug products or food in treatment of physical disorders); general interest (effects of vitamins, minerals and nutrients in improvement of health or afflictions); historical (documentation of experiments or treatment establishing value of nutrients as boon to health); how-to (acquire strength and vitality, improve health of children and prepare tasty health-food meals); inspirational (first-person accounts of triumph over disease through substitution of natural foods and nutritional supplements for drugs and surgery); interview (benefits of research and/or case studies in establishing prevention as key to good health); new product (120-180 words plus 5x7 or 8x10 b&w glossy of product); personal experience ("my story" feature in conquering poor health); personal opinion (views of orthomolecular doctors or their patients on value of health foods toward maintaining good health); profile (background and/or medical history of preventive medicine, MDs or PhDs, in advancement of nutrition); and health food recipes ($5 on publication). "We do not want kookie first-person accounts of experiences with drugs or junk foods, faddist healers or unorthodox treatments." Buys 10-14 mss/issue. Query with clips of published work. Length: 750-2,000 words. Pays $50-250.

Photos: State availability of photos with ms. Pays $17.50-35 for 8x10 b&w glossy prints; $35-60 for 8x10 color prints and 35mm color transparencies. $150 for good cover shot. Captions and model releases required.

Columns/Departments: My Story and Interviews. Buys 1-2/issue. Query. Length: 750-1,200 words. Pays $50-250.

Tips: "We want writers with heavy experience in reseaching non-surgical medical subjects, interviewing authoritative MDs and hospital administrators, with the ability to simplify technical and clinical information for the layman. A captivating lead and structural flow are essential."

LIFE AND HEALTH, 6856 Eastern Ave. NW, Washington DC 20012. Editor: Joyce McClintock. Monthly. Circ. 50,000. Buys all rights. Byline given. Buys 100-150 mss/year. Pays on acceptance. Sample copy $1.25. Free writer's guidelines. Submit seasonal health articles 6 months in advance. Reports on material within 2-3 months. SASE.

Nonfiction: General subject matter consists of "short, concise articles that simply and clearly present a concept in the field of health. Emphasis on prevention; faddism avoided." Approach should be a "simple, interesting style for laymen. Readability important. Medical jargon avoided. Material should be reliable and include latest findings. We are perhaps more conservative than other magazines in our field. Not seeking sensationalism." Buys informational, interview, some humor. "Greatest single problem is returning articles for proper and thorough documentation. References to other lay journals not acceptable." Length: 1,500 words maximum. Pays $50-150.

Photos: Buys 5x7 or larger b&w glossy prints with mss. Color photos usually by staff ("but not always; we'll look at quality color slides from authors").

Poetry: Buys some health-related light verse. Pays $10.

Tips: "Information should be accurate up-to-date, footnoted (when applicable); from reliable sources, but written in lay person's language. Interesting style. Neat copy. Originals not photocopies. Prefer seeing finished manuscript rather than query."

LISTEN MAGAZINE, 6830 Laurel St. NW, Washington DC 20012. (202)723-0800. Editor: Francis A. Soper. 50% freelance written. Drug education for teens. "*Listen* is used in many high school curriculum classes, in addition to use by professionals: medical personnel, counselors, law enforcement officers, educators, youth workers, etc." Monthly magazine, 32 pages. Circ. 200,000. Buys all rights. Byline given. Buys 100-200 mss/year. Pays on acceptance. Free sample copy and writer's guidelines. Reports in 4 weeks. Query. SASE.

Nonfiction: Specializes in preventive angle, presenting positive alternatives to various drug dependencies. Especially interested in youth-slanted articles or personality interviews encouraging nonalcoholic and nondrug ways of life. Teenage point of view is essential. Popularized medical, legal and educational articles. "We don't want typical alcoholic story/skid-row bum, AA stories." Length: 500-1,500 words. Pays 3-6¢/word.

Photos: Purchased with accompanying ms. Captions required. Pays $5-15 per b&w print (5x7, but 8x10 preferred).

Poetry: Blank verse and free verse only. Very little inspirational poetry; short poems preferred. Pays $15 maximum.

Fillers: Word square/general puzzles are also considered. Pays $15.

Tips: "True stories are good, especially if they have a unique angle. Other authoritative articles need a fresh approach. In query, briefly summarize article idea and logic of why you feel it's good."

MUSCLE MAGAZINE INTERNATIONAL, Unit 1, 270 Rutherford Rd. S., Brampton, Ontario, Canada L6W 3K7. Editor: Robert Kennedy. 80% freelance written. For 16- to 30-year-old men interested in physical fitness and overall body improvement. Bimonthly magazine; 84 pages. Circ. 120,000. Buys all rights. Byline given. Buys 80 mss/year. Pays on acceptance. Sample copy $2. Reports in 2 weeks. Submit complete ms. SAE and International Reply Coupons.

Nonfiction: Articles on ideal physical proportions and importance of protein in the diet. Should be helpful and instructional and appeal to young men who want to live life in a vigorous and healthy style. "We would like to see articles for the physical culturist on muscle building or an article on fitness testing." Informational, how-to, personal experience, interview, profile, inspirational, humor, historical, exposé, nostalgia, personal opinion, photo, spot news, new product, merchandising technique articles. Length: 1,200-1,600 words. Pays 6¢/word.

Columns/Departments: Nutrition Talk (eating for top results) and Shaping Up (improving fitness and stamina). Length: 1,300 words. Pays 6¢/word.

Photos: B&w and color photos are purchased with or without ms. Pays $10 for 8x10 glossy exercise photos; $10 for 8x10 b&w posing shots. Pays $100 for color cover and $15 for color used inside magazine (transparencies).

Fillers: Newsbreaks, puzzles, jokes, short humor. Length: open. Pays $5 minimum.

Tips: "Best way to break in is to seek out the muscle-building 'stars' and do in-depth interviews with biography in mind. Picture support essential."

SAN DIEGO COUNTY'S HEALTH AND RESOURCE GUIDE, Community Resource Group, Box 81702, San Diego CA 92138. (714)299-3718. Editor: Patricia F. Doering. Annual book covering health for an audience consisting of anyone interested in health and community resources, and health professionals who purchase a specially bound version of the same guide. Circ. 5,000. Pays on publication. Buys all rights. Local phone queries OK. Submit seasonal material 3 months in advance. Previously published submissions OK. SASE. Reports in 3 weeks on queries; in 1 month on mss. Sample copy $1.25.

Nonfiction: General interest (cancer, heart disease, exercise); how-to (related to health, how-to enter a nursing home, prepare for old age, avoid catastrophic illness and related costs, etc.); interview; profile; new product; and photo feature (drugs, alcohol, mental health and aging). "Nothing offbeat. We are particularly in need of current statistical data which keeps the public informed of current trends and advances within both traditional medicine and holistic medicine. We are not a 'borderline' or 'off-beat' medical publication, but one wishing to keep the public informed of all areas in health." Query with clips of previously published work. Length: 300-1,500 words. Pays $25-500.

Photos: State availability of photos. Pays $25-100/8x10 b&w glossy print or contact sheets. Pays $50-200 for 5x7 and 8x10 color prints and negatives and 5x7 and 35mm color transparencies. Offers no additional payment for photos accepted with ms. Captions preferred; model release required. Buys all rights.

Fillers: Newsbreaks and photos. Length: 100-500 words. Pays 5-10¢/word.

Tips: "We are most open to freelancers in the areas of mental health, aging, child diseases, hospital stories, drugs and alcoholism."

SLIMMER, Health and Beauty for the Total Woman, Playgirl Magazine, 3420 Ocean Park Blvd., Santa Monica CA 90405. (213)450-0900. Editor: Katherine Vaz. Entertainment Editor: Neil Feineman. Monthly magazine covering health and beauty for "college-educated single or married women, ages 18-34, interested in physical fitness and weight loss." Estab. 1980. Circ. 250,000. Pays 30 days after acceptance. Byline given. Buys all rights. Submit seasonal/holiday queries 6 months in advance. Previously published submissions OK ("if author holds all rights we pay half"). SASE. Reports in 1 month. Writer's guidelines for business size SAE and 1 first class stamp.

Nonfiction: Diet, lifestyle and sports. "We look for well-researched material—the newer the better—by expert writers." No fashion or first-person articles. Buys 48 mss/year. Query with clips of published work. Length: 2,500-3,000 words. Pays $300-350.

Photos: State availability of photos.

Columns/Departments: Medicine; Image (beauty); and Diet Corner. Buys 36 mss/year. Query with clips of published work. Length: 900-1,000 words. Pays $200.

TRIO, Trio Publications, 1800 N. Highland Ave., Los Angeles CA 90028. (213)464-4626. Editor: Robert L. Smith. Bimonthly magazine devoted to holistic health for a family oriented readership. Estab. 1979. Circ. 60,000. Pays on publication. Buys first rights. Submit seasonal material 2½ months in advance. Photocopied submissions OK. SASE. Reports on queries in 3 weeks; on mss in 1 month. Sample copy $1.

Nonfiction: Exposé; general interest (family health, nutrition and mental health); how-to (exercise, diet, meditate, prepare natural food); inspirational (meditation); new product (exercise equipment, sports clothing, solar energy, natural foods); and personal experience. No articles on Eastern religions. Buys 48 mss/year. Length: 1,800-2,600 words. Pays $50-75.

Photos: Pays $15 maximum/5x7 and 8x10 b&w glossy print. Pays $25 maximum/5x7 and 8x10 color print. Offers no additional payment for photos accepted with ms. Captions and model release required. Buys one-time rights.

Columns/Departments: Buys 18 mss/year. Send complete ms. Length: 1,000-1,500 words. Pays $50-75.

VITAL, The Magazine of Healthful Living, Signature Publications, 2020 Dempster St., Chicago IL 60202. (312)973-7300. Editor: Karen G. Stevens. Bimonthly magazine covering health and fitness; "designed principally for women (secondary appeal to men and children) between 25-40." Estab. 1981. Circ. approx. 150,000. Pays on acceptance. Byline given. Pays 25-50% kill fee. Buys all rights or "liberal reassignment rights." Submit seasonal/holiday material 6 months in advance. Simultaneous queries and photocopied submissions OK. SASE. Reports in 1 month. Sample copy and writer's guidelines free.

Nonfiction: Contact: Karen Stevens, Rita Rousseau or Paul Kitzke. Book excerpts (general health and fitness, beauty and child-rearing advice, etc.); expos´ (far-reaching: FDA, for example; drug or diet plans); historical/nostalgic (occasional, folk medicine, old world medical quackery); how-to (lose weight; apply makeup, stay fit, etc); humor; interview/profile (usually health-oriented types or celebrities); new product (in the fitness field); personal experience and photo feature (food and fashion spreads). "We want practical information that readers can apply to their lives. Write in a popular, nontechnical informative style." "No highly technical medical papers." Buys 120 mss/year. Query with clips of published work. Length: 800-3,000 words. Pays $300-1,000.

Photos: Betty Petroski, photo editor. State availability of photos. Pays $75-500 for 35mm, 2¼x2¼, or large format color transparencies. Model releases and identification of subjects required. Buys one-time rights.

Columns/Departments: Looking Good (beauty and grooming—makeup, sun protection, hair dyes, male cosmetics); Shaping Up (general fitness, including seasonal tips); Food for Thought (nutrition, but not recipes); On Growing (child-rearing); Consumer Corner (sample subjects: advantages and disadvantages of generic drugs, the cost—efficiency of outpatient surgery, etc.). Buys 50 mss/year. Query with clips of published work. Length: 800-1,500 words. Pays $300-500.

Tips: "Submit thorough queries, i.e., concept, format, style. We want good idea of approach that will be taken. Mention of experts that will be consulted, places visited, etc., is a good idea, too. Also submit previous published work, especially in the health fitness field."

WEIGHT WATCHERS MAGAZINE, 575 Lexington Ave., New York NY 10022. (212)888-9166. Editor: Judith Nolte. Managing Editor: Linda Konner. Monthly publication for those interested in weight loss and weight maintenance through sensible eating and health/nutrition guidance. Circ. 700,000. Buys 3-5 mss/month. Pays on acceptance. Reports in 4 weeks. Sample copy and writer's guidelines $1.25.

Nonfiction: Subject matter should be related to food, health or weight loss, but not specific diets. Would like to see researched articles related to the psychological aspects of weight loss and control and suggestions for making the battle easier. Inspirational success stories of weight loss following the Weight Watchers Program also accepted. Length: 1,500 words maximum. Pays $200-600.

WELL-BEING MAGAZINE, Oak Valley Star Rt., Camptonville, CA 95922. (916)288-3251. Editor: David Copperfield. Reports on "do-it-yourself" health care techniques for readers interested in change for the better, for the individual and the planet. 24 page health care section in *Vegetarian Times.* Pays on publication. Byline given. Submit seasonal/holiday material 4 months in advance. Photocopied and previously published submissions OK. Reports in 1-2 months. Sample copy $2; free writer's guidelines with SASE.

Nonfiction: Reports on various health care techniques, alternative and traditional. Subjects include diet, massage, herbs, exercise, life styles, gardening, wild foods, holistic medicine, home birth, etc. How-to (use recycling methods, garden naturally, conserve, improve health); informational (effects of common foods, drugs, additives, flavorings, colorings); interviews (doctors, midwives, other health practitioners); personal experience (home remedies, home birth, new herbal uses); and technical (how to build health related devices, etc., for the home). Buys 6-8/issue. Length: 500-10,000 words. Pays $20-200.

Photos: Purchased with or without mss, or on assignment. Query. Send b&w glossy prints. Color transparencies by arrangement.

History

AMERICAN HERITAGE, 10 Rockefeller Plaza, New York NY 10020. Editor: Geoffrey C. Ward. Bimonthly. Circ. 125,250. Usually buys all rights. Byline given. Buys 20 uncommissioned mss/ year. Pays on acceptance. Before submitting, "check our five- and ten-year and annual indexes to see whether we have already treated the subject." Submit seasonal material 12 months in advance. Reports in 1 month. Query. SASE.

Nonfiction: Wants "historical articles intended for intelligent lay readers rather than professional historians." Emphasis is on authenticity, accuracy and verve. Style should stress "readability and accuracy." Length: 3,000-5,000 words.

Tips: "Our needs are such that the criteria for a young, promising writer are unfortunately no different than those for an old hand. Nevertheless, we have over the years published quite a few firsts from young writers whose historical knowledge, research methods and writing skills met our standards. Everything depends on the quality of the material. We don't really care whether the author is 20 and unknown, or 80 and famous."

AMERICAN HISTORY ILLUSTRATED, Box 1831, Harrisburg PA 17105. (717)255-7713. Editor: Patrick L. Faust. Aimed at general public with an interest in sound, well-researched history. Monthly except March and September. Buys all rights. Byline given. Pays on acceptance. Sample copy $2; free writer's guidelines. "Do not bind the manuscript or put it in a folder or such. Simply paperclip it. We prefer a ribbon copy, not a carbon or photocopy. No multiple submissions, please. It is best to consult several back issues before submitting any material, in order to see what we have already covered and to get an idea of our editorial preferences. Please include informal annotations and a reading list of materials used in preparing the article." Reports on queries in 2 weeks; mss in 2 months. Query and include suggestions for illustrations. "Prefer concise one-page summaries emphasizing article's unique properties. One or two sources to be used as research are helpful." SASE.

Nonfiction: US history from 1492 times to the Korean War. Topics include biographic, military, social, cultural and political. Need "more human interest material and detailed accounts of battles." Also covers the US in relation to the rest of the world, as in World Wars I and II. Style should be readable and entertaining, but not glib or casual. Slant generally up to the author. No shallow research or extensive quotation. Length: 2,500-5,000 words. Short features 1,500-2,000 words considered. Pays $50-350.

Photos: Occasionally buys 8x10 glossy prints with mss; welcomes suggestions for illustrations. Address to Frederic Ray, Art Director.

Tips: "Query first and be willing to submit on speculation. Be willing to revise if necessary."

THE AMERICAN WEST, Box 40310, Tucson AZ 85717. Managing Editor: Mae Reid-Bills. Editor: Thomas W. Pew, Jr. Published by the Buffalo Bill Memorial Association, Cody WY. Sponsored by the Western History Association. Emphasizes Western American history, the old and the living West. Bimonthly magazine; 80 pages. Circ. 75,000. Pays within 2-4 weeks of acceptance. Buys first North American periodical rights, plus anthology rights. Byline given. Submit seasonal/holiday material 6 months in advance. Photocopied submissions OK. SASE. Reports in 6-8 weeks. Free sample copy and writer's guidelines.

Nonfiction: Historical (lively, nonacademic, but carefully researched and accurate articles of interest to the intelligent general reader, having some direct relationship to Western American history); and pictorial feature (presenting the life and works of an outstanding Old Western painter or photographer). Length: approx. 3,000 words. Shorter regular features range from 850-1,000 words: "Gourmet & Grub" (historical background of a popular western recipe); "Shelters & Households" (history behind a Western architectural form); "Hidden Inns and Lost Trails" (history behind Western landmarks and places to stay—no commercial promotion). Pays $200-800.

Photos: Usually purchased with or without accompanying ms., or assigned. Captions required. Query. Also "Western Snapshots" ("submissions from readers of interesting old photos 'that tell a story of a bygone day'"). Pays $25 on acceptance.

Tips: "We strive to connect what the West was with what it is today and what it is likely to become. We seek dynamic, absorbing articles that reflect good research and thoughtful organization of historical details around a strong central story line. We define 'the West' as the United States west of the Mississippi River, and, in proper context, Canada and Mexico."

ART AND ARCHAEOLOGY NEWSLETTER, 243 East 39 St., New York NY 10016. Editor: Otto F. Reiss. For people interested in archeology; educated laymen, educators, some professional archeologists. Quarterly newsletter, 20 pages. Circ. 1,500. Buys all rights, second serial (reprint) rights. Buys 1-2 mss/year. Pays on publication. Sample copy to writer for $1.80 in 18¢ stamps. Photocopied or simultaneous submissions OK. Reports in 2 weeks. Query. SASE.
Nonfiction: "Ancient history, archeology, new discoveries, new conclusions, new theories. Our approach is similar to the way *Time Magazine* would treat archeology or ancient history in its science section. A lighter tone, less rigidly academic. Don't avoid mystery, glamour, eroticism. Primarily interested in Old World antiquity. No travel articles. Definitely not interested in Indian arrowheads, Indian pots, kivas, etc." Length: 400-2,500 words. Pays $20.
Photos: Offers no additional payment for photos purchased with accompanying ms. Pays $7.50 minimum for b&w glossy prints purchased without mss. Information (data) required for all b&w photos. No color. Will write own captions.
Tips: "Have a passionate, all-consuming interest in antiquity and archeology, be up on its history, and have a journalist's feel for what is interesting and intriguing. We are not interested in 'submission methods'. The techniques of writing are very secondary. If the writer has something intriguing to say, we can always fix up, or edit, the writing. Read books about archeology and ancient history so that you become something of an expert on the subject. Be prepared to give precise sources, with page and paragraph, for factual statements. Some freelance writers, pretending to submit nonfiction, invent their material. Altogether, dealing with freelance people in this field is more trouble than it is worth. But hope blooms eternal. Perhaps there's another enthusiast who sneaked his way into an Alexander's Tomb."

BRITISH HERITAGE, Incorporating British History Illustrated, Historical Times, Inc., Box 1831, Harrisburg PA 17105. (717)255-7755. Editor: Roy Baker. Bimonthly magazine covering British History up to and including the Korean War. "*British Heritage* aims to present aspects of Britain's history and culture in an entertaining and informative manner." Circ. 60,000. Pays on acceptance. Byline given. Makes work-for-hire assignments. Simultaneous queries and simultaneous submissions OK. SASE. Reports in 2 weeks on queries; 10 weeks on mss. Sample copy $3; free writer's guidelines for SAE and 1 first class stamp.
Nonfiction: Historical (British history). Though we insist on sound research for both historical and general interest articles, the sources need not be exclusively primary ones, especially where the field has been thoroughly covered by reliable scholars. We prefer a popular to a scholarly style, but no fictionalization. All thoughts and conversations must be borne out by memoirs or other sound evidence. We advocate simplicity and clarity of style, but not at the cost of over-simplification. Because of the great range of subject matter in Britain's 2,000 year history, we prefer to cover significant rather than trivial aspects of people, issues, events and places. We have, however, no bias against the little-known or controversial subject *per se* as long as it is interesting." No fiction, personal experience type articles, poetry or biography. Buys 36 mss/year. Query with clips of published work. Length: 1,000-5,000 words. Pays $65/1,000 words; $400 maximum.
Photos: State availability of photos or send photocopies. "We use our own photographers mainly, but like to consider work associated with British culture and history. Pays $20 maximum for color transparencies; $10 maximum for b&w prints. Captions and identification of subjects required. Buys one-time rights.
Tips: "No footnotes needed but sources are required. English style and spelling only. Please read the magazine for hints on style and subject matter. "Grab the readers' attention as early as possible, and don't be afraid to use humor, at least in the covering letter. We look for accurate research written in a flowing, interesting style with excellent opportunities for illustration. Provide a list of further reading."

CANADA WEST, Box 3399, Langley, British Columbia, Canada V3A 4R7. (604)534-8222. Editor-in-Chief: T.W. Paterson. 75% freelance written. Emphasizes pioneer history, primarily of British Columbia, Alberta and the Yukon. Quarterly magazine; 40 pages. Circ. 5,000. Pays on publication. Buys first North American serial rights. Phone queries OK. Previously published submissions OK. SASE. Reports in 2 months. Free sample copy and writer's guidelines.
Nonfiction: How-to (related to gold panning and dredging); historical (pioneers, shipwrecks, massacres, battles, exploration, logging, Indians and railroads). No American locale articles. Buys 28 mss/year. Submit complete ms. Length: 2,000-3,500 words. Pays 4¢/word.
Photos: All mss must include photos or other artwork. Submit photos with ms. Pays $5 maximum

for 5x7 or larger b&w glossy prints. Captions preferred. "Photographs are kept for future reference with the right to re-use. However, we do not forbid other uses, generally, as these are historical prints from archives."
Columns/Departments: Open to suggestions for new columns/departments.

CHICAGO HISTORY, Chicago Historical Society, Clark St. at North Ave., Chicago IL 60614. (312)642-4600. Editor-in-Chief: Fannia Weingartner. Emphasizes history for history scholars, buffs and academics. Quarterly magazine; 64 pages. Circ. 6,500. Pays on acceptance. Buys all rights, second serial (reprint) rights and one-time rights. Byline given. Ribbon copy preferred. SASE. Reports in 2 months. Sample copy $1; free writer's guidelines.
Nonfiction: Historical (of Chicago and the Old Northwest). "Articles should be well researched, based on original primary source material, analytical, informative, and directed at a popular audience, but one with a special interest in history." No articles on Frontier Chicago, Fort Dearborn or Chicago authors. Buys 4-5 mss/issue. Query. Length: 4,000 words maximum. Pays $75-250. Query should include a clear sketch, outline of the proposed article, with as many major points suggested as possible."
Tips: "The manuscripts we like best were usually done for a college or graduate school class."

CIVIL WAR TIMES ILLUSTRATED, Box 1831, Harrisburg PA 17105. (717)234-5091. Editor: John E. Stanchak. Magazine published monthly except March and September. Circ. 102,000. Pays on acceptance. Buys all rights, first rights or one-time rights, or makes work-for-hire assignments. Submit seasonal/holiday material 1 year in advance. SASE. Reports in 2 weeks on queries; in 1-2 months on mss. Sample copy $1.50; free writer's guidelines.
Nonfiction: Profile, photo feature, and Civil War historical material. "Positively no fiction or poetry." Buys 20 mss/year. Length: 2,500-5,000 words. Query. Pays $50-350.
Photos: Frederic Ray, art director. State availability. Pays $5-25 for 8x10 b&w glossy prints or 4x5 color transparencies.
Tips: "We're very open to new submissions. Querying us after reading several back issues, then submitting illustration and art possibilities along with the query letter is the best 'in.' Never base the narrative solely on family stories or accounts. Submissions must be written in a popular style, but based on solid academic research. Manuscripts are required to have marginal source annotations."

EL PALACIO, QUARTERLY JOURNAL OF THE MUSEUM OF NEW MEXICO, Museum of New Mexico Press, Box 2087, Santa Fe NM 87503. (505)827-2352. Editor-in-Chief: Richard L. Polese. Emphasizes anthropology, history, folk and fine arts, natural history and geography. Quarterly magazine; 48 pages. Circ. 2,500. Pays on publication. We hope "to attract more professional writers who can translate new and complex information into material that will fascinate and inform a general educated readership." Acquires all rights that can be reassigned to the writer. Byline given. Phone queries OK. Submit seasonal/holiday material 1 year in advance. Photocopied submissions OK. SASE. Reports in 4-6 weeks. Sample copy $2.50; free writer's guidelines.
Nonfiction: Historical (on Southwest; technical approach OK); how-to (folk art and craft, emphasis on the authentic); informational (more in the fields of geography and natural history); photo essay; anthropology. Buys 4 mss/issue. Send complete ms and writer's background and credentials. Length: 1,750-5,000 words. Pays $50 honorarium minimum.
Photos: Photos purchased with accompanying ms or on assignment. Captions required. Pays "on contract" for 5x7 (or larger) b&w photos and 5x7 or 8½x11 prints or 35mm color transparencies. Send prints and transparencies. Total purchase price for ms includes payment for photos.
Columns/Departments: The Museum's World, Photo Essay, Books (reviews of interest to *El Palacio* readers). Open to suggestions for new columns/departments.
Tips: "*El Palacio* magazine offers a unique opportunity for writers with technical ability to have their work reach publication and be seen by influential professionals as well as avidly interested lay readers. The magazine is highly regarded in its field. To break in, the writer should live in this region; have a good background in writing and the field written about; and have an eclectic approach in writing. Be able to communicate technical concepts to the average educated reader. We like to have a bibliography, list of sources, or suggested reading list with nearly every submission."

THE HIGHLANDER, Angus J. Ray Associates, Inc., Box 397, Barrington IL 60010. (312)382-1035. Editor: Angus J. Ray. Managing Editor: Ethyl Kennedy Ray. Bimonthly magazine covering Scottish history, clans, genealogy, travel/history, and Scottish/American activities. Circ. 21,000. Pays on acceptance. Byline given. Buys first North American serial rights or second serial (reprint) rights. Submit seasonal/holiday material 6 months in advance. Photocopied and pre-

viously published submissions OK. SASE. Reports in 1 month. Sample copy and writer's guidelines free.
Nonfiction: Historical/nostalgic. "No fiction; no articles unrelated to Scotland." Buys 20 mss/year. Query. Length: 750-2,000 words. Pays $50-100.
Photos: State availability of photos. Pays $5-10 for 8x10 b&w prints. Reviews b&w contact sheets. Identification of subjects required. Buys one-time rights.
Tips: "Submit something that has appeared elsewhere."

HISTORIC PRESERVATION, National Trust for Historic Preservation, 1785 Massachusetts Ave. NW, Washington DC 20036. Editor: Thomas J. Colin. A benefit of membership in the National Trust for Historic Preservation. Read by professional planners and preservationists but more importantly, by well-educated people with a strong interest in preserving America's architectural and cultural heritage. Bimonthly magazine. Circ. 150,000. Pays on publication. May buy all, second serial (reprint), or one-time rights. SASE. Reports in 2-4 weeks. Free writer's guidelines.
Nonfiction: "Willing to review queries from professional writers on subjects directly and indirectly related to historic preservation, including efforts to save buildings, structures and rural and urban neighborhoods of historical, architectural and cultural significance. No local history; must relate to sites, objects, buildings and neighborhoods specifically. Also interested in maritime and archeological subjects relating to heritage preservation. Indirectly related subjects OK, such as old-style regional foods, cultural traditions. Interesting, well-written feature stories with a preservation angle are sought. Most material prepared on a commissioned basis. Writer must be very familiar with our subject matter, which deals with a specialized field, in order to present a unique publication idea." Length: 1,000-2,500 words. Pays $600 maximum.
Photos: Query or send contact sheet. Pays $10-50 for 8x10 b&w glossy prints purchased without mss or on assignment; $40-70 for color.

JOURNAL OF GENEALOGY, Anderson Publishing Co., Inc., Box 31097, Omaha NE 68131. (402)554-1800. Editor-in-Chief: Robert D. Anderson. Emphasizes genealogy and history. Monthly magazine; 48 pages. Circ. 10,000. Pays on publication. Buys all rights. Submit seasonal/holiday material 4 months in advance. Previously published submissions OK. SASE. Reports in 6 weeks. Sample copy $3; writer's guidelines for SASE.
Nonfiction: Historical (on places or obscure pioneers, place names, etc.); how-to (new or different ways to trace ancestors, new ways to keep notes, or new ways to diagram a pedigree chart); interview (of well-known persons involved in genealogy); new product (about innovations in capturing, storing, indexing and retrieving data—such as computers and microfiche relating to historical or genealogical data); personal experience (must have profound impact on genealogical research, not articles on one family); personal opinion (must be in-depth and scholarly dealing with genealogy and/or history); profile; travel (genealogists like to combine a vacation with genealogical research); and scholarly (we need thought provoking articles on the science of genealogy and how it relates to other sciences). Buys 20 mss/year. Query. Length: 750-4,500 words; "longer considered, but need natural breaks for serialization." Pays 2¢/word.
Photos: Purchased with or without accompanying ms or on assignment. Captions required. Query. Pays $5-25 for 8x10 b&w photos. Model release required.
Columns/Departments: Society Station (help for genealogical and historical societies in their day-to-day activities, e.g., "How to Write a News Release" or "Should We File for Non-Profit Status?"). Query. Length: 750-2,000 words. Pays 2¢/word. Open to suggestions for new columns/departments.
Tips: "We want articles that will help the most people find the most genealogy. Always ask yourself, as we do, 'is it meaningful?' We need good articles on researching in foreign countries. Articles of this nature should include information on the location of all archives and other repositories of records and the procedures one uses to research in person and by mail."

MANKIND, The Magazine of Popular History, Mankind Publishing Co., 8060 Melrose Ave., Los Angeles CA 90046. (213)653-8060. Editor: Jared Rutter. Quarterly magazine covering history (also art, anthropology, related fields) in a non-academic manner for readers who are not specialists in the field. Circ. 25,000. Pays on publication. Byline given. Buys first North American serial rights. Submit seasonal/holiday material 6 months in advance. Simultaneous queries and previously published submissions OK. SASE. Reports in 3 weeks on queries; 1 month on mss. Sample copy $2.00; free writer's guidelines.
Nonfiction: Historical/nostalgic. Buys 20-25 mss/year. Query. Length: 1,000-5,000 words. Pays $50-150/article.
Photos: State availability of photos. Pays $150 for color cover; $25 each for other color shots. ("We have color only on front and back cover"); and $10 for each b&w print used.
Columns/Departments: Buys 10-12 mss/year. Query. Length: 500-1,500 words. Pays $50-100/article.

NORTH CAROLINA HISTORICAL REVIEW, Historical Publications Section, Archives and History, 109 E. Jones St., Raleigh NC 27611. (919)733-7442. Editor: Marie D. Moore. Emphasizes scholarly historical subjects for historians and others interested in history, with emphasis on the history of North Carolina. Quarterly magazine; 100 pages. Circ. 2,000. Buys all rights. Phone queries OK. SASE. Reports in 3 months. Free writer's guidelines.
Nonfiction: Mrs. Memory F. Mitchell, nonfiction editor. Articles relating to North Carolina history in particular, Southern history in general. Topics about which relatively little is known or are new interpretations of familiar subjects. All articles must be based on primary sources and footnoted. Length: 15-25 typed pages. Pays $10/article.

NORTH SOUTH TRADER, 8020 New Hampshire Ave., Langley Park MD 20783. (301)434-2100. Editor: Wm. S. Mussenden. For Civil War historians, collectors, relic hunters, libraries and museums. Bimonthly magazine; 52 to 68 (8½x11) pages. Circ. 10,000. Rights purchased vary with author and material. Usually buys all rights. Buys 70 mss/year. Pays on publication. Sample copy and writer's guidelines $1. Photocopied and simultaneous submissions OK. Reports in 2 weeks. Query first or submit complete ms. SASE.
Nonfiction and Photos: General subject matter deals with battlefield preservation, relic restoration, military artifacts of the Civil War (weapons, accoutrements, uniforms, etc.); historical information on battles, camp sites and famous people of the War Between the States. Prefers a factual or documentary approach to subject matter. Emphasis is on current findings and research related to the places, people, and artifacts of the conflict. Not interested in treasure magazine type articles. Length: 500-3,000 words. Pays 2¢/word. B&w photos are purchased with or without ms. Captions required. Pays $2.
Columns/Departments: Includes Relic Restoration, Lost Heritage and Interview. Length: 1,000-1,500 words. Pays 2¢/word.

OLD WEST, Quarterly Western Publications, Inc., Box 3338, Austin TX 78764. (512)444-3674. Editor: Pat Wagner. Byline given. See *True West*.

PAPERBACK QUARTERLY, (Journal of Mass-Market Paperback History), 1710 Vincent, Brownwood TX 76801. (915)643-1182. Editor: Billy C. Lee. For paperback collectors. Quarterly magazine; 60 pages. Circ. 300. Pays on publication. Buys all rights. Pays 50% kill fee. Byline given. Phone queries OK. Photocopied and previously published submissions OK. SASE. Reports in 4 weeks. Sample copy $2; free writer's guidelines.
Nonfiction: Historical (notes or articles on paperback publishers, paperback writers, paperback cover artists, and paperback distributors of used, rare or new paperbacks); interview (with paperback cover artists, paperback publishers, or paperback writers of new, used or rare paperbacks); and nostalgia (as related to the paperback industry of the 1940s-1960s). Buys 2-3 mss/issue. Send complete ms. Length: 1,000-2,000 words. Pays (1¢/word).
Photos: Send photos with ms. Uses 2x3 or 4x6½ b&w prints; offers no additional payment for photos. Captions required.
Columns/Departments: Notes & Queries (500-word ms concerning a paperback publisher, writer, cover artist or distributor, or any aspect of the paperback industry both current and old).

PERSIMMON HILL, 1700 NE 63rd St., Oklahoma City OK 73111. Editor: Dean Krakel. Senior Editor: Sara Dobberteen. For an audience interested in Western art, Western history, ranching and rodeo; historians, artists, ranchers, art galleries, schools, libraries. Publication of the National Cowboy Hall of Fame and Western Heritage Center. Quarterly. Circ. 25,000. Buys all rights. Byline given. Buys 12-14 mss/year. Pays on publication. Sample copy $3. Reporting time on mss accepted for publication varies. Returns rejected material immediately. Query. SASE.
Nonfiction: Historical and contemporary articles on famous Western figures connected with pioneering the American West; Western art; rodeo; cowboys; etc. (or biographies of such people); stories of Western flora and animal life; environmental subjects. Only thoroughly researched and historically authentic material is considered. May have a humorous approach to subject. Not interested in articles that reappraise, or in any way put the West and its personalities in an unfavorable light. No "broad, sweeping, superficial pieces; i.e., the California Gold Rush or rehashed pieces on Billy the Kid, etc." Length: 2,000-3,000 words. Pays $200 minimum.
Photos: B&w glossy prints or color transparencies purchased with or without ms, or on assignment. Pays according to quality and importance for b&w and color. Suggested captions appreciated.

TRUE WEST, Western Publications, Inc., Box 3338, Austin TX 78764. (512)444-3674. Editor: Pat Wagner. Monthly magazine. Circ. 90,000. Pays on acceptance. Buys first North American serial rights. Byline given. "Magazine is distributed nationally, but if not on the newsstands in a particular location will send sample copy for $1. Queries should give proposed length of article, what rights are offered, whether pix are available, and enough information for us to check our file for material covered or on hand. Example: an ageless query, 'Would you like an article on a mountain man?' Without his name, we simply can't say." SASE.

Nonfiction: "Factual accounts regarding people, places and events of the frontier West (1850-1910). Sources are required. If based on family papers, records, memoirs, etc., reminiscences must be accurate as to dates and events. Unless the author is telling of his/her own experiences, please use third person whenever possible; that is, give the people names: 'James Brown,' instead of Grandfather, etc. Family relationship can be stated at end. We strive for stories with an element of action, suspense, heroics and humor, but those about the better-known outlaws, Indians, lawmen and explorers will probably overlap material we have already run. At present we are receiving too much material from the 1920s, '30s and '40s. We regret that many first-hand accounts have to be returned because the happenings are too recent for us. We also receive considerable material which is good local history, but would have limited appeal for a national readership." Length: 750-5,000 words. Pays 3¢/word.

Photos: "We usually buy mss and photos as a package. Photos are returned after publication."

VIRGINIA CAVALCADE, Virginia State Library, Richmond VA 23219. Primarily for Virginians and others with an interest in Virginia history. Quarterly magazine; 48 pages. Circ. 13,000. Buys all rights. Byline given. Buys 15-20 mss/year. Pays on acceptance. Sample copy $1; free writer's guidelines. Rarely considers simultaneous submissions. Submit seasonal material 15-18 months in advance. Reports in 4 weeks to 1 year. Query. SASE.

Nonfiction: "We welcome readable and factually accurate articles that are relevant to some phase of Virginia history. Art, architecture, literature, education, business, technology and transportation are all acceptable subjects, as well as political and military affairs. Articles must be based on thorough, scholarly research. We require footnotes but do not publish them. Any period from the age of exploration to the mid-20th century, and any geographical section or area of the state may be represented. Must deal with subjects that will appeal to a broad readership, rather than to a very restricted group or locality. Articles must be suitable for illustration, although it is not necessary that the author provide the pictures. If the author does have pertinent illustrations or knows their location, the editor appreciates information concerning them." Length: approximately 3,500 words. Pays $100.

Photos: Uses 8x10 b&w glossy prints; color transparencies should be at least 4x5.

VIRGINIA MAGAZINE OF HISTORY AND BIOGRAPHY, Virginia Historical Society, Box 7311, Richmond VA 23221. Acting Editor: E. Lee Shepard. Quarterly for serious students of Virginia history. Usually buys all rights. Byline given. Pays on publication. Reports in 2 months. SASE.

Nonfiction: Carefully researched and documented articles on Virginia history, and well-edited source material relating to Virginia. Must be dignified, lucid and scholarly. Length: 1,500-15,000 words. Appropriate illustrations are used. Pays $2/printed page.

Tips: Articles should offer new information and fresh perspective—not simply retell a familiar story. Contributors should follow guidelines in University of Chicago's *Manual of Style*, and should probably consult a recent issue of the magazine to be familiar with specific style requirements. Footnoots should be typed double-spaced following text."

Hobby and Craft

Publications in this section gear toward collectors, do-it-yourselfers, and craft hobbyists. Look for publications for electronics and radio hobbyists in the Science classification. Magazines designed for owners of personal computers are in the Home Computing section.

AMERICAN BLADE, Beinfeld Publishing, Inc., 12767 Saticoy St., North Hollywood CA 91605. (213)982-3700. Editor: Wallace Beinfeld. For knife enthusiasts who want to know as much as possible about quality knives and edged weapons. Bimonthly magazine; 52 pages. Circ. 15,000. Pays on publication. Buys all rights. Submit seasonal/holiday material 6 months in advance. Previously published submissions OK. SASE. Reports in 6 weeks. Sample copy $1.50.

Nonfiction: Historical (on knives and weapons); how-to; interview (knifemakers); new product; nostalgia; personal experience; photo feature; profile and technical. Buys 6 mss/issue. Query with "short letter describing subject to be covered. We will respond as to our interest in the subject. We do not contract on the basis of a letter. We evaluate manuscripts and make our decision on that basis." Length: 1,000-2,000 words. Pays 5¢/word.

Photos: Send photos with ms. Pays $5 for 8x10 b&w glossy prints; $25-75 for 35mm color transparencies. Captions required.

AMERICAN BOOK COLLECTOR, 274 Madison Ave., New York NY 10016. (212)685-2250. Consulting Editor: Anthony Fair. Bimonthly magazine on book collecting from the 15th century to the present for individuals, rare book dealers, librarians, and others interested in books and bibliomania. Circ. 2,700. Pays on publication. Submit seasonal material 3 months in advance. Photocopied and previously published submissions OK. SASE. Reports in 2 weeks. Sample copy and writer's guidelines for $3.50.

Nonfiction: General interest (some facet of book collecting: category of books; taste and technique; artist; printer; binder); interview (prominent book collectors; producers of contemporary fine and limited editions; scholars; librarians); and reviews of exhibitions. "We absolutely require queries with clips of previously published work." Length: 1,500-3,500 words. Pays 5¢/word.

Photos: State availability of photos. Reviews b&w glossy prints of any size. Offers no additional payment for photos accompanying ms. Captions and model release required. Buys one-time rights.

Columns/Departments: Contact Daniel Traister. Book reviews of books on book collecting, gallery exhibitions.

Tips: "Query should include precise description of proposed article accompanied by description of author's background plus indication of extent of illustrations."

AMERICAN COLLECTOR, 100 E. San Antonio, Kermit TX 79745. Editor: Randy Ormsby. Managing Editor: Frank B. Knight. 80% freelance written. Emphasizes collecting for antique buffs, collectors of all kinds, dealers, and investors. Monthly tabloid; 48 pages. Circ. 100,000. Pays on publication. Buys all rights. Byline given. Submit seasonal/holiday material 3 months in advance of issue date. SASE. Reports in 1 month. Sample copy $1; free writer's guidelines.

Nonfiction: Exposé (fake collectibles and fake antiques); how-to (evaluate, protect an item, tips on finding or buying, and prices); interview; unusual collections and/or collectors; personal experience (related to collecting); and photo feature (related to collecting). No nostalgia pieces. Buys 100 mss/year. Submit complete ms. Length: 500-1,200 words. Pays $1/inch.

Photos: Submit photo material with accompanying ms. Pays $5 for 8x10 b&w glossy prints and $10-20 for 35mm or 2¼x2¼ color transparencies. Captions required. Buys all rights.

Tips: "When submitting, freelancers should include a complete package consisting of ms in final form, any illustrative material and proper captions for any photos. Always include a phone number for the editor's convenience. Before submitting, secure a copy of our Writer's Guide and study it carefully."

AMERICAN CRAFT, American Craft Council Publishers, 22 W. 55th St., New York NY 10019. Editor: Lois Moran. Senior Editor: Patricia Dandignac. Bimonthly. Circ. 38,000. Published by American Craft Council for professional craftspeople, artists, teachers, architects, designers, decorators, collectors, connoisseurs and the consumer public. Pays on publication. Free sample copy. Reports "as soon as possible." Query. SASE.

Nonfiction: Articles on the subject of creative work in ceramics, weaving, stitchery, jewelry, metalwork, woodwork, etc. Discussions of the technology, the materials and the ideas of artists working in the above media. Length: 1,700 words. Pays $200-300.

Photos: Pays $200, cover; $50, photos smaller than ½ page; $75, photos ½ page to full page; $100, one-page multiple-object shot; $150, spread; $100, photos using models (any size). Or pays day rate of $350 plus transportation, film and development.

AMERICAN INDIAN BASKETRY MAGAZINE, Box 66124, Portland OR 97266. (503)771-8540. Editor: John M. Gogol. Quarterly magazine about American Indian basketry for collectors, native Americans, anthropologists, craftspeople and the general public. Estab. 1979. Circ. 5,000. Pays on publication. Buys all rights. Phone queries OK. Simultaneous, photocopied and previously published submissions OK. SASE. Reports in 3 weeks. Sample copy $5.95.

Nonfiction: Historical (of American Indian basketry); how-to (step by step articles on how traditional baskets are made); interview (with basketmakers); profile (of basketmakers); photo feature (of collections and basketmakers); and technical. Buys 8 mss/year. Send complete ms. Pays $10-100.

Photos: Send photos with ms. Reviews 8x10 b&w glossy prints. Offers no additional payment for photos accepted with ms but will purchase individual photos also. Captions and model release preferred. Rights vary.

Tips: "To break in, be knowledgeable about the subject. Write interestingly about the life and craft of the basketmaker."

AMERICANA, 475 Park Ave., S., New York NY 10016. (212)686-6810. Editor: Michael Durham. Bimonthly magazine featuring contemporary uses of the American past for "people who like to adapt historical ways to modern living." Circ. 275,000. Pays on acceptance. Byline given. Buys all rights. Submit seasonal material 6 months in advance. SASE. Reports in 6 weeks. Sample copy $1.95; free writer's guidelines for SASE.
Nonfiction: General interest (crafts, architecture, cooking, gardening, restorations, antiques, preservation, decorating, collecting, people who are active in these fields and museums); and travel (to historic sites, restored villages, hotels, inns, and events celebrating the past). "Familiarize yourself with the magazine. You must write from first-hand knowledge, not just historical research. Send a well-thought idea. Send a few snapshots of a home restoration or whatever you are writing about." Especially needs material for Christmas and Thanksgiving issues. Buys 10 mss/issue. Query with clips of previously published work. Length: 2,000 words minimum. Pays $350 minimum.
Columns/Departments: On Exhibit (short piece on an upcoming exhibit, $75-350); How-to (usually restoration or preservation of an historical object, 2,000 words, $350); Sampler (newsy items to fit the whole magazine, 250 words, $50); In the Marketplace (market analysis of a category of historical objects, 4,000 words, $350); Book Reviews ($50-75); In the Days Ahead (text and calendar of events such as antique shows or craft shows, 200 words, $350).

THE ANTIQUARIAN, Box 798, Huntington NY 11743. (516)271-8990. Editor-in-Chief: Marguerite Cantine. Managing Editor: Elizabeth Kilpatrick. Emphasizes antiques and 19th-century or earlier art. Monthly tabloid magazine; 24-32 pages. Circ. 10,000. Pays on publication. Buys all rights. Pays 10% kill fee. Byline given. Submit seasonal/holiday material 3 months in advance. SASE. Reports in 6 weeks. Sample copy for SASE (8½x11, 98¢).
Nonfiction: How-to (refinish furniture, repair glass, restore old houses, paintings, rebind books, resilver glass, etc.); general interest (relations of buyers and dealers at antique shows/sales, auction reports); historical (data, personal and otherwise, on famous people in the arts and antiques field); interview; photo feature (auctions, must have caption on item including selling price); profile (wants articles around movie stars and actors who collect antiques; query); and travel (historical sites of interest in New York, New Jersey, Connecticut, Pennsylvania and Delaware). Wants no material on art deco, collectibles, anything made after 1900, cutesy things to 'remake' from antiques, or flea markets and crafts shows. Buys 6 mss/year. Submit complete ms. Length: 200-2,000 words. Pays 1¢/word.
Photos: Pays $.50-1 for 3½x5 glossy b&w prints. Captions required. Buys all rights. Model release required.
Fillers: Newsbreaks. Length: 100-200 words. Pays 1¢/word.
Tips: "Don't write an article unless you *love* this field. Antiques belong to a neurotic group. Collecting is a sickness as expensive as gambling, and twice as hard to break, because we are all content in our insanity. Don't write like a textbook. Write as though you were carrying on a nice conversation with your mother. No pretentions. No superiority. Simple, warm, one-to-one, natural, day-to-day, neighbor-over-coffee writing. If you don't follow the instructions regarding the SASE, don't expect a reply."

ANTIQUE & COLLECTORS MART, 15100 W. Kellogg, Wichita KS 67235. (316)772-9750. An antique investors marketplace. Publisher: William Bales, Jr. Pays on publication. Buys first rights. Photocopied submissions OK. SASE. Reports in 1 month. Free sample copy.
Nonfiction: Antique investment topics but must be educational and authenticated. No first-party stories. Prefers active current events, market trends, historical sites and items, etc. Buys 2-4 mss/issue. Query. Length: 500-1,000 words. Pays 50¢/column inch but special articles negotiable.
Photos: State availablity of photos. Pays $5 for 5x7 or 8x10 b&w glossy prints; $10 for 35mm color transparencies.
Columns/Departments: Market trends, book reviews, quality antique items, profile studies, historical places and up to date investment guides. Query. Open to suggestions for new columns/departments.
Fillers: Anecdotes, newsbreaks, auction reports, show reports and price reports. Length: 50-200 words. Pays 50¢/column inch.

ANTIQUE MONTHLY, Boone, Inc., Drawer 2, Tuscaloosa AL 35402. (205)345-0272. Editor/Publisher: Gray D. Boone. Senior Editor: Anita G. Mason. Monthly tabloid covering art, antiques, and major museum shows. "More than half are college graduates; over 27% have postgraduate degrees. Fifty-nine percent are in $35,000 and over income bracket. Average number of years readers have been collecting art/antiques is 20.5/years." Circ. 85,100. Pays on publication.

Buys all rights. Submit seasonal/holiday material 2 months in advance. Photocopied submissions OK. SASE. Reports in 1 month on queries and mss. Free sample copy.

Nonfiction: Historical/nostalgic (pertaining to art, furniture, glass, etc. styles); travel (historic sites, restorations); museum exhibitions; and book reviews. No personal material. Buys 60 mss/year. Length: 1,000-1,500 words. Pays $125 minimum/article.

Photos: "Black and whites stand a better chance of being used than color." State availability of photos. Reviews color transparencies and 5x7 b&w prints. "We rarely pay for photos; usually we pay only for costs incurred by the writer, and this must be on prior agreement." Captions required.

Tips: "Freelancers are important because they offer the ability to cover stories that regular staff and correspondents cannot cover."

THE ANTIQUE TRADER WEEKLY, Box 1050, Dubuque IA 52001. (319)588-2073. Editor: Kyle D. Husfloen. 75% freelance written. For collectors and dealers in antiques and collectibles. Weekly newspaper; 90-120 pages. Circ. 90,000. Buys all rights. Buys about 200 mss/year. Payment at beginning of month following publication. Free sample copy and writer's guidelines. Photocopied and simultaneous submissions OK. Submit seasonal material (holidays) 4 months in advance. Query or submit complete ms. SASE.

Nonfiction: "We invite authoritative and well-researched articles on all types of antiques and collectors' items and in-depth stories on specific types of antiques and collectibles. "We do not pay for brief information on new shops opening or other material printed as service to the antiques hobby." Submissions should include a liberal number of good b&w photos. Pays $5-50 for feature articles; $50-150 for feature cover stories.

Photos: Submit a liberal number of good b&w photos to accompany article. Uses 35mm or larger color transparencies for cover. Offers no additional payment for photos accompanying mss.

Tips: "Send concise, polite letter stating the topic to be covered in the story and the writer's qualifications. No 'cute' letters rambling on about some 'imaginative' story idea. Writers who have a concise yet readable style and know their topic are always appreciated. I am most interested in those who have personal collecting experience or can put together a knowledgeable and informative feature after interviewing a serious collector/authority."

ANTIQUES JOURNAL, Babka Publishing Co., Box 1046, Dubuque IA 52001. Emphasizes antiques and collecting for "experienced and incipient antiques collectors and dealers age 20-80 interested in learning the backgrounds of both the older antiques and the more recent collectible objects." Monthly magazine; 68 pages. Circ. 60,000. Pays on acceptance. Buys first North American serial rights. Byline given. Submit seasonal/holiday material 10 months in advance. SASE. Reports in 2-4 weeks. Sample copy $1.50.

Nonfiction: Historical; informational; interview (only occasionally); and nostalgia (if related to collectible objects of the 1920s-50s). Buys 100 mss/year. Query. Length: 300-2,000 words. Pays $45-130.

Photos: Uses 4x5 or 8x10 b&w glossy prints. Pays $20-35 for 35mm-4x5 color transparencies (for cover). Caption required. Offers no additional payment for b&w photos purchased with accompanying mss. Model release required.

ANTIQUES USA, Collector's Media Inc., Box 1068, Martinez CA 94553. (415)228-1838. Editor: John F. Maloney. Bimonthly covering antique collecting. "We cover the antiques marketplace and the collecting hobby, with a strong regional slant (regional interests, exhibits, auctions)." Circ. 110,000. Pays on publication. Byline given. Offers negotiable kill fee. Buys all rights. Submit seasonal/holiday material 2 months in advance. Simultaneous queries OK. SASE. Reports in 2 weeks. Sample copy for 9x12 SAE and 6 first class stamps; free writer's guidelines.

Nonfiction: Book excerpts (original research); expos´e (antique-related); humor (antique-related); interview/profile (of well-known dealer, curator or collector); personal experience (antique-related); photo feature (antique-related); and travel (historic towns, villages, restorations). No "nostalgia pieces, articles about recent 'collectibles.' Query. Length: 500-1,500 words. Pays $25-300.

Photos: State availability of photos. Pays $10-20 for 4x5 color transparencies; $5 maximum for 5x7 or 8x10 b&w prints. Caption, model release, and identification of subjects required.

Tips: "Query with a good solid, innovative story idea or new information about a specific kind of antique. One writer recently came up with the idea of interviewing dealers at antique shows for

---

Market conditions are constantly changing! If this is 1983 or later, buy the newest edition of *Writer's Market* at your favorite bookstore or use the back-of-the-book order form.

survey of market for a category of antique. Features and news are equally welcome. Human interest (quotes, anecdotes, people in photos) helps sell, as does a strong regional slant with *Antiques USA* issued in 5 regional editions, we are an unusually good prospect for freelancers, since we buy that much more material. But it must be top quality (photos and words)."

BANK NOTE REPORTER, Krause Publications, 700 E. State St., Iola WI 54945. (715)445-2214. Assistant to the Publisher: Bob Lemke. Monthly tabloid for advanced collectors who have chosen to invest in paper money Circ. 4,000. Pays on acceptance. Byline given. Buys first North American serial rights and first reprint rights. Submit seasonal material 4 months in advance. Simultaneous and photocopied submissions OK. SASE. Reports in 2 weeks. Free sample copy.
Nonfiction: "We review articles covering any phase of paper money collection including investing, display, storage, history, art, story behind a particular piece of paper money and the business of paper money." Buys 6 mss/issue. Send complete ms. Length: 500-2,000 words. Pays 3¢/word to first-time contributors; negotiates fee for later articles.
Photos: Pays $5 minimum for 5x7 b&w glossy prints. Captions and model release required. Buys first rights, and first reprint rights.

BOOK BUYER'S GUIDE/MARKETPLACE, Franklin Publishing Co., Box 208, East Millstone NJ 08873. Editor: Kevin K. Kopec. Emphasizes mail order book buying/collecting. Quarterly tabloid; 16 pages. Circ. 5,000. Pays on acceptance. Buys all rights. Byline given. Phone queries OK. Submit seasonal/holiday material 1 month in advance. Simultaneous, photocopied and previously published submissions OK. SASE. Reports in 2 weeks. Sample copy $1.25.
Nonfiction: General interest (buying by mail, sources, tips, reviews); how-to (collect, maintain old books); interview (publishers, authors); and new product (book reviews). Buys 5-6 mss/issue. Send complete ms. Length: 200-500 words. Pays 1¢/word-$5.
Fillers: Clippings and newsbreaks. Buys 8-10/issue. Length: 50-100 words. Pays 1¢/word.

THE BOOK-MART, Box 72, Lake Wales FL 33853. Editor: Robert Pohle. Publisher: Mae Pohle McKinley. 60% freelance written. Emphasizes book collecting and the used book trade. Monthly tabloid; 32 pages. Circ. 2,000. Pays on publication. Buys one-time rights. Submit seasonal/holiday material 6 weeks in advance. Simultaneous, photocopied and previously published submissions OK. SASE. Reports in 6 weeks. Sample copy for 35¢ in postage.
Nonfiction: "Especially need articles of interest to book dealers and collectors containing bibliographical and pricing data." Exposé (literary forgeries); general interest (articles about regional authors, especially those highly collected); historical (about books, authors, publishers, printers, booksellers); how-to (book conservation and restoration techniques, no amateur binding); interview (if in field of interest); nostalgia (articles about paper collectibles, especially those with pricing information); personal experience; and travel (literary landmarks). "No rambling accounts with no specific focus or articles about an unknown poet who has published his/her first book." Buys 3 mss/issue. Query. Length: 1,000-2,500 words. Pays 50¢/column inch.
Photos: State availability of photos with query. Pays $5 minimum for 5x7 or larger b&w glossy or matte finish prints. Buys one-time rights.
Columns/Departments: Books in Review. Query "unless of a timely nature." Pays 50¢/column inch.

COINS, Krause Publications, 700 E. State St., Iola WI 54945. (715)445-2214. Assistant to the Publisher: Bob Lemke. Monthly magazine about United States and foreign coins for all levels of collectors, investors and dealers. Circ. 30,000. Average issue includes 8 features.
Nonfiction: "We'd like to see articles on any phase of the coin hobby; collection, investing, displaying, history, art, the story behind the coin, unusual collections, profiles on dealers and the business of coins." Buys 8 mss/issue. Send complete ms. Length: 500-5,000 words. Pays 3¢/word to first-time contributors; fee negotiated for later articles.
Photos: Pays $5 minimum for b&w prints. Pays $25 minimum for 35mm color transparencies. Captions and model release required. Buys first rights and first reprint rights.

COLLECTIBLES AND ANTIQUES GAZETTE, 1133 71st St., Miami Beach FL 33141. (305)861-9732. Editor-in-Chief: Arthur Brickman. Managing Editor: Nettie Brickman. Emphasizes all collectibles and antiques including rare books. Monthly magazine. Circ. 5,000. Pays on publication. Buys all rights. Phone queries OK. Submit seasonal/holiday material 3 months in advance. Simultaneous and photocopied submissions OK. SASE. Reports in 4 weeks. Free sample copy and writer's guidelines.
Nonfiction: Sal Perrine, articles editor. Informational; historical; interview; nostalgia; personal opinion; photo feature; and technical. Buys 100-120 mss/year. Query or submit complete ms. Length: 300-1,500 words. Pays 3¢/word.

Photos: Lee Gottlieb, photo editor. Pays $2 for b&w photos. Captions required.
Fillers: Clippings, newsbreaks and short humor. Pays $1.

COLLECTOR EDITIONS QUARTERLY, 170 5th Ave., New York NY 10010. Editor: R. C. Rowe. For collectors, mostly 30 to 65 in any rural or suburban, affluent, area; reasonably well-educated. Published 5 times a year, quarterly with an annual issue. Circ. 90,000. Rights purchased vary with author and material. Buys all rights; first North American serial rights; first serial rights; second serial (reprint) rights; simultaneous rights. Buys 15-30 mss/year. "First assignments are always done on a speculative basis." Pays on acceptance. Will send sample copy to writer for $1. Photocopied submissions and simultaneous submissions OK. Query with outline. Reports in 1 month. SASE.
Nonfiction: "Short features about collecting, written in tight, newsy style. We specialize in contemporary (postwar) collectibles. Particularly interested in items affected by scarcity." Informational, how-to, interview, profile, exposé, nostalgia. Length: 500-2,500 words. Pays $50-150. Columns cover stamps, cars, porcelains, glass, western art and graphics. Length: 750 words. Pays $75.
Photos: B&w and color photos purchased with accompanying ms with no additional payment. Also purchased without ms and on assignment. Captions are required. "Wants clear, distinct, full-frame image that says something." Pays $10-50.

COLLECTORS NEWS, Box 156, 606 8th St., Grundy Center IA 50638. (319)824-5456. Editor: Mary E. Croker. For dealers in, and collectors of, antiques. Monthly tabloid newspaper; 80-104 pages. Circ. 30,000. Buys 60 mss/year. Byline given. Pays on publication. Free sample copy. Submit seasonal material (holidays) 2 months in advance. Reports in 4 weeks. Query or submit complete ms. SASE.
Nonfiction: Only factual articles pertaining to some phase of collecting or interesting collections. Informational; profile; nostalgia. Length: 1,200 words minimum; 1,600 words average. Pays 50¢/column inch.
Photos: Offers no additional payment for b&w photos used with mss. Captions required.
Tips: "A freelancer can best contribute by writing for our writers guidelines and a sample copy of our paper to see the length of articles, our style, type of article needed, or where he could fill a gap. He might also ask what subject matter we are in need of at the time and should tell us what subjects he could cover in the collecting field."

CRAFTS 'N THINGS, 14 Main St., Park Ridge IL 60068. (312)825-2161. Editor: Nancy Tosh. Assistant Editor: Jackie Thielen. Bimonthly magazine covering crafts for "mostly women, around age 40." Circ. 274,000. Pays on publication. Byline, photo and brief bio given. Buys one-time rights. Submit seasonal/holiday material 6 months in advance. Simultaneous queries, and photocopied and previously published submissions OK ("if so indicated"). SASE. Reports in 1 month. Free sample copy.
Nonfiction: How-to (do a craft project). Buys 12-14 mss/year. Query with clips of published work and photos ("will be returned"). Length: 1-5 magazine pages. Pays $50-200, "depending on how much staff work is required."
Photos: "Submit photos only as part of query to decide if project will be used."
Tips: "We're looking harder for people who can craft than people who can write."

CREATIVE CRAFTS, Carsten's Publications, Inc., Box 700, Newton NJ 07860. Managing Editor: Wendie R. Blanchard. 80-90% freelance written. Emphasizes crafts for the serious adult hobbyist. Bimonthly magazine; 76 pages. Circ. 100,000. Pays on publication. Buys all rights. Byline given. Submit seasonal/holiday material 7 months in advance. SASE. Reports in 4 weeks. Mss cannot be considered unless accompanied by photos of completed project. Sample copy $1; free writer's guidelines.
Nonfiction: How-to (step-by-step of specific projects or general techniques; instructions must be clearly written and accompanied by b&w procedural photos and/or drawings). Buys 50-60 mss/year. Query. Length: 1,200 words average. Pays $50/magazine page. No human interest articles.
Photos: Purchased with accompanying ms.
Columns/Departments: Going Places (articles dealing with annual fairs, craft "villages" or museums of special interest to craft enthusiasts). Buys 1 ms/issue. Query. Length: 1,200 words average. Pays $50/magazine page without advertising; $25/page mixed. Open to suggestions for new columns/departments.
Tips: "Articles written by knowledgable craftsmen covering projects that can be done at home. Our need is for quality crafts that offer some challenge to the hobbyist. Whenever possible, send good clear photos, drawings and instructions."

EARLY AMERICAN LIFE, Early American Society, Box 1831, Harrisburg PA 17105. Editor: Frances Carnahan. 70% freelance written. For "people who are interested in capturing the warmth and beauty of the 1600 to 1850 period and using it in their homes and lives today. They are interested in arts, crafts, travel, restoration, collecting." Bimonthly magazine; 100 pages. Circ. 400,000. Buys all rights. Buys 50 mss/year. Pays on acceptance. Free sample copy and writer's guidelines. Photocopied submissions OK. Reports in 1 month. Query or submit complete ms. SASE.

Nonfiction: "Social history (the story of the people, not epic heroes and battles); crafts such as woodworking and needlepoint; travel to historic sites; country inns; antiques and reproductions; refinishing and restoration; architecture and decorating. We try to entertain as we inform, but always attempt to give the reader something he can do. While we're always on the lookout for good pieces on any of our subjects, the 'travel to historic sites' theme is most frequently submitted. Would like to see more how-to-do-it (well-illustrated) on how real people did something great to their homes." Length: 750-3,000 words. Pays $50-400.

Photos: Pays $10 for 5x7 (and up) b&w photos used with mss; minimum of $25 for color. Prefers 2¼x2¼ and up, but can work from 35mm.

Tips: "Get a feeling for 'today's early Americans,' the folks who are visiting flea markets, auctions, junkyards, the antiques shops. They are our readers and they hunger for ideas on how to bring the warmth and beauty of early America into their lives. Then, conceive a new approach to satisfying their related interests in arts, crafts, travel to historic sites, and the story of the people of the 1600-1850 period. Write to entertain and inform at the same time, and be prepared to help us with illustrations, or sources for them."

FIBERARTS, The Magazine of Textiles, 50 College St., Asheville NC 28801. (704)253-0467. Editor: Jane Luddecke. Bimonthly magazine covering textiles as art and craft (weaving, quilting, surface design, stitchery, knitting, crochet, etc.) for textile artists, craftspeople, hobbyists, teachers, museum and gallery staffs, collectors and enthusiasts. Circ. 20,000. Pays on acceptance. Byline given. Rights purchased are negotiable. Submit seasonal/holiday material 6 months in advance. SASE. Reporting time varies. Sample copy $3.

Nonfiction: Book excerpts; historical/nostalgic; how-to; humor; interview/profile; opinion; personal experience; photo feature; technical; travel (for the textile enthusiast, i.e., collecting rugs in Turkey); and education, trends, exhibition reviews and textile news. Buys 50 mss/year. Query. "Please be very specific about your proposal. Also an important consideration in accepting an article is the kind of photos—35mm slides and/or b&w glossies—that you can provide as illustration. We like to see photos in advance." Length: 250-1,200 words. Pays $20-100/article.

Fillers: Clippings, jokes, gags, anecdotes, short humor and newsbreaks. Length: 125 words. Pays $5-10.

Tips: "Our writers are very familiar with the textile field and this is what we look for in a new writer. The writer should also be familiar with *Fiberarts*, the magazine. We outline our upcoming issue in a column called '50 College St.' far enough in advance for a prospective writer to be aware of our future needs in proposing an article."

THE FRANKLIN MINT ALMANAC, Franklin Center PA 19091. (215)459-7016. Editor: Samuel H. Young. Associate Editor: Rosemary Rennicke. Bimonthly magazine covering collecting, emphasizing numismatics, philatelics, porcelain, crystal, books, records and graphics for members of Franklin Mint Collectors Society who are regular customers and others who request. Circ. 500,000. Pays on acceptance. Byline given. Pays negotiable kill fee. Buys one-time rights. Submit seasonal/holiday material 6 months in advance. Simultaneous queries, and simultaneous, photocopied, and previously published submissions OK. Reports in 1 week on queries. Free sample copy.

Nonfiction: General interest (topics related to products offered by the Franklin Mint); interview/profile (with well-known people who collect or Franklin Mint collectors); and types of collections. Buys 25 mss/year. Query. Length: 1,500-2,000 words. Pays $500 average/article.

Photos: State availability of photos.

Fillers: Newsbreaks related to collecting. Pays negotiable fee.

Tips: "We do make an effort to give beginning writers a break. We're looking for writers away from the Philadelphia area."

GEMS AND MINERALS, Box 687, Mentone CA 92359. (714)794-1173. Editor: Jack R. Cox. Monthly for the amateur gem cutter, jewelry maker, mineral collector and rockhound. Buys first North American serial rights. Byline given. Buys 150-200 mss/year. Pays on publication. Free sample copy and writer's guidelines. Query. Reports in 4 weeks. SASE.

Nonfiction: Material must have how-to slant. No personality stories. Field trips to mineral or gem collecting localities used; must be accurate and give details so they can be found. Instructions on how to cut gems; design and creation of jewelry. Four to eight typed pages plus illustrations preferred, but do not limit if subject is important. Frequently good articles are serialized if too long for one issue. Pays 50¢/inch for text.

Photos: Pays for b&w prints as part of text. Pays $1 inch for color photos as published.

Tips: "Because we are a specialty magazine, it is difficult for a writer to prepare a suitable story for us unless he is familiar with the subject matter: jewelry making, gem cutting, mineral collecting and display, and fossil collecting. Our readers want accurate instructions on how to do it and where they can collect gemstones and minerals in the field. The majority of our articles are purchased from freelance writers, most of whom are hobbyists (rockhounds) or have technical knowledge of one of the subjects. Infrequently, a freelancer with no knowledge of the subject interviews an expert (gem cutter, jewelry maker, etc.) and gets what this expert tells him down on paper for a good how-to article. However, the problem here is that if the expert neglects to mention all the steps in his process, the writer does not realize it. Then, there is a delay while we check it out. My best advice to a freelance writer is to send for a sample copy of our magazine and author's specification sheet which will tell him what we need. We are interested in helping new writers and try to answer them personally, giving any pointers that we think will be of value to them. Let us emphasize that our readers want how-to and where-to stories. They are not at all interested in personality sketches about one of their fellow hobbyists."

HANDWOVEN, From Interweave Press, 306 N. Washington, Loveland CO 80537. (303)669-7672. Editor: Linda C. Ligon. Bimonthly magazine (except July) covering handweaving, spinning and dyeing. Audience includes "practicing textile craftsmen. Article should show considerable depth of knowledge of subject, though tone should be informal and accessible." Circ. 25,000. Pays on publication. Byline given. Pays 50% kill fee. Buys first North American serial rights. Simultaneous queries and photocopied submissions OK. SASE. Sample copy for $3.50 and 8½x11 SAE; free writer's guidelines.

Nonfiction: Historical and how-to (on weaving and other craft techniques; specific items with instructions); interview/profile (of successful and/or interesting textile craftsmen); and technical (on handweaving, spinning and dyeing technology). "All articles must contain a high level of in-depth information. Our readers are very knowledgeable about these subjects." Query. Length: 2,000 words. Pays $35-100.

Photos: State availability of photos. Identification of subjects required.

LAPIDARY JOURNAL, Box 80937, San Diego CA 92138. Editor: Pansy D. Kraus. For "all ages interested in the lapidary hobby." Monthly. Circ. 61,617. Rights purchased vary with author and material. Buys all rights or first serial rights. Byline given. Pays on publication. Free sample copy and writer's guidelines. Photocopied submissions OK. Query. SASE.

Nonfiction: Publishes "articles pertaining to gem cutting, gem collecting and jewelry making for the hobbyist." Buys informational, how-to, personal experience, historical, travel and technical articles. Pays 1¢/word.

Photos: Buys good contrast b&w photos. Contact editor for color. Payment varies according to size.

LOOSE CHANGE, Mead Publishing Corp., 21176 Alameda St., Long Beach CA 90810. (213)549-0730. Publisher: Daniel R. Meed. Managing Editor: Mel Gilden. Monthly magazine covering collecting and investing in antique coin-operated machines. "Our audience is mainly male. Readers are all collectors or enthusiasts of antique coin-operated machines, particularly antique slot machines. Subscribers are, in general, not heavy readers." Circ. 3,000. Pays on acceptance. Byline given. Buys all rights; "we may allow author to reprint upon request in noncompetitive publications." Photocopied submissions OK. Previously published submissions must be accompanied by complete list of previous sales, including sale dates. SASE. Reports in 1 month on queries; 6 weeks on mss. Sample copy $1; free writer's guidelines.

Nonfiction: Historical/nostalgic, how-to, interview/profile, opinion, personal experience, photo feature and technical. "Articles illustrated with clear, black and white photos are always considered much more favorably than articles without photos (we have a picture-oriented audience). The writer must be knowledgeable about his subject because our readers are knowlegeable and will spot inaccuracies." Buys 36-60 mss/year. Length: 900-6,000 words; 3,500-12,000, cover stories. Pays $150 maximum, inside stories; $250 maximum, cover stories.

Photos: "At best, captions should tell a complete story without reference to the body text." Send photos with ms. Reviews 8x10 b&w glossy prints. Captions required. "Purchase price for photos includes payment for photos."

Fiction: "All fiction must have a gambling/coin-operated-machine angle." Buys maximum 12 mss/year. Send complete ms. Length: 800-2,500 words. Pays $60.

LOST TREASURE, 15115 S. 76th E. Ave., Bixby OK 74008. Editor: Michael Rieke. 95% freelance written. For treasure hunting hobbyists, bottle and relic collectors, amateur prospectors and miners. Monthly magazine; 72 pages. Circ. 55,000. Buys all rights. Byline given. Buys 100 mss/

year. Pays on publication. Free sample copy and writer's guidelines. Will consider photocopied submissions. No simultaneous submissions. Reports in 6-8 weeks. Submit complete ms. SASE.
Nonfiction: How-to articles about treasure hunting, coinshooting, personal profiles stories about actual hunts. Avoid writing about the more famous treasures and lost mines. Length: 100-3,000 words. Pays 3¢/word.
Photos: Pays $5-10 for b&w glossy prints purchased with mss. Captions required. Pays $100 for color transparencies used on cover; 2¼x2¼ minimum size.

McCALL'S NEEDLEWORK & CRAFTS MAGAZINE, 825 7th Ave. (7th fl.), New York NY 10019. Editor: Margaret Gilman. Bimonthly. All rights bought for original needlework and handicraft designs. SASE.
Nonfiction: Submit preliminary color photos for editorial consideration. Accepted made-up items must be accompanied by directions, diagrams and charts. Payment ranges from a few dollars to a few hundred dollars.

THE MAGAZINE ANTIQUES, Straight Enterprises, 551 5th Ave., New York NY 10177. (212)682-8282. Editor/Publisher: Wendell Garrett. Managing Editor: Alfred Mayor. Monthly magazine covering art, antiques and architecture for collectors, dealers, scholars and institutions. Circ. 70,000. Pays on publication. Byline given. Buys all rights. Submit seasonal/holiday material 6 months in advance. SASE. Reports in 6 months on mss.
Nonfiction: "Articles generally present new research results that pertain to art, architecture, fine arts, artists or towns, and that either correct or add to the existing record. We lean toward American art, but include some European art with an American connection." Special issues include: May, *American Furniture* and November, *American Painting.* Buys 48 mss/year. Send complete ms "and photos to give an idea." Length: 1,500-2,000 words. Pays 10¢/published word.
Photos: Reviews 4x5 transparencies and 8x10 glossy prints. "Generally we assign photos to freelancers who work with us regularly." Pay "varies widely."
Columns/Departments: Collector's Notes, Karen M. Jones (updates on the record); Current and Coming, Sarah B. Sherrill (exhibitions, forums, symposiums); Clues & Footnotes, Eleanor H. Gustafson (footnoteworthy quotations on the arts, crafts and architecture of an earlier era, from historical sources printed on manuscript); Museum Accessions, Eleanor H. Gustafson; Letters from London. "Contributors to Clues & Footnotes are paid $10 lawful money on publication." Book reviews and queries, Allison M. Eckardt.

MAKE IT WITH LEATHER, Box 1386, Fort Worth TX 76101. (817)335-4161. Editor: Earl F. Warren. Buys all rights. Byline given except for news releases or if ghosted or written on assignment with predetermined no byline. Bimonthly. Circ. 60,000. Buys 60 or more mss/year. Pays on publication. Free sample copy and writer's guidelines. Reports in 6-8 weeks. SASE.
Nonfiction: "How-to-do-it leathercraft stories illustrated with cutting patterns, carving patterns. First-person approach even though article may be ghosted. Story can be for professional or novice. Strong on details; logical progression in steps; easy to follow how-to-do-it." Length: 2,000 words or less suggested. Payment normally starts at $50 plus $10 per illustration. "All articles judged on merit and may range to '$250 plus' per ms. Depends on project and work involved by author."
Photos: 5x7, or larger, b&w photos of reproduction quality purchased with mss. Captions required. Color of professional quality is used on cover at $50/accepted photo. Ektachrome transparencies or sheet film stock. Negatives needed with all print film stock. All photos are used to illustrate project on step-by-step basis and finished item. "We can do photos in our studio if product sample is sent. No charge, but no payment for photos to writer. Letting us 'do it our way' does help on some marginal story ideas and mss since we can add such things as artist's sketches or drawings to improve the presentation."
Fillers: "Tips and Hints." Short practical hints for doing leathercraft or protecting tools, new ways of doing things, etc. Length: 100 words maximum. Pays $10 minimum.
Tips: "There are plenty of leathercraftsmen around who don't feel qualified to write up a project or who don't have the time to do it. Put their ideas and projects down on paper for them and share the payment. We need plenty of small, quick, easy-to-do ideas; things that we can do in one page are in short supply."

MINIATURE COLLECTOR, Acquire Publishing Co., Inc., 170 5th Ave., New York NY 10010. (212)989-8700. Editor: Peter Dwyer. Bimonthly magazine; 60 pages. Circ. 60,000. Pays 20% kill fee. Byline given. Pays on publication. Submit seasonal/holiday material 4 months in advance. Photocopied and previously published submissions OK. SASE. Reports in 1 month. Sample copy $1.
Nonfiction: How-to (detailed furniture and accessories projects in 1/12th scale with accurate patterns and illustrations); interview (with well-established collectors, museum curators with

pictures); new product (very short-caption type pieces—no payment); photo feature (show reports, heavily photographic, with captions stressing pieces and availability of new and unusual pieces); and profile (of collectors with photos). Buys 3-6 mss/issue. Query. Length: 600-1,200 words. Pays $65-175.

Photos: Send photos with ms. Pays $20-100 for 5x7 or 8x10 b&w glossy prints; $30-125 for color transparencies. Buys one-time rights. Captions required.

THE MINIATURE MAGAZINE, Box 700, Newton NJ 07860. (201)383-3355. Editor: Wendie R. Blanchard. *"The Miniature Magazine* is edited for the miniaturist working in 1"-1' scale dollhouse miniatures, including the collector, scratch builder, kit user and inquisitive beginner." Quarterly magazine. Circ. 40,000. Pays on publication. Buys all rights. Submit seasonal/holiday material 7 months in advance. SASE. Reports in 4 weeks. Sample copy $1; free writer's guidelines.

Nonfiction: "I am in the market for articles dealing with dollhouse construction, furniture making and all types of craft techniques which can be applied to the creation of miniatures. The magazine covers both the crafting and collecting aspects of the hobby, with emphasis upon scale and quality. It does not cover dollhouses as children's playthings, but regards them as a serious, three-dimensional art form."

Photos: Purchased with accompanying ms.

Columns/Departments: Going Places in Lilliput covers places to visit to see fine miniatures. "We desire articles that are written by craftsmen (or collectors) knowledgeable about the hobby."

Tips: "When photographing miniatures, be sure to include some photos that have a scale relationship, i.e., a coin or a hand next to the miniature to give an idea of proportion."

MODEL RAILROADER, 1027 N. 7th St., Milwaukee WI 53233. Editor: Russell G. Larson. For hobbyists interested in scale model railroading. Monthly. Buys exclusive rights. Study publication before submitting material. Reports on submissions within 4 weeks. Query. SASE.

Nonfiction: Wants construction articles on specific model railroad projects (structures, cars, locomotives, scenery, benchwork, etc.). Also photo stories showing model railroads. First-hand knowledge of subject almost always necessary for acceptable slant. Pays base rate of $45/page.

Photos: Buys photos with detailed descriptive captions only. Pays $7.50 and up, depending on size and use. Color: double b&w rate. Full color cover: $210.

NEEDLE & THREAD, Happy Hands Publishing, 4949 Byers, Ft. Worth TX 76107. (817)732-7494. Editor: Janet Fawcett. Bimonthly magazine covering home sewing of all types for people interested in sewing fashions, home decorations and gifts. Estab. 1981. Circ. 400,000. Pays on acceptance. Byline given. Buys negotiable rights. Simultaneous queries and simultaneous and previously published submissions OK (if indicated where else they were submitted). Reports in 6 weeks. Sample copy $3.

Nonfiction: How-to (on sewing projects); and interview/profile (of outstanding seamstresses and designers). Buys 2-4 mss/year. Query with clips of published work or resume of sewing experience. Length: 1,000-2,000 words. Pays negotiable fee depending on the project.

Photos: State availability of photos.

Tips: "All projects must be original designs. On garments a manufactured pattern may be used with original decorative techniques."

NEEDLECRAFT FOR TODAY, Happy Hands Publishing, 4949 Byers, Ft. Worth TX 76107. (817)732-7494. Editor: Sandra Wright. Bimonthly magazine for needlecraft enthusiasts. Circ. 800,000. Pays on acceptance "of total project." Byline given "either with story or photo." Buys negotiable rights. Submit seasonal/holiday material 1 year in advance. Simultaneous queries and simultaneous and previously published submissions OK ("if indicated where else they were submitted"). SASE. Reports in 1 week. Sample copy $3.

Nonfiction: "Crochet, needlepoint, crewel, knitting and dollmaking, are used every issue. Any fiber project is of interest to us. How-to must be originally designed project. Provide a finished sample, chart, pattern, list of material and instructions." Buys 300 mss/year. Length: average 1,500 words. Pays "by arrangement, depending on the project."

Photos: "We photograph most finished projects ourselves." Send photos with query.

Columns/Departments: Forum, guest speaker on any subject of interest to needlecrafters. Needlecraft Principles explains a craft to a beginner. Buys 6 mss/year. Send complete ms. Pays $100-200.

Tips: "Writer must be able to write very clear step-by-step instructions for original projects, from small bazaar items to advanced projects made from commercially available materials. Be an experienced needlecrafter."

99 IC PROJECTS, Davis Publications, Inc., 380 Lexington Ave., New York NY 10017. (212)557-9100. Associate Publisher/Editor-in-Chief: Julian S. Martin. Editor: Gordon Sell. 100% freelance written. Emphasizes home hobby projects and theory. Annual magazine; 96 pages. Estab. January 1979. Pays on acceptance. Buys all rights. Pays 100% kill fee. Byline given. Previously published submissions OK. SASE. Reports in 1 month.

Nonfiction: "We are looking for brief, simple IC construction ideas that authors have assembled and operated. Refer to *101 Electronic Projects* or *99 IC Projects* for style and size." Buys 100 mss/issue. Query. Length: 100-150 words. Pays $30-50/project. Buys all rights. "In most cases, we give permission for author and/or photographer to use material in other publications after publication date. Authorization given in writing only."

Fillers: Jokes, gags, anecdotes. Buys 3/issue. Pays $20-30.

NOSTALGIAWORLD, for Collectors, Northeast International, Box 231, North Haven CT 06473. (203)239-4891. Editor: Bonnie Roth. Managing Editor: Stanley N. Lozowski. Bimonthly tabloid covering entertainment collectibles. Estab. 1979. Circ. 5,000-10,000. Pays on publication. Byline given. Buys all rights. Submit seasonal/holiday material 6 months in advance. Simultaneous queries, and simultaneous, photocopied, and previously published submissions OK. SASE. Reports in 4 weeks on queries; 6 weeks on mss. Sample copy $2; writer's guidelines for legal size SAE and 1 first class stamp.

Nonfiction: Historical/nostalgic; how-to (get started in collecting); and interview/profile (of movie, recording, or sport stars). "Articles must be aimed toward the collector and provide insight into a specific area of collecting. *Nostalgiaworld* readers collect records, sheet music, movie magazines, posters and memorabilia, personality items, comics, baseball, sports memorabilia. We do *not* cater to antiques, glass, or other non-entertainment collectibles. All submissions must be double-spaced and typewritten."

Photos: Send photos with ms. Pays $10-25 for 5x7 b&w prints; reviews b&w contact sheets. Captions and identification of subjects required. Buys all rights.

Columns/Departments: Video Memories (early TV); and 78 RPM-For Collectors Only (advice and tips for the collector of 78 RMP recordings; prices, values, outstanding rarities). Buys varying number of mss/year. Query or send complete ms. Length: 500-1,500 words. Pays $10-25.

Tips: "Most readers are curious to find out what their collectibles are worth. With inflation running at such a high rate, people are investing in nostalgia items more than ever. *Nostalgiaworld* provides a place to buy and sell and also lists conventions and collectors' meets across the country. Our publication is interested in the entertainment field as it evolved in the twentieth century. Our readers collect anything and everything related to this field."

NUMISMATIC NEWS, Krause Publications, 700 E. State St., Iola WI 54945. (715)445-2214. Editor: Bob Lemke. Weekly magazine about United States and Canadian paper money, tokens, old checks and collecting for beginning and advanced collectors. Estab. 1979. Circ. 15,000. Pays on acceptance. Byline given. Buys first North American serial rights. Simultaneous and photocopied submissions OK. SASE. Reports in 2 weeks. Free sample copy.

Nonfiction: "We're seeking features on people who are actively involved in any phase of coin or paper money collecting and investing." Buys 3-4 mss/issue. Send complete ms. Length: 2,000-5,000 words. Pays first time contributors 3¢/word; negotiates fees for others.

Photos: Send photos with ms. Pays $5 minimum for 5x7 b&w glossy prints. Pays $25 minimum for 35mm color transparencies. Captions and model release required. Buys first rights and first reprint rights.

NUTSHELL NEWS, Boynton and Associates, Clifton House, Clifton VA 22024. (703)830-1000. Editor: Ann Ruble. Monthly magazine about miniatures for miniatures enthusiasts, collectors, craftspeople and hobbyists. "*Nutshell News* is the only magazine in the miniatures field which offers readers comprehensive coverage of all facets of miniature collecting and crafting." Circ. 30,000. Pays on publication. Buys all rights in the field. Phone queries OK, "but would prefer letters and photos." Submit seasonal material 4 months in advance. Previously published submissions OK ("if they did not appear in a competing magazine"). Reports in 2 months. Sample copy $2.50; free writer's guidelines for SASE.

Nonfiction: Interview/profile of craftspeople specializing in miniatures. Research articles on design periods and styles. Articles on private and museum collections of miniatures. How-to articles on decorating, building miniature furniture, dollhouses, rooms, accessories. Show reports, book reviews, new product information. "We need stringers nationwide to work on an assignment basis, preferably freelancers with knowledge in the miniatures field to cover interviews with craftspeople and report on miniature shows." Buys 10 mss/issue. Query with "photos of the work to be written about. We're looking for craftspeople doing fine quality work, or collectors with top notch collections. Photos give us an idea of this quality." Length: 1,500-2,000 words. Pays 10¢/published word.

Photos: Pays $7.50 minimum for 5x7 b&w glossy prints. Pays $10 maximum for 35mm or larger color transparencies. Captions required.

OHIO ANTIQUE REVIEW, Box 538, Worthington OH 43085. (614)885-9757. Managing Editor: Charles Muller. (614)885-9757. 60% freelance written. For an antique-oriented readership, "generally well-educated, interested in folk art and other early American items." Monthly tabloid; 90-110 pages. Circ. 10,000. Pays on publication date assigned at time of purchase. Buys first North American serial rights and one-time rights. Byline given. Phone queries OK. Submit seasonal/holiday material 2 months in advance. Simultaneous, photocopied and previously published submissions OK. SASE. Reports in 1 month. Free sample copy and writer's guidelines.
Nonfiction: "The articles we desire concern history and production of furniture, pottery, china, and other antiques of the period prior to the 1880s. In some cases, contemporary folk art items are acceptable. We are also interested in reporting on antique shows and auctions with statements on conditions and prices. We do not want articles on contemporary collectibles." Buys 5-8 mss/issue. Query with clips of published work. Query should show "author's familarity with antiques and the kinds of antiques, and an interest in the historical development of artifacts relating to early America." Length: 200-2,000 words. Pays $75-100.
Photos: State availability of photos with ms. Payment included in ms price. Uses 3x5 or 5x7 glossy b&w prints. Captions required. Articles with photographs receive preference.
Tips: "Give us a call and let us know of specific interests. We are more concerned with the background in antiques than in writing abilities. The writing can be edited, but the knowledge imparted is of primary interest."

THE OLD BOTTLE MAGAZINE, Box 243, Bend OR 97701. (503)382-6978. Editor: Shirley Asher. For collectors of old bottles, insulators, relics. Monthly. Circ. 7,000. Buys all rights. Byline given. Buys 35 mss/year. Pays on acceptance. Will send a sample copy to a writer on request. No query required. Reports in 1 month. SASE.
Nonfiction, Photos and Fillers: "We are soliciting factual accounts on specific old bottles, canning jars, insulators and relics." Stories of a general nature on these subjects not wanted. "Interviews of collectors are usually not suitable when written by noncollectors. A knowledge of the subject is imperative. Would highly recommend potential contributors study an issue before making submissions. Articles that tie certain old bottles to a historical background are desired." Length: 250-2,500 words. B&w glossy prints and clippings purchased separately.

OLD CARS NEWSPAPER, Krause Publications, 700 E. State St., Iola WI 54945. (715)445-2214. Editors: LeRoi Smith, Richard Johnson and R.C. Halla. 40% freelance written. "Our readers collect, drive and restore everything from 1899 locomobiles to '76 Cadillac convertibles. They cover all age and income groups." Weekly tabloid; 60 pages. Circ. 95,000. Pays on acceptance. Buys all rights. Phone queries OK. Byline given. SASE. Reports in 2 months. Sample copy 50¢.
Nonfiction: Historical (sites related to auto history, interesting oldsters from the automobile past, etc.); how-to (good restoration articles); interview (with important national-level personages in the car hobby); nostalgia (auto-related, and only occasionally); and photo feature (by knowing hobby reporters, definite query). No "local man restores Model T Ford, local club sponsors parking lot show or local couple takes trip in Model A" stories. Buys 4 mss/issue. Query. Pays 3¢/word.
Photos: State availability of photos with query. Pays $5 for 5x7 b&w glossy prints. Captions required. Buys all rights.
Columns/Departments: Book reviews (new releases for hobbyists). Buys 1 ms/issue. Query. Pays 3¢/word.
Fillers: Newsbreaks. Buys 50/year. Pays 3¢/word.
Tips: "Must know automotive hobby well. One writer caught the editor's eye by submitting excellent drawings with his manuscript."

QUILTER'S NEWSLETTER MAGAZINE, Box 394, Wheatridge CO 80033. Editor: Bonnie Leman. Monthly. Circ. 100,000. Buys first or second North American serial rights. Buys 15 mss/year. Pays on acceptance. Free sample copy. Reports in 3-4 weeks. Submit complete ms. SASE.
Nonfiction: "We are interested in articles on the subject of quilts and quiltmakers *only*. We are not interested in anything relating to 'Grandma's Scrap Quilts,' but could use material about contemporary quilting." Pays 2¢/word minimum.
Photos: Additional payment for photos depends on quality.
Fillers: Related to quilts and quiltmakers only.
Tips: "Be specific, brief, and professional in tone. Study our magazine to learn the kind of thing we like. Send us material which fits into our format, but which is different enough to be interesting. Realize that we think we're the best quilt magazine on the market and that we're aspiring to be even better, then send us the cream off the top of your quilt material."

RAGGEDY ANN REVIEW, The Midwestern Periodical for Doll and Toy Collectors, 4781 Aberdeen Rd., Mound MN 55364. (612)472-4054. Editor: Sandy Andrews. Quarterly magazine covering Midwestern (central USA) doll and toy collectors (magazine emphasizes dolls)—both new and long-time, sophisticated collectors. Estab. 1980. Circ. 200 charter subscribers. Payment is negotiable. Kill fee not yet established. Buys one-time rights. Reprints should acknowledge us. Submit seasonal/holiday material 6 months in advance. Photocopied submissions and previously published work OK (if so indicated). SASE. Reports in 1 month. Sample copy $1 for SAE and 36¢ postage.

Nonfiction: Expose (e.g., museum in Wisconsin that closed); humor (doll hospital); historical/nostalgic (in-depth, comprehensive articles on historical side of collecting well-written, thorough, well-organized); technical (specific dolls, dollmaking, doll clothes, doll dishes, doll furniture); doll artists, sights in Midwest (museums, shows, etc.), obscure dolls—not doll topics that have been overworked. Buys 4-16 mss/year. Query with clips of published work or send complete ms. Length: 2,000 words average. Pays $35 average—negotiable.

Photos: Photo stories on doll museums (photos w/article); photos taken in the 30s to be printed in sepia-toned ink and used for cover. Pays $10. Send photos with accompanying ms. Prefers any size b&w glossy prints. Captions, model releases and identification of subjects required. Buys all rights but will negotiate.

Columns/Departments: The Book Nook (reviews of new books on doll collecting or dolls). Buys 3 mss/year. Send complete ms. Length: 300-500 words. Pays $10 minimum.

Poetry: Light verse and traditional. Must be directly related to subject of the magazine in a historical or other sense; seasonal is good. Buys 1-2/issue. Amount of poems to be submitted is open. Length: open. No payment at this time.

Tips: "Research methods are important—be sure not to violate copyright laws. List your written sources; we won't necessarily print them, but we want to know what they are. Query and ask for specific needs. At present, we need articles on soap dolls; in-depth articles on any topic related to doll collecting, e.g., articles providing new insights into old dolls, are most needed. Request a copy of the magazine to see what kind of material I'm using. We're looking for correspondents for 'Raggedy Ann Rag Sheet,' a semiannual newsletter supplement. *Raggedy Ann Review* has been locally piloted with favorable response—will go to color as soon as possible."

RAILROAD MODEL CRAFTSMAN, Box 700, Newton NJ 07860. (201)383-3355. Managing Editor: William C. Schaumburg. 75% freelance written. For "model railroad hobbyists, in all scales and gauges." Monthly. Circ. 97,000. Buys all rights. Buys 50-100 mss/year. Pays on publication. Sample copy $1.50. Submit seasonal material 6 months in advance. SASE requested for writer's and photographer's information.

Nonfiction: "How-to model railroad features written by persons who did the work are preferred. Almost all our features and articles are written by active model railroaders familiar with the hobby. It is difficult for non-modelers to know how to approach writing for this field." Minimum payment: $1.75/column inch of copy ($50/page).

Photos: Purchased with or without mss. Buys sharp 8x10 glossy prints and 35mm or larger color transparencies. Pays $10 for photos or $2/diagonal inch of published b&w photos, $3 for color transparencies and $100 for covers which must tie in with article in that issue. Captions required.

RARITIES, The Magazine of Collectibles, Behn-Miller Publishers, Inc., 17337 Ventura Blvd., Encino CA 91316. (213)788-7080. Senior Editor: W.R.C. Shedenhelm. Quarterly magazine covering collectibles for fun and profit for people with a broad interest in collecting. Estab. 1980. Circ. 80,000. Pays on publication. Byline given. Buys first North American serial rights. Submit 6 months in advance. Simultaneous queries and photocopied submissions OK. SASE. Reports in 1 week. Sample copy $2; writer's guidelines for business size SAE and 1 first class stamp.

Nonfiction: General interest (on collectible and profitable items); and how-to (assemble a collection). No antiques; no single collection or collector. Buys 40-50 mss/year. Query. Length: 2,000-10,000 words. Pays $50/printed page.

Photos: "We're heavy users of photos, and expect the writer to provide photos or find a photographer to shoot pictures." State availability of photos. Reviews 35mm color transparencies and b&w or color glossy prints. Pays $50/printed page. Captions required. Buys one-time rights.

RECORD COLLECTORS AUCTION, Country Sound Publishing, 100 Lancaster St., Marietta OH 45750. (614)374-5322. Editor: Lawrence Koon. Monthly newspaper covering record collecting for record collectors worldwide. Estab. 1980. Circ. 5,000. Pays on publication. Byline given. Buys all rights. Submit seasonal/holiday material 3 months in advance. Simultaneous queries, and simultaneous and photocopied submissions OK. SASE. Reports in 6 weeks. Sample copy $2.50.

Nonfiction: General interest, how-to and record collecting. "We need record collectors' for-sale lists and want lists." Buys 6 mss/year. Length: 500-2,500 words.

Photos: "We're looking for photos of 1950s recording artists." Send photos with ms. Reviews b&w contact sheets and 5x7 prints. Identification of subjects required.
Columns/Departments: Send complete ms. Pays $50-300.
Fiction: Send complete ms.

ROCK & GEM, Behn-Miller Publishers, Inc., 17337 Ventura Blvd., Encino CA 91316. (213)788-7080. Senior Editor: W.R.C. Shedenhelm. 95% freelance written. For amateur lapidaries and rockhounds. Monthly magazine; 100 pages. Circ. 75,000. Rights purchased vary with author and material. May buy first North American serial rights or first serial rights. Byline given. Pays on publication. Sample copy $2. Reports in 1 month. Query or submit complete ms. SASE.
Nonfiction: Knowledgeable articles on rockhounding and lapidary work; step-by-step how-to articles on lapidary and jewelry making. Length: open. Pays $50/published page.
Photos: No additional payment for 5x7 or larger b&w glossy prints used with mss. Color for cover (4x5 transparencies) is by assignment only.

JOEL SATER'S ANTIQUES & AUCTION NEWS, 225 W. Market St., Marietta PA 17547. (717)426-1956. Managing Editor: Joel Sater. Editor: Denise Murphy. For dealers and buyers of antiques, nostalgics and collectibles; and those who follow antique shows and shops. Biweekly tabloid; 24 pages. Circ. 80,000. Pays on publication. Buys all rights. Phone queries OK. Submit seasonal/holiday material 3 months in advance. Simultaneous (if so notified), photocopied and previously published submissions OK. SASE. Reports in 6 weeks. Free sample copy (must identify *Writer's Market*).
Nonfiction: Historical (related to American artifacts or material culture); how-to (restoring and preserving antiques and collectibles); informational (research on antiques or collectibles; "news about activities in our field"); interview; nostalgia; personal experience; photo feature; profile; and travel. Buys 100-150 mss/year. Query or submit complete ms. Length: 500-2,500 words. Pays $5-25.
Photos: Purchased with or without accompanying ms. Captions required. Send prints. Pays $2-10 for b&w photos. Offers no additional payment for photos purchased with mss.

SCOTT'S MONTHLY STAMP JOURNAL, 3 E. 57th St., New York NY 10022. (212)371-5700. Editor: Ira S. Zweifach. For stamp collectors, from the beginner to the sophisticated philatelist. Monthly magazine; 72 pages. Circ. 30,000. Rights purchased vary with author and material. Byline given. Usually buys all rights. Buys 24-36 mss/year. Pays within 1 month after acceptance. Submit seasonal or holiday material 3 months in advance. Reports in 4 weeks. Query. SASE.
Nonfiction: "We want articles of a serious philatelic nature, ranging in length from 1,500-2,500 words. We are also in the market for articles, written in an engaging fashion, concerning the remote byways and often-overlooked aspects of the hobby. Writing should be clear and concise, and subjects should be well-researched and documented. Illustrative material should also accompany articles whenever possible." Pays $50-250.
Photos: State availability of photos. Offers no additional payment for b&w photos used with mss.
Tips: "*Scott's Monthly Stamp Journal* is undergoing a complete change. Although all material deals with stamps, new writers are invited to seek assignments. It is not necessary to be a stamp collector or a published professional. You must be a good writer, and be willing to do careful research on strong material. Because our emphasis is on lively, interesting articles about stamps, including historical perspectives and human interest slants, we are open to writers who can produce the same. Of course, if you are an experienced philatelist, so much the better. We do *not* want to see finished manuscripts. Submit query as above with an attractive idea that has depth and is not a simple survey of an overworked topic. We do not want, for instance, stories about the picture on a stamp taken from a history book or an encyclopedia and dressed up to look like research. We want articles written from a philatelic standpoint. If idea is good and not a basic rehash, we are interested."

THE SPINNING WHEEL, Everybody's Press, Inc., Hanover PA 17331. (717)632-3535. Editor: A. Christian Revi. For antique collectors and dealers. 6 times a year. Pays on publication. Buys exclusive rights unless author wishes some reservations. Byline given. SASE.
Nonfiction: Authentic, well-researched material on antiques in any and all collecting areas; home decorating ideas with antiques. Prefers combined scholar-student-amateur appeal. No first-person or family history. Prefers draft or outline first. Requires bibliography with each ms. Quality illustrations. Length: 500-1,500 words. Pays minimum $1/published inch, including pictures.
Photos: Photos and professional line drawings accepted. Photos should be top quality b&w, no smaller than 5x7. If of individual items shown in groups, each should be separated for mechanical expediency. Avoid fancy groupings. 4-color transparencies for illustrations must also be top quality (35mm or 4x5).
Tips: "Find out what young collectors are buying at modest prices and write about it."

TREASURE, Jess Publishing, 16146 Covello St., Van Nuys CA 91406. (213)988-6910. Editor-in-Chief: David Weeks. Managing Editor: Jim Williams. Emphasizes treasure hunting and metal detecting. Monthly magazine; 74 pages. Circ. 100,000. Pays on publication. Buys all rights. Byline given. Phone queries OK. Submit seasonal/holiday material 4 months in advance. Previously published submissions OK. SASE. Reports in 1 month. Free writer's guidelines.
Nonfiction: Jim Williams, articles editor. How-to (coinshooting and treasure hunting tips); informational and historical (location of lost treasures with emphasis on the lesser-known); interviews (with treasure hunters); profiles (successful treasure hunters and metal detector hobbyists); personal experience (treasure hunting); technical (advice on use of metal detectors and metal detector designs). Buys 6-8 mss/issue. Send complete ms. Length: 300-3,000 words. Pays $15-150. "Our rate of payment varies considerably depending upon the proficiency of the author, the quality of the photographs, the importance of the subject matter, and the amount of useful information given."
Photos: Offers no additional payment for 5x7 or 8x10 b&w glossy prints used with mss. Pays $50 minimum for color transparencies (120 or 2¼x2¼). Color for cover only. Model release required.
Tips: "Clear photos and other illustrations are a must."

THE WOODWORKER'S JOURNAL, Madrigal Publishing Co., Inc., 25 Town View Dr., Box 1629, New Milford CT 06776. (203)355-2697. Editor: James J. McQuillan. Managing Editor: Thomas G. Begnal. Bimonthly magazine covering woodworking for woodworking hobbyists of all levels of skill. Circ. 41,000. Pays on acceptance. Byline given. Buys all rights. Submit seasonal/holiday material 3 months in advance. SASE. Reports in 5 weeks. Free sample copy and writer's guidelines.
Nonfiction: "In each issue, we try to offer a variety of plans—some selected with the novice in mind, others for the more experienced cabinetmaker. We also like to offer a variety of furniture styles, i.e., contemporary, colonial, Spanish, etc. We are always in the market for original plans for all types of furniture, wood accessories, jigs, and other shop equipment. We are also interested in seeing carving and marquetry projects." Buys 20-30 mss/year. Send complete ms. Length "varies with project." Pays $80-120/page. "Payment rate is for a complete project submission, consisting of dimensioned sketches, a write-up explaining how the project was built, and at least one high-quality b&w photo."
Photos: Send photos with ms. Reviews 5x7 b&w prints. "Photo payment is included in our basic payment rate of $80-120/page for a complete project submission." Captions required. Buys all rights.
Tips: "Submit projects that are well designed and constructed. Include clear and complete plans, a detailed write-up explaining how the project was built, and at least one high-quality b&w photo."

THE WORKBASKET, 4251 Pennsylvania Ave., Kansas City MO 64111. Editor: Roma Jean Rice. Issued monthly except bimonthly June-July and November-December. Buys first rights. Pays on acceptance. Query. Reports in 6 weeks. SASE.
Nonfiction: Interested in articles of 400-500 words of step-by-step directions for craft projects and gardening articles of 200-500 words. Pays 5¢/word.
Photos: Pays $5-7 for 8x10 glossies with ms.
Columns/Departments: "With the Cooks" (original recipes from readers); "Women Who Make Cents" (short how-to section featuring ideas for pin money from readers).

WORKBENCH, 4251 Pennsylvania Ave., Kansas City MO 64111. (816)531-5730. Editor: Jay W. Hedden. 90% freelance written. For woodworkers. Circ. 650,000. Pays on publication. Buys all rights. Byline given if requested. Reports in 2 weeks. Query. SASE. Free sample copy and writer's guidelines.
Nonfiction: "In the last couple of years, we have increased our emphasis on home improvement and home maintenance, and now we are getting into alternate energy projects. Ours is a nuts-and-bolts approach, rather than telling how someone has done it. Because most of our readers own their own homes, we stress 'retrofitting' of energy-saving devices, rather than saying they should rush out and buy or build a solar home. Energy conservation is another subject we cover thoroughly; insulation, weatherstripping, making your own storm windows. We still are very strong in woodworking, cabinetmaking and furniture construction. Projects range from simple toys to complicated reproductions of furniture now in museums." Pays: $125 minimum/published page.
Columns/Departments: Shop tips bring $20 maximum with drawing and/or photo.
Tips: "If you can consistently provide good material, including photos, your rates will go up, and you will get assignments. The field is wide open, but only if you produce quality material and clear, sharp b&w photos. If we pay less than the rate, it's because we have to supply photos, information, drawings or details the contributor has overlooked. Contributors should look over the published story to see what they should include next time. Our editors are skilled woodworkers, do-it-yourselfers and photographers. We have a complete woodworking shop at the office and we use it often to check out construction details of projects submitted to us."

WORLD COIN NEWS, Krause Publications, 700 E. State., Iola WI 54945. (715)445-2214. Managing Editor: Russ Rulau. Weekly newspaper about non-United States coin collecting for novices and advanced collectors of foreign coins, medals, and paper money. Circ. 15,000. Pays on acceptance. Byline given. Buys first North American serial rights; first reprint rights. Submit seasonal material 4 months in advance. Simultaneous and photocopied submissions OK. Reports in 2 weeks. Free sample copy.
Nonfiction: "Send us timely news stories related to collecting foreign coins and current information on coin values and markets." Send complete ms. Length: 500-2,000 words. Pays 3¢/word to first-time contributors; fees negotiated for later articles.
Photos: Send photos with ms. Pays $5 minimum for b&w prints. Captions and model release required. Buys first rights and first reprint rights.

YESTERYEAR, Yesteryear Publications, Box 2, Princeton WI 54968. (414)295-3969. Editor: Michael Jacobi. For antique dealers and collectors, people interested in collecting just about anything, and nostalgia buffs. Monthly tabloid; 28 pages. Circ. 6,000. Pays on publication. Buys one-time rights. Byline given. Submit seasonal/holiday material 3 months in advance. Simultaneous, photocopied and previously published submissions OK. SASE. Reports in 2 weeks for queries; 1 month for mss. Sample copy $1.
Nonfiction: General interest (basically, anything pertaining to antiques, collectible items or nostalgia in general); historical (again, pertaining to the above categories); how-to (refinishing antiques, how to collect); nostalgia; and personal experience. "We do not want opinion articles." Buys 4 mss/issue. Send complete ms. Pays $5-25.
Photos: Send photos with ms. Pays $5 for 5x7 b&w glossy or matte prints; $5 for 5x7 color prints. Captions preferred.
Columns/Departments: "We will consider new column concepts as long as they fit into the general areas of antiques, collectibles, nostalgia. These can include book reviews." Buys 3/issue. Send complete ms. Pays $5-25.

Home and Garden

AUSTIN HOMES AND GARDENS, Diversified Productions, 1204 Nueces, Austin TX 78701. (512)474-7666. Associate Editor: Jean Trimble. Monthly magazine emphasizing Austin, Texas homes and gardens for current, former and prospective residents. Estab. 1979. Circ. 20,000. Average issue includes 10-12 articles. Pays on publication. Byline given. Buys first North American serial rights. Phone queries OK. Photocopied submissions OK. SASE. Reports in 1 month. Sample copy $1.
Nonfiction: General interest (interior decorating; trends in furniture and landscaping; arts and crafts); nostalgia; historical (on local houses); profile; how-to (on home or garden); new product (on gardening products); and photo feature. Buys 5 mss/issue. Query. Length: 700-1,500 words. Pays $100 minimum.
Columns/Departments: Departments include Good Cooking (outstanding local cooks); Breakaway (nearby travel in or near Austin); and Profiles (interesting people). Query. Length: 500-1,000 words. Pays $100 minimum.

BETTER HOMES AND GARDENS, 1716 Locust St., Des Moines IA 50336. (515)284-9011. Editor: Gordon G. Greer. For "middle-and-up income, homeowning and community-concerned families." Monthly. Circ. 8,000,000. Buys all rights. Pays on acceptance. Query preferred. Submit seasonal material 1 year in advance. Mss should be directed to the department where the story line is strongest. SASE.
Nonfiction: "Freelance material is used in areas of travel, health, cars, money management, and home entertainment. Reading the magazine will give the writer the best idea of our style. We do not deal with political subjects or areas not connected with the home, community and family." Length: 500-2,000 words. Pays top rates based on estimated length of published article; $100-2,000.
Photos: Shot under the direction of the editors. Purchased with mss.
Tips: "Follow and study the magazine, to see what we do and how we do it. There are no secrets, after all; it's all there on the printed page. Having studied several issues, the writer should come up with one or several ideas that interest him, and, hopefully, us. The next step is to write a good query letter. It needn't be more than a page in length (for each idea), and should include a good stab at a title, a specific angle, and a couple of paragraphs devoted to the main points of the article. This

method is not guaranteed to produce a sale, of course; there is no magic formula. But it's still the best way I know to have an idea considered."

COLORADO HOMES & LIFESTYLES, 2550 31st St., Suite 154, Denver CO 80216. (303)433-6533. Editor: Garrett Giann. Associate Editor: Dianne Shindler-Burks. Bimonthly magazine covering Colorado homes and lifestyles for interior decorators of upper-middle-class incomes. Estab. 1980. Circ. 30,000. Pays on publication. Byline given. Buys all rights. Submit seasonal/holiday material 6 months in advance. Simultaneous queries and photocopied submissions OK. SASE. Reports in 1 month.
Nonfiction: The arts in the home, gardening and plants, decorating and design, and fine food and entertainment. Buys 24 mss/year. Send complete ms. Length: 1,200-1,500 words. Pays average 20¢/word.
Photos: Send photos with ms. Reviews 35mm color transparencies and 5x7 b&w glossy prints. Identification of subjects required.

THE FAMILY FOOD GARDEN, 1999 Shepard Rd., St. Paul MN 55116. (612)690-7478. Editor: Sharon Ross. For vegetable gardeners. Magazine published 6 times/year; 80 pages. Circ. 300,000. Buys all rights. Byline given. Buys 60 mss/year. Pays on acceptance. Writer's guidelines for SASE. Sample copy $2. Submit seasonal material 5-6 months in advance. Reports on queries in 4 weeks; reports on submissions in 6 weeks. Query. SASE.
Nonfiction: "We look for straightforward, practical and technically accurate writing about food growing in the home garden or orchard. We do not cover flower gardening, commerical growing or small farming. Recipe stories are by assignment only. We prefer to buy ms, photographs and illustrations as a package." Length: 500-2,000 words. Pays $50-300 for illustrated articles.
Photos: Submit large b&w glossy prints or any size color transparency. "Be sure they are professional quality. This is a must."
Tips: "Be sure article is applicable to home gardeners all across the country."

FAMILY HANDYMAN, Webb Co., 1999 Shepard Rd., St. Paul MN 55116. Editor: Gene Schnaser. Emphasizes do-it-yourself home maintenance, repair and improvement. Publishes 10 issues yearly. Magazine; 100 plus pages. Circ. 1,000,000. Pays on acceptance. Buys all rights. Submit seasonal material 6 months in advance. SASE. Reports in 4-6 weeks. Free sample copy and writer's guidelines.
Nonfiction: How-to home, lawn and garden maintenance; repairs; remodeling; and shop projects. Buys 5 mss/issue. Query or send complete ms. Length: 700-1,200 words. Pays $150-1,000 depending on length, whether color or b&w photos used, and quality of entire piece.
Photos: Send photos with ms. Uses 5x7 or 8x10 b&w glossy or 35mm or larger color transparencies. Offers no additional payment for photos purchased with mss. Captions and model releases required.

FLOWER AND GARDEN MAGAZINE, 4251 Pennsylvania, Kansas City MO 64111. Editor-in-Chief: Rachel Snyder. For home gardeners. Bimonthly. Picture magazine. Circ. 450,000. Buys first rights. Byline given. Pays on acceptance. Free writer's guidelines. Query. Reports in 6 weeks. SASE.
Nonfiction: Interested in illustrated articles on how to do certain types of gardening, descriptive articles about individual plants. Flower arranging, landscape design, house plants, patio gardening are other aspects covered. Especially needs articles about food gardening. "The approach we stress is practical (how-to-do-it, what-to-do-it-with). We try to stress plain talk, clarity, economy of words. We are published in 3 editions: Northern, Southern, Western. Some editorial matter is purchased just for single edition use. Most, however, is used in all editions, so it should be tailored for a national audience. Material for a specific edition should be slanted to that audience only." Length: 500-1,500 words. Pays 6¢/word or more, depending on quality and kind of material.
Photos: Pays up to $12.50/5x7 or 8x10 b&w prints, depending on quality, suitability. Also buys color transparencies, 35mm and larger. "We are using more 4 color illustrations." Pays $30-125 for these, depending on size and use.
Tips: "Prospective author needs good grounding in gardening practice and literature. Then offer well-researched and well-written material appropriate to the experience level of our audience. Use botanical names as well as common. Illustrations help sell the story. Describe special qualifications for writing the particular proposed subject."

GARDEN MAGAZINE, The Garden Society, A Division of the New York Botanical Garden, Bronx Park, Bronx NY 10458. Editor: Ann Botshon. Emphasizes horticulture, environment and botany for a diverse readership, largely college graduates and professionals united by a common interest in plants and the environment. Many are members of botanical gardens and arboreta.

Bimonthly magazine; 44 pages. Circ. 23,000. Buys all rights. Submit seasonal/holiday material 4 months in advance. Photocopied submissions OK. SASE. Reports in 2 months. Sample copy $2.
Nonfiction: Ann Botshon, editor. "All articles must be of high quality, meticulously researched and botanically accurate." Exposé (environmental subjects); how-to (horticultural techniques, must be unusual and verifiable); general interest (plants of interest, botanical information); humor (pertaining to botany and horticulture); photo feature (pertaining to plants and the environment); and travel (great gardens of the world). Buys 1-2 mss/issue. Query with clips of published work. Length: 500-2,500 words. Pays $50-300.
Photos: James Cooper, designer. Pays $35-50/5x7 b&w glossy print; $40-150/4x5 or 35mm color transparency. Captions preferred. Buys one-time rights.
Tips: "We appreciate some evidence that the freelancer has studied our magazine and understands our special requirements."

GARDENS FOR ALL NEWS, Newsmagazine of the National Association for Gardening, Gardens for All, 180 Flynn Ave., Burlington VT 05401. (802)863-1308; 863-1321. Editor: Ruth W. Page. Bimonthly tabloid covering food gardening and food trees. "We publish not only how-to-garden techniques, but also news that affects gardeners and items on gardens for special purposes like therapy, education, feed the hungry, etc." Circ. 25,000. Pays on acceptance. Byline given. Buys one-time rights. Submit seasonal/holiday material 4 months in advance. Photocopied and previously published submissions OK. SASE. Reports in 2 weeks on queries; 1 month on mss. Free sample copy and writer's guidelines.
Nonfiction: How-to, humor, inspirational, interview/profile, new product, personal experience, photo feature, and technical. "All articles must be connected with food-gardening." Buys 50 mss/year. Query. Length: 300-3,500 words. Pays $15-90/article.
Photos: Lorraine Lilja, photo editor. Send photos with ms. Pays $5-15 for b&w photos; $15-35 for color photos. Captions, model releases and identification of subjects required.

GREAT AMERICAN HOME DESIGNS, (formerly *Decor Magazine*), Great American Publishing, Inc., 57 E. Oakland, Salt Lake City UT 84115. (801)486-1700. Editor: Jayne Muir. Emphasizes home decorating ideas for new or potential home buyers. Monthly magazine. Circ. 105,000. Pays on acceptance. Byline given. Buys all rights, first rights, second serial rights, first North American serial rights and one-time rights. Phone queries OK. Simultaneous, photocopied and previously published submissions OK. SASE. Reports in 2 weeks. Free sample copy and writer's guidelines.
Nonfiction: General interest (home decorating, landscaping and remodeling); how-to; new product; and photo feature. "No amateur photos with pedantic tones on decorating. No do-it-yourself projects. We want a single idea, not a whole home being decorated." Color photos only. Buys 100 mss/year. Query. Length: 100-1,800 words. Pays $50-250.
Photos: Send photos with ms. Pays $20-50 minimum for 3x5 or larger color transparencies. Captions preferred. Model release required. Buys one-time rights.
Tips: "We want short, but pertinent pieces that give the reader new ideas. Articles must be general in scope and timeless in appeal, short yet meaty."

GURNEY'S GARDENING NEWS, A Family Newspaper for Gurney Gardeners, Gurney Seed and Nursery Co., 2nd and Capitol, Yankton SD 57079. (605)665-4451. Managing Editor: David B. McCreary. Bimonthly tabloid covering gardening, horticulture and related subjects for a family audience. Estab. 1980. Circ. 30,000. Pays on acceptance. Byline given. Buys first North American serial rights, second serial (reprint) rights, and makes work-for-hire assignments. Submit seasonal/holiday material 6 months in advance. Simultaneous queries, and photocopied and previously published submissions OK. SASE. Reports in 1 month on queries; 2 months on mss. Sample copy for 9x12 SAE; writer's guidelines for business size SAE.
Nonfiction: How-to (raise vegetables, flowers, bulbs, trees); interview/profile (of gardeners); photo feature (of garden activities); and technical (horticultural-related). Buys 130 mss/year. Query. Length: 700-2,500 words. Pays $50-375.
Photos: Send photos with ms. Pays $10-85 for 5x7 or 8x10 b&w prints or contact sheets. Caption, model release and identification of subjects required. Buys one-time rights.
Fiction: "We're interested in read aloud stories for family reading section." No sex or violence. Buys 6 mss/year. Send complete ms. Length: 500-1,000 words. Pays $50-100.
Tips: "Please time articles to coincide with the proper season. We like to see articles that are interesting, fresh, organized, and easy to understand. A word of caution: Our readers know gardening. If you don't, don't write for us."

HERB QUARTERLY, Box 275. New Fane VT 05345. (802)365-4392. Editor: Sallie Ballantine. Quarterly magazine about herbs for enthusiasts interested in herbal aspects of gardening or cooking, history and folklore. Estab. 1979. Circ. 11,000. Pays on publication. Buys first North

American serial rights. Phone queries OK. SASE. Reports in 1 month. Sample copy $3.50.

Nonfiction: General interest (plant sciences, landscaping); historical (concerning the use and folklore of herbs); how-to (related to crafts, cooking and cultivation); humor; interview (of a famous person involved with herbs); profile; travel (looking for herbs); personal experience; and photo feature. Send complete ms. Length: 1,500-3,000 words. Pays $25 minimum.

Photos: "Cover quality." Pays $25/layout minimum for 8x10 b&w prints.

Fiction: Adventure; fantasy; historical; humorous; mystery; romance; suspense; and religious (herbs of the Bible).

Bryan Publications, Inc., 3355 Via Lido, Newport Beach CA 92663. Editor: Janie Murphy. Emphasizes new homes available for homebuyers and homebuilders. Monthly magazine; 112 pages. Estab. 1960. Circ. 115,000. Pays on publication. Buys first North American serial rights. Photocopied submissions OK. Previously published work OK, but state where and when it appeared. SASE. Reports in 2 months.

Nonfiction: General interest (taxes, insurance, home safety, mortgages); how-to (beat high prices, build a patio, select wallpaper, set up a tool bench, panel a wall, landscape); and opinion (by experts in a field, e.g., a CPA on taxes). "Gear all material to the California homeowner and consumer. Write in an informative yet entertaining style. Give examples the reader can identify with." Buys 2 mss/issue. Send complete ms. Length: 500-1,500 words. Pays $75-200.

Photos: Send photos with ms. Uses b&w 8x10 glossy prints and 4x5 color transparencies. Offers no additional payment for photos accepted with ms. Captions preferred, model release required. Buys one-time rights.

Columns/Departments: Energy, Taxes, Finance, Landscape, Home Safety, Home Improvement; new products; and Personalizing Your Home (how homeowners have customized development homes). Buys 2 mss/issue. Send complete ms. Length: 500-1,200 words. Pays $75-200.

HOME ENERGY DIGEST, Investment Rarities, Inc., 8009 34th Ave. S., Minneapolis MN 55420. (612)853-0777. Editor: Carey Bohn. Managing Editor: Terry Brown. Bimonthly magazine covering alternative energy as applied to homeowners. "Our audience is composed of college-educated, upper-middle-class, professionally-employed homeowners. They're ambitious enough to take a personal approach to energy conservation, and they're willing, within reason, to spend some money as a means to saving in the future. A smaller percentage of readers lives on farms or in the country." Circ. 60,000. Pays on publication. Byline given. Pays 50% kill fee. Buys first North American serial rights. Submit seasonal/holiday queries 6 months in advance. SASE. Reports in 2 weeks. Sample copy $3; writer's guidelines for business size SAE and 1 first class stamp.

Nonfiction: How-to ("We're interested in energy saving techniques. Explain in laymen's terms, but demonstrate facility with technical aspects. If it's innovative, effective, and economical, chances are we'll be interested."); interview/profile ("We're always looking for people living the ideas we promote. If they have an interesting outlook, an odd situation, or an especially effective method for surviving economically in a home, whether in energy terms or merely through wise management of the homestead, they may have a place in the magazine."); and technical ("Most such articles are assigned to regular contributors, but someone with demonstrable expertise in a given relevant area, and the right idea, who also can write may find a spot in the magazine.) Writers should bring a perspective favorable to energy conservation to the magazine, naturally, and demonstrate a sense for the satisfaction and benefits of living self-sufficiently."

Photos: "We prefer to assign photos to regular contributors, but we will take photos with mss to illustrate stories for our purposes. If they turn out to be publishable, we can negotiate payment. Most important to discuss visuals in the query letter."

Tips: "The best way for a freelancer to break in with us is through detailed, competent queries. The writer who can give us a fresh idea thoroughly thought out, plus an indication why he or she is the right one to assign the piece to (including a writing sample or two), will stand head and shoulders above most of those who query us. One admonition about query style: Try to write like a journalist, and not an advertising copywriter. We know our needs and the worth of an idea if it's described in sufficient detail. The more to-the-point and professional the query, and the less self-congratulatory about the idea, the better. The best place to break in with us probably is the Home Energy Hotline section, which is composed of generally short pieces of a newsy nature, as a rule. The same criteria apply here that apply to general features, though practical items should be simpler and more concise. The writer who can give us a tight, useful item (250-1,250 words) about a new development in energy or household economy, a practical tip, and the like will stand a better chance of being assigned a longer feature. If your neighbor Sam has an efficient energy trick going in his house, don't query us unless his trick is applicable to other homes, and then present it as a concise, instructive vignette with a good technical foundation."

HOME MAGAZINE, (formerly *Hudson Home Magazine*), Hudson Publishing Company, 690 Kinderkamack Rd., Oradell NJ 07649. (201)967-7520. Editor: James A. Reynolds. Managing

Editor: James G. Keough. Monthly magazine covering home remodeling, home improving and home building. "*Home* tells homeowners how to remodel or improve an existing home, build a new home, and deal effectively with architects, contractors, and building supply dealers." Circ. 250,000. Pays on acceptance. No byline given. Pays negotiable kill fee. Buys all rights and makes work-for-hire assignments. Submit seasonal/holiday material 4 months in advance. SASE. Reports in 3 weeks on queries; 6 weeks on mss. Sample copy $2..

Nonfiction: How-to (homeowner-oriented, do-it-yourself projects); and financial subjects of interest to homeowners, e.g., taxes, insurance, etc. Buys 6-18 mss/year. Query with clips of published work. Length: 200-2,500 words. Pays $150-1,000.

HOMEOWNERS HOW TO HANDBOOK, The Make-It, Fix-it, Improve-it Magazine, 380 Madison Ave., New York NY 10017. Editor: Jim Liston. A publication of Times Mirror Magazines. Bimonthly. Circ. 400,000. Buys first rights. Pays 50% kill fee. Byline given. Pays on acceptance. Sample copy $1.50; address request to Warren Braren, *Homeowners How To Handbook* Circulation Department. Submit seasonal material 7 months in advance. Reports in 3 weeks. SASE.

Nonfiction: Wants how-to information based on facts and experience—not theory. No material on gardening or decorating. "Design ideas should be original and uncomplicated. They should be directed at young homeowners working with simple tools, and if possible, the kind of project that can be completed on a weekend. Likes articles on good before-and-after remodelings. All articles should contain a list of necessary materials and tools." Length: 1,800 words maximum. Pays $150/published page maximum.

Photos: Offers no additional payment for b&w photos used with mss. "Photos are as important as words. B&w preferred. 4x5's are OK, but 8x10's are better."

Fillers: Problem Solvers, a regular filler feature, pays $25 per captioned photo that contains a work-saving hint or solves a problem.

Tips: Send snapshots or even pencil sketches or plans of remodeling projects with query. "To break in a writer should show a willingness to submit the proposed article on speculation. (Once a writer has proved himself to us, this is not required)."

HOMEOWNER'S MONTHLY, INSIGHTS, ECM Newsletters, Inc., Box 92085, Houston, TX 77206. (713)691-1192. Editor-in-chief: G.R. Didow. Managing Editor: Joan Holst. Monthly newsletters covering real estate and housing interests. Purchased by real estate sales associates to be given at no charge to consumers. Estab. 1979. Circ. 400,000. Pays on acceptance. Buys all rights. Submit seasonal material 3 months in advance. Photocopied submissions OK. SASE. Reports in 1 month on queries. Sample copy and writer's guidelines for business size SASE.

Nonfiction: General interest; how-to (home repair, gardening, etc.); travel; other (health, unusual recipes, short anecdotes, quotes from well-know persons). "No controversial subject matter, no opinionated articles on current issues, and no brand names." Material should be informative without being overly sales-oriented. Buys 20-25 mss/issue. Query. Length: 20-200 words. Pays 10¢/word minimum.

Photos: State availability of photos. Pays $10 for b&w 8x10 prints. Captions preferred. Buys all rights.

HORTICULTURE, 300 Massachusetts Ave., Boston MA 02115. Editor: Thomas C. Cooper. Published by the Massachusetts Horticultural Society. Monthly. "We buy only first North American serial rights to mss; one-time use rights for photos." Byline given. Pays after publication. Query. Reports in 6 weeks. SASE.

Nonfiction and Photos: Uses articles from 500-5,000 words on plant science, practical gardening and the environment, and noteworthy gardens and gardeners. Study publication. Photos: color transparencies and good quality b&w prints, preferably 8x10; "accurately identified."

HOUSE & GARDEN, The Condé Nast Bldg; 350 Madison Ave., New York NY 10017. Editor-in-Chief: Louis Oliver Gropp. Editors: Denise Otis and Martin Filler. For homeowners and renters in middle and upper income brackets. Monthly. Circ. 1,136,444. Buys all rights. Pays on acceptance. "Study magazine before querying." Reports immediately. Query with clips of published work. SASE.

Nonfiction: Subjects of interest to "families concerned with their homes. Nothing for young marrieds specifically." Anything to do with the house or garden and affiliated subjects such as music, art, books, cooking, travel, health, etc. Length: about 1,500 words. Payment varies. Jerome H. Denner, managing editor, is department editor.

Photos: Photos purchased with mss only.

Tips: "This is a very tough market to break into. We very seldom use unsolicited material, but if anything is going to have a chance of making it here, it should be on a news breaking item. It must be something which has not already been covered in the other major magazines. It must have a new slant. Read the magazine closely for style and avoid things we've already done. We get too many freelancers sending us material on subjects for which the crest of wave has already passed. There's no guarantee that providing a short item (say, for Gardener's Notes or Living, which are mostly staff-written) will be an easier way in, but if you understand our needs and provide something that's really good, there's always a chance. It's best to send a query and a sample of previous writing."

HOUSE BEAUTIFUL, The Hearst Corp., 717 5th Ave., New York NY 10022. Editor: JoAnn Barwick. Executive Editor: Margaret Kennedy. Emphasizes design, architecture and building. Monthly magazine; 200 pages. Circ. 925,000. Pays on acceptance. Pays 25% kill fee. Byline given. Submit seasonal/holiday material 4 months in advance of issue date. SASE. Reports in 5 weeks. **Nonfiction:** Lois Perschetz, Copy Editor. Historical (landmark buildings and restorations); how-to (kitchen, bath remodeling service); humor; interview; new product; profile. Submit complete ms. Length: 300-1,000 words. Pays $150-400.
Photos: State availability of photos with ms. Offers no additional payment for photos.

HOUSTON HOME/GARDEN, Bayland Publishing, Inc., Box 25386, Houston TX 77005. Editor: Carol Sama. Emphasizes shelter. Monthly magazine; 200 pages. Circ. 80,000. Pays on publication. Buys all rights. Byline given. Submit seasonal/holiday material 4-6 months in advance. SASE. Reports in 1 month. Sample copy $3.25; free writer's guidelines.
Nonfiction: Wendy Meyer, managing editor. How-to (home maintenance and repairs); informational (city, tax information) and new product (short description). Needs Houston angle. Buys 20 mss/year. Query. Length: 1,000-2,000 words. Pays $2.50/published inch.
Photos: Photos purchased with accompanying ms. Captions required. Pays $15-20/8x10 b&w glossy print. Model release required.

LOG HOME GUIDE FOR BUILDERS & BUYERS, Muir Publishing Company Ltd., 1 Pacific Ave., Gardenvale, Quebec, Canada H9X 1B0. (514)457-2045. Editor: Doris Muir. Quarterly magazine covering the buying and building of log homes. "We publish for persons who want to buy or build their own log home. The writer should always keep in mind that this is a special type of person—usually a back-to-the-land, back-to-tradition type of individual who is looking for practical information on how to buy or build a log home." Circ. "50,000 and rising." Pays on publication. Byline given. Buys one-time rights. Submit seasonal/holiday material 4 months in advance. Simultaneous queries, and simultaneous ("writer should explain"), photocopied, and previously published submissions OK. SASE. Reports in 2 weeks. Sample copy $2.50 (postage included).
Nonfiction: Fred G. Dafoe, assistant editor. General interest; historical/nostalgic (log home historic sites; restoration of old log structures); how-to (anything to do with building log homes); inspirational (" 'Sweat equity—encouraging people that they can build their own home for less cost"); interview/profile (with persons who have built their own log homes); new product ("or new company manufacturing log homes—check with us first"); personal experience ("authors own experience with building his own log home, with photos is ideal); photo feature (on author or on anyone else building his own log home); technical (for "Techno-log" section; specific construction details, i.e. truss sections); also, "would like photo/interview/profile stories on famous persons and their log homes—how they did it, where they got their logs, etc."). "Please no exaggeration— this is a truthful, back-to-basics type of magazine trying to help the person interested in log homes." Buys 25 mss/year. Query with clips of published work or send complete ms. "Prefer queries first." Length: open. Pays $50 minimum.
Photos: State availability of photos. Send photos with mss "if possible. It would help us to get a real idea of what's involved." Pays $5-25 for b&w or color prints. "All payment are arranged with individual authors/submitters." Captions and identification of subjects required. Buys one-time rights.
Columns/Departments: Pro-Log (short news pieces of interest to the log-building world); Techno-Log (technical articles, i.e. solar energy systems; any illustrations welcome); and Book-Log (book reviews only, on books related to log building and alternate energy). Buys "possible 50-75 mss/ year. Query with clips of published work or send complete ms. Prefer queries first. Length: 100-1,000 words. All payment are arranged with individual authors/submitters."
Fillers: "Mainly interested in feature-news stories."

LOG HOUSE MAGAZINE, Box 1205, Prince George, British Columbia, Canada V2L 4V3. Editor-in-Chief: B. Allan Mackie. "For a middle- to upper-income audience; well-educated, men and women of all ages. Everyone needs a home, but these are the people who have the energy, the drive, the intelligence to want to create a superior home with their own hands." Annual magazine; 96 pages. Estab. 1974. Circ. 20,000. Pays on publication day.

Nonfiction: Historical (on excellent log construction methods), how-to (do any part/portion of a good solid timber house), informational, humor, inspirational, interview (with a practicing, professional builder, or a factual one on an individual who built a good house), new product (if relevant), personal experience (house building), photo feature (on good log buildings of a permanent residential nature; absolutely no cabins or rotting hulks), and technical (preservatives, tools). Query. Lenth: Open. Pays $50 minimum.

Photos: Mary Mackie, Photo Editor. Purchased with accompanying ms. Captions required. Send contact sheet. Pays $3 minimum/5x7 b&w glossy prints photo (negatives appreciated); $10 minimum for 2¼x2¼ transparencies.

METROPOLITAN HOME, (formerly *Apartment Life*), 750 3rd Ave., New York NY 10017. Editor: Joanna Krotz. For city dwellers. Monthly magazine; 110 pages. Circ. 850,000. Buys all rights. Buys 60-100 mss/year. Pays on acceptance. Submit seasonal material 6 months in advance. Reports in 2 months. Query. SASE.
Nonfiction: "Service material specifically for people who live in cities on interior designs, collectibles, equity, food, travel, health and housing. Thorough, factual, informative articles." Buys 60-100 mss/year. Query. Length: 300-1,000 words. Pays $250-400.
Photos: B&w photos and color are purchased only on assignment.
Columns/Departments: Travel, Wheels, Good Spirits (wine and liquor), Food and Real Estate. Length: 300-1,000 words. Pays $250-400.

NEW SHELTER, Rodale Press, 33 E. Minor St., Emmaus PA 18049. (215)957-5171. Executive Editor: Lawrence R. Stains. Managing Editor. Kim A. Mac Leod. Magazine published 9 times/year about energy-efficient homes. Estab. 1980. Circ. 500,000. Pays on acceptance. Buys all rights. Phone queries OK. Submit seasonal material at least 6 months in advance. SASE. Reports in 1 month.
Nonfiction: "We are the how-to magazine for the post-petroleum age. Roughly half our articles will tell people how to incorporate energy efficiency and alternate energy into both new and existing homes. The balance of the editorial will deal with other home improvement and do-it-yourself topics. We don't want the run-of-the-mill wooden how-to prose. We want lively writing about what the real people have done with their homes, telling how and why our readers should do the same." Query with clips of previously published work. Length: 1,000-5,000 words. Payment starts at 10¢/word.
Photos: Art director: John Johanek. State availability of photos. Pays $15-25 for b&w contact sheets with negatives and 8x10 glossy prints with ms. Pays $25 minimum for 2x2 or 35mm color transparencies. Captions and model release required.

1001 HOME IDEAS, Family Media, 149 Fifth Ave., New York NY 10010. (212)598-0800. Editor: Evan Frances Agnew. Managing Editor: Errol Croft. Monthly magazine covering interior design and decorating, remodeling and building, food, pet news, crafts and travel for middle-income, college educated homeowners, ages 35-40. Circ. 1.1 million. Pays on publication. Byline given. Buys all rights. Submit seasonal/holiday material 6 months in advance. Photocopied submissions OK. SASE. Reports in 1 month. Sample copy $1.
Nonfiction: How-to (decorate your home yourself); travel ("we generally feature a large city"); remodeling projects; and crafts ("new and original designs with instructions"). Buys 24 mss/year. Query. Length: open. Pays $100-300.
Photos: "Mss must be accompanied by b&w photos of the home featured in the article."
Columns/Departments: How America Copes ("problem that is solved by decorating or remodeling"); and Can Do ("repairs or decorating projects that a woman can do"). Query. Length: open. Pay varies.

ORGANIC GARDENING, Rodale Press Publications, 33 E. Minor St., Emmaus PA 18049. (215)967-5171. Managing Editor: Jack Ruttle. For a readership "interested in health and conservation, in growing plants, vegetables and fruits without chemicals, and in protecting the environment." Monthly magazine; 160-240 pages. Circ. 1,200,000. Buys all rights and the right to reuse in other Rodale Press Publications with agreed additional payment. Pays 25% kill fee, "if we agree to one." Byline given. Buys 400-500 mss/year. Pays on publication (actually, on preparation for publication). Free sample copy and writer's guidelines. Reports in 4-6 weeks. Query or submit complete ms. "Query with full details, no hype." SASE.
Nonfiction: "Factual and informative articles or fillers, especially on backyard gardening and family self-sufficiency, stressing organic methods. Interested in all crops, soil topics, indoor gardening, greenhouses; natural foods preparation, storage, etc.; biological pest control; variety breeding, nutrition, recycling, energy conservation; community and club gardening. Strong on specific details, step-by-step how-to, adequate research. Good slant and interesting presentation

always help. We do not want to see generalized garden success stories. And some build-it-yourself topics are often repeated. We would like to see material on development, techniques, different approaches to organic methods in producing fruit crops, grains, new and old vegetables; effective composting, soil building, waste recycling, food preparation, and insect control. Emphasis is on interesting, practical information, presented effectively and accurately." Length: 1,000-2,000 words for features. Pays $200-450.

Photos: B&w and color purchased with mss or on assignment. Enlarged b&w glossy print and/or negative preferred. Pays $15-25. 2¼x2¼ (or larger) color transparencies.

Fillers: Fillers on above topics are also used. Length: 150-500 words. Pays $50-100.

Tips: "Read the magazine regularly, like a hawk. Then write to suit the reader's needs."

PERFECT HOME MAGAZINE, 427 6th Ave. SE, Cedar Rapids IA 52401. Editor: Donna Nicholas Hahn. For "homeowners or others interested in building or improving their homes." Monthly. Buys all rights. "Only bylined feature is celebrity editorial which is written in first-person format." Pays on acceptance. Study magazine carefully before submitting. No seasonal material used. Submit editorial material at least 6 months in advance. Reports "at once." Query. SASE. Free sample copy.

Nonfiction: "Ours is a nationally syndicated monthly magazine sponsored in local communities by qualified home builders, real estate companies, home financing institutions, and lumber and building supply dealers. We are primarily a photo magazine that creates a desire for an attractive, comfortable home. We need homebuilding, decorating and remodeling features; decorating idea photographs, complete home coverage, and plans on homes." No do-it-yourself features. Length: 1-3 paragraphs. No set price.

Photos: Purchases photos with articles on home building, decorating and remodeling; also purchases photos of interest to homeowners with, captions only. Buys either b&w or color; color 3¼x4¼ up. "We return color; keep b&w unless return is requested as soon as issue has been printed. May hold photos 1 year." Photos must be well-styled and of highest professional quality. No models in pictures. Interested in series (for example, several pictures of gates, bay windows, window treatment, fireplaces, etc.). Pays $35 minimum for color.

Columns/Departments: What Home Means to Me. "Each month we feature one nationally known guest editor on this topic. Check with us before contacting a celebrity, since we have had so many of them." Length: 500-1,000 words. Pays $100, including copy, photos, signature, and signed release from individual.

Tips: "We love to find new sources but freelancers are seldom professional enough for us. We are primarily photo-oriented. Most letters reveal the writer has never seen the magazine. It would help so much if he would send for a free copy."

PHOENIX HOME/GARDEN, Arizona Home Garden, Inc., 1001 North Central, Suite 601, Phoenix AZ 85004. (602)258-9766. Editor: Manya Winsted. Associate Editors: Nora Burba and Joe Kullman. Monthly magazine covering homes, entertainment and gardening for Phoenix area residents interested in better living. Estab. 1980. Circ. 26,000. Pays "within 30 days of acceptance." Byline given. Buys all rights. Submit seasonal/holiday material 6 months in advance. Simultaneous queries OK. SASE. Reports in 6 weeks on queries. Sample copy $1.50.

Nonfiction: Book excerpts; general interest (on gardening, entertainment, food); historical (on furnishings related to homes); how-to (on home improvement or decorating); new product (for the home or garden); photo feature; and travel (of interest to Phoenix residents). Buys 100 or more mss/year. Query with clips of published work. Length: 2,000 words maximum. Pays $75-300 minimum/article.

Columns/Departments: Book Reviews (800-1,000 words); Crafts; and Homeworks (decorative how-to projects). Buys 200 mss/year. Query.

Fillers: Newsbreaks ("Sampler" describes "neat new products for the home in local stores"; "All's Fare" describes "food-related items of local interest, such as products or eateries"). Pays $20-25 (item and photo).

Tips: "I need so much material because this is a brand new magazine. It's not a closed shop. I want the brightest, freshest material available."

REAL ESTATE, Box 1689, Cedar Rapids IA 52406. (319)366-1597. Editor: C.K. Parks. "A publication sponsored by real estate brokers for distribution to homebuyers, clients, and community leaders." Bimonthly magazine; 16 pages. Special Christmas issue. Circ. 80,000. Buys all rights. No byline. Buys 24 mss/year. Pays on acceptance. Photocopied submissions OK. Submit seasonal material 4 months in advance. Reports in 30 days. SASE. Free sample copy.

Nonfiction: "The work of freelance writers fits particularly well into this type of publication because we are looking for nontechnical material of interest to the general public." Wants mss about how-to projects that can be done around the home, decorating in the home, and investing in

real estate. Length: 700-1,200 words. Pays $100.
Photos: Prefers articles with b&w photos.

SAN DIEGO HOME/GARDEN, Westward Press, 432 F St., San Diego CA 92101. (714)233-4567. Editor: Payne Johnson. Managing Editor: Peter Jensen. Associate Editors: Mary-Ann Courtenaye, Mary White. Monthly magazine covering homes and gardens and nearby travel for 20 to 40 year old residents of San Diego city and county and Northern Baja, California. Estab. 1979. Circ. 30,000. Pays on publication. Byline given. Buys all rights. Submit seasonal material 3 months in advance. Photocopied submissions OK. Reports in 1 month. Free writer's guidelines for SASE.
Nonfiction: General interest (service articles with plenty of factual information, prices and "where to buy" on home needs); how-to (save energy, garden, cook); new product (for the house); photo feature (on houses and gardens); and architecture; home improvement; remodeling and real estate. Articles must have local slant. Buys 10-20 mss/issue. Query with clips of previously published work. Length: 1,000 words minimum. Pays $50-200.

SELECT HOME DESIGNS, 382 W. Broadway, Vancouver, British Columbia, Canada V5Y 1R2. (604)879-4144. Editor: Ralph Westbrook. Publisher: Brian Thorn. Emphasizes building, renovation and interior design of single-family homes. Quarterly magazine. Circ. 150,000. Pays on acceptance. Buys all rights. Byline given. Submit 60 days in advance. Simultaneous, photocopied, and previously published submissions OK. SASE. Reports in 2 weeks. Sample copy and writer's guidelines 50¢ postage.
Nonfiction: General interest (explaining new products or innovations in methods relating to home and cottage); how-to (pertaining to home or cottaging); new product (energy sources, interior design products, lighting, etc.); photo feature (furniture, interiors, housing in general); and technical (new products or techniques relative to home or cottage). Buys 4-5 mss/issue. Query. Length: 250-2,000 words. Pays 10¢/word.
Photos: Geoffrey Noble, artistic director. "We are a 4-color consumer magazine. We prefer color photography for maximum effect." Pays $5 minimum/for 8x10 glossy b&w print; $10 minimum/ 35mm color transparency. Captions preferred. Buys all rights. Model release required.
Columns/Departments: "We have no established columns or departments, but are open to their establishment on a continuing basis." Query. Length: 250-1,000 words. Pays 10¢/word.

SOUTHERN ACCENTS, W.R.C. Smith Publishing Co., 1760 Peachtree Rd. NW, Atlanta GA 30357. (404)874-4462. Editor: James A. Hooton. Managing Editor: Diane Burrell. Emphasizes interior design and gardens of Southern homes for upper middle class and above. Most, but not all, readers live in the South. Read by interior designers and landscape architects "but most are simply people with varied vocations who are interested in mteriors, collections, gardens and in the Southern cultural heritage and places of beauty." Quarterly magazine; 144 pages, mostly photographs. Circ. 105,000. Pays on publication. Buys all rights. Phone queries OK. Submit seasonal/ holiday material 3 months in advance. SASE. Reports in 2-3 weeks. Sample copy $3.50; free writer's guidelines.
Nonfiction: Historical ("each issue carries at least one story on the renovation of a Southern home or historical garden; we're also interested in histories of certain decorative art, forms—Chinese export porcelains and American coin silver are two we have covered in the past. These articles depend less on illustration and can run considerably longer than 600 words"); "the didactic articles should help our readers learn to be more sophisticated collectors, e.g: 'A Primer for the Buyer of English Antique Furniture' "; interview ("a brief, regular feature called 'Inside Decorating' lets an interior designer tell how he or she approached and solved the problems of decorating a particular space"); and photo feature ("the majority of our articles describe the architecture and interior design of a house and simply tell how it got to look that way; text should tell the story and explicit captions should spell out names of manufacturers of fabrics, furniture, etc., origins of decorative articles. We use mostly color photos."). Buys 2-3 mss/issue. Query with clips of published work. Length: 500-600 words.
Photos: "We need to see photos in order to be able to judge whether or not we would be interested in the story." Rarely uses b&w photos. Payment varies for 4x5 or 2¼x2¼ color transparencies. Captions required.
Tips: Writers should have some expertise and credentials in the area in which they are writing, such as knowledge of period furniture and interior design.

YOUR HOME, Meridian Publishing, Box 2315, Ogden UT 84404. Editor: Mrs. Bermuda Dawson. Monthly magazine; 12 pages. Circ. 650,000. Distributed to businesses, with their inserts, as house organs. A pictorial magazine with emphasis on home and garden decorating and improvement. We prefer manuscripts with photos, color and/or b&w. 400-1,000 words. Pays 10¢/word. $20 for b&w, $25 for color transparencies or slides. Buys all rights. Credit line given. Payment on

acceptance. 10 month lead time. Send SASE for guidelines. 50¢ for sample copy.
Tips: "To break in a lot depends on the 'quality' photos which accompany the submissions."

Home Computing

This section lists publications for the owners of personal computers. Publications for data processing personnel are listed in that section of Trade Journals.

BYTE MAGAZINE, 70 Main St., Peterborough NH 03458. (603)924-7217. Editor: Christopher P. Morgan. Monthly magazine covering personal computers for college-educated users of computers. Circ. 190,000. Pays on acceptance. Buys all rights. Photocopied submissions OK. SASE. Reports on rejections in 3 months; in 6 months if accepted. Sample copy $2.75; writer's guidelines for SASE.
Nonfiction: How-to (technical information about computers) and technical. Buys 240 mss/year. Submit complete ms. Length: 20,000 words maximum. Pays $50/typeset magazine page maximum.
Tips: "Almost all *Byte* authors are regular readers of the magazine, and most use a computer of some size, either at home or at work. Back issues of the magazine give prospective authors an idea of the type of article published in *Byte*. Articles can take one of several forms: tutorial articles on a given subject, how-to articles detailing a specific implementation of a hardware or software project done on a small computer, survey articles on the future of some aspect of computer science, and sometimes academic articles describing original work in computer science (if written in an informal, 'friendly' style. Authors with less of a technical orientation should consider writing for our sister publication *Popular Computing Magazine.*

COMPUTER & PROGRAMMING, Davis Publications, 380 Lexington Ave., New York NY 10017. (212)557-9100. Editor: Alan Rose. Managing Editor: Paul Margolis. Bimonthly magazine covering the use, theory and application of computers (hardware and software) for hobbyists, small businessmen, scientists and computer buffs. Estab. 1981. Circ. 250,000. Pays on acceptance. Byline given. Buys all rights. SASE. Reports in 2 weeks. Sample copy free.
Nonfiction: Computer application, theory, use, hardware, hardware reviews, software reviews, original programs, tutorials and games. "We like to see some sort of artwork, graphs, photos or circuits with every ms." Buys 120 mss/year. Query. Length: 1,000-5,000 "and up." Pays $100-275.
Photos: Reviews 5x7 b&w glossy prints. Photos are paid for with payment for ms. Captions and model releases required. Buys one-time rights.

CREATIVE COMPUTING, 39 E. Hanover Ave., Morris Plains NJ 07950. Publisher/Editor-in-Chief: David Ahl. Editor: Elizabeth Staples. Monthly magazine covering the use of computers in homes, businesses and schools for students, faculty, hobbyists—everyone interested in the effects of computers on society and the use of computers in school, at home or at work. Circ. 100,000. Pays on acceptance. "Buys first rights and usually first reprint rights so as to publish in 'Best of' volumes; then rights automatically revert to author." Pays 20% kill fee. Byline given. Submit seasonal/holiday material at least 4 months in advance. SASE. Reports in 2 weeks. Sample copy $2.50.
Nonfiction: How-to (building a computer at home, personal computer applications and software); informational (computer careers; simulations on computers; problem-solving techniques; use in a particular institution or discipline such as medicine, education, music, animation, space exploration, business or home use); historical articles (history of computers, or of a certain discipline, like computers and animation); interviews (with personalities in the hobbyist field, old-timers in the computer industry or someone doing innovative work); personal experience (first-person accounts of using hardware or software are actively sought); and technical (programs, games and simulations with printouts). Buys 300 mss/year. Length: 500-3,000 words. Pays $35-50/printed page.
Photos: Usually purchased with mss, with no additional payment, but sometimes pays $3-50 for b&w glossy prints or $10-150 for any size color.
Columns/Departments: Compendium uses interesting, short articles about crazy, silly, unfortunate or interesting uses of computers (some human interest) about use in menu planning, pole vaulting, exploring, mistakes in computer programming, etc. Length: 50-500 words. Pays $5-30. Pays in copy of publication for book reviews (all books on computer use). New Products section accepts only press releases on new products. Query Betsy Staples.

Fiction: Humorous fiction, mysteries and science fiction. "Fiction must be specifically related to robots or computers. Interesting stories that show how computers can benefit society are sought. Writers must keep in mind that people program computers and should program them for people's benefit. Stories dealing with new field of computers in the home are also sought." Buys 30 mss/year. Submit complete ms. Length: 500-3,000 words. Pays $15-400.

Fillers: Jokes, gags, anecdotes, puzzles, short humor. Buys 100/year. Pays $5-50.

80 MICROCOMPUTING, 80 Magazine St., Peterborough NH 03458. (603)924-3873. Publisher: Wayne Green. Editor: Michael Comendul. Monthly magazine about microcomputing for "owners and users of TRS-80 by Radio Shack." Estab. 1980. Circ. 65,000. Pays on acceptance. Buys all rights. Phone queries OK. Photocopied submissions OK. SASE. Reports in 2 months. Sample copy $2.50; writer's guidelines for SAE.

Nonfiction: General interest (application for business, education, home and hobby); how-to (program); humor; and technical (programs and uses). "We are looking for articles pertaining to TRS-80 microcomputers, their hardware and software. There are sections for beginners and those in advanced levels." Buys 30 mss/issue. Query. Length: 3,000 words minimum. Pays $50/printed page.

Reviews: Writers interested in reviewing current available software are asked to query the review editor, stating areas of interest and equipment owned. Buys 8-15 reviews per issue.

Photos: Offers no additional payment for photos accepted with ms. Captions and model release required. Buys all rights.

HOBBY COMPUTER HANDBOOK, Davis Publications, Inc., 380 Lexington Ave., New York NY 10017. (212)557-9100. Associate Publisher/Editor-in-Chief: Julian S. Martin. Editor: Gordon Sell. Annual magazine covering home hobby computers and theory. Pays on acceptance. Buys all rights. Pays 100% kill fee. Byline given. Previously published submissions OK. SASE. Reports in 6 weeks. Free writer's guidelines.

Nonfiction: "The nature of the magazine's title limits the manuscript contributions to the subject matter. Aim at the hobbyist who is a beginner, or working with his first computer. Stick to theory articles, how-to ideas that are universal to hobby computers and simple project ideas. If you know nothing about hobby computers, have not worked with a hobby computer, don't write to us! You can't fake it in this field." Buys 60 mss/year. Query. Length: 1,000-3,500 words. Pays $150-250.

Photos: State availability of photos with query. Offers no additional payment for b&w negatives with proof sheet. Buys all rights. "In most cases, we give permission for author and/or photographer to use material in other publications after publication date." Authorization given in writing only.

Fillers: Jokes, gags, anecdotes. Buys 3/issue. Pays $20-$30.

KILOBAUD MICROCOMPUTING, 73 Magazine St., Peterborough NH 03458. (603)924-3873. Publisher: Wayne Green. Assistant Publisher: Jeff Detray. Monthly magazine about microcomputing for microcomputer hobbyists, businessmen interested in computer systems and students who want to learn about computers. Circ. 80,000. Pays on acceptance. Buys all rights. Phone queries OK. Submit seasonal/holiday material 4 months in advance. Photocopied submissions OK. SASE. Reports in 3 weeks. Sample copy $2.95; writer's guidelines for SASE.

Nonfiction: General interest (the how and why of design, programs, algorithms, program modules, and experimental work in advanced fields); how-to (use for a hobby, in educational programs, business, etc.); humor; new product (evaluations); and technical (all related to microcomputers, with diagrams included on a separate sheet). Buys 25-35 mss/issue. Query. Length: 3,000 words minimum. Pays $35-50/page.

Photos: Reviews 5x7 and 8x10 b&w glossy prints. Pays $150 minimum for 8x10 color glossy prints and transparencies. Especially needs microcomputer with a person in the picture (vertical). Offers no additional payment for photos accepted with ms. Captions and model release required.

Fiction: Query.

Tips: "Use as few buzzwords as possible. Remember that *Kilobaud Microcomputing* is trying to interest newcomers in this field, not scare them away. Use the first person and subheadings."

PERSONAL COMPUTING, 1050 Commonwealth Ave., Boston MA 02215. (617)232-5470. Editor: Harold G. Buchbinder. Managing Editor: Don Wood. Monthly magazine covering small business, office, home and school computing. Monthly magazine; 116 pages. Estab. 1977. Circ. 35,000. Pays on publication. Buys all rights. Byline given. Phone queries OK. Submit seasonal/holiday material 4 months in advance. Photocopied submissions OK, but state if material is not multiple submission. SASE. Sample copy $3; free writer's guidelines.

Nonfiction: Comparison pieces, product reviews and evaluations; general interest (related to microcomputers); historical (original pieces concerning computer history); how-to (program and use computers; "especially articles with programs our readers can use in business, office, home and school"); humor (fiction relating to computers and personal stories concerning computers); interview (with prominent figures in the field); new product (review, but not puff piece, must be objective); nostalgia (only if related to computing); computer chess and computer bridge; personal experience (someone who has worked with a specific system and has learned something readers can benefit from); opinion (editorials, or opinion of someone in field); photo feature (only if accompanied by article); profile (of prominent person in field); and technical (program writing, debugging; especially good are applications for business, education, or home use). No articles on product hype, personal experiences that don't pass anything on to the reader, games that have been published in similar form already, and puzzles. Buys 10 mss/issue. Query with a listing and sample runs. Complete ms preferred. Length: 1,000 words minimum. Pays $20/printed page minimum.

Photos: State availability of photos with query or ms. Offers no additional payment for b&w or color pictures. Captions preferred. Buys all rights.

Columns/Departments: Editorials (on any topic in the field); Future Computing (a detailed look at one or more aspects of what's going on in the field and what's projected); *PC* Interview (of prominent figures in the field); Random Access (unusual applications, goings on, or stories about computers); Computer Chess (and other games) and What's Coming Up (product reviews, comments on, criticism of, and comparison). Query but complete ms preferred. Length: 500 words minimum. Pays $20/printed page; Random Access pieces are paid anywhere from $5-$25. Rewritten press releases are not acceptable.

Fiction: "Fiction should relate to computers—especially microcomputers. Science fiction showing computer uses in the future also acceptable." Humor and nostalgia related to computer. Buys 1 ms/issue. Submit complete ms. Length: 750 words minimum. Pays $20/printed page.

POPULAR COMPUTING MAGAZINE, (formerly *On Computing Magazine*),70 Main St., Peterborough, NH 03458. (603)924-9281. Editor: Stanley M. Miastkowski. McGraw-Hill monthly magazine covering personal computers directed particularly at beginners and professional people such as educators, attorneys, doctors and so on. Estab. May 1979. Circ. 10,000. Pays on acceptance. Buys all rights. Photocopied submissions OK. SASE. Reports in 3 months. Sample copy $2.75; writer's guidelines for SASE.

Nonfiction: "Articles should contain information about buying personal computers plus reviews of computers and other material related to personal computers." No tic-tac-toe or biorhythm programs. Buys 200 mss/year. Submit complete ms. Length: 4,000 words maximum. Pays $60/page and up.

Tips: "Visit personal computer stores or read any of the books on the market pertaining to personal computers. *Popular Computing Magazine* is similar to *Byte Magazine* in some ways but will be at a lower technical level, designed for the mass market. The ideal *Popular Computing Magazine* article popularizes personal computer concepts without talking down to the reader. Articles should be free of computer jargon as much as possible. Requesting our author's guide and following its guidelines are two good ways to increase your chances of acceptance."

PROGRAMMERS SOFTWARE EXCHANGE, 2110 N. 2nd Street, Cabot AR 72023. (501)843-6037. Editor: Linda Brown. Quarterly magazine covering personally owned computers. Circ. 3,000. Pays on acceptance. Buys all rights. Pays 25% kill fee. Byline given. Phone queries OK. Submit seasonal/holiday material 1 month in advance. Simultaneous, photocopied and previously published submissions OK. SASE. Reports in 2 weeks. Free sample copy and writer's guidelines.

Nonfiction: Exposé (computer crime); general interest (game programs); historical; how-to (program computers); humor; inspirational; nostalgia; opinion; profile; and travel. "All articles must be related to personal computers in various uses and configurations." Buys 2 mss/issue. Send complete ms. Length: 100-600 words. Pays 15¢/word.

Photos: State availability of photos. Pays $10-$50 for b&w contact sheets; $10-$50 for color contact sheets; offers no additional payment for photos accompanying ms. Buys one-time rights. Captions preferred.

Columns/Departments: Why Not Do It In Software. Send complete ms. Length: 100-600 words. Pays 15¢/word.

Fiction: Adventure, erotica, fantasy, experimental, historical, humorous and mainstream. "All articles must be slanted to computer use by people." Send complete ms. Length: 200-600 words. Pays $30-$90.

Poetry: Free verse, haiku, light verse and traditional. Submit in batches of 10. Length: 5-20 lines. Pays $10-$50.

Fillers: Clippings, jokes, gags, anecdotes and puzzles. Buys 5/issue. Length: 10-100 words. Pays $5-$20.

Tips: "Don't limit your story to what is now common knowledge, but think of future uses of home computers; e.g., children being monitored 24 hours a day by wearing wrist bands, etc. You must have a precise knowledge of an advancing industry and understand what computers are capable of doing (which is left to the imagination)."

SYNTAX ZX80, Syntax ZX80, Inc., Rd. 2 Box 457, Bolton Rd., Harvard MA 01451. (617)456-3661. Editor: Ann L. Zevnik. Monthly newsletter covering ZX80 and MicroAce microcomputers for owners of all levels of expertise. Estab. 1980. Circ. 1,700. Pays on acceptance. Byline given. Buys all rights; "nonexclusive." Submit seasonal/holiday material 2 months in advance. Photocopied submissions OK. SASE. Reports in 2 weeks. Free sample copy.

Nonfiction: How-to (hardware projects, software tutorials); new product (ZX80-related peripherals); technical (programs: business, educational or game programs written in BASIC or Z80 machine language. Explanations of machine technical workings). "We need clearly written stories and reviews to both interest experts and educate beginners. An extremely tight style is especially important to our newsletter format. No long, chatty stories. We are a newsletter whose main purpose is to give readers as much information as possible in a minimum space. Set them to thinking rather than drowning them in explanation." Buys 48 mss/year. Length: 100-900 words. Pays $5-60; "additional for accompanying programs."

Columns/Departments: "We need reviews of ZX80 and ZX80-related books on hardware and programming. Again, the piece must be user-oriented, but objective. No advertising." Query. Length: 100-900 words. Pays $5-60.

Fillers: Newsbreaks (short-short information, such as 1-2 line commands to access computer memory). "Mostly staff-written but would buy 30/year if available." Length: 15-100 words. Pays $2-7.

Tips: "Demonstrate knowledge of ZX80 computer, electronics, or programming and be able to express technical concepts clearly and simply. We have no strict submission requirements but prefer typed copy and listing. Hardware projects and software stories are about 80% submitted. Make sure instructions are specific and clear, and writing should be super-tight. Of course, all project and programs must work."

Humor

Publications herein specialize in cartoon panel humor, gaglines or prose humor. Other publications that use humor can be found in nearly every category in this book. Some of these have special needs for major humor pieces; some use humor as fillers; many others are simply interested in material that meets their ordinary fiction or nonfiction requirements but has a humorous slant.

CHEAP LAUGHS/COMEDY UPDATE, Comedy Comedy Comedy, 408 Clement St., San Francisco CA 94118. (415)397-5962 or 928-5189. Comedy/Update, Editor-in-Chief: Paul Giles; Cheap Laughs, Editor-in-Chief: Karen Warner. Buys 30 jokes/issue. "Bulk of our subscribers are comedians, DJ's, speechwriters, publications using quips or jokes., i.e., Phyllis Diller, Joey Adams, Norma Canfield, *Readers Digest*, Jim Allen *National Enquirer*, Herb Caen *SF Chronicle*, Gary Owens, Bill Rafferty, Tony DePaul, etc." Prefers submissions double-spaced on 3x5 cards or slips of paper. "However, we will also consider material submitted on 8x11 sheets of typing paper. You can single space or double space the joke but it makes it easier for us to read if you type in all caps and you leave space between each joke." Reports in 2 weeks on unused material; 3 months on published material. Pays $2/joke on acceptance; buys all rights. SASE.

Humor: "Especially need jokes on sports in season. Also material that can be used by toastmasters/business speakers/or anyone who performs in front of a live audience (i.e., heckler stoppers; mike failure; lights out; small crowd; large crowd; etc).

Tips: "Be original. Don't waste your postage and our time sending us old jokes you've heard from others. Study joke books that specialize in oneliners, as opposed to joke books that have funny stories. Listen to comedians like Phyllis Diller, Joan Rivers, Johnny Carson."

MAD MAGAZINE, 485 Madison Ave., New York NY 10022. Editor: Al Feldstein. Buys all rights. Byline given.

Humor & Satire: "You know you're almost a *Mad* writer when: You include a self-addressed, stamped envelope with each submission. You realize we are a visual magazine and we don't print prose, text or first/second/third-person narratives. You don't send us stuff like the above saying,

'I'm sure one of your great artists can do wonders with this.' You first submit a 'premise' for an article, and show us how you're going to treat it with three or four examples, describing the visuals (sketches not necessary). You don't send in 'timely' material, knowing it takes about 6 months between typewriter and on-the-stands. You don't send poems, song parodies, fold-ins, movie and/or TV show satires, Lighter Sides or other standard features. You understand that individual criticism of art or script is impossible due to the enormous amount of submissions we receive. You don't ask for assignments or staff jobs since *Mad* is strictly a freelance operation. You concentrate on new ideas and concepts other than things we've done (and over-done), like 'You Know You're a . . . When. . . .' "

ORBEN'S CURRENT COMEDY, 1200 N. Nash St., #1122, Arlington VA 22209. (703)522-3666. Editor: Robert Orben. For "speakers, toastmasters, businessmen, public relations people, communications professionals." Biweekly. Buys all rights. Pays at the end of the month for material used in issues published that month. "Material should be typed and submitted on standard size paper. Please leave 3 spaces between each item. Unused material will be returned to the writer within a few days if SASE is enclosed. We do not send rejection slips. If SASE is not enclosed, all material will be destroyed after being considered except for items purchased."
Fillers: "We are looking for funny, performable one-liners, short jokes and stories that are related to happenings in the news, fads, trends and topical subjects. The accent is on comedy, not wit. Ask yourself, 'Will this line get a laugh if performed in public?' Material should be written in a conversational style and, if the joke permits it, the inclusion of dialogue is a plus. We are particularly interested in material that can be used by speakers and toastmasters: lines for beginning a speech, ending a speech, acknowledging an introduction, specific occasions, anything that would be of use to a person making a speech. We can use lines to be used at sales meetings, presentations, conventions, seminars and conferences. Short, sharp comment on business trends, fads and events is also desirable. Please do not send us material that's primarily written to be read rather than spoken. We have little use for definitions, epigrams, puns, etc. The submissions must be original. If material is sent to us that we find to be copied or rewritten from some other source, we will no longer consider material from the contributor." Pays $5.
Tips: "Follow the instructions in our guidelines. Although they are quite specific, we have received everything from epic poems to serious novels."

SMILE AND CHUCKLE INC., Smile and Chuckle, Inc., 108 S. Iris St., Alexandria VA 22304. (703)370-2085. Editor: Dan Boger. Monthly humor tabloid distributed to all residents in a zip code area. Estab. 1979. Circ. 10,000. Pays on publication. Buys all rights. Phone queries OK. Submit seasonal material 2 months in advance. Simultaneous and photocopied submissions OK, if so indicated. SASE. Reports in 2 months. Free sample copy and writer's guidelines. "Due to the large volume of requests, I must receive postage and an envelope large enough to handle a 24-page tabloid."
Nonfiction: Humor. No sex, violence, politics or controversial subjects. Buys 150 mss/year. Send complete ms. Length: 100-1,200 words. Pays 5¢/word.
Columns/Departments: Light humor. Send complete ms.
Fiction: Humorous. No sex, violence, politics or controversial subjects.
Poetry: Humor. Buys 2 mss/issue. Submit maximum 5 poems. Pays 5¢/word.
Fillers: Jokes, gags and short humor. Buys 100/year. Pays $2 maximum.

In-Flight

This list consists of publications read by commercial airline passengers. They use general interest freelance material such as travel articles, etc., as well as general interest material on aviation and other subjects.

AIRCAL, (formerly *Air California Magazine*), Box 707, South Laguna CA 92677. (714)494-1727. Editor-in-Chief: Michael McFadden. Emphasizes all aspects of the West for airline passengers on AirCal. Monthly magazine; 128 pages. Estab. 1967. Circ. 350,000. Pays on publication. Buys one-time rights. 35% freelance written. Submit seasonal/holiday material 3 months in advance. Simultaneous, photocopied and previously published submissions OK. SASE. Reports in 2 months. Sample copy $2. "We get 50-75 queries a month and almost an equal number of manuscripts. We will not be responsible for unsolicited manuscripts or art. If we want to assign a piece we will answer a query. Otherwise they will go unanswered."

Nonfiction: Address queries to Cristofer Gross, Managing Editor. Historical; humor; informational (travel); inspirational (if not sentimental); interview (West Coast personalities); nostalgia; photo feature; profile; and travel (West Coast). Buys 35-40 mss/year. Query to be short and to the point. Length: 1,500-5,000 words. Pays $50-150.

Photos: Photos purchased with accompanying ms or on assignment. Captions required. Pays $10-25 for 8x10 b&w photos; $25-50 for 35mm color photos. No additional payment for photos accepted with accompanying ms. Model release required.

ALASKAFEST, Seattle Northwest Publishing Co., 1932 1st Ave., Suite 503, Seattle WA 98101. (206)682-5871. Editor: Ed Reading. For travelers on Alaska Airlines. Monthly magazine; 64-80 pages. Circ. 25,000-35,000 (depending on season). Pays within 2 weeks of publication. Buys first rights. Byline given. Phone queries OK. Submit seasonal/holiday material 4 months in advance. SASE. Query with clips of published work. "A smart query begins with the lead of the story and is written in the style of the story. We don't get many like that." Free sample copy and writer's guidelines.

Nonfiction: The audience is predominantly male, business travelers. We cover not only Alaska, but the whole West Coast. Editorial content includes general-interest, adventure travel, business, life-style, and think pieces. We continue to look for humor and fiction. Buys 6 mss/issue. Length: 800-2,500 words. Pays $75-400.

Photos: State availability of photos with mss or send photos with ms. Pays $25-100 for b&w prints; $40-200 for color transparencies. Captions required.

Tips: "Read a copy of the magazine. Then send something I would pubish. Show, don't tell."

AMERICAN WAY, Box 61616, DFW Airport, TX 75261. (214)355-1583. The inflight magazine for American Airlines. Monthly magazine. Pays on acceptance. Buys various rights depending on author and material. Sometimes pays kill fee. Byline given. Submit seasonal/holiday material 7 months in advance. Reports in 4 months. SASE. Free sample copy.

Nonfiction: Broadly oriented rather than travel-oriented. "Seek timely articles that deal with almost any subject. Avoid controversial subjects or advocacy articles." Query (phone queries discouraged). "We would like writing samples that show a writer's abilities and scope. These will not be returned. We have no patience with writers who haven't familiarized themselves with the magazine." Submit Attn: Articles Editor. Nearly all articles written by a well-established group of freelancers. Length: 1,500-1,750 words for think pieces, interviews, profiles, humor, nostalgia, travel pieces, sports articles and how-to. Pays $300 minimum.

Tips: "Write interestingly and populate articles with real people who have something to say. Show a special concern for spelling of proper names. Send a query letter that is inherently interesting. It can almost be like a letter telling a friend about something interesting. Don't tell me *why* I should be interested."

CAMINOS DEL AIRE, Titsch Publishing, 2500 Curtis St., Suite 200, Denver CO 80205. (303)573-1433. Editor: Dawn Alba Denzer. Bimonthly magazine about destinations and information of interest to people who fly Mexicana Airlines, 60% of whom are Mexican Nationals. Estab. 1980. Circ. 120,000. Pays on publication. Byline given. Buys first North American serial rights. Phone queries OK. Submit seasonal material 2 months in advance. Simultaneous and previously published work OK if so indicated. SASE. Reports in 2 months. Free sample copy and writer's guidelines.

Nonfiction: "We are interested in articles related to shopping and travel advice, destination articles, events, festivals, cultural activities of Mexican and American interest. All of our magazine is freelance written. We feel we can get a much better variety that way. All articles are printed in both English and Spanish. We're anxious to hear from anyone who is bilingual or can translate articles into Spanish." Buys 10 mss/issue. Send complete ms. Length: 1,000-1,500 words. Pays 10¢/word minimum.

Photos: Reviews 2¼x2¼ color transparencies. Offers no additional payment for photos accepted with ms. Captions and model release required. Buys one-time rights plus rights for one reprint.

DELTA SKY, Halsey Publishing, 12955 Biscayne Blvd., N. Miami FL 33181. (305)653-1723. Editor: Donna Dupuy. Audience is Delta Air Lines passengers. Monthly magazine. Circ. 3.25 million monthly. "Unsolicited materials are rarely used, and only text/photo packages are considered." For details and Guidelines, send SASE to Donna Dupuy, Managing Editor.

EAST/WEST NETWORK, INC., 34 E. 51st St., New York NY 10022. Editor-in-Chief: Fred R. Smith. Executive Editors: Joseph Poindexter and John Johns. Publishes monthly inflight publications: *Extra*, (Continental Arilines), *Flightime* (Ozark Airlines), *Mainliner* (United Airlines), *PSA*

Magazine (Pacific Southwest Airlines), *ReView* (Eastern Airlines), and *Texas Flyer*, (Texas International). Combined circ. 18 million. Pays within 60 days of acceptance. Buys all East/West Network Publications: author retains other rights. Pays 50% kill fee. Byline given. SASE. Reports in 1 month.

Nonfiction: "Magazines publish articles of interest to consumer magazine audience that are timely and have national significance." Queries with published work for *Mainliner* and *ReView* should be sent to New York office. Queries for all other publications should be sent to the West Coast office to Editor and name of publication at 5900 Wilshire Blvd., Los Angeles CA 90036. Length: 1,000-2,500 words. Pays $300-700.

Photos: Wants no photos sent by writers.

EXTRA, East/West Network, 5900 Wilshire Blvd., Suite 300, Los Angeles CA 90036. Magazine is a showcase of the best feature journalism appearing in major American newspapers. Reprints articles from these papers written both by staff reporters and freelancers. Uses original travel stories focused on Continental Airlines' destinations. Length: 1,500-2,500 words. Pays $300-600. For other requirements, see East/West Network.

Tips: "For feature articles, newspaper clips serve as manuscripts if writer owns rights; query letter is not necessary. For travel, the query must illustrate the writer's broad knowledge of a destination, not just one aspect, and should serve as a sample of the writer's style as well. Familiarity with the publication and the airlines route system is crucial. Writers who have sold features to newspapers, features that will not be old news in a month or two, may submit clips directly for consideration. Phone calls are not welcome. Articles must not be too local in focus; must not be too dated (we have three-month lead time on features); should be between 1,000 and 3,000 words. Profiles of noted people, celebrities, etc., are always welcome, particularly if these people are or will be in the news."

FLIGHTIME, 5900 Wilshire Blvd., Suite 300, Los Angeles CA 90036. For requirements, see: *East/West Network*.

FLYING COLORS, Halsey Publishing, 12955 Biscayne Boulevard, N. Miami FL 33181. (305)893-1520. Publisher: Seymour Gerber. Editor: Steve Winston. Monthly magazine about Braniff destination cities, sports and culture for Braniff passengers who are mostly affluent, upper management people who do a great deal of traveling. Circ. 200,000. Pays on publication. Byline given. Buys first North American serial rights. Simultaneous submissions OK, if so indicated. SASE. Reports in 2 months. Sample copy $2; writer's guidelines for SASE.

Nonfiction: General interest; historical (only pertaining to Braniff destination cities); travel (Braniff destination cities and surrounding areas); energy; and sports. "Send a story idea with a unique angle and a unique style. Offbeat stories included one on a graveyard for antique aircraft, the history and distilling of champagne and interesting rides in New York City. Most travel pieces are given on assignment, rather than query." No stories on companies or products. Buys 9-15 mss/issue, most on assignment. Query with clips of previously published work. Length: 1,600-2,000 words. Pays $250-300 for photo-text package.

Photos: State availability of photos. Offers no additional payment for photos accepted with ms. Model release required. Buys one-time rights.

Tips: In query, list Braniff cities you are familiar with, availability of color transparencies, and send a few clips. For other stories, send brief bio and few clips. Please enclose SASE (and sufficient postage).

FRONTIER, In-Flight Publishing Co., 1637 S. Oakland Court. Aurora CO 80012. Editor: C.A. Stevens. Bimonthly magazine promoting aviation and the Christian ethic, as well as entertaining and informing an affluent audience of both seasoned air travelers and first-timers. Annual special emphasis sections include Summertime Vacations in the Rockies (April) and Skiing Frontier's Rockies (September). Circ. 6,000,000. Pays on acceptance for mss; on publication for photos. Buys one-time rights and non-exclusive reprint rights. Offers 25% kill fee on assigned material. Submit seasonal material 4 months in advance. SASE. Reports in 6 weeks.

Nonfiction: General interest ("there are few limitations"—aviation lore; ethics and Christianity; patriotism and national security); historical (of a Western or aviation nature); humor; profile (personalities); health; science; sports; travel; the outdoors. Query. Length: 300-1,000 words (shorts); 1,500-2,500 (features). Pays $75-250.

Photos: Pays $10-40 for b&w and color photos; double for covers and spreads.

Tips: "Stories should build on substance and fact, rather than abstract ideas or intangible concepts. Avoid dullness—we like a good yarn or a tall tale. When the subject demands it, even first-person treatment is occasionally used. Good photos—both b&w and color—are also cherished."

INFLIGHT, Meridian Publishing Co., Box 2315, Ogden UT 84404. (801)394-9446. Editor: Dick Harris. Bimonthly magazine covering general-interest topics. Readers are "business-oriented, predominantly male, age 30-50, middle-to-high income, well-educated, who travel extensively in connection with business and personal affairs, like sports, and are moving up professionally. Our magazine aims at providing short, brightly-written articles that inform and entertain." Pays on acceptance. Byline given. Buys first North American serial rights and second serial (reprint) rights. Submit seasonal/holiday material 6 months in advance. SASE. Reports in 2 weeks on queries and mss. Sample copy 50¢ with 9x12 SAE and 40¢ postage; writer's guideline free for #10 SAE and 18¢ postage.
Nonfiction: General interest, historical/nostalgic, how-to, humor, inspirational, interview/profile, photo feature and travel. No "exposés, think pieces, off-color humor or politics." Buys 50 mss/year. Query. Length: 400-1,200 words. Pays up to 10¢/word.
Photos: State availability of photos. Pays $25-50 for 35mm or 4x5 color transparencies; $20 for 8x10 b&w prints. Captions and identification of subjects required. Buys one-time rights.
Fillers: Short humor. "This is the most accessible section to freelancers. We're looking for short, humorous pieces of 300-400 words or 1-page humor features of about 800 words." Buys 20-30/year. Length: 300-400 words.

NORTHWEST PASSAGES, The Webb Co., 1999 Shepard Rd., St. Paul MN 55116. Editor-in-Chief: Jean Marie Hamilton. Columns Editor: Paul Froiland. 80% freelance written. For Northwest Orient Airlines passengers. Monthly magazine. Pays on acceptance. Buys first magazine rights and nonexclusive reprint rights. Buys 61 mss/year. Reports in 1 month. Query with clips of published work. SASE. Sample copy $1; free writer's guidelines.
Nonfiction: How-to (on business, health, etc.,—no crafts); informational (sports, business trends, lifestyle, current issues); interviews and profiles (on interesting people who are saying things of significance); entertainment (television, movies, the arts); science; politics; travel (no what-to-see, where-to-stay pieces); and business management. Length: 2,000-3,000 words. Pays $300-1,000.
Photos: Purchased with mss and on assignment. Query. Pays $25-75/b&w; $50-100/color; $200/cover shots. For photos purchased with mss, "the package price is negotiated ahead of time." Model release required.
Columns/Departments: Sports and Health, The Arts, Pop psychology quizzes, Science, Travel and Finances. Buys 2-4 mss/issue. Length 800-1,200 words. Pays $100-200.

PAN-AM CLIPPER, Ziff-Davis Publishing, 1 Park Ave., New York NY 10016. (212)725-3454. Editor: Ruth Kelton. Senior Editor: Martha Lorini. Monthly magazine for passengers of Pan-Am airlines (50% American, 50% foreign men travelling on business). Circ. 300,000. Pays on acceptance. Buys first world serial rights. Submit seasonal material 4 months in advance. Photocopied submissions OK. SASE. Reports in 1 month on queries; in 2 weeks on mss.
Nonfiction: General interest; interview (internationally important); profile; travel (destination pieces on unusual people and events of interest); humor (of worldwide appeal); technical (science and medical); other (great stories of sports of international interest). Buys 7-10 mss/issue. Length: 1,500 words maximum. Query with clips of previously published work. Pays $700 minimum.
Photos: Photo Editor: G. Woodford Pratt. State availability of photos. Reviews 8x10 b&w glossy prints and 35mm color transparencies. Pays $200/page rate; $400/full page. Captions and model release required. Buys one-time rights.
Fiction: Adventure, humorous, suspense, condensed novels, historical and mainstream. Buys 3 mss/year. Length: 1,500 words minimum. Pays $700 minimum.

PSA MAGAZINE, East/West Network, Inc., 5900 Wilshire Blvd., Suite 300, Los Angeles CA 90036. (213)937-5810. Editor: John Johns. Managing Editor: Cori Reminick. 90% freelance written. Monthly magazine; 160 pages. Pays within 60 days after acceptance. Buys first rights. Pays 25% kill fee. Byline given. Submit seasonal/holiday material 4 months in advance of issue date. Simultaneous and photocopied submissions OK. SASE. Sample copy $2.
Nonfiction: Prefers California/West Coast slant. General interest; interview (top-level government, entertainment, sports figures); new product (trends, survey field); profile; and business (with California and West Coast orientation). Buys 10 mss/issue. Query. Length: 500-2,000 words. Pays $150-700.
Photos: State availability of photos with query. Pays $50-100 for b&w contact sheets or negatives; pays $75-250 for 35mm or 2¼x2¼ color transparencies. Captions required. Buys one-time rights. Model release required.
Columns/Departments: Business Trends. Buys 1 ms/issue. Query. Length: 700-1,500 words. Pays $100-400.
Fiction: Humorous. No esoteric or historic fiction. Buys 1 ms/year. Submit complete ms. Length: 500-1,500 words. Pays $100-400.

REPUBLIC SCENE, Ziff-Davis Publishing Co., One Park Ave., New York NY 10016. Editor-in-Chief: Marguerite Tarrant. Articles Editor: Germaine Nicoll. Monthly in-flight magazine of Republic Airlines covering general nonfiction for predominantly male business travelers. Circ. 100,000 copies. Pays on acceptance. Byline given. Pays ⅓ kill fee. Buys first North American serial rights. Submit seasonal/holiday material at least 3 months in advance. SASE. Reports in 2 weeks on queries; 1 month on mss. Free sample copy and writer's guidelines.
Nonfiction: General interest, humor, interview/profile, photo feature and travel. "Material must be non-controversial." No reviews. Buys 96 mss/year. Query with clips of published work. Length: 2,000-3,000 words. Pays $250-600.
Photos: Ezra Shapiro, art director. State availability of photos. Pays $75 minimum for color transparenices; $25 minimum for 8x10 b&w glossy prints. Captions preferred. Model releases required "where applicable." Buys one-time rights.
Columns/Departments: "Columns cover wine, personal finance, science, health and fitness. No reviews, but subjects vary widely. We mostly use writers whose work we know." Buys 24 mss/year. Length: 750-1,500 words. Pays $200-400.

TAILWINDS, Titsch Publishing, Box 5400 TA, Denver CO 80217. (303)573-1433. Editor: William Ender. Designer: Diana Graham. In-flight magazine published 5 times/year for passengers of Rocky Mountain Airways including businessmen, vacationers and skiers. Estab. 1978. Circ. 14,000. Pays on publication. Byline given. Buys first North American serial rights. Phone queries OK. Simultaneous, photocopied and previously published submissions OK if so indicated. SASE. Reports in 1 month. Free writer's guidelines with SASE.
Nonfiction: "We look for general lifestyle articles and photo features that showcase people, events, issues and trends in the Rocky Mountain region, particularly Colorado. No articles on 'my summer vacation.' " Buys 3-5 mss/issue. Query with clips of previously published work. Length: 1,500-2,000 words.
Photos: State availability of photos. Reviews 35mm and larger color transparencies. Payment negotiable. Captions and model release required. Buys one-time rights or makes work-for-hire assignments.

TAKE ME AWAY, The In-flight Magazine of Wien Air Alaska, Printmore Corporation, 920 Whitney Rd., Anchorage AK 99501. (907)276-0575. Editor: P.W. Benediktsson. Managing Editor: Ray Haley. Monthly magazine covering Wien Air Alaska's destinations in Alaska, Washington, Oregon and Canada. Estab. 1980. Circ. "subject to passenger count." Pays on publication. Byline given. Buys one-time rights. Submit seasonal/holiday material 3 months in advance. Simultaneous queries, and simultaneous, photocopied, and previously published submissions OK. SASE. Reports in 2 months. Free sample copy and writer's guidelines.
Nonfiction: Book excerpts, historical/nostalgic, interview/profile, personal experience, photo feature, technical and travel. "We prefer mss with photographic support. No articles dealing with topics other than Alaskana." Buys 60 mss/year. Send complete ms. Length: 1,000-1,500 words. Pays $75 or part page percentage.
Photos: Send photos with ms. Reviews 35mm transparencies. Identification of subjects required.

TEXAS FLYER, East/West Network, 5900 Wilshire Ave., Suite 300, Los Angeles CA 90036. For requirements, see: *East/West Network*.

TWA AMBASSADOR, (for Trans World Airlines), The Webb Co., 1999 Shepard Rd., St. Paul MN 55116. Editor-in-Chief: David Martin. 90% freelance written. "For TWA passengers, top management executives, professional men and women, world travelers; affluent, interested and responsive." Monthly magazine. Circ. 263,000. Pays on acceptance. Buys all rights. Pays 30% kill fee. Byline given. Submit seasonal/holiday material 6 months in advance. SASE. Reports in 1 month. Sample copy $2.
Nonfiction: Subjects dealing with substantive issues, the arts, in-depth profiles, business concerns, straight reporting on a variety of subjects and service pieces. Query. Length: 2,500-5,000 words. Pays $600-1,000.
Columns/Departments: Destinations, Outdoors, Science, Business, Personal Finance, The Arts, Media, Books and The Law. Query to William J. Reynolds, senior editor. Length: 1,800-2,000 words. Pays $150-300.

USAIR MAGAZINE, Ziff-Davis, 1 Park Ave., New York NY 10016. Editor: Richard Busch. Senior Editor: James A Frank. A monthly general interest magazine published for airline passengers, many of whom are business travelers, male, with a high income and college education. Estab. 1979. Circ. 150,000. Pays on acceptance. Buys first rights. Submit seasonal material 6 months in advance. Photocopied submissions OK. SASE. Reports in 2 weeks. Sample copy $1.50; free writer's guidelines with SASE.

Nonfiction: General-interest (sports individuals and teams, financial outlook and investments); how-to; profile (of athletes, business people, celebrities and little known personalities); travel (traditional destinations and off-beat places); new product; photo (portfolio); the arts, science, and nature. "No downbeat stories or controversial articles." Buys 100 mss/year. Query with clips of previously published work. Length: 750-2,000 words. Pays $300-700.

Photos: Send photos with ms. Pays $75-150/b&w print, depending on size; color from $100-200/print or slide. Captions preferred; model release required. Buys one-time rights.

Columns/Departments: Sports, food, money, health, business, living, and photography. Buys 3-4 mss/issue. Query. Length: 1,000-1,500 words.

Tips: "Send irresistible ideas and proof that you can write."

VOYAGER, 63 Shrewsbury Lane, Shooters Hill, London, England SE18 3JJ. Editor: Dennis Winston. 80% freelance written. 20% of material from American/Canadian writers. Emphasizes travel for "a reasonably sophisticated audience, middle- to upper-income and intelligence, both sexes, all ages." For passengers of British Midland Airways. Quarterly magazine; 36 pages. Circ. 25,000. Pays on publication. Buys one-time rights. Byline given unless author requests otherwise. Submit seasonal/holiday material 6 months in advance. Photocopied and previously published submissions OK ("if not previously published in UK"). SAE and International Reply Coupons. Reports in 1 month.

Nonfiction: Humor (real-life travel experiences); informational (articles concerning business and/or holidays in areas with which magazine is concerned); and travel (relevant to area served by magazine). "*Voyager* is the free inflight magazine for passengers of British Midland Airways, which has several domestic routes within the UK, and international routes to France, Holland, Majorca, and the Republic of Ireland. Our need is for well-informed, entertaining articles about business, tourism, and facets of life in those countries and in others for which those countries are gateways." No fiction, poetry, jokes or whimsy. Buys 6 mss/issue. Submit complete ms. Length: 800-1,500 words maximum. Pays 30-45 pounds.

Photos: Purchased with accompanying ms. Captions required. Submit b&w prints or transparencies. Pays 3-12 pounds for 8x6 b&w glossy prints; 7-20 pounds for color transparencies. Total purchase price for ms includes payment for photos.

Tips: "Articles must be informative, specific (e.g., name hotels and restaurants, give prices), not outdated, entertaining. First-person material is welcomed."

WESTERN'S WORLD, 141 El Camino, Beverly Hills CA 90212. (213)273-1990. Editor: Frank M. Hiteshew. Assistant Editor/Art Director: Tom Medsger. Published by Western Airlines for the airline traveler. Magazine published 6 times/year. Circ. 250,000. Buys all rights. Pays 50% kill fee. Byline given. Buys 40-50 mss/year. Pays on publication. Photocopied submissions OK. Submit seasonal material 1 year in advance of issue date. Reports within one month. Query. SASE.

Nonfiction: "Articles should relate to travel, dining, or entertainment in the area served by Western Airlines: London, Hawaii, Minneapolis/St. Paul, Alaska to Mexico, Miami, Washington DC and between. General interest (nontravel) articles are welcome too, as a change of pace. Compared to other airline magazines, *Western's World* strives for a more editorial approach. It's not as promotional-looking; all articles are bylined articles. Some writers are the top names in the field." Buys photo features, travel, pop psychology and human behavior pieces. No personality profiles. Length: 1,000-2,000 words. Pays 10¢/word.

Photos: Department Editor: Tom Medsger. Purchased with or without mss or on assignment; captions required. Uses 8x10 b&w glossy prints. Pays $35. Uses 35mm, 4x5 or larger color transparencies. Pays $50-200; "possibly more for cover, subject to negotiation."

Fiction: Short stories, fantasy and humor. "Rarely printed because we've seen so few good ones. Should relate to the geographic areas served by Western Airlines." Length: 1,000-2,000 words. Pays 10¢/word.

Jewish

The following publications use material on topics of general interest slanted toward a Jewish readership. Publications using Jewish-oriented religious material are categorized in Religious Publications.

THE AMERICAN ZIONIST, Zionist Organization of America, 4 E. 34th St., New York NY 10016. Managing Editor: Paul Flacks. 15% freelance written. Political journal pertaining to Israel, Middle East and Jewish affairs. Monthly magazine; 32 pages. Circ. 46,000. Pays "some time after publication." Buys all rights. Byline given. Photocopied submissions OK. SASE.
Nonfiction: Expose, historical, humor, informational, inspirational, interview, profile and travel. Buys 48 mss/year. Length: 2,000-3,000 words. Pays $25-100.
Fiction: Dealing with Israel or Judaic experiences. Buys 4-6 mss/year. 500-1,500 words. Pays $25.
Poetry: "Mainly used as filler material." Buys 4 poems/year. Pays $15.

BALTIMORE JEWISH TIMES, 2104 N. Charles St., Baltimore MD 21218. (301)752-3504. Editor: Gary Rosenblatt. Weekly magazine covering subjects of interest to Jewish readers. "*Baltimore Jewish Times* reaches 20,000 Baltimore-area Jewish homes, as well as several thousand elsewhere in the US and Canada; almost anything of interest to that audience is of interest to us. This includes reportage, general interest articles, personal opinion, and personal experience pieces about every kind of Jewish subject from narrowly religious issues to popular sociology; from the Mideast, to the streets of Brooklyn, to the suburbs of Baltimore. We run articles of special interest to purely secular Jews as well as to highly observant ones. We are Orthodox, Conservative, and Reform all at once. We are spiritual and mundane. We are establishment and we are alternative culture." Circ. 20,000. Pays on publication. Byline given. Buys one-time rights, first rights, or second serial (reprint) rights. Submit seasonal/holiday material 2 months in advance. Simultaneous queries, and photocopied and previously published submissions OK. "We will not return submissions without SASE." Reports in 6 weeks. Sample copy $2.
Nonfiction: Robert Kanigel, special projects editor. Book excerpts, expose, general interest, historical/nostalgic, humor, interview/profile, opinion, personal experience and photo feature. "We are inundated with Israel personal experience and Holocaust-related articles, so submissions on these subjects must be of particularly high quality." Buys 100 mss/year. "Established writers query; others send complete ms." Length: 1,200-6,000 words. Pays $25-250.
Photos: Kim Muller-Thym, graphics editor. Send photos with ms. Pays $10-35 for 8x10 b&w prints.
Fiction: Robert Kanigel, special projects editor. "We'll occasionally run a high quality short story with a Jewish theme." Buys 6 mss/year. Send complete ms. Length: 1,200-6,000 words. pays $25-250.

CANADIAN ZIONIST, 1310 Greene Ave., Montreal, Quebec, Canada H3Z 2B2. Editor-in-Chief: Dr. Leon Kronitz. Associate Editor: Rabbi Sender Shizgal. 40% freelance written. Emphasizes Zionism. Published 7-8 times/year; 40-48 pages. Circ. 34,000. Byline given. Pays on publication. Submit seasonal/holiday material 2 months in advance. Photocopied submissions OK. Reports in 3 weeks. Free sample copy.
Nonfiction: General interest (Jewish or Zionist current events); historical (Jewish or Zionist history); interview (with prominent figures in Israeli politics, art or science); profile (on Israeli political figures); and technical (Zionism, Jewish interest, Middle East politics). No stories on personal experiences or travel to Israel. Buys 10 mss/year. Query with clips of published work. Length: 1,500-2,500. Pays $125 minimum.
Photos: State availability of photos with query. No additional payment for b&w prints.

CONGRESS MONTHLY, A Journal of Opinion and Jewish Affairs, American Jewish Congress, 15 E. 84th St., New York NY 10028. (212)879-4000. Managing Editor: Nancy Miller. Magazine published 10 times/year covering Jewish opinion for members of the American Jewish Congress; readers are intellectual, Jewish and educated. Circ. 35,000. Pays on publication. Byline given. Not copyrighted. Buys one-time rights. Submit seasonal/holiday material 2 months in advance. Photocopied and previously published submissions OK. Reports in 2 months. Free sample copy.
Nonfiction: General interest ("current topical issues geared toward our audience"). No technical material. Buys 30 mss/year. Send complete ms. Length: 3,500 words maximum. Pays $50-75/article.
Photos: State availability of photos. Reviews b&w prints. "Photos are paid for with payment for ms."

Columns/Departments: Book Reviews. Buys 12 mss/year. Send complete ms. Length: 1,500 words maximum. Pays $50-75/article.
Fiction: Mainstream ("must have some kind of a 'hook' for a Jewish magazine"). Buys 6 mss/year. Send complete ms. Length: 3,000 words. Pays $50-75/article.
Poetry: Light verse and traditional. Buys 6/year. Pays $15.

JEWISH POST AND OPINION, National Jewish Post, Inc., 611 N. Park Ave., Indianapolis IN 46204. (317)634-1307. Editor: Gabriel Cohen. Weekly tabloid covering only news of Jewish interest. Circ. 112,000. Pays on publication. Byline given
Nonfiction: "Straight reporting of hard news and human interest feature stories involving Jews." Length: 500-750 words for features. Pays 4¢/word. "No articles now, please, but we use stringers (correspondents) all throughout North America at 4¢ a word for news, etc. published." Information to involve Jewish person or incident.

JEWISH TELEGRAPH, Telegraph House, Bury Old Rd., Manchester M25 8HH, England. Editor: Paul Harris. Weekly. Circ. 11,500. Copyrighted. Pays on publication. SAE and International Reply Coupons. Free sample copy.
Nonfiction: Exclusive news and humorous and historical articles of Jewish interest. Pays 5 pounds minimum.

MIDSTREAM, A Monthly Jewish Review, 515 Park Ave., New York NY 10022. Editor: Joel Carmichael. Monthly. Circ. 14,000. Buys first rights. Byline given. Pays on publication. Reports in 4 weeks. SASE.
Nonfiction: "Articles offering a critical interpretation of the past, searching examination of the present, and affording a medium for independent opinion and creative cultural expression. Articles on the political and social scene in Israel, on Jews in Russia and the US; generally it helps to have a Zionist orientation. If you're going abroad, we would like to see what you might have to report on a Jewish community abroad." Buys historical and think pieces, primarily of Jewish and related content. Pays 5¢/word.
Fiction: Primarily of Jewish and related content. Pays 5¢/word.
Tips: "A book review would be the best way to start. Send us a sample review or a clip, let us know your area of interest, suggest books you would like to review. The author should briefly outline the subject and theme of his article and give a brief account of his background or credentials in this field. Since we are a monthly, we look for critical analysis rather than a 'journalistic' approach."

MOMENT MAGAZINE, 462 Boylston St.; Boston MA 02116. (617)536-6252. Editor: Leonard Fein. Emphasizes Jewish affairs. Monthly magazine; 64 pages. Circ. 25,000. Pays on publication. Buys all rights. Pays 25% kill fee on commissioned articles. Byline given. Phone queries OK. Submit seasonal/holiday material 6 months in advance. Reports in 6 weeks. Sample copy $2.50.
Nonfiction: Expose, how-to, informational, historical, humor, nostalgia, profile and personal experience. "We have a heavy backlog of poetry. A very high percentage of the material we receive deals with the Holocaust; we also get a large number of articles and stories focusing on grandparents. It's not that we don't want to see them, but we accept very few." Top literary quality only. Buys 100 mss/year. Query or submit complete ms. Length: 1,000-5,000 words. Pays $50 minimum.
Fiction: "We use only the highest quality fiction. Stories should have high Jewish content." Buys 8 mss/year. Submit complete ms. Length: 1,000-5,000 words. Pays $100-400.
Tips: Read the magazine. Submit relevant material. Send "a comprehensive letter that will outline elements to be covered as well as overall thrust of the article. It is helpful to include sources that will be used, and a brief summary of your experience (other publications, relevant credentials)."

THE NATIONAL JEWISH MONTHLY, 1640 Rhode Island NW, Washington DC 20036. (202)857-6645. Editor: Marc Silver. Published by B'nai B'rith. Monthly magazine. Buys North American serial rights. Pays on publication. SASE.
Nonfiction: Articles of interest to the Jewish community: economic, demographic, political, social, biographical. No travelogues or immigrant reminiscences. Query (with clips of published work) should be direct, well-organized and map out the story. Length: 4,000 words maximum. Pays up to 10¢/word maximum.

RECONSTRUCTIONIST, 432 Park Ave. S., New York NY 10016. (212)889-9080. Editor: Dr. Ira Eisenstein. A general Jewish religious and cultural magazine. Monthly. Circ. 6,000. Buys all rights. Buys 10 mss/year. Pays on publication. Query. SASE. Free sample copy.
Nonfiction: Publishes literary criticism, reports from Israel and other lands where Jews live, and material of educational or communal interest. Preferred length is 3,000 words. Pays $15-25.
Fiction: Uses a small amount of fiction as fillers.
Poetry: Used as fillers.

SOUTHERN JEWISH WEEKLY, Box 3297, Jacksonville FL 32206. (904)355-3459. Editor: Isadore Moscovitz. 10% freelance written. For a Jewish audience. General subject matter is human interest and short stories. Weekly. Circ. 28,500. Pays on acceptance. Not copyrighted. Buys all rights. Submit seasonal/holiday material 1 month in advance. SASE. Reports in 1 week. Free sample copy and writer's guidelines.
Nonfiction: "Any type of article as long as it is of Southern Jewish interest." Buys 15 mss/year. Length: 250-500 words. Pays $10-100.
Photos: State availability of photos. Pays $5-15 for b&w prints.

Juvenile

This section of *Writer's Market* includes publications for children aged 2-12. Magazines for young people 12-26 appear in a separate Teen and Young Adult category.

Most of the following publications are produced by religious groups, and wherever possible, the specific denomination is given. For the writer with a story or article slanted to a specific age group, the sub-index which follows is a quick reference to markets for his story in that age group.

Those editors who are willing to receive simultaneous submissions are indicated. (This is the technique of mailing the same story at the same time to a number of low-paying religious markets of nonoverlapping circulation. In each case, the writer, when making a simultaneous submission, should so advise the editor. In fact, some editors advise a query over a complete manuscript when you're considering making a simultaneous submission.) The few mass circulation, nondenominational publications included in this section that have good pay rates are not interested in simultaneous submissions and should not be approached with this technique. Magazines that pay good rates expect, and deserve, the exclusive use of material.

Writers will also note in some of the listings that editors will buy "second rights" to stories. This refers to a story which has been previously published in a magazine and to which the writer has already sold "first rights." Payment is usually less for the re-use of a story than for first-time publication.

Juvenile Publications Classified by Age

Two- to Five-Year-Olds: *Children's Playmate, Children's Service, The Friend, Highlights for Children, Humpty Dumpty, Odyssey, Our Little Friend, Primary Treasure, Ranger Rick's Nature Magazine, Story Friends, Wee Wisdom.*
Six- to Eight-Year-Olds: *Children's Playmate, Children's Service, Dash, Ebony Jr!, The Friend, Highlights for Children, Humpty Dumpty, Jack and Jill, My Devotions, Odyssey, Our Little Friend, Primary Treasure, R-A-D-A-R, Ranger Rick's Nature Magazine, Story Friends, Touch, Trails, Video-Presse, Wee Wisdom, Wonder Time, The Young Crusader, Young Judaean.*
Nine- to Twelve-Year-Olds: *Action, Child's Life, Children's Service, Cobblestone, Comin' Up Magazine, Crusader Magazine, Dash, Discoveries, Ebony Jr!, The Friend, Highlights for Children, Jack and Jill, Junior Trails, Kidbits, My Devotions, On the Line, R-A-D-A-R, Ranger Rick's Nature Magazine, Story Friends, 3-2-1 Contact, Touch, Trails, Video-Presse, The Vine, Wee Wisdom, The Young Crusader, Young Judaean, Young Musicians.*

ACTION, (formerly *Discovery*), Dept. of Christian Education, Free Methodist Headquarters, 901 College Ave., Winona Lake IN 46590. (219)267-7656. Editor: Vera Bethel. For "57% girls, 43% boys, age 9-11; 48% city, 23% small towns." Weekly magazine; 8 pages. Circ. 15,000. Pays on acceptance. Rights purchased vary; may buy simultaneous rights, second serial rights or first

North American serial rights. Submit seasonal/holiday material 3 months in advance. Simultaneous and previously published submissions OK. Reports in 1 month. Free sample copy and writer's guidelines.

Nonfiction: How-to (craft articles, how to train pets, party ideas, how to make gifts); informational (nature articles with pix); historical (short biographies except Lincoln and Washington); and personal experience (my favorite vacation, my pet, my hobby, etc.). Buys 50 mss/year. Submit complete ms. Length: 200-500 words. Pays 2¢/word. SASE must be enclosed; no return without it.

Photos: Purchased with accompanying ms. Captions required. Submit prints. Pays $5-10 for 8x10 b&w glossy prints. $2 for snapshots.

Fiction: Adventure, humorous, mystery and religious. Buys 50 mss/year. Submit complete ms. Length: 1,000 words. Pays 2¢/word. SASE must be enclosed; no return without it.

Poetry: Free verse, haiku, light verse, traditional, devotional and nature. Buys 100/year. Limit submissions to batches of 5-6. Length: 4-16 lines. Pays 25¢/line.

Tips: "Send interview articles with children about their pets, their hobbies, a recent or special vacation—all with pix if possible. Kids like to read about other kids."

CHILD LIFE, Benjamin Franklin Literary & Medical Society, Inc., 1100 Waterway Blvd., Box 567B, Indianapolis IN 46206. Editor: John D. Craton. For youngsters 8-11. Monthly (except bimonthly issues in April/May, June/July and August/September) magazine; 48 pages. Pays on publication. Buys all rights. Byline given. Submit seasonal/holiday material 8 months in advance. Photocopied submissions OK. SASE. Reports in 10 weeks. Sample copy 50¢; writer's guidelines for SASE.

Nonfiction: Specifically need articles dealing with health, safety, nutrition, and exercise (including group sports). "We prefer not to sound encyclopedic in our presentation and therefore are always on the lookout for innovative ways to present our material. Articles on sports and sports figures are welcome, but they should try to influence youngsters to participate and learn the benefits of participation, both from a social and a physical point of view." In addition to health, seasonal articles are needed. Buys about 10 mss/issue. Submit complete ms; query not necessary. Length: 1,200 words maximum. Give word count on ms. Pays approximately 3¢/word.

Photos: Purchased only with accompanying ms. Captions and model release required. B&w glossies 3x5 or larger or color transparencies 35mm or larger only (no instant-print photos, please). Pays $3/photo used in publication. Buys one-time rights on most photos.

Fiction: Should emphasize some aspect of health, but not necessarily as a main theme. Seasonal stories also accepted. Buys about 2 mss/issue. Submit complete ms; query not necessary. Length: 500-1,800 words. Give word count on ms. Pays approximately 3¢/word.

CHILDREN'S DIGEST, Benjamin Franklin Society, Box 567B, Indianapolis IN 46206. (317)636-8881. Editor: Christine French. Magazine published 9 times/year covering children's health for children ages 9-12. Estab. 1980. Circ. 300,000. Pays on publication. Byline given. Buys all rights. Submit seasonal/holiday material 8 months in advance. Photocopied submissions OK (if clear). SASE. Reports in 2 months. Sample copy 75¢; writer's guidelines for business size SAE and 1 first class stamp.

Nonfiction: Historical/nostalgic; interview/profile (biographical); craft ideas; health; nutrition; hygiene; exercise and safety. Buys 15-20 mss/year. Send complete ms. Length: 1,200 words maximum. Pays 3¢/word.

Photos: State availability of photos. Pays $5-10 for 5x7 b&w glossy prints. Model release and identification of subjects required. Buys one-time rights.

Fiction: Adventure, humorous, mainstream and mystery. "We're looking for stories that incorporate one of our five areas of emphasis. We like a light or humorous approach." Buys 15-20 mss/year. Length: 500-1,800 words. Pays 3¢/word.

Poetry: "We accept only poetry that is age-appropriate and that emphasizes one of our health themes." Pays $5 minimum.

CHILDREN'S PLAYMATE, 1100 Waterway Blvd., Box 567B, Indianapolis IN 46206. (317)634-1100, ext. 296. Editor: Beth Wood Thomas. "We are looking for articles, stories, and activities with a health, safety, exercise, or nutritionally oriented theme. Primarily we are concerned with preventative medicine. We try to present our material in a positive—not a negative— light, and we try to incorporate humor and a light approach wherever possible without minimizing the seriousness of what we are saying." Write for guidelines. For children, ages 5-8. Magazine published 9 times/year. Buys all rights. Byline given. Pays on publication. Sample copy 50¢; free writer's guidelines with SASE. No query. "We do not consider resumes and outlines. Reading the whole ms is the only way to give fair consideration. The editors cannot criticize, offer suggestions, or review unsolicited material that is not accepted." Submit seasonal material 8 months in advance. Reports in 2 months. Sometimes may hold mss for up to 1 year, with author's permission.

"Material will not be returned unless accompanied by a self-addressed envelope and sufficient postage."

Nonfiction: Beginning science, 600 words maximum. Monthly "All about . . ." feature, 300-500 words, may be an interesting presentation on animals, people, events, objects or places, especially about good health, exercise, proper nutrition and safety. "Include number of words in articles." Pays about 3¢/word.

Fiction: Short stories, not over 700 words for beginning readers. No inanimate, talking objects. Humorous stories, unusual plots. Vocabulary suitable for ages 5-8. Pays about 3¢/word. "Include number of words in stories."

Fillers: Puzzles, dot-to-dots, color-ins, mazes, tricks, games, guessing games, and brain teasers. Payment varies.

Tips: Especially interested in stories, poems and articles about special holidays, customs and events.

CHILDREN'S SERVICE PROGRAMS, Concordia Publishing House, 3558 S. Jefferson Ave., St. Louis MO 63118. (314)664-7000. Issued annually by The Lutheran Church—Missouri Synod, for children, aged three through eighth grade. Buys all rights. Receipt of children's worship scripts will be acknowledged immediately, but acceptance or rejection may require up to a year. All mss must be typed, double-spaced on 8½x11 paper. SASE. Write for details.

Nonfiction: "Two Christmas worship service programs for congregational use published yearly. Every script must include usual elements embodied in a worship service. Children lead the worship with adults participating in singing some of the hymns. Youth and adult choir selections optional. Every script must emphasize the Biblical message of the Gospel through which God shares His love and which calls for a joyful response from His people. Services requiring elaborate staging or costumes not accepted." Pays $125, but buys few mss.

Fiction: Drama. See guidelines for nonfiction. Buys few mss.

COBBLESTONE, Cobblestone Publishing, Inc., 28 Main St., Peterborough NH 03458. (603)924-7209. Editor: Frances Nankin. Monthly magazine covering American history for children 8-13 years old. "Each issue presents a particular theme, approaching it from different angles, making it exciting as well as informative." Estab. 1980. Circ. 25,000. Pays on publication. Byline given. Buys first North American serial rights, second serial rights, or all rights. Makes some assignments on a work-for-hire basis. All material must relate to monthly theme. Simultaneous and previously published submissions OK. SASE. Reports in 1 month on queries; 10 weeks on mss. Sample copy $2; writer's guidelines for SASE.

Nonfiction: Historical/nostalgic, how-to, interview and personal experience. "Request a copy of the writer's guidelines to find out specific issue themes in upcoming months." No Revolutionary War memorabilia, particularly hometown guides to monuments. Buys 5-8 mss/issue. Length: 500-1,200 words. Query with clips of previously published work. Pays up to 15¢/word.

Fiction: Adventure, historical, humorous, mystery, western. Buys 1-2 mss/issue. Length: 800-2,000 words. Query or send clips of previously published work. Pays up to 25¢/word.

Poetry: Free verse, light verse and traditional. Buys 6 mss/year. Submit maximum 2 poems. Length: 5-100 lines. Pays $2/line.

Fillers: Word puzzles and mazes. Buys 1/issue. Pays $75 maximum.

Tips: "All material is considered on the basis of merit and appropriateness to theme. Query should state idea for material simply, with rationale for why material is applicable to theme. Self-addressed postcard enclosed with 'yes, go ahead' and 'no, don't go ahead' for editor to check off."

COMIN' UP MAGAZINE, The Magazine for Today's Boys & Girls, Windell Publishing Corp., 94 3rd Ave., New York NY 10003. (212)473-1860. Editor: Terry Schindell. Monthly magazine covering "anything of interest to children age 8-15. We provide entertainment as well as information. Do not speak down to our audience just because they're young." Estab. 1980. Circ. 100,000. Pays on publication. Byline given. Buys one-time rights, simultaneous rights, all rights, first rights and makes work-for-hire assignments. Submit seasonal/holiday material 6 months in advance. Simultaneous queries, simultaneous and photocopied submissions OK. SASE. Reports in 1 week on queries; 3 weeks on mss. Sample copy $1.50; free writer's guidelines for SAE.

Nonfiction: Felicia Onofrietti. General interest; historical/nostalgic; how-to (make/build/create); humor; interview/profile; new product; opinion; personal experience; photo feature; and travel. No religious viewpoints. Buys 200 mss/year. Query with outline. Length: 500-2,000 words. Pays $25-125/article.

Photos: State availability of photos. Reviews b&w contact sheets and color transparencies. Captions, model releases and identification of subjects required.

Columns/Departments: Buys 30 mss/year. Query. Length: 300-800 words.

Fiction: Adventure, fantasy, historical, humorous, mystery, science fiction and suspense. No "cute stories." Buys 50 mss/year. Query. Length: 500-1,000 words. Pays $20-50/article.

Poetry: Felicia Onofreitti. Free verse, light verse and traditional. Buys 10-15 mss/year. Pays $5-25.

Fillers: Carol Laufer. Clippings, jokes, gags, anecdotes and short humor. Buys 100 mss/year. Pays $5-25.

Tips: "Submit concepts on articles first so that photography and art may be easily coordinated. We are most open to nonfiction of interest to our age group."

CRUSADER MAGAZINE, Box 7244, Grand Rapids MI 49510. Editor: David Koetje. "*Crusader Magazine* shows boys (9-14) how God is at work in their lives and in the world around them." Magazine published 7 times/year; 24 pages. Circ. 13,000. Rights purchased vary with author and material. Byline given. Buys 15-20 mss/year. Pays on acceptance. Free sample copy and writer's guidelines. Photocopied and simultaneous submissions OK. Submit seasonal material (Christmas, Easter) at least 5 months in advance. Reports in 1 month. Query or submit complete ms. SASE.

Nonfiction: Articles about young boys' interests: sports, outdoor activities, bike riding, science, crafts, etc., and problems. Emphasis is on a Christian perspective, but no simplistic moralisms. Informational, how-to, personal experience, interview, profile, inspirational, humor. Length: 500-1,500 words. Pays 2-5¢/word.

Photos: Pays $4-25 for b&w photos purchased with mss.

Fiction: "Considerable fiction is used. Fast-moving stories that appeal to a boy's sense of adventure or sense of humor are welcome. Avoid 'preachiness.' Avoid simplistic answers to complicated problems. Avoid long dialogue and little action." Length: 500-1,500 words. Pays 2¢/word minimum.

Fillers: Uses short humor and any type of puzzles as fillers.

DASH, Box 150, Wheaton IL 60187. Editor: Michael Chiapperino. 50% freelance written. For boys 8-11 years of age. Most subscribers are in a Christian Service Brigade program. Monthly magazine except for combined issues in April-May, July-August, October-November, January-February. Circ. 32,000. Rights purchased vary with author and material. Buys 8-10 mss/year. Pays on publication. Submit seasonal material 6 months in advance. Reports in 3 weeks. Query. SASE. Sample copy $1.

Nonfiction: "Our emphasis is on boys and how their belief in Jesus Christ affects their everyday lives." Uses short articles about boys of this age, problems they encounter. Interview, profile. Length: 1,000-1,500 words. Pays $30-70.

Photos: Pays $25 for 8x10 b&w photos for inside use.

Fiction: Avoid trite, condescending tone. Needs adventure, mystery with Christian message. Length: 1,000-1,500 words. Pays $60-90.

Tips: "I like queries that begin with a 'grabbing' sentence. Queries must be succinct, well-written, and exciting to draw my interest. Send for sample copies, get a feel for our publication, then write something tailored specifically for us."

DISCOVERIES, 6401 The Paseo, Kansas City MO 64131. Editor: Mark York. 100% freelance written. For boys and girls 9-12 in the Church of the Nazarene. Weekly. Buys first rights and some second rights. "Minimal comments on pre-printed form are made on rejected material." SASE.

Nonfiction: Articles on Christian faith, biography of Christian leaders, Bible manners and customs, family projects. Should be informal and aimed at 4th grade vocabulary. Sharp photos and artwork help sell features. Submit complete ms. Length: 400-800 words. Pays 3¢ for first rights and 2¢/word for reprint.

Photos: Sometimes buys pix submitted with mss. Buys them with captions only if subject has appeal. Send quality photos, 8x10.

Fiction: Stories with Christian emphasis on high ideals, wholesome social relationships and activities, right choices, Sabbath observance, church loyalty, and missions. Informal style. Submit complete ms. Length: 800-1,000 words. Pays 3¢/word for first rights and 2¢/word for reprint.

Poetry: Nature and Christian thoughts or prayers, 4-16 lines. Pays $1 for each 4 lines, minimum of $2.

Tips: "The freelancer needs an understanding of the doctrine of the Church of the Nazarene and the Sunday School material for 3rd-6th graders."

EBONY JR!, Johnson Publishing Co., 820 S. Michigan Ave., Chicago IL 60605. (312)322-9272. Managing Editor: Marcia V. Roebuck. For all children, but geared toward black children, ages 6-12. Monthly magazine (except bimonthly issues in June/July and August/September); 48 pages. Circ. 75,000. Pays on acceptance. Buys all rights, second serial (reprint) rights or first North American serial rights. Byline given. Submit seasonal/holiday material 4 months in advance. Previously published work OK. SASE. Acknowledges receipt of material in 3 weeks. Sample copy 75¢; free writer's guidelines.

Nonfiction: How-to (make things, gifts and crafts; cooking articles); informational (science experiments or articles explaining how things are made or where things come from); historical (events or people in black history); inspirational (career articles showing children they can become whatever they want); interviews; personal experience (taken from child's point of view); profiles (of black Americans who have done great things—especially need articles on those who have not been recognized). Buys 3/issue. Query or submit complete ms. Length: 500-1,500 words. Pays $75-200.

Photos: Purchased with or without mss. Must be clear photos; no Instamatic prints. Pays $10-15/b&w; $25 maximum/color. Send prints and transparencies. Model release required.

Columns/Departments: *Ebony Jr!* News uses news of outstanding black children, reviews of books, movies, TV shows, of interest to children. Pays $25-400.

Fiction: Must be believable and include experiences black children can relate to. Adventure, fantasy, historical (stories on black musicians, singers, actors, astronomers, scientists, inventors, writers, politicians, leaders; any historical figures who can give black children positive images). Buys 2 mss/issue. Query or submit complete ms. Length: 300-1,500 words. Pays $75-200.

Poetry: Free verse, haiku, light verse, traditional forms of poetry. Buys 2/issue. No specific limit on number of submissions, but usually purchase no more than two at a time. Length: 5-50 lines; longer for stories in poetry form. Pays $15-100.

Fillers: Jokes, gags, anecdotes, newsbreaks and current events written at a child's level. Brain teasers, word games, crossword puzzles, guessing games, dot-to-dot games; games that are fun, yet educational. Pays $15-85.

Tips: "Those freelancers who have submitted material featuring an event or person who is/was relatively unknown to the general public, yet is the type of material that would have great relevance and interest to children in their everyday lives, are usually the successful writers."

THE FRIEND, 50 East North Temple, Salt Lake City UT 84150. Managing Editor: Lucile C. Reading. 75% freelance written. Appeals to children ages 4-12. Publication of the Church of Jesus Christ of Latter-day Saints. Issues feature different countries of the world, their cultures and children. Special issues: Christmas and Easter. Monthly. Circ. 200,000. Pays on acceptance. "Submit only complete ms—no queries, please." Submit seasonal material 6 months in advance. SASE. Free sample copy and guidelines for writers.

Nonfiction: Subjects of current interest, science, nature, pets, sports, foreign countries, and things to make and do. Length: 1,000 words maximum. Pays 5¢/word minimum.

Fiction: Seasonal and holiday stories; stories about other countries and their children. Wholesome and optimistic; high motive, plot, and action. Also simple, but suspense-filled mysteries. Character-building stories preferred. Length: 1,200 words maximum. Stories for younger children should not exceed 700 words. Pays 5¢/word minimum.

Poetry: Serious, humorous and holiday. Any form with child appeal. Pays 35¢/line minimum.

Tips: "Do you remember how it feels to be a child? Can you write stories that appeal to children ages 4-12 in today's world? We're interested in stories with an international flavor and those that focus on present-day problems. Send material of high literary quality slanted to our editorial requirements. Let the child solve the problem—not some helpful, all-wise adult. No overt moralizing. Nonfiction should be creatively presented—not an array of facts strung together. Beware of being cutesy."

HIGHLIGHTS FOR CHILDREN, 803 Church St., Honesdale PA 18431. Editor: Kent L. Brown Jr. For children 2-12. Magazine published 11 times/year. Circ. 1,200,000. Buys all rights. Pays on acceptance. Free writer's guidelines. Reports in 2 months. SASE.

Nonfiction: "We prefer factual features, including history and science, written by persons with rich background and mastery in their respective fields. Contributions always welcomed from new writers, especially science teachers, engineers, scientists, historians, etc., who can interpret to children useful, interesting and authentic facts, but not of the bizarre or 'Ripley' type; also writers who have lived abroad and can interpret the ways of life, especially of children, in other countries, and who don't leave the impression that US ways are always the best. Sports material, biographies, articles about sports of interest to children. Direct, simple style, interesting content, without word embellishment; not rewritten from encyclopedias. State background and qualifications for writing factual articles submitted. Include references or sources of information. Length: 900 words maximum. Pays $65 minimum. Also buys original party plans for children 7-12, clearly described in 400-700 words, including drawings or sample of items to be illustrated. Also, novel but tested ideas in crafts, with clear directions and made-up models. Projects must require only free or inexpensive, easy-to-obtain materials. Especially desirable if easy enough for early primary grades. Also, fingerplays with lots of action, easy for very young children to grasp and parents to dramatize. Avoid wordiness. Pays minimum $30 for party plans; $15 for crafts ideas; $25 for fingerplays.

Fiction: Unusual, wholesome stories appealing to both girls and boys. Vivid, full of action and word-pictures, easy to illustrate. Seeks stories that the child 8-12 will eagerly read, and the child 2-6 will like to hear when read aloud. "We print no stories just to be read aloud; they must serve this two-fold purpose. We encourage authors not to hold themselves to controlled word lists. Avoid suggestion of material reward for upward striving. Moral teaching should be subtle. The main character should preferably overcome difficulties and frustrations through her or his own efforts. The story should leave a good moral and emotional residue. We especially need stories in the suspense-adventure-mystery category, and short (200 words and under) stories for the beginning reader, with an interesting plot and a number of picturable words. Also need stories with urban settings, animal stories for beginning readers (500 words), humorous stories, and horse stories. We also need more material of one page length (300-500 words), both fiction and factual. We need creative-thinking puzzles that can be illustrated, optical illusions, body teasers, and other 'fun' activities. War, crime and violence are taboo. Some fanciful stories wanted." Length: 400-900 words. Pays 7¢ word/minimum.

Tips: "We are pleased that many authors of children's literature report that their first published work was in the pages of *Highlights*. It is not our policy to consider fiction on the strength of the reputation of the author. We judge each submission on its own merits. With factual material, however, we do prefer either authorities in their fields or people with first-hand experience. In this manner we can avoid the encyclopedic article that merely restates information readily available elsewhere. A beginning writer should first become familiar with the type of material which *Highlights* publishes. We are most eager for easy stories for very young readers, but realize that this is probably the most difficult kind of writing. Query with simple letter to establish whether the *subject* is likely to be of interest. Include special qualifications, if any, of author. Write for the child, not the editor."

HUMPTY DUMPTY'S MAGAZINE, 1100 Waterway Blvd., Box 567, Indianapolis IN 46226. Magazine published 9 times/year stressing health, nutrition, hygiene, exercise, and safety for children ages 4 to 7. Combined issues: April/May, June/July, and August/September. Pays on publication. Buys all rights. Submit seasonal material 8 months in advance. Sample copy 50¢; writer's guidelines for SASE.

Nonfiction: "Material with a health theme: nutrition, safety, hygiene. Short biographies of well-known people in the medical field. Simple scientific articles dealing with the body." Submit complete ms. "Include number of words in manuscript and Social Security number." Length: 600 words maximum. Pays 4¢/word.

Fiction: "We're primarily interested in stories in rhyme and easy-to-read stories for the beginning reader. Preferred stories should employ a health theme. We try to present our material in a positive light, incorporating humor and a light approach wherever possible, without minimizing the seriousness of our message." Submit complete ms. "Include number of words in manuscript and Social Security number." Length: 600 words maximum. Pays 4¢/word.

Poetry: Short, simple poems. Pays $5 minimum.

JACK AND JILL, 1100 Waterway Blvd., Box 567B, Indianapolis IN 46206. (317)634-1100. Editor: William Wagner. For children 7-10. Magazine published 9 times/year. Buys all rights. Byline given. Pays on publication. Sample copy 50¢; writer's guidelines for SASE. Submit seasonal material 8 months in advance. Reports in about 2 months. May hold material seriously being considered for up to 6 months. "Material will not be returned unless accompanied by self-addressed envelope with sufficient postage."

Nonfiction: "*Jack and Jill*'s primary purpose is to encourage children to read for pleasure. The editors are actively interested in material that will inform and instruct the young reader and challenge his intelligence, but it must first of all be enjoyable reading. Submissions should appeal to both boys and girls." Current needs are for articles, stories, and activities with a health, safety, exercise, or nutritionally oriented theme. "We try to present our material in a positive—not a negative—light, and we try to incorporate humor and a light approach wherever possible without minimizing the seriousness of what we are saying. Fiction stories that deal with a health theme need not have health as the primary subject but should include it in some way in the course of events. Activities should be enjoyable to youngsters and encourage them to practice better health habits or teach them scientific facts about the body or nutrition. Articles should try not to be 'preachy,' but should be informative and appealing to young readers." Length 500-1,200 words. Pays approximately 3¢/word.

Photos: When appropriate, should accompany mss. 35mm color transparencies or sharp, contrasting b&w glossy prints. Pays $2.50 for each b&w photo, $5 for each color photo.

Fiction: "May include, but is not limited to, realistic stories, fantasy, adventure—set in the past, present, or future. All stories need plot structure, action and incident. Humor is highly desirable." Length: 500-1,200 words, short stories; 1,200 words/installment, serials of 2 or 3 parts. Pays approximately 3¢/word.

Fillers: "Short plays, puzzles (including varied kinds of word and crossword puzzles), poems, games, science projects and creative construction projects. Instructions for activities should be clearly and simply written and accompanied by models or diagram sketches. Payment varies for fillers. Pays approximately 3¢/word for drama.

Tips: "We have been accused of using the same authors over and over again, not keeping an open mind when it comes to giving new authors a chance. To some extent, perhaps we do lean a little heavier toward veteran authors. But there is a good reason for this. Authors who have been published in *Jack and Jill* over and over again have shown us that they can write the kind of material we are looking for. They obtain *current* issues of the magazine and *study* them to find out our present needs, and they write in a style that is compatible with our current editorial policies. That is the reason we use them over and over; not because they have a special 'in.' We would reject a story by the world's best known author if it didn't fit our needs. After all, our young readers are more interested in reading a good story than they are in reading a good byline. We are constantly looking for new writers who have told a good story with an interesting slant—a story that is not full of outdated and time-worn expressions. If an author's material meets these requirements, then he stands as good a chance of getting published as anyone."

JUNIOR TRAILS, Gospel Publishing House, 1445 Boonville Ave., Springfield MO 65802. (417)862-2781. Editor: John Maempa. Weekly tabloid covering religious fiction; and biographical, historical, and scientific articles with a spiritual emphasis for boys and girls, ages 10 and 11. Circ. 95,000. Pays on acceptance. Byline given. Not copyrighted. Buys simultaneous rights, first rights, or second serial (reprint) rights. Submit seasonal/holiday material 1 year in advance. Simultaneous and previously published submissions OK. SASE. Reports in 6 weeks on queries; 2 months on mss. Sample copy for 9x12 SAE and 2 first class stamps; writer's guidelines for 9x12 SAE and 2 first class stamps.

Nonfiction: Biographical, historical, scientific (with spiritual lesson or emphasis). Buys 30-40 mss/year. Send complete ms. Length: 500-1,000 words. Pays $10-30.

Fiction: Adventure (with spiritual lesson or application); and religious. "We're looking for fiction that presents believable characters working out their problems according to Biblical principles. No fictionalized accounts of Bible stories or events." Buys 50-70 mss/year. Send complete ms. Length: 1,000-1,500 words. Pays $20-45.

Poetry: Free verse and light verse. Buys 6-8 mss/year. Pays 2¢/line.

Fillers: Anecdotes (with spiritual emphasis). Buys 15-20/year. Length: 200 words maximum. Pays $6.

Tips: "Junior-age children need to be alerted to the dangers of drugs, alcohol, smoking, etc. They need positive guidelines and believable examples relating to living a Christian life in an ever-changing world."

KIDBITS, A Children's Magazine, Hug Verlag AG (Co.), Zurich, Switzerland. US Address: Ross House, Suite 305, Head House Sq., 401 S. 2nd St., Philadelphia PA 19147. (215)925-0642. Editor: Hiley H. Ward. General Manager: Andrea G. Snyder. Monthly magazine covering "subjects of interest—and of help—to pre-teens and early teens, and appealing generally to the 8- to 14-year-old crowd." Estab. 1981. Circ. 75,000. Pays on acceptance. Byline given. Buys "all rights for 1 year." Submit seasonal/holiday material 5 months in advance. SASE. Reports in 1 month on queries; 2 months on mss. Free sample copy and writer's guidelines.

Nonfiction: Historical/nostalgic (some children's products; we have used history of sneakers, ice cream, jeans, etc."); how-to (make something, solve problems, play games/sports); humor; interview/profile (of young celebrities—generally staff-written); photo feature; and science. "Science, sports and how-to features are the areas most accessible to freelancers. Strive for utility as well as entertainment." No "general short stories (we use some short—500-word—mysteries)." Buys 100+ mss/year. Query. Length: 100-700 words. Pays $25-125.

Photos: "We place an emphasis on identity and real people." State availability of photos. Reviews color transparencies. Captions, model releases, and identification of subjects required. Buys all rights for 1 year.

Columns/Departments: "All columns currently assigned." Query. Length: 200-400 words.

Fiction: Mystery (intelligent, short). "Will not consider any other type." Query.

Poetry: "Only if part of a puzzle—or humorous; must be very brief."

Fillers: Jokes, gags and short humor. "We really don't have fillers as such (we plan every line), and miscellaneous material often is grouped by theme."

Tips: "Study an issue (free) and query; understand children and don't talk down to them. Good humor and creative puzzles (no crosswords, mazes or dot connecting) are jewels that go rewarded by us."

MY DEVOTIONS, Concordia Publishing House, 3558 S. Jefferson Ave., St. Louis MO 63118. For young Christians, 8-13. Buys little freelance material. Guidelines for #10 SASE. Material is rejected here because of poor writing, lack of logic, and lack of Lutheran theology. Byline given. Pays $12.50/printed devotion.

ODYSSEY, AstroMedia Corp., 411 E. Mason St., Milwaukee WI 53202. Editor: Nancy Mack. Emphasizes astronomy and outer space for children of ages 8-12. Monthly magazine; 32 pages. Estab. January 1979. Circ. 64,000. Pays on publication. Buys all or first North American serial rights. Submit seasonal/holiday material 3-4 months in advance. Photocopied and published submissions OK. SASE. Reports in 4-6 weeks. Free sample copy.
Nonfiction: General interest (astronomy, outer space, spacecraft, planets, stars, etc.); how-to (astronomy projects, experiments, etc.); and photo feature (spacecraft, planets, stars, etc.). "We do not want science fiction articles." Buys 2-3 mss/issue. Query with clips of previously published work. Length: 750-2,000 words. Pays $100.
Photos: State availability of photos. Pays $10 for 8x10 b&w glossy prints; $15 for any size color transparencies. Buys one-time rights. Captions preferred; model release required.
Tips: "Since I am overstocked and have a stable of regular writers, a query is very important. I often get several mss on the same subject and must reject them. Write a very specific proposal and indicate why it will interest kids. If the subject is very technical, indicate your qualifications to write about it."

ON THE LINE, Mennonite Publishing House, 616 Walnut Ave., Scottdale PA 15683. (412)887-8500. Editor: Helen Alderfer. For children 10-14. Weekly magazine; 8 pages. Circ. 17,650. Pays on acceptance. Buys one-time rights. Byline given. Submit seasonal/holiday material 6 months in advance. Simultaneous, photocopied and previously published submissions OK. SASE. Reports in 2 weeks.
Nonfiction: How-to (things to make with easy-to-get materials); and informational (500-word articles on wonders of nature, people who have made outstanding contributions). Buys 25-40 mss/issue. Length: 500-1,200 words. Pays $10-24.
Photos: Photos purchased with or without accompanying ms. Pays $10-25 for 8x10 b&w photos. Total purchase price for ms includes payment for photos.
Columns/Departments: Fiction, adventure, humorous and religious. Buys 52 mss/year. Send complete ms. Length: 800-1,200 words. Pays $15-24.
Poetry: Light verse and religious. Length: 3-12 lines. Pays $5-15.
Tips: "Study the publication first. State theme and length of material in query."

OUR LITTLE FRIEND, PRIMARY TREASURE, Pacific Press Publishing Association, 1350 Villa St., Mountain View CA 94042. (415)961-2323, ext. 335. Editor: Louis Schutter. Published weekly for youngsters of the Seventh-day Adventist church. *Our Little Friend* is for children ages 2-6; *Primary Treasure*, 7-9. Buys first serial rights (international); or second serial (reprint) rights (international). Byline given. "The payment we make is for one magazine right. In most cases, it is for the first one. But we make payment for second and third rights also." Simultaneous submissions OK. "We do not purchase material during June, July and August." SASE.
Nonfiction: All stories must be based on fact, written in story form. True to life, character-building stories; written from viewpoint of child and giving emphasis to lessons of life needed for Christian living. True to life is emphasized here more than plot. Nature or science articles, but no fantasy; science must be very simple. All material should be educational or informative and stress moral attitude and religious principle.
Fiction: Should emphasize honesty, truthfulness, courtesy, health, and temperance, along with stories of heroism, adventure, nature and safety. 700-1,000 works for *Our Little Friend*, 600-1,200 words for *Primary Treasure*. Fictionalized Bible stories are not used. Pays 1¢/word.
Photos: 8x10 glossy prints for cover. "Photo payment: sliding scale according to quality."
Poetry Juvenile poetry. Up to 12 lines.
Fillers: Uses puzzles as fillers.
Tips: "We are in need of 1,200 word mss for the cover of *Primary Treasure*—an adventure story that has a premise or lesson embroidered into the plot. We use stories that are thematic with the Bible lesson for the week. The cover story must have a scene that our illustrator can put his teeth into."

PRIMARY TREASURE, Pacific Press Publishing Association, 1350 Villa St., Mountain View CA 94042. See *Our Little Friend*.

R-A-D-A-R, 8121 Hamilton Ave., Cincinnati OH 45231. (513)931-4050. Editor: Dana Eynon. 75% freelance written. For children 8-11 in Christian Sunday schools. Weekly. Rights purchased vary with author and material. Buys first serial rights or second serial (reprint) rights. Occasionally overstocked. Pays on acceptance. Submit seasonal material 12 months in advance. Reports in 4-6 weeks. SASE. Free sample copy.

Nonfiction: Articles on hobbies and handicrafts, nature, famous people, seasonal subjects, etc., written from a Christian viewpoint. No articles about historical figures with an absence of religious implication. Length: 500-1,000 words. Pays 2¢/word maximum.

Fiction: Short stories of heroism, adventure, travel, mystery, animals and biography. True or possible plots stressing clean, wholesome, Christian character-building ideas, but not preachy. Make prayer, church attendance, Christian living a natural part of the story. "We correlate our fiction and other features with a definite Bible lesson. Writers who want to meet our needs should send for a theme list." No talking animal stories, science fiction, Halloween stories or first-person stories from an adult's viewpoint. Length: 900-1,100 words; 2,000 words complete length for 2-part stories. Pays 2¢/word maximum.

RANGER RICK'S NATURE MAGAZINE, National Wildlife Federation, 1412 16th St. NW, Washington DC 20036. (202)797-6800. Editorial Director: Trudy D. Farrand. For "children from ages 6-12, with the greatest concentration in the 7-10 age bracket." Monthly. Buys all world rights. Byline given but "occasionally, for very brief pieces, we will identify author by name at the end. Contributions to regular departments usually are not bylined. Pays on acceptance. Anything written with a specific month in mind should be in our hands at least 10 months before that issue date." Query. SASE.

Nonfiction: "Articles may be written on any phase of nature, conservation, environmental problems, or natural science."

Photos: "Photographs, when used, are paid for separately. It is not necessary that illustrations accompany material."

Fiction: "Do not humanize wildlife. We limit the attributing of human qualities to animals in our regular feature, 'Ranger Rick and His Friends.' The publisher, The National Wildlife Federation, discourages wildlife pets." Length: 900 words maximum. Pays from $10-300, depending on length.

Tips: "Include in query details of what manuscript will cover; sample lead; evidence that you can write playfully or with great enthusiasm, purpose and excitement (formal, serious, dull queries indicate otherwise). Think of an exciting subject we haven't done recently, sell it effectively with query, produce manuscript of highest quality. Read past issues to learn successful styles and unique approaches to subjects. If your submission is commonplace in any way we won't want it."

STORY FRIENDS, Mennonite Publishing House, 616 Walnut Ave., Scottdale PA 15683. (412)887-8500. Editor: Marjorie Waybill. For children 4-9 years of age. Published monthly in weekly parts. Not copyrighted. Byline given. Pays on acceptance. Submit seasonal/holiday material 6 months in advance. SASE. Free sample copy.

Nonfiction: "The over-arching purpose of this publication is to portray Jesus as a friend and helper—a friend who cares about each happy and sad experience in the child's life. Persons who know Jesus have values which affect every area of their lives."

Fiction: "Stories of everyday experiences at home, at church, in school or at play can provide models of these values. Of special importance are relationships, patterns of forgiveness, respect, honesty, trust and caring. Prefer short stories that offer a wide variety of settings, acquaint children with a wide range of friends, and mirror the joys, fears, temptations and successes of the readers. *Story Friends* needs stories that speak to the needs and interests of children of a variety of ethnic backgrounds. Stories should provide patterns of forgiveness, respect, integrity, understanding, caring, sharing; increase the children's sense of self-worth through growing confidence in God's love for them as they are; help answer the children's questions about God, Jesus, the Bible, prayer, death, heaven; develop awe and reverence for God the Creator and for all of His creation; avoid preachiness, but have well-defined spiritual values as an integral part of each story; be plausible in plot; introduce children to followers of Jesus Christ; and develop appreciation for our Mennonite heritage." Length: 300-800 words. Pays 2½-3¢/word.

Poetry: Traditional and free verse. Length: 3-12 lines. Pays $5.

3-2-1 CONTACT, Children's Television Workshop, One Lincoln Plaza, New York NY 10023. (212)595-3456. Editor: Andrew Gutelle. Associate Editor: Joanna Foley. Magazine published 10 times/year covering science for children 8-12. Estab. 1979. Circ. 150,000. Pays on acceptance. Submit seasonal material 6 months in advance. Simultaneous, photocopied and previously published submissions OK if so indicated. Reports in 1 month. Free writer's guidelines. Sample copies not available.

Nonfiction: General interest (space exploration, the human body, animals, current issues); profile (of interesting scientists or children in age group); photo feature (centered around a science theme); and role models of women scientists. No articles on travel not related to science. Buys 1 ms/issue. Query with clips of previously published work. Length: 700-1,000 words. Pays $150-200.

Photos: Reviews 8x10 b&w prints and 35mm color transparencies. Model release preferred.

Tips: "I prefer a short query, without manuscript, that makes it clear that an article is newsworthy and unique and gives the writer's point of view and intentions."

TOUCH, Box 7244, Grand Rapids MI 49510. Editor: Joanne Ilbrink. 50-60% freelance written. Purpose of publication is to show girls ages 8-15 how God is at work in their lives and in the world around them. Monthly magazine; 24 pages. Circ. 14,000. Pays on acceptance. Buys simultaneous, second serial and first North American serial rights. Byline given. Submit seasonal/holiday material 3-5 months in advance. Simultaneous, photocopied or previously published submissions OK. SASE. Reports in 3 weeks. Free sample copy and writer's guidelines.
Nonfiction: How-to (crafts girls can make easily and inexpensively); informational (write for issue themes); humor (needs much more); inspirational (seasonal and holiday); interview; travel; personal experience (avoid the testimony approach); and photo feature (query first). "Because our magazine is published around a monthly theme, requesting the letter we send out twice a year to our established freelancers would be most helpful. We do not want easy solutions or quick character changes from bad to good. No pietistic characters. Constant mention of God is not necessary, if the moral tone of the story is positive. We do not want stories that always have a good ending." Buys 20 mss/year. Submit complete ms. Length: 100-1,000 words. Pays 2¢/word, depending on the amount of editing.
Photos: Purchased with or without ms. Submit 3x5 clear glossy prints. B&w only. Pays $5-25.
Fiction: Adventure (that girls could experience in their hometowns or places they might realistically visit), humorous, mystery (believable only), romance (stories that deal with awakening awareness of boys are appreciated), suspense (can be serialized) and religious (nothing preachy). Buys 20 mss/year. Submit complete ms. Length: 300-1,500 words. Pays 2¢/word.
Poetry: Free verse, haiku, light verse and traditional. Buys 10/year. Length: 50 lines maximum. Pays $5 minimum.
Fillers: Puzzles, short humor and cartoons. Buys 6/issue. Pays $2.50-7.

TRAILS, Pioneer Girls, Inc., Box 788, Wheaton IL 60187. Editor: LoraBeth Norton. Assistant Editor: Lorraine Mulligan. Emphasizes the development of a Christian lifestyle for girls, 6-12, most of whom are enrolled in the Pioneer Girls club program. It is kept general in content so it will appeal to a wider audience. Bimonthly magazine; 32 pages. Circ. 20,000. Pays on acceptance. Buys first, second, or simultaneous rights. Byline given. Submit seasonal/holiday material 6 months in advance. SASE. Reports in 4-8 weeks. Sample copy and writer's guidelines $1.50.
Nonfiction: How-to (crafts and puzzles); humor; informational; inspirational; and biography. Submit complete ms. Length: 800-1,500 words. Pays $25-50.
Fiction: Adventure, fantasy, historical, humorous, mainstream, mystery and religious. Buys 6 mss/issue. Submit complete ms. Length: 800-1,500 words. Pays $25-40.
Fillers: Jokes, gags, cartoons and short humor. Pays $5-15.

VIDEO-PRESSE, 3965 est, boul. Henri-Bourassa, Montreal, Quebec, Canada H1H 1L1. Editor: Pierre Claude. For "French Canadian boys and girls of 8-15." Monthly. Circ. 45,000. Buys all rights. Buys 20-30 mss/year. Pays on publication. Free sample copy. Reports in 2 weeks. SAE and International Reply Coupons.
Nonfiction: "Material with a French-Canadian background. The articles have to be written in French, and must appeal to children aged 8 to 15." Buys how-to, personal experience articles, interviews, profiles, humor, historical articles, photo features and travel pieces. Length: 1,500-3,000 words. Pays 3¢/word.
Photos: B&w glossy prints, color transparencies; with captions only. Pays $13.50.
Fillers: Puzzles, jokes and short humor.

WEE WISDOM, Unity Village MO 64065. Editor: Colleen Zuck. Magazine published 10 times/year. A Christian magazine for boys and girls aged 13 and under dedicated to the truths: that each person is a child of God and that as a child of God each person has an inner source of wisdom, power, love and health from their Father that can be applied in a practical manner to everyday life." Free sample copy, editorial policy on request. Buys first North American serial rights. Byline given. Pays on acceptance. SASE.
Nonfiction: Entertaining nature articles or projects, activities to encourage appreciation of all life. Pays 3¢/word minimum.
Fiction: "Character-building stories that encourage a positive self-image. Although entertaining enough to hold the interest of the older child, they should be readable by the third grader. Characters should be appealing but realistic; plots should be plausible, and all stories should be told in a forthright manner but without preaching. Life itself combines fun and humor with its more serious lessons, and our most interesting and helpful stories do the same thing. Language should be universal, avoiding the Sunday school image." Length: 500-800 words. Pay 3¢/word minimum.
Poetry: Very limited. Pays 50¢/line. Prefers short, seasonal or humorous poems. Also buys rhymed prose for "read alouds" and pays $15 minimum.
Fillers: Pays $3 minimum for puzzles and games.

WONDER TIME, 6401 The Paseo, Kansas City MO 64131. (816)333-7000. Editor: Evelyn Beals. Published weekly by Church of the Nazarene for children ages 6-8. Free sample copy. Buys first rights. Byline given. Pays on acceptance. SASE.
Fiction: Buys stories portraying Christian attitudes without being preachy. Uses stories for special days—stories teaching honesty, truthfulness, kindness, helpfulness or other important spiritual truths, and avoiding symbolism. "God should be spoken of as our Father who loves and cares for us; Jesus, as our Lord and Savior." Length: 400-600 words. Pays 3¢/word on acceptance.
Poetry: Uses verse which has seasonal or Christian emphasis. Length: 4-12 lines. Pays 25¢/line minimum-$2.50.
Tips: "Any stories that allude to church doctrine must be in keeping with Nazarene beliefs. Any type of fantasy must be in good taste and easily recognizable. Overstocked now with poetry and stories with general theme. Brochure with specific needs available with free sample."

WORLD OVER, 426 W. 58th St., New York NY 10019. Editor: Stephen Schaffzin. 50% freelance written. Buys first serial rights. Byline given. Pays on acceptance. Reports in 4-6 weeks. SASE.
Nonfiction, Photos and Fiction: Uses material of Jewish interest, past or present for ages 8-13 and up. Articles up to 1,000 words. Fiction should be Jewish in content. Length: 600-800 words. Query. Pays 12¢/word minimum. B&w glossy prints purchased with mss.
Tips: "Please consider our age group (8-13) in terms of vocabulary and syntax as well as content. We read everything and accept on the individual story's merit."

THE YOUNG CRUSADER, 1730 Chicago Ave., Evanston IL 60201. (312)864-1396. Managing Editor: Michael Vitucci. For children ages 6-12. Monthly. Not copyrighted. Pays on publication. Submit seasonal material 6 months in advance. SASE. Free sample copy.
Nonfiction: Uses articles on total abstinence, character-building, love of animals. Also science stories. Length: 650-800 words. Pays ½¢/word.
Fiction: Should emphasize Christian principles and world friendship. Also science stories. Length: 650-800 words. Pays ½¢/word.

YOUNG JUDAEAN, 50 W. 58th St., New York NY 10019. (212)355-7900, ext. 464, 465. Editor: Barbara Gingold. Editorial Assistant: Toby Snopkovski. For Jewish children aged 8-13, and members of Young Judaea. Publication of Hadassah Zionist Youth Commission. All material must be on some Jewish theme. Special issues for Jewish/Israeli holidays, or particular Jewish themes which vary from year to year; for example, Hassidim, Holocaust, etc. Monthly (November through June). Circ. 8,000. Buys all rights, first North American serial rights or first serial rights. Byline given. Buys 10-20 mss/year. Payment in contributor's copies or small token payment. Sample copy and annual list of themes for 50¢. Prefers complete ms. Will consider photocopied and simultaneous submissions. Submit seasonal material 4 months in advance. Reports in 3 months. SASE.
Nonfiction: "Articles about Jewish-American life, Jewish historical and international interest. Israel and Zionist-oriented material. Try to awaken kids' Jewish consciousness by creative approach to Jewish history and religion, ethics and culture, politics and current events. Style can be didactic, but not patronizing." Informational (300-1,000 words), how-to (300-500 words), personal experience, interview, humor, historical, think articles, photo, travel, and reviews (books, theater and movies). Length: 500-1,200 words. Pays $5-25. "Token payments only, due to minuscule budget."
Photos: Photos purchased with accompanying mss. Captions required. 5x7 maximum. B&w prefered. Payment included with fee for article. Illustrations also accepted.
Fiction: Experimental, mainstream, mystery, suspense, adventure, science fiction, fantasy, humorous, religious and historical fiction. Length: 500-1,000 words. Pays $5-25. Must be of specific Jewish interest.
Poetry and Fillers: Traditional forms, blank verse, free verse, avant-garde forms and light verse. Poetry themes must relate to subject matter of magazine. Length: 25-100 lines. Pays $5-15. Newsbreaks, jokes and short humor purchased for $5.
Tips: "Think of an aspect of Jewish history/religion/culture which can be handled in a fresh, imaginative way, fictionally or factually. Don't preach; inform and entertain."

YOUNG MUSICIANS, 127 9th Ave. N., Nashville TN 37234. Editor: Jimmy R. Key. 5-10% freelance written. For boys and girls age 9-11, and their leaders in children's choirs in Southern Baptist churches (and some other churches). Monthly magazine; 52 pages. Buys all rights. Buys 5-6 mss/year. Pays on acceptance. Free sample copy. No photocopied or simultaneous submissions. Query. SASE.
Nonfiction: "All material is slanted for use with and by children in church choirs. Music study materials related to study units in *The Music Leader*. Ours is a curriculum magazine written almost

entirely on assignment." Informational, how-to, historical. Length: 300-900 words. Pays approximately 3½¢/word.
Fiction: Child-centered stories related to church music and music in the home. Length: 600-900 words. Pays approximately 3½¢/word.
Tips: "Submit a unit of study (4-6 sessions) using large and small group activities relating to music; how-to, theory, singing. The unit of study must relate to *Young Musicians Magazine*, which is the companion piece that is used by children—stories, games, theory and music."

Literary and "Little"

Many of the publications in this category do not pay except in contributor's copies. Nonpaying markets are included because they offer the writer a vehicle for expression that often can't be found in the commercial press. Many talented American writers found first publication in magazines like these. Writers are reminded that many "littles" remain at one address for a limited time; others are sometimes unbusinesslike in their reporting on or returning of submissions. University-affiliated reviews are conscientious about manuscripts but some of these are also slow in replying to queries or returning submissions.

Magazines that specialize in publishing poetry or poetry criticism are found in the Poetry category. Many "little" publications that offer contributors a forum for expression of minority opinions are classified in the listings for Alternative Publications.

For more information about fiction technique—and some specialized markets—see *Fiction Writer's Market*, published by Writer's Digest Books.

THE AMERICAN BOOK REVIEW, The Writers' Review, Inc., Box 188, New York NY 10003. Publisher: Ronald Sukenick. Editors: Rochelle Ratner, Charles Russell, John Tytell and Suzanne Zavrian. For anyone interested in contemporary literature. Bimonthly tabloid; 20 pages. Circ. 9,000. Pays $25. Buys all rights. Photocopied submissions OK. SASE. Reports in 2 months. Free sample copy and writer's guidelines.
Nonfiction: Book Reviews only. Query. Length: 300-1,500 words. Pays $25.

AMERICAN NOTES AND QUERIES, Erasmus Press, 225 Culpepper, Lexington KY 40502. (606)266-1058. Editor: John Cutler. Ten times a year. No payment. Byline given. SASE.
Nonfiction: Historical, literary, bibliographical, linguistic and folklore matters; scholarly book reviews and reviews of foreign reference books; items of unusual antiquarian interest.
Tips: "We don't buy anything. We publish significant scholarly notes on the basis of the readers' advice."

AMERICAN QUARTERLY, Van Pelt Library, University of Pennsylvania, 303 College Hall, Philadelphia PA 19104. (215)243-6252. Editor: Dr. Bruce Kuklick. For college professors, teachers, museum directors, researchers, students, college and high school libraries. Readers professionally interested in American studies. Acquires all rights. Byline given. Does not pay. Reports in 2-4 months. SASE and 2 copies of article.
Nonfiction: Scholarly, interdisciplinary articles on American studies, about 20 pages. Bibliography issue contains bibliographic essays, dissertation listings, American Studies programs.
Photos: Occasionally uses photos.

THE AMERICAN SCHOLAR, 1811 Q St. NW, Washington DC 20009. (202)265-3808. Editor: Joseph Epstein. "For college-educated, mid-20s and older, rather intellectual in orientation and interests." Quarterly magazine, 144 pages. Circ. 32,000. Buys right to publish; rights stay in author's possession. Byline given. Buys 20-30 mss/year. Pays on acceptance for publication. Sample copy $4; free writer's guidelines. No simultaneous submissions. Reports in 1 month. Query, with samples, if possible. SASE.
Nonfiction: "The aim of *The Scholar* is to fill the gap between the learned journals and the good magazines for a popular audience. We are interested not so much in the definitive analysis as in the lucid and creative exploration of what is going on in the fields of science, art, religion, politics, and

national and foreign affairs. Advances in science particularly interest us." Informational, interview, profile, historical, think articles, and book reviews. Length: 3,500-4,000 words. Pays $350/article and $100 for reviews.

Poetry: Pays $50 for poetry on any theme. Approximately 5 poems published per issue. "We would like to see poetry that develops an image or a thought or event, without the use of a single cliché or contrived archaism. The most hackneyed subject matter is self-conscious love; the most tired verse is iambic pentameter with rhyming endings. The usual length of our poems is 30 lines. From 1-4 poems may be submitted at one time; *no more* for a careful reading. We urge prospective contributors to familiarize themselves with the type of poetry we have published by looking at the magazine."

Tips: "See our magazine in your public library before submitting material to us. Know what we publish and the quality of our articles."

THE ANTIGONISH REVIEW, St. Francis Xavier University, Antigonish, Nova Scotia, Canada B2G 1C0. Editor: R.J. MacSween. For "those with literary interests." Quarterly magazine; 100 pages. Circ. 500. Pays in copies only. Not copyrighted. Photocopied submissions OK. SASE. Reports in 6 weeks. Free sample copy.

Nonfiction: Literary articles of general interest. Submit complete ms.

Fiction: Fantasy, experimental and mainstream. No erotica. Submit complete ms.

Poetry: Avant-garde and traditional. Uses 30/issue.

Tips: "We could use more reviews of literary books."

ANTIOCH REVIEW, Box 148, Yellow Springs OH 45387. Editor: Robert S. Fogarty. For general, literary and academic audience. Quarterly. Buys all rights. Byline given. Pays on publication. Reports in 4-6 weeks. SASE.

Nonfiction: "Contemporary articles in the humanities and social sciences, politics, economics, literature and all areas of broad intellectual concern. Somewhat scholarly, but never pedantic in style, eschewing all professional jargon. Lively, distinctive prose insisted upon." Length: 2,000-8,000 words. Pays $10/published page.

Fiction: Prefers a strong narrative line with strong, fresh insights into the human condition. No science fiction, fantasy, confessions. Pays $10/published page.

Poetry: Concrete visual imagery. No light or inspirational verse. Contributors should be familiar with the magazine before submitting.

APALACHEE QUARTERLY, Box 20106, Tallahassee FL 32304. Collective Editorship. For an artistic/critical audience; over 16 years of age. Quarterly magazine; 44-60 pages. Circ. 450. Acquires all rights. Uses 80 mss/year. Pays in contributor's copies. Sample copy for $1.50. No simultaneous submissions. Reports in 10 weeks. Submit complete ms. SASE.

Nonfiction: Emphasis is on creative writing, rather than criticism. Uses interviews and reviews of fiction and poetry. Length: 300-3,000 words.

Photos: B&w photos purchased without ms. Captions optional.

Fiction: Short stories, experimental or mainstream. Length: 300-6,000 words.

Poetry: Traditional forms of poetry, blank verse, free verse, avant garde forms. Length: 8-100 lines.

Tips: "Our publication can be enjoyed by anyone with even a basic background in literature, but is not for the barely literate. We publish things that our editors would take pride in having written. Therefore, take pride in what you submit. We like avant garde writing and traditional writing, yet the traditional is difficult to master and the avant garde is impossible to attempt until the traditional has been mastered."

THE ARK RIVER REVIEW, c/o A. Sobin, English Department, Wichita State University, Wichita KS 67208. Editors-in-Chief: Jonathan Katz, A.G. Sobin. 100% freelance written. For "the well-educated, college age and above; poets, writers, and the readers of contemporary poetry and fiction." Published biannually. Magazine; 85-150 pages. Circ. 1,000. Pays on publication. Buys all rights. Byline given. Photocopied submissions OK. Reports in 1 month; finalists may take considerably longer. Sample copy, appropriate to your genre $2.50.

Fiction: "We print one fiction issue/year featuring chapbook-sized collections of the work of 3 writers. We will read manuscripts of 75-125 pages (short fiction or novella or novel excerpt), up to ⅓ of which may have been previously published in magazine form. We will consider only writers who have yet to publish a full-length book. Conventional fiction stands little chance. We are interested only in highly innovative and sophisticated material. Type and subject matter are far less important to us than the way in which the story is written. We are looking for freshness in approach, style and language. We suggest strongly that you read back issues before submitting." Buys 3 mss/issue. Send complete ms (no novels). Pays $250/manuscript and contributor's copies.

Poetry: "Poetry should be substantial, intelligent and serious (this doesn't mean it can't be funny). Any form is OK, though we almost never print rhyming poems or haiku. As in fiction, we print one poetry issue/year, which contains chapbook-sized collections of the work of 3 poets. We will read manuscripts of 15-30 pages, up to ⅓ of which may have been previously published in magazine form." Pays $250. Buys 3/issue.
Tips: "Your work should demonstrate to us that you know what has gone on in literature in the last 50 years, and that you're working toward something better. The best way to find out what we're after is to read back issues. Send complete ms and $2.50 handling fee, receive a free copy of the next issue appropriate to your genre. (No reading fee required of subscribers)." Queries and ms must be accompanied by SASE.

ART AND LITERARY DIGEST, Summer address: Madoc-Tweed Art Centre, Tweed, Ontario, Canada. Winter address: 1109 N. Betty Lane, Clearwater FL 33515. Editor: Roy Cadwell. "Our readers are the public and former students of the Art and Writing Centre. As an educational publication we welcome new writers who have something to say and want to see their name in print and get paid for it." Quarterly. Circ. 1,000. Not copyrighted. Byline given. Pays on publication. Sample copy $1. "Photocopied mss are accepted, but not returned. You may submit elsewhere after 1 month. Original mss must be accompanied by return envelope and unattached postage." SASE. "We are no longer accepting unsolicited material other than poetry."

ASPEN ANTHOLOGY, Aspen Leaves, Inc., Box 3185, Aspen CO 81612. (303)925-8750. Editor: Donald A. Child. For poets, short fiction writers, novelists, teachers and literate readers. Biannual magazine; 130 pages. Circ. 1,000. Pays in contributor's copies. Acquires all rights. Phone queries OK. SASE. Reports in 4 weeks. Sample copy $3.50.
Fiction: Address Fiction Editors. Experimental. Uses 2-4 mss/issue. Submit complete ms. Length: 10,000 words maximum. Pays in 2 copies.
Poetry: Address Poetry Editors. Any style. Uses 30-40/issue. No length limit. Pays in 2 copies.
Tips: Selection cycles usually end September 15 and March 15. "Be familiar with quality contemporary writing; send small bunches of poetry (not more than 5 poems/submission)."

BIOGRAPHY: An Interdisciplinary Quarterly, Biographical Research Center and University Press of Hawaii, 2840 Kolowalu St., Honolulu HI 96822. (808)948-8803. Editor: George Simson. Associate Editor: Anthony Friedson. Review Editor: W. Gerald Marshall. Emphasizes biographical studies. Quarterly magazine; 96 pages. Circ. 400. Holds all rights unless negotiated otherwise. Byline given. Photocopied submissions OK. SASE. Reports in 3 months. Sample copy $3.50 in US; $4, elsewhere; free writer's guidelines.
Nonfiction: All scholarship: interdisciplinary, historical, psychological, literary, interview, personal experience and profile. Query or send complete ms. Length: 2,500-10,000 words. Pays 5 copies of issue in which article appears.
Photos: Must be camera-ready. State availability of photos. Offers no additional payment for photos accepted with accompanying ms. Captions required.
Columns/Departments: Yearly index, annual bibliography and communications. Query or send complete ms.

BLACK AMERICAN LITERATURE FORUM, Indiana State University, Parsons Hall 237, Terre Haute IN 47809. (812)232-6311, ext. 2760. Editor: Joe Weixlmann. Emphasizes black American literature. Quarterly magazine; 40-48 pages. Circ. 990. Pays in copies. Acquires simultaneous rights. Byline given. Phone queries OK. Submit seasonal/holiday material at least 3 months in advance. SASE. Reports in 3 months. Sample copy $2.50; free writer's guidelines.
Nonfiction: "We publish scholarly criticism and bibliographies of black American writers, also pedagogical articles and curricular evaluations. We also use poetry by black writers and original graphic work by black artists."
Photos: Sketches and photos used without accompanying ms. Pays $15/graphic work.

BLACK SCHOLAR, Box 908, Sausalito CA 94966 Editor: Robert Allen. Mainly for black professionals, educators, and students. Bimonthly journal of black studies and research; 96 pages. Circ. 20,000. Acquires all rights. Uses about 60 mss/year. Pays in contributor's copies. Free sample copy and writer's guidelines. Photocopied submissions and simultaneous submissions OK, "but must be so informed." Reports in 2 months. Query about upcoming topics. SASE.
Nonfiction: "We seek essays discussing issues affecting the black community (education, health, economics, psychology, culture, literature, etc.). Essays should be reasoned and well-documented. Each issue is organized around a specific topic: black education, health, prisons, family, etc., with a variety of viewpoints." Informational, interview, profile, historical, think articles, and book and film reviews. Length: 1,500-7,000 words.

THE BLACK WARRIOR REVIEW, The University of Alabama, Box 2936, University AL 35486. (205)348-7839. Editor: Michael Pettit. Emphasizes fiction and poetry. Semiannual magazine; 128 pages. Circ. 1,000. Pays in copies. Acquires all rights. Phone queries OK. Submit material for fall by Oct. 1; for spring by Feb. 1. SASE. Reports in 2 months. Sample copy $2.50.
Nonfiction: Interview and criticism of contemporary literature. Buys 4 mss/year. Query.
Fiction: Jon Hershey, fiction editor. Experimental and mainstream. "Acceptance depends on quality, not subject matter, genre or treatment." Buys 1-4 mss/issue. Submit complete ms.
Poetry: Dev Hathaway, poetry editor. Free verse and traditional. Buys 20/issue.

BLOOMSBURY REVIEW, Box 8928, Denver CO 80201. (303)455-0593. Editor: Tom Auer. Managing Editor: J. Vinay. Bimonthly magazine covering book reviews, and stories of interest to residents of the western states. Estab. 1980. Circ. 5,000. Pays on publication. Byline and one-line biography given. Buys one-time rights. Simultaneous queries OK. SASE. Reports in 2 months on queries and mss. Sample copy 75¢; free writer's guidelines.
Nonfiction: Historical/nostalgic (related to books and publishing); interview/profile (of prominent people in the book business such as authors and publishers); essays; and book reviews. "Submitting a book review is the best way to break into *Bloomsbury Review*." Query with clips of published work. Length: average 750 words. Pays $10 minimum."
Fiction: Adventure, ethnic, experimental, fantasy, historical, horror, humorous, mainstream, mystery, science fiction, suspense, and western.
Poetry: Avant-garde, free verse, haiku, light verse, traditional and all others. Buys 24/year. Pays $5 average.

BOOK ARTS NEWSLETTER, (formerly *Book Arts*) The Center for Book Arts, 15 Bleecker St., New York NY 10012. (212)260-6860. Managing Editor: Mindell Dubansky. Emphasizes bookbinding and exploring the arts of the book. Quarterly newsletter; 6 pages. Circ. 1,000. Pays in copies. Acquires all rights. Byline given. Submit seasonal/holiday material 3 months in advance. Simultaneous, photocopied and previously published submissions OK. Reports in 2 months. Free sample copy.
Nonfiction: Exposé (on banning books in schools, other censorship, etc.); historical (bookburnings, looking at the history of watermarks and any other book experience); interview (with book artists) and technical (e.g., "William Blake's Method of Printing"). Query. Pays in copies.

BOOK FORUM, Hudson River Press, 38 E. 76th St., New York NY 10021. (212)861-8328. Editor: Marshall Hayes. Editorial Director: Marilyn Wood. Emphasizes contemporary literature, the arts, and foreign affairs for "intellectually sophisticated and knowledgeable professionals: university-level academics, writers, people in government, and the professions." Quarterly magazine; 192 pages. Circ. 5,200. Pays on publication. Buys all rights. Pays 33⅓% kill fee. Byline given. Phone queries OK. Photocopied submissions OK. SASE. Reports in 2 weeks. Sample copy $3.
Nonfiction: "We seek highly literate essays that would appeal to the same readership as, say, the *London Times Literary Supplement* or *Encounter*. Our readers are interested in professionally written, highly literate and informative essays, profiles and reviews in literature, the arts, behavior, and foreign and public affairs. We cannot use material designed for a mass readership, nor for the counterculture. Think of us as an Eastern establishment, somewhat snobbish literary and public affairs journal and you will have it right." General interest, interview (with select contemporary writers), profiles, and essays about contemporary writers. Buys 20 mss/year. Query. Length: 1,400-3,000 words. Pays $25-100.
Tips: "To break in send with the query letter a sample of writing in an area relevant to our interests. If the writer wants to contribute book reviews, send a book review sample, published or not, of the kind of title we are likely to review—literary, social, biographical, art."

C.S.P. WORLD NEWS, Editions Stencil, Box 2608, Station D, Ottawa, Ontario, Canada K1P 5W7. Editor-in-Chief: Guy F. Claude Hamel. Emphasizes book reviews. Monthly literary journal. Circ. 200,000. Buys all rights. Photocopied submissions OK. SAE and International Reply Coupons. Reports in 2 months. Sample copy $1.
Nonfiction: Publishes on sociology and criminology. Buys 12 mss/year. Send complete ms. Length: 2,600-5,000 words. Pays $1-2/typewritten, double-spaced page.
Columns/Departments: Writer's Workshop material. Buys 12 items/year. Send complete ms. Length: 20-50 words. Pays $1-2.
Poetry: Publishes avant-garde forms. Buys 12/year. Submit complete ms; no more than 2 at a time. Length: 6-12 lines. Pays $1.
Fillers: Jokes, gags and anecdotes. Pays $1-2.

THE CALIFORNIA QUARTERLY, 100 Sproul, University of California, Davis CA 95616. Editor: Elliot Gilbert. 95% freelance written. "Addressed to an audience of educated, literary, and general readers, interested in good writing on a variety of subjects, but emphasis is on poetry and fiction." Quarterly. Usually buys first North American serial rights. Reports in 2 months but the editorial office is closed from June 1 to September 30. SASE.

Nonfiction: Original, critical articles, interviews and book reviews. Length: 8,000 words maximum. Pays $2/published page.

Fiction: Department Editor: Diane Johnson. "Short fiction of quality with emphasis on stylistic distinction; contemporary themes, any subject." Experimental, mainstream. Length: 8,000 words maximum. Pays $2/published page.

Poetry: Department editor: Sandra M. Gilbert. "Original, all types; any subject appropriate for genuine poetic expression; any length suitable to subject." Pays $3/published page.

CANADIAN FICTION MAGAZINE, Box 946, Station F, Toronto, Ontario, Canada M4Y 2N9. Editor: Geoffrey Hancock. Emphasizes Canadian fiction, short stories and novel excerpts. Quarterly magazine; 148 pages. Circ. 1,800. Pays on publication. Buys first North American serial rights. Byline given. SASE (Canadian stamps). Reports in 4-6 weeks. Back issue $4.00 (in Canadian funds). Current issue $5.50 (in Canadian funds).

Nonfiction: Interview (must have a definite purpose, both as biography and as a critical tool focusing on problems and techniques) and book reviews (Canadian fiction only). Buys 35 mss/year. Query. Length: 1,000-3,000 words. Pays $10/printed page plus one-year subscription.

Photos: Purchased on assignment. Send prints. Pays $5 for 5x7 b&w glossy prints; $20 for cover. Model release required.

Fiction: "No restrictions on subject matter or theme. We are open to experimental and speculative fiction as well as traditional forms. Style content and form are the author's prerogative. We also publish self-contained sections of novel-in-progress and French-Canadian fiction in translation, as well as an annual special issue on a single author such as Mavis Gallant, Leon Rooke, Robert Harlow or Jane Rule. Please note that *CFM* is an anthology devoted exclusively to Canadian fiction. We publish only the works of writers and artists residing in Canada and Canadians living abroad."

CANADIAN LITERATURE, University of British Columbia, Vancouver, British Columbia, Canada V6T 1W5. Editor: W.H. New. Quarterly. Circ. 2,500. Not copyrighted. Pays on publication. Query "with a clear description of the project." SAE and International Reply Coupons.

Nonfiction: Articles of high quality on Canadian books and writers only. Articles should be scholarly and readable. No fiction, fillers, or thematic studies. Length: 2,000-5,500 words. Pays $5/printed page.

CAROLINA QUARTERLY, University of North Carolina, Greenlaw Hall 066A, Chapel Hill NC 27514. (919)933-0244. Editor: Davis A. March. Managing Editor: Dani Thompson. Literary journal published 3 times/year. Circ. 1,200. Pays on publication. Byline given. Buys first North American serial rights. Photocopied submissions OK. SASE. Reports in 4 months. Sample copy $4 (includes postage); writer's guidelines for SAE and 1 first class stamp.

Nonfiction: Book excerpts and photo feature. "Nonfiction articles are not commissioned; used at Editor's discretion." Buy 1-2 mss/year. Send complete ms. Length: 6,000 words.

Fiction: "We are interested in maturity and all that that implies: control over language; command of structure and technique; understanding of the possibilities and demands of prose narrative, with respect to stylistics, characterization, and point of view. What we want is precisely to discourage that which merely *pretends*. We publish a good many unsolicited stories; and *CQ* is a market for newcomer and professional alike." No pornography. Buys 12-18 mss/year. Send complete ms. Length: 7,000 words maximum. Pays $3/printed page.

Poetry: "*CQ* places no specific restrictions on the length, form or substance of poems considered for publication, though limited space makes inclusion of works of more than 300 lines impracticable." Submit 2-6 poems. Buys 60 mss/year. Pays $5/printed poem.

Tips: "*One* fiction ms at a time; no cover letter is necessary. Address to appropriate editor, not to general editor. Look at the magazine, a recent number if possible."

CHELSEA, Box 5880, Grand Central Station, New York NY 10163. Editor: Sonia Raiziss. Acquires first North American serial rights. Pays in copies. SASE.

Nonfiction: Occasional nonfiction articles, interviews, artwork.

Fiction: Short fiction. Accent on style. "Also interested in fresh, contemporary translations."

Poetry: Poetry of high quality.

Tips: "Best thing to do: Read several issues of the magazine to get the tone/content, themes, penchants, and range of contributions." No guidelines.

CHICAGO REVIEW, University of Chicago, Faculty Exchange Box C, Chicago IL 60637. (312)753-3571. Editor: Molly McQuade and John Sutton. Readership interested in contemporary literature and criticisms. Quarterly magazine; 140 pages. Circ. 2,000. Pays in copies. Acquires all rights. Photocopied submissions OK. SASE. Reports in 3 months. Sample copy $3.00, plus postage (75¢).

Nonfiction: Ted Shen and Ellen Tuckev, nonfiction editors. Informational and interview. "We consider essays on and reviews of contemporary writing and the arts." Submit complete ms. Length: 500-5,000 words.

Fiction: Jan Deckenbach and Sarah E. Lauzen, fiction editors. Experimental and mainstream. "We welcome the work of younger, less established writers." Uses 3-12/issue. Submit complete ms.

Poetry: Thomas Bonnell and Keith Tuma, poetry editors. Avant-garde, free verse, translations and traditional. Uses 12/year. Limit submissions to batches of 3-5.

Tips: "Try short book reviews, and query first, with brevity and wit."

CHICAGO SUN-TIMES SHOW/BOOK WEEK, *Chicago Sun-Times,* 401 N. Wabash Ave., Chicago IL 60611. (312)321-2131. Editor: Barbara Haese. Emphasizes entertainment, arts and books. Weekly newspaper section; 10 pages. Circ. 750,000. Pays on publication. Buys all rights. Pays negotiable kill fee, except on speculative articles. Submit seasonal/holiday material at least 2 months in advance. Photocopied and previously published work OK. SASE. Reports in 3 weeks.

Nonfiction: "Articles and essays dealing with all the serious and lively arts—movies, theater (pro, semipro, amateur, foreign), filmmakers, painting, sculpture, music (all fields, from classical to rock—we have regular columnists in these fields). Our Book Week columns have from 6-8 reviews, mostly assigned. Material has to be very good because we have our own regular staffers who write almost every week. Writing must be tight. No warmed-over stuff of fan magazine type. No high-schoolish literary themes." Query. Length: 800-1,000 words. Pays $75-100.

CHILDREN'S LITERATURE, The Children's Literature Foundation, Box 370, Windham Center CT 06280. (203)456-1900. Editor: Francelia Butler. Managing Editor: John C. Wandell. Annual journal; 250-300 pages. Circ. 3,500. Pays in reprints. Byline given. Phone queries OK. Submit seasonal/holiday material 1 year in advance. SASE. Reports in 1 month.

Nonfiction: Scholarly or critical essays. Uses 20 mss/issue. Query or send complete ms. Length: 7,500 words.

Photos: State availability of photos. Uses 4x5 or 8x10 b&w glossy prints. Captions and permission to publish required.

Columns/Departments: Book Review Articles (send to David L. Greene, Chairman, English Department, Piedmont College, Demorest GA). Uses 20/year. Query. Length: 3,000 words. Open to suggestions for new columns/departments.

CIMARRON REVIEW, Oklahoma State University, Stillwater OK 74078. Editor-in-Chief: Neil J. Hackett. Managing Editor: Jeanne Adams Wray. 100% freelance written. For educated readers, college- and university-oriented. Quarterly magazine, small and humanistic, 72 pages, (6x9). Circ. 500. Acquires all rights. Byline given. Pays contributor's copies. Reports in 3 weeks. Submit only complete ms. SASE. Free sample copy.

Nonfiction: Articles and essays. Occasional theme issues. "We are particularly interested in articles and essays on topics of contemporary concern and significance."

Fiction: Short stories. "We wish to publish works of vision and high quality dealing with a wide variety of themes."

CONFRONTATION, Long Island University, 1 University Plaza, Brooklyn NY 11201. (212)834-6170. Editor: Martin Tucker. 90% freelance written. Emphasizes creative writing for a "literate, educated, college-graduate audience." Semiannual magazine; 190 pages. Circ. 2,000. Pays on publication. Buys all rights. Pays 50% kill fee. Byline given. Phone queries OK. Simultaneous and photocopied submissions OK. SASE. Reports in 2 months. Sample copy $1.50.

Nonfiction: "Articles are, basically, commissioned essays on a specific subject." Memoirs wanted. Buys 6 mss/year. Query. Length: 1,000-3,000 words. Pays $10-50.

Fiction: Ken Bernard, fiction editor. Fantasy, experimental, humorous, mainstream. Buys 20 mss/year. Submit complete ms. Length: "completely open." Pays $15-75.

Poetry: W. Palmer, poetry editor. Avant-garde, free verse, haiku, light verse, traditional. Buys 40/year. Limit submissions to batches of 10. No length requirement. Pays $5-40.

Tips: "At this time we discourage fantasy and light verse. We do, however, read all mss."

CONTEMPORARY LITERATURE, Dept. of English, Helen C. White Hall, University of Wisconsin, Madison WI 53706. Editor: L.S. Dembo. Quarterly. A scholarly journal that examines various aspects of contemporary literature, including generalizations on current trends and themes in both criticism and literature, studies of individual writer's techniques and/or the place of a specific work in his or her whole canon, and the placing of writer or his work in a particular literary or critical context. "All details should conform to those recommended by the MLA Style Sheet." Does not encourage contributions from freelance writers without academic credentials.

Tips: "We are not interested in simple readings of novels, or explications of poems—we want material with a definite theoretical or critical base."

CREAM CITY REVIEW, Department of English, Box 413, University of Wisconsin-Milwaukee, Milwaukee WI 53201. Editor: Ned Williams. 100% freelance written. Emphasizes poetry, fiction, criticism, reviews, graphics and interviews. Published 2 times/year. Magazine; 120 pages. Circ. 800 at present. Pays in copies. Obtains all rights. Byline given. Direct each submission to the editor of the appropriate department: fiction, poetry, nonfiction or art. Photocopied and previously published submissions OK. SASE. Reports in 4 months. Sample copy $2.50.

Nonfiction: Experimental writing, literary reviews, cultural criticism.

Photos: B&w photos should be proportioned for a 6x9 format (to cover 1 full page).

Fiction: Any kind of excellent fiction, parts of novels. Uses 5-7 mss/issue.

Poetry: All kinds. Uses 90-100/year.

CRITIQUE: STUDIES IN MODERN FICTION, Department of English, Georgia Institute of Technology, Atlanta GA 30332. Editor: James Dean Young. For college and university teachers and students. Triannual. Circ. 1,500. Acquires all rights. Pays in contributor's copies. Submit complete original ms. Writers should follow the *MLA Style Sheet*. Reports in 4-6 months. SASE.

Nonfiction: "Critical essays on writers of contemporary fiction. We prefer essays on writers from any country who are alive and without great reputations. We only rarely publish essays on well-known, established writers such as James, Conrad, Joyce and Faulkner." Uses informational articles and interviews. Length: 4,000-8,000 words.

CROP DUST, Crop Dust Press, Rt. 2, Box 392, Bealeton VA 22712. (703)439-2140. Editor: Edward C. Lynskey. Managing Editors: Wayne Kline and Cameron Yeatts. Magazine published 2 times/year "for a widespread readership, found within the university as well as outside of academia." Estab. 1979. Circ. 500. Pays on publication. Buys first North American serial rights. Photocopied submissions OK. SASE. Reports in 2 weeks on queries; 3 months on mss. Sample copy $1.50; free writer's guidelines.

Nonfiction: Interview/profile. "We publish only one interview and/or profile per issue. No more farm pieces. You must query first." Buys 4 mss/year. Query. "Submit a short letter describing what the intent is. We appreciate some background info as means of introduction. Always include SASE." Length: 250-750. Pays in copies.

Columns/Departments: "We welcome well-written reviews of magazines and recently published books. Special emphasis is on small press publications." Buys 30 mss/year. Length: 250-750 words. Pays in copies.

Fiction: Adventure, experimental, fantasy, mainstream, mystery, science fiction, and suspense. "Please do not send juvenile or religious-oriented material." Buys 5 mss/year. Send complete ms. Length: 750-3,500 words. Pays in copies.

Poetry: Avant-garde, free verse, haiku, light verse, and traditional. "We will consider any style or form of poetry that is well-done. We hardly ever publish newspaper, inspirational, or religious verse." Buys 80/year. Submit maximum 3-6 poems. Length: 3 lines-2 pages. Pays in copies.

Tips: "Please put the correct postage on SASE or will return postage due. Though our name implies a rural outlook, we are dedicated to reading well-written, literary material."

CROSSCURRENTS, 2200 Glastonbury Rd., Westlake Village CA 91361. Editor: Linda Brown Michelson. Quarterly magazine covering fiction and poetry for an educated audience. Estab. 1980. Circ. 650. Average issue includes 5-7 pieces of short fiction, 7-10 pieces of poetry and 1-2 pieces of nonfiction. Pays on acceptance. Byline given. Offers 50% kill fee. Buys first North American serial rights. Submit seasonal material 4 months in advance. Photocopied submissions OK. SASE. Reports in 2 weeks on queries; in 6 weeks on mss. Sample copy $2.50; free writer's guidelines for SASE. No simultaneous submissions.

Nonfiction: Historical, interview, profile, memoirs and film. "Our only concern is well-crafted work; the new writer is as welcome as the established writer. We have scheduled a special issue for May 1982; we will study 'Men, Women and the Arts!" Buys 4-7 mss/year. Query. Pays $35 minimum.

Photos: Photo editor: Michael Hughes. State availability of photos. Pays $10 minimum for b&w negative plus prints. Model release required. Buys one-time rights.

Fiction: "We try to remain open to all types of fiction." Buys 20-25 mss/year. Send complete ms. Length: 8,000 words maximum. Pays $35 minimum. Also pays in copies.

Poetry: Poetry editor: Pamela Camille. "We try to remain open to all types of poetry." Buys 35

mss/year. Submit maximum 5 poems. Pays $10 minimum. Also pays in copies.
Tips: "Study a sample issue of our publication, then send us something terrifically appropriate. We receive quite a bit of material that is well-done, but just not quite right for us."

DANDELION, Dandelion Magazine Society, 922 9th Ave. SE, Calgary, Alberta, Canada T2G 0S4. (403)265-0524. Editors: Robert Hilles and Beverly Hocking. Literary magazine published twice/year covering fiction, poetry and visual arts. Strives for "quality writing which leaves the reader with something to remember; superior use of language in poetry or prose." Circ. 500. Pays on publication. Byline given. Buys first North American serial rights and one-time rights. SAE and International Reply Coupons. "US mss without Canadian SASE should not attach US return stamps. Leave loose." Sample copy $3.
Photos: Art editor. "In the past, we've used high contrast b&w scenes with highly poetic content: statement or symbol." Send photos with ms. Pays $10-20 for 5x7 or 8x10 b&w prints. Buys one-time rights.
Fiction: Beverly Hocking, fiction editor. Experimental, fantasy, mainstream and novel excerpts; "short stories (of the beginning, middle and end sort). No poorly conceived, 'overly popular' material." Buys 8 mss/year. Send complete ms. "No established minimum or maximum word length." Pays $50-100.
Poetry: Robert Hilles, poetry editor. Avant-garde, free verse, haiku, traditional and long poems. No "first drafts (mailed prior to review for typos, etc.)." Buys 50 mss/year. Submit 20 mss pages maximum (as a guide). There is no policy on this." Length: open. Pays $10-20.
Tips: "A good storyteller with superior skills in using the language can break in here. Often an extremely short piece fits between the cracks. Non-Canadians *don't* get top priority, however. To date, we've taken about one US manuscript per year."

DARK HORSE, Box 9, Somerville MA 02413. Editor: June Gross. Quarterly. Circ. 3,000. Each issue contains average 30 poems, 1-2 short stories, 3-4 reviews of small press books. Pays in contributor's copies. Sample copy $2. Reports in 3 months. No simultaneous submissions. SASE.
Nonfiction: "We welcome reviews of small press books of poetry or fiction and articles about literary scene. Length: 600-800 words.
Photos: B&w photos used.
Fiction: Favor plots. No science fiction. Identify each page with name.
Poetry: Favor well-crafted, emotionally intense and honest poems; include name and address on each page.
Tips: We highly recommend reading a sample copy before submitting. Submissions of different categories should be sent separately, each with own SASE, contents marked on outside of envelope. Include brief bio information with each submission. "Include name and address on every poem, name on every page of story/article. Always looking for new ideas on small press, the literary community, state-of-re-art, high-quality poetry, well-plotted fiction."

DE KALB LITERARY ARTS JOURNAL, 555 N. Indian Creek Dr., Clarkston GA 30021. (404)292-1520. Editor: William S. Newman. For those interested in poetry, fiction and/or art. Quarterly magazine. Circ. 5,000. Acquires first serial rights. Pays in contributor's copies. Sample copy for $3 (cost plus postage). "Look for announcements of special issues." Seeking material for National Poets Issue. Submit complete ms. Reports in 3 months. SASE.
Nonfiction: Subject matter is unrestricted.
Photos: B&w photos are used with mss; 8x10 glossy prints preferred.
Fiction: "Our decisions are based on quality of material."
Poetry: Traditional, blank verse, free verse, light verse and avant-garde forms of poetry.

THE DENVER QUARTERLY, University of Denver, Denver CO 80208. (303)753-2869. Editor: Leland H. Chambers. For an intellectual/university readership. Quarterly magazine; 125-160 pages. Circ. 500. Pays on publication. Buys first North American serial rights. Phone queries OK. Photocopied (if explained as not simultaneous) submissions OK. SASE. Reports in 10 weeks. Sample copy $2. "Each issue may focus on a topic of contemporary, literary, and cultural concern. For example, Winter, 1980: Native American literature; future issues: Chicano literature, American translators, and contemporary Arabic poetry. Submissions need not coincide with these topics."
Nonfiction: Modern culture, literary analysis, theory and translations of same. Buys 10-12 mss/year. Send complete ms. Pays $5/printed page.
Fiction: Experimental, historical, traditional and translations of same. Buys 8-10 mss/year. Send complete ms. Pays $5/printed page.
Poetry: Avant-garde, free verse, traditional and translations of same. Buys 30 poems/year. Send poems. Pays $10/printed page.

Tips: "We decide on the basis of quality only. Prior publication is irrelevant. Promising material, even though rejected, will receive some personal comment from the editor; some material can be revised to meet our standards through such criticism. I receive more good stuff than *DQ* can accept, so there is some subjectivity and a good deal of luck involved in any final acceptance."

DESCANT, Texas Christian University Press, Department of English, TCU, Fort Worth TX 76129. (817)921-7240. Editor: Betsy Feagan Colquitt. Quarterly magazine; 48 pages. Circ. 650. Pays in contributor's copies on publication. Acquires first rights. Phone queries OK. Simultaneous and photocopied submissions OK. SASE. Reports in 6 weeks. Sample copy $2.
Nonfiction: Informational (articles used are literary criticism, with examination of modern literature as principal concern of the essay). Uses 4 mss/year. Submit complete ms. Length: 3,000-5,000 words.
Fiction: Fantasy, confession, experimental, historical. Uses 10-12 mss/year. Submit complete ms. Length: 2,000-6,000 words.
Poetry: Avant-garde, free verse, traditional. Uses 40/year. Limit submissions to batches of 6. Length: 10-40 lines.

EVENT, c/o Kwantlen College, Box 9030, Surrey, B.C., Canada, V3T 5H8. Managing Editor: Vye Flindall. For "those interested in literature and writing." Biannual magazine; 176-192 pages. Circ. 900. Uses 65-75 mss/year. Small payment and contributor's copies. Byline given. Photocopied and simultaneous submissions OK. Reports in 4 months. Submit complete ms. SAE and International Reply Coupons.
Nonfiction: "High-quality work." Reviews of Canadian books and essays.
Fiction: Short stories and drama.
Poetry: Submit complete ms. "We are looking for high quality modern poetry."

EXPLORATIONS IN ETHNIC STUDIES, National Association of Interdisciplinary Ethnic Studies (NAIES), Ethnic Studies Dept., California State Polytechnic University. 3801 W. Temple Ave., Pomona CA 91768. Editor: Charles Irby. Emphasizes the study of ethnicity, ethnic groups, intergroup relations, and the cultural life of ethnic minorities. Biannual (January and July) journal; 90 pages. Circ. 300. Phone queries OK. Byline given. Submit seasonal/holiday material 2 months in advance. Simultaneous and photocopied submissions OK. SASE. Reports in 3 weeks (queries); 6 months (mss). Free sample copy.
Nonfiction: Research (involving pursuit of explorations and solutions within the context of oppression as it relates to the human experience). Send complete ms; length: 10 pages.
Poetry: "To reflect intent of journal." Submit in batches of 2. Length: 10 words minimum.

THE FAULT, 33513 6th St., Union City CA 94587. (415)489-8561. Editor: Terrence McMahon. Emphasizes innovative literature for the small press collector, libraries, anyone interested in experimental and contemporary works of art. Semiannual magazine; 125 pages. Circ. 500. Pays in copies. Buys one-time and reprint rights. Byline given. Phone queries OK. Submit seasonal/holiday material 2 months in advance. Photocopied and previously published submissions OK. SASE. Reports in 4 weeks. Sample copy $2.25; free writer's guidelines.
Photos: Purchased without accompanying manuscript. Send prints.
Fiction: Science fiction, dada, visual, erotica, experimental, fantasy and mainstream. Uses 10 mss/year. Send complete ms. Length: 100-5,000 words.
Poetry: Avant-garde and free verse. Uses 40 poems/year. Limit submissions to batches of 10. Length: 2-100.
Fillers: Collages. Uses 10/year. Length: 1-100 words.
Tips: "No need for formula fiction filled with clichés and unimaginative writing; poetry with end rhymes filled with abstractions and archaic ideas; any work that lacks style, invention, originality. Each issue is constructed around a particular theme, subject or style. Send SASE for future guidelines."

FICTION, City College, 138th St. and Convent Ave., New York NY 10031. (212)690-8170. Editor: Mark Mirsky. Published by a cooperative of writers. For individual subscribers of all ages; and college libraries, bookstores and college bookstores. Published 2 times a year. Book; 150-250 pages. Circ. 5,000. Acquires all rights. Byline given. Payment in contributor's copies only. Submit complete ms. Mss not accepted between June 1st and September 15th. Allow 3 months for report, "hopefully less." SASE.
Fiction: "We publish only fiction." Length: 15 pages or less.
Photos: Photos purchased without accompanying ms. Photo Editor: Inger Grytting.

FICTION INTERNATIONAL, St. Lawrence University, Canton NY 13617. Editor: Joe David Bellamy. For "readers interested in the best writing by talented writers working in new forms or working in old forms in especially fruitful new ways; readers interested in contemporary literary developments and possibilities." Published annually in the summer;—150-300 pages in perfect-bound book format. Pays on publication. Copyrighted; rights revert to author. Reports in 1-3 months. SASE. Mss considered only from September through December of each year.
Fiction: Study publication. Previous contributors include: Asa Baber, Russell Banks, Jonathan Baumbach, T. Coraghessan Boyle, Rosellen Brown, Jerry Bumpus, David Madden, Joyce Carol Oates, Ronald Sukenick, Gordon Weaver and Robley Wilson Jr. Highly selective. Not an easy market for unsophisticated writers. No length limitations but "rarely use short-shorts or mss over 30 pages." Portions of novels acceptable if self-contained enough for independent publication.
Interviews: Seeking interviews with well-known or innovative fiction writers "able to discuss their ideas and aesthetic predilections intelligently."
Reviews: Review Editor: G. E. Murray. By assignment only. No payment. *Fiction International* also sponsors the annual $1,000 St. Lawrence Award for Fiction for an outstanding first collection of short fiction published in North America.

THE FIDDLEHEAD, University of New Brunswick, The Observatory, Box 4400, Fredericton, New Brunswick, Canada E3B 5A3. (506)454-3591. Editor: Roger Ploude. Quarterly magazine covering poetry, short fiction, photographs and book reviews. Circ. 1,045. Pays on publication. Not copyrighted. Buys first North American serial rights. Submit seasonal/holiday material 6 months in advance. Simultaneous queries, and photocopied submissions (if legible) OK. SAE and International Reply Coupons. Reports in 3 weeks on queries; 2 months on mss. Sample copy $3, Canada; $3.25, US.
Fiction: Michael Taylor and Ted Colson. "Stories may be on any subject—acceptance is based on quality alone. Because the journal is heavily subsidized by the Canadian government, strong preference is given to Canadian writers." Buys 20 mss/year. Pays $5/page; $50/article.
Poetry: Robert Gibbs. "Poetry may be on any subject—acceptance is based on quality alone. Because the journal is heavily subsidized by the Canadian government, strong preference is given to Canadian writers." Buys average of 60/year. Submit maximum 10 poems. Pays $5/page; $50 maximum.
Tips: "Quality alone is the criterion for publication. Return postage (Canadian, or International Reply Coupons) should accompnay all mss."

FIRELANDS REVIEW, (formerly *Firelands Arts Review*), Firelands College, Huron OH 44839. Editor: Joel Rudinger. Sample copy $3. Query first with SASE.

FORMS, The Review of Anthropos Theophoros, Box 3379, San Francisco CA 94119. Editor: Emily McCormick. 90% freelance written. For adults interested in ideas, especially as related to all forms of art. Quarterly magazine; 100 pages. Circ. 500. Pays on publication. Buys one-time rights. Submit seasonal/holiday material 6 months in advance of issue date. Simultaneous and photocopied submissions OK. SASE. Reports in 3 months. Sample copy $1.
Nonfiction: General interest, humor, historical, interview, opinion, philosophical, profile, religious, travel "and music, art, and book reviews of more than topical interest." Buys 10 mss/issue. Submit complete ms. Length: 500-20,000 words. Pays in contributor's copies and membership in Anthropos Theophoros.
Fiction: Adventure; experimental; fantasy; humorous; and mainstream. No science fiction. Buys 6 mss/issue. Submit complete ms. Length: 500-20,000 words. Pays in contributor's copies and AT membership.
Poetry: Avant-garde, free verse, haiku, light verse and traditional. Buys 10/issue. Limit submissions to batches of 10. Length 4-1,000 words. Pays in contributor's copies and AT membership.

GREAT RIVER REVIEW, Box 14805, Minneapolis MN 55414. (612)378-9076. Editors: Jean Ervin, Fiction; Chet Corey, Poetry and Book Reviews; Heidi Schwabacher, Art. Published 2 times/year. Magazine; 145 pages. Pays on publication. Photocopied submissions OK. SASE. Reports in 2-4 months. Sample copy: back issues $3; current issues: $3.50.
Nonfiction: Articles on Midwestern authors. Submit complete ms. Pays $20-50.
Fiction: Experimental and mainstream, but not mass-circulation style. Midwestern writers only. Buys 6 mss/issue. Submit complete ms. Length: 2,000-10,000 words. Pays $20-50; $200 award for best fiction each issue.
Poetry: Avant-garde; free verse; and traditional. No newspaper poetry. Buys 30 poems/issue. Limit submissions to batches of 10-15. Pays modest rates for poetry.
Tips: "We are publishing fiction and poetry largely."

GUSTO MAGAZINE, Gusto Press, Box 1009, Bronx NY 10465. Editor: M. Karl Kulikowski. Quarterly magazine featuring poetry and literary articles. Circ. 500. Average issue includes 75% poetry and 25% short stories. Byline given. Acquires first North American serial rights. Submit seasonal material 3 months in advance. Photocopied submissions OK. SASE. Reports in 2 weeks on queries; in 3 weeks on mss. Sample copy $2.50; free writer's guidelines.
Nonfiction: General interest, historical, humor and literary. Buys 10 mss/year. Send complete ms. Length: 500-5,000 words. "We are constantly on the alert for quality. Send 4-5 poems or up to 3 short stories or articles. We will judge from that."
Fiction: Adventure, humorous, suspense, condensed novels, confession, experimental, historical, mainstream and serialized novels. Buys 15 mss/year. Send complete ms. Length: 500-5,000 words.
Poetry: Avant-garde, free verse, haiku, light verse, traditional and eclectic. "No adolescent porn." Buys 600 mss/year. Submit maximum 6 poems. Length: 2-400 lines.
Tips: "Although we do not pay cash for what we print, we believe that the 'payment' we have made to some writers is invaluable. In 1979, we printed 6 books of poetry in our *Discovery Series* for contributors, 60 pages or more, at no cost to them; 1 book, chapbook, 36 pages, and 1 book of short stories in our *Short Story Discovery* Series of 163 pages—something that poets and short story writers find almost impossible to achieve in today's market. In 1980 we did 10 books for writers, one of which was a book of short stories; we will do the same number in 1981."

HANGING LOOSE, 231 Wyckoff St., Brooklyn NY 11217. Editors: Dick Lourie, Ron Schreiber, Robert Hershon. Quarterly. Acquires first serial rights. Pays in copies. Sample copy $3. Reports in 2-3 months. SASE.
Poetry and Fiction: Fresh, energetic poems of any length. Excellent quality. Experimental fiction. "Space for fiction very limited."
Tips: "We strongly suggest that writers read the magazine before sending work, to save our time and theirs. Also note that artwork and book mss are by invitation only."

THE HUDSON REVIEW, 65 E. 55th St., New York NY 10022. Managing Editor: Richard B. Smith. Quarterly. Pays on publication. Reports in 6-8 weeks. SASE for return of submissions.
Nonfiction: Articles, translations and reviews. Length: 8,000 words maximum.
Fiction: Uses "quality fiction". Length: 10,000 words maximum. Pays 2½¢/word.
Poetry: 50¢/line for poetry.
Tips: Unsolicited mss. are not read during the months of June, July, August and September.

HUNGRY YEARS, Box 7213, Newport Beach CA 92660. Editor/Publisher: Les Brown. Biannual magazine featuring the work of new talent for creative people of all ages and interests. Circ. 500. Pays in copies. Buys one-time rights. Photocopied and previously published submissions OK. SASE. Reports in 6 months. Free sample copy and writer's guidelines.
Nonfiction: General interest (reprints of surveys made by institutions or organizations and findings of interest to philosophy and art and cultural enrichment); and inspirational (journal entries or notations expressing interesting and relevant information and insights).
Fiction: Adventure, fantasy, confession, experimental, historical, humorous, mystery, romance, suspense, mainstream, science fiction, western and serialized novels. No religious material. Length: 1 page minimum. Pays in copies.
Poetry: Avant-garde, free verse, haiku, light verse and traditional. Pays in copies.

IN A NUTSHELL, Hibiscus Press, Box 22248, Sacramento CA 95822. Editor: Margaret Wensrich. 99% freelance written. Emphasizes poetry and fiction. Quarterly magazine; 32 pages. Circ. 5,000. Pays on publication. Buys one-time rights. Submit seasonal/holiday material 6 months in advance. Photocopied submissions OK. SASE. Reports in 4 weeks. Sample copy $3; writer's guidelines for SASE #10 envelope.
Fiction: Adventure, fantasy, confession, experimental, historical, humorous, mystery, romance, suspense, mainstream, science fiction and western. No slapstick. Buys 12 mss/year. Submit complete ms. Length: 1,500-3,500 words. Pays $10 minimum.
Poetry: Joyce Odam, poetry editor. No line or subject limit. Buys 40-60/year. Limit submissions to batches of 4-6. Pays $2 minimum. Send #10 envelope, or larger, for return of ms.
Tips: "Clean copy ensures a fair reading."

INTER-AMERICAN REVIEW OF BIBLIOGRAPHY, Organization of American States, Washington DC 20006. Editor: Dr. Roberto Etchepareborda. Quarterly magazine; 120-150 pages. Circ. 3,000. Pays in subscription to magazine. Byline given. Sample copy $2; free writer's guidelines.
Nonfiction: Scholarly material only in the social sciences and the humanities, in the area of Latin America and the Caribbean. Uses 16 mss/year. Query.
Columns/Departments: Book reviews, recent books, recent articles, recent doctoral dissertations

completed in US universities, recent publications of the US Congress, OAS publications. (All of the above in the disciplines and area described above). Length: 20-30 pages for articles; 400-500 words for book reviews; 1 paragraph for news. Pays in copy of book to be reviewed.

THE INTERCOLLEGIATE REVIEW, Intercollegiate Studies Institute, 14 S. Bryn Mawr Ave., Bryn Mawr PA 19010. (215)525-7501. Editor: Robert A. Schadler. Emphasizes intellectual conservatism on cultural, economic, political, literary and philosophical issues. Quarterly magazine; 64 pages, Circ. 30,000. Pays on publication. Buys all rights. Byline given. Phone queries OK. SASE. Reports in 6 months. Free sample copy.
Nonfiction: Political; historical; informational; and personal. Buys 4 mss/issue. Query. Length: 1,000-5,000 words. Pays $50-150.

THE IOWA REVIEW, 308 EPB, The University of Iowa, Iowa City IA 52242. (319)353-6048. Editors: David Hamilton and Fredrick Woodard with the help of colleagues, graduate assistants, and occasional guest editors. Quarterly magazine. Buys first rights. Photocopied submissions OK. SASE. Reports in 3 months.
Nonfiction: "We publish essays, stories and poems and would like for our essays not always to be works of academic criticism. We are particularly open to reviews of small press publications." Buys 100 mss/year. Submit complete ms. Pays $1/line for verse; $10/page for prose.
Tips: "It is not difficult to 'break in'—we read very carefully all submissions."

JAPANOPHILE, Box 223, Okemos MI 48864. Editor: Earl Snodgrass. For literate people who are interested in Japanese culture anywhere in the world. Quarterly magazine. Pays on publication. Buys first North American serial rights. Previously published submissions OK. SASE. Reports in 4 weeks. Sample copy $2.
Nonfiction: "We want material on Japanese culture in *North America or anywhere in the world,* even Japan. We want articles, preferably with pictures, about persons engaged in arts of Japanese origin: a Michigan naturalist who is a haiku poet, a potter who learned raku in Japan, a vivid 'I was there' account of a Go tournament in California. We use some travel articles if exceptionally well-written, but we are *not* a regional magazine about Japan. We are a little magazine, a literary magazine. Our particular slant is a certain kind of culture wherever it is in the world: Canada, the US, Europe, Japan. The culture includes flower arranging, haiku, religion, art, photography, fiction. It is important to study the magazine." Buys 8 mss/issue. Query or send complete ms. Length: 800-2,000 words. Pays $8-15.
Photos: State availability of photos. Pays $5 for 8x10 b&w glossy prints.
Fiction: Short stories to 5,000 words with a setting in Japan. Pays $20 and sometimes more. Best to see a sample copy, $2.
Columns/Departments: "We are looking for columnists to write about cultural activities in Chicago, New York, Los Angeles, San Francisco, Tokyo and Honolulu. That is, one columnist for each city." Query. Length: 600-1,200 words. Pays $7-15.
Tips: Prefers to see more articles about Japanese culture in the US, Canada and Europe.

JOHNSONIAN NEWS LETTER, 610 Philosophy Hall, Columbia University, New York NY 10027. Editor: John H. Middendorf. For scholars, book collectors and all those interested in 18th-century English literature. 4 times a year. No payment. Acknowledgment given. Reports "immediately." SASE.
Nonfiction: Interested in news items, queries, short comments, etc., having to do with 18th-century English literature. Must be written in simple style. Length: maximum 500 words.

THE JOURNAL OF MEXICAN AMERICAN HISTORY, Box 13861-UCSB, Santa Barbara CA 93107. (805)968-5915. Editor-in-Chief: Joseph Peter Navarro. Emphasizes history for specialists in Mexican-American history, including professors, graduate and undergraduate students. Annual magazine; 150-200 pages. Circ. 1,500. No payment. Acquires simultaneous rights. Phone queries OK. Submit seasonal/holiday material 6-12 months in advance. Photocopied submissions OK. SASE. Reports in 2 weeks. Sample copy $17.50.
Nonfiction: Historical (Mexican-American history from 1848 to present); interview; personal experience (documented carefully); personal opinion; photo feature (if historical and pertinent). Send complete ms. Length: 1,500-4,500 words. Prize of $100 for best article. Captions required for b&w photos used.

JOURNAL OF MODERN LITERATURE, Temple University, 1241 Humanities Bldg., Philadelphia PA 19122. (215)787-8505. Editor-in-Chief: Maurice Beebe. Managing Editor: Kathleen Quinn. Emphasizes scholarly studies for academics interested in literature of the past 100 years.

Quarterly magazine; 160-200 pages. Circ. 2,000. Buys all rights. Phone queries OK. Photocopied submissions OK. SASE. Reports in 8 weeks. Free sample copy.
Nonfiction: Historical (20th-century literature); informational (20th-century literature); and photo feature on art and literature. Buys 30 mss/year. Query or send complete ms. Pays $50-100.
Photos: Purchased only with accompanying nonfiction manuscript. Total purchase price for ms includes payment for photos.

JOURNAL OF THE NORTH AMERICAN WOLF SOCIETY, Rt. 2, Troy Pike, Versailles KY 40383. Editor: Sandra Gray Thacker. For audience with interest in "conservation issues and a strong concern for the preservation, and promotion, of the wolf and its habitat, and other wild canids of North America." 3 issues per year. Circ. 400. Rights acquired vary with author and material. Payment in contributor's copies. Sample copy $2; free editorial guidelines sheet. Simultaneous and photocopied submissions OK. Reports in 6 weeks. Query not necessary. SASE.
Nonfiction: "Subject matter must be relevant to wolves, or other wild canids such as coyotes, their prey, their habitat, or activities of individuals or groups on their behalf. Our approach is factual and objective. We try to provide space for as many positions as possible in this complex and emotional subject, as long as these positions have their bases in fact, and are rationally presented. We always like to see sources and references though these may not be published with the article." Series articles: Interested in queries proposing minimum of 2 articles, maximum of three, which could be run as one article per issue for consecutive issues. Articles must have a central theme. Examples: Wolves in US Legends; Interviews with Wild Canid Conservationists; Histories of Wild Canid Various Regions; Development of Conservation Education Programs, etc. Length: 1,000-2,000 words per article.
Fiction: Published under regular column entitled, "Post Scripts." Creative fiction based in sound ecological fact. Must relate to wild canids. Length: 1,000-2,000 words.
Columns/Departments: "Views & Reviews" (original poetry/literature reviews); "Wolves in Legend" (folklore concepts).
Photos and Fillers: Photos and/or original artwork submitted must be black-and-white. Also uses newsbreaks and clippings. Payment in contributor's copies. Contributors also listed in "About the Author" and "About the Artist/Photographer" section.

JOURNAL OF POPULAR CULTURE, University Hall, Bowling Green State University, Bowling Green OH 43402. (419)372-2610. Editor: Ray B. Browne. 100% freelance written. For students and adults, interested in popular culture, TV, films, popular literature, sports, music, etc. Quarterly magazine, 192 pages. Circ. 3,000. Acquires all rights. Payment in copies. Sample copy $5. Original copies only. Reports in 3-6 months. SASE.
Nonfiction and Photos: "Critical essays on media, books, poetry, advertising, etc." Informational, interview, historical, think pieces, nostalgia, reviews of books, movies, television. Length: 5,000 words maximum. Pays in contributor's copies (25 reprints). Uses b&w glossy prints.

JUMP RIVER REVIEW, Jump River Press, Inc., 819 Single Ave., Wausau WI 54401. (715)842-8243. Editor: Mark Bruner. Quarterly magazine covering a literary review of the basics, behavior and human culture. Estab. 1979. Circ. 400. Pays on publication in copies. Acquires one-time rights. Phone queries OK. Submit seasonal material 3½ months in advance. Photocopied submissions OK, if not submitted elsewhere. SASE. Reports in 1-2 weeks. Sample copy $2.50; free writer's guidelines.
Nonfiction: Historical ("articles relating either historical or contemporary events to the nature of our cultural fabric"); how-to (article should be related to writing and publishing); interview (of literary figures); nostalgia (but no overly sentimental approaches); photo feature (query); and essays on the spiritual aspects of culture ("not religious, spiritual"). Especially in need of opinion (in essay form and related to culture, literature and human behavior). Buys 2-3 mss/issue. Send complete ms. Length: approx. 900 words preferred. Pays in copies. "Poetry is most open to freelancers because we publish so much of it. We don't want driveling sentiment, confessions or pretense. Feel free to experiment. We would like to see some more forms of concrete poetry and poetry related to myth, folklife, enchantment, primalism."
Fiction: Erotica; fantasy; experimental; historical; humorous; mainstream; religious (spiritual, not sentimental; should be nondenominational). "No self-centered confessional type fiction." Buys 9 mss/year. Send complete ms. Length: 900-1,000 words preferred. Pays in copies.
Poetry: Avant-garde; free verse; traditional; and concrete. Buys 90 mss/year. Pays in copies.
Fillers: Puzzles. Buys 9 mss/year. Pays in copies.
Tips: "Read *Jump River Review*. We devote a portion of each issue to young writers. If you're a high school or elementary aged writer, tell us. Right now the best chance of getting accepted is with essays, drama, criticism and short prose. If there is anyone out there who can produce a 5-6 page short drama, you have a good chance of getting our interest. Letting me know if you're young or

unpublished somtimes makes me more apt to spend time with your work. And read the magazine—not only does that help us keep solvent, but it saves everyone much time in correspondence."

JUST PULP, Box 243, Narragansett RI 02882. Editor: Robert E. Moore. Fiction Editor: Stephen Strang. Poetry Editor: Pat Leitch. For a general, educated readership. Quarterly magazine. Circ. 600. Acquires all rights. Pays ¼¢/word for fiction; $5/poem. Pays on publication. Photocopied submissions OK. SASE. Reports in 6-12 weeks. Sample copies $2.
Fiction: Mainstream, mystery, suspense, adventure, fantasy, science fiction and "shades between." Serialized novels and continuing sagas considered. "We're interested in all the 'pulp' forms-those of today and 5 years from now." Length: 15,000 words maximum. Uses 7-8/issue. Limit submission to 1 ms. Submit complete ms.
Poetry: All forms. Limit submissions to batches of 5. Uses 10-15/issue.

KANSAS QUARTERLY, Dept. of English, Kansas State University, Manhattan KS 66506. (913)532-6716. Editors: Harold W. Schneider, Ben Nyberg, W.R. Moses. For "adults interested in creative writing, literary criticism, Midwestern history, and art." Quarterly. Circ. 1,200. Acquires all rights. Pays in contributor's copies. Sample copy $3. Query for nonfiction. "Follow *MLA Style Sheet* and write for a sophisticated audience." Reports in about 2-4 months. SASE.
Nonfiction: Art, history and literary criticism on special topics. "We emphasize but do not limit ourselves to the history, culture and lifestyle of the Mid-Plains region. We do not want 'slick' material or special interest material not in keeping with our special numbers." Historical articles on "special topics only."
Photos: Photos should have captions; 4x6 b&w preferred.
Fiction: Experimental and mainstream fiction. Length: 250-10,000 words.
Poetry: Traditional and avant-garde forms of poetry, blank verse and free verse. Poetry themes open.

KARAMU, English Department, Eastern Illinois University, Charleston IL 61920. (217)345-5013. Editor: Bruce Guernsey. For literate, university-educated audience. Annually. Circ. 500. Acquires first North American serial rights. Uses 25 mss/year. Pays in 2 contributor's copies. Submit complete ms. Reports on poetry, 2-4 weeks; fiction, 1 month. SASE. Sample copy $1.50.
Nonfiction: Articles on contemporary literature. Length: open.
Fiction: Experimental, mainstream. Length: 2,000-8,000 words.
Poetry: Traditional forms, free verse and avant-garde. Dept. Editor: Bruce Guernsey.

L'ESPRIT CREATEUR, Dept. of French & Italian, Louisiana State University, Baton Rouge LA 70803. (504)388-6713. Editor: John D. Erickson. Bilingual journal for persons interested in French literature (educators, critics). Quarterly; 95 to 100 pages. Circ. 1,200. Acquires all rights but will reassign rights to author after publication. Uses about 30-35 mss/year. Payment in 5 contributor's copies. Sample copy $3. Prefers the *MLA Style Sheet* style. "All issues are devoted to special subjects, though we print book reviews and review articles of critical works that do not correspond to the issue subject. Please note subjects of coming issues, listed in each issue. Submit June 1 for spring issue, October 1 for summer issue, February 1 for fall issue, and May 1 for winter issue." Reports in 3-6 months. Query ahead or submit complete ms. "Query with incisive description of the article topic, its contribution to scholarship in the author's judgment, acknowledgment of its suitability for a particular issue." SASE.
Nonfiction: "Criticism of French literature centered on a particular theme each issue; interviews with French writers or critics that appear irregularly; book reviews of critical works on French literature. Critical studies of whatever methodological persuasion that observe the primacy of the text. We notice a bit too much emphasis on extra-literary matters and a failure to note the special issues scheduled. Interested in new critical practices in France. We prefer articles that are direct and honest, avoid pedantry, respect the integrity of the literary work and have something intelligent to say. Please keep footnotes to a reasonable limit." Length: about 15 double-spaced typed pages, or 4,500 words.

LETTERS, Mainspring Press, Box 82, Stonington ME 04681. (207)367-2484. Editor-in-Chief: Helen Nash. Publication of the Maine Writers' Workshop. For general literary audience. Quarterly magazine; 4-10 pages. Circ. 6,500. Pays on acceptance. Buys all rights. Submit seasonal/holiday material 5 months in advance. SASE. Reports in 1 month. SASE for free sample copy and submissions. Back copies are not free.
Nonfiction: "Any subject within moral standards and with quality writing style." Query. Length: 100-500 words. Pays 5¢/word.
Fiction: No pornography, confession, religious or western. Buys 5 mss/year. Pays 5¢/word.
Poetry: G.F. Bush, poetry editor. Light verse, traditional, blank verse, humorous, narrative, avant-garde, free verse and haiku. Buys 15/year. Length: 30-42 lines. Pays maximum $1/line.

LITERARY REVIEW, Fairleigh Dickinson University, 285 Madison Ave., Madison NJ 07940. (201)377-4050. Editors: Martin Green, Harry Keyishian. For international literary audience, largely libraries, academic readers and other poets and writers. Quarterly magazine; 128 pages. Circ. 1,000. Pays in copies. Acquires first North American serial rights. Photocopied submissions OK. Reports in 2-3 months. Sample copy $3.50.
Nonfiction: Literary criticism on contemporary American and world literature; themes, authors and movements aimed at nonspecialist audience. "Review essays of recent books on above topics welcome." Uses 2-3 mss/issue.
Fiction: Experimental or traditional. "We seek literary stories, not slick types." Uses 3-4/issue. Special fiction issue, fall.
Poetry: Avant-garde, free verse and traditional. Uses 5-10/issue. Special poetry issue, spring. Translations from contemporary non-English literature.
Tips: "We are generally open to newcomers. Quality will tell."

LITERARY SKETCHES, Box 711, Williamsburg VA 23185. (804)229-2901. Editor: Mary Lewis Chapman. For readers with literary interests; all ages. Monthly newsletter; 14 pages. Circ. 500. Not copyrighted. Byline given. Buys about 12 mss/year. Pays on publication. Sample copy for SASE. Photocopied and simultaneous submissions OK. Reports in 1 month. Submit complete ms. SASE.
Nonfiction: "We use only interviews of well-known writers and biographical material on past writers. Very informal style; concise. Centennial or bicentennial pieces relating to a writer's birth, death or famous works are usually interesting. Look up births of literary figures and start from there." Length: 1,000 words maximum. Pays ½¢/word.

THE LONDON COLLECTOR, 1005 Bond St., North Manchester IN 46962. (219)982-8750. Editor: Dennis E. Hensley. Managing Editor: Richard Weiderman. 80% freelance written. For students, book collectors, readers, fans and professors who are interested in the career and life of Jack London. Magazine published 2 times/year; 32 pages. Circ. 322. Pays in bylines and copies. Acquires first North American serial rights. SASE. Reports in 2 weeks. Sample copy $2.
Nonfiction: Book reviews (any and all reviews of books and monographs written about Jack London); general interest (literary analysis of London's writings); historical (London family history); humor (articles on London's use of humor in his articles, novels and short stories). Buys 10 mss/year. Submit complete ms with clips of published work. Length: 250-1,400 words. Pays 4 copies.
Photos: State availability of photos with ms. Offers no additional payment for 5x7 b&w glossy prints. Captions preferred. Acquires one-time rights. Model release required.
Fillers: Clippings and newsbreaks. Buys 7/year. Length: 50-175 words.
Tips: "Don't be loose with facts or research—we *know* London's life and writings and we will reject anything even slightly exaggerated or inaccurate."

LOONFEATHER: MINNESOTA NORTH COUNTRY ART, Loonfeather, Inc., Box 48, Hagg-Sauer Hall, Bemidji State University, Bemidji MN 56601. Regional Editor: William Elliott. Tabloid published 3 times/year covering art and literature for artists and writers, particularly in the North Central Minnesota region. Estab. 1979. Circ. 2,000. Pays in copies. Acquires one-time rights. Phone queries OK. Submit seasonal material 4 months in advance. Simultaneous, photocopied and previously published submissions OK. SASE. Reports in 3 weeks on queries; in 1 month on mss.
Nonfiction: Reviews of small press books.
Fiction: Fantasy; experimental and serialized novels. Buys 2 mss/issue. Send complete ms. Length: 2,000 words maximum. Pays 2 copies of magazine.
Poetry: Avant-garde and free verse. No inspirational poems. Buys 15 mss/issue. Length: 16 lines maximum. Pays 2 copies of magazine.

LOVECRAFT STUDIES, Necronomicon Press, 101 Lockwood St., West Warwick RI 02893. Editor: S.T. Joshi. Biannual magazine covering the criticism of the work of H.P. Lovecraft for Lovecraft scholars, fans, enthusiasts and university libraries. Estab. 1979. Circ. 400. Pays on publication. Byline given. Acquires all rights for 1 year. Photocopied submissions OK. SASE. Reports in 2 weeks. Sample copy $2.50.
Nonfiction: Scholarly literary criticism. Buys 3-5 mss/issue. Send complete ms. Length: 6,000 words maximum. Pays in copies. "We are concerned only with articles directly concerning the life, work and thought of H.P. Lovecraft. Articles must be of the highest scholarly quality and must center upon Lovecraft himself; articles discussing Lovecraft only tangentially should be sent to journals which publish general fantasy or science fiction criticism."
Tips: "We are particularly trying to avoid low-level of 'fan' criticism of Lovecraft and making a

serious effort to make Lovecraft an academically recognized figure. A writer ought to be familiar with the critical work done on Lovecraft over the past 40 years so that his article does not merely cover old ground. We need to know 1) what previous scholarly work (in any field) you have done; & 2) what scholarly work on Lovecraft in particular (if any) you have done. Please be up-to-date on modern advances in Lovecraft criticism-this is imperative. Too many unsolicited articles do not take into consideration the important, almost revolutionary work done during the last 5-10 years."

MAGICAL BLEND MAGAZINE, Box 11303, San Francisco CA 94101. Co-editors: Michael Peter Langevin and Katherine Zunic. Quarterly magazine covering spiritual growth. "Our readers are creative, growing people interested in alternative lifestyles and philosophies. We stress positive, uplifting, inspiring, spiritual and occult material." Estab. 1980. Circ. 6,000. Pays on publication. Byline given. Buys one-time rights. Submit seasonal/holiday material 2 months in advance. Simultaneous, photocopied and previously published submissions OK. SASE. Reports in 1 month on queries; 1 month on mss. Sample copy $2; free writer's guidelines for SAE.
Nonfiction: General interest (on magic, spiritual, psychic); how-to (become more self-reliant, self-sufficient); inspirational ("writing that makes people want to go out and make this world better"); interview/profile (with persons who are excited about life and the potential we all have); personal experience (with magic, psychic phenomena, spiritual growth); photo feature (photos of a beautiful nature); and any other material that deals with the occult, spiritual or psychic. No "dark, negative, sexist or racist material." Buys 28 mss/year. Length: 500-2,500 words. Pays in copies.
Fiction: Fantasy (magical, positive); and science fiction (magical, positive). No "dark, sexist, negative or racist material." Buys 20 mss/year. Send complete ms. Length: 500-2,500 words. Pays in copies.
Poetry: Joe Blondo, poetry editor. Free verse, haiku, light verse and traditional. No dark, depressing or sexist poems. Buys 60/year. Length: 3-150 lines. Pays in copies.
Tips: "It's best to write material that makes one feel better about him/herself, and/or the world. We're open to new formats (reviews, columns, etc.). We cover a broad spectrum of spiritual manifestation; however, we are basically positive and human potential-oriented."

MANHATTAN BOOK HOUND, The Monthly Guide to Literary Manhattan, Butler Communications, Box 5347, FDR Station, New York NY 10150. (212)888-6059. Editor: Lorna Butler. Monthly magazine covering literary events and news of books, especially low-profile books not usually found in bookstores. "*MBH* is styled as a service to its readers, and prints news of books and periodicals about books for the serious reader/collector/professional. Designed for a literate readership seeking to be informed about little-known books and sources—both bookstores and publishers—of such books." Estab. 1980. Circ. 2,000. Pays on acceptance. Byline "depends on the material used." Pays negotiable kill fee. Buys all rights. Submit seasonal/holiday material 3 months in advance. Photocopied and previously published submissions OK. SASE. Reports in 1 month on queries; 2 months on mss. Sample copy for business size SAE and 3 first class stamps; writer's guidelines for business size SAE and 1 first class stamp.
Nonfiction: Special issues include: A Book Hound's Guide to Manhattan (bookstores, literary landmarks, etc); book collecting for the neophyte; book fairs around the US; books about books. "No ponderous, wordy material on any subject; book reviews of bestsellers or widely reviewed books; opinionated observations not documented in some manner; or lengthy announcements of books except nonfiction books." Query with clips of published work. Length: 750 words maximum. Pays "honorarium only or 25 copies of issue, depending on material used."
Photos: "Photos used only on cover (b&w) and only of New York." Identification of subjects required. Buys all rights; "will reassign most times."
Columns/Departments: Can use material on "Books about Books," "Books about New York," "Bargain Books," "New (literary-related) Products," "Mail Order Books," "Book Collecting for the Neophyte," "Literary Periodicals," "Best Books Lists," "Book Search Services," "Bookstore Profiles—New York and Environs," "New Literary Prizes," small presses and reprint publishers. Send complete ms. Length: 50-200 words. Pays "honorarium or free copies."
Fillers: Clippings, newsbreaks and quotations re: books and writing, literature.
Tips: "Knowledge of the Manhattan bookstore scene is invaluable—profiles of shops, personnel; citations of little-known and meritorious books about New York City, books, researching and writing, etc. We are a small publication geared to information, not flash. If something is a useful tip and we don't already know of it, chances are we'll want to use it, but our budget is very small. All areas are open to freelancers. Our editorial requirements are good, tight writing style; documentation of claims made; accuracy; and an interest in the use and enjoyment of books, both fiction and nonfiction."

MARK TWAIN JOURNAL, Kirkwood MO 63122. Editor: Cyril Clemens. For those interested in American and English literature. Semiannual magazine. Not copyrighted. SASE. Sample copy $1. Pays in contributor's copies. Reports in 2 weeks. "Queries welcome."
Nonfiction: Critical and biographical articles dealing with Mark Twain and other American, English and foreign authors.

THE MARKHAM REVIEW, Horrmann Library, Wagner College, Staten Island NY 10301. (212)390-3000. Editor: Joseph W. Slade. For academics; specialists in American culture. Newsletter; 20 pages. Quarterly. Circ. 1,000. Rights purchased vary with author and material. Byline given. Usually buys all rights. Buys 15-20 mss/year. Pays in contributor's copies. Will send free sample copy to writer on request. No photocopied or simultaneous submissions. Reports in 4 weeks. Query or submit complete ms. SASE.
Nonfiction: Scholarly approach following *MLA* style. Does not want articles on Henry James or Ernest Hemingway or other major writers. Would consider material on the history of science and technology. Length: 6,000 words maximum.

THE MASSACHUSETTS REVIEW, Memorial Hall, University of Massachusetts, Amherst MA 01003. Editors: John Hicks and Robert Tucker. Quarterly. Buys first North American serial rights. Pays on publication. Reports "promptly." Mss will not be returned unless accompanied by a self-addressed stamped envelope. Sample copy $4.
Nonfiction: Articles on literary criticism, women, public affairs, art, philosophy, music and dance. Average length: 6,500 words. Pays $50.
Fiction: Short stories or chapters from novels when suitable for independent publication. Pays $50.
Poetry: 35¢/line or $15 minimum.

MAXY'S JOURNAL, Truedog Press, Inc., 216 W. Academy St., Lonoke AR 72086. Editor: Mac Bennett. Managing Editor: Craig Chambers. Irregularly published magazine featuring poetry, fiction and criticism for members of the English-speaking community who are interested in contemporary literature. Circ. 500. Pays on publication. Buys all rights. Submit seasonal material 8 months in advance. Photocopied submissions OK. SASE. Reports in 6 weeks. Sample copy $2.
Nonfiction: Short reviews of contemporary poets. Buys 3 mss/issue. Send complete ms. Length: 500-2,000 words. Pays in copies.
Fiction: Adventure, erotica, fantasy, confession, experimental, historical, humorous, condensed novels, mainstream and science fiction. Buys 2-3 mss/issue. Send complete ms. Length: open. Pays in copies.
Poetry: Avant-garde, free verse, haiku and traditional. Buys 35 mss/issue. Submit maximum 10 poems. Length: open. Pays in copies. "We are primarily a poetry journal and have published many well-known British and American poets, but our main interest, from whatever source, is good poetry and short fiction."

MICHIGAN QUARTERLY REVIEW, 3032 Rackham Bldg., University of Michigan, Ann Arbor MI 48109. Editor: Laurence Goldstein. Quarterly. Circ. 2,000. Pays on acceptance. Buys first rights. Reports in 4 weeks for mss submitted in September-May; in summer, 8 weeks. SASE. Sample copy $2.
Nonfiction: "*MQR* is open to general articles directed at an intellectual audience. Essays ought to have a personal voice and engage a significant subject. Scholarship must be present as a foundation but we are not interested in specialized essays directed only at professionals in the field. We prefer ruminative essays, written in a fresh style, which reach interesting conclusions." Length: 2,000-5,000 words. Pays $100-175, sometimes more.
Fiction and Poetry: No restrictions on subject matter or language. "We publish about 10 stories a year and are very selective." Pays $8-10/published page.
Tips: "Read the journal and assess the range of contents and the level of writing. We have no guidelines to offer or set expectations; every ms is judged on its unique qualities. On essays—query with a very thorough description of the argument, and a copy of the first page. Do not query for fiction and poetry. Watch for announcements of special issues, which are usually expanded issues and draw upon a lot of freelance writing. Study a copy of a recent issue. Be aware that this is a university quarterly that publishes a limited amount of fiction and poetry; that it is directed at an educated audience, one that has done a great deal of reading in all types of literature."

THE MIDWEST QUARTERLY, Pittsburg State University, Pittsburg KS 66762. (316)231-7000. Editor: James B. Schick. 95% freelance written. Published "for an educated adult audience interested in contemporary thought in a variety of scholarly disciplines." Magazine; 100 pages. July issue is all literary analysis. Quarterly. Circ. 1,000. Acquires all rights. Byline given. Uses 24 articles; 48 poems/year. Pays in contributor's copies. Photocopied submissions OK. Submit sea-

sonal material 6-9 months in advance. Reports in 3 months. SASE.
Nonfiction and Poetry: "Literary analysis, history, social sciences, art, musicology, natural science in nontechnical language. Write standard literary English without jargon or pedantry. We do not use fiction. Would like to see more history and social science." No unsolicited poetry. Length: 3,500-5,000 words. Publishes traditional forms of poetry, blank verse, free verse, avant-garde forms and haiku. Subject: open. Length: 4-200 lines. Poetry Editor: Michael Heffernan.

MISSISSIPPI REVIEW, Center for Writers, University of Southern Mississippi, Southern Station, Box 5144, Hattiesburg MS 39401. (601)266-4169. Editor: Frederick Barthelme. For general literary audiences, including students, libraries and writers. Published 3 times/year; 120 pages. Buys all rights. Byline given. Pays in copies. SASE. Reports in 8-10 weeks. No submissions in June or July. Sample copy $3.50.
Fiction: All types considered.
Poetry: All types considered.

MISSISSIPPI VALLEY REVIEW, Department of English, Western Illinois University, Macomb IL 61455. Editor: Forrest Robinson. For persons active in creating, teaching or reading poetry and fiction. Magazine; 64 pages. Published twice a year. Circ. 400. "Permission to reprint must be gained from individual authors." Accepts 80-100 mss/year. Payment in 2 contributor's copies, plus a copy of the next 2 issues. Sample copy $2 plus postage. "Only excellent" photocopied submissions OK. Will consider simultaneous submissions only if the author "notifies us immediately upon receipt of an acceptance elsewhere. We try to return mss within 3 months. We do not mind writers asking for progress reports if we are a bit late. Allow for no ms reading during summer." Submit complete ms. SASE.
Fiction and Poetry: Publishes stories and poems. Tries to provide a range and variety of style and subject matter. "*Writer's Market* guidelines for ms submission suggested. We publish no articles. We usually solicit our reviews." Fiction Editor: Loren Logsdon. Poetry Editor: John Mann.
Tips: "We prefer that mss be accompanied by a letter. Query letters are rarely helpful to us. Although we have published some fine work by beginners, our contributors have usually published elsewhere. Afer acceptance, we ask the contributor for credits, not before."

MODERN FICTION STUDIES, Dept. of English, Purdue University, West Lafayette IN 47907. (317)493-1684. Editors: William T. Stafford, Margaret Church. For students and academic critics and teachers of modern fiction in all modern languages. Quarterly magazine; 160-200 pages. Circ. 4,000. Acquires all rights, but with written stipulated agreement with author permitting him or her to republish anywhere, any time as long as *MFS* is cited, and splitting 50/50 with him reprints by others of his agreed-to-be-reprinted material. Byline given. No payment. Reports in 2-4 months. "Every other issue is a special issue. See current copy for future topics. Submit material any time before announced deadline for special issue." SASE.
Nonfiction: Interested in critical or scholarly articles on American, British, and Continental fiction since 1880. Length: notes, 500-2,500 words; articles, 3,000-7,000 words.

MOVING OUT, Wayne State University, 4866 3rd, Detroit MI 48202. (313)898-7972. Editors: Margaret Kaminski, Gloria Dyc, Joan Gartland, Paula Rabinowitz, Amy Cherry. Feminist literary and arts journal for college and career women and others interested in women's studies and writing. Magazine; 2 times a year; 100 pages. Circ. 800. Pays in contributor's copies. Acquires all rights. Byline given unless writer wants name withheld. Phone queries OK. SASE. "Queries/mss without postage usually are not returned." Reports in 6-12 months. Sample copy $2.50.
Nonfiction: Literary criticism (not too academic in style); reviews of women's books; magazines, records or film reviews of interest to women. Historical (papers on famous women writers, artists, etc.). Interviews and personal experience (diary excerpts). Photo features (portfolios of fine art photography or artwork, graphics, paintings, etc.); uses 1/issue. "We like nonfiction and criticism that are illustrated." Query or submit complete ms. Maximum length: about 20 pages.
Fiction: Must be related to women's experience. Also uses novel excerpts. Query or submit complete ms. Maximum length: 20 pages.
Poetry: Free verse, haiku, prose poems, feminist poetry.
Tips: "Query should specify the topic of article or paper, length, etc."

MUNDUS ARTIUM, A Journal of International Literature and the Arts, University of Texas at Dallas, Box 688, Richardson TX 75080. Editor: Rainer Schulte. 30-50% freelance written. For all levels "except the scholarly, footnote-starved type." Semiannual magazine; 160 pages. Circ. 2,000. Buys all rights. Buys about 50 mss/year. Pays on publication. Sample copy $3.50. Photocopied submissions OK. No simultaneous submissions. Reports in 90 days. Submit complete ms. SASE.
Nonfiction and Photos: "In articles, we look for people who are able to talk about our nontradi-

tional, conceptual kind of orientation from a broad, esthetic point of view. We like interdisciplinary emphasis. We don't want scholarly articles, kitsch, or social-political material, or descriptive, representational work." Length: open. Pays $15-100. Only avant-garde photography is acceptable.

Fiction: Experimental and fantasy. Must be nontraditional and conceptual. Length: open. Pays $5/page minimum.

Poetry: Avant-garde forms. Prefers to publish young, outstanding poets from the international and American scene who, as yet, are unrecognized. Pays $5 per page.

Tips: "Since we have a bilingual format, translations of contemporary international poets is a good way to break in. Otherwise, creative work which goes beyond description and regional, national restrictions. We are looking for imaginative essays in the field of interdisciplinary studies within the humanities."

NAMES, American Name Society, North Country Community College, Saranac Lake NY 12983. Editor: Murray Heller. Emphasizes onomatology (the study of names). Quarterly magazine; 72 pages. Circ. 1,000. Submit material 6 months in advance. Byline given. SASE. Reports in 8 weeks. Sample copy $5.

Nonfiction: General interest (general or specialized interest, may be very erudite); and historical (general or specialized interest, may be erudite). "We want articles to be scholarly, documented, presenting new facts or old facts with a new interpretation, not before published, in area of name-study. We do not want anything that is nonscholarly: subjectivity per se; genealogies, except when incident to the research of a name and its history. Nothing 'creative' or imaginative. Send complete ms. The journal offers no remuneration whatsoever."

NEBULA, 970 Copeland St., North Bay, Ontario, Canada P1B 3E4. (705)472-5127. Editor: Ken Stange. Managing Editor: Ursula Stange. Emphasizes literature for an intellectually sophisticated readership. Quarterly magazine; 88 pages. Circ. 750. Pays on publication in copies and grants. Buys first North American serial rights. Byline given. Phone queries OK. SAE and International Reply Coupons. Reports in 5 weeks. Sample copy and writer's guidelines $1.

Nonfiction: Interview (with literary figures); and opinion (critical essays). Submit complete ms.

Fiction: Erotica; experimental; fantasy; mainstream; and science fiction. Submit complete ms.

Poetry: Quality poetry of all kinds.

Tips: "We do thematic issues, the themes announced in preceding issues, so a would-be contributor is advised to send for a recent sample. Seeing the type of material we generally publish and learning what specific themes we will be exploring in future issues is the best guide to any writer considering our publication."

NEW BOSTON REVIEW, 10 B Mt. Auburn St., Cambridge MA 02138. Editors: Gail Pool, Lorna Condon. Bimonthly magazine for people interested in the arts. Circ. 12,000. Acquires all rights, unless author requests otherwise. Byline given. Photocopied and simultaneous submissions OK. SASE. Reports in 6 weeks. Sample copy $1.

Nonfiction: Critical essays and reviews in all the arts: literature, painting, music, film, theater, photography, dance. Length: 1,000-3,000 words.

Fiction: Length: 2,000-4,000 words. Pays in copies.

Poetry: Pays in copies.

NEW ORLEANS REVIEW, Box 195, Loyola University, New Orleans LA 70118. (504)865-2294. Editor: John Biguenet. Emphasizes art and literature "for anyone who likes literature and is interested in current culture." Magazine published 3 times/year. Circ. 1,500. Pays on publication. Buys first North American serial rights. Byline given. SASE. Reports in 1 month. Sample copy $2.50.

Nonfiction: Interviews with writers, photographers, film directors, producers and artists. "We are also interested in articles dealing with science and the humanities. These must be directed to an educated lay audience." 12 mss/year. Query. Length: 2,000-5,000 words.

Fiction: Quality fiction. Buys 9 mss/year. Under 40 pages. Submit complete ms. Pays $25.

Poetry: "All types, as long as the poem is good." Buys 50 poems/year. Pays $10.

NEW VIRGINIA REVIEW, New Virginia Review, Inc., Box 415, Norfolk VA 23501. Managing Editor: Ms. Childrey W. Farber. Biannual book covering literary and visual arts in Virginia for "a literary audience interested in serious fiction and poetry." Estab. 1979. Circ. 1,500. Pays shortly after publication. Buys rights held jointly by publisher and individual contributors. SASE. Reports on queries in 6 weeks; on mss in 6 months. Sample copy $12; free writer's guidelines.

Nonfiction: "Each issue features an in-depth interview with a major writer or writers; e.g., our first issue had a joint interview with the poets W.D. Snodgrass and Richard Wilbur." No articles unrelated to the literary or visual arts. Buys 2 mss/issue. Query with clips of previously published work. "Length determined on a case-by-case basis." Pays $10-150.

Photos: State availability of photos. Reviews b&w 8x10 glossy prints. Offers no additional payment for photos accompanying ms. Model release required. Buys rights held jointly by publisher and photographer.

Columns/Departments: Articles editor. "Briefs" (200-500 word pieces on literary and visual arts organizations, projects, institutions, etc., in Virginia). No criticism. Buys 8 mss/issue. Query. Length: 200-500 words. Pays $5-25. Open to suggestions for new columns/departments; query articles editor.

Fiction: "We are willing to consider any serious, well-written work of fiction." Buys 6 mss/issue. Send complete ms. "No rules regarding length." Pays $10-200.

Poetry: "We are willing to consider any serious, well written work of poetry." Buys 25-30 mss/issue. No limit on number of submissions. Length: open. Pays $10-50.

Tips: "The *New Virginia Review* is a book-length publication that specializes in the work of first-rate Virginia writers. We also publish writers from outside the state who have contributed to Virginia's literary life, such as visiting writers at Virginia universities. We try for a balance between established writers and promising newcomers. Though we solicit much of our material, we are always very interested in unsolicited fiction and poetry. We try to encourage freshness and diversity by appointing new fiction, poetry, and articles editors each year."

NEW YORK LITERARY FORUM, Box 262, Lenox Hill Station, New York NY 10021. Editor: Jeanine P. Plottel. For teachers, scholars, college students of literature, philosophy, and the humanities and the general reader interested in keeping abreast of current serious, academic literary work. Published 2 times/year. Book format; 322 pages. Byline given. SASE. Reports in 6 weeks. Sample copy $8.50; free writer's guidelines.

Nonfiction: Interview (with important writers) and any article about literature. Query. Length: 2,500-3,750 words.

Columns/Departments: Texts and Documents. Buys 2 mss/year. Query. Length: 4,000 words maximum.

Fiction: "We have not yet included any fiction, but may do so in our Texts and Documents section." Query. Length: 3,500 words maximum.

Poetry: "We do not normally include poetry but are considering doing so in future issues."

Tips: "Each volume deals with just one topic."

NEWSART, 5 Beekman St., New York NY 10038. Editor: Harry Smith. Newspaper. Published 2 times/year, as a supplement to *Pulpsmith*. Circ. 5,000. Buys first rights. Byline given. Pays on acceptance. Sample copy $1. Reports in 4 weeks. Query for nonfiction. Submit complete ms for fiction and poetry. SASE.

Nonfiction: Essays, humor, interviews. Pays $15 minimum for nonfiction.

Photos: Purchased with accompanying ms with extra payment. B&w only. "8x10 best but not exclusively used." Pays $5-25.

Fiction: Fiction "should be reasonably short for newspaper format—newsy element helpful." Pays $15 minimum for fiction.

Poetry: Poetry should be short, though occasional long poems are used. Pays $5-10 for poetry. Titles often changed to headlines for newspaper effect.

NIMROD, 2210 S. Main Tula OK 74114. (918)583-8716. Editor: Francine Ringold. For readers and writers interested in good literature and art. Semiannual magazine; 120 (6x9) pages. Circ. 1,000. Acquires all rights. Byline given. Payment in contributor's copies and $5/page when funds are available. Photocopied submissions OK, but they must be very clear. No simultaneous submissions. Reports in 3 to 6 months. Query or submit complete ms. SASE.

Nonfiction: Interviews and essays. Length: open.

Fiction and Poetry: Experimental and mainstream fiction. Traditional forms of poetry; blank verse, free verse and avant-garde forms. "We are interested in quality and vigor. We often do special issues. Writers should watch for announced themes and/or query."

NIR/NEW INFINITY REVIEW, Box 804, Ironton OH 45638. (614)533-9276. Editor: James R. Pack. Manuscript Editor: Ron Houchin. Art Editor: Ariyan. For the lovers of new writing with "pizzazz and verve." Quarterly magazine; 60 pages. Circ. 500. Acquires North American serial rights. Pays in copies or gift subscriptions. Sample copy and writer's guidelines $1. Photocopied submissions OK "if readable." All submissions should be accompanied by a brief autobiography, stressing the individual and his/her unique personality, and including current activities and publication credits. Reports in 2 months. SASE.

Nonfiction and Photos: "Short essays that chronicle new perspectives, the mysterious and fantastic. Subjects can range from the psychic to the sociological." Length: 3,000 words maximum. Accompanying photos or illustrations are welcome.
Fiction: "We seek stories that are mentally exciting and germinal with ideas. Mystery, science fiction and fantasy find an eager eye." Length: 4,000 words maximum.
Poetry: "Send as large a sample as possible (4-20). We try to feature one poet every issue, using 4-8 or more poems. Free verse; experimental; avant-garde; and all poetry approaching the visual are encouraged. What we seek most is clear voice and lots of energy. No length limit."
Tips: "We especially need good short fiction, 3-6 pages, that deals with the new and the strange."

NORTH AMERICAN MENTOR MAGAZINE, 1745 Madison St., Fennimore WI 53809. (608)822-6237. Editors: John Westburg, Mildred Westburg. 95% freelance written. For "largely mature readers, above average in education, most being fairly well-to-do; many being retired persons over 60; college personnel and professional writers or aspirants to being professional." Quarterly. A small press non-commercial publication, primarily supported by the editors, other contributors and donors. Acquires all rights. Byline given. Pays in contributor's copies. Sample copy $2. Photocopied and simultaneous submissions OK. Reports in 1 week to 6 months. SASE.
Nonfiction: "We desire writing in reasonably good taste; traditional is preferable, but emphasis should be on creativity or scholarship. I know of no other of the small magazine genre that is like this one. We make no claim to being avant-garde, but have been accused of being a rear-guard periodical, for we try to follow the general traditions of western civilization (whatever that might be). Would be interested in readable but well-documented articles on anthropology, archeology, American Indians, black or white Africa. Do not want vulgarity or overworked sensationalism. No stuff on riots, protests, drugs, obscenity or treason. We do not want to discourage a writer's experimental efforts. Let the writer send what he thinks best in his best style. This is very, very essential: Study a current issue first, before submitting any work!" Length: "maximum about 4,000 words."
Fiction: "Short stories should have a plot, action, significance, and depth of thought, elevating rather than depressing; would be glad to get something on the order of Dickens, Thackeray or Dostoyevsky rather than Malamud, Vidal or Bellow. Sustained wit without sarcasm would be welcome; propaganda pieces unwelcome. Would like to see fiction about young people who behave as responsible persons." Length: 1,000-4,000 words.
Poetry: Accepts traditional, blank and free verse, avant-garde forms and light verse. "Poetry from many cultures. We would like to see more poetry by new writers." Length: 50 lines maximum.

THE NORTH AMERICAN REVIEW, University of Northern Iowa, Cedar Falls IA 50614. (319)273-2681. Editor: Robley Wilson Jr. Quarterly. Circ. 3,000. Buys all rights for nonfiction and North American serial rights for fiction and poetry. Pays on publication. Sample copy $1.50. Familiarity with magazine helpful. Reports in 8-10 weeks. Query for nonfiction. SASE.
Nonfiction: No restrictions, but most nonfiction is commissioned by magazine. Rate of payment arranged.
Fiction: No restrictions; highest quality only. Length: open. Pays minimum $10/page. Fiction department closed (no manuscripts read) from April 1 to October 1.
Poetry: Department Editor: Peter Cooley. No restrictions; highest quality only. Length: open. Pays 50¢/line minimum.

THE NORTHEAST OHIO CIRCLE MAGAZINE, 2685 Euclid Hts. Blvd., Apt. #6, Cleveland Heights OH 44106. (216)932-5538. Assistant Editor: Bill Sones. Quarterly magazine for a general audience. Estab. 1980. Circ. 1,000. Pays on acceptance. Byline given. Buys first rights for Northeastern Ohio. Simultaneous queries and photocopies and previously published submissions OK ("if publication and date indicated"). SASE. Reports in 1 week on queries; 1 month on mss. Sample copy for 15¢ or one first class stamp.
Nonfiction: Needs "anything that is thoughtful and worth reading in the Consciousness III vein, such as politics, science, the arts, travel, theater, movies, gardening and personality profiles. Send good, thought-provoking material." Buys 8 mss/year. Query. Length: 4,000 words maximum. Pays 2¢/word.
Fiction: Adventure, erotica, ethnic, experimental, fantasy, historical, horror, humorous, mainstream, romance and science fiction. Buys 12mss/year. Length: 4,000 words maximum. Pays 2¢/word.
Poetry: Avant-garde, free verse, haiku, light verse and traditional. Buys 8/year. Submit maximum 5 poems. Length: open. Pays 2¢/word minimum.
Fillers: Math puzzles, organic diets, food tips and gardening. Buys 8/year. Length: Up to 1,500 words. Pays 2¢/word.
Tips: "We try for a balanced approach. We're not afraid to set think pieces alongside recipes, puzzles, crafts, trivia. And fiction is not a dying art here. Good stories set in the Cleveland-Akron

area have an excellent chance with us. A query that shows some facility with language, as well as staking out the burden of the article is recommmended. We're very receptive to new writers. Try us!"

NORTHWEST REVIEW, 369 P.L.C., University of Oregon, Dept. of English, Eugene OR 97403. (503)686-3957. Editor-in-Chief: John Witte. 85% freelance written. For literate readership. "We have one issue per year with Northwest emphasis; the other two are of general interest to those who follow American/world poetry and fiction." Published 3 times/year; 130 pages. Circ. 2,000. Pays on publication in copies. Buys all rights. Phone queries OK. Photocopied submissions OK. SASE. Reports in 6-8 weeks. Sample copy $2.50; free writer's guidelines.
Nonfiction: John Witte, editor-in-chief. Essays, interviews, and book reviews considered, generally with a literary orientation. Uses 5 mss/issue.
Artwork: Deb Casey, art editor. B&w graphics, drawings, prints. Send transparencies of 10+ pieces with SASE.
Fiction: Deb Casey, fiction editor. All types. Uses 5 mss/issue. Send complete ms.
Poetry: John Addiego, poetry editor. Uses 20-30 poems/issue. Limit submissions to batches of 6-10.
Tips: "Persist: the more we can see of an author's work, the better we're able to assess it."

THE OHIO JOURNAL, A Magazine of Literature and the Visual Arts, Department of English, Ohio State University, 164 W. 17th Ave., Columbus OH 43210. Editor: William Allen. Magazine; 2 times a year. Circ. 1,000. Pays in contributor's copies. Acquires all rights. Byline given. Photocopied and simultaneous submissions OK. SASE. Reports in 6 weeks.
Nonfiction and Photos: Norma Bradley Allen, art editor. Material of interest to an audience knowledgeable about literature and the arts, but not of an academic nature. Interviews and photo essays welcome. No color reproductions. Fiction: William Collen. Poetry: Thomas Young. No restrictions as to category or type. Maximum length for fiction: 6,000 words.

THE OHIO REVIEW, Ellis Hall, Ohio University, Athens OH 45701. (614)594-5889. Editor: Wayne Dodd. "A balanced, informed engagement of contemporary American letters, special emphasis on poetics." Published 3 times/year. Circ. 1,800. Rights acquired vary with author and material. Acquires all rights or first North American serial rights. Submit complete ms. Unsolicited material will be read only September-June. Reports in 6 to 8 weeks. SASE.
Nonfiction, Fiction and Poetry: Buys essays of general intellectual and special literary appeal. Not interested in narrowly focused scholarly articles. Seeks writing that is marked by clarity, liveliness, and perspective. Interested in the best fiction and poetry. Pays minimum $5/page, plus copies.
Tips: "Make your query very brief, not gabby, one that describes some publishing history, but no extensive bibliographies."

OHIOANA QUARTERLY, Ohioana Library Association, 65 S. Front St., 1105 Ohio Departments Bldg., Columbus OH 43215. (614)466-3831. Editor: James Barry. Quarterly magazine; 60 pages. Circ. 1,800. No payment. Byline given. Phone queries OK. Reports in 2 weeks.
Nonfiction: "Limited to articles about Ohio authors, musicians or other artists, and current book reviews; or articles by published Ohio authors." Query. Length: 500-3,000 words.

OPINION, Box 3563, Bloomington IL 61701. Editor: James E. Kurtz. 80% freelance written. For readers 18 and older; people who have an appetite for invigorating, inspiring, thought-provoking articles. Numerous teachers, clergymen and professional people. Monthly magazine, 16 (8½x11) pages. Circ. 3,700. Not copyrighted. Pays 25% kill fee. Byline given. Uses about 38 mss/year. Pays in contributor's copies. Sample copy 30¢. Photocopied submissions and simultaneous submissions OK. Submit complete ms. Reports in 3 to 5 weeks. SASE.
Nonfiction: "We publish articles dealing with social problems, philosophical themes, theological studies. Our articles are on current subjects but inspirational as well. Controversy but not just for the sake of being 'different.' Our writers believe in what they write. Be yourself. Take a deep subject and make it simple—don't write down to people but lift people up to a higher level of understanding. *Opinion* is down to earth. We carry some in-depth essays but for the most part we present to our readers, articles that hit the nail on the head. We are informal but we adhere to the old principles of good writing. Articles on marriage problems are a bit heavy and we prefer to see more material on philosophy and theology. Common sense philosophy. Particularly we want articles on religious adventure, new trends, new happenings." Informational, personal experience, profile, inspirational, historical, think articles, expose, nostalgia, opinion, spot news and new product. Length: 1,500 words maximum.
Photos: Uses 5x7 or 8x10 b&w glossy prints. Captions optional.
Poetry: Traditional forms, free verse and light verse.

PARABOLA, 150 5th Ave., New York NY 10011. (212)924-0004. Executive Editor: Susan Bergholz. Managing Editor: Lee Ewing. "Audience shares an interest in exploring the wisdom and truth transmitted through myth and the great religious traditions." Quarterly magazine; 128 pages. Circ. 14,000. Buys all rights. Pays 33⅓% kill fee. Byline given. Pays on publication. Photocopied submissions OK. SASE. Reports in 3-5 weeks. Free writer's guidelines.
Nonfiction: "We handle work from a wide range of perspectives—from comparative religion and anthropology to psychology and literary criticism. We seek to use these disciplines in the quest for meaning. Don't be scholarly, don't footnote, don't be dry. We want fresh approaches to timeless subjects." Length: 5,000 words maximum. Buys 30 mss/year. Query. Pays $25-150.
Photos: Purchased with or without accompanying ms. No color. Pays $25.
Fiction: Prefers retellings of traditional stories, legends, myths. Length: 3,000 words maximum. Pays "negotiable rates."

THE PARIS REVIEW, 45-39 171st Place, Flushing NY 11358. Editor: George A. Plimpton. Quarterly. Buys all rights. Pays on publication. Address submissions to proper department. SASE.
Fiction: Study publication. No length limit. Pays up to $150. Makes award of $500 in annual fiction contest.
Poetry: Study publication. Pays $10 to 25 lines; $15 to 50 lines; $25 to 100 lines; $50 thereafter. Poetry mss must be submitted to Jonathan Galassi at 541 E. 72nd St., New York NY 10021. Sample copy $4.25.

PHOEBE, The George Mason Review, George Mason University, 4400 University Dr., Fairfax VA 22030. Contact: *Phoebe*. For the literary community. Quarterly magazine; 64-80 pages. Circ. 3,500. Pays in 2 contributor's copies on publication. Byline given. SASE. Reports in 6 weeks. Sample copy $3.
Nonfiction: General interest. Rarely used. Send complete ms. Pays in contributor's copies.
Photos: General interest. Uses 5-10 b&w any size prints/issue. Pays in contributor is copies.
Fiction: Adventure, experimental, fantasy, historical, humorous, mystery, romance, suspense, science fiction, western and serialized novels. "We use only exceptionally well-written material." Accepts 6-10 mss/issue. Send complete ms. Length: no limit. Pays in contributor's copies.
Columns/Departments: Reviews of new novels, particularly first novels and chapbooks. Pays in contributor's copies.
Poetry: Avant-garde, free verse, haiku and traditional. Accepts 20-30 poems/issue. Length: no limit. Pays in contributor's copies.
Tips: "We are interested in stories that give us a feeling of living inside a person's head—the rhythms of existence recreated through words."

PIEDMONT LITERARY REVIEW, Piedmont Literary Society, Box 3656, Danville VA 24541. Editor: John P. Dameron. Quarterly magazine featuring poetry, short fiction and reviews. Circ. 350. Pays in copies. Acquires one-time rights. Submit seasonal material 4 months in advance. Photocopied and previously published submissions OK. SASE. Reports in 2 weeks on queries; in 3 months on mss. Sample copy $2; writer's guidelines for SASE.
Nonfiction: "All submissions are given equal consideration, quality being the key factor in judging submissions. Since our editorial board consists of 3-5 different Piedmont Literary Society members for each issue, we suggest poetry be of a type that would have broad appeal." General interest (reviews of poetry books and poetry publications); how-to (articles related to poetry and poetry analysis); and interview (with poets or writers). Buys 1-3 prose pieces/issue. Send complete ms. Length: 1,500 words maximum. Pays in copies.
Fiction: Fantasy, experimental, historical, romance, suspense and science fiction. "No religious, political or erotic pieces or long short stories." Buys 4 mss/year. Send complete ms. Length: 1,500 words maximum. Pays in copies.
Poetry: Contact: Don Conner and Hal D. Rhoads. Avant-garde, free verse, haiku, light verse and traditional. "We will consider any type of poetry. Lengthy poems do not stand a good chance of being published." Buys 20 mss/issue. Submit maximum 5 poems. Length: 40 lines maximum. Pays in 1 contributor's copy.
Tips: "We publish the best from the material submitted. We try to give special attention to works of students and previously unpublished poets. Writers should indicate if they are students or previously unpublished. Submit 3-5 well written poems on several occasions if rejected initially. We use most types of poetry; our selection board varies from issue to issue. We generally reject all manuscripts that use an overabundance of profanity or gutter language. We prefer work that elevates rather than denigrates mankind."

PIERIAN SPRING, Box 5, Brandon University, Manitoba Canada R7A 6A9. Chief Editor: Dr. Robert W. Brockway. Quarterly (January, April, July, October). Magazine; 50 pages. Circ. 350.

Pays in copies. $25 prize for best poem and best story/issue; book prizes for second place. Special featured poet section in some issues by invitation. "We are international and do not have a national or regional emphasis. We are primarily interested in quality and effectiveness of submissions rather than the address of the writer." Both beginning and established writers welcome. Submit complete ms. Sample copy and writer's guidelines for $1. All rights revert to author. Byline given. SASE requested but not required (Canadian postage or International Reply Coupons). Reprints seldom accepted; originals preferred.

Fiction: Any type of short story up to 3,000 words.

Poetry: "We are not particularly experimental or avant-garde although we will consider all submissions."

Tips: "Prefers mainstream material; fine literary style, excellent language, imagery, comprehensibility."

PIG IRON MAGAZINE, Pig Iron Press, Box 237, Youngstown OH 44501. (216)744-2258. Editor-in-Chief: Jim Villani. 70% freelance written. Emphasizes literature/art for writers, artists and intelligent lay audience with bias towards social responsibility in the arts. Semiannual magazine; 96 pages. Circ. 1,500. Pays on publication. Buys one-time rights. Byline given. Submit seasonal/holiday material 4 months in advance of issue date. Photocopied and previously published submissions OK. SASE. Reports in 3 months. Sample copy $2.50; free writer's guidelines.

Nonfiction: General interest, interview, personal opinion, profile, political or alternative lifestyle/systems. Buys 3 mss/year. Query. Length: 8,000 words maximum. Pays $2/page minimum.

Photos: Submit photo material with accompanying query. Pays $2 minimum for 5x7 or 8x10 b&w glossy prints. Buys one-time rights.

Columns/Departments: Fascia: explores alternative lifestyles and systems. Buys 3 mss/year. Query. Pays $2. minimum.

Fiction: Rose Sayre, fiction editor. Fantasy, avant-garde, experimental, psychological fiction and science fiction. Buys 4-8 mss/issue. Submit complete ms. Length: 8,000 words maximum. Pays $2 minimum.

Poetry: Terry Murcko and Joe Allgren, poetry editors. Avant-garde and free verse. Buys 25-50/issue. Submit in batches of 10 or less. Length: open. Pays $2 minimum.

Tips: "Make query simple and direct. Send modest batches of material at frequent intervals (3-4 times per year). Let us see the range of your talent and interests by mixing up styles, subject matter. We are interested in modernistic, surreal, satirical, futuristic, political subjects."

PLOUGHSHARES, Box 529, Dept. M, Cambridge MA 02139. Editor: DeWitt Henry. For "readers of serious contemporary literature; students, educators, adult public." Quarterly magazine; 188 pages. Circ. 3,000. Rights purchased vary with author and material. Usually buys all rights or may buy first North American serial rights. Buys 50-100 mss per year. Pays on publication. Sample copy $3.50. Photocopied submissions OK. No simultaneous submissions. Reports in 3 months. SASE.

Nonfiction, Poetry and Fiction: "Highest quality poetry, fiction, criticism." Interview and literary essays. Length: 5,000 words maximum. Pays $50. Reviews (assigned). Length: 500 words maximum. Pays $15. Fiction. Experimental and mainstream. Length: 300-6,000 words. Pays $5-50. Poetry. Buys traditional forms, blank verse, free verse, avant-garde forms. Length: open. Pays $10/poem.

PRAIRIE SCHOONER, Andrews Hall, University of Nebraska, Lincoln NE 68588. Editor: Hugh Luke. Quarterly. Usually acquires all rights, unless author specifies first serial rights only. Small payment, depending on grants, plus copies of the magazine, offprints and prizes. Reports usually in 1-2 months. SASE.

Nonfiction: Uses 1 or 2 articles per issue. Subjects of literary or general interest. Seldom prints extremely academic articles. Length: 5,000 words maximum.

Fiction: Uses several stories per issue.

Poetry: Uses 20-30 poems in each issue of the magazine. These may be on any subject, in any style. Occasional long poems are used, but the preference is for the shorter length. High quality necessary.

PRIMAVERA, University of Chicago, 1212 E. 59th St., Chicago IL 60637. (312)752-5655. Editor: Janet Ruth Heller. Managing Editor: Karen Peterson. Annual magazine covering literature and art by women for readers high school age and up interested in contemporary literature and art. Circ. 800. Average issue includes 6 short stories and 45 poems. Pays on publication. Byline given. Acquires first North American serial rights. Phone queries OK. SASE. Reports in 2 months on queries; in 6 months on mss. Sample copy $3.90; free writer's guidelines.

Photos: Send photos with ms. Pays 2 free copies and discount on other copies for 8½x11 b&w

prints. Offers no additional payment for photos accepted with ms. Captions preferred; model release required. Acquires one-time rights.

Fiction: Contact: Ruth J. Young. Adventure, fantasy, humorous, mystery, romance, suspense, experimental, historical, mainstream and science fiction. Buys 6 mss/year. Send complete ms. Length: 25 pages double spaced maximum. Pays 2 free copies.

Poetry: Editor: Mary Biggs. Avant-garde, free verse, haiku, light verse and traditional. Buys 45 mss/year. Submit maximum 6 poems. Length: 10 page maximum. Pays 2 free copies.

Tips: "Read a recent issue. We publish a wide range of material, all by women. We're looking for new ideas and interesting styles. We do not publish scholarly articles or formula-type fiction. Read one of our issues."

PRISM INTERNATIONAL, Department of Creative Writing, University of British Columbia, Vancouver, British Columbia, Canada V6T 1W5. Editor-in-Chief: John Schoutsen. Managing Editor: Stephen Barnett. Emphasizes contemporary literature, including translations. For university and public libraries, and private subscribers. Tri-annual magazine; 130 pages. Circ. 1,000. Pays on publication. Buys first North American serial rights. Photocopied submissions OK. SAE and International Reply Coupons. Reports in 10 weeks. Sample copy $4.

Fiction: Experimental and traditional. Buys 8 mss/issue. Send complete ms. Length: 5,000 words maximum. Pays $10/printed page and 1 yr. subscription.

Poetry: Avant-garde and traditional. Buys 60 poems/issue. Limit submissions to batches of 6. Pays $10/printed page and 1 yr. subscription.

Drama: 1-Acts preferred. Pays $10/printed page and 1 yr. subscription.

PTERANODON, Lieb and Schott, Box 229, Bourbonnais IL 60914. Editors: Patricia Lieb and Carol Schott. Quarterly magazine featuring short stories, poetry and writer's workshops for poets and writers. Estab. 1979. Circ. 500. Pays on publication. Acquires first rights. Photocopied submissions OK. SASE. Reports in 2 weeks on queries; in 2 months on mss. Sample copy $2.50; free writer's guidelines.

Nonfiction: Interview and profile. "Only articles about writers accepted (living or dead). Query." Pays in copies.

Photos: "Only photos with articles about authors. Query."

Columns/Departments: "Query with column ideas. They should be by professional writers." Pays in copies.

Fiction: Adventure, fantasy, experimental, historical, suspense and mainstream. "We are not interested in romance confession style. We are interested in quality fiction with literary value. We are interested in modern fiction." Send complete ms. Length: 500-2,000 words. Pays in copies.

Poetry: Avant-garde, free verse, haiku, light verse, traditional and modern. Submit maximum 4 poems. Length: 3-175 lines. Pays in copies.

PUB, Ansuda Publications, Box 158, Harris IA 51345. Editor: Daniel Betz. Quarterly magazine of poetry and fiction allowing writers to express their gut-feelings and concerns. Estab. 1979. Circ. 200. Pays in copies. Acquires first North American serial rights. Submit seasonal material 6 months in advance. Simultaneous, photocopied and previously published submissions OK if so indicated. SASE. Reports in 1 day on queries; in 2 months on mss. Sample copy $1; free writer's guidelines with SASE.

Columns/Departments: Editor: Alexander Gold. Query. Pays in copies.

Fiction: Adventure, fantasy, mystery, suspense, and science fiction (no technical pieces). Send complete ms. Length: 8,000 words maximum. Pays in copies.

Poetry: Free verse, traditional and blank verse. "No haiku and senseless rhyming." Submit maximum 6 poems. Pays in copies.

Tips: "We are especially interested in new writers and other writers who cannot get published anywhere else. Let us know about you; you may have what we want. The poets are the ones we have trouble with. We would like to have more poetry in each issue, but many poetry submissions are just 'beautiful words' that leave no image in our minds; we'd like more concrete poetry."

PULP, c/o Sage, 720 Greenwich St., New York NY 10014. Editor: Howard Sage. For writers and any persons interested in quality fiction, poetry, art. Quarterly tabloid; 16 pages. Circ. 2,000. Acquires all rights. Payment in contributor's copies. Sample copy $1, check payable to Howard Sage. Will consider photocopied submissions. No simultaneous submissions. Reports in 1 month. Submit complete ms. SASE.

Fiction and Poetry: "Fiction topics of human relations (especially intercultural relations). Quality fiction is especially needed and welcome. Translations of poetry and fiction welcome. Submit clear, publishable copy of original with translation. Brief biography should accompany all submissions." Experimental fiction and serialized novels. Length: open. "Poems on all topics as long as subject is well handled and control is deft." Traditional and avant-garde forms; free verse. Length: open.

PULPSMITH, 5 Beekman St., New York, NY 10038. Managing Editor: Tom Tolnay. Editor: Harry Smith. Roving Editor: Sidney Bernard. Digest-sized pulp-paper, four-color cover magazine that "turns a good read into a genre." Quarterly magazine. Estab. 1981. Circ. 10,000. Pays on publication. Byline given. Buys 200 mss/year. Buys first North American serial rights and second serial (reprint) rights. Reports in 2 months. Sample copy $1.50. SASE.
Nonfiction: Timely, topical, speculative articles on phenomena today and tomorrow—religion, sciences, sports, social, political, crime, medicine. Science Editor: Schmael Prager. Shorter pieces have better chance, but fine longer pieces will be bought. A few book reviews that are essays with broader areas of investigation. Pays $25-75.
Fiction: Special interest in stories within traditional genres—detective, science fiction, western, fantasy—but of a literary quality with strong story value: a good read. "True Story" page seeks fiction-like actual experiences, with strong flavor and lively style. Occasional genre novel may be serialized. Pays $25-75. More for novels.
Poetry: Special interest in "story poems," with long ballads and short lyric poems of popular interest and style. Pays $5-25 (higher for longer ballads).

REVISTA/REVIEW INTERAMERICANA, G. Box 3255, San Juan, Puerto Rico 00936. (809)763-9622. Editor: John Zebrowski. For "mostly college graduates and people with higher degrees." Publication of the Inter American University of Puerto Rico. Quarterly. Circ. 2,000. Acquires all rights, "but will pay 50% of money received if reprinted or quoted." Byline given. Uses about 75 mss/year. Payment in reprints (25) mailed to author. Free sample copy. Query or submit complete ms. Will consider photocopied submissions. No simultaneous submissions. Submit seasonal material at least 6 months in advance. Reports in 6 months. SASE.
Nonfiction: "Articles on the level of educated laymen; bilingual. Also book reviews. Preference to Puerto Rican and Caribbean and Latin American themes from multidisciplinary approach." Length: maximum 10,000 words.
Photos: B&w glossy prints, 4x5 minimum. Captions required. No color.
Fiction and Poetry: "Bilingual; Spanish or English." Experimental, fantasy, humorous and historical fiction. Blank verse, free verse, experimental, traditional and avant-garde forms of poetry.

ROMANCE PHILOLOGY, University of California, Berkeley CA 94720. Editor: Yakov Malkiel, Department of Linguistics. For college and university professors, including graduate students. Quarterly magazine, 120 pages. Circ. 1,250. No payment. Write for copy of editorial guidelines for writers. Query. Reports in 6 weeks. SASE.
Nonfiction: "Scholarly articles, notes, review articles, book reviews, briefer reviews, editorial comments, necrologies and technical essays. Examine very carefully some of the recent issues." General linguistics, theory of literature, historical grammar; dialectology, textual criticism applied to older Romance materials.

THE ROMANTIST, F. Marion Crawford Memorial Society, Saracinesca House. 3610 Meadowbrook Ave., Nashville TN 37205. (615)292-9695 or 292-2918. Editor: John C. Moran. Associate Editors: Don Herron and Steve Eng. Emphasizes modern Romanticism; especially fantastic literature and art. Annual magazine. Circ. 300. Buys all rights. Byline given. Photocopied and previously published submissions OK. SASE. Reports in 4 weeks. Free writer's guidelines.
Nonfiction: General interest (Romanticism, fantasy, weird, horror); interview (with authors writing in the Romantic tradition, mainly fantasy and horror); nostalgia (about authors); personal opinion (about authors); and profile (about authors). "We do not want unrestrained, emotional articles or cliché-ridden, overly academic articles." Uses 5-10 mss/issue.
Columns/Departments: Lost Crawfordiana (reprints undiscovered or forgotten items by and about Francis Marion Crawford). Book reviews on assignment. Query.
Poetry: Free verse and traditional. "We much prefer rhymed and metered poems, no experimental or concrete verse." Uses 10-15/issue.

THE ROSE'S HOPE, 394 Lakeside Rd., Ardmore PA 19003. (215)642-9353. Editor: Peter Langman. Quarterly magazine featuring poetry for writers, high school and college students, teachers and anyone who likes poetry. Estab. 1979. Circ. 175. Pays in copies. Phone queries OK. Submit seasonal material 1 month in advance. Simultaneous, photocopied, and previously published submissions OK. SASE. Reports in 1-2 months on mss.
Nonfiction: Historical (articles about various trends or periods in poetry or about a specific poet); how-to (read or write poetry); opinion (ideas or views about poetry or poets); and personal experience (with poetry: teaching it, being taught, trying to get published). Buys 1-2 mss/issue.

Send complete ms. Length: 1,000 words maximum. Pays in copies.

Poetry: Free verse, haiku, light verse and traditional. "No originality for originality's sake. Strangeness does not mean quality. We are not interested in poets who try to write like their contemporaries. No versified sermons or poems that preach." Buys 20 mss/issue. Length: 60 lines maximum. Pays in copies. "Free verse should not be cheap shredded prose. Poems should express an idea or feeling; they should be about something, not simply a fragment of words. Rather than diffuse and wandering, poems should be intense."

Tips: "Looking for the communication of something real and sincere born out of human experience. Not into difficult, obscure, or overly intellectual material—from published or unpublished poets."

RUNESTONE, Asatru Free Assembly, 3400 Village Ave., Denair CA 95316. Editor: Stephen A. McNallen. Quarterly newsletter about the religion and culture of pre-Christian Scandinavia and the Germanic lands generally, for people who follow the religion of the Vikings and related peoples, or are interested in Neo-Paganism. Circ. 300. Pays on publication. Acquires all rights. Submit seasonal material 3 months in advance. Photocopied and previously published submissions OK. SASE. Reports in 2 weeks. Free sample copy.

Nonfiction: Exposé (of the repression of pagans by authorities in today's world); general interest (mythology and religion of the pagan Scandinavia/Germany, or on the ethic and conduct implied); historical (of the Vikings or other early Germanic peoples, especially anything debunking the "uncouth barbarian" stereotype); travel (dealing with historical sites); and personal experience. Buys 8 mss/year. Query. Length: 600-2,000 words. Pays in copies.

Poetry: Free verse and traditional. "We are especially interested in skaldic poetry in the Old Norse style. Nothing too esoteric." Buys 3 mss/year. Submit maximum 5 poems. Length: 10-20 lines. Pays in copies.

Tips: "Study a sample copy carefully to gain an understanding of our rather unorthodox views."

RUSSIAN LITERATURE TRIQUARTERLY, 2901 Heatherway, Ann Arbor MI 48104. (313)971-2367. Editors: Carl R. and Ellendea Proffer. For "readers of material related to Russian literature and art." 3 times a year. Circ. 1,400. Acquires all rights. Byline given. Uses about 50 mss/year. Except for photographs, payment is made in contributor's copies. Will send sample copy for $5. Query or submit complete ms. Will consider photocopied and simultaneous submissions. Reports on material in 1 to 2 months. SASE.

Nonfiction and Photos: Translations of Russian criticism, bibliographies, parodies, texts and documents from English literature. Critical articles. All in English. Interviews and reviews of Russia-related books. Payment by arrangement for b&w glossy prints or negatives. "Only requirement is relation of some kind to Russian art, literature."

THE RUSSIAN REVIEW, Hoover Institution, Stanford CA 94305. (415)497-2067. Editor: Terence Emmons. Quarterly journal; 128 pages. Circ. 1,850. Will consider photocopied submissions. No simultaneous submissions. Reports in 6-8 weeks. Query. SASE.

Nonfiction: A forum for work on Russia past and present. Uses material of high quality in the fields of Russian history, politics and society, literature and the arts. Scholarly reviews. Length: 2,500-7,500 words.

SACKBUT REVIEW, Sackbut Press, 2513 E. Webster Place, Milwaukee WI 53211. Editor: Angela Peckenpaugh. Quarterly magazine for those interested in poetry, fiction and art. Circ. 250. Pays in copies. Simultaneous and photocopied submissions OK. SASE. Reports in 1 month. Sample copy $1.50.

Nonfiction: Interview (with literary figures, comparative religion experts and people in the realm of consciousness research); journal entries, essays. "No articles that are pornographic, warlike, enervating or about trivia." Query. Pays in copies.

Photos: Reviews b&w prints. Pays in copies.

Fiction: Experimental and mainstream. "Nothing long, too much like a soap opera." Query. Length: 1,000 words maximum. Pays in copies.

Poetry: Free verse and prose poem, translation. No greeting card verse. Submit maximum 5 poems. Length: 1-80 lines. Pays in copies.

Tips: Is not taking much fiction now or any reviews.

ST. CROIX REVIEW, Religion Society, Inc., Box 244, Stillwater MN 55082. Editor-in-Chief: Angus MacDonald. For an audience from college presidents to students. Bimonthly magazine; 48 pages. Circ. 2,000. Pays in copies. Buys all rights. Submit seasonal/holiday material 2 months in advance. Simultaneous, photocopied and previously published submissions OK. SASE. Reports in 2 weeks. Sample copy 50¢.

Nonfiction: "Articles must be germane to today's problems." Scholarly, but not pedantic articles for intelligent and concerned American and foreign audience. Must analyze and evaluate current problems in terms of West European intellectual heritage. Editorial viewpoint is classical liberalism. Length: 5,000 words maximum.
Tips: "Have an adequate knowledge of subject matter, common sense, simplicity of style. No purple passages."

SALT LICK PRESS, Box 1064, Quincy IL 62301. Editor-in-Chief: James Haining. Emphasizes literature. Published irregularly; magazine; 68 pages. Circ. 1,500. Pays in copies. Photocopied and previously published submissions OK. SASE. Reports in 2 weeks. Sample copy $3.
Nonfiction: Informational and personal opinion. Send complete ms.
Photos: Send contact sheet.
Fiction: Experimental. Send complete ms.
Poetry: Open to all types.
Fillers: Query.

SAN FRANCISCO REVIEW OF BOOKS, 1111 Kearny St., San Francisco CA 94133. Editor: Ron Nowicki. For a college-educated audience interested in books and publishing. Monthly magazine 40 pages. Circ. 20,000. Acquires all rights. Byline given. Uses about 180 mss/year. Payment in contributor's copies and subscription. Sample copy $1. No photocopied or simultaneous submissions. Reports on material accepted for publication in 4-6 weeks. Query for nonfiction; submit complete ms for book reviews. SASE.
Nonfiction: Book reviews; articles about authors, books and their themes. "No glib, slick writing. Primarily serious; humor occasionally acceptable. No restrictions on language provided it is germane to the book or article." Interviews, profiles, historical and think articles. Length: 1,000 words maximum for reviews; 2,000 words maximum for articles.

SAN JOSE STUDIES, San Jose State University, San Jose CA 95192. (408)277-3460. Editor: Selma Burkom. For the educated, literate reader. Interdisciplinary, scholarly journal; 112 pages. Three times a year: February, May and November. Circ. 500. Acquires first serial rights. Uses about 40 mss/year. $100 annual prize for the best contribution published during the year. Pays in contributor's copies. Sample copy $3.50. Reports in 2-3 months. Submit complete ms. SASE.
Nonfiction and Photos: In-depth, erudite discussions of topics in the arts, business, humanities, sciences, and social sciences. Review essays of authors. Informational, interview, profile, humor. Photo essays can be free-wheeling. "We need more science articles and more in-depth review essays of significant, but little known, contemporary writers." Recently published articles include previously unpublished letters of William James; "Deriddling Tillie Olsen's Writings," "Of Mice and Marshes," "The Use of IQ Tests in Blaming the Victims," and "Christianity and the Aztecs." Length: 5,000 words maximum. Payment consists of 2 copies of the journal.
Fiction and Poetry: Experimental, mainstream, fantasy, humorous, mystery and science fiction. Length: 5,000 words maximum. Traditional and avant-garde forms of poetry; blank verse and free verse. Themes and length are open.

SECOND COMING, Box 31249, San Francisco CA 94131. Editor-in-Chief: A.D. Winans. Semiannual magazine; 80-120 pages. Circ. 1,000. Pays in copies. Acquires one-time rights. Not accepting unsolicited mss through winter of '81. Query first with an "honest statement of credits." SASE. Reports in 1-4 weeks. Sample copy $2.
Fiction: Experimental (avant-garde) and humorous. Uses 6-10 mss/year. Submit complete ms. Length: 1,000-3,000 words. Pays in copies.
Poetry: Avant-garde, free verse, and surrealism. Uses 100-150/year. Limit submissions to batches of 6. No length requirement. Pays in copies.
Photos: Pays $5 token plus copies for b&w photos.
Tips: "We publish mostly veterans of the small press scene. Read at least 2 back issues."

SEWANEE REVIEW, University of the South, Sewanee TN 37375. (615)598-5931. Editor: George Core. For audience of "variable ages and locations, mostly college-educated and with interest in literature." Quarterly. Circ. 3,500. Buys all serial rights. Pays on publication. Sample copy $4.50. Returns in 4-8 weeks. SASE.
Nonfiction and Fiction: Short fiction (but not drama); essays of critical nature on literary subjects (especially modern British and American literature); essay-reviews and reviews (books and reviewers selected by the editors). Payment varies: averages $10 per printed page.
Poetry: Selections of 4 to 6 poems preferred. In general, light verse and translations are not acceptable. Maximum payment is 60¢ per line.

SHAW. THE ANNUAL OF BERNARD SHAW STUDIES, (formerly *Shaw Review*), S-234 Burrowes Bldg., University Park PA 16802. (814)865-4242. Editor: Stanley Weintraub. For scholars and writers and educators interested in Bernard Shaw and his work, his milieu, etc. Published annually. Circ. 2,000. Pays $50 for articles on publication. Will consider photocopied submissions. Submit complete ms. Reports in 6 weeks. SASE.
Nonfiction: "Articles must pertain to G.B. Shaw, his writing life and milieu." Uses informational and historical articles and interviews. Length: open.

SIGNS: JOURNAL OF WOMEN IN CULTURE & SOCIETY, Center for Research on Women, Serra House, Stanford University, Stanford CA 94305. Editor: Barbara Charlesworth Gelpi. For academic and professional women; women and men interested in the study of women. Journal; 196 pages. Quarterly. Circ. 7,000. Acquires all rights. Payment in copies and offprints. Write for copy of guidelines for writers. Will consider photocopied submissions. Reports in 2-6 months. SASE.
Nonfiction: "Scholarly essays exploring women, their roles and culture, their relations with society, etc. We are especially looking for articles with larger theoretical implications." Length: 20-45 typed, double-spaced pages.

THE SMALL POND MAGAZINE OF LITERATURE, Box 664, Stratford CT 06497. (203)378-4066. Editor: Napoleon St. Cyr. For some "high school students, the rest college and college grad students who read us in college libraries, or, in general, the literati." Published 3 times a year. 40 pages. Circ. 300. Acquires all rights. Uses about 100 mss/year. Payment in contributor's copies. Sample copy $2. Will consider photocopied submissions. No simultaneous submissions. Query or submit complete ms. Reports in 10-30 days. SASE.
Nonfiction, Fiction, and Poetry: "About ⅔ poetry; the rest is open to any and all subjects, essays, articles, and stories. We've had an uncanny knack for discovering talent which has gone on and risen rapidly in the literary field. We don't want anything on the high school and college drug scene, or fiction based on *Love Story*. Particularly interested in authoritative inside exposés (not rabid yellow journalism) of some aspect of business, government, international affairs, or even the world of literature and performing arts." Nonfiction length: 2,500 words maximum. Experimental, mainstream, fantasy, historical and humorous fiction. Length: 200-2,500 words. Traditional and avant-garde forms of poetry, blank, free and light verse. Length: 100 lines maximum.

SMALL PRESS REVIEW, Box 1056, Paradise CA 95969. Editor: Len Fulton. Associate Editor: Ellen Ferber. For "people interested in small presses and magazines, current trends and data; many libraries." Monthly. Circ. 3,000. Accepts 50-200 mss/year. Byline given. Free sample copy. "Query if you're unsure." Reports in 1 to 2 months. SASE.
Nonfiction and Photos: "News, short reviews, photos, short articles on small magazines and presses. Get the facts and know your mind well enough to build your opinion into the article." Uses how-to's, personal experience articles, interviews, profiles, spot news, historical articles, think pieces, photo pieces, and coverage of merchandising techniques. Length: 100-200 words. Uses b&w glossy photos.

SOUTH ATLANTIC QUARTERLY, Box 6697, College Station, Durham NC 27708. Editor: Oliver W. Ferguson. Primarily for the academic profession. Quarterly. No payment. Proceeds of sale of rights to reprint divided with author. Reports in 6 weeks. SASE.
Nonfiction: Articles on current affairs, literature, history and historiography, art, education, essays on most anything, economics, etc.—a general magazine. No taboos. Length: 4,500 words maximum.

SOUTH CAROLINA REVIEW, English Dept., Clemson University, Clemson SC 29631. (803)656-3229. Editor: R. Calhoun. Managing Editor: F. Day. Publishes in spring and fall. Magazine; 72 pages. Circ. 500. Pays in copies. Acquires all rights. Phone queries OK. Simultaneous and photocopied submissions OK. SASE. Reports in 2 months.
Nonfiction: Literary criticism, literary history and history of ideas. Submit complete ms. Pays in copies.
Fiction: "We have no set types; if it's fiction, we'll look at it." Submit complete ms.
Poetry: "If it's poetry, we'll look at it."

SOUTH DAKOTA REVIEW, Box 111, University Exchange, Vermillion SD 57069. (605)677-5229. Editor: John R. Milton. For a university audience and the college educated, although reaches others as well. Quarterly. Acquires North American serial rights and reprint rights. Byline given. Pays in contributor's copies. Reports in 4 weeks or less, except when has a guest editor. SASE.

Nonfiction: Prefers, but does not insist upon, Western American literature and history; especially critical studies of Western writers. Open to anything on literature, history, culture, travel, the arts, but selection depends on patterns and interests of individual numbers within each volume. Contents should be reasonably scholarly, but style should be informal and readable. All well-written mss will be considered. Length: 5,000 words maximum, but at times has used longer.

Fiction: Contemporary Western setting preferred (Great Plains, Rockies, Southwest), but receptive to almost anything that is disciplined and original. Quality is more important than subject or setting. No excessive emotions. Rarely uses hunting, fishing, or adolescent narrator or subject studies. Length: 5,000 words maximum, but has used longer at times.

Poetry: Prefers poetry which is disciplined and controlled, though open to any form (tends to prefer traditional free verse). Any length considered, but prefers 10-30 lines.

THE SOUTHERN REVIEW, Drawer D, University Station, Baton Rouge LA 70893. (504)388-5108. Editors: Donald E. Stanford and Lewis P. Simpson. For academic, professional, literary, intellectual audience. Quarterly. Circ. 3,000. Buys first rights. Byline given. Pays on publication. Will send sample copy to writer for $1.50. No queries. Reports in 2 to 3 months. SASE.

Nonfiction: Essays; careful attention to craftsmanship and technique and to seriousness of subject matter. "Willing to publish experimental writing if it has a valid artistic purpose. Avoid extremism and sensationalism. Essays exhibit thoughtful and sometimes severe awareness of the necessity of literary standards in our time." Emphasis on contemporary literature, especially Southern culture and history. Minimum number of footnotes. Length: 4,000-10,000 words. Pays 3¢/word minimum.

Fiction and Poetry: Short stories of lasting literary merit, with emphasis on style and technique. Length: 4,000-8,000 words. Pays minimum of 3¢/word. Pays $20/page for poetry.

SOUTHWEST REVIEW, Southern Methodist University, Dallas TX 75275. (214)692-2263. Editor: Margaret L. Hartley. For adults and college graduates with literary interests and some interest in the Southwest, but subscribers are from all over America and some foreign countries. Quarterly magazine; 120 pages. Circ. 1,200. Buys all rights. Byline given. Buys 65 mss/year. Pays on publication. Sample copy $1. Query for nonfiction. Submit only complete ms for fiction and poetry. Reports in 3 months. SASE.

Nonfiction and Photos: "Articles, literary criticism, social and political problems, history (especially Southwestern), folklore (especially Southwestern), the arts, etc. Articles should be appropriate for a literary quarterly; no feature stories. Critical articles should consider a writer's whole body of work, not just one book. History should use new primary sources or a new perspective, not syntheses of old material. We're regional but not provincial." Interviews with writers, historical articles, and book reviews of scholarly nonfiction. Length: 1,500-5,000 words. Pays ½¢/word. Regular columns are Regional Sketchbook (Southwestern) and Points of View (personal essays). Uses b&w photos for cover and occasional photo essays.

Fiction: No limitations on subject matter for fiction. No experiences of adolescents—that's overworked. Experimental (not too far out), and mainstream fiction. Length: 1,500-5,000 words. Pays ½¢/word. The John H. McGinnis Memorial Award is made in alternate years for fiction and nonfiction pieces published in *SR*.

Poetry: No limitations on subject matter. "We don't care for most religious and nature poetry." Free verse, avant-garde forms (not too far out), and open to all serious forms of poetry. Length: prefers 18 lines or shorter. Pays $5 per poem.

SOU'WESTER, Department of English, Southern Illinois University, Edwardsville IL 62026. Editor: Dickie Spurgeon. For "poets, fiction writers, teachers, and anyone else connected with or interested in the small press." Magazine published three times/year. Circ. 400. Acquires all rights. Uses about 70 mss/year. Payment in contributor's copies. Sample copy $1.50. Will consider photocopied submissions. Will "reluctantly" consider simultaneous submissions. Reports in 4 to 6 weeks except in the summer. "We do not read mss during June, July and August." Submit complete ms. SASE.

Fiction and Poetry: "We publish fiction, poetry and letters. We do not have any particular editorial bias, but we do insist on meaningful, imaginative development and technical proficiency. No doggerel; no old-fashioned magazine fiction aimed at old-fashioned housewives." Experimental, mainstream, fantasy, historical and science fiction. Length: 10,000 words maximum. Traditional and avant-garde forms of poetry; blank verse, free verse, haiku. Length: 80 lines maximum.

SUN AND MOON: A JOURNAL OF LITERATURE AND ART, 4330 Hartwick Rd., #418, College Park MD 20740. (301)864-6921. Editors: Douglas Messerli and Howard N. Fox. For those interested in contemporary issues of literature and art, and experimental works. Publishes 1-3 issues/year. Magazine; 150 pages. Circ. 500. Buys all rights. Photocopied submissions OK. SASE. Reports in 1-4 weeks. Sample copy $4.50.

Nonfiction: Interview (with art and literary figures) and critical essays on literature and art. "We want only those mentioned above." Buys 1-2 mss/issue. Query or send complete ms. Length: 15 typed pages maximum. Pays in copies.

Fiction: Experimental (any good experimental fiction); mainstream (if the story is of high quality). "We want only those mentioned above." Buys 3-4 mss/issue. Send complete ms. Pays in copies.

Poetry: Avant-garde and free verse. "No traditional or light verse." Buys 40-50 poems/issue. Pays in copies.

13TH MOON, Drawer F, Inwood Station, New York, NY 10034. Editor-in-Chief: Ellen Marie Bissert. A feminist literary magazine. Emphasizes quality work by women for a well-read audience. Semiannual magazine; 80-120 pages. Pays in copies. Acquires all rights. SASE. Reports in 2 months. Sample copy $4.50 plus 75¢ postage and handling.

Nonfiction: Literary criticism, aesthetics and reviews. Query.

Photos: Photos used without accompanying ms. Uses b&w photos. Send 5x7 prints.

Fiction: Woman-oriented. Open to all styles. "Send complete ms, but study magazine first."

Poetry: Open to all styles.

THOUGHT, The Quarterly of Fordham University, Fordham University Press, Box L, Fordham University, The Bronx NY 10458. Editor: G. Richard Dimler, S.J. Acquires all rights. Byline given. Payment in copies. Reports in 4 months. SASE.

Nonfiction: A review of culture and idea, *Thought* discusses questions of permanent value and contemporary interest in every field of learning and culture in a scholarly but not excessively technical way. Articles vary from 5,000 to 8,000 words.

TRI-QUARTERLY, Fiction Editor, 1735 Benson Ave., Northwestern University, Evanston IL 60201. (312)492-3490. Editor: Elliott Anderson. 3 times yearly. For an intellectual and literary audience. "Our format is extremely eclectic. The tone and intentions of each issue may vary." Buys first serial rights. Reports on unsolicited mss within 4-6 weeks; solicited mss immediately. Pays on publication. Study publication before submitting mss; enclose SASE.

Fiction and Photos: No length limits. "We are not committed to the short story as the only publishable form of fiction. Frequently excerpts from longer works tell us more about an author and his work." Payment at $10 per page, if possible. Occasionally uses photos.

UNICORN, A Miscellaneous Journal, Box 118, Salisbury VT 05769. Editor: Karen S. Rockow. 75% freelance written. Mainly for college and graduate school students and faculty. "Well-educated and sophisticated. Not jaded." Published irregularly. Circ. 700. Acquires all rights. Byline given. Uses 15 to 25 freelance mss a year. Pays an honorarium only for nonfiction. Submit complete ms. Generally reports in 3 to 4 weeks, longer over summer. Sample copy $1.50. Will consider photocopied submissions. SASE.

Nonfiction and Photos: "*Unicorn* is a community of writers and readers brought together to share their favorite books and topics. Primarily, we publish essays. These range from personal essays to graceful, scholarly papers directed at a general audience. Areas of greatest interest are folklore, popular culture (especially fantasy literature, detective fiction, children's books) and medieval studies, but we will consider mss on any subject. Scholarly and semischolarly papers may include footnotes (use *MLA* form). The supporting scholarship must be rigorous, but avoid 'intellectualese.' Also have a very offbeat foods column, The Galumphing Gourmet, and publish many reviews, long and short. We are looking for crisp, honest prose and stand committed against pretentiousness. We pay $5 honorarium for each article and essay accepted." B&w glossy prints, any size. Payment in cost of film plus extra roll and offprints. Optimum length: 2,500-5,000 words; 7,500 words maximum, but will break longer articles and consider series.

Tips: No poetry or fiction. "Query for articles. Send a review. Read the magazine before doing anything."

UNIVERSITY OF TORONTO QUARTERLY, University of Toronto Press, 63 A St. George Street, Toronto, Ontario M5S 1A6. Editor-in-Chief: W.J. Keith. Emphasizes literature and the humanities for the university community. Quarterly magazine. Pays on publication. Buys all rights. Byline given. Photocopied submissions OK. SAE and International Reply Coupons. Sample copy $4.50.

Nonfiction: Scholarly articles on the humanities; literary criticism and intellectual discussion. Buys 15 mss/year. Pays $50 maximum.

UNIVERSITY OF WINDSOR REVIEW, Windsor, Ontario, Canada N9B 3P4 (519)253-4232. Editor: Eugene McNamara. For "the literate layman, the old common reader." Biannual. Circ.

300 plus. Acquires first North American serial rights. Accepts 50 mss/year. Sample copy $3 plus postage. Follow *MLA Style Sheet*. Reports in 4 to 6 weeks. Enclose SAE and International Reply Coupons.

Nonfiction and Photos: "We publish articles on literature, history, social science, etc. I think we reflect competently the Canadian intellectual scene, and are equally receptive to contributions from outside the country; I think we are good and are trying to get better. We are receiving too many poems, too many short stories. Everybody in the world is writing them. Too many articles on literature itself. Not enough in the other areas: history, etc." Seeks informational articles. Length: about 6,000 words. Pays $25. For photos, please inquire to Evelyn McLean.

Fiction: Department Editor: Alistair MacLeod. Publishes mainstream prose with open attitude toward themes. Length: 2,000-6,000 words. Pays $25.

Poetry: Department Editor: John Ditsky. Accepts traditional forms, blank verse, free verse, and avant-garde forms. No epics. Pays $10.

UNMUZZLED OX, 105 Hudson St., New York NY 10013. (212)226-7170. Editor-in-Chief: Michael Andre. Emphasizes art and poetry. Quarterly magazine; 140 pages. Circ. 6,000. Pays on publication. Buys all rights. Photocopied submissions OK. SASE. Reports in 1 month. Sample copy $5.75.

Nonfiction: Interviews (artists, writers and politicians). Buys 1 ms/issue. Query. Pays $1-50.

Photos: Photos purchased on assignment only. Pays $1-25 for photos. Model release required.

Fiction: Experimental. Buys 1 ms/issue. Mostly solicited. Pays $1-50.

Poetry: Avant-garde. Pays $1.50.

THE VILLAGER, 135 Midland Ave., Bronxville NY 10708. (914)337-3252. Editor: Amy Murphy. Publication of the Bronxville Women's Club. For club members and families; professional people and advertisers. Monthly, October through June. Circ. 750. Acquires all rights. Uses 40 mss/year. Pays in copies only. Sample copy .75¢. Submit seasonal material (Thanksgiving, Christmas, Easter) 3 months in advance. Submit only complete ms. Reports in 2 weeks. SASE. "We will accept mss *only* from US; no foreign mail." Send publications to Mrs. Anton Tedesko, (nonfiction, fiction).

Nonfiction: Short articles about interesting homes, travel, historic, pertinent subjects, sports, etc. Informational, personal experience, inspirational, humor, historical, nostalgia, travel.

Fiction: Mainstream, mystery, suspense, adventure, humorous, romance, and historical fiction. Length: 900-2,500 words. "We prefer mss under 1,800 words."

Poetry: Traditional forms of poetry, blank verse, free verse, avant-garde forms, light verse. Length: 20 lines.

VILTIS (Hope), Box 1226, Denver CO 80201. (303)839-1589. Editor: V.F. Beliajus. For teenagers and adults interested in folk dance, folk customs and folklore; all professions and levels of education. Bimonthly magazine; 40 pages. Circ. 2,500. Acquires all rights. No payment. Free sample copy. Query. SASE.

Nonfiction: Uses articles on folklore, legends, customs and nationality backgrounds. Folkish (not too erudite) but informative. Can be any length. Everything must be based on custom, interview, profile, humor, exposé reportage. Length: 500-3,500 words.

THE VIRGINIA QUARTERLY REVIEW, 1 W. Range, Charlottesville VA 22903. (804)924-3124. Editor: Staige Blackford. Quarterly. Pays on publication. Reports in 4 weeks. SASE.

Nonfiction: Articles on current problems, economic, historical; literary essays. Length: 3,000-6,000 words. Byline given. Pays $10/345-word page.

Fiction: Good short stories, conventional or experimental. Length: 2,000-7,000 words. Pays $10/350-word page. Prizes offered for best short stories and poems published in a calendar year.

Poetry: Generally publishes 10 pages of poetry in each issue. No length or subject restrictions. Pays $1/line.

WALT WHITMAN REVIEW, Editorial Office: Journalism Program, Communication Arts Department, Oakland University, Rochester MI 48063. Editors: William White and Charles E. Feinberg. For specialists in American literature. Quarterly. Payment in contributor's copies. Wayne State University Press and author share all rights. Byline given unless author requests otherwise. Reports in a few days. SASE.

Nonfiction: All articles and book reviews, notes and queries should deal with Walt Whitman and his writings. "No poems to or about Whitman." Length: 500-6,000 words.

Tips: Well stocked now with contributions.

WASCANA REVIEW, University of Regina, Saskatchewan, Canada. Editor-in-Chief: W. Howard. Emphasizes literature and the arts for readers interested in serious poetry, fiction and

scholarship. Semiannual magazine; 90 pages. Circ. 300. Pays on publication. Buys all rights. Photocopied submissions OK. SAE and International Reply Coupons. Reports in 6-8 weeks.
Nonfiction: Literary criticism and scholarship in the field of English, American, Canadian, French or German literature and drama; reviews of current books (2,000-6,000 words). Buys 1-4 mss/issue. Send complete ms. Pays $3-4/page.
Fiction: Quality fiction with an honest, meaningful grasp of human experience. Any form. Buys 2-5 mss/issue. Send complete ms. Length: 2,000-6,000 words. Pays $3/page.
Poetry: Avant-garde, free verse, haiku, light verse and traditional. Buys 10-15 poems/issue. Length: 2-100 lines. Pays $10/page.

WAVES, 79 Denham Dr., Thornhill, Ontario L4J 1P2. (416)889-6703. Editor: Bernice Lever. For university and high school English teachers and readers of literary magazines. "Our main focus is publishing poetry and fiction." Magazine published 3 times/year; 90-100 pages. Circ. 1,000 plus. Acquires first North American serial rights. Byline given. Payment in contributor's copies. Sample copy $1. Photocopied submissions OK. No simultaneous submissions. Reports in 3-6 weeks. Submit complete ms. SAE and International Reply Coupons.
Nonfiction and Photos: Robert Billings, reviews editor. "Intelligent, thorough, unique, humanitarian material. Good quality; yet wide variety of genres and styles." Uses interviews, essays, literary think pieces and book reviews. Length: 250-7,000 words. B&w photos and graphics are used.
Fiction: Marvyne Jenoff, fiction editor. Experimental, mainstream, fantasy, humorous and science fiction. Length: 500-5,000 words.
Poetry: Contact: Pier Giorgio. Formal and free verse. Length: 5-150 lines.
Tips: "Read a few issues to see the level of language—intelligent academic dryness—in reviews. In poetry and fiction, we look for subtle control of technique, with emotion and thought input. *Waves* aims to print mss of the quality one reads in *The Atlantic* or *Paris Review*."

WEBSTER REVIEW, Webster College, Webster Groves MO 63119. (314)432-2657. Editor: Nancy Schapiro. For "academics, students, all persons interested in contemporary international literature." Magazine; 96 pages. Semiannually. Circ. 800. Not copyrighted. Byline given. Uses 200 mss/year. Pays in copies. Free sample copy. Photocopied and simultaneous submissions OK. Reports in 1 month. SASE.
Fiction and Poetry: "Stories, poems, excerpts from novels, essays and English translations of foreign contemporary literature. Subject matter is not important, but quality is. Our emphasis is on international as well as American contemporary quality writing." No restrictions on length.

WESTERN HUMANITIES REVIEW, University of Utah, Salt Lake City UT 84112. (801)581-7438. Editor-in-Chief: Jack Garlington. For educated readers. Quarterly magazine; 96 pages. Circ. 1,000. Pays on acceptance. Buys all rights. Phone queries OK. Simultaneous and photocopied submissions OK. SASE. Reports in 4 weeks.
Nonfiction: Authoritative, readable articles on literature, art, philosophy, current events, history, religion, anything in the humanities. Interdisciplinary articles encouraged. Departments on film and books. Pays $50-150.
Fiction: Any type or theme. Buys 2 mss/issue. Send complete ms. Pays $25-150.
Poetry: Avant-garde; free verse and traditional. "We seek freshness and significance." Buys 5-10 poems/issue. Pays $50.
Tips: Do not send poetry without having a look at the magazine first.

WIND/LITERARY JOURNAL, R.F.D. 1, Box 809K, Pikeville KY 41501. (606)631-1129. Editor: Quentin R. Howard. For literary people. Magazine; 80 pages. Quarterly. Circ. 500. Uses 500 mss/year. Payment in contributor's copies. Sample copy $1.50. No photocopied or simultaneous submissions. Reports in 10-20 days. Submit complete ms. SASE.
Nonfiction, Fiction, Drama and Poetry: Short essays and book reviews (preferably from small presses) are used, as well as short stories and 1-act plays. Blank verse, traditional and avant-garde forms of poetry, free verse, haiku.

WISCONSIN REVIEW, Box 276, Dempsey Hall, University of Wisconsin-Oshkosh, Oshkosh WI 54901. (414)424-2267. Editors: Perry Peterson, Ann M. Hayes and Kathy Lucas. Quarterly magazine; 32 pages. Circ. 2,000. Acquires first rights. Pays in contributor's copies. Sample copy $1.50. Reports in 5 months. Submit complete ms. SASE.
Fiction: Uses very little.
Poetry: Mainly uses poetry and art.

WOMEN ARTISTS NEWS, Midmarch Associates, Box 3304 Grand Central Station, New York NY 10163. Editor-in-Chief: Cindy Lyle. For "artists and art historians, museum and gallery

personnel, students, teachers, crafts personnel, art critics, writers." Bimonthly magazine; 32 pages. Circ. 5,000. "Token payment as funding permits." Byline given. Submit seasonal material 1-2 months in advance. SASE. Reports in 1 month. $2.50 for sample copy.
Nonfiction: Features; informational; historical; interview; opinion; personal experience; photo feature; and technical. Query or submit complete ms. Length: 500-2,500 words.
Photos: Used with or without accompanying ms. Captions required. Query or submit contact sheet or prints. Pays $5 for 5x7 b&w prints when money is available.

WORLD LITERATURE TODAY, 630 Parrington Oval, Room 110, University of Oklahoma, Norman OK 73019. "A review of contemporary literary activity throughout the world. Read by libraries, scholars, specialists, foreign journals, area studies specialists, 'common readers' in US and abroad. Emphasizes book reviewing (300/issue) and critical-descriptive-evaluative commentary on contemporary writers and trends." Editor: Ivar Ivask. University of Oklahoma holds all rights to materials published unless otherwise noted. SASE.
Nonfiction: Articles (maximum length 3,000 words) concerned with contemporary literature; book reviews of 200-300 words on new, important, original works of a literary nature in any language; "no unrequested reviews. With a staff of some 800 active reviewers, we prefer to handle reviews solely on a requested basis." All contributions in English. Pays only in offprints (25) of a major article, plus 3 complimentary copies.
Tips: "Query should inquire about the possible usefulness of an essay on a particular contemporary writer, group of writers, or specific topic relating to current world literature or literary activity in some area of the world. We also strongly suggest that writers look over several back issues of the journal to familiarize themselves with the type of articles we run and with specific topics and writers covered in recent years."

WRIT MAGAZINE, 2 Sussex Ave., Toronto, Ontario, Canada M5S 1J5. Editor: Roger Greenwald. Circ. 700. Annual literary magazine covering fiction, poetry, and translations of high quality. Pays in copies only. SAE and International Reply Coupons or Canadian postage.
Nonfiction: "Occasional reviews only." Query. Pays in 2 copies.
Fiction: "Stories or parts of novels, any length from 1-60 pages." Send complete ms. Pays in 2 copies.
Poetry: Send complete ms. Pays in 2 copies.

WRITERS FORUM, University of Colorado, Colorado Springs CO 80907. (303)593-3155. Editor: Alex Blackburn. Emphasizes quality fiction and poetry. For people of all ages interested in excellence in creative writing and in contemporary American literature, especially from regions west of the Mississippi. Annual book; 250 pages. Circ. 1,000. Authors retain rights. Byline given. Simultaneous, photocopied and previously published submissions OK. "Send 2 copies of all submissions, brief bio in cover letter, and SASE." Reports in 3-6 weeks. Sample copy discounted 33% to $5.95 for *Writer's Market* readers; free writer's guidelines, SASE with request.
Fiction: Confessions (genuine autobiography); experimental ("any technique that reveals truth of the human heart"); and mainstream (short fiction, novella, coherent excerpt from a novel-in-progress). Buys 12 mss/year. Send complete ms. Length: 1,000-15,000 words. Payment with free copy.
Poetry: Avant-garde, free verse, and traditional, including poetic drama. Publishes 40/year. Submit in batches of 5. Length: 10-2,000 words. Payment with free copy.
Tips: "Query to have bio with career data of previous publication, professional awards, studies, and activities involving literature and creativity. We look for originality, verbal excitement, knowledge of forms, avoidance of 'commercial' themes and approaches, also acquaintance with *Writer's Forum* itself. We give special attention to work submitted on a writer's behalf by a professional writer, teacher of writers, agent, or publisher."

THE YALE REVIEW, 1902A Yale Station, New Haven CT 06520. Editor: Kai T. Erikson. Managing Editor: Sheila Huddleston. Buys all rights. Pays on publication. SASE.
Nonfiction and Fiction: Authoritative discussions of politics, literature and the arts. Pays $75-100. Buys quality fiction. Length: 3,000-5,000 words. Pays $75-100.

Men's

ADAM, Publishers Service, Inc., 8060 Melrose Ave., Los Angeles CA 90046. For the adult male. General subject: "Human sexuality in contemporary society." Monthly. Circ. 500,000. Buys first

North American serial rights. Occasionally overstocked. Pays on publication. Writer's guidelines for SASE. Reports in 6 weeks, but occasionally may take longer. SASE.

Photos: All submissions must contain model release including parent's signature if under 21; fact sheet giving information about the model, place or activity being photographed, including all information of help in writing a photo story, and SASE. Photo payment varies, depending upon amount of space used by photo set.

BEAVER, QMG Corp., 235 Park Ave., S., New York NY 10003. Editor: Biff Norganski. 80% freelance written. For men, age 18-40; high school education; interested in sex, cars, scandal in government, etc. Magazine; 80 pages. Monthly. Circ. 200,000. Buys all rights. Byline given. Pays on acceptance. Multiple submissions OK. Must have clean photocopy. Reports in 1 month. SASE.
Nonfiction and Photos: "Articles of interest to our male readers." Informational, investigative reporting, humor and historical. Query. Length: 2,500-5,000 words. Pays $250-500. Sets of nudes are purchased without mss. Pays $500 for 35mm Kodachrome transparencies.
Fiction: "The approach should be fresh, explicit and very erotic. We don't want to see anything like the typical fiction run in other men's books." Erotic mysteries, science fiction and fantasy, but the sex must be germane to the plot. Submit complete ms. Length: 2,500-4,000 words. Pays $250-500.

CAVALIER, Suite 204, 2355 Salzedo St., Coral Gables FL 33134. Editor: Douglas Allen. For "young males, 18-29, 80% college graduates, affluent, intelligent, interested in current events, ecology, sports, adventure, travel, clothing, good fiction." Monthly. Circ. 250,000. Buys first rights. Byline given. Buys 35-40 mss/year. Pays on publication or before. See past issues for general approach to take. Submit seasonal material at least 3 months in advance. Reports in 3 weeks. SASE.
Nonfiction: Personal experience, interviews, humor, think pieces, expos'e and new product. "Frank—open to dealing with controversial issues." No material on Women's Lib, water sports, hunting, homosexuality or travel, "unless it's something spectacular or special." Query. Length: 2,800-3,500 words. Pays maximum $400 with photos.
Photos: Photos purchased with mss or with captions. No cheesecake.
Fiction: Department Editor: Nye Willden. Mystery, science fiction, humorous, sex, adventure and contemporary problems. Send complete ms. Length: 2,500-3,500 words. Pays $250 maximum, "higher for special."
Tips: "Our greatest interest is in originality—new ideas, new approaches; no tired, overdone stories—both feature and fiction. We do not deal in 'hack' sensationalism but in high-quality pieces. Keep in mind the intelligent 18- to 29-year-old male reader."

CHIC MAGAZINE, Larry Flynt Publications, 2029 Century Park E., Suite 3800, Los Angeles CA 90067. Executive Editor: Donald Evans. For affluent men, 20-35 years old, college-educated and interested in current affairs, luxuries, entertainment and sports. Monthly magazine. Circ. 450,000. Pays 1 month after acceptance. Buys first North American and anthology rights. Pays 20% kill fee. Byline given unless writer requests otherwise. Submit seasonal/holiday material 6 months in advance. SASE. Reports in 1 month.
Nonfiction: Expose (national interest only); how-to (male-oriented consumer interest); humor (parody, satire); informational (entertainment, fashion, etc.); interview (personalities in news and entertainment); celebrity profiles; and travel (rarely used, but will consider). Buys 50 mss/year. Query. Length: 3,000-4,000 words. Pays $500-1,000.
Photos: Bob Elia, photo editor. Purchased with or without mss or on assignment. Query or send transparencies. Pays $35-100/8x11 b&w glossy; $50-150/transparency. Model release required.
Columns/Departments: Steve Campbell, managing editor in charge of Dope, Sex Life. Pays $300. Dave Spector, associate editor in charge of Odds and Ends (front of the book shorts; study the publication first). Pays $50. Length: 100-300 words. Close Up (short profiles) columns. Length: 1,000 words. Pays $100.
Fiction: Erotic, strongly plotted. Buys 12 mss/year. Send complete ms. Length: 2,500-3,500 words. Pays $500 minimum.

DUDE, 2355 Salzdo St., Coral Gables FL 33134. (305)443-2378. Editor: John Fox. "Primarily a photo magazine for men 21 to ?; adventure and sex are their interests." Male-oriented subject matter. Bimonthly. Buys first North American serial rights. Byline given. Buys 100 mss/year. Pays on publication. Submit complete ms. Reports on material in 2 months. SASE.
Nonfiction: "Articles that are male-oriented; primarily concerning sex or adventure." Informational, how-to, personal experience, interview, humor, historical, opinion and travel. Length: 1,500 words maximum. Pays $100-150.
Photos: B&w single photos purchased with mss. Captions required. Length: 100 words.

Fiction: Adventure, erotica, science fiction and humorous. "Fiction should be *very* erotic and sexually explicit." Length: 1,500 words maximum. Pays $100-150.

Tips: "First, study copies of the magazine to see our format and editorial slant. The most original ideas get first consideration. Material must be short (1,000-2,000 words) and professionally presented, clean, original, typewritten ms with SASE. Provocative is the key word . . . something to whet our interest on a subject that has not been over-done, or a new slant on a familiar subject."

EAGLE, Adventure, Survival and Truth, Harris Publications, 79 Madison Ave., New York NY 10026. (212)686-4121. Managing Editor: Angus McTaggert. Bimonthly magazine covering adventure, the military, and the paramilitary for men. Estab. 1980. Circ. 200,000. Pays on acceptance. Byline given. Pays varying kill fee. Buys first North American serial rights. Submit seasonal/ holiday material 4 months in advance. Simultaneous queries, and sumultaneous and photocopied submissions OK. Reports in 3 weeks. Free sample copy; writer's guidelines for business size SAE and 1 first class stamp.

Nonfiction: Book excerpts (military adventure); exposé; historical (combats remembered, inside stories of battles); how-to (pertaining to personal defense or survival); interview/profile (of controversial or interesting figures); new product (unique items); personal experience (combat action, adventure, first-person, or "as-told-to"); photo feature (military events); technical (arms, weaponry); travel (adventure); spy; espionage; conflict around the world; and nature on the rampage. No position pieces. Buys 60 mss/year. Query or send complete ms. Length: 2,000-4,000 words. Pays $300-600.

Photos: State availability of photos or send photos with ms. Pays $25-100 for 35mm color transparencies; $25-100 for 8x10 b&w glossy prints or contact sheets. Captions and model releases required. Buys one-time rights.

Fillers: Buys 25/year. Length: 200-1,000 words. Pays $50-200.

Tips: "Study the book very carefully. We're very interested in seeing material and consider everything."

ELITE MAGAZINE, MINK, AND RUSTLER, 234 Eglington Ave. E., #401, Toronto, Ontario, Canada M4P 1K5. Editor-in-Chief: David Wells. Managing Editor: Andrew Dowler. Emphasizes male entertainment. Monthly magazines. Circ. 500,000. Pays on publication. Buys all rights or First North American serial rights or second rights. Byline given. Submit seasonal/holiday material 6 months in advance. Simultaneous and photocopied submissions OK. SASE. Reports in 3 months. Sample copy $1; free writer's guidelines.

Nonfiction: Expose; general interest (anything topical); interview (topical personalities); and photo feature. "We want material that will appeal to the Canadian reader." Buys 3 mss/issue. Submit complete ms. Length: 2,000-4,000 words. Pays $100-400.

Photos: Purchased with or without accompanying ms. Send contact sheet or transparencies. Pays $20-100 for standard size b&w photos; $100-400 for 35mm or 2¼x2¼ transparencies. Submit at least 20 transparencies. Offers no additional payment for photos accepted with ms. Model release required.

Columns/Departments: "Fantasy Tapes (1,500 words) and Shameless Tales (2,500 words) are departments containing pure erotica; these are the best areas for a freelancer to begin working with us." Submit complete ms. Length: 500-1,000 words. Pays $50-100. Open to suggestions for new column/departments.

Fiction: Adventure, erotica, fantasy and humorous. Buys 12 mss/year. Submit complete ms. Length: 1,500-3,000 words. Pays $100-300.

Fillers: Jokes and gags. Pays $20-50.

ESCAPADE MAGAZINE, Escapade Corp., 210 E. 35th St., New York NY 10016. Editor-in-Chief: Christopher Watson. Emphasizes sophisticated sex. Readers are 18-40, high school educated, interested in sexual entertainment. Monthly magazine. Estab. 1955. Circ. 150,000. Pays 3 weeks after scheduling for specific issue. Buys first North American serial rights. Byline given. Submit seasonal/holiday material 6 months in advance. SASE. Reports in 3 weeks.

Nonfiction: "Material in keeping with contemporary 'sophisticate' magazine standards; must be frank in sexual detail without being tasteless (racist, etc.). Exposé (of sexual nature); interviews (with sex personalities); and photo features (nudes). Buys about 6 mss/issue. Send complete ms. Length: 2,500-3,500 words. Pays $100-150.

Photos: B&w and color purchased with or without mss. Send contact sheet or transparencies. Pays $10 minimum for b&w contacts; $15-20 for 2¼x2¼ or 35mm color. Model release required. All photos must relate to theme of magazine.

Columns/Departments: Offbeat sex news, sex puzzles (crossword), pieces with reader involvement (sexual). Buys 1-2/issue. Length: 1,000-1,500 words. Pays $35-50. Open for suggestions for new columns or departments.

Fiction: Adventure, erotica, fantasy, confession (all sexual). Buys 2 mss/issue. Send complete ms. Length: 2,500-3,000 words. Pays $100.

ESQUIRE, 2 Park Ave., New York NY 10016. Executive Editor: Priscilla Flood. Editor: Phillip Moffitt. Monthly. Usually buys most rights. Pays on acceptance. Reports in 3 weeks. "We depend chiefly on solicited contributions and material from literary agencies. Unable to accept responsibility for unsolicited material." Query. SASE.
Nonfiction: Articles vary in length, but usually average 3,000 words and rarely run longer than 4,000 words. Articles should be slanted for sophisticated, intelligent readers; however, not highbrow in the restrictive sense. Wide range of subject matter. Rates run roughly between $200 and $1,500, depending on length, quality, etc. Expenses are allowed, depending on the assignment.
Photos: Art Director, Robert Priest. Buys all rights. Payment depends on how photo is used, but rates are roughly $25 for single b&w; $100-200 for b&w full page; $150 to $350 for full color page. Guarantee on acceptance. Gives assignments and pays expenses.
Fiction: Rust Hills, Fiction Editor. "Literary excellence is our only criterion." Length: about 1,000-6,000 words. Payment: $350-1,500.

FLING, 1485 Bayshore Blvd., San Francisco CA 94124. Editor/Publisher: Arv Miller. For male readership, 18-40 years old, college-educated and "hip in the sense that he knows what rings true and what sounds phony." Monthly magazine. Buys first rights (additional payment if reprinted in *Fling* special annual editions). Pays on acceptance. SASE. Sample copy for $3 in postage; free writer's guidelines with SASE.
Nonfiction: "We want contemporary subjects that have a special interest to men. Areas such as crime, xxx-rated film reviews, sport figures, personality profiles, new sexual activities, foreign travel, pornography, health-diets, making money and sexual news items are currently needed. 80% of the material we buy has a sex slant. *Fling* is the premier sophisticated men's magazine that specializes in featuring the big-bosomed woman. Any and all items concerning the female breast are a special and continuing need. Style of text should reflect a modern-day, sophisticated approach to prose. No long-winded, scholarly sentences or paragraphs. We want the writer's personal feelings to come through." Quotes and anecdotes important to mss. "No straight fiction." Also buys humor-fillers, personalities and investigative reporting. Query. The query should specify (1) exactly what the article proposes to tell us (the who, what, where, when, why and how), using nouns and verbs; (2) specifically how the writer intends to slant it to *Fling*'s needs; and (3) details of length, photos or illustrations, etc.; also, it should demonstrate an ability to write acceptable English." Length: 1,500-2,500 words. Pays $125-350 on acceptance.
Photos: Buys first or second rights, with additional payment for reprint use.
Fillers: Filler humor also used. Also: short quizzes, sex news clips, satiric items, and brief sex items (one paragraph and up). Send complete ms.
Tips: "Read the publication and make sure anything you send us fits in with our needs and our slant. Query first. Be willing and able to make changes we request in mss to fit them to our current needs. We prefer making assignments; come up with ideas we can use and demonstrate ability to write acceptably and we will try you with an assignment."

GALLERY, Montcalm Publishing Corp., 800 2nd Ave., New York NY 10017. (212)986-9600. Editor/Publisher: Leon Garry. Editorial Director: Eric Protter. Executive Editor: F. Joseph Spieler. Managing Editor: Barbara Cronie. Design Director: Derek Burton. "We are similar to *Playboy* and *Penthouse*. Monthly magazine; 128 pages. Circ. 700,000. Pays 50% on acceptance, 50% on publication. Buys first North American serial rights or will make assignments on a work-for-hire basis. Pays 25% kill fee. Byline given. Submit seasonal/holiday material 6 months in advance. Photocopied submissions OK. SASE. Reports in 1 month on queries; in 6 weeks on mss. Sample copy $2.95.
Nonfiction: Investigative pieces, general interest, how-to, humor, interview, new products and profile. "We do not want to see articles on pornography." Buys 6-8 mss/issue. Query or send complete mss. Length: 1,000-6,000 words. Pays $200-1,000. "Special prices negotiated."
Photos: Send photos with accompanying mss. Pay varies for b&w contact sheets or color contact sheets and negatives. Buys one-time rights. Captions preferred; model release required.
Fiction: Adventure, erotica, experimental, humorous, mainstream, mystery and suspense. Buys 1 ms/issue. Send complete ms. Length: 500-3,000 words. Pays $250-750.

GENESIS MAGAZINE, 770 Lexington Ave., New York NY 10021. Editor: Joseph Kelleher. Monthly magazine. Circ. 600,000. Query. Reports in 3 weeks. SASE.
Nonfiction: "Newsmaking articles, interviews with celebrities—political and entertainment."
Photos: "Erotic photo essays of beautiful women."
Fiction: "Remember that we are oriented toward male entertainment. We want top quality first and foremost. Nothing downbeat, depressing or nostalgic."

GENT, Suite 204, 2355 Salzedo St., Coral Gables FL 33134. (305)443-2378. Editor: John C. Fox. Monthly magazine "for men from every strata of society." Circ. 200,000. Buys first North American serial rights. Byline given. Pays on publication. Submit complete fiction ms. Query first on non-fiction. Reports in 3-6 weeks. SASE.
Nonfiction: Length: 1,500-2,500 words. Buys 70 mss/year. Pays $100-200.
Photos: B&w and color photos purchased with mss. Captions (preferred). Length: 100 words.
Fiction: Erotic. Length: 1,500-3,000 words. Pays $100-200.

GENTLEMAN'S COMPANION, Larry Flynt Publications, 2029 Century Park E., Suite 3800, Los Angeles CA 90067. (213)556-9200. Managing Editor: Thomasine Lewis. Monthly men's magazine. Estab. 1980. Pays on acceptance. Byline given. Buys all rights. Submit seasonal/holiday material 3 months in advance. Simultaneous, photocopied, and previously published submissions OK. SASE. Reports in 1 month on queries. Writer's guidelines furnished upon request.
Columns/Departments: Private Affairs (sexual experience from a woman's point of view.) Buys 12 mss/year. Length: 1,500 words. Pays $50 minimum/article.
Fiction: Contact: Tommi Lewis. "We will consider all fiction with a fully developed plot and characterization that includes one major erotic scene. Plot and characterization should not be subordinated to sexual activities. The latter must grow logically from the story, rather than be forced or contrived. *GC* favors surprise endings." Buys 24 mss/year. Send complete ms. Length: 3,000-4,000 words. Pays $300 minimum.
Tips: "The editorial staff is open to queries from writers who can fulfill column assignments on a regular basis. Read samples of fiction already appearing in magazine."

GENTLEMEN'S QUARTERLY, Conde Nast, 350 Madison Ave., New York NY 10017. Editor-in-Chief: Jack Haber. Managing Editor: Roger C. Sharpe. Circ. 400,000. Emphasizes fashion and service features for men in their late 20s, early 30s, with a large amount of discretionary income. Monthly magazine. Pays $200 kill fee. Byline given. Pays on publication. Submit seasonal/holiday material 4-6 months in advance. Photocopied submissions OK. SASE. Reports in 3 weeks.
Nonfiction: "Content is mostly geared toward self-help and service areas. Subject should cover physical fitness, grooming, nutrition, psychological matters (different types of therapy, etc.), health, travel, money and investment, business matters—all geared to our audience and filling our format." Buys 6-10 mss/issue. Query with outline of story content. Length: 1,500-2,500 words. Pays $300-450.
Columns/Departments: Peter Simon, Associate Editor. Looking Good (physical fitness, diet, nutrition and grooming); Money (investments); Lifelines (self-help); Destinations and Adventure (travel); Health; and Living (catchall for various stories that fit magazine format). Buys 5-8/issue. Query with outline of story content. Length: 1,500-2,500 words. Pays $300-400.
Tips: "The best procedure to break in is really the outline and formulating a proposal structurally in terms of content and information."

HUSTLER MAGAZINE, 2029 Century Park E., Floor 38, Los Angeles CA 90067. (213)556-9200. Articles Editor: Richard Warren Lewis. Monthly magazine. Circ. 3 million. Rights purchased vary with author and material. Usually buys all rights, or buys first world serial rights. Buys 36 full-length mss/year. Pays on acceptance. Write for editorial guidelines. Photocopied submissions (although original is preferred) OK. Reports in 2 months. Query for nonfiction. Query or submit complete ms for other material. SASE.
Nonfiction: Will consider expose, profiles, interviews. Should be hard-hitting, probing, behind-the-scenes material. "We do not want fluff pieces or PR releases. Avoid overly complex sentence structure. Writing should nonetheless be sophisticated and contemporary, devoid of any pretensions, aggressive and down-to-earth, exhibiting no-nonsense attitude. We deal in a realistic world where people sweat and pick their noses. We mirror the reality of our times." The publication is "sexually explicit but no pornography. No interviews or profiles on porno actors or actresses." Wants expose material, particularly exposes in political/celebrity/business world. Length: 5,000 words. Pays $1,000 minimum. Material also needed for regular columns, "Kinky Korner" and "Sex Play." Length: 2,000 words for "Korner"; 1,500-2,000 words for "Play." Pays $150 for "Korner"; $350 for "Play."
Photos: Photos used with mss with no additional payment. Size: 35mm Kodachrome. Buys "total exclusive rights." Pays $300/page for color. "Check a recent copy to see our style. Slides should be sent in plastic pages. Soft-focus and diffusion are not acceptable."
Fiction: Considers all fiction with fully developed plot and characterization that includes at least one major erotic scene. Plot and characterization should not be subordinated to sexual activites. No humor or satire. Length: 5,000 words. Pays $1,000 minimum.

1994, Warren Publishing Co., 145 E. 32nd St., New York NY 10016. (212)683-6050. Editor: Bill DuBay. Bimonthly b&w comic book covering provocative illustrated adult fantasy for an adult market. Pays on acceptance. Byline given. Buys all rights. Photocopied submissions OK. SASE. Reports in 2 months on queries. Free sample copy and writer's guidelines free for business size SAE and 1 first class stamp.

Fiction: Erotica. "Scripts broken down into comic book format: pages, panels and balloons. Each story should be complete in one issue." Buys 36 mss/year. Pays $25/printed page.

NUGGET, Suite 204, 2355 Salzedo St., Coral Gables FL 33135. (305)443-2378. Editor: John Fox. Magazine "primarily devoted to fetishism." Buys first North American serial rights. Byline given. Pays on publication. Submit complete ms. Reports in 2 months. SASE.

Nonfiction: Articles on fetishism—every aspect. Length: 2,000 words maximum. Buys 20-30 mss/year. Pays $100-200.

Photos: Erotic pictorials of women—essay types in fetish clothing (leather, rubber, underwear, etc.,) or women wrestling or boxing other women or men, preferably semi- or nude. Captions or short accompanying manuscript desirable. Color or b&w photos acceptable.

Fiction: Erotic and fetishistic. Should be oriented to *Nugget's* subject matter. Length: 1,500 words maximum. Pays $100-200.

Tips: "We require queries on articles only and the letter should be a brief synopsis of what the article is about. Originality in handling of subject is very helpful. It is almost a necessity for a freelancer to study our magazine first, be knowledgable about the subject matter we deal with and able to write explicit and erotic fetish material."

PENTHOUSE, 909 3rd Ave., New York NY 10022. Editorial Director: James Goode. For male (18-34) audience; upper-income bracket, college-educated. Monthly. Circ. 5,350,000. Buys all rights. Pays 25% kill fee. Byline given. Buys 70-80 mss/year. Pays on acceptance. Photocopied submissions OK. Reports in 1 month. Query. SASE.

Nonfiction: Department Editor: Peter Bloch. Articles on general themes: money, sex, humor, politics, health, crime, etc. Male viewpoint only. Length: 5,000 words. General rates: $2,000 minimum.

Photos: Purchased without mss and on assignment. Pays $200 minimum for b&w; $350 for color. Spec sheet available from Art Director Joe Brooks.

Fiction: Editor: Kathryn Green. Quality fiction. Experimental, mainstream, mystery, suspense and adventure with erotic flavor; erotica; and science fiction. Length: 3,500-6,000 words. Pays $1,500 minimum.

PENTHOUSE VARIATIONS, Viva International, 909 3rd Ave., New York NY 10022. 593-3301. Editor: Victoria McCarty. Monthly magazine. *Variations* is a pleasure guide for everyone who wants to expand his horizons of enjoyment. All forms of sensuality and eroticism appear in its pages, from monogamy to menaging, from bondage to relaxation, from foreplay to romance." Circ. 400,000. Pays on acceptance. No byline given. Buys all rights. Submit seasonal/holiday material 7 months in advance. Simultaneous queries OK. Reports in 1 month on queries; 2 months on mss. Free writer's guidelines.

Nonfiction: Personal experience. "We are looking for 2,500-3,000-word, first-person, true accounts of erotic experiences, squarely focused within *one* of the pleasure variations." "No fiction, articles, or short stories. No porno, favorite erotica; we are not a dirty-story clearing house." Buys 120 mss/year. Query. Length: 2,500-3,000 words. Pays $400.

Tips: "I am easily swayed by professionally neat mss style: clean ribbon, non-erasable paper, double-spacing, margins. I look for complete sentences and an electrically erotic mind sold in a business-like manner."

PLAYBOY, 919 N. Michigan, Chicago IL 60611. Managing Editor: Don Gold. Monthly. Reports in 1 month. Buys first rights and others. SASE.

Nonfiction: James Morgan, articles editor. "We're looking for more timely, more topical pieces. There will be more emphasis on romance. Articles should be carefully researched and written with wit and insight; a lucid style is important. Little true adventure or how-to material. Check magazine for subject matter. Pieces on outstanding contemporary men, sports, politics, sociology, business and finance, music, science and technology, games, all areas of interest to the urban male." Query. Length: 4,000-6,000 words. On acceptance, pays $2,000 minimum. If a commissioned article does not meet standards, will pay a turn-down price of $400. The *Playboy* interviews run between 8,000 and 15,000 words. After getting an assignment, the freelancer outlines the questions, conducts and edits the interview, and writes the introduction. Pays $3,000 on acceptance. For interviews contact G. Barry Golson, Executive Editor, 747 3rd Ave., New York NY 10017.

Photos: Rene Karlin. photography director, suggests that all photographers interested in contributing make a thorough study of the photography currently appearing in the magazine. Generally

all photography is done on assignment. While much of this is assigned to *Playboy*'s staff photographers, approximately 50% of the photography is done by freelancers and *Playboy* is in constant search of creative new talent. Qualified freelancers are encouraged to submit samples of their work and ideas. All assignments made on an all rights basis with payments scaled from $600/color page for miscellaneous features such as fashion, food and drink, etc.; $300/b&w page; $800/color page for girl features; cover, $1,000. Playmate photography for entire project: $9,000. Assignments and submissions handled by associated editors: Jeff Cohen, Janice Moses, and James Larson, Chicago; Marilyn Grabowski, Los Angeles. Assignments made on a minimum guarantee basis. Film, processing, and other expenses necessitated by assignment honored.
Fiction: Alice Turner, Fiction Editor. Both light and serious fiction. Entertainment pieces are clever, smoothly written stories. Serious fiction must come up to the best contemporary standards in substance, idea and style. Both, however, should be designed to appeal to the educated, well-informed male reader. General types include comedy, mystery, fantasy, horror, science fiction, adventure, social-realism, "problem" and psychological stories. *Playboy* has serialized novels by Ian Fleming, Vladimir Nabokov, Graham Greene, Michael Crichton and Irwin Shaw. Other fiction contributors include Saul Bellow, John Cheever, Bernard Malamud and Kurt Vonnegut. Fiction lengths are 3,000-6,000 words; short-shorts of 1,000 to 1,500 words are used. Pays $2,000; $1,000 short-short. Rates rise for additional acceptances. Rate for Ribald Classics is $200.
Fillers: Party Jokes are always welcome. Pays $50 each on acceptance. Also interesting items for Playboy After Hours, front section (best check it carefully before submission). The After Hours front section pays anywhere from $50 for humorous or unusual news items (submissions not returned) to $350 for original reportage. Subject matter should be new trends, fads, personalities, cultural developments. Has movie, book, record reviewers but solicits queries for short (1,000 words or less) pieces on art, places, people, trips, adventures, experiences, erotica, television—in short, open-ended. Book and record reviews are on assignment basis only. Ideas for Playboy Potpourri pay $75 on publication. Query. Games, puzzles and travel articles should be addressed to New York office.

PLAYERS MAGAZINE, Players International Publications, 8060 Melrose Ave., Los Angeles CA 90046. (213)653-8060. Editor: Raymond Locke. Associate Editor: Leslie Gevsicoff. For the black male. Monthly magazine. Circ. 400,000. Pays on publication. Buys all rights. Submit seasonal/holiday material 6 months in advance. Photocopied submissions OK. SASE. Reports in 3 weeks.
Nonfiction: "*Players* is *Playboy* in basic black." Exposé; historical; humor; inspirational; sports; travel; reviews of movies, books and records; profile and interview on assignment. Length: 1,000-5,000 words. Pays 6¢/word. Photos purchased on assignment (pays $25 minimum for b&w; $500 and expenses for 100 shots). Model release required.
Fiction: Adventure, erotica, fantasy, historical (black), humorous, science fiction and experimental. Length: 1,000-4,000 words. Pays 6¢/word.
Tips: "Follow current style with novel theme in query or article. Looking for: city, night life of cities other than New York, Chicago, Los Angeles; interviews with black political leaders; black history."

RESPONSE MAGAZINE, Can-Am Media, Box 238, West Hempstead NY 11552. Contact: Editor. Emphasizes adult relationships heavy in erotic content. Monthly. Pays on publication. Buys all rights. Byline given unless unwanted. Submit seasonal/holiday material 5 months in advance. SASE. Reports in 3 weeks. Free writer's guidelines.
Nonfiction: General interest (marriage and sex); how-to (sexual expertise, regenerate a marriage, have a special affair, etc.); humor (marriage, relationships, sex); current trends in sex; strange and unusual (sexually oriented); nostalgia (sexually oriented); personal experience; personal opinion (sexually oriented); and warm human interest stories that relate to sexual experiences among adults. Query with short proposal/outline of story intentions. "Do not send unsolicited manuscripts." Length: 1,500-2,500 words. Pays $100-150.

ROOK, Warren Publishing Co., 145 E. 32nd St., New York NY 10016. (212)683-6050. Editor: Bill DuBay. Bimonthly black-and-white adventure comic book for adult males.
Fiction: "I'm especially interested in new character ideas. Our publication is like a men's magazine in comic book form."

SAGA, Lexington Library, Inc., 355 Lexington Ave., Brooklyn NY 10017. (212)391-1400. Editor-in-Chief: David J. Elrich. General interest men's magazine. "We offer an alternative to the many 'skin' magazines across the country in that we give an exciting, contemporary look at America today without the porn. A man's magazine that can be read by the entire family." Monthly magazine. Circ. 300,000. Pays on acceptance. Buys first North American serial rights. Byline given.

Phone queries OK. Submit seasonal/holiday material 3 months in advance. SASE. Reports in 1 month. Sample copy $1.50.

Nonfiction: Expose (government), how-to (save money), humor (topical), interview, new product, profile and travel. Buys 12 mss/issue. Query. Length: 1,500-3,500 words. Pays $250-600.

Photos: Photos purchased with accompanying ms or on assignment. Captions required. Pays $35 minimum for b&w photos; $75 minimum for 35mm color photos. Query for photos. Model release required.

SCREW, Box 432, Old Chelsea Station, New York NY 10011. Managing Editor: Richard Jaccoma. For a predominantly male, college-educated audience; 21 through mid-40s. Tabloid newspaper. Weekly. Circ. 125,000. Buys all rights. Byline given. Buys 150-200 mss/year. Pays on publication. Free sample copy and writer's guidelines. Reports in 1 month. Submit complete ms for first-person, true confessions. Query on all other material. SASE.

Nonfiction: "Sexually related news, humor, how-to articles, first-person and true confessions. Frank and explicit treatment of all areas of sex; outrageous and irreverent attitudes combined with hard information, news and consumer reports. Our style is unique. Writers should check several recent issues." Length: 1,000-3,000 words. Pays $100-200. Will also consider material for "Letter From . . .", a consumer-oriented wrapup of commercial sex scene in cities around the country; and "My Scene," a sexual true confession. Length: 1,000-1,200 words. Pays about $40.

Photos: B&w glossy prints (8x10 or 11x14) purchased with or without mss or on assignment. Pays $10-50.

Tips: "All mss get careful attention. Those written in *Screw* style on sexual topics have the best chance."

STAG, The Original Party Magazine, Swank Corp., 888 7th Ave., New York NY 10016. Editor: John Tido. Monthly magazine covering men's entertainment with an emphasis on sex for men 18-35. Circ. 170,000. Pays on publication. Byline given. Offers 25% kill fee. Buys all rights. Submit seasonal/holiday material 6 months in advance. Photocopied and previously published submissions OK. SASE. Reports in 1 month. Sample copy $2.95.

Nonfiction: Interview (music celebrities and people in slightly offbeat or dangerous professions); photo features. "We're looking for anything the national news magazines won't print. Subject matter of any article should lend itself to 4-6 pages of photos." Buys 70 mss/year. Query with clips of published work. Length: 2,500-3,000 words. Pays $350 minimum/article.

Photos: State availability of photos. Reviews 35mm Kodachrome transparencies. Payment varies according to usage rights.

Fiction: Buys 12 mss/year. Send complete ms. Length: 3,000 words average. Pays $350 minimum.

Tips: "We like a query that tips us off to a new sex club, strip joint, love commune etc., that would cooperate with the writer and our photographers for a feature story. For all our articles, photographs or illustrations are essential. Sex is the funniest thing in the world, so don't take it so seriously. Crazy ideas attract our attention. (We recently printed in-depth interviews with Santa Claus and The Ayatollah, probing them for their sex lives.)" Read the magazine.

SWANK, 888 7th Ave., New York NY 10106. Editor-in-Chief: Myles Eric Ludwig. Managing Editor: D. Dichter. For urban men, ages 18-40. "*Swank* is a sophisticated men's interest magazine which attempts to service not only its readers' libidos, but their entire lifestyles." Monthly magazine; 100 pages. Circ. 350,000. Pays on publication. Buys first North American serial rights or second serial (reprint) rights (for books). Pays 25% kill fee. Byline given unless otherwise requested. Submit seasonal/holiday material 4 months in advance. SASE. Reports in 1 month. Sample copy $3.

Nonfiction: Exposé (of government, big business and organized crime); how-to (get a raise, find a divorce lawyer, seduce women); humor; interview (must be established names); photo feature (usually nude sets); profile; and travel (with a strong men's slant). Buys 5-6 mss/issue. Length: 3,000 words maximum (except for *very* strong investigative pieces). Pays $300 minimum.

Photos: Norman Oberlander, Art Director. Purchased without accompanying ms. Send transparencies. Pays $800/set for 2¼x2¼ or 35mm color transparencies. Model release required. "The photos we're looking for are female nudes, not your kids, your puppy, your vacation, etc."

Fiction: Contact: Bruce Foster. "Our greatest need is for sexually-oriented fiction that's well-turned and tasteful." Humor, erotica, mystery, science fiction and suspense. Buys 1 ms/issue. Length: 3,000 words. Pays $300 minimum.

Tips: "The best way to break in is to read several issues which will give you an idea of what we do. Local events and celebrities that are singular enough to be of national interest are usually good query material. With your query, enclose tearsheets of pieces you've written that are fairly close in style to what you'd like to do for us. Don't just list your credits. We have to know if you can write."

VAMPARILLA, Warren Publishing Co., 145 E. 32nd St., New York NY 10016. (212)683-6050. Editor: Chris Adames. Comic book published 9 times/year featuring science fiction, adventure, fantasy and horror for 18-year-old males. Pays on acceptance. Byline given. Buys all rights. Photocopied submissions OK. SASE. Reports in 2 months on queries. Sample copy and writer's guidelines free for business size SAE and 1 first class stamp.
Fiction: Adventure, horror, science fiction, and "beautiful women having exciting adventures. Scripts are broken down into comic book format-pages, panels and balloons. Stories should stand alone but be suitable for follow from issue to issue." Buys 36 mss/year. Send complete ms. Pays $25/page of art.

Military

Technical and semitechnical publications for military commanders, personnel and planners, as well as those for military families and civilians interested in Armed Forces activities are listed here. All of these publications require submissions emphasizing military subjects or aspects of military life.

AIR UNIVERSITY REVIEW, United States Air Force, Air University, Bldg. 1211, Maxwell Air Force Base AL 36112. (205)293-2773. Editor: Lt. Col., USAF. Professional military journal for military supervisory staff, command leadership personnel and top level civilians. Circ. 20,000. Not copyrighted. Byline given. Buys no mss, but gives cash awards on publication. Reports in 6 weeks. Query.
Nonfiction: "Serves as an open forum for exploratory discussion. Purpose is to present innovative thinking and stimulate dialogue concerning Air Force doctrine, strategy, tactics, and related national defense matters. Footnotes as needed. Prefer the author to be the expert. Reviews of defense-related books. Expository style." Length: 1,500-3,500 words. Cash awards up to $150.
Photos: B&w glossy prints or charts to supplement articles are desired.
Tips: "We look for clear, concise writing."

ARMED FORCES JOURNAL, 1414 22nd St. NW, Washington DC 20037. Editor: Benjamin F. Schemmer. For "senior career officers of the US military, defense industry, Congressmen and government officials interested in defense matters, international military and defense industry." Monthly. Circ.25,000. Buys all rights. Buys 10-20 mss/year. Pays on publication. Sample copy $2.75. Photocopied submissions OK. Reports in 1 month. Submit complete ms. SASE.
Nonfiction: Publishes "national and international defense issues: weapons programs, research, personnel programs, international relations (with emphasis on defense aspect). We do not want broad overviews of a general subject; more interested in detailed analysis of a specific program or international defense issue. Our readers are decision-makers in defense matters—hence, subject should not be treated too simplistically. Be provocative. We are not afraid to take issue with our own constituency when an independent voice needs to be heard." Buys informational, profile and think pieces. No poetry or biographies. Length: 1,000-3,000 words. Pays $50-100/page.

ARMY MAGAZINE, 2425 Wilson Blvd., Arlington VA 22201. (703)841-4300. Editor-in-Chief: L. James Binder. Managing Editor: Poppy Walker. Emphasizes military interests. Monthly magazine. Circ. 121,000. Pays on publication. Buys all rights. Byline given except for back-up research. Submit seasonal/holiday material 3 months in advance of issue date. Photocopied submissions OK. SASE. Free sample copy and writer's guidelines.
Nonfiction: Historical (military and original); humor (military feature-length articles and anecdotes); interview; new product; nostalgia; personal experience; photo feature; profile; and technical. No rehashed history. "We would like to see more pieces about interesting military personalities. We especially want material lending itself to heavy, contributor-supplied photographic treatment. The first thing a contributor should recognize is that our readership is very savvy militarily. 'Gee-whiz' personal reminiscences get short shrift, unless they hold their own in a company in which long military service, heroism and unusual experiences are commonplace. At the same time, Army readers like a well-written story with a fresh slant, whether it is about an experience in a foxhole or the fortunes of a corps in battle." Buys 12 mss/issue. Submit complete ms. Length: 4,000 words. Pays 8-12¢/word.
Photos: Submit photo material with accompanying ms. Pays $15-50 for 8x10 b&w glossy prints;

$25-150 for 8x10 color glossy prints or 2¼x2¼ color transparencies, but will accept 35mm. Captions preferred. Buys all rights.

Columns/Departments: Military news; books, comment (*New Yorker*-type "Talk of the Town" items). Buys 8/issue. Submit complete ms. Length: 1,000 words. Pays $30-100.

ASIA-PACIFIC DEFENSE FORUM, Commander-in-Chief, Pacific Command (US Military), Editor, CINCPAC Staff, Box 13, Camp H. M. Smith HI 96861. (808)477-6128. Executive Editor: Lt. Col. Fred W. Walker. Editor: Phillip P. Katz. Managing Editor: Lt. Col. Soot M. Jew. For military officers in Pacific and Indian Ocean regions; all services—Army, Navy and Air Force. Secondary audience—government officials, business and industry personnel and academicians concerned with defense issues. "We seek to enhance international professional dialogue on training, force employment, leadership, strategy and tactics, policy matters and international exchange and cooperation." Quarterly magazine. Circ. 32,000. Pays on acceptance. Buys simultaneous, second serial (reprint) or one-time rights. Byline given. Phone queries OK. Simultaneous, photocopied and previously published submissions OK. SASE. Reports in 3 weeks on queries; in 10 weeks on mss. Free sample copy and writer's guidelines.

Nonfiction: General interest (strategy and tactics, descriptions of type forces and weapons systems, strategic balance and security issues); historical (occasionally used, if relation to present-day defense issues is apparent); how-to (training, leadership, force employment procedures, organization); interview and personal experience (in terms of developing professional military skills). "We do not want highly technical weapons/equipment descriptions or controversial policy and budget matters, nor do we seek discussion of in-house problem areas. We do not deal with military social life, base activities or PR-type personalities/job descriptions." Buys 1-2 mss/issue. Query or send complete ms. Length: 1,000-4,000 words. Pays $25-100.

Photos: State availability of photos with ms. "We provide nearly all photos; however, will consider good quality photos with mss." Uses 5x7 or 8x10 b&w glossy prints or 35mm color transparencies. Offers no additional payment for photos accompanying mss. Buys one-time rights. Captions required.

Tips: "Develop a 'feel' for our foreign audience orientation and provide material that is truly audience-oriented in our view."

AT EASE, Division of Home Missions, Assemblies of God, 1445 Boonville Ave., Springfield MO 65802. Editor: T. E. Gannon. Managing Editor: Ruby M. Enyart. For military personnel. Bimonthly magazine. Circ. 15,000. Buys all rights. "We are quite limited in what we would accept from freelance writers. Everything has to be slanted to Assemblies of God readers." Pays on publication. Free sample copy and writer's guidelines. "If we can't use a submission and we think another department can, we usually let them see it before replying. Otherwise, as soon as we reject it, we return it." Query first. SASE.

Nonfiction and Photos: Materials that will interest military men and women. Must have religious value. Length: 500 to 800 words. Pays minimum of 1½¢ a word.

Tips: "Give a clear statement of background faith in your query. Military experience helpful."

INFANTRY, Box 2005, Fort Benning GA 31905. (404)545-2350. Editor: LTC Edward C. Smith. Published primarily for combat arms officers and noncommissioned officers. Bimonthly magazine. Estab. 1921. Circ. 25,000. Not copyrighted. Pays on publication. Payment cannot be made to US employees. Free sample copy and writer's guidelines. Reports in 1 month.

Nonfiction: Interested in current information on US military organization, weapons, equipment, tactics and techniques; foreign armies and their equipment; lessons learned from combat experience, both past and present; solutions to problems encountered in the active Army and the Reserve components. Departments include Letters, Features and Forum, Training Notes, Book Reviews. Length of articles: 1,500-3,500 words. Length for Book Reviews: 500-1,000 words. Query. Accepts 75 mss/year.

Photos: Used with mss.

Tips: Start with letters to editor, book reviews to break in.

LADYCOM, Downey Communications, Inc., 1800 M St. NW, Suite 650 S., Washington DC 20036. Editor: Sheila Gibbons. For wives of military men who live in the US or overseas. Published eight times a year. Magazine. Circ. 450,000. Pays on publication. Buys first North American serial rights. Submit seasonal/holiday material 4 months in advance. SASE. Reports in 3 weeks. Sample copy 75¢ and writer's guidelines.

Nonfiction: All articles must have special interest for military wives. "No general interest articles or articles on moving from one home to another." How-to (crafts, food), humor, interview, personal experience, personal opinion, profile and travel. Buys 10-12 mss/issue. Query "letter should name sources, describe focus of article, use a few sample quotes from sources, indicate length, and should describe writer's own qualifications for doing the piece." Length: 800-2,000 words. Pays $35-500/article.

Photos: Purchased with accompanying ms and on assignment. Uses 5x7 or 8x10 b&w glossy prints; 35mm or larger color transparencies; modest additional payment for photo with accompanying ms. Captions and model releases are required. Query Claudia Burwell, Design Director.

Columns/Departments: "It Seems to Me"—personal experience pieces by military wives. Travel Column—highlights of life at various bases and posts. Query. Length: 1,100-1,800 words. Rates vary.

Fiction: Mystery, romance and suspense. "Military themes only, please!" Buys 3-4 mss/year. Query. Length: 1,500-2,500 words. Pays $100-250.

Tips: "Our ideal contributor is a military wife who can write. However, I'm always impressed by a writer who has analyzed the market and can suggest some possible new angles for us. Sensitivity to military issues is a must for our contributors, as is the ability to write good personality profiles and/or do thorough research about military life."

LEATHERNECK, Box 1775, Quantico VA 22134. (703)640-3171. Editor: Ronald D. Lyons. Managing Editor: Tom Bartlett. 10% freelance written. Emphasizes all phases of Marine Corps activities. Monthly magazine. Circ. 70,000. Pays on acceptance. Buys all rights. Phone queries OK. Submit seasonal/holiday material 3 months in advance of issue date. SASE. Reports in 2 weeks. Free sample copy and writer's guidelines.

Nonfiction: "All material submitted to *Leatherneck* must pertain to the U.S. Marine Corps and its members." General interest; how-to; humor; historical; interview; nostalgia; personal experience; profile; and travel. No articles on politics, subjects not pertaining to the Marine Corps, and subjects that are not in good taste. Buys 24 mss/year. Query. Length: 1,500-3,000 words. Pays $50 and up per magazine page.

Photos: "We like to receive a complete package when we consider a manuscript for publication." State availability of photos with query. No additional payment for 4x5 or 8x10 b&w glossy prints. Captions required. Buys all rights. Model release required.

Fiction: Adventure; historical; and humorous. All material must pertain to the U.S. Marine Corps and its members. Buys 3 mss/year. Query. Length: 1,000-3,000 words. Pays $50 and up per magazine page.

Poetry: Free verse; light verse; and traditional. No poetry that does not pertain to the U.S. Marine Corps. Buys 40 mss/year. Length: 12 lines. Pays $10-20.

MARINE CORPS GAZETTE, Marine Corps Association, Box 1775, MCB, Quantico VA 22134. Editor: Col. John E. Greenwood. U.S.M.C. (Ret.). May issue is aviation-oriented. November issue is historically-oriented. Monthly. Circ. 28,500. Buys first rights. Buys 170-200 mss/year. Pays on publication. Free sample copy and writer's guidelines. Submit seasonal or special material at least 3 months in advance. Query with outline of idea in detail. Reports in 2 months. SASE.

Nonfiction: Uses articles up to 5,000 words pertaining to the military profession. Does not want copy advocating political positions. Wants practical articles on military subjects, especially amphibious warfare, close air support and helicopter-borne assault. Also uses any practical article on artillery, communications, leadership, etc. Particularly wanted are articles on combined arms tactics, personnel management, in-depth coverage of problem areas of the world, foreign military strategy and tactics. Also historical articles about Marines are always needed for the November issue, the anniversary of the Marine Corps. In addition, seeks news stories up to 500 words about US military, particularly Navy/Marine Corps. All offerings are passed on by an editorial board as well as by the editor. *Gazette* is a professional magazine for Marine Corps officers and cannot use "Sunday supplement" or "gee whiz" material. Pays 3-6¢/word.

Photos: Purchased with mss. Pays $5 each. 8x10 or 5x7 glossy prints preferred.

Tips: "We require strong Marine Corps background or equivalent or related military experience, and factual, professional material."

THE MILITARY ENGINEER, 607 Prince St., Alexandria VA 22314. (703)549-3800. Editor: John J. Kern. Bimonthly magazine. Circ. 22,000. Pays on publication. Buys all rights. Byline given. Phone queries OK. SASE. Reports in 1 month. Sample copy and writer's guidelines $4.

Nonfiction: Well-written and illustrated semi-technical articles by experts and practitioners of civil and military engineering, constructors, equipment manufacturers, defense contract suppliers and architect/engineers on these subjects and on subjects of military biography and history. "Subject matter should represent a contribution to the fund of knowledge, concern a new project or method, be on R&D in these fields; investigate planning and management techniques or problems in these fields, or be of militarily strategic nature." Buys 40-50 mss/year. Length: 1,000-2,500 words. Query.

Photos: Mss must be accompanied by 6-8 well-captioned photos, maps or illustrations; b&w, generally. Pays approximately $25/page.

MILITARY LIVING, Box 4010, Arlington VA 22204. (703)521-7703. Editor: Ann Crawford. For military personnel and their families. Monthly. Circ. 30,000. Buys first serial rights. "Very few freelance features used last year; mostly staff-written." Pays on publication. Sample copy for 50¢ in coin or stamps. "Slow to report due to small staff and workload." Submit complete ms. SASE.
Nonfiction: "Articles on military life in greater Washington DC area. We would especially like recreational features in the Washington DC area. We specialize in passing along morale-boosting information about the military installations in the area, with emphasis on the military family—travel pieces about surrounding area, recreation information, etc. We do not want to see depressing pieces, pieces without the military family in mind, personal petty complaints or general information pieces. Prefer 700 words or less, but will consider more for an exceptional feature. We also prefer a finished article rather than a query." Payment is on an honorarium basis, 1-1½¢/word.
Photos: Photos purchased with mss. 8x10 b&w glossy prints. Payment is $5 for original photos by author.

MILITARY LIVING R&R REPORT, Box 4010, Arlington VA 22204. Publisher: Ann Crawford. For "military consumers worldwide." Bimonthly newsletter. "Please state when sending submission that it is for the *R&R Report Newsletter* so as not to confuse it with our monthly magazine which has different requirements." Buys first rights, but will consider other rights. Pays on publication. Sample copy $1. SASE.
Nonfiction: "We use information on little-known military facilities and privileges, discounts around the world and travel information. Items must be short and concise. Stringers wanted around the world. Payment is on an honorarium basis. 1-1½¢/word."

MILITARY REVIEW, US Army Command and General Staff College, Fort Leavenworth KS 66027. (913)684-5642. Editor-in-Chief: Col. John D. Bloom. Managing Editor: Lt. Col. Dallas Van Hoose, Jr. Business Manager: Lt. Stephen M. Weicht. Emphasizes the military for senior military officers, students and scholars. Monthly magazine. Circ. 24,000. Pays on publication. Buys one-time rights. Byline given. Phone queries OK. Photocopied submissions OK. SASE. Reports in 1 month. Free writer's guidelines.
Nonfiction: Historical, humor, informational, new product, opinion and technical. Buys 8-10 mss/issue. Query. Length: 2,000-4,000 words. Pays $25-100.

NATIONAL DEFENSE, 1700 N. Moore St., Suite 900, Arlington VA 22209. (703)522-1826. Editor: D. Ballou. For members of industry and U.S. Armed Forces. Publication of the American Defense Preparedness Association. Monthly magazine. Circ. 34,000. Buys all rights. Pays 100% kill fee. Byline given. Buys 12-18 mss a year. Pays on publication. Sample copy $4; free writer's guidelines. Photocopied submissions OK. No simultaneous submissions. Reports in 1 month. Query or submit complete ms. SASE.
Nonfiction: Military-related articles: weapons, systems, management and production. "We emphasize industrial preparedness for defense and prefer a news style, with emphasis on the 'why.' " Length: 1,500-2,500 words. Pays $25/published page. Book reviews are sometimes used, but query is required first and no payment is made.

NATIONAL GUARD, (formerly the *National Guardsman*), 1 Massachusetts Ave. NW, Washington DC 20001. (202)789-0031. Editor: Raymond E. Bell Jr. For officers of the Army and Air National Guard. Monthly. Circ. 62,000. Rights negotiable. Byline given. Buys 10-12 mss/year. Pays on acceptance. Query. SASE.
Nonfiction: Military policy, strategy, training, equipment, logistics, personnel policies: tactics, combat lessons learned as they pertain to the Army and Air Force (and impact on Army National Guard and Air National Guard). Material must be strictly accurate from a technical standpoint. Does not publish expos´es, cartoons or jokes. Length: 2,000-3,000 words. Payment ($75-300/article) depends on originality, amount of research involved, etc.
Photos: Photography pertinent to subject matter should accompany ms.

OFF DUTY, US: 3303 Harbor Blvd., Suite C-2, Costa Mesa CA 92626. Editor: Bruce Thorstad; Europe: Eschersheimer Landstrasse 69, Frankfurt/M, West Germany. Editor: Robert Burns; Pacific: Box 9869, Hong Kong. Editor: Jim Shaw. Monthly magazine for US military personnel and their families stationed around the world. Most readers 18-35 year old. Combined circ. 550,000. Buys first serial or second serial rights. Pays on acceptance. Free sample copy and writer's guidelines.

Nonfiction: Three editions—American, Pacific and European. "Emphasis is on off duty travel, leisure, military shopping, wining and dining, sports, hobbies, music, and getting the most out of military life. Overseas editions lean toward foreign travel and living in foreign cultures. Also emphasize what's going on back home. In travel articles we like anecdotes, lots of description, color and dialogue. American edition uses more American trends and how-to/service material. Material with special US, Pacific or European slant should be sent to appropriate address above; material useful in all editions may be sent to US address and will be forwarded to our Hong Kong editorial headquarters." Buys 12-15 mss/issue for each of three editions. Query. Length: 1,500 words average. Also needs 500-word shorties. Pays 10¢/word for use in one edition; 13¢/word for use in 2 or more.

Photos: Bought with or without accompanying ms. Pays $25 for b&w glossy prints; $50 for color transparencies; $100 for full page color; $200 for covers. "Covers must be vertical format, 35mm at minimum; larger format transparencies preferred. We don't get enough good ms/photo packages."

Tips: "We get far too many tales of personal experiences that are neither very typical nor highly unusual. All our military readers are to some extent in the same boat, but they need to relate their experiences in a way that helps the average reader get through the same situations (as: being sent overseas for the first time, for instance). We aren't hard to write for once the writer adjusts to our special audience, an audience which has circumstances, rather than interests, in common, for the most part."

OVERSEAS LIFE, Postfach 29, 6382 Friedrichsdorf 2, West Germany. Managing Editor: James Kitfield. General entertainment magazine serving American and Canadian military personnel stationed throughout Europe. Specifically directed to males 18-35. Monthly magazine. Circ. 82,000. Pays on publication. Buys rights to military communities in Europe. Submit seasonal/holiday material 4 months in advance of issue date. Simultaneous and previously published submissions OK. SAE and International Reply Coupons (not US postage). Sample copy for 1 International Reply Coupon.

Nonfiction: "We are a slick commercial giveaway magazine looking for flashy, sexy, young-male-interest writing and photography. In the past we've bought how-to (travel by bike, van, foot, motorcycle; how to photograph women, rock stars, traveling subjects); interview and profile articles on music and sport celebrities; and do-it-yourself-sports (skiing, kayaking, sailing, soccer, tennis). Also need some music features—rock, soul, C&W, especially on musicians soon coming to Europe. We're looking for a new kind of travel article: the 'in scenes' of Europe written up especially for our young GIs. Should include nightlife, discos, bars, informal eating out, good music scenes, rather than fancy restaurants, cathedrals, or museums. Above all, tell our servicemen where the girls are. Query with a good idea that has not been worked to death, and give a lead paragraph that indicates the style and angle to be adopted, backed by a brief outline of where the article will go. All articles must be pertinent to someone living and working in Europe, or with a slant that is neutral—i.e; profile on celebrity." Buys 80 mss/year. "Writer should be able to deliver a complete package (which means he or she has a means to find photos and any other additional info pertinent to the article) on time." Length: 800-1,500 words. Pays 10¢/word.

Photos: Purchased with accompanying ms. Captions required. Pays $20 for b&w; $35 minimum for color and $150 for covers.

Tips: "Interesting travel stories with anecdotes are a good vehicle to break in, as are profiles of Americans making their mark in Europe. We are willing to consider any material that puts a premium on good, brisk and whenever possible, humorous, writing, that is written with our audience in mind."

PARAMETERS: JOURNAL OF THE U.S. ARMY WAR COLLEGE, U.S. Army War College, Carlisle Barracks PA 17013. (717)245-4943. Editor: Col. Lloyd J. Matthews, U.S. Army. Readership consists of senior leadership of U.S. defense establishment, both uniformed and civilian, plus members of the media, government, industry and academe interested in scholarly articles devoted to national and international security affairs, military strategy, military leadership and management, art and science of warfare, and military history (provided it has contemporary relevance). Most readers possess graduate degree. Quarterly. Circ. 8,500. Not copyrighted; unless copyrighted by author, articles may be reprinted with appropriate credits. Byline given. Pays on publication. Reports in 6 weeks.

Nonfiction: Articles preferred that deal with current security issues, employ critical analysis, and provide solutions or recommendations. Liveliness and verve, consistent with scholarly integrity, appreciated. Theses, studies, and academic course papers should be adapted to article form prior to submission. Documentation in endnotes. Submit complete ms. Length: 5,000 words or less, preferably less. Pays $50 minimum; $100 average (including glossy prints and other visuals).

Photos: Purchased with ms.

Tips: "Research should be thorough; documentation should be complete."

PERIODICAL, Council on Abandoned Military Posts, 4970 N. Camino Antonio, Tucson AZ 85718. Editor-in-Chief: Dan L. Thrapp. Emphasizes old and abandoned forts, posts and military installations; military subjects for a professional, knowledgeable readership interested in onetime defense sites or other military installations. Quarterly magazine. Circ. 1,500. Pays on publication. Buys one-time rights. Simultaneous, photocopied and previously published (if published a long time ago) submissions OK. SASE. Reports in 3 weeks.
Nonfiction: Historical; personal experience; photo feature; technical (relating to posts, their construction/operation and military matters); and travel. Buys 4-6 mss/issue. Query or send complete ms. Length: 300-4,000 words. Pays minimum $2/page.
Photos: Purchased with or without accompanying ms. Captions required. Query. Glossy, single-weight, b&w up to 8x10. Offers no additional payment for photos accepted with accompanying ms.

THE RETIRED OFFICER MAGAZINE, 201 N. Washington St., Alexandria VA 22314. (703)549-2311. Editor: Colonel Minter L. Wilson Jr., USA-Ret. For "officers of the 7 uniformed services and their families." Monthly. Circ. 300,000. May buy all rights or first serial rights. Byline given. Pays on publication. Free sample copy and editorial requirements sheet. Photocopied submissions OK "if clean and fresh." Submit seasonal material (holiday stories in which the Armed Services are depicted) at least 4 months in advance. Reports on material accepted for publication within 6 weeks. Submit complete ms. SASE.
Nonfiction: History, humor, cultural, travel, second-career opportunities and current affairs. "Current topical subjects with particular contextual slant to the military; historical events of military significance; features pertinent to a retired military officer's milieu (second career, caveats in the business world/wives' adjusting, leisure, fascinating hobbies). True military experiences are also useful, and we tend to use articles less technical than a single-service publication might publish." Length: 1,000-2,500 words. Pays $50-300.
Photos: 8x10 b&w photos (normal halftone). Pays $10. Color photos must be suitable for color separation. Pays $50 if reproduced in color; otherwise, same as b&w. Associate editor: Marjorie J. Seng.

RUSI JOURNAL, Royal United Services Institute for Defence Studies, Whitehall SW1A 2ET, England. Editor: Jenny Shaw. Emphasizes defense and military history. Quarterly magazine. For the defense community: service officers, civil servants, politicians, academics, industrialists, etc. Circ. 6,500. Pays on publication. Buys all rights. Photocopied submissions OK. SAE and International Reply Coupons. Sample copy $8.50.
Nonfiction: Learned articles on British and US defense; historical military articles with particular reference to current defense problems; weapon technology; international relations and civil/military relations. Buys 10/issue. Query. Length: 2,500-6,000 words. Pays 12.50 pounds/printed page.
Photos: No additional payment is made for photos, but they should accompany articles whenever possible.

SEA POWER, 818 18th St. NW, Washington DC 20006. Editor: James D. Hessman. Issued monthly by the Navy League of the US for naval personnel and civilians interested in naval maritime and defense matters. Buys all rights. Pays on publication. Will send free sample copy to a writer on request. Reports in 6 weeks. Query first. SASE.
Nonfiction: Factual articles on sea power in general, and the US Navy, the US Marine Corps, US Coast Guard, US merchant marine and naval services and other navies of the world in particular. Should illustrate and expound the importance of the seas and sea power to the US and its allies. Wants timely, clear, nontechnical, lively writing. Length: 500-2,000 words. No historical articles, commentaries, critiques, abstract theories, poetry or editorials. Pays $50-300, depending upon length and research involved.
Photos: Purchased with ms.

SERGEANTS, Air Force Sergeants Association, Box 31050, Washington DC 20031. (301)899-3500. Editor: Karen Thuermer. Monthly magazine for the "air force enlisted (retired, active duty, reserve and guard). Features on all aspects of the Air Force and legislation affecting it." Circ. 140,000. Pays on publication. Byline given. Makes work-for-hire assignments. Submit seasonal/holiday material 2 months in advance. Simultaneous queries, and simultaneous, photocopied, and previously published submissions OK. Reports in 1 week on queries; 1 month on mss. Free sample copy and writer's guidelines.
Nonfiction: Historical/nostalgic (war stories in Air Force involvement enlisted Air Force personnel); interview/profile (of Air Force enlisted people in high positions); personal experience (accounts of interesting Air Force experiences); technical (advances in Air Force technology); and

travel (what to see and do in and around Air Force bases). No "opinion pieces on legislation or government." Buys 24 mss/year. Query with clips of published work. Length: 500-3,000 words. Pays $50/printed page.

Photos: Send photos with ms. Pays $25-250 for color transparencies; $25-50 for b&w prints. Captions, model releases and identification of subjects required. Buys one-time rights.

THE TIMES MAGAZINE, Army Times Publishing Company, 475 School St., SW, Washington, DC 20024. (202)554-7170. Editor: Marianne Lester. Managing Editor: Barry Robinson. Monthly magazine covering current lifestyles and problems of career military families around the world. Circ. 330,000. Pays on publication. Byline given. Offers negotiable kill fee. Buys all rights. Submit seasonal/holiday material 6 months in advance. SASE. Reports in 1 month. Sample copy and writer's guidelines free for SAE.

Nonfiction: Expose (current military); how-to (military wives); interview/profile (military); opinion (military topic); personal experience (military only); travel (of military interest). No poetry or historical articles. Buys 100 mss/year. Query with clips of published work. Length: 1,000-3,000 words. Pays $50-300.

Photos: State availability of photos or send photos with ms. Reviews 35mm color contact sheets and prints. Caption, model releases, and identification of subjects required. Buys all rights.

Tips: "In query write a detailed description of story and how it will be told. A tentative lead is nice. Just one good story 'breaks in' a freelancer."

US NAVAL INSTITUTE PROCEEDINGS, Annapolis MD 21402. (301)268-6110. Editor-in-Chief: Clayton R. Barrow Jr. Senior Editor: Paul Stillwell; Managing Editor: Fred Rainbow. Emphasizes sea services (Navy, Marine Corps, Coast Guard) for sea services officers and enlisted personnel, other military services in the US and abroad, and civilians interested in naval/maritime affairs. Monthly magazine. Circ. 73,000. Pays on acceptance. Buys all rights. Byline given. Phone queries OK, but all material must be submitted on speculation. Submit seasonal/anniversary material at least 6 months in advance. Photocopied submissions OK. SASE. Reports in 2 weeks (queries); 3 months (manuscripts). Free sample copy.

Nonfiction: Informational, analytical, historical (based on primary sources, unpublished and/or first-hand experience); humor; personal opinion; photo feature; technical; professional notes; and book reviews. Query. Length: 4,000 words maximum. Pays $200-400.

Photos: Purchased with or without accompanying ms or on assignment. Captions required. Query. Pays $15 maximum for b&w 8x10 glossy prints. "We pay $2 for each photo submitted with articles by people other than the photographer."

Columns/Departments: Fred Rainbow, managing editor. Comment and discussion (comments 500-700 words on new subjects or ones previously covered in magazine); Professional Notes; Nobody Asked Me, But . . . (700-1,000 words, strong opinion on naval/maritime topic); and Book Reviews. Buys 35 Book Reviews; 35 Professional Notes; 100 Comment and Discussion and 10 NAMB columns a year. Pays $25-50.

Fillers: Miss Nancy B. Smith, fillers editor. Anecdotes should be humorous actual occurrences, not previously published. Buys 25 fillers/year. Length: maximum 200 words. Pays $25 flat rate.

Tips: "The Comment and Discussion section is our bread and butter. It is a glorified letters to the editor section and exemplifies the concept of the *Proceedings* as a forum. We particularly welcome comments on material published in previous issues of the magazine. This offers the writer of the comment an opportunity to expand the discussion of a particular topic and to bring his own viewpoint into it. This feature does not pay particularly well, but it is an excellent opportunity to get one's work into print. Magazine is geared in large part to personnel of sea services so they are often in best position as result of their work to be knowledgeable as authors. Complete outsiders have less chance of breaking in."

Miscellaneous

AERO SUN-TIMES, Grassroots Renewable Energy, Alternative Energy Resources Organization (AERO), 424 Stapleton Bldg., Billings MT 59101. (406)259-1958. Editor: Wilbur Wood. Monthly magazine covering alternative energy and renewable resources for members of *AERO*, a nonprofit public interest group that gathers and disseminates information on renewable energy, laws, projects, conservation ideas, etc. "Our primary focus is Montana, but we use a great deal of material from other regions also." Circ. 1,100. Pays on publication. Byline given. Buys first North American serial rights. Submit seasonal/holiday material 2-4 months in advance. Simultaneous queries, simultaneous, photocopied, and previously published submissions OK. SASE. Reports in 3-5 weeks. Sample copy $1.

Nonfiction: How-to (on conservation and alternative energy projects such as retrofits on existing structures); interview/profile (of interesting people in solar and alternative energy); new product; personal experience; technical; and book reviews, on query. "This is the section that is most accessible to freelancers. We're most interested in articles on alternative energy that are of special interest to residents of the northern US and Canada. There is a trend toward homeowner and community-oriented articles." Buys 5-10 mss/year. Query or send complete ms. Length: 200-2,500 words. Pays $10-50 article "if monetary payment is arranged. Often we pay with a subscription to our magazine, particularly for short articles or poems."

Photos: State availability of photos or send photos with ms. Pays $4-8 for 3x5 or 8x10 b&w prints. Captions required. Buys one-time rights.

Fiction: Fantasy (relating to energy or environmental themes).

Poetry: Avant-garde, free verse, haiku, light verse, traditional. "We'll consider any kind of poem. We're very eclectic as long as the theme is, in general, related to energy or environmental concerns." Buys 10-15 mss/year. "Generally, payment is with a subscription."

ALTERNATIVE SOURCES OF ENERGY MAGAZINE, 107 S. Central Ave., Milaca MN 56353. Executive Editor: Donald Marier. Emphasizes alternative energy sources and the exploration and innovative use of renewable energy sources. Audience is predominantly male, age 36, college educated and concerned about energy and environmental limitations. Bimonthly magazine. Circ. 23,000. Pays on acceptance. Phone queries OK. Simultaneous, photocopied, and previously published submissions OK, "if specified at time of submission." SASE. Reports in 6 weeks. Sample copy $2.95.

Nonfiction: Larry Stoiaken, editor. How-to (plans, kits); informational (new sources of data, products); interview (any active person in field); and technical (plans, kits, designs). "We're especially interested in wind and hydro-power stories. A story (with photo support) detailing installation of low-head hydro or wind-generator with follow-up on the energy produced is higher on our readership survey than most topics." Submit an outline before complete ms. Length: 500-3,000 words. Pays 5¢/word.

Photos: Pays $7.50, prefers b&w.

Tips: "We need well-researched articles emphasizing the practical application of alternative sources of energy: solar, water, wind, biofuels, etc. Always include addresses of all products and/or publications listed. Stay away from philosophical underpinnings; stick to how-to-do-it or rules of thumb."

AMERICAN DANE MAGAZINE, Danish Brotherhood in America, Box 31748, Omaha NE 68131. (402)341-5049. Administrative Editor: Howard Christensen. Submit only material with Danish ethnic flavor. Monthly magazine. Circ. 11,000. Pays on publication. Buys all rights. Submit seasonal/holiday material 4 months in advance (particularly Christmas). Photocopied or previously published submissions OK. SASE. Byline given. Reports in 1 month. Sample copy $1. Free writer's guidelines.

Nonfiction: Historical; humor (satirical, dry wit notoriously Danish); informational (Danish items, Denmark or Danish-American involvements); inspirational (honest inter-relationships); interview; nostalgia; personal experience; photo feature and travel. Buys 20-25 mss/year. Query. Length: 1,500 words maximum. Pays $25-50.

Photos: Purchased on assignment. Query. Pays $10-25 for b&w. Total purchase price for ms includes payment for photos. Model release required.

Fiction: Danish adventure, historical, humorous, mystery, romance and suspense. Must have Danish appeal. Buys 12 mss/year. Query. Length: 500-1,500 words. Pays $25-50.

Fillers: Danish clippings, jokes, gags, anecdotes, puzzles (crossword, anagrams etc.) and short humor. Query. Length: 50-300 words.

ARARAT, The Armenian General Benevolent Union of America, 585 Saddle River Rd., Saddle Brook NJ 07662. Editor-in-Chief: Leo Hamalian. Emphasizes Armenian life and culture for Americans of Armenian descent and Armenian immigrants. "Most are well-educated; some are Old World." Quarterly magazine. Circ. 2,400. Pays on publication. Buys first North American serial rights. Submit seasonal/holiday material at least 3 months in advance. Photocopied and previously published submissions OK. SASE. Reports in 6 weeks. Sample copy $2.50.

Nonfiction: Historical (history of Armenian people, of leaders, etc.); interviews (with prominent or interesting Armenians in any field, but articles are preferred); profile (on subjects relating to Armenian life and culture); personal experience (revealing aspects of typical Armenian life); travel (in Armenia and Armenian communities throughout the world and the US). Buys 3 mss/issue. Query. Length: 1,000-6,000 words. Pays $25-100.

Columns/Departments: Reviews of books by Armenians or relating to Armenians. Buys 6/issue. Query. Pays $25. Open to suggestions for new columns/departments.
Fiction: Any stories dealing with Armenian life in America or in the old country. Buys 4 mss/year. Query. Length: 2,000-5,000 words. Pays $35-75.
Poetry: Any verse that is Armenian in theme. Buys 6/issue. Pays $10.
Tips: "Read the magazine, and write about the kind of subjects we are obviously interested in, e.g., Kirlian photography, Aram Avakian's films, etc. Remember that we have become almost totally ethnic in subject matter, but we want articles that present the Armenian to the rest of the world in an interesting way."

ASIA, A Magazine for American Readers, The Asia Society, Inc., 725 Park Ave., New York NY 10021. (212)288-6400. Editor: Joan Ogden Freseman. Managing Editor: Corinne Hoexter. Bimonthly magazine for "Americans interested in the background of Asian current events. *Asia* views current problems against the backdrop of traditional Asian cultures and folkways and the beauty of a great art heritage." Circ. 30,000. Pays on acceptance. Byline given. Pays variable kill fee. Buys all rights; "writer may request rights returned." Submit seasonal/holiday material 6 months in advance. Interested in first time rights on book mss. Reports in 1 month. Sample copy $3.50; writer's guidelines for business size SAE and 1 first class stamp.
Nonfiction: "We're looking for articles on business, economic and political topics; Asians in America; exploring Asia; and extremely unusual travel articles." Buys 50 mss/year. Query with clips of published work. Length: 2,500-3,500 words. Pays $300 minimum.
Photos: "We have very high standards for photos." State availability of photos. Pays $75 minimum for 35mm color transparencies; $45 minimum for 8x10 glossy prints. Captions required. Buys one-time rights.
Fiction: "We're looking for translations by Americans of Asian literature—short stories and novel excerpts. Writers should have lived in Asia or studied at length an aspect of Asia."

ATTENZIONE, Paulucci Publications, Inc., 10 E. 49th St., New York NY 10017. Editor: Donald Dewey. Senior Editors: Gwenda Blair, Stephen Hall, and Joseph Mancini. Monthly magazine emphasizing Italian-Americans for people who have an interest "in Italy and Italian-Americans, in their political, social and economic endeavors. We are a general interest magazine for a special interest group". Estab. 1979. Circ. 165,000. Pays 2 months after acceptance of article. Buys first North American serial rights. Submit seasonal material 5 months in advance. SASE. Reports in 1 month on queries.
Nonfiction: Expose; general interest; historical (relating to something of current interest); humor; interview; profile; and travel (1 issue/year devoted extensively to travel in Italy). Buys 11 mss/issue. Query. Length: 1,500-3,000 words. Pays $500-750.
Fiction: "All fiction submissions must have an Italian or Italian-American theme." Buys 6 mss/year. Send complete ms. Length: 3,000 words maximum. Pays $350 maximum.

A BETTER LIFE FOR YOU, The National Research Bureau, Inc., 424 N. 3rd St., Burlington IA 52601. (319)752-5415. Editor-in-Chief: B. Beck. Editor: M. Cuppy. For industrial workers of all ages. Quarterly magazine. Circ. 30,000. Pays on publication. Buys all rights. Previously published submissions OK. SASE. Reports in 3 weeks. Free sample copy and writer's guidelines.
Nonfiction: General interest (steps to better health, on the job attitudes); how-to (perform better on the job, do home repair jobs, and keep up maintenance on a car). Buys 4-5 mss/issue. Query or send outline. Length: 400-600 words. Pays $20 minimum.

CAMPAIGN, Lowry Enterprises, Box 896, Fallbrook CA 92028. Editor: Don Lowry. Emphasizes wargaming and military history. Bimonthly magazine. Circ. 2,200. Pays on publication. Buys all rights. Byline given. Photocopied and previously published submissions OK but must be identified as such. SASE. Reports in 3 weeks queries; in 2 months on mss. Sample copy $2.60; free writer's guidelines.
Nonfiction: Historical (military); how-to (create a game, play well, design game); interview (with game designer, publisher); new products (reviews); personal experiences (description of game played to illustrate strategy); personal opinion (on game reviews); and photo feature (new games, coventions). Buys 4-6 mss/issue. Query or send complete ms. Pays $6/printed page.
Photos: State availability of photos or send photos with ms. Pays $6/printed page for b&w glossy prints; and color will be printed as b&w. Captions preferred.
Tips: "A conversational style is best, like a letter to a friend. Prefer to see entire manuscripts."

CLUB LIVING, Club Living Magazine, Inc., 250 Station Plaza, Hartsdale NY 10530. (212)298-1503, (914)472-9191. Editor: Diana Lyons. For private club members. Monthly magazine. Circ. 52,000. Pays on publication. Buys all rights. Byline given. Submit seasonal/holiday material 2 months in advance. Simultaneous and photocopied submissions OK. SASE. Reports in 2 weeks. Sample copy $1.50; free writer's guidelines.

Nonfiction: New products and travel. "*Club Living* concerns private country and city club members and club life. All features must be geared for clubs—that includes travel at exclusive resorts; profiles on prestigious club members; coverage of sport tournaments and social and charity activities; interviews with club chefs; club architecture and renovations; products that are unique, unusually expensive, etc.; financial columns about clubs." Query with clips of published work. Length: 500-1,500 words. Pays $25-125.

Photos: Send photos with ms. Pays $5-50 for b&w contact sheets and prints; $15-75 for color transparencies; no additional payment for photos with accompanying ms. Buys one-time rights. Captions preferred; model releases required.

Columns/Departments: Good Spirits (wine and liquor comment); Bridge (club tournaments, member participation in tournaments); Chef's Choice (special recipes and menus from clubs); Members Speak Out (Members' comments and suggestions); Travel (oriented towards club member interest) and Pro-Scribed (tennis and golf tips). Buys 2/issue. Query. Length: 1,000-1,500 words. Pays $50-100.

Fillers: Intercom: Brief newsbreaks; country club personality news; what's going on at country clubs; future plans; brief sports items of interest to country clubs; and national club policy. Pays $5/printed item.

COUPLES, Playgirl Magazine, 3420 Ocean Park Blvd., Santa Monica CA 90405. (213)450-0900. Editor: Neil Feineman. Quarterly digest magazine covering human relationships for a general audience ("more women than men"), ages 25-40. Estab. 1979. Circ. 250,000. Pays 30 days after acceptance. Byline given. Buys all rights. Submit seasonal/holiday queries 6 months in advance. Simultaneous queries and previously published submissions OK. ("Indicate where and when published.") Reports in 3 weeks. Sample copy $2.95; write to Subscription Department.

Nonfiction: "Articles should appeal to both men and women, and include some aspect of human relationships. Present sexuality in a tasteful manner. A self-help approach is desired." Buys 16 mss/year. Query with clips of published work. Length: 2,000 words minimum. Pays $250 "for first article."

Tips: "I like to keep things as open as possible. All ideas will be considered."

THE DEAF CANADIAN MAGAZINE, Box 1291, Edmonton, Alberta, Canada T5J 2M8. Editor-in-Chief: Roger Carver. For "general consumers who are deaf, parents of deaf children/adults, professionals on deafness, teachers, ministers, and government officials." Monthly magazine. Circ. 141,000. Pays on publication. "Although the publication is copyrighted, we do not purchase any rights which are reserved to the individual contributor." Byline given. Submit seasonal/holiday material 2 months in advance. Simultaneous, photocopied and previously published submissions OK. *Contributions cannot be acknowledged or returned.* Sample copy $2.

Nonfiction: Exposé (education), how-to (skills, jobs, etc.), historical, humor, informational (deafness difficulties), inspirational, interview, new product, personal experience, personal opinion, photo feature (with captions), profile, technical and travel. "Mss must relate to deafness or the deaf world." Buys 1-10 mss/issue. Submit complete ms. Length: 3,000 words maximum. Pays $20-150. "Articles should be illustrated with at least 4 good b&w photos."

Photos: Purchased with accompanying ms or on assignment. Captions required (not less than 15 words). Query. Pays $20 for 2½x3 (preferably) and 5x7 b&w glossy prints; $100 for color transparencies used as cover. Total purchase price for ms includes payment for photos.

Columns/Departments: Here and There, Sports and Recreation, Foreign, Cultural Events and Books. Submit complete ms. Length: 1 page maximum. Pays $50-125. Open to suggestions for new columns/departments.

Fiction: Adventure, experimental, historical, humorous, mystery, mainstream, religious, romance, science fiction, suspense, condensed novels and serialized novels. Buys 1-10 mss/issue. Length: 3,000 words maximum. Pays $50-150.

Fillers: Clippings, jokes, gags, anecdotes, newsbreaks, puzzles and short humor. Must be related to deafness or the deaf world. Buys 1-20 mss/issue. Submit complete ms. Length: 1 page maximum. Pays $1-50.

DELAWARE VALLEY AGENDA, The Magazine for Non-Profit Enterprise, Regional Publications, 1316 Arch St., Philadelphia PA 19107. (215)563-3313. Editor: Gary Brooten. Managing Editor: Arlene Martin. Biweekly tabloid covering nonprofit organizations for education, government, foundations, planning and policy agencies, theatrical and cultural organizations, neighborhood organizations and others. Estab. 1980. Circ. 5,000. Pays on acceptance. Byline given. Buys first North American serial rights. Submit seasonal/holiday material 2 months in advance. Reports in 3 weeks on queries. Free sample copy and writer's guidelines for business size SAE and 1 first class stamp.

Nonfiction: "Three major considerations must be included in each article—money, mission, and people having to do with nonprofit organizations in southeastern Pennsylvania or southern New Jersey. We have an upbeat, newsy style with lots of usable information." Buys 24 long mss/year and 12 short mss/year. Query with outline. Length: 500-2,000 words. Pays $50-350 article.

Photos: State availability of photos. Pays $15-25 for 8x10 glossy prints. Captions and model releases required. Buys one-time rights.

ENCANTO, The Journal of Human Development, El Encanto, 13138 Momtoma Ln, Wilton CA 95693. (916)687-7375. Editor: Burt Liebert. Quarterly magzine covering human development for members of El Encanto, a personal growth center near Sacramento, California; readers are educated, middle income and sophisticated. Estab. 1980. Circ. 1,000. Pays on acceptance. Byline given. Buys all rights, "but will consider reassigning after publication." Submit seasonal/holiday material 6 months in advance. Simultaneous queries and photocopied submissions OK. SASE. Reports in 1 month. Sample copy $1.50; writer's guidelines for 3⅜x6⅝ SAE and 1 first class stamp.

Nonfiction: General interest (on human development or alternative lifestyles); humor; inspirational; interview/profile; opinion; personal experience; photo feature; "education; holistic health; nutrition and natural foods; open/group marriage; human sexuality; community living; ecology; communication skills; social change; spirituality; getting in touch with feelings; dealing with emotions; interpersonal relationships; finding love and companionship; or anything else that relates to finding a free, open, healthy, and fully satisfying life; also, think pieces and vignettes. Factual material, such as information about health and nutrition, should carry some documentation (firsthand research or a source reference). This need not be in the article, but should be made available for our files." No partisan politics or established religion. Buys 6-8 mss/year. Send complete ms. Length: 300-900 words. Pays $10-25.

Photos: Send photos with ms. Pays $5 for b&w snapshots. Identification of subjects required.

Fiction: Humorous, mainstream and science fiction. Buys 4 mss/year. Send complete ms. Length: 800-2,000 words. Pays $25-50.

Poetry: Light verse and traditional. Buys 4-6 mss/year. Submit maximum 2 poems. Length: open. Pays $5-10.

Fillers: Jokes, gags, anecdotes and short humor. Buys 8-20/year. Length: 100 words maximum. Pays $5-10.

Tips: "We are a new publication, and all areas are wide open. We look for material that is warm and human, and that illustrates some phase of personal growth or human relationships."

ENERGY WEST, 200 Sante Fe Dr., Denver CO 80223. (303)893-5165. Publisher: John Waddell. Monthly magazine covering the energy situation for business, professional and government people in a non-technical setting who deal with energy production. Estab. 1980. Circ. 10,000. Average issue includes 8 feature articles and 1-2 columns. Pays on publication. Byline given. Buys first North American serial rights. Phone queries OK. Submit seasonal material 2 months in advance. Simultaneous submissions OK. SASE. Reports in 2 weeks. Sample copy $1.

Nonfiction: "We are interested in articles on energy production that take a new look at old and new developments throughout the entire Western Hemisphere." Submit a good story idea with a creative title aimed at businessmen and executives already in the energy field. We seek non-technical writing; informative rather than chatty and professionally handled all the way through. Articles in the April '81 issue included nuclear, windfall profit tax, plutonium, gasohol, economics and energy, animal waste in a zoo and energy policy. We're also looking for articles on wind, geothermal, solar, biomass, and coal." Query with full outline and creative title. Length: 1,500-3,000 words. Pays 10¢/word.

Photos: State availability of photos. Reviews 5x7 b&w prints and color transparencies. Captions and model release required. Buys one-time rights.

Columns/Departments: Access to energy, opinion, interview, energy news, calendar and editorial.

FAR WEST, Wright Publishing Co., Inc., 2949 Century Pl., Costa Mesa CA 92626. (714)979-2560. Editor: Scott McMillan. Emphasizes "western fiction for a wide field of interest groups—everything from MDs to ditch diggers. They're mostly conservative, but hard to pin down." Quarterly magazine. Circ. 125,000. Pays on publication. Buys all rights. Phone queries OK. Submit seasonal/holiday material 6 months in advance. Previously published submissions OK. SASE. Reports in 3 months. Sample copy $2; writer's guidelines for SASE.

Fiction: Historical and western. "We are looking for fast-moving, well-crafted fiction dealing with the old West, 1840-1900. The common denominator in all stories used is fast-moving action, with well-developed characters and plot. *Believability* is the watchword here. No avant-garde stuff.

Avoid over-violence and explicit sex. Try not to write like Zane Grey." Buys 10 mss/issue. Send complete ms. Length: 1,500-35,000 words. Pays $150-500.

FLORIDA SINGLES MAGAZINE AND DATE BOOK, Box 83, Palm Beach FL 33480. Editor: Harold Alan. Bimonthly magazine covering "singles' problems with life, dating, children, etc., for single, divorced, widowed and separated persons who compose over 40% of the adult population over 18." Circ. 10,000. Pays on publication. Buys second serial rights and one-time rights. Simultaneous, photocopied and previously published submissions OK. SASE. Reports in 2 weeks. Free sample copy.
Nonfiction: "We want any article that is general in nature dealing with any aspect of single life, dating, problems, etc." Buys 1-3 mss/issue. Send complete ms. Length: 800-1,400 words. Pays $10-30. "We are associated with 3 other singles magazines: the Washington/Baltimore, Philadelphia area and Atlanta *Singles Magazine*. We pay up to $30 for the first time use of an article in the first publication and $15 each for each time reprinted in the other magazines."
Photos: Offers no additional payment for photos accepted with ms. Model release required.
Fiction: "We will look at any ms that is general in nature dealing with any aspect of single life, dating, problems, etc."

GREEK ACCENT, Greek Accent Publishing Corp., 257 Park Ave. S., New York NY 10010. (212)477-2550. Editor: Evanthia Allen. Magazine published 11 times/year (combined July-August issue). "We are a publication for and about Greek-Americans and philhellenes." Estab. 1980. Circ. 40,000. Pays on publication. Byline given. Offers 20% kill fee. Buys first North American serial rights. Submit seasonal/holiday material 1 year in advance. Photocopied submissions OK. Previously published submissions OK "only if published in academic journals or small newspapers." SASE. Reports in 1 month on queries; 3 months on mss. Sample copy $2.50 for 9x12 SAE and 83¢ postage.
Nonfiction: Orania Papazoglou, articles editor. Book excerpts; expose; historical/nostalgic (historical more than nostalgic); how-to (only with a Greek slant, about Greece or Greeks); humor; interview/profile; new product (made or manufactured by Greeks or Greek-Americans); travel. No " 'My Trip to Samathraki,' articles or 'Greece Through the Eyes of a Non-Greek.' We publish articles on Greeks and Greece, on Greek-Americans who have succeeded at their work in some important way or who are doing unusual things, and on general interest subjects that might specifically interest our audience, such as the role of Greek Orthodox priests' wives, the crisis in Greek-US political relations, the Cyprus problem, Greek school education in the US, and large Greek-American communities like Astoria, New York." Query with clips of published work. Length: 1,000-3,000 words. Pays $75-200/article.
Photos: Theodore Kalomirakis, art director. State availability of photos. Pays $10 for 8x10 prints or contact sheets; $15 for color transparencies. Model release and identification of subjects required. Buys one-time rights.
Fiction: Ethnic, fantasy, historical, humorous, mainstream, mystery. No novels, Greek or Greek-American stereotyping. Send complete ms. Length: 1,500-3,000 words. Pays $100-200 article.
Fillers: Clippings and newsbreaks. Pays $5-15.
Tips: "Try to deal with problems and concerns peculiar to or of specific interest to Greek-Americans, rather than concentrating solely on Greece. With regard to Greece, heritage-historical-genealogical articles are of interest. We'd rather have investigative, informative articles than paens to the glory that was Greece or puff-pieces on how wonderful everything is for everyone. Also, we do a semi-regular feature (not a department) called 'Profile of a Parish,' spotlighting different parishes throughout the country. We'd especially like to see 'Profiles' of parishes outside the New York, New Jersey, Connecticut area. We'd like pieces on neighborhoods or communities outside this area, too. Probably the easiest way to get published here is to do a good, in-depth piece on a large, active Greek-American community in the Midwest, West, or South, and back it up with pictures. The more we get from outside the tri-state area, the happier we'll be."

INTRO MAGAZINE, "The Single Source", Douglas Publishing, Inc., 3518 Cahuenga Blvd. W., Los Angeles CA 90063. (213)876-7221. Editor: James Michael Yeager. Managing Editor: Nancy Hill-Holtzman. Monthly magazine covering single living for affluent single people, aged 35-55. Estab. 1980. Circ. 150,000. Pays on acceptance. Byline given. Pays variable kill fee. Buys all rights. Submit seasonal/holiday material 4 months in advance. SASE. Reports in 2 weeks on queries. Sample copy $2.50; writers guidelines for business size SAE and 1 first class stamp.
Nonfiction: General interest, how-to, humor, inspirational, interview/profile, opinion and personal experience. "Articles aimed at socially active single people. Looking to simplify the complications of being a single person—the problems and joys of being alone, co-existence with the opposite sex, how to adjust to 'singlehood,' etc. Area of interest covers the entire spectrum of

relationships in contemporary society. Topical interest. Some satire and humor." Buys 48 mss/ year. Length: 2,000 minimum words. Payment varies.
Columns/Departments: Length: 1,000 words.
Tips: Query to be concise and clearly focused. "I want relevant, provocative topics pertaining to my magazine. Fresh approaches."

JADE, The Asian American Magazine, 3932 Wilshire Blvd., Suite 208, Los Angeles CA 90010. (213)388-2571. Editor/Publisher: Gerald Jann. Managing Editor: Edward T. Foster. Quarterly magazine covering Asian-American people and events for Asian-Americans. Circ. 30,000. Pays on publication. Byline given. Offers 25% kill fee. Buys first North American serial rights. Submit seasonal/holiday material 6 months in advance. Simultaneous queries and photocopied submissions OK. SASE. Reports in 3 weeks. Sample copy $1; writer's guidelines for business-size SAE and 1 first class stamp.
Nonfiction: Interview/profile (Asian-Americans in unusual situations or occupations especially successful people active in communities). Buys 40 mss/year. Send complete ms. Length: 4,000 words maximum. Pays $25-200.
Photos: Send photos with ms. Reviews 35mm color transparencies and 5x7 color and b&w glossy prints. Model releases and identification of subjects required. Buys one-time rights.
Columns/Departments: Open to new suggestions for columns/departments.
Fillers: Newsbreaks. Pays $10-25.
Tips: "We're especially interested in hearing from writers who are not on the West Coast."

JOURNAL OF GRAPHOANALYSIS, 111 N. Canal St. Chicago IL 60606. Editor: V. Peter Ferrara. For audience interested in self-improvement. Monthly. Buys all rights. Pays negotiable kill fee. Byline given. Pays on acceptance. Reports on submissions in 1 month. SASE.
Nonfiction: Self-improvement material helpful for ambitious, alert, mature people. Applied psychology and personality studies, techniques of effective living, etc.; all written from intellectual approach by qualified writers in psychology, counseling and teaching, preferably with degrees. Length: 2,000 words. Pays about 5¢/word.

MUSEUM MAGAZINE, 260 Madison Ave., New York NY 10016. Publisher: Jules Warshaw. Managing Editor: Thomas O'Neil. Bimonthly consumer magazine covering museums of art, science, history, sports, etc., for museum enthusiasts. Estab. 1980. Circ. 120,000. Pays on acceptance. Byline given. Average issue includes 10-12 feature articles and 4 departments. Offers 25% kill fee. Buys all rights. Submit seasonal and other timely material 6 months in advance. Simultaneous and photocopied submissions OK, if so indicated. SASE. Reports in 3 weeks on queries; in 1 month on mss. Sample copy $2; free writer's guidelines.
Nonfiction: General interest (art shows at major museums, science museums, outdoor museums); profile (of prominent people in the art or museum world); travel (foreign museums); humor and offbeat possible; photo feature (6-10 pages on a collection or tour of a museum); and major travelling exhibitions. Buys 8-9 mss/issue. Query with clips of previously published work. Length: approximately 2,500 words. Pays $750 maximum. "We are always looking for exceptionally well-written articles on anything to do with the world of museums—art, science, whatever. Always looking for 'eccentric,' offbeat museums."
Photos: Reviews b&w glossy prints. Pays $75 minimum/35mm color transparency.
Fillers: Short features. Buys 5-7 mss/issue. Length: 750 words. Pays $100 minimum.
Tips: "Please fewer stately homes and general major fine arts museums. And for heavens sake, no more queries on the American Museum at Bath, England, or Hyde Park in New York. Query should be informative and anecdotal."

THE NEW YORK ANTIQUE ALMANAC, The New York Eye Publishing Co., Inc., Box 335, Lawrence NY 11559. (516)371-3300. Editor-in-Chief: Carol Nadel. Emphaszies antiques, art, investments and nostalgia. Tabloid published 10 times/year. Circ. 42,000. Pays on publication. Buys all rights. Byline given. Phone queries OK. Submit seasonal/holiday material "whenever available." Previously published submissions OK but must advise. SASE. Reports in 6 weeks. Free sample copy.
Nonfiction: Expose (fraudulent practices); historical (museums, exhibitions, folklore, background of events); how-to (clean, restore, travel, shop, invest); humor (jokes, cartoons, satire); informational; inspirational (essays); interviews (authors, shopkeepers, show managers, appraisers); nostalgia ("The Good Old Days" remembered various ways); personal experience (anything dealing with antiques, art, investments, nostalgia); opinion; photo feature (antique shows, art shows, fairs, crafts markets, restorations); profile; technical (repairing, purchasing, restoring); travel (shopping guides and tips) and investment; economics, and financial reviews. Also purchase puzzles and quizzes related to antiques or nostalgia. Pays $25. Buys 9 mss/issue.

Query or submit complete ms. Length: 3,000 words maximum. Pays $15-50. "Expenses for accompanying photos will be reimbursed."

Photos: "Occasionally, we have photo essays (auctions, shows, street fairs, human interest) and pay $5/photo with caption."

Fillers: Personal experiences, commentaries, anecdotes. "Limited only by author's imagination." Buys 45 mss/year. Pays $5-15.

Tips: "Articles on shows or antique coverage accompanied by photos are definitely preferred."

OPTIMIST UNLIMITED, Health and Happiness Through Proper Thinking, News Publishing, Box 17068, Pittsburgh PA 15235. (412)823-7163. Editor: Terry Smiley. Monthly newsletter for "people who are interested in positive mental attitude: many business people who want to set goals." Estab. 1980. Circ. 1,000. Pays on acceptance. Buys one-time rights. Submit seasonal/holiday material 3 months in advance. Simultaneous, photocopied, and previously published submissions OK. SASE. Reports in 6 weeks on mss. Free sample copy for SAE and 1 first class stamp.

Nonfiction: General interest; how-to (have happiness and good health through proper thinking); humor (related to positive thinking); inspirational; personal experience. Buys more than 100 mss/year. Send complete ms. Length: 200 words maximum. Pays 10¢/word.

Columns/Departments: Book reviews. Buys 12 mss/year. Send complete ms. Length: 200 words maximum. Pays 10¢/word.

PILLOW TALK, 215 Lexington Ave., New York NY 10016. Editor: I. Catherine Duff. "For people interested in all areas of human relationships—meetings, dating, arguing, making up, sex (in all aspects). We're a light, fun, but helpful and reliable publication—a counselor, a friend, a shoulder to lean on, and an entertainment." Monthly magazine. Pays on publication. Buys all rights. Byline given unless author requests otherwise. No simultaneous or photocopied submissions. SASE. Reports in 1 week. Sample copy $1.75; free writer's guidelines for SASE.

Nonfiction: How-to (romantic and sexual techniques, meeting new people, handling relationships, overcoming emotional hurdles); humor (sexual, romantic); interview (maybe in rare cases); personal experience (sexual/romantic scenarios if they illustrate a specific topic); and medical/technical (lightly done on sex-related health topics). "No out-and-out pornography unless incorporated in our new sexual fantasy department. Should be top-class." Buys 11 mss/issue. Query. Length: 1,000-3,000 words. Pays $80-300.

Photos: State availability of photos with query. Pays $25-50 for b&w; $250 for color covers. Buys all rights. Model release required.

Columns/Departments: Front Entry, unusual and interesting news items. The Centerfold, puzzles, crosswords, games and anything out of the ordinary. Healthworks, health related topics; Rear Entry, sexual fantasy. Regular columns on alternate lifestyles: The Gay Life, The Swinging Life and The Kinky Life. Query with clips of published work. Length: 1,250 words. Pays $100. Open to suggestions for new columns/departments.

Fiction: "Only sexual fantasy for our new Rear Entry department." Length: 2,000 words. Pays $100-150.

Fillers: Clippings and newsbreaks (funny, unusual items relating to the broad area of sex). Buys 6 clippings/issue. Pays $5.

Tips: A query letter to *Pillow Talk* should convince the editor that "the writer can write without pleading: poverty, humor or the issue. Query anything—especially researched pieces—giving a one-paragraph outline of the intended angle."

PRACTICAL KNOWLEDGE, 111 N. Canal St., Chicago IL 60606. Editor: Lee Arnold. Bi-monthly. A self-advancement magazine for active and involved men and women. Buys all rights, "but we are happy to cooperate with our authors." Pays on acceptance. Reports in 2-3 weeks. SASE.

Nonfiction and Photos: Uses success stories of famous people, past or present, applied psychology, articles on mental hygiene and personality by qualified writers with proper degrees to make subject matter authoritative. Also human interest stories with an optimistic tone. Up to 5,000 words. Photographs and drawings are used when helpful. Pays 5¢/word minimum; $10 each for illustrations.

READERS REVIEW, The National Research Bureau, Inc., 424 N. 3rd St., Burlington IA 52601. Editor-in-Chief: B. Beck. Editor: M. Cuppy. "For industrial workers of all ages." Quarterly magazine. Circ. 42,000. Pays on publication. Buys all rights. Previously published submissions OK. SASE. Reports in 3 weeks. Free sample copy and writer's guidelines.

Nonfiction: General interest (steps to better health, attitudes on the job); how-to (perform better on the job, do home repairs, car maintenance); and travel. No articles on car repair, stress and tension. Buys 4-5 mss/issue. Query with outline. Length: 400-600 words. Pays $20 minimum.

REVIEW, Center for Inter-American Relations, 680 Park Ave., New York NY 10021. (212)249-8950. Editor: Luis Harss. Assistant Editor: Wilfrido Howard Corral. Emphasizes "views, reviews, interviews, news on Latin-American literature and arts." Published spring, fall and winter. Magazine. Circ. 2,000. Pays on publication. Buys all rights. Phone queries OK. Previously published submissions OK (if originally published in Spanish). Reports in 2 months. Free sample copy.
Nonfiction: Interview, personal opinion, personal experience, literary essays on Latin American authors, art, film. Buys 30 mss/year. Length: 8-14 pages. Pays $35-75.
Fiction: "All types—but has to be by Latin Americans." Buys 3/issue. Query. No length requirement. Pays $50.
Poetry: Uses all types. Buys 3/issue. Limit submissions to batches of 3.

ROMANTIC TIMES, The Complete Newspaper for Readers of Romantic Fiction, Romantic Times, Inc., 163 Joralemon St., Suite 1234, Brooklyn Heights NY 11201. (212)875-5019. Editor: Renee Rubin. Managing Editor: Kathryn Falk. Bimonthly newspaper covering romantic fiction for readers and writers of romantic novels. Estab. 1981. Circ. 30,000. Pays on publication. Byline given. Pays $20 kill fee. Rights purchased vary. Submit seasonal/holiday material 6 months in advance. Simultaneous queries, and simultaneous, photocopied, and previously published submissions OK. SASE. Reports in 3 weeks. Sample copy $2; writer's guidelines for SASE.
Nonfiction: Book excerpts; historical/nostalgic (pertaining to historical novels); how-to (write romantic novels); interview/profile (with romance writers); and personal experience (How I write Romantic Novels). "Submit an interesting, revealing interview with a long-time reader of those novels, explaining his enjoyment and recommendations. An interview with a famous author, present or past, would be most welcomed." Special issues include: Regency Issue and Romantic Suspense Issue. "At this time, no romantic fiction manuscripts. Just *articles about* this subject." Buys "at least 12" mss/year. Query. Length: 1,000-2,500 words. Pays $30-50.
Photos: "We need photos of writers at work or at home." State availability of photos. Pays $10 for b&w prints. Captions, model releases, and identification of subjects required. Buys one-time rights.
Columns/Departments: Book reviews, gossip and historical tidbits. Query. Length: 500-1,000 words. Pays $20-30.
Fillers: Jokes. Buys 12/year. Pays $20.
Tips: "The best freelancer would be one who reads or writes romantic fiction, and has a feel for what the average romantic novel fan would like to read in a newspaper devoted to this subject. We like to see in-depth, but not academic-sounding, articles on the genres of romantic fiction—historical, Regency, suspense, contemporary, and category."

ROSICRUCIAN DIGEST, Rosicrucian Order, AMORC, Rosicrucian Park, San Jose CA 95191. (408)287-9171, ext. 213. Editor-in-Chief: Robin M. Thompson. Emphasizes mysticism, science and the arts. For "men and women of all ages, seeking answers to life's questions." Monthly magazine. Circ. 70,000. Pays on acceptance. Buys first rights and rights to reprint. Byline given. Submit seasonal or holiday material 5 months in advance. Photocopied and previously published submissions OK. SASE. Reports in 1 month. Free sample copy and writer's guidelines.
Nonfiction: How to deal with life's problems and opportunities in a positive and constructive way. Informational articles—new ideas and developments in science, the arts, philosophy and thought. Historical sketches, biographies, human interest, psychology, philosophical and inspirational articles. No religious or political material or articles promoting a particular group or system of thought. Buys 40-50 mss/year. Query. Length: 1,000-1,500 words. Pays 6¢/word.
Photos: Purchased with accompanying ms. Send prints. Pays $3.50/8x10 b&w glossy print.
Fillers: Short inspirational or uplifting (not religious) anecdotes or experiences. Buys 6/year. Query. Length: 25-250 words. Pays 2¢/word.
Tips: "Be specific about what you want to write about—the subject you want to explore—and be willing to work with editor. Articles should appeal to worldwide circulation."

SAVING ENERGY, Box 75837 Sanford Station, Los Angeles CA 90075. (213)874-1453. Editor/ Publisher: Larry Liebman. Emphasizes energy conservation, ideas and case histories aimed at business, industry and commerce. Monthly newsletter. Estab. February 1977. Pays on acceptance. Buys all rights. No byline given. Phone queries OK. SASE. Reports in 2 weeks. Free writer's guidelines.
Nonfiction: "I need good, tightly written case histories on how industry and commerce are saving energy, listing problems and solutions. The item should present an original energy saving idea. Include full name and address of business so readers can contact for follow-up." How-to (conserving energy, what the problem was, how it was resolved, cost, how fast the payback was, etc.); and

technical (case histories). Buys 5 mss/issue. Submit complete ms. Length: 200-800 words. Pays $10-25.

Tips: "Take potluck with a well-written item that meets specs, since the item could be shorter than the query letter after editing."

SCANDINAVIAN REVIEW, American-Scandinavian Foundation, 127 E. 73rd St., New York NY 10021. (212)879-9779. Editor-in-Chief: Nadia Christensen. "The majority of our readership is over 30, well-educated, and in the middle income bracket. Most similar to readers of *Smithsonian* and *Saturday Review.* Have interest in Scandinavia by birth or education." Quarterly magazine. Circ. 7,000. Pays on publication. Buys all rights. Byline given. Submit seasonal/holiday material 9 months in advance. Previously published material (if published abroad) OK. SASE. Reports in 1 month. Sample copy $4. Free writer's guidelines.
Nonfiction: Historical, informational, interview, photo feature and travel. "Modern life and culture in Scandinanvia." Buys 40 mss/year. Send complete ms. Length: maximum 2,500 words. Pays $50-100.
Photos: Purchased with accompanying ms. Captions required. Submit prints or transparencies. Prefers sharp, high contrast b&w enlargements. Total purchase price for ms includes payment for photos.
Fiction: Adventure, fantasy and historical. Prefers work translated from the Scandinavian. Buys 8-12 mss/year. Send complete ms. Length: 2,000 words maximum. Pays $50-100.
Poetry: Translations of contemporary Scandinavian poetry and original poems with a Scandinavian theme. Buys 5-20 poems/year. Pays $10.

SELECTED READING, The National Research Bureau, Inc., 424 N. 3rd St., Burlington IA 52601. Editor-in-Chief: B. Beck. Editor: M. Cuppy. For industrial workers of all ages. Quarterly magazine. Circ. 32,000. Pays on publication. Buys all rights. Previously published submissions OK. SASE. Reports in 3 weeks. Free sample copy and writer's guidelines.
Nonfiction: General interest (economics, health, safety, working relationships); how-to; and travel (out-of-the way places). Buys 2-3 mss/issue. Query. "A short outline or synopsis is best. Lists of titles are no help." Length: 400-600 words. Pays $20 minimum.

SMITHSONIAN MAGAZINE, 900 Jefferson Drive, Washington DC 20560. Articles Editor: Marlane A. Liddell. For "associate members of the Smithsonian Institution; 85% with college education." Monthly. Circ. 1,800,000. Payment for each article to be negotiated depending on our needs and the article's length and excellence. Pays on acceptance. Submit seasonal material 3 months in advance. Reports in 6 weeks. Query. SASE.
Nonfiction: "Our mandate from the Smithsonian Institution says we are to be interested in the same things which now interest or should interest the Institution: cultural and fine arts, history, natural sciences, hard sciences, etc." Length: 750-4,500 words; pay negotiable.
Photos: Purchased with or without ms and on assignment. Captions required. Pays $350/full page.

SOLAR LIVING, Solar Engineering Publishing, Inc., 2636 Walnut Hills Ln., Suite 257, Dallas TX 25229. (214)350-1370. Editor: Richard Curry. Managing Editor: Sally Towlen. Bimonthly magazine covering solar technology for the lay person interested in solar energy. Estab. 1981. Circ. 25,000. "No payment policy has yet been set." Buys all rights. Submit seasonal/holiday material 6 months in advance. SASE. Reports in 1 month.
Nonfiction: "We're looking for articles on products, methods and installations—anything pertaining to ways that people are using solar energy in their homes and in the workplace." Buys 24 mss/year. Query "by mail or phone." Length: 800-3,500 words. Pays negotiable fee.

STRATEGY & TACTICS, Simulation Publications, Inc., 257 Park Ave., New York NY 10010. (212)673-4103. Managing Editor: David J. Ritchie. Bimonthly magazine covering military history for "professionally-oriented people into the hobby of adventure gaming." Circ. 35,000. Pays on publication. Byline given. Buys all rights. Submit seasonal/holiday material 18 months in advance. Reports in 1 month. Free sample copy.
Nonfiction: Historical/nostalgic ("Concentrate on one aspect of military history such as a battle, weapon, single person using hard data"). "No general history and historical narrative-type articles not dealing with specific battles or campaigns." Buys 12 mss/year. Query. Length: 10,000 words maximum. Pays $800 maximum/article.
Photos: State availability of photos. Reviews 8x10 b&w glossy prints.
Columns/Departments: Book reviews, game reviews, historical trivia. Buys 50-200 mss/year. Send complete ms. Length: 500-1,000 words. Pays $10-15.
Tips: "The best way to break in is to thoroughly read a sample copy and play the game. It is awfully hard to understand the kind of information my readers want (and I need in an article) unless you

have at least tried a game. Any writer who exhibits some knowledge of what a game is, has some historical knowledge or background, and can write in English has a very good chance of being commissioned by us. We are specifically looking for military (not general) historians and writers, and those who have no interest in or knowledge of military history and terminology would probably be wasting our time and theirs by submitting material."

SUCCESS MAGAZINE, (formerly *Success Unlimited*), 401 N. Wabash Ave., Chicago IL 60611. Contact: Articles Editor. "Average reader is 25-40, married with 2 children; working in professional, sales or management capacity; college-educated (85%) and has a strong motivation to go into business for himself. Financially, he's doing fine—but he wants to do even better." Monthly magazine. Circ. 210,000. Pays on acceptance. Rights purchased vary with author and material. Free sample copy and writer's guidelines with SASE.
Nonfiction: *Success* emphasizes the importance of a positive mental attitude. We publish three general categories of articles. The first is success profiles. These can be of nationally known individuals in business or industry or less recognizable people who have overcome obstacles in order to achieve success. These profiles can be either full-length—1,500-2,500 words—or short—800-1,000 words. The short profiles, which should have a topical "hook," fit our "Achievers" department. The second type of article is the behavior piece. It deals with the philosophy and psychology of success as applied to social trends and family problems. Written in laymen's language, behavior articles should focus on the latest research and developments. The third type of article is motivational and how-to. These topics include: how to overcome fear, how to start a business, how to stay healthy, goal-setting and time management. Authors of these articles must have expertise. Length: 1,500-2,500 words. Pays $250 minimum, negotiable to $1,000. Query.

TAT JOURNAL, Box 236, Bellaire OH 43906. Editor: Louis Khourey. Quarterly magazine for readers from 20-65 years old, professional and lay, who are interested in self-awareness and self-development, esoteric philosophy, psychology, holistic health, and ancient cultures and sciences. Circ. 5,000. Pays on publication. Buys all rights and first North American serial rights. Simultaneous, photocopied and previously published submissions OK. SASE. Reports in 3 weeks. Sample copy $2; free writer's guidelines.
Nonfiction: Editor: Mark Jaqua. Exposé (occult rip-offs, cults and spiritual gimmicks); historical (ancient cultures, sciences and religions); how-to (innovative meditation techniques and holistic health guidelines); interview (of psychologists, philosophers and scientists, both professional and lay); opinion; and personal experience (new insights into the unsolved mysteries of the universe). "No articles that proselytize any one belief." Buys 3 mss/issue. Send complete ms. Length: 1,500-5,000 words. Pays $10-100.
Columns/Departments: Editor: Mark Jaqua. Book Reviews. Buys 2 mss/year. Send complete ms. Length: 500 words minimum. Pays $5 minimum.
Tips: "We want material that stimulates the reader's curiosity, allowing him to come to his own conclusions."

TREASURE FOUND, 16146 Covello St., Van Nuys CA 91406. (213)988-6910. Editor: Dave Weeks. Managing Editor: Jim Williams. For "all ages, all levels of education. The magazine appeals to all metal detector users, scuba divers, miners, bottle diggers, coin collectors—in short, anyone interested in treasure, especially treasure that has been found." Quarterly magazine. Byline given. Submit seasonal/holiday material 3 months in advance. Photocopied and previously published submissions OK. SASE. Reports in 6 weeks. Sample copy $1; free writer's guidelines.
Nonfiction: Stories of discovered treasure, illustrated with clear photos, maps or drawings. Submit complete ms. Pays approximately $25/magazine page.
Photos: 35mm or 2¼x2¼ color transparencies for cover photos; subject should be of something found (e.g., someone with a collection of bottles; the bottles effectively arranged; coins found, etc.).
Tips: "Our main emphasis is on illustration. Photos are a must. Writer should realize readers are mostly experienced treasure hunters, and thus avoid general newspaper-type introductions. Emphasis is on technique (how does subject find treasure, etc.) and depth."

UFO REVIEW, Global Communications, 303 5th Ave., Suite 1306, New York NY 10016. (212)685-4080. Editor: Timothy Beckley. Emphasizes UFOs and space science. Published 6 times/ year. Tabloid. Circ. 50,000. Pays on publication. "We syndicate material to European markets and split 50-50 with writer." Phone queries OK. Photocopied submissions OK. SASE. Reports in 3 weeks. Sample copy $1.
Nonfiction: Expose (on government secrecy about UFOs). "We also want articles detailing on-the-spot field investigations of UFO landings, contact with UFOs, and UFO abductions. No lights-in-

the-sky stories." Buys 1-2 mss//issue. Query. Length: 1,200-2,000 words. Pays $25-75.
Photos: Send photos with ms. Pays $5-10 for 8x10 b&w prints. Captions required.
Fillers: Clippings. Pays $2-5.

VEGETARIAN TIMES, 124 N. Austin Blvd., Oak Park IL 60302. (312)848-8120. Editor: Paul Barrett Obis Jr. For "nonmeat eaters and people interested in organic food." Monthly magazine. Circ. 60,000. Rights purchased vary with author and material. Will buy first serial or simultaneous rights ("always includes right to use article in our books or 'Best of' series"). May pay 20% kill fee. Byline given unless extensive revisions are required or material is incorporated into a larger article. Buys 50 mss/year. Pays on acceptance. Sample copy $2. Photocopied and simultaneous submissions OK. Submit seasonal material 6 months in advance. Reports in 1 month. Query. SASE.
Nonfiction: Features concise articles related to vegetarianism, animal welfare and liberation, healthfoods, and articles about vegetarians. "All material should be well-documented and researched. It would probably be best to see a sample copy—remember that despite our name, we are beholden to our readers and we do not necessarily care if the health food stores sell more vitamins. We are not in the business of selling health foods. We are strongly pro consumer. We are not interested in personal pet stories or wonder cure-all foods." Informational, how-to, experience, interview, profile, historical, exposé, opinion, successful health food business operations and restaurant reviews. Length: average 1,500 words. Pays 5¢/word minimum. Will also use 500- to 1,000-word items for regular columns.
Photos: Pays $15 for photos and cartoons. No color; b&w ferrotype preferred.
Tips: Write query with "brevity and clarity."

WESTERN & EASTERN TREASURES, People's Publishing, Inc., 1440 W. Walnut St., Box 7030, Compton CA 90224. (213)537-0896. Editor: Ray Krupa. Emphasizes treasure hunting for all ages, entire range in education, coast-to-coast readership. Monthly magazine. Estab. 1966. Circ. 70,000. Pays on publication. Buys all rights. SASE. Reports in 3 weeks. Sample copy and writer's guidelines for 50¢.
Nonfiction: How-to (use of equipment, how to look for rocks, gems, prospect for gold, where to look for treasures, rocks, etc., "first-person" experiences). Buys 150 mss/year. Submit complete ms. Length: maximum 1,500 words. Pays 2¢/word maximum.
Photos: Purchased with accompanying ms. Captions required. Submit prints or transparencies. Pays $5 maximum for 3x5 and up b&w glossy prints; $10 maximum for 35mm and up color transparencies. Model release required.
Columns/Departments: Treasures in the Headlines, Tip of the Month. Buys 50/year. Send complete ms. Length: 800-1,500 words. Pays 2¢/word maximum. Open to suggestions for new columns or departments; address Ray Krupa.

WHAT MAKES PEOPLE SUCCESSFUL, The National Research Bureau, Inc., 424 N. 3rd St., Burlington IA 52601. Editor-in-Chief: B. Beck. Editor: M. Cuppy. For "industrial workers of all ages." Published quarterly. Magazine. Circ. 25,000. Pays on publication. Buys all rights. Previously published submissions OK. SASE. Reports in 3 weeks. Free sample copy and writer's guidelines.
Nonfiction: How-to (be successful); general interest (personality, employee morale, guides to successful living, biographies of successful persons, etc.); experience; opinion. Buys 2-3 mss/issue. Query with outline. Length: 400-600 words. Pays $20 minimum.
Tips: "Say what you have to say and then stop. Obvious padding makes an article sound clumsy and it is almost always removed."

Music

ACCENT Magazine, 1418 Lake St., Evanston IL 60204. (312)328-6000. Executive Editor: Kenneth L. Neidig. "Our readers are serious junior and senior high school musicians. The magazine focuses on styles of music ranging from classical to jazz." Published bimonthly during the school year. Magazine. Pays on publication. Buys all rights. Phone queries OK. Submit seasonal/holiday material at least 3 months in advance. Photocopied submissions OK. SASE. Reports in 2 months. Free sample copy and writer's guidelines.
Nonfiction: General interest (areas of music related to young musicians, including interviews with artists); historical (some areas of music history, not straight biography of Bach, Mozart, etc.); how-to (improve playing technique, take care of instruments, enjoy music more); humor (anything relating to the experience of a high school musician); interview (performers, composers, teachers);

photo feature (featuring a musical event or process, such as building an instrument). "No condescending articles for grade-school-level students. Emphasis is on instrumental students. Articles shouldn't be written like a textbook—they should be lively and practical." No bubble-gum rock. Buys 40 mss/year. Query or submit complete ms. Pays $25-30/magazine page.

Photos: "Good photos can be helpful, although they're not essential. Payment is calculated into overall payment for article." Submit color transparencies or b&w prints. Captions preferred. Buys all rights. Color covers $50-75. Inside color poster $50-75.

Columns/Departments: Checking Out Colleges; Good Vibrations (a potpourri column of newsbriefs, musical jokes and puzzles, new product descriptions, and book and record reviews). Pays $5 minimum. Musical Brain Teaser (a full-page music note exercise). Query. Length: 1,000-2,500 words.

Tips: "Get to know high school band members and write about things they need to know about music that they do not get enough of in their school programs."

AUDIO, CBS Publications, 1515 Broadway, New York NY 10036. (212)975-7270. Editor: Eugene Pitts III. Monthly magazine covering audio equipment and technology for advanced hi-fi buffs and professionals in the industry. Circ. 125,000. Pays on publication. Byline given. Pays negotiable kill fee. Buys all rights. Photocopied and previously published submissions OK ("if publication and date are indicated"). SASE. Reports in 2 months on queries. Free sample copy.

Nonfiction: How-to (construct sets or components); interview/profile (of professionals in hi-fi technology); and technical (concerning hi-fi technology and design). "This is a very technical magazine. Writers must be thoroughly knowledgeable in the field of hi-fi technology." No general or beginner articles. Buys 12-20 mss/year, "mostly from regular contributors." Query with clips of published work and résumé. Length: 2,000-4,000 words. Pays $100-1,000 ($50-150/published page).

Photos: Reviews 35mm color transparencies and prints. "Photos are paid for with payment for ms." Identification of subjects required.

AUDIOSCENE CANADA, MacLean-Hunter, Ltd., 481 University Ave., Toronto, Ontario, Canada M5W 1A7. (416)596-5896. Editor-in-Chief: Ian G. Masters. Emphasizes high fidelity and music. Monthly magazine. Circ. 25,000. Pays on publication. Buys all rights. Byline given. Phone queries OK. Submit seasonal/holiday material 2 months in advance. SAE and International Reply Coupons. Reports in 1 month. Free sample copy.

Nonfiction: How-to (must have firsthand technical knowledge); interview; and technical. No record reviews/music features. Buys 6-8 mss/year. Query. Length: 1,500-2,500 words. Pays 10¢/word.

Photos: Wants photos for personality pieces and appropriate artwork for technical material. Pays $15 minimum for 4x5 or 8x10 b&w glossy prints. Captions preferred. Buys all rights. Model release required.

BAM, THE CALIFORNIA MUSIC MAGAZINE, BAM Publications, 5951 Canning St., Oakland CA 94609. Editor: Dennis Erokan. Managing Editor: Blair Jackson. Biweekly tabloid covering "the music and musicians of California for an audience made up primarily of musicians and music consumers. We cover contemporary music, mainly rock and roll and jazz. We like to emphasize coverage on up-and-coming talent in San Francisco and Los Angeles." Circ. 100,000. Pays 2 weeks after publication. Buys first rights. Photocopied submissions OK. SASE. Reports in 2 weeks. Sample copy $1.

Nonfiction: Exposé (music industry related "though we're not really interested in muckraking crusades"); general interest (personality pieces on musicians off-stage, at play, with family, on-the-road); how-to (technical pieces on musical instruments); interview (musicians and industry figures); nostalgia (musician's childhood); profile; photo feature (California music-related); and technical (on amplifiers, guitars, recording studios and sessions). "No heavily opinionated or egocentric articles or features on performers which are not based on interviews." Buys 2-3 mss/issue. Query. Length: 800-2,000 words. Pays $20/feature.

Photos: State availability of photos. Pays $10/8x10 b&w glossy print.

Tips: "Be familiar with the magazine before sending a query. Clips should show skill in writing interview features (and we don't mean Q&A style). A cover letter describing the kinds of music you like best is helpful."

BEATLEFAN, The Goody Press, Box 33515, Decatur GA 30033. Editor: E.L. King. Managing Editor: Jonathan Parry-King. Bimonthly magazine about the Beatles, John Lennon, Paul McCartney, George Harrison and Ringo Starr for a readership averaging 22 years of age, 55% males and 45% females. Circ. 1,700. Average issue includes 12 articles and 10 departments. Pays on publication. Byline given. Buys all rights. Submit seasonal material 2 months in advance. Simultaneous, photocopied and previously published submissions OK. SASE. Reports in 1 month. Sample copy $1.25.

Nonfiction: Historical (factual articles concerning the early Beatles tours in the US and anything to do with the band's early career); interview (with Beatles and any associates); nostalgia (articles on collecting Beatles memorabilia and trivia); personal experience (stories of meetings with the Beatles and associates); and photo feature (current photos of McCarthy, Harrison and Starr and latterday photos of Lennon). Buys 1 ms/issue. Send complete ms. Length: 350-3,500 words. Pays $5-25. "We are looking for regular correspondents. We also need articles with tips on memorabilia collecting, record collecting, book and record reviews. We have an anniversary issue each December, a Beatlemania issue each February (accounts of the days of the Beatlemania 1964-1966 especially needed) and in event of tours or appearances by any of the Beatles, reports from each city visited will be needed." No essays on the death of John Lennon; no poems of any type.

Photos: Send photos with ms. Pays $1.50-10/5x7 b&w glossy print. Offers no additional payment for photos accepted with ms. Captions required identifying subjects, places, date and photographer's name.

Columns/Departments: Book Review (any books published concerning the Beatles, foreign or domestic); Record Reviews (the Beatles together or individually; domestic or foreign; official or bootleg); Those Were the Days (articles about the Beatles that deal with generally unknown aspects or details of career together or personal lives); collecting (articles with tips for collectors of rare records and memorabilia); Thingumybob (columns of opinion). Buys 1 ms/issue. Send complete ms. Length: 500 words maximum. Pays $5-25.

Fillers: Clippings (not wire service stories) and puzzles having to do with the Beatles. Buys 3 mss/issue. Pays 50¢-$5.

Tips: "We get too many submissions that are general in nature and aimed at a general audience, repeating well-worn facts and events our readers already know by heart. We need articles that are specific, detailed and authoritative and that will tell confirmed Beatlemaniacs something they don't know. Articles should not be simple rewrites of reference book chapters. Among our contributing editors are noted Beatles authors Nicholas Schaffner and Wally Podrazik and former *Mersey Beat* editor Bill Harry. This shows the level of familiarity with the subject we expect."

THE BIG BANDWAGON, 3055 Hull Ave., Bronx NY 10467. Editor: Roselle T. Scaduto. Emphasizes nostalgic music "for persons interested in the sounds of the early jazz and swing eras of the 20's, 30's and 40's." Bimonthly journal. Circ. 4,600. Pays on publication. Buys all rights. SASE "a must." Reports in 3 weeks on queries; in 6 weeks on mss. Sample copy $1.50.

Nonfiction: How-to (collect, buy, sell, trade lp's, 78's, sheet music); nostalgia (bios on well-known bandleaders, musicians and vocalists); opinion (book, record, concert reviews); profiles on new or established jazz clubs, societies, current nostaglia radio programming, etc. Buys 30 mss/year. Send complete ms. 350-650 words. Pays $10 maximum; pays in copies for all reviews.

Columns/Departments: The Sinatra Spot (news on the performer); Book Shelf (nostalgia music and film books); Record Review (swing and jazz recordings); Those Were the Days (the soaps and old-time radio stars); Lights, Camera, Action (30's and 40's films, biographies of stars, big on band filmographies). Buys 30 mss/year. Send complete ms. Length: 100-500 words. Pays $3-5.

Fillers: "We are always in need of nostalgia fillers." Clippings; newsbreaks; puzzles (trivia, quizzes, crosswords, match-ups, fill in blanks on bands and films); and spot news (on where bands and vocalists are appearing). Buys 20 mss/year. Length: 50-150 words. Pays $1/clip and $2-5/puzzle.

Tips: "The best way to break in would be with a short piece on a favorite nostalgia personality, citing background, personal and professional and listing their credits. Bring the subjects to life. We heartily welcome freelancers but will only consider material of a nostalgic nature. Study the journal and become better acquainted with our style and content. Creative ideas and new angles will catch our eye. Only will consider BIG BAND or FILM related nostalgic pieces. We get lots of material we can't use. Follow-up a reject—we may only be temporarily overstocked."

BLUEGRASS UNLIMITED, Box 111, Broad Run VA 22014. (703)361-8992. Editor-in-Chief: Peter V. Kuykendall. Managing Editor: Marion C. Kuykendall. Emphasizes old-time traditional country music for musicians and devotees of bluegrass, ages from teens through the elderly. Monthly magazine. Circ. 15,000. Pays on publication. Buys all rights. Pays variable kill fee. Byline given. Phone queries OK. Submit seasonal/holiday material 3 months in advance. Photocopied and previously published submissions OK. SASE. Reports in 1 month. Free sample copy and writer's guidelines.

Nonfiction: Historical, how-to, humor, informational, interview, nostalgia, personal experience, opinion, photo feature, profile and technical. Buys 20-40 mss/year. Query. Length: 500-5,000 words. Pays 4-5¢/word.

Photos: Purchased with or without accompanying ms. Query for photos. Pays $15-20/page for 5x7

or 8x10 b&w glossy prints, 35mm or 2¼x2¼ color transparencies; $50 for covers.
Columns/Departments: Record and book reviews. Buys 5-10/year. Query. Length: 100-500 words. Pays 4-5¢/word.
Fiction: Adventure and humorous. Buys 5-7 mss/year. Length: 500-2,500 words. Pays 4-5¢/word.

CANADIAN MUSICIAN, Norris Publications, 97 Eglington Ave. E., Suite 302, Toronto, Ontario, Canada M4P 1H4. (416)485-8284. Editor: Kathy Whitney. Bimonthly magazine; for professional and amateur musicians, music students and teachers, music industry people, recording and audio enthusiasts, music enthusiasts. Material must be factual in content, stressing technical and professional aspects of music. Estab. 1979. Circ. 21,000. Pays on acceptance. Buys all rights. Phone queries OK. SASE. Reports in 1 month. Free sample copy and writer's guidelines.
Nonfiction: How-to (projects for building or repairing musical, audio and recording equipment); interviews or articles (with Canadian music people or of Canadian origin); and technical (articles on recording, musical equipment, audio equipment). Buys 4-6 mss/issue. Query. Length: 1,500-2,000 words. Pays $100-150.
Photos: Send photos with ms. Pays $5-25 for 8x10 b&w glossy prints; $25-100 for 2¼ color transparencies. Buys one-time rights.
Columns/Departments: Profile (on Canadian music people less known or behind the scenes with pictures, 700-800 words). Buys 1-2/issue. Query. Pays $20-75.
Tips: "Especially seeking writers who are musicians or experts in their field."

COMPLETE BUYER'S GUIDE TO STEREO/HI-FI EQUIPMENT, Service Communications, Ltd., 50 Rockefeller Plaza, New York NY 10020. Editor: David A. Drucker. For people interested in buying audio equipment; the demographics are probably similar to the audio equipment purchaser profile. Published 8 times/year. Magazine. Circ. 65,000. Pays on publication. Buys all rights. Byline given "on request only." Photocopied submissions OK. SASE. Reports in 6 weeks. Free sample copy.
Nonfiction: General interest, how-to, new product and technical. Buys 2-3 mss/issue. Send complete ms. Length: 1,000-3,000. Pays $75-300.

CONTEMPORARY CHRISTIAN MUSIC, CCM Publications, Inc., Box 6300, Laguna Hills CA 92653. (714)951-9106. Editor/Publisher: John W. Styll. Associate Editor: Karen Marie Platt. Monthly magazine covering Christian music (especially contemporary). "We are a Christian publication dedicated to the arts and the support of contemporary art forms and artists who present a Christian world-view." Circ. 25,000. Pays on publication. Byline given. Pays $25 kill fee. Buys simultaneous rights. Submit seasonal/holiday material 4 months in advance. Simultaneous queries OK. SASE. Reports in 3 months. Sample copy $1.75; writer's guidelines for SAE and 24¢ postage.
Nonfiction: Book excerpts, how-to, humor, inspirational, interview/profile, new product and personal experience. No articles unrelated to music and/or Christianity. Query with resume and clips of published work. Length: 50-2,500 words. Pays 10¢/word ($25 minimum).
Photos: State availability of photos. Pays $10-50 for b&w contact sheets; $25-200 for color transparencies. Identification of subjects required. Buys one-time rights and all rights.
Columns/Departments: Needs information on events, persons and news of the contemporary Christian music scene in the US, Canada and Europe. Query. Length: 10-500 words. Pays $50 maximum.
Poetry: Avant-garde, free verse, haiku, light verse and traditional. "All must relate to contemporary Christian art forms, especially music." Buys 0-6 mss/year. Submit maximum 2 poems. Length: 1-25 lines. Pays $10-50.
Fillers: Jokes, anecdotes and short humor. Buys 0-6/year. Length: 250-500 words. Pays $15-50.

CONTEMPORARY KEYBOARD MAGAZINE, 20605 Lazaneo, Cupertino CA 95014. (408)446-1105. Editor: Tom Darter. For those who play piano, organ, synthesizer, accordion, harpsichord, or any other keyboard instrument. All styles of music; all levels of ability. Monthly magazine. Circ. 70,000. Pays on acceptance. Buys all rights. Byline given. Phone queries OK. SASE. Reports in 2 weeks. Free sample copy and writer's guidelines.
Nonfiction: "We publish articles on a wide variety of topics pertaining to keyboard players and their instruments. In addition to interviews with keyboard artists in all styles of music, we are interested in historical and analytical pieces, how-to articles dealing either with music or with equipment, profiles on well-known instrument makers and their products. In general, anything that amateur and professional keyboardists would find interesting and/or useful." Buys 3-4 mss/issue. Query; letter should mention topic and length of article, and describe basic approach. "It's nice (not necessary) to have a sample first paragraph." Length: approximately 2,000-4,500 words. Pays $75-175.

Tips: "Query first (just a few ideas at at time, rather than twenty). A musical background helps, and a knowledge of keyboard instruments is valuable."

CORNHUSKER COUNTRY, 106 Navajo, Council Bluffs IA 51501. Editor: Robert Everhart. Emphasizes traditional country music. Monthly magazine. Circ. 2,000. Pays on acceptance. Buys one-time rights. Byline given. Submit seasonal/holiday material 3 months in advance of issue date. Simultaneous, photocopied and previously published submissions OK. SASE. Reports in 1 month. Free sample copy.
Nonfiction: Historical (relating to country music); how-to (play, write, or perform country music); inspirational (on country gospel); interview (with country performers, both traditional and contemporary); nostalgia (pioneer living); personal experience (country music); and travel (in connection with country music contests or festivals). Buys 6 mss/year. Query. Length: 200-2,000 words. Pays $20-50.
Photos: State availability of photos with query. Payment is included in ms price. Uses 5x7 b&w prints. Captions and model release required. Buys one-time rights.
Poetry: Free verse and traditional. Buys 1/issue. Length: 3-15 lines. Limit submissions to batches of 3. Pays in copies.
Tips: "Material must be concerned with what we term 'real' country music as opposed to today's 'pop' country music. Freelancer must be knowledgeable of the subject; many writers don't even know who the father of country music is, let alone write about him."

COUNTRY MUSIC MAGAZINE, Country Music, Inc., 475 Park Ave. S., New York NY 10016. Editor-in-Chief: Russell D. Barnard. 80% freelance written. Monthly magazine. Circ. 500,000. Pays on publication. Buys all rights. Submit seasonal/holiday material at least 4 months in advance of issue date. Photocopied and previously published (book excerpts) OK. SASE. Reports in 3-4 weeks. Free sample copy and writer's guidelines.
Nonfiction: General interest ("about country music or subjects of interest to a country music audience"); humor (some, but must be taken article by article); historical (about music, items of interest to our audience); interview (country artist, craftsman, etc.); photo feature; profile; and travel. Buys 6-10 mss/issue. Query with clips of published work. Length: 1,500-3,500 words. Pays $250-400.
Photos: Richard Erlanger, photo editor. State availability of photos with query. Pays $25 minimum/b&w glossy print; $50 minimum/35mm color transparency. Captions required. Buys all rights.
Columns/Departments: Record reviews. Buys 5-10/issue. Query. Length: 100-250 words. Pays $25.

COUNTRYSTYLE, 11058 W. Addison, Franklin Park IL 60131. (312)455-7178. Managing Editor: Jim Albrecht. Emphasizes country music and country lifestyle. Monthly magazine. Circ. 65,000. Pays on publication. Buys all rights. Phone queries OK. Submit seasonal/holiday material 3 months in advance. Photocopied submissions and previously published work OK. SASE. Reports in 2 weeks. Sample copy $1.25. Free writer's guidelines.
Nonfiction: Exposé, informational, interview, nostalgia, profile and photo feature. Buys 100 mss/year. Query. Length: 500-2,000 words. Pays minimum of $10/ms page.
Photos: Purchased with or without ms, or on assignment. Send contact sheet, prints or transparencies. Pays $15-100 for 8x10 b&w glossy prints; $35-250 for color. Prefers 2¼x2¼, but color negatives OK.
Columns/Departments: Country Music. Record Review. Send complete ms. Length: 100-500 words. Pays 5-10¢/word.
Fillers: Newsbreaks. Buys 40/year. Length: 100-300 words. Pays $5-15.
Tips: "Best way to break in is with a timely (in the sense that the artist has a hot song on the charts) feature with good color art. Get good angles on the stars—stories with controversy; fast-breaking news stories."

CREEM, 187 S. Woodward Ave., Suite 211, Birmingham MI 48011. (313)642-8833. Editor: Susan Whitall. Estab. 1969. Buys all rights. Pays on publication. Query. Reports in 6 weeks. SASE.
Nonfiction: Short articles, mostly music-oriented. "Feature-length stories are mostly staff-written, but we're open for newcomers to break in with short pieces. Freelancers are used a lot in the Beat Goes On section. Please send queries and sample articles to Mark J. Norton, submissions editor. We bill ourselves as America's Only Rock 'n' Roll Magazine." Pays $35 minimum for reviews, $125 minimum for full-length features.
Photos: Freelance photos.
Tips: "You can't study the magazine too much—our stable of writers have all come from the ranks of our readers. The writer can save his time and ours by studying what we do print—and producing

similar copy that we can use immediately. Short stuff—no epics on the first try. We really aren't a good market for the professional writer looking for another outlet—a writer has to be pretty obsessed with music and/or pop culture in order to be published in our book. We get people writing in for assignments who obviously have never even read the magazine and that's totally useless to us."

FRETS MAGAZINE, GPI Publications, 20605 Lazaneo, Cupertino CA 95014. (408)446-1105. Editor: Roger H. Siminoff. "For amateur and professional acoustic string music enthusiasts; for players, makers, listeners and fans. Country, jazz, classical, blues, pop and bluegrass. For instrumentalists interested in banjo, mandolin, guitar, violin, upright bass, dobro, dulcimer and others." Monthly magazine. Estab. 1979. Circ. open. Pays on acceptance. Buys first rights. Phone queries OK. Submit material 4 months in advance. SASE. Reports in 3 weeks. Free sample copy and writer's guidelines.
Nonfiction: General interest (artist-oriented); historical (instrument making or manufacture); how-to (instrument craft and repair); interview (with artists or historically important individuals); profile (music performer); travel (if in conjunction with music event); photo feature (in conjunction with music event); and technical (instrument making, acoustics, instrument repair). Buys 35 mss/year. Query with clips of published work and "letter that reveals writer's ability and style." Length: 1,000-2,500 words. Pays $75-125. Experimental (instrument design, acoustics). Pays $50-75.
Photos: State availability of photos. Pays $20 minimum for b&w prints (reviews contact sheets); $150 for cover shot color transparencies. Additional payment for photos accepted with ms. Captions and model release required. Buys one-time rights.
Columns/Departments: Repair Shop (instrument craft and repair); and *FRETS* Visits (on-location visit to manufacturer). Buys 10 mss/issue. Query. Length: 1,200-1,700 words. Pays $75-100.
Fillers: Newsbreaks, upcoming events, music-related news.

GUITAR PLAYER MAGAZINE, 20605 Lazaneo, Cupertino CA 95014. (408)446-1105. Managing Editor: Tom Wheeler. For persons "interested in guitars and guitarists." Monthly magazine. Circ. 150,800. Buys all rights. Byline given. Buys 60-80 mss/year. Pays on acceptance. Free sample copy to a writer on request. Reports in 1 week. Query. SASE.
Nonfiction: Publishes "wide variety of articles pertaining to guitars and guitarists: interviews, guitar craftsmen profiles, how-to features—anything amateur and professional guitarists would find fascinating and/or helpful. On interviews with 'name' performers, be as technical as possible regarding strings, guitars, techniques, etc. We're not a pop culture magazine, but a magazine for musicians." Also buys features on such subjects as a guitar museum, the role of the guitar in elementary education, personal reminiscences of past greats, technical gadgets and how to work them, analysis of flamenco, etc." Length: open. Pays $50-200.
Photos: Photos purchased with mss. B&w glossy prints. Pays $25-50. Buys 35mm color transparencies. Pays $150 (for cover only). Buys one time rights.

HIGH FIDELITY, The Publishing House, State Road, Great Barrington MA 01230. Editorial Director: Robert Clark. For well-educated, young, affluent readers, interested in home recording and playback systems (all disc and tape formats) and music. Special issues: August, tape; June, speakers; September, new recordings and new equipment; December, year's best recordings. Monthly magazine. Circ. 365,000. Buys all rights. Kill fee varies. Byline given. Buys 36-42 mss/year. Pays on acceptance. Photocopied submissions OK, "if they are legible." Submit seasonal material 5 months in advance. Reports in 1 month. Query or submit complete ms. SASE.
Nonfiction: Regular columns include interviews with noted music and recording personalities about their work; and Behind the Scenes, reports of in-progress recording sessions here and abroad. "Material for feature articles is divided between consumer and semipro audio equipment and music makers. Equipment articles should be backed up with as much technical sophistication as possible and appropriate and readily understandable to the lay reader. Music articles should be slanted toward the classical or popular musician's recording career or recordings of his works or aimed at increasing the reader's understanding of music. Articles are sophisticated, detailed and thoroughly backgrounded." Length: 1,000-3,000 words. Pays $200-500.
Photos: Purchased with accompanying manuscripts. Captions required. 8x10 b&w glossy payment included in ms payment. Color rarely used; inquire first.

HIGH FIDELITY/MUSICAL AMERICA, 825 7th Ave., New York NY 10019. Editor: Shirley Fleming. Monthly. Circ. 25,000. Buys all rights. Pays on publication. SASE.
Nonfiction: Articles, musical and audio, are generally prepared by acknowledged writers and authorities in the field, but does use freelance material. Query with clips of published work.

Length: 3,000 words maximum. Pays $100 minimum.

Photos: New b&w photos of musical personalities, events, etc.

HIT PARADER, Charlton Publications, Charlton Bldg., Derby CT 06418. (203)735-3381. Editor: John Shelton Ivany. Managing Editor: Mary Jane Canetti. Monthly magazine. *Hit Parader* covers the field of popular music with interviews and articles on pop stars and musical trends." Circ. 100,000. Pays on publication. Byline given. Offers 50% kill fee. Buys all rights. Simultaneous queries and photocopied submissions OK. SASE. Reports in 3 weeks. Sample copy $1.50.

Nonfiction: Interview/profile, personal experience and photo feature. Buys 100 mss/year. Query with clips of published work. Length: 250-170 words. Pays $50-250.

INTERNATIONAL MUSICIAN, American Federation of Musicians, 1500 Broadway, New York NY 10036. (212)869-1330. Editor: J. Martin Emerson. For professional musicians. Monthly. Byline given. Pays on acceptance. Reports in 2 months. SASE.

Nonfiction: Articles on prominent instrumental musicians (classical, jazz, rock or country). Send complete ms. Length: 1,500-2,000 words.

THE LAMB, 2009 Arthur Ln., Austin TX 78704. (512)443-8416. Editor-in-Chief: Michael Point. Emphasizes music for a readership interested in the current shape and future course of contemporary music. Primary readership lies in the 20-30-year-old bracket with some college affiliation (past or present) and a serious interest in music. Monthly tabloid. Circ. 30,000. Pays on publication. Buys all rights. Pays 50% kill fee. Byline given. Phone queries OK. Photocopied (if clean and clear) submissions OK. SASE. Reports in 1 month. Sample copy $1.

Nonfiction: Historical, informational, interview, nostalgia, opinion, photo feature and profile. "All articles must deal with music, musicians or the music world." Buys 50 mss/year. Query. Length varies. Pays minimum $10.

Photos: Geary Davis, Photo Editor. Purchased with or without accompanying ms or on assignment. Captions required. Pays minimum $5 for 8x10 b&w glossy prints. Send contact sheet or prints. Total purchase price for ms includes payment for photos.

Poetry: Nancy McKinney, poetry editor. Avant-garde, free verse, haiku, light verse and traditional. Buys 50 poems/year. Send poems. Pays minimum $5.

Tips: *"The Lamb* is not a teen or pop music publication. It deals with 'progressive music' of all styles (jazz, rock, classical, etc.) and requires writers able to communicate to an audience of musically informed and interested readers. *The Lamb* is open to all forms of alternative expression dealing with music and invites writers, photographers, etc., to use their creativity when submitting material. Remember that this is a music magazine and, as such, concentrates almost exclusively on the permutations of the music world. Album reviews and performance reviews are customary starting points for new writers."

MODERN DRUMMER, 1000 Clifton Ave., Clifton NJ 07013. (201)778-1700. Editor-in-Chief: Ronald Spagnardi. Features Editor: Rick Mattingly. Managing Editor: Scott K. Fish. For "student, semi-pro and professional drummers at all ages and levels of playing ability, with varied specialized interests within the field." Published 9x yearly. Circ. 40,000. Pays on publication. Buys all rights. Phone queries OK. Photocopied and previously published submissions OK. SASE. Reports in 3 weeks. Sample copy $2; free writer's guidelines.

Nonfiction: How-to, informational, interview, personal opinion, new product, personal experience and technical. "All submissions must appeal to the specialized interests of drummers." Buys 5-15 mss/issue. Query or submit complete ms. Length: 3,000-6,000 words. Pays $100-500.

Photos: Purchased with accompanying ms. Considers 8x10 b&w and color glossy prints. Submit prints or negatives.

Columns/Departments: Jazz Drummers Workshop, Rock Perspectives, Rudimental Symposium, Complete Percussionist, Teachers Forum, Drum Soloist, Show & Studio, Strictly Technique, Book Reviews and Shop Talk. "Technical knowledge of area required for most columns." Buys 10-20 mss/issue. Query or submit complete ms. Length: 500-1,500 words. Pays $25-150. Open to suggestions for new columns and departments.

MODERN RECORDING & MUSIC, Cowan Publishing, 14 Vanderventer Ave., Port Washington NY 11050. (516)883-5705. Editor: Hector LaTorre. Managing Editor: Pamela Highton. Monthly magazine covering semi-pro and professional recording of music for musicians, soundmen and recording engineers. Circ. 70,000. Pays second week of publication month. Buys all rights. Submit seasonal/holiday material 3 months in advance. Photocopied submissions OK. SASE. Reports in 1 week. Provides sample copy "after assignment."

Nonfiction: Historical/nostalgic (recording industry); how-to (basic construction of a device using readily available parts to duplicate an expensive device in a small budget studio or at home);

humor; interview/profile (musician, engineer, producer or someone in an affiliated field). Also publishes an annual buyers' guide listing products, specs, and prices of equipment. Buys 40 mss/year. Query with clips of published work and an outline. Length: 2,000 words minimum. Pays $150-200/article.

Photos: Reviews 2¼x2¼ or 35mm color transparencies; 8x10 glossy prints or contact sheets. Pays $25 inside color; $15 inside b&w; $75 for color cover; or package payment of $150.

MUSIC CITY NEWS, 1302 Division St., Nashville TN 37203. (615)244-5187. Editor: Lee Rector. Emphasizes country music. Monthly tabloid. Circ. 100,000. Buys all rights. Phone queries OK. Submit seasonal or holiday material 2 months in advance. Photocopied submissions OK. SASE. Reports in 10 weeks. Free sample copy.

Nonfiction: "Interview type articles with country music personalities: question/answer, narrative/ quote, etc. Focusing on new and fresh angles about the entertainer more than biographical histories." Buys 4-5 mss/issue. Query. Length: 500-1,250 words. Pays $125/feature, $75/junior feature, and $50/vignettes.

Photos: Purchased on acceptance by assignment. Query. Pays $10 maximum for 8x10 b&w glossy prints.

MUSIC JOURNAL, 60 E. 42nd St., Rm. 3415, New York NY 10017. (212)682-7320. Editor: Bert Wechsler. 70% freelance written. Emphasizes serious music for college and conservatory faculty and students, professional and amateur musicians, and music lovers. Bimonthly magazine. Pays on publication. Submit seasonal/holiday material 4 months in advance of date. Simultaneous and photocopied submissions OK. SASE. Reports in 6 weeks. Sample copy $2.50.

Nonfiction: General interest (composers, performers, music festivals, instruments, new trends, recordings, music business and audio); interview (important figures in the music world); profile (important figures in the music world); and travel (as related to classical music or jazz). Buys about 10 mss/year. Query with 3 clips of published work. Length: 1,000-3,000 words. Pays $75-200.

Photos: State availability of photos with query. No additional payment for b&w prints. Buys one-time rights.

MUSIC MAGAZINE, Barrett & Colgrass Inc., 56 The Esplanade, Suite 202, Toronto, Ontario, Canada M5E 1A7. (416)364-5938. Editor: Ulla Colgrass. Emphasizes classical music. Bimonthly magazine. Circ. 11,000. Pays on publication. Buys all rights. Byline given. Phone queries OK. Submit seasonal/holiday material 4 months in advance. Photocopied and previously published submissions (book excerpts) OK. SAE and International Reply Coupons. Reports in 3 weeks. Sample copy and writer's guidelines $2.

Nonfiction: Interview, historical articles, photo feature and profile. "All articles should pertain to classical music and people in that world. We do not want any academic analysis or short pieces of family experiences in classical music." Query with clips of published work. Length: 1,500-3,500 words. Pays $50-150.

Photos: State availability of photos. Pays $15-25 for 8x10 b&w glossy prints or contact sheets; $100 for color transparencies. No posed promotion photos. "Candid lively material only." Buys one-time rights. Captions required.

Tips: Send sample of your writing, suggested subjects. Off-beat subjects are welcome, but must be thoroughly interesting to be considered. A famous person or major subject in music are your best bet.

OPERA CANADA, 366 Adelaide St. E., Suite 433, Toronto, Ontario Canada M5A 1N4. (416)363-0395. Editor: Ruby Mercer. For readers who are interested in serious music; specifically, opera. Quarterly magazine. Circ. 5,000. Not copyrighted. Byline given. Buys 10 mss/year. Pays on publication. Sample copy $3. Photocopied and simultaneous submissions OK. Reports on material accepted for publication within 1 year. Returns rejected material in 1 month. Query or submit complete ms. SAE and International Reply Coupons.

Nonfiction: "Because we are Canada's opera magazine, we like to keep 75% of our content Canadian, i.e., by Canadians or about Canadian personalities/events. We prefer informative and/or humorous articles about any aspect of music theater, with an emphasis on opera. The relationship of the actual subject matter to opera can be direct or barely discernible. We accept record reviews (*only* operatic recordings); book reviews (books covering any aspect of music theater) and interviews with major operatic personalities. Please, no reviews of performances. We have staff reviewers." Length (for all articles except reviews of books and records): 350-5,000 words. Pays $25-50. Length for reviews: 50-100 words. Pays $10.

Photos: No additional payment for photos used with mss. Captions required.

OVATION, 320 W. 57th St., New York NY 10019. Editor: Sam Chase. Monthly magazine for classical music listeners covering classical music and the equipment on which to hear it. Estab.

1980. Average issue includes 4 features plus departments. Pays on publication. Byline given. Buys all rights. Submit seasonal material 4 months in advance, SASE. Reports in 1 month. Sample copy $2.79.

Nonfiction: "We are primarily interested in interviews with and articles about the foremost classical music artists. Historical pieces will also be considered." Buys 4 mss/issue. Query with clips of previously published work. Length: 800-4,500 words. Pays $5/inch.

Photos: State availability of photos. May offer additional payment for photos accepted with ms. Captions required. Buys one-time rights.

POLYPHONY MAGAZINE, Box 20305, 1020 W. Wilshire, Oklahoma City OK 73156. (405)842-5480. Bimonthly magazine about electronic music and home recording for readers who are interested in building and using electronic music instruments to perform in bands or to make amateur recordings in their home studios. Circ. 4,000. Pays on publication. Buys all rights or by arrangement. Phone queries OK. Submit seasonal material 3 months in advance. Simultaneous, photocopied and previously published submissions OK. SASE. Reports in 2 weeks on queries; in 3 weeks on mss. Free sample copy.

Nonfiction: General interest (music theory, electronics theory, acoustics); how-to (design and build electronic music devices, record music); interview (with progressive musicians using electronic techniques or designers of electronic music equipment); new product; and technical. No mainstream type music and artist review articles. Buys 4 mss/issue. Query with clips of previously published work. "The feature stories we use are the best area for freelancers. We need construction projects, modifications for commercial equipment, computer software for music use, and tutorials dealing with electronic music and recording studio techniques, performance, design and theory. Freelancers should write in a conversational manner; provide enough details in project articles to allow novices to complete the project; provide informative charts, graphs, drawings or photos; present material which is practical to someone working in this medium." Length: 1,000-5,000 words. Pays $10 minimum.

Photos: State availability of photos or send photos with ms. Pays $10 minimum/5x7 b&w glossy print. Captions preferred; model release required. Buys all rights or by arrangement.

Columns/Departments: Patches (patch charts for music synthesizers showing how to get different sounds and effects). Buys 4 mss/issue. Query with clips of previously published work. Length: 100-1,000 words. Pays $10 minimum.

RECORD REVIEW, Ashley Communications, Inc., Box 91878, Los Angeles CA 90009. Editor: Brian J. Ashley. Bimonthly magazine covering the music world for young men, mostly in the Midwest. Circ. 50,000. Pays on publication. Byline given. Buys all rights. Simultaneous ("if so indicated") and photocopied submissions OK. "Do not send anything that requires return." Reports "if interested" in 2 weeks.

Nonfiction: Interview (of rock artists). Buys 75 mss/year. Send complete ms. Length: 3,000 words average. Pays $60-70.

Photos: Send photos with accompanying ms. Pays $10 for 8x10 b&w glossy prints. "We pay for original photos only." Captions required. Buys one-time rights.

Tips: "Typically, we're looking for people who are heavily involved in music first, and writers second. We like to see the author suggest pull quotes and titles."

ROLLING STONE, 745 5th Ave., New York NY 10022. Editor: Jann S. Wenner. "Seldom accept freelance material. All our work is assigned or done by our staff." Pays 33% kill fee. Byline given.

THE SENSIBLE SOUND, 403 Darwin Dr., Snyder NY 14226. Editor/Publisher: John A. Horan. "All readers are high fidelity enthusiasts, and many have a high fidelity industry-related job." Quarterly magazine. Circ. 5,200. Pays on acceptance. Buys all rights. Byline given. Simultaneous, photocopied and previously published submissions OK. SASE. Reports in 2 weeks. Sample copy $2.

Nonfiction: Exposé, how-to, general interest, humor, historical, interview (people in hi-fi business, manufacturers or retail); new product (all types of new audio equipment); nostalgia (articles and opinion on older equipment); personal experience (with various types of audio equipment); photo feature (on installation, or how-to tips); profile (of hi-fi equipment); and technical (pertaining to audio). "Subjective evaluations of hi-fi equipment make up 70% of our publication. Will accept 10/issue." Buys 2 mss/issue. Submit outline. Pays $25 maximum.

Columns/Departments: Bits & Pieces (short items of interest to hi-fi hobbyists); Ramblings (do-it-yourself tips on bettering existing systems); Record Reviews (of records which would be of interest to audiophiles). Query. Length: 25-400 words. Pays $5 maximum.

Fillers: Clippings, jokes, gags, anecdotes and newsbreaks. Buys 2/issue. Length: 25-400 words. Pays $10 maximum.

SHEET MUSIC MAGAZINE, Sheet Music Magazine, Inc., 223 Katonah Ave., Katonah NY 10536. Editor: Joseph L. Knowlton. Emphasizes music and the home musician. Published 9 times/year. Magazine. Circ. 200,000. Pays on publication. Buys all rights. Pays 20% kill fee. Byline given. Submit seasonal/holiday material 4 months in advance. Simultaneous and previously published submissions OK. SASE. Reports in 1 month. Sample copy $2.
Nonfiction: General interest, how-to and nostalgia. Buys 3 mss/issue. Send complete ms. Length: 1,000-3,500 words. Pays $50-300.

STEREO, ABC Leisure Magazines, Inc., The Publishing House, State Rd., Great Barrington MA 01230. (413)528-1300. Editor-in-Chief: William Tynan. Emphasizes high-quality home audio equipment. Quarterly magazine. Circ. 50,000. Pays on acceptance. Buys all rights. Byline given. Phone queries OK. Submit seasonal/holiday material 6 months in advance. Photocopied submissions OK. SASE. Reports in 2 weeks. Free writer's guidelines.
Nonfiction: How-to (technically expert articles dealing with audio equipment), humor, interview (with personalities in audio field) and technical (workings of audio equipment). Buys 1-2 mss/year. Query. Length: 2,000-5,000 words. Pays 10-22½¢/word.
Tips: "We are interested in the small minority of freelancers who are genuine audio experts with the training and experience that qualifies them to write with real authority. *Stereo* is almost entirely staff-written. At the moment, we buy very few manuscripts. However, we would buy more if material meeting our very high technical standards were available. Because every issue is themed to a specific aspect of audio, and all articles are written on assignment, it is *imperative* that freelancers query us before writing. We are not interested in record buffs with 'golden ears.' "

STEREO REVIEW, Ziff-Davis Publishing Co., 1 Park Ave., New York NY 10016. Monthly magazine covering stereo equipment and classical and popular music for music enthusiasts. Circ. 540,000. Average issue includes 2-3 feature articles. Pays on acceptance. Byline given. Offers $100 kill fee. Buys first North American serial rights. Submit seasonal material 4 months in advance. Simultaneous and previously published submissions OK, if so indicated. Reports in 1 week.
Nonfiction: General interest (basic library of music, 5,000 words); interview (musical artists, 4,000 words); and humor (music related, 1,000 words). Buys 1 ms/issue. Query with clips of previously published work. "You must have an extremely acute knowledge of the field and you must have gained a thorough knowledge of the magazine by reading many issues." Pays $50-$150.
Photos: State availability of photos. Negotiates payment.

TROUSER PRESS, Trans-Oceanic Trouser Press, Inc., 212 5th Ave., New York NY 10010. (212)889-7145. Editor: Scott Isler. Monthly magazine covering rock music for young, college-oriented readers. Circ. 60,000. Pays after publication. Byline given. Buys all rights. Submit seasonal/holiday material 3 months in advance. Simultaneous queries, photocopied and previously published submissions OK. SASE. Reports in 2 weeks on queries. Sample copy $1.50.
Nonfiction: Interview/profile (of band, group, or artists) and movements and new developments. Buys 90-100 mss/year. Query with clips of published work. Length: 3,000 words maximum. Pays $50-75/article.
Photos: State availability of photos. Pays $15 minimum for 8x10 glossy prints, more for color slides.
Columns/Departments: Media Eye. Length: 1,000 words maximum. Pays $25-30/article.
Fillers: Concert reviews, LP reviews. Buys 100-150/year. Length: 300-350 words. Pays $5-10.
Tips: "I'm very concerned with quality of writing. If someone has a good portfolio of clippings and a good knowledge of music, I'm impressed. Although *Trouser Press* doesn't offer much in the way of monetary reward, our writers appreciate an outlet for intelligent articles on a very popular subject. With a new national distribution deal just begun, the magazine's visibility (and rates?) should catch up with its reputation."

VOICE, THE MAGAZINE OF VOCAL MUSIC, Leo Publications, Box 1444, Honolulu HI 96806. (808)526-0064. Editor: Charles J. Speake. Bimonthly magazine for serious vocal musicians, professional and amateur. Includes features, articles, and information on performing, teaching, conducting, composing, and accompanying for the human voice. Estab. 1980. Circ. 22,500. Pays on publication. Buys first rights and second serial (reprint) rights. Phone queries OK. Previously published submissions OK. SASE. Reports in 2 weeks on queries; in 3 weeks on mss. Free sample copy and writer's guidelines.
Nonfiction: General interest (to the field of vocal music); historical (related to vocal music); how-to (in any aspects of vocal field: care for your voice, audition); interview; nostalgia; new product; personal experience; and technical. "No gossip or private life material." Buys 30 mss/year. Query with clips of previously published work. Length: 6-15 typewritten pages, double-spaced. Pays $50-$150.

Photos: Send photos with ms. Pays $10-$25 minimum for 5x7 or 8x10 b&w matte/glossy prints. Pays $35-$150 for 35mm or 2¼x2¼ color transparencies. Offers additional payment for photos accepted with ms. Buys all rights.

Mystery

ALFRED HITCHCOCK'S MYSTERY MAGAZINE, Davis Publications, Inc., 380 Lexington Ave., New York NY 10017. Editor: Eleanor Sullivan. Associate Editor: Susan Calderella Groarke. Emphasizes mystery fiction. Magazine published 13 times a year. Circ. 280,000. Pays on acceptance. Buys all rights. Byline given. Submit seasonal/holiday material 7 months in advance. Simultaneous and photocopied submissions OK. SASE. Reports in 1 month or less. Free writer's guidelines.
Fiction: Original and well-written mystery, suspense and crime fiction. Occasionally buys reprints. "A 'now' feeling is preferred for every story, both as to plot urgency and today's world. Plausibility counts heavily even in supernatural stories." Length: 1,000-10,000 words.
Tips: "Think Hitchcock. It's the master's brand of suspense that we want. Avoid gore, which we rarely buy, profanity and explicit sex. *AHMM* publishes fiction of a non-horror nature—it is read by mystery fans, who don't like horror. The emphasis is on twist endings. Use a professional, straightforward approach; have a knowledge of the kind of story we publish."

ELLERY QUEEN'S MYSTERY MAGAZINE, Davis Publications, Inc., 380 Lexington Ave., New York NY 10017. Editor-in-Chief: Ellery Queen. Managing Editor: Eleanor Sullivan. Magazine published 13/year. Circ. 415,000. Pays on acceptance. Byline given. Submit seasonal/holiday material 7 months in advance. Simultaneous, photocopied and previously published submissions OK. SASE. Reports in 1 month. Free writer's guidelines.
Fiction: Elana Lore, associate editor. Special consideration will be given to "anything timely and original. We publish every type of mystery: the suspense story, the psychological study, the deductive puzzle—the gamut of crime and detection from the realistic (including the policeman's lot and stories of police procedure) to the more imaginative (including 'locked rooms' and impossible crimes). We need private-eye stories, but do not want sex, sadism or sensationalism-for-the-sake-of-sensationalism." No parodies or pastiches. Buys 13 mss/issue. Length: 6,000 words maximum; occasionally higher but not often. Pays 3-8¢/word.
Tips: "We have a department of First Stories to encourage writers whose fiction has never before been in print. We publish an average of 24 first stories a year."

MIKE SHAYNE MYSTERY MAGAZINE, Renown Publications, Inc., Box 178, Reseda CA 91335. Editor: Charles E. Fritch. Monthly magazine. Buys non-exclusive World Magazine serial rights. Photocopied submissions OK. Obvious rejects returned within a week; possible acceptances take longer.
Fiction: All kinds of mystery/suspense stories; prefers the offbeat and unusual rather than the conventional and clichéd; horror is OK. Pays 1½¢/word on publication.
Tips: "Avoid the clichés—the hard boiled private eye, the spouse-killer, the little old lady being threatened, the standard hitperson, the investigator miraculously solving the case by making unverified conclusions, the criminal confessing at the last minute when there's no reason for him to do so, the culprit caught by some last minute revelation no one but the author knew about, the poor sap who gets clobbered for no reason. Make it short and unusual, something we can't get anyplace else. *MSMM* frequently publishes first stories."

MYSTERY MAGAZINE, Mystery Magazine, Inc., 411 N. Central Ave., Suite 203, Glendale CA 91203. (213)661-0526. Editor: Thomas Godfrey. Bimonthly magazine covering mystery-suspense-adventure-fantasy literature, TV, films, theater, games, events, etc. Estab. 1979. Circ. 250,000. Pays on publication. Byline given. Pays $25 kill fee. Buys first North American serial rights. Submit seasonal/holiday material 4 months in advance. Simultaneous queries and photocopied submissions OK. SASE. Reports in 6 weeks on queries; 3 months on mss. Sample copy $3; writer's guidelines for business size SAE and 1 first class stamp.
Nonfiction: Expose, historical/nostalgic, how-to, interview-profile, new product, and photo feature—all pertaining to mystery. Special issues include: Christmas, Film Noir, Social Issues, Bruce Lee, Medical Examiner, Nero Wolfe, and New York City. No opinion pieces or unsolicited interviews. Buys 30 mss/year. Query with clips of published work. Length: 1,000-4,000 words. Pay varies.

Photos: Send photos with ms. Reviews various types of photos. Pays negotiable fee. Model releases and identification of subjects required. Buys one-time rights.
Columns/Departments: "We need correspondents in big cities for our column 'World of Mystery.' " Query with clips of published work. Length: 500-1,500 words. Pays $50.
Fiction: Fantasy, horror, mystery and suspense. "No sloppily typed hack pieces with many corrections; no mss over 7,500 words; no cardboard characters in predictable situations." Buys 36 mss/year. Send complete ms. Length: 7,500 words maximum. Pays $50-150 ("some exceptions").
Poetry: Light verse. "We are not hot about running poetry—it has to be very special." Buys 1 mss/year. Submit maximum 1 poem.
Fillers: Short humor, newsbreaks. Buys 30/year. Pay varies.
Tips: "Query for a well-researched piece on some aspect of the field, or send a good short story. We are receptive to new ideas, but query first, and be as complete as possible. Know the field, and look at it imaginatively. We are always looking for new, dependable writers."

ROD SERLING'S THE TWILIGHT ZONE MAGAZINE, TZ Publications, 800 Second Ave., New York NY 10017. (212)986-9600. Editorial Director: Eric Protter. Editor: T.E.D. Klein. Managing Editor: Jane Bayer. Monthly magazine covering "stories in the tradition of Rod Serling's *The Twilight Zone* series." Estab. 1981. Circ. 191,000. Pays one-half on acceptance; one-half on publication. Byline given. Buys first North American serial rights and non-exclusive international rights. Submit seasonal/holiday material 6 months in advance. Simultaneous and photocopied submissions OK. SASE. Reports in 2 months on mss. "We acknowledge receipt with a postcard immediately."
Nonfiction: Interview/profile (of well-known writers and movie directors). No pact-with-the-devil stories; no misunderstood girls with super-normal powers. "We can't cope with query letters because of short staff; send good writing."
Fiction: "Ordinary people caught up in extraordinary circumstances. Stories of the supernatural, horror, fantasy, suspense and science fiction." No "stories containing a lot of science fiction hardware and gadgetry." Buys 120 mss/year. Send complete ms. Length: 500-15,000 words. "Most stories purchased are between 2,000-5,000 words." Pays $150-750.
Tips: "We always suggest reading the magazine—it's the best guide. Send a story we will like: we have and do publish new writers."

Nature, Conservation, and Ecology

The publications in this section exist for the furtherance of the natural environment—wildlife, nature preserves and the ecobalance. They do not publish recreational or travel articles except as they relate to conservation or nature. Other markets for this kind of material will be found in the Regional, Sport and Outdoor, and Travel, Camping, and Trailer categories, although the magazines listed there require that nature or conservation articles be slanted to their specialized subject matter and audience.

AMERICAN FORESTS, American Forestry Association, 1319 18th St. NW, Washington DC 20036. (202)467-5810. Editor: Bill Rooney. "We are an organization for the advancement of intelligent management and use of our forests, soil, water, wildlife, and all other natural resources necessary for an environment of high quality and the well-being of all citizens." Monthly magazine. Circ. 80,000. Pays on acceptance. Buys one-time rights. Byline given. Phone queries OK, but written queries preferred. Submit seasonal/holiday material 5 months in advance. SASE. Reports in 6 weeks. Free sample copy and writer's guidelines.
Nonfiction: General interest, historical, how-to, humor and inspirational. "All articles should emphasize trees, forests, wildlife or land use." Buys 5 mss/issue. Query. Length: 2,000 words. Pays $100-350.
Photos: State availability of photos. Offers no additional payment for photos accompanying mss. Uses 8x10 b&w glossy prints; 35mm or larger color transparencies. Buys one-time rights. Captions required.
Tips: "Query should have honesty, information on photo support."

AUDUBON, 950 3rd Ave., New York NY 10022. "Not soliciting freelance material; practically all articles done on assignment only. We have a backlog of articles from known writers and contributors. Our issues are planned well in advance of publication and follow a theme." Pays negotiable kill fee. Byline given.

BIRD WATCHER'S DIGEST, Pardson Corp., Box 110, Marietta OH 45750. Editor: Mary B. Bowers. Focuses on birds and bird watching. Bimonthly magazine. Circ. 20,000. Pays on publication. Buys first North American serial rights and second serial rights. Simultaneous, photocopied and previously published submissions OK. SASE. Reports in 1 month on queries. Sample copy $2; writer's guidelines for SASE.
Nonfiction: General interest (features on species, environmental issues involving birds, endangered and threatened species); historical; how-to; humor (essays); interview (and reports on research); nostalgia; opinion; profile (outstanding or unusual bird watchers); travel (where to go to see birds); personal experience (rare sightings); photo feature; technical (individual species); and accompanying artwork. Buys 18-22 mss/issue. Send complete ms or send clips of previously published work with query. Length: 600-3,000 words. Pays $25/reprint and $50/original.
Photos: State availability of photos. Reviews 5x7 and up b&w glossy prints and 35mm and up color transparencies. Pays $10 for each photo used (returnable).
Poetry: Avant-garde, free verse; light verse; and traditional. Buys 12-20 mss/year. Maximum of 5. Pays $15.
Fillers: Anecdotes. Buys 3-6 mss/issue. Length: 50-225 words. Pays $5.
Tips: "We want good ornithology, good writing. Articles on birds suited for a general interest magazine may be too basic for us. Our audience is quite knowledgeable about birds. Writers must be at least as knowledgeable."

DEFENDERS, Defenders of Wildlife, 1244 19th St., NW, Washington DC 20036. (202)659-9510. Editor: James Deane. Bimonthly magazine for members of Defenders of Wildlife, "a national organization dedicated to the preservation of all forms of wildlife." Circ. 50,000. Pays on publication. Byline given. Buys first North American serial rights. Submit seasonal/holiday material 4 months in advance. Photocopied submissions OK. SASE. Reports in 1 month. Sample copy free; writer's guidelines for business size SAE and 1 first class stamp.
Nonfiction: Michael Lipske, articles editor. Historical (natural history); how-to; photo feature; wildlife, usually North American; "threats to individual species, habitat, wilderness; and newsworthy efforts to alleviate such threats. No scientific pieces, encyclopedia extracts or natural history accounts of creatures you have not personally observed." Buys 35 mss/year. Query. Length: 1,500 words average. Pays $350 minimum.
Photos: Cecilia J. Parker, photo editor. State availability of photos. Pays $35 minimum for b&w glossy prints. Captions required. Buys one-time rights.
Tips: "We like to see quotes from persons talking about and doing the things they know best. We want more articles telling readers what they, as individuals, can do to help wildlife."

ENVIRONMENT, 4000 Albemarle St. NW., Washington DC 20016. Managing Editor: Barbara Ferkiss. For citizens, scientists, business and government executives, teachers, high school and college students interested in environment or effects of technology and science in public affairs. Magazine published 10 times/year. Circ. 15,000. Buys all rights. Byline given. Pays on publication to professional writers. Sample copy $3. Photocopied submissions OK. Reports in 6-8 weeks. Query or submit complete ms. SASE.
Nonfiction: Scientific and environmental material; effects of technology on society. Preferred length: 2,500-4,500 words. Pays $100-300, depending on material.

ENVIRONMENTAL ACTION, 1346 Connecticut Ave., Washington DC 20036. Editors: Francesca Lyman, Janet Marinelli and Gail Robinson. 20% freelance written. Emphasizes grass-roots citizen action and congressional/governmental activity affecting the environment for a well-educated, sophisticated, politically oriented readership. Monthly magazine; 32 pages. Circ. 20,000+. Pays on publication. Buys all rights. Byline given. Simultaneous (if so identified), photocopied and previously published submissions OK. SASE. Reports in 6 weeks. Free sample copy.
Nonfiction: Expose; general interest; news feature; essay (on such issues as the urban environment, chemical pollution, public health, alternative energy, and the public interest movement); and profile. Less interested in wilderness and wildlife issues. Buys 20 mss/year. Query with clips of published work. Length: 1,000-2,500 words. Pays according to length.
Photos: State availability of photos. Pays $15-50 for 8x10 b&w glossy prints. Buys all rights.
Tips: "We are frequently in the market for local stories which have national significance. Because we have virtually no travel budget, we are most receptive to articles that the editors cannot do from Washington."

THE EXPLORER, Cleveland Museum of Natural History, Wade Oval, University Circle, Cleveland OH 44106. (216)231-4600. Editor: Bill Baughman. 50% freelance written. For readers with a strong interest in natural history and science. Quarterly. Circ. 32,000. Audience is members of 32 natural history museums and many library subscribers. Acquires one-time rights. Byline given. Payment in contributor's copies. Submit seasonal material 6 months in advance. Reports in 3-4 weeks. SASE. Editorial requirements outline and/or photo guidelines available on request.
Nonfiction and Photos: "We are especially concerned with interpreting the natural history and science of North America, but mostly US. We endeavor to give a voice to the natural scientists and naturalists functioning within these geographical boundaries and feel an obligation to make our readers aware of the crucial issues at stake in the world regarding conservation and environmental problems. Now assigning most articles, but will consider articles by scientists, naturalists and experts in nature, ecology, and environmental areas. Writing should have a lively style and be understandable to scientists of all ages. Exploring nature can be exciting. Your writing should reflect and encourage the exploring mind." Length: 1,000-3,000 words. B&w (8x10) photos. Some color transparencies are used. 35mm Kodachrome color, 2¼x2¼ and 4x5 transparencies are acceptable for inside editorial and cover illustrations. All photos, particularly close-ups of plants, birds and animals, must be needle-sharp. Also interested in b&w photo essays (12 photos maximum) on natural history topics. Format measures 8¼x11.

INTERNATIONAL WILDLIFE, 225 E. Michigan, Milwaukee WI 53202. Editor: John Strohm. 80% freelance written. For persons interested in natural history, outdoor adventure and the environment. Bimonthly. Buys all rights to text; usually one-time rights to photos and art. Pays on acceptance. Query. "Now assigning most articles but will consider detailed proposals for quality feature material of interest to broad audience." Reports in 2 weeks. SASE.
Nonfiction and Photos: Focus on world wildlife, environmental problems and man's relationship to the natural world as reflected in such issues as population control, pollution, resource utilization, food production, etc. Especially interested in articles on animal behavior and other natural history, little-known places, first-person experiences, timely issues. "Payment varies according to value and use of feature articles, but usually begins at $750. Purchase top-quality color and b&w photos; prefer 'packages' of related photos and text, but single shots of exceptional interest and sequences also considered. Prefer Kodachrome transparencies for color, 8x10 prints for b&w."

JOURNAL OF FRESHWATER, Freshwater Biological Research Foundation, 2500 Shadywood Rd., Box 90, Navarre MN 55392. (612)471-7467. Editor: Karen Thompson. 50% freelance written. Always emphasizes freshwater issues. Annual (November) magazine; 64 pages. Pays on publication. Buys all rights and one-time rights. Byline given. Phone queries OK. SASE. Reports in 4-6 weeks. Sample copy $5; free writer's, artist's and photographer's guidelines.
Nonfiction: Scientific, yet easy to read; how-to; general interest; humor; interview; nostalgia; photo feature; and technical. "We will consider virtually any material dealing with freshwater environment as long as it is well-written and interesting. Entries must clearly and quickly answer the reader's question 'So what's that got to do with me, my pocketbook, or my relatives?'." No "bumper-sticker" philosophies, encyclopedia articles or unresearched material, please. No articles about dam controversies, personal travelogues, fish-catching stories, or long pieces of poetry. Buys 10-15 mss/year. Submit complete ms. Length: "However long it takes—and not a word more." Pays $100 (more with photos or art), per 800 words used.
Photos: Submit photos with accompanying ms. Payment for photos can be included in purchase price of article. Uses 5x7 minimum b&w glossy photos or 35mm, 2¼x2¼ or larger color transparencies. Captions preferred. Buys all rights for cover photos and all or one-time rights for others. Model release required.
Fiction: Experimental and humorous. "We purchase little fiction. But we're always open to it as long as it's very water related." Pays $50-300.
Poetry: Short; free verse; haiku; or light verse. "Prefer poetry illustrated with *excellent* photos." Buys 4-6/issue. Limit submissions to batches of 5-10. Pays $20-50.
Tips: "Study at least 2 past issues of the journal. Query us before you write the article, to save your time and ours. Introduce yourself, state story idea and why we should be interested. Give a few key facts, state main sources you expect to use, propose a deadline you can meet, and offer to round up excellent photos to illustrate."

THE LIVING WILDERNESS, 1901 Pennsylvania Ave. NW., Washington DC 20006. (202)828-6662. Editor: James G. Deane. For members of the Wilderness Society, libraries and educational institutions. Circ. 55,000. Quarterly. "There may be a considerable wait for return of unsolicited materials." Pays on publication. SASE. Sample copy $2; free writer's guidelines.
Nonfiction, Poetry and Photos: Articles on wilderness preservation and appreciation and on

wildlife conservation. Special interest in threats to North American wild areas. Occasional articles on other environmental issues and natural history; occasional nature-oriented essays and high-caliber wilderness-oriented poetry. Some book reviews are assigned. Mss should be of professional quality. Payment depends on character of material. Editors consider only highest quality photographs relevant to the foregoing subjects, usually to illustrate specific articles. Pays $25 minimum/ b&w; $75 minimum/color, except when bought in article/photo package.
Tips: "Demonstrate an accurate awareness about public land issues and policies." Show priority and urgency of coverage for your subject.

NATIONAL PARKS, (formerly *National Parks & Conservation Magazine*), 1701 18th St. NW, Washington DC 20009. (202)265-2717. Editor: Eugenia Horstman Connally. For a highly educated audience interested in preservation of natural areas and protection of wildlife habitat. Monthly magazine; 32 pages. Circ. 33,000. Pays on acceptance. Buys first North American serial rights. Submit seasonal/holiday material 4 months in advance. SASE. Reports in 4-6 weeks. Sample copy $2; free writer's guidelines.
Nonfiction: Exposé (on threats, wildlife problems to national parks); descriptive articles about new or proposed national parks and wilderness parks; "adventures" in national parks (crosscountry skiing, bouldering, mountain climbing, kayaking, canoeing, backpacking); travel tips to national parks. No poetry or philosophical essays. Buys 2-3 mss/issue. Query or send complete ms. Length: 1,000-1,500 words. Pays $75-200.
Photos: State availability of photos or send photos with ms. Pays $20-50 for 8x10 b&w glossy prints; $25-75 for color transparencies; offers no additional payment for photos accompanying ms. Buys one-time rights. Captions required.

NATIONAL WILDLIFE, 225 E. Michigan Ave., Milwaukee WI 53202. Editor-in-Chief: John Strohm. Emphasizes wildlife. Bimonthly magazine; 52 pages. Circ. 900,000. Pays on acceptance. Buys all rights. Submit seasonal/holiday material 6 months in advance. Previously published submissions OK. SASE. Reports in 2 weeks. Free writer's guidelines.
Nonfiction: Mark Wexler, Nonfiction Editor. How-to; humor; informational; interview; personal experience; photo feature and profile. Buys 8 mss/issue. Query. Length: 2,000-3,000 words. Pays $750 minimum.
Photos: John Nuhn, Photo Editor. Photos purchased with or without accompanying ms or on assignment. Pays $50-100 for 8x10 b&w glossy prints; $100 minimum for 35mm color Kodachromes.

NATURAL HISTORY, Natural History Magazine Circulation Dept., 79th and Central Park W., New York NY 10024. Editor: Alan Ternes. For "well-educated, ecologically aware audience. Includes many professional people, scientists, scholars." Monthly. Circ. 460,000. Buys 50 mss/ year. Kill fee varies. Byline given. Pays on publication. Sample copy $2.50. Submit seasonal material 6 months in advance. Query or submit complete ms. SASE.
Nonfiction: Uses all types of scientific articles except chemistry and physics—emphasis is on the biological sciences and anthropology. Prefers professional scientists as authors. "We always want to see new research findings in almost all the branches of the natural sciences—anthropology, archeology, zoology, ornithology. We find that it is particularly difficult to get something new in herpetology (amphibians and reptiles) or entomology (insects) and we would like to see material in those fields. We lean heavily toward writers who are scientists or professional science writers. High standards of writing and research. Favor an ecological slant in most of our pieces, but do not generally lobby for causes, environmental or other. Writer should have a deep knowledge of his subject. Then submit original ideas either in query or by ms. Should be able to supply high-quality illustrations." Length: 2,000-4,000 words. Pays $300-750, plus additional payment for photos used.
Photos: Uses some 8x10 b&w glossy photographs; pays $125/page maximum. Much color is used; pays $250 for inside and up to $350 for cover. Photos are purchased for one-time use.
Tips: "Learn about something in depth before you bother writing about it."

OCEANS, 315 Fort Mason, San Francisco CA 94123. Editor-in-Chief: Keith K. Howell. 100% freelance written. Publication of The Oceanic Society. For people interested in the sea. Bimonthly magazine; 72 pages. Circ. 65,000. Pays on publication. Buys one-time rights. Byline given. Submit seasonal/holiday material 4 months in advance. Simultaneous and photocopied submissions OK. SASE. Reports in 8 weeks. Sample copy $1. Free writer's guidelines.
Nonfiction: "Want articles on the worldwide realm of salt water; marine life (biology and ecology), oceanography, maritime history, geography, undersea exploration and study, voyages, ships, coastal areas including environmental problems, seaports and shipping, islands, food-fishing and aquaculture (mariculture), peoples of the sea, including anthropological materials. Writing should be simple, direct, factual, very readable (avoid dullness and pedantry, make it lively and interest-

ing but not cute, flippant or tongue-in-cheek; avoid purple prose). Careful research, good structuring, no padding. Factual information in good, narrative style. *Oceans* is authoritative, but less technical than *Scientific American.* We do not want articles on scuba; adventuring, travel tends to be overworked. Prefer no sport fishing, boating, surfing, or other purely sport-type matter. Diving okay if serious in purpose, unusual in results or story angle. We want articles on rarely visited islands, ports or shores that have great intrinsic interest, but not treated in purely travelogue style. Can use more on environmental concerns." Length: 1,000-6,000 words. Pays $100/page.

PACIFIC DISCOVERY, California Academy of Sciences, Golden Gate Park, San Francisco CA 94118. (415)221-5100. Editor: Bruce Finson. 100% freelance written. "A journal of nature and culture around the world, read by scientists, naturalists, teachers, students, and others having a keen interest in knowing the natural world more thoroughly." Published bimonthly by the California Academy of Sciences. Circ. 16,000. Buys first North American serial rights of articles; one-time use of photos. Usually reports within 3 months; publishes accepted articles in 3-6 months. Pays on publication. Query with 100-word summary of projected article for review before preparing finished ms. SASE.
Nonfiction and Photos: "Subjects of articles include behavior and natural history of animals and plants, ecology, anthropology, geology, paleontology, biogeography, taxonomy, and related topics in the natural sciences. Occasional articles are published on the history of natural science, exploration, astronomy and archeology. Types of articles include discussions of individual species or groups of plants and animals that are related to or involved with one another, narratives of scientific expeditions together with detailed discussions of field work and results, reports of biological and geological discoveries and of short-lived phenomena, and explanations of specialized topics in natural science. Authors need not be scientists; however, all articles must be based, at least in part, on firsthand fieldwork." Length: 1,000-3,000 words. Pays 7½¢/word. B&w photos or color transparencies must accompany all mss or they will not be reviewed. Send 15-30 with each ms. Photos should have both scientific and aesthetic interest, be captioned in a few sentences on a separate caption list keyed to the photos and numbered in story sequence. Some photo stories are used. Pays $15/photo. All transparencies, negatives, and prints are returned soon after publication.

PACIFIC NORTHWEST, (Formerly *Pacific Search*), 222 Dexter Ave. N., Seattle WA 98109. Editor: Peter Potterfield. Emphasizes the arts, culture, recreation, service, and urban and rural lifestyle in the Pacific Northwest. Monthly magazine (except January and August). Pays on acceptance. Buys first rights. Simultaneous and previously published submissions OK. SASE. Reports in 6 weeks. Will send writer's guidelines.
Nonfiction: Editorial material should entertain, inform or contribute to an understanding of the Pacific Northwest, including BC and Alaska. Subject matter includes travel and exploration, outdoor activities, issues in the region's development, science and the environment, arts, history, profiles of places and people, and current issues, ideas and events that concern the Northwest. Buys 4 mss/issue. Query with clips of published work. Length: 600-3,000 words. Pay starts at 10¢/word.
Photos: Send photos with or without ms. Pays $15-50 for b&w prints; $50-125 for color transparencies, 35mm or larger. Buys one-time rights. Captions preferred.
Columns/Departments: Skywatch (astronomy, sky events); Scannings (news items); Books; Closer Look (regional issues and profiles); Who Knows; (questions and answers); Food and Lodging; Back Page (photo); Calendar of Events; Letters. Query.
Tips: "Query should have clear description of topic and relevance to Northwest with clips if writer is new to us. We look for entertaining as well as informative style and format plus original or unusual information and research. Many native, outdoors, or history submissions assume a more narrowly interested audience than we are aiming for."

SIERRA, The Sierra Club Bulletin, 530 Bush Street, San Francisco CA 94108. (415)981-8634. Editor-in-Chief: Frances Gendlin. Managing Editor: David Gancher. 70% freelance written. Emphasizes conservation and environmental politics for people who are well-educated, activist, outdoor-oriented, and politically well-informed with a dedication to conservation. Magazine published 6 times/year; 80 pages. Circ. 200,000. Pays on publication. Byline given. Simultaneous and photocopied submissions OK. SASE. Reports in 6 weeks. Writer's guidelines.
Nonfiction: Exposé (well-documented on environmental issues of national importance such as energy, wilderness, forests, etc.); general interest (well-researched pieces on areas of particular environmental concern); historical (relevant to environmental concerns); how-to (on camping, climbing, outdoor photography, etc.); interview (with very prominent figures in the field); personal experience (by or about children and wilderness); photo feature (photo essays on threatened areas); and technical (on energy sources, wildlife management land-use, solid waste management,

etc.). No "My trip to . . ." or why we must save wildlife/nature articles; no poetry or general superficial essays on environmentalism and local environmental issues. Buys 2-3 mss/issue. Query with clips of published work. Length: 800-3,000 words. Pays $200-350.

Photos: Gerald Klein, production manager. State availability of photos. Pays $100 maximum for color transparencies; $200 for cover photos. Buys one-time rights.

Columns/Departments: Book Reviews. Buys 5 mss/year. Length: 800-2,000 words. Query. Submit queries to Mary Lou Van Deventer, associate editor.

Tips: "Queries should include an outline of how the topic would be covered, and a mention of the political appropriateness and timeliness of the article. Statements of the writer's qualifications should be included."

SNOWY EGRET, 205 S. 9th St., Williamsburg KY 40769. (606)549-0850. Editor: Humphrey A. Olsen. For "persons of at least high school age interested in literary, artistic, philosophical and historical natural history." Semiannual. Circ. less than 500. Buys first North American serial rights. Byline given. Buys 40-50 mss/year. Pays on publication. Sample copy $2. Usually reports in 2 months. SASE.

Nonfiction: Subject matter limited to material related to natural history, especially literary, artistic, philosophical, and historical aspects. Criticism, book reviews, essays, biographies. Pays $2/printed page.

Fiction: "We are interested in considering stories or self-contained portions of novels. All fiction must be natural history or man and nature. The scope is broad enough to include such stories as Hemingway's 'Big Two-Hearted River' and Warren's 'Blackberry Winter.' " Length: maximum 10,000 words. Pays $2/printed page. Send mss and books for review to Dr. William T. Hamilton, Dept. of English, Otterbein College, Westerville OH 43081. "It is preferable to query first."

Poetry: No length limits. Pays $4/printed page, minimum $2. Send poems and poetry books for review to Dr. Hamilton, Literary Editor.

TERRA, Natural History Museum Alliance, 900 Exposition Blvd., Los Angeles CA 90007. Editor: Dorothy H. Seligman. Quarterly published by the Alliance of the Natural History Museum of Los Angeles County covering new findings of both scientific and popular interest for an 85% college-educated audience. Readership: 100,000. Pays on acceptance. "We do not accept reprints. Our material is automatically copyrighted. In case of second rights, *Terra* retains half, and the rest goes to the writer." Submit seasonal material 6 months in advance. SASE. Reports in 3 months.

Nonfiction: *Terra's* focus is on the natural sciences and history, particularly of the West. However, there is some leeway for timely subjects of wider geographical range. Photos and/or other illustrative material must accompany articles. No political or religious articles. Length: 1,000-5,000 words. Pays $250 maximum.

Photos: Some photo essays with captions are accepted. Pays $200.

Tips: "Good articles about natural history subjects accompanied by visuals will get us every time."

Newspapers and Weekly Magazine Sections

The grouping below includes the lifestyle, travel, and editorial sections of daily newspapers as well as Saturday and Sunday magazine sections of daily newspapers. They are listed geographically by state headings although some cover wide areas (for example, *Michiana* serves both Michigan and Indiana).

Arizona

ARIZONA MAGAZINE, Box 1950, Phoenix AZ 85001. (602)271-8291. Editor: Jim Cook. For "everyone who reads a Sunday newspaper." Weekly; 60 pages. Circ. 425,000. Kill fee varies. Byline given. Buys 250 mss/year. Pays when article is scheduled for publication. For sample copy and guidelines for writers send 50¢. Photocopied submissions OK. Simultaneous submissions OK if exclusive regionally. Reports in 2 weeks. Query or submit complete ms. SASE.

Nonfiction and Photos: "General subjects that have an Arizona connection, are of interest to the West, or are of universal interest. Should have a bemused, I-don't-believe-it approach. Nothing is that serious. Should have an abundance of quotes and anecdotes. Some travel and entertainment.

"We are interested in Arizona, the West, and universal subjects, not always in that order. W to be topical and lively. We want stories that show some creativity in their approach." His subjects are being overworked. No "routine historical pieces; willing to see *the* dynamite story of how it really happened, but not any more routine stuff." Length: 1,000-3,000 words. State availability of photos. Pays $50-350. B&w and color photos purchased with or without mss or on assignment. Pays $15-25 for 8x10 b&w glossy prints; $25-80 for color (35mm or larger).

Tips: "Find a good personal subject and write about him so the reader will feel he is with the subject. Describe the subject in anecdotes and let him reveal himself by his quotes. Please include social security and telephone numbers."

California

CALIFORNIA LIVING, Los Angeles Herald Examiner, 1111 S. Broadway, Los Angeles CA 90015. (213)744-8454. Editor: Linda Hasert. Weekly magazine covering lifestyle and trends in Southern California for newspaper readers. Estab. 1979. Circ. 275,000. Pays on publication. Byline given. Buys one-time rights. Submit seasonal/holiday material 2 months in advance. Simultaneous queries, and simultaneous, photocopied, and previously published submissions OK. SASE. Reports in 2 weeks on queries; 3 weeks on mss.

Nonfiction: General interest (relating to Southern California lifestyles); humor; interview/profile; and personal experience (first-person pieces on very unusual experiences). Buys 150 mss/year. Query with clips of published work. Length: 2,000-4,000 words. Pays $100-300.

Columns/Departments: A Conversation With . . . (Q-and-A-format interviews of people who are well-known and have a philosophy of interest to Southern Californians). Buys 50 mss/year. Query with clips of published work. Pays $100.

CALIFORNIA LIVING, San Francisco Examiner, 110 Fifth St., San Francisco CA 94103. (415)777-7905. Editor: Hal Silverman. Managing Editor: Jane Ciabattari. Weekly magazine covering lifestyle, leisure, service and untold stories with a Bay area and/or regional focus, for newspaper readers. Circ. 750,000. Pays on publication. Byline given. Buys one-time rights. Submit seasonal/holiday material 3 months in advance. Photocopied submissions OK. SASE. Reports in 3 weeks. Sample copy "available on newsstands."

Nonfiction: Lifestyle, leisure and service articles, untold stories, and behind-the-scenes news stories; must have a Bay area and/or regional focus. Buys 150 mss/year. Send complete ms. Length: 1,500-2,500 words. Pays $200.

Photos: Send photos with ms. Reviews 35mm color transparencies and 8x10 glossy prints. Pays "open fee." Captions and model releases required. Buys one-time rights.

Fiction: Novel excerpts (relating to the Bay area).

CALIFORNIA TODAY, 750 Ridder Park Dr., San Jose CA 95190. (408)289-5602. Editor: John Parkyn. For a general audience. Weekly rotogravure newspaper-magazine, published with the *San Jose Mercury News*. Circ. 290,000. Byline given. Buys 100 mss/year. Pays on acceptance. Free sample copy. Will consider photocopied and simultaneous submissions, if the simultaneous submission is out of their area. Submit seasonal material (skiing, wine, outdoor living) 3 months in advance. Reports in 4 weeks. Query. SASE.

Nonfiction and Photos: A general newspaper-magazine requiring that most subjects be related to California and interests in that area. Will consider subjects outside California if subject is of broad or national appeal. Length: 1,000-4,000 words. Pays $100-400. Payment varies for b&w and color photos purchased with or without mss. Captions required.

OAKLAND TRIBUNE/EASTBAY TODAY, Gannett Co., Box 24424, Oakland CA 94623. (415)645-2547. Daily newspaper for the greater San Francisco/Oakland Bay area. Circ. 210,000. Pays on publication. Byline given. Not copyrighted. Buys one-time rights. Submit seasonal/holiday material 6 weeks in advance. Simultaneous queries and simultaneous, photocopied, and previously published submissions OK. SASE.

Nonfiction: Opinion. Length: 800 words maximum. Pays $50 maximum.

THE SACRAMENTO BEE, Box 15779, Sacramento CA 95813. For a general readership; higher-than-average education; higher-than-average interest in politics and government; oriented toward outdoor activity. Newspaper; 60 pages. Daily. Circ. 214,000 daily; 245,000 Sunday. Not copyrighted. Buys 200 mss/year. Pays on publication. Will consider simultaneous submissions if they are not duplicated in Northern California. Reports in 2 weeks. Query or submit complete ms to Features Editor. SASE.

Nonfiction and Photos: Human interest features, news background. Prefers narrative feature style. Does not want to see sophomoric humor. Will consider interviews, profiles, nostalgic and historical articles; exposé; personal experience. Length: 100-1,500 words. Pays $20-100. B&w glossy prints and color (negatives) purchased with or without mss. Pays $15-75 for b&w; $25-100 for color. Captions required.

SUNDAY MAGAZINE, *Daily News* of Los Angeles, 14539 Sylvan St., Van Nuys CA 91401. (213)873-2051. Editor: Debbie Goffa. Weekly magazine. Circ. 250,000. Pays on publication. Byline given. Buys one-time rights. Submit seasonal/holiday material 6 weeks in advance. SASE. Reports in 1 month. Writer's guidelines for business size SAE and 1 first class stamp.
Nonfiction: General interest; historical/nostalgic; humor; interview/profile; opinion (essay); personal experience ("extremely unusual"); political stories; sports features; and investigative pieces. Buys 175 mss/year. Query with clips of published work. Length: 1,500-3,000 words. Pays $100-300.

Colorado

BOULDER DAILY CAMERA FOCUS MAGAZINE, Box 591, Boulder CO 80306. (303)442-1202. Editor-in-Chief: Barbara Baumgarten. 50% freelance written. Emphasizes subjects of particular interest to Boulder County residents. Weekly tabloid; 40 pages. Circ. 28,000. Pays on first of month following publication. Buys one-time rights. Byline given. Phone queries OK. Submit seasonal/holiday material 6-8 weeks in advance. Photocopied submissions OK. SASE. Reports in 2 weeks.
Nonfiction: Exposé (anything relevant to Boulder County that needs exposing); informational (emphasis on good writing, warmth and impact); historical (pertaining to Boulder County or Colorado in general); interview and profile (stress local angle); photo feature (featuring Boulder County or areas in Colorado and Rocky Mountain West where Boulder County residents are apt to go). Buys 100 mss/year. Query. Length: 700-2,000 words. Pays 40-80¢ a column inch.
Photos: Purchased with or without mss, or on assignment. Captions required. Query. Pays $5 for 8x10 b&w glossy prints; $8 for 35mm or 2¼x2¼ (or larger) color transparencies.

CONTEMPORARY MAGAZINE, Sunday supplement to *The Denver Post*, 650 15th St., Denver CO 80201. Editor: Katie Dean. For "young, professional, sophisticated people aware of today's issues and lifestyles." Newspaper format. Buys first rights. Pays on publication. No query required. "We are selective. Want humorous, or bright upbeat material." No commentary. Submit seasonal material 3 months in advance. Reporting time varies. SASE.
Nonfiction: Length of 500-1,500 words. Pays $50-75.
Tips: "We are looking for humor and stories that appeal to young, professional people with sophisticated tastes in the age group 20-50."

EMPIRE MAGAZINE, *The Denver Post*, Box 1709, Denver CO 80201. (303)820-1687. Editor: Carl Skiff. Weekly. Buys 250 mss/year. Buys first rights. Byline given. Pays on acceptance for nonfiction; on publication for photos. Query. SASE.
Nonfiction and Photos: "A rotogravure magazine covering the general scene in our circulation area. We are looking for material of national magazine quality in interest and writing style, but with a strong, regional peg. Our region focuses on Colorado, Wyoming, Utah, New Mexico, Montana, Idaho, western Kansas and Nebraska. We need solidly researched articles about exciting things, personalities and situations. We also need light humor and reminiscences." Length: 2,500 words maximum. Pays about 7¢/word. "Photographs can help sell a story." B&w photos are purchased with ms or as singles or series or as picture stories (500 words). Picture stories use 5-8 photos; query. Pays $75 for color transparencies used for cover; $100 for double spread; $25 for singles (color) used inside; $15 for b&w.

NOW, *Rocky Mountain News*, 400 W. Colfax Ave., Denver CO 80204. (303)892-5000. Feature Editor: Brad Thompson. Sunday supplement of daily newspaper covering general interest topics; newspaper circulates throughout Colorado and southern part of Wyoming. Circ. 300,000. Pays on publication. Byline given. Buys one-time rights. Submit seasonal/holiday material 1 month in advance. Simultaneous and previously published submissions OK ("if outside circulation area—Colorado and Southern Wyoming"). SASE. Reports in 1 month.
Nonfiction: Investigative; general interest; historical; photo feature; articles with Western angle on an out-of-the-way place; and the arts (with a Denver angle). Also looking for commentary pieces for Sunday newspapers; query Jay Ambrose. Buys 20 mss/year. Send complete ms. Length: 1,500-2,000 words. Pays $30-100.

Photos: State availability of photos or send photos with ms ("if article covers an event we can't cover ourselves"). Reviews color transparencies and 8x10 b&w glossy prints. Pay varies. Captions required. Buys one-time rights.

Connecticut

THE HARTFORD COURANT MAGAZINE, 285 Broad St., Hartford CT 06115. (203)241-6200. Editor: Joel Lang. Weekly magazine for a Connecticut audience. Circ. 280,000. Pays on publication. Byline given. Buys one-time rights. Submit seasonal/holiday material 2 months in advance. Previously published work OK. Reports in 2 weeks.
Nonfiction: General interest; historical/nostalgic; interview/profile (of people of local interest); photo feature (of local interest); and essays (anecdotal and personal). "Eighty-five percent of articles have a Connecticut angle." Buys 60-100 mss/year. Query. Length: 1,500-3,000 words. Pays $300 maximum.
Photos: "Photos are usually assigned." State availability of photos.
Fillers: Anecdotes and personal essays. Buys 35/year. Length: 300-600 words. Pays $75.

District of Columbia

HOME/LIFE AND GARDEN, Washington Star, 225 Virginia Ave., SE, Washington DC 20061. (202)484-4319. Editor: John Montorio. Associate Editor: Constance Kurz. Weekly magazine covering lifestyles, home gardening, architecture, food, entertaining and crafts; shelter magazine for newspaper readers. Circ. 326,000. Pays on publication. Byline given. Buys first North American serial rights. Submit seasonal/holiday material 3 months in advance. Simultaneous queries, and simultaneous (if so indicated) and photocopied submissions OK. SASE. Reports in 1 month.
Nonfiction: Historical/nostalgic (architecture- and design-related); how-to (improve a home); new product (gadgets, housewares, books); photo feature (home-related); and technical (home computers, video and household appliances). No articles on fashion. Buys 25 mss/year. Send complete ms. Length: 750-2,000 words. Pays $100-300.
Photos: Send photos with ms. Reviews 8x10 b&w glossy prints. "Photos are paid for with payment for ms." Captions required; model release preferred. Buys one-time rights.
Columns/Departments: The Home Life (essays). Buys 12-50 mss/year. Send complete ms. Length: 1,000 words minimum. Pays $100-300.

PRESERVATION NEWS, 1785 Massachusetts Ave., NW, Washington DC 20036. (202)673-4074. Publisher: Terry B. Morton. Editor: Carleton Knight, III. Monthly newspaper for members of the National Trust for Historic Preservation. Circ. 165,000. Tabloid format, 12-16 pages. Pays on publication. Reports in 6 weeks. Free sample copy with guidelines. Not copyrighted. Previously published work OK. "The National Trust is a diverse group of individuals interested in preserving America's built environment and concerned with the physical fabric of our cities and its preservation."
Articles: Carleton Knight III, Editor. "The newspaper is quite small and the amount of news is inordinately large. Thus most of the stories are done in-house. We do have occasion to use freelance writers, however, for specialized feature stories. They must be familiar with the field and able to write concisely about a specific subject. At the present time we are looking for stories on how various cities are responding to preservation issues, such as neighborhood conservation, energy, economics, and recycling of old buildings. All authors must query first." Length: 750-1,000 words. Pays $100-150. Buys about 10-12 mss/year. Buys one-time or reprint rights.
Photos: Additional payment not usually made for photos used with mss. Pays $15-25 purchased without ms (captions required). Query first.

WASHINGTON POST MAGAZINE, *Washington Post*, 1150 15th St., NW, Washington D.C. 20071. Acting Editor: Stephen Petranek. Weekly rotogravure featuring regional and national interest articles (Washington DC, Southern Pennsylvania, Delaware, Maryland, West Virginia and Northern Virginia) for people of all ages and all interests. Circ. 827,000. Average issue includes 3-4 feature articles and 4-5 columns. Pays on acceptance. Byline given. Buys all rights or first North American serial rights depending on fee. Submit seasonal material 4 months in advance. Photocopied submissions OK. SASE. Reports in 6 weeks on queries; in 2 weeks on mss. Free sample copy.
Nonfiction: "Controversial and regional interest articles. We want everything from politics to the outdoors, trends and issues." Photo feature. Buys 1 ms/issue. Query with clips of previously

published work. Length: 1,500-4,500 words. Pays $200-up.
Photos: Reviews 4x5 or larger b&w glossy prints and 35 mm or larger color transparencies. Offers no additional payment for photos accepted with ms. Model release required. Buys one-time rights.
Columns/Departments: Passing Show (850 word statement about life in the Washington D.C. area). Buys 1 ms/issue. Send complete ms. Length: 850 words minimum. Pays $200 minimum.
Fiction: Fantasy, humorous, mystery, romance, historical, mainstream and science fiction. Buys 6 mss/year. Send complete ms. Length: 3,000 words maximum. Pays $200-$750.

Florida

THE FLORIDIAN, Box 1211, St. Petersburg FL 33731. Editor: Judy Sedgeman. For middle-income readers with contemporary outlook. Weekly magazine; 24-40 pages. Circ. 200,000. Pays on acceptance. Buys first North American serial, second serial or simultaneous rights; exclusive rights within Florida. Simultaneous and photocopied submissions OK. SASE. Free writer's guidelines.
Nonfiction: Incisive articles should focus on Florida. Subject areas include government and politics, consumer issues, business and finance, health, leisure and recreation, food, fashion, interior design, architecture, and profiles of high-interest personalities. "Presentation should be crisp, original, innovative. No once-over-lightly features. Articles must be validated by substantial research and a high degree of professionalism is expected. Style is as important as substance." Buys 125 mss/year. Length: 1,000-3,000 words. Pays $75-800.
Tips: "We place an emphasis on professionalism, experience and quality of writers. We're not looking for stories on 'how I spent my last vacation.' We want experienced journalists and we pay well for high quality."

TROPIC MAGAZINE, Sunday Magazine of the Miami Herald, Knight Ridder, 1 Herald Plaza, Miami FL 33101. (305)350-2036. Editor: Lary Bloom. Managing Editor: Heath Merriwether. Weekly magazine covering general interest, locally-oriented topics for local readers. Circ. 500,000. Pays on publication. Byline given. Buys first rights. Submit seasonal/holiday material 2 months in advance. SASE. Reports in 6 weeks.
Nonfiction: Doug Balz, articles editor. General interest; interview/profile (first-person); and personal experience. No fiction. Buys 20 mss/year. Query with clips of published work or send complete ms. Length: 1,500-3,000 words. Pays $200-600/article.
Photos: Leon Rosenblatt, photo editor. State availability of photos.

Georgia

ATLANTA JOURNAL-CONSTITUTION, Box 4689, Atlanta GA 30302. (404)526-5151. Travel Editor: Colin Bessonette. Weekly section of daily newspaper, covering travel. Circ. 509,000. Byline given. Submit seasonal/holiday material 1 month in advance. Simultaneous queries OK. SASE.
Nonfiction: Travel (to the Southeastern US, the Caribbean, Canada, Mexico or Western Europe—any mode of transportation). Buys 20 mss/year. Query. Length: 1,200-1,600 words. Pays $50-100.
Photos: Reviews any size b&w glossy prints. Identification of subjects required. Buys one-time rights.
Tips: "We have an extensive network of writers now. Not seeking a lot of material."

Indiana

MICHIANA, Sunday Magazine of *The South Bend Tribune*, Colfax at Lafayette, South Bend IN 46626. (219)233-6161. Editor: Bill Sonneborn. 70% freelance written. For "average daily newspaper readers; perhaps a little above average since we have more than a dozen colleges and universities in our area." Weekly. Circ. 125,000. May buy first North American serial rights or simultaneous rights providing material offered will be used outside of Indiana and Michigan. Byline given. Buys 200 mss/year. Pays on publication. Will consider photocopied submissions if clearly legible. Submit special material for spring and fall travel sections at least 1 month in advance. Reports in 2 weeks. Submit complete ms. SASE.
Nonfiction and Photos: "Items of general and unusual interest, written in good, clear, simple sentences with logical approach to subject. We like material oriented to the Midwest, especially Indiana, Michigan, Ohio and Illinois. We avoid all freelance material that supports movements of a political nature. We seldom use first-person humor. We can use some offbeat stuff if it isn't too far out." Length: 800-3,000 words. Payment is $50-60 minimum, with increases as deemed suit-

able. All mss must be accompanied by illustrations or b&w photos or 35mm or larger color transparencies.

Iowa

DES MOINES SUNDAY REGISTER PICTURE MAGAZINE, *Des Moines Register*, 715 Locust St., Des Moines IA 50309. Editor: Ronald G. Linn. 15% freelance written. For mass newspaper audience, metropolitan and rural. Weekly. Circ. 400,000. Buys first rights. Pays $50 maximum kill fee. Byline given. Buys 25 mss/year. Pays on publication. Submit seasonal material 8-12 weeks in advance. SASE.
Nonfiction and Photos: "Articles heavily concentrated on Iowa, mostly picture stories. Anything interesting in Iowa, or interesting elsewhere with some kind of tie to Iowans." No travel articles. Submit complete ms and photos. Length: 750-1,000 words maximum. Material must lend itself to strong photographic presentation. If the idea is good, a photographer will be assigned if writer does not have professional quality photos. Pays $75-150/ms. Photos purchased with or without mss. Captions required. Prefers 8x10 b&w glossy prints. Pays $15 minimum. 35mm or larger transparencies. Pays $75 minimum for cover; $25 for inside use.

Kentucky

THE COURIER-JOURNAL MAGAZINE, 525 W. Broadway, Louisville KY 40203. Publisher: Barry Bingham Jr. Editor: James Pope. 25% freelance written, mostly from regular professional sources. For general readership in Kentucky and Indiana. Weekly magazine; 52 pages. Circ. 350,000. Pays on publication. Buys one-time rights. Byline given. Submit seasonal/holiday material 2 months in advance of issue date. Simultaneous, photocopied and previously published submissions OK. SASE. Reports in 4 weeks.
Nonfiction: General interest but some link to Kentucky-Indiana region almost mandatory; photo feature; and profile. Buys 80 mss/year. Query. Length: 1,500-3,000 words. Pays $100-300.
Photos: State availability of photos. Pays $15-25 for 10x12 b&w glossy prints and $20-40 for color transparencies. Captions required. Buys one-time rights.

THE VOICE NEWSPAPERS, (formerly *The Voice-Jeffersonian*), 3818 Shelbyville St., Matthews KY 40207. (502)897-0106. Publisher: William Matthews. For middle- and upper-income suburban audience. Family readership, but no taboos. Weekly. "No copyright unless the story is super-special and exclusive to us." SASE.
Nonfiction and Photos: News and Features departments. 300-1,500 words on local (east and south Jefferson County) subjects. "Manuscripts must have a local angle. Writers persistently ignore this fundamental standard." 5x7 b&w glossy prints. Pays 2¢-$1/inch; $5-15 for photos.

Louisiana

DIXIE, *New Orleans Times-Picayune*, 3800 Howard Ave., New Orleans LA 70140. (504)586-3620. Editor: Terry Smith. Weekly rotogravure covering general-interest topics. Circ. 325,000. Pays on publication. Byline given. Buys first North American serial rights. Submit seasonal/holiday material 2 months in advance. Simultaneous queries, and simultaneous, photocopied, and previously published submissions OK. SASE. Reports in 1 month. Writer's guidelines for business size SAE and 1 first class stamp.
Nonfiction: General interest (with a local angle); interview/profile (of local personalities); and photo feature (of New Orleans area people, places and events). No articles on hobbies or crafts. Buys 50 mss/year. Query or send complete ms. Length: 800-1,000 words. Pays $50-300.
Photos: Send photos with ms. Pays $10 minimum for 35mm color transparencies; $10 minimum for b&w prints; $50 bonus for cover photo. Model release and identification of subjects required. Buys one-time rights.

SUNDAY ADVOCATE MAGAZINE, Box 588, Baton Rouge LA 70821. (504)383-1111, ext. 319. Editor: Charles H. Lindsay. Byline given. Pays on publication. SASE.
Nonfiction and Photos: Well-illustrated, short articles; must have local, area or Louisiana angle, in that order of preference. Photos purchased with mss. Rates vary.

Maryland

PERSPECTIVE, *The Baltimore Sun*, 501 N. Calvert St., Baltimore MD 21203. Editor: Leo Coughlin. 50% freelance written. Emphasizes current affairs, national and international politics, social issues, etc. Length: 1,000-1,500. Weekly newspaper section; 3 pages. Circ. 375,000. Pays on publication. SASE. Free sample copy on request.

Massachusetts

BOSTON GLOBE MAGAZINE, *Boston Globe*, Boston MA 02107. Editor-in-Chief: Al Larkin. 25% freelance written. Weekly magazine; 44 pages. Circ. 714,528. Pays on publication. Buys one-time rights. Submit seasonal/holiday material 3 months in advance. Reports in 2 weeks. SASE must be included with ms or queries for return.
Nonfiction: Exposé (variety of issues including political, economic, scientific, medicine and the arts); interview; and profile. Buys 65 mss/year. Query. Length: 1,000-3,000 words. Pays $200-750.
Photos: Purchased with accompanying ms or on assignment. Captions required. Send contact sheet. Pays $35-100 for b&w photos; $100-300 for color.

THE CHRISTIAN SCIENCE MONITOR, 1 Norway St., Boston MA 02115. (617)262-2300, ext. 2303. Editor: Earl W. Foell. International newspaper issued daily except Saturdays, Sundays and holidays in North America; weekly international edition. Special issues: travel, winter vacation and international travel, summer vacation, autumn vacation, and others. February and September: fashion. Circ. 184,000. Buys all newspaper rights for 3 months following publication. Buys 2,500 mss a year. Pays on acceptance or publication, "depending on department." Submit seasonal material 2 months in advance. Reports in 4 weeks. Submit only complete original ms. SASE.
Nonfiction: Managing Editor, Features: Robert P. Hey. In-depth features and essays. "Style should be bright but not cute, concise but thoroughly researched. Try to humanize news or feature writing so reader identifies with it. Avoid sensationalism, crime and disaster. Accent constructive, solution-oriented treatment of subjects. Feature pages use colorful human interest material usually not exceeding 800 words. Home Forum page buys essays of 400-800 words. Pays $500. Buys poetry of high quality in a wide variety (traditional, blank and free verse). Pays $20 average. Education, arts, real estate, travel, living, garden, furnishings, and science pages will consider articles not usually more than 800 words appropriate to respective subjects." Pays $40-65. Some areas covered in travel pages include: Switzerland, Britain, Canada and the Caribbean.

SUNDAY MORNING MAGAZINE, *Worcester Sunday Telegram*, 20 Franklin St., Worcester MA 01613. (617)793-9100. Sunday Editor: Robert Z. Nemeth. 25% freelance written. Sunday supplement serving a broad cross-section of Central Massachusetts residents; 20 pages. Circ. 110,000. Pays on publication. Buys first North American serial rights. Byline given. Phone queries OK: Submit seasonal/holiday material 2 months in advance. SASE. Free sample copy.
Nonfiction: Expose (related to circulation area); informational (should have broad application); personal experience (something unusual); photo feature; and profile. Buys 2 mss/issue. Query. Length: 600-2,400 words. Pays $50-100. "All pieces must have a local angle. Also travel pieces and humor."
Photos: Photos purchased with or without accompanying ms or on assignment. Captions required. Pays $5 for 5x7 b&w glossy prints.
Columns/Departments: Open to suggestions for new columns and departments.

Michigan

DETROIT MAGAZINE, *The Detroit Free Press*, 321 Lafayette Blvd., Detroit MI 48231. (313)222-6477. Editor: Polk Laffoon IV. For a general newspaper readership; urban and suburban. Weekly magazine. Circ. 714,000. Pays within 6 weeks of publication. Buys first rights. Kill fee varies. Byline given. Reports in 3-4 weeks. SASE. Sample copy for SASE.
Nonfiction: "Seeking quality magazine journalism on subjects of interest to Detroit and Michigan readers: lifestyles and better living, trends, behavior, health and body, business and political intrigue, crime and cops, money, success and failure, sports, fascinating people, arts and entertainment. *Detroit Magazine* is bright and cosmopolitan in tone. Most desired writing style is literate but casual—the kind you'd like to read—and reporting must be unimpeachable. We also use guides or service pieces." Buys 65-75 mss/year. Query or submit complete ms. "If possible, the letter

should be held to one page. It should present topic, organizational technique and writing angle. It should demonstrate writing style and give some indication as to why the story would be of interest to us. It should not, however, be an extended sales pitch." Length: 3,500 words maximum. Pays $125-300.

Photos: Purchased with or without accompanying ms. Pays $25 for b&w glossy prints or color transparencies used inside; $100 for color used as cover.

Tips: "Try to generate fresh ideas, or fresh approaches to older ideas. Always begin with a query letter and not a telephone call. If sending a complete ms, be very brief in your cover letter; we really are not interested in previous publication credits. If the story is good for us, we'll know, and if the most widely published writer sends us something lousy, we aren't going to take it."

DETROIT NEWS SUNDAY MAGAZINE, 615 Lafayette, Detroit MI 48231. (313)222-2000. Articles Editor: David Good. Weekly rotogravure featuring the state of Michigan for general interest newspaper readers. Circ. 830,000. Average issue includes 6 feature articles, departments and staff written columns. Pays on publication. Byline given. Kill fee varies. Buys first North American serial rights. Phone queries OK. Submit seasonal material 2 months in advance. Simultaneous and previously published submissions OK, if other publication involved is outside of Michigan. Reports in 3 weeks on queries; in 2 weeks on mss.

Nonfiction: General interest (issue-related topics: environment, consumer issues, trends in population, trends in human rights); interview (with prominent people in Michigan or of national interest); profile; travel (international); and new product. Buys 2 mss/issue. Query with clips of previously published work. Length: 3,000 words minimum. Pays $200 minimum.

Photos: Pays $50 minimum/5x7 b&w glossy print. Pays $100-$250/35mm or larger color transparency. Captions required. Buys first rights.

Columns/Departments: Reflections (essays on topical issues). Buys 1 ms/issue. Send complete ms. Length: 750 words maximum. Pays $100 minimum.

Tips: "In query be brief as possible and include writers qualifications on subjects. Writing style is of primary importance, even more so than the subject matter."

Minnesota

ST. PAUL PIONEER PRESS, 55 E. 4th St., St. Paul MN 55101. (612)222-5011. Feature Editor: Russ Johnson. Sunday edition of daily newspaper. Circ. 600,000. Pays on publication. Byline given. Buys one-time rights. Submit seasonal/holiday material 6 months in advance. Simultaneous ("if outside our area") and previously published submissions ("if outside our area") OK. SASE. Reports in 2 weeks.

Nonfiction: "Especially looking for articles on travel in the Midwest." Buys 25 mss/year. Send complete ms. Length: 1,000-2,000 words. Pays $50-80.

Photos: Pays $50 maximum for 35mm color transparencies; $15 maximum for 8x10 b&w glossy prints. Captions required.

Missouri

STAR MAGAZINE, Kansas City Star, 1729 Grand Ave., Kansas City MO 64108. (816)234-4400. Editor: Giles M. Fowler. Assistant Editor: Christie Cater. Weekly rotogravure featuring Kansas City area stories for affluent, well-educated readers from 20-45. Circ. 430,000. Average issue includes 3-6 features and 3-4 standard features. Pays on publication. Byline given. Buys first North American serial rights. Phone queries OK. Submit seasonal material 2 months in advance. Simultaneous, photocopied and previously published submissions OK, if so indicated. SASE. Reports in 1 week. Free sample copy.

Nonfiction: "I like articles that deal in a sophisticated provocative way with issues of long-range interest. We go for indepth reporting and intelligent writing. We also carry articles dealing with good living, home, food, fashion and art. Recent articles have covered political figures, singles life, boxing, the handgun controversy, medicine, and historical periods in Kansas City. While general-interest stories *must* have a local peg, I do not rule out the possibility of using non-local stories in our lifestyle departments, so long as the information can be applied by Kansas City people." No commonplace, trivial, shallow or travel pieces. Buys 1-3 mss/issue. Query with clips of previously published work. Length: 1,250-2,000 words. Pays $130-200.

Photos: State availability of photos. Reviews contact sheets, 8x10 b&w glossy prints and 35mm or 4x5 color transparencies. Offers no additional payment for photos accepted with ms. Captions and model release required. Buys one-time rights.

Columns/Departments: Bite (readers commentary on frustrations of daily life). Buys 1 ms/issue. Send complete ms. Length: 400 words minimum. Pays $25.
Tips: "Our feeling is that unpublished or little-experienced authors should not bother with queries, but send finished manuscripts only. Experienced writers might save themselves time by sending queries, but finished manuscripts are welcome."

Nevada

THE NEVADAN, *The Las Vegas Review Journal*, Box 70, Las Vegas NV 89101. (702)385-4241. Editor-in-Chief: A.D. Hopkins. 15% freelance written. For Las Vegas and surrounding small town residents of all ages "who take our Sunday paper—affluent, outdoor-oriented." Weekly tabloid; 28 pages. Circ. 95,000. Pays on publication. Buys one-time rights. Byline given. Phone queries OK. Submit seasonal/holiday material 2 months in advance of issue date. Photocopied and previously published submissions OK. SASE. Reports in 3 weeks. Free sample copy and writer's guidelines; mention *Writer's Market* in request.
Nonfiction: General interest (contemporary off-beat features on Nevada's outdoors, mining towns and back country); historical (more of these than anything else, always linked to Nevada, southern Utah, northern Arizona and Death Valley); how-to (on nostalgic arts, e.g., article on how to play mumbledy-peg); nostalgia (about small-town life in Nevada mining camps); personal experience (any with strong pioneer Nevada angle, pioneer can be 1948 in some parts of Nevada); and travel (interesting new Nevada destinations). "No articles on history that are based on doubtful sources; no current showbusiness material; no commercial plugs." Buys 52 mss/year. Query. Length: 600-2,400 words. Pays $50.
Photos: State availability of photos. Pays $6 for 5x7 or 8x10 b&w glossy prints; $15 for 35 or 120mm color transparencies. Captions required. Buys one-time rights.
Tips: "Offer us well-written material, in our subject area, from geographic areas we cover but which are well-removed from Las Vegas and thus hard for us to write about. Offer us articles on little-known interesting incidents in Nevada history, and good historic photos. In queries come to the point. Tell me what sort of photos are available, whether historic or contemporary, black-and-white or color transparency. Be specific in talking about what you want to write."

New Jersey

OCEAN COUNTY TIMES OBSERVER, 8 Robbins St., Toms River NJ 08753. (201)349-3000. Newspaper published 6 times/week for "a high proportion of senior citizens in retirement villages and a high concentration of summer resort visitors." Circ. 26,000. Pays on publication. Byline given. Buys one-time rights. Submit seasonal/holiday material 1 month in advance. Photocopied submissions preferred; simultaneous and previously published submissions OK. SASE. Reports in 1 week.
Nonfiction: General interest (trends, topics); and articles of special interest to residents of resort communities and retirement villages. Buys 10 mss/year. Send complete ms. Length: 800 words minimum. Interested in short articles (approx. 800 words) that could be developed into series of four. Pay is negotiable.
Photos: Send photos with ms. Pays negotiable fee for 8x10 b&w glossy prints. Captions and model releases required. Buys one-time rights.

PRINCETON SPECTRUM, Jade Communications, Box 3005, Princeton NJ 08540. Editor: Geraldine Hutner. Weekly newspaper covering consumer articles, arts and entertainment for a middle class, educated 18 to 65-year-old audience. Circ. 38,000. Pays on publication. Buys first rights. Submit seasonal material 1 month in advance. Simultaneous and photocopied submissions OK. SASE. Reports in 3 weeks. Sample copy 75¢.
Nonfiction: Exposé (related to New Jersey or important national issues); general interest (interviews and consumer-oriented pieces); historical (only about New Jersey); how-to (arts related articles); interview (personalities or New Jersey people); nostalgia (only for holidays); opinion (holiday material only); profile; travel; and new product (if it has a broad appeal to a certain age group). Buys 5 mss/issue. Query. Length: 1,000-3,000 words. Pays $5-$75.
Columns/Departments: "We are starting a travel column and possibly an all-year gardening column." Buys 2 mss/issue. Query with clips of previously published work. Length: 150-250 words. Pays $5-$20.
Poetry: Editor: Jean Hollander. All types. Submit maximum 3 poems. "This is a poetry section devoted to poets who are interested in a good editor and no payment for their work."

New York

LI MAGAZINE, *Newsday,* Long Island NY 11747. (516)454-2038. Managing Editor: Stanley Green. For well-educated, affluent suburban readers. Weekly. Circ. 550,000. Buys all rights. Byline given. Pays on publication. Query. SASE.
Nonfiction and Photos: Graphics Director: Miriam Smith. "Stories must be about Long Island people, places or events." Length: 600-2,500 words. Pays $100-600. B&w contacts and 35mm transparencies purchased on assignment. Pays $100/page maximum for b&w; $200/page maximum for color, including cover.

THE NEW YORK TIMES, 229 W. 43rd St., New York NY 10036. SASE.
Nonfiction and Photos: *The New York Times Magazine* appears in *The New York Times* on Sunday. Views should be fresh, lively and provocative writing on national and international news developments, science, education, family life, social trends and problems, arts and entertainment, personalities, sports and the changing American scene. Freelance contributions are invited. Articles must be timely. They must be based on specific news items, forthcoming events or significant anniversaries, or they must reflect trends. Our full-length articles run approximately 4,000 words, and for these we pay $850 on acceptance. ($1,000 after two prior acceptances). Our shorter pieces run from 1,500-2,500 words, and for these we pay $500 on acceptance. Unsolicited articles and proposals should be addressed to Articles Editor. *Arts and Leisure* section of *The New York Times* appears on Sunday. Wants "to encourage imaginativeness in terms of form and approach—stressing ideas, issues, trends, investigations, symbolic reporting and stories delving deeply into the creative achievements and processes of artists and entertainers—and seeks to break away from old-fashioned gushy, fan magazine stuff." Length: 4,000 words. Pays $100-250, depending on length. Pays $75 minimum for b&w photos. Send to Photo Editor. *Arts and Leisure* Editor: William H. Honan.
Tips: "The Op Ed page is always looking for new material and publishes many people who have never been published before. We want material of universal relevance which people can talk about in a personal way. When writing for the Op Ed page, there is no formula, but the writing itself should have some polish. Don't make the mistake of pontificating on the news. We're not looking for more political columnists. Op Ed length runs about 750 words, and pays about $150."

NEWSDAY, Melville, LI, New York NY 11747. Travel Editor: Steve Schatt. Assistant Travel Editor: Barbara Shea. Travel Columnist: Jane Morse. Travel Writer: Eileen Swift. For general readership of Sunday Travel Section. Newspaper. Weekly. Circ. 750,000. Buys all rights for the New York area only. Buys 150 mss/year. Pays on publication. Will consider photocopied submissions. Simultaneous submissions considered if others are being made outside of New York area. Reports in 4 weeks. Submit complete ms. SASE.
Nonfiction and Photos: Travel articles with strong focus and theme for the Sunday Travel Section. Emphasis on accuracy, honesty, service, and quality writing to convey mood and flavor. Destination pieces must involve visit or experience that typical traveler can easily duplicate. Skip diaries, "My First Trip Abroad" pieces or compendiums of activities; downplay first person. Length: 600-1,750 words; prefers 800- to 1,000-word pieces. Pays 10¢/word. Also, regional "weekender" pieces of 700-800 words plus service box, but query Eileen Swift first.

SUBURBIA TODAY, Gannett Newspapers, One Gannett Dr., White Plains NY 10604. (914)694-5024. Editor: Hugh Wachter. Weekly Sunday supplement of the Gannett Westchester Rockland Newspapers. Estab. 1981. Circ. 200,000. Pays between acceptance and publication. Buys one-time rights. Submit seasonal/holiday material 3 months in advance. Simultaneous queries, and simultaneous ("out of circulation area") and previously published submissions OK. SASE. Reports in 2 weeks.
Nonfiction: General interest (lifestyle); historical (well-written local area history); interview/profile (of well-known and less well-known personalities); and trends. Special issues include: June—summer activities; October—house design; November—jewelry and diamonds; and December—sight and sound. Buys 25 mss/year. Query with clips of published work. Length: 1,000-4,000 words. Pays $100-300.
Photos: "Most photos are taken by newspaper staff photographers." State availability of photos. Pay is open.
Tips: "We'd like to hear from specialty writers in fashion, home furnishings, leisure activities and home entertainment."

SUNDAY, *Buffalo Courier-Express,* 795 Main St., Buffalo NY 14240. (716)855-6565. Acting Editor: Mitch Gerber. Weekly magazine with a local slant. Circ. 260,000. Pays on publication. Byline given. Buys "first local serial rights." Submit seasonal/holiday material 2 months in advance. Simultaneous queries, and simultaneous and previously published submissions (outside circulation area) OK. SASE. Reports in 1 month. Sample copy for 9x12 SAE and 3 first class stamps.

Nonfiction: General interest (topics with a strong Buffalo or western New York angle); historical/nostalgic (local and lively); interview/profile (of interesting people—not necessarily celebrities); and photo feature (with strong local interest). "Most articles are either written by local persons or generated by the staff, but we will look at good writing from anywhere." Buys 150 mss/year. Query or send complete ms. Length: 1,000-1,600 words. Pays $100-125.

Photos: State availability of photos.

Poetry: "Accepted only from current or former residents of western New York."

UPSTATE NEW YORK, *Gannett Rochester Democrat and Chronicle*, 55 Exchange St., Rochester NY 14614. (716)232-7100. Editor: Marcia Bullard. Assistant Editor: Dan Olmsted. Weekly magazine covering general interest topics for area residents. Circ. 230,000. Pays on publication. Byline given. Buys first North American serial rights. Submit seasonal/holiday material 3 months in advance. SASE. Reports in 1 month.

Nonfiction: Investigative; general interest (places and events of local interest); historical/nostalgic; humor; interview/profile (of outstanding people in local area); personal experience; photo feature (with local angle); and travel (regional). Buys 50-75 mss/year. Query. Length: 2,000-3,000 words. Pays $50-325.

Fiction: Adventure, condensed novels, ethnic, experimental, fantasy, historical, horror, humorous, mainstream, mystery, novel excerpts, religious, romance, science fiction, and suspense. Buys 4-5 mss/year. Send complete ms. Length: 2,000-3,000 words. Pays $50-325.

Fillers: Short takes. Buys 100/year. Length: 200 words maximum. Pay varies.

Ohio

THE BLADE TOLEDO MAGAZINE, 541 Superior St., Toledo OH 43660. (419)259-6132. Editor: Tom Gearhart. General readership. Weekly magazine; 32 pages. Circ. 210,000. Pays on publication. Buys one-time rights. Byline given. Phone queries OK. Submit seasonal/holiday material 6 months in advance. Simultaneous, photocopied and previously published submissions OK. SASE.

Nonfiction: Historical (about northwestern Ohio); informational; interview; personal experience; and photo feature. Buys 1 ms/issue. Query. Length: 600-2,000 words. Pays $35-150.

Photos: Photos purchased with accompanying ms. Captions required. Pays $15-30 for 8x10 b&w glossy prints; $10-45 for 35mm, 2¼x2¼ or 8x10 color glossy prints. Total purchase price for ms includes payment for photos. Model release required.

Tips: "Stories should pertain to our circulation area: Toledo, northwestern Ohio and southern Michigan."

COLUMBUS DISPATCH SUNDAY MAGAZINE, 34 South 3rd St., Columbus OH 43216. (614)461-5250. Editor: Carol Ann Lease. 50% freelance written. Buys one-time rights. Byline given. Payment after publication. SASE.

Nonfiction: "We accept offerings from beginning writers, but they must be professionally written. A good picture helps." Strong Ohio angle is preferable. Buys illustrated and non-illustrated articles. Length: 1,000-1,500 words. Pays $8/page minimum. B&w photos only. Pays $10 maximum/photo.

DAYTON LEISURE, *Dayton Daily News*, 4th and Ludlow Sts., Dayton OH 45401. (513)225-2240. Editor: Jack M. Osler. Sunday supplement. Circ. 225,000. Byline given. Pays on publication. Usually reports in 1 week. SASE.

Nonfiction and Photos: Magazine focuses on leisure-time activities—particularly in Ohio—that are interesting and unusual. Emphasis is on photos supplemented by stories. No travel. Length: 1,000 words maximum. Photos should be glossy. "*The Daily News* will evaluate articles on their own merits. Likewise with photos. Average payment per article: $30." Payments vary depending on quality of writing.

THE ENQUIRER MAGAZINE, 617 Vine St., Cincinnati OH 45201. (513)721-2700. Editor: Mary McDonald. Art Director: Marty Eggerding. Weekly newspaper supplement; 52 pages. Circ. 290,000. Pays on publication. Free writer's guidelines. Photocopied and simultaneous submissions OK. Submit "dated" material at least 2 months in advance. SASE.

Nonfiction: Local articles, current subjects, issues, trends, personalities, topical material, "think"

pieces. Will use some local nostalgia/history. "Will not accept manuscripts about any organization or event written by anyone connected with that organization or event, except in unusual first-person cases." Buys 100 mss/year. Query. Length: 1,500-2,000 words. Pays $50-200.
Photos: Will buy photos with ms; must be of professional quality. Pays $20 for 8x10 b&w prints.

MIDWEST ROTO, Quest Publishing Co., 1601 Brookpark Rd., Cleveland OH 44109. Publisher: Hugh Chronister. Managing Editor: Joan Krzys. Emphasizes "hometown Midwest America. A newspaper supplement which carries human interest articles about the Midwest and Midwest people. Circulates in 175 newspapers." Monthly magazine; 16 pages. Circ. 750,000. Pays on publication. Buys simultaneous rights. Submit seasonal/holiday material 6 months in advance. Simultaneous and previously published submissions OK. SASE. Reports in 1 week.
Nonfiction: Historical, humor, interview, nostalgia, photo feature and profile. Mss must relate to Midwest people and places. Buys 4-6/issue. Submit complete ms. Length: 1,000-3,000 words. Pays $50-300.
Photos: Purchased with accompanying ms. Captions required. Send prints. Pays $15-150 for 8x10 b&w glossy prints. Total purchase price for ms includes payment for photos. Model release required.

Oklahoma

TULSA WORLD, Box 1770, Tulsa OK 74102. (918)583-2161. Editor: Bob Haring. Sunday magazine of daily newspaper, covering travel. Pays on publication. Buys one-time rights. Simultaneous and previously published submissions OK. SASE. Reports in 2 weeks "if rejected."
Nonfiction: General interest (features); interview/profile (of Oklahoma people making good elsewhere); and travel ("lean toward locally produced material on exotic or nearby destinations"). Buys 15 mss/year. Send complete ms. Length: 300-500 words; 600-1,200 words for general-interest features and interview/profiles. Pays $30-75; $150 average for general-interest features and interview/profiles.
Photos: Pays $10 minimum for any size b&w glossy prints. Captions required.

Oregon

NORTHWEST MAGAZINE, *The Sunday Oregonian*, 1320 SW Broadway, Portland OR 97201. Editor: Joseph R. Bianco. For a family audience with somewhat higher education level in Oregon than average. Weekly Sunday supplement magazine; 28-40 pages. Circ. 420,000. Buys all rights. Buys 600-650 mss/year. Pays in the closest period to the 15th of the month following publication. No photocopied submissions. Will consider simultaneous submissions. Reports in 2 weeks. Query or submit complete ms. SASE.
Nonfiction and Photos: "Articles of interest to the Northwest. Topical and (sometimes) controversial. Periodically, an issue is devoted to a theme. For example, the theme of 'Outdoors' is how-to. How to do the hockey stop in skiing, how to find a remote hiking ridge, etc. Keep Northwest articles short, topical, and of interest to the Northwest. Ecology, environment and social mores are always subjects of interest. Also, personality profiles of people of interest." Length: 800-1,500 words. Pays $75-100. 8x10 b&w glossy prints are purchased with mss or on assignment. Captions required.
Poetry: Avant-garde, free verse, Haiku, light verse and traditional. Buys 200-300 mss/year. Pays $5 minimum.
Fillers: Short pieces. Buys 300/year. Length: 500 words maximum. Pays $15-50.
Tips: "Writing quality, rather than subject matter, is our primary criterion. If the story has not been written, query the magazine editor first, to see if it is a topic of interest."

Pennsylvania

THE PITTSBURGH PRESS, 34 Blvd. of Allies, Pittsburgh PA 15230. (412)263-1100. Features Editor: Louis J. Laurenzi. For general newspaper readers. Publishes 3 weekly magazines. Circ. 700,000. Not copyrighted. Byline given. Buys 25-50 mss/year. Pays on publication. Reports in 2 weeks. Submit complete ms. SASE.
Nonfiction and Photos: Picture-oriented material for the *Roto Magazine*; family type stories for *Family Magazine*. Must be local subjects with good general interest. Informational, how-to, per-

sonal experience, profile, inspirational, humor, historical and nostalgia. Pays $25/published page. Some additional payment for b&w photos used with mss.
Tips: "Submit good copy. We prefer receiving the actual manuscripts rather than suggestions for stories. We base our judgment on the whole content."

TODAY MAGAZINE, *Philadelphia Inquirer*, 400 N. Broad St., Philadelphia PA 19101. Editor-in-Chief: David Boldt. Managing Editor: Mary Lowe Kennedy. Sunday magazine section for city and suburban readers. Weekly; 36 pages. Circ. 850,000. Pays on publication. Buys first North American serial rights. Submit seasonal/holiday material 3 months in advance of issue date. Photocopied submissions OK. SASE. Reports in 2 months. Free sample copy.
Nonfiction: "Most of our material is written by freelance writers. Major feature articles generally run 3,000-7,000 words. Also buy some shorter articles (500-1,000 words) for the *Our Town* section, and, occasionally short humorous articles with local angle. We use mainly articles that consist of reporting on, and analysis of, local issues and personalities. Blatant bias in favor of local writers." Query. Pays $250-350 for major articles from first-time contributors.
Tips: "Query should have a dynamite idea, evidence of an effective writing style, clear concept of story structure and reporting plan, with good clips."

Rhode Island

SUNDAY JOURNAL MAGAZINE, (formerly *Rhode Islander*), *The Providence Journal*, Providence RI 02902. (401)277-7263. Co-editors: Wayne Worcester, Maureen Croteau. Sunday magazine section. Circ. 230,000. Buys first rights. Pays on acceptance. Free sample copy. Reports in 2 weeks. Query or submit complete ms. SASE.
Nonfiction and Photos: "Always looking for new writers with real talent. Prefer anecdotal, highly descriptive, thought-provoking articles concerning Rhode Island and southern New England." Photos purchased with mss. "Our weekly feature 'The Back Page' needs essays, humor, nostalgia, etc., intelligently written and thought-provoking. Length: 1,000 words maximum. Pays $100.
Tips: "A phone call is better than a query letter. If you have some specific story ideas, you are always welcome. Read the magazine first; sample copies sent on request. We're always looking for new talent in southern New England. No single photographs, fiction, poetry or commentary on national events."

Tennessee

MID SOUTH MAGAZINE, Commercial Appeal, 495 Union Ave., Memphis TN 38101. (901)529-2111. Editor: Karen Brehm. Sunday newspaper supplement. Circ. 260,000. Pays after publication. Byline given. Buys one-time rights. Simultaneous queries, and photocopied and previously published submissions (if so indicated) OK. SASE. Reports in 3 weeks.
Nonfiction: General interest (with regional tie-in). Buys 12 mss/year. Query with clips of published work. Length: 1,500-2,000 words. Pays $100.
Photos: State availability of photos. Reviews color transparencies and 5x7 b&w glossy prints. "Photos are paid for with payment for ms." Buys one-time rights.
Columns/Departments: Viewpoints (political background, economic commentary, psychological issues, social issues). Buys 50 mss/year. Send complete ms. Length: 1,500-2,000 words. Pays $100.

Texas

SAN ANTONIO EXPRESS-NEWS, Box 2171, San Antonio TX 78297. (512)225-7411. Daily newspaper. Circ. 400,000. Pays on publication. Byline given. Buys one-time rights. Submit seasonal/holiday material 2 months in advance. Simultaneous, photocopied, and previously published ("exclusive to us in South Texas") submissions OK. Reports in 1 month.
Nonfiction: Sunday Editor: Ron White. Travel Editor: John Goodspeed. General interest (anything with a regional angle); and travel (any place in the world). Buys 75 mss/year. Send complete ms. Length: 1,000-5,000 words. Pays $30-100 ("sometimes higher").
Photos: State availability of photos. Reviews 35mm color transparencies (accompanying travel articles); and b&w glossy prints. Captions required.

SCENE MAGAZINE, Sunday Magazine of *The Dallas Morning News*, Belo Corporation, Communications Center, Dallas TX 75265. (214)745-8432. Editor: Betty Cook. Weekly magazine. "We are a lively, topical, sometimes controversial magazine devoted to informing, enlightening and entertaining our urban sunbelt readers with material which is relevant to their lifestyles and interests." Circ. 351,000. Pays on "scheduling." Byline given. Buys first North American serial rights or simultaneous rights. Submit seasonal/holiday material 3 months in advance. Simultaneous queries and simultaneous submissions OK ("if not competitive in our area"). SASE. Reports in 1 month on queries; 6 weeks on mss. Sample copy $1.

Nonfiction: Exposé ("anything Dallas- or Texas-related that is fully substantiated"); general interest; historical/nostalgic (used occasionally); how-to (home, shelter and garden); humor (short); interview/profile; new product (for the home and garden); opinion (reader column department); and uncommon adventure articles. "We look for an exciting style in short, lively, fresh material that is written to indulge the reader rather than the writer. All material must have either a regional or a specific universal frame of reference." Special issues include: Spring and fall home furnishings theme issues. Buys 125-175 mss/year. Query with clips of published work or send complete ms. Length: 750-3,000 words. Pays $75-500.

Photos: State availability of photos. Pays $15-25 for b&w contact sheets; and $25-150 for 35mm or larger color transparencies. Captions, model release, and identification of subjects required. Buys one-time rights.

Columns/Departments: Trina Stovall, HomeScene editor. Buys 75-100 mss/year. Query with clips of published work or send complete ms. Length: 750-1,500 words. Pays $75-200.

WESTWARD, *Dallas Times-Herald*, 1101 Pacific, Dallas TX 75202. Editor: Chris Wohlwend. Weekly magazine. "We tend to cover hard news stories like those found in the national magazines." Estab. 1980. Circ. 400,000. Pays on publication. Byline given. Buys first North American serial rights or one-time rights. Submit seasonal/holiday material 3 months in advance. Simultaneous queries, and simultaneous (if outside circulation area) and previously published submissions OK. SASE. Reports in 2 months.

Nonfiction: Investigative (of local interest); historical/nostalgic; interview/profile (outstanding people of local interest); opinion (essays); photo feature (album style); and discovery pieces on out-of-the-way place. No service articles. Buys 50 mss/year. Query. Length: 1,500-3,000 words. Pays $250-750.

Photos: State availability of photos. Reviews 35mm color transparencies and 8x10 b&w glossy prints. Pays negotiable fee. Captions required. Buys one-time rights.

Tips: "Our only criterior is that we find the material interesting and well-written, although most accepted submissions have a Southwest slant."

Washington

SUNDAY MAGAZINE, *Tacoma News Tribune*, Box 11000, Tacoma WA 98411. (206)597-8671. Editor: Dick Kunkle. 15% freelance written. Sunday supplement. Circ. 100,000. Pays on publication. Byline given. Query. Reports "immediately." SASE.

Nonfiction and Photos: Articles and photos about Pacific Northwest, particularly the Puget Sound area. Historical, biographical, recreational stories. Length: 1,000 words maximum. Pays $50/printed tabloid page, whether pictures, text or both. Also occasionally buys a color cover transparency for $60. Northwest subjects only.

TOTEM MAGAZINE, *The Daily Olympian*, Box 407, Olympia WA 98507. Editor: Rob Schorman. For newspaper readers. Sunday tabloid; 12 pages. Weekly. Circ. 31,000. Not copyrighted. Byline given. Buys 50 mss/year. Pays on publication. Free sample copy to writer on request if postage is included. No photocopied or simultaneous submissions. Reports in 30 days. Query. SASE.

Nonfiction and Photos: Regionally-oriented features and news features. Must be bright and fast-paced material. People, places or things—but no first-person articles. Historical and topical pieces dealing with the immediate area, interview, profile, humor, historical and travel. Length: 800-2,000 words. Pays $35-60. Buys color transparencies or b&w (8x10) prints with mss. Pays $5 for both b&w and color.

Tips: "We prefer to see ms. Only publish on spec and won't make any promises until the story is in our hands."

VENTURE, (formerly *Leisure Places to Go, Things to Do*), Sunday Magazine, Leisure Department, *The Herald*, Box 930, Everett WA 98206. (206)259-5151. Editor: Nancy Erickson. Weekly tabloid Sunday supplement. Circ. 63,000. Pays on publication. Buys one-time rights. Byline given. Simultaneous, photocopied and previously published material OK. SASE. Query first. Reports in 1 month.

Nonfiction: Outdoor recreation; offbeat leisure activities, boating, places to go, things to do. Mini-trips; one or two day trips from Everett-Seattle area of interest to families; getaways; indoors or out: museums, parks, tours, scenic drives, shopping or browsing; also, travel, books, celebrity features, music, home entertainment equipment. Pays $45-70. How-to features for outdoors, leisure, hobbies. How-to stories pay $45-55. Query.

Photos: Color (transparencies only), $35/published photo. B&w photos, $20-25 with ms.

West Virginia

STATE MAGAZINE, *Sunday Gazette-Mail,* 1001 Virginia St. E., Charleston WV 25330. Editor: Diane Lytle. 95% freelance written. For family newspaper readers. Weekly newspaper magazine. Estab. 1952. Circ. 100,000. Not copyrighted. Byline given. Buys 100-125 mss/year. Pays on publication. Sample copy for SASE. Photocopied submissions OK. Simultaneous submissions are considered, if not made to other West Virginia newspapers. Reports in 30-90 days. Query. SASE.

Nonfiction and Photos: Articles and photo essays. "Simple, lucid, tight writing with a logical organization. Subjects: travel, recreation, fashion, food, interior design, trends, consumer issues, health, science, education, arts and entertainment." Length: 800-2,000 words. Pays $10-50. B&w photos with captions, good contrast, good composition, and sharp focus purchased with or without ms. Pays $10. Ultra-sharp, bright, 35mm (or up to 4x5) color transparencies purchased with or without ms. Pays $20.

Tips: "Send ms with SASE. Include phone number."

Wisconsin

INSIGHT MAGAZINE, *Milwaukee Journal,* Box 661, Milwaukee WI 53201. (414)224-2341. Editor: Beth Slocum. Emphasizes general interest reading for a cross-section of Wisconsin and upper Michigan. Weekly magazine; 24-88 pages. Estab. 1969. Circ. 530,000. Pays shortly after publication. Buys one-time rights. Byline given. Submit seasonal/holiday material at least 2 months in advance. SASE. Reports in 2-3 weeks. Free sample copy.

Nonfiction: Humor; profiles; personal experience; provocative essays; and nostalgia. Buys 50-100 mss/year. Length: 1,000-3,000 words. Pays $100-350.

Tips: "Read the magazine and get a feel for its content. Then you might try a personal experience article, a thought-provoking essay or a lively profile. We also need 750-1,000 word fillers—examples of which you'll find in the magazine. Much of our material comes from Wisconsin writers. Generally, we're not a good market for out-of-state writers, although we may buy originals or reprints from time to time from established writers. Query with specific outline of proposed story."

Canada

TODAY MAGAZINE, 2180 Yonge, Suite 1702, Toronto, Ontario, Canada M4S 3A2. (416)485-1552. Editor: Walter Stewart. Buys first North American serial rights. Pays on acceptance. Query. SAE and International Reply Coupons.

Nonfiction: Managing Editor: Peter Sypnowich. "Looking for articles of interest to Canadians from coast to coast, on Canadian subjects, written in a lively and informative manner with plenty of human interest. Effective use of anecdotes quite frequently provides this human interest; so does the narrative form employed in the modern short story. Articles submitted may cover a wide range of topics—human affairs, religion, science, politics, personalities, humor and sport, hobbies, cookery and fashion. Looking for good literary quality. Strongly recommend an outline letter, of 200-300 words." Length: 400-2,500 words. Pays $500-1,600.

THE WESTERN PRODUCER, Box 2500, Saskatoon, Saskatchewan, Canada. (306)665-3500. Publisher: R.H.D. Phillips. Editor: R.H.D. Phillips. 6% freelance written. Emphasizes agriculture for Western Canadian farm families. Weekly newspaper; 56-80 pages. Also publishes *Western People* magazine insert. Magazine Editor: Mary L. Gilchrist. Circ. 140,000. Pays on acceptance. Buys first North American serial rights. Byline given. Submit seasonal/holiday material 2 months in advance of issue date. SASE. Reports in 2 weeks. Free writer's guidelines.

Nonfiction: General interest; historical (Western Canada); personal experience; photo feature and profile. Buys 1,200 mss/year. Submit complete ms. Pays $5-300.

Photos: Submit photos with ms. Pays $5-25 for 5x7 b&w prints. Captions and model release required. Buys one-time rights.

Fiction: Adventure, historical, humorous, mainstream, mystery, suspense, and Western Canadian subjects. Buys 40 mss/year. Length: 1,500 words maximum. Pays $25-100.

Poetry: Traditional. Buys 51/year. Pays $5-15.

Tips: "Write a story of interest to non-urban readers—and realize that 'non-urban' doesn't mean 'dodo.' "

Op-Ed Pages

Within the last few years, a new forum for opinion and observation (and freelance opportunity) has emerged—the op-ed page. The op-ed page is that page in a newspaper opposite the editorial page which solicits commentary on any subject concerning its readers.

Here are the requirements for some of the largest and best-known newspapers that solicit material for their op-ed pages. Be warned that even though these newspapers cover national and international events, they often work primarily with local freelancers. Be sure to check with your own local newspaper to see if it contains an op-ed page, or if it solicits freelance material for use on its editorial page.

THE BALTIMORE NEWS AMERICAN, Box 1795, Baltimore MD 21203. (301)752-1212. Editor: Sara Engram. "News backgrounders and other commentary are most attractive to us when the local angle is plain to see. We are seldom interested in publishing the work of remote contributors on remote topics." Buys 3-4 mss/month. Byline given. Query. SASE. Length: 800 words maximum. Pays $50.

NEW YORK TIMES, 229 W. 43rd St., New York NY 10036. Op-Ed Page Editor: Charlotte Curtis. Daily. Copyrighted, if requested. Submit complete ms. SASE. "No limit to topics, just something of interest to the public. However, it should be an opinion or commentary. No news reports. We are always looking for new and exciting writers to add to the page." Length: 700 words maximum. Pays $150 maximum.

NEWSDAY, Melville NY 1147. Editorial Page Editor: Sylvan Fox. Daily. Copyrighted. SASE. Seeks "opinion on current events, trends, issues—whether national or local government or lifestyle. Must be timely, pertinent, articulate and opinionated. Strong preference for authors within the circulation area, and it's best to consult before you start writing." Byline given. Length: 600-2,000 words. Pays $50-500.

THE SAN DIEGO UNION, Box 191, San Diego CA 92112. Op-Ed Page Editors/Sunday Opinion Editor: Ed Nichols. "The bulk of the material we buy is for our Sunday opinion section, World Currents. Optimum pieces are analytical essays on international, geo-political developments or commentary on domestic social, economic, scientific and political trends. We're looking for in-depth research, some original material in the article, and cogency of thought." Length: 1,200 words. Byline given. Pays $100 on publication. Op-ed page: interested in material on a broad range of topics related to current events and in-depth pieces on world events. Uses the whole spectrum of original writing—but piece must have a purpose (such as humor) or throw new light on an issue. Length: 750 words.

THE SCRANTON TIMES-SUNDAY TIMES, Penn Ave. and Spruce St., Scranton PA 18501. (717)348-9113. Op-Ed Page Editor/Sunday: Gar Kearney. "Our Op-Ed page (Sundays only) is devoted now to columns on local topics by staff columnists!"

Market conditions are constantly changing! If this is 1983 or later, buy the newest edition of *Writer's Market* at your favorite bookstore or use the back-of-the-book order form.

Photography

CAMERA ARTS, Ziff Davis, One Park Ave., New York NY 10016. (212)725-7713. Editor: Jim Hughes. Bimonthly magazine "dedicated to the aesthetics of photography and excellence in image making" for "advanced amateurs and professional photographers." Estab. 1980. Circ. 100,000. Pays "between acceptance and publication." Byline given. Kill fee varies. Buys first North American serial rights or one-time rights. Queries requested, submissions of finished mss accepted, photocopied submissions OK ("neat and clean"); previously published submissions OK ("if publication and date are indicated"), but publication not likely. Reports in 1 month on queries; 2 weeks on mss. Sample copy "available on newsstands." Writer's guidelines free for business size SAE.
Nonfiction: Historical; interview/profile (outstanding individuals in the world of photography); photo feature (exhibit reviews, photographers); technical (tools of the art on an esthetic level); and serials and book reviews. Buys 30-40 mss/year. Send detailed query with clips of published work. Length: 4,000 words. Pays $350 to 750 and up.
Photos: State availability of photos.
Columns/Departments: Perspectives; opinion (strong feelings well expressed); currents; process (technical); and books (book reviews).
Tips: "The writer must be very knowledgeable about photography as an aesthetic experience, in addition to being thoughtfully articulate in his work."

CAMERA 35, Palisades Publishing, Inc., 714 5th Ave., New York NY 10019. (212)582-9510. Editor: Willard Clark. "A very special magazine within a vertical field, directed at thinking photographers." Monthly magazine. Circ. 115,000. Buys first North American serial rights. Kill fee varies. Byline given. Pays on publication. Query. Reports in 1-3 months. SASE.
Photos: "Photography published in form of portfolios and essays. No taboos for either words or pictures, as long as they fit our needs. To determine needs, study at least 3 recent issues. Good literate writing mandatory." Payment rates negotiable prior to acceptance.

PETERSEN'S PHOTOGRAPHIC MAGAZINE, Petersen Publishing Co., 8490 Sunset Blvd., Los Angeles CA 90069. (213)657-5100. Publisher: Paul R. Farber. Editor: Karen Geller-Shinn. Emphasizes how-to photography. Monthly magazine; 108 pages. Circ. 285,000. Pays on publication. Buys one-time rights. Submit seasonal/holiday material 5 months in advance. Photocopied submissions OK. SASE. Reports in 2 months. Sample copy $2.
Nonfiction: Karen Geller-Shinn, editor. How-to (studio photography). "We don't cover personalities or the outstanding career of any one photographer." No material on nature or close-up techniques. Buys 3 mss/issue. Send story, photos and captions. Pays $60/printed page.
Photos: Gallery Editor. Photos purchased with or without accompanying ms. Pays $25-35 for b&w and color photos. Model release and technical details required.

PHOTO INSIGHT, Suite 2, 169-15 Jamaica Ave., Jamaica NY 11432. Managing Editor: Parris Lucas. 82% freelance written. Emphasizes up-to-date photography contests. For amateur and professional photographers. Bimonthly newsletter; 12 pages. Circ. 2,005. Pays on publication. Buys one-time rights. Submit seasonal or holiday material 3 months in advance. Simultaneous and previously published submissions OK. SASE. Reports in 2 months. Sample copy $1.
Nonfiction: How-to on winning contests, humor, inspirational and new products (related to photography). No material on the copyright law for photographers. Buys 6-12 mss/issue. Length: 800-2,000 words. Pays $35 for photo-text package. Captions required.
Photos: Portfolios accepted for publication based on themes. One photographer's portfolio/issue: 6-10 photos.
Columns/Departments: Gallery Insight (photo show reviews) and In The News (new products or seminars). Buys 2 mss/issue. Query. Length: 100-300 words. Pays $15. Open to suggestions for new columns/departments.
Poetry: Contact: Poetry Editor. Traditional. Length: 4-12 lines. Pays $5.
Fillers: Jokes, gags and anecdotes. Pays $5.

PHOTOGRAPHER'S FORUM, 25 W. Anapamu, Santa Barbara CA 93101. (805)966-9392. Editor-in-Chief: Glen Serbin. 50% freelance written. Emphasizes college photographic work. Quarterly magazine; 64 pages. Pays on publication. Buys all rights. Byline given. Simultaneous and previously published submissions OK. SASE. Reports in 3 weeks.
Nonfiction: Expose; interview; general interest; and historical. "Articles must deal with some aspect of photography or student photography." Interviews (how one got started, views on the

different schools); profile (of schools); and photo feature. "No technical articles." Submit complete ms. Length: 1,000-3,000 words. Pays $40.
Photos: State availability of photos with ms. 5x7 or 8x10 b&w matte prints. Buys one-time rights. Model release is recommended.
Columns/Departments: Book Review; Historical Analysis; Interview; and School Profile. Buys 6 mss/issue. Submit complete ms. Length: 1,000-3,000 words. Pays $35. Open to suggestions for new columns/departments.

PHOTOGRAPHY, Model and Allied Publications, Ltd., 130-35 Bridge St., Hemel Hempstead, Herts, England. Editor: John Wade. Monthly magazine: 80 pages. Circ. 48,000. Pays on publication. Buys first British serial rights. Phone queries OK. Submit seasonal/holiday material 3 months in advance. Photocopied submissions OK. SASE. Reports in 4 weeks.
Nonfiction: How-to (photographic topics); photo feature; and technical. "We do not want picture portfolios." Buys 2-3 mss/issue. Query. Length: 500-3,000 words.
Photos: State availability of photos. Offers no additional payment for 8x10 b&w glossy prints or 35mm color transparencies. Buys one-time rights. Captions and model releases required.

PHOTOMETHODS, Ziff-Davis Publishing Co., 1 Park Ave., New York NY 10016. (212)725-3942. Editor-in-Chief: Fred Schmidt. Managing Editor: Richard Cooper. 80% freelance written. Emphasizes photography (still, cine, video) as a tool; most readers are college or technical school graduates, many readers are in science, engineering or education. Monthly magazine; 80-96 pages. Circ. 50,000. Pays on publication. Buys one-time rights. Pays 100% kill fee. Byline given. Phone queries OK. SASE. Reports in 6 weeks. Free sample copy and writer's guidelines; mention *Writer's Market* in request.
Nonfiction: How-to (application stories to help readers in his/her work); interview (emphasis on technical management); personal experience (that will benefit the reader in his/her work); photo feature (rare, but will consider); profile (emphasis on technical management); and technical (always interested in 'popularizing' highly technical applications). No material dealing with amateur photography or snapshooters. Buys 60-70 mss/year. Query. Length: 1,500-3,000 words. Pays $75-300.
Photos: Steven Karl Weininger, art director. State availability of photos with query. Offers no additional payment for photos accepted with ms. Uses 5x7 and up matte-dried or glossy b&w prints and 35mm and up color transparencies. Captions required. Buys one-time rights. Model release required.

POPULAR PHOTOGRAPHY, 1 Park Ave., New York NY 10016. Editor: Kenneth Poli. "Mostly for advanced hobby photographers; nearly 90% are men." Monthly. Circ. 825,000. Also publishes a picture annual and a product directory edited by Jim Hughes. "Rights purchased vary occasionally but usually buy one-time." Byline given. Buys 35-50 mss/year, "mostly from technical types already known to us." Pays on acceptance. Submit material 4 months in advance. Reports in 1 month. Query. SASE.
Nonfiction: This magazine is mainly interested in instructional articles on photography that will help photographers improve their work. This includes all aspects of photography, from theory to camera use and darkroom procedures. Utter familiarity with the subject is a prerequisite to acceptance here. It is best to submit article ideas in outline form since features are set up to fit the magazine's visual policies. "Style should be easily readable but with plenty of factual data when a technique story is involved. We're not quite as 'hardware'-oriented as some magazines. We use many equipment stories, but we often give more space to cultural and aesthetic aspects of the hobby than our competition does." Buys how-to, interviews, profiles, historical articles, photo essays. Length: 500-2,000 words. Pays $125/b&w display page; $200/color page.
Photos: Photo Editor: Monica Cipnic. Interested in seeing b&w prints of any type finish that are 8x10 or larger. Also uses any size color transparency. Usually buys one-time rights except when other agreement is made. No additional payment is made except for occasional reuse of color in "annuals." Gives few assignments.
Fillers: Uses featurettes that run from 1-2 columns to 1-pagers which are short how-to-do-its, illustrated possibly by a single picture. Featurette length should be from 500-1,000 words. Pays $25-75 for featurettes, depending on use.

PRACTICAL PHOTOGRAPHY, EMAP National Publications, Ltd., Bushfield House, Orton Centre, Peterborough England PE2 0UW. 0733-264-666. Editor: Robert Scott. Emphasizes amateur photography. Monthly magazine; 120 pages. Circ. 72,587. Pays on publication. Buys one-time rights. Phone queries OK. Submit seasonal/holiday material 3 months in advance. Photocopied submissions OK. SASE. Reports in 3 weeks.
Nonfiction: How-to (any aspect of photography) and humor (related to photography). No

travelog-type articles. Buys 3-4 mss/issue. Send complete ms. Length: 300-3,000 words. Pays 20 pounds minimum/1,000 words.
Photos: 10 pounds/8x10 b&w glossy print and 35mm color transparency. Captions preferred; model release required.

TODAY'S PHOTOGRAPHER, Performance Publications, Inc., 19 Arden Dr., Amawalk NY 10501. (914)962-7570. Editor: Michael Duffy. Managing Editor: Tina Amicucci. Quarterly magazine covering photography. Estab. 1980. Circ. 90,000. Pays on publication. Byline given. Pays $100 kill fee. Buys one-time rights. Submit seasonal/holiday material 3 months in advance. Photocopied submissions OK "only to view the type of work of photographer and/or writer." SASE. Reports in 1 month. Sample copy $2; free writer's guidelines.
Nonfiction: Expose (photography-oriented); historical/nostalgic (photo-oriented); how-to (achieve quality results, different effects, etc.); interview/profile (on photographers); new product (cameras, photos, etc.); photo feature (techniques, profiles, etc.); technical (on photo material and techniques); travel (photography-oriented); tests ran on equipment; making money; and applying photography to the world. Buys 20 mss/year. Query with clips of published work or send complete ms—photocopies preferred. Length: 1,000-2,000 words. Payment "decided upon submission."
Photos: Reviews b&w or color negatives, transparencies and prints. "Price determined upon submission."
Fiction: Experimental (photo-oriented).

Poetry

Publications in this category publish poetry and articles about poetry for an audience that includes poets, students and fans of the form. A few newspapers and other special media using poetry are also included. Many publications in the Literary and Little category are also interested in poetry submissions. Various other poetry markets are listed in other categories throughout the Consumer section. The Greeting Card Publishers section is another source for poets' material.

Many of the markets that follow pay in contributor's copies, prizes or some form of remuneration other than money. Some publications may even require that you pay for the copy which features your poetry. We have included such markets because there are limited commercial outlets for poetry and these at least offer the poet some visibility.

Poetry manuscripts should have the poet's name and address typed in the upper left-hand corner. Total number of lines in the poem should appear in the upper right-hand corner. Center the title of the poem 8 to 10 lines from the top of the page. The poem should be typed, single-spaced. The poet's name should again appear at the end of the poem. In the case where the poet submits more than one poem to the editor, each poem should always be typed on a separate sheet of paper. Always enclose SASE with poetry submissions.

ALURA: POETRY QUARTERLY, 29371 Jacquelyn, Livonia MI 48154. (313)427-2911. Co-editors: Ruth Lamb, Dorothy Aust. 50 pages. U.S. circ. 325. Reports 1 to 2 months. Sample copy $1.50. Pays 2 copies. Photocopied, simultaneous and previously published submissions OK. Byline given. Standard business envelopes with 4 stamps instead of SASE as only unused material will be returned. 1 page is 52 lines including title, spaces, byline and town. Will use longer if exceptional. Send 6 to 8 poems. "We use 70-80 poems and average 38 poets per issue."
Poetry: Light verse, free verse, blank verse, traditional and haiku. No vulgarity, racial, didactic, religious or uninterpretable symbolism. We want poems that communicate with the reader using imaginative, fresh approaches to universal themes. Some one-page articles on poetry-related subjects."

ARCHER, Camas Press, Box 41, Camas Valley OR 97416. (503)445-2327. Editor: Wilfred Brown. Quarterly magazine for people who enjoy reading and/or writing poetry. There is no special slant or philosophy. Circ. 500. Pays in copies. Frequent prize contests (no entry fees). Buys one-time rights. Submit seasonal material 6 months in advance. Simultaneous and photocopied submissions OK. SASE. Reports in 1 week. Sample copy $1.

Poetry: Avant-garde, free verse, haiku, light verse and traditional. "We're looking for imaginative and colorful verse that is relatively brief, with intended meaning not so obscure as to be unintelligible to the average reader. Brevity is usually an asset, but we do not like lines of only one or two words or only a punctuation mark, which we think detracts from what the poet is trying to say." No long poems. Buys 200-250 mss/year. Submit maximum 4 poems. Length: 2 lines minimum.

Tips: "Read thoroughly at least one copy of *The Archer*, and re-study each poem to be submitted to see if improvements might be made. Re-check carefully the typing, grammar, structure of sentences and historic, literary or other allusions to be certain that they are accurate. Do not be adverse to using punctuation marks if they add to the clarity of what is being said."

BELOIT POETRY JOURNAL, Box 2, Beloit WI 53511. Editors: David Stocking, Marion Stocking, Robert Glauber. "Our readers are people of all ages and occupations who are interested in the growing tip of poetry." Quarterly magazine; 40 pages. Circ. 1,100. Pays in copies of publication. Acquires all rights. Byline given. Photocopied submissions OK. SASE. Reports in 4 months; "actually most rejections are within a week; four months would be the maximum for a poem under serious consideration." Sample copy $1; SASE for writer's guidelines.

Poetry: Avant-garde; free verse; and traditional. Uses 60/year. Limit submissions to batches of 6. "We publish the best contemporary poetry submitted, without bias as to length, form, school or subject. We are particularly interested in discovering new poets, with strong imagination and intense, accurate language."

Tips: "Most of the unsatisfactory submissions show no acquaintance with the high quality of the poems we publish."

BITTERROOT, International Poetry Magazine, Blythebourne Station, Box 51, Brooklyn NY 11219. Editor: Menke Katz. Quarterly. Payment in 1 contributor's copy. SASE. Regular letter-sized envelopes. Please notify of change of address immediately.

Poetry: "We need good poetry of all kinds. If we think a poem is very good, we will publish a two-page poem; mostly however, we prefer shorter poems, not longer than one page. We always discourage stereotyped forms which imitate fixed patterns and leave no individual mark. We inspire all poets who are in harmony with their poems which may be realistic or fantastic, close to earth and cabalistic. We have three annual contests with awards amounting to $425. December 31 of each year is the deadline for the Kaitz award, William Kushner award and Heershe-Dovid Badanna awards. We do not return contest entries. The winners are published."

BLUE UNICORN, 22 Avon Rd., Kensington CA 94707. Editors: Ruth G. Iodice, B. Jo Kinnick, Harold Witt. "We appeal especially to the discriminating lover of poetry, whatever his/her taste runs to." Published 3 times/year. Magazine; 48-60 pages. Circ. 500. Pays in copies on publication. Buys one-time rights. Clear photocopied submissions OK. SASE. Reports in 3-4 months. Sample copy $3.

Poetry: "The main criterion is excellence. We like poems which communicate in a memorable way whatever is deeply felt by the poet—ones which delight with a lasting image, a unique twist of thought, and a haunting music. We don't want the hackneyed, the trite, or the banal." Uses 150 poems/year. Limit submissions to batches of 3-4. Prefers shorter verse; "rarely use poetry over 1 page in length." Pays 1 copy.

BRUSSELS SPROUT, A Journal of Haiku, Bookfactory, Box 175 M, Morristown NJ 07960. (201)539-5028. Editor: Alexis Kaye Rotella. Biannual journal covering haiku and senryu. Estab. 1980. Circ. 300. Byline given. Acquires first North American serial rights. SASE. Reports in 2 weeks on queries. Sample copy $3.

Nonfiction: Articles on haiku. "No regular poetry or poems that try to be passed off as haiku." Send complete ms. Length: open. No payment.

Poetry: Haiku. "No material that is not haiku or senryu." Submit maximum 10 poems. No payment.

THE CAPE ROCK, Southeast Missouri State University Press, English Department, Cape Girardeau MO 63701. (314)651-2151. Editor: Ted Hirschfield. For libraries and persons interested in poetry. Semiannual. Circ. 1,000. Uses 100 mss/year. Pays in contributor's copies. Sample copy $1; writer's guidelines for SASE. Photocopied submissions OK. No simultaneous submissions. Reports in 1-4 months. SASE.

Poetry: "We publish poetry—any style, subject. Avoid cuteness, sentimentality, didacticism. We have summer and winter issues and try to place poetry in the appropriate issue, but do not offer strictly seasonal issues." Photos acquired with accompanying ms with no additional payment; also used without accompanying ms. B&w only. Length: 70 lines maximum.

CEDAR ROCK, 1121 Madeline, New Braunfels TX 78130. (512)625-6002. Editor-in-Chief: David C. Yates. For "persons with an active interest in literature." Quarterly tabloid; 24-32 pages. Circ. 2,000. Pays on acceptance. Buys all rights. Byline given. Phone queries OK. Photocopied submissions OK. SASE. Reports in 3 weeks. Sample copy $1.50; free writer's guidelines with SASE.
Poetry: Avant-garde, free verse, haiku, light verse and traditional. "No deliberately obscure or nature poems." Buys 200 poems/year. Limit submissions to 6 at one time. Length: 3-75 lines. Pays $2-100.
Fiction: Buys 2-4/issue. Pays $2-100. Submit to Pat Ellis Taylor, Box 141122, Dallas, TX 75204.
Tips: "We like stories and poems that are 'deep' (i.e., mean somehting important) but at the same time, readable."

CONNECTIONS MAGAZINE, Bell Hollow Rd., Putnam Valley NY 10579. Editor-in-Chief: Toni Ortner-Zimmerman. Annual magazine; 70 pages. Covers fine quality modern poetry, especially by women. Circ. 600. Pays in copies. SASE. Reports in 2 weeks. Sample copy $3.50. $3.50.
Poetry: Avant-garde, free verse and traditional. Limit submissions to batches of 5. Length: 50 lines maximum.
Tips: "We cannot consider new material til March 1982. We do not accept cliché verse, sexist poetry, or 'cute' poems (overly sentimental)."

CREATIVE REVIEW, 1718 S. Garrison, Carthage MO 64836. Editor: Glen Coffield. For hobbyists, educated, retired, handicapped, educators. Quarterly mimeographed magazine; 14 to 18 pages. Not copyrighted. Uses 250 poems/year. Payment in contributor's copies. Sample copy 50¢. Reports in 3 months. Submit complete ms; "one poem to a page (8½x11)." SASE.
Poetry: "Poems on creativity, good description, local history, examples of good writing, pictures of life, positive approach, good taste, simple and clear. Good grammar and punctuation, logical structure, understandable to the average reader; interesting beginnings, strong endings, objective imagery, not too abstract. We're perhaps more selective and demanding; more traditional in a knowledgeable sense. We don't want anything risque, no negativism or tearing down, no difficult typographical experiments, no excess verbosity and repetition, no intellectual snobbery or trite sophistication. No personal frustrations. Not especially interested in the topical, except positive suggestions on current problems." Length: 32 lines maximum. "Quality demands are greater the longer the poem."

DRAGONFLY: A QUARTERLY OF HAIKU, 4102 NE 130th Place, Portland OR 97230. Editor-in-Chief: Lorraine Ellis Harr. Quarterly magazine; 68 pages. Circ. 500. Cash and book awards. SASE. Reports in 1 month. Sample copy $2.50; free writer's guidelines for SASE.
Nonfiction: 300-word articles on haiku or related matter. "Must be concise and have something to say." Uses 2-3 mss/issue.
Poetry: Mostly haiku. Uses some senryu and oriental forms. Uses 150/issue. Limit submissions to batches of 5.

EARTHWISE: A JOURNAL OF POETRY, Earthwise Publishing Co., Box 680-536, Miami FL 33168. (305)688-8558. Editor: Barbara Holley. Co-editor: Herman Gold. Quarterly magazine covering eclectic poetry for writers and poets. Circ. 300. Pays on publication. Buys first North American serial rights. Phone queries OK. Submit seasonal material 3 months in advance. Photocopied and previously published submissions OK. SASE. Reports in 1 month on queries; in 3 months on mss. Sample copy $2.50; free writer's guidelines.
Nonfiction: Contact: Lisa Chutro. Interview (of poets, artists and writers); profile; travel (places pertaining to the media); and how-to (pertinent to poetry). Buys 4-6 mss/year. Query with SASE. "We like to have a letter that gets to the point immediately, tells what the writer has to offer, and what he expects in return. We can deal with a person like that. Also, always enclose SASE or don't expect a reply!" Length: 1,000 words maximum. Pays $20 maximum. "We especially need brevity, imagery; dislike breast-beating and groin-groaning. Avoid didacticism, use good taste. Good English and punctuation a must. Our *Earthwise Newsletter* is a good place to break in. No submissions read from June 15 to September 15."
Fiction: Kaye Carter, editor. "We like short stories and we love fables, and will be doing an issue on fables this coming fall." Buys 6 mss/year. Query with clips of previously published work. Length: 500-1,000 words. Pays $5 minimum.
Poetry: Sally Newhouse, editor. Avant-garde, free verse, haiku, light verse, traditional and eclectic. "No porno, religious, depressive or downbeat poetry; no poems about love or nature." Buys

200-250 mss/year. Submit maximum 6 poems. Pays $2 minimum.
Fillers: Anecdotes, newsbreaks and recipes of a specific locale (for newsletter). Buys 50 mss/year. Length: 250 words maximum. Pays $1 minimum.
Tips: "Again, send SASE and *be sure* your name and address appear on *each* sheet of work. We are holding right now, some lovely poetry which we cannot publish as we don't know its author! We accept only quality work, well-structured, we ask that you send for a sample copy ($2.50). Our editors/publishers have been published themselves and in the better mags, so we must keep our criteria top-notch. We have an *Earthwise Newsletter* to which one can subscribe for $5.60/year, which tells of all poetry happenings, contests, markets, subscription rates, etc."

ENCORE, A Quarterly of Verse and Poetic Arts, 1121 Major Ave. NW, Albuquerque NM 87107. (505)344-5615. Editor: Alice Briley. For "anyone interested in poetry from young people in high school to established poets. Good poetry on any theme." Quarterly. Circ. 500. Acquires First American rights. Byline given. Uses 300 mss/year. Pays in contributor's copies. Sample copy 75¢. Photocopied submissions OK, "provided the author is free to assign rights to *Encore*. Will require assurance if poem is accepted." Submit seasonal material 6-9 months in advance. Reports on material within a month. Submit complete poetry ms. Query, for short reviews. SASE.
Nonfiction, Poetry and Photos: "Particularly like poetry which illustrates the magazine's theme that poetry is a performing art. Fresh approach greatly desired." Traditional forms, blank verse, free verse, avant-garde and light verse. Limit submissions to batches of 3. Some articles on poetry related subjects. Profiles of poets, poetry reviews, technical verse writing. Length: open, but "very long articles rarely used." Prefers no larger than 5x8 b&w glossy prints with good contrast. Pays in contributor's copies. Also has poetry contests. "My poetry contests have grown considerably. Continuous contests have November 1 and May 1 deadlines. In addition, there are often very good special contests."

FAIRFAX FOLIO, Intermedia Productions, 3039 Shasta Circle S., Los Angeles CA 90065. (213)255-9825. Editor: Marc Steven Dworkin. Associate Editor: Mark Henke. Poetry magazine published twice/year. Circ. 250. Pays on publication. Byline given. All rights revert to author. Photocopied submissions OK. SASE. Reports in 1 month. Sample copy for $1.50 and 6x9 SAE; writer's guidelines for SAE.
Poetry: Avant-garde, free verse, haiku, light verse and traditional. "We are open to all forms and styles of poetry. Having grown out of a grassroots beginning, we encourage the unpublished as well as the more experienced poet to submit work. The unpretentious poem, beyond imitation, is something we seek." Buys 30 mss/year. Submit 5 poems maximum. Length: 60 lines maximum. Pays in 2 copies.

FIELD MAGAZINE, CONTEMPORARY POETRY AND POETICS, Oberlin College, Rice Hall/OC, Oberlin OH 44074. (216)775-8408. Co-editors: David Young and Stuart Friebert. Magazine published twice/year covering "the best in contemporary poetry and essays by poets on poetics." Circ. 2,700. Pays on publication. Byline given. Buys first rights. SASE. Reports in 2 weeks. Sample copy $3 postpaid.
Poetry: David Young, Stuart Friebert, David Walker, Patricia Tkeda and Alberta Turner, poetry editors. "All sort of poetry." Buys 100-150 mss/year. Submit 10 poems maximum number. Pays $20/page.

THE FREE LANCE, A Magazine of Poetry & Prose, 6005 Grand Ave., Cleveland OH 44104. Editors: Russell Atkins, Casper L. Jordan. For college students, teachers and persons who practice the creative arts. Published irregularly. Circ. 600. Pays in contributor's copies. No sample copies. No photocopied or simultaneous submissions. Reports in 6 months. Query for book reviews. SASE.
Nonfiction, Fiction and Poetry: "Largely avant-garde, emphasis on literary techniques and ideas, should be experimental. Book reviews. We are more creative than 'topical,' consequently there are not many themes we would single out." Fiction. Length: 3,000 words maximum. Poetry: mainstream, contemporary and avant-garde forms. "Not in the market for poetry or verse that rhymes, or verse that has a message on social problems, or work that is rigidly traditional in form, etc." Length: open.
Tips: "Send more than one poem but not more than five; on occasion, recommendation by a well-known author will cause us to regard your work with more attention."

GOLDEN ISIS, Wilva, Box 3717, Granada Hills CA 91344. Editor: Gerry Nova. Quarterly magazine for "persons aged 20 and older who are interested in cosmic, metaphysical, occult, and Egyptian/mythological poetry and short fiction." Estab. 1980. Circ. 350. "No payment or free copies." Byline given. Acquires first North American serial rights. Simultaneous and photocopied submissions OK. SASE. Reports in 1 month on queries and mss. Sample copy $1.95; free writer's guidelines.

Fiction: Fantasy, humorous, mystery, science fiction, and supernatural and occult. No "pornographic or religious material." Buys 8 mss/year. Send complete ms. Length: 300-500 words. No payment.

Poetry: Avant-garde, free verse, haiku and blank verse. "Send us material that is mystical, cosmic and/or surrealistic." No "funny or cute poems about flowers, children or little animals. Erotic, religious, racist, vulgar and poorly-written poems are also not wanted. We do not want to see poetry dealing with contemporary controversial problems." Submit maximum 5 poems. Length: 2-15 lines. No payment.

HAPPINESS HOLDING TANK, 1790 Grand River Ave., Okemos MI 48864. Editor: Albert Drake. For "poets of various ages, interests; other editors; students." Triannual magazine; 45 pages, (8½x11). Circ. 300-500. All rights revert to author automatically. Byline given. Payment in contributor's copies. Reports in 1-3 weeks. Not reading during summer months. Submit complete ms. SASE. Sample copy $1.50.

Nonfiction and Poetry: Publishes "poems of various kinds, somewhat eclectic—looking for 'excellence.' Essays and articles on modern poetry. Emphasis on younger but unestablished poets: their work to date. Emphasis on information of various kinds—to make magazine useful. Interested in printing methods of all kinds." Buys informational, how-to, and poetry book reviews. Uses all forms of poetry except light verse. Now doing chapbooks and poetry posters.

Tips: "What we see repeatedly, and do not want, is a kind of poem which can best be described as a 'beginner's poem.' It's usually entitled 'Reflections' or 'Dust' or 'Spring' and has to do with death, love, etc. These are abstractions and the poet treats them in an abstract way. This kind of poem has to be written, but shouldn't be published."

HIRAM POETRY REVIEW, Box 162, Hiram OH 44234. (216)569-3211. Editors: David Fratus and Carol Donley. Published 2 times a year; magazine, 40 to 60 pages, (6x9). "Since our chief subscribers are libraries in major cities or libraries of colleges and universities, our audience is highly literate and comprises persons who are actively interested in poetry of high quality." Circ. 500. Copyrighted. Acquires all rights. Byline given. Uses approximately 75 poems a year. Payment in 2 contributor's copies plus one year's subscription. Free sample copy. Reports in 8 weeks. Submit only complete ms. SASE.

Poetry: "All forms of poetry used. No special emphasis required. Length: open, but we have printed few very long poems." Limit submissions to 4-6 to a batch.

KUDZU, A POETRY MAGAZINE, Kudzu, Inc., 166 Cokesdale Rd., Columbia SC 29210. Editors: Stephen Gardner and Andy Williams. Poetry magazine published twice/year. Circ. 500. Pays on publication. Byline given. Acquires one-time rights. SASE. Reports in 1 week on queries; 1 month on mss. Sample copy $2; writer's guidelines for business size SAE and 1 first class stamp.

Poetry: Avant-garde, free verse, haiku, light verse and traditional. "We're willing to look at most anything, but we tend to shy away from poetry that is religious, self-conscious, abstracted beyond comprehension or into platitudes or cliches; we like images, clear and clean ones." Submit 8 poems maximum. Length: open. Pays in 2 copies of magazine.

Tips: "We see perhaps too much poetry written about poems, about the writing of poetry. Also, angst has become too easy. It's fine to suffer, but we do love poems that suffer in new ways."

LIGHT: A POETRY REVIEW, Box 1295M, Stuyvesant PO, New York NY 10009. Editor-in-Chief: Roberta C. Gould. Annual magazine; 64 pages. Circ. 800. Pays in copies. Acquires first North American serial rights. SASE. Reports in 1 year. Sample copy $1.50. Suggest writers read sample issue before contributing. Uses graphics and some 7½x5 b&w photos. "All correspondence should include SASE."

Poetry: Avant-garde, free verse and formal. Uses 40 poems/issue. Limit submissions to batches of 4. "Please mail work in normal sized business envelopes only." Length: 5-40 words.

Tips: "We're looking for work by writers with experience. Send best works. Please—no first poems or occasional poems by teenagers or others. Writers should have read a lot of poetry."

THE LITTLE REVIEW, Box 205, Marshall University, Huntington WV 25701. Editor: John McKernan. Biannual. Circ. 1,000. Acquires first rights. No payment. "We are not accepting any new material until January 1982." Sample copy $2. Reports in 2 months or more. SASE.

Nonfiction and Poetry: "Poetry, translations, critical reviews of contemporary poets, parodies, and satire. We are mainly a poetry magazine."

THE LYRIC, 307 Dunton Dr. SW, Blacksburg VA 24060. Editor: Leslie Mellichamp. Quarterly magazine; 26 pages. Circ. 1,000. Pays in prizes only: $25-100. Acquires first North American serial

rights. Submit seasonal/holiday material 3-6 months in advance. Photocopied submissions OK. SASE.
Poetry: Traditional, preferably rhymed, several light pieces/issue. Uses 45 poems/issue. Limit submissions to batches of 5. Length: 40 lines maximum.

MILKWEED CHRONICLE, Box 24303, Edina MN 55424. (612)941-5993. Editor: Emilie Buchwald. Tabloid published 3 times/year featuring poetry and graphics. Estab. 1980. Circ. 5,000. Pays on publication. Buys first North American serial rights. Simultaneous and photocopied submissions OK. SASE. Reports in 1 month on queries; in 2 months on mss. Sample copy $2.
Nonfiction: Photo feature (in collaboration with poetry).
Photos: Reviews contact sheets. Pays $25 for double-page graphic designs. Pays $5-$10 photo.
Poetry: Avant-garde, free verse, haiku, traditional and concrete. No religious, inspirational or poems for children. Buys 60 mss/issue. Submit 5 poems maximum. Pays $5.
Tips: "Poetry will be presented in a visually advantageous format. The whole issue will be through design. We are interested in seeing collaborative projects."

MODERN HAIKU, Modern Haiku, Box 1752, Madison WI 53701. Editor: Robert Spiess. Triannual magazine featuring haiku poetry and related articles and book reviews for poets and appreciators of haiku. Circ. 525. Acquires first North American serial rights. Photocopied submissions OK. SASE. Reports in 1 week on queries; in 6 weeks on mss. Sample copy $2.35; free writer's guidelines.
Nonfiction: General interest (articles of a reasonably scholarly nature related to haiku). Uses 1-3 mss/issue. Send complete ms. Pays in copies.
Poetry: Haiku and senryu. No tanka or non-haiku poetry. Uses 130-150 mss/issue. Cash prizes. "Keep in mind: A haiku is not just a mere image, it must express the thing-in-itself and have insight into the nature of the event/experience being expressed."
Tips: "Study what the haiku is from authoritative books on the subject, read *Modern Haiku*, and don't write sentimental, pretty, ego-centered, or superficial little poems under the impression that these are haiku. Submit poems on ½ sheet of paper, with one haiku on each, with name and address on each sheet. Contributors should have a basic knowledge of the inner aspects of haiku beyond the mere knowledge of its form. Simply learn what a haiku really is before submitting material. The magazine has received three consecutive award-grants for excellence from the National Endowment for the Arts."

THE MODULARIST REVIEW, Wooden Needle Press, 52-78 72nd Place, Maspeth NY 11378. Director: R.C. Morse. 96 page national literary arts magazine. Circ. 1,000. Pays in contributor's copies. Acquires all rights. Byline given. SASE. Reports in 6 months. A $2 submission fee is required to accompany all unsolicited mss. Checks should be made payable to the Wooden Needle Press.
Fiction, Photos, Poetry: "All literary, visual and plastic arts." Length: Short fiction mss preferred, but will consider long poems. "We're looking for the best in contemporary poetry and fiction whether from established or unknown talent."

NEW COLLAGE MAGAZINE, 5700 N. Trail, Sarasota FL 33580. (813)355-7671, ext. 203. Editor: A. McA. Miller. For poetry readers. Magazine; 24 pages minimum. Triquarterly. Circ. 2,000. Acquires all rights. Uses 80 poems per year. Token payment or 3 contributor's copies. Sample copy $2, together with editorial guidelines sheet. Photocopied submissions OK. No simultaneous submissions. Reports in 3 weeks. SASE.
Poetry: "We want poetry as a fresh act of language. No tick-tock effusions about everyday sentiments, please. First, read a sample copy. Then, and only then, send us poems. We especially want strong poems, more in Yeats' vein than in W.C. Williams, but we are open to any poem that sustains clear imagery and expressive voice." Length: 150 lines maximum.

NEW WORLDS UNLIMITED, Box 556-WM, Saddle Brook NJ 07662. Editor-in-Chief: Sal St. John Buttaci. Managing Editor: Susan Linda Gerstle. For "professional and aspiring poets of all ages from here and abroad. We've published high school students, college students, graduates, and people from all walks of life who write good poetry." Annual hardcover anthology; 130 pages. Circ. 500-700. No payment. Obtains all rights, but may reassign following publication. Photocopied submissions OK. SASE. Reports in 6 months. Writer's guidelines and contest rules for annual poetry contest for SASE.
Poetry: "We want previously unpublished poems rich in imagery, poems that show intelligent treatment of universal themes and reveal the poet's understanding, even limited, of the poetry craft." Avant-garde; free verse; haiku; light verse; and traditional. No "overly sentimental poems or contrived rhymes." Uses 400/issue. Limit submissions to batches of 5. Length: 2-14 lines.

NORTHERN LIGHT, 605 Fletcher Argue Bldg., University of Manitoba, Winnipeg, Manitoba, Canada R3T 2N2. (204)474-9720. Editor-in-Chief: Douglas Smith. Audience is poets, libraries, professors, teachers and English students. Semiannual magazine; 64 pages. Circ. 1,000. Pays in contributor's copies. Buys all rights. Byline given. Phone queries OK. SAE and International Reply Coupons. Reports in 4 weeks. Sample copy $2.25.
Nonfiction: Reviews of recent poetry publications and interviews with poets. Buys 3 mss/issue. Send complete ms. Length: 1,000-1,800 words.
Photos: Photos purchased without accompanying ms. Uses 8x10 b&w photos.
Poetry: Avant-grade, free verse and traditional. Buys 30 poems/issue. Pays in contributor's copies.
Tips: "We prefer to publish Canadians, so Americans have to be good."

OUTPOSTS, 72 Burwood Rd., Walton-on-Thames, Surrey KT124AL, England. Editor-in-Chief: Howard Sergeant. Quarterly magazine; 40 pages. Circ. 1,500. Pays on publication. Buys first serial rights. Photocopied submissions OK. SAE and International reply coupons. Reports in 2 weeks. Sample copy $3.
Nonfiction: Articles on poetry or critical studies of poetry. Buys 4/year. Length: 1,000-2,500 words. Pays about 3 pounds/page.
Poetry: Any type of poetry, but not of epic length. Buys 25-50/issue. Limit submissions to 6. Length: 80 lines maximum. Pays about 3 pounds/page.

PACIFIC POETRY & FICTION REVIEW, Dept. of English and Comparative Literature, San Diego State University, San Diego CA 92183. (714)265-5443. Editors: Dave Zielinski and Cris Mazza. Biannual literary magazine including fiction and poetry. Circ. 500. Byline given. Not copyrighted. "Author retains rights." Photocopied submissions OK. SASE. Reports in 2 months. Sample copy $3.
Fiction: Experimental and mainstream. No erotica, fantasy/science fiction, religious moralism or mystery/crime. Buys 20 mss/year. Length: 5,000 words maximum. Pays in copies.
Poetry: Avant-garde, free verse and traditional. "No poetry in shapes, no moralism or overt politics." Buys 20 mss/year. Length: one page maximum. Pays in copies.
Tips: "Send good, solid, original work with themes that aren't moralistic or overworked. Everything is carefully read. If material is good, we publish it. Credentials and/or previous success of author make no difference."

POEM, c/o U.A.H., Huntsville AL 35899. Editor: Robert L. Welker. For adults; well-educated, interested in good poetry. Published 3 times/year; magazine, 65 pages. Circ. 500. Acquires all rights. Byline given. Uses 200 poems a year. Payment in contributor's copies. Reports in 2 months. Submit complete ms only. SASE.
Poetry: "We use nothing but superior quality poetry. Good taste (no pornography for its own sake) and technical proficiency. We give special attention to young and less well-known poets. Do not like poems about poems, poets, and other works of art." Traditional forms, blank verse, free verse, and avant-garde forms. Length and theme: open.
Tips: "All our contributors are unsolicited."

POETRY, The Modern Poetry Association, Box 4348, 601 S. Morgan St., Chicago IL 60680. Editor-in-Chief: John F. Nims. Monthly magazine; 64 pages. Circ. 6,700. Pays on publication. Buys all rights. Byline given. Submit seasonal/holiday material 9 months in advance. SASE. Reports in 4-6 weeks. Sample copy $2.25; writer's guidelines for SASE.
Poetry: "We consistently publish the best poetry being written in English. All forms may be acceptable." Buys 500/year. Limit submissions to batches of 6-8. Pays $1/line.

POETRY AUSTRALIA, South Head Press, The Market Place, Berrima, NCW Australia 2577. (048)911407. Editor: Grace Perry. Managing Editor: John Millett. Quarterly magazine emphasizing poetry. Circ. approximately 2,000. Pays on publication. No byline given. Buys Australian rights. Submit seasonal/holiday material 3 months in advance. Simultaneous queries, and simultaneous and photocopied submissions OK. SASE. Reports in 1 month. Free sample copy.
Poetry: Avant-garde, free verse, haiku, light verse and traditional. Buys "200 and more" mss/year. Submit maximum 4 poems. Length: 3-200 lines. Pays $5-10.

POETRY NORTHWEST MAGAZINE, *The Oregonian*, 1320 SW Broadway, Portland OR 97201. Editor: Penny Avila. Poetry column in Sunday magazine of newspaper. Pays on 15th of month following publication. Buys first newspaper rights which revert to poet after publication. Submit holiday material 2 months in advance. SASE. Reports in 2-3 weeks.
Poetry: "We publish 4 poems/week from many schools and disciplines old and new. Rarely use religious poems. Seek fresh metaphor and imagery in issue and ethic-oriented poems. Welcome

the new and experimental, but in good taste." Length: "14-21 lines or so." Pays $5.
Tips: "Mss lacking SASE make the round file. Use an oblique approach to theme and subject, especially for holiday material. Make sure poems are titled and dictionaries consulted."

POETRY SCOPE, (formerly *Poetry View*), 1125 Valley Rd., Menasha WI 54952. Editor: Dorothy Dalton. Published weekly in the Lifestyle section of the *Post-Crescent*. Circ. 60,000. Not copyrighted. Buys 250 poems per year. Pays on 10th of month following publication. Prefers original submissions; no photocopies. No simultaneous submissions. Submit seasonal material 2 to 3 months in advance. Reports in 2 to 3 months. SASE with submissions and queries. Tearsheets are sent to out-of-town contributors.
Poetry: Well-written poetry, showing a fresh use of language. No religious poetry or poetry that is overly sentimental. Uses some traditional forms, free verse, and light verse. Length: serious poetry, to 24 lines; light verse, 4-8 lines. Pays $5 per poem, month following publication.

PUDDING, In cooperation with the National Association for Poetry Therapy Regional Ohio Valley Training Center and Library, 2384 Hardesty Drive South, Columbus OH 43204. (614)279-4188. Editor: Jennifer Groce Welch. Quarterly magazine covering poetry and the creative arts in therapy, self-help, and the human services. Subscribers are poets, psychologists, psychiatrists, nurses, doctors, mental health professionals, teachers, members of the clergy, and those interested in self-help. Poetry of high quality (or, for a special section of the magazine, interesting/revealing writing by patients/clients/inmates). Articles on poetry and creative writing as discovery and therapy and poems that could evoke strong response for the reader are solicited. Authors are paid by 2 copies/piece accepted and the Featured Poet is paid $10 plus 2 author copies. Estab. 1980. Circ. 1,000. Pays on publication. Byline given. Buys one-time rights or first rights. Submit seasonal/holiday material 12 months in advance. Photocopied and previously published submissions OK. SASE. Reports in 2 weeks on queries; 3 weeks on mss. Sample copy $2.50; writer's guidelines for business size SAE and 1 first class stamp.
Nonfiction: Book excerpts; general interest; how-to (conduct/facilitate creative writing groups); inspirational; interview/profile; opinion; personal experience; technical; and creative writing/the writing process, etc. Looking for poems of, for or by the learning disabled; poems for the "children's section" in *Pudding*; poems on addictions of any kind; and poems by fine art, music and poetry therapists. Query with letter indicating "your thought on poetry as therapy, your own poems, and/or your experience with poetry as a discovery tool. Large batches appreciated." Buys "up to 16" mss/year. Send complete ms. Length: 100-2,000 words. Pays $10, only if article is featured.
Poetry: Avant-garde, free verse, light verse, traditional and freewriting. No sentimental or trite themes. Buys 200 mss/year. Submit maximum 25 poems. Pays in copies or cash plus copies.
Fillers: Clippings, jokes, gags, anecdotes, short humor and newsbreaks. Buys a varying number/year. Length: 100 words maximum.

SAN FERNANDO POETRY JOURNAL, Kent Publications, 18301 Halsted St., Northridge CA 91325. (213)349-2080. Editor: Richard Cloke. Managing Editors: Lori C. Smith, Shirley J. Rodecker. More or less quarterly poetry magazine devoted to encouraging and promoting the literary arts. Not regional. Interested in social-content and current technical and scientific advances, or regressions, in poetic form. "Interested in space-age Zeitgeist. This is a general preference; we will not reject quality poetry of any form, or genre. But our crystal ball warns of trouble ahead." Circ. 500. Pays on publication. Acquires one-time rights. Photocopied and previously published submissions OK. SASE. Reports in 2 weeks on queries; in 5 weeks on mss. Sample copy $2 (20% off to libraries and poets who offer for publication); free writer's guidelines for SASE.
Poetry: Social protest-free verse. Buys 50 mss/issue. Submit maximum 10 poems. Length: 10-50 lines preferred. Will print up to 300 lines if exceptional. Pays in copies of magazine for each entry published.
Tips: "Our poetry is keyed to our space in time. No bias against meter and rhyme, if not forced or intrusive. To us, the 'me' generation is passé. The 'we' generation is emerging."

SEVEN, 3630 N.W. 22, Oklahoma City OK 73107. Editor: James Neill Northe. Published 4 times a year on an irregular basis. Circ. 1,000. Pays on acceptance. Buys all rights. No photocopied submissions; simultaneous submissions OK. Reports on material accepted for publication in 10 days. Returns rejected material immediately. Submit complete ms. SASE. Sample copy $1.50.
Poetry: "We strive to present only the most sheerly lyrical, poignant and original material possible. Seven poems and 1 reprint are used in each issue. We prefer the classical sonnet over the variations, accenting adherence to the form. Free verse is acceptable, but not as chopped prose. Good ballads are always acceptable. We like titles, punctuation and capitalization where needed. We like well-written and finely expressed spiritual poems, but they must be spiritual (not religious).

We prefer the universal approach, rather than the personal. We want lines that communicate; not rambling, disjointed, chopped prose in or out of rhyme, lacking the rhythm and power of free verse." No restrictions as to form or subject. "We are not interested in chopped prose or conversational prose." Length: open. Pays $5/poem.

SPARROW POVERTY PAMPHLETS, (formerly *Sparrow*), Sparrow Press, 103 Waldron St., West Lafayette, IN 47906. Editor-in-Chief: Felix Stefanile. Triannual magazine; 32 pages, one poet an issue. Circ. 800. Pays on publication. Buys first North American serial rights. "We share anthology rights. Some previously published submissions OK, but major portion of ms should be first-time original." SASE. "We read only in April and May of each year. Do not send at other times." Reports in 6 weeks. Sample copy $2.
Poetry: "No form bias. Mature, serious work in the modern manner. Poetry must be human and relevant. Only interested in mss typescript of from 20-32 pages." Buys 20-30 poems/issue, each issue devoted to one poet. Pays $25 plus royalties; 20% after cost.
Tips: "We are read monthly by poets of standing. We emphasize the modernist tradition of clarity, intellectual vigor, and experiment with language. We are not faddist, not ideological, not NEA-funded. We are simply not a market for novices. Our authors are now in all anthologies—Untermeyer, Norton, Meridian, etc. The would-be contributor should get to know our taste, and study past issues. Only 5% of people who send bother to buy and inspect issues. This, we understand, is a better record than for most poetry journals. Poets don't seem to study markets, as prose writers learn to do."

STONE COUNTRY, 20 Lorraine Rd., Madison NJ 07940. (201)377-3727. Box 132, Menemsha MA 02552, (617)645-2829 (effective Jan. 1, 1982). Editor: Judith Neeld. "If you are just beginning to write poetry, do not submit to us, please. Read the magazine carefully before submitting; it is our only accurate guideline." Magazine published 2 times/year; 80 pages. Circ. 800. Acquires first North American serial rights. Byline given. Accepts 100-150 poems/year. Payment in contributor's copy plus Phillips Poetry Award ($25) for best poem published in each issue. $10 for reviews and essays. Sample copy $3.50. Reports in 1 month, "more or less." Submit complete ms. "SASE, required, or we will destroy ms."
Poetry and Reviews: Reviews Editor: Robert Blake Truscott. "We publish poetry, poetry criticism and commentaries. No thematic or stylistic limitations, but we are unable to publish long narrative poems in full. All themes must be handled in depth and with a search for language. We must be made to see new!" Free verse, traditional forms, blank verse, avant-garde forms. Length: 40 lines maximum. Limit submissions to 5 poems at a time.

TAR RIVER POETRY, East Carolina University, Department of English, Greenville NC 27834. Editor: Peter Makuck. Biannual magazine "with mix of established poets and newcomers. Quality poetry, paper, layout, drawings, in-depth reviews." 52 pages. Circ. 1,000. Pays in contributor's copies. No fee. SASE. Reports in 6-8 weeks. Sample copy $2.
Poetry: Free verse and fixed forms. "We do not want sentimental or flat-statement poetry. We look for skillful use of figurative lanquage." Uses 40 poems/issue. Submit in batches of 6. Length: 50 lines maximum.

TENDRIL, Tendril, Box 512, Green Harbor MA 02041. (617)834-4137. Co-Editors: Moira Linehan, George Murphy, Chuck Ozug. Poetry magazine published 3 times/year. Circ. 1,500. Pays on publication. Acquires first North American serial rights and second serial reprint rights. Publishes the annual Poet's Choice anthologies. Photocopied submissions OK. SASE. Sample copy $3.
Poetry: We are open to poetry of any genre or length. Buys 200 mss/year. Submit maximum 4 poems. Pays in copies.
Tips: "We're very picky. We reject 100 poems for every one we take. If you're unsure of yourself as a poet, we're not for you; but we often are proud to publish 'first' poets—which we have done in every issue."

TIGHTROPE, Swamp Press, 323 Pelham Rd., Amherst MA 01002.(413)253-2270. Editor: Ed Rayher. Magazine published 2 times/year for readers interested in poetry, reviews of poetry and short fiction. Circ. 200. Pays on publication. Buys one-time rights. Phone queries OK. Photocopied submissions OK. SASE. Reports in 2 weeks on queries; in 6 weeks on mss. Sample copy $2.
Nonfiction: Historical (poetry and writing in fiction); interview (with creative writers and artists); and opinion (reviews of poetry). Buys 40 mss/year. Send complete ms. Pays $5/page.
Photos: Send photos with ms. Pays $5 minimum for b&w prints. Pays $5 minimum/color prints or 35mm color transparencies.
Columns/Departments: Reviews (of poetry books and prose-poetry). Send complete ms. Pays $5/page.

Fiction: Experimental, historical and mainstream. Query. Pays $250.

Poetry: Avant-garde, free verse, haiku, traditional and imagist. "No prolix abstractivism." Buys 20 mss/issue. Pays $5/page.

Tips: "We take the liberty of writing comments upon any material submitted (except art work), unless otherwise instructed."

UP AGAINST THE WALL, MOTHER . . ., 6009 Edgewood Ln., Alexandria VA 22310. (703)971-2219. Editor: Lee-lee Schlegel. Assistant: Pat Hayward. Art Director: Sibyl Lowen. Quarterly magazine covering "women's thoughts and feelings, especially during crisis" for "women across the country—all kinds of women." Estab. 1980. Circ. 200. Byline given. Acquires one-time rights. Previously published submissions OK. SASE. Reports in 3 weeks. Sample copy $2.50.

Poetry: Avant-garde, free verse, haiku, and traditional. Submit maximum 1-10 poems. Length: 30 lines. Pay: "none yet."

VOICES INTERNATIONAL, 1115 Gillette Dr., Little Rock AR 72207. Editor-in-Chief: Clovita Rice. Quarterly magazine; 32-40 pages. Pays in copies on publication. Acquires all rights. Submit seasonal/holiday material 1 year in advance. SASE. Reports in 3 weeks. Sample copy $2.

Poetry: Free verse. Uses 50-60 poems/issue. Limit submissions to batches of 5. Length: 3-40 lines. Will consider longer ones if good.

Tips: "We accept poetry with a new approach, haunting word pictures and significant ideas. Language should be used like watercolors to achieve depth, to highlight one focal point, to be pleasing to the viewer, and to be transparent, leaving space for the reader to project his own view."

WELLSPRING, 228 A, O'Connor St., Menlo Park CA 94025. (415)326-7310. Editor: Tim Chown. Bimonthly magazine featuring poetry written from a Christian perspective; a forum for Christian poets and artists. Circ. 250. Pays on publication. Acquires one-time rights. Phone queries OK. Submit seasonal material 3 months in advance. Simultaneous, photocopied and previously published submissions OK. SASE. Reports in 6 weeks. Free sample copy and writer's guidelines.

Poetry: Free verse, traditional, avant-garde and haiku. "No poetry with jokes, silly play on words, meaningless clichés, stale imagery or language, or greeting card homilies." Buys 125-150 mss/year. Submit maximum 10 poems. Pays in copies.

Tips: "Seek to write and to submit poetry that is powerful both in its communication to the spirit and artistic beauty. Use fresh imagery, language and sound that works on more than one level; the emotional as well as the spiritual. Send 4 to 6 poems. Learn to carefully critique your own work before submitting."

WEST COAST POETRY REVIEW, 1335 Dartmouth Dr., Reno NV 89509. Editor-in-Chief: William L. Fox. Experimental literature only. Irregular magazine. Circ. 750. Pays in copies on publication. Acquires first North American serial rights. Byline given. SASE. Reports in 1 week. Sample copy $5.

Nonfiction: Criticism of experimental poetry only. Query with short biography and publication credits.

Fiction: Short experimental pieces.

Poetry: Avant-garde. Uses 50 poems/issue. Limit submissions to batches of 5.

THE WINDLESS ORCHARD, English Department, Indiana-Purdue University, Ft. Wayne IN 46805. Editor: Dr. Robert Novak. For poets and photographers. Quarterly. Circ. 300. Acquires all rights. Payment in contributor's copies. Reports in 3 to 14 weeks. Submit complete ms. SASE.

Poetry and Photos: Avant-garde forms of poetry, free verse and haiku. Use of photos restricted to b&w.

THE WORMWOOD REVIEW, Box 8840, Stockton CA 95204. Editor: Marvin Malone. Quarterly. Circ. 700. Acquires all rights. Pays in copies or cash equivalent. Pays on publication. Sample copy $2.00. Reports in 2-8 weeks. SASE.

Poetry: Modern poetry and prose poems that communicate the temper and depth of the human scene. All styles and schools from ultra avant-garde to classical; no taboos. Especially interested in prose poems or fables. 3-500 lines.

Tips: "Be original. Be yourself. Have something to say. Say it as economically and effectively as possible. Don't be afraid of wit and intelligence."

XANADU, Box 773, Huntington NY 11743. Editors: Virginia Barmen, Mildred Jeffrey, Lois Walker and Anne-Ruth Baehr. "For an audience interested in reading the best new poetry being written." Biannual magazine; 64 pages. Circ. 1,000. Acquires all rights. Uses about 90 poems/year.

Pays $5/poem plus contributor's copies. Sample copy $2. No photocopied or simultaneous submissions. Reports in 3 months. Submit no more than 5 poems. SASE.
Poetry, Graphics and Photos: "Our main criteria for poetry are excellence of craft and clarity and force of vision. Only the highest quality contemporary poetry. We like to see up to 5 poems by a contributor at one time. Strongly realized poems rooted in human experience have an edge."

Politics and World Affairs

These publications emphasize politics for the general reader interested in current events. Other categories in *Writer's Market* include publications that will also consider articles about politics and world affairs. Some of these categories are Business and Finance, Regional Magazines, General Interest, and Newspapers and Weekly Magazine Sections.

For listings of publications geared toward the professional involved in some branch of government, see Trade Journals/Government and Public Service.

ADA REPORT, Box 5, Ada MI 49301. Editor: Piet Bennett. Emphasizes the humorous side of government: federal, state and local. Newsletter published 8 times/year. Circ. 5,000. Pays on publication. Buys all rights. Photocopied submissions OK. SASE. Reports in 2-3 weeks. Free sample copy.
Columns/Departments: Guest Speaker (provides an open forum to speak-out on government spending, The Congress, job safety, environmental protection, regulation, inflation, cost of living, etc.); Flu Report ("will contain examples of how the Washington bureaucratic flu virus is spreading—and showing up in laws and rules enacted by state governments and county councils"); Tape Worm ("articles on incredible encounters with government red tape"); and Whistle Blower ("stories that will 'blow the whistle' on government excesses or abuse"). Query. Length: 200-500 words. Pays $75-100.
Tips: "Good writing on our type of topic is the only criterion. All submissions are read. Focus more on the follies rather than strengths. Avoid painfully prolonged puns. Our interest is in quality political satire."

AFRICA REPORT, 833 United Nations Plaza, New York NY 10017. (212)949-5731. Editor: Anthony J. Hughes. 60% freelance written. For US citizens, residents with a special interest in African affairs for professional, business, academic or personal reasons. Not tourist-related. Bimonthly. Circ. 10,500. Rights purchased vary with author and material. Usually buys all rights. Negotiable kill fee. Byline given unless otherwise requested. Buys 70 mss/year. Pays on publication. Sample copy for $2.25; free editorial guidelines sheet. SASE.
Nonfiction and Photos: Interested in mss on "African political, economic and cultural affairs, especially in relation to US foreign policy and business objectives. Style should be journalistic but not academic or light. Articles should not be polemical or long on rhetoric but may be committed to a strong viewpoint. I do not want tourism articles." Would like to see in-depth topical analyses of lesser known African countries, based on residence or several months' stay in the country. Pays $150 for nonfiction. Photos purchased with or without accompanying mss with extra payment. B&w only. Pays $25. Submit 12x8 "half-plate."
Tips: "Read *Africa Report* and other international journals regularly. Become an expert on an African or Africa-related topic. Make sure your submissions fit the style, length, and level of *Africa Report*."

AMERICAN OPINION MAGAZINE, Belmont MA 02178. Managing Editor: Scott Stanley Jr. "A conservative, anti-communist journal of political affairs." Monthly except August. Circ. 35,000. Buys all rights. Kill fee varies. Byline given. Pays on publication. Sample copy $1.50. SASE.
Nonfiction: Articles on matters of political affairs of a conservative, anti-communist nature. "We favor highly researched, definitive studies of social, economic, political and international problems that are written with verve and originality of style." Length: 3,000-4,000 words. Pays $25/published page.

AMERICAS, Organization of American States, Washington DC 20006. Contact: Editorial Board. 60% freelance written. Official cultural organ of Organization of American States. Audience is persons interested in inter-American topics. Editions published in English and Spanish. Monthly. Circ. 150,000. Buys first publication and reprint rights. Byline given. Pays on publication. Free sample copy. Articles received only on speculation. Include cover letter with writer's background. Reports in two months. Not necessary to enclose SASE.
Nonfiction: Articles of general hemisphere interest on travel, history, art, literature, theater, development, archeology, travel, etc. Emphasis on modern, up-to-date Latin America. Taboos are religious and political themes or articles with non-international slant. Photos required. Length, about 2,000 words. Pays about $125.
Tips: "Send excellent photographs in both color and b&w, keep the article short and address an international readership, not a local or national one."

CALIFORNIA JOURNAL, The California Center. 1617 10th St., Sacramento CA 95814. (916)444-2840. Editor-in-Chief: Ed Salzman. Managing Editor: Alice Nauman. Emphasizes analysis of California politics and government. Monthly magazine; 40 pages. Circ. 19,000. Pays on publication. Buys all rights. Byline given. Phone queries OK. SASE. Reports immediately. Free sample copy.
Nonfiction: Profiles and state and local government and political analysis. No outright advocacy pieces. Buys 75 mss/year. Query. Length: 900-6,000 words. Pays $50/printed page.
Tips: "You can break in with a phone call. But you must show deep knowledge of subject."

CAMPAIGNS & ELECTIONS, The Journal of Political Action, Stanley Foster Reed, publisher, Suite 602, National Press Bldg., Washington DC 20045. (202)347-2380. Editor: Beryl A. Reed. "Ours is the only publication on political campaigning—the art of getting elected." Quarterly journal covering political campaign management—how to get elected. "*C&E* is a nonpartisan 'how-to' journal on the effective management of political campaigns—be they national, state or local." Estab. 1980. Circ. 1,100. Pays within 3 weeks of publication. Byline given. Buys all rights. Submit seasonal/holiday material 4 months in advance. SASE. Reports in 2 weeks on queries; 3 weeks on mss. Sample copy $10; free writer's guidelines.
Nonfiction: Book excerpts (from books on political campaigning techniques); expose (on political campaign techniques used at any level that worked); how-to (organize specific parts of a political campaign; for example, GOTV, walking precincts, etc.); interview/profile (with top political consultants, media experts). "Writing should be highly factual, on specific campaign techniques and preferably submitted by professionals in the field of political consulting." No "partisan pieces on politics, for example, 'why the Democrats have to rally' or 'why Republicans know what America wants,' etc. Only *technique*." Buys 10 mss/year. Query with clips of published work. Length: 2,500-5,000 words. Pays $100-300/article.
Photos: Pays $10-20 for 5x7 b&w prints.
Columns/Departments: "We only buy guest editorials from syndicated, political journalists or from public officials." Buys 3 mss/year. Query. Length: 2,500-3,500 words. Pays $250-350/article.
Tips: Writers should be "experienced in political campaigning and see an area in the consulting world that needs explication. Articles on how current political consulting trends have been applied at the state or local level in a campaign may be useful."

CONSERVATIVE DIGEST, 7777 Leesburg Pike, Suite 317, Falls Church VA 22043. (703)893-1411. Editor-in-Chief: John Lofton. 10% freelance written. Monthly magazine; 48 pages. Circ. 80,000. Pays on publication. Buys second serial and one-time rights. Pays 10% kill fee. Byline given. SASE. Simultaneous and previously published submissions OK. Reports in 3 weeks. Sample copy $1.50.
Nonfiction: Exposé (government); how-to (political ideas); and interview. Buys 1 ms/issue. Submit complete ms. Length: 750-1,200 words. Pays 10¢/word.
Fillers: Susan Fourt, assistant editor. Clippings and bureaucratic blunders. Buys 20 fillers/issue. Pays $15-25.

CURRENT HISTORY, 4225 Main St., Philadelphia PA 19127. Editor: Carol L. Thompson. Monthly for students at high school through graduate school level. Pays on publication. Reports in 1-2 weeks. Query preferred. "All articles contracted for in advance." SASE.
Nonfiction: Uses articles on current events, chiefly world area studies, stressing their historical, economic, and political background, 3,500-4,000 words in length. Academician contributions almost exclusively. Pays an average of $100.

EUROPE, 2100 M St. NW, 707, Washington DC 20037. Editor: Webster Martin. For anyone with a professional or personal interest in Western Europe and European—US relations. Bimonthly

magazine; 60 pages. Circ. 60,000. Copyrighted. Buys about 50 mss/year. Pays on acceptance. Free sample copy. Submit seasonal material 3 months in advance. Reports in 4 weeks. Query or submit complete ms. Include resume of author's background and qualifications with query or ms. SASE.
Nonfiction and Photos: Interested in current affairs (with emphasis on economics and politics), the Common Market and Europe's relations with the rest of the world. Publishes occasional cultural pieces, with European angle. High quality writing a must. "Please, no more M.A. theses on European integration. We're looking for European angle in topics current in the US." Length: 500-2,000 words. Average payment is $75-250. Photos purchased with or without accompanying mss. Also purchased on assignment. Buys b&w and color. Average payment is $25-35 per b&w print, any size; $50 for inside use of color transparencies; $200-300 for color used on cover.

FOREIGN AFFAIRS, 58 E. 68th St., New York NY 10021. (212)734-0400. Editor: William P. Bundy. For academics, businessmen (national and international), government, educational and cultural readers especially interested in international affairs of a political nature. Published 5 times/year. Circ. 75,000. Buys all rights. Pays kill fee. Byline given. Buys 45 mss/year. Pays on publication. Sample copy $5 postpaid. Photocopied submissions OK. Reports in 4-6 weeks. Submit complete ms. SASE.
Nonfiction: "Articles dealing with international affairs; political, educational, cultural, philosophical and social sciences. Develop an original idea in depth, with a broad basis on topical subjects. Serious, in-depth, developmental articles with international appeal." Length: 2,500-6,000 words. Pays $400.
Tips: "We like the writer to include his/her qualifications for writing on the topic in question (educational, past publications, relevant positions or honors), and a clear summation of the article: the argument (or area examined), and the writer's policy conclusions."

THE FREEMAN, 30 S. Broadway, Irvington-on-Hudson NY 10533. (914)591-7230. Editor: Paul L. Poirot. 60% freelance written. For "fairly advanced students of liberty and the layman." Monthly. Buys all rights, including reprint rights. Byline given. Buys 44 mss/year. Pays on publication. SASE.
Nonfiction: "We want nonfiction clearly analyzing and explaining various aspects of the free market, private enterprise, limited government philosophy, especially as pertains to conditions in the United States. Though a necessary part of the literature of freedom is the exposure of collectivistic clichés and fallacies, our aim is to emphasize and explain the positive case for individual responsibility and choice in a free economy. Especially important, we believe, is the methodology of freedom; self-improvement, offered to others who are interested. We try to avoid name-calling and personality clashes, and find satire of little use as an educational device. Ours is a scholarly analysis of the principles underlying a free market economy. No political strategy or tactics." Length: 3,500 words maximum. Pays 5¢/word.
Tips: "Facts, figures, and quotations cited should be fully documented, to their original source, if possible."

THE LIBERTARIAN REVIEW, Libertarian Review, Inc., 1320 G St., SE, Washington DC 20003. Editor: Roy A. Childs Jr. West Coast Editor: Jeff Riggenbach. Libertarian political analysis of current events and trends. Monthly magazine; 48 pages. Circ. 18,000. Pays on publication. Buys all rights. Original plus one photocopy submission. SASE. Send manuscripts to Joan Kennedy Taylor, Senior Editor. Sample copy $1.50.
Nonfiction: Expose (of government malfeasance); historical (on background and root causes of social problems—must be related to current events); and interview (with newsmakers and opinion makers, especially those in conflict with the state). "Articles and reviews must emphasize the relevance of libertarian ideas to the issues and events of the day." Buys 35 mss/year. Length: 2,000-3,750 words. Pays $200-300.
Photos: State availability of photos. Pays $15-50/photo. Supply b&w contact sheets and negatives. Buys one-time rights.
Columns/Departments: Book Reviews (literally anything of possible interest to libertarians; stress on relevance of libertarian ideas to almost everything—750-1,500 words). Buys 40/year. Submit or query, with clips of published work. Pays $100-200.

THE NATION, 72 5th Ave., New York NY 10011. Editor: Victor Navasky. Weekly. Query. SASE.
Nonfiction and Poetry: "We welcome all articles dealing with the social scene, particularly if they examine it with a new point of view or expose conditions the rest of the media overlooks. Poetry is also accepted." Length and payment to be negotiated. Modest rates.
Tips: "We are absolutely committed to the idea of getting more material from the boondocks. If you live somewhere where you think nothing is going on, look again! We tackle issues such as labor, national politics, consumer affairs, environmental politics, civil liberties, and foreign affairs."

NATIONAL DEVELOPMENT (DESAROLLO NACIONAL), Intercontinental Publications, Inc., 15 Franklin St., Westport CT 06880. (203)226-7463. Editor-in-Chief: Martin Greenburgh. Emphasizes 3rd world infrastructure. For government officials in 3rd world—technocrats, planners, engineers, ministers. Published 9 times/year; 120 pages. Circ. 50,000. Pays on acceptance. Buys all rights. Byline given. Phone queries OK. Previously published submissions OK. SASE. Reports in 4 weeks. Free sample copy and writer's guidelines.
Nonfiction: Technical (tourism, construction, government management, planning, power, telecommunications); informational (agriculture, economics, public works, construction management); interview; photo feature and technical. Buys 6-10 mss/issue. Query with "inclusion of suggestions for specific article topics; point out your area of expertise." Length: 1,800-5,000 words. Pays $150-250.
Photos: B&w and color. Captions required. Query. Total price for ms includes payment for photos.
Columns/Departments: Power technology, telecommunications, technology, water treatment, Financial Technology (finances as they might affect 3rd world governments). Buys 4 mss/issue. Query. Length: 750-1,500 words. Pays $75-150. Open to suggestions for new columns/departments.

NATIONAL JOURNAL, 1730 M St. NW, Washington DC 20036. (202)857-1400. Editor: Richard Frank. "Very limited need for freelance material because fulltime staff produces virtually all of our material." Pays negotiable kill fee. Byline given.

NATIONAL REVIEW, 150 E. 35th St., New York NY 10016. (212)679-7330. Editor: Wm. F. Buckley Jr. Issued fortnightly. Buys all rights. Pays 50% kill fee. Byline given. Pays on publication. Will send sample copy. Reports in a month. SASE.
Nonfiction: Kevin Lynch, articles editor. Uses articles, 1,000-3,500 words, on current events and the arts, which would appeal to a politically conservative audience. Pays $100/magazine page (900 words per page). Inquiries about book reviews, movie, play, TV reviews, or other cultural happenings, or travel should be addressed to Chilton Williamson Jr., 150 E. 35th St., New York NY 10016.

NEW GUARD, Young Americans for Freedom, Woodland Rd., Sterling VA 22170. (703)450-5162. Editor-in-Chief: Richard F. LaMountain. Emphasizes conservative political ideas for readership of mostly young people with a large number of college students. Age range 14-39. Virtually all are politically conservative with interests in politics, economics, philosophy, current affairs. Mostly students or college graduates. Quarterly magazine; 48 pages. Circ. 7,000. Pays on publication. Buys all rights. Byline given. Phone queries OK. Submit seasonal/holiday material 2-3 months in advance. SASE. Reports in 1 month. Free sample copy.
Nonfiction: Exposé (government waste, failure, mismanagement, problems with education or media); historical (illustrating political or economic points); interview (politicians, academics, people with conservative viewpoint or something to say to conservatives); personal opinion; and profile. Buys 40 mss/year. Submit complete ms. Length: 3,500 words maximum. Pays $40-100.
Photos: Purchased with accompanying manuscript.

THE NEW REPUBLIC, A Weekly Journal of Opinion, 1220 19th St. NW, Washington DC 20036. Managing Editor: Dorothy Wickenden. 50% freelance written. Circ. 95,000. Buys all rights. Byline given. Pays on publication. SASE.
Nonfiction: This liberal, intellectual publication uses 1,000- to 1,500-word comments on public affairs and arts. Pays 10¢/published word.

NEWSWEEK, 444 Madison Ave., New York NY 10022. Staff-written. Unsolicited mss accepted for "My Turn," a column of opinion. Length: 1,100 words maximum.

POLITICAL PROFILES, 1202 National Press Building, Washington DC 20045. Publisher: Robert J. Guttman. Managing Editor: Sofia Yank Bassman. Publishing company featuring a newsletter and magazine style monographs on current political issues, election and campaign information. Newsletter published biweekly. Magazine varies. Estab. 1979. Pays on acceptance. Byline given. Buys all rights.
Nonfiction: Exposé (investigative pieces); historical (current history); and profile (political). Query. "We are interested in assigning stories to well-established political reporters. Write a letter outlining your credentials and your availability for assignments."

POLITICAL REPORTER, SRF Publications, Box 447, Great Neck NY 11021. (516)487-2811. Editor: Steven R. Ferber. Managing Editor: Blanche Ferber. Monthly magazine. "Our readers are interested in the lighter and informative sides of politics—no crusading or electioneering. They are looking for the stories behind the news reports we read in our daily newspapers and hear on radio and TV." Circ. 3,000. Pays on publication. Byline given. Pays negotiable kill fee. Buys one-time rights. Submit seasonal/holiday material 3 months in advance. Simultaneous queries and submissions OK. SASE. Reports in 2 weeks on queries; 2 months on mss. Sample copy $1.

Nonfiction: Steve Ferber, articles editor. General interest (of interest to collector of political memorabilia); historical/nostalgic (as it relates to past presidents and political personalities); and interview/profile (political personalities with national or international appeal). No opinion on a candidate or politician not supported by facts. Buys 5 mss/year. Send complete ms. Length: 500-2,000 words. Pays $10-75.

Photos: Blanche Ferber, photo editor. Send photos with ms. Pays $5-100 for b&w 8x10 prints. Prefers photos of political personalities. Captions, model release and identification of subjects required. Buys one-time rights.

Fillers: Anecdotes and newsbreaks. Buys 50/year. Length: 25-200 words. Pays $5-20.

Tips: "Think ahead about rising young candidates with interesting or novel approaches to campaigning or politics. Look for new and different slants to stories about well-known politicians that would be of interest to a general readership. Be concise, don't stretch a 500-word article into a monograph. It will only hurt your chances of being published in our publication."

PRESENT TENSE: THE MAGAZINE OF WORLD JEWISH AFFAIRS, 165 E. 56th St., New York NY 10022. (212)751-4000. Editor: Murray Polner. For college-educated, Jewish-oriented audience interested in Jewish life throughout the world. Quarterly magazine. Circ. 45,000. Buys all rights. Byline given. Buys 60 mss/year. Pays on publication. Sample copy $3. Reports in 6-8 weeks. Query. SASE.

Nonfiction: Quality reportage of contemporary events (a la *Harper's, New Yorker*, etc.). Personal experience, profiles and photo essays. Length: 3,000 words maximum. Pays $100-250.

THE PROGRESSIVE, 408 W. Gorham St., Madison WI 53703. (608)257-4626. Editor: Erwin Knoll. Monthly. Buys all rights. Byline given. Pays on publication. Reports in 2 weeks. Query. SASE.

Nonfiction: Primarily interested in articles which interpret, from a progressive point of view, domestic and world affairs. Occasional lighter features. Length: 3,000 words maximum. Pays $50-200.

Tips: "Display some familiarity with our magazine, its interests and concerns, its format and style. We want query letters that fully describe the proposed article without attempting to sell it—and that give an indication of the writer's competence to deal with the subject."

PUBLIC OPINION, American Enterprise Institute, 1150 17th St. NW, Washington DC 20036. (202)862-5800. Managing Editor: Karlyn Keene. Bimonthly magazine covering public opinion for the public policy community, journalists, and academics interested in public opinion data and its meanings. Circ. 16,000. Pays on publication. Byline given. Buys all rights. Simultaneous queries OK. Reports in 1 month on queries. Sample copy $3.50.

Nonfiction: Historical (dealing with polling industry); "public policy issues, opinion polls and their meaning in relation to public policy." Buys 30-35 mss/year. Query with outline. Length: 2,500-3,000 words. Payment varies widely.

REASON MAGAZINE, Box 40105, Santa Barbara CA 93103. (805)963-5993. Editor: Robert Poole Jr. 50% freelance written. For a readership interested in individual liberty, economic freedom, private enterprise alternatives to government services and protection against inflation and depressions. Monthly; 52 pages. Circ. 24,000. Rights purchased vary with author and material. May buy all rights, first North American serial rights, or first serial rights. Pays 35% kill fee. Byline given. Buys 40 mss/year. Pays on publication. Sample copy $2; free guidelines for writers. "Manuscripts must be typed, double- or triple-spaced on one side of the page only. The first page (or a cover sheet) should contain an aggregate word count, the author's name and mailing address, and a brief (100- to 200-word) abstract. A short biographical sketch of the author should also be included." Photocopied submissions OK. Reports in 3 months. Query. SASE.

Nonfiction and Photos: "*Reason* deals with social, economic and political problems, supporting both individual liberty and economic freedom. Articles dealing with the following subject areas are desired: analyses of current issues and problems from a libertarian viewpoint (e.g., education, energy, victimless crimes, regulatory agencies, foreign policy, etc.). Discussions of social change, i.e., strategy and tactics for moving toward a free society. Discussions of the institutions of a free society and how they would deal with important problems. Articles on self-preservation in today's economic, political and cultural environment. Case studies of unique examples of the current application of libertarian/free-market principles." Length: 1,500-5,000 words. Book reviews are needed.

REVIEW OF THE NEWS, 395 Concord Ave., Belmont MA 02178. (617)489-0600. Editor: Scott Stanley Jr. Weekly magazine covering the news with a conservative and free market orientation. Circ. 60,000. Average issue includes capsulated news items, bylined sports, films, economic advice and overseas and congressional activities. Pays on acceptance or on publication. Byline given. Kill fee negotiated. Buys all rights. Photocopied submissions OK. SASE. Reports in 1 month on queries; in 3 weeks on mss. Free sample copy.

Nonfiction: Expose (of government bungling); general interest (current events and politics); interview (with leading conservatives and newsmakers, heads of state, congressmen, economists and politicians); humor (satire on the news); and commentary on the news. Buys 3-4 mss/year. Query with clips of previously published work. Length: 1,500-3,000 words. Pays $150-$250.

THE SPOKESWOMAN MAGAZINE, 858 National Press Bldg., Washington DC 20045. (202)347-3553. Editor: Mary Blake French. 10-15% freelance written. Emphasizes "legislative, judicial and political actions by and affecting women at federal, state, and local levels for professionals and women activists of all ages and occupations." Monthly feminist magazine; 16-24 pages. Circ. 8,000. Pays on publication. Buys all rights. Phone queries OK. Submit seasonal/ holiday material 6 weeks in advance of issue date. Simultaneous and photocopied submissions OK. SASE. Reports in 6 weeks. Free sample copy.

Nonfiction: Expose ("we are looking for the inside story on any governmental or political action affecting women; just the facts, no opinion"); general interest (innovative government or political actions; stories on the group or individual who has adopted new strategies to bring about change); interview (occasionally if interpretive); and profile (interpretive). "We do not want personal opinion pieces. Our emphasis is on current news of national interest." Buys 1-2 mss/issue. Query. Length: 750-1,500 words. Payment negotiable.

Columns/Departments: "We currently run a monthly syndicated column by Ellen Goodman and are considering the development of other regular features written by freelancers. Writers must be experts in the fields they write about. We are open to ideas for regular features."

TIME MAGAZINE, Rockefeller Center, New York NY 10020. Staff-written.

TODAY'S PATRIOT, Proud Eagle Press, Box 8453, Riverside CA 92515. (714)785-5180. Publisher: Warren Birch. Editor: Alana Cross. Bimonthly newspaper covering politics and Christianity from a conservative viewpoint. Audience includes activist readers. Estab. 1980. Circ. 2,000. Pays on acceptance. Byline given. Buys all rights. Submit seasonal/holiday material 2 months in advance. Simultaneous queries, and photocopied and previously published submissions OK. SASE. Reports in 2 weeks. Sample copy $1; writer's guidelines for business size SAE and 1 first class stamp.

Nonfiction: Howard Christopher, articles editor. Expose (of government from a conservative viewpoint); general interest; inspirational (from a Christian viewpoint); interview/profile (of government or business leaders); new product (on energy or consumer-related); opinion; travel (unique, interesting, inexpensive). "We are beginning a youth feature. Outstanding achievement by a youth. Write: Michael Donahue, youth editor." No racist, bigoted or immoral material. Buys 3-5 mss/issue. Query. Length: 100-1,000 words. Pays $5-25.

Photos: State availability of photos. Pays $5-15 for b&w or color 8x10 prints. Captions, model release, and identification of subjects required.

Columns/Departments: Alana Cross, column/department editor. Buys 8 mss/year. Query. Length: 1,000 maximum. Pays $25. "We will feature an appropriate book review in every issue. Also, any political 'thought' piece which fits our format is carefully considered."

Fiction: J. Sulsenbir, fiction editor. Political satire. Limited market but will consider. No racist or immoral fiction. Buys 2 mss/year. Query. Length: 500 words maximum. Pays $5-25.

Fillers: Howard Christopher, fillers editor. Anecdotes, short humor and newsbreaks. Buys 3 mss/issue. Length: 25-100 words. Pays $5-10. "Newsbreaks or interesting factual pieces are most desired."

Tips: "We are an excellent publication for unpublished writers. We want circulation-boosting pieces. Please document material and avoid sensationalism. We look first at material that has photos—but photos are not mandatory. Recent court decisions make it imperative that the writer be very accurate and can document material. Please, no phone queries. We are somewhat general in format, but specific in viewpoint. Steady income can be had for writing to meet our needs—even for new writers whom we encourage."

US NEWS & WORLD REPORT, 2300 N St. NW, Washington DC 20037. "We are presently not considering unsolicited freelance submissions."

WASHINGTON MONTHLY, 2712 Ontario Rd., NW, Washington DC 20009. (202)462-0128. Editor: Charles Peters. For "well-educated, well-read people in politics and government."

Monthly. Circ. 30,000. Rights purchased depend on author and material. Buys all rights or first rights. Buys 30-40 mss/year. Pays on publication. Sample copy $2.25. Sometimes does special topical issues. Query or submit complete ms. Tries to report in 2-4 weeks. SASE.

Nonfiction and Photos: Responsible investigative or evaluative reporting about the US government, business, society, the press and politics. "No editorial comment/essays, please." Length: "average 2,000-6,000 words." Pays 5-10¢/word. Buys b&w glossy prints.

Tips: "Best route to break in is to send ½ page proposal describing article and angle."

WORLD POLITICS, Corwin Hall, Princeton NJ 08544. Editors: Cyril E. Black, Gerald Garvey, Lynn T. White, III, and Henry S. Bienen. Quarterly for academic readers in social sciences. Pays on publication. Buys all rights. Reports in 1-6 months. SASE.

Nonfiction: Elsbeth Lewin, executive editor. Uses articles based on original scholarly research on problems in international relations and comparative politics. "World Politics is a scholarly journal, not a magazine. We do not publish journalistic accounts, current events, or articles of strictly historical interest." Mss should be double-spaced throughout (including footnotes), and have wide margins. Footnotes should be placed at the end of article. Length: 5,000-8,000 words. Pays $50.

WORLD RESEARCH INK, World Research, Inc., 11722 Sorrento Valley Rd., San Diego CA 92121. (714)755-9761. Executive Editor: Stuart Craig Smith. 80-90% freelance written quarterly news magazine for students, faculty members, business men, women, and individuals who are interested in in-depth coverage, and sometimes alternative perspective of current national topics. Circ. 65,000. Pays on publication. Usually buys all rights. Byline and biographical information given. All submissions must be as a result of an initial query. Previously published material considered. SASE. Sample copy $1.

Nonfiction: "We are looking for quality freelance material by writers who have good ideas and the discipline to turn them into first-class articles. Articles emphasize current topics, highlighting the principles of individual liberty, personal and economic freedoms, and the problem solving capacity of the free market system. Each issue of the magazine gives special attention to a current topic in a cover focus section. Previous cover topics have included inflation, energy, environment and politics. (Contact for planned cover topics, or to suggest one.)" Length: 1,000-2,500 words. Pays $75-250.

Photos: Interested in quality photographs that will enhance the article. B&w 5x7 or 8x10 glossy prints, 35mm and larger color transparencies. Model release and captions required. Pays $5-25.

WORLDVIEW, 170 E. 64th St., New York NY 10021. (212)838-4120. Managing Editor: Susan Woolfson. For "the informed and concerned reader who insists that discussion of public issues must take place within an ethical framework." Monthly. Buys all rights. Pays on publication. Study the magazine and query first.

Nonfiction: Articles on public issues, religion, international affairs, world politics and "moral imperatives." The editors believe that any analysis of our present cultural and political problems which ignores the moral dimension is at best incomplete—at worst, misleading. *Worldview* focuses on international affairs, puts the discussion in an ethical framework, and relates ethical judgment to specifically religious traditions. "We don't want pieces on purely domestic issues ('The IRS & Me'); poetry; or historical rambles ('19th Century Polish Unionism & Its Lessons for Today')." Article length: 1,500-3,500 words; "Excursus": 300-1,000 words; book reviews: 1,000 words. Payment depends on length and use of material.

Tips: "Short pieces for the 'Excursus' section must be as well written and have the same degree of ethical orientation as the longer ones, but it is one way to break in. Book reviews are also a possibility. If a writer sends some samples of previous work and a list of the types of literature he is interested in, we might try him out with an assignment, though with the understanding it is on speculation."

Puzzle

This category includes only those publications devoted entirely to puzzles. The writer will find many additional markets for crosswords, brain teasers, acrostics, etc., by reading the *Filler* listings throughout the Consumer, Trade and Company Publications sections of this book. Especially rich in puzzle markets are the Religious, Juvenile, Teen and Young Adult, and General Interest classifications in the Consumer section.

GAMES, Playboy Enterprises, Inc., 515 Madison Ave., New York NY 10022. Editor: Michael Donner. Bimonthly magazine featuring games, puzzles, mazes and brainteasers for people 18-49 interested in paper and pencil games. Circ. 600,000. Average issue includes 5-7 feature articles, paper and pencil games and fillers, bylined columns and 1-3 contests. Pays on publication. Byline given. Offers 25% kill fee. Buys all rights. Submit seasonal material 6 months in advance. Book reprints considered. Reports in 6 weeks. Free writer's guidelines with SASE.
Nonfiction: "We are looking for visual puzzles, rebuses, brainteasers and logic puzzles. We also want newsbreaks, new games, inventions, and news items of interest to game players." Buys 4-6 mss/issue. Query. Length: 500-2,000 words. Usually pays $110/published page.
Columns/Departments: Wild Cards (25-200 words, short brainteasers, $25-100 words plays, number games, anecdotes and quotes on games). Buys 6-10 mss/issue. Send complete ms. Length: 25-200 words. Pays $25-100.
Fillers: Editor: Will Shortz. Crosswords, cryptograms and word games. Pays $25-50.

OFFICIAL CROSSWORD PUZZLES, DELL CROSSWORD PUZZLES, POCKET CROSSWORD PUZZLES, DELL WORD SEARCH PUZZLES, DELL PENCIL PUZZLES AND WORD GAMES, DELL CROSSWORD ANNUALS, DELL CROSSWORD PUZZLES PAPERBACK BOOK SERIES, Dell Puzzle Publications, 245 E. 47th St., New York NY 10017. Editor: Kathleen Rafferty. For "all ages from 8-80—people whose interests are puzzles, both crosswords and variety features." Buys all rights. SASE.
Puzzles: "We publish puzzles of all kinds, but the market here is limited to those who are able to construct quality pieces which can compete with the real professionals. See our magazines. They are the best guide for our needs. We publish quality puzzles, which are well-conceived and well-edited, with appeal to solvers of all ages and in about every walk of life. We are the world's leading publishers of puzzle publications and are distributed in many countries around the world in addition to the continental US. However, no foreign language puzzles, please! Our market for crosswords and anacrostics is very small, since long-time contributors supply most of the needs in those areas. However, we are always willing to see material of unusual quality, or with a new or original approach. Since most of our publications feature variety puzzles in addition to the usual features, we are especially interested in seeing quizzes, picture features, and new and unusual puzzle features of all kinds. Please do not send us remakes of features we are now using. We are interested only in new ideas. Kriss Krosses are an active market here. However, constructors who wish to enter this field must query us first before submitting any material whatever. Prices vary with the feature, but ours are comparable with the highest in the general puzzle field."

ORIGINAL CROSSWORD PUZZLES, EASY-TIMED CROSSWORD PUZZLES, 575 Madison Ave., New York NY 10022. (212)838-7900. Editorial Director: Arthur Goodman. Bimonthly. Buys all rights. Pays on acceptance. Refer to current issue available on newsstand as guide to type of material wanted. Submissions must be accompanied by SASE for return.
Puzzles: Original adult crossword puzzles; sizes 15x15 and 13x13; easy, medium and hard. Pays $10-12.

WORD HUNT, WORD SCAN, MAKE-A-WORD, COMPLETE-A-WORD, 575 Madison Ave., New York NY 10022. Editorial Director: Arthur Goodman. Original word-finding topics; 16x16. All bimonthly publications. See current issues for guide to word length and presentation. Query before sending other sizes. Pays on acceptance. SASE.

Regional

General interest publications slanted toward residents of and visitors to a particular region are grouped below in geographical order: city first, then state. Because they publish little material that doesn't relate to the area they cover, they represent a limited market for writers who live outside their area. Many buy manuscripts on conservation and the natural wonders of their area; additional markets for such material will be found under the Nature, Conservation, and Ecology, and Sports headings.

Publications that report on the business climate of a region are grouped in the regional division of the Business and Finance category. Newspapers and weekly magazine sections, which also buy material of general interest to area residents, are classified separately under that category heading. Recreational and travel publications specific to a geographical area are listed in the Consumer/Travel section.

City

Arizona

PHOENIX LIVING, 4621 N. 16th St., Phoenix AZ 85016. (602)279-2394. Editor: Pat Adams. Bimonthly magazine covering housing for newcomers and prospective home buyers. Circ. 80,000. Pays on acceptance. Byline given. Buys all rights. Submit seasonal/holiday material 4 months in advance. Simultaneous queries and photocopied and previously published submissions OK. Reports in 1 month. Sample copy free; writer's guidelines for business size SAE and 1 first class stamp.
Nonfiction: Retirement living, real estate, Arizona Business, employment overviews, custom buildings and apartment living—all locally oriented. Buys 30 mss/year. Query with clips of published work. Length: 700-1,000 words; "longer features are assigned locally." Pays 10¢/word.
Photos: State availability of photos. Pays negotiable fee for 8x10 b&w glossy prints. Captions and model release required. Buys all rights.

PHOENIX MAGAZINE, 4707 N. 12th St., Phoenix AZ 85014. (602)248-8900. Editor/Publisher: Kenneth A. Welch. 75% freelance written. For professional, general audience. Monthly magazine. Circ. 40,000. Buys all rights. Pays 50-75% kill fee. Byline given except for regular columns. Buys 60 mss/year. Pays on publication. Sample copy $1.25 plus postage. January issue: Superguide to what to see and do in area; February issue: Real Estate; March issue: Arizona Lifestyle; June issue: Salute to Summer; August issue: Annual Phoenix Progress Report. Submit special issue material 3 months in advance. Reports in 1 month. Query or submit complete ms. SASE.
Nonfiction and Photos: Predominantly features subjects unique to Phoenix life; urban affairs, arts, lifestyle, etc. Subject should be locally oriented. Informational, how-to, interview, profile, historical, photo, successful local business operations. Each issue also embraces 1 or 2 in-depth reports on crucial, frequently controversial issues that confront the community. Length: 1,000-3,000 words. Payment is negotiable. Photos are purchased with ms with no additional payment, or on assignment.

California

BOULEVARDS, The Magazine of San Francisco, Kevin Jenkins and Assoc., 1008 Sutter St., San Francisco CA 94109. (415)441-3597. Editor/Publisher: Kevin Jenkins. Managing Editor: Michael Goldberg. Monthly magazine covering general interest topics, with a focus on the Bay Area. "Stylish, irreverent and opinionated, *Boulevards* is a monthly, general-interest, large-format (10½ inches by 15 inches) magazine focused on the San Francisco Bay Area. We reach a young (18-35), sophisticated, urban audience." Circ. 20,000. Pays "one month following publication." Byline given. Pays $15-20 kill fee. Buys first rights. Submit seasonal/holiday material 3 months in advance. Simultaneous queries and photocopied submissions OK. SASE. Reports in 2 months. Sample copy $3; writer's guidelines for 50¢, business size SAE and 1 first class stamp.
Nonfiction: Michael Goldberg, articles editor. Book excerpts (fiction); expose (emphasizes on all aspects of the Bay Area); historical/nostalgic (relating to Bay Area); how-to (we run a guide each month; e.g., Chinese and Japanese movie theaters in the Bay Area); humor (satire, e.g., takeoff on *Apocalypse Now*); interview/profile (one each month on pop celebrities, e.g., Deborah Harry, Jack

Nicholson); personal experience (query); photo feature (fashion plus photo concept spreads); and travel (where people in Bay Area can go for a cheap but exciting vacation). "We combine the writing quality of *Esquire* with the style of *Rolling Stone* and the regionalism of *New York*. We are interested in presenting our readers with well-written, in-depth stories that provide new insights into the culture, politics or lifestyle of the San Francisco Bay area. Writing should be clear and to-the-point. At the same time, we want exciting writing that 'turns on' our readers." Buys 72 mss/year. Query with clips of published work. Length: 2,000-6,000 words. Pays $40-175.

Photos: Jessica Brackman, photo editor. State availability of photos. Pays $10-20 for 8x10 b&w prints; reviews b&w contact sheets. Buys one-time rights.

Fiction: "We are looking for contemporary fiction, particularly with a Bay Area setting." Buys 4 mss/year. Send complete ms. Length: 3,000-5,000 words. Pays $60-100.

Newsbreaks: "We need 6 short pieces each month for our 'Briefs' section. These can be about unusual Bay Area characters, places, things to buy, etc." Buys 72/year. Length: 300-600 words. Pays $15.

EXPRESS, The East Bay's Free Weekly, Express Publishing Co., Box 3198, Berkeley CA 94703. (415)653-7332. Editor: John Raeside. Weekly tabloid. Circ. 31,000. Pays on publication. Byline given. Buys one-time rights. Simultaneous queries, and simultaneous photocopied and previously published submissions OK. SASE. Reports in 2 weeks on queries; 2 months on mss. Free sample copy.

Nonfiction: "We are a general interest weekly and will consider feature writing of any length as long as it is local to a Berkeley/Oakland, California readership." Book excerpts ("will be considered if they deal with a Berkeley/Oakland subject"); exposé; general interest; historical/nostalgic; humor; interview/profile; opinion ("only rarely"); personal experience, photo feature (occasionally); technical; and travel ("seldom"). No "consumer guides of any kind." Buys 65 mss/year. Query with clips of published work or send complete ms. Length: open. Pays $50-100.

Tips: "Our feature pages are most open to freelancers. We tend to publish longer and more detailed features than newspapers. They should emphasize local personalities and should be written with attention to narrative detail."

LOS ANGELES MAGAZINE, 1888 Century Park E., Los Angeles CA 90067. Editor: Geoff Miller. Monthly. Buys first North American serial rights. Pays 50% kill fee. Byline given except for short "Peoplescape" personality profiles. Query. SASE.

Nonfiction: Uses articles on how best to live (i.e., the quality of life) in the "changing, growing, diverse Los Angeles urban-suburban area; ideas, people, and occasionally places. Writer must have an understanding of contemporary living and doing in Southern California; material must appeal to an upper-income, better-educated group of people. Fields of interest include urban problems, pleasures, personalities and cultural opportunities, leisure and trends, candid interviews of topical interest; the arts. Solid research and reportage required. No essays." Length: 1,000-3,500 words. Also uses some topical satire and humor. Pays 10¢/word minimum.

Photos: Most photos assigned to local photographers. Occasionally buys photographs with mss. B&w should be 8x10. Pays $25-50 for single article photos.

SACRAMENTO MAGAZINE, 1207 Front St., Sacramento CA 95814. Editor: Hank Armstrong. Monthly magazine emphasizing a strong local angle on politics, local issues, human interest and consumer items for readers in the middle to high income brackets. Pays on acceptance within a 30-day billing period. Buys all rights. Original manuscripts only (no previously published work). Absolutely no phone calls; query by letter. Reports in 6 weeks. SASE. Writer's guidelines for SASE.

Nonfiction: Local issues vital to Sacramento quality of life. Past articles have included "Gasping at Straws" (rice straw burning and its resultant air pollution) and "Life on the Stroll" (the prostitution problem in downtown Sacramento). Buys approximately 10 mss/issue. Query first. Length: 200-3,000 words, depending on author, subject matter and treatment.

Photos: State availability of photos. Payment varies depending on photographer, subject matter and treatment. Captions (including ID's, location and date) required.

Columns/Departments: Media, the Gourmet, people, sports, city arts, and Fools Rush In (humor with a strong local peg).

SAN DIEGO MAGAZINE, Box 81809, San Diego CA 92138. (714)225-8953. Editor-in-Chief: Edwin F. Self. 65% freelance written. Emphasizes San Diego. Monthly magazine; 250 pages. Circ. 50,892. Pays on publication. Buys all rights. Pays negotiable kill fee. Byline given. Submit seasonal/holiday material 3 months in advance of issue date. Simultaneous and photocopied submissions OK. SASE. Reports in 2 months. Sample copy $3.

Nonfiction: Exposé (serious, documented); general interest (to San Diego region); historical (San

Diego region); interview (with notable San Diegans); nostalgia; photo essay; profile; service guides; and travel. Buys 7 mss/issue. Query with clips of published work, or submit complete ms. Length: 3,000 words. Pays $500 maximum.

Photos: State availability of photos with query. Pays $7.50-45 for b&w contact sheets or 8x10 glossy prints; $25-100 for color transparencies; $150 for cover. Captions required. Buys all rights. Model release required.

SAN FRANCISCO MAGAZINE, 973 Market St., San Francisco CA 94103. (415)777-5555. Editor: Tracy Kristen Farrell. Monthly magazine covering general-interest topics for San Francisco and Bay Area residents. Circ. 45,000. Pays on publication. Byline and brief bio given. Pays 50% kill fee. Buys first North American serial rights. Submit seasonal/holiday material 2 months in advance. Photocopied submissions OK. Reports in 2 weeks.
Nonfiction: General interest (lifestyles, fashion); humor; interview/profile (of person with a Northern California connection); personal experience (first-person pieces); photo feature; consumer; and science. "Topics may be of national scope. We want well-researched, well-written articles with a Northern California fix." Buys 50-60 mss/year. Query with clips of published work or send a complete ms. Length: 3,500-5,000 words. Pays $500 average.
Photos: State availability of photos. Reviews 35mm color transparencies and 8x10 b&w glossy prints. Negotiates pay separately for package of photos or ms/photo package.
Columns/Departments: Back Page. Buys 12 mss/year. Send complete ms. Length: 800-900 words. Pays $200-300.
Fiction: Mainstream; other types ("could be anything"). "Most of fiction is material from new writers. We like to use experimental material." Buys 12/mss year. Send complete ms. Length: 800-1,500 words. Pays $150.

Colorado

DENVER LIVING, Baker Publications, 2280 S. Xanadu Way, Aurora CO 80014. (303)695-8440. Editor: Patt Dodd. Bimonthly magazine covering housing for newcomers and others looking for new housing or upgrading their existing residence. Circ. 90,000. Pays on publication. Byline given. Buys all rights. Submit seasonal/holiday material 3 months in advance. Simultaneous queries and previously published submissions OK. SASE. Reports in 2 weeks. Sample copy free; writer's guidelines for business size SAE and 1 first class stamp.
Nonfiction: Products, services, events, landscaping, decorating, and food indigenous to the area. Buys 14 mss/year. Query with clips of published work. Length: 200-1,000 words. Pays 10¢/word.
Photos: State availability of photos. Pays negotiable fee for 8x10 glossy prints. Captions and model release required. Buys all rights.
Columns/Departments: Discoveries (special products and services, events, book reviews, restaurant openings, the arts, shopping). Buys 42 mss/year. Query with clips of published work. Length: 150-200 words. Pays 10¢/word.
Tips: "National assignments on decorating, financing, etc., for all of Baker's city magazines are made by Cary Campbell, editor-in-chief. Payment is 20¢/word. Query her at Living, 5757 Alpha Rd., Suite 400, Dallas TX 75240."

DENVER MONTHLY, 1763 Williams, Denver CO 80218. (303)399-5931. Editor and Publisher: John W. Hoffman. Managing Editor: Marjie Lundstrom. For an urban, sophisticated, well-educated audience interested in community events, sports and entertainment. Monthly magazine; 96 pages. Circ. 25,000. Pays on publication. Buys all rights. Byline given except for very short articles or ones requiring extensive rewrite. Submit seasonal/holiday material 4 months in advance. Photocopied submissions OK. SASE. Reports in 2 months.
Nonfiction: Expose (anything that is a "genuine scoop"); informational (Denver and Colorado residents); and interviews and profiles (famous Coloradians). No articles on "timeless energy conservation." Buys 25 mss/year. Query. Length: 800-1,500 words. "Payment varies depending on story quality, length, and author. Base rates range from $50 to $150."
Photos: B&w and color transparencies used with mss or by assignment. Payment negotiable. Query.

Connecticut

NEW HAVEN INFO MAGAZINE, Box 2017, 53 Orange St., New Haven CT 06521. (203)562-5413. Editor: Sol D. Chain. For those interested in art, music, theater, recreational activities, etc. Monthly magazine; 64 pages. Circ. 5,000. Not copyrighted. Byline given. Buys 20 mss/year. Pays on publication. Sample copy 50¢. Will consider photocopied and simultaneous submissions. Reports in 1 month. Query. SASE.

Nonfiction: "Most of our material is on assignment. We publish articles dealing with New Haven area events and people." Personal experience, interview, profile, historical, nostalgia. Length: 350-700 words. Pays $15/page (about 350 words).

District of Columbia

THE WASHINGTONIAN MAGAZINE, 1828 L St. NW, Washington DC 20036. Editor: John A. Limpert. For active, affluent, well-educated audience. Monthly magazine; 250 pages. Circ. 111,000. Buys first rights. Buys 75 mss/year. Pays on publication. Simultaneous and photocopied submissions OK. Reports in 4-6 weeks. Query or submit complete ms. SASE.

Nonfiction and Photos: *"The Washingtonian* is written for Washingtonians. The subject matter is anything we feel might interest people interested in the mind and manners of the city. The style, as Wolcott Gibbs said, should be the author's—if he is an author, and if he has a style. The only thing we ask is thoughtfulness and that no subject be treated too reverently. Audience is literate. We assume considerable sophistication about the city, and a sense of humor." Buys how-to, personal experience, interviews, profiles, humor, coverage of successful business operations, think pieces and exposes. Length: 1,000-7,000 words; average feature, 3,000 words. Pays 10¢/word. Photos rarely purchased with mss.

Fiction and Poetry: Department Editor: Howard Means. Must be Washington-oriented. No limitations on length. Pays 10¢/word for fiction. Payment is negotiable for poetry.

Florida

JACKSONVILLE MAGAZINE, Drawer 329, Jacksonville FL 32201. (904)353-0300. For civic-minded, concerned community types. Bimonthly. Circ. 10,000. Buys all rights. Buys 20-25 mss/year. Pays on publication. Query. Submit seasonal material 3-6 months in advance. Reports in 3 weeks. SASE.

Nonfiction and Photos: Buys historical, photo and business articles pertaining specifically to Jacksonville. Length: usually 1,500-3,000 words. Pays $50-$150. "We accept b&w glossy prints, good contrast; color transparencies." Pays $15 minimum for b&w; color terms to be arranged.

MIAMI MAGAZINE, Box 340008, Coral Gables FL 33134. (305)856-5011. Executive Editor: Richard Covington. For affluent, involved citizens of south Florida; generally well educated. Monthly magazine. Circ. 30,000. Rights purchased vary with author and material. Usually buys first publication rights. Buys about 200 mss/year. Pays on publication. Sample copy $1.75. Reports in 60 days. Query or submit complete ms. SASE.

Nonfiction: Investigative pieces on the area; thorough, general features; exciting, in-depth writing. Informational, how-to, interview, profile, and expose. Strong local angle and fresh, opinionated and humorous approach. Length: 5,000 words maximum. Pays $100-1,500. Departments: Film, business, books, art and travel. Length: 1,500 words maximum. Payment ranges from $100-150.

TAMPA MAGAZINE, City Magazines, Inc., 4100 W. Kennedy Blvd., Tampa FL 33609. (813)872-7449. Editor: Frank Bentayou. Articles Editor: Robert Casterline. Monthly magazine for upscale Tampa Bay Area readers. Estab. 1980. Circ. 15,000+. Pays on publication. Byline given. Pays negotiable kill fee. Buys first North American serial rights. Submit seasonal/holiday material 2½ months in advance. Simultaneous queries OK. SASE. Reports in 1 month. Sample copy $1.50; writer's guidelines for SAE.

Nonfiction: Exposé, general interest, historical/nostalgic, and interview/profile—all pertaining to the Tampa Bay Area. "We have an editorial mix from soft fashion and food features to hard investigative reports. The emphasis is on good writing and more specifically on good, detailed reporting." Occasionally needs get-away pieces for Bay area residents, fashion pieces, and food/drink articles. "No puff profiles, puff travel, sappy nostalgia or uncritical features. Buys 24-36 mss/year. Query with clips of published work. Length: "300-500 for shorts; 3,000-5,000 for 'well' stories." Pays $30-500.

Photos: Brian Noyes, art director. State availability of photos. Reviews b&w contact sheets. Captions, model releases, and identification of subjects required. Buys one-time rights and all rights.

Fiction: "No fiction mss have been bought yet—undecided about the future." Query with clips of published work. Length: 5,000 words maximum. Pays $200-500.

Tips: "The best place to start is 'Crosstown,' and Around-the-Bay section with short, grabby features under 500 words. They must be sharp, well- and accurately researched, and brightly written. Contact Robert Casterline with query. Humorous, insider-type material is most likely to work in the 'Crosstown' section.

Georgia

ATLANTA MAGAZINE, 6285 Barfield Rd., Atlanta GA 30328. (404)256-9800. Editor: John W. Lange. Emphasizes general consumer interest for metro Atlanta with some circulation in the state. Monthly magazine. Pays on acceptance. Buys first publication rights and right to reprint 1 time. Pays 10% kill fee. Byline given. SASE. Reports in 6-8 weeks. Sample copy $3.

Nonfiction: "The majority of articles in any issue must relate to metro Atlanta. Statewide, regional and national articles are acceptable." Query. Length: 2,000-4,000 words. Pays $200 minimum.

Photos: State availability of photos. Buys 8x10 b&w prints or 35mm color transparencies; pay varies. Captions preferred.

AUGUSTA SPECTATOR, Box 3168, Augusta GA 30902. (404)733-1476. Publisher: Faith Bertsche. Magazine published 3 times/year about the Augusta, Georgia and Aiken, South Carolina area for readers who are upper middle class residents, Ft. Gordon army post and medical complex personnel and visitors to the Masters Golf Tournament. Estab. 1980. Circ. 5,000. Pays on publication. Byline given. Buys one-time rights. Submit seasonal material 6 months in advance. Simultaneous, photocopied and previously published submissions OK. SASE. Reports in 1 month. Sample copy $1; free writer's guidelines for SASE.

Nonfiction: General interest (for people interested in golf, horses and local topical issues); historical (issues concerning the southeast coast); interview (of outstanding people of local interest); nostalgia (with a Southern flavor); profile; travel (worldwide); humor (related to the Masters, polo, birddog trials); photo feature. Query. Length: 1,200 words minimum. Pays $25-50.

Photos: State availability of photos. Reviews 5x7 b&w glossy prints. Offers no additional payment for photos accepted with ms. Captions and model release required. Buys one-time rights.

Fiction: Adventure, humorous, mystery, romance, suspense, historical. No unnecessary violence. Buys 2 mss/issue. Send complete ms. Length: 3,000 words maximum. Pays $50 maximum.

Poetry: Editor: Barri Armitage. Free verse and traditional. Submit maximum 6 poems. Pays in copies.

Illinois

CHICAGO MAGAZINE, 500 N. Michigan Ave., Chicago IL 60611. Editor-in-Chief: Allen H. Kelson. Editor: John Fink. 40% freelance written. For an audience which is "95% from Chicago area; 90% college-trained; upper income; overriding interests in the arts, dining, good life in the city and suburbs. Most are in 25 to 50 age bracket and well-read and articulate. Generally liberal inclination." Monthly. Circ. 200,000. Buys first rights. Buys about 50 mss/year. Pays on acceptance. For sample copy, send $3 to Circulation Dept. Submit seasonal material 3 months in advance. Reports in 2 weeks. Query; indicate "specifics, knowledge of city and market, and demonstrable access to sources." SASE.

Nonfiction and Photos: "On themes relating to the quality of life in Chicago; past, present, future." Writers should have "a general awareness that the readers will be concerned, influential longtime Chicagoans reading what the writer has to say about their city. We generally publish material too comprehensive for daily newspapers or of too specialized interest for them." Buys personal experience and think pieces, interviews, profiles, humor, spot news, historical articles, travel, and exposés. Length: 1,000-6,000 words. Pays $100-$750. Photos purchased with mss. Uses b&w glossy prints, 35mm color transparencies or color prints.

Fiction: Christine Newman, articles editor. Mainstream, fantasy and humorous fiction. Preferably with Chicago orientation. No word-length limits, but "no novels, please." Pays $250-500.

Tips: "Submit plainly, be businesslike and avoid cliché ideas."

CHICAGO READER, Box 11101, Chicago IL 60611. (312)828-0350. Editor: Robert A. Roth. "The *Reader* is distributed free in Chicago's lakefront neighborhoods. Generally speaking, these are Chicago's best educated, most affluent neighborhoods—and they have an unusually high concentration of young adults." Weekly tabloid; 120 pages. Circ. 110,000. Pays "by 15th of month following publication." Buys all rights. Byline given. Phone queries OK. Photocopied submissions OK. SASE. Reports in 1 year, "if you're lucky."

Nonfiction: "We want magazine features on Chicago topics. Will also consider reviews." Buys 500 mss/year. Submit complete ms. Length: "whatever's appropriate to the story." Pays $35-550.
Photos: By assignment only.
Columns/Departments: By assignment only.

Indiana

INDIANAPOLIS, 320 N. Meridian, Indianapolis IN 46204. (317)635-4747. Editor: Pegg Kennedy. Emphasizes any Indianapolis-related problems/features or regional related topics. Monthly magazine; 68-140 pages. Circ. 15,000. Pays on publication. Buys first North American serial rights. Byline given. Queries or manuscripts. Submit seasonal/holiday material 4 months in advance. Simultaneous, photocopied and previously published submissions OK. SASE. Reports in 1 month. Sample copy $1.75.
Nonfiction: Exposé (interested, but have no specifics; "we're interested in any Indianapolis-related topic including government and education"); historical (Indianapolis-related only); how-to (buying tips); humor ("broad-category for us"); inspirational (not generally but will read submitted ms); interview (Indianapolis-related person, native sons and daughters); nostalgia (Indianapolis-related); personal experience (Indianapolis-related); photo feature (human interest, Indianapolis-related); profile (Indianapolis-related); and travel (within a day's drive of Indianapolis). "We only want articles with Indianapolis ties, no subjects outside of our region. We aren't very interested in broad-based, national topics either. Our magazine is supplemented by special guides which require general basic information: Guide to Living (in Indianapolis)—a comprehensive directory aobut city services, facilities, organizations; Habitats—a guide to houses, apartments, condos; Indiana Guide—features about people, places, events in the state that make you feel like you know a neat person or want to visit a special thing/place; Sports Guide—all kinds of local sports information stories; Office Guide—background about the commercial side of the city, growth rates, etc." Buys 3-5 mss/issue. Query with clips of published work. Length: 500-3,500 words. Pays $20-140.
Photos: State availability of photos. Pays $10 for b&w; $5-35 for color transparencies. Buys one-time rights. Captions preferred.
Fiction: Fantasy, experimental, humorous, mainstream and science fiction. "We haven't used much fiction in the past but we are open for some, depending on quality and content." Send complete ms. Length: 500-2,500 words. Pays $40-85.
Tips: "I'm big on sidebars."

Kansas

KANSAS CITY MAGAZINE, 5350 W. 94th Terrace, Suite 204, Prairie Village, KS 66207. (913)648-0444. Editor: David Firestone. Monthly; 48-96 pages. Circ. 15,000. Magazine staff and 8-10 contributing writers write 95% of each issue; outside freelance material is considered and occasionally accepted. Written queries only; manuscripts should be accompanied by SASE. Sample copy $1.50. Reports in 1 month. No simultaneous, photocopied, or previously published submissions accepted.
Nonfiction: Editorial content is hard news, investigative reporting, profiles, or lengthy news features. Generally not interested in light features, service items, or humor; no fiction. Short items of 500-1,250 words are considered for "City Window" column; pays $35-75. Longer stories of 2,000-8,000 words pay from $100-500, plus expenses. Columns, which include politics, film, home, art, and a "Postscript" essay, are from 1,500-3,000 words and pay $125-200. These are not generally open to freelancers, although; "Postscript" suggestions are accepted. All material must have a demonstrable connection to Kansas City. Photos and illustrations to accompany stories are assigned by the magazine, and freelance submissions of this kind are not generally considered. Byline are always given, except for "City Window" material; all rights are purchased. Freelancers should show some previous reporting or writing experience of a professional nature.

Louisiana

NEW ORLEANS MAGAZINE, Flambeaux Publishing Co., 6666 Morrison Rd., New Orleans LA 70126. (504)246-2700. Editor: Jean Stewart. 50% freelance written. Monthly magazine; 125 pages. Circ. 60,000. Pays on publication. Buys all rights. Pays 50% kill fee. Byline given. Submit seasonal/holiday material 4 months in advance. SASE. Reports in 3 weeks.

Nonfiction: General interest; interview and profile. Buys 6 mss/issue. Submit complete ms. Length: 1,200-3,000 words. Pays $100-500.

Photos: John Maher, art director. State availability of photos with ms. Offers no additional payment for b&w photos accepted with accompanying ms. Captions required. Buys one-time rights. Model release required.

Maryland

BALTIMORE MAGAZINE, 131 E. Redwood St., Baltimore MD 21202. (301)752-7375. Editor: Stan Heuisler. Managing Editor: Jane Crystal. Monthly magazine; 150 pages. Circ. 50,000. Pays on publication. Buys all rights. Pays 33⅓% kill fee, except for first-time writer. Byline given. Written queries OK. Submit seasonal/holiday material 4 months in advance. SASE. Reports in 6 weeks. Sample copy $2; free writer's guidelines.

Nonfiction: Expose, how-to, interview, profile and consumer guides. Must have local angle. "We do not want to see any soft, non-local features." Buys 7 mss/issue. Send complete ms or clips of published work. Length: 1,000-5,000 words. Pays $50-350.

Photos: State availability of photos with ms. Uses b&w glossy prints. Captions preferred.

Columns/Departments: Hot Stuff (local news tips); and Tips & Touts (local unusual retail opportunities). Query.

Massachusetts

BOSTON MAGAZINE, Municipal Publications, 1050 Park Square Bldg., Boston MA 02116. (617)357-4000. Editor-in-Chief: Terry Catchpole. For upscale readers; majority are professionals, college-educated and affluent. Monthly magazine; 200 pages. Pays on publication. Buys all rights. Pays 20% kill fee. Byline given unless article has to be rewritten by a staff member. Submit seasonal/holiday material 3 months in advance. SASE. Reports in 2 weeks.

Nonfiction: Expose (subject matter varies); profiles (of Bostonians; sometimes, New Englanders); travel (usually only in New England); personal experience. Buys about 40 mss/year. Query. Length: 1,000-10,000 words. Pays $100-750.

Photos: Valerie Bessette, art director. B&w and color purchased on assignment only. Query. Specifications vary. Pays $25-150 for b&w; payment for color (used on cover only) averages $275.

Tips: "If we are unfamiliar with a writer's work, we want to see clips that are representative of his/her style and range of interest and expertise. Remember, we consider ourselves in the entertainment business, so the emphasis here is on compelling, entertaining writing. The one thing that this or any other magazine can never afford to do is bore the reader."

THE BOSTON MONTHLY, Klaber Publications, Inc., 20 Newbury St., Boston MA 02116. (617)536-6606. Editor: Alice Van Buren. Assistant Editor: Julie Agoos. Monthly magazine emphasizing feature and literary writing for middle-class, prosperous, well-educated, sophisticated professionals. Circ. 60,000. Pays on publication. Byline given. Pays 33% kill fee. Buys first North American serial rights. Submit seasonal/holiday material 3 months in advance. Simultaneous queries and photocopied submissions OK. SASE. Reports in 2 weeks. Sample copy $1; writer's guidelines for business size SAE and 1 first class stamp.

Nonfiction: General interest; historical (must be Boston-based or of national interest); humor; interview/profile (of persons of significant ethical or personal stature—not celebrities); personal experience; photo feature; literary and cultural essays; and social commentary. "Controversial pieces welcome." No pornography or religion. Buys 50 mss/year. Query with clips of published work. Length: 1,200-3,500 words. Pays $100-150.

Photos: State availability of photos.

Columns/Departments: Keynotes (short pieces—anecdotes, cameos; writing must be deft—can be whimsical or ironic). Buys 36 mss/year. Length: 900 words maximum. Pays $40.

Fiction: "We're looking for intelligent, closely written short stories—comic or tragic. No pornography, no slush." Buys 8 mss/year. Send complete ms. Length: 4,000 words maximum. Pays $100.

Poetry: Avant-garde, free verse, haiku and light verse. "We accept all forms but only top quality is considered." Buys 12 mss/year. Submit maximum 6 poems. Length: 35 lines. Pays $15.

Michigan

ANN ARBOR OBSERVER, Ann Arbor Observer Company, 206 S. Main, Ann Arbor MI 48104. Editors: Don and Mary Hunt. Monthly magazine featuring stories about people and events in Ann Arbor. Circ. 37,000. Pays on publication. Byline given. Buys one-time rights. Reports in 3 weeks on queries; 4 weeks on mss. Sample copy $1.
Nonfiction: Expose, historical/nostalgic, interview/profile, personal experience and photo feature. Buys 75 mss/year. Query. Length: 100-7,000 words. Pays 8-12¢/word.
Tips: "If you have an idea for a story, write us a 100-200 word description telling us why the story is interesting and what its major point is. We are most open to investigative features of 5,000-7,000 words. We are especially interested in well-researched stories that uncover information about some interesting aspect of Ann Arbor."

GRAND RAPIDS MAGAZINE, 17 Fountain St., NW, Grand Rapids MI 49503. (616)459-4545. Editor and Publisher: John H. Zwarensteyn. Managing Editor: John J. Brosky Jr. Monthly magazine featuring people, issues and industry for educated 25-40 year olds with a high income. Circ. 12,000. Pays 15th of month of publication. Buys all rights. Phone queries OK. Submit seasonal material 4 months in advance. Photocopied and previously published submissions OK. SASE. Reports in 2 months.
Nonfiction: Western Michigan writers preferred. Exposé (of government, labor, education, etc. at the local level); general interest (varied, local subjects have precedence); historical (local or regional); how-to (in all areas); humor (specific to region); inspirational (local or regional significance); interview (local or regional subjects); nostalgia; profile; personal experience, photo feature (local or regional subject). Buys 25 mss/year. Query with clips or phone query. Length: 500-2,000 words. Pays $15-125. Clean copy considered a courtesy.
Photos: State availability of photos or send photos with ms. Pays $10+/5x7 glossy print and $22+/35 or 120mm color transparencies. Captions and model release required. Buys first-run exclusive rights.
Fiction: Stories set in Michigan only; only works of Western Michigan writers, please. Phone queries preferred. Buys 2 mss/year. Send complete ms. Length: 1,500-3,500 words. Pays $35-90.
Tips: "Break in with phone call. Live in West Michigan. Bring ideas for stories that show understanding of our editorial format. Take on assignments. Start with 500 word pieces for 'Grand Stand' sections."

MONTHLY DETROIT MAGAZINE, Detroit Magazine Inc., 1404 Commonwealth Bldg., Detroit MI 48226. (313)962-2350. Editor: Kirk Cheyfitz. Emphasizes Detroit area for an audience of city and suburban residents. Monthly magazine; 136 pages. Circ. 44,000. Pays on publication. Buys first North American serial rights. Kill fee by negotiation only. Byline given. Written queries preferred. Submit seasonal/holiday material 3 months in advance. SASE. Reports in 2 weeks. Sample copy $2.25; free writer's guidelines.
Nonfiction: Features, guides, service pieces, investigations and nostalgia on Detroit history, institutions, politics, neighborhoods and profiles of important metro Detroiters or ex-Detroiters. Art, music and business columns. Query with clips of published work. Buys 10 mss/issue. Length: 200-5,000 words. Pays $50-500 or 10¢/published word for feature articles.
Tips: "We are more receptive to shorter pieces on music, arts and history from first-time freelancers. Query letters should be as specific as possible; the writer's point of view should be stated clearly; the style of the letter should mirror the sytle of the proposed article; the writer's credentials to do the piece should be spelled out."

Minnesota

MPLS. ST. PAUL MAGAZINE, 512 Nicollet Mall, Suite 615, Minneapolis MN 55402. (612)339-7571. Editor-in-Chief: Brian Anderson. Associate Editor: Ingrid Sundstrom. 90% freelance written. For "professional people of middle-to-upper-income levels, college educated, interested in the arts, dining and the good life of Minnesota." Monthly magazine; 125-225 pages. Circ. 40,000. Pays on publication. Buys all rights. Pays 25% maximum kill fee. Byline given except for extremely short pieces and stories that require considerable rewriting. Submit seasonal/holiday material 4 months in advance. SASE. Reports in 3 weeks.
Nonfiction: Investigative; how-to; informational; historical; humor; interview; profile and photo feature. "We can use any of these as long as they are related to Minneapolis-St. Paul." Query. Length: 300-3,000 words. Pays $20-300.
Photos: Maureen Ryan, art director. Purchased on assignment. Query. Pays $25-100 for b&w; $25-175 for color.

Tips: Best way for freelancer to break in is by sending a "short people feature on a local and interesting person. I like short, to-the-point, even informal queries; I hate cute, beat-around-the-bush, detailed queries. I often suggest that the writer develop a lead, followed by a couple graphs saying where the story would go. If I want to read more after the lead, then so might one of our readers, or many of them. Submission of a 300-500 word profile on spec. should be followed in a couple weeks by a phone call. If I send a ms back I usually make suggestions for improving or scrapping the piece. If improvements are made and I see potential in the writer, then I'll make an appointment to discuss the writer's ideas for future stories. He/she may get a larger assignment on spec. at this point. If we like each other, they've got it made."

Missouri

METRO, The Tabloid, Hemlock Press, 1312 Washington Ave., St. Louis MO 63103. (314)231-3353. Editor: Richard A. Wachter. Monthly tabloid "appealing to the upward-oriented middle class—baby boomers and dual income families." Circ. 27,000. Pays on publication. Byline given. Offers 50% kill fee. Buys "flexible" rights. Submit seasonal/holiday material 3 months in advance. Simultaneous queries, and simultaneous and previously published submissions OK. SASE. Reports in 1 month. Sample copy for $1 and 9x12 SASE; writer's guidelines for business size SASE and 1 first class stamp.
Nonfiction: C.T. Dogge, articles editor. Book excerpts, general interest, interview/profile, opinion, photo feature and technical. "Many issues have a theme, but we have constant need for articles relating to sight and sound, film and the arts. No religious or self help. Buys 80 mss/year. Length: 150-10,000 words. Pays $15-250.
Photos: Richard A. Wachter, photo editor. Send photos with ms. Pays $5-25 for b&w. Captions, model release and identification of subjects required.
Columns/Departments: Charles Leonard, column/department editor. Reviews of stage, film, art, books. "Frankly critical material by the highly qualified." Buys 50 mss/year. Query with clips of published work. Length: 150-600 words. Pays $15-100.
Fiction: Max Wells, fiction editor. Erotica ("if handled for adult, but refined market"); experimental ("slight interest"); fantasy; historical; humorous; mainstream; mystery; novel excerpts; romance ("sophisticated and interesting to both men and women"); and science fiction ("infrequently"). No religion, western, confession, ethnic. Buys 6-7 mss/year. Query with clips of published work. Length: 600-10,000 words. Pays $25 minimum.
Poetry: F.E. Malone, poetry editor. Avant-garde, free verse and haiku. No "sweet" poetry. Buys 6-12 mss/year. Submit 10 poems maximum. Length: open. Pays $15-50.
Fillers: Charles Leonard, fillers editor. Clippings, anecdotes and newsbreaks. Buys 25/year. Length: 150 words maximum. Pays $5-15.

ST. LOUIS, 7110 Oakland Ave., St. Louis MO 63117. (314)781-8787. Editor: John Heidenry. For "those interested in the St. Louis area, recreation issues, etc." Monthly. Circ. 50,000. Buys all and second serial (reprint) rights. Buys 60/mss year. Pays on publication. Photocopied submissions OK. Submit seasonal material 4 months in advance. Reports on material in 1 month. Query or submit complete ms. SASE.
Nonfiction and Photos: "Articles on the city of St. Louis, metro area, arts, recreation, media, law, education, politics, timely issues, urban problems/solutions, environment, etc., generally related to St. Louis area. Looking for informative writing of high quality, consistent in style and timely in topic." Informational, how-to, personal experience, humor, historical, think pieces, expose, nostalgia, personal opinion, travel. Length: 1,000 to 5,000 words. Pays $250-700 for 8x10 b&w glossy prints purchased on assignment. "Shooting fee plus $25 minimum print used. All color on individual basis."

Nebraska

OMAHA MAGAZINE, Omaha, The City Magazine, Inc., 8424 West Center Rd., Suite 207, Omaha NE 68124. (402)393-3332. Editor: Art Siemering. Emphasizes people, events and urban survival issues for Omahans active in their city's life. Monthly magazine; 80 pages. Circ. 12,000. Pays on publication. Buys first North American serial rights. Byline given. Phone queries OK. Submit seasonal/holiday material 3 months in advance. Simultaneous, photocopied and previously published submissions OK. SASE. Reports in 6 months. Sample copy $2; writer's guidelines for SASE.
Nonfiction: Exposé (about local issues); general interest (local or native sons in these categories:

entertainment, sports, lifestyle, people, arts, consumer, food, drink, politics, business, personal finance); historical (on assignment only—usually about Omaha); how-to (throw a party, cure boredom, improve quality of life—any topic, but should have specific local application); profile (of famous or controversial Omahans); travel (emphasis on destinations); and photo feature (local). Buys 3-5 mss/issue. Query with clips of published work. Length: 1,000-3,500 words. Pays $50-150.
Photos: State availability of photos or send samples with ms. Pays $35-100 for b&w contact sheets and negatives, and for color transparencies. Captions required. Buys one-time rights.

New Jersey

ATLANTIC CITY MAGAZINE, Menus International, Inc., 1637 Atlantic Ave., Atlantic City NJ 08401. Editor: Donna Andersen. For residents and tourists, as well as people interested in investing in Atlantic City. Bimonthly magazine; 150 pages. Circ. 50,000. Most work done on assignment; rarely purchases unsolicted mss. Pays on publication. Buys one-time rights. Byline given. Submit seasonal/holiday ideas 2 months in advance. SASE. Reports in 4 weeks. Sample copy $2.
Nonfiction: Exposé, general interest, how-to, entertainment, interview, photo feature and profile. "Articles should be related to South Jersey shore area in general and Atlantic City in particular. We will especially need city-related profiles, trend pieces and investigative articles. No confession articles." Buys 28 mss/year. Query and/or send clips of published work. Length: 500-3,000 words. Pays $25-500.
Photos: State availability of photos. Buys 8x10 b&w prints and 2¼x2¼ color transparencies. Pay varies. Captions preferred.
Columns/Departments: Art, Business, Entertainment, Environment, Sports and Real Estate. Buys 30 articles/year. Query and/or send clips of published work. Length: 1,000-3,000 words. Pays $25-500.
Tips: "Story idea must have a local angle. Letter itself should be energetic. No nostalgia. Include samples of published work."

New York

BUFFALO SPREE MAGAZINE, Box 38, Buffalo NY 14226. (716)839-3405. Editor: Johanna V. Shotell. For "a highly literate readership." Quarterly. Circ. 20,000. Buys first serial rights. Buys 5-8 mss/year. SASE.
Nonfiction and Fiction: Department Editor: Gary Goss. "Intellectually stimulating prose exploring contemporary social, philosophical and artistic concerns. We are not a political magazine. Matters of interest to western New York make up a significant part of what we print." Length: 1,800 words maximum. Pays $75 for a lead article. "We print fiction, but it must be brilliant." Pays approximately $75.
Poetry: Department Editor: Janet Goldenberg. "Serious, modern poetry of nature and of man's relationship with nature interests us, provided it is of the highest quality." Pays approximately $15.

EAST END MAGAZINE, The East End Corp., (of Eastern Long Island and The Hamptons). The Long Wharf at Sag Harbor, NY 11963. (516)725-0658. Editor-in-Chief: Andrew Boracci. Emphasizes education, homes, gardens, food, books and East End lifestyle for an affluent and retired affluent audience of locals, tourists, second-home owners, professors and college administrators. Monthly magazine. Estab. 1979. Circ. 15,000. Pays on publication. Makes work-for-hire assignments. Phone queries OK. Submit seasonal material 4 months in advance. Simultaneous, photocopied and previously published submissions OK. SASE. Reports in 2 weeks. Free sample copy and writer's guidelines.
Nonfiction: Exposé, general interest, historical, how-to, humor, inspirational, interview, personal experience, photo feature and technical. "All of these are acceptable, but with a specific East End slant and must be well-researched." Buys 2-3 mss/issue. Query. Length: 750-1,500 words. Pays $25-50/page.
Photos: State availability of photos. Pays $10-50/8x10 b&w glossy print. Pays $50-100 for color transparencies. Captions preferred. Model release required. Buys all rights or negotiates rights.
Tips: "Query first with a specific idea that reveals familiarity with an area or subject matter, then negotiate a 'go ahead' assignment."

FOCUS, 375 Park Ave., New York NY 10022. (212)628-2000. Editor: Steven Arikie. Managing Editor: Barbara Volker. Annual publication featuring a guide to New York City and to New York shops for hotel guests and New York residents. Circ. 250,000. Pays on acceptance. Buys one-time rights. Phone queries OK. Sample copy $1.25.

Nonfiction: "We want reviews of antique shops, art galleries, home furnishing stores, women's shops, men's shops and restaurants. The writer must interview an owner and write a description to be approved by the owner. This is all done on assignment." Buys 120 mss/issue. Query with clips of previously published work. Length: 110 words minimum. Pays $35 minimum.

METROPOLITAN ALMANAC, New York's Complete Day by Day Calendar of Events, 80 E. 11th St., New York NY 10003. Publisher: Marvin Tabak. Managing Editor: Amy Braziller. Weekly tabloid for people in metropolitan New York. Circ. 8,000. Pays on acceptance. Byline given. Buys first North American serial rights. Simultaneous queries and photocopied submissions OK. SASE. Reports in 1 month. Free sample copy.

Nonfiction: "Articles relating to metropolitan New York—cultural, recreational, educational, singles, history, geography and lore—will be used." Query with clips of published work. Length: open. Pay: open.

Photos: State availability of photos.

NEW BROOKLYN, Motivational Communications, 175 Fifth Ave., New York NY 10010. (212)260-0800. Assistant Editor: Allen Grossman. Managing Editor: Tom Bedell. Quarterly magazine covering locally oriented general-interest topics for residents of Brooklyn. Circ. 25,000. Pays on publication. Byline given. Pays average 50% kill fee. Buys first North American serial rights. Submit seasonal/holiday material 3 months in advance. Simultaneous queries, and simultaneous and previously published submissions OK. SASE. Reports in 1 month. Sample copy $2.50.

Nonfiction: Historical/nostalgic (local); humor; interview/profile (of a business or a business person in Brooklyn); the arts; survey pieces; health; home; community services; shopping sprees. "We're looking for light, upbeat, feature pieces of local interest. We want to present a positive image of Brooklyn. No topics without a link to the burrough." Buys 50 mss/year. Query. Length: 1,200 words minimum. Pays $50.

Photos: State availability of photos.

Columns/Departments: Restaurant Reviews; Wavelengths (record reviews). Send complete ms. Length: 500 words minimum. Pays $35.

Fillers: Short humor (with a Brooklyn link). Length: 500 words minimum. Pays $35.

NEW YORK AFFAIRS, 419 Park Ave. S., New York NY 10016. (212)689-1240. Editor-in-Chief: Dick Netzer. Emphasizes urban problems. "Readers tend to be academics, public officials, corporation presidents and intellectual types." Quarterly magazine; 128 pages. Circ. 5,000. Pays on publication. Buys all rights. Phone queries OK. Photocopied submissions OK. SASE. Reports in 1 month. Sample copy $3; free writer's guidelines.

Nonfiction: Michael Winkleman, executive editor. Expose; interview (figures who are key to urban policymaking); and personal opinion. Buys 8 mss/year. Query. Length: 3,000-7,500 words. Pays $50-200. "We also have a section for short articles (250-3,000 words) called 'Side Streets' in which we run what is good about cities—humor especially. Most of our authors are academics whom we don't pay. For those whom we can't afford to pay, which includes authors of most articles and Side Streets, we pay in copies of the magazine."

Columns/Departments: Book reviews. "We don't pay reviewers. They just get to keep the book." Uses 30 pages/year. Query.

Tips: "We are looking for hard-hitting, well-written articles on general urban problems. We especially like articles that take the unconventional approach—that transit fares should be raised, or that the cost of welfare should *not* be picked up by the federal government."

NEW YORK MAGAZINE, New York Magazine Co., 755 2nd Ave., New York, NY 10017. (212)880-0700. Editor: Edward Kosner. Managing Editor: Laurie Jones. "We limit our coverage to the New York metropolitan area." Weekly magazine. Pays on acceptance. Buys all rights. Submit seasonal/holiday material 2 months in advance. Photocopied submissions OK. SASE. Reports in 1 month.

Nonfiction: Exposé, general interest, interview, profile, new product, behavior/lifestyle, health/medicine and photo feature. Query. Pays $300-1,500.

Columns/Departments: Humorous. Length: 1,000 words. Pays $300-1,500.

OUR TOWN, East Side/West Side Communications Corp., 1751 2nd Ave., Suite 202, New York NY 10028. (212)289-8700. Editor: Katy Morgan. Weekly tabloid covering neighborhood news of Manhattan (96th St.-14th St.). Circ. 135,000. Pays on publication. Byline given. Buys all rights. Submit seasonal/holiday material 1 month in advance. SASE.

Nonfiction: Expose (especially consumer ripoffs); historical/nostalgic (Manhattan, 14th St.-96th

St.); interview/profile (of local personalities); photo feature (of local event); and animal rights. "We're looking for local news (Manhattan only, mainly 14th St.-96th St.). We need timely, lively coverage of local issues and events, focusing on people or exposing injustice and good deeds of local residents and business people. (Get *full names, spelled right!*)" Special issues include Education (January, March and August); and Summer Camps (March). Query with clips of published work. Length: 1,000 words maximum. Pays "70¢/20-pica column-inch as published."
Photos: Pays $2-5 for 8x10 b&w prints. Buys all rights.
Tips: "Come by the office and talk to the editor. (Call first.) Bring samples of writing."

STATEN ISLAND, Motivational Communications, 175 Fifth Ave., New York NY 10010. (212)260-0800. Assistant Editor: Allen Grossman. Managing Editor: Tom Bedell. Quarterly magazine covering local residents of Staten Island. Circ. 25,000. Pays on publication. Byline given. Pays average 50% kill fee. Buys first North American serial rights. Submit seasonal/holiday material 3 months in advance. Simultaneous queries, and simultaneous and previously published submissions OK. SASE. Reports in 1 month. Sample copy $2.50
Nonfiction: Historical/nostalgic (locally oriented); humor; interview/profile (of a business or a business person in State Island); the arts (survey pieces); health; home; in-service pieces (schools, hospitals, public institutions); and shopping sprees. Also needs light feature pieces of local interest. "No topics without a link to the burrough." Buys 50 mss/year. Query. Length: 1,200 words minimum. Pays $50.
Photos: State availability of photos.
Columns/Departments: Restaurant Reviews; and Wavelengths (record reviews of local artists). Send complete ms. Length: 500 words. Pays $35.
Fillers: Short humor (with a Staten Island link).

North Carolina

CHARLOTTE MAGAZINE, Box 221269, Charlotte NC 28222. (704)588-2120. Editor: Rob Whaley. Emphasizes probing, researched articles on local people and local places. Bimonthly magazine. Circ. 10,000. Pays on publication. Buys first rights. SASE. Reports in 3 weeks. Sample copy $1.75 from Kathy Bell.
Nonfiction: Departments: lifestyles (alternative and typical); business (spotlight successful, interesting business and people); town talk (short, local articles of interest); theater, arts. No PR promos. "We are seeking articles indicating depth and research in original treatments of subjects. Our eagerness increases with articles that give our well-educated audience significant information through stylish, entertaining prose and uniqueness of perspective. Remember our local/regional emphasis." Send complete ms. Length: 2,500-5,000 words. Pays $150-500.
Photos: State availability of photos. Buys b&w and color prints; pay negotiable. Captions preferred; model releases required.
Columns/Departments: "Will consider all types of articles." Buys 6 columns/issue. Query. Length: 1,000-2,000 words. Pays $75-200.
Fillers: Anecdotes, newsbreaks, and Carolina consumer bargains. Buys 6-8/issue. Length: 250-500 words. Pays 7½¢/word.

Ohio

CINCINNATI MAGAZINE, Greater Cincinnati Chamber of Commerce, 120 W. 5th St., Cincinnati OH 45202. (513)721-3300. Editor: Laura Pulfer. Emphasizes Cincinnati living. Monthly magazine; 88-120 pages. Circ. 25,000. Pays on acceptance. Buys all rights. Pays 33% kill fee. Byline given. Submit seasonal/holiday material 3 months in advance. Simultaneous, photocopied and previously published submissions OK. SASE. Reports in 3 weeks.
Nonfiction: How-to; informational; interview; photo feature; profile; and travel. Buys 4-5 mss/issue. Query. Length: 2,000-4,000 words. Pays $150-400.
Photos: Kay Walker, art director. Photos purchased on assignment only. Model release required.
Columns/Departments: Travel; How-To; Sports and Consumer Tips. Buys 5 mss/issue. Query. Length: 750-1,500 words. Pays $75-150.
Tips: "It helps to mention something you found particularly well done. It shows you've done your homework and sets you apart from the person who clearly is not tailoring his idea to our publication. Send article ideas that probe the whys and wherefores of major issues confronting the community, making candid and in-depth appraisals of the problems and honest attempts to seek

solutions. Have a clear and well-defined subject about the city (the arts, politics, business, sports, government, entertainment); include a rough outline with proposed length; a brief background of writing experience and sample writing if available. We are looking for critical pieces, smoothly written, that ask and answer questions that concern our readers. We do not run features that are "about" places or businesses simply because they exist. There should be a thesis that guides the writer and the reader. We want balanced articles about the city—the arts, politics, business, etc."

COLUMBUS MONTHLY, 171 E. Livingston Ave., Columbus OH 43215. (614)464-4567. Editorial Director: Lenore E. Brown. Emphasizes subjects of general interest primarily to Columbus and central Ohio. Monthly magazine. Pays on publication. Buys all rights. Byline given. SASE. Reports in 1 month. Sample copy $2.65.
Nonfiction: "We want general articles as long as they pertain to Columbus or central Ohio area." Buys 6 mss/issue. Query. "I like query letters which: 1. are well-written; 2. indicate the author has some familiarity with *Columbus Monthly*; 3. give me enough detail to make a decision; 4. include at least a basic bio of the writer." Length: 100-4,500 words. Pays $15-400.
Photos: State availability of photos. Pay varies for b&w or color prints. Model releases required.
Columns/Departments: Art, Business, Food and Drink, Movies, Politics, Sports and Theatre. Buys 2-3 columns/issue. Query. Length: 1,000-2,000 words. Pays $100-175.
Tips: "It makes sense to start small: something for our "Around Columbus" section, perhaps. Stories for that section run between 400-1,000 words."

Oklahoma

TULSA MAGAZINE, Box 1620, Tulsa OK 74101. (918)582-6000. Editor: Kitty G. Silvey. Audience is primarily medium- to upper-income-level Tulsans. Monthly. Circulation: 6,000. Byline given. Pays on acceptance. Sample copy $1. Deadlines are at least 6 weeks prior to publication date, the second Monday of each month. Reports immediately. Query; "indicate name, address and phone number; specific story suggestions or types of stories you prefer; and sample of writing for style and clarity." SASE.
Nonfiction and Photos: Articles must revolve around people or how subject affects people and must have a Tulsa area slant. Style desired is informal and lively. Length: 1,000-4,000 words. Payment is negotiable, $50-150, depending on length and research. Photos usually taken by staff or on assignment. May be purchased with mss.
Tips: "Give me an in-depth, well-researched article on a social problem facing the city of Tulsa— something we haven't already seen in the newspapers a half-dozen times. We do not print fashion or society news unless it is really out-of-the-ordinary. We prefer articles that are issue-oriented, but we are a Chamber of Commerce publication and are somewhat limited in the stands we can take."

Pennsylvania

ERIE MAGAZINE, Dispatch Printing, Box 7159, Erie PA 16510. (814)452-6724. Publisher: E. Joseph Mehl. Co-Editor: Pam Larson. Bimonthly magazine about the Erie, Pennsylvania area for middle to high income residents of Northwest Pennsylvania. Estab. 1979. Circ. 20,000. Pays on publication. Byline given. Buys first North American serial rights. Phone queries OK. Submit seasonal material 3 months in advance. Simultaneous, photocopied and previously published submissions OK if so indicated. SASE. Reports in 1 month. Sample copy $1.25; free writer's guidelines for SASE.
Nonfiction: "We'd like to see articles dealing with the implications of national topics on Erie, Pennsylvania. Articles may deal with trends, local personalities, events and issues." Photo feature. Buys 5 mss/issue. Query with clips of previously published work. Length: 2,000-4,000 words. Pays $35/magazine page with descending scale.
Photos: State availability of photos. Reviews 5x7 b&w glossy prints and 35mm color transparencies. Payment negotiable. Captions and model release required. Buys one-time rights.
Columns/Departments: Short features on health, business, sports, people, the kitchen, arts, agriculture, leisure, education, and travel. Buys 6-7 mss/issue. Query. Length: 1,500-2,000 words. Pays $35 minimum.

PHILADELPHIA MAGAZINE, 1500 Walnut St., Philadelphia PA 19102. Editor: Art Spikol. 35-50% freelance written. For sophisticated middle- and upper-income people in the Greater Philadelphia/South Jersey area. Monthly magazine. Circ. 140,000. Buys first rights. Pays 20% kill fee. Byline given. Buys 50 mss/year. Pays on publication, or within 2 months. Free writer's guidelines for SASE. Reports in 4 weeks. Queries and mss should be sent to Polly Hurst, managing editor. SASE.

Nonfiction and Photos: "Articles should have a strong Philadelphia focus, but should avoid Philadelphia stereotypes—we've seen them all. Lifestyles, city survival, profiles of interesting people, business stories, music, the arts, sports, local politics, stressing the topical or unusual. No puff pieces. We offer lots of latitude for style, but before you make like Norman Mailer, make sure you have something to say." Length: 1,000-7,000 words. Pays $75-500. Photos occasionally purchased with mss at additional payment of $35-150.

Tips: "Almost all that we buy from freelancers comes from the unique perspective of an outsider, things that our own staff might overlook. There's a good market here for first-person experience if it's told right."

PITTSBURGH MAGAZINE, Metropolitan Pittsburgh Public Broadcasting, Inc., 4802 5th Ave., Pittsburgh PA 15213. (412)622-1360. Editor-in-Chief: Randy Rieland. "The magazine is purchased on newsstands and by subscription and is given to those who contribute $20 or more a year to public TV in western Pennsylvania." Monthly magazine; 100 pages. Circ. 55,000. Pays on publication. Buys all rights. Pays 33% kill fee. Byline given. Submit seasonal/holiday material 6 months in advance. SASE. Reports in 6 weeks. Sample copy $1.50; free writer's guidelines.

Nonfiction: Expose, lifestyle, sports, humor, informational, service, interview, nostalgia, personal experience, personal opinion, profile and travel. No historical features. Buys 6 mss/issue. Query or send complete ms. Length: 2,500 words. Pays $50-500.

Photos: Purchased with accompanying ms or on assignment. Captions required. Uses b&w and color. Query for photos. Model release required.

Columns/Departments: Postscript (column of short essays and humor pieces); travel; books, films; dining; and sports. "All must relate to Pittsburgh or western Pennsylvania."

Puerto Rico

WALKING TOURS OF SAN JUAN, Magazine/Guide, Caribbean World Communications, Inc., First Federal Building, Office 301, Santurce PR 00909. (809)722-1767. Editor: Al Dinhofer. Managing Editor: Julie Jewel. Magazine published 2 times/year (winter and summer). Estab. 1980. Circ. 22,000. Pays on publication. Byline given. Buys second serial (reprint) rights. SASE. Reports in 1 month. Sample copy $4 for 9x12 SAE and $2 postage.

Nonfiction: Historical/nostalgic. "We are seeking historically based articles on San Juan. Any aspect of Spanish colonial culture, art, architecture, etc., would probably satisfy our needs. We must have sources—in fact, we will publish source material at the end of each article for reader reference." Buys 2 mss/year. Query. Length: 2,000-3,000 words. Pays $100.

Tennessee

MEMPHIS, Towery Press, 1535 E. Brooks Rd., Memphis TN 38116. (901)345-8000. Executive Editor: Kenneth Neill. Circ. 20,000. Pays on publication. Buys all rights. Pays $35 kill fee. Byline given. Phone queries OK. Simultaneous, photocopied and previously published submissions OK. SASE. Reports in 3 weeks. Sample copy $1.50.

Nonfiction: Exposé, general interest, historical, how-to, humor, interview and profiles. "Virtually all our material has strong Memphis connections." Buys 2 mss/issue. Query or submit complete ms or clips of published work. Length: 1,500-5,000 words. Pays 5¢/published word to first-time writers.

Tips: "The kinds of manuscripts we most need have a sense of story (i.e., plot, suspense, character), an abundance of evocative images to bring that story alive and a sensitivity to issues at work in Memphis. Tough investigative pieces would be especially welcomed."

Texas

D MAGAZINE, Dallas Southwest Media Corp., 1925 San Jacinto, Dallas TX 75201. Editor: Rowland Stiteler. 40% freelance written. For readers in the Dallas-Fort Worth area; primarily the middle to upper income group. Monthly magazine; 198 pages. Circ. 65,000. Pays on acceptance. Buys all rights. Pays 30% kill fee. Byline given. Submit seasonal/holiday material 3 months in advance. Photocopied submissions OK. SASE. Reports in 1 month. Sample copy $2.

Nonfiction: Informational; political; profile; travel; and business. Buys 2-3 mss/issue. Query. Length: 750-4,000 words. Pays $50-400.

Photos: Photos purchased with accompanying ms or on assignment. Pays $25-150 for 8x10 b&w glossy prints; $50-150 for color transparencies. Model release required.

Columns/Departments: Previews (arts, entertainment, books, movies, and concert reviews); Inside Dallas (business and gossip); Dining (reviews); and Windfalls (special products and services). "All pieces must relate to Dallas and the Fort Worth area." Open to suggestions for new columns/departments.

DALLAS/FORT WORTH LIVING, Baker Publications, 5757 Alpha Rd., Suite 400, Dallas TX 75240. (214)239-2399. Managing Editor: Catherine Simpson. Bimonthly magazine covering housing and relocation for persons in the market for houses, apartments, townhouses and condominiums. Circ. 90,000. Pays on publication. Byline given. Buys all rights. Submit seasonal/holiday material 4 months in advance. Simultaneous queries OK. SASE. Reports in 6 weeks. Free sample copy; writer's guidelines for business size SAE and 1 first class stamp.

Nonfiction: How-to (decorate); new product (local "discoveries"); and technical (energy-saving devices/methods). Buys 30 mss/year. Query with clips of published work "that show flexibility of writing style." Length: 1,000-3,000 words. Pays 10¢/word.

Photos: State availability of photos. Pays negotiable fee for color transparencies and 8x10 b&w glossy prints. Identification of subjects required. Buys all rights.

Columns/Departments: Luxury Living (customizing a new or old home). Query with clips of published work. Length: 1,000 words minimum. Pays 10¢/word.

Tips: "I would strongly suggest that any freelancer contact us for our guidelines, which cover both writing and photography. National assignments on decorating, financing, etc. for all of Baker's city magazines are made by Cary Campbell, editor-in-chief. Payment is 20¢/word. Query her at: Living, 5757 Alpha Rd., Suite 400, Dallas TX 75240."

DALLAS MAGAZINE, Dallas Chamber of Commerce, 1507 Pacific Ave., Dallas TX 75201. (214)651-1020. Editor: Sheri W. Rosen. Emphasizes business and other topics of interest to Dallas upper income business people. Monthly magazine; 84 pages. Circ. 20,000. Pays on acceptance. Buys all rights. Pays 100% kill fee "but kill fee is not offered on stories where quality is poor or editor's directions are not followed." Byline given. Submit seasonal/holiday material 3 months in advance. Photocopied submissions OK. SASE. Reports in 1 month. Sample copy $1.25.

Nonfiction: General interest (of interest to successful work-oriented men and women); historical (only on Dallas); humor (rarely accepted, but will use exceptional articles); interview (of Dallas executive or Dallas resident in an important government job or the like); profile (same as interview); and business features. "We do not want stories that underestimate our readers. Controversies involving technique or practices, not people, can be acceptable." Business issues are explored with solutions offered where appropriate. Buys 3-5/mss issue. Query with "an outline that reflects preliminary research." Length: 1,000-2,500 words. Pays $100-250.

Photos: State availability of photos. Pays $75-200 for 8x10 b&w glossy prints; $75-200 for color transparencies. Captions required.

Columns/Departments: Portraits (see "interview" above); enterprise (profile of a local company and its new product, new program, new approach, etc.); ideas (how-to/self-help for business executives at work or at leisure); reviews (includes traditional cultural topics, but also critical reviews of business practices or activities).

HOUSTON, Houston Chamber of Commerce, 1100 Milam Bldg., 25th Floor, Houston TX 77002. Editor: Richard Stanley. Emphasizes the Houston business community. The median reader is 48 years old, a college graduate in a top management position with an income of $54,700. Monthly magazine; 64-90 pages. Circ. 18,000. Pays on acceptance or publication. Buys all rights. Pays 100% kill fee. Byline given. Prefers mail queries. Photocopied submissions OK but must be neat. Reports "in a few weeks."

Nonfiction: Informational (on economy, businesses, people, etc.); historical (on Houston); interview and profile (business people). Query. Pays $350 maximum.

HOUSTON LIVING, Baker Publications, 5444 Westheimer, #450, Houston TX 77056. (713)626-2812. Editor: Ellen Manzur. Bimonthly magazine covering housing for newcomers and other prospective home buyers in the Houston area. Circ. 91,000. Pays on acceptance. Byline and brief bio given. Buys all rights. Submit seasonal/holiday material 4 months in advance. Simultaneous queries, and photocopied and previously published submissions OK. SASE. Reports in 1 month. Free sample copy; writer's guidelines for business size SAE and 1 first class stamp.

Nonfiction: "Articles should be slanted toward buying a home. We want to run solid articles on trends, specifically slanted for the Houston area market." Buys 6 mss/year. Query with clips of

published work. Length: 500-1,500 words. Pays 10¢/word (of 3 or more letters).
Photos: State availability of photos. Reviews any size b&w glossy prints.
Tips: "The writer should demonstrate lively, informative style and personal qualifications for writing on the subject. National assignments on decorating, financing, etc., for all of Baker's city magazines are made by Cary Campbell, editor-in-chief. Payment is 20¢/word. Query her at: Living, 5757 Alpha Rd., Suite 400, Dallas TX 75240."

SAN ANTONIO LIVING, Baker Publications, 84 NE Loop 410, #182 W, San Antonio TX 78216. (512)349-3870. Editor: Kathryn Cocke. Bimonthly magazine covering housing for newcomers and other persons looking for new homes. Circ. 50,000. Pays on publication. Byline given. Buys all rights. Submit seasonal/holiday material 4 months in advance. Simultaneous queries OK. SASE. Reports in 6 weeks. Free sample copy; writer's guidelines for business size SAE and 1 first class stamp.
Nonfiction: How-to (set up a new house, find a bank, choose a neighborhood). "We are interested only in articles of local interest." Buys 3-4 mss/year. Query or send complete ms. Length: 1,250 words minimum. Pays 10¢/word.
Photos: Pays negotiable fee for color transparencies and b&w prints. Identification of subjects required.
Tips: "National assignments on decorating, financing, etc., for all of Baker's city magazines are made by Cary Campbell, editor-in-chief. Payment is 20¢/word. Query her at Living, 5757 Alpha Rd., Suite 400, Dallas TX 75240."

SAN ANTONIO MAGAZINE, Greater San Antonio Chamber of Commerce, Box 1628, San Antonio TX 78296. (512)227-8181. Editor: Alice Costello. 50% freelance written. Emphasizes business and quality of life articles about San Antonio. Monthly magazine; 88 pages. Pays on publication. Buys all rights. Phone queries OK. Photocopied submissions OK. SASE. Reports in 1 month. Free sample copy and writer's guidelines.
Nonfiction: "The magazine's purpose is to inform, educate and entertain readers about the quality of life in San Antonio. We're looking for community and business articles and to inform the business community of current trends." Informational; historical; humor; nostalgia; personal opinion; profiles (personality profiles of people who are interesting, colorful and quotable—must be a San Antonian or have ties to the city); personnel management; business tips; business trends; and photo features. "No material about the Alamo, cowboys and Indians, cable TV, or any non-San Antonio topic." Buys 65 mss/year. Query or send complete ms, "query should be readable, typed and give me an element of the story, as well as some idea of the person's writing ability." Length: 800-3,000 words. Pays $50-300.
Photos: Purchased with mss or on assignment. Captions required. Query. Pays $10-25 for 8x10 b&w glossy prints. Prefers to pay according to the number of photos used in an article, a bulk rate.
Tips: "The best way to break in is to be a resident of San Antonio and, therefore, able to write on assignment or to query the editor personally. Again, we are looking for material which is related to the city of San Antonio, its people, and the business community. We consider all possible angles and tie-ins. We like to see writers who can tie national economic or business events to San Antonio and support information with figures."

Virginia

RICHMOND LIFESTYLE, 701 E. Franklin, Suite 1100, Richmond VA 23219. Managing Editor: Joseph R. Slay. For anyone interested in the affairs of the Richmond metropolitan area. Monthly magazine. Estab. October 1979 from a merger of *Richmond* and *Virginia LifeStyle* magazines. Circ. 20,000. Pays 5¢/word on publication. Buys first North American serial rights. Queries accepted by phone but preferred in writing. Submit seasonal/holiday material 3 months in advance of issue date. SASE. Byline usually given.
Nonfiction: All articles must be of immediate interest and concern to Richmonders. Investigative (only by experienced professionals); guides; how-to; general interest and topical stories; interview; opinion (by recognized figures); and historical. Query with "ideas first; then resume/background on a separate sheet." Length: 750-3,000.

THE ROANOKER, The Magazine of Western Virginia, Leisure Publishing Co., 3424 Brambleton Ave., Box 12567, Roanoke VA 24026. (703)989-6138. Editor: Brenda McDaniel. Monthly magazine covering people and events of Western Virginia. *"The Roanoker* is a general-interest city magazine edited for the people of Roanoke, Virginia, and the surrounding area. Our readers are primarily upper-income, well-educated professionals between the ages of 35 and 60. Coverage ranges from hard news and consumer information to restaurant reviews and local history." Circ. 10,000. Pays on publication. Byline given. Buys all rights and makes work-for-hire assignments. Submit seasonal/holiday material 3 months in advance. Simultaneous queries OK. SASE. Reports in 6 weeks. Sample copy $2.

Nonfiction: Expose (of government tax-supported agencies); historical/nostalgic; how-to (live better in Western Virginia); interview/profile (of well-known area personalities); photo feature; and travel (Virginia and surrounding states). "We are attempting to broaden our base and provide more and more coverage of Western Virginia, i.e., that part of the state west of Roanoke. We place special emphasis on consumer-related issues and how-to articles." Periodic special sections on fashion, real estate, media, banking, investing. Buys 100 mss/year. Query with clips of published work or send complete ms. Length: 3,000 words maximum. Pays $35-100.

Photos: "Each issue carries a four-color thematic photo spread on such themes as 'Wildflowers of Western Virginia,' 'Skiing in Virginia,' and 'Autumn in Western Virginia.' " Send photos with ms. Pays $5-10 for 5x7 or 8x10 b&w prints; $10 maximum for 5x7 or 8x10 color prints. Reviews color transparencies; "no pay for this, but exposure for the photographer is tremendous." Captions and model release required. Rights purchased vary.

Tips: "It helps if freelancer lives in the area."

Washington

SPOKANE MAGAZINE, Box 520, Spokane WA 99210. (509)838-2012. Co-publisher/Editor: Judith Laddon. Editor-in-Chief: Lawrence Shook. 75% freelance written. "*Spokane Magazine* is designed as an editorial vehicle for exploring the color, vitality and quality of life in Spokane and the Northwest." Monthly magazine; 80 pages. Circ. 13,000. Pays on publication. Buys one-time rights. Pays 50% kill fee. Byline given. Submit seasonal/holiday material 4 months in advance. Photocopied submissions OK. SASE. Reports in 8 weeks. Sample copy $1.50; free writer's guidelines.

Nonfiction: "Regular coverage includes politics, the environment, business, the economy, energy, education, the arts, medicine, law, architecture, followup or unique angles on news stories with a distinct Northwest identity, the gamut of sports and recreation, profiles of interesting people, travel throughout the West, and fact pieces on subjects of interest to Northwesterners. Humor is always welcome." Buys 10 mss/issue. Query. ("We need some detail, not just a general idea. Specifically what kind of information is available? What direction and tone does the writer anticipate?") Length: 500-3,000 words. Pays $65/1,000 words.

Photos: State availability of photos with query. Captions preferred. Buys one-time rights.

Tips: "Be alert to the stories in Spokane and the Northwest that we cannot know about. Who's the most interesting person you have ever met in the area? What significant insights do you have about how things work in Spokane? Don't worry as much about what is an 'article idea' as what you would like to tell every citizen of Spokane. Unlike newspaper editors, magazine editors do not have reporters out on beats—city hall, the courthouse, medicine, minorities. We depend upon freelancers for that kind of early warning. Writers should look carefully around to see if you know of something we should know of."

Wisconsin

MADISON MAGAZINE, Box 1604, Madison WI 53701. Editor: James Selk. General city magazine aimed at upscale audience. Magazine; 76-104 pages. Monthly. Circ. 18,500. Buys all rights. 100 mss/year. Pays on publication. Sample copy $3. Reports on material accepted for publication 10 days after publication. Returns rejected material immediately. Query. SASE.

Nonfiction and Photos: General human interest articles with strong local angles. Length: 1,000-5,000 words. Pays $25-100. Offers no additional payment for b&w photos used with mss. Captions required.

Canada

TORONTO LIFE, 59 Front St. E., Toronto, Ontario, Canada M5E 1B3. (416)364-3333. Editor Don Obe. Emphasizes local issues and social trends, short humor/satire, and service features for upper-income, well-educated and, for the most part, young Torontonians. Monthly magazine. Pays on acceptance. Buys first North American rights. Pays 50% kill fee "for commissioned articles

only." Byline given. Phone queries OK. Reports in 3 weeks. SAE and International Reply Coupons. Sample copy $1.50.
Nonfiction: Uses most all types articles. Buys 17 mss/issue. Query with clips of published work. Length: 1,000-5,000 words. Pays $250-1,200.
Photos: State availability of photos. Uses good color transparencies and clear, crisp black b&w prints. They seldom use submitted photos. Captions and model release required.
Columns/Departments: "We run about five columns an issue. They are all freelanced, though most are from regular contributors. They are mostly local in concern and cover politics, money, fine art, performing arts, movies and sports." Length: 1,200 words. Pays $250-400.

WINDSOR THIS MONTH MAGAZINE, Box 1029, Station A, Windsor, Ontario, Canada N9A 6P4. (519)256-7162. Editor: Laura Rosenthal. 75% freelance written. *"Windsor This Month* is mailed out in a system of controlled distribution to 19,000 households in the area. The average reader is a university graduate, middle income, and active in leisure areas." Circ. 22,000. Pays on publication. Buys first North American serial rights. Phone queries OK. Submit seasonal/holiday material 3-4 months in advance. SAE and International Reply Coupons. Reports in 4 weeks.
Nonfiction: "Windsor-oriented editorial: issues, answers, interviews, lifestyles, profiles, photo essays, opinion. How-to accepted if applicable to readership. Special inserts: design and decor, gourmet and travel featured periodically through the year." Buys 5 mss/issue. Query. Length: 500-5,000 words. Pays $25-100.
Photos: State availability of photos with query. Pays $10 for first-published and $5 thereafter for b&w prints. Captions preferred. Buys all rights.
Tips: "If experienced—arm yourself with published work and a list of 10 topics that demonstrate knowledge of the Windsor market, and query the editor. If experience is sought, don't be bashful...compile a list of at least 10 story ideas and make an appointment with the editor. Odds are that one of the ideas will be suitable for publication and your first byline."

State

Alaska

THE ALASKA JOURNAL, Alaska Northwest Publishing Co., Box 4-EEE, Anchorage AK 99509. (907)243-1723. Editor-in-Chief: Robert A. Henning. 90% freelance written. Annual magazine; 256 pages. Circ. 10,000. Pays on publication. Buys one time serial rights. Byline given. SASE. Reports in 2 months. Sample copy $2.
Nonfiction: Historical (Alaska, Northern Canada, Arctic). Buys 35-40 mss/year. Query with "specific details, perhaps a sample lead, and a good description of the photos available for the article. Also, include background about the proposed author: information about other articles published, etc". Length: 500-4,000 words.
Photos: Purchased with accompanying ms. Captions required. Pays $15 for 5x7 or 8x10 b&w photos.
Tips: "We're in the market for well-written and well-research articles on the history of Alaska, Northwestern Canada, and the Arctic. Articles should be accompanied by b&w prints."

ALASKA MAGAZINE, Box 4-EEE, Anchorage AK 99509. Editor/Publisher: Robert A. Henning. 80% freelance written. Monthly magazine. Pays on publication. Buys first North American serial rights. Byline given. SASE.
Nonfiction: *"Alaska Magazine's* subtitle is 'The Magazine of Life on the Last Frontier,' and, as implied, our interests are broad. Feature subjects include backpacking, resource management, sport fishing, wildlife encounters, kayaking and canoeing, trapping, cross-country skiing, snowshoeing, hunting, travel in Alaska, commercial fisheries, native affairs, mining, arts and crafts, mountaineering, bush-country life, profiles of Alaskans, history, town profiles, and wilderness photo essays. Manuscripts may run up to about 4,000 words, but we prefer shorter photo-illustrated pieces in the 1,000- to 2,000-word range. Rates for illustrated material range from $50-400, depending on length."
Photos: "We're heavy on sharp color photographs of Alaska and northwestern Canada, buying about 1,000 transparencies each year. Photos should ideally be Kodachrome slides—no duplicates, please. One-time rates are $100 for covers, $75 for 2-page spreads, $50 for full-page; and $25 for half-page. We also purchase photos outright for $150, providing a duplicate slide for the contributor's files."
Columns/Departments: "Regular monthly features include full-page color photos, letters, book reviews, personality profiles, bush-living tips, and short factual stories on Alaskan creatures."

NEW ALASKAN, Rt. 1, Box 677, Ketchikan AK 99901. Publisher: R.W. Pickrell. 75% freelance written. For residents of southeast Alaska. Tabloid magazine; 28 pages. Monthly. Circ. 9,000. Rights purchased vary with author and material. May buy all rights or second serial (reprint) rights. Byline given. Buys 40 mss/year. Pays on publication. Sample copy 50¢. Photocopied submissions OK. Submit complete ms. SASE.

Nonfiction and Photos: Bill Ostlund, articles editor. Feature material about southeast Alaska. Emphasis is on full photo or art coverage of subject. Informational, how-to, personal experience, interview, profile, inspirational, humor, historical, nostalgia, personal opinion, travel, successful business operations, new product. Length: 1,000 words minimum. Pays 1½¢/word. B&w photos purchased with or without mss. Minimum size: 5x7. Pays $5 per glossy used. Pays $2.50 per negative. Negatives are returned. Captions required.

Fiction: Bill Ostlund, articles editor. Historical fiction related to southeast Alaska. Length: open. Pays 1½¢/word.

Arizona

ARIZONA HIGHWAYS, 2039 W. Lewis Ave., Phoenix AZ 85009. (602)258-6641. Editor: Gary Avey. State-owned publication designed to help attract tourists into and through the state. Magazine. Pays on acceptance.

Nonfiction: "Article categories include first and third-person narratives dealing with contemporary events, history, anthropology, nature, special things to see and do, outstanding arts and crafts, travel, profiles, etc.; all must be Arizona oriented." Buys 6 mss/issue. Query with "a lead paragraph and brief outline of story. We deal with professionals only, so include list of current credits." Length: 2,000 words. Pays 10-20¢/word.

Photos: Picture editor. Pays $25/8x10 b&w print; $40-150 for 4x5 or larger transparencies. Buys one-time rights. "We will use 120mm (2-¼)and 35 mm when it displays exceptional quality or content. We prefer Kodachrome in 35mm. Each transparency *must* be accompanied by information attached to each photograph: where, when, what. No photography will be reviewed by the editors unless the photographer's name appears on *each* and *every* transparency."

Tips: "Writing must be professional quality, warm, sincere, in-depth, and well-peopled. Romance of the Old West feeling is important. Avoid themes that describe first trips to Arizona, Grand Canyon, the desert etc. Emphasis to be on romance and themes that can be photographed."

Arkansas

ARKANSAS TIMES, Arkansas Writers' Project, Inc., 500 E. Markham, Suite 110 C, Little Rock AR 72201. (501)375-2985. Editor: Bill Terry. Monthly magazine. "We are an Arkansas magazine. We seek to appreciate, enliven and, where necessary, improve the quality of life in the state." Circ. 23,000. Pays on publication, "but with exceptions." Byline given. Pays negotiable kill fee. Not copyrighted. Buys first North American serial rights. Submit seasonal/holiday material 2 months in advance. Simultaneous, photocopied, and previously published submissions OK. SASE. Reports in 1 week on queries; 1 month on mss. Sample copy $1.75; writer's guidelines for business size SAE and 1 first class stamp.

Nonfiction: Eugene Richard, articles editor. Book excerpts; expose (in investigative reporting vein); general interest; historical/nostalgic; humor; interview/profile; opinion; recreation; and entertainment, all relating to Arkansas. "The Arkansas angle is all-important." Buys 24 mss/year. Query. Length: 250-6,000 words. Pays $15-300.

Photos: Ira Hocut, photo editor. State availability of photos. Pays $5-10 for 8x10 b&w or color prints. Identification of subjects required. Buys one-time rights.

Columns/Departments: Eugene Richard, column editor. Arkansas Reporter ("articles on people, places and things in Arkansas or with special interest to Arkansans"). "This is the department that is most open to freelancers." Buys 25 mss/year. Query. Length: 250-750 words. Pays $10-20.

Fiction: Adventure, historical, humorous, mainstream and romance. "All fiction must have an Arkansas angle." Buys 4 mss/year. Send complete ms. Length: 1,250-5,000 words. Pays $200-300.

Poetry: Miller Williams, poetry editor. Avant-garde, free verse, haiku, light verse, traditional and ballad. Buys 30-40 mss/year. Submit maximum 5 poems. Pays $50 maximum; "poems are generally without payment."

California

BAJA CALIFORNIA BULLETIN, J L Publications, Apdo. Postal 127, La Paz, Baja California Sur, Mexico. Co-Editors: Luisa Porter, Jerry Klink. Emphasizes tourism in Baja California. Bimonthly magazine; 32 pages. Circ. 10,000. Pays on acceptance. Buys one-time rights. Pays 100% kill fee. Byline given. Submit seasonal/holiday material 4 months in advance of issue date. Previously published submissions OK. SASE. Reports in 4 weeks. Sample copy $1.
Nonfiction: Historical (pre-Columbian Baja California and Baja Indian lore, mission stories, revolutionary highlights); how-to (and where-to on camping, scuba-diving, shopping for bargains); humor (anything humorous about travel in Baja, but nothing about poverty); informational (towns visited, off-beat areas); interview (with famous person who travels in Baja California, related to his experiences on the peninsula); nostalgia (Baja in earlier times, personal experience only); and photo feature (sports, bullfights, off-road racing, boat racing); and animal and plant life of Baja. Buys 12 mss/year. Submit complete ms. Length: 500-1500 words. Pays $15-35.
Photos: Purchased with accompanying ms, no additional payment. Submit 5x7 or larger b&w prints. Captions optional.

BAJA TIMES, Editorial Playas De Rosarito, S.A., Rosarito Beach Hotel Shopping Center III, Rosarito Beach, Baja California. Editor: Hugo Torres. Current Baja information for Americans visiting or living in northern Baja California, Mexico. Monthly tabloid; 16 pages. Circ. 15,000-25,000 (depending on season). Byline given. Pays on acceptance. Makes work-for-hire assignments. Submit seasonal/holiday material 2 months in advance. Simultaneous, photocopied and previously published submissions OK. Reports in 2-3 weeks. Free sample copy.
Nonfiction: Historical (Baja); travel (in Baja); money-saving Baja advice; and personal experience (of those familiar with Baja). Buys 2 mss/issue. Send complete ms. Length: 300-700 words. Pays $30-60; longer ms somewhat higher.
Photos: Send photos with ms. Pays $4-20 for b&w. Captions required. Buys one-time rights.
Tips: "All over the US are descendants of men who explored or invested in Baja during the 19th century and the first 35 years of the 20th. Deeds, photographs, maps, any memorabilia their heirs can assemble would be valuable subject matter for us. We'll work with and carefully develop any such material submitted to us. We are also looking for a book reviewer and women who can write a shopper column."

CALIFORNIA MAGAZINE, (formerly *New West Magazine*), 9665 Wilshire Blvd., Beverly Hills CA 90212. (213)273-7516. Editor-In-Chief: William Broyles, Jr. Executive Editor: Meredith A. White. Publishes 12 issues/year. Buys first rights. Pays 20% kill fee. Byline given. SASE. Reports in 6 weeks. Sample copy $1.50.
Nonfiction: "Articles should be based on California—how to live well, but also hard in-depth features on politics, business, crime, lifestyle, food, restaurants, etc.," Query with clips of published work. Length: 800-4,000 words. Pays $250-1,500.
Photos: State availability of photos. "We assign almost all photos." Buys first rights. Captions preferred; model releases required.
Columns/Departments: Art, Architecture, Business, Food, Health, Law, Music, Politics, Religion, Restaurants, Theater, Travel and Westword." Buys 10/issue. Send complete ms. Length: 900-1,800 words. Pays $250-500.

HUMBOLDT COUNTY MAGAZINE, Box 3150, Eureka CA 95501. (707)445-9038. Editor and Publisher: Craig J. Beardsley. Quarterly magazine covering travel and tourism in Humboldt County, Northern California. This county, roughly the size of Delaware and Rhode Island combined, encompasses more than half of all the world's redwoods. Circ. 30,000. Estab. fall 1979. Pays on acceptance. Buys first rights only. Submit seasonal material 3 months in advance. SASE. Reports in 10 days. Sample copy $2.
Nonfiction: Reason for the publication's existence: "To educate, entertain and inform the 2.5 million visitors who travel through Humboldt County each year. Freelancers welcomed with open arms . . . if they know their subject matter." Recent articles include "Where to Go for Gifts," "The Filming of 'Salem's Lot'—When Warner Bros. Visited Humboldt," "Touring Scotia Mill," "When the Stars Stayed at Benbow Inn," etc. Query. Length: 1,500-3,000 words. Pays $200-500.
Photos: Pays $50 minimum for b&w and color.
Tips: "It's the subject matter that catches an editor's eye rather than the approach."

PACIFIC, Box 751, San Francisco CA 94101. (415)469-9429. Co-Editors: John Brandt and Terri Brandt. Monthly magazine covering the history and culture of northern California for professional people. Circ. 25,000. Pays on publication. Byline given. Offers 50% kill fee. Buys all rights. Submit seasonal/holiday material 3 months in advance. Simultaneous queries, and simultaneous and previously published submissions OK. SASE. Reports in 1 month. Free sample copy; writer's guidelines for business size SAE and 1 first class stamp.

Nonfiction: "*Pacific* is interested primarily in two kinds of material: historical—items about almost any aspect of Northern California and especially San Francisco's past: politics, famous figures, architecture, social events, laws, outlaws, theater, transportation, recreation, and business, to name a few. Articles should stress objective facts rather than personal reminiscence, primary sources of information should be used whenever possible, and subject should be treated in a lively manner. Cultural—Contemporary items about San Francisco and Northern California culture, where culture is defined as a set of traits that makes one group of people different from another, in areas including (but not limited to) literature, music, dance, drama, visual arts, fashion, social customs, language and leisure activities." Buys 70 mss/year. Query with clips of published work. Length: 5,000 words maximum. Pays $50-250.

Photos: Pays $10 minimum for 35mm color transparencies and 8x10 b&w glossy prints; $100 for cover. Model release and identification required.

Fillers: Short items on history or culture of the area. Buys 10/year. Length: 250-500 words. Pays $25 minimum.

Tips: "Show us an article of true quality. Originality and innovation are very important. Also articles that are not self indulgent or subjective. We need exciting, relevant, well written material. Also perfect copy."

THE SAN GABRIEL VALLEY MAGAZINE, Miller Books, 2908 W. Valley Blvd., Alhambra CA 91803. (213)284-7607. Editor-in-Chief: Joseph Miller. For upper to middle-income people who dine out often at better restaurants in Los Angeles County. Bimonthly magazine; 52 pages. Circ. 3,400. Pays on publication. Buys simultaneous, second serial (reprint) and one-time rights. Phone queries OK. Submit seasonal/holiday material 1 month in advance. Simultaneous, photocopied and previously published submissions OK. SASE. Reports in 2 weeks. Sample copy $1.

Nonfiction: Exposé (political); informational (restaurants in the valley); inspirational (success stories and positive thinking); interview (successful people and how they made it); profile (political leaders in the San Gabriel Valley); and travel (places in the valley). Buys 2 mss/issue. Length: 500-10,000 words. Pays 5¢/word.

Columns/Departments: Restaurants, Education, Valley News and Valley Personality. Buys 2 mss/issue. Send complete ms. Length: 500-1,500 words. Pays 5¢/word.

Fiction: Historical (successful people) and western (articles about Los Angeles County). Buys 2 mss/issue. Send complete ms. Length: 500-10,000 words. Pays 5¢/word.

Tips: "Send us a good personal success story about a valley or a California personality. We are also interested in articles on positive thinking and people who have made it."

SOUTH BAY MAGAZINE, South Bay Magazine Publications, 210 Avenue I, Redondo Beach CA 90277. Editor: Rick Pamplin. Managing Editor: Sarah Lancaster. Emphasizes the coastal communities in the southwest region of LA basin: Marina del Rey south to Long Beach. "We're basically a news/feature magazine with hard-hitting articles, but we also cover the arts." Monthly magazine; 96 pages. Circ. 30,000. Pays on publication. Buys first North American serial rights. SASE. Sample copy $2.50.

Nonfiction: Social and political issues (referred to as investigative articles); general interest/interview; historical; how-to (live the good life, improve your environment, quality of social life, health, mind); humor (slanted toward Southern California living); service pieces ("goods and services in our region"); photo feature (b&w and color). No articles on travel or cuisine. Query first, with resume and two clips.

Poetry: Avant-garde, free verse, haiku, light verse and traditional. Length: 25 words minimum. Pays $10.

Tips: " 'Scanner' is a good place to start. This section contains 250-word pieces of newsworthy interest, strictly pertaining to the South Bay. We work only with writers from the South Bay, because we like to deal with them personally and they must know the area they're writing for."

WESTWAYS, Box 2890, Terminal Annex, Los Angeles CA 90051. (213)741-4410. Managing Editor: Mary Ann Cravens. For "fairly affluent, college-educated, mobile and active Southern California families. Average age of head of household is 42. Monthly. Buys first rights. Byline given. Pays on acceptance for mss; on publication for most photos. Reports in 4-6 weeks. Query. SASE.

Nonfiction: "Informative articles, well-researched and written in fresh, literate, honest style." This publication "covers all states west of the Rockies, including Alaska and Hawaii, western Canada and Mexico. We're willing to consider anything that interprets and illuminates the American West—past or present—for the Western American family. Employ imagination in treating subject. Avoid PR hand-out type style and format, and please know at least something about the magazine." Subjects include "travel, history and modern civic, cultural and sociological aspects of the

West; camping, fishing, natural science, humor, first-person adventure and experience, nostalgia, profiles, and occasional unusual and offbeat pieces. Some foreign travel." Length: 1,000 to 1,500 words. Pays 10¢/word minimum.

Photos: Buys color and b&w photos with mss. Prefers 35mm color glossy prints. Pays $25 minimum "for each b&w used as illustration"; $50/transparency.

Poetry: Publishes 2-4 poems/year. Length: up to 24 lines; pays $25.

Colorado

THE COLORADO EXPRESS, Box 18214, Capitol Hill Station, Denver CO 80218. Editor-in-Chief: Karl Kocivar. 80% freelance written. Emphasizes "the outdoors, travel, food, consumer information, crafts, essential living, nature and science for educated, well-informed people of all ages who *read* rather than skim." Semiannual magazine; 96 pages. Pays on publication. Buys all rights. Byline given. Submit seasonal/holiday material 6 months in advance. Simultaneous, photocopied and previously published submissions OK. SASE. Reports in 12-15 weeks. Sample copy $3.50.

Nonfiction: *"The Express* covers a wide range of interest areas. Features might fall under the headings of how-to, personal experience, nostalgia and travel all at once. They are complete to the extent that a reader must rarely feel the need to go elsewhere for more information. But should he feel that need, he can find 'elsewhere' in *the Express.* Each feature is a complete reference and each volume is designed to be kept, read and used. So timely pieces about something that happened last week are not what we're looking for. What we search for is readable, literate (but not literary) writing about almost anything educated, active people who participate in life might enjoy involving themselves with thorough reading. Our readers are looking for useful information that often isn't readily available through other sources. Features have included glaciers, lightning and winter camping for example; consumer pieces on banking services and charge cards and how they work. How-to pieces should not be limited to a dozen candlemaking recipes; they should include historical and anecdotal information as well. Travel pieces shouldn't be limited to the ten best hotels in your favorite city." Buys 5 mss/issue. Submit complete ms. Length: 1,000-7,000 words. Payment varies.

Photos: Send photo material with accompanying ms. Pays $10-50 for 8x10 b&w glossy prints. Captions required. Buys all rights.

ROCKY MOUNTAIN MAGAZINE, Rocky Mountain Country, Ltd., 1741 High St., Denver CO 80218. (303)393-0911. Editor: Bob Wallace. Bimonthly magazine covering Montana, Wyoming, Idaho, Colorado, Utah, Arizona, Nevada and New Mexico for people sharing a general interest lifestyle. Circ. 130,000. Pays on publication. Buys First North American serial rights. Simultaneous submissions OK. SASE. Reports in 2 months. Sample copy $2.75; free writer's guidelines for SASE.

Nonfiction: Exposé (political); general interest (politics, environment, culture, social); interview (celebrities and noteworthy people); nostalgia; profile; travel (only in 8 state area); photo feature (essays); other (recreational activities, fashion, consumer tips, special events). Buys 4-8 mss/issue. Length: 3,000-5,000 words. Query or send complete ms to Manuscripts Editor.

Photos: State availability of photos. Reviews 5x7 b&w glossy prints, prefers 35mm color transparencies. Pays ASMP rates.

Columns/Departments: Straight Shots, Western Report, Short Subjects—shorter, topical pieces of interest and reviews pertinent to Rocky Mountain region.

Fiction: Humorous, condensed novels, experimental, mainstream, serialized novels and contemporary. Buys 1 ms/issue. Send complete ms.

Connecticut

CONNECTICUT MAGAZINE, 636 Kings Hwy., Fairfield CT 06430. (203)576-1205. Editor: Beth Conover. Monthly magazine for an affluent, sophisticated suburban audience. Pays on publication. Buys all rights. Reports in 2 months. Sample copy $2.

Nonfiction: "We want only those features which pertain specifically to Connecticut, with emphasis on service, investigative and consumer articles." Buys 50 mss/year. Query with clips of published work and "a full, intelligent, *neat* outline of the proposed piece. The more information offered, the better the chance of an assignment." Pays $100-500.

Photos: State availability of photos. Pays $35-75 for b&w prints; $75-200 for color transparencies. Captions and model releases required.

Columns/Departments: General features, history, politics pertaining to Connecticut. Buys 30 columns/year. Query. Length: 1,000 words minimum. Pays $100-350.
Tips: "Read past issues of the magazine and submit queries relevant to our state and style. Have good solid ideas and present them in a clear and interesting manner."

FAIRFIELD COUNTY MAGAZINE, County Communications, Inc., Box 269, Westport CT 06881. (203)227-0809. Editor-in-Chief: Elizabeth Hill O'Neil. Emphasizes regional material of interest to high-salaried, well-educated readers. Monthly magazine. Circ. 40,000. Pays on publication. Buys all rights. Phone queries OK. Submit seasonal/holiday material 3 months in advance. Photocopied submissions OK. SASE. Reports in 2 weeks. Sample copy $1.50.
Nonfiction: How-to, informational, historical, interview, profile and travel. "All articles should relate to readers in the Fairfield Country area which stretches from Greenwich to Danbury and includes Stamford, Bridgeport and surrounding towns." Buys 100 mss/year. Query. Length: 750-2,000 words. Pays $50-400.
Photos: State availability of photos. Competitive prices for b&w 4x6 glossy prints or contact sheets; 35mm color transparencies, $400 for cover only. Captions preferred.
Columns/Departments: Art, Books, Education, Music, Profiles and Sports. Buys 2 columns/issue. Query. Length: 750-1,500 words. Pays $50-300.

Delaware

DELAWARE TODAY MAGAZINE, 206 E. Ayre Street, Wilmington DE 19804. (302)995-7146. Editor: John Taylor. 80% freelance written. Monthly magazine covering the most well-known people, places and events in the area; 68 pages. Circ. 13,000. Pays on publication. Buys all rights. Submit seasonal/holiday material 3 months in advance. Photocopied submissions OK. SASE. Reports in 4-6 weeks.
Nonfiction: Exposé, profile, human interest, investigative, lifestyles, photo essays and off-the-wall subjects. "The material must always relate to Delaware; it must have substance and holding power. *Delaware Today* is a magazine that wants first and foremost to be entertaining. The style is upbeat; the flavor contemporary. The reader is between 25 and 40 and wants to see himself in each story. Articles on social or political issues will be considered as well as consumer, ecological and economic pieces that are bright in style and locally oriented, especially in-depth, well-researched work. All material must be oriented to the region and be conversational in flavor. Please don't send articles on flowers, energy or history." Buys 65 mss/year. Query or send complete ms. Length: 1,300-4,000 words. Pays $50-250.
Photos: Purchased with accompanying manuscript. Captions required. Pays $25-100 for b&w; $50-300 for color. Query for photos. Total purchase price for ms includes payment for photos. Model release required.
Fiction: Contact: Rolf Rykken. Published on a monthly basis. Length: 1,300-4,000 words. Pays $50-250.
Tips: "It impresses me when a freelancer knows something about this magazine before he contacts me. I prefer to talk to each writer before he or she starts working so there is only a limited chance the writer can misinterpret our personality."

Florida

BROWARD LIFE, Brenda Publishing Co., 3081 E. Commercial Blvd., Fort Lauderdale FL 33308. (305)491-6350. Editor-in-Chief: W.D. Luening. 50% freelance written. Emphasizes leisure activities in Broward County. Monthly magazine. Circ. 15,000. Pays on acceptance. Buys first North American serial rights. Pays 25% kill fee. Byline given "except if there is a lot of rewriting or research." Phone queries OK. Submit seasonal/holiday material 1 month in advance. Simultaneous, photocopied and previously published submissions OK. SASE. Reports in 6 weeks. Sample copy for $2.
Nonfiction: Exposé (must pertain to persons or events in Broward County); how-to (must appeal to high-income lifestyles); interview (Broward County-oriented); profile (Broward County resident); travel; new product; and photo feature. Buys 2 mss/issue. Submit complete ms. Length: 1,000-3,000 words. Pays $50-500. "We will consider students' work for credit only. Writers previously published in other magazines will be given preference."
Photos: Purchased with accompanying ms or on assignment. Pays $10-500 for b&w or 35mm color transparencies. Query or send contact sheet. Model release required.

CENTRAL FLORIDA SCENE MAGAZINE, Box 7624, Orlando FL 32854. Editor/Publisher: Nancy N. Glick. Emphasizes people, local concerns, fashion, dining, entertainment, gardening and sports for Central Floridians. Monthly magazine. Pays on publication. Buys all rights. Byline given. Previously published work OK. SASE. Reports in 2-3 weeks. Sample copy $2.50.
Nonfiction: Personality features on Central Floridians, national personalities who have a Central Florida tie-in, investigative reporting on a topic of interest to Floridians, financial articles, sports, fashion and interior decorating. "All articles should have a Central Florida connection." Send complete ms. Length: 1,000-3,000 words. Pays $25-100.
Photos: Send photos with ms; offers additional payment of $5 for b&w glossy prints or color transparencies. Captions preferred. Model releases required.

FLORIDA GULF COAST LIVING MAGAZINE, Baker Publications Corp., 402 Reo, Suite 208, Tampa FL 33609. National Editor-in-Chief: Cary Campbell. Managing Editor: Milana McLead Petty. Bimonthly magazine covering real estate and related subjects for "newcomers and local residents looking for new housing in the area we cover." Estab. 1979. Circ. 80,000. Pays on acceptance. Buys all rights. Submit seasonal/holiday material 3 months in advance. Photocopied submissions OK. SASE. Reports in 2 months. Sample copy $2; free writer's guidelines.
Nonfiction: General interest (on housing-related subjects, interior decorating, retirement living, apartment living, plants, landscaping, moving tips); historical (area history); how-to (build a greenhouse, decks, etc.); and travel (interesting trips around Florida, particularly near the area we cover). Buys 42 mss/year. Query with clips of published work or send complete ms. Length: 500-1,200 words. Pays $15-125.
Photos: State availability of photos or send photos with ms. "Your package will be more valuable to us if you provide the illustrations. For color work, 35mm is acceptable, 2¼x2¼ is nice, 4x5 is wonderful." Pays $3-10 for color transparencies; $3-5 for 8x10 glossy prints. "I prefer to include photos in the total package fee." Captions and model release required. Buys one-time rights or all rights, "depending on the subject."
Columns/Departments: Query with suggestions for new columns or departments.
Tips: "Retirement Living, Interiors, Apartment Living and other ideas, are the departments most open to freelancers. Be sure the subject is pertinent to our magazine. Know our magazine's style and write for it."

GULFSHORE LIFE, Gulfshore Publishing Co., Inc., 3620 Tamiami Tr. N., Naples FL 33940. (813)262-6425. Editor: Merri Pate. For an upper-income audience of varied business and academic backgrounds. Monthly magazine published October through June. Circ. 18,000. Buys all rights, with permission in writing to reproduce. Byline given. Buys 35 mss/year. Pays on publication. Photocopied or simultaneous submissions OK. Submit seasonal material 3 months in advance. Reports in 2 months. Query. SASE.
Nonfiction: "People, sports, homes, boats; pinpointing all features to seasonal residents, year-round residents and visitors of Southwest Florida. Travel, fishing and environmental articles are also used. Emphasis on at home lifestyles. Yachting, personality profiles; some historical material. Everything must be localized to the southwest coast of Florida." Length: 500-1,000 words. Pays 5¢/word.
Photos: Photos bought separately. Annual contest with deadline of April 15. Color transparenices or b&w glossy prints. Each entry must convey the theme of "Life Along the Gulfshore." Grand prize each category $50; 2nd prize $25.
Fiction: "Now featuring one fiction story each issue. Must have a Florida setting." Length: 3,000 words. Pays $50. Annual Fiction Contest deadline March 1. SASE. Prizes of $100, $75, $50.
Tips: "Familiarize yourself with the magazine and the location: Naples, Marco Island, Ft. Myers, Ft. Myers Beach, Sanibel-Captiva, Whiskey Creek, Punta Gorda Isles and Port Charlotte. No submissions out of season (May-August)."

ORLANDO-LAND MAGAZINE, Box 2207, Orlando FL 32802. (305)644-3355. Editor-in-Chief: E.L. Prizer. Managing Editor: Carole De Pinto. Emphasizes central Florida information for "a readership made up primarily of people new to Florida—those here as visitors, traveling business-men, new residents." Monthly magazine; 144 pages. Circ. 26,000. Pays on acceptance. Buys all rights or first North American serial rights. Byline given. Phone queries OK. Submit seasonal/holiday material 2 months in advance. Photocopied and previously published submissions OK. SASE. Reports in 6 weeks. Sample copy $1.25.
Nonfiction: Historical, how-to and informational. "Things involved in living in Florida." Pay $25-75.
Tips: "Always in need of *useful* advice-type material presented as first-person experience. Central Florida subjects only. Also, travel (excursion) pieces to places open to general public within 1 day's (there and back) journey of Orlando or experience pieces (hobbies, sports, etc.) that would not be

practical for staff writers—sky diving, delta kites, etc. Must be available in Central Florida."
Photos: B&w glossy prints. Pays $5.

PALM BEACH LIFE, Box 1176, Palm Beach FL 33480. (305)655-5755. Managing Editor: Ava Van de Water. "*Palm Beach Life* caters to a sophisticated, high-income readership and reflects its interests. Readers are affluent . . . usually over 40, well-educated." Special issues on travel, the arts (March), and elegant living, interiors, etc. Monthly. Circ. 18,000. Buys first North American rights. Pays on acceptance. Photocopied submissions OK. Submit seasonal material 5 months in advance. Reports in 3 weeks. Query with outline. SASE. Sample copy $2.33.
Nonfiction and Photos: Subject matter involves "articles on fashion, travel, music, art and related fields; subjects that would be of interest to the sophisticated, well-informed reader, including people profiles. "We feature color photos, but are crying for good b&w." Buys informational, interview, profile, humor, historical, think, photo and travel articles. Length: 1,000-2,500 words. Pays $100-300. Purchases photos with and without mss, or on assignment. Captions are required. Buys 8x10 b&w glossy prints at $15 each. Also buys 35mm or 2¼x2¼ transparencies and photo stories. Pay is negotiable.
Tips: "Please consider our magazine format—send for a sample copy and peruse magazine. We like stories (including good, well-written features) that appeal to upper-income, sophisticated readers."

SOUTH FLORIDA LIVING, Baker Publications, Inc., 700 W. Hillsboro Blvd., Suite 109, Deerfield Beach FL 33441. (305)428-5602. Editor: Cynthia Marusarz. Bimonthly magazine covering real estate market in Broward and Palm Beach counties, for newcomers and home buyers. Estab. 1981. Circ. 90,000. Pays on acceptance. Byline given. Makes work-for-hire assignments. Submit seasonal/holiday material 4 months in advance. Photocopied and previously published submissions OK. SASE. Reports in 2 weeks. Sample copy and writer's guidelines free.
Nonfiction: General interest (entertainment, fine arts); historical; how-to (finance, move, build, design); moving tips; landscaping and gardening; banking; interior decorating; retirement living; and apartment living. Buys 18-20 mss/year. Query. Length: 1,500-2,000 words. Pays 10¢/word.
Photos: State availability of photos. Pays negotiable fee for 35mm color transparencies and 5x7 b&w prints. Captions and model releases required. Buys all rights.
Columns/Departments: Retirement Living; Townhouse & Condo Living; Choices (events); Cultural Crossroads; Landscaping; and Banking. Buys 100 mss/year. Length: 100-150 words. Pays 10¢/word.
Tips: "National assignments on decorating, financing, etc., for all of Baker's city magazines are made by Cary Campbell, editor-in-chief. Payment is 20¢/word. Query her at: *Living*, 5757 Alpha Rd., Suite 400, Dallas TX 75240."

Hawaii

ALOHA, THE MAGAZINE OF HAWAII, Coral Publishing Co., 828 Fort Street Mall, Honolulu HI 96813. Editor: Rita Gormley. For those who have been to Hawaii or those who would like to know more about Hawaii; new places to stay, eat or visit. Bimonthly magazine; 96 pages. Circ. 85,000. Pays on publication. Buys all rights. Byline given. Submit seasonal/holiday material 8 months in advance. Photocopied submissions OK. SASE. Reports in 6 weeks. Sample copy $2.75.
Nonfiction: Art, business, historical, interview, personal experience, photo feature, profile, sports and travel. "All articles must be Hawaii-related. Please, no articles on impressions of romantic sunsets or articles aimed at the tourist." Buys 6 mss/issue. Query or send clips of published work. Length: 1,500-4,000 words. Pays 10¢/word.
Photos: State availability of photos. Pays $25 for 8x10 b&w glossy prints; $50 for color transparencies or $150 for covers. Buys one-time rights. Captions and model releases required for covers.
Fiction: "Any type of story as long as it has a Hawaii-related theme." Buys 1 ms/issue. Send complete ms. Length: 4,000 words maximum. Pays 10¢/word.
Poetry: Free verse, haiku and traditional. Buys 6 poems/year. Submit no more than 6. Pays $25.

Idaho

HIGH COUNTRY, *The Idaho Mountain Record*, Box 494, Council ID 83612. (208)253-4551. Editor-in-Chief: Leo Peurasaari. Editor: Ron Christensen. Monthly tabloid: 32 pages. Circ. 3,000. Pays on publication. Buys one-time rights. Phone queries OK. Submit seasonal/holiday material 3 months in advance of issue date. Simultaneous, photocopied and previously published submissions OK. "Submissions must be accompanied by SASE." Reports in 2 months. Sample copy 50¢; free writer's guidelines.

Nonfiction: Historical ("we are interested in historical articles pertaining to the Old West with a new slant"); how-to ("rural lost arts, 'back-to-Mother Earth-type' skills"); interviews (with local Idaho or well-known figures in the West); and offbeat and unusual inventions and products. Humor always welcome. Survivalism stories and photos needed. Articles with photos have best chance. "Keep in mind we are a rural magazine appealing to a rural audience." Buys 75 mss/year. Submit complete ms. Length: 400-1,500 words. Pays 3-5¢/word.

Photos: Minimum $10/8x10 b&w glossy. Captions and model release required.

Fiction: Historical, humorous and western. Buys 6 mss/year. Length: 400-1,000 words. Pays 3-5¢/word.

Poetry: Light verse, traditional and western. Buys 20/year. Limit submissions to batches of 3. Pays $2-5.

Fillers: Clippings, jokes, gags, anecdotes, newsbreaks, puzzles, short humor or unusual facts. Buys 60/year. Length: 25-200 words. Pays $2-5.

Columns/Departments: Always seeking novel column ideas, 500-700 words monthly. Pays $25.

Tips: "It helps to have good photos related to the story. Material should be of *rural* interest for Idaho residents."

Illinois

ILLINOIS ISSUES, Sangamon State University, Springfield IL 62708. Publisher: J. Michael Lennon. Editor: Caroline Gherardini. Emphasizes Illinois government and issues for state and local government officials and staff plus citizens and businessmen concerned with Illinois and its government (local government also). Monthly magazine; 36 pages. Circ. 6,000. Pays on publication. Buys all rights. SASE. Reports in 8 weeks. Sample copy $2.25.

Nonfiction: How-to (use state services and processes as a citizen); informational (explaining state/local government agency in Illinois, detailing new process initiated by state legislation, city or county ordinance); interview (Illinois government or political leaders); and technical (related to government policy, services with issues stressed, e.g., energy). Buys 3 mss/issue. Query. Length: 800-2,500 words (best chance: 1,200 words). Pays 4-10¢/word.

Tips: "Local issues tied to state government in Illinois have a good chance, but writer must research to know state laws, pending legislation and past attempts that relate to the issue."

Indiana

OUTDOOR INDIANA, Room 612, State Office Bldg., Indianapolis IN 46204. (317)232-4005. Editor: Herbert R. Hill. 2% freelance written. For subscribers who seek information regarding programs, projects, services and facilities of the Indiana Department of Natural Resources. Published 10 times/year. Circ. 44,000. Buys first serial rights. Byline given. Pays on publication. Reports in 2-4 weeks. Query. SASE.

Nonfiction and Photos: Informative, concise, illustrative, bright articles on Indiana outdoor, recreation and natural resource-related topics only. No fiction, essays, verse or non-Indiana topics. Length: 1,000-2,000 words. Usually pays 2¢/word. Photos of Indiana interest only; purchased with mss or with captions only. B&w photos, 8x10; color transparencies, 2¼x2¼ or larger. Pays $5 for b&w; $25 for color; $50 for color cover.

Tips: "Study the magazine. Single copies 75¢; no samples."

Kansas

KANSAS!, Kansas Department of Economic Development, 503 Kansas Ave., 6th Floor, Topeka KS 66603. (913)296-3806. Editor: Andrea Glenn. 60% freelance written. Emphasizes Kansas "faces and places for all ages, occupations and interests." Quarterly magazine; 32 pages. Circ. 38,000. Pays on acceptance. Buys one-time rights. Byline given. Submit seasonal/holiday material 8 months in advance. Simultaneous or photocopied and previously published submissions OK. SASE. Reports in 2 months. Free sample copy and writer's guidelines.

Nonfiction: "Material must be Kansas-oriented and well-written. We run stories about people, places, and events that can be enjoyed by the general public. In other words, events must be open to the public, places also. People featured must have interesting crafts etc." General interest; interview; photo feature; profile; and travel. No exposés. Query. "Query letter should clearly outline story in mind. I'm especially interested in freelancers who can supply their own photos." Length: 5-7 pages double-spaced, typewritten copy. Pays $75-125.

Photos: "We are a full-color photo/manuscript publication." State availability of photos with query. Pays $10-25 ("generally included in ms rate") for 35mm color transparencies. Captions required.

Tips: "History and nostalgia stories do not fit into our format because they can't be illustrated well with color photography."

Louisiana

LOUISIANA LIFE, Magazine of the Bayou State, Louisiana Life, Ltd., 1033 Pleasant St., New Orleans LA 70115. (504)897-1396. Editors: Nancy K. Marshall, Thomas C. Marshall. Associate Editor: Paul F. Stahls, Jr. Bimonthly magazine covering "general interest articles specifically for residents of Louisiana, designed to enlighten and entertain people who want to know about the state and its people." Estab. 1980. Circ. 23,000. Pays on publication. Byline given. Offers negotiable kill fee. Buys first North American serial rights. Submit seasonal/holiday material 6 months in advance. Simultaneous queries, and simultaneous and photocopied submissions OK. SASE. Reports in 6 weeks. Sample copy $3.50; free writer's guidelines.

Photos: Nancy K. Marshall, Paul F. Stahls, photo editors. State availability of photos. Pays $50-100 for b&w contact sheets, negatives or 8x10 prints; $50-200 for color transparencies. Captions, model release and identification of subjects required. Buys one-time rights "with additional right to negotiate for additional use, all photos used in the magazine."

Columns/Departments: Paul F. Stahls, Jr., column/department editor. Art, Music, Perspective (opinion), Just Folks (profile of an interesting, non-publicized person). Buys 30 mss/year. Query with clips of published work or send complete ms. Length: 700-1,000 words. Pays $125-200.

Tips: "Please send us a friendly letter, accompanied by at least five clippings of published work (or, if not published, by a manuscript or two) and any story queries you may have. We are very interested in finding good, dependable freelance talent—people who can come up with creative ideas, solidly written stories and do all on time. We are a new publication and will welcome inquiries."

Maine

DOWN EAST MAGAZINE, Camden ME 04843. (207)594-9544. Editor: Davis Thomas. Emphasizes Maine people, places, events and heritage. Monthly magazine; 116 pages. Circ. 70,000. Pays on acceptance for text; on publication for photos. Buys first North American serial rights. Pays 15% kill fee. Byline given. Phone queries OK. Submit seasonal/holiday material 6 months in advance. SASE. Reports in 1 month. Sample copy $1.75; free writer's guidelines if SASE provided.

Nonfiction: Submit to Manuscript Editor. "All material must be directly related to Maine: profiles, biographies, nature, gardening, nautical, travel, recreation, historical, humorous, nostalgic pieces, and photo essays and stories." Length: 600-2,500 words. Pays up to $250, depending on subject and quality.

Photos: Purchases on assignment or with accompanying ms. Each photo or transparency must bear photographer's name. Captions required. Pays page rate of $50. Accepts 35mm color transparencies and 8x10 b&w. Also purchases single b&w and color scenics for calendars. Model release required.

Columns/Departments: Short travel (600- to 1,500-word, tightly written travelogs focusing on small geographic areas of scenic, historical or local interest); I Remember (short personal accounts of some incident in Maine, less than 1,000 words); and It Happened Down East (1- or 2-paragraph, humorous Maine anecdotes). Pay depends on subject and quality.

MAINE LIFE, Sedgwick ME 04676. Editors: Pat and Tom Schroth. For readers of all ages in urban and rural settings. 70% of readers live in Maine; balance are readers in other states who have an interest in Maine. Monthly magazine; 64-96 pages. Circ. 25,000. Pays on publication. Buys first rights. Sample copy $1. Photocopied submissions OK. Submit seasonal/holiday material 4 months in advance. Reports in 1 month. SASE.

Nonfiction: Interview, profile, humor, historical, nostalgia and poetry. Buys 120 mss/year. Query. Length: 500-2,000 words. Pays $10-50.

Photos: B&w and color photos purchased with or without accompanying ms. Captions required.

Fiction: Length: 500-2,000 words. Pays $10-50.

Maryland

CHESAPEAKE BAY MAGAZINE, 1819 Bay Ridge Ave., Suite 200, Annapolis MD 21403. (301)263-2662. Editor: Betty D. Rigoli. 45% freelance written. *"Chesapeake Bay Magazine* is a regional publication for those who enjoy reading about the Bay and its tributaries. Our readers are yachtsmen, boating families, fishermen, ecologists—anyone who is part of Chesapeake Bay life." Monthly magazine; 64-72 pages. Circ. 15,000. Pays either on acceptance or publication, depending on "type of article, timeliness and need." Buys all or first North American serial rights. Submit seasonal/holiday material 3 months in advance of issue date. Simultaneous (if not to magazines with overlapping circulations) and photocopied submissions OK. SASE. Reports in 1 month. Sample copy $1.50; writer's guidelines for SASE.

Nonfiction: "All material must be about the Chesapeake Bay area—land or water." How-to (fishing, hunting, and sports pertinent to Chesapeake Bay); general interest; humor (welcomed, but don't send any 'dumb boater' stories where common safety is ignored); historical; interviews (with interesting people who have contributed in some way to Chesapeake Bay life: authors, historians, sailors, oystermen, etc.); nostalgia (accurate, informative and well-paced. No maudlin ramblings about "the good old days"); personal experience (drawn from experiences in boating situations, adventures, events in our geographical area); photo feature (with accompanying ms); profile (on natives of Chesapeake Bay); technical (relating to boating, hunting, fishing); and Chesapeake Bay Folklore. "We do not want material written by those unfamiliar with the Bay area, or general sea stories. No personal opinions on environmental issues." Buys 3 mss/issue. Query or submit complete ms. Length: 1,000-2,500 words. Pays $45-85.

Photos: Virginia Leonard, art director. Submit photo material with ms. Uses 8x10 b&w glossy prints; pays $50 for 35mm, 2¼x2¼ or 4x5 color transparencies used for cover photos; $15/color photo used inside. Captions required. Buys one-time rights with reprint permission. Model release required.

Fiction: "All fiction must deal with the Chesapeake Bay, and be written by persons familiar with some facet of bay life." Adventure; fantasy; historical; humorous; mystery; and suspense. "No general stories with Chesapeake Bay superimposed in an attempt to make a sale." Buys 8 mss/year. Query or submit complete ms. Length: 1,000-2,500 words. Pays $45-85.

Poetry: Attention: Poetry Editor. Free verse or traditional. Must be about Chesapeake Bay. "We want well-crafted, serious poetry. Do not send in short, 'inspired' sea-sick poetry or 'sea-widow' poems." Buys 2/year. Limit submissions to batches of 4. Length: 5-30 lines. Pays $10-25. Poetry used on space available basis only.

Tips: "We are a regional publication entirely about the Chesapeake Bay and its tributaries. Our readers are true 'Bay' lovers, and look for stories written by others who obviously share this love. We are particularly interested in material from the Lower Bay (Virginia) area and the Upper Bay (Maryland-Delaware) area."

Massachusetts

GLOUCESTER, 11 Pleasant St., Gloucester MA 01930. Publisher: Joe Kaknes. Managing Editor: Lincoln S. Bates. Quarterly magazine primarily focusing on the North Shore of Massachusetts." Pays within 1 month of publication. Submit seasonal material 6 months in advance. SASE. Reports in 1 month. Sample copy $1.50; free writer's guidelines.

Nonfiction: Social, political and natural history; biography and people profiles; environmental and other pertinent public policy issues; boating, commercial fishing, and other maritime-related businesses; travel; art; education; lifestyles. Query. Length: 1,500-2,000 words. Pays 6¢/word.

Photos: Prefers 8x10 b&w glossy prints and 35mm color transparencies. Pays on publication; negotiable fee. Captions and credit lines required.

Fiction: "This magazine occasionally runs short fiction up to 3,000 words. Such manuscripts should have some connection to the sea, to the coast, or to New England's history or character. No restrictions on style; the main criterion is quality. Query or send complete ms. Pays 6¢/word.

Tips: "We look for the unusual story or angle, the fresh approach, the review/assessment of complex issues. Avoid overwriting and turgid style; stories should be crisp, well-researched, lively and concise. We'd like to see more contemporary type pieces about events, issues or people with whom readers can identify."

NEW ROOTS, Northeast Appropriate Technology Network, Inc., Box 548, Greenfield MA 01302. (413)774-2257. Editor: Rob Okun. Managing Editor: Patricia Greene. Magazine published 8 times/year covering "alternative energy/environmental and cultural issues giving particular emphasis to the Northeastern United States. Written by and for people who want a decentralized, cooperative culture, it offers a positive and realistic vision of society. Reader mean age 37.7." Circ. 40,000. Pays 30 days following publication. Byline given. Offers 30% of assigned word length kill fee. Buys first North American serial rights. Submit seasonal/holiday material 4 months in advance. Simultaneous queries, and photocopied and previously published submissions OK. SASE. Reports in 1 month on queries; 6 weeks on mss. Sample copy $1.50.

Nonfiction: Michael Gery, articles editor. Book excerpts, exposé (solar fraud, nuclear politics, environmental cover-up); general interest; how-to (energy, gardening, conservation, building); humor; interview/profile; new product; opinion; personal experience; photo feature; technical (solar energy); and feminism with environmental/anti-nuclear slant. Special issues include Solar in the City and Ecotopian Visions. "If you picked wild berries, attended a highly technical conference or posited a Latin American conspiracy theory—and want to write about it—try another market." Buys 15-25 mss/year. Query with clips of published work. Length: 600-3,500 words. Pays variable fee.

Photos: Joan Linden, photo editor. State availability of photos. Pays variable fee for b&w contact sheet, and 3¼x3¼ color transparencies and 5x7 prints. Captions, model release, and identification of subjects required. Buys one-time rights.

Columns/Departments: The editors. Books; Health (self-care, holistic); Food (natural); Nuclear (anti); Music (folk, jazz, environmental); Undercurrents (short funny news); Arts (environmental, Northeast culture); Resource (products, books, plans groups in energy, agriculture, community . . .); and Endroot (op/ed, commentary). Buys 30-45 mss/year. Query with clips of published work. Length: 800-1,800 words. Pays variable fee.

Michigan

MICHIGAN ENVIRONS, West Michigan Environmental Action Council, 1324 Lake Drive SE, Grand Rapids MI 49503. (616)451-3051. Managing Editor: Deborah Meadows. Bimonthly magazine covering Michigan's environmental issues. "*Michigan Environs* is a statewide, issue-oriented environmental publication for environmentalists. Packed with news and views on all environmental fronts, *Michigan Environs* scrutinizes legislation, litigation and action shaping Michigan's environmental future." Estab. 1980. Circ. 1,500. Pays on acceptance. Byline given. Currently undergoing copyright process. Submit seasonal/holiday material 2 months in advance. Simultaneous queries; simultaneous, photocopied and previously published submissions OK. SASE. Reports in 2 weeks on queries; 1 months on mss. Sample copy $1; writer's guidelines for business size SAE and 1 first class stamp.

Nonfiction: Exposé (of government/private industry practices); general interest (environmental topics); interview/profile; technical; travel (in the Michigan outdoors); and book reviews (assigned). Articles must be environmentally-oriented and Michigan-related. Buys 30 mss/year. Query with clips of published work. "Focus on an issue, your expertise to handle that issue, and the focus of the article." Length: 500-2,000 words. Pays $25-100.

Columns/Departments: Book Reviews (books about Michigan's environment, or books by Michigan authors on the environment). Buys 8 mss/year. Length: 500-750 words. Pays $25.

Tips: "Send query letter. Follow with a phone call."

Micronesia

GLIMPSES OF MICRONESIA AND THE WESTERN PACIFIC, Box 3191, Agana, Guam 96910. Editor: Mike Malone. 90% freelance written. "A regional publication for Micronesia lovers, travel buffs and readers interested in the United States' last frontier. Our audience covers all age levels and is best described as well-educated and fascinated by our part of the world." Quarterly magazine; 100 pages. Circ. 25,000. Pays on proof. Buys first rights. Pays 10% kill fee on assignments. Byline given. Submit seasonal/holiday material 8 months in advance. SASE. Reports in 2 weeks. Sample copy $2; free writer's guidelines.

Nonfiction: "Range of subjects is broad, from political analysis of Micronesia's newly emerging governments to examination of traditional culture; historical (anything related to Micronesia that is lively and factual); personal experience (first-person adventure, as in our recently published piece about a sailing expedition to the uninhabited islands of the Northern Marianas); interviews/personality profiles of outstanding Micronesian or Western Pacific individuals; scientific/natural history (in lay terms); photo features (we're very photo-oriented—query us on island or Pacific themes); travel (we use one/issue about destinations in Asia and the Pacific)." Buys 30 mss/year. Query. Length: 1,500-5,000 words. Pays 5-10¢/word.

Photos: Purchased with or without accompanying ms. Pays minimum $10 for 8x10 b&w prints or

$15 for 4x5 color transparencies or 35mm slides. Pay $200-300 for photo essays; $100 for covers. Captions required.

Columns/Departments: Short think-pieces on contemporary Micronesia are accepted for the "Island Views" section. Opinions are welcomed, but must be well-founded and must reflect the writer's familiarity with the subject. Length: 500-1,200 words. Pays $30.

Poetry: "Use very little, but willing to look at Pacific-related themes to be used with photos." Only traditional forms. Pays minimum $10.

Tips: "Writers living in or having first-hand experience with Micronesia and the Western Pacific are scarce. If you have that experience, have made yourself familiar with *Glimpses*, and have a good story idea, then we're willing to work with you in developing a good article."

Mississippi

DELTA SCENE, Box B-3, Delta State University, Cleveland MS 38733. (601)846-1976. Editor-in-Chief: Dr. Curt Lamar. Managing Editor: Ms. Sherry Van Liew. For an art-oriented or history-minded audience wanting more information (other than current events) on the Mississippi Delta region. Quarterly magazine; 32 pages. Circ. 800. Pays on publication. Buys one-time rights. Byline given. Submit seasonal/holiday material at least 4 months in advance. Simultaneous, photocopied and previously published submissions OK. SASE. Reports in 4 weeks. Sample copy 50¢.

Nonfiction: Historical and informational articles; interviews, profiles and travel articles; technical articles (particularly in reference to agriculture). "We have a list of articles available free to anyone requesting a copy." Buys 2-3 mss/issue. Query. Length: 1,000-2,000 words. Pays $5-20.

Photos: Purchased with or without ms, or on assignment. Pays $5-15 for 5x7 b&w glossy prints or any size color transparency.

Fiction: Humorous and mainstream. Buys 1/issue. Submit complete ms. Length: 1,000-2,000 words. Pays $10-20.

Poetry: Traditional forms, free verse and haiku. Buys 1/issue. Submit unlimited number. Pays $5-10.

Tips: "The freelancer should follow our magazine's purpose. We generally only accept articles about the Delta area of Mississippi, the state of Mississippi, and South in general. We are sponsored by a state university so no articles, poetry, etc. containing profanity or other questionable material. Nonfiction has a better chance of making it into our magazine than short stories or poetry."

Missouri

FOCUS/MIDWEST, 928A N. McKnight, St. Louis MO 63132. (314)991-1698. Editor/Publisher: Charles L. Klotzer. For an educated audience in Illinois, Missouri and the Midwest. Bimonthly magazine; 28-42 pages. Circ. 5,000. Buys all rights. Pays on publication. Reports in 4-6 weeks. SASE.

Nonfiction: Controversial articles; main emphasis on Illinois and Missouri. Facts, interpretation, analyses presenting political, social, cultural and literary issues on the local, regional and national scene of direct interest to the reader in or observer of the Midwest. Investigative, informational, interview, profile, think pieces. Length: open. Pays minimum of $25.

Poetry: Blank verse and free verse. Length: open. Pays minimum of $10.

New Hampshire

NEW HAMPSHIRE PROFILES, Profiles Publishing Co., 2 Steam Mill Ct., Concord NH 03301. Editor: Brenda Joziatis. Managing Editor: David Anderson. Emphasizes the state of New Hampshire for 30- to 40-year-olds in the middle-income bracket who are relatively active in enjoying sports such as skiing, etc. About a 50-50 in-state vs. out-of-state readership. Magazine published 6 times/year. 100 plus pages. Circ. 20,000. Pays on publication. Buys one-time rights. SASE. Reports in 2 months. Sample copy $2; free writer's guidelines.

Nonfiction: General interest; historical (on little-known New Hampshire characters or incidents); humor; interview; nostalgia; opinion; profile; personal experience; photo feature; arts and crafts; and interesting activities. "All should be oriented to New Hampshire; even New England is too broad an area to interest us. Except for opinion and experience pieces, we prefer articles in the third person. No general articles on how pretty the state is. No historical articles, i.e., biographies of Revolutionary War generals, etc., culled directly from history texts." Buys 7-8 mss/issue. Query with clips of published work. Length: 500-2,000 words. Pays $50-200.

Photos: State availability of photos. Pays $15-25 for b&w 5x7 or 8x10 glossy prints; $25-50 for 2¼x2¼ or 35 mm color transparencies—$150 for cover. Captions preferred; model release required if submitting for cover consideration. Buys one-time rights for color and for b&w.

Columns/Departments: Generally staff-written.

Fillers: Anecdotes and short humor. Length: maximum 300 words. Pays with contributor's copies.

Tips: "It's almost impossible for a writer who has not been in New Hampshire to write for us. We get too many pieces that are on a general topic (gardening, for example, or antiques) and not state-oriented. Don't call me—write; my time is limited. I accept queries, but a completed manuscript from a beginner has a better chance—some subjects sound dull but can be transformed by a skilled stylist (particularly when it comes to humor)."

YANKEE, Dublin NH 03444. (603)563-8111. Editor-in-Chief: Judson D. Hale. Managing Editor: John Pierce. Emphasizes the New England region. Monthly magazine; 176 pages. Circ. 850,000. Pays on acceptance. Buys all, first North American serial or one-time rights. Byline given. Submit seasonal/holiday material at least 4 months in advance. SASE. Reports in 2-4 weeks. Free sample copy and writer's guidelines.

Nonfiction: Historical (New England history, especially with present-day tie-in); how-to (especially for "Forgotten Arts" series of New England arts, crafts, etc.); humor; interview (especially with New Englanders who have not received a great deal of coverage); nostalgia (personal reminiscence of New England life); photo feature (prefer color, captions essential); profile; travel (to the Northeast only, with specifics on places, prices, etc.); current issues; antiques to look for; food. No articles on nature. Buys 50 mss/year. Query with "brief description of how article will be structured (its focus, etc.); articles must include a New England 'hook.' "Length: 1,500-3,000 words. Pays $50-700.

Photos: Purchased with accompanying ms or on assignment. (Without accompanying ms for "This New England" feature only; color only). Captions required. Send prints or transparencies. Pays $15 minimum for 8x10 b&w glossy prints. $125/page for 2¼x2¼ or 35mm transparencies; 4x5 for cover or centerspread. Total purchase price for ms includes payment for photos.

Columns/Departments: New England Trip (with specifics on places, prices, etc.); Antiques to Look For (how to find, prices, other specifics); At Home in New England (recipes, gardening, crafts). Buys 10-12 mss/year. Query. Length: 1,000-2,500 words. Pays $150-350.

Fiction: Deborah Karr, fiction editor. "Emphasis is on character development." Buys 12 mss/year. Send complete ms. Length: 2,000-4,000 words. Pays $600-750.

Poetry: Jean Burden, poetry editor. Free verse and modern. Buys 3-4 poems/issue. Send poems. Length: 32 words maximum. Pays $35 for all rights, $25 for first magazine rights. Annual poetry contest with awards of $150, $100 and $50 for 1st, 2nd and 3rd prizes.

YANKEE MAGAZINE'S TRAVEL GUIDE TO NEW ENGLAND, (formerly *Yankee Magazine's Guide to New England*), Main St., Dublin NH 03444. (603)563-8111. Editor: Sharon Smith. Emphasizes travel and leisure for a readership from New England area and from all states in the union. Annual magazine; 192 pages. Circ. 150,000. Pays on acceptance. Buys first North American serial rights. Pays 25% kill fee. Byline given. Submit seasonal/holiday material 6-12 months in advance. Simultaneous and photocopied submissions OK. SASE. Reports in 3 weeks. Sample copy $1.50; free writer's guidelines.

Nonfiction: "Unusual activities, places to stay, restaurants, shops, the arts, annual events, towns or areas to visit. Strict emphasis on travel discoveries within New England. Since the *Guide* is set up on a state-by-state basis, each story must be confined to activities or attractions within a single state." Buys 15-25 mss/issue. Query. Length: 500-2,500 words. Pays $50-300.

Photos: Michael Schuman, assistant editor. Purchased with or without accompanying ms or on assignment. Send contact sheet or transparencies plus list of stock photos on file. Pays $25-75 for b&w 8x10 glossy prints; $50-150 for 35mm or 2¼x2¼ color transparencies.

Tips: "Send us a letter letting us know where you have been in New England and what ideas you think best fit our publication. Please don't send in suggestions if you have not bothered to obtain a copy of the magazine to see what we are all about! Send a query letter for your ideas, and explain why you are qualified to write about a given subject. Include samples. Ask for a copy of our writer's guidelines."

New Jersey

NEW JERSEY MONTHLY, 1101-I State Rd., Princeton NJ 08540. Editor: Michael Aron. Managing Editor: Barbara Blake. 40% freelance written. Emphasizes New Jersey interests.

Monthly magazine; 100-150 pages. Circ. 95,000. Pays on publication. Buys all rights. Submit seasonal/holiday material 4 months in advance. SASE. Reports in 6 weeks.

Nonfiction: Exposé (government or any institution in New Jersey); general interest (people doing unusual things, in-depth look at situations which define a community); how-to (service pieces must cover entire state; should concentrate on living the 'better' life at reasonable cost); interview (people who are living and doing something in New Jersey—something that affects our readers, as opposed to someone who is from New Jersey and hasn't lived here in years); and personal experience (only if it sheds light on something going on in the state). We're interested in high-quality magazine writing and original thinking." Buys 4-6 mss/issue. Query. Length: 1,500-6,000 words. Pays $250-1,000.

Columns/Departments: Departments run shorter than articles and include sports, media, politics, money and others. "Also have an arts section—800- to 1,200-word pieces on a subject concerning movies, music, art, dance, and theater—no reviews, just pieces that deal with the ongoing arts scene in New Jersey." Buys 3 mss/issue. Query. Length: 1,000-2,000 words. Pays $50-200.

Tips: To break into *New Jersey Monthly,* "either write an impressive query letter or begin supplying good items to our gossip section *The New Jersey Informer*, or better still, promise a good, statewide service piece."

New Mexico

NEW MEXICO MAGAZINE, Bataan Memorial Bldg., Santa Fe NM 87503. (505)827-2642. Editor-in-Chief: Sheila Tryk. Executive Editor: Richard Sandoval. Managing Editor: Scottie King. 75% freelance written. Emphasizes the Southwest, especially New Mexico, for a college-educated readership, above average income, interested in the Southwest. Monthly magazine; 64-80 pages. Circ. 80,000. Pays on acceptance for mss; on publication for photos. Buys first North American serial or one-time rights for photos/compilation. Submit seasonal/holiday material 8 months in advance. SASE. Reports in 10 days to 4 weeks. Sample copy $1.50.

Nonfiction: "New Mexico subjects of interest to travelers. Historical, cultural, humorous, nostalgic and informational articles." Buys 5-7 mss/issue. Query. Length: 500-2,000 words. Pays $25-300.

Photos: Purchased with accompanying ms or on assignment. Captions required. Query, or send contact sheet or transparencies. Pays $20-40 for 8x10 b&w glossy prints; $30-75 for 35mm; prefers Kodachrome; (photos in plastic-pocketed viewing sheets). Model release required. SASE.

Tips: "Send a superb short (1,000 words) manuscript on a little-known event, aspect of history or place to see in New Mexico. Faulty research will immediately ruin a writer's chances for the future. Good style, good grammar, please! No generalized odes to the state or the Southwest. No sentimentalized, paternalistic views of the Indians or of the Hispanos. No glib, gimmicky 'travel brochure' writing."

New York

ADIRONDACK LIFE, Box 137, Keene NY 12942. Editor-in-Chief: Bernard R. Carman. Emphasizes the Adirondack region of New York State for a readership aged 30-60, whose interests include outdoor activities, history, and natural history directly related to the Adirondacks. Bimonthly magazine; 64 pages. Circ. 50,000. Pays on publication. Buys one-time rights. Pays 20% kill fee. Byline given. Submit seasonal/holiday material 4 months in advance. Previously published book excerpts OK. SASE. Reports in 4 weeks. Sample copy $1; free writer's guidelines.

Nonfiction: Outdoor recreation (Adirondack relevance only); how-to (should relate to activities and lifestyles of the region, e.g., managing the home woodlot; informational (natural history of the region); interview (Adirondack personalities); photo feature (Adirondack relevance required); profile; and historical (Adirondacks only). Buys 6-8 mss/issue. Query. Length: 2,500-3,500 words. Pays $100-300.

Photos: Purchased with or without mss or on assignment. Captions required (Adirondacks locale must be identified). Submit contact sheet or transparencies. Pays $15 for 8x10 glossy, semi-glossy or matte photos; $40 for 35mm or larger color transparencies, $150 for covers (color only).

Tips: "Start with a good query that tells us what the article offers—its narrative line and, most importantly, its relevance to the Adirondacks, which is the essential ingredient in every article. We are especially interested in material reflecting qualities of life and recreation in 'the East's last wilderness.' "

WESTCHESTER ILLUSTRATED, 16 School St., Yonkers NY 10701. (914)472-2061. Editor-in-Chief: Stephen H. Acunto. Emphasizes life in Westchester County, New York, for active, sophisticated, college-educated, 25- to 49-year-old suburbanites living within the New York Metropolitan area. "Interests range from participatory sports to the safety and convenience of Westchester's highways, from where to get the best cheesecake in the county to what our famous and not-so-famous neighbors are up to." Monthly magazine; 80 pages. Circ. 37,000. Buys all rights. Phone query OK "sometimes—especially when a story is of a particular moment." Submit seasonal/holiday material 3 months in advance. Simultaneous and photocopied submissions OK. SASE. Reports in 3-5 weeks. Sample copy $1.50; free writer's guidelines.
Nonfiction: "*Westchester Illustrated's* essential function is to support and showcase Westchester lifestyles. We inform and entertain readers in the process. We like how-to articles, reports on new developments in county lifestyles, and profiles of local personalities and celebrities. Consumer-oriented articles receive high priority—we're always looking for fresh material that people can use—material with practical value. Other favored topics are home care and home design, local controversy, the arts in Westchester and feature news. We do not want opinion, puffery or booster pieces, travel and technical writings. Some articles not about Westchester County are accepted, particularly Manhattan-related entertainment material. Buys about 60 mss/year. Query or submit complete ms. Length: 800-4,000 words. Pays $75-350.
Fiction: Good objective fiction now accepted. Pay varies. Submit complete ms. Length: 800-1500 words. Poetry, too.
Photos: Purchased with or without accompanying ms, or on assignment. Detailed captions required. Pays $10-40 for minimum 5x7 b&w glossy or matte prints. Send query and contact sheet. Model release required.
Poetry: Uses some poetry.
Tips: "Query. Spell it out in 3 paragraphs. Don't call. Outline. 1 freelancer clinched a sale by writing an honest outline with clearly movable parts."

North Carolina

SOUTHERN EXPOSURE, Box 531, Durham NC 27702. (919)688-8167. Editor: Bob Hall. 70% freelance written. For Southerners interested in "left-liberal" political perspective and the South; all ages; well-educated. Magazine; 100-230 pages. Quarterly. Circ. 7,500. Buys all rights. Pays kill fee. Byline given. Buys 20 mss/year. Pays on publication. Will consider photocopied and simultaneous submissions. Submit seasonal material 2-3 months in advance. Reports in 1-2 months. "Query is appreciated, but not required." SASE.
Nonfiction and Photos: "Ours is probably the only publication about the South *not* aimed at business or the upper-class people; it appeals to all segments of the population. *And,* it is used as a resource-sold as a magazine and then as a book-so it rarely becomes dated." Needed are investigative articles about the following subjects as related to the South: politics, energy, institutional power from prisons to universities, women, labor, black people and the economy. Informational interview, profile, historical, think articles, exposé, opinion and book reviews. Length: 6,000 words maximum. Pays $50-200. "Very rarely purchase photos, as we have a large number of photographers working for us." 8x10 b&w preferred; no color. Payment negotiable.
Fiction and Poetry: "Fiction should concern the South, e.g., black fiction, growing up Southern, etc." Very little fiction used. Length: 6,000 words maximum. Pays $50-100. All forms of poetry accepted, if they relate to the South, its problems, potential, etc. Length: open. Pays $15-100.

THE STATE, "Down Home in North Carolina," Box 2169, Raleigh NC 27602. Editor: W.B. Wright. Monthly. Buys first rights. Free sample copy. Pays on acceptance. Deadlines 1 month in advance. SASE.
Nonfiction and Photos: "General articles about places, people, events, history, nostalgia, general interest in North Carolina. Emphasis on travel in North Carolina; (devote features regularly to resorts, travel goals, dining and stopping places)." Will use humor if related to region. Length: average of 1,000-1,200 words. Pays $15-50, including illustration. B&w photos. Pays $3-20, "depending on use."

Ohio

BEND OF THE RIVER MAGAZINE, Box 239, Perrysburg OH 43551. (419)874-7534. Publishers: Christine Raizk Alexander and Lee Raizk. For readers interested in Ohio history, antiques, etc. Monthly magazine; 24 pages. Circ. 2,000. Buys first rights. Byline given. Buys 50-60 mss/year.

Pays on publication. No photocopied or simultaneous submissions. Submit seasonal material 2 months in advance; deadline for holiday issue is October 15. Reports in 2 months. Submit complete ms. SASE. Sample copy 50¢.

Nonfiction and Photos: "We deal heavily in Ohio history. We are looking for articles about modern day pioneers, doing the unusual. Another prime target is the uplifting feature, spiritual and/or religious sketch or interview. Don't bother sending anything negative; other than that, we can appreciate each writer's style. We'd like to see interviews with historical (Ohio) authorities; travel sketches of little-known but interesting places in Ohio; grass roots farmers; charismatic people. Nostalgic pieces will be considered. Our main interest is to give our readers happy thoughts. We strive for material that says 'yes' to life, past and present." Length: 1,500 words. Pays $5 minimum. Purchases b&w photos with accompanying mss. Pays $1 minimum. Captions required.

Tips: "Any Toledo-area, well-researched history will be put on top of the heap! Send us any unusual piece that is either cleverly humorous, divinely inspired or thought provoking. We like articles about historical topics treated in down-to-earth conversational tones. We pay a small amount but usually use our writers often and through the years. We're loyal."

OHIO MAGAZINE, O Magazine, Inc., Subsidiary of Dispatch Printing Co., 40 S. 3rd St., Columbus OH 43215. Editor-in-Chief: Robert B. Smith. Managing Editor: Ellen Stein. Emphasizes news and feature material of Ohio for an educated, urban and urbane readership. Monthly magazine; 96-156 pages. Circ. 55,600. Pays on publication. Buys all rights, second serial (reprint) rights, or one-time rights. Pays 20% kill fee. Byline given "except on short articles appearing in sections." Submit seasonal/holiday material 2 months in advance. Simultaneous, photocopied and previously published submissions OK. SASE. Reports in 8 weeks. Free writer's guidelines.

Nonfiction: Features: 2,000-8,000 words. Pays $250-700. Cover pieces $600-850; Reporter and People (should be offbeat with solid news interest; 50-250 words, pays $15-50); Short Cuts (on Ohio or Ohio-related products including mail ordering and goods or people that perform a service that are particularly amusing or offbeat; 100-300 words, pays $15-20); Ohioguide (pieces on upcoming Ohio events, must be offbeat and worth traveling for; 100-300 words, pays $10-15); Diner's Digest ("we are still looking for writers with extensive restaurant reviewing experience to do 5-10 short reviews each month in specific sections of the state on a specific topic. Fee is on a retainer basis and negotiable"); Money (covering business-related news items, profiles of prominent people in business community, personal finance—all Ohio angle; 300-1,000 words, pays $50-250); and Living (embodies dining in, home furnishings, gardening and architecture; 300-1,000 words, pays $50-250). "Send submissions for features to Robert B. Smith, editor-in-chief, or Ellen Stein, managing editor; Reporter and People sections to Michael Castranova, associate editor; Short Cuts, Living Ohioguide and Diner's Digest to Maryann Reilly, services editor; and Money to Ellen Stein, managing editor.

Columns & Departments: Sports, Politics, Media and Last Word to Michael Castranova; and Travel, Fashion, Wine, to Ellen Stein. Open to suggestions for new columns/departments.

Photos: MaryLynn Blasutta, design director. Rate negotiable.

Tips: "Freelancers should send a brief prospectus prior to submission of the complete article. All articles should have a definite Ohio application."

THE WESTERN RESERVE MAGAZINE, Box 243, Garrettsville OH 44231. (216)527-2030. Editor-in-Chief: Mary Folger. 40% freelance written. Emphasizes historical, where-to-go, what-to-do, crafts and collectibles for Northeastern Ohioans. Published 6 times/year; 80-120 pages. Circ. 10,000. Pays on publication. Buys all rights.

Nonfiction: Historical (northeastern Ohio); how-to (crafts with history); and humor (if northeastern Ohio historical slant). No poetry or nostalgia.

Tips: "Our goal is to help preserve the heritage of the Western Reserve. The average reader has three-plus years of college; 70% have advanced degrees—write for this market. This is not a beginning writer's market."

Oregon

CASCADES EAST, 716 NE 4th St., Box 5784, Bend OR 97701. (503)382-0127. Editor: Geoff Hill. 90% freelance written. For "all ages as long as they are interested in outdoor recreation in Central Oregon: fishing, hunting, sight-seeing, hiking, bicycling, mountain climbing, backpacking, rock-hounding, skiing, snowmobiling, etc." Quarterly magazine; 48 pages. Circ. 5,000 (distributed throughout area resorts and motels and to subscribers). Pays on publication. Buys all rights. Byline given. Submit seasonal/holiday material 6 months in advance of issue date. SASE. Reports in 6 weeks. Sample copy $1.50.

Nonfiction: General interest (first-person experiences in outdoor Central Oregon—with photos, can be dramatic, humorous or factual); historical (for feature, "Little Known Tales from Oregon History," with b&w photos); and personal experience (needed on outdoor subjects: dramatic, humorous or factual). "No articles that are too general, sight-seeing articles that come from a travel folder, or outdoor articles without the first-person approach." Buys 5-10 mss/issue. Query. Length: 1,000-3,000 words. Pays 3-6¢/word.

Photos: "Old photos will greatly enhance chances of selling a historical feature. First-person articles need black and white photos, also." Pays $5-10 for b&w; $15-50 for color transparencies. Captions preferred. Buys one-time rights.

Tips: "Submit stories a year or so in advance of publication. We are seasonal and must plan editorial for summer '82 in the spring of '81, etc., in case seasonal photos are needed."

Pennsylvania

SUSQUEHANNA MAGAZINE, Susquehanna Times and Magazine, Box 75A, R.D.1, Marietta PA 17547. (717)426-2212. Editor: Richard S. Bromer. Monthly magazine about regional Lancaster County, Pennsylvania for people in the upper middle socio-economic level who are college educated, aged 25-60, home and family and community oriented, conservative and interested in local history and customs. Circ. 6,000. Pays on publication. Buys all rights. Phone queries OK. Submit seasonal material 2 months in advance. Simultaneous and photocopied submissions OK. SASE. Reports in 6 weeks. Sample copy $1.50.

Nonfiction: General interest (history, customs, personalities, business, agriculture and lifestyle); historical (local events and personalities); how-to (do arts and crafts); humor (sophisticated, educated and psychological); interview; nostalgia; opinion; profile; and technical. "This material must have a special relationship to the area we cover: Lancaster County and nearby areas in Southeast Pennsylvania." Buys 60 mss/year. Send complete ms. Length: 750-2,500 words. Pays $35-$50.

Photos: Offers no additional payment for photos accepted with ms. Captions preferred; model release required.

Fiction: "We use very little fiction. We would accept only if there is an obvious regional relationship."

Poetry: "We would only use if there were an obvious regional relationship."

Tips: "Read several copies of *Susquehanna Magazine* to get a feel for our style and preferred material. Write up fresh material or fresh approach to old material, e.g., historical incidents. We accept 'class' material only (informative, intellectually stimulating, accurate)—nothing trite or 'term paper.' "

South Carolina

COAST, Box 2448, Myrtle Beach SC 29577. Editor: Karen Dover. For tourists to the Grand Strand. Weekly magazine; 180 pages. Circ. 17,500. Buys all rights. Byline given "only on feature stories and featurettes." Buys 5-6 mss/year. Pays on acceptance. Free sample copy. Photocopied and simultaneous submissions OK. Reports in 60-90 days. Query. SASE.

Nonfiction and Photos: "Timely features dealing with coastal activities and events, and an occasional historical article related to the area. Submit an idea before a manuscript. It should be directly related to this coastal area. No vague, general articles." Emphasis is on informational and historical articles. Length: 800-1,000 words. Pays $25-30. B&w photos purchased with mss. Prefers 5x7. Pays $5-10 for b&w. Buys some color for editorial purposes. Must relate to area. Pays $25-50.

SOUTHERN WORLD, Southern World Publishing, Box 5665, Hilton Head SC 29938. (803)785-5010. Editor: John Blakeslee. Bimonthly magazine covering general-interest topics with an emphasis on the South, for an upscale audience. Estab. 1979. Circ. 100,000. Pays on publication. Byline given. Pays kill fee "in some circumstances." Buys all rights, "but may reassign rights and share reprint rights." Submit seasonal/holiday material 4 months in advance. Simultaneous queries and photocopied submissions OK. SASE. Reports in 1 month. Sample copy $1.50; writer's guidelines for SAE.

Nonfiction: Humor; interview/profile (of celebrities with a Southern connection); travel; business; sports; food; nature; the arts; and "any topical issues of current interest to Southern residents." Buys 80-100 mss/year. Query or send complete ms. Length: 1,500-6,000 words. Pays average 10-15¢/word.

Photos: State availability of photos or illustrations. Reviews 35mm color transparencies and 5x7 b&w glossy prints.
Fiction: Condensed novels, ethnic, historical, humorous, mainstream, novel excerpts and serialized novels.
Poetry: Free verse, light verse and traditional. Pay varies.
Fillers: Anecdotes ("You All"); and newsbreaks ("Dixie Notes"). Pays $20 maximum.

South Dakota

BLACK HILLS MONTHLY MAGAZINE, Box 1082, Rapid City SD 57709. (605)342-1993. Editor: Linda Miller. Monthly tabloid covering the art and history of the Black Hills for upper income well-educated people aged 25-40 with an interest in the Black Hills. Estab. 1980. Circ. 20,000. Pays on publication. Byline given. Buys first North American serial rights. Submit seasonal/holiday material 3 months in advance. Simultaneous queries, simultaneous, photocopied, and previously published submissions OK. Reports in 2 weeks on queries. Free sample copy.
Nonfiction: Exposé (on politics, energy, tourism); general interest (current issues of concern to South Dakota); historical/nostalgic; how-to (outdoor sports); humor; interview/profile (people and families of the Black Hills); personal experience (reminiscences); photo feature, technical (related to mining and energy); travel (to encourage tourism in the Black Hills); and art. Buys 100 mss/year. Query. Length: 1,200-1,800 words. Pays $10 minimum.
Photos: State availability of photos. Reviews 8x10 glossy prints. Captions, model release, and identification of subjects required. "Photo payment included in payment for article."
Fiction: Adventure, condensed novels, American Indian, experimental, fantasy, historical, horror, humorous, mainstream, mystery, novel excerpts, romance, science fiction, serialized novels, suspense and western. Buys 25-30 mss/year. Query. Length: 1,200-1,800. Pays $10 minimum.

Tennessee

CUMBERLAND, Cumberland Magazine Co., Box 3085, Clarksville TN 37040. Publisher: James D. Lester. Monthly magazine about Tennessee for an affluent, general audience interested in articles and photos on life in Tennessee. Circ. 17,500. Pays on publication. Buys first North American serial rights. Phone queries OK. Submit seasonal material 3 months in advance. Simultaneous and photocopied submissions OK. SASE. Reports in 1 month. Sample copy $1; free writer's guidelines.
Nonfiction: General interest (crafts, folklore, music, the fashion business, cooking, tours, homes, sports and recreation); historical (anything with a Tennessee or Southern angle); how-to (live better in Tennessee); humor; interview (of celebrities and outstanding Tennessee people); nostalgia; profile; travel (with Tennessee slant); personal experience; and photo feature. Buys 10 mss/issue. Query or send complete ms. Length: 500-3,000 words. Pays 7¢/word to published writers.
Photos: State availability of photos. Reviews any size b&w glossy prints, negatives and contact sheets; any size color transparencies, prints and negatives. Captions and model release required. Buys one-time rights.
Fiction: Historical (with a Southern flavor), humorous and mystery. Buys 5 mss/year. Send complete ms. Length: 2,000 words maximum. Pays 7¢/word.
Poetry: Free verse, light verse and traditional. Buys 4 mss/year. Submit maximum 10 poems. Payment negotiable.

Vermont

VERMONT LIFE MAGAZINE, 61 Elm St., Montpelier VT 05602. (802)828-3241. Editor: Brian Vachon. Quarterly magazine; 64 pages. Circ. 150,000. Buys first rights. Pays 25% kill fee. Byline given. Buys 80 mss/year. "Query is essential." SASE.
Nonfiction: Wants articles on Vermont, those which portray a typical or, if possible, unique, attractive aspect of the state or its people. Style should be literate, clear and concise. Subtle humor favored. No nature close-ups or ecology stories, no Vermont dialect attempts as in "Ayup," or an outsider's view on visiting Vermont. No horses, women farmers or small-town portraits. Length: average 1,500 words. Pays average 10-20¢/word.
Photos: Buys photographs with mss and with captions and seasonal photographs alone. Prefers b&w contact sheets to look at first on assigned material. Color submissions must be 4x5 or 35mm transparencies. Buys one-time rights, but often negotiates for re-use rights also. Rates on accept-

ance; b&w, $10; color, $75 inside, $200 for cover. Gives assignments but not on first trial with photographers. Query.

Tips: "Writers who have read our magazine are given more consideration. Team up with a competent photographer and offer to present a package."

Virginia

COMMONWEALTH, 1011 E. Main St., Richmond VA 23219. (804)649-9000. Editor-in-Chief: Susan Harb. Emphasizes Norfolk, Virginia. Monthly magazine. Circ. 12,000. Pays within 1 month of publication. Buys all rights. Byline given. Submit seasonal/holiday material 4 months in advance. Photocopied submissions OK. SASE. Reports in 6 weeks. Sample copy $1.50.

Nonfiction: Informational; historical; humor; interview; nostalgia; profile; travel; and photo feature. Buys 25-30 mss/year. Query or submit complete ms. Length: 1,200-3,000 words. Pays $150-300.

Photos: Purchased with or without accompanying ms or on assignment. Captions required. Query. Pays $20-50 for 8x10 b&w glossy prints; $150 maximum for 35mm color transparencies.

Tips: "Very difficult for a non-Virginian, or one not familiar with the magazine to break in. We always need good ideas but find most outside freelancers want to provide subjects which are cliches to our readers."

METRO, THE MAGAZINE OF SOUTHEASTERN VIRGINIA, Metro Magazine, Inc., Box 1995, Norfolk VA 23501. (804)622-4122. Editor: William H. Candler. For urban adults interested in lifestyles and important issues in Southeastern Virginia. Monthly magazine; 96 pages. Circ. 18,500. Pays on publication. Buys all rights. Pays negotiable kill fee. Byline given. Phone queries OK. Submit seasonal/holiday material 6 months in advance. Photocopied and previously published submissions OK. SASE. Reports in 4-6 weeks. Sample copy $1.79; free writer's guidelines.

Nonfiction: Expose (must be related to Southeastern Virginia issues); general national interest; how-to (on anything consumer-oriented); humor (particularly related to people and their experiences); interview (prefers interviews with Virginia-related personalities); opinion (on issues pertinent to Southeastern Virginia or issues of general interest); photo; and travel. Buys 10 mss/issue. Query. Length: 750-2,500 words. Pays $35-150.

Photos: State availability of photos. Pays $5 minimum/5x7 b&w glossy print; offers no additional payment for photos accompanying ms. Captions preferred; model releases required.

Columns/Departments: Arts/Entertainment; Business; Outdoors; People; Health; Gourmet; Lifestyle; and Travel (prefers inside story on popular or unusual local or regional spots). Buys 4 columns/issue. Query. Length: 800-1,200 words. Pays $20-100.

Fiction: "No fiction unless exceptional piece by local author or about area."

Fillers: "No limericks or humorous ditties, please. We use them but we generate them locally."

Tips: "Visit with the editor, establish a rapport, show genuine interest in and prior knowledge of the magazine, be prepared with good ideas, show an eagerness to dig for a good story, keep in touch."

NORTHERN VIRGINIAN, 127 Park St., Box 334, Vienna VA 22180. (703)938-0666. Reports in 30 days. Sample copy $1 (to cover postage and handling); free writer's guidelines.

Nonfiction: "Freelance manuscripts welcomed on speculation. Particularly interested in historical articles about or related to Northern Virginia."

Photos: "B&w photos as appropriate, with mss enhance publication probability."

Wisconsin

FOX RIVER PATRIOT, Fox River Publishing Co., Box 54, Princeton WI 54968. (414)295-6252. Editor: Michael Jacobi. For country folks of all ages. Bimonthly tabloid; 36 pages. Circ. 6,000. Pays on publication. Buys first North American serial rights and one-time rights. Byline given. Submit seasonal/holiday material 2 months in advance. Simultaneous, photocopied and previously published submissions OK. SASE. Reports in 4 weeks. Sample copy $1.

Nonfiction: Exposé, general interest, historical, how-to, humor, interview, nostalgia, personal experience, photo feature, profile, and travel. "In general, we are a country-oriented publication— we stress environment, alternative energy technology, alternative building trends, farming and gardening, etc.—submissions should be in this general area." Buys 4 mss/issue. Send complete ms. Pays $5-25.

Photos: Send photos with ms. Pays $5 for 5x7 b&w prints; $5 for 5x7 color prints. Captions preferred.

WISCONSIN TRAILS, Box 5650, Madison WI 53705. (608)831-3363. Editor: Howard Mead. For readers interested in Wisconsin; its natural beauty, history, recreation and personalities; and the arts. Quarterly magazine; 44 pages. Circ. 25,000. Rights purchased vary with author and material. Byline given. Buys 30-40 mss/year. Pays on publication. Free sample copy and writer's guidelines. Photocopied submissions OK. Submit seasonal material at least 1 year in advance. Reports in 1 month. Query or send outline. SASE.
Nonfiction: "Our articles focus on some aspect of Wisconsin life; an interesting site or event, a person or industry, or history and the arts. We do not use first-person essays (reminiscences are sometimes OK), ecstasies about scenery, or biographies about people who were born in Wisconsin, but made their fortunes elsewhere. No cartoons, crosswords or fillers. Poetry exclusively on assignment." Length: 1,000 to 3,000 words. Pays $50-250, depending on length and quality.
Photos: Purchased without mss or on assignment. Captions preferred. B&w photos usually illustrate a given article. Color is mostly scenic. Pays $10 each for b&w on publication. Pays $50 for inside color; pays $100 for covers and center spreads. Transparencies; 2¼x2¼ or larger are preferred.
Tips: "Best queries tell me 1) *what* the topic is; 2) *why* the topic is appropriate for my magazine's audience; and 3) *how* the writer plans to develop the topic into an article, i.e., what approach or form the article will take. Because we're a seasonal magazine, it's also helpful to know if one season is most appropriate for the piece."

Canada

CANADIAN GEOGRAPHIC, 488 Wilbrod St., Ottawa, Ontario Canada K1N 6M8. Editor: David Maclellan. Executive Editor: Ross Smith. Managing Editor: Enid Byford. Circ. 105,000. Bimonthly magazine; 84+ pages. Pays on publication. Buys first Canadian rights; interested only in first time publication. Leaflet for guidance of contributor available on request.
Nonfiction: Buys authoritative geographical articles, in the broad geographical sense, written for the average person, not for a scientific audience. Predominantly Canadian subjects by Canadian authors; non-Canadian subjects have positive Canadian involvement or appeal. Length: 1,200-2,500 words. Pays 12¢ minimum/word. Usual payment for articles with illustrations, $150-500 and up. Higher fees reserved for commissioned articles on which copyright remains with publisher unless otherwise agreed.
Photos: 35mm slides, 2¼x2¼ transparencies or 8x10 glossies. Pays $25-100+ for color shots, depending on published size; $12.50-40 for b&w.
Tips: "Refer to our leaflet for guidance of contributors, and pay attention to our requirements."

RAINCOAST CHRONICLES, Box 219, Madeira Park, British Columbia, Canada V0N 2H0. Editor: Howard White. Biannual magazine covering regional culture of the Pacific Northwest coast. Circ. 5,000. Pays on acceptance. Buys serial and reprint rights. SAE and International Reply Coupons.
Nonfiction: History, reviews, art. Send complete ms. Length: 1,500-5,000 words. Pays 5¢/word.
Photos: Pays $25 for 5x7 b&w prints.
Fiction: Must be related to the Pacific Northwest coast of Canada. Send complete ms.
Poetry: Must be regionally related.
Tips: "Learn something about Canada. Don't forget that most Canadian publications are specialty publications addressed to the national and local issues overlooked by the major US media which we are exposed to."

Religious

Educational and inspirational material of interest to church members, workers and leaders within a denomination or religion is the primary interest of publications in this category. Publications intended to assist lay and professional religious workers in teaching and managing church affairs are classified in Church Administration and Ministry in the Trade Journals section. Religious magazines for children and teenagers will be found in the Juvenile, and Teen and Young Adult classifications. Jewish publications whose main concern is with matters of general Jewish interest (rather than religious interest) are listed in the Jewish Publications category. Publications for the inspirational music fan can be found in the Consumer/Music section.

ALIVE NOW!, The Upper Room, 1980 Grand Ave., Nashville TN 37202. (615)327-2700. Editor: Mary Ruth Coffman. Bimonthly magazine including short prose pieces, poetry, and essays relating to a theme concerned with Christian life and action, for a general Christian audience interested in reflection and meditation. Circ. 75,000. Pays on publication. Byline given. Pays "negotiated kill fee, when applicable." Rights purchased are negotiated ("may be one-time rights, or newspaper and periodical"). Submit seasonal/holiday material 8 months in advance. Previously published work OK. SASE. Reports in 2 months on queries; 6 months on mss. Sample copy and writer's guidelines free.
Nonfiction: Book excerpts, humor, inspirational and personal experience. Especially needs material on energy (spiritual and physical). "Send a typed, interesting story or poem that deals with personal faith journey, relations with other people and the world, questions of meaning, responsibility for the natural world, and/or thoughts on the meaning of existence. Writing should be for the young adult or mature adult, or the adult with a growing faith awareness." No polemic articles. Buys 120 mss/year. Send complete ms. Length: 500 words maximum. Pays $5-40.
Photos: Marie Livingston Roy, photo editor. Send photos with ms. Pays $50-100 for 4x5 color transparencies; $15-25 for 8x10 b&w prints. Buys one-time rights.
Columns/Departments: Excerpts from devotional classics. Buys 4 mss/year. Query with clips of published work. Length: 350-800 words. Pays $25-40.
Fiction: Fantasy, humorous and religious. No confession, erotica, horror, romance or western. Buys 10 mss/year. Query with clips of published work. Length: 100-450 words. Pays $25-40.
Poetry: Avant-garde and free verse. Buys 30 poems/year. Submit maximum 5 poems. Length: 10-45 lines. Pays $5-25.
Fillers: Anecdotes and short humor. Buys 6/year. Length: 25-150 words. Pays $5-15.

AMERICA, 106 W. 56th St., New York NY 10019. (212)581-4640. Editor: Joseph A. O'Hare. Published weekly for adult, educated, largely Roman Catholic audience. Usually buys all rights. Byline given. Pays on acceptance. Reports in 2-3 weeks. Free writer's guidelines. SASE.
Nonfiction and Poetry: "We publish a wide variety of material on politics, economics, ecology, and so forth. We are not a parochial publication, but almost all of our pieces make some moral or religious point. We are not interested in purely informational pieces or personal narratives which are self-contained and have no larger moral interest." Articles on literature, current political and social events. Length: 1,500-2,000 words. Pays $50-100. Poetry length: 15-30 lines. Address to Poetry Editor.

THE ANNALS OF SAINT ANNE DE BEAUPRE, Basilica of St. Anne, Quebec, Canada G0A 3C0. (418)827-4538. Editor-in-Chief: E. Lefebvre. Managing Editor: Francois J. Plourde. 60% freelance written. Emphasizes the Catholic faith for the general public, of average education; mostly Catholic; part of the audience is made up of people who came to The Shrine of St. Anne de Beaupre. Monthly magazine; 32 pages. Circ. 70,000. Pays on acceptance. Buys first North American serial rights. Phone queries OK. Submit seasonal/holiday material 2 months in advance. SAE and International Reply Coupons. Reports in 3-4 weeks. Free sample copy and writer's guidelines.
Nonfiction: Humor (short pieces on education, family, etc.); inspirational; interview; and personal experience. Buys 10 mss/issue. Query. Length: 700-1,700 words. Pays $25-35.
Photos: Purchased with or without accompanying ms. Submit prints. Pays $5-15 for b&w glossy prints; $25-40 for color transparencies. "We buy very few color photos." Total purchase price for ms includes payment for photos.

Columns/Departments: Query. Length: 700-1,700 words. Pays $25-35. Open to suggestions for new columns/departments.
Fiction: Religious (Catholic faith). Buys 1 ms/issue. Query. Length: 700-1,700 words. Pays $25-35.
Poetry: Light verse. Buys 12 poems/year. Limit submissions to batches of 6. Pays $5 minimum.
Fillers: Jokes, gags, anecdotes and short humor. "We buy few fillers." Pays $5 minimum.
Tips: The freelancer can best break in by offering a special column or "submitting articles that fit our needs: popular Catholic life".

ASPIRE, 1819 E. 14th Ave., Denver CO 80218. Editor: Jeanne Pomranka. 50% freelance written. For teens and adults: "those who are looking for a way of life that is practical, logical, spiritual or inspirational." Monthly; 64 pages. Circ. 2,900. Buys all rights. Byline given. Buys 100 mss/year. Pays following publication. Sample copy 20¢ in stamps. Submit seasonal material 6-7 months in advance. Reports in 2 weeks.
Nonfiction: Uses inspirational articles that help to interpret the spiritual meaning of life. Needs are specialized, since this is the organ of the Divine Science teaching. Personal experience, inspirational, think pieces. Also seeks material for God at Work, a department "written in the form of letters to the editor in which the writer describes how God has worked in his life or around him. Teen Talk includes short articles from teenagers to help other teenagers find meaning in life." Length: 100-1,000 words. Pays maximum 1¢/published word.
Fiction: "Anything illustrating spiritual law at work in life." Length: 250-1,000 words. Pays maximum 1¢/published word.
Poetry: Traditional, contemporary, light verse. "We use very little poetry." Length: average 8-16 lines. Pays $1-2/page.
Tips: "Avoid 'churchiness' as opposed to man's true relationship with God and his fellowmen. The latter is what we need—articles on prayer, consciousness building, faith at work, spiritual law, etc. We want good, simple, clear writing—no tired, overused phrases, no overemphasis of tragedy, but emphasis on positive, constructive attitudes that overcome such situations. Must be inspirationally written."

BAPTIST HERALD, 1 S. 210 Summit Ave., Oakbrook Terrace IL 60181. (312)495-2000. Contact: Barbara J. Binder. For "any age from 15 and up, any educational background with mainly religious interests." Monthly. Circ. 9,000. Buys all rights. Byline given. Pays on publication. Occasionally overstocked. Free sample copy. Submit seasonal material 3-4 months in advance. SASE.
Nonfiction and Fiction: "We want articles of general religious interest. Seeking articles that are precise, concise, and honest. We hold a rather conservative religious line." Buys personal experience, interviews, inspirational and opinion articles. Length: 600-1,200 words. Pays $10. Buys religious and historical fiction. Length: 600-1,250 words. Pays $10.

BAPTIST LEADER, Valley Forge PA 19481. (215)768-2158. Editor: Vincie Alessi. For ministers, teachers, and leaders in church schools. Monthly; 64 pages. Buys first rights. Pays on acceptance. Deadlines are 8 months prior to date of issue. Reports immediately. SASE.
Nonfiction: Educational topics. How-to articles for local church school teachers. Length: 1,500-2,000 words. Pays $25-40.
Photos: Church school settings; church, worship, children's and youth activities and adult activities. Purchased with mss. B&w, 8x10; human interest and seasonal themes. Pays $15-20.

BIBLICAL ILLUSTRATOR, The Sunday School Board, 127 9th Ave. N., Nashville TN 37234. Editor: William H. Stephens. For members of Sunday School classes that use the International Sunday School Lessons and other Bible study lessons, and for adults seeking in-depth Biblical information. Quarterly. Circ. 90,000. Buys all rights. Byline given. Rarely purchases freelance material. Pays on acceptance. Reports in 2 weeks. Query. SASE.
Nonfiction and Photo: Journalistic articles and photo stories researched on Biblical subjects, such as archeology and sketches of Biblical personalities. Material must be written for laymen but research quality must be up-to-date and thorough. Should be written in a contemporary, journalistic style. Pays 3½¢/word. B&w and color photos occasionally purchased with ms or on assignment. Captions required. Pays $25 for b&w, more for color.

BRIGADE LEADER, Box 150, Wheaton IL 60187. Managing Editor: Michael Chiapperino. 50% freelance written. For men associated with Christian Service Brigade programs throughout US and Canada. Quarterly magazine; 32 pages. Buys all rights or second serial (reprint) rights. Buys 6-8 mss/year. Pays on acceptance. Submit seasonal material 5 months in advance. Photocopied submissions OK. Reports in 2 months. Query. SASE. Sample copy $1.
Nonfiction and Photos: "Articles about men and things related to them. Relationships in home,

church, work. Specifically geared to men with an interest in boys. Besides men dealing with boys' physical, mental, emotional needs—also deals with spiritual needs." Informational, personal experience, inspirational. Length:· 900-1,500 words. Photos purchased with or without ms. Pays $25 for b&w, inside; $50-75 for b&w, cover.

CANADIAN CHURCHMAN, 600 Jarvis St., Toronto, Ontario, Canada M4Y 2J6. Editor: Jerrold F. Hames. 20% freelance written. For a general audience; Anglican Church of Canada; adult, with religio-socio emphasis. Monthly tabloid newspaper; 24-28 pages. Circ. 270,000. Pays on publication. Photocopied submissions and simultaneous submissions OK. Query. SAE and International Reply Coupons.
Nonfiction: "Religion, news from churches around the world, social issues, theme editions (native rights, abortion, alcoholism, etc.). Newsy approach; bright features of interest to Canadian churchmen. Prefer rough sketch first; freelance usually on assignment only. Our publication is Anglican-slanted, progressive, heavily socially oriented in presenting topical issues." Informational, interview, spot news. Length: 750-1,200 words. Pays $50-150.
Tips: Query should give background of proposed subject and tell why it would interest Canadian Anglican readers.

CARITAS, Editorial Office, St. Augustine's, Blackrock, County, Dublin, Ireland. Phone: 880509. Editor: Br. Bernardine Edwards. Quarterly magazine "published by the Hospitaller Order of St. John of God, Ireland. The Order has founded hospitals for the mentally and physically handicapped in most parts of the world." Pays on acceptance. Reports in 1 month. Sample copy for $2, SAE and International Reply Coupons.
Nonfiction: "We would welcome original articles suitable for family reading; features on youth, family stories and case histories; biographies and memoirs of celebrities; and articles of religious and topical interest." Query. Length: 750-1,800 words. Pays 5-35 pounds.

CATHOLIC DIGEST, Box 43090, St. Paul MN 55164. Editor: Henry Lexau. Managing Editor: Richard Reece. Monthly magazine covering the daily living of Roman Catholics for an audience that is 60% female, 40% male; 37% is college educated. Circ. 650,000. Byline given. Buys first North American serial rights or one-time reprint rights. Submit seasonal material 6 months in advance. Previously published submissions OK, if so indicated. SASE. Reports in 2 weeks.
Nonfiction: General interest (daily living and family relationships); interview (of outstanding Catholics, celebrities and locals); nostalgia (the good old days of family living); profile; religion; travel (shrines); humor; inspirational (overcoming illness, role model people); and personal experience (adventures and daily living). Buys 20 articles/issue. No queries. Send complete ms. Length: 500-3,000 words, 2,000 average. Pays on acceptance $200-400 for originals, $100 for reprints.
Photos: State availability of photos. Reviews 5x7 and 8x10 b&w glossy prints. Pays $150/color photo. Offers no additional payment for photos accepted with ms. Captions and model release required. Buys one-time rights.
Columns/Departments: "Check a copy of the magazine in the library for a description of column needs. Payment varies and is made upon publication. We buy about 5/issue."
Fillers: Jokes, anecdotes and short humor. Buys 10-15 mss/issue. Length: 10-300 words. Pays $3-50 on publication.

CATHOLIC LIFE, 35750 Moravian Dr., Fraser MI 48026. Editor-in-Chief: Robert C. Bayer. 75% freelance written. Emphasizes foreign missionary activities of the Catholic Church in Burma, India, Bangladesh, the Philippines, Hong Kong, Africa, etc., for middle-aged and older audience with either middle incomes or pensions. High school educated (on the average), conservative in both religion and politics. Monthly (except July or August) magazine; 32 pages. Circ. 23,500. Pays on publication. Buys all rights. Byline given. Submit seasonal/holiday material 3-4 months in advance. Simultaneous submissions OK. SASE. Reports in 2 weeks.
Nonfiction: Informational; inspirational (foreign missionary activities of the Catholic Church; experiences, personalities, etc.). Buys 30 mss/year. Query or send complete ms. Length: 1,000-1,500 words. Pays 4¢/word.
Tips: "Query with short, graphic details of what the material will cover or the personality involved in the biographical sketch. Also, we appreciate being advised on the availability of good b&w photos to illustrate the material."

CATHOLIC NEAR EAST MAGAZINE, Catholic Near East Welfare Association, 1011 1st Ave., New York NY 10022. (212)826-1480. Editor: Claudia McDonnell. For a general audience with interest in the Near East, particularly its religious and cultural aspects. Quarterly magazine; 24 pages. Circ. 163,000. Buys first North American serial rights. Byline given. Buys 16 mss/year. Pays on publication. Free sample copy and writer's guidelines. Photocopied submissions OK if legible. Submit seasonal material (Christmas and Easter in different Near Eastern lands or rites) 6 months in advance. Reports in 3-4 weeks. Query or submit complete ms. SASE.

Nonfiction and Photos: "Cultural, territorial, devotional material on the Near East, its history, peoples and religions (especially the Eastern Rites of the Catholic Church). Style should be simple, factual, concise. Articles must stem from personal acquaintance with subject matter, or thorough up-to-date research. No preaching or speculations." Length: 1,200-1,800 words. Pays 10¢/word. "Photographs to accompany ms are always welcome; they should illustrate the people, places, ceremonies, etc., which are described in the article. We prefer color but occasionally use b&w. Pay varies depending on the quality of the photos."

Tips: "Writers please heed: stick to the Near East. Send factual articles; concise, descriptive style preferred. Not too flowery. Pictures are a big plus; if you have photos to accompany your article, please send them at the same time."

CHICAGO STUDIES, Box 665, Mundelein IL 60060. (312)566-1462. Editor: George J. Dyer. 50% freelance written. For Roman Catholic priests and religious educators. Magazine; published 3 times/year; 112 pages. Circ. 10,000. Buys all rights. Buys 30 mss/year. Pays on acceptance. Sample copy $2. Photocopied submissions OK. Submit complete ms. Reports in 6 weeks. SASE.

Nonfiction: Nontechnical discussion of theological, Biblical and ethical topics. Articles aimed at a nontechnical presentation of the contemporary scholarship in those fields. Length: 3,000-5,000 words. Pays $35-100.

THE CHRISTIAN CENTURY, 407 S. Dearborn St., Chicago IL 60605. (312)427-5380. Editor: James M. Wall. For ecumenically-minded, progressive church people, both clergy and lay. Weekly magazine; 24-32 pages. Circ. 33,000. Pays on publication. Usually buys all rights. Query appreciated, but not essential. SASE. Reports in 1 month. Free sample copy.

Nonfiction: "We use articles dealing with social problems, ethical dilemmas, political issues, international affairs, and the arts, as well as with theological and ecclesiastical matters. We focus on concerns that arise at the juncture between church and society, or church and culture." Length: 2,500 words maximum. Payment varies, but averages $20/page.

CHRISTIAN HERALD, 40 Overlook Dr., Chappaqua NY 10514. (914)769-9000. Editor: David E. Kucharsky. 80% freelance written. Emphasizes religious living in family and church. Monthly magazine; 64 pages. Circ. 285,000. Pays on acceptance. Buys all rights. Submit seasonal/holiday material 5-6 months in advance. Photocopied submissions OK. SASE. Sample copy $2; free writer's guidelines.

Nonfiction: How-to; informational; inspirational; interview; profile; and evangelical experience. Buys 50-75 mss/year. Query first. Length: 1,000-2,500 words. Pays $50 minimum.

Photos: Purchased with or without accompanying ms. Send transparencies. Pays $10 minimum for b&w; $25 minimum for 2¼x2¼ color transparencies.

Poetry: Meaningfully Biblical. Buys 30 poems/year. Length: 4-20 lines. Pays $10 minimum.

CHRISTIAN LIFE MAGAZINE, 396 E. St. Charles Rd., Wheaton IL 60187. Editor-in-Chief: Robert Walker. Executive Editor: Janice Franzen. 75% freelance written. Monthly religious magazine; 88 pages. Circ. 100,000. Pays on publication. Buys all rights. Submit seasonal/holiday material 8-12 months in advance. SASE. Free sample copy and writer's guidelines.

Nonfiction: Adventure articles (usually in the first-person, told in narrative style); devotional (include many anecdotes, preferably from the author's own experience); general features (wide variety of subjects, with special programs of unique benefit to the community); inspirational (showing the success of persons, ideas, events and organizations); personality profiles (bright, tightly-written articles on what Christians are thinking); news (with human interest quality dealing with trends); news feature (providing interpretative analysis of person, trend, event and ideas); and trend (should be based on solid research). Pays $175 maximum.

Fiction: Short stories (with good characterization and mood); pays $175 maximum.

CHRISTIAN LIVING, Mennonite Publishing House, 616 Walnut Ave., Scottdale PA 15683. (412)887-8500. Editor: J. Lorne Peachey. For Christian families. Monthly. Buys first or second rights. Pays on acceptance. Submit complete ms. SASE.

Nonfiction and Photos: Articles about Christian family life, parent-child relations, marriage, and family-community relations. Material must address itself to one specific family problem and/or concern and show how that problem/concern may be solved. If about a family activity, it should deal only with one such activity in simple, direct language. All material must relate to the adult members of a family, not the children. Length: 1,000-1,500 words. Pays $70 maximum. Additional payment for b&w photos used with mss.

Fiction and Poetry: Short stories on the same themes as above. Length: 1,000-2,000 words. Poems related to theme. Length: 25 lines. Pays $70 maximum for fiction; $5 minimum for poetry.

CHRISTIAN SINGLE, Family Ministry Dept., Baptist Sunday School Board, 127 9th Ave. North, Nashville TN 37234. (615)251-2228. Editor: Cliff Allbritton. Monthly magazine covering items of special interest to Christian single adults. "*Christian Single* is a contemporary Christian magazine that seeks to give substantive information to singles for living the abundant life. It seeks to be constructive and creative in approach." Estab. 1979. Circ. 85,000. Pays on acceptance "for immediate needs"; on publication "for unsolicited manuscripts." Byline given. Buys all rights or makes work-for-hire assignments. Submit seasonal/holiday material 12 months in advance. SASE. Reports in 6 weeks. Sample copy and writer's guidelines free.
Nonfiction: Humor (good, clean humor that applies to Christian singles); how-to (specific subjects which apply to singles; query needed); inspirational (of the personal experience type); personal experience (of single adults); photo feature (on outstanding Christian singles; query needed); and travel (appropriate for Christian singles; query needed). No "shallow, uninformative mouthing off. This magazine says something and people read it cover to cover." Buys 120-150 mss/year. Query with clips of published work. Length: 300-1,200 words. Pays 3½¢/word.
Tips: "We give preference to Christian single adult writers but publish articles by *sensitive* and *informed* married writers also. Remember that you are talking to educated people who attend church."

CHRISTIANITY & CRISIS, 537 W. 121st St., New York NY 10027. (212)662-5907. Editor: Wayne H. Cowan. For professional clergy and laymen; politically liberal; interested in ecology, good government, minorities and the church. Journal published every 2 weeks; 16 pages. Circ. 19,000. Rights purchased vary with author and material. Usually buys all rights. Buys 5-10 mss a year. Pays on publication. Free sample copy. Will consider photocopied and simultaneous submissions. Reports on material in 3 weeks. SASE.
Nonfiction: "Our articles are written in depth, by well-qualified individuals, most of whom are established figures in their respective fields. We offer comment on contemporary, political and social events occurring in the US and abroad. Articles are factual and of high quality. Anything whimsical, superficial, or politically dogmatic would not be considered." Interested in articles on bio-medical ethics, new community projects; informational articles and book reviews. Length: 500-5,000 words. Pays $25-$50.
Tips: "It is difficult for a freelancer to break in here but not impossible. Several authors we now go to on a regular basis came to us unsolicited and we always have a need for fresh material. Book reviews are short (800-1,500 words) and may be a good place to start, but you should query first. Another possibility is Viewpoints which also runs short pieces. Here we depend on people with a lot of expertise in their fields to write concise comments on current problems. If you have some real area of authority, this would be a good section to try."

CHRISTIANITY TODAY, 465 Gundersen Dr., Carol Stream IL 60187. Editor: Kenneth Kantzer. Emphasizes orthodox, evangelical religion. Semimonthly magazine; 55 pages. Circ. 190,000. Pays on acceptance. Usually buys all rights. Submit seasonal/holiday material 8 months in advance. SASE. Reports in 4-8 weeks. Free sample copy and writer's guidelines.
Nonfiction: Theological, ethical and historical and informational (not merely inspirational). Buys 4 mss/issue. Query or send complete ms. Length: 1,000-2,000 words. Pays $100 minimum.
Columns/Departments: Ministers' Workshop (practical and specific, not elementary). Buys 12 mss/year. Send complete ms. Length: 900-1,100 words. Pays $75.

CHURCH & STATE, Americans United for Separation of Church and State, 8120 Fenton St., Silver Spring MD 20910. (301)589-3707. Editor: Edd Doerr. 15% freelance written. Emphasizes religious liberty and church-state relations matters. Readership "includes the whole religious spectrum, but is predominantly Protestant and well-educated." Monthly magazine; 24 pages. Circ. 50,000. Pays on acceptance. Buys all rights. Simultaneous, photocopied and previously published submissions OK. SASE. Reports in 4 weeks. Free sample copy and writer's guidelines.
Nonfiction: Expose; general interest; historical; and interview. Buys 15 mss/year. Query. Length: 3,000 words maximum. Pays 3¢/word.
Photos: State availability of photos with query. Pays $10 for b&w prints. Captions preferred. Buys one-time rights.

THE CHURCH HERALD, 1324 Lake Dr. SE, Grand Rapids MI 49506. Editor: Dr. John Stapert. Publication of the Reformed Church in America. Biweekly magazine; 32 pages. Circ. 71,000. Buys all rights, first serial rights, or second serial (reprint) rights. Buys about 60 mss/year. Pays on acceptance. Sample copy 50¢; free writer's guidelines. Photocopied and simultaneous submissions

OK. Submit material for major Christian holidays 2 months in advance. Reports in 4 weeks. Query or submit complete ms. SASE.

Nonfiction and Photos: "We expect all of our articles to be helpful and constructive, even when a point of view is vigorously presented. Articles on subjects such as Christianity and culture, government and politics, forms of worship, the media, ethics and business relations, responsible parenthood, marriage and divorce, death and dying, challenges on the campus, evangelism, church leadership, Christian education, Christian perspectives on current issues, spiritual growth, etc." Length: 400-1,500 words. Articles for children, 750 words. Pays 4½¢/word. Photos purchased with or without accompanying ms. Pays $10 minimum/8x10 b&w glossy print.

Fiction and Fillers: Religious fiction. Length: 400-1,500 words. Children's fiction, 750 words. Pays 4¢/word.

Poetry: Length: 30 lines maximum. Pays $10 minimum.

COLUMBIA, Drawer 1670, New Haven CT 06507. Editor: Elmer Von Feldt. For Catholic families; caters particularly to members of the Knights of Columbus. Monthly magazine. Circ. 1,296,000. Buys all rights. Buys 50 mss/year. Pays on acceptance. Free sample copy and writer's guidelines. Submit seasonal material 6 months in advance. Reports in 4 weeks. Query or submit complete ms. SASE.

Nonfiction and Photos: Fact articles directed to the Catholic layman and his family and dealing with current events, social problems, Catholic apostolic activities, education, ecumenism, rearing a family, literature, science, arts, sports and leisure. Length: 1,000-3,000 words. B&w glossy prints are required for illustration. Articles without ample illustrative material are not given consideration. Payment ranges from $300-500, including photos. Photo stories are also wanted. Pays $15/photo used and 10¢/word.

Fiction and Humor: Written from a thoroughly Christian viewpoint. Length: 3,000 words maximum. Pays $400 maximum. Humor or satire should be directed to current religious, social or cultural conditions. Length: 1,000 words. Pays $150.

COMMONWEAL, 232 Madison Ave., New York NY 10016. (212)683-2042. Editor: James O'Gara. Biweekly. Edited by Roman Catholic laymen. For college-educated audience. Special book and education issues. Circ. 20,000. Pays on acceptance. Submit seasonal material 2 months in advance. Reports in 3 weeks. "A number of our articles come in over-the-transom. I suggest a newcomer either avoid particularly sensitive areas (say, politics) or let us know something about yourself (your credentials, tearsheets, a paragraph about yourself)." SASE. Free sample copy.

Nonfiction: "Articles on timely subjects: politics, literature and religion." Original, brightly written mss on value-oriented themes; think pieces. Buys 75 mss/year. Length: 1,000-3,000 words. Pays 2¢/word.

Poetry: Department editors: Rosemary Deen and Marie Ponsot. Contemporary and avant-garde. Length: maximum 150 lines ("long poems very rarely"). Pays $7.50-25.

COMMUNICATE, Box 600, Beaverlodge, Alberta, Canada T0H 0C0. Editor: K. Neill Foster. Monthly tabloid covering family and church activities for "a Christian (Protestant) and generally quite conservative readership; average age is about 45." Circ. 26,500. Pays on publication. Buys first-time rights. Previously published submissions OK. SAE and International Reply Coupons.

Nonfiction: News ("we're always open to short news items of international or Canadian interest"); inspirational/devotional articles, 1,500-2,000 words (on how to apply Biblical principles to daily living"); and news features/human interest (on unusual religious events, activities, personalities). No material with no Christian/moral/ethical significance or features on American politicians, entertainers, etc., who are Christians." Query or send complete ms. Length: 200-2,000 words. Pays $40 maximum.

Photos: Reviews 5x7 b&w prints.

Fiction: "Any fiction we would use would illustrate the application of Christian values, or perhaps the lack thereof, in the life of an individual."

Poetry: "We're looking for poetry that is inspirational, short, and understandable."

Tips: "We are very receptive to American writers. Your best bet is to write along lines of general interest to North Americans and to avoid making your 'Americanness' obvious."

THE COMPANION OF ST. FRANCIS AND ST. ANTHONY, Conventual Franciscan Friars, Box 535, Postal Station F, Toronto, Ontario, Canada M4Y 2L8. (416)924-6349. Editor-in-Chief: the Rev. Nicholas Weiss, OFM Conv. 75% freelance written. Emphasizes religious and human values. Monthly magazine; 32 pages. Circ. 10,000. Pays on acceptance. Buys all rights. Phone queries OK. Submit seasonal/holiday material 6 months in advance. SASE. Reports in 3 weeks. Free writer's guidelines.

Nonfiction: Historical; how-to (medical and psychological coping); informational; inspirational;

interview; nostalgia; profile; and travel. Buys 6 mss/issue. Send complete ms. Length: 1,200-1,500 words. Pays 5¢/word.

Photos: Photos purchased with accompanying ms. Captions required. Pays $7/5x7 (but all sizes accepted) b&w glossy print or color photo. Send prints. Total purchase price for ms includes payment for photos.

Fiction: Adventure; humorous; mainstream; and religious. Buys 1 ms/issue. Send complete ms. Length: 1,200-1,500 words. Pays 5¢/word.

Tips: "Mss on human interest with photos are given immediate preference." Backlog of poetry and short stories.

CONTACT, United Brethren Publishing, 302 Lake St., Box 650, Huntington IN 46750. (219)356-2312. Editor-in-Chief: Stanley Peters. Assistant Editor: Steve Dennie. Sunday School weekly; 4 pages. Circ. 6,000. For conservative evangelical Christians, ages 16 and up. Buys simultaneous, second serial (reprint) and first rights. Byline given. Pays on acceptance; 1¢/word for first rights, ¾¢ otherwise. Submit seasonal/holiday material 9 months in advance. Photocopied and previously published submissions OK. SASE. Reports in 4-8 weeks. Buys at least 2 mss/issue. Free sample copy and writer's guidelines.

Nonfiction: Historical; how-to; humor; informational; inspirational; personal experience. Must have religious slant. Length: 1,300 words maximum.

Fiction: All types, but religious slant necessary. Length: 1,300 words maximum.

Poetry: Buys "a few poems, preferably rhyming." Pays 7¢/line.

Fillers: Jokes; gags; puzzles; cartoons. Buys 2/issue. Pays 1¢/word; $2 for puzzles.

Photos: Bought normally accompanying manuscript. B&w glossy prints only. Pays $3/8x10 photo; $2, all others.

THE COVENANT COMPANION, 5101 N. Francisco Ave., Chicago IL 60625. (312)784-3000. Editor-in-Chief: James R. Hawkinson. 25% freelance written. Emphasizes Christian life and faith. Semimonthly (monthly issues July and August) magazine; 32 pages. Circ. 28,000. Pays on publication. Buys all rights. Submit seasonal/holiday material 3 months in advance. Simultaneous, photocopied and previously published submissions OK. SASE. Reports in 2 months. Sample copy $1.

Nonfiction: Humor; informational; inspirational (especially evangelical Christian); interviews (Christian leaders and personalities); and personal experience. Buys 20-30 mss/year. Length: 100-110 lines of typewritten material at 70 characters/line (double-spaced). Pays $15-35.

DAILY MEDITATION, Box 2710, San Antonio TX 78299. Editor: Ruth S. Paterson. Quarterly. Rights purchased vary. Byline given. Submit seasonal material six months in advance. Sample copy sent to writer on receipt of 50¢.

Nonfiction: Inspirational, self-improvement, nonsectarian religious articles, 500-1,900 words, showing path to greater spiritual growth; new Mayan archeological discoveries. Fillers, to 400 words. Pays 1-1½¢/word for articles.

Poetry: Inspirational. Length: 16 lines maximum. Pays 14¢/line.

DECISION MAGAZINE, 1300 Harmon Place, Minneapolis MN 55403. (612)338-0500. Editor: Roger C. Palms. Conservative evangelical monthly publication of the Billy Graham Evangelistic Association. Magazine; 16 pages. Circ. 3,000,000. Buys first rights on unsolicited manuscripts. Byline given. Pays on publication. Reports in 2 months. SASE.

Nonfiction: Uses some freelance material; best opportunity is in testimony area (1,800-2,200 words). Also uses short narratives, 400-800 words. "Our function is to present Christ as Savior and Lord to unbelievers and present articles on deeper Christian life and human interest articles on Christian growth for Christian readers. No tangents. Center on Christ in all material."

Poetry: Uses devotional thoughts and short poetry in Quiet Heart column. Positive, Christ-centered.

Tips: "The purpose of *Decision* is: 1) To set for the Good News of salvation with such vividness and clarity that the reader will feel drawn to make a commitment to Christ; 2)To strengthen the faith of believers and to offer them hope and encouragement; and 3)To report on the ministries of the Billy Graham Evangelical Association."

THE DISCIPLE, Box 179, St. Louis MO 63166. Editor: James L. Merrell. 30% freelance written. Published by Christian Board of Publication of the Christian Church (Disciples of Christ). For ministers and church members, both young and older adults. Semimonthly. Circ. 69,100. Buys all rights. Pays month after publication. Pays for photos at end of month of acceptance. Sample copy 35¢; free writer's guidelines. Photocopied and simultaneous submissions OK. Submit seasonal material at least 6 months in advance. Reports in 2 weeks to 3 months. SASE.

Nonfiction: Articles and meditations on religious themes; short pieces, some humorous. Length: 500-800 words. Pays $10-20.

Photos: B&w glossy prints, 8x10. Occasional b&w glossy prints, any size, used to illustrate articles. Pays $10-25. Pays $35/cover. No color.

Poetry: Uses 3-5 poems/issue. Traditional forms, blank verse, free verse and light verse. All lengths. Themes may be seasonal, historical, religious, occasionally humorous. Pays $3-10.

Tips: "We're looking for personality features about lay disciples, churches. Give good summary of story idea in query."

EMPHASIS ON FAITH & LIVING, 336 Dumfries Ave., Kitchener, Ontario, Canada N2H 2G1. Editor: Dr. Everek R. Storms. 25% freelance written. Official organ of the Missionary Church. For church members. Magazine is published twice a month in US but serves the Missionary Church in both the US and Canada. Circ. 12,000. Not copyrighted. Buys "only a few" mss/year. Photocopied and simultaneous submissions OK. Uses a limited amount of seasonal material, submitted 3 months in advance. Reports in 1 month. Submit only complete ms. SAE and 20¢ in coin for Canadian postage.

Nonfiction: Religious articles, presenting the truths of the Bible to appeal to today's readers. "We take the Bible literally and historically. It has no errors, myths or contradictions. Articles we publish must have this background. No poetry, please. Especially would like articles covering the workings of the Holy Spirit in today's world." Length: approximately 500 words—"not too long." Pays $5-10.

ENGAGE/SOCIAL ACTION, 100 Maryland Ave. NE, Washington DC 20002. (202)488-5632. Editor: Lee Ranck. 30% freelance written. For "United Methodist clergy and lay people interested in in-depth analysis of social issues, with emphasis on the church's role or involvement in these issues." Monthly. Circ. 6,000. Rights purchased vary with author and material. May buy all rights. Buys 50-60 mss/year (freelance and assigned). Pays on publication. Free sample copy and writer's guidelines. Photocopied submissions OK, but prefers original. Returns rejected material in 2-3 weeks. Reports on material accepted for publication in several weeks. Query or submit complete ms. "Query to show that writer has expertise on a particular social issue, give his credentials, and reflect a readable writing style." SASE.

Nonfiction and Photos: "This is the social action publication of the United Methodist Church published by the denomination's Board of Church and Society. We publish articles relating to current social issues as well as church-related discussions. We do not publish highly technical articles or poetry. Our publication tries to relate social issues to the church—what the church can do, is doing; why the church should be involved. We only accept articles relating to social issues, e.g., war, draft, peace, race relations, welfare, police/community relations, labor, population problems, drug and alcohol problems. Reviews of books should focus on related subjects." Length: 2,000 words maximum. Pays $75.

Tips: "Write on social issues, but not superficially; we're more interested in finding an expert (e.g., on human rights, alcohol problems, peace issues) who can write than a writer who attempts to research a complex issue."

EPIPHANY JOURNAL, Epiphany Press, Box 14727, San Francisco CA 94114. (415)431-1917. Editor: Gary Anderson. Quarterly magazine covering religious topics for the contemplative Christian. Estab. 1980. Circ. 3,000. Pays on publication. Byline given. Buys one-time rights and makes work-for-hire assignments. Submit seasonal/holiday material 6 months in advance. Simultaneous queries, and simultaneous and previously published submissions OK. SASE. Reports in 2 weeks on queries; 2 months on mss. Free sample copy and writer's guidelines.

Nonfiction: Book excerpts (from forthcoming or recently published spiritual or religious works); inspirational (examinations of aspects of the contemplative life, and of the Christian's role and responsibility in the modern world); interview/profile (interviews with current Christian figures; profiles of past and present figures in Christian life); and photo feature (series of artistic photos expressing a theme, e.g., "Transformation," "A Sense of the Divine," "The House of the Lord," and linked with poetry and prose). Buys 20-25 mss/year. Query or send complete ms. Length: 2,000-8,000 words. Pays 2¢/word $100 maximum.

Columns/Departments: Book reviews (any current literature of interest to the Christian thinker). Buys 8-10 mss/year. Query or send complete ms. Length: 1,000-2,500 words. Pays 2¢/word ($30 maximum).

Tips: "Ask for a sample copy and assignment suggestions."

THE EPISCOPALIAN, 1930 Chestnut St., Philadelphia PA 19103. (215)564-2010. Editor: Henry L. McCorkle. Managing Editor: Judy Mathe Foley. Monthly tabloid covering the Episcopal Church for Episcopalians. Circ. 285,000. Pays on publication. Byline given. Submit seasonal/

holiday material 2 months in advance. Previously published submissions. OK. SASE. Reports in 1 month. Sample copy for SAE and 2 first class stamps.

Nonfiction: Inspirational; and interview/profile (of Episcopalians participating in church or community activities). "I like action stories about people doing things and solving problems." No personal experience articles. Buys 24 mss/year. Send complete ms. Length: 1,000-1,500 words. Pays $25-200.

Photos: Pays $10 for b&w glossy prints. Identification of subjects required. Buys one-time rights.

Fillers: Newsbreaks. Buys 30/year. Length: 1,000 words minimum. Pays $25.

THE EVANGELICAL BEACON, 1515 E. 66th St., Minneapolis MN 55423. (612)866-3343. Editor: George Keck. 30% freelance written. For Evangelical and conservative Protestant audience. Demoninational magazine of the Evangelican Free Church of America. Issued twice monthly. Rights purchased vary with author and material. Buys first rights, second serial (reprint) rights, or all rights. Byline given "except when the author requests not to be mentioned or if we feel it best to remain anonymous." Pays on publication. Free sample copy. Reports on submissions in 6-8 weeks. SASE must be included.

Nonfiction and Photos: Devotional material; articles on the church, people and their accomplishments. "Crisp, imaginative, original writing desired—not sermons put on paper." Length: 250-1,800 words. Pays 2¢/word. Prefers 8x10 photos. Pays $6 minimum.

Fiction and Poetry: "Not much fiction used, but will consider if in keeping with aims and needs of magazine." Length: 100-1,500 words. Pays 2¢/word. "In poetry, content is more important than form." Length: open. Pays $2.50 minimum.

Tips: "We receive too much 'off the top of the head' devotional material. We need evidence of real research, thought and study. Articles on current issues of interest to Christians must evidence research, thought, Evangelical perspective."

EVANGELIZING TODAY'S CHILD, 3118 Hiawatha Dr., Loveland CO 80537. (303)669-4810. Production Manager: Kent Rickard. No unsolicited articles being used at this time.

Photos: Submissions of photos on speculation accepted. Need photos of children or related subjects. Please include SASE. Pays $10-25 for 8x10 b&w glossy prints; $50-150 for color transparencies.

FAITH AND INSPIRATION, Seraphim Publishing Group, Inc., 720 White Plains Rd., Scarsdale NY 10583. (914)472-5500. Editor: D.M. Sheehan. 50% freelance written. Emphasizes religious and secular inspirational material for a family readership. Bimonthly magazine. Circ. 75,000. Pays on publication. Buys all rights with exceptions. Byline given. Submit seasonal/holiday material 4 months in advance of issue date. Photocopied submissions OK. SASE. Reports in 2 months. Sample copy and writer's guidelines $1.50.

Nonfiction: Inspirational; interview; personal experience (moving articles of inspiration, does not have to be religious); and profile. Buys 20 mss/issue. Submit complete ms. Length: 50-1,200 words. Pays 5¢ a word.

Poems: Light verse and traditional. Buys 3 poems/issue. Limit submissions to batches of 3. Length: 5-20 lines. Pays $5-15.

Fillers: Short humor, religious, anecdotes and inspirational material. Buys 10/issue. Length: 25-100 words. Pays $5-15.

FAMILY LIFE TODAY MAGAZINE, 2300 Knoll Dr., Ventura CA 93003. (805)644-9721. Editor: Phyllis Alsdurf. 70% freelance written. Emphasizes "building strong marriages and helping families develop a Christian lifestyle." Monthly magazine with July/August combined issue; 48 pages. Circ. 50,000. Pays on acceptance. Byline given. Submit seasonal/holiday material 5 months in advance of issue date. Simultaneous and previously published submissions OK, "but we're accepting few reprints these days." SASE. Reports in 2 months. Send 9x12 SASE for free sample copy and writer's guidelines; mention *Writer's Market* in request.

Nonfiction: How-to (any family-related situation with narrow focus: how to help the hyperactive child, etc.); humor (if wholesome and family related); interview (with person who is recognized authority in area of marriage and family life); personal experience ("when my husband lost his job," etc.); and photo feature (family-related). Buys 6 mss/issue. Query. Length: 300-1,500 words. Pays 4-5¢/word for original; 3¢/word for reprints.

Photos: State availability of photos with query. Pays $15-30 for 8x10 b&w glossy print; $35-85 for 35mm color transparencies. Buys one-time rights. Model release preferred.

Tips: "Don't send ms that offer 'pat' answers ('and they lived happily ever after') to complex family problems. Articles that show the struggle a family or couple has experienced in a realistic manner are what we look for. All mss are carefully read so no gimmicks are needed to get our attention, except a clear writing style and a timely topic. We need more articles by fathers and husbands on parenting and marriage."

FRIDAY (OF THE JEWISH EXPONENT), 226 S. 16th St., Philadelphia PA 19102. (215)893-5745. Editor: Jane Biberman. 95% freelance written. For the Jewish community of Greater Philadelphia. Monthly literary supplement. Circ. 100,000. Buys first rights. Pays 25% kill fee. Byline given. Buys 70 mss/year. Pays after publication. Free sample copy and writer's guidelines. Photocopied submissions OK. No simultaneous submissions. Submit special material 3 months in advance. Reports in 3 weeks. SASE.

Nonfiction and Photos: "We are interested only in articles on Jewish themes, whether they be historical, thought pieces, Jewish travel or photographic essays. Topical themes are appreciated. No Holocaust material." Length: 6-20 double-spaced pages. Pays $30 minimum.

Fiction: Short stories on Jewish themes. Length: 6-20 double-spaced pages. Pays $30 minimum.

Poetry: Traditional forms, blank verse, free verse, avant-garde forms, light verse; must relate to a Jewish theme. Length varies. Pays $10 minimum.

Tips: "Pieces on Jewish personalities—artists, musicians, authors—are most welcome." Include illustrative material.

GOOD NEWS, The Forum for Scriptural Christianity, Inc., 308 E. Main St., Wilmore KY 40390. (606)858-4661. Editor: James V. Heidinger II. Managing Editor: Ann L. Coker. For United Methodist lay people and pastors, primarily middle income; conservative and Biblical religious beliefs; broad range of political, social and cultural values. "We are the only evangelical magazine with the purpose of working within the United Methodist Church for Biblical reform and evangelical renewal." Bimonthly magazine; 88 pages. Circ. 15,000. Pays on acceptance. Byline given. Phone queries OK. Submit seasonal/holiday material 6 months in advance. Simultaneous, photocopied and previously published submissions OK. SASE. Reports in 2 months. Sample copy $1; free writer's guidelines.

Nonfiction: Historical (prominent people or churches from the Methodist/Evangelical United Brethren tradition); how-to (build faith, work in local church); humor (good taste); inspirational (related to Christian faith); personal experience (case histories of God at work in individual lives); and any contemporary issues as they relate to the Christian faith and the United Methodist Church. No sermons. Buys 36 mss/year. Query with a "brief description of the article, perhaps a skeleton outline. Show some enthusiasm about the article and writing (and research). Tell us something about yourself (though not a list of credentials); whether you or the article has United Methodist tie-in." Pays $10-50.

Photos: Photos purchased with accompanying ms or on assignment. Captions required. Uses fine screen b&w glossy prints. Total purchase price for ms includes payment for photos. Payment negotiable.

Columns/Departments: Good News Book Forum. Query.

Fillers: Clippings, jokes, gags, anecdotes, newsbreaks and short humor. Buys 20 fillers/year. Pays $5-10.

GOOD NEWS BROADCASTER, Box 82808, Lincoln NE 68501. (402)474-4567. Editor: Theodore H. Epp. Interdenominational magazine for adults from 17 years of age and up. Monthly. Circ. 190,000. Buys first rights. Buys approximately 125 mss/year. Pays on acceptance. Free sample copy and writer's guidelines. Send all mss to Thomas S. Piper, managing editor. Submit seasonal material at least 6 months in advance. Reports in 5 weeks. Query preferred, but not required. SASE.

Nonfiction and Photos: Articles which will help the reader learn and apply Christian Biblical principles to his life. From the writer's or the subject's own experience. "Especially looking for true, personal experience 'salvation,' church, missions, 'youth' (17 years and over), 'parents,' and 'how to live the Christian life' articles." Nothing dogmatic, or preachy, or sugary sweet, or without Biblical basis. Details or statistics should be authentic and verifiable. Style should be conservative but concise. Prefers that Scripture references be from the *New American Standard Version* or the *Authorized Version* or the *New Scofield Reference Bible*. Length: 1,500 words maximum. Pays 4-10¢/word; "more when you can get us to assign an article to you." Photos sometimes purchased with mss. Pays $15 for b&w glossies; $35-50 for color transparencies.

Tips: "The basic purpose of the magazine is to explain the Bible and how it is relevant to life because we believe this will accomplish one of two things—to present Christ as Saviour to the lost or to promote the spiritual growth of believers, so don't ignore our primary purposes when writing for us. Nonfiction should be Biblical and timely; at the least Biblical in principle. Use illustrations of your own experiences or of someone else's when God solved a problem similar to the reader's. Be so specific that the meanings and significance will be crystal clear to all readers."

GOSPEL CARRIER, Messenger Publishing House, Box 850, Joplin MO 64801. (417)624-7050. Editor-in-Chief: Roy M. Chappell, D.D. Denominational Sunday School take-home paper for adults, ages 20 through retirement. Quarterly publication in weekly parts; 104 pages. Circ. 3,500.

Pays quarterly. Buys simultaneous, second serial and one-time rights. Byline given. Submit seasonal/holiday material 1 year in advance. Simultaneous, photocopied and previously published submissions OK. SASE. Reports in 3 months. Sample copy 50¢; free writer's guidelines.
Nonfiction: Historical (related to great events in the history of the church); informational (may explain the meaning of a Bible passage or a Christian concept); inspirational (must make a Christian point); nostalgia (religious significance); and personal experience (Christian concept). No puzzles, poems, filler material. Buys 50-80 mss/year. Pays 1¢/word.
Photos: Purchased with accompanying ms. Send prints. Pays $2 for b&w glossy prints.
Fiction: Adventure; historical; romance; and religious. Must have Christian significance. Buys 13-20 mss/issue. Submit complete ms. Length: 800-2,000 words. Pays ½¢/word.
Fillers: Short inspirational incidents from personal experience or the lives of great Christians. Buys 52-80/year. Length: 200-500 words. Pays 6¢/word.

GUIDEPOSTS MAGAZINE, 747 3rd Ave., New York NY 10017. Editorial Director: Arthur Gordon. 40-50% freelance written. "*Guideposts* is an inspirational monthly magazine for all faiths in which men and women from all walks of life tell how they overcame obstacles, rose above failures, met sorrow, learned to master themselves, and became more effective people through the direct application of the religious principles by which they live." Buys all rights. Pays 25% kill fee for assigned articles. Byline given "most of our stories are first-person ghosted articles, so the author would not get a byline unless it was his/her story." SASE.
Nonfiction and Fillers: Articles and features should be written in simple, anecdotal style with an emphasis on human interest. Short mss of approximately 250-750 words ($25-100) would be considered for such features as "Quiet People" and general one-page stories. Full-length mss, 750-1,500 words ($200-300). All mss should be typed, double-spaced and accompanied by a stamped, self-addressed envelope. Annually awards scholarships to high school juniors and seniors in writing contest.
Tips: "The freelancer would have the best chance of breaking in by aiming for a 1-page or maybe 2-page article. That would be very short, say 2½ pages of typescript, but in a small magazine such things are very welcome. A sensitively written anecdote that could provide us with an additional title is extremely useful. And they are much easier to just sit down and write than to have to go through the process of preparing a query. They should be warm, well-written, intelligent and upbeat. We like personal narratives that are true and have some universal relevance, but the religious element does not have to be hammered home with a sledge hammer." Address short items to Van Varner.

HIGH ADVENTURE, 1445 Boonville Ave., Springfield MO 65802. (417)862-2781, ext. 1497. Editor: Johnnie Barnes. For boys and men. Quarterly; 16 pages. Circ. 53,000. Rights purchased vary with author and material. Buys 10-12 mss/year. Pays on acceptance. Free sample copy and writer's guidelines. Query or submit complete ms. SASE.
Nonfiction, Fiction, Photos and Fillers: Camping articles, nature stories, fiction adventure stories and jokes. Nature study and campcraft articles about 500-600 words. Buys how-to, personal experience, inspirational, humor and historical articles. Length: 1,200 words. Pays 2¢/word. Photos purchased on assignment. Adventure and western fiction wanted. Puzzles, jokes and short humor used as fillers.

INSIGHT, The Young Calvinist Federation, Box 7244, Grand Rapids MI 49510. (616)241-5616. Editor: John Knight. Assistant Editor: Martha Kalk. For young people, 16-21, Christian backgrounds and well-exposed to the Christian faith. Monthly (except June and August) magazine; 32 pages. Circ. 23,000. Pays on publication. Buys simultaneous, second serial (reprint) and first North American serial rights. Byline given. Phone queries OK. Submit seasonal/holiday material 6 months in advance. Simultaneous, photocopied and previously published submissions OK. SASE. Report in 4 weeks. Sample copy and writer's guidelines for 9x12 SASE.
Photos: Photos purchased without accompanying ms or on assignment. Pays $15-25/8x10 b&w glossy print; $50-200 for 35mm or larger color transparencies. Total purchase price for ms includes payment for photos.
Fiction: Humorous, mainstream and religious. "Looks for short stories that lead our readers to a better understanding of how their Christian beliefs apply to their daily living. They must do more than entertain—they must make the reader see things in a new light." Buys 1-2 mss/issue. Send complete ms. Length: 1,000-3,000 words. Pays $45-100.
Poetry: Free verse; light verse, and traditional. Buys 10 poems/year. Length: 4-25 lines. Pays $20-25.
Fillers: Youth-oriented cartoons, jokes, gags, anecdotes, puzzles and short humor. Length: 50-300 words. Pays $10-35.

INTERLIT, David C. Cook Foundation, Cook Square, Elgin IL 60120. (312)741-2400, ext. 322. Editor-in-Chief: Gladys J. Peterson. 90% freelance on assignment. "Please study publication and query before submitting mss." Emphasizes Christian communications and journalism especially for editors, publishers, and writers in the Third World (developing countries). Also goes to missionaries, broadcasters, and educational personnel in the U.S. Quarterly newsletters; 24 pages. Circ. 9,000. Pays on acceptance. Buys all rights. Photocopied submissions OK. SASE. Reports in 2 weeks. Free sample copy.
Nonfiction: Technical and how-to articles about communications, media, and literacy. Also photo features. Buys 7 mss/issue. Length: 500-1,500 words. Pays 4¢/word.
Photos: Purchased with accompanying ms only. Captions required. Query or send prints. Uses b&w.

LIBERTY, A Magazine of Religious Freedom, 6840 Eastern Ave. NW, Washington DC 20012. (202)723-0800, ext. 745. Editor: Roland R. Hegstad. For "responsible citizens interested in community affairs and religious freedom." Bimonthly. Circ. 500,000. Buys first rights. Buys approximately 40 mss/year. Pays on acceptance. Sample copy $1. Writer's guidelines for SASE. Photocopied submissions OK. Submit seasonal material in our field 6-8 months in advance. Reports in 1-3 weeks. Query not essential, but helpful. SASE.
Nonfiction: "Articles of national and international interest in field of religious liberty and church-state relations. Current events affecting above areas (Sunday law problems, parochial aid problems, religious discrimination by state, etc.). Current events are most important; base articles on current events rather than essay form." Buys how-to's, personal experience and think pieces, interviews, profiles in field of religious liberty. Length: maximum 2,500 words. Pays up to $150.
Photos: "To accompany or illustrate articles." Purchased with mss; with captions only. B&w glossy prints, color transparencies. Pays $15-35. Cover photos to $150.

LIGHT AND LIFE, Free Methodist Publishing House, 999 College Ave., Winona Lake IN 46590. Editor: G. Roger Schoenhals. 35% freelance written. Emphasizes evangelical Christianity with Wesleyan slant for a cross-section of adults. Published monthly. Magazine; 36 pages. Circ. 60,000. Pays on publication. Prefers first rights. Byline given. Submit seasonal/holiday material 6 months in advance. Previously published submissions OK. SASE. Reports in 6 weeks. Sample copy $1; writer's guidelines for SASE.
Nonfiction: "Each issue uses a lead article (warm, positive first-person account of God's help in a time of crisis; 1,500 words); a Christian living article (a fresh, lively, upbeat piece about practical Christian living; 750 words); a Christian growth article (an in-depth, lay-level article on a theme relevant to the maturing Christian; 1,500 words); a discipleship article (a practical how-to piece on some facet of Christian discipleship; 750 words)." Buys 75 mss/year. Submit complete ms. Pays 3¢/word.
Photos: Purchased without accompanying ms. Send prints. Pays $7.50-20 for b&w photos. Offers additional payment for photos accepted with accompanying ms.

LIGUORIAN, Liguori MO 63057. Editor: the Rev. Norman Muckerman. 50% freelance written. For families with Catholic religious convictions. Monthly. Circ. 560,000. Byline given "except on short fillers and jokes." Buys 60 mss/year. Pays on acceptance. Submit seasonal material 5-6 months in advance. Reports in 6-8 weeks. SASE.
Nonfiction and Photos: "Pastoral, practical and personal approach to the problems and challenges of people today. No travelogue approach or unresearched ventures into controversial areas." Length: 400-2,000 words. Pays 7-10¢/word. Photos purchased with mss; b&w glossy prints.

LILLENAS PROGRAM BUILDERS, Lillenas Publishing Company, Box 527, Kansas City MO 64141. Editor: Evelyn Stenbock. Booklets covering program ideas for the Sunday School and church. "We look for unique program ideas for use in Sunday Schools and churches, large and small, with an evangelical slant." Bookstore circulation. Pays on acceptance. Byline given. Buys all rights. Submit seasonal/holiday material 12 months in advance. "Only original material, no previously published submissions." SASE. Reports in 1 month. Free writer's guidelines for SAE and 15¢ postage.
Nonfiction: "Some inspirational and devotional articles suitable for readings. Skits, devotional messages, emcee ideas, banquet plans, church-related humor. Christmas is overworked; Thanksgiving is wide open. Any program you might present in your own church would have a chance in this market." No "secular subjects, such as Santa Claus, ecology, etc." Send complete ms. Payment depends on length and quality.
Poetry: "Recitations; poems suitable for reading aloud before an audience. Sacred poetry, only." Pays 25¢/line.
Fillers: "Church-related items which might be used on a program, such as a banquet emcee might

use." Jokes, anecdotes, short humor, and newsbreaks (missions, etc.).

Tips: "This is a good market for beginning Christian writers. We answer rejections personally, and offer suggestions for better luck next time. Since our program booklets are tied in with a major publisher of sacred music, we buy all rights. Dozens of manuscripts are waiting for a spot, so beginners specifying rights, or copyrighting their material have less of a chance. I'm appalled at how many writers neglect SASE! We still return their manuscripts and reply to their letters, but don't look kindly on such writers, if done regularly. I personally prefer to see the manuscript. Writing a fantastic query is okay, but few can cough up a good finished product. A covering letter can be disastrous, too. The worst thing to give me is a list of meaningless credentials."

LIVING FAITH, 276 W. Cherry Ln., Souderton PA 18964. Acting Editor: Barbara Weller. Magazine published by the United Church People for Bibilical Witness (a United Church of Christ affiliate). "Our magazine is aimed at opening a new avenue for the communication and exchange of viewpoints, and at reaching the widest possible audience with resources for church renewal and growth." Estab. 1980. Pays on acceptance. Buys first rights. SASE. Reports "immediately" on rejections; 6 months on acceptance.

Nonfiction: Biblical, theological, inspirational, UCC news and views. "While *Living Faith* remains centered in the theological vision of the UCC Constitution, which confesses Jesus Christ, Son of God and Savior, as sole head of the church, it is open to various theological and social views." Length: 2,000 words maximum. Pays 6¢/word.

Photos: "Good quality 5x7 b&w photos accompanying mss are encouraged when pertinent. However, we cannot offer extra payment for photos at the present time."

Poetry: Biblical, theological and inspirational.

LIVING MESSAGE, Box 820, Petrolia, Ontario, N0N 1R0, Canada. Editor: Rita Baker. For "active, concerned Christians, mainly Canadian Anglican." Publication of the Anglican Church of Canada. Monthly except July and August. Circ. 14,000. Not copyrighted. Byline given. Pays on publication. Free sample copy. Photocopied submissions OK. Submit seasonal material 5 months in advance. Reports on material in 4 weeks. Submit complete ms. SAE and International Reply Coupons or Canadian stamps.

Fiction, Nonfiction and Photos: "Short stories and articles which give readers an insight into other lives, promote understanding and stimulate action in areas such as community life, concerns of elderly, handicapped, youth, work with children, Christian education, poverty, the Third World, etc. No sentimentality or moralizing. Readers relate to a warm, personal approach; uncluttered writing. 'Reports' or involved explanatory articles are not wanted. The lead-in must capture the reader's imagination. A feeling of love and optimism is important." Length: 2,000 words maximum. Pays $10-25. 8x10 b&w prints (with article). Pays $5. Fiction length: 1,000-1,500 words. Pays $15-25.

LIVING WITH TEENAGERS, Baptist Sunday School Board, 127 9th Ave., Nashville TN 37234. (615)251-2273. Editor: E. Lee Sizemore. Quarterly magazine about teenagers for the Baptist parents of teenagers. Circ. 35,000. Pays 1 month after acceptance. Buys all rights. Phone queries OK. Submit seasonal material 1 year in advance. Previously published submissions OK for a non-competing market. Reports in 1 month. Free sample copy and writer's guidelines.

Nonfiction: "We are looking for a unique Christian element. We want a genuine insight into the teen-parent relationships." General interest (on communication; emotional problems; growing up; drugs and alcohol; leisure; sex education; spiritual growth; working teens and parents; money; family relationships; and church relationships); inspirational; interview; opinion; profile; travel; personal experience. Buys 8-10 mss/issue. Query with clips of previously published work. Length: 600-2,400 words. Pays 3¢/published word.

Photos: Pays $15 minimum/5x7 b&w glossy print. Reviews b&w contact sheets and 2¼x2¼ and 35mm color transparencies. "We need cover transparencies of parents with youth." Captions preferred; model release required.

Fiction: Humorous and religious. "No stories from the teen's point of view." Buys 2 mss/issue. Query with clips of previously published work. Length: 600-2,400 words. Pays 3½¢/published word.

Poetry: Free verse, light verse, traditional and devotional and inspirational. Buys 3 mss/issue. Submit 5 poems maximum. Length: 33 characters maximum. Pays $1.50 plus 85¢/line for 1-7 lines; $4.30 plus 50¢/line for 8 lines minimum.

Tips: "Write in the first person. Make liberal use of illustrations and case studies. Write from the parent's point-of-view."

LOGOS JOURNAL, Logos International Fellowship, Inc., 201 Church St., Plainfield NJ 07060. (201)754-0745. Managing Editor: Harold Hostetler. For a readership interested in charismatic renewal. Bimonthly magazine; 80 pages. Circ. 50,000. Pays on publication; on acceptance if assigned. Buys all rights. Submit seasonal/holiday material 3 months in advance of issue date. Photocopied submissions OK. SASE. Reports in 6 weeks. Sample copy $1.50; free writer's guidelines.

Nonfiction: "The *Logos Journal* is an interdenominational magazine which seeks to communicate the renewal, through the Holy Spirit, of individuals and the church. Our emphasis is on teaching, inspiration, and reconciliation in the body of Christ. Some of our standing feature sections are: Saints, Church, Family, Health and Spirit. All of these will be brief profiles of people, laymen and clergy, famous or obscure, anyone with an inspiring ministry to share with others in Christ. In addition we have a feature called Interview, which highlights well-known personalities sharing details, in dialogue format, of how they live, think and relate the Holy Spirit to their everyday lives." Buys 20-25 mss/year. Length: 800-2,000 words. Pays $75-200.

Photos: Must accompany ms. Pays $15-25 for 2¼x2¼ color transparencies or 5x7 b&w glossy prints.

Columns/Departments: "Desire first-hand reports of charismatic-oriented events/people plus news of spiritual significance." Also Essay column (informed person addressing subject significant to a sizable element in the church). Buys 1/issue. Query. Length: 800-1,000 words.

THE LOOKOUT, 8121 Hamilton Ave., Cincinnati OH 45231. (513)931-4050. Editor: Mark A. Taylor. 50% freelance written. "We are one of the most widely circulated *weekly* religious magazines in the world. (Many others are printed in weekly parts and mailed quarterly. We are mailed weekly.)" For the adult and young adult of the Sunday morning Bible school. Weekly. Pays on acceptance. Byline given. Simultaneous submissions OK. SASE. Reports in 6 weeks. Sample copy and writer's guidelines 50¢.

Nonfiction: "Seeks stories about real people or Sunday-School classes; items that shed Biblical light on matters of contemporary controversy; and items that motivate, that lead the reader to ask, 'Why shouldn't I try that?' or 'Why couldn't our Sunday-School class accomplish this?' Should tell how real people are involved for Christ. In choosing topics, *The Lookout* considers timeliness, the church and national calendar, and the ability of the material to fit the above guidelines. Tell us about ideas that are working in your Sunday School and in the lives of its members. Remember to aim at laymen." Submit complete ms. Length: 1,200-1,800 words. Pays 2-3¢/word, occasionally higher.

Fiction: "A short story is printed in most issues; it is usually between 1,200-1,800 words long, and should be as true to life as possible while remaining inspirational and helpful. Use familiar settings and situations."

Fillers: Inspirational or humorous shorts. "About 400-800 words is a good length for these. Relate an incident that illustrates a point without preaching. Pays 2-4¢/word.

Photos: B&w prints, 4x6 or larger. Pays $5-25. Pays $50-125 for color transparencies for covers. Needs photos of people, especially adults in a variety of settings.

THE LUTHERAN, 2900 Queen Lane, Philadelphia PA 19129. (215)438-6580. Editor: Edgar R. Trexler. General interest magazine of the Lutheran Church in America. Twice monthly, except single issues in July and August. Buys first rights. Pays on acceptance. Free sample copy and writer's guidelines. SASE.

Nonfiction: Popularly written material about human concerns with reference to the Christian faith. "We are especially interested in articles in 4 main fields: Christian ideology; personal religious life, social responsibilities; Church at work; human interest stories about people in whom considerable numbers of other people are likely to be interested." Write "primarily to convey information rather than opinions. Every article should be based on a reasonable amount of research or should explore some source of information not readily available. Most readers are grateful for simplicity of style. Sentences should be straightforward, with a minimum of dependent clauses and prepositional phrases." Length: 500-2,000 words. Pays $75-200.

Photos: Buys pix submitted with mss. Good 8x10 glossy prints. Pays $15-25. Also color for cover use. Pays up to $150.

Tips: "We need informative, detailed query letters. We also accept manuscripts on speculation only and we prefer not to encourage an abundance of query letters."

LUTHERAN FORUM, 308 W. 46th St., New York NY 10036. (212)757-1292. Editor: Glenn C. Stone. 70% freelance written. For church leadership, clerical and lay. Magazine; 40 pages. Quarterly. Circ. 5,400. Rights purchased vary with author and material. Buys all rights, first North American serial rights, first serial rights, second serial (reprint) rights, simultaneous rights. Byline given. Buys 12-15 mss/year. Pays on publication. Sample copy $1. Will consider photocopied and simultaneous submissions. Reports in 4-6 weeks. Query or submit complete ms. SASE.

Nonfiction: Articles about important issues and developments in the church's institutional life and in its cultural/social setting. Payment varies; $20 minimum. Length: 1,000-3,000 words. Informational, how-to, interview, profile, think articles and exposé. Length: 500-3,000 words. Pays $20-50.

Photos: Purchased with mss or with captions only. Prefers 8x10 prints. Uses more vertical than horizontal format. Pays $10 minimum.

THE LUTHERAN JOURNAL, 7317 Cahill Rd., Edina MN 55435. Editor: The Rev. Armin U. Deye. Family magazine for Lutheran church members, middle age and older. Quarterly magazine; 32 pages. Circ. 115,000. Copyrighted. Byline given. Buys 12-15 mss/year. Pays on publication. Free sample copy. Submit Christmas, Easter, other holiday material 4 months in advance. Will consider photocopied and simultaneous submissions. Reports in 8 weeks. Submit complete ms. SASE.

Nonfiction and Photos: Inspirational, religious, human interest, and historical articles. Interesting or unusual church projects. Informational, how-to, personal experience, interview, humor, think articles. Length: 1,500 words maximum; occasionally 2,000 words. Pays 1-1½¢/word. B&w and color photos purchased with accompanying ms. Captions required. Payment varies.

Fiction and Poetry: Mainstream, religious and historical fiction. Must be suitable for church distribution. Length: 2,000 words maximum. Pays 1-1½¢/word. Traditional poetry, blank verse, free verse, related to subject matter.

THE LUTHERAN STANDARD, 426 S. 5th St., Box 1209, Minneapolis MN 55440. (612)330-3300. Editor: The Rev. Lowell G. Almen. 50% freelance written. "We are assigning more projects to specific writers in our editorial planning." For families in congregations of the American Lutheran Church. Semimonthly. Circ. 602,000. Buys first rights or multiple rights. Byline given. Buys 30-50 mss/year. Pays on acceptance. Free sample copy. Reports in 3 weeks. SASE.

Nonfiction and Photos: Inspirational articles, especially about members of the American Lutheran Church who are practicing their faith in noteworthy ways, or congregations with unusual programs. "Should be written in language clearly understandable to persons with a mid-high school reading ability." Also publishes articles that discuss current social issues and problems (crime, family life, divorce, etc.) in terms of Christian involvement and solutions. Length: limit 1,200 words. Pays 5¢/word.

Poetry: Uses very little poetry. The shorter the better. 20 lines. Pays $10/poem.

Tips: "We are interested in personal experience pieces with strong first-person approach. The ms may be on a religious and social issue, but with evident human interest using personal anecdotes and illustrations. How has an individual faced a serious problem and overcome it? How has faith made a difference in a person's life? We prefer letters that clearly describe the proposed project. Excerpts from the project or other samples of the author's work are helpful in determining whether we are intrested in dealing with an author. We would appreciate it if more freelance writers seemed to have a sense of who our readers are and an awareness of the kinds of manuscripts we in fact publish."

LUTHERAN WOMEN, 2900 Queen Lane, Philadelphia PA 19129. Editor: Terry Schutz. 40% freelance written. 10 times yearly. Circ. 40,000. Decides acceptance within 2 months. Prefers to see mss 6 months ahead of issue, at beginning of planning stage. Can consider up to 3 months before publication. SASE.

Nonfiction: Anything of interest to mothers—young or old—professional or other working women related to the contemporary expression of Christian faith in daily life, community action, international concerns. Family publication standards. No recipes or housekeeping hints. Length: 1,500-2,000 words. Some shorter pieces accepted. Pays up to $50 for full-length ms and photos.

Photos: Purchased with or without mss. Women; family situations; religious art objects; overseas situations related to church. Should be clear, sharp b&w. No additional payment for those used with mss. Pays $25-40 for those purchased without mss.

Fiction: Should show deepening of insight; story expressing new understanding in faith; story of human courage, self-giving, building up of community. Length: 2,000 words. Pays $30-40.

Poetry: Very little is used. "Biggest taboo for us is sentimentality. We are limited to family magazine type contributions regarding range of vocabulary, but we don't want almanac-type poetry." No limit on number of lines. Pays $10 minimum/poem.

MARIAN HELPERS BULLETIN, Eden Hill, Stockbridge MA 01262. (413)298-3691. Editor: the Rev. Walter F. Pelczynski, MIC. 90% freelance written. For average Catholics of varying ages with moderate religious views and general education. Quarterly. Circ. 625,000. Not copyrighted. Byline given. Buys 18-24 mss/year. Pays on acceptance. Free sample copy. Reports in 4-8 weeks. Submit seasonal material 6 months in advance. SASE.

Nonfiction and Photos: "Subject matter is of general interest on devotional, spiritual, moral and social topics. Use a positive, practical and optimistic approach, without being sophisticated. We would like to see articles on the Blessed Virgin Mary." Buys informational and inspirational articles. Length: 300-900 words. Pays $25-35. Photos are purchased with or without mss; captions optional. Pays $5-10 for b&w glossy prints.

MARRIAGE & FAMILY LIVING, St. Meinrad IN 47577. (812)357-8011. Editor: Ila M. Stabile. 75% freelance written. Monthly magazine. Circ. 60,000. Pays on acceptance. Buys first North American serial rights, first book reprint option and control of other reprint rights. Byline given. Query. SASE. Reports in 3-4 weeks. Sample copy 50¢.
Nonfiction: Uses 1) Articles aimed at enriching the husband-wife and parent-child relationship by expanding religious and psychological insights or sensitivity. (Note: Ecumenically Judeo-Christian but in conformity with Roman Catholicism.) Length: 1,000-2,000 words. 2) Informative articles aimed at helping the couple cope, in practical ways, with the problems of modern living. Length: 2,000 words maximum. 3) Personal essays relating amusing and/or heart-warming incidents that point up the human side of marriage and family life. Length: 1,500 words maximum. Pays 7¢/word.
Photos: Mark Laurenson, art director. B&w glossy prints (5x7 or larger) and color transparencies or 35mm slides (vertical preferred). Pays $150/4-color cover photo; $50/b&w cover photo; $35/2-page spread in contents, $30 for 1 page in contents; $10 minimum. Photos of couples, families and individuals especially desirable. Model releases required.
Tips: "Query with a brief outline of article's contents and the opening couple of paragraphs. Make sure the subject matter is pertinent to our guidelines. Stay within the word limit. We prefer material to be backed up by the *facts*."

MARYKNOLL MAGAZINE, Maryknoll NY 10545. Editor: Moises Sandoval. Managing Editor: Frank Maurovich. 15% freelance written. Foreign missionary society magazine. Monthly. Pays on acceptance. Byline given. Query before sending any material. Reports in several weeks. SASE. Free sample copy.
Nonfiction: Articles and pictures concerning foreign missions. Articles developing themes such as world hunger, environmental needs, economic and political concerns. Length: 800-1,500 words. Send an outline before submitting material. Pays $50-150.
Photos: "We are a picture/text magazine. All articles must either be accompanied by top-quality photos, or be easily illustrated with photos." Pays $15-25 for b&w; $25-50 for color. Payment is dependent on quality and relevance.

MATURE CATHOLIC, 1100 W. Wells, Milwaukee WI 53233. (414)271-8926. Editor: Carol Johnston. Emphasizes involvement in all aspects of living—cultural, political, emotional, religious, etc.—for the mature reader. Quarterly magazine; 24 pages. Circ. 6,000. Pays on publication. Byline given. Submit seasonal/holiday material 3 months in advance. SASE. Reports in 6 weeks. Sample copy sent.
Nonfiction: Historical, how-to, humor, personal experience, technical and travel (only exceptional nostalgia). Buys 12 mss/year. Length: 2,000 words maximum. Pays 1¢/word.
Tips: "Our readers are retired Catholics. Our philosophy is that age is a natural part of living. We frown on labels like 'senior citizens.' We encourage participation in life and mental and spiritual growth."

MEDIA SPOTLIGHT, 1102 E. Chestnut Ave., Dept. SW-2, Santa Ana CA 92701. (714)547-3740. Editor and Publisher: Albert James Dager. Address all correspondence to Assistant Editor: Steve Wergeland. Quarterly magazine covering the media from a scriptural viewpoint for Christians concerned about the media's effect on people. Circ. 8,000. Pays on publication. Byline given. Buys one-time rights. Submit seasonal material 4 months in advance. Simultaneous, photocopied, and previously published submissions OK. SASE. Reports in 3 months. Sample copy $1. Writer's guidelines for loose 1st-class stamp.
Nonfiction: "We are a ministry to the body of Christ examining and reviewing media and entertainment from a scriptural perspective." Review of anything in TV; films; books; music; news; periodicals; advertising (including billboards and bumper stickers); entertainment; recreation; and popular games. Interview and profile (Christians' impact on media—before and after conversion). Buys 2-4 mss/issue. Query. Length: 200-2,000 words. Pays negotiable fee.
Photos: State availability of photos. Pays negotiable fee for 5x7 b&w glossy prints. Buys one-time rights.
Poetry: Free verse, haiku, light verse and traditional. "Must have a scriptural/media tie-in; or be about disciplined Christian living. Content is more important than form." Buys 3 mss/year. Length: open. Pays $2.50 minimum.

Fillers: Anecdotes; short humor ("if the point is good") and newsbreaks. Must be media-related. Buys 1-3 mss/issue. Length: open. Pays negotiable fee.

Tips: "Freelancers can best break in by first studying our magazine, then matching our approach with 100-1,000 words. Articles must have a strong scriptural/media tie-in. That applies to poetry as well. Describe what a scriptural response to media productions should be. Please, no sentimental poetry."

MENNONITE BRETHREN HERALD, 159 Henderson Hwy., Winnipeg, Manitoba, Canada R2L 1L4. Editor: Harold Jantz. Family publication "read almost entirely by people of the Mennonite faith, reaching a wide cross-section of professional and occupational groups, but also including many homemakers. A substantial segment of our readers is found within farming communities." Biweekly. Circ. 10,600. Pays on publication. Not copyrighted. Byline given. Sample copy 40¢. Reports in 1 month. SAE and International Reply Coupons.

Nonfiction and Photos: Articles with a Christian family orientation; youth directed, Christian faith and life, current issues. Wants articles critiquing the values of a secular society, attempting to relate Christian living to the practical situations of daily living; showing how people have related their faith to their vocations. 1,500 words. Pays $20-35. Photos purchased with mss; pays $5.

THE MESSENGER OF THE SACRED HEART, 833 Broadview Ave., Toronto, Ontario, Canada M4K 2P9. Editor: the Rev. F.J. Power, S.J. 10% freelance written. For "adult Catholics in Canada and the US who are members of the Apostleship of Prayer." Monthly. Circ. 22,000. Buys first rights. Byline given. Pays on acceptance. Free sample copy. Submit seasonal material 3 months in advance. Reports in 1 month. SAE and International Reply Coupons.

Nonfiction: Department Editor: Mary Pujolas. "Articles on the Apostleship of Prayer and on all aspects of Christian living." Current events and social problems that have a bearing on Catholic life, family life, Catholic relations with non-Catholics, personal problems, the liturgy, prayer, devotion to the Sacred Heart. Material should be written in a popular, nonpious style. Buys 12 mss/year. Length: 1,800-2,000 words. Pays 2¢ word.

Fiction: Department editor: Mary Pujolas. Wants fiction which reflects the lives, problems, preoccupations of reading audience. "Short stories that make their point through plot and characters." Length: 1,800-2,000 words. Pays 2¢/word.

THE MIRACULOUS MEDAL, 475 E. Chelten Ave., Philadelphia PA 19144. Editorial Director: the Rev. Robert P. Cawley, C.M. Quarterly. Buys first North American serial rights. Buys articles only on special assignment. Pays on acceptance. SASE. Free sample copy.

Fiction: Should not be pious or sermon-like. Wants good general fiction—not necessarily religious, but if religion is basic to the story, the writer should be sure of his facts. Only restriction is that subject matter and treatment must not conflict with Catholic teaching and practice. Can use seasonal material. Christmas stories. Length: 2,000 words maximum. Occasionally uses short-shorts from 750-1,250 words. Pays 2¢/word minimum.

Poetry: Maximum of 20 lines, preferably about the Virgin Mary or at least with religious slant. Pays 50¢/line minimum.

MODERN LITURGY, Box 444, Saratoga CA 95070. Editor: William Burns. For artists, musicians, and creative individuals who plan group worship; services; teachers of religion. Magazine; 40-48 pages. Eight times/year. Circ. 15,000. Buys all rights. Byline given. Buys 10 mss/year. Pays on publication. Sample copy $3; free writer's guidelines. Reports in 6 weeks. Query. SASE.

Nonfiction and Fiction: Articles (historical, theological and practical) which address special interest topics in the field of liturgy; example services; liturgical art forms (music, poetry, stories, dances, dramatizations, etc.). Practical, creative ideas; and art forms for use in worship and/or religious education classrooms. Length: 750-2,000 words. Pays $5-30.

NEW COVENANT MAGAZINE, Servant Publications, Box 8617, Ann Arbor MI 48107. (313)761-8505. Editor: Bert Ghezzi. Managing Editor: Nick Cavnar. Emphasizes the charismatic renewal of Christian churches. Ecumenical, with a higher percentage of Roman Catholic readers. Monthly magazine; 36 pages. Circ. 73,000. Pays on publication. Buys all rights. Photocopied submissions OK. SASE. Reports in 6-8 weeks. Free sample copy.

Nonfiction: Historical; informational (coverage of recent and upcoming events in the charismatic renewal); inspirational; interview and personal experience (life testimonials relating to the charismatic experience). Buys 2-3 mss/year. Query. Length: 1,000-3,000 words. Pays 2½-3½¢/word.

Photos: Photos purchased with or without accompanying ms., or on assignment. Pays $10-35/8x10 b&w glossy print. Send contact sheet and prints. No additional payment for photos accepted with accompanying ms. Model release required.

THE NEW ERA, 50 E. North Temple, Salt Lake City UT 84150. (801)531-2951. Editor: Brian K. Kelly. 40-60% freelance written. For young people of the Church of Jesus Christ of Latter-Day Saints (Mormon); their church leaders and teachers. Monthly magazine; 51 pages. Circ. 180,000. Buys all rights. Byline given. Buys 100 mss/year. Pays on acceptance. Sample copy 50¢. Submit seasonal material 1 year in advance. Reports in 30 days. Query preferred. SASE.
Nonfiction and Photos: "Material that shows how the Church of Jesus Christ of Latter-Day Saints is relevant in the lives of young people today. Must capture the excitement of being a young Latter-Day Saint. Special interest in the experiences of young Mormons in other countries. No general library research or formula pieces without the *New Era* slant and feel." Uses informational, how-to, personal experience, interview, profile, inspirational, humor, historical, think pieces, travel, spot news. Length: 150-3,000 words. Pays 3-6¢/word. *For Your Information* (news of young Mormons around the world). Uses b&w photos and color transparencies with mss. Payment depends on use in magazine, but begins at $10.
Fiction: Experimental, adventure, science fiction and humorous. Must relate to young Mormon audience. Pays minimum 3¢/word.
Poetry: Traditional forms, blank verse, free verse, avant-garde forms, light verse and all other forms. Must relate to their editorial viewpoint. Pays minimum 25¢/line.

NEW WORLD OUTLOOK, 475 Riverside Dr., Room 1351, New York NY 10115. (212)678-6060. Editor: Arthur J. Moore. For United Methodist lay people; not clergy generally. Monthly magazine; 46 pages. Circ. 40,000. Buys all rights; first North American serial rights. Buys 15-20 mss/year. Pays on publication. Free sample copy and writer's guidelines. Query or submit complete ms. SASE.
Nonfiction: "Articles about the involvement of the church around the world, including the US in outreach and social concerns and Christian witness. Write with good magazine style. Facts, actualities important. Quotes. Relate what Christians are doing to meet problems. Specifics. We have too much on New York and other large urban areas. We need more good journalistic efforts from smaller places in US. Articles by freelancers in out-of-the-way places in the US are especially welcome." Length: 1,000-2,000 words. Usually pays $50-150.
Tips: "A freelancer should have some understanding of the United Methodist Church, or else know very well a local situation of human need or social problem which the churches and Christians have tried to face. Too much freelance material we get tries to paint with broad strokes about world or national issues. The local story of meaning to people elsewhere is still the best material. Avoid pontificating on the big issues. Write cleanly and interestingly on the 'small' ones."

NORTH AMERICAN VOICE OF FATIMA, Fatima Shrine, Youngstown NY 14174. Editor: Steven M. Grancini, C.R.S.P. 75% freelance written. For Roman Catholic readership. Circ. 15,000. Not copyrighted. Pays on acceptance. Free sample copy. Reports in 6 weeks. SASE.
Nonfiction, Photos and Fiction: Inspirational, personal experience, historical and think articles. Religious and historical fiction. Length: 700 words. B&w photos purchased with mss. All material must have a religious slant. Pays 1¢/word.

ONE, 6401 The Paseo, Kansas City MO 64131. (816)333-7000, ext. 210. Editor: Mike Estep. 50% freelance written. Published by the Beacon Hill Press of Kansas City for the 18- to 23-year-old college student and career single. Monthly magazine. Circ. 18,000. Pays on acceptance. Buys first rights or second rights. Byline given. Submit seasonal material 6 months in advance. SASE. Free sample copy.
Nonfiction: Articles which speak to students' needs in light of their spiritual pilgrimage. How they cope on a secular campus from a Christian lifestyle. First-person articles have high priority since writers tend to communicate best that which they are in the process of learning themselves. Style should be evangelical. Material should have "sparkle." Wesleyan in doctrine. Buys interviews, profiles, inspirational and think pieces, humor, photo essays. Length: 1,500 words maximum. Pays 3¢/word.
Photos: B&w glossy prints. Pays $5-25. Interested in photo spreads and photo essays.
Tips: "Be willing to write the article lengthwise according to our editorial needs. (Usually a one or two page article.) Be willing to send a manuscript on speculation. Be concise with description of the theme or content."

THE OTHER SIDE, Box 12236, Philadelphia PA 19144. Co-Editors: John Alexander, Mark Olson. Associate Editor: Alfred Krass. Publisher: Philip Harnden. "A magazine on justice rooted in Christian discipleship, radical in tone and outlook, with a definite point of view but open to other opinions." Monthly. Circ. 10,000. Pays on publication. Buys first serial or simultaneous rights. Byline given. SASE. Reports in 1 month. Sample copy $1. Writer's guidelines available.
Nonfiction: Eunice Amarantides Smith, articles editor. "Articles are not encouraged unless they

are highly creative descriptions of personal experiences relative to Christian discipleship amidst current issues of society or interviews or profiles which don't just 'grind an axe' but communicate personality." Length: 250-2,500 words. Pays $25-250.

Photos: "Shots depicting 'the other side' of affluence or the juxtaposition of affluence and poverty are needed." Photo essays on social issues will be considered. Pays $15-25 for b&w photos.

Fiction: Eunice Amarantides Smith, fiction editor. "Short pieces of creative writing on hard social issues. A Christian perspective should be clear." Especially interested in humor. Length: 300-2,800 words. Pays $25-50.

OUR FAMILY, Oblate Fathers of St. Mary's Province, Box 249, Battleford, Saskatchewan, Canada S0M 0E0. (306)937-2131, 937-7344. Editor-in-Chief: Albert Lalonde, O.M.I. For average family men and women of high school and early college education. Monthly magazine; 36 pages. Circ. 14,633. Pays on acceptance. Generally purchases first North American serial rights; also buys all rights; or simultaneous, second serial (reprint); or one-time rights. Pays 100% kill fee. Byline given. Phone queries OK. Submit seasonal/holiday material 4 months in advance. Simultaneous, photocopied and previously published submissions OK. SASE. Reports in 2-4 weeks. Sample copy $1; free writer's guidelines.

Nonfiction: Humor (related to family life or husband/wife relations); inspirational (anything that depicts people responding to adverse conditions with courage, hope and love); personal experience (with religious dimensions); and photo feature (particularly in search of photo essays on human/religious themes and on persons whose lives are an inspiration to others).

Photos: Photos purchased with or without accompanying ms. Pays $25 for 5x7 or larger b&w glossy prints and color photos (which are converted into b&w). Offers additional payment for photos accepted with ms (payment for these photos varies according to their quality). Free photo spec sheet.

Fiction: Humorous and religious. "Anything true to human nature. No moralizing or sentimentality." Buys 1-2 ms/issue. Send complete ms. Length: 750-3,000 words. Pays 3-5¢/word minimum for original material. Free fiction requirement guide.

Poetry: Avant-garde; free verse; haiku; light verse; and traditional. Buys 4-10 poems/issue. Length: 3-30 lines. Pays 40-60¢/line.

Fillers: Jokes, gags, anecdotes and short humor. Buys 2-10 fillers/issue.

OUR SUNDAY VISITOR MAGAZINE, Noll Plaza, Huntington IN 46750. (219)356-8400. Executive Editor: Robert Lockwood. For general Catholic audience. Weekly. Circ. 340,000. Byline given. Buys 25 mss/year. Pays on acceptance. Submit seasonal material 2 months in advance. Reports in 3 weeks. Query. SASE. Free sample copy.

Nonfiction: Uses articles on Catholic-related subjects. Should explain Catholic religious beliefs in articles of human interest; articles applying Catholic principles to current problems, Catholic profiles, etc. Payment varies depending on reputation of author, quality of work and amount of research required. Length: 1,000-1,200 words. Minimum payment for major features is $100 and a minimum payment for shorter features is $50-75.

Photos: Purchased with mss; with captions only. B&w glossy prints, color transparencies, 35mm color. Pays $125/cover photo story, $75/b&w story; $25/color photo. $10/b&w photo.

PARISH FAMILY DIGEST, Our Sunday Visitor, Inc., 200 Noll Plaza, Huntington IN 46750. (219)356-8400. Editor: Patrick R. Moran. "*Parish Family Digest* is geared to the Catholic family, and to that family as a unit of the parish." Bimonthly magazine; 48 pages. Circ. 140,399. Pays on acceptance. Buys all rights on a work-for-hire basis. Byline given. Submit seasonal/holiday material 3 months in advance. Photocopied and previously published submissions OK. SASE. Reports in 1 week for queries; 2 weeks for mss. Free sample copy and writer's guidelines.

Nonfiction: General interest, historical, inspirational, interview, nostalgia (if related to overall Parish involvement); and profile. Send complete ms. Buys 100 mss/year. Length: 1,000 words maximum. Pays $5-50.

Photos: State availability of photos with ms. Pays $10 for 3x5 b&w prints. Buys all rights. Captions preferred. Model release required.

Fillers: Anecdotes and short humor. Buys 6/issue. Length: 100 words maximum.

Tips: "Know thy publication. Query with outline, title, approximate word length and possible photos. Read the magazine, get the feel of our parish family unit, or involvement, and keep manuscripts to no more than 1,000 maximum. Original ideas usually come through as winners for the beginning writer. Avoid reference book biographicals, and write of real persons."

PENTECOSTAL EVANGEL, The General Council of the Assemblies of God, 1445 Boonville, Springfield MO 65802. (417)862-2781. Editor: Robert C. Cunningham. Managing Editor: Richard G. Champion. 33% freelance written. Emphasizes news of the Assemblies of God for members of the Assemblies and other Pentecostal and charismatic Christians. Weekly magazine; 32 pages. Circ. 285,000. Pays on publication. Buys first rights, simultaneous, second serial (reprint) or one-time rights. Byline given. Submit seasonal/holiday material 6 months in advance. Simultaneous, photocopied and previously published submissions OK. SASE. Reports in 3 months. Free sample copy and writer's guidelines.

Nonfiction: Informational (articles on home life that convey Christian teachings); inspirational; and personal experience. Buys 5 mss/issue. Send complete ms. Length: 500-2,000 words. Pays 2¢/word maximum.

Photos: Photos purchased without accompanying ms. Pays $7.50-15/8x10 b&w glossy prints; $10-35/35mm or larger color transparencies. Total purchase price for ms includes payment for photos.

Poetry: Religious and inspirational. Buys 1 poem/issue. Limit submissions to batches of 6. Pays 15-30¢/line.

Tips: "Break in by writing up a personal experience. We publish first-person articles concerning spiritual experiences; that is, answers to prayer for help in a particular situation. We publish personal testimonials of unusual conversions or healings through faith in Christ. All articles submitted to us should be related to religious life. We are Protestant, evangelical, Pentecostal, and any doctrines or practices portrayed should be in harmony with the official position of our denomination (Assemblies of God)."

THE PENTECOSTAL TESTIMONY, 10 Overlea Blvd., Toronto, Ontario, Canada M4H 1A5. Editor: Joy E. Hansell. Monthly. For church members and general readership. Circ. 20,000. Not copyrighted. Free sample copy. Submit seasonal material at least 3 months in advance. Query. SAE and International Reply Coupons.

Nonfiction: Must be written from Canadian viewpoint. Subjects preferred are contemporary public issues, events on the church calendar (Reformation month, Christmas, Pentecost, etc.) written from conservative theological viewpoint. Preferred lengths are 800-1,200 words.

Photos: Occasionally buys photographs with mss if they are vital to the article. Also buys b&w photos if they are related to some phase of the main topic of the particular issue. Should be 8x10 b&w prints.

POWER FOR LIVING, Scripture Press Publications, Inc., 1825 College Ave., Wheaton IL. 60187. (312)668-6000. Editor: Anne Harrington DeWolf. Quarterly (in weekly parts) 8-page digest covering "true stories showing how God gives individual Christians power for living." Aim is to make Christ relevant to adults in everyday life situations and to offer evidence that Christianity really works. Circ. 400,000. Pays on acceptance. Offers $25 kill fee. Buys first rights and second serial (reprint) rights. Submit seasonal/holiday material 1 year in advance. Simultaneous queries, and simultaneous or previously published submissions OK. SASE. Reports in 2 weeks on queries, 6 weeks on mss. Free sample copy and writer's guidelines.

Nonfiction: Anne Harrington DeWolf, articles editor. General interest, humor, inspirational, personal experience and photo feature. No fiction. Buys 150 mss/year. Query or send complete ms. Length: 1,000-1,500 words. Pays $40-105.

Photos: State availability of photos or send photos with ms. Pays $5-25 for b&w 5x7 or 8x10 prints. Captions, model releases, and identification of subjects required. Buys one-time rights.

Columns/Departments: Turning Point and Viewpoint. Query. Length: 300-500 words. Pays $25-35.

Poetry: Free verse (evangelical). No ordinary run-of-the-mill poetry. ("We use very little poetry.") Buys 3-4 mss/year.

Tips: Prefers "true stories featuring unusual or colorful Christians—strong, emotional true stories with a Christian message. Anecdotes are a must. Pack stories with human interest."

PREPARED!, Christian Preparation Network, Box 628, Grand Rapids MN 55744. (218)326-8475. Editor: Dominick Genovese. Managing Editor: Gale Folsom. Newsletter published 10 times/year covering "preparation for difficulties in all areas of living via *practical* tips, helps, info. A Christian Bible-based viewpoint is helpful, but not essentail, provided material isn't overtly anti-Christian. Audience is primarily, but not exclusively, dedicated Christians looking for ethcial ways to beat inflation, unemployment and other growing ills in the US and Canada." Estab. 1981. Circ. 300+. Pays on acceptance. Byline given. Buys first rights. Submit seasonal/holiday material 3 months in advance. Simultaneous submissions OK. SASE. Reports in 1 month. Sample copy $1; free writer's guidelines.

Nonfiction: Book excerpts; expose (of government, conspiracy); how-to; and humor. "All articles must practically relate to helping people in some area of living. Humor pieces, however, have greater latitude of appeal." No "gloom and doom, uncertifiable hysteria (or *any* kind, for that matter), unsubstantiated warnings, self-aggrandizement, esoteric Bible studies, gossamer and impractical whiz-kid prognostications." Length: 300-1,000 words. Pays 3-5¢/word.

Fillers: "All should relate to theme of preparing and informing people." Clippings, jokes, gags, anecdotes, short humor and newsbreaks. Length: 20-150 words. Pays 5-10¢/word.

Tips: "Including a resume of preparation background and experience may be helpful. We *publish* with a minimum of expense and illustration. Ms should be written with minimum of verbiage and hyperbole."

PRESBYTERIAN JOURNAL, Southern Presbyterian Journal Co, Inc., Box 3108, Asheville NC 28802. Editor: the Rev. G. Aiken Taylor. Managing Editor: Joel Belz. "Emphasis is Presbyterian, although material appeals to religious conservatives. Highly educated readership." Weekly magazine; 24 pages. Circ. 30,000. Pays on publication. Not copyrighted. Submit seasonal/holiday material at least 2 months in advance. Simultaneous and photocopied submissions OK; might consider previously published work. SASE. Reports in 2-6 weeks. Free sample copy.

Nonfiction: General interest (must have a religious slant); how-to (teach Sunday School more effectively—whatever would appeal to readers of religious publications); humor; interview; opinion (does not necessarily have to agree with editorial policy); and personal experience (testimonials welcome). Buys 1-2 mss/issue. Send complete ms. Length: 3,000 word maximum. Pays $20.

Columns/Departments: Under My Palm Tree is directed toward women. No recipes or household hints. Anything else of particular interest to women. Buys 20 mss/year. Send complete ms. Length: 650-1,500 words. Pays $5-25. Open to suggestions for new columns/departments.

Tips: Reads, evalutates and comments on every ms. "Pieces should be *thoughtful*, embodying fresh theological insights, or fresh way of looking at old theological insights."

PRESBYTERIAN RECORD, 50 Wynford Dr., Don Mills, Ontario, Canada M3C 1J7. (416)444-1111. Editor: the Rev. James Dickey. 40-50% freelance written. For a church-oriented, family audience. Monthly magazine. Circ. 84,000. Buys 10 mss/year. Pays on publication. Free sample copy. Submit seasonal material 3 months in advance. Reports on manuscripts accepted for publication in 1 month. Returns rejected material in 6 weeks. Query. SAE and Canadian stamps.

Nonfiction and Photos: Material on religious themes. Check a copy of the magazine for style. Also, personal experience, interview, and inspirational material. Length: 800-1,600 words. Pays $30-50. Pays $10-15 for b&w glossy photos. Captions required. Uses positive color transparencies for the cover. Pays $50.

PURPOSE, 616 Walnut Ave., Scottdale PA 15683. Editor: David E. Hostetler. 85% freelance written. "For adults, young and old, general audience with interests as varied as there are persons. My particular readership is interested in seeing Christianity work in tough situations and come out on top." Monthly magazine. Circ. 21,500. Buys first serial rights; second serial (reprint) rights; simultaneous rights. Byline given. Buys 200 mss a year. Pays on acceptance. Free sample copy and writer's guidelines. Submit seasonal material 5 months in advance. Photocopied and simultaneous submissions OK. Reports in 6 weeks. Submit complete ms. SASE.

Nonfiction and Photos: Inspirational articles from a Christian perspective. "I want material that goes to the core of human problems—morality on all levels, or lack of it in business, politics, religion, sex and any other area—and shows how Christian answers resolve some of these problems. I don't want glib, sweety-sweet, or civil religion pieces. I want critical stuff that's upbeat. *Purpose* is a story paper and as such wants truth to be conveyed either through quality fiction or through articles that use the best fiction techniques to make them come alive. Our magazine has an accent on Christian discipleship. Christianity is to be applied to all of life and we expect our material to show this. We're getting too much self-centered material. I would like to see articles on how people are intelligently and effectively working at some of the great human problems such as overpopulation, food shortages, international understanding, etc., motivated by their faith." Length: 200-1,200 words. Pays 1-3¢/word. Photos purchased with ms. Captions optional. Pays $5-35/b&w, depending on quality. Normal range is $7.50-15. Must be sharp enough for reproduction; prefers prints in all cases. Can use color for halftones at the same rate of payment.

Fiction, Poetry and Fillers: Humorous, religious and historical fiction related to the theme of magazine. "Should not be moralistic." Traditional poetry, blank verse, free verse and light verse. Length: 3-12 lines. Pays 25-75¢/line. Jokes, short humor, and items up to 400 words. Pays 1¢ minimum/word.

Tips: "We are looking for articles which show Christianity slugging it out where people hurt but we want the stories told and presented professionally. Good photographs help place material with us."

QUEEN, Montfort Missionaries, 26 S. Saxon Ave., Bay Shore NY 11706. (516)665-0726. Editor: James McMillan, S.M.M. Managing Editor: Roger Charest, S.M.M. Emphasizes doctrine and devotion to Mary. Bimonthly magazine; 40 pages. Circ. 8,500. Pays on acceptance. Buys all rights.

Phone queries OK. Submit seasonal/holiday material 4 months in advance. SASE. Reports in 1 month.
Nonfiction: Expose (doctrinal); historical; informational; inspirational and interview. Buys 5 mss/issue. Send complete ms. Length: 1,500-2,000 words. Pays $30-40.
Poetry: Free verse and traditional forms. Marian poetry only. Buys 2/issue. Limit submissions to batches of 2. Pays in free subscription for 2 years.

REVIEW FOR RELIGIOUS, 3601 Lindell Blvd., Room 428, St. Louis MO 63108. (314)535-3048. Editor: Daniel F.X. Meenan, S.J. 100% freelance written. Bimonthly. For Roman Catholic priests, brothers and sisters. Pays on publication. Byline given. Reports in about 8 weeks. SASE.
Nonfiction: Articles on ascetical, liturgical and canonical matters. Length: 2,000-8,000 words. Pays $6/page.
Tips: Writer must know about religious life in the Catholic Church, be familiar with prayer, vows and problems related to them.

ST. ANTHONY MESSENGER, 1615 Republic St., Cincinnati OH 45210. Editor-in-Chief: Jeremy Harrington. For a national readership of Catholic families, most of them have children in grade school, high school or college. Monthly magazine; 59 pages. Circ. 330,000. Pays on acceptance. Buys first North American serial rights. Byline given. Submit seasonal/holiday material 4 months in advance. SASE. Free sample copy and writer's guidelines.
Nonfiction: How-to (on psychological and spiritual growth; family problems); humor; informational; inspirational; interview; personal experience (if pertinent to our purpose); personal opinion (limited use; writer must have special qualifications for topic); profile. Buys 12 mss/year. Length: 1,500-3,500 words. Pays 10¢/word.
Fiction: Mainstream and religious. Buys 12 mss/year. Submit complete ms. Length: 2,000-3,500 words. Pays 10¢/word.
Tips: "The freelancer should ask why his/her proposed article would be appropriate for us, rather than for *Redbook* or *Saturday Review*. We treat human problems of all kinds, but from a religious perspective. Get authoritative information (not merely library research; we want interviews with experts). Write in popular style."

ST. JOSEPH'S MESSENGER & ADVOCATE OF THE BLIND, Sisters of St. Joseph of Peace, St. Joseph's Home, Box 288, Jersey City NJ 07303. Editor-in-Chief: Sister Ursula Maphet. 50% freelance written. Quarterly magazine; 30 pages. Circ. 55,000. Pays on acceptance. Buys all rights but will reassign rights back to author after publication asking only that credit line be included in next publication. Submit seasonal/holiday material 3 months in advance (no Christmas issue). Simultaneous and previously published submissions OK. Reports in 3 weeks. Free sample copy and writer's guidelines.
Nonfiction: Humor; inspirational; nostalgia; personal opinion; and personal experience. Buys 24 mss/year. Submit complete ms. Length: 300-1,500 words. Pays $3-15.
Fiction: "Fiction is our most needed area." Romance; suspense; mainstream; and religious. Buys 30 mss/year. Submit complete ms. Length: 600-1,600 words. Pays $6-25.
Poetry: Light verse, traditional. Buys 25/year. Limit submissions to batches of 10. Length: 50-300 words. Pays $5-20.

SANDAL PRINTS, 1820 Mt. Elliott, Detroit MI 48207. Editor: William La Forte. For people who are interested in the work of the Capuchins. Circ. 8,000. Not copyrighted. Pays on acceptance. Free sample copy. Reports in 1 week. Query. SASE.
Nonfiction and Photos: Material must be specifically on the contemporary apostolates and life-style of Capuchins (especially in the Midwest). "We do not use any general religious material; no topical subjects or themes accepted." Length: 2,500 words. Pays $25-50. Pays $5/b&w photo.
Tips: "Write about actually living Capuchins and their work. Query before writing the first word."

SCOPE, 426 S. 5th St., Box 1209, Minneapolis MN 55440. (612)330-3413. Editor: Constance W. Lovaas. 30% freelance written. For women of the American Lutheran Church. Monthly. Circ. 300,000. Buys first rights. Byline given. Buys 200-300 mss/year. Occasionally overstocked. Pays on acceptance. Submit seasonal material 4-5 months in advance. Reports in 4 weeks. SASE. Free sample copy.
Nonfiction and Photos: "The magazine's primary purpose is to be an educational tool in that it transmits the monthly Bible study material which individual women use in preparation for their group meetings. It contains articles for inspiration and growth, as well as information about the mission and concerns of the church, and material that is geared to seasonal emphasis. We are interested in articles that relate to monthly Bible study subject. We also want articles that tell how faith has affected, or can influence, the lives of women or their families. But we do not want

preachy articles. We are interested in any subject that concerns women." Submit complete ms. Length: 400-800 words. Pays $15-50. Buys 3x5 or 8x10 b&w photos with mss or with captions only. Pays $10-30.

Poetry and Fillers: "We can use interesting, brief, pithy, significant or clever filler items, but we use very little poetry and are very selective. We do not buy cute sayings of children." Pays $5-15.

Tips: "Examine a copy of *Scope* and submit a well-written manuscript that fits the obvious slant and audience. No articles built around non-Lutheran teaching and practices but may be written by non-Lutherans. I am interested in articles by and about singles and working mothers."

SEEK, Standard Publishing, 8121 Hamilton Ave., Cincinnati OH 45231. (513)931-4050, ext. 165. Editor: R.W. Baynes. 60% freelance written. For young and middle-aged adults who attend church and Bible classes. Sunday School paper; 8 pages. Quarterly, in weekly issues. Circ. 60,000. Rights purchased vary with author and material. Byline given. Prefers first serial rights. Buys 100-150 mss/year. Pays on acceptance. Free sample copy and writer's guidelines. Submit seasonal (Christmas, Easter, New Year's) material 9-12 months in advance. Reports in 30-60 days. Query not necessary; submit complete ms. SASE.

Nonfiction and Photos: "We look for articles that are warm, inspirational, devotional, of personal or human interest; that deal with controversial matters, timely issues of religious, ethical or moral nature, or first-person testimonies, true-to-life happenings, vignettes, emotional situations or problems; communication problems, and examples of answered prayers. Article must deliver its point in a convincing manner, but not be patronizing or preachy. Must appeal to either men or women. Must be alive, vibrant, sparkling and have a title that demands the article be read. We will purchase a few articles that deal with faith or trials of blacks or other racial groups. Always need stories of families, marriages, problems on campus, and life testimonies." Length: 400-1,200 words. Pays 1-2½¢/word. B&w photos purchased with or without mss. Pays $7.50 minimum for good 8x10 glossy prints.

Fiction: Religious fiction and religiously slanted historical and humorous fiction. Length: 400-1,200 words. Pays 1-2½¢/word.

Tips: Submit mss which tell of faith in action or victorious Christian living as central theme.

THE SIGN, Union City NJ 07087. (201)867-6400. Editor: the Rev. Patrick McDonough, C.P. 75% freelance written. Magazine; 56 pages. 10 issues/year. Buys all rights. Free sample copy. Reports in 3 weeks. SASE.

Nonfiction and Photos: Prime emphasis on religious material: prayer, sacraments, Christian family life, religious education, liturgy, social action—especially "personal testimony" genre. Length: 3500 words maximum. Pays $75-300. Uses photos and artwork submitted with articles.

Fiction: Uses, at most, 1 story/month. Length: 3500 words maximum. Pays $75-300.

Tips: Prefers a query letter "simple and straightforward stating the academic and experiential background of the author. Articles arising from personal experience or personal observation seem to have a better chance."

SIGNS OF THE TIMES, 1350 Villa, Mountain View CA 94042. Editor: Lawrence Maxwell. Seventh-Day Adventist. For religiously inclined persons of all ages and denominations. Monthly. Buys first rights only. Reports in 1 week to several months. SASE.

Nonfiction: Uses articles of interest to the religiously inclined of all denominations. Most material furnished by regular contributors, but freelance submissions carefully read. Sincerity, originality, brevity necessary. Length: 700-1,800/words.

SISTERS TODAY, The Liturgical Press, St. John's Abbey, Collegeville MN 56321. Editor-in-Chief: Sister Mary Anthony Wagner, O.S.B. Associate Editor: Sister Barbara Ann Mayer, O.S.B. 90% freelance written. For religious women of the Roman Catholic Church, primarily. Monthly magazine; 72 pages. Circ. 14,000. Pays on publication. Buys all rights. Byline given. Submit seasonal/holiday material 4 months in advance. SASE. Reports in 2-3 months. Sample copy, $1.50.

Nonfiction: How-to (pray, live in a religious community, exercise faith, hope, charity etc.); informational; and inspirational. Also articles concerning religious renewal, community life, worship and the role of Sisters in the world today. Buys 6-8 mss/issue. Query. Length: 500-2,500 words. Pays $5/printed page.

Poetry: Free verse; haiku; light verse; and traditional. Buys 3 poems/issue. Limit submissions to batches of 4. Pays $10.

SOCIAL JUSTICE REVIEW, 3835 Westminister Place, St. Louis MO 63108. (314)371-1653. Editor: Harvey J. Johnson. Issued bimonthly. Not copyrighted; "however special articles within the magazine may be copyrighted, or an occasional special issue has been copyrighted due to author's request." Query. SASE.

Nonfiction: Wants scholarly articles on society's economic, religious, social, intellectual and political problems with the aim of bringing Catholic social thinking to bear upon these problems. 2,500-3,500 words. Pays about $4/column.

SOLO MAGAZINE, Solo Ministries, Inc., 8740 E. 11th St., Suite Q, Tulsa OK 74112. (918)835-5560. Editor: Jerry Jones. Bimonthly magazine about today's single adults who desire to live within the framework of Christ's teachings. Circ. 20,000. Pays on publication. Buys simultaneous rights. Submit seasonal material 4 months in advance. Simultaneous, photocopied and previously published submissions OK. SASE. Reports in 3 months on queries; in 5 months on mss. Sample copy and writer's guidelines free with SASE.

Nonfiction: Expose (showing how any group, organization or person is taking advantage of or abusing single adults); general interest (articles on travel, adventure appealing to single adults); historical (outstanding single adults in history; views of or on single adults of the past); how-to (repair, cook, garden, etc.); humor (anything that helps us laugh with others and at ourselves); inspirational (outstanding single adults who have done something inspirational); nostalgia; opinion (from a wide range of people on any topics of interest to singles; divorce, sexual attitudes and habits, viewpoints, etc.); profile (a look at outstanding Christian single adults in the *People Magazine* style); travel; new product; and personal experience. "No articles that are not in harmony with Christian principles and Christ's teachings." Buys 12-16 mss/year. Send complete ms. Length: 200-2,000 words. Pays $10-$50.

Photos: Send photos with ms. Pays $5-$25 for 3x5 and 4x7 b&w glossy prints. Pays $10-$75 for 4x7 color glossy prints. Captions preferred; model release required. Buys one-time rights.

Columns/Departments: Relationships (how to build healthy ones, how to argue; how to break up; how to start new ones); Devotional/Bible Study (anything that would assist in the single adult's spiritual growth and development); Single Parenting (anything helpful to the single parent); and Personal Motivation/Self-Help (anything that would help motivate and challenge people to reach for their maximum). Buys 6-12 mss/year. Send complete ms. Length: 200-600 words. Pays $10-$35.

Fiction: "To date, we have published no fiction, however, we would be open to looking at any that is not out of harmony with Christian principles or Christ's teaching." Adventure, fantasy, confession, experimental, humorous, mystery, romance, suspense, condensed novels, mainstream and religious. Send complete ms. Length: 500-2,000 words. Pays $15-$40.

Poetry: Avant-garde, free verse, haiku, light verse and traditional. Buys 6-12 mss/year. Submit maximum 6 poems. Length: 5-40 lines. Pays $5-$25.

Fillers: Clippings, jokes, gags, anecdotes, short humor and newsbreaks. Buys 36 mss/year. Length: 10-100 words. Pays $5-$20.

Tips: "Get a copy of our magazine to know our market *before* submitting article. Ask single friends what kinds of things they would most want to see in a magazine specifically for them, and write about it. Wherever their greatest needs and interests are, there are our stories."

SONLIGHT CHRISTIAN NEWSPAPERS, (includes *Sonlight, Good News, Revival, Solo News,* etc.), Multi-Ministries Fund, 4867 Gulfstream Rd., Lake Worth FL 33461. (305)968-2923. Editor: Dennis Lombard. Monthly tabloids (*Sonlight*: to churches; *Good News*: to the general public; *Revival*: to prayer groups; *Solo*: to Christian singles). "*Sonlight Christian Newspapers* are generally free-distribution tabloids ministering to churches and the public, reaching all denominations, with articles by writers of all backgrounds sharing their Christian experiences and viewpoints." Estab. 1980. Circ. 10,000. Pays on publication. Byline given. Not copyrighted. Buys one-time rights, simultaneous rights and second serial (reprint) rights. Submit seasonal/holiday material 3 months in advance. Simultaneous queries, and simultaneous, photocopied and previously published submissions OK. SASE. Reports in 2 weeks. Sample copy 50¢ or 9x12 SAE and 2 first class stamps.

Nonfiction: Book reports, historical/nostalgic, how-to, humor, inspirational, interview/profile, personal experience, photo feature, testimonies and interviews. "Our publications do *not* debate doctrine, but represent the best and the brightest of all groups. Good, bright, readable writing style is paramount, while source is not important. Self-help articles; testimonies of Christian experience; stories of how God has changed lives; articles on unusual ministries, churches and/or individuals; personality stories of well-known Christians; articles on prayer, revival, harvest of souls, and end-times prophesy are all being sought. The reading level is non-theological, general public. Stories about examples of Christian unity (churches and ministries and individuals working together, especially across denominational lines) are particularly desired at present. No theological tomes or doctrinal arguments." Query with clips of published work or send complete ms. Length: 100-1,500 words. Pays $5-100.

Photos: "Photos are welcome." Send photos with accompanying ms. Pays $1-5 for 5x7 or 8x10 b&w prints. Captions, model release, and identification of subjects required. Buys one-time rights and reprint rights.

Poetry: Free verse, light verse, traditional and inspirational. "No long or deep poems." Buys 10-12 mss/year. Submit maximum 3-5 poems. Length: 4-60 lines. Pays $3-30.

Fillers: Clippings, anecdotes and newsbreaks. Length: 15-150 words. "We generally do not pay for fillers."

Tips: "Read the newspapers, then correspond freely with the editor about your ideas and capabilities of getting specific stories. Write short pieces for hurried readers and tight printing budgets. *Note*: We do not pay well yet but want to develop regulars for better pay."

SPIRITUAL LIFE, 2131 Lincoln Rd. NE, Washington DC 20002. (202)832-6622. Editor: the Rev. Christopher Latimer, O.C.D. 80% freelance written. "Largely Catholic, well-educated, serious readers. High percentage are priests and religious, but also some laymen. A few are non-Catholic or non-Christian." Quarterly. Circ. 17,000. Buys first rights. Buys 20 mss/year. Pays on acceptance. "Brief autobiographical information (present occupation, past occupations, books and articles published, etc.) should accompany article. Follow *A Manual of Style* (University of Chicago)." Reports in 2 weeks. SASE. Free sample copy and writer's guidelines.

Nonfiction: Serious articles of contemporary spirituality. Quality articles about man's encounter with God in the present-day world. Language of articles should be college-level. Technical terminology, if used, should be clearly explained. Material should be presented in a positive manner. Sentimental articles or those dealing with specific devotional practices not accepted. "*Spiritual Life* tries to avoid the 'popular,' sentimental approach to religion and to concentrate on a more intellectual approach. We do not want first-person accounts of spiritual experiences (visions, revelations, etc.) nor sentimental treatments of religious devotions." Buys inspirational and think pieces. No fiction or poetry. Length: 3,000-5,000 words. Pays $50 minimum. "Five contributor's copies are sent to author on publication of article." Book reviews should be sent to Brother Edward O'Donnell, O.C.D., Carmelite Monastery, Box 189, Waverly NY 14892.

SPIRITUALITY TODAY, Aquinas Institute, 3642 Lindell Blvd., St. Louis MO 63108. Editor: the Rev. Christopher Kiesling O.P. 25% freelance written. "For those interested in a more knowing and intense Christian life in the 20th century." Buys all rights, but right to re-use the material is assigned back without charge if credit line is given to *Spirituality Today*. Byline given. Pays on publication. Query or submit complete ms. SASE.

Nonfiction: "Articles that seriously examine important truths pertinent to the spiritual life, or Christian life, in the context of today's world. Scriptural, biographical, doctrinal, liturgical and ecumenical articles are acceptable." Length: 4,000 words. Pays 1¢/word.

Tips: "Examine the journal. It is not a typical magazine. Given its characteristics, the style of writing required is not the sort that regular freelance writers usually employ."

SUNDAY DIGEST, 850 N. Grove Ave., Elgin IL 60120. Editor: Gregory D. Cook. 50% freelance written. Issued weekly for Christian adults. *Sunday Digest* provides a weekly combination or original articles and reprints, selected to help adult readers better understand the Christian faith, to keep them informed of issues and happenings within the Christian community, and to challenge them to a deeper personal commitment to Christ." Prefers to buy all rights. Pays on acceptance. Reports in 1 month. SASE. Free sample copy and writer's guidelines.

Nonfiction and Photos: Needs articles applying the Christian faith to personal and social problems, articles of family interest and on church subjects, personality profiles, inspirational self-help articles, personal experience articles and anecdotes. "No articles on 'How I Got Sick,' 'How My Child Got Sick,' 'Let Me Tell You About My Operation.'" Length: 500-1,800 words. "Study our product and our editorial requirements. Have a clear purpose for every article or story—use anecdotes and dialogue—support opinions with research." Pays 5¢/word minimum. Currently running the series, "Christianity on the Job." Query. "A query letter should demonstrate to me that the writer has read my publication and is offering an article that fits our editorial style or a particular standing feature. *It should be detailed*." Photos purchased only with mss. Pays minimum $10 each, depending on quality. Color transparencies or b&w prints preferred. Return of prints cannot be guaranteed.

Fiction: Interested in fiction that is hard-hitting, fast-moving, with a real woven-in, not "tacked on," Christian message. Length: 1,000-1,500 words. Pays 5¢/word minimum.

Poetry: Only occasionally if appropriate to format. Pay 5¢/word minimum.

Fillers: Anecdotes of inspirational value, jokes and short humor; must be appropriate to format and in good taste. "We have a regular need for short (500 words) pieces that are personally inspiring." Pays 5¢/word minimum.

Tips: "I don't care if a writer is well-known. What is crucial is that the writer is committed to high-quality Christian communication. Show me you care about detail. Offer to write what I obviously have a regular need for as discovered by reading the publication."

THE TEXAS METHODIST/UNITED METHODIST REPORTER, Box 221076, Dallas TX 75222. (214)630-6495. Editor/General Manager: Spurgeon M. Dunnam III. For a national readership of United Methodist pastors and laypersons. Weekly newspaper. Circ. 518,000. Pays on acceptance. Not copyrighted. Byline given. SASE. Free sample copy and writer's guidelines.
Nonfiction: "We welcome short features, approximately 500 words, focused on United Methodist persons, churches or church agencies. Write about a distinctly Christian response to human need or how a person's faith relates to a given situation." Pays 3¢/word.
Photos: Purchased with accompanying ms. "We encourage the submission of good action photos (5x7 or 8x10 b&w glossy prints) of the persons or situations in the article." Pays $10.
Poetry: "Poetry welcome on a religious theme; blank verse or rhyme." Length: 2-20 lines. Pays $2.
Fillers: Crossword, word-find and other puzzles on religious or Biblical themes. Pays $5.

THESE TIMES, Review and Herald Publishing Association, 6556 Eastern Ave. NW, Washington DC 20012. (202)723-3700. Editor: Kenneth J. Holland. For the general public; adult. Monthly magazine; 32 pages. Circ. 215,000. Rights purchased vary with author and material. May buy first North American serial rights, second serial (reprint) rights or simultaneous rights. Pays 33⅓% kill fee. Byline given. Buys 75 mss/year. Pays on acceptance. Photocopied and simultaneous submissions OK. Submit seasonal material 6 months in advance. Reports in 2 weeks. Query. SASE. Free sample copy and writer's guidelines.
Nonfiction and Photos: Material on the relevance of Christianity and everyday life; inspirational articles. How-to; home and family problems; health; drugs, alcohol, gambling, abortion, Bible doctrine. Marriage; divorce; country living or city living. "We like the narrative style. Find a person who has solved a problem. Then, tell how he did it." Length: 250-2,500 words. Pays 8-12¢/word. B&w and color photos are purchased with or without ms, or on assignment. Pays $20-25 for b&w; $75-150 for color.
Tips: "Have two or three persons read your article, do your research thoroughly, and make your lead super-appealing."

TODAY'S CHRISTIAN PARENT, 8121 Hamilton Ave., Cincinnati OH 45231. (513)931-4050. Editor: Mrs. Mildred Mast. Quarterly. Rights purchased vary with author and material. Buys first North American serial rights and first serial rights. Pays on acceptance. Free sample copy. Reports on submissions within 6 weeks. SASE.
Nonfiction: Devotional, inspirational and informational articles for the family. Also articles concerning the problems and pleasures of parents, grandparents and the entire family, and Christian childrearing. Timely articles on moral issues, ethical and social situations. Length: 600-1,200 words. Can use short items on Christian living; and fillers serious or humorous. Very little poetry. Study magazine before submitting. Pays 2¢/word.
Tips: "Write about familiar family situations in a refreshingly different way, so that help and inspiration shine through the problems and pleasures of parenthood. Avoid wordiness, trite situations or formats. Slant: from a Christian perspective."

"TRUTH ON FIRE!", The Bible Holiness Movement, Box 223, Station A, Vancouver, British Columbia, Canada V6C 2M3. (604)683-1833. Editor-in-Chief: Wesley H. Wakefield. 20% freelance written. Emphasizes Evangelism and Bible teachings. Bimonthly magazine; 60 pages. Circ. 5,000. Pays on acceptance. Buys all rights. Byline given unless author requests otherwise. Simultaneous, photocopied and previously published submissions OK. SASE. Reports in 4 weeks. Free sample copy and writer's guidelines.
Nonfiction: "Evangelical articles; articles dealing with social reforms (pacifism, civil rights, religious liberty); expose (present-day slavery, cancer, tobacco, etc.); first-person testimonies of Christian experience; doctrinal articles from Wesleyan interpretation. Must observe our evangelical taboos. Nothing favoring use of tobacco, alcohol, attendance at dances or theaters; nothing in favor of abortion, divorce or remarriage; no hip language or slang; no devotional materials. Also, we do not accept Calvinistic religious or right-wing political material. Would like to see material on Christian pacifism, anti-semitism, present-day slavery, marijuana research, religious issues in Ireland, and religious articles." Length: 300-2,500 words. Pays $5-35.
Photos: Photos purchased with or without accompanying ms. Pays $5-15/5x7 b&w photos. "Subjects should conform to our mores of dress (no jewelry, no makeup, no long-haired men, no mini-skirts, etc.).
Fillers: Newsbreaks, quotes. Length: 30-100 words. Pays $1-2.50.
Tips: "Recognize older evangelical emphasis and mores. Be direct and concise."

TWIN CIRCLE, Twin Circle Publishing, 1901 Avenue of the Stars, Los Angeles CA 90067. (213)553-4911. Executive Editor: Mary Louise Frawley. Weekly tabloid covering Catholic personalities and Catholic interest topics for a mostly female Catholic readership. Circ. 76,000.

Average issue includes 6-7 feature articles. Pays on publication. Byline given. Buys all rights. Submit seasonal material 1 month in advance. Simultaneous and photocopied submissions OK, if so indicated. SASE. Reports in 2 weeks on queries; in 1 week on mss. Free writer's guidelines with SASE.

Nonfiction: "We are looking for articles about prominent Catholic personalities in sports, entertainment, politics and business; ethnic stories about Catholics from other countries and topical issues of concern to Catholics. We are interested in writers who are experienced and write on an ongoing basis." No theological issues. Buys 3-4 mss/issue. Length: 250-1,000 words. Pays 8¢/word.

Photos: State availability of photos. Reviews 5x7 b&w glossy prints. Price negotiated. Captions required. Rights vary.

THE UNITED CHURCH OBSERVER, 85 St. Clair Ave. E., Toronto 7, Ontario, Canada M4T 1M8. (416)925-5931. Editor: Hugh McCullum. A 60-page newsmagazine for persons associated with the United Church of Canada. Monthly. Byline usually given. Deals primarily with events, trends, and policies having religious significance. Most coverage is Canadian, but reports on international or world concerns will be considered.

Nonfiction: Occasional opinion features only. Extended coverage of major issues usually assigned to known writers. Submissions should be written as news, no more than 900 words length, accurate and well researched. Queries preferred. Pays after publication. Rates depend on subject, author, and work involved.

Photos: Buys photographs with mss. B&w should be 5x7 minimum; color 35mm or larger format. Payment varies.

Tips: "Include samples of previous *news* writing with query. Indicate ability and willingness to do research, and to evaluate that research. Don't burden us with samples of brilliant insight in opinion pieces, or poetry."

UNITED EVANGELICAL ACTION, Box 28, Wheaton, IL 60187. (312)665-0500. Editor: Harold Smith. 5% freelance written. "The magazine for 24-hour Christians." Written for men and women concerned about the practical expression of their Christian faith in all aspects of life (including social, political and economic). Quarterly magazine; 40 pages. Circ. 10,000. Pays on publication. Buys all rights. Phone queries OK. SASE. Reports in 4 weeks. Free sample copy and writer's guidelines.

Nonfiction: Harold Smith, editor. Issues and trends in the Church and society that affect the ongoing witness and outreach of evangelical Christians. Content should be well thought through, and should provide practical suggestions for dealing with these issues and trends. Buys 6-8 mss/year. Query. Length: 1,500-2,000 words. Pays 5-8¢/word.

UNITY MAGAZINE, Unity Village MO 64065. Editor: Thomas E. Witherspoon. Publication of Unity School of Christianity. Magazine; 66 pages. Monthly. Circ. 360,000. Buys first serial rights. Buys 200 mss/year. Pays on acceptance. No photocopied or simultaneous submissions. Submit seasonal material 6-8 months in advance. Reports in 4 weeks. Submit complete ms. SASE. Free sample copy and writer's guidelines.

Nonfiction and Photos: "Inspirational articles, metaphysical in nature, about individuals who are using Christian principles in their living." Personal experience and interview. Length: 3,000 words maximum. Pays minimum of 2¢/word. 4x5 or 8x10 color transparencies purchased without mss. Pays $75-100.

Poetry: Traditional forms, blank verse and free verse. Pays 50¢-$1/line.

Tips: "Be innovative and use new twists on old truths."

THE UPPER ROOM, DAILY DEVOTIONAL GUIDE, The Upper Room, 1908 Grand Ave., Nashville TN 37202. (615)327-2700. Editor: Maxie D. Dunnam. Managing Editor: Mary Lou Redding. Bimonthly magazine "offering a daily inspirational message which includes a Bible reading, text, prayer, and 'Thought for the Day.' Each day's meditation is written by a different person and is usually a personal witness about discovering meaning and power for Christian living through some experience from daily life." Circ. 2,225,000 (US) + 385,000 outside US. Pays on publication. Byline given. Offers negotiable kill fee. Buys first North American serial rights and translation rights. Submit seasonal/holiday material 1 year in advance. SASE. Reports in 3 weeks on queries; 6 months on mss. Free sample copy and writer's guidelines.

Nonfiction: Mary Lou Redding, articles editor. Inspirational and personal experience. No poetry, lengthy "spiritual journey" stories. Buys 360 mss/year. Send complete ms. Length: 250 words maximum. Pays $10 minimum.

Columns/Departments: Mary Lou Redding, column/department editor. Prayer Workshop—"a 2-page feature which suggests some meditation or prayer exercise. For 1983, we are considering continuing the 1981 themes of spiritual classics, excerpting and updating material from Christian mystics and thinkers such as St. Francis, Teresa of Avila, Augustine, etc." Buys 6 mss/year. Query with clips of published work. Length: 400-600 words. Pays $50-100. "All material used must be documented through standard footnote material for verification. Writer should obtain permission for use of previously copyrighted material which is quoted."

Tips: "The best way to break into our magazine is to send a well-written manuscript that looks at the Christian faith in a fresh way. Standard stories and sermon illustrations are immediately rejected. We very much want to find new writers and welcome good material. Daily meditations are most open. 'Prayer Workshops' are usually assigned. Good repeat meditations can lead to assignment work for our other publications, which pay more. We encourage theological diversity and especially welcome faith-perspective approaches to current social problems and controversial issues within the Christian faith."

VERONA MISSIONS (COMBONI MISSIONS), 8108 Beechmont Ave., Cincinnati OH 45230. (513)474-4997. Editor: Jo Anne Moser Gibbons. For those interested in Third World topics and mission efforts of the Comboni Missionaries and Comboni Missionary Sisters (formerly Verona Fathers and Sisters). Bimonthly; 36 pages. Distribution over 65,000. Buys all rights; first rights; or second serial (reprint) rights. Byline given. Pays on acceptance. Free sample copy. Reports in 6 weeks. SASE.

Nonfiction: Background information, human interest articles, interviews, profiles, personal experience articles, and photo features on the work of Comboni Missionaries, especially in the developing countries of Africa and Latin America and among US minority groups. Should be written knowledgeably, in a popular, conversational style, and reflect a positive outlook on efforts in social and religious fields. Length: 250-1,000 words, shorter features; 3,000 words maximum, major articles. Pays $25-200.

Photos: B&w (5x7 minimum) photos and color transparencies purchased with ms or on assignment. "We want grabbing 'people photos' with a good sense of place. We'd consider purchasing photos without ms if of a people or area (foreign) served by Comboni Missionaries. All the better if a Comboni appears in the photo and is identified by his/her complete name, native country, and mission country." Captions required. Pays $8 minimum/b&w glossy print; $30/color transparency.

Tips: "We treat Third World subjects sympathetically and multi-dimensionally, and always in a Christian context. No pious, saccharine treatments, please! We want good, solid handling of facts and balanced, realistic stuff. We're a good market for second rights if the article fits our needs and photos are available."

VIRTUE, 850, Sisters OR 97759. (503)549-8261. Managing Editor: Lori Masten. Bimonthly magazine about Christian womanhood for Christian mothers and wives and some single women. Circ. 55,000. Average issue includes 12 feature articles. Pays on publication. Byline given. Buys all rights. Submit seasonal material 4 months in advance. Simultaneous and previously published submissions OK, if so indicated. SASE. Reports in 2 weeks on queries; in 6 weeks on ms. Sample copy $2. Free writer's guidelines.

Nonfiction: Interview (of Christian women); nostalgia (spiritually enriching); profile; how-to (upkeep and organizational tips for home); inspirational (spiritual enrichment); personal experience; and family teaching for husbands, wives and children. "No mystical, preachy articles." Buys 6 mss/issue. Query or send complete ms. Length: 1,000-1,500 words. Pays 3-5¢/words.

Photos: Reviews 3x5 b&w glossy prints. Offers additional payment for photos accepted with ms. Captions required. Buys all rights or first rights.

Columns/Departments: Family (short articles on Christian family life); Special features (interviews and miscellaneous); Foods (recipes and entertaining); and fun (crafts, decorating, creative projects). Buys 4 mss/issue. Send complete ms. Length: 500-1,000 words. Pays 5¢/word.

Fiction: Adventure, humorous, romance and religious. Buys 1 ms/issue. Send complete ms. Length: 1,000-1,500 words. Pays 5¢/word.

Fillers: Anecdotes, short humor, newsbreaks and thought provoking family stories. Buys 2-3 mss/issue. Pays 5¢/word.

VISTA, Wesleyan Publishing House, Box 2000, Marion IN 46952. Address submissions to Editor of Sunday School Magazines. Publication of the Wesleyan Church. For adults. Weekly. Circ. 63,000. Not copyrighted. "Along with mss for first use, we also accept simultaneous submissions, second rights, and reprint rights. It is the writer's obligation to secure clearance from the original publisher for any reprint rights." Pays on acceptance. Byline given. Submit material 9 months in advance. Reports in 6 weeks. "SASE for sample copy and with all manuscripts."

Nonfiction: Devotional, biographical, and informational articles with inspirational, religious, moral or educational values. Favorable toward emphasis on: "New Testament standard of living as applied to our day; soul-winning (evangelism); proper Sunday observance; Christian youth in action; Christian education in the home, the church and the college; good will to others; world-wide missions; clean living, high ideals, and temperance; wholesome social relationships. Disapprove of liquor, tobacco, theaters, dancing. Mss are judged on the basis of human interest, ability to hold reader's attention, vivid characterizations, thoughtful analysis of problems, vital character message, expressive English, correct punctuation, proper diction. Know where you are going and get there." Length: 500-1,500 words. Pays 2¢/word for quality material.

Photos: Pays $12.50-25/5x7 or 8x10 b&w glossy print portraying action, seasonal emphasis or scenic value. Various reader age-groups should be considered.

Fiction: Stories should have definite Christian emphasis and character-building values, without being preachy. Setting, plot and action should be realistic. Length: 1,500-1,800 words; also short-shorts and vignettes. Pays 2¢/word for quality material.

WAR CRY, The Official Organ of the Salvation Army, 120-130 W. 14th St., New York NY 10011. (212)691-8780. Editor: Henry Gariepy. Weekly magazine for "persons with evangelical Christian background; members and families of the Salvation Army; the 'man in the street.'" Circ. 280,000. Buys first rights. Pays on acceptance. SASE. Reports in 2 months. Free sample copy.

Nonfiction: Inspirational and informational articles with a strong evangelical Christian slant, but not preachy. In addition to general articles, needs articles slanted toward most of the holidays including Easter, Christmas, Mother's Day, Father's Day, etc. Buys 100 mss/year. Length: approximately 1,000-2,000 words. Pays $15-35.

Photos: Occasionally buys photos submitted with mss, but seldom with captions only. Pays $4-20 for b&w glossy prints.

Fiction: Prefers complete-in-one issue stories, with a strong Christian slant. Can have modern or Biblical setting, but must not run contrary to Scriptural account. Length: 1,500-2,000 words. Pays 2¢/word.

Poetry: Religious or nature poems. Length: 4-24 lines. Pays $2.50-15.

THE WITTENBERG DOOR, 1224 Greenfield Dr., El Cajon CA 92021. (714)440-2333. Contact: Mike Yaconelli. Bimonthly magazine for men and women, usually connected with the church. Circ. 16,000. Pays on publication. Buys all rights. SASE. Reports in 2 months. Free sample copy.

Nonfiction: Satirical or humorous articles on church renewal, Christianity, organized religion. Some book reviews. Buys about 50 mss/year. Query or submit complete ms. Length: 1,000 words maximum, 500-750 preferred. Pays $20-$50.

Tips: "We look for someone who is clever, on our wave length and has some savvy about the evangelical church."

WORLD ENCOUNTER, 2900 Queen Lane, Philadelphia PA 19129. (215)438-6360. Editor: The Rev. William A. Dudde. For persons who have more than average interest in, and understanding of, overseas missions and current human social concerns in other parts of the world. Quarterly magazine; 32 pages. Circ. 7,000. Buys all rights. Pays 35% kill fee. Byline given. Buys 10 mss/year. Pays on publication. Free sample copy. Photocopied, and simultaneous submissions OK, if information is supplied on other markets being approached. Reports in 1 month. Query or submit complete ms. SASE.

Nonfiction and Photos: "This is a religious and educational publication using human interest features and think pieces related to the Christian world mission and world community. Race relations in southern Africa; human rights struggles with tyrannical regimes; social and political ferment in Latin America; resurgence of Oriental religions. Simple travelogues are not useful to us. Prospective writers should inquire as to the countries and topics of particular interest to our constituents. Material must be written in a popular style but the content must be more than superficial. It must be theologically, sociologically and anthropologically sound. We try to maintain a balance between gospel proclamation and concern for human and social development. We focus on what is happening in Lutheran groups. Our standards of content quality and writing are very high." Length: 500-1,800 words. Pays $35-175. B&w photos are purchased with or without accompanying mss or on assignment. Pays $10-20. Captions required.

Tips: "Contact Lutheran missionaries in some overseas country and work out an article treatment with them. Or simply write the editor, outlining your background and areas of international knowledge and interest, asking at what points they converge with our magazine's interests. Study the publication before submitting a manuscript. Too many of the pieces we receive are quite inappropriate."

Retirement

DYNAMIC YEARS, 215 Long Beach Blvd., Long Beach CA 90802. Executive Editor: James Wiggins. Managing Editor: Carol Powers. 90% freelance written. "*Dynamic Years* is the official publication of Action for Independent Maturity (AIM). AIM members are the 40-60 age bracket, pre-retirees." Bimonthly. Circ. 458,000. Rights purchased vary with author and material. Buys first-use or first North American rights. Pays negotiable kill fee. Byline given. Pays on acceptance. Submit seasonal material 6 months in advance. Reports in 2 weeks. Query or submit complete ms. "Submit only 1 ms at a time." SASE. Free sample copy.

Nonfiction: General subject matter is "health , pre-retirement planning, second careers, personal adjustment, well-developed hobbies, 'people in action' with unusual activities, exciting use of leisure, finance, travel and sports. We like the 'you' approach, nonpreachy, use of lively examples. We try to slant everything toward our age group. We do not want pieces about individuals long retired. No poetry, fiction or inspirational preachments." Buys how-to, personal experience, profile, humor and travel articles. Buys 100 mss/year. Length: 1,000-2,000 words. Pays $500 minimum.

Photos: State availability of photos with ms. Photos purchased with and without mss for covers. Captions required. Pays $25 minimum for professional quality 5x7 or 8x10 b&w photos. Pays $100 minimum for professional quality color photos (35mm or 2¼x2¼ transparencies).

50 PLUS, (formerly *Retirement Living*), 850 3rd Ave., New York NY 10022. (212)593-2100. Editor: Jess Gorkin. Executive Editor: Meg Whitcomb. "A service-oriented publication for men and women (age 50 and up). Readers are active, forward-looking, interested in all aspects of meaningful living in the middle and later years." Monthly. Buys all rights. Pays kill fee. Byline given. Buys 10-12 mss/year. Pays on acceptance. Sample copy $1.25 and 18¢ postage. Study magazine and needs before submitting ms or query (indexed in *Readers' Guide*). Submit seasonal and holiday material 6 months in advance. Reports in 6-8 weeks. Queries preferred, but will look at complete ms. "Manuscripts must be accompanied by SASE; otherwise not returned."

Nonfiction: "We want articles with a strong, timely service value or features about personalities or activities for people over 50 not covered in other general-interest magazines. Personal experiences, humor, income ideas, unusual hobbies, self-fulfillment, celebrity interviews, food, fashion and controversial issues." Unusual travel stories, directly relevant to people over 50, only. Length: 1,000-2,500 words. Pays $100-750 an article. "We reserve all rights to edit and rewrite to our style and space requirements.

Photos: "Photos and color transparencies must be of professional quality." Pays $25 minimum.

Fillers: Spot news, anecdotes and personality items. Pays $25-50.

Tips: "Profile a dynamic person over 50 who has news value to readers over 50, and whose current activities are meaningful or unusual to a wide range of readers."

MATURE LIVING, The Sunday School Board of the Southern Baptist Convention, 127 9th Ave. N., Nashville TN 37234. (615)251-2274. Editor: Jack Gulledge. Assistant Editor: Zada Malugen. A Christian magazine for retired senior adults 60 + . Monthly magazine; 52 pages. Pays on acceptance. Buys all rights. Byline given. Submit seasonal/holiday material at least 12-15 months in advance. SASE. Reports in 6 weeks. Free sample copy and writer's guidelines.

Nonfiction: How-to (easy, inexpensive craft articles made from easily obtained materials); informational (safety, consumer fraud, labor-saving and money-saving for senior adults); inspirational (short paragraphs with subject matter appealing to elders); nostalgia; unique personal experiences; and travel. Buys 7-8 mss/issue. Send complete ms. Length: 400-1,400 words; prefers articles of 875 words. Pays $14-49.

Photos: Some original photos purchased with accompanying ms. Pays about $5-15 depending on size, b&w glossy prints. Model release required.

Fiction: Everyday living, humor and religious. "Must have suspense and character interaction." Buys 1 ms/issue. Send complete ms. Length: 875-1,400 words. Pays 3½¢/word.

Fillers: Short humor, religious or grandparent/grandchild episodes. Length: 125 words maximum. Pays $5.

Tips: "We want warm, creative, unique manuscripts. Presentations don't have to be moralistic or religious, but must reflect Christian standards. Don't write down to target audience. Speak *to* senior adults on issues that interest them. They like contemporary, good-Samaritan, and nostalgia articles. We buy some light humor. We use 140-word profiles of interesting unusual, senior adults worthy of recognition, when accompanied by a quality action b/w photo. Pays $25. Query should emphasize the uniqueness of proposed copy. Study back issues and guidelines, research and come up with creative material, that hits a need. Rewrite and refine to proper word count."

MATURE YEARS, 201 8th Ave., S., Nashville TN 37202. Editor: Daisy D. Warren. 55% freelance written. For retired persons and those facing retirement; persons seeking help on how to handle problems and privileges of retirement. Quarterly. Rights purchased vary with author and material; usually buys all rights. Buys 50 mss/year. Pays on acceptance. Submit seasonal material 14 months in advance. Reports in 6 weeks. Submit complete ms. SASE. Free writer's guidelines.

Nonfiction: "*Mature Years* is different from the secular press in that we like material with Christian and church orientation. Usually we prefer materials that have a happy, healthy outlook regarding aging, although advocacy (for older adults) articles are at times used. Each issue is developed on a specific theme and the majority of theme-related articles are solicited. However, many freelance materials are used. Articles dealing with all aspects of pre-retirement and retirement living. Short stories and leisure-time hobbies related to specific seasons. Examples of how older persons, organizations, and institutions are helping others. Writing should be of interest to older adults, with Christian emphasis, though not preachy and moralizing. No poking fun or mushy, sentimental articles. We treat retirement from the religious viewpoint. How-to, humor and travel also considered." Length: 1,200-2,000 words.

Photos: 8x10 b&w glossy prints purchased with ms or on assignment.

Fiction: "We buy fiction for adults. Humor is preferred. Please, no children's stories and no stories about depressed situations of older adults." Length: 1,000-2,000 words. Payment varies.

MODERN MATURITY, American Association of Retired Persons, 215 Long Beach Blvd., Long Beach CA 90801. Editor-in-Chief: Hubert C. Pryor. Managing Editor: Ian Ledgerwood. 75% freelance written. For readership over 55 years of age. Bimonthly magazine; 72 pages. Circ. 10 million. Pays on acceptance. Buys all rights. Byline given. Submit seasonal/holiday material 6 months in advance. Photocopied submissions OK. SASE. Reports in 2 weeks. Free sample copy and writer's guidelines.

Nonfiction: Historical, how-to, humor, informational, inspirational, interview, new product, nostalgia, personal experience, opinion, photo feature, profile and travel. Query or send complete ms. Length: 1,000-2,000 words. Pays $200-750.

Photos: Photos purchased with or without accompanying ms. Pays $25/minimum for 8x12 b&w glossy print, "much more for color transparencies or prints."

Fiction: Buys some fiction, but must be suitable for older readers. Buys 2-3 mss/year. Send complete ms. Length: 1,000-2,000 words. Pays $300 minimum.

Poetry: All types. Length: 40 lines maximum. Pays $10-50.

Fillers: Clippings, jokes, gags, anecdotes, newsbreaks, puzzles (find-the-word, not crossword) and short humor. Length: 200-500 words. Pays $10 minimum.

NEW ENGLAND SENIOR CITIZEN/SENIOR AMERICAN NEWS, Prime National Publishing Corp., 470 Boston Post Rd., Weston MA 02193. Editor-in-Chief: Ira Alterman. 50% freelance written. For men and women aged 60 and over who are interested in travel, finances, retirement life styles, special legislation, nostalgia, etc. Monthly newspaper; 24-32 pages. Circ. 60,000. Pays on publication. Buys all rights. Pays 100% kill fee. Byline given. Submit seasonal/holiday material 3 months in advance. Previously published material OK. SASE. Reports in 6 weeks. Sample copy 50¢.

Nonfiction: General interest; how-to (anything dealing with retirement years); inspirational; historical; humor; interview; nostalgia; profile; travel; personal experience; photo features; and articles about medicine relating to gerontology. Buys 10-15 mss/issue. Submit complete ms. Length: 500-1,500 words. Pays $25-50.

Photos: Purchased with ms. Captions required. Pays $5-15/5x7 or 8x10 b&w glossy print. Captions and model releases required.

Columns/Departments: Humor. Buys 1/issue. Submit complete ms. Length: 500-1,000 words. Pays $25-50. Open to suggestions for new columns and departments.

Fiction: Adventure, historical, humorous, mystery, romance, suspense and religious. Buys 1 ms/issue. Submit complete ms. Length: 500-1,500 words. Pays $25-50.

Tips: "Clean, typed, top-quality copy aimed at older tastes, interests, lifestyles and memories."

NRTA JOURNAL, 215 Long Beach Blvd., Long Beach CA 90801. (213)432-5781. Editor: Hubert Pryor. 75% freelance written. Publication of the National Retired Teachers Association. For retired teachers. Bimonthly. Buys all rights. Byline given. Pays on acceptance. Free sample copy. Reports in 2 weeks. SASE.

Nonfiction: Service pieces for the retired teacher relating to income, health, hobbies, living; Americana, nostalgia, reminiscence, personality pieces, inspirational articles, current trends; also holiday material. Length: 1,000-2,000 words. Pays $100-500.

Fiction: Buys fiction occasionally. Length: 1,000-2,000 words. Pays $100-500.

Photos: "Special consideration for picture stories, photographic portfolios, etc." Pays $50 and up each; much more for color and covers.
Fillers: Puzzles, jokes, short humor. Pays $10 and up.

PRIME TIME, Prime Time Publications, Inc., 1700 Broadway, New York NY 10019. (212)246-6969. Editor: Bayard Hooper. Executive Editor: Peter Young. Monthly magazine about people in their prime for men and women 45-65 with a focus on pleasures and problems of the midlife years. Estab. 1979. Circ. 150,000. Pays on acceptance. Buys first North American serial rights. Submit seasonal material 5 months in advance. Simultaneous and photocopied submissions OK; "do not submit original copies of slides or mss." SASE. Reports in 1 month. Sample copy $2.50; writer's guidelines free with SASE.
Nonfiction: Shari E. Hartford, editorial manager. General interest (money, financial planning, home buying, decorating, health and beauty, continuing education, people and personalities, the psychology of successful living); and humor. No health-related, travel or personal experience articles. Buys 10 mss/issue. Query with clips of previously published work and legal size SASE. Length: 2,500-3,500 words. Pays $750-$1,000.
Columns/Departments: Health; Finance; Second Acts (career changes); Buys 3 mss/issue. Query with clips of previously published work. Length: 1,500-2,000 words. Pays $750 minimum.
Fiction: Shari E. Hartford, editorial manager. "We are interested in anything that will appeal to a mid-life audience." Buys 4 mss/year. Query. Length: 2,500-3,500. Pays $750-$1,000.
Tips: "The largest problem with submissions is the lack of understanding the author has about the publication that they are submitting to. In order to insure a working relationship between author and publication they should read all available copies of the publication and totally familiarize themselves with the product."

PRIME TIMES, Narcup, Inc., Editorial offices: 433 W. Washington Ave., Suite 503, Madison WI 53703. Executive Director: Steve Goldberg. Managing Editor: Glenn Deutsch. Quarterly magazine for uncommon retirees and people who want to redefine retirement. The audience is primarily retirees and people over 50 who were or are credit union members and want to plan and manage their retirement. Estab. 1979. Circ. 50,000. Pays on publication. Makes work-for-hire assignments. Buys first rights and second serial (reprint) rights. Submit seasonal material 3 months in advance. Previously published submissions OK. SASE. Reports in 1 month on queries; in 6 weeks on mss. Free sample copy with 9x12 SAE and 5 first-class stamps postage; free writer's guidelines for SASE.
Nonfiction: Exposé (of Sunbelt retirement condominium communities, insurance and medical rip-offs and mail-order investment frauds); how-to (related to financial planning methods; consumer activism; health; travel; and working after retirement); interview (of people over 50 who are leading active or important retirements); opinion; profile; travel; personal experience; and photo feature. "No rocking chair reminiscing." Buys 16-30 mss/year. Query with clips of previously published work. Length: 500-2,500 words. Pays $50-500. SASE.
Photos: Pays $50/8x10 b&w glossy high contrast prints. Pays $50/35mm color transparency; $7.50/cutline. Captions and model release required. Buys one-time rights. SASE.
Tips: "Query should state qualifications (expertise). And put five Ws and H in first paragraph (who, what, when, where, why and how). Freelancers should submit copy—double-spaced and typed 60 characters/line. They should also send photos, copies of photos, or other art accompanying the articles. Special issues requiring freelance work include publications on medical practice in the United States (geared to elders); money management; travel; and retirement communities. Whether urban or rural, male or female, if attempts at humor, lightness or tongue-in-cheek seem off-target to you, they will to me, too. Our only good humor is good-natured. And we don't gloss over important matters. If you identify a problem, we want you to identify a solution."

SENIOR EXCHANGE, S.E. Publishing Co., Box 249, Highwood IL 60040. (312)433-4550. Editor: Kirk Landers. Emphasizes the interests of retired and pre-retired persons, 55 years old and over. "We are changing the editorial format from a newsletter to a fast reading service magazine." Bimonthly magazine. Estab. 1977. Circ. 50,000. Pays on acceptance. Pays 25-50% kill fee. Buys all rights. Phone queries OK. Submit seasonal/holiday material 3 months in advance. Previously published work OK if accompanied by written permission from copyright owner. SASE. Send label and 25¢ for sample copy.
Nonfiction: Diet, health, recreation, retirement, travel, consumer advice, medicine, law, government, moneysaving tips, recipes/menus, entertainment and retirement communities. No condescending remarks, phony quotes, faked research, or sources of information whose qualifications are not clear. Buys 1-2 mss/issue. Query. Length: 1,500-2,000 words. Pays $100 maximum, "depending on merit."
Photos: State availability of photos with query or send photos with ms. Uses b&w 5x7 glossy prints.

Does not yet print color, but has used color prints for b&w reproduction. Offers no additional payment for photos accepted with ms. Captions required. Buys one-time rights.
Columns/Departments: Diet, health, recreation, retirement, travel, consumer adivce, medicine, law, government, money saving tips, recipes/menus, entertainment and retirement communities. Buys 7/year. Query. Length: 750-1,000 words. Pays $50 minimum.

SENIOR WORLD, Senior World Publications, Inc., 4640 Jewell St., San Diego CA 92109. (714)270-8181. Editor: Leonard J. Hansen. Managing Editor: Laura Impastato. Monthly tabloid about senior citizens for active older adults and senior citizens living in San Diego County. Circ. 83,000. Pays on publication. Rights vary. Submit seasonal material 3 months in advance. Simultaneous and photocopied submissions OK. SASE. Reports in 6 weeks. Sample copy $1; free writer's guidelines.
Nonfiction: Exposé (government bungling of senior citizen programs or concerns); general interests; how-to (save money; fix things around the house; make money; cook for one or two); humor and cartoons (positive representation of senior citizens); interview; profile (of remarkable seniors and celebrities who are now senior citizens and still active); new product; and photo feature (query). "No 'pity the poor senior' stories or 'walking 12 miles to school' stories or talking down to senior citizens." Query. Length: 200-900 words. Pay $15-75.
Photos: State availability of photos or send photos with ms. Pays $10-30 for 8x10 b&w prints. Offers no additional payment for photos accepted with ms. Captions prefered; model release required. Rights vary.
Columns/Departments: "All columns currently are staff written, but we will look at proposals." Query.
Tips: "Read the publication, see the very active news styles; realize that older adults and senior citizens are very active, alive and alert people. You're writing to senior citizens, not down to them. They read well and understand. Make query brief—no more than one page. A good clear explanation of the article proposed and information on photos or other illustrations to go with it plus a brief paragraph or two on the writer's background and other writing credits. We are always on the lookout for good celebrity profiles of seniors and remarkable seniors who are still working and making a contribution to society. Also innovative stories about new programs, projects etc. for seniors."

SEPTEMBER DAYS, Days Inns of America, Inc., 2751 Buford Hwy., NE Atlanta GA 30324. (404)325-4000. Editor: Tom Eppes. Quarterly magazine primarily covering travel, with some personalities, and human interest articles for members of the September Days Club, who are 55 and older and whose primary interest is travel. Circ. 260,000. Pays on publication. Submit seasonal material 6 months in advance. Simultaneous and photocopied submissions OK. SASE. Reports in 3 weeks. Sample copy $2; free writer's guidelines with SASE.
Nonfiction: General interest (for people 55 years and older; personality and celebrity profiles); travel (in the continental United States, destination stories); and photo feature (of the United States). No poems or historical pieces. Buys 4-5 mss/issue. Send complete ms. Length: 250-1,600 words. Pays 15¢/word; $240 maximum.
Photos: "Good, color transparencies or slides are a major factor in the decision to use or not to use a story. Limited black and white photos are acceptable." Pays $15 and up for 8x10 b&w prints. Pays $15 minimum for standard color transparencies. Captions preferred; model release required. Buys one-time rights.
Tips: "Send complete ms on spec only; must include photos."

Science

Publications classified here aim at laymen interested in technical and scientific developments and discoveries, applied science, and technical or scientific hobbies. Publications of interest to the personal computer owner are listed in the Home Computing category. Journals for professional scientists, engineers, repairmen, etc., will be found in Trade Journals.

ASTRONOMY, AstroMedia Corp., 411 E. Mason St., Box 92788, Milwaukee WI 53202. (414)276-2689. Editor: Richard Berry. Emphasizes the science of astronomy. Monthly magazine; 88 pages. Circ. 122,000. Pays on publication. Reports in 6-8 weeks. Sample copy $2; free writer's guidelines.

Nonfiction: How-to (build a telescope; grind a mirror); informational (latest research; what you can observe using a specific type or size of equipment, etc.). "We do not accept articles on UFOs, astrology or religion." Buys 40-50/year. Submit complete ms. Length: 1,500-3,000 words. Pays 5-10¢/word.

Photos: Purchased with or without mss, or on assignment. B&w and color. Send prints and transparencies. Pays $10/b&w; $10 minimum for color.

Columns/Departments: Astro News and Astronomy Reviews (books), and Forum. Buys 20-30/year. Query. Length: 150-500 words. Pays $3/typeset line; $35/review; $100/Forum.

CB MAGAZINE, 531 N. Ann Arbor, Oklahoma City OK 73127. Managing Editor: Gordon West. (405)947-6113. For operations of citizens band 2-way radio for personal and business communications. Monthly. Circ. 180,000. Pays on publication. Buys all rights. Byline given "except if there is major rewriting or additional research required." Free sample copy. SASE.

Nonfiction: Case histories of use of citizens band radio in disaster, crime or public service. Semitechnical articles about equipment installation, operation and repair. Interested in true-life stories where CB radio was used to render public service. Uses informational, how-to, personal experience, expose and technical. Buys 4 mss/issue. Query. Length: 500-1,500 words. Payment varies.

Photos: Send photos with ms. Offers no additional payment for photos accepted with ms. Uses b&w prints.

CQ: THE RADIO AMATEUR'S JOURNAL, 76 N. Broadway, Hicksville NY 11801. (516)681-2922. Editor: Alan Dorhoffer. For the amateur radio community. Monthly journal. Circ. 100,000. Pays on publication. Buys first rights. Phone queries OK. Submit seasonal/holiday material 3 months in advance. SASE. Reports in 2-3 weeks. Free sample copy.

Nonfiction: "We are interested in articles that address all technical levels of amateur radio. Included would be basic material for newcomers and intermediate and advanced material for oldtimers. Articles may be of a theoretical, practical or anecdotal nature. They can be general interest pieces for all amateurs or they can focus in on specific topics. We would like historical articles, material on new developments, articles on projects you can do in a weekend, and pieces on long-range projects taking a month or so to complete." Length: 6-10 typewritten pages. Pays $35/published page.

ELECTRONICS HOBBYIST, 380 Lexington Ave., New York NY 10017. (212)557-9100. Associate Publisher: Julian S. Martin. Editor: Gordon Sell. 100% freelance written. For "guys who like to build electronic projects from simple one-transistor jobs to complex computer dences." Annual magazine; 96 pages. Circ. 135,000. Buys all rights. Pays 100% kill fee. Byline given. Buys 60-80 mss/year. Pays on acceptance. No photocopied or simultaneous submissions. Reports in 1 month. Query. SASE.

Nonfiction: Construction projects only. "Write a letter to us telling details of proposed project." Length: open. Pays $150-250.

ELECTRONICS TODAY INTERNATIONAL, Unit 6, 25 Overlea Blvd., Toronto, Ontario, Canada M4H 1B1. (416)423-3262. Editor: Halvor Moorshead. 40% freelance written. Emphasizes audio, electronics and personal computing for a wide-ranging readership, both professionals and hobbyists. Monthly magazine; 76 pages. Circ. 27,000. Pays on publication. Buys all rights. Byline given. Phone queries OK. Submit seasonal/holiday material 4 months in advance. Photocopied submissions OK. SAE and International Reply Coupons. Reports in 4 weeks. Sample copy $2; free writer's guidelines.

Nonfiction: How-to (technical articles in electronics field); humor (if relevant to electronics); new product (if using new electronic techniques); and technical (on new developments, research, etc.). Buys 3-4 mss/issue. Query. Length: 600-3,500 words. Pays $30-70/1,000 words.

Photos: "Ideally we like to publish 2 photos or diagrams per 1,000 words of copy." State availability of photo material with query. Offers no additional payment for photos accepted with accompanying ms. Captions required. Buys all rights.

Fillers: Puzzles (mathematical). Buys 10/year. Length: 50-250 words. Pays $6-10.

FREY SCIENTIFIC COMPANY CATALOG, 905 Hickory Lane, Mansfield OH 44905. Published annually. Buys all rights. Buys 70-100 rhymes/year. Pays "on acceptance, between October 1 and January 1. Rhymes that arrive after the latter date are held and paid for about October 1, the start of our next publication season." SASE.

Poetry: Contact: Rhyme Editor. "We use humorous quatrains and limericks in our annual school science materials catalog, which is sent to every high school and college in the US. Each rhyme—limerick, quatrain, or couplet—is matched as best as possible to the appropriate section of our catalog. Rhymes pertaining to physics are included in the physics section, biology in the biology section, chemistry in the chemistry section, earth science to earth science, etc." Interested in buying material from writers "who can combine, in a single rhyme, our requirements of proper rhyme construction, distinct scientific reference, and humor. Generally, we will waive any of the three requirements if the rhyme is strong in the other two." Pays $5/rhyme.

FUSION MAGAZINE, Fusion Energy Foundation, Suite 2404, 888 7th Ave., New York NY 10019. (212)265-3749. Editor: Dr. Steven Bardwell. Managing Editor: Marjorie Mazel Hecht. Monthly magazine about fusion energy and nuclear energy for both lay and technical readers. Circ. 200,000. Pays on publication. Buys all rights and makes work-for-hire assignments. Phone queries OK. Photocopied and previously published submissions OK. SASE.
Nonfiction: Exposé (energy, science, research, environment and anti-science); general interest (epistemology and science education); historical (science, research, technology, economics, discoveries and industrial development); humor (political satire); interview (science figures); new product (high technology and medical technology); personal experience; photo feature (advanced energy technologies); and technical (advanced technology in biology, physics, medicine, fusion, fission research, breakthroughs and international scientific work); and conference reports. Query. Length: 500-3,500 words. Pays $100 minimum.
Photos: State availability of photos. Captions and model release required. Buys all rights.
Tips: "Look through back issues to see the range of topics and styles."

FUTURE LIFE, Starlog Press, 475 Park Ave., S., New York NY 10016. (212)689-2830. Editor: Bob Woods. Managing Editor: Barbara Krasnoff. Magazine published every 6 weeks covering futurism, space travel, popular science, etc.; for "intelligent, inquisitive persons interested in the possibilities of the future." Circ. 80,000. Pays on publication. Byline given. Buys first North American serial rights "with the option to publish in foreign edition." Simultaneous queries and photocopied submissions OK; previously published submissions "occasionally accepted." SASE. Reports in 1 month. Sample copy $2.50; free writer's guidelines for business size SAE and 1 first class stamp.
Nonfiction: Book excerpts, interview/profile, photo feature and technical. Buys 25 mss/year. Query. Length: 1,500-3,000 words. Pays $200 minimum.
Photos: State availability of photos. Pays $35-200 for 35mm color transparencies; $25 for 4x5 b&w prints. Captions and identification of subjects required. Buys one-time rights "with the option for publication in foreign edition."
Fillers: Newsbreaks. Buys 25/year. Length: 200-500 words. Pays $25-50.
Tips: "We are definitely open to newcomers. It helps if the writer has some background in the field."

HAM RADIO MAGAZINE, Greenville NH 03048. (603)878-1441. Editor: Alfred Wilson. For amateur radio licensees and electronics experimenters. Special May issue: antenna. Monthly. Circ. 80,000. Buys all rights. Buys 10 mss/month. Pays on acceptance. Submit special issue material 6 months in advance. Reports in 1 month. Query helpful, but not essential. SASE. Free sample copy and writer's guidelines.
Nonfiction: "Technical and home construction articles pertaining to amateur radio. Stress is placed on new developments. Technical articles of interest to the radio amateur, or home construction articles pertaining to amateur radio equipment. Experience has shown that writers who are not licensed amateur radio operators cannot write successfully for this publication." Length: 500-5,000 words. Pays approximately $35/magazine page. No fiction or operating news.
Photos: Sharp, clear glossy prints (4x5 to 8x10) purchased with accompanying mss.
Tips: "There are no special tricks; just offer good material. Every issue has articles from previously unpublished authors."

HIGH TECHNOLOGY, Technology Publishing Co., 38 Commercial Wharf, Boston MA 02110. (617)227-4700. Editor: Robert Haavind. Bimonthly magazine covering "all areas of high technology for managers, professionals and investors—technical and non-technical readers." Estab. 1981. Circ. 200,000. Pays on acceptance. Byline given. Offers negotiable kill fee. Buys all rights. SASE. Reports in 3 weeks. Free sample copy.
Nonfiction: "We're interested in important advances in high technology—where it's going, what's standing in the way, market factors, how does it work, and how does it compare with other technologies and economic factors and typical applications. *High Technology* is primarily written by technical specialists but edited for comprehension by nontechnical readers. No 'gee whiz' school of writing. No philosophy or speculation." Buys 36-48 mss/year. Query with clips of published work. Length: 3,000-4,000 words. Pays average $1,400.
Photos: Must be high quality photos." State availability of photos. Reviews 35mm and larger color transparencies and 8x10 b&w glossy prints. "Payment for photos is part of article payment." Captions required. Buys first rights.

Columns/Departments: Perspectives—new developments in high technology. Buys 20-40 mss/ year. Query. Length: 300-800. Pays $200-500.
Fillers: Updates. "Significant develpments in technology." Newsbreaks. Buys 60/year. Length: 2-4 sentences. Pays $50-100.

MECHANIX ILLUSTRATED, 1515 Broadway, New York NY 10036. (212)975-4111. Editor: David E. Petzal. Home and Shop Editor: Burt Murphy. Managing Editor: Paul M. Eckstein. Special issues include new cars (October). Monthly magazine; 106-180 pages. Buys all rights except for picture sets. Byline given. Pays on acceptance. Send SASE for copy of guidelines for writers. Reports "promptly." Query. SASE.
Nonfiction: Feature articles about science, inventions, electronics, alternative energy. We are seeking "more and more energy-related material." Length: 1,500-2,500 words. Pays $400 minimum. Also uses home workshop projects, kinks, etc., for Home and Shop section. Pays $75-700, and higher in exceptional circumstances. "We offer a varied market for all types of do-it-yourself material, ranging from simple tips on easier ways to do things to major construction projects, Furniture construction, painting, photography, gardening, concrete and masonry work or any type of building construction or repair are just a few of the subjects that interest." Pays minimum of $15 for a tip submitted on a post card without an illustration. Pays $20-25 for an illustrated and captioned tip.
Photos: Photos should accompany mss. Pays $400 and up for transparencies of interesting mechanical or scientific subjects accepted for cover; prefers 4x5, but 2¼x2¼ square is acceptable. Inside color: $300/1 page, $500/2, $700/3, etc. Pays $35/single (b&w) feature photo involving new developments, etc., in the field. Home and Shop tips illustrated with 1 photo, $25. Captions are required. B&w picture sets, $350 maximum. Requires model releases.
Fillers: Pays $75 for half-page fillers.
Tips: "If you're planning some kind of home improvement and can write, you might consider doing a piece on it for us. Good how-to articles on home improvement are always difficult to come by. Aside from that, no particular part of the book is easier to break into than another because we simply don't care whether you've been around or been published here before. We don't care who you are or whether you have any credentials—we're in the market for good journalism and if it's convincing, we buy it."

OMNI, 909 3rd. Ave., New York NY 10022. (212)593-3301. Executive Editor: Ben Bova. Editor: Bob Guccione. Monthly magazine of the future covering science fact, fiction, and fantasy for readers of all ages, backgrounds and interests. Circ. 1,000,000. Average issue includes 6 nonfiction articles and 2-3 fiction articles. Pays on acceptance. Offers 25% kill fee. Buys exclusive worldwide and first English rights and rights for *Omni* Anthology. Submit seasonal material 4 months in advance. Photocopied submissions OK. SASE. Reports in 1 month. Free writer's guidelines with SASE (request fiction or nonfiction).
Nonfiction: "We want articles with a futuristic angle, offering readers alternatives in housing, energy, transportation, medicine and communications. Executive editor Ben Bova explains that scientists can affect the public's perception of science and scientists by "opening their minds to the new possibilities of science journalism. People want to know, want to understand what scientists are doing and how scientific research is affecting their lives and their future. *Omni* publishes articles about science in language that people can understand. We seek very knowledgeable science writers who are ready to work with scientists to produce articles that can inform and interest the general reader." Buys 6 mss/issue. Send complete ms. Length: 2,500-3,500 words. Pays $850-1,250.
Photos: Art Director: Frank DeVino. State availability of photos. Reviews 5x7 b&w glossy prints. Captions required.
Columns/Departments: UFO Update; Explorations (unusual travel or locations on Earth); Innovations (new products; Mind (by and about psychiatrists and psychologists); Earth (environment); Life (biomedicine); Space (astronomy); Arts (theater, music, film, technololgy); Interview (of prominent person); People (prominent people in science); and Continuum (newsbreaks). Query with clips of previously published work. Length: 1,500 words maximum. Pays $500 minimum.
Fiction: Contact: Robert Sheckley. Fantasy and science fiction. Buys 2-3 mss/issue. Send complete ms. Length: 10,000 words maximum. Pays $850-1,250.
Tips: "Consider science fact and science fiction pictorials. We're interested in thematic composites of excellent photos or art with exciting copy."

POPULAR ELECTRONICS, 1 Park Ave., New York NY 10016. (212)725-3566. Editor-in-Chief: C.P. Gilmore.80% freelance written. For electronics experimenters, hi-fi enthusiasts, computer hobbyists, CB'ers, hams. Monthly. Estab. 1954. Circ. 400,000. Buys all rights. Pays 50% kill fee.

Byline given. Buys about 100 mss/year. Pays on acceptance. No photocopied or simultaneous submissions. Reports in 2-4 weeks. Query. SASE. Free writer's guidelines.

Nonfiction: "State-of-the-art reports, tutorial articles, construction projects, etc. The writer must know what he's talking about and not depend on 'hand-out' literature from a few manufacturers or research laboratories. The writer must always bear in mind that the reader has some knowledge of electronics." Informational, how-to, and technical articles. Query; if a project, include a block diagram or schematic and approximate cost to builder. Length: 500-3,000 words. Pays $80-150/published page with photo illustration, rough diagrams. B&w glossy prints preferred, though color transparencies are sometimes used.

Fillers: Electronics circuits quizzes, circuit and bench tips. Length: 100-1,000 words. Pays $10-100.

POPULAR MECHANICS, 224 W. 57th St., New York NY 10019. (212)262-4815. Editor: John A. Linkletter. Executive Editor: Robin Nelson. Managing Editor: William Hartford. Home and Shop Editor: Harry Wicks. Monthly magazine; 200 pages. Circ. 1,671,216. Buys all rights. Byline given. Pays "promptly." Query. SASE.

Nonfiction: Needs material on "ingenious ways readers are coping with growing energy shortages—both in their homes and in their automobiles. Principal subjects are automotive (new cars, car maintenance) and how-to (woodworking, metalworking, home improvement and home maintenance). In addition, we use features on new technology, sports, electronics, photography and hi-fi." Exciting male interest articles with strong science, exploration and adventure emphasis. Looking for reporting on new and unusual developments. The writer should be specific about what makes it new, different, better, cheaper, etc. "We are always looking for fresh ideas in home maintenance, shop technique and crafts for project pieces used in the back part of the book. The front of the book uses articles in technology and general science, but writers in that area should have background in science." Length: 300-2,000 words. Pays $300-800 and up.

Photos: Dramatic photos are most important, and they should show people and things in action. Occasionally buys picture stories with short text block and picture captions. The photos must tell the story without much explanation. Topnotch photos are a must with Craft Section articles. Can also use remodeling of homes, rooms and outdoor structures. Pays $25 minimum.

Fillers: How-to articles on craft projects and shop work well-illustrated with photos and drawings. The writer must provide the drawings, diagrams, cutaways, and/or photos that would be appropriate to the piece. Finished drawings suitable for publication are not necessary; rough but accurate pencil drawings are adequate for artist's copy. Pays $15.

POPULAR SCIENCE MONTHLY, 380 Madison Ave., New York NY 10017. Editor-in-Chief: C.P. Gilmore. For the well-educated adult, interested in science, technology, new products. Monthly magazine; 200 pages. Circ. 1,850,000. Buys all rights. Pays negotiable kill fee. Byline given. Buys several hundred mss a year. Pays on acceptance. Free guidelines for writers. No photocopied or simultaneous submissions. Submit seasonal material 4 months in advance. Reports in 3 weeks. Query. SASE.

Nonfiction: "*Popular Science Monthly* is devoted to exploring (and explaining) to a nontechnical but knowledgeable readership the technical world around us. We are a 'thing'-oriented publication: things that fly or travel down a turnpike, or go on or under the sea, or cut wood, or reproduce music, or build buildings, or make pictures, or mow lawns. We are especially focused on the new, the ingenious and the useful. We are consumer-oriented and are interested in any product that adds to a man's enjoyment of his home, yard, car, boat, workshop, outdoor recreation. Some of our 'articles' are only a picture and caption long. Some are a page long. Some occupy 4 or more pages. Contributors should be as alert to the possibility of selling us pictures and short features as they are to major articles. Freelancers should study the magazine to see what we want and avoid irrelevant submissions." Length: 2,000 words maximum. Pays $200 a published page minimum. Prefers 8x10 b&w glossy prints. Pays $25.

Fillers: Uses shortcuts and tips for homeowners, home craftsmen, car owners, mechanics and machinists.

Tips: "Probably the easiest way to break in here is by covering a news story in science and technology that we haven't heard about yet. We need people to be acting as bird-dogs for us out there and we are willing to give the most leeway on these performances. What impresses us the most in a freelance piece—when we're thinking about uncovering a good contributor for the future—is the kind of illustrations the writer supplies. Too many of them kiss off the problem of illustrations. Nothing impresses us more than knowing that the writer can take or acquire good photos to accompany his piece. We probably buy the most freelance material in the do-it-yourself and home improvement areas."

QUEST/STAR, The World of Science Fiction, MW Communications Inc., 247 Fort Pitt Blvd., Pittsburgh PA 15222. (412)562-0362. Publisher: William G. Wilson Jr. Managing Editor: Paul D.

Adomites. Magazine published 9x/year covering all aspects of science fiction, fantasy, horror and science for "upscale readers who want more than just entertainment; people who are looking to the future with a positive attitude and a smile." Circ. 130,000. Pays publication. Byline given. Offers 25% kill fee. Buys first North American serial rights or makes work-for-hire assignments. Photocopied and previously published submissions ("if published overseas") OK. SASE. Reports in 1 month. Sample copy $2; free writer's guidelines.

Nonfiction: General interest (unique looks at how science fiction is a look into the future); nostalgic (looks at great science fiction and genre films of the past); humor (science fiction-oriented satires and spoofs but "steer clear of personality attacks"); profile (film directors, technical people, etc.); and technical ("using science fiction as a springboard into views of the future"). Buys 12-15 mss/year. Query with clips of published work and brief biography. Length: 1,000-5,000 words. Pays 2½¢-5¢/word.

Photos: State availability of photos. Pays $10 minimum for 4x5 color transparencies; $5 minimum for 8x10 b&w glossy prints. Captions required. Must include "names and places (check spelling) and all pertinent copyright and release information." Buys one-time rights.

Columns/Departments: Prism (news, views, people-style featurette). Buys 30 mss/year. Length: 100-250 words. Pays $10-30.

Fiction: "Send no unsolicited fiction. We are currently buying all our fiction via special assignment."

Tips: "Our 'Prism' department is a great way for us to get to know each other, because we like writers who, like us, are curious, involved and easily bored with 'typical' articles and stories. We like to think of ourselves as the *Life* magazine of science fiction. We want a wide range of subjects treated, but all with high levels of quality and freshness. Query should include good background information from the writer on his experience and credentials; good, thoughtful suggestions and questions regarding our audience and our needs."

RADIO-ELECTRONICS, 200 Park Ave. S., New York NY 10003. (212)777-6400. Managing Editor: Art Kleiman. For electronics professionals and hobbyists. Monthly magazine, 128 pages. Circ. 185,000. Buys all rights. Byline given. Pays on acceptance. Submit seasonal/holiday material 6-8 months in advance. SASE. Reports in 3 weeks. Send for "Guide to Writing."

Nonfiction: Interesting technical stories on all aspects of electronics, including video, radio, computers, communications, and stereo written from viewpoint of the electronics professional, serious experimenter, or layman with technical interests. Construction (how-to-build-it) articles used heavily. Unique projects bring top dollars. Cost of project limited only by what item will do. Emphasis on "how it works, and why." Much of material illustrated with schematic diagrams and pictures provided by author. Also high interest in how-to articles. Length: 1,000-1,500 words. Pays about $50-500.

Photos: State availability of photos. Offers no additional payment for b&w prints or 35mm color transparencies. Model releases required.

Columns/Departments: Pays $50-200/column.

Fillers: Pays $15-35.

Tips: "The simplest way to come in would be with a short article on some specific construction project. Queries aren't necessary; just send the article, 5 or 6 typewritten pages."

SCIENCE & ELECTRONICS, Davis Publications, 380 Lexington Ave., New York NY 10017. (212)557-9100. Associate Publisher: Dr. Julian S. Martin. Editor: Alan Rose. For all computer hobbyist types and electronics hobbyists. Bimonthly magazine; 100 pages. Circ. 250,000. Buys all rights. Pays 100% kill fee. Byline given. Pays on acceptance. No photocopied or simultaneous submissions. SASE. Reports in 2 weeks. Free sample copy and writer's guidelines.

Nonfiction: "Our need for the eighties will be in the computer hardware and software areas. Hobbycomputing will be the major topic of interest in S&E. All software programs submitted as part of a story should be presented in the 'list' form on a computer printout, plus the program on a printout as a 'run.' Should you not understand these instruction, your experience in computers is insufficient to consider writing for us." How-to and technical articles. "The writer should read our book and decide whether he can be of service to us; and then send us a precis of the story he wishes to submit." Buys 15 mss/issue. Query. Length: 1,000-5,000 words. Pays $150 minimum.

Photos: No additional payment for photos used with mss.

Tips: "I would make three suggestions. First, "how-to" instructional pieces are always winners. The same goes for construction projects. But they must be to fulfill some need, not just for the sake of selling an article. Finally, installation stories are very good—something that you buy and where the installation takes some degree of know-how that can be illustrated with step-by-step photos. The author will have to take the photos as he does the job. Theory pieces are tougher—you have to really know us and sense our needs and the sorts of things our readers want to learn about. Feeling and timing are key. Please read the magazine first!"

SCIENCE & MECHANICS, Davis Publications, 380 Lexington Ave., New York NY 10017. Editor-in-Chief: Joseph Daffron. Managing Editor: Stephen Wagner. Published quarterly. Pays on acceptance. Buys all rights. Submit seasonal material 5 months in advance of issue date. SASE. Reports in 2 weeks.
Nonfiction: How-to (wood, mechanical, electronic and outdoor projects; home fix-up and repair); general interest (science, mechanics, technology, energy saving); and technical (what's new, inventions, electronics, science, technology, automotive and mechanical). Buys 10-12 mss/issue. Length: 2,500-4,000 words. Query first; rates negotiable.
Photos: "Technical and how-to material must be illustrated; would like to see drawings and diagrams, if applicable." State availability of photos with query. Captions preferred.

SCIENCE DIGEST, Hearst Magazines Division, Hearst Corp., 224 W. 57th St., New York NY 10019. (212)262-4161. Editor-in-Chief: Scott DeGarmo. Emphasizes sciences and technologies for all ages with a scientific bent. Monthly magazine; 140 pages. Circ. 500,000. Pays on acceptance. Buys all rights. Pays kill fee. Byline given. Submit seasonal/holiday material 3 months in advance.
Nonfiction: Informational (authentic, timely information in all areas of science). Buys 100 mss/year. Query.
Photos: Purchased with or without accompanying ms or on assignment. Captions required. Query.
Fillers: Amazing Scientific Facts. Length: 50-250 words. Pays $25-50.

SCIENCE NEWS, Science Service, Inc., 1719 N St. NW, Washington DC 20036. Editor-in-Chief: Robert Trotter. For scientists and science-oriented laymen. Weekly magazine; 16 pages. Circ. 175,000. Pays on acceptance. Buys all rights. SASE.
Nonfiction: Profile and technical news. Buys 4 mss/year. Query or send complete ms. Pays $75-200. "Freelancers should study the magazine to see what we want and avoid irrelevant submissions." Length: 2,000 words maximum. Pays a minimum of about $150/published page. "We are primarily staff-written for two reasons: (1) Being a weekly newsmagazine, we work very close to deadline. Communications and coordination are crucial. Everyone must note what we've previously reported on the same subject and then add what's new. (2) Quality control. We have really gotten burned in the past by freelance articles that were factually inaccurate. We are occasionally in the market for prepublication excerpts from books, especially those involving a thoughtful, humanistic approach toward science, by noted scientists of established reputation; but again this is seldom."
Photos: Prefers 8x10 b&w glossy prints. Pays $75-200.
Tips: "Acceptance occurs when the writer is either covering a newsworthy scientific meeting that for some reason we have no reporter attending, or has a topical news-feature article (1,500-1,800 words) on a specific science topic that we haven't already covered. For them to work for us, writers must be very familiar with *Science News* (suitable for scientists and the scientifically interested lay public) and for the subjects we already cover thoroughly. These include, generally, physics, astronomy, the space sciences, behavioral sciences and medical sciences. Articles must have both news and science value."

SCIENTIFIC AMERICAN, 415 Madison Ave., New York NY 10017. Articles by professional scientists only.

73 MAGAZINE, Peterborough NH 03458. (603)924-3873. Publisher: Wayne Green. For amateur radio operators and experimenters. Monthly. Buys all rights. Pays on acceptance. Reports on submissions within a few weeks. Query. SASE.
Nonfiction: Articles on anything of interest to radio amateurs, experimenters and computer hobbyists—construction projects. Pays $40-50/page.
Photos: Photos purchased with ms.
Tips: Query letter "should be as specific as possible. Don't hold back details that would help us make a decision. We are not interested in theoretical discussions, but in practical ideas and projects which our readers can use."

TECHNOLOGY REVIEW, Alumni Association of the Massachusetts Institute of Technology, Room 10-1040, Massachusetts Institute of Technology, Cambridge MA 02139. Editor-in-Chief: John I. Mattill. Managing Editor: Steven J. Marcus. 10% freelance written. Emphasizes technology and its implications for scientists, engineers, managers and social scientists. Magazine published 8 times/year. Circ. 65,000. Pays on publication. Buys all rights. Phone queries OK. Submit seasonal/holiday material 6 months in advance of issue date. Simultaneous and photocopied submissions OK. SASE. Reports in 6 weeks. Sample copy $2.50.
Nonfiction: General interest, interview, photo feature and technical. Buys 3-5 mss/year. Query. Length: 1,000-10,000 words. Pays $75-300.

Columns/Departments: Book Reviews; Trend of Affairs; Society; Technology and Science and "Prospects" (guest column). Also special reports on other appropriate subjects. Buys 1 ms/issue. Query. Length: 750-1,500 words. Pays $75-150.

Science Fiction

ANALOG SCIENCE FICTION & SCIENCE FACT, 380 Lexington Ave., New York NY 10017. Editor: Dr. Stanley Schmidt. 100% freelance written. For general future-minded audience. Monthly. Buys first North American and nonexclusive foreign serial rights. Byline given. Pays on acceptance. Reports in 3-4 weeks. SASE.
Nonfiction: Illustrated technical articles dealing with subjects of not only current but future interest, i.e., with topics at the present frontiers of research whose likely future developments have implications of wide interest. Query. Length: 5,000 words. Pays 5¢/word.
Photos: Buys photos with mss only. Pays $5.
Fiction: "Basically, we publish science fiction stories. That is, stories in which some aspect of future science or technology is so integral to the plot that, if some aspect were removed, the story would collapse. The science can be physical, sociological or psychological. The technology can be anything from electronic engineering to biogenetic engineering. But the stories must be strong and realistic, with believable people doing believable things things—no matter how fantastic the background might be." Send complete ms on short fiction; query about serials. Length: 2,000-60,000 words. Pays 3.5-4.6¢/word for novelettes and novels; 5.75-6.9¢/word for shorts under 7,500 words.
Tips: "In query give clear indication of central ideas and themes and general nature of story line—and what is distinctive or unusual about it. We have no hard-and-fast editorial guidelines, because science fiction is such a broad field that I don't want to inhibit a new writer's thinking by imposing 'Thou Shalt Not's.' Besides, a really good story can make an editor swallow his preconceived taboos. *Analog* will consider material submitted from any writer and consider it solely on the basis of merit. We are definitely anxious to find and develop new, capable writers."

ARES, SPI, 257 Park Ave., S., New York, NY 10010. (212)673-4103. Editor: Redmond A. Simonsen. Managing Editor: Michael Moore. Bimonthly magazine for people interested in science fiction, fantasy and simulation games. Estab. 1980. Circ. 15,000. Average issue includes 1-3 fiction articles, 1-2 nonfiction articles and 3 columns. Pays on acceptance. Byline given. Buys first English language serial rights. Phone queries OK. Submit seasonal material 4 months in advance. Simultaneous (if so indicated) and photocopied submissions ok. SASE. Reports in 6 weeks. Sample copy $4; free writer's guidelines with SASE.
Nonfiction: "We are interested in science and historical magic and myth as they relate to science fiction and fantasy." Buys 1-2 mss/issue. Send complete ms. Length: 3,000-6,000 words. Pays 3¢-4¢/word depending on the experience of the writer.
Fiction: Fantasy and science fiction. "We want action-oriented fiction with identifiable protagonists and antagonists; problem solving, hard science fiction; adventure/survival; quest; battle; challenge/mission; and empire building. Especially interested in stories that tie-in with the adventure game in that issue. We do not want 'better mousetrap' and interesting gadget stories." Buys 1-3 mss/issue. Send complete ms. Length: 2,500-5,000 words. Pays 3¢-6¢/word depending on the experience of the writer.
Tips: "Query letter should tie in story article idea with style of magazine's content; it should not be a shot in the dark that has nothing to do with the kinds of material used previously. Know the magazine and what is in keeping with past issues. At the same time, come up with original ideas. We have heavy backlog of fantasy short fiction. Would prefer to see more science fiction."

ISAAC ASIMOV'S SCIENCE FICTION MAGAZINE, Davis Publications, Inc., 380 Lexington Ave. New York NY 10010. (212)557-9100. Editor-in-Chief: George H. Scithers. 100% freelance written. Emphasizes science fiction. 13 times a year magazine; 176 pages. Circ. 150,000. Pays on acceptance. Buys first North American serial rights and foreign serial rights. Photocopied submissions OK. SASE. Reports in 2-3 weeks. Writer's guidelines for SASE.
Nonfiction: Science. Query first.
Fiction: Science fiction only. "At first, each story must stand on its own; but as the magazine progresses, we want to see continuing use of memorable characters and backgrounds." No UFO stories or computers gone berserk. Buys 12 mss/issue. Submit complete ms. Length: 100-15,000 words. Pays 3-5¢/word.
Tips: Query letters not wanted, except for non-fiction.

GALILEO: Magazine of Science & Fiction, Avenue Victor Hugo, Inc., 339 Newbury St., Boston MA 02115. Editor: Charles C. Ryan. Bimonthly magazine; 96 pages. Circ. 70,000. Pays on publication. Buys first world serial rights and nonexclusive options on anthology rights and foreign serial rights. Byline given. Submit seasonal/holiday material 6-8 months in advance. Photocopied submissions OK. SASE. Reports in 4-8 weeks. Sample copy $1.95.

Nonfiction: Interview and technical. "We are interested in articles which examine in clear, easy-to-understand, but eloquent language the theoretical limits of science. Also articles which examine future developments as well as interviews with top science fiction authors or top scientists." Buys 3-4 mss/issue. Query with SASE, brisk outline and sample of 1-2 pages of article. Length: 2,500 words maximum.

Columns/Departments: Book and Movie Reviews. Query with SASE. Buys 5/issue. Length 350-500 words. Pays $10-25.

Fiction: Science fiction and serialized novels. "Be imaginative, rather than imitative." Buys 30-42 mss/year. Send complete ms. Length: 1,500-20,000 words. Pays 3-10¢/word.

Poetry: Avant-garde, free verse, haiku, light verse and traditional. "Poems must be about science or science fiction in nature." Buys 1/issue. Pays 3-10¢/word.

Fillers: Jokes, gags and anecdotes of science or science fiction. Pays 3¢/word.

NIGHT VOYAGES, The Last Angry Zine, Creative Images, Box 175, Freeburg IL 62243. (618)397-7059. Publisher/Literary Editor: Gerald J. Brown. Art Editor: Charles Pitts. Magazine published "approximately twice yearly" covering science fiction, fantasy fiction, illustration, and supplementary material offering perspectives on professional writing and illustrating. Circ. 1,300. Pays on publication. Byline given. Buys first North American serial rights, or first rights. Submit seasonal/holiday material 3 months in advance. SASE. Reports "as quickly as possible." Sample copy for 8½x11 SAE and 52¢ postage; free writer's guidelines.

Nonfiction: Expose and interview/profile; possibly historical/nostalgic and humor. "Trick ending not a requisite, but quality is. Exceeding of 2,000-word limit must be justifiable. No unsolicited reviews of anything; no personal experience pieces on things that happen at conventions unless it directly ties in with professional writer/artist, who should be the main focus." Buys 3-5 mss/year. Query. Length: 5,000 words. Pays "¼-2¢/word, negotiable, with $60 maximum."

Photos: State availability of photos. Pays $3-10 for b&w prints. Identification of subjects required. Buys one-time rights.

Fiction: Experimental, fantasy, horror, science fiction; possibly adventure, mainstream, mystery and suspense. "No overly long fiction. I have a particular aversion to overly cute satire and thinly veiled autobiographical vignettes." Buys 15-20 mss/year. Send complete ms. Length: 2,000 words. Pays "¼-2¢/word negotiable, with $60 maximum."

Poetry: "We are *very* limited on this, and we only use exceptionally good material in rare instances." Buys 2-3 mss/year. Submit maximum 2 poems. Length: open. Pays $5/accepted poem.

Tips: "Quality, entertaining stories are what we are looking for, with or without clever endings. Material should conform to our thematic concentration, be well researched where necessary, and accurate in slant on human nature. We exist for the sole purpose of supplementing the freelance literary market, regardless of what our thematic concentration may be. Stories and illustrations we cannot use we will at least try to give valid reasons as to why we can't. We wish to cooperate and assist newcomers getting started with their chosen avocations. We're looking for good semi-professionals who enjoy writing and illustrating, not overly concerned with monetary aspect—at least not as much as with the prospect of seeing their work in print and reaching a wider audience. All contributors whose work sees print will receive one complimentary copy of the book their work appears in."

PARSEC Fanzine of Science Fiction & Fantasy, SLB Communications, 48466 Jasper Dr., Oakridge OR 97463. (503)782-3029. Editor: Stanley L. Blumenthal. Annual newsletter covering science fiction and fantasy. "We try to reach those who are just breaking into the SF/Fantasy market." Estab. 1979. Pays on acceptance. Byline given. Buys all rights. Photocopied and previously published submissions OK. Reports in 1 month. Sample copy available $3.50; writer's guidelines for business size SAE and 1 first class stamp.

Fiction: Fantasy and science fiction only. Deadline for all copy is April 15. "We are in the market for hardcore science fiction, science fantasy and space opera type stories." Buys 10 mss/year. Send complete ms. Length: 3,000-5,000 words. Pays $5-25.

Tips: "Don't be discouraged if we reject your material first time around. Just keep writing and keep sending it in. Get published now, for tommorrow nobody will be reading anything anymore!"

SPACE AND TIME, 138 W. 70th St., New York NY 10023. Editor: Gordon Linzner. Quarterly magazine covering fantasy fiction, with a broad definition of fantasy that encompasses science fiction, horror, swords and sorcery, etc. Circ. 300. Pays on acceptance. Byline given. Buys first

North American serial rights. Photocopied submissions OK. SASE. Reports in 3 months. Sample copy $2.

Fiction: Fantasy, horror and science fiction. "Submit skillful writing and original ideas. We lean toward strong plot and character. No fiction based on TV shows or movies (*Star Trek*, *Star Wars*, etc.) or popular established literary characters (i.e., Conan) except as satire or other special case. No UFO, gods from space, or material of that ilk, unless you've got a drastically new slant." Buys 24 mss/year. Length: 15,000 words maximum. Pays ¼¢/word plus contributor's copies.

Poetry: Free verse, haiku, light verse, traditional and narrative. "No poetry without a definite fantastic theme or content." Buys 12 mss/year. Submit maximum 5 poems. Length: open. Pays in contributor's copies.

Tips: "All areas are open to freelancers, but we would particularly like to see more hard science fiction, and fantasies set in 'real' historical times."

STARWIND, The Starwind Press, Box 3346, Columbus OH 43210. Editors: Dave Powell, Louis Kennedy, Eric Nickels. 70-80% freelance written. Interested in science fiction and fantasy. Magazine; 50-60 pages. Twice a year (fall and spring). Circ. 2,500. Rights purchased vary with author and material. May buy first North American serial rights or second serial (reprint) rights. Buys about 25 mss/year. Pays on publication. Will consider photocopied submissions. No simultaneous submissions. Reports in 6-8 weeks. Submit complete ms. SASE. Sample copy $2; free writer's guidelines with SASE.

Nonfiction: "Interested in analyses of works of well-known science fiction authors and genres in sf and fantasy, or interviews with sf authors or publishers. Reviews of sf books. Also interested in articles dealing with current developments or research in space exploration or colonization, artificial intelligence, genetics, bioengineering, or other subjects. Emphasis should be on extrapolations which are of interest to readers of science fiction." Length: 2,000-10,000 words. Pays 1¢/word.

Fiction: "Both hard and soft science fiction, including extrapolative and speculative stories. "We will consider science fantasy, dark fantasy, sword and sorcery and occult material only if it is both original in content and competent in execution. We are looking for interesting, imaginative story-telling. We like to showcase the work of new authors and welcome stylistic experimentation." Length: 10,000 words maximum. Pays 1¢/word.

Tips: "Our magazine is geared to writers who are trying to break into the publishing field. We include articles about where to submit mss, etc. We are interested in good satire and parody. We emphasize originality and new ideas."

WEIRDBOOK, Box 35, Amherst Branch, Buffalo NY 14226. Editor-in-Chief: W. Paul Ganley. Emphasizes weird fantasy (swords and sorcery, supernatural horror, pure fantasy) for educated, mature readers of all ages, a readership teen-age and up. Irregularly published magazine; 64 pages. Circ. 900. Pays on publication. Buys first North American serial rights and right to reprint as part of entire issue. Photocopied submissions OK. SASE. "Best time to submit is in December or May if quick response is desired." Sample copy $3; writer's guidelines for SASE.

Fiction: Adventure (with weird elements); experimental (maybe, if in fantasy or horror area). Buys 6 mss/year. Submit complete ms. "No unsolicited manuscripts accepted until after January 1983." Length: 20,000 words maximum. Pays ¼¢/word minimum.

WHISPERS, Box 904, Chapel Hill NC 27514. Editor: Dr. Stuart David Schiff. 100% freelance written. For intelligent adults with an interest in literate horror, terror, fantasy, and heroic fantasy. Many readers collect first edition books and the like in these fields. Magazine; 164 pages. An approximate biannual schedule. Circ. 3,000. Buys first North American serial rights only. Buys 15-20 mss/year. Pays half of fee on acceptance; balance on publication. Photocopied submissions OK. No simultaneous submissions. Reports in 3 months. Submit complete ms. SASE.

Fiction: Stories of fantasy, terror, horror and heroic fantasy. No science fiction such as rocket ships, futuristic societies, bug-eyed monsters or the like. Authors whose work is most related to their needs include H. P. Lovecraft, Lord Dunsany, Edgar Allan Poe, Algernon Blackwood, Robert Bloch, Fritz Leiber, Ray Bradbury and Clark Ashton Smith. Length: 500-5,000 words. Pays 1¢/word.

Social Science

PARAPSYCHOLOGY REVIEW, 228 E. 71st St., New York NY 10021. (212)751-5940. Editor: Betty Shapin. Emphasizes psychic research, parapsychology, research and experiments pertaining to extrasensory perception. For the scientific community, academic community, lay audience with special interest in psychical research and the paranormal. Bimonthly. Circ. 2,500. Buys all rights. Byline given. Buys 20-30 mss/year. Pays on acceptance. Reports in 2 weeks. Query or submit complete ms. SASE. Sample copy $1.50.

Nonfiction: Articles, news items, book reviews in this general subject area. Must approach psychical research in scientific, experimental fashion. Length: 500-3,000 words. Pays $50 minimum.

Tips: "We are not interested in personal experiences or most anecdotal material. We need well-documented theory and reports of experiments or other studies."

PSYCHOLOGY TODAY, 1 Park Ave., New York NY 10016. (212)725-2500. For intelligent laymen concerned with society and individual behavior. Monthly. Buys all rights. Pays 10% kill fee. Byline given. Each ms will be edited by staff and returned to author prior to publication for comments and approval. Author should retain a copy. Reports in 1 month. Address all queries to Articles Editor. SASE.

Nonfiction: Most mss are based on scientific research and written by scholars; freelancers are used very rarely. Primary purpose is to provide the nonspecialist with accurate, surprising and/or fresh readable information about society and behavior. Technical and specialized vocabularies should be avoided except in cases where familiar expressions cannot serve as adequate equivalents and technical expressions, when necessary, should be defined carefully for the nonexpert. References to technical literature should not be cited within article. One-page queries should usually be accompanied by one or more of the scholarly presentations or papers on which suggested story is based. Usual length of finished articles: 3,000 words. Usual payment is $550.

Tips: "Be a researcher with talent, imagination and a solid grasp of social science methodology—or a trained science journalist thoroughly knowledgeable in the field being reported."

SEXOLOGY TODAY (formerly *Sexology*), 313 W. 53rd St., New York NY 10019. For a lay readership. Monthly magazine; 96 pages. Circ. 100,000. Pays on acceptance. Buys all rights, first serial rights or second serial (reprint) rights. SASE. Reports in 4 weeks.

Nonfiction: "We are seeking articles to bring frank information that will help readers in their sexual experiences and relationships. Themes must be solidly educational or informative and, at the same time, entertaining. Our editorial aim is to provide helpful, accurate guidance and advice. We eschew sensationalism, but any solid attempt to bring information to our public is reviewed. We regularly publish how-to themes with specific advice, including sexual acts. We seek articles about sexuality, psychology, sexual lifestyles, singles, new scientific breakthroughs, sociological/philosophical perspectives, first person pieces and modern appraisals of the relationship/sex theme." Query with outline (Please include a writing sample). Length: 1,500-3,000 words. Pays $200 minimum.

Tips: "We are open to completed manuscripts, no copies please, that run our word length and are compatible with our magazine's content and style. We aren't particularly concerned with name authors, rather good ones. Too many writers obviously are looking for an 'easy' sell or a guaranteed column that really expresses nothing new or original. Good writing is a must. Don't press for a long-term commitment before we know you are a writer who is understanding of our editorial goals and values."

THE SINGLE PARENT, Parents Without Partners, Inc., 7910 Woodmont Ave., Washington DC 20014. (301)654-8850. Editor-in-Chief: Kathryn C. Geruing. Emphasizes marriage, family, divorce, widowhood and children. Distributed to members of Parents Without Partners, plus libraries, universities, psychologists, psychiatrists, etc. Magazine, published 10 times/year; 48 pages. Circ. 220,000. Pays on publication. Rights purchased vary. Phone queries OK. Submit seasonal/holiday material 3 months in advance of issue date. Simultaneous, photocopied and previously published submissions OK. SASE. Reports in 6-8 weeks. Free sample copy and writer's guidelines.

Nonfiction: Informational (parenting, career development, money management, day care); interview (with professionals in the field, with people who have successfully survived the trauma of divorce); how-to (raise children alone, travel, take up a new career, home/auto fix-up). Buys 4-5 mss/issue. Query. Length: 1,000-2,000 words. Pay is negotiable.

Photos: Purchased with accompanying ms. Query. Pays $10-50 for any size b&w glossies. Model release required.

Rejects: "No first-hand accounts of bitter legal battles with former spouses."

TRANSACTION/SOCIETY, Rutgers University, New Brunswick NJ 08903. (201)932-2280, ext. 83. Editor: Irving Louis Horowitz. For social scientists (policymakers with training in sociology, political issues and economics). Every 2 months. Circ. 45,000. Buys all rights. Byline given. Pays on publication. Free sample copy and writer's guidelines. Will consider photocopied submissions. No simultaneous submissions. Reports in 4 weeks. Query. SASE.

Nonfiction and Photos: Articles Editor: Karen Osborne. Photo Editor: Joan DuFault. "Articles of wide interest in areas of specific interest to the social science community. Must have an awareness of problems and issues in education, population and urbanization that are not widely reported. Articles on overpopulation, terrorism, international organizations. No general think pieces." Payment for articles is made only if done on assignment. *No payment for unsolicited articles.* Pays $200 for photographic essays done on assignment or accepted for publication.

Tips: "Submit an article on a thoroughly unique subject, written with good literary quality."

VICTIMOLOGY: An International Journal, Box 39045, Washington DC 20016. (703)528-8872. Editor-in-Chief: Emilio C. Viano. "We are the only magazine specifically focusing on the victim, on the dynamics of victimization; for social scientists, criminal justice professionals and practitioners, social workers and volunteer and professional groups engaged in prevention of victimization and in offering assistance to victims of rape, spouse abuse, child abuse, natural disasters, etc." Quarterly magazine. Circ. 2,500. Pays on publication. Buys all rights. Byline given. SASE. Reports in 6-8 weeks. Sample copy $5; free writer's guidelines.

Nonfiction: Expose, historical, how-to, informational, interview, personal experience, profile, research and technical. Buys 10 mss/issue. Query. Length: 500-5,000 words. Pays $50-150.

Photos: Purchased with accompanying ms. Captions required. Send contact sheet. Pays $15-50 for 5x7 or 8x10 b&w glossy prints.

Poetry: Avant-garde, free verse, light verse and traditional. Length: 30 lines maximum. Pays $10-25.

Tips: "Focus on what is being researched and discovered on the victim, the victim-offender relationship, treatment of the offender, the bystander-witness, preventive measures, and what is being done in the areas of service to the victims of rape, spouse abuse, neglect and occupational and environmental hazards and the elderly."

Sports

The publications listed in this category are intended for sports activists, sports fans, or both. They buy material on how to practice and enjoy both team and individual sports, material on conservation of streams and forests, and articles reporting on and analyzing professional sports.

Writers will note that several editors mention that they do not wish to see "Me 'n Joe" stories. These are detailed accounts of one hunting/fishing trip taken by the author and a buddy—starting with the friends' awakening at dawn and ending with their return home, "tired but happy."

For the convenience of writers who specialize in one or two areas of sport and outdoor writing, the publications are subcategorized by the sport or subject matter they emphasize. Publications in related categories (for example, Hunting and Fishing; Archery and Bowhunting) often buy similar material (in this case articles on bow and arrow hunting). Consequently, writers should read through this entire Sport and Outdoor category to become familiar with the subcategories and note the ones that contain markets for their own type of writing.

Publications concerned with horse breeding, hunting dogs or the use of other animals in sport are classified in the Animal category. Publications dealing with automobile or motorcycle racing will be found in the Automotive and Motorcycle category. Outdoor publications that exist to further the preservation of nature, placing only secondary emphasis on preserving nature as a setting for sport, are listed in the Nature, Conservation, and Ecology category. Newspapers and Magazine sections, as well as Regional magazines, are frequently interested in conservation or sports material with a local angle. Camping publications are classified in the Travel, Camping, and Trailer category.

Archery and Bowhunting

ARCHERY WORLD, 225 E. Michigan, Milwaukee WI 53202. Editor: Robert Brandau. 30-50% freelance written. For "archers of average education, hunters and target archers, experts to beginners." Subject matter is the "entire scope of archery—hunting, bowfishing, indoor target, outdoor target, field." Bimonthly. Circ. 105,000. Buys first serial rights. Buys 30-35 mss/year. Pays on publication. Will send a free sample copy to a writer on request. Tries to report in 2 weeks. Query. SASE.

Nonfiction: "Get a free sample and study it. Try, in ms, to entertain archer and show him how to enjoy his sport more and be better at it." Wants how-to, semitechnical, and hunting where-to and how-to articles. "Looking for more good technical stories and short how-to pieces." Also uses profiles and some humor. Length: 1,000-2,200 words. Payment is $50-200.

Photos: B&w glossies purchased with mss and with captions. "Like to see proofsheets and negatives with submitted stories. We make own cropping and enlargements." Color transparencies purchased. Pays $100 for color transparencies; $15 minimum for b&w.

BOW AND ARROW, Box HH/34249 Camino Capistrano, Capistrano Beach CA 92624. Managing Editor: Roger Combs. 75% freelance written. For archery competitors and bowhunters. Bimonthly. Buys all rights, "but will relinquish all but first American serial rights on written request of author." Byline given. Pays on acceptance. Reports on submissions in 6-8 weeks. Author must have some knowledge of archery terms. SASE.

Nonfiction: Articles: bowhunting, major archery tournaments, techniques used by champs, how to make your own tackle, and off-trail hunting tales. Likes a touch of humor in articles. Also uses one technical article per issue. Submit complete ms. Length: 1,500-2,500 words. Pays $50-200.

Photos: Purchased as package with mss; 5x7 minimum or submit contacts with negatives (returned to photographer). Pays $75-100 for cover chromes, 35mm or larger.

Tips: "Good b&w photos are of primary importance. Don't submit color prints."

BOWHUNTER MAGAZINE, 3808 S. Calhoun St., Fort Wayne IN 46807. (219)744-1373 or 432-5772. Editor: M. R. James. For "readers of all ages, background and experience. All share two common passions—hunting with the bow and arrow and a love of the great outdoors." Bimonthly magazine; 96 pages. Circ. 135,000. Buys all rights. Buys 55 mss/year. Pays on acceptance. Will send sample copy to writer on request. Write for copy of guidelines for writers. No photocopied or simultaneous submissions. "We publish a special deer hunting issue each August. Submit seasonal material 6-8 months in advance." Reports in 4-6 weeks. Query or submit complete ms. SASE.

Nonfiction, Photos and Fillers: "Our articles are written for, by and about bowhunters and we ask that they inform as well as entertain. Most material deals with big or small game bowhunting (how-to, where to go, etc.), but we do use some technical material and personality pieces. We do not attempt to cover all aspects of archery—only bowhunting. Anyone hoping to sell to us must have a thorough knowledge of bowhunting. Next, they must have either an interesting story to relate or a fresh approach to a common subject. We would like to see more material on what is being done to combat the anti-hunting sentiment in this country." Informational, how-to, personal experience, interview, profile, humor, historical, think articles, expose, nostalgia, personal opinion, spot news, new product and technical articles. No "See what animal I bagged" articles. Length: 200-5,000 words. Pays $25-250. Photos purchased with accompanying ms or without ms. Captions optional. Pays $10-25 for 5x7 or 8x10 b&w prints; $50 minimum for 35mm or 2¼x2¼ color. Also purchases newsbreaks of 50-500 words for $5-25.

Tips: "The answer is simple if you know bowhunting and have some interesting, informative experiences or tips to share. Keep the reader in mind. Anticipate questions and answer them in the article. Weave information into the storyline (e.g., costs involved, services of guide or outfitter, hunting season dates, equipment preferred and why, tips on items to bring, etc.) and, if at all possible, study back issues of the magazine. We have no set formula, really, but most articles are first-person narratives and most published material will contain the elements mentioned above."

Basketball

BASKETBALL WEEKLY, 17820 E. Warren, Detroit MI 48224. (313)881-9554. Publisher: Roger Stanton. Editor: Mark Engel. 20 issues during season, September-May. Circ. 45,000. Buys all rights. Pays on publication. Sample copy for SASE. Reports in 2 weeks. SASE.

Nonfiction, Photos and Fillers: Current stories on teams and personalities in college and pro basketball. Length: 800-1,000 words. Payment is $30-50. 8x10 b&w glossy photos purchased with mss. Also uses newsbreaks.

EASTERN BASKETBALL, Eastern Basketball Publications, Inc., 7 May Court, West Hempstead NY 11552. (516)483-9495. Managing Editor: Rita Napolotano. Emphasizes basketball in the East for high school and college basketball enthusiasts from Maine to North Carolina. Published 12

times/year (November-May); magazine. Circ. 23,000. Pays on publication. Buys one-time rights. Phone queries OK. Reports in 6 weeks on mss. Free sample copy.
Nonfiction: "We are interested in feature stories on Eastern teams, players, coaches and issues related to the sport. Also in sports medicine, the role of the college recruit, choosing a college carefully and player profiles. Buys 1-2 mss/issue. Query or send complete ms. Length: open. Pays $35-50.
Photos: State availability of photos or send photos with ms.
Tips: "We are open to suggestions for articles on equipment, training, psychology of the star player vs. an ordinary player. Also articles such as 'What happens on the court is the end result of a lot of other things.' "

HOOP, Professional Sports Publications, 600 3rd Ave., New York NY 10016. (212)697-1460. Vice President: Pamela L. Blawie. 32-page color insert that is bound into the local magazines of each of the NBA teams. Buys all rights. "For the most part, assignments are being made to newspapermen and columnists on the pro basketball beat around the country. Features are subject to NBA approval." Sample copy $2.00. Reports in 1 week. SASE.
Nonfiction: Features on NBA players, officials, personalities connected with league. Length: 800-1,000 words. Pays $75.
Tips: "The best way for a freelancer to break in is to aim something for the local team section. That can be anything from articles about the players or about their wives to unusual off-court activities. The best way to handle this is to send material directly to the PR person for the local team. They have to approve anything that we do on that particular team and if they like it, they forward it to me. They're always looking for new material—otherwise they have to crank it all out themselves."

Bicycling

BICYCLING, (Incorporating *Bike World*), Rodale Press, Inc., 33 E. Minor St., Emmaus PA 18049. Editor and Publisher: James C. McCullagh. 9 issues/year (6 monthly, 3 bimonthly); 80 pages. Circ. 170,000. Pays on publication. Buys all rights. Pays negotiable kill fee. Byline given. Submit seasonal/holiday material 5 months in advance. SASE. Free sample copy and writer's guidelines.
Nonfiction: How-to (on all phases of bicycle touring, bike repair, maintenance, commuting, riding technique, nutrition for cyclists, conditioning); travel (bicycling must be central here); photo feature (on cycling events of national significance); and technical (component review—query). "We are strictly a bicycling magazine. We seek readable, clear, well-informed pieces. We rarely run articles that are pure humor or inspiration but a little of either might flavor even our most technical pieces." Buys 5 mss/issue. Query. Length: 2,500 words maximum. Pays $200 for color cover photo. Offers no
Photos: State availability of photos with query letter or send photo material with ms. Pays $10-15 for b&w negatives and $15-30 for color transparencies. Pays $200 for color cover photo. Offers no additional payment for photos accepted with ms. Captions preferred; model release required.
Fillers: Anecdotes. Buys 1-2/issue. Length: 150-200 words. Pays $15-25.

VELO-NEWS, A Journal of Bicycle Racing, Box 1257, Brattleboro VT 05301. (802)254-2305. Editor: Ed Paveilka. Monthly tabloid. (October-March, biweekly April-September) covering bicycle racing. Circ. 8,000+. Pays on publication. Byline given. Buys all rights. Simultaneous queries, and simultaneous, photocopied and previsouly published submissions OK. SASE. Reports in 2 weeks. Sample copy for 9x12 SAE.
Nonfiction: How-to (on bicycle racing); interview/profile (of people important in bicycle racing); opinion; photo feature; and technical. Most open to race reports and short features. Buys 50 mss/year. Query. Length: 300-3,000 words. Pays $1.50/column inch.
Photos: State availability of photos. Pays $15-30 for 8x10 b&w prints. Captions and identification of subjects required. Buys one-time rights.

Boating

BAY & DELTA YACHTSMAN, Recreation Publications, 2019 Clement Ave., Alameda CA 94501. (415)865-7500. Managing Editor: John J. Bray. 80% freelance written. Emphasizes recreational boating for small boat owners and recreational yachtsmen in northern California. Monthly tabloid newspaper; 90 pages. Circ. 17,000. Pays on publication. Buys all rights. Byline given. Phone queries OK. Submit seasonal/holiday material 2 months in advance. Photocopied submissions OK. SASE. Reports in 1 month. Free writer's guidelines.
Nonfiction: Historical (nautical history of northern California); how-to (modifications, equip-

ment, supplies, rigging etc., aboard both power and sailboats); humor (no disaster or boating ineptitude pieces); informational (government legislation as it relates to recreational boating); interview; new product; nostalgia; personal experience ("How I learned about boating from this" type of approach); personal opinion; photo feature (to accompany copy); profile; and travel. Buys 10-15 mss/issue. Query. Length: 750-2,000 words. Pays $1/column inch.

Photos: Photos purchased with accompanying ms. Captions required. Pays $5 for b&w glossy or matte finish photos. Total purchase price for ms includes payment for photos.

Fiction: Adventure (sea stories, cruises, races pertaining to West Coast and points South/South West.);fantasy; historical; humorous; and mystery. Buys 2 mss/year. Query. Length: 500-1,750 words. Pays $1/column inch.

Tips: "Think of our market area: the waterways of northern California and how, why, when and where the boatman would use those waters. Think about unusual onboard application of ideas (power and sail), special cruising tips, etc. We're very interested in local boating interviews—both the famous and unknown. Write for a knowledgeable boating public."

BOATING, 1 Park Ave., New York NY 10016. (212)725-3972. Editor: Jeff Hammond. For power-boat enthusiasts—informed boatmen, not beginners. Publishes special Boat Show issue in January; Fall show issue in September; New York National Boat Show issue in December; annual maintenance issue in April. Monthly. Circ. 200,000. Buys first periodical rights. Buys 100 mss/year..Pays on acceptance. Submit seasonal material 6-8 months in advance. Reports in 2 months. Query. SASE.

Nonfiction: Uses articles about cruises in powerboats with b&w or color photos, that offer more than usual interest; how-to pieces illustrated with good b&w photos or drawings; piloting articles, seamanship, etc.; new developments in boating; profiles of well-known boating people. "Don't talk down to the reader. Use little fantasy, emphasize the practical aspects of the subject." Length: 300-3,000 words. Pays $25-500, and varies according to subject and writer's skill.

Photos: Prefers 25 Kodachrome transparencies of happenings of interest to a national boating audience, for both cover and interior use. Pays $100-300 for one-time use "but not for anything that has previously appeared in a boating publication."

Fillers: Uses short items pertaining to boating that have an unusual quality of historical interest, timeliness, or instruction. Pays $50-100.

CANADIAN YACHTING MAGAZINE, 425 University Ave., 6th Floor, Toronto, Ontario, Canada M5G 1T6. Editor: John Turnbull. Monthly magazine aimed at owners of power and sail boats of between 20 and 40 ft., both cruising and racing. Most but not all of the audience is Canadian. Circ. 30,000. Pays on acceptance. Buys first North American rights. Previously published submissions OK, but remember "our obligation not to duplicate material published in larger American magazines available in our reader area." SAE and International Reply Coupons.

Nonfiction: "Much of our 'entertainment' coverage of important racing events must be handled by US freelancers. Cruise stories are welcome from anyone." Also uses technical pieces, especially on motor maintenance. Send complete ms. Length: 1,800-2,500 words. Pays $150-450.

Photos: Pays $15-40 for 8x10 b&w prints; $25-150 for 35mm color transparencies.

Tips: "Query should contain writer's experience and reassurance of photo quality (usually sample)."

CANOE MAGAZINE, Voyager Publications Inc., 2410 N. Clinton, Fort Wayne IN 46805. Editor and Publisher: John Viehman. "*Canoe* represents the self-propelled water traveler." For an audience ranging from weekend canoe-camper to Olympic caliber flatwater/whitewater racing, marathon, poling, sailing, wilderness tripping types. Six times/year; 72 pages. Circ. 45,000. Buys all rights. Pays 25% kill fee. Byline given. Buys 30 mss/year. Pays on acceptance or on publication. Free sample copy and writer's guidelines for $1 and 9x12 SASE. Reports in 60 days. Query or submit complete ms. SASE.

Nonfiction and Photos: "We publish a variety of canoeing and kayaking articles, striving for a balanced mix of stories to reflect all interests in this outdoor activity, recreational or competitive. Also interested in any articles dealing with conservation issues which may adversely affect the sport. Writing should be readable rather than academic; clever rather than endlessly descriptive. Diary type first-person style not desirable. A good, provocative lead is considered a prime ingredient. We want stories about canoeing/kayaking activities in the 50 states and Canada with which canoeists/kayakers of average ability can identify. Also interested in articles discussing safety aspects or instructional items. Occasional call for outdoor photography feature as relates to water accessible subjects. Please pick up and study a recent issue before querying. Also study back issues and each published issue index to avoid duplication." Length: 1,500-3,000 words. Pays $50-300. Will consider relevant book reviews (pays $15 on publication); length, 200-350 words.

CRUISING WORLD, Box 452, Newport RI 02840. (401)847-1588. Executive Editor: C. Dale Nouse. 75% freelance written. For all those who cruise under sail. Monthly magazine; 180 pages. Circ. 82,000. Rights purchased vary with author and material. May buy first North American serial rights or first serial rights. Pays on publication. Reports in about 8 weeks. Submit complete ms. SASE.
Nonfiction and Photos: "We are interested in seeing informative articles on the technical and enjoyable aspects of cruising under sail. Also subjects of general interest to seafarers." Length: 500-3,500 words. Pays $50 minimum. B&w prints (5x7) and color transparencies purchased with accompanying ms.

LAKELAND BOATING, 412 Longshore Dr., Ann Arbor MI 48105. Editor: Freeman Pittman. Emphasizes pleasure boating on fresh-water lakes; both sail and power boats. Monthly magazine. Pays on publication. Buys first publication, with one reprint rights. SASE. Reports in 3-4 weeks. Sample copy 50¢.
Nonfiction: 2-3 "Cruise" stories/issue. Personal experience stories of power and/or sailboat cruises on freshwater lakes or rivers. Query first on stories on special events. Include sketches, maps, lists of marinas, access ramps, harbors of refuge. Length: 1,000-2,000 words. Technical articles on both sail and power boats, maintenance. Length: 200-1,500 words.
Photos: Send photos with mss. 5x7 or 8x10 b&w can also be submitted separately. Original transparency for color stories. Offers no additional payment for photos accepted with accompanying ms. Captions required or identification of all pictures, prints, or transparencies. "Please stamp every transparency with name and address."

MOTORBOATING AND SAILING, 224 W. 57th St., New York NY 10019. (212)262-8768. Editor: Oliver S. Morre III. Monthly magazine covering powerboats and cruising sailboats for people who own their own boats and are active in a yachting lifestyle. Circ. 140,000. Average issue includes 8-10 feature articles. Pays on acceptance. Byline given. Buys one-time rights. SASE. Reports in 3 months.
Nonfiction: General interest (navigation, adventure, cruising); and how-to (maintenance). Buys 5-6 mss/issue. Query. Length: 2,000 words.
Photos: Reviews 5x7 b&w glossy prints and 35mm or larger color transparencies. Offers no additional payment for photos accepted with ms. Captions and model release required.

PLEASURE BOATING MAGAZINE, Wet Set Publishing, Inc., 1995 NE 150th St., North Miami FL 33181. (305)945-7403. Editor: Bob Stearns. Managing Editor: Jean Lang. For high-income persons interested in all types of Southern boating and fishing. Monthly tabloid; 40-48 pages. Circ. 40,000. Pays on publication. Buys all rights. Phone queries OK. Submit seasonal/holiday material 3 months in advance. SASE. Reports in 2 weeks. Free sample copy.
Nonfiction: "Anything dealing with boating and fishing on a how-to, technical, first-person or humorous basis." Buys 6-8 mss/issue. Send complete ms. Length: 500-2,000 words. Pays 5-10¢/word.
Photos: Send photos with ms. Pay is open for b&w contact sheets or 2¼x2¼. Buys all rights. Captions and model releases required.

POWERBOAT MAGAZINE, 15917 Strathern St., Van Nuys CA 91406. Editor: Mark Spencer. 30% freelance written. For performance-conscious boating enthusiasts. January and February, Boat Performance Reports; March, Water Ski issue; April, Tow Vehicle issue; June and July, Big Boat Reports; September, Outboards; amd October, Stern Drive issue. Monthly circ. 75,000. Buys all rights or one-time North American serial rights. Pays on publication. Free sample copy. Reports in 2 weeks. Query required. SASE.
Nonfiction and Photos: Uses articles about power boats and water skiing that offer special interest to performance-minded boaters, how-to-do-it pieces with good b&w pictures, developments in boating, profiles on well-known boating and skiing individuals, competition coverage of national and major events. Length: 1,500-2,000 words. Pays $150-250/article. Photos purchased with mss. Prefers 8x10 b&w, 2¼x2¼ color transparency preferred for cover; top quality vertical 35mm considered. Pays $50-100 for one-time use.

RUDDER, Petersen Publishing Co., 151 River Rd., Cos Cob CT 06807. (203)622-8232. Editor: Wayne Carpenter. Managing Editor: Judy Pepler. Monthly magazine covering recreational boating. Circ. 64,000. Pays on publication. Byline given. Offers standard or negotiated kill fee. Buys first North American serial rights in *Rudder* region. Submit seasonal/holiday material 6 months in advance. Simultaneous queries OK. SASE. Reports in 6 weeks on queries; 3 months on mss. Free sample copy and writer's guidelines.
Nonfiction: Historical/nostalgic, how-to, interview/profile, opinion, personal experience and

technical. Buys 60 mss/year. Send complete ms. Length: 750-2,500 words. Pays $50-350.
Photos: Chris Larson, photo editor. State availability of photos or send photos with ms. Pays $25-300 for 35mm color transparencies; $10-50 for 8x10 b&w prints. Model release and identification of subjects required. Buys one-time rights.

SAIL, 34 Commercial Wharf, Boston MA 02110. (617)227-0888. Editor: Keith Taylor. For audience that is "strictly sailors, average age 35, better than average education." Special issues: "Cruising issues, chartering issues, fitting-out issues, special race issues (e.g., America's Cup), boat show issues." Monthly magazine. Pays on publication. Buys first North American serial rights. Submit seasonal or special material at least 3 months in advance. Reports in 6 weeks. SASE. Free sample copy.
Nonfiction: Patience Wales, managing editor. Wants "articles on sailing: technical, techniques and feature stories." Interested in how-to, personal experience, profiles, historical, new products and photo articles. "Generally emphasize the excitement of sail and the human, personal aspect." Buys 200 mss/year. Length: 1,500-3,000 words. Pays $100-800.
Photos: State availability of photos. Offers additional payment for photos. Uses b&w glossy prints or color transparencies. Pays $400 if photo is used on the cover.

SAILING MAGAZINE, 125 E. Main St., Port Washington WI 53074. (414)284-3494. Editor: William F. Schanen III. For readers 25-44, majority professionals. About 75% of them own their own sailboat. Monthly magazine; 82 pages. Circ. 35,000. Not copyrighted. Buys 24 mss/year. Pays on publication. Write for copy of guidelines for writers. Photocopied and simultaneous submissions OK. Reports in 6 weeks. Query or submit complete ms. SASE.
Nonfiction: Micca Leffingwell Hutchins, managing editor. "Experiences of sailing, whether cruising, racing or learning. We require no special style. We're devoted exclusively to sailing and sailboat enthusiasts, and particularly interested in articles about the trend toward cruising in the sailing world." Informational, personal experience, profile, historical, travel and book reviews. Length: open. Payment negotiable. Must be accompanied by photos.
Photos: B&w and color photos purchased with or without accompanying ms. Captions required. Flat fee for article.

SMALL BOAT JOURNAL, Highland Mill, Camden, ME 04843. (207)236-8523. Editor: Jim Brown. Bimonthly magazine about small boats which emphasizes the elements of grace, function, utility, performance and economy for small boat owners, designers and builders. Estab. 1979. Circ. 35,000. Pays on acceptance. Byline given. Buys one-time rights. Phone queries OK. Submit seasonal material 4 months in advance. Simultaneous and photocopied submissions OK, if so indicated. SASE. Reports in 2 weeks. Free sample copy and writer's guidelines.
Nonfiction: General interest (boat care, boating activities); interview (of celebrities and outstanding people in boating); how-to (care of boats); new product (for boats); personal experience (adventures and boatbuilding); photo feature (if accompanied by good text); and technical (care and maintenance). Query. Length: 500-2,500 words. Pays 10¢/word minimum.
Photos: Pays $10 minimum/5x7 b&w glossy print. Pays $50 minimum/35mm and larger color transparency. Captions required.
Columns/Departments: Small Talk (news and notes on boating safety, design, equipment and accessories); Small Boat Library (book reviews of interest to boating enthusiasts; fiction and nonfiction, 1,000 words); Bitts and Pieces (new products, 200-300 words, home built equipment, modifications, 500 words). Send complete ms. Pays 10¢/word minimum.

SOUTHERN BOATING MAGAZINE, Southern Boating & Yachting, Inc., 1975 NW South River Dr., Miami FL 33125. (305)642-5350. Publisher and Editor: Skip Allen. Associate Editor: Eden Yount. Monthly magazine; 75 pages. Circ. 25,000. Pays on publication. Buys all rights. Byline given. Phone queries OK. Submit seasonal/holiday material 2 months in advance. Photocopied submissions OK. SASE. Reports in 3 weeks.
Nonfiction: Historical, how-to, personal experience and travel, navigation. "All articles should be related to yachting. We do want technical articles." Buys 4 mss/issue. Send complete ms. Length: 2,000-5,000 words. Pays $35-75.
Photos: State availability of photos or send photos with ms. Captions and model releases required.
Tips: "The best query device is to ask a question or series of questions that a boat owner/operator might ask, then explain how the proposed article answers those questions. Send cover letter with manuscript. Specify anticipated payment and state whether open to negotiation. Send accompanying artwork with ms. Include address and phone number where to be reached during the day. If possible, include name and address on back of photos or on slide covers."

TEXAS SAILING, Box 14643, Austin TX 78761. (512)451-5390. Editor: Bruce Renfro. Monthly tabloid covering sailing for beginners and advanced sailors of Texas. *Texas Sailing* sets out to cover the full range of sailing activity in the state—racing, cruising, daysailing, and boardboating on our lakes and coastal waters." Estab. 1981. Circ. 11,000. Pays on publication. Byline given. Buys one-time rights. Submit seasonal/holiday material 3 months in advance. Photocopied and previously published submissions OK. SASE. Reports in 1 week on ms. Free sample copy and writer's guidelines.

Nonfiction: Personal experience, photo feature and racing. Query or send complete ms. Length: 2,500 maximum. Pays $40-80.

Photos: Reviews 5x7 or 8x10 glossy prints. Captions required. "Photo payment is included in price of ms."

Fillers: How-to (boat and sail care and racing techniques).

Tips: "We're new. Write, call, come by. Tell us exactly what you will write and photograph. We want to know where the Texas slant is."

TRAILER BOATS MAGAZINE, Poole Publications, Inc., 1440 W. Walnut, Compton CA 90220. (213)537-1037. Editor: Ralph Poole. Managing Editor: Jim Youngs. Emphasizes legally trailerable boats and related activities. Monthly magazine (Nov./Dec. issue combined); 80 pages. Circ. 80,000. Pays on publication. Buys all rights. Byline given. Phone queries OK. Submit seasonal/holiday material 3 months in advance. SASE. Reports in 4 weeks. Free sample copy and writer's guidelines.

Nonfiction: General interest (trailer boating activities); historical (places, events, boats); how-to (repair boats, installation, etc.); humor (almost any subject); nostalgia (same as historical); personal experience; photo feature; profile; technical; and travel (boating travel on water or highways). Buys 4 mss/issue. Query or send complete ms. Length: 500-3,000 words. Pays $50 minimum.

Photos: Send photos with ms. Pays $7.50-30/5x7 or 8x10 b&w glossy print; $10-100/35mm color transparency. Captions required.

Columns & Departments: Boaters Bookshelf (boating book reviews); Over the Transom (funny or strange boating photos); and Patent Pending (an invention with drawings). Buys 2/issue. Query. Length: 100-500 words. Pays $15. Mini-Cruise (short enthusiastic approach to a favorite boating spot). Need map and photographs. Length: 500-750 words. Pays $50. Open to suggestions for new columns/departments.

Fiction: Adventure, experimental, historical, humorous and suspense. "We do not use too many fiction stories but we will consider them if they fit the general editorial guidelines." Query or send complete ms. Length: 500-1,500 words. Pays $50 minimum.

Tips: "Query should contain short general outline of the intended material; what kind of photos; how the photos illustrate the piece. Write with authority covering the subject like on expert. Use basic information rather than prose, particularly in travel stories."

WATERWAY GUIDE, 93 Main St., Annapolis MD 21401. (301)268-9546. Associate Editor: Jerri Anne Hopkins. A pleasure-boater's cruising guide to the Intracoastal Waterway, East Coast waters and the Great Lakes. Annual magazine.

Nonfiction: "We occasionally have a need for a special, short article on some particular aspect of pleasure cruising—such as living aboard, sailing vs. powerboating, having children or pets on board—or a particular stretch of coast—a port off the beaten track, conditions peculiar to a certain area, a pleasant weekend cruise, anchorages and so on." Query with ms.

Photos: State availability of photos. "We have a need for good photographs, taken from the water, of ports, inlets and points of interest. Guidelines on request with SASE."

Tips: "Keep the query simple and friendly. Include a short bio and boating experience. Prefer to see manuscript sample attached. No personal experiences, i.e., we need information, not reminiscences."

WOODENBOAT, Box 78, Brooklin ME 04616. Editor-in-Chief: Jonathan Wilson. Readership is composed mainly of owners, builders and designers of wooden boats. Bimonthly magazine; 160 pages. Circ. 58,000. Pays on publication. Buys first North American serial rights. Byline given "except if the material published were substantially revised and enlarged." Photocopied and previously published submissions OK. SASE. Reports in 2 months. Sample copy $3; writer's guidelines for SASE.

Nonfiction: Historical (detailed evolution of boat types of famous designers or builders of wooden boats); how-to (repair, restore, build or maintain wooden boats); informational (technical detail on repairs/restoration/construction); new product (documented by facts or statistics on performance of product); opinion (backed up by experience and experimentation in boat building, restoring, maintaining, etc.); photo feature (with in-depth captioning and identification of boats);

and technical (on adhesives and other boat-building products and materials, or on particular phases of repair or boat construction). Buys 85 mss/year. Submit complete ms. Length: 1,200-3,500 words. Pays $3/column inch.

Photos: Purchased with or without (only occasionally) accompanying ms. Captions required. Send prints, negatives or transparencies. Pays $10 for 8x10 high contrast b&w glossy prints; $25 minimum for color transparencies. Put name and address on all photos, slides or illustrations.

Columns & Departments: "Tidings" (seeking news on developments and contemporary trends of wooden boat construction); and Book Reviews (on wooden boats and related subjects). Buys 1 ms/issue. Length: 300-800 words. Pays $3/column inch.

Tips: "Because we are bimonthly, and issues are scheduled well in advance, freelancers should bear in mind that if their material is accepted, it will inevitably be some time before publication can be arranged. We seek innovative and informative ideas in freelancers' manuscripts, and the degree to which research and careful attention has been paid in compiling an article must be apparent. We're not looking for scholarly treatises, rather detailed and thought-out material reflecting imagination and interest in the subject. It is important to: a) become familiar with the magazine first; read back issues to see what kinds of articles we use. b) submit a detailed query letter; be knowledgeable, not superficial, in dealing with your subject. We relate to experience, not conjecture."

YACHTING, Yachting Publishing Corp., 1 Park Ave., New York NY 10016. Editor: Wolcott Gibbs Jr. For yachtsmen interested in powerboats and sailboats. Monthly. Circ. 150,000. Buys North American serial rights. Reports in 3 weeks. SASE.

Nonfiction: Nuts-and-bolts articles on all phases of yachting; good technical pieces on motors, electronics, and sailing gear. Length: 2,500 words maximum. Article should be accompanied by 6-8 color transparencies.

Photos: Pays $50 for b&w photos, "more for color when used." Will accept a story without photos, if story is outstanding.

YACHT RACING/CRUISING MAGAZINE, North American Publishing Co., Box 902, 23 Leroy Ave., Darien CT 06820. Managing Editor: Pamela Polhemus. Magazine published 10 times/year; 120 pages. Circ. 50,000. Pays on publication. Buys First North American serial rights. Byline given. SASE. Reports in 2 months. Sample copy $2.

Nonfiction: How-to for racing/cruising sailors, personal experience, photo feature, profile and travel. Buys 10 mss/issue. Query. Length: 1,000-2,500 words. Pays $100 minimum.

Tips: "Send thorough letter on what you can offer, with your experience."

Bowling and Billiards

BILLIARDS DIGEST, National Bowlers Journal, Inc., 875 N. Michigan Ave., Suite 2564, Chicago IL 60611. (312)266-7179. Editor: Michael Panozzo. 25% freelance written. Emphasizes billiards/pool for "readers who are accomplished players and hard core fans—also a trade readership." Bimonthly magazine; 48-70 pages. Circ. 7,000. Pays on publication. Buys all rights. Byline given. Phone queries OK. Submit seasonal/holiday material 2 months in advance of issue date. Simultaneous, photocopied and previously published submissions OK. SASE. Reports in 2 weeks. Sample copy $2; free writer's guidelines.

Nonfiction: General interest (tournament results, features on top players); historical (features on greats of the game); how-to (how to improve your game, your billiard room, billiards table maintenance); humor (anecdotes, any humorous feature dealing with billiards); interview (former and current stars, industry leaders); new product (any new product dealing with billiards, short 'blip' or feature); and profile (former and current stars—prefer current stars). No basic news stories. "We want features that provide in-depth material, including anecdotes, atmosphere and facts." Buys 3 mss/issue. Query. Length: 1,000-1,500 words. Pays $75-150.

Photos: State availability of photos with query. Pays $10-25 for 8x10 b&w glossy prints; $15-25 for 35mm or 2¼x2¼ color transparencies. Cover negotiable. Captions preferred. Buys all rights.

Tips: "The best way to break in at *Billiards Digest* is a simple query with day and night phone numbers, so we can get in touch for suggestions. Worst way is to submit ms that starts with a cliche, 'The stranger walked into the pool room. . .' We are *very* interested in tips from stars (past and present). But query, first."

BOWLERS JOURNAL, 875 N. Michigan, Chicago IL 60611. (312)266-7171. Editor-in-Chief: Mort Luby. Managing Editor: Jim Dressel. 30% freelance written. Emphasizes bowling. Monthly magazine; 100 pages. Circ. 18,000. Pays on acceptance. Buys all rights. Phone queries OK. Submit

seasonal/holiday material 2 months in advance of issue date. Photocopied submissions OK. SASE. Reports in 2 weeks. Sample copy $2.
Nonfiction: General interest (stories on top pros); historical (stories of old-time bowlers or bowling alleys); interview (top pros, men and women); and profile (top pros). Buys 3 or 4 mss/issue. Query. Length: 1,200-3,500 words. Pays $50-150.
Photos: State availability of photos with query. Pays $5-15 for 8x10 b&w prints; and $5-20 for 35mm or 2¼x2¼ color transparencies. Buys one-time rights.

BOWLING, 5301 S. 76th St., Greendale WI 53129. (414)421-6400, ext. 230. Editor: Bob Johnson. Official publication of the American Bowling Congress. Monthly. Rights purchased vary with author and material. Usually buys all rights. Byline given. Pays on publication. Reports in 30 days. SASE.
Nonfiction and Photos: "This is a specialized field and the average writer attempting the subject of bowling should be well-informed. However, anyone is free to submit material for approval." Wants articles about unusual ABC sanctioned leagues and tournaments, personalities, etc., featuring male bowlers. Nostalgia articles also considered. No material on history of bowling. Length: 500-1,200 words. Pays $25-100 per article; $10-15 per photo.
Tips: "Submit feature material on bowlers, generally amateurs competing in local leagues, or special events involving the game of bowling. Should have connection with ABC membership. Queries should be as detailed as possible so that we may get a clear idea of what the proposed story would be all about. It saves us time and the writer time. Samples of previously published material in the bowling or general sports field would help. Once we find a talented writer in a given area, we're likely to go back to him in the future. We're looking for good writers who can handle assignments professionally and promptly."

JUNIOR BOWLER, 5301 S. 76th St., Greendale WI 53129. (414)421-4700. Official publication of American Junior Bowling Congress. Editor: Jean Yeager. 30% freelance written. For boys and girls ages 21 and under. Estab. 1946 as *Prep Pin Patter*; in 1964 as *Junior Bowler*. Monthly, November through April. Circ. 89,000. Buys all rights. Byline given "except if necessary to do extensive rewriting." Pays on publication. Reports in 10 days. Query. SASE.
Nonfiction and Photos: Subject matter of articles must be based on tenpin bowling and activities connected with American Junior Bowling Congress only. Audience includes youngsters down to 6 years of age, but material should feature the teenage group. Length: 500-800 words. Accompanying photos or art preferred. Pays $30-100/article. Photos should be 8x10 b&w glossy prints related to subject matter. Pays $5 minimum.
Tips: "We are primarily looking for feature stories on a specific person or activity. Stories about a specific person generally should center around the outstanding bowling achievements of that person in an AJBC sanctioned league or tournament. Articles on special leagues for high average bowlers, physically or mentally handicapped bowlers, etc. should focus on the unique quality of the league. *Junior Bowler* also carries articles on AJBC sanctioned tournaments, but these should be more than just a list of the winners and their scores. Again, the unique feature of the tournament should be emphasized."

THE WOMAN BOWLER, 5301 S. 76th St., Greendale WI 53129. (414)421-9000. Editor: Linda Krupke. Emphasizes bowling for women bowlers, ages 8-90. Monthly (except for combined July/August, December/January issues) magazine; 48 pages. Circ. 150,000. Pays on acceptance. Buys all rights. Byline given "except on occasion, when freelance article is used as part of a regular magazine department. When this occurs, it is discussed first with the author." Phone queries OK. Submit seasonal/holiday material 2 months in advance. Photocopied and previously published submissions OK. SASE. Reports in 1 month. Free sample copy and writer's guidelines.
Nonfiction: Historical (about bowling and of national significance); interview; profile; and spot news. Buys 25 mss/year. Query. Length: 1,500 words maximum (unless by special assignment). Pays $15-50.
Photos: Purchased with accompanying ms. Identification required. Query. Pays $5-10 for b&w glossy prints. Model release required.

Football

ALL SOUTH CAROLINA FOOTBALL ANNUAL, Box 3, Columbia SC 29202. (803)796-9200. Editor: Mike Monroe. Associate Editor: Dennis Nichols. Issued annually, August 1. Buys first rights. Pays on publication. Deadline for material each year is 10 weeks preceding publication date. Query. SASE.

Nonfiction and Photos: Material must be about South Carolina high school and college football teams, players and coaches. Pays 3¢ minimum a word. Buys photos with ms. Captions required. 5x7 or 8x10 b&w glossy prints; 4x5 or 35mm color transparencies. Uses color on cover only. Pays $5 minimum for b&w; $10 minimum for color.

FOOTBALL NEWS, 17820 E. Warren, Detroit MI 48224. Publisher: Roger Stanton. 25% freelance written. For avid grid fans. Weekly tabloid published during football season; 24 pages. Circ. 100,000. Not copyrighted. Pays 50% kill fee. Byline given. Buys 12 to 15 mss a year. Pays on publication. Will send sample copy to writer for $1. Reports in 1 month. Query. SASE.
Nonfiction: Articles on players, officials, coaches, past and present, with fresh approach. Highly informative, concise, positive approach. Interested in profiles of former punt, pass and kick players who have made the pros. Interview, profile, historical, think articles, and exposés. Length: 800-1,000 words. Pays $35-75/ms.

PRO QUARTERBACK, Arden C, Box 99, Amawalk NY 10501. (914)962-7570. Publisher: John McCluskey. Magazine published 3 times/year about professional quarterbacks for male football fans from 15-60 years old. Circ. 150,000. Average issue includes 10-15 articles. Pays on publication. Byline given. Buys first North American serial rights. Simultaneous, photocopied and previously published submissions OK if so indicated. SASE. Reports in 1 week.
Nonfiction: "We want in-depth profiles and personal history articles about professional quarterbacks in the NFC and AFC. Buys 10-15 mss/issue. Query. Length: 1,500-2,000 words. Pays $300-450.
Photos: "We must have photos to accompany articles." Reviews 5x7 b&w glossy prints and 35mm color transparencies. Offers no additional payment for photos accepted with ms. Captions required.

Gambling

CASINO & CABARET, Luxury Resorts/Fashions/Entertainment,Publishers Development Corporation, Suite 200, 591 Camino de la Reina, San Diego CA 92108. (714)297-5352. Editor: Charles Hennegan. Monthly magazine covering posh resorts, their stage shows and extravaganzas, their casinos and unique wining and dining experiences for the affluent single, couples and families with discretionary income available for leisure activities who are in the mood to say "will we enjoy it?" rather than "can we afford it?" Estab. 1981. Circ. 165,000. Pays on acceptance. Byline given. Pays negotiable kill fee. Buys first North American serial rights. Submit seasonal/holiday material 6 months in advance. Simultaneous, photocopied, and previously published submissions OK if so indicated. SASE. Reports in 2 weeks on mss. Sample copy $2.
Nonfiction: Articles cover "the entertainment of the lounge and dinner shows; the games people are playing at the casinos; the top-rated fashions for day and night; cruises that combine all of the resort and casino pleasures; and a potpourri of practical, informative, and entertaining features for those planning their 'great escape,' be it for a week, a month, or a lifetime. We plan to concentrate on the gaming industry throughout the world, exploring in depth those places that offer casino style gambling." Buys 60 mss/year. Send complete ms. Length: 1,000-4,000 words. Pays $500 maximum.
Photos: Send photos with accompanying ms. "Excellent photos are the key to selling articles here." Reviews 35mm and up color transparencies, and 8x10 b&w prints. Captions and model release required. Buys one-time rights. Photos included in price paid for ms.
Fiction: Must be top quality writing related to the magazine's theme. Buys 12 mss/year. Send complete ms. Length: 1,000-5,000 words. Pays $500 maximum.
Tips: "The writer does not have to be well-traveled but must have intimate knowledge of the subject matter." Submit "simple and clear, well-written articles on casinos, nightclubs, and interesting personalities. Good photographs are a necessity."

CHIPS, For the Winners, 49 W. 45th St., New York NY 10036. (212)944-1790. Executive Editor: William H. Thomas. Bimonthly magazine covering lifestyle topics with an emphasis on gambling for the older successful executive type. Estab. 1980. Circ. 100,000. Pays on publication. Byline and brief bio given. Buys first North American serial rights. Submit seasonal/holiday material 4 months in advance. Simultaneous queries and simultaneous, photocopied, and previously published submissions OK. Reports in 1 month.
Nonfiction: How-to (win); humor; interview/profile (of sports celebrities); and personal experience (on offbeat themes). Buys 100+ mss/year. Query or send complete ms. Length: 2,500-3,000 words. Pays $500 maximum.

Photos: State availability of photos. Pays $100/page for 35mm color transparencies; $25 minimum for b&w glossy prints. Captions and model release required.
Columns/Departments: On the Town (city tours featuring dining and night spots). Send complete ms. Length: 1,200-1,500 words. Pays $250 (includes b&w photos).
Fillers: "Last Shuffle" (how to spot cheaters). Length: 750 words minimum. Pays $200 maximum.

GAMBLING TIMES MAGAZINE, 1018 N. Cole Ave., Hollywood CA 90038. (213)463-4833. Editor: Len Miller. Address mss to Pat Chleboroski, Associate Editor. 50% freelance written. Monthly magazine; 100 pages. Circ. 70,000. Pays shortly after publication. Buys first North American serial rights. Byline given. Submit seasonal/holiday material 5-6 months in advance of issue date. SASE. Double-space all submissions, maximum 10 pp. Reports in 4-6 weeks. Free writer's guidelines; mention *Writer's Market* in request.
Nonfiction: How-to (related to gambling systems, betting methods, etc.); humor; photo feature (racetracks, jai alai, casinos); and travel (gambling spas and resort areas). "Also interested in investigative reports focusing on the political, economical and legal issues surrounding gambling in the US and the world and new gambling developments. No cutesy stuff. Keep your style clean, hard-edged and sardonic (if appropriate)." Buys 100 mss/year; prefers pictures with mss. Query. Pays $50-150.
Fiction: "We only use heavily gambling-related material." Buys 12 mss/year. Submit complete ms double spaced, maximum 9 pp. Pays $50-100.
Tips: "Be sure to keep xerox of the mss sent. Know gambling thoroughly. We like short sentences and paragraphs; clear, precise, instructional material; and well-written, to-the-point material. Pictures with mss will add $50 to the payment. Action shots—always people shots. Photographs must show something unique to the subject in article."

General Interest

BC OUTDOORS, Special Interest Publications Division, Maclean-Hunter, Ltd., 202, 1132 Hamilton St., Vancouver, British Columbia, Canada V6B 2S2. (604)687-1581. Editor: Henry L. Frew. Emphasizes any outdoors activity which is not an organized sport. "We're interested in family recreation." Monthly magazine, 64-96 pages. Circ. 35,000. Pays on acceptance. Buys first rights or first North American serial rights. Phone queries OK. Submit seasonal/holiday material 3 months in advance. Previously published work "occasionally" OK. SAE and International Reply Coupons. Reports in 2-4 weeks. Free sample copy and writer's guidelines.
Nonfiction: General interest (about British Columbia outdoors); historical (about British Columbia and the Yukon only); how-to (canoe, choose your RV, plant a wild-flower garden, catch a rainbow trout in British Columbia, build a cabin, photograph mountain goats, find British Columbia jade, save the environment, etc.); interview (with British Columbia people involved in outdoors and others involved in British Columbia affairs); profile; travel (in British Columbia and the Yukon); new product (for outdoors activities); personal experience; photo feature; and technical. Buys 6 mss/issue. Query or send complete ms. Length: 800-1,500 words, but maximum is usually 2,000. Pays 10¢/word minimum.
Photos: "We want photos for every story." Send photos with ms. Pays $15 for b&w 8x10 glossy prints; and $15-75 for color transparencies or prints (not silk). Captions and model release required. Buys one-time rights except for covers; purchase includes further possible use or reproduction for promotional purposes anywhere by SIP-Maclean-Hunter, Ltd.
Columns/Departments: Buys very few. Length: 800 words maximum. Open to suggestions for new columns/departments.

CHICAGO SPORT SCENE, Action Sport Scene Publishing, Inc., 1521 Jarvis Ave., Elk Grove Village IL 60007. (312)981-0100. Editor: Bill Troller. Associate Publisher: Gloria Telander. Monthly magazine covering "sports (pros, college, prep) and special sports interests in the metropolitan Chicago area for the everyday sports fan in Chicagoland. We cover both spectator and participation sports, the teams and the individuals, plus new and unusual leisure sports pursuits." Estab. 1980. Circ. 50,000. Pays on publication. Byline given. Offers $50 kill fee. Buys one-time rights. Submit seasonal/holiday material 4 months in advance. Simultaneous and photocopied submissions OK. SASE. Reports in 1 month on queries; 2 weeks on mss ("assigned mss only"). Sample copy $2.50 with 8x11 SAE.
Nonfiction: Book excerpts (based on accounts written about a Chicago player and/or teams); general interest (introduction to new clubs or sports); historical/nostalgic (on historic sports events or persons from the Chicago area); interview/profile (of Chicago pro, prep, and collegiate personalities); opinion (in-depth looks at problems facing athletics which contain a Chicago angle);

personal experience (as a viewer, spectator, or participant at a Chicago sporting event); photo feature ("nearly any suitable sports topic; photographer must check with editor for definite assignments"); and travel (on camping, hiking, recreating in Midwest states areas). "No special issues are planned, but we will be needing one strong article each month profiling a new or unusual sports pursuit in the Chicago area." No "articles attacking or in poor taste concerning teams and/or players in the Chicago area. Positive-oriented articles have a far better chance for publica-·tion." Buys 30-40 mss/year. Query with clips of published work. Length: 600-1,200 words. Pays $75-200.

Photos: State availability of photos. Reviews 35mm color transparencies and b&w prints. "All payments are negotiable." Model release and identification of subjects required.

Tips: "We are most open to general personality features, in-depth focus articles on sports problems or a dilemma that can be used for Chicago sports coverage. Historical articles on teams or players are also sought—articles must be well researched to provide new, fresh material to the reader."

CITY SPORTS MONTHLY, "All the news that keeps you fit," Box 3693, San Francisco CA 94119. Editor: Maggie Cloherty in northern California and 1120 Princeton Dr., Marina del Rey CA 90291. Editor: Terry Mulgannon. Monthly controlled circulation tabloid covering participant sports for avid sports participants. Circ. in California 167,000. Two editions published monthly—one covering sports in northern California and the other for southern California's participant sportsmarket. "For the most part, we use separate writers for each magazine." Pays on publication. Byline and brief bio given. Pays negotiable kill fee. Buys one-time rights. Submit seasonal/holiday material 3 months in advance. Simultaneous queries OK; previously published submissions ("from outside readership area") OK. SASE. Reports in 1 month on queries. Sample copy $1.

Nonfiction: Interview/profile (of athletes); travel; and instructional and service pieces on sports. No "first person accounts on mastery of a sports challenge, e.g., running ones' first marathon." Special issues include: April, Tennis; May, Running; June, Backpacking and Camping; July, Biking; October, Skiing; November, Cross Country Skiing. Buys 60 mss/year. Query with clips of published work. Length: 1,500-2,400 words. Pays $75-175.

Photos: Pays $35-100 for 35mm color; $25 for 8x10 glossy prints. Model release and identification of subjects required.

INFOAAU, (formerly *AAU News*), Amateur Athletic Union of the United States, AAU House, 3400 W. 86th St., Indianapolis IN 46268. (317)872-2900. Editor: Leslie A. King. Emphasizes AAU activities and amateur sports. Monthly magazine; 20-28 pages. Circ. 5,000. Pays on publication. Buys one-time rights. Sometimes give bylines; "Etcetera section profiles are not bylined, but assigned sports news articles are." SASE. Free sample copy.

Nonfiction: "General subject matter is profiles of top amateur athletes and athletic volunteers or leaders. Reports on AAU championships, previews of coming seasons, etc." Buys interviews, profiles, photo features. Length: 1,000 words maximum. Pays $10-50.

Photos: Photo purchased with or without accompanying ms or on assignment. Captions required. Pays $5-25 for 8½x11 b&w glossy prints; $10-25 for any size color transparencies. No additional payment for photos accepted with accompanying ms. Model release not required.

Tips: "Stay within the framework of AAU sports: Basketball, baton twirling, bobsledding, boxing, gymnastics, handball, horseshoe pitching, judo, karate, luge, taekwondo, volleyball, weightlifting; also AAU Junior Olympics and all matters pertaining to Olympic development in AAU sports."

INSIDE SPORTS, Newsweek, 444 Madison Ave., New York NY 10022. (212)350-2000. Monthly magazine for a sophisticated, mostly male audience. Estab. 1980. Circ. 550,000. Pays on acceptance "and after a written agreement has been signed." Reports in 1 week on queries; 1 month on mss.

Columns/Departments: Business, Medicine, Gambling, Style, Inside Track, Food, Media. Buys 1-2 mss/year for each column. Length: 3,000 words maximum. Pays $500-750.

Fillers: Updates and lists (newsworthy topics with a news slant); Numbers (ideas, new or offbeat statistics).

OUTDOOR CANADA MAGAZINE, 953A Eglinton Ave. E., Toronto, Ontario, Canada M4G 4B5. (416)429-5550. Editor-in-Chief: Sheila Kaighin. 50% freelance written. Emphasizes noncompetitive outdoor recreation. Published 7 times/year; magazine; 64-96 pages. Circ. 61,134. Pays on publication. Buys all rights. Submit seasonal/holiday material 5-6 months in advance of issue date. Byline given. Originals only. SASE or material not returned. Reports in 4 weeks. Sample copy $1; writer's guidelines, 50¢; mention *Writer's Market* in request.

Nonfiction: Exposé (only as it pertains to the outdoors, e.g. wildlife management); and how-to (in-depth, thorough pieces on how to select equipment for various subjects, or improve techniques only as they relate to outdoor subjects covered). Buys 35-40 mss/year. Submit complete ms.

Length: 1,000-3,500 words. Pays $75-150. $300 for cover story—e.g., when one of the author's color transparencies is used as the cover to lead into his story.
Photos: Submit photo material with accompanying ms. Pays $5-30 for 8x10 b&w glossy prints and $50 for 35mm color transparencies; $150/cover. Captions preferred. Buys all rights. Model release required.
Fillers: Outdoor tips. Buys 10/year. Length: 350-500 words. Pays $25.
Tips: All submissions *must* include SASE or International Reply Coupon.

OUTSIDE, (formerly *Mariah/Outside*), Mariah Publication Corp., 3401 W. Division St., Chicago IL 60651. (312)342-7777. Emphasizes outdoor subjects. Eight issues/year; 112 pages. Circ. 200,000. Pays on publication or before. Buys first North American serial rights. Submit seasonal/holiday material 4 months in advance. SASE. Reports in 4 weeks (queries); 6 weeks (ms). Sample copy $2; free writer's guidelines.
Nonfiction: Exposé (environmental/political and consumer outdoor equipment); general interest (as pertains to the outdoors); historical (profiles of early pioneers and expeditions); how-to (photography, equipment, techniques used in outdoor sports); humor (as pertains to outdoor activities); profiles (leaders and major figures associated with sports, politics, ecology of the outdoors); new product (hardware/software, reviews of performance of products used in camping, backpacking, outdoor sports, etc.); personal experience (major and minor expeditions and adventures); photo feature (outdoor photography); technical (of outdoor equipment); and travel (to exotic regions and cultures rarely visited). Buys 40 mss/year. Query with clips of published work. Length: 1,000-4,000 words. Pays $350-1,200.
Photos: Send photos with ms. Pays $50-200 for 35mm color transparencies. Buys one-time rights. Captions required.
Columns/Departments: Dispatches (news items); Equipage (articles on broad categories of outdoor equipment); Hardware/Software (short equipment reviews, slant to new innovative products, must include evaluation); Natural Acts (natural sciences); Reviews (books). Buys 3-4/issue. Query with clips of published work. Length: 200-1,500 words. Pays $150-400.
Fiction: Adventure, fantasy and humorous. Query with clips of published work or send finished manuscript. Length: 1,000-4,000 words. Pays $250-1,000.

REFEREE, Referee Enterprises, Inc., Box 161, Franksville WI 53126. (414)632-8855. Managing Editor: Tom Hammill. For well-educated, mostly 26- to 50-year-old male sports officials. Monthly magazine; 60 pages. Circ. 42,000. Pays on acceptance of completed manuscript. Buys all rights. Submit seasonal/holiday material 6 months in advance. Photocopied and previously published submissions OK. SASE. Reports in 4 weeks. Sample copy for 9x12 SASE with 41¢ postage.
Nonfiction: How-to, informational, humor, interview, profile, personal experience, photo feature and technical. Buys 54 mss/year. Query. Length: 700-2,000 words. Pays 4¢/word up to a maximum of $100. "No general sports articles or stories on successful pro or major college officials/umpires." Recent article titles: "Rating Systems—Are They Counterproductive?", "Disaster Along the Toutle River," and "Welcome to Referees Anonymous."
Photos: Tom Hammill, managing editor. Purchased with or without accompanying ms or on assignment. Captions required. Send contact sheet, prints, negatives or transparencies. Pays $15 for each b&w used; $25 for each color used; $75-100 for color cover.
Columns/Departments: Arena (bios); Library (book reviews); and Law (legal aspects). Buys 24 mss/year. Query. Length: 200-800 words. Pays 4¢/word up to $50 maximum for Library and Law. Arena pays no fee, but full author credit is given.
Fillers: Tom Hammill, managing editor. Jokes, gags, anecdotes, puzzles and referee shorts. Query. Length: 50-200 words. Pays 4¢/word in some cases; others offer only author credit lines.
Tips: "Queries with a specific idea appeals most. It is helpful to obtain suitable photos to augment story. Don't send fluff—we need hard hitting, incisive material tailored just for our audience. Anything smacking of PR is a no sale."

SOUTHWEST SPORTS, 113 Girard SE, Albuquerque NM 87106. Editor: Richard H. Rogers. 75% freelance written. "The only publication located in the heart of the Southwestern US covering major indoor and outdoor events and key personalities. Emphasizes regional sports, recreation and physical fitness of prime interest to large masses of active people including, but not limited to, participants, spectators, promoters, developers and coaches." Monthly magazine: 56 pages. Circ. 50,000. Pays on publication. Buys all rights. Byline given. Submit seasonal/holiday material 4 months in advance of issue date. Photocopied and previously published (in different region) submissions OK. SASE. Reports in 4-6 weeks. Free writer's guidelines; mention *Writer's Market* in request.
Nonfiction: Competitive sports (key events, all types); rodeo and horse-related activities; horse racing; outdoors (all types, including hunting, fishing, camping and backpacking and conserva-

tion); how-to (something unique, not trite advice column); general interest; humor; inspirational; interviews (stars or other athletes with something to say, coaches); new product (sports equipment, recreational travel); personal experience; opinion (how to improve sports or recreational facilities); photo feature; profile; and travel (Southwest recreational). "We use very little material that does not fit our *regional* approach." Buys 5-10 mss/issue. Query on major projects; submit complete ms on short articles. Length: 500-5,000 words. Pays $25-200.

Photos: Submit photo material with accompanying query or ms. Pays $10-100 for 5x7 or 8x10 b&w glossy prints; $10-150 for 5x7 or 8x10 matte color prints or 2¼x2¼ transparencies. Captions and model release required. Buys all rights.

Columns/Departments: Book reviews (sports and Southwest); editor's page (opinion or sidelights); equipment (evaluation of sports, travel and equipment); profiles (200 words of sports achievements); and schools (sports programs and facilities at Southwest colleges). Submit complete ms. Length: 200-1,000 words. Pays $10-50. Open to suggestions for new columns/departments.

SPORT, Sports Media Corp., 641 Lexington Ave., New York NY 10022. (212)872-8010. Contact: Neil Cohen. Managing Editor: Wade Leftwich. Monthly magazine covering primarily college and pro sports—baseball, football, basketball, hockey, soccer, tennis, others—for sports fans. Circ. 1.25 million. Pays on acceptance. Byline given. Offers 25% kill fee. Buys first North American serial rights. Submit seasonal/holiday material 3 months in advance. SASE. Reports in 2 weeks.

Nonfiction: General interest; interview (sport interview in Q&A format); photo feature (on minor and major sports); and investigative reports on the world of sports. Buys 75 mss/year. Query with clips of published work. No telephone queries. Length: 1,000-2,500 words. Pays $1,000 minimum.

Columns/Departments: Back Page (humorous essays on sport); Sport Talk (briefs on news or offbeat aspects of sport). Buys 48+ mss/year. Length: 250-1,000 words. Pays $100-500, depending on length and type of piece.

SPORTING NEWS, 1212 N. Lindbergh Blvd., St. Louis MO 63132. "We do not actively solicit freelance material."

SPORTS ILLUSTRATED, Time & Life Bldg., Rockefeller Center, New York NY 10020. Articles Editor: Robert W. Creamer. Primarily staff-written, with small but steady amount of outside material. Weekly. Reports in 4 weeks. Pays on acceptance. Buys all North American rights or first North American publication rights. Pay varies for kill fee. Byline given "except for Scorecard department." SASE.

Nonfiction: "Material falls into two general categories: regional (text that runs in editorial space accompanying regional advertising pages) and national text. Runs a great deal of regional advertising and, as a result, considerable text in that section of the magazine. Regional text does not have a geographical connotation; it can be any sort of short feature: Shopwalk, Footloose, Viewpoint and Sideline (500 or 1,000 words, not in-between); Yesterday, Nostalgia, Reminiscence, Perspective, First Person, On the Scene (1,200-2,000 words), but it must deal with some aspect of sports. National text (1,500-6,000 words) also must have a clear sporting connection; should be personality, personal reminiscence, knowing look into a significant aspect of a sporting subject, but national text should be written for broad appeal, so that readers without special knowledge will appreciate the piece." Pays $400-750 for regional pieces, $1,000 and up for national text. Smaller payments are made for material used in special sections or departments.

Photos: "Do not submit photos or artwork until story is purchased." No fiction, no poetry.

Tips: "Regional text is the best section for a newcomer. National text is difficult as many of the national sections are staff-written."

THE SPORTS JOURNAL, B4-416 Meridian Rd. SE, Calgary, Alberta, Canada T2A 1X2. (403)273-5141. Editor-in-Chief: Barry A. Whetstone. 80% freelance written. Monthly tabloid; 32 pages. Circ. 30,000. Pays on publication. Buys all rights. Byline given. Phone queries OK. Submit seasonal/holiday material 1 month in advance of issue date. Simultaneous, photocopied and previously published submissions OK. SASE. Reports in 1 month. Free sample copy and writer's guidelines; mention *Writer's Market* in request.

Nonfiction: General interest; interview (sports figures); nostalgia (sports history); personal opinion (on sports-related topics); and profile. Buys 15-25 mss/issue. Submit complete ms. Length: 300-350 words. Pays $20.

Photos: "We do not pay extra for photos accompanying mss, but the ms stands a much better chance for publication if photos are included." Submit photos with ms. Uses b&w prints. Buys one-time rights.

Columns/Departments: "We cover all major sports; coverage can be by league, team, or invividual players." Submit complete ms. Length: 200-600 words. Pays $20.

Tips: "We will review any and all matter received, excluding quizzes, puzzles and cartoons."

SPORTS PARADE, Meridian Publishing Co., Inc., Box 2315, Ogden UT 84404. (801)394-9446. Editor: Dick Harris. Monthly magazine covering sports and general interest items. "*Sports Parade* covers all sports, but gives emphasis to participant activities including racquetball, tennis, swimming, jogging, surfing, skiing, softball, volleyball, motorcycling, boating, horseback riding, snowmobiling, and even horseshoes and wrist wrestling." Pays on acceptance. Byline given. Buys first North American serial rights. SASE. Reports in 2 weeks. Sample copy 50¢.
Nonfiction: How-to, humor, inspirational, interview/profile and success stories. "We're looking for the different twist, the unusual, the down-to-earth, and the kinds of activities that families can get involved in. Articles should have wide appeal." Query. Length: 900-1,200 words for features; 600-800 words for others. Pays 10¢/word.
Photos: "We want good, sharp, in-action photos. No snapshots. keep in mind opportunities for cover (vertical color)." Pays $20/b&w photo; $25/color photo; "more (to be negotiated) for cover photos."
Fillers: Shorts. Buys 24/year. Length: 200-400 words.

WOMEN'S SPORTS MAGAZINE, Women's Sports Publications, Inc., 314 Town & Country Village, Palo Alto CA 94301. Editor: Sue Hoover, Senior Editor: Amy Rennert. Emphasizes women's sports, fitness and health. Monthly magazine; 72 pages. Estab. January 1979. Circ. 105,000. Pays on publication. Buys all rights. Submit seasonal/holiday material 3 months in advance. SASE. Reports in 1 month (queries); 6 weeks (ms). Sample copy $2.00; SASE for writer's guidelines.
Nonfiction: Exposé, general interest, how-to, humor, interview, new product, nostalgia, personal experience, personal opinion, profile and travel. "All articles should pertain to women's sports, fitness and health. All must be of national interest" Buys 5 mss/issue. Query with clips of published work. Length: 250-3,000 words. Pays $25 minimum.
Photos: State availability of photos. Pays about $25 for b&w prints; about $50 for 35mm color transparencies. Buys one-time rights.
Columns/Departments: Buys 3/issue. Query with clips of published work. Length: 500-1,500 words. Pays $25 minimum.
Fillers: Clippings, anecdotes, short humor, newsbreaks and health and fitness articles. Length: 25-250 words.
Tips: "The best query letters often start with a first paragraph which could be the first paragraph of the article the writer wants to do. It immediately gets the editor curious. Queries should indicate that the writer has done the preliminary research for the article. Published clips help too. Freelancers can best break into Women's Sports by submitting fillers for the Sidelines and Active Woman's Almanac sections. We are not looking for profiles of athletes which lack depth or a real understanding of the athlete."

Golf

CAROLINA GOLFER, Box 3, Columbia SC 29202. (803)796-9200. Editor: Sydney L. Wise. Associate Editor: Larry Booker. Bimonthly. Buys first rights. Pays on publication. Free sample copy. Reports in 3-8 weeks. SASE.
Nonfiction and Photos: Articles on golf and golfers, clubs, courses, tournaments, only in the Carolinas. Stories on the various courses should be done "in the manner that would give the reader a basic idea of what each course is like." Length: 1,200-1,500 words. Pays according to quality of ms; 3¢ minimum/word. Buys photos with mss. 5x7 or 8x10 b&w glossy prints. Color should be 4x5 or 35mm transparencies. Pays $5 minimum for b&w; $25 for color transparencies used for cover.

COUNTRY CLUB GOLFER, 2171 Campus Dr., Irvine CA 92715. (714)752-6474. Editor: Edward F. Pazdur. For private country club members and club golfers; professional, affluent, college-educated. Monthly magazine; 64 pages. Circ. 70,000. Pays on publication. Buys all rights.
Poetry: Humorous golf poems. Buys 4/issue. Submit in batches of 12. Length: 6-12 lines. Pays $10.
Tips: "We are interested in full length golf oriented articles that would appeal to *private* country club golfers. Rates are negotiable. Maximum payment is between $100-150."

GOLF DIGEST, 495 Westport Ave., Norwalk CT 06856. (203)847-5811. Editor: Nick Seitz. Emphasizes golfing. Monthly magazine; 130 pages. Circ. 1 million. Pays on publication. Buys all rights. Byline given. Submit seasonal/holiday material 4 months in advance. Photocopied submissions OK. SASE. Reports in 4-6 weeks.
Nonfiction: Exposé, how-to, informational, historical, humor, inspirational, interview, nostalgia,

opinion, profile, travel, new product, personal experience, photo feature and technical; "all on playing and otherwise enjoying the game of golf." Query. Length: 1,000-2,500 words. Pays 20¢/edited word minimum.

Photos: Pete Libby, art editor. Purchased without accompanying ms. Pays $10-150 for 5x7 or 8x10 b&w prints; $25-300/35mm color transparency. Model release required.

Poetry: Lois Haines, poetry editor. Light verse. Buys 1-2/issue. Length: 4-8 lines. Pays $10-25.

Fillers: Lois Haines, fillers editor. Jokes, gags, anecdotes. Buys 1-2/issue. Length: 2-6 lines. Pays $10-25.

GOLF JOURNAL, United States Golf Association, Far Hills NJ 07931. (201)234-2300. Editor: Robert Sommers. For golfers of all ages and both sexes. Official publication of the U.S. Golf Association. "Our focus is on service and historical information, enterainingly presented, about the game itself, its history, its rules, its courses, and the amateur players." Magazine; 32 pages. 8 times/year. Circ. 100,000. Buys all rights. Byline given. Buys 30 mss/year. Pays on acceptance. Free sample copy. No photocopied or simultaneous submissions. Reports in 2 weeks. Query. "Sell your idea in your query, and write it as though it is your manuscript. A poorly written query is a turn-off." SASE.

Nonfiction and Photos: Contact: George Eberl. "As the official publication of the United States Golf Association, our magazine is strong on decisions on the Rules of Golf, USGA Championships, history of the game, and on service articles directed to the club golfer. All facets of golf, its history, courses, and clubs. Instruction. Humor, but not jokes." Length: 500-2,000 words. Pays $400 maximum. Pays $15 minimum for b&w photos. Captions required.

Tips: "Golf isn't sacred, but it can be lovable. Write with a twinkle, a sense of joy, with knowledge, and an awareness of a complete sentence. Our readers expect it. Acquaint yourself with *Golf Journal*—its approach, its tone, its feel. Keep in mind its readership is highly literate; this same virtue must be present in those hoping to sell articles to the magazine. Tired topics and poor writing are the two major reasons for rejections."

GOLF MAGAZINE, Times Mirror Magazines, Inc., 380 Madison Ave., New York NY 10017. (212)687-3000. Editor: George Peper. 20% freelance written. Emphasizes golf for males, ages 15-80, college-educated, professionals. Monthly magazine; 150 pages. Circ. 750,000. Pays on acceptance. Buys all rights. Byline given. Submit seasonal/holiday material 4 months in advance. Photocopied submissions OK. SASE. Reports in 4 weeks. Sample copy $1.25.

Nonfiction: How-to (improve game, instructional tips); informational (news in golf); humor; profile (people in golf); travel (golf courses, resorts); new product (golf equipment, apparel, teaching aids); and photo feature (great moments in golf; must be special. Most photography on assignment only). Buys 4-6 unsolicited mss/year. Query. Length: 1,200-2,500 words. Pays $350-500.

Photos: Purchased with accompanying ms or on assignment. Captions required. Query. Pays $50 for 8½x11 glossy prints (with contact sheet and negatives); $75 minimum for 3x5 color prints. Total purchase price for ms includes payment for photos. Model release required.

Columns/Departments: Golf Reports (interesting golf events, feats, etc.). Buys 5-10 mss/year. Query. Length: 250 words maximum. Pays $35. Open to suggestions for new columns/departments.

Fiction: Humorous, mystery. Must be golf-related. Buys 1-2 mss/year. Query. Length: 1,200-2,000 words. Pays $350-500.

Fillers: Short humor. Length: 20-35 words. Pays $25.

Tips: "Best chance is to aim for a light piece which is not too long and is focused on a personality. Anything very technical that would require a consummate knowledge of golf, we would rather assign ourselves. But if you are successful with something light and not too long, we might use you for something heavier later. Probably the best way to break in would be by our Golf Reports section in which we run short items on interesting golf feats, events and so forth. If you send us something like that, about an important event in your area, it is an easy way for us to get acquainted."

Guns

AMERICAN HANDGUNNER, Publishers Development Corp., 591 Camino De La Reina, Suite 700, San Diego CA 92108. (714)297-5352. Editor: Jerome Rakusan. Bimonthly magazine about combat shooting, metallic silhouette shooting, target shooting and big game shooting with handguns. Circ. 100,000. Pays on publication. Buys first North American serial rights. Reports in 3 weeks. Free sample copy and writer's guidelines.

Nonfiction: Historical (relating to guns and ammunition); how-to (conversions and alterations); interview (with gunsmiths or manufacturers); opinion (pros and cons of styles of combat shooting); new product (objective text reports); photo feature (of competitions); and technical. This is a "highly technical field. You must know what you're writing about. Nothing on periphery of shooting subjects." Query. Length: 800-2,000 words. Pays $150-250.

Photos: Pays $50-150 for 4x5 or 8x10 b&w prints, or color negatives and prints; offers no additional payment for photos accepted with ms. Buys one-time rights.

Columns/Departments: Combat Course, Pistol Smithing, Taking Air (opinion) and Cops Talk (about law enforcement). Buys 5 mss/issue. Query. Length: 400-800 words. Pays $150 minimum.

THE AMERICAN SHOTGUNNER, Box 3351, Reno NV 89505. Publisher: Bob Thruston. Monthly tabloid; 48 pages. Circ. 80,000. Buys all rights. Buys 24-50 mss/year. Pays on publication. Free sample copy and writer's guidelines. Submit special material (hunting) 3-4 months in advance. Reports on material accepted for publication in 30 days. Returns rejected material. Submit query. SASE.

Nonfiction and Photos: Paula DelGiudice, senior editor. All aspects of shotgunning trap and skeet shooting and hunting, reloading, shooting clothing and shooting equipment. Emphasis is on the how-to and instructional approach. "We give the sportsman actual material that will help him to improve his game, fill his limit, or build that duck blind, etc. Hunting articles are used in all issues, year round." Length: open. Pays $75-250. No additional payment for photos used with mss. "We also purchase professional cover material. Send transparencies (originals)."

BLACK POWDER TIMES, Box 842, Mount Vernon WA 98273. (206)336-2969. Editor: Fred Holder. 25-30% freelance written. For people interested in shooting and collecting black powder guns, primarily of the muzzle-loading variety. Tabloid newspaper; 24 pages. Monthly. Not copyrighted. Byline given. Pays on publication. Sample copy $1.25. Will consider photocopied and simultaneous submissions. Reports in 2-4 weeks. Query. SASE.

Nonfiction: Articles on gunsmiths who make black powder guns, on shoots, on muzzle-loading gun clubs, on guns of the black powder vintage, and anything related to the sport of black powder shooting and hunting. Emphasis is on good writing and reporting. Informational, how-to, personal experience, interview, profile, historical articles and book reviews. Length: 500-2,000 words. Pays 2¢/word.

COMBAT HANDGUNS, Harris Publications Outdoor Group, 79 Madison Ave., New York NY 10016. (212)686-4121. Managing Editor: Harry Kane. Bimonthly magazine covering use of handguns in combat situations and in military, police and personal defense. Readers are persons in law enforcement and the military and those interested in the uses and the history of combat firearms. Estab. 1980. Circ. 80,000. Pays on acceptance. Byline given. Buys all rights. Submit seasonal/holiday material 4 months in advance. Simultaneous queries, and photocopied and previously published submissions OK. SASE. Reports in 1 month. Free sample copy.

Nonfiction: Book excerpts; general interest (modifications and uses in combat situations; also gun use in every area of personal defense); how-to; profile (of gunsmith schools); opinion; personal experience ("moment of truth"); photo feature and technical. Buys 60 mss/year. Query. Length: 1,500-3,500 words. Pays $150-400.

Photos: "What I really like is photos and plenty of good ones." State availability of photos or send photos with ms. Reviews color transparencies and b&w prints. Captions required. Buys first rights.

Columns/Departments: Police Armory and Combat Ammo. Buys 6 mss/year. Query. Length: 500-1,000 words. Pays $100 maximum.

GUN JOURNAL, Charlton Publications, Charlton Bldg., Derby CT 06418. (203)735-3381. Editor: John Bartimole. Bimonthly magazine covering the gun market. Estab. 1980. Circ. 100,000. Pays on publication. Byline given. Buys all rights, but will reassign on request. Submit seasonal/holiday material 4 months in advance. SASE. Reports in 1 month. Sample copy $1.50; writer's guidelines for business size SAE and 1 first class stamp.

Nonfiction: Historical/nostalgic; how-to (collect, field, or become proficient in building, using and collecting guns and related items); interview/profile (of persons who are outstanding in anything related to firearms); and technical (testing articles). Buys 60 mss/year. Query with clips of published work or resumé. Length: 1,000-3,000 words. Pays 8¢/word.

Photos: State availability of photos. Reviews 35mm or 2¼x2¼ transparencies, and 8x10 b&w glossy prints. No extra fee for b&w. Pays minimum $125 per color cover. Captions required.

Tips: "Give us some reason that you're in a position to write this particular article."

GUN WEEK, Hawkeye Publishing, Inc., Box 411, Station C, Buffalo NY 14209. (716)885-6408. Executive Editor/Publisher: Joseph P. Tartaro. Emphasizes gun hobby; sports, collecting and news. Weekly newspaper; 28 pages. Circ. 30,000. Pays on publication. Buys first North American serial rights. Phone queries OK. Submit seasonal/holiday material 6 weeks in advance. Simultaneous and photocopied submissions OK. SASE. Reports in 6 weeks. Free sample copy and writer's guidelines.

Nonfiction: Historical (history of firearms or how they affected an historical event); how-to (dealing with firearms, construction, care, etc.); informational (hunting, firearms, legislative news—national and all states); interview (gun-related persons, heads of college shooting programs, etc.); new product (firearms, ammunition, cleaners, gun-related products, knives, hunting accessories); photo feature (conservation interests); profile (hunters, gun buffs, legislators, writers, conservationists, etc.); book reviews (technical). Buys 500 mss/year. Query or send complete ms. Length: 125-2,000 words. Pays 50¢/column inch.

Photos: Usually purchased with accompanying ms. Hunting and legislative news photos separately. Captions required. Send contact sheet, prints and/or transparencies. Usually pays $3 for 5x7 or 8x10 b&w glossy prints; $5 for 35mm color transparencies. (50¢/column inch with manuscript). Total purchase price for ms includes payment for photos. Model release required.

Columns/Departments: Buys 150-300 mss/year. Query or submit complete ms. Length: 500-1,500 words. Pays $20-35. Open to suggestions from freelancers for new columns/departments; address to Joseph P. Tartaro. "Many freelance writers are now writing under one designated column, 'Muzzle Loading'—Don Davis, etc. We are looking for possible columns and articles for new departments on collecting, hunting, rifles, shotguns, handguns, reloading, books, gun shops, benchrest, etc."

GUN WORLD, Box HH, 34249 Camino Capistrano, Capistrano Beach CA 92624. Editorial Director: Jack Lewis. 50% freelance written. For ages that "range from mid-20s to mid-60s; many professional types who are interested in relaxation of hunting and shooting." Monthly. Circ. 136,000. Buys all rights. Byline given. Buys 50 mss/year. Pays on acceptance. Copy of editorial requirements for SASE. Submit seasonal material 4 months in advance. Reports in 6 weeks, perhaps longer. SASE.

Nonfiction and Photos: General subject matter consists of "well-rounded articles—not by amateurs—on shooting techniques, with anecdotes; hunting stories with tips and knowledge integrated. No poems or fiction. We like broad humor in our articles, so long as it does not reflect upon firearms safety. Most arms magazines are pretty deadly and we feel shooting can be fun. Too much material aimed at pro-gun people. Most of this is staff-written and most shooters don't have to be told of their rights under the Constitution. We want articles on new development; off-track inventions, novel military uses of arms; police armament and training techniques; do-it-yourself projects in this field." Buys informational, how-to, personal experience and nostalgia articles. Pays $300 maximum. Purchases photos with mss and captions required. Wants 5x7 b&w.

Tips: "To break in, offer an anecdote having to do with proposed copy."

GUNS & AMMO MAGAZINE, Petersen Publishing Co., 8490 Sunset Blvd., Los Angeles CA 90069. Editor-in-Chief: Howard E. French. Managing Editor: E.G. Bell. Emphasizes the firearms field. Monthly magazine; 108 pages. Circ. 450,000. Pays on publication. Buys all rights. Submit seasonal/holiday material 4 months in advance. SASE. Reports in 1 month. Free writer's guidelines.

Nonfiction: Informational and technical. Especially needs semi-technical articles on guns, shooting and reloading. Buys 7-10 mss/issue. Send complete ms. Length: 1,200-3,000 words. Pays $125-350.

Photos: Purchased with accompanying ms. Captions required. Uses 8x10 b&w glossy prints. Total purchase price for ms includes payment for photos. Model release required.

GUNS MAGAZINE, 591 Camino de la Reina, San Diego CA 92108. (714)297-5352. Editor: J. Rakusan. Monthly for firearms enthusiasts. Circ. 135,000. Buys all rights. Buys 100-150 mss/year. Pays on publication. Will send free sample copy to a writer on request. Reports in 2-3 weeks. SASE.

Nonfiction and Photos: Test reports on new firearms; how-to on gunsmithing, reloading; roundup articles on firearms types. Historical pieces. Does not want to see anything about "John and I went hunting" or rewrites of a general nature, or controversy for the sake of controversy, without new illumination. "More short, punchy articles will be used in the next year. Payments will not be as large as for full length features, but the quantity used will give more writers a chance to get published." Length: 1,000-2,500 words. Pays $75-175. Major emphasis is on good photos. No additional payment for b&w glossy prints purchased with mss. Pays $50-$100 for color; 2¼x2¼ minimum.

HANDLOADER, Wolfe Publishing Co., Inc., Box 3030, Prescott AZ 86302. (602)445-7810. Editor: Ken Howell. Bimonthly magazine covering handloading ammunition for sporting use in rifles, handguns and shotguns for readers who are technically very knowledgeable. Circ. 35,000. Pays on publication. Buys first North American serial rights. Phone queries OK. Submit seasonal material 3 months in advance. SASE. Free sample copy and writer's guidelines.

Nonfiction: Technical (on ammunition, loading and shooting). "No general, negative or critical articles. Study the magazine, its coverage, style, tone and limitations. Sound technical knowledge is absolutely necessary; our readers have it and quickly spot weak or thin presentations by writers who have insufficient knowledge or experience. Field-test data are also vital." Buys 3-5 mss/issue. Send complete ms. Length: 2,000-4,000 words. Pays $150-300.

Photos: Send photos with ms. Reviews 5x7 and 8x10 b&w glossy and semi-glossy prints. Pays $50 minimum for 2¼x2¾ and 4x5 color transparencies. Offers no additional payment for photos accepted with ms. Captions required. Buys one-time rights.

Columns/Departments: Reader Research (short technical articles of same general type as features but not as extensive). Buys 3-4 mss/year. Send complete ms. Length: 1,000-2,000 words. Pays $25 maximum.

Tips: "Avoid 'technical' style, coldness or distance in tone and an elegant variation. Write simply, straightforwardly. Report technical facts with little or no editorial commentary. Don't try to be clever, cute, folksy or scientific. Present the facts and let them bear their own weight."

RIFLE, Wolfe Publishing Co., Inc., Box 3030, Prescott AZ 86302. (602)445-7810. Editor: Ken Howell. 50% freelance written. Bimonthly. For advanced rifle enthusiasts. Pays on publication. Buys North American serial rights. No simultaneous submissions. Reports in 30 days. SASE.

Nonfiction and Photos: Articles must be fresh and of a quality and style to enlighten rather than entertain knowledgeable gun enthusiasts. Subject matter must be technical and supported by appropriate research. "We are interested in seeing new bylines and new ideas, but if a writer doesn't have a solid knowledge of firearms and ballistics, he's wasting his time and ours submitting." Length: 2,000-4,000 words. Pays $150-300. Photos should accompany ms. Buys ms and photos as a package.

SHOOTIN' TRAP, Keepin' Track, Inc., Box 5400, Reno NV 89513. (702)329-4519. Editor: Frank Kodl. Managing Editor: Fredi Kodl. Monthly magazine covering the sport of trapshooting. Circ. 25,000. Pays on publication. Byline given. Buys one-time rights. Submit seasonal/holiday material 3 months in advance. SASE. Reports in 1 month. Free sample copy and writer's guidelines.

Nonfiction: Book excerpts, expose, general interest, historical/nostalgic, how-to, humor, inspiration, interview/profile, new product, opinion, personal experience, photo feature, technical and travel; "all articles must be related directly to trapshooting." Buys 50-70 mss/year. Query or send complete mss. Length: open. Pays $50-200.

Photos: State availability of photos or send photos with ms. Reviews 5x7 b&w prints. "Photos included in payment for ms." Captions required.

Horse Racing

THE BACKSTRETCH, 19363 James Couzens Hwy., Detroit MI 48235. (313)342-6144. Editor: Ruth LeGrove. For thoroughbred horse trainers, owners, breeders, farm managers, track personnel, jockeys, grooms and racing fans who span the age range from very young to very old. Publication of United Thoroughbred Trainers of America, Inc. Quarterly magazine; 100 pages. Circ. 25,000.

Nonfiction: "*Backstretch* contains mostly general information. Articles deal with biographical material on trainers, owners, jockeys, horses and their careers on and off the track, historical track articles, etc. Unless writer's material is related to thoroughbreds and thoroughbred racing, it should not be submitted. Articles accepted on speculation basis—payment made after material is used. If not suitable, articles are returned immediately. Articles that do not require printing by a specified date are preferred. No special length requirement and amount paid depends on material. Advisable to include photos if possible. Articles should be original copies and should state whether presented to any other magazine, or whether previously printed in any other magazine. Submit complete ms. SASE. Sample copy $1. We do not buy crossword puzzles, cartoons, newspaper clippings, fiction or poetry."

HUB RAIL, Hub Rail, Inc., 6320 Busch Blvd., Columbus OH 43229. (614)846-0770. Editor: David M. Dolezal. Emphasizes harness horse racing or breeding. Quarterly magazine; 120 pages. Circ. 10,000. Pays on publication. Buys all rights. Phone queries OK. Submit seasonal/holiday material 3 months in advance. Simultaneous and photocopied submissions OK. SASE. Reports in 4 weeks. Free sample copy and writer's guidelines.

Nonfiction: General interest, historical, humor and nostalgia. "Articles should pertain to harness racing." Buys 10 mss/year. Send clips of published work. Length: 1,000-5,000 words. Pays $50-200.

Fiction: "We use short stories pertaining to harness racing." Buys 2 mss/year. Send clips of published work. Length: 2,500-7,000 words. Pays $50-200.

RACING DIGEST, Racing Digest Publishing Co., Inc., Box 101, Dover PA 17315. (717)292-5608. Editor: Cole Atwood. Managing Editor: Robin Fidler. Weekly newspaper covering thoroughbred horse racing and breeding. Circ. 58,000. Pays on publication. Byline given. Makes work-for-hire assignments. Submit seasonal/holiday material 2 months in advance. Simultaneous queries, and simultaneous and photocopied submissions OK. SASE. Reports in 2 weeks. Sample copy for $2 and 9x12 SAE.
Nonfiction: Query. Length: 500-2,000 words. Pay "depends on article, assignment, etc."
Photos: State availability of photos. Reviews b&w contact sheets and prints. Captions and identification of subjects required. Buys one-time rights.

SPUR, Box 85, Middleburg Va 22117. (703)687-6314. Editor: Connie Coopersmith. Managing Editor: Annette C. Penney. Bimonthly magazine covering thoroughbred horses "and the amazing people who inhabit this world." Circ. 8,000. Pays on publication. Byline given. Copyrighted. Buys all rights. Submit seasonal/holiday material 2½ months in advance. Simultaneous queries, and simultaneous, photocopied, and previously published submissions OK. SASE. Reports in 2 weeks on queries; 1 month on mss. Sample copy $2; writer's guidelines for business size SAE and 1 first class stamp.
Nonfiction: Historical/nostalgic, humor, interview/profile, new product, opinion, personal experience, photo feature and travel. "We are looking for fresh, interesting approaches to entertaining and instructing our readers. The world of the thoroughbred has many facets, including stories about personalities (e.g., how they live and play). No tasteless or sex types of articles." Buys 30 mss/year. Query with clips of published work, "or we will consider complete mss." Length: 300-2,500 words. Pays $25-500 and up.
Photos: State availability of photos. Reviews color or b&w contact sheets. Captions, model releases and identification of subjects required. Buys all rights "unless otherwise negotiated."
Columns/Departments: Deborah Pritchard, senior editor. Query or send complete ms. Length: 100-500 words. Pays $25-50 and up.
Fillers: Anecdotes, short humor. Length: 50-100 words. Pays $25 and up.
Tips: "Writers must have a knowledge of horses, horse owners, breeding, training, racing, and riding—or the ability to obtain this knowledge from a subject and to turn out a good article."

TROT, 233 Evans Ave., Toronto, Ontario, Canada M8Z 1J6. Executive Editor: Michel Corbeil. Editor: Renée St. Louis. Official publication of the Canadian Trotting Association. "Quite a number of our readers derive all their income from harness racing." Circ. 19,000. Pays on acceptance. Buys first North American serial rights. Previously published submissions OK. SAE and International Reply Coupons.
Nonfiction: "General material dealing with any aspect of harness racing or prominent figures in the sport. We would appreciate submissions of any general material on harness racing from anywhere in the US. Nothing dealing with strictly US subjects." Query. Length: 1,000-1,500 words. Pays $100-200.
Photos: Pays $15 for 8x10 b&w prints; $40 for 2¼x2¼ color transparencies.

TURF & SPORT DIGEST, 511 Oakland Ave., Baltimore MD 21212. Editor: Allen Mitzel Jr. For an audience composed of thoroughbred horseracing fans. Bimonthly magazine; 80 pages. Circ. 40,000. Buys all rights. Phone queries OK. Submit seasonal/holiday material 3 months in advance. Photocopied submissions and previously published submissions OK. SASE. Reports in 3 weeks. Free sample copy.
Nonfiction: Historical, humor, informational and personal experience articles on racing; interviews and profiles (racing personalities). Buys 4 mss/issue. Query. Length: 300-3,000 words. Pays $60-220.
Photos: Purchased with or without mss. Send contact sheet. Pays $15-25/b&w, $100/color.

Hunting and Fishing

ALABAMA GAME & FISH, GEORGIA SPORTSMAN, TENNESSEE SPORTSMAN, Game & Fish Publications, Inc., Box 741, Marietta GA 30061. (404)434-0807. Editor: David Morris.

Assistant Editor: Priscilla Crumpler. Monthly magazine covering game and fish indigenous to each state. Estab. 1980. Circ. 10,000 (*Alabama*); 45,000 (*Georgia*); 10,000 (*Tennessee*). Pays on publication. Byline given. Buys one-time rights. Submit seasonal material "at least 4 months in advance." Simultaneous queries OK. SASE. Reports in 2 months on queries. Sample copy $1.75; free writer's guidelines.

Nonfiction: How-to, interview/profile, personal experience, technical, travel—"if pertinent to 'where-to-go.' " No poems, general interest or historical. Query. Length: 1,200-2,800 words. "Payment depends on if run in one magazine only, or 2 magazines, or 3 combination."

Photos: State availability of photos or send photos with mss. Pays negotiable fee for 35mm or 2¼x2¼ color transparencies or 8x10 b&w prints. Captions required.

Tips: "Be a how-to, where-to-go, when-to-go-technical writer. Have an expertise in game and fish areas—and experience."

AMERICAN FIELD, 222 W. Adams St., Chicago IL 60606. Editor: William F. Brown. Weekly. Buys first publication rights. Pays on acceptance. Free sample copy. Reports in 20 days. SASE.

Nonfiction and Photos: Interested in factual articles on breeding, rearing, development and training of hunting dogs, how-to material written to appeal to upland bird hunters, sporting dog owners, field trialers, etc. Also wants stories and articles about hunting trips in quest of upland game birds. Length: 1,000-2,500 words. Pays $50-200. Uses photos submitted with manuscripts if they are suitable; also photos submitted with captions only. Pays $5 minimum for b&w.

Fillers: Very infrequently uses some 100- to 250-word fillers. Pays $5 minimum.

THE AMERICAN HUNTER, 1600 Rhode Island Ave. NW, Washington DC 20036. Editor: Earl Shelsby. 90% freelance written. For sport hunters who are members of the National Rifle Association; all ages, all political persuasions, all economic levels. Circ. over 700,000. Buys first North American serial rights "and the right to reprint our presentation." Byline given. Pays on acceptance. Free sample copy and writer's guidelines. Reports in 1-3 weeks. SASE.

Nonfiction: "Factual material on all phases of sport hunting and game animals and their habitats. Good angles and depth writing are essential. You have to *know* to write successfully here." Not interested in material on fishermen, campers or ecology buffs. Buys 200 mss/year. Query or submit complete ms. Length: 1,500-2,500 words. Pays $25-400.

Photos: No additional payment made for photos used with mss. Pays $10-25 for b&w photos purchased without accompanying mss. Pays $40-200 for color.

THE AMERICAN RIFLEMAN, 1600 Rhode Island Ave. NW, Washington DC 20036. Editor: William F. Parkerson, III. Monthly. Official journal of National Rifle Association of America. Buys first North American serial rights, including publication in this magazine, or any of the official publications of the National Rifle Association. Residuary rights will be returned after publication upon request of the author. Pays on acceptance. Free sample copy and writers' guidelines. Reports in 1-4 weeks. SASE.

Nonfiction: Factual articles on hunting, target shooting, shotgunning, conservation, firearms repairs and oddities accepted from qualified freelancers. Articles should be informative and interesting. No fiction. Nothing that "winks" at lawbreaking, or delineates practices that are inimical to the best interests of gun ownership, shooting, or good citizenship. Articles should run from one to four magazine pages. Pays $100-600.

Photos: Full-color transparencies for possible use on cover and inside. Photo articles that run one to two magazine pages. Pays $15 minimum for inside b&w photo; $100 minimum for cover; payment for groups of photos is negotiable.

ANGLER, Box 12155, Oakland CA 94604. Managing Editor: Dan Blanton. 50% freelance written. Fishing magazine for western US. Bimonthly magazine. Circ. 15,000. Pays on acceptance. Buys one-time rights. Byline given. Submit seasonl/holiday material 4 months in advance of issue date. Photocopied submissions OK. SASE. Reports in 2 weeks. Sample copy $2.50; free writer's guidelines for SASE.

Nonfiction: How-to; humor; inspirational; and travel. Buys 24 mss/year. Query. Length: 1,000-3,000 words. Pays $125-250.

Fiction: Buys 3 mss/year. Query. Length: 1,000-2,000 words. Pays $35-100.

BASS MASTER MAGAZINE, B.A.S.S. Publications, Box 17900, Montgomery AL 36141. (205)272-9530. Editor: Bob Cobb. Bimonthly magazine about largemouth, smallmouth, spotted bass and striped bass for dedicated beginning and advanced bass fishermen. Circ. 365,000. Pays on acceptance. Byline given. Buys all rights. Submit seasonal material 6 months in advance. Simultaneous and photocopied submissions OK, if so indicated. SASE. Reports in 1 week. Sample copy $2; free writer's guidelines with SASE.

Nonfiction: Historical; interview (of knowledgeable people in the sport); profile (outstanding fishermen); travel (where to go to fish for bass); how-to (catch bass and enjoy the outdoors); new product (reels, rods and bass boats); and conservation related to bass fishing. "No 'Me and Joe Go Fishing' type articles." Query. Length: 400-2,100 words. Pays $100-300.

Photos: "We want a mixture of black and white and color photos." Pays $15 minimum for b&w prints. Pays $100-150 for color cover transparencies. Captions required; model release preferred. Buys all rights.

Fillers: Anecdotes, short humor and newsbreaks. Buys 4-5 mss/issue. Length: 250-500 words. Pays $100 minimum.

FIELD AND STREAM, 1515 Broadway, New York NY 10036. Editor: Jack Samson. 50% freelance written. Monthly. Buys all rights. Byline given. Reports in 4 weeks. Query. SASE.

Nonfiction and Photos: "This is a broad-based outdoor service magazine. Editorial content ranges from very basic how-to stories that tell either in pictures or words how an outdoor technique is done or a device is made. Articles of penetrating depth about national conservation, game management, resource management, and recreation development problems. Hunting, fishing, camping, backpacking, nature, outdoor, photography, equipment, wild game and fish recipes, and other activities allied to the outdoors. The 'me and Joe' story is about dead, with minor exceptions. Both where-to and how-to articles should be well-illustrated." Especially needs conservation and environmental stories. Prefers color to b&w. Submit outline first with photos. Length: 2,500 words. Payment varies depending on the name of the author, quality of work, importance of the article. Pays 18¢/word minimum. Usually buys photos with mss. When purchased separately, pays $200 minimum for color. Buys all rights to photos.

Fillers: Buys "how it's done" fillers of 150-500 words. Must be unusual or helpful subjects. Pays $250.

FISHING AND HUNTING NEWS, Outdoor Empire Publishing Co., Inc., 511 Eastlake Ave. E., Box C-19000, Seattle WA 98109. (206)624-3845. Managing Editor: Vence Malernee. Emphasizes fishing and hunting. Weekly tabloid; 12-28 pages. Estab. 1944. Circ. 135,000. Pays on acceptance. Buys all rights. Submit seasonal/holiday material 3 months in advance. Photocopied submissions OK. Free sample copy and writer's guidelines.

Nonfiction: How-to (fish and hunt successfully, things that make outdoor jaunts more enjoyable/productive); photo feature (successful fishing/hunting in the Western US); informational. Buys 70 or more mss/year. Query. Length: 100-1,000 words. Pays $10 minimum.

Photos: Purchased with or without accompanying ms. Captions required. Submit prints or transparencies. Pays $5 minimum for 8x10 b&w glossy prints; $10 minimum for 35mm or 2¼x2¼color transparencies.

FISHING WORLD, 51 Atlantic Ave., Floral Park NY 11001. Editor: Keith Gardner. Bimonthly. Circ. 265,000. Buys first North American serial rights. Byline given. Pays on acceptance. Free sample copy. Photocopied submissions OK. Reports in 2 weeks. Query. SASE.

Nonfiction and Photos: "Feature articles range from 1,000-2,000 words with the shorter preferred. A good selection of color transparencies and b&w glossy prints should accompany each submission. Subject matter can range from a hot fishing site to tackle and techniques, from tips on taking individual species to a story on one lake or an entire region, either freshwater or salt. However, how-to is definitely preferred over where-to, and a strong biological/scientific slant is best of all. Where-to articles, especially if they describe foreign fishing, should be accompanied by sidebars covering how to make reservations and arrange transportation, how to get there, where to stay. Angling methods should be developed in clear detail, with accurate and useful information about tackle and boats. Depending on article length, suitability of photographs and other factors, payment is up to $250 for feature articles accompanied by suitable photography. Color transparencies selected for cover use pay an additional $250. B&w or unillustrated featurettes are also considered. These can be on anything remotely connected with fishing. Length: 1,000 words. Pays $25-100 depending on length and photos. Detailed queries accompanied by photos are preferred. Cover shots are purchased separately, rather than selected from those accompanying mss. The editor favors drama rather than serenity in selecting cover shots."

FLY FISHERMAN MAGAZINE, Ziff-Davis Publishing Co., Dorset VT 05251. (802)867-5951. Editor: Donald D. Zahner. Managing Editor: John Randolph. Associate Editor: John Barstow. Published 6 times/year; 116 pages. Circ. 130.000. Pays on publication. Buys first North American magazine rights and one-time periodical rights. Written queries preferred. Submit seasonal/holiday material 6 months in advance. SASE. Reports in 6 weeks. Free sample copy and writer's guidelines.

Nonfiction: How-to or where-to-go, new product, personal experience, photo feature, profile, technical and travel. Buys 10-12 mss/issue. Query or submit complete ms. Length: 100-3,000 words. Pays $35-400.

Photos: Send photos with ms. Pays $30-75 for 8x10 b&w glossy prints; $40-100 for 35mm, 2¼x2¼ 4x5 color transparencies; $200 maximum for cover. Buys one-time rights. Captions required.

Columns/Departments: Casting About (where-to-go shorts); Fly Fisherman's Bookshelf (book reviews); Fly-Tier's Bench (technical how-to); and Rod Rack (technical how-to). Buys 5/issue. Query or submit complete ms. Length: 100-1,500 words. Pays $35-200.

Fiction: Adventure and humorous. Query or submit complete ms. Length: 1,000-3,000 words. Pays $100-400.

Fillers: Mini-articles (technical or nontechnical). Buys 5/issue. Length: 100-300 words. Pays $35-100.

THE FLYFISHER, 390 Bella Vista, San Francisco CA 94127. (415)586-8332. Editor: Michael Fong. "*The Flyfisher* is the official publication of the Federation of Flyfishermen, a nonprofit organization of member clubs and individuals in the US, Canada, United Kingdom, France, New Zealand, Chile and other nations. It serves an audience of sophisticated anglers." Quarterly magazine; 48 pages. Circ. 8,500. Pays on acceptance for solicited material. Buys first North American serial rights. Byline given. Submit seasonal/holiday material 150 days in advance of issue date. SASE. Reports in 4 weeks. Sample copy $1.50, available from Box 1088, West Yellowstone MT 59758; writer's guidelines for SASE.

Nonfiction: How-to (fly fishing techniques, fly tying, tackle, etc.); general interest (any type including where to go, conservation); historical (places, people, events that have significance to fly fishing); inspirational (looking for articles dealing with Federation clubs on conservation projects); interview (articles of famous fly fishermen, fly tiers, teachers, etc.); nostalgia (articles of reminiscences on flies, fishing personalities, equipment and places); photo feature (preferably a combination of 35mm slides and b&w prints about places and seasons); technical (about techniques of fly fishing in salt and fresh waters). "Our readers are pretty sophisticated fly fishermen and articles too basic or not innovative do not appeal to us." Buys 8-10 mss/issue. Query. Length: 1,500-3,500 words. Pays $50-200.

Photos: Pays $15-25 for 8x10 b&w glossy prints; $20-40 for 35mm or larger color transparencies for inside use. $100 for covers. Captions required. Buys one-time rights. Prefers a selection of transparencies and glossies when illustrating with a manuscript, which are purchased as a package.

Fiction: (Must be related to fly fishing). Adventure; confession; fantasy; historical; humorous; and suspense. Buys 2 mss/issue. Query. Length: 1,500-2,500 words. Pays $50-125.

Tips: "We make it a purpose to deal with freelancers breaking into the field. Our only concern is that the material be in keeping with the quality established."

FUR-FISH-GAME, 2878 E. Main, Columbus OH 43209. Editor: A. R. Harding. For outdoorsmen of all ages, interested in fishing, hunting, camping, woodcraft, trapping. Magazine; 64 pages. Monthly. Circ. 200,000. Byline given. Buys 150 mss/year. Pays on acceptance. Sample copy 60¢; free writer's guidelines. No simultaneous submissions. Reports in 4 weeks. Submit complete ms. SASE.

Nonfiction and Photos: Articles on outdoor-related subjects. Articles on hunting, fishing, trapping, camping, boating, conservation. Must be down-to-earth, informative and instructive. Prefers first person. Informational, how-to, personal experience, inspirational, historical, nostalgia, personal opinion, travel, new product, technical. Length: 2,000-3,000 words. Pays $60-75. Also buys shorter articles for Gun Rack, Fishing, Dog and Trapping departments. Length: 1,000-2,000 words. Pays $20-50. Offers no additional payment for 8x10 b&w glossy prints used with ms.

GRAY'S SPORTING JOURNAL, 42 Bay Road, So. Hamilton MA 01982. Editor/Publisher: Ed Gray. 95% freelance written. Emphasizes hunting, fishing and conservation for sportsmen. Published 4 times/year. Magazine; 128 pages. Estab. November 1975. Circ. 60,000. Buys first North American serial rights. Byline given. Phone queries OK. Submit seasonal material 4 months in advance of issue date. SASE. Reports in 3 months. Sample copy $5; writer's guidelines for SASE.

Nonfiction: Articles on hunting and fishing experiences. Humor; historical; personal experience; opinion; and photo feature. Buys 7/issue. Submit complete ms. Length: 500-5,000 words. Pays $500-1,000 on publication.

Photos: Submit photo material with accompanying ms. Pays $50-300 for any size color transparencies. Captions preferred. Buys one-time rights.

Fiction: Adventure (mostly thoughtful and low-key); and humor. Submit complete ms. Length: 500-5,000 words. Pays $500-1000.

Poetry: Free verse; light verse; and traditional. Buys 1/issue. Pays $50-75.

Tips: Write a query letter that shows you are "someone who knows his material but is not a self-acclaimed expert; someone who can write well and with a sense of humor; someone who can share his experiences without talking down to the readers; someone who can prepare an article with focus and a creative approach to his prose."

GREAT LAKES FISHERMAN, Great Lakes Fisherman Publishing Co., 3400 Kenny Rd., Columbus OH 43221. (614)451-9307. Editor: Woody Earnheart. Managing Editor: Ottie M. Snyder, Jr. Monthly magazine covering how, when and where to fish in the Great Lakes region. Estab. 1979. Circ. 68,000. Pays on acceptance. Byline given. Offers $40 kill fee. Buys first North American serial rights. Submit seasonal/holiday material 3 months in advance. SASE. Reports in 5 weeks. Free sample copy and writer's guidelines.
Nonfiction: How-to (where to and when to freshwater fish). "No humor, me and Joe or subject matter outside the Great Lakes region." Buys 84 mss/year. Query with clips of published work. "Letters should be tightly written, but descriptive enough to present no surprises when the ms is received. Prefer b&w photos to be used to illustrate ms with query." Length: 1,500-2,500 words. Pays $125-200.
Photos: Send photos with ms. "Black and white photos are considered part of manuscript package and as such receive no additional payment." Prefers 99% of cover shots to be verticals with fish and fisherman action shots. "We consider b&w photos to be a vital part of a ms package and return more packages because of poor quality photos than any other reason. We look for four types of illustration with each article: scene (a backed off shot of fisherman); result (not the typical meat shot of angler grinning at camera with big stringer but in most cases just a single nice fish with the angler admiring the fish); method (a lure shot or illustration of special rigs mentioned in the text); and action (angler landing a fish, fighting a fish, etc.). Illustrations (line drawings) need not be finished art but should be good enough for our artist to get the idea of what the author is trying to depict." Pays $100 minimum for 35mm color transparencies; reviews 8x10 b&w prints. Captions, model release and identifications of subjects required. Buys one-time rights.
Tips: "Our feature articles are 99.9 percent freelance material. The magazine is circulated in the eight states bordering the Great Lakes, an area where one-third of the nation's licenced anglers reside. All of our feature content is how, when or where, or a combination of all three covering the species common to the region. Fishing is an age-old sport with countless words printed on the subject each year. A fresh new slant that indicates a desire to share with the reader the author's knowledge is a sale. We expect the freelancer to answer any anticipated questions the reader might have (on accommodations, launch sites, equipment needed, etc.) within the ms. We publish an equal mix each month of both warm- and cold-water articles."

HUNTERS WORLD, Deer Hunting Annual, Harris Publications Outdoor Group, 79 Madison Ave., New York NY 10026. (212)686-4121. Editor: Lamar Underwood. Annual magazine covering deer hunting for deer hunters. Estab. 1980. Circ. 100,000. Pays on acceptance. Byline given. Pays varying kill fee. Buys first North American serial rights. Simultaneous queries, and simultaneous and photocopied submissions OK. SASE. Reports in 3 weeks. Free sample copy; writer's guidelines for business size SAE and 1 first class stamp.
Nonfiction: Nostalgic; how-to (or where-to); personal experience ("Me and Joe" stories); and photo feature (with accompanying test). "Unlike other publications, we like the 'Me and Joe' stuff. Everything is considered carefully." Buys 15 mss/year. Query or send complete ms. Length: 2,000-4,000 words. Pays $250-500.
Photos: State availability of photos or send photos with ms. Pays $25-100 for 35mm color transparencies; $25-100 for 8x10 b&w glossy prints or contact sheets. Captions and model releases required. Buys one-time rights.

HUNTING DIGEST, Harris Publications Outdoor Group, 79 Madison Ave., New York NY 10026. (212)686-4121. Editor: Lamar Underwood. Magazine published 2 times/year (late summer and late fall) covering all aspects of hunting for hunters. Estab. 1980. Circ. 100,000. Pays on acceptance. Byline given. Pays varying kill fee. Buys first North American serial rights. Submit seasonal/holiday material 4 months in advance. Simultaneous queries, and simultaneous and photocopied submissions OK. SASE. Reports in 3 weeks. Free sample copy; writer's guidelines for business size SAE and 1 first class stmap.
Nonfiction: Nostalgic; how-to (or where-to); personal experience ("Me and Joe" stories); and photo feature (with accompanying text). Buys 30 mss/year. Query or send complete ms. Length: 2,000-4,000 words. Pays $250-500.
Photos: State availability of photos or send photos with ms. Pays $25-100 for color transparencies (35mm and larger); $25-100 for 8x10 b&w glossy prints or contact sheets. Captions and model releases required. Buys one-time rights.
Tips: "Study the magazine carefully before submitting. We buy almost all our material over-the-transom."

ILLINOIS WILDLIFE, Box 116-13005, S. Western Ave., Blue Island IL 60406. (312)388-3995. Editor: Tom Mills. 35% freelance written. For conservationists and sportsmen. "Tabloid newspaper utilizing newspaper format instead of magazine-type articles." Monthly. Circ. 35,000. Buys one-time rights. Byline given. Pays on acceptance. Will send a sample copy to a writer for 50¢. Reports in 2 weeks. SASE.

Nonfiction and Photos: Wants "material aimed at conserving and restoring our natural resources." How-to, humor, photo articles. Length: "maximum 2,000 words, prefer 1,000-word articles." Pays 1½¢/word. B&w glossy prints. Prefers 8x10. Pays $7.50.

MICHIGAN OUT-OF-DOORS, Box 30235, Lansing MI 48909. (517)371-1041. Editor: Kenneth S. Lowe. 50% freelance written. Emphasizes outdoor recreation, especially hunting and fishing; conservation; environmental affairs. Monthly magazine; 116 pages. Circ. 110,000. Pays on publication. Buys first North American serial rights. Byline given. Phone queries OK. Submit seasonal/holiday material 6 months in advance. Photocopied and previously published (if so indicated) submissions OK. SASE. Reports in 1 month. Sample copy 50¢; free writer's guidelines.

Nonfiction: Expose, historical, how-to, informational, interview, nostalgia, personal experience, personal opinion, photo feature and profile. "Stories *must* have a Michigan slant unless they treat a subject of universal interest to our readers." Buys 8 mss/issue. Send complete ms. Length: 1,000-3,000 words. Pays $10-75.

Photos: Purchased with or without accompanying ms. Pays $10 minimum for any size b&w glossy prints; $60 maximum for color (for cover). Offers no additional payment for photos accepted with accompanying ms. Buys one-time rights. Captions preferred.

Tips: "Top priority is placed on true accounts of personal adventures in the out-of-doors—not simple narratives of hunting or fishing trips but well-written tales of very unusual incidents encountered while hunting, fishing, camping, hiking, etc."

MICHIGAN SPORTSMAN, Sportsman Group Publications, Box 2483, Oshkosh WI 54903. (414)231-9338. Editor: Gordon Charles. Managing Editor: Tom Petrie. Bimonthly magazine covering fishing, hunting and general outdoor recreation in Michigan. Circ. 50,000. Pays on publication. Byline given. Buys first North American serial rights. Submit seasonal/holiday material 6 months in advance. Simultaneous queries OK. SASE. Reports in 1 month on queries; 2 months on mss. Sample copy $1.50; writer's guidelines for business size SAE and 1 first class stamp.

Nonfiction: Carol Krenke, articles editor. Exposé, historical/nostalgic, how-to, interview/profile, new product, photo feature and technical. "All of these must relate to hunting and fishing in Michigan." No personal experience. Buys 12 mss/year. Query. Length: 300-2,000 words. Pays $25-300.

MID WEST OUTDOORS, Mid West Outdoors, Ltd., 111 Shore Drive, Hinsdale (Burr Ridge) IL 60521. (312)887-7722. Editor: Gene Laulunen. Emphasizes fishing, hunting, camping and boating. Monthly tabloid; 100 pages. Circ. 96,000. Pays on publication. Buys simultaneous rights. Byline given. Submit seasonal material 2 months in advance. Simultaneous, photocopied and previously published submissions OK. SASE. Reports in 3 weeks. Sample copy $1; free writer's guidelines.

Nonfiction: How-to (fishing, hunting, camping in the Midwest) and where-to-go (fishing, hunting, camping within 500 miles of Chicago). "We do not want to see any articles on 'my first fishing, hunting or camping experiences.' " Buys 20/mss issue. Send complete ms. Length: 1,000-1,500 words. Pays $15-25.

Photos: Offers no additional payment for photos accompanying ms; uses b&w prints. Buys all rights. Captions required.

Columns/Departments: Archery, Camping, Dogs, Fishing and Hunting. Open to suggestions for columns/departments. Send complete ms. Pays $20.

Tips: "Break in with a great unknown fishing hole within 500 miles of Chicago. Where, how, when and why."

NORTH AMERICAN HUNTER, North American Hunting Club, Inc., Box 35557, Minneapolis MN 55435. (612)835-5542. Editor: Mark LaBarbera. Bimonthly magazine covering "hunting for North American Hunting Club members, who are dedicated hunters." Circ. 70,000. Pays on acceptance. Byline given. Buys one-time rights. Submit seasonal/holiday material 6 months in advance. SASE. Reports in 1 month. Writer's guidelines for 9x12 SAE and 1 first class stamp.

Nonfiction: How-to (improve hunting skills, increase enjoyment of outdoors while hunting); and travel (where-to-go pieces). Buys 25 mss/year. Send query with brief bio. Length: 1,700-2,500 words. Pays $300 maximum.

Photos: State availability of photos or illustrations. Reviews 35mm color transparencies and 8x10

b&w glossy prints. "Photos are paid for with payment for ms." Captions required.
Tips: "We like to keep our articles both entertaining and informative, with emphasis on things that make a hunter successful."

OHIO FISHERMAN, Ohio Fisherman Publishing Co., 3400 Kenny Rd., Columbus OH 43221. (614)451-5769. Editor: Woody Earnheart. Managing Editor: Ottie M. Snyder, Jr. Monthly magazine covering the how, when and where of Ohio fishing. Circ. 45,000. Pays on publication. Byline given. Offers $40 kill fee. Buys first rights. Submit seasonal/holiday material 3 months in advance. SASE. Reports in 5 weeks. Free sample copy and writer's guidelines.
Nonfiction: How-to (also where to and when to fresh water fish). "Our feature articles are 99% freelance material, and all have the same basic theme—sharing fishing knowledge." "No humorous or 'me and Joe' articles." Buys 84 mss/year. Query with clips of published work. Letters should be "tightly written, but descriptive enough to present no surprises when the ms is received. Prefer b&w photos to be used to illustrate ms with query." Length: 1,500-2,500 words. Pays $100-150.
Photos: 99% of covers purchased are verticals involving fishermen and fish—action preferred." Send photos with query. "We consider b&w photos to be a vital part of a ms package and return more mss because of poor quality photos than any other reason. We look for four types of illustration with each article: scene (a backed off shot of fisherman); result (not the typical meat shot of angler grinning at camera with big stringer, but in most cases just a single nice fish with the angler admiring the fish); method (a lure or illustration of special rigs mentioned in the text); and action (angler landing a fish, fighting a fish, etc.). Illustrations (line drawings) need not be finished art but should be good enough for our artist to get the idea of what the author is trying to depict." Pays $100 minimum for 35mm color transparencies (cover use); also buys 8x10 b&w prints as part of ms package—"no additional payments." Captions and identification of subjects required. Buys one-time rights.
Tips: "The specialist and regional markets are here to stay. They both offer the freelancer the opportunity for steady income. Fishing is an age-old sport with countless words printed on the subject each year. A fresh new slant that indicates a desire to share with the reader the author's knowledge is a sale. We expect the freelancer to answer any anticipated questions the reader might have (on accommodations, launch sites, equipment needed, etc.) within the ms."

ONTARIO OUT OF DOORS, 3 Church St., Toronto, Ontario, Canada M5E 1M2. (416)361-0434. Editor-in-Chief: Burton J. Myers. 75% freelance written. Emphasizes hunting, fishing, camping, and conservation. Monthly magazine; 72 pages. Circ. 55,000. Pays on acceptance. Buys all rights. Phone queries OK. Submit seasonal/holiday material 3 months in advance of issue date. Photocopied submissions OK. Reports in 6 weeks. Free sample copy and writer's guidelines; mention *Writer's Market* in request.
Nonfiction: Expose of conservation practices; how-to (improve your fishing and hunting skills); humor; photo feature (on wildlife); travel (where to find good fishing and hunting); and any news on Ontario. "Avoid 'Me and Joe' articles." Buys 120 mss/year. Query. Length: 150-3,500 words. Pays $15-200.
Photos: Submit photo material with accompanying query. No additional payment for b&w contact sheets and 35mm color transparencies. "Should a photo be used on the cover, an additional payment of $150-200 is made."
Fillers: Outdoor tips. Buys 24 mss/year. Length: 20-50 words. Pays $10.

OUTDOOR AMERICA, 1800 N. Kent St., Arlington VA 22209. (703)528-1818. Editor: Judith Hijikata. Bimonthly magazine about natural resource conservation and outdoor recreation for 50,000 members of the Izaak Walton League and members of Congress. Circ. 50,000. Pays on publication. Byline given. Buys first North American serial rights. Submit seasonal material 6 months in advance. Simultaneous and photocopied submissions OK, if so indicated. SASE. Reports in 2 weeks. Sample copy 50¢; free writer's guidelines with SASE.
Nonfiction: "We are interested in current, issue-oriented articles on resource topics, conservation, government activities that hurt or improve the land, and articles about outdoor recreation such as hunting, fishing, canoeing, wilderness activities." Query with clips of previously published work. Length 2,000-2,300 words. Pays $75-100.
Photos: Reviews 5x7 b&w glossy prints and 35mm and larger color transparencies. Offers no additional payment for photos accepted with ms. Caption and model release required. Buys one-time rights.

PENNSYLVANIA GAME NEWS, Box 1567, Harrisburg PA 17120. (717)787-3745. Editor-in-Chief: Bob Bell. 85% freelance written. Emphasizes hunting in Pennsylvania. Monthly magazine; 64 pages. Estab. 1929. Circ. 210,000. Pays on acceptance. Buys all rights. Byline given. Phone queries OK. Submit seasonal/holiday material 6 months in advance. Photocopied submissions

OK. SASE. Reports in 1 month. Free sample copy and writer's guidelines.
Nonfiction: Historical, how-to, informational, personal experience, photo feature and technical. "Must be related to outdoors in Pennsylvania." Buys 4-8 mss/issue. Query. Length: 2,500 words maximum. Pays $250 maximum.
Photos: Purchased with accompanying ms. Pays $5-20 for 8x10 b&w glossy prints. Model release required.

PENNSYLVANIA SPORTSMAN, Box 388, Boiling Springs PA 17007. Editor: Dave Wolf. Covering hunting, fishing, camping, boating and conservation in Pennsylvania. Pays on publication. Buys one-time rights. Byline given. Simultaneous and previously published submissions OK. SASE. Reports in 3 weeks. Sample copy 75¢.
Nonfiction: How-to and where-to articles on hunting, fishing, camping and boating. Buys 2-3 mss/issue. Submit complete ms or query with photos. Length 800-1,200 words. Pays $40.
Photos: Pays $10 for 5x7 b&w prints; $75/color cover; $20/color inside.Prefers 35mm slides. Captions and model releases are required.
Columns/Departments: Staff-written.
Fillers: "Fillers welcome. Subjects should be different, e.g., 'How to Make A Fishy Pegbored,' 'A Camp Toaster.' We are also looking for helpful hints." Length: 300-400 words. Pays $25 each; $10 additional for b&w used with article.

PETERSEN'S HUNTING, Petersen Publishing Co., 8490 Sunset Blvd., Los Angeles CA 90069. (213)657-5100. Editor-in-Chief: Basil Bradbury. Emphasizes sport hunting. Monthly magazine; 84 pages. Circ. 250,000. Pays on acceptance. Buys all rights. Submit seasonal/holiday material 6 months in advance. SASE. Reports in 2 months. Sample copy $1.50. Free writer's guidelines.
Nonfiction: How-to (how to be a better hunter, how to make hunting-related items); personal experience (use a hunting trip as an anecdote to illustrate how-to contents). Buys 3 mss/issue. Query. Length: 1,500-2,500 words. Pays $200-300.
Photos: Photos purchased with or without accompanying ms. Captions required. Pays $25 minimum for 8x10 b&w glossy prints; $50-150 for 2¼x2¼ or 35mm color transparencies. Total purchase price for ms includes payment for photos. Model release required.
Tips: "Write an unusual hunting story that is not often covered in other publications."

SALT WATER SPORTSMAN, 10 High St., Boston MA 02110. (617)426-4074. Editor-in-Chief: Frank Woolner. Managing Editor: Rip Cunningham. 85% freelance written. Emphasizes saltwater fishing. Monthly magazine; 120 pages. Circ. 115,000. Pays on acceptance. Buys first North American serial rights. Pays 100% kill fee. Byline given. Submit seasonal material 8 months in advance. No photocopied submissions. SASE. Reports in 4 weeks. Free sample copy and writer's guidelines.
Nonfiction: How-to, personal experience, technical and travel (to fishing areas). Buys 8 mss/issue. Query. "It is helpful if the writer states experience in salt water fishing and any previous related articles. We want 1, possibly 2 well-explained ideas per query letter—not merely a listing." Length: 1,500-2,000 words. Pays 5¢/word.
Photos: Purchased with or without accompanying ms. Captions required. Uses 5x7 or 8x10 b&w prints and color slides. Pays $300 minimum for 35mm, 2¼x2¼ or 8x10 color transparencies for cover. Offers additional payment for photos accepted with accompanying ms.

SOUTH CAROLINA WILDLIFE, Box 167, Rembert Dennis Bldg., Columbia SC 29202. (803)758-6291. Editor: John Davis. Associate Editor: Nancy Coleman. For South Carolinians interested in wildlife and outdoor activities. Bimonthly magazine; 64 pages. Circ. 60,000. Copyrighted. Pays 10¢/word kill fee. Byline given. Pays on acceptance. Free sample copy. Reports in 1 month. Submit 1 page outline and 1 page explanation.
Nonfiction and Photos: Articles on outdoor South Carolina with an emphasis on preserving and protecting our natural resources. "Realize that the topic must be of interest to South Carolinians and that we must be able to justify using it in a state government publication, published by the wildlife department—so if it isn't directly about hunting, fishing, a certain plant or animal, it must be somehow related to the environment and conservation. Query with "a one-page outline citing sources, giving ideas for graphic design, explaining justification and giving an example of the first two paragraphs." Length: 1,000-3,000 words. Pays 10¢/word. Pays $35 for b&w glossy prints purchased with or without ms, or on assignment. Pays $75 for color, $100 back cover, $200 front cover.

SOUTHERN ANGLER'S GUIDE, SOUTHERN HUNTER'S GUIDE, Box 2188, Hot Springs AR 71901. Editor: Don J. Fuelsch. Covers the Southern scene on hunting and fishing completely. Buys all rights. Byline given. Issued annually. Query. SASE.
Nonfiction: Hunting, fishing, boating, camping articles. Articles that have been thoroughly re-

searched. Condensed in digest style. Complete how-to rundown on tricks and techniques used in taking various species of fresh and saltwater fish and game found in the Southern states. Interested in new and talented writers with thorough knowledge of their subject. Not interested in first-person or "me and Joe" pieces. Length: flexible; 750 and 1,800 words preferred, although may run as high as 3,000 words. Pays 5-30¢/word.

Photos: Buys photographs with mss or with captions only. Fishing or hunting subjects in Southern setting. No Rocky Mountain backgrounds. B&w only—5x7 or 8x10 glossy prints.

SPORTS AFIELD, 250 W. 55th St., New York NY 10019. Editor: Tom Paugh. For people of all ages whose interests are centered around the out-of-doors (hunting and fishing) and related subjects. Monthly magazine. Circ. 600,000. Buys first North American serial rights. Byline given. Pays on acceptance. "Our magazine is seasonal and material submitted should be in accordance. Fishing in spring and summer; hunting in the fall; camping in summer and fall." Submit seasonal material 6 months in advance. Reports in 1 month. Query or submit complete ms. SASE.

Nonfiction and Photos: "Informative articles and personal experiences with good photos on hunting, fishing, camping, boating and subjects such as conservation and travel related to hunting and fishing. We want first-class writing and reporting." Length: 500-2,500 words. Pays $650 minimum, depending on length and quality. Photos purchased with or without ms. Pays $25 minimum for 8x10 b&w glossy prints. Pays $50 minimum for 2¼x2¼ or larger transparencies; 35mm acceptable.

Fillers: Payment depends on length. Almanac pays $10 and up depending on length, for newsworthy, unusual, how-to and nature items.

SPORTSMAN'S HUNTING, Harris Publications Outdoor Group, 79 Madison Ave., New York NY 10026. (212)686-4121. Editor: Lamar Underwood. Magazine published 2 times/year (early and late fall) covering hunting for hunters. Estab. 1980. Circ. 100,000. Pays on acceptance. Byline given. Pays varying kill fee. Buys first North American serial rights. Submit seasonal/holiday material 4 months in advance. Simultaneous queries, and simultaneous and photocopied submissions OK. SASE. Reports in 3 weeks. Free sample copy; writer's guidelines for business size SAE and 1 first class stamp.

Nonfiction: Nostalgic; how-to (and where-to); personal experience ("Me and Joe" stories); and photo feature (with accompanying text). Buys 30 mss/year. Query or send complete ms. Length: 2,000-4,000 words. Pays $250-500.

Photos: State availability of photos or send photos with ms. Pays $25-100 for color transparencies (35mm and larger); $25-100 for 8x10 glossy prints or glossy contact sheets. Captions and model releases required. Buys one-time rights.

Tips: Study the magazine carefully. We are very interested in freelance submissions and consider everything."

THE TEXAS FISHERMAN, Voice of the Lone Star Angler, Cordovan Corp., 5314 Bingle Road, Houston TX 77092. Editor: Larry Bozka. For freshwater and saltwater fishermen in Texas. Monthly tabloid; 56-64 pages. Circ. 100,000. Rights purchased vary with author and material. Byline given. Usually buys second serial (reprint) rights. Buys 6-8 mss/month. Pays on publication. Free sample copy and writer's guidelines. Will consider simultaneous submissions. Reports in 4 weeks. Query. SASE.

Nonfiction and Photos: General how-to, where-to, features on all phases of fishing in Texas. Strong slant on informative pieces. Strong writing. Good saltwater stories (Texas only). Length: 2,000-3,000 words, prefers 2,500. Pays $35-150, depending on length and quality of writing and photos. Mss must include 8-10 good action b&w photos or illustrations.

Tips: "Query should be a short, but complete description of the story that emphasizes a specific angle. When possible, send black and white photos with manuscripts. Good art will sell us a story that is mediocre, but even a great story can't replace bad photographs. How-to stories are preferred."

TEXAS SPORTSMAN MAGAZINE, Box 10411, San Antonio TX 78210. (512)533-8991. Editor: John Kollman. Senior Editor: Ginny Kollman. Monthly magazine covering Texas fishing and hunting. Circ. 45,000. Pays on publication. Byline given. Buys one-time rights. Submit seasonal/holiday material 4-6 months in advance. Simultaneous queries and photocopied submissions OK. SASE. Reports in 2 weeks on queries; in 1 month on mss. Sample copy for 10x12 SAE and 6 first class stamps; writer's guidelines for 10x12 SAE and 3 first class stamps.

Nonfiction: General interest, historical/nostalgic, how-to, humor, interview/profile, personal experience, photo feature, technical and travel. No articles not relating to Texas. Buys 90 mss/year. Query with clips of published work. Length: 1,800-3,000 words. Pays $75-150.

Photos: Send photos with ms. Reviews b&w contact sheets and 35mm color transparencies. Captions required.

Columns/Departments: Hunting, Shooting, Freshwater, Saltwater, Boating, Travel, Bowhunting, Conservation, and Good Old Days. Buys 90 mss/year. Query with clips of published work. Length: 1,800-2,000 words. Pays $75-100.
Fillers: Clippings, jokes, gags, anecdotes, short humor and newsbreaks. Buys 200/year. Length: 25-100 words. Pays $5-15.

TURKEY CALL, Wild Turkey Bldg., Box 467, Edgefield SC 29824. (803)637-3106. Editor: Gene Smith. 30% freelance written. An educational publication for the wild turkey enthusiast. Bimonthly magazine. Circ. 30,000. Buys one-time rights. Byline given. Buys 20 mss/year. Pays on publication. Free sample copy when supplies permit. Reports in 3 weeks. Query with "one-page letter indicating story line and objective (e.g., education, entertainment, shock value, inspiration, etc.), and describing available illustratons"; or submit complete ms (typewritten originals only). SASE.
Nonfiction and Photos: "Feature articles dealing with the history, management, restoration, harvesting techniques and distribution of the American wild turkey. These stories must consist of accurate information and must appeal to the dyed-in-the-wool turkey hunter as well as to management personnel and the general public. No "first-person hunt experiences, unillustrated. e.g., 'My First Turkey.' " Length: 1,200-1,500 words. Pays $50 minimum; $250-275 for illustrated feature. "Seeking how-to and where-to-go articles, along with 'how the wild turkey became re-established' articles with specific information and practical hints for success in harvest and management of the wild turkey. We use color transparencies for the cover. We want action photos submitted with feature articles; mainly b&w. For color, we prefer transparencies. We can use 35mm slides. We prefer 8x10 b&w glossy prints for inside illustrations, but will settle for smaller prints if they are of good quality. We want action shots, not the typical 'dead turkey' photos. We are allergic to posed photos. Photos on how-to should make the techniques clear." Pays $10 minimum for b&w gloss.
Tips: To break in you "must write above the reader/member's own level of special knowledge about wild turkeys, wild turkey management, biology, and hunting; must have 'been there.' Find fresh approaches to familiar themes."

VIRGINIA WILDLIFE, Box 11104, Richmond VA 23230. (804)257-1000. Editor: Harry L. Gillam. 70% freelance written. For sportsmen and outdoor enthusiasts. Pays on acceptance. Buys first North American serial rights. Byline given. Free sample copy. SASE.
Nonfiction: Uses factual outdoor stories, especially those set in Virginia. "Currently need boating subjects, women and youth in the outdoors, wildlife and nature in urban areas. Always need good fishing and hunting stories—not of the 'Me and Joe' genre, however. Slant should be to enjoy the outdoors and what you can do to improve it. Material must be applicable to Virginia, sound from a scientific basis, accurate and easily readable." Submit photos with ms. Length: prefers approximately 1,200 words. Pays 5¢/word.
Photos: Buys photos with mss; "and occasionally buy unaccompanied good photos." Prefers color transparencies, but also has limited need for 8x10 b&w glossy prints. Captions required. Pays $10/b&w photo; $10-15 for color.
Tips: "We are currently receiving too many anecdotes and too few articles with an educational bent—we want instructional, 'how-to' articles on hunting, fishing and outdoor sports, and also want semi-technical articles on wildlife. We are not receiving enough articles with high-quality photographs accompanying them. Catering to these needs will greatly enhance chances for acceptance of manuscripts. We have more 'backyard bird' articles than we could ever hope to use, and not enough good submissions on trapping or bird hunting."

WASHINGTON FISHING HOLES, Snohomish Publishing Co., Inc., 114 Avenue C, Snohomish WA 98290. (206)568-4121. Editors: Milt Keizer, Terry Sheely. 45-65% freelance written. For anglers from 8-80, whether beginner or expert, interested in the where-to and how-to of Washington fishing. Magazine published every two months; 80 pages. Circ. 8,500. Pays on publication. Buys first North American serial rights. Submit material 30 days in advance. SASE. Reports in 3 weeks. Free sample copy and writer's guidelines.
Nonfiction: How-to (angling only); informational (how-to). "Articles and illustrations *must* be local, Washington angling or readily available within short distance for Washington anglers." Buys 18-32 mss/year. Query. Length: 800-1,200 words. Pays $50.
Photos: Purchased with accompanying ms at $10 each extra. Captions required. Buys 5x7 b&w glossy prints or 35mm color transparencies with article. Model release required.
Fillers For '82: "Would like to see some pieces on striped bass fishing, angling north of Skagit River, and Olympic Peninsula steelheading."

WATERFOWLER'S WORLD, Waterfowl Publications, Ltd., Box 38306, Germantown TN 38138. (901)749-8589. Editor: Cindy Dixon. Bimonthly magazine covering duck and goose hunting for the serious hunter and experienced waterfowler, with an emphasis on improvement of skills. Circ. 25,000. Pays on publication. Buys first North American serial rights. SASE. Reports in 6 weeks. Sample copy $2.50; free writer's guidelines.

Nonfiction: General interest (where to hunt); how-to (market hunter's art; make regional decoys; do layout gunning); new product; and technical. Query. Length: 1,500 words. Pays $75-200.

Photos: Reviews 8x10 b&w prints and 35mm color transparencies. Pays $25/cover.

Columns/Departments: Fowlweather Gear (outdoor clothes and supplies).

WESTERN OUTDOORS, 3197-E Airport Loop, Costa Mesa CA 92626. (714)546-4360. Editor-in-Chief: Burt Twilegar. Emphasizes hunting, fishing, camping, boating for 11 Western states only, Canada and Alaska. Monthly magazine; 88 pages. Circ. 150,000. Pays on publication. Buys one-time rights. Query (in writing). Submit seasonal material 4-6 months in advance. Photocopied submissions OK. SASE. Reports in 4-6 weeks. Sample copy $1.50; free writer's guidelines for SASE.

Nonfiction: How-to (catch more fish, bag more game, improve equipment, etc.); informational; photo feature; and technical. Buys 130 mss/year. Query or send complete ms. Length: 1,000-2,000 words maximum. Pays $100-250.

Photos: Purchased with accompanying ms. Captions required. Uses 8x10 b&w glossy prints; prefers Kodachrome II 35mm slides. Offers no additional payment for photos accepted with accompanying ms.

Tips: "Provide a complete package of photos, map, trip facts and manuscript written according to our news feature format. Stick with where-to type articles. Both b&w and color photo selections make a sale more likely."

WESTERN SPORTSMAN, (formerly *Fish and Game Sportsman*), Box 737, Regina, Saskatchewan, Canada S4P 3A8. (306)352-8384. Editor: J.B. (Red) Wilkinson. 90% freelance written. For fishermen, hunters, campers and others interested in outdoor recreation. "Please note that our coverage area is Alberta and Saskatchewan." Quarterly magazine; 64-112 pages. Circ. 23,000. Rights purchased vary with author and material. May buy first North American serial rights or second serial (reprint) rights. Byline given. Pays on publication. Sample copy $1.50; free writer's guidelines. "We try to include as much information as possible on all subjects in each edition. Therefore, we usually publish fishing articles in our winter magazine along with a variety of winter stories. If material is dated, we would like to receive articles 2 months in advance of our publication date." Will consider photocopied submissions. Reports in 4 weeks. SAE and International Reply Coupons.

Nonfiction: "It is necessary that all articles can identify with our coverage area of Alberta and Saskatchewan. We are interested in mss from writers who have experienced an interesting fishing, hunting, camping or other outdoor experience. We also publish how-to and other informational pieces as long as they can relate to our coverage area. Our editors are experienced people who have spent many hours afield fishing, hunting, camping etc., and we simply cannot accept information which borders on the ridiculous. The record fish does not jump two feet out of the water with a brilliant sunset backdrop, two-pound test line, one-hour battle, a hole in the boat, tumbling waterfalls, all in the first paragraph. We are more interested in articles which tell about the average guy living on beans, guiding his own boat, stalking his game and generally doing his own thing in our part of Western Canada than a story describing a well-to-do outdoorsman traveling by motorhome, staying at an expensive lodge with guides doing everything for him except catching the fish, or shooting the big game animal. The articles that are submitted to us need to be prepared in a knowledgeable way and include more information than the actual fish catch or animal or bird kill. Discuss the terrain, the people involved on the trip, the water or weather conditions, the costs, the planning that went into the trip, the equipment and other data closely associated with the particular event in a factual manner. We like to see exciting writing, but leave out the gloss and nonsense. We are very short of camping articles and how-to pieces on snowmobiling, including mechanical information. We generally have sufficient fishing and hunting data but we're always looking for new writers. I would be very interested in hearing from writers who are experienced campers and snowmobilers." Buys 80 mss/year. Submit complete ms. Length: 1,500-3,000 words. Pays $40-225.

Photos: Photos purchased with ms with no additional payment. Also purchased without ms. Pays $7-10/5x7 or 8x10 b&w print; $100-150/35mm or larger transparency for front cover.

WISCONSIN SPORTSMAN, Box 2266 Oshkosh WI 54903. Editor: Tom Petrie. 30% freelance written. Emphasizes Wisconsin fishing, hunting, and outdoors. Bimonthly magazine. Circ. 73,000. Pays on publication. Buys all rights. Submit seasonal/holiday material 5 months in advance of issue date. Previously published submissions OK. SASE. Reports in 2-3 weeks.

Nonfiction: Historical (Wisconsin state history); how-to (fishing/hunting/camping-oriented, with photos or illustrations if applicable); photo feature (color transparencies on Wisconsin wildlife, outdoor recreation, scenics or touring); and travel (with pix). No 'why-I-hunt' or 'what the outdoors means to me' style articles. Buys 28 mss/year. Query or submit complete ms. Length: 300-2,000 words. Pays $50-300.

Photos: Submit photos with query or ms. Offers no additional payment for photos accepted with ms unless used as cover photo or with sister publications, *Minnesota Sportsman* and *Michigan Sportsman*. Uses 8x10 glossy b&w prints and 35mm color transparencies. Captions preferred.

Martial Arts

BLACK BELT, Rainbow Publications, Inc., 1845 W. Empire, Burbank CA 91504. (213)843-4444. Publisher: Michael James. Emphasizes martial arts for both practitioner and layman. Monthly magazine; 100 pages. Circ. 75,000. Pays on publication. Buys all rights. Submit seasonal/holiday material 6 months in advance. Simultaneous and photocopied submissions OK. SASE. Reports in 4 weeks. Free sample copy.

Nonfiction: Exposé, how-to, informational, interview, new product, personal experience, profile, technical and travel. Buys 6 mss/issue. Query or send complete ms. Length: 500-1,200 words. Pays $10/page of manuscript.

Photos: Purchased with or without accompanying ms. Captions required. Pays $4-7 for 5x7 or 8x10 b&w or color transparencies. Total purchase price for ms includes payment for photos. Model release required.

Fiction: Historical. Buys 1 ms/issue. Query. Pays $35-100.

Fillers: Send fillers. Pays $5 minimum.

FIGHTING STARS, Rainbow Publications, 1845 W. Empire Ave., Burbank CA 91504. (213)843-4444. Executive Editor: Ben Singer. Bimonthly magazine about the martial arts and action adventure films. Circ. 80,000. Pays on publication. Buys first North American serial rights. Submit seasonal material 4 months in advance. Simultaneous and photocopied submissions OK. SASE. Reports in 6 weeks. Free sample copy; free writer's guidelines for SASE.

Nonfiction: General interest (concerning martial arts films); historical (detailing life history of a martial artist); interview (of martial artists); profile (of celebrities in martial arts, and teachers and trainers); and photo feature (on set and candids). Buys 2-3 mss/issue. Send complete ms. Length: 1,200-2,000 words. Pays $40-200.

Photos: Editor: David M. King. State availability of photos. Reviews 5x7 and 8x10 b&w glossy prints and 5x7 and 8x10 color glossy prints. Offers no additional payment for photos accepted with ms. Model release required. Buys all rights.

Tips: "We are specifically concerned with action/adventure, martial arts films, their stars, personalities, the stuntmen and stuntwomen in them. We generally have a beat on all the studios and filmmakers and the projects they are doing. Therefore, more comparative pieces on various films, actors and their styles stand a better chance of being published. Because we are a bimonthly, timeliness is of the essence. Also, stories on women in the martial arts/action-adventure film market stand a good chance with us."

INSIDE KUNG-FU, The Ultimate In Martial Arts Coverage!, Unique Publication, 7011 Sunset Blvd., Hollywood CA 90028. (213)467-1300. Editor: Paul Maslak. Monthly magazine covering martial arts for those with "traditional, modern, athletic and intellectual tastes. The magazine slants toward little-known martial arts, and little-known aspects of established martial arts." Circ. 100,000. Pays on publication. Byline given. Offers $35 kill fee. Buys first North American serial rights. Submit seasonal/holiday material 4 months in advance. Simultaneous queries, and simultaneous and photocopied submissions OK. SASE. Reports in 3 weeks on queries; 6 weeks on mss. Sample copy $1.75 with 9x12 SAE and 5 first class stamps; free writer's guidelines.

Nonfiction: Expose (topics relating to the martial arts); historical/nostalgic; how-to (primarily technical materials); humor; interview/profile; personal experience; photo feature; and technical. "Articles must be technically or historically accurate." No "sports coverage, first-person articles, or articles which constitute personal aggrandizement." Buys 100 mss/year. Query or send complete ms. Length: 10-15 pages, typewritten. Pays $75-100.

Photos: Send photos with accompanying ms. Reviews b&w contact sheets, b&w negatives and 8x10 b&w prints. "Photos are paid for with payment for ms." Captions and model release required. Buys one-time rights.

Fiction: Adventure, historical, humorous, mystery and suspense. "Fiction must be short (500-2,00 words) and relate to the martial arts." Buys 10 mss/year. Length: 500-2,000 words. Pays $75.

KARATE ILLUSTRATED, Rainbow Publications, Inc., 1845 W. Empire Ave., Burbank CA 91504. (213)843-4444. Publisher: Michael James. Emphasizes karate and kung fu from the tournament standpoint. Monthly magazine; 64 pages. Circ. 67,000. Pays on publication. Buys all rights. Submit seasonal/holiday material 6 months in advance. Simultaneous and photocopied submissions OK. SASE. Reports in 4-6 weeks. Free sample copy.
Nonfiction: Expose, historical, how-to, informational, interview, new product, personal experience, personal opinion, photo feature, profile, technical and travel. Buys 6 mss/issue. Query or submit complete ms. Pays $35-150.
Photos: Purchased with or without accompanying ms. Submit 5x7 or 8x10 b&w or color photos. Total purchase price for ms includes payment for photos.
Columns/Departments: Reader's Photo Contest and Calendar. Query. Pays $5-25. Open to suggestions for new columns/departments.
Fiction: Historical. Query. Pays $35-150.
Fillers: Newsbreaks. Query. Pays $5.

KICK ILLUSTRATED, The Magazine for Today's Total Martial Artist, Unique Publications, 7011 Sunset Blvd., Hollywood CA 90028. (213)467-1300. Editor: John Corcoran. Assistant Editor: Lucille Tajiri. Monthly magazine covering the martial arts. Estab. 1980. Circ. 120,000. Pays on acceptance for preferred writers. Byline given. Offers $25 kill fee. Buys first North American serial rights. Submit seasonal/holiday material 4 months in advance. Simultaneous queries, and simultaneous and photocopied submissions OK. SASE. Reports in 3 weeks on queries; in 6 weeks on mss. Sample copy for $1.50 and 9x12 SAE and 5 first class stamps; free writer's guidelines.
Nonfiction: Book excerpts; exposé (of martial arts); historical/nostalgic; humor; interview/profile (with approval only); opinion; personal experience; photo feature; and technical (with approval only). *Kick Illustrated* deals specifically with all aspects of the gi disciplines of the martial arts, not with the Chinese arts or the lesser known esoteric practices which are slanted more toward *Kick's* sister publication, *Inside Kung Fu. Kick Illustrated* seeks a balance of the following in each issue: tradition, history, glamour, profiles and/or interviews (both by assignment only), technical, philosophical and think pieces. To date, most 'how to' pieces have been done in-house." No "sports coverage, first person pieces, or articles constituting personal aggrandizement." Buys 70 mss/year. Query. Length: 1,000-2,500 words: "preferred—10-12 page ms." Pays $25-100.
Photos: Send photos with ms. Reviews b&w contact sheets, negatives and 8x10 prints. Captions and identification of subjects required. Buys one-time rights.
Tips: "Request a copy of the style guide, then follow its directions precisely. Or query with one or more ideas, and a style guide will be sent with the editor's reply."

OFFICIAL KARATE, 351 W. 54th St., New York NY 10019. Editor: Al Weiss. For karatemen or those interested in the martial arts. Monthly. Circ. 100,000. Rights purchased vary with author and material; generally, first publication rights. Pays 50% kill fee. Byline given. Buys 60-70 mss/year. Pays on publication. Free sample copy. Will consider photocopied submissions. Reports in 1 month. Query or submit complete ms. SASE.
Nonfiction and Photos: "Biographical material on leading and upcoming karateka, tournament coverage, controversial subjects on the art ('Does Karate Teach Hate?', 'Should the Government Control Karate?', etc.) We cover the 'little man' in the arts rather than devote all space to established leaders or champions; people and happenings in out-of-the-way areas along with our regular material." Informational, how-to, interview, profile, spot news. Length: 1,000-3,000 words. Pays $50-150. B&w contacts or prints. Pays $10-15.

Miscellaneous

ACTION NOW, (formerly *Skateboarder Magazine*), Surfer Publications, Box 1028, Dana Point CA 92629. (714)496-5922. Editor: D. David Morin. Emphasizes all action sports: i.e. skateboarding, surfing, boogie boarding, bicycles (BMX and cruisers) motocross, skiing, snowboarding, etc. and more; some rock 'n roll coverage with monthly feature and album reviews. Monthly magazine; 68 pages. Circ. 100,000. Pays on publication. Submit seasonal/holiday material 3-4 months in advance. SASE. Reports in 2 months. Free sample copy.
Nonfiction: Exposé, general interest, historical, how-to, humor, inspirational, interview, new product, nostalgia, personal experience, photo feature, profile, technical and travel. Buys 3 mss/issue. Send complete ms. Length: 300-800 words. Payment rates available on request.
Photos: Send photos with ms. Pays $10-100 for 5x7 or 8x10 b&w contact sheets, negatives or glossy prints; $20-300 for 35mm color transparencies. Buys one-time rights. Model release required.

ALASKA OUTDOORS, Swensen's Publishing, Box 6324, Anchorage AK 99502. (907)276-2670. Editor: Christopher Batin. Bimonthly magazine covering outdoor recreation in Alaska. Circ. 70,000. Pays on acceptance. Byline given. Submit seasonal/holiday material 6 months in advance. SASE. Reports in 1 week. Sample copy $2; writer's guidelines for 4¼x9½ SASE and 1 first class stamp.
Nonfiction: How-to, investigative reports on outdoor issues in Alaska, and articles on any type of outdoor recreation engaged in Alaska. "Articles should include a sidebar that will aid the reader in duplicating your adventure. No survival-type articles or personal brushes with death." Buys 60 mss/year. Query. Length: 800-1,800 words. Pays $50-300; "$250 minimum for article with photographic support."
Photos: Adela Johnson Ward, photo editor. Send photos with ms. Pays $10-25 for b&w contact sheets; $25-200 for 2½x2¼ or 35mm color transparencies. Captions required. Buys one-time rights.
Columns/Departments: Fly Fishing Only ("tips, techniques and methods concerning flyfishing in Alaska"). Buys 6 mss/year. Query with clips of published work. Pays $125.
Fiction: Adventure ("all types of outdoor recreation practiced in Alaska"); and humorous (outdoor-related).
Tips: "Include more information and more descriptive writing, and less storytelling and Me 'n Joe type articles. Most of our writers have visited or live in Alaska. We are more than just a regional publication; we're distributed nationally."

BODYBUILDER, MUSCLE UP, Charlton Publications, Inc., Charlton Bldg., Derby CT 06418. Editor: Alan Paul. "These bimonthlies have similar formats." Not exclusively for body builders. Pays 2 weeks prior to publication. Buys first North American rights. Reports in 1 month. SASE.
Nonfiction: Nutrition; training tips; personalities; and some weight lifting tips. Query, but "we prefer to see complete manuscript." Length: 1,500-2,500 words. Pays $50-$150.
Photos: Pays $5-$10/b&w photo; $100/color cover; $50 for full-page color inside; $75 for color centerfold.

THE BOSTON MARATHON, The Official Magazine of the B.A.A. Marathon, Marathon Publications, 7 Water St., Boston MA 02109. (617)367-8600. Editor: Peter Morrissey. Magazine published semiannually covering running/marathon sports. Estab. 1979. Circ. 125,000. Pays on publication. Byline given "sometimes." Buys first North American serial rights and one-time rights. Submit seasonal/holiday material 5 months in advance. Photocopied and previously published submissions OK. SASE. Reports in 1 month. Sample copy $2.
Nonfiction: General interest, how-to, humor, personal experience, photo feature, and technical. "No unsolicited manuscripts." Query with clips of published work. Length: 800-1,200 words. Pays negotiable fee.
Photos: State availability of photos. Pays negotiable fee for 35mm color transparencies. Caption, model release and identification of subjects required. Buys one-time rights and all rights.

CLUB SCENE, Southern California Racquet ClubScene Magazine, 6400 Westminster Ave., Suite 106, Westminster CA 92683. (714)891-2217. Editor: John Brumm. National monthly magazine covers racquetball and tennis for male and female racquet club members. The average reader is 35, upper middle income, and maintains an active lifestyle. Estab. 1980. Circ. 105,000. Pays on acceptance. Byline given. Buys first North American serial rights and occasionally buys second serial (reprint) rights. Submit seasonal/holiday material 5 months in advance. Simultaneous queries and photocopied submissions OK. SASE. Reports in 4 weeks. Sample copy $2.50; writer's guidelines free for SAE and 1 first class stamp.
Nonfiction: General interest (pertaining to racquet sports, health, nutrition, and medicine); historical/nostalgic; humor; interview/profile (outstanding players and celebrity players); photo feature; and travel (places to play racquet sports around the world). Query with clips of published work or send complete ms. Length: 1,500 words average. Pays $200.
Photos: Send photos with accompanying ms. Reviews 35mm and larger color transparencies and 5x7 glossy b&w prints. "Photos are paid for with payment for ms." Caption and model release required. Buys one-time rights.
Columns/Departments: "Open for ideas."
Fillers: Newsbreaks. Buys 2/year. Length: 500 words. Payment varies.

FLYING DISC MAGAZINE, Palmeri-Guernsey Publications, Box 4035, Rochester NY 14610. (716)442-6910. Editor: Jim Palmeri. Managing Editor: Carol Moldt. Bimonthly magazine covering Frisbee sports and games. "Our readers are high-school-aged through age 60 (median age, mid-20s); 80% male, 20% female.) Our editorial material pervades of health, vitality, physical fitness and humor." Estab. 1980. Circ. 1,800. Pays on publication. Byline given. Pays negotiable kill fee. Buys first North American serial rights. Submit seasonal/holiday material 6 months in advance. Photocopied, simultaneous and previously published submissions OK. SASE. Reports in 6 weeks. Sample copy and writer's guidelines free.

Nonfiction: Historical/nostalgic (history of the sport; early events of Frisbee throwing); how-to (techniques on Frisbee skills, strategies for winning the various competitive games); humor (anything that makes people laugh); interview/profile (of person involved with the sport); new product (new Frisbees on the market); opinion, personal experience; photo feature; technical; and travel (good places to play Frisbee). "Wit and humor as a vehicle for a message or opinion is of top priority. Articles should be light and amusing, and at the same time, informative." Buys 12-18 mss/year. Query with clips of published work or send complete ms. Length: 1,000-15,000 words. Pays 3¢ word/minimum.

Photos: Mike Guernsey, photo editor. "If an article's subject matter pertains to specific photos, we'd like to see them accompany the manuscript; otherwise, it doesn't matter." Send photos with ms. Pays $6 minimum for b&w contact sheets or 5x7 glossy prints. Model release required. Buys one-time rights; sometimes other types, "depending on nature of photo."

Columns/Departments: Opinion, Disc Golf Course of the Month, Word Puzzle, Canine, Years Ago. Buys 30 or more mss/year. Send complete ms. Length: 800-1,100 words. Pays $50 minimum.

Fiction: Adventure, humorous, mystery and science fiction. No erotica, religion, serialized novels or romance. Buys 6 mss/year. Send complete ms. Length: 1,000-10,000 words.

Fillers: Jokes, anecdotes, short humor and newsbreaks. Buys 12-36/year. Length: 50-1,000 words. Pays $5 minimum.

GEORGIA SPORTSMAN MAGAZINE, Box 741, Marietta GA 30061. Editor: David Morris. Emphasizes hunting and fishing and outdoor recreational opportunities in Georgia. Monthly magazine; 64 pages. Circ. 45,000. Pays on publication. Byline given. Query. Submit seasonal material 4 months in advance. Simultaneous, "very legible" photocopied and previously published submissions OK. Source must be identified for previously published work. SASE. Reports in 4 weeks. Sample copy $1.75; free writer's guidelines.

Nonfiction: Exposé; how-to; informational; historical (acceptable on a very small scale); humor; interviews with fishermen or hunters known statewide; nostalgia (antique weapons such as percussion guns); and articles concerning major legislation and environmental issues affecting Georgia. Length: 2,000-2,800 words. Pays $150 maximum.

Photos: B&w and color purchased with or without mss or on assignment. Pays $150 for cover use.

HANG GLIDING, United States Hang Gliding Association, Box 66306, Los Angeles CA 90066. (213)390-3065. Editor: Gilbert Dodgen. Monthly magazine; 72 pages. Circ. 12,000. Buys all rights. Phone queries OK. Submit seasonal/holiday material 6 weeks in advance. SASE. Reports in 2 months. Free sample copy.

Nonfiction: Technical articles on both powered and non-powered hang gliders, instruments, aerodynamics, exposé, general interest, historical, how-to, humor, inspirational, interview, nostalgia, new product, experience, opinion, photo feature, profile and travel. Buys 1-2 mss/issue. Query with detailed description of subject, type of treatment, and clips of published work or send complete ms. Length: 500-2,000 words. Payment negotiable.

Photos: State availability of photos or send photos with ms. Pays $3.50 for b&w negatives. Buys one-time rights. Captions and model releases required.

Fiction: Adventure, fantasy, experimental, historical, humorous, mystery and suspense. "We prefer short, to-the-point articles. We do not want anything other than articles about hang gliding." Query with clips of published work or send complete ms. Payment negotiable.

Poetry: "Anything that pertains to hang gliding." Submit in batches of 4 or 5. Length: 25 lines maximum. No pay.

Fillers: Clippings, jokes, gags, anecdotes, newsbreaks, short humor, comic strips, photos and letters to the editor.

Tips: "We need technical and how-to articles, on design, building, modifications, flying techniques, powered ultralights, maintenance, weather, instruments, propellers and engines, etc. We don't need 'My First Flight' or similar type articles."

HOCKEY MAGAZINE, The Quality Hockey Magazine, Hockey Magazine, Inc., Box 629, Landmark Sq., Norwalk Ct 06852. (203)866-2321. Editor: Keith A. Bellows. Magazine published 8 times/year (October-May) covering hockey for "a Canada-US readership. It is edited for the top end of a 10- to 30-year-old audience." Circ. 30,000. Pays on publication. Byline given. Kill fee varies up to 50%. Buys first North American serial rights. Submit seasonal/holiday material at least 4 months in advance. Will consider simultaneous queries and previously published work (published book excerpts and some reprints). Reports in 2 weeks on queries; 3 weeks on ms. Free sample copy for 8½x11 SAE and $1 postage; free writer's guidelines for 4x8 SAE and 15¢ postage.

Nonfiction: Book excerpts, expose, how-to, humor, interview/profile. opinion, personal experience, photo feature, technical and travel. No articles on "My Son, the Youth Hockey Player"; no clichés or cliché subjects. Buys 40 mss/year. Query with clips of published work. Length: 1,000-3,500 words. Pays $100-400.

Photos: Peter Mecca, photo editor. State availability of photos. Pays $25-100/b&w, $50-125/color contact sheet; reviews 2x2 color transparencies. Identification of subjects required. "Purchase rights varies but usually buys one-time rights."

Columns/Departments: "Our departments are either staff written or assigned to regular columnists who work on annual contracts."

Fiction: Hockey. "We'll look at anything but it better be good—and different." Buys 2 mss/year. Send complete ms. Length: 1,000-2,500 words. Pays $100-400.

Fillers: "We don't generally buy fillers, but we now consider crossword puzzles and the like and sophisticated cartoons in the Tank McNamara vein."

Tips: "Non-pro articles are the best bet. We'll work with beginners if they show promise, are willing to research, and have a good idea. Stay away from big-name profiles; they're done by regulars. Like most magazines, we look for people-oriented material. Many of our instructional material is tied to personalities. Readers want punchy, entertaining prose, good anecdotes and inside information. We deliver. So must you if you want to write for us."

INSIDE RUNNING, 8100 Bellaire Blvd., No. 1301, Houston TX 77036. Editor/Publisher: Joanne Schmidt. Monthly tabloid covering "news and features of interest to joggers, racewalkers, and track and field athletes. We are a *Texas* magazine and our focus is on runners and running in the state." Circ. 5,000. Buys one-time rights. Pays on acceptance. SASE. Reports "within a month or less." Sample copy 50¢; writer's guidelines for SASE.

Nonfiction: "Strongly researched service pieces, profiles, race reports, and coverage of developments in the sport. We would like to discover correspondents and writers in Texas who run or have a familiarity with the sport and are looking for assignments in their area. We want very much to include capsule accounts of races from around the state for our Texas Round-up section. No personal 'How I Ran the Marathon' pieces, please." Query, and explain your background and photographic experience. Include writing samples, if possible. Pays 2¢/word. "We may pay more if a query is sent beforehand and the writer shows strong writing ability and offers special research."

Photos: "Strong photos earn extra payment." Pays $5 for b&w 5x7 prints "when inclusion of race results (top 10 and age group winners at least) and caption material are included."

Fiction: Pays $15-50, "depending on length, quality and originality."

Tips: "Report on races in your area or profile a local runner doing something different. Emphasize a Texas locale. Quotes and good b&w photos will give you the edge."

INTERNATIONAL OLYMPIC LIFTER, Box 65855, Los Angeles CA 90065. Editor: Bob Hise. Monthly magazine covering international lifting results for serious lifters and hard-core fans. Pays on publication. Buys all rights. Reports in 2 months. SASE.

Nonfiction: Diet; historical; exercise of the month; human interest (about Olympic weight lifters; accompanied by good b&w photos). "We publish a story re: Olympic lifting occasionally—most writing is done by the staff." Pays $25-150.

Poetry: "At present all we are in the market for are poems about the sport of 'Olympic' (competition) weightlifting and weightlifters. Prefer rhyming, metered verse. All rejected poems returned if a stamped return envelope is enclosed." Length: 8-16 lines. Pays $10-25.

JOGGER, 2420 K St., NW, Washington D.C. 20037. (212)965-3430. Editor: Glenn Petherick. Bimonthly tabloid covering jogging for members of the National Jogging Association interested in health, physical fitness and nutrition. Circ. 35,000. Pays on publication. Buys all rights. Reports in 1 month. Free sample copy.

Nonfiction: General interest (health and jogging-related activities); interview (of joggers); profile (women joggers or unusual people jogging); personal experience (effects of running on marriage and emotional, psychological and mental health); and events (marathons). "We are especially interested in articles by medical experts on physical and psychological effects of jogging and medical treatment for injuries." Buys 1-3 mss/issue. Send complete ms. Length: 1,000-3,000 words. Pays 10¢/word maximum.

Photos: State availability of photos. Pays $25 for 8x10 b&w prints.

Fiction: Short stories on running. Query. Length: 1,000-3,000 words.

Poetry: Free verse, light verse and traditional. Buys 1 ms/issue. Length: open.

THE MAINE SPORTSMAN, Box 365, Augusta ME 04330. Editor: Harry Vanderweide. 80-90% freelance written. Monthly tabloid; 32 pages. Circ. 17,000. Pays "shortly after publication." Byline given. SASE. Reports in 2-4 weeks.

Nonfiction: "We publish only articles about Maine outdoor activities. Any well-written, researched, knowledgeable article about that subject area is likely to be accepted by us." Expose; how-to; general interest; interview; nostalgia; personal experience; personal opinion; profile; and technical. Buys 25-30 mss/issue. Submit complete ms. Length: 200-3,000 words. Pays $20-80.

Photos: "We can have illustrations drawn, but prefer 1-3 b&w photos." Submit photos with accompanying ms. Pays $5-35 for b&w print.

MOUNTAIN STATES RECREATION, 2124 S. Dayton St., Denver CO 80231. (303)695-6252. Editor: Jay Lutsky. Emphasizes outdoor recreation (skiing, camping, fishing, racquet sports, running, bicycling and other participant-oriented sports). Monthly magazine. Circ. 50,000. Pays on publication. Buys all rights. Submit material 4 months in advance. SASE required. Reports in 1 month. Sample copy $1.25; free writer's guidelines.

Nonfiction: General interest to outdoor enthusiasts (inside story of what is going on in an activity); how-to; interviews; unique experiences. Buys 6-8 mss/issue. Length: 500-2,500 words. Pays $25-150.

Fiction: "We're open, but it must deal with recreation in some form."

Photos: Pays $10-25 for b&w prints; $25-150 for color transparencies. Captions and model release required. Photo essays accepted, price to be negotiated.

MUSCLE DIGEST, 10317 E. Whittier Blvd., Whittier CA 90606. Editor: Jon Meade. Bimonthly body building magazine whose purpose is "to inform, educate and inspire." Pays on publication. Buys exclusive rights. Reports in 2 weeks. SASE.

Nonfiction: Weight training, nutrition, personalities, posing tips, specific body workouts, health research, rising stars and articles for and about women. Query or send complete ms. Length: 500-2,000 words. Payment varies from $1.25/col inch. to $3/col inch.

Tips: "We challenge the 'free-thinking' writers of America who feel they have talent to send in their mss. It is an 'easy market to break into right now!' Submit, in-depth, credible articles. No personal 'success stories' unless very unusual and unique."

NATIONAL RACQUETBALL, United States Racquetball Association, 4101 Dempster, Skokie IL 60076. Managing Editor: Carol Brusslan. For racquetball players of all ages. Monthly magazine; 88 pages. Circ. 50,000. Pays on publication. Buys all rights. Byline given. Submit seasonal/holiday material 2-3 months in advance. SASE. Reports in 2 months. Sample copy $1.50.

Nonfiction: How-to (play better racquetball or train for racquetball); interview (with players or others connected with racquetball business); opinion (usually used in letters but sometimes fullblown opinion features on phases of the game); photo feature (on any subject mentioned); profile (short pieces with photos on women or men players interesting in other ways or on older players); health (as it relates to racquetball players—food, rest, eye protection, etc.); and fashion. Buys 4 mss/issue. Query with clips of published work. Length: 500-2,500 words. Pays $25-200.

Photos: State availability of photos or send photos with ms. Offers no additional payment for photos accompanying ms. Uses b&w prints or color transparencies. Buys one-time rights. Captions and model releases required.

Fiction: Adventure, humorous, mystery, romance, science fiction and suspense. "Whatever an inventive mind can do with racquetball." Buys 3 mss/year. Send complete ms. Pays $25-200.

Poetry: Light verse. Buys 1/year. Pays $10-25.

Fillers: Puzzles. Buys 2/year. Pays $10-25.

Tips: "Break into *National Racquetball* by writing for monthly features—short pieces about racquetball players you know for 'Who's Playing Racquetball?' or 'Beyond the Open.' "

PRORODEO SPORTS NEWS, 101 Prorodeo Dr., Colorado Springs CO 80919. (303)593-8840. Professional Rodeo Cowboys Association. Editor: Bill Crawford. Semimonthly tabloid for rodeo contestants, contract members, committeemen and rodeo fans. Published every other Wednesday (1 issue in January; none in December). Circ 30,000. Publishes the Annual Championship Edition, a 120-page slick paper magazine, following the National Finals Rodeo each December. Offers $15 kill fee on assigned material. Buys all rights. SASE. Reports in 2 weeks. Sample copy $1; free writer's guidelines.

Nonfiction: News of professional rodeo, columns, interviews, features about PRCA contestants, rodeo animals, contract members and committeemen; appropriate photographs. Material must focus on a single issue; emphasis on professionalism. All material must be accurate and attributable. Avoid countrified dialect. All material must relate directly to PRCA rodeos. Length: 18 column inches maximum. Query or send complete ms.

Photos: Pays $6 for b&w 8x10 glossy prints. Rodeo action, wrecks, PRCA members involved in other activities, such as competing in other sports, receiving awards, working with disabled persons, etc. Should have complete information written on the front in the white borders. Action photos should give name and hometown of rider, score made on the ride, name or number and owner of the animal, date and place photo taken. Wreck photos should contain information as to outcome. Continuous need for mugshots, candid, unposed. Particular needs are rodeo action in all events. Pays $30 for color transparencies; $130 for color transparency used on front cover of annual.

Fiction: "Professionally written and plotted authentic rodeo fiction." Length: 40 column inches maximum.

RACING PIGEON PICTORIAL, Coo Press, Ltd. 19 Doughty St., London, England WCIN 2PT. Editor-in-Chief: Colin Osman. Emphasizes racing pigeons for "all ages and occupations; generally 'working class' backgrounds, both sexes." Monthly magazine. Circ. 13,000. Pays on publication. Buys first rights. Submit seasonal/holiday material 3 months in advance. Photocopied and previously published submissions OK. SAE and International Reply Coupons. Reports in 5 weeks. Sample copy $2; free writer's guidelines.

Nonfiction: Michael Shepherd, Articles Editor. How-to (methods of famous fanciers, treatment of diseases, building lofts, etc.); historical (histories of pigeon breeds); informational (practical information for pigeon fanciers); interview (with winning fanciers); and technical (where applicable to pigeons). "Don't bother, if you're not a specialist!" Buys 4 mss/issue. Submit complete ms. Length: 6,000 words minimum. Pays $30/page minimum.

Photos: Rick Osman, Photo Editor. Purchased with or without accompanying ms or on assignment. Captions required. Send 8x10 b&w glossy prints or 2¼x2¼ or 35mm color transparencies.

RACQUETBALL, Towery Publishing Co., Inc., Box 16566, 1535 E. Brooks Rd., Memphis TN 38116. (901)345-8000. Editor: Nancy K. Crowell. For the amateur racquetball player. Official publication of the American Amateur Racquetball Association. Monthly magazine; 52 pages. Circ: 35,000. Pays on publication. Buys all rights. Byline given. Submit seasonal/holiday material 2 months in advance. Photocopied submissions OK. SASE. Reports in 3 weeks. Sample copy $1.

Nonfiction: General interest (an unusual court club, a look at racquetball training camps, new developments in racquetball, etc.); most interested in how-to (improve your backhand, return serves, play a lefthander, make lob shots, etc.); profile (of interesting people in racquetball—a top amateur player, a racquetball association official, etc.); new product (racquetball-related); health articles (particularly by people with backgrounds in the field of health, medicine). No "personal accounts of 'Experiences of a first-time player' and no sexist humor." Buys 5 mss/issue. Query with lists of credentials and clips of published work. Length: 2,000-3,000 words. "Payment negotiable."

Tips: "Most interested in good investigative reporters who are familiar with racquetball, and good instructional writers."

RACQUETBALL EVERYONE, 5724 W. Diversey, Chicago IL 60639. (312)745-9400. Editor: Raymond Mitchell. Monthly tabloid for Chicago and Illinois racquetball players. Circ. 25,000. Pays on publication. Buys one-time rights. Phone queries OK. Simultaneous, photocopied and previously published submissions OK. SASE. Reports in 1 week. Free sample copy.

Nonfiction: How-to; interview; profile (of professional celebrities); travel; new product (equipment and buildings); photo feature; technical; and events (amateur and professional); and instruction. Send complete ms. Length: 400-600 words. Pays $25-75.

Photos: Reviews any size b&w glossy prints. Offers no additional payment for photos accepted with ms. Captions required.

Columns/Departments: Instructional, travel, fashion and exercise. Length: 600-800 words. Pays $25-$75.

RACQUETBALL ILLUSTRATED, 7011 Sunset Blvd., Hollywood CA 90028. (213)467-1300. Editor: Ben S. Kalb. Monthly magazine about racquetball for an audience that is 18-65 years old. 55% male, upper middle class, members of private clubs. Circ. 105,000. Pays after acceptance. Buys first rights. Submit seasonal material 3 months in advance. Photocopied submissions OK. Reports in 1 month. Sample copy $1.50.

Nonfiction: Expose (politics of the racquetball industry); general interest; historical; how-to (turn a loser into a winner, psych out an opponent); humor; interview (of pros, unusual characters, celebrities); profile; travel; photo feature (kids in racquetball; racquetball in interesting cities; celebrities). No first person or puff pieces. Instruction done only by touring pros or qualified instructors. "Find a celebrity or a pro interesting on a national level and query. Also, we have annual special issues on shoes, racquets, balls, accessories, travel, health and instruction." No "'first time on the court' stories." Buys 5 mss/issue. Query explaining subject matter in detail and giving background information on persons. Length: 1,500-3,000 words. Pays $100-300.

Photos: Editor: Dave King. State availability of photos. Pays $15-30 for 8x10 b&w prints. Reviews color transparencies. Offers $25-50 additional payment for photos accepted with ms. Captions preferred; model release required. Buys one-time rights.

Fiction: "We are interested in general fiction with racquetball as the theme." Buys 6 mss/year. Send complete ms. Length: 3,000 words minimum. Pays $100-300.

Fillers: Short humor. Pays $15 minimum.

Tips: "I want a variety of articles to appeal to beginners as well as advanced players, the general player as well as the hard-core player. I'm not afraid to run a controversial article. Almost sure sellers are medical or psychological stories for 'Rx for winning' column."

RACQUETS CANADA, 425 University Ave., Toronto, Ontario, Canada M5G 1T6. Editor: Clive Hobson. Magazine published 6 times/year covering all racquet sports, with an emphasis on Canada. Circ. 110,000. Pays within 1 month of acceptance. Buys first rights. SAE and International Reply Coupons.

Nonfiction: General interest (on all racquet sports in Canada); also uses "specific feature material dealing with American or international topics. Photo coverage of same. No overly American-oriented material or material of a topical or news nature." Query. Length: 1,500-4,000 words. Pays $150-1,000.

Photos: Pays $50-200 for color transparencies.

Tips: "It's essential that the writer be familiar with the nature of our Canadian readership. What's news to Americans is not necessarily so with Canadian readers. Certain familiarity with Canadian personalities and adjacent areas of interest, plus awareness of Canadian issues helps."

THE RUNNER, 1 Park Ave., New York NY 10016. Editor-in-Chief: Marc Bloom. Emphasizes the world of running in the broadest scope with its main thrust in jogging, roadrunning and marathoning/fitness and health. Monthly magazine. Circ. 205,000. Pays on acceptance. Buys first North American serial rights. Pays 20% kill fee. Byline given. Submit seasonal/holiday material 3 months in advance. SASE. Reports in 2-3 weeks. Free sample copy.

Nonfiction: Profiles, body science, historical, event coverage, training, lifestyle, sports medicine, phenomena and humor. Buys 5-6 mss/issue. Query with clips of published work. Length: 1,500 words and up. Pays $250 and up, usually $500 or so for 3,000 words.

Photos: State availability of photos. Pay is negotiable for b&w contact sheets and 35mm color transparencies. Buys one-time rights. Captions required.

Columns/Departments: Reviews (books, film, etc.); people; statistical listings; humor; food; medicine; and training. Regular columnists used. Buys 3-4/issue. Length: 900-1,200 words. Pays $150 and up.

Warmups: Short news items and whimsical items. Length: 100-400 words. Pays $25-50.

Fiction: Senior Editor: Frederika Randall. Theme should be running. Buys 2 mss/year. Send complete ms. Length: 1,500 words minimum. Price negotiable.

RUNNER'S WORLD MAGAZINE, World Publications, Box 366, Mountain View CA 94040. (415)965-8777. Executive Editor: Richard Benyo. Managing Editor: Mark Levine. 50% freelance written. Emphasizes the sport of running, and health, fitness and nutrition for beginning and experienced runners, coaches, equipment manufacturers and salesmen, race promoters, etc. Monthly magazine; 112-160 pages. Circ. 475,000. Pays on publication. Buys all rights. Pays 25-45% kill fee. Byline given. Submit seasonal/holiday material 3-4 months in advance. SASE. Reports in 1 month. Free sample copy and writer's guidelines.

Nonfiction: Exposé; historical (where-are-they-now articles, primarily); how-to (improving one's own running, fitness and health); humor; informational; inspirational; interview; technical and profile. No stories written in the first person such as "How I completed my first marathon." Buys 8 mss/issue. Query "send a concise, typewritten, well-documented letter that projects that you do, indeed 'know' the magazine." Length: 200-5,000 words. Pays $25-650.

Photos: Photos purchased with or without accompanying ms or on assignment. Pays $15-40 for 5x7 or 8x10 b&w glossy prints; $50-100 for 35mm or 2¼x2¼ color transparencies. Query and send photos. Total purchase price for ms includes payment for photos.

Columns/Departments: Claire Colemen, copy editor. Looking at People (short profiles with pictures of celebrities or very unusual personalities involved in running, health and fitness activities). Length: 200-300 words. Pays $35 for each photo accepted; $15 for the ms. Runner's Forum (800 words maximum). Buys 6 mss/issue. Pays $25/ms.

Tips: "Know the magazine and analyze the type of stories that have been published in the past. Have a real good handle of the types of stories we publish; everything from nutrition and health to 'hardcore' running sports features. And, know the subject. Many writers call any long race a marathon; a marathon is 26 miles, 385 yards."

RUNNING TIMES, Running Times, Inc., 12808 Occoquan Rd., Woodbridge VA 22192. (703)550-7799. Editor: Edward Ayres. Emphasizes running, jogging, holistic health and fitness.

Monthly magazine; 72 pages. Circ. 100,000. Pays on publication. Buys all rights. Byline given. Submit seasonal/holiday material 3 months in advance. Simultaneous and photocopied submissions OK. SASE. Reports in 1 month. Sample copy $1.75.

Nonfiction: How-to (training techniques, racing techniques, self-treatment of injuries, etc.); humor; interview; photo feature; profile; and technical (written for a general readership). "We do not want opinions or ideas which are not backed up by solid research." Buys 1-2 mss/issue. Query or send complete ms. Length: 500-2,500 words. Pays $25-400.

Photos: State availability of photos. Pays $5-25 for 5x7 or 8x10 b&w glossy prints; $30-200 for color transparencies. Captions preferred.

Fiction: Adventure, erotica, fantasy and humorous. "Subjects must involve runners or running." Buys 4 mss/year. Send complete ms or clips of published work. Length: 700-2,500 words. Pays $50-200.

SIGNPOST MAGAZINE, 16812 36th Ave. W., Lynnwood WA 98036. Publisher: Louise B. Marshall. Editor: Ann L. Marshall. About hiking, backpacking and similar trail-related activities, mostly from a Pacific Northwest viewpoint. Monthly. Will consider any rights offered by author. Buys 12 mss/year. Pays on publication. Sample copy $1. Will consider photocopied submissions. Reports in 3 weeks. Query or submit complete ms. SASE.

Nonfiction and Photos: "Most material is donated by subscribers or is staff-written. Payment for purchased material is low, but a good way to break into print or spread a particular point of view."

SKYDIVING, Box 189, Deltona FL 32725. (904)736-9779. Editor: Michael Truffer. Monthly tabloid featuring skydiving for sport parachutists, worldwide dealers and equipment manufacturers. Estab. 1979. Circ. 6,000. Average issue includes 3 feature articles and 3 columns of technical information. Pays on publication. Byline given. Buys one-time rights. Simultaneous, photocopied and previously published submissions OK, if so indicated. SASE. Reports in 1 month. Sample copy $2; free writer's guidelines with SASE.

Nonfiction: "Send us news and information on equipment, techniques, events and outstanding personalities who skydive. We want articles written by people who have a solid knowledge of parachuting." No personal experience articles. Query. Length: 500-1,000 words. Pays $25-100.

Photos: State availability of photos. Reviews 5x7 and larger b&w glossy prints. Offers no additional payment for photos accepted with ms. Captions required.

Fillers: Newsbreaks. Length: 100-200 words. Pays $25 minimum.

SOUTHERN OUTDOORS MAGAZINE, B.A.S.S. Publications, Number 1 Bell Rd., Montgomery AL 36141. (205)277-3940. Editor: Dave Precht. Emphasizes Southern outdoor activities, including hunting, fishing, boating, travel, shooting, camping. "Competition is greater in the outdoors field, so only imaginative, well-written pieces will be purchased by *Southern Outdoors*." Published 8 times/year. Circ. 200,000. Pays on acceptance. Buys all rights. Submit seasonal/holiday material 10 months in advance. SASE. Reports in 1 month. Writers should be thoroughly familiar with "To Know Us Is To Sell To Us," a comprehensive, free writers'/photographers' manual available from *Southern Outdoors*.

Nonfiction: Must have obvious, legitimate Southern outdoors slant. Subjects can vary widely. No travel or environmental. All submissions must be compatible with guidelines; seldom are first-person stories purchased. Article should inform and entertain. Buys 100+/manuscripts a year. Query with one- or two-page sample from ms. Length: up to 3,500 words with sidebars and photos. Pays $200-700.

Photos: Purchased with or without accompanying ms. Captions required. Pays $10 minimum for 8x10 b&w glossy prints or 35mm color transparencies and larger. Offers no additional payment for photos accepted with accompanying ms, unless cover is obtained, then additional payment, on publication, of $150-300 is remitted.

Fillers: Needs short articles of 50-500 words written in a bright, clever style, on Southern outdoor topics. Emphasis on irony and humor, with a newsy slant. Pays about 15¢/word.

Tips: "Start with shorts. Don't expect a major assignment, even on spec, if we don't know you. We need good 'how-to' stories on new techniques for fishing, hunting or shooting, with a Southern slant. If you send a manuscript, make sure it has a catchy title and excellent lead. Stories most likely to sell: bass fishing, deer hunting, other freshwater fishing, inshore saltwater fishing, dove and quail hunting, waterfowl hunting, small game hunting, shooting, camping and boating, in that order."

STRENGTH & HEALTH MAGAZINE, S&H Publishing Co., Inc., Box 1707, York PA 17405. (717)848-1541. Editor-in-Chief: Bob Hoffman. Managing Editor: John Grimek. 35% freelance written. Emphasizes Olympic weightlifting and weight training. Bimonthly magazine; 74 pages. Circ. 100,000. Submit seasonal/holiday material 4-5 months in advance. SASE. Reports in 2 months.

Nonfiction: Robert Dennis, Articles Editor. How-to (physical fitness routines); interview (sports figures); and profile. Buys 15 mss/year. Submit complete ms. Length: 1,500-3,000 words. Pays $50-100.

Photos: Ms. Sallie Sload, Photo Editor. Purchased with accompanying ms. Captions required. Query. Pays $5-10 for b&w glossy or matte finish; $50-100 for 2¼x2¼ color transparencies (for cover). Model release preferred.

Columns/Departments: Jan Dellinger, Department Editor. Barbells on Campus (weight training program of college or university; captioned photos required, at least one photo of prominent building or feature of campus); In the Spotlight (profile of a championship-caliber weightlifter, training photos as well as casual, family & "other sports" shots). Buys 1-2/issue. Submit complete ms. Length: 1,500-2,500 words. Pays $50-100.

TEXAS SPORTS, The Sports Magazine of the Lone Star State, Windsor Communications, Box 402086, Dallas TX 75240. (214)931-8440. Editor: David Hadeler. Managing Editor: Larry Meeks. Monthly magazine for "athletes, athletic teams and/or events from Texas or with Texas ties. Our magazine is aimed at the sports fans (participant and/or observer) in Texas." Estab. 1979. Circ. 96,000. Pays on publication. Byline given. Pays a varying kill fee. Buys all rights. Phone queries OK. Submit seasonal material 4 months in advance. Simultaneous queries OK. SASE. Reports in 5 weeks on queries; in 2 months on mss. Sample copy and writer's guidelines free.

Nonfiction: Scott White, associate editor. General interest (athletes, teams, owners, managers, collegiate sports, high school sports, leisure sports, amateur sports, women in sports and hunting and fishing); interview; and profile. "We are looking for really good in-depth features on sports-related topics such as injuries, player contracts, negotiations, sports gambling, equipment and political issues. In our magazine, the trend is toward tighter, crisper writing and increased use of illustration." Special issues include Football Preview, July; Basketball Preview, November; Baseball Preview, April; and Fishing Preview, March. No "personal experience ('my best friend is . . .') articles." Buys 50-75 mss/year. Query or send complete ms. Length: 1,500-4,000 words. Pays $200-500.

Photos: State availability of photos or send photos with ms. Pays $20-150 for color transparencies; $20-75 for 8x10 b&w prints. Captions required. Buys all rights.

Columns/Departments: Cathee Cran, editorial assistant. Pro (professional sports); College (college sports); Leisure (participant sports); Amateur (amateur sports); "The Amateur and Leisure departments are easiest to break in with. Aim the articles toward personalities involved in participant sports (running, racquet sports, golf, bowling, hunting/fishing). In many cases, after writers have proven to be dependable and capable in writing for departments, we assign them to major features." Buys 50-80 mss/year. Query or send complete ms. Length: 500-1,500 words. Pays $75-150.

Fillers: Scott White, associate editor. Clippings, anecdotes, short humor. Buys 80-100/year. Length: 75-250 words. Pays $25-75.

Tips: "Don't give up if you're rejected. Eventually you'll come up with an idea we like. The best way to break into our publication is through the departments which contain general interest or analysis articles of no more than 1,500 words on subjects such as professional, amateur; college, women's, leisure and high school sports. We don't want articles that are padded with clichés or articles that are little more than a lot of quotes strung together with a transitional phrase here and there."

THE WORLD OF RODEO AND WESTERN HERITAGE, Rodeo Construction Agency, Box 660, Billings MT 59103. Editor-in-Chief: Jack Tanner. "We reach all these facets of rodeo: Professional, all-girls rodeo, little britches, college, regional, high school rodeo, Canadian rodeo, and oldtimers rodeo. Audience age: 9-90." 12 times/year. Tabloid; 40-80 pages. Estab. 1977. Circ. 18,000. Buys one-time rights. Byline given. Phone queries OK. Previously published submissions OK. SASE. Free sample copy and writer's guidelines.

Nonfiction: Exposé (personality), historical (oldtimers and famous rodeo animals); humor (pertaining to cowboys or Western history); informational (reports on current rodeo events); interview (with controversy or strong message); photo feature (emphasis on quality rodeo action and/or drama); profile (short in-depth sketch of person or persons); Western heritage (stories of the West and Western way of life). Buys 15 mss/issue. Query or submit complete ms. Length: 500-2,000 words. Pays $15-150.

Photos: B&w purchased with or without mss. Captions required. Send prints. Pays $5/8x10 b&w glossy with good contrast; $35-50/2¼x2¼, 35mm or 8x10 matte or glossy with good color balance.

Skiing and Snow Sports

CANADIAN SKATER, Canadian Figure Skating Association, 333 River Rd., Ottawa, Ontario, Canada K1L 8B9. (613)746-5953. Editor: Teresa C. Moore. 60% freelance written. "*Canadian Skater* appeals to skaters and skating fans of all ages—children, teenagers and adults who skate for fun; coaches, skating officials and parents. Published 6 times/year in both English and French. Magazine; 48 pages. Circ. 8,000. Pays on publication. Buys first North American serial rights or one-time rights. Byline given. Phone queries OK. Submit seasonal/holiday material 2½ months in advance. SAE and International Reply Coupons. Reports in 2-3 months. Free sample copy and writer's guidelines.
Nonfiction: "Articles dealing with Canada and the world's best amateur figure skaters, and the amateur figure skating scene in general." How-to (produce skating carnivals, raise funds, administer a skating club); general interest; humor; historical (Canadian figure skating); interview (top world and Canadian skaters, skating personalities actively involved in the amateur skating world); nostalgia; personal experience; personal opinion; photo feature; profile (special club activities); technical (figure skating skills) and competition reports or evaluations. No articles concentrating on professional rather than amateur skaters. Buys 5-8 mss/issue. Query. Length: 700-2,500 words. Pays $2/printed inch; $80 maximum.
Photos: "We do not have photographers on staff, and sometimes find it difficult to obtain the photos we wish." Pays $15-25 for 8x10 b&w glossy prints; $25-45 for color prints and $50-75 for cover (2¼x2¼ color transparencies). Captions required. Buys one-time rights. Model release required.
Columns/Departments: Former Canadian Champions; You and Your Instructor; Carnival Productions; Clubs in Canada (special activities); and Book Reviews. Buys 4/issue. Query with clips of published work. Length: 500-1,500 words. Pays $20-50.
Fiction: "Fiction relating to figure skating, especially children's stories." Adventure; fantasy; historical; and humorous. Buys 1/issue. Query with clips of published work. Length: 500-2,500. Pays $20-50.
Poetry: Free verse; light verse; traditional. "All poetry must relate to skating." Buys 1/issue. Pays $15-30.
Fillers: Anecdotes, newsbreaks and short humor. Buys 6/issue. Length: 75-150 words. Pays $10-15.
Tips: "We depend on freelancers and so are always on the lookout for new contributors. We appreciate seeing samples of previously published submissions when inquiries are made."

NORDIC SKIING, Nordic Skiing, Inc., Box 106, West Brattleboro VT 05301. (802)254-9080. Editor: Barbara Brewster. Emphasizes cross country skiing. Monthly (September-Feb/March) magazine; 80 pages. Circ. 30,000. Pays on publication. Buys all North American serial rights. Pays 40% kill fee. Byline given. Submit seasonal/holiday material 6-9 months in advance. SASE. Reports in 3 weeks (queries); 4 weeks (mss). Sample copy $1.
Nonfiction: Exposé (of legislative action affecting federal land use relating to cross country skiing); general interest (vacation areas or places to ski complete with description of facilities); how-to (technique articles on cross country skiing accepted only from qualified people in the field); humor (related to cross country skiing experiences or training); photo feature and travel. Buys 3 mss/issue. Query with clips of published work. Length: 900-3,000 words. Pays $50-200.
Photos: State availability of photos with ms. Pays $10-25/8x10 b&w glossy print; $25-200/35mm color transparency. Buys first-time rights. Captions preferred.
Columns/Departments: Trail Smackers (recipes for day or overnight ski tours) and Helpful Hints (any information that might be helpful or useful to a cross country skier). Buys 2-3/issue. Send complete ms. Length: 50-200 words. Pays $5.

NORTHWEST SKIER AND NORTHWEST SPORTS, Box 5029, University Station, Seattle WA 98105. (206)634-3620. Publisher: Ian F. Brown. Published 14 times/year. Circ. 16,000. Some issues copyrighted. Byline given. Pays on publication. Will send sample copy to writer for $1. Reports "immediately." SASE.
Nonfiction: Grant Alden, editor. Well-written articles of interest to outdoor sports participants in the Pacific Northwest and Western Canada, or pieces of a general scope which would interest all of the winter sporting public. Character studies, unusual feats or activities. Must be authoritative, tightly-constructed and convincingly thorough. Humor accepted. "Politics are occasionally considered, along 'speaking out' lines. No "profiles of destination ski resorts, especially in Colorado or Europe. The inclusion of photos or graphics generally improves prospects for acceptance."Length: 350 words minimum. Pays $10 minimum/article; $1.25/column inch.
Photos: Purchased almost exclusively with ms and with captions only. Needs strong graphics of

winter outdoor sports scene, preferably not posed shots. 8x10 or 4x5 prints. Pays $5 minimum/photo.

Fiction: Grant Alden, editor. Uses very little, depending on quality and uniquity. Will use humorous fiction. Length: 350 words plus. Pays $1.25/column inch.

Tips: "We are open to all forms of outdoor sports, particularly those ventures of a radical or desperate nature, on a year-round basis. We like to encourage a slightly offbeat approach to the presentation."

POWDER MAGAZINE, Box 1028, Dana Point CA 92629. (714)496-5922. Publisher: Neil Stebbins. Editors: David Moe and Pat Cochran. 7/year, including two special issues; pre-season equipment review and photo annual. Circ. 100,000. Rights purchased vary with author and material. May buy all rights, but will reassign rights to author after publication; or first North American serial rights; or simultaneous rights. Buys 25-30 mss a year. Pays on publication. Sample copy for 50¢. Will consider simultaneous submissions. Submit material late spring, early summer for publication the following season. Reports on material accepted for publication in 6 weeks. Phone or written query preferred. Enclose SASE.

Nonfiction and Photos: "We want material by or about people who reach out for the limits of the ski experience. Avoid classical ski-teaching technique problems, specific equipment tests, travel guides, or beginner-oriented articles. We try to emphasize the quality of the ski experience rather than its mechanics, logistics, or purely commercial aspects." Length: 500-2,500 words. Pays approximately 10¢/word. *Top Quality* b&w and color transparencies purchased with or without mss or on assignment. Pays approximately $25-75 b&w, full or partial page, $40-150 for color, full or partial page; $300 cover.

Fiction: Humorous, mainstream adventure and experimental fiction. Must relate to subject matter. Length: open. Pays 7-10¢/word.

SKATING, United States Figure Skating Association, 20 First St., Colorado Springs CO 80906. (303)635-5200. Editor-in-Chief: Ian A. Anderson. Monthly magazine; 64 pages. Circ. 31,000. Pays on publication. Buys all rights. Byline given "only if requested." Phone queries OK. Submit seasonal/holiday material 3 months in advance. Photocopied and previously published submissions OK. SASE. Reports in 1 month. Writer's guidelines for SASE.

Nonfiction: Historical; how-to (photograph skaters, train, exercise); humor; informational; interview; new product; personal experience; personal opinion; photo feature; profile (background and interests of national-caliber skaters); technical; and competition reports. Buys 4 mss/issue. Query or send complete ms. Length: 500-1,000 words. Pays $50.

Photos: Shawn Doherty, Art Director. Photos purchased with or without accompanying ms. Pays $10 for 8x10 or 5x7 b&w glossy prints and $35/color transparencies. Query.

Columns/Departments: European Letter (skating news from Europe); Ice Abroad (competition results and report from outside the US); Book Reviews; People; Club News (what individual clubs are doing); and Music column (what's new and used for music for skating). Buys 4 ms/issue. Query or send complete ms. Length: 100-500 words. Pays $35. Open to suggestions for new columns/departments.

Fillers: Newsbreaks, puzzles (skating-related) and short humor. Buys 2 fillers/issue. Query. Length: 50-250 words. Pays $20.

SKI, 380 Madison Ave., New York NY 10017. (212)687-3000. Editor: Dick Needham. 15% freelance written. 7 times/year, September through March. Buys first-time rights in most cases. Pays 50% kill fee. Byline given "except when report is incorporated in 'Ski Life' department." Pays on publication. Reports in 1 month. SASE.

Nonfiction: Prefers articles of general interest to skiers, travel, adventure, how-to, budget savers, unusual people, places or events that reader can identify with. Must be authoritative, knowledgeably written, in easy, informative language and have a professional flair. Cater to middle to upper income bracket readers who are college graduates, wide travelers. No fiction. Length: 1,500-2,000 words. Pays $100-250.

Photos: Buys photos submitted with manuscripts and with captions only. Good action shots in color for covers; pays minimum $300. B&w photos, pays $40 each; minimum $150 for photo stories. (Query on these.) Color shots. Pays $50 each; $150/page.

Tips: "We also publish *Cross Country Ski Magazine,* for which we need individual text and photo stories on cross-country ski touring and centers. We're looking for 1,000-2,000 words on a particular tour and it's an excellent way for us to get acquainted with new writers. Could lead to assignments for *Ski.* Photos are essential. Another possibility is our monthly column, Ski People, which runs 300-400-word items on unusual people who ski and have made some contribution to the sport. For another column, Personal Adventure, we welcome 2,000- to 2,500-word 'It Happened to Me' stories of unique (humorous, near disaster, etc.) experiences on skis. Payment is $100.

We want to see outline of how author proposes to develop story, sample opening page or paragraph; include previous clippings or published writing samples. Humor is welcome."

SKI AMERICA, Ski America Enterprise, Inc., 8 Bank Row, Box 1140, Pittsfield MA 01201. (413)442-6953. Editor: Barry Hollister. Managing Editor: Jim Hollister. Published 4 times/year. Magazine; 32-64 pages. Circ. 300,000. Pays on publication. Buys one-time rights or makes assignments on work-for-hire basis. Pays 25-50% kill fee. Byline given. Phone queries OK. Submit seasonal/holiday material 1 month in advance. SASE. Reports in 1 month. Free sample copy.
Nonfiction: General interest, humor, new product, photo feature and travel. Buys 4 mss/issue. Query. Length: 1,000-1,500 words.
Photos: State availability of photos. Pays $10-125/8x10 b&w print; $50-250/35mm color transparency. Captions preferred.
Fiction: Adventure and humorous. Query. Length: 1,000-1,500 words. Pays $75-250.

SKI SOUTH, The Magazine of Southern Skiers, Leisure Publishing Co., 3424 Brambleton Ave., Box 12567, Roanoke VA 24026. (703)989-6138. Managing Editor: Richard Wells. Magazine published twice/year covering skiing in the south. "*Ski South* reaches an affluent, young adult audience of recreational skiing enthusiasts. Emphasis on Southern ski resorts, technique, equipment, fashion, etc." Circ. 18,000. Pays on publication. Byline given. Makes work-for-hire assignments. Simultaneous queries OK. SASE. Reports in 6 weeks. Free sample copy.
Nonfiction: Interview/profile, opinion, personal experience, photo feature and travel. Buys 6-8 mss/year. Send complete ms. Length: 500-1,500 words. Pays $35-150.
Photos: Send photos with ms. Pays $50-100 for 35mm color transparencies. Captions required. Buys one-time rights.

SKIING MAGAZINE, Ziff-Davis Publishing Co., 1 Park Ave., New York NY 10016. Editor-in-Chief: Alfred H. Greenberg. Executive Editor: Dinah B. Witchel. Published 7 times/year (September-March). Magazine; 175 pages. Circ. 430,000. Pays on acceptance. Buys first rights. Byline given. Submit seasonal/holiday material 4 months in advance. SASE. Sample copy $1.50.
Nonfiction: "This magazine is in the market for any material of interest to skiers. Material must appeal to and please the confirmed skier. Much of the copy is staff-prepared, but many freelance features are purchased provided the writing is fast-paced, concise and knowledgeable." Buys 10 mss/year. Submit complete ms. Length: 1,500-3,000 words. Pays 10¢/word minimum.
Photos: Rick Fiala, Art Director. Purchased with or without accompanying ms or on assignment. Send contact sheet or transparencies. Pays $100/full page for 8x10 b&w glossy or matte photos; $125 minimum/full page for 35mm transparencies, pro-rated. Model release required.

SNOW GOER, The Webb Co., 1999 Shephard Rd., St. Paul MN 55116. (612)690-7269. Editor: Jerry Bassett. Managing Editor: Bill Monn. For snowmobilers. Magazine published 5 times seasonally, covering snowmobiling. Magazine, 60-104 pages. Circ. 2,600,000. Buys all rights. Byline given. Pays on acceptance. Submit special issue material 1 year in advance. Reports in 2 months. Query or submit complete ms. SASE.
Nonfiction: General interest; historical/nostalgic; how-to (mechanical); interview/profile; personal experience; photo feature; technical; and travel. Features on snowmobiling with strong secondary story angle, such as ice fishing, mountain climbing, snow camping, conservation, rescue. Also uses features relating to man out-of-doors in winter. " 'Me and Joe' articles have to be unique for this audience." Buys 2-3 mss/issue. Length: 800-1,500 words. Pays $100-250.
Photos: State availability of photos; send photos with ms. Pays $5-25 for 5x7 or 8x10 b&w glossy contact sheets; $15-50 for 35mm color transparencies. Offers no additional payment for photos with accompanying ms. Captions, model releases, and identification of subjects required. Buys all rights.

SNOWMOBILE MAGAZINE, Winter Sports Publications, Inc., 225 E. Michigan, Milwaukee WI 53202. (414)276-6000. Editor: Cynthia Swanson. Associate Editor: Dick Hendricks. Magazine published 5 times/year covering snowmobiling for snowmobilers throughout North America. Estab. 1980. Circ. 500,000. Pays on publication. Byline given. Buys all rights, but "author may request return." Simultaneous and previously published submissions OK ("if publication and date are indicated"). SASE. Reports in 1 month on mss. Free sample copy and writer's guidelines.
Nonfiction: "We want articles on anything involving snowmobiling or winter recreation." Humor; interview/profile; and travel (places to go and things to do on snowmobiles). Buys 15-20 mss/year. Send complete ms. Length: 1,800-3,000 words. Pays $175-350.
Photos: Send photos with or without accompanying ms. Reviews 35mm color transparencies.
Columns/Departments: ETC. (short items pertaining to snowmobiling). Buys 10 mss/year. Send complete ms. Length: 200-500 words. Pays $25-50.

SNOWMOBILE WEST, 521 Park Ave., Box 981, Idaho Falls ID 83401. Editor: Darryl Harris. 50% freelance written. For recreational snowmobile riders and owners of all ages. Magazine; 48 pages. Publishes six issues each winter. Circ. 125,000. Buys first North American serial rights. Pays kill fee if previously negotiated at time of assignment. Byline given on substantive articles of two pages or more. Buys 10 mss/year. Pays on publication. Free sample copy and writer's guidelines. Reports in 2 months. Articles for one season are generally photogaphed and written the previous season. Query. SASE.

Nonfiction and Photos: Articles about snowtrail riding in the Western US; issues affecting snowmobilers; and maps of trail areas with good color photos and b&w. Pays 3¢/word; $5/b&w; $10/color. B&w should be 5x7 or 8x10 glossy print; color should be 35mm transparencies or larger, furnished with mss. With a story of 1,000 words, typically a selection of 5 b&w and 5 color photos should accompany. Longer stories in proportion. Length: 500-2,000 words.

Soccer

AMERICAN SOCCER MAGAZINE, 211 Culver Blvd., Playa del Rey CA 90291. Editor-in-Chief: Donald R. Edgington. 25% freelance written. Bimonthly magazine; 32 pages. Circ. 322,000. Pays on publication. Buys all rights. Simultaneous and previously published submissions OK. SASE. Reports in 2 weeks. Sample copy 50¢ and free writer's guidelines; mention *Writer's Market* in request.

Nonfiction: How-to (soccer drills, skills); humor (cartoons); interview (pro players of national stature); photo feature (action of championship calibre games-youth); and profile (pro and youth players of national stature). Buys 8 mss/year. Query. Length: 650-1,800 words. Pays $25-50.

Photos: State availability of photos with query. Offers no additional payment for 8x10 b&w glossy prints or 35mm color transparencies. Captions and model release required. Buys one-time rights.

B.C. SOCCER MAGAZINE, Holden-Lea Soccer Publications, Ltd., 17231 57A Ave., Surrey, British Columbia, Canada V3S 5A8. (604)576-1611. Editor: David Leach. Magazine published 6 times/year covering "all aspects of amateur and professional soccer in British Columbia Canada." Estab. 1980. Circ. 15,000. Pays on publication. Byline given. Buys one-time rights. Submit seasonal/holiday material 3 months in advance. Simultaneous, photocopied and previously published submissions OK. SASE. Sample copy $1.50.

Nonfiction: Short book excerpts (soccer); general interest (soccer); historical/nostalgic (British Columbia soccer); humor (shorter pieces relating to soccer); interview/profile (of soccer pro with British Columbian background); and photo feature (of traveling British Columbia teams). "Traveling teams from British Columbia, general soccer articles, e.g., the soccer mother, life of a junior coach. We need B.C. player profiles and humorous articles. We are expanding fast!" No articles on American soccer (USA) or eastern Canadian soccer, at the moment. Buys 25 mss/year. Send complete ms. Length: 250-5,000 words. Pays 3-10¢/published word.

Photos: Send photos with ms. Pays $5 Canadian for b&w prints. Caption, model release, and identification of subjects required. Buys one-time rights.

Fillers: Anecdotes and short humor. "We need soccer biased material." Buys 50/year. Length: 25-100 words. Pays 3¢/word.

SOCCER AMERICA, Box 23704, Oakland CA 94623. (415)549-1414. Editor-in-Chief: Ms. Lynn Berling. For a wide range of soccer enthusiasts. Weekly tabloid. Circ. 6,000. Pays on publication. Buys all rights. Byline given. Submit seasonal/holiday material 14 days in advance. SASE. Reports in 1 month. Sample copy and writer's guidelines, $1.

Nonfiction: Expose (why a pro franchise isn't working right, etc.); historical; how-to; informational (news features); inspirational; interview; photo feature; profile; and technical. Buys 1-2 mss/issue. Query. Length: 200-2,000 words. Pays 50¢/inch minimum.

Photos: Photos purchased with or without accompanying ms or on assignment. Captions required. Pays $5-15 for 5x7 or larger b&w glossy prints. Query. Total purchase price for ms includes payment for photos.

Columns/Departments: Book Reviews. Buys 25 mss/year. Send complete ms. Length: 200-1,000 words. Pays 1¢/word minimum. Open to suggestions for new columns/departments.

Market conditions are constantly changing! If this is 1983 or later, buy the newest edition of *Writer's Market* at your favorite bookstore or use the back-of-the-book order form.

SOCCER MONTHLY, US Soccer Federation, 370 Lexington, New York NY 10017. (212)679-1060. Editor: Kenneth Ross. Monthly magazine covering soccer for enthusiasts and people involved in the soccer movement. Circ. 5,000. Average issue includes 4 feature articles and 3 columns. Pays on publication. Byline given. Buys all rights. Free sample copy.
Nonfiction: "We are interested in articles covering American youth soccer and youth soccer competitors here and abroad; the women's leagues; professionals—regular and indoor; college, U.S. Olympic, and World Cup scenes. We rely primarily on freelancers. All articles are done on assignment." Special issues include March, soccer camp; April, pro preview; September, college preview; and December, indoor soccer. Buys 6 mss/issue. Query with clips of previously published work. "No unsolicited manuscripts will be considered." Length: 1,000-1,500 words. Pays $75-100.
Photos: State availability of photos. Pays $15 minimum for 5x7 b&w glossy prints. Pays $35 minimum ($100 for cover) for 35mm color transparencies. Captions required. Buys one-time rights.

Tennis

NEW ENGLAND TENNIS JOURNAL, Grassroots Publishing Co., Inc., 376 Bolyston St., Suite 504, Boston MA 02116. (617)266-5125. Publisher: Steffi Karp. Editor: Jeffrey Tarter. Monthly magazine about tennis, raquetball, and other racquet sports in the six New England states, New York and New Jersey. Circ. 25,000. Pays on publication. Buys first North American serial rights. Phone queries OK. Submit seasonal material 3 months in advance. Simultaneous, photocopied and previously published submissions OK. SASE. Reports in 1 month. Free sample copy.
Nonfiction: General interest (equipment, fashion, travel, camps) historical; how-to (instruction); humor; interview; opinion; profile (not-so-famous players doing well in New England); travel; personal experience; photo feature; technical (buildings, tennis court surface and racquet products); and the business of running tennis clubs; racquet sport parties; and physical fitness programs. Buys 2-3 mss/issue. Query with clips of previously published work. Length: 500-2,000 words. Pays $75-100.
Photos: State availability of photos. Reviews contact sheets and 5x7 b&w glossy prints.
Columns/Departments: Players Notebook (instruction, racquet reviews and health ideas). Buys 2-3 mss/issue. Send complete ms. Length: 500 words maximum. Pays $35 minimum.
Fillers: Clippings, jokes, gags, anecdotes, short humor, newsbreaks and puzzles.

TENNIS, 495 Westport Ave., Norwalk CT 06856. Publisher: Howard R. Gill Jr. Editor: Shepherd Campbell. For persons who play tennis and want to play it better. Monthly magazine. Circ. 460,000. Buys all rights. Byline given. Pays on publication. SASE.
Nonfiction and Photos: Emphasis on instructional and reader service articles, but also seeks lively, well-researched features on personalities and other aspects of the game, as well as humor. Query. Length varies. Pays $200 minimum/article, considerably more for major features. Pays $15-75/8x10 b&w glossies or color transparencies.

TENNIS EVERYONE, 5724 W. Diversey, Chicago IL 60639. (312)745-9400. Editor: Raymond Mitchell. Monthly tabloid for Chicago and Illinois tennis players. Circ. 25,000. Pays on publication. Buys one-time rights. Phone queries OK. Simultaneous, photocopied and previously published submissions OK. SASE. Reports in 1 week. Free sample copy.
Nonfiction: How-to; interview; profile (of celebrities and professionals); new product; photo feature; technical; and events. Send complete ms. Length: 400-600 words. Pays $20 minimum.
Photos: Reviews 8x10 b&w glossy prints. Offers no additional payment for photos accepted with ms. Captions required.
Columns/Departments: Instructional, travel, fashion and exercise. Length: 400-600 words. Pays $25-$75.

TENNIS USA, Contact Consumer, a Division of CBS Inc., 1515 Broadway, New York NY 10036. Publisher: Bruce W. Gray.

TENNIS WEEK, Tennis News, Inc., 1107 Broadway, New York NY 10010. (212)741-2323. Publisher and Founder: Eugene L. Scott. Managing Editor: Linda Pentz. Weekly newspaper; 16-24 pages. Circ. 25,000. Byline given. Pays on acceptance. Photocopied submissions OK. SASE. Reports in 2 weeks. Sample copy 50¢.
Nonfiction: "Articles should concentrate on players' lives off the court." Buys 100 mss/year. Send complete ms. Pays $25-100.
Photos: Send photos with ms. Pays $10/8x10 b&w glossy print.

THE TOURNAMENT TIMES, Western Tennis Publications, a div. of ITA, Box 4577, Santa Fe NM 87502. (505)988-7252. Editor/Publisher: Bob Raedisch. Newspaper issuing 12 main volumes with 2-4 supplements annually, covering "tennis tournaments, etc. for tennis pros and players of all levels. We mainly focus on local, national and international tournaments." Estab. 1979. Circ. varies with issues. Pays on publication. Copyright pending. Makes work-for-hire assignments "but not always." Submit seasonal/holiday material 3 months in advance. Simultaneous, photocopied, and previously published work OK. SASE. Reports in 1 month. Free sample copy and writer's guidelines.
Nonfiction: Book excerpts, general interest (on players, etc.); historical/nostalgic (on tennis in the past); how-to (improve tennis strokes and play in general); humor (tennis jokes); interview/profile (of players, officials, etc.); new product (tennis items); and travel (tennis resorts). Special issues include travel, camps, equipment (all tennis) plus an explanation of tennis world structure. Buys 16 mss/year. Query. Length: 200-1,000 maximum, 50 words minimum for tennis tips. Pays $20 minimum.
Photos: State availability of photos. Pays $2 or more for b&w contact sheets. Captions preferred; model release required. Buys all rights.
Columns/Departments: "We're open to suggestions for new columns or departments." Query. Pays $20 minimum.
Tips: "We welcome coverage of tournaments and stories on national tennis happenings and players."

WORLD TENNIS MAGAZINE, CBS Consumer Publishing, a Division of CBS Inc., 1515 Broadway, New York NY 10036. Publisher: Bruce W. Gray.

Water Sports

ATLANTIC COASTAL DIVER, RCS Publishing, 5205 York Rd., Baltimore MD 21212. (301)323-3550. Editor: Joseph Dorsey. Executive Editor: Rick Swanson. Bimonthly magazine covering diving for sport divers from Maine to Florida and throughout the Caribbean. Circ. 43,000. Pays on publication. Byline given. Buys all rights, "but may reassign rights to author." Submit seasonal/holiday material 4 months in advance. Simultaneous queries, and simultaneous and photocopied submissions OK. SASE. Reports in 2 weeks. Sample copy for 9x12 SAE and 40¢ postage.
Nonfiction: Buys 9 mss/year. Query or send complete ms. Length: 1,200 words or 2,500 words. Pays $50 average; "we sometimes negotiate a higher amount."
Photos: Send photos with ms. Reviews 35mm color transparencies and any size b&w glossy prints. "Photos are paid for with payment for mss." Captions required; model release preferred.

DIVER, Seagraphic Publications, Ltd., Boaters Village, 1601 Granville St., Vancouver, British Columbia V6Z 2B3. (604)689-8688. Publisher: Peter Vassilopoulos. Editor: Neil McDaniel. 60% freelance written. Emphasizes scuba diving, ocean science and technology (commercial and military diving) for a well-educated, outdoor-oriented readership. Published 8 times/year. Magazine; 56-72 pages. Circ. 25,000. Payment "follows publication." Buys first North American serial rights. Byline given. Query (by mail only). Submit seasonal/holiday material 3 months in advance of issue date. SAE and International Reply Coupons. Reports in 6 weeks.
Nonfiction: How-to (underwater activities such as photography, etc.); general interest (underwater oriented); humor; historical (shipwrecks, treasure artifacts, archeological); interview (underwater personalities in all spheres—military, sports, scientific or commercial); personal experience (related to diving); photo feature (marine life); technical (related to oceanography, commercial/military diving, etc.); and travel (dive resorts). No subjective product reports. Buys 40 mss/year. Submit complete ms. Length: 800-2,000 words. Pays $2.50/column inch.
Photos: "Features are mostly those describing dive sites, experiences, etc. Photo features are reserved more as specials, while almost all articles must be well illustrated with b&w prints supplemented by color transparencies." Submit photo material with accompanying ms. Pays $7 minimum for 5x7 or 8x10 glossy b&w prints; $15 minimum for 35mm color transparencies. Captions required. Buys one-time rights.
Columns/Departments: Book reviews. Submit complete ms. Length: 200 words maximum. Pays to $25. Open to suggestions for new columns/departments.
Fillers: Anecdotes, newsbreaks and short humor. Buys 8-10/year. Length: 50-150 words. Pays $10.

H2O POLO SCOREBOARD, H2O Polo Revue Enterprises, Box 5236, Long Beach CA 90805. (213)423-7026 or (213)861-6390. Editor: Ron Arendas. Quarterly magazine covering the growing sport of water polo for water polo players, coaches and enthusiasts. Estab. 1980. Circ. 10,000. Pays on publication. Byline given. Pays 50% kill fee. Buys first North American serial rights. Previously published work OK. Reports in 2 weeks. Sample copy $1, 1 No. 9 SAE, and 1 first class stamp.

Nonfiction: General interest, hisorical/nostalgic, how-to, humor, inspirational, interview/profile, new product, opinion, personal experience, photo feature, technical, travel, and news information about the sport. "We are open to anything that relates (even slightly) to water polo—especially an interview with a well-known player or coach." Buys 10 mss/year. Query. Length: 750-1,500 words. Pays $25-50.

Photos: Bill Hughes, photo editor. Send photos with accompanying ms. Pays $10 maximum for b&w or color contact sheets; $10 maximum for b&w negatives; $10 maximum for 35mm b&w or color transparencies; $10 maximum for any size b&w or color prints. Captions required. Buys all rights.

Columns/Departments: Back to Basics (technical material; water polo fundamentals); Polo People (interesting water polo personalities); and Places to Water Polo (interesting reports of a city or area with water polo teams or events). "We are currently developing two new departments called 'Places to H2O Polo' and 'Polo People.' These are simple, short, human-interest pieces which will serve to introduce our readers to other people and places in the water polo world." Buys 20-30 mss/year. Query. Length: 500-1,000 words. Pays $25 maximum.

Fiction: Experimental, humorous and suspense. No material unrelated to water polo. Buys 1-4 mss/year. Send complete ms. Length: 750-1,500 words. Pays $25 maximum.

Fillers: Clippings, anecdotes, short humor and newsbreaks (shorts). Buys 30/year. Length: 25-500 words. Pays $5-20.

Tips: "The freelancer must familiarize himself with the sport of water polo. The sport is in a state of growth and change in the US. Our main purpose is to show this growth in a positive way and provide a medium of communication for poloists nationwide. New writers will be given a break with us! We are growing and will allow budding writers to grow with us."

SCUBA TIMES, The Active Diver's Magazine, MWP Publishing Co., Box 6268, Pensacola FL 32503. (904)478-5288. Editor: Meta Leckband. Managing Editor: M. Wallace Poole. Monthly magazine covering skin diving. "Our reader is the young, reasonably affluent skin diver looking for a more exciting approach to diving than he could find in the other diving magazines." Estab. 1979. Circ. 15,000. Pays after publication. Byline given. Buys first North American serial rights. Simultaneous queries OK. SASE. Reports in 1 month. Sample copy $2. Writer's guidelines for business size SAE and 1 first class stamp.

Nonfiction: General interest; how-to; interview profile ("Of 'name' people in the sport, especially if they're currently doing something radical"); new product (how to more effectively use them); personal experience (good underwater photography pieces); and travel (pertaining to diving). No articles without a specific theme. Buys 18 mss/year. Query with clips of published work. Length: 500-1,200 words. Pays $35-150.

Photos: Jo Dee Williams, photo editor. Pays $25-250 for 35mm color transparencies; reviews 8x10 prints. Captions, model release, and identification of subjects required. Buys one-time rights.

Tips: "Our current contributors are among the top writers in the diving field. A newcomer must have a style that draws the reader into the article, leaves him satisfied at the end of it, and makes him want to see something else by this same author soonest! Writing for diving magazines has become a fairly sophisticated venture. The 'me and Joe went diving' type of article just won't do anymore. Writers must be able to compete with the best in order to survive."

SKIN DIVER, 8490 Sunset Blvd., Los Angeles CA 90069. (213)657-5100. Editor/Publisher: Paul J. Tzimoulis. Circ. 180,000. "The majority of our contributors are divers turned writers." Buys only one-time rights. Byline given. Pays on publication. Acknowledges material immediately. All model releases and author's grants must be submitted with mss. Manuscripts reviewed are either returned to the author or tentatively scheduled for future issue. Time for review varies. Mss considered "accepted" when published; all material held on "tentatively scheduled" basis subject to change or rejection up to time of printing. Submit complete ms with photos. SASE.

Nonfiction and Photos: Contact: Bonnie J. Cardone. Stories and articles directly related to skin diving activities, equipment or personalities. Features and articles equally divided into following categories: adventure, equipment, underwater photography, wrecks, treasure, spearfishing, undersea science, travel, marine life, do-it-yourself, technique and archeology. No "articles on marine life or fish-of-the-month candidates." Length: 1,000-2,000 words, well-illustrated by photos; b&w at ratio of 3:1 to color. Pays $50/printed page. Photos purchased with mss; b&w 8x10 glossy prints; color 35mm, 2¼x2¼ or 4x5 transparencies; do not submit color prints or negatives. All photos must be captioned and marked with name and address. Pays $50/published page for inside photos; $300/cover photo.

Tips: "The best way to get published in *Skin Diver* is to write an article on a dive spot or subject familiar to the writer, and submit good clear photos with it. We are photo-oriented; thus, sharp colorful photos often mean the difference between acceptance or rejection."

SPRAY'S WATER SKI MAGAZINE, Box 4779, Winter Park FL 32793. (305)671-0655. Editor: Harvey W. McLeod Jr. Magazine published 10 times/year for recreational through competition water skiers. Circ. 80,000. Pays on publication. Byline given. Buys all rights. Submit seasonal material 3 months in advance. Photocopied and previously published submissions OK. SASE. Reports in 2 weeks. Free sample copy; writer's guidelines for SASE.
Nonfiction: Expose; general interest on speed skiing, barefoot, kite flying, tubing, knee board skiing, slalom, tricks, jump and recreational); historical; nostalgia; profile (recreational skiers who do something unique in unusual locations or situations); travel (unique places worldwide, preferably in US); how-to (by experts); humor (short and long); personal experience (first-person motivational); and technical (from experienced person). Buys 1-2 mss/issue. Query with clips of previously published work. Pays $35-100 for short features on safety, how-to (500-1,500 words); $50-300 for longer features (3,000-4,500 words).
Photos: Reviews 35mm and larger transparencies. Offers no additional payment for photos accompanying ms. Captions and model release required. Buys all rights.

SURFER, Box 1028, Dana Point CA 92629. (714)496-5922. Editor: Paul Holmes. For teens and young adults. Slant is toward the contemporary, fast-moving and hard core enthusiasts in the sport of surfing. Monthly. Rights purchased vary with author and material. Pays on publication. Sample copy $2. Reports on submissions in 2 weeks. SASE.
Nonfiction: "We use anything about surfing if interesting and authoritative. Must be written from an expert's viewpoint. We're looking for good comprehensive articles on any surfing spot—especially surfing in faraway foreign lands." Length: preferrably not more than 2 pages typewritten. Pays 6-10¢/word.
Photos: Buys photos with mss or with captions only. Likes 8x10 glossy b&w proofsheets with negatives. Also uses expert color 35mm and 2¼x2¼ transparencies carefully wrapped. Pays $10-75 b&w; $25-125/35mm color transparency.

SWIMMING WORLD, 1130 Florence Ave., Inglewood CA 90301. (213)641-2727. Editor: Robert Ingram. 2% freelance written. For "competitors (10-24), plus their coaches, parents, and those who are involved in the enjoyment of the sport." Monthly. Circ. 40,000. Buys all rights. Byline given. Buys 10-12 mss/year. Pays on publication. Reports in 1-2 months. Query. SASE.
Nonfiction: Articles of interest to competitive swimmers, divers and water poloists, their parents and coaches. Can deal with diet, body conditioning or medicine, as applicable to competitive swimming. Nutrition and stroke and diving techniques. Psychology and profiles of athletes. Must be authoritative. Length: 1,500 words maximum. Pays $100 maximum.
Photos: Photos purchased with mss. Does not pay extra for photos with mss. 8x10 b&w only. Also photos with captions. Pays $50 maximum for b&w.

UNDERCURRENT, Box 1658, Sausalito CA 94965. (415)332-3684. Managing Editor: Ben Davison. 20-50% freelance written. Emphasizes scuba diving. Monthly consumer-oriented newsletter; 10 pages. Circ. 11,200. Pays on publication. Buys first rights. Pays $50 kill fee. Byline given. Simultaneous (if to other than diving publisher), photocopied and previously published submissions OK. SASE. Reports in 4-6 weeks. Free sample copy and writer's guidelines; mention *Writer's Market* in request.
Nonfiction: Equipment evaluation; how-to; general interest; new product; and travel review. Buys 2 mss/issue. Query. Length: 2,000 words maximum. Pays $50-250.
Fillers: Buys clippings and newsbreaks. Buys 20/year. Length: 25-500 words. Pays $5-20.

THE WATER SKIER, Box 191, Winter Haven FL 33880. (813)324-4341. Editor: Thomas C. Hardman. Official publication of the American Water Ski Association. 15% freelance written. Published 7 times/year. Circ. 21,000. Buys North American serial rights only. Byline given. Buys limited amount of freelance material. Pays on acceptance. Free sample copy. Reports on submissions within 10 days. SASE.
Nonfiction and Photos: Occasionally buys exceptionally offbeat, unusual text/photo features on the sport of water skiing. Pays $35 minimum.

Teen and Young Adult

The publications in this category are for young people aged 12 to 26. Publications aimed at 2- to 12-year-olds are classified in the Juvenile category. Publications for college alumni, students and friends are listed in College, University, and Alumni.

ALIVE FOR YOUNG TEENS, Christian Board of Publications, Box 179, St. Louis MO 63166. Editor: Mike Dixon. Ecumenical, mainline publication with a Protestant slant; aimed at young teens. "We especially appreciate submissions of useable quality from 12- 15-year-olds. Those in this age range should include their age with the submission. We appreciate use of humor that early adolescents would appreciate. Please keep the age group in mind." Sample copy 50¢.
Nonfiction: "Articles should concern interesting youth, church youth groups, projects and activities. There is little chance of our taking an article not accompanied by at least 3-4 captioned b&w photos." Length: 800-1,000 words. Pays 2¢/word; photos $3-5.
Fiction: "Give us fiction concerning characters in the *Alive for Young Teens* readers' age group (12-15), dealing with problems and situations peculiar to that group." Length: 100-1200 words. Pays 2¢/word. Uses 6-10 photos features/issue. Pays $5 maximum for photos.
Photos: Send photos with ms. Submit in batches. Pays $7-10 for b&w prints.
Poetry: Length: 20 lines maximum. Pays 25¢/line.
Fillers: Puzzles, riddles, tongue twisters and daffy definitions. Pays $10 maximum.

AMERICAN NEWSPAPER CARRIER, American Newspaper Boy Press, 915 Carolina Ave. NW, Winston-Salem NC 27101. Editor: Charles F. Moester. 10% freelance written. Buys all rights. Pays on acceptance. Will send list of requirements on request. Reports in 10 days. SASE.
Fiction: Uses a limited amount of short fiction, 1,500-2,000 words. "It is preferable, but not required, that the stories be written around newspaper carrier characters. Before writing this type of fiction for this market, the author should consult a newspaper circulation manager and learn something of the system under which the independent 'little merchant' route carriers operate generally the country over. Stories featuring carrier contests, prize awards, etc., are not acceptable. Humor and mystery are good. Stories are bought with the understanding that *American Newspaper Carrier* has the privilege of reprinting and supplying the material to other newspaper carrier publications in the US, and such permission should accompany all mss submitted." Pays $15 minimum.

THE BLACK COLLEGIAN, 1240 South Broad St., New Orleans LA 70125. (504)821-5694. Editor: Kalamu Ya Salaam. 40% freelance written. For black college students and recent graduates with an interest in black cultural awareness, sports, news, personalities, history, trends, current events and job opportunities. Published bimonthly during school year; 200 pages. Circ. 250,000. Rights purchased usually first North American serial rights. Byline given. Buys 25 mss/year. Pays on publication. Will send free sample copy to writer on request. Write for copy of guidelines for writers. Will consider photocopied and simultaneous submissions. Submit special material three months in advance of issue date (Careers in Electronics, August; Health, November; Engineering and Travel/Summer Programs, January; Science and Jobs, March; Women and Government, May). Returns rejected material in 1½ months. Query. SASE.
Nonfiction and Photos: Material on careers, sports, black history, news analysis. Articles on problems and opportunities confronting black college students and recent graduates. Informational, personal experience, profile, inspirational, humor, think pieces, travel. Length: 500-4500 words. Pays $25-350. B&w photos or color transparencies purchased with or without mss. 5x7 *and* 8x10 preferred. Pays $35/b&w; $50/color.

BOYS' LIFE, Boy Scouts of America, Magazine Division, National Office, Box 61030, Dallas/Fort Worth Airport, TX 75261. (214)659-2000. Editor: Robert Hood. Monthly magazine covering Boy Scout activities for "ages 8-18—Boy Scouts, Cub Scouts, and others of that age group." Circ. 1.5 million. Pays on publication. Byline given.
Nonfiction: "Almost all articles are assigned. We do not encourage unsolicited material."
Columns/Departments: Hobby How's (1-2 paragraphs on hobby tips). Buys 60 mss/year. Send complete ms. Pays $5 minimum.
Fillers: Jokes (Think and Grin—1-3 sentences). Pays $1 minimum.

BREAD, 6401 The Paseo, Kansas City MO 64131. Editor: Gary Sivewright. Christian leisure reading magazine for junior and senior high students, published by the Division of Christian Life,

Church of the Nazarene. Monthly. Pays on acceptance. Accepts simultaneous submissions. Buys first rights; sometimes second rights. Byline given. Free sample copy and editorial specifications sheet.

Nonfiction: Helpful articles in the area of developing the Christian life; first-person, "this is how I did it" stories about Christian witness. Length: up to 1,500 words. Articles must be theologically acceptable. Looking for fresh approach to basic themes. Also needs articles dealing with doctrinal subjects such as the Holy Spirit, written for the young reader. Pays 3¢/word for first rights and 2¢/word for second rights. Works 6 months ahead of publication.

Photos: 8x10 b&w glossy prints of teens in action. Payment is $15 and up. Also considers photo spreads and essays. Uses 1 color transparency/month for cover.

Fiction: "Adventure, school, and church-oriented. No sermonizing." Length: 1,500 words maximum. Pays 3¢/word for first rights and 2¢/word for second rights.

Tips: Send complete ms by mail for consideration. Reports in 6 weeks. SASE.

BUSINESS TODAY, Foundation for Student Communication, Inc., Aaron Burr Hall, Princeton NJ 08540. (609)921-1111. Editor: Timothy G. Ewing. Managing Editor: Markus Renschler. Emphasizes general business and political economy for college juniors and seniors at top colleges and universities. "Articles must be general enough for the non-business major, yet detailed enough for a very intelligent and inquisitive audience." Magazine published 3 times annually. Circ. 210,000. Pays on publication. Buys all rights. Submit seasonal material 3 months in advance. Simultaneous, photocopied and previously published submissions OK. SASE. Reports in 3 weeks on queries; in 6 weeks on mss. Sample copy $2; writer's guidelines with SASE.

Nonfiction: Expose (topics on general business, including government regulation, energy, multinationals, entrepreneurs and specific industries); historical (pertaining to business, such as history of a particular industry); interview (with toplevel corporate officers or government regulators); opinion (on general business); profile (on business figures that would interest college students); personal experience (on company employment or alternative economic systems). "No articles for business people on how to do their jobs effectively, or how to get jobs, choose careers, etc." Buys 1-5 mss/issue. Send complete ms or clips of previously published work. Length: 1,000-6,000 words. Pay depends on quality of article.

Photos: State availability of photos or send photos with ms. Pays $10 for glossy or lustre b&w prints or contact sheets. Pays $25 minimum for 35mm color transparencies or contact sheets. Captions preferred. Buys one-time rights.

Columns/Departments: "Usually 800-1,000 words, on any controversial, business-related topics." Buys 2 mss/issue. Send complete ms or clips of previously published work. Length: 600-1,200 words. Pays $25 minimum.

Tips: "Some typical material we are seeking from freelancers is: articles on Third World countries; articles on corporate support of the arts; and articles on credit cards for college students."

CAMPUS LIFE MAGAZINE, Youth for Christ International, Box 419, Wheaton IL 60187. Editor: Gregg Lewis. Managing Editor: Jim Long. Associate Editors: S. Rickly Christian, Verne Becker. For a readership of young adults, high school and college age. "Though our readership is largely Christian, *Campus Life* reflects the interests of all kids—music, bicycling, photography, cars and sports." Largely staff-written. "*Campus Life* is a Christian magazine that is *not* overtly religious. The indirect style is intended to create a safety zone with our readers and to reflect our philosophy that God is interested in all of life. Therefore, we publish message stories side by side with general interest, humor, etc." Monthly magazine. Circ. 250,000. Pays on acceptance. Buys one-time rights. Byline given. Submit seasonal/holiday material 4 months in advance. Simultaneous, photocopied and previously published submissions OK. SASE. Reports in 1 month. Sample copy $2; writer's guidelines for SASE.

Nonfiction: Contact: Margie Testin. Personal experiences; photo features; humor; short items—how-to, college or career, travel, etc. No "sappy, unbelievable anything. It has to be real and it has to be well-written." Query or submit complete manuscript. Length: 500-3,000 words. Pays $100-250.

Photos: S. Rickly Christian, photo editor. Pays $35 minimum/8x10 b&w glossy print; $65 minimum/color transparency; $200/cover photo. Buys one-time rights.

Fiction: Contact: Margie Testin. Stories about problems and experiences kids face. Sappy religious stories are not acceptable, though well-written first-person stories of changed lives are given careful consideration."

Tips: "Most manuscripts that miss us fail in the aspect of style. Sappy, simplistic religious stuff just won't go. Also lacking is good, quality writing. Most mss are very unprofessional. Study good writing and strive for excellence in expressing yourself. Then study *Campus Life* to get an understanding of our audience and style. But don't submit unless you have *at least* read the magazine."

CHRISTIAN ADVENTURER, Messenger Publishing House, Box 850, Joplin MO 64801. (417)624-7050. Editor-in-Chief: Roy M. Chappell, D.D. Managing Editor: Mrs. Rosmarie Foreman. A denominational Sunday School take-home paper for teens, 13-19. Quarterly; 104 pages. Circ. 3,500. Pays quarterly. Buys simultaneous, second serial (reprint) or one-time rights. Byline given. Submit seasonal/holiday material 1 year in advance. Photocopied and previously published submissions OK. SASE. Reports in 4-6 weeks. Sample copy 50¢. Free writer's guidelines with sample copy.
Nonfiction: Historical (related to great events in the history of the church); informational (explaining the meaning of a Bible passage or a Christian concept); inspirational; nostalgia; and personal experience. Buys 13-20 mss/issue. Send complete ms. Length: 500-1,000 words. Pays 1¢/word.
Photos: Photos purchased with accompanying ms. Pays $2 for any size b&w glossy prints.
Fiction: Adventure; historical; religious and romance. Buys 13-20 mss/issue. Length: 800-2,000 words. Pays 1¢/word.
Fillers: Puzzles (must be Bible-based and require no art). Buys 13-20 fillers/issue. Length: 200-500 words. Pays 1¢/word.

CHRISTIAN LIVING FOR SENIOR HIGHS, David C. Cook Publishing Co., 850 N. Grove, Elgin IL 60120. (312)741-2400. Editor: John Conaway. "A take-home paper used in senior high Sunday School classes. We encourage Christian teens to write to us." Quarterly magazine; 4 pages. Pays on acceptance. Buys all rights. Byline given. Phone queries OK. Reports in 3-5 weeks. SASE. Free sample copy and writer's guidelines.
Nonfiction: How-to (Sunday School youth projects); historical (with religious base); humor (from Christian perspective); inspirational and personality (nonpreachy); personal teen experience (Christian); poetry written by teens and photo feature (Christian subject). Buys 6 mss/issue. Submit complete ms. Length: 900-1,200 words. Pays $60-75; $30 for short pieces.
Fiction: Adventure (with religious theme); historical (with Christian perspective); humorous; mystery and religious. Buys 2 mss/issue. Submit complete ms. Length: 900-1,200 words. Pays $60-75. "No preachy experiences."
Photos: Sue Greer, Photo Editor. Photos purchased with or without accompanying ms or on assignment. Send contact sheet, prints or transparencies. Pays $20-35 for 8½x11 b&w photos; $50 minimum for color transparencies.

CIRCLE K MAGAZINE, 101 E. Erie St., Chicago IL 60611. Executive Editor: Greg Stanmar. "Our readership consists almost entirely of college students interested in the concept of voluntary service. They are politically and socially aware and have a wide range of interests." Published 5 times/year. Magazine; 16 pages. Circ. 14,500. Pays on acceptance. Normally buys first North American serial rights. Byline given. Submit seasonal/holiday material 6 months in advance. SASE. Reports in 4 weeks. Free sample copy and writer's guidelines.
Nonfiction: Informational (general interest articles on any area pertinent to concerned college students); travel (Ft. Worth, 1982; Atlanta, 1983); community concerns (volunteerism, youth, medical, underprivileged). No "first-person confessions or history." Buys 10-12 mss/year. Query or submit complete ms. Length: 1,500-2,500 words. Pays $100-175.
Photos: Purchased with accompanying ms. Captions required. Query. Total purchase price for ms includes payment for photos.
Tips: "Query must be typed," and should indicate "familiarity with the field and sources."

CO-ED, Scholastic Magazines, Inc., 50 W. 44th St., New York NY 10036. For girls and boys ages 13-18. Monthly. Buys all rights. Pays on acceptance. Send $1 for sample copy.
Fiction: "Stories dealing with problems of contemporary teenagers. (We prefer stories about older teenagers, 16, 17, 18 years old.) Emphasis on personal growth of one or more characters as they confront problems with friendships, dating, family, social prejudice. Suggested themes: finding identity, reconciling reality and fantasy, making appropriate life decisions. Although we do *not* want stories with a preachy, moralistic treatment, we do look for themes that can be a starting point for class discussion, since our magazine is used as a teaching tool in home economics classrooms. Try for well-rounded characters and strong, logical plots. Avoid stereotyped characters and clichéd, fluffy romances. If girls with conventional 'feminine' interests are portrayed, they should nonetheless be interesting, active and realistic people." Length: 3,000 words maximum. Pays $300 maximum.

CREEPY, Warren Publishing Co., 145 E. 32nd St., New York NY 10016. (212)683-6050. Editor: Chris Adames. Black and white comic book published 10 times/year for 15-year-old males. Pays on acceptance. Byline given. Buys all rights. Photocopied submissions OK. SASE. Reports in 2 months on queries. Free sample copy; writer's guidelines for business size SAE and 1 first class stamp.

Fiction: Adventure, horror and science fiction. No mummy or werewolf stories. "Scripts broken down into comic book format: pages, panels and balloons. Each story should be complete in one issue." Buys 36 mss/year. Submit fully panelized scripts; no plot outlines. Pays $25/printed page.

EERIE, Warren Publishing Co., 145 E. 32nd St., New York NY 10016. (212)683-6050. Editor: Chris Adames. Black and white comic book published 10 times/year for 15-year-old males. Pays on acceptance. Byline given. Buys all rights. Photocopied submissions OK. SASE. Reports in 2 months on queries. Free sample copy; writer's guidelines for business size SAE and 1 first class stamp.
Fiction: Adventure, horror and serials ("stories carry over from issue to issue"). Buys 36 mss/year. "Scripts broken down into comic book format: pages, panels and balloons. Each story should be an episode that could stand alone and carry over to the next issue." Pays $25/printed page.

18 ALMANAC, 13-30, 505 Market St., Knoxville TN 37902. (615)637-7621. Managing Editor: Don Akchin. Annual magazine for graduating high school seniors. Circ. 600,000. Pays on acceptance. Byline given. Offers 33⅓% kill fee. Buys first North American serial rights. Reports in 1 month on written queries; in 3 weeks on mss. Free sample copy with 9x12 SASE (30¢ postage); free writer's guidelines with SASE. March best time to query.
Nonfiction: "Typical topics are 'how to apply to colleges'; 'how to apply for financial aid'; 'coping with the campus'; 'how to apply for a job'; 'what the work world is like'; 'staying healthy'; and 'dealing with legal hassles.' " Query with clips of previously published work. Length: 1,000-2,500 words. Pays 10¢-20¢/word. "We want fact-filled articles to help students make decisions about their futures after high school. We primarily cover college careers and practical living. We use a conversational tone that is helpful, but not condescending. New angles on old topics are encouraged."
Photos: State availability of photos.
Tips: "We rarely accept unsolicited mss."

EVANGEL, Dept. of Christian Education, Free Methodist Headquarters, 901 College Ave., Winona Lake IN 46590. (219)267-7161. Editor: Vera Bethel. 100% freelance written. Audience is 65% female, 35% male; married, 25-31 years old, mostly city dwellers, high school graduates, mostly nonprofessional. Weekly magazine; 8 pages. Circ. 35,000. Pays on acceptance. Buys simultaneous, second serial (reprint) or one-time rights. Submit seasonal/holiday material 3 months in advance. Simultaneous and previously published submissions OK. SASE. Reports in 4 weeks. Free sample copy and writer's guidelines.
Nonfiction: Interview (with ordinary person who is doing something extraordinary in his community, in service to others); profile (of missionary or one from similar service profession who is contributing significantly to society); personal experience (finding a solution to a problem common to man; coping with handicapped child, for instance, or with a neighborhood problem. Story of how God-given strength or insight saved a situation). Buys 100 mss/year. Submit complete ms. Length: 300-1,000 words. Pays 2¢/word.
Photos: Purchased with accompanying ms. Captions required. Send prints. Pays $5-10 for 8x10 b&w glossy prints; $2 for snapshots.
Fiction: Religious themes dealing with contemporary issues dealt with from a Christian frame of reference. Story must "go somewhere." Buys 50 mss/year. Submit complete ms. Length: 1,200-1,800 words. Pays 2¢/word. SASE required.
Poetry: Free verse, haiku, light verse, traditional, religious. Buys 50/year. Limit submissions to batches of 5-6. Length: 4-24 lines. Pays 35¢/line. SASE required.
Tips: "Seasonal material will get a second look (won't be rejected so easily) because we get so little. Write an attention-grabbing lead, followed by a body of article that says something worthwhile. Relate the lead to some of the universal needs of the reader—promise in that lead to help the reader in some way. Remember that everybody is interested most in himself. Lack of SASE brands author as a nonprofessional; I seldom even bother to read the script. If the writer doesn't want the script back, it must have no value for me, either."

FACE-TO-FACE, 201 8th Ave. S., Nashville TN 37202. (615)749-6224. Editor: Eddie L. Robinson. For United Methodist young people, ages 15-18 inclusive. Published by the Curriculum Resources Committee of the General Board of Discipleship of The United Methodist Church. Quarterly magazine; 48 pages. Circ. 30,000. Rights purchased vary with author and material. Buys first North American serial rights or simultaneous rights. Byline given. Buys about 8 mss/year. Pays on acceptance. Submit Christmas, Easter and summertime material 8-9 months in advance. Reports in 1-2 months. SASE.
Nonfiction: "Our purpose is to speak to young persons' concerns about their faith, their purpose in life, their personal relationships, goals, and feelings. Articles and features (with photos) should be

subjects of major interest and concern to high school young people. These include home and family life, school, extracurricular activities, vocation, etc. Satires, lampoons, related to the themes of an issue are also used." Submit complete ms. Length: 2,500 words maximum. Pays 4¢/word.

Photos: Uses 8x10 b&w glossy prints with high impact and good contrast. Pays $15 for one-time use of b&w. "We buy stock photos and those especially taken to illustrate articles."

Fiction: Must deal with major problems and concerns of older teens, such as finding one's own identity, dealing with family and peer-group pressures, and so forth. No straight moral fiction or stories with pat answers or easy solutions used. Story must fit themes of issue. No serials. Submit complete ms. Length: 2,500-3,000 words. Pays 4¢/word.

Poetry: Related to the theme of an issue. Free verse, blank verse, traditional and avant-garde forms. Length: 10-150 lines. Pays 50¢/line.

4-H TEEN, National 4-H Council, 7100 Connecticut Ave., Washington DC 20015. (301)656-9000. Editor: Suzanne C. Harting. Managing Editor: Larry L. Krug. Supplement to *National 4-H News*. Published 5 times/year. Covers readership and personal development for older 4-H members, ages 15-19. Estab. 1980. Circ. 225,000. Pays on acceptance. Byline given. Pays negotiable kill fee. Not copyrighted. Buys first North American serial rights and one-time rights. Submit seasonal/holiday material 1 year in advance. Simultaneous queries, and simultaneous and photocopied submissions OK. SASE. Reports in 1 month. Free sample copy and writer's guidelines.

Nonfiction: How-to (crafts); interview/profile (of 4-H alumni and personalities of interest to teens); personal experience (4-H related); educational philosophy; psychology; and consumer education pertaining to a teen audience. No poetry or humor. Buys 20 mss/year. Query with clips of published work. Length: 300-1,200 words. Pays $100 maximum.

Photos: State availability of photos. Reviews contact sheets, 35mm transparencies, and 5x7 or larger prints. Pays negotiable fee (minimum $25). Model release and identification of subjects required. Buys one-time rights.

Columns/Departments: A Look at the Job Scene (career education and exploration; specific occupations—employment outlook, working conditions, earnings, etc.); and Buy Wise (consumerism for teens). Buys 5-10 mss/year. Query with clips of published work. Length: 400-1,000 words. Pays $100 maximum.

Tips: "We are a special-interest publication, seeking writers familiar with the 4-H program, or experienced in working with older teenagers. Write from personal experience in an informal style."

FREEWAY, Scripture Press, Box 513, Glen Ellyn IL 60137. Publication Editor: John Duckworth. For "young adults of high school and college age." Weekly. Circ. 70,000. Prefers either first rights or all rights, "but passes along reprint fees on all rights material to author, when material is picked up after publication." Buys 100 mss/year. Byline given. Free sample copy and writer's guidelines. No photocopied submissions. Reports on material accepted for publication in 4-6 weeks. Returns rejected material in 2-3 weeks. Query or submit complete ms. "Define narrowly the topic you intend to tackle; tell us why you're qualified to write about it (education or personal experience); describe the Christian message you'll get across; and show us what kind of writer you are (brief resume and/or sample of related work)." SASE.

Nonfiction and Photos: "Mostly person-centered nonfiction with photos. Subject must have had specific encounter with Christ. Direct tie-in to faith in Christ. No simply religious or moral stories; subjects must be specifically Christ-centered. No "singsongy poetry, fiction with unreal characters or plots that depend on unlikely events, stories that promote organizations instead of individuals, material with no Christian message, anything that preaches, or anything too young or old for our readers." Christian message must be woven naturally into a good, true, dramatic, human interest story. Current interest is in sports, social problems (teen alcoholism) and battles by Christians against grief, tragedy, loneliness, etc." Thought articles on Biblical themes. Study *FreeWay*. Send for our guidelines and sample copy. Then try a 1,200- to 1,500-word true experience (first-person) about how God has changed the life of someone who will appeal to young people (preferably a young person age 15-25). This could be the story of how the subject received Christ as Saviour or later matured as a Christian through a crisis. Don't just tell the story, show it through anecdotes. And, if at all possible, send good, relevant, b&w photos that illuminate your manuscript. Length: 500-1,500 words. Pays $25-120. Pays $5-30 for 5x7 and 8x10 b&w photos.

Fiction: Same themes, lengths and rate of payment as nonfiction.

GRADUATE, 13-30 Corp., 505 Market St., Knoxville TN 37902. (615)637-7621. Managing Editor: Don Akchin. Annual magazine for graduating college seniors about life after college. Circ. 450,000. Pays on acceptance. Byline given. Offers 33⅓% kill fee. Buys first North American serial rights. SASE. Reports in 1 month on written queries; in 3 weeks on mss. Free sample copy with 9x12 SASE (30¢ postage); free writer's guidelines with SASE. July-August best time to query.

Nonfiction: General interest (careers, job hunting, practical living, travel, working life, and graduate and professional programs); interview; and personal experience (emotional and practical adjustments that graduates must make on the job, in a new city and with life goals). "We look for informative overviews of career prospects and lifestyle concerns packed with plenty of expert advice ideas and sources. We want unique angles on the job hunting/job interviewing process and on graduate and professional schools. We like a conversational tone and usable information." Query with clips of previously published work. Length: 1,000-4,000 words. Pays 10¢-20¢/word.
Photos: State availability of photos.

GROUP, Thom Schultz Publications, Box 481, Loveland CO 80537. (303)669-3836. Editor-in-Chief: Thom Schultz. 60% freelance written. For members and leaders of high-school-age Christian youth groups; average age 16. Magazine published 8 times/year; 48 pages. Circ. 40,000. Pays on publication. Buys all rights. Byline given. Phone queries OK. Submit seasonal/holiday material 5 months in advance. Special Easter, Thanksgiving and Christmas issues and college issues. Simultaneous, photocopied and previously published submissions OK. SASE. Reports in 3-4 weeks. Sample copy $1; writer's guidelines for SASE.
Nonfiction: How-to (fund-raising, membership-building, worship, games, discussions, activities, crowd breakers, simulation games); informational; (drama, worship, service projects); inspirational (issues facing young people today); interview and photo feature (group activities). Buys 3 mss/issue. Query. Length: 500-1,500 words. Pays $25-100.
Photos: Photos purchased with or without accompanying ms or on assignment. Captions required. Pays $15 minimum for 8x10 b&w glossy prints, $30 minimum for 35mm color transparencies.
Columns/Departments: Try This One (short ideas for games; crowd breakers, discussions, worships, fund raisers, service projects, etc.). Buys 6 mss/issue. Send complete ms. Length: 500 words maximum. Pays $10.

GUIDE, 6856 Eastern Ave., NW, Washington DC 20012. (202)723-3700. Editor: Lowell Litten. 90% freelance written. A Seventh-Day Adventist journal for junior youth and early teens. "Its content reflects Seventh-Day Adventist beliefs and standards. Another characteristic which probably distinguishes it from many other magazines is the fact that all its stories are nonfiction." Weekly magazine; 32 pages. Circ. 60,000. Buys first serial rights. Byline given. Buys about 350 mss/year. Pays on acceptance. Reports in 6 weeks. SASE.
Nonfiction and Poetry: Wants articles and nonfiction stories of character-building and spiritual value. All stories must be true and include dialogue. Should emphasize the positive aspects of living—faithfulness, obedience to parents, perseverance, kindness, gratitude, courtesy, etc. "We do not use stories of hunting, fishing, trapping or spiritualism." Send complete ms (include word count). Length: 1,500-2,500 words. Pays 2-4¢/word. Also buys serialized true stories. Length: 10 chapters. Buys traditional forms of poetry; also some free verse. Length: 4-16 lines. Pays 50¢-$1/line.

HI-CALL, Gospel Publishing House, 1445 Boonville Ave., Springfield MO 65802. (417)862-2781, ext. 1207. Editor-in-Chief: Dr. Charles W. Ford. Youth Editor: Ed Wright. Sunday School take-home paper for church-oriented teenagers, 12-17. Weekly magazine; 8 pages. Circ. 160,000. Pays on acceptance. Buys first and reprint rights. Submit seasonal/holiday material 12 months in advance. Simultaneous and previously published submissions OK. SASE. Reports in 3 weeks. Free sample copy and writer's guidelines.
Nonfiction: Historical; humor; informational; inspirational; and personal experience. "All pieces should stress Christian principles for everyday living." Buys 125-150 mss/year. Send complete ms. Length: 500-1,000 words. Pays 2-3¢/word.
Photos: Photos purchased with or without accompanying ms. Pays $20-25/8x10 b&w glossy print; $20-35/35mm or 4x5 color transparency.
Fiction: Adventure (strong Biblical emphasis, but not preachy); humorous; mystery; religious; romance; suspense; and western. Buys 130 mss/year. Send complete ms. Length: 500-1,800 words. Pays 2-3¢/word.

HIS, 5206 Main St., Downers Grove IL 60515. (312)964-5700. Editor: Linda Doll. Issued monthly from October-June for collegiate students, faculty, administrators and graduate students interested in the evangelical Christian persuasion. "It is an interdenominational, Biblical presentation, combining insights on Scripture and everyday life on campus." Buys first rights. Pays on acceptance. Reports in 3 months. SASE.
Nonfiction and Fiction: "Articles dealing with practical aspects of Christian living on campus, relating contemporary issues to Biblical principles. Should show relationship between Christianity and various fields of study, Christian doctrine, or missions." Submit complete ms. Length: 2,000 words maximum. Pays $35-70.

Poetry: Pays $10-20.
Tips: "Direct your principles and illustrations at the college milieu. Avoid preachiness; share your insights on a peer basis."

IN TOUCH, Wesleyan Publishing House, Box 2000, Marion IN 46952. For teens, ages 13-18. Weekly. Special issues for all religious and national holidays. Not copyrighted. Byline given. Pays on acceptance. Queries discouraged. Submit holiday/seasonal material 9 months in advance. SASE. Reports in 6 weeks. Free sample copy.
Nonfiction: Features of youth involvement in religious and social activity; true life incidents and articles on Christian growth. Avoid implied approval of liquor, tobacco, theaters, and dancing. Length: 1,500-1,800 words. Pays 2¢/word.
Fiction: Stories with definite Christian emphasis and character-building values, without being preachy. Setting, plot and action should be realistic. Length: 1,200-1,600 words. Pays 2¢/word.
Photos: Portraying action or the teenage world, or with seasonal emphasis. Pays $15-20 for 5x7 or 8x11 b&w glossy prints.

KEYNOTER MAGAZINE, 101 E. Erie St., Chicago IL 60611. (312)943-2300, ext. 274. Executive Editor: David Dee. 50% freelance written. An organizational publication of Key Club International. For a high school audience, male and female, 15 to 18, members of Key Club, a Kiwanis International sponsored youth organization; service-oriented. Published 7 times/year; magazine, 16 pages. Circ. 100,000. Buys about 20 mss/year. Pays on acceptance. Free sample copy and writer's guidelines. Prompt reports on material accepted for publication. Returns rejected material in about a month. Query. SASE.
Nonfiction and Photos: "Topical material directed to mature, service-oriented teenagers. Our readers are intelligent school leaders; write to them, not down to them. We're looking for fresh approaches to contemporary social problems and problems that directly affect the teenager's life. Also interested in self-help and consumer features. Recently published articles include 'Abusive parents: getting away with murder,' 'Tuning out the TV habit,' 'Teen volunteers learn by doing,' and 'Teen suicide: Can we stop the killing?' Study sample and guidelines. For the year ahead we especially need stories that show teens ways they can be a positive influence on junior high and younger age students." Pays $175 maximum.
Tips: "While we receive many more manuscripts than we can buy, writers should realize that at least 90% should not have been sent to the *Keynoter* in the first place. A writer who has an idea we can use has every opportunity of getting published. We work closely with writers."

LIGHT 'n' HEAVY, 1445 Boonville Ave., Springfield MO 65802. Editor: Carol A. Ball. Quarterly publication for Assemblies of God high school teens. Purpose is to provide spiritual nurture for Assemblies of God youth, to supply information regarding youth activities, and to promote the ministries of the National Youth Department of the Assemblies of God. Buys some first rights, but "we are interested in multiple submissions, second rights and other reprints." Pays on acceptance. Will send a free sample copy to a writer on request. Reports in 6 weeks. SASE.
Nonfiction, Photos and Poetry: "We can use b&w photos of teen-related subjects, biographical features, reports on outstanding Christian youth, some poems, humor, news, motivational articles, and personal experiences. Avoid cliches, unexplained theological terms, sermonizing, and 'talking down' to youth." Length of articles: 300-1,000 words. Payment is 1½-5¢ word; poetry is minimum $5 or 20¢/line.

LIVE, 1445 Boonville Ave., Springfield MO 65802. (417)862-2781. Editor: Kenneth D. Barney. 100% freelance written. For adults in Assemblies of God Sunday Schools. Weekly. Circ. 225,000. Not copyrighted. Buys about 100 mss/year. Pays on acceptance. Free sample copy and writer's guidelines. Submit seasonal material 10 months in advance. Reports on material within 6 weeks. SASE.
Nonfiction and Photos: "Articles with reader appeal, emphasizing some phase of Christian living, presented in a down-to-earth manner. Biography or missionary material using fiction techniques. Historical, scientific or nature material with a spiritual lesson. Be accurate in detail and factual material. Writing for Christian publications is a ministry. The spiritual emphasis must be an integral part of your material." Length: 1,000 words maximum. Pays 3¢/word for first rights; 2¢/word for second rights, according to the value of the material and the amount of editorial work necessary. Color photos or transparencies purchased with mss, or on assignment. Pay open.
Fiction: "Present believable characters working out their problems according to Bible principles; in other words, present Christianity in action, without being preachy. We use very few serials, but we will consider 4- to 6-part stories if each part conforms to average word length for short stories. Each part must contain a spiritual emphasis and have enough suspense to carry the reader's interest from one week to the next. Stories should be true to life, but not what we would feel is bad

to set before the reader as a pattern for living. Stories should not put parents, teachers, ministers or other Christian workers in a bad light. Setting, plot and action should be realistic, with strong motivation. Characterize so that the people will live in your story. Construct your plot carefully so that each incident moves naturally and sensibly toward crisis and conclusion. An element of conflict is necessary in fiction. Short stories should be written from one viewpoint only. We do not accept fiction based on incidents in the Bible." Length: 1,200-2,000 words. Pays 3¢/word for first rights; 2¢/word for second rights.

Poetry: Buys traditional, free and blank verse. Length: 12-20 lines. "Please do not send large numbers of poems at one time." Pays 20¢/line, for first rights.

Fillers: Brief, purposeful, usually containing an anecdote, and always with a strong evangelical emphasis.

THE MODERN WOODMEN, 1701 1st Ave., Rock Island IL 61201. (309)786-6481. Editor: Robert E. Frank. For members of Modern Woodmen of America, a fraternal insurance society. Quarterly magazine; 24 pages. Circ. 325,000. Not copyrighted. Pays on acceptance. Sample copy and writer's guidelines for SASE. Photocopied and simultaneous submissions OK. Reports in 3-4 weeks. SASE.

Nonfiction: "Nonfiction may be either for children or adults. Fiction should be slanted toward children up to age 16. Our audience is broad and diverse. We want clear, educational, inspirational articles for children and young people. We don't want religious material, teen romances, teen adventure stories." Buys informational, how-to, historical, and technical articles. Submit complete ms. Length: 1,500-2,000 words. Pays $40 minimum depending on quality.

Photos: B&w photos purchased with ms. Captions optional. Prefers vertical, b&w glossy photos for cover use. Payment varies with quality and need.

Fiction: Mainstream and historical fiction. Length: 1,500-2,500 words. Pays $40. No poetry.

NUTSHELL, 13-30 Corp., 505 Market St., Knoxville TN 37902. (615)637-7621. Managing Editor: Don Akchin. Annual magazine covering all facets of the college experience, from academics, health, financial aid, career training, to entertainment, sports and fashion. The audience is college students, ages 18-22. Circ. 1.25 million. Pays on acceptance. Byline given. Offers 33% kill fee. Buys first North American serial rights. Simultaneous and photocopied submissions OK if so indicated. SASE. "We welcome written queries from college journalists and recent graduates. Be sure to submit ideas that have national application and enclose clips." Reports in 3 weeks. Free sample copy with 9x12 SASE; free writer's guidelines with SASE. January best time to query.

Nonfiction: "Recent articles have explored the future prospects for careers in space industries; highlighted the most unique campus festivals from coast to coast; examined the new boom in student businesses and followed a day in the life of a college dance major. We also use how-to articles that relate to the problems and experiences of college students, from learning how to study more efficiently to handling health or emotional problems." Query with clips of previously published work. Length: 1,500-3,500 words. Pays 10¢-20¢/word.

Photos: State availability of photos.

Columns/Departments: Campus Chronicle (100-500 words on activities taking place on campus and items of special interest to a college audience such as campus pranks; the increasing popularity of war games among college students; and term paper mills); major features (1,000-3,000 words dealing with wide-ranging campus trends, or providing information of special use to students such as upcoming films; current efforts to raise the drinking age; a first person account of a computer dating experience and series of profiles of student cartoonists). Pays 10¢-20¢/word.

PROBE, Baptist Brotherhood Commission, 1548 Poplar Ave., Memphis TN 38104. (901)272-2461. Editor-in-Chief: James B. Johnson. 5% freelance written. For "boys age 12-17 who are members of a missions organization in Southern Baptist churches." Monthly magazine; 32 pages. Circ. 48,000. Byline given. Pays on acceptance. Buys one-time rights. Phone queries OK. Submit seasonal/holiday material 6 months in advance. Simultaneous submissions OK. SASE. Reports in 1 month. Free sample copy and writer's guidelines.

Nonfiction: How-to (crafts, hobbies); informational (youth, religious especially); inspirational (personalities); personal experience (any first-person by teenagers—especially religious); photo feature (sports, teen subjects). Submit complete ms. Length: 500-1,500 words. Pays 3¢/word.

Photos: Purchased with accompanying ms or on assignment. Captions required. Query. Pays $10 for 8x10 b&w glossy prints.

REFLECTION, Pioneer Ministries, Inc., Box 788, Wheaton IL 60187. Editor: Lora Beth Norton. Assistant Editor: Lorraine Mulligan. 50% freelance written. Emphasizes the development of a Christian life-style for the teenage girl in today's world. Bimonthly magazine; 32 pages. Circ. 10,000. Pays on acceptance. Buys first, second or simultaneous rights. Submit seasonal/holiday

material 6 months in advance. Simultaneous and previously published submissions OK. SASE. Reports in 4-8 weeks. Sample copy and writer's guidelines $1.50. Submit complete manuscripts.
Nonfiction: How-to (crafts geared especially to teenage girls); humor; inspirational; biography; and personal experience. No nature articles. Buys 6 mss/issue. Length: 800-1,500 words. Pays $20-35.
Fiction: Adventure; fantasy; historical; humorous; mystery; religious; romance; and suspense. Length: 900-1,500 words. Pays $20-35.
Fillers: Jokes, puzzles. Buys 12/year. Submit complete ms. Pays $5-15.

SCHOLASTIC SCOPE, Scholastic Magazines, Inc., 50 W. 44th St., New York NY 10036. Editor: Katherine Robinson. Circ. 1,100,000. Buys all rights. Byline given. Issued weekly. 4-6th grade reading level; 15-18 age level. Reports in 4-6 weeks. SASE.
Nonfiction and Photos: Articles with photos about teenagers who have accomplished something against great odds, overcome obstacles, performed heroically, or simply done something out of the ordinary. Prefers articles about people outside New York area. Length: 400-1,200 words. Pays $125 and up.
Fiction and Drama: Problems of contemporary teenagers (drugs, prejudice, runaways, failure in school, family problems, etc.); relationships between people (interracial, adult-teenage, employer-employee, etc.) in family, job, and school situations. Strive for directness, realism, and action, perhaps carried through dialogue rather than exposition. Try for depth of characterization in at least one character. Avoid too many coincidences and random happenings. Although action stories are wanted, it's not a market for crime fiction. Looking for material about American Indian, Chicano, Mexican-American, Puerto Rican, and black experiences, among others. Occasionally uses mysteries and science fiction. Length: 400-1,200 words. Uses plays up to 3,000 words. Pays $150 minimum.

SEVENTEEN, 850 3rd Ave., New York NY 10022. Executive Editor: Ray Robinson. Monthly. Circ. 1,500,000. Buys first rights for nonfiction, features and poetry. Buys first rights on fiction. Pays 25% kill fee. Byline given. Pays on acceptance. SASE.
Nonfiction and Photos: Articles and features of general interest to young women who are concerned with the development of their own lives and the problems of the world around them; strong emphasis on topicality and helpfulness. Send brief outline and query, including a typical lead paragraph, summing up basic idea of article. Also like to receive articles and features on speculation. Length: 2,000-3,000 words. Pays $50-500 for articles written by teenagers but more to established adult freelancers. Articles are commissioned after outlines are submitted and approved. Fees for commissioned articles generally range from $350-1,500. Photos usually by assignment only. Tamara Schneider, art director.
Fiction: Cathy Winters, fiction editor. Top-quality stories featuring teenagers—the problems, concerns and preoccupations of adolescence, which will have recognition and identification value for readers. Does not want "typical teenage" stories, but high literary quality. Avoid oversophisticated material; unhappy endings acceptable if emotional impact is sufficient. Humorous stories that do not condescend to or caricature young people are welcome. Best lengths are 2,500-3,000 words. "We publish a novelette every July (not to exceed 30 doubled-spaced manuscript pages)—sometimes with a suspenseful plot." Pays $50-500. Conducts an annual short story contest.
Poetry: By teenagers only. Pays $5-25. Submissions are nonreturnable unless accompanied by SASE.
Tips: "The best way for beginning teenage writers to crack the *Seventeen* lineup is for them to contribute suggestions and short pieces to the Free-For-All column, a literary format which lends itself to just about every kind of writing: profiles, puzzles, essays, exposes, reportage, and book reviews."

SPRINT, 850 N. Grove, Elgin IL 60120. (312)741-2400. Editor: Kristine Miller Tomasik. For junior high school age students who attend Sunday School. Weekly. Buys all rights. Buys 20-30 mss/year. Pays on acceptance. Free sample copy and writer's guidelines. SASE. Rarely considers photocopied or simultaneous submissions. Submit seasonal material for Christmas, Easter and Thanksgiving issues 1 year in advance. Reports in 3 months.
Nonfiction: Wants "very short, catchy articles (800-1,000 words) reporting on teen involvement in church/community projects; interviewing outstanding teens, or personalities and emotional needs of teens; etc. We are using the photo feature format increasingly to treat these topics." All mss should present a Christian approach to life. Query first for nonfiction. Pays $65-75.
Fiction: "Fiction must be believable, with realistic characters and dialogue. If your sole purpose in writing is to preach, please don't send your story to us." Stories should be 1,000-2,000 words. Pays $65-75. Submit only complete manuscripts for fiction and poetry. SASE.
Photos: Photo editor: Christine Pearson. Photos purchased with or without mss on assignment.

Captions optional. Pays $20 for b&w glossy prints. Pays $50 for color transparencies. Color photos rarely used.

STARTING LINE, Starting Line Publications, Box 878, Reseda CA 91335. (213)345-3769. Editor/ Publisher: Max Zucker. Quarterly magazine covering sports for youngsters under age 18 who participate in active sports. Circ. 8,000. Pays on publication. Byline given. Buys first North American serial rights. Submit seasonal/holiday material 6 months in advance. Previously published submissions OK "if from non-competing publication." Reports in 1 week (August-May); in 1 month (summer); "if query is of interest to us." Free sample copy.
Nonfiction: "Well-researched articles written for young people, coaches and teachers, and pertaining to running and other physically active sports. We like to have illustrations, charts or photos to use as a basis for our art department to create graphics." Buys 8-12 mss/year. Query with clips of published work and brief bio. Length: 200-2,000 words. Pays $100 minimum.
Photos: Send photos with ms "to be used as basis for graphics. Would pay about $10 extra."
Tips: "We're looking for a few writers whom we can depend on from issue to issue."

STRAIGHT, Standard Publishing Co., 8121 Hamilton Ave., Cincinnati OH 45231. (513)931-4050. Editor: Dawn Brettschneider. "Teens, age 12-19, from Christian backgrounds generally receive this publication in their Sunday School classes or through subscriptions." Weekly (published quarterly) magazine; 12 pages. Pays on acceptance. Buys all rights, or second serial (reprint) rights. Byline given. Submit seasonal/holiday material 1 year in advance. Reports in 3-6 weeks. Free sample copy; writer's guidelines with SASE. Include Social Security number on ms. SASE.
Nonfiction: Religious-oriented topics, general interest, humor, inspirational, interview (religious leaders, Christian teens, musicians); personal experience. "We want articles that promote Christian ethics and ideals." No puzzles. Query or submit complete ms. Length: 800-1,100 words. Pays 2¢/word.
Fiction: Adventure, historical, humorous, religious and suspense. "All fiction should have some message for the modern Christian teen." Fiction should deal with all subjects in a forthright manner, without being preachy and without talking down to teens. No tasteless manuscripts that promote anything adverse to Bible's teachings. Submit complete ms. Length: 1,000-2,000 words. Pays 2¢/word; less for reprints.
Photos: May submit photos with ms. Pays $10-20 for 8x10 b&w glossy prints. Captions required; model release should be available. Buys one-time rights.
Tips: "Don't be trite. Use unusual settings or problems. Use a lot of illustrations, a good balance of conversation, narration, and action. Style must be clear, fresh—no sermonettes or sicky-sweet fiction. Take a realistic approach to problems. Be willing to submit to editorial policies on doctrine; knowledge of the *Bible* a must. Also, be aware of teens today, and what they do. Language, clothing, and activities included in mss should be contemporary."

THE STUDENT, 127 9th Ave. N., Nashville TN 37234. Editor: W. Howard Bramlette. Publication of National Student Ministries of the Southern Baptist Convention. For college students; focusing on freshman and sophomore level. Published 12 times during the school year. Circ. 25,000. Buys all rights. Payment on acceptance. Mss should be double spaced on white paper with 70-space line, 25 lines/page. Prefers complete ms rather than query. Reports usually in 6 weeks. SASE. Free sample copy.
Nonfiction: Contemporary questions, problems, and issues facing college students viewed from a Christian perspective: the need to develop high moral and ethical values. The struggle for integrity in self-concept and the need to cultivate interpersonal relationships directed by Christian love. Length: 800-1,000 words. Length: 1,100 words maximum. Pays 3½¢/word after editing with reserved right to edit accepted material.
Fiction: Satire and parody on college life, humorous episodes; emphasize clean fun and the ability to grow and be uplifted through humor. Contemporary fiction involving student life, on campus as well as off. Length: 1,000-1,500 words. Pays 3½¢/word.

TEEN MAGAZINE, 8490 Sunset Blvd., Hollywood CA 90069. Editor: Roxanne Camron. For teenage girls. Monthly magazine; 100 pages. Circ. 1,000,000. Buys all rights. Predominantly staff-written. Freelance purchases are limited. Reports in 6-8 weeks. SASE.
Fiction: Stories up to 3,500 words dealing specifically with teenagers and contemporary teen issues. More fiction on emerging alternatives for young women. Suspense, humorous and romance. No prom or cheerleader stories. "Young love is all right, but teens want to read about it in more relevant settings." Length: 2,000-3,000 words. Pays $100.

TEENS TODAY, Church of the Nazarene, 6401 The Paseo, Kansas City MO 64131. (816)333-7000. Managing Editor: Gary Sivewright. 80% freelance written. For junior and senior high teens, to age 18, attending Church of the Nazarene Sunday School. Weekly magazine; 8 pages. Circ. 70,000. Pays on acceptance. Buys all rights. Byline given. Submit seasonal/holiday material 10 months in advance. Simultaneous, photocopied and previously published submissions OK. SASE. Reports in 6-8 weeks. Free sample copy and writer's guidelines upon request.

Nonfiction: How-to (mature and be a better person in Christian life); humor (cartoons); personal experience; and photo feature. Buys 1 ms/issue. Send complete ms. Length: 500-1,500 words. Pays $10-30.

Photos: Photos purchased with or without accompanying ms or on assignment. Pays $10-25 for 8x10 b&w glossy prints. Additional payment for photos accepted with accompanying ms. Model release required.

Fiction: Adventure (if Christian principles are apparent); humorous; religious; and romance (keep it clean). Buys 1 ms/issue. Send complete ms. Length: 1,500-2,500 words. Pays 3¢/word.

Poetry: Free verse; haiku; light verse; and traditional. Buys 15 poems/year. Pays 20-25¢/line.

Fillers: Puzzles (religious). Buys 15 fillers/year. Pays $5-10.

Tips: "We're looking for quality nonfiction dealing with teen issues: peers, self, parents, vocation, Christian truths related to life, etc. Would also like to see more biographical sketches of outstanding Christians."

TIGER BEAT MAGAZINE, Laufer Publishing, 7060 Hollywood Blvd., #800, Hollywood CA 90028. (213)467-3111. Editoral Director: Sharon Lee. Editor: Kerry Laufer. For young teenage girls and subteens. Median age: 13. Monthly magazine; 100 pages. Circ. 700,000. Buys all rights. Buys 10 mss/year. Pays on acceptance.

Nonfiction: Stories about young entertainers; their lives, what they do, their interests. Quality writing expected, but must be written with the 12-16 age group in mind. Length: depends on feature. Pays $50-100.

Photos: Pays $15 for b&w photos used with mss: captions optional. $50 for color used inside; $75 for cover. 35mm transparencies preferred.

Tips: "We're mostly staff-written; a freelancer's best bet is to come up with something original and exclusive that the staff couldn't do or get."

TIGER BEAT STAR, Laufer Publishing, 7060 Hollywood Blvd., #800, Hollywood CA 90028. (213)467-3111. Editor: Doreen Lioy. Associate Editor: Debi Fee. Bimonthly teenage fan magazine for young adults interested in movie, TV and recording stars. "It differs from other teenage fan magazines in that we feature many soap opera stars as well as the regular teenage TV, movie and music stars." Circ. 400,000. Average issue includes 20 feature interviews, gossip columns and fashion and beauty columns. Pays on acceptance. No byline given. Offers 50% kill fee. Buys first North American serial rights. Submit seasonal material 10 weeks in advance. Previously published submissions OK, if so indicated. SASE. Reports in 2 weeks.

Nonfiction: Interview (of movie, TV and recording stars). Buys 1-2 mss/issue. Query with clips of previously published work. "Write a good query indicating your contact with the star. Investigative pieces are preferred." Length: 200-400 words. Pays $75-200.

Photos: State availability of photos. Pays $15 minimum for 5x7 and 8x10 b&w glossy prints. Pays $35 minimum for 35mm and 2¼ color transparencies. Captions and model release required. Buys all rights.

Fillers: Anecdotes and celebrity oriented newsbreaks. Buys 5 mss/issue. Length: 100 words minimum. Pays $25 minimum.

Tips: "Be aware of our readership (teenage girls, generally ages 9-17), be 'up' on the current TV, movie and music stars, and be aware of our magazine's unique writing style (it's not geared down *too* far for the young readers or we lose attention of older girls)."

VENTURE MAGAZINE, Box 150, Wheaton IL 60187. Editor: Michael J. Chiapperino. 50-70% freelance written. Publication of Christian Service Brigade. For young men 12-18 years of age. Most participate in a Christian Service Brigade program. Monthly magazine. Circ. 22,000. Published 8 times/year. Buys first rights on unsolicited material. Buys 1-3 mss/issue. Pays on publication. Submit seasonal material 7 months in advance. Usually reports in 2-3 weeks. Query. SASE. Sample copy $1; writer's guidelines for SASE.

Nonfiction: "Family-based articles from boys' perspective; family problems, possible solutions. Interested in photo features on innovative teenage boys who do unusual things, also true-story adventures. Assigned articles deal with specific monthly themes decided by the editorial staff. Most material has an emphasis on boys in a Christian setting. No trite 'Sunday school' mss." Length: 400-1,200 words. Pays $50-100.

Photos: No additional payment is made for 8x10 b&w photos used with mss. Pays $25 for those purchased on assignment; $50-75 for b&w cover photos of boys.

Fiction: "Action-packed, suspense thrillers with Christian theme or lesson. No far-out plots or trite themes/settings." Length 1,000-1,800 words. Pays $50-100.

WORKING FOR BOYS, Box A, Danvers MA 01923. Editor: Brother Alphonsus Dwyer, C.F.X. 37% freelance written. For junior high, parents, grandparents (the latter because the magazine goes back to 1884). Quarterly magazine; 28 pages. Circ. 16,000. Not copyrighted. Buys 30 mss/year. Pays on acceptance. Submit special material (Christmas, Easter, sports, vacation time) 6 months in advance. Reports in 1 week. Submit only complete ms. Address all mss to the Associate Editor, Brother Alois, CFX, St. John's High School, Main St., Shrewsbury MA 01545. SASE. Free sample copy.
Nonfiction: "Conservative, not necessarily religious, articles. Seasonal mostly (Christmas, Easter, etc.). Cheerful, successful outlook suitable for early teenagers. Maybe we are on the 'square' side, favoring the traditional regarding youth manners: generosity to others, respect for older people, patriotism, etc. Animal articles and tales are numerous, but an occasional good dog or horse story is okay. We like to cover seasonal sports." Buys informational, how-to, personal experience, historical and travel. Length: 800-1,200 words. Pays 4¢/word.
Photos: 6x6 b&w glossy prints purchased with ms for $10 each.
Fiction: "Fiction should be wholesome and conservative." Mainstream, adventure, religious, and historical fiction. Theme: open. Length: 500-1,000 words. Pays 4¢/word.
Poetry: Length: 24 lines maximum. Pays 40¢/line.

YOUNG AMBASSADOR, The Good News Broadcasting Association, Inc., Box 82808, Lincoln NE 68501. (402)474-4567. Editor-in-Chief: Melvin A. Jones. Managing Editor: James D. Wallace. Emphasizes Christian living for church-oriented teens, 12-16. Monthly magazine. Circ. 80,000. Buys second serial (reprint) and first North American serial rights. Byline given. Phone queries OK. Submit seasonal/holiday material at least 6 months in advance. Previously published submissions OK. SASE. Reports in 6 weeks. Free sample copy and writer's guidelines.
Nonfiction: James D. Wallace, managing editor. How-to (church youth group activities); interview; personal experience; photo features; a few inspirational and informational features on spiritual topics. Buys 1-2 mss/issue. Query or send complete ms. Length: 800-1,500 words. Pays 4-7¢/word for unsolicited mss; 7-10¢ for assigned articles. "Material that covers social, spiritual and emotional needs of teenagers. Interviews with teens who are demonstrating their faith in Christ in some unusual way. Biographical articles about teens who have overcome obstacles in their lives."
Fiction: James D. Wallace, managing editor. "Must be about teens in everyday contemporary situations. Not interested in historical fiction or any fiction without a spiritual lesson." Buys 30 mss/year. Query or send complete ms. Length: 2,000 words maximum. Pays 4-7¢/word. "Stories of interest to early teenagers with strong, well-developed plot and a definite spiritual tone. Prefer not to see 'preachy' stories. Seasonal stories needed. Should have a realistic, contemporary setting and offer scriptural answers to the problems teens are facing."
Fillers: "Accepted mostly from teens." Jokes and puzzles. Send complete mss. Pays $3-10 for puzzles.
Tips: "Request our themes for the year and write articles and stories accordingly."

YOUNG AND ALIVE, Christian Record Braille Foundation, Inc., Editorial Dept., 4444 S. 52nd St., Lincoln NE 68506. Editor: Richard Kaiser. Monthly magazine for blind and visually impaired young adults (16-20) published in braille and large print for an interdenominational Christian audience. Pays on acceptance. SASE. Free writer's guidelines.
Nonfiction: Adventure, biography, camping, health, history, hobbies, nature, practical Christianity, sports and travel. "From a Christian point of view, *Young and Alive* seeks to encourage the thinking, feelings, and activities of people afflicted with sight impairment. While it's true that many blind and visually impaired young adults have the same interests as their sighted counterparts, the material should meet the needs for the sight-impaired, specifically." Length: 1,800-2,000 words. Query. Pays 3¢-5¢/word.
Fiction: "All forms of stories (such as serials, parables, satire) are used. Their content, however, must be absolutely credible." Length: 1,800-2,000 words. Query. Pays 3¢-5¢/word.
Photos: Pays $3-$4 for b&w glossy prints.

YOUNG MISS, 685 3rd Ave., New York NY 10017. Editor-in-Chief: Phyllis Schneider. 75-80% freelance written. Published 10 times/year for teen girls, aged 12-17. Buys first rights. Byline given. Pays on acceptance. Editorial requirement sheet for SASE. Query on nonfiction. Reports on submissions in 3-4 weeks. All mss must be typed, double-spaced. SASE.
Nonfiction: Deborah Purcell, features/fiction editor. Hobbies, unusual projects, humor, self-improvement and personal growth; how-to articles on all possible subjects; profiles of sports, TV, film and music figures appealing to teens. Length: 1,500-2,000 words. Pays $75 minimum. No illustrations.
Fiction: Deborah Purcell, features/fiction editor. "All fiction should be aimed at teen girls. When

in doubt, go older rather than younger. Stories may be set in any locale or time—urban, western, foreign, past, contemporary or future. Romance, mystery and adventure stories are welcomed, as well as more traditional types of stories. Stories of today are particularly desirable. Length: 2,000-2,500 words. Pays $350-600.

Tips: "Query should express original thought; desire and ability to do thorough research where applicable; clear understanding of the interests and needs of 12-17 year olds; fresh angles. We are not interested in lightweight material or style except where applicable (e.g., humor)."

Theater, Movie, TV, and Entertainment

This category features publications covering live and filmed or videotaped entertainment. For those publications whose emphasis is on music and musicians, see the section on Music Publications. Nonpaying markets for similar material are listed in the Literary and "Little" Publications category. Some Alternative and Art Publications also cover films.

ADAM FILM WORLD, 8060 Melrose Ave., Los Angeles CA 90046. (213)653-8060. Editor: Edward S. Sullivan. For fans of X- and R-rated movies. Bimonthly magazine; 76 pages. Circ. 250,000. Buys first North American serial rights. Buys about 12 mss/year. Pays on publication. No photocopied or simultaneous submissions. Reports on mss accepted for publication in 1-2 months. Returns rejected material in 2 weeks. Query. SASE. Sample copy $1.50.

Nonfiction: "All copy is slanted for fans of X and R movies and can be critical of this or that picture, but not critical of the genre itself. Some art. Publication's main emphasis is on pictorial layouts, rather than text; layouts of stills from erotic pictures. Any article must have possibilities for illustration. We go very strong in the erotic direction, but *no* hard-core stills. We see too many fictional interviews with a fictitious porno star, and too many fantasy suggestions for erotic film plots. No think pieces or interviews with porn stars. We would consider articles on the continuing erotization of legitimate films from major studios, and the increasing legitimization of X and R films from the minors." Length: 1,000-3,000 words. Pays $80-210.

Photos: Most photos are bought on assignment from regular photographers with studio contacts, but a few 8x10 b&w's are purchased from freelancers for use as illustrations. Pays minimum of $10/photo.

AFTER DARK, 161 W. 54th St., Suite 1202, New York NY 10019. (212)246-7979. Editor: Louis Miele. For a sophisticated audience 20-55 years old, "visually oriented, who wants to know what's news and who's making the news in the world of entertainment." Monthly. Circ. 74,000. Buys first rights. Buys about 10 mss/year. Pays on publication. Sample copy $3.00. Submit seasonal material 4 months in advance. Reports in 3-4 weeks. Query, including copies of previously published work; some mention of access to illustrative materials is always useful.

Nonfiction: Articles on "every area of entertainment—films, TV, theater, nightclubs, books, records. No 'think' or survey pieces about the social or psychological implications to be gleaned from some entertainment trend. The fastest approach would be to offer access to some hard-to-reach entertainment celebrity who customarily has not given interviews. However, we do not want lurid, tasteless accounts laced with sexual anecdote." Length: 500-1,500 words. Pays $150-300.

Photos: Photos with captions only. B&w glossy prints, color transparencies. Pays $20-75.

Tips: "The best way to crack *After Dark* is by doing a piece on some new trend in the entertainment world. We have people in most of the important cities, but we rely on freelancers to send us material from out-of-the-way places where new things are developing. Some of our contributing editors started out that way. Query."

AFTERNOON TV, Roband Publications, 2 Park Ave., Suite 910, New York NY 10016. Editor: Connie Passalacqua. Twelve times a year. For soap opera viewers. Byline given.

Nonfiction: Interviews with afternoon TV stars. "Daytime TV is a very specialized market. We're only interested in in-depth, intelligent and well-written interviews with daytime actors on any of the 13 soap operas in New York and Los Angeles. We're looking for good writers who can do bright personality profiles with new angles or thoughtful, informed feature pieces on soap operas and daytime TV in general. New writers considered on spec only." Pays $100/6-page story.

Photos: Pays $50-75/photo shooting.

AMAZING CINEMA, Cinema Enterprises, 12 Moray Ct., Baltimore MD 21236. Editor: Don Dohler. Managing Editor: Pam Dohler. Monthly magazine covering special effects films, production and filmmakers. "Our readers are horror/science fiction film fans and filmmakers with an insatiable appetite for information about all aspects of special effects movies—from classics of yesteryear to today's modern epics." Estab. 1981. Circ. 10,000-20,000. Pays on publication. Byline given. Buys all rights "unless arranged otherwise in advance." Submit seasonal/holiday material 2 months in advance. Simultaneous queries, and simultaneous and photocopied submissions OK. SASE. Reports in 2 weeks on queries; 1 month on mss. Sample copy $3; free writer's guidelines.
Nonfiction: How-to (nontechnical information on how special effects were achieved on independent and Hollywood features); interview/profile; new product; personal experience; and photo feature. "*Amazing Cinema* is a photo-oriented magazine devoted to the world of special effects in film. We are looking for stories about independent, amateur, and professional filmmakers (including directors, producers, technicians, etc.) who are creating or have created films in the horror/fantasy/science fiction genre. A revealing, behind-the-scenes slant is desired; photos, frame clips, and color slides are a must to illustrate such pieces. Interviews should be meaty and the interviewer should thoroughly research the filmmaker and his films. *Amazing Cinema* is written in a friendly, down-to-earth style; highly technical jargon (about filming techniques) should be avoided. A simple, layman's approach to describing technical effects is preferred." No criticism, personal opinion, or poorly research "exclusives." Buys 80-120 mss/year. Send complete ms. Length: 300-5,000 words. Pays $10/printed page (or part of), including photos and art.
Photos: Send photos with ms. Pays $2-25 for color transparencies; $1-5 for 5x7 or 8x10 b&w prints.
Tips: "We are not as demanding as most magazines, since we are used to dealing with inexperienced writers; as long as the material is accurate and interesting, we will happily edit and polish it. All departments are staff-written, and assignments are made to staff writers only. We are most interested in freelance features and articles. Writers should see a sample copy of the magazine, and send a SASE for free 'Guidelines To Submitting Articles.' "

AMERICAN FILM, American Film Institute, Kennedy Center, Washington DC 20566. (202)828-4060. Editor: Peter Biskind. 80% freelance written. For film professionals, students, teachers, film enthusiasts, culturally oriented readers. Monthly magazine; 80 pages. Circ. 100,000. Buys First North American serial rights. Pays kill fee. Byline given. Pays on acceptance. Sample copy $1. Will consider photocopied submissions. Submit material 3 months in advance. Reports in 1 month. Query. SASE.
Nonfiction: In-depth articles on film and television-related subjects. "Our articles require expertise and first-rate writing ability." Buys informational, profile, historical and "think" pieces. No film reviews. Buys 20-30 mss/year. Length: 2,000-3,000 words. Pays $100-600.

BALLET NEWS, The Metropolitan Opera Guild, Inc., 1865 Broadway, New York NY 10023. (212)582-7500. Editor: Robert Jacobson. Managing Editor: Karl Reuling. Monthly magazine. Covering dance and the related fields of films, video and records. Estab. 1979. Circ. 50,000. Average issue includes 6-7 feature articles. "All are accompanied by many photos and graphics. We are writing for a dance audience who wants to better appreciate the art form. We include reviews, calendar and book reviews." Pays on publication. Byline given. Kill fee negotiable. Buys first rights. Phone queries OK. Photocopied submissions OK. SASE. Reports in 1 month. Sample copy $1.75.
Nonfiction: General interest (critical analysis, theaters); historical; interview (dancers, choreographers, entrepreneurs, costumers, stage designers); profile; travel (dance in any location); and technical (staging, practice). Buys 6 mss/issue. Query, send complete ms or send clips of previously published work. Length: 3,000 words. Pays 10¢/word.
Photos: State availability of photos or send photos with ms. Payment negotiable for b&w contact sheets.

BLACK STARS, Johnson Publishing Co., Inc., 820 S. Michigan Ave., Chicago IL 60605. (312)322-9311. Managing Editor: Ariel P. Strong. 20% freelance written. Emphasizes entertainment. Monthly magazine; 74 pages. Circ. 350,000. Pays on publication. Buys all rights. Seasonal/holiday material should be submitted 3 months in advance. SASE. Reports in 3 weeks. Sample copy $1.25; free writer's guidelines.
Nonfiction: Personal experience and photo feature. "Only articles on black entertainers including sports figures." Buys 600 mss/year. Query. Length: 3,000 words maximum. Pays $100-200.
Photos: Purchases 8x10 b&w or transparencies. Query, submit prints or transparencies.
Tips: "All of our articles are assigned. Freelancers should submit their subjects to us by request and we will let them know if 'subject' is assigned. We basically deal with black entertainers in the field of drama, TV, singers (records), sports, etc."

CANADIAN THEATRE REVIEW, 4700 Keele St., Downsview, Ontario, Canada M3J 1P3. (416)667-3768. Editor-in-Chief: Don Rubin. Business Manager: Gail Thomson. 80% freelance written. Emphasizes theater for Canadian academics and professionals. No "non-Canadian material." Quarterly magazine; 144 pages. Circ. 5,000. Pays on publication. Buys one-time rights. Pays 50% kill fee. Byline given. SAE and International Reply Coupons. Reports in 10-12 weeks. Sample copy $3.50
Nonfiction: Historical (theater in Canada); interview (internationally known theater figures); and photo feature (theater worldwide). Buys 40 mss/year. Length: 1,500-5,000 words. Query or submit complete ms. Pays $15/published page.
Photos: State availability of photos with query or mss.

CHANNELS MAGAZINE, Media Commentary Council, Inc., 1515 Broadway, New York NY 10036. (212)398-1300. Editor: Les Brown. Senior Editor: Valerie Brooks. Bimonthly magazine covering television and radio communication for professionals, academics, and people in the media business. Estab. 1981. Circ. 50,000. Pays on acceptance. Byline given. Pays 25% kill fee. Buys first North American serial rights. Simultaneous queries, and photocopied and previously published submissions OK ("indicate where and when published"). Reports in 3 weeks. Sample copy $3.
Nonfiction: Articles on the business of TV and radio communications. No reviews or personality pieces. Buys 35-40 mss/year. Query with clips of published work. Length: 2,000-4,000 words. Pays $300-1,000.
Columns/Departments: Book reviews. Buys 30 mss/year. Query. Length: 800 words. Pays $100.
Fillers: Newsbreaks. Buys 60-100/year. Length: 300-500 words. Pays $150.

CINEASTE MAGAZINE, A Magazine on the Art and Politics of the Cinema, 419 Park Ave. S., New York NY 10016. Editors: Gary Crowdus, Dan Georgakas, Lenny Rubenstein, Melanie Wallace. Quarterly magazine covering films for filmmaking students, film lovers, and people involved in making or distributing films. Circ. 6,500. Pays on publication. Byline and brief bio given. Buys first North American serial rights. SASE. Reports in 1 month on queries. Sample copy $1; writer's guidelines for business size SAE and 1 first class stamp.
Nonfiction: Interview (of filmmakers, actors, screenwriters and directors); and social issues raised by films. Buys 6-10 mss/year. Query with clips of published work "if relevant. Query with letter should state the exact project the author wishes to undertake and his qualifications." Length: 3,000-5,000 words. Pays $10 minimum.
Columns/Departments: A Second Look (occasional feature reviewing a movie); and book reviews. Buys 6 mss/year. Send complete ms. Buys 1,000-3,000 words. Pays $5 minimum.
Tips: "Familiarity with the magazine is a must. Otherwise authors are wasting their time. We seek only high level intellectual material from people who have read the magazine and agree with its general orientation."

CINEFANTASTIQUE, Box 270, Oak Park IL 60303. Publisher/Editor: Frederick S. Clarke. Managing Editor: Michael Kaplan. For persons interested in horror, fantasy and science fiction films. Magazine; 52 pages. Bimonthly. Circ. 25,000. Rights purchased are all magazine rights in all languages. Pays on publication. Photocopied submissions OK. Reports in 4 weeks. SASE.
Nonfiction: "We're interested in articles, interviews and reviews which concern horror, fantasy and science fiction films." Query with clips, writing sample and developed outline. Pays 25¢/line, 30-40 spaces.

CITY LIMITS, 101 Tremont, Boston MA 02108. (617)482-3880. Editor: Bill Barol. Monthly magazine covering the New England area for young people, aged 18-34. Estab. 1981. Circ. 35,000. Pays on publication. Byline given. Offers 25% kill fee. Buys all rights. Simultaneous queries, and simultaneous, photocopied submissions OK. Reports in 2 weeks on queries.
Nonfiction: Lifestyle, arts and entertainment. "We're trying to reach the young market. The writing style is light, upbeat, irreverent." Buys 100-125 mss/year. Query with clips of published work. Length: 3,000-5,000 words. Pays 7-10¢/word.
Columns/Departments: Books (essays or reviews); Food and Drink (essays or reviews); Music (essays); Stage and Screen (essays); and Back Page (humor). "Material must be Boston-oriented." Length: 1,000 words minimum. Pays $100 minimum.
Poetry: Avant-garde, free verse, haiku, light verse, traditional and limericks. Buys 12-20 mss/year. Pays $10 minimum.
Fillers: Almanac (soft news, trends, very short fiction, humor). Length: 500-700 words. Pays $10 minimum.
Tips: "Queries should include mention of the topic and contacts for the story. Discuss several possible approaches for the story, including personal interest in, and familiarity with subject

matter. A phone call alerting us to a submission will usually have the best results. We're not looking for pieces or story ideas that have appeared elsewhere. As long as a submission is original, and treated professionally, we think it's worth a look."

THE CURTAIN, International Thespian Society, 3368 Central Pkwy., Cincinnati OH 45225. (513)559-1996. Editor-in-Chief: S. Ezra Goldstein. Associate Editor: Donald Corathers. For theater arts students, teachers, and others interested in theater arts education. Bimonthly tabloid supplement to *Dramatics Magazine*; published in October, December, February, April and June. Circ. 50,000. Pays on acceptance. Buys first North American serial rights. Byline given. Phone queries OK. Submit seasonal/holiday material 3 months in advance. Simultaneous, photocopied and previously published submissions OK. SASE. Reports in 3 weeks. Sample copy $1; free writer's guidelines.
Nonfiction: Historical; how-to (technical theater); informational; interview; photo feature; profile; and technical. Submit complete ms. Length: 2,500 words minimum. Pays from contributor's copies to $30.
Photos: Purchased with accompanying ms. Uses b&w photos. Query. Total purchase price for ms includes payment for photos.
Tips: "The best way to break in is to know our audience—drama students and teachers and others interested in theater—and to write for them. Writers who have some practical experience in theater, especially in technical areas, have a leg-up here, but we'll work with anybody who has a good idea. We like for writers to read us before they try to write for us."

DANCE MAGAZINE, 1180 Avenue of the Americas, New York NY 10036. (212)399-2400. Editor: William Como. Managing Editor: Richard Philp. Monthly. For the dance profession and members of the public interested in the art of dance, all areas of the performing art—stage performances, concerts, history, teaching, personalities—while retaining the format of an art publication. Buys all rights. Pays on publication. Sample copy $2. Query with outline of knowledge of dance. SASE.
Nonfiction: Personalities, knowledgeable comment, news. No personality profiles or personal interviews. Length: 2,000-2,500 words. Pays $300 maximum.
Photos: Purchased with articles or with captions only. Pays $5-15.
Tips: "Query first, preferably by mail. Do a piece about a local company that's not too well known but growing; or a particular school that is doing well which we may not have heard about; or a local dancer who you feel will be gaining national recognition."

DANCE SCOPE, American Dance Guild, 1133 Broadway, Rm. 1427, New York NY 10010. Editor-in-Chief: H.B. Kronen. 95% freelance written. Emphasizes dance and related performing/visual/musical arts. For performers, university teachers and students, general public audiences, other artists, arts administrators, critics, historians. Quarterly magazine; 80 pages. Circ. 7,000. Pays on publication. Buys all rights. Submit seasonal or holiday material 6 months in advance. Photocopied submissions OK. SASE. Reports in 1 month. Sample copy $4.
Nonfiction: Informational (contemporary developments, trends, ideas); historical (synthesis of ideas, not narrowly academic); inspirational (documentation and think pieces); interviews (with commentary, intros, etc.); personal experience (with broad relevance). Buys 12 mss/year. Query. Length: 1,500-3,000 words. Pays $25-50.
Photos: No additional payment for b&w glossy prints used with mss. Captions required. Query. Model release required.

DANCE TEACHER NOW, SMW Communications, Inc., 1333 Notre Dame Dr., Davis CA 95616. (916)756-6222. Editor: Susan Wershing. For professional teachers of stage and ballroom dance in private studios and colleges. Bimonthly magazine. Estab. 1979. Circ. 4,000. Average issue includes 5-6 feature articles, departments, and 3 calendar sections. Pays on acceptance. Byline given. Buys all rights. Submit seasonal material 6 months in advance. Previously published submissions OK; specify where and when. Reports in 2 months. Sample copy $1; free writer's guidelines.
Nonfiction: "Legal issues, health and dance injuries, dance techniques, business, advertising, taxes and insurance, curricula, student/teacher relations, government grants, studio equipment, concerts and recitals, departmental budgets, etc." Buys 5-6 mss/issue. Query with clips of previously published work. Length: 1,000-3,000 words. Pays $100-300.
Photos: State availability of photos. Pays $20 minimum for 5x7 b&w glossy prints. Model release required. Buys all rights.
Columns/Departments: Practical tips (3-4 paragraphs, short items of immediate practical use to the teacher), and profiles of successful teachers.
Tips: "We like complete reportage of the material with all the specifics, but personalized with

direct quotes and anecdotes. The writer should speak one-to-one to the teacher, but keep the national character of the magazine in mind."

DAYTIME STARS, 2 Park Ave., New York NY 10016. Editor: Sherry Amatenstein. 70% freelance written. For daytime television viewers. Monthly. Circ. 200,000. Buys all rights. Pays on publication. Query. SASE.
Nonfiction: "I'd like some new ideas, such as round-ups (i.e., 'my most embarrassing moment on a soap opera'); information on *how* the show is put together; why so many people get caught up in daytime drama, etc. I'd also like stories on interesting storylines such as the wife abuse plot on *All My Children*, or alcoholism in teenagers on the soaps." Personality pieces with daytime TV stars of serials and quiz shows; main emphasis is on serial stars. Also interested in some women's interest material. Buys interviews, personality pieces, round-up articles, analysis of the serials for "Soapbox" column—especially crticism, and personal experience articles related to daytime TV only. Length: approximately 1,500 words. Pays $100 minimum.
Tips: "The key thing for breaking in here is to have access to one of the daytime TV personalities or a fresh idea about the soap world. Try to choose a character whose story line is evolving into a bigger and more important role. But query first; don't waste your time doing a story on a character who will be going off the show soon. For writers who don't have this kind of access, the best bet is a career retrospective on one of the major characters who has been on for years. You'll need to check a library for clippings. Or do issue-oriented pieces such as bed hopping or mental breakdowns on the soaps."

THE DRAMA REVIEW, New York University, 721 Broadway, 6th Floor, New York NY 10003. (212)598-2597. Editor: Michael Kirby. 75% freelance written. Emphasizes avant-garde performance art for professors, students and the general theater and dance-going public as well as professional practitioners in the performing arts. Quarterly magazine; 144 pages. Circ. 10,000. Pays on publication. Phone queries OK. Submit seasonal/holiday material 4 months in advance. Photocopied and previously published (if published in another language) submissions OK. SASE. Reports in 3 months. Sample copy $4; free writer's guidelines.
Nonfiction: Terry Helbing, managing editor. Historical (the historical avant-garde in any performance art, translations of previously unpublished plays, etc.) and informational (documentation of a particular performance). Buys 10-20 mss/issue. Query. Pays 1¢/word for translations; 2¢/word for other material.
Photos: Terry Helbing, managing editor. Photos purchased with or without accompanying ms or on assignment. Captions required. Pays $10 for b&w photos. No additional payment for photos accepted with accompanying ms.
Tips: "No criticism in the sense of value judgments—we are not interested in the author's opinions. We are only interested in documentation theory and analysis."

DRAMATICS MAGAZINE, International Thespian Society, 3368 Central Pkwy., Cincinnati OH 45225. (513)559-1996. Editor-in-Chief: S. Ezra Goldstein. Associate Editor: Donald Corathers. 25-30% freelance written. For theater arts students, teachers and others interested in theater arts education. Magazine published bimonthly in September, November, January, March and May; 48-56 pages. Circ. 50,000. Pays on acceptance. Buys first North American serial rights. Byline given. Phone queries OK. Submit seasonal/holiday material 3 months in advance. Simultaneous, photocopied and previously published submissions OK. SASE. Reports in 3 weeks. Sample copy $1; free writer's guidelines.
Nonfiction: Historical; how-to (technical theater); informational; interview; photo feature; humorous; profile; and technical. Buys 30 mss/year. Submit complete ms. Length: 2,500 words minimum. Pays $30-150.
Photos: Purchased with accompanying ms. Uses b&w photos and color transparencies. Query. Total purchase price for ms includes payment for photos.
Columns/Departments: Technicalities (theater how-to articles); Tag Line (editorials on some phase of the theater); and Promptbook (entertainment arts news relevant to an educational magazine). Buys 15 mss/year. Send complete ms. Length: 250-1,000 words. Pays $30-60.
Fiction: Drama (one-act plays). Buys 5 mss/year. Send complete ms. Pays $50-150.

DRAMATIKA, 429 Hope St., Tarpon Springs FL 33589. Editors: John and Andrea Pyros. Magazine; 40 pages. For persons interested in the theater arts. Published 2 times/year. Circ. 500-1,000. Buys all rights. Pays on publication. Sample copy $2. Query. SASE. Reports in 1 month.
Fiction: Wants "performable pieces—plays, songs, scripts, etc." Will consider plays on various and open themes. Query first. Length: 20 pages maximum. Pays about $25/piece; $5-10 for smaller pieces.
Photos: B&w photos purchased with ms with extra payment. Captions required. Pays $5. Size: 8x11.

THE ENTERTAINER, 1347 S. 3rd St., Louisville KY 40208. (502)636-2541. Editor: Charles Hunter. Biweekly magazine distributed free through record stores and clothing stores. Covers music and entertainment-related events for men and women aged 21-45 interested in leisure activities. Circ. 80,000. Pays on acceptance. Byline given. Buys all rights. Submit seasonal/holiday material 2 months in advance. SASE. Reports in 2 weeks. Free sample copy.

Nonfiction: Expose (of the entertainment field); general interest (pertaining to leisure activities); historical/nostalgic (involving entertainment events or musical instruments); humor; interview/profile (of pop, rock or country artists); personal experience (firsthand stories about the author's involvement with an artist); and entertainment events. Buys 300 mss/year. Send complete ms. Length: 1,500-2,000 words. Pays 4¢/word.

Photos: Send photos with accompanying ms. Pays negotiable fee for 35mm color transparencies; $7.50 minimum for 5x7 glossy prints. Identification of subjects required. Buys one-time rights.

Fiction: Short stories. Buys 24 mss/year. Send complete ms. Length: 2,000 word average. Pays 4¢/word.

FANTASTIC FILMS, The Magazine of Imaginative Media, Blake Publishing Corp., 21 W. Elm St., Chicago IL 60610. (312)943-2233. Magazine published 9 times/year, covering science fiction films and fantasy animation, for adherents of science fiction and nostalgia, ages 7-40. Circ. 110,000. Pays "shortly after publication." Byline given. Buys first North American serial rights. Submit seasonal/holiday material 3 months in advance. Simultaneous queries OK; photocopied submission preferred. SASE. Reports in 1 month.

Nonfiction: General interest (human side of filmmaking); interview/profile (of persons involved in making films); and technical (dealing with filmmaking). Buys 3 mss/year. Query with clips of published work. Length: 7,000-10,000 words. Pays 5¢/word.

Photos: State availability of photos or send photos with accompanying ms. "Writer must supply all graphics to accompany article. All material will be returned."

Tips: "I prefer to deal with writers who are knowledgeable in area written about or have connections with directors, producers and special effects people."

FILM QUARTERLY, University of California Press, Berkeley CA 94720. (415)642-6333. Editor: Ernest Callenbach. 100% freelance written. Quarterly. Buys all rights. Byline given. Pays on publication. Query; "sample pages are very helpful from unknown writers." SASE.

Nonfiction: Articles on style and structure in films, articles analyzing the work of important directors, historical articles on development of the film as art, reviews of current films and detailed analyses of classics, book reviews of film books. Must be familiar with the past and present of the art; must be competently, although not necessarily breezily, written; must deal with important problems of the art. "We write for people who like to think and talk seriously about films, as well as simply view them and enjoy them. We use no personality pieces or reportage pieces. Interviews usually work for us only when conducted by someone familiar with most of a film-maker's work. (We don't use performer interviews.)" Length: 6,000 words maximum. Pay is about 2¢/word.

Tips: "*Film Quarterly* is a specialized academic journal of film criticism, though it is also a magazine (with pictures) sold in bookstores. It is read by film teachers, students, and die-hard movie buffs, so unless you fall into one of those categories, it is very hard to write for us. Currently, we are especially looking for material on independent, documentary, etc. films not written about in the national film reviewing columns."

HIFI BUYER'S REVIEW, Box 684, Southampton NY 11968. (516)283-2360. Editor: Tom Farre. For the hi-fi enthusiast. Emphasizes "fact-filled buying and using information about hi-fi equipment." Bimonthly publication of Hampton International Communications, Inc. Magazine; 68 pages. Circ. 60,000. Buys all rights. Byline given. Buys about 36 mss/year. Pays after publication. Query with sample of work. No photocopied or simultaneous submissions. Reports in 6 months. SASE.

Nonfiction: Publishes hi-fidelity information, equipment stories and laboratory reports. Length: informational, 3,000 words. Pays $140.

Photos: Photos purchased with ms for no additional payment.

Tips: "Prospective writers must be expert in technical aspects of field, with hands-on experience with products."

HOME VIDEO, United Business Publications, 475 Park Ave., S., New York NY 10016. Editor: Robert Vare. Managing Editor: Diana Loevy. Monthly magazine about video; all forms of home entertainment center around television, including hardware and software for an audience who either owns video equipment (video cassette recorders, cameras, projection TVs or cable), is planning to buy, or is interested in new forms of entertainment. Estab. 1979. Circ. 100,000. Pays on acceptance. Rights vary. Submit seasonal material 6 months in advance. Simultaneous and photocopied submissions OK, if so indicated. SASE. Reports in 2 weeks.

Nonfiction: How-to (use a video camera, set up video equipment, be innovative with video cassette recorders); interview/profile (of personalities who have video equipment, top industry people or wry observers of the entertainment scene, e.g., Pauline Kael and Fran Lebowitz); nostalgia (photos of rooms or factories with old televisions); opinion (on the nature of TV); profile; new product; humor; essays; personal experience; photo feature (of rooms designed with video equipment in them); technical; and articles on the genres of films available on video cassettes. "No articles on film production or on the commercial applications of video." Query with clips of published work. Length: 2,500 words maximum. Pays $200-750.

Photos: State availability of photos or send photos with ms. Captions preferred; model release required.

Tips: "Write a trend piece on what is happening in the area of home video, who is buying, what and why. Something in-depth that solves a problem, poses questions, then answers them. We are most interested in great photos accompanying a manuscript describing how people use video and design around/for it."

IN CINEMA, 919 3rd Ave., New York NY 10022. (212)758-5580. Editor: Harlan Jacobson. Associate Editor: Hildy Johnson. Magazine published 10 times/year covering movies for 300 movie theaters in New York, Connecticut, New Jersey and Los Angeles area. Estab. 1980. Circ. 600,000. Pays on publication (within 2 weeks). Byline given. Offers variable kill fee. Buys all rights. Simultaneous queries, and photocopied and previously published submissions OK. SASE. Reports "when assignment is available." Sample copy for 7x9 SAE and 2 first class stamps.

Nonfiction: "Topical features and Q & A interviews with major individuals in front of or behind camera." No personality articles. Buys 20-30 mss/year. Query with clips of published work; "may not return." Length: 1,000-1,500 words. Pays to $400.

Photos: State availability of photos.

Columns/Departments: Books; Behind the Scenes; Nostalgia; Music; and Restaurant. Query with clips of published work; "send photocopies." Length: 375-750 words. Pays $100-250.

Fillers: Newsbreaks: "film news on future releases." Length: 50 words minimum.

Tips: "Features require some knowledge of the film business as well as film as art."

MARTIAL ARTS MOVIES, Unique Publications, 7011 Sunset Blvd., Hollywood CA 90028. (213)467-1300. Editor: Sandra Segal. Monthly magazine covering "new martial arts movies or movies that include extensive martial arts sequences in the American, Japanese and Chinese film industries. It is not a fan magazine, but an intelligent, well-written, and accurate look at a specialty cinema." Estab. 1981. Circ. 60,000. Pays on publication. Byline given. Buys first North American serial rights. Submit seasonal/holiday material 4 months in advance. Simultaneous queries, and simultaneous and photocopied submissions OK. SASE. Reports in 3 weeks on queries; 6 weeks on mss. Sample copy $1.50; free writer's guidelines.

Nonfiction: Buys 25-50 mss/year. Query with clips of published work or send complete ms (review). Length: 1,000-2,500 words. Pays $50-100.

Photos: Send photos with accompanying ms. Reviews b&w or color contact sheets, negatives or 8x10 prints. "Photos are paid for with payment for ms." Model release and identification of subjects required.

MEDIA HISTORY DIGEST, Media Digest History Corp., Box 867, William Penn Annex, Philadelphia PA 19105. (215)787-1906. Editor: Hiley H. Ward. Managing Editor: John P. Hayes. Quarterly magazine covering media history—newspapers, books, film, radio-TV and magazines—for "both a specialized (history, journalism) and a general market. Articles must have high popular interest." Estab. 1980. Circ. 2,000. Buys first rights. Submit seasonal/holiday material 6 months in advance. SASE. Reports in 1 month on queries; 2 months on mss. Sample copy $2.

Nonfiction: Exposé (of the media); historical/nostalgic; humor (related to the media, present or historical); and interview/profile (older people's oral history). No "unreadable academic articles of narrow interest." Buys 12 mss/year. Query. Length: 500-1,500 words. Pays $50-100.

Photos: "Most of our photos would come from historical files." State availability of photos.

Fillers: Puzzles (media history quizzes, crosswords on specific topics). Pays $25-35.

MOTIF, An Exploration of the Arts, The Vineyard Arts Fellowship, Box 7816, Atlanta GA 30309. (404)952-4035. Editor: Frank Thompson. Bimonthly magazine covering the arts from a Christian perspective. "It is our aim to offer an intelligent, thought provoking exploration of the arts that reflects a Christian's attitude and standard." Estab. 1981. Pays on acceptance. Byline given. Buys one-time rights. Submit seasonal/holiday material 6 months in advance. Simultaneous queries, and simultaneous, photocopied, and previously published submissions OK. SASE. Reports in 1 month on queries; 2 months on mss. Sampe copy for 9x12 SAE and 70¢ postage.

Nonfiction: Book excerpts, historical/nostalgic, humor, interview/profile and photo feature. "We are planning a special dance issue for winter of 1982. Submissions could take the form of photo essays of particular dancers, historical articles, interviews with Christian dancers in major companies, profiles, or overviews of books that deal with dance from a biblical or spiritual slant." Buys 12 mss/year. Query with clips of published work or send complete ms. Length: 1,000-5,000 words. Pays $50-200.

Columns/Departments: Book, film and record reviews. Buys appoximately 15 mss/year. Query with clips of published work or send complete ms. Length: 500-1,000 words. Pays $10-50.

Fiction: Buys 2 mss/year. Send complete ms. Length: 1,000-5,000 words.

Tips: "Since we have no writer's guidelines at present, freelancers would do best to study an issue of *Motif* to determine the sort of articles we're looking for. We're open to a very wide variety of ideas and we'd like to encourage freelancers to let their imaginations run wild. We're a young magazine and we can therefore go in any direction. All the magazine's sections are open to submissions, and new departments will open as we grow."

NEW ENGLAND ENTERTAINMENT DIGEST, Box 735, Marshfield MA 02050. Editor/Publisher: P.J. Reale. Semimonthly tabloid covering all facets of entertainment for professional and amateur actors, theater owners, nightclub owners and dancers. Estab. 1980. Circ. 13,000. Pays on publication. Makes work-for-hire assignments. Buys one-time rights. SASE. Reports in 1 week on queries; in 2 weeks on mss. Sample copy $1.

Nonfiction: Expose (nothing too strong); general interest (stories that will make people in entertainment better able to achieve their goals); historical (theater lore); interview (personality pieces, particularly New England related); nostalgia; opinion; profile; travel; new product (theaters); personal experience; photo feature (for a centerfold of photos featuring a theater group or entertainer). Pays $10-30. "We'll be publishing play and nightclub reviews for the six New England states, both professional and amateur; theater crafts and theater lore stories; book reviews of theater-related books; personality pieces; a 'people' column; hard news related to entertainment; and audition notices."

Photos: Send photos with ms. Reviews 8x10 b&w glossy prints. Captions and model release required. Buys one-time rights.

Columns/Departments: People column (of short, snappy items about people who are in any way involved in entertainment; news, anecdotal or human interest); and notices of tryouts in New England. Buys 1 ms/issue. Send complete ms. Pays $10 maximum.

Poetry: Light verse. Buys 2 mss/issue. Pays $2.

Fillers: Short humor, newsbreaks and puzzles. Pays $2.

NEW YORK THEATRE REVIEW, 55 W. 42 St., #1218, New York NY 10036. (212)929-7723. Editor: Ira J. Bilowit. Associate Editor: Debbi Wasserman. Emphasizes theater only. 10 issue/year magazine; 52 pages. Circ. 20,000. Pays on publication. Buys all rights. Photocopied submissions OK. SASE. Reports in 6 months. Sample copy $2.

Nonfiction: Interview, nostalgia, photo feature, profile and technical. "We consider only articles which relate to the theater and which enlighten the reader on theater techniques, the work of theater personalities or the theater process. We do not want humor, personality or personal experiences of unknowns." Query with clips of published work. Buys 2 mss/issue. Length: 750-3,000 words. Pays $25/magazine page.

Photos: State availability of photos. Uses b&w prints. Offers no additional payment for photos accepted with ms. Captions are required.

Columns/Departments: Theater nostalgia, picture stories of new plays and people who make theater. Query with clips of published work. Buys 1/issue. Length: 700 words. Pays $25. Open to suggestions for new columns/department.

PERFORMING ARTS IN CANADA, 52 Avenue Rd., 2nd Fl., Toronto, Ontario, Canada M5R 2G3. (416)921-2601. Editor: Linda Kelley. For professional performers and general readers with an interest in Canadian theater, dance and music. Covers "all three major fields of the performing arts (music, theater and dance), modern and classical, plus articles on related subjects (technical topics, government arts policy, etc.)." Quarterly magazine. Circ. 66,000. Pays 1 month following publication. Buys first rights. Pays 30-50% kill fee. Byline given. Reports in 3-6 weeks. SAE and International Reply Coupons. Sample copy 50¢.

Nonfiction: "Lively, stimulating, well-researched articles on Canadian performing artists or groups. We tend to be overstocked with theater pieces; most often in need of good classical music articles." Buys 30-35 mss/year. Query. Length: 1,500-2,000 words. Pays $150.

Tips: "Query with a good idea for an article—at the very least, state field of interest and two or three broad subjects that could be worked into a specific proposal for an article. Writers new to this publication should include clippings."

PERFORMING ARTS MAGAZINE, Performing Arts, Inc., 11 Greenway Plaza, Suite 620, Houston TX 77046. (713)621-2787. Publisher: Carter Rochelle. Editor: Scott Heumann. Managing Editor: David Kaplan. Emphasizes music, dance and theater. "Unlike many other publications in the field, *Performing Arts* is ecumenical and can be read with interest by non-specialists." Monthly magazine. Circ. 58-84,000. Pays on publication. Will negotiate rights. Byline given. Submit seasonal/holiday material 3 months in advance. SASE. Reports in 4 weeks. Sample copy $1; writer's guidelines for SASE.
Nonfiction: General interest ("need features on music, dance and theater that are informative and aimed at a well-read audience; local slant preferred but not required"); historical (same as general interest); humor (short features related to the performing arts); interview/profile (must be relevant to events in Houston—will send schedule on request). "We do not want reviews, opinion pieces, didactic or highly technical pieces of specialized interest, harangues on the subject of audience behavior, or stories about 'making it' in New York or L.A. theater scene." Buys 1-2 mss/issue. Send complete ms or query with clips of published work. Length: 500-2,000 words. Pays 10¢/word. Short theater-related features (500 words) may be retained for publication in our playbill, *Tonight!*. Pays 10¢/word.
Photos: State availability of photos or send photos with ms. Pays $50 (3 or more photos) for 8x10 b&w glossy prints. Buys one-time rights. Model release required.

PERFORMING ARTS MAGAZINE & PLAYBILL, (formerly *Applause*), **San Diego Magazine of the Performing Arts**, 3680 5th Ave., San Diego CA 92130. Managing Editor: Deborah O'Keefe. Distributed at performances of the San Diego opera, symphony and other cultural events. Monthly magazine; 52 pages. Total circ. 90,000. Pays on publication. Buys all rights. Submit seasonal/holiday material 3 months in advance. SASE. Reports in 2 weeks. Sample copy $1; writer's guidelines for SASE.
Nonfiction: "Primary editorial emphasis is on the San Diego opera, symphony and Old Globe Theatre. We look for articles that will get an 'I-didn't-know-that' reaction from our readers. We also cover other aspects of both performing and visual arts. Our pages are open to your suggestions." Length: 1,000-2,000 words. Pays $1.04/column inch.
Tips: "We are interested in matters relating to the San Diego arts scene—the people, organizations, and events that shape the milieu. The writer should be on the alert for future San Diego happenings and performers."

PHOTO SCREEN, Sterling's Magazines, Inc., 355 Lexington Ave., New York NY 10017. (212)391-1400. Editor: Marsha Daly. 50-60% freelance written. Emphasizes TV and movie news of star personalities. Bimonthly magazine; 75 pages. Circ. 300,000. Pays on publication. Buys all rights. SASE. Reports in 6 weeks.
Nonfiction: Exposes (on stars' lives); informational (on Hollywood life); interviews (with stars); photo features (on stars' personal lives). Buys 5-6 mss/month. Length: 1,500 words. Query. No unsolicited mss, fiction or local personality stories. Pays $75-200.
Photos: Roger Glazer, department editor. Purchased without ms; mostly on speculation. Pays $25-35 for 8x10 b&w (glossy or matte); $50 minimum for color. Chromes only; 35mm or 2¼x2¼.

PLAYBILL MAGAZINE, 100 Avenue of the Americas, New York NY 10013. Editor-in-Chief: Ms. Joan Alleman Rubin. Monthly; free to theatergoers. "It is the only magazine in Manhattan that focuses entirely on the New York Theater." Buys first and second US magazine rights. Pays 25% kill fee. Byline given. SASE.
Nonfiction: "The major emphasis is on current theater and theater people. Wants sophisticated, informative prose that makes judgments and shows style. Uses unusual interviews, although most of these are staff-written. Article proposal must be about a current Broadway show or star, or playwright, director, composer, etc. We do not use parody or satire. We occasionally publish 'round-up' articles—stars who play tennis, or who cook, etc. Style should be worldly and literate without being pretentious or arch; runs closer to *New Yorker* than to *Partisan Review*. Wants interesting information, written in a genuine, personal style. Humor is also welcome. Between 1,000 and 2,500 words for articles." Pays $100-400.
Tips: "We're difficult to break into and most of our pieces are assigned. We don't take any theater pieces relating to theater outside New York. The best way for a newcomer to break in is with a 750-word article for *A View From The Audience* describing how a Broadway play or musical deeply affected the writer." Pays $100.

PRE-VUE, Box 31255, Billings MT 59107. Editor-Publisher: Virginia Hansen. "We are the cable-TV guide for southern and western Montana; our audience is as diverse as people who subscribe to cable TV." Weekly magazine; 32-40 pages. Circ. 15,000. Not copyrighted. Byline given. Pays on publication. Reports in 8 weeks. Query. SASE.

Nonfiction and Photos: Valerie Hansen, department editor. "Subject matter is general, but must relate in some way to television or our reading area (Montana). We would like articles to have a beginning, middle and end; in other words, popular magazine style, heavy on the hooker lead." Informational, how-to, interview, profile, humor, historical, travel, TV reviews. Feature length: 500 words. Pays minimum of 2¢/word. 8x10 (sometimes smaller) b&w photos purchased with mss or on assignment. Pays $3-6. Captions required.

Fillers: Short humor, local history and oddities. Buys 10/year. Length: 50-200 words. Pays minimum of 2¢/word.

Tips: "We're looking for work from experienced writers; we prefer writing that is short and peppy, or very informative, or humorous."

PROLOG, 104 N. St. Mary, Dallas TX 75204. (214)827-7734. Editor: Mike Firth. 10% freelance written. For "playwrights and teachers of playwriting." Quarterly newsletter; 8 pages. Circ. 300. Not copyrighted. Buys 4 mss/year. Pays on acceptance; "may hold pending final approval." Sample copy $2. Photocopied and simultaneous submissions OK. Reports in "over 3 months." SASE.

Nonfiction: Wants "articles and anecdotes about writing, sales and production of play scripts. Style should be direct to reader (as opposed to third-person observational)." No general attacks on theater, personal problems, problems without solutions, or general interest. Pays 1¢/word.

RONA BARRETT'S HOLLYWOOD, Laufer Publications, 7060 Hollywood Blvd., Suite 800, Hollywood CA 90028. (213)467-3111. Editor: Diane Dalbey. Monthly magazine featuring TV, movie and music personalities; primarily for women 14-35. "We're the only entertainment monthly to originate in Hollywood. We are very strong therefore in firsthand, behind-the-scenes stories and a wide variety of photos." Circ. 400,000. Average issue includes 6-8 feature articles, Rona's column, Las Vegas column and fashion. Pays on acceptance. Byline given. Buys first North American serial rights. Submit seasonal material 3 months in advance. Simultaneous submissions OK. SASE. Reports in 1 month.

Nonfiction: Interview (of celebrities in Hollywood); investigative reports on a controversial issue in show business. "All articles should funnel down into highly recognizable celebrities. We're very strong on exclusive interviews and investigative stories." Buys 3-6 mss/issue. Query with clips of previously published work. Length: 800-1,600 words. Pays $200-750.

Tips: Freelance writers should be persistent "in pushing not what they think we need but what we explain we need. Please keep in mind we have a staff of writers, so freelancers are used only in instances where our people can't get the story. Often good ideas are submitted to *RBH* but are unusable by us because they're too esoteric or 'inside' for our pop, middle of the road, middle American readers."

SCENE CHANGES, 8 York St., 7th Floor, Toronto, Ontario, Canada M5J 1R2. (416)366-2938. Editor: Jeniva Berger. Magazine published 9 times/year covering live theater for both professionals in the theatrical field and a general theater going public who simply enjoy being observers. We also have a good many readers who are actively involved in community theater, as well as educators in theater arts. Circ. 14,000. Average issue includes 6 features and 4-8 theater (drama) reviews. Pays within 1 month of acceptance. Pays 50%-100% kill fee, depending upon circumstances. Buys first North American serial rights. Phone queries OK. Submit seasonal material 4 months in advance. Photocopied (if clear) and previously published submissions OK. SAE and International Reply Coupons. Reports in 3 weeks. Free sample copy and writer's guidelines.

Nonfiction: "Our mandate is to cover professional, community, and educational theater and within those guidelines, we hope and strive to be entertaining and provocative. Most of our material is Canadian oriented—about 80%—but recent articles which have dealt with theater elsewhere include *Joseph Papp's Empire in the Park, What's Peter Brooks up to Now?* and *Japan's New Theatre.*" No "interviews with local people who are not particularly well known outside the area or local stories from writers out of country." Query with clips of previously published work. "We cannot use academic material, so the writers must show in the query that they know *our* magazine and know what magazine writing is all about. Writers that can capture the personality of the performer they want to interview in the query, that can sell me on that personality (or subject) and do not try to hit me with fifteen ideas for articles in two pages, are just fine." Length: 2,000 words. Pays $50-200.

Columns/Departments: Book review. Query with clips of previously published work. Length: 750 words. Pays $50. Open to suggestions for new columns and departments.

Tips: "New writers outside Canada must query first since our choice of material is quite specific. Canadian writers are advised to query also. I like resumes, especially if writers have good theater backgrounds. Our magazine is slick; pictures are large and plentiful; layout is extremely careful and imaginative. We like writers who love theater and love writing about it."

SELECTIVE VIEWING, A Video Home Review, Regal, Inc., 104 Charles St., Boston MA 02114. Editor: H.S. Taylor. Managing Editor: Paul Regal. Monthly magazine covering the adult home video field. Estab. 1979. Pays on acceptance. Byline given. Offers $50 kill fee. Buys first North American serial rights or simultaneous rights; makes work-for-hire assignments. Submit seasonal/holiday material 8 months in advance. Simultaneous submissions OK. SASE. Reports in 1 month on queries; 7 weeks on mss. Sample copy $4.

Nonfiction: New product (video) and video news items. Query.

Columns/Departments: Video Product Review Dept.; Video tape/disc ads; video player/recorder; editorials. Query.

Fillers: Clippings and newsbreaks. Pays $25-40.

Tips: Prefers "well-researched pieces on new products (tapes/discs, video accessories) *with sample of product or tape*, etc."

SOAP OPERA DIGEST, 254 W. 31st St., New York NY 10001. Executive Editor: Ruth J. Gordon. 5% freelance written. Biweekly magazine; 144 pages. Circ. 740,000. Pays on publication. Buys all rights. Submit seasonal/holiday material 4 months in advance of issue date. Photocopied submissions OK. SASE. Reports in 1 month.

Nonfiction: "Articles only directly about daytime personalities or soap operas." Interview (no telephone interviews); nostalgia; photo feature (must be recent); and profile. No summaries, personal opinions or analyses of shows. Buys 1-2 mss/issue. Query with clips of previously published work. Length: 1,000-2,000 words. Pays $75-100.

Photos: State availability of photos with query. Offers no additional payment for photos accepted with ms. Captions preferred. Buys all rights.

SUPER-8 FILMAKER, PMS Publishing Co., 609 Mission St., San Francisco CA 94105. Editor-in-Chief: Richard J. Jantz. 90% freelance written. Emphasizes filmmaking in Super-8 for amateur and professional filmmakers, students and teachers of film. Magazine (8 times a year); 66 pages. Circ. 46,000. Pays on publication. Buys all rights. Submit seasonal/holiday material 8 months in advance. SASE. Reports in 1 month. Sample copy $2.50; free writer's guidelines.

Nonfiction: How-to; informational; and technical (dealing with filmmaking only). Buys 5 mss/issue. Query. Length: 2,000-3,000 words.

Tips: "We are a consumer publication, not a trade publication. Articles written for *Super-8 Filmaker* should contain technical information, but they should not be written in technical terminology. All technical terms and concepts should be defined simply and concisely."

TUNED IN MAGAZINE, Jetpro Inc., 9420 Farnham St., Suite 105, San Diego CA 92123. (714)268-3314. Editor: Bernadette Guiniling. Weekly magazine covering TV, including cable, radio and entertainment for "entertainment-oriented San Diegans, usually between the ages of 18 and 50, of a middle-income background." Estab. 1980. Circ. 30,000. Pays on publication. Byline given. Offers kill fee. Buys one-time rights. Submit seasonal/holiday material 6 weeks in advance. Simultaneous and photocopied submissions OK. SASE. Reports in 2 weeks on queries; 1 month on mss. San Diego writers only.

Nonfiction: General interest (personal stories, TV/radio articles, entertainment); how-to (get involved in the media; to interact and be a part of it); humor (lighthearted looks at the media and entertainment technology, etc.); interview/profile (of San Diegans who made good; visiting celebrities); new product (technological updates; services such as radio for the blind); opinion (anything for opinion column, "Open Channels"); personal experience (on what it was like on an editorial rebuttal, running into the media); and photo feature ("We'd have to see it."). "We're looking for sharp, snappy articles that deal with some aspect of the San Diego entertainment field, or entertainment (TV, radio, film) as it *impacts* San Diego. We run 3 freelance articles per issue, and 5 columns (3 staff-written). Query. Mss length: 1,200-1,500 words. Pays $75.

Photos: Send photos with accompanying ms. Captions required.

Columns/Departments: Dining Out (restaurant reviews); San Diego Nights (club/concert guides, staff-written); What's Happening (guide, staff-written); plus two other staff columns.

Tips: "Think in terms of national trends as they affect the local community, entertainment options that don't get much coverage, public-service articles, and guides."

TV GUIDE, Radnor PA 19088. Editor: David Sendler. Managing Editor: R.C. Smith. Weekly. Circ. 20 million. Study publication. Query to Andrew Mills, Assistant Managing Editor. SASE.

Nonfiction: Wants offbeat articles about TV people and shows. This magazine is not interested in fan material. Also wants stories on the newest trends of television, but they must be written in clear, lively English. Length: 1,000-2,000 words.

Photos: Uses professional high-quality photos, normally shot on assignment, by photographers chosen by *TV Guide*. Prefers color. Pays $250 day rate against page rates—$350 for 2 pages or less.

TV GUIDE, (Canada, Inc.), 112 Merton St., Toronto, Canada M4S 2Z7. Editor: W.A. Marsano. Weekly magazine covering TV listings and related articles. Circ. 1,000,000. Pays on acceptance. Buys first North American rights and promotional use. SAE and International Reply Coupons.
Nonfiction: TV personality profiles. Query. Length: 1,000-1,750 words. Pays $500-1,000.
Photos: Pays $150-500 for 35mm color transparencies.

TV PICTURE LIFE, 355 Lexington Ave., New York NY 10017. (212)391-1400. Creative Director: Robert Schartoff. Editor: Fran Levine. Bimonthly magazine; 72 pages. 100% freelance written. Rights purchased vary with author and material. Usually buys all rights. Pays negotiable kill fee. Byline given. Pays on acceptance. Reports "immediately." Query. SASE.
Nonfiction and Photos: Celebrity interviews, profiles and angles that are provocative, enticing and truthful. Length: 1,000-1,500 words. Pays $100 minimum. Photos of celebrities purchased without ms or on assignment. Pays $25 minimum for photos.

TV TIME AND CHANNEL, Cable Communications Media, Inc., Box 2108, Lehigh Valley PA 18001. (215)865-6600. Production Manager: Jeff Bittner. For television and other entertainment forms. Weekly magazine; 44 pages. Pays on publication. Buys all rights. Byline given "when requested." Phone queries OK. Submit seasonal/holiday material one month in advance. Simultaneous, photocopied and previously published submissions OK. SASE. Reports in 2 weeks. Sample copy for 50¢.
Nonfiction: Expose (entertainment world and behind-the-scenes); general interest (TV related); how-to (things a TV watcher would like to know); humor; interviews (stars, producers and directors); and photo feature; fiction; opinion or whimsical humor. Pays 2-7¢/word.
Photos: Uses 8x10 b&w prints. Offers no additional payment for photos accepted with ms. Captions preferred.

VIDEO, Reese Publishing Co., Inc., 235 Park Ave., S., New York NY 10003 (212)777-0800. Editor: Bruce Apar. Managing Editor: Donald Pohl. Monthly magazine about home video for the person who wants to get the most from his home video equipment and keep abreast of the new products and developments in the video field. Circ. 100,000. Pays on acceptance. Buys first North American serial rights. Submit seasonal material 4 months in advance. Photocopied submissions OK. SASE. Reports in 1 month. Free sample copy.
Nonfiction: How-to (use the equipment to integrate video into your lifestyle); humor; interview (with people using video in an innovative way); nostalgia (TV related); opinion; profile (celebrities who use video); travel (documenting a trip on videotape); personal experience (use of the equipment or video solving community problems); photo feature (of interior design); technical (daily use solutions); satellite stations in the backyard; and churches and Sunday schools using video. "Report on video clubs in your community. Tell us how video is used at the grassroots level or unusual specific applications of video." No trade or business articles. Buys 8 mss/issue. Query with clips of previously published work. Length: 1,000-1,500 words.
Photos: State availability of photos. Buys 8x10 b&w prints and 35mm and 2¼x2¼ color transparencies. Views contact sheets. Pays negotiable fee. Captions and model release required. Buys one-time rights.
Columns/Departments: TV Den (understanding the equipment); Video Environment (people's home installations and interior decorating); Video Forum (short items on experiences and solutions). Query with clips of previously published work. Length: 1,000-3,000 words. Pays $200 minimum.

VIDEO ACTION, Video Action, Inc., 21 W. Elm, Chicago IL 60610. (312)743-2233. Editor: Mike Gold. Monthly magazine. "*Video Action* magazine covers the entire world of video, emphasizing developments in the areas of tape, disc, cable and games, and covering the areas of satellites, traditional broadcast and teletext. Editorial is written for the consumer rather than the TV repariman or electronics genius." Estab. 1980. Circ. 75,000. Pays on publication. Byline given. Pays 50% kill fee. Buys first North American serial rights. Submit seasonal/holiday material 3 months in advance. Simultaneous queries OK. SASE. Reports in 1 week on queries; 1 month on mss. Sample copy $2.
Nonfiction: Expose (consumer fraud); general interest; how-to (home video systems—repair, etc.); interview/profile; new product; personal experience (with home video systems); and technical (written from a consumer perspective). No articles on celebrities. Buys 85 mss/year. Query with clips of published work. Length: 1,500-3,500 words. Pays $75-350.
Photos: State availability of photos. Pays negotiable fee. Captions, model release, and identification of subject required. Buys one-time rights.

VIDEO REVIEW, The World Authority on Home Video, CES Publishing, 325 E. 75th St., New York NY 10021. (212)794-0500. Editor: Roy Hemming. Managing Editor: David Hajdu. Monthly magazine covering home video for owners and prospective owners of home video equipment. Estab. 1980. Circ. 100,000. Pays on publication. Offers 25% kill fee. Buys all rights. Submit queries for seasonal/holiday material 6 months in advance. Previously published submissions OK "if indicated where and when published." SASE. Reports in 6 weeks on queries.

Nonfiction: Think pieces on technology and the video arts. How-to (on imaginative ways of using home video); interview/profile (of personalities who appear on tapes); technical; and surveys of trends in upcoming programming. Buys 80 mss/year. Query with clips of published work. "We suggest that a writer study our magazine thoroughly before sending a query." Length: 1,000-2,000 words. Pays $200-300.

Columns/Departments: Reviews of programs on video cassettes and discs by assignment only. Seeks short, anecdotal items of light nature. Pays $25-50.

Tips: "Write, do not phone. Enclose photocopies of published material, or a reasonable sample manuscript or excerpt from a manuscript that shows your style."

VIDEO TODAY AND TOMORROW, ABC Leisure Magazines, Inc., 825 7th Ave., New York NY 10019. (212)887-8472. Editor: William Tynan. Monthly supplement bound in *High Fidelity* and *Modern Photography* covering home video. Estab. 1980. Circ. 1,000,000. Pays on acceptance. Byline given. Buys all rights. Submit seasonal/holiday material 6 months in advance. Simultaneous queries and photocopied submissions OK. SASE. Reports in 1 month. Free sample copy.

Nonfiction: General interest (on creative things being done with video); how-to (use video equipment, set-up); personal experience ("video vignettes"—must have accompanying photos); and nuts and bolts pieces on video. Buys 12-15 mss/year. Query with clips of published work. Length: 2,000 words maximum. Pays $450-600.

Photos: State availability of photos. Reviews 8x10 b&w glossy prints. Captions and model release required.

VIDEOGRAPHY, United Business Publications, 475 Park Ave. S., New York NY 10016. (212)725-2300. Editor: Marjorie Costello. Monthly magazine for professional users of video and executives in the videotape and videodisc industries. Circ. 25,000. Pays 1 month after publication. Buys all rights. Phone queries OK. SASE. Reports in 1 month. Sample copy $2.

Nonfiction: Any article about the use of video in business, education, medicine, etc. Especially interested in stories about the use of new video technology to solve production problems. Also stories about cable TV and pay TV services. No "personal reflections or stories about one company." Buys 4 mss/issue. Query with clips of previously published work. Length: 1,000-2,500 words. Pays $50-$100.

Photos: Submit photo material with accompanying query. Offers no additional payment for 5x7 b&w glossy prints or color transparencies. Captions required. Buys all rights.

Travel, Camping, and Trailer

Publications in this category tell campers and tourists the where-to's and how-to's of travel. Publications that buy how-to camping and travel material with a conservation angle are listed in the Nature, Conservation, and Ecology classification. Newspapers and Weekly Magazine Sections, as well as Regional Publications, are frequently interested in travel and camping material with a local angle. Hunting and fishing and outdoor publications that buy camping how-to material will be found in the Sport and Outdoor category. Publications dealing with automobiles or other vehicles maintained for sport or as a hobby will be found in the Automotive and Motorcycle category. Many publications in the In-Flight category are also in the market for travel articles and photos.

AAA WORLD, (Wisconsin AAA), (formerly *Travel Magazine*), 433 W. Washington Ave., Madison WI 53703. (608)257-711. Editor: Hugh P. (Mickey) McLinden. 10% freelance written. Aimed at an audience of domestic and foreign motorist-travelers. Bimonthly magazine. Pays on publication. Buys all rights. Reports "immediately." SASE.

Nonfiction: Domestic and foreign travel; motoring, safety, highways, new motoring products. Length: 1,500 words maximum. Pays $75 minimum.

Photos: Photos purchased with ms or separately. Captions required. B&w and color. Pays $20 minimum.

ACCENT, 1720 Washington Blvd., Box 2315, Ogden UT 84404. Editor: Dick Harris. 90% freelance written. Travel-oriented. Monthly. Circ. 600,000. "*Accent* is sold to business and industrial firms coast-to-coast who distribute it with appropriate inserts as their house magazines." Buys first rights. Buys 120-140 mss/year, 200-300 photos/year. Pays on acceptance. Sample copy, 50¢; free guidelines with SASE. Query with SASE.
Nonfiction and Photos: "We want travel articles—places to go, advice to travelers, new ways to travel, money-saving tips, new resorts, famous travelers, and humor. Stories and photos are often purchased as a package. Pictures are important to us in our decision on buying or rejecting material." No foreign (exotic) travel. Uses b&w glossies and color transparencies. Captions required. Feature article length: 500-1000 words. Payment: 10¢/word, $20/b&w photo, $25/color transparency, more for color covers.
Tips: "Pictures are a very important part of our magazine. Sharp, good contrast, (colorful for colorshots) often sell the piece, so make sure super-quality photos are available. Please remember we work 10 months in advance, and submit seasonal material accordingly."

AWAY, 888 Worcester St., Wellesley MA 02181. (617)237-5200. Editor: Gerard J. Gagnon. For "members of the ALA Auto & Travel Club, interested in their autos and in travel. Ages range from approximately 20-65. They live primarily in New England." Slanted to seasons. Quarterly. Circ. 195,000. Buys first serial rights. Pays on acceptance. Submit seasonal material 6 months in advance. Reports "as soon as possible." Although a query is not mandatory, it may be advisable for many articles. SASE. Free sample copy.
Nonfiction: Articles on "travel, tourist attractions, safety, history, etc., preferably with a New England angle. Also, car care tips and related subjects." Would like a "positive feel to all pieces, but not the chamber of commerce approach." Buys both general seasonal travel and specific travel articles, for example, travel-related articles (photo hints, etc.); outdoor activities; for example, gravestone rubbing, snow sculpturing; historical articles linked to places to visit; humor with a point, photo essays. "Would like to see more nonseasonally oriented material. Most material now submitted seems suitable only for our summer issue. Avoid pieces on hunting and about New England's most publicized attractions, such as Old Sturbridge Village and Mystic Seaport." Length: 800-1,500 words, "preferably 1,000-1,200." Pays approximately 10¢/word.
Photos: Photos purchased with mss. Captions required. B&w glossy prints. Pays $5-10/b&w photo, payment on publication based upon which photos are used. Not buying color at this time.

CAMPERWAYS, 550 Penllyn Pike, Blue Bell PA 19422. (215)643-1988. Editor-in-Chief: Charles E. Myers. 60% freelance written. Emphasis on recreation vehicle camping and travel. Monthly (except Dec. and Jan.) tabloid; 36 pages. Circ. 25,000. Pays on publication. Buys simultaneous, second serial (reprint) or regional rights. Byline given. Submit seasonal/holiday material 3-4 months in advance. Simultaneous, photocopied and previously published submissions OK. SASE. Reports in 1 month. Free sample copy and writer's guidelines.
Nonfiction: Historical (when tied in with camping trip to historical attraction or area); how-to (selection, care, maintenance of RVs, accessories and camping equipment); humor; personal experience; and travel (camping destinations within 200 miles of Philadelphia-DC metro corridor). No "material on camping trips to destinations outside stated coverage area." Buys 40 mss/year. Query. Length: 800-1,500 words. Pays $40-75.
Photos: "Good photos greatly increase likelihood of acceptance. Don't send snapshots, polaroids. We can't use them." Photos purchased with accompanying ms. Captions required. Uses 5x7 or 8x10 b&w glossy prints. Total purchase price for ms includes payment for photos.
Columns/Departments: Camp Cookery (ideas for cooking in RV galleys and over campfires. Should include recipes). Buys 10 mss/year. Query. Length: 500-1,000 words. Pays $25-50.
Tips: "Articles should focus on single attraction or activity or on closely clustered attractions within reach on the same weekend camping trip rather than on types of attractions or activities in general. We're looking for little-known or offbeat items. Emphasize positive aspects of camping: fun, economy, etc. We want feature items, not shorts and fillers."

CAMPING JOURNAL, Davis Publications, 380 Lexington Ave., New York NY 10017. (212)557-9100. Editor-in-Chief: Andrew J. Carra. Managing Editor: Lee Schreiber. 75% freelance written. Emphasizes outdoor recreation. Published 8 times/year. Magazine; 64 pages. Circ. 300,000. Pays on acceptance. Buys all rights. Byline given. Submit seasonal/holiday material 4-6 months in advance of issue date. Photocopied submissions OK. SASE. Reports in 6 weeks. Sample copy $1; free writer's guidelines.
Nonfiction: General interest (travel); how-to (equipment); humor (personal experience); new product; personal experience; photo feature; and travel. Buys 100 mss/year. Query. Length: 1,500-3,500 words. Pays $100-300.
Photos: State availability of photos with query. No additional payment for 8x10 b&w glossy prints

and 2¼x2¼ or 35mm color transparencies. Pays $200-250 for cover photos. Captions preferred. Buys all rights. Model release required.
Fillers: Buys 1/issue. Length: 500-1,000 words. Pays $50-150.

CHECKPOINT, United States Auto Club, Box 67, Motoring Div., South Bend IN 46624. (219)232-5901. Editor: Thom Villing. Assistant Editor: Liz Peralta. Quarterly magazine covering travel and automotive subjects for United States Auto Club members. Circ. 100,000. Average issue includes 6-8 articles. Pays on publication. Buys first North American serial rights and makes work-for-hire assignments. Submit seasonal/holiday material 5 months in advance. Photocopied and previously published (if reworked) submissions OK. SASE. Reports in 6 weeks. Free writer's guidelines.
Nonfiction: General interest and historical (travel-related); how-to (automotive); new product (automotive/energy-related); travel (all types; prefer less known places, predictable car maintenance, events, attractions); photos feature (on travel); and technical (automotive). "No common places, predictable car maintenance, first person, sex, or think pieces." Buys 2 mss/issue. Query. Length: 350-1,200 words. Pays $35-200.
Photos: State availability of photos. Pays $20-100 for 35mm or larger color transparencies. Captions preferred; model release required. Buys one-time rights.
Tips: "Give me an idea I've not seen before. Be fresh, upbeat, lively. Prose must be vigorous, not flabby. If the query is poorly written. I wouldn't dream of asking for the entire article."

CHEVRON USA, Box 6227, San Jose CA 95150. (408)296-1060. Editor: Helen Bignell. Associate Editor: Therese Beaver. 80% freelance written. For members of the Chevron Travel Club. Quarterly. Buys first North American serial rights. Pays for articles on acceptance. Pays for photos on publication. Reports in 2 months. SASE. Free sample copy, writer's guidelines and coverage map.
Nonfiction: "We need lively, well-organized articles with sense of place and history, yet packed with see-and-do information geared toward families. No long-distance travel or driving information. State seasonal or specific slant early. Enthusiasm for, and knowledge of, subject should show. We carry stories with theme subjects (such as circuses) but also need material on handicrafts, energy, conservation, museums, sports and the outdoors. No public relations, brochure approach; no historical treatises." Length: 500-1,500 words. Pays 15¢/word and up.
Photos: Subject matter same as for nonfiction. No empty scenics. Majority of photos must have active people in them. Prefers top quality 35mm, 2¼ or 4x5—all color. Pays $150/page maximum, $75 minimum.
Fillers: Anecdotal material. Must be about travel, personal experiences. Must be original. Length: about 75-100 words. Pays $25 each.

CONNECTICUT MOTORIST, Connecticut Motor Club, 2276 Whitney Ave., Hamden CT 06518. (203)288-7441. Director of Publications: Donald K. Walker. Bimonthly magazine covering domestic and foreign travel and auto safety and maintenance for AAA members in Litchfield, Fairfield, and New Haven counties in southwestern Connecticut. Circ. 154,000. Pays on acceptance. Byline given. Buys all rights. Submit seasonal/holiday material 6 months in advance. Photocopied and previously published submissions OK ("if not published or circulated within our area"). SASE. Reports in 2 weeks on queries; 6 weeks on mss. Free sample copy.
Nonfiction: Book excerpts (from travel books); photo feature; travel; and automotive (but not how-to or repair); and auto and bike safety. "Our travel abroad and travel in New England sections are most accessible to freelancers. Send an article on people, places, activities or events—but *not* just a rehash of tour brochure copy. No 'My Summer Vacation' stories, with pictures of hubby standing next to an historical monument; no auto repair stories." Buys 6-8 mss/year. Send complete ms. Length: 500-1,500 words. Pays $50-300.
Photos: "Photos are usually essential to a travel story." Send photos with ms. Pays $10-25 for 2¼x2¼ color transparencies; $5-15 for 8x10 b&w prints. Reviews b&w contact sheets ("returned after prints selected"). Captions and identification of subject required. Buys all rights.
Tips: "Study the articles in other magazines—*Travel/Holiday, Signature, Adventure Travel, National Geographic.* Don't forget to enclose SASE."

DESERT MAGAZINE, Box 1318, Palm Desert CA 92261. (714)568-2781. Editor: Don MacDonald. Emphasizes Southwest travel, lifestyles and history. "Our magazine covers all of the southwestern desert, including Sonora and Baja in Mexico." For recreation-minded families—middle class income, RV owners, off-roaders, and backpackers. Readers are present, future or immediate past residents of the Southwest. "We welcome writers who are new to the profession or new to us." Monthly magazine. Circ. 75,000. Pays on acceptance. Buys all rights. Submit seasonal or holiday material 6 months in advance. SASE. Reports in 4 weeks. Free writer's guidelines.
Nonfiction: Historical, informational, personal experience, travel, natural sciences and solutions

to problems of desert living. Buys 8 articles/issue. Query. Length: 1,000-2,500 words. Pays $100-400.

Photos: Photo Editor: Tom Threinen. Professional quality photos purchased with or without accompanying ms. Captions required. Pay negotiable.

Tips: "We are not for the typical tourist. Start from the nearest paved road or airport. Fill any piece with interesting/tragic/funny fact and anecdote, historical or current. No lecturing, cautions, politicking or starry-eyed visits to Death Valley. We want the out-of-the-way but still accessible places. Our biggest concern, and cause for rejection, is photo quality."

DISCOVERY MAGAZINE, Allstate Plaza, Northbrook IL 60062. Editor: Sarah Hoban. 75% freelance written. For motor club members; mobile families with above-average income. Quarterly. Circ. 1,000,000. Buys first North American serial rights. Buys 35 mss/year. Pays on acceptance. Free sample copy and writer's guidelines. Submit seasonal material 8-12 months in advance. Reports in 3 weeks. Query; don't send manuscripts. SASE.

Nonfiction and Photos: "The emphasis is on fuel-conscious travel features. Also automotive safety and consumer-related articles. Short pieces on restaurants must include recipes from the establishment. We're looking for polished magazine articles with useful information—not narratives of people's vacations. Query must be literate—clean and free from misspelling, grammatical errors; concise; enthusiastic—the writer must care about the subject and want to sell it to our publication." Day rate is paid; rates for existing photos depend on how the photos are used. Color transparencies (35mm or larger) are preferred. Photos should show people doing things; captions required. Send transparencies by registered mail, with plenty of cardboard protection. Buys one-time rights for photography. Color photos are returned after use. Length: 1,000-2,500 words. "Rates vary, depending on type of article, ranging from $125-750 for full-length features."

Fillers: True, humorous travel anecdotes. Length: 50-150 words. Pays $10.

EXPEDITION, The Magazine of the Americas, 2216 4th St., N., St. Petersburg FL 33704. (813)821-1038. Editor: Andrea Favara. Bimonthly magazine covering travel and cultural experiences for "international businessmen, travellers, retired executives and travel-oriented agencies." Circ. 30,000. Pays on publication. Buys one-time rights. Simultaneous and previously published submissions OK. SASE. Reports in 2 weeks. Sample copy $2; free writer's guidelines.

Tips: Concentrate on Western hemisphere.

FAMILY MOTOR COACHING, 8291 Clough Pike, Cincinnati OH 45244. (513)474-3622. Managing Editor: Greg Clouse. 75% freelance written. Emphasizes travel with motorhome, and motorhome modifications. Monthly magazine; 130 pages. Circ. 26,500. Pays on acceptance. Buys all rights. Byline given. Phone queries OK. Submit seasonal/holiday material 3 months in advance. SASE. Reports in 2 months. Sample copy $2; free writer's guidelines.

Nonfiction: Motorhome travel and living on the road; travel (various areas of country accessible by motor coach); how-to (modify motor coach features); bus conversions, and nostalgia. Buys 3 mss/issue. Query. Length: 1,500 words minimum. Pays $50-200.

Photos: State availability of photos with query. Offers no additional payment for b&w contact sheet(s) 35mm or 2¼x2¼ color transparencies. Captions required. Buys first rights.

GOING PLACES, Signature Publications, 2020 Dempster, Evanston IL 60202. Contact: Editor. Bimonthly magazine covering travel. "The complete travel magazine." Estab. 1980. Circ. 100,000. Pays on acceptance. Byline given. Buys all rights. Submit seasonal/holiday material 6 months in advance. Photocopied and previously published submissions OK "if indicated where." SASE. Reports in 6 weeks on queries. Sample copy for 9x12 SAE and 2 first class stamps; writer's guidelines for business size SAE and 1 first class stamp.

Nonfiction: All aspects of travel. Buys 40+ mss/year. Query with clips of published work. Length: 3,000 maximum. Pays 20¢/word.

Photos: State availability of photos. Reviews color transparencies. "Photos are considered a separate contract."

Columns/Departments: Buys 18 mss/year. Query with clips of published work. Length: 1,000 words maximum. Pays 20¢/word.

HOME & AWAY, Box 3985, Omaha NE 68103. Editor: Barc Wade. Official publication of Midwestern AAA Clubs. Bimonthly covering travel by auto and regional interest. Query. Submit seasonal/holiday material 1 year in advance. Simultaneous and photocopied submissions OK. Previously published work OK, if published in a different region. Reports in 3 weeks. Sample copy and writer's guidelines for 9x12 SASE.

Nonfiction: General interest pieces related to cars or Midwest tourist region; how-to; personal travel experiences; photo features about travel; technical pieces; and international and domestic travel articles. No "lists of things to see and do at a destination." Length: 1,200-1,800 words. Pays $300-400.

Photos: Pays $25 minimum for color.

JOURNAL OF CHRISTIAN CAMPING, Christian Camping International, Box 400, Somonauk IL 60552. Editor: Gary L. Wall. Managing Editor: Charlyene Wall. Emphasizes the broad scope of organized camping with emphasis on Christian camping. "Leaders of youth camps and adult conferences read our magazine to get practical help in ways to run their camps." Bimonthly magazine; 32-48 pages. Circ. 6,000. Pays on acceptance. Buys all rights. Pays 25% kill fee. Byline given. SASE. Reports in 4 weeks. Sample copy $2; writer's guidelines for SASE.

Nonfiction: General interest (trends in organized camping in general and Christian camping in particular); how-to (anything involved with organized camping from repairing refrigerators, to motivating staff, to programming, to record keeping, to camper follow-up); inspirational (limited use, but might be interested in practical applications of Scriptural principles to everyday situations in camping, no preaching); interview (with movers and shakers in camping and Christian camping in particular, submit a list of basic questions first); and opinion (write a letter to the editor). Buys 50-60 mss/year. Query desired, but accept unsolicited mss. Length: 600-2,500 words. Pays 5¢/word.

Photos: Send photos with ms. Pays $10/5x7 b&w contact sheet or print; price negotiable for 35mm color transparencies. Buys all rights. Captions required.

LEISUREGUIDE, 29901 Agoura Rd., Agoura, CA 91301. Managing Editor: Bob Howells. An in-room hotel guidebook emphasizing information for travelers in Chicago, Boston, Houston, Puerto Rico, Florida Gold Coast (Miami to Palm Beach), Central Florida (Orlando area), South Carolina's Grand Strand (Myrtle Beach) and Louisville. "We try to establish a feeling of intimacy with each of our markets, so the traveler has confidence in the information we present. And we present it in a lively, readable manner. We also strive for excellence in graphics and photography." Each edition is an annual hardcover magazine; 84-200 pages. Pays on publication. Buys all rights. Byline given. Reports in 6 weeks. Sample copy $2.

Nonfiction: "We seek articles that capture the true essence of each of our cities for the sophisticated traveler who stays in luxury hotels. We occasionally publish articles of general interest to all travelers, but most articles focus on the cities themselves. We also publish a photo essay in each edition that captures an aspect or aspects of the city in a highly unique fashion." Buys about 25 mss/year. Query. "We want to know that the writer is intimately familiar with the city involved, and that he has seen our publication and knows our sophisticated approach." SASE. Length: 1,000-2,500 words. Pays $125-300.

Photos: Purchased without ms or on assignment. Pays $50/page for b&w, $100/page for color.

Tips: "Prove to us that you can write about the city involved in a highly knowledgeable, lively fashion. Writing ability means everything. Submitting top quality color transparencies is a plus, but not necessary."

THE LUFKIN LINE, Lufkin Industries, Inc., Box 849, Lufkin TX 75901. Editor: Miss Virginia R. Allen. For men in oil and industrial and marine gear industries; readers mostly degreed engineers. Each issue devoted to different areas where division offices located; that is, West Coast, Canada, Mid-Continent, Rocky Mountain, Texas, Gulf Coast, International. Quarterly. Circ. 12,000. Not copyrighted. Buys 4-8 mss/year. Pays on acceptance. Submit seasonal material 4 months in advance. Reports in 1 month. Query showing prose style as well as subject matter. SASE. Free sample copy and writer's guidelines.

Nonfiction and Photos: "Travel articles. Subjects dealing with US and Canada, and (rarely) foreign travel subjects. Product articles staff-written. Length: 1,000-1,200 words. Pays $100/ms with illustrating photos. Color transparencies purchased for front cover (no seasonal subjects); pays $50. Illustrations for travel articles may be color prints or transparencies (no smaller than 2¼x2¼). No b&w photos are purchased. Color photos for travel articles may be secured from state tourist or development commissions.

MICHIGAN LIVING/AAA MOTOR NEWS, Automobile Club of Michigan, Auto Club Dr., Dearborn MI 48126. (313)336-1504. Editor: Len Barnes. 50% freelance written. Emphasizes travel and auto use. Monthly magazine; 48 pages. Circ. 820,000. Pays on acceptance. Buys first North American serial rights. Pays 100% kill fee. Byline given. Submit seasonal/holiday material 3 months in advance. SASE. Reports in 4-6 weeks. Buys 120 mss/year. Free sample copy and writer's guidelines.

Nonfiction: Marcia Danner, Managing Editor. Travel articles on US and Canadian topics, but not on California, Florida or Arizona. Send complete ms. Length: 800-1,800 words. Pays $75-300.

Photos: Photos purchased with accompanying ms. Captions required. Pays $25-150 for color transparencies; total purchase price for ms includes payment for b&w photos.

Tips: "In addition to descriptions of things to see and do, articles should contain accurate, current information on costs the traveler would encounter on his trip. Items such as lodging, meal and entertainment expenses should be included, not in the form of a balance sheet but as an integral part of the piece. We want the sounds, sights, tastes, smells of a place or experience so someone will feel he has been there and knows if he wants to go back."

THE MIDWEST MOTORIST, The Auto Club of Missouri, 201 Progress Pkwy., Maryland Heights MO 63043. (314)576-7350. Editor: Michael J. Right. Associate Editors: Carolyn Callison, Tim Sitek. For the motoring public. Bimonthly magazine; 32 pages. Circ. 300,000. Pays on acceptance or publication depending on the situation. Not copyrighted. Pays kill fee as agreed. Byline given. Submit seasonal/holiday material 3-4 months in advance. Simultaneous, photocopied and previously published submissions OK. SASE. Reports in 1 month. Free sample copy and writer's guidelines.

Nonfiction: General interest; historical (of Midwest regional interest); humor (motoring slant); interview, profile, travel and photo feature. No technical auto or safety stories. Buys 3 mss/issue. Query with list of credits or clips of published work. Length: 1,000-1,800 words. Pays $50-200.

Photos: Send photos with ms. Uses b&w contact sheets or prints and color transparencies for cover. Offers no additional payment for photos accepted with ms. Captions preferred.

Tips: "We are tired of cliche-ridden travel stories and articles on the well-known vacation spots."

MOTORHOME LIFE, Trailer Life Publishing Co., Inc., 29901 Agoura Rd., Agoura CA 91301. (213)991-4980. Managing Editor: Michael Schneider. For owners and prospective buyers of motorhomes. Published 9 times/year. Circ. 125,000. Buys all rights. Byline given. Buys 50 mss/year. Pays on publication. Submit seasonal material 3 months in advance. Reports in 1 month. SASE. Sample copy $1; free writer's guidelines.

Nonfiction and Photos: "Articles which tell the owner of a self-propelled RV about interesting places to travel, interesting things to do. Human interest and variety articles sought as well. All material must be tailored specifically for our audience." Information, personal experience, humor, historical, opinion, travel, new product and technical articles. Length: 2,500 words maximum. Pays $75-200. Photos purchased with accompanying ms with no additional payment.

NATIONAL MOTORIST, National Automobile Club, 1 Market Plaza, #300, San Francisco CA 94105. (415)777-4000. Editor: Jane M. Offers. 75% freelance written. Emphasizes motor travel in the West. Bimonthly magazine; 32 pages. Circ. 265,000. Pays on acceptance for article, layout stage for pix. Buys first publication rights. Byline given. Submit seasonal/holiday material 3 months in advance SASE. Reports in 2 weeks.

Nonfiction: Well-researched articles on care of car, travel by car. Profile/interview (of someone in transportation/energy field); and travel (interesting places and areas to visit in the 11 Western states). Buys 2-3 mss/issue. Query. Length: "around 1,100 words." Pays 10¢/word and up.

Photos: "Suggestions welcome. May accompany with ms, but considered separately. Payment either with ms or separately, depending on source. Often procured from source other than author." Captions optional, "but must have caption info for pix." Send prints or transparencies. Pays $20 maximum/8x10 b&w glossy print; $30 minimum/35mm, 2¼x2¼ or 4x5 color transparency. Model release required.

NORTHEAST OUTDOORS, Box 2180, Waterbury CT 06722. (203)755-0158. Editor: John Florian. 70% freelance written. Monthly. Circ. 20,000. Buys all rights. Byline given. Pays on publication. "Queries are not required, but are useful for our planning and to avoid possible duplication of subject matter. If you have any questions, contact the editor." Deadlines are on the 1st of the month preceding publication. Reports in 15-30 days. SASE. Free sample copy.

Nonfiction and Photos: Interested in articles and photos that pertain to outdoor activities in the Northeast. Recreational vehicle tips and campgrounds are prime topics, along with first-person travel experiences in the Northeast while camping. "While the primary focus is on camping, we carry some related articles on outdoor topics like skiing, nature, hiking, fishing, canoeing, etc. In each issue we publish a 'Favorite Trip' experience, submitted by a reader, relating to a favorite camping experience, usually in the Northeast. Payment for this is $20 and writing quality need not be professional. Another reader feature is My Favorite Campground. Payment is $10. Our pay rate is flexible, but generally runs from $30-40 for features without photos, and up to $80 for features accompanied by 2 or more photos. Features should be from 300-1,000 words. Premium rates are paid on the basis of quality, not length. Pays $10/8x10 b&w print."

ODYSSEY, H.M. Gousha Publications, Box 6227, San Jose CA 95150. (408)296-1060. Editor: Pat Ford. Bimonthly magazine devoted to travel and leisure travel with national and international coverage. Pays on acceptance. Buys first North American serial rights. Submit seasonal material 1 year in advance. SASE. Reports in 1 month. "If no response to query within 6 weeks, writer should feel free to offer idea elsewhere." Free sample copy and writer's guidelines.

Nonfiction: Travel and travel-related features; how-to (get started in a new sport, hobby or recreation); and unusually interesting industrial tours open to the general public. "We want lively, well-researched articles packed with helpful information, such as what to see and do in a given city or destination, as well as how to see it so visitors can enjoy it more fully. The style should be friendly and informal. We don't object to personalization or anecdotes if skillfully done. Please study magazine beore sending submission." Buys 6-7 mss/issue. Query with clips of previously published work. Length, major feature: 1,200-1,600 words. Pays $220-$300 (first-time contributors) for major features.

Photos: Lisa Worthington, photo editor. State availability of color photos or send photos with ms. Pays $75-$150 for 2¼, 4x5 or 35mm color transparencies. Pays $350 for a front cover that is article-related and $200 for a back cover not article related. Buys one-time rights. "Send photos featuring people enjoying leisure and travel."

Columns/Departments: Cities and Sights (500-600 words about US towns, museums, zoos, marketplaces, historic sights or scenic attractions); People in Travel (500-600 words about someone who travels a great deal in pursuit of career or hobby; must have color vertical photo); and Driver's Seat (about driving safety, auto maintenance). Buys 3 mss/issue. Send complete ms on spec or query with clips of previously published work. Length: 500-600 words. Pays $100 (first-time contributors) for Cities and Sights and People In Travel; $150 for solid, informative Driver's Seat articles and/or auto/safety quizzes.

OHIO MOTORIST, Box 6150, Cleveland OH 44101. Editor: A. K. Murway Jr. 10-15% freelance written. For AAA members in 8 northeast Ohio counties. Monthly. Circ. 265,000. Buys one-time publication rights. Byline given. Buys 30 mss/year. Pays on acceptance. Submit seasonal material 2 months prior to season. Reports in 2 weeks. Submit complete ms. SASE. Free sample copy.

Nonfiction and Photos: "Travel, including foreign; automotive, highways, etc.; motoring laws and safety. No particular approach beyond brevity and newspaper journalistic treatment. Articles for travel seasons." Length: 2,000 words maximum. Pays $50-200/article including b&w photos. $125-250 for articles with color photos, transparencies any size. 8x10 b&w photos preferred. Purchased with accompanying mss. Captions required. Ohioana is major need.

Poetry: Humorous verse. Length: 4-6 lines. Pays $8-15.

PACIFIC BOATING ALMANAC, Box Q, Ventura CA 93002. (805)644-6043. Editor: William Berssen. For "Western boat owners." Published in 3 editions to cover the Pacific Coastal area. Circ. 30,000. Buys all rights. Buys 12 mss/year. Pays on publication. Sample copy $6.95. Submit seasonal material 3 to 6 months in advance. Reports in 4 weeks. Query. SASE.

Nonfiction and Photos: "This is a cruising guide, published annually in 3 editions, covering all of the navigable waters in the Pacific coast. Though we are almost entirely staff-produced, we would be interested in well-written articles on cruising and trailer-boating along the Pacific coast and in the navigable lakes and rivers of the Western states from Baja, California to Alaska inclusive." Pays $50 minimum. Pays $10/8x10 b&w glossy print.

Tips: "We are also publishers of boating books that fall within the classification of 'where-to' and 'how-to.' Authors are advised not to send mss until requested after we've reviewed a 2-4 page outline of the projected books."

RV'N ON, 10417 Chandler Blvd., North Hollywood CA 91601. (213)763-4515. Editor/Publisher: Kim Ouimet. Monthly mini-newspaper, 16-22 pages, about recreational vehicles (motorhomes, campers and trailers, etc.) Official publication of the International Travel and Trailer Club, Inc. Estab. 1979. Circ. 550. Pays on publication. Buys one-time rights. Submit seasonal material 3 months in advance. Simultaneous and photocopied submissions OK. SASE. Reports in 6 weeks. Sample copy 95¢; free writer's guidelines with SASE.

Nonfiction: General interest; historical; how-to; humor; interview; nostalgia; opinion; travel; new product; personal experience; and technical. Buys 30 mss/year. Send complete ms. Length: 100-300 words. Pays in copies.

Photos: State availability of photos. Pays $5 maximum for 5x7 b&w glossy prints. Captions preferred; model release required. Buys one-time rights.

Columns/Departments: Campfire Tales (fiction or humorous, anecdotes or short bedtime stories for children); Roadwise Driving Tips; Rolling Kitchen; An Unusual Place—places (off the road worth visiting); A Most Unusual Person (release required if name used). Buys 12 mss/year. Send complete ms. Length: 100-500 words. Pays 3¢/word-$15.

Fiction: Adventure, fantasy, historical, humorous, and suspense. No lengthy items. Buys 6 mss/year. Length: 200-400 words. Pays 3¢/word minimum.

Fillers: Jokes, anecdotes, short humor and newsbreaks. Buys 12 mss/year. Length: 25-50 words. Pays $2 maximum.

Tips: "Know motorhomes, campers, etc. and what will be of interest to owners, such as storage tips, repairs, tips of traveling with animals and children. We are anxious to have actual RVers submit material."

SOUTHERN RV, Intra-South Publications, 6637 Superior Ave., Sarasota FL 33581. (813)921-5687. Editor-in-Chief: George J. Haborak. Emphasizes recreational vehicles and the outdoors. Monthly tabloid; 72 pages. Circ. 30,000. Pays 1 month after publication. Buys all rights. Submit seasonal/holiday material 2 months in advance. Simultaneous (but not to another publication in the Southeast), photocopied and previously published submissions OK. SASE. Reports in 1 month. Free sample copy.

Nonfiction: General interest (anything related in some way to the great Southeastern outdoors scene, fishing, camping, but not hunting); how-to (get the most out of a camping trip, cook camp meals, do something 'outdoorsy' and do it easily); historical (short articles on historical areas of the South are welcome); humor (any tidbit of humor related to camping out or using an RV); personal experience (camping experiences not based on specific locales); photo feature (on the Southeast—any area); technical (semi-technical how-to-fix-it articles would fit well occasionally); and travel (any travel experience relating to the Southeast and RV's). Buys 6 mss/issue. Submit complete ms. Length: 800-2,000 words. Pays $15-50.

Photos: State availability of photos with query. Offers no additional payment for photos accepted with ms, "they just make for a better article and better chances of being published." Uses 3x5 glossy b&w prints. Captions required. Buys all rights.

TRAILER LIFE, TL Enterprises, Inc., 29901 Agoura Rd., Agoura CA 90301. (213)991-4980. Editorial Director: Alice Robison. Monthly magazine for owners and potential buyers of trailers, campers and motor homes. Circ. 324,906. Pays on publication. Buys all rights. Phone queries OK. Submit seasonal material 4 months in advance. SASE. Reports in 2 weeks on queries; in 3 weeks on mss. Free sample copy and writer's guidelines.

Nonfiction: Art of using a trailer, camper or motor home and the problems involved. Length: 2,000 words maximum. Also uses how-to articles with step-by-step photos a necessity. Length: 800 words maximum. Combine as many operations in each photo or drawing as possible. Personal experience stories must be truly interesting. Merely living in or traveling by trailer is not enough. Uses travel articles with 3-6 good 8x10 glossy prints on trips that are inexpensive or unusual, into areas which are accessible by a travel trailer or pickup camper. Length: 1,000-2,000 words. Also uses short travel pieces, with a couple of photos of interesting places off the established routes. Length: 100-250 words. Allied interest articles are one of main interests, things that trailerists do, like boating, hiking, fishing and spelunking hobbies. A definite tie-in with travel trailers, motor homes or pickup campers is essential. Tell the reader how their trailers fit into the sport and where they can park while there. All travel articles should include basic information on trailer parking facilities in the areas, costs, location, and time of year, etc. Payment varies "based on the quality of the material submitted and how it's used, but $125-$175 is the present rate."

Photos: "We are often asked by photographers about submissions of single photos. We seldom, if ever, buy photos alone; we suggest that if a photographer has a series of related good pictures either black and white or color—involving RV activity, that he wrap a story around the photos and submit the pictures and manuscript as a package. Photos should be 8x10 glossy. Prints should be numbered and the photographer identified on the back, with numbers corresponding to a caption sheet. Photos should show action and should be as close up as the subject matter will allow."

TRANSITIONS, 18 Hulst Rd., Amherst MA 01002. (413)256-0373. Editor and Publisher: Prof. Clayton A. Hubbs. Travel Editor: Bill Gertz. Managing Editor: Max Hartshorne. Emphasizes educational travel. *Transitions* is a resource guide to work, study and travel abroad, for students travel advisors and low budget travelers. Bound magazine. Circ. 10,000. Pays on publication. Rights revert to writer. Byline given. Phone queries OK. SASE. Reports in 4 weeks. Sample copy $1.50; free writer's guidelines.

Nonfiction: How-to (find courses, inexpensive lodging and travel); interview (information on specific areas and people); personal experience (evaluation of courses, study tours, economy travel); and travel (what to see and do in specific areas of the world, new learning and travel ideas). No travel pieces for businessmen; no "hitching across Europe" or grape picking stories. Buys 12 mss/issue. Query with credentials. Length: 500-1,500 words. Pays $25-75.

Photos: Send photos with ms. Pays $5-15 for 8x10 b&w glossy prints, higher for some covers. No color. Offers no additional payment for photos accompanying ms. Buys one-time rights. Captions required.

Columns/Departments: Studynotes (evaluation of courses or programs); Travel notes (new ideas for offbeat independent travel); and Jobnotes (how to find it and what to expect). Buys 8/issue. Send complete ms. Length: 1,000 words maximum. Pays $10-50.

Fillers: Newsbreaks (having to do with travel, particularly offbeat educational travel and work or study abroad). Buys 5/issue. Length: 100 words maximum. Pays $5-20.

Tips: "We like nuts and bolts stuff. Real practical information, especially on how to work abroad."

THE TRAVEL ADVISOR, Box 716, Bronxville NY 10708. Editor-in-Chief: Hal E. Gieseking. 55% freelance written. Monthly newsletter; 12 pages. Owned by *Travel/Holiday* magazine. Circ. 800,000 (published as part of *Travel/Holiday*). Pays on publication. Buys all rights. Pays kill fee sometimes; depends on work done. Byline given on destination reports but not on short travel items. SASE. Reports in 4 weeks. Free sample copy and writer's guidelines. No photos used.

Nonfiction: "Send us short, *very candid* items based on the writer's own travel experience—*not* written first-person. Example: a baggage rip-off in Rome; a great new restaurant in Tokyo (with prices)." Expose (candid look at the travel industry); and how-to (good, inside information on how travelers can avoid problems, save money, etc.). "No typical travel articles that extol the setting sun." Buys 100 mss/year. Submit complete ms. Length: 20-150 words. Pays $20/item. Also buys candid destination reports which are assigned (based on query and writer's reputation). Length: 2,500 words. Query. Pays $250 maximum.

389-5640

TRAVEL AND LEISURE, 1350 Avenue of the Americas, New York NY 10019. (212)399-2500. Editor-in-Chief: Pamela Fiori. Monthly. Circ. 925,000. Buys first North American serial rights. Pays 25% kill fee. Byline given unless material is assigned as research. Pays on acceptance. Reports in 2 weeks. Query. SASE.

Nonfiction: Uses articles on travel and vacation places, food, wine, shopping, sports. Nearly all articles are assigned. Length: 2,000-3,000 words. Pays $750-2,000.

Photos: Makes assignments mainly to established photographers. Pays expenses.

Tips: "New writers might try to get something in one of our regional editions (East, West, South and Midwest). They don't pay as much as our national articles ($600), but it is a good way to start. We have a need for pieces that run no more than 800-1,200 words. Regionals cover any number of possibilities from a profile of an interesting town in a certain state to unusual new attractions."

TRAVEL/HOLIDAY MAGAZINE, Travel Magazine, Inc., 51 Atlantic Ave., Floral Park NY 11001. (516)352-9700. Editor: Barbara Lotz. Managing Editor: Jim Ferri. For the active traveler with time and money to travel several times a year. Monthly magazine; 100 pages. Circ. 800,000. Pays on acceptance. Buys first North American serial rights. Byline given. Submit seasonal/holiday material 6 months in advance. SASE. Reports in 3 weeks. Free sample copy and writer's guidelines.

Nonfiction: Interested in any travel-related item. Buys 100 mss/year. Query by letter and include clips of previously published work. "Don't ask if we want anything on France, Italy, etc. Pick a specific area and tell us what make sit so interesting that we should denote space to it. Is it a new and upcoming resort area? Are there interesting museums, superb restaurants, spectacular vistas, etc.? Let us know how you plan to handle the piece—give us the mood of the city, area, etc., about which you plan to write." Length: 1,500-2,500 words. Pays $200 minimum.

Photos: Pays $25 minimum for b&w 5x7 or larger prints; and $50 for 35mm or larger color transparencies used inside (more for covers). Offers no additional payment for photos accepted with ms. Captions required. Buys one-time rights.

Tips: "Feature stories should be about major destinations: cities, states, regions, etc. Featurettes can be about individual attractions, specific festivals, side trips, etc. Either could be critical, including both positive and negative aspects. We welcome sidebar service information. Stimulate reader interest in the subject as a travel destination through lively, entertainng writing. A good way to break in if we're not familiar with your writing is to send us a good idea for a featurette (a walking tour of historic montreal, a famous castle open to tourists, etc., are items we've run in the past). We are looking for the highest quality photography to accompany articles. If you do not have quality photography, let us know where we can obtain pictures. Convey the mood of a place without being verbose; although we like good anecdotal material, our primary interest is in the destination itself, not the author's adventures."

TRAVEL SMART, Communications House, Inc., Dobbs Ferry NY 10522. (914)693-4208. Editor/Publisher: H.J. Teison. Managing Editor/Publisher: Mary L. Hunt. Covers information on "budget, good-value travel." Monthly newsletter. Pays on publication. Buys all rights. Photocopied submissions OK. SASE. Reports in 6 weeks. Free sample copy and writer's guidelines for #10 SASE and 28¢ postage.

Nonfiction: Mary L. Hunt, managing editor. "Interested primarily in great bargains or little-known deals on transportations, lodging, food, unusual destinations that won't break the bank.

Please, no destination stories on major Caribbean islands, London, New York, no travelogues, my vacation, poetry, fillers. No photos or illustrations. Just hard facts." Query first. Length: 100-500 words. Pays $5-10.

Tips: "Send clippings of ads for bargain airfares, package tours, hotel deals in your area (outside New York only). When you travel, check out small hotels offering good prices, little known restaurants, and send us brief rundown (with prices, phone numbers, addresses) of at least 4 at one location. Information must be current and backed up with literature, etc. Include your phone number with submission, because we sometimes make immediate assignments."

TRAVELHOST, America's Number 1 Travel Magazine, Omni Industries, 6116 N. Central, Suite 1020, Dallas TX 75206. (214)691-1163. Managing Editor: J. Nelson Black. In-room weekly magazine of general interest to American travelers. Circ. 1,000,000+. Byline given. Buys all rights. Submit seasonal/holiday material 2 months in advance. Simultaneous queries OK. SASE. Reports in 2 weeks. Sample copy for 9x12 SAE and 3 first class stamps.

Nonfiction: General interest and travel. No "puff pieces, travel articles of purely local interest, or dull and humorless pieces appealing to isolated and parochial interest." Buys 3 mss/year. "We use less than 5% freelance work/year; 95% staff written." Send complete ms. Length: 500-2,400 words. Pays 20¢/word.

Tips: "Query us and convince us of your ability to write a piece of broad national appeal that will amuse, inform and delight our readers better than we can. Because of our format and readership, articles for *Travelhost* must have nationwide appeal within the context of the 63 cities and local editions in which the national section appears."

TRAVELORE REPORT, 225 S. 15th St., Philadelphia PA 19102. Editor: Ted Barkus. For affluent travelers; businessmen, retirees, well-educated; interested in specific tips, tours, and bargain opportunities in travel. Monthly newsletter; 4 pages. Buys all rights. Buys 25-50 mss/year. Pays on publication. Sample copy $1. Submit seasonal material 2 months in advance.

Nonfiction: "Brief insights (25-200 words) with facts, prices, names of hotels and restaurants, etc., on offbeat subjects of interest to people going places. What to do, what not to do. Supply information. We will rewrite if acceptable. We're candid—we tell it like it is with no sugar coating. Avoid telling us about places in United States or abroad without specific recommendations (hotel name, costs, rip-offs, why, how long, etc.)." Pays $5.

VISTA/USA, Box 161, Convent Station NJ 07961. (201)538-7600. Editor: Patrick Sarver. Managing Editor: Kathleen Caccavale. Quarterly magazine for the one million members of the Exxon Travel Club. "Our publication uses articles on North American areas without overtly encouraging travel. We strive to use as literate a writing as we can in our articles, helping our readers to gain an in-depth understanding of cities, towns and areas as well as other aspects of American culture that affect the character of the nation." Circ. 1,050,000. Pays on acceptance. Buys first North American serial rights. Query about seasonal subjects 18 months in advance. SASE. Reports in 1 month. Free sample copy and writer's guidelines.

Nonfiction: General interest (geographically-oriented articles on North America focusing on the character of an area; also general articles related to travel and places); humor (related to travel or places); and photo features (photo essays on subjects such as autumn, winter, highly photogenic travel subjects; and special interest areas). "We buy feature articles on North America, Hawaii, Mexico and the Caribbean that appeal to a national audience." No articles that mention driving or follow routes on a map or articles about hotels, restaurants or annual events. Uses 7-10 mss/issue. Query with outline and clips of previously published work. Length: 1,200-2,500 words. Pays $500 minimum.

Photos: Keith Slack, art director. Send photos with ms. Pays $100 minimum for color transparencies. Captions preferred. Buys one-time rights.

Columns/Departments: Places of Interest ("on places in the US that do not have enough national significance to rate as features, along with non-North American areas; tight, straightforward prose to give the reader a vignette impression of places with as much information as is practical within a short length"). Uses 5 mss/issue. Query with clips of previously published work. Length: 400-600 words. Pays $125-$150.

Tips: "We are looking for readable pieces with good writing that will interest armchair travelers as much as readers who may want to visit the areas you write about. Articles should have definite themes and should give our readers an insight into the character and flavor of an area. Stories about personal experiences must impart a sense of drama and excitement or have a strong human-interest angle. Stories about areas should communicate a strong sense of what it feels like to be there. Good use of anecdotes and quotes should be included. Study the articles in the magazine to understand how they are organized, how they present their subjects, the range of writing styles, and the specific types of subjects used. Then query and enclose samples of your best writing."

WOODALL'S CAMPING HOTLINE, (formerly *Woodall's Trailer & RV Travel*), 500 Hyacinth Place, Highland Park IL 60035. (312)433-4550. Editor: Larry Green. 25% freelance written. For camping families whose interests include travel in North America, and buying, maintaining, customizing and using their recreation vehicles and tents. Monthly magazine. Estab. 1981. Circ. 50,000. Rights purchased vary with author and material. Usually buys all rights. Pays 25-50% kill fee, depending on the assignment. Byline given. Buys 30 mss/year. Pays on acceptance. No photocopied or simultaneous submissions. Submit seasonal material 6 months in advance. Reports in 4 weeks. Query or submit complete ms. SASE. Free sample copy.
Nonfiction: "Travel guides and narratives providing comprehensive views of great camping areas. Also, humor, profiles (especially of those who live and work on the road); recipe and menu ideas; money-saving tips; vehicle maintenance and improvement; insurance, equipment, etc. Our greatest joy is a thoroughly researched article in which facts, figures, quotes and conclusions are presented in clear, concise prose, and in a logical sequence. We avoid material that is slanted exclusively to the raw beginner. Best areas of query: unusual travel destinations with camping tie-in, tips gained from experience, and new developments in industry, conservation and camping. Pays $75-200; more on assignment.
Photos: B&w and color purchased with mss.
Tips: "A background in this special interest field is a must; so is a familiarity with our editorial style and format. The ripest subject areas are probably general interest material and off-the-beaten-path travel destinations."

WORLD TRAVELING, Midwest News Service, Inc., 30943 Club House Lane, Farmington Hills MI 48018. Editor: Theresa Mitan. Bimonthly magazine. Circ. 8,000-9,000. Pays on publication. Buys all rights. Byline given. Submit seasonal/holiday material 6 months in advance. Simultaneous submissions OK. SASE. Reports in 2 weeks. Sample copy $2.
Nonfiction: General interest, how-to (on any travel experience that might help other travelers, e.g., adventure travel, hang-gliding); humor; photo feature and travel. Buys 6 mss/issue. Send complete ms. Length: 1,000 words. Pays $100 for 1,000 words.
Photos: Send photos with ms. Pays $10 for b&w prints; $10 for color transparencies. Buys one-time rights.
Columns & Departments: Good Restaurant Guide and Question and Answers about travel. Query or send complete ms. Length: 500 words.
Fillers: Jokes, gags, anecdotes and short humor. Pays 10¢/word.

Union

OCAW UNION NEWS, Box 2812, Denver CO 80201. (303)893-0811. Editor: Jerry Archuleta. Official publication of Oil, Chemical and Atomic Workers International Union. For union members. Monthly tabloid newspaper; 12 pages. Circ. 155,000. Not copyrighted. Byline given. Pays on acceptance. Reports in 30 days. Query. SASE. Free sample copy.
Nonfiction: Labor union materials, political subjects and consumer interest articles, slanted toward workers and consumers, with liberal political view. Interview, profile, think pieces and exposes. Most material is done on assignment. Length: 1,500-1,800 words. Pays $50-75.
Photos: No additional payment is made for 8x10 b&w glossy photos used with mss. Captions required.

UTU NEWS, United Transportation Union, 14600 Detroit Ave., Cleveland, OH 44107. (216)228-9400. Editor: Jim Turner. For members of the union (250,000) working in the crafts of engineer, conductor, firemen and brakemen on North American railroads. Weekly newspaper; 4 pages. (Also one monthly tabloid; 8 pages). Pays on publication. Buys photos only. Buys all rights. Phone queries OK. Reports "at once."
Photos: Current news shots of railroad or bus accidents, especially when employees are killed or injured. Captions required. Pays $20 minimum for any size b&w glossy prints.

Market conditions are constantly changing! If this is 1983 or later, buy the newest edition of *Writer's Market* at your favorite bookstore or use the back-of-the-book order form.

Women's

The publications listed in this category specialize in material of interest to women. Other publications that occasionally use material slanted to women's interests can be found in the following categories: Alternative; Business and Finance; Child Care and Parental Guidance; Confession; Education; Food and Drink; Hobby and Craft; Home and Garden; Military; Religious; and Sports publications.

THE AMERICAN MIZRACHI WOMAN, American Mizrachi Women, 817 Broadway, New York NY 10003. (212)477-4720. Executive Editor: Ruth Weinfeld. Editor: Agatha I. Leifer. Magazine published 8 times/year "concerned with Jewish and Israeli themes, i.e., Jewish art, Jewish sociology, Jewish communities around the world to an audience with an above average educational level, a commitment to Jewish tradition and Zionism and a concern for the future of the Jewish community the world over." Circ. 50,000. Pays on publication. Buys all rights. Submit seasonal material 6 months in advance. SASE. Reports in 1 month. Free sample copy and writer's guidelines.
Nonfiction: General interest; historical; interview (with notable figures in Jewish and Israeli life); nostalgia; travel; and photo feature (particularly Jewish holiday photos). "We do special holiday features for all Jewish holidays." Buys 32 mss/year. Query. Length: 1,000-2,000 words. Pays $50 minimum.
Photos: State availability of photos. Reviews 5x7 b&w glossy prints. Offers no additional payment for photos accepted with ms. Captions preferred. Buys one-time rights.
Columns/Departments: Jews Around the World (1,000-2,000 words); Life in Israel (1,000-2,000 words); Book Reviews (500-1,000 words); and Jewish Holiday Recipes (4 recipes). Buys 32 mss/year. Query. Length: 1,000-2,000 words. Pays $50 minimum.
Poetry: Free verse and traditional. Buys 5/year. Submit 3 maximum. Length: 10-50 lines. Pays $10 minimum.
Tips: "We are interested in adding to our stable of freelance writers. The best way to break in is to send a detailed query about a subject you would like to handle for the magazine. All queries will be carefully considered and answered."

BLUEGRASS WOMAN, The Magazine for Women of Kentucky, 449 S. Ashland, Lexington KY 40502. (606)259-5676. Editor: Suzanne Cassidy. Managing Editor: Anne Cassidy. Bimonthly magazine for "well-educated, upwardly mobile Kentucky women interested in local, regional, and national trends that influence their lives." Circ. 6,000. Pays on publication. Byline given. Buys first North American serial rights. Submit seasonal/holiday material 4 months in advance. Simultaneous queries and submissions, photocopied submissions OK ("if so indicated"). Reports in 6 weeks on queries; 1 month on mss. Sample copy $1.
Nonfiction: Anne Cassidy, managing editor. Expose (of Kentucky issues); general interest (current issues); how-to (on home, personal grooming, crafts, gardening, smart shopping); humor; interview/profile (of outstanding women residing in Kentucky or originally from Kentucky; new product (of interest to women); personal experience; photo feature (on homes, events, people); travel (anywhere); and the arts (performing or visual). Buys 30 mss/year. Query with clips of published work. Length: 1,000-3,000 words. Pays $50-150.
Photos: State availability of photos. Reviews 35mm color transparencies and 5x7 b&w prints. "Photos are paid for with payment for ms." Model release and identification of subjects required.
Fiction: Anne Cassidy, managing editor. Fantasy; historical (Kentucky-oriented); humorous; mainstream; mystery; serialized novels; and suspense. Buys 6 mss/year. Send complete ms. Length: 2,000-4,000 words. Pays $50-150.

BRIDE'S, Conde Nast Bldg., 350 Madison Ave., New York NY 10017. (212)880-8533. Editor-in-Chief: Barbara D. Tober. For the first- or second-time bride in her early twenties, her family and friends, the groom and his family. Magazine published 6 times/year. Circ. 300,000. Buys all rights. Pays 15% kill fee, depending on circumstances. Byline given. Buys 30 mss/year. Pays on acceptance. Reports in 8 weeks. Query or submit complete ms. Address mss to Copy and Features Department. Free writer's guidelines.
Nonfiction: "We want warm, personal articles, optimistic in tone, with help offered in a clear, specific way. All issues should be handled within the context of marriage. How-to features on all aspects of marriage: communications, in-laws, careers, money, sex, family planning, religion; informational articles on the realities of marriage, the changing roles of men and women, the kinds

of troubles in engagement that are likely to become big issues in marriage; stories from couples or marriage authorities that illustrate marital problems and solutions to men and women both; and how-to features on wedding planning that offer expert advice. We're using less of the first-person piece and requiring more that articles be well researched, relying on quotes from authorities in the field." Length: 1,000-3,000 words. Pays $200-550.

Tips: "Send us a well-written article that is both easy to read and offers real help for the bride as she adjusts to her new role. No first-person narratives on wedding and reception planning, home furnishings, cooking, fashion, beauty, travel. For examples of the kinds of features we want, study any issue; read articles listed in table of contents under 'Planning for Marriage.'"

CHATELAINE, 481 University Ave., Toronto, Canada M5W 1A7. Editor-in-Chief: Mildred Istona. General interest magazine for Canadian women, from age 20 up. Monthly magazine. Circ. over 1 million. Pays on acceptance. Buys first North American serial rights in English and French. Byline given. Free writer's guidelines.

Nonfiction: Elizabeth Parr and Liz Primeau, articles editors. Length: 2,000-3,600 words. Pays $750 minimum.

Fiction: Barbara West, fiction editor. Relationships; humorous; mainstream; romance; and condensed novels. No short shorts. Length: 3,000-4,500 words. Pays $1,000 minimum.

COSMOPOLITAN, Hearst Corp., 224 W. 57th St., New York NY 10019. Editor: Helen Gurley Brown. Managing Editor: Guy Flatley. For career women, ages 18-34. Monthly. Circ. 2,500,000. Buys all rights. Pays on acceptance. Not interested in receiving unsolicited manuscripts. Most material is assigned to established, known professional writers who sell regularly to top national markets, or is commissioned through literary agents.

Nonfiction: Not interested in unsolicited manuscripts; for agents and top professional writers, requirements are as follows: "We want pieces that tell an attractive, 18-34-year-old, intelligent, good-citizen girl how to have a more rewarding life—'how-to' pieces, self-improvement pieces as well as articles which deal with more serious matters. We'd be interested in articles on careers, part-time jobs, diets, food, fashion, men, the entertainment world, emotions, money, medicine and psychology and fabulous characters." Uses some first-person stories. Logical, interesting, authoritative writing is a must, as is a feminist consciousness. Length: 1,000-3,000 words. Pays $200-500 for short pieces, $500-750 for longer articles.

Photos: Photos purchased on assignment only.

Fiction: Department Editor: Nancy Coffey. Not interested in unsolicited manuscripts; for agents and top professional writers, requirements are as follows: "Good plotting and excellent writing are important. We want short stories dealing with adult subject matter which would interest a sophisticated audience, primarily female, 18-34. We prefer serious quality fiction or light tongue-in-cheek stories on any subject, done in good taste. We love stories dealing with contemporary man-woman relationships. Short-shorts are okay but we prefer them to have snap or 'trick' endings. The formula story, the soap opera, skimpy mood pieces or character sketches are not for us." Length: short-shorts, 1,500-3,000 words; short stories, 4,000-6,000 words; condensed novels and novel excerpts. "We also use murder or suspense stories of about 25,000-30,000 words dealing with the upper class stratum of American living. A foreign background is acceptable, but the chief characters should be American." Has published the work of Agatha Christie, Joyce Carol Oates, Evan Hunter, and other established writers. Pays $1,000 minimum and up for short stories and novel excerpts; $4,500 minimum for condensed novels.

COSMOPOLITAN LIVING, Hearst Corp., 224 W. 57th St., New York NY 10019. (212)262-4111. Editor: Ellen Levine. Executive Editor: Ruth Fitzgibbons. Quarterly magazine about lifestyles for young women for a home oriented audience from 25-45 years old. Estab. 1980. Circ. 400,000. Average issue includes 18 features and 6 columns. Pays on acceptance. Byline given. Offers 10% kill fee. Buys all rights. SASE.

Nonfiction: "We are a special edition of *Cosmopolitan Magazine* aimed at young urban women. We are called a 'citified shelter magazine' and articles cover decorating and home furnishings, food, entertaining, lifestyles, products, art, money, travel, living together, etc. Look at the magazine to get a drift of the desired articles. We have a long assignment list and wouldn't mind seeing copies of previously published work so that we could make assignments in the writer's area of expertise." Buys 15-20 mss/issue. Query with clips of previously published work. Length: 3,000 words maximum. Payment negotiable.

Columns/Departments: Beauty, Health, Travel and Indulgences. Buys 4 mss/issue. Query with clips of previously published work. Length: 500-1,000 words. Payment varies.

Fillers: Buys 2-4 mss/issue. Length: 500 words minimum. Pays $100 minimum

FAMILY CIRCLE GREAT IDEAS, Family Circle Magazine, 488 Madison Ave., New York NY 10022. (212)593-8181. Editor: Marie T. Walsh. Managing Editor: Susan Kiely Tierney. Emphasizes how to: decorating, fashion and crafts. Bimonthly magazine; 128 pages. Circ. 1,000,000. Pays on publication. Buys all rights. Submit seasonal/holiday material 9 months in advance. Reports in 4 weeks. Sample copy $1.95.
Nonfiction: How-to (fashion, decorating, crafts, food and beauty) and new product (for home and family). Buys 2 mss/issue. Query. Length: 500-1,500 words. Pays $150-350.

FAMILY CIRCLE MAGAZINE, 488 Madison Ave., New York NY 10022. (212)593-8000. Editor: Arthur Hettich. 60% freelance written. For women/homemakers. Published 17 times/year. Usually buys all rights. Pays 25% kill fee. Byline given. Pays on acceptance. Reports in 6-8 weeks. Query. "We like to see a strong query on unique or problem-solving aspects of family life, and are especially interested in writers who have a solid background in the areas they suggest." SASE.
Nonfiction: Contact: Babette Ashby. Women's interest subjects such as family and social relationships, children, humor, physical and mental health, leisure-time activities, self-improvement, popular culture, travel. Service articles. For travel, interested mainly in local material, no far-flung foreign or extensive travel. "We look for human stories, told in terms of people. We like them to be down-to-earth and unacademic." Length: 1,000-2,500 words. Pays $250-2,500.
Fiction: Contact: Constance Leisure. Occasionally uses fiction related to women. Buys short stories, short-shorts, vignettes. Length: 2,000-2,500 words. Payment negotiable. Minimum payment for full-length story is $500.
Tips: Query letters should be "concise and to the point. We get some with 10 different suggestions—by the time they're passed on to all possible editors involved, weeks may go by." Also writers should "keep close tabs on *Family Circle* and other women's magazines to avoid submitting recently run subject matter."

FARM WIFE NEWS, Box 643, Milwaukee WI 53201. (414)423-0100. Managing Editor: Ruth Benedict. For farm and ranch women of all ages; nationwide. "We are the one and only completely-dedicated-to-farm/ranch-women's magazine. Unlike some, which only dedicate a few pages to rural women's interests, we try to make each and every issue appropriate to their busy, unique and important lives." Circ. 395,000. Byline given. Buys 180 mss/year. Pays on publication. Sample copy $1; free writer's guidelines. Submit seasonal material 8 months in advance. No photocopied submissions. Reports in 6 weeks. Query stating availability of photos, etc., or submit complete ms. SASE.
Nonfiction: "We are always looking for good freelance material. Our prime consideration is that it is farm-oriented, focusing on a farm woman or a subject that would appeal especially to her. So much about rural living has been said before—'it's the best place to raise children, work together with the family, etc.'—I'm quite interested in hearing from people with a new point of view." Uses a wide variety of material: daily life, sewing, gardening, decorating, outstanding farm women, etc. Topic should always be approached from a rural woman's point of view. Informational, how-to, personal experience, interview, profile, inspirational, humor, think pieces, nostalgia, opinion, successful sideline business operations from farm and/or ranches. No "nostalgia pieces on Mom's old cookstove, the first time someone drove the Model T, etc. Looking for more unique reflections and nostalgia—new angles." Length: 1,000 words maximum. Departments and columns which also use material are: A Day in Our Lives, Besides Farming, Country Crafts, Sewing and Needlecraft, Gardening, Decorating, and I Remember When. Pays $45-180.
Photos: B&w photos are purchased with or without accompanying mss. Color slides and transparencies are also used. "We look for scenic color photos and shots of farm wives at work and at play which show the life on the farm." Captions required. Payment depends on use, but begins at $30 for b&w photos; at $40 and up for color slides or transparencies.
Fiction: Mainstream, humorous. Themes should relate to subject matter. Length: 1,000 words maximum. Pays $40-100.
Poetry: Farm life related. Pays $25-60.
Fillers: Word puzzles and short humor. Pays $20-45.
Tips: "Supply enough facts and your article stands a good chance of making it. Articles that require correspondence and calls for better photos, pertinent names, quotes, places or even added shaping don't survive very well."

FLARE, 481 University Ave., Toronto, Canada M5W 1A7. (416)596-5453. Editor: Keitha McLean. Associate Editor: Julie Beddoes. Special interest magazine published 10 times/year for 18-34-year-old Canadian women, most of whom are working. Covers fashion, beauty, health, careers, lifestyle features. Estab. 1979. Circ. 170,000. Pays on acceptance. Byline given. Buys first North American serial rights; Career pages, buys all rights. Submit seasonal material 3 months in advance. Simultaneous, photocopied and previously published submissions OK. Reports in 1

month. Sample copy 80¢; free writer's guidelines.
Nonfiction: General interest and profile (up and coming Canadians in arts, sports, politics and sciences, etc.). "We want soundly researched and perceptively written articles on human relationships (the shortage of desirable men; living together vs. marriage; how to cope with aging parents); offbeat recreational activites (rock-climbing, river-rafting); problems of modern living (anxiety; the new woman alcoholic); women's legal and health issues (birth control). We also buy a limited amount of information-packed travel material for the budget-minded woman who favors an active vacation." Buys 2 mss/issue. Query with clips of previously published work. Length: 3,500 words maximum. Pays $200-900.
Columns/Departments: Wavelength (personal essays, preferably lively and opinionated); Options (emerging trends such as shared home ownership). Buys 2 mss/issue. Length: 1,000 words. Career News: clippings, ideas and news items for working women. Courses, conferences, solutions to problems, research findings, breakthroughs. Printable items, 200 words maximum. Pays $10-30.
Fiction: "We are a showcase for new Canadian literary talent. We look for quality, not formula romances, and find most of our fiction through an annual competition announced each fall. We accept fiction only from Canadian citizens or landed immigrants."
Fillers: "Zippy news reports on noteworthy Canadian people, places, things and events, from the socially important to the unabashedly zany. Our lead time is two months, and we welcome submissions from across Canada. We're also interested in Canadians achieving break-throughs in the United States. Length: 75 words. Pays $30/item.
Tips: "Usually start with small items, e.g., Career News, etc."

GLAMOUR, Conde Nast, 350 Madison Ave., New York NY 10017. (212)692-5500. Editor-in-Chief: Ruth Whitney. Articles Editor: Sue Mittenthal. For women, 18-35-years old. Circ. 1.9 million; 6.5 million readers. SASE. Pays on acceptance. Pays 20% kill fee. Byline given. Reports in 5 weeks.
Nonfiction: Sue Mittenthal, articles editor. "Editorial approach is 'how-to' with articles that are relevant in the areas of careers, health, psychology, interpersonal relationships, etc. We look for queries that are fresh and include a contemporary, timely angle. Fashion, beauty, decorating, travel, food and entertainment are all staff-written." Buys 10-12 mss/issue. Query "with letter that is well-focused; well-organized; and documented with surveys, statistics and research." Short articles (1,500-2,000 words) pay $500-750; longer mss (2,500-3,000 words) pay $850 minimum.

GOOD HOUSEKEEPING, Hearst Corp., 959 8th Ave., New York NY 10019. Editor-in-Chief: John Mack Carter. Executive Editor: Mina Mulvey. Managing Editor: Mary Fiore. Mass women's magazine. Monthly; 250 pages. Circ. 5,000,000. Pays on acceptance. Rights vary with author and material. Pays 25% kill fee. Byline given. Submit seasonal/holiday material 8 months in advance. SASE. Reports "as soon as possible." Sample copy $1.25.
Nonfiction: Shirley Howard, articles editor. Exposé; how-to-informational; inspirational; interviews; nostalgia; personal experience; profiles. Regional Editor: Shirley Howard. Local interest pieces; some travel. Pays $250-350. Buys 8-10 mss/issue. Query. Length: 1,000-5,000 words. Pays $500-5,000.
Photos: Herbert Bleiweiss, art director. Photos purchased on assignment mostly. Some short photo features with captions. Pays $50-250 for b&w; $50-350 for color photos. Query. Model release required.
Columns/Departments: Light Housekeeping & Fillers, edited by Mary Ann Littell. Humorous short-short prose and verse. Jokes, gags, anecdotes. Pays $25-100. The Better Way, edited by Bob Liles. Ideas and in-depth research. Query. Pays $25-35. "Only outstanding material has a chance here."
Fiction: Naome Lewis, fiction editor. Romance, mainstream, suspense, condensed novels and serialized novels. "Presently overstocked." Buys 3 mss/issue. Send complete mss. Length: 1,000 words (short-shorts); 10,000 words (novels); average 4,000 words. Pays $1,000 minimum.
Poetry: Leonhard Dowty, poetry editor. Light verse and traditional. "Presently overstocked." Buys 3 poems/issue. Pays $25 minimum.

GRADUATE WOMAN (formerly *AAUW Journal*), 2401 Virginia Ave. NW., Washington DC 20037. (202)785-7727. Publication of American Association of University Women. Editor: Patricia Jenkins. For women of all ages who have a healthy intellectual curiosity. Published 6 times/year. Circ. 190,000. Buys all rights. Byline given. Pays on acceptance. Sample copy $1.50. SASE.
Nonfiction: "Material used is usually related to broad themes with which AAUW is concerned, including equity for women, laws and public policies affecting women, education, community issues, cultural affairs and international relations. Special concentration next year on economic issues and taking hold of technology. Emphasis is on women and their efforts to improve society.

Articles (250 to 2,500 words) must be thoroughly researched, well thought through, and competently written. Pays "generally $50-200."
Photos: We pay extra for high-quality photos, b&w or color related to the article."

HADASSAH MAGAZINE, 50 W. 58th St., New York NY 10019. Chairman: Charlotte Jacobson. Executive Editor: Alan M. Tigay. For members of Hadassah. Monthly, except combined issues (June-July and August-September). Circ. 370,000. Buys US publication rights. Pays on publication. Reports in 6 weeks. SASE.
Nonfiction: Contact: Sol Sverdlin. Primarily concerned with Israel, the American Jewish community and American civic affairs. Length: 1,500-2,000 words. Pays $200-400.
Photos: "We buy photos only to illustrate articles, with the exception of outstanding color from Israel which we use on our covers. We pay $100 and up for a suitable color photo."
Fiction: Contact: Roselyn Bell. Short stories with strong plots and positive Jewish values. No personal memoirs, "schmaltzy" fiction, or women's magazine fiction. Length: 3,000 words maximum. Pays $300 minimum.
Tips: Of special interest are "strong fiction with a Jewish orientation; unusual experience with a Jewish community around the world—or specifically Israel."

HARPER'S BAZAAR, 717 5th Ave., New York NY 10022. Editor-in-Chief: Anthony Mazzola. For "women, late 20s and above, middle income and above, sophisticated and aware, with at least 2 years of college. Most combine families, professions, travel, often more than one home. They are active and concerned over what's happening in the arts, their communities, the world." Monthly. All rights purchased. Query first. SASE.
Nonfiction: "We publish whatever is important to an intelligent, modern woman. Fashion questions plus beauty and health—how the changing world affects her family and herself; how she can affect it; how others are trying to do so; changing life patterns and so forth. Query us first."

LADIES' HOME JOURNAL, Charter Corp., 641 Lexington Ave., New York NY 10022. Editor: Lenore Hershey. Articles Editor: Sandra Forsyth Enos. Senior Editor: Jan Goodwin. Monthly magazine; 200 pages. Pays on publication. Simultaneous and photocopied submissions OK. "We only accept manuscripts that are submitted to us through literary agents." Submit seasonal/holiday material 6 months in advance. SASE. Reports in 6 weeks. Free writer's guidelines.
Nonfiction: Expose, general interest and profile. No personal essays and memories or travel pieces. Buys 3 mss/issue. Query. Length: 2,000 words minimum. Pays $500 minimum.
Fiction: Does not consider short stories sent through the mail. "We do not have facilities that permit proper handling. Please do not send in manuscripts as we will be unable to return them."
Poetry: Poetry editor. Light verse and traditional. Buys 30-50/year. Submit in batches of 6. Length: 8-15 lines. Pays $5/line.

LADY'S CIRCLE MAGAZINE, Lopez Publications, Inc., 23 W. 26th St., New York NY 10010. Editor: Ardis Sandel. Service Editor: Barbara Jacksier. For homemakers. Monthly. Buys all rights. Byline given. Pays on publication. Submit seasonal/holiday material 6 months in advance. Reports in 3 months. Query with brief outline. SASE.
Nonfiction: Particularly likes first-person or as-told-to pieces about health and doing good. Also how homemakers and mothers make money at home. Hobbies and crafts; ways to save time and/or money. Also articles on baby care, home management, gardening, as well as problems of the homemaker. Also, stories of people who have overcome illnesses or handicaps. Articles must be written on specific subjects and must be thoroughly researched and based on sound authority. Length: 2,500 words. Pays $125 minimum.
Photos: Pays $15 for quality b&w photos accompanying articles.
Fiction: Short, humorous or emotional fiction pieces.

McCALL'S, 230 Park Ave., New York NY 10017. Editor: Robert Stein. "Study recent issues." Our publication "carefully and conscientiously services the needs of the woman reader—concentrating on matters that directly affect her life and offering information and understanding on subjects of personal importance to her." Monthly. Circ. 6,200,000. Pays on acceptance. Pays 20% kill fee. Byline given. Reports in 6 weeks. SASE.
Nonfiction: Senior Editor: Janet Chan. No subject of wide public or personal interest is out of bounds for *McCall's* so long as it is appropriately treated. The editors are seeking meaningful stories of personal experience. They are on the lookout for new research that will provide the basis for penetrating articles on the ethical, physical, material and social problems concerning readers. They are most receptive to humor. *McCall's* buys 200-300 articles/year, many in the 1,000- to 1,500-word length. Mrs. Helen Del Monte and Andrea Thompson are Editors of Nonfiction Books, from which *McCall's* frequently publishes excerpts. These are on subjects of interest to

women: biography, memoirs, reportage, etc. Almost all features on food, household equipment and management, fashion, beauty, building and decorating are staff-written. Query. "All manuscripts must be submitted on speculation and *McCall's* accepts no responsibility for unsolicited manuscripts."

Columns/Departments: Address queries for Right Now column to Mrs. Merrill Skrocki. Subjects can be education, medicine, social and community affairs (new ideas and trends), problems being solved in new ways, ecology, women doing interesting things, women's liberation, any timely subject. Short pieces with a news or service angle. Length: 300-500 words. Payment is up to $300. The magazine is not in the market for new columns.

Fiction: Department Editor: Helen DelMonte. "Again the editors would remind writers of the contemporary woman's taste and intelligence. Most of all, fiction can awaken a reader's sense of identity, deepen her understanding of herself and others, refresh her with a laugh at herself, etc. *McCall's* looks for stories which will have meaning for an adult reader of some literary sensitivity. *McCall's* principal interest is in short stories; but fiction of all lengths is considered." Length: about 4,000 words. Length for short-shorts: about 2,000 words. Payment begins at $1,250.

Tips: "Your best bet is our monthly newsletter section, Right Now. It's an 8-page section and we buy a lot of freelance material for it, much of that from beginning writers. Some people have gone on from Right Now to do feature material for us."

McCALL'S WORKING MOTHER MAGAZINE, McCall's Publishing Co., 230 Park Ave., New York NY 10017. (212)551-9500. Editor: Vivian Cadden. Managing Editor: Mary McLaughlin. For the working mothers in this country whose problems and concerns are determined by the fact that they have children under 18 living at home. Monthly magazine; 140 pages. Circ. 200,000. Pays on acceptance. Buys all rights. Pays 20% kill fee. Byline given. Submit seasonal/holiday material 8 months in advance. Simultaneous and photocopied submissions OK. SASE. Reports in 8 weeks. Sample copy $1.50.

Nonfiction: How-to (save time, find a day care center, balance job and housework, find time for yourself) and humor (anything that may be amusing to the working mother). "Don't just go out and find some mother who holds a job, and describe how she runs her home, manages her children and feels fulfilled. Find a unique angle." Buys 9-10 mss/issue. Query. Length: 750-2,000 words. Pays $300-500.

Columns/Departments: Take Care of Yourself (health) and What's In Your Lunchbox (readers' ideas for midday meals). Uses 2-3/issue. Query.

Fiction: "We are interested in fiction if the right piece comes along, but we're still more interested in nonfiction pieces."

Poetry: Light verse and traditional. Uses 1-2/year.

MADEMOISELLE, 350 Madison Ave., New York NY 10017. Editor-in-Chief: Amy Levin. 90% freelance written. Directed to college-educated women 18-34. Circ. 1,000,000. Reports in 3-4 weeks. Buys first North American serial rights and all Australian rights. Pays on acceptance. Prefers written query plus samples of work, published or unpublished. SASE.

Nonfiction: Katherine Ball Ross, articles editor. Particular concentration on articles of interest to the intelligent young woman that concern the arts, health, careers, travel, current women-oriented problems. Articles should be well-researched and of good quality. Length: "Opinion" essay column, 1,300 words; articles, 1,500-6,000 words. Pays $300 for "Opinion" essay column; article $300 minimum.

Photos: Department editor: Ann Shakshaft. Commissioned work assigned according to needs. Photos of fashion, beauty, travel; career and college shots of interest to accompany articles. Payment ranges from no-charge to an agreed rate of payment per shot, job series, or page rate. Buys all rights. Pays on publication for photos.

Fiction: Department editor: Susan Schneider. High-quality fiction by both name writers and unknowns. Length: 1,500-3,000 words. Pays $300 minimum. Uses short-shorts on occasion. "We are particularly interested in encouraging young talent, and with this aim in mind, we conduct a college fiction contest each year, open to men and women undergraduates. A $500 prize is awarded for each of the two winning stories which are published in our August issue. However, our encouragement of unknown talent is not limited to college students or youth. We are not interested in formula stories, and subject matter need not be confined to a specific age or theme." Annually awards 2 prizes for short stories.

MODERN BRIDE, 1 Park Ave., New York NY 10016. Executive Editor: Cele G. Lalli. Bi-monthly. Buys first periodical publishing rights. Byline given. Pays on acceptance. Reports in 2 weeks. SASE.

Nonfiction: Uses articles of interest to brides-to-be. "We prefer articles on etiquette, marriage and planning a home. Travel is staff-written or specially assigned. We edit everything, but don't rewrite without permission." Length: about 2,000 words. Payment is about $200 minimum.

Poetry: Occasionally buys poetry pertaining to love and marriage. Pays $15-25 for average short poem.

MS. MAGAZINE, 119 W. 40th St., New York NY 10018. (212)725-2666. Editor-in-Chief and Publisher: Patricia Carbine. Editor: Gloria Steinem. For "women predominantly; varying ages, backgrounds, but committed to exploring new life styles and changes in their roles and society." Monthly. Circ. approximately 500,000. Rights purchased vary with author and material. Pays on acceptance. Will consider photocopied submissions. Submit seasonal material at least 3 months in advance. Reports in 5-6 weeks. SASE.

Photos: Purchased with mss, without mss, or on assignment. Payment "depends on usage." Address to Art Department.

Tips: "The Gazette section which features short news items is the easiest way to get published here, and is especially receptive to regional material from New York but much has to be rejected because of space limitations and lack of professional standards. We use a lot of material from all over the country on politics, the women's movement, human interest features. It is possible to move from the Gazette to do other work for *Ms.*"

PLAYGIRL, 3420 Ocean Park Blvd., Santa Monica CA 90405. (213)450-0900. Editor: Dianne Grosskopf. Senior Editor: Pat McGilligan. Monthly magazine covering entertainment, fiction, reviews, beauty, fashion, cooking and travel for 18-40 year old females. Circ. 850,000. Average issue includes 4 articles and 1 interview. Pays 1 month after acceptance. Byline given. Offers 15% kill fee. Buys all rights. Submit seasonal material 4 months in advance. Simultaneous and photocopied submissions OK, if so indicated. SASE. Reports in 1 month on queries; in 2 months on mss. Free writer's guidelines with SASE.

Nonfiction: Expose (related to women's issues); interview (Q&A format using celebrities); humor (related to the modern woman); sexuality; hard information on credit; finances; medical breakthroughs; relationships; coping; and career pieces. Buys 4 mss/issue. Query with clips of previously published work. Length: 2,500 words. Pays $500-850.

REDBOOK MAGAZINE, 230 Park Ave., New York NY 10017. (212)850-9300. Editor-in-Chief: Sey Chassler. Monthly magazine; 200 pages. Circ. 4,300,000. Rights purchased vary with author and material. Reports in 4 weeks. Pays on acceptance. SASE. Writer's guidelines on writing fiction for Redbook free for SASE.

Nonfiction: Silvia Koner, articles editor. Articles relevant to the magazine's readers, who are young women in the 18-34-year-old group. Also interested in submissions for "Young Mother's Story." "We are interested in stories offering practical and useful information you would like to share with others on how you, as a mother and a wife, are dealing with the changing problems of marriage and family life, such as the management of outside employment, housework, time, money, the home and children. Stories also may deal with how you, as a concerned citizen or consumer, handled a problem in your community. For each 1,000-2,000 words accepted for publication, we pay $500. Mss accompanied by a large, stamped, self-addressed envelope, must be signed, and mailed to: Young Mother's Story, c/o *Redbook Magazine*. Length: articles, 3,000-3,500 words; short articles, 2,000-2,500 words. Young Mother's reports in 10-12 weeks.

Fiction: Eileen Schnurr, fiction editor. "Out of the 36,000 unsolicited manuscripts that we receive annually, we buy about a third of the stories (about 50/year) that appear in *Redbook* over the course of a year. We find many more stories that, for one reason or another, are not suited to our needs, but are good enough to warrant our encouraging the author to send others. Often such an author's subsequent submission turns out to be something we can use. So we take our 'slush pile' very seriously, and each of the editors in the department spends several hours a week reading these manuscripts that come in 'over the transom.' There are among the stories by and about men and women, realistic stories and fantasies, funny and sad stories, stories of people together and people alone; stories with familiar and exotic settings, love stories and work stories. But there are a few things common to all of them, that made them stand out from the crowd. The high quality of their writing, for one thing. The distinctiveness of their characters and plots—stock characters and sitcom stories are not for us. A definite emotional satisfaction, or resonance, whether the emotion be delight, wistfulness, amusement, grief, triumph, hope, contentment—cool intellectual or stylistic experiments are more of interest, we feel, to readers of literary magazines than of a magazine like *Redbook* that tries to offer insights into the hows and whys of day-to-day living. And all the stories reflect some aspect of the experience, the interests, or the dreams of *Redbook's* particular readership: young women." Short-short stories (7-9 pages, 1,400-1,600 words) are always in demand; but short stories of 10-15 pages, (3,000-5,000 words) is an acceptable length. Stories 20 pages and over have a "hard fight, given our tight space limits— but we have bought longer stories that we loved." Manuscripts must be typewritten, double-spaced, and accompanied by SASE the size of the manuscript. Payment begins at $850 for short shorts; $1,000 for short stories.

Tips: "It is very difficult to break into the nonfiction section, although Young Mother's, which publishes short personal experience pieces (1,000-2,000 words), does depend on freelancers."

SAVVY, The Magazine for Executive Women, Alan Bennett, 111 8th Ave., New York NY 10011. (212)255-0990. Editor: Judith Daniels. Assistant-to-the Editor: Lisa Enfield. Monthly magazine covering the business and personal aspects of life for highly educated, professional career women. Estab. 1980. Circ. 200,000. Average issue includes 5 features. Pays on publication. Byline given. Buys first North American serial rights. Simultaneous and photocopied submissions OK. SASE. Reports in 1 month on queries; in 2 months on mss.

Nonfiction: Elizabeth Alvarez, nonfiction editor. General interest (articles should be slanted toward sophisticated women who have a wide range of interests with an emphasis on how their professional lives affect their personal lives); how-to (handle business situations) and personal experience. No "food, home, decorating or 'helpful hint' articles. Send in one or two well-developed ideas and some previously published work to show how you carry out your ideas. We require articles on speculation before we make an assignment to a writer not known to us." Query with clips of previously published work; letters should be "concise and to the point, with the angle of the proposed article made very specific." Length: 1,500-3,500 words. Pays $300-750.

Photos: Art Director: Carol Carson.

Columns/Departments: Tools of the Trade (ideas and strategies for doing business better, 500-1,500 words); and 1,000 Words (essays on anything of general interest to executive women, 1,000 words).

SELF, Conde-Nast, 350 Madison Ave., New York NY 10017. (212)880-8834. Editor: Phyllis Starr Wilson. Managing Editor: Valorie Weaver. Monthly magazine emphasizing self improvement of mental and physical well-being for women of all ages. Estab. 1979. Circ. 900,000. Average issue includes 12-20 feature articles and 3-4 columns. Pays on acceptance. Byline given. Offers 20% kill fee. Buys first North American serial rights. Submit seasonal material 4 months in advance. Simultaneous and photocopied submissions OK. SASE. Reports in 1 month. Free writer's guidelines.

Nonfiction: General interest (self improvement; beauty; mind; the psychological angle of daily activities; health; careers; and current issues). "We don't want anything one dimensional. Everything should relate to the whole person." Buys 6-10 mss/issue. Query with clips of previously published work. Length: 1,000-2,500 words. Pays $700-1,200. "We are always looking for any piece that has a psychological or behavioral side. We rely heavily on freelancers who can take an article on interior decorating, for example, and add a psychological aspect to it."

Photos: Editor: Susan Niles. State availability of photos. Reviews 5x7 b&w glossy prints.

Columns/Departments: Self games (psychological issues); Self issues (800-1,000 words on current topics of interest to women); Health Watch (800-1,000 words on health topics); and Career and Money (800-1,000 words on finance topics). Buys 1-2 mss/issue. Query. Pays $700-1,200.

SUNDAY WOMAN, The King Features Syndicate, 235 E. 45th, New York NY 10017. Associate Editor: Elaine Liner. Syndicated weekly magazine-tabloid aimed at women's interests. Circ. 3 million. Pays on acceptance. Buys second serial (reprint) rights and first North American serial rights. Previously published work OK. SASE. Reports in 4 weeks.

Nonfiction: Expose, how-to, interview, personal experience and profile (show-business, especially TV and movies). No craft or food articles. "We do not want any articles that are not of specific interest to women." Query short and to the point. Attach one or two clips of published material. Length: 500-1,500 words. Pays $50-300.

Tips: "Submit previously published pieces for second serial publication by us."

VOGUE, 350 Madison Ave., New York NY 10017. Editor: Grace Mirabella. Monthly magazine for highly intelligent women. Pays on acceptance. Byline given. SASE.

Nonfiction: Feature Editor: Leo Lerman. Uses articles and ideas for features. Fashion articles are staff-written. Material must be of high literary quality, contain good information. Query. Length: 2,000-2,500 words. Pays $300 minimum.

W, *Women's Wear Daily*, 7 E. 12th St., New York NY 10003. Completely staff-written newspaper.

WOMAN LOCALLY MAGAZINE, 97 Columbia St., Albany NY 12210. (518)465-8508. Editor: Cheryl Funbeck. Managing Editor: Cathy Cholakis. Monthly magazine; 48 pages. Circ. 2,000. Pays no later than publication of next issue. Buys all rights. Byline given. Submit material 2 months in advance. Simultaneous and photocopied submissions OK.

Nonfiction: Buys 10 mss/issue. Query. Length: 300-1,500 words. Pays $5-50.

Photos: Send photos with ms. Pays 5-15 for b&w prints; model release required.
Columns/Departments: Clinic, Creative Expressions, Job Forum, Sports and Women in Focus. Query. "Mostly consignment with publisher."

WOMAN'S DAY, 1515 Broadway, New York NY 10036. Editor: Geraldine Rhoads. 15 issues/ year. Circ. over 8,000,000. Buys first and second North American serial rights. Pays negotiable kill fee. Byline given. Pays on acceptance. Reports in 2 weeks on queries; longer on mss. Submit detailed queries first to Rebecca Greer, Articles Editor. SASE.
Nonfiction: Uses articles on all subjects of interest to women—marriage, family life, child rearing, education, homemaking, money management, careers, family health and leisure activities. Also interested in fresh, dramatic narratives of women's lives and concerns. Length: 500-3,500 words, depending on material. Payment varies depending on length, whether it's for regional or national use, etc.
Fiction: Department editor: Eileen Herbert Jordan. Uses high-quality, genuine human interest, romance and humor, in lengths between 1,500 and 3,000 words. Payment varies. "We pay any writer's established rate, however."
Fillers: Brief (500 words maximum), factual articles on contemporary life, community projects, unusual activities are used—condensed, sprightly, and unbylined—in "It's All in a Woman's Day" section. "Neighbors" column also pays $25/each letter and $5/each brief practical suggestion on homemaking or child rearing. Address to the editor of the appropriate section.

WOMAN'S WORLD, The Woman's Weekly, Heinrich Bauer North American, Inc., 177 N. Dean St., Englewood NJ 07631. (201)569-0006. Editor-in-Chief: Barbara Bright. Weekly magazine covering women's issues for women across the nation aged 25-60, low- to middle-income. Estab. 1981. Circ. 600,000. Pays on acceptance. Byline given. Offers negotiable kill fee. Buys first North American serial rights. Submit seasonal/holiday material 4 months in advance. Simultaneous queries, and simultaneous, photocopied and previously published submissions OK. SASE. Reports in 6 weeks on queries. Sample copy $1; writer's guidelines for business size SAE and 1 first class stamp.
Nonfiction: Report (issues and trends of vital interest to women, 2,200 words); Cover (low- and middle-income career topics); Careers Interview (celebrity); Self help (psychology); Lay physiology ("scientific pieces written in lay language"); Medicine and health (topics of interest to women); Dollars and sense (economics of home and daily life); "At home with" (celebrity); Travel (emphasis U.S.); and American Woman (first-person accounts). Query appropriate editor with clips of published work. Pays $350 minimum for 1,000 words; $550 minimum for 2,000 words.
Photos: State availability of photos. "State photo leads. Photos are assigned to freelance photographers." Buys one-time rights.
Fiction: Mainstream (short story); and mini-mystery (one page, 1,200 words). Length: 1,000-2,000 words. Pays $350-550.
Tips: "Come up with good queries. We have a strong emphasis on well-researched material. We require a hard news edge and topics of national scope. Writers must send research with ms including book references and phone numbers for double checking."

WOMEN IN BUSINESS, Box 8728, Kansas City MO 64114. (816)361-6621. Editor: Sharon K. Tiley. 50% freelance written. For working women in all fields and at all levels; largely middle-aged women in traditional "women's" fields. Bimonthly magazine; 44 pages. Circ. 109,000. Pays on acceptance. Buys all rights. Phone queries OK. Submit seasonal/holiday material 3 months in advance. SASE. Reports in 2 months. Free sample copy and writer's guidelines.
Nonfiction: General interest, how-to, new product and simplified technical. No interviews or profiles of individuals. Articles should be slanted toward the average working woman. No articles on women who have made it to the top, resumes, the jobhunt or investment. "We also avoid articles based on first-hand experiences (the 'I' stories)." Buys 25 mss/year. Query or submit complete ms. Length: 1,000-2,000 words. Pays $100-200.
Photos: State availability of photos with query or submit with accompanying ms. Pays $50-75/8x10 b&w glossy contact sheet; $100-200/cover color transparency. Captions preferred. Buys all rights. Model release required.
Columns/Departments: Books Briefly (short reviews); Personal Business (financial); The Manager's Outlook (tips); and Your Personality (pop psychology); The Small Business Owner (tips); and The Business Woman (tips for the non-manager/business owner). Buys 6/year. Query. Length: 1,000-1,500 words. Pays $100-200.

WOMEN'S CIRCLE, Box 428, Seabrook NH 03874. Editor: Marjorie Pearl. Monthly magazine for women of all ages. Buys all rights. Byline given. Pays on acceptance. Submit seasonal material 7 months in advance. Reports in 3 months. SASE. Sample copy 75¢.

Nonfiction: How-to articles on hobbies, handicrafts, etc. Also food, needlework, dolls, home, family and children. Informational approach. Needs Christmas crafts for Christmas annual. Buys 200 mss/year. Query or submit complete ms. Length: open. Pays 3¢/word.

WORKING WOMAN, Hal Publications, Inc., 1180 Avenue of the Americas, New York NY 10036. Editor-in-chief: Kate Rand Lloyd. Editor: Gay Bryant. Articles Editor: Julia Kagan. Monthly magazine; 112 pages. "We offer sophisticated, practical advice to the career-oriented working woman. Readers are not career beginners." Circ. 440,000. Pays on acceptance. Buys all rights. Pays 20% kill fee. Byline given. Submit seasonal/holiday material 6 months in advance. SASE. Reports in 6 weeks. Sample copy $1.75; free writer's guidelines.

Nonfiction: How-to (career strategies, managing personal life/work life, etc.); finance (personal money management, some pieces on national economic issues—especially those affecting women); social trends—(two-career couple, generation gap in the office, etc.); health (physical and psychological); humor (related to work and work situations); interview (with women in various career areas, experts in various fields); and profile. "We want subjects that have special application to career-oriented working women or are of particular interest to them." No articles on getting started, working at home, or managing a career and children/husband. "No more women truck drivers. No stale advice on getting ahead." Buys 6 mss/issue. Query with clips of published work or send complete ms. Explain why the subject is important to our readers and why now; also, indicate how you would handle the idea and why you would be especially good to write it (i.e., what is your background?). Length: 1,500-2,500 words. Pays $300-500.

Photos: State availability of photos with ms.

Columns/Departments: Consumer Advice, Mind & Body, Money Talks, Learning Your Way, Success Story, Your Business, Job Market, My Side, Education, Traveling Easy and Working Your Way Up. "All columns/departments are geared to specific problems/pluses of working women." Buys 5/issue. Query with clips of published work. Length: 850-1,200 words. Pays $200-350.

Tips: "Send query letter as described above with clips of previously published work. Describe background—even if the submission is a manuscript rather than a query. What we need to know is why this article and why you? If profile, should include specific business information about the woman's work. We include much more financial how-to in our profiles of working women, not just 'nice' interview quotes. Pictures (if interview/profile) of subject helpful. We are interested only in polished, professional-level writing. Financial advice must be sophisticated—our readers know what a CD is. We have a 4-month lead time."

Gag Writing

Humor is everywhere: in current events, in the street, at social functions, and probably at your own backyard barbecue.

Translating that humor to the gag that accompanies a cartoon requires a good ear, the ability to invoke reader identification, and an awareness of the world around you.

To write gags for a cartoonist, you need not be an artist yourself. If you can draw a stick figure, you will have your cartoon rough sketch well at hand.

Captions—if used—should be simple and fairly universal. You can get more mileage out of a gag by initially directing it toward a specific audience (a medical journal, for example) and altering it somewhat for a more general market, such as a family magazine.

Be brief—and amusing. Avoid "talking heads" gags: two people talking, not really doing or saying anything funny. Go for the big laugh—and not one that has been done so many times it belongs in the Smithsonian.

Next time you're browsing the library or bookstore, look for cartoonists' work in books and magazines. Get a feel for their styles. Consult their requirements in *WM* and write accordingly.

Submit gags on 3x5 cards or slips, one per card. Include an identification number on the upper left-hand corner, and type your name and address on the back of the card. Submitting between 10 and 20 gags at one time is standard. But—it's better to send five *great* gags than 15 mediocre (translated: unsalable) and five great ones.

This is one field where imitation is the sincerest form of flattery—and that's about all. Cartoonists look for an original approach and fresh humor, plus some topicality.

The cartooning business is steady to better than it has been in years, so the gagwriter who submits his best work—and who can make people laugh and wonder why they didn't think of that—should do well.

Opportunities increase as articles, syndicated columns, and children's books are increasingly illustrated with cartoons.

For more information on gagwriting, read *The Cartoonist's and Gag Writer's Handbook*, by Jack Markow (Writer's Digest Books).

RAE AVENA, 36 Winslow Rd., Trumbull CT 06611. Has sold to *National Enquirer, New York Times*, and Pyramid Publications (paperbacks). "Gagwriters should send around 12 gags. Keep descriptions short." Pays 25% commission. Returns rejected material "as soon as possible." SASE. Likes to see all types of gags.

HARVEY BOSCH, 7925 Densmore N., Seattle WA 98103. (206)525-6438. Holds 200-300 gags/year. Sells to general, male, family, and women's magazines. Has sold to *National Enquirer, Saturday Evening Post, Rotarian*, King Features, *New Woman, Forum* and *American Legion*. Submit on 3x5 slips, 20-40 gags/batch. Reports in 2 days. Pays 25% commission. SASE.
Needs: Mostly male gags. General, family and women's gags also. "I will look at anything."

BILL BOYNANSKY, Apt. 13/20, Ansonia Hotel, 2109 Broadway, New York NY 10023. (212)787-7690, "Please phone after 2 pm." Holds over 1,000 gags/year; sells between 800-900 cartoons/year. Submit 15-20 gags at one time. Reports in 3 days to 2 months. Pays "25% for regular, 35% for captionless; all others—regular payment." SASE.
Needs: General, male, female, sexy, girlie, family, children's, adventure, medical. "No overdone girlie gags, overdone family gags, TV, parking the car, woman nagging husband, etc. Prefer to see captionless gag ideas on all subject matters, but no beginners; only those who know their business. I prefer to deal with cartoonists by letter or phone because it saves me time. However, I will respect and consider all mail replies."

ASHLEIGH BRILLIANT, 117 W. Valerio St.. Santa Barbara CA 93101. Buys 150 gags maximum/year; sold about 315 cartoons last year. Sells regularly to the Chicago Tribune-New York Times News Syndicate. Reports in 2 weeks. Pays $10.
Needs: "My work is so different from that of any other cartoonist that it must be carefully studied before any gags are submitted. Any interested writer not completely familiar with my work should first send $1 for my catalog of 1,000 examples. Otherwise, their time and mine will be wasted."

COMEDY UNLIMITED, Suite 625, Jack Tar Office Bldg., 1255 Post St., San Francisco CA 94109. Contact: Jim Curtis. Buys over 3,000 gags/year. Pays $1-3/line, on acceptance, and "considerably" more for zany, new premise ideas and sight gags. Reports in 2 weeks. If SASE is not enclosed with submission, all material will be destroyed after being considered, except items purchased.
Needs: "Because we probably sell more original comedy material than any other company in America, we are always looking for fresh, new premise ideas for unique and creative standup comedy monologues, as well as clever and original sight gags, and crazy pieces of business. We also buy original one-liners tailored especially for any of the following: comedians, public speakers, singers, magicians, or jugglers. Since we build everything from night club acts to humorous corporate speeches, it would be advisable not to submit any material until you have sent an SASE and requested our current projects list to find out exactly what we're most interested in buying during any given quarter. No mother-in-law jokes, airline routines, 'my wife is such a bad cook', etc."
Tips: "Keep in mind we are exclusively concerned with material intended for oral presentation."

THOMAS W. DAVIE, 1407 S. Tyler, Tacoma WA 98405. Buys 100 gags/year; sold 175 cartoons last year. Has sold to *Medical Economics*, *Sports Afield*, King Features, *Chevron USA*, *Rotarian*, *Saturday Evening Post*, *Ladies' Home Journal*, *Playgirl* and *Boys' Life*. Gags should be typed on 3x5 slips. Prefers batches of 5-25. Pays 25% commission. Reports in 1 month. SASE.
Needs: General gags, medicals, mild girlies, sports (hunting and fishing), business and travel gags. No pornography.
Tips: "Generals are coming back."

LEE DeGROOT, Box 115, Ambler PA 19002. Pays 25% on sales.
Needs: Interested in receiving studio greeting card ideas. "I draw up each idea in color before submitting to greeting card publishers, therefore, giving the editors a chance to visualize the idea as it would appear when printed . . . and thus increasing enormously the chances of selling the idea. Also returning to gag cartooning on a limited basis after a period of inactivity. Interested in receiving all types of gags, but do not wish to be overwhelmed by huge amounts of ideas at a time. Established writers only. Have sold previously to *Saturday Evening Post*, *Holiday*, *Saturday Review*, etc." Pays 25%. Please enclose SASE.

MIGUEL ESPARZA, 17157 E. Milan Circle, Aurora CO 80013. (303)693-9296. Holds 50 gags/year. Has sold to both men's and women's publications, general interest magazines, some trade journals. Submit on 3x5 cards, 12 gags/batch. Reports in 2 weeks. Pays 25% commission. SASE.
Needs: "Sophisticated material for larger markets such as *Playboy*, *Wall St. Journal*, *Changing Times*. Also more graphic gags for *National Enquirer*. For creative purposes would like gagwriter to provide all *National Enquirer* material in one batch. In other words, don't mix them up. Welcome market suggestions for material from gagwriter. I have a rather basic style and would prefer basic gags to go with it. Don't need anything for *Hustler* or *Penthouse*."

CHARLES HENDRICK JR., Old Fort Ave., Kennebunkport ME 04046. (207)967-4412. Buys several gags/year; sold 50-60 cartoons last year. Sells to local markets. Submit 10 gags at a time. Pays 50% of commission. Reports in 10-30 days. SASE.
Needs: General family, trade (hotel, motel, general, travel, vacationers). Safe travel ideas—any vehicle. Gags must be clean; no lewd sex.

DAVID R. HOWELL, Box 170, Porterville CA 93258. (209)781-5885. Buys about 150 gags/year; sold about 500 last year. Has sold to *Writer's Digest*, *New Woman*, *Modern Medicine*, *Mechanix Illustrated*, *Popular Electronics* and the other electronic newsstand magazines and computer slants, *Ag World* and the other farm magazines, the horse magazines, dental magazines, business magazines, general markets, and many technical journals. Pays 25-30% commission. Returns rejected gags same day received. SASE.
Needs: Medical (fresh and topical), dental, electronic, farm, business, family, teenager, current slants and auto mechanics. "I will always look at any to be slanted toward a particular technical journal market." No "husband downing the wife—old cliches, corny puns."
Tips: "Try to write gags for special markets that can, if need be, also sell to general markets."

LARRY (KAZ) KATZMAN, 101 Central Park W., Apt. 4B, New York NY 10023. (212)724-7862. Purchased over 100 gags last year. Has sold to *Modern Medicine* and *Medical Economics*. Submit 12-15 gags at one time. Pays 25% commission. Reports in 1 week. SASE.
Needs: "I use only medical (doctor, nurse, hospital) gags; no others." Must be submitted on numbered, separate slips.

STEVE KELL, 733 Waimea Dr., El Cajon CA 92021. (714)444-6769. Buys 53 gags/year; sold 150 cartoons last year. Has sold to *Playgirl, Penthouse, Esquire*, etc. Submit gags in batches of 10-15. Reports in 1 week. Pays 25%. SASE.
Needs: "All fresh and surprising slants accepted. "I'll also buy gags for syndicated comic strip *The Captain and Mandy* (slant towards airline travel)."

REAMER KELLER, 4500 Ocean Blvd., S. Palm Beach FL 33480. (305)582-2436. Buys 225 gags/year; sold "plenty of cartoons" last year. Has sold to *Cosmopolitan, Medical Economics, National Enquirer, American Legion, Good Housekeeping*, etc. Submit gags in batches of 20-30. Reports in 2 weeks. Pays 25%. SASE.
Needs: "Action, short captions and captionless. Topical gags, sight gags with captions—action in the cartoon, not just 2 people talking." General; medical; hospital; girlie; "timely stuff, homey."

MILO KINN, 1413 SW Cambridge St., Seattle WA 98106. Holds approximately 200 gags/year; sells 100-200 cartoons/year. Has sold to *Medical Economics, Modern Medicine, Farm Wife News, Private Practice, Wallace's Farmer,* etc. Pays 25% commission. SASE.
Needs: Medical, dental, farm, male slant, girlie, captionless, adventure and family gags. Sells girlie, farm, medical, office and general cartoons.
Tips: "The cartoon should be a funny picture or situation—not just 2 people talking. The gag should be a single caption-(not 'he' or 'she')—not just a joke, but a 'comic picture'! Gags demeaning or putting down females (dumb wife; dumb blonde type) do not seem to sell as well as others."

LO LINKERT, 1333 Vivian Place, Port Coquitlam, British Columbia, Canada V3C 2T9. Has sold to most major markets. Prefers batches of 10-15 gags. Returns rejected material in 1 week. Enclose SAE and 18¢ US postage. Pays 25% commission; $50 for greeting card ideas.
Needs: Clean, general, topical, medical, family, office, outdoors gags; captionless sophisticated ideas; greeting card ideas. "Make sure your stuff is funny. No spreads." Wants "action gags—not two people saying something funny. No puns, dirty sex, drugs, drunks, racial."

ART McCOURT, Box 210346, Dallas TX 75211. (214)339-6865. Sells 700 cartoons/year. Has sold to *Arizona Republic, Wallace's Farmer, Independent Banker, National Enquirer, Changing Times, American Legion, Mechanix Illustrated* and King Features. Submit 10-15 gags at one time. Reports in 1 week. Pays 25% commission. SASE.
Needs: "Something unique and up-to-date." No "crowds, TV, mothers-in-law, talking animals or desert islands."

HAROLD B. MONEY ("HALM"), 1206 Dover Ave., Wilmington DE 19805. (302)994-0272. Holds 400 gags/year; sold 260 cartoons last year. Has sold to *Nugget, Dude, Gent, Beaver* and *Hustler.* Submit "brief, concise, neatly-typed gags"; 10-15/batch. Reports in 3-4 days. Pays 25% on sales to $15; 30% thereafter. SASE.
Needs: "Strictly girlie slant gags with a fresh viewpoint on what is essentially a limited human activity, and 'punchy' gaglines. No general or trade journal gags. No orgy scenes, VD gags, flashers, bride and groom, or multi-panel ideas."

RAY MORIN, 140 Hamilton Ave., Meriden CT 06450. (203)237-4500. Holds 5+ gags/year; sells 90+ cartoons/year. Has sold to *Boys' Life, Wall Street Journal,* McNaught Syndicate and King Features. Submit 7-10 gags at one time. SASE. Pays 25% commission. Holds gags "indefinitely," trying to redraw the cartoon from a different angle.
Needs: General, family, children's, medical and business. "I do 95% of my own gags, but am willing to look."

BOB NELSON, 910 Bay St., #4, San Francisco CA 94109. Holds 50+ gags/year. Sells to general interest magazines; trade journals; newspapers. Has sold to *San Francisco Bay Guardian, Inside Detective, Ampersand, The SF Paper, The San Franciscans Magazine, Writer's Digest, Modern Cartooning.* Submit on 3x5 cards, 12 maximum gags/batch. Reports in 2 days. Pays 25% commission on publication. SASE.
Needs: "I prefer off-beat, whimsical humor. Weird but not violent or grotesque. Word-play and puns OK. The above humor style is acceptable in any topic context."

MICHAEL J. ("ZIP" & "SKI") PELLOWSKI, Box 726, Bound Brook NJ 08805. Buys 25-50 gags/year; sells hundreds of jokes and cartoons every year. Buys mostly gags for joke books compiled for publishers. Bought hundreds of jokes last year from a select few writers. Sometimes buys juvenile gags and riddles for 25¢ each for use in joke books. Has sold to *Sick* magazine, *Trucking, Cracked, Trash, Parody, Wacko, Playboy, Pub, Gem, Crazy* and most men's and humor magazines. Submit gag slips or gags typed on a page with triple spacing. Pays $1-5 outright purchase. SASE. "No SASE—no return."
Needs: Panel-to-panel material for publication in illustrated humor magazines. Sells jokes, gags, and one-liners to well-known stand up comedians. Buys performable comedy material for outright fee and polishes same for sale. Will look at clean material that can be performed in night clubs or on TV. "I use few if any cartoon ideas. I will always look at jokes, gags, one-liners, panel to panel pieces of 1-3 pages for illustrated humor publications. Original gags only. My need is for material for comedians and joke books, not for speakers or DJs. I am not a monthly comedy service. I build comedy routines and do joke books." No routines, sketches, or TV sitcom material. "I am not a producer or an agent."
Tips: "These days I'm doing more writing than drawing. I'm interested in teaming with artists on possible syndicated projects or working as a writer on established cartoon features. I always give tips to newcomers. Returns always get a personal reply and sometimes another market suggestion if I like the material but can't use it. My buying spells run hot and cold depending on whether I'm doing a book, building a routine for a comic, working on a TV project or sitting around biting my nails."

IRV PHILLIPS, 2807 E. Sylvia St., Phoenix AZ 85032. Pays 25% commission; $10 minimum on syndication. SASE.
Needs: General, pantomime and word gags. Submit on 3x5 cards.

DOM RINALDO, 29 Bay, 20 St., Brooklyn NY 11214. Holds 80 gags/year. Buys 30-40 gags/year. Has sold to *Cavalier, Oui, Saturday Evening Post, Hustler,* etc. Submit gags on 3x5 cards, numbered or coded. "Keep gag brief." Reports immediately. Pays 25%.
Needs: "Girlie," family and trade. No golf gags, or making fun of religion.
Tips: "I like to see gags that are no good without the picture (cartoon). Pays 25%, enclose SASE. Also interested in a comic strip, with the writer supplying strip ideas. Also editorial type cartoons about any subject."

FRANK ("DEAC") SEMATONES, 5226 Mt. Alifan Dr., San Diego CA 92111. (714)279-7178. Has sold to *National Enquirer* and male and girlie magazines. Pays 25% commission. Reports "immediately, but will keep unsold gags going forever unless return is requested." SASE.
Needs: Male, sexy, girlie. Must be new, fresh and funny. "I need a gagwriter to collaborate on new developing daily panel, comic 'tentatively' named: 'Amen' (priests, nuns, rabbis, assorted religious angle)."

JOSEPH SERRANO, Box 42, Gloucester MA 01930. Has sold to most major and middle markets. Pays 25% commission. SASE.
Needs: General and topical material.

E.G. SHIPLEY, 4725 Homesdale Ave., Baltimore MD 21206. Sold 24 cartoons last year. Has sold to *Computerworld, Industrial Machinery News, American Machinist, Metlfax,* etc. Submit gags typed on 3x5 cards; 15-20 to a batch. May hold unsold gags indefinitely. Pays 25% of sale price, and 30% to anyone who writes machine shop gags.
Needs: General, computer, office and machine shop gags. "I am doing mostly trade journal cartoons." No medical gags.

JOHN W. SIDE, 335 Wells St., Darlington WI 53530. Interested in "small-town, local happening gags with a general slant." Pays 25% commission. Sample cartoon $1. Returns rejected material "immediately." SASE.

SCOTT SMITH, 170 Madison Ave., Danville KY 40422. (606)236-9390. Holds 150-200 gags/ year; sells 500 cartoons/year. Has sold to *Independent Banker, Saturday Evening Post, New Woman* and *Changing Times.* Submit gags on 3x5 cards; 10-15/batch. Reports "immediately." Pays 25%. SASE.
Needs: General topics suitable for *National Enquirer, Saturday Evening Post,* etc. No "small island in the middle of the ocean type subjects, husband/wife dumb jokes, guru types, old magazine-in-doctor's office, woman driver, IRS, politics."

JOHN STINGER, 4 Hillcrest Rd., Mt. Lakes NJ 07046. Interested in general, family and general business gags. Interested in business-type gags first. Would like to see more captionless sight gags. Currently doing a syndicated panel on business, for which funny ideas are needed. Has sold to major markets. "Index cards are fine, but please keep short." Pays 25% commission; "more to top writers." Bought about 50 gags last year. Can hold unsold gags for as long as a year. SASE.

BOB THAVES, Box 67, Manhattan Beach CA 90266. Pays 25% commission. Returns rejected material in 1-2 weeks. May hold unsold gags indefinitely. SASE.
Needs: Gags "dealing with anything except raw sex. Also buy gags for syndicated (daily and Sunday) panel, *Frank & Ernest*. I prefer offbeat gags for that, although almost any general gag will do."

MARVIN TOWNSEND, 631 W. 88th St., Kansas City MO 64114. Holds 25-30 gags/year; sells 300 cartoons/year. Sells to trade and business publications and church and school magazines. Prefers batches of 12 gags. Pays 25% commission. SASE.
Needs: Interested in gags with a trade journal or business slant. Such as office executives, professional engineers, plant managers, doctors, etc. "Religious and children gags also welcome. Captioned or captionless. *No general gags wanted*. Don't waste postage sending general gags or worn-out material."

BARDULF UELAND, Halstad MN 56548. Has sold to *Parade, Legion, New Woman*, King Features, McNaught Syndicate. Submit 12-15 gags/batch. Pays 25% commission. Reports in 1-3 days, but holds unsold gags indefinitely unless return is requested. SASE.
Needs: General, family, medical and farm gags. No sex.

ART WINBURG, 21 McKinley Ave., Jamestown NY 14701. Has sold to *National Star, VFW Magazine, Physician's Management, American Legion, Modern Medicine, New Woman* and *Highlights for Children*. Pays 25% commission. Returns rejected material "usually within a week, sometimes same day received." Will return unsold gags "on request. Always a possibility of eventually selling a cartoon." SASE.
Needs: All types of gags; general, family, trade and professional journals, adventure, sports, medical, children's magazines. Gagwriter should "use variety, be original, and avoid old cliches." Would prefer not to see gags about "smoke signals, flying carpets, moon men, harems, or cannibals with some person in cooking pot."

ANDY WYATT, 155 W. 68th St., Apt. 408, New York NY 10023. (212)595-7694. Buys several dozen gags/year; sold several hundred cartoons last year. Returns rejected material in "1-2 weeks if I definitely can't use; sometimes longer if I feel there's a possibility." May hold unsold gags "until I sell, unless a writer specifies he wants gags back at a certain time." Pays 25% commission. SASE.
Needs: General, topical, family, business and animal. "I like visual gags, but any good gag is OK. No girlie or sex gags."
Tips: "Most submissions just not funny. Study the markets you write for."

Greeting Card Publishers

Why do people send cards? To communicate thoughts they don't have time to put on paper. You can be the card buyer's savior if you think of a greeting card as a produced *message* instead of a letter.

To achieve this distinction, you must write a basic sentiment or sophisticated greeting that speaks to an audience largely composed of women between the ages of 18 and 60.

It's a tough market to crack. You'll have to compete with blank note cards, along with comic book and trade book specialty line tie-ins. In general, it is best to steer away from overwriting, unfunny lines, and insensitive or unsophisticated messages.

Browse the card racks at your bookstore or department store to get an idea of what has been done and what remains to be done. Publishers report that sex and booze are old themes, though they still sell. Recently there has been a need for birthday cards for the 18-30 crowd.

While at the card shop, look for new card lines, particularly during the holiday periods. Keep ahead of publishers' seasonal needs by asking for a "current needs list" from markets that follow. *Greetings Magazine* (Mackay Publishing Corp., 95 Madison Ave., New York City 10016) lists addresses of greeting card publishers, and the National Association of Greeting Card Publishers (600 Pennsylvania Ave. SE, #300, Washington, D.C. 20003) has a membership roster available to writers. Consulting *A Guide to Greeting Card Writing*, edited by Larry Sandman (Writer's Digest Books), is also wise.

To submit conventional greeting card material, type or neatly print your verses on either 4x6 or 3x5 slips of paper or file cards. For humorous or studio card ideas, either fold sheets of paper into card dummies about the size and shape of an actual card, or use file cards. For ideas that use attachments, try to get the actual attachment and put it on your dummy; if you can't, suggest the attachment. For mechanical card ideas, you must make a workable mechanical card dummy. Most companies will pay more for attachment and mechanical card ideas.

Neatly print or type your idea on the dummy as it would appear on the finished card. Type your name and address on the back of each dummy or card, along with an identification number (which helps both you and the editor in keeping records). Always maintain records of where and when ideas were submitted; use a file card for each idea.

Submit 10-15 ideas at a time (this constitutes a "batch"). Keep the file cards for each batch together until rejected ideas are returned.

Listings below cover publishers' requirements for verse, gags and other product ideas. Artwork requirements are also covered when a company is interested in a complete package of art and idea. You will encounter these terms when using listings:

Contemporary card: upbeat greeting; studio card belonging to the present time; always rectangular in shape.
Conventional card: general card; formal or sentimental, usually verse or simple one-line prose.
Current needs list: see *market letter.*
Cute card: informal, gentle humor; slightly soft card in which the text is closely tied to the illustration.
Everyday card: for occasions occurring every day of the year, such as birthdays and anniversaries.
Humorous card: card in which the sentiment is expressed humorously; text may be either verse or prose, but usually verse; illustrations usually tied closely to the

text, and much of the humor is derived from the illustration itself; often illustrated with animals.

Informal card: see *cute card.*

Inspirational card: slightly more poetic and religious-oriented card within the conventional card line; purpose is to inspire, and is usually poetical and almost Biblical in nature.

Juvenile card: designed to be sent to children up to about age 12; text is usually written keeping in mind that an adult will send the card.

Market letter: current needs list; list of categories and themes of ideas and kinds of cards an editor currently needs; some companies publish monthly market letters; others only when the need arises.

Mechanical: card that contains action of some kind.

Novelty: refers to ideas that fall outside realm of greeting cards, but sent for the same occasion as greeting cards; usually boxed differently and sold at prices different from standard greeting card prices.

Other product lines: booklets, books, bumper stickers, buttons, calendars, figurines, games, invitations and announcements, mottos, note papers, placemats, plaques, post cards, posters, puzzles, slogans, stationery and wallhangings.

Pop-up: a mechanical action in which a form protrudes from the inside of the card when the card is opened.

Promotions: usually a series or group of cards (although not confined to cards) that have a common feature and are given special sales promotion.

Punch-outs: sections of a card, usually in juvenile cards, that are perforated so they can be easily removed.

Risque card: one that jokes about sex.

Seasonal card: published for the several special days that are observed during the year, such as Christmas, Hanukkah, Easter, graduation and Halloween.

Sensitivity card: beautiful, sensitive, personal greeting.

Soft line: gentle, "me-to-you message" in greeting form.

Studio: contemporary cards using short, punchy gags in keeping with current trends in humor; always rectangular in shape; often irreverent.

Topical: ideas or cards discussing current subjects.

Visual gags: a gag in which most, if not all, the humor depends upon the drawing or series of drawings used in the card, similar to captionless cartoons.

AMBERLEY GREETING CARD CO., Box 37902, Cincinnati OH 45222. (513)242-6630. Editor: Ned Stern. Submit ideas on regular 3x5 cards. "We always take a closer look if artwork (a rough sketch) is submitted with the gag. It gives us a better idea of what the writer has in mind." No conventional cards. Reports in 3-4 weeks. Buys all rights. SASE. Free market list revised about every 6 months.
Humorous, Studio and Promotions: Buys all kinds of studio and humorous everyday cards. Birthday studio is still the best selling caption. We never get enough. We look for belly laugh humor. All types of risque are accepted. No ideas with attachments. We prefer short and snappy ideas. The shorter gags seem to sell best. No seasonal cards. Buys 200 items/year. Pays $40. Occasionally buys promotion ideas. Payment negotiable, "depending entirely upon our need, the quantity, and work involved."

AMERICAN GIFTLINE CORP., Box 432, Cambridge MA 02139. (617)961-3400. President: V.G. Badoian. Submit ideas in letter/samples (no more than 2-3/batch) 1 year in advance. SASE. Reports in 2 months. Buys all rights. Pays on acceptance.
Needs: Promotions, posters, calendars, bumper stickers. Pays $200/minimum.
Tips: "Your idea must be entirely new and different—something to excite the imagination, or don't submit."

AMERICAN GREETINGS CORP., 10500 American Rd., Cleveland OH 44144. Does not accept unsolicited material. Will look at ideas for new concepts, promotions, unusal humorous directions, but query first. Editorial Director: Carl Goeller.

ARTFORMS CARD CORPORATION, 3150 Skokie Valley Rd., #7, Highland Park IL 60035. (312)433-0532. Editor: Ms. Bluma K. Marder. Buys "about 60-70 messages"/year. Submit seasonal/holiday material 6 months in advance. SASE. Reports in 3 weeks. Buys common law and statutory copyright rights. Market list available for legal size SASE.
Needs: Conventional; humorous; informal; inspirational; sensitivity; studio; messages for Jewish Greeting Cards such as Bar/Bat Mitzvah, Jewish New Year and Chanukah; Wedding, Sympathy, Anniversary, Get Well and Birthday. No insults or risque greetings. Pays $15-25/card idea.
Other Product Lines: Puzzles. Pays $25-50.
Tips: "Do research on Judaism so greeting is not questionable to a religious market; also if Biblical quotes are used, make sure references are correct. We look for simple messages that pertain directly to subject matter."

BARKER GREETING CARD CO., 950 Airport Rd., West Chester PA 19380. Contact: Humor Dept. Submissions should be typed or neatly printed on separate 3x5 cards or folded paper. Name, address and a code number should be on back of each idea submitted. SASE must accompany each batch. Artwork on ideas is not necessary. Reports in 1-3 weeks. Buys all rights. Pays on acceptance. Send SASE for *Market Letter*.
Needs: Studio card ideas for all everyday and seasonal captions; special need for card ideas involving the use of mechanicals and attachments. Specific needs are detailed in their periodic *Market Letter*. Seasonal needs include Christmas, Hanukkah, Valentine's Day, St. Patrick's Day, Mother's Day, Father's Day, graduation, Halloween and Thanksgiving. Everyday captions are birthday, friendship and get well. "All verse should be as concise as possible." Promotions, mottoes, etc., may be submitted at any time. No "extremely risque, sarcastic or masculine ideas." Pays $25 minimum.
Tips: "Our typical customers are women between the ages of 18 and 35. Writers should not so much write feminine ideas as edit their material, so as not to *exclude* this group."

BLUE MOUNTAIN ARTS, INC., Box 4549, Boulder CO 80306. Contact: Editorial Staff. Buys 50-75 items/year. SASE. Reports in 2 months. Buys all rights. Pays on publication.
Needs: Inspirational (without being religious); and sensitivity ("primarily need sensitive and sensible writings about love, friendships, families, philosophies, etc.—written with originality and universal appeal"). Pays $25-150.
Other Product Lines: Calendars, gift books and greeting books. Payment varies.
Tips: "A small amount of informal, 'cute' material will be considered. Seasonal needs (primarily Christmas) are relatively small. A very limited amount of freelance material is selected each year, either for publication on a notecard or in a gift anthology, and the selection prospects are highly competitive. But new material is always welcome and each manuscript is given serious consideration."

BRILLIANT ENTERPRISES, 117 W. Valerio St., Santa Barbara CA 93101. Editor: Ashleigh Brilliant. Buys all rights. Submit seasonal material any time. "Submit words and art in black on 5½x3½ horizontal, thin white paper. Regular bond okay, but no card or cardboard." Reports "usually in 2 weeks." SASE. Catalog and sample set for $1.
Other Product Lines: Post cards. "All our cards are everyday cards in the sense that they are not intended only for specific seasons, holidays, or occasions." Messages should be "of a highly original nature, emphasizing subtlety, simplicity, insight, wit, profundity, beauty, and felicity of expression. Accompanying art should be in the nature of oblique commentary or decoration rather than direct illustration. Messages should be of universal appeal, capable of being appreciated by all types of people and of being easily translated into other languages. Since our line of cards is highly unconventional, it is essential that freelancers study it before submitting." No "topical references, subjects limited to American culture, or puns." Limit of 17 words/card. Buys 200 items maximum/year. Pays $30 for "complete ready-to-print word and picture design."

CUSTOMCARD, 1239 Adanac St., Vancouver, British Columbia, Canada V6A 2C8. (604)253-4444. Editor: E. Bluett. Submit ideas on 3x5 cards or small mock-ups in batches of 10. Reports in 3-6 weeks. Buys world rights. Pays on acceptance. Current needs list for SAE and International Reply Coupon.
Needs: All types, both risque and nonrisque. "The shorter, the better." Birthday, belated birthday, get well, anniversary, thank you, congratulations, miss you, new job, etc. Seasonal ideas needed for Christmas by March; Valentine's Day (September); graduation (December); Mother's Day and Father's Day (December). Pays $50 minimum.

DRAWING BOARD GREETING CARDS, INC., 8200 Carpenter Freeway, Dallas TX 75247. (214)637-0390. Editorial Director: Jimmie Fitzgerald. Submit ideas on 3x5 cards, typed, with

name and address on each card. Submit query letter first. SASE. Reports in 2 weeks. Pays on acceptance. Market list available to writer on mailing list basis.
Needs: Conventional, humorous, informal, inspirational, everyday, seasonal, and studio cards. No 'blue' or sex humor. Pays $30-50.
Other Product Lines: Calendars. Pays $200-600.

THE EVERGREEN PRESS, Box 4971, Walnut Creek CA 94596. (415)825-7850. Editor: Malcolm Nielsen. Submit Christmas material any time. "Initial offering may be in the rough. Will not publish risque or 'cute' art." Reports in 2 weeks. SASE. Buys all rights. Pays on publication. Write for specifications sheet.
Needs: Interested in submissions from artists. "Our major line is Christmas. We avoid the Christmas cliches and attempt to publish offbeat types of art. For Christmas cards, we do not want cute Santa Claus, Christmas trees, wreaths, poodle dogs or kittens. We don't want sentimental, coy or cloying types of art. For everyday greeting cards we are interested in series of cards with a common theme. We are not interested in single designs with no relation to each other. We can use either finished art which we will separate or can use the artist's separations. We do not try to compete in the broad studio line, but only with specialized series. We do not purchase verse alone, but only complete card ideas, including verse and art." Payment for art on "royalty basis, depending on the form in which it is submitted."
Other Product Lines: Bookplates, note papers, invitations, children's books, stationery. Payment negotiated.

THE FENCE POST PUBLISHING CO., 21753 Birch Hill Dr., Diamond Bar CA 91765. (714)595-2938. Editor: Tom Boyle. SASE. Reports in 3 weeks. Buys all rights. Pays on acceptance. Current market list for any size SAE and 1 first class stamp.
Needs: Humorous (if adaptable to plaques); and studio (if adaptable to plaques). "No seasonal/holiday material. No artwork—only short copy, maximum of 6 lines of 32 characters and spaces. Nothing raunchy or pornographic." Pays $15 for each acceptance.
Other Product Lines: Bumper stickers and plaques. Pays $15.
Tips: "Send SASE for current list now selling. Also, look through files for material that has strong humor. Vulgarity in short, honest context is acceptable, but material should not be raunchy or pornographic." Sendability is very important. 'Saying it like it is' seems to be popular with our buyers."

FRAN MAR GREETING CARDS, LTD., Box 1057, Mt. Vernon NY 10550. (914)664-5060. President: Stan Cohen. Buys 100-300 items/year. Submit ideas in small batches (no more than 15 in a batch) on 3x5 sheets or cards. SASE. "Copy will not be returned without SASE enclosed with submissions." Reports in 1-2 weeks. Buys all rights. Pays on the 15th of the month following acceptance.
Needs: Invitations (all categories), thank you notes (all categories).
Other Product Lines: Stationery (novelty and camp), camp concepts, captions, novelty pad captions.

HALLMARK CARDS, INC., Contemporary Design Department, 25th and McGee, Kansas City MO 64141. Editor, Contemporary: Nancy Saulsbury. Submit ideas either on card mock-ups or 3x5 cards; 10-20/batch. SASE. Reports in 2-3 weeks. Buys all rights. Pays on acceptance. Market list for SASE.
Needs: Studio cards. Pays $66 maximum. "Avoid heavily masculine humor as our buyers are mostly female."
Tips: "Don't send non-humorous material thinking as long as it's here, we'll read it and buy it. This is a waste of our time and yours. Don't be afraid to analyze your material and throw it out or redo it. Most submissions lack a me-to-you sending situation."

WHITNEY McDERMUT, INC., 35 Market St., Box 385, Elmwood Park NJ 07407.
Needs: Fine art greeting cards. Personalized greeting cards, boxed Christmas cards, blank notes. Pay is open.

ALFRED MAINZER, INC., 27-08 40th Ave., Long Island City NY 11101. (212)392-4200. Art Director: Arwed Baenisch. Buys all rights. SASE.
Needs: Conventional, inspirational, informal and juvenile. All types of cards and ideas. Traditional material. All seasonals and occasionals wanted. Payment for card ideas negotiated on individual basis only.

MARK I GREETING CARDS, 1733 W. Irving Park Rd., Chicago IL 60613. Editor: Alex H. Cohen. Buys all rights. Reports in 2 weeks. SASE.

Needs: Sensitivity, humorous, studio, invitations and announcements. "The verse should fit the cards; humorous for the studio cards; sensitive for the 'Tenderness' line. Also interested in Christmas (both sensitivity and studio), and Valentine's Day (sensitivity and studio), Mother's Day and Father's Day (studio and sensitivity), graduation (studio)." Pays $35 for studio ideas; $35-50 for sensitivity ideas; and $125-150 for photographs.

NORCROSS-RUST CRAFT, 950 Airport Rd., West Chester PA 19380. (215)436-8000. Contact: Editorial Department. Submit ideas on 3x5 individual coded cards (one for each sentiment); writer's name on each card with SASE. Reports in 3 weeks. Buys all rights. Pays on acceptance. Market letter sent upon request with SASE.
Needs: Everyday and seasonal verse; studio and humorous ideas; greeting cards for birthday, illness, friendship, etc., both humorous and general. Pays from $15 for informal and cute cards with strong illustration possibilities; from $10 for imaginative sentimental prose; from $25 for juvenile and humorous, on acceptance.

PANACHE PAPETERIE PRODUCTS, Bank Village, New Ipswich NH 03071. Director of Product: Lew Fifield. For the sophisticated professional, 25-40 years old. Uses seasonal and everyday material. Buys all rights. Photocopied submissions OK. "Material will not be returned unless a SASE is included." Reports on queries in 2 months.
Needs: Avant-garde, haiku and light verse poetry in the traditional (not sugary, super sentimental) card text. Submit no more than 12 poems at one time. Length: 5-10 lines. Pays $25-50.
Tips: Textual postcards, where text rather than image says it, is the area most open to freelancers. Need expressive material.

THE PARAMOUNT LINE, INC., Box 678, Pawtucket RI 02862. Editor: Bernice Gourse. Submit seasonal/holiday material 10 months in advance. SASE. Reports in 3 weeks. Buys all rights. Pays on acceptance. Instruction sheet for SAE and 1 first class stamp.
Needs: Announcements (everyday—all titles); conventional (everyday, seasonal 4-, 6-, and 8-line verses, general and family); humorous (everyday, seasonal, general and family titles); informal (everyday, seasonal, general and family titles); inspirational (religious and non-religious); invitations (everyday, all titles, Christmas, confirmation, communion); juvenile (everyday, seasonal, general and family titles); sensitivity (contemporary prose: love, general, wish, inspirational, compliment, etc.); studio (everyday, seasonal, general titles); and contemporary promotions. Rates upon request.
Other Product Lines: Greeting books, postcards and promotions.
Tips: "Study the market; use conversational, contemporary language; include SASE; send 10-12 items at a time, on 3x5 cards."

RED FARM STUDIO, 334 Pleasant St., Pawtucket RI 02860. Editor: Claudia Scott. Send 6-12 submissions at 1 time. Submit on 3x5 index cards. SASE. Reports in 1-2 weeks. Pays on acceptance. Pay varies.
Needs: Material for announcements, humorous, inspirational, conventional, informal, sensitivity, Mother's Day, Father's Day, Easter and Christmas (relative or general). Pay varies.
Other Product Lines: Coloring books, paintables, placemats, gift wrap and note paper. No studiotype or related subjects.

REED STARLINE CARD CO., 3331 Sunset Blvd., Los Angeles CA 90026. (213)663-3161. Submit seasonal/holiday material 1 year in advance. SASE. Reports in 2 weeks. Pays on acceptance. Free market list.
Needs: Announcements, humorous, informal, invitations and studio. No verse or jingles-type material. Pays $40/card idea.
Tips: "Study the current trends on card racks to determine the type of card that is selling."

STRAND ENTERPRISES, 1809½ N. Orangethorpe Park, Anaheim CA 90630. (714)871-4744. President: S. S. Waltzman. SASE. Reports in 2 weeks. Buys all rights. Pays on acceptance.
Needs: Notecards that express one's feelings about love and friendship, philosophical and inspirational; religious verse on marriage, children, human relationships, nature and faith in short, poetic form (not too deep), prose or statement. Length: 16 lines maximum.
Payment: Soft line, sensitivity, humorous, inspirational, $5-15.

VAGABOND CREATIONS, 2560 Lance Dr., Dayton OH 45409. Editor: George F. Stanley Jr. Buys all rights. Submit seasonal material any time; "we try to plan ahead a great deal in advance." Submit on 3x5 cards. "We don't want artwork—only ideas." Reports in same week usually. May hold ideas 3 or 4 days. SASE for return of submissions.

Needs: Christmas, Valentine's, graduation, everyday, Mother's Day and Father's Day verse. "The current style of the new 'Sophisticates' greeting card line is graphics only on the front with a short tie-in punch line on the inside of the card. General rather than specific subject matter." Buys 120 items/year. Pays $10 "for beginners; up to $15 for regular contributors."

Other Product Lines: Interested in receiving copy for mottoes and humorous buttons. "On buttons we like double-entendre expressions—preferably short. We don't want the protest button or a specific person named. We pay $10 for each button idea." Mottoes should be written in the first-person about situations at the job, about the job, confusion, modest bragging, drinking habits, etc. Pays $10 for mottoes.

Tips: "Our audience includes college students and their contemporaries . . . and young moderns. Writers can tailor their efforts by checking racks in college bookstores and discussing what college students are requesting with card buyers in these stores."

Scriptwriting

Scriptwriting opportunities avail themselves to the freelancer in one of two areas: audiovisual materials for business and educational communities, and theatrical scripts (stage, film and TV).

Although you might dream of adding "screenwriter" to your reśumé, the best place to break into this market is in business or educational scriptwriting. In fact, you may find the opportunities so bountiful that you won't have time to write for the more competitive stage, screen or TV markets.

Although writing for all three media involves some of the same technical skills, primarily in terms of script format, there are some vast differences among these media. Analyzing individual *WM* listings will define the best approach to these markets, as well as variations in content and style.

Business and Educational Writing

Writing a script for a multimedia presentation, slide show, or 16mm or 35mm film often requires face-to-face discussions with the show's producer. In many cases, producers tell us that local writers only need apply. Writers might be required to meet with the clients as the script develops, meet with the producer in script conferences, or do in-house research.

Whether working from a distance or in the producer's city, be professional in all your dealings. In business or educational writing, experience works in your favor. If you're writing for the school market, teaching experience helps. For business writing, prior business employment and a specialization will get you off on the right foot.

Know your material. Do your research—don't leave holes that will raise doubts about your thoroughness.

Express yourself clearly. Be brief, whether your first contact is through a query letter or through a sample script exemplifying your style. Producers do not appreciate writers who unload a trunk of scripts, or lengthy, verbose scripts. They look for fast-paced scripts with short sentences, with an occasional longer, slower sentence to balance the script's rhythm.

Be original. Don't risk your script's life with a rewrite—whether it's conscious or unconscious—of old material the company has already produced. To avoid this, do some research in your public library. Find out what films the firm has produced, and see if you can arrange screenings.

Try to show that "something extra" in your script. Make it come alive through drama and innovation in style. Know how to use dialogue to keep the audience's attention.

Match the market's needs. Oddly enough, a common complaint business and educational producers voice is that writers send *fiction*. Study carefully the WM listings that follow and submit your best material to the appropriate market. Identify yourself as a writer in the upper right-hand corner of your résumé.

A/V CONCEPTS CORP., 30 Montauk Blvd., Oakdale NY 11769. (516)587-7229. Editor: Sharon Diane Orlan. Produces material for el-hi language arts students, both those on grade level and in remedial situations. Query with resume and samples. SASE. Reports on outline in 2 weeks; on final scripts in 1 month. Buys all rights. Catalog for SASE.
Needs: "Authors must receive a set of our specifications before submitting material. Manuscripts must be written using our lists of vocabulary words, and must meet readability formula requirements provided by us. Length of manuscript and subjects will vary according to grade level for

which material is prepared. Basically, we want articles and stories that will motivate people to read. Authors must be highly creative and highly disciplined." No "history lessons. We are interested in mature content material." Pays $75.

Tips: "If possible, contact the editor or editorial department by phone and 'meet' the company through 'personal' contact."

ADVISION COMMUNICATIONS LTD., 10012 105th St., Edmonton, Alberta, Canada T5J 1C4. (403)423-1318. President: Ray Schwartz. Produces material for "professionals, general public, etc. depending on the project." Submit resume and completed script. SASE. Reports in 3 weeks. Material is not copyrighted.

Needs: "Most AVs are 10-15 minutes in length and subject matter is naturally dependent upon the project. Incentive and training programs are very popular, as well as programs showing a new product. Government departments have also requested programs on energy, coal, and general PR." Produces multimedia kits, tapes and cassettes, slides and TV commercials (16mm or videotape). Pays by "hourly rate, percentage of budget dependent upon project."

AERO PRODUCTS RESEARCH, INC., 11201 Hindry Ave., Los Angeles CA 90045. (213)641-7242. Contact: J. Parr. Produces material for pilot training and schools (private and public schools from K through college). SASE.

Needs: Aviation/aeroscience/aerospace education material and "developing and editing both technical and nontechnical material. Charts, silent filmstrips, models, multimedia kits, overhead transparencies, phonograph records, prerecorded tapes and cassettes, slides and study prints. Royalty arrangements are handled on an individual project basis. Writers should have flight instructor and ground school instructor experience."

AFRICAMERA LTD., Box 975, Cary NC 27511. Contact: H. Kent Craig. Estab. 1981. Produces material for "primarily secondary and post-secondary educational markets; also business/ overseas commerce, and some general public audiences. We currently have a cadre of five writers who produce most of our material on an as-needed basis." Rights purchased are negotiable. SASE. Reports in 1 week. Catalog for SASE.

Needs: "Subject matter *must* be limited strictly to subjects related to Africa. Examples: filmstrips scripts about African geography, movie/play scripts on African social commentary, African language texts, translations, manuscripts on pre-1900 Western European African Imperialism, profiles of current African leaders, biographies of any African leader past or present, wildlife/ tourism/photography guides, possible weekly or fortnightly column ideas, and texts on scientific Africana. Please don't send rambling texts on the problems of racism in Africa, or political attacks on the right or left in current African leadership. Length: open, except possible columns, which must be under 250 words. All manuscripts must be typed, double-spaced, with wide margins, on one side of the paper. Slant *must* be apolitical in every case." Charts, 8mm and 16mm film loops, 8mm and 16mm films, silent filmstrips, sound filmstrips, models, multimedia kits, overhead transparencies, phonograph records, slides, study prints, and tapes and cassettes. Query with samples and completed script. Pays 50% royalty or in outright purchase of $50-500.

DOM ALBI ASSOCIATES, INC., 40 E. 34th St., New York NY 10016. (212)679-0979. President: Dom Albi. Produces material for corporate and government audiences. Buys 20-30 scripts/year. Query or submit resume listing types of clients. Buys all rights.

Needs: Produces charts, 8mm and 16mm film loops, sound filmstrips, models, 16mm films, multimedia kits, overhead transparencies, tapes and cassettes, and slides. Payment negotiable.

Tips: "We expect our writers to spend as much tme on concept and purpose, as they do on finished script."

ALLEGRO FILM PRODUCTIONS, INC., Box 25195, Tamarac FL 33320. President: Mr. J. Forman. Produces for the general and school markets. Buys 3-20 scripts/year. Submit resume. Buys all rights.

Needs: Science films for education, films for industry and government, and documentaries. Produces 16mm and 35mm films. Pays negotiable fee.

AMVID COMMUNICATION SERVICES, INC., 2100 Sepulveda Blvd., Manhattan Beach CA 90266. (213)545-6691. Production Manager: Larry Meyers. Produces material for industry and education. Query with samples. SASE. Reports in 2 weeks. Buys all rights.

Needs: Produces silent and sound filmstrips; 16mm films; videotape; tapes and cassettes; and teaching machine programs. Pays in outright purchase.

ANCO/BOSTON, INC., 441 Stuart St., Boston MA 02116. (617)267-9700. Director, Instructional Systems: R. Hoyt. Produces for the industrial and business communities. Submit resume. SASE. Reports in 1 week. Buys all rights.
Needs: "Technical or business-oriented material on specific subjects for specific customized needs." Produces charts, sound filmstrips, multimedia kits, overhead transparencies and cassettes and slides. Pays by outright purchase price of $400-800.

ANIMATION ARTS ASSOCIATES, INC., 2225 Spring Garden St., Philadelphia PA 19130. (215)563-2520. Contact: Harry E. Ziegler Jr. For "government, industry, engineers, doctors, scientists, dentists, general public, military." Send "resume of credits for motion picture and filmstrip productions. The writer should have scriptwriting credits for training, sales, promotion, public relations." SASE.
Needs: Produces 3½-minute, 8mm and 16mm film loops; 16mm and 35mm films (ranging from 5-40 minutes); 2¼x2¼ or 4x5 slides; and teaching machine programs for training, sales, industry and public relations. Pay dependent on client's budget.
Tips: "Send us a resume listing writing and directing credits for films and sound/slide programs."

ARZTCO PICTURES, INC., 15 E. 61st St., New York NY 10021. (212)753-1050. President/Producer: Tony Arzt. Produces material for industrial, education, and home viewing audiences (TV specials and documentaries). Buys 8-10 scripts/year. Buys all rights. Previously produced material OK ("as sample of work only"). SASE, "however, we will only comment in writing on work that interests us." Reports in 3 weeks.
Needs: Business films, sales, training, promotional, educational. "Also interested in low-budget feature film scripts." 16mm and 35mm films and video tapes and cassettes. Submit synopsis/outline or completed script and resume. Pays in accordance with Writers Guild standards.
Tips: "We would like writers to understand that we cannot find time to deal with each individual submission in great detail. If we feel your work is right for us, you will definitely hear from us. We're looking for writers with originality, skill in turning out words, and a sense of humor when appropriate. We prefer to work with writers available in the New York metropolitan area."

AUDIO-VIDEO CORP., 55 Delaware Ave., Delmar NY 12054. (518)439-7611. Producer: Lee Bowden. Produces material for TV commercial audiences, and sales and informational film screenings. "We purchase 20 scripts annually, with our need increasing." Query with samples or submit resume. SASE. Reports in 6 weeks. Buys first rights.
Needs: Scripts for 10- to 30-minute programs for audiences ranging from educational, business and consumer groups to nonprofit organizations. "At least half of the material is of a humorous nature, or is otherwise informative and thought-provoking. We seek imagination, motivation, experience, and after receiving numerous responses from this listing, we would prefer to narrow down our writers' file to those in the New York State-New England area. Delmar is a suburb of Albany, New York and we will be providing production services to our offices across the rest of the state. While our market primarily encompasses the Northeast, our requirements span a spectrum of subjects. With our recent expansion, we need access to a pool of freelance writers experienced in producing film scripts that are creative and practical." Produces videotapes, 16mm films, multimedia kits and slide sets. Pays $30-80/minute of finished program.
Tips: "The realities of budgets in the current economy naturally restrict production extravaganzas. It is essential to come up with a clever, concise script that lends itself well to the location and studio budget priorities of the project. Having a visual sense is a bonus and sometimes essential for a 'fresh' approach, but inexperience in this realm should not be a restraint to a good writer."

A.V. MEDIA CRAFTSMAN, INC., 110 E. 23rd St., Suite 600, New York NY 10010. (212)228-6644. Vice President: Carolyn Clark. Produces training material for corporations and educational material for publishers. Works with New York area writers only. Buys 15-20 scripts/year. Query with samples and resume. Reports immediately. Buys all rights.
Needs: "Most of our projects are 10-15 minute training scripts with related study materials for corporations and educational publishers. We create multi-screen presentations for conferences as well." Produces slide shows, sound filmstrips, multiscreen shows, multimedia kits, overhead transparencies, phonograph records, tapes and cassettes, films in many formats, and teaching machine programs. Pays in outright purchase of $350-500, for scripts.
Tips: "Accept changes, do accurate research, and enjoy the subject matter to a point of becoming creatively playful with our scripts."

BACHNER PRODUCTIONS, INC., 45 W. 45th St., New York NY 10036. (212)354-8760. Produces 16mm and 35mm films; videotape programs; and 2-inch, 1-inch, and ¾-inch cassettes. Not copyrighted. Does not accept unsolicited material. Prospective writer usually must have experience in subject related to proposed film, and needs knowledge of videotape or film requirements. Sometimes will use good writer without specialized experience and then supply all necessary research. SASE.

Needs: Produces training and sales films and documentaries. Subject matter and style depend on client requirements. "Sometimes clients supply outlines and research from which our writers work. We usually pay Writers Guild scale, depending on usage and what is supplied by us. Price varies with assignments."

Tips: "Writer should have knowledge of film dialogue writing, and recognize that there is "less money available for experimentation. You must write with budgets in mind."

BARR FILMS, 3490 E. Foothill Blvd., Pasadena CA 91107. (213)793-6153. "Produces material for all age levels; grades K through college level as well as in the public library market to the same age span and adult audience. We also have interest in materials aimed at business and industry training programs." Catalog $1. Query with samples. "We will assign projects to qualified writers. We require previous experience in film writing and want to see samples of films previously written and completed for sale in the market." SASE. Reports in 1 month.

Needs: "We produce and distribute 16mm films in all curriculum and subject areas. We prefer a semi-dramatic form of script with a moral or informational point. Avoid excess verbiage—we produce films, not books. The length of our films is 15-18 minutes. We will also consider pure informational subjects with voice over narration. Fees are entirely negotiable. We will accept film treatments and/or completed visual and dialog scripts. Please inquire prior to sending your materials to us."

Tips: "Meet the producer; share previous films; talk film; and be available."

BLACKSIDE, INC., 238 Huntington Ave., Boston MA 02115. President: Henry Hampton. Produces material for "all types" of audiences. "Query only. No scripts are accepted unless they're requested." Buys all rights.

Needs: Produces silent and sound filmstrips, kinescopes, 16mm and 35mm films, multimedia kits, overhead transparencies, phonograph records, tapes and cassettes, slide sets, and teaching machine programs.

BNA COMMUNICATIONS, INC., 9417 Decoverly Hall Rd., Rockville MD 20850. (301)948-0540. Producer/Director: Pare Lorentz Jr. Produces material primarily for business, industry and government; "client-sponsored films approach specific audiences." Buys 7-12 scripts, works with 3-4 writers/year. Buys "usually all rights—but other arrangements have been made." Reports in 1 month. Free catalog.

Needs: "Presently under control." 16mm films, slides, and tapes, cassettes and videodiscs. Query with samples. "Find out what we do before you query." Pays negotiable fee.

Tips: "We're looking for writers with the ability to grasp the subject and develop a relatively simple treatment, particularly if the client is not motion-savvy. Don't overload with tricks . . . unless the show is about tricks. Most good scripts have some concept of a beginning, middle and end. We are interested in good *dialogue* writers."

BOARD OF JEWISH EDUCATION OF NEW YORK, 426 W. 58th St., New York NY 10019. (212)245-8200. Director, Multimedia Services and Materials Development: Yaakov Reshef. Produces material for Jewish schools, youth groups, temples and synagogues; for audience from kindergarten to old age. Buys 12-15 scripts/year. Submit outline/synopsis or resume. SASE. Reports in 3 months. Buys first rights or all rights.

Needs: General, educational and informational. "Generally, length is up to 20-25 minutes maximum; most material geared to 10-12 years old and up. Jewish background needed." Produces sound filmstrips, 16mm films, tapes and cassettes, and slide sets. Pays 10-15% royalty or $500 minimum/outright purchase.

BOBBS-MERRILL EDUCATIONAL PUBLISHING, 4300 W. 62nd St., Indianapolis IN 46268. (317)298-5400. Manager of Acquisitions: Charlie Dresser. Query; include information about what makes the proposal unique, and define potential markets. Enclose SASE.

Needs: Educational scripts for "vocational/technical, business education, English and speech, and allied health subjects at the technical school, junior and senior college levels. Many of the submissions we receive are outside of our stated educational disciplines." Payment by royalty arrangement.

Tips: Writers who can take their own photographs are given higher consideration. "They can better conceptualize the end product."

BOUCHARD, WALTON PRODUCTIONS, Bishop's Rd., Kingston MA 02364. (617)585-8069. Script Supervisor: Betsy B. Walton. Produces material on contract base for business and industrial clients. Works with 4-6 writers/year. Buys "specific rights for intended use." SASE. Reports in 3 weeks on queries; 2 weeks on mss.

Needs: "We are currently researching the production of generic materials in marine related fields, i.e., safety, training." Sound filmstrips (LaBelle Commpaks). Query with samples. Pays negotiable fee, "per project/budget."

Tips: "Our requirements are usually technical and specific. Flexibility and good research habits, combined with the ability to logically present targeted subject matter, are more essential than off-the-wall creativity. We prefer experienced writers with excellent technical skills, a simple, direct style, and the ability to write for the ear, and with the eye. We do not interview freelance writers until we have a specific need. We welcome samples with cover letters for our files. No phone calls, please."

ROBERT J. BRADY CO., Routes 197 & 450, Bowie MD 20715. AV Production Manager: Richard M. Brady. Produces material for professionals and paraprofessionals in medical, allied health, nursing, emergency medicine, fire service, vocational and business fields. Buys all rights. Free catalog. "We are always eager to develop new writers who can blend both book skills and audiovisual skills. Since most of our writing needs would be commissioned, all submissions should be in the form of resumes, sample materials, and client and title lists." Query. Produces sound filmstrips, films, videotapes, overhead transparencies, audio tapes and cassettes, 35mm slides, and books and manuals.

Needs: Educational (35mm sound/slide programs, 35mm sound filmstrips—instructional); subject areas: business (training, skills, general); medicine (allied health, nursing, emergency medicine); and fire service training. "Our company deals with instructional rather than informational-type programs." Pays $200-1,200/script.

Tips: "Send a resume with samples of writing ability and grasp of subject."

BILL BRITTAIN ASSOCIATES, 130 Lakeside Park, Hendersonville TN 37075. (615)824-1593. President: Bill Brittain. Produces material for various audiences, but mostly business-industry/educational. Works with "in-house writers mostly except on special projects." Buys all rights "to products we produce." SASE. "We don't answer unsolicited scripts or material." Query with resume. "Send letter-resume for our files."

Tips: Be able to "re-write from print media for audio/visual media, and prepare radio and TV copy."

CALIFORNIA COMMUNICATIONS, 6900 Santa Monica Blvd., Los Angeles CA 90038. (213)466-8511. Editorial Director: Bill Muster. Produces material for corporations, industry and service industry. Submit resume. "No unsolicited manuscripts." SASE. Reports in 2 weeks. Buys all rights.

Needs: Produces industrial sound filmstrips, 16mm films, multimedia kits, slides, and AV multi image shows and videotapes. "We work on assignment only." Pays in outright purchase of "approximately $100/minute minimum."

PAUL CARTER PRODUCTIONS, INC., 638 Congress St., Portland ME 04101. (207)775-1008. President: Paul Carter. Produces material for industry and education. Query with samples and resume. SASE. Reports in 1 week. Buys all rights.

Needs: Interested in "energy education, appropriate technology, environment—15-30 minutes, documentary." Produces sound filmstrips and 16mm films. Pays in outright purchase of $100-250/minute (negotiable).

Tips: Looking for writers with "understanding of the audience, subject and filmmaking process. Clearly understood and defined objectives for the piece."

CLEARWATER PRODUCTIONS, 45 W. Broadway, Suite 201, Eugene OR 97401. (503)683-5200. Owner: Douglas C. Daggett. Produces training, sales, and PR sound-slide shows. Buys 10-20 AV scripts/year; works with 3-6 writers/year. Query with samples and resume. SASE. Buys all rights.

Needs: Slides. Pays in outright purchase.

Tips: Seeks "writers with imagination, humor and the ability to let the visuals tell the story."

COCHRAN FILM PRODUCTIONS, INC., 110 Tiburon Blvd., Mill Valley CA 94941. (415)388-2371. President: Ted Cochran. Produces material for educational, medical and general TV audiences. Buys 3 scripts/year. Query; specify purpose, intended audience, marketing proposal. SASE. Reports in 2 weeks. Buys all rights or first rights.

Needs: Nontheatrical, travel, industrial and medical scripts, and specials for TV/cable. "We seek enthusiasm, a working knowledge of specific subjects, experience in the technical field, and experience with writing nontheatrical films." Produces 16mm films. Pays according to Writers Guild standards.
Tips: "Avoid past trends: negative subjects that are anti-everything."

COMART ASSOCIATES, INC., 122 E. 42nd St., New York NY 10168. Producer: Richard Gottlieb. Produces material for a variety of audiences, including internal sales forces, trainees, industrial plant workers, and people attending international exhibits. Buys 20-30 scripts/year. Query with samples or submit resume. SASE. Reports in 6 weeks. Not copyrighted.
Needs: "AV needs depend entirely upon the clients. They can include business, technical, general or educational. We look for visual sense, clarity, economy, speed, flexibility, and an understanding of the differing requirements of various media." Produces sound filmstrips, 16mm films, multimedia kits, tapes and cassettes, slides and videotapes. Pays by outright purchase of $750-3,000.

COMMAND PRODUCTIONS, 99 Lafayette Ave., White Plains NY 10603. Executive Producer: G. Stromberg. Produces material for business clients. Works with 10 writers/year. Submit resume, sample script and long range goals. SASE. Buys all rights.
Needs: Technical and nontechnical business presentations and customized training programs. Produces sound filmstrips, multimedia kits, overhead transparencies, slides, booklets and brochures. Pays by outright purchase.

COMMUNICATION CORPORATION, INC., 711 4th St. NW, Washington DC 20001. (202)638-6550. Vice President: Juris Lazdins. Produces material for corporations, federal agencies, schools, industry and broadcast industry. Query with samples. SASE. Reports in 2 weeks. Buys all rights.
Needs: Material needs include "5-30 minute expository films and slide shows. Voice-over narrations, proposals and treatments." Produces 8mm film loops, silent and sound filmstrips, 16mm films, multimedia kits, tapes and cassettes, and slides. Pays in outright purchase of $100-3,000.

COMPASS FILMS, 6 Florence Ln., Newton NJ 07860. Executive Producer: Robert Whittaker. Produces material for educational, industrial and general adult audiences. Specializes in Marine films, stop motion and special effects with a budget . . . and worldwide filming in difficult locations. Works with 4 writers/year. Query with samples or submit resume. SASE. Reports in 3 weeks. Buys all rights.
Needs: Scripts for 10- to 30-minute business films, and general documentary and theatrical feature films. "We would like to consider theatrical stories for possible use for feature films. We also would like to review writers to develop existing film treatments and ideas with strong dialogue." Also needs (ghost writers) editors and researchers. Produces 16mm and 35mm films. Pays according to Writers Guild standards.
Tips: Writer/photographers receive higher consideration "because we could also use them as still photographers on location and they could double-up as rewrite men . . . and ladies."

COMPRENETICS, INC., 5821 Uplander Way, Culver City CA 90230. (213)204-2080. President: Ira Englander. "Target audience varies, however, programs are designed for health care audiences only. This ranges from entry level health workers with minimal academic background to continuing education programs for physicians and health professions. In the cultural area, all levels." Buys approximately 10-20 scripts/year. Query with samples or submit resume. SASE. Reports in 1 month. Buys all rights.
Needs: "Films are generally 10 to 20 minutes in length and tend to have a dramatic framework. Subject topics include all educational areas with emphasis on health and medical films, manpower and management training and multi-cultural education. Our staff normally does subject matter research and content review which is provided for the writer who is then required to provide us with an outline or film treatment for review. Due to the extensive review procedures, writers are frequently required to modify through three or four drafts before final approval." Produces sound filmstrips, 16mm films, and tapes and cassettes. Pays $1,000-5,000.

DAVID C. COOK PUBLISHING CO., 850 N. Grove Ave., Elgin IL 60120. Editor: Anne Blischke. Produces material for preschool, K-3. Buys 12 scripts/year. Query with samples or submit outline. "Send a resume and samples of work accepted by other publishers in the same field." SASE. Reports in 2 weeks. Buys all rights. Free catalog.
Needs: Education (various topics with pictures and stories for children; manual for teachers).
Tips: No textbook materials, negative subjects, poetry or 1,000-word stories. Pays $35-60/print. "In many submissions the authors cannot write for children—or the subjects are much too silly, or they want more money than we can afford."

CORY SOUND CO., 310 Townsend St., San Francisco CA 94107. (415)543-0440. Owner: Phil Markinson. Produces material for various audiences. Buys all rights. SASE. Reports in 1 week. **Needs:** Tapes and cassettes. Query. Pays in outright purchase.

THE CREATIVE ESTABLISHMENT, 50 E. 42nd St., New York NY 10017. (212)682-0840. Executive Producer: Ted Schulman. Produces material for business meetings and industrial audiences. Works with approximately 10 writers/year. Buys all rights. SASE. "We don't return unsolicited material; material is held on file." Reports "when needed. Material is always specific to project. We cannot project future needs." 8mm and 16mm film loops, 16mm and 35mm films, sound filmstrips, slides, and multi-image and live shows. Submit synopsis/outline or completed script and resume. Pays in outright purchase.

CREATIVE MEDIA, 7271 Garden Grove Blvd., Suite E, Garden Grove CA 92641. (714)892-9469. Owner/Manager: Tim Keenan. Produces material for trainees, employees, general public, and technical personnel. Query with samples and resume. SASE. Reports in 2 weeks. Buys first and all rights.
Needs: Produces multimedia kits, tapes and cassettes, slides and videotape (non-commercial—industrial, training, sales presentations). Pays in outright purchase of $50-500.

CREATIVE PRODUCTIONS, INC., 200 Main St., Orange NJ 07050. (212)290-9075. Contact: Gus Nichols, Bill Griffing. Produces material for industrial, business and medical clients. Query with resume and "background that is appropriate for specific project we may have." SASE. Buys all rights.
Needs: "We can use staff writers/associate producers with AV experience. We may consider help from time to time on a project basis. The writer must have the ability to create visual sequences as well as narrative. Flexibility is a must; treatments might be technical, humorous, etc." Produces sound filmstrips, 16mm films, slides, video and multi-image shows. Pays salary to writers added to the staff; a negotiable fee to freelancers.

CREATIVE VISUALS, Division of Gamco Industries, Inc., Box 1911, Big Spring TX 79720. (915)267-6327. Vice President, Research and Development: Judith Rickey. Free catalog and author's guidelines. "Provide a list of your educational degrees and majors. Explain your teaching experience, including subjects taught, grades taught, and the number of years you have taught. Please describe any writing experience, and, if possible, include a sample of your published educational material currently on the market. We ask for this information because we have found that our best authors are usually experienced classroom teachers who are writing in their subject area. Once we have information about your background, we will ask you for the subject and titles of your proposed series." Produces sound filmstrips, overhead transparencies, cassettes, study prints, posters, games and reproduceable books.
Needs: Education (grades K-12, all subjects areas). Pays royalty; usually 5 or 10% of net sales.

RAUL DA SILVA & OTHER FILMMAKERS, 1400 East Ave., Rochester NY 14610. Creative Director: Raul da Silva. Produces material for business, industry, institutions, education and entertainment audiences. "We strive for excellence in both script and visual interpretation. We produce quality only, and bow to the budget-conscious clients who cannot or will not afford quality." Submit resume. "Generally works on assignment only. Cannot handle unsolicited mail/scripts." Rights purchased vary. "If possible, we share profits with writers, particularly when resale is involved."
Needs: "We produce both types of material: on assignment from clients (one-shot communications) and proprietary AV materials which resell." Produces 8mm and 16mm film loops, silent and sound filmstrips, 16mm and 35mm films, multimedia kits, phonograph records, tapes and cassettes and slides. Pays 10% royalty; also pays in outright purchase of 10% of total budget. Pays in accordance with Writers Guild standards.
Tips: "We are impressed with scripts that have received recognition in writing competition. We also welcome resumes from writers. From these we will select our future writers." Looks for "knowledge of medium, structure, style, cohesiveness (mastery of continuity), clarity, obvious love for the language and intelligence."

NICHOLAS DANCY PRODUCTIONS, INC., 276 5th Ave., New York NY 10001. (212)684-0376. President: Nicholas Dancy. Produces material for general audiences, employees, members of professional groups, members of associations, and special customer groups. Buys 5-10 scripts/year; works with 5-10 writers/year. Buys all rights. Reports in 1 month.
Needs: "We need scripts for films or videotapes from 15 minutes to 1 hour for corporate communi-

cations, sales, orientation, corporate image, medical, documentary, training." 16mm films, slides, and tapes and cassettes (audio tapes and videotapes). Query with resume. "No unsolicited material. Our field is too specialized." Pays in outright purchase of $800-5,000.
Tips: "Writers should have knowledge of business and industry and professions, ability to work with clients and communicators, fresh narrative style, creative use of dialogue, good skills in accomplishing research, and a professional approach to production."

ALFRED DE MARTINI EDUCATIONAL FILMS, 414 4th Ave., Haddon Heights NJ 08035. (609)547-2800. President: Alfred De Martini. Produces material for schools, colleges, universities, libraries and museums. "We're informal, creative, earthy, realistic, productive and perfection-oriented." Submit synopsis/outline or completed script. SASE. Reports in 1 month. Buys all rights. Free catalog for SASE.
Needs: Subject topics include "educational material on art, travel and history from secondary to adult level." Produces silent and sound filmstrips, multimedia kits, and tapes and cassettes. Pays in outright purchase of $100-$2,500. "Fee is established in advance with writers."
Tips: Interested in "imagination, brevity, uniqueness of style and ascertaining objectives."

DEFENSE PRODUCTS CO., Audiovisual Div., 645 Azalea Dr., Rockville MD 20850. (301)279-0808. Manager: Harry A. Carragher. Produces material for industrial and public relations clients and the general public. Buys 4 scripts/year. Submit outline/synopsis, submit complete ms, or query with resume. Does not return unsolicited submissions. Reports in 2 weeks. Buys first rights. Free catalog.
Needs: Sample treatments in business, technical and general material; also exhibit design and fabrication. Produces sound filmstrips; 16mm films; multimedia kits; and slide sets. Pays 5% royalty; or by outright purchase of $100 minimum.

DIVISION OF AV ARTS, NATIONAL PARK SERVICE, Harpers Ferry Center, Harpers Ferry WV 25425. Production Manager: Bob Morris. Produces materials for the general public. Buys 5-25 scripts/year. Buys all rights. SASE. Reports in 1 month.
Needs: 16mm and 35mm films, multimedia kits, slide shows, and tapes and cassettes. Submit resume. Pays in outright purchase; negotiable.
Tips: "We're looking for writers with an understanding and appreciation of the wildlife environment; ability for interpretation and historical reenactments."

MARK DRUCK PRODUCTIONS, 300 E. 40th St., New York NY 10016. Produces audiovisuals for "mostly industrial audiences or women's groups." Produces 16mm films, multimedia kits and videotape industrials. Subjects: retail items, drugs, travel, industrial products, etc. Material is sometimes copyrighted. "The whole production belongs to the client. No unsolicited scripts; only resumes, lists of credits, etc. The freelance writer must have some expertise in the subject, and in writing AV scripts." SASE.
General: Pays $500/reel minimum. "Writer will be expected to produce outline, treatment and shooting script."

THE DURASELL CORPORATION, 360 Lexington Ave., New York NY 10017. (212)687-1010. Produces material for sales presentations, and training programs—primarily for consumer package goods companies. Buys 30-50 scripts/year; works with 6-10 writers/year. Buys all rights. Previously produced material (motivational AV modules) OK. Reports within weeks.
Needs: 16mm films, sound filmstrips, slides and tapes and cassettes. Query with samples and resume. Pays in outright purchase. ("Freelancer sets fee.")
Tips: "Freelancers must be fast, creative, enthusiastic, experienced talent. Demonstrate heavy experience in AV sales meetings scripts and in creative multi-image sales meetings."

DYNACOM COMMUNICATIONS INTERNATIONAL, Box 702, Snowdon Station, Montreal, Quebec, Canada H3X 3X8. (514)342-5200. Director: David P. Leonard. Produces material for industrial and business management training and development and exhibits (entertainment, PR, motivation). Buys 12 10- to 20-minute scripts/year. Submit resume. SAE and International Reply Coupons. Reports in 1 month. Buys all rights. Brochure/presentation $4.
Needs: Business (sales and marketing presentations); industry (technical and nontechnical training programs in motivation, management, etc.); education (learning modules for elementary and high school and college); and general (exhibit audiovisuals for museums, conferences, meetings). Produces charts, dioramas, Super 8mm and 16mm films, color television videocassettes, multimedia kits, overhead transparencies, phonograph records, tapes and cassettes, slide sets, and teaching machine programs. Pays in outright purchase "based on length and complexity of project, and the research required."

EDUCATIONAL DIMENSIONS GROUP, Box 126, Stamford CT 06904. Managing Editor: Gregory A. Byrnes. Produces material for K-12 levels. Query. Catalog $1.
Needs: 40-80 frames geared to proper grade level; all educational disciplines. Produces sound filmstrips, video, multimedia kits and 2¼x2¼ slides. Pays $100 minimum for consultation. Script writing fees vary.

EDUCATIONAL FILM CENTER, 5401 Port Royal Rd., Springfield VA 22151. (703)321-9410. Chief Writer: Ruth Pollak. Produces material for family, schools/communities. Works with 5-20 writers/year. Buys all rights. SASE. Reports in 1 month.
Needs: "Action adventure for children/drama format/incorporating educational objectives." 16mm films and tapes and cassettes. Query with samples. Pays in ourtright purchase of $100-150/minute.
Tips: "We're interested in visually-oriented film scripts; the ability to structure the story and develop characters economically; and the ability to take an instructional objective and weave it subtly into a dramatic film."

EDUCATIONAL IMAGES LTD., Box 367, Lyons Falls NY 13368. (315)348-8211. Executive Director: Dr. Charles R. Belinky. Produces material for schools, K-college and graduate school, public libraries, parks, nature centers, etc. Buys all AV rights. Free catalog. Query with a meaningful sample of proposed program. Produces sound filmstrips, multimedia kits and slide sets.
Needs: Slide sets and filmstrips on science, natural history, anthropology and social studies. "We are looking primarily for complete AV programs; will consider slide collections to add to our files. This requires high quality, factual text and pictures." Pays $150 minimum.
Tips: The writer/photographer is given high consideration. "Once we express interest, follow up! Potential contributors lose many sales to us by not following up on initial query. Don't waste our time and yours if you can't deliver."

EFFECTIVE COMMUNICATION ARTS, INC., 47 W. 57th St., New York NY 10019. (212)688-6225. Vice President: W.J. Comcowich. Produces "imaginative technical films" for the general public; and sales training, medical education and science students. Buys 30 scripts/year. Query with resume of specific titles and descriptions of scripts written—objectives, format, audience, etc. "Explain what the films accomplished—how they were better than the typical." Buys all rights.
Needs: "Primarily 10- to 30-minute films on science, medicine and technology. We also need 3- to 5-minute films on product promotion. A writer must have the ability to 'translate' technical material and supply scripts with detailed visuals. Films on science and medicine are becoming even more technically oriented. Writers must have ability to do independent research." Produces sound filmstrips, models, 16mm films, multimedia kits, tapes and cassettes, slides, and allied print materials. Pays by negotiation based on the project's budget.

EMC CORP., 180 E. 6th St., St. Paul MN 55101. Production Editor: Rosemary Barry. Senior Editor: Northrop Dawson Jr. Produces material for children and teenagers in the primary grades through high school. "We sell strictly to schools and public libraries. Because much of school buying is affected by school funding, our market changes as school funding changes." Buys world rights. Catalog for 9x12 SASE. "The writer, via submitted sample, must show the capability to write appropriately for the educational market." Query. "No unsolicited manuscripts accepted."
Needs: Career education, consumer education, special education (as related to language arts especially), low vocabulary but high interest fiction and nonfiction for problem readers at secondary grade levels. "No standard requirements, due to the nature of educational materials publishing." No nature or environmental topics. Payment varies.

THE EPISCOPAL RADIO-TV FOUNDATION, INC., 3379 Peachtree Rd. NE, Atlanta GA 30326. (404)233-5419. Executive Director: Dr. Theodore Baehr. Produces materials for educational and religious organizations. Catalog for SASE.
Needs: 16mm films and tapes and cassettes.

MARTIN EZRA & ASSOCIATES, 48 Garrett Rd., Upper Darby PA 19082. (215)352-9595 or 9596. Producer: Martin Ezra. Produces material for business, industry and education. Works with 4-5 writers/year. Buys all rights and first rights. SASE. Reports in 3 weeks.
Needs: Educational and informational work. Film loops, films, silent filmstrips, sound filmstrips, multimedia kits, slides, and tapes and cassettes. Query with samples or submit completed script "in writing only." Payment "varies with project."

FAMILY FILMS, 14622 Lanark St., Panorama City CA 91402. Company Director: Rev. Norman E. Walter. Produces 16mm films and sound filmstrips for interdenominational church market for all age levels from preschool through adult. Query. Free catalog.
Needs: "The majority of the projects are assigned and developed to our specifications. Writers may submit their credentials and experience or outlines; ideas and story treatments of specific projects may be submitted. Some experience in writing film and filmstrip scripts is desired. Motion pictures vary from 10 minutes to 30-40 minutes. Filmstrips are about 50-60 frames with running time of 7-10 minutes. The emphasis is on the application of Christian values to everyday living and person-to-person relationships. No royalty arrangements. Outright payment depends on project and available budget. As an example, our usual filmstrip project requires four scripts, for which we pay $200-250 each; motion picture scripts through final draft, $1,500-2,000."
Tips: "An up-to-date understanding of the nature and ministry of the average mainstream church is desirable."

FILM COMMUNICATION, INC., Outer Winthrop Rd., Hallowell ME 04347. (207)623-9466. President: Paul J. Fournier. "Not making assignments to writers."

FILM COMMUNICATORS, 11136 Weddington St., North Hollywood CA 91601. Senior Production Administrator: Pat Davies. Produces material on fire science, police science, fire education for children, and emergency medical care training for fire service, law enforcement, industrial and educational audiences. Buys 3-10 scripts/year. Submit resume of related writing experience to the production department. "Resumes are retained in our files. We do not solicit writing samples as a first contact. If a resume is of interest, we may initiate a request for samples." Buys all rights.
Needs: "Writers should be based in Los Angeles, since we require consultations on our premises. Our educational films are all slanted towards the various safety markets—fire prevention, fire survival, fire education, emergency medical care, law enforcement, industrial safety. Most films are high in dramatic content. They are hard-core training with a high entertainment value, as well. They are generally 10-25 minutes long. The writer must be very heavily into research. Total accuracy in fire/medical procedures is extremely critical. We frequently go into the fourth or fifth drafts of a script before arriving at a final shooting script. We look for originality, the ability to take a dry, technical, demanding subject and turn it into an entertaining script. Basically, we look for writers who are also all-around filmmakers, i.e., they are also able to direct and edit film." Produces 16mm films. Pays by outright purchase.

FILMS FOR CHRIST ASSOCIATION, INC., 5310 N. Eden Rd., Elmwood IL 61529. (309)565-7266. Production Manager: Paul Taylor. Produces material for use by churches (interdenominational), schools (both secular and parochial), and missions. Most films are 20-90 minutes in length. Previously published submissions OK. Free catalog.
Needs: Produces 16mm films, sound filmstrips, slides and books. Documentaries and dramas. Particularly interested in scripts or script ideas dealing with such subjects as: Creation vs. evolution, archaeology, science and the Bible, apologetics, Christian living and evangelism. Also interested in good scripts for evangelistic children's films. Query. Prefers brief one-page synopsis. Payment negotiable.

FLORIDA PRODUCTION CENTER, (formerly Com 21/Ted Johnson Productions), 150 Riverside Ave., Jacksonville FL 32202. (904)354-7000. Vice President: Lou DiGiusto. Produces material for business, industry, government and education. Buys 24 scripts/year. Query with samples and resume. SASE. Buys all rights. Previously produced material OK.
Needs: "General script needs. Training programs and industrial motivation. Six training of 10 minutes and 10 industrial—some with image-type slant, others with informational slant." Produces 8mm film loops, silent and sound filmstrips, 16-35mm films, multimedia kits, tapes and cassettes, slides, teaching machine programs and videotape presentations. Pays in outright purchase "depending on project."

PAUL FRENCH & PARTNERS, INC., Rt. 5, Gabbettville Rd., LaGrange GA 30240. (404)882-5581. Contact: B.L. Bryan or Mike Chambliss. Query or submit resume. SASE. Reports in 2 weeks. Buys all rights.
Needs: Wants to see multi-screen scripts (all employee attitude related) and/or multi-screen AV sales meeting scripts or resumes. Produces silent and sound filmstrips, 16mm films, multimedia kits, phonograph records, tapes and cassettes, and slides. Pays in outright purchase of $500-$5,000. Payment is in accordance with Writers Guild standards.

JOEL FRIED AUDIOVISUALS, INC., Box 61, Simsbury CT 06070. President: Joel Fried. Executive Producer: Wendy Rappaport. Vice President, Industrial Division: Pat Fox. Production Assistant: R.T. Daley. "We produce filmstrips/multimedia packages that are aimed at the high school/college market." Query; "tell us what your idea is, and why you can write on this particular subject." SASE. Buys all rights.

Needs: "Vocational education is very important to us. You should be familiar with the market and what subjects are of interest to today's students. We are open to any good idea." Subjects include vocational education and academics, including high school chemistry, career awareness, physics and biology, horticulture and home management/home economics. Produces sound filmstrips, 16mm films, videotape, overhead transparencies, slides, study prints, teaching machine programs and multimedia kits. Pays about $300-450/program.

FRIEDENTAG PHOTOGRAPHICS, 356 Grape St., Denver CO 80220. (303)333-7096. Contact: Harvey Friedentag. Estab. 1957. Produces training and information material for commercial, industrial and governmental audiences. Buys 24 scripts from 22 writers each year. Submit outline/synopsis or completed script. "We often work with writers to produce audiovisuals or films." SASE. Reports in 1 month. Not copyrighted.

Needs: "We need good ideas for training and information for business productions, either ordered or submitted on speculation. We're looking for someone qualified and easy to get along with, who can communicate. *Deadlines are a must*." Produces silent and sound filmstrips, kinescopes, 16mm films, overhead transparencies, slide sets, study prints, videotapes and videocassettes. Pays by outright purchase; assignments are determined "based on bids from the writer, or by 50% speculation on unordered projects."

GATEWAY PRODUCTIONS INC., 18 E. 50th St., New York NY 10022. (212)371-8535. Vice President Personnel Administration: Ms. Judy Hinichs. Produces material for corporate communications, over-the-air commercial television, cable and the international business community. Submit resume. SASE. Buys "non-theatrical rights under corporation client's name."

Needs: "Scripts are developed through research of each client's needs. Length is usually 10-30 minutes. Subject matter and style vary." Produces 16mm films and video. Payment is "based on overall production budget and negotiation of flat fee."

Tips: Interested in "strong visualization capability, fresh concepts, research capability, client rapport and especially professionalism. Most people who write for us come to us through referrals and are actually working in the New York metropolitan area."

GENERAL EDUCATIONAL MEDIA, INC., 701 Beaver Valley Rd., Wilmington DE 19803. (302)478-1994. President: David Engler. Produces for schools, colleges, business and industry, and general adult audiences. Buys 30-40 scripts/year from 5-6 writers. Query with samples. SASE. Reports in 3 weeks. Buys all rights.

Needs: Typical length, 12- to 25-minute scripts; subjects, style and format variable. Produces films; video; sound filmstrips; multimedia kits; tapes and cassettes; slides; computer-based programs; and teaching machine programs. Pays $200-500.

ROBERT GILMORE ASSOCIATES, INC., 990 Washington St., Dedham MA 02026. (617)329-6633. Produces materials for industrial training and sales promotion. "We are interested to learn of writers in the New England area with experience in writing for videotape and film industrial production."

Needs: 16mm and 35mm films and slides.

HANDEL FILM CORP., 8730 Sunset Blvd., West Hollywood CA 90069. Contact: Peter Mertens. Produces material for a variety of audiences, depending on the film. Query. SASE. Buys all rights.

Needs: Material for educational and documentary films in science, history and other areas. Produces 16mm films. Payment negotiable.

HAYES SCHOOL PUBLISHING CO., INC., 321 Pennwood Ave., Wilkinsburg PA 15221. (412)371-2373. 2nd Vice President: Clair N. Hayes III. Produces material for school teachers, principals, elementary and junior high school students. Buys all rights. Catalog for SASE. Query. Produces charts, workbooks, teachers' handbooks, posters, bulletin board material, and liquid duplicating books.

Needs: Education material only ("we will consider all types of material suitable for use in elementary schools"). Pays $25 minimum.

IDEAL SCHOOL SUPPLY CO., Affiliate of Westinghouse Learning Corp., 11000 S. Lavergne Ave., Oak Lawn IL 60453. (312)425-0800. Manager, Product Development: Barbara Stiles. Produces material for preschool, primary, elementary, and high school students. "The majority of our product line comes from outside sources, most of them practicing classroom teachers." Occasionally these products are edited by freelance talent. Writers and editors are also used for some special development projects. Query with resume which will be filed for future reference. Free catalog.

Needs: "Style, length and format vary according to grade level and subject matter of material." Produces manipulatives, games, models, printed material, multimedia kits, and cassette programs.

IMAGE INNOVATIONS, INC., 14 Buttonwood Dr., Somerset NJ 08873. President: Mark A. Else. Produces material for business, education and general audiences. Query with samples. SASE. Reports in 2 weeks. Buys all rights.

Needs: Subject topics include education, sales and public relations. Produces sound filmstrips, 16mm films, multimedia kits, 8 inch video, and tapes and cassettes. Pays in outright purchase of $500-2,000.

IMAGE MARKETING SERVICES, INC., 97 Compark Rd., Centerville OH 45459. (513)434-3974. President: Dale R. Mercer. Produces material for business, industry, institutions, and the general public. Arrange "advance appointment with samples." Buys all rights.

Needs: Produces silent and sound filmstrips; multimedia kits; tapes and cassettes; and slides. Pays negotiable outright purchase "based on assignment budget."

IMAGE MEDIA, 3532 Humboldt Ave. S, Minneapolis MN 55408. (612)827-6500. Creative Director: A.M. Rifkin. Query with samples. SASE. Reports in 2 weeks. Rights purchased "depend on project."

Needs: Produces silent and sound filmstrips, 16mm films, tapes and cassettes, and slides. Pays in outright purchase.

IMARC CORP., Box H, Newtown Square PA 19073. (215)356-2000. President: Bob Barry. Produces material for management, sales people, customers and trainees. "In the past 8 months we have worked with 7 writers and produced 16 audiovisual projects." Query with resume. SASE. Reports in 1 week. Buys all rights; some material is not copyrighted.

Needs: "We are very broad-based—from speech writing to full-length industrial films, brochures, technical writing, presentation formats, training and learning manuals and audiovisual projects, etc. We cover all fields, e.g., chemical, services, telephone, insurance, banks, manufacturers, etc." Produces charts, dioramas, film loops, silent and sound filmstrips, models, 16mm and 35mm films, phonograph records, tapes and cassettes, and slide sets. Pays $300-4,000/project.

IMPERIAL INTERNATIONAL LEARNING CORP., Box 548, Kankakee IL 60901. Director of Manuscript Development: Joanne Dressler. Educational AV publisher producing a variety of instructional aids for grades K through high school. Draws mainly from freelance sources on an assignment basis. Seeks authors skilled in writing sound filmstrips, cassette tape and multimedia programs. "Writers should submit a query letter which includes background and professional writing experience. Indicate that you understand our particular market." Reports in 6 weeks.

Needs: Sound filmstrips; slides; tapes and cassettes; Spirit master worksheets and teacher's manuals. Reading and math are main areas of concentration. Pays fee within 1 month after acceptance of ms. Contract provided.

Tips: "Offer concrete evidence that specific needs and requirements of the company would be met. Manuscripts need to be well researched. Stories should be intriguing with modern themes and illustrations."

INSGROUP, INC., 16052 Beach Blvd., Huntington Beach CA 92647. Senior Producer: Sharyn M. Case. Produces material for industrial, military (both enlisted men and officers), public schools (K-graduate level), police, nurses, and public administrators. Criteria for writers are determined on a project by project basis. Query with resume; be prepared to submit copies of previous efforts. "Please do not submit existing proprietary materials." SASE.

Needs: General material. Produces charts, silent and sound filmstrips, multimedia kits, overhead transparencies, tapes and cassettes, 35mm slides, study prints, teaching machine programs, and videotapes. "Insgroup develops objective-based validated audiovisual instructional programs both for commercial customers and for publication by Insgroup. These programs cover the entire range of subject areas, styles, formats, etc. Most writing is on a fee basis.

Tips: "There is a need in the AV field for writers who understand the needs of not only videotape, but videodisc and micro-computer learning machines and playback units. Often this equipment has time limitations or pulsing requirements that affect the materials produced for them."

INSIGHT ASSOCIATES, 1341 Hamburg Tpke., Wayne NJ 07470. Creative Director: Jim Cordes. Produces business programs, meetings, training and safety films, business theater, multi-

mixed media, VTR and films. "We strive to develop an agency relationship with clients." Buys 10-15 scripts or speeches/year. Works with 5 writers/year. Buys all rights. SASE. Reports in 2 weeks; "never, if not interested."
Needs: "We're looking for bright meeting modules that are philosophical or humorous, e.g., chemical safety programs, general media." 16mm films, sound filmstrips, multimedia kits, slides and tapes and cassettes. Query with resume. Pays "as per budget, length, research time."
Tips: Writer should have a "creative background in a range of industries."

INSTRUCTIONAL DYNAMICS INC., 666 N. Lake Shore Dr., Suite 924, Chicago IL 60611. Chief Executive Officer: L. Reiffel. For early learning through college level. "Writer should have valid background and experience that parallels the specific assignment. Would like to have vita as first contact. We keep on file and activate as needs arise. We use a substantial group of outside talent to supplement our in-house staff." SASE. Buys all rights.
Needs: Silent filmstrips, sound filmstrips, multimedia kits, overhead transparencies, phonograph records, prerecorded tapes and cassettes, 2x2 slides, study prints and hard copy. "Requirements for these vary depending upon assignments from our clients. Payment depends on contractual arrangements with our client and also varies depending on medium or multimedia involved."

INSTRUCTOR CURRICULUM MATERIALS, 7 Bank St., Dansville NY 14437. (716)335-2221. Editorial Director: Rosemary Alexander. "US and Canadian school supervisors, principals, and teachers purchase items in our line for instructional purposes." Buys all rights. Writer should have "experience in preparing materials for elementary students, including suitable teaching guides to accompany them, and demonstrate knowledge of the appropriate subject areas, or demonstrable ability for accurate and efficient research and documentation." Query. SASE. Free catalog.
Needs: "Elementary curriculum enrichment—all subject areas. Display material, copy and illustration should match interest and reading skills of children in grades for which material is intended. Production is limited to printed matter: posters, charts, duplicating masters, resource handbooks, teaching guides." Length: 6,000-12,000 words. "Standard contract, but fees vary considerably, depending on type of project."
Tips: "Writers who reflect current educational practices can expect to sell to us."

JEAN-GUY JACQUE ET COMPAGNIE, 1463 Tamarind Ave., Hollywood CA 90028. (213)462-6474. Owner: J.G. Jacque. Produces TV commercials. Query with samples. SASE. Reports in 3 weeks. Buys all rights.
Needs: Produces 16mm and 35mm films. Pays according to Writers Guild standards.

KAPCO COMMUNICATIONS, 5221 N. Elston Ave., Chicago IL 60630. (312)545-2544. President: K.L. Rubel. Produces material for general and business management audiences. "Most of our material comes from freelancers. Query to find out our specific needs, or about projects in the making. Do not submit stories or outlines; we want to see script ideas and finished scripts." Phone queries OK. SASE. Reports in 3 weeks. Buys all rights.
Needs: General interest, humorous (10-20 minutes), interview (related to business management), new product, technical, and travel (about the US, with visual appeal) subjects, and education subjects for students. Produces videotapes. Pays $100-750.
Tips: "Know what projects we're considering—or are in the process."

PAUL S. KARR PRODUCTIONS, Box 11711, 2949 W. Indian School Rd., Phoenix AZ 85017. Utah Division Box 1254, 1024, No. 250 Orem UT 84057. (801)225-8485/226-8209. (602)266-4198. Produces films and materials for industry, business and education with some TV and theater spots. Query. "Do not submit material unless requested." Buys all rights.
Needs: Produces 16mm films. Payment varies.
Tips: "One of the best ways for a writer to become a screenwriter is to create a situation with a client that requires a film. He then can assume the position of an associate producer, work with an experienced professional producer in putting the film into being and in that way learn about filmmaking and chalk up some meaningful credits."

KEN-DEL PRODUCTIONS, INC., 111 Valley Rd., Richardson Park, Wilmington DE 19804. (302)655-7488. President: Ed Kennedy. Produces material for "elementary, junior high, high school, and college level, as well as interested organizations and companies." Query. SASE.
Needs: "Topics of the present (technology, cities, traffic, transit, pollution, ecology, health, water, race, genetics, consumerism, fashions, communications, education, population control, waste, future sources of food, undeveloped sources of living, food, health, etc.); topics of the future; how-to series (everything for the housewife, farmer, banker or mechanic, on music, art, sports, reading, science, love, repair, sleep—on any subject); and material handling." Produces sound

filmstrips; 8mm, 16mm, and 35mm films; 16mm film loops; phonograph records; prerecorded tapes and cassettes; slides.

KIMBO EDUCATIONAL-UNITED SOUND ARTS, INC., 10-16 N. 3rd Ave., Box 477, Long Branch NJ 07740. (201)229-4949. Contact: James Kimble or Amy Laufer. Produces materials for the educational market (early childhood, special education, music, physical education, dance, and preschool children 6 months and up). Buys approximately 12-15 scripts/year; works with approximately 12-15 writers/year. Buys all rights or first rights. Previously produced material OK "in some instances." SASE. Reports in 1 month. Free catalog.
Needs: "For the next two years we will be concentrating on a few new special education products, general early chilhood-movement-oriented products, new albums in the dance field and more. Each will be an album/cassette with accompanying teacher's manual and, if warranted, manipulatives." Phonograph records and cassettes; "all with accompanying manual or teaching guides." Query with samples and synopsis/outline or completed script. Pays 5-7% royalty on lowest wholesale selling price, and in outright purchase. Both negotiable.
Tips: "We look for creativity first. Having material that is educationally sound is also important. Being organized is certainly helpful. Fitness is growing rapidly in popularity and will always be a necessary thing. Children will always need to be taught the basic fine and gross motor skills. Capturing interest while reaching these goals is the key."

KNOWLEDGE TREE GROUP, INC., 360 Park Ave., New York NY 10010. (212)689-1500. President/Editorial Director: H. Nagourney. Produces for the elhi and college market. Works with 10-15 writers/year. Query with samples or submit resume. SASE. Reports in 3 weeks. Buys all rights. Catalog for SASE.
Needs: Elhi and college material in various subject areas: language arts, social studies, science, math, etc. Produces charts, sound filmstrips, 16mm films, multimedia kits, tapes and cassettes, and study prints. Pays 5-10% royalty, or by outright purchase.

L & M STAGECRAFT, 2110 Superior, Cleveland OH 44114. (216)621-0754. Contact: Craig Lynch. Produces material for large corporate meetings. Buys all rights. SASE.
Needs: Multi-image. Multimedia kits, slides, and tapes and cassettes. Query with samples and resume. Pays in outright purchase on a "per-job basis."

LANSFORD PUBLISHING CO., Box 8711, San Jose CA 95155. (408)287-3105. Managing Editor: Mary Chatton. Produces material for college, adult, industrial and business audiences. Buys 10-30 scripts/year. Query "with outline of product, its intended market, clear overall description of topic, and use for product." SASE. Reports in 1 month. Buys all rights. Free catalog.
Needs: "Our chief sales area is in the fields of management, communication, psychology, and social problems. Please note the intended audience. We produce material for adult students—not elementary or secondary." Produces multimedia kits; overhead transparencies (10-20 visuals plus booklet); tapes and cassettes (2-6 one-hour tapes/set); and slides (20 or more slides). Pays royalty.
Tips: "Keep up with 'people problems.' Be careful with management how-to's—these are often redundant or overworked."

WILLIAM V. LEVINE ASSOCIATES, INC., 31 E. 28th St., New York NY 10016. (212)683-7177. President: William V. Levine. Presentations for business and industry. Firm emphasizes "creativity and understanding of the client's goals and objectives. We have the ability to create totally tailored presentations to fulfill these objectives." Buys 1-2 scripts/month. Previously published material OK. Query with resume. "We prefer New York City-area based writers only." SASE. Reports in 3 weeks. Buys all rights.
Needs: Business-related scripts on assignment for specific clients for use at sales meetings or for desk-top presentations. Also uses theme-setting and inspirational scripts with inherent messages of business interest. Produces charts, sound and silent filmstrips, 16 mm films, multimedia kits, tapes and cassettes, slide sets and live industrial shows. Pays $500-2,500.

LIGHTHOUSE PRODUCTIONS, 2345 Symmes St., Cincinnati OH 45206. (513)721-9900. Director of Operations: Mark Ackley. Produces materials for sales forces. Works with 10 writers/year. Buys 25-50 scripts/year. Buys all rights. SASE. Reports in 2 weeks.
Needs: "Generally we produce 4-6 annual conventions which are national in scope and client size (plus hundreds of smaller projects)." Slides and multimedia presentations. Query with samples and resume. Pays on a contract basis.
Tips: "There are more freelance opportunities, along with more competition. Production experience is helpful; dramatic abilities, a must. Our writers must be able to visualize the final product and understand the medium technically in order to write for it."

J.B. LIPPINCOTT CO., Audiovisual Media Department, East Washington Sq., Philadelphia PA 19105. (215)574-4235. Contact: H.M. Eisler. Produces materials for nursing students and medical students. Works with approximately 25 writers/year. Buys all rights. SASE. Reports in 2 weeks on queries; 4 weeks on submissions. Free catalog.
Needs: "High-level instruction in medical/surgical topics for pre-service and in-service professional education." 16mm films, sound filmstrips, slides (rarely) and video materials. Query. Negotiates pay.

LORI PRODUCTIONS, INC., 6430 Sunset Blvd., Hollywood CA 90028. (213)466-7567. Vice President, Administration: Emmy Cresciman. Produces material for industrial clients. Buys 5-10 scripts/year. Query with resume. SASE. Reports in 3 weeks. Buys all rights.
Needs: "We produce industrial films (sales, corporate image, training, safety), which generally run from 6-20 minutes in length." Seeks writers with a "clean, concise writing style; a familiarity with film production; and experience with industrial films." Works with local writers. Produces silent and sound filmstrips, 16mm films, multimedia kits, tapes and cassettes, and slide sets. Pays by outright purchase of $500-2,000.

LYONS STUDIOS, INC., 200 W. 9th St., Wilmington DE 19801. (302)654-6146. Creative Director: Ben Lisenby. Produces material for business and industry. Submit completed script with resume. SASE. Reports in 2 weeks. Buys all rights.
Needs: Subject topics include "business/industrial presentations-both educational and motivational." Produces multimedia presentations, video programs and collateral materials. Pays in outright purchase of $200-$1,000.
Tips: "Submit complete scripts with description of objectives, audience, time and budget required. We want honest estimates of time and budget needs; clean, terse style—conversational copy."

THE MCMANUS COMPANY, Box 446, Greens Farms CT 06436. (203)255-3301. President: John F. McManus. National Advertising, Marketing and Public Relations Agency. Produces material for consumers, corporate management and trade associations. Query with resume. Rights purchased "depend upon project and usage."
Needs: "Our needs are based on specific assignment, mostly business oriented." Produces 16mm and 35mm films, radio commercial tapes and cassettes.
Tips: "We maintain a complete and up-to-date file of talent availabilities." Interested in creativity, originality and realism.

MAGNETIX CORP., 770 W. Bay St., Winter Garden FL 32787. (305)656-4494. President: John Lory. Produces material for the general public. "Personal contact must be made due to wide variety of very specific scripts we require." Buys all rights.
Needs: Produces tapes and cassettes: 20- to 30-minute audio programs with sound effects written to be sold to general public as a souvenir with some educational value. "Writers must have the ability to dramatize our subjects using sound effects, etc." Pays $300 minimum.

MAJOR MEDIA, INC., 747 Lake Cook Rd., Deerfield IL 60015. (312)498-4610. President: Jay Steinberg. Produces industrial/training material. Buys 20 scripts and works with 3 writers/year. Buys all rights. Previously produced material OK. SASE. Reports in 3 months.
Needs: Educational, industrial and training, and sales meetings (new product launch). 8mm and 16mm film loops; 8mm and 16mm films; silent and sound filmstrips; kinescopes; microfilm; multimedia kits; overhead transparencies; phonograph records; realia; slides; study prints; tapes and cassettes; teaching machine programs; and video tape and live shows. Submit synopsis/outline and resume. Pays in negotiable outright purchase.

MARSHFILM ENTERPRISES, INC., Box 8082, Shawnee Mission KS 66208. (816)523-1059. President: Joan K. Marsh. Produces material for elementary and junior/senior high school students. Buys 8-16 scripts/year. Buys all rights.
Needs: 50 frame; 15 minutes/script. Sound filmstrips. Query "only." Pays in outright purchase of $250-500/script.

ED MARZOLA & ASSOCIATES, 839 N. Highland Ave., Hollywood CA 90038. (213)469-1961. Creative Director: William Case. Produces material for educational and industrial audiences. Query with samples or submit resume. SASE. Reports in 2 weeks. Buys all rights.
Needs: "We now produce shows for the grammar school levels; also feature-length films for theatrical release." Produces sound filmstrips, 16mm and 35mm films and videotaped presentations. Pays by outright purchase; "we negotiate each case individually." Pays according to Writers Guild standards.

Tips: "Multimedia and multi-image trends will make most writers think and plan in several planes at the same time."

MASTER MEDIA, INC., 4228 1st Ave., Atlanta/Tucker GA 30084. (404)491-0330. President: Dave Causey. Produces materials for "a wide variety of audiences. In addtion to regular commercial production, we have a unique relationship with Christian audiences in single showings, workshops and seminars." Buys approximately 18 scripts/year. Buys variable rights, "depending upon use and the economics involved." Previously produced material OK. SASE. Reports in 2 weeks.
Needs: Devotional topics, narrative, human interest, travel, hunger and human rights; Christian perspective; 12-28 minutes in length. "We are very interested at this point in scripts dealing with human conditions, social problems and human rights. Religious, especially Christian, content material is needed. We need, now, a script with impact on world hunger." 16mm films, multimedia kits, slides, tapes and cassettes and multi-image materials. Submit synopsis/outline or completed script. Pays negotiable fee.
Tips: "Writers need to think visually, that is, subject development should not be too abstract. The multi-image medium is becoming more content-oriented instead of the initial visual excitement from graphics syndrome. We see an increasing need for scripts with a 'message,' or emotional and entertainment values in the 12-28 minute range."

MAXFILMS, INC. 2525 Hyperion Ave., Los Angeles CA 90027. (213)662-3285. Vice President: Sid Glenar. Produces educational material for audiences "from high-school to college graduate level in our educational film division, and to all business and technical people in our industrial division. We also produce made-for-television movies and documentaries, and quality scripts and ideas in these areas are actively sought. The amount of material we use varies greatly from year to year, but on the average, perhaps 5-10 educational/industrial scripts are bought each year, with an additional 15-20 story ideas and scripts for TV movies or documentaries." Query or submit outline/synopsis, "a statement about the audience for which it is intended and the present extent of its development." SASE. Reports in 3 weeks. Rights purchased vary.
Needs: "The primary criterion for educational material is that the subject matter have entertainment as well as educational value. This does not preclude straight educational-informational scripts, but they must be entertainingly presented. Scripts or concepts for television movies must have appeal for an adult audience and have a story concept that is either unique or of current social interest. If the same concept has appeal for children as well, so much the better." Produces 16mm and 35mm films. Payment varies according to rights purchased.
Tips: "We are willing to work with new writers who show promise. About one-half of the story concepts and scripts we buy are from new writers."

MEDIA 2001, 5643 Paradise Dr., Corte Madera CA 94925. (415)924-5311. Managing Editor: Richard Pinkerton. Produces material for general business and professionals. Query with resume and samples or synopsis/outline. SASE. Reports in 2 months. Buys all rights. Catalog for SASE.
Needs: "We publish multimedia materials for 30-60 minute presentations in the motivational and public relations fields." Produces charts, 35mm film loops, silent and sound filmstrips, 16mm films, multimedia kits, tapes and cassettes, slides, and videotape recordings. Pays 10% royalty or in accordance with Writers Guild standards.
Tips: "We constantly utilize freelance writers in order to effect a national scope for our projects. Material should be directed toward a specific audience and topic area."

MEDIACOM, INC., 2049 Century Park E., Suite 2020, Los Angeles CA 90067. (213)552-9988. Vice President/Program Development: Stephen Strosser. Query with samples. SASE. Reports in 1 month. Buys all rights or first rights.
Needs: Produces charts; sound filmstrips; 16mm films; multimedia kits; overhead transparencies; tapes and cassettes; slides and videotape with programmed instructional print materials. Negotiates payment depending on project.
Tips: "Send short samples of work. Especially interested in flexibility to meet clients' demands, creativity in treatment of precise subject matter."

MEDICAL MULTIMEDIA CORP., 211 E. 43rd St., New York NY 10017. (212)986-0180. Administrative Assistant: Vanessa Reed-Edwards. Produces for the medical and paramedical professions. Buys 10-12 scripts/year. Query with résumé; "scripts are purchased on assignment." Buys all rights.
Needs: "Style and format vary; however, all writing is for the medical health sciences profession." Produces charts, sound filmstrips, 16mm film, multimedia kits, tapes and cassettes, videotapes, slides and teaching machine programs. Pays $200-2,000.

ARTHUR MERIWETHER, INC., Box 457, Downers Grove IL 60515. "We put a large emphasis on participation—or 'hands-on' ideas." Produces material for high school students. "Prior professional experience is required. Query with synopsis. Background as an educator is often helpful." SASE. Catalog 75¢.
Needs: Educational material. "We prefer items applying to language arts, English, speech and drama studies to be used as a supplement to regular curriculum materials." Filmstrips (silent and sound), films and multimedia kits. Games for learning also considered. "We will also consider 1-act plays and filmstrip scripts that deal with subjects of contemporary religious interest for elementary and high school religious education groups. Liberal approach preferred. Professional quality only. Scripts purchased outright, or by royalty arrangement." Also needed are business-oriented mss or scripts on marketing and staff training. Pays negotiated royalty.

MICHAELJAY COMMUNICATIONS, INC., 802 Wabash Ave., Chesterton IN 46304. (219)926-7615. President: Michael J. Griffin. Produces material for business and industry. Submit resume. SASE. Reports in 2 weeks. Buys all rights.
Needs: "Michaeljay is a full service communications company specializing in the development of marketing, advertising and training programs for a wide variety of business and industrial clients. The vast majority of our audiovisual presentations must be motivational or inspirational as much as informational. Our programs encompass various media including films, filmstrips, multi-image presentations, brochures, media advertising, training manuals, point-of-purchase displays, etc. Each of our programs is designed to achieve specific objectives. We do not produce generic programs for mass distribution. Each communication program is custom designed and produced." Produces charts; sound filmstrips; films; multimedia kits; overhead transparencies; tapes and cassettes; and slides. "Because of complex array of programs, payment varies on assignment."
Tips: "Those writers with the best chance of breaking in with our company will have multiple talents in a wide variety of applications. Show your best work in different media. Potential contributors should show a unique ability to approach communication problems with fresh, exciting ideas. The 'poetic ego' should not get in the way of the express objective. There is tremendous amount of room for creativity, but it must be channeled toward specific business goals."

MODE-ART PICTURES, INC., 3075 W. Liberty Ave., Pittsburgh PA 15216. (412)343-8700. Chairman: James L. Baker. Produces material for "all" audiences. Buys 5-10 scripts/year, but "each year is different." Query; "we write by contract." SASE. Reports in 3 weeks. Buys all rights.
Needs: Produces sound filmstrips, 16mm and 35mm films, slide sets, and teaching machine programs. "We seek writers who are flexible and willing to work. Good writers in our field are hard to find." Pays $1,000-5,000.

MONTAGE COMMUNICATIONS, 1556 N. Fairfax Ave., Los Angeles CA 90046. (213)851-8010. President: Stan Ono. Produces material for corporate audiences. Query with samples and resume. SASE. Reports in 1 month. Buys all rights.
Needs: Subject topics include 10-15 minute scripts of training and orientation. Produces training materials, e.g. workbooks; sound filmstrips; 16mm films; multimedia kits; tapes and cassettes; slides; and video. Pays in outright purchase.

MARCELO MONTEALEGRE, INC., 512 Broadway, 3rd Fl., New York NY 10012. Contact: Marcelo Montealegre. Produces material for students, institutions, community organizations, commercial clients, business. Works with 5-7 writers/year. Buys negotiable rights. SASE. Reports in 1 month on queries; 6 weeks on mss. Flyer for business size SAE and 1 first class stamp.
Needs: Human rights questions, slide shows (5-8 minutes). Sound filmstrips, slides, sound tapes and cassettes. Submit synopsis/outline and resume. Pays negotiable royalty or in outright purchase of $500-2,000.
Tips: "We look for writers with visual capabilities—the ability to preview the finished idea *on* screen."

BENJAMIN MORSE INC., 16 Aberdeen St., Boston MA 02215. (617)262-1550. President: Nat Morse. Produces material for industry and education. Query with samples and resume. Does not return unsolicited material-"cannot handle volume." Reports in 2 weeks. Buys all rights. Free catalog.
Needs: Produces charts; 16mm and 35mm film loops; silent and sound filmstrips; models; multimedia kits; overhead transparencies; tapes and cassettes; slides; study prints; teaching machine programs; and special effects. Pays "depending on job."
Tips: Especially interested in "someone who writes for 'the ear' and not 'the eye.' "

MOTIVATION MEDIA, INC., 1245 Milwaukee Ave., Glenview IL 60025. (312)297-4740. Executive Producer: Frank Stedronsky. Produces material for salespeople, customers, corporate/industrial employees and distributors. Query with samples. SASE. Reports in 1 month. Buys all rights.
Needs: Material for all audiovisual media—particularly marketing-oriented (sales training, sales promotional, sales motivational) material. Produces sound filmstrips, 16mm films, multimedia sales meeting programs, tapes and cassettes and slide sets. Pays $150-5,000.

M.P.K. OMEGA CO., 3615 Carson, Amarillo TX 79109. (806)355-9369. President/Producer: Mike Kiefer. Produces material for industry and education. Query. SASE. Reports in 2 weeks.
Needs: Subject topics include "all aspects of educating laymen on biology, biophysics, ecology, and geology." Produces 8 and 16mm films. Pays in outright purchase: negotiable.

MRC FILMS, Div. McLaughlin Research Corp., 71 W. 23rd St., New York NY 10010. Executive Producer: Larry Mollot. "Audience varies with subject matter, which is wide and diverse." Writer "should have an ability to visualize concepts and to express ideas clearly in words. Experience in film or filmstrip script writing is desirable. Write us, giving some idea of background. Submit samples of writing. We are looking for new talent. No unsolicited material accepted. Work upon assignment only." Query. SASE.
Needs: "Industrial, documentary, educational and television films. Also, public relations, teaching and motivational filmstrips. Some subjects are highly technical in the fields of aerospace and electronics. Others are on personal relationships, selling techniques, ecology, etc. A writer with an imaginative visual sense is important." Produces 16mm films, silent and sound filmstrips, video programs, and tapes and cassettes. "Fee depends on nature and length of job. Typical fees: $600-1,200 for script for 10-minute film; $1,200-2,000 for script for 20-minute film; $1,500-3,000 for script for 30-minute film. For narration writing only, the range is $300-600 for a 10-minute film; $500-900 for a 20-minute film; $600-1,200 for a 30-minute film. For scriptwriting services by the day, fee is $80-150 per day. All fees may be higher on specific projects with higher budgets."

MULTI-MEDIA PRODUCTIONS, INC., Box 5097, Stanford CA 94305. Program Director: Mark Vining. Produces material for elementary (grades 4-6) and secondary (grades 9-12) school students. Buys 24 scripts/year. Query with samples, if available. Reports in 6 weeks. Buys all rights. Free catalog.
Needs: "Material suitable for general high school and elementary school social studies curricula: history, biography, sociology, psychology, anthropology, archeology and economics. Style should be straightforward, lively and objective." Approximate specifications: 50 frames, 10 minutes/program part; 2 sentences and 1 visual per frame; 1- or 2-part programs. Writer supplies script, slides for filmstrip, and teacher's manual (as per our format). Pays royalties quarterly, based on 12½% of return on each program sold. "We like to avoid programs geared to a travelogue, generalized approach to foreign countries, and programs that deal with nebulous, values-oriented subject matter. Programs with a central academic theme sell best."
Tips: "Submit creative ideas for filmstrip programs covering major curriculum topics as well as treating interesting areas that larger, more inflexible companies will not touch. History, sociology, and remedial materials in 'reading, writing and arithmetic'-type subjects remain in demand." Writer/photographers are given higher consideration. "Many of the programs *without* proposed visuals, supplied by the writer, are useless to me."

HENRY NASON PRODUCTIONS, INC., 555 W. 57th St., New York NY 10019. President: Henry Nason. Produces custom audiovisual presentations for corporate clients. Query with samples or contact for personal interview. SASE. Reports in 1 month. Buys all rights.
Needs: "Usually 10- to 15-minute scripts on corporate subjects, such as sales, marketing, employee benefits, products, systems, public affairs, etc. Usually freestanding audiovisual modules. The style should be clear and relaxed, well-researched and organized. Writers must live in the New York City area." Produces slide and multimedia presentations. Pays "an average of 8-10% of the production budget."

NEW ORIENT MEDIA, 103 N. 2nd St., W. Dundee, IL 60118. (312)428-6000. Producer: Darlene Anderson. Produces material for pharmaceutical, automotive, communications and industrial audiences. Submit resume. SASE. Reports in 2 weeks. Buys all rights.
Needs: "Primarily sales oriented multi-image programs—training oriented films and slide programs." Produces sound filmstrips; 8mm and 16mm films; phonograph records; tapes and cassettes; slides and multi-image. Buys "40-50 scripts/year. We also buy research from writers." Pays in outright purchase by negotiation.

Tips: "We like unusual approaches that reflect a futuristic approach to communications. Writers have to be willing to come to us for input."

NORTHLIGHT PHOTOGRAPHIC LIMITED, Box 5873, St. John's, Newfoundland, Canada A1C 5X4. (709)579-1919. AV Manager: Scott Strong. Produces material for a general employee audience, corporate management, and engineering and other technical fields. Buys approximately 15-20 scripts/year. Buys all rights. Previously produced material OK. SAE and International Reply Coupons. Reports in 3 weeks. Free catalog.
Needs: "Stock scripts on energy conservation and other general concern material will receive the most attention." Charts, 8mm film loops, 16mm films, silent filmstrips, sound filmstrips, models, multimedia kits, overhead transparencies, slides, study prints, tapes and cassettes and video. Query with samples. Pays in outright purchase of $300-2,000.
Tips: "We look for conversational style in general, some engineering/technical background. Our emphasis is on technical subjects and allied research."

NYSTROM, 3333 Elston Ave., Chicago IL 60618. Editorial Director: Laura B. Parish. Produces material for school audiences (kindergarten through 12th grade). Required credentials depend on topics and subject matter and approach desired. Query. SASE. Free catalog.
Needs: Educational material on social studies, earth and life sciences, career education, reading, language arts and mathematics. Produces charts, sound filmstrips, models, multimedia kits, overhead transparencies and realia. Pays according to circumstances.

OCEAN REALM VIDEO PRODUCTIONS, 1995 NE 150th St., N. Miami FL 33160. President: Richard H. Stewart. Produces material for broad and narrow-cast audience. Works with 8 writers/year. Buys all rights and first rights. Previously produced material OK. SASE. Reports in 2 weeks.
Needs: Tapes and cassettes. Query with samples.

ORIGIN, INC., 4466 Laclede, St. Louis MO 63108. (314)533-0010. President: Carla Lane. Creative Director: George Johnson. Produces material for corporate training, sales POP, conventions, magazine videoformat, personnel, financial, paperwork, procedures and communications testing. Rights purchased by assignment. SASE. Reports in 2 weeks.
Needs: "All material is produced according to client needs." Charts, 35mm films; silent and sound filmstrips; slides; tapes and cassettes; teaching machine programs; video and videodisc; and stage. Query or query with samples and resume. Pays by contract.
Tips: Looks for writers with "imagination, creativity and logical progression of thought. Have the ability to understand complicated business functions in minimum time."

OUR SUNDAY VISITOR, INC., Audiovisual Dept., 200 Noll Plaza, Huntington IN 46750. Audiovisual Manager: Richard D. Hawthorne. Produces material for students (kindergarten through 12th grade), adult religious education groups and teacher trainees. "We are very concerned that the materials we produce meet the needs of today's church." Query. SASE. Free catalog.
Needs: "Proposals for projects should be no more than 2 pages in length, in outline form. Programs should display up-to-date audiovisual techniques and cohesiveness. Broadly speaking, material should deal with religious education, including liturgy and daily Christian living, as well as structured catechesis. It must not conflict with sound Catholic doctrine, and should reflect modern trends in education." Produces charts, sound filmstrips, phonograph records, tapes and cassettes and multimedia kits. "Work-for-hire and royalty arrangements possible."
Tips: "We're interested in two types of background: audiovisual and religious education. Very few people have both, and cannot be expected to perform equally well in each area. We want the best in either field."

PAN AUDIOVISUAL LTD., 11 Ely Pl., Dublin 2, Ireland. (01)760124. Director: Keith Nolan. Produces material for various audiences. Buys 15-20 scripts/year. Buys all rights. Previously produced material OK. SASE. Reports in 1 month on queries; 2 months on mss. Free catalog.
Needs: Charts, 16mm film loops, sound filmstrips, slides and video materials. Query with samples and synopsis/outline. Pays $1,000 minimum in outright purchase.

THE PERFECTION FORM CO., 8350 Hickman Rd., Des Moines IA 50322. Editor-in-Chief: Wayne F. DeMouth. Produces original manuscripts, sound filmstrips, cassette programs and learning packages for use in secondary language arts and social studies education. Reports in 1 month. Write for catalog.
Needs: Prefers manuscripts of approximately 30,000-40,000 words—novels written for young adult audiences ages 12-18. Fiction only. Pays on publication. Buys all rights. Adventure stories, humor,

school problems, personal conflict and choice, sports, family, courage and endurance. Interested also in curriculum materials, especially workbooks.

PHOENIX FILMS, INC., 470 Park Ave. S, New York NY 10016. (212)684-5910. Director of Promotion: Gina Blumenfeld. Produces material for educational and TV audiences. "We are a small independent distributor of high quality educational films. We distribute mostly to schools and libraries." Query with samples and resume. SASE. Reports in 6 weeks. Buys all rights. Catalog for $5.
Needs: "Short study guides for films on wide variety of subjects." Distributes 16mm films. Buys 50-75 films/year for promotion. Pays in outright purchase of $35-$90.
Tips: Wants writers with "ability to be concise and organized with some knowledge of educational film audiences."

PHOTOCOM PRODUCTIONS, Box 3135, Pismo Beach CA 93449. Creative Services Director: B. L. Pattison. Produces material for schools, junior high to university level. Query with samples or submit outline/synopsis. SASE. Reports in 3 weeks. Buys filmstrip rights. Free guidelines.
Needs: "We're most interested in how-to's in vocational areas that can be used in high school shop classes or adult education classes. We are also adding social science and natural history materials to our line. Material that we've been buying is 60-70 frames long." Produces sound filmstrips, multimedia kits, cassettes, and slide sets. Pays 10-15% royalty or $200 minimum/script.
Tips: Writer/photographers receive high consideration. So do beginning AV writers. "We're small and so can give special attention to first timers who show potential: we're a good place to get your start."

PHOTO-SYNTHESIS, INC., 450 Lincoln, Denver CO 80203. (303)777-1300. Head Copywriter: Sherry White. Produces material for internal and external industrial and corporate audiences. Query with samples, submit outline/synopsis, or submit resume. SASE. Reports in 2 weeks. Rights purchased vary.
Needs: Material about business ("with a motivational, educational, or thought-provoking slant on current issues"), communications, and technology and its impact. "We look for the ability to think and organize visually. Writers should understand practical business uses and applications." Produces multimedia kits; slide sets; and multi-image, multiscreen corporate cinema. Payment varies, but pays according to Writers Guild standards; may pay royalty or by outright purchase.

PREMIER FILM & RECORDING CORP., 3033 Locust, St. Louis MO 63103. (314)531-3555. Secretary/Treasurer: Grace Dalzell. Produces material for the corporate community; religious organizations; political arms; and hospital and educational groups. Buys 50-100 scripts/year. Buys all rights; "very occasionally the writer retains rights." Previously produced material OK; "depends upon original purposes and markets." SASE. Reports "within a month or as soon as possible."
Needs: "Our work is all custom-produced with the needs being known only as required." 35mm film loops, super 8mm and 35mm films; silent and sound filmstrips; multimedia kits; overhead transparencies; phonograph records; slides; tapes and cassettes; and "LaBelle Filmstrips (a specialty)." Submit complete script and resume. Pays in accordance with Writers Guild standards or by outright purchase of $100 to "any appropriate sum."
Tips: "Always place *occupational pursuit*, name, address, and phone number in upper right hand corner of resume without fail. We're looking for writers with creativity, good background, and a presentable image."

PRIME TIME DESIGN, 1911 Classen Blvd., Oklahoma City OK 73106. (405)521-8956. Managing Director: Steve Shockey. Producer: Jay Kruger. Produces material for industry, education and general audiences. Query. Reports in 1 month. Buys all rights.
Needs: "Might use scripts on corporate subjects such as sales, marketing, employee benefits, products, systems, etc. Most tapes run 20 minutes. Produces video material for industry; feature tapes; TV specials; documentaries; TV pilots; TV commercials; and medical and general educational productions." Payment "varies with production requirements."
Tips: "Writers should live in Oklahoma City or Tulsa area. Broadcast copywriting experience helpful. Rejections result from material which is not original enough."

PRIMEDIA CONCEPTS, LTD., 201 E. Erie St., Chicago IL 60611. (312)222-9480. Producer: Mr. J. Hassen. Produces material for governmental, business, industrial and syndicated TV audiences. Submit synopsis/outline and completed script. Does not return unsolicited material. Reports in 1 month. Buys first rights. Free catalog.
Needs: "15-20 minute informative; educational promotional and marketing for business, govern-

ment and corporate communications." Produces 16mm and 35mm films and videotape. Pays in outright purchase of $1,500 minimum.

Tips: Wants to see "humorous yet effective scripts for presentations. Be willing to thoroughly research topic and audiences."

PRODUCERS GROUP, LTD., 405 N. Wabash Ave., Suite 3404, Chicago IL 60611. (312)467-1830. Produces audiovisual material and films for general audiences. "Do not submit scripts. First, we get the assignment; then we go into creative work. Unsolicited mss are wasteful, inappropriate. If the writer has a proven record, we match the project to the writer's skills and expertise. We originate most of our own creative material here. We prefer any writer to have at least a B.A., or equivalent experience. Must have a record in AV writing, and hopefully, production."

Needs: Film loops and sound filmstrips, 16mm films, and multimedia kits. Business-oriented multimedia shows, educational films, and talk demonstrations. Fees negotiable. No royalty arrangements. Straight buy out.

Tips: "We require a clean shooting script, with all visuals completely designated."

PULLIN PRODUCTIONS LTD., Suite 102, 617-11th Ave., SW, Calgary, Alberta, Canada T2R 0E1. (403)261-5883. Creative Director: Edie Tusor. Produces material for industrial clients. Buys average of 20 scripts/year. Buys all rights. Reports in 1 month.

Needs: "Scripts for multi-image programs on an individual basis." 16mm films and slides. Query with samples. Pays in outright purchase, or determines pay by "individual negotiation."

Q-ED PRODUCTIONS, INC., Box 4029, Westlake Village CA 91359. President: Edward D. Eagle. Produces material for grade levels K-12. Buys all rights. Free catalog. "Knowledge of the field and experience as a writer of filmstrips for education required. Also, demonstrated ability in research required." Query. SASE.

Needs: "We are interested in reviewing completed filmstrip packages (2-6 filmstrips in a set) for distribution on royalty basis, or outright buy." Grade levels K-12. Interested in core curriculum materials. Historically strong in values. Materials should be inquiry-oriented, open-ended, strong objectives (cognitive, affective, psycho-motor). Royalties open on original materials. Fees range from $450 for a 10-minute filmstrip.

Tips: "We look for the new approach. Unique ways of imparting information so that children will want to learn more and on their own. Definitely not interested in didactic, mundane approaches to learning."

RAMIC PRODUCTIONS, Box 7530, 4910 Birch St., Newport Beach CA 92660. (714)833-2444. Executive Vice President: Evan Aiken. Produces material for schools, business and industry. Buys all rights. Previously produced material OK. SASE. Reports in 3 weeks.

Needs: 16mm, 30-minute films on human behavior—instructional films. "Must be aimed at motivating personal achievement." Query with background. Pays in accordance with Writers Guild standards.

REGENTS PUBLISHING CO., 2 Park Ave., New York NY 10016. President: Patrick Dubs. "Send all applications and queries to Ms. Mary Vaughn, Managing Editor." Copyrighted material. Query with description of material, table of contents and sample portions, and suggested marketing strategy. Free catalog.

Needs: English as a second language. Spanish, French, German. Supplementary materials, cultural aspects of wide appeal in foreign language classes. Vocabulary within the range of foreign 'language students. Prerecorded tapes and cassettes.

RESCO, 99 Draper Ave., Meriden CT 06450. (203)238-4709. Producer: Mr. Ronald F. LaVoie. Produces material for "all types of audiences based on subject matter—no pornography of any type." Submit resume. SASE. Reports immediately. Buys all rights. "Contingencies between writer, producer and/or client can be negotiated as well."

Needs: "Scripting for sound slide productions 16-18 minutes long. Subject topics include education, religion, business, technical, medical and general." Produces 8mm film loops (special request); sound filmstrips, overhead transparencies; tapes and cassettes; and sound slides. Pays 5% royalties; outright purchase of $25-$2,500; by negotiation or pre-contract. Pays in accordance with Writers Guild standards.

Tips: Writers should demonstrate "flexible grammarian interface with subject material, self starter creativity, intuitiveness, in-depth detail with minimal use of grammar and immense imagination as well as conceptual visualization."

RHYTHMS PRODUCTIONS, Whitney Bldg., Box 34485, Los Angeles CA 90034. President: R.S. White. "Our audience is generally educational, with current projects in early childhood." Query. "We need to know a writer's background and credits and to see samples of his work." SASE.

Needs: Teacher resource books; phonograph records. "Content is basic to the resource books; educational background is a necessity. For our phonograph records, we accept only fully produced tapes of a professional quality. If tapes are sent, include return postage."

JIM SANT 'ANDREA MIDWEST INC., 875 N. Michigan Ave., Chicago IL 60611. General Manager: W.R. Kaufman. Associate Creative Director: Shirley Shannon. Produces business communications presentations of all kinds. Submit resume. "We like to keep resumes on file." Buys all rights.

Needs: Subject types include business; technical; medical; and general. Produces multimedia, films, slides, videotape and live shows. Pays by project requirements.

Tips: Writers should show "originality, marketing savvy, good grasp of subject matter and be able to work with producer and client well."

SAVE THE CHILDREN, 48 Wilton Rd., Westport CT 06880. (203)226-7272. Producer: Joseph Loya. Generally buys all rights, "but it depends on project. We use work only written for specific assignments." Produces 16mm films, tapes and cassettes, 2¼x2¼ slides and posters and displays.

Needs: General (radio and TV); and education (high school, college and adult). Pays $250-500 minimum/assignment.

SAXTON COMMUNICATIONS GROUP LTD., 605 3rd Ave., New York NY 10016. (212)953-1300. Co-creative Director: Charles Reich. Produces material for industrial, consumer and theatrical audiences. Submit resume. SASE.

Needs: "We work with more than 10 outside writers regularly. We buy copy and scripts for approximately 30 projects/year."

SCREENSCOPE, INC., 3600 M St. NW, #204, Washington DC 20007. (202)965-6900. Production Manager: Jim Hristagos. Produces material for schools, industry and libraries. Submit resume. SASE. Reports in 1 month. Buys all rights.

Needs: "For education we need a script which can communicate to many grade levels. Style, format, length, etc. are discussed with producer and client." Produces 16mm and 35mm films and slides. Buys 20 scripts/year. Pays in outright purchase.

SEVEN OAKS PRODUCTIONS, 9145 Sligo Creek Pkwy., Silver Spring MD 20901. (301)587-0030. Production Manager: M. Marlow. Produces material for students, civic and professional groups, and PTA chapters. Buys 30 scripts from 10 writers/year. Query with samples, submit outline/synopsis or submit completed script. SASE. Reports in 2 months. Buys all rights or first rights, but rights purchased are negotiable.

Needs: Educational, medical, safety and general entertainment material. "We look for clarity in style, imagination with the ability to get information across and accomplish objectives, the ability to meet deadlines and to dig if necessary to get sufficient information to make the script better than another on the same subject. Writers should know the film format." Produces 16mm films, multimedia kits, phonograph records, tapes and cassettes, and slide sets. Payment negotiable according to project.

PHOEBE T. SNOW PRODUCTIONS, INC., 240 Madison Ave., New York NY 10016. (212)679-8756. Creative Director: Pennie Wilfong. Produces material for corporate uses, sales force, in-house training, etc. Buys 20-40 scripts/year. Buys all rights. SASE. Reports in 2 weeks on queries; 1 month on mss.

Needs: 16mm films, sound filmstrips and slides. Query with samples and resume. Pays in outright purchase.

Tips: "Have some understanding of AV for corporations. This is not the educational field. We're looking for creative writers who work with speed and can take direction. Be aware of short deadlines and some low budgets."

JOE SNYDER & COMPANY LTD., 155 W. 68th St., New York City NY 10023. (212)595-5925. Chairman: Joseph H. Snyder. Produces material for corporations, management seminars and employee training. Submit resume. SASE. Reports in 1 month. Buys all rights.

Needs: Subject topics include "education; motivation; management; productivity; speaking and writing. Produces multimedia kits, tapes and cassettes, and slides. Payment is in accordance with Writers Guild standards.

Tips: Especially interested in "sharpness and clarity."

SORGEL-LEE, INC., 205 W. Highland Ave., Milwaukee WI 53203. (414)224-9600. Creative Director: Brien Lee. Produces custom audiovisual material for business; industry; arts/non-profit; advertising and public relations agencies; business associations; special entertainment oriented projects. Submit an example of your scripting ability as well as a resume. SASE. Reports in 1 month, sometimes leading to an interview and an assignment. Buys all rights.
Needs: "People who understand what 'AV' is all about . . . words, pictures, sound. Motivational, informational, clear-cut, straightforward . . . writing that is literate, but never so good it could stand on its own without the pictures or sound. Usually writing for one narrator, plus additional voices and/or characters. No hype." Produces filmstrips, multi-image presentations, and mixed media presentations, slide-sound programs.

SOUNDCEPT AUDIO-VISUAL, Box 68, Silver Spring MD 20907. (202)269-6144. Executive Producer: Tom Colvin. Produces slide shows and multi-image programs for non-profit agencies, hospitals, colleges and government agencies. Buys 8-10 scripts/year. Buys all rights. SASE. Reports in 1 month.
Needs: "We specialize in matters pertaining to social policy and human development, education and training, recruitment and public relations (fundraising, etc.) Generally our scripts run from 8-15 minutes." 8mm film loops, 8mm and 16mm films, silent and sound filmstrips, multimedia kits, slides, and tapes and cassettes. Query with samples. Pays in outright purchase of $400-1,200.
Tips: "Writers must be experienced with slide/tape format, knowing how to co-ordinate script with visuals. We prefer writers who can incorporate imaginative use of sound into script and who understand the potentials of spoken narrative. A sense of humor helps, too."

SOUTH CAROLINA EDUCATIONAL TELEVISION NETWORK, Drawer L, Columbia SC 29250. (803)758-7261. Associate Director for State Agencies: Ms. Sandie Pedlow. Produces material for the general public; training and career development for business and industry; college courses; and on-going adult education in fields of medicine, dentistry and technical education. Query or submit resume. SASE. Reports in 2 weeks. Buys all rights.
Needs: "The Division of Continuing Education works in all media. Since, as a state agency, we work with other state agencies of varying needs, style, format, length, etc. are determined for each individual project." Produces kinescopes, 16mm films, multimedia kits, overhead transparencies, tapes and cassettes, slides, videotape and live in-studio television productions, also related printed materials for training programs. Payment "depends on funding governed by South Carolina state law guidelines."
Tips: "If possible come in for an interview and bring in samples of previous work."

SPACE PRODUCTIONS, 451 West End Ave., New York NY 10024. (212)986-0857. Producer: J. Alexander. Produces material for broadcast and industrial firms. Works with 10-25 scripts and/or writers/year. Buys all rights or first rights, "depending on assignment." Previously produced material OK. SASE. Reports in 2 months.
Needs: Documentary/news features and other types of scripts for TV. Sound filmstrips, multimedia kits, slides, tapes and cassettes, teaching machine programs and videotapes. Query with samples, synopsis/outline and resume. Pay varies, "depending on use of material."

SPENCER PRODUCTIONS, INC., 234 5th Ave., New York NY 10001. (212)697-5895. General Manager: Bruce Spencer. Produces material for high school students, college students and adults. Occasionally uses freelance writers with considerable talent. Query. SASE.
Needs: 16mm films, prerecorded tapes and cassettes. Satirical material only. Pay is negotiable.

SPOTLIGHT PRESENTS, INC., 20 E. 46th St., New York NY 10017. Producer: Carmine Santandrea. Produces material for corporate employees, trade association members and the general public. Query with samples and resume. SASE. Reports in 3 weeks. Buys all rights. Free catalog for SASE.
Needs: "We specialize in multi-image productions (3-30 projectors), 5-15 minutes in length. Subject topics: business, corporate image, new product introductions, and general. Frequently need proposals written." Produces sound filmstrips; 16mm and 35mm films; multimedia kits; overhead transparencies; slides and video. "Freelancers supply approximately 20 scripts/year and approximately 60 proposals/year." Pays in outright purchase of $50-$125/running minute.
Tips: "Submit samples indicative of range of writing experience, e.g., proposals, multimedia and film." Writers should show "reliability, thoroughness, creativity and responsiveness to suggestions."

SPOTTSWOOD STUDIOS, 2524 Old Shell Rd., Box 7061, Mobile AL 36607. (205)478-9387. Co-owner: M.W. Spottswood. "We normally work for sponsors (not always) who seek public

attention." Query with resume and samples. SASE. Reports in 2 weeks. Buys all rights.
Needs: Business; religious; and general. Produces 16mm films and 8mm loops; sound filmstrips; videotape and slide sets. Pays in outright purchase price.

AL STAHL ANIMATED, 1600 Broadway, New York NY 10019. (212)265-2942. President: Al Stahl. Estab. 1950. Produces industrial, sales promotion, educational and television commercial material. Query. SASE. Buys first rights. Free catalog.
Needs: "We specialize in making movies from slides, and in converting slide shows and multimedia (three or more screens) into a one-screen movie." Produces 8mm and 16mm films, and multimedia kits. Pays by outright purchase.

E.J. STEWART, INC., 525 Mildred Ave., Primos PA 19018. (215)626-6500. Creative Director: David Lindquester. "Our firm is a television production house providing programming for the broadcast, industrial, educational and medical fields. Government work is also handled." Buys 100 scripts/year. Buys all rights. SASE. Reports "when needed."
Needs: "We produce programming for our clients' specific needs. We do not know in advance what our needs will be other than general scripts for commercials and programs depending upon requests that we receive from clients." Videotapes. Submit resume only. Pays in negotiable outright purchase.

STUDIO CENTER CORP., 200 W. 22nd St., Norfolk VA 23517. (804)622-2111. Executive Producer: Fred Donour. Creative Director: Vince Ahern. Produces material for all audiences except medical. Submit completed script and resume. SASE. Reports in 3 weeks. Buys all rights.
Needs: "All topics except medical with emphasis on corporate image scripts. All styles (comedy dialogue to documentary), 8-15 minutes average times." Produces silent and sound filmstrips; multimedia kits; phonograph records; tapes and cassettes; and slides. Pays in outright purchase of $250-$1,000.
Tips: "We don't like straight narrations." Wants to see "thematic approach with creativity."

SUNTREE PRODUCTIONS, LTD., 220 E. 23rd St., New York NY 10010. (212)686-4111. President: D.W. Funt. Produces material for commercial, industrial and educational audiences. "We bought 11 scripts last year from 5 writers. Submit resume; we will call writers with interesting resumes when projects are available." Buys all rights.
Needs: "We are contract producers. Our needs vary from big-budget multimedia shows to educational filmstrips. We look for speed, accuracy, flexibility, wit and intelligence." Produces charts, sound filmstrips, multimedia shows, tapes and cassettes, and slide sets. "Payment varies according to the project and the writer's experience."
Tips: To keep pace with trends in this field, "writers must be conceptual as well as verbal."

SUPER 8 FILMS BY SUTHERLAND, 28 Smith Terrace, Staten Island NY 10304. (212)447-3908. General Manager: Don Sutherland. "Ours are made-for-hire films that serve specific functions for our clients, usually firms or institutions that benefit from expedient, low-cost motion picture communication. Sales demos, personnel training, fundraising and sociological documentations are typical. Nearly all our scripts are created in-house, on assignment from clients; however, possible expansion into the videocassette field may broaden future requirements." Query. SASE. Reports "as soon as possible." Rights purchased depend on the application of the completed production.
Needs: "There is a possibility of our entering the home-distribution videocassette market. We may do so through materials that represent non-mainstream points of view in dramatic programming. Thus our bad guys may be good, our good guys bad, our sexy stuff more erotic than hamburger; but hamburger is what we may make of assorted sacred cows. We think that most sacred cows, whether traditional or 'now,' comprise a lot of bull. We tend to favor themes and concepts that encourage optimism and people's pride in themselves. Activism and self-determination are values we like to hold as ideals; self-pity, though generally fashionable these days, will not find its way into any catalog we produce. We subscribe to the philosophy that people of various races, religions, sexes and sexual inclinations are different from one another, and that such differences should be played to the hilt. We look for the ability and willingness to do as promised." Produces super 8mm films. Payment is negotiable.

TALCO PRODUCTIONS, 279 E. 44th St., New York NY 10017. (212)697-4015. President: Alan Lawrence. Produces for TV, also videotape and film programming for schools, foundations, industrial organizations and associations. Buys all rights. "We maintain a file of writers and call on those with experience in the general category. We do not accept unsolicited mss. We prefer to receive a writer's resume listing credits. If his experience merits, we will be in touch when a project seems right." Produces sound filmstrips, films, videotapes, phonograph records, tapes and cassettes, and slide sets.

Needs: General (client-oriented productions to meet specific needs); education (peripheral market); business (public relations, documentaries, industrial); foreign language (we sometimes dub shows completed for clients for a specific market). Payment runs $500 and up; usually Writers Guild minimums apply.

TAPE 'N TEXT, Tape 'n Text Publishing Co., Box 250, Fredonia NY 14063. Editor-in-Chief: William R. Parks. Publishes printed text closely coordinated with narration on cassette tape and home computer software. Offers royalty contract of 10% minimum. Published 9 Tape 'n Text titles last year and 9 disc-based home computer programs. Marketing currently through direct mail to schools, libraries, retail stores and through distributors. Photocopied submissions OK. Query. Reports in 6 weeks. SASE.

Education and Training: "The kind of Tape 'n Text material we want from prospective authors is either a narration on tape with printed text which is very closely coordinated, or taped lectures or talks. We are now in English, computer science, mathematics and home and hobby computing, software, courseware and instruction. We must have inquiries first before writers or programmers send in their material. We also request that writers consider that their educational background and experience are important factors. Authors should examine the existing Tape 'n Text titles and computer software packages. Follow our format for their development of material. It is important that the writer and/or programmer establish what his target audience is, i.e., level: elementary school, junior high school, high school, junior college, university, or the general trade markets." Current titles include *Basic English Language Usage*, by Dr. G.H. Poteet; *Programming in Basic*, by W.R. Parks; and *Home Computer Software Packages* (Apple-2 and TRS-80), by John H. Barnes and W.R. Parks..

TEL A TRAIN, Box 4752, Chattanooga TN 37405. (615)624-2628. President: Perry V. Lane. Produces materials for engineers and maintenance personnel in industrial plants. Purchases approximately 7 scripts/year. Buys all rights. SASE. Reports in 2 weeks. Free catalog.

Needs: Pneumatics: 10 programs approximately 20 minutes long. 8mm and 16mm films and tapes and cassettes. Query. Pays in outright purchase.

TEL-AIR INTERESTS, INC., 1755 N.E. 149th St., Miami FL 33181. (305)944-3268. President: Grant H. Gravitt. Produces material for groups and theatrical and TV audiences. Submit resume. SASE. Buys all rights.

Needs: "Documentary films on education, travel and sports." Produces films and videotape. Pays in outright purchase.

TELSTAR PRODUCTIONS, INC., 366 N. Prior Ave., St. Paul MN 55104. Editor: Dr. Victor Kerns. Produces video material for adult, college-level audience, in industry and continuing education. Buys video recording rights. Query. Produces instructional videotapes not intended for broadcast.

Needs: Education (curricular materials for small group or independent study); business (training and development material); and medicine (paramedical topics). Pays $100 plus royalties.

Tips: Writer/photographers receive high consideration because "they are aware of some video limitations."

BOB THOMAS PRODUCTIONS, Box 1787, Wayne NJ 07470. (201)696-7500. New York Office: 55 W. 42nd St., New York NY 10036. (212)221-3602. President: Robert G. Thomas. Buys all rights. "Send material with introductory letter explaining ideas. Submit outline or rough draft for film or business matter. If possible, we will contact the writer for further discussion." SASE.

Needs: "We produce 2 types of material for 2 types of audiences: 8mm and 16mm films for business (educational, distributed by agencies); 35mm films for entertainment for a general audience (theater type). General subject matter may be of any style, any length." Produces material for the future, 35mm theatrical shorts for distribution. Pays "dependent on agreements between both parties. On 8mm and 16mm matter, one fee arrangement. On 35mm shorts, percentage or fee."

FRANCIS THOMPSON, INC., 231 E. 51st St., New York NY 10022. Vice President: Byron McKinney. Produces films for varied audiences. Commissions scriptwriting only.

ROGER TILTON FILMS, INC., 241 W. "G" St., San Diego CA 92101. (714)233-6513. Production Manager: Robert T. Hitchcox. Audience "varies with client." Submit resume. SASE. "We do not accept unrequested scripts. We will request samples if a writer is being considered." Reports in 2 weeks. Buys all rights.

Needs: "Scripts are all on contract basis with specific details supplied by us or our clients. Subjects run full spectrum of topics and audiences." Produces sound filmstrips, 16mm, 35mm and 65mm films and video cassettes. Pays in outright purchase; "depends on project, quoted in advance."
Tips: Writers must demonstrate "ability to work within the constraints of the client."

TRIDENT COMMUNICATIONS/INTERNATIONAL AUDIOVISUAL DESIGNERS, INC., 114 E. 32nd St., New York NY 10016. (212)685-2770. Executive Producer: Manos Angelakis. Produces material for "consumer and trade in travel, food services, flavors and fragrances. Also corporate image and employee orientation." Submit resume. "No unsolicited scripts accepted." Buys all rights.
Needs: "We only work on assignment and therefore our needs vary with the subject with which the current assignment deals." Produces 8mm film loops; sound filmstrips; 16mm films; slides; and multiscreen/multi-image/multimedia.Pays in outright purchase of $300-$3,000; "⅓ in advance, ⅓ on delivery, ⅓ within 30 days from delivery for scripts $600-up. $600-under pays on delivery.
Tips: Writers should be "creative, exciting and well versed in the subject" undertaken.

TROLL ASSOCIATES, 320 Rt. 17, Mahwah NJ 07430. (201)529-4000. Contact: M. Schecter. Produces material for elementary and high school students. Buys approximately 200 scripts/year. Query or submit outline/synopsis. SASE. Reports in 3 weeks. Buys all rights. Free catalog.
Needs: Produces silent and sound filmstrips, multimedia kits, tapes and cassettes, and books. Pays royalty or by outright purchase.

TUTOR/TAPE, 107 France St., Toms River NJ 08753. President: Richard R. Gallagher. Produces and publishes cassettes, filmstrips and visual aids including slides and transparencies for the college market. "We are the largest publisher of pre-recorded educational cassettes to the college market. We are capable of handling everything from writer to recording to packaging to marketing in a totally vertically integrated production-marketing publishing organization." SASE. Reports in 1 week.
Needs: 10- to 25-page scripts for 15- to 30-minute educational messages on college topics, including business, management, marketing, personnel, advertising, accounting, economics, and other related material. We also seek remedial and study skills material useful to college students and suitable for audio presentation. Send brief synopsis or short outline stating credentials, education or experience. Pays 15% royalty or in outright purchase.
Tips: "Writers should submit material relevant to students in college who need assistance in passing difficult courses, or interesting material which supplements college textbooks and enhances class work."

UNIVERSAL TRAINING SYSTEMS CO., 3201 Old Glenview Rd., Wilmette IL 60091. (312)251-8700. Creative Director: Paul W. Jensen. Produces complete training programs for business and industry. "We work with 10-12 freelance writers on a fairly steady basis." Works only with Chicago area writers. Submit resume. Reports in 1 month. Buys all rights.
Needs: "We produce custom training programs in a variety of media. Subject areas include sales training, management development, technical skills, data entry and word processing, and customer service. Experience in training and/or subject matter expertise are almost essential. We do not use 'pure creative' writers for freelance assignments. Potential new sources may be asked to complete a brief test assignment for which no fee is paid." Produces workshops, self-instructional programs, sound filmstrips, motion pictures, videotapes, audio cassettes, manuals, texts, study guides, workbooks, etc. Pays $300-3,000.
Tips: "Submit a letter and resume, with a description of the projects and request the company's application for freelance assignments. After returning the completed application be prepared to submit typewritten manuscript of requested samples of work."

UNIVERSITY OF WISCONSIN STOUT TELEPRODUCTION CENTER, 800 S. Broadway, Menomonie WI 54751. (715)232-1649. Director of Instructional Television: David Conyer. Produces "TV material for primary; secondary; post secondary; and general audiences. We produce instructional and public television programs for national, regional and state distribution." Query with resume and samples of TV scripts. SASE. Reports in 3 weeks. Buys all rights. Free catalog.
Needs: "Our clients fund programs in a 'series' format which tend to be 4-6 programs each. The subject matter can range from 'hard' content (science, math, reading) to documentary approach." Produces 16mm films for TV. "I need materials from writers who have experience in instructional TV. At present, we are looking for writers who have instructional television writing experience in early childhood with an emphasis in writing for kindergartners. We also have a need for writers in

Wisconsin and Minnesota whom we can call on to write one or multi program/series in instructional television."

Tips: Especially interested in "experience, time commitment to the project, willingness to work with producer/director(s) to meet content committee requests."

VIDEOCOM, INC., 502 Sprague St., Dedham MA 02026. (617)329-4080. Executive Vice President: W.S. Taylor. Vice president of production and creative services: L.A. Lessard. Produces materials for broadcast, industrial and educational audiences. Buys 25 scripts/year. Query with samples. Buys all rights.

Needs: "Scripts and copy for broadcast and industrial clients ranging from commercials to marketing and training programs and printed materials. We look for originality in the ability to understand problems and in the design of a solution." Produces videotape (all formats), films, slide presentations and printed materials. Pays by outright purchase.

VISUAL EDUCATION CORP., Box 2321, Princeton NJ 08540. Vice President: William J. West. Produces material for elementary and high schools. Query with resume, samples, and range of fees. Submissions will not be returned; "we like to keep a file of freelancers on whom we can call." Reports in 1 month. Buys all rights.

Needs: "Most of our audiovisual work is in filmstrips of about 80 frames (10 minutes). Topics range from language arts to social studies and home economics. A recent development is the editorial management of high school textbooks." Produces sound filmstrips, films, teacher's guides and student activity material, multimedia kits, and tapes and cassettes. Pays $250 minimum.

Tips: "The ability to write clearly and to the grade level is more important than knowledge of the content area. We need an example of how you think out a project."

VISUAL HORIZONS, 180 Metro Park, Rochester NY 14623. (716)424-5300. President: Stanley Feingold. Produces material for general audiences. Buys 20 programs/year. Query with samples. SASE. Reports in 5 months. Buys all rights. Free catalog.

Needs: Business, medical and general subjects. Produces silent and sound filmstrips, multimedia kits, slide sets, and videotapes. Payment negotiable.

VOCATIONAL EDUCATION PRODUCTIONS, California Polytechnic State University, San Luis Obispo CA 93407. Supervising Editor: Mary Williver. "We specialize in agricultural media." Query. SASE.

Needs: Produces sound filmstrips, multimedia kits, tapes and cassettes, and 35mm slide sets. "We usually furnish script development pages for the typing of final drafts, just to make it easier to work with the script. Our productions deal almost exclusively with agricultural subjects. Since we sell around the world, we cannot focus on a limited regional topic. Total length of our filmstrips is about 10 minutes, or 50-70 frames. Avoid talking down to the viewer. Technical accuracy is an absolute must." Pays $300/script for a series of 3-6; $400-600 for a single script.

JERRY WARNER & ASSOCIATES, 300 A1A, Bldg. 0406, Jupiter FL 33458. Produces material for business, government, school and television audiences. Copyright depending on client situation. "We buy full rights to writers' works for sponsored films. Writer must be a professional screenwriter or within the discipline of the special area of subject matter. Do not submit single copy material. Have the material registered for datemark, or Writers Guild protection. We accept no responsibility of unsolicited manuscripts." Will answer inquiries within the boundaries of production interest. SASE.

Needs: Scripts on business and general topics. Produces sound filmstrips; multimedia kits; tapes and cassettes; sponsored business and government films; and training, public information, public relations, sales promotion, educational and report films. Royalties are paid on proprietary films that writers take equity in rather than full fee, participations. "We read concepts for educational and documentary films and properties for feature films, but do not solicit scripts as a general rule. Fees vary and depend upon individual client or agency. We frequently pay from $75-100 per day for research periods and from $650-2,000 per reel of script. The wide variance is indicative of how each project has different scope and must be approached on the basis of talent requirement."

WREN ASSOCIATES, INC., 208 Bunn Dr., Princeton NJ 08540. (609)924-8085. President: Karl Faller. Produces material for corporate personnel and sales audiences. Buys 35-40 scripts/year. Query or submit resume. Not copyrighted.

Needs: Business, sales, public relations and training scripts. "We look for experience in our field." Produces sound filmstrips, 16mm films, tapes and cassettes, slide sets and videotapes. Pays $500-6,000.

XICOM, Sterling Forest, Tuxedo NY 10928. (914)351-4735. Director of Marketing: Arthur J. Blazek. Produces materials for business and industry; audiences are adults of all ages, from college age up. Buys all rights. SASE. Free catalog.
Needs: "Will be discussed at interview." Multimedia kits and tapes and cassettes. Query with resume. Pay is "based on project."

THE YANKEE GROUP, 2815 Michigan NE, Grand Rapids MI 49506. (616)57-2340. Creative Director: Steve Yankee. Estab. 1980. "We produce films, radio and TV commercials and multi-image presentations for business and industry: furniture, electronics, manufacturing, consumer products. We are professional communicators, dealing with clients who *demand* perfection, and, for the most part, will settle for nothing but the very best presentation we can produce." Buys "about 24 scripts/year." Buys all rights. SASE. Reports in 2 weeks.
Needs: "We are heavily involved with office furniture manufacturers and need writers that have previously worked with multi-image presentations. We are interested in resumes and samples, not queries or submissions." Super 8mm film loops; 16mm films; slides; and tapes and cassettes. Submit resume. Pays in outright purchase of $500-2,500.
Tips: "We are not looking for beginners. We would consider working with writers with experience. Writers should have a sense of humor, a definite style, an ability to communicate visually, willingness to travel if necessary, and patience to make sure the job is well done."

ZELMAN STUDIOS LTD., 623 Cortelyou Rd., Brooklyn NY 11218. (212)941-5500. General Manager: Jerry Krone. Produces material for business, education and fund raising audiences. Query with samples and resume. SASE. Reports in 1 month. Buys all rights.
Needs: Produces film loops; silent and sound filmstrips; films; tapes and cassettes; and slides. Pays in outright purchase "by agreement, based on talent and turnaround."

Playwriting

Writing for the stage is not like writing for any other medium—certainly not like films or TV. For one thing, the audience is much smaller. It could be as few as 75 or as many as 6,000. But it would never reach the vastness of a film or TV audience. Because of its size, it is also a much more intimate medium, so that flaws in scripting are much more apparent than in other media.

A common mistake beginning playwrights make is submitting their plays before they are ready for production. The scripts may be overplotted (or underplotted), lack strong central characters, or smack of "talkiness."

The cure? Read—or better yet—*see* as many plays as possible to gauge what works for the audience. Even better: Work in theater. A logical way to break in is to act, *then* write.

Be sure your play engages the interest of the audience. Keep the action moving. Work on dialogue.

Don't write your autobiography. What interests you and your six brothers may lose the audience, unless you seek a unique approach. Be unique but don't be absurd, especially when it comes to budget-inflating special effects, multiple sets, and large casts. Less is more on stage.

If you're writing for children's theater, consider your audience very carefully. Don't write down to children; they have real joys, fears and expectations—just like the rest of us. Keep in mind, too, that although you're writing for a younger audience, the actors will usually be adults.

Other tips: Patience is nowhere more of a virtue than in theater. Sometimes collaboration helps. Definitely, the ability to revise will aid your manuscript's survival. And, a word about the manuscript: Submit it typed and bound. Recognize the importance of a good title that telegraphs the play's theme. Remember these things, and when the curtain goes up, that title will be *your* play.

ACTORS THEATRE OF LOUISVILLE, 316 W. Main St., Louisville KY 40202. Producing-Director: Jon Jory. Actors Theatre of Louisville is a resident professional theater operating under a L.O.R.T. contract for a 35-week season from September to June. Subscription audience of 18,000 from extremely diverse backgrounds. "Plays with a strong story line and a basically positive life view. We are not interested in situation comedies or 'absurdists' work. We are particularly interested in new musicals and small-cast straight plays. No more than 12 to 15 actors. There are two theaters, one a 640-seat thrust and one seating 200. Multiple-set shows are impossible here." Produces 35 plays a year; 50% are originals. Payment is negotiated. Submit mss to ElizaBeth King, literary manager. SASE. Reports in 6 months.

ALLEY THEATRE, 615 Texas Ave., Houston TX 77002. A resident professional theater; large stage seating 798; arena stage seating 296.
Needs: "Good plays, with no length restrictions. No musicals." Pays variable royalty arrangements. Send complete script. SASE. Reports in 6-12 weeks. Produces 6-8 plays/year.
Recent Play Productions: *Indulgences in a Louisville Harem*, by Orlock; *Black Coffee*, by Christie; *To Grandmother's House We Go*, by Glass.

ALLIANCE THEATRE, 15 16th St., Atlanta GA 30309. (404)898-1132. Artistic Director: Fred Chapell. "We are a professional Equity Theater." Produces 16 plays/year for a general audience— "We also have sj ason directed at children." Submit complete ms. Reports in 3 months. Buys variable rights. Pays royalty or variable fee/performance. SASE.
Needs: "Full-length; 10 cast members or less; drama, comedy or musical." No "situation comedy of the dinner theater mentality."
Tips: "We are particularly interested in finding plays with good female roles."

AMERICAN STAGE FESTIVAL, Box 225, Milford NH 03055. Artistic Director: Harold Defelice. "The ASF is a central New England professional theater (professional equity company) with a 3 month summer season (June-August)" for audience of all ages, interests, education and sophistication levels. Query with synopsis. Produces musicals (20%) and nonmusicals (80%) (5 are mainstage and 10 are children's productions); 40% are originals. Royalty option and subsequent amount of gross: optional. SASE. Reports in 1 month.
Needs: "The Festival can do comedies, musicals and dramas. However, the most frequent problems come from plays not fitting into the resident acting company system (all men, all young, for examples) and/or that are bolder in language and action than a general mixed audience will accept. We emphasize plays that move; long and philosophical discussion-oriented plays are generally not done. We have 40 foot proscenium stage with 30 foot wings, but no fly system. Festival plays are chosen to present scale and opportunities for scenic and costume projects far beyond the 'summer theater' type of play. No saga/heavy dramas." Length: Mainstage: 2-3 acts; children's productions: 50 minutes.
Recent Productions: *Artichokes*, by Joanna Glass; and *Troupers*, by Harold DeFevre.
Tips: Writers could improve submissions with "dramatic action, complexity, subplot and a unique statement. Try to get a staged reading of the script before submitting the play to us. Our audiences prefer plays that deal with human problems presented in a conventional manner."

THE ANCHORAGE PRESS, INC., Box 8067, New Orleans LA 70182. (504)283-8868. Editor: Mr. Orlin Corey. Publishes 5-8 plays/year. Query with synopsis, or submit complete ms "with proof of production by someone *other* than the playwright—reviews, programs, etc." Pays 10% royalty on retail playbook sales; 50% production royalty. Buys publication rights for the playbook, including anthology and translation rights; and amateur and professional rights for the stage, television, cinema and radio. Reports in 1 week on queries, in 30-45 days on unsolicited mss, and 2-3 weeks on solicited mss. Free catalog.
Needs: "Adaptations of beloved classics of the world; original plays inclusive of children in their appeal and development (*not* exclusive of adult interest, of course); musicals concerned with either of the above; and any material that honors the child as intelligent, caring, questioning, searching, trusting, hoping. No plays that are essentially cabaret in feeling, that is, utilizing a children's story for purposes of travesty, ridicule or adult-only implications; such plays may be excellent for cabaret, where audiences have an established frame of reference, but when aimed at children, they insult, ignore, underestimate and overlook the child's world, a world of wonder, of new possibilities, of models. Our chief admonishment is that 'theater for children is not different from adult, only better' (Stanislavski). He was obviously not speaking of what is ordinarily written or produced. He was speaking of the ideal. By 'better' he really meant, among other matters, that theater for young audiences is inclusive (it includes the adult, too, who, after all, is—or better be—a child within his adultness), whereas adult theater is essentially exclusive—i ealing with problems of maturity that children may perceive but are unlikely to fully grasp: anxieties, competition, social

and political issues, sex, age. Too many authors underestimate the child. Too many write beneath their own ability when they write for children. Fine playwrights neither underestimate nor write down." Length: 1 hour minimum; prefers "full-length (that is, 90-120 minutes); with options for cutting by producers who desire a shorter length."

RAN AVNI/JEWISH REPERTORY THEATRE, 344 E. 14th St., New York NY 10003. (212)674-7200. Artistic Director: Ran Avni. "We are an Equity non-profit theater, Code Tier II." Produces 6 plays/year. Query with synopsis. Reports in 1 month. Pays $25-50/performance. SASE.
Needs: "Plays in English that relate to the Jewish experience."

BAKER'S PLAY PUBLISHING CO., 100 Chauncy St., Boston MA 02111. Editor: John B. Welch. Plays performed by amateur groups, high schools, children's theater, churches and community theater groups. "We are the largest publisher of chancel drama in the world." Submit complete script. Publishes 18-25 straight plays; all originals. Pay varies; outright purchase price to split in production fees. SASE. Reports in 2-3 months.
Needs: "One-acts (specifically for competition use). Quality children's theater scripts. Chancel drama for easy staging—voice plays ideal. Long plays only if they have a marketable theme. Include as much stage direction in the script as possible." Emphasis on large female cast desired. No operettas for elementary school production.
Recent Titles: *Captain Fantastic*, by Tim Kelly (2-act spoof); *A New Sunrise*, by Herman Coble (1-act comedy); *Noodle Doodle Box*, by Anita Page and Paul Maar (children's comedy); and *Watch at the World's End*, by Philip Turner.

BARTER THEATRE, Main St., Abingdon VA 24210. Producer: Rex Partington.
Needs: "Good plays, particularly comedies." Two or three acts, preferably, but will consider good quality plays of shorter length. Pays 5% royalties. Send complete script. SASE.

BERKSHIRE THEATRE FESTIVAL, INC., E. Main St., Stockbridge MA 01262. Artistic Director: Josephine R. Abady. Submit complete ms. Reports in 4-6 months. Produces 10-14 plays a year (5 are mainstage and 5-9 are second spaces). Pays in royalties for full production, in fees for reading. "Scripts not returned without SASE."
Needs: "Main stage productions are classic plays from the American theatre experience. For our second stage, we seek new plays which can be performed by a uniformly young company. Small cast musicals are especially welcome. Send cassette tape. All scripts must be bound and should contain complete cast description and a brief synopsis." No historical dramas; costume epics; or gratuitous nudity, obscenity or profanity.
Recent Productions: *Heebie Jeebies* (musical about the Boswell sisters).

GERT BUNCHEZ AND ASSOCIATES, INC., 7730 Carondelet, St. Louis MO 63105. President: Gert Bunchez. "We feel that the time is propitious for the return of stories to radio. It is our feeling that it is not necessary to 'bring back' old programs, and that there certainly should be contemporary talent to write mystery, detective, suspense, children's stories, soap operas, etc. We syndicate radio properties to advertisers and stations. Requirements are plays with sustaining lead characters, 5 minutes to 30 minutes in length, suitable for radio reproduction. Disclaimer letter must accompany scripts. Produces nonmusicals only, send complete script. SASE. Produces 10 plays a year. Rates from $100 per script if acceptable for radio production and actually produced." SASE.

CASA MANANA MUSICALS, INC., 3101 W. Lancaster, Box 9054, Fort Worth TX 76107. (817)332-9319. Producer/General Manager: Bud Franks. Produces 12 plays/year. "All performances are staged at Casa Manana Theatre, and are community funded." Query. Reports in 2 months. Produces Summer Musicals (uses Equity people only), Theatre for Youth and new plays. Theater-in-the-round or proscenium.
Needs: Scripts suitable for family productions.

THE CHANGING SCENE THEATER, 1527½ Champa St., Denver CO 80202. Director: Alfred Brooks. Year-round productions in theater space. Cast may be made up of both professional and amateur actors. For public audience; age varies; but mostly youthful, and interested in taking a chance on new and/or experimental works. No limit to subject matter or story themes. Emphasis is on the innovative. "Also, we require that the playwright be present for at least one performance of his work, if not for the entire rehearsal period. We have a small stage area, but are able to convert to round, semi-round or environmental. Prefer to do plays with limited sets and props." 1-act, 2-act and 3-act. Produces 8-10 nonmusicals a year; all are originals. "We do not pay royalties, or sign contracts with playwrights. We function on a performance share basis of payment. Our theater seats 76; the first 38 seats go to the theater, the balance is divided among the participants in the production. The performance share process is based on the entire production run, and not determined by individual performances. We do not copyright our plays." Send complete script. SASE. Reporting time varies; usually several months.

Recent Productions: *Signs of Life*, by Joan Schenkar (Victorian treatment of women); and *The Sand Rats*, by William Lang (comedy about a returned Vietnam veteran).

Tips: "We are experimental: open to young artists who want to test their talents and open to experienced artists who want to test new ideas/explore new techniques. Dare to write 'strange and wonderful' well-thought-out scripts. We want upbeat ones. Consider that we have a small performance area when submitting."

CHELSEA THEATER CENTER, 407 W. 43rd St., New York NY 10036. Artistic Director: Robert Kalfin. Looking for full-length plays "that stretch the bounds of the theater in form and content. No limitation as to size of cast or physical production." Pays for a 6-month renewable option for an off-Broadway production. Works 10 months in advance. No unsolicited mss. Essential to submit advance synopsis. SASE.

Recent Productions: *Hijinks!*, adapted from Clyde Fitch's *Captain Jinks of the Horse Marines*; *Monsieur Amilcar*, by Yves Jamiaque (emotional bankruptcy of the leisure class); and *Dona Rosita*, by Federico Garcia Lorca (withering of the human spirit).

THE CLEVELAND PLAY HOUSE, Box 1989, Cleveland OH 44106. Dramaturg: Peter Sander. Plays performed in professional LORT theater for the general public. "Ours is a long-standing resident company performing in 3 theaters presenting an eclectic season of commercial plays, musicals, and contemporary and traditional classics with occasional American and world premieres." Submit complete script. Produces 8 musicals (12%) and nonmusicals (88%) a year; 25% are originals. Buys stock rights, and sometimes first class options. Payment varies. SASE. Reports in 6 months.

Needs: "No restrictions. Vulgarity and gratuitous fads are not held in much esteem. Cast size should be small to moderate. Plays intended for arena stages are not appropriate. Musicals should be geared for actors, not singers. One-act plays are rarely performed. Plays of an extremely experimental nature are almost never selected." No first drafts; works-in-progress; unfinished manuscripts. Length: 3 acts.

Recent Productions: *Images—The Music of Serge Lama*, by Joseph J. Garry Jr. and David O. Frazier; *Peanuts and Cracker Jack*, by Jerry Slaff (2-character baseball play); and *Wuthering Heights*, adapted from the classic by Paul Lee.

CONTEMPORARY DRAMA SERVICE, Box 457, Downers Grove IL 60515. Editor: Arthur Zapel. Plays performed in churches and schools with amateur performers for age level high school to adult. "We publish reader's theater and other modern forms of drama." Publishes 25-30 plays/year; (5%) musicals and (95%) 1-act plays; originals and adaptations. Submit synopsis or complete script. Usually buys amateur rights only. Pays negotiable royalty up to 10%. SASE. Reports in 1 month.

Needs: "We prefer scripts that can be produced in schools or churches where staging materials are limited. In the church field we are looking for chancel drama for presentation at various holidays: Thanksgiving, Mother's Day, Christmas, Easter, etc. School drama materials can be reader's theater adaptations, drama rehearsal scripts, simple dialogues and short action plays. Emphasis on humor. We like a free and easy style. Nothing formal. Short sentences and fast pace." No 3-act serious drama. "We specialize in 1-act plays but we do publish 3-act comedy plays. We are not interested in musicals." SASE. Length: 1-act, skits or short games. Prefers casts not to exceed 9 players.

Recent Titles: *Unidentified Flying High School*, by Tim Kelly; *An Old Fashioned Soap Opera*, by Paul Leslie; and *Ten Practice Monologs for Stand-Up Comedians*, by Bill Majeski.

CRESSON LAKE PLAYHOUSE, Box 767, Spangler PA 15775. Artistic Director: Kenny Resinski. Produces 1 original play/year; performed in 200-seat summer barn theater for 13 performances. Submit query and synopsis. Reports in 1 month. Pays $50/performance. SASE.

Needs: "Original works dealing with occupations, trades, or professions or life styles, that would relate to a rural mountainous area. Minimal set, minimal number of men, maximal number of women." No Broadway comedies.

THE CRICKET THEATRE, 528 Hennepin Ave., Minneapolis MN 55403. (612)333-5241. Literary Manager: John Orlock. Estab. 1971. Audiences consist of adults and students. Submit complete ms. "Must include SASE." Reports in 7 months. Buys production rights for selected dates. Produces 6 plays, main stage; 6 plays, works-in-progress; musicals (14%) and nonmusicals (86%) a

year; 64% are originals. Produces plays by living American playwrights only. Only full-length plays will be considered for production.
Needs: "There are no content or form restrictions for scripts of the main season. For works-in-progress, any kind of a script is welcomed provided there is a spark of a good play in it. Works-in-progress productions are seminars, readings and staged readings depending on the availability of the playwright. The focus is on the text and not the fully staged, polished performance as with the main season. All works-in-progress playwrights are brought to Minneapolis to join in the play's rehearsal and revision process. Works-in-progress cannot use plays currently under option or that have had full professional productions. Such plays will be considered only for the main season." No children's plays or large Broadway-type musicals. Cast limit: 10.

DODD, MEAD & CO., 79 Madison Ave., New York NY 10016. Executive Editor: Allen T. Klots. "We're only interested in playwrights after professional production, who promise to contribute to the literature of the theater." Royalty negotiated. Buys book rights only. Reports in about 4 weeks. SASE.

THE DRAMATIC PUBLISHING CO., 4150 N. Milwaukee Ave., Chicago IL 60641. (312)545-2062. Produces about 50 new titles/year. "We have a larger amateur market than most companies (i.e. schools, churches, small community theaters)." Submit complete ms. Reports in 4-6 weeks. Buys amateur and stock theatrical rights. Pays royalty or by outright purchase. SASE.
Needs: "Props, staging, etc., should be simple so that any school could perform it no matter how limited the budget or space. Casts can be any size. No risque language or material. We do not want to have to clean up plays so that they can be presented to any audience."
Tips: Create a "sympathetic character, one that people can identify with. Language should be natural, the way people really talk."

DAVID EASTWOOD, Box 266, Lake George NY 12845. Plays will be for professional casts in summer theater. Audience: public, tourists. Would like to see "Neil Simon-type comedies." Send synopsis. No drama. Maximum of 8 characters; 2 sets. Will consider 3-act plays; 2½ hours in length. Produces 4 plays/year; musicals (25%) and straight plays (75%); 10% originals. Payment flexible. Not copyrighted. Query with synopsis. SASE.

ELDRIDGE PUBLISHING CO., Drawer 209, Franklin OH 45005. (513)746-6531. Editor/ General Manager: Kay Myerly. Plays performed in high schools and churches; some professional—but most are amateur productions. Publishes plays for all age groups. Publishes 15-20 plays/year; (2%) musicals; 100% originals. Send synopsis or complete script. Buys all rights "unless the author wishes to retain some rights." Pays $75-100 for 1-act plays; $350 for 3-acts. Also royalty contracts for topnotch plays. SASE. Reports in 60-90 days.
Needs: "We are looking for good straight comedies which will appeal to high and junior-high age groups. We do not publish anything which can be suggestive. Most of our plays are published with a hanging indentation, 2 ems. All stage, scenery and costume plots must be included." No run-of-the-mill plots. Length: 1-acts from 25-30 minutes; 2-acts of around 2 hours; and skits of 10-15 minutes.
Recent Titles: *North of the Moon*, by Guy Gayon (mystery/comedy); *Lost in Space*, by Tim Kelly (space spoof); and *King Lud*, by Guy Guyon (comedy).

ZELDA FICHANDLER, c/o Arena Stage, 6th and M Sts. SW, Washington DC 20024. Wants original plays preferably (but not necessarily) submitted through agents. "Plays with relevance to the human situation—which cover a multitude of dramatic approaches—are welcome here." Produces 12 musicals (15%) and nonmusicals (85%) a year; 50% are originals. Pays 5% of gross. Query. Reports in 3 months. SASE.

H.D. FLOWERS, Dept. of Fine and Performing Arts, Bowie State College, Bowie MD 20715. Summer educational theater for college and community audience. Plays with black themes are needed. Style does not matter. Will consider 1-, 2- and 3-act plays. Pays $50-75/performance. Produces 4-6 plays/year. Send complete script only. SASE.

FOLGER THEATRE GROUP, 201 E. Capitol St., Washington DC 20003. Produced in professional theater, AEA LORT Contract, for general public. All kinds of plays. "Since we produce several Shakespeare productions a season, we would rather not read classical adaptations or historical plays which are not contemporary in theme or treatment." No limitations in cast, props; Folger stage is small but flexible; Terrace Theatre at the Kennedy Center can accommodate larger productions, including small musicals. Any length play. Produces 7 plays/year; 40% are new plays. Payment negotiable. Send synopsis or submit through agent. SASE. Reports "as soon as possible, usually 8-10 weeks."

Recent Productions: *Whose Life is It, Anyway?*, by Brian Clark; *Custer*, by Robert E. Ingham (contemporary interpretation of the Custer myth); and *Charlie and Algernon*, by David Rogers and Charles Strouse (musical version of *Flowers for Algernon*).

FORTUNE THEATRE, 362 N. "D" St., San Bernardino CA 92401. Artistic Director: Harvey Friedman. Produces 7 plays/year. "Plays are preformed on the community theater level using both area talent and professional actors. The theater is located approximately 50 miles from Los Angeles and serves a community of over 100,000 people." Query. SASE. Reports in 3-4 weeks. Buys one-time production rights. Pays 3-5% royalties.
Needs: "The Fortune Theatre is dedicated to producing new plays in the comedic genre. There is an emphasis on 'culturally relevant' material that is 'above board.' Small casts and simple sets are a basic necessity. No dramas or musicals. Payment negotiable."

SAMUEL FRENCH, INC., 25 W. 45th St., New York NY 10036. Editor: Lawrence Harbison. "We publish 10-15 manuscripts a year from freelancers. We are the world's largest publisher of plays. In addition to publishing plays, we also act as agents in the placement of plays for professional production—eventually in New York (hopefully)." Pays on royalty basis. Submit complete ms (bound). Require a minimum of 2 months to report." SASE.
Needs: "Willing at all times to read manuscripts of plays from freelancers, we prefer simple-to-stage, small cast, light romantic full-length comedies or mysteries. One-act plays must be something that high school groups can do, so: nothing 'controversial'. We also eschew all- or mostly-male-character plays. These must have a New York City success before we can publish them." No 25-page "full-length" plays; children's plays to be performed *by* children; adaptations of familiar children's stories in the public domain; verse plays, large-cast historical plays; puppet plays; television plays; translations of foreign plays requiring large casts; seasonal or religious plays; or "high school" plays.

GEORGETOWN PRODUCTIONS, 7 Park Ave., New York NY 10016. Producers: Gerald Van De Vorst and David Singer. Produces 1-2 plays/year for a general audience. Submit complete ms only. Standard Dramatists Guild contract. SASE.
Needs: Prefers plays with small casts and not demanding more than one set. Interested in new unconventional scripts dealing with contemporary issues, comedies, mysteries, musicals or dramas. No first-drafts; outlines; 1-act plays; historical plays; or plays about the end of the world.
Recent Productions: *Night Fever*, by Sebastian Stuart (comedy-drama about hitch-hikers along a California highway); and *Attention Fragile*, by André Ernotte and Elliot Tiber (two-character musical).

GOODMAN THEATRE, 200 S. Columbus Dr., Chicago IL 60603. (312)443-3811. Artistic Director: Gregory Mosher. Produces 8-10 plays/year. "Ours are professional productions, done during the theater season—until the end of June—for the benefit of Chicago theater goers. Many of the members of our audience are subscribers to the full season of main stage plays. We also have a studio theater in which we produce." Submit complete ms. Reports in 6 weeks. Buys variable rights. SASE.
Needs: "We are particularly interested in finding playwrights capable of adaptations and material in which playwrights have taken risks. Our interest in the material depends on the success the playwright has had in shaping that risk. Gregory Mosher, the artistic director, looks for plays which ask large questions—social, political, emotional. We have a large stage to fill. We hope to challenge our audiences. No standard domestic dramas, musicals (highly unlikely we will produce a musical which comes in cold—no previous history with the writer)."
Tips: "If a writer, simply looking for work, is able to read and write equally well in French, German, Italian and English, we are often looking for playwrights who can translate and adapt."

HEUER PUBLISHING CO., 233 Dows Bldg., Box 248, Cedar Rapids IA 52406. Publishes 15-20 plays/year. Amateur productions for schools and church groups. Audience consists of junior and senior high school students and some intermediate groups. Needs 1- and 3-act plays. Prefers comedy, farce, mystery and mystery/comedy. Uses 1-act plays suitable for contest work (strong drama). "We suggest potential authors write for our brochure on types of plays." No sex, controversial subjects or family scenes. Prefers 1 simple setting and noncostume plays. Current need is for plays with a large number of characters (16-20). One-act plays should be 30-35 minutes long; 3-act, 90-105 minutes. Most mss purchased outright, with price depending on quality. Minimum of $500 usually. Copyrighted, however, contract stipulates amateur rights only, so author retains professional rights to TV, radio, etc. Query with synopsis only. SASE. Reports in 1 week to 10 days.
Recent Titles: *Pick A Boy—Any Boy*, by Frank Priore (plot line along humorous witchcraft); *Requiem for a Small Town*, by Donald Payton (demise of a small town); and *Never Fear—Strongheart's Here*, by Sneed Hearn (dastardly deeds melodrama).

HIGH TOR THEATRE, Ashby West Rd., Fitchburg MA 01420. (617)342-6592. Director: Eugene S. Casassa. Produces 8 plays/year. Submit complete ms. Reports as soon as possible. Buys one week's production rights. Pays negotiable fee. SASE.
Needs: Produces a very wide range of plays in a small theater and limited budget. Small casts preferred. No 1-act plays or absurdists.

HONOLULU THEATRE FOR YOUTH, Box 3257, Honolulu HI 96801. Produces plays of "1 hour without intermission. Plays are produced in Honolulu in various theater buildings and throughout Hawaii. Casts are professional with a complement of actors from the community; adult actors, with children as needed. Plays are produced for family audiences and school children." Interested in new plays, plays about Pacific countries, Pacific legends, Asian legends and Asian history. Plays must have strong character with whom young people can identify, with stress on action rather than exposition, but not at the expense of reality. Plays should be reasonably simple technically and use primarily adult characters. Elaborate musicals requiring large orchestras are not recommended. Casts up to 10, preferably. Technical requirements should be reasonably simple. Produces 5 plays/year; 2-3 are originals. Royalty fee is based on number of performances. Query with synopsis only. Reports in 1-2 months. SASE.

WILLIAM E. HUNT, 801 West End Ave., New York NY 10025. Interested in reading scripts for stock production, off-Broadway and even Broadway production. "Small cast, youth-oriented, meaningful, technically adventuresome; serious, funny, far-out. Must be about people first, ideas second. No political or social tracts." No individual 1-act, anti-black, anti-Semitic, or anti-gay plays. "I do not want 1920, 1930, or 1940 plays disguised as modern by 'modern' language. I do not want plays with 24 characters, plays with 150 costumes, plays about symbols instead of people. I do not want plays which are really movie or TV scripts." Pays royalties on production. Off-Broadway, 5%; on Broadway, 5%, 7½% and 10%, based on gross. No royalty paid if play is selected for a showcase production. Reports in "a few weeks." SASE.
Recent Productions: *Miss Stanwyck is Still in Hiding*, by Larry Puchall and Reigh Hagen; *Variable Lengths*, by various authors, including Kopit, Guare, Beckett, Ginsberg, Mailer, et al. (vaudeville of short works by major "today" playwrights and poets, some poems set to music).

THE MAC-HAYDN THEATRE, INC., Box 204, Chatham NY 12037. (518)392-9292 (summer). Producers: Lynne Haydn, Linda MacNish. Produces 6-15 plays/year. "This is a resort area, and our audiences include rural residents and summer residents from the metropolitan New York City and Albany areas who demand professional quality productions. Submit complete ms; we can only consider a complete script and written score, and would prefer that at least a piano tape be included of the score." Reports in 8 months. Buys exclusive rights to stage production. Pays $25-100/performance. SASE.
Needs: "We are interested in musicals which are wholesome family entertainment; these should be full-length musicals, although we might consider one-act musicals in the future. There is no limitation as to topic, so long as the object is to entertain. We will consider original material as well as adaptations, but any adaptations of copyright material must include proper clearances. We are most interested in legitimate music for trained voices; no rock or fad music. We are looking for scripts which have a story to tell, and which build to a climax; no vignettes, slice of life or character study. We prefer a fast pace and good emotional content, and the score should extend the action, not cause it to stop. We are not interested in political muck-raking or controversy unless it has high entertainment value, and we will not consider obscenity, nudity or bad writing."
Recent Productions: *South Pacific*, by Rodgers and Hammerstein; *Minnie's Boys*, (based on the life of the Marx brothers); *On the 20th Century*, by Comden and Green, music by Cy Coleman.

MAGIC THEATRE, INC., Bldg. 314, Fort Mason, San Francisco CA 94123. (415)441-8001. General Director: John Lion. Administrative Director: Rossi Snipper. Dramaturg: Martin Esslin. "Oldest experimental theater in California." For public audience, generally college-educated. General cross-section of the area with an interest in alternative theater. Plays produced in the off-off Broadway manner. Cast is part Equity, part non-Equity. Produces 8 plays/year. Submit complete ms. SASE.
Needs: "The playwright should have an approach to his writing with a specific intellectual concept in mind or specific theme of social relevance. We don't want to see scripts that would be television or 'B' movies-oriented. 1- or 2-act plays considered. We pay 5% of gross; $100 advance."
Recent Productions: *Buried Child* and *True West*, by Sam Shepard; *Winterplay*, by Adele Edling Shank; *All Night Long*, by John O'Keefe; and *The Man Who Killed the Buddha*, by Martin Epstein.

MANHATTAN THEATRE CLUB, 321 E. 73 St., New York NY 10021. Literary Manager: Jonathan Alper. A three-theater performing arts complex classified as Off-Broadway, using professional actors. "We present a wide range of new work, from this country and abroad, to a subscription audience. We want plays about contemporary problems and people. No special requirements. No verse plays or historical dramas or large musicals. Very heavy set shows or multiple detailed sets are out. We prefer shows with casts not more than 15. No skits, but any other length is fine." Payment is negotiable. Query with synopsis. SASE. Reports in 6 months. Produces 20 plays/year.

TOM MARKUS, (formerly Loraine Slade), Artistic Director, Virginia Museum Theatre, Boulevard and Grove Ave., Richmond VA 23221. For public, well-educated, conservative, adventurous audiences. Professional resident theater. Looking for biography, experimental styles. Standard format of presentation. Light comedies, musicals. 2-act and 3-act plays considered. No 1-acts. Payment is negotiable. For a premiere, theater requires share in future income. Produces one new script/year. Send complete script. Reports in 3-5 months. SASE.

NASHVILLE ACADEMY THEATRE, Box 100047, Nashville TN 37210. (615)254-6020. Contact: Artistic Director. Produces both amateur and professional productions in a studio situation and in a 696-seat theater. Age groups performed for are: Kindergarten through 4th grade, 5th grade through 8th, and 9th grade to adult. "We are considered a family theater. Although we select plays for different age groups, we feel that any age should enjoy any play we do on some level. In the past we have produced murder mysteries, Shakespeare, plays of the supernatural, fairy tales, *The Mikado* dance-drama, musical comedy, serious drama, chamber theater, contemporary children's drama—almost anything you can think of." Reports in 2 months. Produces 6 musicals (15%) and nonmusicals (85%) a year; 15% are originals. Buys exclusive performance rights for middle Tennessee, one year prior to and during their production. Pays $10-35/performance. SASE.
Needs: "We prefer a variety of styles and genres. Length is usually limited to one hour. We are interested in quality new scripts of the old fairy tales for our younger audiences. There is no limit on topics. Interested in musicals also." Wants a richness of language and mood in their productions. No intermissions. Fluid and fast moving. Must have at least some literary merit. No or little obscenity. Cast size: 5-20 players. No limits in staging.

NEW JERSEY SHAKESPEARE FESTIVAL, Madison NJ 07940. Director: Paul Barry. Looks for plays on any subject. Pays standard Dramatists Guild royalty percentage. All scripts must be free and clear of subsidiary rights commitments. No musicals or one-acts. Submit synopsis or full-length play. SASE.

NEW PLAYS, INC., Box 273, Rowayton CT 06853. Publisher: Patricia Whitton. Publishes 2-4 plays/year. "We are publishers of children's plays; for colleges, high schools, community theater groups, junior leagues, summer camps, etc." Query with synopsis. Reports in 1-2 months. Buys "exclusive rights to publish acting scripts and act as agent for productions—but the author remains the owner of the script." Pays 50% of performance royalties; "we charge our customers a royalty of $35 for the first performance and $30 for each subsequent performance. The author gets one-half of this."
Needs: "Generally, plays of approximately 45 minutes up to 1½ hours long, for teenagers and adults to perform for children. No plays for children to perform, such as assembly skits. We're looking for originality in form or content. We don't want adaptations of material that has already been done a great deal such as *Rumplestiltskin* and *Sleeping Beauty*. Plays have to have been successfully produced by at least one organization before being published."
Recent Titles: *Molly Whuppie*, by Joella Brown (contemporary story woven into an English folk tale dream sequence); and *Circus Home*, by Joanna Kraus (a "freak" young man finds acceptance in the world of the circus).

THE NEW PLAYWRIGHTS' THEATRE OF WASHINGTON, 1742 Church St. NW, Washington DC 20036. (202)232-4527. Producing Director: Harry M. Bagdasian. Literary Manager: Lloyd Rose. Produces 1 musical and straight plays and 20 readings/year. "Plays are produced in professional productions for general Washington audiences." Submit complete ms, "typed to form, suitably bound." Reports in 1 year. "Rights purchased and financial arrangements are individually negotiated." SASE.
Needs: "All styles, traditional to experimental, straight plays to musicals and music-dramas, revues and cabaret shows, one-acts and full-lengths. Plays must ultimately have an affirmative point-of-view. No plays that have had major, full-scale, professional productions, or that have been published." Cast: "no more than 15." Staging: Performance space adaptable.

NORTH LIGHT REPERTORY, 2300 Green Bay Rd., Evanston IL 60201. (312)869-7732. Associate Art Director: Mary F. Monroe. "We are a LORT theater using professional artistic personnel with a season that runs from September through June, located just outside Chicago with a subscription audience. We are committed to producing new plays of high quality rather than pure entertainment or more commercial fare. Audience is college age and over, broad range of socioeconomic and religious backgrounds." Query with synopsis. Reports in 2 months. Produces 5 nonmusicals a year; 50-75% are originals. Rights purchased vary. Pays 4% minimum royalty. SASE.

Needs: "New plays of high quality. Plays may vary in genre and topic. We are most interested in contemporary rather than classic material. Full-length and of a cast size of 10 or less. Though accessibility is an issue, we rate substance as a higher concern for our audience. We prefer and stress 10 characters or less with doubling. We have a 298 seat house with a small proscenium/thrust stage allowing for some use of multiple sets but only the suggestion of levels, e.g., a second story home, etc. Our budget and other resources restrict very elaborate staging but we are fortunate to have talented and creative designers. Solely commercial work or dinner theater material is not appropriate for our audiences. We emphasize work which speaks to the human condition and is often contemporary. Musicals often require larger budgets than we are able to provide and are not favored by us unless their requirements are minimal."

Tips: "Many of the submissions we receive are simply void of skill in structuring a play, language and characterization. The style and form of a play are not as great a concern to us as the honesty of the text and often we find stereotyping or basic ignorance of human relations. I would urge playwrights to seek out workshops or refresher courses in playwrighting."

OLD LOG THEATER, Box 250, Excelsior MN 55331. Producer: Don Stolz. Produces 2-act and 3-act plays for "a professional cast. Public audiences, usually adult. Interested in contemporary comedies. No more than 2 sets. Cast not too large." Produces about 14 plays/year. Payment by Dramatists Guild agreement. Send complete script. SASE.

O'NEILL THEATER CENTER'S NATIONAL PLAYWRIGHTS CONFERENCE, 1860 Broadway, Suite 601, New York NY 10023. (212)246-1485. Artistic Director: Lloyd Richards. Produces 12 stage plays, 4 teleplays/year for a general audience. "Our theater is located in Waterford, Connecticut and we operate under an Equity LORT(C) Contract. We have 3 theaters: Barn-250 seats, Amphitheatre-300 seats, Instant Theater-150." Submit complete ms. Decisions in approximately 2 months. "We have an option on the script from time of acceptance until one month *after* the four-week summer conference is completed. After that all rights revert to the author." Pays $200 stipend plus room, board and transportation. SASE. "Interested writers should send us a self-addressed-stamped envelope and request our updated guidelines. We accept script submissions from September 15-December 1st of each year. Conference takes place during four-weeks in July and August each summer."

Needs: "We do staged readings of new American plays. We use modular sets for all plays, minimal lighting, minimal props and no costumes. We do script-in-hand readings with professional actors and directors."

OPERA VARIETY THEATER, 3944 Balboa St., San Francisco CA 94121. Director: Violette M. Dale. Plays to be performed by professional and amateur casts for a public audience; all ages, generally families; upper educational level. Submit complete script. Produces 2-3 musicals (50% or more) and nonmusicals (1-2) a year; all are originals. "Everyone (cast, author, technical people, publicity, etc.) receives equal percentage." SASE. Reports in 6 months.

Needs: "Prefer musicals (but must have musically challenging, singable, tuneful material; arranged, ready to cast). Plays or music on most any theme that conservative audiences would enjoy. Must have substantial, believable plot and good characterizations. Must be simple to produce; fairly small cast, easy setting, etc. (small backstage area limits cast, props, staging, etc.). Emphasis is on entertainment rather than social reform." Length: 1, 2 or 3 acts. "No vulgarity in language or action; no wordy preaching."

Recent Productions: *The Making of Perpeople*, by Hulsebus (comedy on creation story); and *The Innkeeper & The Mermaid*, by Tom Hogue (comedy on Shakespeare's early life in London).

PALISADES THEATRE COMPANY, Box 10717, St. Petersburg FL 33733. (813)823-1600. Dramaturg: Neil DeGroot. Produces 4-6 plays/year. "Palisades Theatre Company is a resident professional theater in St. Petersburg, Florida, and a touring theater operating up and down the East Coast." Query or submit complete ms. Reports in 3 months. "Rights are negotiated on an individual basis with the author." Pays $8 minimum/performance. SASE.

Needs: "We are interested in plays for a universal audience and specifically for young audiences (touring program), the latter usually being 45-50 minutes in length. We prefer plays for small casts, but will consider each play on its own merits."

JOSEPH PAPP PRODUCER, New York Shakespeare Festival, 425 Lafayette St., New York NY 10003. (212)598-7100. Gail Merrifield, Director, Play Department. Interested in full-length plays and musical works. No restrictions as to style, historical period, traditional or experimental forms, etc. New works produced on 6 stages at the Public Theater. Produces about 25 plays/year; 90% are originals. Unsolicited material accepted *only* if recommended by legitimate source in theater, music or other professionally related fields." Standard option and production agreements. Reports in 6 weeks. SASE.

PERFORMANCE PUBLISHING CO., 978 N. McLean Blvd., Elgin IL 60120. Editor: Virginia Butler. "We publish one-, two- and three-act plays and musicals suitable for stock, community, college, high school and children's theater. We're looking for comedies, mysteries, dramas, farces, etc. with modern dialogue and theme. Plays for and about high school students are usually the most remunerative and we publish 50% high school, 15% children's theater and 35% for the balance of the market. The new writer is advised to obtain experience by limiting himself to one-acts until he has been published. We offer a standard royalty contract for amateur, stock, and community theater licensing rights." Publishes 40 plays/year; (15%) musicals and (85%) straight plays. Authors should retain a copy of any script mailed. Include SASE. Reports in 3 months.
Needs: "Budgets are limited and production costs are escalating. Sets should be kept simple but innovative."
Recent Titles: *Nashville Jamboree*, by Tim Kelly, music and lyrics by Jim and Mary Stuart (country western theme); *You Gotta Charleston!*, by Cynthia Mercati (nostalgia campus comedy); and *How the West Was Fun*, by James Seay (western comedy/melodrama).
Tips: "Our interest in the new writer and editorial guidance is unique in the field. The new writer needs to read more successful plays and see more to learn technique. Plot structure should be a primary concern."

PETERBOROUGH PLAYERS, Box 1, Peterborough NH 03458. Artistic Director: Charles Morey. Professional summer theater (Equity). Query with synopsis or submit complete ms. "Submissions will be accepted September-February of the year. Mss should be submitted during that period to Charles Morey, Peterborough Players, 718 W. 171st St., #51, New York NY 10032." Produces 5 nonmusicals a year; 20% are originals. Buys single production rights only (10 performances). Pays $500 minimum. SASE.
Needs: "Interested in all types of material. Quality is the only guideline."

PIONEER DRAMA SERVICE, 2171 S. Colorado Blvd., Box 22555, Denver CO 80222. (303)759-4297. Publisher: Shubert Fendrich. Plays are performed by high school, junior high and adult groups, colleges, and recreation programs for audiences of all ages. "We are one of the largest full-service play publishers in the country in that we handle straight plays, musicals, children's theater and melodrama." Publishes 15 plays/year; (40%) musicals and (60%) straight plays. Submit synopsis or complete script. Buys all rights. Pays "usually 10% royalty on copy sales; 50% of production royalty and 50% of subsidiary rights with some limitations on first-time writers." SASE. Reports in 30-60 days.
Needs: "We are looking for adaptations of great works in the public domain or plays on subjects of current interest. We use the standard 1-act and 3-act format, 2-act musicals, melodrama in all lengths and plays for children's theater (plays to be done by adult actors for children)." Length: 1-acts of 30-45 minutes; 2-act musicals and 3-act comedies from 90 minutes to 2 hours; and children's theater of 1 hour. No "heavily domestic comedy or drama, simplistic children's plays, shows with multiple sets or that hang heavily on special effects, plays with a primarily male cast, highly experimental works, or plays which lean strongly on profanity or sexual overtones."
Recent Titles: *Airline*, by Tim Kelly (comedy); *Paul Bunyan and the Hard Winter*, by Wil Denson (children's theater); *A Golden Fleecing*, by R. Eugene Jackson (melodrama); and *Ransom of Red Chief*, by Pam Nagle and George Wingerter (musical).

PLAYERS PRESS, INC., Box 1132, Studio City CA 91604. Senior Editor: Robert W. Gordon. "We deal in all areas and handle works for film, television as well as theater. But all works must be in stage play format for publication." Submit complete ms. "Must have SASE or play will not be returned. All submissions must have been produced and should include a flyer and/or program with dates of performance." Reports in 3 months. Buys negotiable rights. "We prefer all area rights." Pays variable royalty "according to area; approximately 10-75% of gross receipts." Also pays in outright purchase of $100-25,000 or $5-5,000/performance.
Needs: "We prefer comedies, musicals, and children's theater, but are open to all genres. We will rework the ms after acceptance. We are interested in the quality, not the format."

PLAYS, *The Drama Magazine for Young People*, 8 Arlington St., Boston MA 02116. Editor: Sylvia K. Burack. Publishes approximately 80 1-act plays each season to be performed by junior and senior high, middle grades, lower grades. Can use comedies, farces, melodramas, skits, mysteries and dramas, plays for holidays and other special occasions, such as Book Week; adaptations of classic stories and fables; historical plays; plays about other lands; puppet plays; folk and fairy tales; creative dramatics; and plays for conservation, ecology or human rights programs. Mss should follow the general style of *Plays*. Stage directions should not be typed in capital letters or underlined. No incorrect grammar or dialect. Characters with physical defects or speech impediments should not be included. Desired lengths for mss are: Junior and Senior high—20 double spaced ms pages (25 to 30 minutes playing time). Middle Grades—12 to 15 pages (25 to 20 minutes playing time). Lower Grades—6 to 10 pages (8 to 15 minutes playing time). Pays "good rates on acceptance." Reports in 3-4 weeks. SASE. "Manuscript specification sheet sent on request."

READ MAGAZINE, 245 Long Hill Rd., Middletown CT 06457. (203)347-7251. Editor: Edwin A. Hoey. 10% freelance written. For junior high school students. Biweekly magazine; 32 pages. Circ. 796,305. Rights purchased vary with author and material. May buy second serial (reprint) rights or all rights. Byline given. Buys 20 mss/year. Pays on publication. Free sample copy and writer's guidelines. Will consider photocopied submissions. No simultaneous submissions. Reports in 6 weeks. Submit complete ms. SASE.
Drama and Fiction: First emphasis is on plays; second on fiction with suspense, adventure, or teenage identification themes. "No preachy material. Plays should have 12 to 15 parts and not require complicated stage directions, for they'll be used mainly for reading aloud in class. Remember that we try to be educational as well as entertaining." No kid detective stories or plays. No obscenity. Pays $50 minimum.

REPERTORY THEATER OF AMERICA/ALPHA-OMEGA PLAYERS, Box 1296, Rockport TX 78382. Director: Drexel H. Riley. Plays performed on the college and country club circuit (professional national tour); arts councils; and civic groups. For a private audience, college age and over; majority are college graduates; wide range of geographic and religious backgrounds and tastes. Query with synopsis. *Send no scripts until requested. Scripts not requested will be returned to sender unread.* Produces 3-4 musicals (50%) and nonmusicals (50%) a year; 25% are originals. Pays $10-20/performance; averages approximately 100 performances per play per year. SASE. Reports in 3 weeks.
Needs: "Revues, possibly old-fashioned melodramas for 4 persons, vaudeville-type shows; a dinner theater setting. Length: 2-acts; total running time 1½ hours. No plays with casts larger than 4 (2 men, 2 women). Limited sound facilities, minimum props. "No guerrilla theater, obscenity, intellectualizing or bad writing."

SCORPIO REPERTORY THEATRE, 426 N. Hoover St., Los Angeles CA 90004. Contact: Louise Newmark. For an audience of selected theater buffs. "Scorpio Repertory Theatre is dedicated to the works of new playwrights, and winner of Los Angeles Drama Critics' Circle Award. Looking for all kinds of plays, but prefer contemporary themes. We don't want any situation comedies or Broadway type musicals. Simple cast, props, stage, etc. 1-act, 2-act, 3-act, but open to all." Also interested in developmental work with playwrights-in-residence. Buys amateur performance rights. Produces 8-12 musicals (50%) and nonmusicals (50%); 80-90% are originals. Payment to be negotiated. Send complete script. Reports in 2-3 months. SASE.
Recent Productions: *A New England Weekend*, by Richard Steele (domestic comedy/drama); *Man in His Birthday Suit*, by Marylou Chavez and Mark Leach (musical revolving around a true-life incident in the city); *Electra's Song*, by Louise Newmark (an original adaptation of the classical piece); and *Saints* (a musical adaptation of *The Balcony*, by Jean Genet).

CHARLES STILWILL, Managing Director, Community Playhouse, Box 433, Waterloo IA 50704. (319)235-0367. Plays performed at Waterloo Community Playhouse with a volunteer cast. "We are one of few community theaters with a commitment to new scripts. We do at least one a year. We are the largest community theater per capita in the country." We have 5,606 season members. Average attendance at main stage shows is 5,663; at studio shows 2,247. We try to fit the play to the theater. We do a wide variety of plays. Looking for good plays with more roles for women than men. Our public isn't going to accept nudity, too much sex, too much strong language. We don't have enough black actors to do all-black shows. We have done plays with as few as 3 characters, and as many as 56." Produces 9 plays; 1 musical and 8 nonmusicals a year; 12½% originals. "On the main stage we usually pay between $300 and $500. In our studio we usually pay between $50 and $300." Send synopsis or complete script. SASE. "Reports negatively within 9 months, but acceptance takes longer because we try to fit a wanted script into the balanced season."
Recent Productions: *The Penultimate Problem of Sherlock Holmes* (psychological mystery); *The Headhunters*, by Henry Denker (political prosecution); *Towards the Morning*, by John Fenn

(communication between young and old); and *Harry and Sylvia*, by Richard Strand (communication between the clown and the world).

JOE SUTHERIN, c/o St. Bart's Playhouse, 109 E. 50th St., New York NY 10022. Plays will be produced at St. Bart's Playhouse, a 350-seat community theater. "I am also looking for material to produce in other (professional) situations." For public/commercial "sophisticated" audience. Looking for revue, comedy material, or writer who likes to do same. No material that relies heavily on sex, four-letter words, etc., to make it viable. Produces 5-7 shows; 2 musicals and 2-4 nonmusicals a year. Originals, one every 2-3 years. Payment varies. Copyright negotiable. Send synopsis or complete script. SASE. Reports in "3 months if I'm not snowed under."

SYRACUSE STAGE, 820 E. Genesee St., Syracuse NY 13210. (315)423-4008. Dramaturg: Tom Walsh. "We are the only professional theater in central New York state." A professional regional theater; uses Equity performers, professional directors and designers. Audience is from the Syracuse community. Reports in 4 months. Produces 6 plays, of which at least one is original. Negotiates rights with playwright and/or agent. Pays royalties. SASE.
Needs: "New American plays (one or two per season—the remainder of the plays, four or five, are from the standard international repertoire.) We are looking for talented work, preferably with a cast of fewer than 12. We are less interested in musicals than in dramas, but consider small-scale musicals upon occasion. We are looking for plays that will have importance, not merely clever or gimmicky ideas. We are particularly interested in plays that experiment with form while maintaining strong characterizations and believable situations. No classroom exercises. Biblical adaptations, large musicals or TV scripts. We also do a series of staged readings/playwrights workshops for unproduced scripts."
Recent Productions: *Loved*, by Olwen Wymark; *The Griffin and the Minor Cannon* (children's play); and *Paradise is Closing Down*, by Pieter Dirk Uys.

THEATRE OF WESTERN SPRINGS, Box 29, Western Springs IL 60558. (213)246-4043. Artistic Director: Ted Kehoe. Produces 7 adult and 2 children's plays a year; 100% nonmusicals. Plays are performed in advanced community theater, main stage or workshops. Submit complete ms. SASE.

THEATRE RAPPORT, 8128 Gould Ave., Hollywood CA 90040. Artistic Director: Crane Jackson. Equity company. Produces full-length plays only (no one-act plays) using one set. Produces gutsy, relevant plays on highly artistic level and true subjects. No unjustified homosexuality, nudity or profanity; realistic acceptable—also hard hitting biographical. For a sophisticated, educated, non-fad, conservative (although venturesome) audience looking for something new and different. Not avant-garde, but a strong point of view is an asset. Approach must be unique. All plays must be West Coast premieres. Pays 20% of gross. Send complete script with past reviews, if available (good or bad). Response if interested. All mss read, but *none are returned*. Produces 6 plays a year.
Recent Productions: *Man in the Deadpan*, by Joseph Gangi (play about Buster Keaton); and *Last Rites for the Boys*, by J. Robert Nash (play about famous gangsters: Capone, Siegel and Moran).

UNIVERSITY OF MINNESOTA DEPARTMENT OF THEATRE, Marshall Performing Arts Center, Duluth MN 55812. (218)726-8562. Department Head: Rick Graves. Estab. 1851. Plays are performed in the theater of the Marshall Arts Performing Center; audience is about 50% students and 50% community adults. Submit query and synopsis. Reports in 1 month. Produces 12-20 musicals (25%) and nonmusicals (75%) a year; originals vary each year. Buys "the right to perform the script for a single engagement. Pays $25-50/performance and occasionally fees to bring the playwright on campus during rehearsals." SASE.
Needs: "The department is committed to the development of young playwrights whose works have not attracted wide commercial attention." Opera; dance; "and all types of drama and musical theater."
Recent Productions: *Ubu Roi*, by Alfred Jarry; *Macbeth*, by William Shakespeare; *Man With Bags*, by Ionesco; and *Red Ryder*, by Mark Medof.

Screenwriting

It is true that a West Coast location—*and* an agent—are usually required of the screenwriter. But, as video technology advances and cable TV and independent producers vie for innovative programming, the demand for scriptwriters across the country gallops.

Many smaller production companies—because of potential legal entanglements—prefer that you register your script with the Writers Guild of America prior to submitting it. Often ideas, rather than entire scripts, are sold to networks or producers—so don't be suprised if *your* dialogue doesn't make it to the screen.

Some producers seek only scripts submitted through agents. (See the Authors' Agents section for more information.)

Format for the screenplay calls for a typed, single-spaced (triple-spaced between the dialogue of different characters) manuscript. Set margins at 15 and 75 (pica)—18 and 90 (elite)—and allow 125-150 pages for a two-hour feature film (90 pages for 90 minutes).

A good screenplay avoids stereotypes and cliches. It features originality and a solid story idea. It proves the writer can handle characterization, dialogue, plot construction, conflict and resolution.

For more information on writing for television, consult *The TV Scriptwriter's Handbook*, by Alfred Brenner (Writer's Digest Books). For copyright details, see *Films/TV Law*, by Walter E. Hurst, Johnny Minus and William Storm Hale (Seven Arts Press, 6605 Hollywood Blvd., Hollywood, California 90028).

KEN ANDERSON FILMS, Box 618, Winona Lake IN 46590. (219)267-5774. President: Ken Anderson. Produces material for church-related libraries with evangelical bias; films for all ages, with particular interest in children and teenagers. Previously published submissions OK. Considers brief, 1-page story synopses only. "We try to maintain a very warm attitude toward writers and will try to give careful consideration to queries. Unsolicited mss will be returned unread. We only produce 4-6 films/year, so our quantity needs are limited." Free catalog.
Needs: Religious material only. "We are constantly looking for good material that is positively Christian and relates realistically to today's lifestyle. We want true stories for young people and adults; fiction for children." Pays "as low as $100 for basic story idea, which the author could then market elsewhere. But general payment runs more between $250-1,000, depending upon story quality and adaptability for audiovisual production."

SAMUEL Z. ARKOFF CO., 9200 Sunset Blvd., P.H. 3, Los Angeles CA 90069. (213)278-7600. Contact: Joe Akerman. "We do not accept unsolicited manuscripts. We work through agents and attorneys only."

BATJAC PRODUCTIONS, INC., 9570 Wilshire Blvd., Beverly Hills CA 90212. (213)278-9870. Story Editor: Thomas Kane. Agented submissions only.

BONIME ASSOCIATES, LTD., 60 E. 42nd St., New York NY 10017. (212)490-2910. President: Andrew Bonime.. Estab. 1979. Produces "feature motion pictures, primarily; television secondarily. We develop high quality, moderate-to high-budget feature film projects. We either purchase scripts, book manuscripts, or hire writers on the average of 6 projects per year (includes rewrites of presently owned material)." Buys theatrical motion picture rights. "We accept only material submitted through recognized agents."
Needs: Submit "through recognized agents." Pays in accordance with Writers Guild standards.
Tips: "We are always looking for new writing talent, but because of sheer time and volume and because of legal reasons, we cannot accept unsolicited material or any material that does not come through recognized agents. We're interested in writers who have an understanding of motion picture technique for writing scripts, ability to create character—drama/or comedy—and an understanding of the visual process of film."

BRAVERMAN PRODUCTIONS, 1237 7th St., Santa Monica CA 90401. Agented submissions only.

BRYNA COMPANY, 141 El Camino Dr., Beverly Hills CA 90212. (213)274-5294. Contact: Sophie Alexis. Buys all rights. Previously produced material OK. SASE. Reporting time "depends on number of scripts received."

Needs: "We are open as to topics and slant." 35mm films. Submit complete script. Pays in accordance with Writers Guild standards.

CAMBRIDGE FILM CORP., 123 Thorndike St., Cambridge MA 02141. Producer: Richard MacLeod. Produces material for general theatrical and TV audiences. "Films range from G-rated children's pictures to R-rated sex and action." Buys "not more than four feature-length scripts per year." Query, with outline/synopsis. *Do not* send complete scripts. "We are not interested in receiving resumes." SASE. Reports in 6 weeks. Usually buys film and TV rights.
Needs: "All our releases are 35mm films or videotapes for subscription and cable TV. We don't employ writers; all scripts are freelanced. The easiest approach is with a short synopsis, plus a cover indicating the highlights and the major selling features (the sales handles, as it were) of the film as the author sees it."

THE CHAMBA ORGANIZATION, 230 W. 105th St. (2A), New York NY 10025. President: St. Clair Bourne. Produces material for "the new hip, activist-oriented audience; the general audience (PG), and in the educational film market, we aim at high school and adult audiences, especially the so-called 'minority' audiences. Assignments are given solely based upon our reaction to submitted material. The material is the credential." Query with a brief description of plot, thumbnail descriptions of principal characters and any unusual elements. SASE.
Needs: "I concentrate primarily on feature film projects. However, I am always interested in a unique feature-length documentary film project. We prefer submission of film treatments first. Then, if the idea interests us, we negotiate the writing of the script." Payment negotiable according to Writers Guild standards.

THE CHANNING DEBBIN LOCKE CO., 8833 Sunset Blvd., Suite 302, Los Angeles CA 90069. Agented submissions only.

CHEROKEE/MARTIN PRODUCTIONS, Box 2151, Beverly Hills CA 90213. (213)275-4791. Contact: Rick Martin. Buys first rights. Previously produced material OK.
Needs: "Basically drama." 35mm films. Submit synopsis/outline "or a treatment we can quickly read and get the main idea." Pays in accordance with Writer's Guild standards.

CINE/DESIGN FILMS, INC., 255 Washington St., Denver CO 80203. (303)777-4222. Producer/Director: Jon Husband. Produces educational material for general, sales training and theatrical audiences. Buys 10-15 scripts/year. Phone query OK; "original solid ideas are encouraged." Rights purchased vary.
Needs: "Motion picture outlines in the theatrical, documentary, sales or educational areas. We are seeking theatrical scripts in the low-budget area that are possible to produce for under $1,500,000. We seek flexibility and personalities who can work well with our clients." Produces 16mm and 35mm films. Pays $100-200/screen minute on 16mm productions. Theatrical scripts negotiable.
Tips: "Understand the marketing needs of film production today."

CINETUDES FILM PRODUCTIONS, LTD., 377 Broadway, New York NY 10013. (212)966-4600. President: Christine Jurzykowski. Director: Neal Marshad. Produces material for TV. Works with 20 writers/year. Query with samples or submit resume. SASE. Reports in 2 weeks. Buys all rights.
Needs: Feature length screenplays (theatrical/TV); theatrical shorts; children's programming. "We look for the willingness to listen, and past experience in visual writing." Produces 16mm and 35mm films and videotape. Pays by outright purchase, or pays daily rates.

COMPASS INTERNATIONAL PICTURES, 9229 Sunset Blvd., Los Angeles CA 90069. (213)273-9125. Contact: Donna Wells. "We accept approximately 1 script from each 50 submitted." Buys all rights. Previously published material OK, (if so advised). Reporting time "varies, depending upon workload."
Needs: Submit complete script. Pays in accordance with Writers Guild standards.

CONCORDIA PUBLISHING HOUSE, Product Development Division, 3558 S. Jefferson Ave., St. Louis MO 63118. (314)664-7000. Produces religious material for preschool through adult audiences, for institutional and home use. "Writer must have demonstrated skills in writing produceable material for print and the audio and visual fields. Competence in the content area is necessary. Initial query is preferred in view of existing production commitments and necessity to maintain a satisfactory product mix. Do not send completed manuscripts or multiple submissions." SASE. Free catalog.
Needs: Manuscripts and scripts for educational and religious subjects. "The content areas relate to

the requirements of religious and moral guidance instruction. The emphasis may be curricular, quasi-curricular or enriching." Produces books, silent and sound filmstrips, 16mm films, multimedia kits, overhead transparencies, phonograph records, tapes and cassettes, 35mm slides and study prints. "Writing fees are negotiated in consideration of such factors as type of production, configuration, complexity of assignment, research required, field tests and production deadlines."
Tips: "Send a prospectus of project to be evaluated as to produceability, market, etc."

PIERRE COSSETTE CO., 8899 Beverly Blvd., Los Angeles CA 90048. (213)278-3366. Contact: Dan DiStefano. Writers worked with "varies from year to year." Rights purchased "depends on situation." Previously produced material OK. SASE. Reports on queries.
Needs: TV. "Query first, then if we're interested we will ask for a submission." Pay "depends on situation."

DARINO FILMS, 222 Park Ave. S., New York NY 10013. Creative Director: Ed Darino. Produces material for education and youngsters. Submit synopsis/outline. SASE. Reports in 2 months "only if we see possibility for the future. Then we use SASE for report." Buys educational/TV first rights.
Needs: Subject topics include "children's and youngsters' films, animated short stories and legends of the world. 1-2 pages maximum outline. Simple, direct style. Non-verbal preferred on animation. Minimum dialogue always." Produces silent filmstrips, 16mm and 35mm films, phonograph records (few songs only) and videotape. Payment is in accordance with Writers Guild standards—"if producer has royalties basis, so do we."
Tips: "Our firm has over 24 awards. We only look for the best: new style, original approach, the message, education or human aspect of the work we do, considering always the people we do it for. We are looking for original material only, topnotch quality. We respect and love children, so do not send commercial junk."

DBA ENTERTAINMENT, 3211 Cahuenga Blvd. W., Hollywood CA 90028. Producer: Wayne Threm. "We read unsolicited scripts and those received through people we know. If we are interested, we will follow up."
Needs: Most ideas are "generated within. The producers do a lot of writing themselves. This firm does a lot of documentary work, but we're also branching out into other areas. We do not do many sponsored films. We work up our own ideas first and then sell them."

WALT DISNEY PRODUCTIONS, 500 S. Buena Vista St., Burbank CA 91521. (213)840-1000. Executive Story Editor: David Ehrman. Produces material for an audience of children through adults. Buys 20 scripts/year. Buys all rights. SASE. Reports in 2 weeks on queries; 1 month on submissions.
Needs: Screenplays, teleplays, treatments, outlines, fantasies, high adventure, optimistic dramas and comedies. 35mm films and TV. Query. Pays in accordance with Writers Guild standards.
Tips: "Disney will only entertain G- or PG-rated material. We look for strong characters, an unusual storyline and strong dialogue. A good many scripts suffer from episodic story construction. In other words the writer tells the story in a 'and then they did this' fashion. Characters sometimes tend to be cardboard or stereotypes. Writers should strive for original tales or perhaps a new variation on an old theme."

ECHO FILM PRODUCTIONS, 413 Idaho St., #200, Boise ID 83702. (208)336-0349. Producer: Norman Nelson. Produces material for "local TV audiences, national TV audiences concerned with the environment, national and worldwide audiences concerned with sports and action film documentaries." Buys 2-6 scripts/year. Query. SASE. Reports in 1 week. Buys all rights.
Needs: Material for action sports documentaries, wildlife documentaries, short dramas, and promotional films. Avoid "overwriting and flowery wording." Produces 16mm films. Pays $500-2,000.

EMI TELEVISION, INC., 4024 Radford Ave., Studio City CA 91604. Agented submissions only.

GOLDEN IMAGE MOTION PICTURE CORP., 9465 Wilshire Blvd., Suite 511, Beverly Hills CA 90212. (213)550-8710. Contact: Sandy Cobe. "We did 4 pictures in 1980 and expect to do 3-4 in 1981." Buys all rights. Previously produced material OK "if from another medium."
Needs: Submit synopsis/outline "with SASE for return." Pays in outright purchase.

GRAND CENTRAL PICTURES, INC., 12 E. 46th St., New York NY 10017. (212)687-4312. President: Richard M. Spitalny. Produces material for a "mass theatrical audience, those moviegoers 18-34 years of age." Query with samples, submit completed script, or submit resume. SASE. "Only those submissions with adequate return postage will be returned." Buys all rights or first rights.

Needs: "Feature-length film scripts, treatments, synopses based on concepts developed by Grand Central Pictures, writers' concepts, and adaptations of existing properties (only if optioned and/or owned by writer or GCP)." Length: scripts, 100-135 pages; treatments, 15-30 pages; synopses, 1-6 pages. "We look for a professional approach to deadlines." Produces 35mm feature films.

GARY GRIFFIN PRODUCTIONS, 12667 Memorial Dr., Houston TX 77024. (713)465-9017. Produces material for general audiences. Buys half of material used from outside writers. Submit outline/synopsis or submit resume. SASE. Reports in 2 weeks. Buys all rights.
Needs: "We offer a broad entertainment package and can provide our clients with any of the services required, from concept to finished product. We prefer general-interest topics, but we also have many clients that require technical, medical, industrial, etc., material. We look for the ability to work in a flexible range, creative and innovative ideologies, and an amiable personality." Produces 16mm and 35mm films, TV commercials, videotape specials, commercial and TV pilots. Pays $100-75,000; pays according to Writers Guild standards.

INSTAR PRODUCTIONS, INC., 145 W. 55th St., New York NY 10019. Executives in Charge: John Gentile and Anthony Gentile. Produces material for the general moviegoing public. Query with completed script and synopsis. SASE. Reports in 2 months. Buys all rights.
Needs: "Intelligent feature film screenplays only—comedy, horror, action-thrillers. We look for the utmost professionalism." Produces 35mm films. Pays according to Writers Guild standards.

INTERGROUP PRODUCTIONS, INC., 300 E. 59th St., New York NY 10022. (212)832-8169. Executive Producer: Rudolf Gartzman. Produces material for industry; theatrical release feature films; TV specials and documentaries; and dramatic nonfiction and fiction. Buys 12-15 scripts/ year. Query with samples and brief resume with clear definitions of projects. SASE. Will not return by mail script copies sumbitted. Reports in 6 weeks. Buys all rights.
Needs: Industrial films; general sales and promotional material; and sales training material. Produces 16mm and 35mm films. Pays $1,200-1,700 for 15-minute script with 1 draft and 3 rewrites; "individual company standard contract for industrial material; Writers Guild standards for film."
Tips: Beware of over-narration. "A strong literal sense impedes visual imagination."

KINGS POINT FILMS, 9336 Washington Blvd., Culver City CA 90230. (213)954-6602. Contact: Ken Yates. Buys maximum 3 scripts/year. Buys all rights.
Needs: Submit synopsis/outline. Pays in outright purchase and in accordance with Writers Guild standards.

THE KOENIGSBURG CO., 10201 W. Pico Blvd., CA 90064. Agented submissions only.

KRACO PRODUCTIONS, 1112 Sherbourne, Los Angeles CA 90069. (213)854-4400. Contact: John. Agented submissions only.

JERRY LEIDER PRODUCTIONS, 1041 N. Formosa Ave., Los Angeles CA 90046. (213)650-2888. Story Editor: Diana Brent. Agented submissions only.

LIROL TV PRODUCTIONS, 6335 Homewood Ave., Los Angeles CA 90028. (213)467-8111. Contact: Morlene Keller. Writers worked with "varies from year to year." Buys all rights.
Needs: TV syndication only. Submit synopsis/outline. Pays in accordance with Writers Guild standards.

MARGIE-LEE ENTERPRISES, 56 W. 56th St., New York NY 10022. (212)581-4982. President: Lee Levinson. Produces material for network television and motion picture audiences. Buys 25 scripts/year. Buys TV and motion picture rights. SASE. Reports in 1 week on queries; 2 weeks on submissions.
Needs: Screenplays, treatments, outlines. 35mm films. Query with samples, or submit synopsis/ outline or completed script. Pays in accordance with Writers Guild standards.

MARKOWITZ/CHESLER PRODUCING CORP., 9200 Sunset Blvd., #520, Los Angeles CA 90069. (213)655-6983. Contact: Lew Chesler. Produces variety and comedy television material, movies of the week, and theatrical films for Canadian productions. Works with approximately 100 writers/year. Buys all rights. Previously produced material OK. SASE. Reports in 3 weeks.
Needs: 35mm films and tapes and cassettes. Submit complete script. Pays royalty, in outright purchase, in accordance with Writers Guild standards, or by other arrangement.

BRAD MARKS PRODUCTIONS, INC., 9124 Sunset Blvd., Los Angeles CA 90069. (213)278-8360. Director of Program Development: Gary Grossman. "We have an open policy on submissions." Reports on submissions.
Needs: Wholesome family entertainment. Family-oriented TV movies; specials; and concept specials. Query with a paragraph capsule of the idea. "If interested, we will request a larger treatment of the idea. All submissions must be prior-registered with the Writers Guild of America." Pays in accordance with Writers Guild standards.

METROMEDIA PRODUCERS CORP., 5746 Sunset Blvd., Hollywood CA. (213)462-7111. Contact: Ms. Toni Woodward, assistant to the President, or Jay Wolpert. "We use a lot of material." Buys negotiable rights; "depends on the project." Previously produced material OK, "as we are also a distributing company." Reporting time "depends on volume. If it's something we really like, we may call the writer the day material is received."
Needs: Wide variety. TV. Query with samples and resume, or submit synopsis/outline or completed script. Pays in accordance with Writers Guild standards.

DOUG MOODY MYSTIC RECORDS, Box 2434, Hollywood CA 90028. Coordinator: Nancy Faith. For home entertainment, all ages. Query with synopsis. SASE.
Needs: Produces work on phonograph albums and audiovisual records. Pays depending upon royalties to artists and musical copyright royalties. Buys phonograph and audiovisual rights.
Tips: "We are looking for works capable of being performed within one hour. Can be nonvisual. Can rely on sound effects to replace visual effects. Think about the medium."

MULTI-MEDIA INTERNATIONAL, 8915 Yolanda Ave., Northridge CA 91324. (213)993-7816. Contact: Bob Cawley. Vice President: Rena Winters. Works with 10 writers/year and buys 3-5 scripts and synopses/year. Buys all rights or arranges package deal with writers for creator fees throughout series in TV, or for film. "We contact writers whose ideas we like as soon as possible. Please enclose SASE with submissions for return of material, in case we can't use it."
Needs: 35mm films and TV. "We're looking for 2 kinds of material: top drawer action-adventure, and warm subject matters with commentary on our times (about people trying to get their lives back together, e.g., *Kramer Vs. Kramer*). We're interested in material that can be produced for between $3 million and $6 million." Submit synopsis/outline or complete script. Pays ("depending on the situation") royalty, in outright purchase, or in accordance with Writers Guild standards.
Tips: "If we can't use a script or synopsis that we feel has potential, *sometimes* we will make notations with suggestions as to how the script could be made stronger, or if we aren't using that particular kind of material at the time, we may refer the writer to someone who is."

NEW PLAYERS COMPANY, INC., 914 N. Charles St., Baltimore MD 21201. (301)837-6071. Contact: Ray Hamby. Buys 6 scripts/year. "We will be negotiating cable TV rights on a percentage of gross basis with each author." Reports in 1 month.
Needs: "Scripts that can be produced with simple sets, modern dress and small casts preferred. Subject matter open. Full-length only. No one-acters, explicit sex, costume epics, multi-sets, theater of the absurd—minimal vulgarity. Cable TV." Query with synopsis. Pays 5% minimum royalty.
Tips: "We do not want material that competes with *Alice*, *M*A*S*H*, *Shirley* and *Whoever*. We want plays with writing quality—comedies or dramas."

OMSTAR PRODUCTIONS, 1714 N. Ivar, Los Angeles CA 90028. (213)464-6699. Contact: Edmund Penney. Works with variable number of writers/year. Buys all rights. SASE.
Needs: "We are open. We're now in production in 2 comedies, an adventure film and a mystery." Submit synopsis/outline. Pays in accordance with Writer's Guild standards.

PACE FILMS, INC., 411 E. 53rd St., New York NY 10022. President: Mr. R. Vanderbes. Produces material for "TV and theatrical audiences in the US and worldwide." Writing assignments are handled through agencies, but independent queries or submissions are considered. SASE. Buys all rights.
Needs: "Feature films for TV and theaters." Pays according to Writers Guild standards.

PAULIST PRODUCTIONS, Box 1057, Pacific Palisades CA 90272. (213)454-0688. Contact: Thomas Holahan. Produces material for adult and teen audiences. Submit "5 page treatment." SASE. Reports in 2 months. Reserves TV and educational film rights. Free info for SASE.
Needs: "We use 28½ minute format for *Insight*: A modern dramatic TV series that explores human values and current issues. We also use 24½ minute format for *Reflections*: A modern dramatic TV series for teenagers, 14-18, stressing human values." Produces 16mm films and TV. Payment is

"based on current agreement with syndicator for *Reflections, Insight* series uses donated scripts: only 13 episodes/year."
Tips: Looking for writers with "good ear for dialogue and ability to grasp the message of the story and make it dramatically satisfying, realistic and humane."

PENTHOUSE FILMS INTERNATIONAL, 909 3rd Ave., New York NY 10022. (212)593-3301. Contact: Peter Bloch (nonfiction), Kathy Green (fiction). Works with variable number of writers/ year. Buys all rights. "You must send SASE for reply. We send a standard form letter for rejection. If we want something on spec, we'll write a short letter."
Needs: 35mm films. "Queries must be typed. Synopsis or scripts must be typed and double-spaced. We have a standard contract."

EDWARD R. PRESSMAN PRODUCTIONS, 4000 Warner Blvd., Burbank CA. (213)843-6000. Contact: Edward R. Pressman. Works with variable number of writers/year. Buys all rights. SASE.
Needs: Open as to slant and subject topics. 35mm films. Submit complete script. Pays in outright purchase.

MARTIN RANSOHOFF PRODUCTIONS, INC., Columbia Plaza West, Burbank CA 91505. (213)843-6000. Contact: Debbie. Agented submissions only.

THE SNELLER CO., 1888 Century Park East, #1218, Los Angeles CA 90067. (213)553-4144. Contact: Karen Shapiro. Uses freelance writers for rewrites. Buys all rights. Screenplays based on books are OK. SASE. Reports on synopses and scripts.
Needs: 35mm feature films. Submit synopsis/outline or complete script.
Tips: "We are looking for all different kinds of material."

TANDEM PRODUCTIONS/T.A.T. COMMUNICATIONS, 5752 Sunset Blvd., Los Angeles CA 90028. (213)856-1500. "Our shows are mainly staff-written. Occasionally we use outside writers, but legally we can only accept work from writers whose material is submitted through accredited agents."

20TH-FOX FEATURES, 10201 W. Pico Blvd., Los Angeles CA 90064. (213)277-2211. Story Editor: David Madden. Agented submissions only.

UNITED PRODUCTIONS, LTD., Box 5942, Sherman Oaks CA 91403. (213)986-6644. Contact: Richard Summers. Buys "several" scripts/year. Previously produced material OK.
Needs: "We're interested in everything." 35mm films and TV. Submit synopsis/outline or complete script. Pays in accordance with Writers Guild standards.

UNIVERSAL PRODUCTIONS CANADA, INC., 38 Prince Arthur Ave., Toronto, Ontario, Canada M5R 1A9. (416)968-2704. Associate Producer: Alma Lee. Produces feature films for theatrical release. Buys all rights. SASE. Reports "right away on queries"; 5 weeks on mss.
Needs: Outlines, treatments, scripts for feature length films. We do not accept unsolicited scripts." 35mm films. "Telephone inquiries only as we do not accept unsolicited scripts." Pays in accordance with Writers Guild standards.

Syndicates

Syndicated columns are among the most widely read material in the US—and a successful column can prove very profitable to a writer.

Syndicates sell editorial copy (columns, feature articles, news, puzzles and cartoons) for a commission. The author receives from 40% to 60% of the gross proceeds, though some syndicates pay the writer a salary and others buy material outright. The syndicate's percentage covers costs of promotion, mailing, staff, etc. Writers of top syndicated columns can earn more than $50,000 a year, though most syndicated writers can't expect to see anything near that figure.

To be a successful syndicated columnist, keep your ideas fresh. For instance, if you can show people how to save money on a consistent basis, you may be a natural for column writing. Everyone wants to read about shortcuts and money-savers. Whether the subject is self-improvement, home repairs, household hints, or children's activities, if it beats inflation, it could sell. But people also enjoy an occasional escape from the day-to-day concerns of modern life, thus the popularity of syndicated celebrity biographies.

Syndicated material should be short (500-1,000 words/column), objective, and carefully documented. Since syndicates sell primarily to newspapers, you must employ a terse "newspaper style," even when writing features. This means a "grabber" lead, animated quotes and anecdotes, and lean sentences that come straight to the point.

Study acceptable syndicate style by reading as many examples of syndicated work as you can. A bundle of syndicated material is delivered to most writers every morning or evening: the newspaper. Read syndicated features and columns, paying careful attention to style, length, the audience they are apparently aimed at, and what syndicates handled them. Carefully note the subjects covered in the material, especially in regular columns. Take care to not duplicate an already existing column: create something fresh. Don't even consider doing an astrology column or an Erma Bombeck type of column, for instance—every syndicate interested in carrying one probably already has one. Be original.

Consult the following listings for the topic and form of submissions preferred by various syndicates. Some deal with regular features, some with article series, some with individual features. Listings also cover the syndicate's outlets. Most, as mentioned above, sell to newspapers, but many also sell to magazines, and to radio stations that use syndicated material as "brights"—that is, lively, interesting facts and anecdotes. For more information about the titles of columns and features handled by particular syndicates, consult *Editor and Publisher Syndicate Directory* (575 Lexington Ave., New York City 10022).

Most syndicate editors prefer that you query them with about six sample columns or features. Enclose a self-addressed, stamped envelope with all queries and submissions.

Some writers self-syndicate their material, earning 100% of the income, but also bearing the expense of soliciting clients, reproducing and mailing the features, billing, etc.

AMERICAN FEATURES SYNDICATE, 964 3rd Ave., New York NY 10155. Editor: Robert Behren. Copyrights material. Will consider photocopied submissions. Reporting time "varies." Query. SASE.
Nonfiction: Travel and true adventure. Buys single features and article series. Does not contract for columns. Length: 1,000-5,000 words. Pays $100-$750. Usual outlets are newspapers and regional magazines, including some trade publications.

AP NEWSFEATURES, 50 Rockefeller Plaza, New York NY 10020. Assistant General Manager: Dan Perkes. SASE.

Nonfiction: Buys column ideas "dealing with all areas that can be expanded into book form. Do not buy single features."

ARKIN MAGAZINE SYNDICATE, 761 NE 180th St., North Miami Beach FL 33162. Editor: Joseph Arkin. "We regularly purchase articles from several freelancers, most of whom belong to ABWA, for syndication in trade and professional magazines." Submit complete ms. SASE. Reports in 3 weeks. Buys all North American magazine and newspaper rights. Previously published submissions OK, "if all rights haven't been sold."
Needs: Magazine articles (nonfiction; 800-1,800 words, directly relating to business problems common to several (not just one) business firms, in different types of businesses); and photos (purchased with written material). "We are in dire need of the 'how-to' business article." Will not consider article series. Pays 3-10¢/word; $5-10 for photos; "actually line drawings are preferred instead of photos." Pays on acceptance.
Tips: "Study a representative group of trade magazines to learn style, needs and other facets of the field."

AUTHENTICATED NEWS INTERNATIONAL, ANI, 29 Katonah Ave., Katonah NY 10536. (914)232-7726. Editor: Sidney Polinsky. Syndication and Features Editor: Helga Brink. Supplies book review material to national magazines, newspapers, and house organs in the United States and important countries abroad. Buys exclusive and non-exclusive rights. Previously published "at times." Submissions OK. Reports in 3 months. SASE.
Nonfiction and Photos: Can use photo material in the following areas: hard news, photo features, ecology and the environment, science, medical, industry, education, human interest, the arts, city planning, and pertinent photo material from abroad. 750 words maximum. Prefers 8x10 b&w glossy prints, color transparencies (4x5 or 2¼x2¼, 35mm color). Where necessary, model releases required. Pays 50% royalty.

AUTO NEWS SYNDICATE, Box 2085, Daytona Beach FL 32015. (904)439-2747. Editor: Don O'Reilly. Unsolicited material is acknowledged or returned within a few days, "but we cannot be responsible for loss." SASE.
Nonfiction and Photos: Syndicated articles, photos on automotive subjects and motor sports. Newspaper articles ("Dateline Detroit" and "Inside Auto Racing"). Magazine articles. Radio broadcasts ("Motorcade USA"). 50% commission. "Payment is made between acceptance and publication." No flat fees.

BUDDY BASCH FEATURE SYNDICATE, 771 West End Ave., New York NY 10025. Publisher: Buddy Basch. Buys all rights. Will consider photocopied submissions, but not of anything previously printed. Query or submit complete ms. Reports in 1 week to 10 days. Must enclose SASE.
Nonfiction, Humor, Photos, and Fillers: News items, nonfiction, humor, photos, fillers, puzzles, and columns and features on travel and entertainment. "Mostly staff written at present. Query."
Tips: "Come up with something really unique. Most writers have the same old hackneyed ideas (*they* think are original) which no one can use. Just because someone in the family or a friend said, 'What a great idea,' doesn't make it so."

CANADIAN SCENE, Suite 305, 2 College St., Toronto, Ontario, Canada M5G 1K3. Editor: Miss Ruth Gordon. Query. Submit seasonal material 3 months in advance. Reports in 1 week. Pays on acceptance. Enclose SAE and International Reply Coupons for reply to queries.
Nonfiction: "Canadian Scene is a voluntary information service. Its purpose is to provide written material to democratic, ethnic publications, and radio and television stations broadcasting in languages other than English and French in Canada. Translations are provided in 15 foreign languages. The material is chosen with a view to directing readers to an understanding of Canadian political affairs, foreign relations, social customs, industrial progress, culture, history, and institutions. In a 700-word article, the writer can submit almost any subject on Canada, providing it leaves the newcomer with a better knowledge of Canada. It should be written in a simple, tightly knit, straightforward style." Length: 500-1,000 words. Pays 5¢/word.

CHICAGO TRIBUNE-NEW YORK NEWS SYNDICATE, INC., 220 E. 42nd St., New York NY 10017. Editor: Don Michel. Supplies material to Sunday supplements and newspapers in North America and abroad. Buys worldwide rights, where possible; must have North American rights to be interested. Submit at least 6 samples of any submission for continuing feature. SASE for return of submissions.
Columns, Puzzles: No fiction. Material must be extremely well-written and must not be a copy of something now being marketed to newspapers. Length varies, though columns should generally be

500 words or less. Pay varies, depending on market; usually 50-50 split of net after production on contractual material.

CITY DESK FEATURES, 110-45 71st Rd., Forest Hills NY 11375. (212)261-4061. President: Sylvia Fenmore. Estab. 1979. Uses syndicated material for newspapers all over the country and for national and regional magazines. Submit complete ms. SASE. Reports in 1-2 months. Buys all rights.
Needs: Magazine features, newspaper features, magazine columns, newspaper columns and fillers. Pays $35-50 for 500-700 word features. No additional payment for photos accompanying ms. "Submissions should be original, creative, exclusive, well-researched, verified, newsworthy and of national and broad human interest. Include a self-addressed, stamped envelope if return of material is requested. Payment arrangements with writers upon acceptance."

COLLEGE PRESS SERVICE, 2629 18th St., Denver CO 80211. (303)458-7216. Editor: Bill Sonn. "We work with about 10-15 freelancers a year." Initial written query is imperative. SASE. Reports in 2-4 weeks. Material is not copyrighted.
Needs: Magazine and newspaper features; news items. Material must be related to college life. Pays 5¢/word.

COLUMBIA FEATURES, INC., 36 W. 44 St., New York NY 10036. President: Joseph M. Boychuk. (212)840-1812. Vice President, Executive Editor: Kurt Lassen. Associate Editor: Helen M. Staunton. Syndicates to daily newspapers. Buys all rights, and world rights, all media. Will consider photocopied submissions. Submit complete ms. Pays on a regular monthly basis for continuing column or contract. Reports in 3 months. SASE.
Needs: Long-term panel cartoons, comic strips and columns on a continuing basis. "Highly salable items only from topnotch professionals. No random thoughts or one-shots." Features for special sections: family, home, women's, Sunday supplements or short serializations. No single features, except series of 6-12 parts, about 750-1,000 words/article. Lengths vary according to features. Columns: 500-750 words. Pays standard 50% syndicate contract.

COMMUNITY AND SUBURBAN PRESS SERVICE, Box 639, Frankfort KY 40602. Editor: Kennison Keene. Buys second serial (reprint) rights. Pays on acceptance. SASE.
Humor and Photos: Cartoons, gag panels, human interest photos. No personalized columns. 8x10 glossy photos purchased without features. Captions required. Pays $15 per cartoon or photo.

COMMUNITY FEATURES, Dept. A, Box 1062, Berkeley CA 94704. Editor: Tamar Wise. Works with 150 writers. Syndicates material to newspapers. Writer's guidelines for SASE and $1. Reports in 2-6 weeks. Buys various rights; buys reprints.
Nonfiction, Reviews, Photos Stories and Columns: "We distribute newspaper and magazine features on women, family, education, senior affairs, science, technology, the environment, consumer protection, nutrition and health; ethnic traditions and cuisine; travel; advice and opinion columns; book and film reviews; educational features; and a small number of quizzes, games and illustrated panels." Buys single features and article series 400-1,500 words; prefers 400-800 words. Buys human interest photo stories and captioned photo essays on the above topics. Pays $10-50 for b&w 8x10 glossy prints with cartoons; photos must include full range of greys for newspaper reproduction. Pays 3-10¢/word. Pays 50% of net sales for weekly features. Proposals for weekly features should include three or more samples and a brief description of follow-up installments. Helpful to include samples of previously published work.
Tips: "We want well written science, technology and health features, reviews and opinion columns (see below). We can also use good reprints and previous publications. Material must be direct and simply stated, not condescending. We do not use inspirational articles, fiction, celebrity or astrology columns; material that denigrates women or any other group. Nothing special or strictly local in interest, verbose or overwritten. For style we follow Rudolf Flesch's *The Art of Readable Writing* and Strunk and White's *Elements of Style*. Lively, direct, active writing is a must. We return material on subjects that have already been widely treated in print. If you read about it somewhere else, there's a good chance our readers have, too. Adhere to Guidelines. Address your article to a national newspaper readership. We will accept 500-1,000 word Opinion pieces. These must be of excellent quality on issues of national or international interest for syndication to Op-Ed Sections in the United States, Canada and Western Europe. Send mss to Opinion Page, Community Features. Ensure a prompt reply by including a #10 or larger SASE with all correspondence."

CURIOUS FACTS FEATURES, 6B Ridge Ct., Lebanon OH 45036. (513)932-1820. Editor: Donald Whitacre. Buys 175 articles, features and fillers/year. Syndicates to newspapers. SASE.

Reports in 6 weeks. Buys all rights. Writer's guidelines for 4½x9½ SAE and 2 first class stamps.
Needs: Fillers (maximum 50 words; oddities of all types); and newspaper features (maximum 400 words; strange laws of the world; strange animals of the world). "We are always interested in 'Strange Anomalies of Medicine'—Questions and Answers dealing with Oddities in the World. We purchase all kinds of oddities (no copyrighted material)." Submit complete ms. Pays 50% commission.
Photos: No additional payment for photos accepted with ms. Currently syndicates *Curious Facts . . .*, by Donald Whitacre (oddities of all kinds); *Cooking Around the World*, by Mary C. Sherman (cooking oddities); and *Little Known Facts About the World*, by DuMont White (foreign countries' oddities).

DORN-FREDRICKS PUBLISHING CO., 35 E. 35th St., Suite 7-H, New York NY 10016. Editor: Dona Davis Grant. Buys all rights, worldwide, foreign rights. Query. SASE.
Nonfiction, Humor, Poetry, and Fillers: Gossip columns of worldwide interest; material for feminine markets; fashion, beauty, etc. Single features include: "Harvest Time of Life" (column), "Mighty Mixture" (column), "Famous Mothers," "Your Key to Courage," "How the West Was Won," "Crafts" and "Homemaker's New Ideas." Interested in humor columns of approximately 800 words. Famous personalities, and beauty. Column length: 800 words. Pays 3¢/word minimum, depending on name value.

EDITORIAL CONSULTANT SERVICE, Box 524, West Hempstead NY 11552. Editorial Director: Arthur A. Ingoglia. "We work with 75 writers in the US and Canada." Syndicates material to newspapers, magazines, and radio stations. Query. SASE. Reports in 3-4 weeks. Buys all rights. Writer's guidelines for SASE.
Needs: Magazine and newspaper columns and features; news items; and radio broadcast material. Prefers carefully documented material with automotive slant. Also considers trade features. Will consider article series. No horoscope, child care, lovelorn or pet care. Author's percentage varies; usually averages 50%. Additional payment for 8x10 b&w and color photos accepted with ms. Currently syndicates *Let's Talk About Your Car*, by R. Hite; *Book Talk*, by L. Stevens; and *Car World*, by A. Ingoglia.

ERWIN LYNN ADVERTISING FEATURES, 9 Deb St., Plainview NY 11803. Editor: Erwin Lynn. Estab. 1979. "I plan to buy from 3-5 writers/year." Syndicates to newspapers. SASE. Reports in 1 month. Buys all rights or second serial (reprint) rights.
Needs: Newspaper columns and newspaper features (do-it-yourself; quizzes/puzzles; sports; food; medicine, etc.). "Features are sold to newspaper advertising departments. Features are then sponsored by local companies. Buys article series. "Topics, as listed above, 750 words each article." Query with clips of published work or submit complete ms. Pays 50% commission.
Photos: No additional payment for photos accepted with ms.
Tips: "Features must be family- and community-oriented in order to enable us to acquire local sponsorship."

FACING SOUTH, Box 531, Durham NC 27702. (919)688-8167. Co-Editors: Chris Mayfield and Kathleen Zobel. Buys 52 columns/year for syndication to newspapers. Query or submit complete ms. SASE. Reports in 5 weeks. Buys all rights.
Needs: "700-750-word columns focusing on a Southern individual, allowing that person to tell a story. We need portraits of activists, innovators and artists; also of ordinary Southerners creatively involved in their communities. Each week a different writer does a column, although we will use more than one column by the same writer—just spread them over several months." No Horatio Alger themes, Southern sterotypes, or "sentimental glorifications of Southern life 'the way it used to be'; or slick tributes to the wonders of Sun Belt prosperity. Writers should avoid these simplistic extremes." Pays $50. "Writers must send for our guidelines before attempting a column." No payment for photos; "we just need some kind of a snapshot that our artist can use to do an illustration."
Tips: "Use lots of quotes; make it clear why the person profiled would be interesting to all Southerners; take a serious tone if the story warrants it (or humorous). We particularly need stories about people working for positive social change in their communities; also about young people."

FEATURE ASSOCIATES, 3334 Kerner Blvd., San Rafael CA 94901. (415)457-1947. Editor: Peter Menkin. Purchases 10 features annually from freelance writers. Uses syndicated material primarily for newspapers. Submit complete ms, 100 word synopsis of column ideas and 75-100 word biography and resume. SASE. Reports in 4 weeks. Buys all rights or second serial rights.
Needs: Newspaper features. Purchases single features for current issues. Special features for domestic and overseas distribution; illustrated features. Query first. Occasionally buys article

series. Pays 50-50 author's percentage. No photos purchased with ms. Currently syndicates *Future Think, Silver Screen* and *Women at Work*.

FIELD NEWSPAPER SYNDICATE, 1703 Kaiser Ave., Irving CA 92714. President/Chief Executive Officer: Steven Jehorek. Syndicates material to newspapers. Submit "examples of work with explanatory letter." SASE. Reports in 1-2 months. Rights purchased vary. Free writer's guidelines.
Needs: Newspaper columns (should be 500-800 words in length and should appeal to a wide audience. Subject matter should not be too specialized because syndicates sell columns to newspapers all over the US and Canada). Currently syndicates *Ann Landers*, by Ann Landers; *At Wit's End*, by Erma Bombeck; and *Inside Report*, by Rowland Guans and Robert Novak.

GENERAL NEWS SYNDICATE, 147 W. 42nd St., New York NY 10036. (212)221-0043. Works with 12 writers/year. Syndicates to newspaper and radio. SASE. Reports in 3 weeks. Buys one-time rights.

GLOBAL SYNDICATION & LITERARY AGENCY, LTD., 120 Westmont, Hemet CA 92343. Editor: Stephanie Greene. Estab. 1980. Works with 6 feature writers/year. Syndicates to international newspapers and magazines (material distributed through agents overseas). Small percent distributed in the US. SASE. Reports in 1 week. Buys second serial (reprint) rights and foreign reprint rights. Writer's guidelines $1.
Needs: Fiction (science fiction, sophisticated romance); fillers (home repair, household hints, auto repair and upkeep); magazine columns (health and exercise); magazine features (celebrity interviews, nonfiction of interest to women readers); juvenile activity pages (dot-to-dots, mazes, puzzles, games); newspaper columns (automotive repair and upkeep; household hints and home repair); newspaper features (celebrity interviews); and news itmes (latest advances in medicine). Submit complete ms with SASE. Pays commission. Currently syndicates *Legal Limits*, by L. Sturgiss (newspaper column); *Firsts*, by C. Crist (newspaper column—trivia); and *Travel Articles*, by B. Horngren.
Tips: "Have at least 26 of anything submitted available if submitting a column. Since we are an international syndicate, bear in mind that items must have global appeal."

DAVE GOODWIN & ASSOCIATES, P.O. Drawer 54-6661, Surfside FL 33154. Editor: Dave Goodwin. Rights purchased vary with author and material. May buy first rights or second serial (reprint) rights. Will handle copyrighted material. Buys about 25 features a year from freelancers. Query or submit complete ms. Reports in 3 weeks. SASE.
Nonfiction: "Money-saving information for consumers: how to save on home expenses; auto, medical, drug, insurance, boat, business items, etc." Buys article series on brief, practical, down-to-earth items for consumer use or knowledge. Rarely buys single features. Currently handling "Insurance for Consumers." Length: 300-5,000 words. Pays 50% on publication.

HARRIS & ASSOCIATES PUBLISHING DIVISION, 247 South 800 East, Logan UT 84321. (801)753-3587. President: Dick Harris. Rights purchased vary with author and material. Buys first rights. Does not purchase many mss per year since material must be in special style. Pays on acceptance. Not necessary to query. Send sample or representative material. Reports in less than 30 days. SASE.
Nonfiction, Photos, and Humor: Material on driver safety and accident prevention. Humor for modern women (not women's lib); humor for sports page. "We like to look at anything in our special interest areas. Golf and tennis are our specialties. We'll also look at cartoons in these areas. Will buy or contract for syndication. Everything must be short, terse, with humorous approach." Action, unposed, 8x10 b&w photos are purchased without features or on assignment. Captions are required. Pays 10¢ minimum per word and $15 minimum per photo.
Tips: "Submit *good* photos or art with text."

HER SAY, Box 11010, San Francisco CA 94101. (415)495-3881. Editors: Marlene Edmunds, Shelley Buck, Ann Milner. Query; submissions will not be returned. Reports in 3 weeks. Writer's guidelines for SASE.
Needs: "*Her Say* is a national women's weekly news service, going out to a number of radio news outlets and publications around the country, in Canada, and in Europe. We are looking for input from researchers, writers and reporters from everywhere to help us keep posted on events concerning women. We would like items which can be rewritten to 75-250 word stories for both print and radio outlets. Keep an eye on the major news of the country and look for the holes in the news. Current status of legislation, socio-political research on, by, or for women, humorous items, new breakthroughs in medicine, scientific studies, and Third World news—these are the types of stories we would like to see. No news which demeans women. Have an editorial focus which is relevant to women." Pays $5/item.

HOLLYWOOD INSIDE SYNDICATE, Box 49957, Los Angeles CA 90049. Editor: John Austin. Purchases mss for syndication to newspapers in San Francisco, Philadelphia, Detroit, Montreal, London, and Sydney, etc. Query or submit complete ms. Previously published submissions OK, if published in the US and Canada only." SASE. Reports in 4-6 weeks. Buys first rights or second serial (reprint) rights.

Needs: News items (column items concerning entertainment—motion picture—personalities and jet setters for syndicated column; 750-800 words). Also considers series of 1,500-word articles; "suggest descriptive query first." Pay negotiable. Pays on acceptance "but this is also negotiable because of delays in world market acceptance."

Tips: "Study the entertainment pages of Sunday (and daily) newspapers to see the type of specialized material we deal in. Perhaps we are different from other syndicates, but we deal with celebrities and particularly not 'I' journalism such as when 'I spoke to Cloris Leachman.' Many freelancers submit material from the 'dinner theater' and summer stock circuit of 'gossip type' items from what they have observed about the 'stars' or featured players in these productions—how they act off stage, who they romance, etc. We use this material."

INDEPENDENT NEWS ALLIANCE, 200 Park Ave., New York NY 10166. Executive Editor: Sidney Goldberg. Supplies material to leading US and Canadian newspapers, also to South America, Europe, Asia and Africa. Rights purchased vary with author and material. May buy all rights, first rights, or second serial (reprint) rights. Pays "on distribution to clients." Previously published submissions OK "on occasion." Query or submit complete ms. Reports in 2 weeks. SASE.

Nonfiction and Photos: In the market for background, investigative, interpretive and news features. Life style, trends, the arts, national issues that affect individuals and neighborhoods. The news element must be strong and purchases are generally made only from experienced, working journalists and authors. Wants timely news features of national interest that do not duplicate other coverage but add to it, interpret it, etc. Wants first-class nonfiction suitable for feature development. The story must be aimed at newspapers, must be self-explanatory, factual and well condensed. It must add measurably to the public's information or understanding of the subject, or be genuinely entertaining. Broad general interest is the key to success here. Length: 500 to 1,500 words, on occasion longer. Rarely buys columns. Looking for good 1-shots and good series of 2 to 7 articles. Where opinions are given, the author should advise, for publication, his qualifications to comment on specialized subjects. The news must be exclusive to be considered at all. Rate varies depending on interest and news value. Average payment is $150, but will go considerably higher for promotable copy. Buys 8x10 glossy photos when needed to illustrate story, pays $25-50.

INTERNATIONAL EDITORIAL SERVICES/NEWSWEEK, INC., 444 Madison Ave., New York NY 10022. Vice President: R.J. Melvin. Offers on speculation to listing of *Newsweek* worldwide associates first rights or second serial (reprint) rights. Offers 50 to 100 features, over 1,000 photos and graphics a year. Will consider photocopied submissions. Query. Reports in 3 months. SASE.

Nonfiction and Photos: News items, backgrounders, personalities in the news. News-related features suitable for international syndication. No investigation pieces. Prefers approximately 1,200 words for features. Pays 50% on publication. Photos purchased with features. Pays $35-100 for b&w if purchased separately.

INTERPRESS OF LONDON AND NEW YORK, 400 Madison Ave., New York NY 10017, (212)832-2839. Editor: Jeffrey Blyth. Buys British and European rights mostly, but can handle world rights. Will consider photocopied submissions. Previously published submissions OK "for overseas." Query or submit complete ms. Pays on publication, or agreement of sale. Reports immediately or as soon as practicable. SASE.

Nonfiction and Photos: "Unusual stories and photos for British and European press. Picture stories, for example, on such 'Americana' as a five-year-old evangelist; the 800-pound 'con-man'; the nude-male calendar; tallest girl in the world; interviews with pop celebrities such as Yoko Ono, Bob Dylan, Sen. Kennedy, Margaret Trudeau, Priscilla Presley, Cheryl Tiegs, Liza Minelli; cult subjects such as voodoo, college fads, anything amusing or offbeat. Extracts from books such as Earl Wilson's *Show Business Laid Bare*, inside-Hollywood type series ('Secrets of the Stuntmen,' 'My Life with Racquel Welch'). Real life adventure dramas ('Three Months in an Open Boat,' 'The Air Crash Cannibals of the Andes'). No length limits—short or long, but not too long. Payment varies; depending on whether material is original, or world rights. Pay top rates, up to several thousand dollars, for exclusive material. Photos purchased with or without features. Captions required. Standard size prints. Pay $50 to $100, but no limit on exclusive material."

KING FEATURES SYNDICATE, INC., 235 E. 45th St., New York NY 10017. (212)682-5600. Editor: Allan Priaulx. "We have about 55 regular text features, and add one to five new features annually." Syndicates material to newspapers. Submit "brief cover letter with samples of feature proposals." Previously published submissions OK. SASE. Reports in 2-3 weeks. Buys all rights.
Needs: Newspaper features and columns. Will consider article series. No travel, wine or general humor columns; restaurant, theater or movie reviews; or fad-oriented subjects. Pays "revenue commission percentage" or flat fee. Special single article opportunity is *Sunday Woman* a weekly supplement distributed nationally. Buys one-time rights to articles on beauty, health, grooming, fashion, coping, money management for women, career guidance etc. Query with SASE Elaine Liner, associate editor.
Tips: "Be brief, thoughtful and offer some evidence that the feature proposal is viable. Read newspapers—lots of them in big and small markets—to find out what already is out there. Don't try to buck established columns which newspapers would be reluctant to replace with new and untried material."

KNOWLEDGE NEWS & FEATURES SYNDICATE, Kenilworth IL 60043. (312)256-0059. Executive Editor: Dr. Whitt N. Schultz. Rights purchased vary with author and material. Will consider photocopied submissions. Previously published submissions OK.
Business Features, Photos and Nonfiction: News items; humor; fillers; business, knowledge and education articles; "success stories." Payment negotiable. Photos purchased with features and also on assignment. Captions required. Buys 8x10 glossy photos. Payment negotiable.
Fillers: Short humorous articles. "We like definitions, epigrams, puns, etc." Pays negotiable fee.
Tips: "Clear, crisp, concise, cogent writing—easy to read—Open—Spotlight success, inspiration; positive news features. Material should be typed and submitted on standard size paper. Please leave 3 spaces between each item. Unused material will be returned to the writer within a few days if SASE is enclosed. We do not send rejection slips. Please do not send us any material that has been sent to other publications. If SASE is not enclosed, all material will be destroyed after being considered except for items purchased."

MIKE LeFAN FEATURES, 1802 S. 13th, Temple TX 76501. Editor: Mike LeFan. Buys "about 50 items annually. Much of the outside material used is submitted by readers of my features, but I'm quite willing to pay for suitable pieces from freelancers. My syndicated features appear in both magazines, and in daily and weekly newspapers." Submit complete ms; 1 item to a page. SASE. Reports in 3 weeks. Material is not copyrighted.
Needs: Fillers (practical, usable items on how people can get more for their money, up to 250 words). "An acceptable filler tells the average man or woman how to get more for their money on food, utilities, travel, clothing, auto, household needs, entertainment, or any other area of daily life, but the ideas must be practical and useful. There are no bylines as such, but items will be credited within the text of a particular column to identify the writer." Pays $2/filler. Currently syndicates More For Your Money (a weekly column) and More For Your Money Fillers to a readership of about 400,000.
Tips: "I do not want to see general household tips. All the items must relate to column's theme—more for your money."

MEDIA PRESS INTERNATIONAL, 6464 Sunset Blvd., Suite 735, Hollywood CA 90028. (213)463-3984. Features Editor: Kathe Brockman. Buys 360 mss/year. (Does not purchase material outright; works on a commission basis). Distributes to over 1,500 magazines in Europe and Asia. SASE. Reports in 3 weeks. Buys international rights. "Only photojournalist guidelines available."
Needs: Magazine features (human interest and celebrity features). Buys one-shot features. "Human interest and celebrity material. We syndicate material for high quality photojournalists on a 50-50 basis. Use mostly originals, will consider reprints if rights revert back to photojournalist." Query with clips of published work or submit complete ms with photos. "Local photojournalists are welcome to visit the office and look over the *MPI* portfolio." Pays 50% commission.
Photos: No additional payment for photos accepted with ms.
Tips: "The combination of excellent visuals and text sells our features. International publications look to us for material they cannot obtain in their own countries."

NATIONAL CATHOLIC NEWS SERVICE, 1312 Massachusetts Ave. NW, Washington DC 20005. Editor: Richard W. Daw. "We are served by a number of stringers as well as freelancers. We provide a daily service and have a fairly constant market. Inquiries are welcomed, but they should be both brief and precise. Too many inquiries are coy and/or vague. Will consider photocopied submissions." Pays on publication. Reports in 4-5 weeks. SASE.

Nonfiction: Short news and feature items of religious or social interest, particularly items with a Catholic thrust. Buys single features and article series. Feature examples: FCC plagued by letters about non-existent petition from atheist; clown tours America as God's Good Humor Man; bishop lives in house heated 20 degrees cooler than White House. Series examples: Moral implications and religious involvement in capital punishment issue; Catholic schools and integration. Contracts for columns: "This is a highly competitive market and we are extremely selective. Our columns range from labor concerns to the liturgy." Length for single features: no minimum, maximum of 800 words. Article series: maximum of 3 parts, about 700 words each. Columns: open in length; generally, the shorter the better. Generally pays a maximum of 5¢ a word for news and feature copy. Buys book reviews at a rate of 3¢ a word for a maximum of 500 words. Does not buy *unsolicited* reviews, but welcomes queries. "We market primarily to more than 100 Catholic weekly newspapers. We also serve foreign Catholic agencies and U.S. Catholic weekly newspapers."

Photos: Purchased with or without features. Captions helpful but not required. News and feature photos of interest to Catholic periodicals. Also other religions, family, humor and seasonal. No churches, travel, scenes, animals or flowers. "We buy 1,000 photos a year. Pay $20/b&w 8x10 only. SASE. Samples must accompany queries for assignment. Pay negotiable."

NATIONAL FEATURES SYNDICATE, INC., c/o National Medical Enterprises Inc., 11620 Wilshire Blvd., 10th floor, Los Angeles CA 90025. Executive Editor: Fred Rosenblatt. "Subscribers are the media, especially if involved in the health industry." Submit complete ms. SASE. Reports in 2 weeks. Buys first North American serial rights. Writer's guidelines for SASE.
Needs: Newspaper features and news items concerning the health industry. Will consider single features and articles series. Pays $5-100.

NEW YORK TIMES SYNDICATION SALES CORP., 200 Park Ave., New York NY 10017. (212)972-1070. Acquistions Editor of Special Features: Alexandra Wells. Syndicates "about one book or feature per week primarily in newspapers." Also included in foreign newspapers and magazines. Prefers world rights but often buys North American second serial rights; for books, "first, second or both" rights.
Needs: Wants magazine and newspaper features; magazine and newspaper columns; and book series. Recently ran the Kissinger memoirs and Norman Mailer's *The Executioner's Song*. Usually offers the author a 50-50 split of the profit. Total purchase price includes payment for photos. "If you don't have to include photos, don't."

NEWS FLASH INTERNATIONAL, INC., 508 Atlanta Ave., North Massapequa NY 11758. Editor: Jackson B. Pokress. Supplies material to Observer newspapers and overseas publications. "Contact editor prior to submission to allow for space if article is newsworthy." Photocopied submissions OK. Pays on publication. SASE.
Nonfiction: "We have been supplying a 'ready-for-camera' sports page (tabloid size) complete with column and current sports photos on a weekly basis to many newspapers on Long Island as well as pictures and written material to publications in England and Canada. Payment for assignments is based on the article. It may vary. Payments vary from $20 for a feature of 800 words. Our sports stories feature in-depth reporting as well as book reviews on this subject. We are always in the market for good photos, sharp and clear, action photos of boxing, wrestling, football, baseball and hockey. We cover all major league ball parks during the baseball and football seasons. We are accredited to the Mets, Yanks, Jets and Giants. During the winter we cover basketball and hockey and all sports events at the Nassau Coliseum."
Photos: Purchased on assignment; captions required. Uses "good quality 8x10 b&w glossy prints; good choice of angles and lenses." Pays $7.50 minimum for b&w photos.
Tips: "Submit articles, which are fresh in their approach, on a regular basis. Articles should have a hard-hitting approach and plenty of quotes and short terse sentences."

NEWSPAPER ENTERPRISE ASSOCIATION, INC., 200 Park Ave., New York NY 10166. (212)557-5870. Vice-president and Editorial Director: David Hendin. Assistant Managing Editor: M.E. Barbara McDowell. Syndicates material to newspapers. Query or submit complete ms. SASE. Reports in 3 weeks. Buys all rights.
Needs: Newspaper columns and features, fillers and comics. Will consider article series. No "fluff" or "fillers." Pay varies according to purchase. Photos should accompany all submissions; no additional payment.

NUMISMATIC INFORMATION SERVICE, Rossway Rd., Rt. 4, Box 237A, Pleasant Valley NY 12569. Editor: Barbara White. Buys 5 features/year. Query. SASE. Reports in 1-2 weeks. Buys all rights.

Needs: Newspaper columns (anything related to numismatics and philately, particularly the technical aspects of the avocations); news items (relative to the world of coin and stamp collecting); and fillers (on individual coins or stamps, or the various aspects of the hobbies). No fiction or get rich schemes. Pays $5/500 word article; 50¢ additional payment for b&w photos accepted with ms.

OCEANIC PRESS SERVICE, Box 4158, 4717 Laurel Canyon Blvd., North Hollywood CA 91607. (213)980-6600. Editor: John Taylor. Buys from 12-15 writers annually, "using their published work" for use in magazines, newspapers or books. Query with clips of published work. SASE. Reports in 3 weeks. Buys all rights, or second serial (reprint) rights. Writer's guidelines $1.
Needs: "We like authors and cartoonists but, for our mutual benefit, they must fit into our editorial policies. The following list will give an idea of the kind of materials we want: interviews or profiles (world figures only); recipes, with color transparencies or b&w pictures; home building and home decoration features with photos; hairstyle features with photos; interviews with movie and TV stars with photos; current books to be sold for translation to foreign markets: mysteries, biographies, how to do, self improvement, westerns, science fiction, romance, psychological, and gothic novels; features on family relations, modern women, heroism, and ecology; features on water sports, with color transparencies; and newspaper columns with illustrations. We are always happy to obtain reprint rights, especially book excerpts or serializations. Payment is outright or on a 50/50 basis. We take care of foreign language translations."

THE REGISTER AND TRIBUNE SYNDICATE, INC., 715 Locust St., Des Moines IA 50304. President: Dennis R. Allen. Buys material for syndication in newspapers. Submit complete ms. SASE. Photocopied submissions preferred. Reports in 6 weeks. Buys all rights.
Needs: News items (nonfiction); and photos (purchased with written material). Buys article series "from 500-700 words on current topics such as the metric system, motorcycles, self-improvement programs, seasonal series for Christmas and Easter. Most submissions require at least 6-weeks worth of column copy or artwork in near finish form. Don't send original work." Pays in royalties. Pays on publication.
Tips: "Work must have pulse for what is occuring now and to come—too often submissions reflect past popular trends. Read newspapers to see what they are currently running, the styles and formats they like . . . originality in thought and the complete execution of these ideas in sample material form is essential."

RELIGIOUS NEWS SERVICE, 43 W. 57th St., New York NY 10019. Editor and Director: Gerald Renner. Supplies material to "secular press, religious press of all denominations, radio and TV stations." Previously published submissions OK. SASE for return of submissions.
Nonfiction and Photos: "Good news stories on important newsworthy developments. Religious news." Will buy single features "if they have news pegs. Most of our article series are produced by our own staff." Length: 200-1,000 words. Pays 3¢ a word. Photos purchased with and without features and on assignment; captions required. Uses b&w glossy prints, preferably 8x10. Pays $12.50 minimum.

SCI/SINGER COMMUNICATIONS, INC., 3164 W. Tyler Ave., Anaheim CA 92801. (714)527-5650. Acting President: Natalie Carlton. Syndicates to newspapers, magazines, and book publishers. Query with clips of published work. SASE. Reports in 3 weeks. Buys all rights, or domestic and foreign reprint rights. Writer's guidelines $1.
Needs: Magazine and newspaper features with international interest; fiction slanted to women readers; and features (juvenile puzzles, interviews, mazes, games, and how-to's). Will consider article series if previously published. Especially needs "sophisticated short stories for women's magazines for the German, Dutch and Scandinavian markets" and "out of print romance books to be reissued for publication in both United States and foreign countries." Pays 50% on features to author. Currently syndicates *Solv-A-Crime*, by A.C. Gordon (mystery series); and *Celebrities Speak*, by J. Finletter (interviews). Serializes books (romance, Western, mysteries, war, historical romance, doctor-nurse books). Pays author 90% for US book rights and 80% for foreign rights. Purchasing agent for German, Australian, Norwegian and Mexican publishers.

SPOTLIGHT INTERNATIONAL, 346 W. 15th St., New York NY 10011. (212)929-8266. President/Executive Editor: Bert Goodman. Fifty features *with photos* are accepted for syndication annually for magazines. Submit query or complete ms and sample photos with SASE. Reports in 3 wks. Buys all rights, first North American, and second and third domestic and foreign reprint rights.
Needs: Magazine features with b&w or color slides (upbeat, compelling or controversial stories—need contemporary, celebrity, supernatural, rock 'n roll, erotic, investigative, entertainment, "real people"/"that's incredible!"-type human-interest stories with good photos). 1,000-3,000 words.

"We'll syndicate short fillers if accompanied by a strong set of pictures." Purchase single features; no article series. Pays author's percentage (1st rights: 65-75% and 2nd rights: 50%), and $50-100 flat rate. Pays $20-50 for photos. Currently syndicates *Vacations In Space, The Wizards of Hollywood, Blondie, Nude Mud Wrestling, Bob Marx Treasure Diver, Marlon Brando,* and *Alligator Farm.*

TEENAGE CORNER, INC., 70-540 Gardenia Ct., Rancho Mirage CA 92270. President: David J. Lavin. Buys 122 items/year for use in newspapers. Submit complete ms. Reports in 1 week. Material is not copyrighted.
Needs: 500-word newspaper features. Pays $25.

TRANS-WORLD NEWS SERVICE, INC., Box 66, Denver CO 80201. (303)831-0897. President/Managing Editor: C.D. Fleet, Jr. SASE. Reports immediately.
Needs: Newspaper features (400-750 words, prefers balanced articles); newspaper columns (400-800 words; most any subject with continuity); radio broadcast material (recorded programs for syndication or scripts 2-5 minutes in length). Offers syndication contract. "No single articles instead of columns."

UNITED FEATURE SYNDICATE, 200 Park Ave., New York NY 10017. Editorial Director: David Hendin. Executive Editor: Sidney Goldberg. Supplies material to newspapers throughout the world. Will handle copyrighted material. Buys 25 to 50 series per year, preferably 3 to 7 articles (world rights preferred). Buys first and/or second rights to book serializations. Query with outline. Reports in 3 weeks. SASE.
Nonfiction, Comic Strips and Puzzles: News, features, series, columns, comic strips, puzzles. Current columnists include Jack Anderson, Marquis Childs, Ben Wattenberg, Martin Sloane, Barbara Gibbons. Comic strips include *Peanuts, Nancy, Garfield, Drabble* and *Ben Swift.* Rates negotiable for one-shot purchases. Standard syndication contracts are offered for columns and comic strips.

UNITED PRESS INTERNATIONAL (UPI), 220 E. 42nd St., New York NY 10017. Editor-in-Chief: H.L. Stevenson. "We seldom, if ever, accept material from outside our own ranks."

U.S. NEW SERVICE, Box 483, Washington DC 20044. Bureau Chief: Dr. Walter Fish. Buys all rights. May handle copyrighted material. May not return rejected material. SASE for return of submissions.
Nonfiction, Humor, Fiction, Photos, Fillers: Buys single features and column ideas. Length varies. Payment varies. 8x10 single weight glossy prints purchased with features, without features, and on assignment. Captions required.

UNIVERSAL PRESS SYNDICATE, 4400 Johnson Dr., Fairway KS 66205. Buys syndication rights. Reports normally in 1 month. Returned postage required.
Nonfiction: Looking for features—columns for daily and weekly newspapers. "Any material suitable for syndication in daily newspapers." Currently handling the following: *Doonesbury* by G.B. Trudeau, Garry Wills column, *Dear Abby* etc. Payment varies according to contract.

WORLD-WIDE NEWS BUREAU, 309 Varick St., Jersey City NJ 07302. Editor: Arejas Vitkauskas. SASE for return of submissions.
Nonfiction: "Our multiple writeups (separate, and in our weekly columns) start in greater New York publications, then go simultaneously all over the US and all over the world where English is printed. News from authors, literary agents or publishers on books planned, or ready or published. Anything from poetry and children's books, to space technology textbooks. We cover over eighty different trade fields." No complete book mss.

ZODIAC NEWS SERVICE, 54 Mint St., #510, San Francisco CA 94103. (415)956-3555. Editor: Jon Newhall. "We purchase about 1,000 pieces of material from a loose network of 100+ stringers in the United States and Canada, for radio use mainly, with a few magazines, newspapers, and TV stations." Submissions returned "if specifically requested. We assume, however, that SASEs are for payment, not return of submissions, so please note otherwise." Previously published submissions OK but in condensed form. Buys first North American serial rights; "we want exclusive rights for 48 hours." Writer's guidelines for SASE.
Needs: "We are a reliable source of up-to-date news which is often ignored, overlooked, or misinterpreted by the major wire services. Our clients are primarily radio stations, ranging from progressive FM and college radio outlets to top-40 and all-news formats. Although we are based in San Francisco, our coverage is international, and so we are looking for stringers worldwide. If you

have story leads, ideas or news items that can be reported in a radio format (i.e., within the frustrating confines of 200 words), please telephone or mail them to our San Francisco office. We pay $10 for each story lead or item used. Most of our successful stringers receive regular payments by spotting ZNS-type items, which are often overlooked by the major wire services in daily or weekly publications."

Tips: "Scan all the newspapers, magazines and other publications at your disposal, clipping out and sending to ZNS all items that might conceivably be of particular interest to younger audiences (i.e., 15-35). The greater the number of submissions, the more likely that at least some will be accepted."

Trade, Technical, and Professional Journals

The trade of many freelance writers is writing for trade journals and other professional publications. Yet, these magazines are often overlooked by the writer looking for a chance to be published in "glamorous" consumer publications. But what the trade journals lack in glamour, they make up for with acceptance letters.

A professional submission to a trade journal means a solid, accurate, in-depth approach to writing. Although some trade publications are probably too specialized for the general writer, others are open to the freelancer who can grasp a subject quickly, and write clearly and tightly.

Most trade journals appeal to one of three audiences: 1) *retailers*, who are interested in unusual store displays, successful sales campaigns, and other ways of making money or managing businesses efficiently (included in this group are businesspeople who perform *services*); 2) *manufacturers*, who want stories on solving industry problems, equipment reports, and other such coverage; and 3) *professionals and industry experts*, interested in technical and other developments. Whatever its audience, the trade journal has one purpose: to help its reader to do his job better. These publications are read for profit, not pleasure. Editors want to tell their readers about trends and solutions to problems, and offer advice on how to conduct business more profitably.

For solid tips on approaching magazines in general, consult the introduction to the Consumer Publications section, but remember that writing for trade publications demands more specialization than does writing for consumer magazines.

Of course, a nonspecialist writer who does careful research can sell to these magazines. In fact, such a writer can often take technical material and communicate it in layman's terms, avoiding the jargon a specialist might fall into. Everyday language and a touch of humor—too often lacking in manuscripts for trade journals—are needed by editors.

Most of the magazines listed here want to see queries. A few will accept complete manuscripts, but because of the specialized nature of the material, a query will generally save time and effort.

One way to break into this market is by regularly submitting short, informative items. Prove yourself to the editor by tracking down news items or information the magazine needs for another story. Then, after the editor sees you are reliable and interested in doing a good job, he may trust you with a larger story. Reliability is important to editors.

Many trade and professional publications have special theme issues or year-end issues. Ask for a copy of the magazine's editorial schedule, if available, and tailor your submissions to special issues.

Freelancing to trade journals means helping magazine readers run their businesses. Minding the other guy's business can be good business for you.

Accounting

CA MAGAZINE, 250 Bloor St., E., Toronto, Ontario, Canada M4W 1G5. Editor: Nelson Luscombe. Monthly magazine for accountants and financial managers. Circ. 45,000. Pays on publication for the article's copyright.
Nonfiction: Accounting, business, management and taxation. "We accept whatever is relevant to our readership, no matter the origin as long as it meets our standards. No inflation accounting articles." Length: 3,000-5,000 words. Pays $100.

CASHFLOW, Coordinated Capital Resources, Inc., 1807 Glenview Rd., Glenview IL 60025. (312)998-6688. Managing Editor: Hellena Smejda. Magazine published 10 times/year, covering treasury professionals in organizations or "professionals who are called upon to fulfill corporate treasury functions." Almost half hold the 'Treasurer' title and the remainder are either directly or peripherally involved in treasury activities. A good number hold CPAs or other professional designations. Estab. 1980. Circ. 16,000. Pays on publication. Byline sometimes given. Pays $100 or 25% kill fee. Buys negotiable rights. Submit seasonal/holiday material 3 months in advance. SASE. Reports in 2 weeks on queries; 1 month on mss. Sample copy $4; free writer's guidelines.
Nonfiction: Accepts no material "without a query first." Buys 5 mss/year. Query or query with clips of published work. Length: 2,500-3,000 words. Pays variable fee.
Photos: Reviews b&w and color contact sheets, negatives, transparencies and prints. Model release and identification of subjects required.

CGA MAGAZINE, 7th Floor, 1176 W. Georgia St., Vancouver, British Columbia, Canada V6E 4A2. (604)681-3538. 25% freelance written. For accountants and financial managers. Magazine published 9 times/year; 44 pages. Circ. 28,000. Pays on acceptance. Buys one-time rights. Byline given. Phone queries OK. Simultaneous and photocopied submissions OK. SASE. Reports in 2-4 weeks. Free sample copy and writer's guidelines.
Nonfiction: "Accounting and financial subjects of interest to highly qualified professional accountants as opposed to accountants in public practice. All submissions must be relevant to Canadian accounting. All material must be of top professional quality, but at the same time written simply and interestingly." How-to; humor; informational; personal experience; personal opinion; and technical. Buys 36 mss/year. Query with outline and estimate of word count. Length: 1,500-2,000 words. Pays $100-500.
Photos: State availability of photos with query. Offers no additional payment for 8x10 b&w glossy prints.

Advertising and Marketing

Trade journals for professional advertising executives, copywriters and marketing professionals are listed in this category. Those whose main interests are the advertising and marketing of specific products (such as Beverages and Bottling and Hardware) are classified under individual product categories.

AD FORUM, for Consumer Marketing Management, MIN Publishing, 75 E. 55th St., New York NY 10022. (212)888-1793. Managing Editor: Elizabeth J. Berry. Monthly magazine covering consumer marketing for "top management down through the marketing divisions of the leading 1,000 national advertisers." Estab. 1980. Circ. 6,000. Pays on publication. Byline given; "writer is listed in masthead as contributor." Pays 50% kill fee. Buys all rights; "reprints must be credited to *Ad Forum*." Submit seasonal/holiday material 3 months in advance. SASE. Reports in 1 month. Sample copy free.
Nonfiction: Profile (of a specific industry); and trend stories in lifestyles or markets management. Buys 24 mss/year. Query with clips of published work. Length: 800-1,200 words. Pays $200-500.
Photos: State availability of photos. Reviews any size b&w glossy prints. Identification of subjects required. Buys one-time rights.

ADVERTISING AGE, 740 N. Rush, Chicago IL 60611. Managing Editor: L.E. Doherty. Currently staff-produced. Includes weekly sections devoted to one topic (i.e., marketing in Southern California; agribusiness/advertising; TV syndication trends). Much of this material is done freelance—on assignment only. Pays kill fee "based on hours spent plus expenses." Byline given "except short articles or contributions to a roundup."

ADVERTISING TECHNIQUES, ADA Publishing Co., 10 E. 39th St., New York NY 10616. (212)889-6500. Managing Editor: Lawrence Oberwager. 10% freelance written. For advertising executives. Monthly magazine; 50 pages. Circ. 4,500. Pays on acceptance. Not copyrighted. Reports in 1 month. Sample copy $1.75.
Nonfiction: Articles on advertising techniques. Buys 10 mss/year. Query. Pays $25-50.

ADWEEK/WEST, 415 Shatto Place, Los Angeles CA 90020. Editor: Lee Kerry. For "people involved in advertising: media, agencies, and client organizations as well as affiliated businesses."

Weekly. Buys all rights. Pays on acceptance. Reports in 1 month. Query. SASE.
Nonfiction and Photos: "Advertising in the West. Not particularly interested in success stories. We want articles by experts in advertising, marketing, communications." Length: 1,000-1,750 words. Pays $100. Photos purchased with mss.

AMERICAN DEMOGRAPHICS, American Demographics, Inc., Box 68, Ithaca NY 14850. (607)273-6343. Editor: Bryant Robey. Managing Editor: F. Jill Charboneau. For private business executives, market researchers, media and communications people, public policymakers and those in academic world. Monthly magazine; 48 pages. Estab. 1979. Circ. 2,200. Pays on publication. Copyrighted. Buys all rights. Phone queries OK. Submit seasonal/holiday material 5-6 months in advance. Simultaneous, photocopied and previously published submissions OK. SASE. Reports on queries 1 month; mss/2 months. Include self-addressed stamped postcard for return word that ms arrived safely. Sample copy $4; free writer's guidelines.
Nonfiction: General interest (on demographic trends, implications of changing demographics, profile of business using demographic data); how-to (on the use of demographic techniques, understand projections, data, apply demography to business and planning); humor (about demographers).
Columns/Departments: "We are writing departments in-house now, but would consider contributors for sources, techniques, and book reviews. Writers with ideas should call (607)273-6343, those with book review suggestions (607)277-4878.
Fillers: Clippings, anecdotes and newsbreaks. Length: 200-1,000 words. Pays $5-25.

ART DIRECTION, Advertising Trade Publications, Inc., 10 E. 39th St., New York NY 10016. (212)889-6500. Managing Editor: Laurence Oberwager. 15% freelance written. Emphasis on advertising design for art directors of ad agencies (corporate, in-plant, editorial, freelance, etc.). Monthly magazine; 100 pages. Circ. 12,000. Pays on publication. Buys one-time rights. SASE. Reports in 3 months. Sample copy $1.75.
Nonfiction: How-to articles on advertising campaigns. Pays $25 minimum.

CO-OP NEWS, Standard Rate & Data Service, 5201 Old Orchard Rd., Skokie IL 60077. (312)470-3462. Editor: Dorothy Jerome. Biweekly tabloid covering co-operative advertising for media, ad agencies, manufacturers and retailers. Estab. 1980. Circ. 5,000. Pays on publication. Byline given. Pays $50 kill fee. Buys all rights. Submit seasonal/holiday material 2 months in advance. Simultaneous, photocopied, and previously published submissions OK. SASE. Reports in 6 weeks. Free sample copy; writer's guidelines for business size SAE and 1 first class stamp.
Nonfiction: How-to (run a co-op program; increase co-op linage in print publications); interview/profile ("of a consultant or any other personality in our readership"); and photo feature (ad layouts). "We like tight, fact-filled stories." Buys 20 mss/year. Query with clips of published work. Length: 1,000 words minimum. Pays $75-200.
Photos: State availability of photos. Pays $50 maximum for b&w 8x10 glossy prints. Captions required. Buys one-time rights.
Fillers: Newsbreaks. Buys 100/year. Length: average 200 words. Pays average $25.

THE COUNSELOR MAGAZINE, Advertising Specialty Institute, NBS Bldg., 1120 Wheeler Way, Langhorne PA 19047. (215)752-4200. Editor: Charles Pahl. For executives, both distributors and suppliers, in the ad specialty industry. Monthly magazine; 250 pages. Circ. 5,000. Pays on publication. Copyrighted. Buys first rights. No phone queries. Submit seasonal/holiday material 3 months in advance. Simultaneous submissions, photocopied submissions and previously published work OK. Reports in two months.
Nonfiction: Contact: Managing Editor. How-to (promotional case histories); interview (with executives and government figures); profile (of executives); travel (business and technical industry material only). No "cutesy poems that attempt to spoof radio and TV advertising. We won't use them, so don't bother sending them." Buys 30 mss/year. Length: 1,000 words minimum. Query with samples. Pays $75-150.
Photos: State availability of photos. B&w photos only. Prefers contact sheet(s) and 5x7 prints. Offers no additional payment for photos accepted with ms. Captions and model releases required. Buys one-time rights.
Tips: "If a writer shows promise, we can modify his suggestions to suit our publication and provide leads. Writers must be willing to adapt or rewrite their material for a specific audience. If an article is suitable for 5 or 6 other publications, it's probably not suitable for us. The best way to break in is to write for *Imprint*, a quarterly publication we produce for the clients of ad specialty counselors. *Imprint* covers promotional campaigns—safety programs, trade show exhibits, traffic builders and sales incentives—all with specialty advertising tie-in."

CREATIVE SELLING, (formerly *Professional Salesman's Letter*, Januz Marketing Communications, Inc., Evergreen 41 Executive Plaza, Box 1000, Lake Forest IL 60045. President: L.R. Januz. Emphasizes professional selling techniques for "professional salesmen in industry, finance, automobiles, travel, etc.—our subscriber is the sales manager who buys bulk copies for his salesmen." Semimonthly newsletter; 4-6 pages. Circ. 3,000. Pays on publication. Buys all rights. "No submissions will be returned—will be held for permanent consideration. If the item is not used (and paid for) within one year the writer can probably figure we won't use it." Sample copy $3.50.
Nonfiction: Interview ("must be actual stories by a salesman/writer of how he/she sold the big one or cracked the difficult account). The only thing we want are 1-5 paragraphs (if it is over 5 paragraphs long we cannot use it) articles about how a salesman successfully closed a sale, or a selling technique that has resulted in selling. We have no use for any other material and will not read or return it." Buys 3-4 mss/issue. Send complete ms; doesn't answer queries. Length: 1-5 paragraphs. Pays $5-10.

DM NEWS, THE NEWSPAPER OF DIRECT MARKETING, DM News Corp., 156 E. 52nd St., New York NY 10022. (212)935-2980. Editor: Joe Fitz-Morris. Monthly tabloid about direct response marketing for users and producers of direct response marketing throughout the nation. Estab. 1979. Circ. 21,000. Pays on acceptance. Byline given. Makes work-for-hire assignments. Phone queries OK. SASE. Reports in 1 week on queries; in 2 weeks on mss.
Nonfiction: "Come up with a newsbeat scoop and check it out with the editor." Query. Pays $50-100.
Photos: Send photos with ms. Reviews 8x10 b&w glossy prints. Offers no additional payment for photos accepted with ms. Captions and model release required. Buys one-time rights.

imprint, the magazine of specialty advertising ideas, Advertising Specialty Institute, 1120 Wheeler Way, Langhorne PA 19047. (215)752-4200. Editor: Charles A. Pahl III. Managing Editor: Robin Moore. Quarterly magazine covering specialty advertising. Circ. 50,000+. Pays on acceptance. Byline given. Pays $25 kill fee. Buys one-time rights. Submit seasonal/holiday material 6 months in advance. Simultaneous queries OK. Reports in 1 month. Free sample copy.
Nonfiction: Robin Moore, articles editor. How-to (case histories of specialty advertising campaigns); and photo feature (how ad specialties are distributed in promotions). "Emphasize effective use of specialty advertising. Avoid direct-buy situations. Stress the distributor's role in promotions. No generalized pieces on print, broadcast or outdoor advertising." Buys 10-12 mss/year. Query with clips of published work. Length: 750-1,500 words. Pays $50-100.
Photos: State availability of photos. Pays $10-25 for 5x7 b&w prints. Captions, model release and identification of subjects required.
Tips: "Query with a case history suggestion and writing samples. We can provide additional leads. All articles must be specifically geared to specialty advertising (and sometimes, premium) promotions."

INCENTIVE MARKETING, Bill Communications, Inc., 633 3rd Ave., New York NY 10017. (212)986-4800. Editor: James Hogg. For buyers of merchandise and travel used in motivational promotions. Monthly magazine; 200 pages. Circ. 37,000. Pays on acceptance. Buys all rights. No byline. SASE. Reports in 2 weeks. Free sample copy and writer's guidelines.
Nonfiction: Informational, case histories. "No bank premium stories, please!" Buys 200 mss/year. Query. Length: 1,000-3,000 words. Pays $125-145.
Tips: "We need coverage in the West, the South and Chicago."

INDUSTRIAL MARKETING, Crain Communications, Inc., 708 3rd Ave., New York NY 10017. (212)986-5050. Editor: Bob Donath. Managing Editor: John A. Roberts. Monthly magazine covering the advertising, sales and promotion of industrial products and services for an audience in marketing/sales middle management and corporate top management in companies selling products and services to other businesses. Circ. 30,000. Pays on publication. Rights reserved. Submit seasonal material 3 months in advance; 1½ months in advance for spot news. SASE. Reports in 2 weeks on queries; in 3 weeks on mss. Sample copy $2.
Nonfiction: Exposé (of marketing industry); how-to (advertise, do sales management promotion, do strategy development); interview (of industrial marketing executives); opinion (on industry practices); profile; and technical (advertising/marketing practice). "No self promotion or puff pieces." Buys 5 mss/year. Query. Length: 1,000-2,000 words. Pays $50 minimum.
Photos: State availability of photos. Reviews 8x10 b&w glossy prints and color transparencies. Offers no additional payment for photos accepted with ms. Captions preferred; model release required.
Columns/Departments: Query. Length: 500-1,000 words. "Column ideas should be queried, but generally we have no need for paid freelance columnists."

Fillers: Newsbreaks. Buys 2 mss/issue. Length: 100-500 words. Pays $5 minimum/printed column inch.

MAGAZINE AGE, 225 Park Ave., New York NY 10169. (212)986-7366. Editor: Wallis Wood. Monthly magazine from advertisers and advertising agencies designed to examine how they use a wide range of publications, including consumer, business, trade, farm, etc. Estab. 1980. Circ. 39,000. Pays on acceptance. Buys all rights. Reports in 2 weeks. Free sample copy and writer's guidelines.
Nonfiction: "We are interested in magazine advertising success and failure stories. We want marketing pieces, case histories, effective use of magazine advertising and current trends." Buys 4 mss/issue. Query. Length: 3,000 words maximum. Pays $500 maximum.
Photos: Pays $25/layout for b&w photos.
Tips: "Find an unusual aspect of print advertising."

MARKETING COMMUNICATIONS, United Business Publications, Inc., 475 Park Ave., S., New York NY 10016. Editor-in-Chief: Ronnie Telzer. 70% freelance written. Emphasizes marketing and promotion. Monthly magazine; 90 pages. Circ. 27,000. Pays on publication. Buys all rights. Byline given. Submit seasonal or holiday material 2-3 months in advance. Photocopied submissions OK (if exclusive). Reports in 2 months. Sample copy $1.50; free writer's guidelines.
Nonfiction: "The preferred format for feature articles is the case history approach to solving marketing problems. Critical evaluations of market planning, premium and incentive programs, point-of-purchase displays, direct mail campaigns, dealer/distributor meetings, media advertising, and sales promotion tools and techniques are particularly relevant." How-to articles (develop successful product campaigns); informational (marketing case histories); personal opinion (guest editorials by marketing executives); profiles (on a given industry, i.e., tobacco, razors, food); technical articles (technology updates on a field of interest to marketing people). Buys 7 mss/issue. Length: 750-1,250 words. Pays $75-300.
Photos: Prefers 8x10 b&w glossies with mss, or 2¼x2¼ color transparencies; other formats acceptable. Submit prints and transparencies. Captions required. No additional payment.
Tips: "Read our magazine and understand that we only cover major campaigns and corporations. Make specific suggestions and enclose clip samples that are appropriate and well-written."

TELEPHONE MARKETING REPORT, 3-D, 200 S. Roberts Rd., Rosemont PA 19010. (215)525-2069. Editor: Jim Atkins. Monthly newsletter about telecommunication and phone marketing for companies that have an 800 number, use direct response or sell by phone. Estab. 1979. Circ. 3,000. Pays on publication. Buys one-time rights. Phone queries OK. Simultaneous, photocopied and previously published submissions OK. SASE. Reports in 2 weeks. Sample copy $1.
Nonfiction: Interview, new product, technical, and how-to sell by phone. Buys 36 mss/year. Query. Length: 10-1,000 words. Pays 10¢/word.
Tips: "Watch local newspapers. When you see some company doing phone marketing, or doing direct response marketing, call them and see if they use the telephone in marketing. Do a short interview and send me the article. The article must show how to increase sales with the telephone, or at least cut costs."

VISUAL MERCHANDISING, S.T. Publications, 407 Gilbert Ave., Cincinnati OH 45202. Editor: Pamela Gramke. Emphasizes store design and display. Monthly magazine; 72 pages. Circ. 10,000. Pays on publication. Simultaneous and previously published submissions OK. SASE. Reports in 1 month.
Nonfiction: Exposé; how-to (display); informational (store design, construction, merchandise display); interview (display directors and shop owners); profile (new and remodeled stores); new product; photo feature (window display); technical (store lighting, carpet, wallcoverings, fixtures). Buys 24 mss a year. Query or submit complete ms. Length: 500-3,000 words. Pays $50-200.
Photos: Purchased with accompanying ms or on assignment.
Tips: "Be fashion and design conscious and reflect that in the article. Submit finished mss with photos always. Look for stories on department and specialty store visual merchandisers (profiles, methods, views on the industry, sales promotions and new store design or remodels)."

ZIP MAGAZINE, North American Publishing, 545 Madison Ave., New York NY 10011. (212)371-4100. Editor: Ray Lewis. Emphasizes marketing, list selection and testing, circulation, communications, and direct mail/mailing systems for mail-oriented professionals in business, industry and direct marketing. Typical articles published recently were on marketing to children; improved business-to-business communications, and justifying mailroom equipment purchases in a tight economy. Some ideas they would be interested in are "Fufure of Communications in General," mail-order, fund raising, publication mail programs, and articles dealing with mail

handling/processing. Interested in freelance stories on equipment and methods used to mail, process mail, transfer names onto and out of computers, labeling and packaging. Published 9 times/year; 88 pages. Circ. 37,500. Pays on publication in some cases, acceptance in others. Copyrighted. Rights purchased vary. Phone queries OK. Simultaneous, photocopied and previously published submissions OK. Reports in 2 weeks. Free sample copy.
Nonfiction: General interest (about magazine circulation or direct-mail stories); how-to: (improve mailroom operation, direct-marketing case histories); interview, profile and photo features should be about mail-oriented executives and professionals. "We are not interested in personal opinion or experience articles." Buys 4 mss/issue. Query or send complete ms. Length: 500-1,000 words. Pays $100-200.
Photos: State availability of photos or send with ms. Accepts only b&w photos and prefers contact sheet and 4x5 glossy prints. Pays $20-100. Captions preferred. Buys one-time rights.

Agricultural Equipment and Supplies

CUSTOM APPLICATOR, Little Publications, 6263 Poplar Ave., Suite 540, Memphis TN 38119. Editor: Tom Griffin. For "firms that sell and custom apply agricultural chemicals." Circ. 17,000. Buys all rights. Pays on publication. "Query is best. The editor can help you develop the story line regarding our specific needs." SASE.
Nonfiction and Photos: "We are looking for articles on custom application firms telling others how to better perform jobs of chemical application, develop new customers, handle credit, etc. Lack of a good idea or usable information will bring a rejection." Length: 1,000-1,200 words "with 3 or 4 b&w glossy prints." Pays 15¢/word.

FARM SUPPLIER, Watt Publishing Co., Sandstone Bldg., Mount Morris IL 61054. (815)734-4171. Editor-in-Chief: Jim Klatt. For retail farm supply dealers and managers over the US. Monthly magazine; 64 pages. Circ. 20,000. Pays on acceptance. Buys all rights in competitive farm supply fields. Byline given. Phone queries OK. Submit seasonal material or query 2 months in advance. SASE. Reports in 2 weeks.
Nonfiction: How-to; informational; interview; new product; and photo feature. "Articles emphasizing product news, and how new product developments have been profitably resold or successfully used. No material on successful farm dealers, particularly involving custom application, fertilizer, herbicides, etc." Buys 20 mss/year. Query. Length: 300-1,500 words. Pays $30-125. "Longer articles must include photos, charts, etc."
Photos: Purchased with accompanying ms. Submit 5x7 or 8x10 b&w prints; 35mm or larger color transparencies. Total purchase price for a ms includes payment for photos.
Tips: "Because of a constantly changing industry, *FS* attempts to work only two months in advance. Freelancers should slant stories to each season in the farm industry—examples: herbicides in January-March, application equipment in September—and should provide vertical color photos whenever possible with longer features."

Architecture

Journals in this category edit for architects and city planners whose primary concern is the design of buildings and urban environments. Those that emphasize choice of materials, structural details, and methods of constructing buildings are classified in the Construction and Contracting category.

PROGRESSIVE ARCHITECTURE, 600 Summer St., Stamford CT 06904. Editor: John M. Dixon. Monthly. Buys first-time rights for use in architectural press. Pays on publication. SASE.
Nonfiction and Photos: "Articles of technical professional interest devoted to architecture, interior design, and urban design; planning and illustrated by photographs and architectural drawings. Also use technical articles, which are prepared by technical authorities and would be beyond the scope of the lay writer. Practically all the material is professional, and most of it is prepared by writers in the field who are approached by the magazine for material." Pays $50-$250. Buys one-time reproduction rights to b&w and color photos.

Auto and Truck

The journals below aim at automobile and truck dealers, service department personnel, or fleet operators. Publications for highway planners and traffic control experts are classified in the Government and Public Service category.

AMERICAN TRUCKER MAGAZINE, MTN Publications, Box 6391, San Bernardino CA 92412. (714)889-1167. Co-Publishers: Bud Feldkamp and Steve Krieger. Senior Editor: K.C. Richardson. Pays within 30 days of publication. "First time rights requested." Monthly magazine for professional truck drivers, owners, management and other trucking personnel. Articles, fillers and other materials should be generally conservative and of particular interest to the readership, of an informative or entertaining nature relating to the trucking industry. Circ. 71,000. Phone queries OK. Submit seasonal/holiday material 3 months in advance. SASE. Reports in 3 weeks. Free sample copy and writer's guidelines.
Nonfiction: "Articles directed to professional truck drivers, owner-operators, company drivers, fleets and management, with the intention of presenting a realistic reflection of truckers, while promoting a positive image. General and human interest, historical, nostalgia, humorous, travel. Short reporting-type articles should be at least 450 words in length and feature copy items to 2,500 words." Buys 120 articles/year. Pays standard column inch rate.
Photos: State availability of photos or send captioned photos with ms. Model release required.
Fiction: Humorous material of general interest to the specific readership. Query. Length: 1,200-2,500 words. Pays standard column inch rate.
Fillers: Jokes and short humor. Length: 50-500 words. Pays standard column inch rate.

AUTO LAUNDRY NEWS, Columbia Communications, 370 Lexington Ave., New York NY 10017. (212)532-9290. Editor-in-Chief: Ralph Monti. For sophisticated carwash operators. Monthly magazine; 52 pages. Circ. 18,000. Pays on publication. Buys all rights. Phone queries OK. Submit seasonal/holiday material 60 days in advance. SASE. Reports in 4 weeks. Free sample copy.
Nonfiction: How-to; historical; humor; informational; new product; nostalgia; personal experience; technical; interviews; photo features; and profiles. Buys 40 mss/year. Query. Length: 1,000-2,000 words. Pays $75-175.
Tips: "Read the magazine; notice its style and come up with something interesting to the industry. Foremost, the writer has to know the industry."

AUTOMOTIVE BOOSTER OF CALIFORNIA, Box 765, LaCanada CA 91011. (213)790-6554. Editor: Don McAnally. 3% freelance written. For members of Automotive Booster clubs, automotive warehouse distributors and automotive parts jobbers in California. Monthly. Circ. 4,000. Not copyrighted. Byline given. Pays on publication. Submit complete ms. SASE.
Nonfiction and Photos: Will look at short articles and pictures about successes of automotive parts outlets in California. Also can use personnel assignments for automotive parts people in California. Pays $1/column inch (about 2¢/word); $5 for b&w photos used with mss.

AUTOMOTIVE MARKETER, 109 Vanderhoof Ave., Suite 101, Toronto, Ontario, Canada M4G 2JR. Editor: Dick Nolan, Quarterly magazine for "big mass-marketing chains (e.g., Canadian Tire, K-Mart, etc.), specialty chains (e.g., Midas Muffler), tire chains, car dealerships, performance distributors and oil companies." Circ. 10,000. Pays on acceptance. Buys first North American rights. SAE and International Reply Coupons.
Nonfiction: "We're looking for lively features that stress the merchandising aspects of the business. This could include stories on US firms, e.g., Montgomery Ward. No vague how-to features." Query with letter indicating "a detailed knowledge of the automotive aftermarket, American or Canadian." Length: 600-1,500 words. Pays $150-200.
Tips: "Know retailing per se. Learn as much as possible about the Canadian aftermarket, i.e., how parts are sold and distributed in Canada, the U.S.-Canadian Auto Pact. Visit an auto department in a chain store or a service bar and learn how it works. Read back issues of *AM* in a library; get a feel for the trends and the problems. Concentrate on American companies."

AUTOMOTIVE REBUILDER MAGAZINE, Babcox Publications, Inc., 11 S. Forge St., Akron OH 44304. (216)535-6117. Editor-in-Chief: Andrew J. Doherty. Associate Editor: David Champion. Emphasizes the automotive and heavy duty mechanical/parts rebuilding industry and jobber machine shops. Monthly magazine: 108 pages. Circ. 17,000. Pays on publication. Buys all rights. Phone queries OK. Submit seasonal/holiday material 6 weeks in advance of issue date.

Simultaneous, photocopied and previously published submissions OK. SASE. Reports in 2 weeks. Free sample copy.

Nonfiction: "How-to (technical writing); humor (we particularly like humor, must be relevant to rebuilders); historical (historical automotive); inspirational (concentrate on how a rebuilder overcomes disaster or personal handicap); interview (concentrate on growth or success stories); nostalgia (only if it applies to rebuilding); personal experience (experiences with rebuilding); personal opinion (comment on legislation affecting rebuilders); photo feature (on machine shops; try to get people in photos, we want photojournalism, not photo illustration); profile (about individual rebuilder; perhaps the small rebuilder); technical (you must know what you're talking about, rebuilders don't just fall off Christmas trees) and articles on regulation at the state and local level (conservation of resources, air and water pollution)." Buys 8 mss/year. Query. Length: 500-1,500 words. Pays 4-6¢/word.

Columns & Departments: People (profile or close-up of industry figures welcome); Tech Notes (this entails technical how-to writing); new product ("we generally do this ourselves"); and The Forum Guest (opinions on current events relevant to rebuilders). Buys 1 ms/year. Query. Length: 200-1,500 words. Pays 4-6¢/word. Open to suggestions for columns/departments.

THE BATTERY MAN, Independent Battery Manufacturers Association, Inc., 100 Larchwood Dr., Largo FL 33540. (813)586-1409. Editor: Celwyn E. Hopkins. Emphasizes SLI battery manufacture, applications, new developments. For battery manufacturers and retailers (garage owners, servicemen, fleet owners, etc.). Monthly magazine; 28 pages. Circ. 6,200. Pays on acceptance. Buys all rights. Byline given. Submit seasonal/holiday material 2 months in advance. Simultaneous, photocopied and previously published submissions OK. SASE. Reports in 2 weeks. Sample copy $2.50.

Nonfiction: Technical articles. Submit complete ms. Length: 1,200-1,500 words. Pays $70-90.

BRAKE & FRONT END, 11 S. Forge St., Akron OH 44304. (216)535-6117. Editor: Jeffrey S. Davis. 5-10% freelance written. For owners of automotive repair shops engaged in brake, wheel, suspension, chassis and frame repair, including: specialty shops; general repair shops; new car and truck dealers; gas stations; mass merchandisers and tire stores. Monthly magazine; 68 pages. Circ. 28,000. Pays on publication. Buys exclusive rights in field. Byline given. SASE. Reports immediately. Sample copy and editorial schedule $3.

Nonfiction and Photos: Specialty shops taking on new ideas using new merchandising techniques; growth of business, volume; reasons for growth and success. Expansions, and unusual brake shops. Query. Length: about 800-1,500 words. Pays 7-9¢/word. Pays $8.50 for b&w glossy prints purchased with mss.

CANADIAN AUTOMOTIVE TRADE MAGAZINE, MacLean—Hunter, Ltd., 481 University Ave., Toronto, Ontario, Canada M5W 1A7. (416)596-5784. Editor-in-Chief: Edward Belitsky. 30% freelance written. Emphasizes the automotive aftermarket for mechanics, service station and garage operators, new car dealers and parts jobbers. Monthly magazine; 60 pages. Circ. 31,000. Pays on acceptance. Buys all rights. Byline given. Phone queries OK. Submit seasonal/holiday material 2 months in advance. Photocopied submissions OK. SAE and International Reply Coupons. Reports in 2 months.

Nonfiction: Informational; new product; technical; interviews; and profiles. "We can use business articles every month from the 4 corners of Canada. Service articles can come from anywhere. We need Canadian business profiles most. No general business articles." Buys 3 mss/issue. Length: 600-1,400 words. Pays $60-200.

Photos: Purchased with accompanying ms. Captions required. Send contact sheet and/or transparencies. Pays $5-20 for 4x5 b&w prints or 35mm color transparencies. Model release required.

THE CHEK-CHART SERVICE BULLETIN, Box 6227, San Jose CA 95150. Editor: Leslie Wiseman. 20% freelance written. Emphasizes trade news and how-to articles on automobile service for professional mechanics. Monthly newsletter; 8 pages. Circ. 20,000. Pays on acceptance. Buys all rights. No byline. Submit seasonal/holiday material 3-4 months in advance of issue date. SASE. Reports in 2 weeks. Free sample copy and writer's guidelines; mention *Writer's Market* in request.

Nonfiction: "The *Service Bulletin* is a trade newsletter, *not* a consumer magazine. How-to articles and service trade news for professional auto mechanics, also articles on merchandising automobile service. No 'do-it-yourself' articles." Buys 1-2 mss/issue. Query with samples. Length: 700-1,100 words. Pays $75-125.

Photos: State availability of photos with query. Offers no additional payment for photos accepted with ms. Uses 8x10 b&w glossy photos. Captions and model release required. Buys all rights.

Tips: "Be willing to work in our style. Ask about subjects we would like to have covered in the future."

COLLISION, Info-Quest, Inc., Box M, Franklin MA 02038. Editor: Jay Kruza. For auto dealers, auto body repairmen and managers, and tow truck operators. Magazine published every 6 weeks; 52 pages. Pays on acceptance. Buys all rights. Submit seasonal/holiday material 4 months in advance. Simultaneous, photocopied and previously published submissions OK. SASE. Reports in 2-3 weeks. Sample copy $1; free writer's guidelines.

Nonfiction: Exposé (on government intervention in private enterprise via rule making and notable failures; also how big business skims the cream of profitable business but fails to satisfy needs of motorist); how-to (fix a dent, a frame, repair plastics, run your business better); personal experience (regarding automotive success or failure). Query before submitting interview, personal opinion or technical articles. "Journalism of newsworthy material in local areas pertaining to auto body is of interest." Buys 20 articles/year. Length: 100-1,500 words. Pays $15-100.

Photos: "Our readers work with their hands and are more likely to be stopped by photo with story." Send photos with ms. Pays $15/first, $5/each additional for 5x7 b&w prints; $15/first, $5/each additional for color. Captions preferred. Model release required if not news material.

Columns & Departments: Personalities in Auto Dealership, Auto Body Repair Shops, Association News and Lifestyle, dealing with general human interest hobbies or past times. Almost anything that would attract readership interest. "Photos are very important. Stories that we have purchased are: 'Clearing the Farm . . . of Rattlesnakes'; 'Annual Mule Convention in Bishop, California'; and 'Cochise's Hidden Treasure.' " Buys 20/year. Query. Length: 50-500 words. Pays $25-75.

COMMERCIAL CAR JOURNAL, Chilton Way, Radnor PA 19089. Editor: James D. Winsor. Monthly. Buys all rights. Pays on acceptance. "Query with article outline." SASE.

Nonfiction: "Articles and photo features dealing with management, maintenance, and operating phases of truck and bus fleet operations. Material must be somewhat specialized and deal with a specific phase of the operation." Length: open. Pays $50 to $150.

Photos: "Occasionally use separate photos with captions." Pays $10-25.

CONOCO TODAY, Conoco, Inc., Box 2197, Houston TX 77001. Editor: Lynn E. Hohensee. Bimonthly. Buys all rights. Pays on acceptance. Free sample copy. Query. Reports at once. SASE.

Nonfiction: Conoco service station operation and wholesale distributor operations, news and ideas. Length: 1,000 words. Pays 7¢ a word.

Photos: Purchased with mss. B&w 8x10, pays $10.

FLEET MAINTENANCE & SPECIFYING, 7300 N. Cicero, Lincolnwood IL 60646. (312)588-7300. Editor: Tom Gelinas. For those directly responsible for specification, purchase, repair and maintenance of on-road vehicles of 10,000 GVW or more. Monthly magazine. Circ. 50,000. Buys all rights. No byline. Pays on publication. Free sample copy. Photocopied submissions OK. Reports as soon as possible. SASE.

Nonfiction and Photos: Articles on troubleshooting repair and maintenance of trucks. Articles on fleets and their maintenance programs; management technique stories. "Our publication is technically oriented. Our only interest is in generally superior work." Does not want to see product-oriented job stories, but will consider industry reports or articles on safety. Length: 2,000 to 5,000 words. Pays $25 per printed page minimum, without photos. Pays extra for 4-color transparencies. No additional payment is made for large format transparencies used with articles.

GO WEST MAGAZINE, 1240 Bayshore Hwy., Burlingame CA 94010. Managing Editor: James Sterling. Editor: Bill Fitzgerald. 20% freelance written. Emphasizes truck transport for the truck operator who is concerned with operation, maintenance and purchase of trucks and related equipment, and running a profitable business. Monthly magazine; 80 pages. Circ. 51,000. Pays on acceptance. Buys all rights. Pays full kill fee. Byline given except "series using same format, but different locations and subjects." Phone queries OK. Submit seasonal/holiday material 6 months in advance of issue date. SASE. Reports in 2 weeks. Free sample copy; mention *Writer's Market* in request.

Nonfiction: Exposé; general interest; how-to; interview; and new product. Buys 2 mss/issue. Query. Length: 500-3,500 words. Pays $200-600.

Photos: State availability of photos with query. Pays $5-15 for b&w photos; $100 for 2¼x2¼ color transparencies. Captions required. Buys all rights.

HEAVY DUTY MARKETING, Babcox Publications, 11 S. Forge St., Akron OH 44304. (216)535-6117. Editor: Jeffrey S. Davis. Bimonthly magazine about heavy duty truck parts and service. Circ. 15,500. Pays on publication. Byline given. Buys first North American serial rights. Submit seasonal material 2 months in advance. Simultaneous and photocopied submissions OK. SASE. Reports in 1 week. Sample copy $2.50.

Nonfiction: Interview (related to heavy duty truck parts and service); profile; and technical. No

stories about truck fleets. Buys 12 mss/year. Query. Length: 750-3,000 words. Pays 7¢-9¢/word. "We need feature stories on established businesses in heavy duty aftermarket, including truck dealers and factory branches, trailer dealers, parts distributors and repair facilities. We also need interviews with high level executives in heavy duty parts and service."
Photos: State availability of photos. Pays $8.50 maximum for b&w negatives and contact sheets. Reviews color negatives and contact sheets. Payment negotiated. Captions required. Buys all rights.

JOBBER NEWS, Wadham Publications, Ltd., 109 Vanderhoof Ave., Toronto, Ontario, Canada M4G 2J2. (416)425-9021. Editor-in-Chief: Sam Dixon. Emphasizes auto parts merchandising and management for owners and managers of automotive wholesaling establishments, warehouse distributors, and engine rebuilding shops in Canada. Monthly magazine; 58 pages. Circ. 8,000. Pays on acceptance. Buys all rights. Pays 100% kill fee. Byline given. Phone queries OK. Submit seasonal/holiday material 2 months in advance. Simultaneous, photocopied, and previously published submissions OK. SAE and International Reply Coupons. Reports in 2 weeks. Free sample copy and writer's guidelines.
Nonfiction: How-to articles. Must have authentic Canadian application. Query. Length: 2,000-3,000 words. Pays $50-125.

JOBBER/RETAILER, Bill Communications, Box 5417, Akron OH 44313. Editor: Sarah Frankson. 10% freelance written. "Readership is the automotive parts jobber who has entered the world of retailing to the automotive do-it-yourselfer and also wholesales to dealer trade. Editorial slant is business, merchandising/marketing-oriented with news secondary." Monthly tabloid; 56 pages. Circ. 31,000. Pays on publication. Buys all rights. Submit seasonal/holiday material 1-2 months in advance of issue date. Simultaneous, photocopied and previously published submissions in noncompetitive publications OK. SASE. Free sample copy and writer's guidelines; mention *Writer's Market* in request.
Nonfiction: How-to (merchandising do-it-yourself auto parts, store layout and design, transforming traditional jobber facilities to retail operations as well); interview (of jobber/retailers who have done an excellent job in retail merchandising or a particular item or product line); and technical (on do-it-yourself repairs). Submit complete ms. Length: 500-1,500 words maximum. Pays $125-200.

JOBBER TOPICS, 7300 N. Cicero Ave., Lincolnwood IL 60646. (312)588-7300. Articles Editor: Jack Creighton. "A digest-sized magazine dedicated to helping its readers—auto parts jobbers and warehouse distributors—succeed in their business via better management and merchandising techniques; and a better knowledge of industry trends, activities and local or federal legislation that may influence their business activities." Monthly. Buys all rights. No byline given. Pays on acceptance. Query with outline. SASE.
Nonfiction and Photos: Most editorial material is staff-written. "Articles with unusual or outstanding automotive jobber procedures, with special emphasis on sales and merchandising; any phase of automotive parts and equipment distribution. Especially interested in merchandising practices and machine shop operation. Most independent businesses usually have a strong point or two. We like to see a writer zero in on that strong point(s) and submit an outline, (or query) advising us of those points and what he intends to include in a feature. We will give him, or her, a prompt reply." Length: 2,000 words maximum. Pays based on quality and timeliness of feature. 5x7 or 8x10 b&w glossies or 4-color transparencies purchased with mss.

MERCHANDISER, Amoco Oil Company, Box 6110-A, Chicago IL 60680. Editor: Owen C. Wavrinek. For Amoco service station dealers, jobbers. Quarterly. Circ. 30,000. Buys all rights. Buys 1-2 mss/year. Pays on publication. Query recommended. SASE.
Nonfiction and Photos: Short, to-the-point, success stories and how-to stories, that will trigger creative thinking by the reader. Storylines are most often in the merchandising, motivational, and educational areas. "We're looking for articles about specific dealers, rather than general marketing concepts." Length: 750 words maximum. Payment varies, with minimum of $100. Uses b&w and color photos, which can be submitted upon acceptance of story.

MILK AND LIQUID FOOD TRANSPORTER, Dairy Marketing Communications, N80 W12878 Fond du Lac Ave., Box 878, Menomonee Falls WI 53051. (414)255-0108. Editor: Karl F. Ohm III. Monthly magazine about milk and liquid food transportation for owners, operators and management people who haul milk and other liquid food products. Circ. 16,871. Pays on acceptance. Byline given. Buys all rights. Submit seasonal material 3 months in advance. SASE. Reports in 2 weeks on queries; in 1 month on mss. Free sample copy and writer's guidelines.
Nonfiction: Expose (government regulation, state and federal); historical; interview; profile;

how-to (maintenance); new product (staff written); and technical (truck maintenance). No personal opinion, humor, first-person nostalgia, travel or inspirational. "We do interpretative reporting on timely issues affecting the business of transporting milk and other liquid food products. We prefer articles that cover problems unique to haulers in a particular state. Articles about innovative milk and liquid food transporters stand a better chance of being accepted." Buys 6-8 mss/year. Query. "I like to know why the writer thinks his/her story is pertinent to my publication. I also would like to know why the writer chose a particular slant." Length: 1,500-2,500 words. Pays $90-200.

Photos: State availability of photos. Pays $10-20 for b&w contact sheets. Captions and model release required. Buys all rights.

Tips: "Freelancers should become familiar with our audience by reading several past issues of the publication."

MODERN TIRE DEALER, Box 5417, 77 N. Miller Rd., Akron OH 44313. (216)867-4401. Editorial Director: Charles S. Slaybaugh. For independent tire dealers. Monthly tabloid, plus quarterly special emphasis issue magazines; 50-page tabloid, 80-page special issues. Published 16 times annually. Buys all rights. Photocopied submissions OK. Query. Reports in 1 month. SASE. Free writer's guidelines.

Nonfiction, Photos, and Fillers: "How independent tire dealers sell tires, accessories and allied services, such as brakes, wheel alignment, shocks, mufflers. The emphasis is on merchandising and management. We prefer the writer to zero in on some specific area of interest; avoid shotgun approach." Length: 1,500 words. Pays $100-250. 8x10, 4x5, 5x7 b&w glossy prints purchased with mss. Buys 300-word fillers. Pays $5-10.

MOTOR MAGAZINE, Hearst Corp., 224 W. 57th St., New York NY 10019. (212)262-8616. Editor: Joe Oldham. Emphasizes auto repair. "Readers are professional auto repairmen or people who own auto repair facilities." Monthly magazine; 80-90 pages. Circ. 135,000. Pays on acceptance. Buys all rights. Pays 100% kill fee. Byline given. SASE. Reports in 1 month. Free sample copy.

Nonfiction: How-to. "Writers should be able to relate their own hands-on experience to handling specific repair and technical articles." Buys 6 mss/issue. Query. Length: 1,000-2,000 words. Pays $150-300.

Photos: "Photos and/or rough artwork must accompany how-to articles." State availability of photos. Uses 5x7 glossy prints. Offers no additional payment for photos accepted with ms. Captions and model releases required.

MOTOR SERVICE, Hunter Publishing Co., 950 Lee, Des Plaines IL 60016. Editor: Larry W. Carley. Monthly magazine for professional auto mechanics and the owners and service managers of repair shops, garages and fleets. Circ. 137,000. Pays on acceptance. Buys all rights. Pays 100% kill fee. Byline given. Free sample copy.

Nonfiction: Technical how-to features in language a mechanic can enjoy and understand; management articles to help shop owners and service managers operate a better business; technical theory pieces on how something works; new technology roundups, etc. No "generic business pieces on management tips, increasing sales, employee motivation, etc." Recent articles include "Workman's Compensation Insurance; Is It A Ripoff?," "Understanding Synthetic Oils," "Diesel Diagnosis," "Servicing MacPherson Struts." Length: 1,500-2,500 words. Pays $150-300. Buys 25-30 mss/year. Query first. "Writers must know our market."

Photos: Photos and/or diagrams must accompany technical articles. Uses 5x7 b&w prints or 35mm transparencies. Offers no additional payment for photos accepted with ms. Captions and model releases required. Also buys color transparencies for cover use. Pays $50-200.

Tips: "Ask for a sample issue, then submit a query after seeing what type of articles we use."

MUFFLER DIGEST, Box 10467, Springfield MO 65808. (417)866-3917. Editor: J. M. Ryan. For professional installers and manufacturers of exhaust systems and exhaust system components. Monthly magazine; 60-80 pages. Circ. 10,000. Pays on acceptance. Buys all rights. Byline given. Simultaneous and photocopied submissions OK. SASE. Reports in 1 week.

Nonfiction: How-to; humor (in the muffler field); informational; interview (good interviews with shop owners); profile (industry people); photo feature; and technical. "We're not interested in 'How I Got Ripped Off at . . .' types of features." Buys 6-10 mss/year. Query. Length: 100-1,000 words. Pays 5-10¢/word.

Photos: Gary Kennon, photo editor. Purchased with accompanying ms. Captions required. Query. Pays $5 for b&w photos.

Columns & Departments: How-To column (could be a shop-talk type of article). Query. Length: 500 words. Pays 5-10¢/word.

Tips: "We are covering the professional exhaust system installer in the US, Mexico and Canada. When we talk about professional we are talking about muffler specialty shops—Midas, Tuffy and other franchise chain operators as well as independents. We are not interested in service stations, Sears, Wards, etc. We would prefer to see more stories on successful independent installers; how did they get started, what special tricks have they picked up, what is their most successful merchandising tool, etc."

NTDRA DEALER NEWS, 1343 L St. NW, Washington DC 20005. Editor: C.D. "Tony" Hylton III. 1-2% freelance written. For tire dealers and retreaders. Publication of the National Tire Dealers & Retreaders Association. Monthly magazine. Circ. 7,500. Occasionally copyrighted, depending on content. Byline given. Buys 10 to 15 mss a year. Will send free sample copy on request. Will consider photocopied and simultaneous submissions. Reports immediately. Query. SASE.
Nonfiction: Articles relating to retailing and marketing, with special emphasis on the tire dealer, retreader and small business sector in general. "Industry news, business aids, new products. Dealer and consumer comments regarding this industry. Most articles recewed are of too general interest." Uses informational, technical, how-to, interview, think pieces and material on successful business operations and merchandising techniques. Pays $150-200.

O AND A MARKETING NEWS, Box 765, LaCanada CA 91011. (213)790-6554. Editor: Don McAnally. 5% freelance written. For "service station dealers, garagemen, TBA (tires, batteries, accessories) people, oil company marketing management." Bimonthly. Circ. 15,000. Not copyrighted. Pays on publication. Reports in 1 week. SASE.
Nonfiction and Photos: "Straight news material; management, service, and merchandising applications; emphasis on news about or affecting markets and marketers within the publication's geographic area of the 11 Western states. No restrictions on style or slant. We could use straight news of our industry from some Western cities, notably Las Vegas, Reno, and Salt Lake City. Query with a letter that gives me a capsule treatment of what the story is about." Query. Length: maximum 1,000 words. Pays $1.25/column inch (about 2½¢ a word). Photos purchased with or without mss; captions required. No cartoons. Pays $5.

OHIO TRUCK TIMES, Mezzanine Floor, Neil House Hotel, Columbus OH 43215. Editor: David F. Bartosic. Publication of the Ohio Trucking Association read by management, safety, government, law enforcement media and allied industries. Quarterly. Buys material for exclusive publication only. Pays on publication. Free sample copy. Reports in 30 days. SASE.
Nonfiction: Modern developments in truck transportation, particularly as they apply to Ohio industry and truck operators. Submit complete mss. Length: 1,500 words. Pay negotiable.
Photos: With mss or with captions only. Transportation subjects. Pay negotiable.

OWNER OPERATOR MAGAZINE, Chilton Co., 1 Chilton Way, Radnor PA 19089. (215)687-8200. Executive Editor: Brant Clark. Managing Editor: Leon E. Witconis. 20% freelance written. For one-truck owner/operators. Bimonthly magazine; 160 pages. Circ. 100,000. Pays on publication. Buys all rights. Submit seasonal/holiday material 6 months in advance of issue date. Previously published submissions OK. SASE. Reports in 3 weeks. Sample copy $1.50.
Nonfiction: Expose (government, unions, trucking companies, brokers, trucking associations); historical (trucking industry); how-to (perform maintenance, repairs or fix-up on heavy duty trucks); humor; interview (top trucking officials or unusual occupations in trucking); personal experience (only from truckers); photo feature (occupational, with pix); profile; and technical (truck). Buys 3-4 mss/issue. Submit complete ms and clips of previously published work. Length: 600 words maximum. Pays $50-300.
Photos: Submit photos with accompanying ms. Payment included in ms price. Uses 8x10 b&w prints. Buys all rights. Model release required.
Columns & Departments: Chatterbox (interviews with owner/operators at truck stops with pix). Buys 6/year. Query. Length: 300-450 words. Pays $150-250.

REFRIGERATED TRANSPORTER, 1602 Harold St., Houston TX 77006. (713)523-8124. 5% freelance written. Monthly. Not copyrighted. Byline given "except articles which must be extensively rewritten by our staff." Pays on publication. Reports in 1 month. SASE.
Nonfiction and Photos: "Articles on fleet management and maintenance of vehicles, especially the refrigerated van and the refrigerating unit; shop tips; loading or handling systems, especially for frozen or refrigerated cargo; new equipment specifications; conversions of equipment for better handling or more efficient operations. Prefer articles with illustrations obtained from fleets operating refrigerated trucks or trailers." Pays variable rate.
Fillers: Buys newspaper clippings. "Do not rewrite."

SERVICE STATION AND GARAGE MANAGEMENT, 109 Vanderhoof Ave., Suite 101, Toronto, Ontario Canada M4G 2J2. Editor: Gene Lethbridge. For "service station operators and garagemen in Canada only." Monthly. Circ. 26,000. Buys first Canadian serial rights. Buys 1 or 2 articles a year. Pays on acceptance. Sample copy for 50¢. Query. Reports in 2 days. Enclose SAE and International Reply Coupons.
Nonfiction and Photos: "Articles on service station operators in Canada only; those who are doing top merchandising job. Also on specific phases of service station doings: brakes, tune-up, lubrication, etc. Solid business facts and figures; information must have human interest angles. Interested in controversial legislation, trade problems, sales and service promotions, technical data, personnel activities and changes. No general, long-winded material. The approach must be Canadian. The writer must know the trade and must provide facts and figures useful and helpful to readers. The style should be easy, simple, and friendly—not stilted." Length: 1,000 words. Payment negotiable. Photos purchased with mss and without mss "if different or novel"; captions required. Pays $5 for 5x7 or 8x10 b&w glossies.

SOUTHERN MOTOR CARGO, Box 4169, Memphis TN 38104. Editor: Mike Pennington. For "trucking management and maintenance personnel of private, contract, and for-hire carriers in 16 Southern states (Ala., Ark., Del., Fla., Ga., Ky., La., Md., Miss., N.C., Okla., S.C., Tenn., Tex., Va., and W. Va.) and the District of Columbia." Special issues include "ATA Convention," October; "Transportation Graduate Directory," January; "Mid-America Truck Show," February. Monthly. Circ. 53,000. Buys first rights within circulation area. Pays on publication (or on acceptance in certain cases). Free sample copy to sincere, interested contributors. SASE.
Nonfiction: "How a Southern trucker builds a better mousetrap. Factual newspaper style with punch in lead. Don't get flowery. No success stories. Pick one item, i.e. tire maintenance, billing procedure, etc., and show how such-and-such carrier has developed or modified it to better fit his organization. Bring in problems solved by the way he adapted this or that and what way he plans to better his present layout. Find a segment of the business that has been altered or modified due to economics or new information, such as 'due to information gathered by a new IBM process, it has been discovered that an XYZ transmission needs overhauling every 60,000 miles instead of every 35,000 miles, thereby resulting in savings of $$$ over the normal life of this transmission.' Or, 'by incorporating a new method of record keeping, claims on damaged freight have been expedited with a resultant savings in time and money.' Compare the old method with the new, itemize savings, and get quotes from personnel involved. Articles must be built around an outstanding phase of the operation and must be documented and approved by the firm's management prior to publication." Length: 1,000-3,000 words. Pays minimum 8¢ a word for "feature material."
Photos: Purchased with cutlines; glossy prints. Pays $10.

SPECIALTY & CUSTOM DEALER, Babcox Publications, 11 S. Forge St., Akron OH 44304. (216)535-6117. Editor/Publisher: Gary Gardner. "Audience is primarily jobbers and retailers of specialty automotive parts and accessories. Average reader has been in business for 10 years, and is store owner or manager. Educational background varies, with most readers in the high school graduate with some college category." Monthly magazine; 56 pages. Circ. 22,000. Pays on publication. Buys all rights. Submit seasonal or holiday material 4 months in advance. SASE. Reports in 6 weeks. Sample copy $1.50.
Nonfiction: Publishes informational (business techniques), interview, new product, profile, and technical articles. "No hyperbolic accounts of business or those that read like public relations releases. No broad generalizations concerning a 'great product' without technical data behind the information. Lack of detail concerning business operations." Buys 10 mss/year. Query. Length: 1,000-2,000 words. Pays $50-150.
Tips: "For the most part, an understanding of automotive products and business practices is essential. Features on a specific retailer, his merchandising techniques and unique business methods are most often used. Such a feature might include inventory control, display methods, lines carried, handling obsolete products, etc."

THE SUCCESSFUL DEALER, Kona-Cal, Inc., 707 Lake Cook Rd., Deerfield IL 60015. (312)498-3180. Editor: Jay T. Branson. Managing Editor: Thea J. Berg. Magazine published 9 times/year covering dealership management of medium and heavy duty trucks; construction equipment; forklift trucks; diesel engines; and truck trailers. Circ. 17,000. Pays on publication. Byline sometimes given. Buys first rights. Simultaneous queries, and simultaneous and photocopied submissions OK. SASE. Reports in 2 weeks.
Nonfiction: How-to (solve problems within the dealership); interview/profile (concentrating on business, not personality); new product (exceptional only); opinion (by readers—those in industry); personal experience (of readers); photo feature (of major events); and technical (vehicle

componentry). Special issues include: September—parts and service and November/December—finance. Query. Length: open. Pays $100-150/page.

Tips: "Phone first, then follow up with a detailed explanation of the proposed article. Allow two weeks for our response. Know dealers and dealerships, their problems and opportunities; heavy-equipment industry."

TIRE REVIEW, 11 S. Forge St., Akron OH 44304. (216)535-6117. Editor: William Whitney. For "independent tire dealers and retreaders, company stores, tire company executives, some oil company executives." Monthly. Circulation: 32,500. Buys first rights. Buys 6 or 7 mss a year. Pays on publication. Will send a free sample copy to a writer on request. Query. Reports in 1 week. SASE.

Nonfiction and Photos: Features on independent tire dealers and retreaders, news of trade shows and conventions, tire and related service and accessory merchandising tips. All articles should be straightforward, concise, information-packed, and not slanted toward any particular manufacturer or brand name. Must have something to do with tires or the tire industry, particularly independent dealers doing brake and front-end and tune-up services." Length: "no limitations." Pays 4-6¢/word. B&w and color glossies purchased with and without mss. Pays "$5 a photo with story, $8.50 for photos used alone."

TODAY'S TRANSPORT INTERNATIONAL/TRANSPORTE MODERNO, Intercontinental Publications, Inc., Box 5017, Westport CT 06881. (203)226-7463. Editor: Martin Greenburgh. 100% freelance written. Emphasizes "fleet operations and materials handling for vehicle fleet operators and materials handling executives in 150 developing countries in Africa, Asia, Middle East, and Latin America." Bimonthly magazine; 96 pages. Circ. 39,000. Pays on acceptance. Buys all rights. Offers negotiable kill fee. Byline given. Phone queries OK. Previously published submissions OK. SASE. Free sample copy and writer's guidelines.

Nonfiction: How-to (run a fleet, specify equipment, etc.); informational (fleet operations, new technologies); interview (with fleet executives discussing problem solving); photo feature (fleets and materials handling); and technical (vehicle/bus/truck systems, fork lifts, materials handling) articles. Buys 24-30 a year. Query. Length: 1,500-3,000 words. Pays $200-250. No articles about US or developed countries without direct relevance to the 3rd world.

Photos: Purchased with accompanying ms. Captions required. Query.

Columns & Departments: Materials Handling (tips and methods for materials handling personnel). Buys 1 ms/issue. Query. Length: 750-1,500 words. Pays $100-150. Open to suggestions for new columns or departments.

Tips: "Articles must be written for readers in the 3rd world. Avoid US-oriented approach. Our readers are administrators and executives—address them."

TOW-AGE, Info-Quest, Inc., Box M, Franklin MA 02038. Editor: J. Kruza. For readers who run their own towing service business. Published every 6 weeks. Circ. 12,000. Buys all rights. Buys about 12 mss/year. Pays on acceptance. Sample copy $1; free writer's guidelines. Photocopied and simultaneous submissions OK. Reports in 1-4 weeks. SASE.

Nonfiction and Photos: Articles on business, legal and technical information for the towing industry. "Light reading material; short, with punch." Informational, how-to, personal experience, interview, profile. Query or submit complete ms. Length: 200-800 words. Pays $20-50. Spot news and successful business operations. Length: 100-500 words. Technical articles. Length: 100-1,000 words. Up to 8x10 b&w photos purchased with or without mss, or on assignment. Pays $15 for first photo; $5 for each additional photo in series. Captions required.

TRUCK CANADA, Sentinel Business Publications, 6725 Darlington Ave., Suite 200, Montreal, Quebec, Canada H3S 2J7. (514)731-3524. Editor: Keith Fredricks. For members of the heavy trucking industry. Monthly magazine; 40 pages. Circ. 21,500. Pays on publication. Buys first Canadian rights. Phone queries OK. Submit seasonal/holiday material 3 months in advance. Photocopied submissions and previously published work (if not previously published in Canada) OK. SAE and International Reply Coupons. Reports in 3 weeks. Free sample copy and writer's guidelines.

Nonfiction: General interest; historical; how-to (on truck maintenance); interview, profile and technical. Buys 18 articles/year. Query. Length: 1,500-2,500. Pays 7¢/word.

Photos: "We feel articles with photos illustrating them are better accepted by readers." State availability of photos. Pays $5 for b&w contact sheets and $7.50 for color transparencies.

WARD'S AUTO WORLD, 28 W. Adams, Detroit MI 48226. (313)962-4433. Editor-in-Chief: David C. Smith. Executive Editor: Albert E. Fleming. Senior Editor: Richard L. Waddell. Associate Editor: Daniel F. McCosh. 10% freelance written. For top and middle management in all phases of auto industry. Monthly magazine; 72 pages. Circ. 65,000. Pays on publication. Buys all rights. Pay varies for kill fee. Byline given. Phone queries OK. Submit seasonal/holiday material 1 month in advance of issue date. SASE. Reports in 2 weeks. Free sample copy and writer's guidelines.

Nonfiction: Expose; general interest; historical; humor; interview; new product; nostalgia; personal experience; photo feature; and technical. Few consumer-type articles. No "nostalgia or personal history type stories (like 'My Favorite Car')." Buys 12 mss/year. Query. Length: 700-5,000 words. Pay $100-600.

Photos: "We're heavy on graphics." Submit photo material with query. Pay varies for 8x10 b&w prints or color transparencies. Captions required. Buys one-time rights.

Tips: "Don't send poetry, how-to and 'My Favorite Car' stuff. It doesn't stand a chance. This is a business newsmagazine and operates on a news basis just like any other newsmagazine."

WAREHOUSE DISTRIBUTION, 7300 N. Cicero Ave., Lincolnwood, Chicago IL 60646. (312)588-7300. Editor: Larry Moore. For "businessmen in the auto parts distribution field who are doing above one million dollars business per year." Published 10 times/year. Circ. 30,000. Buys all rights. Pays on publication. Most material is staff-written. Reports "within a reasonable amount of time." SASE.

Nonfiction and Photos: "Business management subjects, limited to the automotive parts distribution field." Query. Length: 1,500-2,000 words. Pays 4¢-10¢ a word, "based on value to industry and the quality of the article." Photos purchased with and without mss; captions required. Wants "sharp 5x7 prints." Pays maximum $6.

WAREHOUSE DISTRIBUTOR NEWS, 11 S. Forge St., Akron OH 44304. Editor: John B. Stoner. 10% freelance written. For warehouse distributors and redistributing jobbers of automotive parts and accessories, tools and equipment and supplies (all upper management personnel). Magazine; 60 pages. Monthly. Circ. 12,000. Rights purchased vary with author and material. May buy exclusive rights in field. Byline given. Buys about 12 mss/year. Pays on publication. Sample copy $2.50. Photocopied and simultaneous submissions OK. Reports at once. SASE.

Nonfiction and Photos: Automotive aftermarket distribution management articles and those on general management, success stories, etc., of interest to the industry. Articles on manufacturers and their distributors. Must be aftermarket-oriented. Each issue centers around a theme, such as rebuilt parts issue, import issue, materials handling issue, etc. Schedule changes yearly based on developments in the industry. Does not want to see freelance material on materials handling, or product information. Would be interested in merchandising articles; those on EDP startup, and interviews with prominent industry figures. Query. Length: open. Pays 5-9¢/word. B&w (5x7) photos purchased with or without ms. Captions required.

WISCONSIN MOTOR CARRIER, Wisconsin Motor Carriers Association, 125 West Doty St., Madison WI 53703. (608)255-6789. Director, Public Relations: Janice H. Thieme. Assistant Editor: Linda Scheel. Quarterly magazine covering trucking and related information. "Our readers are from the regulated for-hire and private trucking community, governmental agencies, and safety personnel." Circ. 5,000. Pays on publication. Byline given. Buys one-time rights. Submit seasonal/holiday material 3 months in advance. Simultaneous queries, and photocopied and previously published submissions ("with copyright clearance only") OK. SASE. Reports in 6 weeks. Free sample copy.

Nonfiction: Book excerpts; historical/nostalgic; how-to (on engine care, driving tips, cargo control); humor; new product (alternative fuels, safety equipment); technical (tires, road building/surface testing; transportation planning; engines; future truck prototypes; fuel economy; hazardous shipments management); and fuel, safety, small communities, hazardous materials/wastes. "All must be truck or trucking/safety regulations related. We are especially interested in technical articles relating to transportation and in exploring the potential for quarterly columns on workers' compensation/insurance, safety, and equipment specifications." Special issues include safety/fuel economy—deadline September 1, 1981. No opinions or general interest. Query. Length: 750-2,000 words. Pays $25-200.

Photos: Pays $10-25 for 5x7 b&w prints. Captions required.

Columns/Departments: Cab-over Commentary—driver's viewpoint. Buys 4 mss/year. Query. Length: 200-750 words. Pays $20-75.

Fiction: Humorous—about trucking. Query. Length: 750-1,500 words. Pays $75-150.

Fillers: Jokes, anecdotes and short humor. Length: 50-75 words. Pays $5-7.50.

Aviation and Space

In this category are journals for aviation business executives and airport operators and technical aviation and space journals. Publications for professional and private pilots are classified with the Aviation magazines in the Consumer Publications section.

AG-PILOT INTERNATIONAL MAGAZINE, Agri-Aviation Publishing Co., 10 N.E. Sixth, Milton-Freewater OR 97862. (503)938-5502. Editor: Tom J. Wood. Executive Editor: Don Carraway. Emphasizes aerial agricultural application (crop dusting). "This is intended to be a fun-to-read, technical, as well as humorous and serious publication for the pilot and operator. They are our primary target. We will enlarge our field in the future, to near related areas." Monthly (except January and February) magazine; 48 pages. Circ. 8,300. Pays on publication. Buys all rights. Byline given unless writer requested holding name. Phone queries OK. Simultaneous, photocopied, and previously published (if not very recent) submissions OK. SASE. Reports in 1 week. Sample copy $1.
Nonfiction: Expose (of EPA, OSHA, FAA or any government function concerned with this industry); general interest; historical; interview (of well-known ag/aviation person); nostalgia; personal opinion; new product; personal experience; and photo feature. "If we receive an article, in any area we have solicited, it is quite possible this person could stay on our staff indefinitely. The international input is what we desire. Industry-related material is a must." Send complete ms. Length: 300-1,500 words. Pays $20-100.
Photos: "We would like one b&w 5x7 (or smaller) with the manuscript, if applicable—but it will not hurt, nor help, the chance of utilization." Four color. Offers no additional payment for photos accepted with ms. Captions preferred, model release required.
Columns/Departments: International (of prime interest, as they need to cultivate this area—aviation/crop dusting-related); Embryo Birdman (should be written, or appear to be written, by a first-year spray pilot); The Chopper Hopper (by anyone in the helicopter industry—not necessarily related to agriculture); Trouble Shooter (ag aircraft maintenance tips); BioGraphical Interview Type (of well-known person in aviation related position, but not necessarily agricultural aviation related); and Catchin' The Corner (written by a person obviously skilled in the crop dusting field of experience or other interest-capturing material related to the industry). Send complete ms. Length: 700-1,500 words. Pays $20-100.
Poetry: Interested in all types of Agri-Aviation related poetry. Buys 1/issue. Submit no more than 5 at one time. Length: one 10 inch x 24 picas maximum. Pays $20-40.
Fillers: Short jokes, short humor and industry-related newsbreaks. Length: 10-100 words. Pays $5-20.
Tips: "Writers should be witty, and knowledgeable about the crop dusting aviation world. Material *must* be agricultural/aviation-oriented. Crop dusting, or nothing!"

BUSINESS AND COMMERCIAL AVIATION, Hangar C-1, Westchester County Airport, White Plains NY 10604. Editor: John Olcott. For "corporate pilots and business aircraft operators." Monthly. Circ. 52,000. Buys all rights. Buys "very little" freelance material. Pays on acceptance. Sample copy $1. Reports "as soon as an evaluation is made." SASE.
Nonfiction and Photos: "Our readers are pilots and we have found general articles to be inadequate. Writers with a technical knowledge of aviation would be most suitable." Wants "reports on business aviation operations, pilot reports, etc." Query. Length: "no limits." Pays $100-300. B&w photos of aircraft purchased with mss. Pays $15-20. Pays $300 for cover color photos. Uses very little freelance photography.

HELICOPTERS IN CANADA, Corvus Publishing Group, Ltd., Suite 158, 1224 53rd Ave. NE, Calgary, Alberta, Canada T2E 7E2. (403)275-9457. Editor: Wayne D. Ralph. Quarterly magazine covering the helicopter community across Canada, for professionally employed members of helicopter aviation, such as pilots, engineers and senior management. Concerned with business, flight safety, technical advances in the helicopter industry, marketing and finance, newsworthy events in helicopter activities, and noteworthy individuals and programs involving Canadians and Canadian companies. Estab. 1980. Circ. 5,000. Pays on publication. Byline given. Pays $75 kill fee. Buys first North American serial rights and one-time rights. SASE. Reports in 3 weeks on queries; 2 months on mss. Sample copy $2.
Nonfiction: General interest; historical/nostalgic (mostly historical); how-to (requires expert knowledge of aviation); interview/profile (used occasionally); new product; opinion (from indus-

try or government executives only); personal experience (used rarely); photo feature; technical (used often); travel (used rarely); and flight tests. "We're interested in stories on the Canadian helicopter community, companies in helicopter flying across Canada, persons of noteworthy significance to that industry sector." No humor, "How I See It," poetry, political diatribes, or personal anecdotal accounts. Buys 5-10 mss/year. Query; "include phone number." Length: 500-2,000 words. Pays $75-300.

Photos: State availability of photos. Pays $10-25 for 35mm b&w transparencies; $50-100 for 35mm color transparencies; $10-25 for 5x7 b&w prints; $50-100 for 5x7 color prints. Captions required. Buys one-time rights.

Columns/Departments: "All columns are handled internally and are rarely farmed out to freelancers."

Tips: *"Helicopters In Canada* is aimed at the professionally employed helicopter expert, pilots, enginers, management, and writers must have a thorough knowledge of this technical field in order to provide realistic and insightful copy."

INTERLINE REPORTER, 2 W. 46th St., New York NY 10036. (212)575-9000. Editor: Eric Friedheim. An inspirational and interesting magazine for airline employees. Buys first serial rights. Query. SASE.

Nonfiction and Photos: Wants nontechnical articles on airline activities; stories should be slanted to the sales, reservations and counter personnel. Articles on offbeat airlines and, most of all, on airline employees—those who lead an adventurous life, have a unique hobby, or have acted above and beyond the call of duty. Personality stories showing how a job has been well done are particularly welcome. Length: up to 1,200 words. Pays $50-75 for articles with photographic illustrations.

INTERNATIONAL AVIATION MECHANICS JOURNAL, 211 S. 4th St., Basin WY 82410. (307)568-2413. Editor: Dale Hurst. For governmentally licensed airframe and powerplant mechanics involved in maintaining general aviation airplanes, and students. Monthly magazine; 72 pages. Circ. 16,500. Buys all rights. Pays within 30 days of publication. Free sample copy. Photocopied submissions OK. Reports in 30 days. SASE.

Nonfiction and Photos: Technical articles on aircraft maintenance procedures and articles helping the mechanics to be more efficient and productive. All material should be written from the point of view of an aircraft mechanic, helping him solve common field problems. Buys 30-40 mss/year. Query or submit complete ms. Informational (length: 500-2,000 words; pays $25-100); how-to (length: 100-500 words; pays $25); photo articles (length: 50-100 words; pays $20); and Technical (length: 500-4,000 words; pays $25-150).

JET CARGO NEWS, 5314 Bingle Rd., Houston TX 77092. (713)688-8811. General Manager: Rich Hall. For "traffic and distribution managers, marketing executives, sales executives, and corporate management who use or may sometime use air transportation to ship their company's products." Monthly. Circ. 20,333. Buys all rights. Buys 6 to 10 mss a year. Pays on publication. Will send a sample copy to a writer on request. Write for copy of guidelines for writers. Will not consider photocopied submissions. Submit seasonal material 2 weeks in advance of issue date. Reports in a month, if postage is included. Submit complete ms. SASE.

Nonfiction and Photos: "Air marketing success stories, cargo rate changes, new ideas on packaging and/or sales. The writer's message should be to the shipper, not to or about airlines. We feel the shipper wants to know how an airline can help him, and that he's not particularly interested in the airline's economics. Use a tight magazine style. The writer must know marketing. We want depth, how-to material. We don't like the 'gee whiz' approach to product marketing by air. We are not particularly interested in rare items moving by air freight. Rather, we are interested in why a shipper switches from surface to air transportation." Buys informational articles, how-to's, interviews, and coverage of successful business operations. Length: maximum 2,500 words. Pays $3/inch. 8x10 b&w glossy prints purchased with and without mss; captions required. Pays $7.50.

Baking

BAKING TODAY, Maclaren Publishers, Ltd., Box 109, Davis House, 69-77 High St., Croydon, CR9 1QH, England. (01)688-7788. Editor: Chris Whitehorn. Up to 40% freelance written. For managers and proprietors throughout the baking industry. Monthly magazine. Circ. 3,500. Copyrighted, SAE and International Reply Coupons. Sample copy $1.

Nonfiction: Features on baking and allied subjects. Length: 1,000-3,000 words. Submit complete ms. Pays $120/1,000 words.

Photos: B&w glossies used with mss. Captions required. Query.

PACIFIC BAKERS NEWS, Route 2, Belfair WA 98528. (206)275-6421. Publisher: Leo Livingston. 50% freelance written. Business newsletter for commercial bakeries in the Western states. Monthly. Pays on publication. No byline given; uses only one-paragraph news items.
Needs: Uses bakery business reports and news about bakers. Buys only brief "boiled-down news items about bakers and bakeries operating only in Alaska, Hawaii, Pacific Coast and Rocky Mountain states. Welcome clippings. Need monthly news reports and clippings about the baking industry and the donut business. No pictures, jokes, poetry or cartoons." Length: 10-200 words. Pays 6¢/word for clips and news used.

Beverages and Bottling

The following journals are for manufacturers, distributors and retailers of soft drinks and alcoholic beverages. Publications for bar and tavern operators and managers of restaurants are classified in the Hotels, Motels, Clubs, Resorts and Restaurants category.

BEER WHOLESALER, Dogan Publications, 75 SE 4th Ave., Delray Beach FL 33444. (305)272-1223. Editor: Kenneth Breslauer. Bimonthly magazine about the beer industry for beer wholesalers, importers and brewers. Circ. 5,000. Pays on publication. Byline given. Buys all rights. Reports in 3 weeks on queries; in 2 months on mss. Sample copy $5.
Nonfiction: General interest, interview, profile, how-to and technical. "Submit articles that are business-oriented and presented in an organized manner. Dig for the unusual; what makes this beer wholesaler different? What new ideas can be used? No consumer-oriented articles such as stories on beer can collecting." Buys 3 mss/issue. Query. Length: 1,200-5,000 words. Pays $70-150.
Photos: Send photos with ms. Offers no additional payment for photos accepted with ms. Captions required. Buys all rights.

LIQUOR STORE MAGAZINE, Jobson Publishing Corp., 448 Madison Ave., New York NY 10022. (212)758-5620. Editor: Peter Wulff. Magazine published 9 times/year about liquor retailing for retailers in the business. Circ. 50,000. Average issue includes 6 departments and 4 articles. Pays on acceptance. Buys first North American serial rights. Phone queries OK. Submit seasonal material 4 months in advance. SASE. Reports in 1 week on queries; in 1 month on mss. Sample copy $2.
Nonfiction: "Articles focus on case history studies of stores, and features on security, selling and equipment, etc. No general articles." Buys 3-4 mss/year. Send complete ms. Length: 1,000-2,000 words. Pays $150-200.
Photos: Send photos with ms. Reviews 5x7 b&w glossy prints. Offers no additional payment for photos accepted with ms. Captions preferred, model release required. Buys all rights.

MICHIGAN BEVERAGE NEWS, 24681 Northwestern Hwy., Suite 408, Southfield MI 48075. Editor: Larry Stotz. For "owners of bars, taverns, package liquor stores, hotels, and clubs in Michigan." Semimonthly. Buys exclusive rights to publication in Michigan. Byline given. Pays on publication. Free sample copy. Reports "immediately." SASE.
Nonfiction and Photos: "Feature stories with pictures. Unusual attractions and business-building ideas in use by Michigan liquor licensees. Profit tips, success stories, etc., slanted to the trade, not to the general public. Especially interested in working with freelancers in Grand Rapids, Flint, Kalamazoo, Marquette, Sault Ste. Marie, and Bay City areas." Query. Length: 500-750 words. Pays 75¢/column inch. Buys photos of Michigan licensees engaged in business activities. Pays 75¢/column inch.

MID-CONTINENT BOTTLER, 1900 W. 47th Place, Westwood KS 66205. (913)384-0770. Publisher: Floyd E. Sageser. 3% freelance written. For "soft drink bottlers in the 20-state Midwestern area." Bimonthly. Not copyrighted. Pays on acceptance. Free sample copy. Reports "immediately." SASE.
Nonfiction and Photos: "Items of specific soft drink bottler interest with special emphasis on sales and merchandising techniques. Feature style desired." Length: 2,000 words. Pays $15-$50. Photos purchased with mss.

MODERN BREWERY AGE, Box 5550, East Norwalk CT 06856. Editorial Director: Howard Kelly. For "brewery and beer distribution executives on the technical, administrative, and market-

ing levels." Buys North American serial rights. Pays on publication. Reports "at once." SASE.
Nonfiction and Photos: "Technical and business articles of interest to brewers." Query. Length: 5-8 double-spaced typewritten pages. Pays $50/printed page (about 3 to 3½ pages double-spaced typewritten ms)." Pays $15/published photo. Captions required.

REDWOOD RANCHER, 756 Kansas St., San Francisco CA 94107. (415)824-1563. Editor: Sally Taylor. 50% freelance written. For grape growers, and other California north coast ranchers. Magazine; 48 pages. Special issues: Vintage (July). Monthly. Circulation: 7,000. Buys 20-35 mss/year. Byline given. Pays on publication. Free sample copy (to writers "in our area"). Photocopied and simultaneous submissions OK. Submit special issue material at least 2 months in advance. Reports in 2-4 weeks. Query. SASE.
Nonfiction and Photos: "All material must be locally oriented." Technical articles on viticulturists, and country people. "Down-to-earth, humorous, with technical savvy." Articles on pest control, carbonic maceration, pruning, chemical control, new equipment. Informational, personal opinion, how-to, interview, profile, exposés run from 100-3,000 words. Pays $15-300. Pays $10-150 for historical articles of 100-2,000 words. Pays $10-50 for spot news, articles on successful business operations, new products, merchandising techniques; technical. Length: 25-200 words. 8x10 b&w glossies and color (separations preferred) purchased with mss or on assignment. Pays $7.50 for b&w; $25 for cover.

SOUTHERN BEVERAGE JOURNAL, Box 561107, Miami FL 33156. (305)233-7230. Managing Editor: Raymond G. Feldman. 25% freelance written. For owners of package stores, bars and restaurants throughout the South. Monthly magazine; 100 pages. Circ. 21,000. Pays on publication. Buys all rights. Submit seasonal/holiday material 4 months in advance of issue date. Reports in 2 months. Free sample copy and writer's guidelines.
Nonfiction: Contact: Eliot Levin. How-to articles on improving business practices, etc. No "window displays, inventory, or phone selling; we want specifics—success stories in our markets." Buys 12 mss/year. Submit complete ms. Pays 4-6¢/word.
Photos: State availability of photos with ms. Pays $5 for b&w or color prints. Captions preferred. Buys all rights.
Tips: "Our readers are in the trade; articles must be written for them. Ideas must be specific. Stories on successful establishments within our circulation area are desired."

WINES & VINES, 703 Market St., San Francisco CA 94103. Editor: Philip Hiaring. For everyone concerned with the wine industry including winemakers, wine merchants, suppliers, consumers, etc. Monthly magazine. Circ. 6,000. Buy first North American serial rights or simultaneous rights. Pays on acceptance. Free sample copy. Submit special material (brandy, January; vineyard, February; export-import, May; champagne, June; statistical, July; marketing, September; equipment and supplies, November) 3 months in advance. Reports in 2 weeks. SASE.
Nonfiction and Photos: Articles of interest to the trade. "These could be on grapegrowing in unusual areas; new winemaking techniques; wine marketing, retailing, etc." Interview, historical, spot news, merchandising techniques and technical. No stories with a strong consumer orientation as against trade orientation. Author should know the subject matter, i.e., know proper winegrowing/winemaking terminology. Buys 4-5 ms/year. Query. Length: 1,000-2,500 words. Pays $25-50. Pays $5-$10 for 4x5 or 8x10 b&w photos purchased with mss. Captions required.

Book and Bookstore Trade

AB BOOKMAN'S WEEKLY, Box AB, Clifton NJ 07015. (201)772-0020. Editor-in-Chief: Jacob L. Chernofsky. For professional and specialist booksellers, acquisitions and academic librarians, book publishers, book collectors, bibliographers, historians, etc. Weekly magazine; 200 pages. Circ. 8,500. Pays on publication. Buys all rights. Byline given. Phone queries OK. Submit seasonal or holiday material 1-2 months in advance. Simultaneous and photocopied submissions OK. SASE. Reports in 1 month. Sample copy $3.
Nonfiction: How-to (for professional booksellers); historical (related to books or book trade or printing or publishing). Personal experience, nostalgia, interviews, profiles. Query. Length: 2,500 words minimum. Pays $40 minimum.
Photos: Photos used with mss.

AMERICAN BOOKSELLER, Booksellers Publishing, Inc., 122 E. 42nd St., New York NY 10168. (212)867-9060. Editor: Ginger Curwen. This publication emphasizes retail bookselling and goes to the 5,700 members of the American Booksellers Association and to more than 2,400 other readers nationwide, most of whom are involved in publishing. Monthly magazine; 48 pages. Circ. 8,700. Pays on acceptance. Buys all rights. Pays 25% kill fee. Byline given "except on small news stories." Submit seasonal/holiday material 3 months in advance. Simultaneous, photocopied and previously published submissions OK. SASE. Reports in 3 weeks. Sample copy $3.

Nonfiction: General interest (on publishing and bookselling); how-to (run a bookstore, work with publishers); interview (on authors and booksellers); and photo feature (on book-related events). Buys 6 mss/issue. Query with clips of published work and background knowledge of bookselling. Length: 750-2,000 words. Pays $40-100.

Photos: State availability of photos. Uses b&w 5x7 matte prints and contact sheets. Pays $10-20. Uses 35mm color transparencies. Pays $10-50. Captions and model releases required.

CHRISTIAN BOOKSELLER, 396 E. St. Charles Rd., Wheaton IL 60187. (312)653-4200. Stephen R. Clark. 50% freelance written. Emphasizes "any products that are found in the religious bookstore." Monthly magazine; 68 pages. Circ. 10,000. Pays on publication. Buys first rights. Phone queries OK. Submit seasonal/holiday material 4 months in advance of issue date. SASE. Reports in 4-6 weeks. Free sample copy and writer's guidelines.

Nonfiction: "*Christian Bookseller* is a trade magazine serving religious bookstores. Needs successful business stories—reports of Christian bookstores that are utilizing unique methods of merchandising promotions, have unique departments, etc." Query. Length: 1,000-2,000 words. Pays $25-85.

Photos: "Photos are to accompany successful business stories." State availability of photos with query. Reviews 5x7 b&w glossy prints and contact sheets. Offers no additional payment for photos accompanying ms. Uses 2-3 b&w photos/story. Captions preferred. Buys all rights.

Tips: "In queries get to the point; cut the hype; state credentials factually—tell me what you're going to write. All mss must be substantial in content, authoritatively written, and well documented where called for. Writers must exhibit knowledge and understanding of the religious retailing business and industry."

COLLEGE STORE EXECUTIVE, Box 1500, Westbury NY 11590. (516)334-3030. Editor: Marcy Kornreich. 5% freelance written. Emphasizes merchandising and marketing in the college store market. Publishes 10 issues/year tabloid; 40 pages. Circ. 8,500. Pays on publication. Buys all rights. Byline given. Submit seasonal/holiday material 2 months in advance of issue date. Photocopied submissions OK. SASE. Reports in 2 weeks. Written queries a must.

Nonfiction: Expose (on inadequate stores; problems in college market); general interest (to managers); how-to (advertise, manage a store, store profile); inspirational (how to be successful in the college store market); interview (with bookstore managers); personal experience (someone who worked for a publisher selling to bookstores); personal opinion (from those who know about the market); photo feature (on specific colleges in the country or outside); and technical (how to display products). No articles on the typical college student. Buys 8 mss/year. Query. Length: 1,000 words. Pays $2/column inch.

Photos: State availability of photos with query. Pays $5-10 for any size b&w prints or contact sheets. Captions preferred. Buys all rights.

PUBLISHERS WEEKLY, 1180 Avenue of the Americas, New York NY 10036. (212)764-5153. Editor-in-Chief: John F. Baker. Weekly. Buys first North American rights only. Pays on publication. Reports "in several weeks." SASE.

Nonfiction and Photos: "We rarely use unsolicited mss because of our highly specialized audience and their professional interests, but we can sometimes use news items about publishers, publishing projects, bookstores and other subjects relating to books." Payment negotiable; generally $100/printed page. Photos purchased with and without mss "occasionally."

Brick, Glass, and Ceramics

AMERICAN GLASS REVIEW, Box 2147, Clifton NJ 07015. (201)779-1600. Editor-in-Chief: Donald Doctorow. 10% freelance written. Monthly magazine; 24 pages. Pays on publication. Byline given. Phone queries OK. Buys all rights. Submit seasonal/holiday material 2 months in advance of issue date. SASE. Reports in 2-3 weeks. Free sample copy and writer's guidelines; mention *Writer's Market* in request.

Nonfiction: Glass plant and glass manufacturing articles. Buys 6 mss/year. Query. Length: 1,500-3,000. Pays $40-50.

Photos: State availability of photos with query. No additional payment for b&w contact sheets. Captions preferred. Buys all rights.

BRICK AND CLAY RECORD, 5 S. Wabash Ave., Chicago IL 60603. (312)372-6880. Editor: Phil Jeffers. For "the heavy clay products industry." Monthly. Buys all rights. Pays on publication. Query first. Reports in 15 days. SASE.
Nonfiction and Photos: "News concerning personnel changes within companies; news concerning new plants for manufacture of brick, clay pipe, refractories, drain tile, face brick, glazed tile, lightweight clay aggregate products and abrasives; news of new products, expansion, new building." Length: 1,500-2,000 words. Pays minimum 8¢/published line. "Photos paid for only when initially requested by editor."
Fillers: "Items should concern only news of brick, clay pipe, refractory, or clay lightweight aggregate plant operations. If news of personnel, should be only of top-level plant personnel. Not interested in items such as patio, motel, or home construction using brick; of weddings or engagements of clay products people, unless major executives; obituaries, unless of major personnel; items concerning floor or wall tile (only structural tile); of plastics, metal, concrete, bakelite, or similar products; items concerning people not directly involved in clay plant operation." Pays $6 "per published 2- or 3-line brief item." Pays minimum $6 for "full-length published news item, depending on value of item and editor's discretion. Payment is only for items published in the magazine. No items sent in can be returned."

CERAMIC INDUSTRY, 5 S. Wabash, Chicago IL 60603. Editor: J.J. Svec. For the ceramics industry; manufacturers of glass, porcelain, enamel, whitewares and electronic/industrial newer ceramics. Magazine; 50-60 pages. Monthly. Circ. 7,500. Buys all rights. Byline given. Buys 10-12 mss/year (on assignment only). Pays on acceptance. Will send free sample copy to writer on request. Reports immediately. Query first. SASE.
Nonfiction and Photos: Semitechnical, informational and how-to material purchased on assignment only. Length: 500-1,500 words. Pays $50/published page. No additional payment for photos used with mss. Captions required.

CERAMIC SCOPE, Box 48497, Los Angeles CA 90048. (213)935-1122. Editor: Mel Fiske. Associate Editor: Nancy J. Lee. Monthly magazine covering hobby ceramics business. For "ceramic studio owners and teachers, operating out of homes as well as storefronts, who have a love for ceramics, but meager business education." Also read by distributors, dealers, and supervisors of ceramic programs in institutions. Circ. 6,800. Pays on acceptance. Buys all rights. Byline given unless it is a round-up story with any number of sources. Phone queries OK. Submit seasonal/holiday material 5 months in advance. SASE. Reports in 2 weeks. Sample copy $1.
Nonfiction: "Articles on operating a small business specifically tailored to the ceramic hobby field; photo feature stories with in-depth information about business practices and methods that contribute to successful studio operation. We don't need articles dealing primarily with biographical material or how owner started in business."
Photos: State availability of photos or send photos with ms. Pays $5/4x5 or 5x7 glossy b&w print; $25-50/color contact sheets. Captions required.

GLASS DIGEST, 110 E. 42nd St., New York NY 10017. (212)682-7681. Editor: Oscar S. Glasberg. Monthly. Buys first rights. Byline given "only industry people—not freelancers." Pays on publication "or before, if ms held too long." Will send a sample copy to a writer on request. Reports "as soon as possible." Enclose SASE for return of submissions.
Nonfiction and Photos: "Items about firms in glass distribution, personnel, plants, etc. Stories about outstanding jobs accomplished—volume of flat glass, storefronts, curtainwalls, auto glass, mirrors, windows (metal), glass doors; special uses and values; who installed it. Stories about successful glass/metal distributors, dealers, and glazing contractors—their methods, promotion work done, advertising, results." Length: 1,000-1,500 words. Pays 7¢/word, "usually more. No interest in bottles, glassware, containers, etc., but leaded and stained glass good." B&w photos purchased with mss; "8x10 preferred." Pays $7.50, "usually more."
Tips: "Find a typical dealer case history about a firm operating in such a successful way that its methods can be duplicated by readers everywhere."

NATIONAL GLASS BUDGET, LJV Corp., Box 7138, Pittsburgh PA 15213. (412)682-5136. Managing Editor: Liz Scott. Semimonthly magazine covering glass manufacturing, and glass industry news for glass manufacturers, dealers and people involved in the making, buying and selling of glass items and products. Circ. 1,200. Pays on publication. Makes work-for-hire assignments. Phone queries OK. Submit seasonal material 3 months in advance. Simultaneous and photocopied submissions OK. SASE. Reports in 2 weeks on queries; in 2 months on mss. Free sample copy.

Nonfiction: Historical (about glass manufacturers, trademarks and processes); how-to (concerning techniques of glass manufacturers); interview (with glass-related people); profile; new product (glass use or glass); and technical (glass manufacture or use). Special needs include a 100th Anniversary Edition coming in 1984. Buys 5-10 mss/year. Query. Length: 500-10,000 words. Pays $25 minimum.

Photos: State availability of photos. Pays $10 minimum for 8x10 b&w glossy prints. Offers no additional payment for photos accepted with ms. Captions preferred; model release required. Buys one-time rights.

Fillers: Anecdotes, short humor, newsbreaks and puzzles. Buys 5 mss/year. Pays $10 minimum.

Tips: "Get to know a lot about glass, how it is made and new developments."

Building Interiors

LIGHTING DIMENSIONS MAGAZINE, 31706 S. Coast Hwy., Suite 302, South Laguna CA 92677 (714)499-2233. Managing Editor: Barbara Hall. Magazine published seven times/year featuring entertainment lighting (for theaters, films, TV, disco, touring and laser shows) for lighting designers in all areas of entertainment, production managers, technical directors, technicians, instructors, laser specialists, holographers and manufacturers and suppliers. Circ. 10,000. Byline given. Buys first North American serial rights. Phone queries OK. Submit seasonal material 2 months in advance. Simultaneous, photocopied and previously published submissions OK. SASE. Reports in 2 weeks. Free sample copy and writer's guidelines.

Nonfiction: Interview (with well-known lighting designers); profile; how-to; photo feature; and technical. "Articles may be technical, describing new equipment or techniques. They can also be on lighting in a specific play, opera, dance production, film, TV show or nightclub installation. We also like interviews with designers and cinematographers." Buys 3 mss/issue. Send complete ms. Pays $25-150.

Photos: State availability of photos or send photos with ms. Reviews b&w glossy prints and 8x10 color glossy prints. Offers no additional payment for photos accepted with ms. Model release required. Buys one-time rights.

Tips: "It would be tremendously helpful if the writer had some theater background, knowledge of film production, etc."

MODERN FLOOR COVERINGS, Charleson Publishing Co., 124 E. 40th St., New York NY 10016. (212)953-0274. Editor: Bob Barrett. Monthly tabloid featuring floor coverings, for the retail community. Circ. 30,000. Pays on acceptance. Byline given. Makes work-for-hire assignments. Submit seasonal material 6 months in advance. SASE. Reports in 2 weeks.

Nonfiction: Interview. Buys 2 mss/year. Send complete ms. Length: 1,000-10,000 words. Pays $50-250.

Photos: Send photos with ms. Pays $10-20 for b&w contact sheets. Pays $10-20 for color slide transparencies. Captions preferred. Buys one-time rights.

PROFESSIONAL DECORATING & COATING ACTION, Painting and Decorating Contractors of America, 7223 Lee Hwy., Falls Church VA 22046. (703)534-1201. Editor/Manager: Heskett K. Darby. Emphasizes professional decorating, painting, wallcovering and sandblasting for painting contractors and their top assistants. Monthly magazine; 40-48 pages. Circ. 15,000. Pays on acceptance. Buys all rights. Submit seasonal or holiday material 2 months in advance. SASE. Reports in 3 weeks. Free sample copy.

Nonfiction: Publishes how-to and informational articles. Buys 17-20 mss/year. Query. Length: preferably under 1,000 words. Pays 10¢/word maximum.

Photos: Purchased with accompanying ms. Captions required. Pays $7.50 for professional quality 8½x11 or 4x5 glossy b&w prints. Model release required.

Tips: "Gear your writing to our specializations. Query us first with precis."

PROFESSIONAL REMODELING, Harcourt Brace Jovanovich, 757 3rd Ave., New York NY 10017. Editor: Frank Giammanco. For professional remodeling contractors, distributors and dealers engaged in home and light commercial remodeling. Monthly tabloid with magazine format. Circ. 30,000. Pays on publication. Buys all rights. No phone queries. Submit seasonal/holiday material 3 months in advance. SASE. Reports in 1 month. Free sample copy and writer's guidelines.

Nonfiction: How-to (on remodeling projects from inception to completion); interview and profiles on key industry figures. Solid service information only. Query. Pays $100.
Photos: "*PR* is strong on four-color graphics." Prefers 5x7 b&w glossy prints and 4x5 color transparencies. Also reviews 35mm color. Pays $10. Captions required.

TILE AND DECORATIVE SURFACES, Tile and Decorative Surfaces Magazine Publishing Co., Inc., 18327 Sherman Way, Suite 104, Reseda CA 91335. (213)344-4200. Editor: Jerry Fisher. Monthly magazine covering the ceramic tile industry for manufacturers, distributors, dealers and contractors in the ceramic and quarry tile, marble and terrazzo field, as well as design architects, interior designers and landscape designers. Circ. 14,000. Pays on acceptance. Byline given. Buys all rights. Phone queries OK. Submit seasonal material 2 months in advance. Simultaneous, photocopied and previously published submissions OK. SASE. Reports in 1 week on queries; in 2 weeks on mss. Free sample copy.
Nonfiction: Timely business topics. "Articles must be pertinent to the industry." Buys 4 mss/issue. Send complete ms. Length: 1,000-2,000 words. Pays $100 maximum.
Columns & Departments: Send complete ms. Length: 1,000-2,000 words. Pays $100 maximum.

WALLS & CEILINGS, 14006 Ventura Blvd., Sherman Oaks CA 91423. (213)789-8733. Editor-in-Chief: Robert Welch. Managing Editor: Don Haley. 10% freelance written. For contractors involved in lathing and plastering, drywall, acoustics, fireproofing, curtain walls, movable partitions together with manufacturers, dealers, and architects. Monthly magazine; 32 pages. Circ. 10,000. Pays on publication. Buys first North American serial rights. Byline given. Phone queries OK. Submit seasonal/holiday material 3 months in advance of issue date. SASE. Reports in 3 weeks. Sample copy $1.
Nonfiction: How-to (drywall and plaster construction and business management); and interview. Buys 5 mss/year. Query. Length: 200-1,000 words. Pays $75 maximum.
Photos: State availability of photos with query. Pays $5 for 8x10 b&w prints. Captions required. Buys one-time rights.

Business Management

The publications listed here are directed at owners of businesses and top level business executives. They cover business trends and general theory and practice of management. Publications that use similar material but have a less technical or professional slant are listed in Business and Finance in the Consumer Publications section. Journals dealing with banking, investment, and financial management are classified in the Finance category in this section.

Publications dealing with lower level management (including supervisors and office managers) will be found in Management and Supervision. Journals for industrial plant managers are listed under Industrial Management, and under the names of specific industries such as Machinery and Metal Trade or Plastics. Publications for office supply store operators will be found with the Office Equipment and Supplies Journals.

ADMINISTRATIVE MANAGEMENT, Geyer-McAllister Publications, 51 Madison Ave., New York NY 10010. Editor: Walter A. Kleinschrod. Executive Editor: Walter J. Presnick. 33% freelance written. Emphasizes office systems and their management. Monthly magazine; 120 pages. Circ. 53,000. Pays on publication. Buys all rights. Byline given. Photocopied submissions OK. Reports in 8 weeks. Sample copy $2; free writer's guidelines.
Nonfiction: Exposé (what's wrong with certain management theories or office products); general interest (business operations); and how-to (run an efficient office operation of some kind).
Photos: State availability of photos with query or submit photo material with accompanying query. Possible additional payment for b&w prints or contact sheets or color contact sheets. Captions preferred. Buys one-time rights.

BETTER COMMUNICATION, Information Plus, Inc., Box 602, Livingston NJ 07039. (201)334-9598. Editor: Linn Page. Managing Editor: Scott Benson. Weekly newsletter covering business communication for managers, administrators, accountants, engineers, secretaries and other professionals. Estab. 1979. Circ. 1,600. Pays on acceptance. Byline sometimes given. Buys all rights. Submit seasonal/holiday material 3 months in advance. Simultaneous queries, and photocopied and simultaneous submissions OK. SASE. Reports in 3 weeks on queries; 5 weeks on mss. Sample copy for business size SAE and 1 first class stamp.

Nonfiction: How-to, humor, and personal experience, all relating to communication. "We're looking for articles on how to write a better letter, memo, or report; how to communicate effectively with co-workers, bosses, employees; how to make an effective speech or presentation; how to run meetings, how to negotiate, sell your ideas, motivate people; how to listen, speak, use the telephone—anything to do with effective business communication. All articles should give practical, down-to-earth advice, and also be interesting to read." Buys 10-20 mss/year. Send complete ms. Length: 300-1,200 words. Pays $15-75.

Fillers: Jokes, anecdotes and short humor "relating to communication only." Buys 10/year. Length: 25-300 words. Pays $5-25.

Tips: "Read sample issues, and provide us with similar material, but with a new slant. Uses lots of anecdotes and examples from real life, to show how communication has been successful or unsuccessful in various organizations."

BOARDROOM REPORTS, 500 5th Ave., New York NY 10110. (212)354-0005. Senior Editor: Donald Ediger. Executive Editor: Marion Buhagiar. Biweekly magazine covering business advice for business executives at the managerial level. Pays on acceptance. Byline sometimes given "if writer is also expert in the field." Buys one-time rights. Submit seasonal/holiday material 3 months in advance. Previously published work OK. Reports in 1 week on queries. Free sample copy and writer's guidelines.

Nonfiction: Needs articles giving "advice to business executives on such subjects as taxes, investments, management, management psychology, personnel and law." Also personal executive advice on health, travel, etc. Query. Length: 400 words maximum. Pays "competitive rates."

EXECUTIVE REVIEW, 224 S. Michigan Ave., Chicago IL 60604. (312)922-4083. Editor-in-Chief: Harold Sabes. 10% freelance written. For management of small and middle-class companies, middle management in larger companies and enterprises. Monthly magazine; 32 pages. Circ. 25,000. Pays on publication. Buys one-time and second rights. Byline given. Submit seasonal/holiday material 6 months in advance of issue date. Simultaneous, photocopied, and previously published submissions OK. SASE. Reports in 6 weeks. Free sample copy and writer's guidelines; mention *Writer's Market* in request.

Nonfiction: How-to (how to do it articles that will be of interest to businessmen in the operation of their companies, and ideas that can be adapted and successfully used by others); interview; personal experience (business); profile; and travel. Buys 7 mss/issue. Submit complete ms. Length: 1,000-1,500 words. Pays $15-50.

HARVARD BUSINESS REVIEW, Soldiers Field, Boston MA 02163. (617)495-6800. Editor: Kenneth R. Andrews. For top management in US industry, and in Japan and Western Europe; younger managers who aspire to top management responsibilities; policymaking executives in government, policymakers in noncommercial organizations, and professional people interested in the viewpoint of business management. Published 6 times/year. Buys all rights. Byline given. Pays on publication. Reports in 2 to 6 weeks. SASE.

Nonfiction: Articles on business trends, techniques and problems. *"Harvard Business Review* seeks to inform executives about what is taking place in management, but it also wants to challenge them and stretch their thinking about the policies they make, how they make them, and how they administer them. It does this by presenting articles that provide in-depth analyses of issues and problems in management and, wherever possible, guidelines for thinking out and working toward resolutions of these issues and problems." Length: 3,000-6,000 words. Pays $500.

IN BUSINESS, JG Press, Inc., Box 323, Emmaus PA 18049. (215)967-4010. Editor: Jerome Goldstein. Managing Editor: Ina Pincus. Bimonthly magazine covering small businesses, their management, and new developments for small business owners or people thinking about starting out. Estab. 1979. Circ. 15,500. Pays on publication. Buys first North American serial rights. Submit seasonal material 3 months in advance. SASE. Reports in 3 weeks. Sample copy $2; free writer's guidelines.

Nonfiction: Exposé (related to small business, government regulations and economic climate); how-to (advertise, market, handle publicity, take inventory); profile (of an innovative small-scale business); new product (inventions and R&D by small businesses). "Keep how-to's in mind for feature articles; capture the personality of the business owner and the effect of that on the business operations." Buys 6-7 mss/issue. Query with clips of published work. Length: 1,000-2,000 words. Pays $75-200.

Photos: State availability of photos. Pays $25-75. Reviews contact sheets. Captions preferred; model release required.
Tips: "Get a copy of the magazine and read it carefully so you can better understand the editorial focus. Send several specific article ideas on one topic, so we can sharpen the focus. Keep in mind that the reader will be looking for specifics and transferrable information."

MANAGING, Graduate School of Business, University of Pittsburgh, 1917 Cathedral of Learning, Pittsburgh PA 15260. (412)624-6667. Editor-in-Chief: Karen Burgio Hoy. Associate Editor: Chris Regan. Art Director: Barbara U. Dinsmore. Emphasizes business and management issues. Many of the readers are Graduate School of Business alumni; others are upper- and middle-level managers and executives in the city, tri-state region and country. Magazine published three times/year (February, June and October); 48 pages. Estab. 1979. Circ. 5,000. Pays on acceptance. Buys all rights and one-time rights. Submit seasonal/holiday material 3 months in advance. Photocopied submissions OK; previously published submissions OK, but not for full-length features. SASE. Reports in 1 month. Free sample copy and writer's guidelines.
Nonfiction: Profile (on corporate executive to give full picture of man and his work) and business or management-oriented features which stem from a regional base, but the story should have national impact. No "articles on personnel, sales or creativity." Buys 3-4 mss/issue. Length: 1,500-4,000 words. Query with samples. "Queries should include information about the author's previously published works and why he/she is qualified to handle the assignment. Prefer information on angle (direction) article will take, persons to be interviewed, subjects explored." Pays $100-300.
Photos: State availability of photos. Pays $10-40 for b&w contact sheets.
Columns/Departments: Your Turn (a column on personal views toward a business or management issue written with a background in the area); Management (medium-length article dealing with a particular management problem and how to solve it). Buys 1/issue. Send complete ms. Length: 500-1,500 words. Brief Cases (short synopses of interesting management research topics with humorous twist). Length: 50-100 words. Pays $25 if used.
Tips: "Our magazine is not writen for the average business person. It is published three times/year so articles are in-depth and are meant to be referred to by our readers. Articles *must* have an unusual slant and contain a lot of information—information our readers can't get from the popular business publications."

MAY TRENDS, 111 S. Washington St., Park Ridge IL 60068. (312)825-8806. Editor: J.J. Coffey Jr. 100% freelance written. For chief executives of businesses, hospitals and nursing homes, trade associations, government bureaus, Better Business Bureaus, educational institutions, newspapers. Publication of George S. May International Company. Magazine published without charge 3 times a year; 28-30 pages. Circulation: 15,000. Buys all rights. Byline given. Buys 15-20 mss/year. Pays on acceptance. Will send free sample copy to writer on request. Reports on material accepted for publication in 1 week. Returns rejected material immediately. Query or submit complete ms. SASE.
Nonfiction: "We prefer articles dealing with problems of specific industries (manufacturers, wholesalers, retailers, service businesses, small hospitals and nursing homes) where contact has been made with key executives whose comments regarding their problems may be quoted." Avoid material on overworked, labor-management relations. Interested in small business success stories vs. the "giants"; automobile dealers coping with existing dull markets; contractors solving cost—inventory problems. Will consider material on successful business operations and merchandising techniques. Length: 2,000-3,000 words. Pays $100-250.
Tips: Query letter should tell "type of business and problems the article will deal with. We specialize in the problems of small (35-500 employees, $500,000-2,500,000 volume) business and hospitals and nursing homes."

NATION'S BUSINESS, Chamber of Commerce of the United States, 1615 H St., NW, Washington DC 20062. (202)659-6010. Editor: Grover Heiman. Monthly magazine covering business as related to government for business owners and executives. Circ. 1.2 million. Pays on acceptance. Byline given. Buys all rights. Submit seasonal/holiday material 3 months in advance. SASE. Reports in 1 month.
Nonfiction: "Trends in business and business relations with the federal government. We only occasionally take unsolicited freelance mss." Query. Length: 1,500 words average. "Payment is subject to agreement."
Photos: State availability of photos.

NEWSBEAT, Newsletter for Executives of Small Business, Best Employers Association, 5950 Roe Blvd., Shawnee Mission KS 66205. (913)262-4000. Editor: Donald L. Campbell. Monthly newsletter covering small businesses' voice to government for small business operators averaging 3-5 employees. Estab. 1980. Circ. 35,000. Pays on publication. No byline given. Not copyrighted. Buys one-time rights. Submit seasonal/holiday material 2 months in advance. Simultaneous queries, and simultaneous, photocopied, and previously published submissions OK. SASE. Reports in 1 month on mss. Sample copy for business size SAE and 1 first class stamp.

Nonfiction: "We seek productivity, personal motivation, training, financing, sales, planning management skills, advertising and promotion topics." No financial planning, insurance or legal articles accepted. Query. Length: 500-600 word installments; up to three installments. Pays $100/installment; $225 for 3 installments.

SMALL BUSINESS NEWSLETTER, 7514 N. 53rd St., Milwaukee WI 53223. Editor/Publisher: Don Ristow. For small business owners and managers. Monthly newsletter; 4 pages. Circ. 500. Pays on publication. Buys one-time rights. Submit seasonal/holiday material 3 months in advance of issue date. Simultaneous, photocopied and previously published submissions OK. SASE. Reports 1 month prior to publication. Sample copy and writer's guidelines for $1.

Nonfiction: General interest; how-to (cut taxes, improve management, advertise/promote, etc.); inspirational; new product (for small business use); and technical (taxes, administration, other small business interests). Submit complete ms. Pays $10-100.

Fillers: Jokes, gags, and anecdotes (tax or business related). Pays $5.

Church Administration and Ministry

THE CHRISTIAN MINISTRY, 407 S. Dearborn St., Chicago IL 60605. (312)427-5380. Editorial Director: James M. Wall. 10% freelance written. For the professional clergy (primarily liberal Protestant). Bimonthly magazine; 40 pages. Circ. 12,000. Buys all rights. Buys 50 mss/year. Pays on publication. Free sample copy. Reports in 2 weeks. SASE.

Nonfiction: "We want articles by clergy-theologians who know the clergy audience. We are interested in articles on local church problems and in helpful how-to as well as 'think' pieces." Query. Length: 1,200-1,800 words. Pay varies, $10/page minimum.

CHURCH ADMINISTRATION, 127 9th Ave. N., Nashville TN 37234. (615)251-2060. Editor: George Clark. For Southern Baptist pastors, staff and volunteer church leaders. Monthly. Buys all rights. Byline given. Will also consider second rights. Uses limited amount of freelance material. Pays on acceptance. Free sample copy and writer's guidelines upon request. SASE.

Nonfiction and Photos: "Ours is a journal for effectiveness in ministry, including church programming, organizing, and staffing; administrative skills; church financing; church food services; church facilities; communication; pastoral ministries and community needs." Length: 1,200-1,500 words. Pays 3½¢/word.

Tips: "A beginning writer should first be acquainted with organization and policy of Baptist churches and with the administrative needs of Southern Baptist churches. He should perhaps interview one or several SBC pastors or staff members, find out how they are handling a certain administrative problem such as 'enlisting volunteer workers' or 'sharing the administrative load with church staff or volunteer workers.' I suggest writers compile an article showing how *several* different administrators (or churches) handled the problem, perhaps giving meaningful quotes. Submit the completed manuscript, typed 54 characters to the line, for consideration."

CHURCH MANAGEMENT—THE CLERGY JOURNAL, Box 1625, Austin TX 78767. (512)452-0443. Editor: Manfred Holck Jr. 100% freelance written. For professional clergy and church business administrators. Monthly (except June and December) magazine; 38 pages. Circ. 12,000. Pays on publication. Buys all rights. Pays 50% kill fee. Byline given. Submit seasonal/holiday material 6 months in advance of issue date. Photocopied submissions OK. SASE. Reports in 2 months. Sample copy $1.50.

Nonfiction: How-to (be a more effective minister or administrator); and inspirational (seasonal sermons). No poetry or personal experiences. Buys 4 mss/issue. Submit complete ms. Length: 1,000-1,500 words. Pays $25-35.

Columns/Departments: Stewardship; Church Administration; Sermons; Tax Planning for Clergy; and Problem Solving. Buys 2/issue. Send complete ms. Length: 1,000-1,500 words. Pays $20-35. Open to suggestions for new columns/departments.

Tips: "Send completed mss. Avoid devotional, personal stories, interviews. Readers want to know how to be more effective ministers."

CHURCH PROGRAMS FOR PRIMARIES, (formerly *Children's Church: The Leader's Guide*), 1445 Boonville Ave., Springfield MO 65807. Editor: James E. Erdmann. Assistant Editor: Diana Ansley. "For teachers of primary-age children in a children's church, extended session story hour or Bible club setting." Quarterly magazine. Circ. 6,500. Pays on acceptance. Buys one-time rights or first North American serial rights. Phone queries OK. Submit seasonal/holiday material 12-15 months in advance. Previously published submissions OK "if you tell us." Reports in 6 weeks. SASE. Free sample copy and writer's guidelines.

Nonfiction: How-to ("Get Seven Helpers Out of an Old Sock," worship through music, etc.); inspirational; and practical help for the teacher. The spiritual must be an integral part of your material and articles should reflect actual experience or observations related to working with 6- to 7-year-olds. "Articles and stories should be oriented both to children and to a church programs setting. Some how-to articles are helpful." Buys 12 mss/year. Submit complete ms. Length: 500-1,200 words. Pays $8-20.

Photos: Purchased with mss about handcrafted items. Offers no additional payment for photos accepted with ms.

Fiction: Most religious stories done on assignment. Buys 13 mss/issue. Query. Length: 2,000-2,200 words.

Tips: "Write, requesting a sample of our publication and a copy of our writer's guidelines."

CHURCH TRAINING, 127 9th Ave. N., Nashville TN 37234. (615)251-2843. Publisher: The Sunday School Board of the Southern Baptist Convention. Editor: Richard B. Sims. For all workers and leaders in the Church Training program of the Southern Baptist Convention. Monthly. Circulation: 40,000. Buys all rights. Byline given. Buys 25 mss/year. Pays on acceptance. Will send sample copy to writer on request. Write for copy of guidelines for writers. No photocopied or simultaneous submissions. Reports in 6 weeks. Query with rough outline. SASE.

Nonfiction: "Articles that pertain to leadership training in the church. Success stories that pertain to Church Training. Associational articles. Informational, how-to's that pertain to Church Training." Length: 500-1,500 words. Pays 3½¢/word.

Tips: "Write an article that reflects the writer's experience of personal growth through church training. Keep in mind the target audience: workers and leaders of Church Training organizations in churches of the Southern Baptist Convention."

THE EDGE on Christian Education, Nazarene Publishing House, 6401 The Paseo, Kansas City MO 64131. Editor: Melton Wienecke. Assistant Editor: Nina Beegle. Emphasizes Christian/ religious education for Sunday school teachers, pastors, Sunday school superintendents, supervisors and workers. Quarterly magazine; 48 pages. Circ. 40,000. Pays on acceptance. Buys all rights, second serial (reprint) rights, or one-time rights. Byline given. Submit seasonal/holiday material 12 months in advance. Simultaneous, photocopied and previously published submissions OK. SASE. Reports in 10 weeks. Free sample copy and writer's guidelines.

Nonfiction: Publishes how-to, humor, informational, inspirational, new product, personal experience and technical articles; interviews, profiles of trends, photo features, and articles on philosophy of Christian education. Send complete ms. Length: 1,500 words maximum. Buys 80-100 mss/year. Pays 3¢/word for first rights; 2¢/word for reprints.

Photos: B&w and color purchased with or without mss, or on assignment. Send prints and transparencies. Pays $20 maximum b&w. Include your asking price with submissions.

Fiction: Considered if it is short and deals with a problem in the field. Submit complete ms. Length: 1,500 words maximum. Pays 3¢/word for first rights; 2¢/word for reprints.

Poetry: Publishes light verse or poetry in traditional forms. Buys 10 a year. Pays 25¢/line, $2.50 minimum.

EMMANUEL, 194 E. 76th St., New York NY 10021. (212)861-1076. Editor: the Rev. Paul J. Bernier, S.S.S. Monthly. Emphasizes recent theological and spiritual development for the Catholic clergy. Circ. 13,000. Rights to be arranged with author. Buys 5-6 mss/year. Pays on publication. Will consider photocopied submissions. Submit seasonal material 3-4 months in advance. Reports in 8 weeks. SASE.

Nonfiction: Articles of Catholic (especially priestly) spirituality; can be biographical, historical or critical. Articles on Eucharistic theology, and those which provide a solid scriptural and/or theological foundation for priestly spirituality (prayer, applied spirituality, etc.). Aims at providing today's priest and involved Catholics with an adequate theology and philosophy of ministry in today's church. Length: 1,500-3,000 words. Usually pays $50.

Tips: "Send a letter inquiring about topical material and asking whether we're interested in the topic, and how we'd like to see it treated. It's difficult for people without a theological and scriptural background to write an article we'd use. A phone call to the editor might save a lot of time and trouble."

ENDURING WORD ADULT TEACHER, 6401 The Paseo, Kansas City MO 64131. (816)333-7000. Editor: John B. Nielson. 10% freelance written. For teachers of adults. Quarterly. Buys first and second rights; will accept simultaneous submissions. Pays on acceptance. Will consider photocopied submissions. Reports in 6 weeks. SASE.
Nonfiction: "Articles of interest to teachers of adults and articles relevant to the Enduring Word Series Sunday school lesson outline." Length: 1,000 words maximum. Pays minimum $30/1,000 words.
Photos: Purchased with captions only. Pays minimum $5; 4-color up to $100.
Poetry: Inspirational, seasonal or lesson-related poetry. Length: 24 lines maximum. Pays minimum 25¢/line.

KEY TO CHRISTIAN EDUCATION, Standard Publishing, 8121 Hamilton Ave., Cincinnati OH 45231. (513)931-4050. Editor-in-Chief: Virginia Beddow. 50% freelance written. For "church leaders of all ages; Sunday-school teachers and superintendents; ministers; Christian education professors; youth workers." Quarterly magazine; 48 pages. Circ. 70,000. Pays on acceptance. Buys first North American serial rights. Byline given. Phone queries OK. Submit seasonal/holiday material 15 months in advance. Photocopied and previously published submissions OK. SASE. Reports in 4 weeks. Free sample copy and writer's guidelines.
Nonfiction: How-to (programs and projects for Christian education); informational; interview; opinion; and personal experience. Buys 10 mss/issue. Query or submit complete ms. Length: 700-2,000 words. Pays $20-60.
Photos: Purchased with accompanying ms. Submit prints. Pays $5-25 for any size glossy finish b&w prints. Total price for ms includes payment for photos. Model release required.
Fillers: Purchases short ideas on "this is how we did it" articles. Buys 10 mss/issue. Submit complete ms. Length: 50-250 words. Pays $5-10.
Tips: "Write for guidelines, sample issue and themes. Then write an article that fits one of the themes following the guidelines. Be practical. If the article pertains to a specific age group, address the article to that department editor."

MINISTRIES, 1201 E. David Rd., Dayton OH 45429. (513)294-0844. Editor: Rod Brownfield. Magazine published 9 times/year for Catholic and other Christian ministers, both ordained and not ordained professionals with special skills or areas of competence. Estab. 1980. Circ. 8,000. Pays on acceptance. Buys all rights. Phone queries OK. Submit seasonal material 2 months in advance. Prefers brief statement of topic and treatment prior to submission. Photocopied submissions OK. SASE. Reports in 4 weeks. Free sample copy.
Nonfiction: "We want articles that seriously profile and probe special ministries such as the sick, dying, minorities; parish models of ministry; liturgy; religious education; experimental communities; and freelance ministries. Buys 6 mss/issue. Query. Length: 1,500-1,800 words. Pays $125-150.
Photos: Pays $20 minimum for 8x10 b&w glossy prints. Captions and model release required. Buys one-time rights.

PASTORAL LIFE, Society of St. Paul, Route 224, Canfield OH 44406. Editor: Victor L. Viberti, S.S.P. Emphasizes priests and those interested in pastoral ministry. Magazine; 64 pages. Monthly. Circ. 8,800. Buys first rights. Byline given. Pays on acceptance. Will send sample copy to writer on request. Query with a outline before submitting ms. "New contributors are expected to include, in addition, a few lines of personal data that indicate academic and professional background." Reports in 7-10 days. SASE.
Nonfiction: "*Pastoral Life* is a professional review, principally designed to focus attention on current problems, needs, issues and all important activities related to all phases of pastoral work and life. Avoids merely academic treatments on abstract and too controversial subjects." Length: 2,000-3,400 words. Pays 3½¢/word minimum.

THE PRIEST, Our Sunday Visitor, Inc., 200 Noll Plaza, Huntington IN 46750. (219)356-8400. Editor: Father Vincent J. Giese. Managing Editor: Robert A. Willems. Monthly magazine (July-August combined issue) covering the priesthood. "Our magazine is basically for priests, by priests, although much is now being accepted from laypeople." Circ. 10,050. Pays on acceptance. Byline given. Not copyrighted. Buys one-time rights. Submit seasonal/holiday material 5 months in advance. SASE. Reports in 1 week on queries; 2 weeks on mss. Free sample copy.
Nonfiction: How-to, inspirational, interview/profile, opinion, personal experience and technical. "Material must deal with the day-to-day problems of the priest in his work in the parish. Don't pad articles." Buys 66-70 mss/year. Send complete ms. Length: 500-3,000 words. Pays $25-150.
Fillers: Anecdotes and short humor.

SUCCESS, Box 15337, Denver CO 80215. Editor: Edith Quinlan. 90% freelance written. Quarterly magazine. Byline given. Reports in 2-3 weeks. SASE. Free sample copy and writer's guidelines.
Nonfiction: "Articles should be from 500-2,000 words in length, and should provide ideas helpful to workers in Christian education. We are more interested in receiving articles from people who know Christian education, or workers who have accomplished something worthwhile in Sunday sch ool and youth work, than from experienced writers who do not have such backgr Qund. A combination of both, however, is ideal. Articles may be of a general nature, or be slanted to specific age groups, such as preschool, elementary, youth and adult." Pays 3¢/word.

SUNDAY SCHOOL COUNSELOR, General Council of the Assemblies of God, 1445 Boonville Ave., Springfield MO 65802. (417)862-2781, ext. 1426. Editor: Sylvia Lee. "Our audience consists of local church school teachers and administrators. These are people who, by and large, have not been professionally trained for their positions but are rather volunteer workers. Most would have not more than a high school education." Monthly magazine; 32 pages. Circ. 40,000. Pays on acceptance. Social security number required before check can be issued. Buys all rights or simultaneous rights. Byline given. Submit seasonal/holiday material 9 months in advance. Simultaneous and previously published submissions OK. SASE. Reports in 4-6 weeks. Free sample copy and writer's guidelines.
Nonfiction: How-to (Sunday school teaching, crafts, discipline in the Sunday school, building student-teacher relationships); inspirational (on the teaching ministry); and personal experience (as related to teaching ministry or how a Sunday school teacher handled a particular situation). Buys 70 mss/year. Submit complete ms. Length: 400-1,000 words. Pays 1-3¢/word.
Photos: Purchased with accompanying ms or on assignment. Send prints or transparencies. Pays $10-15 for 5x7 b&w photos; $25-70 for 2¼x2¼ color transparencies. Model release required.
Tips: "A freelancer can break into our publication by submitting a first-person account of a Sunday school experience. This must be actual, and contain a new slant or insight on an old topic. We are a good freelance market providing the person has taken time to study our publication first and to see our needs and slant."

YOUR CHURCH, Religious Publishing Co., 198 Allendale Rd., King of Prussia PA 19406. Editor: Phyllis Mather Rice. Production & Design Director: Norman Lock. 30% freelance written. Bimonthly magazine; 56 pages. Circ. 188,000. Pays on publication. Buys all rights. Pays 50% kill fee. Photocopied submissions OK. SASE. Reports in 2-3 months.
Nonfiction: "Articles for pastors, informative and cogently related to some aspect of being a pastor (counseling, personal finance, administration, building, etc.). No articles about newsletters; no preaching, sermons or devotional material." Buys 20-40 mss/year. Length: 5-15 typewritten pages. Pays $5/page, not to exceed $75.
Tips: "Always send a covering letter with some information about the article and the author."

THE YOUTH LEADER, 1445 Boonville Ave., Springfield MO 65802. Editor: Glen Ellard. For church leaders of teenagers (other than in Sunday school): staff, volunteer, appointed lay workers, adult sponsors, counselors, youth ministers. Evangelical Christianity. Secular and sacred holiday emphasis. Monthly. Circ. 4,500. Buys any rights; pays accordingly. Byline given. Buys 35-40 mss/year. Pays on acceptance. Free sample copy. Photocopied submissions OK. Submit seasonal material 4 months in advance. Reports in 6 weeks. SASE.
Nonfiction: How-to articles (e.g., "Basics of Backpacking," "Handling the Bus Trip," "Ten Ways to Better Understand Youth"); skits and role-plays; scripture choruses, ideas for youth services, projects, fund raising and socials; Bible studies and Bible study know-how; discussion starters; simulation games and activities. Avoid cliches (especially religious ones); practical rather than inspirational emphasis. Submit complete ms. Length: 500-2,000 words. Pays 2.5-3.75¢/word.
Tips: "Lead time is three and a half to four months; writing in summer, think fall, etc. Because the title of our publication is *The Youth Leader*, we get submissions for workers with children as well as teens. Because writers are more familiar with Sunday school than any other phase of church work, they write for S.S. workers. We use neither type of submission."

Clothing and Knit Goods

APPAREL INDUSTRY MAGAZINE, 6226 Vineland Ave., North Hollywood CA 91606. (213)766-5291. Executive Editor: Carolyn Pressler. For executive management in apparel companies with interests in equipment, government intervention in the garment industry; finance, management and training in industry. Monthly magazine; 70-100 pages. Circ. 20,000. Not copyrighted. Byline given. Buys 40-50 mss/year. Pays on publication. Sample copy $1. Will consider legible photocopied submissions. Reports in 3-4 weeks. Query. SASE.

Nonfiction and Photos: Articles dealing with equipment, training, finance; state and federal government, consumer interests, etc., related to the industry. "Use concise, precise language that is easy to read and understand. In other words, because the subjects are technical, keep the language comprehensible. Material must be precisely related to the apparel industry." Informational, interview, profile, successful business operations, technical articles. Length: 2,000 words maximum. No additional payment for b&w photos.

APPAREL SOUTH, Communication Channels, 6285 Barfield Rd., Atlanta GA 30238. (404)256-9800. Editor: Karen Schaffner. Managing Editor: Penny Kron. Tabloid published 9 times/year about the women's and children's apparel industry for retailers in 11 states of the Southwest. Estab. 1979. Average issue includes 6-10 features. Pays on publici tion. Byline given. Buys all rights. Written queries only. Submit seasonal material 2 months in advance. Simultaneous and previously published submissions OK if so indicated. Reports in 1 month on queries; in 2 weeks on mss.

Nonfiction: General interest (trends in fashion retailing); profile (of individuals and stores); and how-to (run an apparel retail store; display; manage personnel, energy, accounting and buying). Buys 2-3 mss/issue. Query with clips of previously published work. Length: 750-1,000 words. Pays 10¢/word.

Photos: State availability of photos. Pays $10 minimum for 5x7 b&w glossy prints. Captions and model release required. Buys one-time rights.

Tips: "Query should be a brief description of the article proposed and why the writer feels it should interest me. State availability of photos with a brief explanation of why the writer is capable of doing the article. Must know the fashion retail field."

BODY FASHIONS/INTIMATE APPAREL, Harcourt Brace Jovanovich Publications, 757 3rd Ave., New York NY 10017. (212)888-4364. Editor-in-Chief: Jill Jacobson. Emphasizes information about men's and women's hosiery and underwear; women's undergarments, lingerie, sleepwear, robes, hosiery, leisurewear. For merchandise managers and buyers of store products, manufacturers and suppliers to the trade. Monthly tabloid insert, plus 7 regional market issues called *Market Maker*; 24 pages minimum. Circ. 13,500. Pays on publication. Buys all rights. Phone queries OK. Submit seasonal/holiday material 2 months in advance. Previously published submissions OK. SASE. Reports in 4 weeks.

Columns/Departments: New Image (discussions of renovations of *Body Fashions/Intimate Apparel* department); Creative Retailing (deals with successful retail promotions); Ad Ideas (descriptions of successful advertising campaigns). Buys 6 features/year. Query. Length: 500-2,500 words. Pays 15¢/word as edited. Open to suggestions for new columns and departments.

Photos: B&w (5x7) photos purchased without mss. Captions required. Send contact sheet, prints or negatives. Pays $5-25. Model release required.

FOOTWEAR FOCUS, National Shoe Retailers Association, 200 Madison Ave., Room 1409, New York NY 10016. (212)686-7520. Magazine published 4 times/year about shoes for shoe swore owners, buyers and managers from all over the United States. The publication features articles pertaining to new methods, creative ideas, and reliable information to help them better operate their businesses. Circ. 20,000. Average issue includes 5 articles and 4 departments. Pays on acceptance. Byline given. Makes work-for-hire assignments. SASE. Reports in 2 weeks on queries; in 1 month on mss. Free sample copy and writer's guidelines.

Nonfiction: Contact: Editor, *Footwear Focus*. Interview (with buyers and store owners); how-to (advertise, display, create interiors, do inventory accounting, and manage data processing systems); new product (shoes and accessories); and technical (new methods of hide tanning and shoe manufacturing). "No generic-type articles that can be applied to any industry. No articles on salesmanship, management training or computers." Buys 2 mss/year. Query with resume and clips of previously published work. "We do not accept mss." Length: 900-1,500 words. Pays $100-200. "We want feature articles that are personality interviews or how-to articles. They must be closely related to the shoe industry. All how-to's must pertain to some aspect of shoe retailing such as developing advertising plans, interior displays, setting up an open-to-buy or fashion merchandising."

Tips: "Freelancers must have knowledge, experience or background in fashion merchandising and retailing, preferably in shoes. Other areas open are advertising and promotion, customer services, and buying and inventory control. We prefer article suggestions to actual manuscripts, as most freelance writing is assigned according to the editor's choice of subject and topic areas. Those writers interested in doing personal interviews and covering regional events in the shoe industry have the best opportunity, since NYC staff writers can cover only local events."

IMPRESSIONS, Windsor Communications, Inc., 17311 Dallas North Pkwy., Dallas TX 75248. Editor: Christine B. Caperton. Associate Editor: Susan L. Anderson. Monthly magazine about the imprinted sportswear industry for retailers, printers, wholesalers, manufacturers and suppliers. Circ. 18,000. Average issue contains 2 features and 10 departments. Seasonal submissions should be 3 months prior to publication month. Competitive rates, pay upon acceptance for unpublished, original materials. Increased rates when photos or illustrations available. 1,500 word minimum. Written or phone queries encouraged. Free sample and writer's guidelines. Buys 12 or more mss/year.
Nonfiction: Technical or general interest related to imprinted sportswear industry. Examples: screen printing of textiles (techniques, materials, etc.), direct or heat transfers printing (methods, mediums, etc.); manufacturing of equipment, imprintables (T-shirts, caps, uniforms, etc.), supplies, etc.; business management (employee management, accounting and credit, inventory control, computers, etc.); legal materials (copyright and trademark rulings, sales contracts, etc.); art (preparation for transfers, screen printing, advertising, etc.); sales techniques; retailing; merchandising.

INFANT & TODDLER WEAR, Columbia Communications, 370 Lexington Ave., New York NY 10017. (212)5)2-9290. Editor: Lisa Keith. Bimonthly magazine covering retailing and manufacturing of prol ucts for infants, for retailers and manufacturers. Estab. 1980. Circ. 13,000. Pays on publication. Byline given. Buys first North American serial rights. Submit seasonal/holiday material 6 months in advance. Simultaneous queries and photocopied submissions OK. Reports in 2 weeks. Free sample gopy; writer's guidelines for business size SAE and 1 first class stamp.
Nonfiction: Profile (of stores or manufacturers); and new product. No how-to material. Buys 6 mss/year. Query with clips of published work (trade). Length: 1,200-2,000 words. Pays $200 minimum.
Photos: State availability of photos. Reviews 35mm color transparencies. "Photos are paid for with payment for ms." Captions required. Buys one-time rights.
Tips: "We are keeping a file of freelancers and articles for future use. Writers may not hear from us immediately."

KNITTING TIMES, National Knitted Outerwear Association, 51 Madison Ave., New York NY 10010. (212)683-7520. Editor: Eric Hertz. For the knitting industry, from the knitter to the cutter and sewer to the machinery manufacturer, to the fiber and yarn producer, chemical manufacturer, and various other suppliers to the industry. Weekly magazine; 58 pages. Circ: 6,100. Pays on publication. Buys all rights. Submit seasonal or holiday material 1 month in advance. SASE. Reports in 4 weeks. Free sample copy and writer's guidelines.
Nonfiction: Historical (various parts of the knitting industry; development of machines, here and abroad); how-to (cut and sew various outer garments; knit, dye and finish; needle set-outs for various knit constructions); informational (market or show reports, trends, new fabrics, machine, fiber, yarn, chemical developments); interviews (with leading figures in the industry; may be knitter, head of fiber company, etc. Must say something significant such as new market development, import situation, projections and the like). New product (on anything in the industry such as machines, fibers, yarns, dyeing and finishing equipment, etc.). Photo features (on plants or plant layouts, how to cut and sew sweaters, skirts, etc.). Profiles (can be on industry leaders, or on operation of a company; specifically plant stories and photos). Technical (on machines, chemical processes, finishing, dyeing, spinning, texturing, etc.). Length: 750 words minimum. Query first. Pays $.70-1 an inch.
Photos: B&w glossies (8x10) purchased with mss. Query first. Pays $3 for glossies; $5/diagram.

MEN'S WEAR, Fairchild Publications, 7 E. 12th St., New York NY 10003. Editorial Director: Kevin Doyle. Emphasizes men's and boy's apparel for retailers. Semimonthly magazine; 50 pages. Circ. 26,700. Pays on acceptance. Buys all rights. SASE. Reports in 3 weeks. Free sample copy.
Nonfiction: In-depth analysis (pertaining to men's wear industry companies or issues); how-to (on making men's wear retailing more profitable; sales promotions; advertising; displays). Buys 2-3 mss/year. Query. Unsolicited ms not considered. Length: 1,000 words minimum. Pays $100-300.

TACK 'N TOGS MERCHANDISING, Box 67, Minneapolis MN 55440. Editor: Doug Dahl. For "retailers of products for horse and rider and Western and English fashion apparel." Monthly. Circ. 16,000. Rights purchased vary with author and material; may buy alyrights. Byline given "except on simultaneous submissions, or non-exclusive articles that may appear in slightly edited form in other publications." Buys 5-10 mss/year. Pays on acceptance. Will send a sample copy to a writer on request. Write for copy of guidelines for writers. Query; "style isn't important, but substance has to be something I need—suggest angle from which writer will cover the story." SASE.

Nonfiction and Photos: "Case histories, trends of industry." Buys informational articles, how-to's, interviews, profiles, coverage of successful business operations, and articles on merchandising techniques. No boiler-plate articles. Length: open. Pays "up to $150." B&w glossies and color transparencies purchased with mss.

Tips: "Write a letter describing a geographic area you can cover. Show some ex' ertise in a particular phase of retail management."

TEENS & BOYS, 7l W. 35th St., New York NY 10001. Market Editor: Robin Kerr. 20% freelance written. For retailers, manufacturers, resident buying offices in male apparel trade. Monthly magazine; 48-100 pages. Pays on publication. Buys one-time rights. Byline given. Submit seasonal/holiday material 6 months in advance. SASE.

Nonfiction: "*Teens & Boys* is edited for large and small retailers of apparel for boys and male teenage students, aged 4-18. It forecasts style trends, reports on all aspects of retailing. All factual, carefully researched, pertinent articles presented in a lively style will be considered. No tax articles." Buys 2 mss/issue. Query with "well-detailed outline and writing samples. Retail related stories most appreciated." Length: 1,000-2,000 words. Pays $30-150.

Photos: State availability of photos with query. Pays $7.50-10 for contact sheets, negatives or 5x7 b&w glossy prints. Captions required. Buys one-time rights.

Tips: "Phone inquiries followed up in writing are most successful. We strive for regional representation of retailers, so geographic distribution is good."

WESTERN OUTFITTER, 5314 Bingle Rd., Houston TX 77092. (713)688-8811. Editor: Tad S. Mizwa. For "owners and managers of retail stores in all 50 states and Canada. These stores sell clothing for riders and equipment for horses, both Western and English style." Monthly. Buys all rights. Pays on publication. Query. SASE.

Nonfiction: Method stories: "in-depth treatment of subjects each merchant wrestles with daily. We want stories that first describe the problem, then give details on methods used in eliminating the problem. Be factual and specific." Subjects include merchandising, promotion, customer contact, accounting and finance, store operation, merchandise handling and personnel. "To merit feature coverage, this merchant has to be a winner. It is the uniqueness of the winner's operation that will bi nefit other store owners who read this magazine." Length: 1,000-1,500 words for full-length feature; 500-600 words for featurette. Pays 7¢/published word for shortcut featurettes; 7¢ published word for full-length feature and featurettes. "Send us copies of stories you have done for other trade magazines. Send us queries based on visits to Western dealers in your territory."

Photos: "Excellent photos make excellent copy much better. Plan photos that bring to life the key points in your text. Avoid shots of store fixtures without people. Submit photos in glossy finish, in 8x10 size or smaller. Sharp focus is a must." Captions required. "Cover photos: We will pay $50 for a color transparency if used for a cover (2¼x2¼ or 35mm). Your 35mm shots are fine for interior b&w art." Pays $10/b&w photo used with ms. Also uses "single photos, or pairs of photos that show display ideas, tricks, promotional devices that are different and that bring more business." Pays $10.

Tips: "The queries that have thought out the subject, advance some angles on which the story is built, and show that the writer has digested our detailed guidelines statement are a real pleasure to respond to."

WESTERN WEAR AND EQUIPMENT MAGAZINE, Bell Publishing, 2403 Champa, Denver CO 80205. (303)572-1777. Editor: Alan Bell. Managing Editor: Joy Heckendorf. For "Western wear and equipment retailers, manufacturers and distributors. The magazine features retailing practices such as marketing, merchandising, display techniques, buying and selling to help business grow or improve, etc. Every issue carries feature stories on Western wear and equipment stores throughout the US and occasionally foreign stores." Monthly magazine; 50 pages. Circ. 13,000. Pays on publication. Not copyrighted. Byline given unless extensive rewriting is required. Phone queries OK. Submit seasonal/holiday material 3 months in advance. Simultaneous (to noncompeting publications), photocopied and previously published submissions OK. SASE. Reports in 3 weeks. Free sample copy and writer's guidelines.

Nonfiction: Exposé (of government as related to industry or people in industry); general interest (pertaining to Western lifestyle); interview (with Western store owners or Western personalities); new product (of interest to Western clothing or tack retailers—send photo); and photo feature (on Western lifestyle or Western retailing operation). Buys 2 mss/issue. Query with outline. Length: 800-3,600 words. Pays $50-150.

Photos: "We buy photos with manuscripts. Occasionally we purchase photos that illustrate a unique display or store with only a cutline." State availability of photos. Captions required with "names of people or products and locations." Buys one-time rights.
Columns/Departments: "We accept freelance material for a profile column. The material should feature the operations of a Western wear or equipment retailer. We prefer accompanying photos."
Fiction: "We use very little fiction. Writer should query with ideas." Buys 1-2 mss/year. Length: open. Pays $50-75.

Coin-Operated Machines

AMERICAN COIN-OP, 500 N. Dearborn St., Chicago IL 60610. (312)337-7700. Editor: Ben Russell. For owners of coin-operated laundry and drycleaning stores. Monthly magazine; 42 pages. Circ. 19,000. Rights purchased vary with author and material but are exclusive to the field. No byline. Buys 25 mss/year. Pays two weeks prior to publication. Free sample copy. Reports as soon as possible; usually in 2 weeks. SASE.
Nonfiction and Photos: "We emphasize store operation and use features on industry topics: utility use and conservation, maintenance, store management, customer service and advertising. A case study should emphasize how the store operator accomplished whatever he did—in a way that the reader can apply to his own operation. Mss should have no-nonsense, businesslike approach." Uses informational, how-to, interview, profile, think pieces, successful business operations articles. Length: 500-3,000 words. Pays 5¢/word minimum. Pays $5 minimum for 8x10 b&w glossy photos purchased with mss. (Contact sheets with negatives preferred.) Must be clear and have good contrast.
Fillers: Newsbreaks, clippings. Length: open. Pays 3¢/word; $3 minimum.
Tips: "Query about subjects of current interest. Be observant of coin-operated laundries—how they are designed and equipped; how they serve customers; how (if) they advertise and promote their services. Most general articles turned down because they are not aimed well enough at audience. Most case histories turned down because of lack of practical purpose (nothing new or worth reporting)."

COINAMATIC AGE, 5 Beekman St., Room 401, New York NY 10038. (212)349-3754. Editor: C.F. Lee. For operators/owners of coin-operated laundries; dry cleaners. Bimonthly. Buys all rights. Pays on publication. "Queries get same-day attention."
Nonfiction and Photos: "We are currently considering articles on coin-operated laundries, and/or in combination with drycleaners. Slant should focus on the unusual, but at the same time should stress possible adaptation by other coinamat operators. Particular interest at this time centers on energy conservation methods. We are interested in promotional and advertising techniques; reasons for expansion or additional locations; attached sidelines such as carwashes and other businesses; Main Street vs. shopping center operations; successes in dealing with permanent press garment laundering and cleaning; ironing services; and, primarily, financial success, personal satisfaction, or any other motivation that the owner derives from his business. Give the story punch, details, and applicability to the reader. Include a list of specifications, detailing the number of units (washers, dryers, etc.), the different pound-loads of each machine and the make and model numbers of all these, as well as any vending machines, changemakers, etc. Three action photos (preferably a minimum of 6) must accompany each article. At this time, we are especially interested in combined laundry-cleaning articles. Submitted photos must include an exterior shot of the installation and interior shots showing customers. Where possible, a photo of the owner at work is also desired. If you have a far-out slant, query first." Pays 3-4¢/word, depending on need to rewrite. Length: 1,200-2,000 words. No "plugola" for manufacturers' products. Photos purchased with mss. Pays $12 for 3 photos and $6 for each additional photo.

GAME MERCHANDISING, Boynton & Associates, Inc., Clifton House, Clifton VA 22024. (703)830-1000. Editor: Rick Ludwick. Monthly magazine covering the retail sale of games and related supplies. "*Game Merchandising* helps retailers and buyers stay informed on new products, industry trends, and effective sales techniques." Estab. 1981. Circ. 9,000. Pays on publication. Byline given. Buys all rights. Submit seasonal/holiday material 3 months in advance. Photocopied submissions and previously published work ("negotiable") OK. SASE. Reports in 3 weeks. Sample copy for 9x12 SAE; writer's guidelines for legal size SAE and 1 first class stamp.
Nonfiction: How-to (sell games most effectively); and interview/profile (of store owners/managers and industry figures). "We are slanted toward the retailer, so we prefer articles embody-

ing hard information on the industry or the experience of successful retailers. No detailed reviews of games." Buys "estimating 20" mss/year. Query. Length: 1,500 words. Pays 10¢/word.
Photos: State availability of photos. Pays $7.50 for 5x7 b&w prints. Identification of subjects required. Buys all rights.
Columns/Departments: Tabletop Games (puzzles, board games, etc.); Electronic Games; Gaming Miniatures; and Role-playing Games. "All departme, ts use survey articles or articles on how a particular store effectively sells that type of product." Query. Length: 1,500 words. Pays 10¢/word.
Tips: "Freelancers can best break in by querying for necessary details and writing a 'Retailer Profile' on a successful game store or game department. Once a writer has identified a suitable store, he should be able to write a good interview by adding a few questions to our standard interview form."

LEISURE TIME ELECTRONICS, Charleson Publishing Co., 124 E. 40th St., New York NY 10016. (212)953-0230. Editor: Bob Citelli. Tabloid published 5 times in 1981, monthly in 1982, covering electronic games and toys, personal computers and software, audio and video hardware and software, and personal electronics for retailers of leisure electronics. Estab. 1980. Circ. 46,000. Pays on acceptance. Byline and brief bio given. Buys "all rights in the trade." Photocopied submissions OK. Reports "promptly." Free sample copy.
Nonfiction: Technical (state-of-the-art explaining technology); and merchandising (all aspects). Buys 20 mss/year. Query with clips of published work and resume. Length: 1,500 words average. Pays rates "competitive with any national magazine."
Photos: "We ask writers to request photos from storeowners. Product photos come from manufacturers." Reviews color transparencies and 8x10 b&w glossy prints. Identification of subjects required.
Fillers: Newsbreaks. Length: 100 words maximum. Pays varying fee.

PLAY METER MAGAZINE, Skybird Publishing Co., Inc., Box 24170. New Orleans LA 70184. Publisher: Ralph Lally. Editorial Director: David Pierson. Managing Editor: Ray Tilley. 25% freelance written. Trade publication for owners/operators of coin-operated amusement machine companies, e.g., pinball machines, video games, arcade pieces, jukeboxes, etc. Bimonthly magazine; 90 pages. Circ. 8,300. Pays on publication. Buys all rights. Byline given. Submit seasonal/holiday material 2 months in advance of issue date. Photocopied and previously published submissions OK. SASE. Reports in 1 month. Sample copy $2; free writer's guidelines.
Nonfiction: How-to (get better locations for machines, promote tournaments, evaluate profitability of route, etc.); interview (with industry leaders); new product (if practical for industry, not interested in vending machines); and photo features (with some copy). "No 'puff' or 'plug' pieces about new manufacturers. Our readers want to read about how they can make more money from their machines, how they can get better tax breaks, commissions, etc. Also no stories about *playing* pinball. Our readers don't play the game per se; they buy the machines and make money from them." Buys 1-2 mss/issue. Submit complete ms. Length: 250-3,000 words. Pays $10-150.
Photos: "The photography should have news value. We don't want 'stand 'km up-shoot 'em down' group shots." Pays $10 minimum for 5x7 or 8x10 b&w prints; $50 for color cover pictures. Captions preferred. Buys all rights.

VENDING TIMES, 211 E. 43rd St., New York NY 10017. Editor: Arthur E. Yohalem. For operators of vending machines. Monthly. Circ. 13,500. Buys all rights. Pays on publication. Query: "we will discuss the story requirements with the writer in detail." SASE.
Nonfiction and Photos: Feature articles and news stories about vending operations; practical and important aspects of the business. "We are always willing to pay for good material."

Confectionery and Snack Foods

CANDY AND SNACK INDUSTRY, 747 3rd Ave., New York NY 10017. (212)838-7778. Editor: Myron Lench. For confectionery and snack manufacturers. Monthly. Buys all rights. Reports in 2 weeks. SASE.
Nonfiction: "Feature articles of interest to large-scale candy, cookie, cracker, and other snack manufacturers that deal with activities in the fields of production, packaging (including package design), merchandising; financial news (sales figures, profits, earnings), advertising campaigns in all media, and promotional methods used to increase the sale or distribution of candy and snacks." Length: 1,000-1,250 words. Pays 5¢/word; "special rates on assignments."

Photos: "Good quality glossies with complete and accurate captions, in sizes not smaller than 5x7." Pays $5. Color covers.
Fillers: "Short news stories about the trade and anything related to candy and snacks." Pays 5¢/word; $1 for clippings.

CANDY MARKETER, 747 3rd Ave., New York NY 10017. (212)838-7778. Publisher: Mike Lench. Editor: Louis J. Lassus. For owners and executives of wholesale and retail businesses. Monthly magazine. Circ. 14,000. Buys all rights. Byline given. Buys 20 mss/year. Pays on acceptance. Free sample copy. Photocopied submissions OK. Submit seasonal material at least 6 months in advance. Reports in 2 weeks. SASE.
Nonfiction: News and features on the candy trade. "Describe operation, interview candy buyer or merchandise manager; quote liberally. More interested in mass operations, than in unusual little shops." Informational, how-to, interview, profile, spot news, successful business operations, merchandising techniques. Annual issues on Halloween merchandising, Christmas merchandising and Easter merchandising are published in May, June and November (respectively). Length: 1,000-2,500 words. Pays 10¢/word.
Photos: 5x7 or 8½x11 b&w photos and color transparencies or prints purchased with mss. Captions required. Pays $5 for b&w; $15 for color.
Fillers: Pays $1 for each clipping used.

Construction and Contracting

Journals aimed at architects and city planners will be found in the Architecture category. Those for specialists in the interior aspects of construction are listed under Building Interiors.

ABC AMERICAN ROOFER AND BUILDING IMPROVEMENT CONTRACTOR, Shelter Publications, Inc., 5006 Washington St., Downers Grove IL 60515. (312)964-6200. Aspects of construction for contractors who do roofing and exterior remodeling and improvement work. Monthly magazine; 20-32 pages. Circ. 28,800. Pays on publication. Buys all rights. Byline given. Submit seasonal/holiday material 4 months in advance. SASE. Reports in 1 week. Free sample copy, if SASE (9x12) is sent.
Nonfiction: Publishes how-to (apply various kinds of material on roofs, preferably unusual kinds of data); historical; humor (if original); interview; photo feature (unusual types of roofing); profile (on industry men); and technical. "No generalized industry articles; no women-in-industry stories unless the job is the important part of the article." Buys 5 mss/year. Query. Length: 1,500 words maximum. Pays $10-50. Editorial schedule available.
Photos: Purchased with accompanying ms. Captions required. Pays $5-25 for b&w glossy prints. Query or submit prints.
Tips: "Mss must pertain to our industry. Be concise and brief. Spaced-out wordings are not tolerated—articles must be well condensed, yet carry all the pertinent facts. The story is the only thing that gets our interest. The content must address itself to readers' interests very, very specifically (not in general). It must feature a roofing contractor by name (with full addresses) and full details on the main feature points."

ARCHITECTURAL METALS, National Association of Architectural Metal Manufacturers, 221 N. LaSalle St., Chicago IL 60601. (312)346-1600. Editor: Jim Nowakowski. Managing Editor: August L. Sisco. Semiannual magazine covering architectural metal applications for architects, specifiers, and other engineers involved in using architectural metal products. Circ. 15,000. Pays on acceptance. Byline given. Buys first North American serial rights and simultaneous rights on work-for-hire assignments. Submit seasonal material 2 months in advance. Simultaneous queries, and simultaneous, photocopied and previously published submissions OK. Reports in 2 weeks on queries; 1 month on mss. Sample copy 50¢; free writer's guidelines.
Nonfiction: "No articles that are too general." Number of mss bought/year "depends on need." Query with clips of published work or send complete ms. Phone queries OK. Length: 1,000 words minimum. Pays $150-400/article.
Photos: Send photos with ms. Pays $10 maximum for 5x7 b&w prints. Captions required.
Tips: "Have a knowledge of architectural metals and write clearly. Applications of hollow metal/flagpoles/metal bar grating/architectural metals are all open. Keep the subject matter clear and interesting. Technical details are a must."

AUTOMATION IN HOUSING & SYSTEMS BUILDING NEWS, CMN Associates, Inc., Box 126, Carpinteria CA 93013. (805)684-7659. Editor-in Chief: Don Carlson. Specializes in management for industrialized (manufactured) housing and volume home builders. Monthly magazine; 88 pages. Circ. 23,000. Pays on acceptance. Buys first North American or one-time rights. Phone queries OK. SASE. Reports in 2 weeks. Free sample copy and writer's guidelines.
Nonfiction: Case history articles on successful home building companies which may be 1) production (big volume) home builders; 2) mobile home manufacturers; 3) modular home manufacturers; 4) prefabricated home manufacturers or; 5) house component manufacturers. Also uses interviews, photo features and technical articles. Buys 6-8 mss/year. Query. Length: 2,500 words maximum. Pays $250 minimum.
Photos: Purchased with accompanying ms. Captions required. Query. No additional payment for 4x5, 5x7 or 8x10 b&w glossies or 35mm or larger color transparencies (35mm preferred).

CALIFORNIA BUILDER & ENGINEER, 4110 Transport St., Palo Alto CA 94303. Editor: John S. Whitaker. "For contractors, engineers, machinery distributors for the construction industry, and civic officials concerned with public works. Our coverage is limited to California, Hawaii, western Arizona and western Nevada." Published twice a month. Circ. 12,500. Pays on publication. Makes work-for-hire assignments. Not copyrighted. Reports in 3 weeks. SASE. Free sample copy.
Nonfiction: "We are particularly interested in knowledgeable articles on nonconstruction issues that affect the large and small contractor in our region. For example, accounting for the contractor, labor issues, pending legislation or ecology. These articles must be written with rigid accuracy, often requiring specialized knowledge. We are also interested in job stories from Hawaii on heavy public construction. We are not interested in residential construction. Field experience and in-depth knowledge of the industry are essential in writing for us." Query. Length: 1,500-2,200 words. Pays $60/page.
Photos: Send photos with ms. Reviews 5x7 b&w glossy prints. Offers no additional payment for photos accompanying ms. Captions and model release required. Buys one-time rights.

CONSTRUCTION EQUIPMENT OPERATION AND MAINTENANCE, Box 1689, Cedar Rapids IA 52406. (319)366-1597. Editor: C.K. Parks. 15% freelance written. For users of heavy construction equipment. Bimonthly. Buys all rights. Pays on acceptance. Query. Reports in 1 month. SASE.
Nonfiction and Photos: "Articles on selection, use, operation, or maintenance of construction equipment; articles and features on the construction industry in general; job safety articles." Length: 1,000-2,000 words. Also buys a limited number of job stories with photos, and feature articles on individual contractors in certain areas of US and Canada. Length varies. Pays $50-200.

CONSTRUCTION SPECIFIER, 1150 17th St. NW, Washington DC 20036. (202)833-2160. Editor: Jack Reeder. 100% freelance written. Professional society magazine for architects, engineers, specification writers and contractors. Monthly. Circ. 14,000. Buys one-time North American serial rights. Pays on publication. Free sample copy. Deadline: 60 days preceding publication on the 5th of each month. Reports in 2-3 weeks. SASE. Model releases, author copyright transferral requested.
Nonfiction and Photos: "Articles on selection and specification of products, materials, equipment and methods used in construction projects, specifications as related to construction design, plus legal and contractual subjects." Query. Length: 3,600-5,100 words. Pays 5¢/published word, plus art. Photos critical to consideration for publication; line art, sketches, diagrams, charts and graphs also desired. Full color transparencies may be used. Prices negotiable. 8x10 glossies, 3¼ slides preferred.

CONSTRUCTION WEST, Box 34080, Station 'D', Vancouver, British Columbia, Canada V6J 4M8. Editorial Director: Brian Martin. Monthly. Serving the heavy construction industry of western Canada. Buys first Canadian rights. Pays on acceptance. Query first.
Nonfiction and Photos: Specialized stories for specific audience. Average length: 1,500 words. Pays 14¢/word (Canadian). Pays $5 for 5x7 photos.

CONSTRUCTIONEER, 1 Bond St., Chatham NJ 07928. Editor: Ken Hanan. 10% freelance written. For contractors, distributors, material producers, public works officials, consulting engineers, etc. Biweekly. Circ. 18,000. Buys all rights. Byline given "only on rare occasions. Our general policy is 'no byline for either staff-written or supplied material.' " Buys 10 mss/year. Pays on acceptance. Sample copy $1. Photocopied submissions OK. Submit seasonal material 2 months in advance. Reports in 1-2 months. SASE.
Nonfiction: Construction job stories; new methods studies. Detailed job studies of methods and equipment used; oriented around geographical area of New York, New Jersey, Pennsylvania and

Delaware. Winter snow and ice removal and control; winter construction methods. Current themes: public works, profiles, conservation. Query; "contact by phone as to potential job story in area that might be of interest." Length: 1,500-1,800 words. Pays $100-200.
Photos: B&w photos purchased with or without accompanying ms or on assignment. Pays $5-8.

CONSTRUCTOR MAGAZINE (The Management Magazine for the Construction Industry), 1957 E St. NW, Washington DC 20006. Editor: Diane B. Snow. Publication of the Associated General Contractors of America for "men and women in the age range of approximately 25-70 (predominantly 40s and 50s), most with a college education. Most own or are officers in their own corporations." Monthly. Circ. 27,500. Buys all rights. Buys 15 mss/year. Pays on publication. Query or submit complete ms. "Often telephone query first is best." Reports in 2 months. SASE. Sample copy $2; free writer's guidelines.
Nonfiction: "Feature material dealing with labor, legal, technical and professional material pertinent to the construction industry. We deal only with the management aspect of the construction industry." Buys informational articles, interviews, think pieces, exposes, photo features, coverage of successful business operations, and technical articles. "Please no new product plugs, technical articles, or AGC construction project stories where the contractor wasn't an AGC member." Length: "no minimum or maximum; subject much more important than length." Pays $150 minimum.
Photos: State availability of photos. Reviews 8x10 b&w semi-glossy prints and 35mm color transparencies. Offers no additional payment for photos accompanying ms. Captions required with "action description, date, location, names of persons, general contractor's firm's name, location and AGC chapter affiliation, if applicable. Model release required. Buys all rights.

DIXIE CONTRACTOR, Box 280, Decatur GA 30031. (404)377-2683. Editor: Russell K. Paul. 20% freelance written. For contractors, public officials, architects, engineers, and construction equipment manufacturers and dealers. Biweekly magazine; 125 pages. Circ. 9,000. Pays on publication. Buys all rights. Phone queries OK. Submit seasonal/holiday material 2 months in advance of issue date. Photocopied submissions OK. SASE. Reports in 2 weeks. Free sample copy.
Nonfiction: How-to (articles on new construction techniques and innovations); and interview (with government officials influencing construction, or prominent contractors). Buys 7 mss/year. Query or submit complete ms. Length: 1,500-2,000 words. Pays $50 minimum.
Photos: State availability of photos with query or ms. Captions and model release required. Buys all rights.
Columns/Departments: Labor-Management Relations in Construction. Buys 26 mss/year. Submit complete ms. Length: 1,000-1,500 words. Pays $50 minimum.
Tips: "We are interested only in freelancers who have a business writing background and who reside in the Southeast. We won't reply to people who live on the West Coast, in the Midwest or Upper Northeast. It's a waste of our time."

ENGINEERING AND CONTRACT RECORD, 1450 Don Mills Road, Don Mills, Ontario, Canada M3B 2X7. (416)445-6641. Editor: Nick Hancock. For contractors in engineered construction and aggregate producers. Monthly. Circ. 23,100. Buys Canadian rights. Pays on publication. Free sample copy. Reports in 2 weeks. SAE and International Reply Coupons.
Nonfiction: "Job stories. How to build a project quicker, cheaper, better through innovations and unusual methods. Articles on construction methods, technology, equipment, maintenance and management innovations. Management articles. Stories are limited to Canadian projects or Canadian construction firms working on projects overseas." Buys 12-15 mss/year. Query. Length: 1,000-1,200 words. Pays 15¢/printed word.
Photos: B&w 8x10 glossy prints purchased with mss. Pays $10/photo.

EQUIPMENT ADVERTISER DIGEST, 100 N. 7th St., Suite 207, Minneapolis MN 55403. (800)328-7170. Editor: Chris Lee. Monthly tabloid about the construction and heavy equipment industries for contractors and users of heavy equipment. Circ. 45,000. Average issue includes 2 feature articles, 2 columns, and profiles of companies. Pays on publication. Byline given. Offers $25 kill fee. Buys all rights. Phone queries OK. Photocopied and previously published submissions OK if so indicated. SASE. Reports in 2 weeks. Free sample copy.
Nonfiction: "We're looking for articles that cover people in the construction industry, legislation affecting the industry, regulations, finance, and operating a small business. Submit a story idea from your region that the editorial office in Minneapolis would not know about." Buys 1-2 mss/issue. Query with clips of previously published work and resume. Pays $150 minimum.
Photos: Reviews b&w glossy prints and negatives. Captions required. Buys one-time rights.

EXCAVATING CONTRACTOR, Cummins Publishing Co., 3221 W. Big Beaver Rd., Suite 204, Troy MI 48084. (313)362-4650. Editor: Andrew J. Cummins. Monthly magazine about earthmoving/small business management for small earthmoving contractors and entrepreneurs. Circ. 30,000. Pays on publication. Byline given. Makes work-for-hire assignments. Phone queries OK. Submit seasonal material 2 months in advance. Previously published submissions OK; "state where." SASE. Reports in 1 month. Free sample copy and writer's guidelines.

Nonfiction: Expose (of government rip-offs of the small businessman); historical (anything on old earthmoving machines); how-to (maintain machines; move dirt more effectively); new product (innovations in the industry); and photo feature (job stories). Buys 8 mss/year. Query with clips of previously published work. Length: 500-1,500 words. "We are a national construction publication that goes exclusively to the small earthmoving contractor. We have five departments: one is devoted to the woman's side of the business, written in an Erma Bombeck style. We also feature a good deal of articles on small business management, tax advice, etc. Read a few copies of the publication and talk to a few small contractors. Contact us and discuss the story idea. Your best bet would be a job article on how a certain small contractor tackled a particularly tough situation or used a unique approach to a problem. Special issues needing work are on winter work, and how to keep busy in the off season."

Photos: State availability of photos or send photos with ms. Reviews b&w contact sheets. Pays $25-50 for cover color contact sheets. Offers no additional payment for photos accepted with ms. Captions preferred. Buys one-time rights.

Columns/Departments: Excavator's Wife (humorous but hard-hitting articles on running a small business); Book Review (of small business or contracting-related book). Buys 12 mss/year. Query with clips of previously published work. Length: 1,000-1,800 words. Pays $25-$50.

Fillers: Jokes. Buys 5 mss/year. Length: 50-100 words. Pays $5 maximum.

FENCE INDUSTRY, 6285 Barfield Rd., Atlanta GA 30328. (404)393-2920. Editor/Associate Publisher: Bill Coker. For retailers of fencing materials. Monthly magazine; 54-80 pages. Circ. 13,000. Buys all rights. Buys 25-35 mss/year. Pays on publication. Free sample copy. Reports in 3 months. Query or submit complete ms. SASE.

Nonfiction and Photos: Case histories, as well as articles on fencing for highways, pools, farms, playgrounds, homes, industries. Surveys, and management and sales reports. Interview, profile, historical, successful business operations, and articles on merchandising techniques. Length: open. Pays 10¢/word. Pays $10 for 8x10 b&w photos purchased with mss. Captions required.

JOURNAL OF COMMERCE, Box 34080, Station D, Vancouver, B.C., Canada, V6J 4M8. Editorial Director: Brian Martin. Twice-weekly tabloid aimed at a general construction and development audience in western Canada. Circ. 14,000. Buys first Canadian rights. Payment on acceptance. Query first. Enclose SAE and International Reply Coupons.

Nonfiction and Photos: Specialized stories for specific audiences. Average length: 1,500 words. Pays 14¢/word (Canadian). Pays $5 for 5x7 photos.

RESTAURANT DESIGN MAGAZINE, Bill Communications, 633 3rd Ave., New York NY 10017. (212)986-4800, ext. 338, 355. Editor: Regina Baraban. Associate Editor: Barbara Knox. Quarterly magazine about contract design and the restaurant business for architects, designers and restaurant and hotel executives. Estab. 1979. Circ. 30,000. Pays on acceptance. Byline given. Buys first North American serial rights. Phone queries OK. Photocopied and previously published submissions OK. SASE. Reports in 1 month on queries; in 2 months on mss. Free sample copy.

Nonfiction: Profile. Buys 8 mss/year. Query with clips of previously published work. Length: 1,500-2,500 words.

Columns/Departments: Length: 250-500 words. Pays $50-75.

Tips: "We generally work very closely with a writer, directing research and focusing articles. We ask for rewriting frequently. As a result, unsolicited works seldom suit our format. Query should have clarity, brevity, knowledge of the magazine and design language. Submit quality photography with any project query so that we can determine whether or not we can use the story."

WORLD CONSTRUCTION, 666 5th Ave., New York NY 10019. (212)489-4652. Editor: Henry Mozdzer. 10-20% freelance written. For "English-speaking engineers, contractors, and government officials everywhere except the US and Canada." Monthly. Buys all rights. Byline given unless "the article is less than one page long." Pays on publication. Free sample copy. Query. Reports in 1 month. SASE.

Nonfiction: "How-to articles that stress how contractors can do their jobs faster, better or more economically. Articles are rejected when they tell only what was constructed, but not how it was constructed and why it was constructed in that way. No clippings from newspapers telling of construction projects." Length: 1,000-6,000 words. Pays $75/magazine page, or 5 typed ms pages.

Photos: State availability of photos. Photos purchased with mss; uses 4x5 or larger b&w glossy prints.

Tips: "At present time, we would only consider buying articles dealing with construction projects in overseas locations."

Dairy Products

DAIRY SCOPE, Box 547, Penngrove CA 94951. Editor: Chase W. Hastings. 50% freelance written. Bimonthly magazine; 20 pages. Circ. 1,500. Pays on publication. Buys one-time rights. Photocopied submissions OK. SASE. Reports in 4 weeks. Free sample copy and writer's guidelines.
Nonfiction: How-to (new or interesting techniques in dairying and dairy processing); general interest (to the Western dairy processing industry); historical (Western dairy industry); technical (Western dairy processing); and dairy of the month. Buys 24 mss/year. Query. Length: 100-2,000 words. Pays $2.50/column inch.
Photos: State availability of photos in query. Pays $5-25 for 8x10 b&w glossy prints, contact sheets and negatives. Captions preferred. Buys one-time rights. Model release required.
Fillers: Clippings. Pays $2.

Data Processing

CANADIAN DATASYSTEMS, 481 University Ave., Toronto, Ontario, Canada M5W 1A7. (416)596-5907. Editor: Tom Weissmann. For data processing managers, computer systems managers, systems analysts, computer programmers, corporate management and similar people concerned with the use of computers in business, industry, government and education. Monthly magazine; 70 pages. Circ. 15,000. Buys first Canadian rights. Pays on acceptance. Free sample copy. No photocopied or simultaneous submissions. Reports in 1 month. Enclose SAE and International Reply Coupons.
Nonfiction: Articles of technical, semi-technical and general interest within the general area of data processing. How-to features, application reports, descriptions of new techniques, surveys of equipment and services. Emphasis should be placed on the use of data processing equipment and services in Canada. Articles must be technical enough to satisfy an informed readership. Buys 20 mss/year. Query or submit complete ms. Length: 2,000 words maximum. Pays $200/feature article.

COMPUTER CONSULTANT, Battery Lane Publications, Box 30214, Bethesda MD 20014. (301)770-2726. Editor: Eric Balkan. Monthy newsletter covering data processing consulting, contracting and freelancing. "*Computer Consultant* tries to help independent DP professionals improve their business; it includes tax/legal/marketing tips, software writer's market guide, and software wanted notices." Estab. 1979. Pays on acceptance. Byline given. Rights purchased are negotiable. Simultaneous queries, and simultaneous, photocopied, and previously published submissions OK. Reports in 1 week queries; 2 weeks on mss. Sample copy for business size SAE and 2 first class stamps.
Nonfiction: Book excerpts; how-to (especially marketing); interview/profile; new product; opinion; personal experience; technical; legal tips; and tax tips. "We're open to freelance submissions in any area—interviews with consultants or people who hire consultants especially welcome." Query with clips of published work or send complete ms. Length: flexible. Pays $40-120.
Fillers: Clippings and newsbreaks. Pays $5-25.
Tips: "Call or write with an article idea."

COMPUTER DEALER, Gordon Publications, Inc., 20 Community Place, Morristown NJ 07960. (201)267-6040. Editor: David Shadovitz. Sales and marketing of computer products and services for dealers, software producers, systems houses, consultants, consumer electronics outlets and business equipment dealers. Monthly magazine: 48-64 pages. Circ. 10,000. Pays on publication. Buys all rights. Phone queries OK. Submit seasonal/holiday material 6 months in advance. Previously published submissions OK. SASE. Reports in 1 month. Free sample copy.
Nonfiction: How-to (sell, market, etc.); interview (with computer notables or/and where market information is revealed); and articles on capital formation, etc. Writers "must have a knowledge of

marketing and the computer industry, and the ability to ferret information or restate information known in other fields in a usable, interesting and particularly applicable way to those persons engaged in selling computers and peripheral products." Buys 3-6 mss/issue. Query. Length: 1,000-4,000 words. Pays $50 minimum/page; 8¢/word maximum.

Photos: "Photos (artwork) provide and spark greater reader interest, and are most times necessary to explicate text." Send photos with ms. Uses b&w 8½x11 glossy prints or 3x5 color transparencies. Offers no additional payment for photos accepted with ms. Captions and model releases required.

Columns/Departments: "Columns are solicited by editor. If writers have suggestions, please query."

COMPUTER DECISIONS, 50 Essex St., Rochelle Park NJ 07662. Editor: Mel Mandell. 10% freelance written. For computer-involved managers in industry, government, finance, academia, etc. with "emphasis on the pragmatic—here and now. Audience is well-educated, sophisticated and highly paid." Monthly. Circ. 117,000. Buys first serial rights. Pays 30% kill fee. Byline given. Pays on acceptance. Free sample copy to writer "who has a good background." Photocopied submissions OK. Reports in 4 weeks. SASE.

Nonfiction: "Mainly serious articles about raising effectiveness of information handling. Interviews. Informational, technical, think pieces, spot news. News pieces about computers and their business use. Articles should be clear and not stylized. Assertions should be well-supported by facts. We are business-oriented, witty, more interested in the widely applicable story, and less technical than most. We'll run a good article with a computer peg even if it's not entirely about computers. Business analysis done by people with good backgrounds." Buys 12-24 mss/year. Length: 300-1,000 words for news; 1,000-5,000 words for features. Pays 3-10¢/word. "Supply professional pictures with story."

COMPUTER DESIGN, 11 Goldsmith St., Littleton MA 01460. Managing Editor: Sydney F. Shapiro. 35% freelance written. For digital electronic design engineers and engineering managers. Monthly. Buys all rights. Pays on publication. Byline given. Free sample copy. Reports in 12 weeks. SASE.

Nonfiction: Engineering articles on the design and application of digital equipment and systems used in computing, data processing, control, automation, instrumentation and communications. Query. Pays $30-50/page.

Tips: "Send query letter before outline or manuscript. Know the subject intimately before attempting to write an article. List suggested title, scope, and length of article and why *CD* readers would be interested."

COMPUTER GRAPHICS WORLD, Cygnus Publications, Inc., 54 Mint St., San Francisco CA 94103. (415)543-0978. Publisher/Editor: Randall Stickrod. Monthly magazine covering computer graphics for managers in business, government and institutions; readers are interested in maps, graphs, charts, industrial design, animation, video effects and computer engineering. Circ. 6,000. Pays on publication. Byline and brief bio with picture given. Buys first North American serial rights; "reprints should give us credit." Simultaneous queries and photocopied submissions OK. Reports immediately. Free sample copy; "Editorial Highlights" available.

Nonfiction: Case studies, success stories in using computer graphics to solve problems. "Articles must be relevant to the needs of persons interested in applying computer graphics." Buys 12 mss/year. Query by phone or brief letter. Length: 1,500 words minimum. Pays $50-300.

Photos: "We prefer reflective color photos." State availability of photos or graphics. Reviews 35mm color transparencies and 8x10 b&w glossy prints. Captions required. Buys all rights.

COMPUTER RETAILING, W.R.C. Smith Publishing, 1760 Peachtree Rd., Atlanta GA 30357. (404)874-4462. Editor: Mike Witter. Emphasizes retailing microcomputers. Monthly tabloid; 80 pages. Circ. 8,500. Pays on acceptance. Buys first rights. Pays 50% kill fee. Byline given. Phone queries OK. Submit seasonal/holiday material 2 months in advance. SASE. Reports in 2 weeks. Free sample copy and writer's guidelines.

Nonfiction: Interested in interviews with local computer specialty retailers with photos as feature. Also interested in editorial and photo essay of local microcomputer shows. Buys 2-3 mss/issue. Query. Length: 750-2,000 words. Pays $100-200.

Photos: State availability of photos with ms. Pays $5-25 for 8x10 b&w prints; $15-40 for color transparencies. Buys one-time rights. Captions required.

Tips: "With a little basic industry knowledge, it should be very easy for a freelancer to fulfill either a retailer interview (we supply guideline questions) or a photo assignment for a show."

COMPUTER TIMES, OEM Business and Technical News, Hayden Publishing Co., Inc., 50 Essex St., Rochelle Park NJ 07662. (201)843-0550. Editor: David Gabel. Senior Editor: Susan Foster.

Monthly tabloid covering computers for management, software and hardware agencies in the original equipment market. Estab. 1980. Circ. 45,000. Pays on publication. Byline given. Pays a varying kill fee. Buys all rights. Submit seasonal/holiday material 2 months in advance. Photocopied submissions OK. SASE. Reports "immediately." Free sample copy.

Nonfiction: Articles cover new equipment and government activities affecting the computer industry and conferences. Query by phone. Length: 500-1,500 words. Pays $200-400.

Photos: Reviews prints of any size. "Photos are paid for with payment for ms." Captions required.

COMPUTERWORLD, 375 Cochituate Rd., Box 880, Framingham MA 01701. (617)879-0700. Editor: E. Drake Lundell Jr. 10% freelance written. For management-level computer users, chiefly in the business community, but also in government and education. Weekly. Circ. 120,000. Buys all rights. Pays negotiable kill fee; "we have to initiate the assignment in order to pay a kill fee." Pays on publication. Free sample copy, if request is accompanied by story idea or specific query; free writer's guidelines. Photocopied submissions OK, if exclusive for stated period. Submit special issue material 2 months in advance. Reports in 2-4 weeks. SASE.

Nonfiction: Articles on problems in using computers; educating computer people; trends in the industry; new, innovative, interesting uses of computers. "We stress impact on users and need a practical approach. What does a development mean for other computer users? Most important facts first, then in decreasing order of significance. We would be interested in material on factory automation and other areas of computer usage that will impact society in general, and not just businesses. We prefer *not* to see executive appointments or financial results. We occasionally accept innovative material that is oriented to unique seasonal or geographical issues." Buys 100 mss/year. Query, "or call specific editor to ask what's needed at a particular time, establish phone rapport with individual editor." Length: 250-1,200 words. Pays 10¢/word.

Photos: B&w (5x7) glossy prints purchased with ms or on assignment. Captions required. Pays $10 minimum.

Fillers: Newsbreaks and clippings. Query. Length: 50-250 words. Pays 10¢/word.

DATAMATION, Technical Publishing D & B, 666 5th Ave., New York NY 10103. (212)489-2515. Editor: John Kirkley. Articles Editor: Wendy Crisp. Monthly magazine for scientific, engineering and commercial data processing professionals. Circ. 130,000. Pays on publication. Byline given. Pays negotiable kill fee. Buys all rights. Submit seasonal/holiday material 3 months in advance. Photocopied submissions and previously published submissions ("if indicated where") OK. SASE. Reports as soon as possible on queries. Free sample copy and writer's guidelines. "Request our list of themes for the coming year."

Nonfiction: Wendy Crisp, articles editor. "Horizontal publication covering all aspects of technical, managerial and sociological concerns, as well as computer industry news analysis." No general articles on computers. Buys 30 mss/year. Query with clips of published work. Length: 2,000-4,000 words. Pays $300-1,000/article.

Photos: Reviews 35mm color transparencies and 8x10 b&w prints. "No extra payment for photos—included in payment for manuscript."

Fiction: Science fiction (computer related).

ICP INTERFACE SERIES, International Computer Programs, Inc., 9000 Keystone Crossing, Indianapolis IN 46240. (317)844-7461. Editor-in-Chief: Dennis Hamilton. Editors: Louis Harm and Sheila Cunningham. Seven quarterly magazines covering computer software applications and program use in the business and scientific community. Circ. 198,000. Pays on acceptance. Byline given. Buys all rights. Phone queries OK. Submit seasonal material 3 months in advance. Simultaneous and photocopied submissions OK. Reports in 3 weeks. Free sample copy and writer's guidelines.

Nonfiction: Expose (waste, corruption, misuse of computers); interview (of major computer industry figures); opinion (of computer applications); how-to (computer solutions); humor (computer-related); new product; personal experience (case studies); and technical (application). Buys 50 mss/year. Length: 1,000-3,000 words. Pays $50-$250.

INFORMATION SYSTEMS NEWS for Information Systems Management, CMP Publications, 333 E. Shore Rd., Manhasset NY 11030. (516)829-5880. Editor: James Moran. Biweekly tabloid covering computer communication and office automation for managers and staff of major computer installations at US corporations. Estab. 1979. Circ. 100,000. Pays "within 30 days of acceptance." Byline given. Buys all rights. SASE. Reports in 1 month.

Nonfiction: "We're looking for articles of business-oriented news for managers of information systems." Buys 50 mss/year. Query by phone or mail. Length: 500 words minimum. Pays $150 minimum/article.

Photos: State availability of photos.

Tips: "Unsolicited manuscripts are discouraged, but clippings, queries and resumes are considered carefully. Be sure to include a phone number."

INTERFACE, The Computer Education Quarterly, Mitchell Publishing, Inc., 116 Royal Oak, Santa Cruz CA 95066. (408)438-5018. Editor: Kris Johnson. Managing Editor: Roger Howell. Quarterly magazine covering computers. Estab. 1979. Circ. 1,000. Pays on publication. Byline given. Makes work-for-hire assignments. Simultaneous queries OK. SASE. Reports in 2 weeks. Free sample copy.
Nonfiction: Steve Mitchell, articles editor. Humor, new product and technical. Query with clips of published work. Pay is negotiable.
Columns/Departments: Query with clips of published work.
Fillers: Steve Mitchell, fillers editor. Buys 20/year. Pay is negotiable.

INTERFACE AGE, Computing for Business and Home, McPheters, Wolfe & Jones, 16704 Marquardt Ave., Cerritos CA 90701. (213)926-9544. Managing Editor: Kathy Tekawa. Monthly magazine covering microcomputers in business and consumer electronics for small business owners, engineers, teachers and home users. "Although *Interface Age* has a wide range of readers from engineers to hobbyists, there is a distinct focus toward the small businessman. Readers receive up-to-the-minute reports on new products, applications for business and home, and programs they can apply to their own personal computer." Circ. 90,000. Pays "$25 on acceptance and balance on publication." Buys first North American serial rights. Submit seasonal/holiday material 4 months in advance. Reports in 6 weeks on mss. Sample copy $3; free writer's guidelines for 4x9 SAE and 1 first class stamp.
Nonfiction: "Articles should pertain to microcomputing applications in business, law, education, medicine, robotics, software, unique breakthroughs, future projections. We seek interviews/profiles of people well-known in the industry or making unusual use of microcomputers. Computer programs and sample listings must be printed with a new ribbon to get the best quality reproduction in the magazine." Send complete ms. Length: 1,500-3,000 words. Pays $20-50/printed page including photos, charts, programs and listings.
Photos: Send photos, charts, listings and programs with ms.
Fillers: Book reviews (on anything concerning microcomputers). Length: 250 words minimum. Pays $20 each.
Tips: "The more manuscripts we receive from an author, the more his chances improve to be published. Once we publish a couple of his articles and he keeps in touch with us through letters or other articles he's submitted, we recognize his name after awhile and develop a steady relationship. An author who is consistent, conscientious and puts out the effort to keep in touch with us will most likely become a regular contributor."

JOURNAL OF SYSTEMS MANAGEMENT, 24587 Bagley Road, Cleveland OH 44138. (216)243-6900. Publisher: James Andrews. 100% freelance written. For systems and procedures and management people. Monthly. Buys all serial rights. Byline given. Pays on publication. Free sample copy. Reports "as soon as possible." SASE.
Nonfiction: Articles on case histories, projects on systems, forms control, administrative practices and computer operations. No computer applications articles. Query or submit ms in triplicate. Length: 3,000-5,000 words. Pays $25 maximum.

MINI-MICRO SYSTEMS, Cahners Publishing Co., 221 Columbus Ave., Boston MA 02116. (617)536-7780. Editor-in-Chief: Lawrence J. Curran. Executive Editor: Alan R. Kaplan. Monthly magazine covering minicomputer and microcomputer industries for manufacturers and users of small computers, related equipment and software. Circ. 94,000. Pays on publication. Byline given. Buys all rights. Submit seasonal/holiday material 2 months in advance. Simultaneous queries and photocopied submissions OK. SASE. Reports in 1 month on queries. Free sample copy; free writer's guidelines for 4x9 SAE and 1 first class stamp.
Nonfiction: Peter P. Hayhow, managing editor. "Articles about highly innovative applications of computer hardware and software, 'firsts' or with broad human-interest appeal." Buys 60-100 mss/year. Query with clips of published work. Length: 500-2,500 words. Pays $70/printed page, including illustrations.
Photos: Send line art, diagrams, photos or color transparencies.
Tips: "The best way to break in is to be affiliated with a computer company or the public relations agency of such a company."

SMALL SYSTEMS WORLD, Hunter Publishing, 53 W. Jackson, Rm. 550, Chicago IL 60604. (312)322-8950. Editor: John Hansen. Assistant Editor: Linda Habjan. Monthly magazine covering applications of small computer systems in business. Circ. 40,000. Pays on acceptance. Byline given.

Buys all rights. Submit seasonal/holiday material 4 months in advance. Reports in 2 weeks on queries. Free sample copy.
Nonfiction: How-to (use the computer in business); and technical (organization of a data base or file system). "A writer who submits material to us should be an expert in computer applications. No material on large-scale computer equipment." Buys 30 mss/year. Query. Length: 3,000-4,000 words. Pays $100 minimum/article.
Photos: State availability of photos.
Poetry: Payment varies/poem.
Fillers: Needs "management-oriented articles for small computer installations." Buys 12/year. Length: 800-1,500 words. Pays $75 average.

Dental

CONTACTS, Box 407, North Chatham NY 12132. Editor: Joseph Strack. For laboratory owners, managers, and dental technician staffs. Bimonthly. Circ. 1,200. Pays on acceptance. Byline given. Free sample copy. Reports in 1-2 weeks. SASE.
Nonfiction and Photos: Writer should know the dental laboratory field or have good contacts there to provide technical articles, how-to, and successful business operation articles. Query. Length: 1,500 words maximum. Pays 3-5¢/word. Willing to receive suggestions for columns and departments for material of 400-800 words. Payment for these negotiable.

DENTAL ECONOMICS, Box 1260, Tulsa OK 74101. Editor: Pat Muchmore. 60% freelance written. Emphasizes "practice management for dentists." Monthly magazine; 90 pages. Circ. 103,000. Pays on acceptance. Buys all rights. Byline given. "Occasionally no byline is given when it's an article combining talents of several authors, but credit is always acknowledged." Submit seasonal/holiday material 4 months in advance of issue date. SASE. Reports in 4 weeks. Free sample copy and writer's guidelines.
Nonfiction: Expose (closed panels, NHI); how-to (hire personnel, bookkeeping, improve production); humor (in-office type); investments (all kinds); interview (doctors in the news, health officials); personal experience (of dentists, but only if related to business side of practice); profile (a few on doctors who made dramatic lifestyle changes); and travel (only if dentist is involved). Buys 120 mss/year. Query or submit complete ms. Length: 600-3,500 words. Pays $50-500.
Photos: State availability of photos with query or submit photos with ms. Pays $10 minimum for 8x10 glossy photos; $25 minimum for 35mm color transparencies. Captions and model release required. Buys all North American rights.
Columns/Departments: Viewpoint (issues of dentistry are aired here). Buys 1 ms/issue. Submit complete ms. Length: 600-1,500 words.
Tips: *DE's* advice to freelancers is: "Talk to dentists about their problems and find an answer to one or more of them. Know the field. Read several copies of *DE* to determine slant, style and length. Write for 1 dentist, not 100,000."

DENTAL MANAGEMENT, Harcourt Brace Jovanovich, 757 3rd Ave., New York NY 10017. Editor: K.A. Moss. 25% freelance written. "*Dental Management* is the national business publication for dentists." Monthly magazine; 100 pages. Circ. 100,000. Pays on acceptance. Buys all rights. Pays 50% kill fee. Byline given. Submit seasonal/holiday material 4 months in advance of issue date. Photocopied and simultaneous submissions OK. SASE. Reports in 2 weeks. Free writer's guidelines.
Nonfiction: "The editorial aim of *Dental Management* is to help the dentist to build a bigger, more successful practice, to help him conserve and invest his money, and to help him keep posted on the economic, legal and sociological changes that affect him." Exposé; general interest; how-to; and interview. Buys 2-4 mss/issue. Query. Length: 1,000-2,500 words. Pays 15¢/word.

PROOFS, The Magazine of Dental Sales and Marketing, Box 1260, Tulsa OK 74101. (918)835-3161. Publisher: Joe Bessette. Editor: Mary Elizabeth Good. Monthly. Pays on publication. Byline given. Will send free sample copy on request. Query. Reports in 2 weeks. SASE.
Nonfiction: Uses short articles, chiefly on selling to dentists. Must have understanding of dental trade industry, and problems of marketing and selling to dentists and dental laboratories. Pays about $75.

TIC MAGAZINE, Box 407, North Chatham NY 12132. (518)766-3047. Editor: Joseph Strack. For dentists, dental assistants, and oral hygienists. Monthly. Buys first publication rights in the dental

field. Byline given. Pays on acceptance. Reports in 2 weeks. SASE.
Nonfiction: Uses articles (with illustrations, if possible) as follows: 1. Lead feature: Dealing with major developments in dentistry of direct, vital interest to all dentists. 2. How-to-do-it pieces: Ways and means of building dental practices, improving professional techniques, managing patients, increasing office efficiency, etc. 3. Special articles: Ways and means of improving dentist-laboratory relations for mutual advantage, of developing auxiliary dental personnel into an efficient office team, of helping the individual dentist to play a more effective role in alleviating the burden of dental needs in the nation and in his community, etc. 4. General articles: Concerning any phase of dentistry or dentistry-related subjects of high interest to the average dentist. "Especially interested in profile pieces (with b&w photographs) on dentists who have achieved recognition/success in nondental fields—business, art, sport or whatever. Interesting, well-written pieces a sure bet." Query. Length: 800-3,200 words. Pays 4¢ minimum/word.
Photos: Photo stories: 4-10 pictures of interesting developments and novel ideas in dentistry. B&w only. Pays $10 minimum/photo.
Tips: "We can use fillers of about 300 words or so. They should be pieces of substance on just about anything of interest to dentists. A psychoanalyst broke in with us recently with pieces relating to interpretations of patients' problems and attitudes in dentistry. Another writer broke in with a profile of a dentist working with an Indian tribe."

Department Store, Variety, and Dry Goods

MILITARY MARKET, Army Times Publishing Co., 475 School St. SW, Washington DC 20024. (202)554-7180. Editor: Nancy Tucker. For store managers, headquarters personnel, Pentagon decision-makers, Congressional types, wholesalers to the military, manufacturers. Monthly magazine; 68 pages. Circ. 10,500. Pays on acceptance. Buys all rights. Byline given. Phone queries OK. SASE. Reports in 2 months. Free sample copy.
Nonfiction: Publishes how-to articles (directed toward improving management techniques or store operations); humor (funny aspects of the business); informational (implementation of policies and directions); interviews (notables in the field); technical (store operations). No general material. Buys 1 ms/year. Length: 1,000-4,000 words. Query with account of experience with the military's retailing systems. Pays $75-300.

SEW BUSINESS, 666 5th Ave., New York NY 10019. Editor: Christina Holmes. For retailers of home-sewing, quilting and needlework merchandise. "We are the only glossy magazine format in the industry—including homesewing, art needlework and a new *Quilt Quarterly* supplement." Monthly. Circ. 17,000. Not copyrighted. Pays on publication. Free sample copy and writer's guidelines. Reports in 3 weeks on queries; in 1 month on ms. SASE.
Nonfiction and Photos: Articles on department store or fabric shop operations, including coverage of art needlework, piece goods, patterns, quilting, sewing accessories and all other notions. Interviews with buyers—retailers on their department or shop. "Stories must be oriented to provide interesting information from a *trade* point of view. Unless they are doing something different or offbeat, something that another retailer could put to good use in his own operation, there is no sense wasting their or your time in doing an interview and story. Best to query editor first to find out if a particular article might be of interest to us." Buys 100 mss/year. Query. Length: 750-1,500 words. Pays $85 minimum. Photos purchased with mss. "Should illustrate important details of the story." Sharp 5x7 b&w glossies. Offers no additional payment for photos accompanying ms. Pays $5.

Drugs, Health Care, and Medical Products

THE APOTHECARY, HealthCare Marketing Services, 330 2nd St., Box AP, Los Altos CA 94022. (415)941-3955. Editor: Jerold Karabensh. Managing Editor: Lois Krauss. Magazine published 10 times/year covering pharmacy. "*The Apothecary* aims to provide practical information to community retail pharmacists." Circ. 65,000. Pays on acceptance. Byline given. Buys all rights. Submit seasonal/holiday material 6-8 months in advance. Simultaneous queries and photocopied submissions OK. SASE. Reports in 6 weeks on queries; 3 months on mss. Free sample copy and writer's guidelines.

Nonfiction: Cathryn D. Evans, articles editor. How-to (e.g., manage a pharmacy); opinion (of registered pharmacists); technical (related to drug therapy); and health-related feature stories. "We publish general health articles, but only those with some practical application for the pharmacist. No general articles not geared to our pharmacy readership; no fiction." Buys 10 mss/year. Query with clips of published work. Length: 750-3,000 words. Pays $100-350.

Columns/Departments: Cathryn D. Evans, column/department editor. Commentary (views or issues relevant to the subject of pharmacy or to pharmacists). Send complete ms. Length: 750-1,000 words. "This section unpaid; will take submissions with byline."

Fillers: Cathryn D. Evans, fillers editor. Clippings. Unpaid; usually supplied from within.

Tips: "Write according to our policy, i.e., health-related articles with emphasis on practical information for a community pharmacist, or business articles of specific relevance to a pharmacist. Suggest reading several back issues and following general feature-story tone, depth, etc. Stay away from condescending use of language. Though our articles are written in simple style, they must reflect knowledge of subject and reasonable respect for the readers' professionalism and intelligence."

CANADIAN PHARMACEUTICAL JOURNAL, 101-1815 Alta Vista Dr., Ottawa, Ontario, Canada K1G 3Y6. (613)523-7877. Associate Editor: S. Jessup-Petticrew. For pharmacists. Monthly journal; 40 pages. Circ. 13,500. Pays on acceptance. Buys all rights. Phone queries OK. Reports in 2 months. Free sample copy and writer's guidelines.

Nonfiction: (relevant to Canadian pharmacy); publishes exposés (pharmacy practice, education and legislation); how-to (pharmacy business operations); historical (pharmacy practice, Canadian legislation, education); interviews with an profiles on Canadian and international pharmacy figures. Buys 4-8 mss/year. Length: 400-800 words (for news notices); 1,000-2,000 words (for articles). Query. Payment is contingent on value; usually 10¢/word.

Photos: B&w (5x7) glossies purchased with mss. Captions required. Pays $5/photo. Model release required.

Tips: "Query with complete description of proposed article, including topic, sources (in general), length, payment requested, suggested submissions date, whether photographs will be included. It is helpful if the writer has read a *recent* (1980-81) copy of the journal; we are glad to send one if required. Canadian writers are especially welcome to contribute. The letter should describe the proposed article thoroughly. References should be included where appropriate (this is vital where medical and scientific information is included). Send two copies of each ms. Author's degree and affiliations (if any) should be listed; author's writing background should be included (in brief form)."

DRUG SURVIVAL NEWS, Do It Now Foundation, Box 5115, Phoenix AZ 85010. (602)257-0797. Editor: Jim Parker. For workers in drug abuse and alcoholism field; schools, counselors, nurses, state and local mental health agencies and military involved with drug and alcohol programs; and those concerned with the problems of drug and alcohol abuse. Bimonthly tabloid newspaper. Circ. 10,000. Buys all rights and retains the option of publishing later as a pamphlet or part of a collection. Pays 50% kill fee. Byline given. Pays on publication. Photocopied submissions OK. Simultaneous submissions are considered only if you provide the name of publication to which other submission was sent. SASE. Reports in 1 month. Free sample copy.

Nonfiction: Research, news and articles about the effects of various chemicals, and in-depth articles about prominent programs and the people who run them. Writers should have experience with these subjects, either professionally or subjectively (as a former user, etc.—but not prejudiced against the topics beforehand). No articles by ex-addicts or alcoholics describing their lives. Informational, interview, profile, historical, opinion, photo features, book reviews, successful program operations, new product and technical. Query. Length: 100-2,000 words. Pays $1/column inch, usually; $250 maximum for assigned work.

Photos: Pays $5-10 for b&w photos purchased with ms or on assignment.

Fillers: Drug-related news or health and science pieces. "No drug-bust articles, please." Length: 100-300 words. Pays 50¢-$1/column inch, usually; $250 maximum for assigned work.

DRUG TOPICS, 680 Kinderkamack Rd., Oradell NJ 07649. (201)262-3030. Editor: Valentine Cardinale. Executive Editor: Ralph M. Thurlow. For retail drug stores and wholesalers, manufacturers. Semimonthly. Circ. over 70,000. Buys all rights. Pay varies for kill fee. Byline given "only for features." Pays on acceptance. SASE.

Nonfiction: News of local, regional, state pharmaceutical associations, legislation affecting operation of drug stores, news of pharmacists and store managers in civic and professional activities, etc. Query on drug store success stories which deal with displays, advertising, promotions, selling techniques. Query. Length: 1,500 words maximum. Pays $5 and up for leads, $25 and up for short articles, $100-300 for feature articles, "depending on length and depth."
Photos: May buy photos submitted with mss. May buy news photos with captions only. Pays $10-20.

NARD JOURNAL, The National Association of Retail Druggists, 1750 K St. NW, Washington DC 20006. (202)347-7495. Editor: Jim Roberts. For the independent retail pharmacist, aimed at improving his competitive position in the marketplace and his professional standing. Monthly magazine; 64 pages. Circ. 24,000. Subscription is included in membership. Pays on publication. Buys first North American rights; will consider industry exclusive. Phone queries OK. Submit seasonal/holiday material 6 months in advance. Photocopied submissions OK. Reports in 2-4 weeks. Free sample copy and writer's guidelines.
Nonfiction: How-to (solve small business problems); interview (with pharmaceutical industry and regulatory personages); and profile (successful pharmacists). Buys 20-25 mss/year. Query; "outline the proposed article with specifics." Length: 750-1,000 words. Negotiates pay depending on ms.
Photos: "Photos are welcome if they help clarify material in the article. Don't send merely to pad the package. For space reasons articles should be capable of standing alone, if convenient." State availability of photos with query. Pays $5 for 5x7 b&w glossy prints; $15-25 for 35mm color transparencies. Captions and model release required. Buys first North American rights; will consider industry exclusive.
Fillers: Newsbreaks.
Tips: "Because of a change of policy, the *Nard Journal* will be seeking more freelance articles on a regular basis than ever before. Would like to see 15-20 good articles come across my desk every month."

PATIENT AID DIGEST, 2009 Morris Ave., Union NJ 07083. (201)687-8282. Editor: David Cassak. For pharmacists, home health care managers and manufacturers of patient aid products. Bimonthly. Circ. 11,000. Buys all rights. Pays on publication. Free sample copy and writer's guidelines. Photocopied and simultaneous submissions OK. Reports in 8 weeks. SASE.
Nonfiction and Photos: "Articles about existing home health care centers or opportunities for proprietors; articles about new technologies in the home care field; helpful hints for the pharmacist engaged in serving the booming consumer/home health care field. It is essential to understand your reading audience. Articles must be informative, but not extremely technical." Buys informational, how-to, interview, photo articles. Query. Length: 1,000-1,500 words. Pays 5¢/word. Photos purchased with accompanying ms with no additional payment. Captions optional.

WHOLESALE DRUGS, 1111 E. 54th St., Indianapolis IN 46220. Editor: William F. Funkhouser. Bimonthly. Buys first rights. Query. SASE.
Nonfiction and Photos: Wants features on presidents and salesmen of full line wholesale drug houses throughout the country. No set style, but article should tell about both the subject and his/her company—history, type of operation, etc. Pays $50 for text and pictures.

Education

Professional educators, teachers, coaches and school personnel—as well as other people involved with training and education—read the journals classified here. Publications for parents or the general public interested in education-related topics are listed under Education in the Consumer Publications section.

AMERICAN EDUCATOR, 11 Dupont Circle NW, Washington DC 20036. Editor: Linda Chavez. Professional journal of the American Federation of Teachers and other members of the education community. Published quarterly in February, May, August, and November. Replaces "Changing Education" supplement to the AFT's newspaper, *American Teacher*. Circ. 530,000. Buys all rights. Pays on publication. Free sample copy and writer's guidelines. Reports in 3 weeks. SASE.
Nonfiction: "We are interested in articles on a wide range of topics, including new trends in

education, politics, international affairs of interest to teachers and labor movement, well-researched features on current problems in education, education law, professional ethics, 'think' pieces and essays that explore current social issues relevant to American education and society. Each issue is centered around a theme; it is advisable to call or write us first to find out the themes of upcoming issues. No jargon-filled research papers and theses. Query first. Length: 750-3,000 words. Pays $200 minimum. Buys 8-10 mss/year.
Photos: B&w glossy prints, 8x10. Occasional photo essays; stock photos of classroom scenes. Buys one-time rights. Model release required.

THE AMERICAN SCHOOL BOARD JOURNAL, National School Boards Association, 1055 Thomas Jefferson St. NW, Washington DC 20007. (202)337-7666. Editor-in-Chief: David Martin. Emphasizes public school administration and policymaking. For elected members of public boards of education throughout the US and Canada, and high-level administrators of same. Monthly magazine; 64 pages. Circ. 50,000. Pays on acceptance. Buys all rights. Phone queries OK. Submit seasonal/holiday material 4-6 months in advance. Photocopied submissions OK. SASE. Reports in 3 weeks. Free sample copy.
Nonfiction: Publishes how-to articles (solutions to problems of public school operation including political problems); interviews with notable figures in public education. Buys 20 mss/year. Query. Length: 400-2,000 words. Payment varies, "but never less than $100."
Photos: B&w glossies (any size) and color purchased on assignment. Captions required. Pays $10-50. Model release required.

ARTS & ACTIVITIES, 591 Camino de la Reina, San Diego CA 92108. (714)297-5352. Editor-in-Chief: Dr. Leven C. Leatherbury. 90% freelance written. Emphasizes art education. Monthly (except July and August) magazine; 60 pages. Circ. 36,000. Pays on publication. Buys first rights. Phone queries OK. Submit seasonal/holiday material 4 months in advance of issue date. Reports in 1 month. Free sample copy and writer's guidelines.
Nonfiction: How-to (describing specific lessons and projects which have proved successful and emphasizing aesthetic learnings and lesson motivation and objectives); and articles on art history and art education. Buys 8-12 mss/issue. Submit complete ms. Length: 500 words average. Pays $50-150.
Photos: Submit photo material with accompanying ms. No additional payment for 5x7 b&w glossy prints or color transparencies. Captions preferred. Buys first rights.

CATECHIST, Peter Li, Inc., 2451 E. River Rd., Dayton OH 45439. Editor: Patricia Fischer. Emphasizes religious education for professional and volunteer religious educators working in Catholic schools. Monthly (September-May) magazine; 70 pages. Circ. 82,000. Pays on publication. Buys all rights. Submit seasonal/holiday material 3 months in advance. SASE. Reports in 2 months. Sample copy $1; free writer's guidelines.
Nonfiction: Publishes how-to articles (methods for teaching a particular topic or concept); informational (theology and church-related subjects, insights into current trends and developments); personal experience (in the religious classroom). Buys 45 mss/year. Query. Length: 1,500 words maximum. Pays $30-75.
Photos: Pays $15-25 for b&w 8x10 glossy prints purchased without mss. Send contact sheet.
Tips: "We like to see articles that would be of practical use for the teacher of religion or an article that results from personal experience and expertise in the field."

COACH AND ATHLETE MAGAZINE, Coach and Athlete Publishing Co., Inc., Box 657, Needham MA 02192. (617)449-5040. Editor-in-Chief: Jay H. Elliott. Managing Editor: Margaret Hebb. Magazine published 7 times/year for high school and college athletic coaches, trainers, and athletic directors. "Published articles deal with areas that will be helpful to the coach in the areas of techniques, physiology, psychology, management, training, etc." Circ. 48,000. Pays on publication. Byline given. Buys all rights. Submit seasonal/holiday material 3 months in advance. Simultaneous, photocopied, and previously published submissions OK. SASE. Reports in 1 week on queries and mss. Free sample copy; writer's guidelines available.
Nonfiction: Expose (coaching, athletic administration, government regulations, salaries, etc.); general interest (on coaching); how-to; historical/nostalgic (on sports, coaching); inspirational; interview/profile (on coaching, sports); new product; personal experience; photo feature; and technical (coaching, management, training, etc.). "No opinion articles." Buys 40 mss/year. Query or send complete ms. Length: 1,500-4,000 words. Pays $25-50/article.
Photos: "Photographs are used whenever feasible as an implement to an article or in a 'how-to' fashion." State availability of photos or send photos with ms. Reviews b&w contact sheets; pays $7.50-12.50/5x7 or 8x10 matte b&w prints.

COACHING REVIEW, Coaching Association of Canada, 333 River Rd., Ottawa, Ontario Canada K1L 8B9. (613)741-0036. Editor: Vic MacKenzie. For volunteer, community and paid coaches, high school and university sports personnel. Bimonthly magazine in seperate English and French issues; 64 pages. Circ. 15,000. Pays on acceptance. Buys first North American rights. Pays 50-75% kill fee. Byline given unless author requests otherwise. Phone queries OK. Submit seasonal/ holiday material 3 months in advance. Reports in 3 weeks. Free sample copy and writer's guidlines.
Nonfiction: How-to (coach-related of a general interest to all sports); humor (in coaching situations); inspirational (coaching success stories); interview (with top successful coaches); and new product (new ideas and ways of coaching). Wants "authoritative original material on coaching topics." Does not want sports stories with little or no relevance to coaching. Buys 6 mss/issue. Query with complete ms. Length: 1,500-2,500 words. Pays up to $200.
Photos: State availability of photos. Pays $5-25 for b&w contact sheets; $15-30 for slide size color transparencies. Captions required. Buys one-time rights.

COACHING: WOMEN'S ATHLETICS, Intercommunications, Inc., 1353 Boston Post Road, Madison CT 06443. (203)245-3000. Publisher/Editor: William J. Burgess. For administrators of women's athletic and/or physical education departments of public, private and parochial junior and senior high schools, preparatory schools, junior colleges and universities. Bimonthly (except July/August) magazine; 90 pages. Circ. 10,000. Pays on publication. Buys all rights. Byline given. Phone queries OK. Reports in 2 weeks. Sample copy $5; free writer's guidelines.
Nonfiction: How-to, sports news, personal experience and profile. Buys 100 mss/year. Length: 2,200 words maximum. Pays $75-125 for technique articles; competitively for features.
Photos: Uses 4x5 or larger b&w glossy prints to accompany ms; 35mm, 2¼x2¼ or 4x5 color transparencies for covers. Pays $200-300 for cover color transparencies.

CURRENT: THE JOURNAL OF MARINE EDUCATION, National Marine Education Association, College of Education, University of Delaware, Newark DE 19711. Editor: Dr. Les Picker. Quarterly magazine emphasizing marine education for teachers at all grade levels; administrators; directors of aquaria; zoos; and federal and state marine education projects. Circ. 1,500. Pays on publication. Buys first rights. SASE. Reports in 2 weeks on queries; in 1 month on mss. Free sample copy and writer's guidelines. Mention *Writer's Market* in query.
Nonfiction: General interest (about the marine environment; facts; features; and little-known facts); historical (maritime history as it applies to teaching); how-to (plan activities with kids and adults and make equipment); humor; interview (with people in marine education); opinion; profile (of people prominent in marine education); new product; personal experience; photo feature (b&w only); and technical (especially in the education area). Buys 8-12 mss/year. Query. Length: 250-3,000 words. pays $25-50.
Photos: State availability of photos or send photos with ms. Pays $5 minimum for 5x7 b&w prints. Captions and model release required. Buys one-time rights.
Poetry: Free verse, haiku, light verse and traditional. Buys 4-6 mss/year. Submit maximum 5 poems. Pays $5-10.
Tips: "We are always interested in classroom activities which teachers can put into use immediately. These must be realistic, tried and successful how-to's. Also, the life history of an interesting fresh water or marine plant or animal, including a pen and ink drawing."

CURRICULUM REVIEW, Curriculum Advisory Service, 500 S. Clinton St., Chicago IL 60607. (312)939-3010. Editor-in-Chief: Irene M. Goldman. For K-12 superintendents, curriculum planners, teachers, librarians, schools of education. 5 times yearly magazine; 80 pages. Circ. 2,500. Pays on publication. Buys all rights. Byline given. Phone queries OK. Photocopied submissions OK. Reports in 2 months. Free sample copy and writer's guidelines.
Nonfiction: Charlotte H. Cox, articles editor. Informational (on K-12 curriculum, current trends, methods, theory). Buys 30 essay mss/year. Query. Length: 1,000-2,000 words. Pays $30-75. Also publishes 300-400 book reviews/year on an assigned basis; classroom text materials in language arts, mathematics, science, social studies. Pays $10-50 a review depending on scope and difficulty of materials. Send educational vita. "We are especially interested in innovative articles on materials selection, curriculum design, and controversial educational trends. Writing style should be succinct, fresh and direct; no educational jargon. Please include two copies of ms and SASE."
For '82: "We will feature values education, career education, health, and study and reference skills, as well as basic skills improvement. Schedule available on request."

EDUCATIONAL DEALER MAGAZINE, Peter Li, Inc., 2451 East River Rd., Suite 200, Dayton OH 45439. (513)294-5785. Editor-in-Chief: Ruth A. Matheny. Editor: Jay S. Sweeney. Bimonthly magazine covering school supplies, audiovisual and office products and retail stores; a how-tooriented, trade publication concentrating on small businesses. Circ. 10,000. Pays on publication. Byline given. Buys first North American serial rights. Phone queries OK. Previously published submissions OK. SASE. Reports in 2 weeks on queries; in 3 weeks on mss. Sample copy $1; free writer's guidelines.

Nonfiction: Expose (bad government practices as related to dealers' abilities to function competitively); interview (of industry personalities); opinion (of government regulation, economic policies and business techniques); profile (of retailers involved in sales to education; communication and training markets); how-to (direct mail; sales calls; phone sales; increasing business to new markets; and collections); and personal experience (starting a business dealership related to audiovisuals, school supply, office products stores). No "general information—we need specific articles related directly to our audience." Buys 6-10 mss/year. Query with clips of previously published work. Send letter "proposing a specific benefit or group of benefits to our readers." Length: 1,000-3,500 words. Pays $50-200. "We are interested in portraits of dealers/distributors and letting our readers see how other small-to-large businesses cope with today's challenges. This is the magazine's most important function: to serve as a how-to source for our readers in these industries."

Columns/Departments: Book Reviews (management, how-to books related to education; communication and training markets; and legislative developments affecting education budgets and small business). Buys 3-4 mss/year. Query with clips of previously published work. Length: 800-1,800 words. Pays $15-75.

FORECAST FOR HOME ECONOMICS, 50 W. 44th St., New York NY 10036. (212)867-7700. Editorial Director: Kathy Gogich. Senior Editor: Elizabeth Tener. 10% freelance written. Monthly (September-June) magazine; 80 pages. Circ. 78,000. Pays on publication. Buys first rights. Pays negotiable kill fee. Byline given. Submit seasonal/holiday material 6-8 months in advance of issue date. SASE. Free writer's guidelines.

Nonfiction: Current consumer/home economics-related issues, especially energy, careers, family relations/child development, teaching techniques, health, nutrition, metrics, mainstreaming the handicapped, appealing to both boys and girls in the classroom, money management, housing, crafts, bulletin board and game ideas. Buys 3 mss/issue. Query. Length: 1,000-3,000 words. Pays $100 minimum.

Photos: State availability of photos with query. No additional payment for b&w glossy prints. Captions required. Model release required.

Tips: "Contributors to *Forecast* should be professional home economists, and *should* query editorial director before submitting an article. Be sure to include in your query letter "some information about your background, and a list of potential articles with a 2-3 line descriptive blurb about what will be included in each article."

HOSPITAL/HEALTH CARE TRAINING MEDIA PROFILES, Olympic Media Information, 70 Hudson St., Hoboken NJ 07030. (201)963-1600. Publisher: Walt Carroll. 100% freelance written. For hospital education departments, nursing schools, schools of allied health, paramedical training units, colleges, community colleges, local health organizations. Serial, in loose-leaf format, published every 2 months. Circulation: 1,000 plus. Buys all rights. Buys 240 mss/year. Pays on publication. Sample copies and writer's guidelines sent on receipt of your resume, background, and mention of audiovisual hardware you have access to. Reports in 1 month. Query. SASE.

Nonfiction: "Reviews of all kinds of audiovisual media. We are the only review publication devoted exclusively to evaluation of audiovisual aids for hospital and health training. We have a highly specialized, definite format that must be followed in all cases. Samples should be seen by all means. Our writers should first have a background in health sciences; second, have some experience with audiovisuals; and third, follow our format precisely. Besides basic biological sciences, we are interested in materials for nursing education, in-service education, continuing education, personnel training, patient education, patient care, medical problems. We will assign audiovisual aids to qualified writers and send them these to review for us. Unsolicited mss not welcome." Pays $15/review.

INDUSTRIAL EDUCATION, 757 3rd Ave., New York NY 10017. Editor: Paul Cuneo. For administrators and instructors in elementary, secondary, and post-secondary education in industrial arts, vocational, industrial and technical education. Monthly, except July and August and combined May-June issue. Buys all rights. Pays on acceptance. Free writer's guidelines. Reports in 5 weeks. SASE.

Nonfiction and Photos: "Articles dealing with the broad aspects of industrial arts, vocational, and technical education as it is taught in our junior and senior high schools, vocational and technical high schools, and junior colleges. We're interested in analytical articles in relation to such areas as curriculum planning, teacher training, teaching methods, supervision, professional standards, industrial arts or vocational education, industrial practice, relationship of industrial education to industry at the various educational levels, current problems, trends, etc. How-to-do, how-to-teach, how-to-make articles of a very practical nature that will assist the instructor in the laboratory at every level of industrial education. Typical are the 'activities' articles in every instructional area. Also typical is the article which demonstrates to the teacher a new or improved way of doing something or of teaching something or how to utilize special teaching aids or equipment to full advantage—activities which help the teacher do a better job of introducing the industrial world of work to the student." Photos or rough drawings generally necessary. Pays $30/magazine page minimum.

Fillers: Short hints on some aspect of shop management or teaching techniques. Length: 25-250 words.

INSTRUCTOR MAGAZINE, 757 3rd Ave., New York NY 10017. Editor-in-Chief: Leanna Landsmann. 30% freelance written. Emphasizes elementary education. Monthly magazine; 180 pages. Circ. 256,605. Pays on acceptance. Buys all rights. Phone queries OK. Submit seasonal/holiday material 6 months in advance of issue date. Photocopied submissions OK. SASE. Reports in 6 weeks. Free sample copy and writer's guidelines; mention *Writer's Market* in request.
Nonfiction: How-to articles on elementary classroom practice—practical suggestions as well as project reports. Buys 10-15 mss/year. Query. Length: 750-2,500 words.

LEARNING, The Magazine for Creative Teaching, 530 University Ave., Palo Alto CA 94301. Editor: Morton Malkofsky. 45% freelance written. Emphasizes elementary and junior high school education topics. Monthly during school year. Magazine; 150 pages. Circ. 225,000. Pays on acceptance. Buys all rights. Submit seasonal/holiday material 6 months in advance of issue date. Photocopied submissions OK. SASE. Reports in 2 months. Writer's guidelines sent upon request.
Nonfiction: "We publish manuscripts that describe innovative teaching strategies or probe controversial and significant social/political issues related to the professional and classroom interest of preschool to 8th grade teachers." How-to (classroom management, specific lessons or units or activities for children—all at the elementary and junior high level, and hints for teaching math and science); interview (with teachers who are in unusual or innovative teaching situations); new product; personal experience (from teachers in elementary and junior high schools); and profile (with teachers who are in unusual or innovative teaching situations). Strong interest in articles that deal with discipline, gifted and talented (regular classroom), motivation and working with parents. Buys 6 mss/issue. Query. Length: 1,000-3,500 words. Pays $100-350.
Photos: State availability of photos with query. Offers no additional payment for 8x10 b&w glossy prints or 35mm color transparencies. Captions preferred. Buys all rights. Model release required.

MEDIA & METHODS, 1511 Walnut St., Philadelphia PA 19102. Editor: Donald Kersey. For teachers who have an abiding interest in humanistic and media-oriented education, plus a core of librarians, media specialists, filmmakers; the cutting edge of educational innovators. Magazine; 16-20 (8½x11) pages. Monthly (September through May). Circ. 25,000. Normally buys all rights. About half of each issue is freelance material. Pays on publication. Free writer's guidelines with SASE. Will consider photocopied submissions. Reports in 1-2 months. Submit complete ms or query. SASE.
Nonfiction: "We are looking for the middle school, high school or college educator who has something vital and interesting to say. Subjects include practical how-to articles with broad applicability to our readers, and innovative, challenging, conceptual stories that deal with educational change. Our style is breezy and conversational, occasionally offbeat. We make a concentrated effort to be nonsexist; mss filled with 'he,' 'him' and 'mankind' (when the gender is unspecified) will pose unnecessary barriers to acceptance." Length: 1,800 words maximum. Pays $15-75.
Tips: "We look for articles that talk to educators about methods that they can put to work in the classroom. Theorizing and heavy academic philosophizing are not welcome."

MOMENTUM, National Catholic Educational Association, 1 Dupont Circle, Suite 350, Washington DC 20036. (202)293-5954. Editor: Patricia Feistritzer. For Catholic administrators and teachers, some parents and students, in all levels of education (preschool, elementary, secondary, higher). Quarterly magazine; 48-64 pages. Circ. 14,500. Buys first magazine publishing rights only. Buys 28-36 mss/year. Pays on publication. Free sample copy. Submit special issue material 3 months in advance. Query with outline of article. Reports in 4 weeks. SASE.
Nonfiction and Photos: "Articles concerned with educational philosophy, psychology, methodology, innovative programs, teacher training, research, etc. Catholic-oriented material. Book reviews on educational-religious topics. Innovative educational programs; financial and public relations programs; management systems applicable to nonpublic schools. Avoid general topics, such as

what's right (wrong) with Catholic education. In most cases, we look for a straightforward, journalistic style with emphasis on practical examples but are also interested in scholarly writing and statistical. Emphasis on professionalism." Length: 1,500-2,000 words. Pays 2¢/word. Pays $7 for b&w glossy photos purchased with mss. Captions required.

NATIONAL ON-CAMPUS REPORT, 621 N. Sherman Ave., Suite 4, Madison WI 53704. (608)249-2455. Editor: Carol Wilson. 15% freelance written. For education administrators, college student leaders, journalists, and directors of youth organizations. Monthly. Pays 25% kill fee. Pays on publication. Sample copy and writer's guidelines for SASE. Photocopied submissions OK. Reports in 1 month. SASE.
Nonfiction and Fillers: Short, timely articles relating to events and activities of college students. "No clippings of routine college news, only unusual items of possible national interest." Also buys newsbreaks and clippings related to college students and their activities. "We particularly want items about trends in student media: newspapers, magazines, campus radio, etc." Buys 100 mss/year. Submit complete ms. Length: 25-800 words. Pays 10-12¢/word.

NJEA REVIEW, New Jersey Education Association, 180 W. State St., Box 1211, Trenton NJ 08607. Editor-in-Chief: George Adams. 20% freelance written. For members of the association employed in New Jersey schools: teachers, administrators, etc. Monthly (September-May) magazine; 48-72 pages. Circ. 110,000. Pays on acceptance. Buys all rights. Byline given. Previously published submissions OK. SASE. Reports in 1-2 months. Free sample copy and writer's guidelines.
Nonfiction: How-to (classroom ideas), informational (curriculum area), opinion articles (on educational issues) and interviews with "names" in education. Length: 2,500-3,000 words maximum. Buys 15-20 mss/year. Query or submit complete ms. Pays $35 minimum.
Photos: B&w (5x7 or 8x10) glossies purchased with ms. Query. Pays $5 minimum. Model release required.
Tips: "Needed are well-researched articles (but no footnotes, please) on new trends in education (such as teaching and curriculum experimentation) and subject area articles. These are especially suitable if they grow directly out of experience in a New Jersey school or college. Human interest stories about people, teaching situations, or education in general also often acceptable."

PHI DELTA KAPPAN, Box 789, Bloomington IN 47402. Editor: Robert W. Cole, Jr. For educators, especially those in leadership positions, such as administrators; mid-40s; all hold BA degrees; one-third hold doctorates. Monthly magazine; 72 pages. Circ. 140,000. Buys all rights. Pays on publication. Free sample copy. Reports in 1-2 months. SASE.
Nonfiction and Photos: Feature articles on education, emphasizing policy, trends, both sides of issues, controversial developments. Also, informational, how-to, personal experience, interview, profile, inspirational, humor, think articles, expose. "Our audience is scholarly but hard-headed." Buys 10-15 mss/year. Submit complete ms. Length: 500-5,000 words. Pays $25-$250. "We pay a fee only occasionally, and then it is usually to an author whom *we* seek out. We do welcome inquiries from freelancers, but it is misleading to suggest that we buy very much from them." Pays average photographer's rates for b&w photos purchased with mss, but captions are required. Will purchase photos on assignment. Sizes: 8x10 or 5x7 preferred.

SCHOOL ARTS MAGAZINE, 72 Printers Bldg., Worcester MA 01608. Editor: David W. Baker. Services arts and craft education profession, K-12, higher education and museum education programs. Monthly, except June, July and August. Will send a sample copy to a writer on request. Pays on publication. Reports in 90 days. SASE.
Nonfiction and Photos: Articles, with photos, on art and craft activities in schools. Query or send complete ms. Length: 600-1,400 words. Pays $15-85.

SCHOOL FUND RAISER, Sedgwood Publishing Corp., Box 1226, Escondido CA 92025. (714)743-2715. Editor: Gene Michals. Quarterly magazine covering school fund raising for an audience of business and school fund raisers. Estab. 1979. Circ. 215,000. Average issue includes 6-10 articles. Pays on acceptance. Byline given. Buys one-time rights. Phone queries OK. Submit seasonal material 6 months in advance. Simultaneous, photocopied and previously published submissions OK. SASE. Reports in 3 months. Sample copy $1.50.
Nonfiction: General interest (related to setting up new, interesting school programs); interview (with successful fund raisers); opinion; profile; how-to (raise funds; organize fund drives); humor; inspirational (successful fund raising); new product (that schools can sell); personal experience; and photo feature (fund drives in progress). Buys 2 mss/issue. Query. Length: 600-2,500 words. Pays $10-150.
Photos: State availability of photos. Pays $10-20 for 3x4 b&w glossy prints. Pays $10-20 for 3x3 color transparencies. Captions preferred.

SCHOOL SHOP, Box 8623, Ann Arbor MI 48107. Editor: Lawrence W. Prakken. For "industrial and technical education personnel." Special issue in April deals with varying topics for which mss are solicited. Published 10 times/year. Circ. 45,000. Buys all rights. Pays on publication. Prefers authors who have "direct connection with the field of industrial and/or technical education." Submit mss to Howard Kahn, managing editor. Submit seasonal material 3 months in advance. Reports in 6 weeks. SASE.

Nonfiction and Photos: Uses articles pertinent to the various teaching areas in industrial education (woodwork, electronics, drafting, machine shop, graphic arts, computer training, etc.). "Outlook should be on innovation in educational programs, processes, or projects which directly apply to the industrial-technical education area." Buys how-to's, personal experience and think pieces, interviews, humor, coverage of new products and cartoons. Length: 500-2,000 words. Pays $15-50. B&w photos purchased with ms.

SIGHTLINES, Educational Film Library Association, Inc., 43 W. 61st St., New York NY 10023. (212)246-4533. Editor: Nadine Covert. 80% freelance written. Emphasizes the nontheatrical film and video world for librarians in university and public libraries, independent filmmakers and video makers, film teachers on the high school and college level, film programmers in the community, university, religious organizations, film curators in museums. Quarterly magazine; 44 pages. Circ. 3,000. Pays on publication. Buys all rights. Byline given. Phone queries OK. SASE. Reports in 2 months. Free sample copy.

Nonfiction: Informational (on the production, distribution and programming of nontheatrical films), interview (with filmmakers who work in 16mm, video; who make documentary, avant-garde, children's, and personal films), new product, and personal opinion (for regular Freedom To View column). No fanzine material. Buys 4 mss/issue. Query. Length: 4,000-6,000 words. Pay 2½¢/word.

Photos: Purchased with accompanying ms. Captions required. Offers no additional payment for photos accepted with accompanying ms. Model release required.

Columns/Departments: Who's Who in Filmmaking (interview or profile of filmmaker or video artist who works in the nontheatrical field); Book Reviews (reviews of serious film, media, and/or library-related books); Members Reports (open to those library or museum personnel, film teachers, who are members of the Educational Film Library Association and who have creative ideas for programming films or media in institutions, have solved censorship problems, or other nuts-and-bolts thoughts on using film/media in libraries/schools). Buys 1-3 mss/issue. Query. Pays 2½¢/word. Open to suggestions for new columns or departments.

SPECIAL EDUCATION: FORWARD TRENDS, 12 Hollycroft Ave., London NW3 7QL, England. Editor: Margaret Peter. Quarterly. Circ. 6,500. Pays token fee for commissioned articles. SAE and International Reply Coupons.

Nonfiction: Articles on the education of all types of handicapped children. "The aim of this journal of the National Council for Special Education is to provide articles on special education and handicapped children that will keep readers informed of practical and theoretical developments not only in education but in the many other aspects of the education and welfare of the handicapped. While we hope that articles will lead students and others to further related reading, their main function is to give readers an adequate introduction to a topic which they may not have an opportunity to pursue further. References should therefore be selective and mainly easily accessible ones. It is important, therefore, that articles of a more technical nature (e.g., psychology, medical, research reviews) should, whenever possible, avoid unnecessary technicalities or ensure that necessary technical terms or expressions are made clear to nonspecialists by the context or by the provision of brief additional explanations or examples. Send query that summarizes the proposed content of the article in some detail, i.e., up to 500 words." Length: 2,200-3,300 words. Payment by arrangement for commissioned articles only.

Tips: "It's not easy for freelancers to break in unless they are practitioners and specialists in special education. If they have the appropriate specialized knowledge and experience, then articles in easily understood, jargon-free language are welcome, provided the depth of analysis and description are also there."

TODAY'S CATHOLIC TEACHER, 2451 E. River Rd., Dayton OH 45439. (513)294-5785. Editor-in-Chief: Ruth A. Matheny. 25% freelance written. For administrators, teachers, parents concerned with Catholic schools, both parochial and CCD. Circ. 60,000. Pays on publication. Buys all rights. Byline given. Phone queries OK. Submit seasonal/holiday material 3 months in advance of issue date. SASE. Sample copy $1; free writer's guidelines for SASE; mention *Writer's Market* in request.

Nonfiction: How-to (based on experience, particularly in Catholic situations, philosophy with practical applications); inspirational (tribute to teacher); interview (of practicing educators, edu-

cational leaders); personal experience (classroom happenings); and profile (of educational leader). Buys 35-40 mss/year. Submit complete ms. Length: 800-2,000 words. Pays $15-75.
Photos: State availability of photos with ms. Offers no additional payment for 8x10 b&w glossy prints. Captions preferred. Buys one-time rights. Model release required.

TODAY'S EDUCATION, National Education Association, 1201 16th St. NW., Washington DC 20036. (202)833-5442. Editor-in-Chief: Elizabeth E. Yeary. For elementary, secondary and higher education teachers. Quarterly magazine; 96 pages. Circ. 1,700,000. Pays on acceptance. Buys all rights. Submit seasonal/holiday material 3 months in advance of issue date. SASE. Reports in 4 weeks. Free writer's guidelines.
Nonfiction: How-to (teach); descriptions of exemplary public school programs; and in-depth articles on problems of children and youth, e.g., child abuse, student suicide. Buys 8 mss/year. Submit complete ms. Length: 1,600-3,200 words. Pays $200-1,000 "to recognized freelance writers."
Photos: Submit photo material with accompanying ms. Pays $50 for 8x10 b&w glossy prints; $150 for 35mm color transparencies. Buys one-time rights. Model release required.

TRAINING FILM PROFILES, Olympic Media Information, 70 Hudson St., Hoboken NJ 07030. (201)963-1600. Editor: Walt Carroll. For colleges, community colleges, libraries, training directors, manpower specialists, education and training services, career development centers, audiovisual specialists, administrators. Serial in looseleaf format, published every 2 months. Circ. 1,000. Buys all rights. No byline. Pays on publication. "Send resume of your experience in human resource development to introduce yourself." Reports in 2 months. SASE.
Nonfiction: "Reviews of instructional films, filmstrips, videotapes and cassettes, sound-slide programs and the like. We have a highly specialized, rigid format that must be followed without exception. Ask us for sample *Profiles* to see what we mean. Besides job training areas, we are also interested in the areas of values and personal self-development, upward mobility in the world of work, social change, futuristics, management training, problem solving, and adult education. Tell us what audiovisual hardware you have access to." Buys 200-240 mss/year. Query. Pays $5-15/review.

Electricity

Publications classified here publish for electrical engineers, electrical contractors, and others who build, design, and maintain systems connecting and supplying homes, businesses, and industries with power. Journals dealing with generating and supplying power to users will be found in the Power and Power Plants category. Publications for appliance servicemen and dealers will be found in the Home Furnishings classification.

CEDA CURRENT, Kerrwil Publications, Ltd., 20 Holly St., Suite 201, Toronto, Ontario, Canada M4S 2E8. (416)487-3461. Editor-in-Chief: Karen Dalton. 25% freelance written. For "marketing and operating personnel in electrical maintenance and construction as well as distributors." Monthly magazine; 20 tabloid pages. Circ. 26,000. Pays on acceptance. Buys first North American serial rights. Pays 10% kill fee. Byline given. Phone queries OK. Submit seasonal/holiday material 4 months in advance of issue date. Previously published submissions "sometimes considered." SAE and International Reply Coupons. Reports in 2 weeks. Free sample copy.
Nonfiction: Canadian content only. How-to (problem solving, wiring, electrical construction and maintenance); general interest (to the electrical industry); interview (with electrical distributors and maintenance men); new product ("from manufacturers—we don't pay for news releases"); and technical. Query. Length: 500-1,500 words. Pays 5-10¢/word.
Photos: State availability of photos with query. Pays $5 for b&w photos; "negotiable" payment for color transparencies. Captions required. Buys one-time rights.

ELECTRICAL CONTRACTOR, 7315 Wisconsin Ave., Washington DC 20014. (301)657-3110. Editor: Larry C. Osius. 10% freelance written. For electrical contractors. Monthly. Circ. 49,000. Buys first rights, reprint rights, or simultaneous rights. Byline given. Will send free sample copy on request. Usually reports in 1 month. SASE.
Nonfiction and Photos: Installation articles showing informative application of new techniques

and products. Slant is product and method contributing to better, faster, more economical construction process. Query. Length: 800-2,500 words. Pays $65/printed page, including photos and illustrative material. Photos should be sharp, reproducible glossies, 5x7 and up.

ELECTRICAL CONTRACTOR & MAINTENANCE SUPERVISOR, 481 University Ave., Toronto, Ontario, M5W 1A7, Canada. Contact: Editor. For "men who either run their own businesses or are in fairly responsible management positions. They range from university graduates to those with public school education only." Monthly. Circ. 18,000. Rights purchased vary with author and material. "Depending on author's wish, payment is either on acceptance or on publication." Free sample copy. SAE and International Reply Coupons.
Nonfiction and Photos: Ralph Hainer, managing editor. "Articles that have some relation to electrical contracting or electrical maintenance and related business management. The writer should include as much information as possible pertaining to the electrical field. We're not interested in articles that are too general and philosophical. Don't belabor the obvious, particularly on better business management. We're interested in coverage of labor difficulties, related association business, informational articles, how-to's, profiles, coverage of successful business operations, new product pieces, or technical articles." Length: "no minimum or maximum." Payment depends on pre-established rate according to type of article and technical expertise of the writer. Photos purchased with mss or on assignment; captions optional.

IEEE SPECTRUM, Institute of Electrical and Electronics Engineers, Inc., 345 E. 47th St., New York NY 10017. (212)644-7555. Editor: Donald Christiansen. Senior Editor, Administration: Ronald K. Jurgen. Monthly magazine covering electrical/electronics engineering for executive and staff electrical and electronics engineers in design, development, research, production, operations, maintenance, in the field of electronic and allied product manufacturing, commercial users of electronic equipment, independent research development firms, government and military departments and service/installation establishments. Circ. 200,000. Pays on acceptance. Buys all rights. Phone queries OK. Submit material 4 months in advance. Photocopied submissions OK. Reports in 2 weeks. Free sample copy and writer's guidelines.
Nonfiction: Interview (about socio-technical subjects and energy); technical overviews; historical; opinion (about careers and management). Buys 1 ms/issue. Query. Length: 5,000-6,000 words. Pays $400-$1,500.
Columns/Departments: Relate to meetings; industrial developments and publications in the electrical or electronics engineering field. Most departmental material is staff written.
Tips: "Contact the senior editor with story ideas. Be able to exhibit a working knowledge of the magazine's charter."

Electronics and Communication

Listed here are publications for electronics engineers, radio and TV broadcasting managers, electronic equipment operators, and builders of electronic communication systems and equipment, including stereos, television sets, and radio-TV broadcasting systems. Journals for professional announcers or communicators will be found under Journalism; those for electronic appliance retailers will be found in Home Furnishings; publications on computer design and data processing systems will be found in Data Processing. Publications for electronics enthusiasts or stereo hobbyists will be found in Hobby and Craft or in Music in the Consumer Publications section.

ARIZONA ELECTRONICS, Concept Publishing, Inc., 210 S. 4th Ave., Phoenix AZ 85003. (602)253-9086. Editor: Paul Setzer. Monthly magazine covering a "broad spectrum of electronics as applied to Arizona for middle managers and above associated with the Arizona electronics industry (manufacturing, wholesaling and retailing)." Estab. 1981. Circ. 12,000. Pays on acceptance. Byline given. Rights purchased are negotiable. Submit seasonal/holiday material 3 months in advance. Simultaneous queries and photocopied submissions OK. SASE. Reports in 2 weeks on queries. Sample copy free; writer's guidelines free for business size SAE and 1 first class stamp.
Nonfiction: Historical/nostalgic (electronics-related); how-to (manage business); humor (unique applications of electronic technology); interview/profile (of businesses and business leaders); personal experience (of managers); photo feature; and technical (written in a non-technical

manner and in a marketing style). Buys 40 mss/year. Query with clips of published work. Length: 1,500-3,000 words. Pays 15¢/word minimum.
Photos: State availability of photos. Pays $75-100 for color transparencies; $20 minimum for 8x10 b&w glossy prints; and $125 for color covers. Captions and model releases required. Rights purchased are negotiable.

AUDIO VISUAL DIRECTIONS, Montage Publishing, 5173 Overland Ave., Culver City CA 90230. (213)204-3313. Publisher: Joy McGrath. Associate Publisher: Lloyd McGrath. Magazine published 7 times/year about the uses of audiovisuals for readers who use audiovisuals in their professional capacities in business, industry, government, health care, financial and educational institutions and civil and community service organizations, such as police, fire, museums, libraries and churches. Circ. 30,000. Pays on publication. Byline given. Buys all rights. Phone queries OK. Submit seasonal material 2 months in advance. Simultaneous and photocopied submissions OK. Reports in 3 weeks. Free sample copy and writer's guidelines.
Nonfiction: Nancy Scott, editor. How-to. "In every issue we attempt to publish a wide variety of articles relating to all aspects of audio-visual productions as well as developments in video. We welcome all informed, well-written articles pertaining to slides, sound, video, overheads, multi-image and all attendant applications." Buys 1 ms/issue.
Columns/Departments: Showbill (write-ups on schools, seminars, shows, courses and conferences dedicated to educating the A/V user); Software Solutions (showcase for professionally made software programs for training, education and internal communications); Products on Parade (news articles on "what's new" in equipment, materials and services); Anatomy of a Show (descriptive information on a current audio visual show, what went into producing it, equipment used, and a biography on the producer); and Reviews to Use (review of a current AV book). Send complete ms. Pays $100 minimum.
Tips: "Freelancers should have some direct involvement or experience with audiovisuals—creating or producing AV productions, scripting, using audiovisual equipment, teaching AV courses, running programs, etc. They should have some relevant information which they want to share with readers, to teach to readers, relating to audiovisuals."

BROADCAST ENGINEERING, Box 12901, Overland Park KS 66212. Editor: Bill Rhodes. For "owners, managers, and top technical people at AM, FM, TV stations, cable TV operators, as well as recording studios." Monthly. Circ. 34,000. Buys all rights. Buys 50 mss/year. Pays on acceptance; "for a series, we pay for each part on publication." Free sample copy and writer's guidelines. Reports in 6 weeks. SASE.
Nonfiction: Wants technical features dealing with design, installation, modification, and maintenance of radio and TV broadcast equipment; interested in features of interest to communications engineers and technicians as well as broadcast management, and features on self-designed and constructed equipment for use in broadcast and communications field. "We use a technical, but not textbook, style. Our publication is mostly how-to, and it operates as a forum. We reject material that is far too general, not on target, or not backed by evidence of proof. Our Station-to-Station column provides a forum for equipment improvement and build-it-yourself tips. We pay up to $30. We're especially interested in articles on recording studios and improving facilities and techniques." Query. Length: 1,500-2,000 words for features. Pays $75-200.
Photos: Photos purchased with or without mss; captions required. Pays $5-10 for b&w prints; $10-100 for 2¼x2¼ or larger color transparencies.

BROADCAST MANAGEMENT/ENGINEERING, 295 Madison Ave., New York NY 10017. (212)685-5320. Editor: D. Hawthorne. 10% freelance written. For broadcast executives, general managers, chief engineers and program directors of radio and TV stations. Monthly. Circ. 30,000. Buys all rights. Byline given unless "article is used as backup for staff-written piece, which happens rarely." Buys 12-15 mss/year. Pays on publication. Reports in 4 weeks. Query. SASE.
Nonfiction: Articles on technical trends, business trends affecting broadcasting. Particularly interested in equipment applications by broadcasters in the production of radio and television programs. Emphasis on "competitive advantage. No product puff pieces." Length: 1,200-3,000 words. Pays $25-100.
Tips: "To break in demonstrate a knowledge of the industry we serve. Send for an editorial schedule and sample copy of the magazine; then suggest an idea which demonstrates an understanding of our needs. Pictures, graphs, charts, schematics and other graphic material a must."

BROADCAST TECHNOLOGY, Diversified Publications, Ltd., Box 423, Station J, Toronto, Ontario, Canada M4J 4Y8. (416)463-5304. Editor-in-Chief: Doug Loney. 50% freelance written. Emphasizes broadcast engineering. Bimonthly magazine; 64 pages. Circ. 6,300. Pays on publication. Buys all rights. Byline given. Phone queries OK. SAE and International Reply Coupons. Free writer's guidelines.

Nonfiction: Technical articles on developments in broadcast engineering, especially pertaining to Canada. Query. Length: 500-1,500 words. Pays $50-200.

Photos: Purchased with accompanying ms. Captions required. Query for b&w or color. Total purchase price for a ms includes payment for photos.

BROADCASTER, 7 Labatt Ave., Toronto, Ontario, Canada M5A 3P2. (416)363-6111. Editor: Barbara Byers. For the Canadian "communications industry—radio, television, cable, ETV, advertisers and their agencies." Monthly. Circ. 7,200. Buys all rights. Byline given. Buys 50-60 mss/year. Pays on publication. Writers should submit outlines and samples of published work; sample issue will be sent for style. Photocopied and simultaneous submissions OK. Returns rejected material "as soon as possible." SAE and International Reply Coupons.

Nonfiction: Technical and general articles about the broadcasting industry, almost exclusively Canadian. Length: 1,000-2,000 words. Pays $125-350.

Photos: Rarely purchased.

CABLEVISION, (now including *Watch,* **Television in the '80s**), Titsch Publishing, Inc., Box 5400 T.A., Denver CO 80217. (303)573-1433. Publisher: Barbara Ruger, 75 E. 55th, N.Y. NY 10022. (212)753-2095. Weekly magazine; 100 pages. Circ. 10,000. Pays on publication. Buys all rights. Submit material 2 months in advance of issue date. Simultaneous, photocopied and previously published submissions OK. SASE. Reports in 1 month. Free sample copy.

Nonfiction: Exposé (governmental, financial, educational, dealing specifically with the cable TV industry); how-to (safety methods, field procedures, use of products in cable TV industry); interview (people involved in the cable TV, film, satellite and TV industries); new product (dealing specifically with the cable TV industry); and technical. Buys 6-12 mss/year. Query or submit complete ms. Length: 750-2,000 words. Fee negotiable.

Photos: Offers no additional payment for photos used with accompanying ms. Uses 5x7 glossy b&w prints or color transparencies. Buys all rights.

Tips: "We are interested in coverage in localities of cable TV-related events and issues, more on news than feature basis. Want to establish stringers who call us with tips; stories assigned according to our needs."

CANADIAN ELECTRONICS ENGINEERING, 481 University Ave., Toronto M5W 1A7, Ontario, Canada. (416)596-5731. Editor: Ernie Welling. For makers, marketers and users of professional electronics products. Monthly. Buys Canadian rights. Pays on acceptance. Free sample copy.

Nonfiction: Science and technology involving professional electronic products and techniques. Must have direct relevance to work being done in Canada. Query with brief outline of article. Length: maximum about 1,500 words. Pays 10¢/word minimum depending on importance of subject, amount of research, and ability of writer.

Photos: Purchased with mss. 4x5 to 8x10 b&w glossies; must provide useful information on story subject. Pays average professional rates for time required on any particular assignment.

ELECTRONIC BUYERS' NEWS, 333 East Shore Rd., Manhasset NY 11030. (516)829-5880. Editor: Paul Hyman. The purchasing publication for the electronics industry. Newspaper; 120 pages. Circ. 40,737. Pays on publication. Usually buys first rights. Byline given. SASE. Reports in 2 months. Rejected material not returned unless requested. Free sample copy. Prefer telephone queries.

Nonfiction: "Each issue features a specific theme or electronic component. Articles are usually accepted from companies involved with that component. Other stories are accepted occasionally from authors knowledgeable in that field." All material is aimed directly at the purchasing profession. Length: open. Pays $100 minimum.

Tips: "Writers should have a working knowledge of the electronics marketplace and/or electronics purchasing. We are always interested in ideas for news features that are new, timely and informative in our field."

ELECTRONIC PACKAGING AND PRODUCTION, Kiver Publications, 222 W. Adams St., Chicago IL 60606. (312)263-4866. Editor: Donald J. Levinthal. Managing Editor: Leonard Marks. 40% freelance written. Emphasizes electronic equipment fabrication for engineering and production personnel, including product testing. Monthly magazine; 150 pages. Circ. 27,000. Pays on publication. Buys all rights. Byline given. Phone queries OK. Photocopied submissions OK. SASE. Reports in 3 weeks. Free sample copy and writer's guidelines.

Nonfiction: How-to (innovative packaging, production or testing technique); interview (new features about technological trends in electronics); and technical (articles pertaining to the electronic packaging, production and testing of electronic systems and hybrids). "No single-product-oriented articles of a commercial sales-pitch nature." Buys 40 mss/year. Query or submit complete ms. Length: 1,000-2,500 words.

Photos: State availability of photos with query or submit photos with ms. Offers no additional payment for 4x5 or larger b&w or color prints. Captions preferred. Buys all rights.

ELECTRONIC TECHNICIAN/DEALER, 111 E. Wacker Dr., Chicago IL 60601. (312)467-0670. Editor: Walter H. Schwartz. For owners, managers, technician employees of consumer electronic sales and/or service firms. Magazine; 72 pages. Monthly. Circ. 50,000. Buys all rights. Pays on acceptance. Free sample copy and writer's guidelines. Simultaneous submissions OK. Reports "immediately." SASE.

Nonfiction and Photos: Feature articles of a practical nature about consumer electronic technology and servicing techniques; business profiles and/or business management. No generalization; must have concise, practical orientation; a specific approach. No business management articles which are too general and superficial. Informational, how-to, interview, profile, technical articles and those on successful business operations. Buys 36 mss/year. Query or submit complete ms. Length: 1,200-2,500 words. Pays $100-250. No additional payment for b&w photos purchased with mss. Captions required.

ELECTRONICS, 1221 Avenue of the Americas, New York NY 10019. Editor: Samuel Weber. 10-15% freelance written. Biweekly. Buys all rights. Byline given. Reports in 2 weeks. SASE.

Nonfiction: Uses copy about research, development, design and production of electronic devices and management of electronic manufacturing firms; articles on "descriptions of new circuit systems, components, design techniques, how specific electronic engineering problems were solved; interesting applications of electronics; step-by-step, how-to design articles; monographs, charts, tables for solution of repetitive design problems." Query. Length: 1,000-3,500 words. Pays $30/printed page.

FIBER OPTICS AND COMMUNICATIONS, Information Gatekeepers, Inc., 167 Corey Rd., Suite 111, Brookline MA 02146. (617)739-2022. Editor: Denise Wallace. Monthly newsletter covering fiber optics, communications and related fields. Circ. 500. Pays on acceptance. No byline given. Buys all rights. Submit seasonal/holiday material 1 month in advance. Simultaneous queries OK. SASE. Reports in 1 month. Sample copy $10; free writer's guidelines.

Nonfiction: General interest, interview/profile, new product and technical. "We are most open to US news, military news, international news and news publications." No fiction. Length: 600 words maximum. Pays 10¢/word minimum.

MICROELECTRONICS JOURNAL, Mackintosh Publications, Ltd., Box 28, Mackintosh House, Napier Rd., Luton, England·LU1 5DB. 0582-417438. Publications Director: Philip Rathkey. For electronics engineers engaged in research design, production, applications, sales in commercial or government organizations, academics (teaching, research) and higher degree students. "Writer must be active in the microelectronics industry (including academics or higher degree students) and have either an original observation to make or be able to inform/update readers on the state-of-the-art in a specialty area, or on the activities of an organization." Bimonthly magazine; 48 pages. Circ. 1,500. Pays on publication. Buys all rights. Phone queries OK. Submit seasonal/holiday material 3 months in advance. Photocopied submissions OK. Accepts previously published work only if first English translation of foreign language paper. SAE and International Reply Coupons. Reports in 3 weeks to US. Free sample copy and writer's guidelines.

Nonfiction: Expose (technical critique of manufacturers' products, of government, commercial, trade); general interest (state-of-the-art technical/marketing articles); how-to (on new designs, applications, production, materials, technology/techniques); interview (of eminent captain of industry or government politician); nostalgia (concerning how microelectronics companies got started or techniques were invented); personal opinion (on any relevant technical/commercial subject); profile (of company research activities, university research activities); new product (assessment and evidence of product's importance); photo feature (must include write-up explaining its technical/commercial significance); technical (on integrated circuit technology and systems, memories, microprocessors, optoelectronics, infra-red, hybrid integrated circuits, microwave solid-state devices, CCD and SAW techniques, semiconductor materials and chemicals, semiconductor production equipment and processing techniques, and automatic test techniques and equipment). Buys 10-30 mss/year. Query or submit complete ms. Length: 4,000-6,000 words. Pays $50/published page including diagrams, photos, etc.

Photos: Prefers b&w 6½x4½ prints unless color is technically essential. Offers no additional payment for photos accepted with ms. Captions required.

Columns/Departments: Book reviews. Buys 1 page/issue. Query. Length: 350-1,000 words. Pays $25.

MICROWAVES, 50 Essex St., Rochelle Park NJ 07662. (201)843-0550. Editor: Stacy V. Bearse. 50% freelance written. Emphasizes microwave electronics. "Qualified recipients are those individuals actively engaged in microwave research, design, development, production, and application engineering, engineering management, administration or purchasing departments in organizations and facilities where application and use of devices, systems and techniques involve frequencies from HF through visible light." Monthly magazine; 100 pages. Circ. 40,217. Pays on publication. Buys all rights. Phone queries OK. Photocopied submissions OK. SASE. Reports in 6 weeks. Free sample copy and writer's guidelines; mention *Writer's Market* in request.
Nonfiction: "Interested in material on research and development in microwave technology and economic news that affects the industry." How-to (microwave design); new product; opinion; and technical. Buys 60 mss/year. Query. Pays $30-50/published page.
Fillers: Newsbreaks. Pays $10 (minimum).

MILITARY ELECTRONICS, ICOM of North America, 2065 Martin Ave., Suite 104, Santa Clara CA 95050. (408)727-3330, (800)538-9700. Managing Editor: Judith Anspacher. Monthly magazine for engineers, technical managers, and members of the US government and DoD, covering high technology used in military applications. Circ. 33,000. Pays on publication. Byline given. Buys all rights. Previously published work OK. Report in 6 weeks on queries; 2 months on mss. Free sample copy and writer's guidelines.
Nonfiction: Historical on military electronic applications, how-to use new technology, and explanations of new technology. Special issues on microcircuits, software, simulation, computers, electronic warfare, millimeter wave, space electronics. Buys 12-24 mss/year. Query. Length: 3,000-3,500 words. Pays negotiable fee.
Photos: Murry Shohat, photo editor. Pays $5-10 per 8x10 b&w or color glossy print. Offers no additional payment for photos accepted with accompanying ms. Captions and model release required. Buys all rights.
Tips: "Our freelancers are subject matter experts, without exception. Most have been in the field at least 10 years, usually 15, and are already proven authors. We must know the author's background. It's helpful if he/she submits samples with the query letter."

MOBILE TIMES, Titsch Publishing, Box 5400 TA, Denver CO 80217. (303)573-1433. Editor: Michael McCready. Monthly magazine covering the uses of mobile radios for people working in railroads, utilities, forestry, agriculture, policework. fire departments, health, petroleum industry, industrial delivery, taxis industry, and others whose businesses use radio communications. Circ. 18,000. Average issue includes 2-3 feature articles. Pays on publication. Byline given; also biography and picture. Buys first North American serial rights. Phone queries OK. Submit seasonal material 3 months in advance. Simultaneous, photocopied and previously published submissions OK if so indicated. SASE. Reports in 2 weeks on queries; in 4 weeks on mss. Free sample copy with 9x12 SASE (75¢ postage).
Nonfiction: "We want articles concerned with the application of radio in daily working situations, rather than the hardware of mobile radio. If you know what 'land mobile radio' means, you can write for us. We're looking for more freelance written material to round out our news and features monthly." Buys 1-3 mss/issue. Query. Length: 1,500-3,000 words. Pays $50-$250.
Photos: Reviews 5x7 b&w glossy prints and 35mm and larger color transparencies. Offers no additional payment for photos accepted with ms. Captions and model release required. Buys one-time rights.

ON PAGE, On Page Enterprises, Box 439, Sudbury MA 01776. Editor: Stanley J. Kaplan. Managing Editor: Steve Kravette. Monthly newsletter about the beeper industry (radio pocket paging) for professionals, medical people, sales people, small businessmen, municipal employees and any person whose job takes him away from the telephone and who must maintain communications. Estab. 1979. Circ. 100,000. Pays on acceptance. Buys all rights. Phone queries OK. Submit seasonal material 3 months in advance. Simultaneous, photocopied and previously published submissions OK. SASE. Reports in 2 weeks. Free sample copy and writer's guidelines.
Fillers: Clippings, jokes, gags, anecdotes, short humor and newsbreaks. "We are particularly interested in anecdotes for our On Page Forum column in the first person narrative, stories of people and their beeper experiences, and newsbreaks on a variety of communication subjects of interest to people who use beepers. We especially need freelance help for our Christmas issue." Buys 24 mss/year. Length: 75-150 words. Pays $25 minimum.
Tips: "Submissions should be geared to beeper users (e.g. subject matter must be related to communications or mobility)."

OPTICAL SPECTRA, Optical Publishing Co., The Berkshire Common, Box 1146, Pittsfield MA 01201. (413)499-0514. Editor-in-Chief: Dianne Kelley. Executive Editor: Robert S. Clark. Monthly magazine. "*Optical Spectra* circulates monthly among scientists, engineers and managers who work in the fields of optics, electro-optics, fiber optics, vacuum technology and lasers. The magazine's purpose is to keep its readers abreast of new developments in our specific fields and related ones." Circ. 33,700. Average issue includes 12 departments, 2 or 3 contributed pieces in addition to staff reports. Pays on publication. Offers $50 kill fee "if ms is acceptable." Buys all rights. Submit seasonal material 4 months in advance. Photocopied submissions OK. SASE. Reports in 2 weeks on queries; in 1 month on mss. SASE. Sample copy and writer's guidelines free for SASE.
Nonfiction: "*Optical Spectra* is a technically and scientifically-oriented publication of optics, electro-optics and lasers. We offer a combination of timely news reports and feature articles examining aspects of the industries and related industries." Interview (prominent figures in the industry); profile (prominent figures in the industry); other (trends in the field, specific developments). Buys 2-3 mss/issue. Query with clips of previously published work. Length: 750-3,000 words. Pays $50-$200.
Photos: State availability of photos. Pays $10-20 for 8x10 b&w prints. Pays $20-$40 for color transparencies; higher for covers. Captions required. Buys all rights.
Columns/Departments: Query with clips of previously published work.
Tips: "Query about topic, ask for sample copy of the magazine, write pithily and colorfully—and accurately."

RECORDING ENGINEER/PRODUCER, Box 2449, Hollywood CA 90028. (213)467-1111. Editor: Martin Gallay. 100% freelance written. Emphasizes recording technology and concert sound for "all levels of professionals within the recording industry as well as high-level amateur recording interests." Bimonthly magazine; 120 pages. Circ. 16,023. Pays on publication. Buys first publication rights. Photocopied submissions OK. SASE. Reports in 4 weeks. Sample copy $2.50.
Nonfiction: Interview (known engineering and producing personalities from the recording industry); new product (as related to technological advances within the recording and concert sound industry); and technical (recording and concert sound information, both technical and semi-technical). Buys 6 mss/issue. Query. Pays $100-250.

SATELLITE COMMUNICATIONS, Cardiff Publishing Corp., 3900 S. Wadsworth Blvd., Denver CO 80235. (303)988-4670. Editor: Anthony Chiaviello. Emphasizes satellite communications industry. Readership includes broadcasters, satellite industry personnel, cable television operators, government, educators, medical personnel, common carriers, military and corporate telecommunications management, spacecraft manufacturing companies. Monthly magazine; 70 pages. Circ. 12,500. Pays on publication. Buys all rights. Byline given. Phone queries OK. SASE. Reports in 3 weeks. Free sample copy.
Nonfiction: Interviews (of industry figures); technical features; systems descriptions and application articles; marketing articles; satellite future studies; descriptions of satellite experiments; corporate profiles, technological developments, business news; FCC policy analysis; teleconferencing; current issues in space communication; launches and industry conventions; demonstrations and articles on new products. Buys 5-10 mss/year. Query. Length: 750-2,500. Pays $50/published page.
Photos: Prefers b&w 5x7 glossy prints. Offers no additional payment for photos accepted with ms.
Tips: "We prefer a letter personally addressed, clear, concise, with an idea for a story in it, one page, informal but from a writer who is flexible on terms and prompt with copy. The best way to break in would be for a writer to have his own area of expertise so he would be the best possible source for material on that subject: Then we'd *have* to use him. We regularly print articles by business leaders and engineers who can write, usually gratis with byline only."

SOLUTION, 1 Jake Brown Rd., Old Bridge NJ 08857. (201)679-4000. 20% freelance written. For persons involved in television servicing; most own their own stores. Also for trade school graduates. Publication of Blonder-Tongue Labs. Quarterly. Circ. 30,000. Buys all rights. Buys 6 mss/year. Pays on publication. Free sample copy. Will consider photocopied and simultaneous submissions. Reports in 1 month. SASE.
Nonfiction and Photos: General interest articles on TV and signal distribution, MATV systems, and cable television systems. General knowledge of electronics is a must. Author must be able to talk the language. "Will consider short features." Buys informational, new product and technical articles. Length: 750-1,500 words. Pays $250 minimum. Photos purchased with accompanying mss with no additional payment.

TELEPHONY MAGAZINE, 55 E. Jackson Blvd., Chicago IL 60604. Editor: Del Myers. 5% freelance written. For people employed by telecommunications operating companies. Weekly. Buys all rights. Pays on publication. SASE.
Nonfiction: Technical or management articles describing a new or better way of doing something at a telecommunications company. "Feature articles range from highly technical state-of-the-art presentations to down-to-earth case studies. Case-history articles should cover a new or particularly efficient way of handling a specific job at a specific telecommunications company." Query. Length: 1,500 words. Generally pays $30/published magazine page.

TELEVISION INTERNATIONAL MAGAZINE, Box 2430, Hollywood CA 90028. (213)876-2219. Editor: Al Preiss. For management/creative members of the TV industry. Every 2 months. Circ. 8,000 (USA); 4,000 (foreign). Rights purchased vary with author and material. Pays on publication. Will send sample copy to writer for $2. Will consider photocopied submissions. Reports in 30 days. Query. SASE.
Nonfiction and Photos: Articles on all aspects of TV programming. "This is not a house organ for the industry. We invite articles critical of TV." Pays $150-350. Column material of 600-800 words. Pays $75. Will consider suggestions for new columns and departments. Pays $25 for b&w photos purchased with mss; $35 for color transparencies.

TVC MAGAZINE, Cardiff Publishing Co., 3900 S. Wadsworth Blvd., Suite 560, Denver CO 80235. (303)988-4670. Features Editor: Sally Benson Dulin. News Editor: Chuck Moozakis. Semimonthly magazine about cable television for CATV system operators and equipment suppliers. Circ. 7,000. Pays on publication. Byline given. Makes work-for-hire assignments. Phone queries OK. Reports in 2 weeks on queries; in 1 month on mss. Free sample copy.
Nonfiction: Exposé (of industry corruption and government mismanagement); historical (early days of CATV); interview (of important people in the industry); how-to (manage or engineer cable systems); new product (description and application); and case history. "We use articles on all aspects of cable television from programming through government regulation to technical pieces. We use both color and black and white photos, charts and graphs. A writer should have some knowledge of cable television, then send a letter with a proposed topic." Buys 25 mss/year. Query. Length: 1,800-3,500 words. Pays $50/page of magazine space.
Photos: State availability of photos. Pays $50/page of magazine space for contact sheets. Reviews 35mm color transparencies. Offers no additional payment for photos accepted with ms. Captions required.

TWO-WAY RADIO DEALER, Titsch Publishing, Box 5400TA, Denver CO 80217. (303)573-1433. Editor: Michael McCready. Monthly magazine covering the sales and service of two-way radios for dealers, service people and technicians. Circ. 8,000. Average issue includes 2-3 feature articles. Pays on publication. Byline given. Buys first North American serial rights or one-time rights. Phone queries OK. Simultaneous, photocopied and previously published submissions OK. SASE. Reports in 2 weeks on queries; in 1 month on mss. Free sample copy with 9x12 SASE and 75¢ postage.
Nonfiction: "We need very technical articles which include schematics and problem solving, and business articles concerning marketing, finance and self employment. The writer must have special knowledge of land-mobile radio use or the business of running a dealership. We want to increase the amount of freelance material used." Buys 1-2 mss/issue. Send complete ms. Length: 1,500-3,000 words. Pays $50-$250.
Photos: Reviews 5x7 b&w glossy prints and 35mm and larger color transparencies. Offers no additional payment for photos accepted with ms. Captions and model release required. Buys one-time rights.

VIDEO SYSTEMS, Box 12901, Overland Park KS 66212. (913)888-4664. Publisher: George Laughead. 80% freelance written. For qualified persons engaged in various applications of closed-circuit communications who have operating responsibilities and purchasing authority for equipment and software in the video systems field. Monthly magazine; 60 pages. Circ. 16,000. Pays on acceptance. Buys one-time rights. Submit seasonal/holiday material 2 months in advance of issue date. Photocopied submissions OK. SASE. Reports in 2 months. Free sample copy and writer's guidelines.
Nonfiction: General interest (about professional video); how-to (use professional video equipment); historical (on professional video); new product; and technical. Buys 3 mss/issue. Submit complete ms. Length: 1,000-3,000 words. Pays $125.
Photos: State availability of photos with ms. Pay varies for 8x10 b&w glossy prints; $100 maximum for 35mm color transparencies. Model release required.

Engineering and Technology

Publications for electrical engineers are classified under Electricity; journals for electronics engineers are classified with the Electronics and Communications publications.

CANADIAN CONSULTING ENGINEER, 1450 Don Mills Rd., Don Mills, Ontario, M3B 2X7, Canada. Managing Editor: Louanne Smrke. 60% freelance written. For private engineering consultants. Buys exclusive rights preferably; occasionally exclusive to field or country. Pays on publication. Reports in 15 days. SAE and International Reply Coupons.
Nonfiction: "We serve our readers with articles on how to start, maintain, develop and expand private engineering consultancies. Emphasis is on this management aspect. We are not a how-to magazine. We don't tell our readers how to design a bridge, a high rise, a power station or a sewage plant. Paradoxically, we are interested if the bridge falls down, for engineers are vitally interested in Errors and Omissions claims (much like journalists are about libel suits). We have articles on income tax, legal problems associated with consulting engineering, public relations and interviews with political figures. When we write about subjects like pollution, we write from a conceptual point of view; e.g., how the environmental situation will affect their practices. But because our readers are also concerned citizens, we include material that might interest them from a social, or educational point of view. The word to remember is *conceptual* (new concepts or interesting variations of old ones)." Usually pays $100-200, but this depends on length and extent of research required.
Photos: B&w (any size) photos, where applicable, are appriciated with mss (no extra pay).

CIVIL ENGINEERING-ASCE, Amercian Society of Civil Engineers, 345 E. 47th St., New York NY 10017. (212)644-7507. Editor: Ned Godfrey. Monthly magazine about civil engineering for members of the American Society of Civil Engineers. Circ. 90,000. Average issue includes 5-8 features. Pays on acceptance. Byline given. Makes work-for-hire assignments. Phone queries OK. Previously published submissions OK. Reports in 2 months. Free sample copy and writer's guidelines.
Nonfiction: Technical. "Come up with articles that are timely, well-written and slanted to a Civil Engineering audience. We have an annual special issue in September on the environment." Buys 1-2 mss/year. Query. Pays $300-600.
Columns/Departments (includes new products information): Editor: Charles F. Hemming. "We want reports or news stories on conferences of interest to an engineering audience." Buys 1-2 mss/year. Query. Pays $100 minimum.

DESIGN ENGINEERING, 2 Park Ave., New York NY 10016. (212)340-9700. Editor: Frank Yeaple. Monthly magazine about designing products and parts for design engineers. Circ. 110,000. Average issue includes 5-7 features. Pays on acceptance. Byline given. Buys all rights. Phone queries OK. Submit seasonal material 2 months in advance. Simultaneous and photocopied submissions OK. Reports in 1 week. Free sample copy.
Nonfiction: General interest (what is new in the field of engineering; products to use in design; and changes in technology that affect the design engineer's job); how-to (design machines, vehicles, appliances). Buys 6 mss/year. Query with clips of previously published work. Length: 2,500-5,000 words. Pays $50-1,000.
Photos: Reviews 5x7 b&w glossy prints and 35mm and larger color transparencies. Captions required. Payment varies.

DETROIT ENGINEER, 25875 Jefferson, St. Clair Shores MI 48081. Editor: Jack Grenard. "Our readers are mostly management-level engineers in automotive, construction, medical, technical and educational jobs. Our slant is to show the engineer and scientist as a world hero." Monthly magazine. Circ. 9,000. Pays on acceptance. Buys first North American serial rights. Simultaneous, photocopied and previously published submissions OK. SASE. Reports in 3 weeks. Sample copy $1.25.
Nonfiction: General interest (technical background or basis); humor (occasionally, on automotive subjects); and technical (on the *Scientific American* level). Buys 6 mss/year. Query or submit complete ms. Length: 1,500 words maximum. Pays $20-200.

ELECTRO-OPTICAL SYSTEMS DESIGN MAGAZINE, Room 900, 222 W. Adams St., Chicago IL 60606. (312)263-4866. Editor: Richard Cunningham. Monthly magazine for graduate scientists and engineers. Circ. 30,000. Buys all rights. Byline given unless anonymity requested.

Pays on publication. Will send a sample copy to a writer on request. Write for copy of guidelines for writers. Will consider cassette submissions. Query with "a clear statement of why the article would be important to readers." Editorial deadlines are on the 10th of the 2nd month preceding publication. SASE.

Nonfiction and Photos: Articles and photos on lasers, laser systems and optical systems aimed at electro-optical scientists and engineers. "Each article should serve a reader's need by either stimulating ideas, increasing technical competence or improving design capabilities in the following areas: natural light and radiation sources, artificial light and radiation sources, light modulators, optical components, image detectors, energy detectors, information displays, image processing, information storage and processing, system and subsystem testing, materials, support equipment, and other related areas." Rejects flighty prose, material not written for readership, and irrelevant material. Pays $30/page. Submit 8x10 b&w glossies with ms.

GRADUATING ENGINEER, McGraw Hill, 1221 Avenue of the Americas, New York NY 10020. (212)997-4123. Editor: Howard Cohn. Quarterly magazine "helping graduating engineers make the transition from campus to the working world." Estab. 1979. Circ. 75,000. Pays on acceptance. Byline given. Buys first North American serial rights. Submit seasonal/holiday material 3 months in advance. Reports in 1 week. Free sample copy.
Nonfiction: General interest (on management, human resources); interview/profile (campus report from. . . .); high technology; and careers, ethics, resumes, future. Special issues on women, minorities, etc. Buys 100+ mss/year. Query. Length: 2,000-3,000 words. Pays $300-500.
Photos: State availability of photos, illustrations or charts. Reviews 35mm color transparencies, 8x10 b&w glossy prints. Captions and model release required.
Columns/Departments: Job Prospects (in several categories). "Very difficult to break into this section." Query. Length: 1,000 words. Pays $150.

LIGHTING DESIGN & APPLICATION, 345 E. 47th St., New York NY 10017. (212)644-7922. Editor: Wanda Jankowski. 10% freelance written. For "lighting designers, architects, consulting engineers, and lighting engineers." Monthly. Circ. 13,500. Rights purchased vary with author and material. Pays kill fee. Byline given. Buys 10 mss/year. Pays on acceptance. Query. SASE.
Nonfiction: "Stories on lighting design and application, as the name implies. Specific installations reviewed in depth if they are recent, important and demonstrate good lighting. Techniques for saving energy, improving lighting quality and predicting the effecting of a lighting arrangement are needed. Reports on research and tests of new ideas in lighting. Psychological factors in visibility." Length: 500-4,000 words. Pays $250-1,000.

PARKING MAGAZINE, National Parking Association, Inc., 1101 17th St. NW., Washington DC 20036. (202)296-4336. Executive Editor: Thomas G. Kobus. Editor: Robin Rhodes. 10% freelance written. "The bulk of our readers are owners/operators of commercial, off-street parking facilities in major metropolitan areas. The remainder is made up of architects, engineers, city officals, planners, retailers, contractors and service equipment suppliers." Quarterly magazine; 60 pages. Circ. 6,500. Pays on acceptance. Buys one-time rights. Phone queries OK. Submit seasonal/ holiday material 3 months in advance of issue date. Simultaneous, photocopied and previously published submissions OK. Reports in 1 week. Sample copy $1; free writer's guidelines; mention *Writer's Market* in request.
Nonfiction: General interest (pieces on revitalization of central business districts have a high current priority); how-to (new construction, design, equipment or operational techniques); historical (could deal with some aspect of history of parking, including piece on historic garage, etc.); new product (parking-related equipment); photo feature (range of facilities in a particular city); and travel (parking in other countries). "No general, nebulous pieces or ones not dealing with most current trends in the industry." Query. Length: 1,000-5,000 words. Pays $50-500, or negotiable.
Photos: State availability of photos with query. Pays $5-25 for 8x10 b&w glossy prints and $10-50 for 2¼x2¼ or larger color transparencies. Captions preferred. Buys one-time rights. Model release required.

RESOURCE DEPARTMENT, (formerly *Northern Development*), IBIS Holdings, Inc.; Box 91760, West Vancouver, B.C., Canada V7V 4S1. (604)986-9501. Editor: Duncan Cumming. Monthly magazine covering energy and mineral exploration/development. Circ. 17,000. Pays on publication. Byline given. Pays 50% kill fee. Buys first rights or makes work-for-hire assignments. Simultaneous queries, and simultaneous, photocopied and previously published submissions OK. SASE. Reports in 2 weeks on queries; 1 month on mss. Sample copy $2; free writer's guidelines.
Nonfiction: How-to (pertaining to energy and mineral exploration/development); interview/ profile; new product; and technical (new technology). Buys 12 mss/year. Query. Length: 100-2,000 words. Pays $15-500.

Photos: State availability of photos. Pays $10-100 for 35mm and larger color transparencies; $5-20 for 5x7 and larger b&w prints. Captions required. Buys one-time rights.
Tips: "A high level of technical or engineering writing experience is required."

THE WOMAN ENGINEER and THE MINORITY ENGINEER, Equal Opportunity Publications, Inc., 44 Broadway, Greenlawn NY 11768. (516)261-8899. Editorial Director: Paul Podgus. Editor: Christopher Podgus. Magazines published 3 times/2 years (fall, winter, spring). *Woman Engineer:* for senior year engineering students and the working woman engineer. *Minority Engineer:* written for the college graduate and professional minority engineer. Estab. 1980. Circ. 7,500 each. Pays on publication. Byline given. Buys all rights. Submit seasonal/holiday material 2 months in advance. Simultaneous, photocpied, and previously published submissions OK. SASE. Reports in 1 month. Sample copy and writer's guidelines available on request.
Nonfiction: General interest; how-to (land a job, keep a job, etc.); interview; opinion; personal experience; photo feature; technical (state-of-the art engineering). "We're interested in 7 to 10 articles per issue—articles dealing with career guidance and job getting for women and minority engineers." No articles on how to interview or how to write resumes. Buys 70 mss/year. Query with clips of published work or send complete ms. Length: 2,000-5,000 words. Pays $200-750/article.
Photos: Bob Goetter, photo editor. State availability of photos or send photos with ms. Reviews b&w and color contact sheets and prints. Payment is standard. Caption data required. Buys all rights.
Columns/Departments: Query.
Tips: "We're looking for any indication of special affinities or interests related to our magazines. We are particularly interested in hearing from Black, Hispanic, and American Indian writers."

Farm

Today's farmer wears bib-overalls and claims a six-figure investment in producing foodstuffs for the country and the world. Today's farm magazines reflect this, and the successful farm freelance writer is the person who grasps this fact and turns his attention to the business end of farming.

Do you need to be a farmer to write about farming? The general consensus is yes, and no, depending on just what you're writing about. For more technical articles, most editors feel that you should have a farm background (and not just summer visits to Aunt Rhodie's farm, either) or some technical farm education. But there are plenty of writing opportunities for the general freelancer, too. Easier stories to undertake for farm publications include straight reporting of agricultural events; meetings of national agricultural organizations; or coverage of agricultural legislation. Other ideas might be articles on rural living, rural health care or transportation in small towns.

Always a commandment in any kind of writing, but possibly even more so in the farm field, is the tenet "*Study Thy Market.*" The following listings for farm publications are broken down into seven categories, each specializing in a different aspect of farm publishing: crops and soil management; dairy farming; general interest farming and rural life (both national and local); livestock; miscellaneous; and poultry.

The best bet for a freelancer without much farming background is probably the general interest, family-oriented magazines. These are sort of the *Saturday Evening Posts* of the farm set. The other six categories are more specialized, dealing in only one aspect of farm production.

Where should a writer go for information about farming specialties? Go to a land-grant university; there's one in every state. Also try farming seminars or the county extension offices.

As you can see, there's no room for hayseeds in the farm writing field. But for the freelance writer who is willing to plow in and study, there's a good chance he'll find himself in the middle of a cash crop.

Crops and Soil Management

AVOCADO GROWER MAGAZINE, Rancher Publications, Box 2047, Vista CA 92083. (714)758-4743. Editor: Mark Affleck. Emphasizes avocado and subtropical fruit for growers and professionals (doctors, pilots, investors). Monthly magazine; 64 pages. Circ. 8,000. Pays on publication. Buys all rights. Pays 50% kill fee. Byline given. Phone queries OK. Submit seasonal/holiday material at least 1 month in advance. Simultaneous, photocopied and previously published submissions OK. SASE. Reports in 2-3 weeks. Sample copy $2.00.
Nonfiction: General interest (relative to avocado industry); historical (on avocado industry); how-to (grow avocados, jojoba or kiwi—any interesting cultural aspects); humor (short pieces of agricultural nature); interview (with avocado industry leader); new product (briefs only). Open to suggestions for photo features. Buys 2-3 mss/issue. Query with clips of published work or submit complete ms. Pays $1-2/column inch.
Photos: "If it can be said more explicitly with photos, use them to supplement the manuscript." State availability of photos. Pays $3-4.50 for 4x5 b&w prints or 4x5 or standard color prints. Captions preferred, model releases required for minors.
Tips: "Be thorough in the outline. I must be convinced the article has facts, readability and punch. I'm most interested in quality, completeness and readability."

THE FLUE CURED TOBACCO FARMER, Box 95075, Raleigh NC 27625. Editor: Chris Bickers. For farmers who produce 5 or more acres of flue cured tobacco. Magazine; 40 pages. Published 8 times/year. Circ. 42,000. Buys all rights. Pays on acceptance. Reports in 30 days. Query. SASE.
Nonfiction and Photos: Production and industry-related articles. Emphasis is on a knowledge of the industry and the ability to write specifically for it. All material must be in-depth and be up to date on all industry activities. Informational, how-to, personal experience, interview, profile, opinion, successful business operations. Length: 500-1,500 words for features; 100 words or less for short items. Pays "competitive rates." B&w illustrations desirable with features.

THE PEANUT FARMER, Box 95075, Raleigh NC 27625. Editor: Chris Bickers. For peanut farmers with 15 or more acres of peanuts. Magazine; 32 pages. Published 8 times/year. Circ. 29,000. Buys all rights. Pays on acceptance. Reports in 30 days. Query. SASE.
Nonfiction and Photos: Production and industry-related articles. Must be in-depth and up to date on all industry activities. Writer must know the market and write specifically for it. Informational, how-to, personal experience, interview, profile, opinion, successful business operations. Length: 500-1,500 words for features; 100 words or less for short items. Pays "competitive rates." B&w illustrations desirable with features.

POTATO GROWER OF IDAHO, Harris Publishing, Inc., Box 981, Idaho Falls ID 83401. (208)522-5187. Editor/Publisher: Darryl W. Harris. 25% freelance written. Emphasizes material slanted to the potato grower and the business of farming related to this subject—packing, shipping, processing, research, etc. Monthly magazine; 32-56 pages. Circ. 17,000. Pays on publication. Buys all rights. Byline given. Phone queries OK. Submit seasonal/holiday material 6 weeks in advance. Photocopied submissions and previously published work OK. SASE. Reports in 1 month. Free sample copy and editorial guidelines.
Nonfiction: Expose (facts, not fiction or opinion, pertaining to the subject); how-to (do the job better, cheaper, faster, etc.); informational articles; interviews ("can use one of these a month, but must come from state of Idaho since this is a regional publication, telling the nation 'how Idaho grows potatoes' "); all types of new product articles pertaining to the subject; photo features (story can be mostly photos, but must have sufficient outlines to carry technical information); technical articles (all aspects of the industry of growing, storage, processing, packing and research of potatoes in general, but must relate to the Idaho potato industry). Buys 24 mss/year. Query. Length: 750 words minimum. Pays 3¢/word.
Photos: B&w glossies (any size) purchased with mss or on assignment; use of color limited. Captions required. Query if photos are not to be accompanied by ms. Pays $5 minimum; $25 for color used on cover. Model release required.
Tips: "Choose one vital, but small, aspect of the industry; research that subject, slant it to fit the readership and/or goals of the magazine. All articles on research must have valid source for foundation. Material must be general in nature about the subject or specific in nature about Idaho potato growers. Write a query letter, noting what you have in mind for an article; be specific."

REDWOOD RANCHER, 756 Kansas St., San Francisco CA 94107. (415)824-1563. Editor: Sally Taylor. 50% freelance written. For grape growers, and other California north coast ranchers. Magazine; 48 pages. Special issues: Vintage (September); Viticulture (February). Bimonthly. Circulation: 7,000. Buys 20-35 mss/year. Byline given "at writer's request." Pays on publication.

Free sample copy (to writers "in our area"). Photocopied and simultaneous submissions OK. Submit special issue material at least 2 months in advance. Reports in 2-4 weeks. Query. SASE. **Nonfiction and Photos:** "All material must be locally oriented." Technical articles on viticulturists, and country people. "Down-to-earth, with technical savvy." Articles on pest control, carbonic maceration, pruning, new equipment. Informational, personal opinion, how-to, interview, profile, exposes run from 100-3,000 words. Pays $15-300. Pays $10-150 for historical articles of 100-2,000 words. Pays $10-50 for spot news, articles on successful business operations, new products, merchandising techniques; technical. Length: 25-200 words. 8x10 b&w glossies and color (separations preferred) purchased with mss or on assignment. Pays $10 for b&w; $40 for cover.

SOYBEAN DIGEST, Box 27300, 777 Craig Rd., St. Louis MO 63141. (314)432-1600. Editor: Grant Mangold. 75% freelance written. Emphasizes soybean production and marketing. Monthly magazine; 48 pages. Circ. 150,000. Pays on acceptance. Buys all rights. Byline given. Phone queries OK. Submit seasonal material 2 months in advance of issue date. Photocopied submissions OK. Reports in 3 weeks. Sample copy 50¢; mention *Writer's Market* in request.
Nonfiction: How-to (soybean production and marketing); and new product (soybean production and marketing). Buys 100 mss/year. Query or submit complete ms. Length: 1,000 words. Pays $50-350.
Photos: State availability of photos with query. Pays $15-50 for 5x7 b&w prints and $50-250 for 35mm color transparencies and up to $325 for covers. Captions and/or manuscript preferred. Buys all rights.

Dairy Farming

Publications for dairy farmers are classified here. Publications for farmers who raise animals for meat, wool, or hides are included in the Livestock category. Other magazines that buy material on dairy herds will be found in the General Interest Farming and Rural Life classification. Journals for dairy products retailers will be found under Dairy Products.

BUTTER-FAT, Fraser Valley Milk Producers' Association, Box 9100, Vancouver, British Columbia, Canada V6B 4G4. (604)420-6611. Editor: C.A. Paulson. Managing Editor: T.W. Low. Bimonthly magazine emphasizing dairy farming and marketing for dairy farmers in British Columbia. Circ. 3,000. Pays on acceptance. Byline given. Makes work-for-hire assignments. Phone queries OK. Submit seasonal material 4 months in advance. Simultaneous, photocopied and previously published submissions OK. Reports in 1 week on queries; in 1 month on mss. Free sample copy and writer's guidelines.
Nonfiction: Interview (character profile with industry leaders); local nostalgia; opinion (of industry leaders); profile (of association members); technical (farming); and new techniques, new machinery, and new people.
Photos: Reviews 5x7 b&w negatives and contact sheets. Offers no additional payment for photos accepted with ms. Captions required. Buys all rights.
Columns/Departments: "We want technical and financial information on dairy farming. It must be applicable to British Columbia conditions." Buys 3 mss/issue. Query. Length: 500-1,500 words. Pays 7¢/word.
Fiction: Humorous. Buys 6 mss/year. Query. Length: 700-1,500 words. Pays $49-105.
Poetry: Free verse, light verse and traditional. Buys 1 ms/issue. Submit maximum 10 poems. Pays $10-25.
Fillers: Jokes, short humor and quotes. Buys 5 mss/issue. Pays $10.
Tips: "Make an appointment to come by and see us!"

DAIRY GOAT JOURNAL, Box 1808, Scottsdale AZ 85252. Editor: Kent Leach. 40% freelance written. Monthly for breeders and raisers of dairy goats. Pays on publication. Free sample copy. Reports in 1 month. Query. SASE.
Nonfiction and Photos: Uses articles, items, and photos that deal with dairy goats, and the people who raise them, goat dairies and shows. How-to articles up to 1,000 words. Pays by arrangement. Also buys 5x7 or 8x10 b&w photos for $1-15.
Tips: "In query give the thrust or point of the article, what illustrations may be available, how soon it might be finished—and if payments are expected, state how much or if negotiable."

DAIRY HERD MANAGEMENT, Miller Publishing Co., Box 67, Minneapolis MN 55440. (612)374-5200. Editorial Director: George Ashfield. 50% freelance written. Emphasizes dairy farming. Monthly magazine; 60 pages. Circ. 65,000. Pays on acceptance. Buys first time North American rights. Submit seasonal/holiday material 2 months in advance. Photocopied and previously published submissions OK. SASE. Reports in 3-6 weeks. Free sample copy and writer's guidelines.
Nonfiction: How-to, informational, technical. Buys 6 mss/year. Query. Length: 1,000-3,000 words. Pays $75-200. "Articles should concentrate on useful management information. Be specific rather than general."

THE DAIRYMAN, Box 819, Corona CA 91720. Editor: Dennis J. Halladay. For large herd dairy farmers. Monthly. Buys reprint rights. Pays on publication. Free sample copy. Reports in 3 weeks. SASE.
Nonfiction and Photos: Uses articles on anything related to dairy farming, preferably anything new and different or substantially unique in operation, for US subjects. Acceptance of foreign dairy farming stories based on potential interest of readers. Pays $2/printed inch. Buys photos with or without mss. Pays $10 each.
Tips: "Break in by sending us something . . . we're very informal about freelancers. Just send us the story and a proof, and we'll say yes or no. We only publish material concerning dairying—no pigs, horses, beef cattle or otherwise. We don't care about the Midwest, or East Coast. Our readers are the best dairymen in the world; stories should reflect the modern times of the industry."

DAIRYMEN'S DIGEST (Southern Region Edition), Box 5040, Arlington TX 76011. Editor: Phil Porter. For commercial dairy farmers and their families, throughout the central US, with interests in dairy production and marketing. Magazine; 32 pages. Monthly. Circ. 9,000. Not copyrighted, Byline given. Buys 34 mss/year. Pays on publication. Will send free sample copy to writer on request. Reports in 3 weeks. SASE.
Nonfiction and Photos: Emphasis on dairy production and marketing. Buys articles of general interest to farm families, especially dairy-oriented. Seeks unusual accomplishments and satisfactions resulting from determination and persistence. Must be positive and credible. Needs newsbreaks, fresh ideas, profile, personal experience articles. Buys some historical, inspirational or nostalgia. Also articles of interest to farm wives. Length: 50-1,500 words. Pay varies from $10-125, plus additional amount for photos, depending on quality.

General Interest Farming and Rural Life

The publications listed here aim at farm families or farmers in general and contain material on sophisticated agricultural and business techniques. Magazines that specialize in the raising of crops will be found in the Crops and Soil Management classification; publications that deal exclusively with livestock rasing are classified in the Livestock category; magazines for poultry farmers are grouped under the Poultry classification. Magazines that aim at farm supplies are grouped under Agricultural Equipment and Supplies.

National

AGWAY COOPERATOR, Box 4933, Syracuse NY 13221. (315)477-6488. Editor: James E. Hurley. For farmers. Published 9 times/year. Pays on acceptance. Usually reports in 1 week. SASE.
Nonfiction: Should deal with topics of farm or rural interest in the Northeastern US. Length: 1,200 words maximum. Pays $75, usually including photos.

BLAIR AND KETCHUM'S COUNTRY JOURNAL, William Blair, Box 870, Manchester VT 05255. Editor: Richard Ketchum. Managing Editor: Thomas Rawls. Monthly magazine featuring country living for people who live in the country or who are thinking about moving there, small and part-time farmers. Circ. 220,000. Average issue includes 8-10 feature articles and 6 departments. Pays on acceptance. Byline given. Buys all rights. Submit seasonal material 6 months in advance. Photocopied submissions OK. SASE. Reports in 6 months.
Nonfiction: Opinion (essays); profile (people who are outstanding in terms of country living); how-to (2,000-2,500 words on practial gardening, energy, and animal care); and technical (new

developments in a certain category). Buys 6-8 mss/issue. Query with clips of previously published work. Length: 2,000-2,500 words. Pays $300-400.
Photos: State availability of photos. Reviews 5x7 and 8x10 b&w glossy prints and 35mm or larger color transparencies. Captions and model release required. Buys one-time rights.
Poetry: Free verse, light verse and traditional. Buys 1 ms/issue. Pays $2/line.

THE COUNTRY GENTLEMAN, 1100 Waterway Blvd., Indianapolis IN 46202. Editor & Associate Publisher: Bruce Kinnaird. Emphasizes sophisticated country living. Quarterly magazine. Circ. 200,000. Pays on publication. Usually buys all rights, first rights or second serial (reprint) rights. Pays 33% kill fee. Byline given. Photocopied submissions OK. SASE. Reports in about 2 weeks. Sample copy $1.
Nonfiction: Articles and stories geared to the country life. "We look for how-to's, but also publish articles on personalities, outdoor sports, travel, food and humor. Every issue contains at least one conservation-oriented article, dealing with either wildlife or natural resources. Recent articles have covered home cheese-making, outdoor photography, fly fishing, solar energy, travel in Norway, and interviews with country music personalities." Length: 2,500 words maximum. Pays $75-400.
Photos: "We buy color photographs and illustrations having to do with rural life in America and abroad." Pays $25-150.
Fiction: Mainstream, mystery, adventure, western and humorous stories. Length: 3,000 words maximum. Pays $75-300.

FARM JOURNAL, 230 W. Washington Square, Philadelphia PA 19105. Editor: Lane Palmer. "The business magazine of American agriculture" is published 14 times/year with many regional editions. Material bought for one or more editions depending upon where it fits. Buys all rights. Byline given "except when article is too short or too heavily written to justify one." Payment made on acceptance and is the same regardless of editions in which the piece is used. SASE.
Nonfiction: Timeliness and seasonableness are very important. Material must be highly practical and should be helpful to as many farmers as possible. Farmers' experiences should apply to one or more of these 8 basic commodities: corn, wheat, milo, soybeans, cotton, dairy, beef and hogs. Technical material must be accurate. Query to describe a new idea that farmers can use. Length: 500-1,500 words. Pays 10-20¢/word published.
Photos: Much in demand either separately or with short how-to material in picture stories and as illustrations for articles. Warm human interest pix for covers—activities on modern farms. For inside use, shots of homemade and handy ideas to get work done easier and faster, farm news photos, and pictures of farm people with interesting hobbies. In b&w, 8x10 glossies are preferred; color submissions should be 2¼x2¼ for the cover, and 35mm for inside use. Pays $50 and up for b&w shot; $75 and up for color.

FARM MONEY MANAGEMENT, Box 67, Minneapolis MN 55440. (612)374-5200. Editor: Craig Sabatka. Quarterly magazine covering farm finance and economics for high-income farmers, agricultural lenders, farm managers and agricultural consultants. Estab. 1980. Circ. 60,000. Pays on acceptance. Byline given. Buys first North American serial rights. Submit seasonal/holiday queries 3 months in advance. Simultaneous queries, and simultaneous ("if so indicated"), photocopied, and previously published submissions OK. SASE. Reports in 2 weeks. Sample copy free; writer's guidelines for business size SAE and 1 first class stamp.
Nonfiction: Needs articles on estate planning, tax planning, marketing, hedging, record keeping, computer applications, leasing, off-farm-investment and financing, improvements, as well as features and profiles of industrial farmers or lenders. Buys 15 mss/year. Query or send complete ms. Length: 1,000-2,500 words. Pays average $200.
Photos: Reviews 35mm color transparencies and 5x7 or 8x10 b&w glossy prints.

THE FURROW, Deere & Co., John Deere Rd., Moline IL 61265. Executive Editor: Ralph E. Reynolds. Magazine published 8 times/year. For commercial farmers and ranchers. Circ. 1.1 million. Pays on acceptance. Buys all rights. Submit seasonal/holiday material at least 6 months in advance. SASE. Reports in 2 weeks. Free sample copy and writer's guidelines.
Nonfiction: George R. Sollenberger, North American editor. "We want articles describing new developments in the production and marketing of crops and livestock. These could be classified as how-to, informational and technical, but all must have a news angle. All articles should include some interviews, but we rarely use straight interviews. We publish articles describing farmers' personal experiences with new practices. We occasionally use photo features related to agriculture." Buys 10-15 mss/year. Submit complete ms. Length: 600-1,500 words. Pays $200-500.
Photos: Wayne Burkart, art editor. Original color transparencies (no copies) or color negatives of any size used only with mss. Captions required. Send negatives or transparencies with ms. No additional payment.

THE NATIONAL FUTURE FARMER, Box 15130, Alexandria VA 22309. (703)360-3600. Editor-in-Chief: Wilson W. Carnes. Bimonthly magazine for members of the Future Farmers of America who are students of vocational agriculture in high school, ranging in age from 14-21; major interest in careers in agriculture/agribusiness and other youth interest subjects. Circ. 475,073. Pays on acceptance. Buys all rights. Byline given. Submit seasonal/holiday material 3-4 months in advance. SASE. Usually reports in 2 weeks. Free sample copy and writer's guidelines.
Nonfiction: How-to for youth (outdoor-type such as camping, hunting, fishing); informational (getting money for college, farming; other help for youth). Informational, personal experience and interviews are used only if FFA members or former members are involved. Buys 2-3 mss/issue. Query or send complete ms. Length: 1,200 words maximum. Pays 4-6¢/word.
Photos: Purchased with mss (5x7 or 8x10 b&w glossies; 35mm or larger color transparencies). Pays $5-7.50 for b&w; $30-40 for inside color; $100 for cover.
Tips: "Find an FFA member who has done something truly outstanding that will motivate and inspire others, or provide helpful information for a career in farming, ranching or agribusiness."

REPORT ON FARMING, Free Press, 300 Carlton St., Winnipeg, Manitoba, Canada R3C 3C1. Managing Editor: Leo Quigley. For "upper-income, progressive farmers." Monthly tabloid, Circ. 130,000. Pays on publication. Buys one-time rights. Phone queries OK. Submit seasonal/holiday material 8 weeks in advance. Simultaneous, photocopied and previously published submissions OK. SAE and International Reply Coupons. Reports in 4 weeks. Free sample copy.
Nonfiction: "Will look at ideas for agricultural news features. Most, however, will be done by assignments." Submit complete ms. Length: 1,500 words maximum. Pays 8¢/word.
Photos: Purchased with accompanying ms. Captions required. Pays $10-20 for b&w prints.

SUCCESSFUL FARMING, 1716 Locust St., Des Moines IA 50336. (515)284-2693. Editor: Dick Hanson. Magazine of farm management published for top farmers. 13 times/year. Circ. 750,000. Buys all rights. Pays on acceptance. Reports in 2 weeks. SASE.
Nonfiction: Semi-technical articles on the aspects of farming with emphasis on how to apply this information to one's own farm. "Most of our material is too limited and unfamiliar for freelance writers, except for the few who specialize in agriculture, have a farm background and a modern agricultural education." Query with outline. Length: about 1,500 words maximum. Pays $250-600.
Photos: Ralph Figg, art director, prefers 8x10 b&w glossies to contacts; color should be transparencies, not prints. Buys exclusive rights. Assignments are given, and sometimes a guarantee, provided the editors can be sure the photography will be acceptable. Pays expenses.

Local

BUCKEYE FARM NEWS, Ohio Farm Bureau Federation, Box 479, Columbus OH 43216. (614)225-8906. Editor-in-Chief: S.C. Cashman. Managing Editor: S. Kim Wells. Emphasizes agricultural policy pertaining to Ohio farmers. Monthly magazine; 48 pages. Circ. 90,000. Pays on acceptance. Buys all rights. Byline given. Phone queries OK. Submit holiday/seasonal material 3 months in advance. Simultaneous, photocopied and previously published submissions OK. SASE. Reports in 3 weeks. Free sample copy.
Nonfiction: Exposes (of government, agriculture); humor (light pieces about farm life); informational (but no nuts-and-bolts); inspirational ("as long as they're not too heavy"); opinion; and interview. Buys 20 mss/year. Query. Length: 500-2,000 words. Pays $25-100.
Photos: B&w and color purchased with mss or on assignment. Captions required. Send prints and transparencies. Pays $5-10 for b&w.
Poetry: Traditional forms and light verse. Buys 12/year. Limit submissions to batches of 3. Pays $10-25.
Fillers: Buys about 6 newsbreaks/year. Length: 100-250 words. Pays $10-25.

COUNTRY WORLD, Box 1770, Tulsa OK 74102. (918)583-2161, ext. 230. Editor: Herb Karner. For a rural, urban, and suburban readership. Monthly. Buys first serial rights. Pays on publication. Query. SASE.
Nonfiction and Photos: Wants farm and ranch success stories; also suburban living, homemaking, youth, 4-H, and F.F.A. Effective photo illustrations necessary. Preferred length: 700-800 words. Pays $10 a column, sometimes more for exceptional copy. Photos purchased with mss and occasionally with captions only. Prefers b&w glossies, at least 5x7.

FARM & COUNTRY, Agricultural Publishing Co., Ltd., 950 Yonge St., Suite 700, Toronto, Ontario, Canada M4W 2J4. (416)924-6209. Editor-in-Chief: John Phillips. Managing Editor: Corinne Jeffery. 35% freelance written. Emphasizes farm news, business, and management for

Ontario farmers. Semimonthly tabloid; 60 pages. Circ. 76,000. Pays on publication. Buys first rights. Phone queries OK. Submit seasonal/holiday material 6 weeks in advance of issue date. Simultaneous and photocopied submissions OK. SAE and International Reply Coupons. Reports in 4 weeks. Free sample copy and writer's guidelines; send request to News Editor.

Nonfiction: Exposé (government, education, corporate domination); general interest (what's new in farming); how-to (farm application); new product; photo feature; and technical. No "folksy" material. Buys 10 mss/issue. Query with clips of published work. Length: 300-800 words. Pays $3-5/column inch.

Photos: "We use lots of pix." Pays $15 for 3x5 glossy b&w prints. Captions required. Buys one-time rights.

FARM FOCUS, Box 128 Yarmouth, Nova Scotia, Canada B5A 4B1. Bimonthly magazine read by farmers, people in agribusiness, and in government agricultural agencies. "It is the only farm and agricultural paper that is distributed throughout Atlantic Canada." Circ. 13,500. Pays on publication. Buys first or second rights. SAE and International Reply Coupons.

Nonfiction: "Any American developments that could have an impact on the Canadian agricultural scene." No "re-writes on energy development or grain embargoes." Send complete ms. Length: 800-1,400 words. Pays 3¢-5¢/word.

Photos: Pays $5 for 5x7 b&w prints.

Tips: "At the present time it is not easy for a freelance writer to break into the limited field we service, but copy on any government policies that would affect agriculture, new innovations in agriculture, or about individuals or groups that have been successful by flying in the face of tradition, would be of interest. Articles should be as concise as possible and written so the layman can understand them."

FARMLAND NEWS, Box 7305, Kansas City MO 64116. Editor: Frank C. Whitsitt. For rural members of farmer co-ops. Tabloid newspaper; 16-32 pages. Not copyrighted. Free sample copy. No photocopied or simultaneous submissions. Submit seasonal material 3 months in advance. Reports on material accepted for publication in 1-2 weeks. Returns rejected material in a few days. SASE.

Nonfiction: "We try to personalize and humanize stories of broad significance. We use features of interest to our rural audience, as well as holiday-slanted material (Christmas, Thanksgiving, Easter)." Length: open. Pays $25-150.

FLORIDA GROWER & RANCHER, 17 S. Lake Ave., Orlando FL 32801. Editor: William Deitenbeck. For citrus grove managers and production managers, vegetable growers and managers. Monthly magazine. Circ. 32,500. Buys all rights. Pays on publication. Reports in 30 days. Query. SASE.

Nonfiction and Photos: Articles on production and industry-related topics. In-depth and up-to-date. Writer must know the market and write specifically for it. Informational, how-to, personal experience, interview, profile, opinion, successful business operations. Length: 500-1,500 words for features; 100 words or less for short items. Pays "competitive rates." B&w illustrations desirable with features. Color illustrations purchased only occasionally.

INDIANA PRAIRIE FARMER, a Farm Progress Publication, Box 41281, Indianapolis IN 46241. (317)248-0681. Editor: Thomas Budd. Semimonthly magazine covering farm management, production technology and policy for owners of farms, farm workers, and agribusiness people. Controlled circ. 89,500. Pays on acceptance. No byline given. Buys first North American serial rights. Submit seasonal/holiday material 6 months in advance. Reports in 2 weeks. Free sample copy.

Nonfiction: "We are a farm business magazine seeking articles on farm management and production with emphasis on farmer interviews." Buys 30-40 mss/year. Length: 600-1,200 words. Pays $75-150.

Photos: Send photos with ms. Pays $100-150 for 35mm color transparencies; $15-25 for 8x10 b&w prints. B&w photo payment included in payment for ms. Captions and model release required. Buys first rights.

IOWA REC NEWS, 8525 Douglas, Suite 48, Urbandale IA 50322. (515)276-5350. Editor: Thomas P. Graves. Emphasizes rural energy issues for residents of rural Iowa. Monthly magazine. Circ. 142,000. Pays on publication. Not copyrighted. Simultaneous, photocopied and previously published submissions OK. SASE. Reports in 2 weeks.

Nonfiction: General interest, historical, humor, nostalgia (farm) and photo features. "We especially need humor, well-researched issue pieces, rural history, and articles about rural life with an Iowa, or at least a Midwestern slant." Buys 2 mss/issue. Send complete ms. Pays $40-125.

Tips: "The easiest way to break into our magazine is: query about non-fiction, research a particular rural or energy issue well, or, be very funny. Reading and knowing about farm people is important."

MICHIGAN FARMER, 3303 W. Saginaw St., Lansing MI 48901. (517)321-9393. Editor: Richard Lehnert. 10-20% freelance written. Semimonthly. Buys first North American rights. Byline given. Pays on acceptance. Reports in 1 month. Query. SASE.
Nonfiction: Uses problem solving articles of interest and value to Michigan farmers, which discuss Michigan agriculture and the people involved in it. Also articles for home section about Michigan farm housewives and what they are doing. Lucid, easy-to-understand writing is desired. Length depends on topic. Rates are $1/column inch minimum; special stories bring higher rates.
Photos: Buys some b&w singles; also a few color transparencies, for cover use. Pays $5-10 each for b&w, depending on quality. Pays $60 for selected cover transparencies of identifiable Michigan farm or rural scenes.

MISSOURI RURALIST, Harvest Publishing, 2103 Burlington, Suite 600, Columbia MO 65201. Editor: Larry Harper. Managing Editor: Hank Ernst. Semimonthly magazine featuring Missouri farming for people who make their living at farming. Pays on acceptance. Byline given. Buys first North American serial rights and all rights in Missouri. Photocopied submissions OK. SASE. Reports in 1 month. Sample copy $1.
Nonfiction: "We use articles valuable to the Missouri farmer, discussing Missouri agriculture and people involved in it, including housewives. Technical articles must be writtin in an easy-to-read style. The length depends on the topic." Query. Pays 2¢/word minimum
Photos: State availability of photos. Pays $5-10 for 5x7 b&w glossy prints. Pays $60 maximum for 35mm transparencies for covers. Captions required.
Fillers: Newsbreaks. Length: 100-500 words. Pays $60/printed page.

NEBRASKA FARMER, Box 81208, Lincoln NE 68501. (402)489-9331. Editor-in-Chief: Robert L. Bishop. Managing Editor: Dave Howe. 5% freelance written. For "9 out of 10 Nebraska farmers." Semimonthly magazine; 80 pages. Circ. 80,000. Pays on acceptance. Buys all rights. Byline given. Phone queries OK. Submit seasonal/holiday material 6 months in advance of issue date. SASE. Reports in 2 weeks.
Nonfiction: How-to and new product articles of interest to Nebraska farmers. No human interest material. Buys 10-12 mss/year. Query. Length: 500-2,500 words. Pays $25-150.
Photos: State availability of photos with query. Pays $5-15 for b&w prints; $25-50 for color transparencies. Captions and model release required. Buys one-time rights.

THE OHIO FARMER, 1350 W. 5th Ave., Columbus OH 43212. (614)486-9637. Editor: Andrew Stevens. For Ohio farmers and their families. Biweekly magazine; 50 pages. Circ. 103,000. Usually buys all rights. Buys 15-20 mss/year. Pays on publication. Sample copy $1; free writer's guidelines. Will consider photocopied submissions. Reports in 2 weeks. Submit complete ms. SASE.
Nonfiction and Photos: Technical and on-the-farm stories. Buys informational, how-to, personal experience. Length: 600-700 words. Pays $15. Photos purchased with ms with no additional payment, or without ms. Pays $5-25 for b&w; $35-100 for color. Size: 4x5 for b&w glossies; transparencies or 8x10 prints for color.

RFD NEWS, Gazette Publishing Co., Box 367, Bellevue OH 44811. (419)483-7410. Editor: B. Sberna. Bimonthly tabloid covering rural and suburban living for a general interest, farm and suburban audience. Circ. 80,000. Pays on publication. Byline given. Not copyrighted. Submit seasonal/holiday material 1 month in advance. Simultaneous queries, and simultaneous, photocopied, and previously published submissions OK. SASE. Reports in 2 weeks on queries; 1 month on mss. Sample copy $1.
Nonfiction: General interest, historical/nostalgic, personal experience, and photo feature. Length: 1,500-2,500 words. Pays $70 maximum/article.
Photos: Send photos with ms. Reviews b&w prints. Captions required.

RURAL MONTANA, (formerly *Montana Rural Electric News*), Montana Associated Utilities, Inc., Box 1641, Great Falls MT 59403. (406)454-1412. Managing Editor: Martin L. Erickson. Emphasizes rural life. For farmers, ranchers and rural dwellers. Monthly magazine; 32 pages. Circ. 52,000. Pays on publication. Buys one-time rights. Phone queries OK. Simultaneous, photocopied, and previously published submissions OK. SASE. Reports in 3 weeks.
Nonfiction: How-to, informational, historical, humor, inspirational, nostalgic and travel articles; interviews and photo features. Query. Length: 500-2,000 words. Pays $15 minimum.
Photos: Purchased with mss or on assignment. Captions required. Query. Pays $10 minimum for 8x10 (or 5x7 minimum) b&w glossies. Model release required.

WALLACES FARMER, 1912 Grand Ave., Des Moines IA 50305. (515)243-6181. Editor: Monte N. Sesker. Semimonthly magazine for Iowa farmers and their families. Buys Midwest states rights (Nebraska, Minnesota, Wisconsin, Illinois, Missouri, South Dakota and Iowa). Pays on acceptance. Reports in 2 weeks. SASE.
Nonfiction and Photos: Occasional short feature articles about Iowa farming accompanied by photos. Query. Length: 500-1,000 words. Pays about 4-5¢/word. Photos purchased with or without mss. Should be taken on Iowa farms. Pays $7-15 for 5x7 b&w; $50-100 for 4x5, 2¼x2¼ color transparencies. See recent issue covers for examples.

WYOMING RURAL ELECTRIC NEWS, 340 West B St., Casper WY 82601. (307)234-6152. Editor: Susan LeMaster. For audience of primarily farmers and ranchers. Monthly magazine; 16 pages. Cir. 26,000. Not copyrighted. Byline given. Buys 12-15 mss/year. Pays on publication. Free sample copy. Will consider photocopied and simultaneous submissions. Submit seasonal material 2 months in advance. Reports "immediately." SASE.
Nonfiction, Photos and Fiction: Wants energy-related material, "people" features, historical pieces about Wyoming and the West, things of interest to Wyoming's rural people. Buys informational, humor, historical, nostalgia and photo mss. Submit complete ms. Length for nonfiction and fiction: 1,200-1,500 words. Pays $10-25. Photos purchased with accompanying ms with no additional payment, or purchased without ms. Captions required. Pays $10 for cover photos. B&w preferred. Buys some experimental, western, humorous and historical fiction. Pays $25.
Tips: "Study an issue or two of the magazine to become familiar with our focus and the type of freelance material we're using. Submit entire manuscript. Don't submit a regionally-set story from some other part of the country and merely change the place names to Wyoming. Photos, illustrations (if appropriate) are always welcomed."

Livestock

Publications in this section are for farmers who raise cattle, sheep or hogs for meat, wool or hides. Publications for farmers who raise other animals are listed in the Miscellaneous category; also many magazines in the General Interest Farming and Rural Life classification buy material on raising livestock. Magazines for dairy farmers are included under Dairy Farming. Publications dealing with raising horses, pets or other pleasure animals will be found under Animal in the Consumer Publications section.

BEEF, The Webb Co., 1999 Shepard Rd., St. Paul MN 55116. (612)647-7374. Editor-in-Chief: Paul D. Andre. Managing Editor: Warren Kester. Monthly magazine. For readers who have the same basic interest—making a living feeding cattle or running a cow herd. Circ. 110,000. Pays on acceptance. Buys one-time rights. Byline given. Phone queries OK. Submit seasonal material 3 months in advance. SASE. Reports in 2 months. Free sample copy and writer's guidelines.
Nonfiction: How-to and informational articles on doing a better job of producing feeding cattle, market building, managing, and animal health practices. Buys 8-10 mss/year. Query. Length: 500-2,000 words. Pays $25-250.
Photos: B&w glossies (8x10) and color transparencies (35mm or 2¼x2¼) purchased with or without mss. Captions required. Query or send contact sheet or transparencies. Pays $10-50 for b&w; $25-100 for color. Model release required.
Tips: "Be completely knowledgeable about cattle feeding and cowherd operations. Know what makes a story. We want specifics, not a general roundup of an operation. Pick one angle and develop it fully."

BEEF IMPROVEMENT NEWS, Box 1127, Ames IA 50010. Publisher: Angus Stone. 10% freelance written. Published for the Iowa Beef Improvement Association. For cow-producers (farmers) in the Corn Belt states. "This is a very sophisticated audience—we can use only very professional material." Tabloid style magazine; 24 (11½x17) pages. Monthly. Circ. 63,000. Not copyrighted. Pays on acceptance. Will send free sample copy to writer on request. Will consider photocopied and simultaneous submissions. Returns rejected material immediately. Query first or submit complete ms. Enclose SASE.
Nonfiction and Photos: "Our only interest is genetic improvement of beef cattle and updated cattle raising procedures. Success stories on beef cattle producers (not feeders) who participate in a

program of performance testing. Articles on new equipment, products or procedures applicable to cow-calf operations. We prefer a conservative, typical Midwest farm approach." Interview, profile, successful business operations and technical articles. Length: 1,000-1,500 words. Pays $40-100. Photos are purchased with mss or on assignment. No additional payment is made for those purchased with mss.

BLACKS UNLIMITED INC., Box 578, Webster City IA 50595. Editor: Greg Garwood. Monthly magazine published for North American cattlemen interested in Angus cattle or Angus cross cattle such as Brangus and Chiangus. The publication reaches purebred breeders as well as commercial cattlemen. Estab. 1979. Circ. 12,000. Pays on publication. Rights negotiable. Phone queries OK. Submit seasonal material 2 months in advance. Simultaneous, photocopied and previously published submissions OK. Reports in 2 weeks. Free sample copy and writer's guidelines.
Nonfiction: Expose, general interest, how-to, interview, opinion, profile, travel, new product, photo feature, and research in breeding cattle. Buys 4 mss/issue. Query. Length: 2,000-2,500 words. Pays $25-500.
Photos: State availability of photos. Reviews b&w contact sheets. Payment negotiable.

THE CATTLEMAN MAGAZINE, Texas & Southwestern Cattle Raisers Association, 1301 W. 7th St., Ft. Worth TX 76102. (817)332-7155. Editor-in-Chief: Dale Segraves. Emphasizes beef cattle production and feeding. "Readership consists of commercial cattlemen, purebred feedstock producers, cattle feeders, horsemen in the Southwest." Monthly magazine; 170 pages. Circ. 27,000. Pays on acceptance. Buys all rights. SASE. Reports in 3 weeks. Sample copy $1.50; free writer's guidelines.
Nonfiction: Need informative, entertaining feature articles on specific commercial ranch operations, cattle breeding and feeding, range and pasture management, profit tips and university research. Will take a few historical western lore pieces. Must be well-documented. No first-person narratives or fiction. Buys 15 articles/year. Query. Length open. Pays $25-100. No articles pertaining to areas outside of Southwestern US.
Photos: Photos purchased with or without accompanying ms. Captions required. Pays $10-25 for 8x10 b&w glossies; $25-100 for color photos. Total purchase price for ms includes payment for photos. Model release required.
Tips: "Submit an article dealing with ranching in the Southwest. Too many writers submit stories out of our general readership area."

NATIONAL WOOL GROWER, 600 Crandall Bldg., Salt Lake City UT 84101. (801)363-4484. Editor: Vern Newbold. 1% freelance written. Not copyrighted. A very limited market. Best to query first here. Reports in 4-5 days. SASE.
Nonfiction: Material of interest to sheepmen. Length: 2,000 words. Pays 3¢/word for material used.

POLLED HEREFORD WORLD, 4700 E. 63rd St., Kansas City MO 64130. (816)333-7731. Editor: Ed Bible. For "breeders of Polled Hereford cattle—about 80% registered breeders, 5% commercial cattle breeders; remainder are agribusinessmen in related fields." Monthly. Circ. 20,000. Not copyrighted. Buys "very few mss at present." Pays on publication. Free sample copy. Photocopied submissions OK. Submit seasonal material "as early as possible: 2 months preferred." Reports in 1 month. Query first for reports of events and activities. Query first or submit complete ms for features. SASE.
Nonfiction: "Features on registered or commercial Polled Hereford breeders. Some on related agricultural subjects (pastures, fences, feeds, buildings, etc.). Mostly technical in nature; some human interest. Our readers make their living with cattle, so write for an informed, mature audience." Buys informational articles, how-to's, personal experience articles, interviews, profiles, historical and think pieces, nostalgia, photo features, coverage of successful business operations, articles on merchandising techniques, and technical articles. Length: "varies with subject and content of feature." Pays about 5¢/word ("usually about 50¢/column inch, but can vary with the value of material").
Photos: Purchased with mss, sometimes purchased without mss, or on assignment; captions required. "Only good quality b&w glossies accepted; any size. Good color prints or transparencies." Pays $2 for b&w, $2-25 for color. Pays $25 for color covers.

SIMMENTAL SHIELD, Box 511, Lindsborg KS 67456. Editor: Chester Peterson Jr. Official publication of American Simmental Association. Readers are purebred cattle breeders and/or commercial cattlemen. Monthly; 150 pages. Circ. 7,000. Buys all rights. Pays on publication. Will send free sample copy to writer on request. January is AI issue; August is herd sire issue; December is brood cow issue. Submit material 3-4 months in advance. Reports in 1 week. Query first or submit complete ms. SASE.

Nonfiction, Photos, and Fillers: Farmer experience; management articles with emphasis on ideas used and successful management ideas based on cattleman who owns Simmental. Research: new twist to old ideas or application of new techniques to the Simmental or cattle business. Wants articles that detail to reader how to make or save money or pare labor needs. Buys informational, how-to, personal experience, interview, profile, humor, think articles. Rates vary, but equal or exceed those of comparable magazines. Photos purchased with accompanying ms with no additional payment. Interest in cover photos; accepts 35mm if sharp, well-exposed.
Tips: "Articles must involve Simmental and/or beef breeding cattle."

Miscellaneous

AMERICAN BEE JOURNAL, Dadant and Sons, Inc., 51 S. 2nd St., Hamilton IL 62341. (217)847-3324. Editor: Joe Graham. Monthly magazine about beekeeping for hobbyist beekeepers, commercial beekeepers and researchers. Circ. 22,000. Average issue includes 8-10 nonscientific articles and 1-2 scientific articles by researchers. Pays on publication. Byline given. Buys all rights. Submit seasonal material 2 months in advance. Previously published submissions OK, if so indicated. SASE. Reports in 2 weeks. Free sample copy.
Nonfiction: General interest (articles that deal with beekeeping management; honey packing and handling; bee diseases; other products of the hive such as royal jelly, pollen and beeswax; pesticide hazards to honeybees; and occasional articles on beekeeping as a business). Buys 3-5 mss/issue. Send complete ms. Length: 1,200-1,500 words. Pays 2½¢/word minimum.
Photos: Send photos with ms. Pays $5 minimum for 5x7 b&w glossy prints. Captions and model release required.
Fillers: Newsbreaks. Buys 1-2 mss/issue. Pays 2½¢/word minimum.

GLEANINGS IN BEE CULTURE, 623 W. Liberty St., Medina OH 44256. Editor: Lawrence R. Goltz. For beekeepers. Monthly. Buys first North American serial rights. Pays on publication. Reports in 15-90 days. SASE.
Nonfiction and Photos: Interested in articles giving new ideas on managing bees. Also uses success stories about commercial beekeepers. No "how I began beekeeping" articles. Length: 3,000 words maximum. Pays $23/published page. Sharp b&w photos pertaining to honeybees purchased with mss. Can be any size, prints or enlargements, but 4x5 or larger preferred. Pays $3-5/picture.
Tips: "Do an interview story on commercial beekeepers who are cooperative enough to furnish accurate, factual information on their operations."

THE SUGAR PRODUCER, Harris Publishing, Inc., 520 Park, Box 981, Idaho Falls ID 83401. (208)522-5187. Editor/Publisher: Darryl W. Harris. 25% freelance written. Emphasizes the growing, storage, use and by-products of the sugar beet. Magazine published 7 times a year; 32 pages. Circ. 19,000. Pays on publication. Buys all rights. Byline given. Phone queries OK. Photocopied submissions and previously published work OK. SASE. Reports in 30 days. Free sample copy and writer's guidelines.
Nonfiction: "This is a trade magazine, not a farm magazine. It deals with the business of growing sugar beets, and the related industry. All articles must tell the grower how he can do his job better, or at least be of interest to him, such as historical, because he is vitally interested in the process of growing sugar beets, and the industries related to this." Exposé (pertaining to the sugar industry or the beet grower); how-to (all aspects of growing, storing and marketing the sugar beet); interview; profile; personal experience; technical (material source must accompany story—research and data must be from an accepted research institution). Query or send complete ms. Length: 750-2,000 words. Pays 3¢/word.
Photos: Purchased with mss. Captions required. Pays $5 for any convenient size b&w; $10 for color print or transparency; $25 for color shot used on cover. Model release required.

Poultry

The publications listed here specialize in material on poultry farming. Other publications that buy material on poultry will be found in the General Interest Farming and Rural Life classification.

CANADA POULTRYMAN, 605 Royal Ave., New Westminster, British Columbia, Canada V3M 1J4. Editor: Martin Dyck. For poultry producers and those servicing this industry. Monthly magazine. Circ. 12,000. Buys all rights. Pays on publication. Will send free sample copy to writer on request. Submit seasonal material 2 months in advance. Reports in 1 month. Submit complete ms. Enclose SAE and International Reply Coupons.

Nonfiction and Photos: Canadian market facts, management material, pieces on persons in the industry. Length: 200-2,000 words. Pays 4-5¢ a word. Photos (up to 5x7) purchased with mss for $4. Captions required.

DUCK, GOOSE & SWAN, J. Todd Miles, Publisher, Greystones Farm, Millbury MA 01527. (617)754-4612. Editor: J. Todd Miles. Bimonthly magazine covering care, feeding, breeding, and sales of domestic waterfowl. "Our typical reader is a part-time breeder with 25-30 birds, who would like to read about similar and larger operations." Estab. 1980. Circ. 1,281. Pays on publication. Byline given. Not copyrighted. Buys first rights and second serial (reprint) rights. Submit seasonal/holiday material 3 months in advance. Simultaneous queries, simultaneous, photocopied and previously published submissions OK. SASE. Reports in 2 weeks on queries and mss. Sample copy $2.

Nonfiction: Historical/nostalgic, how-to, interview/profile, new product, opinion, personal experience, photo feature, technical. Some article topics include "Raising Khaki Campbell Ducks for Maximum Production" and "How to Protect Your Stock From Predators." No stories about wild waterfowl. Buys 12 mss/year. Send complete ms. Length: 250-2,000 words. Pays $20/page—500 plus or minus words.

Photos: Send photos with ms. "Clear b&w Polaroid photos are OK. Prefer b&w prints; color will be printed in b&w." Reviews 5x7 b&w prints. Pays $5-20/5x7 b&w and color prints.

Columns/Departments: Book Review, Equipment, Test Report, and Show Report. Buys 6 mss/year. Send complete ms. Length: 250-1,000 words. Pays $5/article. $20/page for first rights includes photos. "For example, a typed page with 250 words copy and 1 b&w picture brings $20 total."

Tips: "We are open to stories and pictures of various duck or goose farms from around the country. It is best if the writer is or has been a waterfowl breeder. If not, you should stick to reports on established waterfowl breeders, i.e., 'John Smith sells eggs retail' or 'How Mary Doe fights the zoning board—and wins.' Talk to some local breeders (there are a few in every town—ask at the local farm supply and grain store). Find out what they want to read and write about it. We are more concerned with content than style. Know what you are talking about; our readers are really sharp!"

Finance

The magazines listed below deal with banking, investment, and financial management. Magazines that use similar material but have a less technical or professional slant are listed in the Consumer Publications under Business and Finance.

ABA BANKING JOURNAL, (formerly *Banking, Journal of the American Bankers Association*), 345 Hudson St., New York NY 10014. (212)966-7700. Editor: Harry L. Waddall. Managing Editor: William Streeter. Executive Editor: Joe W. Kizzia. 15-20% freelance written. Monthly magazine; 150 pages. Circ. 41,000. Pays on publication. Buys all rights. Phone queries OK. Photocopied submissions OK. SASE. Reports in 4-6 weeks. Sample copy sent to writer "only if a manuscript is commissioned."

Nonfiction: How-to; new product; and articles dealing with banking. Buys 24-36 mss/year. Query. Average length: 2,000 words. Pays $100/magazine page, including headlines, photos and artwork.

Photos: State availability of photos with query. Uses 8x10 b&w glossy prints and 35mm color transparencies. Buys one-time rights.

BANK SYSTEMS & EQUIPMENT, 1515 Broadway, New York NY 10036. Editor: Joan Prevete Hyman. For bank, savings and loan association, mutual savings banks and credit union operations executives. Monthly. Circ. 22,000. Buys all rights. Byline given. Pays on publication. Query for style sheet and specific article assignment. Mss should be triple-spaced on one side of paper only with wide margin at left-hand side of the page. SASE.

Nonfiction: Third-person case history articles and interviews as well as material related to systems, operations and automation. Charts, systems diagrams, artist's renderings of new buildings, etc., may accompany ms and must be suitable for reproduction. Prefers one color only. Length: open. Pays $100 for each published page.

Photos: 5x7 or 8x10 single-weight glossies. Candids of persons interviewed, views of bank, bank's data center, etc. Captions required. "We do not pay extra for photos."

Tips: "Writers can break in by covering telecommunications in banks and thefts."

THE CANADIAN BANKER & ICB REVIEW, The Canadian Bankers' Association, Box 282, T-D Centre, Toronto, Ontario, Canada M5K 1K2. Editor: Brian O'Brien. 90% freelance written. Emphasizes banking in Canada. Bimonthly magazine; 72 pages. Circ. 45,000. Buys first North American serial rights. Byline given. SAE and International Reply Coupons. Reports in 1 month. **Nonfiction:** Informational articles on international banking and economics; interviews, nostalgic and opinion articles; book reviews. Query. Length: 750-2,000 words. Pays $100-300. "Freelancer should be an authority on the subject. Most contributors are bankers, economists and university professors."

COMMODITIES MAGAZINE, 219 Parkade, Cedar Falls IA 50613. (319)677-6341. Publisher: Merrill Oster. Editorial Director: Ed Lee. Editor: Darrell Jobman. For private, individual futures traders, brokers, exchange members, agribusinessmen; agricultural banks; anyone with an interest in commodities. Monthly magazine; 48-80 pages. Circ. 50,000. Buys all rights. Byline given. Pays on publication. Free sample copy. Photocopied submissions OK. Reports in 1 month. Query or submit complete ms. SASE.

Nonfiction and Photos: Articles analyzing specific commodity futures trading strategies; fundamental and technical analysis of individual commodities and markets; interviews, book reviews, "success" stories; news items. Material on new legislation affecting commodities, trading, any new trading strategy ("results must be able to be substantiated"); personalities. No "homespun" rules for trading and simplistic approaches to the commodities market. Treatment is always in-depth and broad. Informational, how-to, interview, profile, technical. "Articles should be written for a reader who has traded commodities for one year or more; should not talk down or hypothesize. Relatively complex material is acceptable." Buys 30-40 mss/year. Length: No maximum or minimum; 2,500 words optimum. Pays $50-1,000, depending upon author's research and writing quality. Pays $15-50 for glossy print b&w photos. Captions required.

Tips: "Writers must have a solid understanding and appreciation for futures trading."

FLORIDA BANKER, Box 6847, Orlando FL 32853. Editor: William P. Seaparke. 20% freelance written. Monthly magazine; 52 pages. Circ. 7,300. Pays on publication. Buys all rights. Pays 50% kill fee. Byline given. SASE. Reports in 3 months. Sample copy and writer's guidelines $2 prepaid. **Nonfiction:** General interest (banking-oriented); historical (on banking); how-to (anything in banking industry or trade); inspirational (occasionally, must deal with banking); interview; nostalgia; photo feature; profile; technical; and travel. Buys 2-3 mss/issue. Query. Length: 600-8,000 words. Payment varies.

Photos: State availability of photos with query. Pays $10-100 for 5x7 b&w glossy prints; $20-200 for 35mm color transparencies. Captions and model release required. Buys all rights.

Columns/Departments: Economy; interviews; and energy. Query. Length: 600-3,000 words. Pays $20 minimum. Open to suggestions for new columns/departments.

ILLINOIS BANKER, Illinois Bankers Association, 188 W. Randolph, Chicago IL 60601. (312)984-1505. Editor: Cindy L. Altman. Editorial Assistant: Kelly Cunningham. Monthly magazine about banking for top decision makers and executives, bank officers, title and insurance company executives, elected officials, and individual subscribers interested in banking products and services. Circ. 3,500. Pays on acceptance. Byline given. Buys first rights. Phone queries OK. Submit seasonal material by the 10th of the month prior to publication. Simultaneous submissions OK. Reports in 2 weeks. Free sample copy and writer's guidelines.

Nonfiction: Interview (ranking government and banking leaders); personal experience (along the lines of customer relations); and technical (specific areas of banking). "The purpose of the publication is to educate, inform, and guide its readers in the activities and projects of their banks and those of their fellow bankers, while keeping them aware of any developments within the banking industry and other related fields. Any clear, fresh approach geared to a specific area of banking, such as agricultural bank management, credit, lending, marketing and trust is what we want." Buys 8 mss/year. Send complete ms. Length: 825-3,000 words. Pays $50-150.

Fillers: Jokes, anecdotes and financial puzzles. Buys 8 mss/year. Pays $10-50.

MERGERS & ACQUISITIONS, 229 S. 18th St., Philadelphia PA 19103. Editor-in-Chief: Leonard Zweig. For presidents and other high corporate personnel, financiers, buyers, stockbrokers, accountants and related professionals. Quarterly. Buys all rights. Byline given. Pays 21 days after publication. Will send a free sample copy to a writer on request. Query with outline. Include 50-word autobiography with mss. SASE.

Nonfiction: "Articles on merger and acquisition techniques (taxes, SEC regulations, anti-trust, etc.), case studies or surveys and roundups emphasizing analysis and description of trends and implications thereof. Case histories should contain 20-60 facts/1,000 words (real names, dates, places, companies, etc.). Technical articles should be well researched and documented." Length: maximum 3,000-10,000 words. Pays $100-150/1,000 printed words for articles by professional freelance writers; 200 reprints for articles by professional business persons, such as lawyers and investment analysts.

Tips: "We prefer actual practitioners in the M&A field—investment bankers, auditors, tax lawyers, etc. to write for us. Freelancers with a business writing background are welcome to submit projects for Case Studies of deals."

MONEYFAX, National Association of Financial Consultants, Ivy Publications, Box 1, Ischua NY 14746. (716)557-8900. Editor: Richard Brisky. Monthly newsletter covering financing, loans and mortgages. Byline given. Buys all rights. Submit seasonal/holiday material 2 months in advance. Simultaneous queries, and simultaneous and previously published submissions OK. SASE. Reports in 1 week on queries; 3 weeks on mss. Sample copy and writer's guidelines free for business size SAE and 28¢ postage.

Nonfiction: Expose (of loan frauds); how-to (get loans); and humor (money jokes). "No nonfinancial material." Query. Length: 300-1,000 words. Pay is negotiable.

Columns/Departments: "We're interested in anything regarding financing or loan brokerage." Query. Length: 300-1,000 words. Pay is negotiable.

Fillers: Clippings, jokes, and newsbreaks (anything about financing and money brokerage). Length: open. Pay is negotiable.

Fishing

AQUACULTURE MAGAZINE, Briggs Associates, Box 2451, Little Rock AR 72203. (501)376-1921. Editor: Porter Briggs. Managing Editor: Dorothy Stuck. Bimonthly magazine about aquaculture for aquaculturists in the production, processing and marketing of finfish, shellfish, crustaceans and aquatic plants. The publication is also read by scientists, academicians, local, state and federal government program personnel. Circ. 4,800. Average issue includes 3-4 features and 4 columns. Pays on publication. Byline given. Buys one-time rights. Phone queries OK. Submit seasonal material 2 months in advance. Simultaneous, photocopied, and previously published submissions OK. SASE. Reports in 2 weeks on queries; in 1 month on mss. Free sample copy.

Nonfiction: General interest, profile, how-to, personal experience, photo feature and technical. Buys 12 mss/year. Query. Length: 1,000-3,000 words. Pays $100-300. "Freelancers generally contribute either expanded news stories (usual length: 1,000-1,500 words) or feature articles (1,500-3,000 words). Contact us by phone or letter giving an idea of a proposed article and background as a writer. If we are interested, we will outline points that should be covered and ask for submission of a written outline. If satisfied with the outline, we will make an agreement with the author on the length, photos needed and payment."

Photos: State availability of photos. Reviews b&w glossy prints, and color glossy prints and transparencies. Offers no additional payment for photos accepted with ms. "We do consider interesting color prints or slides which could be used for a cover and will pay separately for these." Buys one-time rights.

COMMERCIAL FISHERIES NEWS, (formerly *Maine Commercial Fisheries*), Box 37, Stonington ME 04681. (207)367-5590. Managing Editor: Bill Donnell. 33% freelance written. Emphasizes commercial fisheries. Monthly newspaper with New England wide coverage; 44 pages. Circ. 6,000. Pays on publication. Byline given. SASE. Reports in 2 weeks. Sample copy $1.

Nonfiction: "Material strictly limited to coverage of commercial fishing, technical and general; occasional environment, business, etc. articles as they relate to commercial fishing." Query. Pays $50-100.

FISHING GAZETTE, Fishing Gazette Publishing Co., 461 8th Ave., New York NY 10001. (212)324-0959. Editor: Jo Brock. Publisher: Stuart Meyers. Monthly magazine covering commercial fishing interests for everyone connected with fishing interests: importers, exporters, commercial manufacturers of all equipment that goes aboard a vessel and equipment that goes into a manufacturing plant. Circ. 19,000. Pays "first week of month of issue." Byline given. Rights purchased vary. Submit seasonal/holiday material 3 months in advance. Simultaneous queries OK; previously published submissions OK ("if copyright permission is available and article appeared in a different market.") Reports in 2 weeks. Free sample copy.

Nonfiction: Human interest stories concerning commercial fishing. "We're interested in any timely story that our audience would be interested in, e.g., new boats, new processes for packaging and freezing fish." Buys 75 mss/year. Query with clips of published work or send complete ms. Length: 1,000-1,500 words. Pays $175 average, "depending on research, time, and distance involved."

Photos: State availability of photos. Reviews 5x7 b&w glossy prints. Pays negotiable fee. Captions and model release required. Buys all rights.

Fillers: Anecdotes. Buys 50/year. Length: 100-200 words. Pays $25-30.

NATIONAL FISHERMAN, Diversified Communications, 21 Elm St., Camden ME 04843. (207)236-4342. Editor-in-Chief: David R. Getchell. Managing Editor: James W. Fullilove. 75% freelance written. For amateur and professional boatbuilders, commercial fishermen, armchair sailors, bureaucrats and politicians. Monthly tabloid; 120 pages. Circ. 63,000. Pays in month of acceptance. Buys one-time rights. Pays negotiable kill fee. Byline given. Phone queries OK. Submit seasonal/holiday material 3 months in advance of issue date. Photocopied submissions OK. SASE. Reports in 4 weeks. Free sample copy and writer's guidelines; mention *Writer's Market* in request.

Nonfiction: Expose; how-to; general interest; humor; historical; inspirational; interview; new product; nostalgia; personal experience; opinion; photo feature; profile; and technical. Especially needs articles on boat-building (commercial fishing boats, sport fishing boats, workboats); commercial fishing techniques (problems, solutions, large catches, busts); gear development; and marine historical and offbeat articles. No articles about sailboat racing, cruising and sportfishing. Buys 40/issue. Submit complete ms. Length: 100-3,500 words. Pays $10 minimum and $125-250 maximum.

Photos: State availability of photos with ms. Pays $5-15 for 5x7 or 8x10 b&w prints. Buys one-time rights.

Columns/Departments: Boatyard news (photos with captions of new boats, commercial fishboats favored); fishing highlights (short articles on catches); marine book review and seafood recipes. Buys 5/issue. Submit complete ms. Length: 50-1,000 words. Pays $10 or 5¢/word minimum, whichever is more. Open to suggestions for new columns/departments.

Florists, Nurseries, and Landscaping

FLORIST, Florists' Transworld Delivery Association, 29200 Northwestern Hwy., Box 2227, Southfield MI 48037. (313)355-9300. Editor-in-Chief: William P. Golden. Managing Editor: Bill Gubbins. 5% freelance written. For retail florists, floriculture growers, wholesalers, researchers and teachers. Monthly magazine; 96 pages. Circ. 25,000. Pays on acceptance. Buys one-time rights. Pays 10-25% kill fee. Byline given "unless the story needs a substantial rewrite." Phone queries OK. Submit seasonal/holiday material 3-4 months in advance of issue date. Simultaneous, photocopied and previously published submissions OK. SASE. Reports in 1 month.

Nonfiction: How-to (more profitably run a retail flower shop, grow and maintain better-quality flowers, etc.); general interest (to floriculture and retail floristry); and technical (on flower and plant growing, breeding, etc.). Buys 10-12 mss/year. Query with clips of published work. Length: 1,200-3,000 words. Pays 6¢/word.

Photos: "We do not like to run stories without photos." State availability of photos with query. Pays $10-25 for 5x7 b&w photos or color transparencies. Buys one-time rights.

Tips: "Send samples of published work with query. Suggest several ideas in query letter."

FLOWER NEWS, 549 W. Randolph St., Chicago IL 60606. (312)236-8648. Managing Editor: Nancy Olderr. For retail, wholesale florists, floral suppliers, supply jobbers, growers. Weekly newspaper; 40 pages. Circ. 13,905. Pays on acceptance. Copyrighted. Byline given. Submit seasonal/holiday material at least 2 months in advance. Photocopied and previously published submissions OK. SASE. Reports "immediately." Free sample copy and writer's guidelines.

Nonfiction: How-to articles (increase business, set up a new shop, etc.; anything floral-related without being an individual shop story); informational (general articles of interest to industry); and technical (grower stories related to industry, but not individual grower stories). No articles on

"protecting your business from crime; how to get past-due accounts to pay; attitudes for salespeople." Submit complete ms. Length: 3-5 typed pages. Pays $10.
Photos: "We do not buy individual pictures. They may be enclosed with ms at regular ms rate (b&w only)."

FLOWERS &, 2400 Compton Blvd., Redondo Beach CA 90278. Publisher and Editor-in-Chief: Barbara Cady. Published by Teleflora Inc., for members of the floriculture industry. Positioned as "The magazine with a new approach to the floriculture industry." Monthly. Circ. 20,000. Buys one-time rights in floral trade magazine field. Byline given unless "article is not thorough enough but portions are included in another article." Most articles are staff-written. Pays on acceptance. Reports in 3 weeks. Must send query letter with proposed, brief outline first. SASE.
Nonfiction: Articles dealing with buying and selling profitably, merchandising of product, sales promotion, management, designing, shop remodeling, display techniques, etc. Also, allied interests such as floral wholesalers, growers, tradespeople, gift markets, etc. Covers general interest stories and news about retail business, finances and taxes. All articles must be thoroughly researched and professionally relevant. Length: 1,000-3,000 words. Pays approximately 14¢/published word.
Tips: "Queries should be brief and to the point, with *no* typos, include author's qualifications and past published experience plus a brief outline detailing the proposed article. We prefer to see no unsolicited manuscripts."

SOUTHERN FLORIST AND NURSERYMAN, Southern Florist Publishing Co., Box 1868, Fort Worth TX 76101. (817)332-8236. Editor: Mike Branch. Weekly magazine about nurserymen and growers for wholesale and retail florists, growers, nurserymen and distributors, concentrated in the Southern states. Circ. 6,313. Average issue includes 15 major articles, schedules of upcoming events, news of interest to the trade, information about tradesmen and features on florists. Pays on publication. Byline given. Buys all serial rights. (Book rights remain with author.) Phone queries OK. Submit seasonal material 2 months in advance. Photocopied and previously published submissions OK. SASE. Reports in 2 weeks on queries; in 3 weeks on mss. Free sample copy and writer's guidelines.
Nonfiction: Historical (a company's anniversary, history of a well-known trade name); nostalgia (by a tradesman); opinion; profile (of someone prominent in the trade or of shops or operations); how-to (design, grow); new product (new concept, not a specific brand); personal experience; and technical (may take the form of an interview with a successful grower/designer). "We write for the trade, not for consumers, so avoid gardening tips and how-to take care of house plants." Buys 5-6 original mss/issue. Send complete ms. Length: 100-2,500 words. Pays $150 maximum. "Watch the newspaper for any information about florists, growers or trends in this area. We pay for material reprinted. Also, visit florists or growers in your area and ask them about special techniques or systems they employ—what has been successful for them—and look for ways to apply to other operations."
Photos: State availability of photos or send photos with ms. Pays $9 minimum for original 5x7 b&w glossy prints. Pays $15 minimum for original color transparencies. Captions preferred. Buys one-time rights.
Fillers: Clippings. Pays $3 minimum.

WEEDS TREES & TURF, Harcourt Brace Jovanovich, 737 3rd Ave., New York NY 10017. Editor: Bruce Shank. For "turf managers, parks; superintendents of golf courses, airports, schools; landscape architects, landscape contractors and sod farmers." Monthly magazine. Circ. 45,000. Pays on publication. Buys all rights. Submit seasonal/holiday material 4 months in advance. Photocopied submissions OK. SASE. Reports in 6 weeks.
Nonfiction: Publishes how-to, informational and technical articles. Buys 24 mss/year. Query or submit complete ms. Length: 750-2,000 words. Pays $200-400.

Food Products, Processing, and Service

In this list are journals for food wholesalers, processors, warehousers, caterers, institutional managers, and suppliers of grocery store equipment. Publications for grocery store operators are classified under Groceries. Journals for food vending machine operators will be found under Coin-Operated Machines.

FAST SERVICE, Harcourt Brace Jovanovich, Inc., 757 3rd Ave., New York NY 10017. (212)888-4324. Editor: Peter Romeo. Monthly. Circ. 50,800. Buys all rights. Pays 50% kill fee. Pays on acceptance. Reports in 2 weeks. Query. SASE.
Nonfiction and Photos: Articles on operations and case histories of all phases of fast service restaurant operations. Length: 1,500-2,000 words. Pays 10-20¢/word. B&w photos (5x7 or 8x10) purchased with mss or with captions only. Color transparencies used for cover and for feature article illustration. Fee is negotiated for all color photography. Will accept 35mm work if of high quality.

FOOD IN CANADA, 481 University Ave., Toronto, Ontario, Canada M5W 1A7. Editor: R.F. (Bob) Barratt. "*Food in Canada* is a business publication serving Canada's food and beverage processing (or manufacturing) industry. Food manufacturing is Canada's largest secondary activity." Circ. 9,000. Pays on acceptance. Buys first Canadian serial rights. Previously published work "possibly OK, but it might need a rewrite." SAE and International Reply Coupons.
Nonfiction: "We would consider US material that contains a high interest or information factor for the Canadian food industrialist. We are always interested in material that discusses truly new US food and beverage processing developments that hold out the promise for profitable application by Canadian based food and beverage processing companies." Query. Length: 1,000-1,500 words. Short pieces about new processing and food research developments should be 250-750 words. Pays 15¢/word minimum.
Photos: Pays $10 for 5x7 or 8x10 b&w prints.

KITCHEN PLANNING, Harcourt Brace Jovanovich, Inc., 757 3rd Ave., New York NY 10017. Editor: Peter Romeo. Buys all rights. Pays on acceptance. Query. SASE.
Nonfiction and Photos: How-to, in-depth articles on designing commercial and institutional kitchens—installations based on actual experience of specific operation—with quotes, facts, figures. Length: 1,000-1,500 words. Kitchen floor plans must accompany ms. B&w glossies purchased with ms. Pays 10-15¢/word.

MEAT PLANT MAGAZINE, 9701 Gravois Ave., St. Louis MO 63123. (314)638-4050. Editor: Tony Nolan. For meat processors, locker plant operators, freezer provisioners, portion control packers, meat dealers, and food service (food plan) operators. Monthly. Pays on acceptance. Reports in 2 weeks. SASE for return of submissions.
Nonfiction, Photos, and Fillers: Buys feature-length articles and shorter subjects pertinent to the field. Length: 1,000-1,500 words for features. Pays 5¢/word. Pays $5 for photos.

PRODUCE NEWS, 2185 Lemoine Ave., Fort Lee NJ 07024. Editor: Melvina Bauer. For "commercial growers and shippers, receivers, and distributors of fresh fruits and vegetables, including chain store produce buyers and merchandisers." Weekly. Circ. 5,300. Not copyrighted. Pays on publication. Free sample copy. "Our deadline is Wednesday afternoon before Friday press day each week." SASE.
Nonfiction, Fillers and Photos: "News is our principal stock in trade, particularly trends in crop growing, distributing, and marketing. Tell the story clearly, simply, and briefly." Buys informational articles, how-to's, profiles, spot news, coverage of successful business operations, new product pieces, articles on merchandising techniques. Query. Length: "no special length." Pays 50¢ a column inch for original material, 40¢ column inch for clippings. 8½x11 b&w glossies purchased with ms.

QUICK FROZEN FOODS, Harcourt Brace Jovanovich, 757 3rd Ave., New York NY 10017. (212)888-3300. Editor: Theodore C. Boytos. Senior Associate Editor: C. Ross Chamberlain. 5-10% freelance written. For executives of processing plants, distributors, warehouses, transport companies, retailers and food service operators involved in frozen foods. Monthly magazine; 100 pages. Circ. 25,000. Pays on acceptance. Buys all rights. Pays kill fee up to full amount if reasons for kill are not fault of author. Byline given unless it is work-for-hire or ghostwriting. Submit seasonal/holiday material 3 months in advance of issue date. SASE. Reports in 1 week. Free sample copy; mention *Writer's Market* in request.
Nonfiction: Interview; new product; photo feature; profile; and technical. Buys 12 mss/year. Query or submit complete ms. Length: 1,500-3,000 words. Pays 5¢/word. "For special circumstances will offer flat rate for package which may be higher than word rate."
Photos: State availability of photos with query or ms. Pays $5 for 4x5 b&w smooth prints. Captions required. Buys all rights.

SNACK FOOD, HBJ Publications, Inc., 1 E. 1st St., Duluth MN 55802. (218)727-8511. Editor-in-Chief: Jerry L. Hess. 10-15% freelance written. For manufacturers and distributors of snack foods. Monthly magazine; 60 pages. Circ. 10,000. Pays on acceptance. Buys first North American serial rights. Occasional byline. Phone queries OK. Photocopied submissions OK. SASE. Reports in 2-3 weeks. Free sample copy and writer's guidelines.
Nonfiction: Informational, interview, new product, nostalgia, photo feature, profile and technical articles. "We use a variety of mini news-features and personality sketches." Length: 300-600 words for mini-features; 1,000-1,500 words for longer features. Pays $100 minimum.
Photos: Purchased with accompanying ms. Captions required. Pays $15 for 5x7 b&w photos; $15-20 for 4x5 color transparencies. Total purchase price for a ms includes payment for photos. Buys all rights.
Tips: "Query should contain specific lead and display more than a casual knowledge of our audience."

THE WISCONSIN RESTAURATEUR, M/S Publishing, 122 W. Washington, Madison WI 53703. (603)251-3663. Editor: Jan La Rue. Emphasizes restaurant industry for restaurateurs, hospitals, institutions, food service students, etc. Monthly magazine "except November/December combined." Circ. 3,200. Pays on acceptance. Buys all rights or one-time rights. Pays 10% kill fee. Byline given. Phone queries OK. Submit seasonal/holiday material 2-3 months in advance. Previously published work OK; "indicate where." SASE. Reports in 3 weeks. Free sample copy and writer's guidelines with large post paid envelope.
Nonfiction: Interested in expose, general interest, historical, how-to, humor, inspirational, interview, nostalgia, opinion, profile, travel, new product, personal experience, photo feature and technical articles pertaining to restaurant industry. "No features on nonmember restaurants." Buys 1 ms/issue. Query with "copyright clearance information and a note about the writer in general." Length: 700-1,500 words. Pays $10-20.
Photos: Fiction and how-to article mss stand a better chance for publication if photo is submitted. State availability of photos. Pays $15 for b&w 8x10 glossy prints. Model releases required, captions are not.
Columns/Departments: Spotlight column provides restaurant member profiles. Buys 6/year. Query. Length: 500-1,500 words. Pays $5-10.
Fiction: Likes experimental, historical and humorous stories related to food service only. Buys 12 mss/year. Query. Length: 1,000-3,000 words. Pays $10-20.
Poetry: Uses all types of poetry, but must have food service as subject. Buys 6-12/year. No more than 5 submissions at one time. Length: 10-50 lines. Pays $5-10.
Fillers: Uses clippings, jokes, gags, anecdotes, newsbreaks, and short humor. No puzzles or games. Buys 12/year. Length: 50-500 words. Pays $2.50-7.50.

Gas

GAS DIGEST, Box 35819, Houston TX 77035. (713)723-7456. Editor: Ken Kridner. 30% freelance written. For operating personnel of the gas industry. Bimonthly magazine; 36 pages. Circ. 9,000. Rights may be retained by the author. Pays on publication. Photocopied submissions OK. Reports in 1 month. Query.
Nonfiction: Applications stories; new developments. All material must be operations-oriented and meaningful to one working in the gas industry. How-to, technical articles. Length: 500-1,000 words. Pays 2¢/word minimum.
Photos: B&w photos purchased with ms. Pays $5 minimum.

LP-GAS, 1 E. 1st St., Duluth MN 55802. Editor: Zane Chastain. For liquefied petroleum gas (propane, 'bottled gas') marketers. Monthly. Buys all rights. No byline. Pays on acceptance. Query. SASE.
Nonfiction: Uses dealer and LP-gas utilization articles, how-to features on selling, delivery, service, etc. Tersely written, illustrated by photo or line for documentation. Length: maximum 2,000 words. Pays 5-10¢/word.
Photos: Pix with mss or captions only; not less than 2¼x2¼. Pays $5-7.

SOONER LPG TIMES, 2910 N. Walnut, Suite 114-A, Oklahoma City OK 73105. (405)525-9386. Editor: John E. Orr. 33% freelance written. For "dealers and suppliers of LP-gas and their employees." Monthly. Not copyrighted. Byline given. Pays on publication. Reports in 3 weeks. SASE.

Nonfiction: "Articles relating to the LP-gas industry, safety, small business practices, and economics; anything of interest to small businessmen." Length: 1,000-2,000 words. Pays $10-15.

Government and Public Service

Below are journals for individuals who provide governmental services, either in the employ of local, state, or national governments or of franchised utilities. Included are journals for city managers, politicians, civil servants, firemen, policemen, public administrators, urban transit managers, utilities managers, etc.

Publications that emphasize the architectural and building side of city planning and development are classified in Architecture. Publications for lawyers are found in the Law category. Journals for teachers and administrators in the schools are found in Education. Publications for private citizens interested in politics, government, and public affairs are classified with the Politics and World Affairs magazines in the Consumer Publications section.

CORRECTIONS, Criminal Justice Publications, 116 W. 32nd St., New York NY 10001. (212)947-2700. Editor: Michael S. Serrill. Bimonthly magazine for corrections professionals. Circ. 10,000. Pays ½ on acceptance. Buys all rights. Photocopied submissions OK. SASE. Reports in 1 month on queries. Free sample copy.
Nonfiction: "We are interested in new strategies and innovative techniques for dealing with corrections problems, prison programs, drug treatment, community-based corrections programs, and changes in laws regarding prisoners and offenders." Runs 5 mss/issue; buys 2-3. Query. Length: 1,000-6,000 words. Pays $400-1,100.
Columns/Departments: In My Opinion (from practitioners in corrections work); Prisons and the Law; News Briefs.
Tips: "We pride ourselves on developing new writers into successful professionals."

FIRE CHIEF MAGAZINE, 625 N. Michigan Ave., Chicago IL 60611. (312)642-9862. Editor: William Randleman. 10% freelance written. For chiefs of volunteer and paid fire departments. Buys all rights. Pays on publication. Reports in 10 days. SASE.
Nonfiction: Wants articles on fire department administration, training or fire-fighting operations. Will accept case histories of major fires, extinguished by either volunteer or paid departments, detailing exactly how the fire department fought the fire and the lessons learned from the experience. "Prefer feature articles to be bylined by a fire chief or other fire service authority." Writing must be simple, clear and detailed, preferably conversational in style. Pays $1-1.50/column inch.
Photos: Used with mss or with captions only. 4x5 or larger; Polaroid or other small prints of individuals or small subjects accepted. Pays up to $35 for acceptable color photos. Pays nothing for public domain photos, up to $5 for exclusives, $1 for mug shots.

FIRE ENGINEERING, 666 5th Ave., New York NY 10103. Editor: Richard Pratt Sylvia. For commissioners, chiefs and senior officers of the paid, volunteer, industrial and military fire departments and brigades. Buys first serial rights. Byline given. Pays on publication. Reports in 3 weeks.
Nonfiction and Photos: Wants articles on fire suppression, fire prevention, and any other subject that relates to fire service. Length: 750-1,500 words. Pays 3¢/word minimum. Inside photos used only with articles. Particular need for color photos for cover; small print or slide satisfactory for submission, but must always be a vertical or capable of being cropped to vertical. Transparency required if accepted. Pays $25 for color shots used on cover, $15 and up for b&w shots.

FIREHOUSE MAGAZINE, 515 Madison Ave., New York NY 10022. (212)935-4550. Editor-in-Chief: Dennis Smith. 75% freelance written. For volunteer firefighters, paid firefighters, their families and fire buffs. Monthly magazine; 72 pages. Circ. 100,000. Pays on publication. Buys all rights. Submit seasonal or holiday material 4 months in advance. Photocopied submissions OK. SASE. Reports in 2 months. Sample copy $1.50. Free writer's guidelines.
Nonfiction: How-to (firefighting); informational (family activities); historical (great fires); profiles (achieving firefighters); new product; personal experience (firefighting); photo features (recent fires); technical (fire science and medicine); puzzles using firefighting terms; and stories on recent large and unusual fires or disasters involving firefighters. Buys 120 mss/year. Query. Length:

500-2,000 words. Pays $100-200/article, depending on length.
Photos: Purchased with or without ms, or on assignment. Captions required. Query. Pays $15-45 for 8x10 glossies or color transparencies.

FOREIGN SERVICE JOURNAL, 2101 E St., NW, Washington DC 20037. (202)338-4045. Editor: Stephen R. Dujack. For Foreign Service officers and others interested in foreign affairs and related subjects. Monthly (July/August combined). Buys first North American rights. Byline given. Pays on publication. SASE.
Nonfiction: Uses articles on "international relations, internal problems of the State Department and Foreign Service, informative material on other nations. Much of our material is contributed by those working in the fields we reach. Informed outside contributions are welcomed, however." Query. Length: 1,000-4,000 words. Pays 2-6¢/word.

OSC CORPORATION, 46 Leo Birmingham Pkwy., Boston MA 02135. (617)787-0005. Managing Editor: Penny Deyoe. Several magazines covering law enforcement for law enforcement personnel, legislators, and local government leaders. Circ. 100,000. Pays on publication. Byline given. Buys all rights. Submit seasonal/holiday material 4 months in advance. Simultaneous queries and photocopied submissions OK. SASE. Reports in 1 week on queries. Writer's guidelines available for business size SAE and 1 first class stamp.
Nonfiction: General interest (consumer, health, trends in law enforcement); historical/nostalgic (if it can be tied to something current); interview/profile (of interesting police and legendary criminals); offbeat crimes; and white collar crime. "We like to cover trends in the profession, such as the current trend toward using more civilians for inside work. Also, our readers like to read about the legendary criminals. No blood and gore." Buys 100 mss/year. Query. Length: 3,000 minimum. Pays 5¢/word.
Photos: Pays $5 minimum for 5x7 or 8x10 b&w glossy prints. Captions and model release required.
Columns/Departments: Criminal justice (new laws, Supreme Court decisions); and Consumer Information (money stretching tips). Send complete ms. Length: 3,000 words minimum. Pays 5¢/word.

PASSENGER TRANSPORT, 1225 Connecticut Ave., NW, Washington DC 20036. Editor: Albert Engelken. Published by the American Public Transit Association for those in mid- to top-level management of urban mass transportation and government officals. Pays on publication. Very little material bought. SASE.
Nonfiction: Uses short, concise articles which can be documented on urban mass transportation. Latest news only. No airline, steamship, intercity bus or railroad news.
Photos: Sometimes buys photographs with mss and with captions only, but standards are high. 8x10's preferred. No color.

PLANNING, American Planning Association, 1313 E. 60th St., Chicago IL 60637. (312)947-2108. Editor: Sylvia Lewis. Emphasizes urban planning for adult, college-educated readers who are university faculty or students; or regional and urban planners in city, state or federal agencies or in private business. Published monthly; 36 pages. Circ. 25,000. Pays on publication. Buys all rights or first serial rights. Byline given. Phone queries OK. Photocopied and previously published submissions OK. SASE. Reports in 5 weeks. Free sample copy and writer's guidelines.
Nonfiction: Expose (on government or business, but on topics related to planning, housing, land use, zoning); general interest (trend stories on cities, land use, government); historical (historic preservation); how-to (successful government or citizen efforts in planning; innovations; concepts that have been applied); profile (only of extraordinary people in our field); photo feature; technical (detailed articles on the nitty-gritty of planning, zoning, transportation but no footnotes or mathematical models). Also needs news stories up to 500 words. "It's best to query with a fairly detailed, one-page letter. We'll consider any article that's well-written and relevant to our audience. Articles have a better chance if they are timely and related to planning and land use, and if they appeal to a national audience. All articles should be written in magazine feature style." Buys 2 features, 1 news story and 2 book reviews/issue. Length: 500-2,000 words. Pays $50-200. "We pay freelance writers and photographers only."
Photos: "We prefer that authors supply their own photos, but we sometimes take our own or arrange for them in other ways." State availability of photos. Pays $25 minimum for 8x10 matte or glossy prints and $125 for color covers (35mm transparencies). Captions preferred. Buys one-time rights.
Columns/Departments: Planners Library (book reviews). Books assigned by book review editor. Buys 1 review/issue. Query. Length: 500-1,000 words. Pays $35.

POLICE MAGAZINE, Criminal Justice Publications, 116 W. 32 St., New York NY 10001. (212)947-2700. Editor: Michael S. Serrill. Bimonthly magazine for law enforcement officers, district attorneys and deputy sheriffs. Circ. 38,000. Pays on acceptance. Buys first North American serial rights. Simultaneous and photocopied submissions OK. SASE. Reports in 1 month. Free sample copy.

Nonfiction: General interest (crime articles; strategies for dealing with crime; innovative law enforcement techniques; in-depth reports on internal police operations; and the incidence of crime); historical (police operations of the past); how-to (deal with crime); interview (of police officials and atypical police officers); profile (of police departments and officials, based on specific incidents); new product (hardware and software, radar, bullet proof vests. etc.); technical (police techniques for prevention and apprehension); and broad articles on specific kinds of crime problems. Buys 4 mss/issue. Query. "The query letter writer should, if he has a story idea, be very specific about what it is and how he would go about reporting it. Daily newspaper experience is almost a must; I always want to see clips before I will take a chance on a person." Length: 1,000-6,000 words. Pays $300-1,000. "All work is done by assignment. Send no unsolicited manuscripts."

Columns/Departments: Viewpoint (only written by law enforcment professionals); Hardware/Software; Police and the Law; Incident Report; Roll Call (short news item); Letters.

Tips: "We use some freelancers who don't have much experience. We pride ourselves on developing new writers into successful professionals."

POLICE PRODUCT NEWS, Dyna Graphics, Inc., 6200 Yarrow Dr., Carlsbad CA 92008. Editor: Denny Fallon. For all law enforcement personnel. Monthly magazine; 72-88 pages. Circ. 50,000. Pays on publication. Buys one time rights. Byline given. Submit seasonal/holiday material 2 months in advance. SASE. Reports in 1 week. Sample copy $2; free writer's guidelines.

Nonfiction: Expose, historical, how-to, humor, interview, profile (of police departments around the country); new product (testing/evaluation/opinion); and technical. "All material must be related to law enforcement in some way and no stories about law enforcement personnel being killed." Buys 4-5 mss/year. Send complete ms. Length: 1,000-4,000 words. Pays $75-400.

Photos: State availability of photos or send photos with ms. Pays $25-40 for b&w 8x10 glossy prints and $35-50 for 2¼x2¼ color transparencies; offers no additional payment for photos accepted with ms. Model release required.

Fiction: Wants law enforcement-related adventure, fantasy, historical, humorous (especially interested in this type), mystery and suspense. Buys 1 ms/issue. Send complete ms. Length: 1,000-4,000 words. Pays $75-400.

POLICE TIMES MAGAZINE, 1100 NE 125th St., North Miami FL 33161. (305)891-1700. Editor: Gerald Arenberg. 90% freelance written. For "law enforcement officers: federal, state, county, local and private security." Monthly. Circ. 87,000. Buys all rights. Buys 10-20 mss/year. Pays on publication. Sample copy for 50¢ postage. Reports "at once." SASE.

Nonfiction and Photos: Interested in articles about local police departments all over the nation. In particular, short articles about what the police department is doing, any unusual arrests made, acts of valor of officers in the performance of duties, etc. Also articles on any police subject from prisons to reserve police. "We prefer newspaper style. Short and to the point. Photos and drawings are a big help." Length: 300-1,200 words. Pays $5-15—up to $25 in some cases based on 1¢/word. Uses b&w Polaroid and 8x10 b&w glossy prints, "if of particular value." Pays $5-15 for each photo used.

RESERVE LAW NEWS, Box 17807, San Antonio TX 78217. Editor: Otto Vehle. 20% freelance written. Publication of Reserve Law Officers Association of America. For sheriffs, chiefs of police, other law enforcement officials and their reserve components. Monthly. Circ. "over 10,000." Not copyrighted. Byline given. Pays on publication. Photocopied submissions OK. SASE. Free sample copy.

Nonfiction: "Articles describing police reserve and sheriff reserve organizations and their activities should be informative and interesting. Style should be simple, straightforward, and with a touch of humor when appropriate. We need current features on outstanding contemporary lawmen, both regular officers and reserves. We are still hoping to attract freelance writers who have some law enforcement orientation as it actually is, not based upon experiences gained from watching TV. Yet, highly technical writing is not sought. Reserve Law Officers are businessmen and women who generally have incomes considerably above that of the average law officer and who find great satisfaction in donating their time to a law enforcement agency. These few hours per month they donate might possibly produce some excitement and adrenalin flow, but such occasions are rare since most police work is rather dull and monotonous. Therefore, articles submitted to us should contain some thrills, excitement, danger (much like a story submitted to a fishing magazine would place the reader in the big game fishing chair as the line spins off the reel)." No profanity, sex exploitation or racial slurs. Submit complete ms. Length: 500-2,000 words.

Photos: "In most cases, the manuscript should be accompanied by high-contrast 8x10 b&w action photos, properly identified and captioned." Pays $10 minimum; plus $5 for first photo and $2.50 for additional photos used in same article.
Columns/Departments: Ichthus (a chaplain's column dealing with Christian law officers—100-500 words); Law-Haw (humorous anecdotes about police work—40-60 words); Fundamentals (basic how-to's of law enforcement—100-500 words). Pays contributor's copies minimum, $50 maximum.
Fiction: "Fictionalized accounts of true police cases involving reserve officers will be accepted if they meet our needs." Length: 200-800 words. Pays $50 maximum.
Fillers: Jokes and short humor "of the law enforcement type." Length: 20-80 words. Pays $10 maximum.

ROLL CALL, 201 Massachusetts Ave. NE, Washington DC 20002. (202)546-3080. Editor: Sidney Yudain. For US Congressmen, political buffs, editors, etc. Weekly newspaper. Circ. 9,000. Buys first North American serial rights. Byline given. Pays on acceptance. Photocopied and simultaneous submissions OK. Tries to report in 1 week. Query or submit complete ms. SASE.
Nonfiction and Photos: Profiles, humor, historical and nostalgic articles. No "treatises on issues such as economy, budget, Social Security, abortion, etc. Political satire material must measure up to the work of the noted satirists we usually publish." Buys 10 mss/year. Length: 500-2,000 words. Pays $5-25. No additional payment for b&w photos used with articles.
Poetry and Fillers: Light verse related to subject matter. Puzzles on a Congressional or political theme and short humor on political topics are used as fillers. Pays $2 minimum.
Tips: "Submissions must be informative/enlightening/entertaining."

STATE LEGISLATURES, National Conference of State Legislatures, 1125 17th St., Suite 1500, Denver CO 80202. (303)623-6600. Editor: Steve Millard. Associate Editor: Dan Pilcher. Emphasizes current issues facing state legislatures for legislators, legislative staff members and close observers of state politics and government. Magazine published 10 times/year; 32 pages. Pays on acceptance. Buys all rights. Byline given. SASE. Reports in 1 month. Free sample copy.
Nonfiction: "We're interested in original reporting on the responses of states (particularly state legislatures) to current problems, e.g., tax reform, health care, energy, consumer protection, etc. We also look for articles on federal actions that affect the states. We're open to a limited number of interviews, but these are always assigned to writers who are thoroughly familiar with the magazine and its audience." Query preferred, but will consider complete ms. Pays $250-400, depending on length.

WESTERN FIRE JOURNAL, 9072 E. Artesia Blvd., Suite 7, Bellflower CA 90706. (213)866-1664. Editor: David K. McKnight. 20% freelance written, "but only because we receive just 20% freelance material. The more we receive, the more we will use." For fire chiefs of paid and volunteer departments in metropolitan and small communities located in the 11 Western states. Also read by other fire department officers and personnel. Monthly magazine; 66 pages. Circ. 5,000. Pays on publication. Buys one-time rights. Offers negotiable kill fee to regular contributors. Byline given, "even in some cases where a writer, unfamiliar with the Fire Service, comes up with a dynamite idea but only compiles the information for us and does not write the actual article." Phone queries OK. Photocopied submissions OK. SASE. Reports in 3 weeks. Sample copy $1; free writer's guidelines; mention *Writer's Market* in request.
Nonfiction: How-to (develop or build a new piece of fire protection equipment or facility); interview (leaders recognized in fire protection with something constructive to say); and technical (new ideas in fire protection techniques, management training and prevention). Topics must concern Western Fire Service activities. No articles on a fire fighter's day. No human interest. Buys 20 mss/year. Query. Pays $1.50-1.75/inch.
Photos: State availability of photos with query. Pays $4-10 for 8x10 b&w matte prints or $10-25 for 35mm color transparencies. Captions preferred. Buys one-time rights.
Tips: "Writers have to remember that most editors are writers, too. Editors understand writers' problems in most cases. Please, writers, try to understand our problems, too. If you send me something that could have been published in the Sunday supplement of your local paper, it's just not going to make it in our magazine. You've got to realize that professional Fire Service people are not interested in reading 'cute' human interest pieces. They've heard the same stories many times already. Call me any Friday and ask for our specific needs (they change monthly). If I am not in the office, try me again the next Friday. Sorry, we simply can't afford to return calls regarding queries. But if you call, I'll be happy to talk with you. Please include an SASE. If we buy your piece, it will more than pay for the stamps; if we don't it will guarantee its return."

YOUR VIRGINIA STATE TROOPER MAGAZINE, Box 2189, Springfield VA 22152. (703)451-2524. Editor: Geraldine A. Lash. Biannual magazine covering police topics for troopers, police, libraries, legislators and businesses. Estab. 1979. Circ. 5,000. Pays on acceptance. Byline given. Buys first North American serial rights and all rights on assignments. Submit seasonal/ holiday material 2 months in advance. Simultaneous and photocopied submissions OK. Reports in 2 weeks on mss. Sample copy $5.

Nonfiction: Book excerpts; expose (consumer or police-related); general interest; historical/ nostalgic; how-to (energy saving); humor; interview/profile (notable police figures); opinion; personal experience; technical (radar); and other (recreation). All articles must be police related. Buys 35 mss/year. Query with clips of published work or send complete ms. Length: 2,500-3,000 words. Pays $250 maximum/article (10¢/word).

Photos: Send photos with ms. Pays $25 maximum/5x7 b&w glossy print. Captions and model release required. Buys one-time rights.

Fiction: Adventure, humorous, mystery, novel excerpts, and suspense. All articles must be police-related. Buys 4 mss/year. Send complete ms. Length: 2,500 words minimum. Pays $250 maximum (10¢/word) on acceptance.

Groceries

The journals that follow are for owners and operators of retail food stores. Journals for food wholesalers, packers, warehousers and caterers are classified with the Food Products, Processing and Service journals. Publications for food vending machine operators are found in the Coin-Operated Machines category.

CANADIAN GROCER, Maclean-Hunter Ltd., 481 University Ave., Toronto, Ontario, Canada M5W 1A7. (416)596-5772. Editor: George H. Condon. Monthly magazine about supermarketing and food retailing for Canadian chain and independent food store managers, owners, buyers, executives, food brokers, food processors and manufacturers. Circ 16,000. Pays on publication. Byline given. Buys first Canadian rights. Phone queries OK. Submit seasonal material 2 months in advance. Previously published submissions OK. SAE and International Reply Coupons. Reports in 2 weeks. Sample copy $4.

Nonfiction: Interview (national trendsetters in marketing, finance or food distribution); technical (store operations, equipment and finance); and news features on supermarkets. "Freelancers should be well versed on the supermarket industry. We don't want unsolicited material. Writers with business and/or finance expertise are preferred. Know the retail food industry and be able to write concisely and accurately on subjects relevant to our readers: food store managers, senior corporate executives, etc. A good example of an article would be 'How a Six Store Chain of Supermarkets Improved Profits 2% and Kept Customers Coming.' " Buys 14 mss/year. Query with clips of previously published work. Pays $25-175.

Photos: State availability of photos. Pays $5-15 for 8x10 b&w glossy prints. Captions preferred. Buys one-time rights.

ENTREE, Fairchild, 7 E. 12th St., New York NY 10003. (212)741-4009. Editor: Paul Camp. Managing Editor: Priscilla Smart. Monthly tabloid covering "trends in cooking, general industry news, new products in the gourmet and lifestyle areas for specialty retailers and buyers of gourmet products and executives and managers in the gourmet product industry." Estab. 1980. Circ. 15,000. Average issue includes 8-11 features, 5 columns, a calendar, news and 50% advertising. Pays on publication. Byline given. Kill fee varies. Buys all rights. Phone queries OK. Photocopied submissions OK. SASE. Reports in 6 weeks on queries; in 1 week on mss. Sample copy $1.50.

Nonfiction: Profile (of retailers); how-to (handle a business situation as explained by retailers of gourmet products); humor; new product ("hot product categories"); photo feature; and technical (cookware in terms retailers can apply to their businesses). Buys 2-3 mss/issue. Query. Length: 1,500-3,000 words. Pays $120-150.

Photos: Editor: Mare Earley. Pays $20 for 8x10 b&w glossy prints. Color photos negotiable. Captions required.

Columns/Departments: Sizzlers (about people); Simmer (on news); Menu Makers (cookware reviews); Gourmania (on "wild stuff about cooking or food, the lighter side of gourmet"); and Bright Ideas (on new products).

FOODSMAN, 1001 E. Main St., Richmond VA 23219. (804)644-0731. Editor: Brian F. Daly. 10% freelance written. For food retailers, wholesalers, distributors. Quarterly magazine; 22-34 pages. Circ. 7,000. Not copyrighted. Pays 20% kill fee. Byline given. Pays on publication. Will send free sample copy to writer on request. Query. "Queries handled immediately." SASE.

Nonfiction and Photos: "Consumer articles; anything of interest to food people. From attitude surveys, operational studies, general interest articles or photo layouts on store design. Emphasis is on Virginia and helpful ideas to be implemented by either food retailers, wholesalers or distributors." Informational, interviews with government officials, profiles, think pieces, training reviews, spot news, successful business operations, new product, merchandising techniques. Length: open. Pays 10¢/word.

GOURMET RETAILER, Industry Publishers, Inc., 1545 NE 23rd St., North Miami FL 33161. (305)893-8775. Executive Editor: Michael J. Keighley. Managing Editor: Joan Whaley. Monthly magazine about design, display, merchandising techniques, retailing procedures and shop layout and lighting. Estab. 1979. Circ. 13,500. Average issue includes 3-4 feature articles and 6 columns. Pays on publication. Byline given. Buys all rights. Submit seasonal material 2 months in advance. Reports in 6 weeks. Sample copy $2.50; free writer's guidelines.

Nonfiction: General interest and how-to. "Learn our format and do general articles of interest to our specialized readers." Send complete ms. Length: 1,500-3,000 words. Pays 5¢/word.

GROCER'S SPOTLIGHT, Shamie Publishing Co., 22725 Mack Ave., St. Clair Shores MI 48080. (313)779-4940. Editor: Joe Scheringer. Monthly tabloid about the supermarket industry for operators, chain and independent wholesalers, food brokers and manufacturers. Circ. 65,000. Pays on publication. Byline given. Buys all rights. Phone queries OK. Submit seasonal material 2 months in advance. Simultaneous and photocopied submissions OK. SASE. Reports in 3 weeks. Free sample copy and writer's guidelines.

Nonfiction: Interview. Query. Pays $2/column inch.

Columns/Departments: Query. Pays $1/column inch.

HEALTH FOODS BUSINESS, Howmark Publishing Corp., 567 Morris Ave., Elizabeth NJ 07208 (201)353-7373. Editor-in-Chief: Alan Richman. 20% freelance written. For owners and managers of health food stores. Monthly magazine; 100 pages. Circ. over 6,000. Pays on publication. Buys simultaneous rights, second serial (reprint) rights or first North American serial rights. Pays 100% kill fee "if kill is our fault, otherwise kill fee is negotiable." No byline given unless a technical article by an authority or other special circumstances. Phone queries OK. "Query us about a good health foods store in your area. We use many store profile stories." Simultaneous and photocopied submissions OK if exclusive to their field. Previously published work OK. SASE. Reports in 1 month. Sample copy $2.

Nonfiction: Exposes (government hassling with health food industry); how-to (unique or successful retail operators); informational (how or why a product works; technical aspects must be clear to laymen); historical (natural food use); interviews (must be prominent person in industry or closely related to the health food industry); and photo features (any unusual subject related to the retailer's interests). Buys 2-3 mss/issue. Query for interviews and photo features. Will consider complete ms in other categories. Length: 1,000 words minimum. Pays $25/published page minimum.

Photos: "Most articles must have photos included"; minimum 5x7 b&w glossies. Captions required. Send prints or contact sheets with negatives. No additional payment.

PENNSYLVANIA GROCER, 3701 N. Broad St., Philadelphia PA 19140. (215)228-0808. Editor: John McNelis. For grocers, their families and employees, store managers; food people in general. Monthly magazine; 16 pages. Circ. 3,000. Byline given. Pays on publication. Sample copy 75¢. Reports in 30 days. SASE.

Nonfiction and Photos: Articles on food subjects in retail food outlets; mainly local, in Pennsylvania and surrounding areas. Informational, interviews, profiles, historical, successful business operations, new product, merchandising techniques and technical articles. Buys 10-15 mss/year. Query or submit complete ms. Length: 500-900 words. Pays $25. Pays $25 maximum for minimum of 2 b&w photos purchased with ms.

PROGRESSIVE GROCER, 708 3rd Ave., New York NY 10017. (212)490-1000. Editor-in-Chief: Edgar B. Walzer. For supermarket operators, managers, buyers; executives in the grocery business. Monthly magazine; 150 pages. Circ. 90,000. May buy all rights; first North American serial rights; first serial rights; second serial (reprint) rights; or simultaneous rights. Pays on acceptance. Photocopied and simultaneous submissions OK. Submit seasonal merchandising material (spring, summer, fall, holiday) 3 months in advance. Reports in 2-3 weeks. SASE.

Nonfiction and Photos: Department Editor: Mary Ann Linsen. Articles on supermarket merchandising; success stories; consumer relations pieces; promotional campaigns; personal pieces about people in the business. How grocers manage to relate and communicate with consumers via smart programs that really work. Tight, direct, informal, colorful writing needed. Does not want to see anything about quaint little "mom and pop" stores or "run of mill" stores with nothing more than half-hearted gourmet sections. Buys 20 mss/year. Query. Length: open. Pays 5¢/word minimum. Pays $15 minimum for b&w glossies; $25 for color. Captions required.

WHOLE FOODS, Hester Communications, Inc., 1700 Dyer Rd., Suite 250, Santa Ana CA 92705. Editor: Pat Brumm. Monthly magazine about the health foods business for retail store operators, organic farmers, natural foods manufacturers and distributors. Circ. 12,000. Average issue includes 4-5 features and 8 departments. Pays on publication. Byline given. Buys first North American rights. Submit seasonal material 3 months in advance. Photocopied submissions OK. SASE. Reports in 1 month. Free sample copy.
Nonfiction: "We are interested in articles with information for the retailer including processing of foods, ingredients, farming, marketing, *merchandising* and the efficient operation of stores." Buys approximately 10 mss/year. Length: 1,200-2,000 words. Pays $200 average.
Photos: State availability of photos. Photos are purchased with ms as a package. Provide captions and model release if appropriate.

Grooming Products and Services

AMERICAN HAIRDRESSER/SALON OWNER, 100 Park Ave., New York NY 10017. (212)532-5588. Editor: Louise Cotter. For beauty salon owners and operators. Monthly. Buys all rights. Pays on publication. Reports "6 weeks prior to publication." SASE.
Nonfiction: "Technical material; is mainly staff-written." Pays $25/magazine page.

BLACK STYLIST, Morrow's Unlimited, 4167 Market St., San Diego CA 92102. (714)263-8141. Editor: Willie Morrow. Managing Editor: Candace Ludlow Trotter. Monthly magazine covering news and educational information for black barbers and hairstylists, beauty schools and beauty supply distributors. Circ. 30,000. Average issue includes 1 short feature. Pays on publication. Byline given. Buys one-time rights. Phone queries OK. Submit seasonal material 3 months in advance. Simultaneous, photocopied and previously published submissions OK. SASE. Reports in 2 weeks on queries; in 2 months on mss. Free sample copy.
Nonfiction: Profile (on individual black barbers and beauticians, shops and schools and distributors); and how-to (increase income, improve methods of operation). Buys 1 ms/issue. Send complete ms. Length: 600-1,500 words. Pays 3¢/word.
Photos: State availability of photos. Pays $4.50 minimum for 8x10 b&w glossy prints. Captions required.
Tips: "We prefer query letters which show an interest in the beauty industry and sensitivity to the needs of the barber/stylist. Although we are an industry magazine, submissions that are directed to a primarily black population will receive greatest consideration."

WOMAN BEAUTIFUL, Allied Publications, Inc., Drawer 189, Palm Beach FL 33480. (305)833-4593. Editor: Anita M. Kirchen. For "students at beauty schools and people who go to beauty salons." Used as a recruiting tool at high school career days also. Bimonthly magazine; 16 pages. Pays on acceptance. Buys one-time rights. Simultaneous submissions OK. Sample copy $1. Free writer's guidelines. Reports in 4 weeks. SASE.
Nonfiction: "Articles on hairstyling, beauty, and women's fashion." Interested in some new product articles; interviews (with famous hairstylists) and anything related to celebrities and hairstyles. Occasionally uses a history piece such as an article on the history of wigs. Buys 2 mss/issue. Length: 400-800 words. Pays 5¢/published word. Send complete ms.
Columns/Departments: Beauty News and Health & Fitness. Pays 5¢/published word.

Hardware

In this classification are journals for general hardware wholesalers and retailers, locksmiths, and retailers of miscellaneous special hardware items. Journals specializing in the retailing of hardware for a certain trade, such as plumbing or automotive supplies, are classified with the other publications for that trade.

CHAIN SAW AGE, 3435 N.E. Broadway, Portland OR 97232. Editor: Norman W. Raies. For "mostly chain saw dealers (retailers); small businesses—typically small town, typical ages, interests, education." Monthly. Circ. 18,000. Not copyrighted. Buys "very few" mss/year. Pays on acceptance or publication—"varies". Free sample copy. Will consider photocopied submissions. Query first. SASE.

Nonfiction and Photos: "Must relate to chain saw use, merchandising, adaptation, manufacture or display." Buys informational articles, how-to's, personal experience articles, interviews, profiles, inspirational articles, personal opinion articles, photo features, coverage of successful business operations, and articles on merchandising techniques. Length: 500-1,000 words. Pays $20-50 ("2½¢/word plus photo fees"). Photos purchased with or without mss, or on assignment; captions required. For b&w glossies, pay "varies."

HARDWARE AGE, Chilton Co., Chilton Way, Radnor PA 19089. (215)687-8200. Editor-in-Chief: Jon Kinslow. Editor: Jay Holtzman. 5% freelance written. Emphasizes retailing, distribution and merchandising of hardware and building materials. Monthly magazine; 180 pages. Circ. 71,000. Buys first North American serial rights. No byline. Submit seasonal/holiday material 3 months in advance of issue date. Simultaneous, photocopied and previously published submissions OK, if exclusive in the field. SASE. Reports in 1-2 months. Sample copy and writer's guidelines $1; mention *Writer's Market* in request.

Nonfiction: Wendy Ampolsk, managing editor. How-to (more profitably run a hardware store or a department within a store). "We particularly want stories on local hardware stores and home improvement centers, with photos. Stories should concentrate on one particular aspect of how the retailer in question has been successful); and technical (possibly will accept stories on retail accounting or inventory management by qualified writers). Buys 1-2 mss/issue. Submit complete ms. Length: 500-3,000 words. Pays $75-150.

Photos: "We like store features with b&w photos. Usually use b&w for small freelance features." Send photos with ms. Pays $25 for 4x5 glossy b&w prints. Captions preferred. Buys one-time rights.

Columns/Departments: Focus on Law, Money Savers and Business in Print (book reviews). Query or submit complete ms. Length: 1,000-1,250 words. Pays $35. Open to suggestions for new columns/departments.

HARDWARE MERCHANDISER, The Irving-Cloud Publishing Co., 7300 N. Cicero, Lincolnwood IL 60646. (312)674-7300. Editor: James W. Stapleton. Administrative Editor: Pamela Paradowski. Monthly tabloid covering hardware, home center and hardlines market for owners and managers of hardware stores, home centers, and executives of businesses serving them. Circ. 75,000. Pays on acceptance. Buys first North American serial rights. SASE. Reports in 1 month on queries. Free sample copy.

Nonfiction: Profile (of hardware business). Buys 10 mss/year. Query or send complete ms "on speculation; enough to tell the story." Pays $300/article.

Photos: Send photos with ms. Reviews 35mm or larger color transparencies. "Photos are paid for as part of article payment."

HARDWARE MERCHANDISING, Maclean-Hunter Co., Ltd., 481 University Ave., Toronto, Ontario, Canada M5W 1A7. (416)596-5797. Editor-In-Chief: Norman Rosen. Canadian freelancers should contact Mr. Rosen at above address for more information.

NORTHERN HARDWARE TRADE, 2965 Broadmoor Valley Rd., Suite B, Colorado Springs CO 80906. Editor: Edward Gonzales. 1% freelance written. For "owners, managers of hardware and discount stores and lumber yards and home centers; hardware, sporting goods, wholesalers." Monthly. Circ. 18,800. Not copyrighted. Pays on publication. Submit seasonal material 3 months in advance of issue date. SASE.

Nonfiction and Photos: "Case histories on successful retail stores." Buys how-to's and articles on successful business operations. Query or submit complete ms. Pays 4¢/word. B&w photos purchased with mss. Pays $5.

OUTDOOR POWER EQUIPMENT, 4915 W. Freeway, Box 1570, Fort Worth TX 76101. Publisher: Bill Quinn. 5-7% freelance written. Monthly. Circ. 12,000. Not copyrighted. Pays on publication. SASE.

Nonfiction and Photos: Rix Quinn, editor. Photo-story on a single outstanding feature of power equipment stores (lawnmower, snowblower, garden tractors, chain saws, tiller, snowmobiles, etc.). Feature can be a good display, interior or exterior; sales or service tip; unusual sign; advertising or promotion tip; store layout; demonstrations, etc. Photos must be vertical. One 8x10 glossy sufficient. Query. "Submit first story with query letter. Freelancers can call us collect anytime they have questions." Length: 200-300 words. Pays $37.50.

SOUTHERN HARDWARE, 1760 Peachtree Rd., N.W., Atlanta GA 30357. (404)874-4462. Editor-in-Chief: Ralph E. Kirby. 50% freelance written. For retailers of hardware and allied lines, located in the Southern states. Monthly magazine; 80 pages. Circ. 16,500. Pays on acceptance. Buys all rights. Phone queries OK. Submit seasonal/holiday material 3 months in advance of issue date. SASE. Free sample copy and writer's guidelines; mention *Writer's Market* in request.
Nonfiction: How-to (how a store can achieve greater results in selling lines or a line of merchandise). "No articles on history of business." Buys 4 mss/issue. Query. Length: 500-1,000 words. Pays $95-200.
Photos: State availability of photos with query. Offers no additional payment for 5x7 or 8x10 b&w prints. Buys all rights.

Home Furnishings and Appliances

APPLIANCE SERVICE NEWS, 110 W. Saint Charles Rd., Lombard IL 60148. Editor: William Wingstedt. For professional service people whose main interest is repairing major and portable household appliances. Their jobs consist of either service shop owner, service manager or service technician. Monthly "newspaper style" publication; 0-32 pages. Circ. 41,000. Buys all rights. Byline given. Pays on publication. Sample copy $1. Will consider simultaneous submissions. Reports in about 1 month. SASE.
Nonfiction and Photos: James Hodl, associate editor. "Our main interest is in technical articles about appliances and their repair. We also consider articles on the business of running a successful service agency. Material should be written in a straightforward, easy-to-understand style. It should be crisp and interesting, with a high informational content. Our main interest is in the major and portable appliance repair field. We are not interested in retail sales." Query. Length: open. Pays 5-7¢/word. Pays $10 for b&w photos used with ms. Captions required.

CHINA GLASS & TABLEWARE, Ebel-Doctorow Publications, Inc., Box 2147, Clifton NJ 07015. (201)779-1600. Editor-in-Chief: Susan Grisham. 30% freelance written. Monthly magazine for buyers, merchandise managers, and specialty store owners who deal in tableware, dinnerware, glassware, flatware, and other tabletop accessories. Pays on publication. Buys one-time rights. Byline given. Phone queries OK. Submit seasonal/holiday material 3 months in advance of issue date. SASE. Reports in 2-3 weeks. Free sample copy and writer's guidelines; mention *Writer's Market* in request.
Nonfiction: General interest (on store successes, reasons for a store's business track record); interview (personalities of store owners; how they cope with industry problems; why they are in table ware); technical (on the business aspects of retailing china, glassware and flatware). "Bridal registry material always welcomed." No articles on how-to or gift shops. Buys 2-3 mss/issue. Query. Length: 1,500-3,000 words. Pays $40-50/page.
Photos: State availability of photos with query. No additional payment for b&w contact sheets or color contact sheets. Captions required. Buys one-time rights.
Fillers: Clippings. Buys 2/issue. Pays $3-5.
Tips: "Show imagination in the query; have a good angle on a story—that makes it unique from the competition's coverage and requires less work on the editor's part for rewriting a snappy beginning."

FLOORING MAGAZINE, 757 3rd Ave., New York NY 10017. Editor: Michael Korsonsky. 10% freelance written. For floor covering retailers, wholesalers, floor covering specifiers, architects, etc. Monthly. Circulation: 22,000. Buys all rights. No byline. Buys 10-12 mss/year. Pays on acceptance. Free sample copy. Query. Reports in 2-4 weeks. SASE.
Nonfiction and Photos: "Merchandising articles, new industry developments, unusual installations of floor coverings, etc. Conversational approach; snappy, interesting leads; plenty of quotes." Informational, how-to, interview, successful business operations, merchandising techniques, technical. Length: 1,500-1,800 words. Pays 10¢/word. 5x7 or 8x10 b&w photos. Pays $5. Color transparencies (when specified). Pays $10. Captions required.
Tips: "It pays to talk to the subject before sending and incorporating some quotes into the letter."

GIFTS & DECORATIVE ACCESSORIES, 51 Madison Ave., New York NY 10010. (212)689-4411. Editor-in-Chief: Phyllis Sweed. Managing Editor: Douglas Gilbert-Neiss. 10% freelance written. Published primarily for quality gift retailers. Monthly magazine; 250 pages. Circ. 33,000. Pays on publication. No byline. Buys all rights. Submit seasonal/holiday material 6

months in advance of issue date. Photocopied submissions OK. SASE. Reports "as soon as possible." Free writer's guidelines.
Nonfiction: "Merchandising how-to stories of quality stores—how they have solved a particular merchandising problem, or successfully displayed or promoted a particularly difficult area." Nothing about discount stores or mass merchants. Buys 12 mss/year. Query or submit complete ms. Length: 500-1,500 words. Pays $25-150.
Photos: "Photos should illustrate merchandising points made in a story." Pays $7.50-10 for good 5x7 glossy b&w prints; $10-20 for 4x5 color transparencies or 35mm transparencies. Captions required. Buys all rights.
Tips: "We're always in the market for a good story from the West or Southwest."

GIFTWARE BUSINESS, 1515 Broadway, New York NY 10036. (212)764-7317. Editor: Rita Guarna. For "merchants (department store buyers, specialty shop owners) engaged in the resale of giftware, china and glass, decorative accessories." Monthly. Circ. 36,800. Buys all rights. Byline given "by request only." Pays on acceptance. Query or submit complete ms. Will consider photocopied submissions. SASE.
Nonfiction: "Retail store success stories. Describe a single merchandising gimmick. We are a tabloid format—glossy stock. Descriptions of store interiors are less important than sales performance unless display is outstanding. We're interested in articles on aggressive selling tactics. We cannot use material written for the consumer." Buys coverage of successful business operations and merchandising techniques. Length: 750 words maximum.
Photos: Purchased with mss and on assignment; captions required. "Individuals are to be identified." Reviews b&w glossy prints (preferred) and color transparencies.

HOME LIGHTING & ACCESSORIES, Box 2147, Clifton NJ 07015. (201)779-1600. Editor-in-Chief: Herb Ballinger. 35% freelance written. For lighting stores/departments. Monthly magazine; 80 pages. Circ. 7,000. Pays on publication. Buys all rights. Phone queries OK. Submit seasonal/holiday material 6 months in advance of issue date. SASE. Free sample copy.
Nonfiction: How-to (run your lighting store/department, including all retail topics); interview (with lighting retailers); personal experience (as a businessperson involved with lighting); opinion (about business approaches and marketing); profile (of a successful lighting retailer/lamp buyer); and technical (concerning lighting or lighting design). Buys 30 mss/year. Query. Pays $50/published page.
Photos: State availability of photos with query. Offers no additional payment for 5x7 or 8x10 b&w glossy prints. Pays additional $75 for 35mm color transparencies used on cover. Captions required. Buys all rights.

LINENS, DOMESTICS AND BATH PRODUCTS, 370 Lexington Ave., New York NY 10017. (212)532-9290. Editor: Rochelle Goldstein. For department stores, mass merchandisers, specialty stores and bath boutiques. Published 6 times/year. Buys all rights. Pays on publication. Reports in 4-6 weeks. SASE.
Nonfiction and Photos: Merchandising articles that educate the buyer on sales and fashion trends, promotions, industry news, styles; in-depth articles with photos on retail stores/departments for bath accessories, linens and sheets, tablecloths, napkins and place mats, towels, and comforters. Especially focusing on interesting promotions and creative displays within these departments. Length: 700-1,500 words. Pays $150-250. Photos purchased with mss.

MART MAGAZINE, 2 Park Ave., New York NY 10016. (212)340-9754. Editor-in-Chief: Cathy Ciccolella. Managing Editor: Ann Medynski. 20% freelance written. For retailers (independent dealers, buyers for department and discount stores, etc.) of major appliances, consumer electronics and electric housewares. Monthly magazine; 75 pages. Circ. 45,000. Pays on acceptance. Buys all rights. Byline given. SASE. Reports in 2 weeks.
Nonfiction: "We are edited for all retailers of these products: independent appliance-TV dealers, department stores, audio specialists, discount chains, video specialists, catalog showrooms, drug chains, hardware stores and buying offices. We want articles about stores large and small, well-known or unknown. The question we ask about every article is: 'How does this help the guy in the store?' One natural story is how a dealer solved some problem. The problem could be almost anything: financial management, direct mail, radio or TV advertising, salesmanship, etc." Buys 1-3 mss/issue. Query. Length: 200-2,500 words. Pays $35-500.
Photos: "We do not run any stories that are all text." Pays $15 minimum for b&w contact sheets or negatives; $50 minimum for 2¼x2¼ color transparencies. Captions required. Buys all rights.

NATIONAL HOME CENTER NEWS, Lebhar-Friedman, Inc., 425 Park Ave., New York NY 10022. (212)371-9400. Editor: Robert Z. Chew. Biweekly tabloid covering "news in the do-it-

yourself retailing industry, also known as the home center industry." Circ. 30,000. Pays on publication. No byline given. Pays negotiable kill fee. Rights purchased are negotiable. Submit seasonal/holiday material 1 month in advance. Simultaneous queries, and simulaneous and photocopied submissions OK. Reports in 2 weeks.
Nonfiction: "We use very little freelance material. Please write first. Query editor on possible story ideas concerning home centers, housing, fixing-up or other industry-related subjects."
Columns/Departments: Lumber, security, law and wholesaling. Buys 5 mss/year. Query. Length: 300-500 words. Pays $50-100.

RETAILER AND MARKETING NEWS, Box 57194, Dallas TX 75207. (214)651-9959. Editor: Michael J. Anderson. For "retail dealers and wholesalers in appliances, TV's, furniture, consumer electronics, records, air conditioning, housewares, hardware and all related businesses." Monthly. Circ. 10,000. Free sample copy. Photocopied submissions OK. SASE.
Nonfiction: "How a retail dealer can make more profit" is the approach. Wants "sales promotion ideas, advertising, sales tips, business builders and the like, localized to the Southwest and particularly to north Texas." Submit complete ms. Length: 100-900 words. Pays $30-50.

SOUTHWEST HOMEFURNISHINGS NEWS, 4313 N. Central Expressway, Box 64545, Dallas TX 75206. (214)526-7757. Editor: Julia McNair. Quarterly magazine for home furnishings retail dealers, manufacturers, their representatives, and others in related fields. Circ. 12,000. Pays on acceptance. No simultaneous submissions. SASE. Reports in 2 weeks. Sample copy for 9x12 SAE and $1.20 postage.
Nonfiction: Informational articles about retail selling; trends in home furnishings styles; construction of/history of furniture; success and problem solving stories in the retail business, etc. Query. Length: open; appropriate to subject and slant. Pays 10¢/word. "Extensive research projects done on assignment negotiated in addition to the per-word rate."
Photos: "Photos with manuscripts are very important—we love it when they can take pictures on an interview." Pays negotiable fee for b&w glossy and four-color prints.
Tips: "While it is difficult to write for an industry publication without some specific background or association with the field, we are very open to freelance submissions from those who study the magazine first and understand its audience/approach. We would be particularly interested in location stringers in the High Point, North Carolina, Atlanta and San Francisco areas."

TOTALLY HOUSEWARES, The Newspaper for Housewares Executives, DINAN Communications, Inc., 122 42nd St., New York NY 10017. (212)490-3224. Editor: Ron Schneiderman. Managing Editor: Phyllis Katz. Biweekly tabloid covering the housewares industry for retailers, wholesalers and manufacturers. Estab. 1980. Circ. 15,000. Pays on acceptance. Byline given. Buys all rights. Submit seasonal/holiday material 3 months in advance. SASE. Reports in 1 week. Free sample copy.
Nonfiction: Interview (of retailers); and "any topic concerning business or merchandising in the housewares field." Special issues include Gourmet, Clocks, Microwaves, Business Outlook and Cookware. Buys 70 mss/year. Query with clips of published work or query by phone. Length: 1,000-1,500 words. Pay varies.
Photos: State availability of photos. Reviews 5x7 b&w glossy prints. Captions required. Buys one-time rights. "Will reimburse expenses for film, etc."
Tips: "Writers who query us should be knowledgeable in retailing and merchandising."

Hospitals, Nursing, and Nursing Homes

In this section are journals for nurses; medical and nonmedical nursing homes; clinical and hospital staffs; and laboratory technicians and managers. Journals for physicians in private practice or that publish technical material on new discoveries in medicine will be found in the Medical category. Publications that report on medical trends for the consumer are in the Health and Science categories.

HOSPITAL SUPERVISOR'S BULLETIN, Bureau of Business Practice, 24 Rope Ferry Rd., Waterford CT 06386. Editor: Pat Ryan. For hospital supervisors. Semimonthly newsletter; 8 pages. Circ. 8,000. Pays on acceptance. Buys all rights. No byline. Submit seasonal/holiday

material 6 months in advance. Photocopied submissions OK. SASE. Reports in 4 weeks. Free sample copy and writer's guidelines.
Nonfiction: Publishes interviews with non-medical hospital department heads. "You should ask supervisors to pinpoint current problems in supervision, tell how they are trying to solve these problems and what results they're getting—backed up by real examples from daily life." Also publishes articles on people problems and good methods of management. People problems include the areas of training, planning, evaluating, counseling, discipline, motivation, supervising the undereducated, getting along with the medical staff, etc., with emphasis on good methods of management. "We prefer 6- to 8-page typewritten articles, based on interviews." Pays 10-15¢/word after editing.

HOSPITALS, American Hospital Publishing, Inc., 211 E. Chicago Ave., Chicago IL 60611. (312)951-1100. Editor: Daniel Schechter. Managing Editor: Wesley Curry. Bimonthly magazine featuring hospitals and health care systems. Circ. 95,000. Average issue includes 9-12 articles. Pays on acceptance. Byline given. Buys first North American serial rights. Phone queries OK. Submit seasonal material 4 months in advance. Photocopied submissions OK. Reports in 2 weeks on queries; in 2 months on mss. Free sample copy and writer's guidelines.
Nonfiction: How-to and new product. "Articles must address issues of the management of health care institutions." Buys 10 mss/year. Query with "reasonably detailed summary or outline of proposed article." Length: 3,000 words maximum. Pays $250-500.
Columns/Departments: "Columns are published on cost containment, architecture and design, and long-term care. Another column includes short features on innovative hospital programs."

JOURNAL OF NURSING CARE, Technomic Publishing Co., 265 Post Rd., W., Westport CT 06880. (203)226-7203. Editor: Gerald C. Melson. Monthly magazine covering nursing and related subject matter for National Federation of Licensed Practical Nurses members. Circ. 70,000. Average issue includes 5-7 departments and 5 articles. Byline given. Submit seasonal material 3 months in advance. Simultaneous and photocopied submissions OK. SASE. Free sample copy and writer's guidelines.
Nonfiction: Historical (patient care); interview; opinion; profile; how-to (health-related matters); humor; inspirational; new product; personal experience; photo feature; and technical. "We prefer at least 4 double-spaced, typed pages or longer. The biggest problem is that articles, while good, are usually too short for publication. Drawings and/or photographs are quite helpful." Buys 20 mss/year. Send complete ms. Length: 800-4,400 words.
Photos: State availability of photos.

NURSING JOB NEWS, Prime National Publishing Corp., 470 Boston Post Rd., Weston MA 02193. Editor: Ira Alterman. Emphasizes career interests for a readership of generally younger nurses interested in new job opportunities, travel and new nursing opportunities. "We are quite eager to receive manuscripts from good writers all over the country who can deal with the helpful aspects of nursing all over the country. We serve the interests of nurses and nursing students, some of whom have never made a move." Monthly tabloid newspaper; 24-72 pages. Circ. 40,000. Pays on publication. Buys one-time rights. Byline given. Phone queries OK. Submit seasonal/holiday material 1-3 months in advance. Previously published work OK. SASE. Reports on queries in 3 weeks; on mss in 1 month. Sample copy $2.
Nonfiction: General interest; how-to; interview (with nurses, students); opinion; profile; travel; personal experience; photo feature; and employment. All articles must be related to nursing or hospitals. Buys 1-2 mss/issue. Send complete ms. Length: 1,000 words maximum. Pays $25 minimum.
Photos: Pays $5-15 each b&w 5x7 or 8x10 glossy print. Captions and model releases required.
Columns/Departments: Open to suggestions for new columns or departments.

RN, 680 Kinderkamack Rd., Oradell NJ 07649. (201)262-3030. Editor: David W. Sifton. For registered nurses, mostly hospital-based but also in physicians' offices, public health, schools, industry. Monthly magazine; 120 pages. Circ. 330,000. Buys all rights. Pays 25% kill fee. Byline given. Pays on publication. Submit seasonal/holiday material 8 months in advance. Free writer's guidelines. Reports in 6-8 weeks. SASE. Sample copy $2.
Nonfiction: "If you are a nurse who writes, we would like to see your work. Editorial content: diseases, clinical techniques, surgery, therapy, equipment, drugs, etc. These should be thoroughly researched and sources cited. Personal anecdotes, experiences, observations based on your relations with doctors, hospitals, patients and nursing colleagues. Our style is simple, direct, not preachy. Do include examples, case histories that relate the reader to her own nursing experience. Talk mostly about people, rather than things. Dashes of humor or insight are always welcome. Include photos where feasible." Buys 100 mss/year. Query or submit complete ms. Length: 1,000-2,000 words. Pays $100-300.

Photos: "We want good clinical illustration." Send photos with ms. Pays $25 minimum/b&w contact sheet; $35 minimum/35mm color transparency. Captions preferred; model release required. Buys all rights.
Columns/Departments: Anthony Lee, columns/departments editor. Leadership at Work (management); and Legally Speaking (legal advice). Query with clips of previously published work. Length: 750-1,000 words. Pays $50-150. Query David W. Sifton with suggestions for new columns/departments.
Fillers: Karen Bardessi, fillers editor. Crossword puzzles. Pays $50 minimum.

Hotels, Motels, Clubs, Resorts, Restaurants

Journals that emphasize retailing for bar and beverage operators are classified in the Beverages and Bottling category. For publications slanted to food wholesalers, processors, and caterers, see Food Products, Processing and Service.

BARTENDER, Bartender Publishing Corp., Box 707, Livingston NJ 07039. (201)736-9579. Publisher: Raymond P. Foley. Editor: Michael Cammarano. Emphasizes liquor and bartending for bartenders, tavern owners and owners of restaurants with liquor licenses. Bimonthly magazine; 50 pages. Estab. June 1979. Circ. 10,000. Pays on publication. Buys all rights. Pays 33⅓% kill fee. Byline given. Phone queries OK. Submit seasonal/holiday material 3 months in advance. Simultaneous, photocopied, and previously published submissions OK. SASE. Reports in 2 months.
Nonfiction: General interest, historical, how-to, humor, interview (with famous ex-bartenders); new products, nostalgia, personal experience, unique bars, opinion, new techniques, new drinking trends, photo feature, profile, travel and bar sports. Send complete ms. Length: 500-1,000 words.
Photos: Send photos with ms. Pays $7.50-50 for 8x10 b&w glossy prints; $10-75 for 8x10 color glossy prints. Caption preferred and model release required.
Columns/Departments: Bar of the Month; Bartender of the Month; Drink of the Month; New Drink Ideas; Bar Sports; Quiz; Bar Art; Wine Cellar Tips of the Month (from prominent figures in the liquor industry); One For The Road (travel); Collectors (bar or liquor related items); Photo Essays. Query. Length: 200-1,000 words. Pays $50-200.
Fillers: Clippings, jokes, gags, anecdotes, short humor, newsbreaks and anything relating to bartending and the liquor industry. Length: 25-100 words. Pays $5-25.
Tips: "To break in, absolutely make sure that your work will be of interest to all bartenders across the country. Your style of writing should reflect the audience you are addressing."

THE CANADIAN INN BUSINESS, Kerch Publications, Ltd., 108 Harvard Rd., Guelph, Ontario, Canada N1G 2Z2. (519)836-4883. Editor: Evelyn Couch. For resort, hotel and motel owners and managers. Bimonthly. Circ. 10,000. Buys one-time rights. Pays on publication. Reports in 6 weeks. SAE or International Reply Coupons.
Nonfiction: Informational, technical and how-to articles. Canadian content required. Interviews; successful business operations, new products; and merchandising techniques. Length: open. Pays 5¢/word.

CHUCK WAGON, Texas Restaurant Association, Box 1429, Austin TX 78767. (512)444-6543. Editor: Teressa Nolin. Magazine published 10 times/year about the Texas food service industry for restaurant owners and operators in Texas. Circ. 6,700. Pays on acceptance. Byline given. Buys one-time rights. Phone queries OK. Submit seasonal material 2 months in advance. Photocopied submissions OK. SASE. Reports in 1 month. Free sample copy.
Nonfiction: Interview, profile, how-to, humor and personal experience. "The magazine spotlights many general categories (economy, energy, labor relations, new products and staff editorials) in short columns. Therefore, we appreciate getting good, terse articles with a how-to-improve-your-business slant. These we prefer with sharp, black and white photos. All articles should be substantiated with plenty of facts or specific examples. Avoid too much vocabulary. Opt for shorter sentences and shorter words." Send complete ms. Length: 1,000-1,500 words. Pays $15-50.
Columns/Departments: Send complete ms. Open to suggestions for new columns or departments.
Tips: "All of our readers are business people, seeking to improve their operations. We like to

feature specific areas of food service, such as hiring mentally disabled workers; serving health food; computers; and catering to the senior citizen market. No restaurant critiques."

CLUBS & RECREATION, Box 7088, Alexandria VA 22307. Editor: Paul E. Reece. 20% freelance written. For military club and leisure-time activities managers. Monthly. Not copyrighted. Pays on publication. Reports in 2 weeks. SASE.
Nonfiction: Articles about food and beverages, design, equipment, promotional ideas, etc. Length: 1,500-2,000 words. Pays 4¢/word.

HOTEL AND MOTEL MANAGEMENT, Harcourt Brace Jovanovich, Inc., 757 3rd Ave., New York NY 10017. (212)888-3531. Editor: Alexandra Roll. Managing Editor: Sandra Beckerman. Monthly magazine about hotels, motels and resorts in North America for general managers, corporate executives, and department heads (such as director of sales; food and beverage; energy; security; front office; housekeeping, etc.) Circ. 36,000. Pays on publication. Byline given. Buys first North American serial rights. Phone queries OK. Submit seasonal material 2 months in advance. SASE. Reports in 3 weeks on queries; in 1 month on mss. Free sample copy.
Nonfiction: Sandra Beckerman, managing editor. Travel, how-to, and hotel, motel and resort-oriented material. "No philosophical or theory-oriented articles." Buys 2 mss/issue. Query with clips of previously published work. "Write a query letter outlining your idea and be specific." Length: 800 words maximum.
Photos: State availability of b&w photos. Captions preferred. Buys one-time rights.
Tips: "We need 'hands on' articles which explain the topic."

INNKEEPING WORLD, Motel Services, Inc., Box 1123, Gainesville FL 32602. Editor/Publisher: Charles Nolte. 50% freelance written. Emphasizes the lodging industry and travel. Bimonthly newsletter; 8 pages. Circ. 2,000. Pays on publication. Buys one-time rights. No byline. Submit seasonal/holiday material 1 month in advance of issue date. Simultaneous and previously published submissions OK. SASE. Reports in 4 weeks. Free sample copy (provide SASE).
Nonfiction: How-to (increase business, cut expenses, treat guests and anything that would help hotel/motel managers); and travel (statistics). Buys 2 mss/issue. Query with "thorough description of article and SASE." Length: 100-500 words. Pays 10¢/word. Special reports: "The Guest Speaks"; interviews with well-traveled people, their positive comments on hotels/motels; and "Management"; interviews with successful hotel managers for innkeeping wisdom. Buys 2/issue. Length: 100-1,000 words. Pays 10¢/word.
Columns/Departments: Advertising/Promotion; Cutting expenses; Increasing business; Energy; Labor incentives/relations; and news, trends and ideas (for fillers). Buys 2/issue. Length: 50-500 words. Pays 10¢/word.

KANSAS RESTAURANT MAGAZINE, 359 S. Hydraulic St., Wichita KS 67211. (316)267-8383. Editor: Neal D. Whitaker. For food service operators. Special issues: Christmas, October Convention, Who's Who in Kansas Food Service, Beef Month, Dairy Month, Wheat Month. Monthly. Circ. 1,400. Not copyrighted. Pays on publication. Sample copy 50¢. Reports "immediately." SASE.
Nonfiction and Photos: Articles on food and food service. Length: 1,000 words maximum. Pays $10. Photos purchased with ms.

LODGING AND FOOD SERVICE NEWS, 131 Clarendon St., Boston MA 02116. Managing Editor: Mrs. Susan G. Holaday. For managers and executives of hotels, motels, restaurants, fast food operations, contract feeders, country clubs, etc. Every 2 weeks. Circ. 8,000. Not copyrighted. Byline rarely given. Pays on publication. Will send sample copy to writer on request. Submit seasonal material 6 months in advance. Reports in 1 month. Query. SASE.
Nonfiction and Photos: News relating to hotels, restaurants, etc. Travel and tourism trends. Features on unusual operations. Stories on new chains and expansions. Must have hard-breaking news orientation. Stories on food service promotions for the holidays and summer merchandising news. Length: 16-80 double-spaced lines. Pays $25 minimum. Pays $5 for 8x10 b&w glossies used with mss.

MANAGING THE LEISURE FACILITY, Billboard Publications, Inc., Box 24970, Nashville TN 37202. (615)748-8120. Editor: Steve Rogers. Emphasizes operational aspects of amusement/recreation facilities for management and department heads. Bimonthly magazine; 36 pages. Circ. 17,000. Pays upon determination of payment based on typeset galleys. Buys all rights. Phone queries OK. Simultaneous, photocopied and previously published submissions OK. SASE. Reports in 2 weeks. Free sample copy and writer's guidelines.
Nonfiction: How-to; informational; photo feature; and technical. "The writing style is straightfor-

ward, based on plain language and logical grammatical construction. Unjustified contractions and breeziness are contrary to our dignified approach. The same inhibition would apply to superlatives and hyperbole." Buys 6 mss/issue. Query or submit complete ms, "but query is a time-saver for original work." Length: 250-2,500 words. Pays $20-250.

Photos: State availability of photos with query. Pays $3-5 for 5x7 or 8x10 b&w glossy prints or color transparencies.

Tips: "After the initial contact, I like to see a freelancer generate one or two story ideas which show me he/she understands the magazine and its audience. I much prefer a letter outlining a story proposal to an unsolicited manuscript. Sloppy typing jobs are likely to be tossed."

NATION'S RESTAURANT NEWS, 425 Park Ave., New York NY 10022. Editor: Charles Bernstein. "National business newspaper for food service chains and independents." Biweekly newspaper. Circ. 65,000. Pays on acceptance.

Nonfiction: "News and newsfeatures, analyses of specific new types of restaurants, mergers and acquisitions, new appointments, commodity reports, personalities. Problem: Most business press stories are mere rehashes of consumer pieces. We must have business insight. Sometimes a freelancer can provide us with enough peripheral material that we'll buy the idea, then assign it to staff writers for further digging." Length: 500 words maximum. Pays $5-75.

Photos: B&w glossies purchased with mss and captions only. Pays $10 minimum.

Tips: "Send most wanted material, such as personality profiles, business-oriented restaurant news articles, but no how-to stories."

RESORT MANAGEMENT, Box 40169, Memphis TN 38104. (901)276-5424. Editor: Allen J. Fagans. 40% freelance written. For "the owners and/or managing executives of America's largest luxury vacation resorts." Monthly. Buys first rights only. Byline sometimes given. Pays on publication. Query. "Editorial deadline is the 1st of the previous month; e.g., January material must be received by December 1." Reports in 10 days. SASE.

Nonfiction and Photos: "This is not a travel or tourist publication. It is a 'how-to-do-it' or 'how-it-was-done' business journal. Descriptive background of any sort used to illustrate the subject matter must be held to a minimum. Our material helps managers attract, house, feed and provide entertainment for guests and their friends, and bring them back again and again. Any facet of the resort operation could be of interest: guest activities, remodeling, advertising and promotion, maintenance, food, landscaping, kitchen, personnel, furnishings, etc. We do not want to see material related to any facet of commercial hotels, motels, motor courts, fishing and hunting camps, housekeeping or other facilities serving transients. Material submitted must be accurate, to the point, and supported by facts and costs, plus pertinent examples illustrating the subject discussed." Length: 800-1,000 words. Pays 75¢/inch for a 20-em column; 50¢/inch for a 13-em column. "Photos of the resort and of its manager, and the subject(s) being discussed are a must." Pays $5/photo.

Fillers: Uses clippings related to resorts and resort area organizations only. Promotions: president, general manager, resident manager (including changes from one resort to another). Resort Obituaries: president, owner, general manager. Resort Construction: changes, additions, new facilities, etc. New Resorts: planned or under construction. Changes in resort ownership. Resort News: factual news concerning specific resorts, resort areas, state tourism development. No clippings about city hotels, roadside motels, motor inns or chain (franchise) operations. Clippings must be pasted on individual sheets of paper, and addressed to Clipping Editor. Your complete mailing address (typed or printed) must be included, as well as the name of the newspaper or magazine and date of issue. Do not send advertisements or pictures. Clippings will not be returned unless a self-addressed envelope and sufficient postage is enclosed. Pays $2/clipping.

RESTAURANT HOSPITALITY, Penton IPC, Penton Plaza, 1111 Chester Ave., Cleveland OH 44114. (216)696-7000. Editor: Stephen Michaelides. Managing Editor: Michael DeLuca. Monthly magazine covering the commercial food service industry for owners and operators of independent restaurants, hotel food services, and executives of national and regional restaurant chains. Circ. 80,000. Average issue includes 10-12 features. Pays on acceptance. Byline given. Buys one-time rights. Phone queries OK. Simultaneous and photocopied submissions OK. SASE. Reports in 1 week. Free sample copy.

Nonfiction: Michael DeLuca, managing editor. General interest (articles that advise operators how to run their operations profitably and efficiently); interview (with operators); profile. No restaurant reviews. Buys 10 mss/issue. Query with clips of previously published work and a short bio. Length: 2,000-2,500 words. Pays $300-500.

Photos: Send photos with manuscript. Captions required.

Tips: "We need new angles on old stories and we like to see pieces on emerging trends, technologies in the restaurant industry. Stories on psychology, consumer behavior, managerial problems and solutions, how-to's on buying insurance, investing (our readers have a high degree of disposable income), design elements. They don't want to read how to open a restaurant."

Industrial Management

Industrial plant managers, executives, distributors and buyers read the journals that follow. Some industrial management journals are also listed under the names of specific industries, such as Machinery and Metal Trade. Publications for industrial supervisors are listed in Management and Supervision.

COMPRESSED AIR, 253 E. Washington Ave., Washington NJ 07882. Editor: Charles Beardsley. 50% freelance written. Emphasizes "the application of energy technologies for middle and upper management personnel in all industries." Monthly magazine; 48 pages. Circ. 150,000. Buys all rights. Submit seasonal/holiday material 6 months in advance of issue date. SASE. Reports in 4-6 weeks. Free sample copy, editorial schedule, and writer's guidelines; mention *Writer's Market* in request.
Nonfiction: "Articles must be reviewed by experts in the field." How-to (save costs with air power); and historical (engineering). "No 'soft' energy articles, i.e., wind, solar, hydro, etc." Buys 20 mss/year. Query with clips of previously published work. Pays negotiable fee.
Photos: State availability of photos in query. Payment for 8x10 glossy b&w photos is included in total purchase price. Captions required. Buys all rights.
Tips: "We are presently looking for freelancers with a proven track record in industrial trade books. Because our editorial schedule is developed well in advance, we prefer to assign stories rather than review queries. Resume and samples help. Writers with access to authorities preferred; prefer interviews over library research. The magazine's name doesn't reflect its contents; suggest writers request sample copies."

CRUCIBLE, Non-Ferrous Founders' Society, 221 N. LaSalle St., Chicago IL 60601. (312)346-1600. Editor: Jim Nowakowski. Managing Editor: August L. Sisco. Bimonthly magazine covering management topics of concern to nonferrous foundry owners. Circ. 1,100. Pays on publication. Byline given. Buys first North American serial rights, simultaneous rights, second serial (reprint) rights and makes work-for-hire assignments. Submit seasonal/holiday material 2 months in advance. Simultaneous queries, and simultaneous, photocopied, and previously published submissions OK. Reports in 2 weeks on queries; 1 month on mss. Sample copy 50¢; free writer's guidelines.
Nonfiction: How-to (run a business more efficiently); new product (nonferrous foundry-related); and technical (casting methods in nonferrous applications). "No articles that are not specific enough on management of foundries." Query with clips of published work or send complete ms. Length: 1,100 words minimum. Pays $75-$250/article.
Photos: Send photos with ms. Pays $10 maximum for 5x7 b&w prints. Captions required. Buys one-time rights.
Tips: "Have a story to say, and say it clearly. Our readers want to know how to operate their businesses more efficiently. They are also interested in foundries in the nonferrous industry that operate efficiently—i.e. a new method for saving time or increasing productivity."

ENERGY NEWS, Energy Publications—division of Harcourt Brace Jovanovich, Box 1589, Dallas TX 75221. (214)748-4403. Editor: Gregory Martin. 5% freelance written. Emphasizes natural gas production, transmission, distribution, regulation and projects for executives or managers of energy, supply and financial companies or the government; particularly utilities. Biweekly newsletter; 4 pages. Circ. 500. Pays on publication. Buys all rights. Phone queries OK. Simultaneous and photocopied submissions OK. SASE. Reports in 4 weeks. Free sample copy and writer's guidelines.
Nonfiction: Interviews with energy industry or government leaders keyed to recent news and technical articles on natural gas projects, trends, prices or new technologies. "Can't use anything not related to natural gas or utilities." Buys 1-2 mss/issue. Length: 250 words maximum. Pays 15¢/word.

ENERGY WEEK, Energy Publications—division of Harcourt Brace Jovanovich, Box 1589, Dallas TX 75221. (214)748-4403. Editor: Gregory Martin. 5% freelance written. Emphasizes energy production, transmission, regulation, prices, etc., for executives or management of energy supply

or financial companies or the government. Biweekly newsletter; 4 pages. Circ. 500. Pays on publication. Buys all rights. Phone queries OK. Simultaneous and photocopied submissions OK. SASE. Reports in 4 weeks. Free sample copy and writer's guidelines.
Nonfiction: Interview (with energy industry trend-setters, should be keyed to recent news); and technical (new energy technologies, feasibility, costs, or technical features). "No stories dealing with the surface rather than the inner core of energy developments. Our readers are aware of news related to energy; they want to know *why* and how *they* are affected." Buys 1-2 mss/issue. Submit complete ms. Length: 250 words maximum. Pays 15¢/word.

HANDLING AND SHIPPING MANAGEMENT, 1111 Chester Ave., Cleveland OH 44114. (216)696-7000. Executive Editor: H.G. Becker Jr. 10-20% freelance written. For operating executives with physical distribution responsibilities in transportation, material handling, warehousing, packaging, and shipping. Monthly. Buys all rights. Byline given unless article requires substantial editing or previous arrangements made. Pays on publication. "Query with 50-word description of proposed article." SASE.
Nonfiction and Photos: Material on aspects of physical distribution management, with economic emphasis. Informational and successful business operations material. Writer must know the field and the publications in it. Not for amateurs and generalists. Length: 1,500-3,000 words. Pays $50/published page minimum. Additional payment is made for b&w photos used with mss, but they must be sharp, for good reproduction. No prints from copy negatives. Any size. Color used may be prints or transparencies.

INDUSTRIAL DISTRIBUTION, 2 Park Ave., New York NY 10016. (212)340-9700. Editor: George J. Berkwitt. Monthly. Buys all rights. Byline given if author is an expert in his field. Will consider cassette submissions. SASE.
Nonfiction: "Articles aimed at making industrial distributor management, sales and other personnel aware of trends, developments and problems and solutions in their segment of industry. Articles accepted range widely; may cover legislation, sales training, administration, Washington, marketing techniques, case histories, profiles on industry leaders, abstracted speeches—any area that is timely and pertinent and provides readers with interesting informative data. Use either roundups or bylined pieces. We're looking for industry breakthroughs." Length: 900 words minimum. Pays "flat fee based on value; usually $100/published page."
Columns/Departments: Open to new ideas for columns. Query. George J. Berkwitt.
Tips: "To break in ms must apply to our unique readership and it must be pertinent and timely. As long as the query letter describes an activity, case history, trend or anything else that our readers might be interested in, the letter (and/or manuscript) will be reviewed."

INDUSTRIAL DISTRIBUTOR NEWS, 1 West Olney Ave., Philadelphia PA 19120. Managing Editor: Jerry Steinbrink. For industrial distributors, industrial equipment wholesalers, business managers and industrial salesmen. Monthly. Circ. 32,000. Free sample copy. Reports on material within 6 weeks. "Freelancers would do well to query before testing the waters of distribution without guidance." SASE. Byline given.
Nonfiction and Photos: "Feature material must be tailored to industrial marketing and demonstrate an understanding of the problems of distribution. Case studies or interviews should cite specifics, quote liberally and be written for an audience of top managers." Length: 1,000-3,000 words. B&w 8x10 only.

INDUSTRIAL FABRIC PRODUCTS REVIEW, Industrial Fabrics Assoc., 350 Endicott Bldg., St. Paul MN 55101. (612)222-2508. Editor: Mike Coughlin. Managing Editor: Brian Becker. Monthly magazine covering industrial textiles for company owners, salespersons, and researchers in a variety of industrial textile areas. Circ. 6,000. Pays on acceptance. Byline given. Buys all rights. Submit seasonal/holiday material 4 months in advance. Simultaneous queries, and photocopied and previously published submissions OK. SASE. Reports in 2 weeks. Sample copy free "after query and phone conversation."
Nonfiction: Technical, marketing, and other topics "related to any aspect of industrial fabric industry from fiber to finished fabric product." Special issues include new products, industrial and equipment. No historical articles. Buys 12 mss/year. Query with phone number. Length: 1,200-3,000 words. Pays $150.
Photos: State availability of photos. Reviews 8x10 b&w glossy prints. Pay is negotiable. Model release and identification of subjects required. Buys one-time rights.

INDUSTRY WEEK, Penton/IPC, Inc., 1111 Chester Ave., Cleveland OH 44114, (216)696-7000. Editor-in-Chief: Stanley Modic. 5-10% freelance written. Emphasizes manufacturing and related industries for top or middle management (administrating, production, engineering, finance, purchasing or marketing) throughout industry. Biweekly magazine; 120 pages. Circ. 300,000. Pays on publication. Buys all rights. Byline given depending on length of article. Phone queries OK. Submit seasonal or holiday material 3 months in advance. Simultaneous and photocopied submissions OK. SASE. Reports in 4 weeks. Sample copy $2.

Nonfiction: Robert W. Gardner, managing editor. How-to and informational articles (should deal with areas of interest to manager audience, e.g., developing managerial skills or managing effectively). "No product news or case histories, please." Length: 1,000-4,000 words. Pays $300/first 1,000 words; $100/additional 1,000 words. Buys 5-10/year. Query. No product news or clippings.

Photos: Nick Dankovich, art director. B&w and color purchased with ms or on assignment. Query. Pays $35 minimum. Model release required.

MANUFACTURING TODAY, Continental Publishing Co., Box 25444, Chicago IL 60625. (312)539-1936. Editor: Wayne Wilson. Bimonthly magazine for personnel of mobile home, modular, component and recreational vehicle manufacturing. Circ 13,000. Average issue includes 2-3 features, several columns and departments. Pays on publication. Byline given. Phone queries OK. Submit seasonal material 3 months in advance. Photocopied and previously published submissions OK. SASE. Reports in 2 weeks. Free sample copy.

Nonfiction: Interview (of plant management); new product (related to the industries covered); and technical (proper use and application). "No puff pieces. Send previously published work, outline of story content and required payment. We are especially interested in feature articles on topics of interest to mobile/manufactured housing, recreational vehicle and component manufacturers—primarily topics on the proper construction and new building techniques." Buys 40 mss/year. Query with clips of previously published work. Length: 1,000-1,800 words. Pays $200-250.

Photos: State availability of photos. Reviews 8x10 b&w prints and color transparencies. Offers no additional payment for photos accepted with ms. Captions required. Buys one-time rights.

Columns/Departments: Washington Review, and Codes and Standards. Buys 24-30 mss/year. Query with clips of previously published work.

Fillers: Clippings and jokes.

METALWORK: Six Magazines in One, Stanger Publications, 303 W. 42nd St., New York NY 10036. (212)265-6417. Editor: Bill Stanger. Managing Editor: Mario Moussa. Monthly magazine covering metalworking; "this is a highly technical magazine for persons in the metalworking field." Estab. 1981. Circ. 4,000. Pays on publication. Byline given. Pays 100% kill fee. Buys first North American serial rights. Simultaneous queries and submissions OK. Reports in 3 weeks. Free sample copy and writer's guidelines.

Nonfiction: Technical (articles covering machining, numerical control, assembly, finishing, metals and press working). "No business-oriented material, e.g., people, promotions, expansion." Buys 12 mss/year. Query. Length: 1,000-2,000 words. Pays negotiable fee.

Photos: Reviews b&w glossy prints. "Photos are paid for with payment for ms." Captions and identification of subjects required.

Columns/Departments: "We need experts to write for us on a regular basis." Pays negotiable fee.

Tips: "I'll talk to anyone who is technically knowledgeable in the field of metalworking."

THE PHILADELPHIA PURCHASOR, 1518 Walnut St., Suite 610, Philadelphia PA 19102. Editor-in-Chief: Howard B. Armstrong Jr. 35% freelance written. For buyers of industrial supplies and equipment, including the materials of manufacture, as well as the maintenance, repair and operating items; and for buyers of office equipment and supplies for banks and other industries. Monthly magazine; 65 pages. Circ. 4,000. Not copyrighted. Pays on acceptance. Free sample copy and writer's guidelines. Photocopied and simultaneous submissions OK. Reports in 1 month. SASE.

Nonfiction and Photos: "We use articles on industrial, service and institutional purchasing—*not* consumer. We also use business articles of the kind that would interest purchasing personnel. Ours is a regional magazine covering the middle Atlantic area, and if material takes this into account, it is more effective." Buys 25-35 mss/year. Query or submit complete ms. Length: 900-1,200 words. Pays minimum of $15. No additional payment for b&w photos used with mss.

PLANT MANAGEMENT & ENGINEERING, MacLean Hunter, 481 University Ave., Toronto, Ontario, Canada M5W 1A7. Editor: William Roebuck. 20% freelance written. For Canadian plant managers and engineers. Monthly magazine. Circ. 23,500. Pays on acceptance. Buys first Canadian rights. SAE and International Reply Coupons. Reports in 2-3 weeks. Free sample copy with SAE only.

Nonfiction: How-to, technical and management technique articles. Must have Canadian slant. Query. Pays 12¢/word minimum.

Photos: State availability of photos with query. Pays $25-50 for b&w prints; $50-100 for 2¼x2¼ or 35mm color transparencies. Captions preferred. Buys one-time rights.

Tips: "Write or call first with a really good idea we haven't already done or thought about. Read the magazine. Know the Canadian readers' special needs. Write well! Use case-history approach (Canadian plants). Must quote real plant managers/engineers."

PRODUCTION ENGINEERING, Penton Plaza, Cleveland OH 44114. (216)696-7000. Editor-in-Chief: Larry Boulden. Executive Editor: John McRainey. 50% freelance written. For "men and women in production engineering—the engineers who plan, design and improve manufacturing operations." Monthly magazine; 100 pages. Circ. 95,000. Pays on publication. Buys exclusive North American first rights. Byline given "unless, by prior arrangement, an author contributed a segment of a broader article, he might not be bylined." Phone queries OK. Photocopied submissions OK, if exclusive. SASE. Reports in 2 weeks. Free sample copy and writer's guidelines.

Nonfiction: How-to (engineering, data for engineers); personal experience (from *very* senior production or manufacturing engineers only); and technical (technical news or how-to). "We're interested in solid, hard-hitting technical articles on the gut issues of manufacturing. Not case histories, but no-fat treatments of manufacturing concepts, innovative manufacturing methods, and state-of-the-art procedures. Our readers also enjoy articles that detail a variety of practical solutions to some specific, everyday manufacturing headache." Buys 2 mss/issue. Query. Length: 800-3,000 words. Pays $25-150.

Photos: "Sell me the manuscript, then we'll talk about photos."

PURCHASING EXECUTIVE'S BULLETIN, Bureau of Business Practice, 24 Rope Ferry Rd., Waterford CT 06386. (203)442-4365. Editor: Claire Sherman. Managing Editor: Wayne Muller. For purchasing managers and purchasing agents. Semimonthly newsletter; 4 pages. Circ. 5,500. Pays on acceptance. Buys all rights. Submit seasonal/holiday material 3 months in advance. Reports in 2 weeks. Free sample copy and writer's guidelines.

Nonfiction: How-to (better cope with problems confronting purchasing executives); and direct interviews detailing how purchasing has overcome problems and found better ways of handling departments. No derogatory material about a company; no writer's opinions; no training or minority purchasing articles. "We don't want material that's too elementary (things any purchasing executive already knows)." Buys 2-3 mss/issue. Query. Length: 750-1,000 words.

Tips: "Make sure that a release is obtained and attached to a submitted article."

ROD, WIRE & FASTENER, Business Information Services, Inc., 20 Pine Mountain Rd., Ridgefield CT 06877. (203)748-6529. Editorial Director: Dick Callahan. Editor: Charles Joslin. Bimonthly magazine covering wire and fastener industries and fiber optics for middle and upper management. Emphasis is on business and personalities. Estab. 1980. Circ. 12,000. Pays on acceptance. Byline given. Buys one-time rights. Reports in 2 months on queries; 3 weeks on mss. Free sample copy.

Nonfiction: Interview/profile, photo feature, and technical. "No how-to or general business topics." Buys 24 mss/year. Query with clips of published work ("preferably bylined"). Length: 1,000-5,000 words. Pays $300-500/article.

Photos: State availability of photos. Pays $50-100 for b&w contact sheets or 5x7 prints.

Tips: "We are most open to profiles of individuals or companies in the wire or fastener business. Writers do not have to have a technical background. We want *Forbes*- or *Barron's*-type articles stressing business aspects of companies."

SEMICONDUCTOR INTERNATIONAL, Cahners Publishing Co., 222 W. Adams St., Chicago IL 60606. (312)263-4866. Editor: Donald J. Levinthal. Monthly magazine covering semiconductor industry processing, assembly and testing technology subjects for semiconductor industry processing engineers and management. "Technology stories that cover all phases of semiconductor product manufacturing and testing are our prime interest." Circ. 18,360. Pays on publication. "News items are paid for upon acceptance." Byline given. Buys all rights and makes work-for-hire assignments. Reports in 2 weeks. Free sample copy and writer's guidelines.

Nonfiction: Technical and news pertaining to the semiconductor industry in the US and overseas. No "articles that are commercial in nature or product oriented." Buys 50 mss/year (including feature articles and news). Query with "your interest and capabilities" or send complete ms. Length: 2,500 words maximum. Pays approximately 15¢/word.

Photos: State availability of photos or send photos with ms. Reviews 8x10 b&w prints. "Payment is part of article payment." Captions and identification of subjects required.

Columns/Departments: "News of the semiconductor industry as it pertains to technology trends is of interest. Of special interest is news of the semiconductor industry in foreign countries such as Japan, England, Germany, France, Netherlands." Buys 30-40 mss/year. Query. Length: 200-1,500 words. Pays 15¢/word for accepted, edited copy.

Insurance

BUSINESS INSURANCE, 740 N. Rush Street, Chicago IL 60611. Editor: Kathryn J. McIntyre. For "corporate risk and employee managers, insurance brokers and agents, insurance company executives, interested in insurance, risk and benefit financing, safety, security, employee benefits." Special issues on safety, pensions, health and life benefits, bracers, reinsured, international insurance. Weekly. Circ. 36,000. Buys all rights. Pays negotiable kill fee. Byline given. Buys 75-100 mss/year. Pays on publication. Submit seasonal or special material 2 months in advance. Reports in 2 weeks. Query. SASE.
Nonfiction: "We publish material on corporate insurance and employee benefit programs and related subjects. We take everything from the buyers' point of view, rather than that of the insurance company, broker or consultant who is selling something. Items on insurance companies, insurance brokers, property/liability insurance, union contract (benefit) settlements, group life/health/medical plans, of interest—provided the *commercial* insurance or benefits angle is clear. Special emphasis on corporate risk management and employee benefits administration requires that freelancers discuss with us their proposed articles. Length is subject to discussion with contributor." Pays $5/column inch or negotiated fee.
Tips: "Send a detailed proposal including story angle and description of sources—or personally visit the editor in Chicago or bureaus in New York, Los Angeles, Dallas, Washington DC."

LINES MAGAZINE, Reliance Insurance Co., 4 Penn Center, Philadelphia PA 19103. Editor: Patricia McLaughlin. 30% freelance written. Emphasizes insurance and business for "Reliance employees and independent insurance agents interested in business trends and opinion." Quarterly magazine; 28 pages. Circ. 11,000. Pays on acceptance. Copyrighted. Submit seasonal/holiday material 2 months in advance of issue date. SASE. Reports in 2 weeks. Free sample copy; mention *Writer's Market* in request.
Nonfiction: Features that relate to insurance, more general pieces about business, and usually 1-2 general interest pieces per issue. Buys 10 mss/year. Query with clips of previously published work. Length: 800-2,000 words.
Fillers: Newsbriefs for wraparound, original or clipped from a newspaper or magazine. Length: 50-200 words.

Jewelry

AMERICAN JEWELRY MANUFACTURER, 825 7th Ave., 8th Floor, New York NY 10019. (212)245-7555. Editor: Steffan Aletti. For manufacturers of supplies and tools for the jewelry industry; their representatives, wholesalers and agencies. Monthly. Circ. 5,000. Buys all rights (with exceptions). Pays negotiable kill fee. Byline given. Buys 2-5 mss/year. Free sample copy and writer's guidelines. Will consider photocopied submissions. Submit seasonal material 3 months in advance. Reports in 1 month. Query. SASE.
Nonfiction and Photos: "Topical articles on manufacturing; company stories; economics (e.g., rising gold prices). Story must inform or educate the manufacturer. Occasional special issues on timely topics, e.g., gold; occasional issues on specific processes in casting and plating. We reject material that is not specifically pointed at our industry; e.g., articles geared to jewelry retailing, not the manufacturers." Informational, how-to, interview, profile, historical, expose, successful business operations, new product, merchandising techniques, technical. Length: open. Payment "usually around $25/printed page." B&w photos purchased with ms; 5x7 minimum.

CANADIAN JEWELLER, 481 University Ave., Toronto, Ontario, Canada M5W 1A7. Editor: Simon Hally. Monthly magazine for members of the jewelry trade, primarily retailers. Circ. 6,000. Pays on acceptance. Buys first Canadian serial rights. SAE and International Reply Coupons.
Nonfiction: Wants "stories on the jewelry industry internationally, primarily on production of gemstones. No stories on the US jewelry business." Query. Length: 200-2,000 words. Pays $30-300.
Photos: Reviews 5x7 and 8x10 b&w prints and 35mm and 2¼x2¼ color transparencies. "We pay more if usable photos accompany ms. Payment is based on space used in the book including both text and photos."

THE DIAMOND REGISTRY BULLETIN, 30 W. 47th St., New York NY 10036. Editor-in-Chief: Joseph Schlussel. 15% freelance written. Monthly newsletter. Pays on publication. Buys all rights. Submit seasonal/holiday material 1 month in advance of issue date. Simultaneous and

previously published submissions OK. SASE. Reports in 3 weeks. Sample copy $5.
Nonfiction: Prevention advice (on crimes against jewelers); how-to (ways to increase sales in diamonds, improve security, etc.); and interview (of interest to diamond dealers or jewelers). Submit complete ms. Length: 50-500 words. Pays $10-150.
Tips: "We seek ideas to increase sales of diamonds."

JEWELER'S CIRCULAR-KEYSTONE, Chilton Co., Radnor PA 19089. Editor: George Holmes. For retail jewelers. Monthly. Circ. 44,000. Buys all rights. Pays on publication. SASE.
Nonfiction: Wants "how-to articles, case history approach, which specify how a given jeweler solved a specific problem. No general stories, no stories without a jeweler's name in it, no stories not about a specific jeweler and his business." Buys 4-6 unsolicited mss/year. Length: 1,000-2,000 words.
Tips: "Can use good, specific management stories—on inventory control, computerization, buying, etc."

MODERN JEWELER, 15 W. 10th St., Kansas City MO 64105. Executive Editor: Bill Allison. For retail jewelers and watchmakers. Monthly magazine. Pays on acceptance. Buys one-time rights. Phone queries OK. Submit seasonal/holiday material 3 months in advance. Simultaneous, photocopied and previously published submissions OK. Will send sample copy only if query interests the editor. Reports in 30 days. SASE.
Nonfiction and Photos: "Articles with 3-4 photos about retail jewelers—specific jewelers, with names and addresses, and how they have overcome certain business problems, moved merchandise, increased store traffic, etc. Must contain idea adaptable to other jewelry operations; 'how-to' slant. Informal, story-telling slant with human interest. We are not interested in articles about how manufacturing jewelers design and make one-of-a-kind jewelry pieces. Our readers are interested in retail selling techniques, not manufacturing processes. No articles with general information about accounting procedures, estate planning, insurance requirements, etc. Photos must include people (not just store shots) and should help tell the story. We reject poor photography and articles written as local newspaper features, rather than for a business publication." Buys 15 mss/year. Query. Length: 5,000-6,000 words. Pays average $100-150 for article and photos.
Tips: "We are interested in freelancers who can cover the many regional jewelry and watchmaking conventions we cover, by assignment, of course. This involves taking pictures and editorial coverage of the events that transpire."

THE NORTHWESTERN JEWELER, Washington and Main Sts., Albert Lea MN 56007. Publisher: John R. Hayek. Monthly magazine "heavy on trade shows, conventions, meetings, etc." Not copyrighted. Pays on publication. SASE.
Nonfiction and Photos: Uses news stories about jewelers in the Northwest and Upper Midwest and feature news stories about the same group. Also buys retail jeweler "success" stories with the how-to angle played up, articles on finance, advertising, ideas, windows and store planning, and occasionally a technical story on jewelry or watchmaking. Pictures increase publication chances. Pays 1¢/published word. Pays $2.50/photo.

PACIFIC GOLDSMITH, 41 Sutter St., San Francisco CA 94104. (415)986-4323. Editor: Robert B. Frier. For jewelers and watchmakers. Monthly magazine. Circ. 14,000. Not copyrighted. Pays on acceptance. Byline given. Sample copy $2. Submit seasonal (merchandising) material 4 months in advance. Reports in 1 week. SASE.
Nonfiction and Photos: "Our main interest is in how Western jewelers can do a better selling job. We use how-to-do-it merchandising articles, showing dealers how to sell more jewelry store items to more people, at a greater profit. Seasonal merchandising articles are always welcome, if acceptable." Buys 12 mss/year. Query or submit complete ms. Length: 1,500-2,000 words. Pays 2¢/word. Pays $5 for b&w photos used with mss; 3x5 minimum. Captions required.

SOUTHERN JEWELER, 75 3rd St. NW, Atlanta GA 30308. (404)881-6442. Editor: Roy Conradi. For Southern retail jewelers and watchmakers. Monthly. Circ. 6,000. Not copyrighted. Pays on publication. Submit seasonal material 2 months in advance. SASE.
Nonfiction: Articles related to Southern retail jewelers regarding advertising, management, and merchandising. Buys spot news about Southern jewelers and coverage of successful business operations. Prefers *not* to see material concerning jewelers outside the 14 Southern states. No articles on general sales techniques. Length: open. Pays $50-150 for features; $1/clipping.
Photos: Buys b&w glossies. Pays $4.
Tips: "Query should describe specifically the type article proposed. Writer should be based in the South. Ideally, he/she should have retail jewelry trade background, but a good writer can pick up technical points from us (samples of features used in past will be sent upon request). Send a sample

of your work related to any trade or industry, along with a couple of b&w pictures of the subject character and the establishment."

WATCH AND CLOCK REVIEW, (formerly *American Horologist and Jeweler*), 2403 Champa St., Denver CO 80205. (303)572-1777. Managing Editor: Jayne L. Barrick. 20% freelance written. The magazine of watch/clock sales and service. Monthly magazine; 68 pages. Circ. 16,000. Pays on publication. Buys first rights. Byline given. Submit seasonal/holiday material 3 months in advance of issue date. SASE. Reports in 2-3 weeks. Free sample copy.
Nonfiction: Articles on successful watch/clock manufacturers and retailers; merchandising and display; profiles of industry leaders. Buys 15 mss/year. Query. Length: 1,000-2,000 words. Pays $50-150.
Photos: Submit photo material with accompanying ms. No additional payment for b&w glossy prints. Captions preferred. Buys first rights. Model release required.
Columns/Departments: Buys 7/issue. Pays $50-150. Open to suggestions for new columns/ departments.
Tips: "Brevity is helpful in a query. Find the right subject—an interesting clock shop, a jewelry store with unique watch displays, a street clock of antiquarian interest, etc."

Journalism

Because many writers are familiar with the journals of the writing profession and might want to submit to them, those that do not pay for contributions are identified in this list. Writers wishing to contribute material to these publications should query about requirements before submitting work.

THE CALIFORNIA PUBLISHER, 1127 St., Suite 1040, Sacramento CA 95814. (916)443-5991. Editor: Jackie Nava. Monthly tabloid read by publishers, editors and managers in newspaper publishing in California. Byline given.
Nonfiction: In-depth stories or articles designed to inform and amuse California newspaper publishers. Sample topics include: newsprint shortage, changing role of papers, historical profiles on California journalism greats, success stories, minorities in the newspaper field and technological advances. Query. Pays $25-30.
Photos: Reviews b&w glossy prints.
Tips: "Go on; query us! Stories used will be read by all the newspaper publishers who count in the state of Cailfornia. We'd like to showcase first-effort, good writing talent."

CANADIAN AUTHOR & BOOKMAN, Canadian Authors' Association, 24 Ryerson Ave., Toronto, Ontario, Canada M5T 2P3. Editor: Sybil Marshall. 75% freelance written. "For writers—all ages, all levels of experience." Quarterly magazine; 32 pages. Circ. 5,000. Pays on publication. Buys first Canadian rights. Byline given. Written queries only.
Nonfiction: How-to (on writing, selling; the specifics of the different genres—what they are and how to write them); informational (the writing scene—who's who and what's what); interview (on writers, mainly leading ones, but also those with a story that can help others write and sell more often); and opinion. No "personal, lightweight writing experiences; no fillers." Query with "immediate pinpointing of topic, length (if ms is ready), and writer's background." Length: 800-1,500 words. Pays 1¢/word.
Photos: "We're after an interesting-looking magazine and graphics are a decided help." State availability of photos with query. Offers no additional payment for b&w photos accepted with ms. Buys one-time rights.
Poetry: "High quality/Canadian only. Major poets publish with us—others need to be as good." Buys 60 poems/year. Pays $2.
Tips: "*CA&B*'s stated aim is to make every article an extension of the writer's—and, more specifically, the reader's—capabilities. We look for professional caliber in nonfiction. Our fiction and poetry sections (emphasis on Canadian) give beginners a chance, but material selected is still required to be of top quality."

THE CATHOLIC JOURNALIST, 119 N. Park Ave., Rockville Center NY 11570. "We are no longer buying freelance material."

COLLEGE PRESS REVIEW, Department of Journalism, University of Mississippi, University MS 38655. (601)232-7146, 232-7147. Editor: John W. Windhauser. For members of the National Council of College Publications staffs, editors and faculty advisers; staff members of student publications, journalism professors and others interested in the student communication media. Quarterly. Circ. 1,500. Acquires all rights. No payment. Sample copy $1.50; free writer's guidelines. Photocopied submissions OK. No simultaneous submissions. Reports in 2-5 months. Query or submit complete ms. SASE.
Nonfiction and Photos: Articles by, about, and of interest to college publication staffs, editors, and faculty advisers. Articles should focus on the editing, advising and production of college newspapers, magazines and yearbooks. "We like to use articles on research and opinion in the student communications media and related areas. We also like to use features on journalism techniques. The writer should write in a readable style. We will accept no manuscripts that read like term papers." Topical subjects of interest include use of new technology on campus publications; case studies of censorship problems at private schools; tips on purchasing new equipment; the adviser's role in revitalizing a dying publication. Length: 3,000 words maximum. B&w glossy photos used with ms. Captions required.

COLUMBIA JOURNALISM REVIEW, 700 Journalism Bldg., Columbia University, New York NY 10027. (212)280-5595. Managing Editor: Gloria Cooper. "We welcome queries concerning the media, as well as subjects covered by the media. *CJR* also publishes book reviews. We emphasize in-depth reporting, critical essays and good writing. All queries are read by editors.

EDITOR & PUBLISHER, 575 Lexington Ave., New York NY 10022. (212)752-7050. Editor: Robert U. Brown. For newspaper publishers, editors, executives, employees and others in communications, marketing, advertising, etc. Weekly magazine; 60 pages. Circ. 28,000. Pays on publication. Sample copy $1. SASE.
Nonfiction: Department Editor: Jerome H. Walker Jr. Uses newspaper business articles and news items; also newspaper personality features and printing technology. Query.
Fillers: "Amusing typographical errors found in newspapers." Pays $2.

FEED/BACK, THE CALIFORNIA JOURNALISM REVIEW, 1600 Holloway, San Francisco CA 94132. (415)469-2086. Executive Editor: David M. Cole. 40-50% freelance written. For the working journalist, the journalism student, the journalism professor and the journalistic layman. Magazine; 60 pages. Quarterly. Circ. 1,750. Byline given. Pays in subscriptions and copies. Sample copy $1. Will consider photocopied and simultaneous submissions. Reports in 1 month. Query. SASE.
Nonfiction and Photos: In-depth views of California journalism. Criticism of journalistic trends throughout the country, but with a local angle. Reviews of books concerning journalism. Informational, interview, profile, humor, historical, think pieces, expose, nostalgia, spot news, successful (or unsuccessful) business operations, new product, technical; all must be related to journalism. "Articles must focus on the news media and be of interest to professional journalists—they are our audience. We like articles that examine press performance—strengths and weaknesses; we also like personality articles on offbeat or little-known editors and journalists who escape national attention." Rejects articles that are not documented, or those in which the subject matter is not pertinent or those which show personal prejudice not supported by evidence. Length: 1,000-5,000 words. B&w glossies (8x10 or 11x14) used with or without mss. Pays in subscriptions and/or copies, tearsheets for all material.

FLORIDA FREELANCE, Osborne Communications, Box 016074, Miami FL 33101. (305)757-4682. Editor/Publisher: Eddie Osborne. Monthly newsletter covering writing and photography for Florida-based writers and photographers. Estab. 1980. Circ. approximately 200. Pays on acceptance. Byline given. Pays 40% kill fee. Buys first rights. Submit seasonal/holiday material 6 months in advance. Photocopied, simultaneous and previously published submissions OK. SASE. Reports in 1 month. Sample copy 50¢; free writer's guidelines.
Nonfiction: Historical/nostalgic (writing and photography); how-to (do anything relating to writing or photography); interview/profile (with Florida writers and photographers); new product; opinion; personal experience; and technical. "No material that does not relate in some way to writing or photography. No poetry!" Buys 12-36 mss/year. Query or send complete ms. Length: 300-600 words. Pays 10¢ word.
Photos: State availability of photos or send photos with ms. Pays $5-10 for 5x7 b&w glossy prints. Captions preferred. Model release required. Buys first serial rights.
Columns/Departments: Fiction, Photography. Buys 12 mss/year. Length: 300-600 words. Pays 10¢/word.

Fiction: No material on how to write fiction. Buys 12 mss/year. Query with clips of published work. Length: 300-600 words. Pays 10¢/word.

Fillers: Anecdotes and newsbreaks. Buys 12-60/year. Length: 25-300 words. Pays 10¢/word.

FOLIO: The Magazine for Magazine Management, 125 Elm St., Box 697, New Canaan CT 06840. Staff written.

THE JOURNALISM EDUCATOR, Department of Journalism and Telecommunication, University of Wyoming, Laramie WY 82071. (307)766-3122. Editor: William Roepke. For journalism professors, administrators, and a growing number of news executives in the US and Canada. Published by the Association for Education in Journalism. Founded by the American Society of Journalism Administrators. Quarterly. Byline given. SASE.

Nonfiction: "We do accept some unsolicited manuscripts dealing with our publication's specialized area—problems of administration and teaching in journalism education. Because we receive more articles than we can use from persons working in this field, we do not need to encourage freelance materials, however. A writer, generally, would have to be in journalism/communications teaching or in some media work to have the background to write convincingly about the subjects this publication is interested in. The writer also should become familiar with the content of recent issues of this publication." Maximum length: 2,500 words. Does not pay.

JOURNALISM QUARTERLY, School of Journalism, Ohio University, Athens OH 45701. (614)594-6710. Editor: Guido H. Stempel III. 100% freelance written. For members of the Association for Education in Journalism and other academicians and journalists. Quarterly. Usually acquires all rights. Circ. 4,800. Photocopied submissions OK. Free writer's guidelines. Reports in 4-6 months. SASE.

Nonfiction: Research in mass communication. Length: 4,000 words maximum. Submit complete ms "in triplicate." No payment.

Tips: "Query letters don't really help either the author or me very much. We can't make commitments on the basis of query letters, and we are not likely to reject or discourage the manuscript either unless it is clearly outside our scope. Do a good piece of research. Write a clear, well-organized manuscript."

LITERARY MARKET REVIEW, 73-47 255th St., Glen Oaks NY 11004. (212)343-7285. Editor: Kunnuparampie P. Punnosse. Managing Editor: K.P. Andrews. Quarterly magazine covering writing, publishing and the book trade. Circ. 2,200. Pays on publication. Byline given. Buys one-time rights and first rights. Simultaneous queries, and simultaneous, photocopied, and previously published submissions OK. Reports in 1 week on queries; 1 month on ms. Free sample copy and writer's guidelines.

Nonfiction: How-to (on publishing, the book trade or writing); interview/profile (of publishers, authors, etc.); personal experience (of publishing or writing); and technical. Buys 50 mss/year. Send complete ms. Length: 500-2,00 words. Pays $25-100.

MEDICAL COMMUNICATIONS, 4404 Sherwood Rd., Philadelphia PA 19131. (215)877-1137. Editor: Edith Schwager. For members of the American Medical Writers Association, physicians, medical libraries, journal and medical news editors, pharmaceutical advertising people, and other communicators in medical and allied fields. Quarterly. 32- to 48-page digest-size magazine. Circ. over 2,000. Acquires first North American serial rights. Byline. Uses 6-8 mss/issue. Pays 3 contributor's copies. Sample copy for $1.25. Reports in 6 weeks. Query. SASE.

Nonfiction: Articles related to any aspect of medical communications. No clinical articles. May be either philosophic or how-to. "We are more of a journal than a magazine, but like to take a less formal approach." Uses fairly serious, simple, straightforward style. Humor and special features accepted. Footnotes if required. Length: 1,500-3,000 words. Tables and figures are used with mss, if needed.

Tips: "We're especially interested in articles on subjects not usually covered in other journals aimed at medical writers/editors: translation, indexing, speaking. Write an article about a topic of interest to our members. True humor is rare; a writer should not be heavyfooted or heavyhanded with it. We accept few articles resting on a humorous base. Most of our members are experienced, literate and literary-minded writers and editors. Only the best writing holds their interest; the topic must be important to them, too."

MILITARY MEDIA REVIEW, Defense Informational School, Bldg. 400, Fort Benjamin Harrison IN 46216. (317)542-2173. Editor-in-Chief: Mary C. Rothgeb. 100% freelance written. For military and Civil Service employees of the Department of Defense and all military branch services in the fields of information/public affairs, print, broadcast and photojournalism. Quar-

terly magazine; 32 pages. Circ. 6,500. Pays in copies on publication. Not copyrighted. Byline given unless author requests otherwise. Phone queries OK. Submit seasonal/holiday material 5 months in advance of issue date. Simultaneous, photocopied and previously published submissions OK. Reports in 4 weeks. Free sample copy and writer's guidelines; mention *Writer's Market* in request.
Nonfiction: "*Military Media Review* prints how-to articles in the fields of military public affairs, print, broadcast and photojournalism. A sample topic might be 'How to Run a Military Press Center,' or 'How to Design a Post Newspaper,' etc. Occasionally, we run an interview with an outstanding figure in our field. Personal opinion and experience features must be informative. They must relate information our readers will find useful in the field. Photo features and technical articles also must relate to the field." Query or submit complete ms. Length: 1,000-4,000 words.
Photos: State availability of photos with query or submit with ms. Uses 8x10 b&w glossy prints.

THE PEN WOMAN MAGAZINE, 1300 17th St. NW, Washington DC 20036. Editor: Wilma W. Burton. For women who are professional writers, artists, composers. Publication of National League of American Pen Women. Magazine; 32-36 pages. Published 9 times/year, October through June. Circ. 6,200. Rights purchased vary with author and material. Byline given. Pays on publication. Sample copy for SASE. Photocopied submissions "sometimes" OK. Submit seasonal material 3-4 months in advance. Reports in 6 weeks. SASE.
Nonfiction: "We are overstocked from our own members. Only on occasion do we accept freelance material which must be of unusual appeal in both information and inspiration to our readers." Mss (slanted toward the professional writer, composer and artist) should be 300-1,500 words.
Fiction: Department Editor: Marie Butler, 6927 NW 78th St., Kansas City MO 64152. "Usually purchase or use reprints from recognized magazines; use some original materials."
Poetry: Department Editor: Catharine N. Fieleke, 312 Ohio St., Momence IL 60954. Uses traditional forms, blank verse, experimental forms, free verse, light verse and haiku. "We encourage shorter poems under 36 lines."

PHILATELIC JOURNALIST, 154 Laguna Court, St. Augustine FL 32084. (914)266-3150. Editor: Gustav Detjen Jr. For "journalists, writers, columnists in the field of stamp collecting. *The Philatelic Journalist* is mainly read by philatelic writers, professionals and amateurs, including all of the members of the Society of Philaticians, an international group of philatelic journalists." Bimonthly. Circ. 1,000. Not copyrighted. Pays on publication. Free sample copy. Will consider photocopied submissions. Submit seasonal material 2 months in advance. Reports in 2 weeks. Query. SASE.
Nonfiction and Photos: "Articles concerned with the problems of the philatelic journalist, how to publicize and promote stamp collecting, how to improve relations between philatelic writers and publishers and postal administrations. Philatelic journalists, many of them amateurs, are very much interested in receiving greater recognition as journalists, and in gaining greater recognition for the use of philatelic literature by stamp collectors. Any criticism should be coupled with suggestions for improvement." Buys profiles and opinion articles. Length: 250-500 words. Pays $15-30. Photos purchased with ms; captions required.

PREMIERE MAGAZINE, Technical Arts Corp., 1211 E. 7th St., St. Paul MN 55106. (612)774-5708. Editor: Gerald Fechner. Managing Editor: Judy Fechner. Quarterly magazine devoted to the preservation of the short story and traditional poetry for people of all ages. Circ. 200. Pays on publication. Buys first North American serial rights. Phone queries OK. Submit seasonal material 4 months in advance. Simultaneous, photocopied and previously published submissons OK. SASE. Reports in 6 weeks. Sample copy $1; free writer's guidelines for SASE.
Nonfiction: Humor; inspirational; profile (of interesting personalities and animals); and personal experience. Pays $20-50.
Fiction: Adventure, fantasy, experimental, historical, humorous, mystery, romance, suspense, mainstream, science fiction and western. "No bizarre or pornographic material." Buys 24 mss/year. Send complete ms. Length: 2,000 words. Pays $20-50.
Poetry: Free verse, light verse and traditional. "No poetry without rhyme or reason." Buys 100 mss/year. Length: 4-40 lines. Pays $5-10.
Tips: "All a writer needs is good-quality material that would appeal to children, middle-aged people and senior citizens. He must also have a reproducible photo because we like to show the reader what the author looks like."

PRO/COMM, (formerly *Matrix*), The Professional Communicator, published by Women in Communications, Inc., Box 9561, Austin TX 78766. (512)345-8922. Editor: Ruth Massingill. Associate Editor: Ellen L. Batt. 95% freelance written; mostly by WICI members and usually without pay. Monthly February-November; expanded annual issue January; 8-12 pages. Estab. 1981 (replacing monthly newsletter and quarterly magazine, *Matrix*). Circ. over 9,000. Pays on publication. Buys one-time rights. Byline given. Photocopied and previously published submissions OK. SASE. Reports in 4 weeks. Sample copy $1.50.

Nonfiction: General interest (media, freedom of information, legislation related to communications); how-to (improve graphics, take better photos, write a better story, do investigative reporting, sell ideas, start a magazine or newspaper, improve journalism education, reach decision-making jobs, etc.); personal experience (self-improvement, steps to take to reach management-level jobs); profile (people of interest because of their work in communications); and technical (advancements in print or electronic media). Buys 1-2 mss/issue. Query. Length: 1,000-1,500 words. Pays $25-150.

Photos: Offers no additional payment for photos accepted with mss. State availability of photos with query. Uses b&w photos. Captions required. Buys one-time rights.

THE QUILL, Magazine for Journalists, 840 N. Lakeshore Dr., Suite 801, Chicago IL 60640. Editor: Naomi Donson. 50% freelance written. For newspaper reporters, editors and photographers; television newsmen and women; magazine journalists; freelance writers; journalism educators and students of journalism. Monthly magazine (except for combined July-August issue); 36 pages. Circ. 30,000. Pays on publication. Buys all rights. Byline given for all feature articles. Submit seasonal/holiday material 2 months in advance of issue date. SASE. Sample copy $1. Free editorial guidelines.

Nonfiction: Expose (ethnical questions related to the practice of journalism and articles dealing with First Amendment questions related to the press); general interest; and opinion ("we have a guest opinion page entitled 'Comment'; of course, we welcome letters to the editor"). Query with clips of published work.

ST. LOUIS JOURNALISM REVIEW, 928 N. McKnight, St. Louis MO 63132. (314)991-1699. Publisher: Charles L. Klotzer. A critique of St. Louis media, print, broadcasting and cable by working journalists. No taboos. Bimonthly. Buys all rights. Byline given. SASE.

Nonfiction: "We buy material which analyzes, critically, local (St. Louis area) institutions, personalities, or trends." Payment depends.

SCIENCE FICTION CHRONICLE, Algol Press, Box 4175, New York NY 10163. (212)643-9011. Editor: Andrew Porter. Monthly magazine about science fiction publishing for science fiction readers, editors, writers, et al., who are interested in keeping up with the latest developments and news in science fiction. Publication also includes market reports and media news. Estab. 1979. Circ. 3,000. Pays on publication. Makes work-for-hire assignments. Phone queries OK. Submit seasonal material 4 months in advance. SASE. Reports in 1 week. Sample copy $1.

Nonfiction: Expose (science fiction which is more investigative than sensational); new product; and photo feature. No articles about UFO's or interviews. Buys 2 mss/issue. Send complete ms. Length: 200-1,000 words. Pays 3¢/word.

Photos: Send photos with ms. Pays $5-15 for 4x5 and 8x10 b&w prints. Captions preferred. Buys one-time rights.

Tips: "News of publishers and booksellers is most needed from freelancers."

WESTERN PUBLISHER, A Trade Magazine, San Francisco Publishing Co., 1111 Kearny St., Suite 4, San Francisco CA 94133. (415)421-9577. Editor: Ronald E. Nowicki. Managing Editor: Chris Goodrich. Monthly tabloid covering book publishing, especially in the Western states. "Our audience is anyone connected to the book trade, in writing, editing, producing, wholesaling, distributing, or retailing. The emphasis is on the business side of things and on current and emerging trends." Estab. 1980. Pays on publication. Byline given. Buys first North American Serial rights. Submit seasonal/holiday material 2-3 months in advance. Simultaneous queries and photocpied submissions OK. SASE. Reports in 3 weeks on queries; 5 weeks on mss. Sample copy $1.

Nonfiction: New product; technical: and trends, news, and ventures in publishing. Special issues include: American Bookseller Association annual, in May of each year. No how-I-did-it (got published/self-published) articles. Buys 12 mss/year. Send complete ms. Length: 800-1,200 words. Pays $20-30.

Tips: "We're a small, growing publication, but relatively specialized; potential writers should see us as an opportunity to break into print, but should be aware that they must know the publishing industry well."

THE WRITER, 8 Arlington St., Boston MA 02116. Editor: Sylvia K. Burack. Monthly. Pays on acceptance. Uses very little freelance material. SASE.

Nonfiction: Articles of instruction for writers. Length: about 2,000 words. Pays good rates, on acceptance.

WRITER'S DIGEST, 9933 Alliance Rd., Cincinnati OH 45242. (513)984-0717. Editor: John Brady. Monthly magazine about writing and publishing. "Our readers write fiction, poetry, non-fiction, plays and all kinds of creative writing. They're interested in improving their writing skills, improving their salesmanship, and finding new outlets for their talents." Circ. 150,000. Pays on acceptance. Buys first North American serial rights for one-time editorial use, microfilm/microfiche use, and magazine promotional use. Pays 20% kill fee. Byline given. Submit seasonal/holiday material 6 months in advance. Previously published and photocopied submissions OK. SASE. Reports in 1 month. Sample copy $1.50; writer's guidelines for SASE.

Nonfiction: "Our mainstay is the how-to article—that is, an article telling how to write and sell more of what you write. For instance, how to sell to horse magazines, how to improve your character descriptions, how to take better pictures. Be alert in spotting the new opportunities for writers and be concise in letting the reader know how to write for that market, and how to market the article once it's written. We like plenty of examples, anecdotes and $$$ in our articles—so other writers can actually see what's been done successfully by the author of a particular piece. We like our articles to speak directly to the reader through the use of the first-person voice. Don't submit an article on what five book editors say about writing mysteries. Instead, submit an article on how you cracked the mystery market, and how our readers can do the same. But don't limit the article to your experiences; include the opinions of those five editors to give your article increased depth and authority." General interest (about writing); how-to (writing and marketing techniques that work); humor (short pieces); inspirational; interview and profile (query first); new product; personal experience (marketing and freelancing experiences). "We could use some articles on fiction technique, and solid articles on poetry or poets are always welcome. We have a separate guideline sheet for articles that tell how to write for specific markets. We also use a 'Money-Marker' feature each month. These articles point out ways to make extra cash doing things such as writing resumes and freelance editing." Buys 85 mss/year. Queries are preferred, but complete mss are OK. Length: 500-3,000 words. Pays 10¢/word.

Photos: "All things being equal, photos do make a difference, especially for interviews and profiles. State availability of photos or send contact sheet with ms." Pays $25 for 5x7 or larger b&w prints. Captions required.

Columns/Departments: And You Can Quote Me, uses authors' quotes; pays $5/quote (include source). Chronicle, first-person narratives of writing adventures; length: 1,200-1,500 words; pays $120-150. The Writing Life; buys 4 items/issue; length: 50-800 words; pays 10¢/word. Trends/Topics, short, unbylined news items about topics and issues that affect writers, pays 10¢/word. Send complete ms.

Poetry: Light verse. "We are also considering poetry other than short light verse—but related to writing, publishing, other poets and authors, etc." Buys 2/issue. Submit poems in batches of 4-6. Length: 2-20 lines. Pays $5-50/poem.

Fillers: Anecdotes and short humor, primarily for use in The Writing Life column. Buys 2/issue. Length: 50-200 words. Pays 10¢/word.

WRITER'S LIFELINE, Cobalt, Ontario, Canada P0J 1C0. Editor: Douglas C. Pollard. Newsletter published twice a month "aimed at freelance writers of all ages and interests." Pays on publication. Acquires first rights. Previously published submissions OK. SAE and International Reply Coupons.

Nonfiction: "Articles on all aspects of writing and publishing." Send complete ms. Length: 500 words maximum. Pays in 1-year subscription to *Writer's Lifeline.*

Fiction: Must be tied in to writing and publishing. Poetry published; payment: 5 free issues in which poems appear.

Tips: "Writer should show evidence of his qualification to write on subject. All articles should be pegged to current concerns of writers: self-publishing, hitting local markets, anecdotes of new writer breaking in, and preparing book reviews are among articles we have published recently."

WRITER'S YEARBOOK, 9933 Alliance Rd., Cincinnati OH 45242. Editor: John Brady. Newsstand annual for freelance writers. "We provide information to help our readers become more successful at writing." Buys first North American serial rights and (occasionally) reprint rights. Pays 20% kill fee. Byline given. Buys about 20 mss/year. Pays on acceptance. Sample copy $2.95. "Writers should query in spring with ideas for the following year." Previously published (book reprints) and high-quality photocopied submissions OK. SASE.

Nonfiction: "We want articles that reflect the current state of writing in America. Trends, inside information, money-saving and money-making ideas for the freelance writer. Material on writer's hardware—typewriters, cameras, recorders, etc.—and how it can be used to make writing easier or more lucrative. We try to touch on the various facets of writing in each issue of the *Yearbook*—from fiction to poetry to playwriting, and any other endeavor a writer can pursue. How-to articles—that is, articles that explain in detail how to do something—are very important to us. For example, you could explain how to establish mood in fiction, how to improve interviewing techniques, or how to construct and market a good poem. We are also interested in the writer's spare time—what she/he does to retreat occasionally from the writing wars; where and how to refuel and replenish the writing spirit. We also want big interviews or profiles, always with good pictures. Articles on writing techniques that are effective today are always welcome." Length: 750-4,500 words. "The manuscripts we use in the *Yearbook* are usually similar to the material we buy for *Writer's Digest*. The extra space available in the *Yearbook*, however, allows us to cover topics in greater length and depth." Pays 10¢/word.

Photos: Interviews and profiles must be accompanied by high-quality photos. B&w only; depending on use, pays $20-50/published photo. Captions required.

Laundry and Dry Cleaning

Some journals in the Coin-Operated Machines category are also in the market for material on laundries and dry cleaning establishments.

AMERICAN DRYCLEANER, 500 N. Dearborn St., Chicago IL 60610. (312)337-7700. Editor: Earl V. Fischer. For professional drycleaners. Monthly. Circ. 28,000. Buys all rights. Pays on publication. Will send free sample copy on request. Reports "promptly." SASE.
Nonfiction and Photos: Articles on merchandising, diversification, sales programs, personnel management, consumer relations, cost cutting, workflow effectiveness, drycleaning methods. "Articles should help the drycleaner build his business with the most efficient utilization of time, money and effort, inform the drycleaner about current developments within and outside the industry that may affect him and his business, introduce the drycleaner to new concepts and applications that may be of use to him, teach the drycleaner the proper methods of his trade. Tight, crisp writing on significant topics imperative. Eliminate everything that has no direct relationship to the article's theme. Select details which add depth and color to the story. Direct quotes are indispensable." Pays a minimum of 5¢/published word. Photos purchased with mss; quality 8x10 or 5x7 b&w glossies. Photos should help tell story. No model releases required. Pays $5.
Tips: "I would like each query letter to state as specifically as possible the proposed subject matter. It would help to get a theme sentence or brief outline of the proposed article. Also helpful would be a statement of whether (and what sort of) photos or other illustrations are available. Anyone with the type of article that our readers would find helpful can break into the publication. Find a successful drycleaner—one with unusually satisfied customers, for example, or one that seems to be making a lot of money. Find out what makes that cleaner so successful. Tell us about it in specific, practical terms, so other cleaners will be able to follow suit. Articles should help our readers operate their drycleaning businesses more successfully; the appropriateness and practical value of information given are more important than writing style."

AMERICAN LAUNDRY DIGEST, American Trade Magazines, Inc., 500 N. Dearborn St., Chicago IL 60610. (312)337-7700. Editor: Larry Kai Ebert. 13-26% freelance written. For a professional laundering, linen supply, uniform rental audience. Monthly magazine; 52 pages. Circ. 17,100. Pays 2 weeks prior to publication. Buys all rights. Phone queries OK. Photocopied submissions OK. SASE. Reports in 2 weeks. Free sample copy and writer's guidelines.
Nonfiction: How-to articles about how laundrymen have cut costs, increased production, improved safety, gained sales, etc. "Interviews with laundrymen about how they run a successful plant would be welcome." Query. Length: 300-3,000 words. Pays minimum of 5¢/word.
Photos: B&w glossies (8x10 preferred; 5x7 acceptable) purchased with mss. Send contact sheet. Pays minimum of $5.

INDUSTRIAL LAUNDERER, 1730 M St. NW, Suite 613, Washington DC 20036. (202)296-6744. Editor: David A. Ritchey. 15-20% freelance written. For decisionmakers in the industrial laundry industry. Publication of the Institute of Industrial Launderers, Inc. Magazine; 124 pages. Monthly. Circ. 2,500. Buys all rights. Buys 15-20 mss/year. Pays on publication. Sample copies $1; limited sample copies available. Write for copy of guidelines for writers. Reports in 1 week. Query. SASE.
Nonfiction and Photos: General interest pieces for the industrial laundry industry; labor news, news from Washington; book reviews on publications of interest to people in this industry. Technical advancements and "people" stories. Informational, personal experience, interview, profile, historical, successful business operations, merchandising techniques. No "general business articles or articles not specifically related to the industrial laundry industry." Length: 750 words

minimum. Payment negotiable. No additional payment for 8x10 b&w glossies used with ms. Pays $5 minimum for those purchased on assignment. Captions required.

WESTERN CLEANER AND LAUNDERER, Box 722, La Canada CA 91011. (213)247-8595. Editor: Monida Urquhart. 15% freelance written. For owner/managers and key employees of drycleaning, laundry, rug cleaning, drapery, and cleaning plants. Monthly tabloid; 36 pages. Circ. 11,000. Pays on publication. Buys all rights. Phone queries OK. Submit seasonal/holiday material 2 months in advance of issue date. SASE. Reports in 4 weeks. Free sample copy.
Nonfiction: General interest (successful operation of drycleaning or laundry business); how-to (operate a cleaning/laundry plant); new product; and profile. Buys 10-12 mss/year. Query. Length: 400-1,200 words. Pays 5¢/word.
Photos: State availability of photos with query. Pays $4 each for 4x5 b&w glossy prints for number used with story. Captions and model release required. Buys all rights.

Law

BARRISTER, American Bar Association Press, 1155 E. 60th St., Chicago IL 60637. (312)947-4072. Managing Editor: Harvey Rudoff. For young lawyers who are members of the American Bar Association, concerned about practice of law, improvement of the profession and service to the public. Quarterly magazine; 64 pages. Circ. 146,000. Pays on acceptance. Buys all rights, first serial rights, second serial (reprint) rights, or simultaneous rights. Photocopied submissions OK. SASE. Reports in 4-6 weeks. Free sample copy.
Nonfiction: "As a magazine of ideas and opinion, we seek material that will help readers in their interrelated roles of attorney and citizen; major themes in legal and social affairs." Especially needs expository or advocacy articles; position should be defended clearly in good, crisp, journalistic prose. "We would like to see articles on issues such as the feasibility of energy alternatives to nuclear power, the possible constitutional convention, the power and future of multinational corporations; national issues such as gun control; aspects of the legal profession such as salary comparisons, use of computers in law practice." Length: 3,000-4,000 words. Query with a working title and outline of topic. "Be specific." Pays $150-400.
Photos: Donna Tashjian, photo editor. B&w photos and color transparencies purchased without accompanying ms. Pays $35-150.

LEGAL ECONOMICS, Box 11418, Columbia SC 29211. Managing Editor/Art Director: Delmar L. Roberts. For the practicing lawyer. Bimonthly magazine; 56-68 pages. Circ. 19,000. Rights purchased vary with author and material. Usually buys all rights. Byline given. Pays on publication. Free writer's guidelines. Sample copy $2.50 (make check payable to American Bar Association). Returns rejected material in 90 days, if requested. Query. SASE.
Nonfiction and Photos: "We assist the practicing lawyer in operating and managing his office in an efficient and economical manner by providing relevant articles and editorial matter written in a readable and informative style. Editorial content is intended to aid the lawyer by conveying management methods that will allow him or her to provide legal services to clients in a prompt and efficient manner at reasonable cost. Typical topics of articles include timekeeping systems; malpractice insurance; word processing systems; client/lawyer relations; office equipment; computerized research; professional compensation; information retrieval; and use of paralegals." Pays $50-200. Pays $25-30 for b&w photos purchased with mss; $35-45 for color; $65 for cover transparencies.

THE NATIONAL LAW JOURNAL, New York Law Publishing Company, 233 Broadway, New York NY 10279. (212)964-9400. Editor: Timothy Robinson. Managing Editor: Tamar Lewin. Weekly newspaper for the legal profession. Circ. 37,000. Pays on publication. Byline given. Offers $75 kill fee. Buys all rights. Reports in 1 month. Simultaneous queries OK. SASE. Reports in 3 weeks on queries; 5 weeks on mss. Sample copy $1.50.
Nonfiction: Expose (on subjects of interest to lawyers); humor (relating to legal topics); and interview/profile (of lawyers or judges of note). "The bulk of our freelance articles are 2,000-2,500 word profiles of prominent lawyers, or trend stories relating to the legal profession. We also buy a steady stream of short, spot-news stories on local court decisions or lawsuits; often, these come from legal affairs writers on local newspapers. No articles without a legal angle." Buys 60 mss/year. Query with clips of published work or send complete ms. Length: 1,500-3,000 words. Pays $300-500.
Tips: "For those who are not covering legal affairs on a regular basis, the best way into *The*

National Law Journal is probably through our 'On Trial' feature. Every week, we print a sort of reporter's notebook on some proceeding currently underway in a courtroom. These stories come from all around the country, and range from gory murder trials to a night in small claims court. They usually run about 1,000 words, and are stylistically quite flexible. We also use op-ed pieces on subjects of legal interest, many of which come from freelancers. Writers interested in doing an op-ed piece should query first."

STUDENT LAWYER, American Bar Association, 1155 E. 60th St., Chicago IL 60637. (312)947-4087. Editor: A.J. Buckingham. Associate Editor: Catherine Cahan. Monthly (during school year) magazine; 60 pages. Circ. 43,000. Pays on publication. Buys all rights. Pays negotiable kill fee. Byline given. Submit seasonal/holiday material 2 months in advance of issue date. Photocopied submissions OK. SASE. Reports in 2 weeks. Sample copy $1; free writer's guidelines.
Nonfiction: Exposé (government, law, education and business); profiles (prominent persons in law-related fields); opinion (on matters of current legal interest); essays (on legal affairs); interviews and photo features. Buys 5 mss/issue. Query. Length: 3,000-5,000 words. Pays $150-450.
Photos: State availability of photos with query. Pays $35-75 for 8x10 b&w prints; $50-150 for color. Model release required.
Columns/Departments: Briefly (short stories on unusual and interesting developments in the law); Legal Aids (unusual approaches and programs connected to teaching law students and lawyers); Legal Ease (highlighting specific products of interest to law students and attorneys); Legal Fictions (short ironic or humorous pieces); Esq. (brief profiles of people in the law); and Status (news stories on legal education, programs and personalities). Buys 4-8 mss/issue. Length: 50-1,500 words. Pays $25-175.
Fiction: "We buy fiction when it is very good and deals with the issues of law in the contemporary world, or offers insights into the inner workings of lawyers. No mystery or science fiction stories accepted." Pays $50-350.
Tips: "*Student Lawyer* actively seeks good, new writers. Legal training definitely not essential; writing talent is. The writer should not think we are a law review; we are a features magazine with the law (in the broadest sense) as the common denominator. Past articles concerned gay rights, prison reform, the media, pornography, capital punishment, and space law. Find issues of national scope and interest to write about; be aware of subjects the magazine has already covered and propose some something new. Write clearly and well."

Leather Goods

LUGGAGE AND LEATHERGOODS NEWS, G.P. Page Publications, Ltd., 380 Wellington St. W., Toronto, Ontario, Canada M5V 1E3. (416)366-4608. Editor: Robin Black. 10-15% freelance written. "The majority of our readers are retailers of luggage, leather goods, handbags, and related products. The remainder are those who supply the luggage retailers with products. 99.9% of all that I buy is of Canadian content." Published 9 times/year. Tabloid; 16 pages. Circ. 4,700. Pays on publication. Buys all rights. Phone queries OK. Submit seasonal/holiday material 3-4 months in advance of issue date. SAE and International Reply Coupons. Reports in 3 weeks.
Nonfiction: How-to (more effectively sell luggage and leather goods; articles must be based on the experiences of a retailer); interview (with Canadian industry leaders only or American companies represented in Canada); and photo features (open to b&w only). Buys up to 9 mss/year. Query. Length: 500-1,200 words. Pays 5¢/word.
Photos: "There's no point in buying an article from a freelancer in another country if I have to go (or send someone) to take photos. Works of art are not necessary—just good b&w photos." State availability of photos with query. Pays $5 for 5x7 or 8x10 b&w prints.
Tips: "It helps if you have an idea in mind. I am not too impressed if a writer simply says, 'I would like to write for your magazine.' Send a concise description of the type of article you intend to write; include names of people you intend to contact. Photos are an asset."

Library Science

AMERICAN LIBRARIES, 50 E. Huron St., Chicago IL 60611. (312)944-6780. Editor: Arthur Plotnik. For librarians. "A highly literate audience. They are for the most part practicing professionals with down-to-earth interest in people and current trends." Published 11 times a year. Circ.

39,000. Buys first North American serial rights. Pays negotiable kill fee. Byline given. Will consider photocopied submissions if not being considered elsewhere at time of submission. Submit seasonal material 6 months in advance. Reports in 10 weeks. SASE.

Nonfiction, Photos and Fillers: "Material reflecting the special and current interests of the library profession. Nonlibrarians should browse recent journals in the field, available on request in medium-sized and large libraries everywhere. Topic and/or approach must be fresh, vital, or highly entertaining. Library memoirs and stereotyped stories about old maids, overdue books, fines, etc., are unacceptable. Our first concern is with the American Library Association's activities, and how they relate to the 39,000 reader/members. Tough for an outsider to write on this topic, but not to supplement it with short, offbeat library stories and features. Will look at all good b&w, well-lit photos of library situations, and at color transparencies for possible cover use." Pays $15-150 for fillers and articles. Pays $5-50 for b&w photos.

Tips: "You can break in with a sparkling, 300-word report on a true, offbeat library event, or with an exciting photo and caption. Though stories on public libraries are always of interest, we especially need arresting material on academic and school libraries."

EMERGENCY LIBRARIAN, Dyad Services, Box 46258, Stn. G, Vancouver, British Columbia, Canada V6R 4G6. Co-Editors: Carol Ann Haycock; Ken Haycock. Bimonthly magazine; 32 pages. Circ. 2,250. Pays on publication. Photocopied submissions OK. SAE and International Reply Coupons. Reports in 4-6 weeks. Free sample copy.

Nonfiction: Emphasis is on improvement of library service for children and young adults in school and public libraries. Also annotated bibliographies. Buys 3 mss/issue. Query. No multiple submissions. Length: 1,000-3,500 words. Pays $25.

Columns/Departments: Book Reviews (of professional materials in education, librarianship and nonsexist children's books). Query. Length: 100-300 words. Payment consists of book reviewed.

THE HORN BOOK MAGAZINE, 31 St. James Ave., Park Square Bldg., Boston MA 02116. (617)482-5198. Editor-in-Chief: Ethel L. Heins. Assistant Editor: Kate M. Flanagan. Very little freelance written. For librarians, teachers, parents, authors, illustrators and publishers. Bimonthly magazine; 128 pages. Circ. 20,500. Pays on publication. Phone queries OK. Submit seasonal/holiday material 8 months in advance of issue date. Photocopied submissions OK. SASE. Free sample copy and writer's guidelines.

Nonfiction: All related to children's books. Historical; humor; inspirational; experience; personal opinion; profile; and travel. Query. Pays $20/page.

Poetry: Free verse, haiku, and traditional. Buys 1-6 mss/year. Pays $20.

LIBRARY JOURNAL, 1180 Avenue of the Americas, New York NY 10036. Editor-in-Chief: John N. Berry III. For librarians (academic, public, special). 115-page magazine published every 2 weeks. Circ. 40,000. Buys all rights. Buys 50-100 mss/year (mostly from professionals in the field). Pays on publication. Submit complete ms. SASE.

Nonfiction and Photos: "*Library Journal* is a professional magazine for librarians. Freelancers are most often rejected because they submit one of the following types of article: 'A wonderful, warm, concerned, loving librarian who started me on the road to good reading and success'; 'How I became rich, famous, and successful by using my public library'; 'Libraries are the most wonderful and important institutions in our society, because they have all of the knowledge of mankind—praise them.' We need material of greater sophistication, dealing with issues related to the transfer of information, access to it, or related phenomena. (Current hot ones are copyright, censorship, the decline in funding for public institutions, the local politics of libraries, trusteeship, etc.)" Professional articles on criticism, censorship, professional concerns, library activities, historical articles and spot news. Outlook should be from librarian's point of view. Length: 1,500-2,000 words. Pays $50-250. Payment for b&w glossy photos purchased without accompanying mss is $25. Must be at least 5x7. Captions required.

MEDIA: LIBRARY SERVICES JOURNAL, 127 9th Ave. N., Nashville TN 37234. (615)251-2752. Editor: Floyd B. Simpson. For adult leaders in church organizations and people interested in library work (especially church library work). Quarterly magazine; 50 pages. Circ. 17,500. Pays on publication. Buys all rights. Byline given. Phone queries OK. Submit seasonal/holiday material 14 months in advance. Previously published submissions OK. SASE. Reports in 1 month. Free sample copy and writer's guidelines.

Nonfiction: "Primarily interested in articles that relate to the development of church libraries in providing media and services to support the total program of a church and in meeting individual needs. We publish personal experience accounts of services provided, promotional ideas, exciting things that have happened as a result of implementing an idea or service; human interest stories that are library-related; media education (teaching and learning with a media mix). Articles should be practical for church library staffs and for teachers and other leaders of the church." Buys 15-20 mss/issue. Query. Pays 4¢/word.

THE PAMPHLETEER MONTHLY, 308 E. 79th St., New York NY 10021. (212)628-1995. Editor: William Frederick. 20% freelance written. A review source for paper-covered materials; from single-page leaflets to booklets and pamphlets/books up to and beyond 160 pages. For the library trade; buying guide for public school, college, university, and special libraries; book review source. Magazine; 48 pages. Monthly except July/August. Circ. 6,000. Buys all rights. No byline. Pays on assignment. Query. Send in a resume and clips of previous reviews or published writing.
Nonfiction: Book reviews on assignment only. Length: 50 words, average. Pays $1. (Usually, 50-100 assigned reviews at a time.)

SCHOOL LIBRARY JOURNAL, 1180 Avenue of the Americas, New York NY 10036. Editor: Lillian N. Gerhardt. For librarians in schools and public libraries. Magazine published 10 times/ year; 88 pages. Circ. 43,000. Buys all rights. Pays on publication. Reports in 3 months. SASE.
Nonfiction: Articles on library services, local censorship problems, how-to articles on programs that use books or films. Informational, personal experience, interview, expose, successful business operations. "Interested in history articles on the establishment/development of children's and young adult services in schools and public libraries." Buys 24 mss/year. Length: 2,500-3,000 words. Pays $100.

WILSON LIBRARY BULLETIN, 950 University Ave., Bronx NY 10452. (212)588-8400. Editor: Milo Nelson. For professional librarians and those interested in the book and library worlds. Monthly (September-June). Circ. 30,000. Buys North American serial rights only. Pays on publication. Sample copies may be seen on request in most libraries. "Ms must be original copy, double-spaced; additional photocopy or carbon is appreciated. Deadlines are a minimum 2 months before publication." Reports in 8-12 weeks. SASE.
Nonfiction: Uses articles "of interest to librarians throughout the nation and around the world. Style must be lively, readable and sophisticated, with appeal to modern professionals; facts must be thoroughly researched. Subjects range from the political to the comic in the world of media and libraries, with an emphasis on the human as well as the technical aspects of any story. No condescension: no library stereotypes." Send complete ms. Length: 2,500-6,000 words. Pays about $50-150, "depending on the substance of article and its importance to readers."
Tips: "The best way you can break in is with a first-rate b&w photo and caption information on a library, library service, or librarian that departs completely from all stereotypes and the common-place. Note: Libraries have changed! You'd better first discover what is now commonplace."

Lumber and Woodworking

B.C. LUMBERMAN MAGAZINE, Box 34080, Station D, Vancouver, British Columbia, Canada, V6J 4M8. (403)731-1171. Editorial Director: Brian Martin. 60% freelance written. For the logging and sawmilling industries of Western Canada and the Pacific Northwest of the United States. Monthly magazine; 75 pages. Circ. 8,500. Pays on acceptance. Buys first Canadian rights. Query first. Submit seasonal/holiday material 2 months in advance of issue date. Reports in 2 weeks. Free sample copy; mention *Writer's Market* in request.
Nonfiction: How-to (technical articles on any aspect of the forest industry); general interest (anything of interest to persons in forest industies in western Canada or US Pacific Northwest); interview (occasionally related to leading forestry personnel); and technical (forestry). Buys 8 mss/issue. Query with clips of published work. Average length: 1,500 words. Pays 14¢/word (Canadian).
Photos: State availability of photos with query. Pays $5-25 for b&w negatives and $50-80 for 8x10 glossy color prints. Captions required. Buys first Canadian rights.

CANADIAN FOREST INDUSTRIES, 1450 Don Mills Rd., Don Mills, Ontario, Canada M3B 2X7. Editor: Keith Atkinson. 25% freelance written. For forest companies, loggers, lumber-plywood-board manufacturers. Monthly. Circ. 12,000. Buys first North American serial rights. Byline given. Pays on publication. Free sample copy. Reports in 1 month. SAE and International Reply Coupons.
Nonfiction: Uses "articles concerning industry topics, especially how-to articles that help business-men in the forest industries. All articles should take the form of detailed reports of new methods,

techniques and cost-cutting practices that are being successfully used anywhere in Canada, together with descriptions of new equipment that is improving efficiency and utilization of wood. It is very important that accurate descriptions of machinery (make, model, etc.) be always included and any details of costs, etc., in actual dollars and cents can make the difference between a below-average article and an exceptional one." Query. Length: 1,200-1,500 words. Pays 20¢/word minimum, more with photos.

Photos: Buys photos with mss, sometimes with captions only. Should be 8x10, b&w glossies or negatives.

LOGGING MANAGEMENT, Vance Publishing Corp., 300 W. Adams, Chicago IL 60606. (312)977-7200. Managing Editor: Harry Urban. Associate Editor: Dave Lenckus. 10-15% freelance written. "For management and operating executives involved in forestry and sawmills, including growing, felling, extraction, loading, shipping, exporting and milling of timber." Bimonthly magazine. Circ. 22,000. Pays on publication. Phone queries OK. Submit seasonal/holiday material 4 months in advance of issue date. Simultaneous, photocopied, and previously published submissions OK (if exclusive in field). SASE. Free sample copy, writer's guidelines and annual story schedule.

Nonfiction: Expose (government activities, upcoming regulations); how-to (increase production, efficiency, improve business operations); humor (if related to industry); interview (industry, government leaders, environmentalists); new product (a product offering truly new technology, not just a new capscrew); and photo feature (unusual or outstanding logging operations). Buys 10 mss/year. Query with clips of published work. Length: 500-1,500 words. Pays $50-150.

Photos: State availability of photos with query. Offers no additional payment for photos accepted with ms. Uses b&w prints and color transparencies. Captions required. Buys one-time rights.

Columns/Departments: Trends & News (news developments). Buys 6/year. Query. Length: 100-500 words. Pays $50-150

Tips: "We want stories to help our loggers, not the manufacturers of logging equipment. We don't want a story about how great titanium is in horse chokers; we want a story about whether horse logging is a practical alternative."

PLYWOOD AND PANEL MAGAZINE, Box 567B, Indianapolis IN 46206. (317)634-1100. Editor: Robert F. Dixon. For manufacturers and industrial fabricators of plywood, veneer and composite board. Monthly. Buys first North American serial rights. Byline given, "but any short industry news item that does not rate full feature treatment would be used at a $5 minimum payment with no byline; this includes clippings from other publications." Pays on publication. Reports in 6 weeks. SASE. Free sample copy and writer's guidelines.

Nonfiction: "Factual and accurate articles concerning unusual techniques or aspects in the manufacturing or processing of veneer, plywood, particleboard, hardboard; detailing successful and/or unusual marketing techniques for wood panel products; or concerning important or unusual industrial end-uses of these materials in the production of consumer goods." Length: 800-2,000 words. Pays maximum 5¢/word.

Photos: Of good quality and directly pertinent to editorial needs. Action photos; no catalog shots. No in-plant photos of machinery not operating or not manned in natural fashion. Must be completely captioned; 5x7 b&w or larger preferred. Pays up to $5-10 per photo.

Fillers: Clippings and newsbreaks. Pays 5¢/word.

WOOD & WOOD PRODUCTS, 300 W. Adams St., Chicago IL 60606. (312)977-7200. Managing Editor: Russ Gager. 10-15% freelance written. For owners and managers of furniture and wood products companies, including plywood mills, particleboard mills, laminated panels or millwork, moulding and cabinet companies. Monthly magazine; 84 pages. Circ. 30,000. Pays on publication. Buys all rights unless otherwise specified. Byline given. Phone queries OK. Submit material 3 months in advance of issue date. SASE. Free sample copy, writer's guidelines, and annual story schedule.

Nonfiction: Exposé (of upcoming government regulations); how-to (increase production, efficiency, and profits); new product (one offering truly new technology, not just a new cap screw); photo feature (how-to, plant story); and technical. No articles on hobbyist woodworking or small woodcraft shops. Buys 15 mss/year. Query with clips of published work; "give full information on story and indicate whether any competition is interested in story or has turned it down." Length: 500-1,500 words. Pays $50-150.

Photos: State availability of photos with query. Offers no additional payment for b&w contact sheets or prints 35mm color transparencies. Captions required.

Columns/Departments: Production Ideas (efficiency tips, how a company solved a problem); and Trends & News (news items). Query. Length: 100-150 words. Pays $50-150.

Tips: "Find a good story and offer us an exclusive, with good color transparencies and snappy writing. Query first. To us, a good story is one about a new product or technique which will help woodworkers save money."

WOODWORKING & FURNITURE DIGEST, Hitchcock Bldg., Wheaton IL 60187. (312)665-1000. Editor: Ren Rooney. For industrial manufacturers whose products employ wood as a basic raw material. Monthly. Buys all rights. Pays on publication. Will send free sample copy to serious freelancer on request. Query. Reports in 10 days. Will sometimes hold ms for further evaluation up to 2 months, if at first it appears to have possibilities. SASE.
Nonfiction and Photos: "Articles on woodworking and furniture manufacturing with emphasis on management concepts, applications for primary raw materials (including plastics, if involved with wood), technology of remanufacturing methods and machines, and news of broad industry interest. Articles should focus on cost reduction, labor efficiency, product improvement, and profit. No handcraft, do-it-yourself or small custom shopwork. Present theme, or why reader can benefit, in first paragraph. Cover 'feeds and speeds' thoroughly to include operating data and engineering reasons why. Leave reader with something to do or think. Avoid mechanically handled case histories and plant tours that do not include management/engineering reasons. Photos, charts and diagrams which tell what cannot be told in words should be included. We like a balance between technical information and action photos." Length: "no length limit, but stop before you run out of gas!" Pays $35-50/published page. Photos purchased with mss. Good technical quality and perception of subject shown. No posed views. Prefers candid action or tight closeups. Full-color cover photo must be story-related.

Machinery and Metal Trade

ASSEMBLY ENGINEERING, Hitchcock Publishing Co., Wheaton IL 60187. Editor: Robert T. Kelly. 30% freelance written. For design and manufacturing engineers and production personnel concerned with assembly problems in manufacturing plants. Monthly. Buys first publication rights. Pays on publication. Sample copy will be sent on request. "Query on leads or ideas. We report on ms decision as soon as review is completed and provide edited proofs for checking by author, prior to publication." SASE.
Nonfiction and Photos: Wants features on design, engineering and production practices for the assembly of manufactured products. Material should be submitted on "exclusive rights" basis. Subject areas include selection, specification, and application of fasteners, mounting hardware, electrical connectors, wiring, hydraulic and pneumatic fittings, seals and gaskets, adhesives, joining methods (soldering, welding, brazing, etc.) and assembly equipment; specification of fits and tolerances; joint design; design and shop assembly standards; time and motion study (assembly line); quality control in assembly; layout and balancing of assembly lines; assembly tool and jig design; programming assembly line operations; working conditions, incentives, labor costs, and union relations as they relate to assembly line operators; hiring and training of assembly line personnel; supervisory practices for the assembly line. Also looking for news items on assembly-related subjects, and for unique or unusual "ideas" on assembly components, equipment, processes, practices and methods. Requires good quality photos or sketches, usually close-ups of specific details. Pays $30 minimum/published page.

AUTOMATIC MACHINING, 228 N. Winton Rd., Rochester NY 14610. (716)654-8964. Editor: Donald E. Wood. For metalworking technical management. Buys all rights. Byline given. Query. SASE.
Nonfiction: "This is not a market for the average freelancer. A personal knowledge of the trade is essential. Articles deal in depth with specific job operations on automatic screw machines, chucking machines, high production metal turning lathes and cold heading machines. Part prints, tooling layouts always required, plus written agreement of source to publish the material. Without personal background in operation of this type of equipment, freelancers are wasting time." Length: "no limit." Pays $20/printed page.

CANADIAN MACHINERY AND METALWORKING, 481 University Ave., Toronto, Ontario, Canada M5W 1A7. (416)596-5714. Editor: J. Davies. Monthly. Buys first Canadian rights. Pays on acceptance. Query. SAE and International Reply Coupons.
Nonfiction: Technical and semitechnical articles dealing with metalworking operations in Canada and in the US, if of particular interest. Accuracy and service appeal to readers is a must. Pays minimum 10¢/word.
Photos: Purchased with mss and with captions only. Pays $10 minimum for b&w features.

CUTTING TOOL ENGINEERING, Box 937, Wheaton IL 60187. (312)653-3210. Managing Editor: Mary W. Brown. For metalworking industry executives and engineers concerned with the metal-cutting/metal-removal/abrasive machining function in metalworking. Bimonthly. Circ. 39,000. Buys all rights. Byline given. Pays on publication. Will send free sample copy on request. Query with outline of article and professional background, or submit complete ms. SASE.
Nonfiction: "Intelligently written articles on specific applications of all types of metal cutting tools, mills, drills, reamers, etc. Articles must contain all information related to the operation, such as feeds and speeds, materials machined, etc. Should be tersely written, in-depth treatment. In the Annual Diamond/Superabrasive Directory, published in May/June, we cover the use of diamond/superabrasive cutting tools and diamond/superabrasive grinding wheels." Length: 1,000-2,500 words. Pays "$35/published page, or about 5¢/published word."
Photos: Purchased with mss. 8x10 b&w glossies preferred.

FOUNDRY MANAGEMENT AND TECHNOLOGY, Penton Plaza, Cleveland OH 44114. (216)696-7000. Editor: J.C. Miske. Monthly. Byline given. Reports in 2 weeks. SASE.
Nonfiction and Photos: Uses articles describing operating practice in foundries written to interest companies producing metal castings. Length: 3,000 words maximum. Pays $35-50/printed page. Uses illustrative photographs with article; uses "a great deal of 4-color photos."

INDUSTRIAL MACHINERY NEWS, 29516 Southfield Rd., C.S. #5002, Southfield MI 48037. (313)557-0100. Editor-in-Chief: Lucky D. Slate. Emphasizes metalworking for buyers, specifiers, manufacturing executives, engineers, management, plant managers, production managers, master mechanics, designers and machinery dealers. Monthly tabloid; 200 pages. Circ. 175,000. Pays on publication. Buys first North American serial rights. Submit seasonal/holiday material 3 months in advance. Simultaneous, photocopied and previously published submissions OK. SASE. Reports in 3-6 weeks. Sample copy $3.
Nonfiction and Photos: Articles on "metal removal, metal forming, assembly, finishing, inspection, application of machine tools, technology, measuring, gauging equipment, small cutting tools, tooling accessories, materials handling in metalworking plants, safety programs. We give our publication a newspaper feel—fast reading with lots of action or human interest photos." Buys how-to's. Pays $25 minimum. Length: open. Photos purchased with mss; captions required. Pays $5 minimum.
Fillers: Puzzles, jokes, short humor. Pays $5 minimum.
Tips: "We're looking for stories on old machine tools—how they're holding up and how they're being used. We're also interested in metalworking machinery and equipment application articles that illustrate techniques geared to improving efficiency and productivity in the plant."

MODERN MACHINE SHOP, 600 Main St., Cincinnati OH 45202. Editor: Ken Gettelman. Monthly. Byline given. Pays 30 days following acceptance. Query. Reports in 5 days. SASE.
Nonfiction: Uses articles dealing with all phases of metal manufacturing and machine shop work, with photos. No general articles. "Ours is an industrial publication, and contributing authors should have a working knowledge of the metalworking industry." Length: 800-3,000 words. Pays current market rate.

N C SHOPOWNER, McGraw Hill Publications, 1221 Avenue of the Americas, New York NY 10020. (212)997-3618. Editor: Charles Emerson. Quarterly magazine covering manufacturing techniques, machine shops and press shops. Estab. 1980. Circ. 48,000. Pays on acceptance. Byline given. Buys all rights. Simultaneous queries, and simultaneous and photocopied submissions OK. Reports in 1 month. Free sample copy.
Nonfiction: General interest (management, training people, financing machines, programming and purchasing); technical (machines, controls, and cutting tools, and how they are used with numerical control); case studies (good examples); and application of new technology in small shops. Buys 12 mss/year. Query or send complete ms. Length: 700-2,000 words. Pays $175-500.
Photos: State availability of photos.

ORNAMENTAL/MISCELLANEOUS METAL FABRICATOR, Suite 109, 2996 Grandview Ave., NE, Atlanta GA 30305. Editor: Blanche Blackwell. For fabricators of ornamental and miscellaneous metals who are interested in their businesses and families, their community and nation. Most are owners of small businesses employing an estimated average of 10 persons, usually including family members. Official publication of the National Ornamental and Miscellaneous Metals Association. Magazine published every 2 months; 24 pages. Circ. 6,000. Not copyrighted. Byline given. Buys 6 mss/year. Pays on acceptance. Will send free sample copy to writer on request. Will not consider photocopied or simultaneous submissions. Submit seasonal material 2 months in advance. Reports "immediately." Query. SASE.

Nonfiction and Photos: "Our publication deals solely with fabrication of ornamental and miscellaneous metals, a more creative and aesthetic aspect of the metals construction industry. Special emphasis on ornamental and miscellaneous metal trade. How-to articles that will help our readers improve their businesses. Articles on use and history of ornamental metal; on better operation of the business; on technical aspects. News about the association and its individual members and about 14 chapters affiliated with the national association. Articles on the effects of steel shortage on ornamental metal fabricator and how a typical firm is handling the problem; the search for qualified employees; successful prepaint treatments and finishes." Prefers not to see "character study" articles. Length: 1,000-5,000 words. Pays 3¢/word. B&w glossy photos purchased with accompanying mss. Pays $4.

POWER TRANSMISSION DESIGN, 614 Superior Ave. W., Cleveland OH 44113. (216)696-0300. Editor: Ro Lutz-Nagey. Features Editor: LaVerne Leonard. 20% freelance written. Emphasizes industrial motion and control systems. Monthly magazine: 96 pages. Circ. 50,600. Pays on publication. Buys first-time publication rights and nonexclusive republication rights. Byline given all features. Phone queries OK. Submit seasonal/holiday material 5 months in advance. Photocopied submissions OK. Reports in 1 month. Free sample copy.
Nonfiction: Articles on design, selection and maintenance of industry power-transmission systems and components. Buys 5 mss/issue. Query with description of technical questions to be answered by article. Include "why new" information. Length: 1,500-7,500 words. Pays $35-200.

PRODUCTION, Box 101, Bloomfield Hills MI 48013. (313)647-8400. Editor: Robert F. Huber. For "managers of manufacturing." Monthly. Circ. 80,000. Buys all rights. Buys "a few" mss/year. Pays on acceptance. Query first. SASE.
Nonfiction and Photos: "Trends, developments, and applicatons in manufacturing." Length: open. Pays $50-350. Photos purchased with mss; captions required.

PRODUCTS FINISHING, 600 Main St., Cincinnati OH 45202. Editor: Gerard H. Poll Jr. Monthly. Buys all rights. Byline given "except on press releases from agencies." Pays within 30 days after acceptance. Reports in 1 week. SASE.
Nonfiction: Uses "material devoted to the finishing of metal and plastic products. This includes the cleaning, plating, polishing and painting of metal and plastic products of all kinds. Articles can be technical and must be practical. Technical articles should be on processes and methods. Particular attention given to articles describing novel approaches used by product finishers to control air and water pollution, and finishing techniques that reduce costs." Pays 8¢ minimum/word.
Photos: Wants photographs dealing with finishing methods or processes. Pays $10 minimum for each photo used.

33 METAL PRODUCING, McGraw-Hill Bldg., 1221 Avenue of the Americas, 36th Floor, New York NY 10020. (212)997-3330. Editor: Joseph L. Mazel. For "operating managers (from turn foreman on up), engineers, metallurgical and chemical specialists, and corporate officials in the steelmaking industry. Work areas for these readers range from blast furnace and coke ovens into and through the steel works and rolling mills. *33*'s readers also work in nonferrous industries and foundries." Monthly. Buys all rights. Pays on publication. Free sample copy. Query. Reports in 3 weeks. SASE.
Nonfiction: Case histories of primary metals producing equipment in use, such as smelting, blast furnace, steelmaking, rolling. "Broadly speaking, *33 Metal Producing* concentrates its editorial efforts in the areas of technique (what's being done and how it's being done), technology (new developments), and equipment (what's being used). Your article should include a detailed explanation (who, what, why, where and how) and the significance (what it means to operating manager, engineer, or industry) of the techniques, technology or equipment being written about. In addition, your readers will want to know of the problems you experienced during the planning, developing, implementing and operating phases. And, it would be especially beneficial to tell of the steps you took to solve the problems or roadblocks encountered. You should also include all cost data relating to implementation, operation, maintenance, etc., wherever possible. Benefits (cost savings, improved manpower utilization, reduced cycle time, increased quality, etc.) should be cited to gauge the effectiveness of the subject being discussed. The highlight of any article is its illustrative material. This can take the form of photographs, drawings, tables, charts, graphs, etc. Your type of illustration should support and reinforce the text material. It should not just be an added, unrelated item. Each element of illustrative material should be identified and contain a short description of exactly what is being presented. We reject material that lacks in-depth knowledge of the technology on operations involved in metal producing." Pays $50/published page. Minimum 5x7 b&w glossies purchased with mss.

Maintenance and Safety

BUILDING SERVICES CONTRACTOR, MacNair-McDorland Co., 101 W. 31st St., New York NY 10001. (212)279-4455. Editor-in-Chief: John Vollmuth. 10% freelance written. Bimonthly magazine; 60 pages. Circ. 6,000. Pays on publication. Buys all rights. Phone queries OK. Submit seasonal/holiday material 2-3 months in advance of issue date. SASE. Reports in 2 weeks. Free sample copy and writer's guidelines.
Nonfiction: General interest, historical, interview, new product, personal experience, photo feature, profile and technical. Submit complete ms. Length: 800-1,500 words. Pays $135-150.
Photos: Submit photo material with accompanying ms. No additional payment for b&w prints. Buys all rights.
Fillers: Clippings. Buys 3/issue. Pays $1-3.

HEAVY DUTY EQUIPMENT MANAGEMENT/MAINTENANCE, 7300 N. Cicero Ave., Lincolnwood IL 60646. (312)588-7300. Editor: Greg Sitek. 10% freelance written. Magazine; 76-110 pages. Monthly. Circ. 51,000. Rights purchased vary with author and material. Usually buys all rights. Buys 12 mss/year. Pays on publication. Free sample copy. No photocopied or simultaneous submissions. Reports in 4 weeks. Query with outline. SASE.
Nonfiction and Photos: "Our focus is on the effective management of equipment through proper selection, careful specification, correct application and efficient maintenance. We use job stories, technical articles, safety features, basics and shop notes. No product stories." Length: 2,000-5,000 words. Pays $25/printed page minimum, without photos. Uses 35mm and 2¼x2¼ or larger color transparencies with mss. Pays $50/printed page when photos are furnished by author.
Tips: "Know the equipment, how to manage it, and how to maintain/service/repair it."

INDUSTRIAL SAFETY PRODUCT NEWS, Ames Publishing Co., 1 W. Olney Ave., Philadelphia PA 19120. (215)224-7000. Editor: Leonard M. Wasserbly. Managing Editor: Dave Johnson. Monthly magazine about safety and health in the industrial plant for safety and health management personnel in charge of safety in over 36,000 large industrial plants. Circ. 52,000. Pays on publication. Byline given. Buys all rights. Phone queries OK. Submit seasonal material 2 months in advance. Simultaneous, photocopied and previously published submissions OK. SASE. Reports in 1 week on queries; in 1 month on mss. Free sample copy.
Nonfiction: New product, personal experience and technical. "We have only recently begun using one or two bylined articles dealing with the area of industrial safety from experts in the field. *We are eager to have more submitted.* Articles should be concise and have graphics included where appropriate. Special issues in the future will be on fire protection; security devices; industrial health problems; regulatory reform; personal protection products; and safety and health programs in industrial plants." Buys 3-5 mss/year. Query; indicate "expertise in subject area and proof of subject's relevancy to reader interests." Length: 200-1,000 words. Pays $100-400.
Photos: Send photos with ms. Pays $20-100 for b&w prints. Reviews color transparencies. Model release required. Buys one-time rights.
Tips: "The freelancer should first call the managing editor to discuss editorial emphasis issues for the coming year. A copy of the publication and demographic information will be sent gratis to help explain the nature of the audience."

MAINTENANCE SUPPLIES, 101 W. 31st St., New York NY 10001. (212)279-4455. Editor-in-Chief: John Vollmuth. Managing Editor: Ed Pasternack. 10% freelance written. For distributors of janitorial supplies. Monthly magazine; 100 pages. Circ. 11,000. Pays on publication. Buys all rights. Phone queries OK. Submit seasonal/holiday material 2-3 months in advance of issue date. Photocopied submissions OK. SASE. Reports in 2 weeks. Free sample copy.
Nonfiction: General interest; historical; interview; new product; personal experience; photo feature; profile; and technical. Buys 2 mss/issue. Submit complete ms. Length: 800-1,500 words. Pays $135-150.
Photos: Submit photo material with accompanying ms. Offers no additional payment for b&w prints. Buys all rights.
Columns/Departments: New Literature and New Products. Buys 1/issue. Submit complete ms. Length: 500-800 words. Pays $50. Open to suggestions for new columns/departments.

OCCUPATIONAL HAZARDS, 614 Superior Ave. W., Cleveland OH 44113. (216)696-0300. Editor: Peter J. Sheridan. "Distributed by function to middle management officials in industry who have the responsibility for accident prevention, occupational health, plant fire protection, and plant security programs. Job titles on our list include: safety directors, industrial hygienists, fire protection engineers, plant security managers and medical directors." Monthly. Buys first rights in field. Pays on publication. Reports in 30 days. SASE.

Nonfiction: "Articles on industrial health, safety, security and fire protection. Specific facts and figures must be cited. No material on farm, home or traffic safety. All material accepted subject to sharp editing to conform to publisher's distilled writing style. Illustrations preferred but not essential. Work is rejected when story is not targeted to professional concerns of our readers, but rather is addressed to the world at large." Length: 300-2,000 words. Pays 5¢/word minimum.

Photos: Accepts 4x5, 5x7 and 8x10 photos with mss. Pays $10.

THE OSHA COMPLIANCE LETTER, Bureau of Business Practice, 24 Rope Ferry Rd., Waterford CT 06386. (203)442-4365, ext. 262. Editor: Gail Heller. For "safety directors or persons with safety responsibilities—in all firms covered by job safety and health regulations." Bimonthly newsletter. Pays on acceptance. Buys all rights. Phone queries OK. SASE. Reports in 2 months. Free sample copy and writer's guidelines.

Nonfiction: Interviews revealing ways in which a company complies with job safety/health regulations. Interview safety directors or other supervisors with safety responsibilities. "Get familiar with the field. In the case of safety management, collar friends, neighbors, acquaintances in the field and pump them with questions. Then, at least, you'll be going to interviews with a good idea of the appropriate questions. Direct interviews along specific, topical lines. And when an interviewee lets fall a statement like: 'people who've had accidents are the best people to make suggestions on how to prevent future mishaps,' don't let the comment hang in air. Get at the why and how—not just the what." No "overviews of company safety programs; safety committee stories; stories that focus on generalities like communicating safety, safety awareness, or safety attitude. We need more meat, more specifics." Buys 2 mss/issue. Query. Length: 1,000-1,300. Pays 10¢/word after editing.

Tips: "Phone queries are the easiest and most productive way of breaking in. By talking to a freelancer, I can best steer him or her in the right direction, provide advice on how to approach an interview and explain what types of problems he/she may encounter with a specific lead. A freelancer must include full name, title and phone number of person interviewed; full name and address of company; and his own phone number."

PEST CONTROL MAGAZINE, 757 3rd Ave., New York NY 10017. (212)888-2563. Editor: John Kerr. For professional pest control operators and sanitation workers. Monthly magazine; 68 pages. Circ. 15,000. Buys all rights. Buys 12+ mss/year. Pays on publication. Submit seasonal material 2 months in advance. Reports in 30 days. Query or submit complete ms. SASE.

Nonfiction and Photos: Business tips, unique control situations, personal experience articles. Must have trade or business orientation. No general information type of articles desired. Length: 4 double-spaced pages. Pays $150 minimum. Regular columns use material oriented to this profession. Length: 8 double-spaced pages. No additional payment for photos used with mss. Pays $50-150 for 8x10 color or transparencies.

Management and Supervision

This category includes trade journals for lower level business and industrial managers, including supervisors and office managers. Journals for business executives and owners are classified under Business Management. Those for industrial plant managers are listed in Industrial Management.

AIRPORT SERVICES MANAGEMENT, Lakewood Publications, 731 Hennepin Ave. S., Minneapolis MN 55403. (612)333-0471. Editorial Director: Philip G. Jones. 20% freelance written. Emphasizes management of airports and airport business. Monthly magazine; 50 pages. Circ. 20,000. Pays on acceptance. Buys all rights. Byline given. Phone queries OK. Submit seasonal/holiday material 3 months in advance of issue date. Photocopied submissions OK. SASE. Reports in 4 weeks. Free sample copy and writer's guidelines.

Nonfiction: How-to (manage an aviation business or service organization, work with local governments, etc.); interview (with a successful operator); and technical (how to manage maintenance shops, snow removal operations, bird control, security operations). "No flying, no airport nostalgia, or product puff pieces. Just plain 'how-to' story lines, please." Buys 20 mss/year. Query. "Send a well-written but informal letter detailing the proposed subject, proposed approach, and what you expect the reader would learn from the piece that might apply to reader's own situation; also send writing sample and brief bio." Length: 500-1,500 words. Pays $85/published page.

Photos: State availability of photos with query. Payment for photos is included in total purchase price. Uses 5x7 or 8x10 glossy b&w photos.
Tips: "No 'gee whiz' approaches, but no bureaucratic, legalistic, convoluted language, either. Keep it lively, straightforward and simple."

THE BUSINESS QUARTERLY, School of Business Administration, University of Western Ontario, London, Ontario N6A 3K7, Canada. (519)679-3222. Editor: Doreen Sanders. For persons in upper and middle management, university education, interested in continuing and updating their management education. Quarterly. Circ. 11,500. Buys all rights. Buys 35 mss/year. Pays on publication. Reports in 3 months. Query with brief outline of article and some biographical material." Enclose SAE and International Reply Coupons.
Nonfiction: Articles pertaining to all aspects of management development. Must have depth. "Think" articles and those on successful business operations. Length: 2,000-5,000 words. Pays $100.
Tips: "The material submitted must be of vital interest to Canadian managers."

CONSTRUCTION FOREMAN'S & SUPERVISOR'S LETTER, Bureau of Business Practice, 24 Rope Ferry Rd., Waterford CT 06386. (203)442-4365. Emphasizes all aspects of construction supervision. Semimonthly newsletter; 4 pages. Buys all rights. Phone queries OK. Submit seasonal or holiday material at least 4 months in advance. SASE. Reports in 4-6 weeks. Free sample copy and writer's guidelines.
Nonfiction: Publishes solid interviews with construction managers or supervisors on how to improve a single aspect of the supervisor's job. Buys 100 mss/year. Length: 360-720 words. Pays 7-10¢/word.
Photos: B&w head and shoulders "mug shots" of person interviewed purchased with mss. Send prints. Pays $10.

EMPLOYEE RELATIONS BULLETIN, Bureau of Business Practice, 24 Rope Ferry Rd., Waterford CT 06386. Supervisory Editor: Barbara Kelsey. For personnel, human resources and employee relations managers on the executive level. Semimonthly newsletter; 8 pages. Circ. 3,000. Pays on acceptance. Buys all rights. No byline. Phone queries OK. Submit seasonal/holiday material 6 months in advance. Photocopied submissions OK. SASE. Reports in 2 weeks. Free sample copy and writer's guidelines.
Nonfiction: Interviews about all types of business and industry such as banks, insurance companies, public utilities, airlines, consulting firms, etc. Interviewee should be a high level company officer—general manager, president, industrial relations manager, etc. Writer must get signed release from person interviewed showing that article has been read and approved by him/her, before submission. Some subjects for interviews might be productivity improvement, communications, compensation, government regulations, safety and health, grievance handling, human relations techniques and problems, etc. Buys 3 mss/issue. Query. Length: 700-2,000 words. Pays 10¢/word after editing.

THE FOREMAN'S LETTER, National Foremen's Institute, 24 Rope Ferry Rd., Waterford CT 06386. (203)442-4365. Editor: Paula Brisco. For industrial supervisors. Semimonthly. Buys all rights. Pays on acceptance. Interested in regular stringers (freelance). SASE. Comprehensive guidelines available.
Nonfiction: Interested primarily in direct in-depth interviews with industrial supervisors in the US and Canada. Subject matter would be the interviewee's techniques for becoming a more effective manager, bolstered by illustrations out of the interviewee's own job experiences. Slant would be toward informing readers how to solve a particular supervisory problem. "Our aim is to offer information which, hopefully, readers may apply to their own professional self-improvement." Length: 600-1,200 words. Pays 8¢-14½¢/word "after editing for all rights."
Photos: Buys photos submitted with mss. "Captions needed for identification only." Head and shoulders, any size b&w glossy from 2x3 up. Pays $10.
Tips: "Study our editorial guidelines carefully. Emulate the style of sample issues. Write a how-to article focusing on one specific topic. A new freelancer should be willing to rewrite submissions if neccessary. Editor will offer suggestions."

LE BUREAU, 625 President Kennedy, Montreal, Quebec, Canada, H3A 1K5. (514)845-5141. Editor: Paul Saint-Pierre. For "office executives." Published 6 times/year. Circ. 7,500. Buys all rights. Byline given. Buys about 10 mss/year. Pays on acceptance. Query or submit complete ms. Submit seasonal material "between 1 and 2 months" in advance of issue date. SAE and International Reply Coupons.
Nonfiction and Photos: "Our publication is published in the French language. We use case

histories on new office systems, applications of new equipment, articles on personnel problems. Material should be exclusive and above-average quality." Buys personal experience articles, interviews, think pieces, coverage of successful business operations, and new product articles. Length: 500-1,000 words. Pays $75-150. B&w glossies purchased with mss. Pays $25 each.

MANAGE, 2210 Arbor Blvd., Dayton OH 45439. (513)294-0421. Editor-in-Chief: Douglas E. Shaw. 60% freelance written. For first-line and middle management and scientific/technical managers. Quarterly magazine; 36 pages. Circ. 65,000. Pays on acceptance. Buys North American magazine rights with reprint privileges; book rights remain with the author. Phone queries OK. SASE. Reports in 1 month. Free sample copy and writer's guidelines.
Nonfiction: "All material published by *Manage* is in some way management-oriented. Most articles concern one or more of the following categories: communications; cost reduction; economics; executive abilities; health and safety; human relations; job status; labor relations; leadership; motivation and productivity; and professionalism. Articles should be specific and tell the manager how to apply the information to his job immediately. Be sure to include pertinent examples, and back up statements with facts and, where possible, charts and illustrations. *Manage* does not want essays or academic reports, but interesting, well-written and practical articles for and about management." Buys 6 mss/issue. Submit complete ms. Length: 600-2,000 words. Pays 5¢/word.
Tips: "Keep current on management subjects; submit timely work."

PERSONNEL ADVISORY BULLETIN, Bureau of Business Practice, 24 Rope Ferry Rd., Waterford CT 06386. (203)442-4365. Supervisory Editor: Barbara Kelsey. Emphasizes all aspects of personnel management for personnel managers in all types and sizes of companies, both white collar and industrial. Semimonthly newsletter; 4 pages. Pays on acceptance. Buys all rights. Phone queries OK. Submit seasonal/holiday material 4 months in advance of issue date. SASE. Reports in 2 weeks. Free sample copy and writer's guidelines.
Nonfiction: Interviews with personnel managers or human resource executives on topics of current interest in the personnel field. No articles on training programs, hiring and interviewing, or management development. Buys 30 mss/year. Query with brief, specific outline. Length: 800-1,000 words. Pays 10¢/word after editing.
Tips: "It's very easy to break in. Just query by phone or letter (preferable phone) and we'll discuss the topic. Especially need writers in the Midwest and West. Send for guidelines and sample first, though, so we can have a coherent conversation."

SALES MANAGER'S BULLETIN, The Bureau of Business Practice, 24 Rope Ferry Rd., Waterford CT 06386. Editor: James Cornell. For sales managers and salespeople interested in getting into sales management. Newsletter published twice a month; 8 pages. Pays on acceptance. Phone queries from regulars OK. Submit seasonal/holiday material 6 months in advance. Original submissions only. SASE. Reports in 2 weeks. Free sample copy and writer's guidelines only when accompanied by SASE.
Nonfiction: How-to (motivate salespeople, cut costs, create territories, etc.); interview (with working sales managers who use innovative techniques); and technical (marketing stories based on interviews with experts). No articles on territory management, saving fuel in the field, or public speaking skills. Break into this publication by reading their guidelines and sample issue. Follow their directions closely and chances for acceptance go up dramatically. One easy way to start is with an interview article ("Here's what sales executives have to say about . . ."). Buys 20-35 mss/year. Query is vital to acceptance; "send a simple postcard explaining briefly the subject matter, the interviewees (if any), slant, length, and date of expected completion, accompanied by a SASE." Length: 800-1,500. Pays 10-15¢/word.
Tips: "Freelancers should always request samples and writer's guidelines, accompanied by SASE. Requests without SASE are discarded immediately. Examine the sample, and don't try to improve on our style. Write as we write. The more time a writer can save the editors, the greater his or her chance of a sale and repeated sales, when queries may not be necessary any longer."

SECURITY MANAGEMENT, Bureau of Business Practice, 24 Rope Ferry Rd., Waterford CT 06386. Editor: Alex Vaughn. Emphasizes security for industry. "All material should be slanted toward security directors, preferably industrial, but some retail and institutional as well." Semimonthly newsletter; 4 pages. Circ. 3,000. Pays on acceptance. Buys all rights. Phone queries OK. Photocopied submissions OK. SASE. Reports in 2 weeks. Free sample copy and writer's guidelines.
Nonfiction: Interview (with security professionals only). "Articles should be tight and specific. They should deal with new security techniques or new twists on old ones." Buys 2 mss/issue. Query. Length: 750-1,000 words. Pays 10¢/word.

SUPERVISION, 424 N. 3rd St., Burlington IA 52601. Editor-in-Chief: Betty Beck. Managing Editor: M.A. Darnall. 65% freelance written. For first-line foremen, supervisors and office managers. Monthly magazine; 24 pages. Circ. 11,778. Pays on publication. Buys all rights. Previously published submissions OK. SASE. Reports in 3 weeks. Free sample copy and writer's guidelines; mention *Writer's Market* in request.

Nonfiction: How-to (cope with supervisory problems, discipline, absenteeism, safety, productivity, goal setting, etc.); personal experience (unusual success story of foreman or supervisor). Buys 7 mss/issue. Query. Length: 1,500-1,800 words. Pays up to 5¢/word.

Tips: "Query to be brief, but long enough to give a clear picture of material and approach being used. We are particularly interested in writers with first-hand experience—current or former supervisors who are also good writers. Following AP stylebook would be helpful, but at least follow some style. We give all submissions the same consideration. The important thing is, do you have something to say?"

TRAINING, The Magazine of Human Resources Development, 731 Hennepin Ave., Minneapolis MN 55403. (612)333-0471. Managing Editor: Dick Schaaf. Monthly magazine for persons who train people in business, industry, government and health care. Circ. 40,000. Rights purchased vary with author and material. Usually buys all rights. Buys 10-20 mss/year; pays on acceptance. Will consider photocopied submissions. No simultaneous submissions. Works three months in advance. Reports in 6 weeks. Query only. SASE. Write for sample copy and editorial guidelines.

Nonfiction and Photos: Articles on management and techniques of employee training. "Material should discuss a specific training problem or need; why the need existed, how it was met, alternatives considered, criteria for success, etc. Should furnish enough data for readers to make an independent judgment about the appropriateness of the solution and identify implications for their own situations. We want names and specific details on all techniques and programs used." Would like to see "articles relating general business concerns to specific training and development functions; interesting examples of successful training and management development programs; articles about why certain types of the above seem to fail; profiles of trainers who have moved into upper-level executive positions." Informational, how-to. Length: 1,200-2,000 words. Training Today: Reports on research, opinions or events of significance to human resources development professionals; length; 300-1,000. No extra payment for photos. Prefers b&w or color transparencies, with captions. Negotiates payment at time of assignment. Pays stipend to training and development professionals, more to qualified freelancers. Details in editorial guidelines.

UTILITY SUPERVISION, Bureau of Business Practice, 24 Rope Ferry Rd., Waterford CT 06386. (203)442-4365. Editor: Peter W. Hawkins. Emphasizes all aspects of utility supervision. Semi-monthly newsletter; 4 pages. Pays on acceptance. Buys all rights. Phone queries OK. Submit seasonal material 4 months in advance. SASE. Reports in 4-6 weeks. Free sample copy and writer's guidelines.

Nonfiction: Publishes how-to (interview on a single aspect of supervision with utility manager/supervisor concentrating on how reader/supervisor can improve in that area). Buys 100 mss/year. Query. Length: 500-1,000 words. Pays 8-12¢/word.

Photos: Purchased with accompanying ms. Pays $7.50 for b&w prints of "head and shoulders 'mug shot' of person interviewed." Total purchase price for ms includes payment for photos.

Tips: "Write solid interview articles on a single aspect of supervision in the utility field. Concentrate on how the reader/supervisor can improve his/her own performance in that area."

Marine Industries and Water Navigation

THE BOATING INDUSTRY, 850 3rd Ave., New York NY 10022. Editor: Charles A. Jones. For "boating retailers and distributors." Monthly. Circ. 26,000. Buys all rights. Byline given. Buys 10-15 mss/year. Pays on publication. "Best practice is to check with managing editor first on story ideas for go-ahead." Submit seasonal material 3-4 months in advance. Reports in 2 months. SASE.

Nonfiction and Photos: No clippings. Pays 7-10¢/word. B&w glossy photos purchased with mss.

CANADIAN SHIPPING AND MARINE ENGINEERING, 5200 Dixie Rd., Suite 204. Mississauga, Ontario, Canada L4W 1E4. Editor: Patrick Brophy. Monthly magazine covering ship building, repair and operation. Circ. 3,800. Pays on publication. Buys first Canadian rights. SAE and International Reply Coupons.

Nonfiction: "*Competent, authoritative*, technical or historical material dealing with maritime subjects of interest to Canadian readers." Query or send complete ms. Length: 1,000-2,000 words. Pays 10¢-12¢/word.

Photos: Uses 5x7 b&w prints and 35mm or larger color transparencies or prints with articles.

MARINE ENGINEERING/LOG, Simmons Boardman Publishing Co., 350 Broadway, New York NY 10013. (212)226-1186. Executive Editor: Lindley R. Higgins. Monthly magazine about marine engineering, naval architecture, and shipping for owners and operators of vessels, shipbuilders, marine engineers and naval architects. Circ. 27,000. Pays on publication. Byline given. Buys all rights. Phone queries OK. Photocopied submissions OK. Reports in 1 week. Free sample copy and writer's guidelines.
Nonfiction: Expose, general interest, interview, opinion, profile, how-to, photo feature and technical. Query. "Always send a short description of story first." Payment varies.
Photos: State availability of photos. Reviews 8x10 b&w glossy prints and color transparencies. Captions required.

SEAWAY REVIEW, The Business Magazine of the Great Lakes/St. Lawrence Seaway, Transportation System, Harbor Island, Maple City Postal Station MI 49664. Senior Editor: Jacques Les-Strang. Associate Editor: Michelle Cortright. 10% freelance written. For "the entire Great Lakes maritime community, executives of companies that ship via the Great Lakes, traffic managers, transportation executives, federal and state government officials and manufacturers of maritime equipment." Quarterly magazine; 108 pages. Circ. 15,500. Pays on publication. Buys first North American serial rights. Submit seasonal material 2 months in advance of issue date. Photocopied submissions OK. SASE. Reports in 3 weeks. Sample copy $2.
Nonfiction: "Articles dealing with Great Lakes shipping, shipbuilding, marine technology, economics of 8 states in Seaway region (Michigan, Minnesota, Illinois, Indiana, Ohio, New York, Pennsylvania and Wisconsin), and Canada, port operation, Seaway's role in economic development, historical articles dealing with Great Lakes shipping, current events dealing with commercial shipping on lakes, etc." Submit complete ms. Length: 1,000-2,000 words. Pay "varies with value of subject matter and knowledgeability of author, up to $250."
Photos: State availability of photos with query. Pays $10-50 for 8x10 glossy b&w prints; $10-100 for 8x10 glossy color prints. Captions required. Buys one-time rights. Buys "hundreds" of freelance photos each year.
Fillers: Clippings and spot news relating to ports and the Seaway system. Buys 3/issue. Length: 50-500 words. Pays $5-50.

THE WORK BOAT, H.L. Peace Publications, Box 2400, Covington LA 70434. (504)893-2930. Publisher/Editor: Harry L. Peace. Monthly. Buys all rights. Pays on acceptance. Query. Reports in 1 month. SASE. Samples copy $3; writer's guidelines for SASE.
Nonfiction: "Articles on waterways, river terminals, barge line operations, work boat construction and design, barges, offshore oil vessels and tugs. Best bet for freelancers: One-angle article showing in detail how a barge line, tug operator or dredging firm solves a problem of either mechanical or operational nature. This market is semitechnical and rather exacting. Such articles must be specific, containing firm name, location, officials of company, major equipment involved, by brand name, model, power, capacity and manufacturer; with color or b&w photos." Length: 1,000-2,000 words. Pays $150 minimum.
Photos: 5x5 or 5x7 b&w; 4x5 color prints only. No additional payment for photos accompanying ms. Captions and model release required. Buys one-time rights.

Medical

Publications aimed at the private physician, or that publish technical material on new discoveries in medicine, are classified here. Journals for nurses, laboratory technicians, hospital resident physicians, and other medical workers will be found with the Hospitals, Nursing, and Nursing Homes journals. Publications for druggists and drug wholesalers and retailers are grouped with the Drugs, Health Care, and Medical Products journals. Publications that report on medical trends for the consumer can be found in Health and Science categories.

AMERICAN FAMILY PHYSICIAN, 1740 W. 92nd St., Kansas City MO 64114. (816)333-9700. Publisher: Walter H. Kemp. Monthly. Circ. 130,000. Buys all rights. Pays on publication. "Most

articles are assigned and written by physicians." Query first "with a clear outline plus author's qualifications to write the article." Reports in 2 weeks. SASE.
Nonfiction: Interested only in clinical articles. Length: 2,500 words. Pays $50-250.

BEHAVIORAL MEDICINE, Magazines for Medicine, Inc., 475 5th Ave., New York NY 10017. (212)889-1050. Editor: Robert McCrie. Managing Editor: Beverly E. Martin. Emphasizes medical aspects of behavior for MDs in general and family practice, psychiatry and neurology. Monthly magazine; 48 pages. Circ. 96,000. Pays on publication. Buys second serial (reprint) rights. Phone queries OK. Simultaneous, photocopied and previously published submissions OK. SASE. Reports in 1 month. Sample copy $2.50; free writer's guidelines.
Nonfiction: Technical pieces; study recent issues. Buys 1-3 unsolicited mss/issue. Query. Pays $150-500.
Photos: "We have one photo article per issue at least." Uses b&w prints and color transparencies. Offers no additional payment for photos accepted with ms; however, photo articles go for higher rates to established sources. Captions required. Buys one-time rights.
Tips: "Submit contributions (queries preferred) in duplicate, if possible, being sure to stress how the article will provide practical, informative, and specific procedures to help PCP's deal more effectively with their patients. MD co-author generally desired. Articles based on new, fresh approaches and behavioral techniques are particularly interesting to us."

CANADIAN DOCTOR, 310 Victoria Ave., Suite 201, Montreal, Quebec, Canada H3Z 2M9. (514)487-2302. Editor-in-Chief: Peter N. Williamson. Assistant Editor: Fran Lowry. Monthly magazine; 100 pages. Circ. 34,000. Pays on publication. Buys all rights. Byline given. SAE and International Reply Coupons are essential for return of material. Reports in 3 weeks. Free sample copy and writer's guidelines.
Nonfiction: How-to (run a physician's practice efficiently); interview (with Canadian doctors, perhaps those who have moved to US); personal experience (from Canadian doctors); personal opinion (from Canadian doctor about the profession); profile (of Canadian doctor); and travel (only on assignment). Query with outline of article, "preferably in point form so that editors can add/change to meet needs." Length: 500-2,500 words. Pays $25-150.
Photos: State availability of photos with query. Pays $15 for b&w glossy prints. Captions required. Buys one-time rights. Model release required.
Tips: "We are a Canadian magazine aimed at a Canadian audience, 34,000+. We have different problems (a health insurance scheme for one, based on fee-for-service), but we can learn about medical business management from anywhere."

DIAGNOSTIC IMAGING, Miller Freeman, 500 Howard St., San Francisco CA 94105. Editor: Thomas Kemp. Managing Editor: Paul Brown. Monthly news magazine covering radiology, nuclear medicine and ultrasound for physicians and chief technicians in diagnostic professions. Estab. 1979. Circ. 26,000. Average issue includes 2-3 features. Pays on acceptance. Byline given. Buys all rights. Phone queries OK. "Written query should be well written, concise and contain a brief outine of proposed article and a description of the approach or perspective the author is taking." Submit seasonal material 1 month in advance. Simultaneous and photocopied submissions OK. SASE. Reports in 2 weeks. Free sample copy.
Nonfiction: "We are interested in topical news features in the areas of radiology, nuclear medicine, and ultrasound, especially news of state and federal legislation, new products, insurance, regulations, medical literature, professional meetings and symposia and continuing education." Buys 10-12 mss/year. Query with clips of previously published work. Length: 1,000-2,000 words. Pays 10¢/word minimum.
Photos: Reviews 5x7 b&w glossy prints and 35mm and larger color transparencies. Offers no additional payment for photos accepted with ms. Captions required. Buys one-time rights.

DRUG THERAPY MEDICAL JOURNAL, Biomedical Information Corp., 800 2nd Ave., New York NY 10017. (212)599-3400. Editorial Directors: Ellen H. Datloff, Edwin S. Geffner. Published in 2 editions: office edition for office based physicians; hospital edition for resident and staff physicians and hospital pharmacists. Emphasizes drug therapy for physicians in all clinical specialties as well as internists, residents and attendants in the hospital setting throughout the US. Monthly magazine; 175 pages. Circ. 140,000, office edition; 100,000, hospital edition. Pays on publication. Phone queries OK. Submit seasonal or holiday material 4 months in advance. Photocopied submissions OK. Previously published graphic material acceptable as long as reprint rights are clear. SASE. Reports in 1-3 weeks. Free sample copy and editorial guidelines.
Nonfiction: How-to (diagnosis and treatment as clinical entity); informational (use of drugs, new drugs, how a drug works, etc.). Technical and new product articles. Buys 10-15 mss/issue. Query. Length: 1,000 words minimum. Pays $300.

Photos: No additional payment for b&w or color used with mss.
Tips: "Most of our major articles are physician-authored. The type of material written by a nonscientist that we would consider might include brief items for our news and features columns (e.g., a 250-400 word report on a national medical meeting, new research breakthrough, etc.)."

FACETS, American Medical Association Auxiliary, Inc., 535 N. Dearborn St., Chicago IL 60610. (312)751-6166. Editor: Kathleen T. Jordan. For physicians' spouses. Magazine published 5 times/year; 32 pages. Circ. 90,000. Pays on acceptance. Buys first rights. Submit seasonal/holiday material 4 months in advance of issue date. Simultaneous, photocopied and previously published submissions OK. SASE. Reports in 6 weeks. Free sample copy and writer's guidelines.
Nonfiction: All articles must be related to the experiences of physicians' wives. Current health issues; financial topics; physicians' family circumstances and business management. No leadership how-to's. Buys 8 mss/year. Query with clear outline of article—what points will be made, what conclusions drawn, what sources will be used. Length: 1,000-2,500 words. Pays $300-600.
Photos: State availability of photos with query. Uses 8x10 glossy b&w prints and 2¼x2¼ color transparencies.
Tips: Uses "articles only on specified topical matter; with good sources, not hearsay or opinion, but credibility. Since we use only nonfiction articles and have a limited readership, we must relate factual material."

GENETIC ENGINEERING NEWS, The Information Source of the Biotechnology Industry, Mary Ann Liebert, Inc., 500 E. 85th St., New York NY 10028. (212)988-0743. Editor: Mr. Chris Weathersbee. Bimonthly tabloid featuring articles on industry and research in all areas of biotechnology such as recombinant DNA and hybridoma technology. Estab. 1981. Circ. 10,000. Pays on publication. Byline given. Buys all rights. Previously published submissions OK. SASE. Reports in 3 weeks on queries; 1 month on mss. Free sample copy and writer's guidelines for 9x12 SAE and 4 first class stamps.
Nonfiction: Interview/profile (of corporate executives, academicians or researchers); new product; technical (any articles relating to biotechnology with emphasis on application); and financial (Wall Street analysis, etc.—of new companies). Buys 75 mss/year. Query with clips of published work. Length: 1,000-1,200 words. Pays $150 minimum. "All negotiable."
Photos: Send photos with ms. Pays negotiable fee for b&w contact sheets. Identification of subjects required.
Tips: "Writers submitting queries must be extremely knowledgeable in the field and have direct access to hard news."

LAB WORLD, North American Publishing Co., 401 N. Broad St., Philadelphia PA 19108. (215)574-9600. Editorial Director and Publisher: A.E. Woolley, PhD. 50% freelance written. Emphasizes laboratory medicine for pathologists, lab chiefs, medical technologists, medical technicians and other staff members of laboratories. Monthly magazine; 100 pages. Circ. 62,000. Pays on acceptance. Buys first North American serial or one-time rights. Submit seasonal/holiday material 4-6 months in advance of issue date. SASE. Reports in 2 weeks. Sample copy $2.50.
Nonfiction: All articles must pertain to the laboratory field. General interest; humor; inspirational; interview; photo feature; and profile. No technical papers. Buys 20-50 mss/year. Query. Length: 750-7,000 words. Pays $100-300.
Photos: State availability of photos with query. Pays $50-150 for 5x7 or 8x10 b&w semigloss photos; $100-200 for 35mm color transparencies. Captions and model release required. Buys one-time rights.

THE MAYO ALUMNUS, Mayo Clinic, 200 SW 1st St., Rochester MN 55901. (507)284-2511. Editor: David E. Swanson. For physicians, scientists, and medical educators who trained at the Mayo Clinic. Quarterly magazine; 40 pages. Circ. 10,000. Pays on acceptance. Buys all rights. Phone queries OK. Submit seasonal/holiday material 6 months in advance of issue date. Previously published submissions OK. SASE. Reports in 2 months. Free sample copy; mention *Writer's Market* in request.
Nonfiction: "We're interested in seeing interviews with members of the Mayo Alumni Association—stories about Mayo-trained doctors/educators/scientists/researchers who are interesting people doing interesting things in medicine, surgery or hobbies of interest, etc." Query with clips of published work. Length: 1,000-3,000 words. Pays 15¢/word, first 1,500 words. Maximum payment is $275.
Photos: "We need art and must make arrangements if not provided with the story." Pays $10 for b&w photos. State availability of photos with query. Captions preferred. Buys all rights.

MEDICAL ECONOMICS, 680 Kinderkamack Rd., Oradell NJ 07649. (201)262-3030. Editor-in-Chief: Don L. Berg. Executive Editor: James D. Hendricks. Emphasizes "the business side of medical practice for office-based physicians in private practice." Biweekly magazine; 200-300 pages. Circ. 170,000. Pays on acceptance. Buys all rights. Pays kill fee. Byline given "except when a story is so poorly done that it has to be extensively rewritten or re-researched." Submit seasonal/ holiday material 4 months in advance of issue date. Previously published submissions OK. SASE. Reports in 4 weeks. Free sample copy and writer's guidelines.

Nonfiction: Lilian Fine, senior editor. "Articles tell the doctor how to manage his practice, his financial affairs, and his dealings with fellow professionals. Major subjects include medicolegal matters, health legislation, office and personnel management, investments, fees, hospital problems, taxes, cars and doctor-patient relations. The subject matter is nonmedical, nonclinical and nondiagnostic." Buys 18 mss/year. Query. Length: 1,000-3,000 words. Pays $500-1,500.

Fillers: Humorous medical anecdotes. Buys 100-150/year. Length: 250 words maximum. Pays $30-35.

Tips: "Clean, brightly written, articles that directly and immediately address our audience and tell doctors why they need this information—these will be the best bet for us."

THE MEDICAL POST, 481 University Ave., Toronto, Ontario, Canada M5W 1A7. Editor: Derek Cassels. For the medical profession. Biweekly. Will send sample copy to medical writers only. Buys first Canadian serial rights. Pays on publication. SAE and International Reply Coupons.

Nonfiction: Uses newsy, factual reports of medical developments. Must be aimed at professional audience, and written in newspaper style. Length: 300-800 words. Pays 14¢/word.

Photos: Uses photos with mss or captions only, of medical interest; pays $10 up.

THE NEW PHYSICIAN, 14650 Lee Rd., Chantilly VA 22021. Editor: Todd Dankmyer. 25% freelance written. For medical students, interns and residents. Monthly magazine; 64 pages. Circ. 75,000. Buys all rights. Buys 6-12 mss/year. Pays on publication. Free sample copy. Will consider simultaneous submissions. Reports in 4-8 weeks. Query. SASE.

Nonfiction and Photos: "Articles on social, political, economic issues in medicine/medical education. Our readers need more than a superficial, simplistic look into issues that affect them. We want skeptical, accurate, professional contributors to do well-researched, comprehensive reports, and offer new perspectives on health care problems." Not interested in material on "my operation," or encounters with physicians, or personal experiences as physician's patient. Occasionally publishes special topic issues, such as those on death and dying and alternatives in medical training. Informational articles, interviews and exposes are sought. Length: 500-2,500 words. Pays $25-300. Pays $10-35 for b&w photos used with mss. Captions required.

Tips: "Our magazine demands real sophistication on the issues we cover because we are a professional journal. Those freelancers we publish reveal in their queries and ultimately in their mss a willingness and an ability to look deeply into the issues in question and not be satisfied with a cursory review of those issues."

PHYSICIAN'S MANAGEMENT, Harcourt Brace Jovanovich Health Care Publications, 757 3rd Ave., New York NY 10017. (212)888-2938. Editor: Jim Hayes. Emphasizes finances, investments, small office administration, practice management and taxes for physicians in private practice. Monthly magazine; 148 pages. Circ. 105,000. Pays on acceptance. Buys all rights. Submit seasonal or holiday material 5 months in advance. SASE. Reports in 2-4 weeks.

Nonfiction: *"Physician's Management* is a socio-economic publication, not a clinical one." Publishes how-to articles (limited to medical practice management); informational (when relevant to audience); personal experience articles (if written by a physician). Length: 500-3,000 words. Buys 15-20/issue. Query. Pays $50-500.

Tips: "Talk to doctors first about their practices, financial interests, and day-to-day nonclinical problems and then query us. Use of an MD byline helps tremendously! Also, the ability to write a concise, well-structured and well-researched magazine article is essential. Most freelancers think like patients and fail with us. Those who can think like MDs are successful."

PRIVATE PRACTICE, Box 12489, Oklahoma City OK 73157. Executive Editor: Terri T. Burke. For "medical doctors in private practice." Monthly. Buys first North American serial rights. "If an article is assigned, it is paid for in full, used or killed." Byline given "except if it was completely rewritten or a considerable amount of additional material is added to the article." Pays on acceptance. Query. SASE.

Nonfiction and Photos: "Articles that indicate importance of maintaining freedom of medical practice or which detail outside interferences in the practice of medicine, including research, hospital operation, drug manufacture, etc. Straight reporting style. No cliches, no scare words, no flowery phrases to cover up poor reporting. Stories must be actual, factual, precise, correct. Copy should be lively and easy-to-read. Also publish travel, sports, leisure, historical, offbeat, and

humorous articles of medical interest." Length: up to 2,500 words. Pays "usual minimum $150."
Photos purchased with mss only. B&w glossies, 8x10. Payment "depends on quality, relevancy of
material, etc."
Tips: "The article we are most likely to buy will be a straight report on some situation where the
freedom to practice medicine has been enhanced, or where it has been intruded on to the detri-
ment of good health."

SURGICAL BUSINESS, Box 1487, Union NJ 07083. Editor: David Cassak. For medical/surgical
dealers and dealer/salesmen. Monthly magazine; 92 pages. Circ. 7,000. Buys exclusive industry
rights. Byline given. Buys 5-10 mss/year. Pays on publication. Free sample copy and writer's
guidelines. Will consider photocopied and simultaneous submissions. Query or submit complete
ms. SASE.
Nonfiction and Photos: "We publish articles touching on all aspects of healthcare supply, from
company and individual profiles to market studies, and from government regulatory action and its
impact to coming trends. We are also interested in new technologies and products, but from a
marketing perspective, not a technical one. Keep in mind that we deal with the marketing (or
selling) of healthcare supplies to hospitals, doctors, and the home healthcare trade, and that our
readers are, for the most part, sophisticated businessmen. We insist that submitted articles demonstrate an understanding of the issues that affect the industry." No general articles on finances
(especially around tax time) or selling that could apply to a variety of fields. No additional
payment for b&w photos used with mss. Length: approximately 2,500 words. Pays 5¢/word.
Tips: "We are always eager to receive quality freelance submissions and would gladly enter into a
long-term arrangement with a freelancer whose work we like. Submitted articles can relieve a
burden on our own staff and give our publication a wider perspective. The problem we encounter
with most freelancers, however, quality of writing aside, is that they want to write general articles
that they can submit to a number of publications, and thus do not want to write articles of
sufficient sophistication for our readers. Simply put, the articles are so general in approach, they
rarely provide any real information at all for anyone even slightly exposed to the field. Know
either the publication or the field. We encourage freelancers to write for a sample copy of our
publication."

Mining and Minerals

AMERICAN GOLD NEWS, Box 457, Ione CA 95640. (209)274-2196. Editor: Cecil L. Helms. 25%
freelance written. For anyone interested in gold, gold mining, gold companies, gold stocks, gold
history, gold coins, the future of gold in our economy. Monthly tabloid newspaper; 20 pages. Circ.
3,500. Not copyrighted. Byline given. Pays on publication. Sample copy and writer's guidelines for
$1. No photocopied or simultaneous submissions. Submit seasonal material (relating to seasonal
times in mining country) 2 months in advance. Reports in 2-4 weeks. Query or submit complete
ms. SASE.
Nonfiction and Photos: "This is not a literary publication. We want information on any subject
pertaining to gold told in the most simple, direct and interesting way. How to build gold mining
equipment. History of mines (with pix). History of gold throughout the US. Financial articles on
gold philosophy in money matters. Picture stories of mines, mining towns, mining country. Would
like to see more histories of mines, from any state. Length: 500-2,000 words. Pays $10-50. B&w
photos purchased with or without ms. Must be sharp (if not old historical photos). Pays $2.50-25.
Captions required.

COAL AGE, 1221 Avenue of the Americas, New York NY 10020. Editor: Joseph F. Wilkinson.
For supervisors, engineers and executives in coal mining. Monthly. Circ. 20,000. Buys all rights.
Pays on publication. Query. Reports in 2-3 weeks. SASE.
Nonfiction: Uses some technical (operating type) articles; some how-to pieces on equipment
maintenance; management articles. Pays $200/page.

KENTUCKY COAL JOURNAL, 115 Tanglewood Dr., Frankfort KY 40601. (502)223-1619. Editor: Ken Hart. Monthly tabloid about coal mining: specifically the constrictions placed on the
industry by federal and state bureaus regulating it, and market conditions. Circ. 9,000. Pays on
publication. Byline given. Buys one-time rights. Phone queries OK. Submit seasonal material 1
month in advance. Photocopied and previously published submissions OK. Reports in 1 week.
Free sample copy.

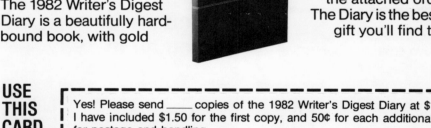

Nonfiction: Exposé (of government); historical (of old coal mines); opinion; profile (of Kentucky coal mines and miners); humor; new product (revolutionary); and photo feature. "We have been called an example of 'personal journalism' meaning we inject comments, viewpoints, etc., into just about anything that's printed. We first took up for the small, independent operator; now we have become the unofficial spokesman for the entire Kentucky coal industry, although our circulation is national." No fictional or highly technical articles. Buys 2-3 mss/issue. Send complete ms. Length: 300 words minimum. Pays $25-300.
Photos: State availability of photos. Pay $15 minimum for any size b&w glossy prints. Captions required. Buys one-time rights.
Tips: "Tell us about a unique coal venture, mine or person. Tell us how to bust a particular bureaucracy. Or write a timely, factual story that fits into our editorial philosophy. We do not object to an adversary point of view, but no diatribes, please. If you have a valid and logical reason for opposing something, fine. Reading a copy of the *Coal Journal* will help."

Miscellaneous

A.I.D. (ALARM INSTALLER AND DEALER), Fortuna Publishing, Inc., Box 9200, Calabasas CA 91302. Editor: Robert J. Bargert. Monthly magazine covering the alarm industry for alarm installers, dealers, distributors and manufacturers. Estab. 1979. Circ. 12,000. Pays on publication. Buys all rights. Submit seasonal material 6 weeks in advance. Reports in 2 weeks. SASE. Free sample copy.
Nonfiction: Exposé; general interest; how-to; interview; new product; photo feature; and technical. "We are interested in articles about state, regional and national legislation, cities considering ordinances, case history success stories, and women in the alarm industry. We are most interested in industry news from the East Coast and the Midwest; also good case history success stories from dealers in these areas." Query. Length: 300-3,000 words. Pays $25-500.
Photos: State availability of photos. Pays $1-20 for 8x10 glossy prints and $15-30 for 4x5 color glossy prints and 35mm transparencies. Captions and model release required. Buys all rights.
Columns/Departments: Interested in industry news. Send complete ms. Length: 150-300 words. Pays $25 minimum.
Fillers: Clippings. Length: 100-300 words. Pays $5-15.

AMERICAN CHRISTMAS TREE JOURNAL, 611 E. Wells St., Milwaukee WI 53202. (414)276-6410. Editors: Phil Jones and Jane A. Svinicki. Quarterly magazine. Circ. 1,800-2,000. Byline given. Pays on publication. Simultaneous, photocopied and previously published submissions OK. Reports in 1 month. Free sample copy and writer's guidelines.
Nonfiction: How-to, interview, job safety (any farm equipment); vocational techniques, new product (chemicals, equipment, tags, shearing knives and chain saws, etc.); personal experience, profile and technical (foresters, researchers). Query. Length: 2,000 words minimum. Pays $50.

THE ANTIQUES DEALER, 1115 Clifton Ave., Clifton NJ 07013. (201)779-1600. Editor: Kathy Moor O'Brien. 90% freelance written. For antiques dealers. Monthly magazine. Circ. 7,000. Average issue includes 4 features, 5 columns. Rights purchased vary with author and material. Buys all rights. Byline given. Buys 40 mss a year. Pays on publication. Submit seasonal/holiday material 4 months in advance. Will send free sample copy to writer on request. Will consider previously published and photocopied submissions "if clear". Reports in 3 weeks. SASE.
Nonfiction: "Remember that we are a trade publication and all material must be slanted to the needs and interests of antique dealers. We publish nothing of a too general ('be a good salesman') or too limited (eastern Pennsylvania chairs) nature." Only articles of national interest to dealers; may be tutorial if by authority in one specific field (how to restore antiques; open a dealership; locate a specific antique); otherwise of broad general interest to all dealers and news of the international antique trade. Emphasis is currently on heirlooms (50-100 years old), as well as antiques (over 100 years old). Buys 2 mss/issue. Length: minimum 500 words; maximum 2-part article, about 7,000 words; 3,500 words if one-part. Pays $50/page for features; $1.50/inch for small items. Columns cover trade news; anything from a couple of sentences to about 200 words, with photo or two.
Photos: Purchased with or without accompanying mss, or on assignment. Pays $5 per b&w used inside, $10 for covers; no smaller than 5x7 (glossy). Professional quality only; no Polaroids.
Fillers: Suitable for professional dealers; any type of fillers. Length: 300-400 words. Pays approximately $15 for half-page.
Tips: "It is more important that the writer knows his subject well, as a specialist or one interviewing

a specialist, than his writing prowess. But I am looking for good business journalists who can cover news and interviews well."

APA MONITOR, 1200 17th St. NW, Washington DC 20036. Editor: Pam Moore. Managing Editor: Karen Schaar. For psychologists and other social scientists and professionals interested in behaviorial sciences and mental health area. Monthly newspaper combined June/July, August/September. Circ. 67,000. Buys all rights. Pays on publication. Free sample copy.
Nonfiction: News and feature articles about issues facing psychology both as a science and a mental health profession; political, social and economic developments in the behavioral sciences area. Interview, profile, humor, historical, interpretive and think pieces. Buys about 35 mss/year. Query. Length; 300-3,000 words.

ASSOCIATION & SOCIETY MANAGER, Brentwood Publishing Corp., 825 S. Barrington Ave., Los Angeles CA 90049. (213)826-8388. Bimonthly magazine covering associations and societies for managers. Pays "between acceptance and publication." Buys all rights. SASE. Reports "when an assignment is available." Send clips of published work and resume. "Do not query with specific article ideas. All articles are assigned."

C & S (Casket and Sunnyside), NB Enterprises, 274 Madison Ave., New York NY 10016. (212)685-8310. Editor: Howard Barnard. 10% freelance written. "This magazine is circulated to funeral directors of all ages, more and more who are becoming college educated." Published 10 times/year; 48 pages. Circ. 8,500. Pays on publication. Buys all rights. Byline given. Phone queries OK. Submit seasonal/holiday material 2 months in advance of issue date. SASE. Reports in 2 weeks.
Nonfiction: General interest (stories on mortuaries); historical (articles dealing with embalming, early funeral vehicles and ambulances, etc.); how-to (handle difficult or unusual restorative art or embalming cases); inspirational (public relations achievements); and "short items or new products in the funeral field." Buys 20 mss/year. Query. Length: 2,500-3,500 words. Pays $75.
Photos: State availability of photos with query. Pays $5 for 5x7 or 8x10 b&w prints. Captions required. Buys all rights.
Fillers: Clippings, obituaries and items concerning various activities of funeral directors. Buys 10-15/issue. Pays $3.
Tips: "We appreciate a straightforward inquiry, indicating concisely what the author proposes to write about. We are interested in receiving stories on new or remodeled mortuaries."

CANADIAN FUNERAL DIRECTOR, Peter Perry Publishing, Ltd., 1658 Victoria Park Ave., Suite 5, Scarboro, Ontario, Canada M1R 1P7. (416)755-7050. Managing Editor: Peter Perry. 15% freelance written. Emphasizes funeral home operation. Monthly magazine; 60 pages. Circ. 1,700. Pays on publication. Buys one-time rights. Byline given. Phone queries OK. Reports in 30-60 days. Simultaneous and photocopied submissions and previously published work OK. SASE. Reports in 3 weeks. Free sample copy.
Nonfiction: Informational, historical, humor, interview, personal opinion, profile, photo feature, technical. Buys 12 mss a year. Query. Length: 200-1,500 words. Pays $75/1,000 words.
Photos: Purchased with or without ms. Captions required. Query or send contact sheet. Pays $5-10/5x7 or 8x10 b&w glossies.
Tips: "Canadian writers only need query, with Canadian subject material."

CHINA BUSINESS REVIEW, National Council for US China Trade, 17th St. NW, Suite 350, Washington DC 20036. (202)828-8300. Editor: Jim Stepanek. Bimonthly magazine covering "US-China trade development, and China's economy and foreign trade policies for firms that engage in US-China trade—primarily members of the National Council for US-China Trade." Circ. 10,000. Pays on publication. Byline given. Buys all rights. SASE. Reports in 2 weeks. Sample copy $10.
Nonfiction: "Writers in the field will know what our interest is." Buys 6 mss/year. Query "by phone or letter." Length: 5,000 words maximum. Pays negotiable fee.
Photos: State availability of photos. Pays negotiable fee for 35mm color transparencies and 8x10 b&w glossy prints. Captions required.

COLLEGE UNION MAGAZINE, 825 Old Country Rd., Box 1500, Westbury NY 11590. Managing Editor: Marcy Kornreich. Emphasizes leisure time aspects of college life for campus activity and service professionals. Published 6 times/year. Estab. 1979. Circ. 10,000. Pays on publication. Buys all rights. Must query. Photocopied submissions OK. Reports in 3 weeks on queries.
Nonfiction: General interest (food service, student alcoholism, vending, refurbishing building); historical (history of a particular school's union); how-to (run or operate any aspect of student activities); interview (director of student activities); profiles (of particular school's operation and

director of college union); personal experience (within college union work); and photo feature (operations, machine room, cultural program, whole building, lobby, theater, ballroom). Query. Length: 1,500 words maximum. Pays $2/column inch.
Photos: Pays $5-10 for 5x7 b&w prints and contact sheets.
Columns/Departments: Pinpoint (trends in campus life). Query. Length: 50-200 words.
Tips: "Submit articles aimed at professional employees who operate college unions, not students."

COLLEGIATE CAREER WOMAN, Equal Opportunity Publications, Inc., 44 Broadway, Greenlawn NY 11740. (516)261-8899. Editorial Director: Paul Podgus. Editor: Chris Podgus. Magazine published 3 times/year ("fall, winter, spring; geared to college year") covering career guidance for college women. Strives "to aid women in developing career abilities to the fullest potential; improve job hunting skills; present career opportunities; provide personal resources; help cope with discrimination." Audience is 85% college juniors and seniors, 15% working graduates. Circ. 10,500. "Controlled circulation, distributed through college guidance and placement offices." Pays on acceptance or publication, "negotiable." Byline given. Kill fee "discussed on individual basis." Buys first North American serial rights; one-time rights; all rights; simultaneous rights; first rights; second serial (reprint) rights; as required. "Deadline dates: fall, July 28; winter, October 27; spring, February 10. Submit seasonal/holiday material 1 month in advance. Simultaneous queries, and simultaneous, photocopied and previously published submissions OK. Reports in 2 weeks on queries; 3 weeks on mss. Free sample copy and writer's guidelines.
Nonfiction: Christopher Podgus, editor. Book excerpts (on self-improvement, role models, success stories, employment helps); general interest (on special concerns of women); historical/nostalgic (on women's achievements, progress, and hopes for the future); how-to (on self-evaluation, job-finding skills, adjustment, coping with the real world); humor (student or career related); inspirational (encouragement and guidance); interview/profile (of successful career women, outstanding students); new product (new career opportunities); opinion (on women's progress, male attitudes, discrimination); personal experience (student and career experiences); technical (on career fields offering opportunities for women); travel (on overseas job opportunities); and contributions to the development of the whole person. Special issues include career opportunities for liberal arts graduates. "Fiction, religion, and politics are not our concern. (Politics in the sense of promotion of any party or politician.)" Buys 15-21 mss/year. Query, query with clips of published work or send complete ms. Length: 1,250-5,000 words. Pays $125-650; "negotiable, according to subject and writer."
Photos: Christopher Podgus, photo editor. Pays $25-150 for color transparencies and prints; $200 maximum for color covers; $25-50 for b&w contact sheets or prints. Captions, model release and identification of subjects required, "if necessary." Buys one-time rights, all rights, and other rights "as needed and available."

EMERGENCY, Box 159, Carlsbad CA 92008. Managing Editor: Donna Mann. 40% freelance written. Emphasizes emergency medical services for anyone involved in emergency services, including ambulance personnel, paramedics, search and rescue personnel, emergency room personnel, law enforcement personnel and firefighters. Monthly magazine; 84 pages. Circ. 40,000. Pays on publication. Buys all rights. Byline and biographical information given. Submit seasonal/holiday material 4 months in advance of issue date. SASE. Reports in 2 months. Free sample copy and writer's guidelines.
Nonfiction: How-to (better execute a certain emergency procedure; guidelines for emergency medical techniques). Buys 3 mss/issue. Query. Length: 800-3,000 words. Pays $50-175.
Photos: State availability of photos with query. Pays $15 minimum for 5x7 b&w glossy prints; $25-35 for 35mm color transparencies. Captions required. Buys all rights. Buys 4-6 cover color transparencies/year. Pays $100-150.
Columns/Departments: News Briefs (short items of interest to emergency personnel); and Funds and Grants (allocated for improvement of emergency care). Buys 10/year. Query. Length: 50-100 words. Pays $1/inch. Open to suggestions for new columns/departments.
Tips: "All articles are carefully reviewed; therefore, any well-written article, especially one including 35mm transparencies, has a good chance of being published."

EQUAL OPPORTUNITY, The Nation's Only Multi-Ethnic Recruitment Magazine for Black, Hispanic, Native American & Asian College Grads, Equal Opportunity Publications, Inc., 44 Broadway, Greenlawn NY 11740. (516)261-8899. Editorial Director: Paul Podgus. Editor: Chris Podgus. Magazine published 3 times/year ("fall, winter, spring; geared to college academic year") covering career guidance for minorities of ethnic origin. "Our audience is 90% college juniors and seniors, 10% working graduates. An understanding of educational and career problems of minorities is essential." Circ. 15,000. "Controlled circulation, distributed through college guidance and placement offices." Pays on acceptance or publication, "negotiable." Byline given. Kill fee "discussed on individual basis." Buys first North American serial rights; one-time rights; all rights; simultaneous rights; first rights; second serial (reprint) rights; others as available. "Deadline dates: fall, August 11; winter, November 10; spring, February 20. Submit seasonal/holiday material 1 month in advance. Simultaneous queries, and simultaneous, photocopied and previously published submissions OK. Reports in 2 weeks on queries; 3 weeks on mss. Free sample copy and writer's guidelines.

Nonfiction: Book excerpts and articles (on self-improvement, role models); general interest (on specific minority concerns); historical/nostalgic; how-to (on job-hunting skills, personal finance, better living, adjustment, coping with discrimination); humor (student or career related); inspirational (on thought, leader encouragement and guidance); interview/profile (minority role models); new product (new career opportunities); opinion (problems of ethnic minorities); personal experience (professional and student study and career experiences); technical (on career fields offering opportunities for ethnic minorities); travel (on overseas job opportunities); and coverage of black, Hispanic, American Indian and Asian interest. Special issues include career opportunities for liberal arts graduates. No "religion, politics and sex (the other kind, not women's rights), rabid racism of any kind." Buys 16-25 mss/year. Query, or query with clips of published work. Length: 1,250-5,000 words. Pays $125-650; "negotiable, art availability is a factor."

Photos: Pays $25-50 for b&w contact sheets or prints; $25-150 for color transparencies or prints (covers additional). Captions, model release and identification of subjects required, "if necessary." Buys one-time rights, all rights, and other rights "as available."

FREELANCE ART MONTHLY, Alexander Publishing Co., 540 Frontage Rd., Suite 303, Northfield IL 60093. (312)446-6190. Editor: Paul A. Casper. Managing Editor: Eileen Sullivan. Monthly magazine covering the entire graphics industry; a marketplace for freelance artists and photographers and art buyers. Pays on acceptance. Byline given. Buys one-time rights. Simultaneous queries, and simultaneous and photocopied submissions OK. SASE. Reports in 2 weeks. Sample copy $3; writer's guidelines for business size envelope and 1 first class stamp.

Nonfiction: Eileen Sullivan, articles editor. General interest (only to the graphics industry); how-to (put together technical illustrations: only commercial art areas); and interview/profile (with unusual or well-known creative illustrators or graphic designers). No fine art. Query with clips of published work. Length: 750 words minimum. Pays $50-100.

Photos: Kathy Casper, photo editor. State availability of photos. Reviews 8x10 b&w prints. Captions required.

Columns/Departments: Query. Length: 300 words minimum.

THE GRANTSMANSHIP CENTER NEWS, The Grantsmanship Center, 1031 S. Grand Ave., Los Angeles CA 90015. (213)749-4721. Acting Editor: Cathleen Collins. Emphasizes funding, philanthropy, grants process and nonprofit management for professionals involved in government or foundation grant making or grant seeking. Bimonthly magazine; 104 pages. Circ. 25,000. Pays on acceptance. Makes assignments on a work-for-hire basis. Pays variable kill fee. Byline given. Simultaneous, photocopied and previously published submissions OK. SASE. Reports in 2 months. Sample copy $3.25.

Nonfiction: Exposé, general interest, how-to and interview. "Familiarity with the field is an asset." Buys 2-3 mss/issue. Query with clips of published work. Length: 1,500-10,000 words. Pays 10¢/word minimum.

Photos: State availability of photos. Uses b&w contact sheets and color transparencies. Offers no additional payment for photos accepted with ms. Captions preferred; model release required. Buys all rights.

HOUSEHOLD AND PERSONAL PRODUCTS INDUSTRY, 26 Lake St., Ramsey NJ 07446. Editor: Hamilton C. Carson. 5-10% freelance written. For "manufacturers of soaps, detergents, cosmetics and toiletries, waxes and polishes, insecticides, and aerosols." Monthly. Circ. 14,000. Not copyrighted. Buys 3 to 4 mss a year, "but would buy more if slanted to our needs." Pays on publication. Will send a sample copy to a writer on request. Will consider photocopied submissions. Submit seasonal material 2 months in advance. Query. SASE.

Nonfiction and Photos: "Technical and semitechnical articles on manufacturing, distribution, marketing, new products, plant stories, etc., of the industries served. Some knowledge of the field is essential in writing for us." Buys informational articles, interviews, photo features, spot news, coverage of successful business operations, new product articles, coverage of merchandising techniques, and technical articles. Query with clips of published work. Length: 500-2,000 words. Pays $10-200. 5x7 or 8x10 b&w glossies purchased with mss. Pays $10.

THE INDIAN TRADER, Box 867, Gallup NM (505)722-3493. Publisher: Chester MacRorie. 70% freelance written. For traders in the Indian arts, crafts and culture. Monthly tabloid; 72 pages.

Circ. 10,000. Pays on publication. Buys all rights. Byline given "if the writer requests it and if their reason is valid. We do not byline short advances—mostly the coverage of events, features, and lengthy how-to-do articles." Phone queries OK. Submit seasonal/holiday material 2 months in advance. Reports in 3-6 weeks. Free sample copy and writer's guidelines.

Nonfiction: Historical (must be accurately researched and of special interest to collectors of Indian artifacts, traders, or those interested in current American activities); informational (characters of historical interest, their descendants, etc.); interviews (with exceptional Indian craftsmen, collectors, shows, pow-wows, etc.); photo features (coverage of Indian affairs, reservation happenings, etc.); and travel (visits to Indian ruins, trading posts, similar material in areas of the Northwest or Northeast, or Canada). Buys 8-10 mss/issue. Pays $1.50/column inch. "This usually works out to about 2-4¢/word, but we do pay by the column inch. We pay between $300-400 for a cover story."

Photos: B&w (8x10) glossies preferred. Purchased with or without mss or on assignment. Captions optional, but information must be included if captionless. Query or send prints. Pays $2-15 when additional payment is made. Total purchase price sometimes includes payment for photos.

Columns/Departments: Buys 1-3 book reviews/issue. Query. Pays $1.50/column inch.

Tips: "Factual material favored. Indian legends, etc., accurately researched and sources are needed."

INDUSTRIAL CHEMICAL NEWS, Bill Communications, 633 3rd Ave., New York NY 10025. (212)986-4800. Editor: Irvin Schwartz. Managing Editor: Suzanne Lavenas. Monthly magazine covering the scientific, business industrial aspects of chemistry for chemists working in industry. Estab. 1980. Circ. 20,000. Pays on publication. Byline given. Pays $100 kill fee. Buys all rights. SASE. Reports within weeks. Free sample copy and writer's guidelines.

Nonfiction: Expose (of government or industry matters); interview/profile (related to the chemical industry); personal experience (of a chemist's work life); photo feature (of a chemical development); and technical (chemical or biological). "The features in *ICN* are written in an informative and fresh style. We do not intend to burden our readers with complex technical jargon when the facts can be told more simply and other publications cover research articles. But neither do we want a basic story; we must tell them something new, something they must know. The features emphasize examples and details of how the research was actually accomplished (equipment used, dollars spent, etc.). Always, the emphasis is our readers: How will the industrial chemist learn from the information?" Buys approximately 20 mss/year. Query with clips of published work. Length: 1,000-3,000 words. Pays $200-500.

Photos: State availability of photos. "It would be helpful if the author could supply the artwork or recommend material that could be used to clearly portray points made in the written material." Buys one-time rights.

Columns/Departments: Book reviews (new books); employment briefs ("news items on chemical careers"); and news ("broad topic of interest to chemists"). Length: 300-3,000 words.

INDUSTRIAL DESIGN, Design Publications, Inc., 717 5th Ave., Room 1201, New York NY 10022. (212)752-4956. Managing Editor: David G. Ellingson. Subject of this publication is industrial design (of products, packaging, graphics and environments) and design management. Bimonthly magazine; 90 pages. Circ. 11,000. Pays on publication. Buys all rights. Byline given. Phone queries OK. Previously published work OK. SASE. Sample copy $5.

Nonfiction: Exposé (design related); how-to (all aspects of design and design management), interview (of important people in business and design); profile (corporate, showing value of design and/or how design is managed); and new product. Buys 5 mss/issue. Length: 1,800 words. Query with point-by-point outline and clips of published work. Pays $100-500.

Photos: State availability of photos. Wants very good quality b&w glossy prints and contact sheets. Offers no additional payment for photos accepted with ms. Captions required.

Columns/Departments: Materials, Components, Processes; New Applications; Design Tools; and Briefs are all short items written from press releases. Other departments include Portfolio (new products); Visual Communications (graphics, packaging); Environments; and News and Views. Query with clips of published work. Pays $5/hour.

Tips: "Show that you are thoroughly backgrounded on the general aspects of your topic, as well as specifics. Read the magazine."

INFO FRANCHISE NEWSLETTER, 11 Bond St., St. Catharines, Ontario, Canada L2R 4Z4 or 736 Center St., Lewiston NY 14092. (716)754-4669. Editor-in-Chief: E.L. Dixon Jr. Managing Editor: Heather Barnes. Monthly newsletter; 8 pages. Circ. 5,000. Pays on publication. Buys all rights. Photocopied submissions OK. SASE. Reports in 4 weeks.

Nonfiction: "We are particularly interested in receiving articles regarding franchise legislation, franchise litigation, franchise success stories, and new franchises. Both American and Canadian items are of interest. We do not want to receive any information which is not fully documented; or articles which could have appeared in any newspaper or magazine in North America. An author with a legal background, who could comment upon such things as arbitration and franchising, collective bargaining and franchising or class actions and franchising would be of great interest to us." Expose; how-to; informational; interview; profile; new product; personal experience and technical. Buys 10-20 mss/year. Length: 25-1,000 words. Pays $10-300.

INSULATION OUTLOOK, National Insulation Contractors Association, 1120 19th St., NW, #405, Washington DC 20036. (202)223-4406. Editor: D.M. Humphrey. Monthly magazine about general business, commercial and industrial insulation for the insulation industry in the United States and abroad. Publication is read by engineers, specifiers, buyers, contractors, and union members in the industrial and commerical insulation field. There is also representative distribution to public utilities, and energy related industries. Pays on publication. Byline given. Buys first rights. Phone queries OK. Written queries should be short and simple, with samples of writing attached. Submit seasonal material 6 months in advance. Simultaneous, photocopied and previously published submissions OK. SASE. Sample copy $2; free writer's guidelines. "Give us a call. If there seems to be compatibility, we will send a free issue sample so the writer can see directly the type of publication he or she is dealing with."
Columns/Departments: Query. Pays $50-300.

JOURNAL OF MICROGRAPHICS, National Micrographics Association, 8719 Colesville Rd., Silver Spring MD 20910. (301)587-8202. Editor. Emphasizes micrographics and related technologies such as facsimile, data processing, word processing and records management. Monthly magazine; 48 pages. Circ. 9,000. Pays on acceptance. Buys all rights. Byline given. Phone queries OK. Photocopied submissions OK. Reports in 4 weeks. Free sample copy and writer's guidelines.
Nonfiction: How-to (applications articles on how organizations interfaced micrographics with other information handling technologies); and technical (new developments in technologies that could interface with micrographics). The number of articles they buy varies with each issue. Query. Length: 6,000 words. Pays $50.
Photos: "In a technical publication like ours, photographs help explain the subject to new readers." Send photos with ms. Wants b&w 5x7 glossy prints. Offers no additional payment for photos accepted with ms. Captions required.

LAWN CARE INDUSTRY, Harcourt Brace Jovanovich, Inc., 757 3rd Ave., New York NY 10017. (212)888-2892. Editor: Bob Earley. 10% freelance written. For lawn care businessmen. Monthly tabloid; 40 pages. Circ. 12,000. Pays on acceptance. Buys all rights. Phone queries OK. Submit seasonal/holiday material 3 months in advance of issue date. Simultaneous and photocopied submissions OK. SASE. Reports in 2 weeks. Free sample copy.
Nonfiction: General interest (articles related to small business operation); how-to (running a lawn care business); interview (with lawn care operator or industry notable); new product (helping to better business practices); and profile (of lawn care businessmen). Buys 3 mss/issue. Query. Length: 500-1,000 words. Pays $50-250.
Photos: State availability of photos with query. Pays $10-100 for 5x7 glossy b&w prints; $50-250 for 35mm color transparencies. Captions required. Buys one-time rights.

MEETINGS & CONVENTIONS, Ziff-Davis Publishing Co., 1 Park Ave., New York NY 10016. Editor-in-Chief: Mel Hosansky. 15% freelance written. For association and corporate executives who plan sales meetings, training meetings, annual conventions, incentive travel trips, and any other kind of off-premises meeting. Monthly magazine; 150 pages. Circ. 73,500. Pays on acceptance. Buys all rights. Photocopied submissions and previously published work (if not published in a competing publication) OK. SASE. Reports in 1-2 months.
Nonfiction: "Publication is basically how-to. We tell how to run better meetings; where to hold them, etc. Must be case history, talking about specific meeting." Query. Length: 250-2,000 words. Pays $35-400.
Photos: Query.

NATIONAL MALL MONITOR, Suite 500, Arbor Office Center, 1321 US 19 S., Clearwater FL 33516. (813)531-5893. Editor: Terry Dunham. 25-40% freelance written. For shopping center industry developers, mall managers, financing institutions, architects, engineers, commercial brokers, and retailers. Bimonthly magazine. Circ. 22,000. Pays on publication. Buys all rights. Phone queries OK. Submit seasonal/holiday material 4 months in advance of issue date. SASE. Reports in 6 weeks. Sample copy $4 plus postage; free writer's guidelines.
Nonfiction: Wants concise, factual, well-written mss that will keep readers informed of the latest happenings within the industry and allied fields. "The pieces should be cleared through the proper

channels for accuracy and authenticity and must be written in a free and easy style, similar to consumer magazines but must be slanted to the insider's special understanding of the industry." Buys how-to articles (such as the best way to build, renovate or maintain a shopping center). Stories about unusual specialty or theme centers always in demand. "Always looking for articles about noted architects, engineers, designers, as long as they have something to say to the industry that it doesn't already know." No articles on pageants, auto shows, band concerts or local promotional activities. Buys 20 mss/year. Query. Length: 500-2,000 words. Pays 7½¢/word for 1st sale and 10¢/word for each subsequent sale.

Photos: State availability of photos with query. Pays $9 minimum for 5x7 b&w glossy prints and 8x10 glossy color prints or 2¼x2¼ mounted transparencies. Captions required. Buys all rights. Model release required.

Columns/Departments: Spotlights leasing, management and promotion. Query. Length: 800-1,200 words. Pays 7½¢/word for 1st sale and 10¢/word for each subsequent sale. Open to suggestions for new columns/departments.

NEWSLETTER OF INTERNATIONAL TRADE, Bureau of International Trade USA, Inc., 240 Commercial St., Suite 400, Boston MA 02109. (617)523-1441. Editor: Garrit Schuurem. Managing Editor: Peter Gray. Monthly newsletter covering international trade for international trade managers, marketing directors in medium- to large-sized firms, international lawyers and accountants, customs brokers and freight forwarders, and individuals involved in the import/export trade. Estab. 1981. Circ. 1,500. Pays on acceptance. Byline given. Pays negotiable kill fee. Buys one-time rights. Simultaneous queries OK; previously published work OK ("if publication and date are indicated"). SASE. Reports on queries in 2 weeks. Sample copy for 9x12 SAE and 2 first class stamps; writer's guidelines for business size SAE and 1 first class stamp.

Nonfiction: "The emphasis is on how other companies might benefit from and initiate certain programs for improving marketing overseas. We are especially seeking articles covering trade fairs, seminars and exhibitions worldwide. Articles should be timely, well-researched and written in a concise, factual manner. We are looking for freelancers overseas who can cover news on the spot." Buys 50-60 mss/year. Send complete ms. Length: 300-3,000 words. Pays 10¢ maximum/published word.

Fillers: Newsbreaks (international trade topics and how-to material). Length: 300-3,000 words. Pays 10¢ maximum/published word.

NON-FOODS MERCHANDISING, Charleson Publishing Co., 124 E. 40th St., New York NY 10024. Editor: Lynne S. Dumas. 10% freelance written. For buyers, manufacturers, and distributors of health and beauty aids and general merchandise (non-food) in the supermarket. Monthly tabloid; 75 pages. Circ. 19,000. Pays on publication. Buys all rights. Byline given on major features. Photocopied submissions OK. SASE.

Nonfiction: "Reports on aspects of our business." Analytical trends, historical, interview, profile, how-to and new product. Buys 6 mss/issue. Query with clips of published work. Length: 2,000-6,000 words. Pays $150-350.

Photos: Pays $50 for 5x7 b&w prints, contact sheets, or negatives; $50-75 for 2¼x2¼ or 35mm color transparencies or 5x7 glossy or silk prints. Captions required. Buys all rights.

PROBLEMS OF COMMUNISM, International Communication Agency, PGM/PMP, Room 964, 1776 Pennsylvania Ave., N.W., Washington DC 20547. (202)724-9801. Editor: Paul A. Smith Jr. For scholars and decision makers in all countries of the world with higher education and a serious interest in foreign area studies and international relations. Circ. 26,000. Not copyrighted. Pays 20% kill fee. Byline given. Buys 60-70 mss/year. Pays on acceptance. Free sample copy. Photocopied submissions OK. Reports in 3 months.

Nonfiction: "*Problems of Communism* is one of a very few journals devoted to objective, dispassionate discourse on a highly unobjective, passionately debated phenomenon: communism. It is maintained as a forum in which qualified observers can contribute to a clearer understanding of the sources, nature and direction of change in the areas of its interest. It has no special emphasis or outlook and represents no partisan point of view. Standards of style are those appropriate to the field of international scholarship and journalism. We use intellectually rigorous studies of East-West relations, and/or related political, economic, social and strategic trends in the USSR, China and their associated states and movements. Length is usually 5,000 words. Essay reviews of 1,500 words cover new books offering significant information and analysis. Emphasis throughout *Problems of Communism* is on original research, reliability of sources and perceptive insights. We do not publish political statements or other forms of advocacy or apologetics for particular forms of belief." Query or submit complete ms. Pays $500/article; $200/essay reviews.

Photos: Pays minimum $35 for b&w glossy prints.

SOLAR AGE MAGAZINE, Solarvision, Inc., Church Hill, Harrisville NH 03450. (603)827-3347. Editor: William D'Alessandro. Editorial Assistant: Mary A. Cummiskey. Monthly magazine covering renewable energy resources for solar professionals, designers, installers, architects, inventors, educators, solar business executives, and state, local and federal employees in research and development. Circ. 75,000. Average issue includes 6 features articles. Pays on publication. Byline given. Buys first magazine rights. Phone queries OK. Photocopied and previously published submissions OK. Reports in 1 week on queries; in 1 month on mss.
Nonfiction: Exposé (of government, consumer and business); interview (of nationally known solar energy or renewable energy personalities); how-to (install solar, conserve energy, retrofit and design systems); new product; personal experience; photo feature; and technical. "Articles for us should be thoroughly researched for technical accuracy but be written without jargon. Writers are encouraged to discuss the submissions and style with the editors before proceeding." Buys 20-25 mss/year. Query. Length: 2,000 words maximum. Pays $125 minimum.
Photos: B&w and color transparencies accepted. Subject matter should parallel editorial subjects listed above. All photo payments are negotiable. Photographers should present portfolios or send samples. Captions and model release required. Buys one-time rights.

SOLAR ENERGY DIGEST, Box 17776, San Diego CA 92117. Editor: William B. Edmondson. 5-10% freelance written. For manufacturers, scientists, engineers, architects, builders, developers, technicians, energy experts, teachers, inventors, and others interested in solar energy conversion. Newsletter. Monthly. Circ. 1,500. Buys all rights. Pays on publication. Sample copy for $1 and SASE. Reports in 1-3 weeks. SASE.
Nonfiction: Wants mss about new developments in any facet of solar energy conversion, including applications in agriculture, architecture, cooking, distillation, mechanical engines and pumps, photo-electricity, steam generation, flat plate and concentrating collectors, sea thermal plants, furnaces, heat and energy storage, photosynthesis, wind power, wave power, etc. "Assume that the reader knows the fundamentals of the subject and plunge right in without a long introduction. Keep it simple, but not simplistic." No generalized papers on solar energy. "We like to cover a specific new development in each story." Buys 60-75 mss/year. Length: 100-1,000 words. Length for regular columns: 1,000 words maximum. Pays 5¢-7¢/word.
Fillers: Shorts and news clippings on solar energy. Length: 25-200 words. Pays $1-5.
Tips: Also makes assignments to rewrite and condense solar energy news. Send resume and rewrite of a sample clipping.

TOBACCO REPORTER, 757 3rd Ave., New York NY 10017. Editor: Peter Sangenito. For tobacco growers, processors, warehousemen, exporters, importers, manufacturers and distributors of cigars, cigarettes, and tobacco products. Monthly. Buys all rights. Pays on publication. SASE.
Nonfiction and Photos: Uses original material on request only. Pays approximately 2½¢/word. Pays $3 for photos purchased with mss.
Fillers: Wants clippings on new tobacco product brands, local tobacco distributors, smoking and health, and the following relating to tobacco and tobacco products: job promotions, obituaries, honors, equipment, etc. Pays minimum 25¢/clipping on use only.

WEIGHING & MEASUREMENT, Key Markets Publishing Co., Box 5867, Rockford IL 61125. (815)399-6970. Editor: David M. Mathieu. For users of industrial scales and meters. Bimonthly magazine; 32 pages. Circ. 25,000. Pays on acceptance. Buys all rights. Pays 20% kill fee. Byline given. Reports in 2 weeks. Free sample copy.
Nonfiction: Interview (with presidents of companies); personal opinion (guest editorials on government involvement in business, etc.); profile (about users of weighing and measurement equipment); and technical. Buys 25 mss/year. Query on technical articles; submit complete ms for general interest material. Length: 750-2,500 words. Pays $45-125.

WESTERN LANDSCAPING NEWS, Hester Communications, Inc., Box 19531, Irvine CA 92713. (714)549-4834. Associate Publisher/Editor: Steve McGonigal. Published for the Western landscaping and irrigation industry. Monthly magazine; 64 pages. Circ. 17,000+. Pays on publication. Buys all rights. Submit seasonal/holiday material 4 months in advance. Photocopied and previously published submissions OK. SASE. Reports in 3 weeks. Free sample copy.
Nonfiction: How-to (ideas for the average contractor on design, product selection, planning, irrigation, selecting nursery stock, management and marketing, etc.); interview (with respected person in industry in the West or someone promoting or improving the industry); personal opinion (government regulations, etc.); profile (Western landscapers who have unusual qualities); personal opinion (only when author is known and respected in industry); and technical (write in lay terms). "If you're intent on writing for us, interview an expert and let him form the basis of your article." Buys 1 ms/issue. Query. Length: 1,200-3,000 words. Pays $50-150.

Photos: "Ours is basically a visual industry. When we're talking about an interesting landscape design, we'd like to picture it." State availability of photos. Pays $5 for b&w 5x7 or 8x10 prints, and $10-25 for 35mm color transparencies. Captions and model releases required.

WIRE JOURNAL, Box H, 1570 Boston Post Rd., Guilford CT 06437. Editor: Arthur L. Slepian. Technical journal for wire and cable manufacturers and for fabricators using wire and cable in their products. Monthly magazine; 120 pages. Circ. 13,000. Pays on publication. Buys all rights. Byline given. Photocopied submissions OK. SASE. Reports in 1 month. Sample copy $3.
Nonfiction: Historical (background on wire and cable manufacturers); personal experience (only if from someone in the wire industry); and technical (wiredrawing, stranding, insulating); case histories on plant engineering and product fabrication. Query stating what photos are avilable. Length: 1,500 words maximum. Pays $100-200.
Tips: Writer should know "something about metals industry and wire manufacturing; also have knowledge of plant engineering and other industrial plant functions including management."

Music

ASCAP IN ACTION, A Publication of the American Society of Composers, Authors and Publishers, 1 Lincoln Plaza, New York NY 10023. (212)595-3050. Editor: Merry Aronson. Magazine published 3 times/year covering music and its creators and publishers, ASCAP members, the music industry, college libraries, and foreign performing rights organizations. Estab. 1979. Circ. 50,000. Pays on acceptance. Byline "generally given." Buys first North American serial rights. Photocopied submissions OK. Reports in 1 month. Free sample copy.
Nonfiction: Profile (of an individual or event); publishing trends; and performing rights issues. No articles on BMI members or music people who are not writers." Buys 10-15 mss/year. Query with clips of published work. Length: 3,000-3,500 words. Pays $350.
Photos: "Whenever possible we get free use of photos through publicity agents; otherwise we buy." State availability of photos. Reviews color transparencies and 8x10 glossy prints. Captions required. Buys one-time rights.
Fillers: Anecdotes and short humor (music-oriented). Pays negotiable fee.

THE CANADIAN COMPOSER, Creative Arts Co., #401, 1240 Bay St., Toronto, Ontario, Canada M5R 2A7. (416)925-5138. Editor-in-Chief: Richard Flohil. For "composers of music in Canada who are CAPAC members; 10% 'serious', the rest involved in various kinds of popular music." Published 10 times/year. Magazine; 48 pages. Pays on publication. Buys one-time rights. Phone queries OK. Submit seasonal/holiday material 3 months in advance. Photocopied submissions OK. SASE. Reports in 1 week. Free sample copy.
Nonfiction: Informational, interview and profile. Buys 4 mss/issue. Query. Length: 2,500 words. Pays $90-125.
Photos: Purchased with accompanying ms or on assignment. Captions required. Query or submit contact sheet. Pays $10-20 for 8x10 b&w glossies.

THE CHURCH MUSICIAN, 127 9th Ave. N., Nashville TN 37234. (615)251-2953. Editor: William Anderson. 30% freelance written. Southern Baptist publication. For Southern Baptist church music leaders. Monthly. Circ. 20,000. Buys all rights. Pays on acceptance. Free sample copy. No query required. Reports in 2 months. SASE.
Nonfiction: Leadership and how-to features, success stories, articles on Protestant church music. "We reject material when the subject of an article doesn't meet our needs. And they are often poorly written, or contain too many 'glittering generalities' or lack creativity." Length: maximum 1,300 words. Pays up to 3½¢/word.
Photos: Purchased with mss; related to mss content only.
Fiction: Inspiration, guidance, motivation, morality with Protestant church music slant. Length: to 1,300 words. Pays up to 3½¢/word.
Poetry: Church music slant, inspirational. Length: 8-24 lines. Pays $5-$10.
Fillers: Puzzles, short humor. Church music slant. No clippings. Pays $3-$10.
Tips: "I'd advise a beginning writer to write about his or her experience with some aspect of church music; the social, musical, and spiritual benefits from singing in a choir; a success story about their instrumental group; a testimonial about how they were enlisted in a choir—especially if they were not inclined to be enlisted at first. A writer might speak to hymn singers—what turns them on and what doesn't. Some might include how music has helped them to talk about Jesus as well as sing about Him. We would prefer most of these experiences be related to the church, of course,

although we include many articles by freelance writers whose affiliation is other than Baptist. A writer might relate his experience with a choir of blind or deaf members. Some people receive benefits from working with unusual children—retarded, or culturally deprived, emotionally unstable, and so forth. Photographs are valuable here."

CLAVIER, 1418 Lake Street, Evanston IL 60204. (312)328-6000. Editor: Lee Prater Yost. Magazine; 48 pages. 10 times a year. Buys all rights. Pays on publication. Free sample copy. No simultaneous submissions. "Suggest query to avoid duplication." Reports in 4 weeks on very good or very bad mss. SASE.
Nonfiction and Photos: Wants "articles aimed at teachers of piano and organ. Must be written from thoroughly professional point of view. Avoid, however, the thesis-style subject matter and pedantic style generally found in scholarly journals. We like fresh writing, practical approach. We can use interviews with concert pianists and organists. An interview should not be solely a personality story, but should focus on a subject of interest to musicians. Any word length. Photos may accompany ms." Pays $35/printed page. Need color photos for cover, such as angle shots of details of instruments, other imaginative photos, with keyboard music themes."

HIGH FIDELITY TRADE NEWS, 6 E. 43rd St., New York NY 10017. For "retailers, salesmen, manufacturers, and representatives involved in the high fidelity/home entertainment market." Monthly. Circ. 26,000. Buys all rights. Pays 50% kill fee. Byline given. Buys 36-50 mss a year. Pays on acceptance. Free sample copy. Query; "all work by assignment only." SASE.
Nonfiction: "Dealer profiles, specific articles on merchandising of high fidelity products, market surveys, sales trends, etc." Length: "open." Pay varies "as to type of article."
Tips: "We prefer to rely on our own resources for developing story ideas. Let us know about your willingness to work and submit, if possible, some samples of previous work. Even if you're a new writer, we're still likely to try you out, especially if you know the business or live in a market area where we need coverage. Articles on merchandising, product reports, and dealer profiles."

THE INSTRUMENTALIST, 1418 Lake St., Evanston IL 60204. Editor: Kenneth L. Neidig. For instrumental music educators. Monthly. Circ. 22,527. Buys all rights. Byline given. Buys 200 mss a year. Pays on publication. Sample copy $1.50. Submit seasonal material 4 months in advance. Sound Reinforcement (January); New Products (February); Summer Camps, Clinics, Workshops (March); Marching Bands (June); Back to School (September); Fund raising (October). Reports on material accepted for publication within 4 months. Returns rejected material within 3 months. Query. SASE.
Nonfiction and Photos: "Practical information of immediate use to instrumentalists. Not articles 'about music and musicians,' but articles by musicians who are sharing knowledge, techniques, experience. 'In-service education.' Professional help for instrumentalists in the form of instrumental clinics, how-to articles, new trends, practical philosophy. Most contributions are from professionals in the field." Interpretive photojournalism. "Query for mss over 1,000 words." Length: 100-1,500 words. Pays according to length (approximately $25-35/printed page), plus 2 contributor's copies. Quality b&w prints. Pays $5-10. Color: 35mm and up. Pays $50-75 if used for cover.

MUSIC EDUCATORS JOURNAL, 1902 Association Dr., Reston VA 22091. (703)860-4000. Editor: Malcolm E. Bessom. Managing Editor: Arthur J. Michaels. For music educators in elementary and secondary schools and universities. Monthly (September-May) magazine; 120 pages. Circ. 62,000. Pays on acceptance. Byline given. SASE. Reports in 6-8 weeks. Free sample copy and 9-page author's guidesheet.
Nonfiction: "We publish articles on music education at all levels—not about individual schools, but about broad issues, trends, instructional techniques. Also articles on music, aside from teaching it. Particularly interested in how-to, solid, heavily researched pieces on individual aspects of American and non-Western music, and interviews with important but lesser known composers. We do not want to see articles about 'the joys of music,' or about personal experiences. We are not a homey type of publication." Length: 1,000-3,000 words. Query the managing editor. Pays $75-200 for assigned articles.
Tips: "We're always interested in how-to material. Our readers are experts in music education, so accuracy and complete familiarity with the subject is essential. A selection of appropriate professional-quality 8x10 b&w glossy prints submitted with a manuscript greatly increases the chances of acceptance."

OPERA NEWS, 1865 Broadway, New York NY 10023. Editor: Robert Jacobson. For all people interested in opera; opera singers, opera management people, administrative people in opera, opera publicity people, artists' agents; people in the trade and interested laymen. Magazine; 32-72 pages. Weekly. (Monthly in summer.) Circ. 105,000. Copyrighted. Pays negotiable kill fee. Byline given. Pays on publication. Will send sample copy to writer for 75¢. Query. SASE.

Nonfiction and Photos: Most articles are commissioned in advance. In summer, uses articles of various interests on opera; in the fall and winter, articles that relate to the weekly broadcasts. Emphasis is on high quality in writing and an intellectual interest in the opera-oriented public. Informational, how-to, personal experience, interview, profile, humor, historical, think pieces, personal opinion; opera reviews. Length: 300 words maximum. Pays 11¢/word for features; 9¢/word for reviews. Pays minimum of $25 for photos purchased on assignment. Captions required.

SYMPHONY MAGAZINE, American Symphony Orchestra League, Box 669, Vienna VA 22180. (703)281-1230. Editor: Robin L. Perry. Editorial Associate: Chester Lane. Bimonthly magazine covering symphony orchestras in North America and the classical music industry for members of the association, including managers, conductors, board members, musicians, volunteer association members, music businesses, schools, libraries, etc. Circ. 14,500. Pays on publication. Byline given. Pays negotiable kill fee. Buys all rights. Simultaneous queries, and photocopied and previously published submissions OK. Reports in 1 month. Free sample copy.

Nonfiction: How-to (put together a symphony); interview/profile (conductors and personalities in the field); technical (budgeting, tour planning); and "thoughtful, reflective looks at the state of the classical music industry." Buys 20 mss/year. Query with clips of published work. Length: 2,500-3,000 words. Pays $50-250.

Photos: "We prefer action shots and informal shots." State availability of photos. Pays $25-50 for 8x10 glossy prints. Captions required.

UP BEAT MAGAZINE, Maher Publications, Inc., 222 W. Adams St., Chicago IL 60606. Editor: Herb Nolan. Associate Editor: Charles Mueller. Magazine published 10 times/year about the musical instrument and sound equipment industry for retailers of musical instruments and sound equipment. Circ. 11,200. Average issue includes 8 features and 3-4 columns. Pays on publication. Byline given. Offers 50%-100% kill fee. Buys all rights. Phone queries OK. Submit seasonal material 2½ months in advance. Simultaneous and photocopied submissions OK. SASE. Reports in 2 weeks. Sample copy $2.50; free writer's guidelines.

Nonfiction: Interview; profile; how-to; new product; and technical. "We want breezy how-to articles dealing with the musical instrument industry, slanted toward retailers. Articles are largely based on phone interviews with successful music industry people (retailers and manufacturers); some interpret trends in musical taste and how they affect the equipment industry. Articles should be clear and incisive, with depth and hard business advice." Buys 40 mss/year. Query with clips of previously published work. Length: 1,000-3,000 words. Pays $75-125.

Photos: Send photos with ms. Pays $15-25 for 8x10 b&w glossy prints. Buys one-time rights.

Columns/Departments: Money, Management, Clinics, Promotions, Education, Selling. "Department articles should be based on interviews with knowledgeable music industry figures." Buys 4 mss/issue. Query with clips of previously published work. Length: 1,000-2,800 words. Pays $50-125.

Tips: "All articles should be well-researched, with quotes from successful retailers and manufacturers of musical instruments and sound equipment."

Oceanography

The journals below are intended primarily for scientists who are studying the ocean. Publications for ocean fishermen will be found under Fishing. Those for persons interested in water and the ocean as a means of travel or shipping are listed with the Marine Industries and Water Navigation journals.

SEA FRONTIERS, 3979 Rickenbacker Causeway, Virginia Key, Miami FL 33149. (305)361-5786. Editor: F.G.W. Smith. 90-95% freelance written. "For anyone with an interest in any aspect of the sea; its conservation, and the life it contains; professional people for the most part; people in executive positions and students." Bimonthly. Circ. 60,000. Buys all rights. Byline given. Buys 45-50 mss/year. Pays on publication. Sample copy and writer's guidelines for 40¢ postage. Query. Will consider photocopied submissions "if very clear." Reports on material within 2 months. SASE.

Nonfiction and Photos: "Articles (with illustrations) covering interesting and little known facts about the sea, marine life, ecology, conservation, explorations, discoveries or advances in our knowledge of the marine sciences, or describing the activities of oceanographic laboratories or expeditions to any part of the world. Emphasis should be on research and discoveries rather than personalities involved." Length: 500-3,000 words. Pays $20-30/page. 8x10 b&w glossy prints and 35mm (or larger) color transparencies purchased with ms. Pays $50 for color used on front and $25 for the back cover. Pays $20 for color used on inside covers.

Tips: "Query to include a paragraph or two that tells the subject, the angle or approach to be taken, and the writer's qualifications for covering this subject or the authorities with whom the facts will be checked."

Office Equipment and Supplies

GEYER'S DEALER TOPICS, 51 Madison Ave., New York NY 10010. (212)689-4411. Editor: C. Edwin Shade. For independent office equipment and stationery dealers, and special purchasers for store departments handling stationery and office equipment. Monthly. Buys all rights. Pays kill fee. Byline given. Pays on publication. Reports "immediately." SASE.

Nonfiction and Photos: Articles on merchandising and sales promotion; programs of stationery and office equipment dealers. Problem-solving articles related to retailers of office supplies, social stationery items, office furniture and equipment and office machines. Must feature specified stores. Minimum payment, $50, but quality of article is real determinant. Query. Length: 300-1,000 words. B&w glossies are purchased with accompanying ms with no additional payment.

OFFICE PRODUCTS DEALER, Hitchcock Bldg., Wheaton IL 60187. (312)665-1000. Editor: Robert R. Mueller. For "independent dealers who sell all types of office products—office machines, systems furniture and supplies." Monthly. Circ. 25,000. Buys all rights. Byline given "except on collaborative articles." Pays on acceptance. Article deadlines are the 1st of the third month preceding date of issue. News deadlines are the 1st of each month. Reports in 3-4 weeks. Query on any long articles. SASE.

Nonfiction: "We're interested in anything that will improve an office product dealer's methods of doing business. Some emphasis on selling and promotion, but interested in all phases of dealer operations." Length: "that which tells the story, and no more or less." Pays $25-150 "based on quality of article."

Photos: Purchased with mss.

PACIFIC STATIONER, 41 Sutter St., San Francisco CA 94104. Editor: Robert B. Frier. Monthly magazine; 60-70 pages. Circ. 6,500. Not copyrighted. Byline given. Buys 12 mss/year. Pays on acceptance. Sample copy $2. No photocopied or simultaneous submissions. Submit seasonal (merchandising) material 4 months in advance. Reports in 1 week. Query or submit complete ms. SASE.

Nonfiction and Photos: "Our main interest is in how Western retailers of stationery and office products can do a better selling job. We use how-to-do-it merchandising articles showing dealers how to sell more stationery and office products to more people at a greater profit. Seasonal merchandising articles always welcome, if acceptable." Informational, how-to, personal experience, interview, successful business operations. Length: 1,000-1,500 words. Pays 2¢/word. Pays $5 for b&w photos used with mss; 3x5 minimum. Captions required.

SOUTHERN OFFICE OUTFITTER, (formerly *Southern Stationer and Office Outfitter*), 75 3rd St. NW, Atlanta GA 30308. Editor: Earl Lines Jr. For retailers of office products in the Southeast and Southwest. Monthly. Not copyrighted. Pays on publication. Free sample copy. Reports "promptly." SASE.

Nonfiction: Can use articles about retailers in the Southeast and Southwest regarding problems solved concerning store layout, inventory, personnel, etc. "We want articles giving in-depth treatment of a single aspect of a dealer's operation rather than superficial treatment of a number of aspects." Query. Must be approved by subject. Length: 1,000-1,400 words. Pays 2-4¢/word.

Photos: Purchased with mss. Pays $5.

Optical

THE DISPENSING OPTICIAN, Opticians Association of America, 1250 Connecticut Ave. NW, Washington DC 20036. Editor: James H. McCormick. 40% freelance written, but only 20% by paid

writers. For dispensing opticians. Published 11 times/year. Magazine; 44-52 pages. Circ. 8,000-9,000. Pays "when issue is locked up." Buys either all rights or industry rights. Byline given. Photocopied submissions OK. SASE. "Reports are slow due to clearance by editorial board (up to 60 days)." Will send sample copy to writer "only when we're interested in an article suggestion."
Nonfiction: Publishes informational, how-to, interview, profile, historical, photo feature, successful business operations, merchandising techniques, and technical articles. "All must specifically pertain to or interest the dispensing optician, and profiles and successful business operations must be of Association members." Query. Buys 20-25 mss/year. Length: 400-2,500 words. Pays 9-16¢/word for original work; 6-12¢/word for industry rights to non-syndicated articles; 4-7¢/word for industry rights to syndicated articles.
Photos: Purchased with or without accompanying ms, or on assignment. Caption material required. Pays $8-60 for 5x7 or 8x10 b&w prints. Query.

Packing, Canning, and Packaging

Journals in this category are for packaging engineers and others concerned with new methods of packing, canning, and packaging foods in general. Other publications that buy similar material will be found under the Food Processing, Products, and Services heading.

FOOD & DRUG PACKAGING, 747 3rd Ave., New York NY 10017. Editor: Ben Miyares. For packaging decision makers in food, drug, cosmetic firms. Biweekly. Will be a monthly publication in January of 1982. Circ. 56,000. Rights purchased vary with author and material. Pays on acceptance. "Queries only." SASE.
Nonfiction and Photos: "Looking for news stories about local and state (not federal) packaging legislation, and its impact on the marketplace. Newspaper style." Length: 1,000-2,500 words; usually 500-700. Payments vary; usually 5¢/word. Photos purchased with mss. 5x7 glossies preferred. Pays $5.
Tips: "1) Get details on local packaging legislation's impact on marketplace/sales/consumer/ retailer reaction; etc. 2) Keep an eye open to *new* packages. Query when you think you've got one. New packages move into test markets every day, so if you don't see anything new this week, try again next week. Buy it; describe it briefly in a query."

PACKAGE PRINTING, North American Publishing Co., 401 N. Broad St., Philadelphia PA 19108. Managing Editor: Hennie Marine. 50% freelance written. Emphasizes "any sort of package printing (gravure, flexo, offset) for the plant superintendent or general manager of the company's package printing department." Monthly magazine; 88 pages. Circ. 10,000. Pays on acceptance. Buys all rights. Pays 33% kill fee. Byline given. Phone queries OK. Simultaneous and photocopied submissions OK. SASE. Reports in 2 weeks. Sample copy $1.
Nonfiction: "Generally a 'plant' story on the operation of the printing department of a packaging concern. The writer may not know a flexographic machine from a gravure machine or any other, but we expect him to interview the plant manager and get all the technical as well as 'people' details. How is the package printed? What is the paper/film/foil used? How many? What kinds? Names and speed of all machines used; number of employees in production; everything relating to the manufacture and printing of any sort of package (look in any supermarket for 1,000 examples of packages)." Query. Pays $75/printed page.
Photos: State availability of photos with query. Pays $10 for 5x7 or 8x10 b&w prints. Captions required. Buys all rights.

THE PACKER, Box 2939, Shawnee Mission KS 66201. (913)381-6310. Editor: Paul Campbell. 5% freelance written. For shippers, fruit and vegetable growers, wholesalers, brokers, retailers. Newspaper; 36 pages. Weekly. Circ. 16,500. Buys all rights. Buys about 10 mss/year. Pays on publication. Will send free sample copy to writer on request. Write for copy of guidelines for writers. Will consider simultaneous submissions. Reports in 2 weeks. Returns rejected material in 1 month. Query or submit complete ms. SASE.
Nonfiction: Articles on growing techniques, merchandising, marketing, transportation, refrigeration. Emphasis is on the "what's new" approach in these areas. Length: 1,000 words. Pays $40 minimum.
Tips: "It's important to be a good photographer, too. Have features on new growing, merchandising or shipping techniques."

Paint

Additional journals that buy material on paint, wallpaper, floor covering, and decorating products stores are listed under Building Interiors.

AMERICAN PAINT & COATINGS JOURNAL, American Paint Journal Co., 2911 Washington Ave., St. Louis MO 63103. (314)534-0301. Editor: Fred Schulenberg. 10% freelance written. For the coatings industry (paint, varnish, lacquer, etc.); manufacturers of coatings, suppliers to coatings industry, educational institutions, salesmen. Weekly magazine; 78 pages. Circ. 7,300. Pays on publication. Buys all rights. Pays kill fee "depending on the work done." Phone queries OK. Simultaneous and photocopied submissions OK. SASE. Reports in 3 weeks. Free sample copy and writer's guidelines.
Nonfiction: Informational, historical, interview, new product and technical articles and coatings industry news. Buys 2 mss/issue. Query before sending long articles; submit complete ms for short pieces. Length: 75-1,200 words. Pays $5-100.
Photos: B&w (5x7) glossies purchased with or without mss, or on assignment. Query. Pays $3-10.

AMERICAN PAINTING CONTRACTOR, American Paint Journal Co., 2911 Washington Ave., St. Louis MO 63103. (314)534-0301. Editor-in-Chief: John L. Cleveland. For painting and decorating contractors, in-plant maintenance painting department heads, architects and paint specifiers. Monthly magazine; 80 pages. Circ. 34,000. Buys all rights. Phone queries OK. Submit seasonal/holiday material 2 months in advance. Simultaneous and photocopied submissions OK. SASE. Reports in 3 weeks. Free sample copy and writer's guidelines.
Nonfiction: Historical, how-to, humor, informational, new product, personal experience, opinion and technical articles; interviews, photo features and profiles. Buys 4 mss/issue. "Freelancers should be able to write well and have some understanding of the painting and decorating industry. We do not want general theme articles such as 'How to Get More Work Out of Your Employee' unless they relate to a problem within the painting and decorating industry. Query before submitting copy." Length: 1,000-2,500 words. Pays $150-200.
Photos: B&w and color purchased with mss or on assignment. Captions required. Send contact sheets, prints or transparencies. Pays $15-35.

DECORATIVE PRODUCTS WORLD, American Paint Journal Co., 2911 Washington, St. Louis MO 63103. (314)534-0301. Editor: Cathy Reilly. Editorial Director: John Cleveland. Monthly magazine about decorating outlets for retailers of paint, wallpaper and related items. Circ. 33,000. Pays on publication. Byline given. Submit seasonal material 3 months in advance. Reports in 1 month. Free sample copy and writer's guidelines.
Nonfiction: Profile (of stores). "Find stories that will give useful information for our readers. We are basically a service to our readers and our articles reflect that." Buys 1-2 mss/issue. Query. Pays $150.
Photos: "Photos must accompany a story in order to be published." State availability of photos. Pays $10 maximum for b&w prints. Pays $25 maximum for color transparencies. Captions required. Buys one-time rights.
Fillers: Short humor. Buys 3 mss/issue. Pays $4 maximum.

Paper

FORET ET PAPIER, 625 President Kennedy Ave., Montreal, Quebec, Canada H3A 1K5. (514)845-5141. Editor: Paul Saint-Pierre, C. Adm. For engineers and technicians engaged in the making of paper. Bimonthly magazine; 50 pages. Circ. 7,000. Rights purchased vary with author and material. Buys first North American serial rights, second serial (reprint) rights, and simultaneous rights. Buys about 12 mss/year. Pays on acceptance. Will consider photocopied submissions. Free sample copy. Reports on mss accepted for publication in 1 week. Returns rejected material in 2 days. SASE.
Nonfiction and Photos: Uses technical articles on papermaking. Buys informational, how-to, personal experience, interview, photo and technical articles. Length: 1,000 words maximum. Pays $25-150. Photos purchased with accompanying ms with extra payment or purchased on assignment. Captions required. Pays $25 for b&w. Color shots must be vertical. Pays $150 maximum for color cover shots.

PAPER TRADE JOURNAL, Vance Publishing Co., 133 E. 58th St., New York NY 10022. Editor: Jeremiah E. Flynn. Managing Editor: Mary Anne Murphy. Semimonthly magazine about the pulp and paper industry for the top management of paper mills. Circ. 11,500. Pays on publication. Byline given. Buys first North American serial rights. Submit seasonal material 3 months in advance. SASE. Reports in 2 weeks. Free sample copy.
Nonfiction: Profile, how-to, new product and technical. Query. Length: 1,500 words. Pays $125.
Columns/Departments: Query.
Fillers: Clippings. Buys 250 mss/year. Pays $1.

PAPERBOARD PACKAGING, 747 3rd Ave., New York NY 10017. (212)838-7778. Editor: Jim Young. For "managers, supervisors, and technical personnel who operate corrugated box manufacturing and folding cartons converting companies and plants." Monthly. Circ. 15,000. Buys all rights. Pays on publication. Will send a sample copy to a writer on request. Will consider photocopied submissions. Submit seasonal material 3 months in advance. Query. SASE.
Nonfiction and Photos: "Application articles, installation stories, etc. Contact the editor first to establish the approach desired for the article. Especially interested in packaging systems using composite materials, including paper and other materials." Buys technical articles. Length: open. Pays "$75/printed page (about 1,000 words to a page), including photos. We do not pay for commercially oriented material. We do pay for material if it is not designed to generate business for someone in our field. Will not pay photography costs, but will pay cost of photo reproductions for article."

Petroleum

ENERGY MANAGEMENT REPORT, Box 1589, Dallas TX 75221. (214)748-4403. Editor-in-Chief: Ernestine Adams. Assistant Editor: Gregory Martin. 7-10% freelance written. Emphasizes energy for operating management of oil/gas operating companies and supply/service companies. Monthly magazine; 16 pages. Circ. 56,916. Pays on publication. Buys all rights. SASE. Free sample copy; mention *Writer's Market* in request.
Nonfiction: Uses energy briefs and concise analysis of energy situations. "Across-the-board interpretive reporting on current energy events." Publishes briefs about energy world news, international design and engineering, offshore energy business, environmental action, energy financing, new products (price information on crude oil and gasoline). Pays 10¢/word.

FUEL OIL NEWS, Publex Corp., Box 308, Whitehouse NJ 08888. (201)534-9023. Editor: George Schultz. Monthly magazine about the home heating oil market. Circ. 17,000. Pays on publication. Byline given. Offers $75 kill fee. Makes work-for-hire assignments. Phone queries OK. Submit seasonal material 3 months in advance. Simultaneous, photocopied and previously published submissions OK. Reports in 2 months. Free sample copy and writer's guidelines.
Nonfiction: Interview (industry); profile (of industry leaders); how-to (on industry methods of delivering fuel or servicing equipment); and technical. No general business articles or new product information. Buys 2 mss/issue. Query. Length: 1,000-3,000 words. Pays $70-200. "Articles should be geared to helping fuel oil dealers maintain viability in the marketplace or to some aspect of home heating or oil delivery."
Photos: State availability of photos. Pays $25 maximum for b&w contact sheets. Captions preferred; model release required. Buys all rights.

FUELOIL AND OIL HEAT, 200 Commerce Rd., Cedar Grove NJ 07009. (201)239-5800. Feature Editor: M. F. Hundley. For distributors of fuel oil, heating and air conditioning equipment dealers. Monthly. Buys first rights. Pays on publication. Reports in 2 weeks. SASE.
Nonfiction: Management articles dealing with fuel oil distribution and oilheating equipment selling. Length: up to 2,500 words. Pays $35/printed page.

HUGHES RIGWAY, Hughes Tool Co., Box 2539, Houston TX 77001. Editor-in-Chief: John Poxon. For oilfield drilling personnel. Quarterly magazine; 32 pages. Circ. 17,000. Pays on acceptance. Buys first North American serial rights. Byline given. Simultaneous and photocopied submissions OK. SASE. Reports in 1 month. Free sample copy and writer's guidelines.
Nonfiction and Photos: "Character-revealing historical narratives about little-known incidents, heroes, or facts, particularly those which contradict conventional concepts. Must be thoroughly documented." Length: 2,000-2,500 words. Pays 10¢/word. Photos purchased with mss.

Fiction: "Top-quality fiction in oilfield and historical settings." Length: 2,000-2,500 words. Pays 10¢/word.
Tips: "Manuscripts should have plenty of dialogue."

HYDROCARBON PROCESSING, Box 2608, Houston TX 77001. Editor: Frank L. Evans. 95% freelance written by industry authors. For personnel in oil refining, gas and petrochemical processing; or engineering-contractors, including engineering, operation, maintenance and management phases. Special issues: January, Maintenance; April, Natural Gas Processing; September, Refining Processes; November, Petrochemical Processes. Monthly. Buys first publication rights. Write for copy of guidelines for writers. SASE.
Nonfiction: Wants technical manuscripts on engineering and operations in the industry that will help personnel. Also nontechnical articles on management, safety and industrial relations that will help technical men become managers. Length: open, "but do not waste words." Pays about $25/printed page.
Tips: "Articles must all pass a rigid evaluation of their reader appeal, accuracy and overall merit. Reader interest determines an article's value. We covet articles that will be of real job value to subscribers. Before writing, ask to see our *Author's Handbook*. You may save time and effort by writing a letter, and outline briefly what you have in mind. If your article will or won't meet our needs, we will tell you promptly."

NATIONAL PETROLEUM NEWS, 225 W. 34th St., New York NY 10001. (212)947-0739. Editor: William Olcott. For businessmen who make their living in the oil marketing industry, either as company employees or through their own business operations. Monthly magazine; 90 pages. Circ. 19,000. Rights purchased vary with author and material. Usually buys all rights. Buys 2 mss/year. Pays on acceptance if done on assignment. Pays on publication for unsolicited material. "The occasional freelance copy we use is done on assignment." Query. SASE.
Nonfiction and Photos: News Editor: Ron Landry. Material related directly to developments and issues in the oil marketing industry and "how-to" and "what-with" case studies. Informational; successful business operations. Length: 2,000 words maximum. Pays $60/printed page. Payment for b&w photos "depends upon advance understanding."

OCEAN INDUSTRY, Gulf Publishing Co., Box 2608, Houston TX 77001. (713)529-4301. Editor-in-Chief: Donald M. Taylor. Associate Editors: Maretta Tubb, Al Trafford. Department Editor: Margaret Cashman. 25% freelance written. "Our readers are generally engineers and company executives in companies with business dealings with off-shore petroleum and deepsea mining interests." Monthly magazine. Circ. 33,000. Pays on publication. Buys all rights. Pays kill fee "if we assign an article and it is not used, we pay full rate on estimated length." Byline given. Phone queries OK. Photocopied and previously published submissions OK. SASE. Reports in 2 months. Free sample copy and writer's guidelines.
Nonfiction: Technical articles relating to hydrocarbon exploration and development, diving, deepsea mining, oil terminals, and oil and LNG shipping. No oceanographic, fisheries, aquaculture or mariculture material. Buys 120-140 mss/year. Query. Length: 300-1,500 words. Pays $35-100/published page.
Photos: "Technical concepts are easier to understand when illustrated." State availability of photos with query. No additional payment for 5x7 or 8x10 glossy b&w or color prints. Captions required. Buys all rights.

PETROLEO INTERNACIONAL, Petroleum Publishing Co., Box 1260, Tulsa OK 74101. (918)835-3161. Editor: Gustavo Pena. Executive Editor: Ms. Dolores Proubasta. Monthly magazine about the Latin American petroleum industry for the management, engineering and technical operating personnel in the oil and gas industry of the Spanish speaking world. Circ. 7,500. Average issue includes 6-7 main articles and several shorter ones. Pays on publication. Byline given. Makes work-for-hire assignments. Phone queries OK. Submit seasonal material 1 month in advance. Simultaneous, photocopied and previously published submissions OK. SASE. Reports in 2 weeks. Free sample copy and writer's guidelines.
Nonfiction: Technical (oil and gas, petrochemical industry and equipment for the petroleum industry). Query. Pays $25 minimum.
Photos: Send photos with ms. Reviews b&w prints and color prints. Offers no additional payment for photos accepted with ms. Captions required. Buys one-time rights.
Columns/Departments: "We have a section on people involved in the industry; new literature out for the industry, business in the industry, and current happenings in the petroleum industry." Pays $25 minimum.
Fillers: Newsbreaks. Pays $25 minimum.

PETROLEUM INDEPENDENT, 1101 16th St. NW, Washington DC 20036. (202)466-8240. Associate Editor: Joe W. Taylor. For "college-educated men and women involved in high-risk petroleum ventures. Our readers find nearly 90% of all the oil this country owns. They pit themselves against the major oil companies, politicians, and a dry hole rate of 9 out of 10 to try to find enough petroleum to offset imports. They are in a highly competitive, extremely expensive business and look to this magazine to help them change the political landscape, to help them make their businesses as profitable as possible, to read about their friends and the activities of the Independent Petroleum Association of America, and to be entertained. Contrary to popular opinion, they are not all Texans. They live in almost every state. These people are politically motivated. They follow energy legislation closely and involve themselves in lobbying and electoral politics." Bimonthly magazine; 64-88 pages. Circ. 14,000. Pays on acceptance. Buys all rights. Byline given "except if part of a large report compiled in-house." Photocopied submissions OK. SASE. Reports in 1 week. Sample copy $1.

Nonfiction: "Articles need not be limited to oil and natural gas—but must tie in nicely." Expose (bureaucratic blunder); informational; historical (energy-related, accurate, with a witty twist); humor ("we look for good humor pieces and have found a few"); interview (with energy decision-makers. Center with questions concerning independent petroleum industry. Send edited transcript plus tape.); opinion; profile (of members of Independent Petroleum Association of America); and photo feature. Buys 30 mss/year. Query with brief outline. SASE. Length: 750-3,000 words. Pays $40-300.

Photos: Purchased with or without accompanying ms or on assignment. Pays $15-75 for b&w and color photos. $200 (for cover only, we are always looking for good oil patch pictures) for 35mm or 2¼x2¼ transparencies. Send contact sheet, prints or transparencies.

Tips: "Call first, then send outline and query. Don't write with a particular slant. Write as if for a mainstream publication."

PIPELINE & GAS JOURNAL, Box 1589, Dallas TX 75221. (214)748-4403. Editor-in-Chief: Dean Hale. 5% freelance written. Emphasizes energy transportation (oil, gas and coal slurry) by pipeline. Monthly magazine; 100 pages. Circ. 26,000. Pays on publication. Buys all rights. Phone queries OK. Photocopied submissions OK. SASE. Reports in 6-10 weeks. Free sample copy.

Nonfiction: Technical. No articles on management. Buys 5-6 mss/year. Query. Length: 800-1,500 words. Pays minimum $35/printed page.

Photos: State availability of photos with query. No additional payment for 8x10 b&w glossy prints and 5x7 or 8x10 color glossy prints. Captions required. Buys all rights. Model release required.

Pets

Listed here are publications for professionals in the pet industry: wholesalers, manufacturers, suppliers, retailers, owners of pet specialty stores, pet groomers, aquarium retailers, distributors, manufacturers and those interested in the fish industry. Publications for pet owners are listed in the Animal section of Consumer Publications.

PET AGE, H.H. Backer Associates, Inc., 207 S. Wabash Ave., Chicago IL 60604. (312)663-4040. Editor: Richard Edel. Monthly magazine about the pet industry for pet retailers. Circ. 18,000. Pays on acceptance. Byline given. Buys all rights. Submit seasonal material 6 months in advance. SASE. Reports in 6 weeks. Free sample copy and writer's guidelines.

Nonfiction: Profile (of a successful, well-run pet retail operation). Buys 10 mss/year. Query. "Query as to the name and location of a pet operation you wish to profile and why the operation is successful, why it would make a good feature." Length: 1,600-2,000 words. Pays $80 minimum.

Photos: State availability of photos. Reviews 5x7 b&w glossy prints and color transparencies. Offers no additional payment for photos accepted with ms. Captions required. Buys all rights.

Columns/Departments: Fish Care, Retailing, Government Action, Bird Care, New Products and Industry News.

PET BUSINESS, Pet Business, Inc., 7330 NW 66th, Miami FL 33166. Publisher: Dr. Bern Levine. Editor: Robert L. Behme. For the complete pet industry—retailers, groomers, breeders, manufacturers, wholesalers and importers. Monthly tabloid; 30 pages. Circ. 18,500. Pays on acceptance. Not copyrighted. Previously published submissions OK. SASE. Reports in 3 weeks. Free sample copy and writer's guidelines.

Nonfiction: General interest (to retailers—what a store is doing, etc.); historical (when there is a reason—death, sale, etc.); how-to (sell more, retailer ideas); interview (with successful stores and manufacturers); opinion (with background); photo feature (on occasion). No news of stores. Buys 2-4 mss/issue. "We will consider anything if queried first." Length: 600-1,500 words. Pays $35-250.
Photos: State availability of photos. Pays $5 for 5x7 or larger b&w prints; and $30 for any size color prints. Captions required.
Columns/Departments: "We're interested in ideas that relate to retailing, e.g., dogs, cats, small animals—but it must be on a retail, not hobby, level." Open to suggestions for new columns/departments. Query. Pays $100.

THE PET DEALER, Howmark Publishing Corp., 567 Morris Ave., Elizabeth NJ 07208. (201)353-7373. Editor-in-Chief: William G. Reddan. Assistant Editor: Charles Horner. 15% freelance written. Emphasizes merchandising, marketing and management for owners and managers of pet specialty stores, departments, and dog groomers and their suppliers. Monthly magazine; 80 pages. Circ. 10,000. Byline given. Pays on publication. Phone queries OK. Submit seasonal/holiday material 3 months in advance of issue date. SASE. Reports in 1 week. Free sample copy and writer's guidelines.
Nonfiction: How-to (store operations, administration, merchandising, marketing, management, promotion, and purchasing). Buys 1 mss/issue. Length: 800-1,200 words. Pays $50-100.
Photos: Submit photo material with ms. No additional payment for 5x7 b&w glossy prints. "Six photos with captions required." Buys one-time rights. Model release required.
Tips: "We're interested in store profiles outside the New York, New Jersey, Connecticut, Pennsylvania metro areas. Photos are of key importance. Articles focus on new techniques in merchandising or promotion. Submit query letter first, with writing background summarized; include samples. We seek one-to-one, interview-type features on retail pet store merchandising. Indicate the availability of the proposed article, your willingness to sumit on exclusive or first-in-field basis, and whether you are patient enough to await payment on publication."

PETS/SUPPLIES/MARKETING, Harcourt Brace Jovanovich Publications, 1 E. 1st St., Duluth MN 55802. (218)727-8511. Editor: Dennis Mitchell. For pet retailers (both small, "mom-and-pop" stores and chain franchisers); livestock and pet supply wholesalers, manufacturers of pet products. Monthly magazine; 100 pages. Circ. 14,200. Pays on publication, occasionally on acceptance. Buys first rights. Phone queries OK. Submit seasonal/holiday material 4 months in advance. Photocopied submissions OK. SASE. Reports in 4-6 weeks. Free sample copy and writer's guidelines.
Nonfiction: How-to (merchandise pet products, display, set up window displays, market pet product line); interviews (with pet store retailers); opinion (of pet industry members or problems facing the industry); photo features (of successful pet stores or effective merchandising techniques and in-store displays); profiles (of successful retail outlets engaged in the pet trade); technical articles (on more effective pet retailing; e.g., building a central filtration unit, constructing custom aquariums or display areas). Length: 1,000-1,500 words. Buys 2-3 mss/issue. Query. Pays 8-10¢/word.
Photos: Purchased with or without mss or on assignment. "We prefer 5x7 or 8x10 b&w glossies. But we will accept contact sheets and standard print sizes. For color, we prefer 35mm transparencies or 2¼x2¼." Pays $7.50-10.00 for b&w; $15-20 for color. Captions and model release required.
Columns/Departments: Short, human interest items on the pet trade for Up Front. Suggestions for new columns or departments should be addressed to the editor.
Fillers: Occasional jokes, gags, anecdotes, newsbreaks, puzzles, short humor; anything concerned with the pet industry. Buys 1-2/issue. Length: 25-100 words. Pays $10-25.
Tips: "Send a letter of introduction and we will send our guidelines for writers and a sample copy of the magazine. After studying each, the freelancer could visit a number of pet stores and if any seem like interesting material for *PSM*, query us. We will check them out through our wholesalers and, if recommended by them, will assign the article to the freelancer. Once we have bought several articles from a writer, we will send the person out on specific assignments."

Photography

AMERICAN CINEMATOGRAPHER, A.S.C. Holding Corp., 1782 N. Orange Dr., Hollywood CA 90028. (213)876-5080. Editor: Herb A. Lightman. Assistant Editor: Lyla Dusing. Specializes in coverage of 16mm and 35mm motion picture production. For an audience ranging from students to retirees; professional interest or advanced amateurs in cinematography. Monthly magazine; 108 pages. Circ. 22,500. Time of payment depends on nature of article. Buys all rights. Phone

queries OK. Simultaneous and photocopied submissions OK. SASE. Free sample copy.
Nonfiction: How-to articles must be unusual type of treatment, or technique used in filming a production. Interviews with cinematographers. New product pieces on 16mm and 35mm cinematographic items. "The articles we use are primarily those submitted by the photographers of motion pictures. Other material is submitted by the manufacturers of equipment important in our industry. The magazine is technical in nature and the writer must have a background in motion picture photography to be able to write for us." Buys 1 ms per issue. Query. Length varies with interest. Pays $75-125.
Photos: B&w and color purchased with mss. No additional payment.
Tips: "Queries must describe writer's qualifications and include writing samples."

AMERICAN PREMIERE, 183 N. Martel, Suite 1, Los Angeles CA 90069. Editor: Michael J. Firmature. Monthly magazine (except July and August) "for and about persons in the film industry—producers, directors, actors, and all others associated." Estab. 1980. Circ. 25,000. Pays on publication. Byline given. Pays negotiable kill fee. Buys all rights, "but will consider reassigning rights." Submit seasonal/holiday material 6 weeks in advance. Simultaneous queries, and photocopied and previously published submissions OK. SASE. Reports in 6 weeks. Sample copy $3 (address request to "Circulation"); writer's guidelines for business size SAE and 1 first class stamp.
Nonfiction: Investigative; historical; how-to (incorporate yourself, read a contract, etc.); humor (satire); inspirational; interview/profile (directors, producers, businesses, persons in the industry); personal experience; photo feature ("Photo Albums"); and other themes associated with the film industry. "We like business-oriented articles." No fan material or gossip. Buys 100-125 mss/year. Query with "limited samples" of published work and resume. Length: 1,200-3,000 words. Pays $50-150.
Photos: State availability of photos. Reviews color transparencies and b&w prints. "Photos are paid for with payment for ms." Captions and model release required.
Fillers: Anecdotes, short humor and newsbreaks. "Must directly relate to film industry." Buys "100+"/year. Length: 50-150 words. Pays $10 maximum.
Tips: "Writers should be well-versed on the workings of the film industry. We're interested in people who can do statistical, but not boring, articles."

BUSINESS SCREEN, 165 W. 46th St., New York NY 10036. For sponsors, producers and users of business, commercial advertising and industrial motion pictures, slidefilms and related audiovisual media. Bimonthly. Buys all rights. ("We could accept an article written for another publication as long as it was not a competing one . . . if it was printed elsewhere, does not preclude our accepting and using it—we must see it first, and will then make up our minds.") Pays on publication. Query first. Reports in 2 weeks. SASE.
Nonfiction: "Short articles on successful application of these 'tools' in industry and commerce, but only when approved by submission of advance query to publisher's office. Technical articles on film production techniques, with or without illustrations, science film data and interesting featurettes about application or utilization of films in community, industry, etc., also welcomed. Usually, we simply pay $50-100 flat for an article, 1 page or 2 pages or 3 pages of a magazine sized publication, now called *Back Stage Magazine Supplement With Business Screen*."
Tips: "Material now being eagerly sought...one page outline will be sufficient to tell us if it would be acceptable. Not interested in feature films, radio or records. Not interested in interviews with actors or stars; not interested in theater or legit. Don't bother us with this stuff! We are interested in interviews with producers/directors/technicians involved in commercials, industrial films, especially those away from major centers of New York, Los Angeles and Chicago. Send outlines with new slants on production and AV-TV application for industry."

FUNCTIONAL PHOTOGRAPHY, PTN Publishing Corp., 250 Fulton Ave., Hempstead NY 11550. (516)489-1300. Editor: Mel Konecoff. Emphasizes scientific photography for scientists, engineers and medical professionals who use photography to document their work. Bimonthly magazine; 60 pages. Circ. 39,000. Pays on publication. Buys first North American serial rights. Photocopied submissions OK. Reports in 4 weeks. Free sample copy and writer's guidelines.
Nonfiction: Interview, personal opinion, profile, photo feature and technical. Buys 4-6 mss/issue. Query. Pays $50-350.
Photos: "We must have photos to explain article." Uses 5x7 or 8x10 b&w glossy prints, glossy color prints (any size), and color transparencies. Offers no additional payment for photos accepted with ms. Captions and model releases required. Buys one-time rights.

INDUSTRIAL PHOTOGRAPHY, United Business Publications, Inc., 475 Park Ave. S., New York NY 10016. (212)725-2300. Editor: Rich Mullin. For "the staff industrial photographer and his daily challenges. Our audience ranges from older, conservative, self-educated photographic personnel to younger, college or university educated aggressive individuals. Writers must keep stories simple, regardless." Monthly magazine. Circ. 40,000. Pays on publication. Buys first North American serial rights. Byline given. Previously photocopied and published submissions OK. SASE. Reports in 4-6 weeks. Free sample copy and writer's guidelines.

Nonfiction: How-to (material of value and interest to staff photographic personnel in non-photographic companies or military or government); interview (of industrial photographers on staff); profile (of successful in-house departments); personal experience (applications of photography in the industrial field); photo feature (as related to how-to); and technical (as related to how-to). "We regularly cover management reform and attitudes, budgeting, related outside activities (and how they may affect the staffer's position within the industry), etc." Buys 10 mss/year. Query. Length: 750-3,000 words. Pays $50-275.

Photos: Photos should be supplied by the subject, not the writer. Uses 5x7 or larger b&w prints, 5x7 or 8x10 glossy color prints and 35mm or larger transparencies. Offers no additional payment for photos accepted with ms. Captions required. Buys one-time rights.

MILLIMETER MAGAZINE, 12 E. 46th St., New York NY 10017. (212)867-3636. Editor: Alice C. Wolf. 75% freelance written. For personnel in motion picture and television industries, ad agencies, and equipment manufacturers/rentals. Monthly magazine. Circ. 21,500. Pays on publication. Buys all rights. Pays 33-50% kill fee. Byline given. Phone queries OK. Submit seasonal/holiday material 6 months in advance of issue date. Photocopied submissions OK. SASE. Reports in 3 weeks. Free sample copy.

Nonfiction: "Production stories that deal with entertainment industries of motion pictures and television programming, including TV commercials. Stories should be somewhat technical, involving equipment used, anecdotal, problems encountered and solved, and should deal with nationally known production figures. Also interviews with heads of production of current motion pictures and television personnel. Examples: directors, producers, cinematographers, scriptwriters. No personality pieces on 'stars.' " Buys 8 mss/issue. Query. Length: 1,500-4,000 words. Pays $175 minimum.

ON LOCATION, On Location, Inc., 6464 Sunset Blvd., Suite 570, Hollywood CA 90028. (213)467-1268. Editor: Ray Herbeck, Jr. Monthly magazine covering film and videotape production for producers, directors, production managers, cinematographers and sound, lighting, motion picture and video equipment suppliers. Circ. 18,200. Pays on t ublication. Byline given. Buys all rights. Submit seasonal/holiday material 4 months in advance. Simultaneous queries and photocopied submissions OK. SASE. Reports in 3 weeks. Free sample copy; writer's guidelines for business size SAE and 1 first class stamp.

Nonfiction: General interest (unique locations); how-to (use innovations and unusual techniques); technical (semi-technical articles, naming equipment brand names). No interviews with performers. Buys 10-12 mss/year. Query with clips of published work. Length 1,500-2,000 words. Pays $100-300.

Photos: State availability of photos. "usually the unit publicist will help get photos."

Fillers: Short humor. "Must be right on target. Writer must know cinematography well." Buys 5/year. Length: 500 words minimum. Pays $50-75.

Tips: "Query should include a strong hook and convince us that the filming location is unique. We like to have a feeling that the writer was on the set when the film was shot. Talk with a director, cinamatographer and set designer to find out how they solved problems down to the finest details. We use many regional correspondents."

PHOTO LAB MANAGEMENT, PLM Publishing, Inc., 1312 Lincoln Blvd., Santa Monica CA 904 6. (213)451-1344. Editor: Charlene Marmer Solomon. Associate Editor: Jacquie Kreiman. Bimonthly magazine covering process chemistries, process control, process equipment and marketing/administration for photo lab owners, managers and management personnel. Estab. 1979. Circ. 10,000. Pays on publication. Byline and brief bio given. Buys first North American serial rights. Submit seasonal/holiday material 4 months in advance. Photocopied submissions OK. SASE. Reports on queries in 6 weeks. Free sample copy and writer's guidelines for business size SAE and 1 first class stamp.

Nonfiction: Book excerpts; general interest; interview/profile (lab or lab managers); personal experience (lab manager); technical; and management or administration. Buys 12-15 mss/year "from freelancers outside the industry." Query with brief biography. Length: 1,200-1,800 words. Pays $150-180/article.

Photos: Reviews 35mm color transparencies and 4-color prints suitable for cover. "We're looking for outstanding cover shots of things to do with photo finishing. Unfortunately, we don't pay for photos that accompany stories, but the photographer gets a contributor's biography inside the magazine."

Tips: "Send a query if you have some background in the industry or a willingness to dig out information and research for a top-quality article that really speaks to our audience."

THE PHOTOLETTER, PhotoSearch International, Dept. 79, Osceola WI 54020. (715)248-3800. Managing Editor: Eileen Hacken. For professional photographers and serious amateurs interested in publishing their pictures. Newsletter published 2 times/month; 4 pages. Circ. 1,300. Pays on acceptance. Buys one-time rights. No byline; "text conforms to a format, authors feed us only details and leave style to our editor." Phone queries OK. Simultaneous, tear sheets, clippings, photocopied and previously published submissions OK. SASE. Reports in 2 weeks. Sample copy $2.

Columns/Departments: Current photos needed. "Since we pair photographers with picture buyers, we are always seeking up-to-the-minute photo needs of magazines, contests, government agencies, book publishers, etc." Buys 10 mss/issue. Phone first, unless deadline for photos will permit correspondence. Length: 25-100 words.

Fillers: Clippings and inventive ways of selling one's photos. Buys 12/year. Length: 25-100 words. Pays 20-25¢/word.

PHOTOMETHODS, Ziff-Davis Publishing Co., 1 Park Ave., New York NY 10016. (212)725-3942. Editor-in-Chief: Fred Schmidt. For professional and in-plant image-makers (still, film, video, AV) and visual communications managers. Monthly magazine; 80-96 pages. Circ. 50,000. Pays on publication. Buys one-time rights. Pays 100% kill fee. Byline given. Phone queries OK. SASE. Reports in 6 weeks. Free sample copy and writer's guidelines.

Nonfiction: How-to and photo features (solve problems with image-making techniques: photography, etc.); technical management; informational (to help the reader use photography, cine and video); interviews (with working pros); personal experience (in solving problems with photography, cine and video); profiles (well-known personalities in imaging); and technical (on photography, cine and video). Buys 5 mss/issue. Length: 1,500-3,000 words. Pays $75 minimum.

Photos: Steven Karl Weininger, art director. B&w photos (5x7 up matte or dried glossy) and color (35mm transparencies minimum or 8x10 print) purchased with or without mss, or on assignment. Captions required. Query or submit contact sheet. Pays $35 for b&w; $50 for color; more for covers. Model release required.

Tips: "You can get my attention by knowing who we are and what we publish. Anything sent must be professionally packaged: neatly typed, well organized; and have patience. Don't come across as a writer we cannot live without. Don't contact us unless you know the magazine and the type of articles we publish. No unsolicited mss. Please query first."

THE RANGEFINDER, 1312 Lincoln Blvd., Santa Monica CA 90406. (213)451-8506. Editor: Jacquie Kreiman. Assistant Editor: Patrice Apodaca. Emphasizes professional photography. Monthly magazine; 100 pages. Circ. 47,500. Pays on publication. Buys first North American serial rights. Phone queries OK. Submit seasonal material 4 months in advance. Byline given. SASE. Reports in 3 weeks. Sample copy $1.50; free writer's guidelines.

Nonfiction: How-to (solve a photographic problem; such as new techniques in lighting, new poses or setups); interview (success stories); new product (test reports of product in use); and technical (roundup style on equipment in use such as light meters, front projection, large format cameras, etc.). "Articles should contain lots of practical, solid information. Issues should be covered in depth. Look thoroughly into the topic." No opinion, experience or biographical articles. Especially needs "stories on new breakthroughs in the field." Buys 3 mss/issue. Query with outline. Length: 800-1,200 words. Pays $48-60/published page.

Photos: State availability of photos with query. Offers no additional payment for 8x10 b&w glossy prints. Captions preferred. Buys one-time rights. Model release required.

Tips: "Exhibit some knowledge of photography. Introduce yourself with a well-written letter and a great story idea."

SHOOTING COMMERCIALS MAGAZINE, Knowledge Industry Publications, Inc., 701 Westchester, White Plains NY 10604. (914)328-9157. Editor: Louise Moore. Emphasizes commercial production for production companies, advertising agencies, equipment houses, clients, animators, actors and sound track composers. Monthly magazine; 32 pages. Circ. 14,000. Pays on publication. Buys one-time rights. Byline given. Phone queries OK. Photocopied submissions OK. Reports "immediately." Free sample copy and writer's guidelines.

Nonfiction: How-to (how a specific commercial was filmed or videotaped); interview (with ad agency people or production people); profile (of persons involved in production of commercials); new product; personal experience; photo feature; and technical. "We are limited in space, therefore our articles must be timely, succinct and capture the reader's attention immediately." Query by phone. Length: 700 words preferred, but longer material is accepted if the subject is interesting. Pays $75.

Photos: B&w glossy prints (any size). Offers no additional payment for photos accepted with ms. Captions required.

STUDIO PHOTOGRAPHY, PTN Publishing Corp., 250 Fulton Ave., Hempstead NY 11550. (516)489-1300. Editor: Frederic W. Rosen. Managing Editor: David Fox. 50% freelance written. Monthly magazine. Circ. 55,000. Pays on publication. Not copyrighted. Submit seasonal/holiday material 5 months in advance of issue date. SASE. Reports in 6 weeks.

Nonfiction: Interview; personal experience; photo feature; communication-oriented; technical; and travel. No business-oriented articles. Buys 2-3 mss/issue. Length: 1,700-3,000 words. Pays $75 minimum/published page.

Photos: State availability of photos with query. Photos and article in one package.

Columns/Departments: Point of View (any aspect of photography dealing with professionals only). Buys 1 ms/issue. Length: 1,700 words minimum. Pays $35 minimum.

Tips: "No handwritten queries will even be looked at. We look for professional quality in writing. No originals, only fine-quality dupes. Prefer layer format, though not essential. Submit b&w photos with all articles. Only people with definite ideas and a sense of who they are need apply for publication."

TECHNICAL PHOTOGRAPHY, PTN Publishing Corp., 250 Fulton Ave., Hempstead NY 11550. Editor-in-Chief: Don Garbera. 50% freelance written. Publication of the "on-staff (in-house) industrial, military and government still, cinema, video and AV professional who must produce (or know where to get) visuals of all kinds." Monthly magazine; 64 pages. Circ. 53,000. Pays on publication. Buys first North American serial rights. Byline given except when it needs complete rewrite or when supplied through public relations agency." SASE. Reports in 4 weeks. Free sample copy and writer's guidelines.

Nonfiction: How-to; interview; photo feature; profile (detailed stories about in-house operations); and technical. "All manuscripts must relate to industrial, military or government production of visuals." Buys 75-110 mss/year. Query. Length: "as long as needed to get the information across." Pays $50-350 minimum/display page.

Photos: Offers no additional payment for photos purchased with ms. Captions required. Query.

Plumbing, Heating, Air Conditioning, and Refrigeration

Publications for fuel oil dealers who also install heating equipment are classified with the Petroleum journals.

AIR CONDITIONING, HEATING AND REFRIGERATION NEWS, Box 2600, Troy MI 48084. (313)362-3700. Editor-in-Chief: Gordon D. Duffy. Managing Editor: John O. Sweet. 20% freelance written. "An industry newspaper that covers both the technology and marketing of air conditioning, heating and refrigeration." Weekly tabloid; 30 pages. Circ. 31,000. Pays on publication. Buys all rights. Phone queries OK. "Query to be a short precis of the story containing a slant writer plans to take—not something vague like 'I'll give you what you want.' We can add or delete from a 'known' letter than a 'maybe.'" Submit seasonal/holiday material 1 month in advance of issue date. Simultaneous and photocopied submissions OK. Reports in 2-3 weeks. Free sample copy.

Nonfiction: How-to (basic business management applied to contracting operations; sophisticated technical problems in heating, air conditioning, and refrigeration); interview (check first); nostalgia; profile; and technical. Buys 2-4 mss/issue. Query. Length: 1,500 words. Pays $1.50-2.25/column inch.

Photos: State availability of photos with query or ms. Pays $10-35 for 5x7 or 8x10 b&w glossy prints. Captions required. Buys all rights.

CONTRACTOR MAGAZINE, Berkshire Common, Pittsfield MA 01201. Editor: Seth Shepard. 20% freelance written. For mechanical contractors and wholesalers. Newspaper; 50 (11x15) pages. Twice monthly. Circ. 43,000. Not copyrighted. Buys 10 mss/year. Pays on publication. Sample copy for $3. Photocopied submissions OK. No simultaneous submissions. Reports in 1 month.

Query first or submit complete ms. SASE.

Nonfiction and Photos: Articles on materials, use, policies, and business methods of the air conditioning, heating, plumbing contracting industry. Topics covered include: interpretive reports, how-to, informational, interview, profile, think articles, expose, spot news, successful business operations, merchandising techniques, labor. Pays $300 maximum. 5x7 b&w glossies purchased with or without ms. Pays $10. Captions required.

DOMESTIC ENGINEERING MAGAZINE, Construction Press, 135 Addison St., Elmhurst IL 60126. Editor: Stephen J. Shafer. Managing Editor: Donald Michard. Emphasizes plumbing, heating, air conditioning and piping for contractors, and for mechanical contractors in these specialties gives information on management, marketing and merchandising. Monthly magazine; 100 pages. Circ. 40,000. Pays on acceptance. Buys all rights, simultaneous rights, or first rights. Simultaneous, photocopied and previously published submissions OK. SASE. Reports in 1 month. Sample copy $2.

Nonfiction: How-to (some technical in industry areas). Expose, interview, profile, personal experience, photo feature and technical articles are written on assignment only and should be about management, marketing and merchandising for plumbing and mechanical contracting businessmen. Buys 12 mss/year. Query. Pays $25 minimum.

Photos: State availability of photos. Pays $10 minimum for b&w prints (reviews contact sheets) and color transparencies.

EXPORT, 386 Park Ave. S., New York NY 10016. Editor: R. Weingarten. For importers and distributors in 167 countries who handle hardware, air conditioning and refrigeration equipment and related consumer hardlines. Bimonthly magazine; 60-80 pages in English and Spanish editions. Circ. 38,500. Buys first serial rights. Byline given. Buys about 10 mss/year. Pays on acceptance. Reports in 1 month. Query. SASE.

Nonfiction: News stories of products and merchandising of air conditioning and refrigeration equipment, hardware and related consumer hardlines. Informational, how-to, interview, profile, successful business operations. Length: 1,000-3,000 words. Pays 10¢/word, maximum.

Tips: "One of the best ways to break in here is with a story originating outside the US or Canada. Our major interest is in new products and new developments—but they must be available and valuable to overseas buyers. We also like company profile stories. Departments and news stories are staff-written."

HEATING/PIPING/AIR CONDITIONING, 2 Illinois Center, Chicago IL 60601. (312)861-0880. Editor: Robert T. Korte. Monthly. Buys all rights. Pays on publication. Query. Reports in 2 weeks. SASE.

Nonfiction: Uses engineering and technical articles covering design, installation, operation, maintenance, etc., of heating, piping and air conditioning systems in industrial plants and large buildings. Length: 3,000-4,000 words maximum. Pays $30/printed page.

Tips: "Query to have facts and an in-depth analysis of unique approaches. Be able to communicate with top level engineers first. Non-engineering trained freelancers really have very little chance of acceptance."

HEATING, PLUMBING, AIR CONDITIONING, 1450 Don Mills Rd., Don Mills, Ontario, Canada M3B 2X7. (416)445-6641. Editor: Ronald Shuker. For mechanical contractors; plumbers; warm air heating, refrigeration, ventilation and air conditioning contractors; wholesalers; architects; consulting and mechanical engineers who are in key management or specifying positions in the plumbing, heating, air conditioning and refrigeration industries in Canada. Monthly. Circ. 12,500. Pays on publication. Free sample copy. Reports in 1-2 months. For a prompt reply, "enclose a sheet on which is typed a statement either approving or rejecting the suggested article which can either be checked off, or a quick answer written in and signed and returned."

Nonfiction and Photos: News, technical, business management and "how-to" articles that will inform, educate and motivate readers who design, manufacture, install, service, maintain or supply all mechanical components and systems in residential, commercial, institutional and industrial installations across Canada. Length: 1,000-1,500 words. Pays 10¢/word. Photos purchased with mss. Prefers 5x7 or 8x10 glossies.

Tips: Topics must relate directly to the day-to-day activities of *HPAC* readers in Canada. Must be detailed, with specific examples, quotes from specific people or authorities, show depth. Specifically want material from other parts of Canada besides Southern Ontario. Not really interested in material from US unless specifically related to Canadian readers concerns. Primarily want articles that show *HPAC* readers how they can increase their sales and business step-by-step based on specific examples of what others have done.

SNIPS MAGAZINE, 407 Mannheim Rd., Bellwood IL 60104. (312)544-3870. Editor: Nick Carter. For sheet metal, warm air heating, ventilating, air conditioning, and roofing contractors. Monthly. Buys all rights. "Write for detailed list of requirements before submitting any work." SASE.
Nonfiction: Material should deal with information about contractors who do sheet metal, warm air heating, air conditioning, ventilation and roofing work; also about successful advertising campaigns conducted by these contractors and the results. Length: "prefers stories to run less than 1,000 words unless on special assignment." Pays 2¢ each for first 500 words, 1¢ each for additional words.
Photos: Pays $2 each for small snapshot pictures, $4 each for usable 8x10 pictures.

THE WHOLESALER, Distribution Voice of the Plumbing, Heating, Air Conditioning and Refrigeration Industry, Scott Periodicals, 135 Addison, Elmhurst IL 60126. (312)530-6160. Editor: Mary Ann Falkman. Monthly tabloid covering business management for wholesalers who carry mechanical systems of the construction industry. Circ. 25,000. Pays on publication. Byline given. Buys one-time rights. Simultaneous queries, and photocopied and previously published submissions OK. SASE. Reports on queries in 1 month.
Nonfiction: How-to (manage a business tied to a specific topic). "No profiles on individuals or businesses." Buys 10-12 mss/year. Query with clips of published work. Length: 2,500 minimum words. Pays $200-300/article.
Photos: State availability of photos. Reviews 5x7 b&w glossy prints. Pays $50 maximum total for photo package. Captions required. Buys one-time rights.
Tips: "Author must be a qualified expert in subject he is writing on."

Power and Power Plants

Publications in this listing aim at company managers, engineers and others involved in generating and supplying power for businesses, homes and industries. Journals for electrical engineers who design, maintain and install systems connecting users with sources of power are classified under Electricity.

DIESEL PROGRESS/DIESEL & GAS TURBINE WORLDWIDE, (formerly *Diesel and Gas Turbine Progress*), Box 26308, Milwaukee WI 52336. Editorial Director: Robert A. Wilson. Senior Editor: J. Kane. Assistant Managing Editor: Mike Osenga. 5% freelance written. Monthly magazine; 88 pages. Circ. 25,000. Pays on publication. Buys first rights. Submit editorial material 6 weeks in advance of issue date. Previously published submissions OK. SASE. Reports in 4 weeks. Sample copy $2.
Nonfiction: "The articles we would consider from freelancers would be technical descriptions of unique diesel or gas turbine engine applications—including extensive technical descriptions of the installation, the method of operations and maintenance." Buys 10 mss/year. Query and submit clips of published work. Length: 1,600-2,400 words. Pay based on use.
Photos: "All stories are illustrated and photos of the engine installation must accompany the text, or it is really of little value." State availability of photos with query. No additional payment for 8x10 b&w glossy prints and 8x10 glossy color prints (cover only). Captions preferred. Buys all rights.

PUBLIC POWER, 2600 Virginia Ave. NW, Washington DC 20037. (202)342-7200. Editor: Vic Reinemer. Bimonthly. Not copyrighted. Byline given "depends upon the copy." Pays on publication. Query.
Nonfiction: News and features on municipal and other local publicly owned electric systems. Payment negotiable.
Photos: Uses b&w glossy prints and color.

Printing

AMERICAN INK MAKER, 101 W. 31st St., New York NY 10001. (212)279-4455. Editor-in-Chief: John Vollmuth. 10% freelance written. Monthly magazine; 70 pages. Circ. 4,000. Pays on publication. Buys one-time rights. Phone queries OK. Submit seasonal/holiday material 2 months in

Writer's DIGEST

Writer's DIGEST

THE WORLD'S LEADING MAGAZINE FOR WRITERS

Would you like to:

- get up-to-the-minute reports on the writing markets?
- receive the advice of editors and professional writers about what to write and how to write it to maximize your opportunities for getting published?
- read interviews of leading authors that reveal their secrets of success?
- hear what experts have to say about writing and selling fiction, nonfiction, and poetry?
- get a $3 discount?

(See other side for details.)

advance of issue date. Photocopied submissions OK. SASE. Reports in 2 weeks. Free sample copy.
Nonfiction: General interest; historical; humor; interview; new product; personal experience; opinion; profile; and technical. Buys 4 mss/year. Submit complete ms. Length: 800-1,500 words. Pays $135-150.
Photos: No additional payment for photos with accompanying ms. Captions preferred. Buys all rights.

AMERICAN PRINTER AND LITHOGRAPHER, 300 W. Adams St., Chicago IL 60606. Editor: Elizabeth G. Berglund. 45-60% freelance written. For qualified personnel active in any phase of the graphic arts industry. Monthly. Circ. 75,000. Buys all rights, unless otherwise specified in writing at time of purchase. Byline given. Pays on publication. Free sample copy. Submit seasonal material 2 months in advance. "Study publication before writing." SASE.
Nonfiction: Management, and technical subjects with illustrations pertinent to the graphic arts industry. Query. Length: 1,500-3,000 words. Pays $50-250.
Photos: Purchased with mss; also news shots of graphic arts occurrences. Uses 5x7 or 8x10 glossy prints. Pays $5-10.
Fillers: Clippings about product installations, plant openings, acquisitions and purchases, business reorganization. Particularly interested in items on newspapers; not interested in personnel announcements. Pays $2-5.

GRAPHIC ARTS MONTHLY, Technical Publishing Co., A Dun & Bradstreet Co., 666 5th Ave., New York NY 10103. Editor-in-Chief: B.D. Chapman. Managing Editor: Lynne Nicholson. 10% freelance written. For "printers and persons in graphic communications, composition, plate-making, color separations, ink, press room chemicals, etc." Monthly magazine; 170 pages. Circ. 80,000. Pays on publication. Buys all rights. Submit seasonal/holiday material 2-3 months in advance of issue date. SASE. Reports in 2 weeks.
Nonfiction: Historical; how-to; interview; new product; photo feature; and technical. "We accept articles directly related to the printing trades. Following criteria to be observed: material should be written objectively, and should stress the savings of cost, enhancement of quality, increased productivity or maximize safety." Query with clips of published work. Length: 1,000-2,500 words. Pays 7-10¢/word.
Photos: State availability of photos with query. Pays $15 for 5x7 or 8x10 b&w prints. Captions for identification. Buys all rights.

IN-PLANT REPRODUCTIONS, North American Publishing Co., 401 N. Broad St., Philadelphia PA 19108. (215)574-9600. Editor: Tom Bluesteen. Assistant Editor: Anita McKelvey. Monthly magazine about in-plant printing management for printing departments in business, government and industry. These graphic arts facilities include art, composition, camera, platemaking, press, and finishing equipment, xerographic and other business communications systems. Circ. 40,000. Pays on publication. Byline given. Buys first North American serial rights or all rights. Phone queries OK. SASE. Reports in 1 month. Sample copy $5.
Nonfiction: Interview, profile, how-to, and technical. Buys 4 mss/issue. Query. Length: 500-2,500 words. Pays $75-200.

NEWSPAPER PRODUCTION, North American Publishing Co., 401 N. Broad St., Philadelphia PA 19108. (215)574-9600. Demographic edition of *Printing Impressions*. Editor-in-Chief: Walter Kubilius. 50% freelance written. For the newspaper industry; production personnel through management to editor and publisher. Bimonthly demographic section magazine; 56 pages. Circ. 17,500. Pays on publication. Buys all rights. Phone queries OK. Photocopied submissions OK, "but please identify if simultaneous elsewhere." SASE. Reports in 3 weeks.
Nonfiction: Publishes production case histories and how-to articles (production techniques). Length: 1,500 words minimum. Query or submit complete ms. Pays $50-175.
Photos: B&w and color purchased with or without mss, or on assignment. Captions required. Query or submit contact sheet or prints. Additional payment for those used with mss computed into article's length. Model release required.

PLAN AND PRINT, 10116 Franklin Ave., Franklin Park IL 60131. (312)671-5356. Editor-in-Chief: James C. Vebeck. 50% freelance written. For commercial reproduction companies and in-plant reproduction, printing, drafting and design departments of business and industry. Monthly magazine. Circ. 23,000. Pays on publication. Buys all rights. Byline given. Submit seasonal/holiday material 4-6 months in advance of issue date. SASE. Reports in 2 weeks. Free sample and writer's guidelines.
Nonfiction: How-to (how certain problems may have been solved; new methods of doing certain kinds of reproduction and/or design/drafting work); and technical (must relate to industry). Buys

50 mss/year. Query with clips of previously published work. Length: 250-5,000 words. Pays $25-300.

Photos: State availability of photos with query. Pays $5-10 for 8x10 b&w glossy prints. Captions required. Buys all rights. Model release required.

Columns/Departments: Open to suggestions for new columns/departments.

Poetry: Light verse related to the industry. Buys 6/year. Length: 4-12 lines. Pays $7.50 maximum.

QUICK PRINTING, Coast Publishing, Inc., 3255 S. US 1, Ft. Pierce FL 33450. (305)465-9450. Editor: Judy Gallagher. Monthly magazine about quick copy and duplicating for owners and managers of quick print shops with 2-5 employees and who average $180,000 in sales annually. Circ. 15,000. Pays on publication. Byline given. Makes work-for-hire assignments. Phone queries OK. Submit seasonal material 4 months in advance. Photocopied and previously published submissions OK. SASE. Reports in 1 month on queries; in 2 months on mss. Free sample copy.

Nonfiction: Interview (with quick print industry suppliers); profile (with successful quick printer); how-to (save money on supplies, set up a darkroom, price printing and art work); technical (press production and typesetting). "Knowledge of quick printing is a must. Photos are usually used with story or product item. Freelancers should submit articles on production, bindery, darkroom, high speed copiers, presses, ink and paper; and typesetting, successful quick printers, purchasing, leasing equipment and management tips." Buys 6 mss/year. Query with outline and clips of previously published work. Length: 500-1,500 words. Pays $25-100.

Columns/Departments: Product News, Industry News and Printing Production Hints.

Tips: "Send us stories relating directly to quick printers rather than articles for general use."

SCREEN PRINTING, 407 Gilbert Ave., Cincinnati OH 45202. (513)421-2050. Editor: Jonathan E. Schiff. For the screen printing industry, including screen printers (commercial, industrial and captive shops), suppliers and manufacturers, ad agencies and allied professions. Monthly magazine; 120 pages. Circ. 10,000. Buys all rights. Byline given. Pays on publication. Free writer's guidelines. Will not consider photocopied submissions. Will consider simultaneous submissions. Reporting time varies. SASE.

Nonfiction and Photos: "Since the screen printing industry covers a broad range of applications and overlaps other fields in the graphic arts, it's necessary that articles be of a significant contribution, preferably to a specific area of screen printing. Subject matter is fairly open, with preference given to articles on administration or technology; trends and developments. We try to give a good sampling of technical business and management articles; articles about unique operations. We also publish special features and issues on important subjects, such as material shortages, new markets and new technology breakthroughs. While most of our material is nitty-gritty, we appreciate a writer who can take an essentially dull subject and encourage the reader to read on through concise, factual, flairful and creative, expressive writing. Interviews are published after consultation with and guidance from the editor." Interested in stories on unique approaches by some shops on how to lick the problems created by the petroleum shortage (the industry relies heavily on petrol products). Length: 1,500-2,000 words. Pays minimum of $150 for major features; minimum of $75 for minor features; minimum of $50 for back of book articles. Cover photos negotiable; b&w or color. Published material becomes the property of the magazine.

WORLD-WIDE PRINTER, North American Publishing Co., 401 N. Broad St., Philadelphia PA 19108. Editor: Walter Kubilius. Emphasizes printing and printing technology for printers; packagers; and publishers of newspapers, books, magazines, any and all printed matter in all parts of the world. Distributed internationally. Bimonthly magazine; 110 pages. Circ. 15,000. Pays on publication. Buys all rights. Phone queries OK. Submit seasonal/holiday material 2 months in advance. Simultaneous, photocopied and previously published submissions OK, if identified as to other possible placement. Reports in 3 weeks. Sample copy $2.

Nonfiction: Technical material only. "Knowledge of printing technology is absolutely necessary in the writer, even if the subject is only an interview or plant story." Buys 2-3 mss/issue. Query. Length: 500-2,000 words. Pays $25-150.

Photos: State availability of photos. Pays $5 for b&w 5x7 prints.

Public Relations

PUBLICIST, Public Relations Aids, Inc., 221 Park Ave. S., New York NY 10003. Editor-in-Chief: Lee Levitt. 25% freelance written. Devoted entirely to professional publicity/public relations. For "a controlled circulation of people engaged in publicity on a national or major regional scale."

Bimonthly tabloid. Circ. 14,000. Pays on acceptance. Pays 100% kill fee. Buys one-time rights . Byline given unless "writer told in response to initial inquiry that material could only be used as part of another article (in which case, of course, he can decide not to submit material); payment also is much lower in such cases." Submit seasonal/holiday material 6 months in advance. Simultaneous, photocopied and previously published material OK. SASE. Reports in 1 month. Free sample copy and writer's guidelines for self-addressed mailing label plus 45¢ in stamps.

Nonfiction: How-to, informational, humor, interview, nostalgia, profile, personal experience, photo feature and technical. "The subject of every article must be publicity, or organizations or persons engaged in publicity. We cover only national projects." Buys 5 mss/issue. Query. Length: 400-2,000 words. Pays $30-250.

Photos: Purchased with or without accompanying ms or on assignment. Captions required. Uses b&w only. Query. Prefers 8x10 prints. Pays $20-50.

Fiction: Humorous, condensed novels, mainstream, serialized novels. "All fiction must concern publicity people in a realistic, professional situation; must exhibit sophisticated comprehension of big time PR practice." Query. Length: 500 words minimum. Pays $50-400.

Fillers: Clippings, jokes, gags, anecdotes, newsbreaks, short humor on professional public relations topics only. Buys 2/issue. Length: 50-400 words. Pays $2-40.

Tips: "We are most likely to accept case histories of national publicity projects; the article must include details of the project's cost; you must send documentation of the project. All our articles are in newspaper style: flat, abrupt leads, attributions for all important statements, no editorial comment. To break in, first: Send a self-addressed label and 45¢ postage for a sample copy and writer's guidelines. Then telephone the editor and discuss with him any story ideas you may have; or write and mail a query, in which case the editor probably will phone you. We are glad to help first-timers in any way we can. The writer must start with a basic understanding of professional public relations work; however—we cannot teach you this on the phone."

Real Estate

AREA DEVELOPMENT MAGAZINE, 432 Park Ave. S., New York NY 10016. (212)532-4360. Editor-in-Chief: Tom Bergeron. 50% freelance written. Emphasizes corporate facility planning and site selection for manufacturing chief executives worldwide. Monthly magazine; 110-190 pages. Circ. 32,000. Pays when edited. Buys first rights. Byline given. Photocopied submissions OK. Reports in 1-3 weeks. Free sample copy and writer's guidelines.

Nonfiction: How-to (case histories of companies; experiences in site selection and all other aspects of corporate facility planning); historical (if it deals with corporate facility planning); interview (corporate executives and professional developers); experience (of corporate executives); personal opinion; and photo feature (pictures of new plants, offices and warehouses). Buys 3-5 mss/issue. Query. Pays $50-60/printed page, including illustrations.

Photos: State availability of photos with query. Additional payment for 8x10 or 5x7 b&w glossy prints. Captions preferred. Buys first rights.

Tips: "Articles must be accurate, objective (no puffery) and useful to our manufacturing executive readers. Avoid any discussion of the merits or disadvantages of any particular areas or communities."

COMMUNITY DEVELOPMENT PUBLICATIONS, 399 National Press Bldg., Washington DC 20045. (202)638-6113. Various newsletters for government officials and industry executives in housing-community development—housing production; housing market; managing housing; community development programs; neighborhoods and home improvement; real estate. Pays end of month after publication. SASE if return desired. Sample copy and writer's guidelines for SASE.

Fillers: Uses contributions of significant newspaper clippings on housing, community development, and real estate; substantive actions and litigations that would be of interest to housing, community development, and real estate professionals beyond immediate area. "We reject news not of interest to our needs which can't hold up until use." Particularly wants regular contributors for multistates, region, or at least a full state, especially state capitals. Normally pays $2.50 for each clipping used.

EMPIRE STATE REALTOR, New York State Association of Realtors, Executive Park Tower, Western Ave. at Fuller Rd., Albany NY 12203. Monthly tabloid covering real estate, housing, general economy/legistation for realtors, associates; also sent to NYS legislators and allied businesses. Estab. 1980. Circ. 24,152. Pays on publication. Byline given. Not copyrighted. Buys all rights. Submit seasonal/holiday material 2 months in advance. Photocopied and previously

published submissions OK. Reports in 2 weeks on queries; 3 weeks on mss. Free sample copy and writer's guidelines.
Nonfiction: Book excerpts and reviews; general interest (feature articles on real estate, housing, and related legislative issues); how-to (list, sell, close); personal experience (of realtors or allied professionals); and technical (financing). "Articles should relate in some way to the real estate industry. Offer new or creative tips, hints, guidelines on sales techniques; or write an article on aspects of creative financing. Styles range from hard news to creative writing. Be concise, yet creative. Share your ideas for success with others." Buys maximum of 12 mss/year ("no set amount"). Send complete ms. Length: 250-1,500 words. Pays $25 maximum/article.

FINANCIAL FREEDOM REPORT, National Institute of Financial Planning, Suite C, 1811 Fort Union Blvd., Salt Lake City UT 84121. (801)943-1280. Editor: Mark O. Haroldsen. Managing Editor: Michael Hansen. For "professional and nonprofessional investors, and would-be investors in real estate—real estate brokers, insurance companies, investment planners, truck drivers, housewives, doctors, architects, contractors, etc. The magazine's content is presently expanding to interest and inform the readers about other ways to put their money to work for them." Monthly magazine; 72 pages. Circ. 50,000. Pays on publication. Buys all rights. Phone queries OK. Simultaneous submissions OK. SASE. Reports in 2 weeks. Sample copy $3; free writer's guidelines.
Nonfiction: How-to (find real estate bargains, finance property, use of leverage, managing property, developing market trends, goal setting, motivational); and interviews (success stories of those who have relied on own initiative and determination in real estate market or other business endeavors, e.g., Ray Kroc of McDonald's). Buys 9 mss/issue. Query with clips of published work or submit complete ms. Length: 1,500-4,500 words. "If the topic warranted a two- or three-parter, we would consider it." Pays 7-10¢/word.
Photos: Send photos with ms. Uses b&w 8x10 matte prints. Offers no additional payment for photos accepted with ms. Captions required.

PROPERTIES MAGAZINE, 4900 Euclid Ave., Cleveland OH 44103. (216)431-7666. Editor: Gene Bluhm. Monthly. Buys all rights. Pays on publication. Query. SASE.
Nonfiction and Photos: Wants articles of real estate and construction news value. Interested primarily in articles relating to northeastern Ohio. Length: up to 900 words. Buys photographs with mss, 5x7 preferred.

REALTOR NEWS, The Advocate Newspaper for Private Property Rights, Public Communications, Inc. (for National Association of Realtors), 35 E. Wacker Dr., Chicago IL 60601. (312)558-1788. Weekly tabloid covering the economy and legislation as pertains to real estate; real estate trends and features; legal decisions. "90% of readership is realtors, members of NAR; any news items, trends, or regional issues that may have national significance for our readers are of interest. The National Association of Realtors is a 700,000 member group dedicated to private property rights. Estab. 1980. Circ. 175,000. Pays on acceptance "whether used or not." No byline given. Submit seasonal/holiday material 1 month in advance. Simultaneous queries OK. Free sample copy and writer's guidelines.
Nonfiction: Expose (of government regulations no-growth issues; rent control); general interest (on trends; features; creative financing; legal decisions—housing related); photo feature (of adaptive re-use of buildings); and technical (energy-saving; home design). Buys 25 mss/year. Query. Length: 300-1,000 words. Pays $75-150.
Photos: State availability of photos. Captions and identification of subject required. Buys all rights.
Tips: "Please submit all queries initially by mail to articles editor of *Realtor News*. Freelancers might think in terms of stories, local and regional, that have national appeal and would improve business for all realtors."

SOUTHWEST REAL ESTATE NEWS, Communication Channels, Inc., 11325 Pegasus, Suite W-158, Dallas TX 75238. (214)348-0739. Editor: Jim Mitchell. Managing Editor: Sheryl Roberts. Monthly newspaper about commercial and industrial real estate for professional real estate people, including realtors, developers, mortgage bankers, corporate real estate executives, architects, contractors and brokers. Circ. 16,000. Average issue includes 4 columns, 20-50 short news items, 2-5 special articles and 10 departments. Pays on publication. Byline given. Buys all rights. Phone queries OK. Submit seasonal material 2 months in advance. Photocopied submissions OK. SASE. Reports in 4-6 weeks. Free sample copy and writer's guidelines.
Nonfiction: "We're interested in hearing from writers in major cities in the states that we cover, which are TX, OK, CO, NM, LA, AZ, AR. We are particularly interested in writers with newspaper experience or real estate background. Assignments are made according to our editorial schedule which we will supply upon request. Most open to freelancers are city reviews and special

articles. Contact the staff to discuss ideas first. No unsolicited material." Buys 3-5 mss/issue. Query. Pays $50-300.

Columns/Departments: Offices; Shopping Centers; Industrials; Multiplexes; Leases; Sales and Purchases; Mortgage and Financial; Realty Operations; Residentials; and People in the News. No newspaper clippings. Buys 3 mss/issue. Query. Length: 1,000-5,000 words. Pays $50-75.

Recreational Park and Campground Management

CAMPGROUND MANAGEMENT, 500 Hyacinth Pl., Highland Park IL 60035. (312)433-4550. Editor: Mike Byrnes. Monthly. Circ. 18,000. Buys all rights. Pays 4-6 weeks after acceptance. Reports in 1 month. Query first. Free sample copy. SASE.

Nonfiction and Photos: Success stories and management information articles for owners of campgrounds and recreation vehicle parks in US, Canada and Mexico. News stories about campgrounds, associations, campground chains and any other subjects helpful or of interest to campground operators. Also uses features about such subjects as a specialized bookkeeping system for campground operations, an interesting traffic circulation system, an advertising and promotion program that has worked well for a campground, efficient trash collection systems. Successful operation of coin-operated dispensing machines, successful efforts by a campground owner in bringing in extra income through such means as stores, charge showers, swimming fees, etc. Use newspaper style reporting for news items and newspaper feature style for articles. Length: 500-700 words, news stories; 300-2,000 words. Pays $20-200. "B&w photos should accompany articles whenever practical."

CAMPGROUND MERCHANDISING, 401 N. Broad St., Suite 904, Philadelphia PA 19108. Managing Editor: Mary Horner. For owners and managers of campgrounds who sell merchandise or equipment to people who vacation at campgrounds. Magazine published 4 times a year; 56 pages. Circ. 14,500. Buys first North American serial rights. No byline. Buys 5 mss/year. Pays on acceptance. Will not consider photocopied or simultaneous submissions. Submit seasonal material 3 months in advance. Reports in 2 weeks. Query or submit complete ms. SASE.

Nonfiction and Photos: "We specialize in RV campgrounds that resell equipment or merchandise to RV'ers who are visiting the RV campground. We use articles about how to best operate a recreation vehicle campground. We want stories on reselling food and souvenirs to guests; also stories on putting in waterslides, tennis and other recreation attractions. The best approach is to interview managers of recreation vehicle campgrounds about their operations. Not interested in RV campgrounds selling bread, milk, ice cream. Main interest is in their sales of equipment or merchandise wanted only by RV'ers, and how the resale of merchandise and equipment in an RV campground made it profitable." Informational, how-to, personal experience, interview, successful business operations, merchandising techniques. Length: 800-1,500 words. Pays about 4¢/word. Prefers 8x10 b&w glossies, but can use 5x7. Pays $10 for each one used with ms. No color. Captions optional.

Fillers: Clippings are purchased only if about RV parks and newsworthy. Pays 80¢/inch used.

TOURIST ATTRACTIONS AND PARKS, 401 N. Broad St., Suite 904, Philadelphia PA 14108. Editor: Paula Scully. 10% freelance written. For managers, owners of amusement parks, theme parks, tourist attractions, carnivals, fairgrounds, arenas, stadiums, booking entertainment, interested in improving promotion and personnel handling in theme parks and tourist attractions. Quarterly. Circ. 17,500. Pays between publication and acceptance. Phone queries OK. Buys first North American serial rights. SASE. Reports in 2 weeks. Writer's guidelines for SASE.

Nonfiction: How-to; new product (must be new and worthwhile); personal experience (only with a management technique or new type of ride, or of system that improves an amusement park or theme park's operations); technical (a device that does job better or less expensively, a description of a new technique that is successful—a ride or a way to attract visitors). "No travel pieces of scenic wonder or a national or state park." Buys 2 mss/issue. Query. Length: 1,000-3,000 words. Pays 1-2¢/inch.

Photos: State availability of photos with query. Pays $10 for 8x10 b&w glossy prints with white borders. Captions preferred. Buys one-time rights.

Secretarial

MODERN SECRETARY, Allied Publications, Drawer 189, Palm Beach FL 33480. Editor: Anita M. Kirchen. Monthly magazine; 16 pages. Pays on acceptance. Buys simultaneous rights. Submit seasonal/holiday material 6 months in advance of issue date. Simultaneous, photocopied and previously published submissions OK. SASE. Reports in 1 month. Sample copy $1; writer's guidelines for SASE.
Nonfiction: Office tips for secretaries and picture stories of secretaries of famous personalities. How-to; general interest; humor; historical; interview; nostalgia; personal experience; profile; technical. Nothing controversial or suggestive. Submit complete ms. Length: 500-800 words. Pays 5¢/accepted word.
Photos: Pays $5 for 8½x11 b&w glossy prints. Captions required. Buys simultaneous rights.

TODAY'S SECRETARY, McGraw-Hill, Inc., 1221 Avenue of the Americas, New York NY 10020. (212)997-2166. Editor: Nhora Cortes-Comerer. 75% freelance written. "For a readership between 15-21, enrolled in high school, junior college and private business school secretarial programs." Monthly (October-May) magazine; 32 pages. Circ. 60,000. Pays on publication. Buys all rights. Submit seasonal/holiday material 6 months in advance of issue date. SASE. Reports in 2-3 months. Free sample copy and writer's guidelines; mention *Writer's Market* in request.
Nonfiction: General interest (women's issues, consumer topics); historical (related to business and offices); how-to (office procedures); humor (office situations); interview (interesting secretaries); new products (office products and supplies). Buys 32 mss/year. Query with clips of published work. Length: 800-3,000 words. Pays $75-350.
Columns/Departments: Word Teasers (grammatical points); Consumer Wise (consumer information); and Think It Out (secretarial procedure). Buys 24 mss/year. Query. Length: 800-2,000 words. Pays $75-200.
Tips: "The best way to break in would be with a short piece (800 words). Keep in mind that our audience is 17-22, in high school or business school. Also, the stories shouldn't be too heavy. Other good freelance possibilities include profiles of secretaries with unusual job responsibilities or in an unusual field, secretaries who have and use shorthand skills, and secretarial procedure stories—tips on filing, making travel arrangements for your boss, etc. Become familiar with the publication. Have unusual angle, and lively but not puffy writing style. Stay away from stereotypes."

Selling and Merchandising

In this category are journals for sales personnel and merchandisers publishing general material on how to sell products successfully. Journals in nearly every other category of this Trade Journal section also buy this kind of material if it is slanted to the specialized product or industry they deal with, such as clothing or petroleum. Publications for advertising and marketing professionals will be found under Advertising and Marketing.

AGENCY SALES MAGAZINE, Box 16878, Irvine CA 92713. (714)752-5231. Editor: Dan Bayless. 60% freelance written. For independent sales representatives and the manufacturers they represent. Publication of Manufacturers' Agents National Association. Magazine; 48-56 pages. Monthly. Circ. 13,000. Rights purchased vary with author and material. May buy all rights or simultaneous rights. Byline given. Buys 35 mss/year. Pays on publication. Free sample copy and writer's guidelines. Will consider photocopied or simultaneous submissions. Reports in 2 months. Query. SASE.
Nonfiction and Photos: Articles on independent sales representatives, the suppliers and customers, and their operations and manufacturers who sell through sales agents. Must be about independent selling from the agent's or manufacturer's point of view. Uses how-to, profile, interview, successful business techniques. "Articles about selling should not be too general—specifics a must." Length: 500-2,500 words. Ideal length is 1,500 words. Pays $50-100. Photos purchased with accompanying ms with extra payment. Captions required. B&w glossies only. Pays $10-15. Size: 3x5, 8x10.

THE AMERICAN SALESMAN, 424 N. 3rd Street., Burlington IA 52601. Editor-in-Chief: B. Beck. Managing Editor: M. Darnall. 95% freelance written. For distribution through company sales representatives. Monthly magazine; 44 pages. Circ. 5,998. Pays on publication. Buys all

rights. Free sample copy and writer's guidelines; mention *Writer's Market* in request.
Nonfiction: Sales seminars, customer service and followup, closing sales, sales presentations, handling objections, competition, telephone usage and correspondence, managing your territory and new innovative sales concepts. Query. Length: 900-1,200 words. Pays 3-5¢/word. Uses no photos or advertising.

ARMY/NAVY STORE AND OUTDOOR MERCHANDISER, 567 Morris Ave., Elizabeth NJ 07208. (201)353-7373. Editor: Alan Richman. 15-20% freelance written. For the owners of army/navy surplus and outdoor goods stores. Circ. 5,400. Pays kill fee. No byline. Buys 30 mss/year. Pays on publication. SASE. Reports in 1 month. Sample copy $2 plus $1.50 postage and handling.
Nonfiction and Photos: Articles on the methods stores use to promote items; especially on how army/navy items have become fashion items, and the problems attendant to catering to this new customer. Sources of supply, how they promote, including windows, newspapers, etc. "If the guy wants to tell his life story, listen and take notes. Use simple words. Stick to a single subject, if possible. Find out how the man makes money and tell us. The true 'success' story is the most frequently submitted and the most dreadful; yet nothing is of more interest if it is done well. No one truly wishes to tell you how he earns money." Length: 1,000 words minimum. Pays $50 minimum. "Most articles—especially on stores—must have photos included; minimum 5x7 b&w glossies with captions."
Tips: "Am anxious to build our coverage of camping departments. The best material always has a unique—but not forced—slant to most routine store stories."

AUTOMOTIVE AGE, Freed-Crown Publishing, 6931 Van Nuys Blvd., Van Nuys CA 92405. (213)873-1320. Editor: Chris Hosford. For owners and management of new car dealerships. Monthly magazine designed to inform readers of management techniques, systems and products to make car dealerships more profitable. Circ. 35,000. Buys all rights. Byline given. Phone queries OK. Simultaneous submissions OK, if list of other publications receiving same or similar story is furnished. SASE. Reports in 2 weeks. Free sample copy.
Nonfiction: Publishes humorous articles related to retail sales, auto repair, or management of new car dealerships; informational articles (sales techniques, dealership/retail promotions). "Clean, sophisticated copy that talks to the audience on a professional level." Buys 1-3 mss/issue. Query with brief bio of author if unfamiliar to editor. Length: 300-2,000 words. Pays $5/column inch.
Photos: Pays $15-25/b&w photo used with articles, columns or departments; $50-150 color.
Tips: "Understand the new car dealer's business needs and interests and address those in accurate, well-researched articles."

CONVENIENCE STORE NEWS, BMT Publications, Inc., 254 W. 31st St., New York NY 10001. (212)594-4120. Editor: Barbara J. Bagley. For convenience-store chain executives, middle-management and owner/operators; franchisors and franchisees; convenience store managers, wholesalers, distributors, service merchandisers, food brokers and manufacturers involved in the food retailing and convenience store business. Twice monthly tabloid; 40 pages. Circ. 40,000. Pays on publication. Buys all rights. Phone queries OK. Query for submission of seasonal/holiday material. Reports on queries in 1-2 weeks. Free sample copy and writer's guidelines.
Nonfiction: General interest, how-to, interview, profile and photo feature. Interested in news about convenience stores and chains, their personnel, operations and product mix trends, promotions and legislative activities on all levels of government that affect the operations of these businesses. Buys 20 mss/issue. Query. Pays $2/column inch.
Photos: Send photos with ms. Pays $5 for b&w glossy prints. Good Polaroid prints acceptable. Captions required.
Columns/Departments: Store Managers Section. Buys 16-20 mss/issue. Query. Length: 6 double-spaced ms pages maximum. Pays $2/column inch.
Fillers: Newsbreaks ("in our industry only"). Length: half page, double-spaced.

CRAFT & ART MARKET, Dept. WM, P.O. Drawer 1, Greenwood MS 38930. (601)453-5822. Managing Editor: John Ashcraft. For retail store owners, wholesalers, mass merchandise buyers of commercial craft supplies. Monthly magazine; 56 pages. Circ. 18,000. Pays on publication. Buys all rights for our industry. Submit seasonal/holiday material 5 months in advance. Simultaneous and photocopied submissions OK. SASE. Reports in 2 months.
Nonfiction: Connie Adams, department editor. Craft industry related business and how-to articles, interviews and photo features. Submit complete ms. Length: 500-3,200 words. Pays $50-200.
Photos: B&w glossies (5x7) purchased with mss. Captions required. Pays $10.

GIFTWARE NEWS, Box 243, Deptford NJ 08096. (609)227-0798. Editor: Anthony Demasi. For retailers, gift stores, florists, stationers, department stores, jewelry and home furnishings stores.

Published 3 times/year plus an annual *Buyers Guide*. Circ. 41,000. Rights purchased vary with author and material. Buys about 24 mss/year. Pays on publication. Sample copy $1.50; free writer's guidelines. Submit seasonal material (related to the gift industry) 2 months in advance. Reports in 1-2 months. Query or submit complete ms. SASE.

Nonfiction and Photos: Trade material. Only informative articles written in a manner applicable to daily business and general knowledge; not mere rhetorical exercises. Articles on store management, security, backgrounds (history) of giftwares, e.g., crystals, silver, (methods, procedures of manufacture); porcelain, etc. Informational, interview, profiles, material on new products and merchandising techniques. Length: 1,000 words minimum. Pays $75 minimum. Pays $15 minimum for b&w photos used with mss. Captions optional.

Tips: "Always interested in security and display stories."

KEY NEWSLETTER, Voice Publications, Goreville IL 62939. (618)995-2027. Editor-in-Chief: Bernard Lyons. 5% freelance written, "but would like to see more." Emphasizes direct marketing/mail order, specifically for those using classified columns of national magazines. Quarterly newsletter; 8 pages. Pays on acceptance. Buys all rights. Submit seasonal/holiday material 4 months in advance of issue date. Photocopied submissions OK. SASE. Reports in 2 weeks. One sample copy, $3; mention *Writer's Market* in request.

Nonfiction: Exposé (fraud in mail order/direct marketing); historical (old classified ads); how-to (write classified ads, match markets, increase response to ads); humor (funny classifieds); inspirational (examples of successful classifieds, personal stories of successful mail order through classifieds); interview (with successful mail order/direct market persons using classifieds); new product (if of help to small business); personal experience (summary of test results); profile (successful users of classifieds, written in first person); and technical (math for mail order/direct marketing). Buys 10 mss/year. Submit complete ms. Length: 50-1,500 words. Pays $10-75.

Tips: "We do not cover want-ads, but only classified ads in the national publications, those that you find on the newsstand. To break in find a consistent mail order advertiser; write up his or her experiences, including start, problems, ad response, etc.; mail it to us today, without anything more than the clearest and simplest language describing the who, why, what, where, when and how."

PHOTO MARKETING, 3000 Picture Place, Jackson MI 49201. Managing Editor: Diane Bair. For camera store dealers, photofinishers, manufacturers and distributors of photographic equipment. Publication of the Photo Marketing Association, International. Monthly magazine; 75 pages. Circ. 15,000. Buys all rights. Pays on publication. Reports in 21 days. Query with outline and story line. SASE.

Nonfiction and Photos: Business features dealing with photographic retailing or photofinishing operations, highlighting unique aspects, promotional programs, special problems. Length: 300-500 typewritten lines. Pays 5-7¢/word minimum. Pays $10-15/published 5x7 glossy photo.

Tips: Query to have: "indications that freelancer understands who our reader is—the businessperson who needs advice; intent by freelancer to tailor article to our market by talking to/interviewing people in photo business. Writers should send us a list of articles they have prepared, with descriptions, and their qualifications/background. If they're doing an article on selling techniques, for example, I'd like to know who they talked with or if they've worked in retailing to get info."

RENTAL EQUIPMENT REGISTER, Miramar Publishing Co., 2048 Cotner Ave., Los Angeles CA 90025. (213)477-1033. Director of Publications: Tim Novoselski. Editor: Richard Cerilli. Monthly magazine covering the rental industry including those firms engaged in the rental of tools, trucks, trailers, contractor equipment, sickroom and party goods, for rental equipment dealers, small and large rental center operators and independent businessmen. Circ. 11,000. Average issue includes 5-20 major articles and 5 columns. Pays on publication. Byline given. Buys all rights. Phone queries OK. Submit seasonal material 3 months in advance. SASE. Reports in 1 month. Sample copy and writer's guidelines free with cost of postage.

Nonfiction: General interest; interview; profile; and technical. "We are looking for articles that will help businessmen in the industry in day-to-day operation and over a long term period. We want stories about how a rentalman can improve his business using another rentalman as an example. Number one on our acceptance list are handy hints; unusual items in the rental industry. We have three major convention issues in July, November and December." No puff pieces. Buys 10-12 mss/year. Send complete ms. Length: 2,000 words maximum. Pays 10¢/word.

Photos: Send photos with ms. Pays $8 minimum for 5x7 b&w glossy prints. Pays $25 for 2¼x2¼ or 5x7 color transparencies. Captions required. Buys all rights.

Fillers: Cartoons, anecdotes and short humor. Pays $10/piece or 10¢/word minimum.

SALESMAN'S OPPORTUNITY MAGAZINE, 6 N. Michigan Ave., Chicago IL 60602. Managing Editor: Jack Weissman. 30% freelance written. "For anyone who is interested in making money, full or spare time, in selling or in independent business program." Monthly magazine. Circ. 190,000. Pays on publication. Buys all rights. Byline given. Submit seasonal/holiday material 6 months in advance of issue date. SASE. Free sample copy and writer's guidelines.

Nonfiction: "We use articles dealing with sales techniques, sales psychology or general self-improvement topics." How-to; inspirational; and interview (with successful salespeople who are selling products offered by direct selling firms, especially concerning firms which recruit salespeople through *Salesman's Opportunity Magazine*). Articles on self-improvement should deal with specifics rather than generalities. Would like to have more articles that deal with overcoming fear, building self-confidence, increasing personal effectiveness, and other psychological subjects. Submit complete ms. Length: 250-900 words. Pays $20-35.

Photos: State availability of photos with ms. Offers no additional payment for 8x10 b&w glossy prints. Captions required. Buys all rights. Model release required.

Tips: "Many articles are too academic for our audience. We look for free-and-easy style in simple language which is packed with useful information, drama and inspiration. Check the magazine before writing. Try to relate the article to the actual work in which the reader is engaged."

SMOKESHOP, BMT Publications, 254 W. 31st St., New York NY 10001. (212)594-4120. Editor: Gerard P. Sullivan. Associate Editor: John A. Borden. For owners of high-quality smokeshops who offer personal service and knowledge of products. "*Smokeshop's* editorial objective is to help the retailer become a more successful businessperson—not by telling him how to run his business, out by explaining how other tobacconists run theirs." Monthly magazine; 50 pages. Circ. 3,250. Pays on publication. Buys all rights. Phone queries OK. Submit seasonal/holiday material 6 weeks in advance. SASE. Reports in 2 weeks.

Nonfiction: How-to (improve sales through increased traffic; display or any innovative means); interview (with shopowners, people with something to offer shopowners); nostalgia (may consider a featurette); profile (of interesting tobacconists); and photo feature. "Don't fall into the trap of writing from a consumer standpoint. We are looking for pieces by experts in display, fixtures, blending, product mix, etc. The tobacconist's business is a relatively simple operation that is conducted in a rather friendly and personal manner. *Smokeshop's* editorial style reflects these same characteristics." Buys 3-4 mss/issue. Query with clips of published work. Length: 500-3,500 words. Pays $2/column inch.

Photos: "Good photos make the piece more interesting and the book more attractive." State availability of photos. Pays $5 for b&w glossy prints and color prints. Captions required.

Fillers: Clippings and newsbreaks. Pays $2/column inch.

Tips: "*Smokeshop* prefers the case history that focuses on a specific retailing function—buying, supplier relations, inventory controls, advertising, sales promotion, display, merchandising, sales training, employee relations, store design, fixturing, diversification, customer service, seasonal promotions, merchandising events, mail-order, private labelling, security, etc. In addition to relating what the tobacconist is doing, the case history should mention: (1) alternative courses of action that were available to him; (2) the rationale for his elected course of action, and (3) the results achieved."

SPECIALTY SALESMAN MAGAZINE, Communications Channels, Inc., 6285 Barfield Rd., Atlanta GA 30328. (404)256-9800. Publisher: Yale A. Katz. Editor: Jan Little. 75% advertising, 25% freelance written. For independent businessmen and women who sell door-to-door, store-to-store, office-to-office and by the party plan method as well as through direct mail and telephone solicitation; selling products and services. Monthly magazine; 70 pages. Circ. 500,000. Pays on publication. Buys all rights. Byline given. Submit seasonal/holiday material 3 months in advance of issue date. SASE. Reports in 3 months. Free sample copy and writer's guidelines.

Nonfiction: How-to (sell better; increase profits); historical (related to the history of various kinds of sales pitches, anecdotes, etc.); inspirational (success stories, "rags to riches" type of stories); with no additional payment. Photos purchased with accompanying ms. Buys 6 mss/issue. Query or submit complete ms. Length: 500-1,500 words. Pays 3¢/word.

Columns/Departments: Ideas Exchange (generated from our readers). Submit complete ms. Open to suggestions for new columns/departments.

Fillers: Jokes, gags, anecdotes and short humor. Buys 2/issue. Length: 150-500 words. Pays 3¢/word.

STORES, National Retail Merchants Association, 100 W. 31st St., New York NY 10001. (212)244-8780. Editor: Joan Bergmann. Managing Editor: Carol Ellen Messenger. Monthly magazine about retail issues for top retail management. Circ. 24,000. Pays on publication. Byline given. Buys all rights. Reports in 2 weeks on queries; in 2 months on mss. Free sample copy and writer's guidelines.

Nonfiction: Buys 8-10 mss/issue. Query with clips of previously published work. Length: 1,000 words minimum. Pays 10¢/word.
Photos: Send photos with ms on assigned story. Pays $5 for each b&w used. Buys all rights.
Tips: "Send writing samples and background; assignments sometimes are given on the basis of writing style."

VIDEO BUSINESS, CES Publications, 325 E. 75th St., New York NY 10021. (212)794-0500. Editor: George Kopp. Managing Editor: Frank Moldstad. Monthly magazine covering video specialty retailers. Estab. 1981. Circ. 18,000. Pays on publication. Byline given. Buys all rights in the industry. Simultaneous queries and previously published submissions OK ("indicate where and when published"). SASE. Reports in 1 month. Free sample copy.
Nonfiction: Informational pieces (on marketing, merchandising and selling themes). No "technical articles." Buys 40 mss/year. Query. Length: 1,500-2,000 words. Pays 12¢/word.
Photos: State availability of photos.

WALLCOVERINGS MAGAZINE, Publishing Dynamics, Inc., 2 Selleck St., Stamford CT 06902. Editor: Martin A. Johnson. Managing Editor: Jody Stone. Monthly trade journal of the flexible wallcoverings industry. Circ. 9,000. Submit query on all nonfiction article ideas. Buys all rights. SASE. Sample copy $4.
Nonfiction: Articles about manufacturers, distributors, retailers who sell flexible wallcoverings. Query with clips of previously published work. Rates negotiable.
Photos: On assignment. 8x10 b&w prints or contact sheets with negatives. Rates negotiable. Model release required.

Show People and Amusements

AMUSEMENT BUSINESS, Billboard Publications, Inc., Box 24970, Nashville TN 37202. (615)748-8120. Editor: Tom Powell. Managing Editor: Tim Taggart. Emphasizes hard news of the amusement and mass entertainment industry. Read by top management. Weekly tabloid; 24-48 pages. Circ. 15,000. Pays on publication. Buys all rights. Byline sometimes given; "it depends on the quality of the individual piece." Phone queries OK. SASE. Submit seasonal/holiday material 2-3 weeks in advance. Free sample copy and writer's guidelines; mention *Writer's Market* in request.
Nonfiction: How-to (case history of successful promotions); interview; new product; and technical (how "new" devices, shows or services work at parks, fairs, auditoriums and conventions). Likes lots of financial support data: grosses, profits, operating budgets, per-cap spending. No personality pieces or interviews with stage stars. Buys 500-1,000 mss/year. Query. Length: 400-700 words. Pays $1-2.50/published inch.
Photos: State availability of photos with query. Pays $3-5 for b&w 8x10 glossy prints. Captions required. Buys all rights. Model release required.
Columns/Departments: Auditorium Arenas; Fairs, Fun Parks; Food Concessions; Merchandise; Shopping Centers; Promotion; Shows (carnival and circus); Talent; Tourist Attractions; and Management Changes.

BILLBOARD, 9000 Sunset Blvd., Los Angeles CA 90069. Publisher: Lee Zhito. Special Issues Editor: Earl Paige. L.A. Bureau Chief: Sam Sutherland. Sound Business/Studios Editor: Jim McCullaugh. Record Review/Campus Editor: Ed Harrison. Talent Editor: Jean Williams. Marketing News Editor: John Sippel. (All Los Angeles.) Managing Editor: Richard White. Radio/TV Editor: Doug Hall. International Editor: Adam Nusser. Publishing & News Editor: Irv Lichtman. Disco Editor: Radcliffe Joe. Editor-in-Chief: Gerry Wood. Executive Editor: Is Horowitz. (All New York.) Country Music Editor: Kip Kirby (Nashville). Classical: Alan Penchansky (Chicago). Weekly. Buys all rights. Pays on publication. SASE.
Nonfiction: "Correspondents are appointed to send in spot amusement news covering phonograph record programming by broadcasters and record merchandising by retail dealers. Concert reviews; interviews with artists; stories on discotheques. We are extremely interested in blank tape, tape playback and record hardware stores." Length: short. Pays 24¢-$1/published inch; $5/published photo. "Special issues rates are competitive and negotiated, as subjects range into every area of music."

BOXOFFICE MAGAZINE, Vance Publishing Corp., 1800 N. Highland Ave., Suite 316, Hollywood CA 90028. (213)465-1186. Editor: Alexander Auerbach. Monthly magazine about the mo-

tion picture industry for members of the film industry: theater owners, film producers, directors, financiers and allied industries. Circ. 16,000. Pays on publication. Byline given. Buys one-time rights. Phone queries OK. Submit seasonal material 2 months in advance. Simultaneous, photocopied and previously published submissions OK. SASE. Reports in 2 weeks. Free sample copy.
Nonfiction: Exposé, interview, nostalgia, profile, new product, photo feature and technical. "We are a general news magazine about the motion picture industry and are looking for stories about trends, developments, problems or opportunities facing the industry. Almost any story will be considered, including corporate profiles, but we don't want gossip or celebrity stuff." Buys 1-2 mss/issue. Query with clips of previously published work. Length: 1,500-2,500 words. Pays $75-150.
Photos: State availability of photos. Pays $10 minimum for 8x10 b&w prints. Captions required.
Tips: "Write a clear, comprehensive outline of the proposed story, and enclose a résumé and clip samples. We welcome new writers but don't want to be a classroom. Know how to write."

G-STRING BEAT, Atlanta Enterprises, Box 007, Gays Mills WI 54631. Editor: Rita Atlanta. Emphasizes burlesque and allied fields of entertainment. Quarterly magazine; 48 pages. Circ. 12,000. Pays on publication. Buys all rights. SASE. Reports in 2-3 weeks.
Nonfiction: Publishes in-depth, hard-edged profiles of performers who are real people with hopes and fears. Buys 6-10 mss/year. Submit complete ms. Length: 1,000-2,500 words. Pays $75-150.
Photos: Query. "We have about 5,000 pix on hand and pix must be exceptional for us to buy."
Fiction: John Bane, Department Editor. Publishes mystery, humorous and suspense fiction. "Very little fiction is accepted because freelance writers have a limited 'feel' (no pun intended) of burlesque. The tensions of the business are rarely understood by outsiders. Would say that this is one of the hardest markets to please." Buys 2-3 mss/year. Submit complete ms. Length: 2,500-5,000 words. Pays $100-250.

THE HOLLYWOOD REPORTER, Publishers Press, 6715 Sunset Blvd., Hollywood CA 90028. (213)464-7411. Publisher: Tichi Wilkerson Miles. Editor: Cynthia Wilkerson Miles. Emphasizes entertainment industry, film, TV and theater and is interested in everything to do with financial news in these areas. Daily magazine. Circ. 2,000. SASE. Reports in 1 month. Sample copy $1.

PERFORMANCE, 2929 Cullen St., Fort Worth TX 76107. (817)338-9444. Editor: Jan Hash. Assistant Editor: Paula Vanderslice. "Performance publishes tour routing information, updated on a weekly basis. These itineraries, along with box office reports, street news, live performance reviews and industry features are of interest to our readers." Weekly magazine; also publishes industry directories once a month. Circ. 51,000. Buys all rights. Phone queries OK. Submit seasonal/holiday material 2 months in advance. Simultaneous, photocopied and previously published submissions OK. SASE. Reports in 1 month. Sample copy and writer's guidelines $3.
Nonfiction: "This is a trade publication, dealing basically with the ins and outs of booking live entertainment. We are interested in adding freelancers from major cities around the US to provide us with 'street news' and spot information on sound lighting, clubs, ticketing, facilities, and college news relevant to live entertainment. Also publish interviews and overviews from time to time." Interviews, opinion and profile.
Photos: State availability of photos with ms. Captions preferred. Buys all rights.

VARIETY, 154 W. 46th St., New York NY 10036. Does not buy freelance material.

Sport Trade

AMERICAN BICYCLIST AND MOTORCYCLIST, 461 8th Ave., New York NY 10001. (212)563-3430. Editor: Stan Gottlieb. For bicycle sales and service shops. Monthly. Circ. 9,700. Buys all rights. "Only staff-written articles are bylined, except under special circumstances." Pays on publication. Reports in 10 days.
Nonfiction: Typical story describes (very specifically) unique traffic-builder or merchandising ideas used with success by an actual dealer. Articles may also deal exclusively with moped sales and service operation within conventional bicycle shop. Emphasis is on showing other dealers how they can follow a similar pattern and increase their business. Articles may also be based entirely on repair shop operation, depicting efficient and profitable service systems and methods. Buys 8 mss/year. Query. Length: 1,000-2,800 words. Pays 4¢/word, plus "bonus for outstanding manuscript."

Photos: Relevant b&w photos illustrating principal points in article purchased with ms; 5x7 minimum. No transparencies. Pays $5 per photo. Captions required. Buys all rights.

AMERICAN FIREARMS INDUSTRY, American Press Media Association, Inc., 7001 N. Clark St., Chicago IL 60626. Specializes in the sporting arms trade. Monthly magazine. Circ. 23,500. Pays on publication. Buys all rights. Submit seasonal/holiday material 60 days in advance. SASE. Reports in 2 weeks. Sample copy, $1.

AMERICAN HOCKEY AND ARENA MAGAZINE, Amateur Hockey Association of the United States, 2997 Broadmoor Valley Rd., Colorado Springs CO 80906. (303)576-4990. Publisher: Hal Trumble. Managing Editor: Mary-Leslie Ullman. Monthly magazine covering hockey equipment and arena components for teams, coaches and referees of the Amateur Hockey Association of the United States, ice facilities in the US and Canada, buyers, schools, colleges, pro teams, and park and recreation departments. Estab. 1979. Circ. 30,000. Pays on publication. Byline given. Makes work-for-hire assignments. Phone queries OK. Submit seasonal material 4 months in advance. Photocopied and previously published submissions OK. SASE. Reports in 1 month. Sample copy $1.
Nonfiction: Managing Editor: Mary-Leslie Ullman. General interest, profile, new product and technical. Query. Length: 500-3,000 words. Pays $25 minimum.
Photos: Editor: Doug Spencer. Reviews 5x7 b&w glossy prints and 5x7 color glossy prints. Offers no additional payment for photos accepted with ms. Captions preferred. Buys one-time rights.
Columns/Departments: Editor: Doug Spencer. Rebounds (miscellaneous); Product Update (hockey equipment and arena component news); and Rink Forum (Q&A on rink operations). Open to suggestions for new columns. Query.

ARCHERY RETAILER, Winter Sports Publishing, Inc., 225 E. Michigan, Milwaukee WI 53202. (414)276-6600. Editor: Robert Brandau. Emphasizes archery retailing. Magazine published 5 times/year; 54 pages. Circ. 14,500. Pays on publication. Buys one-time rights. Byline given. Phone queries OK, "but prefer mail queries." Submit seasonal/holiday material 4 months in advance. SASE. Reports in 3 weeks. Free sample copy and writer's guidelines.
Nonfiction: How-to (better buying, selling, displaying, advertising, etc.); interview; profile. "No stories about dinky shops selling because they love archery but have no idea of profitability." Buys 2-4 mss/issue. Query. Length: 500-2,000 words. Pays $150.
Photos: Purchased with or without accompanying ms. Captions required. Pays $10-25 for 8x10 b&w glossies.

BICYCLE DEALER SHOWCASE, Box 19531, Irvine CA 92713. Associate Publisher: Herb Wetenkamp. Editor: John Francis. For bicycle/moped dealers and industry personnel. Monthly magazine; 90-110 pages. Circ. 13,000. Buys all rights. Buys about 12 mss/year. Pays on publication. Free sample copy and writer's guidelines with SASE. Submit seasonal material 2 months in advance. Reports in 3-4 weeks. Query or submit complete ms. SASE.
Nonfiction: Articles dealing with marketing bicycle products; financing, better management techniques, current trends, as related to bicycle equipment or selling. Material must be fairly straightforward, with a slant toward economic factors or marketing techniques. Informational, how-to, interview, profile, humor, successful business operations, merchandising techniques, technical. Length: 500-1,000 words. Pays $100 "or more, depending on the work involved."
Photos: 8x10 b&w glossy prints purchased with mss. Pays $10 minimum/photo.
Tips: "We judge the writer's style, ability and command of the facts by his query. If the query is good, the writer is good. Know what you're talking about, be open to suggestions and keep in constant touch, whether you have an article in mind or not. We often assign writers to cover story ideas we generate. No simultaneous submissions. Are in desperate need of humor, jokes about bikes and dealers, and cartoons."

BICYCLE JOURNAL, 4915 W. Freeway, Box 1570, Fort Worth TX 76101. Editor: Walt Jarvis. Monthly. Circ. 9,000. Not copyrighted. Pays on publication. SASE.
Nonfiction and Photos: Stories about dealers who service what they sell, emphasizing progressive, successful sales ideas in the face of rising costs and increased competition. Length: 5 double-spaced pages maximum. Also includes moped dealerships. B&w glossy photo a must; vertical photo preferred. "One 8x10 photo is sufficient." Query.

BOWLERS JOURNAL, 875 N. Michigan Ave., Chicago IL 60611. (312)266-7171. Editor-in-Chief: Mort Luby. 30-50% freelance written. For tournament bowlers and a trade audience of proprietors, dealers, distributors. Monthly magazine; 100 pages. Circ. 18,000. Pays on acceptance. Buys one-time rights. Phone queries OK. Submit seasonal/holiday material 2 months in advance

of issue date. Simultaneous and photocopied submissions OK. SASE. Reports in 3 weeks.
Nonfiction: Uses illustrated articles about successful bowling and billiard room proprietors who have used unusual promotions to build business, profiles of interesting industry personalities (including bowlers and billiard players), and coverage of major competitive events, both bowling and billiards. "We publish some controversial matter, seek out outspoken personalities. We reject material that is too general; that is, not written for high average bowlers and bowling proprietors who already know basics of playing the game and basics of operating a bowling alley." Length: 1,500-2,500 words. Pays $75-150.
Photos: B&w (8x10) glossies and color (35mm or 120 or 4x5) transparencies purchased with mss. Captions required. Pays $5-10 for b&w; $15-25 for color.

GOLF BUSINESS, Harvest Publishing Co./Div. of Harcourt Brace Jovanovich, 7500 Old Oak Blvd., Middleburg Hts. OH 44130. (216)243-8100. Managing Editor: Ron Morris. Emphasizes golf course maintenance and management. Monthly magazine; 60 pages. Circ. 17,000. Pays on publication. Buys all rights. Submit seasonal material 4 months in advance. SASE. Reports in 2 months.
Nonfiction: Exposé (may focus on industry problem that would uncover information new and beneficial to business); how-to (find something new that a course is doing that can be applied to whole industry); informational (new concepts in course management); interview (with industry or governmental individual involved in business); new product (also interested in new services which are in the news); photo feature (if it demonstrates a new technique in course maintenance operations). Buys 7 mss/year. Query. Length: 1,500-3,000 words. Pays $100-150.
Photos: Used with ms with no additional payment. Query or send contact sheet. B&w glossies, at least 5x7 or color transparencies.

GOLF INDUSTRY, Industry Publishers, Inc., 915 NE 125th St., Suite 2-C, North Miami FL 33161. (305)893-8771. Executive Editor: Michael J. Keighley. Editor: Joan Whaley. Emphasizes the golf industry for country clubs, pro-owned golf shops, real estate developments, municipal courses, military and schools. Bimonthly magazine; 75 pages. Circ. 17,000. Pays on publication. Buys all rights. Submit seasonal/holiday material 2-3 months in advance. SASE. Reports "usually in 6-8 weeks." Sample copy $2.50. Free writer's guidelines.
Nonfiction: Publishes informational articles "dealing with a specific facet of golf club or pro shop operations, e.g., design, merchandising, finances, etc." Buys 20 mss/year. Submit complete ms. Length: 2,500 words maximum. Pays 5¢/word.
Tips: "Since we don't make freelance assignments, a query is not particularly important. We would rather have a complete ms which conforms to our policy of general, but informative, articles about one specific facet of the business of golf merchandising, financing, retailing, etc. Well-done mss, if not used immediately, are often held in our files for use in a future issue. We never publish articles concentrating on one specific manufacturer, or extolling the virtues of one product over another. We seldom feature one club or retail outlet. We don't deal with the game itself, but with the business end of the game."

GOLF SHOP OPERATIONS, 495 Westport Ave., Norwalk CT 06856. (203)847-5811. Editor: Nick Romano. For golf professionals and shop operators at public and private courses, resorts and driving ranges. Magazine published 6 times/year; 36 pages. Circ. 12,500. Byline given. Pays on publication. Free sample copy. Photocopied submissions OK. Submit seasonal material (for Christmas and other holiday sales, or profiles of successful professionals) 3 months in advance. Reports in 1 month.
Nonfiction: "We emphasize improving the golf professional's knowledge of his profession. Articles should describe how pros are buying, promoting, merchandising and displaying wares in their shops that might be of practical value to fellow professionals. Must be aimed only at the pro audience. We would be interested in seeing material on how certain pros are fighting discount store competition." How-to, profile, successful business operation, merchandising techniques. No profiles of professionals from the Southern US. Buys 8 mss/year. Phone queries preferred. Pays $100-125.
Photos: "Pictures are mandatory with all manuscript submissions." Captions required.
Tips: "I'm less inclined to assign anything unless the person can handle a camera. The profile pieces must have decent photos. We're really looking for the freelancers that understand the golf business. This helps us in that we won't have to rewrite a lot or have the writer go back and ask the obvious questions."

INTERNATIONAL MOTORCYCLE TRADE JOURNAL, Motorcycle Aftermarket Publications, 393 7th Ave., New York NY 10001. (212)563-2747. Editor: Thomas Hudson Sr. Managing Editor: Robert F. Kneller. Bimonthly magazine about the motorcycle business, how dealers can improve their business through better retailing techniques, merchandising, community relations and promotion. Circ. 15,000. Pays on publication. Byline given. Buys all rights. Submit seasonal material 6 months in advance. SASE. Reports in 3 weeks. Sample copy $2.

Nonfiction: Interview (of motorcycle industry figures and unique or successful dealers); and how-to (improve business). Query. Length: 500-5,000 words. Pays $50 minimum.

Photos: State availability of photos. Reviews b&w contact sheets and color transparencies. Model release required. Buys all rights.

MOTORCYCLE DEALER & TRADE, Brave Beaver Pressworks, Ltd., 290 Jarvis St., Toronto, Ontario, Canada M5B 2C5. (416)977-6318. Editor: Christina Montgomery. Managing Editor: Georgs Kolesnikovs. Monthly tabloid covering the Canadian motorcycle business. Circ. 2,500. Pays on acceptance or publication; "depends on the situation." Byline given. Offers 50% kill fee. Buys one-time rights. Submit seasonal/holiday material 2 months in advance. Simultaneous queries, and simultaneous and photocopied submissions OK. SASE. Reports in 2 weeks. Free sample copy and writer's guidelines.

Nonfiction: How-to (relative to retail m/c business); interview/profile (of successful m/c businessmen); and new product (re: motorcycles). "Since most of our readers are dealers, we publish many stories of the how-to variety—how to sell, display, insure your premises, etc." No articles "that pertain solely to US situations." Buys 5 mss/year. Query with clips of published work. Length: 500-1,000 words. Pays $50-100.

Photos: State availability of photos. Pays $10-35 for b&w contact sheets or negatives. Identification of subjects required.

Tips: "We're primarily interested in articles to help motorcycle dealers do their job better. Humorous articles about the business also welcome. We prefer very fast-paced stories jam-packed with useful information. No puff pieces, please."

PGA MAGAZINE, Professional Golfer's Association of America, 100 Avenue of Champions, Palm Beach Gardens FL 33410. (305)626-3600. Editor: Jim Warters. Managing Editor: William A. Burbaum. Monthly magazine about golf for 14,000 club professionals and apprentices nationwide. Circ. 16,000. Average issue includes 8-10 articles and 6 departments. Pays on acceptance. Byline given. Phone queries OK. Submit seasonal material 3 months in advance. Photocopied and previously published submissions OK. Reports in 3 weeks. Free sample copy and writer's guidelines.

Nonfiction: Historical (great moments in golf revisited); profile (success stories); how-to (instructional, PGA member teaching techniques); inspirational (personal success stories); and photo feature (great golf courses). Buys 15 mss/year. Query with outline and clips of previously published work. Length: 900-1,500 words. Pays 15¢/word minimum. "Exhibit knowledge and interest in the professional business and in other needs of today's club professional."

Photos: Pays $10-25/b&w contact sheets. Pays $10-25/35mm color transparencies. Captions and model release required. Buys all rights. Query with clips of previously published work. Length: 600-900 words. Pays 15¢/word minimum.

POOL & SPA NEWS, Leisure Publications, 3923 W. 6th St., Los Angeles CA 90020. (213)385-3926. Editor-in-Chief: J. Field. 40% freelance written. Emphasizes news of the swimming pool and spa industry for pool builders, pool retail stores and pool service firms. Semimonthly magazine. Circ. 10,000. Pays on publication. Buys all rights. Phone queries OK. Photocopied submissions OK. SASE. Reports in 2 weeks.

Nonfiction: Interview, new product, profile, and technical. Length: 500-2,000 words. Pays 5¢/word. Pays $5 per b&w photo used.

POOL INDUSTRY CANADA, 1450 Don Mills Rd., Don Mills, Ontario, Canada M3B 2X7. Editor: Trevor Sissing. Quarterly magazine for pool manufacturers, distributors and retailers; chemical suppliers; and service companies. Pays on publication. Buys all rights. SAE and International Reply Coupons.

Nonfiction: Technical pieces related to chemistry, service, maintenance, sales or business management. Query. Length: 500-2,000 words. Pays $75-200.

Photos: Uses 5x7 or 8x10 b&w prints and color transparencies.

RACQUETBALL INDUSTRY, Industry Publishers, Inc., 1545 NE 123rd St., North Miami FL 33161. (305)893-8771. Executive Editor: Michael J. Keighley. Editor: Joan Whaley. Bimonthly magazine about the business of racquetball for the retailers and business people in the industry. Circ. 15,000. Pays on publication. Byline given. Buys all rights. Submit seasonal material 2 months in advance. SASE. Reports in 6 weeks. Sample copy $2.50; free writer's guidelines.

Nonfiction: "Content must be general, not featuring one specific manufacturing company or individual shop case-study. Articles can feature products, such as an examination of women's racquetball apparel, but must include industry-wide information, not pertaining specifically to the product of one manufacturer. Design, display, merchandising techniques, retailing procedures, shop layout and lighting are among those categories that would be of interest to our readers." Query. Length: 2,000-2,500 words. Pays 5¢/word.

RVD, RECREATIONAL VEHICLE DEALER, 29901 Agoura Rd., Agoura CA 91301. Editorial Director: Alice Robison. 50% freelance written. For men and women of the RV industry, primarily those involved in the sale of trailers, motorhomes, pickup campers, to the public. Also, owners and operators of trailer supply stores, plus manufacturers and executives of the RV industry nationwide and in Canada. Monthly magazine; 100 pages. Circ. 28,000. Buys all rights. Pays on publication. Free sample copy and writer's guidelines. Reports in 4 weeks. SASE.
Nonfiction and Photos: "Stories that show trends in the industry; success stories of particular dealerships throughout the country; news stories on new products; accessories (news section); how to sell; how to increase profits, be a better businessman. Interested in broadbased, general interest material of use to all RV retailers, rather than mere trade reporting." Informational, how-to, personal experience, interview, profile, humor, think articles, successful business operations, and merchandising techniques. Buys 100-150 mss/year. Query. Length: 1,000-2,000 words. Pays $100-175. Shorter items for regular columns or departments run 800 words. Pays $50-75. Photos purchased with accompanying ms with no additional payment. Captions required.
Columns/Departments: Dealer/industry items from over the country; newsbreaks. Length: 100-200 words; with photos, if possible. Payment based on length.

THE SHOOTING INDUSTRY, 291 Camino de la Reina, San Diego CA 92108. (714)297-5352. Editor: J. Rakusan. For manufacturers, dealers, sales representatives of archery and shooting equipment. Monthly. Buys all rights. Byline given. Pays on publication. Free sample copy. Reports in 2-3 weeks. SASE.
Nonfiction and Photos: Articles that tell "secrets of my success" based on experience of individual gun dealer; articles of advice to help dealers sell more guns and shooting equipment. Also, articles about and of interest to manufacturers and top manufacturers' executives. Buys about 135 mss/year. Query. Length: 3,000 words maximum. Pays $50-150. Photos essential; b&w glossies purchased with ms.

SKI BUSINESS, 380 Madison Ave., New York NY 10017. (212) 687-3000. Editor: Seth Masia. Monthly tabloid newspaper; 28 pages. For ski retailers and instructors. Circ. 15,000. Pays $75 kill fee. Byline given, except on "press releases and roundup articles containing passages from articles submitted by several writers." Pays on publication. Submit seasonal material 3 weeks in advance. Reports in 1 month. Photocopied submissions OK. Free writer's guidelines and sample copy. SASE.
Nonfiction: Will consider ski shop case studies; mss about unique and successful merchandising ideas, and ski area equipment rental operations. "All material should be slanted toward usefulness to the ski shop operator. Always interested in interviews with successful retailers." Uses round-ups of preseason sales and Christmas buying across the country during September to December. Would like to see reports on what retailers in major markets are doing. Buys about 150 mss/year. Query or submit complete ms. Length: 800-1,500 words. Pays $50-150.
Photos: Photos purchased with accompanying mss. Buys b&w glossy 8x10 photos. Pays $10-25.

SKIING TRADE NEWS, 1 Park Ave., New York NY 10016. Editor: Rick Kahl. For ski shop owners. Annual magazine; 340 pages. Also publishes a tabloid 10 times/year. Circ. about 11,600. Buys first North American serial rights. Pays on acceptance. Reports in 1 month. SASE.
Nonfiction: Factual how-to or success articles about buying at the ski trade shows, merchandising ski equipment, keeping control of inventory, etc. Buys 14 mss/year. Query. Length: 2,000 words. Pays 12¢/word.
Tips: "Find a ski shop that is a success, one that does something differently and makes money at it. Research the reasons for the shop's success and query."

THE SPORTING GOODS DEALER, 1212 N. Lindbergh Blvd., St. Louis MO 63166. (314)997-7111. Chairman: C.C. Johnson Spink. President: Richard Waters. Managing Editor: Gary Goldman. For members of the sporting goods trade: retailers, manufacturers, wholesalers, representatives. Monthly magazine. Circ. 16,161. Buys second serial (reprint) rights. Buys about 15 mss/year. Pays on publication. Sample copy $1 (refunded with first ms); free writer's guidelines. Will not consider photocopied or simultaneous submissions. Reports in 2 weeks. Query. SASE.
Nonfiction and Photos: "Articles about specific sporting goods retail stores, their promotions, display techniques, sales ideas, merchandising, timely news of key personnel; expansions, new stores, deaths—all in the sporting goods trade. Specific details on how individual successful sport-

ing goods stores operate. What specific retail sporting goods stores are doing that is new and different. We would also be interested in features dealing with stores doing an outstanding job in retailing of baseball, fishing, golf, tennis, camping, firearms/hunting and allied lines of equipment. Query on these." Successful business operations, merchandising techniques. Does not want to see announcements of doings and engagements. Length: open. Pays $2 per 100 published words. Also looking for material for the following columns: Terse Tales of the Trade (store news); Selling Slants (store promotions); Open for Business (new retail sporting goods stores or sporting goods departments). All material must relate to specific sporting goods stores by name, city, and state; general information is not accepted. Pays minimum of $3.50 for sharp clear b&w photos; size not important. These are purchased with or without mss. Captions optional, but identification requested.
Fillers: Clippings. These must relate directly to the sporting goods industry. Pays 1-2¢/published word.

SPORTING GOODS TRADE, Page Publications, Ltd., 380 Wellington St. W., Toronto, Ontario, Canada M5V 1E3. (416)366-4608. Editor: Jamie Howe. For sporting goods retailers, manufacturers, wholesalers, jobbers, department and chain stores, camping equipment dealers, bicycle sales and service, etc. Bimonthly magazine; 50-100 pages. Circ. 9,800. Pays on publication. Buys first rights. Reports in 2 months. SAE and International Reply Coupons.
Nonfiction: Technical and informational articles. Articles on successful Canadian business operations, new products, merchandising techniques; interviews. Query. Length: 1,200-2,000 words. Pays 7¢/word or $40/published page.
Tips: Submit Canadian-oriented articles only; "new sales help techniques are best."

SPORTS MERCHANDISER, W.R.C. Smith Publishing Co., 1760 Peachtree Rd. NW, Atlanta GA 30357. (404)874-4462. Editor: Eugene R. Marnell. For retailers and wholesalers of sporting goods in all categories; independent stores, chains, specialty stores, department store departments. Monthly tabloid; 100 pages. Circ. 40,000. Pays on acceptance, buys all rights. Submit seasonal/holiday material 4-6 months in advance. SASE. Reports in 4 months. Write for writer's guidelines.
Nonfiction: "Articles telling how retailers are successful in selling a line of products, display ideas, successful merchandising programs, inventory operations, and advertising program successes. No articles on business history. Query to be one-page with card (reply) enclosed. Letters to state full name of contact, address, etc. and describe type of business relative to volume, inventory, positioning in local market. Tell particular slant author believes most interesting." Length: 500-1,500 words. Pays $75-175.
Photos: State availability of photos with query. Offers no additional payment for 5x7 or 8x10 b&w prints. Captions required. Buys all rights.
Tips: "The retail order season is almost six months opposite the retail buying season (i.e., consumer buying). Lead time for ordering is six months—sometimes more on hardgoods and softgoods. Other products have full-year ordering cycle. Hence, query will help everyone."

SPORTS RETAILER, (formerly *Selling Sporting Goods*), 717 N. Michigan Ave., Chicago IL 60611. (312)944-0205. Managing Editor: Colleen Cason. For owners and managers of retail sporting goods stores. Monthly. Circ. 15,000. Buys first North American serial rights. Buys 12 mss/year. Pays on publication. Free sample copy and writer's guidelines. Submit seasonal material 4 months in advance. SASE.
Nonfiction and Photos: Articles on "full-line and specialty sporting goods stores. Informational articles, how-to's; articles on retail sporting goods advertising, promotions, in-store clinics/workshops; employee hiring and training; merchandising techniques. Articles should cover one aspect of store operation in depth." Query with clips of previously published work. Length: 1,500-2,000 words. Pays $50-150. B&w glossies purchased with or without accompanying ms. 5x7 minimum. Captions required. Color transparencies acceptable. Pays $100 for cover transparency. Buys one-time rights.
Tips: "Practice photography! Most stories, no matter how good, are useless without quality photos. They can be submitted as contact sheets with negatives to hold down writer's cost."

SWIMMING POOL WEEKLY/AGE, Hoffman Publications, Inc., Box 11299, Fort Lauderdale FL 33339. (305)566-8402. Editor: Sara Rovner Leary. Emphasizes pool industry. Bimonthly tabloid. Circ. 15,000. Pays on acceptance. Buys all rights for industry. Phone queries OK. Submit seasonal/holiday material 1 month in advance. SASE. Reports in 2 weeks. Writer's guidelines for SASE.
Nonfiction: Expose (if in industry, company frauds); how-to (stories on installation techniques done with an expert in a given field); interview (with important people within the industry); photo feature (pool construction or special pool use); technical (should be prepared with expert within

the industry). Buys 40-50 mss/year. Query. Length: 1,000 words maximum. Pays $35-75.
Photos: Purchased with or without accompanying ms or on assignment. Captions required. Query or send contact sheet. Pays $5-20 for any size larger than 5x7 b&w photo; $15-25 for any size above 35mm color transparencies.
Columns/Departments: "Short news on personality items always welcome at about $10-15 for 25-100 words."

TENNIS INDUSTRY, Industry Publishers, Inc., 915 NE 125th St., Suite 2-C, North Miami FL 33161. (305)893-8771. Editor: Michael J. Keighley. Emphasizes the tennis industry for teaching pros, pro shop managers, specialty shop managers, country club managers, coaches, athletic directors, etc. Monthly magazine; 200 pages. Circ. 19,000. Pays on publication. Buys all rights. Submit seasonal/holiday material 2-3 months in advance. Previously published submissions OK. SASE. Reports "usually in 6-8 weeks." Sample copy $2.50; free writer's guidelines.
Nonfiction: Publishes informational articles dealing "with specific facets of the tennis club or pro shop operation, e.g., design, merchandising, finances, etc." Buys 20 mss/year. Submit complete ms. Length: 2,500 words maximum. Pays 5¢/word.
Tips: "Since we do not make freelance assignments, a query is not particularly important. We would rather have a complete ms which conforms to our policy of general, but informative articles about one specific facet of the business of tennis merchandising, financing, retailing, etc. Well-done manuscripts, if not used immediately, are often held in our files for use in a future issue."
Rejects: "We never publish articles concentrating on one specific manufacturer, or extolling the virtues of one product over another. We seldom feature one club or retail outlet. We don't deal with the game itself, but with the business end of the game."

Stone and Quarry Products

CONCRETE, Cement and Concrete Association, 11 Grosvenor Crescent, London SW1X 7EE. (01)245-9744. Editor: R.J. Barfoot. Emphasizes civil engineering and building and construction. Monthly magazine; 60 pages. Circ. 10,500. Pays on publication. Phone queries OK. Photocopied submissions OK. Free sample copy.
Nonfiction: Historical, new product, and technical articles dealing with concrete and allied industries. Buys 12 mss/year. Query or submit complete ms. Length: 1,000-3,000 words. Pays $30-50.

CONCRETE CONSTRUCTION MAGAZINE, 426 South Westgate, Addison IL 60101. Editor: M.K. Hurd. For general and concrete contractors, architects, engineers, concrete producers, cement manufacturers, distributors and dealers in construction equipment, testing labs. Monthly magazine; 80 pages average. Circ. 70,000. Buys all rights. "Bylines are used only by prearrangement with the author." Pays on acceptance. Free sample copy and writer's guidelines. Photocopied and simultaneous submissions OK. Reports in 1-2 months. Submit query with topical outline. SASE.
Nonfiction and Photos: "Our magazine has one major emphasis: cast-in-place (site cast) concrete. Our articles deal with tools, techniques and materials that result in better handling, better placing, and ultimately an improved final product. We are particularly firm about not using proprietary names in any of our articles. Manufacturers and products are never mentioned; only the processes or techniques that might be of help to the concrete contractor, the architect or the engineer dealing with the material. We do use 'bingo cards' that accomplish the purpose of relaying reader interest to manufacturers." Does not want to see job stories or promotional material. Length: 3,500 words. Pays 10¢/published word. Pays $10 for b&w glossy photos and color used with mss. Photos are used only as part of a completed ms.
Tips: "Condensed, totally factual presentations preferred."

CONCRETE INTERNATIONAL: DESIGN AND CONSTRUCTION, American Concrete Institute, 22400 W. Seven Mile Rd., Detroit MI 48219. (313)532-2600. Editor: Alan V. Lambert. Monthly magazine about concrete for design engineers, management and construction people. Estab. 1979. Circ. 17,000. Pays on publication. Buys all rights, first rights, second serial rights, and makes assignments on a work-for-hire basis. Phone queries OK. Submit seasonal material 4 months in advance. SASE. Reports in 2 weeks on queries; in 1 month on mss. Free sample copy and writer's guidelines.
Nonfiction: Historical (concrete structures); how-to (concrete construction, new methods, techniques); new product (concrete-related); and technical (concrete-related). Query. Length: 300-8,000 words. Pays $100/printed page.

Photos: State availability of photos or send photos with ms. Reviews b&w contact sheets and 5x7 and 8x10 prints. Offers no additional payment for photos accepted with ms. Captions and model release required. Buys one-time rights.
Columns/Departments: Legal (related to concrete construction); Problems, solutions and practices; and Management Techniques. Query. Length: 600-1,000 words. Pays $30 maximum.

MINE AND QUARRY, Ashire Publishing Ltd., 42 Gray's Inn Rd., London, England WC1X 8LR. Editor: Keith Whitworth. Monthly magazine; for senior management at mines and quarries. 80 pages. Circ. 4,600. Buys all rights. Phone queries OK. Submit seasonal/holiday material 2 months in advance. Simultaneous, photocopied and previously published submissions OK. SAE and International Reply Coupons. Reports in 2 months. Free sample copy and writer's guidelines.
Nonfiction: Technical and new product articles related to the industry. Buys 20 mss/year. Submit complete ms. Length: 200-1,000 words. Pays $10-20.
Photos: B&w glossy prints and color transparencies purchased with or without mss. Captions required. Send contact sheet, prints or transparencies. Pays $3-6.

STONE IN AMERICA, American Monument Association, 6902 N. High St., Worthington OH 43085. (614)885-2713. Managing Editor: Bob Moon. Monthly magazine for the retailers of upright memorials in the US and Canada. Circ. 2,600. Pays on publication. Buys one-time rights. Phone queries preferred. SASE. Reports in 1 month. Free sample copy and writer's guidelines.
Nonfiction: How-to (run a monument business); informational (major news within the industry, monuments as an art form); profile (successful retailers); and technical. Buys 30-40 mss/year. Length: 2,000-3,500 words. Query. Pays $50-150.
Photos: Pays $20-50 for 5x7 or 8x10 b&w glossy prints.
Columns/Departments: Spectrum. Length: 250-1,000 words.

Textile

TEXTILE WORLD, 1175 Peachtree St. NE, Atlanta GA 30361. Editor-in-Chief: Laurence A. Christiansen. Monthly. Buys all rights. Pays on acceptance. SASE.
Nonfiction and Photos: Uses articles covering textile management methods, manufacturing and marketing techniques, new equipment, details about new and modernized mills, etc., but avoids elementary, historical, or generally well-known material. Pays $25 minimum/page. Photos purchased with accompanying ms with no additional payment, or purchased on assignment.

Toy, Novelty, and Hobby

CREATIVE PRODUCT NEWS, Box 584, Lake Forest IL 60045. (312)234-5052. Editor: Linda F. McKee. Bimonthly tabloid for retailers of crafts, needlework, and art materials for fine art, hobby art, and doll house miniatures. Estab. 1980. Circ. 28,000. Pays on acceptance. Byline given. Buys first North American serial rights. Submit seasonal/holiday material 7 months in advance. Simultaneous queries and photocopied submissions OK. SASE. Reports in 1 month. Free sample copy.
Nonfiction: "We need only one thing: packages containing 4-6 photos and 200- 500-word descriptions. Topic should be demonstration of a new art or craft technique; photos must show finished article, supplies used and procedure." Buys 12 mss/year. Query with clips of published work. Pays $50.
Tips: "Our total concern is what's new. Submit only ideas that are truly new."

MINIATURES DEALER MAGAZINE, Boynton & Associates Inc., Clifton House, Clifton VA 22024. (703)830-1000. Editor: Marla Young. For "retailers in the dollhouse/miniatures trade. Our readers are generally independent, small store owners who don't have time to read anything that does not pertain specifically to their own problems." Monthly magazine; 100 pages. Circ. 6,000. Pays on publication. Buys all rights. Byline given. Phone queries OK. Submit seasonal/holiday material 3 months in advance. Photocopied and previously published submissions OK; simultaneous submissions (if submitted to publications in different fields) OK. SASE. Reports in 2 months. Sample copy $1.50; free writer's guidelines (SASE).
Nonfiction: How-to (unique articles—for example, how to finish a dollhouse exterior—are acceptable if they introduce new techniques or ideas; show the retailer how learning this technique will

help sell dollhouses); profiles of miniatures stores; business information pertaining to small store retailers. Buys 4-6 mss/issue. Query or send complete ms. "In query, writer should give clear description of intended article, when he could have it to me plus indication that he has studied the field, and is not making a 'blind' query. Availability of photos should be noted."Pays 10¢/word.
Photos: "Photos must tie in directly with articles." State availability of photos. Pays $7 for each photo used. Prefers 5x7 b&w glossy prints (reviews contact sheets); and $25 for 2¼x2¼ color transparencies. Buys very few color photos. Captions preferred; model release preferred.
Tips: "The best way for a freelancer to break in is to study several issues of our magazine, then try to visit a miniatures shop and submit an *MD* Visits . . . article. This is a regular feature that can be written by a sharp freelancer who takes the time to study and follow the formula this feature uses. Also, basic business articles for retailers—inventory control, how to handle bad checks, etc., that are written with miniatures dealers in mind, are always needed."

MODEL RETAILER MAGAZINE, Clifton House, Clifton VA 22024. (703)830-1000. Editor-in-Chief: Geoffrey Wheeler. 60-70% freelance written. "For hobby store owners—generally well-established small business persons, fairly well educated, and very busy." Monthly magazine. Circ. 6,700. Pays on publication. Buys "all rights in our field." Byline given. Phone queries OK (no collect calls, please) but prefers written queries. Submit seasonal/holiday material 2-3 months in advance of issue date. Simultaneous, photocopied and previously published submissions OK. SASE. Reports in 2 weeks. Sample copy $1.50; free writer's guidelines.
Nonfiction: Retailer profiles; articles on store management, marketing, merchandising, advertising; and photo feature (if photos tie in with marketing techniques or hobby store operation, etc.). Buys 3-5 mss/issue. Query. Length: 1,200-2,000 words. Pays 10¢/word minimum.
Photos: "Photos that illustrate key points and are of good quality will help the article, particularly if it concerns business operation." Pays $15-25 for b&w prints. Buys all rights.

PROFITABLE CRAFT MERCHANDISING, PJS Publications, Inc., News Plaza, Box 1790, Peoria IL 61656. (309)682-6626. Editor: Michael W. Hartnett. Assistant Editor: Cyndy T. Andrews. Emphasizes making and saving money in craft supply retailing for retailers, manufacturers, wholesalers and publishers. Monthly magazine. Circ. 23,000. Pays on acceptance. Buys all rights. Byline given. Submit seasonal/holiday material 4-6 months in advance. SASE. Free sample copy and writer's guidelines.
Nonfiction: Profile (on unique or unusual craft stores that are successful); and business articles on how to make and save money, accounting, advertising, store layout, security, classroom instruction, merchandising techniques, etc. Buys 5 mss/issue. Query to include copy of a published business article and a letter telling me of the writer's publishing and/or crafts background." Length: 1,800 words maximum. Pays $60-275.
Photos: "If photos can clarify story aspect, they are encouraged. Photos are a must with profiles of craft supply stores." Send photos with ms. Uses b&w 5x7 or 8x10 glossy prints. Offers no additional payment for photos accepted with ms. Captions required.

SOUVENIRS AND NOVELTIES, 401 N. Broad St., Philadelphia PA 19108. Editor: Paula Scully. 20% freelance written. For managers and owners of souvenir shops in resorts, parks, museums, and airports. Magazine published 7 times/year; 88 pages. Circ. 16,500. Pays on publication. Buys first North American serial rights. Phone queries OK. Submit seasonal/holiday material 4 months in advance of issue date. Photocopied and previously published submissions OK. SASE. Reports in 2 weeks. Free writer's guidelines for 6x9 envelope.
Nonfiction: How-to (operate and improve souvenir shops), interview and profile. "No travel articles on the beauty of an area." Buys 20 mss/year. Query. Length: 1,000-2,000 words. Pays 4-6¢/word.
Photos: State availability of photos with query. Pays $10 for 5x7 or 8x10 glossy prints. Captions preferred. Buys one-time rights.
Fillers: Clippings. Pays 80¢/inch.

THE STAMP WHOLESALER, Box 706, Albany OR 97321. Publisher: Jim Magruder. 80% freelance written. For small-time independent businessmen; many are part-time and/or retired from other work. Published 26 times/year; 80 pages. Circ. 9,000. Buys all rights. Byline given. Buys 60 mss/year. Pays on publication. Will send free sample copy to writer on request. Reports in 10 weeks. Submit complete ms. SASE.
Nonfiction: How-to information on how to deal more profitably in postage stamps for collections. Emphasis on merchandising techniques and how to make money. Does not want to see any so-called "humor" items from nonprofessionals. Length: 1,500-2,000 words. Pays 3¢/word minimum.
Tips: "Send queries on business stories. Send manuscript on stamp dealer stories. We need stories to help dealers make and save money."

TOY & HOBBY WORLD, 124 E. 40th St., New York NY 10016. For everyone in the toy and hobby and craft industry from manufacturer to retailer. Magazine. Monthly. Circ. 17,000. Buys 5 mss/year. Pays on publication. Sample copy $2. Will consider photocopied submissions. Returns rejected material when requested. Query. SASE.
Nonfiction and Photos: Merchandising Articles and news. Features about wholesalers, retailers, chains, department stores, discount houses, etc., concerned with their toy operations. Prefers stories on toy wholesalers or retailers who have unusual success with unusual methods. No "mere histories of run-of-the-mill operators. Use a news style." Length: 1,000-3,000 words. Payment commensurate with quality of material. Buys 8x10 b&w photos with mss and with captions only. Must be glossy on singleweight paper. Pays $10 and up plus word rate. Prefers captions. Uses color on occasion; query first.

TOYS & GAMES, G.P. Page Publications, Ltd., 380 Wellington St. W., Toronto, Ontario, Canada M5V 1E3. (416)366-4608. Editor-in-Chief: Robin Black. 10-25% freelance written. For toy retailers, wholesalers and jobbers; owners of department stores, variety stores, hobby and handicraft stores, drug stores; arts and craft suppliers. Bimonthly magazine; 60 pages. Circ. 7,500. Pays on publication. Buys all rights. Phone queries OK (but prefer written). SASE. Free sample copy; mention *Writer's Market* in request.
Nonfiction: How-to (more effectively sell toys and games); interview (with industry leaders in Canada only); photo features (open to suggestions for b&w only); and profile (of retailers in Canada doing a good job or retailing toys and games). "No general articles which can be used anywhere with only the names requiring a change. All articles must be written for this industry." Buys 6 mss/year. Query. Length: 500-1,200/words. Pays $25/page.
Photos: State availability of photos with query. Pays $5 for 5x7 or 8x10 b&w prints. Caption preferred. Buys all rights.

Travel

ASTA TRAVEL NEWS, 488 Madison Ave., New York NY 10022. Editor: Patrick D. O. Arton. Managing Editor: Kathi Froio. 75% freelance written. Emphasizes travel, tourism and transportation. Monthly magazine; 120 pages. Circ. 19,500. Pays on acceptance. Buys all rights. Submit seasonal/holiday material 3 months in advance of issue date. Photocopied submissions OK. Reports in 4 weeks.
Nonfiction: How-to; interview; new product; profile; technical; and travel. No first-person personal experience. Buys 75 mss/year. Query. Length: 500-3,000 words. Pays $50-200.
Photos: Submit photo material with accompanying query. No additional payment for b&w prints or color transparencies. Captions required.

INCENTIVE TRAVEL MANAGER, Brentwood Publishing Corp., 825 S. Barrington Ave., Los Angeles CA 90049. (213)826-8388. Editor: John Buchanan. Monthly magazine covering incentive travel for corporate executives in charge of incentive travel. Circ. 40,000. Pays "on edited word count, which falls between acceptance and publication." Byline given. Buys all rights. SASE. Reports "when an assignment is available."
Nonfiction: General interest (incentive travel, planning, setting up, selecting destinations); interview/profile (of executives); travel (destination updates); and literature. Buys 90 mss/year. Query or send resume. "Do not query with article ideas. All articles are assigned." Length: 2,500 words average. Pays 10¢/word.

PACIFIC TRAVEL NEWS, 274 Brannan St., San Francisco CA 94107. (415)397-0070. Publisher: Frederic M. Rea. Editor: Phyllis Elving. 10% freelance written. For travel trade—travel agencies, transportation companies. Monthly. Circ. 25,000. Buys one-time rights for travel trade publication. Pays on publication unless material is for future use; then on acceptance. Free sample copy. All material purchased on assignment following specific outline. Query about assignment. "Do not send unsolicited mss or transparencies." Reports in 4 weeks. SASE.
Nonfiction: Writer must be based in a country in coverage area of the Pacific—from Hawaii west to India, south to Australia and New Zealand. "We are primarily interested in reporting on destinations in the Pacific Ocean area from the standpoint of their tourism attractions, facilities and plans for the future—written with little essay and more facts so that the information is useful to the travel agent in selling tickets to the Pacific area. We are not interested in how-to articles, such as how to sell, decorate your windows, keep your staff happy, cut costs." Pays $300 maximum.
Photos: Purchased with mss or captions only. Related to travel attractions, activities within Pacific area. Sometimes general travel-type photos, other times specific photos related to hotels, tours,

tour equipment, etc. Buys mainly b&w glossy, 5x7 or larger. Also buys about 18 color transparencies/year, 35mm top quality. Pays up to $15 for b&w; up to $50 for inside color; $75 for color used on cover.

THE STAR SERVICE, Sloane Travel Agency Reports, Box 15610, Fort Lauderdale FL 33318. (305)472-8794. Editor: Robert D. Sloane. Editorial manual sold to travel agencies on subscription basis. Buys all rights. Buys about 2,000 reports/year. Pays on publication. "Write for instruction sheet and sample report form. Initial reports sent by a new correspondent will be examined for competence and criticized as necessary upon receipt, but once established, a correspondent's submissions will not usually be acknowledged until payment is forwarded, which can often be several months, depending on immediate editorial needs." Query. SASE.
Nonfiction: "Objective, critical evaluations of worldwide hotels and cruise ships suitable for North Americans, based on inspections. Forms can be provided to correspondents so no special writing style is required, only perception, experience and judgment in travel. No commercial gimmick—no advertising or payment for listings in publication is accepted." With query, writer should *"outline experience in travel and writing specific forthcoming travel plans, time available for inspections.* Leading travel agents throughout the world subscribe to Star Service. No credit or byline is given correspondents due to delicate subject matter often involving negative criticism of hotels. We would like to emphasize the importance of reports being based on current experience and the importance of reporting on a substantial volume of hotels, not just isolated stops (since staying in hotels is not a requisite) in order that work be profitable for both publisher and writer. Experience in travel writing is desirable." Length: "up to 350 words, if submitted in paragraph form; varies if submittied on printed inspection form." Pays $10 minimum/report used. "Guarantees of acceptance of set numbers of reports may be made on establishment of correspondent's ability and reliability, but always on prior arrangement. Higher rates of payment sometimes arranged, after correspondent's reliability is established."

THE TRAVEL AGENT, 2 W. 46th St., New York NY 10036. Editor: Eric Friedheim. For "travel agencies and travel industry executives." Semiweekly. Circ. 35,000. Not copyrighted. Pays on acceptance. Query. Reports "immediately." SASE.
Nonfiction and Photos: Uses trade features slanted to travel agents, sales and marketing people, and executives of transportation companies such as airlines, ship lines, etc. No travelogues such as those appearing in newspapers and consumer publications. Articles should show how agent and carriers can sell more travel to the public. Length: up to 2,500 words. Pays $50-100. Photos purchased with ms.

TRAVELAGE MIDAMERICA, Official Airlines Guide, Inc., A Dun & Bradstreet Co., Suite 2416 Prudential Plaza, Chicago IL 60601. (312)861-0432. Editor/Publisher: Martin Deutsch. Managing Editor: Linnea Smith Jessup. 5% freelance written. "For travel agents in the 13 midAmerica states and in Ontario, Saskatchewan and Manitoba." Biweekly magazine. Circ. 13,000. Pays on pubication. Buys one-time rights. Submit seasonal/holiday material 3 months in advance of issue date. Simultaneous, photocopied and previously published submissions OK. SASE. Reports in 2 weeks. Free sample copy and writer's guidelines.
Nonfiction: "News on destinations, hotels, operators, rates and other developments in the travel business." No general destination stories, especially ones on "do-it-yourself" travel. Buys 8-10 mss/year. Query. Length: 400-1,500 words. Pays $1.50/column inch.
Photos: State availability of photos with query. Pays $1.50/column inch for glossy b&w prints.

TRAVELAGE WEST, Official Airline Guides, Inc., 582 Market St., San Francisco CA 94104. Managing Editor: Donald C. Langley. 5% freelance written. For travel agency sales counselors in the Western US and Canada. Weekly magazine. Circ. 20,000. Pays on publication. Buys all rights. Pays kill fee. Byline given. Submit seasonal/holiday material 2 months in advance. SASE. Reports in 4 weeks. Free writer's guidelines.
Nonfiction: Travel. Buys 15 mss/year. Query. Length: 1,000 words maximum. Pays $1.50/column inch. "No promotional approach or any hint of do-it-yourself travel. Emphasis is on news, not description."
Tips: "Query to be a straight-forward description of the proposed story, including (1) an indication of the news angle, no matter how tenuous and (2) a recognition by the author that we run a trade magazine for travel agents, not a consumer book. I am particularly turned off by letters that try to get me all work up about the 'beauty' or excitement of some place. Authors planning to travel might discuss with us a proposed angle before they go; otherwise their chances of gathering the right information are slim."

Veterinary

MODERN VETERINARY PRACTICE, American Veterinary Publications, Inc., Drawer KK, 300 E. Canon Perdido, Santa Barbara CA 93102. For graduate veterinarians. Monthly magazine; 90 pages. Circ. 15,500. Pays on publication. Buys all rights. Phone queries OK. Submit seasonal/ holiday material 3 months in advance. SASE. Reports in 4 weeks. Sample copy $2.

Nonfiction: How-to articles (clinical medicine, new surgical procedures, business management); informational (business management, education, government projects affecting practicing veterinarians, special veterinary projects); interviews (only on subjects of interest to veterinarians; query first); technical articles (clinical reports, technical advancements in veterinary medicine and surgery). Buys 25-30 mss/year. Submit complete ms, but query first on ideas for pieces other than technical or business articles. Pays $15/page.

Photos: B&w glossies (5x7 or larger) and color transparencies (5x7) used with mss. No additional payment.

Tips: "Contact practicing veterinarians or veterinary colleges. Find out what interests the clinician, and what new procedures and ideas might be useful in a veterinary practice. Better yet, collaborate with a veterinarian. Most of our authors are veterinarians or those working with veterinarians in a professional capacity. Knowledge of the interests and problems of practicing veterinarians is essential."

VETERINARY ECONOMICS MAGAZINE, 2728 Euclid Ave., Cleveland OH 44115. Editorial Director: John D. Velardo. For all practicing veterinarians in the US. Monthly. Buys exclusive rights in the field. Pays on publication. SASE.

Nonfiction and Photos: Uses case histories telling about good business practices on the part of veterinarians. Also, articles about financial problems, investments, insurance and similar subjects of particular interest to professional men. "We reject articles with superficial information about a subject instead of carefully researched and specifically directed articles for our field." Pays $20-30/printed page depending on worth. Pays $100 maximum. Photos purchased with ms. Pays $7.50.

VETERINARY MEDICINE/SMALL ANIMAL CLINICIAN, 144 N. Nettleton Ave., Bonner Springs KS 66012. (913)441-6167. Executive Editor: Ray Ottinger. 5% freelance written. For graduate veterinarians, student veterinarians, libraries, representatives of drug companies and research personnel. Monthly magazine; 160 pages. Circ. 18,500. Pays on publication. Buys first North American serial rights. Byline given. Phone queries OK. Submit seasonal/holiday material 5-6 months in advance of issue date. Previously published submissions OK. SASE. Reports in 2-3 weeks. Free writer's guidelines.

Nonfiction: Accepts only articles dealing with medical case histories, practice management, business, taxes, insurance, investments. Photo feature (new hospital, floor plan, new equipment; remodeled hospital). No "cutesy" stories about animals. Buys 3 mss/issue. Submit complete ms. Length: 1,500-5,000 words. Pays $30-90.

Photos: State availability of photos with ms. Reviews b&w glossy prints, glossy color prints, and 35mm color transparencies. Captions required. Buys one-time and reprint rights. Model release required.

Water Supply and Sewage Disposal

GROUND WATER AGE, 135 Addison Ave., Elmhurst IL 60126. (312)530-6160. Associate Editor: Kathleen Bryers. 20% freelance written. For water well drilling contractors and water systems specialists. Monthly magazine; 64 pages. Circ. 19,000. Pays on acceptance. Buys first North American serial rights. Submit seasonal/holiday material 4 months in advance of issue date. Simultaneous, photocopied, and previously published submissions OK. SASE. Reports in 3 weeks. Free sample copy and writer's guidelines; mention *Writer's Market* in request.

Nonfiction: General interest; historical; how-to; humor; interview; nostalgia; opinion; photo feature; profile; and technical. Buys 18 mss/year. Query or submit complete ms. Length: 1,000-3,000 words. Pays 4-8¢/word.

Photos: State availability of photos with query or submit photos with ms. Pays $5-15 for 4x5 matte b&w prints; $25-75 for 8x10 matte color prints. Captions and model release required. Buys all rights or one-time rights.

SOLID WASTES MANAGEMENT, Communication Channels, Inc., 185 Madison Ave., New York NY 10016. (212)889-1850. Editor-in-Chief: Shirley Kii. Emphasizes refuse hauling, landfill transfer stations and resource recovery for private haulers, municipal sanitation and consulting engineers. Monthly magazine; 100 pages. Circ. 21,000. Pays on publication. Buys all rights. Phone queries OK. Submit seasonal or holiday material 3 months in advance. Photocopied submissions OK. SASE. Reports in 4 weeks. Sample copy $2. Free writer's guidelines.
Nonfiction and Photos: Case studies of individual solid wastes companies, landfills, transfer stations, etc. Material must include details on all quantities handled, statistics, equipment used, etc. Informational, how-to, interview, historical, think pieces and technical articles. Length: 1,500 words minimum. Pays $100-200.

WATER WELL JOURNAL, Water Well Journal Publishing Co., 500 W. Wilson Bridge Rd., Worthington OH 43085. (614)846-4967. Editor: Jay H. Lehr. Managing Editor: Anita B. Stanley. Magazine published 14 times/year about water well drilling and ground water for contractors, suppliers, and manufacturers of equipment. Circ. 22,000. Pays on publication. Byline given. Makes work-for-hire assignments. Submit seasonal material 6 months in advance. Photocopied submissions OK. SASE. Reports in 1 month. Sample copy $1; free writer's guidelines.
Nonfiction: Interview, photo feature and technical. Buys 1 ms/issue. Query. Pays $50/typeset page. "We need major articles such as personality profiles of drillers and articles on pollution problems. We have special issues on pump and pump installation and rural water districts."
Fillers: Editor: Kevin McCray. Clippings. Buys 1 ms/issue. Pays $5/line.

Services

Authors' Agents

After you have made a reasonable number of article, story or book sales on your own, you may want to use an agent. An agent is a literary broker, a middleman who gets your book manuscript to the right editor at the right time, and who makes the sale and negotiates the best possible deal for you. The agent relies on contacts, experience, and knowing what editors are looking for far in advance of publishing-house announcements. The agent also insulates a writer from the business side of writing, and, ideally, is your partner, someone you can trust and work closely with on projects.

Many writers—among them, novelists John Updike and Joseph Wambaugh—prefer not to have an agent. They do their own deal-making, hire an attorney for contract review, and keep the 10%—or, increasingly, the 15%—for themselves. Others find an agent invaluable and cannot function in the manuscript-marketing world without one. Still others cannot find an agent at all. They lack the credits, the contacts . . . whatever it takes to get an agent's sincere attentions.

Getting an Agent

If you are hunting for an agent, the search won't be easy. But if you have good ideas (preferably book-length ones), and if you are persistent, the search can be successful. The most direct approach is to contact an agent by mail with a brief query letter (not to exceed two single-spaced typewritten pages) in which you describe your work, yourself, and your publishing history. For a nonfiction book, add an outline; for fiction, a few sample chapters (up to 50 typed double-spaced pages) will tell an agent whether the book is no or go. Generally, treatments or even concepts are preferred for television or films. Your letter should be personalized—not a photocopied form letter with the agent's name typed in, *always include SASE* with enough postage for a reply plus return of materials. If you don't hear from an agent within six weeks, send a polite note asking if the material has been received—and include a photocopy of your original query plus materials and another SASE. If you hear nothing within four months, send a note withdrawing the material—and contact another agent using the same method, immediately.

Agents and the Market Today

Literary agencies generally come in three sizes: small (handling up to 60 clients), medium (up to 100), and large (over 100). An agent should not be measured by the number of clients, or even by the number of sales made in a given time period, but rather by the number of deals and dollars that really account for writing success. Agents work for *additional* sales of your manuscripts. No good agent will be satisfied selling your novel to a hardcover publisher, for instance; he'll invest some time in selling it to a paperback house, to a movie producer, to a newspaper syndicate for serialization, to a book club, to a foreign publisher. To do this, the agent exercises energy, ideas, connections and business experience the writer probably doesn't have.

Most agents do not handle magazine articles, poetry, or essays. There is not enough revenue generated from such sales to make them worth an agent's time. Most writers develop their own rapport with the people who edit such publications and sell to them directly. Later, when a writer is doing books, his agent may handle such small sales—as a professional courtesy, not an income maker. Autobiography is almost impossible to sell today, unless you are well known in some area of endeavor. Thin books (manuscripts of less than 200-250 pages) do not sell easily either; most agents refuse to handle them because publishers are not likely to be interested. If you are writing genre fiction—such as mysteries, science fiction or romances—you may have to get a couple of book sales behind you before an agent will handle your work. Most publishers who do genre fiction are generally receptive to hearing from authors directly anyway.

Some agents specialize. A list of play agents, for example, is available from The Dramatists Guild, 234 W. 44th St., New York City 10036 (include SASE when making the request). Other agent specialties are indicated in the listings that follow. Most of the agents in this section are members of the Independent Literary Agents Association (Box 5257, FDR Station, New York City 10150), or the Society of Authors' Representatives (40 E. 49th St., New York City 10017). The SAR publishes a pamphlet called "The Literary Agent," which explains the role of the agent and how to get an agent, and lists the current SAR membership. The pamphlet is free, *if* you send SASE (#10 size envelope) with the request.

Fee-Charging Agents

The SAR stresses what an agent *cannot* do: agents can't "sell unsalable work; teach a beginner how to write salable copy; act as editor of the writer's work; solve the author's personal problems or lend money; be available outside of office hours except by appointment; or perform the functions of press agent, social secretary or travel agent." In other words, having an agent is *not* the final solution to your writing problems. An agent can aid and simplify your career, but ultimately your career is in your hands.

One of the SAR bylaws states that its members may not charge "reading fees"—that is, fees to read and consider a submission. *None of the agents listed here charge such fees.* Some agents, however, do charge fees, claiming that reading new material consumes so much time that might otherwise be spent selling books, they have to charge the fee or stop reading unsolicited material altogether. Here are some questions to ask about reading fees:

Is it a one-time fee, or will you have to pay again on subsequent submissions?

Will you have to pay the fee again when resubmitting a revised manuscript?

Will the fee be refunded if the agent decides to represent you?

Will the agent waive the fee if you have already had work published, or if you have particular expertise in the area you are writing about?

What do you get for the fee? Just a reading, or some criticism and analysis?

Agents may offer suggestions on how a book might be rewritten to be made salable, but under no circumstances do legitimate agents charge a fee for editing your manuscript. *Editing should be done by editors—after the book is sold.*

Remember, though, that most agents *don't* charge a reading fee, and you should try to work with those agents first.

The Pseudo-Agent

Do not confuse true literary agents with other individuals or "agencies" that advertise as "consultants" offering manuscript criticism or "literary services" for a fee that may cover a critique, an edit, or a rewrite of your manuscript. Ask anyone who claims to be an "agent," or who uses agent-like phrasing ("We like your manuscript and we think it is marketable—of course, some revisions will be necessary to make it professionally acceptable," etc.) when discussing a fee of any sort, to give you a list of *recent* book sales. If an agent type has not sold three books to established publishing houses in the previous year, he is probably out of the publishing market mainstream. Make sure you can afford such literary services offered you. Fees may range from several hundred to several *thousand* dollars— and there is no guarantee that the arrangement will result in a sale to recoup your investment. Such firms and individuals may make their profits from reading and criticism and editing fees—not from sales to publishers.

Contract Considerations

Be careful, too, in signing any contract with an agent. Many legitimate agents conduct business with a handshake, believing that a contract will neither solidify a good relationship nor help a bad one. They want to be free to drop (or add) clients as relationships develop. Other agents—and many pseudo-agents—require a contract that should be studied carefully with an attorney before signing. Know what rights the agent is handling for your material, and check that no charges are made for services that you do not fully understand and agree to. Some agencies charge for criticism or impose a "marketing fee" for office overhead, etc. If you pay such a fee, you are entitled to see any correspondence that such a marketing endeavor would produce.

Legitimate agents will discuss marketing problems a manuscript might be having. If you have any doubts about where (or whether) your manuscript is being marketed, ask to see the mail between your agent and the publishers he claims to be showing your work to. If you have paid a marketing fee, it is illegal for the agent to withhold a prepaid service longer than three months—unless the customer is allowed to cancel the order and get a refund. An agent who breaks this law can be sued by the writer.

The best way to avoid such complications—legal or otherwise—is by selecting your agent carefully.

DOMINICK ABEL LITERARY AGENCY, INC., 498 West End Ave., New York NY 10024. (212)877-0710. Obtains new clients through recommendations, solicitation, and blind submissions. Will not read unsolicited mss, will read unsolicited queries and outlines. SASE. Member ILAA. Agent receives 10% commission on US sales; 20% on foreign.
Will Handle: Book-length adult fiction and nonfiction.
Recent Sales: *The Home Front*, by A. Satterfield (Seaview); *Indemnity Only*, novel by S. Paretsky (Dial); and *Bing Crosby: The Hollow Man*, by D. Shepherd and R. Slatzer (St. Martin's).

ADAMS, RAY & ROSENBERG, 9200 Sunset Blvd., Los Angeles CA 90069. Obtains new clients through recommendation only. Will not read unsolicited mss. Agent receives 10% commission.
Will Handle: Novels (motion picture, publication and TV rights), motion pictures, stage plays (film rights), and TV scripts.

AUDREY ADLER LITERARY AGENCY, 1001 Connecticut Ave., Washington DC 20036. (202)296-0630. Represents 75 clients. Will not read unsolicited manuscripts. Agent receives 10% commission. Member ILAA.
Will Handle: Genre fiction, sagas and romance as well as nonfiction books.

AGENCY FOR ARTISTS, 9200 Sunset Blvd., #531, Los Angeles CA 90069. (213)278-6243. Writer's Agent: Bettye McCartt. Obtains clients through referrals. Small agency. Authors who

submit "must have something already published or produced." Will read—at no charge—queries and resumes. SASE. Agent receives 10% commission on domestic sales.
Will Handle: Films (feature); and TV scripts (episodic television feature films).

DOROTHY ALBERT, 162 W. 54th St., New York NY 10019. Obtains new clients through recommendations of editors, educational establishments, contacts in the film industry, and inquiries. Writers should send letter of introduction, description of material, and list of previous submissions, if any. Will not read unsolicited mss; will read unsolicited queries and outlines. SASE. Agent receives 10% on domestic sales; 20% on foreign.
Will Handle: Novels, nonfiction books, motion pictures (completed, no treatments), stage plays (musicals), TV scripts, juvenile and how-to. No poetry, short stories, textbooks, articles, documentaries, or scripts for established episode shows. "We are interested in novels which are well-plotted suspense; quality drama, adult fiction and human relations. The writer should have some foreknowledge of structure and endurance, whether it be motion pictures, television, or books."

MAXWELL ALEY ASSOCIATES, 145 E. 35th St., New York NY 10016. (212)679-5377. Contact: Ruth Aley. Represents 20 clients. Prefers to work with previously published authors. Query with a brief biographical background sketch. SASE. Member ILAA. Agent receives 10% commission domestic sales; 20% on foreign.
Will Handle: Preferably nonfiction books.

MARCIA AMSTERDAM, 41 W. 82nd St., New York NY 10024. (212)873-4945. Obtains new clients through client or editor referrals. Will read queries, partials and outlines. SASE. Agent receives 10% on domestic sales; 15% on British; 20% on foreign.
Will Handle: Novels, nonfiction books, teleplays, screenplays.

THE ASSOCIATES, 8961 Sunset Blvd., Los Angeles CA 90069. Obtains new clients through referrals from clients and producers. Made 200 sales in 1980; plans 300 in 1981. "Writers must be published or have motion picture or TV credits." Will not read unsolicited mss; will read queries and outlines. SASE. Agent receives 10% commission.
Will Handle: Novels (will accept unpublished authors if outline and first 3 chapters are submitted); nonfiction (must see outline and complete mss); motion pictures; and TV scripts.
Recent Sales: *The Howling*, novel by Gary Brandner (AVCO Embassy Films); *Slim Down Camp*, novel by Stephen Manes (ABC Television): and *The Last Frontier*, novel by Patricia and Clayton Matthews (Chuck Fries Productions).

THE BALKIN AGENCY, 403 W. 115th St., New York NY 10025. President: Richard Balkin. Obtains new clients through recommendations, over-the-transom inquiries, and solicitation. Will not read unsolicited mss; will read unsolicited queries, or outlines and 2 sample chapters. SASE. Made 30 sales in 1979; plans 35 in 1980, 40 in 1981. Member ILAA. Agent receives 10% commission on domestic sales, 20% on UK, 25% on foreign.
Will Handle: Magazine articles (only as a service to clients who primarily write books), textbooks (college only), nonfiction books, and professional books (on occasion).
Recent Sales: *A Guide to Backpacking In Canada*, (Doubleday Canada); *Finding Your Family: An Adoptee's Handbook* (Harper and Row); and *Ted Kennedy: The Myth of Leadership* (Houghton Mifflin).
Tips: "Query with: A) Description; B) What is unique about the work; C) How it differs from competing or overlapping titles; D) Audiences/Market; and E) Size, amount of art work, if any; and completion date."

VIRGINIA BARBER LITERARY AGENCY, INC., 353 W. 21st St., New York NY 10011. (212)255-6515. Contact: Virginia Barber or Mary Evans. Represents 80 clients. Author should have a book-length ms finished before querying. Query. SASE. Member ILAA. Agent receives 10% commission.
Will Handle: Book-length fiction and nonfiction.

BILL BERGER ASSOCIATES, INC., 444 E. 58th St., New York NY 10022. (212)486-9588. Contact: William Berger for fiction; Henriette Neatrour for juvenile. Represents 50 clients. Prefers to work with previously published authors. Query with a brief biographical background sketch. Member SAR. Agent receives 10% commission.
Will Handle: Trade fiction, thrillers and juvenile books.
Tips: "Write an intelligent letter giving details of all writing experience and give a description of the material you want to submit. Proof and re-proof your submission; nothing looks worse than a letter written in poor grammar filled with typos."

LOIS BERMAN, 250 W. 57th St., New York NY 10019. (212)581-0607. Obtains new clients by referral. Member SAR. Agent receives 10% commission.
Will Handle: Stage plays, screenplays. "The authors I represent are writers of dramatic material—freelance or on assignment."

SHAUNA BERNACCHI AND ASSOCIATES, Penthouse Suites, 1100 Glendon Ave., Los Angeles CA 90024. (213)824-0542. Contact: Shauna Bernacchi. Estab. 1980. Obtains clients through referrals. Prefers to work with published writers. Will read—at no charge—outline with two chapters. Will not read unsolicited mss. SASE. Agent receives 10% commission on domestic sales; 10% on dramatic sales; 10% on foreign sales.
Will Handle: Films, nonfiction books and novels.

RON BERNSTEIN, 200 W. 58th St., New York NY 10019. (212)265-0705. Contact: Ron Bernstein. Obtains new clients through referrals. Represents 60 clients. Prefers previously published authors. Query with outline of proposal. SASE. Member ILAA. Agent receives minimum 10% commission.
Will Handle: Novels, nonfiction books, film and TV scripts. "The principal agent has extensive experience in selling TV and motion picture rights."

BLOOM, LEVY, SHORR & ASSOCIATES, 8816 Burton Way, Beverly Hills CA 90211. (213)858-7741. Estab. 1979; "however, the forerunner of the firm has been in existence since 1963." Obtains new clients by recommendations of writers, directors, producers, and studio executives. SASE. Agent receives 10% commission.
Will Handle: "We will read only completed motion picture screenplays. This may include screenplays for feature films as well as movies made for television. We will not read outlines, treatments, or scripts for episodic or situation comedy television."
Recent Sales: *Goodbye Idaho Kid*, original screenplay by Durrell Crays (CBS Feature Films); *Good King Harry*, original screenplay by Jeffrey Price/Peter Seaman (Columbia); and *Stray Dogs*, original screenplay by David Smilow (Paramount).

BEVERLY BOND LITERARY AGENT, (Southwest affiliate of Michael Larsen/Elizabeth Pomada Literary Agents), 1725 Wroxton Court, Houston TX 77005. (713)524-4974. Contact: Beverly Bond. Estab. 1979. Obtains clients through referral and *Literary Market Place*. Small agency. "Interested in unpublished, but serious writers. I expect a phone call or query letter and do not read manuscripts that are sent without a query." Will read—at no charge—queries. Will not read unsolicited manuscripts. SASE. Agent receives 10% commission on domestic sales; 20% on dramatic sales; 20% on foreign sales.
Will Handle: Nonfiction books and novels.
Criticism Services: "I critique a manuscript only if I believe that, with certain revisions, it is marketable. I do not critique what I believe to be unsalable."

GEORGES BORCHARDT, INC., 136 E. 57th St., New York NY 10022. (212)753-5785. Obtains new clients "mainly through authors already represented by us who refer others." Potential clients "must be highly recommended by someone we know." Reads unsolicited queries from well-established writers. Made 154 U.S. book sales in 1980; plans 150 in 1981. Member SAR. Agent receives 10% commission.
Will Handle: Magazine articles and fiction, novels, and nonfiction books.
Recent Sales: New novel by John Gardner (Alfred A. Knopf); *World Without End*, by Francine du Plessix Gray (Simon & Schuster); and *Emile Zola*, by Fred Brown (Viking Press).
Tips: "Get your manuscript in the best possible shape and enlist the help of an established author of your acquaintance."

BRANDT & BRANDT LITERARY AGENTS, INC., 1501 Broadway, New York NY 10036. (212)840-5760. Represents approximately 150 clients. Query. SASE. Member SAR. Agent receives 10% commission on domestic rights; 15% on British rights; and 20% on other foreign rights.
Will Handle: Novels and nonfiction books.

JAMES BROOKE, 8255 Beverly Blvd., #205, Los Angeles CA 90048. (213)651-5730. Contact: James Brooke. Obtains clients through recommendations. "We go to a lot of screenings at the film schools." Small agency. Will read—at no charge—screenplays. SASE. Agent receives 10% commission on domestic sales.
Will Handle: Films (feature); TV scripts (movies; no episodic material); and screenplays.
Tips: "It is almost impossible for anyone outside Los Angeles or New York to be successful as a screenwriter. There are so many contacts to be made. A writer should be immersed in the whole

process of how films are made. We look for writers who are good storytellers and who know how to build drama through character development, plot and resolution."

JAMES BROWN ASSOCIATES, INC., 25 W. 43rd St., New York NY 10036. (212)840-8272. Potential clients "must be professional, not necessarily published." Will read unsolicited queries. SASE. Member SAR and ILAA. Agent receives 10% commission on domestic sales, 20% on British and translation countries.
Will Handle: "We handle writers concentrating on books." For writers represented will handle all rights, foreign, performance, etc., and magazine articles and fiction.

CURTIS BROWN, LTD., 575 Madison Ave., New York NY 10022. (212)755-4200. President: Perry H. Knowlton. Books: Steven Axelrod, Emilie Jacobson, Perry H. Knowlton, Marilyn Marlow, Clyde Taylor. Film and TV rights: Timothy Knowlton. Query by letter only. Unsolicited manuscripts will be returned unread. Member SAR. Agent receives 10% commission on domestic rights; 20% on foreign rights; 10% on film rights (film commission sometime varies in particular circumstances).
Will Handle: Novels and nonfiction books.

SHIRLEY BURKE AGENCY, 370 E. 76th St., B-704, New York NY 10021. (212)861-2309. Obtains new clients through recommendations. Potential clients must have published at least one book. Will not read or return unsolicited mss (do not send without approval); will read unsolicited queries. SASE. Agent receives 10% commission.
Will Handle: Magazine fiction, novels, and nonfiction books.
Recent Sales: *Storm Watch*, fiction by Stephen Longstreet (Putnam's); *Temptation*, fiction by Lydia Lancaster (Warner Books); and *Too Deep for Tears*, by Lucy Freeman (Elsevier-Dutton).

RUTH CANTOR, LITERARY AGENT, 156 5th Ave., New York NY 10010. Literary Agent: Ruth Cantor. Foreign Rights: Nurnberg. Movies and Television: Al Jackinson. Obtains new clients through recommendations by writers, publishers, editors, and teachers. Potential clients "must be of proven competence as a writer. This means either some publishing record or a recommendation from someone likely to be a competent critic of his work—a teacher of writing, another writer, etc." Will not read unsolicited mss; will read unsolicited queries and outlines. SASE. "Send a letter giving publishing history and writing experience, plus concise outline of proposed project or of ms you want to send. Do not phone." Agent receives 10% commission on domestic sales; 20% on foreign.
Will Handle: Novels, nonfiction books and children's books.
Recent Sales: *Perky*, by G. Bond (Western); *This Savage Land,* by B. Womack (Fawcett); and *Abigail Scott Dunaway,* by D. Morrison (Atheneum).

CANTRELL-COLAS INC., 229 E. 79th St., New York NY 10021. (212)737-8503. Contact: Maryanne Colas. Obtains new clients by recommendation. Represents 60 clients. Made 51 sales in 1980. Query and send brief biographical background. Member ILAA. Agent receives 10% commission.
Will Handle: Novels and nonfiction books. "Always keen to get strong contemporary fiction. I'm also particularly interested in medicine and psychology related topics for trade publication."
Recent Sales: *Class Act*, nonfiction by Benita Eisler (Harper & Row); *Death on the Eno*, mystery novel by Amanda MacKay (Little-Brown); and *The Courage To Change Your Life*, nonfiction by Kathryn Jason and J.J. McMahon (Doubleday).

BERTHA CASE, 345 W. 58th St., New York NY 10019. Member SAR. Small agency. Will read—at no charge—outlines. "Do not send mss." SASE. Agent receives 10% commission on domestic sales.
Will Handle: Novels and stage plays.

HY COHEN LITERARY AGENCY, LTD., 111 W. 57th St., New York NY 10019. (212)757-5237. President: Hy Cohen. Made 12 sales in 1979. Obtains new clients through recommendations. Will read unsolicited mss, queries and outlines. SASE. Agent receives 10% commission.
Will Handle: Magazine articles and fiction, novels, and nonfiction books.
Recent Sales: *Charleston*, fiction by Alexandra Ripley (Doubleday); *Medusa Conspiracy*, fiction by Ethan Shedley (Viking); and *Naked at the Feast*, biography of Josephine Baker by Lynn Haney (Dodd, Mead).

POLLY CONNELL AND ASSOCIATES, 4605 Lankershim, Suite 213, North Hollywood CA 91602. Contact: Polly Connell. Obtains clients through referrals from producers, directors and

other writers. Small agency. Will read—at no charge—queries. Agent receives 10% commission on domestic sales.
Will Handle: Films (features and documentary); and TV scripts (segment TV, movies of the week).

LOIS DE LA HABA, 142 Bank St., New York NY 10014. (212)929-4838. Prospective clients should be professional writers. Query with a brief biographical background sketch. SASE. Member ILAA. Agent receives 15% commission on domestic rights (which includes overseeing public relations on author's projects) and 20% on foreign.
Will Handle: Novels, nonfiction books and TV scripts.

ANITA DIAMANT: THE WRITERS WORKSHOP, INC., 51 E. 42nd St., New York NY 10017. (212)687-1122. President: Anita Diamant. Associate: Humphrey Evans. Obtains new clients through recommendations by publishers or other clients. Potential clients must have made some professional sales. Will not read unsolicited mss; will read unsolicited queries. SASE. Agent receives 10% commission. Member SAR.
Will Handle: Magazine articles and fiction, novels, nonfiction books, motion pictures, and TV scripts.
Recent Sales: *Flowers in the Attic* and *Petals in the Wind*, by Virginia Cleo Andrews (Pocket Books); *Pin*, by Andrew Neiderman (Pocket Books); and *The Sea Shepherd: The Story of Paul Watson, With Warren Rogers* (Norton).

CANDIDA DONADIO & ASSOCIATES, 111 W. 57th St., New York NY 10019. (212)757-5076. Represents 80 clients. Query with outline and sample chapters. SASE. Member SAR. Agent receives 10% commission.
Will Handle: Magazine articles, magazine fiction, novels and trade nonfiction books.

ANN ELMO AGENCY, INC., 60 E. 42nd St., New York NY 10017. (212)661-2880. Obtains new clients through writers' queries. Sales average about a book a month. Will read queries and outlines at no charge. SASE. Member SAR. Agent receives 10% commission on domestic sales and 20% on foreign sales.
Will Handle: Magazine articles (only strong ideas); magazine fiction (very few short stories); novels, nonfiction books; stage plays; and occasional TV scripts.
Recent Sales: *The Rise of Theodore Roosevelt*, biography by Edmund Morris (Coward, McCann & Geoghegan); *Edith Roosevelt*, biography by Silvia Morris (Coward, McCann & Geoghegan); and *The Six Year Pregnancy*, nonfiction by Al Rosenfeld and Dr. Gil Kleiman (Holt, Rinehart & Winston).

PATRICIA FALK FEELEY, INC., AUTHORS' REPRESENTATIVE, Suite 2004, 1501 Broadway, New York NY 10036. Obtains new clients through referrals by clients and editors and by inquiries. Will not read unsolicited mss; will read unsolicited queries and outlines. SASE. Agent receives 10% commission on domestic sales, 15% on British; 20% on foreign.
Will Handle: Novels and nonfiction books.
Recent Sales: *A Banner Red and Gold*, by Annelise Kamada (Warner); *The Germans*, by Gordon Craig (Putnam); and *Flying Indoor Model Planes*, how-to by Williams (Simon & Schuster).

BARTHOLD FLES LITERARY AGENCY, 501 5th Ave., New York NY 10017. Contact: Barthold Fles or Karen Garthe. Obtains new clients through recommendations of clients and editors, scouting tips, and writers' conferences. Will not read unsolicited mss. Made 40 sales in 1980; plans 40-45 in 1981. Agent receives 10% commission on domestic sales; 15% on British; and 20% on foreign.
Will Handle: Novels and nonfiction books. Specializes in intermediate and teenage juveniles; no picture books.
Recent Sales: *George Michael's Secret for Beautiful Glorious Hair*, (Doubleday); *Murder Most Strange*, by Dell Shannon (Morrow); and *Pictorial History of UFO's*, by David C. Knight (McGraw-Hill).

JAY GARON-BROOKE ASSOCIATES, INC., 415 Central Park West, New York NY 10025. (212)866-3654. President: Jay Garon. Obtains new clients through referrals; "however, we will read and answer query letters wherein material is briefly described." Will not read unsolicited mss; will read queries and outlines. SASE. Agent receives 15% commission.
Will Handle: Novels (general and category fiction suitable for hardcover or paperback publication); textbooks (rarely considers professional and technical material unless there is a clear application to a trade market); nonfiction books (biography, autobiography, self-help and/or improvement, popular history—but generally any nonfiction oriented toward popular appeal or interest);

motion pictures (finished screenplays accompanied by treatment only); stage plays and TV scripts (accompanied by treatment).
Recent Sales: *Flamenco Rose*, by Janet Louise Roberts (Warner); *Midnight Whispers*, by Clayton and Patricia Matthews (Bantam); and *Project Identification*, by Dr. Harley Rutledge (Prentice-Hall).

MAX GARTENBERG, LITERARY AGENT, 331 Madison Ave., New York NY 10017. (212)661-5270. Obtains new clients through referrals and solicitations. Will not read unsolicited mss; will read unsolicited queries. SASE. Agent receives 10% commission.
Will Handle: Novels and nonfiction books.
Recent Sales: *Stan: The Life of Stan Laurel*, by Fred Lawrence Guiles (Stein & Day); *Dracula Was a Woman*, by Raymond T. McNally (McGraw-Hill); and *Nor Any Drop to Drink*, by William Ashworth (Summit Books).
Tips: Try to "persuade the agent of your talent and productivity and of the salability of your material."

GERRITSEN INTERNATIONAL TALENT AGENCY, 8721 Sunset Blvd., Suite 203, Los Angeles CA 90069. (213)659-8414. Small agency. Authors who submit "must be established writers and members of the Writers Guild." Will read—at no charge—queries.
Will Handle: Nonfiction books.

FRANCES GOLDIN, 305 E. 11th St., New York NY 10003. (212)777-0047. Contact: Frances Goldin. Obtains new clients by referral. Represents 40 clients. Query. SASE. Member ILAA. Agent receives 10% commission; 20% for juveniles.
Will Handle: Novels, nonfiction books and juveniles. "I don't handle any racist, sexist, agist or pornographic material."
Recent Sales: *Take Back the Night, Women on Pornography*, by Laura Lederer (William Morrow, Bantam); *Politics of Women's Spirituality*, by Charlene Stretnak (Doubleday); and *Humphrey, The Dancing Pig*, by Arthur Getz (Dial).

GOODMAN ASSOCIATES, 500 West End Ave., New York NY 10024. (212)873-4806. Contact: Arnold P.Goodman, Elise Simon Goodman. Small agency. Query and send a brief biographical background sketch. SASE. Member ILAA.
Will Handle: Adult trade novels and adult trade nonfiction. "The agency principals have extensive backgrounds in motion pictures and television and in selling those rights."

THE GOTLER AGENCY, 9100 Sunset Blvd., Suite 360, Los Angeles CA 90069. Estab. 1979. Obtains clients through referrals of other writers. Small agency. Will read—at no charge—queries. "No unsolicited material accepted." Agent receives 10% commission on domestic sales.
Will Handle: Novels (commercial); TV scripts (long, for TV movies); and screenplays.

GRAHAM AGENCY, 317 W. 45th St., New York NY 10036. Owner: Earl Graham. Obtains new clients through queries and recommendations. "Will accept any playwright whose work I feel is salable, and occasionally will work with a playwright whose initial effort may not be salable, but whom I feel is talented, and whose work I feel merits encouraging." Will not read unsolicited mss; will read unsolicited queries pertaining to stage plays only. Material submitted without SASE will not be returned. Member SAR. Agent receives 10% commission.
Will Handle: Full-length stage plays only.

SANFORD J. GREENBERGER ASSOCIATES, INC., 825 3rd Ave., New York NY 10022. (212)753-8581. Represents 200 clients. Query with outline. SASE. Member ILAA. Agent receives 15% commission.
Will Handle: Novels and nonfiction books.

REESE HALSEY AGENCY, 8733 Sunset Blvd., Los Angeles CA 90069. (213)652-2409. Contact: Doris Halsey. Obtains clients through direct referral from existing clients. Small agency. Will read—at no charge—queries only. "Do not send any material until it is requested." SASE. Agent receives 10% commission on domestic sales.
Will Handle: TV scripts (movies of the week; no episodic series).

HEINLE AND HEINLE ENTERPRISES, 29 Lexington Rd., Concord MA 01742. (617)369-7525. Senior Member: Charles A.S. Heinle. Client contact: Mary Green. Obtains new clients through word-of-mouth, *Writer's Market*, activities as resident agents at Cape Cod Writer's Conference, and recommendations by clients. "We are less concerned that a writer is unpublished, as long as we believe in the writer and the future." Will not read unsolicited mss; will read unsolicited queries and outlines. SASE. Agent receives 10% commission.

Will Handle: Novels, textbooks, and nonfiction books. "We are most interested in materials with a New England theme, past, present, and future, but, of course, good writing is the main consideration. We handle some textbooks in the foreign language area, and some reference materials as bibliographies in selected fields."

Recent Sales: *You've Got It Made*, frozen hors d'oeuvre cookbook by Jane Keyes (Hastings House); *The Flowered Box*, a mystery by Thomas Green (Beaufort Books); and *L'Affaire de la Petite Valise Bleue*, a French reader by Joseph Conroy (EMC Publishing Co.).

Tips: "Develop a solid project with material that can be supplied for review on request. Write query letters to several agents describing the project(s) and including an outline or synopsis. Indicate orientation as a writer, and some background information. Supply sample material only if requested."

HINTZ LITERARY AGENCY, (Associated with Ray Peekner Literary Agency). 2879 N. Grant Blvd., Milwaukee WI 53210. Obtains new clients through queries and referrals from clients and editors. Made 8 sales in 1980; plans 25 in 1981. Will not read unsolicited mss; will read outlines and queries. SASE. Agent receives 10% commission.

Will Handle: Trade fiction and nonfiction; juvenile; and religious nonfiction.

Recent Sales: *To Plant a Tree and Write a Book*, trade religious by Keith Clark, O.F.M. (Ave Maria); and *Vengeance Mountain*, western by Richard C. House (Tower).

Tips: "Writers should put all their enthusiasm into a query or synopsis and should always include an author's sheet on themselves."

HUTTO MANAGEMENT, INC., 110 W. 57th St., New York NY 10019. (212)581-5610. Contact: Michael Powers or Jack Hutto. Represents 15 clients. Made 3 book sales and 2 play sales in 1979. Query. SASE. Member SAR. Agent receives 10% commission.

Will Handle: Novels, nonfiction books and stage plays.

Recent Sales: *Romantic Comedy*, Broadway play by Bernard Slade; and *These Men*, play by Mayo Simon.

INPRA INTERNATIONAL PRESS AGENCY, 411 London Press Centre, 76 Shoe Lane, London England EC4A 3JB. (01)353-0186. Literary Agent: Shelley Power. Clients are obtained "by recommendations from existing clients as well as from the firms' listing in the British *Writers' and Artists' Yearbook*. Made 43 sales in 1980. Will read unsolicited mss, queries and outlines at no charge. Send letter before sending manuscript. Member British Association of Authors' Agents. Receives 10% commission in the UK; 20% in other markets where a sub-agent is used.

Will Handle: Magazine fiction ("the only material salable in Britain and the continent is the better-class women's fiction as published in *Redbook*, *McCall's*, etc. Material must not be too American though"). Novels (most fiction considered except science fiction, westerns, erotic historicals, erotic novels. Will ojfer children's fiction, too). Nonfiction books (will consider all nonfiction which is topical and interesting to an international market. Will offer children's books, too). No poetry or plays.

Recent Sales: *The Headache Book*, by Peter Lambley (Star); *Tears*, by Denise Brinig (Futura); and *Sobukwe: Letters from Prison*, by Benjamin Pogrund (Rex Collings).

Tips: "I personally prefer to receive a letter of introduction first, with a brief description of the work being offered, as well as details of previously published work."

LARRY KARLIN AGENCY, 10850 Wilshire Blvd., Suite 600, Los Angeles CA 90024. (213)475-4828. Contact: Larry Karlin. Member Writers Guild. Obtains clients through recommendation. Small agency. Will read—at no charge—queries. "No unsolicited mss will be considered." SASE. Agent receives 10% commission on domestic sales.

Will Handle: Nonfiction books; novels; TV scripts (movies of the week, episodic); and screenplays.

IRVING KERNER LITERARY AGENCY, 934 Pearl St., Boulder CO 80302. (303)447-8112. Contact: Irving Kerner, Agent Attorney. "New clients are obtained primarily through referrals and inquiries. Writers should send letter of introduction, including description of material and previous writing efforts." Will not read unsolicited mss. Will read unsolicited queries and outlines. SASE. Standard commission is 15%, however, commission is higher on agency-created projects and a 20% commission is taken on revenues derived from merchandise spin-offs and foreign sales.

Will Handle: Novels; nonfiction books; and screenplays.

Criticism Services: "This agency will on occasion supply a writer with a written critique. However, such critiques are supplied at agency discretion. No fees are charged."

VIRGINIA KIDD, WITH JAMES ALLEN, VALERIE SMITH, AND JANE BUTLER, LITERARY AGENTS, 538 E. Harford St., Milford PA 18337. (717)296-6205. Potential client "must be a published writer; should have earned at least $2,000 (from writing) during the previous year." Positively will not read unsolicited mss. The agency's lists are full. Agent receives 10% commission on domestic sales, 15% on dramatic sales, 20% on overseas sales.
Will Handle: Magazine articles and fiction, novels, textbooks, nonfiction books, and science fiction.
Recent Sales: *Hard Words*, poetry collection by Ursula K. Le Guin (Harper & Row); *Crystal Singer*, science fiction novel by Anne McCaffrey (Del Rey Books); and *Spellsinger*, fantasy novel by Alan Dean Foster (Warner Books).
Tips: "Establish a track record first, and prove that you can earn money before seeking representation."

HOWARD KING AGENCY, INC., 6362 Hollywood Blvd., #320, Hollywood CA 90028. (213)462-1745. Estab. 1979. Obtains clients through queries and recommendations. Small agency. Will read—at no charge—queries, outlines, treatments or synopses. Agent receives 10% commission on domestic sales.
Will Handle: Film and TV scripts (pilots, TV ideas).
Tips: "Many tyros are capable of writing material far superior to what professionals are putting out."

LUCY KROLL AGENCY, 390 West End Ave., New York NY 10024. (212)877-0627. Obtains new clients through recommendations. Will not read unsolicited mss. SASE. Agent receives 10% commission.
Will Handle: Novels, nonfiction books and stage plays.

MICHAEL LARSEN/ELIZABETH POMADA LITERARY AGENTS, 1029 Jones St., San Francisco CA 94109. (415)673-0939. Contact: Elizabeth Pomada, fiction; Michael Larsen, nonfiction. Member ILAA. Obtains clients through recommendations from other clients, publishers and writers, listings in *Literary Market Place*, yellow pages, ILAA list, etc. Large Agency. Will read—at no charge—queries. SASE. Agent receives 15% commission "to $75,000 per year income, then 10% commission" on domestic sales; 10% on dramatic sales; 20% on foreign sales.
Will Handle: Nonfiction books ("proposals by authors with published articles are acceptable"); and novels ("send query and first chapter *only*, with SASE—although book must be finished if author has not been published as novelist").
Tips: "Read what you've written before sending it out. Do your homework. Find out what an agent wants to see—and what his track record is—before mailing anything. Use SASEs at *all times*. Write for our brochure."

LENNIGER LITERARY AGENCY, INC., 250 W. 57th St., Suite 2504-06, New York NY 10019. Contact: John K. Payne. New clients by invitation. Made 135 sales in 1980. Query first; will read invited mss only, at no charge. SASE. Agent receives 10% commission.
Will Handle: Nonfiction and fiction books. No articles or short stories.
Recent Sales: *Love Me, Marietta*, by Jennifer Wilde (Warner Books); *Red Is The River*, by T.V. Olsen (Fawcett Books); and *The Wolf and the Buffalo*, by Elmer Kelton (Doubleday).

THE LESCHER AGENCY, 155 E. 71st St., New York NY 10021. (212)249-7600. Contact: Susan Lescher. Represents 115 clients. Made 50 book sales in 1980. Query with outline. SASE. Member SAR. Agent receives a minimum of 10% commission on domestic sales; and 20% on foreign.
Will Handle: Novels and nonfiction books.

PATRICIA LEWIS, 450 7th Ave., Room 602, New York NY 10001. Owner: Patricia Lewis. Obtains new clients through recommendation. Made 8 sales in 1979. Will not read unsolicited mss. SASE for queries and outlines. Agent receives 10% commission.
Will Handle: Novels and nonfiction books.
Recent Sales: *The Census*, young adult by Anderson (Vanguard); *Know Your Rights in Private Industry*, by Merkel (Vanguard); and *The Menelola Report (A New Look at Gay Couples)*, by Crown (Crown).

WENDY LIPKIND, 225 E. 57th St., New York NY 10022. (212)935-1406. Represents 35 clients. Query with synopsis and brief biographical background. SASE. Member ILAA.
Will Handle: Novels and nonfiction books of previously published authors.

THE ROBERT LITTMAN AGENCY, 409 N. Camden, Beverly Hills CA 90210. (213)278-1572. Head of Literary Department: Susan Whipple. Member Writers Guild. Obtains clients through

recommendations of writers, directors, producers and studio executives. Small agency. Will read—at no charge—queries with 1-page outlines. SASE. Agent receives 10% commission on domestic sales.
Will Handle: Feature films.

THE LUND AGENCY, STARMAKERS, UNLIMITED, 7985 Santa Monica Blvd., #201, West Hollywood CA 90046. (213)656-1062. Estab. 1980. "We read everything that comes in the mail—but it must be complete, not just an idea." Small agency. Will read—at no charge—1-2 page synopses; submit also list of characters and resume. SASE. Agent receives 10% commission on domestic sales.
Will Handle: TV scripts (episodic, movies of the week, pilots) and screenplays.

DONALD MacCAMPBELL, INC., 12 E. 41st St., New York NY 10017. (212)683-5580. "Phone queries are preferred but will answer written inquiries that are accompanied by SASE." Agency works on 10% commission basis.
Will Handle: "Now handling book-length fiction exclusively, with emphasis upon the women's markets."
Recent Sales: *Salem's Daughter*, novel by Osborne (Signet); *Griffin's Talon*, novel by Carsley (Gallen/Pocket); and *Boldly They Ride*, western saga by Shirreffs (Fawcett).

ELAINE MARKSON LITERARY AGENCY, 44 Greenwich Ave., New York NY 10011. (212)243-8480. Contact: Elaine Markson. Member ILAA and Writers Guild. Obtains clients through recommendation from editors and other clients. "We prefer people who are previously published, but will also look at other writers with a strong background in writing on their chosen subject." Large agency. Will read—at no charge—queries "with brief biographies." SASE. Agent receives 10% commission on domestic sales.
Will Handle: Nonfiction books ("often with an eclectic viewpoint"); and novels ("serious literary fiction or good literary commercial fiction").

RAYA L. MARKSON, 1888 Century Park E., Los Angeles CA 90067. (213)552-2083. Contact: Raya L. Markson. Member Writers Guild. Obtains clients through recommendations. "We prefer people who have already sold something, though it's not necessary." Will read—at no charge—queries. Small agency. SASE. Agent receives 10% commission on domestic sales.
Will Handle: Feature films and TV scripts (movies of the week).

HAROLD MATSON CO., INC., 22 E. 40th St., New York NY 10016. (212)679-4490. Query. SASE. Member SAR. Agent receives 10% commission.
Will Handle: Novels and nonfiction books.

HELEN MERRILL, 337 W. 22nd St., New York NY 10011. (212)924-6314. Small firm. Query. SASE. Member SAR. Agent receives 10% commission.
Will Handle: Novels, nonfiction books and plays (dramas).

GEORGE MICHAUD AGENCY, 4950 Densmore, #1, Encino CA 91436. (213)981-6680. Literary Agent: Arthur Dreifuss. Obtains clients through Writers Guild publication. "Will consider new writers." Small agency. Will read—at no charge—queries; "will respond with instructions and requirements." SASE. Agent receives 10% commission on domestic sales.
Will Handle: Novels, TV scripts and screenplays, treatments and original stories.

ROBERT P. MILLS, LTD., 156 E. 52nd St., New York NY 10022. President: Robert P. Mills. Represents 75 clients. Obtains new clients through recommendations "of someone I know, or if the writer has a respectable publishing history." Will not read unsolicited mss; will read unsolicited queries. SASE. Member SAR. Agent receives 10% commission.
Will Handle: Novels, nonfiction books, films and syndicated material.
Recent Sales: *The Body Language of Sex Power and Aggression*, by J. Fast (M. Evans & Co.); *Twister*, by J. Bickham (Doubleday & Co.); and *Mockingbird*, by Walter Tevis (Doubleday & Co.).

MULTIMEDIA PRODUCT DEVELOPMENT, INC., 410 S. Michigan Ave., Room 828, Chicago IL 60605. (312)922-3063. President: Jane Jordan Browne. Obtains new clients through recommendations and word-of-mouth. "Multimedia handles only works of professional writers who make their living as authors. The rare exceptions are celebrity autobiographies and the 'new idea' nonfiction book." Will read unsolicited queries and outlines. SASE. Made 250 sales in 1980; plans 250 in 1981. Agent receives 10% commission on domestic sales; 15% on domestic sales for first-book authors; 20% on foreign.

Will Handle: Novels, nonfiction books. No poetry, plays, articles or short stories.
Recent Sales: *Murder Among the Mighty*, by Jay Robert Nash (Delacorte); *Sunshower*, by Karen Kenyon (Richard Marek); and *The Laughter of Time*, by James Kahn (Ballantine).

JEAN V. NAGGAR LITERARY AGENCY, 336 E. 73rd St., New York NY 10021. (212)794-1082. Contact: Jean Naggar. Obtains new clients through recommendations. Query with outline and brief biographical sketch. SASE. Member ILAA. Agent receives 10% for domestic sales; and 20% for foreign sales.
Will Handle: Novels and nonfiction books.
Recent Sales: *The Clan of the Cave Bear*, book I of sweeping prehistoric saga, by Jean M. Auel (Crown and Bantam); *Island Sojourn*, philosophical autobiographical nonfiction, by Elizabeth Arthur (Harper & Row); *The Phoenix Legacy*, science fiction trilogy by M.K. Wren (Berkley); and *Minding My Own Business: Entrepreneurial Women Share Their Secrets for Success*, self-help by Marjorie McVicar and Julia F. Craig (Richard Marek and Playboy Press).

CHARLES NEIGHBORS, INC., 240 Waverly Place, New York NY 10014. (212)924-8296. Obtains new clients "mostly through recommendations of existing clients, but also from editors, other agents, and occasionally from *Writer's Market*." Will not read unsolicited mss; will read unsolicited queries and outlines at no charge. SASE. Member ILAA. Agent receives 10% commission.
Will Handle: Magazine articles and fiction, novels, nonfiction books and motion pictures. No juvenile material.
Recent Sales: *Finished People*, novel by Sandra Hochman (Wyndham); *Computer Games*, nonfiction by Robert Perry (Richard Marek); and *Zion South,* novel by Mark Lieberman (Arbor House).
Tips: "Stop borrowing from successful writers in terms of plot. Read more and re-read and rework and rewrite with the goal of excellence—not just acceptability."

FIFI OSCARD ASSOCIATES, INC., 19 W. 44th St., New York NY 10022. (212)764-1100. Contact: Literary Department. Member SAR. Obtains clients through recommendations. Prefers to work with authors who have previously published articles or books. Medium agency. Will read—at no charge—synopses. SASE. Agent receives 10% commission on domestic sales.
Will Handle: Material in all areas.

RAY PEEKNER LITERARY AGENCY, (associated with Larry Sternig Literary Agency and Hintz Literary Agency), 2625 N. 36th St., Milwaukee WI 53210. Contact: Ray Puechner. Obtains new clients through referrals from clients and editors, some from queries. Will not read unsolicited mss. Made 52 sales in 1980; plans 60 in 1981. Agent receives 10% commission.
Will Handle: Novels, nonfiction books, and young adult material.
Recent Sales: *The Lost and the Fallen*, novel by Hugh and Elizabeth Zachary (Ballantine); *Angel Eyes*, mystery novel by Loren D. Estleman (Houghton-Mifflin); and *Horror House*, novel by J.N. Williamson (Playboy).

ARTHUR PINE ASSOCIATES, INC., 1780 Broadway, New York NY 10019. Vice President: Richard Pine. Obtains new clients through recommendations. "Writers must be professional, and/or have published a book." No unsolicited mss. Agent receives 15% commission.
Will Handle: Novels and nonfiction books (all types with mass market appeal).
Recent Sales: *The Sky's the Limit*, by Dr. Wayne Dyer (Simon & Schuster); *666*, by Jay Anson (Simon & Schuster); and *Virgin* (Edgar Award Winner), by James Patterson (McGraw Hill/Bantam).

THE WALTER PITKIN AGENCY, 11 Oakwood Dr., Weston CT 06883. President: Walter Pitkin. Obtains new clients by referral or direct application. Will read unsolicited queries and outlines. "Writers must write an intelligent letter of inquiry and convince us of ability to write marketable material. Inquiry should include some personal background, plus a statement of what it is that the agency would be trying to place. We will solicit the ms if we like the inquiry." SASE. Made 19 sales in 1980; plans 20 in 1981. Agent receives 10% commission.
Will Handle: Novels and adult nonfiction books.
Recent Sales: *Do What Mama Says*, novel by George McNeil (Bantam); and *Charity's Revenge*, by H.P. Dunne (New American Library); and *Medicinal Herbs*, guidebook by Michelle Mairesse (Arco).

SIDNEY E. PORCELAIN AGENCY, Box J, Rocky Hill NJ 08553. (609)924-4080. Author's Representative: Sidney Porcelain. Associate: Sharon Sottile. Obtains new clients through word-of-mouth and referrals. Will read unsolicited mss, queries and outlines. SASE. Agent receives 10% commission.

Will Handle: Magazine articles and fiction, novels, nonfiction books, and TV scripts.

JULIAN PORTMAN AGENCY, 1680 N. Vine St., Suite 421, Hollywood CA 90028. (213)463-8154. President: Julian Portman. Represents 46 clients. Obtains new clients through recommendations and reputation of the writer. Will not read unsolicited mss. Will read unsolicited queries and outlines. SASE. Agent receives 15% commission.
Will Handle: Novels, textbooks, nonfiction books, motion pictures, TV scripts and syndicated material.
Recent Sales: *RKO Story* (Prentice-Hall); *The Flight of Vin Fiz* (Putnam); *Peter Finch Story* (Pocket Books); and *Tour of Vatican* (Doubleday).
Tips: Submit idea or synopsis before sending an unsolicited manuscript.

CLARKSON N. POTTER, 2 Westwood Rd., Jamestown RI 02835. (401)423-1720. Agent: C.N. Potter. Estab. 1980. Obtains clients "mostly through word of mouth." Small agency. Will read—at no charge—queries, outlines and letters. SASE. Agent receives 10% commission on domestic sales; 10% on dramatic sales; 20% on foreign sales.
Will Handle: Nonfiction books.

THE AARON M. PRIEST LITERARY AGENCY, INC., 150 E. 35th St., New York NY 10016. (212)685-3860. Agents: Aaron Priest and Molly Friedrich. Represents 40 clients. Query with outline and one or two sample chapters. SASE. Member ILAA. Agent receives 10% commission.
Will Handle: Novels and nonfiction books.

PSYCHIATRIC SYNDICATION SERVICE, INC., 22 Greenview Way, Upper Montclair NJ 07043. (201)746-5075. President: Jacqueline Simenauer. Obtains new clients through professional recommendations and advertising. "I only represent psychiatrists and psychologists. Client must either be an MD or a PhD." Will read unsolicited outlines. SASE. Agent receives 10% commission.
Will Handle: "I am only interested in nonfiction—psychiatrically-oriented books aimed at the trade market, written by psychiatrists or psychologists."
Recent Sales: *Husbands and Wives*, nonfiction by Pietropento/Simenauer (Times Book); *Skincore*, nonfiction by Richard Walzer, MD (Simon & Schuster); and *Children's Dreams*, nonfiction by B. Richmond, MD (Dutton).

BARBARA RHODES LITERARY AGENCY, 140 West End Ave., New York NY 10023. (212)580-1300. Owner: Barbara Rhodes. Obtains new clients through recommendation or inquiry letters. Made 15 sales in 1979; plans 25 in 1980. Will not read unsolicited mss; will read unsolicited queries. SASE. Agent receives 15% commission.
Will Handle: Novels, nonfiction books, and stage plays.
Recent Sales: *The Trespasser*, occult by M. Weiser (Avon); *Good Guys-Bad Guys*, forensic psychiatry by Coe and Lubin (McGraw-Hill); and *How to Dine Out*, how-to by K. Ernst (Jove).

MARIE RODELL-FRANCES COLLIN LITERARY AGENCY, 156 E. 52nd St., New York NY 10022. (212)752-2046. Contact: Frances Collin. Query. SASE. Member SAR. Agent receives 10% commission on domestic sales; and 20% on foreign.
Will Handle: Trade novels and trade nonfiction books.

JANE ROTROSEN, 318 E. 51st St., New York NY 10022. (212)752-1038. 4 agents. Represents 60+ clients. "We're looking for people who want to make a career of writing." Query. SASE. Member ILAA.
Will Handle: Novels and nonfiction books.

GLORIA SAFIER, 667 Madison Ave., New York NY 10021. (212)838-4868. Contact: Gloria Safier. Represents 45 clients. Made 50+ sales in 1979. Query. SASE. Member SAR. Agent receives 10% commission.
Will Handle: Trade novels and nonfiction, films and TV scripts.
Recent Sales: *Signs of Life*, fiction by Sumner Locke Elliott (Ticknor & Fields); *Alma Anderson*, fiction by Tad Mosel (Viking); and *High Times, Hard Times*, autobiography by Anita O'Day with George Eells (Putnam).
Tips: "Write a good letter, one that describes the book you want the agent to read (never write a letter that says just, 'I've written a book, would you like to read it?'—this sort of letter is useless) and reveals something about your background."

SUSAN F. SCHULMAN AGENCY, 165 West End Ave., New York NY 10023. (212)877-2216. Represents about 25 clients and projects. Prospective clients must be professional writers. Query.

SASE. Member SAR. Commission ranges from 10-20% (foreign).
Will Handle: Stage plays, fiction and nonfiction books.
Recent Sales: *Passion of Dracula*, play by Bob Hall and David Richmond; *Penquin Primer*, by Dennis Traut (Viking Penquin); and *How to Buy*, by Justin Mamis (Farrar, Straus and Giroux).

ARTHUR SCHWARTZ LITERARY AGENT, 435 Riverside Dr., New York NY 10025. (212)864-3182. Obtains new clients through "letter inquiries from professional writers." Must be established writer. Will read unsolicited queries. SASE. Member ILAA. Agent receives 12½-15% commission (includes normal disbursements).
Will Handle: "We seek any commercially-oriented fiction and nonfiction for books, especially adult-oriented romantic fiction, family sagas, women's historical romantic fiction and commercial nonfiction. We do not handle plays, poetry, articles for magazines or screenplays, but do place motion picture/film rights from book. A letter of inquiry should be made first to our agency. We accept only manuscripts sent by first class mail (do not register, certify, or insure; you must retain the original ms for your file); and enclose a manuscript size SASE. Our agency specializes in representing well-known professionals and professors for both fiction and nonfiction."
Recent Sales: *Feeling Good: A New Approach to Mood Therapy*, popular psychology by Dr. David Burns (William Morrow); *The Cockroach Combat Manual*, popular and humorous science by Dr. Austin Frishman (William Morrow); and *Frenchmen's Mistress*, by Irene Michaels (Dell).

JAMES SELIGMANN AGENCY, 280 Madison Ave., New York NY 10016. (212)679-3383. Contact: James F. Seligmann. Obtains new clients through recommendation, personal contact, or solicitation. Will not read unsolicited mss; will read unsolicited queries and outlines. SASE. Member SAR. Agent receives 15% commission.
Will Handle: Novels and nonfiction books.
Recent Sales: *Flight From Dharan*, nonfiction by John McDonald with Clyde Burleson (Prentice-Hall); *The Dance in Its Time*, nonfiction by Walter Sorell (Doubleday); and *The Only Security Blanket You'll Ever Need*, nonfiction by Sydney Langer, MD, and Julie Rubin (Beaufort).
Tips: "Many mss—if not most—bear the mark of being submitted to a huge number of agents. Some even say or imply as much. A smaller number of submissions at a time, and . . . a more individualized approach would make a better impression."

CHARLOTTE SHEEDY LITERARY AGENCY, 145 W. 86th St., New York NY 10024. (212)873-4768. Contact: Charlotte Sheedy. Represents 125 clients. Query. SASE. Member SAR and ILAA. Agent receives 10% commission.
Will Handle: Novels and nonfiction books.

KEN SHERMAN AND ASSOCIATES, 9507 Santa Monica Blvd., Beverly Hills CA 90210. (213)273-8840. Contact: Ken Sherman. Estab. 1979. Member Writers Guild. Obtains clients through other clients. Small agency. Will read—at no charge—synopsis of screenplay or first 3 chapters and outline of book. SASE. Agent receives 10% commission on domestic sales.
Will Handle: Screenplays, nonfiction books, novels and teleplays.
Tips: "Writer must send release from liability and responsibility. Also, register idea or treatment with Writers Guild."

EVELYN SINGER LITERARY AGENCY, Box 594, White Plains NY 10602. Agent: Evelyn Singer. Obtains new clients through recommendations or if writer has earned $10,000 from freelance writing. Will not read unsolicited mss. SASE. Agent receives 10% commission.
Will Handle: Novels, nonfiction books and children's books (no picture books). "I handle all trade book material and arrange subsidiary and foreign rights. Please type (double-spaced) neatly—do not send hand-written queries. Give any literary background pertinent to your material."
Recent Sales: *No Goodbyes*, nonfiction by Adela Rogers St. Johns (McGraw-Hill); *Position of Ultimate Trust*, suspense novel by William Beechcroft (Dodd, Mead); *Gorillas*, nonfiction juvenile by Mary Elting (Platt and Munk); and *The Launching of Linda Bell*, teen novel by William F. Hallstead (Harcourt Brace Jovanovich).
Tips: "Edit and revise to avoid fiction that is obviously autobiographical, self-conscious: characters that are affected, dialogue stilted. Give yourself a cooling off period so that you can reread objectively. Don't copy the classics. Style and material should be current."

PHILIP G. SPITZER LITERARY AGENCY, 111-25 76th Ave., Forest Hills NY 11375. (212)263-7592. Obtains new clients through recommendations of editors and clients. "No previous publication necessary, but potential clients must be working on a book." Will read unsolicited queries and outlines. SASE. Member SAR. Agent receives 10% commission on domestic sales; 15% on British; 20% for foreign language sales.

Will Handle: Novels, nonfiction books, motion pictures. For clients also writing books, will handle magazine articles and fiction. Specializes in general nonfiction; particular interest in sports and politics. "Because I am a one-man office I can take on few new clients. I will often decline projects I think might be salable, and this should not be taken as a reflection on the author or his presentation."

Recent Sales: *Five Good Boys*, by Leo Rutman (Viking); *Who's Poisoning America*, edited by Ralph Nader and Ronald Brownstein (Sierra Club Books); *An Accidental Woman*, by Richard Neely (Holt, Rinehart & Winston); and *The Craft of the Screenwriter*, by John Brady (Simon & Schuster).

Tips: "In most outlines/proposals, writers often do not anticipate what questions an editor will have. For example, an outline might include a chapter heading, sub-chapter headings, etc., with no explanation of what they mean. Read whatever material you can find on the subject of agents, and the publishing industry, before attempting to write an enticing query letter."

GLORIA STERN, 1230 Park Ave., New York NY 10028. (212)289-7698. Contact: Gloria Stern. Represents 30 clients. "For fiction, I prefer authors who have been published in magazines or have had a book published; for nonfiction, the author must have particular expertise in the field he plans to write about; and for scripts, the author must have credits." Query. SASE. Member ILAA. Agent receives 10% commission.

Will Handle: Novels, trade nonfiction books, films, stage plays and TV scripts.

LARRY STERNIG LITERARY AGENCY, 742 Robertson St., Milwaukee WI 53213. (414)771-7677. "I am unable to take on new clients." Will not read unsolicited mss. Agent receives 10% commission.

Handles: Magazine articles and fiction, novels and nonfiction books.

Recent Sales: *Getting Rid of Marjorie*, by Betty Ren Wright (Holiday House); *The Talisman*, by Gene DeWeese (Playboy Press); and *Horn Crown*, by Andre Norton (DAW).

GUNTHER STUHLMANN, AUTHOR'S REPRESENTATIVE, Box 276, Becket MA 01223. Contact: Ms. Barbara Ward. Obtains new clients through "personal recommendation from clients, publishers, editors." Will not read unsolicited mss. SASE for queries and outlines. Agent receives 10% commission on domestic and Canadian sales; 15% on British and 20% overseas.

Will Handle: Novels, nonfiction books, motion pictures, stage plays, TV scripts and serial rights based on established properties.

Recent Sales: *The People in His Life*, novel by Maia Rodman (Stein & Day); *The Venturer*, novel by Robert Inman (Wyndham Books/Simon & Schuster); and *The Diary of Anais Nin, 1966-1974*, nonfiction (Harcourt, Brace Jovanovich).

TMI, (Talent Management International), (formerly William Schiller Agency), 6380 Wilshire Blvd., Suite 910, Los Angeles CA 90048. (213)273-4000. Agent: Beverly Strong. Obtains clients through referrals. Will read—at no charge—manuscripts, queries and outlines. Small agency. SASE. Agent receives 10% commission on domestic sales.

Will Handle: Feature films and TV scripts ("good stories with real people").

HERB TOBIAS AND ASSOCIATES, INC., 1901 Avenue of the Stars, Los Angeles CA 90067. (213)277-6211. Contact: Randy Herron or Miles Kuhn. Obtains clients through referrals. Small agency. Will read—at no charge—manuscripts. SASE. Agent receives 10% commission on domestic sales.

Will Handle: Feature films and TV scripts.

FRANK VOSS TALENT AGENCY, 1017 N. La Cienega Blvd., Suite 305, Los Angeles CA 90069. (213)628-6857. President: Frank Voss. Estab. 1980. Small agency. Will read—at no charge—manuscripts (80- 120-page screenplays); or synopses. SASE. Agent receives 10% commission on domestic sales.

Will Handle: Screenplays.

ERICA WAIN AGENCY, 1418 N. Highland Ave., Suite 102, Hollywood CA 90028. (213)460-4224. Contact: Erica Wain. Estab. 1979. Obtains clients through referrals. Small agency. Will read—at no charge—queries and/or synopses. SASE. Agent receives 10% commission on domestic sales.

Will Handle: Teleplays, pilots, movies of the week and mini-features.

ANN WRIGHT ASSOCIATES, 8422 Melrose Place, Los Angeles CA 90069. Contact: Dan Wright. Members Writers Guild. Obtains clients through agency's reputation. "I'm interested in new writers, periodically." Small agency. Will read—at no charge—queries with short letter and vita. SASE. Agent receives 10% commission on domestic sales.

Will Handle: "Original or adaptable properties that can be made into books, films or theatrical productions. In the case of an adaptation it's very important that the writer have clear rights to sell the property."

ANN WRIGHT REPRESENTATIVES, INC., 136 E. 57th St., New York NY 10022. Contact: Dan Wright. Member Writers Guild. Obtains clients through agency's reputation. "I'm interested in new writers from time to time." Small agency. Will read—at no charge—queries with short letter and vita. SASE. Agent receives 10% commission on domestic sales.

Will Handle: "Original or adaptable properties that can be made into books, films or theatrical productions. In the case of an adaptation, it is important that the writer have clear rights to sell the property."

WRITERS ROOST AGENCY, 2202B Pico Blvd., Santa Monica CA 90405. (213)450-7052. Estab. 1979. Obtains clients through referrals and Screen Writers Guild list. Will read—at no charge—screenplays and scripts/dialogues. Agent receives 10% commission on domestic sales.

Will Handle: TV scripts (pilots) and full-length feature screenplays.

Tips: "Avoid profanity—it never sold a script. Write about what you know. I'm looking for uplifting, entertaining material."

MARY YOST ASSOCIATES, 75 E. 55th St., New York NY 10022. (212)755-4682. Contact: Mary Yost or Marion Landau. Represents 75 clients. Query with brief biographical background sketch, along with synopsis. SASE. Member SAR. Agent receives 10% commission.

Will Handle: Novels and nonfiction books.

Recent Sales: *Freud Rediscovered*, by Lucy Freeman (Arbor House); *The Awakening*, novel by Ken Grinwood (Doubleday); *Abandoned*, novel by Edwin Silberstang (Doubleday); and *Dear John*, by Susan Lee and Sondra Till Robinson (Richard Marek).

Appendix

The Business of Freelancing

Here are some general guidelines to assist you in the business of being a freelance writer. Some flexibility is required when working with editors at various publications and publishing houses, but by and large the publishing community has come to expect the kind of editorial deportment that is suggested here.

Manuscript Mechanics

It's a grand thing to dream of seeing a story with your byline in one of the major national magazines. The actual *writing* of it may be a bit difficult, but once you have it down in good shape on a rough draft, the rest is a snap . . . you *think*. There is still one very important—though often irksome—chore to do.

Sometimes it's a little difficult to climb off that lofty, creative plane of writing and find the old bugaboo of simple manuscript mechanics staring you in the eye. It's a comedown. It's irritating. It's bothersome. But it's a necessary evil and the quicker you start using the right way, the easier it is to live with.

Type of Paper. One of the things to consider is the paper. It must measure 8½x11 inches. That's a standard size and editors are adamant; they don't want offbeat colors and sizes.

There's a wide range of white, 8½x11 papers. The cheaper ones are all wood content. They will suffice but they are not recommended. Your best bet is a good 25 percent cotton fiber content paper. It has quality feel, smoothness, shows type neatly and holds up under erasing. Editors almost unanimously discourage the use of erasable bond for manuscripts, as it tends to smear when handled. Where weight of the paper is concerned, don't use less than a 16-pound bond, and 20-pound is preferred.

File Copies. Always make a carbon or photocopy of your manuscript before you send it off to a publisher. You might even want to make several photocopies while the original manuscript is still fresh and crisp looking—as insurance against losing a submission in the mails, and as a means of circulating the same manuscript to other editors for reprint sales after the original has been accepted for publication. (Inform editors that the manuscript offered for reprint should *not* be used before it has first appeared in the original publication buying it, of course.) Some writers keep their original manuscript as a file copy, and submit a good-quality photocopy of the manuscript to an editor, with a personal note explaining that it is *not* a simultaneous or multiple submission. They tell the editor that he may toss the manuscript if it is of no interest to him, and reply with a self-addressed postcard (also enclosed). This costs a writer some photocopy expense, but saves on the postage bill—and may speed the manuscript review process in some editorial offices.

Type Characters. Another firm rule: for manuscripts, always type double space, using either elite or pica type. The slightly larger pica type is easier to read and many editors prefer it, but they don't object to elite. They *do* dislike (and often will refuse) hard-to-read or unusual typewritten characters, such as script, italics, Old English, all capitals, unusual letter styles, etc.

Page Format. Do not use a cover sheet; nor should you use a binder—unless you are submitting a play or television or movie script. Instead, in the upper left corner of page one list your name, address and phone number on four single-spaced lines. In the upper right corner, on three single-spaced lines, indicate the approximate word count for the manuscript, the rights you are offering for sale, and your copyright notice (Copyright 1981 Joe Jones). It is *not* necessary to indicate that this is page one. Its format is self-evident.

On every page after the first, type your last name, a dash, and the page number in the upper right corner (page sixteen, for example, would be: Jones—16). Then drop down two double-spaces and begin copy.

How to Estimate Wordage. To estimate wordage, count the exact number of words on the first three pages of your manuscript (in manuscripts up to 25 pages), divide the total by 3 and multiply the result by the number of pages. Carry the total to the nearest 100 words. For example, say you have a 12-page manuscript with totals of 303, 316 and 289 words on the first three pages. Divide your total of 908 by 3 to get 302. Now multiply 302 x 12 pages and you get 3,624. Your approximate wordage, therefore, will be 3,600 words. On manuscripts over 25 pages, count five pages instead of three, then follow the same process, dividing by 5 instead of 3.

Now, flip the lever to double-space and center the title in capital letters halfway down the page. To center, set the tabulator to stop in the exact left-right center of the page. Count the letters in the title (including spaces and punctuation) and back-space half that number. Centered one double-space under that, type "by" and centered one double-space under that, your name or pseudonym.

Margins should be 1½ inches on all sides of each full page of typewritten manuscript. Paragraph indentation is five or six letter spaces, consistently.

Now, after the title and byline block, drop down three double-spaces, paragraph indent and start your story.

Concluding Page. Carry on just as you have on other pages after page one. After your last word and period on this page, however, skip three double-spaces and then center the words "The End" or, more commonly, the old telegrapher's symbol of —30—meaning the same thing.

Special Points to Keep in Mind. Always use a good dark black (*not* colored) typewriter ribbon and clean your keys frequently. If the enclosures in the letters a, b, d, e, g, etc. get inked-in, your keys need cleaning. Keep your manuscript neat *always*. Occasional retyping over erasures is acceptable, but strikeovers are bad and give a manuscript a sloppy, careless appearance. Sloppy typing is viewed by many editors as an index to sloppy work habits—and the likelihood of careless research and writing. Strive for a clean, professional-looking manuscript that reflects pride in your work.

Mailing Your Manuscript. Except when working on assignment from a magazine, or when under contract to do a book for a publisher, always enclose a self-addressed return envelope and the correct amount of postage with your manuscript. Manuscript pages should be held together with a paper clip only—never stapled together. When submitting poetry, the poems should be typed single space (double space between stanzas), one poem per page. Long poems requiring more than a page should be on sheets paper-clipped together.

Most editors won't object too much if manuscripts under five pages are folded in thirds and letter-mailed. However, there is a marked *preference* for flat mailing (in large envelopes) of manuscripts over four pages. You will need two sizes of large gummed or clasped mailing envelopes—9x12 for the return envelope, and 9½x12½ or 10x13 for the one used to send out the manuscript, photos and return envelope.

Mark your envelope, as desired with FIRST CLASS MAIL, or SPECIAL FOURTH CLASS RATE: MANUSCRIPT. First Class mail costs more but assures better handling and faster delivery. Special Fourth Class mail is handled the same as Parcel Post, so

Jones--2

Begin the second page, and all following pages, in this manner--with a page-number line (as above) that includes your name, in case loose manuscript pages get shuffled by mistake.

Joe Jones
1234 My Street
Anytown, U.S.A.
Tel. 123/456-7890

About 3,000 words
First Serial Rights
ⓒ Copyright 1982
Joe Jones

YOUR STORY OR ARTICLE TITLE HERE

by

Joe Jones

The manuscript begins here--about halfway down the first page. It should be cleanly typed, double-spaced, using either elite or pica type. Use one side of the paper only, and leave a margin of about 1-1/2 inches on all four sides.

NEATNESS COUNTS. Here are sample pages of a manuscript ready for submission to an editor. If the author uses a pseudonym, it should be placed on the title page only in the byline position; the author's real name must always appear in the top left corner of the title page—for manuscript mailing and payment purpose.

wrap it well. Also, the Special Fourth Class Rate only applies in the US.

For lighter weight manuscripts, First Class mail is recommended because of the better speed and handling. First Class mail is handled the same as Air Mail.

For foreign publications and publishers, including the expanding Canadian markets, always enclose an International Reply Coupon (IRC), determined by the weight of the manuscript at the post office.

Insurance is available, but payable only on the tangible value of what is in the package, i.e., writing paper, so your best insurance is to keep a copy at home of what you send.

First Class mail is forwarded or returned automatically; however, Special Fourth Class Rate mail is not. To make sure you get your submission back if undeliverable, print "Return Postage Guaranteed" under your return address.

Cover Letters. You may enclose a personal letter with your manuscript sent at the Special Fourth Class Rate, but you must also add enough First Class postage to cover the letter and mark FIRST CLASS LETTER ENCLOSED on the outside.

In most cases, a brief cover letter is helpful in personalizing the submission. Nothing you say will make the editor decide in your favor (the manuscript must stand by itself in that regard), so don't use the letter to make a sales pitch. But you may want to tell an editor something about yourself, your publishing history, or any particular qualifications you have for writing the enclosed manuscript. If you are doing an exposé on, say, nursing home irregularities—it would be useful to point out that you have worked as a volunteer in nursing homes for six years. If you have queried the editor on the article earlier, he probably already has the background information—so the note should be a brief reminder: "Here is the piece on nursing homes we discussed earlier. I look forward to hearing from you at your earliest convenience."

If the manuscript is a photocopy, be sure to indicate whether or not it is a multiple submission. An editor is likely to assume it is, unless you tell him otherwise—and many are offended by writers using this marketing tactic (though when agents use it, that seems to be OK).

When submitting a manuscript to a newspaper—even the Sunday magazine section—be sure to include a cover note inquiring about the paper's rates for freelance submissions. Newspaper editors are deluged regularly by PR offices and "free" writers who submit material for ego and publicity purposes. Make sure your submission is not part of that crowd, or you may find it in print without even an acknowledgment—much less a check.

Submitting Photos by Mail. When submitting black & white prints with your manuscript, send 8x10 glossies unless the editor indicates otherwise. Stamp or print your name, address and phone number on the back of each print or contact sheet. Don't use a heavy felt tip pen because the ink will seep through the print.

Buy some sturdy 9x12 or 10x13 envelopes. Your photo dealer should have standard print mailers in stock; some may be pre-stamped with "Photos—Do Not Bend" and contain two cardboard inserts. You can also pick up corrugated cardboard inserts from your local grocery store. Place your print(s) between two cardboard inserts, wrap two rubber bands around the bundle, and insert it with your manuscript into the envelope.

When sending many prints (say, 25-50 for a photo book), mail them in a sturdy cardboard box; 8x10 print paper boxes are perfect. Add enough cardboard inserts to fill the carton after the prints and manuscript are in place, and cover the box with wrapping paper. Send rare or extremely valuable photos only when an editor specifically requests them; then send them in a fiberboard mailing case with canvas straps, available at most photo stores. Tell the editor to return the photos in the same case or return the empty case itself if the photos are kept.

For color transparencies, 35mm is the universally accepted size. Few buyers will look at color prints. (Check each market listing individually for exact preferences from editors). To mail transparencies, use slotted acetate sheets, which hold twenty slides and offer protection from scratches, moisture, dirt and dust—available in standard sizes from most photo supply houses. Do not use glass mounts. Put your name, address and phone number on each transparency. Mail the transparencies just as you would prints, using corrugated cardboard. If a number of sheets are being sent, use a cardboard box. Because transparencies are irreplaceable (unless you have internegatives or duplicates made), be sure to insure the package.

Photo Captions. Prints and transparencies should always be captioned when submitted for consideration with a manuscript. For prints, type the caption on a sheet of paper and tape it to the bottom of the back of the print. The caption should fold over the front of the photo so that the buyer can fold it back for easy reading. Masking tape allows the editor to easily remove the copy for typesetting.

You can also type the captions on a separate sheet of paper, and assign each an index number corresponding with its photos. A third method, but not generally preferred, is to tape the caption to the back of the print.

Captions for transparencies 2¼x2¼ or larger can be typed on thin strips of paper and inserted in the acetate sleeve protecting the transparency. For 35mm transparencies, type the captions on a separate sheet and assign corresponding numbers.

Enclosing return postage with photos sent through the mail is more than a professional courtesy; it also helps assure that you'll get the photos back. Most writer/ photographers enclose a self-addressed stamped envelope (SASE—same size as the envelope used for the submission) with their material. Never drop loose stamps into the original envelope, nor fasten them to one of the prints with a staple or paper clip. You can, however, enclose a small coin envelope (available at hobby stores) with return postage in it rather than attaching stamps to the return envelope.

Once your photos are properly packaged, speed and safe handling in the mail will be your main concerns. Most writers prefer First Class mail because it ensures both speed and safety of prints, but a cheaper rate can be allowed for the return of the material. A cover letter and manuscript can be mailed with any package sent first class. More information is available from the Postal Service.

Mailing Book Manuscripts. Do not bind your book manuscript pages in any way. They should be mailed loose in a box (a ream-size stationery box is perfect) without binding. To ensure a safe return, enclose a self-addressed label and suitable postage in stamps clipped to the label. If your manuscript is returned, it will either come back in your original box, or—increasingly likely today—in an insulated bag-like mailer, with your label and postage used thereon. Many publishing houses open the box a manuscript is mailed in, and toss the box (if it has not been damaged in the mails, or in the opening already); they then read and circulate the manuscript as necessary for editorial consideration, and finally route it through the mail room back to you with a letter or rejection slip. This kind of handling makes it likely that a freshly typed manuscript will be in rough shape even after one or two submissions. So it is wise to have several photocopies made of a book-length manuscript while it is still fresh—and to circulate those to publishers, rather than risk an expensive retyping job in the midst of your marketing effort. As mentioned above, indicate in a cover note that the submission is not a multiple submission if such is the case.

Book manuscripts can be mailed Fourth Class Manuscript Rate, but that can be slow and have an additional mauling effect on the package in the mails. When doing so, if you include a letter, state this on the outer wrapping and add appropriate postage to your manuscript postal rate. Most writers use First Class, secure in the feeling that their manuscript is in an editorial office within a few days. Some send book manuscripts using the United Parcel Service, which can be less expensive than First Class mail when you drop the package off at UPS yourself. The drawback here is that UPS cannot legally carry First Class mail, so you will have to send your cover letter a few days before giving UPS the manuscript, and both will arrive at about the same time. Check with UPS in your area to see if it has benefits for you. The cost depends on the weight of your manuscript and the delivery distance.

The tips and recommendations made here are based upon what editors prefer. Give editors what they prefer and you won't be beginning with a strike or two against you before the manuscript is even read.

The Waiting Game. The writer who sends off a story, article or book manuscript to an editor should turn immediately to other ideas and try to forget about the submission. Unless you are on assignment, or under contract to do a book—in which case, a phone call to your editor saying the manuscript is in the mail is quite appropriate—it's best to use your time productively on other writing projects, and let the submission take care of itself. But one day you realize it's been too long. According to the *Writer's Market* listing, your editor responds to submissions in a maximum of four weeks—and it's been six already, and you haven't heard a word. Will inquiring about it jeopardize a possible sale? Are they really considering it, or has the editor had an accident and your manuscript is at the bottom of a huge stack of unread mail?

If you have had no report from a publisher by the maximum reporting time given in a *WM* listing, allow six weeks' grace period and then write a brief letter to the editor asking if your manuscript (give the title, a brief description, and the date you mailed it) has in fact reached his office. If so, is it still under consideration? Your concern at this point is the mails: Is the manuscript safely delivered? Don't act impatient with an editor—who may be swamped, or short-handed, or about to give your manuscript a second reading. The wrong word or attitude from you at this point could be hazardous to your manuscript's health. Be polite, be professional. Enclose another SASE to expedite a reply. This is usually enough to stir a decision if matters are lagging in an editorial office, even during rush season (which is year 'round).

If you still hear nothing from a publisher one month after your follow-up, send the editor a short note asking if he received your previous follow-up, and include a photocopy of that second letter. If, after another month, you are still without word, send a polite letter saying that you are withdrawing the manuscript from consideration (include the title, date of submission, and dates of follow-up correspondence), and ask that the manuscript be returned immediately in the SASE your original correspondence included.

Even though matters have not worked out, and you have lost months of precious marketing time—never write in anger. Be cool, professional, and set about the business of finding another publisher for your work. The advantage of having a clean photocopy of the manuscript in your files at this point cannot be overstated. Move on to another publisher with it, using a personal cover letter and the same methods outlined above. In the meantime, continue working on your other writing projects.

At times like these, the advantage of having an agent who can insulate you from such marketing discouragement is considerable. See our section on Agents for guidelines on getting and working with a literary agent, especially if you are working on book-length projects.

The Business of Writing

Writing is an occupation with many hidden costs. In addition to the time a writer spends over a typewriter actually *writing*, many hours and miles are logged doing research, soliciting materials, conducting interviews, communicating with editors, and rounding out the corners of a manuscript. While readers, and to some extent editors, are oblivious to these background tasks, the Internal Revenue Service need not be. Such costs can become deductible writing expenses at income tax time.

For the Records. Though the deadline for filing your tax return is April 15, you should maintain careful records all year. To arrive at verifiable figures, you will need two things: *records and receipts.* For tax purposes, good records are not only helpful; they are *required* by law. Receipts are the foundation that careful record keeping is built upon.

At tax time each year, a freelance writer normally reports his business activities on tax Schedule C ("Profit or Loss From Business or Profession"); the resulting figure for income is entered on Form 1040. In addition, if your writing or editing work nets you $400 or more in earnings, you must file a Schedule SE and pay self-employment tax, which makes you eligible for Social Security benefits. Furthermore, if you think your taxes from freelancing will be $100 or more, you are required to pay your taxes in quarterly installments. To do this, you file a declaration of estimated tax using Form 1040-ES ("Declaration Voucher") and use the envelopes the IRS provides to mail in your estimated taxes every three months.

It's not as complicated as it may sound, but one thing is certain: to document all these tax liabilities at the end of the year, you must have accurate records.

Tax laws don't require any particular type of records, as long as they are permanent, accurate and complete, and they clearly establish income, deductions, credits, etc. It's remarkably easy to overlook deductible expenses unless you record them at the time they are paid and keep receipts for them. Since some assets are subject to depreciation (typewriter, desk, files, tape recorder, camera equipment, etc.), you also need records of the purchase prices you used to determine depreciation allowances.

Finally, you need good records in case the IRS audits you and asks you to explain items reported on your return. Memos, scribbled notes or sketchy records that merely approximate income, deductions, or other pertinent items affecting your taxes are simply *not* adequate. You must have a record supported by sales slips, invoices, receipts, bank deposit slips, canceled checks, and other documents.

Records for Credit Purposes. You and the IRS are not the only ones interested in the well-being of your business. Banks, credit organizations, suppliers of materials, and others often require information on the condition of your finances when you apply for credit—if, for example, you want to buy a house.

In fact, freelance writers, in the eyes of many lending institutions, might as well be totally unemployed. Some writers have taken on fulltime jobs just to qualify for financing for a home, even when the "steady" job might produce less income than freelancing.

A Simple Bookkeeping System. There are almost as many different ways of keeping records as there are record-keepers to keep them. For a freelance writer, normally a simple type of "single-entry" bookkeeping that requires only one account book to record the flow of income and expense is completely adequate. At the heart of this single-entry system is the journal. It is an accounting book, available at any stationery store (the *Writer's Digest Diary* can be used, too), in which all the everyday transactions of your freelance business are recorded. Each transaction is set forth clearly, including the date, a description of the transaction, and the amount entered in the proper column—either "income" or "expense":

Income entries will include whatever funds you receive, either by cash or check. Expense entries might include payments you make for writing supplies, photocopying, postage, repairs, dues paid to writers' organizations, travel expenses, books and magazine subscriptions, photo developing and printing, etc.—whatever you have to spend as a business expense.

The Receipt File. Now comes the really important part: for each income entry you make, keep a copy of a receipt, an invoice, or some other record to substantiate that entry. For each expense entry, keep a canceled check, a receipt, or some other document. By keeping your record complete with some type of document to support *every* entry, your record is foolproof.

A partitioned, envelope-type folder works well for keeping receipts in order. If a receipt does not clearly indicate which entry it refers to, make a note on it and date it before filing it. That way, you can locate it quickly.

Business Banking. To record your income as accurately as possible, it is best to deposit all the money you receive in a separate bank account. This will give you deposit slips to verify the entries in your journal. Furthermore, you should make all payments by check, if possible, so that your business expenses will be well documented. If you have to pay cash, keep receipts on file.

Any record must be retained as long as it may be material to the administration of any law. Statutes of limitations for various legal purposes vary from state to state, but if you keep your records on file for seven to ten years, you will seldom run into difficulty. Records supporting items on a tax return should be kept for at least three years, although keeping them indefinitely is a good idea.

Date	Description	Expense		Income	
JAN. 4	Regional Supply – 1 ream of paper	5	80		
5	Photocopying – _Analog_ story		95		
5	Postage – story sent to Analog	1	75		
8	_Economic Bulletin_ – for March article & photos			450	00
10	Billy's Bookstore – 1980 Writer's Market	14	95		
14	Reed Real Estate – for editing 4th-quarter newsletter			225	00
15	Renewal of _WD_ subscription	12	00		
18	Billy's – 20 manila envelopes	1	80		
21	Mountain Press – for editing _Survival Handbook_			575	00
21	Aardvark & Son – for developing photos for _Am. Horse J._ article	9	55		
25	Regional Supply – Typewriter ribbons	15	20		
28	Fee for Western Writer's Conf.	24	50		
30	_American Horse Journal_ – for February article			325	00
	JAN. TOTALS	86	50	1,575	00

What's Deductible. Among your deductible expenses, don't overlook the following writing-related costs:

● **All writing supplies**, including paper, carbons, pens, ribbons, envelopes, copying costs, postage, photo developing and printing costs, and recording tapes.

● **Repairs and maintenance of writing equipment**, including typewriter, tape recorder and camera.

● **Courses and conferences attended to enhance you as a professional writer.** It's important to realize, though, that you can't deduct courses you take to _become_ a writer. The IRS rule is that courses must be "refresher" or professionally improving in nature to count. Besides deducting the costs of these, also deduct mileage (at 20¢ a mile)—or actual car expenses, whichever is greater—cost of tickets for public transportation; cost of hotel/motel rooms; and costs of meals.

● **Courses taken as research on subjects you are writing about.** To establish that a course is for research, it would help if you had documentation from the potential publisher of your writings—such as a favorable response to a query. Even if

Make sure you have the current edition of Writer's Market

Writer's Market has been the writer's bible for 52 years. Each edition contains hundreds of changes to give you the most current information to work with. Make sure your copy is the latest edition.

This card will get you the 1983 edition... at 1982 prices! ⬇

the magazine should not publish what you write, the response will show the research was done in good faith.

● **Writing books, magazines and other references.**

● **Dues paid for membership in writer organizations.**

● **Home office expenses.** In the past, writers using a portion of their home dining room or living room have been allowed to deduct a percentage of home costs as "office" expenses. This is no longer allowed. To take a home office deduction today, you must have a portion of your dwelling set aside *solely for writing on a regular basis*. The same rule applies to a separate structure on your property. For example, you may not use a portion of your garage for writing and a portion for parking your car. If your car goes in, your home office expense is out.

Example: If you rent a five-room apartment for $200 a month and use one room exclusively for writing, you are entitled to deduct one-fifth of the rent which comes to $40 a month, or $480 a year. Add to this one-fifth of your heating bill and one-fifth of your electric bill and watch the deductions mount up. Keep a list, too, of long-distance phone bills arising from your writing.

If you own your home and use one room for writing, you can deduct the allocated expenses of operating that room. Among these allowable expenses are interest on mortgage, real estate taxes, repairs or additions to the home, cost of utilities, home insurance premiums, and depreciation on the room.

Example: If you own a seven-room house, one room used for writing, one-seventh of the total cost of the house can be depreciated, as well as one-seventh of the above mentioned expenses.

Note: There is a limit to home office expenses. You may not exceed in deductible expenses the amount of your gross income. If you made $1,000 last year, you can't deduct any more than that in home office expenses—no matter how much they came to. Just $1,000 in this case.

● **Mileage.** Take 20¢ a mile for the first 15,000 miles you travel on writing-related missions and 11¢ a mile for miles traveled over 15,000. Or you may take the actual cost of operating your car—gas, oil, tires, maintenance and depreciation. (See below for figuring depreciation.) If you use your car 100 percent for writing, the total cost of operating it is deductible. Compare mileage deduction to cost deduction, and use the one that gives you the bigger break.

What May Be Depreciated. You can count depreciation of your typewriter, desk, chair, lamps, tape recorder, files, camera equipment, photocopier, or anything else related to your writing which costs a considerable amount of money and which has a useful life of more than one year. The easiest, most common method of depreciation for the writer is the straight line method.

In straight line, you take the depreciable basis (original cost of the asset minus the "salvage value"), divide by the number of useful years, and come up with the yearly depreciation deduction. The salvage value is what you could normally sell the item for after its estimated life of usefulness to you is over.

Example: Electric typewriter, purchased January, 1982 for $350. Estimated life, five years. Salvage value at end of five years, $50. Depreciation allowable for the year ending 1982 equals $60. That's what you get when you divide the cost ($350), less salvage value ($50), by the estimated number of useful years (5).

Assets purchased later in the year must be calculated only for the months you had them.

Example: Electric typewriter purchased in May, 1982 for $350. Estimated life, five years. Depreciation allowable for the year is $40. Since the asset was yours for only eight months, you calculate depreciation by dividing 12 (months) into the yearly deduction of $60. This gives you $5 a month. This $5 multiplied by eight months gives you $40 in depreciation.

If salvage value is less than 10 percent of your depreciable basis, you can disregard it for computation. However, you can't depreciate below salvage value.

In addition to deductions and depreciations, you can make some extra gains on purchases made for your "business." For any business equipment purchased during the current tax year, the IRS allows an additional deduction. This deduction, the "investment tax credit" (ITC), is allowed for furniture, equipment, and other depreciable assets, except real estate. It is also subtracted from your total tax liability.

The maximum ITC, 10 percent, occurs when the asset's useful life is seven years or more. If the useful life is only three to five years, take one-third of that 10 percent. Example: A desk with a useful life of three to five years is bought for $100. First take 10 percent ($10), then one-third ($3.33) for the total deduction.

If the asset's useful life is five to seven years, the investment tax credit is calculated on two-thirds of the 10 percent. Thus, your $100 desk, now expected to live longer, has an ITC of $6.66. Of course, once the predicted useful life of an item goes to or beyond seven years, the maximum 10 percent of the total cost may be deducted, and the ITC for your desk would be $10.

You get the investment tax credit on eligible items no matter what time during the year they were purchased.

If after deductions you earn $400 or more, you are required to pay a Social Security tax of .081 of the first $25,900 of your earnings. And you must fill out and submit a Schedule SE (for "self-employment").

Finally, save your rejection slips. Though they may be painful to look at, keep them in a folder—and view them as communiques from publishers. If you are subjected to a tax audit, the slips will help establish you as a working writer.

Rights and the Writer

Selling Rights to Your Writing. Initially, a writer may have little say in the rights sold to an editor. The beginning writer, in fact, can jeopardize a sale by haggling with an editor who is likely to have other writers on call who are anxious to please. As long as there are more writers than there are markets, this situation will remain the same.

As a writer acquires skill, reliability, and professionalism on the job, however, that writer becomes more valued to editors—and rights become a more important consideration. Though a beginning writer will accept modest payment just to get in print, an experienced writer soon learns that he cannot afford to give away good writing just to see a byline. At this point a writer must become concerned with selling reprints of articles already sold to one market, or using sold articles as chapters in a book on the same topic, or seeking markets for the same material overseas, offering work to TV or the movies. Even for the nonfiction writer, such dramatic rights can be meaningful. The hit Broadway musical and movie *The Best Little Whorehouse in Texas*, for example, began as a nonfiction article in *Playboy* magazine.

What Editors Want. And so it is that writers should strive to keep as many rights to their work as they can from the outset, because before you can resell any piece of writing you must own the rights to negotiate. If you have sold "all rights" to an article, for instance, it can be reprinted *without* your permission, and without additional payment to you. What an editor buys, therefore, will determine whether you can resell your own work. Here is a list of the rights most editors and publishers seek.

● **First Serial Rights.** The word serial here does not mean publication in installments, but refers to the fact that libraries call periodicals "serials" because they are published in serial or continuing fashion. *First serial rights* means the writer offers the newspaper or magazine (both of which are periodicals) the right to publish the article, story or poem the first time in their periodical. All other rights to the material belong to the writer. Variations on this right are, for example, First North American Serial rights. Some magazines use this purchasing technique to obtain the right to publish first in both America and Canada since many American magazines are circulated in Canada. If they had purchased only First U.S. Serial Rights, a Canadian magazine could come out with prior or simultaneous publication of the same material. When material is excerpted from a book which is to be published and it appears in a magazine or newspaper prior to book publication, this is also called First Serial Rights.

● **Second Serial (Reprint) Rights.** This gives a newspaper or magazine the opportunity to print an article, poem or story after it has already appeared in some other newspaper or magazine. The term is also used to refer to the sale of part of a book to a newspaper or magazine after a book has been published, whether or not there has been any first serial publication (income derived from second serial rights to book material is often shared 50/50 by author and book publisher).

● **All Rights.** Some magazines, either because of the top prices they pay for material, or the fact that they have book publishing interests or foreign magazine connections, sometimes buy All Rights. A writer who sells an article, story or poem to a magazine under these terms, forfeits the right to use his material in its present form elsewhere himself. If you sign a "work-for-hire" agreement, you sign away all rights and the copyright to the company making the assignment. If the writer thinks he may want to use his material later (perhaps in book form), he must avoid submitting to these types of markets, or refuse payment and withdraw his material if he discovers it later. Or ask the editor whether he's willing to buy only first rights instead of all rights before you agree to an assignment or a sale.

● **Simultaneous Rights.** This term covers articles and stories which are sold to publications (primarily religious magazines) which do not have overlapping circulations. A Baptist publication, for example, might be willing to buy Simultaneous Rights to a Christmas story which they like very much, even though they know a Presbyterian magazine may be publishing the same story in one of its Christmas issues. Publications which will buy simultaneous rights indicate this fact in their listings in *Writer's Market*. Always advise an editor when the material you are sending is a Simultaneous Submission.

● **Foreign Serial Rights.** Can you resell a story you have had published in America to a foreign magazine? If you sold only First U.S. Serial Rights to the American magazine, yes, you are free to market your story abroad. This presumes, of course, that the foreign magazine does buy material which has previously appeared in an American periodical.

● **Syndication Rights.** This is a division of serial rights. For example, a book publisher may sell the rights to a newspaper syndicate to print a book in twelve installments in, say, each of twenty United States newspapers. If they did this prior to book publication it would be syndicating First Serial Rights to the book. If they did this after book publication, they would be syndicating Second Serial Rights to the book.

● **Dramatic, Television and Motion Picture Rights.** This means the writer is selling his material for use on the stage, in television, or in the movies. Often a one-year "option" to buy such rights is offered (generally for 10% of the total price), and the interested party then tries to sell the idea to other people—actors, directors, studios or television networks, etc.—who become part of the project, which then becomes a script. Some properties are optioned over and over again, but fail to become dramatic productions. In such cases, the writer can sell his rights again and again—as long as there is interest in the material. Though dramatic, TV and motion picture rights are more important to the fiction writer than to the nonfiction writer, producers today are increasingly interested in "real-life" material; many biographies and articles that are slices of real life are being dramatized. Gay Talese's nonfiction book *Thy Neighbor's Wife*, for instance, earned some $2.5 million for motion picture rights alone.

Communicate and Clarify. Before submitting material to a market, check its listing in this book to see what rights are purchased. Most editors will discuss rights they wish to purchase before an exchange of money occurs. Some buyers are adamant about what rights they will accept; others will negotiate. In any case, the rights purchased should be stated specifically *in writing* sometime during the course of the sale, usually in a letter or memo of agreement. *Note*: If no rights are transferred in writing, and the material is sold for use in a collective work (that is, a work that derives material from a number of contributors), you are authorizing unlimited use of the piece in that work or in subsequent issues or updates of the work. Thus, you can't collect reprint fees if the rights weren't spelled out in advance, in writing.

Give as much attention to the rights you haven't sold as you do the rights you have sold. Be aware of the rights you retain, with an eye out for additional sales.

Whatever rights you sell or don't sell, make sure all parties involved in any sale understand the terms of the sale. Clarify what is being sold *before* any actual sale, and do it in writing. Communication, coupled with these guidelines and some common sense, will preclude misunderstandings with editors over rights.

Copyrighting Your Writing. The new copyright law, effective since January 1, 1978, protects your writing, unequivocally recognizes the creator of the work as its owner, and grants the creator all the rights, benefits and *privileges* that ownership entails.

In other words, the moment you finish a piece of writing—whether it be short story, article, novel, poem or even paragraph—the law recognizes that only you can decide how it is to be used.

This law gives writers power in dealing with editors and publishers, but they should understand how to use that power. They should also understand that certain circumstances can complicate and confuse the concept of ownership. Writers must be wary of these circumstances, or risk losing ownership of their work.

Here are answers to commonly asked questions about copyright law:

● **To what rights am I entitled under copyright law?** The law gives you, as creator of your work, the right to print, reprint and copy the work; to sell or distribute copies of the work; to prepare "derivative works"—dramatizations, translations, musical arrangement, novelizations, etc.; to record the work; and to perform or display literary, dramatic or musical works publicly. These rights give you control over how your work is used, and assure you that you receive payment for any use of your work.

If, however, you create the work as a "work-for-hire," you *do not* own any of these rights. The person or company that commissioned the work-for-hire owns the copyright. The work-for-hire agreement will be discussed in more detail later.

● **When does copyright law take effect, and how long does it last?** A piece of writing is copyrighted the moment it is put to paper. Protection lasts for the life of the author plus 50 years, thus allowing your heirs to benefit from your work. For material written by two or more people, protection lasts for the life of the last survivor plus 50 years. The life-plus-50 provision applies if the work was created or registered with the Copyright Office after January 1, 1978, when the updated copyright law took effect. The old law protected works for a 28-year term, and gave the copyright owner the option to renew the copyright for an additional 28 years at the end of that term. Works copyrighted under the old law that are in their second 28-year term automatically receive an additional 19 years of protection (for a total of 75 years). Works in their first term also receive the 19-year extension, but must still be renewed when the first term ends.

If you create a work anonymously or pseudonymously, protection lasts for 100 years after the work's creation, or 75 years after its publication, whichever is shorter. The life-plus-50 coverage takes effect, however, if you reveal your identity to the Copyright Office any time before the original term of protection runs out.

Works created on a for-hire basis are also protected for 100 years after the work's creation or 75 years after its publication, whichever is shorter.

● **Must I register my work with the Copyright Office to receive protection?** No. Your work is copyrighted whether or not you register it, although registration offers certain advantages. For example, you must register the work before you can bring an infringement suit to court. You can register the work *after* an infringement has taken place, and *then* take the suit to court, but registering after the fact removes certain rights from you. You can sue for actual damages (the income or other benefits lost as a result of the infringement), but you can't sue for statutory damages and you can't recover attorney's fees unless the work has been registered with the Copyright Office *before* the infringement took place. Registering before the infringement also allows you to make a stronger case when bringing the infringement to court.

If you suspect that someone might infringe on your work, register it. If you doubt that an infringement is likely (and infringements are relatively rare), you might save yourself the time and money involved in registering the material.

● **I have an article that I want to protect fully. How do I register it?** Request the proper form from the Copyright Office. Send the completed form, a $10 registration fee, and one copy (if the work is unpublished; two if it's published) of the work to the Register of Copyrights, Library of Congress, Washington, D.C. 20559. You needn't register each work individually. A group of articles can be registered simultaneously (for a single $10 fee) if they meet these requirements: They must be assembled in orderly form (simply placing them in a notebook binder is sufficient); they must bear a single title ("Works by Joe Jones," for example); they must represent the work of one person (or one set of collaborators); and they must be the subject of a single claim to copyright. No limit is placed on the number of works that can be copyrighted in a group.

● **If my writing is published in a "collective work"—such as a magazine—does the publication handle registration of the work?** Only if the publication owns the piece of writing. Although the copyright notice carried by the magazine covers its contents, you must register any writing to which *you* own the rights if you want the additional protection registration provides.

Collective works are publications with a variety of contributors. Magazines, newspapers, encyclopedias, anthologies, etc., are considered collective works. If you sell something to a collective work, state specifically—*in writing*—what rights you're selling. If you don't, you are automatically selling the nonexclusive right to use the writing in the collective work and in any succeeding issues or revisions of it. For example, a magazine that buys your article without specifying in writing the rights purchased can reuse the article in that magazine—but in no other, not even in another magazine put out by the same publisher—without repaying you. The same is true for other collective works, so always detail *in writing* what rights you are selling before actually making the sale.

When contributing to a collective work, ask that your copyright notice be placed on or near your published manuscript (if you still own the manuscript's rights). Prominent display of your copyright notice on published work has two advantages: It signals to readers and potential reusers of the piece that it belongs to you, and not to the collective work in which it appears; and it allows you to register all published works bearing such notice with the Copyright Office as a group for a single $10 fee. A published work *not* bearing notice indicating you as copyright owner can't be included in a group registration.

Display of copyright notice is especially important when contributing to an uncopyrighted publication—that is, a publication that doesn't display a copyright symbol and doesn't register with the Copyright Office. You risk losing copyright protection on material that appears in an uncopyrighted publication. Also, you have no legal recourse against a person who infringes on something that is published without appropriate copyright notice. That person has been misled by the absence of the copyright notice and can't be held liable for his infringement. Copyright protection remains in force on material published in an uncopyrighted publication without benefit of copyright notice if the notice was left off only a few copies, if you asked (in writing) that the notice be included and the publisher didn't comply, or if you register the work and make a reasonable attempt to place the notice on any copies that haven't been distributed after the omission was discovered.

Official notice of copyright consists of the word "Copyright," the abbreviation "Copr." or symbol ©; the name of the copyright owner or owners; and the year date of creation (for example, "© 1982 by Joe Jones").

● **Under what circumstances should I place my copyright notice on unpublished works that haven't been registered?** Place official copyright notice on the first page of *any* manuscript, a procedure intended not to stop a buyer from stealing your material (editorial piracy is very rare, actually), but to demonstrate to the editor that you understand your rights under copyright law, that you own that particular manuscript, and that you want to retain your ownership after the manuscript is published. Seeing this notice, an editor might be less apt to try to buy all rights from you. Remember, you want to retain your rights to any writing.

● **How do I transfer copyright?** A transfer of copyright, like the sale of any property, is simply an exchange of the property for payment. The law stipulates, however, that the transfer of any exclusive rights (and the copyright is the most exclusive of exclusive rights) must be made in writing to be valid. Various types of exclusive rights exist, as outlined above. Usually it is best not to sell your copyright. If you do, you lose control over use of the manuscript, and forfeit future income from its use.

● **What is a "work-for-hire agreement"?** This is a work that another party commissions you to do. Two types of for-hire works exist: Work done as a regular employee of a company, and commissioned work that is specifically called a "work-for-hire" in writing at the time of assignment. The phrase "work-for-hire" or something close must be used in the written agreement, though you should watch for similar phrasings. The work-for-hire provision was included in the new copyright law so that no writer could unwittingly sign away his copyright. The phrase "work-for-hire" is a bright red flag warning the writer that the agreement he's about to enter into will result in loss of rights to any material created under the agreement.

Some editors offer work-for-hire agreements when making assignments, and expect writers to sign them routinely. By signing them, you forfeit the potential for additional income from a manuscript through reprint sales, or sale of other rights. Be careful, therefore, in signing away your rights in a "work-for-hire" agreement. Many articles written as works-for-hire or to which all rights have been sold are never resold, but if you retain the copyright, you might try to resell the article—something you wouldn't be motivated to do if you forfeited your rights to the piece.

● **Can I get my rights back if I sell all rights to a manuscript, or if I sell the copyright itself?** Yes. You or certain heirs can terminate the transfer of rights 40 years after creation or 35 years after publication of a work by serving written notice to the person to whom you transferred rights within specified time limits. Consult the Copyright Office for the procedural details. This may seem like a long time to wait, but remember that some manuscripts remain popular (and earn royalties and other fees) for much longer than 35 years.

● **Must all transfers be in writing?** Only work-for-hire agreements and transfers of exclusive rights *must* be in writing. However, getting any agreement in writing before the sale is wise. Beware of other statements about what rights the buyer purchases that may appear on checks, writer's guidelines or magazine mastheads. If the publisher makes such a statement elsewhere, you might insert a phrase like "No statement pertaining to purchase of rights other than the one detailed in this letter—including masthead statements or writer's guidelines—applies to this agreement" into the letter that outlines your rights agreement. Some publishers put their terms in writing on the back of a check that, when endorsed by the writer, becomes a "contract." This is a dubious legal maneuver, which many writers sidestep by not signing the check—yet depositing it in their bank accounts with the notation FOR DEPOSIT ONLY.

● **Are ideas copyrightable?** No. Nor can information be copyrighted. Only the actual expression of ideas or information can be copyrighted. You can't copyright the idea to do a solar energy story, and you can't copyright information about building solar energy converters. But you can copyright the article that results from that idea and that information.

● **Where do I go for more information about copyright law?** Write or call (not collect) the Copyright Office (Library of Congress, Washington, D.C. 20559; tel.703/557-8700) for a free Copyright Information Kit. The Copyright Office will answer specific questions, but won't provide legal advice. For more information about copyright and other law, consult *Law and the Writer*, edited by Kirk Polking and Leonard S. Meranus (Writer's Digest Books).

How Much Should I Charge?

Freelance writers are often so busy watching the mailbox for replies from the editors in this book, they sometimes forget there is money to be made as freelance writers in their own hometowns. What follows is a checklist of writing jobs you might want to consider in your own corner of the world—and rates that have been reported to us by freelancers doing similar duties in various parts of the United States. Prices quoted here are by no means fixed; the rates in your own marketplace may be higher or lower, depending on demand and other local variables. Therefore, consider the rates quoted here as guidelines, not fixed fees.

How do you find out what the local going rate is? If possible, contact writers or friends in a related business or agency that employs freelancers to find out what has been paid for certain kinds of jobs in the past. Or try to get the prospective client to quote his budget for a specific project before you name your price.

When setting your own fees, keep two factors in mind: (1)how much you want to earn for your time; and (2)how much you think the client is willing or able to pay for the job. How much you want to earn for your time should take into consideration not only an hourly rate for the time you actually spend writing, but also the time involved in meeting with the client, doing research, and, where necessary, handling details with a printer or producer. One way to figure your hourly rate is to determine what an annual salary might be for a staff person to do the same job you are bidding on, and figure an hourly wage on that. If, for example, you think the buyer would have to pay a staff person $20,000 a year, divide that by 2,000 (approximately 40 hours per week for 50 weeks) and you will arrive at $10 an hour. Then add on another 20% to cover the amount of fringe benefits that an employer normally pays in Social Security, unemployment insurance, paid vacations, hospitalization, retirement funds, etc. Then add on another dollars per hour figure to cover your actual overhead expense for office space, equipment, supplies. (Add up one year's expense and divide by the number of hours per year you work on freelancing. In the beginning you may have to adjust this to avoid pricing yourself out of the market.)

You will, of course, from time to time handle certain jobs at less than desirable rates because they are for a social cause you believe in, or because the job offers you additional experience or exposure to some profitable client for the future. Some clients pay hourly rates, others pay flat fees for the job; both kinds of rates are listed when the data were available so you have as many pricing options as possible. More details on many of the freelance jobs listed below are contained in *Jobs for Writers*, edited by Kirk Polking (Writer's Digest Books)—which tells how to get writing jobs, how to handle them most effectively, and how to get a fair price for your work.

Advertising copywriting: Advertising agencies and the advertising departments of large companies need part-time help in rush seasons; but newspapers, radio and TV stations also need copywriters for their smaller business customers who do not have an agency. Depending on the client and the job, the following rates could apply: $20-$35 per hour, $100 per day, $200 and up per week, $100-$500 as a monthly retainer.

Annual reports: A brief report with some economic information and an explanation of figures, $20-$35 per hour; a report that must meet Securities and Exchange Commission (SEC) standards and reports that use legal language could bill at $40-$50 per hour. Some writers who provide copywriting up to 3,000 words charge flat fees ranging from $1,500-$7,500.

Article manuscript critique: 3,000 words, $30.

Arts reviewing: for weekly newspapers, $5-$15; for dailies, $25 and up; for Sunday supplements, $100-$200; regional arts events summaries for national trade magazines $15-$50; arts calendar compiling for local newspapers, $4 per hour.

Associations: miscellaneous writing projects, small associations, $4-$10 per hour; larger groups, $35-$50 per hour; or a flat fee per project, such as $250-$500 for 10-12 page magazine articles, or $500-$1,000 for a 10-page booklet.

Audio cassette scripts: $150 for 20 minutes.

Audiovisuals: see filmstrips, motion pictures, slide films, video programs.

Book, as-told-to (ghostwriting): author gets full advance and 50% of author's royalties; subject gets 50%. Hourly rate for subjects who are self-publishing.

Book content editing: $10-$25 per hour and up.

Book copyediting: $6-9 per hour and up; occasionally 75¢ per page.

Book indexing: $6-$15 per hour, or a flat fee, or by the entry.

Book jacket blurb writing: $60-$75 for selling front cover copy plus inside and back cover copy summarizing content and tone of the book.

Book manuscript reading, nonspecialized subjects: $20 for a half page summary and recommendation. *Specialized subject:* $100 and up, depending on length of report required.

Book proofreading: $7-$10 per hour and up; sometimes 30-40¢ per page.

Book research: $5-$20 per hour and up, depending on complexity.

Book reviews: byline and the book only, on small papers; to $25-$125 on larger publications.

Book rewriting: $7.50-$12 per hour and up; sometimes $5 per page. Some writers have combination ghostwriting and rewriting short-term jobs for which the pay could be $350 per day and up.

Business writing: On the local or national level, this may be advertising copy, collateral materials, speechwriting, films, public relations or other jobs—see individual entries on these subjects for details. General business writing rates could range from $20-$50 per hour; $50-$200 per day.

Business booklets, announcement folders: writing and editing, $25-$1,000 depending on size, research, etc. Average 8½x11'' brochure, $100-$200.

Business facilities brochure: 12-16 pages, $1,000-$2,000.

Business meeting guide and brochure: 4 pages, $120; 8-12 pages, $200.

Catalogs for business: $60-$75 per printed page; more if many tables or charts must be reworked for readability and consistency.

Collateral materials for business: see business booklets, catalogs, etc.

Comedy writing for night club entertainers: *Gags only*, $2-$7 each. *Routines:* $100-$500 per minute. Some new comics may try to get a five-minute routine for $150; others will pay $1,500 for a five-minute bit from a top writer.

Commercial reports for businesses, insurance companies, credit agencies: $2-$6 per report.

Company newsletters and inhouse publications: writing and editing 2-4 pages, $100-$500; 12-32 pages, $500-$1,000.

Consultation to business: on writing, PR, $25-50 per hour.

Contest judging: short manuscripts, $5 per entry; with one-page critique, $10-$25.

Corporate history: up to 5,000 words, $1,000-$3,000.

Corporate profile: up to 3,000 words, $1,250-$2,500.

Dance criticism: $25-$400 per article (see also Arts reviewing).

Direct mail catalog copy: $10-$30 per page for 3-20 blocks of copy per page of a 24-48 page catalog.

Editing: see book editing, company newsletters, magazines, etc.

Educational consulting and educational grant and proposal writing: $100-$350 per day and up to 1-5% of the total grant funds depending on whether writing only is involved or also research and design of the project itself.

Educational films: see films.

Encyclopedia articles: entries in some reference books, such as biographical encyclopedias, 500-2,000 words and pay ranges from $60-$80 per 1,000 words. Specialists fees vary.

Filmscripts for nontheatrical films for education, business, industry: prices vary depending on the client but some fees which have been paid include $200-$1,200 for one reel (10 minutes); $1,000-$1,500 for 30 minutes; 5-12% of the production cost of films that cost the producers $750-$1,500 per release minute (e.g., $1,500 on a $15,000 film).

Filmstrip script: $50 per minute, $500 minimum.

Financial presentation for a corporation: 20-30 minutes, $1,500-$4,500.

Fund-raising campaign brochure: $2,000 for 20 hours' research and 30 hours to write, get it approved, lay out and produce with printer.

Gags: see comedy writing.

Genealogical research: $5-$25 per hour.

Ghostwriting: $15-$40 per hour; $5-$10 per page. Ghostwritten trade journal article under someone else's byline, $250-400.

Ghostwriting a corporate book: 6 months' work, $13,000-$25,000.

Ghostwriting speeches: see speeches.

Government public information officer: part-time, with local governments, $15 per hour.

House organ editing: see company newsletters and inhouse publications.

Industrial promotions: $15-$40 per hour. See also business writing.

Job application letters: $10-$25.

Lecture fees: $100 and up plus expenses; less for panel discussions.

Magazine column: 200 words, $25. Larger circulation publications pay more.

Magazine editing: religious publications, $200-$500 month.

Magazine stringing: 20¢-$1 per word based on circulation. Daily rate: $200 plus expenses; weekly rate: $750 plus expenses. Also $15-$35 per hour plus expenses.

Manuscript typing: 65¢-$1 per page with one carbon.

Market research survey reports: $2-$6 per report.

Medical editing: $15 per hour.

Medical proofreading: $7-$10 per hour.

Medical writing: $15 per hour.

New product release: $300-$500 plus expenses.

Newsletters: see company newsletters and retail business newsletters.

Newspaper column, local: 80¢ per column inch to $5 for a weekly; $7.50 for dailies of 4,000-6,000 circulation; $10-$12.50 for 7,000-10,000 dailies; $15-$20 for 11,000-25,000 dailies; and $25 and up for larger dailies.

Newspaper reviews of art, music, drama: see Arts reviewing.

Newspaper stringing: 50¢-$2.50 per column inch up to $4-$5 per column inch for some national publications. Also publications like *National Enquirer* pay lead fees up to $250 for tips on page one story ideas.

Newspaper ads for small business: $25 for a small, one-column ad, or $10 per hour and up.

Permission fees to publishers to reprint article or story: $10-$100.

Photo brochures: $700-$15,000 flat fee for photos and writing.

Political writing: see public relations and speechwriting.

Press release: 1-3 pages, $50-$200.

Printers' camera ready typewritten copy: negotiated with individual printers, but see also manuscript typing services above.

Product literature: per page, $100-$150.

Programmed instruction consultant fees: $150-$600 per day; $25 per hour.

Programmed instruction materials for business: $50 per hour for inhouse writing and editing; $500 a day plus expenses for outside research and writing. *Alternate method:* $2,000-$5,000 per hour of programmed training provided, depending on technicality of subject.

Public relations for business: $200-$400 per day plus expenses.

Public relations for conventions: $500-$1,500 flat fee.

Public relations for libraries: small libraries, $5-$10 per hour; larger cities, $35 an hour and up.

Public relations for nonprofit or proprietary organizations: small towns, $100-$300 monthly retainers.

Public relations for politicians: up to 10% of the campaign budget.

Public relations for schools: $10 per hour and up in small districts; larger districts have fulltime staff personnel.

Radio advertising copy: small towns, up to $5 per spot, $100-$250 per week for a four- to six-hour day; larger cities, $250-$400 per week.

Radio continuity writing: $5 per page to $150 per week, part-time.

Radio documentaries: $200 for 60 minutes, local station.

Radio editorials: $10-$30 for 90-second to two-minute spots.

Radio interviews: for National Public Radio, up to 3 minutes, $25; 3-10 minutes, $40-$75; 10-60 minutes, $125 to negotiable fees. Small radio stations would pay approximately 50% of the NPR rate; large stations, double the NPR rate.

Record album cover copy: $100-$200 flat fee.

Recruiting brochure: 8-12 pages, $500-$1,500.

Research for writers or book publishers: $10-$30 an hour and up. Some quote a flat fee of $300-$500 for a complete and complicated job.

Restaurant guide features: short article on restaurant, owner, special attractions, $15; interior, exterior photos, $15.

Resumé writing: $35-$85 per resumé.

Retail business newsletters for customers: $125-$200 for writing four-page publications. Some writers work with a local printer and handle production details as well, billing the client for the total package.

Sales brochure: 12-16 pages, $750-$3,000.

Sales letter for business or industry: $150 for one or two pages.

Services brochure: 12-18 pages, $1,250-$2,000.

Shopping mall promotion: $500 monthly retainer up to 15% of promotion budget for the mall.

Short story manuscript critique: 3,000 words, $30.

Slide film script: $500-$750 for a 10-minute film up to 14% of the production cost (e.g., $1,400 on a $10,000 film).

Slide/single image photos: $75 flat fee.

Slide/tape program: $50 per minute, $500 minimum.

Special news article: for business' submission to trade publication, $250-$400 for 1,000 words.

Slide presentation for an educational institution: $1,000 flat fee.

Speech for owner of a small business: $100 for six minutes.

Speech for owners of larger businesses: $500-$1,500 for 10-15 minutes.

Speech for local political candidate: $150-$250 for 15 minutes.

Speech for statewide candidate: $500-$800.

Speech for national candidate: $1,000 and up.

Syndicated newspaper column, self-promoted: $2-$8 each for weeklies; $5-$25 per week for dailies, based on circulation.

Teaching creative writing in school: $25-$60 per hour of instruction, or $1,200 for a 10 session class of 25 students.

Teaching journalism in high school: proportionate to salary scale for fulltime teacher in the same school district.

Teaching home-bound students: $5 per hour.

Technical writing: $10-$20 per hour.

Technical typing: 65¢ to $1 per double-spaced page.

Translation, commercial: a final draft in one of the common European languages, 2½-4½¢ per English word.

Translation for government agencies: some pay 1½-2¢ per English word.

Translation, literary: $40-$60 per thousand English words.

Translation through translation agencies: less 33⅓% for agency commission.

TV documentary: 30-minute five-six page proposal outline, $250 and up; 15-17 page treatment, $750 and up; less in smaller cities.

TV editorials: $35 and up for 1-minute, 45 seconds (250-300 words).

TV instruction taping: $150 per 30-minute tape; $25 residual each time tape is sold.

TV news film still photo: $3-$6 flat fee.

TV news story: $16-$25 flat fee.

TV filmed news and features: $15 per film clip to $10-$20 per hour for 30-second spot; $15-$20 for 60 seconds.

TV, national and local public stations: $35-$100 per minute down to a flat fee of $100-$500 for a 30- to 60-minute script.

TV scripts: 60 minutes, prime time, Writers Guild March 1981 rates, $6,065; 30 minutes, $4,718.

Videotape program script: $1,000 minimum on a 10-minute program or 10% of the production cost ($1,500 on a 10-minute $15,000 program).

Writer-in-schools: Arts council program, $125 per day plus expenses.

Writer's workshop: lecturing and seminar conducting, $100-$200 per day; local classes $50 per student for 10 sessions.

Glossary

All Rights. See "Rights and the Writer."

Alternative culture. The lifestyles, politics, literature, etc., of those persons with cultural values different from the current "establishment."

Assignment. Editor asks a writer to do a specific article for which he usually names a price for the completed manuscript.

B&W. Abbreviation for black & white photograph.

Beat. A specific subject area regularly covered by a reporter, such as the police department or education or the environment. It can also mean a scoop on some news item.

Bimonthly. Every two months. See also *semimonthly*.

Biweekly. Every two weeks.

Blue-penciling. Editing a manuscript.

Book packager. Draws all the elements of a book together, from the initial concept to writing and marketing strategies, then sells the book package to a book publisher and/or movie producer.

Caption. Originally a title or headline over a picture but now a description of the subject matter of a photograph, including names of people where appropriate. Also called cutline.

Chapbook. A small booklet, usually paperback, of poetry, ballads or tales.

Chicago Manual of Style. A format for the typing of manuscripts as established by the University of Chicago Press.

Clean copy. Free of errors, cross-outs, wrinkles, smudges.

Clippings. News items of possible interest to trade magazine editors.

Column inch. All the type contained in one inch of a typeset column.

Contributor's copies. Copies of the issues of a magazine sent to an author in which his/her work appears.

Co-publishing. An arrangement (usually contractual) in which author and publisher share publication costs and profits.

Copy. Manuscript material before it is set in type.

Copy editing. Editing the manuscript for grammar, punctuation and printing style as opposed to subject content.

Copyright. A means to protect an author's work. See "Rights and the Writer."

Correspondent. Writer away from the home office of a newspaper or magazine who regularly provides it with copy.

Cutline. See *caption*.

El-hi. Elementary to high school.

Epigram. A short, witty, sometimes paradoxical saying.

Erotica. Usually fiction that is sexually-oriented; although it could be art on the same theme.

Fair use. A provision of the copyright law that says short passages from copyrighted material may be used without infringing on the owner's rights.

Feature. An article giving the reader background information on the news. Also used by magazines to indicate a lead article or distinctive department.

Filler. A short item used by an editor to "fill" out a newspaper column or a page in a magazine. It could be a timeless news item, a joke, an anecdote, some light verse or short humor, a puzzle, etc.

First North American serial rights. See "Rights and the Writer."

Formula story. Familiar theme treated in a predictable plot structure—such as boy meets girl, boy loses girl, boy gets girl.

Gagline. The caption for a cartoon, or the cover teaser line and the punchline on the inside of a studio greeting card.

Ghostwriter. A writer who puts into literary form, an article, speech, story or book based on another person's ideas or knowledge.

Glossy. A black & white photograph with a shiny surface as opposed to one with a non-shiny matte finish.

Gothic novel. One in which the central character is usually a beautiful young girl, the setting is an old mansion or castle; there is a handsome hero and a real menace, either natural or supernatural.

Honorarium. A token payment. It may be a very small amount of money, or simply a byline and copies of the publication in which your material appears.

Illustrations. May be photographs, old engravings, artwork. Usually paid for separately from the manuscript. See also *package sale.*

International Postal Reply Coupons. Can be purchased at your local post office and enclosed with your letter or manuscript to a foreign publisher to cover his postage cost when replying.

Invasion of privacy. Cause for suits against some writers who have written about persons (even though truthfully) without their consent.

Kill fee. A portion of the agreed-on price for a complete article that was assigned but which was subsequently cancelled.

Libel. A false accusation; or any published statement or presentation that tends to expose another to public contempt, ridicule, etc. Defenses are truth; fair comment on the matter of public interest; and privileged communication—such as a report of legal proceedings or a client's communication to his lawyer.

Little magazine. Publications of limited circulation, usually on literary or political subject matter.

MLA Handbook. A format for the typing of manuscripts established by the Modern Language Association.

Model release. A paper signed by the subject of a photograph (or his guardian, if a juvenile) giving the photographer permission to use the photograph, editorially or for advertising purposes or for some specific purpose as stated.

Ms. Abbreviation for manuscript.

Mss. Abbreviation for more than one manuscript.

Multiple submissions. Some editors of non-overlapping circulation magazines, such as religious publications, are willing to look at manuscripts which have also been submitted to other editors at the same time. See individual listings for which editors these are. No multiple submissions should be made to larger markets paying good prices for original material, unless it is a query on a highly topical article requiring an immediate response and that fact is so stated in your letter.

Newsbreak. A newsworthy event or item. For example, a clipping about the opening of a new shoe store in a town might be a newsbreak of interest to a trade journal in the shoe industry. Some editors also use the word to mean funny typographical errors.

Novelette. A short novel, or a long short story; 7,000 to 15,000 words approximately.

Offset. Type of printing in which copy and illustrations are photographed and plates made, from which printing is done; as opposed to letterpress printing directly from type metal and engravings of illustrations.

One-time rights. See "Rights and the Writer."

Outline. Of a book is usually a one-page summary of its contents; often in the form of chapter headings with a descriptive sentence or two under each one to show the scope of the book. Of a screenplay or teleplay is a scene-by-scene narrative description of the story (10-15 pages for a ½-hour teleplay; 15-25 pages for a 1-hour teleplay; 25-40 pages for a 90-minute teleplay; 40-60 pages for a 2-hour feature film or teleplay).

Package sale. The editor wants to buy manuscript and photos as a "package" and pay for them in one check.

Page rate. Some magazines pay for material at a fixed rate per published page, rather than so much per word.

Payment on acceptance. The editor sends you a check for your article, story or poem as soon as he reads it and decides to publish it.

Payment on publication. The editor decides to buy your material but doesn't send you a check until he publishes it.

Pen name. The use of a name other than your legal name on articles, stories, or books where you wish to remain anonymous. Simply notify your post office and bank that you are using the name so that you'll receive mail and/or checks in that name.

Photo feature. A feature in which the emphasis is on the photographs rather than any accompanying written material.

Photocopied submissions. Are acceptable to some editors instead of the author's sending his original manuscript. See also *multiple submissions.*

Plagiarism. Passing off as one's own, the expression of ideas, words to another.

Public domain. Material which was either never copyrighted or whose copyright term has run out.

Publication not copyrighted. Publication of an author's work in such a publication places it in the public domain, and it cannot subsequently be copyrighted. See "Rights and the Writer."

Query. A letter to an editor eliciting his interest in an article you want to write.

Reporting times. The number of days, weeks, etc., it takes an editor to report back to the author on his query or manuscript.

Reprint rights. See "Rights and the Writer."

Round-up article. Comments from, or interviews with, a number of celebrities or experts on a single theme.

Royalties, standard hardcover book. 10% of the retail price on the first 5,000 copies sold; 12½% on the next 5,000 and 15% thereafter.

Royalties, standard mass paperback book. 4 to 8% of the retail price on the first 150,000 copies sold.

SAE. Self-addressed envelope.

SASE. Self-addressed, stamped envelope.

Screenplay. Script for a film intended to be shown in theaters.

Second serial rights. See "Rights and the Writer."

Semimonthly. Twice a month.

Semiweekly. Twice a week.

Serial. Published periodically, such as a newspaper or magazine.

Short-short story. Is usually from 500 to 2,000 words.

Sidebar. A feature presented as a companion to a straight news report (or main magazine article) giving sidelights on human-interest aspects, (or) sometimes elucidating just one aspect of the story.

Simultaneous submissions. Submissions of the same article, story or poem to several publications at the same time.

Slant. The approach of a story or article so as to appeal to the readers of a specific magazine. Does, for example, this magazine always like stories with an upbeat ending? Or does that one like articles aimed only at the blue-collar worker?

Slides. Usually called transparencies by editors looking for color photographs.

Speculation. The editor agrees to look at the author's manuscript but doesn't promise to buy it until he reads it.

Stringer. A writer who submits material to a magazine or newspaper from a specific geographical location.

Style. The way in which something is written—for example, short, punchy sentences of flowing, narrative description or heavy use of quotes of dialogue.

Subsidiary rights. All those rights, other than book publishing rights included in a book contract—such as paperback, book club, movie rights, etc.

Subsidy publisher. A book publisher who charges the author for the cost to typeset and print his book, the jacket, etc., as opposed to a royalty publisher which pays the author.

Syndication rights. A book publisher may sell the rights to a newspaper syndicate to print a book in installments in one or more newspapers.

Tabloids. Newspaper format publication on about half the size of the regular newspaper page, such as *National Enquirer.*

Tearsheet. Page from a magazine or newspaper containing your printed story, article, poem or ad.

Teleplay. A dramatic story written to be performed on television.

Think piece. A magazine article that has an intellectual, philosophical, provocative approach to its subject.

Transparencies. Positive color slides; not color prints.

Treatment. Synopsis of a proposed television or film script (40-60 pages for a 2-hour feature film or teleplay). More detailed than an outline.

Uncopyrighted publication. Publication of an author's work in such a publication potentially puts it in the public domain.

Unsolicited manuscript. A story, article, poem or book that an editor did not specifically ask to see.

Vanity publisher. See *subsidy publisher*.
Vignette. A brief scene (500 words or less) offering the reader a flash of illumination about a character as opposed to a more formal story with a beginning, middle and end.

Index

B

E

F

M

U

X, Y, Z

Other Writer's Digest Books

Market Directories
- Artist's Market, 528 pp. $13.95
- Fiction Writer's Market, 504 pp. $15.95
- Photographer's Market, 576 pp. $14.95
- Songwriter's Market, 432 pp. $12.95

General Writing Books
- Beginning Writer's Answer Book, 264 pp. $9.95
- How to Get Started in Writing, 180 pp. $10.95
- Law and the Writer, 240 pp. (paper) $7.95
- Make Every Word Count, 256 pp. (paper) $6.95
- Treasury of Tips for Writers, (paper), 174 pp. $6.95
- Writer's Resource Guide, 488 pp. $12.95

Magazine/News Writing
- Complete Guide to Marketing Magazine Articles, 248 pp. $9.95
- Craft of Interviewing, 244 pp. $9.95
- Magazine Writing: The Inside Angle, 256 pp. $10.95
- Magazine Writing Today, 220 pp. $9.95
- Newsthinking: The Secret of Great Newswriting, 204 pp. $11.95
- 1001 Article Ideas, 270 pp. $10.95
- Stalking the Feature Story, 310 pp. $9.95
- Write on Target, 240 pp. $12.95
- Writing and Selling Non-Fiction, 317 pp. $10.95

Fiction Writing
- Creating Short Fiction, 228 pp. $11.95
- Handbook of Short Story Writing, (paper), 238 pp. $6.95
- How to Write Best-Selling Fiction, 300 pp. $13.95
- How to Write Short Stories that Sell, 212 pp. $9.95
- One Way to Write Your Novel, 138 pp. (paper) $6.95
- Secrets of Successful Fiction, 119 pp. $8.95
- Writing the Novel: From Plot to Print, 197 pp. $10.95

Category Writing Books
- Cartoonist's and Gag Writer's Handbook, (paper), 157 pp. $9.95
- Children's Picture Book: How to Write It, How to Sell It, 224 pp. $16.95
- Confession Writer's Handbook, 173 pp. $9.95
- Guide to Greeting Card Writing, 256 pp. $10.95
- Guide to Writing History, 258 pp. $9.95
- How to Write and Sell Your Personal Experiences, 226 pp. $10.95
- How to Write "How-To" Books and Articles, 192 pp. (paper) $8.95
- Mystery Writer's Handbook, 273 pp. $9.95
- The Poet and the Poem, 399 pp. $11.95
- Poet's Handbook, 224 pp. $10.95
- Sell Copy, 205 pp. $11.95
- Successful Outdoor Writing, 244 pp. $11.95
- Travel Writer's Handbook, 274 pp. $11.95
- TV Scriptwriter's Handbook, 322 pp. $11.95
- Writing and Selling Science Fiction, 191 pp. $8.95
- Writing for Children & Teenagers, 269 pp. $9.95

The Writing Business
- Complete Handbook for Freelance Writers, 391 pp. $14.95
- How to Be a Successful Housewife/Writer, 254 pp. $10.95
- How You Can Make $20,000 a Year Writing: (No Matter Where You Live), 270 pp. (paper) $6.95
- Jobs For Writers, 281 pp. $11.95
- Profitable Part-time/Full-time Freelancing, 195 pp. $10.95
- Writer's Digest Diary, 144 pp. $14.95

Photography Books
How You Can Make $25,000 a Year with Your Camera (No Matter Where You Live), 224 pp.
(paper) $9.95
Sell & Re-Sell Your Photos, 323 pp. $14.95

To order directly from the publisher, include $1.25 postage and handling for 1 book
and 50¢ for each additional book. Allow 30 days for delivery.

For a current catalog of books for writers or information on *Writer's Digest* magazine,
Writer's Yearbook, Writer's Digest School correspondence courses or manuscript
criticism, write to:

Writer's Digest Books, Department B
9933 Alliance Road, Cincinnati OH 45242

Prices subject to change without notice.